The Worker Traits Data Book

Specific details on the 12,741 jobs listed in the *Dictionary of Occupational Titles*

A database of Worker Traits including over 75 separate details for each occupation including: Training Time; Aptitudes; Physical Demands; Environmental Conditions; Temperaments; Work Fields; and Materials, Products, Subject Matter and Services; and cross-walks to SOC, CIP, and OES data bases.

1994 Edition

Compiled by: Don Mayall

Produced by **JIST Works, Inc.** Based on data provided by the U.S. Department of Labor, Employment and Training Administration and the Bureau of Labor Statistics; the U.S. Department of Education; and the North Carolina Occupational Analysis Field Center.

The Worker Traits Data Book

Specific Details on the 12,741 Jobs Listed in the Dictionary of Occupational Titles
© 1994 by JIST Works, Inc.

Published by JIST Works, Inc.
720 N. Park Avenue
Indianapolis, IN 46202-3431
Phone: 317-264-3720 Fax: 317-264-3709 E-mail: JISTWorks@AOL.com

Other Reference Books Provided by JIST

Jist publishes a number of the occupational information books mentioned in this volume:

- *Dictionary of Occupational Titles*
- *Occupational Outlook Handbook*
- *Young Person's Occupational Outlook Handbook*
- *The Enhanced Guide for Occupational Exploration, 2nd Edition*
- *The Complete Guide for Occupational Exploration*

JIST also publishes and distributes hundreds of other career-related books, videos, software, assessment devices and other materials. Please contact the publisher or your distributor for additional details.

Cover Design by Kerry Causey
Data Manipulation and Compilation by Don Mayall

Printed in the United States of America

99 98 97 96   9 8 7 6 5 4 3 2

Library of Congress Cataloging-in-Publication Data
Mayall, Donald, 1932-
     The Worker Traits Data Book Specific Details on the 12,741 Jobs
Listed in the Dictionary of Occupational Titles / compiled by
Donald Mayall. — 1994 ed.
     p.   cm.
  ISBN: 1-56370-110-3 : $49.95
   1. Vocational qualifications—United States.   2. Occupations—United States
I. JIST Works, Inc.   II. Dictionary of Occupational Titles.   III. Title.
HG5382.M368   1994
331.7'02—dc20   93-33412
                                                    CIP

We have been careful to provide accurate information throughout this book, but it is possible that errors and omissions have been introduced. Please consider this in making any career plans or other important decisions. Trust your own judgment above all else and in all things.

ISBN 1-56370-110-3

Foreword

This volume is a supplement to the U.S. Department of Labor's landmark book, the *Dictionary of Occupational Titles* (DOT). While the DOT provides descriptions for more than 12,000 occupations, the Department of Labor keeps track of a variety of occupational data that is not included in the DOT due to space limitations. This volume, *The Worker Traits Data Book* (WTDB), provides much of this information for each of the occupations listed in the DOT that had either not been readily available or available only from researching a variety of hard-to-obtain information sources. With the creation of this volume, the information is readily available from one source for the first time.

The worker traits data provided in this book are quantitative ratings of the requirements placed on workers on such job dimensions as training time, aptitudes, physical demands, environmental conditions, temperaments, workfields, and materials, products, subject matter, and services (MPSMS). This is in contrast to the DOT which consists principally of narrative descriptions of job duties.

Occupational analysts, rehabilitation counselors, and others engaged in serious studies of job requirements have long been aware of the value of worker traits data and have been able to obtain this information only from a variety of specialized sources that were not widely available. The purpose of this publication is to make the worker traits data accessible to a broader spectrum of users such as job changers, career counselors, job developers, educational planners, and personnel analysts.

To enhance the usefulness of this publication, statistical codes link the 12,741 occupations listed in the *Dictionary of Occupational Titles* and the accompanying worker traits data to the Standard Occupational Classification (SOC), the Classification of Instructional Programs (CIP), and the Occupational Employment Statistics (OES) classification systems. These codes will allow simple cross-referencing to other occupational information systems.

The sources for the data in this volume are the U.S. Department of Labor, Employment and Training Administration and Bureau of Labor Statistics; The U.S. Department of Education; and the North Carolina Occupational Analysis Field Center. Their ongoing work makes the creation of this book possible.

Table of Contents

Each of the 12,741 occupations listed in Section 3, the Worker Traits Data Display, provides coded information on more than 75 distinct elements or measures. Each of these elements is defined in Section 1. It is essential that you understand these various elements since the data presented in Section 3 is coded for each of the elements in order to save space. Following is a listing of the various measures.

This section provides information on understanding how to locate a specific occupation within this volume and to complete a special form, the "Worker Traits Profile," on one or more of the selected occupations. Once completed, this form can be used to document all coded information on a specific occupation and compare it to one or more other occupations.

SECTION 3: Worker Traits Data Display ("The Table") . . 29

This is the largest section of the book, providing data for each of the more than 12,000 occupational titles listed in the current *Dictionary of Occupational Titles*, (DOT). There are over 75 separate coded data elements provided for each occupation, arranged in a tabular format. The occupations are organized according to their DOT code number.

Appendix A: DOT Occupational Categories, Divisions, and Groups: 1A

This provides a listing of the major groupings of occupations used by the U.S. Department of Labor. This system of organizing jobs is used in the *Dictionary of Occupational Titles* and is presented as the first three numbers of the DOT code number that is assigned to each occupation listed in the DOT. This appendix will allow you to interpret the specific meaning of these three DOT numbers.

Appendix B: DOT Industry Abbreviations and Titles 1B

To save space, a variety of abbreviations are used throughout this book and in other publications to refer to specific industries where an occupation may be found. While most of these abbreviations are easily understood, this appendix provides the full meaning of each industry abbreviation.

Appendix C: Work Field Codes and Titles (WKF) 1C

A 3-digit code number is used in Section 3 of this book to identify the Work Field (WKF) designation for each occupation. This appendix interprets these codes by providing the Work Field related to each of the 3-digit WKF code.

Appendix D: Materials, Products, Subject Matter, and Services Codes and Titles (MPSMS) 1D

Section 3 of this book provides a 3-digit code that refers to the Material, Products, Subject Matter, and Services for each of the occupations listed. This appendix provides the meaning for each of these codes in numerical sequence.

Appendix E: Guide for Occupational Exploration (GOE) Interest Areas, Work Groups, Subgroups, and Titles 1E

The U.S. Department of Labor has developed a system of organizing occupations into 12 major Interest Areas and increasingly specific subgroups of related jobs. This system is used in the *Guide for Occupational Exploration* (GOE) and each of the occupations listed in Section 3 of this book includes a GOE number. This appendix presents the numerical system of GOE groupings along with their related group names and will help you better interpret the meaning of the GOE number assigned to each occupation in Section 3.

How to Find Your Way Around This Book

The heart of this book is a table showing ratings on more than 70 work characteristics for each of the 12,741 jobs in the *Dictionary of Occupational Titles*. Although this makes a very long tabulation—which can be discouraging to the uninitiated—the information contained in it can help anyone engaged in career choice, change, or job search, as well as the counselor, job developer, educational planner, or personnel analyst. Making effective use of the data requires an understanding of the meaning of the worker traits and how they are presented in the table. Following are some quick directions to help you get started.

If You Are Familiar with the Worker Traits Definitions and Know the DOT Numbers of the Occupations for Which You Want Data

You can turn directly to Section 3—"Worker Traits Data Display." Using a copy of the "Worker Traits Profile" (found at the end of Section 2) you can transcribe the data directly from the book to this form.

If You Need Help Determining the DOT Number of an Occupation or Using the Data Display

You will need a copy of the *Dictionary of Occupational Titles,* 1991 edition. Once you have it, turn to Section 2 of this book—"Developing an Occupational Profile"—for additional suggestions on how to proceed.

If You Want Definitions of the Worker Traits and the Rating Scales

Turn to Section 1—"The Data Elements Defined"— to find descriptions of the more than 70 data measures for each of the over 12,741 occupations listed in this volume. Included are: Training Time; Aptitudes; Physical Demands; Environmental Conditions; Temperaments; Work Fields; Materials, Products, Subject Matter, and Services; and *Guide for Occupational Exploration* (GOE) interest areas.

If You Want Complete Listings of Several of the Coding Systems in This Book

In the appendices you will find a variety of listings and tables of information related to the various coding systems used in this book. For example, there is a complete listing, in logical sequence, of the Classification of Instructional Programs (CIP) codes. Other appendices include listings for Industries; Work Fields; the Materials, Products, Subject Matter and Services category; the *Guide for Occupational Exploration* (GOE) codes; the Standard Occupational Classification (SOC) codes; and the Occupational Employment Statistics (OES) codes.

Introduction

Jobs affect everyone and the thirst for information about occupations is limitless. How much training does it take to be a computer operator? How much lifting does a cake baker do? What skills are required to become a lawyer? The answers to these and many other questions on the entire range of jobs in the U.S. economy are available in a database maintained by the U.S. Department of Labor (DOL).

For more than 40 years, the DOL has maintained a program of research on occupations. In the 1930s the Employment Service, a system of state-run public employment offices, was established under the sponsorship of the DOL. A key mission of this agency was the matching of workers and jobs. This required an understanding of the job requirements put upon workers—in terms of training, abilities, and physical and psychological characteristics.

Among the products of this research is a database on 12,741 jobs found in the American economy. Some parts of this database are better known than others. The *Dictionary of Occupational Titles* (DOT) is a weighty volume that is familiar to almost everyone who works in the career field and contains detailed descriptions of all the jobs in the database. Less well-known are the quantitative ratings which describe the DOT jobs in terms of specific work requirements such as training time required, aptitudes, temperaments, physical demands, environmental conditions, and other characteristics. As a whole, these are called the worker traits data.

The worker traits database has, in the past, been available only to certain specialized users. For instance, researchers who write career information publications may incorporate this data into their descriptions of jobs. A high school student engaged in a career exploration exercise may access a computerized information system that uses the worker traits data as part of an occupational search strategy. A rehabilitation counselor helping a work-injured client choose a new occupation will almost certainly examine the worker traits data on any new jobs under consideration. But, for most people, the information was not readily available.

The purpose of this publication is for the first time to make the worker traits data available to a broad range of users such as job seekers, career counselors, educators, and personnel workers. Anyone considering looking for a job, choosing an occupational program of study, or changing work fields can learn a great deal about job alternatives from the worker traits data. Career counselors can be of more help to their clients with this information at their fingertips. Vocational instructors can use the data to design occupational training programs. Anyone in the business world who writes job descriptions can do a better job using the worker traits data presented here.

The following sections explain the meaning of the database elements and how to use them.

SECTION 1:
The Data Elements Defined

To make full and accurate use of the wealth of occupational information in this book, it is important to understand the meanings of the specific categories and rating schemes it uses. This section contains descriptions and definitions of each of the elements in the database in the order they appear in this volume. The definitions are taken from the 1991 edition of the *Dictionary of Occupational Titles* (DOT) and The *Revised Handbook for Analyzing Jobs*, both published by the U.S. Department of Labor.

There are three types of information in the database—occupational definition, the worker traits, and the statistical codes. The occupational definition includes the DOT code number and title. The first three digits of the code provide information on the occupational categories, the second three digits are the source of the Worker Functions—the Data-People-Things ratings—and the last three digits further categorize jobs in an occupational group. The title includes the "Base Title" (the one most commonly used) and the Industry Designation, which provides information on the location of the occupation, types of duties, products, processes, and raw materials.

The elements referred to as worker traits include Training Time, Aptitudes, Physical Demands, Environmental Conditions, Temperaments, Work Fields, the Materials, Products, Subject Matter, and Services category, and Interests. Information regarding Interests is obtained from the *Guide for Occupational Exploration* (GOE) coding system.

The final set of elements are the statistical codes, including the Standard Occupational Classification codes (SOC), the Classification of Instructional Programs (CIP), and the Occupational Employment Statistics (OES) codes.

The Occupational Definition

Work is organized in a variety of ways. As a result of technological, economic, and sociological influences, nearly every job in the economy is performed slightly differently from any other job. Every job is also similar to a number of other jobs.

In order to look at the millions of jobs in the U.S. economy in an organized way, the DOT groups jobs into "occupations" based on their similarities and defines the structure and content of all listed occupations. Occupational definitions are the result of comprehensive studies of how similar jobs are performed in establishments across the nation and are composites of data collected from diverse sources. The term "occupation," as used in the DOT, refers to this collective description of a number of individual jobs performed, with minor variations, in many establishments.

There are seven basic parts to an occupational definition found in the DOT. Three of these are included here in the *Worker Traits* database, including the occupational code number, the occupational title, and the industry designation.

The first item in an occupational definition is the 9-digit DOT occupational code. In the DOT occupational classification system, each set of three digits has a specific purpose or meaning. Together, they provide a unique identification code for a particular occupation which differentiates it from all others.

Occupational Categories: The First Three DOT Numbers

The first three digits of the DOT occupational code number identify a particular occupational group. All occupations are clustered into one of nine broad "categories" (first digit), such as professional, technical and managerial, or clerical and sales occupations. These categories break down into 83 occupationally-specific "divisions" (the first two digits), such as occupations in architecture and engineering within the professional category, or stenography, typing, and related occupations in the clerical and sales category. Divisions, in turn, are divided into small, homogeneous "groups" (the first three digits). The DOT identifies 564 such groups. The nine primary occupational categories are listed below:

0/1	**Professional, Technical, and Managerial Occupations**
2	**Clerical and Sales Occupations**
3	**Service Occupations**
4	**Agricultural, Fishery, Forestry, and Related Occupations**
5	**Processing Occupations**
6	**Machine Trades Occupations**
7	**Benchwork Occupations**
8	**Structural Work Occupations**
9	**Miscellaneous Occupations**

As an example, in DOT number 652.382-010 **CLOTH PRINTER (any industry)**, the first digit (6) indicates that this particular occupation is found in the category "Machine Trades Occupations."

The second digit refers to a division within that category. The divisions within the "Machine Trades Occupations" category are as follows:

60	**Metal Machining Occupations**
61	**Metalworking Occupations, n.e.c.**
62/63	**Mechanics and Machinery Repairers**
64	**Paperworking Occupations**
65	**Printing Occupations**
66	**Wood Machining Occupations**
67	**Occupations in Machining Stone, Clay, Glass, and Related Materials**
68	**Textile Occupations**
69	**Machine Trades Occupations, n.e.c.**

Note: Some divisions or groups end in the designation "n.e.c." (not elsewhere classified). This indicates that the occupations do not logically fit into precisely defined divisions or groups, or that they could fit into two or more of them equally well.

In the example, 652.382-010 **CLOTH PRINTER (any industry)**, the second digit (5) locates the occupation in the "Printing Occupations" division.

The third digit defines the occupational group within the division. The groups within the "Printing Occupations" division are as follows:

650	**Typesetters and Composers**
651	**Printing Press Occupations**
652	**Printing Machine Occupations**
653	**Bookbinding-Machine Operators and Related Occupations**
654	**Typecasters and Related Occupations**
659	**Printing Occupations, n.e.c.**

In the example, the third digit (2) locates the occupation in the "Printing Machine Occupations" group.

Note: For a listing of all occupational categories, divisions, and groups see Appendix A.

Worker Functions: The Middle Three DOT Numbers

The middle three digits of the DOT occupational code are the Worker Functions ratings of the tasks performed in the occupation. Every job requires a worker functioning to some degree in relation to data, to people, and to things. A separate digit expresses the worker's relationship to each of these three groups:

Data (4th Digit)	**People** (5th Digit)	**Things** (6th Digit)
0 Synthesizing	0 Mentoring	0 Setting Up
1 Coordinating	1 Negotiating	1 Precision Working
2 Analyzing	2 Instructing	2 Operating-Controlling
3 Compiling	3 Supervising	3 Driving-Operating
4 Computing	4 Diverting	4 Manipulating
5 Copying	5 Persuading	5 Tending
6 Comparing	6 Speaking-Signaling	6 Feeding-Off Bearing
	7 Serving	7 Handling
	8 Taking Instruction-Helping	

As a general rule, Worker Functions involving more complex responsibility and judgment are assigned lower numbers in these three lists while functions which are less complicated have higher numbers. For example, "synthesizing" and "coordinating" data are more complex tasks than "copying" data; "instructing" people involves a broader responsibility than "taking instructions-helping;" and "operating" things is a more complicated task than "handling" things.

The Worker Functions code in the example (382) relates to the middle three digits of the DOT occupational code number (352.382-010) and has a different meaning with no connection with group code 652 (the first three digits).

The Worker Functions code (382) may be found in any occupational group. It signifies that the worker is "compiling" (3) in relation to data; "taking instructions-helping" (8) in relation to people; and "operating-controlling" (2) in relation to things. The Worker Functions code indicates the broadest level of responsibility or judgment required in relation to data, people, or things. It is assumed that, if the job requires it, the worker can generally perform any higher-numbered function listed in each of the three categories.

Definitions of Worker Functions

DATA: Information, knowledge, and conceptions; related to data, people, or things obtained by observation, investigation, interpretation, visualization, and mental creation. Data are intangible and include numbers, words, symbols, ideas, concepts, and oral verbalization.

0—Synthesizing: Integrating analyses of data to discover facts and/or develop knowledge concepts or interpretations.

1—Coordinating: Determining time, place, and/or sequence of operations or action to be taken on the basis of analysis of data; executing determinations and/or reporting on events.

2—Analyzing: Examining and evaluating data. Presenting alternative actions in relation to the evaluation is frequently involved.

3—Compiling: Gathering, collating, or classifying information about data, people, or things. Reporting and/or carrying out a prescribed action in relation to the information is frequently involved.

4—Computing: Performing arithmetic operations and reporting on and/or carrying out a prescribed action in relation to them. Does not include counting.

5—Copying: Transcribing, entering, or posting data.

6—Comparing: Judging the readily observable functional, structural, or compositional characteristics (whether similar to or divergent from obvious standards) of data, people, or things.

PEOPLE: Human beings; also animals dealt with on an individual basis as if they were human.

0—Mentoring: Dealing with individuals in terms of their total personality in order to advise, counsel, and/or guide them with regard to problems that may be resolved by legal, scientific, clinical, spiritual, and/or other professional principles.

1—Negotiating: Exchanging ideas, information, and opinions with others to formulate policies and programs and/or arrive jointly at decisions, conclusions, or solutions.

2—Instructing: Teaching subject matter to others, or training others (including animals) through explanation, demonstration, and supervised practice; or making recommendations on the basis of technical disciplines.

3—Supervising: Determining or interpreting work procedures for a group of workers, assigning specific duties to them, maintaining harmonious relations among them, and promoting efficiency. A variety of responsibilities is involved in this function.

4—Diverting: Amusing others, usually through the medium of stage, screen, television, or radio.

5—Persuading: Influencing others in favor of a product, service, or point of view.

6—Speaking-Signaling: Talking with and/or signaling people to convey or exchange information. Includes giving assignments and/or directions to helpers or assistants.

7—Serving: Attending to the needs or requests of people or animals or the expressed or implicit wishes of people. Immediate response is involved.

8—Taking Instructions-Helping: Attending to the work assignment, instructions, or orders of supervisor. (No immediate response required unless clarification of instructions or orders is needed.) Helping applies to "non-learning" helpers.

THINGS: Inanimate objects as distinguished from human beings, substances or materials; and machines, tools, equipment, work aids, and products. A thing is tangible and has shape, form, and other physical characteristics.

0—Setting Up: Preparing machines (or equipment) for operation by planning order of successive machine operations, installing and adjusting tools and other machine components, adjusting the position of workpiece or material, setting controls, and verifying accuracy of machine capabilities, properties of materials, and shop practices. Uses tools, equipment, and work aids, such as precision gauges and measuring instruments. Workers who set up one or a number of machines for other workers or who set up and personally operate a variety of machines are included here.

1—Precision Working: Using body members and/or tools or work aids to work, move, guide, or place objects or materials in situations where ultimate responsibility for the attainment of standards occurs and selection of appropriate tools, objects, or materials, and the adjustment of the tool to the task requires the exercise of considerable judgment.

2—Operating-Controlling: Starting, stopping, controlling, and adjusting the progress of machines or equipment. Operating machines involves setting up and adjusting the machine or material(s) as the work progresses. Controlling involves observing gauges, dials, etc., and turning valves and other devices to regulate factors such as temperature, pressure, flow of liquids, speed of pumps, and reactions of materials.

3—Driving-Operating: Starting, stopping, and controlling the actions of machines or equipment for which a course must be steered or which must be guided to control the movement of things or people for a variety of purposes. Involves such activities as observing gauges and dials, estimating distances and determining speed and direction of other objects, turning cranks and wheels, and pushing or pulling gear lifts or levers. Includes such machines as cranes, conveyor systems, tractors, furnace-charging machines, paving machines, and hoisting machines. Excludes manually powered machines, such as handtrucks and dollies, and power-assisted machines, such as electric wheelbarrows and handtrucks.

4—Manipulating: Using body members, tools, or special devices to work, move, guide, or place objects or materials. Involves some latitude for judgment with regard to precision attained and selecting appropriate tool, object, or material, although this is readily manifest.

5—Tending: Starting, stopping, and observing the functioning of machines and equipment. Involves adjusting materials or controls of the machine, such as changing guides, adjusting timers and temperature gauges, turning valves to allow the flow of materials, and flipping switches in response to lights. Little judgment is involved in making these adjustments.

6—Feeding-Off Bearing: Inserting, throwing, dumping, or placing materials in or removing them from machines or equipment which are automatic or tended or operated by other workers.

7—Handling: Using body members, handtools, and/or special devices to work, move, or carry objects or materials. Involves little or no latitude for judgment with regard to attainment of standards or in selecting appropriate tools, objects, or materials.

Occupational Differentiations: The Last Three DOT Numbers

The last three digits of the occupational code number serve to differentiate a particular occupation from all others. A number of occupations may have the same first six digits, but no two can have the same nine digits. If a 6-digit code is applicable to only one occupational title, the final three digits assigned are always 010 (as in the example). If there is more than one occupation with the same first six digits, the final three digits are usually assigned in alphabetical order of titles in multiples of four (010, 014, 018, 022, etc.). If another printing machine occupation had the same six digits as **CLOTH PRINTER (any industry)** 652.382-010, and began with the letter "D," it would be assigned the occupational code 652.382-014. In order to minimize the number of changes made to the existing occupational classification structure, "new" occupations added to the DOT since the publication of the fourth edition have simply been added sequentially following the previous last entry for each of the 6-digit codes. The full nine digits thus provide each occupation with a unique code suitable for computerized operations.

Base Title

Immediately following the occupational code in every definition is the occupational base title. The base title is always in upper-case boldface letters. It is the most common type of title found in the DOT, and is the title by which the occupation is known in the majority of establishments in which it was found. In the example, **CLOTH PRINTER (any industry)** 652.382-010, "**CLOTH PRINTER**" is a base title.

Industry Designation

The industry designation is in parentheses immediately following the occupational base title. It often differentiates between two or more occupations with identical titles but different duties. Because of this, it is an integral and inseparable part of any occupational title. An industry designation often tells one or more things about an occupation such as:

- location of the occupation (hotel & rest.; machine shop)
- types of duties associated with the occupation (education; forging)
- products manufactured (optical goods; textile)
- processes used (electroplating; petrol. refin.)
- raw materials used (nonfer. metal; stonework)

While a definition usually receives the designation of the industry or industries in which it occurs, certain occupations occur in a large number of industries. When this happens, the industry assigned is a cross-industry designation. For example, clerical occupations are found in almost every industry. To show the broad, cross-industry nature of clerical occupations, "clerical" is an industry designation in itself. Among other cross-industry designations are: "profess. & kin.," "machine shop," and "woodworking."

Occupations which characteristically occur in nearly all industries, or which occur in a number of industries, but not in most industries and which are not considered to have any particular industrial attachment, are assigned the designation of "any industry." The job title in the example is assigned this designation. It should always be identified as **CLOTH PRINTER (any industry)** 652.382-010.

In compiling information for the DOT, analysts were not able to study each occupation in all industries where it occurs. The industry designation, therefore, shows in what industries the occupation was studied but does not mean that it may not be found in others. Therefore, industry designations are to be regarded as indicative of industrial location, but not necessarily restrictive.

Training Time (GED and SVP)

For the purpose of rating jobs, Training Time is defined as the amount of General Educational Development (GED) and Specific Vocational Preparation (SVP) required of a worker to acquire the knowledge and abilities necessary for average performance in a particular job-worker situation. In the data display, the first three numbers refer to the GED divisions of Reasoning, Math, and Language, and the last number reflects the SVP code.

General Educational Development Scale (GED)

GED embraces those aspects of education (formal and informal) which contribute to the worker's (a) reasoning development and ability to follow instructions, and (b) acquisition of "tool" knowledge such as language and mathematical skills. This education is of a general nature which does not have a recognized, fairly specific occupational objective. Ordinarily, such education is obtained in elementary school, high school, or college. However, it derives also from experience and self-study.

The GED Scale comprises three divisions: Reasoning Development, Mathematical Development, and Language Development. The description of the various levels of language and mathematical development are based on the curricula taught in schools throughout the United States. An analysis of mathematics courses in school curricula reveals distinct levels of progression in the primary and secondary grades and in college. These levels of progression facilitated the selection and assignment of six levels of GED for the mathematical development scale.

However, though language courses follow a similar pattern of progression in primary and secondary school, particularly in learning and applying the principles of grammar, this pattern changes at the college level. The diversity of language courses offered at the college level precludes the establishment of distinct levels of language progression for these four years. Consequently, language development is limited to five defined levels of GED since levels 5 and 6 share a common definition even though they are distinct levels.

Reasoning Development

Level 6: Apply principles of logical or scientific thinking to a wide range of intellectual and practical problems. Deal with nonverbal symbolism (formulas, scientific equations, graphs, musical notes, etc.) in its most difficult phases. Deal with a variety of abstract and concrete variables. Apprehend the most abstruse classes of concepts.

Level 5: Apply principles of logical or scientific thinking to define problems, collect data, establish facts, and draw valid conclusions. Interpret an extensive variety of technical instructions in mathematical or diagrammatic form. Deal with several abstract and concrete variables.

Level 4: Apply principles of rational systems* to solve practical problems and deal with a variety of concrete variables in situations where only limited standardization exists. Interpret a variety of instructions furnished in written, oral, diagrammatic, or schedule form. (*Examples of rational systems are: bookkeeping, internal combustion engines, electric wiring systems, house building, farm management, and navigation.)

Level 3: Apply commonsense understanding to carry out instructions furnished in written, oral, or diagrammatic form. Deal with problems involving several concrete variables in or from standardized situations.

Level 2: Apply commonsense understanding to carry out detailed but uninvolved written or oral instructions. Deal with problems involving a few concrete variables in or from standardized situations.

Level 1: Apply commonsense understanding to carry out simple one- or two-step instructions. Deal with standardized situations with occasional or no variables in or from these situations encountered on the job.

Mathematical Development

Level 6: *Advanced calculus:* Work with limits, continuity, real number systems, mean value theorems, and implicit function theorems.
Modern algebra: Apply fundamental concepts of theories of groups, rings, and fields. Work with differential equations, linear algebra, infinite series, advanced operations methods, and functions of real and complex variables.
Statistics: Work with mathematical statistics, mathematical probability and applications, experimental design, statistical inference, and econometrics.

Level 5: *Algebra:* Work with exponents and logarithms, linear equations, quadratic equations, mathematical induction and binomial theorem, and permutations.
Calculus: Apply concepts of analytic geometry, differentiations, and integration of algebraic functions with applications.
Statistics: Apply mathematical operations to frequency distributions, reliability and validity of tests, normal curve, analysis of variance, correlation techniques, chi-square application and sampling theory, and factor analysis.

Level 4: *Algebra:* Deal with systems of real numbers; linear, quadratic, rational, exponential, logarithmic, angle and circular functions, and inverse functions; related algebraic solution of equations and inequalities; limits and continuity; and probability and statistical inference.
Geometry: Deductive axiomatic geometry, plane and solid, and rectangular coordinates.
Shop Math: Practical application of fractions, percentages, ratio and proportion, measurement, logarithms, practical algebra, geometric construction, and essentials of trigonometry.

Level 3: Compute discount, interest, profit, and loss; commission, markup, and selling price; ratio and proportion; and percentage. Calculate surfaces, volumes, weights, and measures.
Algebra: Calculate variables and formulas; monomials and polynomials; ratio and proportion variables; and square roots and radicals.
Geometry: Calculate plane and solid figures, circumference, area, and volume. Understand kinds of angles and properties of pairs of angles.

Level 2: Add, subtract, multiply, and divide all units of measure. Perform the four operations with like common and decimal fractions. Compute ratio, rate, and percent. Draw and interpret bar graphs. Perform arithmetic operations involving all American monetary units.

Level 1: Add and subtract two-digit numbers. Multiply and divide 10's and 100's by 2, 3, 4, and 5. Perform the four basic arithmetic operations with coins as part of a dollar. Perform operations with units such as cup, pint, and quart; inch, foot, and yard; and ounce and pound.

Language Development

Level 6: Same as Level 5.

Level 5: *Reading:* Read literature, book and play reviews, scientific and technical journals, abstracts, financial reports, and legal documents.
Writing: Write novels, plays, editorials, journals, speeches, manuals, critiques, poetry, and songs.
Speaking: Conversant in the theory, principles, and methods of effective and persuasive speaking, voice and diction, phonetics, and discussion and debate.

Level 4: *Reading:* Read novels, poems, newspapers, periodicals, journals, manuals, dictionaries, thesauruses, and encyclopedias.
Writing: Prepare business letters, expositions, summaries, and reports, using prescribed format and conforming to all rules of punctuation, grammar, diction, and style.
Speaking: Participate in panel discussions, dramatizations, and debates. Speak extemporaneously on a variety of subjects.

Level 3: *Reading:* Read a variety of novels, magazines, atlases, and encyclopedias. Read safety rules, instructions in the use and maintenance of shop tools and equipment, and methods and procedures in mechanical drawing and layout work.
Writing: Write reports and essays with proper format, punctuation, spelling, and grammar, using all parts of speech.
Speaking: Speak before an audience with poise, voice control, and confidence, using correct English and well-modulated voice.

Level 2: *Reading:* Passive vocabulary of 5,000 to 6,000 words. Read at a rate of 190 to 215 words per minute. Read adventure stories and comic books, looking up unfamiliar words in dictionary for meaning, spelling, and pronunciation. Read instructions for assembling model cars and airplanes.
Writing: Write compound and complex sentences, using cursive style, proper end punctuation, and employing adjectives and adverbs.
Speaking: Speak clearly and distinctly with appropriate pauses and emphasis, correct punctuation, variations in word order, using present, perfect, and future tenses.

Level 1: *Reading:* Recognize meaning of 2,500 (two- or three-syllable) words. Read at rate of 95 to 120 words per minute. Compare similarities and differences between words and between series of numbers.
Writing: Print simple sentences containing subject, verb, and object, and series of numbers, names, and addresses.
Speaking: Speak simple sentences, using normal word order, and present and past tenses.

Specific Vocational Preparation Scale (SVP)

SVP is the amount of time required to learn the techniques, acquire the information, and develop the facility needed for average performance in a specific job-worker situation. This training may be acquired in a school, work, military, institutional, or vocational environment. It does not include the orientation or training required of a fully-qualified worker to become accustomed to the special conditions of any new job. Specific vocational preparation includes:

- **Vocational Education:** High school commercial or shop training, technical school, art school, and part of college training which is organized around a specific vocational objective.
- **Apprenticeship Training:** Training obtained only in those jobs offering apprenticeships.
- **In Plant Training:** Training given by employer in form of organized class room study.

- **On-the-Job Training:** Instruction given to learner or trainee on the job by a qualified worker.
- **Essential Experience in Other Jobs:** Experience received in less responsible jobs or other job which qualifies for a higher grade job.

The following is an explanation of the various levels of specific vocational preparation:

Level 1: Short demonstration only

Level 2: Anything beyond short demonstration up to and including 1 month

Level 3: Over 1 month up to and including 3 months

Level 4: Over 3 months up to and including 6 months

Level 5: Over 6 months up to and including 1 year

Level 6: Over 1 year up to and including 2 years

Level 7: Over 2 years up to and including 4 years

Level 8: Over 4 years up to and including 10 years

Level 9: Over 10 years

Note: The levels of this scale are mutually exclusive and do not overlap.

Aptitudes

Aptitudes are the capacities or specific abilities which an individual must have in order to learn to perform a given work activity. In the Worker Traits Data Display there are 11 aptitudes, each identified by a code letter. Below are the codes and definitions:

G—General Learning Ability: The ability to "catch on" or understand instructions and underlying principles; the ability to reason, and make judgments. Closely related to doing well in school.

V—Verbal Aptitude: The ability to understand the meaning of words and to use them effectively. The ability to understand relationships between words and to understand the meaning of whole sentences and paragraphs.

N—Numerical Aptitude: The ability to perform arithmetic operations quickly and accurately.

S—Spatial Aptitude: The ability to think visually of geometric forms and to comprehend the two-dimensional representation of three-dimensional objects. The ability to recognize the relationships resulting from the movement of objects in space.

P—Form Perception: The ability to perceive pertinent detail in objects or in pictorial or graphic material. Ability to make visual comparisons and discriminations and see slight differences in shapes and shading of figures and widths and lengths of lines.

Q—Clerical Perception: The ability to perceive detail in verbal or tabular material. Ability to observe differences in copy, to proofread words and numbers, and to avoid perceptual errors in arithmetic computation. A measure of speed of perception is required in many industrial jobs even when the job does not have verbal or numerical content.

K—Motor Coordination: The ability to coordinate eyes and hands or fingers rapidly and accurately in making precise movements with speed. Ability to make movement response accurately and swiftly.

F—Finger Dexterity: The ability to move fingers, and manipulate small objects with fingers, rapidly or accurately.

M—Manual Dexterity: The ability to move hands easily and skillfully. Ability to work with hands in placing and turning motions.

E—Eye-Hand-Foot Coordination: Ability to move the hand and foot coordinately with each other in accordance with visual stimuli.

C—Color Discrimination: The ability to match or discriminate between colors in terms of hue, saturation, and brilliance. Ability to identify a particular color or color combination from memory and be able to perceive harmonious or contrasting color combinations.

Aptitude Levels

Each job in the data display is rated on all eleven aptitudes in the same order presented here. The levels reflect the amount of the aptitude possessed by segments of the working population. Each level is assigned a code number ranging from 1 (the highest) to 5 (the lowest) as follows:

1—The top 10 percent of the population. This segment of the population possesses an extremely high degree of the aptitude.

2—The highest third, exclusive of the top 10 percent of the population. This segment of the population possesses an above average or high degree of the aptitude.

3—The middle third of the population. This segment of the population possesses a medium degree of the aptitude ranging from slightly below to slightly above.

4—The lowest third exclusive of the bottom 10 percent of the population. This segment of the population possesses a below average or low degree of the aptitude.

5—The lowest 10 percent of the population. This segment of the population possesses a negligible degree of the aptitude.

Physical Demands

The Physical Demands Strength Rating reflects the estimated overall strength requirement of the job, expressed in terms of a letter corresponding to the particular strength rating. It represents the strength requirements which are considered to be important for average, successful work performance.

1. **Strength:** The first number in the strength rating is expressed by one of five terms: Sedentary, Light, Medium, Heavy, or Very Heavy. In order to determine the overall rating, an evaluation is made of the worker's involvement in the following activities:

   Standing, Walking, Sitting

   Standing—Remaining on one's feet in an upright position at a work station without moving about.
   Walking—Moving about on foot.
   Sitting—Remaining in a seated position.

   Lifting, Carrying, Pushing, Pulling

   Lifting—Raising or lowering an object from one level to another (includes upward pulling).
   Carrying—Transporting an object, usually holding it in the hands or arms, or on the shoulder.
   Pushing—Exerting force upon an object so that the object moves away from the force (includes slapping, striking, kicking, and treadle actions).
   Pulling—Exerting force upon an object so that the object moves toward the force (includes jerking).

Lifting, pushing, and pulling are evaluated in terms of both intensity and duration. Consideration is given to the weight handled, position of the worker's body, and the aid given by helpers or mechanical equipment. Carrying most often is evaluated in terms of duration, weight carried, and distance carried.

Estimating the Strength Factor rating for an occupation requires the exercise of care on the part of occupational analysts in evaluating the force and physical effort a worker must exert. For instance, if the worker is in a crouching position it may be much more difficult to push an object than if pushed at waist height. Also, if the worker is required to lift and carry continuously or push and pull objects over long distances, the worker may exert as much physical effort as is required to similarly move objects twice as heavy, but less frequently and/or over shorter distances.

Controls

Controls entail the use of one or both hands or arms (hand/arm) and/or one or both feet or legs (foot/leg) to move controls on machinery or equipment. Controls include but are not limited to buttons, knobs, pedals, levers, and cranks.

Strength Ratings Codes

Following are descriptions of the five terms in which the Strength Factor is expressed:

- **S—Sedentary Work:** Exerting up to 10 pounds of force occasionally. (Occasionally: activity or condition exists up to 1/3 of the time) and/or a negligible amount of force frequently (Frequently: activity or condition from 1/3 to 2/3 of the time) to lift, carry, push, pull, or otherwise move objects, including the human body. Sedentary work involves sitting most of the time, but may involve walking or standing for brief periods of time. Jobs are sedentary if walking and standing are required only occasionally and all other sedentary criteria are met.

- **L—Light Work:** Exerting up to 20 pounds of force occasionally, and/or up to 10 pounds of force frequently, and/or a negligible amount of force constantly. (Constantly: activity or condition exists 2/3 or more of the time) to move objects. Physical demand requirements are in excess of those for Sedentary Work. Even though the weight lifted may be only a negligible amount, a job should be rated Light Work: (1) when it requires walking or standing to a significant degree; or (2) when it requires sitting most of the time but entails pushing and/or pulling of arm or leg controls; and/or (3) when the job requires working at a production rate pace entailing the constant pushing and/or pulling of materials even though the weight of those materials is negligible.

Note: The constant stress and strain of maintaining a production rate pace, especially in an industrial setting, can be and is physically demanding of a worker even though the amount of force exerted is negligible.

- **M—Medium Work:** Exerting 20 to 50 pounds of force occasionally, and/or 10 to 25 pounds of force frequently, and/or greater than negligible up to 10 pounds of force constantly to move objects. Physical demand requirements are in excess of those for Light Work.

- **H—Heavy Work:** Exerting 50 to 100 pounds of force occasionally, and/or 25 to 50 pounds of force frequently, and/or 10 to 20 pounds of force constantly to move objects. Physical demand requirements are in excess of those for Medium Work.

- **V—Very Heavy Work:** Exerting in excess of 100 pounds of force occasionally, and/or in excess of 50 pounds of force frequently, and/or in excess of 20 pounds of force constantly to move objects. Physical demand requirements are in excess of those for Heavy Work.

Other Physical Demands Ratings Codes

All other physical demand factors, those numbered from 2 to 20, are coded with a letter that represents the presence and frequency of the activity in the work situation as follows:

N	**Not present**— Activitydoes not exist	
O	**Occasionally**—Activity exists up to one-third of the time	
F	**Frequently**—Activity exists from one-third to two thirds of the time	
C	**Continuously**—Activity exists two thirds or more of the time	

Note: The letters below correspond to the number arrangement in the data display.

2. **Climbing:** Ascending or descending ladders, stairs, scaffolding, ramps, poles, and the like, using feet and legs or hands and arms. Body agility is emphasized.

3. **Balancing:** Maintaining body equilibrium to prevent falling when walking, standing, crouching, or running on narrow, slippery, or erratically moving surfaces; or maintaining body equilibrium when performing gymnastic feats.

4. **Stooping:** Bending body downward and forward by bending spine at the waist, requiring full use of the lower extremities and back muscles.

5. **Kneeling:** Bending legs at knees to rest on knee or knees.

6. **Crouching:** Bending body downward and forward by bending legs and spine.

7. **Crawling:** Moving about on hands and knees or hands and feet.

8. **Reaching:** Extending hand(s) and arm(s) in any direction.

9. **Handling:** Seizing, holding, grasping, turning or otherwise working with hand or hands. Fingers are involved only to the extent that they are an extension of the hand, such as to turn a switch or shift automobile gears.

10. **Fingering:** Picking, pinching, or otherwise working primarily with fingers rather than with the whole hand or arm as in handling.

11. **Feeling:** Perceiving attributes of objects, such as size, shape, temperature, or texture, by touching with skin, particularly that of fingertips.

12. **Talking:** Expressing or exchanging ideas by means of the spoken word to impart oral information to clients or to the public and to convey detailed spoken instructions to other workers accurately, loudly, or quickly.

13. **Hearing:** Perceiving the nature of sounds by ear.

14. **Tasting/Smelling:** Distinguishing, with a degree of accuracy, differences or similarities in intensity or quality of flavors or odors, or recognizing particular flavors or odors, using tongue or nose.

15. **Near Acuity:** Clarity of vision at 20 inches or less.

16. **Far Acuity:** Clarity of vision at 20 feet or more.

17. **Depth Perception:** Three-dimensional vision. Ability to judge distances and spatial relationships so as to see objects where and as they actually are.

18. **Accommodation:** Adjustment of lens of eye to bring an object into sharp focus. This factor is required when doing near point work at varying distances from the eye.

19. **Color Vision:** Ability to identify and distinguish colors.

20. **Field of Vision:** Observing an area that can be seen up and down or to right or left while eyes are fixed on a given point.

Environmental Conditions

All environmental condition factors, except number 5, Noise Intensity Level, are coded with a letter that represents the presence and frequency of the condition in the work situation as follows:

N   **Not present**—Condition does not exist
O   **Occasionally**—Condition exists up to one-third of the time
F   **Frequently**—Condition exists from one-third to two thirds of the time
C   **Continuously**—Condition exists two thirds or more of the time

Note: The letters below correspond to the number arrangement in the data display.

1. **Exposure to Weather:** Exposure to outside atmospheric conditions.

2. **Extreme Cold:** Exposure to nonweather-related cold temperatures.

3. **Extreme Heat:** Exposure to nonweather-related hot temperatures.

4. **Wet and/or Humid:** Contact with water or other liquids or exposure to nonweather-related humid conditions.

5. **Noise Intensity Level:** The noise intensity level to which the worker is exposed in the job environment. This factor is expressed by one of five levels. They are:
   - Very Quiet
   - Quiet
   - Moderate
   - Loud
   - Very Loud

6. **Vibration:** Exposure to a shaking object or surface.

7. **Atmospheric Conditions:** Exposure to conditions such as fumes, noxious odors, dusts, mists, gases, and poor ventilation, that affect the respiratory system, eyes, or skin.

8. **Proximity to Moving Mechanical Parts:** Exposure to possible bodily injury from moving mechanical parts of equipment, tools, or machinery.

9. **Exposure to Electrical Shock:** Exposure to possible bodily injury from electrical shock.

10. **Working in High, Exposed Places:** Exposure to possible bodily injury from falling.

11. **Exposure to Radiation:** Exposure to possible bodily harm from radiation.

12. **Working with Explosives:** Exposure to possible injury from explosions.

13. **Exposure to Toxic or Caustic Chemicals:** Exposure to possible bodily injury from toxic or caustic chemicals.

14. **Other Environmental Conditions:** Other conditions not defined above.

Temperaments

Temperaments are the adaptability requirements imposed on the worker by specific types of jobs. Different jobs or job situations call for different personality traits on the part of the worker. The degree to which a worker can adapt to work situations is often a determining factor in success. A person's dissatisfaction or failure to perform adequately can sometimes be attributed to an inability to adapt to a work situation rather than to an inability to learn and carry out job duties.

Jobs are rated on each of 11 temperament factors. If the factor is considered an important job attribute a code letter for the temperament is assigned. There is no rating indicating degree or level of importance or significance. All occupations in the data display have a least one significant temperament factor and may have as many as five.

D—DIRECTING, Controlling or Planning Activities of Others: Involves accepting responsibility for formulating plans, designs, practices, policies, methods, regulations, and procedures for operations or projects; negotiating with individuals or groups for agreements or contracts; and supervising subordinate workers to implement plans and control activities.

R—Performing REPETITIVE or Short-Cycle Work: Involves performing a few routine and uninvolved tasks over and over again according to set procedures, sequence, or pace with little opportunity for diversion or interruption. Interaction with people is included when it is routine, continual, or prescribed.

I—INFLUENCING People in their Opinions, Attitudes, and Judgments: Involves writing demonstrating, or speaking to persuade and motivate people to change their attitudes or opinions, participate in a particular activity, or purchase a specific commodity or service.

V—Performing a VARIETY of Duties: Involves frequent changes of tasks involving different aptitudes, technologies, techniques, procedures, working conditions, physical demands, or degrees of attentiveness without loss of efficiency or composure.

E—EXPRESSING Personal Feelings: Involves creativity and self-expression in interpreting feelings, ideas, or facts in terms of a personal viewpoint; treating a subject imaginatively rather than literally; reflecting original ideas or feelings in writing, painting, composing, sculpting, decorating, or inventing; or interpreting works of others by arranging, conducting, playing musical instruments, choreographing, acting, directing, critiquing, or editorializing.

A—Working ALONE or Apart in Physical Isolation from Others: Involves working in an environment that regularly precludes face- to-face interpersonal relationships for extended periods of time due to physical barriers or distances involved.

S—Performing Effectively Under STRESS: Involves coping with circumstances dangerous to the worker or others.

T—Attaining Precise Set Limits, TOLERANCES, and Standards: Involves adhering to and achieving exact levels of performance, using precision measuring instruments, tools, and machines to attain precise dimensions; preparing exact verbal and numerical records; and complying with precise instruments and specifications for materials, methods, procedures, and techniques to attain specified standards.

U—Working UNDER Specific Instructions: Performing tasks only under specific instructions, allowing little or no room for independent action or judgment in working out job problems.

P—Dealing with PEOPLE: Involves interpersonal relationships in job situations beyond receiving work instructions.

J—Making JUDGMENTS and Decisions: Involves solving problems, making evaluations, or reaching conclusions based on subjective or objective criteria, such as the five senses, knowledge, past experience, or quantifiable or factual data.

Work Fields

Work Fields are categories of technologies that reflect how work gets done and what gets done as a result of the work activities of a job: the purpose of the job. There are 96 Work Fields in the data display. These range from the specific to the general and are organized into homogenous groups, based on related technologies or objectives, such as the movement of materials, the fabrication of products, the use of data, and the provision of services. Appendix C, Work Field Codes and Titles, provides a listing of these codes.

Materials, Products, Subject Matter, and Services

Materials, Products, Subject Matter, and Services (MPSMS) refers to the objects or outcomes of Work Field activities. Examples include bread, botany, logs, and records. The Department of Labor has identified 386 such categories. Appendix D, Materials, Products, Subject Matter, and Services Codes and Titles, provides a listing of these codes. Titles, definitions, and three-digit codes also may be found in *The Revised Handbook for Analyzing Jobs* (HAJ), published by the U.S. Department of Labor.

Interests (GOE Code Numbers)

An interest is a tendency to become absorbed in an experience and to continue it, according to the U.S. Department of Labor (DOL), which has developed a schema classifying all jobs in terms of 12 interest areas. The 12 Interest Areas are: Artistic, Scientific, Plants and Animals, Protective, Mechanical, Industrial, Business Detail, Selling, Accommodating, Humanitarian, Leading-Influencing, and Physical Performing. These categories make use of some of the widely used Holland Personality typology. Details of this system can be found in a variety of sources including *A Theory of Occupational Choice* by John Holland, Ph.D. The DOL further subdivides the interest areas into work groups and subgroups identified by 6-digit numbers (for example, 06.04.38, Wrapping and Packaging). There are a total of 353 subgroups. This classification system was developed by the U.S. Department of Labor, U.S. Employment Service, and described in the *Guide for Occupational Exploration* (GOE), first published in 1979. This book organizes over 12,000 occupations within the 12 Interest Areas, Work Groups, and Subgroups. More recent books using the same organizational structure but based on jobs listed in the 1991 DOT include *The Complete Guide for Occupational Exploration* (CGOE), 1993, and *The Enhanced Guide for Occupational Exploration* (EGOE), 1992, both published by JIST Works, Inc.

The Guide for Occupational Exploration (GOE) Code Number

Many youths and other jobseekers are unprepared for an effective job search because they lack the knowledge about the kinds of jobs to look for. They have difficulty relating their interests, skills, and potentials to appropriate occupations. To be effective, vocational counselors must have sufficient information to match an individual's interest, temperaments, potential, ability and other personal traits to specific career fields and work requirements.

The *Guide for Occupational Exploration* (GOE) was designed by the U.S. Employment Service to provide career counselors and other *Dictionary of Occupational Titles* (DOT) users with additional information about the interests, aptitudes, entry level preparation, and other traits required for successful performance in various occupations. The GOE, and it's later CGOE and EGOE revisions (described above), are also useful in self-assessment and counselor-assisted settings to help people understand themselves realistically in regard to their ability to meet job requirements. Descriptive information provided for each work group assists the individual in evaluating his or her own interests and relating them to pertinent fields of work.

The 6-digit GOE code assigned to a definition provides a link between the occupation defined and the GOE arrangement of occupations with similar interests, aptitudes, adaptability requirements, and other descriptors.

The GOE coding structure classifies jobs at three levels of consideration. The first level divides occupations according to 12 Interest Areas corresponding to interest factors identified through research conducted by the former Division of Testing in the U.S. Employment Service. The interest factors, identified by a 2-digit code, are defined in terms of broad interest requirements of occupations as well as vocational interests of individuals. This 2-digit code number is used in the first two digits of the GOE code. The 12 Interest Areas are defined as follows:

01—Artistic: An interest in the creative expression of feelings or ideas.

02—Scientific: An interest in discovering, collecting, and analyzing information about the natural world, and in applying scientific research findings to problems in medicine, the life sciences, and the natural sciences.

03—Plants and Animals: An interest in working with plants and animals, usually outdoors.

04—Protective: An interest in using authority to protect people and property.

05—Mechanical: An interest in applying mechanical principles to practical situations by the use of machines or hand tools.

06—Industrial: An interest in repetitive, concrete, organized activities done in a factory setting.

07—Business Detail: An interest in organized, clearly defined activities requiring accuracy and attention to details, primarily done in an office setting.

08—Selling: An interest in bringing others to a particular point of view by personal persuasion and promotional techniques.

09—Accommodating: An interest in catering to the wishes and needs of others, usually on a one-to-one basis.

10—Humanitarian: An interest in helping others with their mental, spiritual, social, physical, or vocational needs.

11—Leading-Influencing: An interest in leading and influencing others by using high-level verbal or numerical abilities.

12—Physical Performing: An interest in physical activities performed before an audience.

The interest areas are then subdivided into work groups (the second set of two digits within the 6-digit GOE code). Each work group contains occupations requiring similar worker traits and capabilities in related work settings. The GOE contains descriptive information for each work group and identifies each occupation in the group with a 4-digit code and title. In many interest areas, occupations that require the most education, training, and experience are in the first group, while those requiring less formal education or experience are listed in the last group.

Work groups are then subdivided into subgroups (the third 2-digit set in the GOE code) of occupations with even more homogeneous interests, aptitudes, and adaptability requirements. Each subgroup is identified by its unique 6-digit code and title. Individual occupations are listed alphabetically within subgroups. Some subgroups contain occupations from more than one industry, listed within alphabetized industries.

Appendix E, GOE Codes for Interest Areas, Work Groups and Subgroups and Titles, provides a complete listing of the GOE schema of Interest Areas, Work Groups and Subgroups.

The Occupational Codes (SOC, CIP, OES)

In addition to the DOT and GOE numbers there are several other systems of classifying occupations referenced in the data display. These are the Standard Occupational Classification code number (SOC), the Classification of Instructional Program code number (CIP), and the Occupational Employment Statistics code number (OES). Each of these code numbers provides a way of referencing other databases and other kinds of information about occupations. Complete listings of these codes are provided in appendices F, G, and H, respectively.

SECTION 2: Developing an Occupational Profile

At the end of this section is a form designed to collect information on the various worker trait data provided in this volume. Titled the "Worker Traits Profile," it was developed to record specific information about the one or more jobs that are of particular interest to you. This section will help you identify occupations and their DOT numbers for further consideration and use of the profile form.

As mentioned earlier, the bulk of this book consists of Section 3, the Worker Traits Data Display. This listing provides coded information on the more than 12,000 occupations described in the *Dictionary of Occupational Titles*. The goal of the Worker Traits Data Display is to help you better understand occupations and their job requirements. Whether you are considering a new career that you would like to train for, are helping a client who wants to change jobs, or writing a job description, you will usually be looking at occupations either one at a time or in small groups.

Finding the DOT Code Number

In using this book, then, your first step will be to find the occupation or occupations in the Worker Traits Data Display that interest you. To do this, you will need to know the *Dictionary of Occupational Titles* (DOT) code number because the data display is arranged numerically in DOT code order.

If you do not know the occupation's DOT code number, there are several ways of determining a DOT code: you can look it up in the alphabetical index of the DOT; you can find it through other listings in the DOT; you can find it in career exploration books like the GOE, EGOE, CGOE, or *Occupational Outlook Handbook*; you can obtain it from taking a career interest test or from some other source; or you can use a computerized guidance system.

Knowing an occupation's DOT code number is essential in using this volume since occupations are arranged by their DOT code number. We did not include an alphabetic listing of occupations in this book due to space limitations and because we felt that most users would only use this book in conjunction with another resource, such as the DOT, EGOE, or other source that provides occupational descriptions. In any case, you should have access to a DOT code number when you develop your occupational profile because you will need to read the description in the DOT carefully to be sure you understand the job associated with the DOT number and verify that is the job you have in mind.

Using the DOT Numbers in the Worker Traits Data Display

The DOT itself provides substantial information on how to identify various occupational titles. The information provided here is a basic overview of how to use the DOT; but you may require additional information from the DOT or other sources in order to better understand the DOT and how best to use it.

The Alphabetical Index of Occupational Titles in the DOT lists all the occupational titles found in the DOT. Descriptions of each of these occupations are located in the main section of the book, with occupations listed in numerical order by their DOT code number.

In the DOT description, the industry designation, which is part of the title, is included in parenthesis, followed by the 9-digit DOT number. Occupational titles with two or more words are treated as one word for purposes of alphabetizing. Three kinds of titles are intermixed in the alphabetic listing; these are base titles, always in upper-case boldface letters (**BASE TITLES**); alternate titles, always in lower-case letters (alternate titles); and undefined related titles, which are in lower-case letters with initial capitals (Undefined Related Titles).

The base title is the title by which the occupation is known in the majority of establishments in which it is found. Each base title is assigned a unique DOT number and is the title by which occupations are identified in the Worker Traits Data Display in this book.

An alternate title is a synonym for a base title. It is not used as commonly as the base title and it has the same code number and industry designation as its base title. Some occupations have large numbers of alternate titles, others have none.

Undefined related titles indicate a variation or specialization of a base occupation. They have the same DOT code as the base and resemble it, but differ enough to require their own unique title and explanatory phrase in the DOT. An unrelated title may have the same industry designation as the base title or it may have a different one. It will have the same DOT code as the base title, and hence be referenced under that code in the Worker Traits Data Display.

The following example from the DOT illustrates the three types of titles: Under base title **STOCK CLERK (clerical)** we find as alternate titles stock checker; stockroom clerk; storekeeper; storeroom clerk; storeroom keeper; stores clerk; supply clerk; and supply-room clerk. All these are simply variants on the base title and have the same industry designation—clerical. At the conclusion of the DOT definition is the comment, "May be designated according to material, equipment, or product stored as Camera-Storeroom Clerk (motion picture); Oil-House Attendant (clerical); Wire Stockkeeper (steel & rel.);" etc. [p. 202]. All these titles will appear in the proper alphabetic location in the DOT's index but all refer to the base title **STOCK CLERK** referenced under DOT number 222.387-058 in the Worker Traits Data Display.

Using the Alphabetical Index

Look through the DOT's alphabetical index for the title of the job as you know it. If you find it, write down the 9-digit code printed to the right of the title. Using this code as a guide, find the definition for the title in the major section of the DOT, the Occupational Group Arrangement. Read the entire definition before deciding whether it is the most appropriate classification.

If you cannot find the job title, or if the definition appears inappropriate, look for another title. Some clues for finding another title are:

1. **Invert the Title:** For example, "maintenance carpenter" is listed as CARPENTER, MAINTENANCE

2. **Contract the Title:** For example, rubber-belt repairer is listed as BELT REPAIRER

3. **Find a Synonym:** For example, car mechanic is listed as AUTOMOBILE MECHANIC

Also, consider such factors as:

4 **Job Location:** As in PARKING LOT ATTENDANT; STOREROOM CLERK

5. **Machines Used:** As in PUNCH-PRESS OPERATOR; MACHINE FEEDER

6. **Materials Used:** As in LOG LOADER; PLASTIC-TILE LAYER

7. **Subject Matter:** As in ACCOUNTING CLERK; CREDIT ANALYST

8. **Services Involved:** As in CLEANER AND PRESSER; BROKER

9. **Activity Performed:** As in TEACHER; INSPECTOR

10. **Job Complexity:** As in MACHINE SETTER; WELDING-MACHINE TENDER

Using the Occupational Group Arrangement

You can also find occupational code numbers by referring to the Occupational Group Arrangement shown in appendix A of this volume. Here are some suggestions for using that appendix:

Step 1. Find the 1-digit occupational category which seems most likely to contain the job.

Step 2. Find the 2-digit occupational division of the category that seems most likely to contain the job.

Step 3. Find the most likely 3-digit group within the division.

Step 4. Use the DOT to examine the occupational definition under the group you have selected and then choose the most appropriate title or titles. Carefully read the definition provided in the DOT or EGOE for the title selected before deciding if this is the best possible classification. If it does not correspond closely with the information you have collected, repeat Steps (1) to (3) to find the most appropriate classification.

In the process of choosing the appropriate occupational category, division, and group (Steps 1 through 3) you will develop information about the job which will be helpful in classifying it. When you are trying to find the most appropriate definition in the occupational group selected (Step 4), remember that jobs requiring more responsibility and independent judgment have lower worker functions numerals and will be found near the beginning of the occupational group, while those requiring less responsibility and independent judgment have higher numbers and will be found nearer the end.

Using the Worker Traits Profile Form

Once you have the DOT number of the occupation or occupations which interest you, the next step is to extract the desired data from the Worker Traits Data Display in Section 3. A convenient tool for doing this is the Worker Traits Profile (WTP) form found at the end of this section. Photocopies of this form can be made for the purpose of transcribing the data when using this book but please do not write on the original.

The Worker Traits Profile form provides space to enter data for several occupations at a time. This allows comparison from one job to another with regard to their worker traits. For example, a student engaged in career exploration could look at the similarities and differences between occupations they are considering. A person contemplating a career change could contrast their current job with a possible alternative job. A rehabilitation counselor could compare physical requirements of a pre-injury job title with post injury possibilities. The form, of course, can also be used to record data on a single occupation.

At the top of the form you can enter the job titles, DOT numbers and duties, and other details from the DOT's description. Be sure that you record the industry along with the title. You can also record other information such as salary and outlook that you may have obtained from sources such as the *Occupational Outlook Handbook*. The rest of the data comes from the Worker Traits Data Display in this book.

Using the form to transcribe data for DOT number 252.152-010 **TRAVEL AGENT (business ser.; motor trans.; retail trade)**, locate this entry, using the DOT number, in the Worker Traits Data Display of this volume. When looking at the coded data in the Worker Traits Data Display, note that the Worker Traits Profile collects information in the same sequence presented in the display.

You may need to refer to Section 1 to refresh your understanding of the various meanings for the codes mentioned here and used on the Worker Traits Profile form. The first three coded entries provided in the data display—Data, People, and Things—come, you may recall, from the fourth, fifth, and sixth numbers of the DOT code itself. Thus you would enter 1 for Data, 5 for People and 2 for Things on the Worker Traits Profile form in the appropriate locations. In a similar way, you can simply transfer the codes from the display table to the appropriate sections of the Worker Traits Profile form.

The next group of codes refers to Training Time. For **TRAVEL AGENT**, we find an entry of 4345, meaning a Reasoning Development level of 4, a Mathematical Development level of 3, a Language Development level of 4, and a Specific Vocational Preparation level of 5. This grouping is followed by the 11 Aptitudes needed for that job, with codes GVNSPQKFMEC. The data for these traits are numbers from 1 to 5.

Then follows a block of 20 entries for Physical Demands. The first is strength and can take a value of S, L, M, H, or V. All the others take values of N, O, F, or C. The next block of 14 traits refer to Environmental Conditions. These all have values of N, O, F, or C also except for number 5, Noise Intensity Level, which takes a value of 1 to 5. In the next block, Temperaments, entries appear only if the temperament is required by the occupation. There will be from 1 to 5 letters, separated by commas as shown in the data display. Thus for **TRAVEL AGENT** we find the letters I,V, indicating that the Temperaments "Influencing Others" and "Variety of Duties" are required. Put checkmarks next to these temperaments on the profile form.

The last six items in the display are code numbers. These code numbers are to be entered on the Worker Traits Profile form and the definition of each can be obtained in the appropriate appendices of this volume. The first, WKF, refers to the Work Field. The next, MPSMS, is the Materials, Products, Subject Matter, and Services code. GOE is the *Guide for Occupational Exploration* Interest Area code number. SOC is the Standard Occupational Classification code number. CIP is the Classification of Instructional Program code number for the occupation. OES is the Occupational Employment Statistics code number.

While all of this coded data on one form can seem a bit overwhelming, we do trust that many people will find it helpful in a variety of ways.

Worker Traits Profile

JOB #1	**JOB #1**
Title: _____	Title: _____
DOT #: _____	DOT #: _____
Industry: _____	Industry: _____
Duties/Other Details: _____	Duties/Other Details: _____
_____	_____
_____	_____
_____	_____
Salary: _____	Salary: _____
Outlook: _____	Outlook: _____

DOT #s 4, 5, and 6	**JOB #1**	**DOT #s 4, 5, and 6**	**JOB #2**
Data	_____	Data	_____
People	_____	People	_____
Things	_____	Things	_____

Training Time	**JOB #1**	**Training Time**	**JOB #2**
R— Reasoning	_____	**R**— Reasoning	_____
M— Mathematical	_____	**M**— Mathematical	_____
L— Language	_____	**L**— Language	_____
S— Spec. Voc. Prep	_____	**S**— Spec. Voc. Prep	_____

Aptitudes	**JOB #1**	**Aptitudes**	**JOB #2**
G— Gen. Learning	_____	**G**— Gen. Learning	_____
V— Verbal	_____	**V**— Verbal	_____
N— Numerical	_____	**N**— Numerical	_____
S— Spatial	_____	**S**— Spatial	_____
P— Form	_____	**P**— Form	_____
Q— Clerical	_____	**Q**— Clerical	_____
K— Motor Coord.	_____	**K**— Motor Coord.	_____
F— Finger	_____	**F**— Finger	_____
M— Manual	_____	**M**— Manual	_____
E— Eye-Hand Coord.	_____	**E**— Eye-Hand Coord.	_____
C— Color Discrim.	_____	**C**— Color Discrim.	_____

Physical Demands	**JOB #1**	**Physical Demands**	**JOB #2**
1— Strength	_____	**1**— Strength	_____
2— Climbing	_____	**2**— Climbing	_____
3— Balancing	_____	**3**— Balancing	_____
4— Stooping	_____	**4**— Stooping	_____
5— Kneeling	_____	**5**— Kneeling	_____
6— Crouching	_____	**6**— Crouching	_____
7— Crawling	_____	**7**— Crawling	_____
8— Reaching	_____	**8**— Reaching	_____
9— Handling	_____	**9**— Handling	_____
10— Fingering	_____	**10**— Fingering	_____
11— Feeling	_____	**11**— Feeling	_____
12— Talking	_____	**12**— Talking	_____
13— Hearing	_____	**13**— Hearing	_____

Physical Demands	JOB #1		Physical Demands	JOB #2
14— Tasting/Smelling			14— Tasting/Smelling	
15— Near Acuity			15— Near Acuity	
16— Far Acuity			16— Far Acuity	
17— Depth Percept.			17— Depth Percept.	
18— Accommodation			18— Accommodation	
19— Color Vision			19— Color Vision	
20— Field of Vision			20— Field of Vision	

Environmental Conditions	JOB #1		Environmental Conditions	JOB #2
1— Weather			1— Weather	
2— Cold			2— Cold	
3— Hot			3— Hot	
4— Wet/Humid			4— Wet/Humid	
5— Noise			5— Noise	
6— Vibration			6— Vibration	
7— Atmospheric Cond			7— Atmospheric Cond	
8— Moving Parts			8— Moving Parts	
9— Electrical Shock			9— Electrical Shock	
10— High, Exposed Places			10— High, Exposed Places	
11— Radiation			11— Radiation	
12— Explosives			12— Explosives	
13— Toxic Chemicals			13— Toxic Chemicals	
14— Other Hazards			14— Other Hazards	

Temperaments	JOB #1		Temperaments	JOB #2
D— Directing Others			D— Directing Others	
R— Repetitive Work			R— Repetitive Work	
I— Influencing Others			I— Influencing Others	
V— Variety of Duties			V— Variety of Duties	
E— Expressing Feelings			E— Expressing Feelings	
A— Working Alone			A— Working Alone	
S— Stress			S— Stress	
T— Precise Tolerances			T— Precise Tolerances	
U— Under Instructions			U— Under Instructions	
P— Dealing with People			P— Dealing with People	
J— Making Judgments			J— Making Judgments	

	JOB #1			JOB #2
WKF Code			WKF Code	
Title			Title	
MPSMS Code			MPSMS Code	
Title			Title	
GOE Code			GOE Code	
Title			Title	
SOC Code			SOC Code	
Title			Title	
CIP Code			CIP Code	
Title			Title	
OES Code			OES Code	

SECTION 3:
Worker Traits
Data Display

DOT #	DOT Title & Industry	Trng	Aptitude	Physical	Environment	Tempra	WKF	MPSMS	GOE	SOC	CIP	OES
001.061-010	ARCHITECT (profess. & kin.)	6668	12111343453	LNNNNNNOOONFFNFOFOON	NNNN3NNNNNNNNNN	D,I,V,T,J	244	701	05.01.07	1610	000000	22302
001.061-014	ARCHITECT, MARINE (profess. & kin.)	6669	11112223354	LNNNNNNFFNFNFNFNON	NNNN3NNNNNNNNNN	V,D,J,T	244	714	05.01.07	1637	000000	22305
001.061-018	LANDSCAPE ARCHITECT (profess. & kin.)	5558	11212233343	LOOOONFFONFFNFNFFON	ONNN2NNNNNNNNNN	D,J,E	264	719	05.01.07	1610	000000	22308
001.167-010	SCHOOL-PLANT CONSULTANT (education)	5556	22222344454	SNNNNNOONNFFNFNONON	NNNN3NNNNNNNNNN	P,J	244	701	05.01.08	1610	000000	22302
001.261-010	DRAFTER, ARCHITECTURAL (profess. & kin.)	4447	23222222354	SNNNNNCCCNOONCNFNON	NNNN2NNNNNNNNNN	T,J	242	701	05.03.02	3720	480102	22514
001.261-014	DRAFTER, LANDSCAPE (profess. & kin.)	4437	23222222353	SNNNNNNCCCNNNNCNFFON	NNNN2NNNNNNNNNN	J,T	242	719	05.03.02	3720	150101	22102
002.061-010	AERODYNAMICIST (aircraft mfg.)	6668	11112333354	LOOOONFFNNOONFOONNN	NNNN3NNNNNNNNNN	D,V,T,J	244	702	05.01.01	1622	000000	22102
002.061-014	AERONAUTICAL ENGINEER (aircraft mfg.)	6668	12113233355	LNNNNNNFFNOONFOONNN	NNNN3NNNNNNNNNN	D,V,T,J	244	702	05.01.07	1622	000000	22102
002.061-018	AERONAUTICAL TEST ENGINEER (aircraft mfg.)	5558	22223333354	LONONONFFONOONFOONON	NNNN3NNNNNNNNNN	V,D,J,T	244	702	05.01.04	1622	000000	22102
002.061-022	AERONAUTICAL-DESIGN ENGINEER (aircraft mfg.)	5558	22222233354	SNNNNNNFFNFFNFNNOON	NNNN3NNNNNNNNNN	V,J,T	244	702	05.01.07	1622	000000	22102
002.061-026	AERONAUTICAL-RESEARCH ENGINEER (aircraft mfg.)	6668	11113333354	LNNNNNNOOFNOONFNNOON	NNNN2NNNNNNNNNN	D,V,T,J	244	702	05.01.01	1622	000000	22102
002.061-030	STRESS ANALYST (aircraft mfg.)	5558	11122323354	SNNNNNNFFNOONFNNFON	NNNN2NNNNNNNNNN	J,T,V	244	702	05.01.04	1622	000000	22102
002.151-010	SALES ENGINEER, AERONAUTICAL PRODUCTS (aircraft mfg.)	5558	22333333354	LNNNNNNOOONFNFNNNON	NNNN2NNNNNNNNNN	D,I,P,J	244	702	05.01.05	4210	000000	49002
002.167-010	VALUE ENGINEER (aircraft mfg.)	6568	22222244454	SNNNNNNOOONOONFNNOON	NNNN2NNNNNNNNNN	D,P,J	244	700	05.01.06	1622	000000	22102
002.167-014	FIELD-SERVICE ENGINEER (aircraft mfg.)	5558	11113333354	LNNNNNNFFONFFNFONNON	NNNN2NNNNNNNNNN	V,T,J	244	702	05.01.04	1622	000000	22102
002.167-018	AERONAUTICAL PROJECT ENGINEER (aircraft mfg.)	6669	11112133354	LNNNNNNOOONFFNFOOON	NNNN3NNNNNNNNNN	D,V,T,P,J	244	702	05.01.08	1622	000000	22102
002.261-010	DRAFTER, AERONAUTICAL (aircraft mfg.)	5547	23222223354	SNNNNNNFOFNOONFNNFFN	NNNN2NNNNNNNNNN	T	242	702	05.03.02	3720	480101	22514
002.261-014	RESEARCH MECHANIC (aircraft mfg.)	4447	23222333354	MOOOOOOFFFOOONFOONON	ONNN4NNFNONOON	V,T,J	102	592	05.03.05	3719	150801	22599
002.262-010	FLIGHT-TEST DATA ACQUISITION TECHNICIAN (aircraft mfg.)	5447	23232332354	LNNNNNNFFNOONFNOFON	NNNN3NNNOONNNNN	J,T,V	233	702	05.03.05	3719	000000	22126
003.061-010	ELECTRICAL ENGINEER (profess. & kin.)	5558	22223333344	LNNNNNNOOFNOONFNNOON	NNNN3NNNNNNNNNN	V,D,T,J	244	703	05.01.08	1633	000000	22126
003.061-014	ELECTRICAL TEST ENGINEER (profess. & kin.)	5558	22223333343	LNNNNNNFFONFFNFNNFON	NNNN2NNNNNNNNNN	V,D,J,T	244	580	05.01.04	1633	000000	22126
003.061-018	ELECTRICAL-DESIGN ENGINEER (profess. & kin.)	5558	22222333344	LNNNNNNNFFONFFNFNNFNN	NNNN3NNNNNNNNNN	V,P,J,T	244	871	05.01.07	1633	000000	22126
003.061-022	ELECTRICAL-PROSPECTING ENGINEER (profess. & kin.)	6668	11112323355	SNNNNNNFFNNFFNNFNNON	NNNN3NNNNNNNNNN	V,J,T	244	703	05.01.07	1633	000000	22126
003.061-026	ELECTRICAL-RESEARCH ENGINEER (profess. & kin.)	5558	22222333343	LNNNNNNFFNNFFNFNNFON	NNNN3NNNNNNNNNN	V,J,T	244	703	05.01.01	1633	000000	22126
003.061-030	ELECTRONICS ENGINEER (profess. & kin.)	5558	11112344455	LNNNNNNFFFNOONFNNOOFN	NNNN3NNNNNNNNNN	V,T,J	244	703	05.01.08	1633	000000	22126
003.061-034	ELECTRONICS-DESIGN ENGINEER (profess. & kin.)	5558	11112233353	LNNNNNNOOFNOONFNNOON	NNNN3NNNNNNNNNN	V,J,T	244	703	05.01.07	1633	000000	22126
003.061-038	ELECTRONICS-RESEARCH ENGINEER (profess. & kin.)	5558	22222333343	LNNNNNNFFONFFNFNNOON	NNNN3NNNNNNNNNN	V,J,T	244	703	05.01.01	1633	000000	22126
003.061-042	ELECTRONICS-TEST ENGINEER (profess. & kin.)	5558	12213333344	LNNNNNNOFONOONFNOOON	NNNN3NNNNNNNNNN	V,D,J,T	244	703	05.01.04	1633	000000	22126
003.061-046	ILLUMINATING ENGINEER (profess. & kin.)	5558	11112333354	SNNNNNNNOOONFFNFNNOON	NNNN3NNNNNNNNNN	D,J,T	244	871	05.01.03	1633	000000	22126
003.061-050	PLANNING ENGINEER, CENTRAL OFFICE FACILITIES (tel. & tel.)	6668	11112344455	SNNNNNNOONNFFNFNNONN	NNNN3NNNNNNNNNN	D,J	244	861	05.01.03	1633	000000	22126
003.131-010	SUPERVISOR, DRAFTING AND PRINTED CIRCUIT DESIGN (profess. & kin.)	4448	22222244455	SNNNNNNNFFONFFNFNNNN	ONNN3NNNNNNNNNN	D,T,P,J	242	703	05.03.02	3720	150303	22514
003.151-010	SALES-ENGINEER, ELECTRICAL PRODUCTS (profess. & kin.)	5558	22233344444	LNNNNNNFFNFNFNFNNN	ONNN2NNNNNNNNNN	D,I,J,T	244	871	05.01.05	4210	000000	49002
003.151-014	SALES-ENGINEER, ELECTRONICS PRODUCTS AND SYSTEMS (profess. & kin.)	5558	22233344443	LNNNNNNOOONFFNFNNOON	ONNN2NNNNNNNNNN	D,I,T,J	244	585	05.01.05	4210	521201	49002
003.161-010	ELECTRICAL TECHNICIAN (profess. & kin.)	4447	22222322244	LNNNNNNFFNNNFNNFFN	NNNN3NNNNNNNNNN	V,J,T	244	703	05.01.01	3711	150303	22505
003.161-014	ELECTRONICS TECHNICIAN (profess. & kin.)	5547	22222322244	LNNNNNNFFFOOONFNOFFN	NNNN3NNNONNNNN	V,T,J	111	703	05.01.01	3711	150303	22505
003.161-018	TECHNICIAN, SEMICONDUCTOR DEVELOPMENT (profess. & kin.)	5548	22222322244	MNNNNNNOOONFNNOOON	NNNN3NONONNNON	D,V,P,J	244	587	05.01.03	3711	150303	22505
003.167-010	CABLE ENGINEER, OUTSIDE PLANT (tel. & tel.)	5558	22222333343	LNNNNNNOOONFFNFNNOON	FNNN3NNNNNNNNNN	V,D,J,T	244	586	05.01.03	1633	000000	22126
003.167-014	DISTRIBUTION-FIELD ENGINEER (utilities)	5558	22222344455	LNNNNNNFFONFFNFNNNN	ONNN2NNNNNNNNNN	V,J,T	244	871	05.01.03	1633	000000	22126
003.167-018	ELECTRICAL ENGINEER, POWER SYSTEM (utilities)	6668	11112333344	LNNNNNNFFONFFNFNNFNN	NNNN2NNNNNNNNNN	V,D,P,J	244	871	05.01.03	1633	000000	22126
003.167-022	ELECTROLYSIS-AND-CORROSION-CONTROL ENGINEER (profess. & kin.)	5558	11122233344	LNNNNNNFFONFFNFNFON	ONNN3NNNNNNNNNN	V,D,T	244	364	05.01.03	1633	000000	22126
003.167-026	ENGINEER OF SYSTEM DEVELOPMENT (utilities)	5558	11122333355	SNNNNNNFFNNOONFNNNN	NNNN2NNNNNNNNNN	V,D,P,J	244	871	05.01.03	1633	000000	22126
003.167-030	ENGINEER-IN-CHARGE, STUDIO OPERATIONS (radio-tv broad.)	5558	22222333355	SNNNNNNOOONFFNONOONN	NNNN3NNNNNNNNNN	D,V,T,J	244	863	05.01.03	1633	099999	22126
003.167-034	ENGINEER-IN-CHARGE, TRANSMITTER (radio-tv broad.)	5558	22223433353	LNNNNNNOOOONFFNOONNNN	NNNN3NNNNNNNNNN	D,V,P,J	244	863	05.01.03	1633	099999	22126
003.167-038	INDUCTION-COORDINATION POWER ENGINEER (utilities)	5558	11113333344	LNNNNNNFFONFFNFNNNN	NNNN2NNNNNNNNNN	V,P,J,T	244	871	05.01.03	1633	000000	22126
003.167-042	OUTSIDE-PLANT ENGINEER (tel. & tel.)	5558	12112333355	LNNNNNNFFNOONFNONNN	NNNN2NNNNNNNNNN	D,J	244	586	05.01.03	1633	000000	22126
003.167-046	POWER-DISTRIBUTION ENGINEER (utilities)	5558	11112322355	SNNNNNNFFONNNNFNFONN	NNNN2NNNNNNNNNN	J,T	244	871	05.01.03	1633	000000	22126
003.167-050	POWER-TRANSMISSION ENGINEER (utilities)	5558	11122333344	LNNNNNNFFNFNFNFNNON	NNNN3NNNNNNNNNN	V,D,P,J	244	871	05.01.03	1633	000000	22126
003.167-054	PROTECTION ENGINEER (utilities)	5558	11112333354	SNNNNNNFFNFFNFNFNON	NNNN3NNNNNNNNNN	V,D,P,J	244	871	05.01.03	1633	000000	22126
003.167-058	SUPERVISOR, MICROWAVE (radio-tv broad.)	5558	11112333354	SNNNNNNFFONFFNFNFOOON	ONNN3NNNNNNNNNN	D,J,P	244	703	05.01.03	1633	000000	22126
003.167-066	TRANSMISSION-AND-PROTECTION ENGINEER (tel. & tel.)	5558	11113344455	LNNNNNNOONNFFNONNNNN	ONNN3NNNNNNNNNN	J,T	244	586	05.01.03	1633	000000	22126
003.167-070	ENGINEERING MANAGER, ELECTRONICS (profess. & kin.)	6659	11112145455	SNNNNNNOONNFFNONNNNN	NNNN3NNNNNNNNNN	D,P,J	295	703	05.01.08	1260	000000	13017

DOT #	DOT Title & Industry	Trng	Aptitude	Physical	Environment	Tempra	WkF	MPSMS	GOE	SOC	CIP	OES
003.187-010	CENTRAL-OFFICE EQUIPMENT ENGINEER (tel. & tel.)	6668	11123344455	SNNNNNNFFONNNNFNNFON	NNNN3NNNNNNNNNN	V,J,T	244	586	05.01.03	1633	099999	22126
003.187-014	COMMERCIAL ENGINEER (radio-tv broad.)	5557	22122344455	LNNNNNNNFFONNFNFNNON	NNNN3NNNNNNNNNN	J,T	244	863	05.01.03	1633	099999	22126
003.187-018	CUSTOMER-EQUIPMENT ENGINEER (tel. & tel.)	5558	22222444455	LNNNNNNNFFONFNFNFOON	NNNN3NNNNNNNNNN	V,D,J	244	861	05.01.08	1633	099999	22126
003.261-010	INSTRUMENTATION TECHNICIAN (profess. & kin.)	5547	22222322244	LNNNNNNNFFNOONFNNOON	NNNN4NNNNNNNNNN	V,J,T	211	700	05.01.01	3711	150403	22505
003.261-014	CONTROLS DESIGNER (profess. & kin.)	5448	22222123355	SNNNNNNFFONOONFOONNN	NNNN3NNNNNNNNNN	T,J	242	719	05.03.02	3720	150805	22514
003.261-018	INTEGRATED CIRCUIT LAYOUT DESIGNER (profess. & kin.)	4448	22222222354	SNNNNNNNFFNOONFNNFFN	NNNN3NNNNNNNNNN	T,J	242	703	05.03.02	3720	150303	22514
003.261-022	PRINTED CIRCUIT DESIGNER (profess. & kin.)	4447	22222222354	SNNNNNNNFFNOONFNNFFN	NNNN3NNNNNNNNNN	T,J,V	242	703	05.03.02	3720	150303	22514
003.281-014	DRAFTER, ELECTRICAL (profess. & kin.)	5547	23222243454	SNNNNNNNFFNOONFNNNON	NNNN3NNNNNNNNNN	J,T	242	703	05.03.02	3720	480104	22514
003.281-014	DRAFTER, ELECTRONIC (profess. & kin.)	5547	23222243454	SNNNNNNNFFNOONFNNNON	NNNN2NNNNNNNNNN	J,T	242	703	05.03.02	3720	480104	22514
003.362-010	DESIGN TECHNICIAN, COMPUTER-AIDED (electron. comp.)	3335	23322223355	SNNNNNNNFFNNNNCNFFFN	NNNN4NNNNNNNNNN	J,T	233	703	05.03.02	3719	480101	22599
005.061-010	AIRPORT ENGINEER (profess. & kin.)	5558	22222233343	LNNNNNNNFFONFFNFOFNNN	FNNN3NNNNNNNNNN	V,D,J,T	244	704	05.01.07	1628	000000	22121
005.061-014	CIVIL ENGINEER (profess. & kin.)	5558	22112233344	LNNNNNNOOONONFOOOON	ONNN3NNNNNNNNNN	D,V,T,J,P	244	704	05.01.07	1628	000000	22121
005.061-018	HYDRAULIC ENGINEER (profess. & kin.)	5557	22222233354	LNNNNNNNNOONNFFNFONNN	FNNN3NNNNNNNNNN	V,D,J,T	244	704	05.01.03	1628	000000	22121
005.061-022	IRRIGATION ENGINEER (profess. & kin.)	5548	22222233333	LNNNNNNNFFOOFFNFONNON	ONNN3NNNNNNNNNN	V,D,J,T	244	704	05.01.03	1628	000000	22121
005.061-026	RAILROAD ENGINEER (profess. & kin.)	5558	22222233333	LNNNNNNNFFONFFNFFNON	FNNN3NNNNNNNNNN	V,D,T	244	704	05.01.07	1628	000000	22121
005.061-030	SANITARY ENGINEER (profess. & kin.)	5558	11122243344	LNNNNNNNFFONFFNFFNON	ONNN3NNNNNNNNNN	V,D,J,T	244	704	05.01.03	1628	000000	22121
005.061-034	STRUCTURAL ENGINEER (construction)	5558	22222233333	LNNNNNNNOOONNNFNNNNN	FNNN3NNNNNNNNNN	J,T,V	244	704	05.01.08	1628	000000	22121
005.061-038	TRANSPORTATION ENGINEER (profess. & kin.)	5558	22222233333	LNNNNNNNNOOONNNFNNNNN	ONNN3NNNNNNNNNN	V,D,J,T	244	704	05.01.08	1628	000000	22121
005.061-042	WASTE-MANAGEMENT ENGINEER, RADIOACTIVE MATERIALS (profess. & kin.)	5558	12112333354	LNNNNNNNFFNFFNFNNFNON	NNNN3NNNNNNNNNN	D,T,J	244	723	05.01.03	1628	000000	22121
005.167-010	CHIEF ENGINEER, WATERWORKS (waterworks)	5559	21112244455	LNNNNNNNFFONFFNFNONNN	NNNN3NNNNNNNNNN	D,P,J,T	244	873	05.01.03	1628	000000	13017
005.167-014	DRAINAGE-DESIGN COORDINATOR (waterworks)	5548	22222444455	SNNNNNNNFFNFFNFNFNNN	NNNN2NNNNNNNNNN	D,J,T	244	369	05.01.03	1628	030101	22121
005.167-018	FOREST ENGINEER (forestry; logging)	5557	11112233344	LNNNNNNNFFNFNFNNOONN	FNNN3NNNNNNNNNN	V,D,J,T	244	704	05.01.06	1628	000000	22121
005.167-022	HIGHWAY-ADMINISTRATIVE ENGINEER (government ser.)	6569	11123244444	SNNNNNNNFFONFFNFNNNON	NNNN3NNNNNNNNNN	D,J,P	244	704	11.05.03	1134	000000	13017
005.167-026	PRODUCTION ENGINEER, TRACK (r.r. trans.)	5349	22444344444	LNNNNNNNFFNFNFNNNON	NNNN3NNNNNNNNNN	D,T,P,J	244	712	05.01.06	1634	000000	22128
005.261-014	CIVIL ENGINEERING TECHNICIAN (profess. & kin.)	4447	22222222354	LNNNNNNNFFNFNFNNOFON	NNNN3NNNNNNNNNN	V,T,J	242	704	05.01.06	3710	150201	22502
005.281-010	DRAFTER, CIVIL (profess. & kin.)	4447	23222333354	SNNNNNNNOFFNNNNFNNNNN	NNNN2NNNNNNNNNN	T,J	242	704	05.03.02	3720	480101	22514
005.281-014	DRAFTER, STRUCTURAL (profess. & kin.)	5547	23222222354	SNNNNNNNCCNNNNCNFFON	NNNN2NNNNNNNNNN	J,T	242	704	05.03.02	3720	150201	22105
006.061-010	CERAMIC DESIGN ENGINEER (profess. & kin.)	5558	22223444443	LNNNNNNNFFNFFNNNOFN	NNNN3NNNNNNNNNN	D,J,T	244	534	05.01.07	1623	000000	22105
006.061-014	CERAMIC ENGINEER (profess. & kin.)	6668	11112143453	LNNNNNNNFFFFFNFNNONON	NNON3NNNNNNNNNN	V,D,J,T	244	705	05.01.07	1623	000000	22105
006.061-018	CERAMIC RESEARCH ENGINEER (profess. & kin.)	5558	22222333343	LNNNNNNNFFNFNFNNOFN	NNNN3NNNNNNNNNN	D,J,T	244	534	05.01.01	1623	000000	22105
006.061-022	CERAMICS TEST ENGINEER (profess. & kin.)	5558	22222333343	SNNNNNNNFFNFNFNNNOON	NNNN3NNNNNNNNNN	D,J,T	244	534	05.01.04	1623	000000	22105
006.151-010	SALES ENGINEER, CERAMIC PRODUCTS (profess. & kin.)	5558	22222333343	LNNNNNNNFFNFNFNNOON	NNNN3NNNNNNNNNN	D,J,T	292	534	05.01.05	4210	000000	49002
006.261-010	SCIENTIFIC GLASS BLOWER (glass products)	4448	22222222252	LNNNNNNNFFNOONFNNFN	NNNN3NONNNNNNNNO	J	102	531	05.05.11	3719	000000	22599
007.061-010	AUTOMOTIVE ENGINEER (auto. mfg.)	5558	22222333353	LNNNNNNNFFNFNFNNOFON	NNNN2NNNNNNNNNN	D,J,T	244	706	05.01.08	1635	000000	22135
007.061-014	MECHANICAL ENGINEER (profess. & kin.)	5558	22123333355	LNNNNNNNFFNFFNFNNOONN	NNNN3NNNNNNNNNN	V,D,T,J	244	706	05.01.08	1635	000000	22135
007.061-018	MECHANICAL-DESIGN ENGINEER, FACILITIES (profess. & kin.)	5558	11212333355	SNNNNNNNFFONFFNFONN	NNNN3NNNNNNNNNN	D,J	244	706	05.01.07	1635	000000	22135
007.061-022	MECHANICAL-DESIGN ENGINEER, PRODUCTS (profess. & kin.)	5558	22222333344	SNNNNNNNFFONFFNFFNONN	NNNN3NNNNNNNNNN	V,D,P,J	244	706	05.01.07	1635	000000	22135
007.061-026	TOOL-DESIGNER (profess. & kin.)	5558	22222333354	LNNNNNNNFFNFNFNFNNON	NNNN4NNNNNNNNNN	J,T	244	706	05.01.07	1635	150805	22135
007.061-030	TOOL-DESIGNER APPRENTICE (profess. & kin.)	4448	22222344454	LNNNNNNNFFNOONFNNFON	NNNN4NNNNNNNNNN	J,T	244	706	05.03.02	3720	150805	22514
007.061-034	UTILIZATION ENGINEER (utilities)	5558	22222344454	SNNNNNNNFFNNNNNNNN	NNNN3NNNNNNNNNN	V,D,J,T	244	706	05.03.02	3720	150805	22514
007.061-038	APPLICATIONS ENGINEER, MANUFACTURING (profess. & kin.)	5558	11222233454	LNNNNNNNOOOONNFNFFFNON	NNNN4NNNNNNNNNN	D,V,P,T,J	244	706	05.01.08	3720	000000	22135
007.061-042	STRESS ANALYST (profess. & kin.)	6658	11121143455	SNNNNNNNNOOFNOONCNOONN	NNNN4NNNNNNNNNN	T,J,P	244	703	05.01.04	1635	150805	22135
007.151-010	SALES ENGINEER, MECHANICAL EQUIPMENT (utilities)	5558	22222333355	LNNNNNNNFFONFFNFNNFN	ONNN3NNNNNNNNNN	V,D,P,I	244	560	05.01.05	4210	080799	49002
007.161-010	DIE DESIGNER (machine shop)	5448	22222322244	LNNNNNNNFFNFNFNFNNOON	NNNN3NNNNNNNNNN	J,T	121	590	05.01.01	3713	150805	22511
007.161-014	DIE-DESIGNER APPRENTICE (machine shop)	4447	22222322254	SNNNNNNNFFNFNFNFNNON	NNNN3NNNNNNNNNN	J	121	603	05.01.01	3713	150699	22511
007.161-018	ENGINEERING ASSISTANT, MECHANICAL EQUIPMENT (profess. & kin.)	5557	22222222254	SNNNNNNNFFONFFNOONFON	NNNN3NNNNNNNNNN	T,J	242	706	05.03.02	3720	480105	22514
007.161-022	MECHANICAL RESEARCH ENGINEER (profess. & kin.)	5558	22222333344	LNNNNNNNFFONFFNFONN	NNNN3NNNNNNNNNN	D,P,J	251	560	05.03.02	3720	150805	22135
007.161-026	MECHANICAL-ENGINEERING TECHNICIAN (profess. & kin.)	5447	22322433354	LNNNNNNNFFNFNFNFNFNN	NNNN3NNNNNNNNNN	J	121	560	05.01.01	3713	150805	22511
007.161-030	OPTOMECHANICAL TECHNICIAN (optical goods; photo. appar.)	5448	22222332244	LNNNNNNNFFNFNFNFNFNN	NNNN3NNNNNNNNNN	J,T	211	603	05.01.04	3713	150699	22511
007.161-034	TEST ENGINEER, MECHANICAL EQUIPMENT (profess. & kin.)	5558	22222333344	SNNNNNNNFFNFNFNFNFFNN	NNNN3NNNNNNNNNN	D,J,T	211	560	05.01.04	1635	000000	22135
007.161-038	SOLAR-ENERGY-SYSTEMS DESIGNER (profess. & kin.)	5445	22222223454	LNNNNNNNFFNNNNFNOOON	NNNN3NNNNNNNNNN	J,T,V	244	553	05.03.07	1635	150505	22135

DOT #	DOT Title & Industry	Trng	Aptitude	Physical	Environment	Tempra	WkF	MPSMS	GOE	SOC	CIP	OES
007.167-010	DIE-DRAWING CHECKER (profess. & kin.)	5547	22222244454	SNNNNNNNCCCNNNNCNFNNN	NNNN3NNNNNNNNNN	J,T	211	706	05.03.02	3713	480101	22511
007.167-014	PLANT ENGINEER (profess. & kin.)	5558	222222344455	LNNNNNNOOONFFNONONNN	NNNN3NNNNNNNNNN	D,J,T,P	244	706	05.01.08	1635	000000	13017
007.167-018	TOOL PROGRAMMER, NUMERICAL CONTROL (any industry)	5447	23222344454	SNNNNNNNFFNOONFNOOFN	NNNN4NNNNNNNNNN	T,J	241	566	05.01.06	3974	110301	25111
007.181-010	HEAT-TRANSFER TECHNICIAN (profess. & kin.)	5557	22222322245	LNNNNNNNFFNOONFNOONN	ONNN3NNNNNNNNNN	V,J,T	212	706	05.03.07	3713	150501	22511
007.261-010	CHIEF DRAFTER (profess. & kin.)	5557	222222329353	SNNNNNNNFONFFNFNOFNN	NNNN3NNNNNNNNNN	V,J,T	242	706	05.03.02	3720	150805	22514
007.261-014	DRAFTER, CASTINGS (profess. & kin.)	4447	22222322255	SNNNNNNNFFNNNNCNOFNN	NNNN3NNNNNNNNNN	J,T	242	706	05.03.02	3720	480101	22514
007.261-018	DRAFTER, PATENT (profess. & kin.)	5557	22222322254	SNNNNNNNFFONNNNCNOFNN	NNNN3NNNNNNNNNN	J,T	242	706	05.03.02	3720	480105	22514
007.261-022	DRAFTER, TOOL DESIGN (profess. & kin.)	5557	22222322255	SNNNNNNNFFONNNNCNOFNN	NNNN3NNNNNNNNNN	J,T	242	706	05.03.02	3720	480101	22514
007.267-010	DRAWINGS CHECKER, ENGINEERING (profess. & kin.)	4446	22212222255	SNNNNNNNOONOOONCNNFON	NNNN3NNNNNNNNNN	T,J	244	559	05.03.02	1635	480101	22135
007.267-014	TOOL DESIGN CHECKER (aircraft mfg.)	5558	222223444444	SNNNNNNNFFNOONFNONNN	NNNN2NNNNNNNNNN	T,J	211	706	05.01.07	3713	000000	22511
007.281-010	DRAFTER, MECHANICAL (profess. & kin.)	5557	23222322354	SNNNNNNNFFNNNNFNOOON	NNNN3NNNNNNNNNN	T,J	242	706	05.03.02	3720	480101	22514
007.362-010	NESTING OPERATOR, NUMERICAL CONTROL (aircraft mfg.)	4336	33332333455	LNNNNNNOOFNOONFNONNN	NNNN3NNNNNNNNNN	T,J	057	566	05.03.02	3974	000000	22511
008.061-010	ABSORPTION-AND-ADSORPTION ENGINEER (profess. & kin.)	6668	1112333354	SNNNNNNNFONFFNFNNNON	NNNN3NNNNNNNNNN	D,J,T	147	707	05.01.07	1626	000000	22114
008.061-014	CHEMICAL DESIGN ENGINEER, PROCESSES (profess. & kin.)	5558	22223333354	SNNNNNNNFFNNNNFNFFN	NNNN3NNNNNNNNNN	D,J,T	147	707	05.01.07	1626	000000	22114
008.061-018	CHEMICAL ENGINEER (profess. & kin.)	6668	1112333354	LNNNNNNNFONFFNFNOFON	ONNN3NNNNNNNNNN	V,D,J,T	244	707	05.01.07	1626	000000	22114
008.061-022	CHEMICAL RESEARCH ENGINEER (profess. & kin.)	5558	22222344444	LNNNNNNNFFONFNFNOFON	NNNN3NNNNNNNNNN	D,J	251	707	05.01.01	1626	000000	22114
008.061-026	CHEMICAL-TEST ENGINEER (profess. & kin.)	5558	22223333354	LNNNNNNNFFONFFNFNNNN	NNNN3NNNNNNNNNN	V,D,J,T	244	500	05.01.04	1626	000000	22114
008.151-010	CHEMICAL-EQUIPMENT SALES ENGINEER (profess. & kin.)	5558	22223344444	LNNNNNNNFFONFFNFNNNN	ONNN3NNNNNNNNNN	D,I,J,T	244	707	05.01.05	4210	000000	49002
008.167-010	TECHNICAL DIRECTOR, CHEMICAL PLANT (profess. & kin.)	6658	12122344455	LNNNNNNNFFNFNFNNNNN	NNNN3NNNNNNNNNN	V,D,J	295	707	05.01.08	1626	410301	13017
008.261-010	CHEMICAL-ENGINEERING TECHNICIAN (profess. & kin.)	5558	22222322234	LNNNNNNNFFONOONFNOFON	NNNN4NNNNNNNNNN	J,T	244	707	05.01.08	1626	000000	22599
010.061-010	DESIGN ENGINEER, MINING-AND-OIL-FIELD EQUIPMENT (profess. & kin.)	5558	22222333344	LNNNNNNNFNFFNFNFFNN	FNNN3NNNNNNNNNN	D,P,T	244	564	05.01.07	1624	000000	22108
010.061-014	MINING ENGINEER (mine & quarry)	5557	12112233355	LNNNOOONOOOONFNFOONNN	ONNN3NONNNNNNNO	D,V,T,J	244	708	05.01.06	1624	000000	22108
010.061-018	PETROLEUM ENGINEER (petrol. & gas)	5558	11112333355	LNNNNNNNFONFNFNOOFNN	NNNN5NNNNNNNNNN	V,D,J,T	244	708	05.01.08	1625	000000	22111
010.061-022	RESEARCH ENGINEER, MINING-AND-OIL-WELL EQUIPMENT (mine & quarry; petrol. & gas)	5558	22233333344	LNNNNNNNFFNFNFNNNNN	NNNN3NNNNNNNNNN	D,P,J	244	564	05.01.01	1624	000000	22108
010.061-026	SAFETY ENGINEER, MINES (mine & quarry)	5558	22222344444	LOOOOOOFFNOONFNFOOFON	OONF3NFNNNNFFN	V,P,I,J	244	712	05.01.02	1624	000000	22108
010.061-030	TEST ENGINEER, MINING-AND-OIL-FIELD EQUIPMENT (mine & quarry; petrol. & gas)	5558	22223333344	LNNNNNNNFFNFNFNNNOON	FNNN3NNNNNNNNNN	D,J,P	212	564	05.01.04	1624	000000	22111
010.131-010	WELL-LOGGING CAPTAIN, MUD ANALYSIS (petrol. & gas)	5547	22233244453	LOOOONNNFONFFNFNFFN	FNNN3NNNNNNNNNN	D,P,T,V,J	211	708	02.04.01	3833	150903	24511
010.151-010	SALES ENGINEER, MINING-AND-OIL-WELL EQUIPMENT AND SERVICES (mine & quarry)	5558	22243344444	LNNNNNNNFONFFNNNNNNN	FNNN3NNNNNNNNNN	V,P,I	244	708	05.01.05	4210	000000	49002
010.161-010	CHIEF ENGINEER, RESEARCH (petrol. & gas)	6668	11112344455	SNNNNNNNFFNFNNNNNNN	NNNN3NNNNNNNNNN	V,D,P,J	244	708	05.01.01	1625	000000	22111
010.161-014	CHIEF PETROLEUM ENGINEER (petrol. & gas)	6669	11112344455	SNNNNNNNOFFNFNNNNNNN	NNNN3NNNNNNNNNN	V,D,J,T	244	708	05.01.08	1625	000000	13017
010.161-018	OBSERVER, SEISMIC PROSPECTING (petrol. & gas)	4447	22233333354	LNNNNNNNFNFFFFNN	FNNN3NNNNNNNNNN	V,D,P	244	708	05.03.04	3833	410399	24511
010.167-010	DISTRICT SUPERVISOR, MUD-ANALYSIS WELL LOGGING (petrol. & gas)	6669	11112323355	LNNNNNNNFFOONFFOONFON	NNNN3NNNNNNNNNN	V,D,J,T	244	708	05.01.04	1625	000000	22111
010.167-014	SUPERINTENDENT, OIL-WELL SERVICES (petrol. & gas)	5558	11112444455	SNNNNNNNOOOONFFNONNNN	NNNN3NNNNNNNNNN	V,D,J	244	708	05.02.03	1625	000000	22111
010.167-018	FIELD ENGINEER, SPECIALIST (petrol. & gas)	5558	22222344455	LNNNNNNNFONFFNOFNONNN	NNNN3NNONNNNNNN	D,J,P,V	244	708	05.02.01	1260	150903	13017
010.261-010	DRAFTER, DIRECTIONAL SURVEY (petrol. & gas)	4447	23232343454	LNNNNNNNFFNFNNNNNNN	FNNN3NNONNNNNN	J,T	242	708	05.03.02	3719	150903	22599
010.261-014	DRAFTER, GEOLOGICAL (petrol. & gas)	4446	23212223255	SNNNNNNNFFNNNNFNNNNN	FNNN3NNNNNNNNNN	V,J,T	242	708	05.03.02	3833	150903	22514
010.261-018	DRAFTER, GEOPHYSICAL (petrol. & gas)	4446	23212322255	LNNNOONFFNOONFNNNNN	NNNN3NNNNNNNNNN	V,J,T	242	708	05.03.02	3720	151102	22514
010.261-022	OBSERVER, ELECTRICAL PROSPECTING (petrol. & gas)	5557	23234343353	LNNOONONFFONNONFNNNNN	FNNN3NNNNNNNNNN	J,V	211	708	05.03.04	3833	150903	24511
010.261-026	OBSERVER, GRAVITY PROSPECTING (petrol. & gas)	4445	23322243354	LNNNNNNFFONFNFNONN	FNNN4NNNNNONNN	J,V	244	708	05.03.04	3833	150903	24511
010.281-010	WELL-LOGGING OPERATOR, MUD ANALYSIS (petrol. & gas)	5557	33332433344	LNNNNNNFFONFNFNNOON	FNNN3NNNNNNNNNN	J,T,V	211	708	05.01.04	3833	150903	24511
010.281-014	SURVEYOR, OIL-WELL DIRECTIONAL (petrol. refin.)	4447	33332433344	LNNNNNNFFOONFFNNFNN	FNNN3NNNNNNNNNN	J,T	211	708	05.01.04	3719	150503	24511
010.281-018	TEST-ENGINE EVALUATOR (petrol. refin.)	5446	22222223355	LNNNNNNNFFFOONFFNNNNNN	FNNN3NNNNNNNNNN	V,P,J	271	501	02.04.01	3719	150503	22599
010.267-010	SCOUT (petrol. & gas)	5557	23212223255	SNNNNNNNFFONOONFNONNN	NNNN3NNONNNNNN	V,J,T	242	708	05.03.02	3720	480103	22514
011.061-010	FOUNDRY METALLURGIST (foundry)	5556	23212223355	LNNNNNNNFFNNNNNNNNN	NNNN3NNNNNNNNNN	V,J,T	242	708	05.03.02	3720	480103	22514
011.061-014	METALLOGRAPHER (profess. & kin.)	5557	23212322255	LNNNNNNNFFNNNNNNNNN	NNNN3NNNNNNNNNN	V,J,T	242	708	05.03.02	3720	151102	24511
011.061-018	METALLURGIST, EXTRACTIVE (profess. & kin.)	4445	23233343353	LNNNNNNFFNFNFNNNNN	FNNN4NNNNNOONN	J,T,V	244	708	02.04.01	3833	150903	24511
011.061-022	METALLURGIST, PHYSICAL (profess. & kin.)	5557	11123333343	LNNNNNNNFFONNONNFNNNN	NNNN3NNNNNNNNNN	V,D,J,T	244	723	05.01.01	1623	000000	22105
011.061-026	WELDING ENGINEER (profess. & kin.)	4447	33332433344	SNNNNNNNFFONOONFNNNN	NNNN3NNNNNNNNNN	V,D,J,T	211	723	05.01.04	1623	000000	22105
011.161-010	SUPERVISOR, METALLURGICAL-AND-QUALITY-CONTROL-TESTING (profess. & kin.)	5558	22233344443	LNNNNNNNFFNOONFNNOON	NNNN3NNNNNNNNNN	D,J,T	211	540	02.04.01	1260	150611	13017
011.261-010	METALLURGICAL TECHNICIAN (profess. & kin.)	4446	33333333343	LNNNNNNNFFNOONFNNFON	NNNN3NNNNNNNNNNO	J,T	211	350	02.04.01	3719	150611	22599

DOT #	DOT Title & Industry	Trmg	Aptitude	Physical	Environment	Tempra	WkF	MPSMS	GOE	SOC	CIP	OES
011.261-014	WELDING TECHNICIAN (profess. & kin.)	4338	33333232354	LNNNNNNFFNFFNFNNNON	NNNN3NNNNNNNNNN	J,T	244	871	05.01.01	3719	150699	22599
011.261-018	NONDESTRUCTIVE TESTER (profess. & kin.)	4336	33333333443	MNNOOONFFONOONFNNOFN	NNNO4NONNNNNONON	V,T,J	211	592	05.07.01	3990	150603	22105
011.261-022	LABORATORY ASSISTANT, METALLURGICAL (steel & rel.)	4447	33334434354	LNNNNNNNFFONFFNFNNNN	NNNN3NNNNNNNNNN	V,J,T	211	540	02.04.01	3719	150611	22599
011.281-014	SPECTROSCOPIST (profess. & kin.)	4447	33333333353	LNNNNNNNFFNNNNNFNOON	NNNN3NNNNNNNNNN	J,T	211	711	02.04.01	3719	150611	22599
011.361-010	TESTER (profess. & kin.)	4435	33333333333	LNNNNNNNFFNNNNFNFON	NNNN3NNNNNNNNNN	J,T	211	540	02.04.01	3719	150702	22599
012.061-010	PRODUCT-SAFETY ENGINEER (profess. & kin.)	6668	22223333354	SNNNNNNNFFNFNFNNNNFN	NNNN3NNNNNNNNNN	V,D,P,J	244	712	05.01.02	1634	000000	22132
012.061-014	SAFETY ENGINEER (profess. & kin.)	6668	22223333354	LNNNNNNOFONFFNOOOOON	NNNN3NNNNNNNNNN	D,P,J,V	244	712	05.01.02	1634	000000	22128
012.061-018	STANDARDS ENGINEER (profess. & kin.)	5558	11112234453	SNNNNNNFFONFFNFNNNFN	NNNN3NNNNNNNNNN	V,J,T	244	719	05.01.06	1634	000000	22128
012.067-010	METROLOGIST (profess. & kin.)	6668	22122223353	SNNNNNNFFNFFNFNNNOFN	NNNN3NNNNNNNNNN	D,J,T	244	719	05.01.04	1634	000000	22128
012.167-010	CONFIGURATION MANAGEMENT ANALYST (profess. & kin.)	5458	22233244455	LNNNNNNNFFNFFNFNNNNN	NNNN4NNNNNNNNNN	V,D,J,T	212	700	05.01.06	1634	000000	22128
012.167-014	MANAGER, QUALITY CONTROL (profess. & kin.)	5558	11223344454	LNNNNNNNOOONFFNFNNOON	NNNN4NNNNNNNNNN	D,J,P,T	211	712	05.02.03	1634	000000	22128
012.167-018	FACTORY LAY-OUT ENGINEER (profess. & kin.)	5558	22223333355	LNNNNNOONFFNOONFNNONN	NNNN3NNNNNNNNNN	D,J,T	244	712	05.01.06	1634	000000	22128
012.167-022	FIRE-PREVENTION RESEARCH ENGINEER (profess. & kin.)	5557	22223344454	SNNNNNNNFFONFFNFNNNNN	ONNN3NNNNNNNNNN	D,P,J	244	712	05.01.01	1634	000000	22132
012.167-026	FIRE-PROTECTION ENGINEER (profess. & kin.)	5557	11122333334	LNNNNNNNFFNNFNCFNOOO	ONNN3NNNNNNNNNN	D,P,J	244	712	05.01.02	1634	000000	22128
012.167-030	INDUSTRIAL ENGINEER (profess. & kin.)	5557	11123344455	SNNNNNNNFFONFFNFNNONN	NNNN2NNNNNNNNNN	D,J,P,V	244	712	05.01.06	1634	000000	22128
012.167-034	INDUSTRIAL-HEALTH ENGINEER (profess. & kin.)	5557	11123344453	SNNNNNNNFFONFFNFNNONN	ONNN3NNNNNNNNNN	D,P,J	244	712	05.01.02	1634	000000	22128
012.167-038	LIAISON ENGINEER (aircraft mfg.)	5547	22222333355	LONOOONOOOFOFFNFNNNNN	NNNN4NNNNNNNNNN	D,V,T,P,J	244	712	05.01.06	1634	150603	22128
012.167-042	MANUFACTURING ENGINEER (profess. & kin.)	5558	12122244455	LNNNNNNNOOONFFNFNNONN	NNNN3NNNNNNNNNN	D,J,P,T,V	244	712	05.01.06	1634	000000	22128
012.167-046	PRODUCTION ENGINEER (profess. & kin.)	5558	22223333355	LNNNNNNOFONFFNFNNNNN	NNNN3NNNNNNNNNN	D,V,P,J	244	712	05.01.06	1634	000000	22128
012.167-050	PRODUCTION PLANNER (profess. & kin.)	5447	22223344455	LNNNNNNOFONFFNONNNNN	NNNN3NNNNNNNNNN	D,V,J	244	712	05.01.06	1634	000000	22128
012.167-054	QUALITY CONTROL ENGINEER (profess. & kin.)	6668	11122333354	LNNNNNNOFFNFNNNNOON	NNNN3NNNNNNNNNN	D,J,P,T	211	712	05.01.04	1634	000000	22128
012.167-058	SAFETY MANAGER (profess. & kin.)	6668	22233333344	SNNONONOOOONFFNOOOOON	NNNN3NNNNNNNNNN	D,V,P,J	244	712	05.01.02	1634	430201	13017
012.167-062	SUPERVISOR, VENDOR QUALITY (any industry)	5557	22344333355	SNNNNNNFFONFFNFNOONN	NNNN3NNNNNNNNNN	D,P,J	211	580	05.03.06	7100	150702	13017
012.167-070	TIME-STUDY ENGINEER (profess. & kin.)	5558	11223344454	LNNNNNNNFFNFFNCONFNN	NNNN3NNNNNNNNNN	D,J	244	712	05.01.06	1634	000000	22128
012.167-074	TOOL PLANNER (any industry)	5558	22223344455	SNNNNNNNFFONFFNFNNNN	NNNN3NNNNNNNNNN	D,J	244	712	05.01.06	1634	150603	22128
012.167-078	DOCUMENTATION ENGINEER (profess. & kin.)	5558	11112144455	LNNNNNOOONFFNFNNOOON	NNNN3NNNNNNNNNN	T,P,J	244	712	05.01.06	1634	000000	22128
012.167-082	MATERIAL SCHEDULER (aircraft mfg.)	5557	22223344455	SNNNNNNNFFONOONFNNFNN	NNNN3NNNNNNNNNN	T,J	232	898	05.03.03	1634	150603	22128
012.187-014	SHOE-LAY-OUT PLANNER (boot & shoe)	5548	33333333353	LNNNNNNFFONNNNNFNOFON	NNNN3NNNNNNNNNN	D,J,P,T	244	522	05.03.02	1634	000000	22128
012.261-010	AIR ANALYST (profess. & kin.)	5545	23233333343	LNNNNNNFFONNNNFNNNNN	NNNN3NNNNNNNNNN	J,T	211	706	05.01.04	3890	150599	24599
012.261-014	QUALITY CONTROL TECHNICIAN (profess. & kin.)	5547	22222333354	LNNNNNNNFFFOOONFNFFFN	NNNN3NONNNNNNNNN	V,J,T	211	712	02.04.01	3890	150603	24599
012.267-010	INDUSTRIAL ENGINEERING TECHNICIAN (profess. & kin.)	5547	22222343454	LNNNNNNNFFNFFNFFNFON	NNNN4NNNNNNNNNO	D,J	244	712	05.03.06	3712	150603	22508
012.281-010	SMOKE TESTER (smelt. & refin.)	4435	33343333354	LNNNNNNNFFNNFNNNNNN	NNNN3NFNNNNNNNN	J,T	211	706	02.04.01	3890	150599	24599
013.061-010	AGRICULTURAL ENGINEER (profess. & kin.)	5558	11123333333	LNNNNNNFFNNNNNFNOOON	FNNN3NNNNNNNNNN	V,D,J	244	713	05.01.08	1632	000000	22123
013.061-014	AGRICULTURAL-RESEARCH ENGINEER (profess. & kin.)	5558	22223333344	LNNNNNNNFFNFFNNNNOON	ONNN3NNNNNNNNNN	D,J,P	251	562	05.01.01	1632	000000	22123
013.061-018	DESIGN-ENGINEER, AGRICULTURAL EQUIPMENT (profess. & kin.)	5558	22223333344	LNNNNNNFFFNFFNNNOON	NNNN3NNNNNNNNNN	D,J,P	244	562	05.01.07	1632	000000	22123
013.061-022	TEST ENGINEER, AGRICULTURAL EQUIPMENT (profess. & kin.)	5558	22223333344	LNNNNNNFFFNFNNNNNN	ONNN3NNNNNNNNNN	D,J,P	211	562	05.01.04	1632	000000	22123
013.151-010	SALES ENGINEER, AGRICULTURAL EQUIPMENT (profess. & kin.)	5558	22223344344	LNNNNNNFFNFNFNNNNON	FNNN3NNNNNNNNNN	D,I,J,P	244	562	05.01.05	4210	080799	49002
013.161-010	AGRICULTURAL-ENGINEERING TECHNICIAN (profess. & kin.)	5547	23222233354	SNNNNNNNFONNNNNFNOFON	FNNN3NNNNNNNNNN	J,T	244	713	05.01.07	3719	020501	22599
014.061-010	DESIGN ENGINEER, MARINE (profess. & kin.)	5558	23222333344	LNNNNNNNFFFNFNFNNOON	NNNN3NNNNNNNNNN	D,J,P	244	593	05.01.07	1637	000000	22138
014.061-014	MARINE ENGINEER (profess. & kin.)	6558	11112343343	LNNNNNNFFFONFFNFNOON	ONNN3NNNNNNNNNN	V,D,J,T	244	714	05.03.02	3720	000000	22514
014.061-018	RESEARCH ENGINEER, MARINE EQUIPMENT (profess. & kin.)	5558	22223333344	LNNNNNNNFFFNFFFNFNNOON	NNNN3NNNNNNNNNN	D,P,J	244	593	05.01.02	1637	000000	22138
014.061-022	TEST ENGINEER, MARINE EQUIPMENT (profess. & kin.)	5558	22223333344	LNNNNNNFFFFNFFNNNOON	NNNN3NNNNNNNNNN	D,J,P	251	593	05.01.01	1637	000000	22138
014.151-010	SALES ENGINEER, MARINE EQUIPMENT (profess. & kin.)	5558	22223333344	LNNNNNNNFFNNFFNNFNNN	NNNN3NNNNNNNNNN	D,J,P	212	593	05.01.05	4210	080799	49002
014.167-010	MARINE SURVEYOR (profess. & kin.)	5448	22233444345	LFOOOOOFFONFFNFFNNN	FNNN3NNNNNNNNNN	J	212	593	05.03.06	1637	000000	22138
014.167-014	PORT ENGINEER (ship-boat mfg.; water trans.)	5438	22222344445	SNNNNNNNFFONNNFNNOONN	NNNN3NNNNNNNNNN	D,J,T	244	706	05.01.06	1637	000000	22138
014.281-010	DRAFTER, MARINE (profess. & kin.)	5547	23222322354	SNNNNNNNFFNNNNNNNN	NNNN3NNNNNNNNNN	J,T	242	714	05.03.02	3720	480101	22514
015.021-010	HEALTH PHYSICIST (profess. & kin.)	6558	11112244454	LNNNNNNNFFONFFNFNNFON	ONNN3NNNNNONNN	D,P,J	293	732	05.01.02	1843	000000	24102
015.061-010	DESIGN ENGINEER, NUCLEAR EQUIPMENT (profess. & kin.)	5558	22223333344	LNNNNNNNFFFNFFNNNOON	NNNN3NNNNNNNNNN	D,J,P	244	725	05.01.07	1627	000000	22117
015.061-014	NUCLEAR ENGINEER (profess. & kin.)	6658	11123333355	SNNNNNNNFFFNFFFFNN	NNNN3NNNNNNFNNN	D,J,T	244	725	05.01.03	1627	080799	22117
015.061-018	RESEARCH ENGINEER, NUCLEAR EQUIPMENT (profess. & kin.)	5558	22223333344	LNNNNNNNFFFNFFNNNN	NNNN3NNNNNNNNNN	D,J,P	251	725	05.01.01	1627	000000	22117
015.061-022	TEST ENGINEER, NUCLEAR EQUIPMENT (profess. & kin.)	5558	22223333344	LNNNNNNNFFFNFNFNNNON	NNNN3NNNNNNNNNN	D,J,P	212	725	05.01.04	1627	000000	22117

DOT #	DOT Title & Industry	Tmg	Aptitude	Physical	Environment	Tempra	WkF	MPSMS	GOE	SOC	CIP	OES
015.061-026	NUCLEAR-FUELS RECLAMATION ENGINEER (profess. & kin.)	6557	11112333355	LNNOOONFFNFFNNFNFNNN	NNNN3NNNNNNNONNN	D,V,J,T	244	715	05.01.03	1627	000000	22117
015.061-030	NUCLEAR-FUELS RESEARCH ENGINEER (profess. & kin.)	6668	11112133344	LNNNNNNFFNFNFOFOON	NNNN3NNNNNNONNN	D,T,J	251	715	05.01.03	1627	000000	22117
015.067-010	NUCLEAR-CRITICALITY SAFETY ENGINEER (profess. & kin.)	6658	11112233455	LNNOOONFFNFFNNFNNNN	NNNN4NNNNNNNONNN	V,T,J	244	715	05.01.02	1627	000000	22117
015.137-010	RADIATION-PROTECTION ENGINEER (profess. & kin.)	5458	22222234455	LNNNNNNOOONFNNFNNNN	NNNN3NNNNNNNONNN	D,V,P,J	211	715	05.01.02	1627	000000	22117
015.151-010	SALES ENGINEER, NUCLEAR EQUIPMENT (profess. & kin.)	5558	22222334444	LNNNNNNFFNFNFNNNNON	NNNN3NNNNNNNONNN	D,J,P	292	725	05.01.05	4210	000000	49002
015.167-010	NUCLEAR-PLANT TECHNICAL ADVISOR (utilities)	6558	11112234444	LNNOOOFFNNFFNFONNON	NNON4NNNNNNNONNN	J,T,V	244	871	05.01.02	1627	000000	22117
015.167-014	NUCLEAR-TEST-REACTOR PROGRAM COORDINATOR (profess. & kin.)	5558	11112223445	LOOOONFFFOFFNFOFFNN	NNNN3NNNNNNNONNN	D,P,T	244	715	05.01.04	1627	410205	22117
015.261-010	CHEMICAL-RADIATION TECHNICIAN (government ser.)	4336	33322423353	LNNOOONFFNOONFNNNON	NNNN4NNNNNNNONNN	J,T	211	715	11.10.03	3832	410205	24508
015.362-010	ACCELERATOR OPERATOR (profess. & kin.)	5457	32332332343	LNNNNNNFFNFNFNNNFFN	NNNN3NNOONONNN	J,T	251	725	02.04.01	3832	000000	24508
015.362-014	GAMMA-FACILITIES OPERATOR (profess. & kin.)	4447	33322422244	MNFFNNFFONOONFNNFNN	NNNN3NNNNNNNNNN	V,J,T	251	725	02.04.01	3832	410204	24508
015.362-018	HOT-CELL TECHNICIAN (profess. & kin.)	4347	33322422244	LNNNNNNCCONOONFFFFOF	NNNN3NNNNNNNNNN	V,J,T	211	725	02.04.01	3832	410205	24508
015.362-022	RADIOISOTOPE-PRODUCTION OPERATOR (profess. & kin.)	4346	33333433334	LNNNNNNCCNNNNFFFOO	NNNN3NNNNNNNNNN	J,T	147	490	02.04.01	3832	410204	24508
015.362-026	REACTOR OPERATOR, TEST-AND-RESEARCH (profess. & kin.)	4447	33333333344	LNNNNNNFFNFNFNNNNNN	NNNN3NNNNNNNNNN	V,J,T	251	725	02.04.01	3832	410205	24508
015.384-010	SCANNER (profess. & kin.)	4346	33322334455	SNNNNNNCCNNNNCNNONN	NNNN3NNNNNNNNNN	J,T	232	715	02.04.01	3832	410204	24508
017.161-010	DRAFTER, CHIEF, DESIGN (utilities)	5558	22222333353	LNNNNNNFFNFNFNFNONN	NNNN3NNNNNNNNNN	D,P,J,T	242	700	05.03.02	3720	150805	22514
017.261-010	AUTO-DESIGN CHECKER (auto. mfg.)	5448	22212223354	LNNNNNNFFNOONFNNFFN	NNNN2NNNNNNNNNN	J,T	242	706	05.03.02	3720	150803	22511
017.261-014	DESIGN DRAFTER, ELECTROMECHANISMS (profess. & kin.)	5547	23222322354	SNNNNNNFCCNFFNCNOFON	NNNN2NNNNNNNNNN	J,T	244	703	05.03.02	3720	480104	22514
017.261-018	DETAILER (profess. & kin.)	4447	22223232255	SNNNNNNFCCNNNNCNOFON	NNNN2NNNNNNNNNN	V,J	242	700	05.03.02	3720	150201	22514
017.261-022	DETAILER, FURNITURE (profess. & kin.)	4447	22222322254	SNNNNNNFCCNNNCNCNOCON	NNNN2NNNNNNNNNN	J,T	242	700	05.03.02	3720	480105	22514
017.261-026	DRAFTER, COMMERCIAL (profess. & kin.)	5546	23222322353	SNNNNNNFFFNNNNFFFFN	NNNN3NNNNNNNNNN	J,T	242	700	05.03.02	3720	480102	22514
017.261-030	DRAFTER, DETAIL (profess. & kin.)	4447	22222222353	SNNNNNNCCNNNNCCCCNN	NNNN2NNNNNNNNNN	J,T	242	700	05.03.02	3720	480101	22514
017.261-034	DRAFTER, HEATING AND VENTILATING (profess. & kin.)	5547	22222222354	SNNNNNNFCCNNNNCCCFON	NNNN2NNNNNNNNNN	J,T	242	706	05.03.02	3720	480102	22514
017.261-038	DRAFTER, PLUMBING (profess. & kin.)	5547	23222222354	SNNNNNNFCCNNNNCCCCON	NNNN2NNNNNNNNNN	J,T	242	706	05.03.02	3720	150101	22514
017.261-042	DRAFTER, AUTOMOTIVE DESIGN (auto. mfg.)	5447	22212223354	LNNNNNNFFNOONFNNFON	NNNN2NNNNNNNNNN	J,T	242	706	05.03.02	3720	480105	22514
017.281-010	AUTO-DESIGN DETAILER (auto. mfg.)	4436	22212223354	LNNNNNNFFNNNNFNNFON	NNNN2NNNNNNNNNN	J,T	242	706	05.03.02	3720	480101	22514
017.281-014	DRAFTER APPRENTICE (profess. & kin.)	5546	22222322353	SNNNNNNFFNNNNFFFFN	NNNN3NNNNNNNNNN	J,T	242	700	05.03.02	3720	480104	22514
017.281-018	DRAFTER, ASSISTANT (profess. & kin.)	4437	34333333354	LNNNNNNFFFNNNNCNNCN	NNNN2NNNNNNNNNN	J,T	244	706	05.03.02	3720	480101	22514
017.281-026	DRAFTER, AUTOMOTIVE DESIGN LAYOUT (auto. mfg.)	4437	22211322254	LNNNNNNFFFNNNNFNNFFN	NNNN2NNNNNNNNNN	J,T	242	708	05.03.02	3720	150903	22514
017.281-030	DRAFTER, OIL AND GAS (petrol. & gas; petrol. refin.)	4437	23222222353	LNNNNNNFFNNNNCNFFFN	NNNN2NNNNNNNNNN	J,T	242	752	05.03.02	3720	480101	22514
017.281-034	TECHNICAL ILLUSTRATOR (profess. & kin.)	5547	23222332353	SNNNNNNFCCNNNNCNCFON	NNNN2NNNNNNNNNN	T,U	264	703	05.03.02	7759	480104	93999
017.684-010	TAPER, PRINTED CIRCUIT LAYOUT (electron. comp.)	2222	44434342355	SNNNNNNFFNFNFNNFNNN	NNNN3NNNNNNNNNN	D,P,J	243	716	05.03.02	3734	150201	22311
018.131-010	SUPERVISOR, CARTOGRAPHY (profess. & kin.)	5558	22222333353	LOONNNNOFFNFFFONN	ONNN3NONNNNNNNNF	D,J,T,P	243	716	05.03.01	1649	150901	22311
018.161-010	SURVEYOR, MINE (profess. & kin.)	5547	23222233345	LFNOONNFFFNFFNFFOFF	CNNN3NONNNNNNNNN	D,J,T	243	716	05.03.01	1649	150201	22521
018.167-010	CHIEF OF PARTY (profess. & kin.)	5546	23222333345	LNNNNNNFFFNNOONFNNNON	FNNN3NNNNNNNNNN	D,J,T	243	716	05.03.01	3739	150201	22311
018.167-014	GEODETIC COMPUTATOR (profess. & kin.)	5547	23222333333	LONOONNFFNFFNFNFFON	FNNN3NNNNNNNNNN	D,J,T	243	716	05.01.06	1643	150201	22311
018.167-018	LAND SURVEYOR (profess. & kin.)	5548	23222333333	LNNNNNNFFNFNFOONON	ONNN3NNNNNNNNNN	D,J,J	295	716	05.02.06	1260	151102	13017
018.167-022	MANAGER, LAND SURVEYING (profess. & kin.)	6658	22211233353	SNNNNNNFCCNFFNCNFFON	NNNN2NNNNNNNNNN	V,D,P,J	243	716	05.03.01	1649	000000	22311
018.167-026	PHOTOGRAMMETRIC ENGINEER (profess. & kin.)	4447	22222244455	SNNNNNNOOOONFNNNFON	NNNN2NNNNNNNNNN	D,J,P	242	716	05.03.02	3734	151102	22521
018.167-030	SUPERVISOR, MAPPING (petrol. & gas; pipe lines)	5547	23222333333	LNNNNNNFFNFNFNNNN	FNNN3NNNNNNNNNN	D,J,T	243	716	05.03.01	3733	151001	22311
018.167-034	SURVEY ASSISTANT, INSTRUMENTS (profess. & kin.)	5547	23222333344	LOONNNNOFFNFFFNNNN	ONNN3NONNNNNNNNF	V,D,J,T	243	716	05.03.01	1649	151102	22311
018.167-038	SURVEYOR, GEODETIC (profess. & kin.)	5446	23222333344	LNNNNNNFFFNNNNCCNNN	FNNN3NNNNNNNNNN	V,D,J,T	243	716	05.03.01	1649	151102	22311
018.167-042	SURVEYOR, GEOPHYSICAL PROSPECTING (petrol. & gas)	5547	23222333333	MNNNNNNFFFNNNNCCNNN	MNNN3NNNNNNNNNN	D,J,T	243	716	05.03.02	1649	400702	22311
018.167-046	SURVEYOR, MARINE (profess. & kin.)	5547	23222333333	SNNNNNNFFNNNNCCCFN	NNNN2NNNNNNNNNN	D,J,T	242	716	05.03.02	3734	151102	22311
018.261-010	DRAFTER, CARTOGRAPHIC (profess. & kin.)	4437	22222222353	LNNNNNNFFFNNNNCNFFON	NNNN3NNNNNNNNNN	J,T	242	716	05.03.02	3734	151102	22521
018.261-018	EDITOR, MAP (profess. & kin.)	4447	23222332343	SNNNNNNFFFNNNNFFON	NNNN2NNNNNNNNNN	J	241	716	05.03.02	3734	151102	22521
018.261-022	MOSAICIST (profess. & kin.)	4447	23222322233	SNNNNNNFFNNNNCNFFON	NNNN2NNNNNNNNNN	J,T	242	716	05.03.02	3739	151102	22521
018.261-026	PHOTOGRAMMETRIST (profess. & kin.)	4336	23222434454	LNNNNNNFFCCNNNNNFON	ONNNNNNNNNNNNNNN	V,J	231	716	05.03.02	1644	150201	22311
018.262-010	FIELD-MAP EDITOR (profess. & kin.)	4447	33322322353	LNNNNNNFFCCNNNCNCFFN	NNNN3NNNNNNNNNN	R,J,T	242	716	05.03.02	3734	151102	22521
018.281-010	STEREO-PLOTTER OPERATOR (profess. & kin.)	6658	11112233353	SNNNNNNFFNFNFFNFOOFN	NNNN3NNNNNNNNNN	D,J,T	244	700	02.02.01	1639	000000	22199
019.061-010	BIOMEDICAL ENGINEER (profess. & kin.)	6658	11112233353	SNNNNNNFFNFNFFNOOOFN	NNNN3NNNNNNNNNN	D,J,T	244	700	02.02.01	1639	000000	22199
019.061-014	MATERIALS ENGINEER (profess. & kin.)	5558	22222233354	SNNNNNNFFNNNNFNNNNN	NNNN3NNNNNNNNNN	V,D,J,T	244	700	05.01.06	1623	150603	22105

DOT #	DOT Title & Industry	Trng	Aptitude	Physical	Environment	Tempra	WkF	MPSMS	GOE	SOC	CIP	OES
019.061-018	OPTICAL ENGINEER (profess. & kin.)	6558	22212244455	SNNNNNNFFNFNFNFFNN	NNNN2NNNNNNNNNNN	D,J	244	606	05.01.07	1639	000000	22199
019.061-022	ORDNANCE ENGINEER (chemical; ordnance)	6658	12122333354	LNNNNNNFFONFFNFNFON	NNNN3NNNNNNNNNNN	D,P,J,T	244	370	05.01.08	1639	000000	22199
019.061-026	RELIABILITY ENGINEER (profess. & kin.)	6658	11122333354	SNNNNNNFFNOONFNNON	NNNN3NNNNNNNNNNN	D,J,T,V	244	719	05.01.04	1639	000000	22199
019.081-010	MAINTAINABILITY ENGINEER (profess. & kin.)	5458	22222333354	SNNNNNNFFNFFNFNNON	NNNN2NNNNNNNNNNN	D,J,T	244	700	05.01.08	1639	000000	22199
019.081-014	PHOTOGRAPHIC ENGINEER (profess. & kin.)	5448	22222233352	LNNNNNNFFONNNFNOONN	NNNN2NNNNNNNNNNN	V,D,J,T	201	753	05.01.07	1639	000000	22199
019.081-018	POLLUTION-CONTROL ENGINEER (profess. & kin.)	6668	11122444254	LNNOONNFFNOONFNNOON	ONNN3NONNNNNNNNNN	D,J,T	244	707	05.01.02	1639	000000	22199
019.161-010	SUPERVISOR, ESTIMATOR AND DRAFTER (utilities)	5558	22222344444	SNNNNNNFFONFFNFNONN	NNNN2NNNNNNNNNNN	V,D,P,J	244	366	05.03.02	3720	150401	85908
019.161-014	TEST TECHNICIAN (profess. & kin.)	5447	22222322244	LNNNNNNFFONFFNFNOON	NNNN3NNNNNNNNNNN	V,J,T	244	560	05.01.04	3719	150805	22599
019.167-010	LOGISTICS ENGINEER (profess. & kin.)	5558	22233344455	SNNNNNNOONFFNFNNNN	NNNN3NNNNNNNNNNN	D,J,T	244	700	05.01.06	1639	150603	22199
019.167-014	PROJECT ENGINEER (profess. & kin.)	5558	22233333355	LNNNNNOFONFFNFNNNN	NNNN3NNNNNNNNNNN	D,V,P,J	244	700	05.01.08	1639	000000	13017
019.167-018	RESOURCE-RECOVERY ENGINEER (government ser.)	6658	12112133354	SNNNNNNFFNFFNFONOON	NNNN3NNNNNNNNNNN	J,P,T	271	719	05.01.02	1628	000000	22121
019.187-010	PACKAGING ENGINEER (profess. & kin.)	5457	33322333353	SNNNNNNFFFNFNFNFNON	NNNN2NNNNNNNNNNN	D,J,P	244	475	05.03.09	1639	000000	22199
019.261-010	BIOMEDICAL EQUIPMENT TECHNICIAN (profess. & kin.)	4446	22222333354	LNNONONFFNNNNFNFFN	NNNN2NNNNNNNNNNN	J,T	111	580	02.04.02	6171	150401	85908
019.261-014	ESTIMATOR AND DRAFTER (utilities)	5557	22222333354	LNNNNNNFFNFFNFNOONN	FNNN3NNNNNNNNNNN	J,T	242	581	05.03.02	3720	480104	22517
019.261-018	FACILITIES PLANNER (any industry)	5557	22233332353	LNNNNNNFFFNFFNCCCCCN	NNNN3NNNNNNNNNNN	D,J	211	719	05.01.06	3719	150101	39999
019.261-022	TEST TECHNICIAN (agric. equip.)	4446	33333333354	LNNNNNNFFONNNNFNOONO	ONNN2NNONNNNNNNN	J,T	211	562	05.03.07	3890	010204	22599
019.261-026	FIRE-PROTECTION ENGINEERING TECHNICIAN (profess. & kin.)	4447	11223344445	LONNNNNCCNOONCOONOO	NNNN3NNNNNNNNNNN	T,J	244	719	05.03.02	3710	150201	22599
019.261-030	LABORATORY TECHNICIAN (auto. mfg.)	4445	33335334355	SNNNNNNFFNFFNFNFFN	NNNN3NNNNNNNNNNN	J,T	212	591	02.04.01	3890	150803	22599
019.261-034	LASER TECHNICIAN (electron. comp.; inst. & app.)	5447	22222322254	MNNOOONCFFNOOOFNFOON	NNNN2NNNNNNFNFNNN	V,T,J	111	580	05.03.02	3719	150304	22599
019.267-010	SPECIFICATION WRITER (profess. & kin.)	5447	22222255555	SNNNNNNOOONNNNFOONNN	NNNN2NNNNNNNNNNN	J,T	244	700	05.03.02	3719	150603	22599
019.281-010	CALIBRATION LABORATORY TECHNICIAN (aircraft mfg.; electron. comp.)	5547	23222432254	LNNONONFFONNNFNFOON	NNNN3NNNONNNNNON	V,T,J	212	601	02.04.01	3711	150303	22505
020.067-014	MATHEMATICIAN (profess. & kin.)	6668	12114444455	SNNNNNNFFNOONFNNONN	NNNN3NNNNNNNNNNN	D,J,T	251	721	02.01.01	1739	000000	25319
020.067-018	OPERATIONS-RESEARCH ANALYST (profess. & kin.)	6667	11233444445	SNNNNNNOOONFFNFNNNN	NNNN2NNNNNNNNNNN	V,J	251	890	11.01.01	1721	000000	25302
020.067-022	STATISTICIAN, MATHEMATICAL (profess. & kin.)	6668	11112344455	SNNNNNNOOONOONFNNFNN	NNNN2NNNNNNNNNNN	J,T	251	721	11.01.01	1733	000000	25312
020.162-010	MATHEMATICAL TECHNICIAN (profess. & kin.)	5557	22234234454	SNNNNNNFFNFFNFNNOON	NNNN3NNNNNNFNFNNN	V,J,T	244	721	11.01.02	3840	000000	25323
020.167-010	ACTUARY (profess. & kin.)	5558	22143144455	SNNNNNNOOONNNNFOONNN	NNNN2NNNNNNNNNNN	D,J,T	232	721	11.01.02	1732	000000	25313
020.167-026	STATISTICIAN, APPLIED (profess. & kin.)	5547	11132244455	SNNNNNNFFNFFNFNNFNN	NNNN3NNNNNNNNNNN	J	251	721	11.01.02	1733	000000	25312
020.167-030	WEIGHT ANALYST (profess. & kin.)	5557	22234244355	MNNNNNNFFNFFNFNNNNN	NNNN3NNNNNNNNNNN	J,T	244	590	07.02.03	1739	000000	25319
021.067-010	ASTRONOMER (profess. & kin.)	6668	11113133453	LNNNNNNNNOOONFNNFNN	NNNN3NNNNNNNNNNN	J	251	722	02.01.01	1842	000000	24102
022.061-010	CHEMIST (profess. & kin.)	6658	11122233352	LNNNNNNFFQOOOFNFFFN	NNNN3NNONNNNNNON	J,T,V	211	723	02.01.01	1845	410301	24105
022.061-014	CHEMIST, FOOD (profess. & kin.)	6557	12132333353	LNNNNNNFFQOOOFNNFFN	NNNN3NNONNNNNNON	D,J	251	732	02.02.03	1845	000000	24105
022.081-010	TOXICOLOGIST (pharmaceut.)	5458	22333233354	LNNNNNNFFQOOOFNNNFN	NNNN3NNNNNNNNNNN	D,J,T	251	732	02.04.02	3820	000000	24308
022.137-010	LABORATORY SUPERVISOR (profess. & kin.)	5547	22233344454	LNNNNNNFFOFFNFNOOON	NNNN3NONNNNNNON	D,J,P,V,T	211	723	02.04.01	1845	000000	24105
022.161-010	CHEMICAL LABORATORY CHIEF (profess. & kin.)	6668	11113333352	LNNNNNNFFOFFOFNOOON	NNNN3NNNNNNNNNNN	D,J,P,T	295	490	02.01.02	1845	000000	24105
022.161-014	COLORIST (profess. & kin.)	5547	22344233351	LNNNNNNFFOFFNFNNFFN	NNNN3NNNNNNNNNNN	J,T	147	490	02.04.02	3831	410301	24505
022.161-018	PERFUMER (chemical)	5547	22244444452	SNNNNNNFFNNNOOFFNNFN	NNNN3NFNNNNNNNN	J	147	494	02.01.02	3831	000000	24505
022.261-010	CHEMICAL LABORATORY TECHNICIAN (profess. & kin.)	6668	22233233354	LNNNNNNFFOOONFNOOON	NNNN3NONNNNNNON	J	147	720	02.04.01	3831	410301	24505
022.261-014	MALT-SPECIFICATIONS-CONTROL ASSISTANT (beverage)	4437	22233244453	SNNNNNNFFQOONFNNON	NNNN3NNNNNNNNNNN	J,T	221	395	05.02.03	3831	150699	24505
022.261-018	CHEMIST, INSTRUMENTATION (profess. & kin.)	5547	22222344454	LNNNNNNFFQOOOFNNOFN	NNNN3NNNNNNNNNNN	J,T	251	874	02.01.01	3831	000000	24505
022.261-022	CHEMIST, WASTEWATER-TREATMENT PLANT (profess. & kin.)	5547	22322344454	SNNNNNNFFOONNNNFNNNON	NNNN3NNNNNNNNNNN	J,T	251	874	02.04.02	3831	000000	24505
022.281-010	ASSAYER (profess. & kin.)	5547	22323333353	LNNNNNNFFONNNNNFNFFN	NNNN2NNNNNNNNNNN	J,T	211	350	02.04.01	3831	410301	24505
022.281-014	CHEMIST, WATER PURIFICATION (waterworks)	6667	22233333353	LNNNNNNFFONOONFNOON	NNNN3NONNNNNNON	J,T	211	491	02.04.01	3831	000000	24505
022.281-018	LABORATORY TESTER (plastic-synth.)	4336	22223343352	LNNNNNNFFNNNNNFNOOFN	NNNN2NNNNNNNNNNN	J,T	147	414	02.04.01	3831	150699	24505
022.381-010	YEAST-CULTURE DEVELOPER (beverage)	4245	33333433354	MNNNNNNNFFOOOFNNFON	OONN3NNNNNNNNNNN	J,V	003	395	02.04.02	3831	150699	24505
023.061-010	ELECTRO-OPTICAL ENGINEER (profess. & kin.)	6668	11112244454	SNNNNNNFFONNNNNFNNNON	NNNN2NNNNNNNNNNN	D,J,T	244	587	05.01.07	1843	000000	24102
023.061-014	PHYSICIST (profess. & kin.)	6668	11111133352	LNNNNNNOOONNNNFNFFN	NNNN2NNNNNNNNNNN	J	251	724	02.01.01	1843	000000	24102
023.067-010	PHYSICIST, THEORETICAL (profess. & kin.)	6667	11111344445	LNNNNNNFFONOONFNNNNN	NNNN2NNNNNNNNNNN	J	251	724	02.01.01	1843	000000	24102
024.061-010	CRYSTALLOGRAPHER (clock & watch)	6668	11233333353	LNNNNNNFFNNNNFNNFFON	NNNN3NNNNNNNNNNN	J	251	725	02.01.02	1847	000000	24111
024.061-014	GEODESIST (profess. & kin.)	6668	11233333344	LNNNNNNFFNNNNNFFFN	ONNN3NNNNNNNNNNN	V,D,J,T	243	725	02.01.01	1649	000000	22311
024.061-018	GEOLOGIST (profess. & kin.)	6668	11122333343	LOOOONNFFNNNNNFFFN	ONNN3NNNNNFNFFN	V,J,T	251	725	02.01.01	1847	000000	24111
024.061-022	GEOLOGIST, PETROLEUM (petrol. & gas)	6658	11212343455	LNNNNNNOOONFFNFFFON	ONNN3NNNNNNNNNN	V,P,J,T	251	725	02.01.02	1847	000000	24111

DOT #	DOT Title & Industry	Trng	Aptitude	Physical	Environment	Tempra	WkF	MPSMS	GOE	SOC	CIP	OES
024.061-026	GEOPHYSICAL PROSPECTOR (petrol. & gas)	6668	11122333343	LNNNNNFFNOONFOOOO	ONNN3NNNNNNNNNN	V,D,J,T	251	725	02.01.02	1847	000000	24111
024.061-030	GEOPHYSICIST (profess. & kin.)	6558	11122334344	LNNNNNFFONFNFFFFO	ONNN3NNNNNNNNNN	V,D,J,T	251	725	02.01.01	1847	000000	24111
024.061-034	HYDROLOGIST (profess. & kin.)	6668	11123333344	LNNOOONFFOONFNFFN	ONNN3NNNNNNNNNN	V,D,J,T	251	725	02.01.01	1847	000000	24111
024.061-038	MINERALOGIST (profess. & kin.)	6668	11223333343	LNOOOOFFOOONFNFFN	ONNN3NNNNNNNNNN	D,J,T	251	725	02.01.01	1847	000000	24111
024.061-042	PALEONTOLOGIST (profess. & kin.)	6668	11312333343	LOOOONFFOOONFNFFN	ONNN3NNNNNNNNNN	V,J,T	251	725	02.01.01	1847	000000	24111
024.061-046	PETROLOGIST (profess. & kin.)	6658	11223333343	LNNOOONFFOOONFNFFN	ONNN3NNNNNNNNNN	D,J,T	251	725	02.01.01	1847	000000	24111
024.061-050	SEISMOLOGIST (profess. & kin.)	6668	11123333343	LNNNNNFFONNNFNFFN	ONNN3NNNNNNNNNN	V,D,J,T	251	725	02.01.01	1847	000000	24111
024.061-054	STRATIGRAPHER (profess. & kin.)	6658	11223333343	LNNNNNFFNNNNFNNFFF	FNNN3NNNNNNNNNN	J	251	725	02.01.01	1847	000000	24111
024.161-010	ENGINEER, SOILS (profess. & kin.)	6567	11223333333	LNNNNNNOOONNFOOFOO	ONNN3NNNNNNNNNN	V,D,J,T	244	704	05.01.08	1847	000000	24111
024.167-010	GEOPHYSICAL-LABORATORY CHIEF (profess. & kin.)	6669	11112444455	LNNNNNNOOONFNFNNFNN	NNNN3NNNNNNNNNN	V,D,P,J	251	725	02.04.01	1847	000000	24111
024.267-010	GEOLOGICAL AIDE (petrol. & gas)	5558	22122223455	LNNNNNNFONFFNFNFNN	NNNN3NNNNNNNNNN	V,I,P	251	725	02.04.01	3833	150903	24511
024.284-010	PROSPECTOR (any industry)	4447	33333344443	HNNOOONFFONNNNOONOON	FNNO4NNNNNNNNNN	J	211	350	05.03.04	3990	000000	39999
024.364-010	PALEONTOLOGICAL HELPER (profess. & kin.)	3226	33343334354	LNNNNNFFFNNNFNNOON	NNNO3NNNNNNNNNN	R	251	725	02.04.01	3890	150903	24599
024.381-010	LABORATORY ASSISTANT (petrol. & gas)	4435	22233432355	LNNNNNFFONNONFNFNN	NNNN3NNNNNNNNNN	J,T	211	340	02.04.01	3833	150903	24511
025.062-010	METEOROLOGIST (profess. & kin.)	5557	22222243434	LNNNNNFOFONONONNOON	NNNN3NNNNNNNNNN	T,P,J	251	725	02.01.01	1846	000000	24108
025.264-010	HYDROGRAPHER (waterworks)	4446	33232253335	MNNNNNOOONNNNFNNFNN	FNNN3NNNNNNNNNN	J	232	725	02.04.01	3890	030101	24599
025.267-010	OCEANOGRAPHER, ASSISTANT (military ser.)	5547	22222333344	MNNNNNFFNFFNFNNOON	ONNN4NNNNNNNNNN	J,T	251	725	02.04.01	3890	400702	24599
025.267-014	WEATHER OBSERVER (profess. & kin.)	4446	33232254555	LNNNNNNOOONNNFNNFNN	NNNN3NNNNNNNNNN	J	232	725	02.04.01	3890	410399	24599
029.067-010	GEOGRAPHER (profess. & kin.)	6667	11233444454	LNNNNNNOOOONFOOFON	ONNN3NNNNNNNNNN	V,D,J	251	729	02.01.01	1849	000000	24199
029.067-014	GEOGRAPHER, PHYSICAL (profess. & kin.)	6667	11233444454	LOOOOOFFNOONFONOON	ONNN3NNNNNNNNNN	V,D,J	251	729	02.01.01	1849	000000	24199
029.081-010	ENVIRONMENTAL ANALYST (profess. & kin.)	6668	11123333344	LNNNNNNOOONFONOON	ONNN3NNNNNNNNNN	D,J,T	251	719	02.01.02	1849	000000	24199
029.081-014	MATERIALS SCIENTIST (profess. & kin.)	6657	11111233343	SNNNNNFFNNNNFNNOFN	NNNN3NNNNNNNNNN	J	251	720	02.01.02	1849	000000	24199
029.167-010	AERIAL-PHOTOGRAPH INTERPRETER (government ser.)	5557	23222344453	SNNNNNNOOONNNFNFFFN	NNNN4NNNNNNNNNN	J,T	271	716	02.01.02	1260	000000	13017
029.167-014	PROJECT MANAGER, ENVIRONMENTAL RESEARCH (profess. & kin.)	5558	33333333343	LNNNNNFFONFFNNNOON	NNNN3NNNNNNNNNN	D,J	251	729	02.01.02	3831	150903	24505
029.261-010	LABORATORY TESTER (any industry)	4446	33333333353	LNNNNNFFNFNNFNFNN	NNNN3NNNNNNNNNN	J,T	211	720	02.04.02	3831	150903	24505
029.261-014	POLLUTION-CONTROL TECHNICIAN (profess. & kin.)	4446	33343334453	LOOOOOFFOFFNFOFOFO	ONNN3NONNNNNNNNO	V,J,T	212	723	05.03.08	3890	030101	24599
029.261-018	TEST-ENGINE OPERATOR (petrol. refin.)	4436	23243444343	LNNNNNFFNFFNFFNFFN	NNNNANONNNNNNNNO	R,J	211	501	05.03.07	3833	150803	24511
029.261-022	TESTER (petrol. refin.)	4436	23233443343	LNNNNNFFFNONFNFFFN	NNNN4NONNNNNNNNO	J,T	152	410	02.04.01	3890	150903	24511
029.261-026	CRIMINALIST (profess. & kin.)	5557	11222244452	LNNNNNNFFOFFNFOFFO	ONNN3NNNNNONNNN	J,P,T,V	271	739	02.04.01	3890	430107	24599
029.280-010	PHOTO-OPTICS TECHNICIAN (profess. & kin.)	5436	22322433354	LNNNNNNFFONNNFOOFOO	NNNN4NNNNNNNNNN	J,T	201	600	02.04.01	3890	100103	24599
029.361-010	BOTTLE-HOUSE QUALITY-CONTROL TECHNICIAN (beverage)	4446	33333333343	LNNNNNFFFNNNFNFFFN	NNNN3NNNNNNNNNN	R,J,T	211	531	02.04.02	3890	150506	24505
029.361-014	FOOD TESTER (any industry)	4335	33333333353	LNNNNNNFFNOOOFNFON	NNNN3NNNNNNNNNN	J,T	211	380	02.04.02	3831	150699	24505
029.361-018	LABORATORY ASSISTANT (utilities)	5556	33323432343	SNNNNNNOOFNOONONONN	NNNN3NNNNNNNNNN	V,J,T	211	720	02.04.01	3972	119999	25105
029.381-010	CLOTH TESTER (garment; textile)	4345	33343333353	LNNNNNNFFONNNONOOFN	NNNN3NNNNNNNNNN	T,J,	211	420	02.04.01	3890	150699	24599
029.381-014	LABORATORY ASSISTANT (textile)	3334	33332433352	LNNNNNNFFONONFNNFFN	NNNN3NNNNNNNNNN	J,T	152	410	02.04.01	3890	150699	24599
029.383-010	PILOT, SUBMERSIBLE (any industry)	5345	22322433323	LNNNNNNFFNOONFONOFF	CONF3NNNNNNNNNF	D,J,S,V	013	725	05.04.02	3890	490304	24599
030.062-010	SOFTWARE ENGINEER (profess. & kin.)	5558	12122233455	SNNNNNNOOFNOONFNNNNN	NNNN3NNNNNNNNNN	V,T,J	233	700	11.01.01	1636	000000	22127
030.162-010	COMPUTER PROGRAMMER (profess. & kin.)	5457	22244144455	SNNNNNNFFNOONFNNONN	NNNN3NNNNNNNNNN	P,J	233	893	11.01.01	3971	521202	25102
030.162-014	PROGRAMMER-ANALYST (profess. & kin.)	5557	12233133455	SNNNNNNOOFFNFFNFNNN	NNNN3NNNNNNNNNN	T,J,P	233	893	11.01.01	1712	000000	25102
030.162-018	PROGRAMMER, ENGINEERING AND SCIENTIFIC (profess. & kin.)	6668	22233244455	SNNNNNNOOFNONONONNN	NNNN3NNNNNNNNNN	J,T	233	700	11.01.01	3972	119999	25105
030.162-022	SYSTEMS PROGRAMMER (profess. & kin.)	5457	12244233355	SNNNNNNFFNFNNNNONN	NNNN2NNNNNNNNNN	T,J,	233	893	11.01.01	1712	119999	25102
030.167-010	CHIEF, COMPUTER PROGRAMMER (profess. & kin.)	5458	22244144455	SNNNNNNFFNFFNFNNNN	NNNN3NNNNNNNNNN	D,T,P,J	233	893	11.01.01	3971	119999	25105
030.167-014	SYSTEMS ANALYST (profess. & kin.)	5457	22244344455	SNNNNNNOOFNFFNFNNNN	NNNN3NNNNNNNNNN	D,P,J	233	893	07.01.02	3990	000000	25102
031.132-010	SUPERVISOR, NETWORK CONTROL OPERATORS (any industry)	4447	22333344455	LNNNNNNOOFNFFNFNFNN	NNNN3NNNNNNNNNN	D,T,P,J	233	893	11.01.01	3990	000000	25199
031.262-010	DATA COMMUNICATIONS ANALYST (profess. & kin.)	5357	22344343354	LNNOOONNOOFNFFNNOON	NNNN3NNNNNNNNNN	P,J	233	893	11.01.01	3990	000000	25199
031.262-014	NETWORK CONTROL OPERATOR (any industry)	4346	33333344454	LNNOONNOOFNFFNFNNOON	NNNN3NNNNNNNNNN	T,P,J	233	893	07.06.01	3990	000000	25199
032.132-010	USER SUPPORT ANALYST SUPERVISOR (profess. & kin.)	4348	22233244455	SNNNNNNFFNCNCNONONN	NNNN3NNNNNNNNNN	P,J,T	233	893	11.01.01	1719	110501	21999
032.262-010	USER SUPPORT ANALYST (profess. & kin.)	4347	22333244455	SNNNNNNOOFNFFNFNNONN	NNNN3NNNNNNNNNN	P,J,T	233	893	11.01.01	1719	110501	21999
033.162-010	COMPUTER SECURITY COORDINATOR (profess. & kin.)	5348	22444234455	SNNNNNNOOFFNFNNNNNN	NNNN3NNNNNNNNNN	T,P,J	233	893	11.10.05	1490	000000	21999
033.162-014	DATA RECOVERY PLANNER (profess. & kin.)	5358	22343244455	LNNNNNNOOFNFFNFNNONN	NNNN3NNNNNNNNNN	D,T,P,J	233	893	11.01.01	1490	000000	21999
033.162-018	TECHNICAL SUPPORT SPECIALIST (profess. & kin.)	5457	22333333355	LNNNNNNOOFNFFNFNONN	NNNN3NNNNNNNNNN	D,T,P,J	233	893	11.01.01	1719	110301	25199

DOT #	DOT Title & Industry	Trng	Aptitude	Physical	Environment	Tempra	WkF	MPSMS	GOE	SOC	CIP	OES
033.167-010	COMPUTER SYSTEMS HARDWARE ANALYST (profess. & kin.)	5557	12223344455	SNNNNNNFFONFFNFNONN	NNNN3NNNNNNNN	D,P,J	244	893	05.01.03	1636	000000	22127
033.262-010	QUALITY ASSURANCE ANALYST (profess. & kin.)	4446	22344133455	LNNNNNNFFNFFNFNNONN	NNNN3NNNNNNNN	T,J	233	893	11.01.01	1719	000000	25102
033.362-010	COMPUTER SECURITY SPECIALIST (profess. & kin.)	4236	22444234455	SNNNNNNOOFNFNCNNCNN	NNNN3NNNNNNNN	T,P	233	893	11.10.05	1490	000000	21999
039.162-010	DATA BASE ADMINISTRATOR (profess. & kin.)	5458	12233144455	SNNNNNNOOONFFNCNNONN	NNNN2NNNNNNNN	J,P,T	233	893	11.01.01	1719	000000	25199
039.162-014	DATA BASE DESIGN ANALYST (profess. & kin.)	5458	12233144455	SNNNNNNOOONFFNCNNONN	NNNN3NNNNNNNN	J,P,T	233	893	11.01.01	1719	000000	25199
039.264-010	MICROCOMPUTER SUPPORT SPECIALIST (profess. & kin.)	4347	23333323354	MONFFFOFFNFNFONNON	NNNN3NNNNNNNN	V,T,P,J	233	571	05.05.05	3990	000000	39999
040.061-010	AGRONOMIST (profess. & kin.)	6668	11244343344	LNNNNNNFFFNNNFNFFN	FNNN3NNNNNNNN	D,J	251	731	02.02.02	1853	049999	24305
040.061-014	ANIMAL SCIENTIST (profess. & kin.)	6668	11222332254	MNNNNNNFFFONNNFNNON	FNNN3NNNNNNNN	V,D,J,T	251	731	02.02.01	1853	000000	24305
040.061-018	DAIRY SCIENTIST (profess. & kin.)	6668	11233422245	LNNNNNNFFOONNNFNOON	NNNN3NNNNNNNN	D,J,T	251	731	02.02.01	1853	000000	24305
040.061-022	DAIRY TECHNOLOGIST (profess. & kin.)	6668	11233342243	LNNNNNNFFNFOONNNFNOFON	NNNN3NNNNNNNN	D,J	251	383	02.02.04	3820	020206	24502
040.061-026	FIBER TECHNOLOGIST (profess. & kin.)	6668	11322433444	LNNNNNNFFOONNNFNOFON	NNNN3NNNNNNNN	D,J,T	251	731	05.01.08	1852	000000	24302
040.061-030	FOREST ECOLOGIST (profess. & kin.)	6668	11233443354	LNNNNNNOOOONNNOOOOOO	FNNN3NNNNNNNN	D,J,T	251	731	02.02.02	1853	030101	24302
040.061-038	HORTICULTURIST (profess. & kin.)	6668	11233343354	MNNOOONFFOFFNFNFFN	ONNN3NNNNNNNN	D,J,T	251	731	02.02.02	1853	000000	24305
040.061-042	POULTRY SCIENTIST (profess. & kin.)	6668	11222333354	LNNNNNNFFONNNNONOON	ONNN3NNNNNNNN	D,J,T	251	731	02.02.01	1853	000000	24305
040.061-046	RANGE MANAGER (profess. & kin.)	6668	11222333344	LNNNNNNOOOOONNOFOFOF	ONNN3NNNNNNNN	V,J,T	251	310	02.02.02	1852	020409	24302
040.061-050	SILVICULTURIST (profess. & kin.)	5557	11233492254	LNNFFNFFNFNFNFNFN	FNNN3NNNNNNNN	D,J,T	251	731	02.02.02	1852	049999	24302
040.061-054	SOIL CONSERVATIONIST (profess. & kin.)	6668	11222433354	LNNOOONFFNOONFOOOOO	FNNN3NNNNNNNN	D,P,J	251	731	02.02.02	1852	049999	24302
040.061-058	SOIL SCIENTIST (profess. & kin.)	6668	11233443353	LNNOOONFFFNNNFNNOON	FNNN3NNNNNNNN	D,J,T	251	731	02.02.02	1853	020501	24305
040.061-062	WOOD TECHNOLOGIST (profess. & kin.)	6558	11233443344	LNNNNNNFFONNNNFNOOON	NNNN4NNNNNNNN	D,J,T	251	459	02.02.02	1852	000000	24302
040.167-010	FORESTER (profess. & kin.)	5558	22233344444	LOOOONOOOOFFNOOOOOO	ONNN3NONNNNNO	D,V,P,J	251	310	03.01.04	1852	030405	24302
040.261-010	SOIL-CONSERVATION TECHNICIAN (profess. & kin.)	5447	22222223334	LNNOOONFFONFNFFOOON	NNNO4NNNNNNNON	J,P,T,V	243	731	02.02.02	1852	020501	24302
040.361-010	LABORATORY TECHNICIAN, ARTIFICIAL BREEDING (agriculture)	4445	33333333353	LNNNNNNFFFNNNNFNOONN	NNNN3NNNNNNNN	J	211	321	02.04.02	3820	010501	24502
040.361-014	SEED ANALYST (profess. & kin.)	4447	33332443453	LNNOONOOOONNNONNOON	NNNN3NNNNNNNN	J,T	211	311	02.04.02	3820	010304	24502
041.061-010	ANATOMIST (profess. & kin.)	6668	11211332244	LNNNNNNFFFNNNFNNFFN	ONNN3NNNNNNNN	V,D,J	251	732	02.02.01	1855	000000	24311
041.061-014	ANIMAL BREEDER (profess. & kin.)	6668	11233433445	LNNNNNNFFFNNNNFOOOO	NNNN3NNNNNNNN	V,D,J,T	251	732	02.02.03	1853	000000	24305
041.061-018	APICULTURIST (profess. & kin.)	6668	11211332243	LNNNNNNNFFFNNNNFOOFOO	ONNN3NNNNNNNN	D,J,T	251	732	02.02.01	1853	000000	24305
041.061-022	AQUATIC BIOLOGIST (profess. & kin.)	6668	12112333343	LNNNNNNFFFONNNFNOOON	FNNO3NNNNNNNN	V,D,J,T	251	732	02.02.03	1854	000000	24308
041.061-026	BIOCHEMIST (profess. & kin.)	6668	12122233353	LNNNNNNFFFNNNNFFN	NNNN3NNNNNNNN	J,T	251	732	02.02.01	1854	000000	24308
041.061-030	BIOLOGIST (profess. & kin.)	6668	11112333343	LNNOOONFFFOONFNFFFN	ONNN3NNNNNNNN	J,T	251	732	02.02.03	1854	000000	24311
041.061-034	BIOPHYSICIST (profess. & kin.)	6668	11111333352	LNNNNNNFFOOONFNFFFN	NNNN3NNNNNNNN	J,T	251	732	02.02.03	1854	000000	24308
041.061-038	BOTANIST (profess. & kin.)	6668	11211333443	LNNOONOOOONNNONNOON	NNNN3NNNNNNNN	J	251	732	02.02.03	1854	000000	24308
041.061-042	CYTOLOGIST (profess. & kin.)	6668	11112333342	LNNOOONOOOOONNNONOON	NNNN3NNNNNNNN	D,J,T	251	732	02.02.02	1854	000000	24308
041.061-046	ENTOMOLOGIST (profess. & kin.)	6668	11222343354	LNNOOONFFNNNNFFOOOO	FNNN3NONNNNNN	D,J	251	732	02.02.03	1853	000000	24308
041.061-050	GENETICIST (profess. & kin.)	6668	11211333355	LNNNNNNNFFNNNNFNFFFN	NNNN3NNNNNNNN	D,J,T	251	732	02.02.01	1854	000000	24305
041.061-054	HISTOPATHOLOGIST (medical ser.)	6668	11211232252	SNNNNNNFFONNNNFNOOON	NNNN2NNNNNNNN	D,T,J	211	732	02.02.01	1855	000000	24311
041.061-058	MICROBIOLOGIST (profess. & kin.)	6668	11222343354	LNNONNNFFFOONFNFFN	NNNN3NNNNNNNN	D,J,T	251	732	02.02.03	1854	000000	24308
041.061-062	MYCOLOGIST (profess. & kin.)	6668	11222333343	LNNNNNNFFONNNFNFFFN	NNNN3NNNNNNNN	D,J,T	251	739	02.02.02	1854	000000	24308
041.061-066	NEMATOLOGIST (profess. & kin.)	6668	11233443354	LNNNNNNFFFOONNNFNFFN	ONNN3NNNNNNNN	D,J	251	732	02.02.02	1854	000000	24308
041.061-070	PARASITOLOGIST (profess. & kin.)	6668	11222343354	LNNNNNNFFFOONNNFNFFN	NNNN3NNNNNNNN	D,J,T	251	732	02.02.01	1854	000000	24311
041.061-074	PHARMACOLOGIST (profess. & kin.)	6668	12111322253	LNNNNNNFFOONNNFNNFFN	NNNN3NNNNNNNN	J,T	251	732	02.02.01	1855	000000	24311
041.061-078	PHYSIOLOGIST (profess. & kin.)	6668	11222422253	LNNNNNNFFOONNNFNFFFN	FNNN3NNNNNNNN	V,J	251	732	02.02.01	1855	000000	24308
041.061-082	PLANT BREEDER (profess. & kin.)	6668	11233433454	LNNOONFFFOONFNNFFFN	NNNN3NNNNNNNN	D,J,T	251	732	02.02.03	1853	000000	24305
041.061-086	PLANT PATHOLOGIST (profess. & kin.)	6668	11222342253	LNNOONFFNNNNFNNFFFN	FNNN3NONNNNNN	D,J,T	251	732	02.02.02	1854	000000	24311
041.061-090	ZOOLOGIST (profess. & kin.)	6668	11222422253	LOOOOOOFFOOONFOOOOO	FNNN3NNNNNNNN	V,J	251	732	02.02.01	1854	020402	24311
041.061-094	STAFF TOXICOLOGIST (government ser.)	6668	11211232351	LNNONNNFFFNFNFNNFCN	NNNN3NNNNNNNN	D,J,T	251	732	02.02.01	1854	000000	24308
041.067-010	MEDICAL COORDINATOR, PESTICIDE USE (government ser.)	6559	11232244452	SNNNNNNFFONFFNFNNFN	NNNN3NNNNNNNN	J,P,T	251	925	02.02.01	1855	000000	24311
041.081-010	FOOD TECHNOLOGIST (profess. & kin.)	6547	12222233353	LNNNNNNFFFNNNNFNNOFN	NNNN3NNNNNNNN	J	251	380	02.02.04	1853	000000	24305
041.167-010	ENVIRONMENTAL EPIDEMIOLOGIST (government ser.)	6658	12122133352	LNNNNNNFFFNNNNFNNOFN	NNNN3NNNNNNNN	D,J,T	251	732	02.02.01	1854	000000	24311
041.261-010	PUBLIC-HEALTH MICROBIOLOGIST (government ser.)	6667	11222332254	LNNNNNNFFONOONNNOOON	NNNN3NNNNNNNN	P,J,T	211	732	02.04.02	1855	000000	24311
041.381-010	BIOLOGY SPECIMEN TECHNICIAN (profess. & kin.)	4337	33422422253	SNNNNNFFNNNNFNNFFN	FNNN3NNNNNNNN	J	136	732	02.04.02	3820	400702	24502
041.384-010	HERBARIUM WORKER (profess. & kin.)	4345	33432333354	LNNONONFFFOOONFNOOON	NNNN3NNNNNNNON	J,T,V	031	310	02.04.02	3990	000000	24502

DOT #	DOT Title & Industry	Trng	Aptitude	Physical	Environment	Tempra	WkF	MPSMS	GOE	SOC	CIP	OES
045.061-010	PSYCHOLOGIST, DEVELOPMENTAL (profess. & kin.)	6657	11233433355	LNNNNNNFFNOONFNNONN	NNNN3NNNNNNNNNNN	V,P,J	251	733	11.03.01	1915	000000	27108
045.061-014	PSYCHOLOGIST, ENGINEERING (profess. & kin.)	6668	11223444455	SNNNNNNNOOONFFNFNNNNN	NNNN2NNNNNNNNNNN	V,J	244	733	11.03.01	1915	000000	27108
045.061-018	PSYCHOLOGIST, EXPERIMENTAL (profess. & kin.)	6658	11233433354	LNNNNNNFFONFFNFNNNNN	NNNN2NNNNNNNNNNN	V,D,J	251	733	11.03.01	1915	000000	27108
045.067-010	PSYCHOLOGIST, EDUCATIONAL (profess. & kin.)	6658	11233444455	LNNNNNNFFFNFFNFNNNNN	NNNN3NNNNNNNNNNN	V,P,I,J	296	733	11.03.01	1915	000000	27108
045.067-014	PSYCHOLOGIST, SOCIAL (profess. & kin.)	6658	11244355455	SNNNNNNFFOOFFNFNNNNN	NNNN2NNNNNNNNNNN	V,P,E	251	733	11.03.01	1915	000000	27108
045.067-018	PSYCHOMETRIST (profess. & kin.)	5557	22233244455	SNNNNNNFFONFNFNNNNN	NNNN2NNNNNNNNNNN	V,J,P,	271	733	11.03.01	1915	000000	27108
045.107-010	COUNSELOR (profess. & kin.)	5557	11244444455	SNNNNNNNOOONFFNFNNNNN	NNNN2NNNNNNNNNNN	J,P,V	298	733	10.01.02	2400	000000	31514
045.107-014	COUNSELOR, NURSES' ASSOCIATION (medical ser.)	5458	21334444455	SNNNNNNNFFNNCCNNNNNNN	NNNN2NNNNNNNNNNN	V,D,P	295	733	10.01.02	2400	000000	31514
045.107-018	DIRECTOR OF COUNSELING (profess. & kin.)	5558	11234444455	SNNNNNNNFFNFFNFNNNNN	NNNN2NNNNNNNNNNN	D,P,I,J	291	733	10.01.02	2400	000000	31514
045.107-022	CLINICAL PSYCHOLOGIST (profess. & kin.)	6568	11343334455	SNNNNNNNOOONFCNONNNNN	NNNN2NNNNNNNNNNN	V,P,J,D	298	733	10.01.02	1915	000000	27108
045.107-026	PSYCHOLOGIST, COUNSELING (profess. & kin.)	6558	11343344455	SNNNNNNNFFONFFNFNNNNN	NNNN2NNNNNNNNNNN	V,P,I,J	298	733	10.01.02	1915	000000	27108
045.107-030	PSYCHOLOGIST, INDUSTRIAL-ORGANIZATIONAL (profess. & kin.)	6658	11233444455	LNNNNNNNNNNNFFNFONONN	NNNN3NNNNNNNNNNN	V,P,I,J	251	733	11.03.01	1915	000000	27108
045.107-034	PSYCHOLOGIST, SCHOOL (profess. & kin.)	6558	11244444455	SNNNNNNNFFONFFNFONONN	NNNN2NNNNNNNNNNN	P,I,J	298	733	10.01.02	1915	000000	31514
045.107-038	RESIDENCE COUNSELOR (education)	5457	11444444455	SNNNNNNNNNNFFNNNNNNN	NNNN2NNNNNNNNNNN	V,P,I,J	298	733	10.01.02	2400	000000	31514
045.107-042	VOCATIONAL REHABILITATION COUNSELOR (government ser.)	5358	22344344455	SNNNNNNNOOONFFNFNNNNN	NNNN2NNNNNNNNNNN	D,J,V,P	298	733	10.01.02	2400	000000	31514
045.107-046	PSYCHOLOGIST, CHIEF (profess. & kin.)	6568	11243344455	SNNNNNNNOOONFFNFNNNNN	NNNN3NNNNNNNNNNN	D,I,V,P,J	294	733	10.01.02	1915	000000	27108
045.107-050	CLINICAL THERAPIST (profess. & kin.)	5557	11144144455	SNNNNNNNOOONFFNFNNNNN	NNNN3NNNNNNNNNNN	I,V,P,J	294	924	10.01.02	3039	000000	32399
045.107-054	COUNSELOR, MARRIAGE AND FAMILY (profess. & kin.)	5358	21344244455	SNNNNNNNOOONCCNONNNNN	NNNN2NNNNNNNNNNN	I,V,P,J	298	733	10.01.02	2400	000000	27302
045.107-058	SUBSTANCE ABUSE COUNSELOR (profess. & kin.)	5358	22344244455	SNNNNNNNOOONCFNNNNNN	NNNN2NNNNNNNNNNN	I,P,J	298	733	10.01.02	2400	000000	31514
045.117-010	DIRECTOR OF GUIDANCE IN PUBLIC SCHOOLS (education)	5558	11244344455	LNNNNNNNNNNFFNFONONN	NNNN2NNNNNNNNNNN	D,P	295	931	11.07.03	2400	000000	31514
049.127-010	PARK NATURALIST (government ser.)	5457	22422234333	MNNNNNNNFFONFFNFOONOO	ONNN4NNNNNNNNNNO	D,J,P,V	282	959	11.07.03	1852	030101	24302
049.364-010	FEED-RESEARCH AIDE (agriculture)	3224	33344344455	MNNNNNNNFFOOOONOONNNN	FNNN3NONNNNNNNN	V	251	731	02.04.02	3820	010302	24502
049.364-014	VECTOR CONTROL ASSISTANT (government ser.)	4235	33333334334	LNNOOONFFNOONFNNON	ONNO3NNNNNNNNN	J	211	920	02.04.02	3820	010302	24502
049.364-018	BIOLOGICAL AIDE (agriculture)	3336	33433434344	MNNOOOOOOOOOOONOOOOO	FOOO3NONNNNNNNN	R	251	300	11.03.05	1912	000000	27102
050.067-010	ECONOMIST (profess. & kin.)	5558	22255255555	SNNNNNNNNOOFNFNNNNN	NNNN3NNNNNNNNNNN	D,I,T,P,J	251	741	11.06.03	1912	521402	27102
050.067-014	MARKET-RESEARCH ANALYST I (profess. & kin.)	5557	22244244455	SNNNNNNNFFNNFNOONNNN	NNNN3NNNNNNNNNNN	J	271	741	11.01.02	1132	000000	19005
050.117-010	DIRECTOR, EMPLOYMENT RESEARCH AND PLANNING (government ser.)	5558	22244244455	SNNNNNNNFFNNFFNFNNNNN	NNNN2NNNNNNNNNNN	D,J	295	959	11.01.02	1914	000000	27199
051.067-010	POLITICAL SCIENTIST (profess. & kin.)	6558	22334244455	SNNNNNNNNNNFFNNNNNNN	NNNN2NNNNNNNNNNN	D,J	251	742	11.03.02	1914	000000	27199
052.067-010	BIOGRAPHER (profess. & kin.)	5257	22344244455	SNNNNNNNNNNFFNNNNNNN	NNNN2NNNNNNNNNNN	D,J	251	743	01.01.02	1913	000000	27199
052.067-014	DIRECTOR, STATE-HISTORICAL SOCIETY (profess. & kin.)	5358	21444244455	SNNNNNNNFFONFFNFNNNNN	NNNN2NNNNNNNNNNN	D,I,J,P	251	743	11.03.03	1913	000000	19999
052.067-018	GENEALOGIST (profess. & kin.)	5257	22344244455	SNNNNNNNFFNNFFNFNNNNN	NNNN2NNNNNNNNNNN	D,J	251	743	11.03.03	1913	000000	27199
052.067-022	HISTORIAN (profess. & kin.)	5257	22344244455	SNNNNNNNFFNNFFNFNNNNN	NNNN2NNNNNNNNNNN	D,J	251	743	11.03.03	1913	000000	27199
052.067-026	HISTORIAN, DRAMATIC ARTS (profess. & kin.)	5458	22433244453	SNNNNNNNOOONFNFNNONN	ONNN2NNNNNNNNNNN	D,P	251	754	11.03.03	1913	000000	27199
052.167-010	DIRECTOR, RESEARCH (motion picture; radio-tv broad.)	6557	11344144455	LNNNNNNNFFONFFNFNNCON	NNNN2NNNNNNNNNNN	D,P	251	941	11.03.02	1916	000000	27199
054.067-010	RESEARCH WORKER, SOCIAL WELFARE (profess. & kin.)	6557	11344344455	SNNNNNNNNNNFFNNNNNNN	NNNN2NNNNNNNNNNN	D,J	251	744	11.03.03	1916	000000	27199
054.067-014	SOCIOLOGIST (profess. & kin.)	5456	22344344455	SNNNNNNNOOOFFNFNNNNN	NNNN3NNNNNNNNNNN	D,V,P,J	294	744	11.03.02	1916	000000	27199
054.067-018	CLINICAL SOCIOLOGIST (profess. & kin.)	6557	11322444445	LNNNNNNNFFONNNFNNNNN	NNNN2NNNNNNNNNNN	J	251	745	11.03.03	1919	000000	27199
055.067-010	ANTHROPOLOGIST (profess. & kin.)	6557	11322444445	LNNNNNNNFFONFFNFNNNNN	NNNN2NNNNNNNNNNN	J	251	745	02.02.01	1919	000000	27199
055.067-014	ANTHROPOLOGIST, PHYSICAL (profess. & kin.)	6557	11322444445	LNNNNNNNFFONFFNFNNCON	ONNN2NNNNNNNNNNN	J	251	745	11.03.03	1919	450301	27199
055.067-018	ARCHEOLOGIST (profess. & kin.)	6557	11322444455	LNNNNNNNFFNNFFNFNNNNN	NNNN2NNNNNNNNNNN	J	251	745	11.03.03	1919	000000	27199
055.067-022	ETHNOLOGIST (profess. & kin.)	4446	33423333454	LNNNNNNNFFONNNNFNNNNN	NNNN2NCNNNNNNNN	J	251	745	01.06.02	1919	450301	27199
059.067-010	PHILOLOGIST (profess. & kin.)	5158	22443244454	LNNNNNNNFFNNFFNFNNFFN	NNNN2NNNNNNNNNNN	J	251	749	11.03.02	1919	000000	27199
059.067-014	SCIENTIFIC LINGUIST (profess. & kin.)	6568	22322244455	SNNNNNNNFFNNFFNFNNNNN	NNNN2NNNNNNNNNNN	P,J	251	745	11.03.02	1919	000000	27199
059.167-010	INTELLIGENCE RESEARCH SPECIALIST (profess. & kin.)	6558	11123444555	SNNNNNNNOOONFFNFNNNNN	NNNN2NNNNNNNNNNN	V,D,E	251	952	11.03.02	1919	000000	27199
059.167-014	INTELLIGENCE SPECIALIST (government ser.)	5447	21333344555	SNNNNNNNFFNFFNFNNNNN	NNNN2NNNNNNNNNNN	V,J,E	211	952	11.03.02	1919	000000	27199
059.267-010	INTELLIGENCE SPECIALIST (military ser.)	4447	22333334453	LNNNNNNNNNNFFNFNNCON	NNNN3NNNNNNNNNNN	J	231	959	04.01.02	1919	000000	27199
070.061-010	PATHOLOGIST (medical ser.)	6568	11211231253	LNNNNNNNFFOFFNCNNFON	NNNN2NCNNNNNNNN	D,J	251	925	02.03.01	2610	000000	32102
070.101-010	ANESTHESIOLOGIST (medical ser.)	6568	12221222253	LNNNNNNNOFFFFNCNNFOFN	NNNN2NNNNNNNNNNN	J,P,S	294	921	02.03.01	2610	000000	32102
070.101-014	CARDIOLOGIST (medical ser.)	6569	11211221243	LNNNNNNNOFFFFNCNNFFN	NNNN2NNNNNNNNNNN	J,P,S	294	921	02.03.01	2610	000000	32102
070.101-018	DERMATOLOGIST (medical ser.)	6568	11221231243	LNNNNNNNOFCFFNCNNFFN	NNNN2NNNNNNNNNNN	J,P,S	294	921	02.03.01	2610	000000	32102

DOT #	DOT Title & Industry	Trng	Aptitude	Physical	Environment	Tempra	WkF	MPSMS	GOE	SOC	CIP	OES
070.101-022	GENERAL PRACTITIONER (medical ser.)	6568	11212221243	LNNNNNNFFFOFFNFNFON	NNNN2NNNNNNNNNN	D,J,P,S	294	921	02.03.01	2610	000000	32102
070.101-026	FAMILY PRACTITIONER (medical ser.)	6568	11211221243	LNNNNNNFFFOFFNFNNOON	NNNN2NNNNNNNNNN	D,J,P,S	294	921	02.03.01	2610	000000	32102
070.101-034	GYNECOLOGIST (medical ser.)	6568	11211231243	LNNNNNNOFFFFNCNNFON	NNNN2NNNNNNNNNN	D,J,P,S	294	921	02.03.01	2610	000000	32102
070.101-042	INTERNIST (medical ser.)	6568	11211221143	LNNNNNNFFFOFFNFNCNFON	NNNN2NNNNNNNNNN	D,J,P,S	294	921	02.03.01	2610	000000	32102
070.101-046	PUBLIC HEALTH PHYSICIAN (medical ser.)	6568	11212232253	LNNNNNNOFFOFFNCNNOON	NNNN2NNNNNNNNNN	D,J,P	294	921	02.03.01	2610	000000	32102
070.101-050	NEUROLOGIST (medical ser.)	6568	11211232243	LNNNNNNOFFOFFNCNNCON	NNNN2NNNNNNNNNN	D,J,P,S	294	921	02.03.01	2610	000000	32102
070.101-054	OBSTETRICIAN (medical ser.)	6568	11211231143	LNNNNNNOFFFFNCNNFON	NNNN2NNNNNNNNNN	D,J,P,S	294	921	02.03.01	2610	000000	32102
070.101-058	OPHTHALMOLOGIST (medical ser.)	6568	11211221242	LNNNNNNOFFFFNCNNFFN	NNNN2NNNNNNNNNN	D,J,P,S	294	921	02.03.01	2610	000000	32102
070.101-062	OTOLARYNGOLOGIST (medical ser.)	6569	11211231243	LNNNNNNOFFFFNCNNFON	NNNN2NNNNNNNNNN	D,J,P,S	294	921	02.03.01	2610	000000	32102
070.101-066	PEDIATRICIAN (medical ser.)	6568	11211221153	LNNNNNNOFFFFNFNNFON	NNNN2NNNNNNNNNN	D,J,P,S	294	921	02.03.01	2610	000000	32102
070.101-070	PHYSIATRIST (medical ser.)	6568	11211222244	MNNNNNNFFFFFNNNNON	NNNN2NNNNNNNNNN	D,J,P,S	294	921	02.03.01	2610	000000	32102
070.101-078	PHYSICIAN, OCCUPATIONAL (medical ser.)	6568	11212221253	LNNNNNNFFFOFFNFNNON	NNNN2NNNNNNNNNN	J,P,S	294	921	02.03.01	2610	000000	32102
070.101-082	POLICE SURGEON (medical ser.)	6568	11212221253	LNNNNNNFFFFFNFNNNON	NNNN2NNNNNNNNNN	P,J,S	294	921	02.03.01	2610	000000	32102
070.101-086	PROCTOLOGIST (medical ser.)	6568	11211221243	LNNNNNNOFFFFNCNNOON	NNNN2NNNNNNNNNN	D,J,P,S	294	921	02.03.01	2610	000000	32102
070.101-090	RADIOLOGIST (medical ser.)	6568	11211221143	LNNNNNNOFFOFFNCNNOON	NNNN2NNNNNONNNN	D,J,P,S	294	921	02.03.01	2610	000000	32102
070.101-094	SURGEON (medical ser.)	6569	11211221143	LNNNNNNOFFFFNCNNFON	NNNN2NNNNNNNNNC	D,J,P,S	294	921	02.03.01	2610	000000	32102
070.101-098	UROLOGIST (medical ser.)	6569	11211221143	LNNNNNNOFFFFNCNNFFN	NNNN2NNNNNNNNNN	D,J,P,S	294	921	02.03.01	2610	000000	32102
070.101-102	ALLERGIST-IMMUNOLOGIST (medical ser.)	6569	11211231143	LNNNNNNOFFFFNCNNFFN	NNNN2NNNNNNNNNN	D,J,P,S	294	921	02.03.01	2610	000000	32102
070.107-014	PSYCHIATRIST (medical ser.)	6568	11212344454	LNNNNNNOOONFFNNNNON	NNNN2NNNNNNNNNN	D,J,P,S	294	921	02.03.01	2610	000000	32102
071.101-010	OSTEOPATHIC PHYSICIAN (medical ser.)	6568	11212221243	LNNNNNNFFFFFNFNFFN	NNNN2NNNNNNNNNN	J,P,S	294	921	02.03.01	2610	000000	32102
072.061-010	ORAL PATHOLOGIST (medical ser.)	6558	12111321143	MNNNNNNFFFFFNNNFFN	NNNN2NNNNNNNNNN	J,P,T,S	294	922	02.03.02	2620	000000	32105
072.101-010	DENTIST (medical ser.)	6558	11212221243	LNNNNNNFFFFFFNFFFN	NNNN2NNNNNNNNNN	J,P,T,S	294	922	02.03.02	2620	000000	32105
072.101-014	ENDODONTIST (medical ser.)	6558	11212221243	LNNNNNNFFFFFFNFFON	NNNN2NNNNNNNNNN	J,P,T,S	294	922	02.03.02	2620	000000	32105
072.101-018	ORAL AND MAXILLOFACIAL SURGEON (medical ser.)	6558	12211221143	LNNNNNNFFFOFFNCNNFON	NNNN2NNNNNNNNNN	J,T,P,S	294	922	02.03.02	2620	000000	32105
072.101-022	ORTHODONTIST (medical ser.)	6558	11213321244	LNNNNNNFFFFNCNNFON	NNNN2NNNNNNNNNN	J,P,T,S	294	922	02.03.02	2620	000000	32105
072.101-026	PEDIATRIC DENTIST (medical ser.)	6558	11212221244	LNNNNNNFFCFFNCNNFON	NNNN2NNNNNNNNNN	J,P,T,S	294	922	02.03.02	2620	000000	32105
072.101-030	PERIODONTIST (medical ser.)	6558	11212221243	LNNNNNNFFCFFNCNNFON	NNNN2NNNNNNNNNN	J,P,T,S	294	922	02.03.02	2620	000000	32105
072.101-034	PROSTHODONTIST (medical ser.)	6558	11212221244	LNNNNNNFFCFFNCNNFON	NNNN2NNNNNNNNNN	J,P,S,T	294	922	02.03.02	2620	000000	32105
072.101-038	PUBLIC-HEALTH DENTIST (medical ser.)	6558	11212221243	LNNNNNNOFFOFFNFNFON	NNNN2NNNNNNNNNN	D,J,P,S	294	922	02.03.02	2620	000000	32105
072.117-010	DIRECTOR, DENTAL SERVICES (medical ser.)	6558	11223233355	SNNNNNNOOONFFNNNNON	NNNN2NNNNNNNNNN	D,J,P,T,V	294	922	02.03.02	2620	000000	32105
073.061-010	VETERINARIAN, LABORATORY ANIMAL CARE (medical ser.)	6458	11111341144	MNNONONFFFOFFOFNNNON	NNNO3NFNNNNNNNF	D,V,J,T,S	294	929	02.02.01	2700	000000	32114
073.061-014	VETERINARY ANATOMIST (profess. & kin.)	5458	11211322154	LNNNNNNFFOONNNFNFOON	NNNN2NFNNNNNNNN	V,J	251	732	02.02.01	2700	000000	32114
073.061-018	VETERINARY MICROBIOLOGIST (profess. & kin.)	6568	11211431153	LNNOOONFFOFFOFFNFFN	NNNN2NFNNNNNNNN	V,J,T	251	732	02.02.01	2700	000000	32114
073.061-022	VETERINARY EPIDEMIOLOGIST (profess. & kin.)	5458	12111441143	LNNNNNNFFONNNFNNOONN	NNNN2NNNNNNNNNN	V,J	251	739	02.02.01	2700	000000	32114
073.061-026	VETERINARY PARASITOLOGIST (profess. & kin.)	5458	11233322454	LNNNNNNFFONNNFNNOON	NNNN2NNNNNNNNNN	J,T	251	732	02.02.01	2700	000000	32114
073.061-030	VETERINARY PATHOLOGIST (medical ser.)	6558	11211431143	MNNONONFFFOOOOFNOOON	NNNF3NFNNNNNNNN	V,J,T	251	732	02.02.01	2700	000000	32114
073.061-034	VETERINARY PHARMACOLOGIST (profess. & kin.)	5448	12111441142	LNNNNNNFFONNNFNONNN	NNNN2NNNNNNNNNN	V,J,T	251	732	02.02.01	2700	000000	32114
073.061-038	VETERINARY PHYSIOLOGIST (profess. & kin.)	5458	12111441143	LNNNNNNFFNFNFNNNOON	NNNN2NNNNNNNNNN	V,J	251	732	02.02.01	2700	000000	32114
073.101-010	VETERINARIAN (medical ser.)	5458	11211321252	MNNOOONFFOFFOFNFFFO	NNNN3NNNNNNNNNF	V,P,J,T	294	929	02.03.03	2700	000000	32114
073.101-014	VETERINARIAN, POULTRY (agriculture)	5458	11312421243	LNNONONFOOOONONNNNN	NNNN3NNNNNNNNNF	J	294	929	02.03.03	2700	000000	32114
073.161-010	ZOO VETERINARIAN (medical ser.)	6568	11211321253	MNNOOOOFFOFFOFOOOOF	ONNNN3NONNNNNNN	D,J,P,S	294	929	02.03.03	2700	000000	32114
073.261-010	VETERINARY LIVESTOCK INSPECTOR (government ser.)	5447	22233332252	MNNNNNNFFOOONONNONOOON	NNNN3NNNNNNNNN	V,J	211	959	02.03.03	2700	000000	32114
073.264-010	VETERINARY VIRUS-SERUM INSPECTOR (government ser.)	5447	22222342254	LNNNNNNFFOONNNONOOON	NNNN3NNNNNNNNN	V,T	211	959	02.03.03	2700	000000	32114
073.264-010	VETERINARY MEAT-INSPECTOR (government ser.)	5458	11211333252	MNNOOONFFNFONOFFO	NNNF3NONNNNNNNN	J,T	211	959	02.03.03	2700	000000	32114
074.161-010	PHARMACIST (medical ser.)	5557	12242232353	SNNNNNNOOONONNNNOO	NNNN3NNNNNNNOO	T,J,V	147	493	02.04.01	3010	000000	32517
074.161-014	RADIOPHARMACIST (medical ser.)	6557	11221222354	LNNNNNNFFNOONFNFNNFN	NJNNN3NNNNONNN	T,J	147	732	02.04.01	3010	000000	32517
074.167-010	DIRECTOR, PHARMACY SERVICES (medical ser.)	6668	11111133452	LNNNNNNFFNFFNFNNOFO	NNNN2NNNNNNNNN	D,V,P,T	294	920	02.04.01	3010	000000	32517
074.381-010	PHARMACIST ASSISTANT (military ser.)	4436	22343433453	LNNNNNNFFOFFNFNNON	NNNN2NNNNNNNNN	J,T	143	493	02.04.01	3690	510805	32999
074.382-010	PHARMACY TECHNICIAN (medical ser.)	3333	33343343353	LNNONNNFFNNONFNNOON	NNNN2NNNNNNNNN	V,T	147	493	05.09.01	5233	510805	32518
075.117-010	CONSULTANT, EDUCATIONAL, STATE BOARD OF NURSING (government ser.)	5458	11244244455	SNNNNNNOOONONONNNNN	NNNN2NNNNNNNNN	V,D,P,J	296	931	11.07.02	1283	000000	15005
075.117-014	DIRECTOR, COMMUNITY-HEALTH NURSING (medical ser.)	5458	22244244455	SNNNNNNNFFNNNNNNNN	NNNN3NNNNNNNNN	V,D,P	295	920	11.07.02	1310	000000	15008

DOT #	DOT Title & Industry	Trng	Aptitude	Physical	Environment	Tempra	WkF	MPSMS	GOE	SOC	CIP	OES
075.117-018	DIRECTOR, EDUCATIONAL, COMMUNITY-HEALTH NURSING (medical ser.)	5458	11233344455	SNNNNNNNNNNFFNNNNNNN	NNNNN2NNNNNNNNNN	V,D,P,J	295	931	10.02.01	1283	000000	15005
075.117-022	DIRECTOR, NURSING SERVICE (medical ser.)	5458	22244244455	SNNNNNNNNOONFFNNNNNN	NNNNN3NNNNNNNNNN	V,D,P	295	924	11.07.02	1310	000000	15008
075.117-026	DIRECTOR, OCCUPATIONAL HEALTH NURSING (medical ser.)	5458	22233244444	NNNNNNNNNNFFNNNNNNN	NNNNN2NNNNNNNNNN	V,D,P,J	295	924	11.07.02	1310	000000	15008
075.117-030	DIRECTOR, SCHOOL OF NURSING (medical ser.)	5458	21234244455	SNNNNNNNNNNFFNNNNNNN	NNNNN2NNNNNNNNNN	V,D,P	295	931	11.07.02	1310	000000	15008
075.117-034	EXECUTIVE DIRECTOR, NURSES' ASSOCIATION (medical ser.)	6468	11144244455	SNNNNNNNNOONCGNNNNNN	NNNNN2NNNNNNNNNN	V,D,P	295	924	11.05.02	1354	000000	19999
075.124-010	NURSE, SCHOOL (medical ser.)	5457	22333233354	LNNNNNNNFFOFFNFNNOON	NNNNN2NNNNNNNNNN	D,J,P,I,S	294	924	10.02.01	2900	000000	32502
075.124-014	NURSE, STAFF, COMMUNITY HEALTH (medical ser.)	5457	22233233343	MNNNNNNNFFOOFFNCNFFFN	NNNNN3NNNNNNNNNN	I,P,J,T	294	920	10.02.01	2900	000000	32502
075.124-018	NURSE, INSTRUCTOR (medical ser.)	5458	21233243454	LNNOONNFFFOFFNFNNOON	NNNNN3NNNNNNNNNN	V,D,P,I	294	924	10.02.01	2232	000000	31114
075.127-010	INSTRUCTOR, PSYCHIATRIC AIDE (education)	5457	22344234455	LNNNNNNNNOONFFNNNNNN	NNNNN3NNNNNNNNNN	D,J,T	296	931	10.02.01	2390	000000	31314
075.127-014	NURSE, CONSULTANT (medical ser.)	5457	22233244455	SNNNNNNNNOONFFNNNNNN	NNNNN3NNNNNNNNNN	V,D,P	282	924	10.02.01	2900	000000	32502
075.127-026	NURSE, SUPERVISOR, COMMUNITY-HEALTH NURSING (medical ser.)	5457	22333334444	SNNNNNNNNOONFFNNNNNN	NNNNN3NNNNNNNNNN	D,P,J	294	920	10.02.01	2900	000000	32502
075.127-030	NURSE, SUPERVISOR, EVENING-OR-NIGHT (medical ser.)	5458	22333233353	LNNNNNNNFFOFFNFONFFN	NNNNN3NNNNNNNNNN	J,D,V,S,P	294	924	10.02.01	2900	000000	32502
075.127-034	NURSE, INFECTION CONTROL (medical ser.)	5457	22243233455	LNNNNNNNOFFNFFNCNNONN	NNNNN2NNNNNNNNNN	D,J,P	294	924	10.02.01	2900	000000	32502
075.137-010	NURSE, SUPERVISOR, OCCUPATIONAL HEALTH NURSING (medical ser.)	5457	22233434344	LNNNNNNNNOOONFFNONNNNN	NNNNN3NNNNNNNNNN	D,P,J	295	924	10.02.01	2900	000000	32502
075.137-014	NURSE, HEAD (medical ser.)	5457	22233233343	MNNFNNNNFFOFFNFNNNFN	NNNNN3NNNNNNNNNN	V,D,P,T,S	294	924	10.02.01	2900	000000	32502
075.167-010	NURSE, SUPERVISOR (medical ser.)	5458	22333233353	LNNNNNNNFFOFFNFONFFN	NNNNN3NNNNNNNNNN	V,D,P,T,S	294	924	10.02.01	2900	000000	32502
075.167-014	QUALITY ASSURANCE COORDINATOR (medical ser.)	5457	22243233455	LNNNNNNNFFFFFFNNNOFN	NNNNN3NNNNNNNNNN	J,P,T	294	924	10.02.01	2900	000000	32502
075.264-010	NURSE PRACTITIONER (medical ser.)	5558	22322233353	LNNONNNFFFFFFNNNNOFN	NNNNN3NNNNNNNNNN	D,J,P	294	924	10.02.01	2900	000000	32502
075.264-014	NURSE-MIDWIFE (medical ser.)	5537	23333333344	MNONNNNFFFFFFNNNNOFN	NNNNN3NNNNNNNNNN	V,P,J	294	924	10.02.01	2900	000000	32502
075.364-010	NURSE, GENERAL DUTY (medical ser.)	5457	22333233344	MNNONNNFFFFFFNNNNOFN	NNNNN3NNNNNNNNNN	P,T,J,S	294	924	10.02.01	2900	000000	32502
075.371-010	NURSE ANESTHETIST (medical ser.)	5558	22222242253	LNNOOONFFFOFFNFNNNFN	NNNNN2NNNNNNNNNN	P,T,S	294	924	10.02.01	2900	000000	32502
075.374-014	NURSE, OFFICE (medical ser.)	5357	23333333354	LNNNNNNNFFOFFNFNNNON	NNNNN2NNNNNNNNNN	P,J,T	294	924	10.02.01	2900	000000	32502
075.374-018	NURSE, PRIVATE DUTY (medical ser.)	5457	22322333344	MNNNNNNNFFNFFNFNNFON	NNNNN3NNNNNNNNNN	P,J,T,S	294	924	10.02.01	2900	000000	32502
075.374-022	NURSE, STAFF, OCCUPATIONAL HEALTH NURSING (medical ser.)	5457	22343333354	LNNNNNNNFFOFFNFNNNOOO	NNNNN3NNNNNNNNNN	V,P,T,J	294	929	02.03.04	3034	000000	32314
076.101-010	AUDIOLOGIST (medical ser.)	5457	22333233354	LNNNNNNNFFFFFFNNNOOO	NNNNN3NNNNNNNNNN	D,J,P	294	920	02.03.04	3034	000000	32314
076.104-010	VOICE PATHOLOGIST (profess. & kin.)	5558	11212233355	LNNNNNNNFFFFFFNNNNFNN	NNNNN3NNNNNNNNNN	D,P,J	294	924	02.03.04	3034	000000	32314
076.107-010	SPEECH PATHOLOGIST (profess. & kin.)	5557	22333333355	LNNNNNNNFFFFFFNNNNNN	NNNNN3NNNNNNNNNN	D,P,J	294	924	11.07.01	3039	000000	32399
076.117-010	COORDINATOR OF REHABILITATION SERVICES (medical ser.)	5558	22344344455	LNNNNNNNNOOFNFFNNNNNN	NNNNN3NNNNNNNNNN	D,J,P,V	295	924	10.02.02	3032	000000	32305
076.121-010	OCCUPATIONAL THERAPIST (medical ser.)	5457	22333343344	MNNOOONFFOFFFFNFNFFOO	NNNNN3NNNNNNNNNN	D,I,J,P,V	294	924	10.02.02	3033	000000	32308
076.121-014	PHYSICAL THERAPIST (education; medical ser.)	5457	22322322244	MONOOOOFFFFFFNFNNOOO	NNNO2NNNNNNNNNNO	D,P,J,I	294	924	10.02.02	3033	000000	32399
076.121-018	EXERCISE PHYSIOLOGIST (medical ser.)	5457	22333333344	MOOOONNFFFFFFNFNOOOO	NNNNN2NNNNNNNNNN	D,I,J,P	231	924	10.02.02	3039	000000	32311
076.124-010	MANUAL-ARTS THERAPIST (medical ser.)	4447	22244422235	LNNNNNNFFNFFNFNFNN	NNNNN3NONNNNNNNN	V,D,P	296	921	10.02.02	3033	000000	32311
076.124-014	RECREATIONAL THERAPIST (medical ser.)	4246	22333233345	LNNNNNNNFFFOFFNFONNNN	NNNNN3NNNNNNNNNN	D,P,V	294	929	10.02.02	3039	512309	32317
076.124-018	HORTICULTURAL THERAPIST (medical ser.)	5457	22343333353	LNNFFNNFFNFNFFNFNFN	FNNN4NNNNNNNNNNN	D,V,P,J	003	924	10.02.02	3039	000000	32399
076.127-010	ART THERAPIST (medical ser.)	5457	22322343343	LNNNNNNFFFFFFFNFNNNFF	NNNNN3NNNNNNNNNN	D,V,P,J	294	924	10.02.02	3039	512301	32317
076.127-014	MUSIC THERAPIST (medical ser.)	5557	22244443345	SNNNNNNNOOONFNFNFNNNNF	NNNNN3NNNNNNNNNN	I,J,P	294	924	10.02.02	3039	512305	32317
076.127-018	DANCE THERAPIST (medical ser.)	5358	22333344415	LNFOONNFFNNFFNNFNNNN	NNNNN3NNNNNNNNNN	D,V,P,J	294	924	10.02.02	3039	512302	32317
076.167-010	INDUSTRIAL THERAPIST (medical ser.)	5557	22333333345	LNNNNNNNFFNFFNFNNNNN	NNNNN3NNNNNNNNNN	V,P,J	294	920	10.02.02	3032	000000	32305
076.224-010	PHYSICAL THERAPIST ASSISTANT (medical ser.)	4346	22333322234	MONFFOFFFFFNNFOO	NNNNN2NNNNNNNNNN	J,P,T,I	294	924	10.02.02	5233	510806	66017
076.224-014	ORIENTATION AND MOBILITY THERAPIST FOR THE BLIND (education; medical ser.; nonprofit org.)	5256	22333333345	LNNNNNNNFFOCOFNNNNO	ONNN3NNNNNNNNNNN	D,V,P	294	931	10.02.02	3039	000000	32399
076.264-010	PHYSICAL-INTEGRATION PRACTITIONER (medical ser.)	3126	33422433344	LNNNNNNNFFFFFFFNNNNN	NNNNN3NNNNNNNNNN	J,P	294	929	10.02.02	3033	512308	32311
076.361-010	CORRECTIVE THERAPIST (medical ser.)	4247	22244422235	MNNONNNFFFOFFNFNNOON	NNNNN3NNNNNNNNNN	V,D,P	294	921	10.02.02	3031	512302	32302
076.361-014	RESPIRATORY THERAPIST (medical ser.)	4336	33333333254	MNNONNNFFNFFNFFNNNNN	NNNNN2NNNNNNNNNN	J,P,T,V	294	924	10.02.02	3031	510908	32302
076.364-010	OCCUPATIONAL THERAPY ASSISTANT (medical ser.)	4346	33333332334	MNNOOONFFFNFFNFOOOOO	NNNO3NNNNNNNNNNN	J,P,T	294	924	10.02.02	5233	511502	66021
077.061-010	DIETITIAN, RESEARCH (profess. & kin.)	6558	11233344452	LNNNNNNFFNFFNFNFNNNN	NNNNN2NNNNNNNNNN	V,P,J	251	732	02.02.04	3020	000000	32521
077.117-010	DIETITIAN, CHIEF (profess. & kin.)	5458	22244344445	SNNNNNNNNNNFFNFNNNNN	NNNNN3NNNNNNNNNN	V,D,J	295	903	11.05.02	3020	000000	32521
077.124-010	DIETETIC TECHNICIAN (profess. & kin.)	5457	23333344354	LNNNNNNNFFONFOFNFNON	NNNNN3NNNNNNNNNN	D,J,P,V	296	924	05.05.17	3020	200404	32523
077.127-010	COMMUNITY DIETITIAN (profess. & kin.)	5458	22333344455	LNNNNNNNNOOOFFNNNNON	NNNNN3NNNNNNNNNN	V,P,J	282	732	11.02.03	3020	000000	32521
077.127-014	DIETITIAN, CLINICAL (profess. & kin.)	5457	22344344454	LNNNNNNNFFONFFNNNNNN	NNNNN2NNNNNNNNNN	D,P,J	295	924	05.05.17	3020	000000	32521
077.127-018	DIETITIAN, CONSULTANT (profess. & kin.)	5458	22233344454	LNNNNNNNNNNNFFNFNNNNN	NNNNN3NNNNNNNNNN	V,D,P	282	732	05.05.17	3020	000000	32521
077.127-022	DIETITIAN, TEACHING (profess. & kin.)	5458	22333344454	LNNNNNNNNNNNFFNFNNNNN	NNNNN3NNNNNNNNNN	P,D,J	296	732	11.02.02	3020	000000	32521

DOT #	DOT Title & Industry	Trng	Aptitude	Physical	Environment	Tempra	WkF	MPSMS	GOE	SOC	CIP	OES
078.121-010	MEDICAL TECHNOLOGIST, TEACHING SUPERVISOR (medical ser.)	5457	21233233345	SNNNNNNNNNNFFNNONN	NNNN3NNNNNNNNN	V,D,P	296	925	02.04.02	3620	000000	32902
078.131-010	CHIEF TECHNOLOGIST, NUCLEAR MEDICINE (medical ser.)	5458	22222233353	LNNNNNNFFNFFNFNNFNNO	NNNN2NNNNNFNNO	D,T,J,P	201	925	02.04.02	3650	510905	32914
078.161-010	MEDICAL TECHNOLOGIST, CHIEF (medical ser.)	5458	12221222342	LNNONNNFFNFFNCNNNOFN	NNNN2NNNNNNNNN	D,P,J,T	211	925	02.04.02	3620	000000	32902
078.161-014	CARDIOPULMONARY TECHNOLOGIST, CHIEF (medical ser.)	5457	22223222342	LNNNNNNFFNFFNNOOOFN	NNNN2NNNNNNNNN	V,P,J	294	921	02.04.02	3690	510901	32925
078.162-010	RADIOLOGIC TECHNOLOGIST, CHIEF (medical ser.)	5458	22222333343	LNNNNNNFFFOOONFNNOOON	NNNN3NNNONONNN	D,P,T	294	925	10.02.02	3650	000000	32917
078.261-010	BIOCHEMISTRY TECHNOLOGIST (medical ser.)	5457	22232332353	LNNONNNFFFOOONFNNONN	NNNN2NNNNNNNNN	V,J,T	294	925	02.04.02	3620	511004	32902
078.261-014	MICROBIOLOGY TECHNOLOGIST (medical ser.)	5457	22231222353	LNNNNNNNOFFNFNCNNFCN	NNNN2NNNNNNNNN	T,J	211	925	02.04.02	3620	511004	32902
078.261-018	ORTHOTIST (medical ser.)	5448	23322443344	MNNOOONFFONFFNFNFOON	NNNN3NNNNNNNNN	P,J,T	294	604	05.05.11	3690	512307	32999
078.261-022	PROSTHETIST (medical ser.)	5448	23322443344	SNNNNNNFFNFFNFNFFN	NNNN3NNNNNNNNN	P,J,T	294	604	05.05.11	3690	512307	32999
078.261-026	CYTOGENETIC TECHNOLOGIST (medical ser.)	5457	22222332253	LNNNNNNFFFOOONFNFFFN	NNNN2NNNNNNNNNO	T,J	211	925	02.04.02	3620	511099	32902
078.261-030	HISTOTECHNOLOGIST (medical ser.)	5456	22232331142	LNNNNNNFFFOOONFNFFFN	NNNN2NNNNNNNNN	T,J	211	925	02.04.02	3620	000000	32902
078.261-034	MEDICAL RADIATION DOSIMETRIST (medical ser.)	5458	22222222354	LNNNNNNFFFOFFNCNNCON	NNNN2NNNNNNNNN	T,P,J	294	925	10.02.02	3650	000000	32914
078.261-038	MEDICAL TECHNOLOGIST (medical ser.)	5457	22231222353	LNNNNNNFFFOFFNFNFON	NNNN3NNNNNNNNN	T,J	211	925	02.04.02	3620	511003	32902
078.261-042	PHERESIS SPECIALIST (medical ser.)	5457	22232322343	LNNFNNNOCCOFFNCNNFFN	NNNN2NNNNNNNNN	P,J,T	294	925	10.02.02	3690	000000	32999
078.261-046	IMMUNOHEMATOLOGIST (medical ser.)	5358	22311322252	LNNNNNNOCCNOONCNNFCN	NNNN2NNNNNNNNN	J,P,T	211	925	02.04.02	3620	511003	32902
078.262-010	PULMONARY-FUNCTION TECHNICIAN (medical ser.)	4446	33333343354	LNNNNNNFFFOCONCNNFON	NNNN2NNNNNNNNN	T,J,P	294	925	10.03.01	3690	510901	32999
078.264-010	HOLTER SCANNING TECHNICIAN (medical ser.)	3336	33344333445	SNNNNNNFFFOOFNCNNFNN	NNNN2NNNNNNNNNC	T,J	294	925	10.03.01	3690	510901	32999
078.281-010	CYTOTECHNOLOGIST (medical ser.)	5456	22311341243	SNNNNNNFFFFFFNFNFFON	NNNN2NNNNNNNNNO	T,J	211	925	02.04.02	3620	511002	32902
078.361-010	DENTAL HYGIENIST (medical ser.)	4346	23323422244	LNNONNNFFFFFNFNFFON	NNNN2NNNNNNNNN	J,P,T	294	925	10.02.02	3690	510602	32908
078.361-018	NUCLEAR MEDICINE TECHNOLOGIST (medical ser.)	5457	22222233244	MNNONONFFFOFFNNOON	NNNN2NNNNCNNNC	T,J,P,V	294	925	10.02.02	3650	510905	32914
078.361-022	ORTHOTICS ASSISTANT (medical ser.)	4447	23322443344	MNNOOONFFFOONFFFON	NNNN3NNNNNNNNN	P,J,T	294	604	05.05.11	3690	000000	32999
078.361-026	PROSTHETICS ASSISTANT (medical ser.)	4447	23322443344	MNNOOONFFNFNFNNOOON	NNNN3NNNNNNNNN	P,J,T	294	604	05.05.11	3690	000000	32999
078.361-034	RADIATION-THERAPY TECHNOLOGIST (medical ser.)	5457	33444334454	LNNONONFFFOOONFNNOON	NNNN2NNNFNFNNN	J,P,T	294	925	10.02.02	3650	510905	32914
078.361-038	OPHTHALMIC TECHNICIAN (medical ser.)	4446	33332333344	LNNNNNNFFFOFFNCONFON	NNNN2NNNNNNNNN	T,P	294	925	10.03.01	3690	000000	32999
078.362-010	AUDIOMETRIST (profess. & kin.)	4346	23343233344	LNNNNNNFOONFFNNFNONN	NNNN2NNNNNNNNN	P,J	211	929	10.03.01	3690	000000	32999
078.362-014	DIALYSIS TECHNICIAN (medical ser.)	4336	33333332344	LNNOONNFFFOFFNCNNFON	NNNN2NNNNNNNNNC	P,T	294	925	10.02.02	3650	510999	32999
078.362-018	ELECTROCARDIOGRAPH TECHNICIAN (medical ser.)	3334	33333333345	LNNONONFFFOFFNFNFNN	NNNN2NNNNNNNNN	J,P,T	294	925	10.03.01	3690	310505	32926
078.362-022	ELECTROENCEPHALOGRAPHIC TECHNOLOGIST (medical ser.)	4446	33333333444	MNNOOOOFFFOONFFFON	NNNN2NNNNNNNNN	J,P,T	294	925	10.03.01	3690	510903	32923
078.362-026	RADIOLOGIC TECHNOLOGIST (medical ser.)	5457	23333333344	LNNNNNNFFFOFFNNOOON	NNNN2NNNNNFFNNN	P,T,J	201	925	10.02.02	3650	510907	32917
078.362-030	CARDIOPULMONARY TECHNOLOGIST (medical ser.)	4447	33332233354	LNNNNNNFFFOOONFNNNON	NNNN2NNNNNFNNN	J,T,P	294	925	10.03.01	3690	510901	32925
078.362-034	PERFUSIONIST (medical ser.)	4347	22333323344	MNNONONCCCOFCNCNCNCON	NNNN2NNNNNNNNNC	S,T,P	294	925	10.03.02	3690	510901	32999
078.362-038	ELECTROMYOGRAPHIC TECHNICIAN (medical ser.)	4445	33333333354	MNNONONNOONNNNFNNONN	NNNN3NNNNNNNNN	T,J	211	925	02.04.02	3690	511003	32905
078.362-042	POLYSOMNOGRAPHIC TECHNICIAN (medical ser.)	4444	33332333344	MNNONNNOFFOOFNCNNFON	NNNN2NNNNNNNNN	T,P,J	294	922	02.04.02	3690	000000	32999
078.362-046	SPECIAL PROCEDURES TECHNOLOGIST, ANGIOGRAM (medical ser.)	5457	23333233344	MNNNNNNFFFOFFNFNFON	NNNN3NNNNNCNNNN	J,P,T	294	929	10.03.02	3690	000000	32917
078.362-050	SPECIAL PROCEDURES TECHNOLOGIST, CARDIAC CATHETERIZATION (medical ser.)	5457	22323233344	MNNNNNNFFOONFFNFNNON	NNNN2NNNNNCNNNN	P,T,J	294	493	02.04.02	3690	000000	32905
078.362-054	SPECIAL PROCEDURES TECHNOLOGIST, CT SCAN (medical ser.)	5457	22323333344	MNNNNNNFFFOFNFON	NNNN2NNNNNFNNN	T,P,J	201	925	10.02.02	3650	000000	32917
078.362-058	SPECIAL PROCEDURES TECHNOLOGIST, MAGNETIC RESONANCE IMAGING (MRI) (medical ser.)	5457	22323233354	MNNNNNNFFFOOFNFNFON	NNNN2NNNNNNNNN	T,P,J	294	925	10.02.02	3650	000000	32917
078.362-062	STRESS TEST TECHNICIAN (medical ser.)	4336	33333333345	LNNNNNNOFFOFFNFNNONN	NNNN2NNNNNNNNN	T,P,J	294	925	10.03.01	3690	000000	32925
078.364-010	ULTRASOUND TECHNOLOGIST (medical ser.)	5447	33322333354	LNNONNNFFFOFFNFNFFON	NNNN2NNNNNNNNN	P,T,J	294	925	02.04.01	3690	510910	32999
078.364-014	ECHOCARDIOGRAPH TECHNICIAN (medical ser.)	4347	33322323344	LNNNNNNFFOOOFNCNNCON	NNNN2NNNNNNNNN	T,P,J	294	925	10.03.01	3690	000000	32925
078.367-010	CARDIAC MONITOR TECHNICIAN (medical ser.)	3225	33444344454	SNNNNNNOOONFFNNNFON	NNNN3NNNNNNNNN	S,U,J	294	925	10.03.01	3690	510902	32999
078.381-014	MEDICAL LABORATORY TECHNICIAN (medical ser.)	4445	33333333353	LNNNNNNFFNNNNFNNOON	NNNN3NNNNNNNNNO	T,J	211	925	02.04.02	3690	511003	32905
078.384-010	CEPHALOMETRIC ANALYST (medical ser.)	4446	33333333354	SNNNNNNOONNNNFNNOON	NNNN3NNNNNNNNN	J,T	242	922	02.04.02	3690	000000	32999
078.664-010	ORTHOPEDIC ASSISTANT (medical ser.)	3234	33344333344	MNNFNNNFONOONFNNONN	NNNN3NNNNNNNNN	J,P,T	294	929	10.03.02	3690	510807	32999
078.687-010	LABORATORY ASSISTANT, BLOOD AND PLASMA (medical ser.; pharmaceut.)	3336	33344333344	LNNNNNNFFNNNNCNNNON	NNNN3NNNNNNNNN	J,R,T	211	493	02.04.02	5233	000000	32905
079.021-014	MEDICAL PHYSICIST (profess. & kin.)	6668	11224444455	LNNNNNNFFFFFFNFNFNN	NNNN2NNNNNNNNN	D,P,J	293	725	02.02.01	1843	000000	24311
079.101-010	CHIROPRACTOR (medical ser.)	5458	22322422244	MNNFNNNFFFFFNFNFON	NNNN2NNNNNNONNN	P,J,	294	923	02.03.04	2890	000000	32113
079.101-014	DOCTOR, NATUROPATHIC (medical ser.)	5457	11222323353	LNNNNNNFFFFFFNFNFON	NNNN2NNNNNNNNN	V,P,J	294	929	02.03.04	2890	000000	32199
079.101-018	OPTOMETRIST (medical ser.)	5457	22212233353	LNNONNNCCFNFFNFNFFON	NNNN2NNNNNNNNN	P,J,T	294	923	02.03.04	2810	000000	32108
079.101-022	PODIATRIST (medical ser.)	5457	23333443355	LNNNNNNFFFNFFNFNOOON	NNNN3NNNNNNNNN	P,J	294	929	02.03.01	2830	000000	32111

DOT #	DOT Title & Industry	Trng	Aptitude	Physical	Environment	Tempra	WkF	MPSMS	GOE	SOC	CIP	OES
079.117-010	EMERGENCY MEDICAL SERVICES COORDINATOR (medical ser.)	4448	22333344455	LNNNNNNOONNFFNFNNNNN	NNNNN3NNNNNNNNNNN	D,P	295	920	11.07.02	1310	000000	15008
079.117-014	PUBLIC HEALTH EDUCATOR (profess. & kin.)	5458	11334344444	LNNNNNNNOONNFFNFNNNNN	ONNNN3NNNNNNNNNNN	D,I,P,J	271	920	11.07.02	2360	510301	31517
079.117-018	SANITARIAN (profess. & kin.)	6568	22333344453	MNNNNNNNOONNFFNFONOON	FNNN4NONNNNNNNNN	D,J,T	293	874	11.10.03	1473	000000	21911
079.127-010	INSERVICE COORDINATOR, AUXILIARY PERSONNEL (medical ser.)	5457	23343344354	LNNNNNNFFNFFNFNNNNNN	NNNNN3NNNNNNNNNN	D,P,I	296	920	10.02.01	1430	000000	21511
079.131-010	DIRECTOR, SPEECH-AND-HEARING (medical ser.)	6558	11212333353	SNNNNNNNFFFFNFNNOON	NNNNN3NNNNNNNNNN	D,I,V,P,J	294	924	11.07.02	1310	000000	15008
079.151-010	TRANSPLANT COORDINATOR (medical ser.)	5557	22322232354	LNNNNNNNFFFCCNCNOFON	NNNN2NNNNNNNNNN	I,T,P	294	924	10.02.01	3690	000000	32999
079.157-010	HYPNOTHERAPIST (profess. & kin.)	4347	22444444455	SNNNNNNNOONNFFNFNNNN	NNNN2NNNNNNNNNN	D,J,P	294	733	10.02.02	2890	000000	32199
079.161-010	INDUSTRIAL HYGIENIST (profess. & kin.)	5458	12111434354	MNNNNNNNFFNFFNFOOFOO	NNNN3NFNNNNNNNN	D,J	244	712	11.10.03	3690	150701	32999
079.167-010	COMMUNITY-SERVICES-AND-HEALTH-EDUCATION OFFICER (government ser.)	6568	22333344555	SNNNNNNNFFNFFNFNNNNN	NNNN3NNNNNNNNNN	D,P,J	295	920	11.07.02	1132	510301	19005
079.167-014	MEDICAL-RECORD ADMINISTRATOR (medical ser.)	6568	12233244455	LNNNNNNNFFNFFNFNNNNN	NNNNN3NNNNNNNNN	D,P,J	295	933	11.07.02	1310	000000	15008
079.267-010	UTILIZATION-REVIEW COORDINATOR (medical ser.)	5457	22244244455	LNNNNNNOOONFFNFNNNNN	NNNNN3NNNNNNNN	D,P,J	295	920	11.07.02	1310	000000	15008
079.271-010	ACUPUNCTURIST (medical ser.)	5456	22322323353	LNNNNNNFFNFFNFNNOOFN	NNNN2NNNNNNNNN	J	294	921	02.03.04	2890	000000	32199
079.271-014	ACUPRESSURIST (medical ser.)	5345	22322322335	MNNNNNNNFFOFFNFNOONN	NNNN3NNNNNNNNN	J,P	294	924	10.02.02	2890	000000	32199
079.361-014	VETERINARY TECHNICIAN (medical ser.)	4346	33333233343	MNNONONFFFOFFOFNNQON	NNNN3NNNNNNNN	S,T,J	294	929	02.03.03	3690	510808	32951
079.361-018	DENTAL ASSISTANT (medical ser.)	4346	33343343344	LNNONNNFFFOOFNFNOOON	NNNN2NNNNNNNN	P,T	294	926	10.03.02	5232	510601	66002
079.362-010	MEDICAL ASSISTANT (medical ser.)	4346	33444333354	LNNNNNNNFFOFFNFNOOON	NNNN3NNNNNNNN	V,T,P	294	926	10.03.02	5233	510705	66005
079.362-014	MEDICAL RECORD TECHNICIAN (medical ser.)	4346	22344343455	LNNOONNNFFNOONFNNONN	NNNN2NNNNNNN	J,T,V	231	929	07.05.03	3640	510707	32911
079.362-018	TUMOR REGISTRAR (medical ser.)	5457	32344344455	SNNNNNNNFFNFFNFNNNNN	NNNN2NNNNNNN	T,J	231	930	07.05.03	3640	000000	32911
079.364-010	CHIROPRACTOR ASSISTANT (medical ser.)	4346	33433323355	MNNNNNNNFFNFFNFNNFNN	NNNN3NNNNNNN	V,P	294	923	10.03.02	5233	510899	66005
079.364-014	OPTOMETRIC ASSISTANT (medical ser.)	4446	33333343333	SNNNNNNNFFOFFNFNFNN	NNNN3NNNNNNN	P,J	294	929	10.03.02	3690	510801	32999
079.364-018	PHYSICIAN ASSISTANT (medical ser.)	5457	22322223353	LNNONNNFFFOOFNCNNFON	NNNN2NNNNNNN	J,T,P	294	924	10.02.01	3040	510807	32511
079.364-022	PHLEBOTOMIST (medical ser.)	3233	33433322254	LNNONNNFFFFFFNFNNOON	NNNN2NNNNNNN	J,P	294	925	02.04.02	5233	511001	66099
079.364-026	PARAMEDIC (medical ser.)	4346	23332222233	VOOFFOOFFOFFOFFFFF	FNNN4NNNNNNNNNC	J,P,T,S	294	929	10.03.02	3690	000000	32508
079.367-018	MEDICAL-SERVICE TECHNICIAN (military ser.)	4337	22323333344	LNNNNNNFFFNFFNFNOOFN	NNNN4NNNNNNNNNF	J,P,S,T	294	924	07.05.03	3690	000000	32999
079.371-014	ORTHOPTIST (medical ser.)	4446	33333232233	LNNNNNNNFFFFNFNNFFFN	NNNN3NNNNNNNN	I,J,P	294	929	10.02.02	3690	000000	32999
079.374-010	EMERGENCY MEDICAL TECHNICIAN (medical ser.)	4345	33332322233	MQOOOOOFFFOFFOFOOFO	FNNN3NNNNNNNN	J,P,S	294	921	10.03.02	3690	510904	32508
079.374-014	NURSE, LICENSED PRACTICAL (medical ser.)	4346	33433333344	MNNFOONFFFOFFNFNNNON	NNNN3NNNNNNNN	V,S,T,P	294	924	10.03.02	3660	511613	32505
079.374-018	PODIATRIC ASSISTANT (medical ser.)	4246	34344233355	LNNNNNNFFFOONFNONNNON	NNNN3NNNNNNN	V,P	231	929	10.03.02	5233	510801	66005
079.374-022	SURGICAL TECHNICIAN (medical ser.)	4436	33444343344	LNNONNNFFFOONFNONNNON	NNNN2NNNNNNNC	J,T,S	294	926	10.03.02	3690	510909	32928
079.374-026	PSYCHIATRIC TECHNICIAN (medical ser.)	4346	33344333345	MNNNNNNFFFFFFNFNNNON	NNNC3NNNNNNNN	J,P,S,V	294	924	10.02.02	3660	511502	32931
090.107-010	FOREIGN-STUDENT ADVISER (education)	5257	21343244455	SNNNNNNFFFNFFNFNNNNN	NNNN3NNNNNNNN	V,D,P,J	298	733	10.01.02	2400	000000	31514
090.117-010	ACADEMIC DEAN (education)	5359	23343244455	SNNNNNNNOONFFNFNNNNN	NNNN3NNNNNNN	D,P,I,J	295	931	11.07.03	1281	000000	15005
090.117-014	ALUMNI SECRETARY (education)	5358	22343244455	SNNNNNNNFONFFNFNNNNN	NNNN3NNNNNNN	D,P,I,J	295	931	11.09.02	1281	000000	15005
090.117-018	DEAN OF STUDENTS (education)	5358	22243244455	SNNNNNNNFFNFFNFNNNNN	NNNN3NNNNNNN	D,P,I	295	931	10.01.02	1281	000000	15005
090.117-022	DIRECTOR, ATHLETIC (education)	5359	22343244455	SNNNNNNNNFFNNNNFFNNNNN	NNNN3NNNNNNN	V,D,P,J	295	931	11.07.03	1281	000000	15005
090.117-026	DIRECTOR, EXTENSION WORK (education)	6359	11243244455	SNNNNNNNOOONFFNFNNNNN	NNNN3NNNNNNN	V,D,P,I,J	295	931	11.07.03	1281	000000	15005
090.117-030	FINANCIAL-AIDS OFFICER (education)	5358	22244244455	SNNNNNNNOOONFFNFNNNNN	NNNN3NNNNNNN	D,P	295	931	11.07.03	1281	000000	15005
090.117-034	PRESIDENT, EDUCATIONAL INSTITUTION (education)	5359	11223244455	SNNNNNNNFFNFFNFNNNNN	NNNN3NNNNNNN	V,D,P,J	295	931	11.07.03	1210	000000	31517
090.164-010	LABORATORY MANAGER (education)	5547	22222244354	LNNNNNNFFONFFNFNOOON	NNNN4NNONNNNNN	P,T,J	296	891	11.07.03	2200	000000	31517
090.167-010	DEPARTMENT HEAD, COLLEGE OR UNIVERSITY (education)	6558	21222244453	MNNNNNNNNFFNFFNFNNNNN	NNNN3NNNNNNN	P,I	295	931	11.07.03	2200	000000	15005
090.167-014	DIRECTOR OF ADMISSIONS (education)	5358	22343244455	SNNNNNNNOOONFFNFNNNNN	NNNN3NNNNNNN	D,P	295	931	11.07.03	1281	000000	15005
090.167-018	DIRECTOR OF INSTITUTIONAL RESEARCH (education)	6558	21243244455	SNNNNNNNNFFNNNNFFNNNNN	NNNN3NNNNNNN	D,J,P	271	931	11.07.03	1281	000000	15005
090.167-022	DIRECTOR OF STUDENT AFFAIRS (education)	5358	22243244455	SNNNNNNNOOONFFNFNNNNN	NNNN3NNNNNNN	D,P,I,J	295	733	11.07.03	1281	000000	15005
090.167-026	DIRECTOR OF SUMMER SESSIONS (education)	5359	22243244455	SNNNNNNNOOONFFNFNNNNN	NNNN3NNNNNNN	D,P,J	295	931	11.07.03	1281	000000	15005
090.167-030	REGISTRAR, COLLEGE OR UNIVERSITY (education)	5558	22222244354	MNNNNNNNNFFNFFNFNNFNN	NNNN3NNNNNNN	D,P,J	232	891	11.07.03	1281	000000	15005
090.167-034	DIRECTOR, FIELD SERVICES (education)	5458	22444344445	SNNNNNNNOOONFFNFNNNNN	NNNN3NNNNNNN	D,I,P	295	931	11.07.03	1281	000000	15005
090.222-010	INSTRUCTOR, BUSINESS EDUCATION (education)	5458	22354123455	LONONNNFFNFNNNNFN	NNNN3NNNNNNN	D,I,P,J	296	931	11.02.01	2233	000000	31314
090.227-010	FACULTY MEMBER, COLLEGE OR UNIVERSITY (education)	6558	11233244455	LNNNNNNNOOONFFNFNNNFNN	NNNN3NNNNNNN	D,P,I,J	296	931	11.02.01	2200	000000	31216
090.227-014	GRADUATE ASSISTANT (education)	6468	22344344454	LNNNNNNNFFNFFNFNNNNN	NNNN3NNNNNNN	P,I	296	931	11.02.01	9900	000000	31117
090.227-018	INSTRUCTOR, EXTENSION WORK (education)	5358	22343244455	SNNNNNNNOOONFFNFONNNN	NNNN3NNNNNNN	D,P,I	296	931	11.02.01	2390	000000	31399
091.107-010	ASSISTANT PRINCIPAL (education)	5358	22344344455	LNNNNNNNOOONFFNFONNNN	NNNN3NNNNNNN	D,P,I,J	295	931	10.01.02	1282	000000	15005

DOT #	DOT Title & Industry	Trmg	Aptitude	Physical	Environment	Tempra	WkF	MPSMS	GOE	SOC	CIP	OES
091.221-010	TEACHER, INDUSTRIAL ARTS (education)	5457	22222333354	LNNNNNNFFOOFFNFOFFOO	NNNN4NNONNNNNNN	D,P,J,V	296	931	11.02.02	2330	000000	31308
091.227-010	TEACHER, SECONDARY SCHOOL (education)	5457	22343244454	LNNNNNNNOFONFFNFONNOO	NNNN3NNNNNNNNNN	D,P,I,J	296	931	11.02.01	2330	000000	31308
092.167-010	DIRECTOR, DAY CARE CENTER (education)	4347	22334344455	SNNNNNNNNNNNNNNNNNN	NNNN3NNNNNNNNNN	D,I,P	295	941	11.07.03	1283	000000	15005
092.227-010	TEACHER, ELEMENTARY SCHOOL (education)	5457	22344244455	LNNONNNOOONCNFONOOO	NNNN3NNNNNNNNNN	D,P,I,J	296	931	11.02.01	2320	000000	31305
092.227-014	TEACHER, KINDERGARTEN (education)	5247	22444333333	LNNONONFFOFFNFNNNON	ONNN4NNNNNNNNNN	D,P,V	296	931	10.02.03	2310	000000	31302
092.227-018	TEACHER, PRESCHOOL (education)	4237	22334344344	LNNOOONFFONFFNOONNON	NNNN3NNNNNNNNNN	D,P	296	931	10.02.03	2310	200203	31302
094.107-010	WORK-STUDY COORDINATOR, SPECIAL EDUCATION (education)	5357	22444344455	LNNNNNNNOOONFFNNNNNN	NNNN3NNNNNNNNNN	D,I,P,J	296	931	10.02.03	2350	510205	31311
094.117-010	DIRECTOR, COMMISSION FOR THE BLIND (government ser.)	5458	22344444555	SNNNNNNNFFNFFNFNNNNN	NNNN3NNNNNNNNNN	V,D,P,J	295	941	11.07.01	1283	000000	15005
094.117-018	VOCATIONAL REHABILITATION CONSULTANT (government ser.)	5458	22334244455	LNNNNNNNOOONFFNFNNNN	NNNN3NNNNNNNNNN	D,I,P,J	251	931	11.07.03	1283	000000	31517
094.167-010	SUPERVISOR, SPECIAL EDUCATION (education)	5458	22344244455	LNNNNNNNOONFFNFNNNNN	NNNN3NNNNNNNNNN	D,I,P,J	296	931	10.02.03	2360	000000	31517
094.167-014	DIRECTOR, SPECIAL EDUCATION (education)	6558	22244244455	LNNNNNNNNOONFFNONNNN	NNNN3NNNNNNNNNN	D,P,J	295	931	11.07.03	1283	000000	15005
094.224-010	TEACHER, HEARING IMPAIRED (education)	5457	22344234455	LNNNNNNNOOFOFFNONNNN	NNNN3NNNNNNNNNN	D,P,I,J	296	931	10.02.03	2350	000000	31311
094.224-014	TEACHER, PHYSICALLY IMPAIRED (education)	5457	22343244455	LNNOOONFFONFFNONNNN	NNNN3NNNNNNNNNN	D,I,P,J,V	296	931	10.02.03	2350	000000	31311
094.224-018	TEACHER, VISUALLY IMPAIRED (education)	5457	22343233455	LNNOOONFFFFFNNNNNO	NNNN3NNNNNNNNNN	D,I,P,J	296	931	10.02.03	2350	000000	31311
094.227-010	TEACHER, EMOTIONALLY IMPAIRED (education)	5457	22344244455	LNNNNNNNOFFNFNONNNNN	NNNN3NNNNNNNNNN	D,P,I,J	296	931	10.02.03	2350	000000	31311
094.227-018	TEACHER, MENTALLY IMPAIRED (education)	5457	22344344455	LNNNNNNNOFONFFNOONNNO	NNNN3NNNNNNNNNN	D,P,I,J	296	931	10.02.03	2350	000000	31311
094.227-026	TEACHER, VOCATIONAL TRAINING (education)	5357	22444344455	LNNONONFFONFFNFNNNNN	NNNN3NNNNNNNNNN	D,P,J	296	931	10.02.03	2350	000000	31311
094.227-030	TEACHER, LEARNING DISABLED (education)	5457	22444344455	LNNNNNNNNFFNFFNOONNNO	NNNN3NNNNNNNNNN	D,I,J,P	296	931	10.02.03	2350	000000	31311
094.267-010	EVALUATOR (education)	5457	22333243455	LNNNNNNNFFFNFNNNNNN	NNNN3NNNNNNNNNN	I,J,P	271	931	10.02.03	2350	000000	31311
096.121-010	COUNTY HOME-DEMONSTRATION AGENT (government ser.)	5357	22333343343	LNNNNNNNFFNFNFOFFOO	NNNN3NNNNNNNNNN	V,D,P,I,J	296	959	11.02.03	2390	000000	31323
096.121-014	HOME ECONOMIST (profess. & kin.)	5357	22333233343	LNNNNNNNFFOFFNFNNFFN	NNNN3NNNNNNNNNN	V,P,J,I	282	931	11.02.03	2390	080102	31323
096.127-010	COUNTY-AGRICULTURAL AGENT (government ser.)	5357	22344344453	LNNNNNNNFFNFFNFNNFON	ONNN3NNNNNNNNNN	V,D,P,I,J	296	959	11.02.03	2390	000000	31323
096.127-014	EXTENSION SERVICE SPECIALIST (government ser.)	5358	22343244453	LNNNNNNNFFNFFNFNNNNN	NNNN3NNNNNNNNNN	V,D,P,I,J	296	959	11.02.03	2390	000000	31323
096.127-018	FEED AND FARM MANAGEMENT ADVISER (agriculture; retail trade)	4347	32344343344	LNNNNNNNFFOFFNFNNNON	ONNN4NNNNNNNNNN	D,P,I,V	296	731	11.02.03	2390	020204	31324
096.127-022	FOUR-H CLUB AGENT (education)	5357	22333344455	LNNNNNNNFFNFFNFNNNNN	NNNN3NNNNNNNNNN	D,P,J,I	296	733	11.02.03	2390	200203	15005
096.161-010	HOME-SERVICE DIRECTOR (profess. & kin.)	5358	22333334453	LNNNNNNNFFNFFNFNNNON	NNNN4NNNNNNNNNN	V,D,P,I	295	931	11.02.03	1283	200501	15005
096.167-010	DISTRICT EXTENSION SERVICE AGENT (government ser.)	5358	22344244453	SNNNNNNNFFNFFNFNNNON	NNNN3NNNNNNNNNN	D,J,P	295	959	11.07.03	1283	000000	15005
096.167-014	SPECIALIST-IN-CHARGE, EXTENSION SERVICE (government ser.)	5358	22344244453	SNNNNNNNOOONFFNFONNNN	NNNN3NNNNNNNNNN	D,I,J,P	296	959	11.02.03	1283	000000	15005
097.167-010	DIRECTOR, VOCATIONAL TRAINING (education)	5358	22343244455	SNNNNNNNFFNFFNFNNNNN	NNNN3NNNNNNNNNN	D,P,J	295	931	11.07.03	1283	000000	19005
097.221-010	INSTRUCTOR, VOCATIONAL TRAINING (education)	5457	22344344453	LNNNNNNNFFNFFNFNONOO	NNNN3NNONNNNNNN	D,P,J	295	931	11.07.03	1283	200203	31517
097.227-010	INSTRUCTOR, FLYING II (education)	6558	22344244455	LNNNNNNNFFOFFNFNNNNN	NNNN3NNNNNNNNNN	D,J	296	931	11.03.04	2390	000000	21511
099.117-010	DIRECTOR, EDUCATIONAL PROGRAM (education)	5358	22324234455	SNNNNNNNFFNFFNFNNNFN	NNNN3NNNNNNNNNN	D,J,P	296	931	11.07.03	1283	200203	15005
099.117-014	EDUCATION SUPERVISOR, CORRECTIONAL INSTITUTION (education)	5358	22333344455	LNNNNNNNFFNFFNFNNNON	NNNN3NNNNNNNNNN	D,P,J	295	931	11.07.03	2360	000000	31517
099.117-018	PRINCIPAL (education)	5358	22322244453	SNNNNNNNOOONFFNFONNNN	NNNN3NNNNNNNNNN	P,I	295	931	11.07.03	1283	000000	15005
099.117-022	SUPERINTENDENT, SCHOOLS (education)	5359	21242244455	SNNNNNNNOOONFFNFONNNN	NNNN3NNNNNNNNNN	D,P,J,V	295	931	11.07.03	1283	000000	15005
099.117-026	SUPERVISOR, EDUCATION (education)	5358	22344244455	LNNNNNNNFFNFFNFNNNNN	NNNN3NNNNNNNNNN	D,I,J	295	931	11.07.03	1282	000000	19005
099.117-030	DIRECTOR, EDUCATION (museums)	5457	22344344453	SNNNNNNNOOONFFNFONNNN	NNNN3NNNNNNNNNN	D,P,J	295	931	11.07.03	2360	200203	31517
099.167-010	CERTIFICATION AND SELECTION SPECIALIST (education)	6558	22344244455	SNNNNNNNFFNFFNFNNNFN	NNNN3NNNNNNNNNN	D,J	211	931	11.03.04	1430	000000	21511
099.167-014	CONSULTANT, EDUCATION (education)	6658	21244144455	LNNNNNNNFFNFFNFNNNNN	NNNN3NNNNNNNNNN	D,J,P	296	931	11.07.03	2360	200203	31517
099.167-018	DIRECTOR, INSTRUCTIONAL MATERIAL (education)	5458	22322244453	LNNNNNNNOOONFFNFNNFFN	NNNN3NNNNNNNNNN	D,E,J,P	296	931	11.07.03	2360	000000	31517
099.167-022	EDUCATIONAL SPECIALIST (education)	6558	11344244455	SNNNNNNNOOONFFNFONNNN	NNNN3NNNNNNNNNN	D,I,J,P	251	931	11.07.03	2360	000000	31517
099.167-026	MUSIC SUPERVISOR (education)	5258	22333244455	SNNNNNNNOOONFFNFNNNNN	NNNN3NNNNNNNNNN	D,I,J,P	295	756	11.07.03	1283	000000	31511
099.167-030	EDUCATIONAL RESOURCE COORDINATOR (museums)	5257	22443344453	LNNONONOOONFFNFNNNNN	NNNN3NNNNNNNNNN	D,I,J,P	295	931	11.07.03	1283	000000	31511
099.167-034	DIRECTOR OF PUPIL PERSONNEL PROGRAM (education)	5458	22344344455	SNNNNNNNFONFFNFNNNNN	NNNN3NNNNNNNNNN	D,P,J	231	931	11.07.03	1283	000000	15005
099.223-010	INSTRUCTOR, DRIVING (education)	4234	33433323324	LNNNNNNNFONFFNFNNFFF	NNNN4NNNNNNNNNO	I,J,S	296	931	09.03.03	2390	000000	31317
099.224-010	INSTRUCTOR, PHYSICAL EDUCATION (education)	5357	22333433314	LOOOOOOFFOOFFNOFOOOF	ONNN3NNNNNNNNNO	D,P,V	296	931	11.02.01	2390	000000	31399
099.224-014	TEACHER, ADVENTURE EDUCATION (education)	5457	22433333334	MFFFFFFFFOFFNOFFNOF	FNNN3NNNNNNNNNN	D,I,J,P	296	931	10.02.03	2390	000000	31317
099.227-010	CHILDREN'S TUTOR (domestic ser.)	4245	33344444455	LNNNNNNNFFNNNNNNNN	NNNN4NNNNNNNNNNO	V,D,P	291	942	10.03.03	2390	200202	31399
099.227-014	INSTRUCTOR, CORRESPONDENCE SCHOOL (education)	5357	22343344455	LNNNNNNNOONFFNFNNNNN	NNNN3NNNNNNNNNN	D,I,J	296	931	11.02.01	2390	000000	31314
099.227-018	INSTRUCTOR, GROUND SERVICES (air trans.)	5357	22223244454	LNNNNNNNOOONFFNFNNNON	NNNN3NNNNNNNNNN	D,P,V	296	855	11.02.02	2390	000000	31314
099.227-022	INSTRUCTOR, MILITARY SCIENCE (education)	5359	22322244455	SNNNNNNNOOONFFNFNNNNN	NNNN3NNNNNNNNNN	D,P,I	296	931	11.02.01	2249	000000	31308

DOT #	DOT Title & Industry	Trng	Aptitude	Physical	Enviroment	Tempra	WkF	MPSMS	GOE	SOC	CIP	OES
099.227-026	INSTRUCTOR, MODELING (education)	4244	32444434343	LNNNNNNFFNFFNFFNFN	NNNN3NNNNNNNNNNN	P,J,E	296	931	01.08.01	2390	000000	31317
099.227-030	TEACHER, ADULT EDUCATION (education)	4247	32333244455	LNNNNNNNFFNFFNFFNFOOONO	NNNN3NNNNNNNNNNN	D,I,J	296	931	11.02.01	2390	000000	31399
099.227-034	TUTOR (education)	5357	22344244455	LNNNNNNNFFNFFNFFNNNNN	NNNN3NNNNNNNNNNN	P,J	296	931	11.02.01	2390	000000	31399
099.227-038	TEACHER (museums)	5457	22333344453	LNNNNNNNFFONFFNFONOON	NNNN3NNNNNNNNNNN	D,P	296	931	11.02.01	2216	000000	31317
099.227-042	TEACHER, RESOURCE (education)	5557	22244244455	LNNNNNNOOONFFNFNNNNN	NNNN3NNNNNNNNNNN	D,P,J	296	931	11.02.01	2300	000000	31311
099.327-010	TEACHER AIDE I (education)	4346	33344344354	LNNNNNNFFONFFNFONNON	NNNN3NNNNNNNNNNN	J,P	296	931	11.02.01	3990	131501	31521
100.117-010	LIBRARY DIRECTOR (library)	6458	11343244455	SNNNNNNNFFNFFNFNNNNN	NNNN3NNNNNNNNNNN	V,D,P,J	295	933	11.07.04	1283	000000	15005
100.117-014	LIBRARY CONSULTANT (library)	6468	11343244455	SNNNNNNNNNNNFFNFNNNNN	NNNN3NNNNNNNNNNN	I,P,V	295	933	11.07.04	2510	000000	21905
100.127-010	CHIEF LIBRARIAN, BRANCH OR DEPARTMENT (library)	5357	22344344455	LNNNNNNNFFNFFNFFNFN	NNNN2NNNNNNNNNNN	D,P,J	221	933	11.07.04	2510	000000	31502
100.127-014	LIBRARIAN (library)	5347	22333322253	LNNONONOFFNFFNFNNNNN	NNNN3NNNNNNNNNNN	V,P,J	282	933	11.02.04	2510	000000	31502
100.167-010	AUDIOVISUAL LIBRARIAN (library)	5337	22333322253	LNNNNNNNFFNFFNFFNNNNN	NNNN3NNNNNNNNNNN	D,P,I,J	221	933	11.02.04	2510	000000	31502
100.167-014	BOOKMOBILE LIBRARIAN (library)	4347	22344344454	LNNNNNNNFFNFFNFNNNON	ONNN3NNNNNNNNNNN	V,D,P	221	933	11.02.04	2510	000000	31502
100.167-018	CHILDREN'S LIBRARIAN (library)	5357	22344344455	LNNNNNNNFFNFFNFNNNNN	NNNN3NNNNNNNNNNN	V,P,J	221	933	11.02.04	2510	000000	31502
100.167-022	INSTITUTION LIBRARIAN (library)	5457	22344344455	LNNOONNFFNFFNFNNNNN	NNNN3NNNNNNNNNNN	V,P,J	221	933	11.02.04	2510	000000	31502
100.167-026	LIBRARIAN, SPECIAL LIBRARY (library)	5458	22233244455	LNNNNNOOONFFNFNNNNN	NNNN2NNNNNNNNNNN	D,V,P,J	221	933	11.02.04	2510	000000	31502
100.167-030	MEDIA SPECIALIST, SCHOOL LIBRARY (library)	5358	22344233354	LNNOONNFFOOFFNFONNON	NNNN2NNNNNNNNNNN	D,I,V,P,J	221	931	11.02.04	2510	000000	31502
100.167-034	YOUNG-ADULT LIBRARIAN (library)	5257	22344344455	LNNNNNNNFFNFFNFFNNNNN	NNNN2NNNNNNNNNNN	D,I,E	282	933	11.02.04	2510	000000	31502
100.167-038	NEWS LIBRARIAN (library)	5457	22943233355	LNNNNNNOOFFNFFNFNNNNN	NNNN2NNNNNNNNNNN	D,V,P,J	282	933	11.02.04	2510	000000	21905
100.267-010	ACQUISITIONS LIBRARIAN (library)	4346	22244344455	LNNOONNFFNFFNFNFNFN	NNNN2NNNNNNNNNNN	V,J	221	933	11.02.04	2510	000000	31502
100.267-014	LIBRARIAN, SPECIAL COLLECTIONS (library)	5258	22343244454	LNNOONNFFNFFNFNNFON	NNNN2NNNNNNNNNNN	D,J	221	933	11.02.04	2510	000000	31502
100.367-010	BIBLIOGRAPHER (profess. & kin.)	4247	11344244455	SNNNNNNNFFNFFNFNFNFN	NNNN2NNNNNNNNNNN	J	231	757	11.02.04	2510	250301	31505
100.367-014	CLASSIFIER (library)	4346	22443244455	LNNNNNNNFFNNFNFNNNNN	NNNN3NNNNNNNNNNN	R,J,T	221	933	11.02.04	2510	250301	31505
100.367-018	LIBRARY TECHNICAL ASSISTANT (library)	4335	33243244455	LNNNNNNNFFNFFNFNNONN	NNNN3NNNNNNNNNNN	P,V	221	933	11.02.01	2510	250301	31505
100.367-022	MUSIC LIBRARIAN (radio-tv broad.)	4246	33343344455	LONOOONFCONOFNONNNNN	NNNN2NNNNNNNNNNN	T,J	221	863	11.02.04	2510	000000	31505
100.367-026	MUSIC LIBRARIAN, INTERNATIONAL BROADCAST (radio-tv broad.)	4346	33343344455	SNNNNNNNFFNFFNFNFNFN	NNNN2NNNNNNNNNNN	J	221	933	11.02.04	2510	000000	31505
100.387-010	CATALOG LIBRARIAN (library)	4245	33343244455	SNNNNNNNFFNFFNFNNNNN	NNNN3NNNNNNNNNNN	R,T	221	933	11.02.04	2510	000000	31505
101.167-010	ARCHIVIST (profess. & kin.)	5358	21233244454	SNNNNNNNFFNFFNFNFNFN	NNNN3NNNNNNNNNNN	V,D,P,J,E	211	933	11.03.03	2520	000000	31511
102.017-010	CURATOR (museums)	6569	11233344453	LNNNNNNNFFNFFNFNNOON	ONNN3NNNNNNNNNNN	D,J	295	939	11.07.04	2520	000000	34035
102.117-010	SUPERVISOR, HISTORIC SITES (government ser.)	5457	21323454454	LNNNNNNNFFNFFNFNFNFN	NNNN3NNNNNNNNNNN	D,P,J,E	295	959	11.05.03	2520	000000	31511
102.117-014	DIRECTOR, MUSEUM-OR-ZOO (museums)	6468	22333344453	SNNNNNNNOOONFFNFNFN	NNNN3NNNNNNNNNNN	D,I,P,V	295	933	11.02.01	2520	000000	31511
102.167-010	ART CONSERVATOR (museums)	5448	12422322251	LNNNNNNNFFFFFNFOOFN	NNNN3NNNNNNNNNNN	D,J	212	751	11.06.02	2520	000000	39999
102.167-014	HISTORIC-SITE ADMINISTRATOR (museums)	5455	22343344454	LNNNNNNOOONFFNONNOON	NNNN3NNNNNNNNNNN	D,P,V	295	939	11.02.01	2520	000000	25102
102.167-018	REGISTRAR, MUSEUM (museums)	5456	11111223444	SNNNNNNOOONOONFNNNFN	NNNN3NNNNNNNNNNN	D,J,V	295	933	11.01.01	1719	110501	25102
102.261-010	CONSERVATION TECHNICIAN (museums)	4446	22922322241	MOOONONFFOOONFNFON	NNNN3NNNNNNNNNNN	J	102	969	07.01.02	2520	000000	31511
102.261-014	PAINTINGS RESTORER (profess. & kin.)	5448	23411331251	LNNNNNNNFFNNNNFFFFN	NNNN2NNNNNNNNNNN	J,E,T	262	751	01.02.02	3250	000000	51002
102.361-010	RESEARCH ASSISTANT I (profess. & kin.)	5447	22333344453	MNNNNNNFFNNNNNFFON	NNNN3NNNNNNNNNNN	J	164	430	01.06.02	2520	000000	31511
102.361-014	RESTORER, LACE AND TEXTILES (museums)	5557	22222422352	LNNNNNNNFFONNNFNFFN	NNNO3NNNNNNNNNNN	J,T	102	530	01.06.02	2520	000000	31511
102.367-010	FINE ARTS PACKER (museums)	4337	22324444554	MNNONONFFNFFNFNONN	NNNF3NNNNNNNNNNN	D,J	041	969	05.03.09	3990	000000	39999
102.381-010	MUSEUM TECHNICIAN (museums)	4347	33422442233	NNNNNNNFFNNNNVFOOOON	NNNN4NNNNNNNNNNO	J,V	102	933	01.06.02	2520	000000	31511
109.067-010	INFORMATION SCIENTIST (profess. & kin.)	5557	21244444455	SNNNNNNOOONOONFNNNFN	NNNN3NNNNNNNNNNO	D,J,T	233	933	11.01.01	1719	110501	25102
109.067-014	RESEARCH ASSOCIATE (museums)	6667	11111223442	SNNNNNNNFFNNNNFFNFN	NNNN3NNNNNNNNNNN	J	251	750	11.03.03	2520	000000	31511
109.137-010	SHELVING SUPERVISOR (library)	4246	33433344455	LNNNNNNNFFNFFNFNNNNN	NNNN2NNNNNNNNNNN	D,P,T	221	933	11.02.04	4519	520204	51002
109.267-010	RESEARCH ASSISTANT I (profess. & kin.)	5447	22323344453	LNNNNNNNFFOOONFFFFF	NNNN3NNNNNNNNNNN	J,T,V	251	750	11.03.03	2520	000000	31511
109.267-014	RESEARCH WORKER, ENCYCLOPEDIA (profess. & kin.)	5356	21332432243	SNNNNNNNFFNFFNFNNNNN	NNNN2NNNNNNNNNNN	J	251	931	11.08.02	2510	000000	31502
109.281-010	ARMORER TECHNICIAN (museums)	5457	33422432243	LNNNNNNNFFNNNNNFOFON	NNNN4NNNNNNNNNNO	J,T	102	440	01.06.02	2520	000000	31511
109.361-010	RESTORER, PAPER-AND-PRINTS (library; museums)	5557	22232322352	SNNNNNNNFFONNNFNOFFN	NNNF3NNNNNNNNNNN	J,V	031	933	01.06.03	2520	000000	31511
109.364-010	CRAFT DEMONSTRATOR (museums)	4244	33333333353	LNNNNNNNFFOONFFNFNF	ONNN3NNNNNNNNNNN	E,J,P,T	282	919	09.01.02	2520	000000	31511
109.367-010	MUSEUM ATTENDANT (museums)	4343	33444334455	LNNNNNNNFFFFFNFONNNF	NNNN3NNNNNNNNNNN	P,V	231	933	07.04.04	2520	000000	31511
110.107-010	LAWYER (profess. & kin.)	6468	11144244455	SNNNNNNNFFNCCNFNNONN	NNNN3NNNNNNNNNNN	V,P,I,J	272	932	11.04.02	2110	000000	28108
110.107-014	LAWYER, CRIMINAL (profess. & kin.)	6468	11144344455	SNNNNNNOOONFFNFNNONN	NNNN3NNNNNNNNNNN	V,P,I	272	932	11.04.02	2110	000000	28108
110.117-010	DISTRICT ATTORNEY (government ser.)	6468	11244344455	SNNNNNNNFFNFFNFNONN	NNNN3NNNNNNNNNNN	P,I,J	272	932	11.04.02	2110	000000	28108

DOT #	DOT Title & Industry	Trmg	Aptitude	Physical	Environment	Tempra	WkF	MPSMS	GOE	SOC	CIP	OES
110.117-014	INSURANCE ATTORNEY (insurance)	6468	11144244455	SNNNNNNOOONFFNFNNONN	NNNN3NNNNNNNNNNN	V,P,J	271	895	11.04.02	2110	000000	28108
110.117-018	LAWYER, ADMIRALTY (profess. & kin.)	6468	11134344455	SNNNNNNOOONFFNFNNONN	NNNN3NNNNNNNNNNN	V,D,P,I,J	272	932	11.04.02	2110	000000	28108
110.117-022	LAWYER, CORPORATION (profess. & kin.)	6468	11144344455	SNNNNNNOOONFFNFNNONN	NNNN3NNNNNNNNNNN	V,D,P,I	272	932	11.04.02	2110	000000	28108
110.117-026	LAWYER, PATENT (profess. & kin.)	6468	11144344455	SNNNNNNFFNFFNFNNFNN	NNNN3NNNNNNNNNNN	V,P,I	272	932	11.04.02	2110	000000	28108
110.117-030	LAWYER, PROBATE (profess. & kin.)	6468	11144444455	SNNNNNNFFNFFNFNNFNN	NNNN3NNNNNNNNNNN	V,D,P,I	272	932	11.04.02	2110	000000	28108
110.117-034	LAWYER, REAL ESTATE (profess. & kin.)	6468	12144244455	SNNNNNNFFNFFNFNNFNN	NNNN3NNNNNNNNNNN	V,D,P,I	272	932	11.04.02	2110	000000	28108
110.117-038	TAX ATTORNEY (profess. & kin.)	6468	11344344455	SNNNNNNFFNFFNFNNFNN	NNNN3NNNNNNNNNNN	V,J	272	932	11.04.02	2110	000000	28108
110.117-042	TITLE ATTORNEY (profess. & kin.)	6468	11344344455	LNNNNNNOOOFFNCNNNNNN	NNNN3NNNNNNNNNNN	P,J,I	272	932	11.04.02	2110	000000	28108
110.167-010	BAR EXAMINER (profess. & kin.)	6469	11344344455	SNNNNNNFFNFFNFNNFNN	NNNN3NNNNNNNNNNN	P,J,E	272	932	11.04.02	2110	000000	28108
111.107-010	JUDGE (government ser.)	6469	11155455555	SNNNNNNOOONFFNFNNONN	NNNN3NNNNNNNNNNN	D,I,P,J	272	932	11.04.01	2120	000000	28102
111.107-014	MAGISTRATE (government ser.)	6469	11155455555	SNNNNNNFFONFFNFNNNNN	NNNN3NNNNNNNNNNN	D,I,J,P	272	932	11.04.01	2120	000000	28102
119.107-010	HEARING OFFICER (government ser.)	6369	12344344455	SNNNNNNFFONFFNFNNFNN	NNNN3NNNNNNNNNNN	D,J	272	959	11.04.01	2120	000000	28105
119.117-010	APPEALS REVIEWER, VETERAN (government ser.)	6559	21343344455	SNNNNNNFFNFFNFNNFNN	NNNN3NNNNNNNNNNN	J,P	271	952	11.04.01	2120	000000	28105
119.167-010	ADJUDICATOR (government ser.)	5457	22244444555	SNNNNNNOOONFFNONNNNN	NNNN3NNNNNNNNNNN	V,P,J	272	932	11.04.03	2120	000000	28105
119.167-014	PATENT AGENT (profess. & kin.)	6567	21223444554	SNNNNNNNNFFNFNNNNNNN	NNNN2NNNNNNNNNNN	I,J,E	272	932	11.04.04	3960	000000	28399
119.167-018	TITLE SUPERVISOR (profess. & kin.)	5358	21333244455	SNNNNNNFFNFFNFNNNNNN	NNNN2NNNNNNNNNNN	D,P,J	271	932	07.01.05	3960	520204	28311
119.267-010	ABSTRACTOR (profess. & kin.)	5356	21444244455	SNNNNNNFFONNNFNNNNNN	NNNN2NNNNNNNNNNN	J,T	271	932	11.04.04	3960	220103	28311
119.267-014	APPEALS REFEREE (government ser.)	6368	22343344455	SNNNNNNOOONFFNONNNNN	NNNN3NNNNNNNNNNN	J	271	959	11.04.01	2120	000000	28105
119.267-018	CONTRACT CLERK (profess. & kin.)	5257	21344344455	SNNNNNNFFONFFNNNNNNN	NNNN3NNNNNNNNNNN	J	272	932	07.01.05	3960	220103	28399
119.267-022	LEGAL INVESTIGATOR (profess. & kin.)	5257	21344344455	SNNNNNNFFNFFNFNNFNN	NNNN3NNNNNNNNNNN	D,I,J,P	271	932	11.04.02	3960	220103	28305
119.267-026	PARALEGAL (profess. & kin.)	5257	21344344455	LNNNNNNFFONNNFNNNNNN	NNNN3NNNNNNNNNNN	P,T,V,J	271	932	11.04.02	3960	220103	28302
119.287-010	TITLE EXAMINER (profess. & kin.)	5357	22344244455	SNNNNNNFFONNNFNNNNNN	NNNN2NNNNNNNNNNN	J	271	932	07.01.04	3960	220103	28311
119.367-010	ESCROW OFFICER (profess. & kin.)	4338	23244233344	SNNNNNNFFNFFNFNNNNNN	NNNN3NNNNNNNNNNN	J,T	231	895	07.01.04	3960	000000	28399
120.107-010	CLERGY MEMBER (profess. & kin.)	6468	11344345455	LNNNNNNOOONFFNNNNNNN	NNNN2NNNNNNNNNNN	E,I,J,P,V	298	944	10.01.01	2042	000000	27502
129.027-010	CANTOR (profess. & kin.)	5148	22343344455	SNNNNNNFFONFFNFNNNNN	NNNN3NNNNNNNNNNN	D,E,P	296	944	11.07.03	2049	000000	27599
129.067-010	CHRISTIAN SCIENCE NURSE (profess. & kin.)	4347	33444244455	LNNNNNNFFONFFNFNNNNN	NNNN3NNNNNNNNNNN	D,J,P	294	944	10.03.02	2049	000000	27599
129.107-014	CHRISTIAN SCIENCE PRACTITIONER (profess. & kin.)	5236	22444444555	SNNNNNNFFNFFNFNNNNNN	NNNN3NNNNNNNNNNN	I,E,P,J	294	896	01.01.02	2049	000000	27599
129.107-018	DIRECTOR OF RELIGIOUS ACTIVITIES (education)	5358	11433444453	SNNNNNNNNNNNFNNNNNNN	NNNN3NNNNNNNNNNN	I,V,E,J	294	944	10.01.01	2049	000000	27505
129.107-022	DIRECTOR, RELIGIOUS EDUCATION (nonprofit org.)	5358	11343333455	SNNNNNNFFNOONFNNNNNN	NNNN2NNNNNNNNNNN	E,J,I,V,P	295	944	01.01.03	2049	000000	27505
129.107-026	PASTORAL ASSISTANT (nonprofit org.)	5356	22344355555	SNNNNNNFFNOONFNNNFNN	NNNN2NNNNNNNNNNN	D,P,I	295	944	11.07.03	2049	000000	27599
129.271-010	MOHEL (profess. & kin.)	4246	22322222253	LNNNNNNOOOFNOONFNNNON	NNNN3NNNNNNNNNNN	D,P,V,J	298	944	10.01.01	2049	000000	27599
131.067-010	COLUMNIST/COMMENTATOR (print. & pub.; radio-tv broad.)	6367	11343334455	LNNNNNNFFNFFNFNNOFON	NNNN2NNNNNNNNNNN	T,P,S	294	944	10.01.01	2049	000000	27599
131.067-014	COPY WRITER (profess. & kin.)	5257	21343334455	SNNNNNNOOONFFNONNONN	NNNN3NNNNNNNNNNN	I,V,E,P,J	261	757	11.08.03	3313	080299	34002
131.067-018	CRITIC (print. & pub.; radio-tv broad.)	6268	11433444453	LNNNNNNFFONFFNFNNNNN	NNNN3NNNNNNNNNNN	I,E,P,J	261	896	01.01.02	3313	000000	34014
131.067-022	EDITORIAL WRITER (print. & pub.)	5358	11343333455	SNNNNNNFFNNNNNFNNNNN	NNNN3NNNNNNNNNNN	I,V,E,J	261	750	01.01.03	3313	000000	34002
131.067-026	HUMORIST (profess. & kin.)	6268	11444244455	SNNNNNNNNNNNNFNNNNNN	NNNN2NNNNNNNNNNN	J,E,P	261	757	01.01.02	3210	000000	34002
131.067-030	LIBRETTIST (profess. & kin.)	6267	11444344455	SNNNNNNFFNOONFNNNNNN	NNNN2NNNNNNNNNNN	J,E,I	261	860	01.01.02	3210	000000	34002
131.067-034	LYRICIST (profess. & kin.)	6267	12444244455	SNNNNNNFFONFFNNNNNNN	NNNN2NNNNNNNNNNN	E,I,J	261	756	01.01.02	3210	000000	34002
131.067-038	PLAYWRIGHT (profess. & kin.)	6268	11444444455	SNNNNNNNNNNNNFNNNNNN	NNNN3NNNNNNNNNNN	I,V,P,J	261	756	01.01.02	3210	000000	34002
131.067-042	POET (profess. & kin.)	6267	11444444455	SNNNNNNFFNNNNNFNNNNN	NNNN3NNNNNNNNNNN	I,P,J	261	754	01.01.02	3210	000000	34002
131.067-046	WRITER, PROSE, FICTION AND NONFICTION (profess. & kin.)	6368	11444444455	SNNNNNNFFNNNNNFNNNNN	NNNN4NNNNNNNNNNN	I,J,E	261	757	01.01.02	3210	000000	34002
131.067-050	SCREEN WRITER (motion picture; radio-tv broad.)	6267	21444444455	SNNNNNNFFNNNNNFNNNNN	NNNN2NNNNNNNNNNN	J,E,P	261	754	01.01.02	3210	000000	34014
131.087-010	CONTINUITY WRITER (radio-tv broad.)	5257	22244444455	SNNNNNNFFNNNNNFNNNNN	NNNN2NNNNNNNNNNN	J,E,I	261	863	01.01.02	3210	000000	34002
131.087-014	READER (motion picture; radio-tv broad.)	5256	21444444455	SNNNNNNFFONFFNNNNNNN	NNNN2NNNNNNNNNNN	E,I,J	261	754	01.01.01	3210	000000	34002
131.262-010	NEWSCASTER (radio-tv broad.)	5257	21344333455	LNNNNNNOOOFNOONFNNNON	NNNN3NNNNNNNNNNN	I,V,P,J	261	863	11.08.03	3313	000000	34014
131.262-014	NEWSWRITER (print. & pub.; radio-tv broad.)	5257	21343334455	SNNNNNNFFONFFNNNNNNN	NNNN3NNNNNNNNNNN	I,P,J	261	757	11.08.02	3313	000000	34002
131.262-018	REPORTER (print. & pub.; radio-tv broad.)	5357	21343334455	LNNNNNNFFNFFNNNNONNN	NNNN3NNNNNNNNNNN	I,P,J	261	757	11.08.02	3313	000000	34011
131.267-022	SCRIPT READER (radio-tv broad.)	4246	32444333355	SNNNNNNFFONFFNCNFNNN	NNNN4NNNNNNNNNNN	J	271	863	07.05.02	3312	000000	34002
131.267-026	WRITER, TECHNICAL PUBLICATIONS (profess. & kin.)	5358	21223244455	SNNNNNNNNFFNFNNNNNNN	NNNN3NNNNNNNNNNN	T,P,J	261	750	11.08.02	3980	000000	34005
132.017-010	EDITOR, MANAGING, NEWSPAPER (print. & pub.)	6368	11333344455	SNNNNNNNNNFFNFNNNNNN	NNNN3NNNNNNNNNNN	V,D,P,I,J	261	757	11.05.01	3312	000000	34002
132.017-014	EDITOR, NEWSPAPER (print. & pub.)	6369	11333334455	SNNNNNNFFNFFNFNNNNNN	NNNN3NNNNNNNNNNN	D,I,J,E,P	295	757	11.08.01	3312	000000	34002

DOT #	DOT Title & Industry	Trng	Aptitude	Physical	Environment	Tempra	WkF	MPSMS	GOE	SOC	CIP	OES
132.017-018	EDITOR, TECHNICAL AND SCIENTIFIC PUBLICATIONS (profess. & kin.)	6369	11333344455	SNNNNNNOONNFFNFNNNNNN	NNNN2NNNNNNNNNNN	D,P,J,E	261	757	11.08.01	3312	000000	34002
132.037-010	CONTINUITY DIRECTOR (radio-tv broad.)	5258	21344344455	SNNNNNNOOONFFNFNNFNN	NNNN3NNNNNNNNNNN	D,P,J	261	863	01.01.01	3312	000000	34002
132.037-014	EDITOR, CITY (print. & pub.)	6368	11343344455	SNNNNNNNNNNFFNFNFNNN	NNNN3NNNNNNNNNNN	V,D,P,J,E	261	757	11.08.01	3312	000000	34002
132.037-018	EDITOR, DEPARTMENT (print. & pub.)	5358	21343344455	SNNNNNNNNNNFFNFNFNNN	NNNN3NNNNNNNNNNN	V,D,P,J,E	261	757	11.08.01	3312	000000	34002
132.037-022	EDITOR, PUBLICATIONS (print. & pub.)	6368	11333334455	SNNNNNNFFONFFNFNNFNN	NNNN3NNNNNNNNNNN	D,P,J,E	261	757	01.01.01	3312	000000	34002
132.037-026	STORY EDITOR (motion picture; radio-tv broad.)	6268	11434344455	SNNNNNNOOONFFNFNNNNNN	NNNN2NNNNNNNNNNN	D,J,E,P	261	754	01.01.01	3312	000000	34002
132.067-010	BUREAU CHIEF (print. & pub.)	5358	21343344455	SNNNNNNNNNNNFFNFNNNNN	NNNN3NNNNNNNNNNN	V,D,P,J,E	261	757	11.08.01	3312	000000	34002
132.067-014	EDITOR, BOOK (print. & pub.)	6368	11333334455	SNNNNNNNOOONFFNFNNNNN	NNNN3NNNNNNNNNNN	D,P,I,J,E	261	757	01.01.01	3312	000000	34002
132.067-018	EDITOR, DICTIONARY (profess. & kin.)	6368	11444444455	SNNNNNNNFFONNNNFNNNNN	NNNN3NNNNNNNNNNN	J,T	261	749	11.08.01	3312	000000	34002
132.067-022	EDITOR, GREETING CARD (print. & pub.)	5256	22344344455	SNNNNNNNFFONNNNFNNNNN	NNNN2NNNNNNNNNNN	J,E	261	485	01.01.01	3312	000000	34002
132.067-026	EDITOR, NEWS (print. & pub.)	5358	21333334455	SNNNNNNNFFONFFNFNNFNN	NNNN3NNNNNNNNNNN	D,J,E,T	261	757	11.08.01	3312	000000	34002
132.067-030	PROGRAM PROPOSALS COORDINATOR (radio-tv broad.)	5357	11344344455	SNNNNNNNOOOFFNFNNFNN	NNNN3NNNNNNNNNNN	D,J,P,V	261	863	11.05.02	3312	000000	34002
132.132-010	ASSIGNMENT EDITOR (radio-tv broad.)	5258	11344343455	SNNNNNNFFNCCNFNNFNN	NNNN2NNNNNNNNNNN	D,P,J	261	863	11.08.01	3312	000000	34056
132.267-010	EDITOR, TELEGRAPH (print. & pub.; radio-tv broad.)	4347	21333344455	SNNNNNNFFNNNNNFNNNNN	NNNN2NNNNNNNNNNN	P,J,T	261	757	11.08.01	3312	000000	34002
132.267-014	EDITORIAL ASSISTANT (print. & pub.)	5357	22333244455	SNNNNNNFFONNNNFNNNNN	NNNN2NNNNNNNNNNN	J	261	757	11.08.01	3312	000000	34002
132.367-010	EDITOR, INDEX (print. & pub.)	5357	22443244455	SNNNNNNFFNOONFNNONN	NNNN2NNNNNNNNNNN	J	261	757	11.08.01	3312	000000	34002
137.137-010	DIRECTOR, TRANSLATION (profess. & kin.)	5358	21244244455	SNNNNNNOOOFFNFNNNNNN	NNNN3NNNNNNNNNNN	D,J,P	295	749	11.08.04	3290	000000	34056
137.267-010	INTERPRETER (profess. & kin.)	5256	21444344455	SNNNNNNFFNCCNNNFNNNNN	NNNN2NNNNNNNNNNN	P,J	281	749	11.08.04	3290	000000	39999
137.267-014	INTERPRETER, DEAF (profess. & kin.)	4345	32443323355	LNNNNNNNFFFNFNNNNNN	NNNN3NNNNNNNNNNN	J,P	282	869	01.03.02	3290	510205	39999
137.267-018	TRANSLATOR (profess. & kin.)	6367	11334344455	SNNNNNNFFONNNNFNNNNN	NNNN2NNNNNNNNNNN	J	261	749	11.08.04	3290	000000	39999
139.087-010	CROSSWORD-PUZZLE MAKER (print. & pub.)	5256	22334344455	SNNNNNNFFONNNNFNNNNN	NNNN3NNNNNNNNNNN	E,T	261	757	01.01.02	3290	000000	39999
139.167-010	PROGRAM COORDINATOR (amuse. & rec.)	4248	22344244455	LNNOONNCCFNFFNFONONO	NNNN3NNNNNNNNNNN	J,I,P,D	295	931	01.03.03	3280	310101	34056
141.031-010	ART DIRECTOR (profess. & kin.)	5358	22322333352	SNNNNNNFFONFFNFNFOFN	NNNN2NNNNNNNNNNN	D,E,I,J,P	264	752	01.02.03	3220	500402	34035
141.051-010	COLOR EXPERT (profess. & kin.)	5247	22443244455	SNNNNNNFFNOONFNNNCN	NNNN2NNNNNNNNNNN	P,I,J,E	264	889	01.02.03	3220	040501	34038
141.061-010	CARTOONIST (print. & pub.)	5247	22422421252	SNNNNNNCCFNNNNCNNONN	NNNN2NNNNNNNNNNN	I,E,J	262	752	01.02.03	3250	500402	34035
141.061-014	FASHION ARTIST (retail trade)	5247	22311321252	SNNNNNNFFNOONFNNOFFN	NNNN2NNNNNNNNNNN	J,E	262	752	01.02.03	3250	500402	34035
141.061-018	GRAPHIC DESIGNER (profess. & kin.)	5347	22322333352	SNNNNNNFFNOONNFFN	NNNN3NNNNNNNNNNN	J,E	264	752	01.02.03	3220	500402	34035
141.061-022	ILLUSTRATOR (profess. & kin.)	5247	22311321251	SNNNNNNFFNNNNNFFFN	NNNN2NNNNNNNNNNN	J,E	262	752	01.02.03	3250	500402	34035
141.061-026	ILLUSTRATOR, MEDICAL AND SCIENTIFIC (profess. & kin.)	5457	22311321251	SNNOOONFFFOOONFNNOFN	NNNN2NNNNNNNNNNN	E,J,T	262	752	01.02.03	3250	500402	34035
141.061-030	ILLUSTRATOR, SET (motion picture; radio-tv broad.)	5348	22311321251	SNNNNNNFFNNNNNFOFOFO	NNNN3NNNNNNNNNNN	J,E	262	752	01.02.03	3250	500402	34035
141.061-034	POLICE ARTIST (government ser.)	5347	22322322253	LNNNNNNFFNFNFFFFFF	NNNN3NNNNNNNNNNN	T,P,J	262	759	01.02.03	3250	000000	34041
141.061-038	COMMERCIAL DESIGNER (profess. & kin.)	5347	22322343352	SNNNNNNCCFNFFNCNCCCO	NNNN2NNNNNNNNNNN	J,E	264	889	01.06.01	3220	500710	34038
141.067-010	CREATIVE DIRECTOR (profess. & kin.)	5358	22322344452	SNNNNNNNFFNFNFNOOON	NNNN2NNNNNNNNNNN	D,E,I,P	264	896	01.02.03	3220	090201	34038
141.081-010	CARTOONIST, MOTION PICTURES (motion picture; radio-tv broad.)	5247	22422421252	LNNNNNNFFFOOONFNFFN	NNNN3NNNNNNNNNNN	J,E	262	752	01.02.03	3250	500402	34035
141.137-010	PRODUCTION MANAGER, ADVERTISING (profess. & kin.)	4347	22322244353	SNNNNNNNFFONOONFNOOFO	NNNN3NNNNNNNNNNN	D,E,T,P	264	896	01.02.03	3220	090201	13011
142.031-014	MANAGER, DISPLAY (retail trade)	5347	22322434452	LNNNNNNFFONFFNFNFFFF	ONNN2NNNNNNNNNNN	D,E,J,P	264	889	01.02.03	3220	200599	34038
142.051-010	DISPLAY DESIGNER (profess. & kin.)	5347	23322432342	SNNNNNNFFNNNNFFNFN	NNNN2NNNNNNNNNNN	J,E	264	752	01.02.03	3220	080299	34038
142.051-014	INTERIOR DESIGNER (profess. & kin.)	5347	22322333352	LONOOONFFONFFNFOFOFO	NNNN3NNNNNNNNNNN	D,P,I,J,E	264	889	01.02.03	3220	040501	34041
142.061-010	BANK-NOTE DESIGNER (government ser.)	4348	22311422351	SNNNNNNFFNFNFNFOFN	NNNN2NNNNNNNNNNN	V,J,E	264	752	05.01.07	3220	500402	34038
142.061-014	CLOTH DESIGNER (profess. & kin.)	4347	22222443352	SNNNNNNCCFNFFNCNCCCO	NNNN2NNNNNNNNNNN	J,E	264	420	01.02.03	3220	150699	34038
142.061-018	FASHION DESIGNER (profess. & kin.)	5347	22322322352	LNNNNNNFFFOOONFNFFN	NNNN3NNNNNNNNNNN	E,J,T,V	264	440	01.02.03	3220	200303	34038
142.061-022	FURNITURE DESIGNER (furniture)	5447	23222333352	SNNNNNNCCNFFNCNFNCN	NNNN3NNNNNNNNNNN	J,E	264	460	01.02.03	3250	500402	34038
142.061-026	INDUSTRIAL DESIGNER (profess. & kin.)	5447	22322332352	SNNNNNNFFNFNFNNOOFN	NNNN2NNNNNNNNNNN	P,J,E	264	700	01.02.03	3220	500402	34035
142.061-030	MEMORIAL DESIGNER (stonework)	4437	23322422254	LNNNNNNCCNOONFNFFFN	NNNN3NOOONNNNNNN	D,J,E	264	537	01.02.03	3250	500402	34038
142.061-034	ORNAMENTAL-METALWORK DESIGNER (struct. metal)	5448	34322432242	LNNNNNNFFONOONFNNFON	NNNN3NOOONNNNNNN	J	102	554	01.02.02	3220	500402	34038
142.061-038	SAFETY-CLOTHING-AND-EQUIPMENT DEVELOPER (profess. & kin.)	5358	22222422355	LNNNNNNCCFNFNCNOONN	NNNN2NNNNNNNNNNN	P,E,T	449	759	01.02.03	3220	000000	34038
142.061-042	SET DECORATOR (motion picture; radio-tv broad.)	5248	22322244451	LONNNNNNOOONFFNOFNFN	NNNN3NNNNNNNNNNN	D,P,J,E	264	759	01.02.03	3220	500402	34038
142.061-046	SET DESIGNER (motion picture; radio-tv broad.)	5348	22322422352	LNNNNNNFFFFFFFFFFF	NNNN3NNNNNNNNNNN	V,E,T,J	242	752	01.02.03	3220	500402	34038
142.061-050	SET DESIGNER (amuse. & rec.)	5348	22312422352	SNNNNNNCCNNNNCNNFFCN	NNNN2NNNNNNNNNNN	D,P,T,J,E	264	701	01.02.03	3220	500402	34038
142.061-054	STAINED GLASS ARTIST (profess. & kin.)	5348	22322332352	SNNNNNNCCCNNNNCNFFCN	NNNN2NNNNNNNNNNN	E,J	264	705	01.02.02	3220	500402	34038
142.061-058	EXHIBIT DESIGNER (museums)	5457	22322333452	SNNNNNNFFNFNFNFOFN	NNNN3NNNNNNNNNNN	D,E,J,P	295	889	01.02.03	3220	000000	34038

DOT #	DOT Title & Industry	Trng	Aptitude	Physical	Environment	Tempra	WkF	MPSMS	GOE	SOC	CIP	OES
142.061-062	ART DIRECTOR (motion picture; radio-tv broad.)	5358	12322422352	SNNNNNNOFONFFNFOFNFN	NNNN3NNNNNNNNNNN	D,E,P,J	264	759	01.02.03	3220	000000	34038
142.081-010	FLORAL DESIGNER (retail trade)	4336	33333333252	LNNNNNNCCNNNNCNFNCN	NNNN2NNNNNNNNNN	J,E	264	889	01.02.03	3220	010603	34038
142.081-014	FUR DESIGNER (fur goods)	4247	22422332343	LNNNNNNFFFOFFNCNNFN	NNNN2NNNNNNNNNN	E,J	264	447	01.02.03	3220	500402	34038
142.081-018	PACKAGE DESIGNER (profess. & kin.)	5347	22322332352	SNNNNNNFFFNNNCNFNCN	NNNN2NNNNNNNNNN	J,E	264	889	01.02.03	3220	500402	34038
142.281-010	COPYIST (garment)	4246	23322432252	LNNNNNNFFONNONFNNFFN	NNNN2NNNNNNNNNN	E,J	262	752	01.02.03	3220	200305	34038
143.062-010	DIRECTOR OF PHOTOGRAPHY (motion picture; radio-tv broad.)	5448	22222444451	LNNNNNNNNNNNFFNCCFOFF	ONNN3NNNNNNNNNNN	D,J,E	201	911	01.02.03	3260	100199	34026
143.062-014	PHOTOGRAPHER, AERIAL (profess. & kin.)	4337	23322433352	LNNNNNNFFFNFFNFFFFF	ONNN4CNNNNNNNNN	J,T	201	753	01.06.01	3260	500406	34023
143.062-018	PHOTOGRAPHER, APPRENTICE (profess. & kin.)	4347	23322433352	LNNOONNFFNOONFFFFFF	ONNN3NNNNNNNNN	P,J,E	201	753	01.02.03	3260	500406	34023
143.062-022	CAMERA OPERATOR (motion picture; radio-tv broad.)	4347	23322433352	MNNONONOFONOFNNNFFN	ONNN3NNNNNNNNN	T,P,J	201	753	01.02.03	3260	100199	34026
143.062-026	PHOTOGRAPHER, SCIENTIFIC (profess. & kin.)	4347	23322433352	LNNNNNNFFNOONNFFFFF	NNNN2NNNNNNONNN	V,J,T	201	720	02.04.01	3260	500406	34023
143.062-030	PHOTOGRAPHER, STILL (profess. & kin.)	4347	23322433352	LNNOONNFFFNOONFFFFF	ONNN3NNNNNNNNN	P,J,E	201	753	01.02.03	3260	500406	34023
143.062-034	PHOTOJOURNALIST (print. & pub.; radio-tv broad.)	4247	33322433355	LNNNNNNCCCNFNFFFFFF	FNNN3NNNNNNNNN	P,J,E	201	753	01.02.03	3260	500406	34023
143.260-010	OPTICAL-EFFECTS-CAMERA OPERATOR (motion picture)	4337	23333333342	LNNONONFFNOONFOOFFN	NNNN3NNNNNNNNN	T,J	201	753	01.02.03	3260	500602	34026
143.362-010	BIOLOGICAL PHOTOGRAPHER (profess. & kin.)	4336	22322433342	LNNNNNNFFNNNNFFFFF	ONNN2NNNNNONNN	V,J,T	201	753	02.04.02	3260	500406	34023
143.362-014	OPHTHALMIC PHOTOGRAPHER (medical ser.)	4446	33332433343	LNNNNNNFFOOFNCFNFON	NNNN2NNNNNNNFN	T,P	201	753	02.04.02	3260	500406	34023
143.382-010	CAMERA OPERATOR, ANIMATION (motion picture)	4336	33332433355	LNNNNNNFFNNNNFFFFF	NNNN2NNNNNNNNN	R,J,T	201	911	05.10.05	3260	100103	34026
143.382-014	PHOTOGRAPHER, FINISH (amuse. & rec.)	4236	34343443355	LNNNNNNFFFNFFFFFNN	NNNN3NNNNNNNNN	T	201	753	05.10.05	3260	500406	34023
143.457-010	PHOTOGRAPHER (amuse. & rec.)	3133	32354444455	LNNNNNNFFFFFNFFFNNN	NNNN2NNNNNNNNN	P,I	292	753	08.03.01	3260	500406	34023
144.061-010	PAINTER (profess. & kin.)	5248	22311421251	LNNNNNNCCCNNNNCCCCC	FNNN1NNNNNNNNN	J,T,E	262	751	01.02.03	3250	000000	34035
144.061-014	PRINTMAKER (profess. & kin.)	5248	22311421252	SNNNNNNFFNOONFNFFN	NNNN3NONNNNNNNN	J,E,T	264	751	01.02.03	3250	500710	34035
144.061-018	SCULPTOR (profess. & kin.)	5348	22311521253	LNNNNNNCCCONNNFFFFO	NNNN2NNNNNNNNN	J,E,T	264	539	01.02.02	3250	000000	34035
149.021-010	TEACHER, ART (education)	5457	22412422251	LNNONNNFFOFFNFOFOFO	NNNN3NNNNNNNNN	D,P,V,I	296	931	01.02.01	2390	000000	31317
149.031-010	SUPERVISOR, SCENIC ARTS (motion picture; radio-tv broad.)	5448	22222332252	LNNNNNNFFNFNFFFOFF	NNNN3NNNNNNNNN	D,J,E,P	262	911	01.02.03	3290	000000	34056
149.041-010	QUICK SKETCH ARTIST (amuse. & rec.)	5136	23422422252	SNNNNNNFFCNNNCNNNFN	FNNN1NNNNNNNNN	T	201	753	08.03.01	3250	500406	39999
149.051-010	SILHOUETTE ARTIST (amuse. & rec.)	5136	23422222255	SNNNNNNCCNNNNCNNOON	ONNN2NNNNNNNNN	J,E	264	759	01.02.02	3290	000000	39999
149.061-010	AUDIOVISUAL PRODUCTION SPECIALIST (profess. & kin.)	5457	22322223353	LNNNNNNFFNFNFNNOON	NNNN3NNNNNNNNN	D,I,P,J,E	201	752	01.02.03	3290	100101	31508
149.261-010	EXHIBIT ARTIST (museums)	5346	22322422252	LNNONONFFOOONFOFFN	NNNN3NNNNNNNNN	E,J,V	262	939	01.02.03	3250	000000	34035
149.281-010	FURNITURE REPRODUCER (furniture)	5347	23322232353	SNNNNNNCCCNNNNCNFFNN	NNNN2NNNNNNNNN	J	242	460	05.03.02	3290	480702	39999
150.027-010	DRAMATIC COACH (profess. & kin.)	5257	22334344455	LNNNNNNNNNNNCCNFFNNOF	NNNN2NNNNNNNNN	D,P,J,E	296	754	01.03.01	3240	000000	34056
150.027-014	TEACHER, DRAMA (education)	5257	22324244453	LNNNNNNFFONCCNFNNNON	NNNN2NNNNNNNNN	V,D,P,J	296	754	01.03.01	2390	000000	31317
150.047-010	ACTOR (amuse. & rec.)	5257	22533444435	LNNNNNNNNNNNNNNNNNN	NNNN3NNNNNNNNN	E,J,P,V	297	754	01.03.02	3240	000000	34056
150.067-010	DIRECTOR, STAGE (amuse. & rec.)	5358	12423344443	LNNNNNNNNNNCCNFFFFF	NNNN3NNNNNNNNN	V,D,P,J,E	295	754	01.03.01	3240	000000	34056
150.147-010	NARRATOR (motion picture)	5255	22344444455	LNNNNNNNNNCCNNNNNNN	NNNN2NNNNNNNNN	E,J	297	911	01.03.03	3240	000000	34056
151.027-010	CHOREOGRAPHER (amuse. & rec.)	5358	22333444323	LNNNNNNNFNFNNFFNNNF	NNNN2NNNNNNNNN	D,E,J,P	263	755	01.05.01	3270	000000	34053
151.027-014	INSTRUCTOR, DANCING (education)	5256	22424423325	HNFNNNNNFOONFFNNFFNNF	NNNN2NNNNNNNNN	D,P,E,T	296	755	01.05.02	2390	000000	31317
151.047-010	DANCER (amuse. & rec.)	4247	23323423314	HFFNNNNFNNNNNNNNNNN	NNNN4NNNNNNNNN	E,J	297	755	01.05.02	3270	000000	34053
152.021-010	TEACHER, MUSIC (education)	5357	22333221255	LNNOONNNOFFOFFNFOOONO	NNNN3NNNNNNNNN	D,E,P	296	931	01.04.01	2390	000000	31317
152.041-010	MUSICIAN, INSTRUMENTAL (amuse. & rec.)	5338	22343222234	LNNNNNNFFONCCNFNFNN	NNNN2NNNNNNNNN	J,E	296	756	01.04.04	3230	000000	34051
152.047-010	CHORAL DIRECTOR (profess. & kin.)	5358	12332223344	LNNNNNNFONNFNFFNNNN	ONNN3NNNNNNNNN	D,P,J,E	297	756	01.04.01	3230	000000	34047
152.047-014	CONDUCTOR, ORCHESTRA (profess. & kin.)	5339	12332223345	LNNNNNNFONNCCNNNNNNN	NNNN3NNNNNNNNN	D,P,J,E	297	756	01.04.01	3230	000000	34047
152.047-018	DIRECTOR, MUSIC (motion picture; radio-tv broad.)	5459	11332322465	LNNNNNNFONCCNNNNNNN	NNNN3NNNNNNNNN	V,D,P,J,E	297	756	01.04.01	3230	000000	34047
152.047-022	SINGER (amuse. & rec.; motion picture; radio-tv broad.)	4348	22344344455	LNNNNNNNNNCCNFNOFNN	NNNN4NNNNNNNNN	J,E	297	756	01.04.03	3230	000000	34047
152.067-010	ARRANGER (profess. & kin.)	6458	11233233355	SNNNNNNOOONFFNNNNNNN	NNNN2NNNNNNNNN	J,E	263	756	01.04.02	3230	000000	34047
152.067-014	COMPOSER (profess. & kin.)	6469	11343244455	SNNNNNNFFNNNNFNNNNN	NNNN2NNNNNNNNN	J,E	263	756	01.04.02	3230	000000	34047
152.067-018	CUE SELECTOR (radio-tv broad.)	6459	13424443455	LNNNNNNNNFFNFNFNNNN	NNNN2NNNNNNNNN	J,T	263	864	01.04.02	3230	000000	34047
152.067-022	ORCHESTRATOR (profess. & kin.)	6458	11233233355	SNNNNNNOONNFFNNNNNNN	NNNN2NNNNNNNNN	J,E	263	756	01.04.02	3230	000000	34047
152.267-010	COPYIST (any industry)	5357	22343343354	LNNNNNNNFFNFNFNNNNF	NNNN2NNNNNNNNN	J,T	263	756	01.04.02	3230	000000	34047
152.367-010	PROMPTER (amuse. & rec.)	4347	32353244445	LNNNNNNNFFNFFNFNNNNF	NNNN3NNNNNNNNN	J	282	754	01.04.02	3230	000000	34047
153.117-010	HEAD COACH (amuse. & rec.)	5449	22334444455	LNNNNNNFNNNNFFNNNNNN	FNNN3NNNNNNNNN	V,D,P,I,J	295	913	12.01.01	3400	000000	34058
153.117-014	MANAGER, ATHLETE (amuse. & rec.)	5557	22244355555	LNNNNNNFONNCNNNNNNN	ONNN2NNNNNNNNN	V,D,P,I,J	292	913	11.12.03	3400	000000	34058
153.117-018	SCOUT, PROFESSIONAL SPORTS (amuse. & rec.)	4348	22433354555	SNNNNNNOOONFFNFFFNF	FNNN3NNNNNNNNN	V,P,J,D,I	211	913	12.01.01	3400	000000	34058

DOT #	DOT Title & Industry	Trng	Aptitude	Physical	Environment	Tempra	WkF	MPSMS	GOE	SOC	CIP	OES
153.117-022	STEWARD, RACETRACK (amuse. & rec.)	5458	22444445555	LNNNNNNNNNNNFFNONNNNN	FNNN3NNNNNNNNNNN	V,D,P,J	295	913	12.01.02	3400	000000	34058
153.137-010	MANAGER, POOL (amuse. & rec.)	3334	33333434334	HNNNNNNFFNFFNFFONFN	ONNO3NNNNNNNNNNN	D,V,P	293	919	11.11.02	1352	310101	27311
153.167-010	PADDOCK JUDGE (amuse. & rec.)	4237	33444444444	LNNNNNOONNFFNFNNNON	FNNN3NNNNNNNNNNN	J,T	211	913	12.01.02	3400	000000	34058
153.167-014	PIT STEWARD (amuse. & rec.)	4346	22344434444	LNNNNNNNFFONFNFNFOQOOO	CNNN4FNNNNNNNNNN	D,J,P	295	913	12.01.02	3400	000000	34058
153.167-018	RACING SECRETARY AND HANDICAPPER (amuse. & rec.)	4448	22355354555	SNNNNNNOOONFFNFNNNNNN	NNNN3NNNNNNNNNNN	V,D,J	211	913	12.01.02	3400	000000	34058
153.167-022	ATHLETIC TRAINER (amuse. & rec.; education)	5448	32433432345	MNNFFNFFOOFFNNNNNNN	FNNN3NNNNNNNNNNN	D,P,S,J	294	913	10.02.02	3400	010505	34058
153.224-010	COACH, PROFESSIONAL ATHLETES (amuse. & rec.)	5348	32433434325	HNNOOONFFNCNCCONNF	FNNN3NNNNNNNNNNN	D,P,J	296	913	12.01.01	3400	000000	34058
153.227-010	INSTRUCTOR, PHYSICAL (amuse. & rec.; education)	3336	33444444425	LNNFNFNFFNFFNNNNNNN	NNNN3NNNNNNNNNNN	D,P	296	919	10.02.02	2390	000000	31321
153.227-014	INSTRUCTOR, SPORTS (amuse. & rec.; education)	4347	22333423224	MNOONONFFNFFNOFFOOO	ONNN3NNNNNNNNNNN	D,P,J	296	913	12.01.01	2390	000000	31321
153.243-010	AUTOMOBILE RACER (amuse. & rec.)	4336	33422422214	MNNNNNNCCCFNFFFFF	ONFN5CNFNNNNNF	S,J,T	297	913	12.01.03	3400	000000	34058
153.243-014	MOTORCYCLE RACER (amuse. & rec.)	3235	33422422214	HNFNNNNFFFOOFNOFFNOF	CNNN4NNNNNNNNNF	S,J	297	913	12.01.03	3400	000000	34058
153.244-010	JOCKEY (amuse. & rec.)	4236	33422533335	MOCNNCNCCNNFFNCCNNNC	FNNN3NNNNNNNNNNC	V,S,J	297	913	12.01.03	3400	000000	34058
153.244-014	SULKY DRIVER (amuse. & rec.)	4236	34434533335	MONNNNNFFNNFFNFFFNF	FNNN3NNNNNNNNNNF	V,S,J	297	913	12.01.03	3400	000000	34058
153.267-010	HORSE-RACE STARTER (amuse. & rec.)	3334	33435544555	LNNNNNNNNNFFNFFFNF	FNNN3NNNNNNNNNNN	V,P,J	282	913	12.01.02	3400	000000	34058
153.267-014	PATROL JUDGE (amuse. & rec.)	4348	32433344443	LFFNNNNOOONFFNFFNF	NNNN3NNNNNNNNNNN	J	211	913	12.01.02	3400	000000	34058
153.267-018	UMPIRE (amuse. & rec.)	4348	22323445445	LNNNNNNNFFNNNFNCCCCC	FNNN2NNNNNNNNNNN	D,P,J	295	913	12.01.02	3400	000000	34058
153.287-010	HOOF AND SHOE INSPECTOR (amuse. & rec.)	4136	34533444455	LNNONNNFFNNNNFNNFNN	ONNN2NNNNNNNNNNN	J,T	211	913	03.03.02	3400	010507	34058
153.341-010	PROFESSIONAL ATHLETE (amuse. & rec.)	4236	33422422214	MFFFFFFFOOONFFFFF	FNNN3NNNNNNNNNNF	P,S,J,T	297	913	12.01.03	3400	000000	34058
153.367-010	CLOCKER (amuse. & rec.)	3222	34333344554	LNNNNNNNFFONNNFFNOFF	FNNN3NNNNNNNNNNN	J,T	211	913	12.01.02	3400	000000	34058
153.367-014	HORSE-RACE TIMER (amuse. & rec.)	3333	44334344454	LNNNNNNNFFNOONFFNOOF	NNNN3NNNNNNNNNNN	J,T	211	913	12.01.02	3400	000000	34058
153.384-010	MARSHAL (amuse. & rec.)	3114	34433534435	HONNNNNFFONNNNOONNNN	CNNN3NNNNNNNNNNF	J,R,S	293	913	12.01.02	3400	000000	34056
153.387-010	IDENTIFIER, HORSE (amuse. & rec.)	3333	34433344453	LNNNNNNNCCCCNNNNNNN	NNNN3NNNNNNNNNNN	J,T	211	913	12.01.02	3400	010505	34056
153.387-014	SCORER (amuse. & rec.)	3334	33343344454	SNNNNNNFFNOONFCCNFC	FNNN4NNNNNNNNNNN	T	231	913	12.01.02	3400	000000	34056
153.467-010	CLERK-OF-SCALES (amuse. & rec.)	3333	34444444455	LNNNNNNNFFNNNNFNNFNN	FNNN3NNNNNNNNNNN	J	212	913	12.01.02	3400	000000	34056
153.667-010	STARTER (amuse. & rec.)	3224	34444444244	LNNNNNNNFFNOONOCCNFC	CNNN4NNNNNNNNNNN	R,J	282	913	12.01.02	3400	000000	34056
153.674-010	EXERCISER, HORSE (amuse. & rec.)	2113	44444534344	MNCNNCNCNNNNNNFFFNF	FNNN3NNNNNNNNNNN	E,J	291	327	03.03.01	3400	010507	34058
153.674-014	LEAD PONY RIDER (amuse. & rec.)	2112	44545533335	MNFNNNNFFNNNNNNFNNNF	FNNN3NNNNNNNNNNN	R	291	327	12.01.02	3400	010505	34058
159.041-010	MAGICIAN (amuse. & rec.)	4346	33433422254	LNNOONCCCNFFNFFFFFF	NNNN3NNNNNNNNNNN	D,E,T,J	297	919	01.03.02	3280	000000	34056
159.041-014	PUPPETEER (amuse. & rec.)	4348	22332422232	LOFFFFOFFOFFNONFOFF	NNNN3NNNNNNNNNNN	S,T,P,J	261	919	01.03.02	3280	000000	34056
159.042-010	LASERIST (amuse. & rec.)	5346	22322322251	LNNOONCCCNOONCCCCCC	NNNN3NNNONNNNNNN	E,J,P,T	297	919	05.03.05	3280	000000	34056
159.044-010	VENTRILOQUIST (amuse. & rec.)	4247	22434533355	LNNNNNNCCCCCNNNNNNN	NNNN3NNNNNNNNNNN	E,P	297	919	01.03.02	3280	000000	34056
159.047-010	CLOWN (amuse. & rec.)	4236	34345523224	LFFNNNNFFNFNFNNNNF	ONNN3NNNNNNNNNNN	P,I,J,T	297	919	01.03.02	3280	000000	34056
159.047-014	COMEDIAN (amuse. & rec.)	5245	32434434455	LNNNNNNNCCNNNNNNN	NNNN3NNNNNNNNNNN	V,P,E	297	919	01.03.03	3280	000000	34056
159.047-018	IMPERSONATOR (amuse. & rec.)	4246	22434444445	LNNNNNNNCCNNNNNNN	NNNN3NNNNNNNNNNN	E,P	297	969	01.03.02	3280	000000	34056
159.047-022	MIME (amuse. & rec.)	5237	23422534424	LNNNNNNCCCNNNNNNNN	NNNN2NNNNNNNNNNN	D,E,J,P	297	754	01.03.02	3280	000000	34056
159.067-010	DIRECTOR, MOTION PICTURE (motion picture)	5458	12333344455	SNNNNNOONNFFNFONNFN	NNNN2NNNNNNNNNNN	V,D,P,J	295	911	01.03.01	3240	000000	34056
159.067-014	DIRECTOR, TELEVISION (radio-tv broad.)	5458	12333344454	LNNNNNNFFONCCNNFOOOO	ONNN3NNNNNNNNNNN	D,V,P,J	295	864	01.03.01	3240	100199	34056
159.117-010	PRODUCER (radio-tv broad.)	6468	11343444454	LNNNNNNOOOFFNNNNFNNNN	NNNN3NNNNNNNNNNN	D,V,E,P,J	295	863	01.03.01	2033	200202	27311
159.124-010	COUNSELOR, CAMP (amuse. & rec.)	4245	22434433334	MOOOOOOOOOFFNOOOOOO	FNNN3NNNNNNNNNNN	V,D,P	282	919	09.01.01	3330	000000	34017
159.147-010	ANNOUNCER (radio-tv broad.)	5346	22344344455	LNNNNNNOOONFFNNNNNN	NNNN3NNNNNNNNNNN	V,T,P,J	282	863	01.03.03	3330	000000	34017
159.147-014	DISC JOCKEY (radio-tv broad.)	5355	32434343455	LNNNNNNOFONOCNNNNNN	NNNN3NNNNNNNNNNN	V,P	282	863	01.03.03	3330	000000	34017
159.147-018	SHOW HOST/HOSTESS (radio-tv broad.)	5356	22344344455	LNNNNNNQOONCCNOONNNO	ONNN3NNNNNNNNNNN	V,P	282	863	01.03.03	3330	000000	34056
159.167-010	ARTIST AND REPERTOIRE MANAGER (amuse. & rec.)	4347	22444444455	LNNNNNNNNCCNNNNNNN	NNNN2NNNNNNNNNNN	D,E,I,J,P	295	869	01.04.01	3280	000000	34056
159.167-014	DIRECTOR, RADIO (radio-tv broad.)	4346	22334343334	SNNNNNNCCCNFFNCNNCCN	NNNN3NNNNNNNNNNN	D,T,P,J	295	863	01.03.01	3240	000000	34056
159.167-018	MANAGER, STAGE (amuse. & rec.; radio-tv broad.)	4347	22334343344	LNNNNNNFFONCCNFNOOOO	NNNN3NNNNNNNNNNN	D,V,P,J	295	910	01.03.01	3240	000000	34056
159.167-022	EXECUTIVE PRODUCER, PROMOS (radio-tv broad.)	5357	22443344454	SNNNNNNOOONFFNNOOOOO	NNNN3NNNNNNNNNNN	D,P,J	261	860	11.09.01	1250	090201	13011
159.207-010	ASTROLOGER (amuse. & rec.)	4444	33344344555	SNNNNNNFFNNNNFNNNNN	NNNN3NNNNNNNNNNN	J	282	733	10.01.02	3280	000000	34056
159.224-010	ANIMAL TRAINER (amuse. & rec.)	4336	22434434334	LNNOOONFFNONFFNOFONOF	ONNN3NNNNNNNNNNO	D,S,J	296	919	03.03.01	3280	000000	34056
159.227-010	INSTRUCTOR, BRIDGE (education)	4448	22244443353	SNNNNNNCCCNFFNCNNCCN	NNNN2NNNNNNNNNNN	V,D,P,J	296	919	09.01.01	2390	000000	31317
159.247-010	ACROBAT (amuse. & rec.)	3225	33323532215	VCCCCNNNNNNNNFFNNNNN	NNNN3NNNNNNNNNNN	V,P,E	297	919	12.02.01	3280	000000	34056
159.247-014	AERIALIST (amuse. & rec.)	3326	33323532215	VFCFNFNFFNNNNNFFNNN	NNNN3NNNNNNNNNNN	V,P,S,E	297	919	12.02.01	3280	000000	34056

DOT #	DOT Title & Industry	Trng	Aptitude	Physical	Environment	Tempra	WkF	MPSMS	GOE	SOC	CIP	OES
159.267-010	DIRECTOR, CASTING (motion picture; radio-tv broad.)	5347	22344255553	LNNNNNNFFNNFFNFNNNNN	NNNNN2NNNNNNNNNNN	V,P,J	297	864	01.03.01	3240	000000	34056
159.341-010	JUGGLER (amuse. & rec.)	3226	33423422215	LNNNNNNCCCCNNNCCCCCC	NNNNN2NNNNNNNNNNN	J,T	297	919	12.02.01	3280	000000	34056
159.341-014	STUNT PERFORMER (amuse. & rec.; motion picture; radio-tv broad.)	3336	33424423115	MOOOOOOOOOOOOFOOOOO	FNNN3NNNNNNNNNNNF	P,T,J,S	297	911	12.02.01	3280	000000	34056
159.344-010	EQUESTRIAN (amuse. & rec.)	3316	33334533225	MFFNNNNCCCNNFNNFNNNF	NNNN3NNNNNNNNNNN	V,P,J,E	297	919	12.02.01	3280	010505	34056
159.344-014	RODEO PERFORMER (amuse. & rec.)	3235	33423523225	HFFFFFFFFFNNNFFFFFF	FNNN3NNNNNNNNNNN	V,J,S	297	913	12.02.01	3280	010507	34056
159.344-018	SHOW-HORSE DRIVER (amuse. & rec.)	3225	33434433335	LOFNNNNFFFFNNNNNNNN	FNNN3NNNNNNNNNNN	P,I	297	327	12.02.01	3280	010505	34056
159.347-010	ANNOUNCER (amuse. & rec)	4246	22434344454	SNNNNNNFFNNCCNFNNNNN	NNNN2NNNNNNNNNNN	P,J	297	919	01.07.02	3330	000000	34021
159.347-014	AQUATIC PERFORMER (amuse. & rec.)	3335	33422423324	MOONNNNNFFNNNNNNNNNN	NNNN3NNNNNNNNNNN	V,P,J	297	919	12.02.01	3280	000000	34056
159.347-018	THRILL PERFORMER (amuse. & rec.)	3225	34423532325	MFFFFFFFFNNNFFFFNF	FNNN3NNNNNNNNNNNF	P,T,J,S	297	919	12.02.01	3280	000000	34056
159.347-022	WIRE WALKER (amuse. & rec.)	3216	33323534215	MFCONONOONNNNCNFNNF	NNNN3NNNNNNNNNNO	V,P,S,E	297	919	12.02.01	3280	000000	34056
159.367-010	RING CONDUCTOR (amuse. & rec.)	4246	32333544455	LNNNNNNNNFFNFNNNNNN	NNNN3NNNNNNNNNNN	P,I,J,T	297	919	01.07.02	3280	000000	34056
159.647-010	AMUSEMENT PARK ENTERTAINER (amuse. & rec.)	2222	33444544455	LNNNNNNFFONFFNNNNNNN	FNNN3NNNNNNNNNNN	P,E	297	919	01.07.03	3280	000000	34056
159.647-014	EXTRA (amuse. & rec.; motion picture; radio-tv broad.)	2222	33444544455	LNNNNNNNNFFNNNNNNN	ONNN3NNNNNNNNNNN	R	297	911	01.08.01	3240	000000	34056
159.647-018	PSYCHIC READER (amuse. & rec.)	3233	33444544455	SNNNNNNOOOOCNNNNNNN	NNNN3NNNNNNNNNNN	E,J	297	919	01.07.01	3280	000000	34056
159.647-022	SHOW GIRL (amuse. & rec.)	2112	44544444435	LNNNNNNFFONNNNNNNN	NNNN3NNNNNNNNNNN	P,R	297	919	01.08.01	3280	000000	34056
160.162-010	ACCOUNTANT, TAX (profess. & kin.)	5558	22244233455	SNNNNNNOOFFNCNNONN	NNNN3NNNNNNNNNNN	T,P,J	232	892	11.06.01	1412	520302	21114
160.162-018	ACCOUNTANT (profess. & kin.)	5558	22244244455	SNNNNNNOOFFNCNNFNN	NNNN3NNNNNNNNNNN	D,T,P,J	232	892	11.06.01	1412	520302	21114
160.162-022	ACCOUNTANT, BUDGET (profess. & kin.)	5558	22244244455	SNNNNNNOOFNOONFNNONN	NNNN3NNNNNNNNNNN	T,P,J	232	892	11.06.01	1412	520302	21114
160.162-026	ACCOUNTANT, COST (profess. & kin.)	5558	22244243455	SNNNNNNOOFNOONCNNONN	NNNN3NNNNNNNNNNN	T,P,J	232	892	11.06.01	1412	520302	21114
160.162-030	AUDITOR, DATA PROCESSING (profess. & kin.)	5457	22244243455	SNNNNNNOOFFNCNNFNN	NNNN3NNNNNNNNNNN	T,P,J	233	892	11.06.01	1412	000000	21114
160.167-022	ACCOUNTANT, PROPERTY (profess. & kin.)	5558	22244244455	SNNNNNNFFONNNNFNNNN	NNNN2NNNNNNNNNNN	V,D,J	232	892	11.06.01	1412	520302	21114
160.167-026	ACCOUNTANT, SYSTEMS (profess. & kin.)	5558	22244244455	SNNNNNNOONNOONONNNNN	NNNN3NNNNNNNNNNN	D,J,P	232	892	11.06.01	1412	520302	21114
160.167-030	AUDITOR, COUNTY OR CITY (government ser.)	5556	22232344455	SNNNNNNOONNOONCNNNNN	NNNN3NNNNNNNNNNN	D,J,P	232	892	11.06.01	1412	000000	21114
160.167-034	AUDITOR, INTERNAL (profess. & kin.)	5557	22244244455	LNNOONOOFNCCNCNNFNN	NNNN3NNNNNNNNNNN	T,P,J	232	892	11.06.01	1412	520302	21114
160.167-038	AUDITOR, TAX (profess. & kin.)	5558	22144244455	LNNNNNNFFNFNFNNNNN	NNNN3NNNNNNNNNNN	D,J,P	271	953	11.06.01	1412	000000	21114
160.167-042	BURSAR (education)	5557	22244244455	SNNNNNNOOONFFNFNNNNN	NNNN2NNNNNNNNNNN	D,J,T	232	892	11.06.01	1412	520302	21114
160.167-046	CHIEF BANK EXAMINER (government ser.)	5558	22244244455	SNNNNNNOOOONFFNFNNONN	NNNN3NNNNNNNNNNN	D,P,J	295	894	11.10.01	1473	000000	21911
160.167-050	REVENUE AGENT (government ser.)	5447	22243344455	LNNNNNNFFNFNFNNNNN	NNNN3NNNNNNNNNNN	P,I,J	232	953	11.06.01	1473	520302	21914
160.167-054	AUDITOR (profess. & kin.)	5558	22144244455	SNNNNNNFFNFNFNNNNN	NNNN2NNNNNNNNNNN	D,J,T,V	295	892	11.06.01	1412	520302	21114
160.167-058	CONTROLLER (profess. & kin.)	5548	12144344455	SNNNNNNNFFONFFNNONN	NNNN2NNNNNNNNNNN	D,P,J	232	890	11.06.02	1220	521401	13002
160.207-010	CREDIT COUNSELOR (profess. & kin.)	5557	22144255455	SNNNNNNFFNFNFNNNNN	NNNN3NNNNNNNNNNN	D,I,J,P	232	890	07.01.01	1419	080401	21199
160.267-010	DIRECTOR, UTILITY ACCOUNTS (government ser.)	5558	22143344455	SNNNNNNFFONNFNNFNN	NNNN2NNNNNNNNNNN	J	232	894	11.06.03	1412	000000	21114
160.267-014	CREDIT ANALYST (financial)	5458	22244244555	SNNNNNNOOONCNNNNNNN	NNNN3NNNNNNNNNNN	J,T	271	894	11.06.03	1419	080401	21105
160.267-022	INVESTMENT ANALYST (financial; insurance)	5558	22244244455	SNNNNNNNOONCNNNNNNN	NNNN2NNNNNNNNNNN	T,J	271	712	11.06.03	1419	000000	25315
161.117-010	BUDGET OFFICER (profess. & kin.)	5558	22143244455	SNNNNNNFFNOONONNNNNN	NNNN3NNNNNNNNNNN	D,P,J	295	892	11.06.05	1419	000000	21117
161.117-014	DIRECTOR, RECORDS MANAGEMENT (profess. & kin.)	5458	22233255553	SNNNNNNFFNFNFNNNNN	NNNN3NNNNNNNNNNN	D,P,J	295	891	11.01.01	1420	521401	21905
161.117-018	TREASURER (profess. & kin.)	5558	22244244455	SNNNNNNFFONFFNNNNON	NNNN3NNNNNNNNNNN	D,J	211	891	11.01.01	1220	000000	13002
161.167-010	MANAGEMENT ANALYST (profess. & kin.)	5557	22233244455	SNNNNNNOOONFFNNONONN	NNNN3NNNNNNNNNNN	P,V,J	232	890	05.01.06	1420	000000	21905
161.167-014	MANAGER, FORMS ANALYSIS (profess. & kin.)	5448	22333255553	SNNNNNNNFFONFFNNNNON	NNNN3NNNNNNNNNNN	D,P,J	212	891	11.06.02	1420	000000	21905
161.167-018	MANAGER, RECORDS ANALYSIS (profess. & kin.)	5448	22322255553	SNNNNNNNFFONFFNNNON	NNNN3NNNNNNNNNNN	D,P,J	295	891	11.06.02	1420	521401	21905
161.167-022	MANAGER, REPORTS ANALYSIS (profess. & kin.)	5448	22333255553	SNNNNNNNFFONFFNNNON	NNNN3NNNNNNNNNNN	D,P,J	295	891	11.06.02	1420	521401	21905
161.267-010	CLERICAL-METHODS ANALYST (profess. & kin.)	5547	22333255553	SNNNNNNFFNFFNFOOFNN	NNNN3NNNNNNNNNNN	V,P,J,T	244	891	05.01.06	1420	000000	21905
161.267-018	FORMS ANALYST (profess. & kin.)	4347	22333255553	SNNNNNNFFNFFNFNNNON	NNNN3NNNNNNNNNNN	V,D,J	211	891	11.01.01	1420	000000	21905
161.267-022	RECORDS-MANAGEMENT ANALYST (profess. & kin.)	4347	22333255553	SNNNNNNFFNFFNFNNNON	NNNN3NNNNNNNNNNN	D,J	212	891	11.06.02	1420	000000	21905
161.267-026	REPORTS ANALYST (profess. & kin.)	4347	22333255553	SNNNNNNFFNFFNFNNNON	NNNN3NNNNNNNNNNN	D,P,J	212	891	11.06.02	1420	000000	21905
161.267-030	BUDGET ANALYST (government ser.)	5347	22244244455	SNNNNNNFFONFFNFNNNNN	NNNN3NNNNNNNNNNN	D,J,T	232	892	11.06.05	1419	000000	21117
162.117-010	CHRISTMAS-TREE CONTRACTOR (any industry)	5357	22343344454	LNNNNNNFFNFNFNNNNN	FNNN4NNNNNNNNNNN	P,I,J	292	312	08.01.03	1443	030401	21305
162.117-014	CONTRACT ADMINISTRATOR (any industry)	5358	22344344455	SNNNNNNNOOONFFNNNNNN	NNNN3NNNNNNNNNNN	D,I,P,J	295	894	11.12.04	1370	080704	13014
162.117-018	CONTRACT SPECIALIST (profess. & kin.)	5358	22344344455	LNNNNNNOOOONFFNNONNN	NNNN3NNNNNNNNNNN	D,I,V,P,J	295	939	11.12.04	1449	080704	21308
162.117-022	FIELD CONTRACTOR (any industry)	5357	22344344454	LNNNNNNOOOONFNFNONOOO	FNNN4NNNNNNNNNNN	V,P,I,J	292	300	03.01.01	1449	010501	21305
162.117-026	FIELD-CONTACT TECHNICIAN (dairy products)	5357	22344444454	LNNNNNNFFNFNFNFNFON	ONNN4NNNNNNNNNNN	V,P,I,J	282	383	08.01.03	1449	080704	21305

DOT #	DOT Title & Industry	Trng	Aptitude	Physical	Environment	Tempra	WKF	MPSMS	GOE	SOC	CIP	OES
162.117-030	RESEARCH-CONTRACTS SUPERVISOR (government ser.)	6558	22344344455	SNNNNNNNNNNFFNONNNNN	NNNN3NNNNNNNNNNN	D,J	251	959	11.12.04	1139	000000	13017
162.157-010	BROKER-AND-MARKET OPERATOR, GRAIN (financial; wholesale tr.)	5447	22233344455	SNNNNNNOOFNFNFNONNN	NNNN2NNNNNNNNNNN	I,J,P	292	882	11.06.04	1443	010501	21305
162.157-018	BUYER (profess. & kin.)	4346	22244344455	LNNNNNNNFFOFFNFNNNNN	NNNN3NNNNNNNNNNN	D,I,V,P,J	292	880	08.01.03	1442	080799	21302
162.157-022	BUYER, ASSISTANT (retail trade)	4336	22333344453	LNNNNNNFFNFFNFNONNONN	NNNN3NNNNNNNNNNN	P,J	292	881	08.01.03	1442	080903	21302
162.157-026	COMMISSION AGENT, LIVESTOCK (wholesale tr.)	4346	22344444454	SNNNNNNNOOONFNFNFNNN	NNNN3NNNNNNNNNNN	P,I,J	292	894	08.01.03	4246	080799	49008
162.157-030	OUTSIDE PROPERTY AGENT (motion picture)	4447	22244344453	SNNNNNNFONFFNFOOOOO	NNNN3NNNNNNNNNNN	P,I,J	292	911	08.01.03	4246	080704	21308
162.157-034	PROCUREMENT ENGINEER (aircraft mfg.)	5557	22233344455	SNNNNNNNOOONFNFNNNNN	NNNN2NNNNNNNNNNN	J,P,T,V	244	702	05.03.03	1449	080704	21308
162.157-038	PURCHASING AGENT (profess. & kin.)	4347	22343344455	LNNNNNNNOOONFFNFNNOON	NNNN2NNNNNNNNNNN	D,I,P,J	292	880	11.05.04	1449	200405	21308
162.167-010	BUYER, GRAIN (grain-feed mills; wholesale tr.)	5348	22233344454	LNNNNNNNFFOFFNFNFNON	NNNN4NONNNNNNNNN	D,J	292	301	08.01.03	1443	010501	41002
162.167-014	BUYER, TOBACCO, HEAD (wholesale tr.)	4347	23344444453	LNNNNNNNNFFOFFNFNNNN	NNNN4NNNNNNNNNNN	D,P,J	292	302	08.01.03	1443	080799	21305
162.167-018	CLEAN-RICE BROKER (grain-feed mills)	5557	22334344455	SNNNNNNNFFNFFNFNNFNN	NNNN3NNNNNNNNNNN	D,J	292	894	11.05.04	1443	010501	21305
162.167-022	MANAGER, PROCUREMENT SERVICES (profess. & kin.)	4447	22244244455	SNNNNNNNFONFFNFNNFNN	NNNN3NNNNNNNNNNN	D,J	292	898	11.05.02	1240	521401	13008
162.167-026	PRIZE COORDINATOR (radio-tv broad.)	4345	33343344454	LNNNNNNNFONFFNFNNNON	NNNN3NNNNNNNNNNN	J,T	221	919	07.01.02	4799	090201	59999
162.167-030	PURCHASE-PRICE ANALYST (profess. & kin.)	5547	22244244455	SNNNNNNNFFNFFNFNNNNN	NNNN3NNNNNNNNNNN	D,J,P	211	899	11.06.03	1449	080704	21308
162.167-034	FLOOR BROKER (financial)	5346	22355243455	LONNNNNNOOONFFNFFNOOO	NNNN3NNNNNNNNNNNO	I,P,J	292	894	11.06.04	4124	000000	43014
162.167-038	SECURITIES TRADER (financial)	5457	22255243455	SNNNNNNNOOFNFFNFNNNNN	NNNN2NNNNNNNNNNN	T,P,J	292	894	11.06.03	4124	080401	43014
162.267-010	TITLE CLERK (petrol. & gas; petrol. refin.; pipe lines)	5456	33344244444	SNNNNNNNFFNFFNFNNFON	NNNN3NNNNNNNNNNN	J,P,V	271	891	07.01.05	3960	220103	28399
163.117-010	MANAGER, CONTRACTS (petrol. & gas; petrol. refin.; pipe lines)	5557	21244344455	SNNNNNNNOOOFFNONNNNN	NNNN3NNNNNNNNNNN	D,J,P,V	292	501	11.05.02	1449	080799	21308
163.117-014	MANAGER, EXPORT (any industry)	5558	22244344455	LNNNNNNNFFNFFNFNNNNN	NNNN3NNNNNNNNNNN	D,J,P,I,V	292	880	11.05.04	1250	521403	13011
163.117-018	MANAGER, PROMOTION (hotel & rest.)	5348	22344344455	LNNNNNNNOOONFNFNNNNN	NNNN3NNNNNNNNNNN	D,J,P,V	295	902	11.09.01	1250	080902	13011
163.117-022	DIRECTOR, MEDIA MARKETING (radio-tv broad.)	5458	22333244454	SNNNNNNNFFNFFNFONNNON	NNNN3NNNNNNNNNNN	D,I,J,P,V	292	864	11.05.04	1250	521401	13011
163.117-026	DIRECTOR, UNDERWRITER SOLICITATION (radio-tv broad.)	5348	22344344455	SNNNNNNNFFONFFNFNNNNN	NNNN3NNNNNNNNNNN	D,I,V,P,J	292	896	11.05.04	1250	521401	13011
163.167-010	MANAGER, ADVERTISING (print. & pub.)	5358	22233344455	SNNNNNNNFFNFFNFNNNNN	NNNN3NNNNNNNNNNN	D,P,J	292	896	11.09.01	1250	090201	13011
163.167-014	MANAGER, CIRCULATION (print. & pub.)	5348	22233344455	SNNNNNNNOOOONFFNFNNNN	NNNN3NNNNNNNNNNN	D,J,P,V	292	896	11.09.01	1250	090201	13011
163.167-018	MANAGER, SALES (any industry)	5358	22233344455	SNNNNNNNOFFNFNFNNNNN	NNNN3NNNNNNNNNNN	D,J,P,V	292	757	11.05.04	1390	520204	19999
163.167-022	MANAGER, UTILITY SALES AND SERVICE (utilities)	5448	22244344455	SNNNNNNOOOONFFNFNNNN	NNNN3NNNNNNNNNNN	V,D,P,I,J	292	860	11.05.04	1250	080799	13011
163.167-026	PROPERTY-DISPOSAL OFFICER (any industry)	5557	22334244454	LNNNNNNNFFNFFNFOOOOO	NNNN3NNNNNNNNNNN	D,P,J	292	871	11.05.04	1250	521401	13014
163.267-010	FIELD REPRESENTATIVE (business ser.; wholesale tr.)	5436	22334344455	LNNNNNNNOOONFFNFNNNNN	NNNN3NNNNNNNNNNN	D,J	292	959	11.05.04	1370	000000	13011
164.117-010	MANAGER, ADVERTISING (any industry)	6558	22344444455	SNNNNNNFFNFFNFNFONNON	NNNN3NNNNNNNNNNN	D,I,J,P	292	899	11.05.04	1250	080299	13011
164.117-014	MANAGER, ADVERTISING AGENCY (business ser.)	5348	22333244453	LNNNNNNNFFOFFNFNNNNN	NNNN3NNNNNNNNNNN	V,D,P,J	295	880	11.09.01	1250	090201	13011
164.117-018	MEDIA DIRECTOR (profess. & kin.)	5458	22233244455	SNNNNNNNFFNFFNFNNNNN	NNNN3NNNNNNNNNNN	D,P,J	295	896	11.09.01	1250	090201	13011
164.167-010	ACCOUNT EXECUTIVE (business ser.)	5348	22333344453	SNNNNNNNOOOONFFNFNNNN	NNNN3NNNNNNNNNNN	D,P,J	295	896	11.09.01	1250	080706	13011
165.017-010	LOBBYIST (profess. & kin.)	5357	33443234453	SNNNNNNNFFNFFNFNNNNN	NNNN3NNNNNNNNNNN	D,P,I,J,E	261	896	11.09.03	3320	000000	34008
165.117-010	DIRECTOR, FUNDRAISING (nonprofit org.)	5448	11244344455	SNNNNNNFFNFFNFNFNNNN	NNNN3NNNNNNNNNNN	D,P,I,J	282	896	11.09.02	1270	000000	19999
165.117-014	DIRECTOR, FUNDS DEVELOPMENT (profess. & kin.)	5457	22255244455	SNNNNNNNOFONFFNFNNNN	NNNN3NNNNNNNNNNN	D,I,V,P,J	295	893	11.09.02	1390	000000	19999
165.157-010	SONG PLUGGER (recording)	4245	32344444455	SNNNNNNNFONCCNNNNNNN	NNNN2NNNNNNNNNNN	D,I,P,J	292	860	08.02.08	4152	000000	43017
165.167-010	SALES-SERVICE PROMOTER (any industry)	5357	22233344444	LNNNNNNNOOONFNFNONNON	NNNN3NNNNNNNNNNN	D,P,I,J,E	295	896	11.09.03	3320	080299	34008
165.167-014	PUBLIC-RELATIONS REPRESENTATIVE (profess. & kin.)	5457	11333344444	SNNNNNNNFFNFFNFNNNON	NNNN3NNNNNNNNNNN	D,I,V,P,J	261	896	11.09.01	3320	080299	34008
166.067-010	OCCUPATIONAL ANALYST (profess. & kin.)	5457	11233344444	LNNNNNNFFONFFNFNNNNN	NNNN3NNNNNNNNNNN	D,P,J	251	919	11.03.04	1430	521001	21511
166.117-010	DIRECTOR, INDUSTRIAL RELATIONS (profess. & kin.)	6458	22344344455	LNNNNNNNOOOONFFNFNNNN	NNNN3NNNNNNNNNNN	D,P,J	295	893	11.05.02	1230	000000	13005
166.117-014	MANAGER, EMPLOYEE WELFARE (profess. & kin.)	5457	22344444455	SNNNNNNNOOOONFNFNNNN	NNNN3NNNNNNNNNNN	D,P	295	712	11.05.02	1430	521001	21511
166.117-018	MANAGER, PERSONNEL (profess. & kin.)	5558	11233344455	SNNNNNNNNFFONFFNFNNN	NNNN3NNNNNNNNNNN	V,D,P,J	295	893	11.05.02	1230	521001	13005
166.167-010	CONTESTANT COORDINATOR (radio-tv broad.)	4345	33443234453	LNNNNNNNOOONFNFNNNON	NNNN3NNNNNNNNNNN	E,J	212	919	07.01.01	1430	000000	21511
166.167-014	DIRECTOR OF PLACEMENT (education)	6558	11244344455	SNNNNNNNFFNNFNNON	NNNN3NNNNNNNNNNN	V,D,P,I,J	295	943	10.01.02	1430	521001	21511
166.167-018	MANAGER, BENEFITS (profess. & kin.)	4447	22255244455	SNNNNNNNOFONFFNFNNNN	NNNN2NNNNNNNNNNN	D,T,P,J	295	893	11.05.02	1230	521001	13005
166.167-022	MANAGER, COMPENSATION (profess. & kin.)	5558	22255355555	SNNNNNNOOOONFFNFNNNN	NNNN3NNNNNNNNNNN	D,P,J	271	712	11.05.02	1430	521001	21511
166.167-026	MANAGER, EDUCATION AND TRAINING (education)	5457	22233345454	LNNNNNNFFNNCCNFONFON	NNNN3NNNNNNNNNNN	D,P,I,J	295	931	11.07.03	1230	521001	13005
166.167-030	MANAGER, EMPLOYMENT (profess. & kin.)	5458	22355355555	SNNNNNNNFFNFFNFNNNNN	NNNN3NNNNNNNNNNN	D,P,J	271	943	11.05.02	1230	521001	13005
166.167-034	MANAGER, LABOR RELATIONS (profess. & kin.)	5458	22344344455	LNNNNNNNOOOONFFNFNNNN	NNNN2NNNNNNNNNNN	D,I,P,J	271	893	11.05.02	1430	521001	21511
166.167-038	PORT PURSER (water trans.)	5448	22244344455	SNNNNNNNFFONFFNFNNNNN	NNNN3NNNNNNNNNNN	V,D,J	295	890	11.11.03	1430	521001	21511
166.167-042	SENIOR ENLISTED ADVISOR (military ser.)	3335	32344233355	LNNNNNNFFNFFNFNFNNNN	ONNN3NNNNNNNNNNN	P,J,V	295	733	11.10.03	1430	000000	21511

DOT #	DOT Title & Industry	Trng	Aptitude	Physical	Environment	Tempra	WkF	MPSMS	GOE	SOC	CIP	OES
166.167-046	SPECIAL AGENT (insurance)	5358	22353244455	SNNNNNNFFNFFNFNNNN	NNNN3NNNNNNNNNN	V,P,I,T,D	295	895	11.05.02	1430	081001	21505
166.167-050	PROGRAM SPECIALIST, EMPLOYEE-HEALTH MAINTENANCE (profess. & kin.)	5356	21344344455	SNNNNNNFFNFFNFNNNN	NNNN3NNNNNNNNNN	D,I,J,P	282	941	11.05.02	1230	511501	13005
166.167-054	TECHNICAL TRAINING COORDINATOR (education)	5358	22343344455	LNNNNNNFFFNCCNCNNNNN	NNNN3NNNNNNNNNN	D,P,J	295	931	11.07.03	1430	000000	21511
166.221-010	INSTRUCTOR, TECHNICAL TRAINING (education)	5458	22222333254	LONNNNNNFFNCCNFNONFO	NNNN3NNOONNNNNN	D,V,T,P,J	296	931	11.02.02	2390	000000	31314
166.227-010	TRAINING REPRESENTATIVE (education)	5457	22233344454	LNNOOONFFONCCNFONOON	NNNN3NNNNNNNNNN	D,P,J,T	296	931	11.02.02	2390	521001	31314
166.257-010	EMPLOYER RELATIONS REPRESENTATIVE (profess. & kin.)	5246	22444344455	LNNNNNNFFNNFFNNNNNN	NNNN3NNNNNNNNNN	I,P	282	896	11.09.03	3320	000000	21511
166.267-010	EMPLOYMENT INTERVIEWER (profess. & kin.)	5356	22344344455	SNNNNNNOFONFFNNNNNN	NNNN2NNNNNNNNNN	I,P,J	271	893	11.03.04	1430	521001	21508
166.267-014	HOSPITAL-INSURANCE REPRESENTATIVE (insurance)	4346	22343244455	SNNNNNNFFNFFNFNNNN	NNNN3NNNNNNNNNN	J	282	895	07.01.05	1430	081001	21511
166.267-018	JOB ANALYST (profess. & kin.)	5456	22233344444	LNNNNNNFFNFFNFNFNN	NNNN3NNNNNNNNNN	D,P,J	295	712	11.03.04	1430	521001	21511
166.267-022	PRISONER-CLASSIFICATION INTERVIEWER (profess. & kin.)	5347	22333355555	SNNNNNNOOONFFNONNNNN	NNNN3NNNNNNNNNN	P,J	271	949	11.03.04	1430	521001	21511
166.267-026	RECRUITER (military ser.)	4235	33444244355	LNNNNNNOOONCCNNNNNNN	NNNN3NNNNNNNNNN	P,J	282	943	11.03.04	1430	521001	21511
166.267-030	RETIREMENT OFFICER (government ser.)	5547	32255355555	SNNNNNNFFNONNNNNNN	NNNN3NNNNNNNNNN	P,J,T	282	894	07.01.01	1430	521001	21511
166.267-034	JOB DEVELOPMENT SPECIALIST (profess. & kin.)	4345	33444445455	SNNNNNNFFONCCNFNNNNN	NNNN3NNNNNNNNNN	I,P,J	298	943	11.03.04	1430	521001	21511
166.267-038	PERSONNEL RECRUITER (profess. & kin.)	5357	22444344455	SNNNNNNFFONCCNFNNNNN	NNNN3NNNNNNNNNN	I,V,P,J	271	943	11.03.04	1430	000000	21511
166.267-042	EMPLOYEE RELATIONS SPECIALIST (profess. & kin.)	4227	22344344455	SNNNNNNFFONCCNFNNNNN	NNNN3NNNNNNNNNN	P,J	271	893	11.03.04	1430	000000	21511
166.267-046	HUMAN RESOURCE ADVISOR (profess. & kin.)	5357	22455355555	LNNNNNNOONNCCNFNNNNN	NNNN3NNNNNNNNNN	D,I,P,J	296	893	11.02.02	1430	000000	21511
168.161-010	CORONER (government ser.)	5547	22222332252	LNNNNNNFFNFFNFNOFON	NNNN3NNNNNNNNNN	D,P,J	295	959	02.02.01	1473	000000	21911
168.161-014	INDUSTRIAL-SAFETY-AND-HEALTH TECHNICIAN (any industry)	5446	33344333344	LNNNNNNFFNFFNFNNOON	NNNN3NNNNNNNNNN	D,T	211	953	11.10.03	1473	150701	21908
168.167-010	CUSTOMS PATROL OFFICER (government ser.)	5348	33333334334	LOOOOOOFFNFNFFFFOF	FNNN3NNNNNNNNNNO	V,P,S,J	271	953	04.01.02	5132	430107	63011
168.167-014	EQUAL-OPPORTUNITY REPRESENTATIVE (government ser.)	5358	23344344444	SNNNNNNFFNFFNFNNNON	NNNN3NNNNNNNNNN	D,J,I,P	295	959	11.10.02	1473	000000	21911
168.167-018	HEALTH OFFICER, FIELD (government ser.)	5356	22343345454	LNNNNNNOOONFFNONNONON	NNNN3NNNNNNNNNN	P,I,J,D	271	920	11.10.03	1473	150701	21911
168.167-022	IMMIGRATION INSPECTOR (government ser.)	4345	32443344454	LNNNNNNOOOONFFNONNONON	ONNN3NNNNNNNNNN	P,J	271	953	11.10.04	1473	000000	21911
168.167-026	INSPECTOR, BOILER (profess. & kin.)	5458	22322244433	LNNOOONOOONFFNFNFOON	NNNN4NNNNNNNNNN	J,T	211	554	05.03.06	1473	150701	21911
168.167-030	INSPECTOR, BUILDING (government ser.)	4447	22323344445	LOOOOONFFONFFNOOOONO	ONNN3NNNNNNNNNNO	T,P,J	211	953	05.03.06	1472	430201	21908
168.167-034	INSPECTOR, ELECTRICAL (government ser.)	5447	22223244434	LOOOOOOFFNOONFOOOOO	ONNN4NNNNNNNNNN	P,J	211	584	05.03.06	1472	150303	21908
168.167-038	INSPECTOR, ELEVATORS (government ser.)	5458	22222344434	LONOOONFFONOONFOFFON	NNNN4NNNNNNNNNNF	D,P,J,T	212	565	05.03.06	1472	150403	21908
168.167-042	INSPECTOR, HEALTH CARE FACILITIES (government ser.)	4346	22333345554	SNNNNNNFFNFFNFNONN	NNNN3NNNNNNNNNN	V,J	271	920	11.10.03	1473	150701	21911
168.167-046	INSPECTOR, HEATING AND REFRIGERATION (government ser.)	5447	22223355534	LONOOONFFONOONFNFFON	NNNN4NNNNNNNNNN	P,J,T	212	553	05.07.02	1472	150501	21908
168.167-050	INSPECTOR, PLUMBING (government ser.)	5447	22223344434	LOOOOOOFFFNFFNFOOOO	ONNN3NNNNNNNNNN	P,J,T	211	364	05.03.06	1472	460501	21908
168.167-058	MANAGER, CUSTOMER SERVICE (tel. & tel.)	5558	22343344455	SNNNNNNOFONFFNFNNNNN	NNNN3NNNNNNNNNN	D,P,I,J	295	862	11.12.01	4514	520204	51002
168.167-062	OCCUPATIONAL-SAFETY-AND-HEALTH INSPECTOR (government ser.)	5556	22333344454	LOOOONFFOFNFFOFNF	ONNN4NNNNNNNNNN	J	271	712	11.10.03	1473	150701	21911
168.167-066	QUALITY-CONTROL COORDINATOR (pharmaceut.)	4446	22234344454	SNNNNNNFFONFFNFNFFN	NNNN3NNNNNNNNNN	D,P,J,T	295	493	05.02.03	1473	410101	15023
168.167-070	REGULATORY ADMINISTRATOR (tel. & tel.)	5558	22444344455	SNNNNNNOOOONFFNNNNNNN	NNNN3NNNNNNNNNN	D,P,J	271	861	11.10.05	1341	000000	15023
168.167-074	REVIEWING OFFICER, DRIVER'S LICENSE (government ser.)	4347	22444344455	SNNNNNNNFFNFFNFNNNN	NNNN3NNNNNNNNNN	P,J	211	959	11.10.03	1473	430107	21911
168.167-078	SAFETY INSPECTOR (insurance)	5458	22233333353	LOOOOOOFFFNFNFNOOFOO	FNNN3NNNNNNNNNN	D,P,I,J	271	895	11.10.03	1473	150701	21911
168.167-082	TRANSPORTATION INSPECTOR (motor trans.; r.r. trans.)	4347	33344354455	LNNNOONNOFFNOONFNNNNN	ONNN4NNNNNNNNNNO	V,J	271	852	11.10.05	1473	460501	21911
168.167-086	SAFETY MANAGER (medical ser.)	5557	22222244355	LNNNNNNNFFNFNFFFFON	NNNN3NNNNNNNNNN	D,I,V,P,J	211	704	11.10.03	1473	150701	21908
168.167-090	MANAGER, REGULATED PROGRAM (government ser.)	5558	12242255555	LONONONOOONFFNONNNNN	NNNN3NNNNNNNNNN	D,V,T,P,J	295	953	11.05.03	1139	000000	21911
168.261-010	RADIATION-PROTECTION SPECIALIST (government ser.)	5458	22323333353	LNNOOONFFNFFNFNNOOFN	NNNN4NNNNNNNNNN	P,T	211	953	11.10.03	1473	000000	21911
168.264-010	INSPECTOR, AIR-CARRIER (government ser.)	5547	23222333244	LNNOOONFFNFNFNFOOO	NNNN5NNNNNNNNNNO	J	211	592	05.03.06	1473	000000	21911
168.264-014	SAFETY INSPECTOR (any industry)	4346	33333344454	LOONNNNFFNFNFFFON	ONNN4NNNNNNNNNN	P,J	271	712	11.10.03	1473	150701	21911
168.264-018	GAS INSPECTOR (utilities)	5457	22243233344	LNNOONONCCONFFNNNNON	NNNN3ONNNNNNNNOON	V,T,P,J	211	953	07.01.07	1473	470501	21911
168.267-010	BUILDING INSPECTOR (insurance)	4347	22334244444	LFOONNNOONNFFNFNFN	FNNN3NNNNNNNNNN	J	211	361	05.03.06	1472	150701	21908
168.267-014	CLAIM EXAMINER (insurance)	5347	22344344455	SNNNNNNNFFNFFNFNFNN	NNNN3NNNNNNNNNN	V,J	271	895	07.02.03	1473	000000	21921
168.267-018	CUSTOMS IMPORT SPECIALIST (government ser.)	5358	22342333343	LNNNNNNFFONFFNNNNNN	NNNN3NNNNNNNNNN	J	271	953	11.10.04	1473	521401	21911
168.267-022	CUSTOMS INSPECTOR (government ser.)	4446	22233233333	LOOOOOOFFNFNFNOOFOO	NNNN4NNNNNNNNNNO	P,J	271	953	11.10.04	1473	430109	21911
168.267-026	DEALER-COMPLIANCE REPRESENTATIVE (retail trade; wholesale tr.)	4336	33344344444	LNNNNNNOFFNFFNFNFFN	NNNN3NNNNNNNNNN	P,J	271	899	11.10.05	1473	081209	21911
168.267-030	DINING-SERVICE INSPECTOR (r.r. trans.)	4237	33443344434	LOONNNNFFNFNFFFFF	NNNN2NNNNNNNNNN	P,J	211	903	11.10.05	1473	200409	21911
168.267-034	DRIVER'S LICENSE EXAMINER (government ser.)	3234	33333333344	LNNNNNNOOONFFNFFNNNN	NNNN2ONNNNNNNNNN	P,J	211	950	07.01.07	1473	000000	21911
168.267-038	ELIGIBILITY-AND-OCCUPANCY INTERVIEWER (government ser.)	4345	33353244444	LNNNNNNFFNFNFNNNNON	NNNN3NNNNNNNNNN	J	271	941	07.01.01	4784	520406	53502
168.267-042	FOOD AND DRUG INSPECTOR (government ser.)	5456	22334344453	LNNNNNNFFFONOONFNOOON	NNNN3NNNNNNNNNNN	J,P,T	271	920	11.10.03	1473	150506	21911

DOT #	DOT Title & Industry	Trng	Aptitude	Physical	Environment	Tempra	WkF	MPSMS	GOE	SOC	CIP	OES
168.267-046	INSPECTOR, FURNITURE AND BEDDING (government ser.)	4346	33343333353	MNNOOONFFFONNNFNOOON	NNNN3NNNNNNNNNN	V,J	271	460	11.10.03	1473	000000	21911
168.267-050	INSPECTOR, GOVERNMENT PROPERTY (government ser.)	4346	22233344454	LNNNNNNNFFNOONFNNNON	FNNN3NNNNNNNNNN	J	271	959	11.10.01	1473	000000	21911
168.267-054	INSPECTOR, INDUSTRIAL WASTE (government ser.)	5456	22333344343	MONONONFFNFFNFNOFFO	FNNN3OONNONNONNF	V,P,J	211	874	05.03.06	1473	150506	21911
168.267-058	INSPECTOR, MOTOR VEHICLES (government ser.)	4345	33433344444	LNNNNNNFFNOONFFFFOF	FNNN3NNNNNNNNNN	J	293	951	11.10.03	1473	000000	21911
168.267-062	INVESTIGATOR (government ser.)	5446	22333355555	LNNNNNNFFNFFNFNNFNN	ONNN3NNNNNNNNNN	P,J	271	950	11.10.01	1473	430107	21911
168.267-066	LICENSE INSPECTOR (government ser.)	4337	22343344455	LNNNNNNOFFNFFNNNNNN	NNNN3NNNNNNNNNN	J,T	271	959	11.10.03	1473	430107	21911
168.267-070	LOGGING-OPERATIONS INSPECTOR (forestry; logging)	5347	22333344455	LOONNNNOOONFFNOOONNN	NNNN3NNNNNNNNNN	P,J	212	712	03.01.04	1473	030405	21911
168.267-074	MINE INSPECTOR (mine & quarry)	4346	33433344434	LFOOONFFONNNNNOFNOF	ONNN4NONNNNNNNNN	J,T	212	369	11.10.03	1473	150701	21911
168.267-078	MORTICIAN INVESTIGATOR (government ser.)	4346	32443444454	LNNNNNNOOONFFNFNNNON	NNNN2NNNNNNNNNN	P,J	271	907	11.10.03	1473	120301	21911
168.267-082	AGRICULTURAL-CHEMICALS INSPECTOR (government ser.)	4237	22344244444	LNNOOONFFNNFFNFNNNNN	NNNN3NNNNNNNNNN	I,J,P	271	953	11.10.03	1473	000000	21911
168.267-086	HAZARDOUS-WASTE MANAGEMENT SPECIALIST (government ser.)	5357	22244244455	SNNNNNNFFONOONFNNNNN	NNNN3NNNNNNNNNN	T,P	271	732	11.10.03	1473	000000	21911
168.267-090	INSPECTOR, WATER-POLLUTION CONTROL (government ser.)	5457	22343344455	LNNNNNNNNNFFNFNNOON	NNNN3NNNNNNNNNN	J,P	211	953	11.10.03	1473	150506	21911
168.267-094	MARINE-CARGO SURVEYOR (business ser.)	4449	22233244455	LOOOOONFFNNFFNFFOONN	ONNN4NNNNNNNNNO	T,P,J	211	953	11.10.03	1473	000000	21911
168.267-098	PESTICIDE-CONTROL INSPECTOR (government ser.)	4237	22444244444	LOOOONNFFNNCCNFONONN	NNNN3NNNNNNNNNN	P,J	271	953	11.10.03	1473	000000	21911
168.267-102	PLAN CHECKER (government ser.)	4447	32222244445	SNNNNNNFFNFNNNNNNN	NNNN3NNNNNNNNNN	P,T	211	953	05.03.06	1472	460403	21908
168.267-106	REGISTRATION SPECIALIST, AGRICULTURAL CHEMICALS (government ser.)	5347	22354244555	SNNNNNNNNFFNFNNNNNN	NNNN3NNNNNNNNNN	J,P	271	953	11.10.03	1473	000000	21911
168.267-110	SANITATION INSPECTOR (government ser.)	3235	33434344454	LNNNNNNFFONFFNFNNOON	FNNN3NNNNNNNNNN	I,J,P	271	953	11.10.02	1473	000000	21911
168.267-114	EQUAL OPPORTUNITY OFFICER (any industry)	5357	22334344455	SNNNNNNOOONFFFNNNNNN	NNNN3NNNNNNNNNN	P,J	271	943	11.10.02	1473	150702	21911
168.287-010	INSPECTOR, AGRICULTURAL COMMODITIES (government ser.)	4347	23332433353	LNNOOONFFFNFFNFOOOON	ONNN4NNNNNNNNNO	V,J	211	300	11.10.03	1473	010401	21911
168.287-014	INSPECTOR, QUALITY ASSURANCE (government ser.)	5557	22233244453	LNNNNNNNNNNFFNFNNOON	NNNN4NNNNNNNNNN	J	211	959	05.03.06	1473	150702	21911
168.287-018	INSPECTOR, RAILROAD (government ser.)	4247	33323333333	MOOOOONFFNNNNFNNFON	FNNN4NNNNNNNNNN	J,T	211	594	05.03.06	1473	000000	21911
168.367-010	ATTENDANCE OFFICER (education)	4247	22444344445	LNNNNNNOOONFFNFNNNNN	ONNN3NNNNNNNNNO	P,J	271	931	07.01.06	1473	000000	21911
168.367-014	RATER, TRAVEL ACCOMMODATIONS (profess. & kin.)	3336	33444444444	LNNNNNNOOOONFFNFNNNN	ONNN3NNNNNNNNNN	D,P,J	211	896	11.10.05	1473	000000	21911
168.367-018	CODE INSPECTOR (government ser.)	3235	33432344455	LNNOONNOOONFFNFNNONN	NNNN3NNNNNNNNNN	P,T	211	953	05.03.06	1473	000000	21911
168.367-022	PERSONNEL QUALITY ASSURANCE AUDITOR (electron. comp.)	3236	33444344554	LNNNNNNOOONFFNFNNFON	NNNN3NNNNNNNNNN	V,P,J	211	587	11.10.05	1473	150702	21911
168.387-010	OPENER-VERIFIER-PACKER, CUSTOMS (government ser.)	3335	34333333353	HNNOOONFFFNNFFNNNNON	NNNN4NNNNNNNNNO	J,T	221	953	05.09.03	1473	000000	21911
169.107-010	ARBITRATOR (profess. & kin.)	5458	21344355555	SNNNNNNOONFFNFNNNNN	NNNN3NNNNNNNNNN	D,I,J,P	271	932	11.04.03	1430	000000	21511
169.117-010	EXECUTIVE SECRETARY, STATE BOARD OF NURSING (government ser.)	5558	21244244455	SNNNNNNFFNFNNNNNNNN	NNNN3NNNNNNNNNN	V,D,P,J	295	959	11.05.03	1132	520402	19005
169.117-014	GRANT COORDINATOR (profess. & kin.)	5458	21244444455	SNNNNNNOONFFNONNNNNN	NNNN3NNNNNNNNNN	D,I,P,J	261	941	11.05.02	1490	000000	21999
169.127-010	CIVIL PREPAREDNESS TRAINING OFFICER (government ser.)	4346	22333444454	LNNNNNNNOOONFFNFOONNO	ONNN3NNNNNNNNNN	I,V	296	959	11.07.02	1131	000000	21911
169.167-010	ADMINISTRATIVE ASSISTANT (any industry)	5357	22343344455	SNNNNNNFFNFNNFNNNNN	NNNN3NNNNNNNNNN	D,J,P,V	295	712	11.05.02	1490	520402	39999
169.167-014	ADMINISTRATIVE SECRETARY (any industry)	5458	22344344455	SNNNNNNOOONFFFNNNNNN	NNNN3NNNNNNNNNN	D,J	295	891	07.01.02	1490	520402	39999
169.167-018	CONTACT REPRESENTATIVE (government ser.)	5356	22344244455	LNNOOOFFNFFNNONNNNN	NNNN3NNNNNNNNNN	I,P,J	271	941	07.01.01	1139	000000	21911
169.167-022	FIRE ASSISTANT (government ser.)	4346	32434344444	SNNNNNNNOOONFFNONONNO	ONNN3NNNNNNNNNN	D,P,J	293	951	04.01.01	1852	430201	24302
169.167-026	LABORATORY ASSISTANT, LIAISON INSPECTION (steel & rel.)	5557	22333344455	LNNNNNNFFNFNNNONONN	ONNN3NNNNNNNNNN	V,P,J	211	540	02.04.01	1131	000000	39999
169.167-030	MANAGER, DATA PROCESSING (profess. & kin.)	5458	11233344455	SNNNNNNNOOONFFNNNONN	NNNN2NNNNNNNNNN	D,P,J	295	893	11.01.01	1260	520204	13017
169.167-034	MANAGER, OFFICE (any industry)	4347	22344343455	SNNNNNNNFFNFNNOONNOON	NNNN3NNNNNNNNNN	D,V,P,J	231	890	07.01.02	1370	520204	13014
169.167-038	ORDER DEPARTMENT SUPERVISOR (any industry)	4347	22344344455	SNNNNNNOOONFFNONONNN	NNNN3NNNNNNNNNN	D,P	232	892	07.05.03	1490	000000	39999
169.167-042	PARK RANGER (government ser.)	4347	33332434324	LOOOOOFFNFFNNFNOOOOO	FNNN4NNNNNNNNNO	V,P,S,J	293	951	04.02.03	1139	030203	21911
169.167-046	PUBLIC HEALTH REGISTRAR (government ser.)	4347	33344344445	LNNNNNNFFONFFNFNNNNN	NNNN3NNNNNNNNNN	J	231	721	07.04.03	1132	000000	21999
169.167-050	SPECIAL AGENT, GROUP INSURANCE (insurance)	5357	22343244455	SNNNNNNNNFFNFNNNNNN	NNNN3NNNNNNNNNN	D,I,J,P	292	895	08.01.02	1490	081001	39999
169.167-054	TOOLING COORDINATOR, PRODUCTION ENGINEERING (aircraft mfg.)	4447	22222243455	LNNNNNNFFNOONFNOONN	NNNN3NNNNNNNNNN	D,J	295	898	05.02.03	1449	150603	21308
169.167-062	COORDINATOR, SKILL-TRAINING PROGRAM (government ser.)	5446	22344344344	SNNNNNNOOONFFNNNOON	NNNN3NNNNNNNNNN	D,I,J,P	295	931	07.01.02	1390	000000	21511
169.167-066	LEGISLATIVE ASSISTANT (government ser.)	5357	22344344455	SNNNNNNNOOONFFNNNNNN	NNNN3NNNNNNNNNN	J,P,V,I	251	939	11.05.03	1139	000000	21999
169.167-070	DIRECTOR, EDUCATIONAL PROGRAMMING (radio-tv broad.)	5457	22343344455	SNNNNNNFFONFFNFONFNN	NNNN3NNNNNNNNNN	D,V,P,J	295	864	11.05.02	1341	000000	15023
169.167-074	PREVENTIVE MAINTENANCE COORDINATOR (any industry)	4337	22233355455	LNNNNNNNFFNFNNNNNNN	NNNN3NNNNNNNNNN	D,V,T,J	271	893	05.01.06	1420	460401	21905
169.167-078	UTILIZATION COORDINATOR (radio-tv broad.)	5357	22444344455	SNNNNNNOOONFFNONNNON	NNNN3NNNNNNNNNN	J,P,V	295	860	11.05.02	1490	090201	21999
169.167-082	MANAGER, COMPUTER OPERATIONS (profess. & kin.)	5448	22333334455	SNNNNNNOOONGCNFNOONN	NNNN3NNNNNNNNNN	D,P,J	295	893	11.01.01	1260	081001	13017
169.167-086	MANAGER, CREDIT AND COLLECTION (any industry)	4448	22355244555	SNNNNNNOOONFFNONNNON	NNNN3NNNNNNNNNN	D,P,J	295	894	11.06.03	1220	080401	13002
169.171-010	GAMEKEEPER (agriculture)	4336	34434443344	HONOOONNNONNONNNNON	FNNN3NNNNNNNNNN	V,J	002	326	03.01.02	5840	020204	79999
169.207-010	CONCILIATOR (profess. & kin.)	5458	21344455555	SNNNNNNOOONFFNONNNNN	NNNN3NNNNNNNNNN	I,J,P	271	733	11.04.03	1430	000000	21511

DOT #	DOT Title & Industry	Trng	Aptitude	Physical	Environment	Tempra	WkF	MPSMS	GOE	SOC	CIP	OES
169.262-010	CASEWORKER (government ser.)	5345	22344223455	SNNOONNFFNFNFNFNN	NNNN3NNNNNNNNNN	J,P	271	893	07.01.06	1139	000000	21999
169.267-010	CLAIMS ADJUDICATOR (government ser.)	5447	22355344455	SNNNNNNFFNFNFNFNN	NNNN3NNNNNNNNNN	J	271	959	11.12.01	2120	000000	28105
169.267-014	EXAMINER (government ser.)	4446	22233344555	SNNNNNNFFNFNFNFNN	NNNN3NNNNNNNNNN	J	271	959	07.01.05	1473	000000	2911
169.267-018	FINANCIAL-AID COUNSELOR (education)	4445	32343244455	SNNNNNOOONFFNONNNNN	NNNN3NNNNNNNNNN	J	271	894	07.01.01	1419	000000	21199
169.267-022	SECRETARY, BOARD-OF-EDUCATION (education)	5557	22242223354	SNNNNNNFFNFNFNFNN	NNNN3NNNNNNNNNN	J	231	892	07.01.02	1283	000000	15005
169.267-026	SUPERVISOR, SPECIAL SERVICES (education)	5456	22244355555	SNNNNNNFFNFNFNFNN	NNNN3NNNNNNNNNN	D,P,I,J	282	733	07.01.01	2400	000000	31514
169.267-030	PASSPORT-APPLICATION EXAMINER (government ser.)	4345	22343344455	LNNNNNNCCONFFNFNFNN	NNNN3NNNNNNNNNN	J,P	271	959	07.01.05	1473	000000	2911
169.267-034	RESEARCH ANALYST (insurance)	5458	22344344455	SNNNNNNFFONOONFNFNN	NNNN3NNNNNNNNNN	P,J	271	895	11.05.02	1490	000000	21999
169.267-038	ESTIMATOR (profess. & kin.)	4447	28233344455	SNNNNNNFFONOONFNNONN	NNNN3NNNNNNNNNN	T,J	232	899	05.03.02	1490	150101	21902
169.267-042	LETTER-OF-CREDIT DOCUMENT EXAMINER (financial)	5447	22255244455	SNNNNNNOOONCCNCNNNNN	NNNN2NNNNNNNNNN	J,P	282	894	11.06.03	1419	080401	21105
169.267-046	UNDERWRITER (insurance)	5457	12244344455	SNNNNNNFFONFFNONNNNN	NNNN2NNNNNNNNNN	J,T	271	895	11.06.03	1414	081001	21102
169.284-010	ADMEASURER (government ser.)	5457	22211334335	SNNNNNNFFNFNFNFNN	NNNN3NNNNNNNNNN	J,T	242	953	05.03.02	1473	000000	2911
169.367-010	EMPLOYMENT-AND-CLAIMS AIDE (government ser.)	3335	33333344453	LONONONFFNOONFOOONO	NNNN3NNNNNNNNNN	V,R,P	282	959	07.04.01	1430	521001	21502
180.117-010	MANAGER, CHRISTMAS-TREE FARM (forestry)	5347	22244455555	SNNNNNNFFNFNFNFNN	NNNN3NNNNNNNNNN	V,D,P,J	295	319	03.01.01	5525	030401	79999
180.161-010	MANAGER, PRODUCTION, SEED CORN (agriculture)	5447	22223444455	LNNNNNNFFNFNFOOOON	ONNN4NNNNNNNNNN	D,P,J,T	301	301	03.01.01	5523	010104	79999
180.161-014	SUPERINTENDENT, HORTICULTURE (museums)	5458	22322323352	LNNNNNNOOONFFNFNNNOFN	NNNN3NNNNNNNNNN	D,J,P	295	310	02.02.02	5525	010603	79999
180.167-010	ARTIFICIAL-BREEDING DISTRIBUTOR (agriculture)	4347	23344333344	LNNNOONFFNFNFNFOOOO	ONNN4NFNNNNNNNN	D,P,I	002	321	03.01.02	5524	020202	79999
180.167-014	FIELD SUPERVISOR, SEED PRODUCTION (agriculture)	5446	23324444454	LNNNNNNFFNFNFFNFFOFF	ONNN4NNNNNNNNNN	D,P,J	003	301	03.02.01	5611	010304	72002
180.167-018	GENERAL MANAGER, FARM (agriculture; wholesale tr.)	5448	22333344444	LNNOONNOOONFFNOONOOO	FNNN3NNNNNNNNNN	D,I,V,P,J	295	300	03.01.01	5522	020202	79999
180.167-022	GROUP LEADER (agriculture)	3227	33444444344	LNNOONOOOONFFNOOONON	FNNN3NNNNNNNNNN	V,D,P,J	003	300	03.01.01	5611	010302	72002
180.167-026	MANAGER, DAIRY FARM (agriculture)	4338	23333344444	LNNONONFFOOFFNFONOOO	ONNN3NNNNNNNNNN	D,J,P	295	383	03.01.01	5524	020204	79999
180.167-030	MANAGER, FISH HATCHERY (fishing & hunt.)	5347	22333344444	LNNNNNNOOONFFNOOOON	FNNN3NNNNNNNNNN	D,J,P,V	295	330	03.01.02	5524	020204	79999
180.167-034	MANAGER, GAME BREEDING FARM (agriculture)	5347	22233344443	LNNNNNNFFONFFNFNNFN	FNNN4NONNNNNNNN	D,J,P,V	295	326	03.01.02	5524	010104	79999
180.167-038	MANAGER, GAME PRESERVE (agriculture)	5448	22333344444	LNNONONFFOOFFNFOOOO	FNNN3NNNNNNNNNN	D,P,J,V	295	326	03.01.01	5524	020409	79999
180.167-042	MANAGER, NURSERY (agriculture; retail trade; wholesale tr.)	5458	22333333344	LNNNNNNFFNFNFFOOOO	FNNN3NNNNNNNNNN	D,V,P,J	295	310	03.01.03	5525	020403	15031
180.167-046	MANAGER, POULTRY HATCHERY (agriculture)	4337	22323344455	LNNNNNNFFNFNFNNONN	NNNN3NNNNNNNNNN	V,D,P	295	324	03.01.01	5524	020203	79999
180.167-050	MIGRANT LEADER (agriculture)	3227	33444344444	LNNOOONFFNFNFNFOOOO	CNNN4NNNNNNNNNN	V,D,P,J	003	300	03.01.01	5611	010304	72002
180.167-054	SUPERINTENDENT (agriculture; can. & preserv.)	5447	22344344455	LNNNNNNFFNFNFNFNOFN	FNNN3NNNNNNNNNN	D,T	295	300	03.01.01	1320	150699	15014
180.167-058	SUPERINTENDENT, PRODUCTION (agriculture)	4337	22233344444	LNNNNNNFFNFNFNFOOOO	NNNN4NNNNNNNNNN	D,P,J	003	304	03.01.01	5523	010304	79999
180.167-062	MANAGER, AERIAL PLANTING AND CULTIVATION (agriculture)	4447	33333344444	SNNNONONOOONFFNOOONOF	NNNN3NONNNNNNNN	D,P,J	295	300	11.11.03	1342	010501	15023
180.167-066	MANAGER, ORCHARD (agriculture)	5458	22333344444	LNNNNNNOOONFFNFNNOON	ONNO3NNNNNNNNNN	D,P,J	899	899	03.01.04	5523	020403	19999
181.117-010	MANAGER, BULK PLANT (petrol. refin.; retail trade)	5448	22233344455	LNNNNNNFFNFNFNFNNNN	NNNN4NNNNNNNNNN	D,P,J	295	501	05.02.07	1320	081209	15014
181.117-014	MINE SUPERINTENDENT (mine & quarry)	5448	22222244455	LNNNNNNOOONFFNFOONNN	ONNN3NONNNNNNNO	D,V,P,J	005	340	05.02.05	1360	150901	15021
181.167-010	MANAGER, FIELD PARTY, GEOPHYSICAL PROSPECTING (petrol. & gas)	4446	22244344455	LNNNNNNFFNFNFNFNN	ONNN3NNNNNNNNNN	V,D,P,J	295	890	11.11.04	1360	150903	15021
181.167-014	SUPERINTENDENT, DRILLING AND PRODUCTION (petrol. & gas)	5548	22333344355	LNNNNNNOONFFNFNFNNNN	FNNN4NNNNNNNNNN	V,D,P,J	295	342	05.02.01	1360	150903	15021
181.167-018	SUPERVISOR, MINE (mine & quarry)	4338	22322344455	LNNNNNNOONNNFNFNNNON	ONNN5NNNNNNNNNO	D,J	005	340	05.03.06	1360	000000	15021
182.167-010	CONTRACTOR (construction)	4447	33222333333	LOOOOOFFOFFNFFFFOF	FNNN4NNNNNNNNNN	V,D,P,J	102	360	11.12.04	1330	000000	15017
182.167-014	LANDSCAPE CONTRACTOR (construction)	4448	33233344453	LNNNNNNFFNFNFFONNFN	FNNN4NNNNNNNNNN	D,J,P,V	295	719	03.01.03	1330	010603	15017
182.167-018	RAILROAD-CONSTRUCTION DIRECTOR (r.r. trans.)	4338	22333344454	LONOOONOONNFFNOOOOO	FNNN5NNNNNNNNNN	D,J	295	367	05.02.02	1330	000000	15014
182.167-022	SUPERINTENDENT, CONCRETE-MIXING PLANT (construction)	4446	22244344455	SONNNNNNFFNFNFONNNN	FNNN4NONNNNNNNN	P	143	536	05.02.03	1320	000000	15014
182.167-026	SUPERINTENDENT, CONSTRUCTION (construction)	5547	23223344445	LNNNNNNFFNFNFONFNN	FNNN3NNNNNNNNNN	V,D,P	295	360	05.02.02	1330	000000	15017
182.167-030	SUPERINTENDENT, MAINTENANCE OF WAY (r.r. trans.)	5448	22334445455	LNNNNNNOONNCCNNONNNO	ONNN3NNNNNNNNNN	D,V,P,J	295	367	05.02.02	1330	000000	15017
182.167-034	SUPERVISOR, BRIDGES AND BUILDINGS (r.r. trans.)	5547	22334443355	LOOOONFFNFNFNOOFOO	FNNN4NNNNNNNNNN	V,D,P,J	295	360	05.02.02	1330	000000	15017
182.267-010	CONSTRUCTION INSPECTOR (construction)	4436	23223444425	LOOOOOFFOFFNFFNOONN	FNNN4NNNNNNNNNN	V,J,T	243	360	05.03.06	1472	150101	21908
183.117-010	MANAGER, BRANCH (any industry)	5448	22244344455	SNNNNNNOOONFFNOONNNN	NNNN3NNNNNNNNNN	D,P,J	295	893	11.05.02	1320	150603	15014
183.117-014	PRODUCTION SUPERINTENDENT (any industry)	5348	23222333343	LNNNNNNFFONFFNFNNONN	NNNO3NNNNNNNNNN	D,J,P,V	295	712	05.02.03	1320	150603	15014
183.161-014	WINE MAKER (beverage)	5448	22233344453	LNNNNNNFFOOFFNNFNN	NNNN3NNNNNNNNNN	D,P,J	146	395	05.02.03	1320	010401	15014
183.167-010	BREWING DIRECTOR (beverage)	5448	22223344445	LNNNNNNFFNFNFONFNN	NNNN3NNNNNNNNNN	D,J,P,T	146	395	05.02.03	1320	020301	15014
183.167-014	GENERAL SUPERINTENDENT, MILLING (grain-feed mills)	5448	22323344455	LNNNNNNOOFNFNFNOOONN	NNNN3NNNNNNNNNN	D,P	295	381	05.02.02	1320	000000	15014
183.167-018	GENERAL SUPERVISOR (any industry)	5448	22233344455	LNNNNNNOOFFNFNNOOONN	NNNN3NNNNNNNNNN	D,J,P,V	295	712	05.02.03	1320	150603	15014
183.167-022	GENERAL SUPERVISOR (beverage)	4348	23333344454	LNNNNNNOOONOFFNONNNON	NNNN3NNNNNNNNNN	V,D,P,T	295	395	05.02.03	1320	000000	15014

DOT #	DOT Title & Industry	Trng	Aptitude	Physical	Environment	Tempra	WkF	MPSMS	GOE	SOC	CIP	OES
183.167-026	MANAGER, FOOD PROCESSING PLANT (can. & preserv.)	5448	22333344454	LNNNNNNFFONFFNFNNNNN	NNNN3NNNNNNNNNN	V,D,P,J	295	300	05.02.03	1320	010401	15014
183.167-030	SERVICE SUPERVISOR, LEASED MACHINERY AND EQUIPMENT (any industry)	4447	22333344455	LNNNNNNNNNNFFNNNNNNN	NNNN3NNNNNNNNNN	V,D,P	111	560	11.11.05	1359	520205	19999
183.167-034	SUPERINTENDENT, CAR CONSTRUCTION (railroad equip.)	5548	22222344455	SNNNNNNNFFONFFNNONNN	NNNN3NNNNNNNNNN	D,P,J,T	295	594	05.02.03	1320	000000	15014
183.167-038	SUPERINTENDENT, LOGGING (logging)	5448	22234344455	LNNNNNOONNFFNFFFNFNF	FNNN3NNNNNNNNNN	D,P,J	295	313	05.02.05	1320	030405	15014
184.117-010	DIRECTOR, PUBLIC SERVICE (radio-tv broad.)	5458	22344344455	LNNNNNNOOONFFNNNNNNN	NNNN3NNNNNNNNNN	D,P,J	295	863	11.09.03	3240	000000	34056
184.117-014	DIRECTOR, TRANSPORTATION (motor trans.)	5558	22344344454	SNNNNNNNNNFFFNNNNNNN	NNNN3NNNNNNNNNN	D,P,J	295	852	11.05.01	1210	520903	15023
184.117-018	DISTRICT SUPERVISOR (motor trans.)	5556	33333334335	LNNNNNNOONNFFNFFNNNN	NNNN3NNNNNNNNNN	D,J,P	295	852	11.12.02	1342	520903	15023
184.117-022	IMPORT-EXPORT AGENT (any industry)	5457	22344355455	SNNNNNNOONNFFNNNNNNN	NNNN3NNNNNNNNNN	D,I,J,P,V	295	850	11.05.02	1342	521403	15023
184.117-026	MANAGER, AIRPORT (air trans.)	5558	22233344454	LNNNNNNFFONFFNNFNNNN	NNNN3NNNNNNNNNN	V,D,P,J	295	855	11.05.01	1342	520903	15023
184.117-030	MANAGER, AREA DEVELOPMENT (utilities)	5348	22244344455	LNNNNNNFFONFFNOONON	NNNN3NNNNNNNNNN	D,I,J,P,V	292	871	11.09.03	1343	000000	15023
184.117-034	MANAGER, AUTOMOTIVE SERVICES (any industry)	5448	22233344455	SNNNNNNOOONFFNONNNNN	NNNN3NNNNNNNNNN	D,P,J	295	591	11.11.03	1342	520903	15023
184.117-038	MANAGER, FLIGHT OPERATIONS (air trans.)	5558	22222334453	SNNNNNNNNFFFNNFFNNNN	NNNN3NNNNNNNNNN	D,J,P	295	855	11.05.02	1342	520903	15023
184.117-042	MANAGER, HARBOR DEPARTMENT (water trans.)	6449	22233344454	SNNNNNNNFFNFFNFNNONN	NNNN3NNNNNNNNNN	D,I,J	295	854	11.05.03	1342	520903	15023
184.117-046	MANAGER, IRRIGATION DISTRICT (waterworks)	5449	11222244455	LNNNNNNOONNFFNOOONNN	NNNN3NNNNNNNNNN	V,D,P	295	873	11.05.03	1343	030101	15023
184.117-050	MANAGER, OPERATIONS (air trans.; motor trans.; r.r. trans.; water trans.)	5458	22244345455	SNNNNNNNNNNCCNFNNNNN	NNNN3NNNNNNNNNN	D,P,J	295	850	11.05.02	1342	520903	15023
184.117-054	MANAGER, REGIONAL (motor trans.)	5558	22244344455	SNNNNNNOONNFFNNNNNNN	NNNN3NNNNNNNNNN	V,D,P	295	852	11.05.02	1342	520903	15023
184.117-058	MANAGER, SCHEDULE PLANNING (air trans.)	5458	11343244455	SNNNNNNNNFFFNONFNNNN	NNNN3NNNNNNNNNN	D,P	295	855	11.05.02	1342	520903	15023
184.117-062	MANAGER, STATION (radio-tv broad.)	5458	22343344455	LNNNNNNOFONFFNNNNNNN	NNNN3NNNNNNNNNN	D,V,P,J	295	863	11.05.02	1341	000000	15023
184.117-066	MANAGER, TRAFFIC (air trans.; motor trans.; water trans.)	5558	22244344455	SNNNNNNFFNFFNFNNNNN	NNNN2NNNNNNNNNN	V,D,P,I,J	295	850	11.11.03	1342	520903	15023
184.117-070	OPERATIONS MANAGER (tel. & tel.)	5558	22232244455	SNNNNNNNNOONFFNNNNNN	NNNN3NNNNNNNNNN	D,P	295	862	11.05.02	1341	000000	15023
184.117-074	REVENUE-SETTLEMENTS ADMINISTRATOR (tel. & tel.)	5558	11244344455	SNNNNNNNOONNFFNNNNNN	NNNN2NNNNNNNNNN	D,P	295	861	11.12.01	1341	000000	15023
184.117-078	SUPERINTENDENT, COMMISSARY (water trans.)	5448	22244344455	SNNNNNNFFNFFNFNNNNN	NNNN3NNNNNNNNNN	V,D,P,J	295	854	11.05.02	1240	520903	13008
184.117-082	SUPERINTENDENT, COMMUNICATIONS (tel. & tel.)	5448	22234444455	SNNNNNNOONNFFNONNNNN	NNNN2NNNNNNNNNN	D,P,J	295	586	05.02.01	1341	000000	15023
184.117-086	MANAGER, CAR INSPECTION AND REPAIR (r.r. trans.)	5458	22344344555	SNNNNNNOOONFFNFNNONN	NNNN3NNNNNNNNNN	D,V,P,J	295	851	11.11.03	1342	470302	15023
184.117-090	REGIONAL SUPERINTENDENT, RAILROAD CAR INSPECTION AND REPAIR (r.r. trans.)	5449	22354354555	SNNNNNNOONNCNCNNNNNN	NNNN3NNNNNNNNNN	D,P,J	295	851	11.11.03	1342	470302	15023
184.161-010	CABLE SUPERVISOR (tel. & tel.)	4248	33333344454	LNNNNNNNFFONFFNNNOON	ONNN3NNNNNNNNNN	D,P,J	111	586	05.05.05	1341	000000	15023
184.161-014	SUPERINTENDENT, WATER-AND-SEWER SYSTEMS (waterworks)	6669	22222333453	SNNNNNNFFONFFNFNNNNN	NNNN3NNNNNNNNNN	D,J,P	244	873	05.02.01	1343	000000	34056
184.162-010	DIRECTOR, PRODUCTION (radio-tv broad.)	5447	22444343444	HNNONONFFONFFNFOOOOO	ONNN3NNNNNNNNNN	D,V,P,J	281	863	11.05.02	3240	000000	34056
184.163-010	TRAFFIC INSPECTOR (motor trans.; r.r. trans.)	4237	22344344444	LNNNNNNFFNFFNFFFFFOF	OONN4NNNNNNNNNN	D,J,P	013	850	11.10.05	1473	520903	21911
184.167-010	BOAT DISPATCHER (water trans.)	4337	22334344555	LNNNNNNOOONFFNFNNNNN	NNNN2NNNNNNNNNN	V,D,P	013	854	07.05.01	1342	520903	15023
184.167-014	DIRECTOR, NEWS (radio-tv broad.)	5358	22344344455	LNNNNNNOOONFFNNNNNNN	NNNN3NNNNNNNNNN	D,P,J	295	860	11.08.01	3240	000000	34056
184.167-018	DIRECTOR, OPERATIONS (radio-tv broad.)	5458	22343344455	SNNNNNNOFONFFNNONNNN	NNNN3NNNNNNNNNN	D,V,P,J	295	863	11.05.02	1341	000000	15023
184.167-022	DIRECTOR, OPERATIONS, BROADCAST (radio-tv broad.)	5358	22444344455	LNNNNNNOOONFFNONNNNN	NNNN3NNNNNNNNNN	D,V,P,J	295	863	11.05.02	3240	000000	34056
184.167-026	DIRECTOR, PHOTOGRAMMETRY FLIGHT OPERATIONS (business ser.)	5448	23322344454	LNNNNNNOONNFFNFNNNNN	NNNN2NNNNNNNNNN	V,D,P,J	295	716	05.03.01	1649	000000	22311
184.167-030	DIRECTOR, PROGRAM (radio-tv broad.)	5458	12344343444	LNNNNNNOOONFFNONNONN	NNNN3NNNNNNNNNN	D,V,P,J	295	756	11.05.02	3240	000000	34056
184.167-034	DIRECTOR, SPORTS (radio-tv broad.)	5458	21333344455	SNNNNNNFFNFFNFNNNNN	NNNN3NNNNNNNNNN	D,J,P	295	863	11.05.02	3240	000000	34056
184.167-038	DISPATCHER, CHIEF I (petrol. & gas; petrol. refin.; pipe lines)	5448	22244344455	SNNNNNNNFFNFFNNFNNNN	NNNN3NNNNNNNNNN	V,D,P,J	295	856	05.02.01	1342	000000	15023
184.167-042	GENERAL AGENT, OPERATIONS (air trans.; motor trans.; r.r. trans.)	4348	22244244455	SNNNNNNNFFONFFNFNNNN	NNNN2NNNNNNNNNN	V,D,P	013	851	11.05.02	1342	520903	15023
184.167-046	INCINERATOR-PLANT-GENERAL SUPERVISOR (sanitary ser.)	4346	22343344455	SNNNNNNNOONNFFNFNNON	NNNN3NNNNNNNNNN	V,D,J	295	874	05.06.04	1342	000000	81008
184.167-050	MAINTENANCE SUPERVISOR (utilities)	4447	22233344445	LONOOOOOONNFFONFFNNON	NNNN3NNNNNNNNNN	D,T,J	111	871	05.02.02	6700	000000	81002
184.167-054	MANAGER, BUS TRANSPORTATION (motor trans.)	4448	23344344454	SNNNNNNFFONFFNFNNNNN	NNNN2NNNNNNNNNN	V,D,P	295	852	11.11.03	6000	520903	15023
184.167-058	MANAGER, CARGO-AND-RAMP-SERVICES (air trans.)	5458	22223344455	SNNNNNNOFONFFNFNNNNN	NNNN3NNNNNNNNNN	D,J,P	295	855	11.11.03	1342	520903	15023
184.167-062	MANAGER, COMMUNICATIONS STATION (tel. & tel.)	5448	22333344455	SNNNNNNOONNFFNFNNONN	NNNN2NNNNNNNNNN	D,J,P	281	860	05.02.04	1342	000000	15023
184.167-066	MANAGER, FLIGHT CONTROL (air trans.)	5448	22334344455	SNNNNNNFFFNFFNFNNNNN	NNNN3NNNNNNNNNN	D,P,J	295	855	05.02.04	1342	520903	15023
184.167-070	MANAGER, FLIGHT-RESERVATIONS (air trans.)	5448	22244344455	SNNNNNNFFONFFNFNNNNN	NNNN3NNNNNNNNNN	D,J,P	295	855	11.11.03	1342	520903	15023
184.167-078	MANAGER, SOLID-WASTE-DISPOSAL (government ser.)	4337	33333344455	LNNNNNNFFONFFNFNONNN	FNNN3NNNNNNNNNN	D,J,P	295	874	05.02.06	1343	000000	15023
184.167-082	MANAGER, STATION (air trans.)	5448	22344344455	SNNNNNNOONNFFNFNONNN	NNNN3NNNNNNNNNN	D,P	295	855	11.11.03	1342	520903	15023
184.167-086	MANAGER, TELEGRAPH OFFICE (tel. & tel.)	4348	22344333354	SNNNNNNNFFONFFNNNONN	NNNN2NNNNNNNNNN	D,P	232	862	07.01.02	1341	000000	15023
184.167-090	MANAGER, TRAFFIC (radio-tv broad.)	5357	22344444455	SNNNNNNNFFONFFNNOON	NNNN3NNNNNNNNNN	V,D,P,J	295	863	11.12.02	1341	090201	15023
184.167-094	MANAGER, TRAFFIC (any industry)	5448	22343344455	SNNNNNNNFFONFFNFNNNN	NNNN3NNNNNNNNNN	D,P,J	221	851	11.05.02	1342	520903	15023
184.167-098	MANAGER, TRAFFIC I (tel. & tel.)	4348	22333344455	SNNNNNNFFONFFNONNNNN	NNNN2NNNNNNNNNN	V,D,P,J	295	862	07.01.02	1341	000000	15023

DOT #	DOT Title & Industry	Trng	Aptitude	Physical	Environment	Tempra	WkF	MPSMS	GOE	SOC	CIP	OES
184.167-102	MANAGER, TRAFFIC I (motor trans.)	5458	22244244455	SNNNNNNNOOONFFNFNNNONN	NNNN3NNNNNNNNNN	D,P	221	853	07.01.02	1342	520903	15023
184.167-106	MANAGER, TRAFFIC II (tel. & tel.)	5458	22223344454	SNNNNNNNFFONFFNNNNNNON	NNNN2NNNNNNNNNN	V,D,P,J	295	861	11.11.03	1341	000000	15023
184.167-110	MANAGER, TRUCK TERMINAL (motor trans.)	4338	33334344455	SNNNNNNNNFFNNFNNNNNNNN	NNNN3NNNNNNNNNN	D,J	295	853	11.11.03	1342	520903	15023
184.167-114	MANAGER, WAREHOUSE (any industry)	4348	22334444455	LNNNNNNNFFNFNNONNNNNNN	NNNN3NNNNNNNNNN	D,V,P,J	221	898	11.11.03	1342	081199	15023
184.167-118	OPERATIONS MANAGER (motor trans.)	4336	33333334335	LNNNNNNNFFNFNNFFFONN	NNNN3NNNNNNNNNN	D,J	295	853	11.11.03	1342	081199	15023
184.167-122	PORT-TRAFFIC MANAGER (water trans.)	5558	22344443455	SNNNNNNNFFNNFFNFNNNNN	NNNN3NNNNNNNNNN	V,D,P,I,J	295	854	11.05.03	1342	521401	15023
184.167-126	SERVICE SUPERVISOR III (utilities)	4448	32333344455	LNNNNNNNNNNFFNFNNONNN	FNNN3NNNNNNNNNN	V,D,P,J	111	581	05.02.02	1343	520205	15023
184.167-130	STATION MANAGER (r.r. trans.)	4337	22344344455	SNNNNNNNNOONNFFNONNNNN	NNNN3NNNNNNNNNN	V,D,P,T	295	851	11.11.03	1342	000000	15023
184.167-134	STATIONS-RELATIONS-CONTACT REPRESENTATIVE (radio-tv broad.)	5458	22344344455	SNNNNNNNOONNNFFNNNNNN	NNNN3NNNNNNNNNN	V,D,P,J	295	863	11.05.02	1341	000000	15023
184.167-138	SUPERINTENDENT OF GENERATION (utilities)	5548	11122244455	SNNNNNNNOONNNONNNNNN	NNNN3NNNNNNNNNN	V,D	244	871	05.02.01	1343	000000	15023
184.167-142	SUPERINTENDENT, COLD STORAGE (any industry)	4338	33334344454	LNNNNNNNONNNNFNNNNFN	NNNN3NNNNNNNNNN	D,J	221	853	05.06.02	7100	521401	81008
184.167-146	SUPERINTENDENT, COMPRESSOR STATIONS (pipe lines)	5448	22222344455	SNNNNNNNFFONFFNFNNNNNN	ONNN2NNNNNNNNNN	V,D,P,J	295	856	05.02.01	1342	000000	15023
184.167-150	SUPERINTENDENT, DISTRIBUTION I (utilities)	5549	11123244444	SNNNNNNNFFONFFNFNNNON	NNNN3NNNNNNNNNN	V,D,P,J	244	871	05.02.01	1343	000000	15023
184.167-154	SUPERINTENDENT, DISTRIBUTION II (utilities)	5448	22223244454	LNNNNNNNFFONFFOFONONN	NNNN3NONNNNNNNNN	V,D,P,J	295	872	05.02.01	1343	000000	15023
184.167-158	SUPERINTENDENT, DIVISION (motor trans.; r.r. trans.)	5358	22344244455	LNNNNNNNFFONFFNFNNONN	NNNN3NNNNNNNNNN	V,D,P,J	295	851	11.05.02	1342	520903	15023
184.167-162	SUPERINTENDENT, ELECTRIC POWER (utilities)	5558	11123244454	SNNNNNNNFFONFFNNNNNNN	NNNN3NNNNNNNNNN	D,V,P,J	244	871	05.02.01	1343	000000	15023
184.167-166	SUPERINTENDENT, GENERATING PLANT (utilities)	5558	22222244444	SNNNNNNNNONONFFNFNNNNN	NNNN4NNNNNNNNNN	D,V,P,J	295	893	05.02.02	1342	000000	15023
184.167-170	SUPERINTENDENT, MAINTENANCE (motor trans.)	4437	33333344455	SNNNNNNNFFNFNNFNNNNNNN	NNNN4NNNNNNNNNN	D,J	295	591	05.02.02	1342	470302	15023
184.167-174	SUPERINTENDENT, MAINTENANCE (air trans.)	5448	22344244444	SNNNNNNNFFONFFNFNNNNN	NNNN4NNNNNNNNNN	V,D,P,J	295	592	05.02.02	1342	000000	15023
184.167-178	SUPERINTENDENT, MAINTENANCE OF EQUIPMENT (motor trans.; r.r. trans.)	4348	22344344455	SNNNNNNNFFONFFNFNNNONN	NNNN3NNNNNNNNNN	D,P,T,V	121	590	11.11.03	1342	000000	15023
184.167-182	SUPERINTENDENT, MARINE (water trans.)	5548	22333344455	SNNNNNNNFFNFNFNFNNNONN	ONNN4NNNNNNNNNN	V,D,P,J	295	854	11.11.03	1342	490399	15023
184.167-186	SUPERINTENDENT, MARINE OIL TERMINAL (water trans.)	4348	12143344454	SNNNNNNNFFNFNFNNNONN	NNNN3NNNNNNNNNN	V,D,P,J	295	501	05.02.07	1342	520903	15023
184.167-190	SUPERINTENDENT, MEASUREMENT (petrol. & gas; pipe lines)	5548	22222344455	SNNNNNNNOOONFFNFNNNNN	NNNN4NNNNNNNNNN	D,P,J	295	364	05.02.01	1342	000000	15023
184.167-194	SUPERINTENDENT, METERS (utilities)	5548	22222333355	LNNNNNNNOONNFFNONNONN	NNNN3NNNNNNNNNN	D,J,P	295	871	05.10.02	6000	150403	81002
184.167-198	SUPERINTENDENT, PIPELINES (pipe lines)	5558	22333244455	SNNNNNNNNNNNNFFNNNNNNN	ONNN4NNNNNNNNNN	V,D,P,J	014	856	05.02.01	1342	099999	81005
184.167-202	SUPERINTENDENT, POWER (r.r. trans.)	5448	22333355555	SNNNNNNNFFONFFNFNNNNN	ONNN2NNNNNNNNNN	D,J	295	871	05.02.01	1342	000000	15023
184.167-206	SUPERINTENDENT, STATIONS (motor trans.; r.r. trans.)	5546	22244244455	SNNNNNNNFFONFFNFNNNNN	NNNN3NNNNNNNNNN	D,J	295	851	11.05.02	1342	520903	15023
184.167-210	SUPERINTENDENT, SYSTEM OPERATION (utilities)	5548	11122244444	LNNNNNNNFFNNFFNFNNFOFNO	NNNN2NNNNNNNNNN	V,D,P,J	244	871	05.02.01	1343	150503	15023
184.167-214	SUPERINTENDENT, TERMINAL (water trans.)	5448	22223344455	SNNNNNNNNOOONFFNONNNNN	NNNN3NNNNNNNNNN	V,D	295	854	11.11.03	1342	520903	15023
184.167-218	SUPERINTENDENT, TESTS (utilities)	5549	22222344444	SNNNNNNFFNFNFNFNNFNN	NNNN4NNNNNNNNNN	V,D,P,J	244	871	05.01.03	1343	150404	15023
184.167-222	SUPERINTENDENT, TRANSMISSION (utilities)	5548	11122244444	LNNNNNNNFFNFNFNFNNOOFNN	ONNN3NNNNNNNNNN	V,D,P,J	244	871	05.02.01	1343	000000	39999
184.167-226	SUPERINTENDENT, TRANSPORTATION (any industry)	5458	22333344455	LNNNNNNNNOOONNFFNNONN	NNNN3NNNNNNNNNN	V,D,P	295	850	11.05.02	1342	520903	15023
184.167-230	SUPERVISOR OF COMMUNICATIONS (any industry)	4448	22343344455	SNNNNNNNNOOONNFFNNNONN	NNNN3NNNNNNNNNN	D,P,J,V	295	860	05.02.04	1341	099999	15023
184.167-234	SUPERVISOR OF WAY (r.r. trans.)	5547	22344244455	SNNNNNNNFFNFNFNFNNFOFNO	ONNN4NNNNNNNNNN	D,J	102	367	05.02.02	6318	000000	81005
184.167-238	SUPERVISOR, SEWER SYSTEM (waterworks)	5558	22222344455	LNNNNNNNFFNFNFNNFOFNNO	ONNN4NNNNNNNNNN	D,P,J,T	295	873	05.02.01	1343	000000	15023
184.167-242	SUPERVISOR, TERMINAL OPERATIONS (motor trans.)	4337	23344344455	LNNNONONOOONFFNFNNNON	NNNN3NNNNNNNNNN	V,D,P,J	295	850	11.05.02	1342	520903	15023
184.167-246	SUPERVISOR, WATERWORKS (waterworks)	5557	22233344454	LNNNNNNNFFFNFNNFNNNNN	ONNN4NNNNNNNNNN	D,P,J	014	873	05.02.01	1343	150506	15023
184.167-250	TARIFF PUBLISHING AGENT (business ser.)	4338	22333344454	SNNNNNNNFFNFNFNNNNFFN	NNNN3NNNNNNNNNN	D,J	282	850	11.04.04	1490	080299	39999
184.167-254	TERMINAL SUPERINTENDENT (r.r. trans.)	4348	22344244455	SNNNNNNNFFNFNFNNFONFON	NNNN4NNNNNNNNNN	D,P,V	295	851	11.11.03	1342	520903	15023
184.167-258	TESTING-AND-REGULATING CHIEF (tel. & tel.)	5448	33334444455	SNNNNNNNFFNFNFNNNNNNN	NNNN3NNNNNNNNNN	D,P	111	586	05.02.01	1341	000000	15023
184.167-262	TRAIN DISPATCHER (r.r. trans.)	4347	23344344454	SNNNNNNNFFNFNFNNNNFFN	NNNN4NNNNNNNNNN	D,J,P	013	851	07.04.05	8113	000000	81011
184.167-266	TRANSPORTATION-MAINTENANCE SUPERVISOR (any industry)	5448	22334344455	SNNNNNNNNOOONNFFNNNON	NNNN4NNNNNNNNNN	V,D,P,J	102	590	05.02.02	1342	000000	15023
184.167-270	WATER CONTROL SUPERVISOR (waterworks)	5448	22334344455	LONNNNNNNFFNFNFNNNFNN	ONNN3NNNNNNNNNN	V,D,P,J	014	873	05.02.01	1343	000000	15023
184.167-274	WHARFINGER, CHIEF (water trans.)	4337	22344334455	SNNNNNNNFFNFNFNNFONFON	NNNN3NNNNNNNNNN	V,D,J	295	854	11.11.03	1342	080709	15023
184.167-278	YARD MANAGER (r.r. trans.)	4348	23344334455	SNNNNNNNFFNFNFNNFNNFOFNO	NNNN4NNNNNNNNNN	V,D,P,J	013	851	11.11.03	8113	000000	19999
184.167-282	DIVISION ROAD SUPERVISOR (r.r. trans.)	4348	22333244444	LNNONONOOOONFFNFNNNON	NNNN4NNNNNNNNNON	D,P,J	295	851	05.02.02	1342	520205	15023
184.167-286	GENERAL CAR SUPERVISOR, YARD (r.r. trans.)	4337	33443354555	LNNNNNNNNOONNFNNNNNN	NNNN4NNNNNNNNNN	D,P,J	295	594	05.02.02	1342	520205	15023
184.167-290	SUPERVISOR, COMMUNICATIONS-AND-SIGNALS (r.r. trans.)	4448	33333344454	LNNNNNNNNOOONNFFNNNON	ONNN4NNNNNNNNNN	D,P,J	295	586	11.11.03	1342	520205	81011
184.167-294	SUPERVISOR, TRAIN OPERATIONS (r.r. trans.)	4348	23344344454	SNNNNNNNFFNFNNFNNNNN	NNNN3NNNNNNNNNN	D,P,J	295	850	05.02.02	1342	080709	15023
184.267-010	FREIGHT-TRAFFIC CONSULTANT (business ser.)	5448	22244334455	SNNNNNNNFFNFNFNNFNNN	NNNN3NNNNNNNNNN	P,I,J	282	850	11.05.02	1342	080709	19999
184.387-010	WHARFINGER (water trans.)	3325	33344334455	LNNNNNNNFFNNFNNNFOONO	FNNN3NNNNNNNNNN	V,J	232	854	07.02.04	4716	521401	55344

DOT #	DOT Title & Industry	Trng	Aptitude	Physical	Environment	Tempra	WkF	MPSMS	GOE	SOC	CIP	OES
185.117-010	MANAGER, DEPARTMENT STORE (retail trade)	5458	22244344455	SNNNNNNFFNNFFNONNNNN	NNNN3NNNNNNNNNN	V,D,J,P	295	881	11.05.02	1210	080705	19005
185.117-014	AREA SUPERVISOR, RETAIL CHAIN STORE (retail trade)	4347	22234243355	LNNNNNNFFNFFNNNNNNN	NNNN3NNNNNNNNNN	D,I,P,J	295	893	11.11.05	1390	080705	13011
185.137-010	MANAGER, FAST FOOD SERVICES (retail trade; wholesale tr.)	4445	33343334455	LNNNNNNFFNFNFNNFNN	NNNN3NNNNNNNNNN	V,D,P,J	146	881	11.11.04	1351	521401	15026
185.157-010	FASHION COORDINATOR (retail trade)	5457	22343344453	LNNNNNNFFOFFNFFFFF	NNNN3NNNNNNNNNN	P,I,J	292	881	11.09.01	1250	080102	13011
185.157-014	SUPERVISOR OF SALES (business ser.)	4447	22244344455	LNNNNNNFFFNFNFNNFNN	NNNN3NNNNNNNNNN	D,P,I	292	882	11.09.01	1250	080299	13011
185.157-018	WHOLESALER II (wholesale tr.)	5457	22244344454	SNNNNNNFFNNFNFNNNN	NNNN3NNNNNNNNNN	D,V,P,I,J	292	881	11.05.04	4020	521403	41002
185.164-010	SERVICE MANAGER (retail trade)	4337	33333433345	HNNNOOONFFONFFNFNNNNN	NNNN4NNNNNNNNNN	D,P,T,V	121	552	05.10.02	6000	089999	81002
185.167-010	COMMISSARY MANAGER (any industry)	4436	23344344455	LNNOOONFFNFFNFNFNN	NNNN3NNNNNNNNNN	V,D,P	292	380	11.11.05	4020	521401	41002
185.167-014	MANAGER, AUTOMOBILE SERVICE STATION (retail trade)	4447	33333333343	MOOOOOOFFOOFFNFNFFON	FOFF3NFNONNNNO	V,D,P,J	292	881	11.11.03	4020	521401	41002
185.167-018	MANAGER, DISTRIBUTION WAREHOUSE (wholesale tr.)	5346	23344344455	SNNNNNNFFNFFNFNNNNN	NNNN3NNNNNNNNNN	V,D,P,J	295	853	11.11.03	4020	081199	41002
185.167-022	MANAGER, FOOD CONCESSION (hotel & rest.)	3336	33334244455	LNNNNNNFFFNFFNFNFNN	NNNN4NNNNNNNNNN	D,P,J	295	903	09.04.01	4030	520902	41002
185.167-026	MANAGER, MACHINERY-OR-EQUIPMENT, RENTAL AND LEASING (any industry)	4446	33344444455	LNNNNNNFFNFNFNFNN	NNNN3NNNNNNNNNN	D,P	292	560	11.11.05	4010	010204	41002
185.167-030	MANAGER, MEAT SALES AND STORAGE (retail trade; wholesale tr.)	4336	33333333353	MNNNNNNFFONFFNFNNONN	NONN2NNNNNNNNNN	D,P,J	292	382	11.11.05	4020	521401	41002
185.167-034	MANAGER, MERCHANDISE (retail trade; wholesale tr.)	4347	22344344455	SNNNNNNFFNFFNFNNNNN	NNNN3NNNNNNNNNN	D,P,J	292	881	11.05.04	1240	080705	13008
185.167-038	MANAGER, PARTS (retail trade; wholesale tr.)	4337	22343344454	LNNNNNNFFFNFNFNFNN	NNNN3NNNNNNNNNN	D,P	292	591	11.11.05	4030	081203	41002
185.167-042	MANAGER, PROFESSIONAL EQUIPMENT SALES-AND-SERVICE (business ser.)	5447	22344344455	SNNNNNNFFNFFNFNFNN	NNNN3NNNNNNNNNN	V,D,P,I	292	589	11.05.04	1390	080299	19999
185.167-046	MANAGER, RETAIL STORE (retail trade)	4447	22344344455	LNNNNNNOFONFFNONNNNN	NNNN3NNNNNNNNNN	D,V,P,J	292	881	11.11.05	4030	080903	41002
185.167-050	MANAGER, TEXTILE CONVERSION (business ser.; wholesale tr.)	4446	23333244452	LNNNNNNFFFFFNFFNNOFN	NNNN4NNNNNNNNNN	D,P,J	292	420	11.11.05	4020	080299	41002
185.167-054	MANAGER, TOBACCO WAREHOUSE (wholesale tr.)	4338	23344344455	LNNNNNNFFNFFNFNNNNN	NNNN4NNNNNNNNNN	D,P,I	292	302	11.11.05	4020	521401	41002
185.167-058	SERVICE MANAGER (automotive ser.)	4346	22344344455	LNNNNNNFFNFFNFNNFNN	NNNN4NNNNNNNNNN	V,D,P,J	111	590	05.10.02	6000	081203	81002
185.167-062	SUPERVISOR, LIQUOR STORES AND AGENCIES (government ser.)	5448	33344445554	SNNNNNNFFNFFNFNNFON	NNNN3NNNNNNNNNN	D,P,J	292	395	11.05.03	1139	080705	19005
185.167-066	VENDING-STAND SUPERVISOR (government ser.)	5447	22333344454	LNNNNNNFFNFFNFNNOON	NNNN3NNNNNNNNNN	V,D,P,J	295	881	09.04.01	4030	080706	41002
185.167-070	WHOLESALER I (wholesale tr.)	5548	22243344455	SNNNNNNFFNFFNFNFNNN	ONNN3NNNNNNNNNN	D,P	292	882	11.05.04	4020	080601	41002
185.167-074	MANAGER, AUTO SPECIALTY SERVICES (automotive ser.)	5447	22343344455	SNNNNNNNNOONFFNONNNNN	NNNN3NNNNNNNNNN	D,P,J	295	591	11.11.04	6000	470604	81002
186.117-010	BUSINESS MANAGER, COLLEGE OR UNIVERSITY (education)	5558	11144244455	SNNNNNNFFNFFNFNNNNN	NNNN3NNNNNNNNNN	D,P,J	295	890	11.05.02	1281	000000	15005
186.117-018	CUSTOMS BROKER (financial)	5457	22254344454	SNNOONOOONCNCNNFON	ONNN3NNNNNNNNNN	T,P,J	232	859	11.04.04	1390	521401	19999
186.117-022	DEPUTY INSURANCE COMMISSIONER (government ser.)	5558	22343344455	SNNNNNNFFNFFNFNNNNN	ONNN3NNNNNNNNNN	V,D,P,J	295	895	11.10.01	1139	000000	19005
186.117-026	GENERAL CLAIMS AGENT (air trans.; motor trans.; r.r. trans.; water trans.)	4448	22344344455	SNNNNNNFFONFFNFNNNNN	NNNN3NNNNNNNNNN	D,J,P	295	895	11.12.01	1490	000000	39999
186.117-030	MANAGER, BROKERAGE OFFICE (financial)	5458	22255244555	SNNNNNNFFNNOOONFFNNN	NNNN2NNNNNNNNNN	D,I,P,J	295	894	11.05.04	1210	521401	19005
186.117-034	MANAGER, LAND DEVELOPMENT (real estate)	5558	21143244455	LNNNNNNFFNFFNFNFOOOOO	ONNN3NNNNNNNNNN	D,I,J,P	295	895	11.05.01	1353	049999	15011
186.117-046	MANAGER, LEASING (petrol. & gas)	5558	12244344455	SNNNNNNNNOONFFNFFNNN	NNNN3NNNNNNNNNN	D,P,J	295	895	11.12.02	1353	521401	15011
186.117-054	PRESIDENT, FINANCIAL INSTITUTION (financial)	6559	11244344455	SNNNNNNOOONFFNFNNNNN	NNNN2NNNNNNNNNN	D,J,P	295	894	11.05.01	1210	000000	19005
186.117-058	REAL-ESTATE AGENT (profess. & kin.)	5558	22233344455	LNNNNNNOOONFFNFNNNNN	ONNN3NNNNNNNNNN	D,P,I,J	295	895	11.12.02	1353	521501	15011
186.117-062	RENTAL MANAGER, PUBLIC EVENTS FACILITIES (business ser.)	5448	22344344455	LNNNNNNNNOONFFNFFNNN	NNNN3NNNNNNNNNN	V,D,P	292	895	11.12.02	1353	080299	15011
186.117-066	RISK AND INSURANCE MANAGER (any industry)	5448	22244344455	SNNNNNNFFNFFNFNNNNN	NNNN3NNNNNNNNNN	D,P	295	895	11.06.03	1419	000000	13002
186.117-070	TREASURER, FINANCIAL INSTITUTION (financial)	5559	22244344455	SNNNNNNNNOONCNFNNONN	NNNN2NNNNNNNNNN	D,J,P	295	894	11.06.05	1220	000000	13002
186.117-074	TRUST OFFICER (financial)	5457	22244344455	LNNNNNNOOFNCCNFNNONN	NNNN2NNNNNNNNNN	D,I,T,P,J	272	894	11.06.05	1419	521401	21199
186.117-078	VICE PRESIDENT, FINANCIAL INSTITUTION (financial)	5558	11244344455	SNNNNNNFFONFFNFNNNNN	NNNN2NNNNNNNNNN	D,P,J	295	894	11.05.02	1220	000000	13002
186.117-082	FOREIGN-EXCHANGE DEALER (financial)	5448	22543244455	SNNNNNNNNOOONCNCNNNNN	NNNN2NNNNNNNNNN	D,J,P	232	894	11.06.03	1419	080401	21199
186.117-086	MANAGER, EXCHANGE FLOOR (financial)	5458	11255244454	SNNNNNNFFONCCNCNNNNN	NNNN3NNNNNNNNNN	D,I,P,J	295	895	11.05.04	4010	000000	13002
186.137-014	OPERATIONS OFFICER (financial)	5447	23344344455	SNNNNNNNNOOONFFNNNONN	NNNN2NNNNNNNNNN	D,P,T,J	232	894	11.06.01	1419	081001	21199
186.167-010	ESTATE PLANNER (insurance)	5457	11244344455	SNNNNNNFFNFFNFNNNNN	NNNN3NNNNNNNNNN	P,J	292	880	08.01.02	1419	081001	21199
186.167-018	MANAGER, APARTMENT HOUSE (real estate)	4345	33344344455	LONONNONFFNFFNFNNNNN	ONNN3NNNNNNNNNN	D,J,V,P	295	895	11.11.01	1353	521401	15011
186.167-030	MANAGER, HOUSING PROJECT (profess. & kin.)	5447	22244244455	SNNNNNNOOONFFNCNNONN	NNNN2NNNNNNNNNN	D,P,I	295	894	11.05.03	1353	080401	13002
186.167-034	MANAGER, INSURANCE OFFICE (insurance)	5458	11255244455	LNNNNNNFFONCNCNNNNNO	NNNN2NNNNNNNNNN	D,J,P	295	895	11.11.04	4010	081001	41002
186.167-038	MANAGER, LAND LEASES-AND-RENTALS (petrol. & gas)	4447	23344344455	SNNNNNNFFNFFNFNNNNN	NNNN3NNNNNNNNNN	D,P,J	232	895	11.05.02	1353	521501	15011
186.167-042	MANAGER, MARKET (retail trade; wholesale tr.)	4337	22333344455	SNNNNNNNOOONFFNNONNNN	NNNN3NNNNNNNNNN	D,P,J	292	880	11.11.05	1353	080601	15011
186.167-046	MANAGER, PROPERTY (real estate)	4348	22244344455	LONONNONFFONFFNFNNNNN	ONNN3NNNNNNNNNN	D,P	295	895	11.11.04	1353	521501	15011
186.167-054	RESERVE OFFICER (financial; insurance)	5549	22244244455	SNNNNNNNNOOONFFNCNNONN	NNNN2NNNNNNNNNN	D,P,J	295	894	11.06.03	1220	080401	13002
186.167-062	CONDOMINIUM MANAGER (real estate)	4347	22343234455	LNNNONONOOONFFNFNNNNN	ONNN3NNNNNNNNNN	D,P,J	295	895	11.11.01	1353	521501	15011
186.167-066	MANAGER, REAL-ESTATE FIRM (real estate)	4348	22233334445	LONNNNNNFFONFFNFNNNNN	ONNN3NNNNNNNNNN	D,I,P,J	295	895	11.11.04	4123	521501	15011

DOT #	DOT Title & Industry	Trng	Aptitude	Physical	Environment	Tempra	WkF	MPSMS	GOE	SOC	CIP	OES
186.167-070	ASSISTANT BRANCH MANAGER, FINANCIAL INSTITUTION (financial)	5457	22244244455	LNNONONOOONCONFONONN	NNNN3NNNNNNNNNN	D,P,J,T	295	894	11.11.04	1419	000000	21199
186.167-074	CLOSER (real estate)	4347	22233223355	SNNNNNNNFFNFNCNNNNNN	NNNN3NNNNNNNNNN	V,P,J,T	232	895	07.01.04	3960	000000	28399
186.167-078	COMMERCIAL LOAN COLLECTION OFFICER (financial)	5458	12344344455	SNNNNNNNOOONCCNCNNNNN	NNNN2NNNNNNNNNN	I,J,P	271	894	11.05.02	1415	000000	21108
186.167-082	FACTOR (financial)	5448	12244344455	SNNNNNNNFFONCNFNONNNN	NNNN2NNNNNNNNNN	J,P	232	894	11.06.03	1419	000000	21199
186.167-086	MANAGER, FINANCIAL INSTITUTION (financial)	5458	22244344455	SNNNNNNNFFONCCNFONONN	NNNN3NNNNNNNNNN	D,P,J	295	894	11.06.03	1220	080401	13002
186.167-090	MANAGER, TITLE SEARCH (real estate)	4447	22243344455	SNNNNNNNFFNFNFNNNN	NNNN3NNNNNNNNNN	D,P,J,V	295	895	11.11.04	1370	000000	15011
186.267-010	BONDING AGENT (business ser.)	4346	33455344455	SNNNNNNNFFNFFNFNNNN	NNNN3NNNNNNNNNN	V,P,J	295	899	07.04.01	1419	000000	21199
186.267-018	LOAN OFFICER (financial; insurance)	5447	23344344455	SNNNNNNNFFONCCNCNNNNN	NNNN2NNNNNNNNNN	P,J	271	894	11.06.03	1415	521401	21108
186.267-022	LOAN REVIEW ANALYST (financial)	5458	22244244455	SNNNNNNNOOONFFNCNNNNN	NNNN2NNNNNNNNNN	T,J	271	894	11.06.03	1419	080401	21108
186.267-026	UNDERWRITER, MORTGAGE LOAN (financial)	5458	12344344455	SNNNNNNNOOONOONCNNNNN	NNNN2NNNNNNNNNN	T,J	271	894	11.06.03	1415	000000	21108
187.117-010	ADMINISTRATOR, HEALTH CARE FACILITY (medical ser.)	5558	12344344455	SNNNNNNNOOOFFNFNNNNN	NNNN2NNNNNNNNNN	V,D,P,J	295	920	11.07.02	1210	000000	15008
187.117-018	DIRECTOR, INSTITUTION (any industry)	5458	12244444455	SNNNNNNNOOONFFNFNNNNN	NNNN2NNNNNNNNNN	D,P,J	295	931	11.07.01	1210	000000	19005
187.117-022	DISTRICT ADVISER (nonprofit org.)	5458	22344444455	SNNNNNNNOOOFFNONNNNN	NNNN3NNNNNNNNNN	D,I,P,V	295	941	11.07.01	1270	000000	19999
187.117-026	EXECUTIVE DIRECTOR, SHELTERED WORKSHOP (nonprofit org.)	5448	33333343455	LNNNNNNNFFNFFNFNNNN	NNNN3NNNNNNNNNN	D,P,J	295	943	11.07.01	1270	000000	19999
187.117-030	EXECUTIVE VICE PRESIDENT, CHAMBER OF COMMERCE (nonprofit org.)	5558	22244444455	SNNNNNNNONONFFNONNNN	NNNN3NNNNNNNNNN	D,I,P,J	295	893	11.05.02	1354	000000	19999
187.117-034	GENERAL MANAGER, ROAD PRODUCTION (amuse. & rec.)	4348	22332344455	SNNNNNNNONONFFNONNNN	NNNN3NNNNNNNNNN	V,D,P,J	295	919	11.11.01	1352	520901	19999
187.117-038	MANAGER, HOTEL OR MOTEL (hotel & rest.)	5447	22244244455	SNNNNNNNOOOFFNFNNNNN	NNNN3NNNNNNNNNN	D,V,P,J	295	902	11.11.01	1351	520901	15026
187.117-042	MANAGER, RECREATION ESTABLISHMENT (amuse. & rec.)	5447	22344344455	LNNNNNNNFFONFNNONNNN	NNNN4NNNNNNNNNN	V,D,P	295	919	11.11.02	1352	520901	19999
187.117-046	PROGRAM DIRECTOR, GROUP WORK (profess. & kin.)	5558	11344444455	LNNNNNNNFFONFFNFNNNN	NNNN3NNNNNNNNNN	V,D,P	295	941	11.07.01	1352	200203	19999
187.117-050	PUBLIC HEALTH SERVICE OFFICER (government ser.)	5558	11222334444	SNNNNNNNOOOFFNFOOOOO	NNNN3NNNNNNNNNN	D,P	295	941	11.07.01	1270	000000	21911
187.117-054	SUPERINTENDENT, RECREATION (government ser.)	5358	11244344455	LNNNNNNNFFNFFNFNNNN	NNNN3NNNNNNNNNN	V,D,P,J	295	920	11.10.03	1132	000000	19005
187.117-058	DIRECTOR, OUTPATIENT SERVICES (medical ser.)	6568	12222233353	SNNNNNNNFFNFFNFNNNFN	NNNN3NNNNNNNNNN	D,P,V	295	941	11.07.04	1132	080903	19005
187.117-062	RADIOLOGY ADMINISTRATOR (medical ser.)	5557	22243254454	SNNNNNNNOOONFFNONNOON	NNNN3NNNNNNNNNN	D,V,P,J	295	920	11.07.02	1310	000000	15008
187.134-010	EXECUTIVE DIRECTOR, RED CROSS (nonprofit org.)	5458	11344344455	LNNNNNNNOOONFFNONNOON	NNNN3NNNNNNNNNN	D,I,P,J	295	925	11.07.02	1310	000000	13014
187.134-014	SUPERVISOR, CONTRACT-SHELTERED WORKSHOP (nonprofit org.)	4337	33333333345	SNNNNNNNOOONFFNFNNNN	NNNN3NNNNNNNNNN	D,V,P,J	296	941	11.07.01	1270	000000	31311
187.137-014	SUPERVISOR, VOLUNTEER SERVICES (profess. & kin.)	4347	22344345455	LNNNNNNNFFNFFNFNNNN	NNNN3NNNNNNNNNN	D,I,V,P,J	298	931	11.07.03	2032	000000	27305
187.137-018	MANAGER, FRONT OFFICE (hotel & rest.)	4446	22344244455	LNNNNNNNFFONFNNONNNN	NNNN3NNNNNNNNNN	D,V,P,J	282	902	11.07.01	1351	080902	15026
187.161-010	EXECUTIVE CHEF (hotel & rest.)	5438	22343244353	LNNNNNNNFFONFNONNNON	NNON3NNNNNNNNNN	V,D,P,J	146	903	11.05.02	1351	120505	15026
187.161-014	MANAGER, HANDICRAFT-OR-HOBBY SHOP (amuse. & rec.)	4447	22323322354	LNNNNNNNFFONFNONNNNN	NNNN4NNNNNNNNNN	V,D,P,J	295	919	11.11.02	1352	520901	19999
187.167-010	APPLIANCE-SERVICE SUPERVISOR (utilities)	4447	22323344454	SNNNNNNNOOOFFNFNNNNN	NNNN3NNNNNNNNNN	D,J,P	295	880	05.02.06	6000	520205	81002
187.167-014	BOOKMAKER (amuse. & rec.)	4336	33344343355	SNNNNNNNOONFFNFNNNNN	NNNN3NNNNNNNNNN	V,D,P,J	295	913	11.06.03	1352	000000	19999
187.167-018	BUSINESS REPRESENTATIVE, LABOR UNION (profess. & kin.)	5348	22334444445	SNNNNNNNFFNFFNFNNNN	NNNN3NNNNNNNNNN	P,V	295	890	11.05.02	1354	000000	19999
187.167-022	COORDINATOR, VOLUNTEER SERVICES (social ser.)	5357	22344244355	SNNNNNNNOOONFFNFNNNN	NNNN3NNNNNNNNNN	D,J,P	295	940	11.07.01	1359	000000	19999
187.167-026	DIRECTOR, FOOD SERVICES (hotel & rest.)	5447	22244344454	SNNNNNNNFFNFFNFNNNN	NNNN3NNNNNNNNNN	D,P,J	295	903	11.11.04	1351	520902	15026
187.167-030	DIRECTOR, FUNERAL (personal ser.)	4447	22333344454	LNNNNNNNFFOFFNFNNNN	NNNN3NNNNNNNNNN	V,D,P,J	291	907	11.11.04	1359	080299	39011
187.167-034	DIRECTOR, NURSES' REGISTRY (medical ser.)	5456	22334244455	SNNNNNNNOOONFFNONNNN	NNNN3NNNNNNNNNN	D,P	295	943	07.01.02	1359	000000	19999
187.167-038	DIRECTOR, VOLUNTEER SERVICES (social ser.)	5447	22344344455	SNNNNNNNFFNFFNFNNNN	NNNN3NNNNNNNNNN	D,P	295	941	11.07.02	1270	000000	19999
187.167-042	DIVISION MANAGER, CHAMBER OF COMMERCE (nonprofit org.)	5457	22344345455	LNNNNNNNFFNFFNFNNNN	NNNN3NNNNNNNNNN	V,D,P	295	953	11.05.02	1354	000000	19999
187.167-046	EXECUTIVE HOUSEKEEPER (any industry)	5448	22333344454	LNNNNNNNFFNCNFNNNON	NNNO4NNNNNNNNNN	D,P,J	295	900	11.11.01	1351	200605	15026
187.167-050	MANAGER, AGRICULTURAL-LABOR CAMP (profess. & kin.)	5447	22344244355	LNNNNNNNOOOFFNFNNNON	ONNN3NNNNNNNNNN	D,P,V	295	940	11.07.01	1351	000000	61099
187.167-054	MANAGER, AQUATIC FACILITY (amuse. & rec.)	5447	22244344454	SNNNNNNNFFNFNFNNNON	NNNN4NNNNNNNNNN	V,D,P	295	919	11.11.02	1352	520901	15026
187.167-058	MANAGER, BARBER OR BEAUTY SHOP (personal ser.)	4447	22233345454	LNNNNNNNFFOFFNFNOOON	NNNN3NNNNNNNNNN	V,D,P,J	295	904	11.11.04	1359	080299	39011
187.167-062	MANAGER, BRANCH OPERATION EVALUATION (hotel & rest.)	4346	33333343454	LNNOOONFFOFFNFNNNON	ONNN4NNNNNNNNNN	D,J	271	902	11.05.02	5251	120403	21911
187.167-066	MANAGER, CAMP (construction; logging)	4336	33333333454	LNNNNNNOOONFFNFNNNN	ONNN3NNNNNNNNNN	D,J	271	900	05.10.04	1473	080902	19999
187.167-070	MANAGER, CASINO (amuse. & rec.)	4447	33344344445	LNNNNNNNOOONFFNFNNNN	ONNN3NNNNNNNNNN	V,D,J	291	919	11.11.02	1359	000000	15026
187.167-074	MANAGER, CEMETERY (real estate)	4447	22333344455	LNNNNNNNOOONCCNFNNNNN	ONNN3NNNNNNNNNN	V,D,P	295	907	11.11.04	1351	521401	19999
187.167-078	MANAGER, CONVENTION (hotel & rest.)	5447	22333334454	LNNNNNNNOOONFFNFOOONO	NNNO4NNNNNNNNNN	V,D,P	295	902	11.11.01	1351	520902	15026
187.167-082	MANAGER, CUSTOMER SERVICES (business ser.; retail trade)	4448	33333334435	LNNNNNNNFFNFNFFOOONO	NNNO4NNNNNNNNNN	D,J,P	295	900	05.10.02	1390	010204	19999
187.167-086	MANAGER, DANCE STUDIO (education)	4346	34343334435	LNNNNNNNOOONCCNFNNNN	NNNN4NNNNNNNNNN	D,I,J,T	292	560	01.05.01	1352	000000	19999
187.167-090	MANAGER, DENTAL LABORATORY (protective dev.)	5447	23333333454	LNNNNNNNFFOFFNFNFOFON	NNNN3NNNNNNNNNN	V,D,P,J	295	925	05.05.11	1359	510603	19999
187.167-094	MANAGER, DUDE RANCH (amuse. & rec.)	4447	33344344454	LNNNNNNNOOONFFNFNNNN	FNNN3NNNNNNNNNN	V,D,P	295	919	11.11.02	1352	520901	19999

DOT #	DOT Title & Industry	Trng	Aptitude	Physical	Environment	Tempra	WkF	MPSMS	GOE	SOC	CIP	OES
187.167-098	MANAGER, EMPLOYMENT AGENCY (profess. & kin.)	4347	22344344455	SNNNNNNOOONFFNONNNNN	NNNN3NNNNNNNNN	D,J,V	295	943	11.11.04	4010	080299	41002
187.167-102	MANAGER, FISH-AND-GAME CLUB (amuse. & rec.)	4446	22344344445	LNNNNNNOOONFFNONNNON	FNNN3NNNNNNNNN	V,D,P,J	001	919	11.11.02	1352	080903	19999
187.167-106	MANAGER, FOOD SERVICE (hotel & rest.; personal ser.)	4447	22244344454	LNNNNNNFFONFFNONNNON	NNNN3NNNNNNNNN	D,V,P,J	295	903	11.11.04	1351	120507	15026
187.167-114	MANAGER, GOLF CLUB (amuse. & rec.)	4446	22244244455	SNNNNNNFFONFFNFNNNNN	NNNN3NNNNNNNNN	V,D,P,J	295	913	11.11.02	1352	080903	19999
187.167-118	MANAGER, GUN CLUB (amuse. & rec.)	4346	22333343455	LNNNNNNFFONFFNFNNNNN	NNNN4NNNNNNNNN	V,D,P,J,T	295	913	11.11.02	1352	521401	19999
187.167-122	MANAGER, HOTEL RECREATIONAL FACILITIES (amuse. & rec.)	4447	22343344455	LNNNNNNFFONFFNFNNNNN	NNNN3NNNNNNNNN	D,P,V	295	919	11.11.02	1351	080903	15026
187.167-126	MANAGER, LIQUOR ESTABLISHMENT (hotel & rest.)	4446	33343344455	LNNNNNNFFONFFNFFOOOO	NNNN4NNNNNNNNN	V,D,P,J	295	903	11.11.04	1351	521401	15026
187.167-130	MANAGER, MARINE SERVICE (ship-boat mfg.)	4338	23322244344	LOOOOOFFOFFNFOOOO	FNNO4NNNNNNNNN	V,D,P,J	102	593	05.05.09	6000	490306	81002
187.167-134	MANAGER, MUTUEL DEPARTMENT (amuse. & rec.)	4445	22224244455	SNNNNNNFFNFFNONNNNN	NNNN3NNNNNNNNN	V,D,P,T	295	892	07.03.01	1352	520204	19999
187.167-138	MANAGER, SALES (laundry & rel.)	4447	22344445554	LNNNNNNOOONFFNONNFNN	NNNN3NNNNNNNNN	D,P,J	291	906	11.11.04	4010	521401	41002
187.167-142	MANAGER, SERVICE DEPARTMENT (wholesale tr.)	4447	22333344455	LNNOOOO4OFNFFNFNNNNN	NNNN4NNNNNNNNN	V,D,J	121	562	11.11.04	6000	010204	81002
187.167-146	MANAGER, SKATING RINK (amuse. & rec.)	4446	32334344445	LNNNNNNFFFNFFNFOOOON	NNNN4NNNNNNNNN	V,D,P,J	295	919	11.11.02	1352	080903	19999
187.167-150	MANAGER, STORAGE GARAGE (automotive ser.)	3336	33344344444	LNNNNNNFFFNFFNFOOOOO	NNNN3NNNNNNNNN	V,D,P	295	961	11.11.03	8111	521401	81011
187.167-154	MANAGER, THEATER (amuse. & rec.)	5347	22344344455	LNNNNNNOOOFCCNONNNNN	NNNN3NNNNNNNNN	D,I,V,P,J	295	911	11.11.02	1352	080903	19999
187.167-158	MANAGER, TRAVEL AGENCY (business ser.; retail trade)	4447	33344344454	LNNNNNNOOONFFNNNNNNN	NNNN3NNNNNNNNN	D,J,P,V	295	850	11.11.04	1359	521401	19999
187.167-162	MANAGER, VEHICLE LEASING AND RENTAL (automotive ser.)	5448	23344345455	LNNNNNNNOONFFNONNNNN	NNNN3NNNNNNNNN	D,I,J,V	295	859	11.11.05	1250	081299	13011
187.167-166	MANAGER, WINTER SPORTS (amuse. & rec.)	4446	22344344445	LNNNNNNOOONFFNFOOONO	ONNN4NNNNNNNNN	V,D,P,J	295	902	11.11.02	1352	520901	19999
187.167-170	MANAGER, WORLD TRADE AND MARITIME DIVISION (nonprofit org.)	5457	22344444455	SNNNNNNOOONFFNFNNNNN	NNNN3NNNNNNNNN	D,I,P	295	741	11.05.02	1354	521401	19999
187.167-174	PRODUCER (motion picture)	6568	12224444455	LNNNNNNFFNFFNFOOOOO	NNNN3NNNNNNNNN	D,P,J	295	754	01.01.01	3240	520901	34056
187.167-178	PRODUCER (amuse. & rec.)	5457	22342444454	LNNNNNNFFNFFNFNNNON	NNNN3NNNNNNNNN	V,D,P,J	295	754	01.03.01	3240	520901	34056
187.167-182	PRODUCER, ASSISTANT (motion picture)	5557	22333444455	SNNNNNNOOONFFNFNNNNN	NNNN3NNNNNNNNN	D,P,V	295	754	11.05.02	3240	000000	34056
187.167-186	RESIDENCE SUPERVISOR (any industry)	4346	33344344455	SNNNNNNFFNFFNONNNNN	NNNN3NNNNNNNNN	V,D,P	295	942	11.07.01	2032	200203	27307
187.167-190	SUPERINTENDENT, BUILDING (any industry)	4447	23223344454	LNNNNNNFFNFFNFOOOON	NNNN3NNNNNNNNN	V,D,P,J	295	900	05.02.02	1353	521401	15011
187.167-194	SUPERINTENDENT, LAUNDRY (laundry & rel.)	4337	22334344455	LNNNNNNFFNFFNFNFNN	NNNN3NNNNNNNNN	D,V,P,J	295	906	11.11.04	1359	200301	39999
187.167-198	VETERANS CONTACT REPRESENTATIVE (nonprofit org.)	5457	22344244455	SNNNNNNFFNFFNFNNNNN	NNNN3NNNNNNNNN	D,P,I	271	941	10.01.02	1490	000000	19999
187.167-202	DIRECTOR, CRAFT CENTER (profess. & kin.)	5457	22232223242	LNNNNNNFFNFFNFNNNNN	NNNN3NNNNNNNNN	D,E,I,P	295	919	11.07.04	1352	000000	19999
187.167-206	DIETARY MANAGER (hotel & rest.)	5558	22233354554	SNNNNNNOOONFFFNNNNNN	NNNN3NNNNNNNNN	D,I,V,P,J	295	903	11.11.04	1351	200409	15026
187.167-210	DIRECTOR, FOOD AND BEVERAGE (amuse. & rec.)	4448	22233344454	LNNNNNNFFNFFNFFNNON	NNNN3NNNNNNNNN	D,T,J,P	295	903	11.11.04	1351	200409	15026
187.167-214	DIRECTOR, SERVICE (nonprofit org.)	5358	12334344355	MNNNNNNFFONFFNFNNNON	NNNN3NNNNNNNNN	D,J,P,V	295	941	11.07.03	1270	000000	19999
187.167-218	MANAGER, ANIMAL SHELTER (nonprofit org.)	5356	22343344455	LNNNNNNFFONFFNFNNNNN	NNNN3NNNNNNNNN	D,J,P,V	295	890	11.07.01	1359	000000	19999
187.167-222	MANAGER, BOWLING ALLEY (amuse. & rec.)	4235	32333344444	LNNNNNNOOONFFNONNNNN	NNNN3NNNNNNNNN	D,P,V	295	919	11.11.02	1352	520901	19999
187.167-226	MANAGER, MARINA DRY DOCK (amuse. & rec.; water trans.)	4336	22334334235	HNNNNNNFFNFFNFNNNNN	NNNN3NNNNNNNNN	D,P,V,J	295	854	05.02.07	1359	520901	19999
187.167-230	MANAGER, RECREATION FACILITY (amuse. & rec.)	4346	22344344455	LNNNNNNFFNNNNFFNNNNN	NNNN3NNNNNNNNN	D,P,V	295	910	11.11.02	1352	520901	19999
187.167-234	DIRECTOR, COMMUNITY ORGANIZATION (nonprofit org.)	5348	22344344455	SNNNNNNOOONFFNFNNNNN	NNNN3NNNNNNNNN	D,V,P,J	295	870	11.07.01	1270	200203	19999
187.167-238	RECREATION SUPERVISOR (profess. & kin.)	5357	11333344444	LNNNNNNOOONFNFFFFOF	NNNN3NNNNNNNNN	J	295	959	11.07.04	1352	080903	27311
188.117-010	APPRENTICESHIP CONSULTANT (government ser.)	5458	22233344454	LNNNNNNFFFNFFNFNNNNN	NNNN3NNNNNNNNN	J	295	959	11.07.03	1132	000000	13005
188.117-014	BUSINESS-ENTERPRISE OFFICER (government ser.)	5456	22222344455	LNNNNNNFFONFFNFNNNNN	NNNN3NNNNNNNNN	D,J	295	941	11.07.01	1132	000000	19005
188.117-018	CHIEF, FISHERY DIVISION (government ser.)	5458	22343344455	LNNNNNNOOONFFNFNNNNN	NNNN3NNNNNNNNN	D,P,J	295	330	03.01.02	1133	030203	19005
188.117-022	CIVIL PREPAREDNESS OFFICER (government ser.)	5356	21333343344	LNNNNNNOOONFFNONNNNN	NNNN3NNNNNNNNN	D,I,V	295	952	11.05.03	1131	000000	19005
188.117-026	COMMISSIONER, CONSERVATION OF RESOURCES (government ser.)	5448	22344344455	SNNNNNNOOONFFNFNNNNN	NNNN3NNNNNNNNN	V,D,P,J,E	295	959	11.05.03	1133	000000	19005
188.117-030	COMMISSIONER, PUBLIC WORKS (government ser.)	5558	22344344455	SNNNNNNOOONFFNFNNNNN	NNNN3NNNNNNNNN	V,D,P,J	295	870	11.05.03	1134	000000	19005
188.117-034	DIRECTOR, AERONAUTICS COMMISSION (government ser.)	5558	22333344555	SNNNNNNOOONFFNNNNNNN	NNNN3NNNNNNNNN	D,P,J	295	959	11.05.03	1139	000000	19005
188.117-038	DIRECTOR, AGRICULTURAL SERVICES (government ser.)	5558	22243344455	LNNNNNNOOONFFNFNNNNN	NNNN3NNNNNNNNN	V,D,P	295	959	11.05.03	1132	000000	19005
188.117-042	DIRECTOR, ARTS-AND-HUMANITIES COUNCIL (government ser.)	5558	22333344455	LNNNNNNOOONFFNFNNNNN	NNNN3NNNNNNNNN	V,D,P	295	959	11.05.03	1132	000000	19005
188.117-046	DIRECTOR, COMPLIANCE (government ser.)	5457	22244344455	LNNNNNNOOONFFNFNNNNN	NNNN3NNNNNNNNN	D,P	295	959	11.10.02	1132	000000	19005
188.117-050	DIRECTOR, CONSUMER AFFAIRS (government ser.)	5558	22244344455	LNNNNNNOOONFFNFNNNNN	NNNN3NNNNNNNNN	D,P,V	295	959	11.10.02	1132	000000	19005
188.117-054	DIRECTOR, CORRECTIONAL AGENCY (government ser.)	6558	11233344455	LNNNNNNOOONFFNFNNNNN	NNNN3NNNNNNNNN	V,D,P	295	959	11.05.03	1131	000000	19005
188.117-058	DIRECTOR, COUNCIL ON AGING (government ser.)	5458	22244344455	SNNNNNNFFFNFFNFNNNNN	NNNN3NNNNNNNNN	D,I,P,J	295	949	11.07.01	1132	000000	19005
188.117-062	DIRECTOR, FIELD REPRESENTATIVES (government ser.)	5558	22443344455	SNNNNNNOOONFFNFNNNNN	NNNN3NNNNNNNNN	D,P,J	295	959	11.07.03	1132	000000	19005
188.117-066	DIRECTOR, LABOR STANDARDS (government ser.)	5558	11233344455	LNNNNNNOOONFFNFNNNNN	NNNN3NNNNNNNNN	V,D,P	295	959	11.10.02	1132	000000	19005
188.117-070	DIRECTOR, LAW ENFORCEMENT (government ser.)	5557	22244344455	LNNNNNNOOONFFNFNNNNN	NNNN3NNNNNNNNN	V,D,P	295	951	11.05.03	1131	000000	19005

DOT #	DOT Title & Industry	Trng	Aptitude	Physical	Environment	Tempra	WkF	MPSMS	GOE	SOC	CIP	OES
188.117-074	DIRECTOR, LICENSING AND REGISTRATION (government ser.)	5558	22244344455	LNNNNNNOONNFFNFNNNNN	NNNN3NNNNNNNNNN	V,P,D	295	959	11.05.03	1135	000000	19005
188.117-078	DIRECTOR, EMPLOYMENT SERVICES (government ser.)	5558	22244344455	LNNNNNNOONNFFNFNNNNN	NNNN3NNNNNNNNNN	D,P,V	295	959	11.05.03	1132	000000	19005
188.117-082	DIRECTOR, MEDICAL FACILITIES SECTION (government ser.)	5558	22344444455	SNNNNNNVNFONFFNFNNNNN	NNNN3NNNNNNNNNN	D,P,J	295	920	11.10.03	1134	000000	19005
188.117-086	DIRECTOR, MERIT SYSTEM (government ser.)	4445	22243344455	LNNNNNNNOONNFFNFNNNNN	NNNN3NNNNNNNNNN	D,P,J	295	712	11.05.03	1370	000000	13005
188.117-090	DIRECTOR, REVENUE (government ser.)	6558	11244344455	LNNNNNNNFFONFFNNNNNN	NNNN3NNNNNNNNNN	V,D,P	295	959	11.05.03	1135	000000	19005
188.117-094	DIRECTOR, UNEMPLOYMENT INSURANCE (government ser.)	5558	11244344455	LNNNNNNNFFONFFNONNNN	NNNN3NNNNNNNNNN	V,D,P	295	959	11.05.03	1132	000000	19005
188.117-098	DISTRICT CUSTOMS DIRECTOR (government ser.)	5558	22344444455	SNNNNNNOONNFFNFNONNNN	NNNN3NNNNNNNNNN	D,V,P,J	295	953	11.10.04	1135	000000	19005
188.117-102	ECONOMIC DEVELOPMENT COORDINATOR (government ser.)	5458	22233344445	LNNNNNNNOONNFFNONFFNN	NNNN3NNNNNNNNNN	D,I,P,V	295	959	11.05.03	1134	000000	19005
188.117-106	FOREIGN-SERVICE OFFICER (government ser.)	5458	21333344455	SNNNNNNFFNFFNFNNNNN	NNNN3NNNNNNNNNN	E,I,J,P,V	295	959	11.09.03	1139	000000	19005
188.117-110	HOUSING-MANAGEMENT OFFICER (government ser.)	5348	22343244455	LNNNNNNOOFNFFNNNNNN	NNNN3NNNNNNNNNN	D,J	295	959	11.05.03	1134	000000	19005
188.117-114	MANAGER, CITY (government ser.)	5458	22344444455	LNNNNNNNOONNFFNFNNNNN	NNNN3NNNNNNNNNN	D,J,P,V	295	959	11.05.03	1120	000000	19002
188.117-118	POLICE COMMISSIONER I (government ser.)	5458	22344444455	SNNNNNNNOONNFFNFNONNNN	NNNN3NNNNNNNNNN	V,D,I,J	295	951	04.01.01	1131	000000	19005
188.117-122	PROPERTY-UTILIZATION OFFICER (government ser.)	5448	22333344454	LNNNNNNNFFONFFNFOONNNN	NNNN3NNNNNNNNNN	I,P,V,D,J	295	959	11.12.02	1370	000000	13014
188.117-126	WELFARE DIRECTOR (government ser.)	5558	22344344445	SNNNNNNNOONNFFNFNNNNN	NNNN3NNNNNNNNNN	V,D,P,J	295	941	11.07.01	1132	000000	19005
188.117-130	COURT ADMINISTRATOR (government ser.)	5458	22234244455	LNNNNNNNOOONFFNFNNNNN	NNNN3NNNNNNNNNN	D,I,J,P	295	959	11.05.03	1131	000000	19999
188.117-134	DIRECTOR, REGULATORY AGENCY (government ser.)	5458	22333244454	SNNNNNNNFFONFFNFNNNNN	NNNN3NNNNNNNNNN	D,P,V,J	295	950	11.05.03	1139	000000	19005
188.137-010	SUPERVISOR (government ser.)	5347	22344344455	LNNNNNNNOOONFFNONOONNN	NNNN3NNNNNNNNNN	D,V,P,J	271	950	11.05.03	9900	000000	19005
188.167-010	APPRAISER (government ser.)	5557	22233244444	LONNNNNNFFNNNNFOONNN	FNNN3NNNNNNNNNN	J	211	895	11.06.03	1473	000000	21917
188.167-014	ASSESSOR-COLLECTOR, IRRIGATION TAX (government ser.)	5558	22234244455	LNNNNNNNOONNFFNONNNN	NNNN3NNNNNNNNNN	D,I,J,P	295	953	11.05.03	1135	000000	19005
188.167-018	CHIEF WARDEN (government ser.)	5446	22344344455	LNNNNNNNOONNFFNONNNN	ONNN3NNNNNNNNNN	D,P,J	295	959	11.05.03	1133	000000	19005
188.167-022	DIRECTOR OF VITAL STATISTICS (government ser.)	5558	12143344455	SNNNNNNOONNFFNFNNNNN	NNNN3NNNNNNNNNN	D,P,J,E	295	721	11.01.02	1139	000000	15005
188.167-026	DIRECTOR, CLASSIFICATION AND TREATMENT (government ser.)	5457	22344344455	SNNNNNNNFFNFFNFNNNNN	NNNN3NNNNNNNNNN	D,P,J,E	295	949	11.07.01	1131	000000	19005
188.167-030	DIRECTOR, FINANCIAL RESPONSIBILITY DIVISION (government ser.)	4446	22344344455	LNNNNNNNOONNFFNFNNNNN	NNNN3NNNNNNNNNN	D,P,J	295	959	11.05.03	1135	000000	19005
188.167-034	DIRECTOR, SAFETY COUNCIL (government ser.)	5558	22333344455	V,D,P,J,I wait	NNNN3NNNNNNNNNN	V,D,P,J,I	295	712	11.05.03	1131	000000	19005
188.167-038	DIRECTOR, SECURITIES AND REAL ESTATE (government ser.)	5457	22444444455	SNNNNNNNOONNFFNFNNNNN	NNNN3NNNNNNNNNN	D,P,J,E	295	894	11.10.01	1473	000000	21911
188.167-042	DIRECTOR, STATE-ASSESSED PROPERTIES (government ser.)	5557	12133344455	SNNNNNNNOONNFFNONNNN	NNNN3NNNNNNNNNN	D,P,J,E	295	895	11.05.03	1135	000000	19005
188.167-046	DISTRICT CUSTOMS DIRECTOR, DEPUTY (government ser.)	5557	22244344455	SNNNNNNNOONNFFNFNNNNN	NNNN3NNNNNNNNNN	V,D,P,J	295	953	11.10.04	1135	000000	19005
188.167-050	ELECTION ASSISTANT (government ser.)	5347	22344344455	SNNNNNNNFFONFFNFNNNNN	NNNN3NNNNNNNNNN	P,D,J	295	959	11.05.03	1139	000000	19005
188.167-054	FEDERAL AID COORDINATOR (government ser.)	5457	22344444455	SNNNNNNFFONFFNFNNNNN	NNNN3NNNNNNNNNN	V,D,P,J	295	954	11.05.03	1133	000000	15002
188.167-058	MANAGER, OFFICE (government ser.)	4448	22233344455	SNNNNNNNFFNFNFNNNNN	NNNN3NNNNNNNNNN	D,J,P,V	271	953	04.01.02	1473	000000	21911
188.167-062	PARK SUPERINTENDENT (government ser.)	5347	22344344434	LOOOOOOFFONFFNFOOOOO	NNNN4NNNNNNNNNN	D,I,J,P,V	295	712	11.07.01	1133	030203	15005
188.167-066	POSTMASTER (government ser.)	4447	22344344455	SNNNNNNNFFONFFNFNNNNN	OOOO3NNNNNNNNNNO	V,D,P,J	295	954	04.01.01	1344	000000	15002
188.167-070	RELOCATION COMMISSIONER (government ser.)	5458	22333344455	LNNNNNNNOONNFFNOONONN	NNNN3NNNNNNNNNN	D,I,P,J	295	895	11.12.02	1134	000000	21999
188.167-074	REVENUE OFFICER (government ser.)	5447	22244344455	LNNNNNNNFFNFFNFNNNNN	NNNN3NNNNNNNNNN	D,I,J,P,S	232	953	11.10.01	1473	000000	21911
188.167-078	ROADS SUPERVISOR (government ser.)	5558	22323344455	SNNNNNNNOONNFFNONNNN	NNNN3NNNNNNNNNN	D,P,J	295	959	11.03.02	1920	000000	27105
188.217-010	COMMISSIONER OF CONCILIATION (government ser.)	5458	21333344455	LNNNNNNOFONFFNFOOONN	NNNN2NNNNNNNNNN	V,I,J	251	932	11.04.03	1139	000000	13005
189.117-010	ASSOCIATION EXECUTIVE (profess. & kin.)	5458	22244344455	LNNNNNNNOONNFFNONNNN	NNNN3NNNNNNNNNN	D,I,P,V	295	893	11.05.01	1354	000000	19999
189.117-014	DIRECTOR, RESEARCH AND DEVELOPMENT (any industry)	5558	22223444454	SNNNNNNNOONNFFNFNNNON	NNNN3NNNNNNNNNN	D,V,P,J	295	700	05.01.01	1260	521402	13017
189.117-018	MANAGER, CUSTOMER TECHNICAL SERVICES (profess. & kin.)	5448	22344344455	SNNNNNNNOONNFFNONNNN	NNNN3NNNNNNNNNN	D,P,J	295	880	05.02.03	1250	080799	13011
189.117-022	MANAGER, INDUSTRIAL ORGANIZATION (any industry)	5458	22233344455	LNNNNNNNOONNFFNFNNNNN	NNNN3NNNNNNNNNN	D,P,J	295	893	11.05.01	1210	000000	19005
189.117-026	PRESIDENT (any industry)	5558	22244344455	SNNNNNNNOONNFFNFNNNNN	NNNN3NNNNNNNNNN	D,V,P,J	295	893	11.05.01	1210	000000	19005
189.117-030	PROJECT DIRECTOR (profess. & kin.)	5558	22244344455	SNNNNNNNOONNFFNFNNNONN	NNNN2NNNNNNNNNN	D,J,P	295	720	11.05.02	1390	000000	19999
189.117-034	VICE PRESIDENT (any industry)	5458	22244344455	SNNNNNNNOONNFFNFNNFNN	NNNN3NNNNNNNNNN	V,D,P,J	295	893	11.05.02	1210	000000	19005

DOT #	DOT Title & Industry	Trng	Aptitude	Physical	Environment	Tempra	WkF	MPSMS	GOE	SOC	CIP	OES
189.117-038	USER REPRESENTATIVE, INTERNATIONAL ACCOUNTING (profess. & kin.)	5558	22132144455	SNNNNNNNFFNFFNFNNONN	NNNN3NNNNNNNNNNN	D,J,P,V	295	893	11.05.02	1390	000000	13002
189.117-042	DIRECTOR, QUALITY ASSURANCE (profess. & kin.)	5558	11144344455	LNNNNNNOOONFFNFNNNNN	NNNN3NNNNNNNNNNN	D,V,P,J	295	893	11.05.02	1320	000000	15014
189.117-046	MANAGER, BAKERY (bakery products)	5448	22244344455	SNNNNNNNNONFFNFNNNNN	NNNN3NNNNNNNNNNN	D,I,V,P,J	295	384	11.05.01	1210	080601	19005
189.157-010	BUSINESS-OPPORTUNITY-AND-PROPERTY-INVESTMENT BROKER (business ser.; real estate)	5447	22334344455	LNNNNNNOOONFFNONNNNN	ONNN3NNNNNNNNNNN	D,P,I,J	292	890	08.01.03	1353	521501	15011
189.167-010	CONSULTANT (profess. & kin.)	5558	22223344455	SNNNNNNNOOONFNFNNNNN	NNNN3NNNNNNNNNNN	D,J,P	244	720	11.01.02	9900	000000	00000
189.167-014	DIRECTOR, SERVICE (retail trade)	5447	22343344455	SNNNNNNNOOONFFNFNNNNN	NNNN3NNNNNNNNNNN	D,J,P	295	881	11.05.02	1390	080705	19999
189.167-018	MANAGEMENT TRAINEE (any industry)	5346	22334344455	LNNNNNNOOONFFNFONONN	NNNN3NNNNNNNNNNN	V,P,J	295	893	11.05.02	1390	521401	19999
189.167-022	MANAGER, DEPARTMENT (any industry)	5447	22333344455	SNNNNNNNOOONFFNFNNNNN	NNNN3NNNNNNNNNNN	D,P,J	295	893	11.05.02	1370	080705	13014
189.167-026	MEMBERSHIP DIRECTOR (profess. & kin.)	5447	22344344455	LNNNNNNNFFONFFNFNNNNN	NNNN3NNNNNNNNNNN	D,I,P,V	282	896	11.09.02	1450	000000	39999
189.167-030	PROGRAM MANAGER (profess. & kin.)	5558	22233244455	SNNNNNNNFFONFFNFNNNNN	NNNN3NNNNNNNNNNN	D,J,P	295	920	11.05.02	1370	520204	13014
189.167-034	SECURITY OFFICER (any industry)	4347	22344444455	SNNNNNNNFFONFNFNNNNN	NNNN3NNNNNNNNNNO	V,D,J	293	951	11.05.02	1490	000000	15023
189.167-038	SUPERINTENDENT, AMMUNITION STORAGE (ordnance)	4448	22233444454	LNNNNNNNFFONFNFOOOOO	FNNN3NNNNNNNNNNN	D,J,P,V	295	969	05.02.07	1342	000000	15014
189.167-042	SUPERINTENDENT, LABOR UTILIZATION (any industry)	4348	22222244444	LNNNNNNOOONFFNFNNNNN	NNNN3NNNNNNNNNON	D,V,P,J	295	893	05.05.02	1320	150603	15014
189.167-046	SUPERINTENDENT, MAINTENANCE (any industry)	5558	22222244444	SNNOONOONNFFNONNNNN	NNNN3NNNNNNNNNNO	V,D,P,J	293	951	11.05.02	1359	430109	19999
189.167-050	SUPERINTENDENT, PLANT PROTECTION (any industry)	5448	22344444455	LNNNNNNOONNFFNFNNNNF	NNNN3NNNNNNNNNNO	V,D,P,J	293	951	11.05.02	1359	430109	19999
189.167-054	SECURITY CONSULTANT (business ser.; personal ser.)	5357	23324344455	LNNNNNNOONNFFNFNNNF	NNNN3NNNNNNNNNNN	D,I,V,S,P	293	951	04.02.02	5144	430109	63035
189.267-010	FIELD REPRESENTATIVE (profess. & kin.)	5458	22344344455	SNNNNNNOONNFFNONNNNN	NNNN3NNNNNNNNNNN	P,I,J	211	940	11.07.01	2032	000000	27305
191.117-010	ARTIST'S MANAGER (amuse. & rec.)	5457	22344344455	SNNNNNNOOONFFNFNNNNN	NNNN4NNNNNNNNNNN	D,I,J,P	295	919	11.12.03	1450	080299	39999
191.117-014	BOOKING MANAGER (amuse. & rec.)	4446	33344244455	SNNNNNNOOONFFNFNNNNN	NNNN4NNNNNNNNNNN	P,I,J	292	910	11.12.03	1450	080903	39999
191.117-018	BUSINESS MANAGER (amuse. & rec.)	5457	22344244454	SNNNNNNNOONNFFNFNNNNN	NNNN3NNNNNNNNNNN	V,D,P,I,J	295	910	11.12.03	1450	080903	39999
191.117-022	CIRCUS AGENT (amuse. & rec.)	4347	22343344455	SNNNNNNOONNFFNONNNNN	NNNN3NNNNNNNNNNN	D,J	295	919	11.12.03	1450	520901	39999
191.117-026	JOCKEY AGENT (amuse. & rec.)	4345	32344344455	SNNNNNNOONNFFNONNNNN	FNNN4NNNNNNNNNNN	P,I,J	295	913	11.12.03	1450	080299	39999
191.117-030	LEASE BUYER (mine & quarry; petrol. & gas)	5457	22343344455	LNNNNNNOONNFFNONNNNN	NNNN3NNNNNNNNNNN	V,P,J,T	272	932	11.12.02	1353	521501	15011
191.117-034	LITERARY AGENT (business ser.)	5457	22333344455	SNNNNNNOOONFFNFNNNNN	NNNN3NNNNNNNNNNN	P,I	292	757	11.12.01	1450	080299	39999
191.117-038	MANAGER, TOURING PRODUCTION (amuse. & rec.)	4347	33344344455	SNNNNNNOOONFFNFNNNNN	NNNN3NNNNNNNNNNN	V,D,P,J	295	910	11.11.04	1450	520901	39999
191.117-042	PERMIT AGENT, GEOPHYSICAL PROSPECTING (petrol. & gas)	5456	22233344455	LNNNNNNOONNFFNFNONNN	ONNN4NNNNNNNNNNN	V,P,J	272	890	11.12.02	1353	521501	15011
191.117-046	RIGHT-OF-WAY AGENT (any industry)	5457	22333344455	LNNNNNNOONNFFNFNNNNN	ONNN3NNNNNNNNNNN	V,P,I	271	870	11.12.02	1353	521501	15011
191.117-050	RIGHT-OF-WAY SUPERVISOR (any industry)	5458	11233244444	LNNNNNNNFFNFFNFNNNNN	NNNN3NNNNNNNNNNN	V,D,P,I,J	272	895	11.12.02	1353	521401	15011
191.157-010	PAWNBROKER (retail trade)	4446	33343344453	LNNNNNNNFFOFNFNFFON	NNNN3NNNNNNNNNNN	V,P,J	211	894	08.01.03	4440	000000	49999
191.167-010	ADVANCE AGENT (amuse. & rec.)	4447	33334344455	LNNNNNNOOONFFNOONNNN	NNNN3NNNNNNNNNNN	D,P,J	291	910	11.12.03	1450	520901	39999
191.167-014	CLAIM AGENT (petrol. & gas; pipe lines)	6367	11344444455	SNNNNNNNFFNFFNFNNFONN	NNNN3NNNNNNNNNNN	V,P,J	271	932	11.12.01	1490	521501	39999
191.167-018	LOCATION MANAGER (motion picture; radio-tv broad.)	4346	22334344455	LNNNNNNOONNFFNONNNNN	ONNN3NNNNNNNNNNN	V,J,E	295	895	11.12.02	1390	521401	19999
191.167-022	SERVICE REPRESENTATIVE (auto. mfg.)	5447	22344344455	SNNNNNNNFFONFFNFNNFNN	NNNN2NNNNNNNNNNN	J,P	271	591	11.12.01	4783	081203	53123
191.267-010	APPRAISER, REAL ESTATE (real estate)	5447	22234244455	LONONONFFNFFNCOOONO	ONNN3NNNNNNNNNNN	P,J,V	211	895	11.06.03	4123	000000	43011
191.287-010	APPRAISER (any industry)	5557	23233344455	SNNNNNNFFONFFNFNNNNN	NNNN3NNNNNNNNNNN	D,T	211	899	11.06.03	4440	081203	49999
191.287-014	APPRAISER, ART (profess. & kin.)	5448	24324244441	LNNNONNFFNOOONFOOOOO	NNNN3NNNNNNNNNNN	J	211	539	01.02.01	4440	000000	49999
191.367-010	PERSONAL PROPERTY ASSESSOR (government ser.)	3334	33344344455	LNNNNNNOONNNNCFNFCN	NNNN2NNNNNNNNNNN	P,J	211	953	11.06.03	1473	000000	21917
193.162-010	AIR-TRAFFIC COORDINATOR (government ser.)	4348	22333344453	SNNNNNNNFFONFFNFONN	NNNN3NNNNNNNNNNN	V,S,J	281	855	05.03.03	3920	490105	39002
193.162-014	AIR-TRAFFIC-CONTROL SPECIALIST, STATION (government ser.)	4348	23344343354	LNNNNNNFFNFFNFNNFFN	ONNN3NNNNNNNNNNN	J,P,S,V,T	295	855	05.03.03	3920	490105	39002
193.162-018	AIR-TRAFFIC-CONTROL SPECIALIST, TOWER (government ser.)	5447	23323343353	LNNNNNNNFFNCCNFFFNFO	NNNN2NNNNNNNNNNN	V,S,T,J,P	281	855	05.03.03	3920	490105	39002
193.162-022	AIRLINE-RADIO OPERATOR, CHIEF (air trans.; business ser.)	4448	22333333344	SNNNNNNNOOONFFNFNNONN	ONNN3NNNNNNNNNNN	D,T	281	860	07.04.05	3930	000000	39008
193.167-010	CHIEF CONTROLLER (government ser.)	5447	22333344453	SNNNNNNFFONFFNFNNNNN	NNNN3NNNNNNNNNNN	D,J,P	281	855	05.03.03	3920	081203	39002
193.167-014	FIELD SUPERVISOR, BROADCAST (radio-tv broad.)	5457	22323333355	LNNNNNNOOONFFNONNONN	NNNN3NNNNNNNNNNN	V,D,P,J	295	860	05.03.05	3930	000000	39002
193.167-018	SUPERINTENDENT, RADIO COMMUNICATIONS (government ser.)	5458	22344344455	LNNNNNNOOONFFNNNNON	ONNN3NNNNNNNNNNN	D,P,J	281	959	05.02.04	3930	100104	15023
193.262-010	AIRLINE-RADIO OPERATOR (air trans.; business ser.)	4447	22343232254	SNNNNNNNFFONFFNFNNNON	NNNN3NNNNNNNNNNN	V,P,J	281	860	07.04.05	3930	490105	39008
193.262-014	DISPATCHER (government ser.)	4346	33444344355	SNNNNNNNOOONFFNFNNNNN	NNNN3NNNNNNNNNNN	V	281	860	07.04.05	1139	100104	34028
193.262-018	FIELD ENGINEER (radio-tv broad.)	5457	23323333353	LNNNNNNNFFNOONNNNON	ONNN3NNNNNNNNNNN	V,T,J	281	860	05.03.05	3930	100104	34028
193.262-022	RADIO OFFICER (water trans.)	4337	22332332244	SNNNNNNNFFONFFNFNNNNN	NNNN3NNNNNNNNNNN	J,T	281	586	07.04.05	3930	000000	34028
193.262-026	RADIO STATION OPERATOR (aircraft mfg.)	5446	22322433354	LNNNNNNNFFNFFNFFFFF	NNNN3NNNNNNNNNNN	T,P,J	281	861	07.04.05	3930	000000	39008
193.262-030	RADIOTELEGRAPH OPERATOR (tel. & tel.)	4237	33444232455	LNNNNNNFFNFFNFNNNNN	NNNN3NNNNNNNNNNN	J	111	860	07.04.05	3930	000000	39008
193.262-034	RADIOTELEPHONE OPERATOR (any industry)	4347	33322333355	LNNNNNNNFFONFFNFNNNNN	NNNN4NNNNNNNNNNN	V,P,T	281	860	05.03.05	3930	000000	39008

DOT #	DOT Title & Industry	Trng	Aptitude	Physical	Environment	Tempra	WkF	MPSMS	GOE	SOC	CIP	OES
193.262-038	TRANSMITTER OPERATOR (radio-tv broad.)	4447	22332432353	MONNNNNOOONONONOCFC	NNNN3NNNNNNNNNN	T,J	281	860	05.03.05	3930	100104	34028
193.362-010	PHOTORADIO OPERATOR (print. & pub.; tel. & tel.)	4446	33333332354	SNNNNNNFFONFFNFNNFFN	NNNN3NNNNNNNNNN	V,J,T	281	863	07.04.05	3930	470103	39008
193.362-014	RADIO-INTELLIGENCE OPERATOR (government ser.)	4346	33334344455	SNNNNNNNFFONFFNFNNNNN	NNNN3NNNNNNNNNN	R,J	281	959	05.03.05	3930	470103	39008
193.382-010	ELECTRONIC INTELLIGENCE OPERATIONS SPECIALIST (military ser.)	4347	22333333355	SNNNNNNNFFNFFNNFNNNN	NNNN3NNNNNNNNNN	J	281	586	05.03.05	3930	470103	39008
194.062-010	TELEVISION TECHNICIAN (radio-tv broad.)	5457	22322333343	HNNONONFFONFFNOOONOOO	ONNN3NNNNNNNNNN	V,E,T,P,J	201	864	01.02.03	3990	100104	34028
194.122-010	ACCESS COORDINATOR, CABLE TELEVISION (radio-tv broad.)	4347	22333433353	HNNONONFFNOONONOOOO	NNNN3NNNNNNNNNN	D,V,P,T,J	281	869	05.03.05	3930	000000	34028
194.162-010	PROGRAM DIRECTOR, CABLE TELEVISION (radio-tv broad.)	5358	22333333353	HNNONONOOONFFNOOOOOO	NNNN3NNNNNNNNNN	D,V,T,P,J	281	869	05.02.04	1341	000000	15023
194.262-010	AUDIO OPERATOR (radio-tv broad.)	4437	33333333355	LNNNNNNOOFNOFNFNNNNN	NNNN3NNNNNNNNNN	T,J	281	864	05.10.05	3930	100104	34028
194.262-014	SOUND CONTROLLER (amuse. & rec.)	4437	22333333345	LNNNNNNFFNFFNFNNNN	NNNN4NNNNNNNNNN	J	281	586	05.10.03	3719	100199	22599
194.262-018	SOUND MIXER (motion picture; radio-tv broad.; recording)	4437	22333433355	SNNNNNNNFCFNFCNFNNNNN	NNNN3NNNNNNNNNN	V,T,J	281	863	05.10.05	3719	100104	22599
194.262-022	MASTER CONTROL OPERATOR (radio-tv broad.)	4348	22344333353	SNNONONFFNNOONFFNNNNN	NNNN3NNNNNNNNNN	T,J	281	864	05.03.05	3930	000000	34028
194.282-010	VIDEO OPERATOR (radio-tv broad.)	4437	22332333352	SNNNNNNONFNNFNNFNFCFN	NNNN3NNNNNNNNNN	T,J	281	864	05.10.05	3930	100104	22599
194.362-010	RECORDING ENGINEER (radio-tv broad.; recording)	3337	33334434355	LNNNNNNFFNFFNFNNONN	NNNN4NNNNNNNNNN	J,T	281	869	05.10.05	3719	100199	22599
194.362-014	RERECORDING MIXER (motion picture; radio-tv broad.)	4447	33335533355	SNNNNNNOOFNOFNOOONNN	NNNN3NNNNNNNNNN	V,T,J	281	911	05.10.05	3930	100104	34028
194.362-018	TELECINE OPERATOR (radio-tv broad.)	4437	33333423354	SNNNNNNCCNOONCNNONN	NNNN3NNNNNNNNNN	J	281	586	05.10.05	3930	100199	34028
194.362-022	TECHNICIAN, NEWS GATHERING (radio-tv broad.)	4338	23343444433	MNNNNNNOOONCNFFOFOC	ONNN3NNNNNNNNNN	T,J	281	864	05.03.05	3930	000000	34028
194.381-010	TECHNICAL TESTING ENGINEER (motion picture)	4436	33332443354	LNNNNNNFFNNFFNFFON	NNNN4NNNNNNNNNN	J,T	111	911	05.10.03	3711	500602	22505
194.382-010	SECTION-PLOTTER OPERATOR (petrol. & gas)	3335	33332443354	LNNNNNNFFNNNFFNFOON	NNNN3NNNNNNNNNN	J,T	231	725	05.10.05	3719	150903	22599
194.382-014	TAPE TRANSFERRER (radio-tv broad.; recording)	3335	33443333355	LNNNNNNFFFNNNNFFNNNN	NNNN3NNNNNNNNNN	R,J,T	281	585	05.10.05	3719	100199	22599
194.382-018	VIDEOTAPE OPERATOR (radio-tv broad.)	4238	34443443353	LNNNNNNNFFFNOONONOON	NNNN3NNNNNNNNNN	T,J	281	864	05.03.05	3930	000000	34028
194.387-010	QUALITY-CONTROL INSPECTOR (recording)	3224	34342444455	SNNNNNNFFFNNFFNFNFNNN	NNNN4NNNNNNNNNN	J	212	585	06.03.01	7820	100199	83005
194.387-014	RECORD TESTER (recording)	3234	33443344455	SNNNNNNFFFNNFFNFNFNN	NNNN4NNNNNNNNNN	J,T	212	585	06.03.01	7830	100199	83005
195.107-010	CASEWORKER (social ser.)	5357	22344233455	SNNNNNNOOONCCNCNNCNN	NNNN2NNNNNNNNNN	D,I,V,P,J	271	941	09.01.01	2032	000000	27305
195.107-014	CASEWORKER, CHILD WELFARE (social ser.)	5357	22344444455	LNNNNNNNOOONFFNONNONN	NNNN3NNNNNNNNNN	I,P,J	271	941	10.01.02	2032	000000	27305
195.107-018	CASEWORKER, FAMILY (social ser.)	5457	22354454455	SNNNNNNNOOONFFNONNONN	NNNN3NNNNNNNNNN	P,I,J	298	941	10.01.02	2032	000000	27305
195.107-022	SOCIAL GROUP WORKER (social ser.)	5358	22344444455	SNNNNNNOOOONFFNONNNNN	NNNN3NNNNNNNNNN	V,D,P,I,J	298	941	10.01.02	2032	000000	27305
195.107-026	SOCIAL WORKER, DELINQUENCY PREVENTION (social ser.)	5358	22344444455	LNNNNNNOOOONFFNFNFNN	NNNN3NNNNNNNNNN	D,P,J	298	941	10.01.02	2032	000000	27305
195.107-030	SOCIAL WORKER, MEDICAL (profess. & kin.)	5357	22344444455	SNNNNNNOOONFFNFNNNNN	NNNN2NNNNNNNNNN	D,P,J	298	941	10.01.02	2032	000000	27302
195.107-034	SOCIAL WORKER, PSYCHIATRIC (profess. & kin.)	5358	22344444455	SNNNNNNOFFNFFNFNNNN	NNNN3NNNNNNNNNN	D,P	298	941	10.01.02	2032	000000	27302
195.107-038	SOCIAL WORKER, SCHOOL (profess. & kin.)	5357	22344334455	LNNNNNNOOOONFFNONNNNN	NNNN2NNNNNNNNNN	V,D,P,I,J	298	941	10.01.02	2032	000000	27305
195.107-042	CORRECTIONAL-TREATMENT SPECIALIST (social ser.)	5357	22344444455	SNNNNNNNOOONFFNONNNNN	NNNN3NNNNNNNNNN	V,D,P,J,I	271	941	10.01.02	2032	000000	27305
195.107-046	PROBATION-AND-PAROLE OFFICER (profess. & kin.)	5357	22344444455	LNNNNNNOOOONFFNONNNNN	NNNN2NNNNNNNNNN	V,D,P,J,I	271	949	10.01.02	2032	000000	27305
195.117-010	ADMINISTRATOR, SOCIAL WELFARE (profess. & kin.)	5358	22344444454	SNNNNNNNOOOONFFNOOOOO	NNNN3NNNNNNNNNN	D,I,J,P	295	941	11.07.01	1270	200203	19999
195.137-010	CASEWORK SUPERVISOR (social ser.)	5357	22354444455	SNNNNNNNOOOONFFNONNONN	NNNN3NNNNNNNNNN	D,I,J,P	298	940	10.01.02	2032	000000	27305
195.164-010	GROUP WORKER (social ser.)	5457	22333433333	LNNNNNNOOONFFNOOOOO	ONNN4NNNNNNNNNN	V,D,P,I,J	298	941	09.01.01	2032	511501	27305
195.167-010	COMMUNITY ORGANIZATION WORKER (social ser.)	5358	22344444455	SNNNNNNOOOONFFNNOOO	NNNN3NNNNNNNNNN	D,I,J,P	282	941	11.07.01	1139	000000	19005
195.167-014	COMMUNITY-RELATIONS-AND-SERVICES ADVISOR, PUBLIC HOUSING (social ser.)	5357	22344444455	SNNNNNNNOOOONFFNONNNNN	NNNN3NNNNNNNNNN	D,P,J	298	941	11.07.01	2032	000000	27305
195.167-018	DIRECTOR, CAMP (social ser.)	5457	22244444455	ONNNNNNOOOONFFNNNNNN	ONNN3NNNNNNNNNN	D,P	295	941	11.11.02	1352	520901	19999
195.167-022	DIRECTOR, FIELD (social ser.)	5457	22344444455	LNNONNNFFFNFFNFNNNOO	NNNN3NNNNNNNNNN	D,P	295	941	11.07.01	1352	520901	19999
195.167-026	DIRECTOR, RECREATION CENTER (social ser.)	5357	22344444455	LNNOONNFFFNFFNFNNNON	ONNN4NNNNNNNNNN	D,P	295	941	11.11.02	1270	520901	19999
195.167-038	REHABILITATION CENTER MANAGER (government ser.)	5457	22344444454	SNNNNNNNOOOONFFNONNNN	ONNN3NNNNNNNNNN	V,D,I,J,E	298	941	11.07.01	2350	000000	19999
195.167-042	ALCOHOL-AND-DRUG-ABUSE-ASSISTANCE PROGRAM ADMINISTRATOR (government ser.)	5357	22344444455	LNNNNNNNOOONFFNFNNNNN	NNNN3NNNNNNNNNN	D,I,P,J	295	940	07.01.01	4784	000000	53502
195.227-010	PROGRAM AIDE, GROUP WORK (social ser.)	5346	22344244455	LNNNNNNOONFFNCCNCNNNN	NNNN3NNNNNNNNNN	D,P,J	294	959	10.01.02	2033	511502	27305
195.227-014	RECREATION LEADER (social ser.)	4346	22433433334	SNNNNNNFFNFFNFNNFNNNO	ONNN3NNNNNNNNNO	V,P,J	291	941	09.01.01	2033	200202	27311
195.227-018	TEACHER, HOME THERAPY (social ser.)	5357	22344333354	SNNNNNNNFFONFFNFONFNN	NNNN3NNNNNNNNNN	D,I,V,P,J	296	941	10.02.03	2350	000000	31311
195.267-010	ELIGIBILITY WORKER (government ser.)	4346	22344214455	SNNNNNNFFONFFNFNNNNN	NNNN3NNNNNNNNNN	J	271	941	07.01.01	4784	000000	53502
195.267-018	PATIENT-RESOURCES-AND-REIMBURSEMENT AGENT (government ser.)	5357	33344244455	LNNNNNNFFNCCNCNNNNN	NNNN3NNNNNNNNNN	P,J	271	941	10.01.02	2032	000000	27305
195.267-022	CHILD SUPPORT OFFICER (government ser.)	5357	22344344455	SNNNNNNFFNFFNFFNNNNN	ONNN3NNNNNNNNNO	V,P,J	271	959	10.01.02	2032	000000	27305
195.367-010	CASE AIDE (social ser.)	4333	33354344455	LNNNNNNOOONFFNONNNNN	NNNN3NNNNNNNNNN	J,P	271	941	10.01.02	2350	511502	27305
195.367-014	MANAGEMENT AIDE (social ser.)	4345	33454444455	LNNNNNNOOONFFNONNNNN	NNNN3NNNNNNNNNN	P,J	282	941	07.01.01	2032	200606	27308
195.367-018	COMMUNITY WORKER (government ser.)	4346	33344334454	LNNNNNNNFFNFFNFOONOO	ONNN3NNNNNNNNNO	D,I,J,P,V	271	941	10.01.02	2032	000000	27305

DOT #	DOT Title & Industry	Trng	Aptitude	Physical	Environment	Tempra	WkF	MPSMS	GOE	SOC	CIP	OES
195.367-022	FOOD-MANAGEMENT AIDE (government ser.)	3233	33444344445	LNNNNNNOONNFFNFNNNNNN	NNNN3NNNNNNNNNN	P	282	941	10.01.02	2032	200601	27308
195.367-026	PREPAROLE-COUNSELING AIDE (government ser.)	4246	33444444455	SNNNNNNNNNNCNFNNNFNN	NNNN3NNNNNNNNNN	P,I,J	271	949	10.01.02	5133	000000	27305
195.367-030	RECREATION AIDE (social ser.)	3232	33344444455	LNNNNNNNFFONFFNNNNNNN	NNNN3NNNNNNNNNN	P,V	291	941	09.01.01	5269	310101	68014
195.367-034	SOCIAL-SERVICES AIDE (social ser.)	4346	33344344455	LNNNNNNOOONFFNFNNFNN	NNNN3NNNNNNNNNN	V,D,P,J	271	941	10.01.02	2032	200602	27308
196.163-010	FLIGHT-OPERATIONS INSPECTOR (government ser.)	5458	21222233324	LNNNNNNFFNFFNFOFOOO	ONNN5NNNNNNNNNN	V,P,S,J	211	855	05.04.01	1473	490102	21911
196.163-014	SUPERVISING AIRPLANE PILOT (government ser.)	5558	12222223313	LNNNNNNNFFNFFNFOOOOO	NNNN4NNNNNNNNNF	D,S,J	211	953	05.04.01	1473	490102	21911
196.167-010	CHIEF PILOT (air trans.)	5459	21233333324	LNNNNNNFFNFFNFFFFF	NNNN4NNNNNNNNNO	D,P,S,J	295	855	05.03.01	8250	490102	97702
196.167-014	NAVIGATOR (air trans.)	5546	23222234334	SNNNNNNFFNNNNNFNFON	NNNN4NNNNNNNNNN	V,S,J,T	243	719	05.03.01	8250	490102	97702
196.223-010	INSTRUCTOR, FLYING I (education)	5457	22222234324	LNNNNNNFFNFNFFFFF	NNNN4NNNNNNNNNF	V,P,S,J,T	296	931	05.04.01	8250	490102	97702
196.223-014	INSTRUCTOR, PILOT (air trans.)	5458	22222334324	LNNNNNNFFNFFFOOFOO	NNNN5NNNNNNNNNF	V,P,S,J,T	296	855	05.04.01	8250	490102	97702
196.263-010	AIRPLANE PILOT (agriculture)	4446	23222232323	LONNNNNFFONFFNFFFFC	ONNN4NNNNNNNNCC	S,T,J	003	300	05.04.01	8250	020408	97702
196.263-014	AIRPLANE PILOT, COMMERCIAL (air trans.)	5448	22233224334	LNNNNNNFFONFNFFFFF	NNNN3NNNNNNNNNN	V,S,T,J	013	855	05.04.01	8250	490102	97702
196.263-018	AIRPLANE PILOT, PHOTOGRAMMETRY (business ser.)	5447	23222323334	LNNNNNNFFNOONFFFFFF	NNNN5NNNNNNNNNN	J,S,T,V	013	716	05.04.01	8250	490102	97702
196.263-022	CHECK PILOT (air trans.)	5458	22343344454	SNNNNNNFFFNOONNOOFOO	NNNN5NNNNNNNNNN	J,S,T	211	855	05.04.01	8250	490102	97702
196.263-026	CONTROLLER, REMOTELY-PILOTED VEHICLE (aircraft mfg.)	5548	22233333324	LNNNNNNFFNFFNFOFOOO	NNNN4NNNNNNNNNO	S,T,J	013	592	05.04.01	8250	490102	97702
196.263-030	EXECUTIVE PILOT (any industry)	5457	22323322324	LNNNNNNFFNFNFFFFF	NNNN5NNNNNNNNNF	D,J	013	855	05.04.01	8250	490102	97702
196.263-034	FACILITIES-FLIGHT-CHECK PILOT (government ser.)	5548	22223333313	LNNNNNNFFNFNFFFFF	NNNN5NNNNNNNNNN	D,S,J,T	211	855	05.04.01	8250	490102	97702
196.263-038	HELICOPTER PILOT (any industry)	4447	23323323324	LONOOOOFFONFFNFFFFOF	NNNN5FNONNNNNNN	T,P,J	013	855	05.04.01	8250	490102	97702
196.263-042	TEST PILOT (aircraft mfg.)	5448	22223434314	MONNNNNFFNFNFFFFFF	NNNN4NNNNNNNNNN	J,T,S	211	592	05.04.01	8250	490102	97702
197.130-010	ENGINEER (water trans.)	4338	33323334344	MOOOOOOFFNFFNFNNNNF	NNFN4NNNNNNNNNF	D,J	021	870	05.06.02	8244	150899	97521
197.133-010	CAPTAIN, FISHING VESSEL (fishing & hunt.)	4447	33322234334	LFFNNNNFFNFNFFFFF	FNNF4NNNNNNNNNF	D,P,S,J,T	001	330	05.04.02	8241	490303	97502
197.133-014	MASTER, YACHT (water trans.)	4448	23322234334	LNNNNNNFFNFFNFOOFOO	ONNN3NNNNNNNNNN	J	013	854	05.04.02	8241	490399	97502
197.133-018	MATE, FISHING VESSEL (fishing & hunt.)	4447	33322434334	MOOFOFNFFNNFNFFFFF	FNNN4NNNNNNNNNF	D,J,T	013	330	03.04.03	8241	490309	97505
197.133-022	MATE, SHIP (water trans.)	4447	33322332334	LOOOOONFFNFFNFOOOOO	NNNN4NNNNNNNNNF	D,J,P	013	854	05.04.02	8241	490399	97505
197.133-026	PILOT, SHIP (water trans.)	4438	21224334334	LOONNNNFFONFFNFFFFF	ONNO4NNNNNNNNNO	D,P,S,J	013	854	05.04.02	8241	490399	97508
197.133-030	TUGBOAT CAPTAIN (water trans.)	4338	22333333344	MONNNNNFFNFFNFFFFFF	ONNO4NNNNNNNNNN	D,P,S,J	013	593	05.04.02	8242	490399	97502
197.133-034	TUGBOAT MATE (water trans.)	4337	33333434334	MOOONONFFNFFNFNFFOOF	ONNO4NNNNNNNNNO	D,J,T	013	593	05.12.01	8242	490399	97505
197.137-010	DREDGE MATE (water trans.)	4437	33333433353	LNNNNNNFFNFFNFNOFOOF	FNNN4NNNNNNNNNF	D,J,T	102	365	05.12.01	8242	490399	97505
197.161-010	DREDGE CAPTAIN (water trans.)	4438	22344344443	LNNNNNNFFNFNFFOOFF	FNNO4NNNNNNNNNF	D,J,P	102	365	05.04.02	8242	490399	97502
197.163-010	FERRYBOAT CAPTAIN (water trans.)	4447	23322334342	LFNNNNNFFNFFNFFOFF	ONNN4NNNNNNNNNN	D,P,J	013	854	05.04.02	8241	490399	97502
197.163-014	MASTER, PASSENGER BARGE (water trans.)	4447	23322334344	LNNNNNNFFNFFNFOFFOFF	ONNO4NNNNNNNNNO	D,J	013	854	05.04.02	8241	490399	97502
197.163-018	MASTER, RIVERBOAT (water trans.)	4447	23322334343	LNNNNNNFFNFFNFFFFOFF	ONNN4NNNNNNNNNN	D,P,J	013	854	05.04.02	8241	490399	97502
197.167-010	MASTER, SHIP (water trans.)	6658	22112233444	LOONNNNFFONFFNFFFFFF	ONNN4NNNNNNNNNO	D,P,S,J,T	013	854	05.04.02	8241	490399	97502
197.167-014	PURSER (water trans.)	4337	22243344455	SNNNNNNFFNFFNFNNFNN	NNNN3NNNNNNNNNN	V,P	232	854	11.11.03	1490	490399	39999
198.167-010	CONDUCTOR, PASSENGER CAR (r.r. trans.)	4348	22344344434	LOONNNNFFONFFNFOOFON	NNNN4NNNNNNNNNN	V,D,P,J	013	851	11.11.03	8113	080709	97302
198.167-014	CONDUCTOR, PULLMAN (r.r. trans.)	4346	33433444444	LNFFNNNFFONFFNNOOONN	NNNN4NNNNNNNNNN	V,D,P	291	851	09.01.04	8113	080709	19005
198.167-018	CONDUCTOR, ROAD FREIGHT (r.r. trans.)	4338	33434344434	LOONNNNFFNFFNNFOOFNN	ONNN4NNNNNNNNNO	V,D,P,J	013	851	11.11.03	8113	080709	97302
199.167-010	RADIATION MONITOR (profess. & kin.)	4446	33344344455	SNNNNNNFFNFFNFNFNNN	NNNN3NNNNNFNNN	P,J,T	211	715	05.03.08	3832	410205	24508
199.167-014	URBAN PLANNER (profess. & kin.)	5458	21222343454	SNNNNNNOONNFFNONNNNN	NNNN3NNNNNNNNNN	V,P,J	244	704	11.03.02	1920	049999	27105
199.167-018	ENERGY-CONTROL OFFICER (education)	4447	33343334455	LNNNNNNFOONFFNFFNNNN	NNNN3NNNNNNNNNN	I,P,T	282	870	05.03.08	3990	150503	39999
199.167-022	ENVIRONMENTAL ANALYST (government ser.)	5348	23334244455	SNNNNNNOONNFFNFNNONN	NNNN3NNNNNNNNNN	D,J,P	295	959	11.05.03	1133	000000	39999
199.171-010	PROOF TECHNICIAN (ordnance)	4446	23232333354	LNNNNNNFFNNNNFOOFNN	NNNN5NNNNNNNNNF	V,J,T	211	370	02.04.01	3990	000000	39999
199.207-010	DIANETIC COUNSELOR (profess. & kin.)	5346	32342444455	SNNNNNNFFNFFNFNNNNN	NNNN3NNNNNNNNNN	J	298	949	10.01.02	2049	000000	27599
199.251-010	TESTER, FOOD PRODUCTS (any industry)	4346	32343344254	LNNNNNNFFNFFNFFFN	NNNN3NNNNNNNNNN	I,J,P	146	380	05.05.17	3990	000000	39999
199.261-010	TAXIDERMIST (profess. & kin.)	5347	22322322251	MNNNNNNFFONNNFNFOFN	NNNN3NFNNNNNNN	V,J,T	136	732	01.06.02	3990	000000	39999
199.261-014	PARKING ANALYST (government ser.)	5457	22223444454	LNNNNNNOOONOONFNONOF	FNNN3NNNNNNNNNN	J	251	719	05.03.06	3990	000000	22502
199.267-010	BALLISTICS EXPERT, FORENSIC (government ser.)	5557	22222333353	LNNNNNNFFNFFNFFFFNN	NNNN5NNNNNNNNNN	J	211	373	02.04.01	3890	430107	24599
199.267-014	CRYPTANALYST (government ser.)	5558	21232344454	SNNNNNNNFFNFFNNNNNN	NNNN3NNNNNNNNNN	V,J,E	271	959	11.08.04	1739	000000	25319
199.267-018	EXAMINATION PROCTOR (government ser.)	4345	32343344455	LNNNNNNFFNFFNNFNNNN	NNNN3NNNNNNNNNN	P,J	295	712	07.01.07	3990	000000	39999
199.267-022	EXAMINER, QUESTIONED DOCUMENTS (government ser.)	5246	21422244454	LNNNNNNOOONNNFNFNN	NNNN3NNNNNNNNNN	J	271	959	02.04.01	3990	430107	39999
199.267-026	POLYGRAPH EXAMINER (profess. & kin.)	5355	21432234354	LNNNNNNFFNFFNFNFNNN	NNNN3NNNNNNNNNN	J	211	951	02.04.02	3990	430107	39999

DOT #	DOT Title & Industry	Trng	Aptitude	Physical	Environment	Tempra	WkF	MPSMS	GOE	SOC	CIP	OES
199.267-030	TRAFFIC TECHNICIAN (government ser.)	5457	22223344454	LNNNNNNFFNFNFFFFFN	ONNN4NNNNNNNNNNN	V,J	251	719	05.03.06	3990	150201	39005
199.267-034	RESEARCH ASSISTANT II (profess. & kin.)	5356	22344244454	SNNNNNNFFFNNNNNNNN	NNNN3NNNNNNNNNNN	V,J	251	939	11.08.02	3990	000000	39999
199.267-038	GRAPHOLOGIST (profess. & kin.)	4336	33442244455	SNNNNNNNOOONFFNCNNNN	NNNN2NNNNNNNNNNN	P,J,I	271	949	02.04.01	3990	000000	39999
199.281-010	GEMOLOGIST (jewelry-silver.)	4347	22322433353	LNNNNNNNFFNNNNFNFFN	NNNN3NNNNNNNNNNN	J,T	211	611	05.05.14	3990	470408	39999
199.361-010	RADIOGRAPHER (any industry)	4445	33333433343	LNNNNNNNFFNNNFNNFOOFON	ONNN4NNNNNNNNNNN	J,T	201	540	05.03.05	3990	410204	39999
199.364-010	CITY PLANNING AIDE (profess. & kin.)	4446	33332233454	LNNNNNNNFFFNFNNFNFFN	NNNN3NNNNNNNNNNN	T,V	271	744	11.03.02	3990	150201	39999
199.364-014	SCIENTIFIC HELPER (profess. & kin.)	4446	33333333333	MNNNNNNNFFNNNNNFFN	ONNN3NNNNNNNNNNN	J,T	251	720	02.04.01	3890	150702	24599
199.382-010	TELEVISION-SCHEDULE COORDINATOR (radio-tv broad.)	4344	33344243455	LNNNNNNNOOFNOONONNFNN	NNNN3NNNNNNNNNNN	T,J	231	863	07.05.01	4752	100104	58008
199.384-010	DECONTAMINATOR (any industry)	3336	33444444355	MNNNNNNNFFFNNNNNFNFNN	NNNF4FFNNNNNNNN	V,J	031	920	02.04.01	3990	410200	39999
199.682-010	AEROSPACE PHYSIOLOGICAL TECHNICIAN (military ser.)	4336	34433433354	SOONNNNNFFNOONFNFNON	NNNN3NNNNNNNNNNN	J,T	281	732	02.04.02	3990	000000	39999
201.162-010	SOCIAL SECRETARY (clerical)	4246	22943333354	SNNNNNNNFFNFNNFNFON	NNNN3NNNNNNNNNNN	V,J,P	231	891	07.01.03	4622	520401	55108
201.362-010	LEGAL SECRETARY (clerical)	4246	22342222354	SNNNNNNNFFFNFNNFFON	NNNN3NNNNNNNNNNN	V,P,J,T	231	891	07.01.03	4622	520403	55102
201.362-014	MEDICAL SECRETARY (medical ser.)	4346	22342222355	SNNONONNFFNFNFNNNNN	NNNN3NNNNNNNNNNN	J,P,T	231	891	07.01.03	4622	510801	55105
201.362-018	MEMBERSHIP SECRETARY (nonprofit org.)	4345	33453233455	SNNNNNNNFFNFNNFNNNN	NNNN3NNNNNNNNNNN	V,P,J	231	891	07.01.02	4622	520401	55108
201.362-022	SCHOOL SECRETARY (education)	4335	33343233355	SNNNNNNNFFFOFFNFNNNF	NNNN3NNNNNNNNNNN	V,T,P	231	891	07.01.03	4622	520401	55108
201.362-026	SCRIPT SUPERVISOR (motion picture; radio-tv broad.)	4246	32344233355	LNNNNNNNFFOFFNFFNNNF	NNNN3NNNNNNNNNNN	V,P,J,T	231	911	01.03.01	4622	520401	55108
201.362-030	SECRETARY (clerical)	4346	32343222355	SNNNNNNNFFNFFNFNNNN	NNNN3NNNNNNNNNNN	V,P,J	231	891	07.01.03	4622	520401	55108
202.132-010	SUPERVISOR, STENO POOL (clerical)	4246	33443222355	SNNNNNNNOOONFFNFNNNNN	NNNN3NNNNNNNNNNN	D,P,T,J	231	864	07.05.03	4513	520401	51002
202.362-010	SHORTHAND REPORTER (clerical)	3236	22442222355	SNNNNNNNOOONNONFNNFNN	NNNN3NNNNNNNNNNN	P,T	231	932	07.05.03	4623	520405	55302
202.362-014	STENOGRAPHER (clerical)	3235	32442222355	SNNNNNNNFFNFNOFNNFNN	NNNN3NNNNNNNNNNN	T	231	891	07.05.03	4623	520401	55302
202.362-018	STENOGRAPHER, PRINT SHOP (print. & pub.)	3235	32442223455	SNNNNNNNFFNFNFNNFNN	NNNN3NNNNNNNNNNN	R,T	231	891	07.05.03	4623	520401	55302
202.362-022	STENOTYPE OPERATOR (clerical)	4245	33443223355	SNNNNNNNCOCNOONFNNNNN	NNNN3NNNNNNNNNNN	R,T	231	891	07.05.03	4623	520401	55302
202.382-010	STENOCAPTIONER (radio-tv broad.)	4248	22431213455	SNNNNNNNOOOCNNFNNNNNN	NNNN3NNNNNNNNNNN	T,J	231	864	07.05.03	4623	000000	55302
203.132-010	SUPERVISOR, TELEGRAPHIC-TYPEWRITER OPERATORS (clerical)	4247	33443233455	LNNNNNNNOOOONFFNONNNNN	NNNN3NNNNNNNNNNN	D,P,T,J	281	862	07.06.02	4523	520204	51002
203.132-014	SUPERVISOR, TRANSCRIBING OPERATORS (clerical)	4246	33433222344	SNNNNNNNNOOONFFNNNNNN	NNNN3NNNNNNNNNNN	D,P,T,J	231	891	07.06.02	4513	520401	51002
203.137-010	SUPERVISOR, WORD PROCESSING (clerical)	4346	22344244455	SNNNNNNNNOOFNONNONNN	NNNN3NNNNNNNNNNN	D,P,J	231	891	07.06.02	4513	520401	51002
203.137-014	TYPING SECTION CHIEF (clerical)	4236	33444223455	LNNNNNNNFFNFNNNNNNN	NNNN3NNNNNNNNNNN	D,P,T,U	231	891	07.06.02	4513	000000	51002
203.362-010	CLERK-TYPIST (clerical)	3334	33343233355	SNNNNNNNFFNFNFNNFNN	NNNN3NNNNNNNNNNN	R,U	231	891	07.06.02	4624	520408	55307
203.362-014	CREDIT REPORTING CLERK (business ser.)	3234	33444333455	SNNNNNNNFFNFNFNNFNN	NNNN3NNNNNNNNNNN	P,R,T	282	899	07.06.01	4649	520407	55305
203.362-026	CAPTION WRITER (motion picture; radio-tv broad.)	4246	32442122334	LNNNNNNNOOFNOFNNNNNON	NNNN3NNNNNNNNNNN	T,J	231	864	07.05.03	3290	000000	34002
203.382-014	CANCELLATION CLERK (insurance)	3335	33343243454	SNNNNNNNFFNNNNFNNNN	NNNN3NNNNNNNNNNN	R,T	231	895	07.02.02	4699	520408	53314
203.382-018	MAGNETIC-TAPE-COMPOSER OPERATOR (print. & pub.)	4335	33322233444	SNNNNNNNFFNNNNCNFFON	NNNN4NNNNNNNNNNN	J,T	191	567	07.06.02	4793	520401	56021
203.382-026	VARITYPE OPERATOR (clerical)	3235	32342222355	SNNNNNNNFFNFNNFNFNN	NNNN3NNNNNNNNNNN	J	231	891	07.06.02	4793	480205	56021
203.382-030	WORD PROCESSING MACHINE OPERATOR (clerical)	3235	33444223355	SNNONONFFCNNFNNNNN	NNNN3NNNNNNNNNNN	J	231	891	07.06.02	4624	520401	55307
203.562-010	WIRE-TRANSFER CLERK (financial)	3334	33344233455	SNNNNNNNOOFNOONCNNCNN	NNNN3NNNNNNNNNNN	T	232	894	07.06.02	4733	520406	57111
203.582-010	BRAILLE OPERATOR (print. & pub.)	3134	33433233345	LNNNNNNNFFNNNNFNNNN	NNNN3NNNNNNNNNNN	R,T	192	567	07.06.02	4793	000000	56017
203.582-014	BRAILLE TYPIST (education; nonprofit organ.; print. & pub.)	4135	33433232355	SNNNNNNNFFNNNNFNNNN	NNNN3NNNNNNNNNNN	R,T	192	567	07.06.02	4793	520401	56017
203.582-018	CRYPTOGRAPHIC-MACHINE OPERATOR (clerical)	4235	33343233455	SNNNNNNNFFNNNNFNNNN	NNNN3NNNNNNNNNNN	J,T	231	869	07.06.02	4793	520407	56017
203.582-038	PERFORATOR TYPIST (clerical)	3134	33443222355	SNNNNNNNFFCCNNNNCNNNNN	NNNN3NNNNNNNNNNN	R,T	231	891	07.06.02	4793	520401	56017
203.582-042	PHOTOCOMPOSING-PERFORATOR-MACHINE OPERATOR (print. & pub.)	4336	33332223354	SNNNNNNNFFNNNNFNNNN	NNNN2NNNNNNNNNNN	T	192	567	07.06.02	4793	520401	56021
203.582-046	PHOTOCOMPOSITION-KEYBOARD OPERATOR (print. & pub.)	3234	33333333355	SNNNNNNNFFNNNNCNNFNN	NNNN3NNNNNNNNNNN	T	231	567	07.06.02	4793	480205	56021
203.582-050	TELEGRAPHIC-TYPEWRITER OPERATOR (clerical)	3234	33443243455	SNNNNNNNFFNNNNFNNONN	NNNN4NNNNNNNNNNN	R,T	281	862	07.06.02	4733	520406	57111
203.582-054	DATA ENTRY CLERK (clerical)	3234	33444223455	SNNNNNNNFFCNNONCNNCNN	NNNN3NNNNNNNNNNN	R,T	231	891	07.06.01	4793	520407	56017
203.582-058	TRANSCRIBING-MACHINE OPERATOR (clerical)	3135	33442224345	SNNNNNNNFFCNNCNFNNNNN	NNNN3NNNNNNNNNNN	R,T,U	231	891	07.06.02	4623	520401	55302
203.582-062	TYPESETTER-PERFORATOR OPERATOR (print. & pub.)	3134	33443222455	SNNNNNNNFFNNNNFNNNNN	NNNN3NNNNNNNNNNN	J,T	192	567	07.06.02	4793	520401	56021
203.582-066	TYPIST (clerical)	3233	33444222355	SNNNNNNNFFNFNFNNFNN	NNNN3NNNNNNNNNNN	T,U	231	891	07.06.02	4624	000000	55307
203.582-078	NOTEREADER (clerical)	3135	33354344455	SNNNNNNNFFNNNNCNNCNN	NNNN3NNNNNNNNNNN	T	231	891	07.06.02	4624	520401	55307
205.137-014	SUPERVISOR, SURVEY WORKERS (clerical)	4336	33354344455	LNNNNNNNFFONFFNFNNNN	NNNN2NNNNNNNNNNN	V,D,P,T,J	231	889	07.04.01	4514	520406	51002
205.162-010	ADMITTING OFFICER (medical ser.)	4237	33434343455	SNNNNNNNNOOFNFFNNONN	NNNN2NNNNNNNNNNN	D,J,P,V	231	929	07.04.01	4514	520406	51002
205.362-010	CIVIL-SERVICE CLERK (government ser.)	3233	33442223455	SNNNNNNNFFFNFNNNNNN	NNNN3NNNNNNNNNNN	P,T	282	891	07.04.04	4692	521001	55314
205.362-014	EMPLOYMENT CLERK (clerical)	4245	22344233455	SNNNNNNNFFNFFNNNNNN	NNNN3NNNNNNNNNNN	V,P,J	231	943	07.04.01	4692	521001	55314

DOT #	DOT Title & Industry	Trng	Aptitude	Physical	Environment	Tempra	WkF	MPSMS	GOE	SOC	CIP	OES
205.362-018	HOSPITAL-ADMITTING CLERK (medical ser.)	3234	33344333455	SNNNNNNFFNFFNFNNNNN	NNNN2NNNNNNNNNNNN	V,P	231	890	07.04.01	4642	520404	55332
205.362-022	IDENTIFICATION CLERK (clerical)	3133	33454323355	SNNNNNNFFNFFNFNNNNN	NNNN3NNNNNNNNNNNN	V,P,T	231	891	07.04.01	4692	521001	55314
205.362-026	CUSTOMER SERVICE REPRESENTATIVE (financial)	4346	33344244455	LNNNNNNFFNCCNFNNFNN	NNNN3NNNNNNNNNNNN	T,P	231	894	07.04.01	4642	520803	53105
205.362-030	OUTPATIENT-ADMITTING CLERK (medical ser.)	3234	33444333355	SNNNNNNFFNFFNFNNNNN	NNNN2NNNNNNNNNNNN	V,P	231	920	07.04.01	4642	520404	55332
205.367-010	ADMISSIONS EVALUATOR (education)	4246	22244344455	SNNNNNNFFNFFNFNNNNN	NNNN3NNNNNNNNNNNN	P,J	271	931	07.01.05	4699	521001	59999
205.367-014	CHARGE-ACCOUNT CLERK (clerical)	3232	33454344455	SNNNNNNFFONFFNONNNNN	NNNN2NNNNNNNNNNNN	P,T	282	894	07.04.02	4782	080705	55332
205.367-018	CLAIMS CLERK II (insurance)	3334	33354344455	SNNNNNNFFNFFNFNNNNN	NNNN2NNNNNNNNNNNN	J	231	895	07.04.02	4642	520803	53311
205.367-022	CREDIT CLERK (clerical)	4344	33355244455	SNNONNNFFNFFNCNNNNNN	NNNN3NNNNNNNNNNNN	T,P	231	894	07.04.01	4642	080401	53121
205.367-026	CREEL CLERK (government ser.)	3332	44444344454	LNNNNNNFFNFNFNNNNON	CNNN3NNNNNNNNNNNN	P,T	231	959	07.04.01	4642	000000	55332
205.367-030	ELECTION CLERK (government ser.)	3222	33454344455	SNNNNNNOOONFFNFNNNNN	NNNN2NNNNNNNNNNNN	J	231	959	07.04.03	4699	520406	59999
205.367-034	LICENSE CLERK (government ser.)	3233	33444344455	LNNNNNNFFNFFNFNNONN	NNNN3NNNNNNNNNNNN	P,J	231	953	07.04.03	4787	520408	53708
205.367-038	REGISTRAR (government ser.)	3235	33444344455	LNNNNNNFFONFFNFNNNNN	ONNN3NNNNNNNNNNNN	V,P	282	959	07.04.03	4645	520406	55305
205.367-042	REGISTRATION CLERK (government ser.)	3233	33453343355	SNNNNNNFFONFFNFNNNNN	NNNN2NNNNNNNNNNNN	R,P,T	271	950	07.04.01	4642	520406	55332
205.367-046	REHABILITATION CLERK (nonprofit org.)	3224	33443233355	SNNNNNNFFNFFNFNNNNNN	NNNN3NNNNNNNNNNNN	P,T	231	733	07.04.01	4642	000000	59999
205.367-050	SUPERVISOR, CONTINGENTS (retail trade)	4246	33444344455	SNNNNNNFFNFFNFNNNNNN	NNNN3NNNNNNNNNNNN	V,J	231	943	07.04.01	4692	520204	55314
205.367-054	SURVEY WORKER (clerical)	3122	33444344455	LNNNNNNFFNFFNFNNNNNN	ONNN2NNNNNNNNNNNN	P,T	231	893	07.04.01	4642	521402	55332
205.367-058	TRAFFIC CHECKER (government ser.)	2222	33333334455	LNNNNNNFFNCCNFNNNNNN	CNNN4NNNNNNNNNNNN	P	231	959	07.04.01	4642	000000	55332
205.367-062	REFERRAL CLERK, TEMPORARY HELP AGENCY (clerical)	3333	33444343455	SNNNNNNOOFNFFNFNNNON	NNNN3NNNNNNNNNNNN	P	231	943	07.05.03	4692	521001	55314
205.567-010	BENEFITS CLERK II (clerical)	3334	33355233355	SNNNNNNFFNFFNFNNNNNN	NNNN3NNNNNNNNNNNN	T,P	231	891	07.05.03	4692	521001	55314
206.137-010	SUPERVISOR, FILES (clerical)	4247	34444344455	LNNNNNNFFNFFNFNNNONN	NNNN3NNNNNNNNNNNN	D,P,J	231	891	07.05.03	4519	520408	51002
206.367-010	ENGINEERING-DOCUMENT-CONTROL CLERK (aircraft mfg.; electron. comp.)	4346	33444343455	LNNNNNNFFNOONFNNONN	NNNN3NNNNNNNNNNNN	T	231	890	07.05.03	4759	520408	58099
206.367-014	FILE CLERK II (clerical)	3233	33443243355	LNNONONFFNFFNFNNNNN	NNNN3NNNNNNNNNNNN	T	231	891	07.05.03	4696	520408	55321
206.367-018	TAPE LIBRARIAN (clerical)	4234	33443233455	LNNONONFFNFFNFNNNNN	NNNN4NNNNNNNNNNNN	T	231	891	07.05.03	4696	520408	55321
206.387-010	CLASSIFICATION CLERK (clerical)	3235	33444344455	SNNNNNNOOFNNONFNNNNN	NNNN3NNNNNNNNNNNN	R,T	231	891	07.05.03	4696	520408	55321
206.387-014	FINGERPRINT CLERK II (government ser.)	4234	33432344455	SNNNNNNFFNNNFNFNNNNN	NNNN2NNNNNNNNNNNN	J,T	231	959	07.05.03	4696	520408	55321
206.387-022	RECORD CLERK (textile)	3223	33443343354	LLNFNNNFFNNNNNFNNNFN	NNNN3NNNNNNNNNNNN	R,T	231	891	07.07.01	4696	520408	55321
206.387-034	FILE CLERK I (clerical)	3123	33442233354	LNNONONFFNNONFNNFON	NNNN3NNNNNNNNNNNN	R,T	231	891	07.07.01	4696	520408	55321
206.587-010	BRAND RECORDER (government ser.)	3124	34432345554	SNNNNNNFFNFFNFNNNNN	NNNN3NNNNNNNNNNNN	T	231	959	07.05.03	4699	520408	59999
207.137-010	CHIEF CLERK, PRINT SHOP (clerical)	4236	33333234455	LNNNNNNFFNFFNFNNNNN	NNNN4NNNNNNNNNNNN	V,D,P,J	191	891	05.10.05	4522	520408	51002
207.682-010	DUPLICATING-MACHINE OPERATOR I (clerical)	3214	33433333355	LNNNNNNFFNNFNFNNNNNN	NNNN3NNNNNNNNNNNN	J,T	191	891	05.10.05	4722	520408	56005
207.682-014	DUPLICATING-MACHINE OPERATOR II (clerical)	2114	34433333354	LNNNNNNFFFNNNONOONN	NNNN3NNNNNNNNNNNN	T	191	891	05.12.19	4722	520408	56005
207.682-018	OFFSET-DUPLICATING-MACHINE OPERATOR (clerical)	3215	34343433354	MNNNNNNFFFNFNFFFN	NNNN4NNNNNNNNNNNN	R,T	191	891	05.10.05	4722	520408	56005
207.685-010	BRAILLE-DUPLICATING-MACHINE OPERATOR (print. & pub.)	2122	44444444355	MNNNNNNFFFNNNNNNNNN	NNNN3NNNNNNNNNNNN	R	192	567	05.12.19	4722	520408	56005
207.685-014	PHOTOCOPYING-MACHINE OPERATOR (clerical)	2112	44443434355	LNNNNNNFFNNNNONNNNN	NNNN3NNNNNNNNNNNN	R	201	891	05.12.19	4722	520408	56005
207.685-018	PHOTOGRAPHIC-MACHINE OPERATOR (clerical)	3222	44444444445	LNNONOCFNNONFNNONN	NNNN3NNNNNNNNNNNN	R	201	899	05.12.19	4722	520408	56005
208.382-010	TERMINAL-MAKEUP OPERATOR (print. & pub.)	3235	33443223455	MNNNNNNFFONNNNFNONN	NNNN3NNNNNNNNNNNN	J,T	231	567	07.06.01	4793	520401	56021
208.462-010	MAILING-MACHINE OPERATOR (clerical)	4235	34333433355	MNNNNNNFFONNNNFFONN	NNNN4NNNNNNNNNNNN	J,T	041	899	06.04.38	4522	000000	56008
208.582-010	ADDRESSING-MACHINE OPERATOR (clerical)	3224	34334444455	LNNNNNNFFONNNNNNNN	NNNN3NNNNNNNNNNNN	R	191	891	05.12.19	4723	520408	56008
208.582-014	EMBOSSING-MACHINE OPERATOR I (clerical)	3124	34433333455	SNNNNNNFFNFFNFFNNNN	NNNN3NNNNNNNNNNNN	T	192	891	06.02.02	4729	520408	56099
208.682-010	EMBOSSING-MACHINE OPERATOR II (clerical)	3124	34433333355	SNNNNNNFFNFFNFFFN	NNNN3NNNNNNNNNNNN	T	192	891	06.02.02	4729	520408	56099
208.685-010	COLLATOR OPERATOR (clerical)	2112	44444344355	LNNNNNNFFFNNNNNNNN	NNNN3NNNNNNNNNNNN	R	231	898	05.12.19	4729	520408	56008
208.685-014	FOLDING-MACHINE OPERATOR (clerical)	2112	44444434355	LNNNNNNFFONNNNNONNN	NNNN3NNNNNNNNNNNN	R	062	891	05.12.19	4723	520408	56008
208.685-018	INSERTING-MACHINE OPERATOR (clerical)	2122	44444344355	LNNNNNNFFONNNNNONNN	NNNN3NNNNNNNNNNNN	R	062	891	05.12.19	4723	520408	56099
208.685-022	MICROFILM MOUNTER (clerical)	2112	44444444454	LNNNNNNFFONNNNNONNN	NNNN3NNNNNNNNNNNN	R,T	063	891	05.12.19	4723	000000	56099
208.685-026	SEALING-AND-CANCELING-MACHINE OPERATOR (clerical)	2222	44443434355	LNNNNNNFFONNNNNONNN	NNNN3NNNNNNNNNNNN	R	063	891	05.12.19	4723	000000	56008
208.685-034	WING-MAILER-MACHINE OPERATOR (print. & pub.)	2112	44534434355	LNNNNNNFFONNNNNONNN	NNNN3NNNNNNNNNNNN	R	063	474	05.12.19	4723	000000	56008
209.132-010	SUPERVISOR, PERSONNEL CLERKS (clerical)	4246	22343223455	SNNNNNNFFNFFNFNONNN	NNNN3NNNNNNNNNNNN	V,P,D,T,J	232	891	07.05.03	4519	520204	51002
209.132-014	TECHNICAL COORDINATOR (government ser.)	4447	32333333354	SNNNNNNFFFNFNOQNN	NNNN2NNNNNNNNNNNN	V,P,J	231	959	07.05.03	4511	520204	51002
209.137-010	MAILROOM SUPERVISOR (clerical)	4346	33344344455	LNNNNNNFFONFFNFNNNNN	NNNN2NNNNNNNNNNNN	D,J,P,V	231	891	07.05.04	4522	520408	51002
209.137-014	METER READER, CHIEF (utilities; waterworks)	4236	33344344455	SNNNNNNFFONFFNFNNNNN	NNNN2NNNNNNNNNNNN	V,P	231	870	07.05.02	4525	000000	51002
209.137-018	SUPERVISOR, AGENCY APPOINTMENTS (insurance)	4347	23344244455	SNNNNNNFFONCCNCNNFNN	NNNN3NNNNNNNNNNNN	D,P,T,J	231	895	07.05.03	4519	520204	51002

DOT #	DOT Title & Industry	Trng	Apitude	Physical	Environment	Tempra	WkF	MPSMS	GOE	SOC	CIP	OES
209.137-026	SUPERVISOR, MARKING ROOM (retail trade)	3236	33444434454	LOOONONFFNFNFNOOON	NNNN3NNNNNNNNNN	D,P,T,J	221	881	05.09.03	4525	080705	51002
209.362-010	CIRCULATION CLERK (print. & pub.)	3233	33344333455	SNNNNNNFFFNNNNFNNNN	NNNN2NNNNNNNNNN	J	231	891	07.05.03	4699	520408	59999
209.362-014	CONTROL CLERK, AUDITING (insurance)	3333	33343233455	SNNNNNNFFONNNNFNNNN	NNNN2NNNNNNNNNN	T	231	891	07.05.03	4699	520803	59999
209.362-018	CREDIT REFERENCE CLERK (financial; retail trade)	3233	33455322355	SNNONONFFNCCNCNNONN	NNNN3NNNNNNNNNN	P,T	271	894	07.05.02	4783	000000	53117
209.362-022	IDENTIFICATION CLERK (government ser.)	3234	33443233354	LNNNNNNOFFNFFNFNNOON	NNNN3NNNNNNNNNN	V,T,P	201	951	07.05.03	4799	520408	59999
209.362-026	PERSONNEL CLERK (clerical)	4244	33344233455	SNNONONFFNFFNFNONN	NNNN3NNNNNNNNNN	V,T,P	231	890	07.05.03	4692	521001	55314
209.362-030	CONGRESSIONAL-DISTRICT AIDE (government ser.)	4345	33344343355	SNNNNNNFFNFFNFNNNNN	NNNN3NNNNNNNNNN	P,V	282	891	07.04.04	4630	520406	55347
209.362-034	CORRESPONDENCE CLERK (clerical)	3226	34444333355	SNNNNNNFFONOONFNNNN	NNNN3NNNNNNNNNN	T,J	231	891	07.04.02	4663	520408	55317
209.367-010	AGENT-LICENSING CLERK (insurance)	4145	33344324355	SNNNNNNCCFNOONFNNNN	NNNN3NNNNNNNNNN	J,T	261	898	07.05.02	4792	520408	53911
209.367-014	BRAILLE PROOFREADER (nonprofit org.; print. & pub.)	4145	22433244455	SNNNNNNFFFFFNFNNNN	NNNN3NNNNNNNNNN	J,T	261	898	07.05.02	4792	520408	53911
209.367-018	CORRESPONDENCE-REVIEW CLERK (clerical)	3135	33444343355	SNNNNNNFFNNNNFNNNNN	NNNN3NNNNNNNNNN	T	231	891	07.05.04	4663	520408	55317
209.367-026	FINGERPRINT CLERK I (government ser.)	3222	33443333455	LNNNNNNFFNFFNFNNNN	NNNN2NNNNNNNNNN	T	231	950	07.04.03	4799	430107	59999
209.367-034	LOST-CHARGE-CARD CLERK (clerical)	3233	33453434455	SNNNNNNFFNFFNFNNFNN	NNNN3NNNNNNNNNN	P	231	894	07.05.03	4699	520406	59999
209.367-038	NEWS ASSISTANT (radio-tv broad.)	4243	33444344455	LNNNNNNFFONFFNFNNNN	NNNN3NNNNNNNNNN	J,T	231	863	07.05.03	4799	520408	59999
209.367-042	RECONSIGNMENT CLERK (clerical)	3334	33344244455	SNNNNNNFFNFFNFNNNN	NNNN3NNNNNNNNNN	P,T	231	850	07.05.04	4753	520499	58028
209.367-046	TITLE SEARCHER (real estate)	3135	33344244455	LNNNNNNFFNOONCNNNNN	NNNN3NNNNNNNNNN	J,T,P	231	895	07.05.02	3960	520408	59999
209.367-050	TRIP FOLLOWER (air trans.)	3333	33343344454	LNNNNNNFFNFFNFNFON	NNNN3NNNNNNNNNN	J	231	855	07.04.05	4799	520499	59999
209.367-054	YARD CLERK (r.r. trans.)	3223	33454333455	SNNNNNNFFNOONFNNNNN	NNNN3NNNNNNNNNN	R,T	231	851	07.05.03	4624	000000	58099
209.382-010	CONTINUITY CLERK (motion picture)	3135	33433233343	SNNNNNNFFNFFNFNNNN	NNNN3NNNNNNNNNN	J,T	231	891	07.05.03	4799	000000	55307
209.382-014	SPECIAL-CERTIFICATE DICTATOR (insurance)	3236	33344333455	SNNNNNNFFNNNNFNNNNN	NNNN3NNNNNNNNNN	J,T	231	895	07.05.03	4799	520803	53314
209.382-022	TRAFFIC CLERK (radio-tv broad.)	3234	34444233355	LNNONNNFFNNNONFNOFNN	NNNN3NNNNNNNNNN	T,J	231	863	07.05.04	4799	520408	59999
209.387-014	COMPILER (clerical)	3234	33454344455	SNNNNNNFFNFFNFNNNN	NNNN3NNNNNNNNNN	T	231	890	07.05.03	4794	000000	55328
209.387-018	CONTACT CLERK (utilities)	3234	33444344455	LNNNNNNFFNFFNFNNNN	NNNN3NNNNNNNNNN	T	231	891	07.05.04	4664	520408	55323
209.387-022	DATA-EXAMINATION CLERK (clerical)	3233	33344344455	SNNONONNFFNNNNFNFNN	NNNN3NNNNNNNNNN	T	231	891	07.05.02	4699	520407	59999
209.387-026	LIBRARY CLERK, TALKING BOOKS (library)	3133	33444344455	LNNNNNNFFNNNNFNNNN	NNNN2NNNNNNNNNN	J	221	933	05.09.01	4694	000000	53902
209.387-030	PROOFREADER (print. & pub.)	4145	22433244454	LNNNNNNFFNNNNCNNNNN	NNNN3NNNNNNNNNN	J,T	261	891	07.07.03	4792	480205	53911
209.387-034	SUGGESTION CLERK (clerical)	3134	33443233455	SNNNNNNFFNNNNFNNNNN	NNNN3NNNNNNNNNN	T	231	891	07.05.03	4699	520408	59999
209.562-010	CLERK, GENERAL (clerical)	3233	33343343455	LNNNNNNFFNOONFNNONN	NNNN3NNNNNNNNNN	T	231	891	07.07.03	4630	520408	55347
209.567-010	METER READER (utilities; waterworks)	3223	33444354554	LNNOOONFFONNNOFNOOOF	CNNN3NNNNNNNNNO	R,T	231	871	05.09.03	4755	000000	58014
209.567-014	ORDER CLERK, FOOD AND BEVERAGE (hotel & rest.)	3122	33454344455	SNNNNNNFFNFFNFNNNNN	NNNN2NNNNNNNNNN	P,T	231	890	07.04.02	4364	120507	49023
209.582-010	MUSIC COPYIST (print. & pub.)	3225	33422223355	SNNNNNNFFNNNNFNNNNN	NNNN3NNNNNNNNNN	R,T	231	891	07.05.03	4799	000000	59999
209.584-010	BRAILLE TRANSCRIBER, HAND (education; nonprofit organ.; print. & pub.)	3134	33443333355	MNNNNNNFFNNNNFNNNNFN	NNNN4NNNNNNNNNN	T	231	756	06.04.26	4757	000000	58017
209.587-010	ADDRESSER (clerical)	2122	44444434355	SNNNNNNFFNNNCCNNNONN	NNNN2NNNNNNNNNN	T	192	480	07.05.03	4799	520401	59999
209.587-014	CREDIT-CARD CLERK (retail trade)	3133	33344343455	SNNNNNNFFNNNCNNNNNN	NNNN3NNNNNNNNNN	R	231	891	07.07.02	4799	520408	59999
209.587-018	DIRECT-MAIL CLERK (clerical)	3124	33354344455	LNNNNNNFFNNNCNNNNNN	NNNN3NNNNNNNNNN	R	231	891	07.07.02	4699	520408	59999
209.587-022	HISTORY-CARD CLERK (utilities)	3234	33344244454	SNNNNNNFFNFFNFNNNN	NNNN2NNNNNNNNNN	R	231	898	07.07.02	4744	000000	57302
209.587-030	MAP CLERK (insurance)	3223	33444344454	SNNNNNNFFOONNNFNNNN	NNNN3NNNNNNNNNN	J	231	895	07.05.03	4699	520408	59999
209.587-034	MARKER (retail trade; wholesale tr.)	2112	44444343455	LNNNNNNFFNNNNFNNNNN	NNNN3NNNNNNNNNN	R,T	231	881	05.09.03	4759	080705	58021
209.587-042	RETURN-TO-FACTORY CLERK (clerical)	3223	33443333354	SNNNNNNFFNNNNFNNNNN	NNNN3NNNNNNNNNN	R,T	231	891	07.05.03	4699	080705	59999
209.587-046	SAMPLE CLERK, PAPER (paper & pulp; paper goods)	3223	33444344444	MNNNNNNFFNNNNFNNNNFN	NNNN4NNNNNNNNNN	T	231	470	06.04.26	4757	520408	58017
209.587-050	WRONG-ADDRESS CLERK (retail trade)	2123	34444344455	SNNNNNNFFNNNFNNNNN	NNNN2NNNNNNNNNN	R	231	880	07.07.02	4759	520408	59999
209.667-010	COPY HOLDER (print. & pub.)	4144	32434234455	SNNNNNNFFONFFNCNNNNN	NNNN3NNNNNNNNNN	R,T	261	891	07.05.02	4792	480205	53911
209.667-014	ORDER CALLER (clerical)	2122	44444444455	LNNNNNNFFNFFNCNNNNN	NNNN3NNNNNNNNNN	R	221	880	05.09.03	4759	000000	58099
209.667-018	CODE AND TEST CLERK (financial)	4345	33353344455	SNNNNNNOOOFNOONCNNONN	NNNN3NNNNNNNNNN	T	231	894	11.08.04	4744	520407	59999
209.687-010	CHECKER II (clerical)	3224	33344344454	SNNNNNNFFONNNNFNNNN	NNNN3NNNNNNNNNN	T	231	890	07.05.02	4792	520408	55338
209.687-014	MAIL HANDLER (government ser.)	3224	34434224355	LNNNNNNFFFNNNNFNNNNN	NNNN2NNNNNNNNNN	R	231	954	07.05.04	4742	000000	57308
209.687-018	REVIEWER (insurance)	3134	33444344455	SNNNNNNFFNNNNFNNNNN	NNNN3NNNNNNNNNN	R	231	895	07.05.02	4699	520803	53314
209.687-022	SORTER (clerical)	2123	44443343354	SNNNNNNFFNNNNFNNNNN	NNNN3NNNNNNNNNN	R	231	890	07.07.02	4699	520408	59999
209.687-026	MAIL CLERK (clerical)	3122	33443344455	LNNNNNNFFNFFNFNNNNN	NNNN3NNNNNNNNNN	R,T	231	891	07.05.04	4744	000000	57302
210.132-010	SUPERVISOR, AUDIT CLERKS (clerical)	4436	22344233455	LNNNNNNFFNFNFNNNNN	NNNN3NNNNNNNNNN	D,P,J	232	892	07.02.01	4521	520302	51002
210.362-010	DISTRIBUTION-ACCOUNTING CLERK (utilities)	3325	33243233354	SNNNNNNFFONFFNFNNNN	NNNN3NNNNNNNNNN	J,T	232	892	07.02.02	4712	520302	55338

DOT # DOT Title & Industry	Trng	Aptitude	Physical	Environment	Tempra	WkF	MPSMS	GOE	SOC	CIP	OES
210.367-010 ACCOUNT-INFORMATION CLERK (utilities)	4336	33344224355	SNNNNNNFFFOCCNFNNNNN	NNNNN3NNNNNNNNNNN	V,P,T	232	892	07.02.03	4712	520302	55338
210.367-014 FOREIGN-EXCHANGE-POSITION CLERK (financial)	4435	33244243355	SNNNNNNOOFNOONCNONNN	NNNNN3NNNNNNNNNNN	T	232	894	07.02.01	4712	520302	55338
210.382-010 AUDIT CLERK (clerical)	4437	33244233355	SNNNNNNFFNNNNFNNFNN	NNNNN3NNNNNNNNNNN	J,T	232	892	07.02.01	4712	520302	55338
210.382-014 BOOKKEEPER (clerical)	4436	33243233355	SNNNNNNFFNNONCNFNN	NNNNN3NNNNNNNNNNN	T	232	892	07.02.01	4712	520302	55338
210.382-030 CLASSIFICATION-CONTROL CLERK (clerical)	4335	33243223355	SNNNNNNFFNNNNCNNNN	NNNNN2NNNNNNNNNNN	R,T	232	892	07.02.02	4712	520302	55338
210.382-038 CREDIT-CARD CLERK (hotel & rest.)	3323	34343223355	SNNNNNNCCFNNNCNNCNN	NNNNN3NNNNNNNNNNN	R,T	232	892	07.02.02	4712	520302	55338
210.382-042 FIXED-CAPITAL CLERK (utilities)	4335	33243223355	SNNNNNNFFONNNNONNNNN	NNNNN3NNNNNNNNNNN	J,T	232	892	07.02.02	4712	520302	55338
210.382-046 GENERAL-LEDGER BOOKKEEPER (clerical)	4435	33243233355	SNNNNNNCCCNNNCNNNNNN	NNNNN2NNNNNNNNNNN	R,T	232	892	07.02.02	4712	520302	55338
210.382-050 MORTGAGE-LOAN-COMPUTATION CLERK (insurance)	3323	33244233355	SNNNNNNCCCNNNNCNNNNN	NNNNN2NNNNNNNNNNN	R,T	232	892	07.02.02	4712	520302	55338
210.382-054 NIGHT AUDITOR (hotel & rest.)	4435	33243233355	SNNNNNNFFFNNNNFNNFNN	NNNNN2NNNNNNNNNNN	R,T	232	892	07.02.02	4712	520302	55338
210.382-062 SECURITIES CLERK (clerical)	4436	33244233455	SNNNNNNFFNNNNFNNNNN	NNNNN3NNNNNNNNNNN	J,T	232	892	07.02.03	4712	520302	55338
211.132-010 TELLER, HEAD (financial)	4348	22243244454	LNNOONFFFOCCNFNNNFON	NNNNN3NNNNNNNNNNN	D,T,P,J	232	894	07.03.01	4529	520803	51002
211.137-010 SUPERVISOR, CASHIERS (hotel & rest.; retail trade)	4337	23344343455	LNNNNNNFFFNFFNFNNNNN	NNNNN3NNNNNNNNNNN	D,J,P	232	899	07.03.01	4529	520204	51002
211.137-014 SUPERVISOR, FOOD CHECKERS AND CASHIERS (hotel & rest.)	4437	23244344455	LNNNNNNFFFNFFNFONN	NNNNN3NNNNNNNNNNN	V,D,P,J	232	903	07.03.01	4529	520902	51002
211.137-018 SUPERVISOR, MONEY-ROOM (amuse. & rec.)	4436	33353243455	LNNNNNNFFFNFFNNNNNN	NNNNN2NNNNNNNNNNN	D,P,T	232	892	07.02.02	4529	520204	51002
211.137-022 SUPERVISOR, TELLERS (utilities)	4448	33344344454	SNNNNNNFFFNFFNFNNNNN	NNNNN2NNNNNNNNNNN	D,P,T,J	232	899	07.03.01	4529	520803	51002
211.362-010 CASHIER I (clerical)	4335	33343233355	SNNNNNNFFNFFNFNNONN	NNNNN3NNNNNNNNNNN	V,P,T	232	899	07.03.01	4364	520803	49023
211.362-014 FOREIGN BANKNOTE TELLER-TRADER (financial)	4445	23243222354	SNNNNNNFFFNFFNFNNNON	NNNNN3NNNNNNNNNNN	T,P	232	894	08.01.03	4791	520803	53102
211.362-018 TELLER (financial)	4335	33343222354	LNNONONCCCOFFNCNNFON	NNNNN3NNNNNNNNNNN	T,P	232	894	07.03.01	4791	520803	53102
211.367-010 PAYMASTER OF PURSES (amuse. & rec.)	4436	33343222455	SNNNNNNFFFNFFNFFNN	NNNNN3NNNNNNNNNNN	P,T	232	899	07.03.01	4364	520803	49023
211.382-010 TELLER, VAULT (financial)	4334	33343222355	MNNOOONCCCNNONCNNCNN	NNNNN3NNNNNNNNNNN	T	232	894	07.03.01	4791	000000	53102
211.462-010 CASHIER II (clerical)	3222	33344333455	LNNNNNNFFFNFFNFNNNNN	NNNNN3NNNNNNNNNNN	T,P	232	880	07.03.01	4364	080601	49023
211.462-014 CASHIER-CHECKER (retail trade)	3223	33344323355	LNNOONCCCNFFNFNONN	NNNNN3NNNNNNNNNNN	P,R,T	221	881	07.03.01	4364	080705	49023
211.462-018 CASHIER-WRAPPER (retail trade)	3223	33344333353	LNNNNNNFFONOONFNNNNN	NNNNN3NNNNNNNNNNN	R,P,T	232	899	09.04.02	4364	080102	49023
211.462-022 CASHIER, GAMBLING (amuse. & rec.)	3324	33344333453	SNNNNNNFFFNNFNNNFN	NNNNN2NNNNNNNNNNN	R,P,T	232	899	07.03.01	4364	000000	49023
211.462-026 CHECK CASHIER (business ser.)	3323	33344344455	SNNNNNNFFNOONFNNNNN	NNNNN2NNNNNNNNNNN	R,P,T	232	899	07.03.01	4364	520803	49023
211.462-030 DRIVERS'-CASH CLERK (motor trans.)	3213	33344333355	LNNNNNNFONFFNONNNN	NNNNN3NNNNNNNNNNN	R,P,T	232	899	07.02.02	4364	520803	49023
211.462-034 TELLER (utilities)	3223	33344333455	LNNNNNNFFNFFNFNNNNN	NNNNN2NNNNNNNNNNN	P,T	232	899	07.03.01	4364	520803	49023
211.462-038 TOLL COLLECTOR (government ser.)	3222	33344333454	LNNNNNNFFONNNNNNNNN	ONNNN2NNNNNNNNNNN	R,T	232	899	07.03.01	4364	000000	49023
211.467-010 CASHIER, COURTESY BOOTH (retail trade)	3223	33344333355	LNNNNNNFFONNNNNNNNN	NNNNN2NNNNNNNNNNN	V,P,T	232	892	09.04.02	4364	080705	49023
211.467-014 MONEY COUNTER (amuse. & rec.)	3334	33343233455	LNNNNNNCCNNNNCFNNNN	NNNNN3NNNNNNNNNNN	J,T	232	892	07.07.02	4718	520803	49023
211.467-018 PARIMUTUEL-TICKET CASHIER (amuse. & rec.)	3222	33353343453	LNNNNNNFFFNNNNNFNNNN	NNNNN2NNNNNNNNNNN	R,P,T	232	899	07.03.01	4364	520803	49023
211.467-022 PARIMUTUEL-TICKET SELLER (amuse. & rec.)	3222	33354343454	LNNNNNNFFNFFNFNNNNN	NNNNN2NNNNNNNNNNN	R,P,T	232	899	07.03.01	4364	520204	49023
211.467-026 SHEET WRITER (amuse. & rec.)	3222	33344343455	LNNNNNNFONFFNONNNN	NNNNN2NNNNNNNNNNN	P,J	232	913	07.02.02	4364	520803	49023
211.467-030 TICKET SELLER (clerical)	3222	33354333454	LOOOOONFFFNFNNFNONN	NNNNN3NNNNNNNNNNN	T,P	292	912	07.03.01	4364	521205	56011
211.467-034 CHANGE PERSON (amuse. & rec.)	2212	4445444455	LNNNNNNFFONNONONNNN	NNNNN3NNNNNNNNNNN	T,P	232	919	07.03.01	4364	000000	49023
211.482-010 CASHIER, TUBE ROOM (retail trade)	3223	33344333454	SNNNNNNFFFNNNNFNNNN	NNNNN3NNNNNNNNNNN	R,T	232	899	07.02.02	4364	080705	49023
211.482-014 FOOD CHECKER (hotel & rest.)	3213	33344343454	SNNNNNNFFONFFNFNNNN	NNNNN3NNNNNNNNNNN	R	232	899	07.06.02	4718	120507	56002
211.482-018 FOOD-AND-BEVERAGE CHECKER (hotel & rest.)	3223	33344333454	LNNNNNNFFNNNNFNNFNN	NNNNN2NNNNNNNNNNN	R,T	232	903	05.09.03	4364	120507	56002
213.132-010 SUPERVISOR, COMPUTER OPERATIONS (clerical)	5447	22233244455	LNNOOONOOONFFNFNNONN	NNNNN3NNNNNNNNNNN	D,P,J,T	233	893	07.06.01	4512	520204	51002
213.362-010 COMPUTER OPERATOR (clerical)	4236	33333233455	LOOOONFFNFFNNFNNONN	NNNNN3NNNNNNNNNNN	T,J	233	894	07.06.01	4612	521205	56014
213.382-010 COMPUTER PERIPHERAL EQUIPMENT OPERATOR (clerical)	3234	34334233355	LNNNNNNFFFNNONONNONN	NNNNN3NNNNNNNNNNN	T	233	893	07.06.01	4613	521205	56014
213.582-010 DIGITIZER OPERATOR (business ser.; petrol. & gas)	3325	33343333355	SNNNNNNFFFNNNNCNCNN	NNNNN3NNNNNNNNNNN	T	231	716	07.06.01	4613	000000	56002
214.137-010 DOCUMENTATION SUPERVISOR (water trans.)	4337	33344344455	LNNNNNNFONFFNFNNNNN	NNNNN3NNNNNNNNNNN	D,J,P	232	890	07.02.04	4521	520204	51002
214.137-014 SUPERVISOR, STATEMENT CLERKS (financial)	4347	33344343355	LNNNNNNFFNFFNFNNNNN	NNNNN3NNNNNNNNNNN	D,P,T	232	894	07.01.04	4519	520302	51002
214.137-018 RATE SUPERVISOR (clerical)	4336	33344344555	SNNNNNNFFONFFNFNNONN	NNNNN2NNNNNNNNNNN	D,V,P	232	850	07.02.02	4525	520204	51002
214.137-022 SUPERVISOR, ACCOUNTS RECEIVABLE (utilities; waterworks)	4438	33344244454	SNNNNNNFFONFFNFNNFON	NNNNN2NNNNNNNNNNN	D,P,J,T	232	892	07.02.02	4521	520204	51002
214.267-010 RATE ANALYST, FREIGHT (air trans.; motor trans.; r.r. trans.; water trans.)	4446	33255344455	SNNNNNNCCCNFFNFNNNNN	NNNNN2NNNNNNNNNNN	J	232	892	11.06.03	4716	520499	55344
214.362-010 DEMURRAGE CLERK (r.r. trans.)	3335	33344333455	SNNNNNNFFONFFNFNFNN	NNNNN3NNNNNNNNNNN	J,T	232	892	07.02.04	4715	520499	55344
214.362-014 DOCUMENTATION-BILLING CLERK (air trans.; motor trans.; r.r. trans.; water trans.)	3334	33343333455	SNNNNNNFFCNOOFNFNNNN	NNNNN2NNNNNNNNNNN	R,T	232	892	07.02.04	4715	520302	55344
214.362-022 INSURANCE CLERK (medical ser.)	4345	33344344455	SNNNNNNFFFNFFNFNNNNN	NNNNN3NNNNNNNNNNN	R,P,T	232	895	07.02.04	4715	510801	55344

DOT #	DOT Title & Industry	Trng	Aptitude	Physical	Environment	Tempra	WkF	MPSMS	GOE	SOC	CIP	OES
214.362-026	INVOICE-CONTROL CLERK (clerical)	4334	33343343455	SNNNNNNFFNFFNNFNFNN	NNNN3NNNNNNNN	T	232	892	07.02.04	4715	520302	55344
214.362-030	RATE CLERK, PASSENGER (motor trans.)	4334	33343343455	SNNNNNNFFNFFNFNNFNN	NNNN3NNNNNNNN	J	232	850	07.04.04	4716	081105	53802
214.362-034	TARIFF INSPECTOR (r.r. trans.)	4445	33353233455	LNNNNNNFFONOONFNNFNN	NNNN2NNNNNNNN	V,J	232	892	11.10.01	4783	520499	53505
214.362-038	TRAFFIC-RATE CLERK (clerical)	4335	33344232455	SNNNNNNFFNOONFNNFNN	NNNN2NNNNNNNN	J,T	232	850	07.02.04	4716	520499	55344
214.362-042	BILLING CLERK (clerical)	4334	33344223454	SNNNNNNCCNNNNCNNCON	NNNN3NNNNNNNN	T	232	899	07.02.04	4715	520302	55344
214.362-046	STATEMENT CLERK (financial)	3234	33343233455	SNNNNNNFFNOONFNNFNN	NNNN3NNNNNNNN	R,T	232	894	07.02.02	4699	520408	53126
214.382-014	BILLING TYPIST (clerical)	3334	33344233355	SNNNNNNFFCNNONFNNONN	NNNN3NNNNNNNN	T	231	892	07.02.04	4715	520302	55344
214.382-018	C.O.D. CLERK (clerical)	3223	33344233455	SNNNNNNFFONNNNFNNFNN	NNNN3NNNNNNNN	R,T	232	892	07.02.04	4715	520302	55344
214.382-022	INTERLINE CLERK (motor trans.; r.r. trans.)	3334	33354333455	SNNNNNNFFNNNNFNNFNN	NNNN2NNNNNNNN	J,T	232	892	07.02.04	4716	520499	55344
214.382-026	REVISING CLERK (motor trans.; r.r. trans.)	3334	33354333455	SNNNNNNCCCNNNNONNONN	NNNN2NNNNNNNN	J,T	232	892	07.02.04	4716	520499	55344
214.382-030	SETTLEMENT CLERK (smelt. & refin.)	3334	33344344455	SNNNNNNFFNNNNFNNNNN	NNNN3NNNNNNNN	J,T	232	892	07.02.04	4715	520302	55344
214.387-010	BILLING-CONTROL CLERK (utilities)	3335	33344233355	SNNNNNNFFFNNNNFNNNNN	NNNN3NNNNNNNN	R,T	231	892	07.02.04	4716	520302	55344
214.387-014	RATE REVIEWER (utilities)	4346	33344344455	SNNNNNNFFNNNNFNNFNN	NNNN2NNNNNNNN	J,T	232	898	11.06.03	4716	520302	55344
214.387-018	SERVICES CLERK (water trans.)	4335	33343333355	SNNNNNNFFNNNNFNNNNN	NNNN2NNNNNNNN	J,T	232	890	07.02.04	4716	520499	56002
214.462-010	ACCOUNTS-ADJUSTABLE CLERK (r.r. trans.)	3333	33354333455	SNNNNNNFFNNNNNONNNNN	NNNN3NNNNNNNN	R,T	232	892	07.02.04	4718	520499	55328
214.467-010	FOREIGN CLERK (clerical).	4435	33344344455	SNNNNNNFFNNNNFNNFNN	NNNN2NNNNNNNN	J	231	891	07.02.04	4716	520302	55344
214.467-014	PRICER, MESSAGE AND DELIVERY SERVICE (business ser.)	3223	33344333355	SNNNNNNFFONFNNNNN	NNNN3NNNNNNNN	T	232	899	07.02.04	4716	520499	56002
214.482-010	BILLING-MACHINE OPERATOR (clerical)	3334	33344233355	SNNNNNNNFFCNNONCNNFNN	NNNN3NNNNNNNN	R,T	232	892	07.06.02	4718	520302	56002
214.482-014	DEPOSIT-REFUND CLERK (utilities)	3334	34344344354	SNNNNNNFFNNNNFNNFON	NNNN3NNNNNNNN	R,T	232	891	07.02.04	4715	520302	55344
214.482-018	MEDICAL-VOUCHER CLERK (insurance)	3233	33344333455	SNNNNNNFFONNNNFNNNNN	NNNN2NNNNNNNN	R,T	232	892	07.02.04	4716	520302	55344
214.482-022	RATER (insurance)	3334	33344233455	SNNNNNNFFNNNNFNNONN	NNNN2NNNNNNNN	R,T	232	895	07.02.04	4716	520803	55344
214.487-010	CHART CALCULATOR (utilities)	4435	33244244454	SNNNNNNFFONNNNFNNNNN	NNNN3NNNNNNNN	J,T	232	892	07.02.04	4794	520302	55328
214.587-010	TELEGRAPH-SERVICE RATER (tel. & tel.)	2222	34454333455	SNNNNNNFFNNNNFNNNNN	NNNN2NNNNNNNN	R	231	890	07.07.03	4716	000000	55344
214.587-014	TRAFFIC CLERK (clerical)	3324	34444343455	SNNNNNNFFNNNNFNNFNN	NNNN2NNNNNNNN	J,T	232	892	07.02.04	4753	520499	58028
215.137-010	CREW SCHEDULER, CHIEF (air trans.)	4347	23344444455	SNNNNNNFONFFNNFNNNNN	NNNN2NNNNNNNN	D,J,P	232	898	07.05.01	4525	520204	51002
215.137-014	SUPERVISOR, PAYROLL (clerical)	4347	33344244455	SNNNNNNFFNFFNFNNFNN	NNNN3NNNNNNNN	D,T,P,J	232	892	07.02.02	4521	520204	51002
215.137-018	SUPERVISOR, FORCE ADJUSTMENT (tel. & tel.)	4347	22343234455	SNNNNNNFFNFFNFNNFON	NNNN3NNNNNNNN	V,D,P,J	232	862	07.05.01	4525	520204	51002
215.167-010	CAR CLERK, PULLMAN (r.r. trans.)	4336	33344344455	SNNNNNNFONFFNNNNNNN	NNNN4NNNNNNNN	D,P	231	851	07.05.01	4752	000000	58005
215.362-010	CREW SCHEDULER (air trans.)	3335	33343343455	SNNNNNNFFNOONFNNNNN	NNNN2NNNNNNNN	R,T	232	898	07.05.01	4752	521001	58008
215.362-014	DISPATCHER CLERK (r.r. trans.)	3224	33344233355	SNNNNNNFFNOONFNNFNN	NNNN3NNNNNNNN	R,T	232	898	07.02.05	4752	521001	58008
215.362-018	FLIGHT-CREW-TIME CLERK (air trans.)	4345	22354242354	SNNNNNNFFNOONFNNFNN	NNNN3NNNNNNNN	J,T	232	898	07.02.05	4713	520302	55341
215.362-022	TIMEKEEPER (clerical)	3223	33344233355	SNNNNNNFFNOONFNNNNN	NNNN3NNNNNNNN	T	232	898	07.02.05	4713	520302	55341
215.367-010	ASSIGNMENT CLERK (motor trans.)	3223	33454344455	SNNNNNNFFNFFFNFNNNNN	NNNN4NNNNNNNN	J,T	231	898	07.05.01	4752	521001	58008
215.367-014	PERSONNEL SCHEDULER (clerical)	4334	33344233455	SNNNNNNFFNNNNFNNNNN	NNNN2NNNNNNNN	J,T	232	898	07.05.01	4752	521001	58008
215.367-018	TAXICAB COORDINATOR (motor trans.)	3225	44444344455	SNNNNNNFFONNNNFNNNNN	NNNN2NNNNNNNN	J,T	232	852	07.05.03	4751	521001	58005
215.382-014	PAYROLL CLERK (clerical)	4334	33344233455	SNNNNNNFFNFFNFNNFNN	NNNN3NNNNNNNN	T	232	892	07.02.05	4713	520302	55341
215.563-010	CALLER (r.r. trans.)	2222	33444334345	LNNNNNNFFNFFNFNNONN	NNNN3NNNNNNNN	P,R	282	899	07.07.03	4745	520406	57311
216.132-010	SUPERVISOR, ACCOUNTING CLERKS (clerical)	4447	22344233455	SNNNNNNOOFNFFNFNNNNN	NNNN3NNNNNNNN	D,T,P,J	232	892	07.02.02	4521	520204	51002
216.132-014	SUPERVISOR, SECURITIES VAULT (financial)	4347	33444343454	SNNNNNNOOFFNFFNCNNFNN	NNNN2NNNNNNNN	D,T,P,J	232	894	07.02.02	4519	520204	51002
216.137-010	COST-AND-SALES-RECORD SUPERVISOR (utilities)	5547	22233243354	SNNNNNNNFFNFFNFNNFON	NNNN2NNNNNNNN	V,P,J,T	232	891	07.02.03	4521	520204	51002
216.137-014	TRANSFER CLERK, HEAD (financial)	4446	32343243455	SNNNNNNNFFONFFNFNNNNN	NNNN3NNNNNNNN	D,P	232	894	07.01.02	4521	520302	51002
216.362-014	COLLECTION CLERK (financial)	4445	33343223455	SNNNNNNFFNOONFNNFNN	NNNN3NNNNNNNN	T	232	894	07.02.02	4718	520302	55338
216.362-022	FOOD-AND-BEVERAGE CONTROLLER (hotel & rest.)	4325	33344333455	SNNNNNNFFNOONCNNNNN	NNNN2NNNNNNNN	R,T	232	892	07.02.02	4718	120507	55338
216.362-026	MORTGAGE-ACCOUNTING CLERK (clerical)	4333	33343243455	SNNNNNNNFFNOONFNNFNN	NNNN2NNNNNNNN	R	232	894	07.02.02	4712	520302	55338
216.362-034	RESERVES CLERK (financial)	4335	33354233355	SNNNNNNOOFNFFNCNNONN	NNNN3NNNNNNNN	T	232	892	07.02.01	4712	520302	55338
216.362-038	ELECTRONIC FUNDS TRANSFER COORDINATOR (financial)	4447	33355223455	LNNNNNNFFNFFNFNNFNN	NNNN3NNNNNNNN	T,P	232	894	07.02.01	4712	000000	55338
216.362-042	MARGIN CLERK I (financial)	3336	33344233455	SNNNNNONOFFNFFNCNNFNN	NNNN2NNNNNNNN	T,P	232	894	07.02.02	4712	000000	53128
216.367-010	TRANSFER CLERK (financial)	3236	33455233455	LNNNNONFFNOONFNNONN	NNNN3NNNNNNNN	T	232	894	07.02.02	4699	000000	59999
216.367-014	TRUST-VAULT CLERK (financial)	4336	33344244455	SNNONNOOFNOONCNNNNN	NNNN2NNNNNNNN	T	232	894	07.02.02	4712	000000	55338
216.382-022	BUDGET CLERK (clerical)	4435	33243233455	SNNNNNNOCCNNNNFNNONN	NNNN3NNNNNNNN	R,T	232	892	07.01.04	4712	520302	55338
216.382-026	CLEARING-HOUSE CLERK (financial)	4335	33343233355	LNNNNNNFFNNNNFNNFNN	NNNN3NNNNNNNN	T	232	894	07.02.01	4712	000000	55338

DOT #	DOT Title & Industry	Trng	Aptitude	Physical	Environment	Tempra	WkF	MPSMS	GOE	SOC	CIP	OES
216.382-034	COST CLERK (clerical)	3334	33344233355	SNNNNNNFFFNONFNFNN	NNNN3NNNNNNNNN	T,J	232	890	07.02.02	4716	520302	55344
216.382-046	MARGIN CLERK II (financial)	4335	33354233455	SNNNNNNFFFNNNNFNNN	NNNN2NNNNNNNNN	T	232	894	07.02.02	4699	000000	53128
216.382-050	POLICY-VALUE CALCULATOR (insurance)	3225	33354233455	SNNNNNNFFFNNNNFNNN	NNNN2NNNNNNNNN	J,T	232	895	07.02.03	4718	520803	55344
216.382-054	RECEIPT-AND-REPORT CLERK (water trans.)	4335	33344233455	SNNNNNNFFFNNNNFNNN	NNNN3NNNNNNNNN	R,J	232	892	07.02.03	4716	520302	55344
216.382-058	RETURNED-ITEM CLERK (financial)	3334	33344233355	SNNNNNNFFFNNNNFNNON	NNNN3NNNNNNNNN	R,T	232	892	07.02.02	4712	520302	55338
216.382-062	STATISTICAL CLERK (clerical)	3334	33343233455	SNNNNNNCCNOONFNNFNN	NNNN3NNNNNNNNN	R,T	232	891	07.02.03	4794	520302	55328
216.382-066	STATISTICAL CLERK, ADVERTISING (retail trade)	3324	34343233355	SNNNNNNFFNNNNFNNFNN	NNNN2NNNNNNNNN	R,T	232	890	07.02.03	4794	520302	55328
216.462-010	BOOKING PRIZER (tobacco)	3333	33343233455	LNNNNNNFFNOONFNNNNN	NNNN3NNNNNNNNN	R,T	232	898	05.09.03	4756	520408	58017
216.482-010	ACCOUNTING CLERK (clerical)	4335	33354233455	SNNNNNNFFFNNNNFNNNN	NNNN3NNNNNNNNN	T	232	892	07.02.02	4712	520302	55338
216.482-018	AUDIT-MACHINE OPERATOR (clerical)	3224	33344233455	SNNNNNNFFFNNONCNNONN	NNNN2NNNNNNNNN	R,T	232	892	07.06.02	4718	520302	56002
216.482-022	CALCULATING-MACHINE OPERATOR (clerical)	3323	33354233455	SNNNNNNFFFNNNNFNNNNN	NNNN3NNNNNNNNN	R,T	232	892	07.02.02	4712	520302	56002
216.482-026	DIVIDEND-DEPOSIT-VOUCHER CLERK (insurance)	3223	33344233355	SNNNNNNFFFNNNNFNNNNN	NNNN3NNNNNNNNN	R,T	232	892	07.02.04	4712	520302	55338
216.482-030	LAUNDRY PRICING CLERK (laundry & rel.)	3323	33344233455	SNNNNNONFFFNNNOONFNN	NNNN3NNNNNNNNN	R	232	892	07.02.02	4363	200301	49017
216.482-034	DIVIDEND CLERK (financial)	3335	33444233455	LNNNNNNFFNOONFNNNNN	NNNN2NNNNNNNNN	T	232	894	07.02.02	4712	000000	53128
216.567-010	TICKET MARKER (wholesale tr.)	3233	33444333455	LNNNNNNFFONNNFNNNNN	NNNN2NNNNNNNNN	R,T	231	898	05.09.03	4759	520499	58021
216.587-010	BOOKING CLERK (wholesale tr.)	2113	34454334455	LNNNNNNFFNNNFNFNNOON	NNNN3NNNNNNNNN	R,T	232	892	05.09.02	4712	520302	55338
216.685-010	GAS USAGE METER CLERK (petrol. refin.; pipe lines; utilities)	3233	34343323343	SNNNNNNNFFONFFNNNNNN	NNNN3NNNNNNNNN	R,T	232	571	05.09.03	4729	000000	56099
217.132-010	PROOF-MACHINE-OPERATOR SUPERVISOR (financial)	4346	22344233355	SNNNNNNCCFNNONCNONN	NNNN3NNNNNNNNN	D,T,P	232	892	07.06.02	4521	520302	51002
217.382-010	PROOF-MACHINE OPERATOR (financial)	3334	33344233355	SNNNNNNFFFNNNNFNNNNN	NNNN3NNNNNNNNN	R,T	232	892	07.06.02	4718	520302	53108
217.485-010	CURRENCY COUNTER (financial)	3223	34343333355	LNNONONFCCNNONONONN	NNNN3NNNNNNNNN	T	232	894	05.12.19	4729	520302	56099
217.585-010	COIN-COUNTER-AND-WRAPPER (clerical)	3223	34344333355	MNNONONFCCNNONCNNONN	NNNN4NNNNNNNNN	T	232	894	05.12.19	4729	520302	56099
219.132-010	SUPERVISOR, POLICY-CHANGE CLERKS (insurance)	4347	23355243455	SNNNNNNFFNFFCNCNNONN	NNNN3NNNNNNNNN	D,J,P	232	895	07.02.02	4519	520803	51002
219.132-014	SUPERVISOR, TRUST ACCOUNTS (financial)	4347	22344244455	SNNNNNNNOOFNCCNCNNONN	NNNN3NNNNNNNNN	D,T,P,J	232	894	07.02.02	4799	080401	51002
219.132-022	SUPERVISOR, UNDERWRITING CLERKS (insurance)	4447	22344243455	LNNNNNNFFNFFFNNNNNN	NNNN2NNNNNNNNN	D,P,T	232	895	07.02.02	4519	520204	51002
219.137-010	FIELD CASHIER (construction)	4334	33344244455	SNNNNNNFFNNNNNNNNNN	NNNN3NNNNNNNNN	D,P,T	231	890	07.02.02	4529	520204	51002
219.267-010	HANDICAPPER, HARNESS RACING (amuse. & rec.)	4334	33344233455	SNNNNNOOONNNNNFNNNNN	NNNN3NNNNNNNNN	J	211	891	11.06.03	3400	000000	34058
219.362-010	ADMINISTRATIVE CLERK (clerical)	4346	33344233455	LNNNNNNFFNFFNFNFNNN	NNNN3NNNNNNNNN	J,P,V	231	890	07.01.02	4630	520408	55347
219.362-014	ATTENDANCE CLERK (education)	3334	33344233355	SNNNNNNFFFNFFNNNNNN	NNNN3NNNNNNNNN	V,P,T	232	891	07.05.03	4699	520408	59999
219.362-018	BROKERAGE CLERK II (financial)	4335	33344333355	LNNNNNNOFFNNONCNNONN	NNNN2NNNNNNNNN	R,T	232	892	07.02.02	4699	080401	53128
219.362-022	CLERK, TELEGRAPH SERVICE (tel. & tel.)	4335	33344233455	SNNNNNNFFFNNNOONFNNN	NNNN3NNNNNNNNN	V,P	232	862	07.02.02	4630	520408	55347
219.362-026	CONTRACT CLERK, AUTOMOBILE (retail trade)	4335	33344233455	SNNNNNNNFFONFNFNNNNN	NNNN2NNNNNNNNN	V,T	232	890	07.02.02	4630	520408	55347
219.362-030	EXTENSION CLERK (utilities)	4345	33354244455	SNNNNNNFFFNNONFNFNNN	NNNN2NNNNNNNNN	J,T	231	898	07.05.03	4752	000000	58008
219.362-038	MORTGAGE-CLOSING CLERK (clerical)	4345	33344244455	SNNNNNNNFFNFFNFNNNNN	NNNN3NNNNNNNNN	P	232	894	07.05.02	4799	000000	53121
219.362-042	POLICY-CHANGE CLERK (insurance)	4335	33244233355	SNNNNNNFFNFFONONCNNONN	NNNN3NNNNNNNNN	T,J	232	895	07.02.02	4699	520803	53314
219.362-046	REAL-ESTATE CLERK (real estate)	3234	33344333355	SNNNNNNFFFNNONFNNNNN	NNNN3NNNNNNNNN	J,T,V	232	895	07.01.04	4630	520408	53914
219.362-050	REVIVAL CLERK (insurance)	4435	33244244455	SNNNNNNFFFNNONFNNNNN	NNNN2NNNNNNNNN	J,T	232	891	07.05.02	4699	520408	53314
219.362-054	SECURITIES CLERK (financial)	4434	33345233455	LNNNNNNOFFNNOONCNNONN	NNNN3NNNNNNNNN	P,T	231	892	07.01.04	4699	000000	53128
219.362-066	VOUCHER CLERK (r.r. trans.)	4346	33344224455	SNNNNNNNFFNNONFNFNNN	NNNN3NNNNNNNNN	J,T	232	892	07.02.04	4712	520302	55338
219.362-070	TAX PREPARER (business ser.)	3323	44334344555	SNNNNNNFFFNNNNFNNCNNN	NNNN3NNNNNNNNN	T,P,J	232	892	07.02.02	4622	520302	21111
219.362-074	TRUST OPERATIONS ASSISTANT (financial)	3334	33344224455	LNNOOONFCNCCNCNNNFNN	ONNN3NNNNNNNNN	T,P,J	231	894	07.01.03	4756	520302	55108
219.367-010	CHECKER, DUMP GROUNDS (business ser.)	3223	33344333455	LNNNNNNFFNNNFFNNNNNN	NNNN3NNNNNNNNN	J,T	212	874	05.09.03	4754	520803	58099
219.367-014	INSURANCE CLERK (financial; insurance)	3335	33343233455	SNNNNNNFFFNNOONFNNNN	NNNN2NNNNNNNNN	T	232	890	07.05.03	4753	520302	53308
219.367-018	MERCHANDISE DISTRIBUTOR (retail trade)	3234	33344334455	LNNNNNNFFFNNOONFNNNN	NNNN2NNNNNNNNN	R,T	232	891	07.05.04	4753	080705	58023
219.367-022	PAPER-CONTROL CLERK (water trans.)	3334	33344333455	SNNNNNNFFFNNOOFFNNNN	NNNN2NNNNNNNNN	J	232	898	07.05.04	4699	520499	58028
219.367-030	SHIPPING-ORDER CLERK (clerical)	4337	33333232354	LNNNNNNFFONFFNFNNNN	NNNN3NNNNNNNNN	R,T	232	895	07.01.04	4699	520499	58028
219.367-038	UNDERWRITING CLERK (insurance)	3334	33344333455	SNNNNNNFFFNCNOONCNNONN	NNNN3NNNNNNNNN	T,J	232	894	07.03.01	4712	520803	59999
219.367-042	CANCELING AND CUTTING CONTROL CLERK (financial)	3334	33333232354	SNNNNNNNFFFNCONOCNNCNFNN	NNNN3NNNNNNNNN	T	231	894	07.05.02	4649	000000	53121
219.367-046	DISBURSEMENT CLERK (financial)	4335	33354333455	SNNNNNNNOOFNOONCNONONN	NNNN3NNNNNNNNN	T	232	894	07.05.02	4712	080401	55338
219.382-010	CHECK WRITER (retail trade)	4423	44344233455	SNNNNNNFFNNNNFNNNNNN	NNNN3NNNNNNNNN	J,T	232	892	07.06.02	4699	520302	59999
219.387-010	ASSIGNMENT CLERK (tel. & tel.)	3334	33343334455	SNNNNNNFFONNNFNNNNNN	NNNN2NNNNNNNNN	R	231	861	07.05.03	4699	000000	59999

DOT #	DOT Title & Industry	Trng	Aptitude	Physical	Environment	Tempra	WkF	MPSMS	GOE	SOC	CIP	OES
219.387-014	INSURANCE CLERK (clerical)	4334	33344344455	SNNNNNNFFNNNNFNNNN	NNNN2NNNNNNNNN	R,T	232	891	07.05.03	4699	520803	59999
219.387-022	PLANIMETER OPERATOR (government ser.)	3213	33343333354	SNNNNNNFFNNNFNNNFON	NNNN2NNNNNNNNN	R,T	232	716	07.07.03	4799	000000	55328
219.387-026	SPACE-AND-STORAGE CLERK (ordnance)	3223	33333343455	LNNNNNNFFNNNNFNNNN	NNNN2NNNNNNNNN	R,T	231	370	07.05.03	4754	520499	58023
219.387-030	STOCK CONTROL CLERK (clerical)	4335	33344344354	LNNNNNNFFNOONFNNONN	NNNN3NNNNNNNNN	T	231	898	07.05.03	4754	080705	58023
219.462-010	COUPON CLERK (financial)	4345	33344233355	SNNNNNNFFNOONFNNFNN	NNNN3NNNNNNNNN	T	232	894	07.02.02	4791	520803	53102
219.462-014	TRAIN CLERK (r.r. trans.)	3223	33354333455	SNNNNNNFFONOONFNNNNN	NNNN3NNNNNNNNN	R,T	231	851	07.05.03	4699	520408	59999
219.467-010	GRADING CLERK (education)	4333	33344344455	SNNNNNNFFONNFNNNNN	NNNN2NNNNNNNNN	T	232	899	07.02.03	4795	521001	53905
219.482-010	BROKERAGE CLERK I (financial)	4335	33355233455	SNNNNNNOFFNNNONCNNONN	NNNN2NNNNNNNNN	T	232	894	07.05.02	4699	000000	53128
219.482-014	INSURANCE CHECKER (insurance)	3335	33355233455	SNNNNNNFFCNNNNFNNONN	NNNN3NNNNNNNNN	T,J	231	895	07.05.02	4699	520803	53314
219.482-018	REINSURANCE CLERK (insurance)	4335	33354233355	SNNNNNNFFCNNNFNNONN	NNNN3NNNNNNNNN	J,T	232	895	07.02.04	4699	520803	59999
219.487-010	TAX CLERK (clerical)	3223	33344333455	SNNNNNNFFNNNFNNONN	NNNN2NNNNNNNNN	R,T	232	892	07.02.04	4712	520302	55338
219.587-010	PARIMUTUEL-TICKET CHECKER (amuse. & rec.)	3332	34343334353	SNNNNNNCCCNNNNCNNCON	NNNN3NNNNNNNNN	J,T	231	891	07.05.02	4712	520302	55338
221.132-010	CHIEF CLERK, MEASUREMENT DEPARTMENT (petrol. & gas; pipe lines)	4447	22243244455	SNNNNNNFFNONNNNN	NNNN2NNNNNNNNN	D,P,T,V	232	898	07.02.03	4525	520204	51002
221.137-010	CONTROL CLERK, HEAD (clock & watch)	4346	33344344455	LNNNNNNFFONFFNFNNNN	NNNN3NNNNNNNNN	D,P,V	221	898	05.09.02	4525	000000	51002
221.137-014	SUPERVISOR, PRODUCTION CLERKS (clerical)	4447	22233244455	SNNNNNNFFNFFNFNNNN	NNNN2NNNNNNNNN	D,J,P	232	898	07.02.03	4525	520204	51002
221.162-010	PRODUCTION CONTROL (clerical)	4348	22333244455	LNNONNNFFNFNFNFNN	NNNN3NNNNNNNNN	D,J	295	898	05.09.02	4525	520204	51002
221.167-010	PRODUCTION SCHEDULER, PAPERBOARD PRODUCTS (paper goods)	4446	33333333355	SNNNNNNFFONNFNNNNN	NNNN2NNNNNNNNN	D,J,P	232	898	05.03.03	4752	150603	58008
221.167-010	COPY CUTTER (print. & pub.)	4338	32432243455	SNNNNNNFFONFNNFNNN	NNNN2NNNNNNNNN	D,P,T	191	898	05.10.05	4752	480205	58008
221.167-014	MATERIAL COORDINATOR (clerical)	4346	33343344454	LNNNONNNFFNFNFNNOON	NNNN3NNNNNNNNN	P,V,J,T	221	898	05.09.02	4752	150603	58008
221.167-018	PRODUCTION COORDINATOR (clerical)	4346	33343344455	SNNNNNNFFONFNNONNNNN	NNNN3NNNNNNNNN	D,T,P,J	231	898	05.09.02	4752	150603	58008
221.167-022	RETORT-LOAD EXPEDITER (wood prod., nec)	3335	33333333345	LNOOOONFFONFFNFOFFNC	NNNN4NNFNFNNNN	D,P,T	231	898	05.09.02	4752	000000	58008
221.167-026	CUSTOMER SERVICES COORDINATOR (print. & pub.)	5446	22333344452	LNNNNNNOOONCNCNONOOON	NNNN3NONNNNNNON	D,P,J	295	899	05.09.02	4752	080299	58008
221.362-010	AIRCRAFT-LOG CLERK (air trans.)	3334	33344344355	SNNOOONFFFNFNNNFNN	NNNN2NNNNNNNNN	J,T	232	898	05.09.03	4759	520408	58099
221.362-014	DISPATCHER, RELAY (pipe lines)	3335	33334333355	SNNNONFFFNFFNNOON	NNNN3NNNNNNNNN	P,J	231	501	07.04.05	4751	520406	58005
221.362-018	ESTIMATOR, PAPERBOARD BOXES (paper goods)	4446	22222233354	LNNNNNNFFFNNFNNNNN	NNNN3NNNNNNNNN	J	232	898	05.09.02	4752	520302	21902
221.362-022	PROGRESS CLERK (construction)	4335	33344333354	LNNNNNNFFNNONNNONNN	NNNN3NNNNNNNNN	R,T	231	891	07.05.03	4752	520408	58099
221.362-026	RAILROAD-MAINTENANCE CLERK (r.r. trans.)	3334	33344333455	SNNNNNNFFNOONFNNNNN	NNNN2NNNNNNNNN	R,T	232	898	07.05.03	4759	520408	58008
221.362-030	COMPUTER PROCESSING SCHEDULER (clerical)	4246	33344233455	SNNNNNNOOFFNFNNFNN	NNNN3NNNNNNNNN	T,P,J	233	893	07.05.01	4752	000000	58008
221.367-010	ALTERATIONS WORKROOM CLERK (retail trade)	3223	33344344455	LNNNNNNFFNOONFNOONN	NNFN4NNNNNNNNN	V,P	232	898	05.09.02	4752	200305	21902
221.367-014	ESTIMATOR, PRINTING (print. & pub.)	4336	23233244454	MNFNNNFFFNFNNFNN	NNNN4NONNNNNNNN	T,P,J	232	898	05.09.02	4752	480208	58008
221.367-018	FOLLOW-UP CLERK (elec. equip.)	4336	33355354454	SNNNNNNFFNOONFNOONN	NNNN2NNNNNNNNN	V,P	221	898	05.09.03	4753	520499	58028
221.367-022	INDUSTRIAL-ORDER CLERK (clerical)	4344	33333333355	SNNNNNNFFONOONFNNNNN	NNNN3NNNNNNNNN	P,T	282	898	05.09.02	4752	000000	58008
221.367-026	LINE-UP WORKER (auto. mfg.)	3223	33344344455	LNNNNNNFFNOONFNNFNN	NNNN3NNNNNNNNN	P,T	231	898	07.05.01	4752	470604	58008
221.367-030	LOCOMOTIVE LUBRICATING-SYSTEMS CLERK (r.r. trans.)	3235	33444344455	SNNNNNNCCCNFNCNOFNN	NNNN3NNNNNNNNN	J	231	851	07.04.05	4752	000000	58005
221.367-034	MACHINE-STOPPAGE-FREQUENCY CHECKER (textile)	3333	33443344455	LNNNNNNFFNOONFONFNN	NNNN4NNNNNNNNN	J,T	231	898	07.05.01	4752	520408	58008
221.367-038	MAINTENANCE DATA ANALYST (military ser.)	3335	33344344455	SNNNNNNFFNFFNFNNNN	ONNN4NNONNNNNNNN	P,V	231	712	05.09.03	4752	000000	58008
221.367-042	MATERIAL EXPEDITER (clerical)	3334	33344344444	MNOONFFNFFNFOOOO	NNNN3NNNNNNNNN	T,P,V	221	864	07.05.04	4751	000000	58008
221.367-046	MILL RECORDER, COMPUTERIZED MILL (steel & rel.)	3235	33333343455	LNNNNNNFFONFFNONNNNN	NNNN3NNNNNNNNN	R,T	232	898	05.09.02	4752	520407	58008
221.367-050	RECORDER (steel & rel.)	3235	33434344455	LNNNNNNFFNNFFNFNNNN	NNFN4NNNNNNNNN	J,T	231	898	07.05.03	4752	520499	58008
221.367-054	RELAY-RECORD CLERK (utilities)	3335	33344344455	SNNNNNNFFNFFNFNNNN	NNNN3NNNNNNNNN	J	231	898	07.05.03	4752	520408	58008
221.367-058	REPRODUCTION ORDER PROCESSOR (clerical)	3235	33344344455	SNNNNNNFFONFNFNFNNN	NNNN3NNNNNNNNN	P,J	191	898	05.09.02	4752	520408	58008
221.367-062	SALES CORRESPONDENT (clerical)	4246	22333344455	LNNNNNNFFONNFNFNNNN	NNNN3NNNNNNNNN	V,P,J	231	898	07.05.01	4663	520408	55317
221.367-066	SCHEDULER, MAINTENANCE (clerical)	3234	33344344455	SNNNNNNFFONFFNONNNNN	NNNN2NNNNNNNNN	P	231	898	05.09.02	4752	520408	58008
221.367-070	SERVICE CLERK (clerical)	3224	33444344455	SNNNNNNFFNFFNFNNNN	NNNN2NNNNNNNNN	V,P	231	898	07.04.05	4751	470604	58005
221.367-078	TRAFFIC CLERK (business ser.)	4234	33444344455	SNNNNNNFFNOOONFNNNNN	NNNN2NNNNNNNNN	V,P	231	898	07.05.01	4752	000000	58008
221.367-082	WORK-ORDER-SORTING CLERK (utilities)	3235	33444344455	SNNNNNNFFNFFNFNNNN	NNNN2NNNNNNNNN	R,T	231	898	07.05.01	4751	520408	58008
221.367-086	CLERK, TELEVISION PRODUCTION (radio-tv broad.)	4336	33443344455	SNNNNNNFFNFNFNFNN	NNNN3NNNNNNNNN	V	232	864	07.05.01	4752	000000	58005
221.367-090	FORMULA CLERK (textile)	3333	33343243455	SNNNNNNFFNNNNFNFNN	NNNN2NNNNNNNNN	T	232	898	05.09.02	4752	150699	58017
221.382-010	CHART CLERK (clerical)	3334	33343233355	SNNNNNNFFONNNNFNNFNN	NNNN2NNNNNNNNN	R,T	232	898	07.02.03	4794	520408	55328
221.382-018	PRODUCTION CLERK (clerical)	3334	33343233355	SNNNNNNCCCNFNFNFNFNN	NNNN2NNNNNNNNN	R,T	232	898	05.03.03	4752	520408	58008
221.382-022	REPAIR-ORDER CLERK (clerical)	3333	33344333355	SNNNNNNFFNNNNFNNNNN	NNNN2NNNNNNNNN	R,T	232	898	07.05.03	4752	000000	58008

DOT #	DOT Title & Industry	Trmg	Aptitude	Physical	Environment	Tempra	WKF	MPSMS	GOE	SOC	CIP	OES
221.382-026	SAMPLE CLERK (furniture)	3335	34333333353	LNNNNNFFFNNNNFNNFFN	NNNNN3NNNNNNNNNN	V,J,T	232	898	05.09.02	4752	000000	58017
221.387-010	BACK-SHOE WORKER (boot & shoe)	3234	33443344454	LNNNNNNFFONNNNFNNNON	NNNNN2NNNNNNNNNN	V,T	221	898	05.09.02	4752	480304	58008
221.387-014	COMPLAINT CLERK (boot & shoe)	3134	44443344454	LNNNNNNFFONNNNFNNNON	NNNNN2NNNNNNNNNN	R,T	221	898	05.09.02	4758	000000	58008
221.387-018	CONTROL CLERK (clock & watch)	3336	33343244355	LNNNNNNFFONNNNFNNNNN	NNNNN2NNNNNNNNNN	V,T	221	898	05.09.02	4752	520408	58008
221.387-022	ESTIMATOR, JEWELRY (jewelry-silver.)	4336	23322344454	SNNNNNNFFNNNNFNNNON	NNNNN3NNNNNNNNNN	J	211	611	05.09.02	4752	470408	58008
221.387-026	EXPEDITER CLERK (optical goods)	3233	33444344454	LNNNNNNFFONNNNFNNNON	NNNNN2NNNNNNNNNN	R	221	898	05.09.02	4758	520499	58008
221.387-030	JACKET PREPARER (print. & pub.)	3233	33444344455	SNNNNNNFFFNNNNFNNNNN	NNNNN2NNNNNNNNNN	R	231	891	07.05.03	4752	000000	58008
221.387-034	JOB TRACER (clerical)	3234	33344344454	LNNNNNNFFONNNNFNNNON	NNNNN2NNNNNNNNNN	R	231	898	05.09.02	4758	520408	58008
221.387-038	LAUNDRY CLERK (clerical)	3233	34344344454	LNNNNNNFFONNNNFNNNNN	NNNNN3NNNNNNNNNN	R,T	231	898	05.09.02	4759	520408	58099
221.387-042	MELTER CLERK (foundry)	3334	33344344355	LNNNNNNFFFNNNNFNNNON	NNON4NNNNNNNNNN	R,T	231	898	05.09.02	4752	000000	58099
221.387-046	ORDER DETAILER (clerical)	3334	33344343354	LNNNNNNFFFNNNNFNNOON	NNNNN3NNNNNNNNNN	R,T	231	898	05.09.02	4752	520408	58008
221.387-050	PRODUCTION ASSISTANT (chemical)	3334	33343244454	LNNNNNNFFONNNNFNNNON	NNNNN3NNNNNNNNNN	R,T	232	898	05.09.02	4752	520499	58008
221.387-054	BATCH-RECORDS CLERK (plastic prod.)	3223	34354344354	SNNNNNNFFONNNNFNNNON	NNNNN3NNNNNNNNNN	T,U	231	898	05.09.02	4752	520499	58008
221.467-010	GIN CLERK (agriculture)	3223	33344333355	LNNNNNNFFFONNNNFNNNON	NNNNN3NNNNNNNNNN	R,T	232	898	05.09.02	4756	000000	58017
221.482-010	FABRIC-AND-ACCESSORIES ESTIMATOR (garment)	3333	33333333354	SNNNNNNFFFNNNNFNNNON	NNNNN2NNNNNNNNNN	R,T	232	898	05.09.02	4752	200303	21902
221.482-014	LUMBER ESTIMATOR (wood. container)	3335	33333333355	SNNNNNNFFFNNNNFNNNNN	NNNNN4NCNNNNNNNN	R,T	232	454	05.09.02	4756	000000	58099
221.482-018	TICKET WORKER (tobacco)	3222	33344333355	LNNOOONFFFNNNNFNOFNN	NNNN4NCNNNNNNNN	R,T	232	898	05.09.02	4756	520499	58099
221.484-010	YARDAGE ESTIMATOR (garment)	3336	33323333344	LNNNNNNFFFNNNNFNNNFON	FNNN3NNNNNNNNNN	J,T	171	440	05.09.02	4752	200306	58008
221.487-010	LUMBER SCALER (woodworking)	3323	34333333354	MNNONNNFFFNNNNFNNNON	NNNNN3NNNNNNNNNN	J,T	232	450	05.09.01	4756	000000	58008
221.584-010	CHART CHANGER (clerical)	3234	34433333354	LNNNNNNFFFNNNNFNNNNN	ONNN3NNNNNNNNNN	R,T	231	898	05.09.03	4794	520408	55328
221.587-010	CHECKER (textile)	2122	44444344455	LNNNNNNFFFNNNNFNNNNN	NNNN4NNNNNNNNNN	R,T	231	898	05.09.02	4756	520499	58099
221.587-014	CHECKER-IN (boot & shoe)	2122	44454344455	MNNNNNNCCNNNNONNNNNN	NNNNN3NNNNNNNNNN	R	231	898	05.09.03	4752	000000	58008
221.587-018	ODD-PIECE CHECKER (knitting)	2122	44444444354	LNNNNNNFFONNNNONNNNNN	NNNN3NNNNNNNNNN	R	221	424	05.09.01	4754	520499	58023
221.587-022	OUTSOLE SCHEDULER (boot & shoe)	2122	44454344455	LNNNNNNFFFNNNNFNNNNN	NNNN2NNNNNNNNNN	R	231	898	05.09.03	4754	520499	58023
221.587-026	RECORDER (knitting)	3122	44434344454	LNNONNNFFFNNNNFNNFON	NNNN4NNNNNNNNNN	R,T	231	898	05.09.01	4756	520499	58017
221.587-030	TALLIER (clerical)	3223	44444344455	LNNONNNFFFNNONFNNNNN	NNNN4NNNNNNNNNN	R,T	231	898	05.09.01	4756	520499	58017
221.587-034	TARE WEIGHER (meat products; sugar & conf.; tobacco)	2223	44444344355	MNNNNNNFFFNNNNFNNNNN	NNNNN3NNNNNNNNNN	R	212	898	05.09.02	4756	520499	58017
221.587-038	TICKET SCHEDULER (boot & shoe)	2223	44444344454	LNNNNNNFFFNNNNFNNNNN	NNNNN2NNNNNNNNNN	R	231	898	05.09.03	4752	000000	58008
222.137-010	FILM-VAULT SUPERVISOR (motion picture)	4337	33333344455	SNNNNNNCCFNNNNFNONFON	NNNN4NNNNNNNNNN	R,T	231	898	07.07.03	4752	000000	58008
222.137-014	LINEN-ROOM SUPERVISOR (laundry & rel.)	4336	33333344455	LNNNNNNFFONFFNONNNNN	NNNN2NNNNNNNNNN	R	231	898	05.09.02	4756	000000	58008
222.137-018	MAGAZINE SUPERVISOR (chemical; ordnance)	4236	33333344455	LNNNNNNFFONFFNONNNNN	NNNN3NNNNNNNCNN	D,J,P,S	221	898	06.02.01	4525	520204	51002
222.137-022	MAILROOM SUPERVISOR (print. & pub.)	4237	33344344455	LNNNNNNFFONFFNFNFNN	NNNN2NNNNNNNNNN	V,D,P,J	221	480	07.07.02	4522	520204	51002
222.137-026	PETROLEUM-INSPECTOR SUPERVISOR (business ser.)	4337	33344344455	SNNONNNFFNFFNNNNNNN	NNNN2NNNNNNNNNN	D,P,J,T	212	501	05.07.05	4525	000000	51002
222.137-030	SHIPPING-AND-RECEIVING SUPERVISOR (clerical)	4346	33333344455	LNNOONNFFNFFNFOOFNN	NNNN3NNNNNNNNNN	D,P,V,J	221	898	05.09.01	4525	080903	51002
222.137-034	STOCK SUPERVISOR (clerical)	4336	33334344455	LNNOOONFFFNFFNFNONNNN	NNNN4NNNNNNNNNN	V,D,P,J	221	898	05.09.01	4525	520499	51002
222.137-038	STOCK-CONTROL SUPERVISOR (clerical)	4336	22243244444	LNNNNNNFFONFFNFNONNNN	NNNN2NNNNNNNNNN	V,D,P	221	898	07.05.03	4525	520499	51002
222.137-042	SUPERVISOR, ASSEMBLY STOCK (clerical)	4236	33333344355	LNNNNNNOOONFFNONONNNN	NNNN3NNNNNNNNNN	D,P,J	221	898	05.09.02	4525	520204	51002
222.137-046	TOOL-CRIB SUPERVISOR (clerical)	4336	33344334454	LNNNNNNFFNFFNFNNNON	NNNN3NNNNNNNNNN	V,D,P,J	221	898	05.09.01	4525	520204	51002
222.137-050	VAULT CASHIER (business ser.)	4335	33343344454	LNNNNNNOOONFFNONNNNN	NNNN4NNNNNNNNNN	D,P,T	221	899	07.01.04	4525	520408	51002
222.167-010	METAL-CONTROL COORDINATOR (nonfer. metal)	4336	33344334454	LNNONONFFNFFNNNNNNN	NNNN4NNNNNNNNNN	V,D,P,J	221	898	05.09.01	4754	000000	58023
222.367-010	CARGO CHECKER (water trans.)	3234	33344344454	LNNNNONFFONONONOOON	ONNN3NNNNNNNNNN	T	221	853	05.09.03	4756	520499	58017
222.367-014	CUT-FILE CLERK (print. & pub.)	3124	33443343455	LNNONONFFFNNNNFNNNNN	NNNNN3NNNNNNNNNN	R,T	221	898	05.09.01	4754	000000	58023
222.367-018	EXPEDITER (clerical)	3336	33343344455	SNNONNNFFFNNFFNNNNN	NNNN2NNNNNNNNNN	P	232	898	07.05.01	4758	000000	58008
222.367-022	EXPRESS CLERK (motor trans.; r.r. trans.)	3334	33434344455	MNNNNNNFFFNFFNNNNNNN	NNNN3NNNNNNNNNN	P	221	850	07.03.01	4744	000000	57302
222.367-026	FILM-OR-TAPE LIBRARIAN (clerical)	3235	33333234455	LONNNNNFFONONONONONNN	NNNN3NNNNNNNNNN	R,T	221	898	11.02.04	4754	520499	58023
222.367-030	FLOOR-SPACE ALLOCATOR (tobacco; wholesale tr.)	3223	33434344455	LNNNNNNOONFFNONONNNN	NNNNN2NNNNNNNNNN	R,P	221	302	05.09.01	4753	081199	58099

DOT #	DOT Title & Industry	Trng	Aptitude	Physical	Environment	Tempra	WkF	MPSMS	GOE	SOC	CIP	OES
222.367-034	LOST-AND-FOUND CLERK (clerical)	3223	33444344454	LNNNNNNFFONFFNONNNON	NNNNN2NNNNNNNNNNN	V,P	221	969	07.07.03	4759	520499	58099
222.367-038	MAGAZINE KEEPER (clerical)	3225	34344344355	MNNNNNNFFONOONFNNNNN	NNNNN2NNNNNNNNNNN	J,S,T	221	499	05.09.02	4754	520499	58023
222.367-042	PARTS CLERK (clerical)	3333	33334343355	HOOONNNFNFNFNNNNNN	NNNNN3NNNNNNNNNNN	R,T	221	898	05.09.01	4754	081203	58023
222.367-046	PETROLEUM INSPECTOR (business ser.)	3225	33443434454	LONONNNFFNNNNFNFON	FNNNN2NNNNNNNNNNO	V,J,T	212	501	05.07.05	4757	000000	58017
222.367-050	PRESCRIPTION CLERK, LENS-AND-FRAMES (optical goods)	3225	33333344354	LNNNNNNFFNOOONFNNON	NNNNN2NNNNNNNNNNN	J,T	221	605	05.09.02	4754	520499	58023
222.367-054	PROPERTY CLERK (government ser.)	3235	33443344455	LNNNNNNFFONOONFNNNN	NNNNN3NNNNNNNNNNN	P,J,T	221	959	07.05.03	4699	520408	59999
222.367-062	TOOL-CRIB ATTENDANT (clerical)	3225	33334334354	MNNOOONFFNFFNFNOOON	NNNNN4NNNNNNNNNNN	T	221	898	05.09.01	4754	520499	58023
222.367-066	TRUCKLOAD CHECKER (construction)	3233	33444344454	LNNNNNNFFNNNNFNNNNN	FNNNN4NNNNNNNNNNN	R	231	898	05.09.03	4754	520499	58028
222.367-070	EXPEDITER, SERVICE ORDER (furniture)	3333	33444344455	LNNNNNNFFONOONFNNNN	NNNNN3NNNNNNNNNNN	P,T	221	898	07.05.01	4758	520499	58008
222.384-010	INSPECTOR, RECEIVING (aircraft mfg.; elec. equip.; electron. comp.)	3235	33333433354	MNNOOONFFFONNNFNOFON	NNNNN4NNNNNNNNNNN	T	212	580	06.03.01	7820	000000	83005
222.387-010	AIRCRAFT-SHIPPING CHECKER (aircraft mfg.)	3335	33333334454	LONOOOOOONNNNFNNOON	ONNN3NNNNNNNNNNN	T	221	898	05.09.03	4756	000000	58017
222.387-014	CAR CHECKER (r.r. trans.)	3232	33443344455	LNNNNNNFFONNNNFNFNN	ONNN3NNNNNNNNNNN	R,T	231	851	05.09.03	4753	520499	58028
222.387-018	FUEL-OIL CLERK (clerical)	3327	33343244455	SNNNNNNFFNFFNFNNFNN	NNNN3NNNNNNNNNNN	J,T	221	898	07.02.03	4754	520499	58023
222.387-022	GUN-REPAIR CLERK (ordnance)	3223	33333333355	LNNNNNNFFONNNNFNNONN	NNNN2NNNNNNNNNNN	V	221	373	05.09.01	4753	000000	58023
222.387-026	INVENTORY CLERK (clerical)	3334	33344244454	MONOOONFFFONNNFNOOON	NNNN3NNNNNNNNNNN	R,T,U	221	898	05.09.01	4754	520499	58023
222.387-030	LINEN-ROOM ATTENDANT (hotel & rest.; medical ser.)	3222	44444344354	MNNNNNNFFONNNNONNNON	NNNN2NNNNNNNNNNN	R,J	221	898	05.09.03	4754	520499	58023
222.387-034	MATERIAL CLERK (clerical)	3335	33344343355	LNNOOONFFFONNNFNNNNN	NNNN3NNNNNNNNNNN	R,U	221	898	05.09.03	4754	520499	58023
222.387-038	PARCEL POST CLERK (clerical)	3233	33343344455	HNNFNNNFFNNNNFNNNNN	NNNN3NNNNNNNNNNN	R,T	232	898	07.05.04	4744	000000	57302
222.387-042	PROPERTY CUSTODIAN (motion picture)	3325	33343344354	LNNONNNFFNNNNFNNNNN	NNNN2NNNNNNNNNNN	J	221	898	05.09.01	4754	520499	58023
222.387-046	RETURNED-TELEPHONE-EQUIPMENT APPRAISER (comm. equip.)	3325	33333344454	LNNNNNNFFNNNNFNNNON	NNNN2NNNNNNNNNNN	J	212	586	06.03.01	4759	520499	58099
222.387-050	SHIPPING AND RECEIVING CLERK (clerical)	3325	33343344455	LNNNNNNFFNNNNFNNNON	NNNN3NNNNNNNNNNN	J,V	221	898	05.09.01	4753	520499	58028
222.387-054	SORTER-PRICER (nonprofit org.)	3324	33333244354	HNNOONNFFNNNNFNNONN	NNNN2NNNNNNNNNNN	V,J	221	898	05.09.03	4753	000000	58023
222.387-058	STOCK CLERK (clerical)	3325	33333344355	LNNNNNNFFNNNNFNNONN	NNNN3NNNNNNNNNNN	T,V,J	221	898	05.09.01	4754	200409	58023
222.387-062	STOREKEEPER (water trans.)	3324	34433333354	LNNOOONFFNOONFNNFON	NNNN4NNNNNNNNNNN	J,T	221	519	05.09.01	4757	520499	58017
222.387-066	SAMPLE CLERK (plastic prod.)	3335	34433333354	LNNOOONFFNOONFNNFON	NNNN2NNNNNNNNNNN	T,J	221	519	05.09.01	4757	520499	58017
222.387-074	SHIPPING-AND-RECEIVING WEIGHER (clerical)	3222	34444344455	LNNNNNNFFNNFFNNNNNN	NNNNN3NNNNNNNNNNN	T	212	898	05.09.01	4756	520499	58028
222.485-010	MILK-RECEIVER, TANK TRUCK (dairy products)	3223	34444444345	MMNONNNFFNNNNFNNNNN	NNNC3NNNNNNNNNNN	R,T	014	383	05.09.01	4753	000000	58017
222.487-010	CHECKER, BAKERY PRODUCTS (bakery products)	2222	44444344444	HNNONNNCCONNNNOOOOON	NNNN3NNNNNNNNNNN	R	221	384	05.09.01	4754	520499	53902
222.487-014	ORDER FILLER (retail trade; wholesale tr.)	3223	33443344354	LNNNNNNFFNNNNFNNFON	NNNN3NNNNNNNNNNN	R,T	221	880	05.09.01	4754	000000	58026
222.567-010	GRAIN ELEVATOR CLERK (beverage; grain-feed mills)	3224	33343344355	LNNNNNNFFNFFNFFNFNN	NNNN2NNNNNNNNNNN	R,T	221	896	07.07.02	4753	080705	58026
222.567-014	SHIP RUNNER (water trans.)	3224	33333344455	LNFFNNNFFNFFNNNONNNN	NNNN2NNNNNNNNNNN	V	231	380	05.09.03	4754	520499	58028
222.567-018	SLOT-TAG INSERTER (clerical)	2222	44554444455	LNNNNNNFFNOONFNNNNN	NNNN4NNNNNNNNNNN	T	221	891	05.09.01	4753	520499	58028
222.585-010	MILK RECEIVER (dairy products)	3223	44444444355	HNNNNNNFFFNNNNFNNONN	NNNO4NNNNNNNNNNN	R	221	898	07.07.02	4744	000000	57302
222.587-014	BRAILLE-AND-TALKING BOOKS CLERK (library)	3233	44443344354	LNNONNNFFNNNNFNNNON	NNNN3NNNNNNNNNNN	R,T	212	933	05.09.01	4756	520499	58017
222.587-018	DISTRIBUTING CLERK (clerical)	3233	33343343354	LNNNNNNFFNNNNFNNNNN	NNNN2NNNNNNNNNNN	R,T	221	896	07.07.02	4753	520499	58023
222.587-022	KITCHEN CLERK (hotel & rest.)	3224	33343344355	MNNNNNNFFFNNNNONNNNN	NNNN2NNNNNNNNNNN	V	231	380	05.09.03	4754	520499	58023
222.587-026	LABORATORY CLERK (clerical)	3223	33343344455	LNNNNNNFFNFONNONNNN	NNNN2NNNNNNNNNNN	R,T	221	891	05.09.01	4759	520499	58099
222.587-030	MAILER (print. & pub.)	2223	34343344355	LNNNNNNFFNNNNFNNNNN	NNNN3NNNNNNNNNNN	R	221	899	05.09.01	4744	000000	57302
222.587-032	MAILER APPRENTICE (print. & pub.)	2223	34344333355	LNNNNNNFFNNNNFNNNNN	NNNN3NNNNNNNNNNN	R	231	899	05.09.01	4744	000000	57302
222.587-034	ROUTE-DELIVERY CLERK (clerical)	2223	33444344454	LNNNNNNFFNNNNNFNNNNN	ONNN2NNNNNNNNNNN	R	221	853	07.05.04	4753	520499	58028
222.587-038	ROUTER (clerical)	2122	44443333355	LNNNNNNFFONNNNONNNNN	NNNN2NNNNNNNNNNN	R	231	898	07.07.02	4759	520499	58099
222.587-042	SAMPLER, WOOL (wholesale tr.)	2223	44444344455	LNNNNNNFFONNNNONNNNN	NNNN2NNNNNNNNNNN	R	231	898	05.09.03	4754	000000	58017
222.587-046	STACKER (leather prod.)	2212	44444443355	MNNNNNNFFNNNNNONNNNN	NNNN2NNNNNNNNNNN	R	041	529	05.09.03	4756	000000	58017
222.587-050	SWATCH CLERK (garment)	2212	44554344454	LNNNNNNFFFONNNNNNNN	NNNN2NNNNNNNNNNN	R	231	891	05.09.03	4754	520499	58017
222.587-054	TRANSFORMER-STOCK CLERK (utilities)	3223	33434444344	LNNNNNNFFNNNNFNNFON	NNNN3NNNNNNNNNNN	R,T	221	581	05.09.01	4754	520499	58023
222.587-058	VAULT WORKER (business ser.)	3223	33444344454	MNNFNFNFFNNNNNONNON	NNNN2NNNNNNNNNNN	J	221	899	07.05.04	4753	520499	58028
222.684-010	MEAT CLERK (retail trade)	2112	44444433354	MNNNNNNFFNNNNNONNOON	NNNN2NNNNNNNNNNN	R,T	146	382	05.09.01	4754	000000	58023
222.687-010	CHECKER I (clerical)	2222	34344344455	LNNNNNNFFNNNNFNNNNN	NNNN3NNNNNNNNNNN	R,T	221	898	07.07.02	4756	000000	58017
222.687-014	GARMENT SORTER (garment)	2212	44544444454	LNNNNNNFFONNNNFNNFON	NNNN3NNNNNNNNNNN	R	221	440	06.03.02	4759	000000	58099
222.687-018	RECEIVING CHECKER (clerical)	3223	34444344355	MNNONNNFFFNNNNFNNNNN	NNNN3NNNNNNNNNNN	R,T	221	898	05.09.03	4756	520499	58017
222.687-022	ROUTING CLERK (clerical)	2222	44444434355	LNNNNNNFFNNNNFNNONN	NNNN2NNNNNNNNNNN	R	221	898	07.07.02	4753	520499	58028

DOT #	DOT Title & Industry	Trng	Aptitude	Physical	Environment	Tempra	WkF	MPSMS	GOE	SOC	CIP	OES
222.687-026	SAMPLE DISPLAY PREPARER (knitting)	3224	3444344353	LNNONNNCCCNNNNFNNFNN	NNNNN3NNNNNNNNN	T	221	446	05.09.01	4754	080199	58017
222.687-030	SHIPPING CHECKER (clerical)	3324	3333334454	LLNNONNNFFFNNNNFNFON	NNNNN3NNNNNNNNN	J,T	221	898	05.09.01	4756	520499	58028
222.687-034	STUBBER (retail trade)	2222	4444323354	MNNNNNNFFONNNNNONNON	NNNN2NNNNNNNNNN	R	221	898	05.09.03	4759	000000	58099
222.687-038	TOOTH CLERK (protective dev.)	3224	3443443453	SNNNNNNNCCONNNNCNNCCN	NNNNN3NNNNNNNNN	R,T	221	898	05.12.19	4754	000000	58023
222.687-042	INSPECTOR, HANDBAG FRAMES (leather prod.)	2222	4444443454	LNNONNNFFONNNNNFNNON	NNNNN3NNNNNNNNN	R	221	525	06.03.02	7820	200303	83005
222.687-046	PROTECTIVE-CLOTHING ISSUER (chemical)	2222	4444444455	LFNFNFFFONNNNNONNNNN	NNNNN3NNNNNNNNN	R	221	898	07.07.02	4754	520499	58023
229.137-010	SACK-DEPARTMENT SUPERVISOR (grain-feed mills)	4326	33344344455	LNNNNNNFONFFNFNNNNN	NNNNN2NNNNNNNNN	D,P,V	221	898	05.09.01	4525	520204	51002
229.137-014	YARD SUPERVISOR (construction)	4347	33333344444	LNNNNNNFONFFNOFFOOF	FNNN3NNNNNNNNNN	V,D,P,J	221	898	05.09.02	4525	000000	51002
229.267-010	PARTS CATALOGER (any industry)	4346	22333343455	SNNNNNNNFFNOONFNNFNN	NNNNN3NNNNNNNNN	V,T,J	231	898	05.03.02	4759	520499	58099
229.367-010	FIELD RECORDER (utilities)	3334	34344343455	LNNNNNNNFFNOONFNNNNN	NNNNN3NNNNNNNNN	R	221	891	05.09.02	4754	000000	58023
229.367-014	PARTS LISTER (electron. comp.)	3334	33333343454	LNNNNNNNOOCNOONONNNON	NNNNN3NNNNNNNNN	P,U	231	898	05.09.01	4754	520499	58023
229.387-010	MATERIAL LISTER (construction)	4345	33333243455	SNNNNNNNFFFNNNNNFNNNN	NNNN2NNNNNNNNNN	J,T	231	898	05.03.02	4752	000000	58008
229.387-014	TANK CALIBRATOR (business ser.)	4435	33233344345	MONONONNFFFNNNNFNNNN	ONNN3NNNNNNNNNN	J,T	212	899	05.09.03	4756	000000	58017
229.587-010	GREIGE-GOODS MARKER (textile)	2122	44454444455	LNNNONNNFFFNNNNNFNNON	NNNNN3NNNNNNNNN	R,T	221	898	07.05.03	4754	520499	58023
229.587-014	QUALITY-CONTROL CLERK (pharmaceut.)	3233	33444344354	LNNNONNNFFFNNNNNFNNFN	FNNN3NNNNNNNNNO	R	231	898	05.09.03	4759	000000	58099
229.587-018	TICKETER (textile)	2122	44444434354	LNNNNNNNCCCNNNNFNNFFN	NNNNN2NNNNNNNNN	R	231	898	05.09.03	4757	000000	58017
229.687-010	SAMPLE CHECKER (carpet & rug; textile)	3123	33443444452	LNNNNNNNFFFNNNNNFFFN	NNNNN3NNNNNNNNN	J,R	212	420	05.09.03	4030	200501	41002
230.137-010	SUPERVISOR, ADVERTISING-MATERIAL DISTRIBUTORS (business ser.)	4246	33344344455	LNNNNNNNFFFNFNNNNNN	ONNN3NNNNNNNNNN	D,P,V	011	896	07.07.02	4030	080299	41002
230.137-014	SUPERVISOR, DELIVERY DEPARTMENT (tel. & tel.)	4236	33344344455	LNNNNNNOOONFFNONNNNN	NNNN3NNNNNNNNNN	V,P	011	862	07.07.02	4525	520204	51002
230.137-018	SUPERVISOR, MAIL CARRIERS (government ser.)	4346	33444244455	LNNNNNNNOOONFFNONNNN	NNNN2NNNNNNNNNN	V,D,P,J	221	954	07.05.04	4524	520204	51002
230.363-010	RURAL MAIL CARRIER (government ser.)	3322	33344344444	MNNNNNNFFFNNNNFNNNFN	ONNN3NNNNNNNNNN	R	221	954	07.05.04	4743	000000	57305
230.367-010	MAIL CARRIER (government ser.)	3234	33444334354	MNNNNNNFFFNOONFFNNNN	FNNN3NNNNNNNNNO	R	221	954	07.04.06	4743	000000	57305
230.647-010	SINGING MESSENGER (business ser.)	3232	33434343313	LNFNNNNNFFONFFNONONON	NNNN3NNNNNNNNNN	P	291	899	07.07.02	2390	000000	31314
230.663-010	DELIVERER, OUTSIDE (clerical)	2122	44444444445	LNNNNNNNFFONOONOFFONF	FNNN3NNNNNNNNNN	R	013	899	07.07.02	4745	520406	59999
230.667-014	TELEPHONE-DIRECTORY DELIVERER (business ser.)	1111	44454444355	HFNFNNNNFFNNNONNNNNN	FNNN2NNNNNNNNNN	R	011	896	07.07.02	8769	000000	98999
230.687-010	ADVERTISING-MATERIAL DISTRIBUTOR (any industry)	1112	44544444355	LNNNNNNFFFNNNNONNNNN	CNNN3NNNNNNNNNN	R	011	896	07.07.02	8769	090201	98999
235.132-010	CENTRAL-OFFICE-OPERATOR SUPERVISOR (tel. & tel.)	4236	33443233355	LNNNNNNNFFNFFNNNNF	NNNN2NNNNNNNNNN	P,J,D	281	861	07.04.06	4523	520406	51002
235.132-014	COMMUNICATION-CENTER COORDINATOR (air trans.)	4345	33443344454	LNNNNNNNFONFFNFNNOON	NNNN3NNNNNNNNNN	D,J,P	281	869	07.04.05	4523	520406	51002
235.137-010	COMMUNICATION-CENTER OPERATOR (air trans.)	4346	33344334455	SNNNNNNNCCFNCCNCNFNNN	NNNN3NNNNNNNNNN	P	281	861	07.04.06	4732	520406	57105
235.137-014	TELEPHONE OPERATOR, CHIEF (clerical)	4246	32344333355	LNNNNNNNFFFNFNNNNNN	NNNN2NNNNNNNNNN	R,P	282	861	07.04.06	4732	520406	57102
235.222-010	PRIVATE-BRANCH-EXCHANGE SERVICE ADVISER (tel. & tel.)	3135	33344233355	SNNNNNNNFFONNNNNFNNN	NNNN2NNNNNNNNNN	V,P,J,T	296	861	07.04.05	2390	520406	59999
235.387-010	RADIO-MESSAGE ROUTER (tel. & tel.)	3133	33344233355	SNNNNNNNFFONNNNNNNNN	NNNN2NNNNNNNNNN	J	231	862	07.05.04	4699	520406	57108
235.462-010	CENTRAL-OFFICE OPERATOR (tel. & tel.)	3234	33334333355	LNNNNNNNCCFNCCNFNNNNN	NNNN2NNNNNNNNNN	R,P	281	861	07.04.06	4732	520406	57199
235.562-010	CLERK, ROUTE (tel. & tel.)	3124	33444433355	SNNNNNNNCCFNCCNFNNNNN	NNNN3NNNNNNNNNN	R,J	231	862	07.05.04	4732	520406	57102
235.562-014	SWITCHBOARD OPERATOR, POLICE DISTRICT (government ser.)	3335	33443333354	LNNNNNNFFNFFNFNNNNNN	NNNN3NNNNNNNNNN	R,P	281	586	07.04.05	4732	081104	00000
235.662-010	COMMAND AND CONTROL SPECIALIST (military ser.)	3235	33443333354	SNNNNNNNFONFFNFNNOON	NNNN4NNNNNNNNNN	P	281	869	07.04.05	4732	520406	57102
235.662-014	COMMUNICATION-CENTER OPERATOR (air trans.)	3233	33443333355	SNNNNNNNCCFNCCNFNNOON	NNNN2NNNNNNNNNN	R,P	282	861	07.04.06	4732	520406	57105
235.662-018	DIRECTORY-ASSISTANCE OPERATOR (tel. & tel.)	3233	33444333455	SNNNNNNNCCFNCCNFNNFNN	NNNN3NNNNNNNNNN	R,P	281	861	07.04.06	4732	520406	57102
235.662-022	TELEPHONE OPERATOR (clerical)	3233	33444433355	LNNNNNNNFFONNNNNNNNN	NNNN2NNNNNNNNNN	R,P	231	861	07.04.06	4739	520406	57102
235.662-026	TELEPHONE-ANSWERING-SERVICE OPERATOR (business ser.)	3233	33445333355	SNNNNNNNCCCNCCNFNNNNN	NNNN3NNNNNNNNNN	R,P	231	861	07.05.03	4152	520406	43017
236.252-010	REPRESENTATIVE, PERSONAL SERVICE (tel. & tel.)	5356	22933333355	LNNNNNNFFONNNNNNNNNN	NNNN3NNNNNNNNNN	P,I	296	862	05.02.06	4152	080299	43017
236.562-010	TELEGRAPHER (r.r. trans.)	4334	33332222355	SNNNNNNFFNCCNFNNNNNN	NNNN3NNNNNNNNNN	R	281	860	07.04.05	4733	520406	57111
236.562-014	TELEGRAPHER AGENT (r.r. trans.)	3235	33355333355	SNNNNNNNFFNCCNFNNNNN	NNNN2NNNNNNNNNN	R,P	282	862	07.04.05	4733	520406	57111
237.137-010	SUPERVISOR, TELEPHONE INFORMATION (motor trans.)	4347	22244244455	SNNNNNNNOOONFFNNNNNN	NNNN4NNNNNNNNNN	D,J,P	282	852	07.04.04	4514	520406	51002
237.137-014	SUPERVISOR, TRAVEL-INFORMATION CENTER (government ser.)	4346	22344244455	LNNNNNNNFFNFFNFNNNNN	NNNN3NNNNNNNNNN	P,D,V,I	282	859	07.04.04	4514	081104	51002
237.267-010	INFORMATION CLERK, AUTOMOBILE CLUB (nonprofit org.)	4345	32344244455	SNNNNNNNOOONFFNNNNN	NNNN3NNNNNNNNNN	J	282	859	07.04.04	4649	520406	55305
237.367-010	APPOINTMENT CLERK (clerical)	3233	33455334455	SNNNNNNNFONFFNFNNNNN	NNNN2NNNNNNNNNN	R,P	231	890	07.04.04	4645	520406	55305
237.367-014	CALL-OUT OPERATOR (business ser.; retail trade)	3232	33445333455	SNNNNNNOOONFFNFNNNNN	NNNN3NNNNNNNNNN	R,P,T	282	894	07.05.03	4783	520406	53117
237.367-018	INFORMATION CLERK (motor trans.; r.r. trans.; water trans.)	4232	32344334355	LNNNNNNNFFONCCNFNNNNN	NNNN3NNNNNNNNNN	R,P	282	850	07.04.04	4649	520406	55305
237.367-022	INFORMATION CLERK (clerical)	4234	33444345455	SNNNNNNNOOONFFNNNNNN	NNNN3NNNNNNNNNN	V,P,J	282	899	07.04.04	4645	520406	55305
237.367-026	LAND-LEASING EXAMINER (government ser.)	4347	33443255455	SNNNNNNNOOONFFNFNNNNN	NNNN3NNNNNNNNNN	J	282	959	07.04.04	4649	520408	55305
237.367-030	MANAGER, TRAFFIC II (motor trans.)	3226	33355534455	SNNNNNNNOOONFFNFNNNNN	NNNN2NNNNNNNNNN	R,P	282	853	07.04.04	4799	520903	59999

DOT #	DOT Title & Industry	Trmg	Aptitude	Physical	Environment	Tempra	WKF	MPSMS	GOE	SOC	CIP	OES
237.367-034	PAY-STATION ATTENDANT (tel. & tel.)	3235	33334434355	LNNNNNNFFNFFNFNNNNNN	NNNNN2NNNNNNNNNN	V,P	282	861	09.04.02	4649	520406	57199
237.367-038	RECEPTIONIST (clerical)	3234	33444344455	SNNNNNNFFONFNNNNNN	NNNNN2NNNNNNNNNN	R,P	282	891	07.04.04	4645	520406	55305
237.367-042	REFERRAL-AND-INFORMATION AIDE (government ser.)	3233	32444344455	SNNNNNNFFNFFNFNNNNNN	NNNNN3NNNNNNNNNN	J,P	282	959	07.04.02	4649	520406	55305
237.367-046	TELEPHONE QUOTATION CLERK (financial)	3232	33443344455	SNNNNNNFFNFFNFNNNONN	NNNNN3NNNNNNNNNN	R,P	282	894	07.04.04	4649	520406	55305
237.367-050	TOURIST-INFORMATION ASSISTANT (government ser.)	4346	32344444455	SNNNNNNNOONNFFNONNNNN	NNNNN3NNNNNNNNNN	V,P,J	282	959	07.04.04	4649	081104	55305
238.137-010	MANAGER, RESERVATIONS (hotel & rest.)	4235	33443334455	LNNNNNNFFNFFNFNNNNNN	NNNNN3NNNNNNNNNN	D,J	291	902	07.05.01	4514	520901	51002
238.137-014	SENIOR RESERVATIONS AGENT (air trans.)	4336	22334344455	LNNNNNNFFNFFNFFNN	NNNNN3NNNNNNNNNN	D,J	013	855	07.05.01	4514	520406	51002
238.137-018	SUPERVISOR, GATE SERVICES (air trans.)	4247	22334344455	LNNNNNNNOONNFFNFNNNNNN	NNNNN5NNNNNNNNNN	D,J,P,V	212	855	09.05.04	4514	080709	51002
238.137-022	SUPERVISOR, TICKET SALES (air trans.)	4346	33344344455	LNNNNNNFFNFFNFFNNONN	NNNNN3NNNNNNNNNN	D,P	292	855	07.03.01	4514	081105	51002
238.167-010	TRAVEL CLERK (government ser.)	4347	22344244455	SNNNNNNFFNFFNFNNNNNN	NNNNN3NNNNNNNNNN	V,P,J	291	859	07.05.01	4644	081105	53802
238.167-014	TRAVEL COUNSELOR, AUTOMOBILE CLUB (nonprofit org.)	4435	33344244455	SNNNNNNNFFNFFNFNNNNNN	NNNNN2NNNNNNNNNN	V,P	291	859	07.05.01	4644	520406	53802
238.362-010	RESERVATION CLERK (clerical)	3335	33334223355	LNNNNNNFFONFNNNNNN	NNNNN5NNNNNNNNNN	V,P,T	291	859	07.05.01	4644	081105	53805
238.367-014	GATE AGENT (air trans.)	3234	33444344455	SNNNNNNFFNFFNFNNNNNN	NNNNN3NNNNNNNNNN	P,J	212	855	09.05.04	4644	080709	53805
238.367-018	RESERVATIONS AGENT (air trans.)	3233	33344333355	SNNNNNNFFNFFNFNNNNNN	NNNNN3NNNNNNNNNN	J	231	851	07.05.01	4644	081105	53805
238.367-022	SPACE SCHEDULER (clerical)	4334	33433333355	SNNNNNNNOOONFFNFNNNNNN	NNNNN3NNNNNNNNNN	R,P,I	291	855	07.04.03	4644	081105	53805
238.367-026	TICKET AGENT (any industry)	4234	33333244455	LNNNNNNFFCNCCNFNNONN	NNNNN3NNNNNNNNNN	J,T	231	931	07.05.01	4649	520406	55305
238.367-030	TRAVEL CLERK (hotel & rest.)	4335	33343333455	SNNNNNNFFNFFNFNNNNNN	NNNNN3NNNNNNNNNN	R,P	292	850	07.03.01	4644	081105	53805
238.367-034	SCHEDULER (museums)	3334	33343244455	SNNNNNNNOOONFFNONNNNN	NNNNN2NNNNNNNNNN	D,P,V	282	859	07.04.04	4644	081104	53802
238.367-038	HOTEL CLERK (hotel & rest.)	3333	33334333355	SNNNNNNNFFNFFNFNNNNNN	NNNNN3NNNNNNNNNN	J,P,V	232	939	07.05.01	4649	000000	55305
239.132-010	SUPERVISOR, TELEPHONE CLERKS (tel. & tel.)	3334	33334343455	LNNNNNNNOOFNFFNFNNNNNN	NNNNN3NNNNNNNNNN	V,P	291	902	07.04.03	4643	080902	53808
239.137-010	COMMERCIAL-INSTRUCTOR SUPERVISOR (tel. & tel.; utilities; waterworks)	4245	33334233455	LNNNNNNNOOFNFFNFNNNNNN	NNNNN2NNNNNNNNNN	D,J,P	281	862	07.04.06	4524	520204	51002
239.137-014	CUSTOMER SERVICE REPRESENTATIVE SUPERVISOR (radio-tv broad.; tel. & tel.; utilities; waterworks)	4348	22343344455	SNNNNNNNOOONFFNONNNNN	NNNNN3NNNNNNNNNN	D,P	296	891	11.07.03	1283	521001	15005
239.137-018	ROUTE SUPERVISOR (tel. & tel.)	4236	33445244455	SNNNNNNNOOONFFNONNNNN	NNNNN3NNNNNNNNNN	V,P	211	869	07.04.01	4516	520204	51002
239.137-022	SERVICE OBSERVER, CHIEF (tel. & tel.)	4236	33554334455	LNNNNNNFFONFNFNNNNNN	NNNNN2NNNNNNNNNN	V,P	231	862	07.05.04	4525	520204	51002
239.137-026	SUPERVISOR, PUBLIC MESSAGE SERVICE (tel. & tel.)	4247	33334343455	LNNNNNNNOOONFFNONNNNN	NNNNN2NNNNNNNNNN	V,P	281	862	07.04.05	4523	520204	51002
239.167-010	COMMUNICATIONS COORDINATOR (medical ser.)	4337	23443344455	SNNNNNNFFONFFNFNNNNNN	NNNNN3NNNNNNNNNN	D,P	281	862	07.04.05	4524	520406	51002
239.167-014	DISPATCHER (tel. & tel.)	4347	33344344355	SNNNNNNFFONFFNFNNNNNN	NNNNN3NNNNNNNNNN	R	231	891	07.04.05	4664	000000	58005
239.227-010	CUSTOMER-SERVICE-REPRESENTATIVE INSTRUCTOR (tel. & tel.; utilities; waterworks)	4236	33344344455	SNNNNNNNOOONFFNONNNNN	NNNNN2NNNNNNNNNN	V,P,J	296	954	07.01.07	1490	000000	57308
239.267-010	PLACER (insurance)	4345	32344244455	SNNNNNNNOOONFFNONNNNN	NNNNN2NNNNNNNNNN	V,D,P,J	296	954	07.04.02	2390	521001	31314
239.362-010	TELEPHONE CLERK, TELEGRAPH OFFICE (tel. & tel.)	3233	33355244455	LNNNNNNFFONFNFNNNNNN	NNNNN2NNNNNNNNNN	P	281	859	08.01.02	4122	080706	43002
239.362-014	CUSTOMER SERVICE REPRESENTATIVE (radio-tv broad.; tel. & tel.; utilities; waterworks)	3235	33444344455	SNNNNNNNOOONFFNCCNONNFNN	NNNNN2NNNNNNNNNN	P,R,T	281	862	07.04.05	4732	520406	57311
239.362-014	DISPATCHER, MAINTENANCE SERVICE (clerical)	3233	33443344455	SNNNNNNNOOOFNCCNONNFNN	NNNNN3NNNNNNNNNN	V,P	231	891	07.04.01	4664	000000	55335
239.367-018	MAIL-DISTRIBUTION-SCHEME EXAMINER (government ser.)	4245	33345244455	SNNNNNNNOOONFFNONNNNN	NNNNN2NNNNNNNNNN	R	231	891	07.04.05	4751	000000	58005
239.367-022	RECEIVER-DISPATCHER (nonprofit org.)	3234	33355244455	LNNNNNNFFONFNFNNNNNN	NNNNN3NNNNNNNNNN	V,P,J	296	859	07.01.07	4742	000000	57308
239.367-026	SERVICE OBSERVER (tel. & tel.)	4244	33355344455	LNNNNNNFFNOFNFNNNNNN	NNNNN2NNNNNNNNNN	P	281	859	07.04.05	4751	000000	58005
239.367-030	DISPATCHER, STREET DEPARTMENT (government ser.)	3123	33444344455	SNNNNNNFFNOFNFNNCNNNNN	NNNNN2NNNNNNNNNN	P,J	281	861	07.04.05	4751	520406	58005
239.367-034	UTILITY CLERK (utilities)	4335	33344234354	LNNONNNCCFNFFNFNNFON	NNNNN3NNNNNNNNNN	P,T	282	870	07.04.05	4649	520406	55335
239.382-010	WIRE-PHOTO OPERATOR, NEWS (print. & pub.)	4235	33432433353	SNNNNNNFFONNFFNOONFNNNN	NNNNN2NNNNNNNNNN	J,T	281	869	05.10.05	4733	000000	55335
239.567-010	OFFICE HELPER (clerical)	2222	34444343355	LNNONNNFFONNNOONN	NNNNN3NNNNNNNNNN	V	231	890	07.07.03	4745	520408	57199
239.677-010	MESSENGER, COPY (print. & pub.)	2122	44444444455	LNNNNNNNFFONNNNNONNNNN	NNNNN2NNNNNNNNNN	P,R	011	899	07.07.02	4745	000000	58005
239.687-010	ROUTE AIDE (tel. & tel.)	2122	34444334355	LNNNNNNNFFONNNNNNONNNNN	NNNNN3NNNNNNNNNN	R	291	899	07.07.02	4745	000000	55335
239.687-014	TUBE OPERATOR (clerical)	2122	33444334355	SNNNNNNFFONNNNFONNNNN	NNNNN2NNNNNNNNNN	R	231	899	07.07.02	4745	000000	57199
241.137-010	SUPERVISOR, CREDIT AND LOAN COLLECTIONS (clerical)	4347	33355344455	SNNNNNNNOOONFFNCNNNNNN	NNNNN3NNNNNNNNNN	R	291	899	07.07.02	4745	000000	57311
241.137-014	SUPERVISOR, CUSTOMER-COMPLAINT SERVICE (clerical)	4346	32344344455	SNNNNNNNOOONFFNFNNNNNN	NNNNN2NNNNNNNNNN	D,I,P,J	231	894	07.04.02	4528	520204	51002
241.137-018	SUPERVISOR, CLAIMS (insurance)	4347	23244244455	SNNNNNNNOOONFFNNNNNN	NNNNN3NNNNNNNNNN	D,J,P	271	890	07.04.02	4528	520204	51002
241.217-010	CLAIM ADJUSTER (business ser.; insurance)	5356	22555344455	LNNNNNNFFONFNFNNNNNN	NNNNN2NNNNNNNNNN	P,I,J	271	895	11.12.01	4528	520204	51002
241.267-010	AGENT-CONTRACT CLERK (insurance)	5145	22555344555	LNNNNNNFFONFNFFNN	ONNNN3NNNNNNNNNN	J	271	895	11.12.01	4782	081001	53302
241.267-014	APPRAISER, AUTOMOBILE DAMAGE (business ser.; insurance)	4247	33332344455	LNNNNNNFFONFNFNNFFNN	ONNNN3NNNNNNNNNN	J	212	961	11.12.01	4692	521001	55314
241.267-018	CLAIM EXAMINER (business ser.; insurance)	4347	22344244455	SNNNNNNFFNFFNFNNNNNN	NNNNN2NNNNNNNNNN	J	271	895	11.12.01	4782	081001	53305

DOT #	DOT Title & Industry	Trng	Aptitude	Physical	Environment	Tempra	WkF	MPSMS	GOE	SOC	CIP	OES
241.267-022	CREDIT ANALYST (clerical)	4347	33344344455	SNNNNNNOOONFFNFNNNNN	NNNNNNNNNNNNNN	J	271	894	07.01.04	1419	080401	21105
241.267-026	DEPOSIT CLERK (utilities)	4346	2235434344455	SNNNNNNOOONFFNFNNNNN	NNNN2NNNNNNNNNN	J	271	871	07.01.04	4716	000000	55344
241.267-030	INVESTIGATOR (clerical)	4345	32355244455	SNNNNNNNFFNFFNFNNNNN	NNNN2NNNNNNNNNN	P,J	271	890	11.06.03	4783	081001	53117
241.267-034	INVESTIGATOR, UTILITY-BILL COMPLAINTS (utilities)	4446	32244244454	LNNNNNNOOONFFNFNNNON	NNNN3NNNNNNNNNN	J	271	891	07.05.02	4783	520408	53123
241.357-010	COLLECTION CLERK (clerical)	4345	33355344455	SNNNNNNNOOFNGCNNONNN	NNNN3NNNNNNNNNN	I,P	271	894	07.04.02	4786	000000	53508
241.362-010	CLAIMS CLERK I (insurance)	4334	33354233455	SNNNNNNNFFNFFNFNNNNN	NNNN2NNNNNNNNNN	J	231	895	07.05.02	4782	520803	53311
241.367-010	COLLECTOR (clerical)	3334	33354344455	LNNNNNNNOOONFFNFNONN	FNNN3NNNNNNNNNN	P,I	271	894	07.03.01	4786	080705	53508
241.367-014	CUSTOMER-COMPLAINT CLERK (clerical)	4345	33344244455	SNNNNNNNOOONFFNONNONN	NNNN3NNNNNNNNNN	J,P,V	271	860	07.05.02	4783	520408	53123
241.367-018	LOAN INTERVIEWER, MORTGAGE (financial)	4336	33345344455	SNNNNNNNFFONCNCNNNNN	NNNN2NNNNNNNNNN	P,J	271	894	07.04.01	1415	080401	53111
241.367-022	REPOSSESSOR (clerical)	3223	34443444434	MNNNNNNNFONFFNONNNON	FNNN2NNNNNNNNNN	P	271	894	04.02.03	4786	000000	53508
241.367-026	SKIP TRACER (clerical)	4244	33454344455	SNNNNNNNFONFFNFNNNNN	NNNN2NNNNNNNNNN	P	271	894	07.04.01	4783	000000	53117
241.367-030	THROW-OUT CLERK (retail trade)	3334	33353244455	SNNNNNNNFONFFNFNNNNN	NNNN3NNNNNNNNNN	P	271	894	07.05.02	4783	000000	53117
241.367-034	TIRE ADJUSTER (retail trade)	3323	33333444455	MNNFNFNFFOOFFNFNNFNN	NNNN2NNNNNNNNNN	P,J	292	511	05.09.01	4783	081203	53123
241.367-038	INVESTIGATOR, DEALER ACCOUNTS (financial)	4342	33343444444	LNNNNNNNOOONFFNFOONOO	ONNN3NNNNNNNNNN	P,T	271	894	07.05.02	4783	080401	53505
241.367-042	PROPERTY-ASSESSMENT MONITOR (government ser.)	4443	33333344444	LNNNNNNNFONFFNOONOON	NNNN3NNNNNNNNNN	P,J	211	959	07.05.02	4799	521501	59999
241.387-010	CLAIMS CLERK (auto. mfg.)	4334	33344333455	SNNNNNNNFFFNNNMFNNFNN	NNNN2NNNNNNNNNN	J	212	591	07.05.02	4783	520408	53123
243.137-010	SUPERVISOR, MAILS (government ser.)	4236	33344234455	LNNNNNNNOOONFFNFNNNNN	NNNN2NNNNNNNNNN	V,D,P,J	221	954	07.05.04	4522	000000	51002
243.362-010	COURT CLERK (government ser.)	4246	33344233355	SNNNNNNNOOONFFNONNNNN	NNNN2NNNNNNNNNN	P,V	231	950	07.01.02	4799	520405	53702
243.362-014	POLICE AIDE (government ser.)	3233	33444333355	SNNNNNNNFFNFFNFNNFNN	NNNN3NNNNNNNNNN	J,T,P	231	951	07.04.05	4630	520408	55347
243.367-010	MAIL CENSOR (government ser.)	4235	33444455555	SNNNNNNNFFNOONFNNFNN	NNNN2NNNNNNNNNN	R,J	271	959	07.05.02	4744	000000	57302
243.367-014	POST-OFFICE CLERK (government ser.)	3334	33343233355	LNNNNNNNFFNFFNFNNNNN	NNNN3NNNNNNNNNN	V,P	221	954	07.03.01	4742	000000	57308
243.367-018	TOWN CLERK (government ser.)	4435	22242244555	SNNNNNNNFFFNOFNFNNNNN	NNNN3NNNNNNNNNN	J	231	890	07.01.02	4799	520402	53705
245.362-010	MEDICAL-RECORD CLERK (medical ser.)	4334	33344323455	LNNNNNNNFFNOONFNNNNN	NNNN3NNNNNNNNNN	T	231	891	07.05.03	4794	510707	55328
245.362-014	UNIT CLERK (medical ser.)	3333	33343333355	LNNNNNNNFFNFFNFNNNNN	NNNN2NNNNNNNNNN	T,V	231	891	07.05.03	4630	520404	55347
245.367-010	ANIMAL-HOSPITAL CLERK (medical ser.)	3234	33344344455	SNNNNNNNFFNFFNFNNNNN	NNNN3NNNNNNNNNN	P	232	929	07.04.03	4630	520408	55347
245.367-014	BLOOD-DONOR-UNIT ASSISTANT (medical ser.)	2122	43443334354	LNNNNNNNFFNOONNNNNNN	NNNN3NNNNNNNNNN	P,T,V	231	929	07.04.01	4630	520404	55347
245.367-018	CALENDAR-CONTROL CLERK, BLOOD BANK (medical ser.)	3223	33345244455	SNNNNNNNFONFFNFNNNNN	NNNN3NNNNNNNNNN	J	231	891	07.05.01	4630	520404	59999
245.367-022	CREDIT CLERK, BLOOD BANK (medical ser.)	3233	33454244455	SNNNNNNNFFFNFFNFNNNNN	NNNN3NNNNNNNNNN	P	231	899	07.05.02	4664	520404	55323
245.367-026	ORDER-CONTROL CLERK, BLOOD BANK (medical ser.; nonprofit organ.)	3233	33344344455	SNNNNNNNFFNFFNFNNNNN	NNNN3NNNNNNNNNN	J	232	899	07.05.04	4664	200404	59999
245.587-010	DIET CLERK (medical ser.)	3333	33343344454	LNNNNNNNFFNNOFNFNNNNN	NNNN3NNNNNNNNNN	U,R	282	903	07.05.03	4699	200404	51002
247.137-010	SUPERVISOR, ADVERTISING-DISPATCH CLERKS (print. & pub.)	4245	33343344454	LNNNNNNNFFNFFNNONNNN	NNNN3NNNNNNNNNN	D,J,P	282	854	07.05.01	4525	090201	51002
247.137-014	SUPERVISOR, CLASSIFIED ADVERTISING (print. & pub.)	4346	32344224455	LNNNNNNNFFNFFNNONNNN	NNNN2NNNNNNNNNN	D,P	261	896	07.05.02	4516	090201	51002
247.367-010	CLASSIFIED-AD CLERK I (print. & pub.)	3235	33344344455	SNNNNNNNFFNFFNFNNNNN	NNNN2NNNNNNNNNN	P,T	231	896	07.04.02	4662	090201	53908
247.382-010	MEDIA CLERK (business ser.)	4335	33343243455	SNNNNNNNFCNNNNFNNNNN	NNNN2NNNNNNNNNN	J,T	232	896	07.02.04	4699	090201	59999
247.387-010	ADVERTISING CLERK (business ser.)	3224	33343233455	SNNNNNNNFFONNNNFNNNN	NNNN3NNNNNNNNNN	T	232	896	07.02.04	4662	090201	53908
247.387-014	ADVERTISING-DISPATCH CLERK (print. & pub.)	3234	33443244455	SNNNNNNNFFONNNNNFNNNN	NNNN2NNNNNNNNNN	R,T	231	896	07.05.01	4752	090201	58008
247.387-018	ADVERTISING-SPACE CLERK (print. & pub.)	3335	33343333354	SNNNNNNNFFONFFNFNNNON	NNNN3NNNNNNNNNN	T	231	896	01.06.01	4662	090201	53908
247.387-022	CLASSIFIED-AD CLERK II (print. & pub.)	3325	33454244455	SNNNNNNNFFNFFNFNNNNN	NNNN3NNNNNNNNNN	R,T	231	898	07.05.02	4662	090201	53908
247.667-010	PRODUCTION PROOFREADER (print. & pub.; retail trade)	3234	33454144455	SNNNNNNNFFNNNCNCNCNN	NNNN3NNNNNNNNNN	J,T	261	896	07.05.02	4792	480205	53911
248.137-010	BOOKING SUPERVISOR (water trans.)	4336	33244344455	LNNNNNNNFFONFFNFNNNNN	NNNN3NNNNNNNNNN	V,D,P	231	891	07.05.01	4529	520204	51002
248.137-014	PURCHASING-AND-CLAIMS SUPERVISOR (water trans.)	4346	22344344455	SNNNNNNNFONFFNFNNNNN	NNNN3NNNNNNNNNN	D,J,P	231	854	07.01.02	4525	520204	51002
248.137-018	SUPERVISOR, CUSTOMER SERVICES (motor trans.)	4346	23333344445	LNNNNNNNOOONFFNFNNNNN	NNNN3NNNNNNNNNN	D,P,I,J	221	853	05.09.02	4525	520204	51002
248.167-010	SUPERCARGO (water trans.)	4337	33333344455	LNNOOOOFFONFFNFOONNN	ONNN3NNNNNNNNNN	D,J,P	011	854	07.02.04	4752	080709	58008
248.362-010	INCOMING-FREIGHT CLERK (water trans.)	3335	33333333355	LNNNNNNNFFONNNNFNNNN	NNNN2NNNNNNNNNN	V,T	232	890	07.02.04	4753	520499	58028
248.362-014	WEATHER CLERK (air trans.)	3233	33343344455	LNNNNNNNFONFFNFNNNNN	NNNN3NNNNNNNNNN	R,T	231	891	07.07.03	4699	520499	59999
248.362-010	AIRPLANE-DISPATCH CLERK (air trans.)	4345	33343244454	LNNNNNNNFFFNFFNFNNNON	NNNN3NNNNNNNNNN	P,V	231	855	07.05.03	4752	520499	58008
248.367-014	BOOKING CLERK (water trans.)	3225	33344344455	SNNNNNNNFFONFFNFNNNNN	NNNN2NNNNNNNNNN	V,P	231	891	07.05.01	4753	520499	58028
248.367-018	CARGO AGENT (air trans.)	3335	33334333344	MNNNNNNNFFNFFNFNONNN	NNNN3NNNNNNNNNN	J	013	855	05.09.01	4753	520499	58011
248.367-022	CONTAINER COORDINATOR (water trans.)	4336	33344233355	SNNNNNNNFFNFFNFNNNNN	NNNN2NNNNNNNNNN	J	231	854	07.05.01	4753	520499	58028
248.367-026	DISPATCHER, SHIP PILOT (water trans.)	3334	33334234455	SNNNNNNNFONFFNFNNNNN	NNNN3NNNNNNNNNN	T	231	854	07.04.05	4751	520499	58005
248.367-030	WATERWAY TRAFFIC CHECKER (water trans.)	3333	33343344554	SNNNNNNNFONFFNFNNOOON	NNNN3NNNNNNNNNN	R,J	281	854	07.04.05	4745	000000	57311

DOT #	DOT Title & Industry	Trng	Aptitude	Physical	Environment	Tempra	WkF	MPSMS	GOE	SOC	CIP	OES
248.382-010	TICKETING CLERK (air trans.)	3334	33344244455	SNNNNNNFFNNNNFNNNN	NNNN3NNNNNNNNNNN	R,T	232	899	07.02.04	4644	081105	53805
248.387-010	FLIGHT OPERATIONS SPECIALIST (military ser.)	3326	33244334455	LNNNNNNFFNNNNFNNNN	NNNN4NNNNNNNNNNN	T,V,J	231	855	07.05.03	4799	520408	00000
248.387-014	TONNAGE-COMPILATION CLERK (water trans.)	4335	33333333355	SNNNNNNFFNNNNFNNONN	NNNN3NNNNNNNNNNN	R,T	232	892	07.02.04	4699	520499	59999
249.137-010	OFFICE SUPERVISOR, ANIMAL HOSPITAL (nonprofit org.)	4346	22344344455	SNNNNNNOOONFFNFNNNN	NNNN3NNNNNNNNNNN	D,V,P	232	899	07.05.03	4511	520204	51002
249.137-014	SUPERVISOR, CONTACT AND SERVICE CLERKS (utilities)	4247	33334244455	SNNNNNNFFONFFNFNNNNN	NNNN2NNNNNNNNNNN	V,D,P	231	871	07.04.02	4516	520204	51002
249.137-018	SUPERVISOR, CORRESPONDENCE SECTION (insurance)	4246	23344244454	SNNNNNNFFONFFNCNNNNN	NNNN3NNNNNNNNNNN	D,P,T,J	231	895	07.05.03	4516	520204	51002
249.137-022	SUPERVISOR, CUSTOMER RECORDS DIVISION (utilities)	4347	33344344455	SNNNNNNOOONFFNFNNNON	NNNN2NNNNNNNNNNN	D,J,P	231	891	07.04.02	4516	520204	51002
249.137-026	SUPERVISOR, ORDER TAKERS (clerical)	4345	33344334455	SNNNNNNFFNFFNFNNNNN	NNNN3NNNNNNNNNNN	D,J,P	231	889	07.04.02	4516	520204	51002
249.137-030	SUPERVISOR, REAL-ESTATE OFFICE (real estate)	4347	22243233355	SNNNNNNNFFNFFNFNNNNN	NNNN3NNNNNNNNNNN	D,P,J	231	894	07.01.04	4529	521501	51002
249.137-034	SUPERVISOR, LENDING ACTIVITIES (financial)	4348	22344243455	SNNNNNNOOONCNCNNONN	NNNN3NNNNNNNNNNN	D,P,T,J	231	894	07.01.02	4514	000000	51002
249.167-010	AUTOMOBILE-CLUB-SAFETY-PROGRAM COORDINATOR (nonprofit org.)	4346	33344344455	SNNNNNNFOONFFNNNNNN	NNNN3NNNNNNNNNNN	D,P	282	961	07.01.01	4751	150201	51002
249.167-014	DISPATCHER, MOTOR VEHICLE (clerical)	3235	33354344455	SNNNNNNFOONFFNNNNNN	NNNN3NNNNNNNNNNN	D,P	231	853	07.05.01	4751	080709	58005
249.167-018	LABOR EXPEDITER (construction)	4345	33354244455	LNNNNNNOOONFFNONNNNN	ONNN2NNNNNNNNNNN	D,P,V	291	850	07.01.02	4758	521001	58008
249.262-010	POLICYHOLDER-INFORMATION CLERK (insurance)	4246	32354244455	SNNNNNNFFFNFNFNNNNN	NNNN3NNNNNNNNNNN	D,P,V	282	895	07.04.04	4649	520408	55305
249.267-010	COPYRIGHT EXPERT (radio-tv broad.)	4247	32344344455	SNNNNNNCCONFFNCNNNNN	NNNN3NNNNNNNNNNN	J	271	863	07.05.02	4799	520408	55305
249.362-010	COUNTER CLERK (tel. & tel.)	4245	33344334455	LNNNNNNFFNFFNFNNNNN	NNNN2NNNNNNNNNNN	R,P,T	232	862	07.03.01	4363	000000	59999
249.362-014	MORTGAGE CLERK (financial)	3335	33343243355	SNNNNNNOOFNOONCNNFNN	NNNN3NNNNNNNNNNN	T,P	231	894	07.01.04	4799	000000	55323
249.362-018	MORTGAGE LOAN CLOSER (financial)	4345	33354233455	SNNNNNNFFNFFNCNNNONN	NNNN3NNNNNNNNNNN	T,P	231	894	07.01.04	4799	080401	53902
249.362-022	MORTGAGE LOAN PROCESSOR (financial)	3335	33344233355	SNNNNNNFFCNOONCNNFNN	NNNN3NNNNNNNNNNN	T	231	894	07.05.02	4799	000000	53121
249.362-026	ORDER CLERK (clerical)	3334	33344244455	LNNNNNNFFNFFNFNNNNN	NNNN3NNNNNNNNNNN	T,P	231	881	07.05.03	4664	080799	55323
249.363-010	BOOKMOBILE DRIVER (library)	3223	33344334334	SNNNNNNOOFNOONCNNFNN	NNNN3NNNNNNNNNNN	V,P	013	862	05.09.01	4363	000000	53902
249.365-010	REGISTRATION CLERK (library)	3135	33344233355	LNNNNNNFFNFFNFNNFNN	NNNN3NNNNNNNNNNN	V,P,T	221	894	07.04.03	4694	000000	53902
249.366-010	COUNTER CLERK (photofinishing)	2222	44444233355	SNNNNNNFFNFFNCNNNONN	NNNN3NNNNNNNNNNN	P	232	899	07.03.01	4363	080705	49017
249.367-010	ANIMAL-SHELTER CLERK (nonprofit org.)	3233	33454244455	LNNNNNNOOONFFNONNNNN	FNNN3NNNNNNNNNNN	P	231	969	07.04.03	4630	520408	55347
249.367-014	CAREER-GUIDANCE TECHNICIAN (education)	4346	33444344455	LNNNNNNFFONFFNOONNN	NNNN3NNNNNNNNNNN	J	282	931	11.02.04	4630	000000	55347
249.367-018	CHARTER (amuse. & rec.)	3233	33323444455	SNNNNNNFFONFFNFNNNNN	NNNN3NNNNNNNNNNN	J	231	891	12.01.02	4799	000000	59999
249.367-022	CREDIT AUTHORIZER (clerical)	3223	33454334455	SNNNNNNFFONFFNFNNNNN	NNNN3NNNNNNNNNNN	J	282	894	07.05.02	4799	080401	53114
249.367-026	CREDIT CARD CONTROL CLERK (financial)	3223	43344233355	SNNNONCCFNOONCNNONN	NNNN3NNNNNNNNNNN	R,T	231	891	07.05.03	4699	520499	59999
249.367-030	DOG LICENSER (nonprofit org.)	3234	33344454455	LONONNNOOONFFNONNONN	FNNN3NNNNNNNNNNN	P	271	953	07.04.03	4787	520408	53708
249.367-034	EVALUATOR (nonprofit org.)	4224	33355244455	SNNNNNNFFNFFNNNNNON	NNNN3NNNNNNNNNNN	J	212	891	05.09.02	47-6	520302	55344
249.367-042	GAS-DISTRIBUTION-AND-EMERGENCY CLERK (utilities)	4336	33343244454	SNNNNNNFFNFFNFNNNON	NNNN2NNNNNNNNNNN	J	282	872	07.04.05	4664	520406	55323
249.367-046	LIBRARY ASSISTANT (library)	3235	33444233355	LNNONONFFNFFNFNNNNN	NNNN3NNNNNNNNNNN	V,P	221	933	11.02.04	4694	520408	53902
249.367-058	PARTS-ORDER-AND-STOCK CLERK (clerical)	3225	33344344455	LNNFFNNNFFNFNNOONN	NNNN2NNNNNNNNNNN	R,T	221	898	05.09.01	4754	520499	58023
249.367-062	PROCESS SERVER (business ser.)	3233	33323444455	SNNNNNNFFONFFNFNNNNN	FNNN3NNNNNNNNNNN	P	282	959	07.07.02	4799	000000	59999
249.367-066	PROCUREMENT CLERK (clerical)	4334	33343243455	SNNNNNNFFNFFNFNNNON	NNNN3NNNNNNNNNNN	V,T,P	232	891	07.01.02	4754	520499	55326
249.367-070	ROUTING CLERK (nonprofit org.)	3233	33453344455	LNNNNNNFFNFFNFONNN	NNNN3NNNNNNNNNNN	J	231	853	07.05.04	4751	520499	58005
249.367-074	TEACHER AIDE II (education)	3333	33343233354	LNNNNNNFFNFFNFONNN	NNNN3NNNNNNNNNNN	P,J,V	296	931	07.01.02	4795	131501	31521
249.367-078	TEST TECHNICIAN (clerical)	3234	33343233354	LNNNNNNFFONNNONONNN	NNNN3NNNNNNNNNNN	J,P,T	296	940	07.01.07	4799	521001	59999
249.367-082	PARK AIDE (government ser.)	4343	33443333354	LNNNNNNOOOONFFNOFOOON	FNNN3NNNNNNNNNNN	P,V	282	919	07.04.03	4645	310101	55305
249.367-086	SATELLITE-INSTRUCTION FACILITATOR (education)	3233	33444344454	SNNNNNNFFONFFNFNNNNN	NNNN3NNNNNNNNNNN	P,T,V	282	869	07.01.02	4795	521001	53905
249.367-090	ASSIGNMENT CLERK (clerical)	3225	33444333455	SNNONNNFFONFFNNNNNN	NNNN3NNNNNNNNNNN	V,P,J	282	891	07.05.03	4692	521001	55314
249.387-010	BROADCAST CHECKER (radio-tv broad.)	3234	33452444455	SNNNNNNFFNFNNNNFNNNNN	NNNN3NNNNNNNNNNN	J	211	863	11.10.02	4799	000000	59999
249.387-014	INTELLIGENCE CLERK (military ser.)	3336	33344244454	MNNNNNNNFFNNNNFNNNON	NNNN3NNNNNNNNNNN	J	231	959	07.05.03	4699	520408	00000
249.387-018	PEDIGREE TRACER (clerical)	3233	33454244455	SNNNNNNFFFNFNNNFNNNNN	NNNN3NNNNNNNNNNN	T	271	891	07.05.02	4783	520408	53505
249.387-022	READER (business ser.)	3134	33344344454	LNNNNNNOOONNNNCNNNNN	NNNN3NNNNNNNNNNN	R,J	231	899	07.05.02	4799	520408	59999
249.467-010	INFORMATION CLERK-CASHIER (amuse. & rec.)	3235	33344244453	LNNNNNNFFONCNCNNNFN	NNNN4NNNNNNNNNNN	P,T	232	899	07.03.01	4364	520803	49023
249.587-010	BOARD ATTENDANT (amuse. & rec.)	3222	34444424454	LNFNNNNNFFONNNONONNNN	NNNN3NNNNNNNNNNN	R,T	231	913	09.05.05	4699	520408	59999
249.587-014	CUTTER-AND-PASTER, PRESS CLIPPINGS (business ser.)	2112	44444424454	SNNNNNNFFONNNNNFNNNNN	NNNN3NNNNNNNNNNN	R	054	899	07.07.03	4759	520408	59999
249.587-018	DOCUMENT PREPARER, MICROFILMING (business ser.)	3122	34434344454	SNNNNNNFFFNNNNNFNNNON	NNNN3NNNNNNNNNNN	V,T	231	891	07.05.03	4759	000000	58099
249.687-010	OFFICE COPY SELECTOR (print. & pub.)	3123	34443444354	LNNNNNNFFFNNNNNFFNNN	NNNN2NNNNNNNNNNN	J,T	212	486	07.05.04	4744	000000	57302
249.687-014	PAGE (library)	2122	33444344455	LNFFNNFFNNNNFNNNNN	NNNN2NNNNNNNNNNN	R	221	933	07.07.02	4694	000000	53902

DOT #	DOT Title & Industry	Trng	Aptitude	Physical	Environment	Tempra	WkF	MPSMS	GOE	SOC	CIP	OES
250.157-010	SUPERINTENDENT, SALES (construction)	5457	22222344454	LNNNINNNOONFFNONNNON	ONNN2NNNNNNNNN	D,I,J,P	292	361	08.02.04	4123	080706	43008
250.257-010	SALES AGENT, INSURANCE (insurance)	4346	22255244455	NNNNNNNNFFNCCNFNNNNN	NNNN2NNNNNNNNN	P,I,J	292	895	08.01.02	4122	080706	43002
250.257-014	FINANCIAL PLANNER (profess. & kin.)	5348	22355255555	SNNNNNNOOONCCNFNFNNN	NNNN3NNNNNNNNN	I,P,J	292	894	08.01.02	4100	521501	43014
250.257-018	REGISTERED REPRESENTATIVE (financial)	4347	22244344455	SNNNNNNOOONFFNNNNNNN	NNNN2NNNNNNNNN	I,P,J	292	894	11.06.04	4124	080401	43014
250.257-022	SALES REPRESENTATIVE, FINANCIAL SERVICES (financial)	5457	22244344455	LNNNNNNFFONCCNFNNNNN	NNNN2NNNNNNNNN	I,P,J	292	894	08.01.02	4124	080706	43014
250.357-010	BUILDING CONSULTANT (wholesale tr.)	4345	22333344455	LNNNNNNFFONFFNFNNNNN	NNNN3NNNNNNNNN	I,J,P	292	895	08.02.04	4123	521501	43008
250.357-014	LEASING AGENT, RESIDENCE (real estate)	4245	22344344455	LONONNNFFNFFNFOOONO	ONNN3NNNNNNNNN	D,P,J	292	895	08.02.04	4123	080706	43008
250.357-018	SALES AGENT, REAL ESTATE (real estate)	4345	22344344455	LONNNNNFFNFFNFOOONN	NNNN3NNNNNNNNN	I,J,P	292	853	08.02.04	4123	080706	43005
250.357-022	SALES REPRESENTATIVE (motor trans.)	3335	22333344455	LONNNNNFFNFFNFOOONN	NNNN3NNNNNNNNN	P,J,I	292	853	08.02.06	4152	080799	43017
250.357-026	SALES AGENT, FINANCIAL-REPORT SERVICE (business ser.)	4345	22344344455	LNNNNNNOOONFFNFNNNN	NNNN3NNNNNNNNN	P,I	292	890	08.01.02	4124	080401	43014
251.157-010	SALES REPRESENTATIVE, DATA PROCESSING SERVICES (business ser.)	5557	22223244455	LNNNNNNOOONFFNFNNNN	NNNN3NNNNNNNNN	I,P,J	292	893	08.01.02	4152	080299	43017
251.257-014	SALES AGENT, PSYCHOLOGICAL TESTS AND INDUSTRIAL RELATIONS (business ser.; print. & pub.)	5457	22344244454	LNNNNNNOOONFFNFNNNNON	NNNN2NNNNNNNNN	V,P,I	292	899	08.01.02	4152	080299	43017
251.357-010	SALES AGENT, BUSINESS SERVICES (business ser.)	4345	33334344454	LNNNNNNOOONFFNNNNON	ONNN3NNNNNNNNN	I,J,P	292	899	08.02.06	4152	120507	43017
251.357-018	SALES AGENT, PEST CONTROL SERVICE (business ser.)	4346	33333344454	LNNONONFFNFFNFFON	NNNN3NNNNNNNNN	I,J,P	292	962	08.02.06	4152	010501	43017
251.357-022	SALES REPRESENTATIVE, FRANCHISE (business ser.)	4345	33344344455	LNNNNNNOOONFFNFNNNNN	NNNN3NNNNNNNNN	I,J,P	292	894	08.02.06	4152	080706	43017
251.357-026	SALES REPRESENTATIVE, HERBICIDE SERVICE (business ser.)	4345	33344344455	LNNNNNNFFNFFNFNNNNN	NNNN3NNNNNNNNN	I,J,P	292	962	08.02.06	4152	080299	43017
252.152-010	SALES REPRESENTATIVE (business ser.; motor trans.; retail trade)	4345	32344233354	SNNNNNNNFFNFFNFNNNON	NNNN3NNNNNNNNN	I,V,P,J	282	850	08.02.06	4369	081105	43021
252.257-010	TRAVEL AGENT (air trans.; motor trans.; r.r. trans.; water trans.)	5347	22343244455	LNNNNNNOOONFFNONNNNN	NNNN3NNNNNNNNN	I,J,P	292	850	08.01.02	4152	080706	43017
252.357-010	TRAFFIC AGENT (air trans.; motor trans.; r.r. trans.)	4345	23223344454	LNNNNNNFFONFFNONONON	NNNN3NNNNNNNNN	I,J,P	292	850	08.01.02	4152	080299	43017
252.357-014	CRATING-AND-MOVING ESTIMATOR (motor trans.; r.r. trans.)	3335	33333344445	LNNNNNNFFONFFNFNNNNN	ONNN3NNNNNNNNN	P,I,J	292	853	08.01.02	4152	080299	43017
252.357-014	SALES REPRESENTATIVE, SHIPPING SERVICES (motor trans.)	5346	22322344455	LNNNNNNOOONCNONNNNN	NNNN3NNNNNNNNN	P,I,J	292	861	08.01.01	4152	099999	43017
253.157-010	COMMUNICATIONS CONSULTANT (tel. & tel.)	5346	22333344455	LNNNNNNOOONFFNNNNNN	NNNN3NNNNNNNNN	I,J,P	292	861	08.01.02	4152	080299	43017
253.257-010	SALES REPRESENTATIVE, TELEPHONE SERVICES (tel. & tel.)	4346	22334344455	LNNNNNNFFONFFNFNNNNN	NNNN3NNNNNNNNN	I,J,P	292	860	08.01.02	4152	080299	43017
254.251-010	SALES REPRESENTATIVE, PUBLIC UTILITIES (tel. & tel.; utilities)	5347	22323333452	LNNNNNNFFONFFNFNNOON	NNNN3NNNNNNNNN	V,P,I,E	292	752	08.01.01	4153	090201	43023
254.251-010	SALES REPRESENTATIVE, GRAPHIC ART (business ser.)	4346	22322344453	LNNNNNNOOONFFFFFFFF	NNNN3NNNNNNNNN	I,J,P	292	896	08.01.01	4153	080299	43023
254.357-010	SALES REPRESENTATIVE, SIGNS AND DISPLAYS (fabrication, nec)	3234	33344344455	LNNNNNNOOONFFNONNNNN	ONNN3NNNNNNNNN	P,I,J	292	885	11.12.02	4153	080299	43023
254.357-010	LEASING AGENT, OUTDOOR ADVERTISING (business ser.)	4346	22323444454	LNNNNNNOOONFFNONONNN	NNNN3NNNNNNNNN	I,J,P	292	882	08.01.02	4153	080299	43023
254.357-014	SALES REPRESENTATIVE, ADVERTISING (print. & pub.)	4345	33343344454	LNNNNNNFFONFFNFNNNNN	NNNN3NNNNNNNNN	I,J,P	292	882	08.01.02	4152	080299	43017
254.357-018	SALES REPRESENTATIVE, PRINTING (wholesale tr.)	4346	33333344453	LNNNNNNOOONFFNONNOON	NNNN3NNNNNNNNN	I,J,P	292	619	08.01.01	4153	090201	43023
254.357-022	SALES REPRESENTATIVE, SIGNS (fabrication, nec)	4346	33344344455	LNNNNNNOOONFFNNNNON	NNNN3NNNNNNNNN	I,J,P	292	911	08.02.06	4369	080299	43099
259.157-010	SALES REPRESENTATIVE, AUDIOVISUAL PROGRAM PRODUCTIONS (motion picture)	4345	22334344455	SNNNNNNOOONFFNFNNNNN	NNNN3NNNNNNNNN	I,J,P	292	902	08.02.06	4152	520902	43099
259.157-014	SALES REPRESENTATIVE, HOTEL SERVICES (hotel & rest.)	4347	22343344455	SNNNNNNOOONFFNFNNNNN	NNNN3NNNNNNNNN	D,I,P,J	292	902	08.01.02	4152	520902	43017
259.257-010	SALES REPRESENTATIVE, EDUCATION COURSES (education)	4345	22333344455	LNNNNNNOOONFFNFNNNNN	NNNN3NNNNNNNNN	P,I,J	292	931	08.01.02	4369	080299	43099
259.257-014	SALES REPRESENTATIVE, ELECTROPLATING (wholesale tr.)	5447	22333344453	LNNNNNNOOONFFNFNNNNN	NNNN3NNNNNNNNN	I,J,P	292	490	08.01.01	4239	080299	49005
259.257-018	SERVICE REPRESENTATIVE, ELEVATORS, ESCALATORS, AND DUMBWAITERS (wholesale)	5445	22233344455	LNNNNNNFFNFFNFNNNONN	NNNN3NNNNNNNNN	P,I,J	292	462	08.01.01	4348	080706	43017
259.257-022	SALES REPRESENTATIVE, SECURITY SYSTEMS (business ser.)	4345	22335344455	LNNNNNNFFNFFNFNNNONN	NNNN3NNNNNNNNN	I,P,J	292	565	08.01.01	4152	080706	43017
259.357-010	GROUP-SALES REPRESENTATIVE (amuse. & rec.)	3233	32354344435	MONOONNOONFFFFNNNNN	NNNN3NNNNNNNNN	P,I	292	586	08.02.08	4152	080299	43099
259.357-014	SALES REPRESENTATIVE, DANCING INSTRUCTIONS (education)	3234	33434344435	LNNNNNNOOONFFNONNNNN	ONNN3NNNNNNNNN	I,J,P,E	292	910	08.02.05	4369	080299	43099
259.357-018	SALES REPRESENTATIVE, RADIO AND TELEVISION TIME (radio-tv broad.)	4346	22334344455	LNNNNNNOOONCCNONOOOONO	NNNN3NNNNNNNNN	I,P,J	292	919	08.01.03	4246	010501	49008
259.357-022	SALES REPRESENTATIVE, TELEVISION CABLE SERVICE (radio-tv broad.)	4343	33343344454	LNNNNNNNFONCCNONNNON	NNNN3NNNNNNNNN	I,P,J	292	863	08.01.02	4153	080706	43023
259.357-026	SALES REPRESENTATIVE, UPHOLSTERY AND FURNITURE REPAIR (retail trade)	4335	33333344453	LNNNNNNOOONFFNFNNNON	NNNN3NNNNNNNNN	I,J,P	292	869	08.02.06	4369	080299	43099
259.357-030	SALES REPRESENTATIVE, WEATHER-FORECASTING SERVICE (business ser.)	4344	33343344454	LNNNNNNOOONFFNFNNNON	NNNN3NNNNNNNNN	I,J,P	292	462	08.01.02	4348	080706	43099
259.357-034	TICKET BROKER (amuse. & rec.)	4346	33333344454	LNNNNNNFFNFFNFNNNNNN	NNNN3NNNNNNNNN	P,I	292	899	08.01.02	4152	080706	43017
259.357-038	TOBACCO-WAREHOUSE AGENT (business ser.)	3233	33444344455	LNNNNNNOOONFFNONNNNN	ONNN3NNNNNNNNN	P,I,J	292	910	11.06.04	4369	010501	43017
260.257-010	SALES REPRESENTATIVE, LIVESTOCK (wholesale tr.)	4345	32354344435	LNNNNNNOOONFFNONNNNN	NNNN3NNNNNNNNN	P,I	292	882	08.01.02	4152	010501	43017
260.357-010	COMMISSION AGENT, AGRICULTURAL PRODUCE (wholesale tr.)	4346	22244344455	SNNNNNNOOONCCNONNNNN	NNNN3NNNNNNNNN	P,I,J	292	300	08.01.03	4246	010501	49008
260.357-014	SALES REPRESENTATIVE, FOOD PRODUCTS (wholesale tr.)	4345	33344344455	LNNNNNNFFONFFNNNNNNN	NNNN3NNNNNNNNN	P,I	292	380	08.02.01	4249	080706	49008
260.357-018	SALES REPRESENTATIVE, MALT LIQUORS (wholesale tr.)	4334	33344344454	LNNNNNNOOONFFNFNNNNN	NNNN3NNNNNNNNN	I,J,P	292	882	08.02.01	4249	080601	49008
260.357-022	SALES REPRESENTATIVE, TOBACCO PRODUCTS AND SMOKING SUPPLIES (retail trade;)	4335	33343344454	LNNNNNNFFNFFNFNNNNNN	NNNN3NNNNNNNNN	P,I	292	403	08.02.03	4249	080601	49008
260.357-026	SALESPERSON, FLOWERS (retail trade)	4334	33333333353	LNNNNNNFFNFFNFNONFNFN	NNNC4NNNNNNNNN	I,J,P,E	292	311	08.02.02	4359	080706	49011
261.351-010	SALESPERSON, WIGS (personal ser.; retail trade)	3334	33423433352	LNNONNNNFFFFFNFNOOFN	NNNN3NNNNNNNNN	I,J,P	292	881	08.02.02	4354	080706	49011

DOT #	DOT Title & Industry	Trng	Aptitude	Physical	Environment	Tempra	WkF	MPSMS	GOE	SOC	CIP	OES
261.354-010	SALESPERSON, CORSETS (retail trade)	4345	33333343354	LNNNNNNNFFONFFNONNNON	NNNN2NNNNNNNNNN	V,P,I,J	292	881	08.02.02	4346	080102	49011
261.357-010	SALES REPRESENTATIVE, APPAREL TRIMMINGS (wholesale tr.)	4345	33333344454	LNNNNNNNOONFFNONNNON	NNNN3NNNNNNNNNN	I,J,P	292	432	08.02.01	4243	080799	49008
261.357-014	SALES REPRESENTATIVE, CANVAS PRODUCTS (wholesale tr.)	4346	33333344454	LNNNNNNNOOONFFNONNNON	ONNN3NNNNNNNNNN	I,J,P	292	882	08.02.01	4249	080706	49008
261.357-018	SALES REPRESENTATIVE, FOOTWEAR (wholesale tr.)	4346	33333344454	LNNNNNNNOOONFFNONNNON	NNNN3NNNNNNNNNN	I,J,P	292	522	08.02.01	4351	080799	49011
261.357-022	SALES REPRESENTATIVE, MEN'S AND BOYS' APPAREL (wholesale tr.)	4346	33333344454	LNNNNNNNOOONFFNONNNON	NNNN2NNNNNNNNNN	I,J,P	292	441	08.02.01	4243	080799	49008
261.357-026	SALES REPRESENTATIVE, SAFETY APPAREL AND EQUIPMENT (wholesale tr.)	4344	33344344455	LNNNNNNNFFOOCNFOONNON	NNNN3NNNNNNNNNN	I,J,P	292	604	08.02.01	4242	080706	49008
261.357-030	SALES REPRESENTATIVE, TEXTILES (wholesale tr.)	4346	22343344453	LNNNNNNNFFOOCNFOOOOO	NNNN3NNNNNNNNNN	I,J,P	292	420	08.02.01	4243	200306	49008
261.357-034	SALES REPRESENTATIVE, UNIFORMS (retail trade; wholesale tr.)	4346	33344344454	LNNNNNNNFONFFNNNON	NNNN3NNNNNNNNNN	I,J,P	292	440	08.02.03	4243	080102	49008
261.357-038	SALES REPRESENTATIVE, WOMEN'S AND GIRLS' APPAREL (wholesale tr.)	4345	33333344454	LNNNNNNNOOONFFNONNNON	NNNN3NNNNNNNNNN	I,J,P	292	440	08.02.01	4243	080706	49008
261.357-042	SALESPERSON, FURS (retail trade)	4345	33333344353	LNNNNNNNFONFFNNNOFN	NNNN2NNNNNNNNNN	I,J,P	292	447	08.02.02	4346	080706	49011
261.357-046	SALESPERSON, INFANTS' AND CHILDREN'S WEAR (retail trade)	4343	33343433354	LNFNNNNNFFNNONFFNONNON	NNNN3NNNNNNNNNN	I,J,P	292	881	08.02.02	4346	080102	49011
261.357-050	SALESPERSON, MEN'S AND BOYS' CLOTHING (retail trade)	3334	33343344453	LNNOONNFCFNFNNFNFN	NNNN3NNNNNNNNNN	I,J,P	292	441	08.02.02	4346	200306	49011
261.357-054	SALESPERSON, MEN'S FURNISHINGS (retail trade)	4344	33343433353	LNNNNNNNFFONFFNONNNFN	NNNN2NNNNNNNNNN	I,J,P	292	881	08.02.02	4346	080102	49011
261.357-058	SALESPERSON, MILLINERY (retail trade)	4343	33343433353	LNNONNNNFFFNFNONFFFN	NNNN2NNNNNNNNNN	I,J,P	292	445	08.02.02	4346	080706	49011
261.357-062	SALESPERSON, SHOES (retail trade)	3234	33344343354	LOOFNFNFCFOFFNFNNNFN	NNNN3NNNNNNNNNN	I,P	292	522	08.02.02	4351	080199	49011
261.357-066	SALESPERSON, WOMEN'S APPAREL AND ACCESSORIES (retail trade)	3233	33344443353	LNNONONFFONFFNNNNNON	NNNN3NNNNNNNNNN	I,P	292	440	08.02.02	4346	080799	49011
261.357-070	SALESPERSON, YARD GOODS (retail trade)	4343	33333433353	LNNNNNNNFFFNFFNNNOFN	NNNN2NNNNNNNNNN	I,J,P	292	420	08.02.02	4359	200306	49011
261.357-074	SALESPERSON, LEATHER-AND-SUEDE APPAREL-AND-ACCESSORIES (retail trade)	3335	33343344453	LNNNNNNNFFOFFNFNNNFN	NNNN3NNNNNNNNNN	I,J,P	292	440	08.02.02	4346	200306	49011
262.157-010	PHARMACEUTICAL DETAILER (wholesale tr.)	5357	22333344454	LNNNNNNNFFONFFNONNNON	NNNN2NNNNNNNNNN	I,J,P	292	493	08.01.01	4236	080706	49005
262.357-010	SALES REPRESENTATIVE, CHEMICALS AND DRUGS (wholesale tr.)	4345	33344344455	LNNNNNNNFFONFFOONNNON	NNNN3NNNNNNNNNN	I,J,P	292	490	08.01.01	4237	080706	49005
262.357-014	SALES REPRESENTATIVE, TOILET PREPARATIONS (wholesale tr.)	4345	33344344454	LNNNNNNNFFONFFOONNNON	NNNN2NNNNNNNNNN	I,J,P	292	494	08.02.01	4354	080705	49011
262.357-018	SALES REPRESENTATIVE, COSMETICS AND TOILETRIES (retail trade)	3334	33333333353	LNNNNNNNFFONFFOONNOON	NNNN2NNNNNNNNNN	I,J,P	292	494	08.02.02	4354	080799	49011
262.357-022	SALES REPRESENTATIVE, WATER-TREATMENT CHEMICALS (wholesale tr.)	3337	32344244443	SONONNNOONFFNONNNON	ONNO3NNNONNNN	I,P,J	292	882	08.02.01	4237	080706	49005
269.357-010	SALES REPRESENTATIVE, FUELS (retail trade; wholesale tr.)	4344	33344344455	LNNNNNNNFFNFFNNNNNNN	NNNN2NNNNNNNNNN	I,J,P	292	341	08.02.03	4249	080706	49008
269.357-014	SALES REPRESENTATIVE, PETROLEUM PRODUCTS (wholesale tr.)	4346	33344344453	LNNNNNNNFFONFFNONNNON	NNNN3NNNNNNNNNN	I,J,P	292	500	08.02.01	4249	080799	49008
269.357-018	SALES-PROMOTION REPRESENTATIVE (wholesale tr.)	4233	33443333344	LNNNNNNNFFONFFNONNNON	NNNN3NNNNNNNNNN	I,J,P	292	882	08.02.01	4153	080799	43023
270.352-010	SALESPERSON, SEWING MACHINES (retail trade)	4346	33333333344	MNNNNNNFNFFNONNNOON	NNNN3NNNNNNNNNN	I,J,P	292	583	08.02.02	4352	080706	49011
270.357-010	SALES REPRESENTATIVE, HOME FURNISHINGS (wholesale tr.)	4345	33333344454	LNNNNNNNOOONFFNONNNON	NNNN2NNNNNNNNNN	I,J,P	292	882	08.02.01	4348	080706	49011
270.357-014	SALES REPRESENTATIVE, HOUSEHOLD APPLIANCES (wholesale tr.)	4345	33344344455	LNNNNNNNOOONFFNONNNON	NNNN3NNNNNNNNNN	I,J,P	292	583	08.02.01	4352	080799	49011
270.357-018	SALESPERSON, CHINA AND SILVERWARE (retail trade; wholesale tr.)	4344	33343333354	LNNNNNNNFFNFNFNONNON	NNNN2NNNNNNNNNN	I,J,P	292	530	08.02.03	4348	080705	49011
270.357-022	SALESPERSON, CURTAINS AND DRAPERIES (retail trade)	4344	33344344453	LNNNNNNNFFNFFNFNNOFN	NNNN2NNNNNNNNNN	I,J,P	292	435	08.02.02	4348	200502	49011
270.357-026	SALESPERSON, FLOOR COVERINGS (retail trade; wholesale tr.)	4344	33344334453	LNNOONNFONFFNFNNNON	NNNN3NNNNNNNNNN	I,J,P	292	431	08.02.01	4348	200501	49011
270.357-030	SALESPERSON, FURNITURE (retail trade)	3334	33333344453	LNNONNNFFONFFNFNNNFN	NNNN3NNNNNNNNNN	I,P	292	460	08.02.02	4348	080809	49011
270.357-034	SALESPERSON, HOUSEHOLD APPLIANCES (retail trade)	4344	33344343354	LNNNNNNNFFONFFNONNNON	NNNN3NNNNNNNNNN	I,J,P	292	562	08.02.02	4352	080705	49011
270.357-038	SALESPERSON, STEREO EQUIPMENT (retail trade)	4344	33343333354	MNNONNNOOONFFNONNNON	NNNN3NNNNNNNNNN	I,J,P	292	562	08.02.02	4352	080809	49011
271.257-010	SALES REPRESENTATIVE, COMMUNICATION EQUIPMENT (wholesale tr.)	4446	22223344454	MNNOONNOOONFFNONNNON	MNNO3NNNNNNNNNN	I,J,P	292	585	08.02.01	4234	080705	49005
271.352-010	SALES REPRESENTATIVE, RADIOGRAPHIC-INSPECTION EQUIPMENT AND SERVICES (wholesale tr.)	4346	22232343354	LNNNNNNNFFONFFNFNNON	NNNN3NNNNNNNNNN	I,J,P	292	586	08.01.01	4235	080706	49005
271.352-014	SALES REPRESENTATIVE, ULTRASONIC EQUIPMENT (wholesale tr.)	4345	22333334355	LNNNNNNNOOONFFNONNNON	NNNN3NNNNNNNNNN	I,J,P	292	589	08.01.01	4234	080799	49005
271.354-010	SALESPERSON, ELECTRIC MOTORS (retail trade; wholesale tr.)	4346	33333343354	LNNNNNNNFFNFFNFNNNON	NNNN3NNNNNNNNNN	I,J,P	292	582	08.02.03	4242	080705	49005
271.357-010	SALES REPRESENTATIVE, HOUSEHOLD APPLIANCES (wholesale tr.)	4346	22333344455	LNNNNNNNOOONFFNONNNON	NNNN2NNNNNNNNNN	I,J,P	292	587	08.01.01	4352	080706	49011
271.357-014	SALES REPRESENTATIVE, ELECTRONICS PARTS (wholesale tr.)	4343	33344344455	LNNNNNNNFFNFNFNNNON	NNNN2NNNNNNNNNN	I,J,P	292	586	08.02.02	4348	080799	49011
271.357-018	SALESPERSON, VIDEOTAPE (wholesale tr.)	4346	33344334453	LNNOONNFONFFNFNNNON	NNNN3NNNNNNNNNN	I,J,P	292	381	08.02.01	4233	080706	49005
272.357-010	SALES REPRESENTATIVE, ANIMAL-FEED PRODUCTS (wholesale tr.)	4346	33334344455	LNNNNNNNOOONFFNONNNON	NNNN3NNNNNNNNNN	I,J,P	292	562	08.02.01	4233	080706	49005
272.357-014	SALES REPRESENTATIVE, FARM AND GARDEN EQUIPMENT AND SUPPLIES (wholesale tr.)	4345	33334344455	MNNNNNNNOOONFFNONNNON	NNNN3NNNNNNNNNN	I,J,P	292	562	08.02.01	4233	010501	49005
272.357-018	SALES REPRESENTATIVE, POULTRY EQUIPMENT AND SUPPLIES (retail trade; wholesale tr.)	4346	22344344454	MNNNNNNNOOONFOFFNONNNON	FNNN3NNNNNNNNNN	I,J,P	292	310	08.02.03	4233	080706	49011
272.357-022	SALESPERSON, HORTICULTURAL AND NURSERY PRODUCTS (retail trade; wholesale tr.)	4344	33444433354	LNNOONNOFONFNNNNNON	NNNN3NNNNNNNNNN	I,J,P	292	592	08.02.03	4353	080503	49011
273.253-010	SALESPERSON, AIRCRAFT (retail trade; wholesale tr.)	5346	22323334334	LNNNNNNNFFONFNFFFFF	ONNN4NNNNNNNNNN	P,I,J	292	591	08.01.01	4232	080799	49005
273.353-010	SALESPERSON, AUTOMOBILES (retail trade)	4346	33333344334	LNNNNNNNFFONFFNOOOO	NNNN3NNNNNNNNNN	I,P	292	342	08.02.02	4342	080705	49011
273.357-010	SALES REPRESENTATIVE, AIRCRAFT EQUIPMENT AND PARTS (wholesale tr.)	4346	22333344455	LNNNNNNNOOONFFNONNNON	NNNN3NNNNNNNNNN	I,J,P	292	592	08.01.01	4232	081208	49005
273.357-014	SALES REPRESENTATIVE, AUTOMOTIVE-LEASING (business ser.)	4345	33344344455	LNNNNNNNOOONFFNONNNON	NNNN3NNNNNNNNNN	I,J,P	292	889	08.02.06	4369	080299	43099
273.357-018	SALES REPRESENTATIVE, BOATS AND MARINE SUPPLIES (retail trade; wholesale tr.)	4345	33333344354	LNNNNNNNFFONFFNONNNON	NNNN2NNNNNNNNNN	I,J,P	292	593	08.02.03	4344	081208	49011

DOT #	DOT Title & Industry	Trng	Aptitude	Physical	Environment	Tempra	WkF	MPSMS	GOE	SOC	CIP	OES
273.357-022	SALES REPRESENTATIVE, MOTOR VEHICLES AND SUPPLIES (wholesale tr.)	4345	22333344455	LNNNNNNOOONFFFNONNNNN	NNNNN2NNNNNNNNNN	I,J,P	292	590	08.02.01	4244	080706	49008
273.357-026	SALES REPRESENTATIVE, RAILROAD EQUIPMENT AND SUPPLIES (wholesale tr.)	4346	22334344455	LNNNNNNNOOONFFFNONNNNN	NNNNN2NNNNNNNNNN	I,J,P	292	594	08.02.01	4235	080799	49005
273.357-030	SALESPERSON, AUTOMOBILE ACCESSORIES (retail trade)	4344	33344344355	LONONNNFFONFFNONNNNN	NNNNN2NNNNNNNNNN	I,J,P	292	591	08.02.03	4342	080705	49011
273.357-034	SALESPERSON, TRAILERS AND MOTOR HOMES (retail trade)	4345	33344344455	LNNNNNNNFFONFFNONNNNN	FNNNN2NNNNNNNNNN	I,J,P	292	590	08.02.02	4342	081208	49011
274.157-010	SALES REPRESENTATIVE, ELEVATORS, ESCALATORS, AND DUMBWAITERS (wholesale)	5445	22223443454	LNNNNNNNFFNFFNFNNNON	NNNN3NNNNNNNNNN	I,J,P	292	565	08.01.01	4242	080706	49005
274.257-010	SALES REPRESENTATIVE, FOUNDRY AND MACHINE SHOP PRODUCTS (wholesale tr.)	5447	33233344455	LNNNNNNNFFONFFNONNNNN	NNNNN3NNNNNNNNNN	I,J,P	292	550	08.01.01	4235	080706	49005
274.357-010	SALES REPRESENTATIVE, ABRASIVES (wholesale tr.)	4346	33333344454	LNNNNNNNNFFONFFNONNNON	NNNN3NNNNNNNNNN	I,J,P	292	538	08.01.01	4235	080799	49005
274.357-014	SALES REPRESENTATIVE, BOTTLES AND BOTTLING EQUIPMENT (wholesale tr.)	4345	32333344455	LNNNNNNNNOOONFFNONNNNN	NNNNN2NNNNNNNNNN	I,J,P	292	882	08.02.01	4249	080706	49005
274.357-018	SALES REPRESENTATIVE, BUILDING EQUIPMENT AND SUPPLIES (wholesale tr.)	4346	33333344444	LNNNNNNNFFONCCNNNNNON	ONNN3NNNNNNNNNN	I,J,P	292	882	08.01.01	4235	080706	49005
274.357-022	SALES REPRESENTATIVE, CONSTRUCTION MACHINERY (wholesale tr.)	4346	22333344455	LNNNNNNNOOOHFFNONNNNN	FNNN3NNNNNNNNNN	I,J,P	292	563	08.01.01	4235	080706	49005
274.357-026	SALES REPRESENTATIVE, CONTAINERS (wholesale tr.)	4345	32333344455	LNNNNNNNFFNFFNFNNNNN	NNNN3NNNNNNNNNN	I,J,P	292	475	08.02.01	4242	080799	49008
274.357-030	SALES REPRESENTATIVE, DAIRY SUPPLIES (wholesale tr.)	4346	23334344454	LNNNNNNNOOONFFFNONNNON	NNNN3NNNNNNNNNN	I,J,P	292	882	08.02.01	4233	080799	49005
274.357-034	SALES REPRESENTATIVE, HARDWARE SUPPLIES (wholesale tr.)	4345	33344344454	LNNNNNNNFFONFFNONNNON	NNNN3NNNNNNNNNN	I,J,P	292	552	08.02.01	4353	080706	49008
274.357-038	SALES REPRESENTATIVE, INDUSTRIAL MACHINERY (wholesale tr.)	4345	33233344455	LNNNNNNNOOONFFNONOONN	NNNN3NNNNNNNNNN	P,I,J	292	560	08.01.01	4235	080799	49008
274.357-042	SALES REPRESENTATIVE, INDUSTRIAL RUBBER GOODS (wholesale tr.)	4346	32343344455	LNNNNNNNOOONFFNOOONNN	NNNN2NNNNNNNNNN	I,J,P	292	509	08.02.01	4242	080706	49008
274.357-046	SALES REPRESENTATIVE, LUBRICATING EQUIPMENT (wholesale tr.)	4345	32333343355	LNNNNNNNOOONFFNOOONNN	NNNN3NNNNNNNNNN	I,J,P	292	882	08.02.01	4235	080706	49005
274.357-050	SALES REPRESENTATIVE, MATERIAL-HANDLING EQUIPMENT (wholesale tr.)	4345	33333344455	LNNNNNNNOOONFFNNONNNON	NNNN3NNNNNNNNNN	I,J,P	292	565	08.02.01	4235	080706	49005
274.357-054	SALES REPRESENTATIVE, METALS (wholesale tr.)	4346	22333344454	LNNNNNNNOOONFFNNONNNON	NNNN3NNNNNNNNNN	P,I,J	292	540	08.01.01	4239	080706	49005
274.357-058	SALES REPRESENTATIVE, OIL FIELD SUPPLIES AND EQUIPMENT (wholesale tr.)	4346	22233344455	LNNNNNNNOOONFFNONNNON	ONNN3NNNNNNNNNN	I,J,P	292	564	08.01.01	4235	080706	49005
274.357-062	SALES REPRESENTATIVE, PRINTING SUPPLIES (wholesale tr.)	4345	32333344454	LNNNNNNNOOONFFFNONNNON	NNNN2NNNNNNNNNN	I,J,P	292	567	08.02.01	4242	080706	49008
274.357-066	SALES REPRESENTATIVE, TEXTILE DESIGNS (wholesale tr.)	4345	32343344453	LNNNNNNNOOONFFNFNFN	NNNN3NNNNNNNNNN	I,J,P	292	567	08.02.01	4242	080799	49008
274.357-070	SALES REPRESENTATIVE, TEXTILE MACHINERY (wholesale tr.)	4346	22333344455	LNNNNNNNOOONFFNONNNNN	NNNN2NNNNNNNNNN	I,J,P	292	567	08.02.01	4235	080706	49005
274.357-074	SALES REPRESENTATIVE, WELDING EQUIPMENT (wholesale tr.)	4346	33333343354	LNNNNNNNOOONFFNONNNNN	NNNN3NNNNNNNNNN	P,I,J	292	566	08.01.01	4235	080706	49005
274.357-078	SALES REPRESENTATIVE, WIRE ROPE (wholesale tr.)	4345	32333434354	LNNNNNNNOOONFFNNOONNON	NNNN3NNNNNNNNNN	I,J,P	292	557	08.02.01	4234	080706	49005
275.257-010	SALES REPRESENTATIVE, COMPUTERS AND EDP SYSTEMS (wholesale tr.)	5446	22334344455	LNNNNNNNFFNFFNFNNNNN	NNNN3NNNNNNNNNN	I,J,P	292	571	08.01.01	4354	080706	49008
275.357-010	SALES REPRESENTATIVE, BARBER AND BEAUTY EQUIPMENT AND SUPPLIES (wholesale)	4345	33333344455	LNNNNNNNOOONFFNONNNON	NNNN2NNNNNNNNNN	I,J,P	292	469	08.02.01	4242	080799	49008
275.357-014	SALES REPRESENTATIVE, CHURCH FURNITURE AND RELIGIOUS SUPPLIES (wholesale)	4345	32343333354	LNNNNNNNOOONFFNONNNON	NNNN2NNNNNNNNNN	I,J,P	292	465	08.02.01	4242	080809	49008
275.357-018	SALES REPRESENTATIVE, COMMERCIAL EQUIPMENT AND SUPPLIES (wholesale tr.)	4344	32444444455	LNNNNNNNOOONFFNNONNNON	NNNN2NNNNNNNNNN	I,J,P	292	617	08.02.01	4242	080706	49008
275.357-022	SALES REPRESENTATIVE, CORDAGE (wholesale tr.)	4345	33344344354	LNNNNNNNOOONFFNNONNNON	NNNN2NNNNNNNNNN	I,J,P	292	413	08.02.01	4242	080799	49005
275.357-026	SALES REPRESENTATIVE, HOTEL AND RESTAURANT EQUIPMENT AND SUPPLIES (wholesale tr.)	4346	32333344455	LNNNNNNNOOONFFNONNNON	NNNN2NNNNNNNNNN	I,J,P	292	882	08.02.01	4242	080706	49008
275.357-030	SALES REPRESENTATIVE, MORTICIAN SUPPLIES (wholesale tr.)	4346	32343344354	LNNNNNNFFFNFNFFNOFON	NNNN3NNNNNNNNNN	I,J,P	292	619	08.02.01	4242	080706	49008
275.357-034	SALES REPRESENTATIVE, OFFICE MACHINES (retail trade; wholesale tr.)	4345	32333333355	MNNNNNNOOONFFNNOOON	NNNN2NNNNNNNNNN	I,J,P	292	881	08.02.03	4242	080810	49008
275.357-038	SALES REPRESENTATIVE, PRESSURE-SENSITIVE TAPE (wholesale tr.)	4344	33344344454	LNNNNNNNFFONFFNFNOONN	NNNN2NNNNNNNNNN	I,J,P	292	882	08.02.01	4245	080706	49008
275.357-042	SALES REPRESENTATIVE, SCHOOL EQUIPMENT AND SUPPLIES (wholesale tr.)	4345	32333344454	LNNNNNNNOOONFFNNONNNON	NNNN2NNNNNNNNNN	I,J,P	292	882	08.02.01	4242	080799	49008
275.357-046	SALES REPRESENTATIVE, SHOE LEATHER AND FINDINGS (wholesale tr.)	4345	33344344455	LNNNNNNNOOONFFNNONNNON	NNNN2NNNNNNNNNN	I,J,P	292	520	08.02.01	4242	080706	49005
275.357-050	SALES REPRESENTATIVE, VENDING AND COIN MACHINES (wholesale tr.)	4346	33444333354	LNNNNNNFFFNFFNFFFOOOOO	NNNN2NNNNNNNNNN	I,J,P	292	572	08.02.01	4249	080706	49008
275.357-054	SALESPERSON, FLORIST SUPPLIES (wholesale tr.)	4344	33344333354	LNNNNNNNOOONFFNNONNNON	NNNN3NNNNNNNNNN	I,J,P	292	882	08.02.01	4236	080706	49008
276.257-010	SALES REPRESENTATIVE, DENTAL AND MEDICAL EQUIPMENT AND SUPPLIES (wholesale)	4346	22344344455	LNNNNNNNOOONFFNONNNON	NNNN2NNNNNNNNNN	I,J,P	292	604	08.01.01	4236	080706	49005
276.257-014	SALES REPRESENTATIVE, WEIGHING AND FORCE- MEASUREMENT INSTRUMENTS (wholesale tr.)	5456	22233344455	SNNNNNNFFNFFNFNNNNN	NNNN3NNNNNNNNNN	I,J,P	292	571	08.01.01	4242	080706	49008
276.257-018	SALESPERSON, ORTHOPEDIC SHOES (retail trade)	4346	23233333354	LNNNNONFFOFFNFNOFON	NNNN2NNNNNNNNNN	I,J,P	292	604	08.02.02	4351	080199	49011
276.257-022	SALESPERSON, SURGICAL APPLIANCES (retail trade)	5346	32333333355	LNNONONFFONFFNFOOON	NNNN2NNNNNNNNNN	I,J,P	292	604	08.02.02	4236	080705	49005
276.354-010	HEARING AID SPECIALIST (retail trade)	4346	33333333355	LNNNNNNFFNFFNFONCNN	NNNN2NNNNNNNNNN	I,J,P	292	589	08.02.02	4359	080706	49011
276.357-010	SALES REPRESENTATIVE, ARCHITECTURAL AND ENGINEERING SUPPLIES (wholesale)	4346	32333333455	LNNNNNNNOOONFFNOONNNN	NNNN2NNNNNNNNNN	I,J,P	292	601	08.02.01	4242	080799	49008
276.357-014	SALES REPRESENTATIVE, PRECISION INSTRUMENTS (wholesale tr.)	4346	33344344455	LNNNNNNNOOONFFNNONNNON	NNNN2NNNNNNNNNN	I,J,P	292	601	08.01.01	4242	080706	49005
276.357-018	SALES REPRESENTATIVE, VETERINARIAN SUPPLIES (wholesale tr.)	4346	32333344454	LNNNNNNNOOONFFNNONNNON	NNNN3NNNNNNNNNN	I,J,P	292	604	08.02.01	4236	080706	49008
277.354-010	SALESPERSON, PIANOS AND ORGANS (retail trade)	4346	23343333354	LNNNNNNFFFNFNFNNNOON	NNNN2NNNNNNNNNN	I,J,P	292	614	08.02.02	4343	080809	49011
277.357-010	SALES REPRESENTATIVE, HOBBIES AND CRAFTS (retail trade; wholesale tr.)	4345	33333333354	LNNNNNNNOOONFFNNONNNON	NNNN2NNNNNNNNNN	I,J,P	292	882	08.02.03	4249	080706	49008
277.357-014	SALES REPRESENTATIVE, MUSICAL INSTRUMENTS AND ACCESSORIES (wholesale tr.)	4346	22344344455	LNNNNNNNOOONFFNNONNNNN	NNNN2NNNNNNNNNN	I,J,P	292	614	08.02.01	4343	080799	49005
277.357-018	SALES REPRESENTATIVE, NOVELTIES (wholesale tr.)	4344	33344344455	LNNNNNNNFFNFFNFNNNNN	NNNN3NNNNNNNNNN	I,J,P	292	610	08.02.01	4249	080706	49008

DOT #	DOT Title & Industry	Trng	Aptitude	Physical	Environment	Tempra	WkF	MPSMS	GOE	SOC	CIP	OES
277.357-022	SALES REPRESENTATIVE, PUBLICATIONS (wholesale tr.)	4345	33344344455	LNNNNNNNFFNFNFNNNNN	NNNN3NNNNNNNNN	I,J,P	292	882	08.02.01	4249	080799	49008
277.357-026	SALES REPRESENTATIVE, RECREATION AND SPORTING GOODS (wholesale tr.)	4345	33333333455	LNNNNNNNNOOONFFNONNNON	NNNN3NNNNNNNNN	I,J,P	292	610	08.02.01	4345	080706	49008
277.357-030	SALES REPRESENTATIVE, WRITING AND MARKING PENS (wholesale tr.)	4343	33344344454	LNNNNNNNNOOONFFNONNNON	NNNN2NNNNNNNNN	I,J,P	292	617	08.02.01	4249	080706	49008
277.357-034	SALESPERSON, BOOKS (retail trade)	4344	32344333455	LNNNNNNNFFNFNFNNNNN	NNNN3NNNNNNNNN	I,J,P	292	881	08.02.02	4347	080706	49011
277.357-038	SALESPERSON, MUSICAL INSTRUMENTS AND ACCESSORIES (retail trade)	4346	23333333354	LNNNNNNNFFFNFNFNNNOON	NNNN2NNNNNNNNN	I,J,P	292	614	08.02.02	4343	080705	49011
277.357-042	SALESPERSON, PETS AND PET SUPPLIES (retail trade)	4344	33344333354	LNNNNNNNFFNFNFONONON	NNNN3NNNNNNNNN	I,J,P	292	320	08.02.02	4359	080705	49011
277.357-046	SALESPERSON, PHONOGRAPH RECORDS AND TAPE RECORDINGS (retail trade)	3333	33333333354	LNNNNNNNFFONFFNONONON	NNNN3NNNNNNNNN	I,J,P	292	881	08.02.02	4343	080705	49011
277.357-050	SALESPERSON, PHOTOGRAPHIC SUPPLIES AND EQUIPMENT (retail trade; wholesale)	4345	33344344455	LNNNNNNNNFFNFNFNNNNN	NNNN3NNNNNNNNN	I,J,P	292	603	08.02.03	4359	080705	49014
277.357-054	SALESPERSON, SHEET MUSIC (retail trade)	4345	23343344455	LNNNNNNNNFFNFNFNNNNN	NNNN2NNNNNNNNN	I,J,P	292	756	08.02.02	4343	080705	49011
277.357-058	SALESPERSON, SPORTING GOODS (retail trade)	4345	33343333354	LNNNNNNNNFFONFFNONNNON	NNNN2NNNNNNNNN	I,J,P	292	616	08.02.02	4345	080903	49011
277.357-062	SALESPERSON, STAMPS OR COINS (retail trade; wholesale tr.)	4345	33344343453	LNNNNNNNNFFNFNFNNNNFN	NNNN3NNNNNNNNN	I,J,P	292	880	08.02.03	4347	080705	49011
277.357-066	SALESPERSON, TOY TRAINS AND ACCESSORIES (retail trade)	4343	33344344454	LNNNNNNNFFNFNFNNNNN	NNNN3NNNNNNNNN	I,J,P	292	881	08.02.02	4359	080705	49011
277.457-010	SALESPERSON, ART OBJECTS (retail trade)	3234	33344334454	LNNNNNNNNFFNFNFNONNNON	NNNN3NNNNNNNNN	I,J,P	292	882	08.02.01	4356	080199	49008
279.157-010	MANUFACTURER'S REPRESENTATIVE (wholesale tr.)	4346	22343344454	LNNNNNNNFFNNFFNFOOOOO	NNNN2NNNNNNNNN	I,J,P	292	882	08.02.01	4249	080706	49008
279.357-010	SALES EXHIBITOR (nonprofit org.)	3233	33344444454	LNNNNNNNNFFNFNFNNNNN	NNNN3NNNNNNNNN	I,P	292	885	08.02.02	4450	080706	49032
279.357-014	SALES REPRESENTATIVE, GENERAL MERCHANDISE (wholesale tr.)	4345	33344344444	LNNNNNNNNFFNFNFNFOOOOO	NNNN3NNNNNNNNN	I,J,P	292	882	08.02.01	4249	080706	49008
279.357-018	SALES REPRESENTATIVE, JEWELRY (wholesale tr.)	4346	33343434453	LNNNNNNNNOOONFFNFNFON	NNNN3NNNNNNNNN	I,J,P	292	611	08.02.01	4356	080199	49008
279.357-022	SALES REPRESENTATIVE, LEATHER GOODS (wholesale tr.)	4346	33344344454	LNNNNNNNNFFONFFNFNNNON	NNNN3NNNNNNNNN	I,J,P	292	882	08.02.01	4249	080799	49008
279.357-026	SALES REPRESENTATIVE, PAPER AND PAPER PRODUCTS (wholesale tr.)	4345	33333345454	LNNNNNNNNOOONNFFNONNNON	NNNN2NNNNNNNNN	I,J,P	292	470	08.02.01	4245	080706	49008
279.357-030	SALES REPRESENTATIVE, PLASTIC PRODUCTS (wholesale tr.)	4344	33333343455	LNNNNNNNNOOONFFNONNNON	NNNN2NNNNNNNNN	I,J,P	292	509	08.02.01	4249	080706	49008
279.357-034	SALES REPRESENTATIVE, WATER-SOFTENING EQUIPMENT (retail trade; wholesale)	4345	33333443353	LNNNNNNNNFFNFNFNNNFN	NNNN3NNNNNNNNN	I,J,P	292	969	08.02.03	4242	080706	49008
279.357-038	SALESPERSON-DEMONSTRATOR, PARTY PLAN (retail trade)	4344	33344344444	LNNNNNNNNFFNFNFNNNNN	NNNN3NNNNNNNNN	I,J,P	292	881	08.02.05	4366	080705	49026
279.357-042	SALESPERSON, BURIAL NEEDS (retail trade)	4345	32344344454	LNNNNNNNNOOONFFNFNNNON	NNNN3NNNNNNNNN	I,J,P	292	881	08.02.02	4369	080199	43099
279.357-046	SALESPERSON, FLYING SQUAD (retail trade)	4346	33343333354	LNNNNNNNNFFNFNFNNNNN	NNNN2NNNNNNNNN	I,J,P	292	881	08.02.02	4369	080706	49011
279.357-050	SALESPERSON, GENERAL HARDWARE (retail trade; wholesale tr.)	3224	33344344454	LNNNNNNNNFFNFNFNNNNN	NNNN3NNNNNNNNN	I,P	292	550	08.02.03	4353	080705	49011
279.357-054	SALESPERSON, GENERAL MERCHANDISE (retail trade; wholesale tr.)	3223	33343333453	LNNNONFFONFFNNNNN	NNNN3NNNNNNNNN	I,P	292	881	08.02.03	4359	080706	49011
279.357-058	SALESPERSON, JEWELRY (retail trade)	4345	33343334454	LNNNNNNNNFFFFNFFNNFFN	NNNN2NNNNNNNNN	I,J,P	292	607	08.02.02	4356	080199	49014
279.357-062	SALESPERSON, PARTS (retail trade; wholesale tr.)	4335	33344333354	LNNONONFFNFFFNFNNFON	NNNN3NNNNNNNNN	I,P,J	292	881	08.02.03	4367	081209	49014
290.477-010	COUPON-REDEMPTION CLERK (retail trade)	3222	33344333355	LNNNNNNNNFFNFNFNNNNN	NNNN3NNNNNNNNN	R,P	221	899	07.03.01	4362	080705	49011
290.477-014	SALES CLERK (retail trade)	3223	33344344454	LNNNNONONFFNFNFNOONNON	NONN3NNNNNNNNN	P	292	881	09.04.02	4362	080601	49011
290.477-018	SALES CLERK, FOOD (retail trade)	3323	33333344455	LNNNNNNNNFFNFNFNNNNN	NNNN3NNNNNNNNN	P	292	884	09.04.02	4030	080208	49011
291.157-010	SUBSCRIPTION CREW LEADER (retail trade)	3235	33344344454	LNNNNNNNNFFNFNFNNNNN	NNNN3NNNNNNNNN	D,J,P	292	884	08.02.08	4366	080705	49026
291.357-010	SALES REPRESENTATIVE, DOOR-TO-DOOR (retail trade)	3232	33344344454	LNNNNNNNNFFNNFFNFOOOOO	FNNN3NNNNNNNNN	P,I	292	881	05.08.03	4366	080705	49026
291.454-010	LEI SELLER (retail trade)	2222	44444444444	LNNNNNNNNFFNFNFNNNNN	FNNN3NNNNNNNNN	P,I	292	311	09.04.02	4365	000000	49026
291.457-010	CIGARETTE VENDOR (hotel & rest.)	2222	44354443335	LNNNNNNNNFFNFNFNNNNN	NNNN3NNNNNNNNN	P	292	884	08.03.01	4366	000000	49026
291.457-014	LOUNGE-CAR ATTENDANT (r.r. trans.)	2222	44354443335	MNFNNNNFFFNFNFNNNNN	NNNN3NNNNNNNNN	R,P	292	903	08.03.01	4366	080706	49026
291.457-018	PEDDLER (retail trade)	2213	44443344443	MMNFNNNNFFOFFNFNNNNF	FNNN3NNNNNNNNN	R,P,I	292	883	09.04.01	8218	120507	97117
291.457-022	VENDOR (amuse. & rec.)	2222	44444444455	MMNFNNNNFFOFFNFNNNNF	FNNN4NNNNNNNNN	P	292	884	08.03.01	4366	000000	49026
292.137-010	COIN-MACHINE-COLLECTOR SUPERVISOR (clerical)	3335	33344344455	LNNNNNNNNFFONFFNFNNNNN	NNNN2NNNNNNNNN	D,J,P	232	899	07.07.03	4529	520204	51002
292.137-014	SUPERVISOR, ROUTE SALES-DELIVERY DRIVERS (retail trade; wholesale tr.)	4345	33344344445	LNNNNNNNNFFNFNFNNNNN	ONNN3NNNNNNNNN	V,D,P,J	013	880	08.02.07	8111	000000	81011
292.353-010	DRIVER, SALES ROUTE (retail trade; wholesale tr.)	3233	33344344334	MNNONNNNFFONFFNOFOFF	ONNN4NNNNNNNNN	I,P	013	880	08.02.07	8218	000000	97117
292.363-010	NEWSPAPER-DELIVERY DRIVER (wholesale tr.)	3224	34444444435	MMNNNNFNNFFFNFFNNF	MNNN3NNNNNNNNN	P	013	883	05.08.03	8218	000000	97117
292.457-010	NEWSPAPER CARRIER (retail trade)	2222	43444444435	LNNNNNNNNFFNFNFNONNNN	FNNN3NNNNNNNNN	I,P	292	883	09.04.02	4365	000000	49026
292.463-010	LUNCH-TRUCK DRIVER (hotel & rest.)	2222	44444434334	MNFNNNNFFNFNFNFF	ONNN3NNNNNNNNN	P	013	903	09.04.01	8218	000000	97117
292.483-010	COIN COLLECTOR (business ser.)	3233	34444334334	MMNFNNNNFFONNNNFNFF	ONNN3NNNNNNNNN	P	011	883	05.08.03	8218	000000	97117
292.667-010	DRIVER HELPER, SALES ROUTE (retail trade; wholesale tr.)	2222	44344444455	LNNNNNNNNFFONFFNFNNNNN	NNNN3NNNNNNNNN	R	011	880	08.02.07	4366	000903	49026
292.687-010	COIN-MACHINE COLLECTOR (business ser.; tel. & tel.)	2122	44444444335	LNNNNNNNNFFONOONONNNNN	FNNN2NNNNNNNNN	R	221	899	07.07.03	4799	000000	59999
293.137-010	SUPERVISOR, BLOOD-DONOR RECRUITERS (medical ser.)	4346	32355244555	SNNNNNNNNFFNFNFNNNNN	NNNN3NNNNNNNNN	D,J,P	282	885	11.09.02	4366	080299	43099
293.157-010	FUND RAISER I (nonprofit org.)	5346	22355354455	MMNNNNFFNNFFNFFNNF	NNNN3NNNNNNNNN	D,I,V,P,J	292	880	11.09.02	4369	080706	43099
293.357-010	BLOOD-DONOR RECRUITER (medical ser.)	4243	32455344555	LNNNNNNNNFFNFNFNONNNNN	NNNN3NNNNNNNNN	I,P	292	885	11.09.02	4369	080706	43099
293.357-014	FUND RAISER II (nonprofit org.)	3232	33344444455	LNNNNNNNNFFNFNFNONNNNN	NNNN3NNNNNNNNN	I,P,J	292	880	08.02.08	4369	080299	43099

DOT #	DOT Title & Industry	Trng	Aptitude	Physical	Environment	Tempra	WkF	MPSMS	GOE	SOC	CIP	OES
293.357-018	GOODWILL AMBASSADOR (business ser.)	3232	33444344455	LNNNNNNFFNFFNFNNNN	NNNN3NNNNNNNNNNN	P,I	292	896	11.09.01	4450	080299	49032
293.357-022	MEMBERSHIP SOLICITOR (any industry)	4344	33455354555	LNNNNNNOOONFFNFONNNN	NNNN3NNNNNNNNNNN	P,I	292	896	08.02.08	4450	080299	43099
294.257-010	AUCTIONEER (retail trade; wholesale tr.)	3236	32453344454	LNNNNNNOOONFFNONONNNN	NNNN4NNNNNNNNNNN	I,J,P,E	211	881	08.02.03	4470	080701	49023
294.567-010	AUCTION CLERK (retail trade; wholesale tr.)	2223	34355344555	SNNNNNNFFNFFNFNFNN	NNNN4NNNNNNNNNNN	P,R	231	881	07.03.01	4364	080701	49023
294.667-010	AUCTION ASSISTANT (retail trade; wholesale tr.)	2122	44444444454	LOOONNFFNFFNFNOFON	NNNN4NNNNNNNNNNN	R,P	221	881	07.07.02	4699	010501	59999
295.137-010	SUPERVISOR, SAFETY DEPOSIT (financial)	4336	33444344455	LNNONONOOONCCNFONONN	NNNN3NNNNNNNNNNN	D,P	231	894	07.01.02	4519	521401	51002
295.357-010	APPAREL-RENTAL CLERK (retail trade)	3333	33344444454	LNNFNONFFONFFNFNNNON	NNNN3NNNNNNNNNNN	I,P,J	292	881	09.04.02	4363	200306	49017
295.357-014	TOOL-AND-EQUIPMENT-RENTAL CLERK (business ser.; retail trade)	3334	33444334444	MNNNNNNNFFNFNFNNNON	NNNN4NNNNNNNNNNN	I,J,P	292	881	09.04.02	4363	080809	49017
295.357-018	FURNITURE-RENTAL CONSULTANT (retail trade)	3222	33444444454	LNNONONOOOFFNFNNOFN	NNNN3NNNNNNNNNNN	I,P	292	881	09.04.02	4363	080809	49017
295.367-010	AIRPLANE-CHARTER CLERK (air trans.)	4343	33343344455	LNNNNNNFFNFFNFNNNNN	NNNN3NNNNNNNNNNN	P	292	881	07.04.03	4363	081105	49017
295.367-014	BABY-STROLLER AND WHEELCHAIR RENTAL CLERK (retail trade)	3232	43344344455	LNNNNNNFFNFFNFNNNNN	NNNN3NNNNNNNNNNN	P,J	292	881	09.04.02	4363	080299	55323
295.367-018	FILM-RENTAL CLERK (business ser.; retail trade)	4345	33343343455	LNNNNNNFFNNOONFNNNNN	NNNN2NNNNNNNNNNN	P,I,J	292	884	11.02.04	4664	080299	59999
295.367-022	SAFE-DEPOSIT-BOX RENTAL CLERK (financial)	3334	33343333355	LNNOONFFNFFNFONONN	NNNN3NNNNNNNNNNN	P	231	894	07.03.01	4799	000000	59999
295.367-026	STORAGE-FACILITY RENTAL CLERK (business ser.; retail trade)	3332	33344344355	LNNOONNFFNFFNFNNNNN	ONNN3NNNNNNNNNNN	P,V	292	889	09.04.02	4363	080299	49017
295.467-010	BICYCLE-RENTAL CLERK (retail trade)	2222	44344344455	LNNNNNNFFNFFNFNNNNN	FNNN3NNNNNNNNNNN	P,J	292	881	09.04.02	4363	080706	49017
295.467-014	BOAT-RENTAL CLERK (amuse. & rec.)	3332	43344444445	LNNONONOOONOONONNNN	FNNN3NNNNNNNNNNN	P	292	919	09.04.02	4363	080706	49017
295.467-018	HOSPITAL-TELEVISION-RENTAL CLERK (business ser.)	2222	43443344454	LNNNNNNFFNFFNFNNNNN	NNNN3NNNNNNNNNNN	P	292	884	09.04.02	4363	080706	49017
295.467-022	TRAILER-RENTAL CLERK (automotive ser.)	3334	33344344455	LNNOOONFFONFFNFNOONN	NNNN3NNNNNNNNNNN	P	292	881	09.04.02	4363	081299	49017
295.467-026	AUTOMOBILE RENTAL CLERK (automotive ser.)	3334	33344344455	LNNNNNNNFFNFFNNOONNNO	ONNN3NNNNNNNNNNN	J,P	292	884	09.04.02	4363	081299	49017
296.357-010	PERSONAL SHOPPER (retail trade)	4335	33344444455	LNNNNNNFFNFFNFNNNNN	NNNN3NNNNNNNNNNN	P,J	291	880	09.04.02	4460	200306	49999
296.367-010	AUTOMOBILE LOCATOR (retail trade)	3233	33444344455	SNNNNNNFFNFFNFNNNNN	NNNN3NNNNNNNNNNN	P	231	899	07.05.03	4460	080706	49999
296.367-014	COMPARISON SHOPPER (retail trade; wholesale tr.)	4233	33453354453	LNNNNNNFFNFFNFNFFFN	NNNN3NNNNNNNNNNN	J	211	889	08.01.03	4460	200306	49999
297.354-010	DEMONSTRATOR (retail trade; wholesale tr.)	3333	33444433344	MNNFOOOFFFONNNFFFFFF	ONNN3NNNNNNNNNNN	P,I,J	292	885	08.02.05	4450	200306	49032
297.354-014	DEMONSTRATOR, KNITTING (retail trade)	4445	33334533355	SNNNNNNFFOFFNFFNN	ONNN3NNNNNNNNNNN	P,T,J	424	889	08.02.05	4450	200306	49032
297.357-010	DEMONSTRATOR, ELECTRIC-GAS APPLIANCES (utilities)	5356	22333343363	LNNNNNNOOONFFNFNNN	NNNN2NNNNNNNNNNN	V,P,I,J	292	583	08.02.05	4450	200306	49032
297.367-010	EXHIBIT-DISPLAY REPRESENTATIVE (any industry)	4245	32343444453	LNNNNNNOOONFFNONNNNN	NNNN3NNNNNNNNNNN	P	293	960	09.01.02	4450	080299	49032
297.451-010	INSTRUCTOR, PAINTING (retail trade)	3334	34344433351	SNNNNNNFFNFFNFNFFN	NNNN3NNNNNNNNNNN	I,E	296	759	01.06.03	4450	000000	49032
297.454-010	DEMONSTRATOR, SEWING TECHNIQUES (retail trade)	3333	34344333334	LNNNNNNFFNFFNFNFFN	NNNN3NNNNNNNNNNN	P,I,J,T	171	880	08.02.05	4450	200306	49032
297.667-014	MODEL (garment; retail trade; wholesale tr.)	3123	35445444443	LNNNNNNFFFNFFNNOONFO	NNNN3NNNNNNNNNNN	P,I	292	885	01.08.01	4450	080102	49032
298.081-010	DISPLAYER, MERCHANDISE (retail trade)	4336	23322444342	MNNFOOOFFONNNFFFFFF	NNNN3NNNNNNNNNNN	E,I,J	264	889	01.02.03	3220	200306	34044
298.381-010	DECORATOR (any industry)	4437	23323333343	LNNFOONFFONNNFFFFFF	NNNN3NNNNNNNNNNN	J,T	102	889	01.06.02	3220	080299	34044
299.137-010	MANAGER, DEPARTMENT (retail trade)	4337	33343344454	MNNONONOFONFFNONNNON	NNNN4NNNNNNNNNNN	D,J,P	221	881	11.11.05	4030	080705	41002
299.137-014	SALES SUPERVISOR, MALT LIQUORS (wholesale tr.)	4345	22344344455	LNNNNNNFFNFFNFNOON	NNNN3NNNNNNNNNNN	D,P,I,J	292	395	08.02.01	4020	521401	41002
299.137-018	SAMPLE-ROOM SUPERVISOR (textile)	4347	32343344453	LNNNNNNFFNFFNFFN	NNNN3NNNNNNNNNNN	D,J,P	292	880	06.02.01	7100	000000	81008
299.137-022	SUPERVISOR, ICE STORAGE, SALE, AND DELIVERY (food prep., nec)	4336	33343344455	LNNNNNNOOONFFNONOONN	NFNN3NNNNNNNNNNN	D,P	292	399	09.04.02	4030	000000	41002
299.137-026	SUPERVISOR, MARINA SALES AND SERVICE (retail trade)	4345	33344344455	LNNFNNNFFNFFNFONNON	FNNF4NNNNNNNNNNN	D,I,J,P	292	881	09.04.02	4030	080706	61099
299.167-010	CIRCULATION-SALES REPRESENTATIVE (print. & pub.)	4346	33444444455	LNNNNNNFFNFFNFNNNON	NNNN3NNNNNNNNNNN	D,I,J,P	292	481	11.09.01	4249	080799	49999
299.251-010	SALES-SERVICE REPRESENTATIVE, MILKING MACHINES (retail trade)	4346	33323333345	MNNONONFONFFNFNONNN	FNNN3NNNNNNNNNNN	I,J,P	121	562	08.02.02	4233	010501	49005
299.357-010	LINEN CONTROLLER (laundry & rel.)	4236	33344344455	SNNNNNNOOFFNONNNON	NNNN3NNNNNNNNNNN	I,P,J	292	906	08.02.06	4490	080706	49026
299.357-014	TELEPHONE SOLICITOR (any industry)	3333	33333333344	LNNNNNNFFOFFNFNNFON	NNNN3NNNNNNNNNNN	I,P,J,V	292	885	08.02.08	4030	080799	49999
299.357-018	WEDDING CONSULTANT (retail trade)	4346	32343344454	LNNNNNNNFFOFFNFFFFF	NNNN3NNNNNNNNNNN	E,I,J,P,V	292	481	11.09.01	4366	080706	49999
299.361-010	OPTICIAN, DISPENSING (optical goods; retail trade)	4347	33322433354	LNNNNNNFFOFFNFFNFFON	NNNN2NNNNNNNNNNN	J,P,T	292	605	05.10.01	4490	000000	32514
299.361-014	OPTICIAN APPRENTICE, DISPENSING (optical goods; retail trade)	4347	33322433354	LNNNNNNFFOFFNFFNFFN	NNNN2NNNNNNNNNNN	J,P,T	292	605	05.10.01	4490	511801	32514
299.364-010	DRAPERY AND UPHOLSTERY MEASURER (retail trade)	3326	33333333354	LONFOONFFNFFNFFNFFN	NNNN3NNNNNNNNNNN	J	292	435	05.09.02	4490	480303	49999
299.364-014	GIFT WRAPPER (retail trade)	3213	44434443454	LNNONNNFFNFFNFNFNON	NNNN3NNNNNNNNNNN	V,P	292	906	08.02.06	4366	080706	49026
299.367-010	CUSTOMER-SERVICE CLERK (retail trade)	3334	33343343453	LNNNNNNFFNFFNFNNNON	NNNN3NNNNNNNNNNN	V,P	291	881	09.04.02	4030	080102	49999
299.367-014	STOCK CLERK (retail trade)	3224	33444334355	HNNONONFFONOONNNON	NNNN3NNNNNNNNNNN	R	221	881	05.09.01	4362	080765	49021
299.367-018	WATCH-AND-CLOCK-REPAIR CLERK (retail trade)	3335	33343333355	LNNNNNNFFONOONFNONNN	NNNN3NNNNNNNNNNN	P,J	212	907	05.09.02	4363	470408	49011
299.377-010	PLATFORM ATTENDANT (food prep., nec)	3223	34343343355	HNNFNNNFFNFFNFNFNN	FFNF3NNNNNNNNNNN	P,R	292	399	09.04.02	4359	000000	49999
299.387-010	DRAPERY AND UPHOLSTERY ESTIMATOR (retail trade)	3325	33333334454	SNNNNNNFFNFFNFNNNFON	NNNN3NNNNNNNNNNN	J,T	212	435	05.09.02	4490	200501	49999
299.387-014	STAMP ANALYST (retail trade)	4236	33442333453	SNNNNNNFFNFFNFNNNON	NNNN3NNNNNNNNNNN	I,J	292	881	07.07.02	4490	000000	49999

DOT #	DOT Title & Industry	Trng	Aptitude	Physical	Environment	Tempra	WkF	MPSMS	GOE	SOC	CIP	OES
299.387-018	STAMP CLASSIFIER (retail trade)	4236	33442344453	SNNNNNNFFNNNFNFFFN	NNNN2NNNNNNNNN	J	211	881	05.09.01	4490	000000	49999
299.467-010	LAYAWAY CLERK (retail trade)	3333	34344344455	LNNNNNNNFFFNNNFNNNN	NNNN3NNNNNNNNN	P,T	232	881	07.03.01	4362	080705	49011
299.477-010	DELIVERER, MERCHANDISE (retail trade)	2222	44344444445	MNOONONFFFNNNNFNNNNN	FNNN3NNNNNNNNN	P	221	881	09.04.02	4490	080705	49999
299.587-010	PRODUCE WEIGHER (retail trade)	1111	44444344454	LNNNNNFFFONNNNFNNFON	NNNN2NNNNNNNNN	R,T	212	881	09.04.02	4756	000000	58017
299.647-010	IMPERSONATOR, CHARACTER (any industry)	3132	33444544455	MFFONONFFNNFFNNNFNNN	ONNN3NNNNNNNNN	P,I	297	885	01.07.02	4450	090201	49032
299.667-010	BILLPOSTER (any industry)	2122	44444544345	MFFONONFFNNFFNNNFNINN	FNNN3NNNNNNNNN	R	062	896	05.12.12	8769	090201	98999
299.667-014	STOCK CHECKER, APPAREL (retail trade)	3122	34344344453	LNNONNNFFFNNNNNFNNNN	NNNN3NNNNNNNNN	R	221	881	05.09.03	4490	080102	49999
299.677-014	SALES ATTENDANT (retail trade)	2223	44444444445	LNNOFNFNFFFNNONNNON	NNNN3NNNNNNNNN	P	221	881	09.04.02	4362	080705	49011
299.677-014	SALES ATTENDANT, BUILDING MATERIALS (retail trade)	2223	44444444445	HNOFNFNFFFNNOONNF	ONNN3NNNNNNNNN	P,V	292	881	09.04.02	4362	089999	49021
299.687-010	PORTER, SAMPLE CASE (wholesale tr.)	2112	44444444344	MNNNNNNFFNNFNNNNNN	CNNN3NNNNNNNNN	R	011	905	09.05.06	4450	080299	98999
299.687-014	SANDWICH-BOARD CARRIER (any industry)	1111	44455544445	LNNNNNFFFNFFFNNNNNN	NNNN3NNNNNNNNN	R	292	896	08.03.02	4450	000000	49032
301.137-010	HOUSEKEEPER, HOME (domestic ser.)	4236	33344444344	MNNOONNCCOOOOOFNNON	NNNN3NNNNNNNNN	V,D,P	291	900	05.12.01	5050	200606	00000
301.474-010	HOUSE WORKER, GENERAL (domestic ser.)	3223	44444444344	MNNONNNOOONFFNNONNNO	NNON3NNNNNNNNN	V	031	901	05.12.18	5070	200606	00000
301.677-010	CHILD MONITOR (domestic ser.)	3123	44555544455	MNNNNNOOONFFNNONNNO	NNNN3NNNNNNNNN	V,P	291	901	10.03.03	5060	200202	00000
301.687-010	CARETAKER (domestic ser.)	2122	44444544345	MOOFFNNFFNNNNNNNNN	ONNN3NNNNNNNNN	V	031	901	05.12.18	5070	200606	00000
301.687-014	DAY WORKER (domestic ser.)	2112	44444544355	MNNOOONFFONNONONONNN	NNNN3NNNNNNNNN	V	031	901	05.12.18	5020	200202	00000
301.687-018	YARD WORKER (domestic ser.)	2222	44444544345	MNNNOONFFONNONNONNN	CNNO3NNNNNNNNN	V	003	909	03.04.04	5622	010605	79999
302.685-010	LAUNDRY WORKER, DOMESTIC (domestic ser.)	2112	44444544454	LNNONNNCCONNNNFNNNON	NNNC3NNNNNNNNN	R	031	909	05.12.18	5030	200606	00000
302.687-010	IRONER (domestic ser.)	1112	44444434345	LNNNONNNCCNNNNCNNNNN	NNNO3NNNNNNNNN	R	032	909	05.10.08	5040	200606	00000
305.281-010	COOK (domestic ser.)	3226	33434344354	LNNONNNFFNNOOFNNNNFN	NNNO3NNNNNNNNN	V,J	146	901	09.01.03	5050	200605	00000
309.137-010	BUTLER (domestic ser.)	4236	33433344345	LNNONNNOOONFFFNNNNNN	NNNN3NNNNNNNNN	V,D,P	291	900	11.02.03	5263	200606	68035
309.354-010	HOMEMAKER (social ser.)	4245	34444444455	LNNFNNNFFNNFNFNFNNNN	NNNN3NNNNNNNNN	I,J,P	298	941	09.05.06	5090	200301	00000
309.367-010	HOUSE SITTER (domestic ser.)	3222	34444444454	LNNNNNNFFFNNOOFOFNNNN	NNNN3NNNNNNNNN	V,J	293	909	05.12.18	5050	200606	00000
309.674-010	BUTLER, SECOND (domestic ser.)	3123	34444444454	LNNNNNNNFFFNNFNNNNNN	NNNN3NNNNNNNNN	V	291	900	09.05.06	5090	200602	00000
309.674-014	PERSONAL ATTENDANT (domestic ser.)	2223	44444444344	LNNFFNNFFNNOONFFFNFF	NNNN3NNNNNNNNN	V,P	291	906	10.03.03	5050	200202	00000
309.677-010	COMPANION (domestic ser.)	3233	44444444345	LNNFNNNFFNOONFFFNFF	NNNN3NNNNNNNNN	V,P	291	942	09.05.06	5090	200301	00000
309.677-014	FOSTER PARENT (domestic ser.)	3233	44444434345	LNNNNNNFFFNOONNNNNNNN	NNNN3NNNNNNNNN	V,P	291	942	10.03.03	5060	200602	00000
310.137-010	HOST/HOSTESS, RESTAURANT (hotel & rest.)	4346	33433344355	MNNOOONFFFNOONNNNNNNN	NNNN3NNNNNNNNN	D,P,J,V	291	903	10.03.03	5211	200202	65002
310.137-018	STEWARD/STEWARDESS (hotel & rest.)	4347	33344344454	LNNNNNNFFONFFOFNNNFON	NNNN3NNNNNNNNN	D,V,P	291	903	09.01.03	5211	200409	61099
310.137-022	STEWARD/STEWARDESS, BANQUET (hotel & rest.)	4337	33344344454	LNNNNNNFFOFFNNFNNON	NNNN4NNNNNNNNN	V,D,P,J	291	903	05.12.01	5211	200409	61099
310.137-026	STEWARD/STEWARDESS, RAILROAD DINING CAR (r.r. trans.)	5448	22233333353	LNFNNNNFFNNFNFNNON	NNNN4NNNNNNNNN	V,D,P,J	146	903	11.11.04	5211	200409	39999
310.267-010	ANALYST, FOOD AND BEVERAGE (hotel & rest.)	3336	22233333353	LNFNNNNFFNNNFNFNNON	NNNN4NNNNNNNNN	D,P,J	212	903	05.05.17	1490	200409	39999
310.357-010	WINE STEWARD/STEWARDESS (hotel & rest.)	3236	33344444444	LNNNNNNFFFONNNNNNON	NNNN3NNNNNNNNN	D,P,J,T	291	903	09.05.02	5213	120507	65008
311.137-010	COUNTER SUPERVISOR (hotel & rest.)	4336	33344344453	LNNNNNFFFONFNFNNNON	NNNN3NNNNNNNNN	J,P	291	903	09.01.03	5211	120507	65008
311.137-014	WAITER/WAITRESS, BANQUET, HEAD (hotel & rest.)	4236	33444444444	LNNNNNFFNFFFNNFNNNON	NNNN4NNNNNNNNN	D,P,V	291	903	09.01.03	5211	120507	61099
311.137-018	WAITER/WAITRESS, CAPTAIN (hotel & rest.)	4346	33444344455	LNNNNNFFFNFNFFNNNON	NNNN3NNNNNNNNN	D,P	291	903	09.01.03	5211	200409	61099
311.137-022	WAITER/WAITRESS, HEAD (hotel & rest.)	2222	44444444444	LNNNNNNFFFNFNFFNNNON	NNNN3NNNNNNNNN	D,P	291	903	09.01.03	5211	120507	61099
311.472-010	FAST-FOODS WORKER (hotel & rest.)	2222	44444434344	LNNONNNCCFNFFOFONNON	FNNN3NNNNNNNNN	D,P,V	291	903	09.04.01	5216	200409	65041
311.477-010	CAR HOP (hotel & rest.)	2222	44444434345	LNNNNNNFFFNFONFNNNON	NNNN3NNNNNNNNN	P,T	291	903	09.04.01	5216	000000	65011
311.477-014	COUNTER ATTENDANT, LUNCHROOM OR COFFEE SHOP (hotel & rest.)	2222	43344444345	LNNONONFFONFFONFNNNON	NNNN3NNNNNNNNN	P	291	903	09.04.01	5217	120507	65017
311.477-018	WAITER/WAITRESS, BAR (hotel & rest.)	3223	33444434335	LNNFNNNFFNFFNFNFNNNN	NNNN4NNNNNNNNN	R,P	291	903	09.04.01	5213	200409	65008
311.477-022	WAITER/WAITRESS, DINING CAR (r.r. trans.)	3223	33343434344	LNNNNNNNFFFNFONFNNNON	NNNN3NNNNNNNNN	P	146	903	09.04.01	5213	120507	61099
311.477-026	WAITER/WAITRESS, FORMAL (hotel & rest.)	3224	33443434344	LNNNNNNFFNFONFFONNNO	NNNN3NNNNNNNNN	R,P	291	903	09.04.01	5213	120507	65008
311.477-030	WAITER/WAITRESS, INFORMAL (hotel & rest.)	3223	34344344345	LNNNNNNFFFNFNFNONNNNO	NNNN3NNNNNNNNN	R,P	291	903	09.04.01	5216	120507	65008
311.477-034	WAITER/WAITRESS, ROOM SERVICE (hotel & rest.)	2223	44444344444	LNNNNNNFFFNNFFFNNNNNO	NNNN3NNNNNNNNN	R,P	291	903	09.05.02	5216	200409	65011
311.477-038	WAITER/WAITRESS, TAKE OUT (hotel & rest.)	2123	44444344455	LNNNNNNFFNNFNNFNNNNN	NNNN3NNNNNNNNN	P	291	903	09.04.01	5216	000000	65017
311.674-010	CANTEEN OPERATOR (any industry)	2122	44444444455	LNNNNNNFFFNNFNNNNNN	NNNN3NNNNNNNNN	P	291	903	09.04.01	5217	120507	65017
311.674-014	RAW SHELLFISH PREPARER (hotel & rest.)	2213	34444434354	LNNFNNNNFFNNFNNFNNNN	NONO3NNNNNNNNN	R,P	146	903	09.05.02	5213	200409	65038
311.674-018	WAITER/WAITRESS, BUFFET (hotel & rest.)	2112	44444434355	LNNONONNFFONONONNNNN	NNNN3NNNNNNNNN	R,P	291	903	09.05.02	5218	120507	65008
311.677-010	CAFETERIA ATTENDANT (hotel & rest.)	2112	44444544345	LNNONONNFFNOONONNNNN	NNNN3NNNNNNNNN	R	291	903	09.05.02	5216	200409	65014
311.677-014	COUNTER ATTENDANT, CAFETERIA (hotel & rest.)	2123	44443433355	LNNFNONFFNOONFNNNNON	NNON4NNNNNNNNN	R,P	291	903	09.05.02	5216	120507	65017

DOT #	DOT Title & Industry	Trng	Aptitude	Physical	Environment	Tempra	WKF	MPSMS	GOE	SOC	CIP	OES
311.677-018	DINING ROOM ATTENDANT (hotel & rest.)	2112	44444444445	MNNONONCCONOONNONNNN	NNNN3NNNNNNNN	R	291	903	09.05.02	5218	120507	65014
312.474-010	BARTENDER (hotel & rest.)	3233	33344334455	LNNONNNFFONFFNFNNNN	NNNN3NNNNNNNN	R,P	291	903	09.04.01	5212	200409	65005
312.477-010	BAR ATTENDANT (hotel & rest.)	2222	33344444355	LNNNNNNFFNFNFFNNNNN	NNNN3NNNNNNNN	R	291	903	09.04.01	5212	200409	65005
312.677-010	TAPROOM ATTENDANT (amuse. & rec.)	2112	44454444355	LNNNNNNFNFNNFFNNNNNN	NNNN3NNNNNNNN	R	291	903	09.05.02	5212	200409	65005
312.687-010	BARTENDER HELPER (hotel & rest.)	2112	44444444445	MNNFNFNFNFNNNNNNNNNN	NONO3NNNNNNNN	R	031	903	05.12.18	5218	200409	65014
313.131-010	BAKER, HEAD (hotel & rest.)	4337	34333344254	LNNNNNNFFOFFNFNNOOO	NNFN3NNNNNNNN	D,J,T	146	384	05.10.08	5211	120501	61099
313.131-014	CHEF (hotel & rest.)	4337	33343334354	LNNNNNNFFOFFOFNONON	NNNN3NNNNNNNN	D,V,P,J	146	903	05.05.17	5211	120505	61099
313.131-018	COOK, HEAD, SCHOOL CAFETERIA (hotel & rest.)	4336	33343344354	MNNONONFFFOFFOFNONON	NNNN3NNNNNNNNO	V,D,P,J	146	903	05.10.08	5211	200409	61099
313.131-022	PASTRY CHEF (hotel & rest.)	4338	33333333253	LNNNNNNFFFOFFNFNFFN	NNFN3NNNNNNNN	D,P,J,E	146	903	05.10.08	5211	120501	61099
313.131-026	SOUS CHEF (hotel & rest.)	4338	33343334354	MNNNNNNFFOFFNFNONON	NNFN3NNNNNNNN	V,D,J,P	146	903	05.05.17	5211	120505	65026
313.281-010	CHEF DE FROID (hotel & rest.)	4337	33322322353	MNNNNNNFONFFNNNNNN	NNNN5NNNNNNNN	V,J,E	146	903	05.05.17	5214	120505	65021
313.361-010	BAKER, SECOND (hotel & rest.)	4337	33333343354	HNNNNNNFFONNNNFNNNON	NNNN3NNNNNNNN	P,J,T	384	384	05.05.17	5214	120501	65026
313.361-014	COOK (hotel & rest.)	3337	33343333354	MNNNNNNFFFNNOOOFNNNON	NNFN3NNNNNNNNF	J,T,V	146	903	05.10.08	5214	120505	65032
313.361-018	COOK APPRENTICE (hotel & rest.)	3337	34443343354	MNNNNNNFFFNNOOFNNNON	NNFN3NNNNNNNN	J,T,V	146	903	05.10.08	5214	120505	65026
313.361-026	COOK, SPECIALTY (hotel & rest.)	3225	34443344354	MNNNNNNFFFNOONFNONON	NNNN3NNNNNNNN	J,T,V	146	903	05.10.08	5214	120505	65032
313.361-030	COOK, SPECIALTY, FOREIGN FOOD (hotel & rest.)	3327	33343344354	MNNNNNNFFFNOONFNONON	NNNN3NNNNNNNN	J,T,V	146	903	05.10.08	5214	120505	65026
313.361-034	GARDE MANGER (hotel & rest.)	3227	34443434354	LNNNNNNFFNOONFNONON	NNNN3NNNNNNNN	V,P,J	146	903	05.10.08	5214	120505	65026
313.361-038	PIE MAKER (hotel & rest.)	3226	34443433254	LNNNNNNFFONNNFNONON	NNNN3NNNNFNONON	J,T	146	903	05.10.08	5214	120501	65021
313.374-010	COOK, FAST FOOD (hotel & rest.)	3225	34443494354	MNNNNNNFFNNOOFNONON	NNFN3NNNNNNNNF	R,T,J	146	903	05.10.08	5215	120505	65032
313.374-014	COOK, SHORT ORDER (hotel & rest.)	3223	33443444354	LNNNNNNFFNFFNFNONON	NNFN3NNNNNNNN	R,P	146	903	05.10.08	5215	120505	65035
313.381-010	BAKER (hotel & rest.)	3226	34433434354	MNNNNNNFFONNFNFNON	NNFN3NNNNNNNNO	J,T	146	384	05.10.08	5214	120501	65021
313.381-014	BAKER, PIZZA (hotel & rest.)	3215	34443444354	MNNNNNNFFONNNFNNON	NNNN3NNNNNNNN	J	146	903	05.10.08	5214	120505	65032
313.381-018	COOK APPRENTICE, PASTRY (hotel & rest.)	4337	33433434254	MNNNNNNFFONNNFNNNON	NNFN3NNNNNNNN	J,E,T	146	384	05.10.08	5214	120501	65021
313.381-022	COOK, BARBECUE (hotel & rest.)	3225	34453434354	MNNONNNFFFONNNNFNNON	NNNN3NNNNNNNN	J,V	146	903	05.10.08	5214	120505	65026
313.381-026	COOK, PASTRY (hotel & rest.)	4337	33433434254	MNNNNNNFFOONNFNNON	NNFN3NNNNNNNN	J,E,T	384	384	05.10.08	5214	120501	65021
313.381-030	COOK, SCHOOL CAFETERIA (hotel & rest.)	3226	34444444354	MNNONONFFNOOFNNOON	NONN3NNNNNNNNO	V,J	146	903	05.10.08	5214	200409	65028
313.381-034	ICE-CREAM CHEF (hotel & rest.)	3225	34443444354	MNNONNNFFNNNNFNNON	NNNN3NNNNNNNN	E,J	146	903	05.10.08	5214	120505	65026
313.684-010	BAKER HELPER (hotel & rest.)	2113	44444544354	MNNNNNNFFONNNONNNON	NNNN3NNNNNNNNF	J,R	146	384	05.12.17	5219	120501	65038
313.687-010	COOK HELPER, PASTRY (hotel & rest.)	2113	44449534354	MNNONNNFFNONNFNNON	NNNN3NNNNNNNN	V	146	903	05.12.17	5219	120501	65038
315.131-010	COOK, CHIEF (water trans.)	4237	33343333354	MNNNNNNFFOFFNFNNNN	NNFF3NNNNNNNNF	D,J,P,E	146	903	05.10.08	5211	120505	61099
315.131-014	PASTRY CHEF (water trans.)	4238	33333332353	LNNNNNNFFNNNNFNNON	NNNN3NNNNNNNN	D,P,J,E	146	903	05.10.08	5211	120501	61099
315.137-010	CHEF, PASSENGER VESSEL (water trans.)	4337	33343344454	LNNNNNNFFNFNFNNNNN	NNNN3NNNNNNNN	D,J,P	146	903	05.05.17	5211	120505	61099
315.137-014	SOUS CHEF (water trans.)	4347	33343444453	LNNNNNNFFNFNFNNNNNFN	NNNN3NNNNNNNN	D,P,J	146	903	05.05.17	5211	120505	61099
315.361-010	COOK (any industry)	3226	34343334354	MNNNNNNFFFOOONFNOOON	NNNF3NNNNNNNNF	V,J,T	146	903	05.10.08	5214	120505	65028
315.361-022	COOK, STATION (water trans.)	3226	34443443354	MNNNNNNFFNNOONFNNNFN	NNNN3NNNNNNNN	J,T	146	903	05.10.08	5214	120505	65026
315.371-010	COOK, MESS (water trans.)	3226	34443343354	MNNONONFFFONNNFNOOON	NNNN3NNNNNNNN	V,J,T	146	903	05.10.08	5214	120505	65028
315.381-010	COOK (fishing & hunt.)	3225	34343434344	MOFONONFFONNNFNONON	NNFN4NNNNNNNN	D,J,T	146	903	05.10.08	5214	120505	65028
315.381-014	COOK, LARDER (water trans.)	4227	34343433354	HNNNNNNFFCFONONFNONON	NNNN2NNNNNNNNF	V,J,T	146	903	05.12.17	5214	120505	65023
315.381-018	COOK, RAILROAD (r.r. trans.)	3226	33343434334	LNCNNNNNFFNNNNFNONON	NONN3NNNNNNNNF	V,J,T	146	903	05.10.08	5214	120505	65026
315.381-022	COOK, THIRD (water trans.)	3126	33443434354	MNNNNNNFFNNNNFNNNFN	NONN3NNNNNNNNF	J,T	146	903	05.10.08	5214	120505	65028
315.381-026	SECOND COOK AND BAKER (water trans.)	3226	33443443354	HOOOONFFONNNFNNNON	NNOO3NNNNNNNNO	J,T	146	903	05.10.08	5214	120505	65028
316.661-010	CARVER (hotel & rest.)	3224	34443434354	LNNNNNNFFNNNNFNNON	NNNN2NNNNNNNNO	R,T	146	903	05.10.08	5217	120506	65038
316.681-010	BUTCHER, MEAT (hotel & rest.)	3226	34433433254	HONNNNNNFFONNNNNCNCCNN	NNNN2NNONNNNNN	J	034	382	05.10.08	6871	120506	65023
316.684-010	BUTCHER, CHICKEN AND FISH (hotel & rest.)	2213	44433533254	LONNNNNNFFONNNNFNONON	NNNN2NNNNNNNNO	R,T	034	324	05.10.08	6871	120506	65028
316.684-014	DELI CUTTER-SLICER (retail trade)	2212	44443433354	MNNNNNNNFFONNNNFNOFON	NNNN2NNNNNNNNF	R,T	054	382	05.12.17	6871	200409	65023
316.684-018	MEAT CUTTER (retail trade; wholesale tr.)	3236	34433434334	HNNNNNNNFCFONONFNONON	NONN3NNNNNNNNF	J,T	034	382	05.10.08	6871	120505	65023
316.684-022	MEAT-CUTTER APPRENTICE (retail trade; wholesale tr.)	3236	34433433254	HNNNNNNNFCFONONFNONON	NONN3NNNNNNNNF	J,T	034	382	05.10.08	6871	120505	65023
317.384-010	SALAD MAKER (water trans.)	3235	34444433354	LNNNNNNFFNNNNFNNNON	NNNN2NNNNNNNNN	R	146	903	05.10.08	5217	200409	65038
317.664-010	SANDWICH MAKER (hotel & rest.)	2112	44444433355	MNNNNNNNCCNFFNCNNCNN	NNNN3NNNNNNNNN	R,T	146	903	05.12.17	5217	200409	65038
317.684-010	COFFEE MAKER (hotel & rest.)	2112	44444443354	MNNNNNNFFONNNNFNNNON	NNNN2NNNNNNNNO	R,T	146	903	05.12.17	5217	200409	65038
317.684-014	PANTRY GOODS MAKER (hotel & rest.)	3224	34444443354	LNNNNNNFFCONNNONNNON	NNNN3NNNNNNNNO	R,T	146	903	05.10.08	5217	200409	65038

DOT #	DOT Title & Industry	Trng	Aptitude	Physical	Environment	Tempra	WkF	MPSMS	GOE	SOC	CIP	OES
317.687-010	COOK HELPER (hotel & rest.)	2112	4444444355	MNNONNNFCFONOOONONNN	NNON3NNNNNNNNNO	R	146	903	05.12.17	5219	200409	65038
318.137-010	KITCHEN STEWARD/STEWARDESS (hotel & rest.)	4346	33344344454	MNNNNNFFFONFFNFONFON	NOFF4NNNNNNNNNF	V,D,P	221	903	05.12.01	5211	200409	61099
318.687-010	KITCHEN HELPER (hotel & rest.)	2112	44544544444	MNNNFNFNCCONNONNNNNON	NOFF4NNNNNNNNNF	R	031	903	05.12.18	5219	200409	65038
318.687-014	SCULLION (water trans.)	2112	44444543355	MNNNNNNCCFNNNNNNNNNN	NONO2NNNNNNNNNN	R	031	911	05.12.18	5219	200409	65038
318.687-018	SILVER WRAPPER (hotel & rest.)	2111	4444444355	LNNNNNNNCCCNNNNNNNNN	NNNN2NNNNNNNNNN	R	041	903	05.12.18	5219	000000	65038
319.137-010	FOOD-SERVICE SUPERVISOR (hotel & rest.)	4336	33344344454	LNNNNNNFFNFFFNNNNFN	NOOO3NNNNNNNNNO	D,V,P,J	146	903	09.05.02	5211	200409	61099
319.137-014	MANAGER, FLIGHT KITCHEN (hotel & rest.)	4337	33343344454	LNNNNNNFFONFFNFNNOON	NNNN2NNNNNNNNNN	V,D,P,J,T	146	903	11.11.04	5211	200405	61099
319.137-018	MANAGER, INDUSTRIAL CAFETERIA (hotel & rest.)	4336	33343344454	LNNNNNNOOONFFNFNNOON	NNNN2NNNNNNNNNN	D,P,J	146	903	11.11.04	5211	200409	61099
319.137-022	SUPERVISOR, COMMISSARY PRODUCTION (hotel & rest.)	4337	33343344454	LNNNNNNFFONFFNFNNNON	NNNN3NNNNNNNNNN	V,D,P,J	146	903	11.11.04	5211	200409	61099
319.137-026	SUPERVISOR, KOSHER DIETARY SERVICE (hotel & rest.)	4237	33433434354	LNNNNNNFFONFFNFNNNON	NNNO2NNNNNNNNNN	D,P,J,T	146	903	05.10.08	5211	000000	61099
319.137-030	KITCHEN SUPERVISOR (hotel & rest.)	4347	33344344454	MNNONONOOONFFNFNNNON	NNNN3NNNNNNNNNN	D,V,P	146	903	05.10.08	5219	200409	61099
319.464-010	AUTOMAT-CAR ATTENDANT (r.r. trans.)	2222	34444444335	LNFNNNNFONFFNNNNNNN	NNNN4NNNNNNNNNN	R,P	291	903	09.04.01	5219	000000	65099
319.464-014	VENDING-MACHINE ATTENDANT (hotel & rest.)	2222	34444444354	LNNNNNNFFONOONFNNNON	NNNN3NNNNNNNNNN	P	291	903	09.04.01	5219	200409	85947
319.467-010	FOOD ORDER EXPEDITER (hotel & rest.)	3223	33344343344	LNNNNNNFFNFFNFNNFON	NNNN2NNNNNNNNNN	P,J	231	903	05.09.03	5219	120507	65099
319.474-010	FOUNTAIN SERVER (hotel & rest.)	2213	44344444355	LNNNNNNFFNFNOFNONNNN	NNNN3NNNNNNNNNN	R,P	146	903	09.04.01	5216	200409	65017
319.484-010	FOOD ASSEMBLER, KITCHEN (hotel & rest.)	2213	44443433354	LNNONNNFFNNNONNNNON	NNNN2NNNNNNNNNN	R,T	146	903	05.12.17	5219	200409	65038
319.677-010	CATERER HELPER (personal ser.)	3223	33443444354	LNNNNNNNFFNFFNFNNNNN	NNNN2NNNNNNNNNN	P	291	903	09.05.02	5217	200405	65099
319.677-014	FOOD-SERVICE WORKER, HOSPITAL (medical ser.)	3222	44444343344	MNNNONONFFONNNNNFNNQOOO	NNGO3NNNNNNNNNO	R,T	146	903	09.05.02	5216	120507	65011
319.687-010	COUNTER-SUPPLY WORKER (hotel & rest.)	2112	44444444354	MNFNNNNFONNNNNNNON	NNNN2NNNNNNNNNN	R	221	903	09.05.02	5218	120507	65014
320.137-010	MANAGER, BOARDING HOUSE (hotel & rest.)	3336	33344344454	LNNNNNNFFONFFNFNNON	NNNN2NNNNNNNNNN	V,D,P	291	902	11.11.01	1351	080902	15026
320.137-014	MANAGER, LODGING FACILITIES (hotel & rest.)	4347	33344344445	MNNNNNNFFNNFFNNNNNNN	NNNN3NNNNNNNNNN	D,V,P	295	902	11.11.01	1351	490399	15026
321.137-010	HOUSEKEEPER (hotel & rest., medical ser., real estate)	3236	33433434355	LNNOONFFONNNNNNNNNN	NNNN2NNNNNNNNNN	V,D,P,J	031	905	05.12.01	5241	200605	61008
321.137-014	INSPECTOR (hotel & rest.)	3236	33333444454	LNNNNNNOOONFFNFNNFON	NNNN2NNNNNNNNNN	V,P,J	031	902	05.12.01	5241	200605	61099
323.137-010	SUPERVISOR, HOUSECLEANER (hotel & rest.)	3236	33333444354	MONFNNNFFONFFNFNNON	NNNN3NNNNNNNNNN	V,D,P	031	902	05.12.01	5242	200604	67002
323.687-010	CLEANER, HOSPITAL (medical ser.)	2122	44544434345	MNNOONFFONFFNNNNNNNN	NNNF2NNNNNNNNNN	R,U	031	905	05.12.18	5242	200605	67002
323.687-014	CLEANER, HOUSEKEEPING (any industry)	1112	44444445455	LNNOOONFFONNNNNNNNNN	NNNN3NNNNNNNNNN	R,U	031	902	05.12.18	5242	200605	67002
323.687-018	HOUSECLEANER (hotel & rest.)	2112	44444344445	HONOOONOFONNONNNNNNNN	NNNN3NNNNNNNNNN	R	011	902	05.12.18	5242	200605	67002
324.137-010	BAGGAGE PORTER, HEAD (hotel & rest.)	3336	33444344445	LNNNNNNFFONFFNONNNN	NNNN2NNNNNNNNNN	V,D,P	291	905	09.05.03	5251	080902	61099
324.137-014	BELL CAPTAIN (hotel & rest.)	3226	33444444445	MNNNNNNFFONFFNONNNN	NNNN2NNNNNNNNNN	V,D,P	291	905	09.05.03	5251	080902	61099
324.477-010	PORTER, BAGGAGE (hotel & rest.)	2222	44444444345	MNNFONNFFONFFNONNNN	NNNN2NNNNNNNNNN	P	291	905	09.05.03	5262	080902	68023
324.577-010	ROOM-SERVICE CLERK (hotel & rest.)	2222	44444343355	LNNNNNNNFFNOONNNNNNN	NNNN2NNNNNNNNNN	V,P	291	899	09.05.03	5269	080902	69999
324.677-010	BELLHOP (hotel & rest.)	2222	44444444345	HONONONFFNOONFFFNNNN	NNNN2NNNNNNNNNN	V,P	291	902	09.05.03	5262	080902	68023
324.677-014	DOORKEEPER (any industry)	2122	44444445455	MNNFNNNFFOFFNFNONON	ONNN2NNNNNNNNNN	V,P	291	905	09.05.04	5269	080902	69999
329.137-010	SUPERINTENDENT, SERVICE (hotel & rest.)	3337	33444344455	LNNNNNNOOONFFNFNONNN	NNNN2NNNNNNNNNN	V,D,P	291	902	09.01.04	5241	520902	61099
329.161-010	MANAGER, CAMP (amuse. & rec.)	4337	33424233544	HOOOOOOFFOFOOONFNONON	ONNN3NNNNNNNNNN	D,V,P,J	295	919	11.11.02	1352	520901	19999
329.467-010	ATTENDANT, LODGING FACILITIES (hotel & rest.)	3236	33424233544	LNNNNNNFFFOFOONFNONON	NNNN3NNNNNNNNNN	T,P,J	291	904	09.02.02	5252	120402	68002
329.677-010	PORTER, MARINA (water trans.)	2123	44443533354	SNNNNNNFFCNNNNCNNCON	NNNN3NNNNNNNNNN	P,J	291	904	09.05.01	5253	120403	68008
329.683-010	ATTENDANT, CAMPGROUND (amuse. & rec.)	2123	44443533354	SNNNNNFFFNNNFNNON	NNNN3NNNNNNNNNN	P,T	291	904	09.05.01	5253	120403	68008
330.371-010	BARBER (personal ser.)	4336	33432433352	LNNNNNNFFOFFNFNONON	NNNO3NFNNNNNNNNN	V,P,J	291	904	09.02.01	5253	120403	68005
330.371-014	BARBER APPRENTICE (personal ser.)	4336	33432433352	LNNNNNNFFOFFNFNONON	NNNO3NFNNNNNNNNN	V,P,J	291	904	09.02.01	5253	120403	68005
331.674-010	MANICURIST (personal ser.)	4336	33433423353	LNNNNNNFFFFFNFNNFFN	NNNN2NNNNNNNNNN	J,P,V	291	904	09.02.01	5253	120406	68005
331.674-014	FINGERNAIL FORMER (personal ser.)	3226	33432423354	LNNNNNNFFFFFFNFNNFFN	NNNN3NNNNNNNNNN	V,J,P,T	264	904	01.06.02	5253	120402	68005
332.271-010	COSMETOLOGIST (personal ser.)	4337	22332433352	LNNFFNCCCCOCONCNNCCN	NNNN3NNNNNNNNNN	V,E,J,P	291	909	01.06.02	5253	120403	68005
332.271-014	COSMETOLOGIST APPRENTICE (personal ser.)	3224	43433433353	LNNNNNNCCCCFFNNNNNON	NNNN2NNNNNNNNNN	V,P,J	291	904	01.06.02	5253	120406	68005
333.071-010	MAKE-UP ARTIST (amuse. & rec.; motion picture; radio-tv broad.)	3234	33433433254	MNNNNNNFFOFOONNNNNON	NNNO2NNNNNNNNNN	V,P,J	291	909	09.05.01	5269	120405	69999
333.271-010	BODY-MAKE-UP ARTIST (amuse. & rec.; motion picture)	2122	44444434355	MNNNNNNNFFOFNNNNNNNN	NNOO2NNNNNNNNNN	P	291	909	09.05.01	5269	120405	69999
334.374-010	MASSEUR/MASSEUSE (personal ser.)	2122	44444444355	LNNONNNFFOFFFNNNNNNN	NNNN2NNNNNNNNNN	R,P	291	909	09.05.01	5269	120405	68032

DOT #	DOT Title & Industry	Trng	Aptitude	Physical	Environment	Tempra	WKF	MPSMS	GOE	SOC	CIP	OES
335.677-014	HOT-ROOM ATTENDANT (personal ser.)	2122	44444444355	LNNNNNNFFOOFFNNNNNN	NNOO2NNNNNNNNNN	V,P	291	909	09.05.01	5269	120405	68032
338.371-010	EMBALMER APPRENTICE (personal ser.)	4447	23332432353	HNNONNNFFONNNNFNNOON	NNNN1NNNNNNNNNFF	V,J,T	291	907	02.04.02	3990	120301	39014
338.371-014	EMBALMER (personal ser.)	4447	23332432353	HNNONNNFFONNNNFNNOON	NNNN1NNNNNNNNNFF	V,J,T	291	907	02.04.02	3990	120301	39014
339.137-010	MANAGER, HEALTH CLUB (personal ser.)	4347	33333334325	LNNFNFNFNFFNFNONOONN	NNNN3NNNNNNNNNN	I,P,J,V	292	909	11.11.02	5251	080299	61099
339.361-010	MORTUARY BEAUTICIAN (personal ser.)	3226	33433433353	MNNNNNNFFONOOONFNNNON	NNNO1NNNNNNNNNN	V,J,T	291	907	01.06.02	5253	120403	68005
339.371-010	ELECTROLOGIST (personal ser.)	3235	33442432345	LNNFNNNFFNFNCNOCNN	NNNN2NNNNNNNNNN	P,J,T	294	904	09.05.01	5253	120403	68005
339.371-014	SCALP-TREATMENT OPERATOR (personal ser.)	3235	33433433354	LNNNNNNFFFFFNFNNNON	NNNN2NNNNNNONNN	V,J,P	294	904	09.02.01	5253	120403	68005
339.571-010	TATTOO ARTIST (personal ser.)	3225	44432422242	SNNNNNNCCCFFFNCNOCCN	NNNN2NNNNNNNNN	V,P,E	291	909	01.06.02	5269	000000	69999
339.687-010	SUPPLY CLERK (personal ser.)	2213	44444444454	LNNFNNNFFFNNNNNONNON	NNNF2NNNNNNNNNN	V	031	904	05.09.01	4754	520499	58023
340.367-010	DESK CLERK, BOWLING FLOOR (amuse. & rec.)	3333	33334344455	LNNNNNNFFONFFNONNNNN	NNNN3NNNNNNNNNN	V,P	291	913	09.04.02	5254	080903	68014
340.477-010	RACKER (amuse. & rec.)	2212	44444443455	LNNNNNNNFFFOOONNNNNN	NNNN2NNNNNNNNNN	R,P	291	913	09.05.05	5254	080903	68014
341.137-010	CADDIE SUPERVISOR (amuse. & rec.)	3226	33444444455	LNNNNNNNNNNFFNNNNNN	ONNN2NNNNNNNNN	D,P	291	913	09.05.06	5251	080903	68014
341.367-010	RECREATION-FACILITY ATTENDANT (amuse. & rec.)	4233	34344334355	LNNNNNNOFONFFNNNNNNN	NNNN3NNNNNNNNN	V,P	291	913	07.04.03	5254	470499	68014
341.464-010	SKATE-SHOP ATTENDANT (amuse. & rec.)	3223	33434434455	LNNNNNNFFFFFNFNNNNN	NNNN3NNNNNNNNN	P,T	292	616	09.04.02	5254	080903	68014
341.665-010	SKI-TOW OPERATOR (amuse. & rec.)	3233	33433444455	LNNNNNNFFNFFNFNNNNN	FNNN2NNNNNNNNNN	R,P	013	913	09.05.08	5254	080903	68014
341.677-010	CADDIE (amuse. & rec.)	2222	44433444455	MNNONNNFFNNFFNNOONNNN	CNNN2NNNNNNNNN	R,P	291	905	09.05.06	5254	080903	68014
341.683-010	GOLF-RANGE ATTENDANT (amuse. & rec.)	2122	44545434345	MNNONNNNFFNNNNFONNNN	FNNN2NNNNNNNNN	R	031	616	05.12.18	5254	080903	68014
342.137-010	SUPERVISOR, RIDES (amuse. & rec.)	4337	33334344455	LOOOONNFFONFFNOOOONO	FNNN4NNNNNNNNN	D,P,V	295	919	05.10.02	5251	080903	61099
342.357-010	WEIGHT GUESSER (amuse. & rec.)	3232	43423455455	LNNNNNNNOOFNCCNFNNNON	CNNN3NNNNNNNNN	I,J,P	297	919	01.07.03	5254	000000	68014
342.657-010	BARKER (amuse. & rec.)	3232	33455535355	LNNNNNNNNNNCNNNNNNNN	CNNN3NNNNNNNNN	P,I,J	292	919	01.07.02	5254	080903	68014
342.657-014	GAME ATTENDANT (amuse. & rec.)	3333	33444444455	LNNNNNNFFFNCFNFNNNNN	NNNN3NNNNNNNNN	I,P	292	919	09.04.02	5254	080903	68014
342.663-010	RIDE OPERATOR (amuse. & rec.)	2223	44444434345	LONNNNNOOONONNONNNNO	NNNN4NNOONNNNNN	R,P	291	919	05.10.02	5254	080903	68014
342.665-010	FUN-HOUSE OPERATOR (amuse. & rec.)	3123	44444434345	LNNNNNNFFNNNNNNNNNN	FNNN3NNNNNNNNN	R,P	292	919	05.12.15	5254	080903	68014
342.667-010	WHARF ATTENDANT (amuse. & rec.)	3233	44444434345	MNOONNNFFNFNFNOFFFNF	CNNO3NNNNNNNNNO	V,P,J	291	919	09.04.02	5254	080903	68014
342.667-014	ATTENDANT, ARCADE (amuse. & rec.)	2222	33344444455	LNNNNNNFFFNNFNNNNNN	NNNN3NNNNNNNNNN	P	282	919	09.04.02	5254	080903	68014
342.677-010	RIDE ATTENDANT (amuse. & rec.)	2122	44444444445	LNNNNNNFFOFFNNCNNNC	FNNN2NNNNNNNNN	R,P	291	919	09.05.08	5254	080903	61099
343.137-010	MANAGER, CARDROOM (amuse. & rec.)	4447	33334444455	LNNNNNNOOONFFNONNNNN	NNNN3NNNNNNNNN	V,D,P,J	295	919	11.11.02	5251	520901	61099
343.137-014	SUPERVISOR, CARDROOM, CARDROOM (amuse. & rec.)	4446	33344443454	LNNNNNNOOONFFNONNNON	NNNN3NNNNNNNNN	D,J,P,V	291	919	09.04.02	5251	080903	61099
343.367-010	CARD PLAYER (amuse. & rec.)	3224	34344443454	SNNNNNNCCCNOONCNNNFN	NNNN2NNNNNNNNN	R,J	297	919	09.04.02	5254	000000	68014
343.367-014	GAMBLING MONITOR (amuse. & rec.)	4337	33343444443	LNNNNNNFFONFFNNNNNNN	NNNN4NNNNNNNNN	J	293	919	04.02.03	5144	430109	63035
343.464-010	GAMBLING DEALER (amuse. & rec.)	3325	33343432354	LNNONNNCOFOFONONNOOF	NNNN3NNNNNNNNN	R,T,P,J	282	919	09.04.02	5256	080903	68014
343.467-010	CARDROOM ATTENDANT I (amuse. & rec.)	3224	33344333455	LNNNNNNFFNFNFNNNNNN	NNNN3NNNNNNNNN	P	291	919	09.04.02	5256	080903	68014
343.467-014	FLOOR ATTENDANT (amuse. & rec.)	2112	44443344455	LNNONNNFFONFFNFNNNNN	NNNN3NNNNNNNNN	R,P	232	919	09.04.02	5254	080903	68014
343.467-022	KENO WRITER (amuse. & rec.)	3334	33334233455	LNNONNNFFNFNFNNNNNN	FNNN3NNNNNNNNNN	R,P	232	919	09.05.05	5254	080903	68014
343.577-010	CARDROOM ATTENDANT II (amuse. & rec.)	2122	44444444455	LNNNNNNFFFNFNFNNNNN	NNNN3NNNNNNNNN	R,P	291	919	09.05.08	5254	080903	68014
343.687-010	PLASTIC-CARD GRADER, CARDROOM (amuse. & rec.)	2124	44442423352	SNNNNNNFFFNNFNNNOFN	NNNN3NNNNNNNNNOFN	R,J,T	212	479	06.03.02	5269	000000	69999
344.137-010	USHER, HEAD (amuse. & rec.)	3234	33344344445	LNNNNNNFFONFFNNNFN	ONNN2NNNNNNNNN	D,P	291	919	09.05.08	5251	000000	61099
344.667-010	TICKET TAKER (amuse. & rec.)	2122	44444455454	LNNNNNNFFNNNFNNNNN	NNNN2NNNNNNNNN	R,P	291	919	09.05.08	5256	080903	68021
344.677-010	PRESS-BOX CUSTODIAN (amuse. & rec.)	2122	44454444455	LNNNONOOOOFFNNFNNNON	NNNN3NNNNNNNNN	P	291	913	09.05.04	5256	080903	68021
344.677-014	USHER (amuse. & rec.)	2112	44454444455	LNNONONOOONFFNNFNONF	NNNN3NNNNNNNNN	R,P	291	910	09.05.08	5256	080903	68021
346.261-010	COSTUMER (motion picture; radio-tv broad.)	4347	22322382353	LNNNNNNCCFNOONFFOFFN	FNNN3NNNNNNNNN	V,J,T	171	911	01.06.02	6859	200305	68032
346.361-010	WARDROBE SUPERVISOR (amuse. & rec.)	3237	33443432343	LNNONONCCCCFFNFNNOON	NNNN3NNNNNNNNN	P,V,J	031	906	09.05.07	5258	200301	68032
346.374-010	COSTUMER ASSISTANT (motion picture; radio-tv broad.)	3234	33343332343	LNNNNNNOOOONOOOOOOO	NNNN3NNNNNNNNNO	V,P,J	221	449	09.05.07	5258	200305	68032
346.667-010	JOCKEY-ROOM CUSTODIAN (amuse. & rec.)	2123	44444455553	LNNNNNNOONNFFNNNNON	NNNN3NNNNNNNNN	V,P,T	291	913	12.01.02	5258	000000	68032
346.674-010	DRESSER (amuse. & rec.)	2223	44444433343	LNNNNNNFFNNNNNNNNNN	NNNN3NNNNNNNNN	V,P	291	906	09.05.06	5258	000000	68032
346.677-010	JOCKEY VALET (amuse. & rec.)	2223	44454544444	LNNNNNNFFNNNNNFNNFN	FNNN3NNNNNNNNN	P	291	906	09.05.06	5258	000000	68032
346.677-014	RIDING-SILKS CUSTODIAN (amuse. & rec.)	2112	44554444454	LNNNNNNFFNNOONFNNNFN	NNNN3NNNNNNNNN	R,T	221	913	09.05.07	5258	000000	68032
346.677-018	SECOND (amuse. & rec.)	2112	44544544444	LONONONFFFFNNNNNNNON	NNNN3NNNNNNNNN	P,J	291	913	09.05.01	5269	000000	66099
349.224-010	ANIMAL-RIDE MANAGER (amuse. & rec.)	4336	33344444345	MNNONNONFFOOFFNNNNNN	FNNN3NNNNNNNNN	V,D,P,J	291	327	03.03.01	5251	010505	61099
349.247-010	DIVER (amuse. & rec.)	3234	33443344444	MONNNNONFFNOONONNNON	FNNF2NNNNNNNNNO	V,P,S	297	330	01.07.02	3280	000000	34056
349.367-010	KENNEL MANAGER, DOG TRACK (amuse. & rec.)	3126	33443344454	LNNNNNNFFNNOONFNNNFN	NNNN3NNNNNNNNN	J	271	913	12.01.02	5269	010505	69999

DOT # DOT Title & Industry	Trng	Aptitude	Physical	Environment	Tempra	WkF	MPSMS	GOE	SOC	CIP	OES
349.367-014 RECEIVING-BARN CUSTODIAN (amuse. & rec.)	3233	33444444445	LNNNNNNOONNFFNNNNNNN	NNNN3NNNNNNNNNN	V,P	293	913	09.05.04	4630	010505	69999
349.477-010 JINRIKISHA DRIVER (amuse. & rec.)	2221	44435434334	NNNNNNCCNNOFNNCCCCCF	CNNN3NNNNNNNNNN	P	291	919	01.07.03	5269	000000	69999
349.664-010 AMUSEMENT PARK WORKER (amuse. & rec.)	2222	33444434354	MNNNNNNOONNFFNOONNON	NNNN3NNNNNNNNNN	P	291	919	09.01.01	5254	080903	68014
349.665-010 SCOREBOARD OPERATOR (amuse. & rec.)	3232	33443435455	SNNNNNNFFNOONNCNNCNC	FNNN3NNNNNNNNNN	R,T	281	913	07.04.05	5269	080903	69999
349.667-010 HOST/HOSTESS, DANCE HALL (amuse. & rec.)	2222	44444444435	LNONNNNNFFONFFNONNNN	NNNN3NNNNNNNNNN	P,J	291	919	09.01.01	5269	080903	69999
349.667-014 HOST/HOSTESS, HEAD (amuse. & rec.)	3232	33444544444	LNNNNNNNNNNFFNNNNNON	NNNN3NNNNNNNNNN	P,J	291	919	09.01.01	5269	080903	69999
349.673-010 DRIVE-IN THEATER ATTENDANT (amuse. & rec.)	2122	43444444455	LNNNNNNNFFNFFNNNFNFF	FNNN3NNNNNNNNNN	R,P	291	912	09.05.04	5256	080903	68021
349.674-010 ANIMAL-RIDE ATTENDANT (amuse. & rec.)	3122	33444434335	HNNONNNFFONFFNFFNFNN	CNNN3NNNNNNNNNN	R,P,J	291	327	03.03.02	5254	080903	68014
349.677-014 CABANA ATTENDANT (amuse. & rec.)	2223	44444444355	LNNONONFFFNFFNNNNNNN	CNNN2NNNNNNNNNN	P	291	919	09.04.02	5269	000000	68014
349.677-014 COACH DRIVER (business ser.)	3113	34443544455	LNNONONFFFNFFNNNNNNN	FNNN3NNNNNNNNNN	P	013	599	01.07.03	5254	080903	68021
349.677-018 CHILDREN'S ATTENDANT (amuse. & rec.)	2112	44444444455	LNNNNNNFFNNFFNFNONN	NNNN3NNNNNNNNNN	P	291	911	09.05.08	5256	200202	68021
349.680-010 TICKET-DISPENSER CHANGER (amuse. & rec.)	3223	33344344454	LNNNNNNOOONNFFNONONN	NNNN3NNNNNNNNNN	R,T	191	567	05.12.15	5269	120507	61099
350.137-010 HEADWAITER/HEADWAITRESS (water trans.)	3237	33344344454	LNNNNNNOOONFFNONNOON	NNNN3NNNNNNNNNN	V,D,P	291	903	09.01.03	5211	120507	61099
350.137-014 STEWARD/STEWARDESS, CHIEF, CARGO VESSEL (water trans.)	4337	33344344454	LOONNNNFFNFFNFNNNNN	NNNN3NNNNNNNNNN	D,P,V	221	854	07.01.02	5211	200409	61099
350.137-018 STEWARD/STEWARDESS, CHIEF, PASSENGER SHIP (water trans.)	4337	33344344454	LOONNNNOOONFFNONNOON	NNNN3NNNNNNNNNN	D,P,V	221	854	05.12.01	5211	200409	61099
350.137-022 STEWARD/STEWARDESS, SECOND (water trans.)	4237	33344344455	LOONNNNOOONFFNONNOON	NNNN3NNNNNNNNNN	D,P,V	291	854	09.01.04	5211	200409	61099
350.137-026 STEWARD/STEWARDESS, THIRD (water trans.)	4237	33444344455	LOONNNNOOONFFNONNONN	NNNN3NNNNNNNNNN	V,D,P	291	854	05.12.01	5241	080709	61099
350.677-010 MESS ATTENDANT (water trans.)	2123	44444434345	MOOONNFFONFFNNNNNNN	NNNN3NNNNNNNNNN	R,P	291	903	09.05.02	5213	200605	65008
350.677-014 PASSENGER ATTENDANT (water trans.)	2122	44444444345	LOONNNNFFNFFNNNNNNN	NNNN3NNNNNNNNNN	R,P	291	900	09.05.02	5257	080709	68028
350.677-018 STEWARD/STEWARDESS, BATH (water trans.)	2113	44444444345	LNOOONNFFONOONNNNNNN	NNNN3NNNNNNNNNN	R,P	291	909	05.12.18	5269	080903	68028
350.677-022 STEWARD/STEWARDESS, WINE (water trans.)	3123	34444444345	LOONNNNFFNFFNNNNNNN	ONNN3NNNNNNNNNN	V,P	291	900	09.01.04	5257	080709	68028
350.677-030 WAITER/WAITRESS (water trans.)	3224	34444434345	MNONNNNFFONFFNNNNNNN	NNNN3NNNNNNNNNN	R,P	291	903	09.05.02	5213	120507	65008
351.677-010 SERVICE ATTENDANT, SLEEPING CAR (r.r. trans.)	3123	43355444455	LNONNNNFFONFFNNNNNNN	NNNN4NNNNNNNNNN	R,P	291	905	09.01.04	5213	120507	65008
352.137-010 SUPERVISOR, AIRPLANE-FLIGHT ATTENDANT (air trans.)	2222	22333344444	LNONNNNNFFFNNFNNNNNN	NNNN4NNNNNNNNNN	V,P	295	855	09.01.04	5269	490106	68028
352.167-010 DIRECTOR, SOCIAL (hotel & rest.; water trans.)	4347	32344344445	LNNNNNNNFFFNNFNNNON	ONNN3NNNNNNNNNN	V,D,P,J	291	855	09.01.04	5269	000000	27311
352.367-010 AIRPLANE-FLIGHT ATTENDANT (air trans.)	4346	33334334334	MNFONNNNFFONFFNNNNON	NNNN4NNNNNNNNNO	V,D,P,J	291	855	09.01.01	5257	080709	68026
352.367-014 FLIGHT ATTENDANT, RAMP (air trans.)	4333	33334244444	MNFONNNNFFONFFNNNNON	NNNN5NNNNNNNNNN	P,J,V	271	855	09.01.01	5251	080709	69999
352.377-010 HOST/HOSTESS, GROUND (air trans.)	4336	33234344455	LNNOONNFFNFFNFNNNNN	NNNN4NNNNNNNNNN	P,V	291	852	09.01.01	5269	080709	69999
352.577-010 BUS ATTENDANT (motor trans.)	3233	33232344335	LNNNNNNFFNFFNFNNNNNN	NNNN3NNNNNNNNNN	V,P	291	909	09.01.04	5257	080709	68028
352.667-010 HOST/HOSTESS (any industry)	3232	33444444455	LNNNNNNFFNNFFNNNNNNN	NNNN3NNNNNNNNNN	V,P	291	909	09.01.01	5269	080903	69999
352.667-014 PARLOR CHAPERONE (hotel & rest.)	3122	31223444444	LNNNNNNFFNFFNNNNNNN	NNNN3NNNNNNNNNN	V,P,J	291	909	09.01.01	5269	000000	69999
352.677-010 PASSENGER SERVICE REPRESENTATIVE I (r.r. trans.)	3233	33444444455	LNOOONNFFONFFNNNNNNN	NNNN4NNNNNNNNNN	V,P,J	291	851	09.01.04	5257	080709	68028
352.677-014 RECEPTIONIST, AIRLINE LOUNGE (air trans.)	4235	43444444455	LNONNNNNFFNFFNNNNNNN	NNNN3NNNNNNNNNN	P	291	903	09.01.03	5269	080709	69999
352.677-018 WAITER/WAITRESS, CLUB (hotel & rest.)	2122	44444444344	LNNNNNNNFFNFFNNONNON	NNNN4NNNNNNNNNN	V,P	291	903	12.01.02	5213	120507	65008
353.137-010 GUIDE, CHIEF AIRPORT (air trans.)	4235	22344344455	LNNNNNNFFNFFNFNNNNNN	NNNN4NNNNNNNNNN	D,P,J	291	909	09.05.02	5251	081104	61099
353.161-010 GUIDE, HUNTING AND FISHING (amuse. & rec.)	4337	33334334444	HOOOOONFFFFFNOFFNOF	CNNN3NNNNNNNNNN	D,J,P,V	291	913	09.01.01	5255	310101	68017
353.164-010 GUIDE, ALPINE (personal ser.)	4347	22422423224	VFFOOOOFFNNFNOOONOO	COOF3NONNFNNNF	V,D,P,J,S	291	919	09.01.01	5255	080903	68017
353.167-010 GUIDE, TRAVEL (personal ser.)	4346	22344344454	LNNNNNNOOONFFNONNNN	NNNN2NNNNNNNNNN	V,P,D	291	859	07.05.01	5255	080903	68017
353.363-010 GUIDE, SIGHTSEEING (amuse. & rec.; personal ser.)	3234	33434434334	LNNOONNFFONFFNNNFF	ONNO2NNNNNNNNNN	V,P	291	919	09.01.02	5255	080903	68017
353.364-010 DUDE WRANGLER (amuse. & rec.)	3234	33443434334	MNNFFNFFFFFNONNNNNON	CNNN3NNNNNNNNNN	D,P,V,J	291	919	12.01.02	5269	000000	69999
353.367-010 GUIDE (personal ser.)	3123	33444443334	LNNNNNNOOONFFNONNON	FNNN3NNNNNNNNNN	V,P	291	909	09.05.02	5255	080903	68017
353.367-014 GUIDE, ESTABLISHMENT (any industry)	3133	33444344445	LOOONONFFONCCNFFNNNN	ONNN3NNNNNNNNNN	P,R,I	282	919	09.01.02	5255	080903	68017
353.367-018 GUIDE, PLANT (any industry)	3233	33444434454	LNNNNNNOOONFFNNNNNON	ONNN3NNNNNNNNNN	V,P	282	931	09.01.02	5255	081104	68017
353.367-022 PAGE (radio-tv broad.)	3232	33444444455	MNNFFNFFFFFNONNNNNN	NNNN3NNNNNNNNNN	P,R	282	931	09.01.02	5255	081104	68017
353.667-010 ESCORT (any industry)	2122	43444444344	LNNNNNNFFONFFNONNNN	FNNN3NNNNNNNNNN	P	291	909	09.05.08	5255	000000	68017
354.374-010 NURSE, PRACTICAL (medical ser.)	3234	33444434355	MNNOOONFFOOFFNNNON	NNNO2NNNNNNNNNN	V,P,S	294	924	10.03.02	3660	511613	66008
354.377-010 BIRTH ATTENDANT (medical ser.)	3124	44433433355	MNNNNNNNFFOOFFNOONNON	NNNN2NNNNNNNNNN	P,J	294	929	10.03.02	5236	511615	66008
354.377-014 HOME ATTENDANT (personal ser.)	3223	33444434344	MNNONONFFOOFFNOOOOOO	ONNO2NNNNNNNNNN	V,P,J	294	942	10.03.03	5236	510904	66011
354.677-010 FIRST-AID ATTENDANT (any industry)	3233	33443333354	LNNNNNNFFOOONFFNNNON	NNNN2NNNNNNNNNN	V,P,S,J	294	929	10.03.02	5236	000000	66008
355.354-010 PHYSICAL THERAPY AIDE (medical ser.)	3234	33444433344	MNNOOOONFFONFFNNNNON	NNNN3NNNNNNNNNN	P,T	294	926	10.03.02	5233	512601	68032

DOT #	DOT Title & Industry	Trng	Aptitude	Physical	Environment	Tempra	WkF	MPSMS	GOE	SOC	CIP	OES
355.374-010	AMBULANCE ATTENDANT (medical ser.)	3233	44444433344	MFFFFNFFONOONONNNON	NNNN2NNNNNNNNNNN	V,P,S,J	294	929	10.03.02	5233	510904	66023
355.374-014	CERTIFIED MEDICATION TECHNICIAN (medical ser.)	3334	33333222344	MNNNNNNFFFOFFNFNONOO	NNNN3NNNNNNNNNNN	P,T,J	294	926	10.03.02	5233	511614	66026
355.377-010	OCCUPATIONAL THERAPY AIDE (medical ser.)	3224	44444443355	MNNNNNNFFFNFFNONNNN	NNNN3NNNNNNNNNNN	U,P	294	926	10.03.02	5233	512302	66021
355.377-014	PSYCHIATRIC AIDE (medical ser.)	3234	33444444355	MNNONNNFFOOFFNFNNNNF	NNNN2NNNNNNNNNNNO	V,S,P	294	926	10.03.02	5236	512601	66014
355.377-018	MENTAL-RETARDATION AIDE (medical ser.)	4336	33444444454	MNNOOONFFONOONONOOON	NNNN3NNNNNNNNNNNO	P,J,V	294	926	10.03.02	5233	511502	66014
355.667-010	MORGUE ATTENDANT (medical ser.)	3224	34434333345	MNNNNNNFFONNNNONNNN	NNNN2NNNNNNNNNNNO	R	291	929	02.04.02	5233	000000	66005
355.674-010	CHILD-CARE ATTENDANT, SCHOOL (personal ser.)	3122	44444444445	MONOOONFFFOOONQNONN	NNNO2NNNNNNNNNNN	V,P,J	291	926	10.03.03	5233	200202	68038
355.674-014	NURSE ASSISTANT (medical ser.)	3224	44444343344	MNNNNNNFFFFNFNNNON	NNNN2NNNNNNNNNNN	V,P,S	294	926	10.03.03	5236	512601	66008
355.674-018	ORDERLY (medical ser.)	3224	44444343344	HNNONONFFOOOONONNON	NNNN2NNNNNNNNNNN	V,P,S	294	926	10.03.02	5236	511614	66008
355.674-022	RESPIRATORY-THERAPY AIDE (medical ser.)	3334	44433333445	MNNONNNFFFNOONFNNNNN	NNNN3NNNNNNNNNNN	J,V	031	926	10.03.02	5233	510908	66099
355.677-014	TRANSPORTER, PATIENTS (medical ser.)	2122	44444444445	MNNNNNNFFONFFNONNNN	NNNN2NNNNNNNNNNN	R,P,U	291	926	10.03.03	5236	000000	66099
355.687-014	GRAVES REGISTRATION SPECIALIST (military ser.)	2223	44444434455	VNNFFNFFONOOONFNNNNN	FNNN3NONNNNNNNNN	R	291	907	02.04.02	5233	000000	69999
357.477-010	BAGGAGE CHECKER (air trans.; motor trans.)	3233	34444344354	MNNFNNNFFONFFNFNNNN	NNNN3NNNNNNNNNNN	P,J	291	850	09.05.03	5262	080709	98999
357.677-010	PORTER (air trans.; motor trans.; r.r. trans.)	2122	44444444445	MNNFNNNFFNFNFNNONN	ONNN3NNNNNNNNNNN	P,R	011	905	09.05.03	5262	080709	98999
358.137-010	CHECKROOM CHIEF (any industry)	3235	33444434444	LNNNNNNFFFNFNFNNON	NNNN3NNNNNNNNNNN	D,P	291	909	09.05.03	5251	080299	61099
358.677-010	CHECKROOM ATTENDANT (any industry)	2222	44444344455	LNNNNNFFNFNFNNNNN	NNNN3NNNNNNNNNNN	R,P	291	909	09.05.03	5269	080903	69999
358.677-014	LOCKER-ROOM ATTENDANT (personal ser.)	2222	44444444455	LNNNONNNFFFNFFNNONNN	NNNN3NNNNNNNNNNN	V,P	291	909	09.05.07	5269	080903	69999
358.677-018	REST ROOM ATTENDANT (any industry)	2112	44454544455	LNNNONNNFFONNNNNNNNN	NNNN3NNNNNNNNNNN	R,P	291	905	09.05.07	5269	000000	68032
358.687-010	CHANGE-HOUSE ATTENDANT (any industry)	2122	44444444345	MNNNNNNFFONNNNNNNNN	NNNF3NNNNNNNNNNN	R	031	905	05.12.18	5244	000605	67005
359.137-010	SUPERVISOR, HOSPITALITY HOUSE (amuse. & rec.)	4346	33344344455	LNNOOONFFONFNFNNOONN	NNNN3NNNNNNNNNNN	V,D,P,J	282	919	09.01.01	5251	520901	61099
359.363-010	HEALTH-EQUIPMENT SERVICER (medical ser.)	3235	39444433344	MNNFNNNFFNFNFNNNOOO	NNNN3NNNNNNNNNNN	T,J	013	929	05.08.03	8214	470106	66099
359.367-010	ESCORT (personal ser.)	3232	33444444444	LNNNNNNOOONFFNONNNNN	NNNN3NNNNNNNNNNN	V,J,P	291	909	09.01.01	5269	000000	69999
359.367-014	WEIGHT-REDUCTION SPECIALIST (personal ser.)	3233	33454344455	LNNNNNNNOONFFNONONN	NNNN3NNNNNNNNNNN	P,J	291	909	09.05.01	5269	200404	69999
359.567-010	REDUCING-SALON ATTENDANT (personal ser.)	2222	44444343345	MMNFNNNFFNFNFNNNON	NNFF4NNNNNNNNNNN	P	291	909	09.05.01	5269	000000	69999
359.573-010	BLIND AIDE (personal ser.)	3223	33434334334	LNNNNNNFFNFNFFFFF	ONNN3NNNNNNNNNNN	V,P	291	909	10.03.03	5263	200202	68035
359.667-010	CHAPERON (personal ser.)	3222	33444444455	LNNNNNNNNNNFNOFNNNF	NNNN3NNNNNNNNNNN	V,P	291	942	04.02.03	5269	200202	69999
359.673-010	CHAUFFEUR (domestic ser.)	2123	34434344434	LNNOONFFNNNNNNFFFF	NNNN3NNNNNNNNNNN	V	850	850	09.03.02	8216	000000	97114
359.673-014	CHAUFFEUR, FUNERAL CAR (personal ser.)	2124	34434534333	VNNONNFFNNNNNFFFFF	NNNN2NNNNNNNNNNN	R,T	013	907	05.08.03	8216	000000	97114
359.677-010	ATTENDANT, CHILDREN'S INSTITUTION (any industry)	3233	33449343444	MNNFNFNFFONFFNFNNOF	NNNN3NNNNNNNNNNN	D,J,J	291	924	10.03.03	5264	200202	68038
359.677-014	FUNERAL ATTENDANT (personal ser.)	2123	44444444454	MMNONNOONFFNNNNNNNN	NNNN2NNNNNNNNNNN	P	291	907	09.01.04	5269	080299	68041
359.677-018	NURSERY SCHOOL ATTENDANT (any industry)	3234	33444444454	LNNFONNFFONFFNNOONO	NNNN3NNNNNNNNNNN	V,P	291	942	10.03.03	5264	200202	68038
359.677-022	PASSENGER SERVICE REPRESENTATIVE (air trans.)	3233	33444434445	LNNONNNFFNFNFNFOONNO	NNNN4NNNNNNNNNNN	V,P	297	855	09.01.04	5257	080709	69999
359.677-026	PLAYROOM ATTENDANT (any industry)	3233	33433433344	LNNQOONFFOMCCNFNNNON	NNNN3NNNNNNNNNNN	V,P,E	291	942	10.03.03	5264	200202	68038
359.677-030	RESEARCH SUBJECT (any industry)	3231	33433333444	LNNNNNNOONNOONNNNNNN	NNCN3NNNNNNNNNNF	U	291	929	09.05.06	5269	000000	69999
359.685-010	CREMATOR (personal ser.)	3223	34444434355	HNNNNNNFFONNNNNONNN	NNON2NNNNNNNNNNN	R,T	031	907	06.04.19	7759	000000	69999
359.687-010	PALLBEARER (personal ser.)	1111	44545444455	MNNNNNNFFQONNNNNNON	ONNN2NNNNNNNNNNN	R	291	907	09.05.03	5269	000000	69999
361.137-010	SUPERVISOR, LAUNDRY (laundry & rel.)	3336	33444434454	MNNNNNNFFFFNFNNNNON	NNFC3NNNNNNNNNNN	D,P,J	031	906	05.09.02	6700	200301	81008
361.587-010	FLATWORK TIER (laundry & rel.)	2222	44454444345	LNNFNNFFFNNNFNNNNN	NNNN3NNNNNNNNNNN	R	062	906	06.04.35	7850	200605	83005
361.665-010	WASHER, MACHINE (laundry & rel.)	3224	44444544355	MMNFNNNFFONOONNNNNNN	NNFF3NNNNNNNNNNN	R,U	031	906	06.04.35	7658	200301	92726
361.682-010	RUG CLEANER, MACHINE (laundry & rel.)	3114	44543544354	MNNONNNFFOONNNNNONOO	NNNF3NNNNNNNNNNNO	R,T	031	906	06.02.18	7658	200309	92726
361.684-010	LAUNDERER, HAND (laundry & rel.)	2122	44443433354	MMNNNNNFFNNNNNNNNN	NNNC3NNNNNNNNNNN	V,J	031	906	06.04.35	7658	200309	92726
361.684-014	LAUNDRY WORKER I (any industry)	2112	44444443344	MNNNNNNFFQONNNNNNON	NNNO3NNNNNNNNNNN	V,J	031	906	05.12.18	7658	200301	92726
361.684-018	SPOTTER I (laundry & rel.)	3113	44543534353	MNNNNNNFFOONNNNNNNN	NNNN3NNNNNNNNNNN	J	031	420	06.02.27	7759	200301	93999
361.685-010	CONDITIONER-TUMBLER OPERATOR (laundry & rel.)	2122	45445444455	LNNNNNNFFNNNNNNNNNN	NNFF3NNNNNNNNNNN	R	141	906	06.04.35	7658	200605	92923
361.685-014	CONTINUOUS-TOWEL ROLLER (laundry & rel.)	2112	44554544355	LNNNNNNFFONNNNNNNNN	NNFF3NNNNNNNNNNN	R	163	906	06.04.35	7658	200605	92726
361.685-018	LAUNDRY WORKER II (any industry)	2112	44444444455	MNNNONNNFFNNNONNNNN	NNFF3NNNNNNNNNNN	R	031	906	06.04.35	7658	200301	92726
361.685-022	PATCHING-MACHINE OPERATOR (laundry & rel.)	1112	44544533353	LNNNNNNFFNNNNNNNNN	NNNN3NNNNNNNNNNN	R	032	906	06.04.35	7658	200605	92726
361.686-010	WASHING-MACHINE LOADER-AND-PULLER (laundry & rel.)	2112	44544544455	HNNNNNNFFNNNNNNNNN	NNNF3NNNNNNNNNNN	R	011	906	06.04.35	8725	200309	98502
361.687-010	ASSEMBLER, WET WASH (laundry & rel.)	2112	44544444455	MNNFNNNFFONNNFNNNNN	NNNF3NNNNNNNNNNN	R	221	906	05.09.03	7850	200309	83005
361.687-014	CLASSIFIER (laundry & rel.)	2122	44554444454	LNNONNNFFONNNNFNNNNN	NNNF3NNNNNNNNNNN	R	221	906	06.03.02	7850	200605	83005
361.687-018	LAUNDRY LABORER (laundry & rel.)	1112	44444444454	MNNNONNNFFONNNONNNNN	NNNF3NNNNNNNNNNN	R	011	906	06.04.35	8769	200309	98999

DOT #	DOT Title & Industry	Trng	Aptitude	Physical	Environment	Tempra	WkF	MPSMS	GOE	SOC	CIP	OES
361.687-022	LINEN GRADER (laundry & rel.)	1112	4444444454	LNNONNNFFNNNNONNNON	NNNN3NNNNNNNNN	J	221	906	06.03.02	7850	200309	83005
361.687-026	SHAKER, WEARING APPAREL (laundry & rel.)	1112	44544544455	LNNNNNNFFNNNNNONNONN	NNNF3NNNNNNNNN	R	062	906	06.04.35	8769	200301	98999
361.687-030	WASHER, HAND (laundry & rel.)	2112	44444544354	LNNFNNNFFONNNNNNNNON	NNNF3NNNNNNNNN	R	031	906	06.04.35	8769	200309	98999
362.381-010	SPOTTER II (laundry & rel.)	3224	34443433353	LNNFNNNFFONNNNNNNNFN	NNFN3NNNNNNNNN	V,J,T	031	906	06.02.16	6855	200301	89514
362.382-010	DRY-CLEANER APPRENTICE (laundry & rel.)	3225	34443444353	MNNONNNFFONNNNONNOON	NNFN3NONNNNNNNN	V,J,T	031	906	06.02.16	7658	200301	92726
362.382-014	DRY CLEANER (laundry & rel.)	3225	34443444353	MNNONNNFFONNNNONNOON	NNFN3NONNNNNNNN	V,J,T	031	906	06.02.16	7658	200301	92726
362.684-010	DRY CLEANER, HAND (laundry & rel.)	2113	44443433353	MNNCNNNCCCCNNNCNNCCN	NNNC3NONNNNNNNN	V	031	906	06.04.35	7759	200309	93999
362.684-014	FUR CLEANER (laundry & rel.)	3225	34443544353	LNNONNNFFOONNFNNFFN	NNNN3NFNNNNNNNN	R,J	031	906	06.02.27	7658	200301	92726
362.684-018	FUR CLEANER, HAND (laundry & rel.)	3125	45443444353	LNNNNNNFFONNNFNNFFN	NNNN3NFNNNNNNNN	R,T	031	447	06.04.35	7759	200301	93999
362.684-022	FURNITURE CLEANER (laundry & rel.)	2123	44443444354	MNNFOONFFONNNCNNCCN	NNNN3NFNNNNNNNN	R	031	906	06.04.35	7759	200501	93999
362.684-026	LEATHER CLEANER (laundry & rel.)	3223	44454444353	LNNFNNNFFNNNNNNNNNN	NNNO4NONNNNNNNN	R,T	031	529	06.04.35	7658	200301	92726
362.685-010	FEATHER RENOVATOR (laundry & rel.)	1112	44544544454	LNNNNNNFFNNNNNNNNNN	NNNN4NNNNNNNNN	R	031	906	06.04.35	7658	200309	98999
362.686-010	DRY-CLEANER HELPER (laundry & rel.)	2112	44544454344	MNNFNNNFFNNNNNNNNON	NNNO4NONNNNNNNN	R	031	906	06.04.35	8617	200301	98999
362.686-014	RUG-CLEANER HELPER (laundry & rel.)	2122	44443444353	MNNONNNFFNNNNNNNNNN	NNNN3NNNNNNNNN	R	031	906	06.04.35	8617	200309	98999
362.687-010	GLOVE CLEANER, HAND (laundry & rel.)	2122	44443444353	LNNONNNFFFNNNFNNFFN	NNNF3NNNNNNNNN	R,J	031	529	06.04.35	8769	200309	98999
362.687-014	LINING SCRUBBER (laundry & rel.)	1112	44543544354	LNNONNNFFONNNNONNON	NNNN3NFNNNNNNNN	R	031	906	06.04.35	8769	200309	98999
362.687-018	SHAVER (laundry & rel.)	1112	45544533455	LNNNNNNFFONNNNNNNNN	NNNF3NNNNNNNNN	R	161	906	06.04.35	8769	200309	98999
363.681-010	SILK FINISHER (laundry & rel.)	3124	34443533344	LNNNNNNFFNNNFNNFFN	NNNF4NFNNNNNNNN	R,T	032	906	06.04.35	6855	200309	89517
363.682-010	LEATHER FINISHER (laundry & rel.)	3124	44443434345	LNNNNNNFFNNNFNOFNN	NNNF4NFNNNNNNNO	R,T	032	529	06.04.35	7657	200309	92728
363.682-014	PRESSER, ALL-AROUND (laundry & rel.)	2213	44443533345	MNNFNNNFFNNNNNNNNNC	NNCC4NCNNNNNNNC	R	032	906	06.04.35	7657	200301	92728
363.682-018	PRESSER, MACHINE (any industry)	2112	44544533345	MNNNNNNFFNNNNFNNNNN	NNFF3NNNNNNNNF	R	032	906	06.04.05	7657	200309	92728
363.684-010	BLOCKER (laundry & rel.)	3213	34433433344	LNNFNNNFFFNNNFNNFFN	NNNF4NONNNNNNNF	R,J,T	032	906	06.02.27	7657	200309	92728
363.684-014	HAT BLOCKER (laundry & rel.)	3114	34433533334	LNNFNNNFFFNNNFNNFN	NNNF3NFNNNNNNNN	R,T	032	906	06.02.27	7657	200309	92728
363.684-018	PRESSER, HAND (any industry)	2112	44534534354	LNNNNNNFFONNNNNNNNN	NNFO3NNNNNNNNN	R	032	906	06.04.35	7759	200301	93921
363.685-010	PRESS OPERATOR (laundry & rel.)	2112	44544544355	LLNONNNNFFNNNNNNNNNN	NNFF3NNNNNNNNN	R	032	906	06.04.35	7657	200309	98502
363.685-014	PRESSER, AUTOMATIC (laundry & rel.)	2113	44544544345	LNNNNNNFFNNNNNNNNNN	NNFF3NNNNNNNNN	R	032	906	06.04.35	7657	200309	92728
363.685-018	PRESSER, FORM (any industry)	2212	44443533335	LNNNNNNNFFNNNNFNNNNN	NNFF3NONNNNNNNO	R,T	032	906	06.04.35	7657	200309	92728
363.685-022	PRESSER, HANDKERCHIEF (laundry & rel.)	1112	44544544345	LNNNNNNNFFONNNNNNNNN	NNFO3NNNNNNNNN	R	032	906	06.04.35	7657	200301	92728
363.685-026	SHIRT PRESSER (laundry & rel.)	2112	44544544355	LNNNNNNNFFNNNNNNNNN	NNFF3NNNNNNNNN	R	032	906	06.04.35	7657	200309	92728
363.686-010	FLATWORK FINISHER (laundry & rel.)	2112	44544534355	LNNNNNNNFOFNNNFNNNNN	NNFF3NNNNNNNNN	R	032	906	06.04.35	7759	200301	98502
363.687-010	GLOVE FORMER (glove & mit.; laundry & rel.)	1113	44444534355	LNOONNNCCFNNNNNNNNN	NNNN3NNNNNNNNF	R,J	032	449	06.04.27	8725	200309	98999
363.687-014	IRONER, SOCK (laundry & rel.)	1111	45544544355	LNNNNNNCCFNNNNNNNNN	NNCF3NNNNNNNNN	R	032	906	06.04.35	8769	200301	98999
363.687-018	PUFF IRONER (laundry & rel.)	1111	45544543355	LNNNNNNFFNNNNNNNNNN	NNNN3NNNNNNNNN	R	032	906	06.04.27	8769	200309	93999
363.687-022	STRETCHER-DRIER OPERATOR (laundry & rel.)	2112	44544543355	LONNNNNNCCCONNNFNNNNN	NNON3NNNNNNNNN	R	141	906	06.04.35	8769	200309	98999
364.361-010	DYER (laundry & rel.)	4327	34343444452	MNNNNNNFFFNNNFNNFFN	NNCC3NNNNNNNNN	J,T	152	420	05.05.16	6855	200309	89521
364.361-014	RUG DYER I (laundry & rel.)	4338	34443444352	MNNNNNNFFNNNNFNNFFN	NNCC3NNNNNNNNN	J	152	431	05.05.16	6855	200309	89521
364.381-010	PAINTER, RUG TOUCH-UP (laundry & rel.)	3126	34532533352	LNNNNNNFFFNNNFNNFFN	NNNN3NNNNNNNNN	J	262	431	01.06.03	6855	200309	89521
364.684-010	RUG DYER II (laundry & rel.)	3225	33443444353	LNOONNNCCFNNNNFNNOFN	NNNO2NNNNNNNNN	R,T	152	431	05.10.07	7658	200309	92726
364.684-014	SHOE DYER (personal ser.)	2213	44453443352	LNNNNNNNFFNNNNFNNFN	NNNN2NNNNNNNNN	J,R,T	152	906	05.12.14	7759	480304	93999
364.684-018	SPRAYER, LEATHER (laundry & rel.)	2124	34543543353	LNNNNNNNFFNNNFNONNFN	NNNF3NNNNNNNNN	R,T	152	906	05.12.14	7759	200309	93999
364.687-010	DYER HELPER (laundry & rel.)	2113	44544544354	HNNNNNNFFNNNNNNNNNN	NNFF3NNNNNNNNN	R	031	420	06.04.35	8769	200309	98999
364.687-014	RUG-DYER HELPER (laundry & rel.)	2113	44544544354	MNOONNNFFONNNNFNNNON	NNCC3NNNNNNNNN	R	152	431	05.12.14	8769	200309	98999
365.131-010	SHOE-REPAIR SUPERVISOR (personal ser.)	3117	33433433234	LNNNNN4NNNNNNNNNNN	NNNN4NNNNNNNNN	D,P,V	102	522	05.05.15	6700	520205	81008
365.361-010	LUGGAGE REPAIRER (any industry)	3226	34433433344	MNNNNNNFFFNFNFNNNON	NNNN3NNNNNNNNN	J,T	102	524	05.10.01	6854	000000	89511
365.361-014	SHOE REPAIRER (personal ser.)	3216	33433433234	LNNNNNFFONNNNNNNNN	NNNN2NNNNNNNNN	R,T,J	102	906	05.05.15	6854	480304	98999
365.674-010	SHOE-REPAIRER HELPER (personal ser.)	2214	44443544354	LNNNNNFFONNNNNNNNN	NNNN2NNNNNNNNN	J,T	102	906	05.05.15	8619	480304	98511
366.677-010	SHOE SHINER (personal ser.)	1112	44554544354	LNNFNNFFONNNNNNNNN	NNNN2NNNNNNNNN	P,R	291	906	09.05.07	5269	000000	69999
369.137-010	SUPERVISOR, DRY CLEANING (laundry & rel.)	4337	33333344453	MNNNNNNFFFNFNFNNNON	NNFF4NNNNNNNNN	V,D,P	031	906	06.04.01	6700	200301	81008
369.137-014	SUPERVISOR, RUG CLEANING (laundry & rel.)	4237	33432344453	LNNNNNNOOONFFNONNON	NNNN3NNNNNNNNN	D,J,P	031	431	05.12.01	6700	200309	81008
369.167-010	MANAGER, LAUNDROMAT (laundry & rel.)	4336	22223344454	SNONNNNFFNOONFNNONO	NNNN3NNNNNNNNN	D,P,J	031	906	11.11.04	7100	521401	81008
369.367-010	FUR-STORAGE CLERK (retail trade)	4336	33343344453	LNNNNNNFFFFNFNNFFN	NNNN3NNNNNNNNN	J,V	211	447	05.09.01	4363	080705	49017

DOT #	DOT Title & Industry	Trng	Aptitude	Physical	Environment	Tempra	WkF	MPSMS	GOE	SOC	CiP	OES
369.367-014	RUG MEASURER (laundry & rel.; retail trade)	3224	34343444453	LNNNNNNFONNNNONNNON	NNNN3NNNNNNNNNN	R,J	231	906	05.09.02	4363	200309	49017
369.384-010	HATTER (laundry & rel.)	3126	34543544353	LNNNNNNCCOONNFNNNON	NNNF3NNNNNNNNNN	J,T	031	906	06.02.27	7759	200301	93999
369.384-014	RUG CLEANER, HAND (laundry & rel.)	3125	44444444344	MNNOONNFONNNNFNNNON	NNNN2NNNNNNNNNN	R,T	031	906	06.02.27	7759	200309	93999
369.387-010	LAUNDRY WORKER III (any industry)	2123	44444444455	LNNNONNNFFNNNNFNNNN	NNNN3NNNNNNNNNN	R,J	221	906	05.09.03	8769	200309	98999
369.467-010	MANAGER, BRANCH STORE (laundry & rel.)	3223	33344434454	LNNNNNNNFFNNFFNNNON	ONNNN3NNNNNNNNNN	D,P,R	292	906	09.04.02	4363	080299	49017
369.477-010	CURB ATTENDANT (laundry & rel.)	2222	44454344455	MNNNNNNFFNFFNFNNNNN	ONNNN2NNNNNNNNNN	R,P	291	906	09.04.02	8769	000000	98999
369.477-014	SERVICE-ESTABLISHMENT ATTENDANT (laundry & rel.; personal ser.)	3223	33444434455	LNNNNNNNFFONFFNFNNNON	NNNN2NNNNNNNNNN	J,P	291	906	09.04.03	4363	200301	49017
369.587-010	VAULT CUSTODIAN (laundry & rel.)	2123	34444334455	MNNNNNNNCCFNNNFNNNNN	NNNN2NNNNNNNNNN	J	221	853	05.09.03	7759	200309	93999
369.677-010	SELF-SERVICE-LAUNDRY-AND-DRY-CLEANING ATTENDANT (laundry & rel.)	3132	44444444454	MNNNNNNNFONFFNFNNNON	NNNN3NNNNNNNNNN	P,V	291	906	09.04.02	4363	200301	49017
369.684-010	FUR GLAZER (fur goods)	2122	44543543353	LONNNNNNCCFNNNCNNOON	NNNN3NNNNNNNNNN	J	153	447	06.04.35	7759	200309	93999
369.684-014	LAUNDRY OPERATOR (laundry & rel.)	2123	44444444344	MNNNNNNNFFONNNFNNNNN	NNOO4NNNNNNNNNN	R	031	906	06.04.35	7658	200309	92726
369.684-018	UMBRELLA REPAIRER (any industry)	2124	34443443355	LNNNNNNNFONNNNONNNNN	NNNN2NNNNNNNNNN	J,T	102	619	05.10.01	7759	000000	93999
369.685-010	FUR BLOWER (retail trade)	2112	44544544454	LNNNNNNNFFONNNNFNNNON	NNNN3NNNNNNNNNN	R,T	031	447	06.04.39	7658	200309	92726
369.685-014	FUR CLEANER, MACHINE (fur goods; laundry & rel.; retail trade; wholesale)	2123	34443444453	LNNNNNNNFFONNNFNNNON	NNNN3NNNNNNNNNN	R,T	031	906	06.04.35	7658	200301	92726
369.685-018	FUR IRONER (laundry & rel.)	3113	34443534335	LNNNNNNNFFONNNFNONNNN	NNNN3NNNNNNNNNN	R,T	032	906	06.04.35	7657	200309	92728
369.685-022	FUR-GLAZING-AND-POLISHING-MACHINE OPERATOR (laundry & rel.)	2113	44443543445	LNNNNNNFFNNNNFNNNNN	NNNN3NNNNNNNNNN	J,T	032	906	06.04.35	7658	200309	92998
369.685-026	RUG-DRY-ROOM ATTENDANT (laundry & rel.)	2112	44544544355	MNNONNNFFNNNNONNNNN	NNNN3NNNNNNNNNN	R	141	906	06.04.35	7659	200309	92923
369.685-030	SHIRT-FOLDING-MACHINE OPERATOR (garment; laundry & rel.)	2122	44544543345	LNNNNNNFFONNNNONONNN	NNNN3NNNNNNNNNN	R	062	440	06.04.05	7659	200303	92998
369.685-034	TUMBLER OPERATOR (laundry & rel.)	2112	44554544455	MNNNNNNNFFONNNNONNNNN	NNOO3NNNNNNNNNN	R	141	906	06.04.35	7659	200309	92923
369.686-010	FOLDING-MACHINE OPERATOR (laundry & rel.)	2112	44444534355	LNNNNNNNFFONNNFNNNNN	NNNN3NNNNNNNNNN	R	062	435	06.04.35	8725	200309	98502
369.687-010	ASSEMBLER (laundry & rel.)	2123	44444444454	LNNNNNNFFNNNNFNNNNN	NNFF3NNNNNNNNNN	R,T	221	906	06.03.02	7850	200301	83005
369.687-014	CHECKER (laundry & rel.)	2112	44454344454	MNNNNNNNFFONNNNONNOON	NNNN3NNNNNNNNNON	R	221	906	05.09.03	7820	200309	83005
369.687-018	FOLDER (laundry & rel.)	2112	44544444454	LNNNNNNFFONNNNFNNNON	NNOC3NNNNNNNNNN	R	061	906	06.04.35	8769	200309	98999
369.687-022	INSPECTOR (laundry & rel.)	2123	44543543453	LNNONNNNFFNNNNFNFON	NNNN3NNNNNNNFON	R,T	212	906	06.03.02	7820	200301	83005
369.687-026	MARKER (laundry & rel.)	2112	44444343344	MNNFNNNFFONNNNFNNNON	NNNF3NNNNNNNNON	R	221	906	05.09.01	8769	200301	83005
369.687-030	RUG INSPECTOR (laundry & rel.)	3124	44542444453	LNNNNNNFFNNNNNFNFFN	NNNN3NNNNNNNNNN	J,T	212	431	06.03.02	7820	200309	83005
371.362-010	DRAWBRIDGE OPERATOR (r.r. trans.)	3124	34423334344	LNNNNNONFFNNFONNNOO	CNNNN3NNNNNNNNNN	R,T	011	859	05.11.04	8245	000000	97802
371.567-010	GUARD, SCHOOL-CROSSING (government ser.)	2223	33445545444	LNNNNNFONNFFNFOOOF	NNNN3NNNNNNNNNN	P	293	959	10.03.03	5142	430109	63044
371.667-010	CROSSING TENDER (any industry)	2223	34433444454	LNNNNNNFFONFFNFOOOF	NNNN3NNNNNNNNNN	R	293	851	05.12.20	5142	430109	63044
372.137-010	CORRECTION OFFICER, HEAD (government ser.)	4236	22444344455	LNNNNNNOOONFFNNNNNNN	NNNN3NNNNNNNNNN	D,J,P,S	293	959	04.01.01	5112	430107	61005
372.167-010	DISPATCHER, SECURITY GUARD (business ser.)	4336	23344344455	LNNNNNNFFNFFNFNOONN	NNNN3NNNNNNNNNN	D,P	293	969	04.02.02	4751	000000	58002
372.167-014	GUARD, CHIEF (any industry)	3236	33433444454	LNNNNNNOOONFFNOFOOOF	ONNN3NNNNNNNNNN	D,P	293	899	04.01.01	5113	430109	61099
372.167-018	JAILER, CHIEF (government ser.)	4347	22234344455	SNNNNNNFFNFFNFNNNNN	ONNNN3NNNNNNNNNO	D,J,P,V	295	951	04.01.01	5112	430109	61005
372.167-022	MANAGER, ARMORED TRANSPORT SERVICE (business ser.)	4346	33344244445	LNNOONNFFNFFNFNNNN	ONNN4NNNNNNNNNO	J	295	899	11.11.04	1342	080299	15023
372.267-010	SPECIAL AGENT (r.r. trans.)	4345	22333444444	LNFNNNNFFNNNNFNNNNN	NNNN4NNNNNNNNNN	P,S,J	271	851	04.02.02	5144	430109	63038
372.363-010	PROTECTIVE OFFICER (government ser.)	3234	33444434344	MONOONNOOONONOONONOO	ONNN2NNNNNNNNNO	V,P,S	293	959	04.02.02	5132	430109	63014
372.367-010	COMMUNITY SERVICE OFFICER, PATROL (government ser.)	3233	33444444455	LNOOONNFFNFFNNNOONNO	CNNNN4NNNNNNNNNO	J,P,S	293	951	04.02.03	5132	430109	63014
372.367-014	JAILER (government ser.)	3224	33443434355	LNNNNNNFFONFFNNOONFNF	NNNN2NNNNNNNNNO	P,S,J	293	959	04.02.01	5133	430109	63017
372.563-010	ARMORED-CAR GUARD AND DRIVER (business ser.)	3223	33334334335	MONONNNFFNONOOFFNNNF	ONNN4NNNNNNNNNO	R,P,S	293	899	04.02.02	5144	430109	63047
372.567-010	ARMORED-CAR GUARD (business ser.)	3223	33343334455	MNNNNNNNFFONOONFNNNNF	NNNN3NNNNNNNNNO	R,P,S	293	899	04.02.01	5144	430109	63047
372.567-014	GUARD, IMMIGRATION (government ser.)	3234	33444334345	MNNNNNNFFNFFNONNNNN	ONNN3NNNNNNNNNN	P,S	293	959	04.02.01	5133	430109	63017
372.667-010	AIRLINE SECURITY REPRESENTATIVE (air trans.)	2122	44433444455	LNNNNNNNOOONFFNOFOOOF	ONNN3NNNNNNNNNF	R,P	293	855	04.02.02	5144	430109	63047
372.667-014	BODYGUARD (personal ser.)	3223	33444343345	MNNNNNNFFNOONFFNNNF	FNNNN3NNNNNNNNOOF	P,S,J	293	909	04.02.02	5144	430109	63047
372.667-018	CORRECTION OFFICER (government ser.)	3224	33443434355	LNNNNNNFFNNNNFNNNNN	NNNN3NNNNNNNNNOF	S,P,J	293	951	04.02.01	5133	430109	63017
372.667-022	FLAGGER (construction)	2122	44444444444	LONONNNFFONOONFFNNOF	CNNNN4NNNNNNNNNF	R	293	850	05.12.20	5142	000000	63044
372.667-026	FLAGGER (amuse. & rec.)	2112	44434545455	LNNNNNNFFNNOONNFNNN	CNNNN3NNNNNNNNNN	T	282	913	12.01.02	8769	000000	63044
372.667-030	GATE GUARD (any industry)	3223	33444444455	LNNNNNNNOONFFNFFNNNNO	FNNNN3NNNNNNNNNF	R,P	293	361	04.02.02	5144	430109	63047
372.667-034	GUARD, SECURITY (any industry)	3123	34344444454	LNNNNNNFFNNOONFOOOOF	FNNNN2NNNNNNNNNO	R,P,S	293	905	04.02.02	5144	430109	63047
372.667-038	MERCHANT PATROLLER (business ser.)	2123	44444444445	LNNNNNNFFONFFNFONNNO	FNNNN2NNNNNNNNNO	J,P,S	293	969	04.02.02	5144	430109	63047
372.667-042	SCHOOL BUS MONITOR (government ser.)	2122	43444444455	LNNNNNNFFNNNNFNNFNF	NNNN3NNNNNNNNNN	P	293	959	04.02.03	5149	430109	63099
372.677-010	PATROL CONDUCTOR (government ser.)	3223	44444343435	LNNNNNNOOONOONOONNNO	NNNN3NNNNNNNNNO	P,R,S	293	951	04.02.01	5133	000000	63017

DOT #	DOT Title & Industry	Trng	Aptitude	Physical	Environment	Tempra	WkF	MPSMS	GOE	SOC	CIP	OES
373.117-010	FIRE CHIEF (government ser.)	5458	22333344453	LNNNNNOOONNFFNFOOOO	FNOO4NONOONONO	V,D,P,J,I	295	951	04.01.01	1131	430203	19005
373.134-010	FIRE CAPTAIN (government ser.)	4347	23324344433	MOOOOONFFONFFNFOOFOO	FNOO4NONOONONO	V,D,P,S,J	293	951	04.01.01	5111	430203	61002
373.167-010	BATTALION CHIEF (government ser.)	5448	22334444432	LOOOONONOOONFFNOOONOO	FNOO3NONOONONO	D,P,S,J	295	951	04.01.01	5111	430203	61002
373.167-014	CAPTAIN, FIRE-PREVENTION BUREAU (government ser.)	5448	22333344444	LONONONOOONFFNOOOFOO	ONNN3NONOONONO	V,D,P,J,I	295	951	04.01.01	5111	430203	61002
373.167-018	FIRE MARSHAL (any industry)	4337	33324344234	MOOOOOOFFNNOONFOOFOO	OOOO3NONOONONO	D,P,J,S	293	951	04.01.01	5111	430201	61002
373.267-010	FIRE INSPECTOR (government ser.)	4347	33433344444	LONOONOOONFFNFOOOFOO	ONNN3NNNNNNNNN	P,J	271	951	11.10.03	5122	430203	63002
373.267-014	FIRE MARSHAL (government ser.)	4347	33333344343	LOOOOOFFFNFFNFOONOO	NNNO3NONNNNNNOF	J,P,V	271	951	04.01.02	5122	430203	63002
373.267-018	FIRE-INVESTIGATION LIEUTENANT (government ser.)	5457	22222333342	MNNOOONFFFOFFNFOFOOO	NNNN4NONONNNNNO	V,J	271	951	11.10.03	5122	430203	63002
373.363-010	FIRE CHIEF'S AIDE (government ser.)	4236	33423344223	HOOOOONFFOOOONFOOOO	FNFF4NONOONOOO	V,S,J	231	951	04.02.04	5123	000000	63008
373.364-010	FIRE FIGHTER (any industry)	4236	33424434223	VOOOOOFFOOFFNFCFOFF	ONFF4NFNOFNFFF	V,S,J	293	951	04.02.04	5123	430203	63008
373.367-010	FIRE INSPECTOR (any industry)	3335	33333344334	MNNNNNNFFONOONFFNNNN	ONNN3NNNNNNNNN	J,T	293	951	04.02.02	5122	430203	63002
375.117-010	POLICE CHIEF (government ser.)	5349	22344344455	SNNNNNNNNNNFNFNNNN	NNNN3NNNNNNNNN	V,D,P,J,I	295	951	04.01.01	1131	430107	19005
375.133-010	POLICE SERGEANT, PRECINCT I (government ser.)	4236	33434343334	LNNNNNNOOONFFNFFOOOO	FNNN3NNNNNNNNO	D,P,S,J	271	951	04.01.01	5112	430107	61005
375.137-010	COMMANDER, IDENTIFICATION AND RECORDS (government ser.)	4338	22323333354	LNNNNNFFFNFFNNOFON	NNNN3NNNNNNNNN	D,J,P	271	951	07.01.06	5112	430107	61005
375.137-014	DESK OFFICER (government ser.)	4237	33344344455	SNNNNNNNOOONNFFNNN	NNNN3NNNNNNNNN	V,D,P	293	951	04.01.01	5112	430107	61005
375.137-018	POLICE LIEUTENANT, COMMUNITY RELATIONS (government ser.)	4338	22344344454	LNNNNNNOOONCNONOOOO	OOON4NNNNNNNNN	D,P,V	293	951	11.09.03	5112	430107	61005
375.137-022	SECRETARY OF POLICE (government ser.)	4347	23243244455	SNNNNNNNFFNFFNNOOO	NNNN3NNNNNNNNN	D,P,J	232	890	07.01.02	4511	520204	51002
375.137-026	TRAFFIC SERGEANT (government ser.)	4237	33433344444	LNNNNNNOOONFFNNOONNOO	FNNN3NNNNNNNNN	P,J	293	951	04.01.01	5112	430107	61005
375.137-030	COMMANDER, POLICE RESERVES (government ser.)	4338	22444344455	LNNNNNNFFNFNNNNONN	NNNN3NNNNNNNNN	D,I,P	293	951	04.01.01	5112	430107	61005
375.137-034	COMMANDING OFFICER, POLICE (government ser.)	4348	22344344455	LNNNNNNOOONNFFNFFNN	NNNN3NNNNNNNNN	D,J,P	271	951	04.01.01	5112	430107	61005
375.137-038	COMPLAINT EVALUATION SUPERVISOR (government ser.)	4238	22444433354	LNNNNNNFFNFNFNNFON	NNNN3NNNNNNNNN	J,S,P	271	951	07.04.05	5112	430107	51002
375.163-010	COMMANDING OFFICER, MOTORIZED SQUAD (government ser.)	4348	22344344455	LNNNNNNOOONFNFFFNF	FNNN3NNNNNNNNF	D,J,P	295	951	04.01.01	5112	430107	61005
375.163-014	PILOT, HIGHWAY PATROL (air trans.)	5346	22322333324	LNNNNNNNFFNFNFFFOF	NNNN5NNNNNNNNO	J,S,T,V	271	951	04.01.02	5132	490102	63014
375.167-010	COMMANDING OFFICER, HOMICIDE SQUAD (government ser.)	4347	22443344434	LNNNNNNOOONNOONNON	NNNN3NNNNNNNNN	D,J,P,S	293	951	04.01.01	5112	430107	63028
375.167-014	COMMANDING OFFICER, INVESTIGATION DIVISION (government ser.)	4237	22344244454	LNNNNNNOOONFFNNNON	NNNN3NNNNNNNNN	V,D,P,J	293	951	04.01.01	5112	430107	61005
375.167-018	COMMANDING OFFICER, MOTOR EQUIPMENT (government ser.)	4348	22344244455	SNNNNNNOOONFFNFOOONN	NNNN3NNNNNNNNN	D,J,P	295	590	11.05.03	1370	470604	81002
375.167-022	DETECTIVE CHIEF (government ser.)	4237	22443344454	LNNNNNNOOONNFFNOOOOO	ONNN3NNNNNNNNO	V,D,P,J	271	951	04.01.01	5112	430107	61005
375.167-026	HARBOR MASTER (government ser.)	5348	22344444455	SNNNNNNNOOONFFNNNNNN	NNNN3NNNNNNNNN	V,D,P,J	295	951	04.01.01	1131	430107	19005
375.167-030	LAUNCH COMMANDER, HARBOR POLICE (government ser.)	4236	33424334444	LONOOOOOOOOFFNFFOONO	FNNN3NNNNNNNNO	D,P,S,J	293	951	04.01.01	5112	430107	61005
375.167-034	POLICE CAPTAIN, PRECINCT (government ser.)	5348	22343344444	LNNNNNNOOONNFFNFFNF	NNNN3NNNNNNNNN	D,P,J	293	931	04.01.01	5132	430107	63011
375.167-038	POLICE LIEUTENANT, PATROL (government ser.)	4348	33343344444	LNNIOONNOOONFFNONOO	ONNN3NNNNNNNNN	D,J,P,S	293	951	04.01.01	5132	430107	31314
375.167-042	SPECIAL AGENT (government ser.)	5557	22223334434	MOOOOOOOFFFFFNFNNOF	FNNN3NNNNNNNNO	J,P,S,V	271	951	04.01.02	5132	430107	63014
375.167-046	TRAFFIC LIEUTENANT (government ser.)	4237	22333334434	MOOOOOOONFFNFFFFF	FNNN3NNNNNNNNF	V,P,S,J	293	951	04.01.01	5112	430107	63014
375.167-050	COMMANDER, INTERNAL AFFAIRS (government ser.)	4348	22344444454	LNNNNNNOOONFFNQONNN	FNNN3NNNNNNNNN	D,J,P	271	951	04.01.01	5112	430107	61005
375.167-054	POLICE ACADEMY PROGRAM COORDINATOR (government ser.)	4347	22494334445	LNNNNNNOOONFFNFFONOO	NNNN3NNNNNNNNN	D,J,P,V	296	931	04.01.01	5132	430107	63011
375.227-010	POLICE-ACADEMY INSTRUCTOR (government ser.)	4237	22333334455	LNNNNNNNOOONFNONONN	NNNN3NNNNNNNNN	V,D,P,J	296	951	04.01.01	2249	430107	31314
375.263-010	ACCIDENT-PREVENTION-SQUAD POLICE OFFICER (government ser.)	4236	22323334354	LNNOONNOOONFFNOOONN	FNNN3NNNNNNNNO	V,D,P,J	271	951	04.01.02	5132	430107	63014
375.263-014	POLICE OFFICER I (government ser.)	4236	33433334334	MOOOOOOOONFFFOFFOO	ONNN3NNNNNNNNO	V,P,S,J	293	951	04.01.02	5132	430107	63014
375.263-018	STATE-HIGHWAY POLICE OFFICER (government ser.)	4236	33433434344	MOOOOOOONFFNFFFFOF	FNNN3NNNNNNNNN	V,P,S,J	293	951	04.01.02	5132	430107	63014
375.267-010	DETECTIVE (government ser.)	4347	33333344444	LNNNNNNOOONFFNFNNOON	FNNN3NNNNNNNNN	V,D,P	271	951	04.01.01	5132	430107	63011
375.267-014	DETECTIVE, NARCOTICS AND VICE (government ser.)	4237	22334334454	LOOOOOOFFOFFNFOFFOO	FNNN3NNNNNNNNO	V,P,S,J	271	951	04.01.02	5132	430107	63011
375.267-018	INVESTIGATOR, NARCOTICS (government ser.)	4237	22443344455	LNNOONNOOONFFNNOONN	FNNN3NNNNNNNNN	J,P,S	271	951	04.01.02	5132	430107	63011
375.267-022	INVESTIGATOR, VICE (government ser.)	4237	22443334354	LNNNNNNNFFNFFNNNON	FNNN3NNNNNNNNN	V,P,S,J	293	951	04.01.02	5132	430107	63011
375.267-026	POLICE INSPECTOR I (government ser.)	4347	22443344455	LNNNNNNOOONFFNFNNON	NNNN3NNNNNNNNN	V,D,P	271	951	04.01.01	5132	430107	21905
375.267-030	POLICE INSPECTOR II (government ser.)	4345	33433434454	LNNNNNNFFNFFNFNNOON	FNNN3NNNNNNNNN	P,S,J	293	951	04.01.01	5132	430107	21905
375.267-034	INVESTIGATOR, INTERNAL AFFAIRS (government ser.)	4347	22344334455	LNNNNNNOOONFFNFNNNN	NNNN3NNNNNNNNO	P,J	271	951	07.01.06	1473	430107	21905
375.267-038	POLICE OFFICER III (government ser.)	4237	33444333355	MNNNNNNFFNFFNFNNNN	NNNN3NNNNNNNNN	J,P,S	271	951	04.01.02	5132	430107	63014
375.267-042	POLICE OFFICER, SAFETY INSTRUCTION (government ser.)	3236	33444444455	LNNNNNNOOONFFNFNNNN	NNNN3NNNNNNNNN	I,P	293	951	04.01.02	5132	430107	63011
375.362-010	POLICE CLERK (government ser.)	4336	33343323455	SNNNNNNNFFNOONFNNNN	NNNN3NNNNNNNNN	T	231	951	07.05.01	4630	520408	55347

DOT #	DOT Title & Industry	Trng	Aptitude	Physical	Environment	Tempra	WkF	MPSMS	GOE	SOC	CIP	OES
375.363-010	BORDER GUARD (government ser.)	3235	33443434445	MOOOOOOOONFFNOOONNN	FNNN3NNNNNNNNNON	J,P,S	293	959	04.02.03	5132	430107	63014
375.367-010	POLICE OFFICER II (government ser.)	3125	33444434355	LNNNNNNFFFOFFNONNNNN	NNNN3NNNNNNNNNNN	P,S	293	959	04.02.01	5133	430107	63017
375.367-014	COMPLAINT EVALUATION OFFICER (government ser.)	4236	33444333354	SNNNNNNFFONFFNFNNNON	NNNN3NNNNNNNNNNN	J,S,P	271	951	07.04.05	5132	430107	63014
375.367-018	POLICE OFFICER, BOOKING (government ser.)	3334	33445344455	LNNNNNNFFNFFNFNNNNN	NNNN3NNNNNNNNNNN	J,P	231	951	04.02.01	5132	430107	63011
375.384-010	POLICE OFFICER, IDENTIFICATION AND RECORDS (government ser.)	4337	33322333354	LNNOOONFFFNNONFFNFON	FNNN5NNNNNNNNNNN	J,T,V	271	951	07.01.06	5132	430107	63011
375.387-010	FINGERPRINT CLASSIFIER (government ser.)	4236	34422344455	LNNNNNNOOONNNNNFFNFNF	NNNN3NNNNNNNNNNN	J,T	271	951	02.04.01	3990	430107	39999
375.587-010	PARKING ENFORCEMENT OFFICER (government ser.)	2122	44444444454	LNNNNNNFFFNNNNONNNON	CNNN3NNNNNNNNNNN	P,R	231	959	04.02.02	5134	430107	63021
376.137-010	MANAGER, INTERNAL SECURITY (business ser.)	4347	22343334454	LONOOOOFFONFFNFFOOFF	ONNN4NNNNNNNNNNO	V,D,P,I,J	293	969	04.01.01	5113	080299	61099
376.167-010	SPECIAL AGENT-IN-CHARGE (r.r. trans.)	4347	22344344455	SONOOONFFFNOONFNONNN	ONNN3NNNNNNNNNNN	V,D,J,P	293	951	04.01.01	5144	430109	63038
376.267-010	INVESTIGATOR, CASH SHORTAGE (retail trade)	4336	33334224455	SNNNNNNFFNOONFONONN	NNNN3NNNNNNNNNNN	P,J	271	969	11.10.01	5144	430109	63035
376.267-014	INVESTIGATOR, FRAUD (retail trade)	4437	33334344454	SNNNNNNFFONFFNFOOONN	NNNN4NNNNNNNNNNN	P,J	271	969	11.10.01	5144	430109	63035
376.267-018	INVESTIGATOR, PRIVATE (business ser.)	4345	33343344454	LNNOOONOOONFFNFOOFOO	FNNN3NNNNNNNNNNO	J,P,S,V	271	969	04.01.02	5144	430109	63035
376.267-022	SHOPPING INVESTIGATOR (business ser.)	3333	33343344455	LNNNNNNOOONFFNFNNNNN	NNNN3NNNNNNNNNNN	P,J	271	899	11.10.05	5144	430109	63035
376.367-010	ALARM INVESTIGATOR (business ser.)	3133	33433343344	LNNNNNNOOONFFNFONOOO	NNNN3NNNNNNNNNNN	S,P	293	969	04.02.04	5144	430109	63035
376.367-014	DETECTIVE I (any industry)	3234	33444444455	LNNOOONFFONFFNFNNNNF	NNNN3NNNNNNNNNNO	P,S,J	271	969	04.02.02	5144	430109	63035
376.367-018	HOUSE OFFICER (hotel & rest.)	3124	33444544444	LNNNNNNOOONFFNFNNNNN	NNNN3NNNNNNNNNNN	P,S	293	969	04.02.03	5144	430109	63047
376.367-022	INVESTIGATOR (utilities)	3236	33444444455	LNNNNNNOOONNNFFNNNNNN	NNNN3NNNNNNNNNNN	P,J	271	969	04.01.02	5144	430109	63035
376.367-026	UNDERCOVER OPERATOR (retail trade)	3234	33444444444	LNNNNNNFFONFFNFNNON	NNNN3NNNNNNNNNNN	P,S,V	293	881	04.02.03	5144	430109	63038
376.667-010	BOUNCER (amuse. & rec.)	2123	33444544445	LNNNNNNOOONFFNFNNNNN	NNNN3NNNNNNNNNNN	J,P,S	293	910	04.02.03	5144	430109	63047
376.667-014	DETECTIVE II (any industry)	3234	33444444455	LNNNNNNOOONNFFNFNNNN	NNNN3NNNNNNNNNNN	P,S	293	969	04.02.03	5144	430109	63035
376.667-018	PATROLLER (r.r. trans.)	2123	33444444445	LNNOOONOONFFNFNNONONO	FNNN3NNNNNNNNNNN	P,S	293	851	04.02.02	5144	430109	63038
377.134-010	SUPERVISOR, IDENTIFICATION AND COMMUNICATIONS (government ser.)	4348	22322343344	LNNOOONFFNFFNFNOOOO	NNNN3NNNNNNNNNNN	J	281	951	07.01.06	5112	430107	61005
377.137-010	DEPUTY SHERIFF, COMMANDER, CIVIL DIVISION (government ser.)	4347	22334344455	SNNNNNNFFFNFNFNFNFNN	NNNN3NNNNNNNNNNN	D,J	271	951	04.01.01	5134	430107	61005
377.137-014	DEPUTY SHERIFF, COMMANDER, CRIMINAL AND PATROL DIVISION (government ser.)	4348	22343344445	SONOOOOFFFOFFNFOOONO	NNNN3NONNNNNNNNNO	D,P,V,J	293	951	04.01.01	5134	430107	61005
377.137-018	DEPUTY, COURT (government ser.)	3236	22343334455	SNNNNNNFFFNFNFNNNNN	NNNN3NNNNNNNNNNN	D,P,V	293	951	04.01.01	5134	430107	61005
377.167-010	DEPUTY SHERIFF, CHIEF (government ser.)	4348	22343334455	SNNNNNNFFNFFNFNNOONN	ONNN3NNNNNNNNNNO	D,P,S,J	293	951	04.01.01	5134	430107	61005
377.263-010	SHERIFF, DEPUTY (government ser.)	3235	33443334335	MOOOOOOFFONFFNFFFFF	ONNN3NNNNNNNNNNN	J,P,S	293	951	04.01.02	5134	430107	63032
377.264-010	IDENTIFICATION OFFICER (government ser.)	4348	22322323344	LNNOOONFFNOONFNOFON	ONNN3NNNNNNNNNNN	J	271	951	07.01.06	5132	430107	63028
377.267-010	DEPUTY UNITED STATES MARSHAL (government ser.)	3235	33443334334	MNNNNNNNNFFNNOONFNNOON	ONNN3NNNNNNNNNNO	J,P,S	293	951	04.01.02	5134	430107	63026
377.363-010	DEPUTY SHERIFF, GRAND JURY (government ser.)	3126	33444444445	LNNNNNNNFFONFFNOOONNO	NNNN4NNNNNNNNNNO	P,J	293	951	04.02.03	5134	430107	63032
377.667-010	BAILIFF (government ser.)	2123	33444443455	VFFFFFFFFOFFFNFFNFO	FNNN3NNNNNNNNNNN	V,P,S	293	951	04.02.03	5134	430109	63023
377.667-014	DEPUTY SHERIFF, BUILDING GUARD (government ser.)	2123	33444434355	LNNNNNNFFFFNNNNON	ONNN3NNNNNNNNNNN	P,S	293	951	04.02.02	5134	430107	63032
377.667-018	DEPUTY SHERIFF, CIVIL DIVISION (government ser.)	3333	33444334355	MNNOOONFFNOONFNOONF	ONNN3NNNNNNNNNNF	P,S	293	959	04.01.02	5134	430107	63032
378.132-010	FIELD ARTILLERY SENIOR SERGEANT (military ser.)	3338	33442334354	LNNNNNNFFFFNFNNNNON	FNNN5NNNNNNNNNNO	D,P,V	293	371	05.03.05	9100	000000	00000
378.137-010	INFANTRY UNIT LEADER (military ser.)	3227	33333334355	VNNFFFNFFNFNFONONN	CNNN5NNNNNNNNNNO	D,P,S,V	293	950	04.02.02	9100	000000	00000
378.161-010	COMBAT SURVEILLANCE AND TARGET ACQUISITION NONCOMMISSIONED OFFICER (military ser.)	3337	33333433355	MNNNNNNFFNFFNFNNNNN	FNNN3NNNNNNNNNNN	D,P,J,V	293	586	05.03.05	9100	000000	00000
378.227-010	MARKSMANSHIP INSTRUCTOR (military ser.)	3234	34344322345	MFNFFFFFFFNFFNNNF	FNNN5NNNNNNNNNNF	D,P	296	373	11.02.01	9100	000000	00000
378.227-014	RECRUIT INSTRUCTOR (military ser.)	3224	34444422245	MNNOOONFFFNFFNFONNNO	FNNN4NNNNNNNNNNN	P,V	296	952	11.02.01	9100	000000	00000
378.227-018	SURVIVAL SPECIALIST (military ser.)	3235	33333433333	VFFFFFFFFOFFNFFFFO	FNNN3NNNNNNNNNNO	D,P,V	296	952	11.02.01	9100	000000	00000
378.267-010	COUNTERINTELLIGENCE AGENT (military ser.)	5457	22344443454	LNNNNNNFFFNFNFNNNON	FNNN3NNNNNNNNNNN	J,P,S,V	271	951	04.01.02	9100	000000	00000
378.267-014	DISASTER OR DAMAGE CONTROL SPECIALIST (military ser.)	4336	33344434355	MNNNNNNFFFFNFNFOONOO	ONNN3NNNNNNNNNNO	V,P,J	271	920	04.02.02	9100	000000	00000
378.281-010	TARGET AIRCRAFT TECHNICIAN (military ser.)	3326	33323433355	MNNOOONFFNOONFNFOON	ONNN4NNNNNNNNNNN	J,T	111	592	05.10.02	9100	000000	00000
378.362-010	SOUND RANGING CREWMEMBER (military ser.)	3335	33323333333	VONOOOOFFFOFFNFOONON	FNNN3NNNNNNNNNNO	J,T,S	281	586	05.03.05	9100	000000	00000
378.363-010	ARMOR RECONNAISSANCE SPECIALIST (military ser.)	3335	33333433235	MNNNNNNFFNFFNFONONN	ONNN4NNNNNNNNNNO	J,V,S	293	370	04.02.02	9100	000000	00000
378.367-010	ARTILLERY OR NAVAL GUNFIRE OBSERVER (military ser.)	3324	33343344444	VNNFFFFFONFFNFNNNN	CNNN3NNNNNNNNNNN	S,J	281	586	05.03.05	9100	000000	00000
378.367-014	FIELD ARTILLERY OPERATIONS SPECIALIST (military ser.)	4435	33223333333	LNNNNNNFFNOONFONNNO	FNNN3NNNNNNNNNNN	J	281	586	05.03.05	9100	000000	00000
378.367-018	FLASH RANGING CREWMEMBER (military ser.)	4435	33333322254	VOOOOOOFFNFFNFFFNFOF	CNNN3NNNNNNNNNNO	J,T,S	281	586	05.03.05	9100	000000	00000
378.367-022	INFANTRY OPERATIONS SPECIALIST (military ser.)	4446	33343344454	MNNNNNNFFFNFFNFNNNON	NNNN3NNNNNNNNNNN	J	231	716	04.02.02	9100	000000	00000
378.367-026	OPERATIONS AND INTELLIGENCE ASSISTANT (military ser.)	3335	32344244454	LNNNNNNFFFNFFNFNNNON	NNNN3NNNNNNNNNNN	J	282	952	04.02.02	9100	000000	00000
378.367-030	RECONNAISSANCE CREWMEMBER (military ser.)	3334	33333433344	VFFFFFFFFNFNFFNFNON	CNNN4NNNNNNNNNNO	J,S	281	869	04.02.02	9100	000000	00000

DOT #	DOT Title & Industry	Trng	Aptitude	Physical	Environment	Tempra	WkF	MPSMS	GOE	SOC	CIP	OES
378.382-010	AIRBORNE SENSOR SPECIALIST (military ser.)	3336	23322322255	VNNNNNNFFNFFNFNNNNN	NNNN4NNNNNNNNNO	J	281	601	05.03.05	9100	000000	00000
378.382-014	DEFENSIVE FIRE CONTROL SYSTEMS OPERATOR (military ser.)	3237	33343444444	SNNNNNNFFNOONFNNNON	NNNN5NNNNNNNNNN	S,J	281	869	05.03.05	9100	000000	00000
378.382-018	UNATTENDED-GROUND-SENSOR SPECIALIST (military ser.)	3336	22333492333	VNNOOOFFNFFNFOONOO	CNNN3NNNNNNNNNO	J,S	281	586	05.03.05	9100	000000	00000
378.464-010	ANTITANK ASSAULT GUNNER (military ser.)	2223	44433333335	HNNFFFFFFNNNNFFNNF	CNNN4NNNNNNNNNO	J,S	293	371	04.02.02	9100	000000	00000
378.663-010	VULCAN CREWMEMBER (military ser.)	2113	44444493335	VNNOOONFFFOOONFFFNNF	CNNN5NNNNNNNNNO	S,J	293	371	05.03.05	9100	000000	00000
378.682-010	REDEYE GUNNER (military ser.)	3333	34433433334	VNNNNNNFFNOONFFFNOF	CNNN4NNNNNNNNNO	J,S	293	370	05.03.05	9100	000000	00000
378.682-014	SMOKE AND FLAME SPECIALIST (military ser.)	3224	34433433334	HNNOOOFFFFFNOOFNOO	FNNN4NNNNNNNNNO	T,S,V	293	372	04.02.02	9100	000000	00000
378.683-010	AMPHIBIAN CREWMEMBER (military ser.)	2113	44434534335	MOONNNNFFNNFNOFFNNF	FNNN4NNNNNNNNNO	V,S	013	593	04.02.02	9100	000000	00000
378.683-014	POWERED BRIDGE SPECIALIST (military ser.)	3335	44434534335	VOOFFFNFFONOONOFONF	FNNF4NNNNNNNNNN	R,T,J	011	363	05.11.04	9100	000000	00000
378.683-018	TANK CREWMEMBER (military ser.)	2224	44433433335	MOONNNNFFNNOONFFFNOF	NNNN4NONNNNNNNNO	V,J,S	293	370	04.02.02	9100	000000	00000
378.684-010	CAMOUFLAGE SPECIALIST (military ser.)	2224	44434443252	HOOFFNFFNNNNNFNNNFN	FNNN4NNNNNNNNNN	J	153	495	04.02.02	9100	000000	00000
378.684-014	COMBAT RIFLE CREWMEMBER (military ser.)	2113	44455533354	VFFFFFFFFNOONFFFNOF	CNNN5NNNNNNNNNO	S,V	293	373	04.02.02	9100	000000	00000
378.684-018	FIELD ARTILLERY CREWMEMBER (military ser.)	2113	44444433355	HNNNNNNFFNNNFFFNOOF	CNNN5NNNNNNNNNO	J,V,S	011	371	04.02.02	9100	000000	00000
378.684-022	INFANTRY INDIRECT FIRE CREWMEMBER (military ser.)	2115	44444433334	VNNFFOFFOOOONFFFNOF	CNNN5NNNNNNNNNO	J,S	011	371	04.02.02	9100	000000	00000
378.684-026	INFANTRY WEAPONS CREWMEMBER (military ser.)	2113	44444433354	VONFFFOFFOOONOFFNOF	CNNN5NNNNNNNNNO	J,S	293	371	04.02.02	9100	000000	00000
378.684-030	LIGHT AIR DEFENSE ARTILLERY CREWMEMBER (military ser.)	2113	44443433335	VNNOOONFFFNOONOFFNNF	CNNN5NNNNNNNNNO	R,S	011	371	04.02.02	9100	000000	00000
378.687-010	COMBAT SURVEILLANCE AND TARGET ACQUISITION CREWMEMBER (military ser.)	2222	44454433344	VNNNNNNFFNOONONONON	CNNN3NNNNNNNNNO	J,S	293	586	05.03.05	9100	000000	00000
379.132-010	SUPERVISOR, TELECOMMUNICATOR (government ser.)	4247	22433233355	SNNNNNNFFNFFNFNNNN	NNNN3NNNNNNNNNN	D,S,P,J	281	861	07.04.05	4525	520406	51002
379.137-010	SUPERVISOR, ANIMAL CRUELTY INVESTIGATION (nonprofit org.)	4247	33444344455	SNNNNNNFFNFNNFFOOOO	FNNN3NNNNNNNNNN	V,D,P	953	953	11.10.03	5113	000000	61099
379.137-014	SUPERVISOR, DOG LICENSE OFFICER (nonprofit org.)	4247	33344344455	LNNNNNNFFNFNFNNNNNN	NNNN3NNNNNNNNNN	V,D,P	271	953	07.04.03	5113	000000	61099
379.137-018	WILDLIFE AGENT, REGIONAL (government ser.)	5447	22344344444	LNNOOOFFNFFNFNNNON	FNNN3NNNNNNNNNN	V,D,J,P	293	326	04.01.02	1133	030203	19905
379.137-022	SUPERVISOR, PROTECTIVE-SIGNAL OPERATIONS (business ser.)	4337	33334344455	LNNNNNNOONFNFNNNNN	NNNN3NNNNNNNNNN	D,J,P	293	951	07.04.05	5113	520406	61099
379.162-010	ALARM OPERATOR (government ser.)	4346	33334343454	SNNNNNNNFONFNFNNNN	NNNN3NNNNNNNNNN	D,P	281	860	07.04.05	4751	520406	58002
379.167-010	FISH AND GAME WARDEN (government ser.)	4346	22344444444	MNNOOOOFFONFFNFFOOOO	FNNN3NNNNNNNNNO	P,S,J	959	959	04.01.02	5134	030601	63041
379.227-010	INSTRUCTOR-TRAINER, CANINE SERVICE (government ser.)	3237	33444444445	LNNNNNNNFFNFNNFFOONO	NNNN3NNNNNNNNNN	D,P,J	329	329	03.03.01	5149	010302	63099
379.263-014	PUBLIC-SAFETY OFFICER (government ser.)	4337	33434444434	VOONNNNOONFFNNFFFOF	FNNN3NNNNNNNNNN	P,S,V	293	951	04.01.02	5149	430107	63014
379.267-010	WILDLIFE CONTROL AGENT (government ser.)	4337	22343433344	MNNFFNFFNFFNFFOFN	CNNN4NNNNNNNONO	J,P,S,V	293	951	03.01.02	5149	010399	63099
379.362-010	DISPATCHER, RADIO (government ser.)	3234	33434334455	SNNNNNNFFNFNNONNNNN	NNNN3NNNNNNNNNN	R,P,S	281	863	07.04.05	4751	520406	58002
379.362-014	PROTECTIVE-SIGNAL OPERATOR (any industry)	3235	33333333453	SNNNNNNFFNFNFNNFFN	NNNN2NNNNNNNNNN	V,S,P	281	899	07.04.05	4739	520406	57199
379.362-018	TELECOMMUNICATOR (government ser.)	4245	22433233355	SNNNNNNFFNCCNFNNFNN	NNNN3NNNNNNNNNN	V,S,P,J	281	861	07.04.05	4751	520406	58002
379.364-010	AUTOMOBILE TESTER (government ser.)	3124	33434344354	LNNOOONFFFNFOONNO	FNNN3NNNNNNNNNN	R,J,T	211	591	05.07.02	7820	470604	83005
379.367-010	ANIMAL TREATMENT INVESTIGATOR (nonprofit org.)	3224	33434444434	VNNNNNNFFFFFFFFFOF	FNNN3NNNNNNNNNN	S,P,J	293	919	04.02.03	5149	000000	63099
379.367-014	SURVEILLANCE-SYSTEM MONITOR (government ser.)	3132	33444444455	SNNNNNNNFFNNNFNNNNN	NNNN2NNNNNNNNNN	U,R,P	293	951	04.02.03	5149	430109	63099
379.384-010	SCUBA DIVER (any industry)	3224	34433443355	HNNNNNNNFFONNNOFFNNF	FNNF3NNNNNNNNNF	J,S	271	969	05.10.01	9900	000000	00000
379.664-010	SKI PATROLLER (amuse. & rec.)	3236	33434533315	HOOOONOOOOOOONOFFNNF	CNNN3NNNNNNNNNF	V,P,J,S	293	913	04.02.03	5149	000000	63099
379.667-010	GOLF-COURSE RANGER (amuse. & rec.)	3234	33444444455	LNNNNNNNFOFFNNNNNN	CNNN3NNNNNNNNNN	V,P	913	913	12.01.02	5144	430109	63047
379.667-014	LIFEGUARD (amuse. & rec.)	3124	33434434334	MONOONNOONFFNNFFNOF	CNNF3NNNNNNNNNO	J,P,S	913	913	04.02.03	5149	000000	63099
379.673-010	DOG CATCHER (government ser.)	3123	44444434335	MNNNNNNNFONFFNOFFNNF	NNNN3NNNNNNNNNO	V,P,S	329	329	03.04.05	5149	000000	63099
379.687-010	FIRE-EXTINGUISHER-SPRINKLER INSPECTOR (any industry)	3224	34434444355	LONOOONOOONNNNFNNFNN	ONNN3NNNNNNNNNN	R,T	212	969	05.07.01	5122	430201	63002
379.687-014	MOSQUITO SPRAYER (government ser.)	1113	44444444355	MNNOONNFFONFFNNNNN	FNNF4NNNNNNNNNN	R	153	962	03.04.05	5246	010501	67008
381.137-010	SUPERVISOR, JANITORIAL SERVICES (any industry)	4236	33443434355	MNNOOONFFONFFNONNNN	NNNN3NNNNNNNNNN	D,P	031	905	05.12.18	5241	200604	61099
381.137-014	SUPERVISOR, CENTRAL SUPPLY (medical ser.)	4347	33334444455	LNNNNNNFFNFNONNNNN	NNNN3NNNNNNNNNN	D,J,P,V	031	929	05.12.01	4525	510799	51002
381.687-010	CENTRAL-SUPPLY WORKER (medical ser.)	1112	33444443354	LNNONNNFFNNNNNNNON	NNNO2NNNNNNNNNN	T,V	031	604	05.12.18	4754	510799	58023
381.687-014	CLEANER, COMMERCIAL OR INSTITUTIONAL (any industry)	2122	44544544345	HONFFFNFFNNOONONNNN	NNNN3NNNNNNNNNN	R	031	905	05.12.18	5244	200604	67005
381.687-018	CLEANER, INDUSTRIAL (any industry)	2212	44444444353	MOOFOFNFFONNNNNNNNN	NNNO3NNNNNNNNNN	R	031	905	05.12.18	5244	200604	67005
381.687-022	CLEANER, LABORATORY EQUIPMENT (any industry)	2212	44444444353	MNNOOONFCONNONONNON	NNNF3NNNNNNNNNN	R	031	601	05.12.18	5244	512601	67005
381.687-026	CLEANER, WALL (any industry)	1112	44544544444	MOOONNOFFNNNNNFNNON	NNNF3NNNNNNNNNN	R	031	905	05.12.18	5244	200604	67005
381.687-030	PATCH WORKER (agriculture)	1112	45444544455	LNNONONFFNNNNNNNNNN	NNNN4NNNNNNNNNN	R	031	361	06.04.40	5244	000000	67005
381.687-034	WAXER, FLOOR (any industry)	1112	44545534444	MNNFFNNFFNNNNNNNNNF	NNNN3NNNNNNNNNF	R,J	031	905	05.12.18	5244	200604	67005
382.137-010	SUPERVISOR, MAINTENANCE (chemical)	4336	33444344355	MNNFFFNFFONFFNFOOONN	NNNN3NNNNNNNNNO	V,D,P,J	031	905	05.12.01	5241	200604	61099

DOT #	DOT Title & Industry	Trng	Aptitude	Physical	Environment	Tempra	WkF	MPSMS	GOE	SOC	CIP	OES
382.664-010	JANITOR (any industry)	3233	34334434344	MOOOOONFFNOONONONON	ONON3NNNNNNNNN	V,T	021	905	05.12.18	5244	460401	67005
383.361-010	FUMIGATOR (business ser.)	4335	33334344344	HONFFFOFFONFFNONOOON	ONNN3NNNNNNNNNF	V,P,J	293	962	05.10.09	5246	010501	67008
383.364-010	EXTERMINATOR, TERMITE (business ser.)	3226	34333333345	HOOFFFFFFNOONOOONNN	FNNN4NNNNNNNNNF	V,D,J	293	962	05.10.09	5246	000000	67008
383.684-010	EXTERMINATOR HELPER (any industry)	3224	44444444334	MNNOOONFFNOOONFNNNON	NNNN3NNNNNNNNN	J	011	960	05.10.09	5246	020408	67008
383.687-010	EXTERMINATOR HELPER, TERMITE (business ser.)	1112	44545544345	HOOFFFFFFNNNNNNNNNN	FNFN3NNNNNNNNNN	R	011	962	05.12.03	5246	000000	61099
388.367-010	ELEVATOR STARTER (any industry)	3226	33434444455	LNNNNNNOOOFFNONNNNNN	NNNN3NNNNNNNNN	J	013	969	09.05.09	5241	000000	61099
388.663-010	ELEVATOR OPERATOR (any industry)	2122	43444434355	LNNNNNNFFFFFNNNNNNN	NNNN3NNNNNNNNNN	R,P	011	969	09.05.09	5245	000000	67011
389.134-010	SUPERVISOR, EXTERMINATION (business ser.)	4336	33334444445	LONOOOOOOOFFNONOOONN	ONNN3NNNNNNNNNF	V,D,P,J	293	962	05.10.09	5241	010501	61099
389.137-010	SUPERVISOR, HOME RESTORATION SERVICE (any industry)	3337	33334444445	MNNNNNNFFNFNFONONN	NNNN3NNNNNNNNNN	D,P,J	031	905	05.12.01	5241	520205	61099
389.664-010	CLEANER, HOME RESTORATION SERVICE (any industry)	2123	34444435345	HONOOOOFFONOONFNNNNN	ONNO3NNNNNNNNNN	U	031	905	05.12.18	5244	200604	67005
389.667-010	SEXTON (nonprofit org.)	2122	44444434334	MNNFNNNNFFONOONNNNNNN	ONNN3NNNNNNNNNN	V	031	905	05.12.18	5244	000000	67005
389.683-010	SWEEPER-CLEANER, INDUSTRIAL (any industry)	1112	44534534335	MNNOOONFFONNNNNNNFNF	NNNN4NNNNNNNNN	R	031	905	05.12.18	5244	200604	67008
389.684-010	EXTERMINATOR (business ser.)	3225	44444444455	LONFFFOFFONNNNONOOONN	NNNN3NFNNNNNNON	V,J	293	962	05.10.09	5246	010501	67008
389.687-014	AIR PURIFIER SERVICER (business ser.)	1112	44445544355	LNNNOOONFFNONNNNFFNNN	NNNN3NNNNNNNNN	R	102	909	05.12.12	5249	000000	67099
389.687-014	CLEANER, WINDOW (any industry)	1112	44445434355	MFFFOOOFFNNNNNNNFNNN	FNNF3NNNNFNNNF	R,S	031	905	05.12.18	5244	200604	67005
389.687-018	LIGHT-FIXTURE SERVICER (any industry)	1112	44545444435	MFFNNNNFFFNNNNNNNNN	NNNN4NNNNNNNNF	R	111	909	05.12.18	5249	000000	67099
401.137-010	SUPERVISOR, AREA (agriculture)	4337	33333334455	LNNFNFNFFFFFNFNNNN	CNNN3NNNNNNNNN	V,D,P,J	003	301	03.02.01	5611	010304	72002
401.137-014	SUPERVISOR, DETASSELING CREW (agriculture)	3296	33493444454	LNNNNNNOOOFFNOONNOF	CNNN3NNNNNNNNN	D,P,V	003	301	03.04.01	5611	010304	72002
401.161-010	FARMER, CASH GRAIN (agriculture)	4337	33333434344	HONOOOOFFOOFFNOOFNOF	FNNN4NNONNNNNN	V,D,J	003	301	03.01.01	5513	020402	79999
401.683-010	FARMWORKER, GRAIN I (agriculture)	3124	34434434344	MONOOOOFFOOOONOFFNOF	FNNN4NNONNNNNN	V	003	301	03.04.01	5616	010304	79021
401.683-014	FARMWORKER, RICE (agriculture)	3225	34434433335	MONOOONFFONNNNNFFNNF	CNNF4NNNNNNNNN	J	003	301	03.04.01	5616	010304	79021
401.687-010	FARMWORKER, GRAIN II (agriculture)	1112	44454544345	MNNNNNNOOOOONFFNNNNNN	CNNN3NNNNNNNNN	V	003	301	03.04.01	5613	010304	79999
402.131-010	SUPERVISOR, VEGETABLE FARMING (agriculture)	4237	33434444344	MONOOONFFFNFNFOONOO	FNNN4NONNNNNNNO	D,J,P	003	303	03.02.01	5611	020402	72002
402.161-010	FARMER, VEGETABLE (agriculture)	4447	23323344444	MONFOONFOOOONOOONOO	FNNN4FONNNNNNNN	D,J,V	003	303	03.01.01	5513	010304	79999
402.663-010	FARMWORKER, VEGETABLE I (agriculture)	3234	33443433345	MONOOONFNNNNNNNFFNNO	CNNN4NFNNNNNNNON	T,V	003	303	03.04.01	5616	010304	79999
402.687-010	FARMWORKER, VEGETABLE II (agriculture)	1112	44444433344	MOOFONFFONNNNNNNNNON	FNNN4FNNNNNNNNN	R	003	303	03.04.01	5613	010304	79999
402.687-014	HARVEST WORKER, VEGETABLE (agriculture)	1111	44544544454	MNNFFFOFFONONFNFNON	NNNN3NNNNNNNNN	R	003	303	03.02.01	5611	010304	79999
403.131-010	SUPERVISOR, TREE-FRUIT-AND-NUT FARMING (agriculture)	4347	33434433344	MOOOOONFFONFFNOOONON	FNNO4NONNNNNNNO	V,D,P,J	003	304	03.02.01	5611	010304	79021
403.131-014	SUPERVISOR, VINE-FRUIT FARMING (agriculture)	4336	33433434344	MONOOONFFFNFFNOONON	FNNN4NNNNNNNNN	D,J,P,V	003	300	03.02.01	5611	010304	79021
403.161-010	FARMER, TREE-FRUIT-AND-NUT CROPS (agriculture)	4447	33333434344	HOOOOONFFOOOONFFNOF	CNNO4NNNNNNNNN	D,J	003	300	03.01.01	5513	010304	79999
403.161-014	FARMER, FRUIT CROPS, BUSH AND VINE (agriculture)	4447	33333434344	HONOOONFFNNFNNOOONOO	ONNO4NONNNNNNNF	D,J,V	003	303	03.01.01	5513	020403	79999
403.683-010	FARMWORKER, FRUIT I (agriculture)	3235	34433534334	MOOONONFFNNOOONOFFNOF	FNNN4NFNNNNNNNF	T,V	003	304	03.04.01	5616	010304	79021
403.687-010	FARMWORKER, FRUIT II (agriculture)	2122	44544544344	MOOFNFNFFONNNNNNONON	FNNO3NNNNNNNNNO	T	003	304	03.04.01	5614	010304	79999
403.687-014	FIG CAPRIFIER (agriculture)	2122	44444434344	MNNNNNNFFNNNNNNNNN	CNNN2NNNNNNNNN	R	003	305	03.04.01	5614	010304	79999
403.687-018	HARVEST WORKER, FRUIT (agriculture)	1112	44544544344	MFFFOONFFONOONOOFNFN	FNNN3NNNNNNNNNF	R	003	304	03.04.01	5614	010304	79999
403.687-022	VINE PRUNER (agriculture)	1111	44455544355	LNNFNNNNFFFONNNFNFNON	CNNN4NFNNNNNNNN	R	003	305	03.01.03	5515	010603	79999
404.131-010	SUPERVISOR, FIELD-CROP FARMING (agriculture)	4337	33433434344	MOOOOONOOOOOFFONFNNOF	NNNN4NNNNNNNNN	D,J,P,V	003	300	03.02.01	5611	020402	72002
404.131-014	SUPERVISOR, SHED WORKERS (agriculture)	4337	33434344354	LNNNNNNNFFNFFNFNON	NNNN3NNNNNNNNN	D,P,J	003	302	03.04.01	5611	010304	72002
404.161-010	FARMER, FIELD CROP (agriculture)	4447	23323344444	MONOOOOFFONFFNOFFNOF	NNNN4NNNNNNNNNF	D,J	003	300	03.01.01	5513	010304	79999
404.663-010	FARMWORKER, FIELD CROP I (agriculture)	3235	34434534334	MOOOOOOOFFNNOONOFFNOF	NNNN4NNNNNNNNN	R,T	003	300	03.04.01	5616	010304	79021
404.685-010	SEED-POTATO ARRANGER (agriculture)	1112	44544544455	LNNFNNNNFFNNOONNNNNNN	NNNN3NNNNNNNNN	R	054	303	03.04.01	5613	010304	79021
404.686-010	SEED CUTTER (agriculture)	1111	45544544355	MNNNNNNFFNNNNNNNNN	ONNN3NNNNNNNNNF	R	054	303	03.04.01	5613	010304	79021
404.687-010	FARMWORKER, FIELD CROP II (agriculture)	1111	44445544344	HOOFFNFNFFONNNNNNNNN	FNNN3NFNNNNNNNN	R	003	300	03.04.01	5613	010304	79999
404.687-014	HARVEST WORKER, FIELD CROP (agriculture)	1111	44445544344	HOOFFNFFONNNNNNNNNO	FNNF3NFNNNNNNN	R	003	302	03.02.03	5611	010606	15031
405.131-010	SUPERVISOR, HORTICULTURAL-SPECIALTY FARMING (agriculture)	4347	33322433344	MNNOOONFFFFFFNONFN	FNNN3NNNNNNNNN	D,J,P,V,T	003	310	03.02.03	5611	010606	79999
405.137-010	SUPERVISOR, ROSE-GRADING (agriculture)	4347	33332432353	MNNONNNFFOFFNFNOOON	NONN3NNNNNNNNN	D,P,V	212	310	03.04.04	5611	010603	72002
405.161-010	BONSAI CULTURIST (agriculture)	4337	33323433354	LNNNNNNNFFFONNNFNFNON	NNNN3NNNNNNNNN	J,E	003	310	03.01.03	5515	010603	79999
405.161-014	HORTICULTURAL-SPECIALTY GROWER, FIELD (agriculture)	4337	33333434333	MOOOONNOFFONFFNFFOOF	NNNN4NNNNNNNNN	D,J	003	310	03.01.03	5515	010607	79999
405.161-018	HORTICULTURAL-SPECIALTY GROWER, INSIDE (agriculture)	4347	23333334343	MNNFOONFOOOONFNFN	NNNF3NNNNNNNNN	D,J	003	300	03.01.03	5515	010604	79999
405.361-010	PLANT PROPAGATOR (agriculture)	4446	33422433353	MNNFOONFFOOONFFFN	NNNN4NNNNNNNNN	J	003	303	03.04.04	5515	010603	79999
405.683-010	FARMWORKER, BULBS (agriculture)	3225	34434434344	MONFNFNFFONNNNNFFNFF	CNNN4NFNNNNNNNO	J,V	003	310	03.04.04	5619	010603	79005

DOT #	DOT Title & Industry	Trng	Aptitude	Physical	Environment	Tempra	WkF	MPSMS	GOE	SOC	CIP	OES
405.683-014	GROWTH-MEDIA MIXER, MUSHROOM (agriculture)	3223	34434534334	MNNNNNFFNNNNNOFFNON	FNNN4NNNNNNNNN	R,T	003	319	03.04.04	5616	010304	79021
405.684-010	BUDDER (agriculture)	2112	44543523355	MNNNNCNCCCNNNNCNCNNN	CNNN3NNNNNNNNN	R,T	003	311	03.04.04	5619	010603	79005
405.684-014	HORTICULTURAL WORKER I (agriculture)	3233	34433444344	HOOOONFFOOOONOOONON	NNNF3NONNNNNNNN	V,J,T	003	310	03.04.04	5619	010603	79005
405.687-010	FLOWER PICKER (agriculture)	1111	44444544354	LNNFFFNFFNNNNNNNNF	CNNN3NNNNNNNNN	R	003	311	03.04.04	5619	010603	79005
405.687-014	HORTICULTURAL WORKER II (agriculture)	2112	44544544344	HNNFFONFFOOOONONFNON	ONNN3NNNNNNNNN	R,U	003	310	03.04.04	5619	010603	79005
405.687-018	TRANSPLANTER, ORCHID (agriculture)	2122	44443433354	MNNNNNNFFNNNNFNFNON	NNNF3NNNNNNNNN	R,T	003	311	03.04.04	5619	010606	79005
406.134-010	SUPERVISOR, CEMETERY WORKERS (real estate)	4336	33433434345	LNNNNONFFNFFNOOONON	CNNN3NNNNNNNNN	D,V,P,J	003	969	03.02.03	5621	010607	72002
406.134-014	SUPERVISOR, LANDSCAPE (museums; waterworks)	4346	33333333343	LNNNNONFFNFFNOOONON	FNNN3NNNNNNNNN	V,D,P,J	003	310	03.02.03	5621	010603	72002
406.137-010	GREENSKEEPER I (any industry)	4336	33333444444	MNNONNNFFONFFNOOONON	FNNN3NNNNNNNNN	V,D,P	003	311	03.04.04	5621	010607	72002
406.137-014	SUPERINTENDENT, GREENS (amuse. & rec.)	4447	23222344444	LNNOONOOOOFFNONNNON	NNNN3NNNNNNNNN	D,P,J	003	310	03.01.03	5621	010607	72002
406.381-010	GARDENER, SPECIAL EFFECTS AND INSTRUCTION MODELS (motion picture; museums)	4335	33433443353	MNNOOONFFNNONFOFFFO	FNNN3NNNNNNNNN	J,T	003	310	03.01.03	5622	010605	79030
406.683-010	GREENSKEEPER II (any industry)	2123	44434534334	MOOOOONFFNNNNNNNONON	CNNN4NNNNNNNNNF	R,T	003	310	03.04.04	5622	010607	79030
406.684-010	CEMETERY WORKER (real estate)	3125	34444444345	HNNFNFNCCONOONNNNNNN	CNNN3NNNNNNNNN	V,T	003	969	03.04.04	5622	000000	79030
406.684-014	GROUNDSKEEPER, INDUSTRIAL-COMMERCIAL (any industry)	2123	44444444345	MOOOOONFFONNNNNOOONO	CNNN4NNNNNNNNN	V	003	310	03.04.04	5622	010605	79030
406.684-018	GARDEN WORKER (agriculture; museums)	3234	34433433343	MOOOOONFFNOONFNNNFN	FNNN4NNNNNNNNN	J,V	003	310	03.04.04	5622	010604	79030
406.687-010	LANDSCAPE SPECIALIST (government ser.)	2122	44544544444	MOOFONFFONOONONOOONON	FNNN4NNNNNNNNN	R,T	003	310	03.04.04	5622	010605	79030
407.131-010	SUPERVISOR, DIVERSIFIED CROPS (agriculture)	4347	33333433344	MNNFOONFFNFFNFNONOON	FNNN4NNNNNNNNN	D,J,P,V	003	300	03.02.01	5611	010304	72002
407.161-010	FARMER, DIVERSIFIED CROPS (agriculture)	4447	23323344344	MONONNNFFONOONFOFNOO	CNNN4NFNNNNNNNO	D,J,V	003	300	03.01.01	5512	020402	79999
407.663-010	FARMWORKER, DIVERSIFIED CROPS I (agriculture)	3234	34434433334	MONFOONFFONOONOOFFNOF	CNNN4NFNNNNNNNF	V,T	003	300	03.04.01	5612	010204	79999
407.687-010	FARMWORKER, DIVERSIFIED CROPS II (agriculture)	1112	44444433344	MOOFONFFFONNNONONON	CNNN4NNNNNNNNN	R	003	300	03.04.01	5612	010304	79999
408.131-010	SUPERVISOR, SPRAY, LAWN AND TREE SERVICE (agriculture)	4447	23334344444	LNNNNNNOOOOFFNFONNOO	ONNN3NNNNNNNNN	D,J	003	300	03.02.03	5621	010699	15032
408.137-010	SUPERVISOR, INSECT AND DISEASE INSPECTION (agriculture)	4446	33333344343	LNNNNNNFFNFFNFOONFO	FNNN3NNNNNNNNN	D,J,P	293	300	03.02.04	5611	010304	72002
408.137-014	SUPERVISOR, TREE-TRIMMING (utilities)	4346	33333344455	MOOONNNFFNOONONFNON	CNNN4NNOONNNN	V,D,R,J	056	969	03.01.03	5622	010603	79038
408.161-010	LANDSCAPE GARDENER (agriculture)	4447	33334433344	HNNFFONFFNOONONFNON	CNNN4NFNNNNNNNF	V,D,J	003	310	03.04.05	5622	010603	79038
408.181-010	TREE SURGEON (agriculture)	4226	23433434223	MFFFFOFFOONNNOFFNOF	CNNF4FNNNNNNNF	V,J,T	003	310	03.01.03	3820	010603	24502
408.364-010	PLANT-CARE WORKER (agriculture)	3233	33443343343	MFNOOONFFFOONFNNFFN	NNNF3NNNNNNNON	J,T	003	310	03.04.05	5619	010604	79005
408.381-010	SCOUT (agriculture)	3234	33444444343	MOONNNNFFONNNNOFFNON	CNNN3NNNNNNNNN	V,T	293	300	03.04.05	5627	010304	79999
408.381-014	WEED INSPECTOR (agriculture)	3235	33443424344	LNNOOONFFONNNNNNNNN	CNNN3NNNNNNFN	J,T	293	962	03.04.05	5627	020408	79999
408.662-010	HYDRO-SPRAYER OPERATOR (agriculture)	3224	34534544325	HOOONONFFNOOONOFFNOO	CNNN4NNNNNNOFNN	J	003	969	03.04.04	5616	010204	79036
408.664-010	TREE TRIMMER (tel. & tel.; utilities)	3224	34534544325	HFFNNNNFFNNNNNFNNNN	CNNN4NNOFNNNNF	R,S	056	312	03.04.05	5730	010699	73099
408.667-010	TREE-TRIMMER HELPER II (utilities)	1112	44545544355	MNNFFFNCONNNNNFNNNN	CNNN4NNNNNNNNN	T	056	312	03.04.05	5730	010699	73099
408.684-010	LAWN-SERVICE WORKER (agriculture)	3224	34434434344	HNNONONFFNNNNOOOONON	CNNN4NNNNNNNNN	T	003	969	03.04.04	5622	010605	79030
408.684-014	SPRAYER, HAND (agriculture)	3224	34433434344	HOOOOONFFNNNNNOFFNOO	CNNF4NFNNNNNNNF	J	003	969	03.04.04	5614	010606	79036
408.684-018	TREE PRUNER (agriculture)	3234	33434444334	MFFONONFFNNNNNNNFNON	NNNN3NNNONNNNN	T	054	300	03.04.05	5614	010304	79033
408.687-010	FIELD INSPECTOR, DISEASE AND INSECT CONTROL (agriculture)	2222	44434443343	LNNFFFNFFNNNNNNNNFN	FNNN3NNNNNNNNN	J,T	293	300	03.02.04	5627	010304	79999
408.687-014	LABORER, LANDSCAPE (agriculture)	2122	44444544344	HNNFFONFFNOONNNNNON	FNNN4NNNNNNNNN	V,T	003	969	03.04.04	5622	010605	79038
408.687-018	TREE-SURGEON HELPER II (agriculture)	2122	44444544444	HOOFOONFFONNNNOFNNF	FNNN4NNNNNNNNN	V,T	003	300	03.04.04	5619	010699	79005
409.117-010	HARVEST CONTRACTOR (agriculture)	4447	33333333344	LNNNONONFFFNFFNFOONOO	CNNN3NFNNNNNNNN	D,V,J,P	003	300	03.01.01	5611	010304	72002
409.131-010	SUPERVISOR, PICKING CREW (agriculture)	4347	33434434344	MOOONONOOOOFFNNONON	FNNN3NNNNNNNNN	V,D,P,J	003	300	03.04.01	5611	010204	72002
409.137-010	IRRIGATOR, HEAD (agriculture)	3235	33343434444	MNNNNNNFFNFNFFFFF	FNNO3NNNNNNNNN	J	003	300	03.04.05	5611	020501	72002
409.137-014	ROW BOSS, HOEING (agriculture)	4347	33434344444	LNNOOONFFNOONONNON	CNNN3NNNNNNNNN	V,D,P,J	003	300	03.04.01	5611	010304	72002
409.667-010	AIRPLANE-PILOT HELPER (agriculture)	2223	44434433434	MONONNNFFONOONOFNNOF	FNNF4NFNNNNNNF	T	003	300	03.04.05	5613	010501	79999
409.683-010	FARM-MACHINE OPERATOR (agriculture)	3223	34333534335	HONFOONFFONNNNOFFNNF	FNNN4NNNNNNNNN	V,J,T	003	969	03.04.01	5616	010204	79021
409.683-014	FIELD HAULER (agriculture)	2223	44534534335	MNNNNNMNFFNNNNNNNNN	FNNN4NNNNNNNNN	R	013	300	03.04.01	5616	010304	79021
409.684-010	IRRIGATOR, VALVE PIPE (agriculture)	2113	34444534345	MMNFFONFFFNNOOONOO	CNNO3NNNNNNNNN	R,T	003	300	03.04.05	5615	010299	79999
409.685-010	FARM-MACHINE TENDER (agriculture)	2122	44545544344	HNNOOONFFONNNNNNONON	FNNN4NNNNNNNNN	R	003	300	03.04.01	5616	010204	79021
409.685-014	IRRIGATOR, SPRINKLING SYSTEM (agriculture)	2122	44434544444	MONFFFNFFNNNNNNFNNNN	FNINF3NNNNNNNNN	T	003	300	03.04.01	5615	010304	79999
409.686-010	FARMWORKER, MACHINE (agriculture)	1111	45544534345	HOOFNFNFFONNNNNFNNN	FNNN4NNNNNNNNN	R	003	300	03.04.01	5616	010204	79021
409.687-010	INSPECTOR-GRADER, AGRICULTURAL ESTABLISHMENT (agriculture)	2222	44545544444	MNNFNFNFFFNNFFNNFN	NNNO3NNNNNNNNN	R,T	212	300	03.04.01	5627	010304	79999
409.687-014	IRRIGATOR, GRAVITY FLOW (agriculture)	2112	44444544455	MNNFNFNFFNNNNNNNNNN	NNNO3NNNNNNNNN	R	003	300	03.04.05	5615	010299	79999
409.687-018	WEEDER-THINNER (agriculture)	1111	44454544445	MNNFFFOFFNNNNNNNNN	CNNN3NNNNNNNNN	R	003	300	03.04.01	5613	010604	79999

DOT #	DOT Title & Industry	Trng	Aptitude	Physical	Environment	Tempra	WkF	MPSMS	GOE	SOC	CIP	OES
410.131-010	BARN BOSS (any industry)	4337	33343444355	LNNNNNNOOOFFNONONNN	NNNN3NNNNNNNNNN	V,D,P	291	327	03.02.04	5611	010302	72002
410.131-014	SUPERVISOR, ARTIFICIAL BREEDING RANCH (agriculture)	4337	33344333333	MNNNONNFFNFFNFNONON	NNNN3NNNNNNNNNO	V,D,J	002	320	03.02.01	5611	020203	72002
410.131-018	SUPERVISOR, DAIRY FARM (agriculture)	4337	33433433334	MNNFOONFFOFFNFNOOON	ONNN3NFNNNNNNNO	D,J,P,V	002	321	03.02.01	5611	020206	72002
410.131-022	SUPERVISOR, STOCK RANCH (agriculture)	4337	34443434334	MOOOOONFFONFFNOOOOO	FNNN4NOONNNNNNN	V,D,P,J	002	320	03.02.01	5611	010302	72002
410.134-010	SUPERVISOR, LIVESTOCK-YARD (any industry)	3336	33433344444	LNNONONFFNFFNFNFNON	FNNN4NNNNNNNNNN	D,J,P	002	320	03.02.04	7100	020201	81008
410.134-014	SUPERVISOR, WOOL-SHEARING (agriculture)	4337	22324334344	HNNFOFNFFNFFNFNNNON	FNNN3NFNNNNNNNN	D,P,I,T	002	323	03.04.01	5611	010302	72002
410.134-018	SUPERVISOR, KENNEL (nonprofit org.)	4234	33333433345	HNNNNNNFFFOFFNOOONNO	FNNO3NONNNNNNNN	D,V,P	291	320	03.02.04	5621	460401	72002
410.134-022	SUPERVISOR, RESEARCH DAIRY FARM (agriculture)	3236	33444344334	HNNNONONOOOFFNFONNON	ONNN3NNNNNNNNNN	D,V,P	002	321	03.02.01	5611	010302	72002
410.137-010	CAMP TENDER (agriculture)	3236	33434544445	LNNFNFNNNOONOFNNNN	FNNN3NNNNNNNNNN	D,J	002	323	03.01.01	5611	020409	72002
410.137-014	TOP SCREW (agriculture)	4337	33434344345	HFFOOONFFOOFFNONNNNN	FNNN4NNNNNNNNNN	D,S	002	321	03.04.01	5611	010302	72002
410.137-018	SUPERVISOR, ANIMAL MAINTENANCE (pharmaceut.)	4336	33334333355	LNNNNNNFFNFFNFNNNNN	NNNN3NNNNNNNNNN	D,V,P	002	320	03.03.02	5621	020203	79015
410.161-010	ANIMAL BREEDER (agriculture)	4336	33343433354	MNNFFNNFFOOONONNOON	ONNN3NNNNNNNNNN	D,J,V	002	329	03.01.02	5514	010302	79999
410.161-014	FUR FARMER (agriculture)	4336	33343433354	LNNNNNNFFOOOONNNNON	ONNN3NNNNNNNNNN	V,D,J	002	325	03.01.02	5514	010302	79999
410.161-018	LIVESTOCK RANCHER (agriculture)	4337	33344434344	HONOOONFFOOOONOOONOO	FNNN4NFNNNNNNNF	V,D,J	002	320	03.01.01	5514	020202	79999
410.161-022	HOG-CONFINEMENT-SYSTEM MANAGER (agriculture)	5447	23222232223	MNNOOONFFOOOOFOFFFN	ONNO3NNNNNNNNNF	D,T,J	002	322	03.01.01	5514	010302	00000
410.357-010	MILK SAMPLER (agriculture)	3234	43444344354	MNNFNNNFFNFFNFNNNON	ONNN3NNNNNNNNNN	R,T	212	969	03.04.05	4757	020206	58017
410.364-010	LAMBER (agriculture)	3123	34434433333	LNNFFFNFFNNNNNONONON	FNNN3NNNNNNNNNN	J	002	323	03.04.01	5617	010302	79999
410.664-010	FARMWORKER, LIVESTOCK (agriculture)	3334	44444434354	HONOOONFFONNNNONONON	FNNN3NFNNNNNNNF	V,J	002	320	03.04.01	5617	010302	79999
410.674-010	ANIMAL CARETAKER (any industry)	2114	34434433354	MNNONONFFOFFNFNNOON	CNNN4NNNNNNNNNN	V,T	002	329	03.03.02	5624	010302	79017
410.674-014	COWPUNCHER (agriculture)	2224	34434434334	MFFOOONFFOONNNOFFNON	CNNN4NNNNNNNNNN	V,S,T	002	321	03.04.01	5617	010302	79999
410.674-018	LIVESTOCK-YARD ATTENDANT (any industry)	3222	34343434344	HOOONONFFNNNNNFNNOON	FNNN4NFNNNNNNNF	R,S	002	320	03.04.01	5617	010302	79999
410.674-022	STABLE ATTENDANT (any industry)	2112	44444444345	HNNOOONFFNNNNNFNNOON	NNNO3NNNNNNNNNO	V,J	002	327	03.03.02	5624	010302	79999
410.684-010	FARMWORKER, DAIRY (agriculture)	2114	44434433344	HNNFOONFFONNNNONONON	FNNN3NFNNNNNNNF	R,J	002	321	03.04.01	5617	010302	79999
410.684-014	SHEEP SHEARER (agriculture)	2113	44544434344	MNNFOFNFFNNNNNNNNNN	NNNN3NFNNNNNNNN	R	002	323	03.04.01	5617	010302	79999
410.685-010	MILKER, MACHINE (agriculture)	2112	44444434344	MNNFFFNFFOONNNFNFOON	NNNN3NNNNNNNNNN	R	002	321	03.04.01	5617	010302	79999
410.687-010	FLEECE TIER (agriculture)	2112	44545444345	MNNFNFNFFNNNNNNNNNN	NNNN3NNNNNNNNNN	R	041	414	03.04.01	5617	010302	79999
410.687-014	GOAT HERDER (agriculture)	2113	44544544455	LNNNNNNFFNNNNNNNNNN	FNNN3NNNNNNNNNN	R	002	323	03.04.01	5617	010302	79999
410.687-018	PELTER (agriculture)	2222	45445543345	MNNNNNNCCNNNNONONON	ONNN4NNNNNNNNNN	R	054	325	03.04.03	5617	010302	79999
410.687-022	SHEEP HERDER (agriculture)	2113	44544544345	MFNFNFNFNNNNNNNNNNN	CNNN3NNNNNNNNNN	V,D	002	323	03.04.01	5617	010302	79999
410.687-026	WOOL-FLEECE SORTER (agriculture)	2113	34444544444	MNNFFFNCCOONNNFNNNON	NNNN3NNNNNNNNNN	R	212	414	03.04.01	5625	000000	79011
411.131-010	SUPERVISOR, POULTRY FARM (agriculture)	4237	33444444444	MNNONONFFOFFNFOOOON	NNNN4NNNNNNNNNN	V,D,P,J	002	324	03.02.01	5611	020209	72002
411.137-010	SUPERVISOR, POULTRY HATCHERY (agriculture)	4236	33443333354	LNNNNNNFFNFFNFOOON	ONNN3NNNNNNNNNN	V,D,P,J	002	324	03.02.01	5611	020209	72002
411.161-010	CANARY BREEDER (agriculture)	4235	33344334344	LNNNNNNFFNFFNFNNNON	NNNN4NNNNNNNNNN	J,V	002	324	03.01.02	5514	010302	79999
411.161-014	POULTRY BREEDER (agriculture)	4337	22393434344	LNNOOONFFONNNNOOON	NNNN4NNNNNNNNNN	R	002	324	03.01.01	5514	020202	79999
411.161-018	POULTRY FARMER (agriculture)	4337	33433444444	MNNONONFFOOONONONON	ONNN4NNNNNNNNNN	D,J,V	002	324	03.01.01	5627	020209	79999
411.267-010	FIELD SERVICE TECHNICIAN, POULTRY (agriculture)	4337	33343344444	LNNNONONFFOOONNCNNON	FNNN3NNNNNNNNNN	J	211	324	03.01.01	5617	020209	79999
411.364-010	BLOOD TESTER, FOWL (agriculture)	3222	33443534354	MNNONONFFOOOONFFNON	ONNN3NNNNNNNNNN	R,J	211	324	03.04.05	3820	010302	24502
411.364-014	POULTRY TENDER (agriculture)	3225	33454444354	HNNNNNNFFONNNFNOON	ONNN3NFNNNNNNNN	T	002	324	03.04.01	5617	020209	79999
411.384-010	POULTRY INSEMINATOR (agriculture)	3223	33443444354	MNNNNNNFFNNNNFFCON	NNNN3NFNNNNNNNN	J,T	002	324	03.04.05	3820	010302	24502
411.584-010	FARMWORKER, POULTRY (agriculture)	2223	34444444354	MONFFFNFFOONNNONON	NNNN4NFNNNNNNNF	J	002	326	03.04.01	5617	010302	79999
411.684-010	CAPONIZER (agriculture)	2112	44545543354	LNNNNNNFFONNNNFNON	NNNN3NNNNNNNNNN	R	002	324	03.04.01	5617	010501	79999
411.684-014	POULTRY VACCINATOR (agriculture)	2112	44554534455	MNNFNFNFFONNNNCNNON	NNNN4NNNNNNNNNN	R,T	002	324	03.04.01	5617	010302	79999
411.687-010	CHICK GRADER (agriculture)	2222	44543543354	MNNNNNNCCCCNNNCNNNON	NNNN3NNNNNNNNNN	J	212	324	03.04.01	5617	010302	79999
411.687-014	CHICK SEXER (agriculture)	2124	44333432353	LNNNNNNCCCCNNNCNCNON	NNNN3NNNNNNNNNN	R	212	324	03.04.01	5617	010302	79999
411.687-018	LABORER, POULTRY FARM (agriculture)	2122	44445534345	MNNFNNNFFNNNNNONONNN	ONNN4NFNNNNNNNN	J	002	324	03.04.01	5617	010302	79999
411.687-022	LABORER, POULTRY HATCHERY (agriculture)	2222	34434434344	MNOFNNNFFNNNNNNONNN	NNNN3NNNNNNNNNN	T,V	002	324	03.04.01	5617	010302	79999
411.687-026	POULTRY DEBEAKER (agriculture)	2113	44434534335	LNNNNNNNCNNNNNCNFNNN	NNNN3NFNNNNNNNF	R	002	324	03.04.01	5617	010302	79999
412.131-010	SUPERVISOR, GAME FARM (agriculture)	4345	33333334334	MNNNFNFNFFNFNFFNNNON	ONNN3NNNNNNNNNO	D,J,P,V	002	324	03.02.01	5611	010399	72002
412.137-010	ANIMAL KEEPER, HEAD (amuse. & rec.)	4337	33333334454	MNNOOONFFOOFFNFONOON	CNNN3NNNNNNNNNO	V,D,P,J	291	329	03.03.02	5621	020203	72002
412.161-010	GAME-BIRD FARMER (agriculture)	4336	33343443354	LNNOONNFFOOOONONNOON	FNNN3NNNNNNNNNO	V,D,J	002	324	03.01.02	5514	010399	79999
412.674-010	ANIMAL KEEPER (amuse. & rec.)	3224	34444533344	MONFFNFFNFFOFFNFONON	FNNO3NNNNNNNNNO	V,J	291	329	03.03.02	5624	010399	79017

DOT #	DOT Title & Industry	Trng	Aptitude	Physical	Environment	Tempra	WkF	MPSMS	GOE	SOC	CIP	OES
412.674-014	ANIMAL-NURSERY WORKER (amuse. & rec.; museums)	3234	33443333354	MNNONONFFONOONFNNNON	NNNN3NNNNNNNNNN	J,P,V	291	329	03.03.02	5624	000000	79017
412.684-010	GAME-FARM HELPER (agriculture)	2223	44444433344	MNNOOONFFNNNNOOONOO	CNNN3NNNNNNNNNNF	V,J	002	326	03.04.01	5617	010399	79999
412.687-010	COMMISSARY ASSISTANT (amuse. & rec.; museums)	2212	44444444335	HNNNONNFFONOOONFNNNN	NNNN3NNNNNNNNNN	V,J	221	380	03.03.02	8726	000000	98799
413.161-010	BEEKEEPER (agriculture)	3337	33333444344	HNNFFFNFFNOONFNOFON	ONNN3NNNNNNNNNNF	J,V	002	329	03.01.02	5514	010302	79999
413.161-014	REPTILE FARMER (agriculture)	4346	22333333345	LNNNOONNFFOOONFNNNNN	FNNN3NNNNNNNNNNF	V,D,J	002	329	03.01.02	5514	010302	79999
413.161-018	WORM GROWER (agriculture)	4336	33443433355	MNNOOONFFOOOONONNNNN	NNNN3NNNNNNNNNN	V,D,J	002	329	03.01.02	5514	010302	79999
413.687-010	WORM PICKER (agriculture)	2111	44544543344	LNNFFFNFFNNNNNNNNN	CNNN3NNNNNNNNNN	R	002	329	03.04.01	5617	010302	79999
413.687-014	WORM-FARM LABORER (agriculture)	2111	45545533455	MNNOOONFFOONNNNNNNNN	NNNN3NNNNNNNNNN	R	002	329	03.04.01	5617	010302	79999
413.687-018	BEE WORKER (agriculture)	2112	44443433455	MONONNNCCFNNNNFNNNNN	NNNN3NNNNNNNNNN	R,U	002	329	03.04.01	5617	010302	79999
418.137-010	SUPERVISOR, LABORATORY ANIMAL FACILITY (agriculture)	4347	22344344455	LNNOOONFFOOFNFNNONN	NNNN3NNNNNNNNNNO	D,V,P,J	251	329	02.04.02	5621	020203	72002
418.137-014	SUPERVISOR, RESEARCH KENNEL (agriculture)	3334	33333344354	MNNOOOONFFONFFNNNCON	NNNN3NNNNNNNNNNN	V,T	251	329	03.02.01	5621	010599	72002
418.381-010	HORSESHOER (agriculture)	3226	34433533254	MNNFNNNNFFNNNNFNOFON	NNNN3NNNNNNNNNNO	J,T	291	969	03.03.02	5624	010599	79017
418.384-010	ARTIFICIAL INSEMINATOR (agriculture)	3323	33433334344	MNNNNNNFFFNNNNONONON	FNNN3NFNNNNNNNNF	V,J	002	321	03.04.05	3820	010302	79015
418.384-014	ARTIFICIAL-BREEDING TECHNICIAN (agriculture)	3326	33332333443	LNNONNNFFONNNFFON	NNNN3NFNNNNNNNFF	V,J,T	002	321	03.02.04	3820	020202	24502
418.674-010	DOG GROOMER (personal ser.)	3234	34433422344	MNNONNNFFNNONFNFNON	NNNN4NNNNNNNNNN	J,P	291	329	03.03.02	5624	010599	79017
418.677-010	DOG BATHER (personal ser.)	3222	34433433344	LNNNNNNFFFNNNNFNOOON	NNNF3NNNNNNNNNN	P,T	291	329	03.03.02	5624	010599	79017
419.224-010	HORSE TRAINER (agriculture; amuse. & rec.)	3227	34433333333	MFFOOOOFFOOOONOFFNOO	FNNN3NNNNNNNNNN	J,V,P	296	327	03.03.01	5617	010501	79016
421.161-010	FARMER, GENERAL (agriculture)	4447	23323344444	HONOOONFFOOOONONFOON	FNNN3NNNNNNNNNNF	V,D,J	003	300	03.01.01	5512	020202	79999
421.683-010	FARMWORKER, GENERAL I (agriculture)	3235	34444433344	HONOOONFFNNNNNNFOON	FNNN3NNNNNNNNNNF	V,J,T	003	300	03.04.01	5612	010204	79855
421.687-010	FARMWORKER, GENERAL II (agriculture)	2112	44545544345	HOOOOONFFNNNNNNNNNNN	FNNN3NNNNNNNNNN	R	003	300	03.04.01	5612	010304	79855
429.387-010	COTTON CLASSER (agriculture; textile)	4337	33333333353	LNNNNNNCCCNNNNCNCFN	NNNN3NNNNNNNNNN	J	211	414	06.01.05	5625	000000	79011
429.587-010	COTTON CLASSER AIDE (agriculture)	2122	44443444455	LNNNNNNOOONONNNNNNNN	NNNN3NNNNNNNNNN	R,T,U	231	302	06.03.02	5625	000000	79011
429.685-010	GINNER (agriculture)	3124	34434444344	LONONONFFOONNOONONON	NNNN4NFNNNNNNNN	R	031	419	05.12.07	5616	010204	79021
429.685-014	THRESHER, BROOMCORN (agriculture)	2112	44544544345	LNNNNNNFFNNNNNNNNN	CNNN4NNNNNNNNNNF	R	003	309	03.04.01	5616	010204	79021
429.686-010	PRESS FEEDER, BROOMCORN (agriculture)	2112	44444444355	LNNNNNNFFNNNNNNFNNN	CNNN4NNNNNNNNNNN	R	003	309	03.04.01	8725	000000	98502
441.132-010	BOATSWAIN, OTTER TRAWLER (fishing & hunt.)	4237	33423433244	HFCFFFOFFFNFNFFFOF	FOON4NNNNNNNNNN	D,P,J	001	330	03.04.01	5830	490303	00000
441.683-010	SKIFF OPERATOR (fishing & hunt.)	3124	34434544335	HFFOOONFFNNNNNNFFNNF	FNNF4NNNNNNNNNNF	S	001	331	03.04.03	5830	000000	79999
441.684-010	FISHER, NET (fishing & hunt.)	2114	34444544435	HFCFFFNFFNNNNNNFFNNF	CNNF4NNNNNNNNNNF	R	001	330	03.04.03	5830	000000	79999
441.684-014	FISHER, POT (fishing & hunt.)	2112	44445544335	VNFFFFNFFNNNNNNNNNN	CNNF4NNNNNNNNNNF	R	001	330	03.04.03	5830	000000	79999
441.684-018	FISHER, TERRAPIN (fishing & hunt.)	2112	44543534334	HOFFNONFFNNNNNNFFNOF	CNNF3NNNNNNNNNN	R	001	339	03.04.03	5830	000000	79999
441.684-022	FISHER, WEIR (fishing & hunt.)	2114	34433534355	HOFFNONFFNNNNNNNFNNN	CNNF3NNNNNNNNNNF	V	001	331	03.04.03	5830	000000	79999
442.684-010	FISHER, LINE (fishing & hunt.)	2113	44444534345	MOFOOONFFONNNNNNNNNN	CONF3NNNNNNNNNNN	R	001	330	03.04.03	5830	000000	79999
443.664-010	FISHER, DIVING (fishing & hunt.)	3224	34433444334	HOFFNCNFFNNOONFFNOF	CNNF3NNNNNNNNNNF	S,J	001	332	03.04.03	5830	000000	79999
443.684-010	FISHER, SPEAR (fishing & hunt.)	2114	44443534334	HOFFNFNFFNNNNNNNFNOF	CNNF3NNNNNNNNNNF	R	001	331	03.04.03	5830	000000	79999
446.133-010	SUPERVISOR, SHELLFISH FARMING (fishing & hunt.)	4236	33433433344	MNNFFONFFNFFNFFONON	CNNF4NNNNNNNNNNO	D,J,P,V	002	332	03.02.01	5611	010303	72002
446.134-010	SUPERVISOR, FISH HATCHERY (fishing & hunt.)	4237	33333343343	MNNNFOONFFFFNFNOFN	CNNF3NFNNNNNNNON	D,J,P,V	002	331	03.02.01	5611	010303	72002
446.161-010	FISH FARMER (fishing & hunt.)	4126	33443443344	MOOFONFFOOOONFOONOO	FONF3NNNNNNNNNNO	D,J	002	331	03.01.02	5514	030301	79999
446.161-014	SHELLFISH GROWER (fishing & hunt.)	4126	33444433335	MNOOFNFFFNNOONONONNN	CNNF4NNNNNNNNNNN	V,D	002	332	03.01.02	5514	010303	79999
446.663-010	SHELLFISH DREDGE OPERATOR (fishing & hunt.)	3225	34433534345	HOFONNFFNNNNNNOFFNNF	FNNF4NNNNNNNNNNF	R,J,T	002	332	03.04.03	5830	010303	79999
446.684-010	FISH HATCHERY WORKER (fishing & hunt.)	3125	34434433343	MOOFFNFFNFFFNNNFOFNFO	FNNF3NNNNNNNNNNF	V,J,T	002	331	03.04.03	5618	010303	79999
446.684-014	SHELLFISH-BED WORKER (fishing & hunt.)	2113	44445534345	HNNFOONFFNFFNNNNNNNN	CNNF3NNNNNNNNNN	R,T	002	332	03.04.03	5618	010303	79999
446.684-018	SOFT CRAB SHEDDER (fishing & hunt.)	2114	44443544345	MNNFNFNFFNNNNNNNNNNN	NNNF3NNNNNNNNNN	R,T	002	332	03.04.03	5618	010303	79999
446.687-010	CLAM SORTER (fishing & hunt.)	2122	44433534345	HNOFORNCCNNNNNNCNNNNN	CNNF3NNNNNNNNNN	R,T	001	332	03.04.03	5625	010303	79011
446.687-014	LABORER, AQUATIC LIFE (fishing & hunt.)	2112	44444534344	HNNFNFNFFNNNNNNNFFNON	CNNF3NNNNNNNNNN	R,T	002	330	03.04.03	5618	010303	79999
447.687-010	SPONGE HOOKER (fishing & hunt.)	1112	44545444444	LNNFFFNFNNNNNNNNNNO	CNNF4NNNNNNNNNN	R	001	339	03.04.03	5830	000000	79999
447.687-010	DULSER (fishing & hunt.)	1112	44454544444	LNNFNFNFNNNNNNNNNNN	CNNF4NNNNNNNNNN	R	003	339	03.04.03	5830	000000	79999
447.687-014	IRISH-MOSS BLEACHER (fishing & hunt.)	1112	44445444445	LNNFNFNFNNNNNNNNNNN	CNNF3NNNNNNNNNNO	R	152	339	03.04.03	5830	000000	79999
447.687-018	IRISH-MOSS GATHERER (fishing & hunt.)	1112	44444544445	LNNFNFNFNNNNNNNNNNN	CNNF3NNNNNNNNNN	R	003	339	03.04.03	5830	000000	79999
447.687-022	KELP CUTTER (fishing & hunt.)	2112	44444543454	HNNNNNNFFFNNNNNNNNNN	CNNF4NNNNNNNNNN	R	003	339	03.04.03	5830	000000	79999
447.687-026	SPONGE CLIPPER (fishing & hunt.; wholesale tr.)	2112	44444543454	LNNNNNNNFFFNNNNNNNNN	ONNN3NNNNNNNNNN	R,T	031	339	03.04.03	5830	000000	79999
449.664-010	NET REPAIRER (fishing & hunt.)	3126	34433533345	HFFFFFNFFOOONFNFNN	CNNF4NNNNNNNNNN	R,T	165	439	05.10.01	5830	490309	79999

DOT #	DOT Title & Industry	Trng	Aptitude	Physical	Environment	Tempra	WkF	MPSMS	GOE	SOC	CIP	OES
449.667-010	DECKHAND, FISHING VESSEL (fishing & hunt.)	2113	44434534334	HNNONNNCCNNNONNNCCNON	CONF4NFNNNNNNF	T,V	001	330	03.04.03	5830	000000	79999
449.674-010	AQUARIST (amuse. & rec.)	3224	33433433344	LNNONONFFNOONFNOOFN	FNNF3NNNNNNNNN	V,J	291	330	03.03.02	5624	010303	79017
449.687-010	OYSTER FLOATER (fishing & hunt.)	1111	44444544455	LNNFNFNFFNNNNNNNNNN	CNNF3NNNNNNNNN	R	001	332	03.04.03	5830	000000	79999
451.137-010	FOREST NURSERY SUPERVISOR (forestry)	4336	33333444454	LNNOOONFFONFFNONONON	FNNO4NNNNNNNNN	D,J,P	003	312	03.02.02	5710	010606	72002
451.137-014	SUPERVISOR, CHRISTMAS-TREE FARM (forestry)	3225	33333444455	LNNNNNNOOONFFNFFNFN	FNNN4NNNNNNNNN	V,D,P	003	319	03.02.01	5710	010603	72002
451.687-010	CHRISTMAS-TREE FARM WORKER (forestry)	1112	45544544335	HNNFFFNFFONNNNNNFNNN	NNNF4NFNNNNNNN	R	003	312	03.04.01	5720	030401	79002
451.687-014	CHRISTMAS-TREE GRADER (forestry)	2113	44434343353	MNNNNNNCCNNNNNNONCNCN	NNNC4NNNNNNNNN	J	212	319	03.04.04	5720	030401	79002
451.687-018	SEEDLING PULLER (forestry)	1111	45544544345	MNNCOONCCNNNNNNNNNNNN	CNNN3NNNNNNNNN	R	003	312	03.04.02	5720	010606	79002
451.687-022	SEEDLING SORTER (forestry)	1112	44543434353	LNNFNNNFFNNONCNNNCN	NNNC4NNNNNNNNN	R,T	212	312	03.04.02	5720	010606	79002
452.134-010	SMOKE JUMPER SUPERVISOR (forestry)	3238	33423434334	VOFFFFFFFFFNOFFNFF	FNFN4NFNNNNNNF	D,P,S,J	293	313	04.02.04	5111	430203	61002
452.167-010	FIRE WARDEN (forestry)	5337	22344444444	LOOFFFNFFONFFOOFFNOF	FNFN4NNNNNNNNF	V,D,P,J	293	313	04.01.02	5122	030203	63005
452.364-010	FORESTER AIDE (forestry)	4336	33333333333	MOOOOOOFFOOFFOOFFNOO	FNFN4NNNNNNNNF	V,P,J	293	313	03.02.02	5720	030101	79002
452.364-014	SMOKE JUMPER (forestry)	3226	33423324223	VOOOOOOFFONFFNOFFNOF	FNFF4NFNNNNNNF	V,S,J	293	313	04.02.04	5123	430203	63008
452.367-010	FIRE LOOKOUT (forestry)	3235	33433444444	LFFNNNNFFNFFNFFFNOF	ONNN3NNNNNNNNN	A,J	293	313	07.04.05	5122	030203	63005
452.367-014	FIRE RANGER (forestry)	3234	33434444434	MOOFFFNFFNFFOOFFNON	FNNN4NNNNNNNNN	V,P,S,J	293	313	04.02.02	5122	030203	63005
452.687-010	FOREST WORKER (forestry)	2112	44434534344	HFFFFFNFFNNNNFNFNFN	CNNN4NNNNNNNNF	V	003	313	03.04.02	5720	030401	79002
452.687-014	FOREST-FIRE FIGHTER (forestry)	2112	44533534334	HFFFFFFFNNNNNNNNON	CNFN4NFNNNNNNF	R,S	293	313	03.04.02	5123	030203	63008
452.687-018	TREE PLANTER (forestry)	1111	45544544445	HFFFFFNCCFNNNNNNNNNN	CNNF3NNNNNNNNN	R	003	312	03.04.02	5720	010606	79002
453.687-010	FOREST-PRODUCTS GATHERER (agriculture; forestry)	2112	44544544444	MNNFFNNFFONNNNFFFNON	CNNN3NNNNNNNNN	R	003	310	03.04.02	5720	030404	79002
453.687-014	LABORER, TREE TAPPING (agriculture; forestry)	1112	44545544445	MNNNNNNFFNNNNFNFNNN	CNNN3NNNNNNNNN	R	003	319	03.04.02	5720	030405	79002
454.134-010	SUPERVISOR, FELLING-BUCKING (logging)	4237	33333445444	LOONNNNFFNFFNFFFNOF	FNNN4NNNNNNNNF	V,D,P,J	004	451	03.04.02	7100	030405	73002
454.384-010	FALLER I (logging)	3126	34343534335	HFOFOFOFFNNNNNFNFNF	CNNN4NNNNNNNNN	V,S,J	004	451	03.04.02	5730	030405	73002
454.683-010	TREE-SHEAR OPERATOR (logging)	3114	34433534335	MONNNNNCCONNNNONFNNF	CNNN4NNNNNNNNN	R	004	451	03.04.02	5730	030405	73011
454.684-010	BUCKER (logging)	2113	44534534335	HFOFOFFNNNNFNFNNF	CNNN4NFNNNNNNF	R	004	451	03.04.02	5730	030405	73002
454.684-014	FALLER II (logging)	2113	44534534345	HNNFOFNFFNNNNNOFFNF	CNNN4NNNNNNNNF	R	004	451	03.04.02	5730	030405	73002
454.684-018	LOGGER, ALL-ROUND (logging)	2214	44344434445	HFOFOFFOONNONFFFNNF	CNNN4NFNNNNNNF	R,J	004	451	03.04.02	5730	030405	73099
454.684-022	RIVER (logging)	2112	44435534345	HNNFFNFFNNNNNFNFNNN	CNNN4NFNNNNNNF	R,T	004	451	03.04.02	5730	030405	73099
454.684-026	TREE CUTTER (agriculture; logging)	2112	44445534345	HFOFOFNFFNNNNNFNFNNF	CNNN4NFNNNNNNF	R	004	451	03.04.02	5730	030405	73002
454.687-010	CHAIN SAW OPERATOR (chemical: logging; millwork-plywood)	3213	34433444444	MNNCNNNCCCNNNNCCCCNC	CNNN4NNNNNNNNN	J	212	451	05.07.06	5790	030404	79008
455.134-010	SUPERVISOR, LOG SORTING (logging; millwork-plywood)	3237	33333333344	LOONNNNFFONFFNNCFNON	CNNF3NNNNNNNNF	V,D,P,S	004	451	03.04.02	5710	030404	72002
455.367-010	LOG GRADER (logging; saw. & plan.)	3326	34433444444	LOFFNFNFFNFFNFFNOF	FNNN4NNNNNNNNN	J	212	451	05.07.06	7850	030404	79008
455.487-010	LOG SCALER (logging; millwork-plywood; paper & pulp: saw. & plan.)	3325	34433334344	LFFFFFNFFNNNNNFNFN	FNNN4NNNNNNNNN	J,T	212	451	05.07.06	5790	030404	79008
455.664-010	RAFTER (logging)	2113	34434534325	HNCFFNCCNNNNNNFFNNF	CNNF4NNNNNNNNF	R,S	004	451	03.04.02	5790	030404	73099
455.684-010	LOG SORTER (logging)	3113	34433533324	LHFNFNFFNNNNFFNFFN	CNNC4NNNNNNNNN	R,S	004	451	03.04.02	5790	000000	73099
455.687-010	LOG MARKER (logging)	2112	44444534334	MFFNNNNFFNNNONNNFNOF	CNNF4NNNNNNNNF	R	231	451	03.04.02	5790	030405	73099
459.133-010	SUPERVISOR, LOGGING (logging)	4237	33434434345	LFONNNNFFONFFNFFFNNF	CNNN4NNNNNNNNN	V,D,P,J	004	451	03.02.02	5710	030405	72002
459.137-010	WOODS BOSS (logging)	4237	33333444455	LNNNNNNFFNNNNFFFNNFF	CNNN3NNNNNNNNO	V,D,P,J	004	451	03.02.01	7100	030405	81008
459.387-010	CRUISER (forestry; logging)	4337	33333434344	MNNNNNNFFNNNNFFFNFF	CNNN3NNNNNNNNN	J	212	313	03.02.02	5790	030101	73099
459.687-010	LABORER, BRUSH CLEARING (any industry)	1112	44544544345	HNNCNNNCCNNNNNNNNNNNN	CNNN4NNNNNNNNN	R	004	310	03.04.02	5730	030101	73099
461.134-010	EXPEDITION SUPERVISOR (fishing & hunt.)	4236	33422424233	VFFOONFFNOFFNFFNOFOOF	CNNN3NFNNNNNNN	J	001	339	03.04.03	5840	030601	79999
461.661-010	PREDATORY-ANIMAL HUNTER (fishing & hunt.)	3115	34433533333	VOOOOOOFFOONNNOFFNFF	CNNN3NFNNNNNNN	V,J	001	325	03.04.03	5840	030601	79999
461.664-010	UNDERWATER HUNTER-TRAPPER (fishing & hunt.)	4235	33433533333	VOOOOOOFFOOONFOFONF	CNNC3NNNNNNNNN	J,S	001	330	03.04.03	5840	030601	79999
461.684-010	SEALER (fishing & hunt.)	2212	44543533334	MNNFFNFFNNNNNNNNNNN	CNNF3NNNNNNNNF	R,J	001	339	03.04.03	5840	000000	79999
461.684-014	TRAPPER, ANIMAL (fishing & hunt.)	3225	34543533333	HOOFOFOFFOONNNOOONOO	CNNO3NNNNNNNNN	V,J	001	325	03.04.03	5840	010399	79999
461.684-018	TRAPPER, BIRD (fishing & hunt.)	3224	34543533333	MOOOOOOFFONNNNNOONON	CNNN4NNNNNNNNN	V,J,T	001	325	03.04.03	5840	010399	79999
500.131-010	SUPERVISOR (electroplating)	4347	33333433354	LNNNNNNFFOFFNFNOFON	NNNF4NNNNNNNNN	D,P,T	154	540	06.02.01	7100	000000	81008
500.132-010	LABORER, SHEET MANUFACTURING (smelt. & refin.)	4337	33333333355	LNNNNNNFFNFFNFNNNNN	NNNN3NNNNNNNNN	V,D,P,J	154	541	06.02.01	7100	000000	81008
500.134-010	SUPERVISOR, MATRIX (recording)	4336	33333444445	LNNNNNNFFONNNNFNNFFN	NNNN3NNNNNNNNN	V,D,P,J	154	556	06.02.01	7100	000000	81008
500.287-010	INSPECTOR, PLATING (electroplating)	3333	33333434353	MNNNNNNFFONNNNFNNFFN	NNNN3NNNNNNNNO	J,T	154	550	06.03.01	7820	000000	83005

DOT #	DOT Title & Industry	Trng	Aptitude	Physical	Environment	Tempra	WkF	MPSMS	GOE	SOC	CIP	OES
500.362-010	ELECTROGALVANIZING-MACHINE OPERATOR (electroplating)	4336	3333343353	HONFFFFFNNNNFNFFFN	NNON4NONNNNNNNO	J,T	154	557	06.02.21	7343	000000	91917
500.362-014	PLATER, BARREL (electroplating)	3335	34434444354	MNNNNNNFFOONNNFNFNON	NNNF4NNNNNNNNN	J,T	154	550	06.02.21	7543	000000	91921
500.380-010	PLATER (electroplating)	4337	33333443334	MNNNNNNFFFONNNFNFFON	NNNF4NFNNNNNNNN	J,T	154	540	06.02.21	7343	000000	91917
500.380-014	PLATER APPRENTICE (electroplating)	4337	34434443354	MNNNNNNFFFONNNFNFFON	NNNF4NFNNNNNNNN	J,T	154	540	06.02.21	7343	000000	91917
500.381-010	CYLINDER GRINDER (print. & pub.)	3337	33433433355	MNNNNNNNFFONNNNFNFNNN	NNNF4NNNNNNNNNN	R,J,T	154	567	05.10.05	6816	480503	89111
500.384-010	MATRIX PLATER (recording)	3224	33443343355	LNNNNNNNFFONNNFNFNNN	NNNF4NNNNNNNNNN	R,T	154	556	06.02.21	7756	000000	91921
500.384-014	MATRIX-BATH ATTENDANT (recording)	3335	34343434355	MNNNNNNNFFNNNNFNFNNN	NNNF3NNNNNNNNNF	J,T	154	556	06.02.21	7549	000000	91921
500.485-010	ZINC-PLATING-MACHINE OPERATOR (electroplating)	3224	34343434354	MNNNNNNNFFNNNNFNFFNN	NNNF3NNNNNNNNNN	J,T	154	544	06.02.21	7543	000000	91921
500.682-010	ANODIZER (any industry)	3234	34433444354	HNNNNNNNFFONNNNFNFNON	ONFF4NFNNNNNNNN	R,T	154	550	06.02.21	7543	000000	91921
500.684-010	ELECTROFORMER (electroplating)	2114	34444443354	LNNNNNNNFFNNNNFNFNON	NNNF3NNNNNNNNNN	R,J	151	619	06.04.33	7759	000000	91921
500.684-014	MATRIX WORKER (recording)	2222	44434444355	LNNNNNNNFFFNNNNFNFNNN	NNNN4NNNNNNNNNN	J,T	031	556	06.04.24	7543	000000	93999
500.684-018	PLATE FORMER (elec. equip.)	3224	34434443354	LNNNNNNNFFNNNNFNFNON	NNNN3NNNNNNNNON	R,T	154	589	06.02.32	7543	000000	91921
500.684-022	SILVER SPRAY WORKER (recording)	2224	34444434354	LNNNNNNNCCONNNNCNCNON	NNNF3NFNNNNNNNN	R	153	585	06.04.33	7756	000000	93947
500.684-026	PLATER, PRINTED CIRCUIT BOARD PANELS (electron. comp.)	2123	44444444355	HNNNNNNNCCONNNNFNFNNN	NNNN4NNNNNNNNON	T,U	154	587	06.02.21	7543	470105	91921
500.684-030	PLATER, SEMICONDUCTOR WAFERS AND COMPONENTS (electron. comp.)	3223	34433434453	HNNNNNNNFFNNNNONOOON	NNNO4NNNNNNNNNF	T	154	587	06.04.19	7543	470105	91921
500.684-034	PLATER (inst. & app.)	3225	34435353355	LNNNNNNNFFOONNNNFNFNN	NNNO4NONNNNNNON	T,U	154	589	06.02.32	7543	000000	91921
500.685-010	ETCHER, ELECTROLYTIC (cutlery-hrdwr.)	2222	44434444355	LNNNNNNNFFNNNNNFNFNNN	NNNN3NNNNNNNNON	R	182	550	06.04.10	7529	000000	92198
500.685-014	PLATING EQUIPMENT TENDER (electroplating)	2223	34434444354	MNNONNNFFONNNNFOFNON	NNNN4NCONNNNNON	R,T	154	540	06.04.21	7543	000000	91921
500.686-010	LABORER, ELECTROPLATING (electroplating)	2222	44444444344	HNNNNNNNFFONNNNONFNON	NNNN4NOONNNNNON	R,U	154	540	06.04.21	8619	000000	98999
500.687-010	PLATE-TAKE-OUT WORKER (elec. equip.)	2112	44444444355	MNNFNNNNFFNNNNNNNNNNN	NNNF3NNNNNNNNNN	R	154	589	06.04.24	8769	000000	98999
501.130-010	SUPERVISOR, HOT-DIP-TINNING (steel & rel.)	4348	33333433355	MNNNNNNNFFONFFNFNFNNN	NNFF4NFNNNNNNNN	V,D,P,J	151	541	06.02.01	7100	000000	81008
501.137-010	SUPERVISOR, HOT-DIP PLATING (galvanizing)	4347	33333433454	LNNNNNNNFFOFFNFNOFON	NNNF4NNNNNNNNNF	V,D,P,J	151	550	06.02.01	7100	000000	81008
501.362-010	COATING-MACHINE OPERATOR (galvanizing)	3337	34343443354	MNNNNNNNFFNNNNNFNFNOO	NNFN4NFNNNNNNNN	R,J,T	151	541	06.02.10	7343	000000	91923
501.485-010	WIRE-COATING OPERATOR, METAL (galvanizing)	2112	44443433345	MNNONONFFFNNNNFNFFNN	NNNN4NNNNNNNNNF	J,T	151	557	06.04.21	7543	000000	91926
501.685-010	PLATER, HOT DIP (galvanizing)	2114	44435443354	HNNNNNNNFFOONNNFNFNON	NNNF4NFNNNNNNNN	R,T	151	550	06.04.21	7543	000000	91926
501.685-014	TINNING-EQUIPMENT TENDER (elec. equip.)	1112	44444444345	MNNNNNNNFFONFFNNNNNNN	NNNN3NNNNNNNNNN	R,T	151	580	06.04.21	7543	000000	91926
501.685-018	BLACK OXIDE COATING EQUIPMENT TENDER (electron. comp.)	2222	44444444455	MONONNNOOONNNNNNNNNN	NNNN4NNNNNNNNNF	R,U	151	587	06.04.21	7543	470105	91926
501.685-022	ELECTROLESS PLATER, PRINTED CIRCUIT BOARD PANELS (electron. comp.)	2222	44444444455	HNNNNNNNFFONNNNFNFFNN	NNNN3NNNNNNNNNN	R,U	151	587	06.04.21	7543	470105	91926
502.130-010	SUPERVISOR, CASTING-AND-PASTING (elec. equip.)	4337	33333433354	LNNNNNNNFFOFFNFNFNON	NNNN4NNNNNNNNNN	V,D,P,J	131	589	06.01.01	7100	520205	81008
502.362-010	SHOT DROPPER (ordnance)	3336	34333344345	MFNNNNNNFFNNOONFNFNNN	NNFN4NFNNNNNNNF	J,T	131	374	06.02.10	7542	480599	91911
502.381-010	CASTER (jewelry-silver.)	3226	34433533355	MNNNNNNNFFONNNNNFNFNN	NNNN3NNNNNNNNNN	R,T	132	611	06.02.24	6822	470408	89126
502.381-014	MOLDER, PUNCH (aircraft mfg.)	4337	33333434355	MNNNOOONFFOONNNONFFNN	NNON4NNNNNNNNNO	T	132	566	06.02.24	6861	480599	89905
502.382-010	BULLET-SLUG-CASTING-MACHINE OPERATOR (ordnance)	3225	34434433355	HNNONONFFFNNNNNFNFONN	NNFN4NNNNNNNNNN	J,T	132	542	06.02.10	7542	480599	91911
502.382-014	FLUOROSCOPE OPERATOR (nonfer. metal)	3335	33432444354	LNNNNNNNFFFNNNNFNFFON	NNNN4NNNNNNNNNF	J,T	211	534	06.03.01	7820	480501	83005
502.382-018	PEWTER CASTER (jewelry-silver.)	3226	34434433355	MNNNNNNONFFONNNNFNFNNN	NNON3NNNNNNNNNN	V,T	132	612	06.02.24	7754	480501	93944
502.482-010	CASTER (nonfer. metal)	2223	34433434354	MNNNNNNNFFFNNNFNFNON	NNFN4NNNNNNNNNF	J,T	131	542	06.02.10	7754	480599	91911
502.482-014	CASTING-MACHINE OPERATOR, AUTOMATIC (elec. equip.)	3224	34443433354	MNNNNNNNFFFNNNFNFNON	NNFN4NNNNNNNNNF	R,J,T	131	589	06.02.10	7542	480599	91911
502.482-018	ROTOR CASTING-MACHINE OPERATOR (elec. equip.)	3225	34434434355	HNNNNNNNFFFNNNNFNFNNN	NNFN4NNNNNNNNNN	J,T	132	582	06.02.10	7342	480599	91908
502.664-010	BLAST-FURNACE KEEPER (steel & rel.)	3226	34434534355	HNNNNNNNFFFNNNNFNFNNN	NNNN4NNNNNNNNNN	R,T	131	541	06.04.10	7759	480599	93999
502.664-014	STEEL POURER (steel & rel.)	3226	34433444345	MNNNNNNNFFOONNNFNFNNN	NNFN4NFNNNNNNNF	J,T	132	541	06.02.24	7754	480599	93941
502.664-018	STEEL-POURER HELPER (steel & rel.)	2225	34434433355	MNNNNNNNFFFNNNNFNFNNN	NNNN4NNNNNNNNNF	J,T	132	541	06.02.24	8620	480501	98999
502.682-010	BULLET-CASTING OPERATOR (ordnance)	3224	34433434355	HONONONFFONNNNNFNFNNN	NNFN4NFNNNNNNNN	J,T	131	540	06.02.10	7542	480599	91911
502.682-014	CASTING-MACHINE OPERATOR (nonfer. metal)	3224	34434444355	MNNNNNNNFFFNNNNFNFNNN	NNFN4NNNNNNNNNN	R,T	132	544	06.02.10	7342	480599	91908
502.682-018	CENTRIFUGAL-CASTING-MACHINE OPERATOR (jewelry-silver.)	3225	34433434355	LNNNNNNNFFFNNNNFNFNNN	NNNN3NNNNNNNNNN	R,T	132	542	06.02.10	7542	470408	91911
502.684-010	LEAD CASTER (elec. equip.)	2223	34433434354	LNNFNNNFFONNNFNFNON	NNFN4NFNNNNNNNN	J,T	131	589	06.04.24	7754	480599	93944
502.684-014	MILL HELPER (nonfer. metal)	2223	44434434355	HNNONONFFFNNNNFNFNNN	NNFN3NFNNNNNNNN	J,T	132	543	06.04.24	7542	480599	91911
502.684-018	MOLD SETTER (elec. equip.)	3333	34343433355	MNNFNNNNFFNNNFNFNNN	NNNN4NFNNNNNNNN	J,T	121	589	06.04.32	7759	480599	93999
502.684-022	NEEDLE LEADER (button & notion)	2222	44434443455	LNNNNNNFFFFNNNNFNFNNN	NNFN3NNNNNNNNNN	R,T	132	618	06.04.32	7754	480599	93944
502.685-010	MOLDER, LEAD INGOT (ordnance)	2222	44444444355	MNNFNNNFFOONNNNNFNNNN	NNFN3NNNNNNNNNN	J,T	132	541	06.04.10	7542	480599	91911
502.685-014	REMELTER (elec. equip.: machinery mfg.; print. & pub.)	2222	44444444355	MNNFNNNFFONNNNNNNNNF	NNFN4NFNNNNNNNF	R	131	541	06.04.10	7542	480599	91911
502.686-010	CASTING-MACHINE-OPERATOR HELPER (elec. equip.)	2112	44444544355	MNNFNNNFFFNNNNNNNNNN	NNNN3NNNNNNNNNN	R	132	589	06.04.10	8614	480599	98999

DOT #	DOT Title & Industry	Trng	Aptitude	Physical	Environment	Tempra	WkF	MPSMS	GOE	SOC	CIP	OES
502.687-010	BLAST-FURNACE-KEEPER HELPER (steel & rel.)	2223	44434534355	HNNNNNNFNNNNNNNNN	NNFN4NNNNNNNNNN	R	131	541	06.04.10	8620	480599	98999
502.687-014	BUSHER (nonmet. min.)	2112	44534344355	HHNFNNNFFNNNNNFNFNNN	NNFN3NNNNNNNNN	R	132	538	06.04.32	8614	480599	98999
502.687-018	LEAD-CASTER HELPER (elec. equip.)	2112	44435544354	LNNNNNNFFONNNFNFON	NNNN3NNNNNNNNN	R,T	131	589	06.04.24	8620	480599	98999
503.137-010	SUPERVISOR, SANDBLASTER (ship-boat mfg.)	4337	33333344355	LONNOOOFFONFFNFFNFNN	FNNN4FNNFNNNNN	D,P,V	051	593	05.12.01	7100	000000	81008
503.362-010	PICKLER, CONTINUOUS PICKLING LINE (any industry)	3326	34333434355	MNNNNNNFFFNNNNFNFNNN	NNNN3NFNNNNNNNN	J,T	031	540	06.02.10	7479	480599	92997
503.362-014	SHOTBLAST-EQUIPMENT OPERATOR (foundry)	3235	33433434344	HNNNNNNFFONOONFONONN	NNNN4NNNNNNNNN	T,J	031	542	06.02.10	7549	480599	92198
503.684-010	CLEANER (ordnance)	2113	44343433354	LNNNNNNFFONNNFNFNFN	NNNF3NFNNNNNNNN	R	031	373	06.04.39	7756	000000	92198
503.685-010	COATER (business ser.)	3224	44434344355	MNNNNNNFFONNNNNOFNNNN	NNON4NNNNNNNNNN	R,T	151	556	06.04.21	7543	000000	91926
503.685-014	DIP-LUBE OPERATOR (ordnance)	2112	44433444355	HNNFNNNFFFNNNFNNNNN	NNNN4NFNNNNNNN	R	151	374	06.04.21	7549	000000	92198
503.685-018	DRIFTER (steel & rel.)	2213	44445544355	MNNNNNNFFNNNNNNNNNN	NNNN4NNNNNNNN	R,T	031	541	06.04.02	7549	000000	92198
503.685-022	FLAME DEGREASER (automotive ser.)	1112	44544544455	MNNNNNNFFNNNNNNNNN	NNFN4NNNNNNNNN	J	031	591	06.04.39	7675	000000	92923
503.685-026	FURNACE-AND-WASH-EQUIPMENT OPERATOR (ordnance)	2222	44443444355	MNNNNNNFFONNNNFNNNNN	NNNN4NNNNNNNNNN	J	141	374	06.04.10	7549	000000	92198
503.685-030	METAL-CLEANER, IMMERSION (any industry)	2212	44444444355	MNNNNNNFFONNNNONFNNN	NNNC4NONNNNNCN	R,T	031	540	06.04.39	7549	000000	92198
503.685-034	METAL-WASHING-MACHINE OPERATOR (svc. ind. mach.)	2222	44434444355	MNNNNNNFFNNNNFNFNNN	NNNF3NNNNNNNNN	R,T	031	573	06.04.21	7549	000000	92198
503.685-038	SANDBLAST OPERATOR (ordnance)	2213	44433544355	MNNNNNNFFFNNNNNNNNN	NNNN3NNNNNNNNNF	R	031	372	06.04.02	7549	000000	92198
503.685-042	SANDBLAST-OR-SHOTBLAST-EQUIPMENT TENDER (any industry)	2212	44444434355	MNNNNNNFFNNNNNNNNN	NNNN5NONNNNNNN	R,U	051	540	05.12.18	7549	000000	92198
503.685-046	STRIP-TANK TENDER (ordnance)	2213	44444434355	MNNNNNNFFFNNNNFNFNNN	NNNF3NFNNNNNNF	R,T	031	373	06.04.10	7549	000000	92198
503.686-010	PICKLER HELPER, CONTINUOUS PICKLING LINE (any industry)	2223	44443434355	MNNNNNNFFONNNNONFNNN	NNNF3NNNNNNNNN	R,T	031	540	06.02.21	8619	000000	98905
503.687-010	SANDBLASTER (any industry)	2212	44445534345	MNNOONNFFONNNFNFNNN	NNNN4NNNNNNNNF	R,T	051	530	05.12.18	8750	480599	98905
504.131-010	HEAT-TREAT SUPERVISOR (heat treating)	4337	33333343353	LNNNNNNFFOFFNFNFEFN	NNFN4NNNNNNNNF	V,D,P,J	133	540	06.01.01	7100	520205	81008
504.281-010	HEAT-TREAT INSPECTOR (heat treating)	4337	33343443353	LNNNNNNFFONNNFNFNFN	NNNN4NNNNNNNNN	J,T	133	540	06.01.05	6881	480503	83002
504.360-010	FLAME-ANNEALING-MACHINE SETTER (heat treating)	4336	34433443353	LNNFNFNFFNOONFNFNFN	NNFN3NNNNNNNNN	J,T	133	374	06.01.02	7344	480503	91928
504.380-010	FLAME-HARDENING-MACHINE SETTER (heat treating)	4337	34433434343	MNNNNNNFFFNNNNFNFNFN	NNNN4NNNNNNNNN	J,T	133	540	06.01.02	7344	480503	91928
504.380-014	INDUCTION-MACHINE SETTER (heat treating)	3337	34433434353	MNNNNNNFFFNNNNFNFNNN	NNNN4NFNNNNNNN	J	133	540	06.01.02	7344	480503	91928
504.382-010	HARDENER (clock & watch)	4336	33333434353	HNNNNNNFFONNNNONNNNN	NNNN4NFNNNNNNN	J,T	133	607	06.02.10	7544	480503	91932
504.382-014	HEAT TREATER I (heat treating)	4337	33343434353	MNNNNNNFFNNNNFNFNFN	NNFN4NFNNNNNNN	V,J,T	133	540	06.02.10	7544	480503	91932
504.382-018	HEAT-TREATER APPRENTICE (heat treating)	4337	33343434353	MNNNNNNFFFNNNNFNFN	NNFN4NFNNNNNNF	V,J,T	133	540	06.02.10	7544	480503	91932
504.387-010	HARDNESS INSPECTOR (heat treating)	3324	34342443355	MNNNNNNFFFNNNNFNFNN	NNNN4NNNNNNNNN	J,T	211	540	06.03.01	7830	480503	83005
504.485-010	RIVET HEATER (heat treating)	3224	34444434353	MONNNNNFFFNNNNONFNFN	ONFN4NNNNNNNNF	R,T	133	555	05.12.10	7675	000000	92923
504.665-010	SLAB-DEPILER OPERATOR (steel & rel.)	3224	34433434355	LNNNNNNNFFNOONFNFNNN	NNON4NNNNNNNNN	J	133	541	06.04.10	7544	480503	97989
504.665-014	CHARGER OPERATOR (steel & rel.)	3224	34434434354	MNNNNNNFFFNNNNFNFNNN	NNFN4NFNNNNNNN	R,T	133	540	06.04.10	7544	480599	91935
504.682-010	ANNEALER (heat treating)	3214	34444434354	MNNNNNNFFFONNNNONOON	NNFN4NNNNNNNNN	J,T	133	540	06.02.10	7544	480503	91932
504.682-014	CASE HARDENER (heat treating)	3324	34444434354	MNNNNNNFFONNNNONONON	NNFN4NNNNNNNN	R,T	133	540	06.02.10	7544	480503	91932
504.682-018	HEAT TREATER II (heat treating)	3324	34443434353	MNNNNNNFFFNNNNNNNFN	NNFN4NNNNNNNNN	R,J,T	133	540	06.02.10	7544	480503	91932
504.682-022	HEAT-TREATING BLUER (heat treating)	3334	34443434353	MNNNNNNFFONNNFNNNNFN	NNFF1NFNNNNNNF	R,J,T	133	373	06.02.10	7544	480503	91932
504.682-026	TEMPERER (heat treating)	3324	34443434353	MNNNNNNFFONNNFNFNNNN	NNFN4NFNNNNNNN	R,J,T	133	540	06.02.10	7544	480503	91932
504.685-010	BASE-DRAW OPERATOR (ordnance)	3223	44444434355	MNNNNNNFFNNNNFNNNNN	NNFN3NNNNNNNNN	R	133	370	06.04.10	7675	480503	91932
504.685-014	FLAME-HARDENING-MACHINE OPERATOR (heat treating)	2212	44444544354	MNNNNNNFFFNNNNFNFNNN	NNFN4NNNNNNNNN	R	133	540	06.04.10	7544	480503	91932
504.685-018	HEAT-TREATER HELPER (heat treating)	2222	44444444355	MNNNNNNFFFNNNNONFNNN	NNFN4NNNNNNNNF	R	133	540	06.04.10	8614	480503	98999
504.685-022	INDUCTION-MACHINE OPERATOR (heat treating)	2212	44444444355	MNNNNNNFFNNNNONONN	NNNN4NNNNNNNNN	R,T	133	540	06.04.10	7544	480503	91932
504.685-026	PRODUCTION HARDENER (heat treating)	2223	44443434355	HNNNNNNFFONNNNNNNNNN	NNFN3NNNNNNNNN	R,J	133	550	06.04.10	7675	480503	91932
504.685-030	REEL-BLADE-BENDER FURNACE TENDER (agric. equip.)	1112	44443434344	LNNNNNNNFFNNNNONNNNN	NNFN4NNNNNNNON	R,T	133	562	06.04.10	7675	000000	92923
504.686-010	CHARGER-OPERATOR HELPER (steel & rel.)	1112	44444444355	MNNNNNNFFFNNNNFNFNNN	NNFN4NNNNNNNNN	R	133	541	06.04.10	8614	000000	98999
504.686-014	FURNACE HELPER (heat treating)	2212	44444444355	MNNNNNNFFFNNNNNFFNNN	NNFN4NNNNNNNNN	R,J	133	541	06.04.10	8725	480503	98502
504.686-018	HARDENER HELPER (clock & watch)	1112	44544545455	HNNNNNNFFONNONFNNNNN	NNNN4NNNNNNNNN	R	133	607	05.09.01	8614	000000	98999
504.686-022	HEAT TREATER (electron. comp.)	1111	45555545455	LNNNNNNNFFONNONFNNNNN	NNON4NNNNNNNN	R,U	133	587	06.04.19	7675	000000	91932
504.687-010	ANNEALER (jewelry-silver.)	2112	44444433355	LNNNNNNFFNFFNFNFNNN	NNNN4NFNNNNNNF	R,T	133	611	06.04.10	7544	470408	91932
505.130-010	SUPERVISOR, METALIZING (any industry)	4448	33322333353	LNNFNFNFFNFFNFNFFN	NNNN4NFNNNNNNN	V,D,P,J	153	541	06.02.01	7100	520205	81008
505.130-014	SUPERVISOR, VACUUM METALIZING (any industry)	4337	33333333354	MNNNNNNFFNFFNFNFNON	NNNN4NNNNNNNNN	V,D,P,J	153	531	06.01.01	7100	520205	81008
505.380-010	METAL SPRAYER, MACHINED PARTS (any industry)	4336	33322434354	MNNONONNFFNNNFNFOON	NNON4NNNNNNNNN	J,T	102	541	06.01.03	7329	480503	92197
505.382-010	METAL-SPRAYING-MACHINE OPERATOR, AUTOMATIC I (any industry)	4327	34332433353	MNNNNNNFFNNNONFNFN	NNFN4NFNNNNNNF	J,T	153	541	06.02.21	7343	000000	91923

DOT #	DOT Title & Industry	Trng	Aptitude	Physical	Environment	Tempra	WkF	MPSMS	GOE	SOC	CIP	OES
505.382-014	WELDING-ROD COATER (elec. equip.)	3326	34343343354	HNNNNNFFFNNNNFNNNON	NNNO3NNONNNNNN	V,J,T	153	557	06.02.21	7543	000000	91926
505.482-010	PASTING-MACHINE OPERATOR (elec. equip.)	3224	34334434355	LNNNNNFFONNNNFNNNNN	NNNN4NFNNNNNNN	R,J,T	151	589	06.02.18	7543	000000	91926
505.682-010	SPRAYER OPERATOR (smelt. & refin.)	3223	33343343334	LNNNNNFFFNNNNFNNNNN	NNFN4NFNNNNNNN	J	153	568	06.02.10	7543	480599	91926
505.684-010	ELECTROLESS PLATER (any industry)	2223	44444534355	MNNNNNFFFNNNNFNNNNN	NNNN4NNNNNNNNN	R,T	151	559	06.04.33	7543	000000	91926
505.684-014	METAL SPRAYER, PRODUCTION (any industry)	2223	44443534354	MNNNNNFFFNNNNFNFNON	NNNN4NNNNNNNNN	R,T	153	541	06.04.33	7543	000000	91926
505.685-010	BROWNING PROCESSOR (ordnance)	2223	44443443353	MNNNNNNFFONNNNFNFNON	NNFO3NNNNNNNOF	R,T	151	373	06.04.10	7543	000000	91926
505.685-014	METAL-SPRAYING-MACHINE OPERATOR, AUTOMATIC II (any industry)	2222	44444544454	MNNNNNNFFONNNNOFNNNNN	NNNN4NNNNNNNNN	R	153	541	06.04.21	7543	000000	91926
505.685-018	VACUUM-METALIZER OPERATOR (any industry)	2223	44444534355	MNNNNNNFFNNNNNFNNNNN	NNNN3NNNNNNNNN	R,T	154	519	06.04.21	7543	000000	91926
509.130-010	SUPERVISOR, POWDERED METAL (nonfer. metal; steel & rel.)	4337	33333494354	LNNNNNFFFNFNOOON	NNON4NNNNNNNNN	V,D,P,T	134	549	06.02.01	7100	520205	81008
509.130-014	SUPERVISOR, POWER-REACTOR (chemical)	4337	22233344354	LNNNNNNFFFNFFNNNON	NNNN3NNNNNNONNN	D,P,J	147	543	06.01.01	6700	000000	81008
509.132-010	SUPERVISOR, SOAKING PITS (steel & rel.)	4338	33333344355	MNNNNNNFFFNFFNNOOFNNO	ONFN4NFNNNNNNN	V,D,P,J	133	541	06.04.01	7100	520205	81008
509.362-010	MIXER OPERATOR, HOT METAL (steel & rel.)	3225	34434444355	LNNNNNNNFONNNNNNONNN	NNFN4NFNNNNNNN	J,T	143	541	06.02.10	7529	480599	92198
509.382-010	COATER OPERATOR (any industry)	3326	33443434343	MNNNNNNFFFNNNNFNFNFN	NNNN4NFNNNNNNF	V,J,T	153	559	06.02.21	7543	000000	91926
509.382-014	DENTAL-AMALGAM PROCESSOR (nonfer. metal)	3224	34433433355	MNNNNNNNFFONNNNONFONN	NNNN4NNNNNNNNN	J,T	147	604	06.02.09	7549	000000	92198
509.384-010	CASE PREPARER-AND-LINER (ordnance)	3224	34433444343	LNNNNNNFFFNNNNFNFOFN	NNNN4NNNNNNNNN	R,T	153	372	06.02.24	7549	000000	92198
509.462-010	ALODIZE-MACHINE OPERATOR (nonfer. metal)	3325	34443434344	MNNNNNNNFFFNNNNFOOOON	NNNF4NNNNNNNNN	R,T	151	543	06.02.10	7343	000000	91923
509.485-010	COMPOUND MIXER (tinware)	3224	34344434345	HNNFNFNFOONNNNNOFNNN	ONNN4NNNNNNNNNF	R,J,T	143	495	06.04.11	7664	000000	92965
509.485-014	SHOT POLISHER AND INSPECTOR (ordnance)	2223	44444444355	LNNNNNNFFFNNNNFNFNNN	NNNN4NNNNNNNNNN	R,J	145	374	06.04.02	7529	000000	92198
509.565-010	KILN OPERATOR (steel & rel.)	2223	44444444355	MNNNNNNFFFNNNNFNNNNN	NNFN4NNNNNNNNN	R,T	147	349	06.04.10	7675	480599	92923
509.566-010	MIXER OPERATOR HELPER, HOT METAL (steel & rel.)	2222	34343444355	MNNNNNNFFFNNNNFNNNNN	NNFN4NFNNNNNNF	R	143	541	06.04.10	8611	480599	98899
509.584-010	TEST PREPARER (nonfer. metal; steel & rel.)	2224	34434434354	MNNNNNNFFFNNNNFNFNNN	NNNN4NNNNNNNNN	R,J,T	054	541	06.04.02	7840	480599	83005
509.666-010	COMPOUND-COATING-MACHINE OFFBEARER (tinware)	2112	45554544355	MNNFNONFFNNOONFNNNNN	NNNN4NNNNNNNNN	R	041	551	06.04.21	8725	000000	98502
509.684-010	ENAMELER (plumbing-heat.)	3225	44335534253	LNNNNNNNFFFONNNNNNFNFN	NNFN4NNNNNNNNN	V	153	553	06.04.33	7543	000000	91926
509.685-010	ALODIZE-MACHINE HELPER (nonfer. metal)	2223	45454534345	MNNFNFNFFNNNNNONFNNN	NNNF3NNNNNNNNN	R,T	163	540	06.04.02	8619	000000	98999
509.685-014	BRANNER-MACHINE TENDER (galvanizing)	3224	44443434355	MNNNNNNFFONNNNFONONN	NNNN4NNNNNNNNN	R,T	031	541	06.04.39	7673	000000	92958
509.685-018	BURNING-PLANT OPERATOR (ordnance)	2112	44544444355	HNNONNNFFNNNNNNNNNN	NNFN4NNNNNNNNNF	R	131	374	05.12.10	7675	000000	92923
509.685-022	CERAMIC COATER, MACHINE (any industry)	2212	44433533354	MNNNNNNFFFNNNNFNFNON	NNFN3NNNNNNNNN	R,T	153	559	06.04.21	7543	000000	91926
509.685-026	GETTERING-FILAMENT-MACHINE OPERATOR (light. fix.)	2213	34443444354	LNNNNNNFFNNNNNFNFNNN	NNNN3NNNNNNNNNF	R	151	584	06.04.21	7543	000000	91926
509.685-030	IMPREGNATOR (nonfer. metal; steel & rel.)	2222	44444444355	MNNNNNNFFONNNNONNNNN	NNNN4NNNNNNNNNF	R,T	152	540	06.04.10	7543	480599	91926
509.685-034	LACQUER-DIPPING-MACHINE OPERATOR (button & notion)	2212	44444444355	MNNFNNNFFONNNNFNNNNN	NNNN3NNNNNNNNN	R	151	618	06.04.21	7543	000000	91926
509.685-038	LUBRICATING-MACHINE TENDER (ordnance)	2212	44444444455	MNNNNNNFFFNNNNFNNNNN	NNFN4NNNNNNNNN	R,J	153	374	06.04.21	7543	000000	91926
509.685-042	LUBRICATOR-GRANULATOR (nonfer. metal; steel & rel.)	2212	44434434355	LNNNNNNNFFNNNNFNNNNN	NNNN4NNNNNNNNN	R,T	147	549	06.04.10	7529	000000	92198
509.685-046	PORCELAIN-ENAMEL LABORER (any industry)	2113	44444544355	MOONNNNFFONNNNFNNNON	ONNN4NONNNNNNO	R	163	549	06.04.02	7529	000000	92974
509.685-050	SCRAP BALLER (nonfer. metal; steel & rel.)	2113	44454544355	LNNNNNNFFONNNNONNNNN	NNNN4NNNNNNNNN	R	145	549	06.04.09	7529	000000	92998
509.685-054	SCRAP HANDLER (any industry)	3223	34444434355	HNNNNNNFFONNNNNNNNNN	NNNN4NNNNNNNNN	R	149	549	06.04.09	7549	000000	92198
509.685-058	TANK TENDER (smelt. & refin.)	3225	34444434355	MNNNNNNFFFNNNNFNNNNN	NNNN3NNNNNNNNN	R,T	031	354	06.04.10	7549	000000	92198
509.686-014	PASTING-MACHINE OFFBEARER (elec. equip.)	1112	44444444455	LNNNNNNCCNNNNNFNNNNN	NNNN3NNNNNNNNN	R	011	589	06.04.09	8725	000000	98502
509.686-018	SCRAP SORTER (nonfer. metal)	2112	44454444355	MNNFNNNFFFOONFNNNNNN	ONFF4NFNNNNNNF	R	011	549	05.12.03	7850	000000	83005
509.687-010	BOTTOM MAKER (steel & rel.)	2113	34444444355	HNONONNFFNNOONFFNNN	NNNN4NNNNNNNNN	R	031	568	06.04.40	8769	480599	85126
509.687-014	PORCELAIN-ENAMEL LABORER (any industry)	1112	44443434355	MONNNNNFFONNNNFNNNON	ONNN4NONNNNNNO	R	031	495	06.04.33	8769	000000	98999
509.687-018	STRINGER (jewelry-silver.)	1111	44444543355	LNNNNNNCCONNNNFFNFNN	NNNN3NNNNNNNNN	R	061	611	06.04.34	7740	000000	93999
509.687-022	WEIGHER, ALLOY (nonfer. metal)	2123	34433444353	MNNFNFNFFNNNNNFNFNFN	NNFN4NFNNNNNNN	J,T	212	540	06.03.02	7850	000000	83005
509.687-026	LABORER, GENERAL (steel & rel.)	2113	44454444355	HONOOONFFONNNNNNNNN	ONEF4NFNNNNNNF	R	011	540	06.04.40	8725	480599	98502
510.465-010	CARBIDE-POWDER PROCESSOR (machine shop)	3225	34444444355	HNONONNFFNNOONFFNN	NNNN4NNNNNNNNN	J,T	147	549	06.02.10	7664	480599	92965
510.465-014	SLURRY-CONTROL TENDER (smelt. & refin.)	3225	34334434334	MONNNNNFFONNNFNNNON	ONNN4NONNNNNNO	J,T	142	355	06.02.10	7664	000000	92965
510.685-010	DUST MIXER (smelt. & refin.)	3214	34433434355	LNNNNNNNCCONNNNFFNFNN	NNNN4NNNNNNNNN	R,T	143	352	06.04.10	7664	480599	92965
510.685-014	MIX-HOUSE TENDER (smelt. & refin.)	2113	44434434354	LNNNNNNNFFNNNNNNNNNN	NNNN3NNNNNNNNN	R,T	143	353	06.04.10	7664	480599	92965
510.685-018	MIXER (nonfer. metal; steel & rel.)	2223	44444434355	MNNNNNNFFFNNNNNNNNN	NNNN4NNNNNNNNN	R,T	143	540	06.04.10	7664	480599	92965
510.685-022	PUG-MILL OPERATOR (smelt. & refin.)	3124	34444434354	LNNNNNNNFFNNNNNNNNON	NNNON3NNNNNNNNON	R	143	350	06.04.10	7664	480599	92965
510.685-026	SINTER-MACHINE OPERATOR (smelt. & refin.; steel & rel.)	3115	34434443355	MNNNNNNNFFFOONFNNNNN	NNNN4NNNNNNNNN	R,T	147	350	06.04.10	7664	480599	92965
510.685-030	SLIME-PLANT OPERATOR I (smelt. & refin.)	3216	34444444344	LNNNNNNFFFNNNNFNNNON	ONNN3NNNNNNNNN	J,T	143	352	06.04.10	7664	480599	92965
511.130-010	ALUMINA-PLANT SUPERVISOR (smelt. & refin.)	4338	33333333355	MNNONONFFFNFFNFNFNN	ONNN3NNNNNNNNN	V,D,P,J	147	355	06.02.01	7100	520205	81008

DOT #	DOT Title & Industry	Trng	Aptitude	Physical	Environment	Tempra	WkF	MPSMS	GOE	SOC	CIP	OES
511.132-010	PRECIPITATOR SUPERVISOR (smelt. & refin.; steel & rel.)	3225	33333344444	LONFNFNFONFFNFNFNFON	FNNN4NCNNNNNNNF	D,J,P	145	350	05.10.02	7100	000000	81008
511.135-010	FILTER-PLANT SUPERVISOR (smelt. & refin.)	4336	33344334344	LNNONOFFNFFNFNNOON	ONNF4NNNNNNNNF	V,D,P,J	145	347	06.04.01	7100	520205	81008
511.382-010	TUNGSTEN REFINER (smelt. & refin.)	3225	33343334354	MONNNNNNFFNNNNNNNNNN	NNNN3NFNNNNNNOF	J,T	147	359	06.02.10	7666	480599	92935
511.385-010	ZINC-CHLORIDE OPERATOR (smelt. & refin.)	3224	34343334354	MNNNNNNFFONNNNFNFNFN	NNNO4NNNNNNNNNN	R,T	145	353	06.02.10	7666	480599	92962
511.462-010	CONCENTRATOR OPERATOR (smelt. & refin.)	4337	33444444454	LFNNNNNNFFOOFFNOFNNFF	FNNC4CCNNNNNNNN	R,T	145	347	06.02.11	7679	000000	92998
511.465-010	TOP-PRECIPITATOR OPERATOR (smelt. & refin.)	3124	34443434355	MNNONNNFFNNOOFONNNN	ONNN4NFNNNNNNNNF	R,T	145	355	06.02.10	7676	000000	92962
511.482-010	CONTROL OPERATOR (smelt. & refin.)	3235	33343344343	LNNNNNNFFNNNNFNFNFN	NNFN3NNNNNNNNNN	J,T	145	541	06.02.10	6940	480599	92944
511.482-014	CRYOLITE-RECOVERY OPERATOR (smelt. & refin.)	3225	34443434354	LFNOOONFFFNNNONNNON	NNFN4NFNNNNNNNN	J,T	147	399	06.02.10	7679	480599	92998
511.482-018	DUST-COLLECTOR OPERATOR (smelt. & refin.)	3113	34443434344	LONOOOOFFOOOONOOONON	ONNN4NNNNNNNNNF	J,T	145	350	06.04.19	7679	000000	92962
511.485-010	MOLYBDENUM-STEAMER OPERATOR (smelt. & refin.)	3224	34344434355	LNNNNNNFFFNNNNNNNN	NNNN3NNNNNNNNNN	R,T	145	359	06.02.10	7676	480599	92962
511.485-014	THICKENER OPERATOR (smelt. & refin.)	3124	34444444344	LNFNFNFFONNNNONNNON	ONNN3NNNNNNNNNN	R,T	145	350	06.04.10	7666	480599	92962
511.562-010	CLASSIFIER OPERATOR (smelt. & refin.)	3225	34444434355	MNNNNNNFFNNNNNNNNN	ONNN3NNNNNNNNNN	R,T	145	355	06.04.10	7666	000000	92962
511.565-010	DEWATERER OPERATOR (smelt. & refin.)	3125	34443434354	MNNNNNNFFNNNNFNNNNN	NNNF3NFNNNNNNNN	R,T	145	355	06.04.10	7666	480599	92962
511.565-014	DRIER TENDER (smelt. & refin.)	3224	34443434354	MNNNNNNFFNNOONFNNNON	NNNN4NNNNNNNNNN	R,T	145	549	06.04.10	7675	480599	92923
511.565-018	IRON-LAUNDER OPERATOR (smelt. & refin.)	3124	34444444444	LNNNONONFFFNFNFNFNON	ONNN3NNNNNNNNNN	R,T	147	352	06.04.10	7666	000000	92962
511.582-010	LEACHER (smelt. & refin.)	3225	34434434344	LONNNNNNFFONNNNNONNNN	NNNN4NNNNNNNNNN	J,T	147	350	06.02.10	7666	480599	92962
511.585-010	HYDRATE-CONTROL TENDER (smelt. & refin.)	3124	34444434355	MONNNNNFFFNNNNFNNNN	NNNN3NFNNNNNNNF	R,T	145	355	06.04.10	7666	000000	92962
511.586-010	TOP-PRECIPITATOR-OPERATOR HELPER (smelt. & refin.)	2112	44444434355	MNNNNNNFFNNNNNFNNN	ONNN4FNNNNNNNNF	R,T	145	355	06.04.10	7676	000000	98999
511.662-010	CLARIFIER OPERATOR (smelt. & refin.)	3224	34344434335	MONONNNFFFONNNNONNNNN	ONNN4NFNNNNNNNN	R,T	145	355	06.04.10	7676	000000	92962
511.664-010	BOTTOM-PRECIPITATOR OPERATOR (smelt. & refin.)	2124	34444434345	MNNNNNNFFNNOONNNNNN	ONNN3NFNNNNNNNN	R,T	145	355	06.04.10	7676	000000	92962
511.667-010	CLARIFIER-OPERATOR HELPER (smelt. & refin.)	2113	44444444355	MNNNNNNFFNOONFNNNNN	ONNN3NFNNNNNNNN	R	145	352	06.04.10	8614	000000	98999
511.667-014	COLOR TESTER (smelt. & refin.)	3123	34434434353	LFNNNNNCCONOONFNNNFN	NNNN4NONNNNNNNN	R,T	212	352	06.03.01	7840	000000	83005
511.682-010	DUST COLLECTOR, ORE CRUSHING (smelt. & refin.)	3123	34434534355	MONOOOOFFNNNNNNNNNN	NNNF4NONNNNNNNN	R,T	031	352	06.02.10	7549	000000	92198
511.685-010	AMALGAMATOR (smelt. & refin.)	3113	34443434334	LNNNNNNNFFNNNNNNNNON	NNNF3NFNNNNNNNN	R,T	145	354	06.04.10	7666	000000	92962
511.685-014	CLASSIFIER TENDER (smelt. & refin.)	3124	34444444345	LNNNNNNFFNFNNNNONNNN	NNNN3NNNNNNNNNN	R,T	145	350	06.04.10	7666	000000	92962
511.685-018	CONDENSER-TUBE TENDER (smelt. & refin.)	2112	44544544345	HNNNNNNFFNNNNNNNNN	ONNN3NNNNNNNNNF	R,T	145	357	06.04.09	7673	000000	92958
511.685-022	DUST-COLLECTOR ATTENDANT (mine & quarry)	3113	34434434345	LNNNNNNFFFNNNNNNNN	NNNF4NNNNNNNNNN	R	031	351	06.04.12	7666	000000	92962
511.685-026	FLOTATION TENDER (smelt. & refin.)	3114	34444444344	LONNNNNNFFNNNNNNNNN	NNNN4NNNNNNNNNON	R,T	145	350	06.04.10	7676	000000	92962
511.685-030	KETTLE TENDER II (smelt. & refin.)	3124	34434544355	MNNNNNNFFNNNNNNNNN	NNFF3NNNNNNNNNN	R,T	147	354	06.04.10	7676	000000	92962
511.685-034	KETTLE TENDER, PLATINUM AND PALLADIUM (smelt. & refin.)	3124	34443434354	LNNNNNNNFFNNNNNNNNN	NNNF3NNNNNNNNNN	R,T	145	350	06.04.10	7676	000000	92962
511.685-038	PRECIPITATOR I (smelt. & refin.)	3114	34443434345	MNNONONFFNNNNNNNNON	NNNN3NNNNNNNNNN	R,T	145	358	06.04.10	7676	000000	92962
511.685-042	PRECIPITATOR II (smelt. & refin.)	3124	34444444345	LNNNNNNFFNNNNNNNNON	NNNN3NNNNNNNNNN	R,T	143	350	06.04.10	7664	000000	92965
511.685-046	REAGENT TENDER (smelt. & refin.)	3114	34444444344	MFNOOONFFONNNNNOONNO	ONNF4NFNNNNNNNN	R,T	145	340	06.04.08	7666	000000	92962
511.685-050	SCREEN OPERATOR (smelt. & refin.)	3124	34443434355	LNNFNFNFFNNNNONNNON	NNNN3NNNNNONNNN	R,T	145	350	06.04.10	7676	000000	92962
511.685-054	SLIME-PLANT OPERATOR II (smelt. & refin.)	3124	34433434344	MNNFOFNFFNNNNNNNNN	ONNF3NNNNNNNNNN	R,T	145	350	06.04.10	8618	000000	98999
511.685-058	SLIME-PLANT-OPERATOR HELPER (smelt. & refin.)	2113	34434434354	MNNNNNNFFONNNNNONNN	NNNN4NFNNNNNNNN	R,T	145	350	06.04.10	7666	000000	92958
511.685-062	TABLE TENDER (smelt. & refin.)	3114	34443434354	MNNNMFNFFNNNNNNNNN	ONNF3NNNNNNNNNN	R,T	145	352	06.04.10	7873	000000	92958
511.685-066	TROMMEL TENDER (smelt. & refin.)	2112	34444544355	MFNFNFNFFNNNNNFNNNN	ONNN3NFNNNNNNNN	R	031	350	06.04.10	8618	000000	98999
511.686-010	REAGENT TENDER HELPER (smelt. & refin.)	2112	44444444355	MNNNNONFFNNNNNNNNNN	NNNN4NNNNNNNNNN	R,T	143	350	06.04.10	8618	000000	98999
511.687-010	BLANKET WASHER (smelt. & refin.)	2112	44444544354	MNNNNNNFFNNNNNNNNON	NNNN4NFNNNNNNNN	R	145	354	06.04.27	8750	000000	98905
511.687-014	DUST COLLECTOR-TREATER (smelt. & refin.)	2113	34443434354	MNNNNNNFFONNNNNONNNN	NNNN4NFNNNNNONNN	R,T	145	352	06.04.09	8618	000000	98999
511.687-018	FLOTATION-TENDER HELPER (smelt. & refin.)	1111	44444444445	MNNFFFOFFNNNNNNNNN	NNNF4NNNNNNNNNN	R	031	350	06.04.34	8618	000000	98999
511.687-022	SKIMMER, REVERBERATORY (smelt. & refin.)	2113	44454434355	MNNNNNNFFONFFNFNFNNF	NNFN4NFNNNNNNNN	R,T	131	352	06.04.34	7759	000000	93999
511.687-026	TAILINGS-DAM LABORER (smelt. & refin.)	2112	44434434355	MNNNNNNFFNNNNNNNNN	CNNF3NNNNNNNNNN	R	014	352	06.04.34	8769	000000	98999
512.130-010	REDUCTION-PLANT SUPERVISOR (smelt. & refin.)	4337	33333333355	LNNNNNNFFONFFNFNFNN	NNFN4NNNNNNNNNNNN	V,D,P,J	131	355	06.04.01	7100	000000	81008
512.132-010	MELTER SUPERVISOR (steel & rel.)	4337	33333344454	LNNNNNNFFONFFNFNFON	NNFN4NNNNNNNNNNNF	V,D,P,J	131	541	06.04.01	7100	520205	81008
512.132-014	RECLAMATION SUPERVISOR (nonfer. metal)	4237	33333334354	LNNNNNNFFNFNFNNNON	NNFN4NFNNNNNNNN	V,D,P,J	131	540	06.04.01	7100	520205	81008
512.132-018	REMELT-FURNACE EXPEDITER (nonfer. metal)	4237	33333333354	MNNNNNNFFONFFNFNNON	NNFN4NFNNNNNNNN	V,D,P,J	131	540	06.04.01	8618	000000	98999
512.132-022	SUPERVISOR, BLAST FURNACE (smelt. & refin.)	4337	33333333354	LNNNNNNNFFONFFNFNFON	NNNF4NNNNNNNNNN	V,D,P,J	131	353	06.04.01	8618	000000	98999
512.135-010	POT-ROOM SUPERVISOR (smelt. & rel.)	4337	33333334355	LNNNNNNNFFONFFNFNFNNF	NNFN3NFNNNNNNON	V,D,P,J	131	355	06.04.01	7100	520205	81008
512.362-010	FIRST HELPER (steel & rel.)	3226	33434444353	HNNNNNNFFNFFNFNFNFN	NNFN4FNNNNNNNF	J,T	131	541	06.02.10	7544	480599	91935

DOT #	DOT Title & Industry	Trng	Aptitude	Physical	Environment	Tempra	WkF	MPSMS	GOE	SOC	CIP	OES
512.362-014	FURNACE OPERATOR (nonfer. metal; smelt. & refin.)	4225	34433343344	MNNNNNNFFNOONFNON	NNFN4NFNNNNNNNF	J,T	131	540	06.02.10	7544	480599	91935
512.362-018	FURNACE OPERATOR (foundry; steel & rel.)	3235	34433434343	MNNOONNFFNOONFNFN	NNFN4NFNNNNNNNF	J,T	131	540	06.02.10	7544	480599	91935
512.382-010	OXYGEN-FURNACE OPERATOR (steel & rel.)	3225	33434434354	MNNNNNNFFNNNNNNNN	NNNN4NNNNNNNNNN	J,T	131	541	06.02.10	7544	480599	91935
512.382-014	STOVE TENDER (steel & rel.)	3125	34443544355	LNNNNNFFFNNNNNNNN	NNON4NNNNNNNNNN	J,T	131	541	06.02.10	7529	480599	92198
512.382-018	TIN RECOVERY WORKER (smelt. & refin.)	3224	34433444355	HNNNNNNFFONNNNNNNN	NNFN4NFNNNNNNNF	J,T	131	540	06.02.10	7529	480599	92198
512.467-010	POTLINE MONITOR (smelt. & refin.)	3224	34433344344	MOOOOOOFFNOONFNOON	NNCN3NNFNNNNNF	J,T	212	568	06.03.01	7830	480599	83005
512.487-010	METAL CONTROL WORKER (foundry)	3223	34344334345	MNNNNNNFFNNNNFNNF	NNNN4NNNNNNNNNN	J,T	212	540	06.03.01	7840	480599	83005
512.662-010	CUPOLA TENDER (foundry)	3224	34443534353	MNNFFNFFNFNFNFN	NNFN4NFNNNNNNNF	J,T	131	541	06.02.10	7544	480599	91935
512.666-010	FURNACE HELPER (nonfer. metal; smelt. & refin.)	2112	44434434355	HNNFNFNFFONOONNNFNNN	NNFN4NFNNNNNNNF	R,T	131	541	06.02.10	8614	480599	98999
512.667-010	TEMPERATURE REGULATOR, PYROMETER (foundry)	2222	44444444454	LNNNNNNFFNNNNNNNN	NNFN4NFNNNNNNNF	J,T	132	541	06.03.02	7830	480599	83005
512.683-010	CHARGING-MACHINE OPERATOR (steel & rel.)	3115	34433534335	LNNNNNNFFNNNNNNNN	NNFN4NNNNNNNNNN	R,T	131	541	06.02.10	7529	480599	92198
512.684-010	SECOND HELPER (steel & rel.)	2113	44434444355	HNNNNNNFFONNNNNNNN	NNFN4NFNNNNNNNF	R	131	541	06.04.10	8614	480599	98999
512.684-014	FURNACE CHARGER (nonfer. metal; smelt. & refin.; steel & rel.)	3224	34334444335	MNNNNNNFFNNNFNNN	NNFN4NFNNNNNNNF	R,T	131	350	06.02.10	7529	480599	91935
512.685-010	FURNACE TENDER (foundry; nonfer. metal)	2113	44434444355	HNNNNNNFFNNNNNNNNNN	NNFN4NNNNNNNNNN	R,T	131	541	06.04.10	7675	480599	91935
512.685-014	NOZZLE TENDER (nonfer. metal)	2123	44434434355	MNNNNNNFFONNNNONNNN	NNFN4NNNNNNNNNN	R,T	131	543	06.04.10	7679	480599	92998
512.685-018	POT TENDER (smelt. & refin.)	3113	44443444354	MNNNNNNFFNNNNNFNON	NNFN4NFNNNNNNNF	R,T	131	541	06.04.10	7675	480599	92923
512.685-022	RECLAMATION KETTLE TENDER, METAL (smelt. & refin.)	2113	44454534354	MNNNNNNFFNNNNNNNNNN	NNNN4NFNNNNNNNF	R,T	131	549	06.04.10	7542	480599	98502
512.686-010	CUPOLA CHARGER (foundry)	2122	44444444355	MNNFNFNFFNOONFNNNN	NNNN4NFNNNNNNNF	R	131	540	06.04.10	7740	480599	93999
512.687-010	CONDENSER SETTER (smelt. & refin.)	2112	44434444455	MNNNNNNFFNNNNNNNNNN	NNFN3NNNNNNNNNN	R,T	144	353	06.04.10	7740	480599	93999
512.687-014	THIRD HELPER (steel & rel.)	2113	44445544355	HNNNNNNFFNNNNNNNNNN	NNFN4NFNNNNNNNF	R	131	540	06.04.10	8769	480599	98999
513.132-010	CONVERTER SUPERVISOR (smelt. & refin.)	4336	33433434344	LFNNNNNFFFNFFNFOONON	NNFN4NFNNNNNNNN	V,D,P,J	141	352	06.04.01	7100	480599	81008
513.362-010	CALCINER OPERATOR (mine & quarry; smelt. & refin.)	3226	34344443454	LONOONNFFFNFFNFONFFN	NNFC4CONNNNNNNF	J	141	347	06.01.01	7679	520205	92998
513.462-010	FURNACE OPERATOR (foundry)	3224	34433534344	MNNFFNNFFNNOONFNON	NNFN4NFNNNNNNNN	J,T	141	350	06.02.10	7675	520205	92923
513.565-010	KILN OPERATOR (smelt. & refin.)	3124	34444434344	LNNNNNNFFFNFNNNON	NNFN4NNNNNNNNNN	R,T	141	355	06.02.10	7675	480599	92923
513.587-010	KILN-OPERATOR HELPER (smelt. & refin.)	2113	34434444345	MNNNNNNFFNNNNNNNNNN	ONFN4NNNNNNNNNN	R,T	141	355	06.04.10	8618	480599	98999
513.667-010	CALCINER-OPERATOR HELPER (mine & quarry; smelt. & refin.)	3114	34434444455	LFNONNNFFOFOONFNNNNN	ONNN4NNNNNNNNNN	T,V	231	898	06.04.01	8618	480599	98999
513.682-010	ROTARY-KILN OPERATOR (smelt. & refin.)	3224	34434443444	MNNONONFFFNNNNNNNN	ONNN3NFNNNNNNNF	R,T	141	357	06.04.10	7675	480599	92923
513.685-010	SINTER FEEDER (steel & rel.)	3224	34443444355	MNNNNNNFFFNNNNNNNNN	NNNN4NFNNNNNNNN	R,T	011	351	06.04.10	8319	480599	97989
514.130-010	PERMANENT-MOLD SUPERVISOR (foundry; nonfer. metal)	4337	23333344355	MNNNNNNFFONFFNFNNNN	NNON4NNNNNNNNNN	V,D,P,J	132	542	06.01.01	7100	520205	81008
514.130-014	SUPERVISOR, DIE CASTING (foundry; smelt. & refin.)	4337	33334333355	MNNNNNFFOFFNFNONNN	NNNN4NFNNNNNNNN	V,D,P,J	132	541	06.01.01	7100	520205	81008
514.131-010	INSPECTOR, CHIEF (foundry)	4337	33333433355	MNNNNNNFFOFFNFNNNN	NNNN4NFNNNNNNNN	V,D,P,J	241	542	06.02.01	6700	520205	81008
514.134-010	TAPPER SUPERVISOR (smelt. & refin.)	4337	33333333355	LNNNNNNNFFFNFNFNNN	NNNN4NFNNNNNNNN	V,D,P,J	131	541	06.04.01	7100	520205	81008
514.137-010	SUPERVISOR, PIG-MACHINE (steel & rel.)	4236	33333344355	MNNNNNNFFFNFNFNNNN	ONFN4NNNNNNNNNN	V,D,P,J	132	541	06.02.01	7100	520205	81008
514.137-014	SUPERVISOR, PIT-AND-AUXILIARIES (steel & rel.)	3236	33344344345	LNNNNNNFFNFFNFNOONN	ONFN4NFNNNNNNNN	V,D,P,J	132	541	06.04.10	7100	520205	81008
514.360-010	DIE-CASTING-MACHINE SETTER (foundry)	4337	33333433344	MNNOOONFFFONNNFNNON	NNNN4NFNNNNNNNN	D,P,J	132	541	06.01.02	7342	480599	91908
514.362-010	PIG-MACHINE OPERATOR (steel & rel.)	3225	34434534355	HNNNNNNFFNNNNNNNNNN	NNFN4NNNNNNNNNN	R,T	132	541	06.02.10	7542	480599	91911
514.362-014	DIE-CASTING-MACHINE OPERATOR I (foundry)	3225	34433434355	MNNNNNNFFONNNONFNNN	NNFN4NNNNNNNNNN	J,T	132	542	06.02.10	7342	480599	91908
514.382-010	CENTRIFUGAL-CASTING-MACHINE OPERATOR III (foundry)	3226	34434434355	MNNNNNNFFNOONFNNNNN	NNFN3NNNNNNNNNN	R,T	132	541	06.02.10	7542	480599	91911
514.562-010	MOLD WORKER (steel & rel.)	2113	44443544355	MFNNNNNNFFNFNFNNN	ONNN4NNNNNNNNNN	R,T	031	541	06.04.32	8769	480599	98999
514.567-010	VACUUM CASTER (foundry)	2125	34433433355	HNNNNNNFFNNNNNNFNON	NNFN3NNNNNNNNNN	J,T	131	541	06.02.10	7542	480599	91911
514.582-010	INGOT HEADER (nonfer. metal; smelt. & refin.)	3114	34434343454	MNNNNNNCCNNNNNNNNON	NNFN4NNNNNNNNFF	R,T	131	541	06.04.10	7542	480599	91911
514.584-010	CASTING OPERATOR (nonfer. metal)	3225	34433433345	MNNNNNNFFNOONFNNNNN	NNFN4NNNNNNNNNN	R,J,T	132	541	06.02.10	7542	480599	91911
514.662-010	CUPOLA TAPPER (foundry)	2222	44445333355	MNNNNNNFFNNNNNNNNNN	NNFN4NNNNNNNNNN	R,T	131	541	06.04.10	7759	480599	93999
514.664-010	TAPPER (nonfer. metal; smelt. & refin.)	2112	44444534354	HNNNNNNFFNNNNNFNONFO	NNCN4NCCNNNNNO	J,T	131	541	06.04.10	7759	480599	93999
514.664-014	CASTING-WHEEL-OPERATOR HELPER (smelt. & refin.)	2112	44545544355	MNNNNNNFFNNFFNNFNNNN	NNFO4NFNNNNNNNF	R,T	132	541	06.04.32	8614	480599	98999
514.667-014	PIG-MACHINE-OPERATOR HELPER (steel & rel.)	2113	44435534355	MNNNNNNFFNFFNNNNNNN	NNON4NNNNNNNNNN	R	132	541	06.04.10	8614	480599	98999
514.667-018	SPOUT WORKER (smelt. & refin.)	2112	44435534355	HNNNNNNFFNNOONFNNNN	NNON4NNFNNNNNN	R	131	352	06.04.10	8614	480599	98999
514.682-010	CASTING-WHEEL OPERATOR (smelt. & refin.)	3224	34433434355	LNNNNNNFFNNNNNNNNNN	NNFN3NNNNNNNNNN	J	132	541	06.02.10	7542	480599	91911
514.682-014	PRESS OPERATOR, CARBON BLOCKS (smelt. & refin.)	3114	34434434345	LNNNNNNFFNNNNNNNNNN	NNFN4NFNNNNNNNF	R,T	132	589	06.02.18	7529	480599	92198
514.684-010	CASTER (smelt. & refin.)	2114	44445534354	MNNNNNNFFNNOONFNNNN	NNFN4NFNNNNNNNF	R,T	011	541	06.04.24	7754	480599	93941
514.684-014	LADLE POURER (smelt. & refin.)	2114	44543534355	MNNNNNNNFFNNNNNNNNNN	NNFN3NCNNNNNNNF	R,T	132	541	06.04.32	7754	480599	93941

DOT #	DOT Title & Industry	Trng	Aptitude	Physical	Environment	Tempra	WkF	MPSMS	GOE	SOC	CIP	OES
514.684-018	NOZZLE-AND-SLEEVE WORKER (nonfer. metal)	2113	44444544355	MNNNNNNFFNNNNNONNONN	NNNN3NNNNNNNNNN	R,T	061	568	06.04.24	6140	480599	85128
514.684-022	POURER, METAL (foundry)	2112	44544534355	HNNNNNNNFFNNNNNNNNNNF	NNCN4NNNNNNNNNNF	R,T	132	541	06.04.10	7754	480599	93941
514.685-010	CENTRIFUGAL-CASTING-MACHINE OPERATOR I (foundry)	3113	44434534355	HNNNNNNNFFNNNNNNNNNNN	NNCN4NNNNNNNNNNF	R,T	132	542	06.04.10	7542	480599	91911
514.685-014	CENTRIFUGAL-CASTING-MACHINE OPERATOR II (foundry)	2113	44544534355	MNNNNNNNFFNNNNNNNNNNN	NNCN4NNNNNNNNNNF	R,T	132	542	06.04.10	7542	480599	91911
514.685-018	DIE-CASTING-MACHINE OPERATOR II (foundry)	2112	44443434355	MNNNNNNNFFFNNNFNFNNFNN	NNCN4NFNNNNNNNNN	R,T	132	542	06.04.10	7542	480599	91911
514.685-022	LIME MIXER TENDER (steel & rel.)	2113	44444544355	MNNNNNNNFFNNNNNFNNNNN	NNNN3NNNNNNNNNN	R,T	143	536	06.04.10	7664	480599	92965
514.685-026	TUBE-CLEANING OPERATOR (foundry)	2112	44544544355	MNNNNNNNFFNNNNNNNNNNN	NNNN3NNNNNNNNNN	R,T	061	542	06.04.02	7542	480599	91914
514.687-010	CASTING INSPECTOR (foundry)	2223	44443444355	LNNNNNNNFFONNNFFNFN	NNNN4NFNNNNNNNN	R,T	212	542	06.03.02	7820	480599	83005
514.687-014	CASTING-HOUSE WORKER (nonfer. metal)	2112	44544544345	HNNNNNNNNNFFONNNNNNNNO	NNCN3NFNNNNNNNO	R	011	540	06.04.24	8769	480599	98999
514.687-018	CASTING-OPERATOR HELPER (nonfer. metal)	2123	44444494355	HNNNNNNNFFNNNNFNFNNNN	NNFN4NNNNNNNNNF	R,T	132	541	06.04.10	8614	480599	98899
515.130-010	MILL SUPERVISOR (smelt. & refin.)	4337	33333333344	LFNNNNNFFNFFNFNONON	NNNN4NFNNNNNNNF	V,D,P,J	142	350	06.02.01	7100	000000	81008
515.132-010	CRUSHER SUPERVISOR (smelt. & refin.)	4337	33333333355	LNNNNNNNFFNFFNFNNNN	ONNN4NNNNNNNNNN	V,D,P,J	011	350	06.02.01	7100	000000	81008
515.382-010	GRINDING-MILL OPERATOR (mine & quarry; smelt. & refin.)	3226	33333333354	LNNNNNNNFFFNNNFNNNON	NNNN4NNNNNNNNNN	R,T	142	350	06.02.08	7677	000000	95099
515.567-010	WEIGHER-AND-CRUSHER (smelt. & refin.)	3114	34434434355	MNNNNNNNFFFNFNNNNNNN	ONNN4NNNNNNNNNN	R,T	142	353	06.04.08	7840	480599	83005
515.585-010	SCALE-RECLAMATION TENDER (smelt. & refin.)	3114	34444444345	MNNNNNNNFFFNNNNNNNNN	ONNN4NFNNNNNNNN	R,T	142	355	06.04.10	7677	480599	92965
515.685-010	BATCH MAKER (nonfer. metal; steel & rel.)	2112	44444534355	LNNNNNNNFFONNNNONNNN	NNNN4NNNNNNNNNN	R	142	549	06.04.10	7677	480599	92965
515.685-014	CRUSHER TENDER (smelt. & refin.)	3113	44534544355	LNNNNNNNFFNNNNNNNNNN	NNNN4NFNNNNNNNF	R,T	142	350	06.04.08	7677	480599	92965
515.685-018	STAMPING-MILL TENDER (smelt. & refin.)	2113	44444534355	LNNNNNNNFFNNNNNNNNNN	NNNN4NNNNNNNNNN	R,T	142	350	06.04.02	7677	480599	92965
515.686-010	BATTERY-WRECKER OPERATOR (nonfer. metal)	2112	45545535345	VNNNNNNNCCONOOONFNNNN	NNNN4NNNNNNNNNN	R,U	142	543	06.04.40	8725	490299	98502
515.687-010	HAMMER-MILL OPERATOR (smelt. & refin.)	2113	44444444355	MNNNNNNNFFNNNNNNNNNN	NNNN4NNNNNNNNNN	R	142	556	06.04.24	7677	480599	92965
518.361-010	MOLDER (aircraft mfg.; concrete prod.; foundry)	4336	33333433355	MNNOOONFFOOOONFOFONO	NNON4OONNNNNNNO	J,T	132	542	06.01.04	6861	480599	89902
518.361-014	MOLDER APPRENTICE (aircraft mfg.; concrete prod.; foundry)	4336	33333433355	MNNOOONFFOOOONFOFONO	NNON4OONNNNNNNO	J,T	132	542	06.01.04	6861	480599	89902
518.361-018	MOLDER, SWEEP (foundry)	4337	33333433355	MNNNNNNNFFOONNNNNFNNN	NNNN4NNNNNNNNNN	J,T	136	566	06.01.04	6861	480599	89902
518.380-010	SETTER, MOLDING-AND-COREMAKING MACHINES (foundry)	3224	33433433355	MNNNNNNNFFOONNFNNFNNN	NNNN4NNNNNNNNNN	J,T	041	566	06.01.02	7342	470408	91908
518.381-010	BENCH-MOLDER APPRENTICE (jewelry-silver.)	4337	33433433355	LNNNNNNNFFNNNNNNFNNN	NNON3NNNNNNNNNN	J,T	132	611	06.01.04	6822	470408	89126
518.381-014	COREMAKER (foundry)	3225	33433433355	MNNFNFNFFNONNNNFNFNNN	NNNN4NNNNNNNNNN	R,J,T	136	566	06.01.04	6861	480599	89902
518.381-018	COREMAKER APPRENTICE (foundry)	3225	33433433355	MNNFNFNFFNONNNFNFNNN	NNON3NNNNNNNNNN	R,J,T	132	566	06.01.04	6822	470408	89126
518.381-022	MOLDER, BENCH (jewelry-silver.)	4337	33433433355	LNNNNNNNFFONNNFFNFNNN	NNNN3NNNNNNNNNN	J,T	132	566	06.02.30	7754	480599	93944
518.484-010	PLASTER MOLDER II (foundry)	3124	34433443355	MNNNONNNFFFONNNFNFNNN	NNNN3NNNNNNNNNN	J,T	132	566	06.02.24	6179	480599	85999
518.664-010	MOLD MAKER (smelt. & refin.)	2124	44444534355	MNNOOONFFOONNNNNNNNN	NNFN4NNNNNNNNNN	R,T	132	568	06.04.17	7675	480599	92923
518.682-010	MACHINE MOLDER (foundry)	3224	34433534345	MNNNNNNNFFFNNNNFNFNNN	NNNN4NFNNNNNNNN	J,T	136	566	06.04.08	7542	480599	91911
518.685-010	SAND-SLINGER OPERATOR (foundry)	2113	45544534355	MNNFNFNFFFNNNNFNNNNN	NNNN4NFNNNNNNNN	R,T	041	566	06.04.08	7667	480599	92971
518.685-018	COREMAKER, MACHINE II (foundry)	2122	44433434355	MNNNNNNNFFFNNNNNNFNNN	NNNN4NFNNNNNNNN	R,T	135	568	06.04.08	8769	480599	98999
518.685-022	COREMAKER, MACHINE III (foundry)	2113	44443534355	MNNNNNNNNONNNNNFNFNNN	NNNN4NFNNNNNNNN	R,T	136	566	06.04.08	7542	480599	91911
518.685-026	SHELL MOLDER (foundry)	2122	44443433345	HNNNNNNNFFFNNNNFNFNNN	NNNN4NFNNNNNNNN	R,T	136	566	06.04.17	7542	480599	91911
518.685-030	SHELL-MOLD-BONDING-MACHINE OPERATOR (foundry)	2112	34433543355	MNNNNNNNFFFNNNNONFNNN	NNNN3NNNNNNNNNF	R,T	063	566	06.04.08	7542	480599	91914
518.687-010	CORE CHECKER (foundry)	2223	34443444355	LNNNNNNNFFONNNFFNNNN	NNNN4NNNNNNNNNN	J,T	212	566	06.03.02	7820	480599	83005
518.687-014	FOUNDRY LABORER, COREROOM (foundry)	2112	44544544355	MNNFFNNFFONNNNNNONNN	NNNN4NNNNNNNNNN	R	011	566	06.04.32	7754	480599	93944
518.687-018	MOLD-MAKER HELPER (smelt. & refin.)	2113	44544544355	MNNVFFNFFNNNNNNNFNNN	NNNN4NNNNNNNNNF	R,T	136	566	06.04.32	8614	480599	98999
518.687-022	WAX-PATTERN COATER (foundry)	2112	44443544355	MNNNNNNNFFNNNNNFNNNN	NNNN4NNNNNNNNNN	R	151	359	06.04.32	7754	480599	93944
519.130-010	CELL-FEED-DEPARTMENT SUPERVISOR (smelt. & refin.)	4337	33333333354	LNNFNFNFFFNFFNFNNNON	NNNN3NNNNNNNNNN	V,D,P,J	147	350	06.02.01	7100	520205	81008
519.130-014	SAMPLER, HEAD (smelt. & refin.)	4337	33333333355	LNNNNNNNFFFNFFNFNNNNN	NNNN4NNNNNNNNNN	V,D,P,J	212	350	06.04.01	7100	520205	81008
519.130-018	SUPERVISOR, LEAD REFINERY (smelt. & refin.)	4338	33333333355	LNNNNNNNFFNFFNFFONNN	NNNN4NFNNNNNNNF	V,D,P,J	131	353	06.01.01	7100	520205	81008
519.130-022	SUPERVISOR, REVERBERATORY FURNACE (smelt. & refin.)	4338	33333333353	LNNNNNNNFFFNFFNFONFN	NNFN4NFNNNNNNNF	V,D,P,J	131	352	06.04.01	7100	520205	81008

DOT #	DOT Title & Industry	Trng	Aptitude	Physical	Environment	Tempra	WkF	MPSMS	GOE	SOC	CIP	OES
519.130-026	SUPERVISOR, SINTERING PLANT (smelt. & refin.)	4338	33333333354	LNNNNNNFFNFFNFNNNON	NNFN4NFNNNNNNNN	D,J,P	147	347	06.02.01	7100	520205	81008
519.130-030	SUPERVISOR, URANIUM PROCESSING (smelt. & refin.)	4338	33333333355	LNNFNFNFFNFFNFNNNNN	ONNN4NFNNNNNNNN	V,D,P,J	147	358	06.01.01	7100	520205	81008
519.131-010	FOUNDRY SUPERVISOR (foundry)	4337	33333333354	MNNNNNNFFOFFNFOFNON	NNFN4NNNNNNNNNN	V,D,P,J	131	566	06.01.01	7100	520205	81008
519.131-014	MILL-LABOR SUPERVISOR (smelt. & refin.)	4337	33333333355	LNNNNNNFFNFFNFFNNNN	NNNN4NNNNNNNNNN	V,D,P,J	031	568	06.04.01	7100	520205	81008
519.132-010	SUPERVISOR, BLAST FURNACE (steel & rel.)	4336	33344333353	LNNNNNNFFNFFNFNFNFN	NNFN4NNNNNNNNNN	V,D,P,J	131	541	06.04.01	7100	520205	81008
519.132-014	SUPERVISOR, BLAST-FURNACE-AUXILIARIES (steel & rel.)	4336	33344333455	LNNNNNNNFFNFFNFNFNN	NNFN4NNNNNNNNNN	V,D,P,J	142	351	06.04.01	7100	520205	81008
519.132-018	SUPERVISOR, CELL OPERATION (smelt. & refin.)	4337	33344334355	LNNNNNNNFFONNNFNFNN	NNFN4NNNNNNNNNN	V,D,P,J	147	359	06.02.01	7100	520205	81008
519.132-022	SUPERVISOR, SOLDER MAKING (nonfer. metal)	4336	33344334354	LNNNNNNFFFNFFFNONON	NNFN4NNNNNNNNNN	V,D,P,J	131	549	06.04.01	7100	520205	81008
519.134-010	POT-LINING SUPERVISOR (smelt. & refin.)	4337	33333333355	LNFNFNFFNFFNFNFNNNN	NNON4NFNNNNNNNN	D,J,P	102	568	06.04.01	7100	520205	81008
519.137-010	SUPERVISOR, MOLD YARD (steel & rel.)	4337	33333344355	LNNNNNNNFFNFFNFNNNN	ONNN4NNNNNNNNNN	V,D,P,J	031	566	06.04.01	7100	520205	81008
519.137-014	SUPERVISOR, SCRAP PREPARATION (steel & rel.)	4336	33334344455	MNNNNNNNFFNFFNFNNNN	FNNN4NNNNNNNNNN	D,P,J,T	011	541	06.04.01	7100	520205	81008
519.362-010	NICKEL-PLANT OPERATOR (smelt. & refin.)	3226	34333444455	MFNFNFNFFONNNNONNNN	NNNF4NNNNNNNNNF	J,T	147	350	06.02.10	7529	480599	92198
519.362-014	TANK-HOUSE OPERATOR (smelt. & refin.)	3226	34333444444	MONFNFNFFONFFNFNONON	NNNF3NNNNNNNNN	J,T	147	352	06.02.10	7529	480599	92198
519.387-010	MANOMETER TECHNICIAN (smelt. & refin.)	3223	34344343455	LNNNNNNFFFONNNNFNNNN	ONNN4NNNNNNNNNN	J,T	212	349	06.03.01	7830	480599	83005
519.484-010	CARNALLITE-PLANT OPERATOR (smelt. & refin.)	2124	34444343355	MNNFNFNFFONNNNNNNNN	NNNN3NNNNNNNNNN	R,T	143	359	06.02.18	7529	480599	92198
519.484-014	RAW SAMPLER (smelt. & refin.)	3114	34444433354	LNNNNNNFFFONNNFNFOON	NNON4NFNNNNNNON	R,T	147	350	02.04.01	7840	480599	83005
519.485-010	GRINDER-MILL OPERATOR (smelt. & refin.)	3114	34433434354	LNNNNNNFFFONNNFNFNON	NNNN4NFNNNNNNNN	R,T	142	350	06.02.08	7677	480599	92965
519.485-014	RECOVERY-OPERATOR HELPER (smelt. & refin.)	2123	34443434355	MFNFNFNFFNNNNNNNNNN	NNNN4NFNNNNNNNF	R,T	145	355	06.04.10	8611	480599	98999
519.565-010	DIGESTION OPERATOR (smelt. & refin.)	2113	44444443355	HONNNNNFFFNNNNNNNNN	ONNN4NFNNNNNNNN	R,T	145	355	06.04.10	7679	480599	92998
519.565-014	TANK-HOUSE-OPERATOR HELPER (smelt. & refin.)	2123	44333444355	HFNFFNNFFNNOONNNNNNN	NNNO4NNNNNNNNNN	R,T	147	352	06.04.10	8611	480599	98999
519.582-010	RECOVERY OPERATOR (smelt. & refin.)	3225	34344343355	MFNFNFNFFNFFNNNNNNN	NNNN4NFNNNNNNNN	J,T	145	355	06.02.10	7529	480599	92198
519.585-010	HARDNESS TESTER (mine & quarry)	3223	34344434355	LNNNNNNFFFONNNFNFNNN	NNNN4NNNNNNNNNN	R,T	212	549	06.03.02	7830	480599	83005
519.585-014	MUD BOSS (smelt. & refin.)	3224	34433434355	MNNNNNNNFFONNNFNFNNN	NNNF4NFNNNNNNNF	R,T	147	350	06.04.10	7679	480599	92998
519.585-018	SAMPLE TESTER-GRINDER (mine & quarry)	3224	34443443355	LNNNNNNNFFNNNNFNFNNN	NNNN4NNNNNNNNNN	R,T	142	341	05.12.07	8611	480599	83005
519.663-010	DOOR-MACHINE OPERATOR (steel & rel.)	3223	34433534345	MNNNNNNNFFNNNNFNFNNN	ONFN4NFNNNNNNNN	R,T	011	505	06.04.12	7529	480599	92198
519.663-014	HOT-CAR OPERATOR (steel & rel.)	2123	44433534345	LNNNNNNNFFNNNFFNNNFNNF	NNFN4NFNNNNNNNF	R,T	013	505	06.04.40	8318	480599	97947
519.663-018	PUSHER OPERATOR (steel & rel.)	2123	44433434345	LNNNNNNNFFNNNFFNNNNNN	ONFN4FNNNNNNNNN	R,T	011	505	06.04.12	7529	480599	92198
519.664-010	ASSEMBLY CLEANER (smelt. & refin.)	3223	34443433345	HONNNNNCCFNOONFNFNNN	NNNN4CCFNNNNNNN	R,T	031	568	06.04.24	8750	480599	98905
519.664-014	POT LINER (smelt. & refin.)	3124	34443534355	HFNFOONFFFNFFNNONFNNN	NNFN4NFNNNNNNNN	R,T	102	568	05.10.01	6140	480599	98999
519.665-010	GRANULATOR TENDER (steel & rel.)	2114	44444444355	MNNNNNNNFFNNFFNNNFNNN	ONFN4NNNNNNNNNF	R,T	147	541	06.04.10	7679	480599	97944
519.665-014	STANDPIPE TENDER (steel & rel.)	2112	44544544345	MFNNNNNFFNNFFNNNNNNN	FNFN4NFNNNNNNNF	R,T	013	505	06.04.12	7675	480599	97947
519.665-018	WET-PLANT OPERATOR (smelt. & refin.)	3224	34434434355	LNNNNNNFFNOONFNNNNNN	NNON4NNNNNNNNNN	R,T	091	350	06.04.10	7676	480599	92962
519.667-010	CARBON SETTER (smelt. & refin.)	3113	44544544355	HNNFFNNFFFNNNNNNNNF	NNNN4NNNNNNNNNN	R	121	568	06.04.34	6140	480599	85128
519.667-014	LABORER, SOLDER MAKING (nonfer. metal)	2113	44444544355	MNNNNNNNFFFNNONNNFNNN	NNFN3NNNNNNNNNF	R	131	543	06.04.24	8769	480599	98999
519.683-010	DROSS SKIMMER (smelt. & refin.)	2114	44543534345	HNNNNNNFFONNNNONNFNNN	NNON4NFNNNNNNNN	R,T	091	534	06.04.30	7720	480599	85126
519.684-010	LARRY OPERATOR (steel & rel.)	2123	44444434345	MNNNFFNFFNNNNFFFNNF	FNFN4NFNNNNNNNF	R,T	142	341	06.04.08	7677	480599	92965
519.684-014	LADLE LINER (foundry; smelt. & refin.)	2113	45545534355	MNNNFFFNFFFNNNFNNNN	NNNN4NFNNNNNNNN	R,T	011	540	06.04.10	8725	480599	98502
519.684-018	LEAF COVERER (smelt. & refin.)	3224	34434434355	MNNNNNNFFONNNFONNNON	NNFN4NNNNNNNNNN	R,T	094	350	06.04.10	7740	480599	93999
519.684-018	MOLD DRESSER (any industry)	3124	34444434354	MNNNNNNFFONNNNFNNFN	NNNN4NNNNNNNNNN	R,T	147	359	06.04.10	7675	480599	93926
519.684-022	STOPPER MAKER (steel & rel.)	2113	44443433355	MNNNNNNNFFNNNNNNNNN	NNFN4NONNNNNNNN	R,T	147	353	06.04.10	7675	480599	93953
519.684-026	TOOL REPAIRER (smelt. & refin.)	2113	44544534355	LNNNNNNNFFNNNNNNONN	NNNO4NFNNNNNNNN	R,T	143	350	06.04.10	7664	480599	92965
519.685-010	BRIQUETTING-MACHINE OPERATOR (smelt. & refin.)	3115	34543533355	LNNNNNNNFFNNNFNNNNNN	NNNN4NFNNNNNNNN	V,T	102	568	06.02.32	6179	490299	85999
519.685-014	GROUT-MACHINE TENDER (smelt. & refin.)	2113	44443434355	LNNNNNNNFFFNNNFNNNNN	NNNN4NNNNNNNNNN	R,T	147	352	06.04.10	7675	480599	92923
519.685-018	KETTLE OPERATOR (smelt. & refin.)	2112	44444444344	MNNNNNNNFFNNNNFNONON	NNNN4NNNNNNNNNN	R,T	094	568	06.04.10	8725	480599	92998
519.685-022	KETTLE TENDER I (smelt. & refin.)	3224	34343434354	MNNNNNNFFONNNNFNNFN	NNNN4NNNNNNNNNN	R,T	147	359	06.04.10	7675	480599	92923
519.685-026	MUD-MILL TENDER (smelt. & refin.)	3124	34444434354	MNNNNNNFFFNNNNNNNNN	NNFN4NFNNNNNNNF	R,T	147	353	06.04.10	7675	480599	93926
519.685-030	ROD-MILL TENDER (cement; smelt. & refin.)	2123	44544534355	LNNNNNNNFFNNNNNONONNN	NNNN4NFNNNNNNNN	R,T	143	350	06.04.10	7677	480599	92965
519.686-010	LABORER, GENERAL (nonfer. metal)	2112	44444434355	HNNNNNNFFFONNNNONONNN	NNNN4NNNNNNNNNN	R	011	540	06.04.08	8725	480599	98502
519.687-010	CELL PLASTERER (smelt. & refin.)	2113	45545544354	LNNNNNNNFFNNNNNNNNON	NNNN3NNNNNNNNNN	R	094	350	06.04.34	7740	480599	93999
519.687-014	DUST PULLER (smelt. & refin.)	2112	45544535345	HNNFOONFFNNNNNNNNNNN	NNNN4NFNNNNNNNN	R	011	350	06.04.10	8726	480599	98799
519.687-018	FLUX-TUBE ATTENDANT (nonfer. metal; smelt. & refin.)	3123	44444434354	MNNNNNNFFNNNNFNNFNQN	NNFN4NFNNNNNNNN	R,T	143	568	06.04.10	7759	480599	93999

DOT #	DOT Title & Industry	Trng	Aptitude	Physical	Environment	Tempra	WkF	MPSMS	GOE	SOC	CIP	OES
519.687-022	FOUNDRY WORKER, GENERAL (foundry)	2112	4444453355	HNNFOFNFFONNNNONFNNN	NNFN4NFNNNNNNNN	R	011	540	06.04.32	8769	480599	98999
519.687-026	LABORER, GENERAL (smelt. & refin.)	2112	4444534345	HNNFFNFFONNNNNNFNNN	ONNN4NNNNNNNNNN	R	011	350	06.04.40	8769	480599	98999
519.687-030	MACHINE-CASTINGS PLASTERER (foundry)	2112	4444534355	LNNNNNNFFONNNNNNFNNN	NNNN4NNNNNNNNNN	R	094	542	06.04.33	7754	480599	93944
519.687-034	RODDING-ANODE WORKER (smelt. & refin.)	2113	4444544345	HNNFFNFFNNNNNNNFNNN	NNFN4NNNNNNNNNNF	R	102	355	06.04.34	7740	480599	93999
519.687-038	STOPPER-MAKER HELPER (steel & rel.)	2112	4444544355	HNNNNNNFFNNNNNNNNNN	NNNO4NNNNNNNNNN	R	091	534	06.04.30	8620	480599	98999
519.687-042	TEST WORKER (foundry)	1112	4454444455	LNNNNNNFFNNNNNFNFNNN	NNFN4NFNNNNNNNNF	R	053	541	06.04.24	7840	480599	83005
520.132-010	BLENDING SUPERVISOR (grain-feed mills)	4336	3334434354	LOONNNNNFFONFFNFNOOON	NNNN4NCCNNNNNNN	V,D,P	143	381	06.02.01	7100	000000	81008
520.132-014	SUPERVISOR, COMPRESSED YEAST (food prep., nec)	4337	3333333353	LNNNNNNFFFFNFNNNFN	NNNN4NNNNNNNNNN	V,D,P,J	146	399	06.02.01	7100	000000	81008
520.136-010	BLENDING SUPERVISOR (tobacco)	4335	3334333454	LNNNNNNFFONFFNNFNNNN	NNNN4NNNNNNNNNN	V,D,P	143	403	06.04.01	7100	000000	81008
520.137-010	SUPERVISOR, LUMP ROOM (tobacco)	4327	3333444454	LNNNNNNFFFNFFNFNNNON	NNNN4NNNNNNNNNN	D,J,T	136	409	06.04.01	7100	000000	81008
520.361-010	HONEY GRADER-AND-BLENDER (food prep., nec)	4336	3333444453	SNNNNNNFFFOFFFFFFFN	NNNN3NNNNNNNNNN	J	143	399	06.01.04	6873	020301	89808
520.362-010	BULK-PLANT OPERATOR (sugar & conf.)	4335	3344433444	LFNNNNNFFNNNNFNFNNN	ONNN4NNNNNNNNNN	T	143	392	06.02.15	7664	000000	89899
520.362-014	DRY-STARCH OPERATOR (grain-feed mills)	3237	3334334354	HONOOONFFNOONFNNNON	NNNN4NOONNNNNNN	J,T	147	381	06.02.15	7664	000000	92965
520.382-010	CISTERN-ROOM OPERATOR (beverage)	3294	3334334455	LNNNNNNFFFNNNNFNNNN	NNNN4NNNNNNNNNN	J,T	143	395	06.02.15	7664	000000	92965
520.382-014	LIQUID-SUGAR MELTER (sugar & conf.)	3224	3434444355	LNNNNNNFONNNNFNFNNN	NNNF4NNNNNNNNNN	J,T	143	392	06.02.15	7664	000000	92965
520.384-010	BENCH HAND (bakery products)	3226	3433343354	MNNNNNNFFONNNNFNFNON	NNNN3NNNNNNNNNN	J,T	146	384	06.02.28	7755	120501	93999
520.385-010	MIXER, WHIPPED TOPPING (food prep., nec)	2223	3434444354	MNNNNNNNFFONNNFNFNON	NNNF4NNNNNNNNNNF	T	146	393	06.04.15	7664	000000	92965
520.387-010	BLENDER (tobacco)	3224	3444444454	LNNFFNNFFFFNNNONNNON	NNNN4NNNNNNNNNN	J	143	403	06.03.01	7850	000000	83005
520.462-010	DOUGH-MIXER OPERATOR (bakery products)	3135	3433443355	LNNFNFNFFFNNNFNFNNN	NNFF4NFNNNNNNNN	J	146	384	06.02.15	7664	120501	92965
520.485-010	FLOUR MIXER (grain-feed mills)	2222	3444444455	HNNFNFNFFNNNNNFNNN	NNNN4NNNNNNNNNN	R,T	143	381	06.04.15	7664	000000	92965
520.485-014	GRAIN MIXER (grain-feed mills)	2112	3444444455	LNNNNNNFFNNNNNFNNN	NNNN4NFNNNNNNNN	R,T	143	381	06.04.15	7664	000000	92965
520.485-018	MINCEMEAT MAKER (can. & preserv.)	3223	3435444355	MNNNNNNFFNNNNONNNNN	NNNN4NNNNNNNNNN	R,T	146	390	06.04.15	7664	000000	92965
520.485-022	REFINED-SYRUP OPERATOR (sugar & conf.)	3334	3333434354	MONNNNNFFNNNNFNNNFN	ONNN4NNNNNNNNNN	J,T	143	392	06.02.15	7664	000000	92965
520.485-026	SYRUP MAKER (beverage)	3234	3434344354	MOONNNNFFFNNNONNNON	NNNC3NNNNNNNNNN	J,T	143	394	06.02.15	7664	000000	92962
520.485-030	STARCHMAKER (grain-feed mills)	3233	3334334354	LNNNNNNFFONNNNONNNOON	NNNF3NNNNNNNNNN	J,T	147	381	06.01.04	7830	000000	83005
520.487-010	CHEESE BLENDER (dairy products)	4436	3334334453	LNNNNNNFFONNNONNNOON	NONN3NNNNNNNNNN	D,J	212	383	05.10.08	5233	200409	66099
520.487-014	FORMULA-ROOM WORKER (dairy products)	2223	3433434353	LNNONNNCCCNNNFNNNNN	NNNN2NNNNNNNNNN	R,T	146	903	06.04.28	7840	120501	83005
520.487-018	PANTRY WORKER (sugar & conf.)	3223	3434334454	LNNFNNNFFNOONFNNNNN	NNNN3NNNNNNNNNN	R,T	212	393	06.04.28	7830	000000	92965
520.565-010	CHURNER (oils & grease)	2112	4444444355	LNNFNNNFFOONFNNNNN	NNNN4NFNNNNNNNN	R,T	143	385	06.04.15	7664	000000	92965
520.585-010	BLENDER (bakery products)	1112	4444444355	HNNFNFNFFNNNNFNNNN	NNNN4NFNNNNNNNN	R,J	143	384	06.04.15	7664	120501	92965
520.585-014	BROTH MIXER (bakery products)	3224	3444444355	HNNNNNNFFNNNNFNFNNN	NNNN4NFNNNNNNNN	J,T	143	392	06.04.15	7664	120501	92965
520.585-018	COOLER TENDER (sugar & conf.)	2114	3444334455	LNNNNNNFFONNNNFNNNN	NNNN4NNNNNNNNNN	J,T	143	392	06.04.15	7664	000000	92965
520.585-022	LIQUID-SUGAR FORTIFIER (sugar & conf.)	2224	4344444353	LNNNNNNFFNNNNFNNNN	NNNN4NNNNNNNNNO	J	143	385	06.02.15	7664	000000	92965
520.585-026	SPICE MIXER (food prep., nec)	1112	4444444353	HNNONNNFFNNNNFNNFFN	NNNN4NCNNNNNNN	R	146	384	06.04.28	7755	120501	92968
520.682-010	BLENDING-PLANT OPERATOR (oils & grease)	3326	3443434354	MNNNNNFFOONFNFNON	NNFF4NNNNNNNNNN	J,T	146	397	06.02.15	7664	000000	92965
520.682-014	CENTER-MACHINE OPERATOR (sugar & conf.)	2113	4444334355	MNNNNNNFFNNFFNNNNNN	NNNN4NNNNNNNNNN	R,T	143	392	06.04.15	7664	120501	92965
520.682-018	EXTRUDER OPERATOR (grain-feed mills)	2112	3343434354	MONNNNNFFNFOONONNONN	NNNO4NNNNNNNNNN	J,T	143	399	06.02.15	7664	120501	92997
520.682-022	GUM-SCORING-MACHINE OPERATOR (sugar & conf.)	3224	3443444354	LNNNNNCCNNNNNNNNNN	NNNO3NONNNNNNNN	J,T	143	389	06.04.15	7664	000000	92965
520.662-010	NOODLE-PRESS OPERATOR (food prep., nec)	3325	3434444354	HONONNNFFOONONONNNN	NNNO4NCNNNNNNN	J,T	135	393	06.02.15	7463	200409	92968
520.665-010	MINGLER OPERATOR (sugar & conf.)	3225	3333343353	MNNNNNFFFNNNNNFNNN	NNNN3NNNNNNNNNN	J,T	135	393	06.02.15	7664	000000	92965
520.665-014	MIXING-MACHINE OPERATOR (food prep., nec)	3225	3443344354	LNNNNNNFFOONNFNFNFN	NNNN5NNNNNNNNNN	J	146	381	06.02.15	7664	000000	92965
520.665-018	STARCH-TREATING ASSISTANT (grain-feed mills)	3215	4444344355	MNNNNNNFFOONNFNFNON	NNNN4NNNNNNNNNN	J	146	393	06.02.15	7664	000000	92965
520.682-010	BLENDING-PLANT OPERATOR (oils & grease)	3236	3333334355	MNNNNNNFFOONNFONNNFN	NNNN4NNNNNNNNNN	R,J,T	132	393	06.02.15	7479	200409	92997
520.682-014	CENTER-MACHINE OPERATOR (sugar & conf.)	3226	4444434354	MNNNNNNFFNNNNNONFNON	NNFN4NNNNNNNNNN	R,T	146	393	06.04.15	7667	200409	92971
520.682-018	EXTRUDER OPERATOR (grain-feed mills)	3225	3443343355	MNNNNNFFONNNFNNNNN	NNNN4NNNNNNNNNN	J,T	146	384	06.02.15	7663	000000	92971
520.682-022	CRACKER-AND-COOKIE-MACHINE OPERATOR (bakery products)	2125	4433433353	LNNNNNNCCCNNNNNNNNFN	NNNN3NNNNNNNNNN	R,J,T	136	393	06.04.32	7755	200409	93999
520.684-010	ALMOND-PASTE MOLDER (sugar & conf.)	3223	3444444354	MNNNNNNFFFNNNNNNNNN	NNNN4NNNNNNNNNN	R,J	136	393	06.04.28	7755	200409	93999
520.684-014	ROLLER (sugar & conf.)	3224	3434344354	LNNFNFFFFNNNNFNFNN	NNNN4NNNNNNNNNN	J,T	143	384	06.04.15	7664	120501	92965
520.685-010	BATTER MIXER (bakery products)	2222	4444444354	HNNNNNNNFFNNNNNNFNON	NNNN3NNNNNNNNNN	R,T	143	384	06.04.15	7664	200409	92965
520.685-018	BLENDER-MACHINE OPERATOR (oils & grease)	2112	4444444355	MNNONONFFNNNNNFNFNNN	NNNN4NNNNNNNNNN	R	143	385	06.04.15	7664	000000	92965

DOT #	DOT Title & Industry	Trng	Aptitude	Physical	Environment	Tempra	WkF	MPSMS	GOE	SOC	CIP	OES
520.685-022	BLENDER, SNUFF (tobacco)	2112	44444444355	LNNNNNFFONNNNFNFNNN	NNFN4NFNNNNNNNNN	R,T	143	404	06.04.15	7664	000000	92965
520.685-026	BLENDING-LINE ATTENDANT (tobacco)	2113	34444444355	MNNNNNNFFNNNNNFNFNNN	NNNNN4NNNNNNNNNN	R,T	143	403	06.04.15	7664	000000	92965
520.685-030	BLENDING-TANK TENDER (beverage; can. & preserv.)	2122	34444444355	HONFNNFFFNNNNNFNFNNN	NNNNN4NNNNNNNNNN	R,T	143	387	06.04.15	7664	000000	92965
520.685-034	BRINE-MIXER OPERATOR, AUTOMATIC (can. & preserv.)	2112	44444444355	LNNNNNNFFNNNNONNNNN	NNNNN4NNNNNNNNNN	R,T	143	387	06.04.15	7664	000000	92971
520.685-038	CAKE FORMER (oils & grease)	2112	44544454445	LNNNNNNFFNNNNNNNNNN	NNNNN4NNNNNNNNNN	R	134	385	06.04.15	7663	000000	92965
520.685-042	CAKE STRIPPER (oils & grease)	2112	44544544445	MNNNNNNFFNNNNNNNNNN	NNNNN4NNNNNNNNNN	R	041	381	06.04.19	7679	000000	92998
520.685-046	CANDY PULLER (sugar & conf.)	3225	44544533354	MNNNNNNFFFNNNNNNNNN	NNNNN4NNNNNNNNNN	R	146	393	06.04.15	7664	000000	92965
520.685-050	CANDY-MAKER HELPER (sugar & conf.)	3214	34344444354	MMNFNNNFFNNNNNFNNNN	NNNNN4NNNNNNNNNF	R,T	146	393	06.04.15	7664	200409	92965
520.685-054	CASING-FLUID TENDER (tobacco)	2113	44443444355	MMNNNNNFFNNNNNFNNON	NNNNN4NNNNNNNNNN	R,T	143	394	06.04.15	7664	000000	92965
520.685-058	CASTING-MACHINE OPERATOR (dairy products)	2213	44443444355	HONNNNNFFFNNNNOOONNN	NNNNN4NNNNNNNNNN	R,T	146	383	06.04.15	7663	000000	92971
520.685-062	CASTING-MACHINE OPERATOR (sugar & conf.)	2112	44444544355	LNNNNNNFFNNNNNNNNN	NNNNN4NNNNNNNNNN	R	135	393	06.04.15	7663	120501	92965
520.685-066	CHOPPING-MACHINE OPERATOR (meat products)	2114	44444444455	MNNNNNNFFNNNNNNNNN	NNNNN4NNNNNNNNNN	R,J,T	146	382	06.04.15	7664	120506	92965
520.685-070	CHURN OPERATOR, MARGARINE (oils & grease)	2222	44444444355	LNNNNNNFFNNNNNFNFNN	NNNNN4NNNNNNNNNN	J,T	146	385	06.04.15	7664	000000	92965
520.685-074	COCOA-POWDER-MIXER OPERATOR (sugar & conf.)	3224	34344444354	MNNNNNNFFNNNFNFNNN	NNNNN4NNNNNNNNNN	R,T	143	393	06.04.15	7664	000000	92965
520.685-078	CONFECTIONERY-DROPS-MACHINE OPERATOR (sugar & conf.)	1112	44444444455	LNNNNNNFFONNNNONFNNN	NNNNN4NNNNNNNNNN	R	135	393	06.04.15	7663	000000	92971
520.685-082	COOKER, CASING (tobacco)	2113	44444444454	MNNNNNNFFNNNNNONNNON	NNNNN3NNNNNNNNNN	R,T	147	394	06.04.15	7664	000000	92917
520.685-086	DIVIDING-MACHINE OPERATOR (bakery products)	3113	34444344355	LNNONNNFFNNOONFNFNNN	NNNNN4NNNNNNNNNN	J,T	146	384	06.04.15	7663	120501	92971
520.685-090	DOUGH-BRAKE-MACHINE OPERATOR (bakery products)	2113	44443443355	MNNNNNNFFNONNNFNNNN	NNNNN4NNNNNNNNNN	R,J	143	384	06.04.15	7664	120501	92965
520.685-094	FEED BLENDER (grain-feed mills)	2112	44444444355	MNNNNNNFFNNFNFNNNNN	NNNF4NNNNNNNNNN	R	143	381	06.04.15	7664	000000	92965
520.685-098	FEED MIXER (grain-feed mills)	2222	44444444355	HNNFNFNFFNNNNFNNNNN	NNNNN4NFNNNNNNNN	R,T	143	381	06.04.15	7664	000000	92965
520.685-102	FLAKING-ROLL OPERATOR (grain-feed mills)	3113	44343434354	LNNNNNNFFFNNNNFNFNON	NNNNN4NNNNNNNNNN	J,T	135	381	06.04.15	7663	200409	92965
520.685-106	FLOUR BLENDER (grain-feed mills)	2113	44444443355	MNNNNNNFFNNNNNNNNN	NNNNN4NFNNNNNNNN	R	143	381	06.04.15	7664	000000	92965
520.685-110	GREEN-COFFEE BLENDER (food prep., nec)	2122	44444444355	HNNFNFNFFNNNNNNNNN	NNNNN4NNNNNNNNNN	R	143	391	06.04.15	7664	000000	92965
520.685-114	ICING MIXER (bakery products)	3123	34344344354	HNNONONFFFNNNNFNFFN	NNNO4NNNNNNNNNN	J,T	143	384	06.04.15	7664	120501	92965
520.685-118	KETTLE TENDER (sugar & conf.)	2112	44434434355	HNNNNNNFFNNNNNFNFNNN	NNNNN4NNNNNNNNNN	R	143	393	06.04.15	7664	000000	92965
520.685-122	LOZENGE-DOUGH MIXER (sugar & conf.)	2224	44444433354	HNNNNNNFFNNNNFNFNNN	NNNNN4NNNNNNNNNN	R,T	143	393	06.04.15	7664	200409	92965
520.685-130	MASH GRINDER (dairy products)	2222	44444444355	HNNNNNNFFNNNNNNNNN	NNNNN4NNNNNNNNNN	J,T	143	393	06.04.15	7664	000000	92965
520.685-134	MILL FEEDER (grain-feed mills)	1112	44444444355	HNNNNNNFFNNNNNFNNNN	NNNNN4NFNNNNNNNN	R,T	146	383	06.04.15	7664	000000	92965
520.685-138	MIXER (food prep., nec)	2213	34433434355	MNNNNNNFFNNNNFNFNNN	NNNNN4NNNNNNNNNN	R	143	381	06.04.15	7664	200409	92965
520.685-142	MIXER OPERATOR II (chemical)	2112	44444444454	MNNNNNNFFNNNNNFNFNN	NNNNN4NFNNNNNNNN	R,T	146	387	06.04.15	7664	200409	92965
520.685-146	MIXER OPERATOR (beverage)	2213	44444444454	LNNNNNNFFNNNNNFNNNN	NNNNN4NNNNNNNNNN	R,T	143	499	06.04.15	7664	000000	92965
520.685-150	MIXER OPERATOR (sugar & conf.)	2213	33344344355	HNNNNNNFFFNNNNNNNNN	NNNNN4NFNNNNNNNN	R,T	143	380	06.04.15	7664	000000	92965
520.685-154	MIXER-AND-BLENDER (food prep., nec)	3224	34344344355	HNNONONFFFNNNNNNNN	NNNNN4NNNNNNNNNN	J,T	143	393	06.04.15	7664	200409	92965
520.685-158	MIXER, CHILI POWDER (food prep., nec)	2213	44444433353	HNNFNNNFFNNNNNFNFNN	NNNNN4NNNNNNNNNNF	J,T	143	389	06.04.15	7664	000000	92965
520.685-162	MIXER, DRY-FOOD PRODUCTS (food prep.,, nec)	2123	34344444445	HNNFNNNFFONNNFNFNNN	NNNNN4NFNNNNNNNN	R,T	143	391	06.04.15	7664	000000	92965
520.685-166	MIXING-MACHINE OPERATOR (can. & preserv.)	1112	44444444355	HNNFNNNFFONNNNONONNN	NNNNN4NNNNNNNNNN	R,T	143	380	06.04.15	7664	000000	92965
520.685-170	MIXING-TANK OPERATOR (oils & grease)	2122	44444544355	MNNNNNNFFNNNFNNNNN	NNNNN4NNNNNNNNNN	R,T	143	387	06.04.15	7664	000000	92965
520.685-174	MOLDER, MEAT (meat products)	2112	44544534355	MNNNNNNFFONNNNFNNNN	NNNNN4NNNNNNNNNN	R	041	385	06.04.15	7664	000000	92965
520.685-178	PELLET-MILL OPERATOR (grain-feed mills)	2112	44444444355	LNNNNNNFFONNNNONFNNN	NFNNN4NFNNNNNNNN	R,J,T	143	382	06.04.15	7662	120506	92974
520.685-182	PRESS OPERATOR, MEAT (meat products)	2112	34444444355	LNNNNNNFFNNNNNFNNNN	NNNNN3NNNNNNNNNN	R,T	135	382	06.04.15	7663	120506	92971
520.685-186	PRESS TENDER (food prep. nec)	1112	44544544355	MNNNFNNFFNNNNNNNNN	NNNNN4NNNNNNNNNN	R	034	382	06.04.15	7664	000000	92965
520.685-190	PRETZEL-TWISTING-MACHINE OPERATOR (bakery products)	3114	34434434353	HONONONFFOONNNONNNNON	NNFF4NNNNNNNNNN	J,T	146	397	06.02.15	7663	000000	92971
520.685-194	RELISH BLENDER (can. & preserv.)	2112	44544544355	LNNFNFNFFNNNNNNNNN	NNNN4NNNNNNNNNN	R,T	146	384	06.04.15	7663	120501	92965
520.685-198	ROLLING-MACHINE OPERATOR (sugar & conf.)	2113	34433434355	MNNNNNNFFNNNNFNFFNF	NNNNN4NNNNNNNNNN	R,T	143	387	06.04.15	7663	000000	92965
520.685-202	SAUSAGE MAKER (meat products)	2122	44444444355	MNNNNNNFFNNNNNNNNN	NNNNN4NNNNNNNNNN	J,T	135	393	06.04.15	7664	120506	92965
520.685-206	SAUSAGE MIXER (meat products)	2123	44444444355	HNNFNFNFFONNNNONNNN	NNNNN4NNNNNNNNNN	R,J,T	143	382	06.04.15	7664	120506	92965
520.685-210	STUFFER (meat products)	2112	44554533355	MNNNNNNFFNNNNNFNNNN	NFNN4NNNNNNNNNN	R,J,T	143	382	06.04.15	7662	120506	92965
520.685-214	SWEET-GOODS-MACHINE OPERATOR (bakery products)	2113	44444443355	MNNNNNNFFONNNNNONNNO	NNNN3NNNNNNNNNN	R	132	382	06.04.15	7662	120506	92974
520.685-218	TRAY-CASTING-MACHINE OPERATOR (dairy products)	2112	34444544455	LNNNNNNFFONNNNONNNNO	NNNNN3NNNNNNNNNN	R	146	384	06.04.15	7663	120501	92971
520.685-222	TUMBLER TENDER (food prep. nec)	1112	44444444455	LNNFNNNFFNNNNNONONN	NNNNN3NNNNNNNNNN	R,T	132	383	06.04.15	7663	000000	92971
520.685-226	UNLEAVENED-DOUGH MIXER (bakery products)	2112	44445434335	LNNONNNFFFNNNNFNFNNN	NNNN4NNNNNNNNNN	R	143	384	06.04.15	7664	200409	92965

DOT #	DOT Title & Industry	Trng	Aptitude	Physical	Environment	Tempra	WkF	MPSMS	GOE	SOC	CIP	OES
520.685-230	MIXER OPERATOR, SNACK FOODS (food prep., nec)	2112	44454444454	MONOOONFFOOOONFNNNON	NNNN4NNNNNNNNNN	R,U	146	399	06.04.15	7664	000000	92965
520.685-234	DOUGH MIXER (bakery products)	3335	34344334354	HNNNNNNFFFNNNNFNFNON	NNNN4NNNNNNNNNN	J,T	143	384	06.02.15	7664	200409	92965
520.686-010	BALL-MACHINE OPERATOR (sugar & conf.)	1112	44544334354	LNNNNNNFFNNNNNNFNNON	NNNN3NNNNNNNNNN	R	146	393	06.04.15	8725	000000	98502
520.686-014	DESSERT-CUP-MACHINE FEEDER (bakery products)	1112	44544533355	LNNNNNNFFONNNNNNNNNN	NNNN3NNNNNNNNNN	R	134	384	06.04.15	8725	120501	98502
520.686-018	FEED-MIXER HELPER (grain-feed mills)	1112	44544444355	HNNFNNNFFNNNNNNNNNNN	NNNN4NNNNNNNNNN	R	143	381	06.04.15	8618	000000	98999
520.686-022	FLOUR-BLENDER HELPER (grain-feed mills)	1112	44444444455	HNNNNNNNFFNNNNNNNNNN	NNNN3NONNNNNNNNN	R,T	143	381	06.04.15	8618	000000	98999
520.686-026	GLUCOSE-AND-SYRUP WEIGHER (sugar & conf.)	1112	44444444455	HNNFNNNFFNNNNNFNNNNN	NNNN3NNNNNNNNNN	R,T	212	393	06.04.28	7840	000000	83005
520.686-030	MOLDING-MACHINE-OPERATOR HELPER (sugar & conf.)	1112	44544544355	MNNNNNNFFNNNNNNNNNNN	NNNN3NNNNNNNNNN	R	146	393	06.04.15	8725	000000	98502
520.686-034	PLUG SHAPER, MACHINE (tobacco)	1112	44544544455	HNNNNNNNCCNNNNNNNNNN	NNNN3NNNNNNNNNN	R	135	403	06.04.15	8725	000000	98502
520.686-038	TAMALE-MACHINE FEEDER (food prep., nec)	1112	44544543355	LNNNNNNFFNNNNNNNNNNN	NNNN3NNNNNNNNNN	R	146	380	06.04.15	7679	000000	92998
520.687-010	BLENDER LABORER (tobacco)	1111	44544444455	VNNONNNFFNNNNNONNNNN	NNNN3NNNNNNNNNN	R	011	403	06.04.40	8726	000000	98799
520.687-014	BLINTZE ROLLER (food prep., nec)	1112	44544544455	MNNNNNNFFNNNNNNNNNNN	NNNN3NNNNNNNNNN	R	146	384	06.04.28	8769	200409	98999
520.687-018	CANDY MOLDER, HAND (sugar & conf.)	2113	44543544455	LNNNNNNFFONNNNNNNNNN	NNNN3NNNNNNNNNN	R,T	132	393	06.04.28	7754	200409	93944
520.687-022	CANDY SPREADER (sugar & conf.)	1112	44444544355	MNNNNNNFFNNNNNNNNNNN	NNNN3NNNNNNNNNN	R	146	393	06.04.28	8769	200409	98999
520.687-026	CASING-MATERIAL WEIGHER (tobacco)	2122	44444444455	HFNNNNNFFNNNNFNFNNN	NNNN3NNNNNNNNNN	R,T	212	394	06.04.28	7840	000000	83005
520.687-030	FILLER MIXER (tobacco)	2112	44444534355	LNNFNNNFFOONNNONNNNN	NNNN3NNNNNNNNNN	R,J	143	403	06.04.28	7759	000000	93999
520.687-034	FOOD MIXER (grain-feed mills)	2222	44444534355	MNNNNNNFFNNNNNNNNNNN	NNNN3NNNNNNNNNN	R,T	143	381	06.04.28	7759	000000	93999
520.687-038	GUM PULLER (sugar & conf.)	2112	44444444455	MNNONNNFFNNNNNNNNNNN	NNNN3NNNNNNNNNN	R	011	393	06.04.15	8726	000000	98799
520.687-042	HOP WEIGHER (beverage)	2123	44443344455	MNNOOONFFNNNNNNNNNNN	NNNN3NNNNNNNNNN	R	212	395	06.03.02	7840	000000	83005
520.687-046	MEXICAN FOOD MAKER, HAND (food prep., nec)	2112	44544543355	LNNNNNNFFNNNNNNNNNNN	NNNN3NNNNNNNNNN	R	146	399	06.04.28	8769	120505	98999
520.687-050	PLUG SHAPER, HAND (tobacco)	1113	44444444455	MNNFNNNFFNNNNNNNNNNN	NNNN4NNNNNNNNNN	R	136	403	06.04.28	7667	000000	92971
520.687-054	SEASONING MIXER (meat products)	2122	44444443355	MNNNNNNFFONNNNNFNNNN	NNNN3NNNNNNNNNN	R,T	212	387	06.04.28	7759	120506	93999
520.687-058	SYRUP-MIXER ASSISTANT (grain-feed mills)	1112	44544544355	VONOOONFFNNNNNNNNNNN	NNNN3NNNNNNNNNN	R	011	392	06.04.40	8618	000000	98999
520.687-062	SPICE MIXER (can. & preserv.)	2222	33355344355	LNNNNNNFFONNNNNNNNNN	NNNN3NNNNNNNNNN	R,T	212	387	06.04.28	7759	000000	93999
520.687-066	BLENDING-TANK TENDER HELPER (can. & preserv.)	2112	44444344355	LNNONNNOONNNNNNNNNNN	NNNN4NNNNNNNNNN	R	011	381	06.04.15	8618	200409	98999
521.130-010	MILLER SUPERVISOR (grain-feed mills)	4237	34443444455	LFNNNNNNFONFFNFFNNNN	NNNN4NCNNNNNNNNN	D,P,J	142	381	06.02.01	7100	000000	81008
521.130-014	SUPERVISOR, POWDERED SUGAR (sugar & conf.)	4337	33344334355	LNNNNNNFFONFFNONNONN	NNNN3NNNNNNNNNN	V,D,P,J	142	392	06.02.01	7100	000000	81008
521.131-010	SUPERVISOR, RICE MILLING (grain-feed mills)	4236	23344344454	LNNOONNFFOFFNFNNNON	NNNN4NONNNNNNNNN	D	146	381	06.02.01	7100	000000	81008
521.132-010	MILL PLATFORM SUPERVISOR (sugar & conf.)	4237	33343334355	MNNNNNNFONFFNFNNNN	NNNN3NNNNNNNNNN	V,D,P,J	142	392	06.02.15	7100	000000	81008
521.132-014	SUPERVISOR, THRESHING DEPARTMENT (tobacco)	4235	33433444455	LNNNNNNFFOOFFNFFNNNO	NNNN4NCNNNNNNNNO	D,P,J,T	054	403	06.02.01	7100	000000	81008
521.137-010	SUPERVISOR, PICKING (tobacco)	4337	33333333354	LNNNNNNFFFFFFNFFNNON	NNNN4NNNNNNNNNN	V,D,P	031	404	06.04.01	7100	000000	81008
521.362-010	CONTINUOUS-ABSORPTION-PROCESS OPERATOR (sugar & conf.)	3224	33444444353	LNNFNFNFFNOONFNNNOFN	NNFN4NNNNNNNNNN	J,T	141	392	06.02.15	7676	000000	95099
521.362-014	MILLER, DISTILLERY (beverage)	3324	33333444345	MNNNNNNFFNNOONFNNNNN	NNNN3NCNNNNNNNNN	V,J,T	142	301	06.02.15	7677	000000	92965
521.362-018	REFINERY OPERATOR (grain-feed mills)	4337	33343333455	LNNNNNNFFONOOONFNNONN	NNNN3NNNNNNNNNN	J,T	146	392	06.02.15	7679	000000	92998
521.365-010	CHAR-FILTER OPERATOR (sugar & conf.)	3225	33443344355	LNNNNNNFFONFFNONNONN	NNON3NNNNNNNNNN	R,T	145	392	06.02.15	7666	000000	92962
521.382-010	EVAPORATOR OPERATOR (can. & preserv.; dairy products; sugar & conf.)	3225	34333433354	LONNNNNFFONNNNFNNFN	NNOO4NONNNNNNNNN	J,T	144	380	06.02.15	7666	000000	92965
521.382-014	SEPARATOR OPERATOR (grain-feed mills)	2224	33343433354	LNNNNNNFFONNNNFNNNON	NNNN3NNNNNNNNNN	J,T	145	381	06.02.15	7666	000000	92962
521.385-010	CRACKING-AND-FANNING-MACHINE OPERATOR (sugar & conf.)	2113	33433444355	MNNNNNNFFNNNNONNNNN	NNNN3NNNNNNNNNN	J,T	142	393	06.04.15	7666	000000	92962
521.462-010	REFINERY OPERATOR, ASSISTANT (grain-feed mills)	3226	33343444343	LNNNNNNFFNNNNNFNNNOOO	NNNN4NNNNNNNNNN	V,J,T	146	392	06.02.15	7679	000000	97989
521.565-010	LIQUOR-BRIDGE OPERATOR (sugar & conf.)	2113	33344444353	MNNNNNNFFNNFFNFNNFNN	NNNN4NNNNNNNNNN	J,T	014	392	06.04.15	7666	000000	92962
521.565-014	MASH-FILTER OPERATOR (beverage)	1112	44444444354	LNNFNFNFFNOONFNNNON	NNFF4NNNNNNNNNN	R	145	395	06.04.15	7676	000000	92962
521.565-018	SOFT-SUGAR OPERATOR, HEAD (sugar & conf.)	3234	33443444344	MNNNNNNFFNFFNFNNNNN	NNNF4NNNNNNNNNN	J,T	145	392	06.02.15	7666	000000	92962
521.582-010	SILICA-FILTER OPERATOR (beverage)	3114	44443434354	MNNNNNNFFNNNNFNNFON	NNNF3NNNNNNNNNN	J,T	145	395	06.02.15	7666	000000	92962
521.585-010	CENTRIFUGAL-STATION OPERATOR, AUTOMATIC (sugar & conf.)	3225	44444344354	LNNNNNNFFNNNNONFOF	NNNC4NNNNNNNNNN	T	145	392	06.02.15	7666	000000	92962
521.585-014	MILLER (beverage)	1112	44444444455	LNNNNNNFFONFFNONNONN	NNNN4NNNNNNNNNN	R	142	301	06.04.15	7677	000000	92965
521.585-018	POWDER-MILL OPERATOR (sugar & conf.)	2224	44443434355	LNNNNNNFFFCONNNNNNNN	NNNN4NNNNNNNNNN	T	142	392	06.04.15	7666	000000	92965
521.662-010	MILLER, WET PROCESS (grain-feed mills)	3237	33433443355	LNNNNNNFFFONNNNNNN	ONNN4NNNNNNNNNN	J,T	142	381	06.02.15	7677	000000	92965
521.665-010	CHAR-FILTER-TANK TENDER, HEAD (grain-feed mills)	3224	44444444454	LNNONONFFNOONFNNNON	NNNN3NNNNNNNNNN	J,T	145	392	06.04.15	7666	000000	92962
521.665-014	EXTRACTOR-MACHINE OPERATOR (can. & preserv.)	1112	44444344345	LONONNNFFNNOONFNNNN	NNNF4NFNNNNNNNNN	R	145	387	06.04.15	7666	000000	92962
521.665-018	FILTER-PRESS TENDER, HEAD (grain-feed mills)	2113	44444434354	MNNNNNNFFNNONONNNNNN	NNFF4NFNNNNNNNNN	J,T	145	392	06.04.15	7667	000000	92971
521.665-022	RICE CLEANING MACHINE TENDER (grain-feed mills)	3113	44444434345	LFNONONFFNNNNNFNNNNN	NNNN4NFNNNNNNNNN	J,T	146	301	06.04.15	7666	000000	92962

DOT #	DOT Title & Industry	Trng	Aptitude	Physical	Environment	Tempra	WkF	MPSMS	GOE	SOC	CIP	OES
521.665-026	SIEVE-GRADER TENDER (can. & preserv.)	2112	44544544355	LNNNNNNNFNNNNNN	NNNN4NNNNNNNNNN	R,T	145	303	06.04.15	7666	000000	92962
521.682-010	CENTRIFUGAL OPERATOR (grain-feed mills; sugar & conf.)	3223	33444534455	MNNNNNNFFNNNNNN	NNNN4NNNNNNNNNN	R	145	392	06.02.15	7666	000000	92962
521.682-014	COCOA-PRESS OPERATOR (sugar & conf.)	3224	34443344355	LNNNNNNFFONNNNN	NNCN4NNNNNNNNNN	J,T	145	393	06.02.15	7666	000000	92962
521.682-018	FILTER OPERATOR (grain-feed mills)	3225	34443344354	LONNNNNFFNNONNNN	NNNN3NNNNNNNNNN	J,T	145	381	06.02.15	7666	000000	92962
521.682-022	FLAKE MILLER, WHEAT AND OATS (grain-feed mills)	3235	33434434355	LONNNNNFFNONNFNN	NNNN4NNNNNNNNNN	J,T	142	381	06.02.15	7677	000000	92965
521.682-026	GRINDER OPERATOR (grain-feed mills)	3127	33443344354	MNNNNNNFFONNNNN	NNNN4NFNNNNNNNN	J,T	142	381	06.02.15	7677	000000	92965
521.682-030	HULLER OPERATOR (grain-feed mills)	3115	34433433344	LOOONONFFFNNNONN	NNNN4NFNNNNNNNN	J,T	145	381	06.02.15	7677	000000	92965
521.682-034	REFINING-MACHINE OPERATOR (sugar & conf.)	3226	34444434354	LNNNNNNFFOONNNON	NNCN4NNCNNNNNNN	J,T	142	393	06.02.15	7677	000000	92965
521.682-038	SHRIMP-PEELING-MACHINE OPERATOR (can. & preserv.)	3125	34343434345	MONOOONFFONNNNON	NNNN4NNCNNNNNNN	R,J,T	142	387	06.02.15	7479	000000	92997
521.685-010	ALMOND HULLER (can. & preserv.)	2112	34433443355	HNNNNNNFFONNNNN	NNNN4NNNNNNNNNN	R	145	306	06.04.15	7666	000000	92962
521.685-014	ALMOND-BLANCHER OPERATOR (can. & preserv.)	2112	44444444455	LNNNNNNFFONNNNN	NNNN4NNNNNNNNNN	R,T	146	306	06.04.15	7666	000000	92962
521.685-018	ALMOND-CUTTING-MACHINE TENDER (can. & preserv.)	2113	44543544355	LNNNNNNFFONNNFNN	NNNN4NNNNNNNNNN	J,T	054	306	06.04.15	7678	000000	92944
521.685-022	BATCH-TANK CONTROLLER (grain-feed mills)	2113	44433344355	LONNNNNFFONNNNN	NNNN3NONNNNNNNN	J,T	145	381	06.04.15	7664	000000	92965
521.685-026	BLEACHER, LARD (meat products; oils & grease)	2112	44445434354	MNNNNNFFFNNNNON	NNNN3NNNNNNNNNN	R,T	145	385	06.04.15	7666	000000	92962
521.685-030	BOLTER (grain-feed mills)	2113	44444444355	LOONNNNFFFNNNFNN	NNNN4NCNNNNNNNN	J	145	381	06.04.15	7666	000000	92962
521.685-034	BREAKING-MACHINE OPERATOR (sugar & conf.)	2112	44545534455	LNNNNNNFFNNNNNN	NNNN3NNNNNNNNNN	R	142	393	06.04.15	7679	000000	92998
521.685-038	BRINE-TANK-SEPARATOR OPERATOR (can. & preserv.)	1112	44444444355	LNNNNNNFFNNNNNN	NNNN4NNNNNNNNNN	R	145	303	06.04.15	7666	000000	92962
521.685-042	CENTRIFUGE OPERATOR (dairy products)	2222	44444444353	HNNNNNNFFONNNNN	NNNO4NNNNNNNNNN	R,T	145	383	06.04.15	7666	000000	92962
521.685-046	CENTRIFUGE OPERATOR (grain-feed mills)	2223	44444444355	LNNIOONFFNNNNON	ONNN3NNNNNNNNNN	R	145	381	06.04.15	7666	000000	92962
521.685-050	CENTRIFUGE OPERATOR (oils & grease)	2213	44444444354	LNNNNNNFFNNNNNON	NNNC4NNNNNNNNNN	J,T	145	385	06.04.15	7677	000000	92965
521.685-054	CLARIFIER (grain-feed mills; oils & grease)	2112	44444444355	LNNNNNNFFONNNFNN	NNNF3NNNNNNNNNN	R	145	385	06.04.15	7676	000000	92962
521.685-058	CLARIFIER (beverage)	2123	44545544455	LNNNNNNFFONNNNN	NNNN3NNNNNNNNNN	R,T	145	395	06.04.15	7679	000000	92962
521.685-062	CLEAN-RICE GRADER AND REEL TENDER (grain-feed mills)	2123	44444444355	LNNNNNNFFONNNNF	NNNN3NNNNNNNNNN	R,T	145	395	06.04.15	7676	000000	92962
521.685-066	COCOA-BEAN CLEANER (sugar & conf.)	2113	44444444355	LNNNNNNFFONNNNF	NNNN4NFNNNNNNNN	R	031	381	06.03.02	7666	000000	92962
521.685-070	COCOA-BUTTER-FILTER OPERATOR (sugar & conf.)	2112	44444444455	MNNNNNNFFONNNNN	NNNN4NFNNNNNNNN	R	031	306	06.04.15	7666	000000	92962
521.685-074	COCOA-ROOM OPERATOR (beverage)	2113	44444444455	HNNNONNFFNNNNNN	NNNN4NFNNNNNNNN	R,T	142	393	06.04.15	7677	000000	92965
521.685-078	COFFEE GRINDER (food prep., nec)	1112	44444444455	LNNNNNNFFNNNNNON	NNNN4NNNNNNNNNN	R,T	142	391	06.04.15	7677	000000	92965
521.685-082	CORN GRINDER (food prep.)	2113	44544544355	MNNNNNNFFOONNNON	NNNF4NNNNNNNNNN	J,R,T	142	301	06.04.15	7677	000000	92965
521.685-086	CORN-GRINDER OPERATOR, AUTOMATIC (grain-feed mills)	2113	34433543455	LNNNNNNFFOONNNN	NNNN3NNNNNNNNNN	J,T	142	381	06.04.15	7677	000000	92965
521.685-090	CRUSHER OPERATOR (sugar & conf.)	2113	44543545455	MNNNNNNFFNNNNNN	NNNN4NNNNNNNNNN	R	142	392	06.04.15	7677	000000	92965
521.685-094	CRUSHING-MACHINE OPERATOR (beverage)	1112	44444544455	LNNNNNNFFNNNNNN	NNNN4NNNNNNNNNN	R	145	395	06.04.15	7677	000000	92965
521.685-098	CUTTER, FROZEN MEAT (can. & preserv.)	2112	44444444455	MFNNNNNFFNNNNOON	NNNN4NCNNNNNNNN	R	142	381	06.04.15	7677	000000	92962
521.685-102	CUTTING-MACHINE OPERATOR (sugar & conf.)	2113	44454544355	MFNNNNNFFNNNNNN	NNNC4NCNNNNNNNN	R,T	145	392	06.04.15	7666	000000	92962
521.685-106	DETHISTLER OPERATOR (can. & preserv.)	3124	44443434355	MFNNNNNFFNNNNONF	ONNN3NNNNNNNNNN	R,T	145	387	06.02.15	7678	000000	92944
521.685-110	DRIED FRUIT WASHER (food prep., nec)	3123	44544544355	MNNNNNNFFNNNNONF	NNNC4NNNNNNNNNN	R,T	145	387	06.04.15	7666	000000	92962
521.685-114	EGG-BREAKING-MACHINE OPERATOR (can. & preserv.)	1112	44544544455	LNNNNNNFFONNNNON	NNNN4NNNNNNNNNN	R	031	387	06.04.15	7673	000000	92958
521.685-118	EXTRACTOR OPERATOR (beverage)	2113	44444444353	LNNNNNNFFNNNNNON	NNNF4NNNNNNNNNN	R	145	382	06.04.15	7666	000000	92962
521.685-122	FEED GRINDER (grain-feed mills)	2123	44444434455	LNNNNNNFFNNNNNN	NNNN4NNNNNNNNNN	R,T	145	395	06.04.15	7667	000000	92971
521.685-126	FILTER OPERATOR (beverage; sugar & conf.)	2112	44444444455	MFNNNNNFFNNNNOONNNNN	NNNN4NCNNNNNNNN	R	142	381	06.04.15	7677	000000	92965
521.685-130	FILTER-PRESS TENDER (beverage)	2113	44454544355	MFNNNNNFFNNNNNN	NNNC4NNNNNNNNNN	R,T	145	395	06.04.15	7666	000000	92962
521.685-134	FILTER-TANK-TENDER HELPER, HEAD (grain-feed mills)	2112	44443434355	MFNNONNFFNNNNNN	ONNN3NNNNNNNNNN	R,T	145	392	06.04.15	7666	000000	92962
521.685-138	FILTERING-MACHINE TENDER (grain-feed mills)	2213	44434444354	MNNONNNFFONNNNON	NNNN3NNNNNNNNNN	R	145	392	06.04.15	7666	000000	92962
521.685-142	FINISHER OPERATOR (can. & preserv.)	2112	44544544355	LNNNNNNFFONNNNON	NNNN3NNNNNNNNNN	R	145	381	06.04.15	7666	000000	92962
521.685-146	FRUIT-PRESS OPERATOR (beverage; can. & preserv.)	1112	44544544355	MNNNNNNFFNNNNONF	NNNF4NNNNNNNNNN	R,T	145	387	06.04.15	7666	000000	92962
521.685-150	GLUTEN-SETTLING TENDER (grain-feed mills)	1112	44544544355	HNNFNNNFFNNNNNN	NNNO3NONNNNNNNN	R,T	145	381	06.04.15	7667	000000	92962
521.685-154	GRADER TENDER (agriculture)	2113	44443444355	HONONONFFNNNNNN	NNNN4NNNNNNNNNN	R,T	145	301	03.04.01	7666	000000	92962
521.685-158	GRANULATING-MACHINE OPERATOR (tobacco)	2112	44444544455	MNNONNNFFNNNNNN	NNNN4NNNNNNNNNN	R	054	404	06.04.15	7678	000000	92944
521.685-162	GRATED-CHEESE MAKER (dairy products)	2223	44444444355	MONONNNFFNNNNNN	NNNN4NFNNNNNNNN	R,T	146	383	06.04.15	7677	000000	92965
521.685-166	GRINDER OPERATOR (grain-feed mills)	2112	34433344355	LNNNNNNFFNNNNNN	NNNN3NNNNNNNNNN	R,T	142	381	06.04.15	7677	000000	92965
521.685-170	HASHER OPERATOR (meat products)	2112	44544544355	HNNFNNNFFONNNNN	NNNN3NCNNNNNNNN	R	034	382	06.04.15	7678	120506	92944
521.685-174	HONEY EXTRACTOR (food prep., nec)	1112	44444444455	MONFNNNFFONNNNNN	NNNN3NNNNNNNNNN	R	145	399	06.04.15	7666	000000	92962

DOT #	DOT Title & Industry	Trng	Aptitude	Physical	Environment	Tempra	WkF	MPSMS	GOE	SOC	CIP	OES
521.685-178	HOP STRAINER (beverage)	2112	44444444455	LNNNNNNFFNNNNNONNN	NNNN3NNNNNNNNN	R,T	145	395	06.04.15	7666	000000	92962
521.685-182	HOPPER ATTENDANT (sugar & conf.)	2112	44444444355	MNNNNNNNNNNNNNNNN	NNNN3NNNNNNNNN	R	011	392	06.04.40	7666	000000	92962
521.685-186	HOT-WORT SETTLER (beverage)	1112	44544444345	LONONNNNFFNNNNONNNNN	NNNO3NNNNNNNNO	R	145	395	06.04.15	7676	000000	92962
521.685-190	ION EXCHANGE OPERATOR (beverage)	2112	44444444445	LONNNNNNFFONOONNNNNNN	NNNN3NNNNNNNNN	R	145	395	06.04.15	7666	000000	92938
521.685-194	LABORATORY MILLER (grain-feed mills)	2113	44344344355	LNNNNNNNNFFNNNNNFNFNN	NNNN4NNNNNNNNN	R	142	381	06.04.15	7677	000000	92965
521.685-198	LINTER TENDER (oils & grease)	2113	44344344355	MNNFNFNFFFNNNONONNN	NNNN4NFNNNNNNNN	R,T	145	302	06.04.19	7677	000000	92962
521.685-202	LIQUOR-GRINDING-MILL OPERATOR (sugar & conf.)	2113	44444443454	LNNNNNNNFFFNNNNNNON	NNFN4NNNNNNNNN	J,T	142	393	06.04.15	7677	000000	92965
521.685-206	LYE-PEEL OPERATOR (can. & preserv.)	1112	44554444455	LONONNNFFFNNNNNNNN	NNNF4NNNNNNNNF	J,T	146	387	06.04.15	7666	000000	92962
521.685-210	MEAL-GRINDER TENDER (grain-feed mills)	1112	44544444345	LNNNNNNNFFNNNNNONNNN	NNNO4NCNNNNNNNN	R	142	301	06.04.15	7677	120506	92965
521.685-214	MEAT GRINDER (meat products)	1112	44544544355	HNNFNNNNFFNNNNNNFNNN	NNNN4NNNNNNNNN	R	142	382	06.04.15	7677	000000	92962
521.685-218	MEAT-GRADING-MACHINE OPERATOR (can. & preserv.)	2112	44444444455	MNNNNNNFFNNNNONFNNN	NNNN4NNNNNNNNN	R,T	145	393	06.04.15	7666	000000	92965
521.685-222	MILK-POWDER GRINDER (dairy products)	1112	44544544355	HNNONNNNFFNNNNNNFNNN	NNNN4NFNNNNNNNN	R	142	383	06.04.15	7677	000000	92962
521.685-226	MILL OPERATOR (grain-feed mills)	1112	44344443355	LFNNNNNNNFFNNNNNFNNN	NNNN4NFNNNNNNNN	J,T	142	381	06.04.15	7677	000000	92962
521.685-230	MONITOR-AND-STORAGE-BIN TENDER (grain-feed mills)	1112	44444454455	LONFNNNNFFNNNNNONNNN	NNNN4NFNNNNNNNN	R	145	301	06.04.15	7677	000000	92965
521.685-234	NUT GRINDER (can. & preserv.)	1112	44444544455	.LNNNNNNNNFFONNNNONONN	NNNN3NNNNNNNNN	R,T	142	306	06.04.15	7677	000000	92962
521.685-238	NUT-SORTER OPERATOR (can. & preserv.)	3113	34433443355	LNNNNNNNNFFNNNNFNNONN	NNNN3NNNNNNNNN	R	145	306	06.04.15	7666	000000	92962
521.685-242	OILSEED-MEAT PRESSER (oils & grease)	2113	44544544455	MNNNNNNNFFNNNNNNNNNN	NNNN4NNNNNNNNN	R	145	385	06.04.19	7667	000000	92971
521.685-246	PEANUT BLANCHER (can. & preserv.)	1112	44433533355	HNNFNFNNFFNNNNFFNNN	NNNN4NNNNNNNNN	R	054	309	06.04.15	7666	000000	92962
521.685-250	POTATO-PEELING-MACHINE OPERATOR (food prep., nec)	2112	44444444455	MNNONNNNFFNNNNONFNNN	NNNN4NNNNNNNNN	R,T	146	387	06.04.15	7666	000000	92962
521.685-254	PROCESSOR, GRAIN (grain-feed mills)	2112	44543444454	LOONNNNNFFNNNNNNONNN	NNNN4NFNNNNNNNN	R,T	145	301	06.04.15	7666	000000	92962
521.685-258	PULP-PRESS TENDER (sugar & conf.)	2113	44444434455	LNNNNNNNFFNNNNNNFNNN	NNNN4NNNNNNNNN	R,T	145	389	06.04.15	7667	000000	92971
521.685-262	PULPER TENDER (can. & preserv.)	1112	44544544355	MNNNNNNNFFONNNNNNNNNN	NNNN4NNNNNNNNN	R	145	387	06.04.15	7666	000000	92962
521.685-266	PULVERIZER (meat products)	1112	44544444455	MONFNFNFFNNNNNFFNFNN	NNNN4NNNNNNNNN	R,T	142	382	06.04.15	7677	000000	92965
521.685-270	RIDDLER OPERATOR (tobacco)	1112	44544544455	HNNFNFNFFNNNNNNNNNN	NNNN4NNNNNNNNN	R	145	403	06.04.15	7666	000000	92962
521.685-274	ROUGH-RICE TENDER (grain-feed mills)	2113	44443444345	LONONNNNFFONNNONNNNN	NNNN4NFNNNNNNNF	J,T	145	301	06.04.15	7666	000000	92962
521.685-278	ROUTING-EQUIPMENT TENDER (grain-feed mills)	2213	44443333355	LNNNNNNNFFNNNNNNNNNN	NNNN4NFNNNNNNNF	R,T	011	381	06.04.40	8319	490299	97989
521.685-282	SCREEN-ROOM OPERATOR (sugar & conf.)	2113	44444444355	MNNNNNNNFFNNNNNNNFNNN	NNNN4NNNNNNNNN	R,T	145	392	06.04.15	7666	000000	92962
521.685-286	SEPARATOR OPERATOR, SHELLFISH MEATS (can. & preserv.)	2112	44443544355	MNNFNNNFFONNNNNNNNN	NNNF4NNNNNNNNN	R,T	145	332	06.04.15	7666	000000	92962
521.685-290	SEPARATOR TENDER II (grain-feed mills)	2113	44444444455	MNNNNNNNFFONNNNONNNNN	NNNF4NFNNNNNNNN	J,T	145	381	06.04.15	7666	000000	92962
521.685-294	SHELLER II (can. & preserv.)	1112	44443544355	HNNNNNNNFFONNNNNNNNNN	NNNN4NNNNNNNNN	R	142	306	06.04.15	7666	000000	92962
521.685-298	SLICE-PLUG-CUTTER OPERATOR (tobacco)	2112	44544544455	LNNNNNNNFFNNNNNNNNNN	NNNN4NNNNNNNNN	R	054	403	06.04.15	7678	000000	92944
521.685-302	SLICING-MACHINE OPERATOR (bakery products)	2112	44443444355	LNNONNNNFFNNNNONONNN	NNNN4NFNNNNNNNN	R,T	054	384	06.04.15	7678	120501	92944
521.685-306	SLICING-MACHINE OPERATOR (dairy products; meat products)	2112	44444444455	MNNNNNNNFFNNNNNFNNN	NNNN4NNNNNNNNNO	R,T	054	382	06.04.15	7678	120506	92944
521.685-310	SMOKING-TOBACCO-CUTTER OPERATOR (tobacco)	2112	44544544355	LNNNNNNNFFNNNNNNNNNN	NNNN4NNNNNNNNN	R	054	403	06.04.15	7678	000000	92944
521.685-314	SNUFF GRINDER AND SCREENER (tobacco)	2114	44544544355	LNNNNNNNFFNNNNNNNNNN	NNNN4NNNNNNNNN	R,T	142	403	06.04.15	7677	000000	92965
521.685-318	SORTING-MACHINE OPERATOR (can. & preserv.)	2112	44443544455	HNNFNNNNFFONNNNONONNN	NNNN3NNNNNNNNN	R	145	387	06.04.15	7666	000000	92962
521.685-322	SPICE CLEANER (food prep., nec)	2112	44444444344	HNNFNNNNFFNNNNNNNNN	NNNN3NNNNNNNNN	R	145	391	06.04.15	7666	000000	92962
521.685-326	SPICE MILLER (food prep., nec)	2113	44444444354	HNNONNNNFFNNNNNONNNON	NNNN4NFNNNNNNNN	R,T	142	391	06.04.15	7677	000000	92965
521.685-330	STEM-ROLLER-OR-CRUSHER OPERATOR (tobacco)	1112	44444444455	MNNONNNFFONNNNNNNNN	NNFN4NNNNNNNNN	R,T	142	404	06.04.15	7666	000000	92971
521.685-334	STEMMER, MACHINE (tobacco)	1112	44444444455	MNNNNNNNFFONNNNNNNNN	NNNN4NNNNNNNNN	R	054	404	06.04.15	7666	000000	92944
521.685-338	STRIP-CUTTING-MACHINE OPERATOR (tobacco)	1112	44444444455	LNNNNNNNFFONNNNNNNNN	NNNN4NNNNNNNNN	R	054	403	06.04.15	7678	000000	92944
521.685-342	STRIPPER-CUTTER, MACHINE (food prep., nec)	2112	44544534345	LNNNNNNNFFONNNNNNNNN	NNNN4NNNNNNNNN	R	054	397	06.04.15	7678	000000	92944
521.685-346	SUGAR GRINDER (sugar & conf.)	2113	44544544355	HNNFNNNNFFONNNNNONONNN	NNNN3NNNNNNNNN	R	142	392	06.04.15	7677	000000	92965
521.685-350	SUGAR PRESSER (grain-feed mills)	1112	44544544355	MNNNNNNNFFNNNNNNNNN	NNNN3NNNNNNNNN	R	145	392	06.04.15	7667	000000	92971
521.685-354	SUGAR-CHIPPER-MACHINE OPERATOR (grain-feed mills)	1112	44544534355	HNNNNNNNFFNNNNNNNNN	NNNN4NNNNNNNNN	R	052	392	06.04.15	7678	000000	92944
521.685-358	SWEET-POTATO DISINTEGRATOR (can. & preserv.)	2112	44544544455	MNNNNNNCCNNNNNNNFNNN	NNNC4NNNNNNNNN	R	142	387	06.04.15	7677	000000	92962
521.685-362	THRESHING-MACHINE OPERATOR (tobacco)	2112	44444444455	LNNNFNNNFFNNNNNNNNN	NNNN4NNNNNNNNN	R	145	392	06.04.15	7666	000000	92962
521.685-366	TIPPLE TENDER (grain-feed mills)	1112	44544544355	MNNONNNNFFNNNNNNNNNN	NNNN4NFNNNNNNNN	R	011	381	06.04.40	8319	490299	97989
521.685-370	WINERY WORKER (beverage)	3113	44444444455	LNNNNNNNFFNNNNNFNNNN	NNNO3NCNNNNNNNN	R,T	146	395	06.04.15	7666	000000	92962
521.685-374	WINTERIZER (oils & grease)	2112	44444444355	LNNNNNNNFFONNNNFNNNN	NFNN3NNNNNNNNN	R,T	147	385	06.04.15	7666	000000	92962
521.685-378	DEBONER, PET FOOD (can. & preserv.)	2122	44544544355	MNNNONNFFONNNNONNNNN	NNNO4NNNNNNNNN	R,U	145	382	06.04.15	7677	010401	92965

DOT #	DOT Title & Industry	Trng	Aptitude	Physical	Environment	Tempra	WkF	MPSMS	GOE	SOC	CIP	OES
521.685-382	FLAVORING OIL FILTERER (beverage)	2124	44443444443	HFNNNNNFFONNNNFNNFN	NNNN4NNONNNNNNN	R,T	145	394	06.04.15	7666	010401	92962
521.685-386	SCALING MACHINE OPERATOR (can. & preserv.)	1112	44544444355	LFNNNNNNOOONNNNNNNN	NNNO4NNONNNNNNN	R	034	386	06.04.15	7678	200409	92944
521.686-010	BOLTER HELPER (grain-feed mills)	2112	44444444355	LFNNNNNFFNNNNNNNNNN	NNNN4NFNNNNNNNN	R	145	381	06.04.15	8618	000000	98999
521.686-014	CAKE PULLER (oils & grease)	1112	44544544455	HNNFNNNFFNNNNNNNNNN	NNNN4NNNNNNNNNN	R	145	381	06.04.19	8725	000000	98502
521.686-018	CHICLE-GRINDER FEEDER (sugar & conf.)	2112	44444444345	MMNONNNFFNNNNNNFNNN	NNNN4NNNNNNNNNN	R,T	142	393	06.04.19	8725	000000	98502
521.686-022	COTTON PULLER (oils & grease)	1111	44544544455	LNNNNNNFFNNNNNNNNNN	NNNN4NFNNNNNNNN	R	145	414	06.04.19	8725	000000	98502
521.686-026	CUSTOM-FEED-MILL-OPERATOR HELPER (grain-feed mills)	1112	44544433355	HNNFNNNFFNNNNNNNNNN	NNNN4NFNNNNNNNN	R	142	381	06.04.15	8618	000000	98999
521.686-030	CUT-IN WORKER (grain-feed mills)	1111	44544544355	HNNNNNNFFNNFFNNNNNN	NNNN4NFNNNNNNNN	R	031	381	06.04.40	8725	000000	98502
521.686-034	FISH-MACHINE FEEDER (can. & preserv.)	2112	44444534354	MMNONNNFFFFNNFFNNNN	NNNN4FNNNNNNNN	R,T	146	331	06.04.15	8725	000000	98502
521.686-038	FLUMER (grain-feed mills)	1111	44544544355	MNNNNNNFFNNNNNNNNNN	NNNN3NNNNNNNNNN	R	031	303	06.04.39	8725	000000	98502
521.686-042	FLUMER II (sugar & conf.)	1111	44544544335	LFNNNNNFFNNNNNNNNNN	ONNF4NNNNNNNNNN	R	031	387	06.04.39	8725	000000	98502
521.686-046	NUT CHOPPER (can. & preserv.; food prep., nec; sugar & conf.)	1112	44544544355	LNNONNNFFONNNNNNNNN	NNNN4NNNNNNNNNN	R	142	393	06.04.15	8725	000000	98502
521.686-050	PROCESSOR HELPER (grain-feed mills)	1112	44544544355	HFNNNNNFFONNNNNNNNN	NNFF4NNNNNNNNNN	R	145	381	06.04.15	8725	000000	98999
521.686-054	SLICE-PLUG-CUTTER-OPERATOR HELPER (tobacco)	1112	44544544455	LNNNNNNFFNNNNNNNNNN	NNNN4NNNNNNNNNN	R	054	403	06.04.15	8618	000000	98999
521.687-010	ALMOND BLANCHER, HAND (can. & preserv.)	1111	44544543355	SNNNNNNFFNNNFFNFNNN	NNNF4NNNNNNNNNN	R	145	306	06.04.28	8769	000000	98999
521.687-014	BINDER CUTTER, HAND (tobacco)	1112	44544544455	LNNNNNNFFNNNNNNNNNN	NNNN3NNNNNNNNNN	R	054	403	06.04.28	8769	000000	98999
521.687-018	BINDER SELECTOR (tobacco)	2112	44544543354	LNNNNNNFFONNNNNFNFON	NNNN3NNNNNNNNNN	J	212	403	06.03.02	7820	000000	83005
521.687-022	BONE PICKER (can. & preserv.)	1111	44543543354	LNNNNNNFFFNNNFNNFN	NNNF4NNNNNNONNF	R,T	031	332	06.04.28	7820	000000	83005
521.687-026	BUNCH TRIMMER, MOLD (tobacco)	1111	45544544455	LNNNNNNFFNNNNNNNNNN	NNNN3NNNNNNNNNN	R	054	402	06.04.28	7820	000000	98999
521.687-030	CHAR PULLER (grain-feed mills; sugar & conf.)	2112	44544544355	HNNFNNNFFONNNNNNNNNN	NNNF3NFNNNNNNNN	R	031	392	06.04.39	8750	000000	98905
521.687-034	CHAR-FILTER-OPERATOR HELPER (sugar & conf.)	2113	44443444355	HNNNNNNFFNNNNNNONNN	NNFN4NNNNNNNNNN	R	147	392	06.04.39	8618	000000	98999
521.687-038	DRIP-BOX TENDER (grain-feed mills)	1111	44544544355	MNNNNNNFFNNNFNNNNNN	NNNF4NNNNNNNNNN	R	041	454	06.04.15	8769	000000	98999
521.687-042	EGG BREAKER (any industry)	1112	44444543454	LNNFNNNFFFFNNNFNNFN	NNNN3NNNNNNNNNN	J	145	382	06.04.28	8769	000000	98999
521.687-046	FILLER SPREADER (tobacco)	1111	45544544455	LNNNNNNFFNNNNNNNNFON	NNNN3NNNNNNNNNN	R	041	409	06.04.28	8769	000000	98999
521.687-050	FILTER CHANGER (beverage)	1112	44443533355	MNNFNNNFFNNNNFFNNNN	NNNN3NNNNNNNNNN	R	031	567	06.04.28	7740	000000	93999
521.687-054	FILTER-SCREEN CLEANER (beverage)	2112	44444534355	MNNNNNNFFFNNNNNNNNN	NNNN3NNNNNNNNNN	R	031	332	06.04.28	8750	000000	98905
521.687-058	FISH CHOPPER, GANG KNIFE (can. & preserv.)	1112	44544534355	MMNNNNNFFFNNNFNNNNN	NNNF4NFNNNNNNNN	R	054	386	06.04.28	8769	000000	98999
521.687-062	FISH-LIVER SORTER (can. & preserv.; fishing & hunt.)	2112	44444544343	MNNNNNNFFFNNNNFNFN	NNNF3NFNNNNNNNF	R	034	331	06.04.28	7850	000000	83005
521.687-066	FRUIT CUTTER (sugar & conf.)	1111	44443433355	LNNNNNNFFNNNNNNNNNN	NNNN3NNNNNNNNNN	R	054	393	06.04.28	8769	200409	98999
521.687-070	HONEYCOMB DECAPPER (food prep., nec)	2113	44444544354	HNNFNONFFNNNNNNNNON	NNNN4NNNNNNNNNN	R	054	399	06.04.28	7759	000000	93999
521.687-074	LABORER, SYRUP MACHINE (grain-feed mills)	1111	44544534355	MNNNNNNFFNNNNNFNNNN	NNNN4NNNNNNNNNN	R	145	392	06.04.39	8769	000000	98999
521.687-078	LIQUOR-BRIDGE-OPERATOR HELPER (sugar & conf.)	2113	44444344345	MNNNNNNFFFNNNNFNNNNN	NNNO3NNNNNNNNNN	R	014	392	06.04.39	8769	000000	98999
521.687-082	MILLER HELPER, DISTILLERY (beverage)	2113	44433444345	MNNNNNNFFFNNNNNFNNN	NNNN4NFNNNNNNNN	R	142	301	06.04.15	8618	000000	98999
521.687-086	NUT SORTER (can. & preserv.)	1112	44554533455	SNNNNNNFFNNNNNNNNNN	NNNN4NNNNNNNNNN	R	145	306	06.03.02	7850	000000	83005
521.687-090	NUT STEAMER (can. & preserv.)	2112	44444533355	HNNONNNFFONNNNOOFNNN	NNNN4NNNNNNONNN	R	152	306	06.04.28	7679	000000	92998
521.687-094	PEELED-POTATO INSPECTOR (food prep., nec)	1112	44543534454	LNNNNNNNFFNNNNFNFNON	NNFF3NNNNNNNNNF	R,T	212	387	06.03.02	7820	200409	83005
521.687-098	PICKER (tobacco)	1112	44545534354	LNNNNNNNFFNNNFFNNNON	NNNN4NNNNNNNNNN	R	031	409	06.03.02	8769	000000	98999
521.687-102	PICKING-TABLE WORKER (sugar & conf.)	1111	44545534355	LNNNNNNFFFNNNNNNNNN	NNNN4NNNNNNNNNN	R	031	565	06.03.02	8769	000000	98999
521.687-106	SAUSAGE-MEAT TRIMMER (meat products)	2212	44444444355	NFNNNONNFFFNNNNNNNN	NFNNN3NFNNNNNNN	R,T	034	382	06.04.28	8769	000000	98999
521.687-110	SHAKER (tobacco)	1111	45544544455	LNNFNNNFFNNNNNNNNNN	NNNN3NFNNNNNNNN	R	145	403	06.04.28	8769	120506	98905
521.687-114	SHAKER WASHER (grain-feed mills)	2112	44544544445	MFNNNNNFFONNNNONONNN	NNNF4NFNNNNNNNN	R	031	567	06.04.39	8769	000000	98999
521.687-118	SHELLER I (can. & preserv.)	1111	44545543355	LNNNNNNFFNNNNNFNNNN	NNNN3NNNNNNNNNN	R	142	306	06.04.28	8750	000000	98999
521.687-122	SHELLFISH SHUCKER (can. & preserv.)	2113	44544544355	LNNNNNNNCCFNNNNNNNNN	NNNF4NNNNNNNNNN	R	034	332	06.04.28	8769	000000	98999
521.687-126	SKIN LIFTER, BACON (meat products)	1111	44435343355	MNNNNNNNFFNNNNNNNNNN	NNNN3NNNNNNNNNN	R	034	382	06.04.28	8769	000000	98999
521.687-130	SKULL GRINDER (meat products)	1112	44454534355	LNNNNNNFFNNNNNNNNNN	NNNN4NNNNNNNNNN	R	031	382	06.04.39	8769	000000	98999
521.687-134	STEMMER, HAND (tobacco)	1112	44544533355	LNNFNNNCCNNNNNNNNNN	NNNN3NNNNNNNNNN	R	145	404	06.04.28	8769	000000	98999
521.687-138	TABLE HAND (tobacco)	1112	44544544455	LNNNNNNNFFNFFNFNONON	NNNN3NNNNNNNNNN	R	011	403	06.04.40	8769	000000	98999
522.130-010	SUPERVISOR, MELT HOUSE (sugar & conf.)	4337	33344334354	LNNNNNNFFNFFNFNONON	NNNF4NNNNNNNNNN	D,P,T	147	392	06.01.01	7100	000000	81008
522.131-010	DISTILLING-DEPARTMENT SUPERVISOR (beverage)	4347	22343344455	LNNNNNNFFNFFNFNNNNN	NNNN4NNNNNNNNNN	V,D,P,J	144	395	06.02.01	7100	000000	81008
522.132-010	SUPERVISOR, MALT HOUSE (beverage)	4347	33333333354	LONNNNNFFNFFNFNNNON	NNNF3NNNNNNNNNN	V,D,P,J	146	395	06.01.01	7100	000000	81008
522.134-010	SUPERVISOR, BRINEYARD (can. & preserv.)	4337	33344344344	HNNNNNNFFONFFNFNNNON	CNNF4NNNNNNNNNN	D,P,T	146	387	06.02.01	7100	010401	81008

DOT #	DOT Title & Industry	Trng	Aptitude	Physical	Environment	Tempra	WkF	MPSMS	GOE	SOC	CIP	OES
522.264-010	TRAINING TECHNICIAN (can. & preserv.)	3226	34343333353	MNNONNFFFFFNFNOOFN	NNNC4NCNNNNNNF	V,T,P,J	146	386	06.04.15	2390	010401	31314
522.362-010	YEAST DISTILLER (beverage)	3234	33333444455	LNNNNNNFFNOONFNNNNN	NNNF3NNNNNNNNNN	R,T	147	395	06.02.15	7679	000000	92917
522.382-010	COTTAGE-CHEESE MAKER (dairy products)	3234	33444444354	MNNNNNNFFFNNNNFNNNON	NNNF4NNNNNNNNNN	J,T	146	383	06.02.15	7679	000000	92998
522.382-014	FERMENTATION OPERATOR (beverage)	4235	33333443455	MNNNNNNFFFNNNNFNNNNN	NNNO4NNNNNNNNNN	J,T	144	395	06.02.15	7679	000000	92962
522.382-018	LIQUOR BLENDER (beverage)	4336	33333443355	LNNNNNNFFNNNNNFNNNNN	NNNN4NNNNNNNNNN	T	146	395	06.02.15	7666	000000	92962
522.382-022	MASH-TUB-COOKER OPERATOR (beverage)	4235	33333443355	MNNNNNNFFFNNNNFNNNNN	NNFN4NNNNNNNNNN	J,T	144	395	06.02.15	7679	000000	92917
522.382-026	STILL OPERATOR II (beverage)	4436	33334444355	LONNNNNNFFFNNNNFNNNNN	NNFN4NNNNNNNNNNF	T	144	395	06.02.15	7676	000000	92962
522.382-030	STILL OPERATOR I (beverage)	3235	33334444355	LONFNNNNFFFNNNNFNNNNN	NNNN4NFNNNNNNNN	R,T	144	395	06.02.15	7676	000000	92917
522.382-034	SUGAR BOILER (sugar & conf.)	3236	33443444445	LNNNNNNNFFFNNNNFNFNN	NNNO3NNNNNNNNNN	V,J,T	144	392	06.02.15	7664	000000	92917
522.382-038	VINEGAR MAKER (food prep., nec)	3234	34334434345	MFFOONNNFFFNNNNFNOFNN	NNNN4NCNNNNNNN	J,T	146	398	06.02.15	7664	000000	92965
522.384-010	FISH ROE TECHNICIAN (can. & preserv.)	3226	34333343355	MNNFNNNNFFFNNNNFNFOFN	NNNC4NCNNNNNNN	T,J	146	386	06.02.28	5625	010401	79011
522.465-010	STEEP TENDER (grain-feed mills)	3224	34333443355	LONONNNNFFFNOONFNNNNN	ONNF4NNNNNNNNN	T	146	301	06.04.15	7676	000000	92962
522.482-010	MASHER (beverage)	3234	34343434354	LNNNNNNNFFFNNNNFNNNFN	NNFF4NNNNNNNNNN	J,T	146	395	06.02.15	7679	000000	92917
522.485-010	PICKLING SOLUTION MAKER (meat products)	2223	44444444455	HNNNNNNNFFFNNNNFNNNNN	NNNF4NNNNNNNNNN	T	143	399	06.04.15	7664	120506	92965
522.584-010	OLIVE BRINE TESTER (can. & preserv.)	2223	44444444353	LNNNNNNNFFFNNFNNFON	FNNN3NNNNNNNNNN	J,T	212	386	06.03.02	7830	000000	83005
522.585-014	GERMINATION WORKER (beverage)	3225	34443444354	MNNFNNNNFFFNNNNFNNNNN	NNNF3NNNNNNNNNN	R,T	146	395	06.02.15	7676	000000	92962
522.587-010	CARBONATION TESTER (beverage)	3222	34443444455	NNNNNNNFONNNNFNFFNN	NNNN3NNNNNNNNNN	R,T	212	395	06.03.02	7830	000000	83005
522.662-010	RECEIVER, FERMENTING CELLARS (beverage)	3224	34443433355	MONONNNFFNOONONNNNN	NNNN3NNNNNNNNNN	J,T	146	395	06.02.15	7664	000000	92965
522.662-014	REDRYING-MACHINE OPERATOR (tobacco)	3225	33444444355	LNNNNNNNFFOFNNFNNNNN	NNNF4NNNNNNNNNN	J,T	141	404	06.04.15	7672	000000	92921
522.665-010	FILTER TENDER (grain-feed mills)	3124	33443444355	LFNNNNNNFFFNNNNNNNNN	NNNF4NNNNNNNNNN	R,T	145	392	06.04.15	7666	000000	92962
522.665-014	YEAST PUSHER (beverage)	2112	44444534355	MNNFNFNNFFFNNNNNNNNN	NFNF3NNNNNNNNNN	R	014	395	06.04.15	8769	000000	98999
522.667-010	LIQUOR INSPECTOR (beverage)	2112	44335444455	LNNNNNNNFFNFFNFNNNN	NNNN4NNNNNNNNNN	R,T	212	395	06.03.02	7820	000000	83005
522.682-010	KETTLE OPERATOR (beverage)	3234	44444444354	LNNNNNNNFFFNNNNFNNNON	NNFF3NNNNNNNNNN	T	144	395	06.02.15	7679	000000	92917
522.682-014	ORDERING-MACHINE OPERATOR (tobacco)	3224	44444444455	LNNNNNNNFFFNNNNFNNNNN	NNNN4NNNNNNNNNN	J,T	152	409	06.02.15	7759	000000	98902
522.684-010	PICKLER (can. & preserv.)	2223	44444444355	HNNFNFNFONNNNNONNNNN	NNNF4NNNNNNNNNN	R,T	146	387	06.04.28	7664	000000	92965
522.685-010	BLENDING-MACHINE OPERATOR (dairy products)	3223	44444434354	MNNONONFFNNNNNFNNNNN	NNNN4NNNNNNNNNN	J,T	146	383	06.04.15	7664	000000	92998
522.685-014	BREWERY CELLAR WORKER (beverage)	2112	44444444355	MNNONONFFFNNNNFNNNNN	NCNF3NNNNNNNNNN	R,T	146	395	06.04.15	7679	000000	92998
522.685-018	BRINE MAKER I (can. & preserv.)	2223	34344434353	MONNNNNNFFFNNNNFNNNNN	NNFF4NNNNNNNNNN	R,T	147	389	06.04.15	7664	000000	92917
522.685-022	BRINE MAKER II (can. & preserv.)	2214	44444434355	MFNNNNNNFFONNNNFNFNNN	FNNN4NFNNNNNNNNF	R,T	147	399	06.04.15	7664	000000	92965
522.685-026	CARBONATION EQUIPMENT TENDER (beverage)	3223	34443343355	LNNONNNFFNNNNNFNNNNN	NNNN3NNNNNNNNNN	R,T	152	395	06.04.15	7676	000000	92965
522.685-030	CASING-MACHINE OPERATOR (tobacco)	2223	44444444355	LNNNNNNNFFFNNNNNNNNN	NNNN4NNNNNNNNNN	R,T	152	403	06.04.15	7679	120506	92998
522.685-034	CORN COOKER (food prep., nec)	2222	44444444355	HNNNNNNNFFFNNNNFNNNNN	NNNO4NNNNNNNNNN	R,T	146	301	06.04.15	7664	200409	92917
522.685-038	CURING-BIN OPERATOR (grain-feed mills)	2223	44443434344	HNNNNNNNFFFNNNNFNFNNN	NNNN4NNNNNNNNNN	R	152	381	06.04.15	7676	000000	92962
522.685-042	DE-ALCOHOLIZER (beverage)	2223	34443434355	LFNNNNNNFFNNNNNONONON	NOON3NNNNNNNNNN	R,T	144	395	06.04.15	7676	000000	92962
522.685-046	DEODORIZER (chemical)	2223	44444444354	MNNONONFFFNNNNONONON	NNOO4NONNNNNNON	J,T	144	385	06.04.15	7676	000000	92962
522.685-050	DORR OPERATOR (sugar & conf.)	2223	34443433355	LNNNNNNNFFFNNNNFNNNNN	NNNN4NNNNNNNNNN	J,T	145	392	06.04.15	7676	000000	92962
522.685-054	DROPPER, FERMENTING CELLAR (beverage)	2122	44443444354	MNNFNNNNFONNNNNNFNON	NNNN3NNNNNNNNNN	J	014	395	06.04.15	7676	000000	92962
522.685-058	DRUM LOADER AND UNLOADER (beverage)	2112	44544544355	HONNONOFFONOONNNNNNN	NNNF3NNNNNNNNNN	R	146	395	06.04.15	7664	000000	92965
522.685-062	FERMENTER, WINE (beverage)	3234	44444434353	LONFNNNNFFFNNNNFNNNNN	NNNN4NFNNNNNNNN	R,T	146	395	06.04.15	7679	000000	92998
522.685-066	FISH SMOKER (can. & preserv.)	2123	44444434353	HNNFNFNNFFFNNNNFNNNNN	NNNF4NFNNNNNNNN	J,T	141	386	06.04.15	7679	000000	92962
522.685-070	HONEY PROCESSOR (food prep., nec)	2113	34443434344	LFNNNNNFFFNNNFNFNON	NNNF4NNFNNNNNNN	R,T	146	399	06.04.15	7676	000000	92962
522.685-074	MALT-HOUSE OPERATOR (beverage)	2223	44434434354	MFOONONFFONNNNONONON	NNFN3NFNVNNNNNN	T	147	395	06.04.15	7676	000000	92962
522.685-078	MOLASSES PREPARER (food prep., nec)	3223	34343434354	MNNNNNNNFFFNNNNVFNNNN	NNNO3NNNNNNNNNN	J,T	146	392	06.04.15	7676	000000	92962
522.685-082	NEUTRALIZER (grain-feed mills)	3223	34343443354	LNNNNNNNFFONNNNFNNNNN	NNNN3NNNNNNNNNN	J,T	147	392	06.04.15	7676	000000	92962
522.685-086	PICKLE PUMPER (meat products)	2223	44444434354	MNNNNNNNFFFNNNNNNNNN	NNNF4NNNNNNNNNN	T	146	382	06.04.15	7679	120506	92998
522.685-090	SEED-YEAST OPERATOR (food prep., nec)	3223	34433433354	LNNNNNNNFFFNNNNFNFNON	NNNN3NNNNNNNNNN	J,T	146	399	06.04.15	7676	000000	92962
522.685-094	STEAM-CONDITIONER OPERATOR (tobacco)	2112	44444444455	HNNNNNNNFFFNNNNFNFNON	NNNN4NNNNNNNNNN	R,T	152	404	06.04.15	7679	000000	92998
522.685-098	STILL OPERATOR (agriculture; can. & preserv.)	3124	33443443354	MOOONONFFONNNNFNFNON	ONNN4NNNNNNNNNN	J,T	144	387	06.04.15	7676	000000	95099
522.685-102	VACUUM-CONDITIONER OPERATOR (tobacco)	3223	34444444455	HNNNNNNNFFFNNNNNNNNN	NNNN4NNNNNNNNNN	R,T	152	403	06.04.15	7679	000000	92998
522.685-106	WRINGER OPERATOR (tobacco)	2112	44444444355	HNNNNNNNFFFNNNNFNNNNN	NNNF4NNNNNNNNNN	R,T	152	403	06.04.15	7676	000000	92962
522.685-110	YEAST-FERMENTATION ATTENDANT (food prep., nec)	2223	34333454455	LNNONNNNFFFNNNNFNONON	NNNN4NNNNNNNNNN	J,T	147	399	06.04.15	7676	000000	92962

DOT #	DOT Title & Industry	Trng	Aptitude	Physical	Environment	Tempra	WKF	MPSMS	GOE	SOC	CIP	OES
522.685-114	BARLEY STEEPER (beverage)	2222	44443434355	MNNNONNFFNNNFNNNNNN	NNNF3NNNNNNNNNN	R,T	152	395	06.04.15	7676	000000	92962
522.686-010	CHIP WASHER (beverage)	1112	44444544355	HNNNNNNFFNNNNNNNNNN	NNNF3NNNNNNNNNN	R	031	395	06.04.39	8725	000000	98502
522.686-014	GENERAL HELPER (food prep., nec)	1112	44444444455	LMNNNNNNFFONNNNNNNNN	NNNN3NNNNNNNNNN	R	011	399	06.04.40	8725	000000	98502
522.687-010	BARREL FILLER I (beverage)	1112	45545544455	HNNNFFNFFNNNNNNNNNN	NNNN4NNNNNNNNNN	R	041	395	06.04.36	8761	000000	98902
522.687-014	BRINER (can. & preserv.)	1112	44444544445	HNNFNNNFFNNNNNNNNNN	NNNF4NFNNNNNNNN	R	152	386	06.04.28	8769	000000	98999
522.687-018	BULKER (tobacco)	1112	44444444355	LFNNNNNNFFONNNNNNNNN	NNNN4NFNNNNNNNN	R	134	403	06.04.28	8761	000000	98902
522.687-022	FILLER ROOM ATTENDANT (tobacco)	1112	44444444455	MNNNNNNFFNNNNNNNNNN	NNNN3NNNNNNNNNN	J	152	403	06.04.28	8769	000000	98999
522.687-026	LEAF CONDITIONER (tobacco)	1112	44445544355	MNNNNNNNFFNNNNNNNNN	NNNO3NNNNNNNNNN	R	152	403	06.04.28	8769	000000	98999
522.687-030	LEAF-CONDITIONER HELPER (tobacco)	1112	44444444355	MNNNNNNNFFNNNNNNNNN	NNNN3NNNNNNNNNN	R	152	403	06.04.28	8620	000000	98999
522.687-034	PICKLER (meat products)	2112	44545454455	MNNFNFNFFONNNFNONNN	NNNF4NNNNNNNNNN	R,J	146	382	06.04.28	7679	120506	98902
522.687-038	TURNER (can. & preserv.)	1112	44444544334	MNNNNNNFFNNNNNNNNNN	NNNN3NNNNNNNNNN	R	011	387	06.04.40	8769	000000	98999
522.687-042	WRAPPER-HANDS SPRAYER (tobacco)	2212	44444444455	LNNNNNNNFFNNNNNNNNN	NNNN3NNNNNNNNNN	J	152	403	06.04.28	8769	000000	98999
523.131-010	FISH ROE PROCESSOR (can. & preserv.)	2112	44444444354	MNNONNNFFONNNFNFOON	NNNC3NNONNNNNNN	R	146	386	06.04.28	8769	000000	93999
523.131-010	TESTING AND ANALYSIS DEPARTMENT SUPERVISOR (can. & preserv.)	4347	33343334345	LNNNNNNNFFOOONFNNNNN	NNNN4NNNNNNNNNN	V,D,P,J	212	306	06.01.01	7100	010401	81008
523.132-010	SUPERVISOR, CHAR HOUSE (sugar & conf.)	4337	33434334355	LNNNNNNFFONFFNONNNNN	NNNO4NNNNNNNNNN	D,P,J,T	141	490	06.02.01	7100	020301	81008
523.137-010	SUPERVISOR, ICE HOUSE (food prep., nec)	4227	33343344455	LNNNNNNNFFNFFNFNNNNN	NFNN3NNNNNNNNNN	V,D,P,J	147	399	06.02.01	7100	000000	81008
523.362-010	COCOA-BEAN ROASTER I (sugar & conf.)	3117	33343433343	LNNNNNNNFFNFFNFNNNNN	NNFN4NNNNNNNNNN	J,T	141	393	06.02.15	7672	000000	92921
523.362-014	DRIER OPERATOR (food prep., nec)	4237	33344434352	LNNNNNNNFFFNNNONNNFN	NNFF3NNNNNNNNNN	J,T	141	397	06.02.15	7672	000000	92921
523.380-010	COCOA-BEAN ROASTER II (sugar & conf.)	4237	33333433353	LNNNNNNNFFONNNFNNNNN	NNFN4NNNNNNNNNN	J,T	146	393	06.01.03	7472	000000	92997
523.382-010	GUNNER (grain-feed mills)	2222	34433433353	LNNNNNNNFFNNNFNNNFN	NNNN4NNNNNNNNNN	J,T	146	381	06.02.15	7672	000000	92921
523.382-014	MAPLE-SYRUP MAKER (food prep., nec)	3225	34345344453	LNNNNNNNFFNNNFNFNFN	NNFF3NNNNNNNNNN	J,T	146	394	06.02.15	7676	000000	92962
523.382-018	MELTER OPERATOR (sugar & conf.)	3224	33344434355	HNNFNNNNFFNNNNNNNNN	NNNF4NNNNNNNNNN	T	146	392	06.02.15	7676	000000	92962
523.382-022	PROCESSOR, INSTANT POTATO (food prep., nec)	3223	33333334454	LFNOONNFFONNNONFNNNN	NNOO3NNONNNNNNN	J,T	146	387	06.02.15	7679	010401	92917
523.385-010	PRESSURE-TANK OPERATOR (chemical)	2113	34444444355	LNNNNNNNFFNFFNNNNNN	NNNN3NNNNNNNNNN	T	145	499	06.04.19	7679	000000	92998
523.562-010	DIFFUSER OPERATOR (sugar & conf.)	3234	33433433343	LNNNNNNNFFNFFNFNNNNN	NNNN4NNNNNNNNNN	T	145	392	06.02.15	7672	000000	92962
523.585-010	BUTTER LIQUEFIER (oils & grease)	2223	44343444355	MNNNNNNNFFFNNNNNNNN	NNNN4NNNNNNNNNN	R,T	146	383	06.04.15	7676	000000	92962
523.585-014	CHILLER TENDER (meat products)	2223	34434444455	LONNNNNNFFONNNNFNNNN	NONN4NNNNNNNNNN	R,T	147	382	06.04.15	7665	120506	92928
523.585-018	CRYSTALLIZER OPERATOR (sugar & conf.)	2222	44444444355	LNNNNNNFFONNNNFNNNNN	NNNF4NNNNNNNNNN	R,T	143	392	06.04.15	7665	000000	92928
523.585-022	DRIER, LONG GOODS (food prep., nec)	2222	44444544455	HNNFNNNNFFNNNNNNNNN	NNFF3NNNNNNNNNN	R,T	141	397	06.04.15	7672	000000	92921
523.585-026	PASTEURIZER (oils & grease)	3222	34344444354	MNNNNNNNFFNNNNNNNON	NNNF4NNNNNNNNNN	T	146	383	06.04.15	7676	000000	92962
523.585-030	PULP-DRIER FIRER (sugar & conf.)	2223	44344444355	LNNNNNNNFFNNNFNNNFN	NNNN3NNNNNNNNNN	J,T	141	389	06.04.15	7672	000000	92921
523.585-034	ROASTER, GRAIN (grain-feed mills)	3224	34433434353	LNNNNNNNFFNFFNNNNNN	NNFN3NNNNNNNNNN	J,T	141	381	06.04.15	7672	000000	92921
523.587-010	DRIER, SHORT GOODS (food prep., nec)	2223	44443334354	LNNNNNNNFFNFFNFNNNN	NNFF3NNNNNNNNNN	J,T	141	397	06.04.15	7672	000000	92921
523.587-014	DRYING-ROOM ATTENDANT (tobacco)	2112	44444444355	LNNNNNNNFFNONFNONON	NNNN3NNNNNNNNNN	T	152	404	06.03.02	8769	000000	98999
523.662-010	BONE-CHAR KILN OPERATOR (grain-feed mills)	3234	34434344355	LONNNNNNFFNOONFNONNN	NNFN3NNNNNNNNNN	R	141	496	06.04.28	7740	000000	93999
523.665-010	SUGAR DRIER (grain-feed mills)	2113	44444444355	LNNONONFFNNOONNNNNNN	NNNO4NNNNNNNNNN	T	141	392	06.02.15	7672	000000	92921
523.666-010	COCOA-BEAN-ROASTER HELPER (sugar & conf.)	2212	44444444354	MNNNNNNFFNNOONFONOON	NNCN4NNNNNNNNNN	R	146	393	06.04.15	8618	000000	98999
523.682-010	CHOCOLATE TEMPERER (sugar & conf.)	3225	34444434455	LNNNNNNNFFNNNNNNNNN	NNNN4NNNNNNNNNN	J,T	146	393	06.02.15	7672	000000	92921
523.682-014	COFFEE ROASTER (food prep., nec)	3225	33444434443	MNNNNNNNFFNNNFNNNNN	NNNN4NNNNNNNNNN	T	146	391	06.02.15	7676	000000	92962
523.682-018	DEXTRINE MIXER (grain-feed mills)	3224	44444444354	LNNONONFFFNNNNNNNON	NNFN3NNNNNNNNNN	J	141	302	06.02.15	7672	000000	92921
523.682-022	DRIER OPERATOR (can. & preserv.; dairy products)	3234	34434344355	MFNONONFFNNNNFNNNFN	NNNF4NNNNNNNNNN	J,T	147	392	06.02.15	7664	000000	92917
523.682-026	DRUM DRIER (grain-feed mills)	3224	34443443353	MNNNNNNFFONNNNFNNNFN	NONF3NNNNNNNNNN	R,T	146	383	06.04.15	7665	000000	92928
523.682-030	KILN OPERATOR, MALT HOUSE (beverage)	3224	44443434355	MNNNNNNNFFONNNFNNNNN	NNFN4NNNNNNNNNN	T	141	395	06.04.15	7679	000000	92998
523.682-034	PERCOLATOR OPERATOR (grain-feed mills)	3224	34434434354	MNNNNNNFFONNNNFNNNNN	NNFN4NNNNNNNNNN	T	141	381	06.04.15	7672	000000	92921
523.682-038	TOBACCO CURER (agriculture)	3113	34443444453	MNNNNNNNFFFNNNNNNON	NNFN3NNNNNNNNNN	J,T	146	381	06.02.15	7676	000000	92921
523.685-010	BATCH FREEZER (dairy products)	2112	44444444355	HNNFNCONFFNNNNFNNNFN	NONF3NNNNNNNNNN	R,T	146	383	06.04.15	7665	200409	92928
523.685-014	BLANCHING-MACHINE OPERATOR (can. & preserv.)	2223	44444444454	HNNFNCONFFNNNNNFNNNN	NNNF4NNNNNNNNNN	J,T	146	387	06.04.15	7665	000000	92921
523.685-018	CHILLING-HOOD OPERATOR (meat products)	1112	45454444455	MNNNNNNNFFONNNNFNNNNN	NNNN3NNNNNNNNNN	T	034	382	06.04.15	7665	120506	92928
523.685-022	CHOCOLATE TEMPERER (bakery products; grain-feed mills)	2113	34454444354	MNNNNNNNFFNNNNNNNON	NNNN3NNNNNNNNNN	T	141	393	06.04.15	7664	200409	92965
523.685-026	COFFEE ROASTER, CONTINUOUS PROCESS (food prep., nec)	2223	44444534355	LNNNNNNNFFNNNONNNNN	NNNN3NNNNNNNNNN	R,T	141	391	06.04.15	7672	000000	92921
523.685-030	COOK-BOX FILLER (meat products)	2112	44544534355	MNNNNNNNFFNNNNNFNNNN	NNFF3NNNNNNNNNN	R,T	146	382	06.04.15	7679	120506	92917

DOT #	DOT Title & Industry	Trng	Aptitude	Physical	Environment	Tempra	WkF	MPSMS	GOE	SOC	CIP	OES
523.685-034	COOKER, MEAL (oils & grease)	2213	44443433354	LFNNNNNFFNNNNONNNON	NNNF4NNNNNNNNNN	J,T	146	385	06.04.15	7679	000000	92917
523.685-038	COOLER TENDER (grain-feed mills)	2212	44443444355	LONNNNNFFNNNNNONNNN	NNNN4NNNNNNNNNN	R,T	146	394	06.04.15	7665	000000	92928
523.685-042	COOLING-MACHINE OPERATOR (beverage)	2112	44444444455	LNNNNNNFFNNNNFNNNNN	NNNN3NNNNNNNNNN	T	146	395	06.04.15	7665	000000	92928
523.685-046	COOLING-PAN TENDER (can. & preserv.)	2112	44454444455	LNNNNNNFFNNNNNNNNNN	NNNN4NNNNNNNNNN	R,T	146	387	06.04.15	7665	000000	92928
523.685-050	CRYSTALLIZER OPERATOR (grain-feed mills)	2223	44433444355	MFNFNFNFNNNNNONNNNN	NNNN4NNNNNNNNNN	T	146	392	06.04.15	7665	000000	92921
523.685-054	DEHYDRATOR TENDER (can. & preserv.)	2223	44433444354	HNNNNNNFFOFNNNFNNNN	NNFN4NNNNNNNNNN	J,T	141	387	06.04.15	7672	000000	92921
523.685-058	DRIER ATTENDANT (can. & preserv.; grain-feed mills)	2113	34433443455	LNNNNNNFFNNNNFNNNNN	NNNN4NNNNNNNNNN	J,T	141	381	06.04.15	7672	000000	92921
523.685-062	DRIER OPERATOR (can. & preserv.)	1112	44544534355	MNNNNNNFFONNNNNNNNN	NNNN4NNNNNNNNNN	R	141	387	06.04.15	7672	000000	92921
523.685-066	DRIER TENDER (can. & preserv.)	2113	34433444355	MNNNNNNFFFNNNONNNNN	ONNN4NNNNNNNNNN	J,T	141	306	06.04.15	7672	000000	92921
523.685-070	DRIER TENDER (grain-feed mills)	2223	34444444355	LNNNNNNFFONNNNFNNNN	NNNN4NNNNNNNNNN	J,T	141	381	06.04.15	7672	000000	92921
523.685-074	DRIER TENDER I (oils & grease)	1112	44444444355	LNNNNNNFFNNNNONNNNN	NNNF3NFNNNNNNNN	T	141	389	06.04.15	7672	000000	92921
523.685-078	FIRER, KILN (sugar & conf.)	2113	34434443355	LNNNNNNNNFNNNNFNNNN	NNFN3NNNNNNNNNN	T	141	499	06.04.15	7672	120501	92921
523.685-082	FREEZER TUNNEL OPERATOR (can. & preserv.)	3123	34444444455	LNNONONFFONOONOONNN	NFNN4NNNNNNNNNN	J,T	146	387	06.04.15	7665	000000	92928
523.685-086	GRAIN DRIER (beverage)	2222	44444444355	HNNFNFNFFNNNNNNNNNN	NNFF3NNNNNNNNNN	J,T	141	381	06.04.15	7672	000000	92921
523.685-090	GRAIN-DRIER OPERATOR (grain-feed mills)	2223	44444444454	LFNNNNNFFNNNNNNNNNN	NNNF4NNNNNNNNNN	T	141	301	06.04.15	7672	000000	92921
523.685-094	GRAIN-WAFER-MACHINE OPERATOR (bakery products)	2123	44433444354	HNNNNNNFFNFNNNNNNFN	NNNN3NNNNNNNNNN	J,T	146	384	06.04.15	7672	120501	92921
523.685-098	GRANULATOR OPERATOR (sugar & conf.)	2113	44444444355	LNNNNNNFFNNNNONNNNN	NNNN3NNNNNNNNNN	J,T	141	392	06.04.15	7672	000000	92921
523.685-102	ICE MAKER (food prep., nec)	2123	44445434355	HNNFFNNFFNNNNNNFNNN	NFNF3NFNNNNNNNN	R,T	147	399	06.04.15	7665	000000	92928
523.685-106	INSTANTIZER OPERATOR (dairy products)	2213	44444444454	LNNNNNNFFOONNNNNNON	NNNN4NNNNNNNNNN	J,T	141	383	06.04.15	7672	000000	92921
523.685-110	PASTEURIZER (beverage; can. & preserv.)	2212	44443444455	LNNNNNNFFONNNFNNNNN	NNNN4NNNNNNNNNN	R,T	146	395	06.04.15	7676	000000	92962
523.685-114	STERILIZER OPERATOR (dairy products)	2223	44443444453	LNNNNNNFFNNNNFNNNFN	NNFN4NNNNNNNNNN	J,T	146	383	06.04.15	7679	000000	92917
523.685-118	TOBACCO-DRIER OPERATOR (tobacco)	2222	44444444455	LNNNNNNFFOONNNNNNNN	NNFN4NNNNNNNNNN	J,T	141	464	06.04.15	7672	120501	92921
523.685-122	VACUUM DRIER OPERATOR (can. & preserv.)	3122	44444444454	HNNFNNNFFONNNNFNNON	NNNN3NCNNNNNNNN	R,T	141	304	06.04.15	7672	000000	92921
523.685-126	WINE PASTEURIZER (beverage)	2213	44444444355	LNNNNNNFFNNNNNFNNNN	NNNN3NNNNNNNNNN	J,T	146	395	06.04.15	7672	000000	92921
523.687-010	COFFEE-ROASTER HELPER (food prep., nec)	1112	44544544454	LNNNNNNFFNNNNFNNNFN	NNNN4NNNNNNNNNN	R	141	391	06.04.28	7850	000000	83005
523.687-014	FISH DRIER (can. & preserv.)	1112	45543543355	HNNNNNNFFNNNNFNNNNN	ONNN3NNNNNNNNNN	R	141	386	06.04.28	8769	000000	98999
523.687-018	KILN LOADER (beverage)	1112	44444544355	MNNFNNNFFNNNNNNNNNN	NNNN3NNNNNNNNNN	R	011	309	06.04.40	8769	000000	98799
523.687-022	FREEZING-ROOM WORKER (can. & preserv.)	2112	33333432353	HNNNNNNFFNNNNNFNNNN	NFNN3NNNNNNNNNN	R	011	382	06.04.40	8726	000000	89899
524.381-010	CAKE DECORATOR (bakery products)	3226	34443433353	LNNNNNNFFNNNNFNNOFN	NNNN2NNNNNNNNNN	J,E	146	384	05.05.17	6879	120501	89899
524.381-014	DECORATOR (dairy products)	4336	34433434354	MNNNNNNFFONNNNFNNNNN	NNNN2NNNNNNNNNN	V,D,E	146	383	01.06.03	6879	000000	92953
524.382-010	COATING-MACHINE OPERATOR (sugar & conf.)	3226	34434344354	MNNNNNNFFONNNNONNNN	NNNN3NNNNNNNNNN	J	151	393	06.02.15	7669	120501	97951
524.382-014	ENROBING-MACHINE OPERATOR (bakery products; sugar & conf.)	3126	34433434354	LNNNNNNFFNNNNFFFFN	NNNN3NNNNNNNNNN	J,T	146	384	06.02.15	7669	120501	92953
524.565-010	TROLLEY OPERATOR (bakery products)	1112	44443444434	MNNONNNFFNNNNNNNNNON	NNNN3NNNNNNNNNN	R,T	011	384	06.04.40	8319	200409	92953
524.665-010	SANDING-MACHINE OPERATOR (sugar & conf.)	1112	44443444455	MNNNNNNFFNNNONONNON	NNNO3NNNNNNNNNN	J,T	151	393	06.04.15	7669	120501	92971
524.682-010	DEPOSITING-MACHINE OPERATOR (bakery products)	3124	44443434354	MNNNNNNFFFNNNFNNNNN	NNNO3NNNNNNNNNN	R,T	151	384	06.02.15	7669	200409	92971
524.684-010	CANDY DIPPER, HAND (sugar & conf.)	2114	44543533354	LNNNNNNFFONNNNNFNNN	NNNN2NNNNNNNNNN	R,T	146	393	06.04.28	7756	120501	92947
524.684-014	DECORATOR (bakery products; sugar & conf.)	2113	44334333253	LNFNNNNFFNNNNNNNNNN	NNNN2NNNNNNNNNN	R,T	146	384	06.04.28	7756	120501	93947
524.684-018	ENROBING-MACHINE CORDER (sugar & conf.)	2114	44533532354	LNNNNNNFFONNNNNNNON	NNNN3NNNNNNNNNN	R	146	393	06.04.28	7756	200409	93947
524.684-022	ICER, HAND (bakery products)	2113	44543543354	LNNNNNNFFNNNNNNNNON	NNNN3NNNNNNNNNN	R	146	384	06.04.28	7756	200409	93947
524.685-010	BREADING MACHINE TENDER (can. & preserv.)	1112	44444444455	MNNONNNFFNNNNNNONNN	NNNN3NFNNNNNNNN	R,T	146	409	06.04.15	7664	000000	92965
524.685-014	CHEESE SPRAYER (sugar & conf.)	1112	44444544455	LNNNNNNFFNNNNNNNNNN	NNNN3NNNNNNNNNN	R,T	146	393	06.04.15	7669	000000	92953
524.685-018	COATING OPERATOR (grain-feed mills)	2113	44443443353	LNNNNNNFFONNNNNOFNN	NNNN4NNNNNNNNNN	J,T	146	381	06.04.15	7669	000000	92953
524.685-022	CRACKER SPRAYER (bakery products)	1112	34343444354	LNNNNNNCCNNNNNCFNON	NNNN3NNNNNNNNNN	R,T	153	384	06.04.15	7669	000000	92953
524.685-026	ENROBING-MACHINE OPERATOR (bakery products)	2112	44443444355	LNNNNNNFFNNNNNNNNON	NNNN4NNNNNNNNNN	R,T	146	384	06.04.15	7669	000000	92953
524.685-030	FILLING MACHINE TENDER (bakery products)	2123	44443444454	LNNNNNNFFONNNNNONNN	NNNN4NNNNNNNNNN	R,T	146	384	06.04.15	7663	120501	92971
524.685-034	ICER, MACHINE (bakery products)	2113	44544544454	MNNNNNNFFONNNNONNON	NNNN3NNNNNNNNNN	R,J	146	384	06.04.15	7669	120501	92953
524.685-038	MEXICAN-FOOD-MACHINE TENDER (food prep., nec)	2112	44444444455	LNNNNNNFFONNNONONNN	NNNN3NNNNNNNNNN	R,T	146	380	06.04.15	7679	000000	92998
524.686-010	ENROBING-MACHINE FEEDER (sugar & conf.)	2112	44443433354	LNNNNNNFFNNNNNNNNON	NNNN3NNNNNNNNNN	R,T	146	393	06.04.15	8725	200409	98502
524.686-014	NOVELTY WORKER (dairy products)	2112	44445433355	LNNNNNNFFNNNNNNNNNN	NNNN4NNNNNNNNNN	R	146	383	06.04.28	8769	200409	98999
524.687-010	CHERRY CUTTER (can. & preserv.)	1111	45544533354	LNNNNNNFFNNNNNNNNON	NNNN3NNNNNNNNNN	R	054	387	06.04.28	8769	000000	98999
524.687-014	GARNISHER (sugar & conf.)	1111	44544533354	LNNNNNNFFNNNNNNNNON	NNNN3NNNNNNNNNN	R	146	393	06.04.28	8769	200409	98999

DOT #	DOT Title & Industry	Trng	Aptitude	Physical	Environment	Tempra	WkF	MPSMS	GOE	SOC	CIP	OES
524.687-018	RACKER (bakery products)	1111	4444544355	LNNNNNCCNNNNNNNNN	NNNN3NNONNNNNNNN	R	011	384	06.04.28	8769	120501	98999
524.687-022	BAKERY WORKER, CONVEYOR LINE (bakery products)	1112	4444444454	LNNNNNNOONNNNONNOON	NNNN3NNONNNNNNNN	R,U	146	384	06.04.28	7759	120501	93999
525.131-010	SUPERVISOR, ABATTOIR (meat products)	4227	33343333343	LNNNNNNNFFNFNFNNFN	NNNF4NNNNNNNNNN	D,P,V	034	382	06.02.01	7100	520205	81008
525.131-014	SUPERVISOR, CUTTING AND BONING (meat products)	4227	33333433354	LNNONONFFONFFNFNNFON	NFNF3NNNNNNNNNN	D,P,V	034	382	06.02.01	7100	520205	81008
525.132-010	SUPERVISOR, CURED MEATS (meat products)	4226	33333333353	LNNNNNNOOOOFFNFNNOFN	NNNO3NNNNNNNNNN	D,P,V	146	382	06.02.01	7100	520205	81008
525.132-014	SUPERVISOR, TANK HOUSE (meat products)	4227	33343333355	MNNNNNNNFFNFFNNOONN	NONN4NNNNNNNNNN	D,P,V	147	382	06.04.01	7100	520205	81008
525.134-010	SUPERVISOR, FISH PROCESSING (can. & preserv.)	4227	33444444355	MNNNONNNFFONFFNFNOONN	NNNF4NNNNNNNNNN	D,P	034	331	06.04.01	7100	000000	81008
525.134-014	SUPERVISOR, POULTRY PROCESSING (meat products)	4227	33433444355	LNNNNNNNFFONFFNFOOONN	NNNC4NCNNNNNNNO	D,P	034	382	06.04.01	7100	520205	81008
525.361-010	SLAUGHTERER, RELIGIOUS RITUAL (meat products)	3225	34443433352	MONONNNNFCOFOONONFOON	OFNO4NNONNNNNNN	J,T	034	382	06.03.01	6871	000000	89802
525.381-010	BUTCHER APPRENTICE (meat products)	3226	33443433354	HNNOONCCCCNNNCNOFFN	NNNC2NNNNNNNNNN	V,T	034	382	06.02.28	6871	120506	89802
525.381-014	BUTCHER, ALL-ROUND (meat products)	3226	33443433354	HNNOONCCCNNNCNNOFFN	NNNC2NNNNNNNNNN	V,T	034	382	06.02.28	6871	120506	89802
525.387-010	GRADER, MEAT (meat products)	3215	34433444452	LNNNNNNNCCONNNNNCNNCCN	NFNF2NNNNNNNNNN	J,T	212	382	06.03.01	7850	010401	83005
525.587-010	SHROUDER (meat products)	1112	4454444355	MNNFNNNFFONNNNNNNNN	NNNF3NNNNNNNNNN	R	041	382	06.04.38	8769	120506	98999
525.587-014	SMOKED MEAT PREPARER (meat products)	2213	44533533354	MNNONNNFFNNNNNNNNNN	NFNF2NNNNNNNNNN	R,T	034	382	06.04.28	7753	120506	93938
525.664-010	MEAT DRESSER (agriculture)	3226	34533433353	MNNFNNNCCFNNNNNNNNN	NNNF3NNNNNNNNNN	R	034	382	03.04.05	6871	120506	89802
525.682-010	SMOKER (meat products)	3214	34444444454	MNNFNNNFFOONNNNNNON	ONNF2NFNNNNNNNO	V,P,T	034	320	06.02.15	7679	120506	92998
525.684-010	BONER, MEAT (meat products)	2124	44533533354	MNNNNNNNCCFONNNFNOOON	NFNF2NNNNNNNNNN	J,T	146	382	06.04.28	7753	120506	93938
525.684-014	BUTCHER, FISH (can. & preserv.)	1112	44544533354	HNNFNFNCCFNNNNFNOFON	NNNF2NFNNNNNNNN	R,T	034	382	06.04.28	7753	120506	93938
525.684-018	CARCASS SPLITTER (meat products)	2213	44533533355	MNNONNNFFNNNNNFNOFNN	NFNF2NNNNNNNNNN	R,T	034	382	06.04.28	7753	120506	93938
525.684-022	CRAB BUTCHER (can. & preserv.)	1112	44533533354	MNNNFNNNCCFNNNNFNOOON	NNNF2NCNNNNNNNO	R	034	332	06.04.28	7753	120506	93938
525.684-026	FINAL-DRESSING CUTTER (meat products)	3114	34443433354	MNNNNNNFFNNNNNCNFCCN	NNNF2NNNNNNNNNN	R,T	034	382	06.04.28	7753	120506	93926
525.684-030	FISH CLEANER (can. & preserv.; fishing & hunt.)	1112	44434533354	MNNFNNNCCCNNNNCNFNFN	NNNC2NCNNNNNNNN	R	034	331	06.04.28	7753	000000	93926
525.684-034	HEAD TRIMMER (meat products)	2113	44433533355	MNNNNNNNCCCNNNNCNFFN	NNNC2NNNNNNNNNN	R	034	382	06.04.28	7753	120506	93926
525.684-038	OFFAL SEPARATOR (meat products)	2112	44544433355	LNNNNNNNFFFNNNFNOONN	NNNC3NCNNNNNNNN	R	034	382	06.04.28	7753	120506	93926
525.684-042	POULTRY KILLER (meat products)	1112	44544534355	LNNNNNNCCNNNNNNNNNN	NNNC3NCNNNNNNNN	R,T	034	382	06.04.28	8769	120506	93999
525.684-046	SKINNER (meat products)	2212	44544534345	MNNCNNNFFONNNNFNFNN	ONNC2NNNNNNNNNO	R,T	034	382	06.04.28	7753	120506	93938
525.684-050	STICKER, ANIMAL (meat products)	2213	44544534355	MNNFNFNFFNNNNNFNFNN	NNNF3NNNNNNNNNN	R,T	034	382	06.04.28	7753	120506	93938
525.684-054	TRIMMER, MEAT (meat products)	2112	44544533354	MNNNNNNNCCFNNNNCNOCON	NONO3NNNNNNNNNN	R,T	034	382	06.04.28	7753	120506	93926
525.685-010	BAND-SAW OPERATOR (meat products)	2112	44444444355	LNNNNNNNCCNNNNNCNCNN	NNNN3NNNNNNNNNN	R	146	382	06.04.15	7678	120506	92944
525.685-014	CASING-RUNNING-MACHINE TENDER (meat products)	1112	45454543355	MNNNNNNFFNNNNNFNFNNN	NNNO4NNFNNNNNNN	R	034	382	06.04.15	7662	120506	92974
525.685-018	DEHAIRING-MACHINE TENDER (meat products)	2213	44544534345	MNNNNNNFFONNNNNNNNNN	NNNC3NCNNNNNNNN	R	062	382	06.04.15	7679	120506	92998
525.685-022	HIDE PULLER (meat products)	2112	44434434344	MNNNNNNNFFNNNNNNNNON	NNNF3NNNNNNNNNN	R	034	382	06.04.15	7666	120506	92962
525.685-026	POULTRY-PICKING MACHINE TENDER (meat products)	2112	44444544455	LNNNNNNNFFNNNNNNFNNN	NNNO4NFNNNNNNNN	R	034	382	06.04.28	7679	120506	92998
525.685-030	SKIN-PEELING-MACHINE OPERATOR (meat products)	2112	44444444355	LNNNNNNNFFNNNNNNNNNN	NNNN3NNNNNNNNNN	R	054	382	06.04.15	7666	120506	92962
525.686-010	CASING CLEANER (meat products)	2112	44544533355	LNNNNNNNFFNNNNNNNNNN	NNNF3NNNNNNNNNN	R	031	382	06.04.15	8725	120506	98502
525.686-014	CONVEYOR LOADER II (meat products)	2112	44445544355	LNNONNNFFNNNNNNNNNN	NNOF4NNNNNNNNNN	R	011	382	06.04.40	8725	120506	98502
525.686-018	HEAD-MACHINE FEEDER (meat products)	2112	44544544355	LNNNNNNNCCNNNNNFNFNNN	NNNC4NNNNNNNNNN	R	034	382	06.04.15	8725	120506	98502
525.686-022	SKINNING-MACHINE FEEDER (meat products)	2112	44544544355	MNNNNNNNFFNNNNNNNNNN	NNNF3NFNNNNNNNN	R	034	382	06.04.15	8725	120506	98502
525.687-010	ANIMAL EVISCERATOR (meat products)	2213	44533534354	MNNONONCCCNNNNCNNCON	NNNC3NNNNNNNNNN	R	034	382	06.04.28	7759	120506	93999
525.687-014	CASING SPLITTER (meat products)	1111	44555544355	LNNNNNNNFFNNNNNNNNNN	NNNN3NNNNNNNNNN	R	034	382	06.04.28	7740	000000	93999
525.687-018	CONVEYOR LOADER I (meat products)	1112	44454444355	HNNNNNNNFFNNNNNFNFNN	NNNC3NNNNNNNNNN	R	145	382	06.04.40	8769	120506	98999
525.687-022	COOLER ROOM WORKER (meat products)	2212	44544444355	LNNNNNNNFFFNNNFNFNN	NFNF3NNNNNNNNNN	R	034	382	06.04.28	8769	120506	98999
525.687-026	DRY CURER (meat products)	2112	44434444354	HNNONNNFFFNNNNNNON	NONN3NNNNNNNNON	R,T	146	382	06.03.02	7759	120506	98999
525.687-030	GAMBRELER (meat products)	1112	44544534345	MNNNNNNFFNNNNNNNNNN	NNNF3NNNNNNNNNN	R	034	382	06.04.28	8769	120506	98999
525.687-034	GAMBRELER HELPER (meat products)	2112	44544544455	HNNFFFNFNNNNNNNNNN	NNNF3ONNNNNNNNN	R	034	382	06.04.27	7820	120506	83005
525.687-038	HIDE HANDLER (meat products; oils & grease)	2123	44554534345	MNNFNFNFFOONNNFOFON	NNNN2NCNNNNNNNN	R,T	152	521	06.03.02	8769	120506	98999
525.687-042	HIDE INSPECTOR (meat products)	2112	45554544355	MNNFNNNNFFNNNNNCNNON	NNNF3NNNNNNNNNN	R	212	521	06.04.39	8769	120506	98999
525.687-046	HIDE TRIMMER (meat products; oils & grease)	2113	44443434344	LNNNNNNFFFNNNNNNNNNN	NNNF3ONNNNNNNNN	R	054	521	06.04.28	8769	120506	98999
525.687-050	NECK SKEWER (meat products)	1112	45555555355	HNNNNNNNFFNNNNNNNNNN	NCNC3NNNNNNNNNN	R	034	382	06.04.28	8769	120506	98999
525.687-054	OFFAL ICER, POULTRY (meat products)	1111	45555555355	HNNNNNNFFNNNNNNNNNN	NONN3NCNNNNNNNN	R	011	382	06.04.40	8726	000000	98799

DOT #	DOT Title & Industry	Trng	Aptitude	Physical	Environment	Tempra	WkF	MPSMS	GOE	SOC	CIP	OES
525.687-058	ORDER RUNNER (meat products)	1112	4444444355	MNNNNNCCONNNNNNNNNN	NCNN3NNNNNNNN	R	011	382	06.04.40	8769	120506	98999
525.687-062	PAINTER, DEPILATORY (meat products)	1111	45554544355	MNNNFNNNFFNNNNNNNNNN	NNNF3NNNNNNNN	R	153	521	06.04.27	8769	000000	98999
525.687-066	POULTRY BONER (meat products)	1112	44444443354	LNNNNNNCCCNNNNNNNNNN	NNNN3NNNNNNNN	R	034	324	06.04.28	8769	120506	98999
525.687-070	POULTRY DRESSER (agriculture; meat products)	1112	44545544355	LNNNNNNNCCNNNNNFNNNN	NNNC3CNNNNNNN	R	034	324	06.04.28	7759	000000	93999
525.687-074	POULTRY EVISCERATOR (meat products)	1112	44545534355	LNNNNNNCCONNNNCNCNN	NNNC3CNNNNNNN	R	034	382	06.04.28	7753	120506	93938
525.687-078	POULTRY HANGER (meat products)	1111	44555543455	MNNONNNCCNNNNNNNNNN	NNNC3NCNNNNNN	R	034	382	06.04.38	8769	000000	98999
525.687-082	POULTRY-DRESSING WORKER (meat products)	1112	44455444355	MNNONNNCCNNNNNFNNNNN	NONC3NCNNNNNN	R	041	382	06.04.38	8761	120506	98902
525.687-086	SHACKLER (meat products)	1112	44545434345	HNNNNNNCCCONNNNNNNNN	NNNC3NCNNNNNN	R	011	382	06.04.40	8726	120506	98799
525.687-090	SHACTOR HELPER (meat products)	1112	44544544455	MNNNNNNFFONNNNNNNNNN	NNNC3NCNNNNNN	R	011	382	06.04.28	8769	000000	98999
525.687-094	SHAVER (meat products)	2112	45544533355	LNNNNNNCCFNNNNCNNCNN	NNNC3NCNNNNNN	R	034	322	06.04.28	8769	120506	98999
525.687-098	SINGER (meat products)	2112	44454534355	LNNNNNNCCNNNNNNNNNN	ONNN3NNNNNNNN	R,T	031	382	06.03.02	7850	120506	83005
525.687-102	SKIN GRADER (meat products)	2122	44444444455	MNNNNNNFFONNNNNNNNNN	NNNN2NNNNNNNN	R	212	521	06.04.34	8769	120506	98999
525.687-106	SLUNK-SKIN CURER (meat products)	2112	44545534355	MNNNNNNCCNNNNNNNNNN	NNNO3NCNNNNNN	R	152	382	06.04.34	8769	120506	98999
525.687-110	STEAMER (meat products)	1111	44454534355	LNNNNNNCCONNNNNNNNNN	ONNC3NNNNNNNN	R	031	382	06.04.39	8769	120506	98999
525.687-114	STUNNER, ANIMAL (meat products)	1112	44545534355	MONFNNNFFNNNNNNNNNN	NNNF3NNNNNNNN	R	034	382	06.04.28	8769	120506	98999
525.687-118	TIER (meat products)	1112	44544544355	LNNNNNNNCCNNNNNNNNNN	NNNC3NNNNNNNN	R	146	382	06.04.28	8761	120506	98902
525.687-122	WASHER, CARCASS (meat products)	1111	44544544455	MNNNNNNCCFNNNNFNNNNN	NNNC3NNNNNNNN	R	031	382	06.04.39	8769	000000	98999
525.687-126	CRAB MEAT PROCESSOR (can. & preserv.)	1112	44444433354	LNNNNNNFFNNNNFNNFON	NNNO3NNNNNNNO	R	034	386	06.04.28	8769	010401	93999
526.131-010	BAKERY SUPERVISOR (bakery products)	4338	33333333354	MNNNNNNNFFFFFNNNNON	NNNN3NNNNNNNN	V,D,P,J,T	146	384	06.01.01	7100	120501	81008
526.134-010	COOK, MEXICAN FOOD (food prep., nec)	4237	33444433355	MNNNNNNNFFFFFNFNNONN	NNNN3NNNNNNNN	V,D,J,T	146	399	06.01.01	7100	120505	81008
526.137-010	POTATO-CHIP-PROCESSING SUPERVISOR (food prep., nec)	4336	33343444454	LNNNNNNNFFNFFNFNNOON	NNNN4NNNNNNNN	V,D,P,J	146	393	06.02.01	7100	200409	81008
526.381-010	BAKER (bakery products)	3227	33343433353	HNNONNNFFFNNOFNNOON	NNNN2NNNNNNNN	V,J,T	146	384	06.02.15	6872	120501	89805
526.381-014	BAKER APPRENTICE (bakery products)	3227	33343433353	HNNONNNFFFNNOFNNOON	NNNN2NNNNNNNN	V,J,T	146	384	06.02.15	6872	120501	89805
526.381-018	BAKER, TEST (grain-feed mills)	3226	34333344453	LNNNNNNFFOONNNFNNNON	NNNO2NNNNNNNN	J,T	146	381	06.02.15	6881	000000	89805
526.381-022	CAKE TESTER (grain-feed mills)	3226	33344444453	LNNNNNNNFFOONNNFNNFFN	NNNN2NNNNNNNN	J,T	146	381	06.02.15	6879	000000	89899
526.381-026	COOK, KETTLE (beverage; can. & preserv.; grain-feed mills)	3226	34444444354	MNNNNNNNFFNNNNFNNONN	NNNF3NNNNNNNN	J,T	146	387	06.01.04	6879	200409	89899
526.382-010	CONCHE OPERATOR (sugar & conf.)	3224	34443533354	MNCONNNNFFONNNNOFNNOON	NNNN4NNNNNNNN	J,T	146	393	06.02.15	7664	000000	92965
526.382-014	CONFECTIONERY COOKER (sugar & conf.)	4237	33343334454	MNNNNNNNFFOONNNFNNNNN	NNNN3NNNNNNNN	J,T	146	393	06.02.15	7672	200409	92899
526.382-018	CONVERTER OPERATOR (grain-feed mills)	3214	34343444354	LNNNNNNNFFONFNONNOON	NNCN3NNNNNNNN	J	146	392	06.02.15	7679	000000	92917
526.382-022	MOLASSES AND CARAMEL OPERATOR (grain-feed mills)	3234	34343344354	MNNNNNNFFNNNNNONNOON	NNCN3NCNNNNNN	J,T	146	384	06.02.15	7679	120501	92921
526.382-026	STEAM-OVEN OPERATOR (can. & preserv.)	2113	34434444355	MNNNNNNNFFFNNNNONONN	NNCC3NCNNNNNN	J	146	331	06.02.15	7672	000000	92998
526.485-010	WORT EXTRACTOR (dairy products)	3113	34444444354	HNNNNNNFFONNNNFNFFON	NNNO4NNNNNNNN	J	146	395	06.04.15	7679	000000	92921
526.585-010	OVEN OPERATOR (grain-feed mills)	2113	34433334353	LNNNNNFFOONNNFNNNOON	NNFN3NNNNNNNN	J,T	146	381	06.04.15	7672	200409	92917
526.665-010	COOKER, PROCESS CHEESE (dairy products)	3223	34444444355	MNNNNNFFONNNNONONNN	NNNC3NNNNNNNN	J,T	146	383	06.04.15	7679	000000	92917
526.665-014	KETTLE TENDER (beverage)	2112	34444434354	LNNNNNNFFOONNNONONNN	NNCF3NNNNNNNN	T	041	395	06.02.15	7479	120501	92997
526.682-010	BATTER SCALER (bakery products)	3224	34343533354	LNNFNNNFFOONNNFNNNNN	NNNO3NNNNNNNN	J,T	146	384	06.02.15	7679	120501	92917
526.682-014	COOK, DOG-AND-CAT FOOD (meat products)	3224	33333344354	MNNNNNNNFFONNNNFNNNNN	NNNC3NCNNNNNN	J	146	394	06.02.15	7679	200409	92998
526.682-018	COOK, SYRUP MAKER (beverage)	3224	34444444354	MONNNNNFFONNNONONNON	NNNN3NNNNNNNN	J	146	384	06.02.15	7679	120501	92917
526.682-022	DOUGHNUT-MACHINE OPERATOR (bakery products)	3234	34443444354	LNNNNNNFFONNNONONOON	NNCN3NNNNNNNN	J,T	146	395	06.02.15	7672	200409	92921
526.682-026	MALT ROASTER (beverage)	3224	34443444354	MNNNNNFFNNNNFNNONNNN	NNNN3NNNNNNNN	J,T	146	387	06.02.15	7679	000000	92921
526.682-034	RETORT OPERATOR (can. & preserv.)	3115	34443444355	HNNNNNNNFFNNNFFNNNNN	NNNF3NNNNNNNN	J,T	146	387	06.02.15	7679	200409	92917
526.684-010	DOUGHNUT MAKER (bakery products)	3114	34443444354	MNNONNNFFFNNNNFNNOON	NNCO3NNNNNNNN	J,T	146	384	06.02.28	7759	120501	93999
526.684-014	LUMPIA WRAPPER MAKER (food prep., nec)	2112	45554533355	HNNONNNFFONNNNFNNOON	NNON3NNNNNNNN	R,U	146	399	05.10.08	7759	120506	93999
526.685-010	COOK (meat products)	3113	34444444355	LNNNNNNFFONNNNNONONNN	NNCC4NNNNNNNN	J,T	146	382	06.04.15	7679	120501	92917
526.685-014	COOK, FRY, DEEP FAT (can. & preserv.; hotel & rest.)	2112	44444545354	MNNNNNFFONNNONNOON	NNNN3NNNNNNNN	R,T	146	386	06.04.15	7679	200409	92917
526.685-018	COOK, VACUUM KETTLE (can. & preserv.)	2112	44444444354	LNNNNNNFFONNNONNOON	NNNF3NNNNNNNN	R,T	146	387	06.04.15	7679	200409	92917
526.685-022	COOKER (grain-feed mills)	2123	44444444354	LNNNNNNFFONNNNFNNOON	NNNN4NNNNNNNN	J,T	146	381	06.04.15	7679	000000	92921
526.685-026	CORN POPPER (sugar & conf.)	1112	44444444455	HNNNNNNFFONNNNFNNOON	NNNN3NNNNNNNN	R	146	393	06.04.15	7672	200409	92921
526.685-030	OVEN TENDER (bakery products)	3114	34443434354	MNNNNNNNFFONNNNFOON	NNCN3NNNNNNNN	J,T	141	384	06.04.15	7672	120501	92921
526.685-034	PAN GREASER, MACHINE (bakery products)	1112	45544534355	LNNNNNNNFFNNNNNNNNNN	NNNN2NNNNNNNN	R	033	384	06.04.21	7679	000000	92998
526.685-038	PIE MAKER, MACHINE (bakery products)	3114	34433433334	MNNNONNNFFFNNNFNNNON	NNNN3NNNNNNNN	J,T	146	384	06.04.15	7679	120501	92998

DOT #	DOT Title & Industry	Trng	Aptitude	Physical	Environment	Tempra	WkF	MPSMS	GOE	SOC	CIP	OES
526.685-042	POPCORN-CANDY MAKER (sugar & conf.)	2213	44444444454	LNNNNNNFFONNNFNFNNNON	NNNO3NNNNNNNNN	J,T	146	393	06.04.15	7679	200409	92917
526.685-046	POTATO-CHIP FRIER (food prep., nec)	2113	44444444354	LNNNNNNFFONNNNNONNNON	NNNN3NNNNNNNNN	J,T	146	387	06.04.15	7679	200409	92917
526.685-050	POTATO-PANCAKE FRIER (food prep., nec)	2112	44544544454	MNNNNNNNFONNNONNONNON	NNCN3NNNNNNNNN	R,T	146	384	06.04.15	7679	200409	92917
526.685-054	PRETZEL COOKER (bakery products)	2113	34443344454	MNNONNNFFONNNNNONNNON	NNON3NNNNNNNNN	J,T	146	384	06.04.15	7672	120501	92921
526.685-058	THERMOSCREW OPERATOR (can. & preserv.)	2113	44444444353	HNNOONNFFONNNNFNNNFON	NNNC4NNNNNNNNN	J,T	146	382	06.04.15	7679	000000	92917
526.685-062	TRIPE COOKER (meat products)	2112	44455445355	MNNMONNFFONNNNNONNFNN	NNNC3NCNNNNNNN	R,T	146	382	06.04.15	7679	120506	92917
526.685-066	WAFER-MACHINE OPERATOR (bakery products)	2113	34444444354	LNNNNNNFFONNNNNONNFON	NNNN3NNNNNNNNN	J,T	146	384	06.04.15	7672	120501	92921
526.685-070	OVEN OPERATOR, AUTOMATIC (bakery products)	3223	44444444454	LNNNNNNFFONNNNFNNFON	NNCN3NNNNNNNNN	J,T	146	384	06.04.15	7672	120501	92921
526.686-010	BAKER HELPER (bakery products)	2112	44444444445	HNNFNNNFFONONNONNNON	NNON3NOONNNNNN	R,T	146	384	06.04.15	8619	120501	98999
526.687-010	POTATO-CHIP SORTER (food prep., nec)	1111	44543533353	LNNNNNNFFNNNNNFNFON	NNNN3NNNNNNNNN	R	212	389	06.03.02	7850	200409	83005
526.687-014	STARCHMAKER (sugar & conf.)	2113	44544444455	LNNNNNNFFNNNNNNNNN	NNNN3NNNNNNNNN	R,T	132	393	06.04.28	7740	000000	93999
529.130-010	SUPERVISOR, CANDY (sugar & conf.)	4237	33333333354	LNNNNNNFFONFFNFNNFON	NNNN3NNNNNNNNN	V,D,P,J,T	146	393	06.02.01	7100	200409	81008
529.130-014	SUPERVISOR, CHOCOLATE-AND-COCOA PROCESSING (sugar & conf.)	4338	22333343354	LONOONFFOOFFNFNNFON	NNNF4NFNNNNNNN	V,D,P,J	146	393	06.01.01	7100	000000	81008
529.130-018	SUPERVISOR, COFFEE (food prep., nec)	4237	33344433354	LNNNNNNFFOOFFNFNNNON	NNON3NCNNNNNNN	V,D,P,T	146	394	06.02.01	7100	000000	81008
529.130-022	SUPERVISOR, FILTRATION (sugar & conf.)	4237	33344334354	LNNNNNNOONFFNNNNNON	NNON3NNNNNNNNN	V,D,P,J	145	392	06.02.01	7100	000000	81008
529.130-026	SUPERVISOR, NUT PROCESSING (can. & preserv.)	4237	33333333355	MONOOONFFNFNFOOONO	ONNN4NNNNNNNNN	V,D,P,J	146	306	06.02.01	7100	000000	81008
529.130-030	SUPERVISOR, PULP HOUSE (sugar & conf.)	4237	33433334355	MNNNNNNFFONNNNNNN	NNNN3NNNNNNNNN	V,D,P,J	141	389	06.02.01	7100	000000	81008
529.130-034	SUPERVISOR, REFINING (sugar & conf.)	4237	33344334354	LNNNNNNFFONFFNNNNN	NNON4NNNNNNNNN	V,D,P,J	147	392	06.01.01	7100	000000	81008
529.130-038	SUPERVISOR, SOFT SUGAR (sugar & conf.)	4237	33344334354	LNNNNNNFFNNFFNNNNN	NNNN3NNNNNNNNN	V,D,P,J	041	392	06.02.01	7100	000000	81008
529.130-042	SUPERVISOR, WHITE SUGAR (sugar & conf.)	4237	33344334355	LNNNNNNFFONFFNONNN	NNNF4NNNNNNNNN	V,D,P,J	145	392	06.02.01	7100	000000	81008
529.131-010	CELLAR SUPERVISOR (beverage)	4238	33333434354	MFNOOONFFNFNFNNNON	NNNF3NNNNNNNNN	V,D,P,J	146	395	06.02.01	7100	000000	81008
529.131-014	SUPERVISOR, DAIRY PROCESSING (dairy products)	4337	33343344355	LONONNNFFOOFFFNNONN	NNNF4NNNNNNNNN	V,D,J,T,P	146	383	06.02.01	7100	200409	81008
529.131-018	CUSTOM-FEED-MILL OPERATOR (grain-feed mills)	4237	34444344455	LNNNNNNFFOFFNNNNN	NNNN3NNNNNNNNN	V,D,J,T	142	381	05.12.01	7100	000000	81008
529.132-014	PLANT SUPERVISOR (grain-feed mills)	4237	34443434354	LNNNNNNNNNFFNNNNFFN	NNNN3NNNNNNNNN	V,D,J,T	141	311	06.01.01	7100	000000	81008
529.132-018	SUPERVISOR, BEET END (sugar & conf.)	4337	33344334354	LNNNNNNFFONFFNNNNN	NNNN4NNNNNNNNN	V,D,P,T	147	392	06.02.01	7100	000000	81008
529.132-022	SUPERVISOR, BOTTLE-HOUSE CLEANERS (beverage)	4337	33333333353	LOOONOOFFONFFNONNOON	NNNO3NNNNNNNNN	D,J	031	567	06.02.01	7100	000000	81008
529.132-026	SUPERVISOR, BREW HOUSE (beverage)	4238	33332333353	LNNNNNNFFNFNFFNFON	NNNF3NNNNNNNNN	V,D,P,J	146	395	06.02.01	7100	000000	81008
529.132-030	SUPERVISOR, CEREAL (grain-feed mills)	4247	33344333454	LONOOONFFOFFNFNNOON	NNON4NNNNNNNNN	D,P,T	146	381	06.02.01	7100	000000	81008
529.132-034	SUPERVISOR, CIGAR-MAKING MACHINE (tobacco)	4237	33433334355	LNNFNFNNNNNFNFNNNN	NNNN4NNNNNNNNN	V,D,P,T	041	402	06.02.01	7100	200409	81008
529.132-038	SUPERVISOR, COOK ROOM (can. & preserv.)	4237	34344344355	LNNNNNNFFNFFNFNNNN	NNNO4NNNNNNNNN	V,D,P,T	146	387	06.02.01	7100	000000	81008
529.132-042	SUPERVISOR, DRIED YEAST (food prep., nec)	4347	33333333355	LNNNNNNFFOFFNNNNN	NNNN3NNNNNNNNN	V,D,P,J	041	399	06.02.01	7100	000000	81008
529.132-046	SUPERVISOR, DRY-STARCH (grain-feed mills)	4237	33344334354	LONNNNNFFONFFNNNNN	NNNN3NNNNNNNNN	V,D,P,T	147	499	06.02.01	7100	000000	81008
529.132-050	SUPERVISOR, FEED HOUSE (grain-feed mills)	4238	33344333355	LFNNNNNFFNNFFNNNNN	CNNN4NNNNNNNNN	D,P,T,J	141	381	06.02.01	7100	000000	81008
529.132-054	SUPERVISOR, FEED MILL (grain-feed mills)	3337	33344343354	LONNNNNFFONFFNFNNNON	NNNN4NFNNNNNNN	D,V,P,J	142	381	06.01.01	7100	000000	81008
529.132-058	SUPERVISOR, FERMENTING CELLARS (beverage)	4237	33333344453	LONNNNNFFONFFFNNNNN	NOON3NNNNNNNNN	V,D,P,T	146	395	06.02.01	7100	000000	81008
529.132-062	SUPERVISOR, GRAIN AND YEAST PLANTS (beverage)	4237	33333343354	LNNNNNNFFNFNFFNFNN	NNNF3NNNNNNNNN	D,P,T	146	395	06.04.01	7100	000000	81008
529.132-066	SUPERVISOR, LIQUID YEAST (food prep., nec)	4337	33343333355	LNNNONONFFONFNFNNNON	NONF3NNNNNNNNN	D,P,J,T	141	397	06.02.01	7100	000000	81008
529.132-070	SUPERVISOR, MALTED MILK (dairy products)	4237	23344333354	MNONONOOOONFFNNNNNNN	NNNN4NNNNNNNNN	V,D,P,J	146	399	06.02.01	7100	000000	81008
529.132-074	SUPERVISOR, MILL HOUSE (grain-feed mills)	4337	33344333355	LONNNNNFFOOFFNNNON	NONF3NNNNNNNNN	V,D,P,J	146	383	06.02.01	7100	020301	81008
529.132-078	SUPERVISOR, NUTRITIONAL YEAST (food prep., nec)	4347	33344333354	LNNNNNNFFONFFNNNON	FNNN4NNNNNNNNN	V,D,P,J	142	381	05.02.07	7100	000000	81008
529.132-082	SUPERVISOR, SOAKERS (beverage)	4347	33344334354	LONNNOONFFNNNFNNNON	NNNC4NNNNNNNNN	D,J,P	146	394	06.02.01	7100	000000	81008
529.132-086	SUPERVISOR, STEFFEN HOUSE (sugar & conf.)	4236	33333433354	LNNNONONFFNONNNNNON	NNNN3NNNNNNNNN	V,D,P,T	031	395	06.02.01	7100	000000	81008
529.132-090	SUPERVISOR, SUGAR HOUSE (grain-feed mills)	4338	33343334353	LNNNNNNFFOOFFNFNNFN	NNNF3NNNNNNNNN	D,T,P,V	141	397	06.02.01	7100	520205	81008
529.132-094	SUPERVISOR, SUGAR REFINERY (grain-feed mills)	4238	33343333355	LNNNNNNOONFFNFNNNN	NNON4NNNNNNNNN	V,D,P	147	404	06.02.01	7100	000000	81008
529.132-098	SUPERVISOR, TANK STORAGE (beverage)	4238	33333323353	LNNNNNNFFOOFFNNNNON	NONF3NNNNNNNNN	V,D,P,J	141	392	06.01.01	7100	000000	81008
529.132-102	SUPERVISOR, TEA AND SPICE (food prep., nec)	4337	33344333354	LNNNONNNFFNONNNNNON	NONF3NNNNNNNNN	V,D,P,J	146	382	06.04.01	7100	000000	81008
529.132-106	SUPERVISOR, WASH HOUSE (beverage)	4347	33332344355	LNNNONNOOONFFNFNNNN	NNNC4NNNNNNNNN	D,J,P	031	395	06.02.01	7100	520205	81008
529.132-110	SUPERVISOR (food prep., nec)	3226	33333334353	LNNONNNFFOOFFNFNOFFN	NNON4NNNNNNNNN	V,D,P,T	141	397	06.02.01	7100	000000	81008
529.135-010	COOKING, CASING, AND DRYING SUPERVISOR (tobacco)	4337	33343444455	LNNNNNNFFONFNFNNFFN	NNNN4NNNNNNNNN	V,D,P	147	404	06.04.01	7100	000000	81008
529.135-014	SUPERVISOR, CURED-MEAT PACKING (meat products)	4227	33333444354	LNNONNNOOONFNFNNFFN	NONN3NNNNNNNNN	D,P	041	382	06.04.01	7100	520205	81008
529.137-010	PREPARATION SUPERVISOR (can. & preserv.)	4237	33333444454	LNNNNNNFFOOFFNFNONON	NNNF4NNNNNNNNN	D,P,V	146	387	06.02.01	7100	000000	81008

DOT #	DOT Title & Industry	Trng	Aptitude	Physical	Environment	Tempra	WkF	MPSMS	GOE	SOC	CIP	OES
529.137-014	SANITARIAN (any industry)	4237	33333344355	LFFFFNFFNFFNFOFOONN	NNNN4NNNNNNNNN	D,P,T	031	380	11.10.03	7100	200409	81008
529.137-018	SUGAR-REPROCESS OPERATOR, HEAD (sugar & conf.)	3236	33344343455	LNNNNNNOOONFNFNFNN	NNNN4NNONNNNNN	D,P,T	041	392	06.02.01	7100	000000	81008
529.137-022	SUPERINTENDENT, GRAIN ELEVATOR (beverage: grain-feed mills)	4346	33344344454	LFOOONOOONFFNOOOOOO	NNNN4NNNNNNNNN	D,P,T,V	221	381	06.01.01	7100	010401	81008
529.137-026	SUPERVISOR (tobacco)	4237	33333443354	LNNNNNNNFFFOFFNFNFNON	NNNN4NNONNNNNN	V,D,P,T	041	401	06.02.01	7100	000000	81008
529.137-030	SUPERVISOR (oils & grease)	4337	33344343453	LONNNNNNOONOONONNNON	NNNN4NNNNNNNNN	V,D,P,J	146	385	06.01.01	7100	000000	81008
529.137-034	SUPERVISOR, CIGAR TOBACCO PROCESSING (tobacco)	4226	33443344454	LNNNNNNFFONFFNFNNNON	NNNN3NNNNNNNNN	D,P,J	212	409	06.02.01	7100	000000	81008
529.137-038	SUPERVISOR, CURING ROOM (tobacco)	4337	33333333354	LNNNONNNOONOFFNONNOON	NNNN4NNNNNNNNN	V,D,P,J	152	403	06.02.01	7100	000000	81008
529.137-042	SUPERVISOR, EGG PROCESSING (can. & preserv.; wholesale tr.)	4337	33333333333	LNNNONNNFFFNFNFNFNN	NONN4NNNNNNNNN	V,P,J,T	041	382	06.01.01	7100	020209	81008
529.137-046	SUPERVISOR, FRUIT GRADING (wholesale tr.)	4236	33443344353	LNNNNNNONNNFFNOONNON	NNNN4NNNNNNNNN	P,J	212	304	06.03.02	7100	010401	81008
529.137-050	SUPERVISOR, MAPLE PRODUCTS (food prep., nec)	4336	33343444453	LNONNNNNOOONFNFFFFF	NNNN4NNNNNNNNN	D,J	146	392	06.02.01	7100	000000	81008
529.137-054	SUPERVISOR, READY-MIXED FOOD PREPARATION (food prep., nec)	4335	23333434454	LNNONNNFFONOONFNOOON	NNNN4NNNNNNNNN	V,D,P	146	399	06.04.01	7100	000000	81008
529.137-058	SUPERVISOR, SYRUP SHED (sugar & conf.)	4336	33344344455	LNNNNNNFFNFFNFNNNNN	NNNN4NNNNNNNNN	D,P,V	146	392	06.02.01	7100	520205	81008
529.137-062	SUPERVISOR, SPECIALTY FOOD PRODUCTS (can. & preserv.; meat products)	4348	33333344455	LNNNONNOOONFFNONNNNN	NONN4NNNNNNNNN	V,D,P	146	382	06.02.01	7100	520205	81008
529.137-066	SUPERVISOR, WHIPPED TOPPING (dairy products)	4237	33344344455	LNNOONNOOONFFNONNNON	NNNN3NNNNNNNNN	V,D,P,J,T	146	383	06.02.01	7100	020301	81008
529.137-070	SUPERVISOR, YARD (beverage)	4228	22223344454	LNNOONNOOONFFNONNNON	OONN3NNNNNNNNN	V,D,P,T	011	851	06.04.01	7100	000000	81008
529.137-074	SUPERVISOR, INSPECTION (sugar & conf.)	4337	33333344455	LNNNNNNNOOONFNFNNFNN	NNNN3NNNNNNNNN	D,T,J	212	393	06.02.01	7100	010401	81008
529.137-078	SUPERVISOR, INSTANT POTATO PROCESSING (food prep., nec)	4337	33344444455	LOONNNNFFNFNFFFOONN	NNOO3NNNNNNNNN	D,P,V,J	146	387	06.02.01	7100	520205	81008
529.137-082	SUPERVISOR, PROCESSING (sugar & conf.)	4337	33343355455	LNNNNNNOOONFNFNNOONN	NNNN3NNNNNNNNN	D,J,P	146	393	06.02.01	7100	150699	81008
529.167-010	FRUIT COORDINATOR (can. & preserv.)	4335	33344344455	LOOCONONOONNFFNFNNNNF	NNNN4NNNNNNNNN	V,P	221	387	05.09.02	7870	000000	83005
529.281-010	TASTER (food prep., nec)	4347	33354344454	LNNONNNFFNNNNNNNNNN	NNNN4NNNNNNNNN	D,V,J,T	146	380	06.01.05	6881	020301	83002
529.361-010	ALMOND-PASTE MIXER (sugar & conf.)	4238	33333433354	MNNNNNNFFFFNNNNNNNFN	NNNN4NNNNNNNNN	J,T	146	393	06.01.04	6873	200409	89808
529.361-014	CANDY MAKER (sugar & conf.)	4347	33333433353	MNNONNNNFFOOFFOFNNNFN	NNON4NNNNNNNNN	V,J,T	212	393	06.02.28	6873	200409	89808
529.361-018	CHEESEMAKER (dairy products)	4347	33343444354	LNNNNNNNFFOONNFFNFNON	NNNN4NNNNNNNNN	D,J	146	383	06.01.04	6873	020301	89808
529.361-022	BUTTERMAKER (dairy products)	3326	33344433353	HNNFNFNFFFNNNNNNNNN	NONO4NNNNNNNNN	J	146	383	06.02.15	7666	020301	92962
529.362-014	DRY-STARCH OPERATOR, AUTOMATIC (grain-feed mills)	3227	33344444354	MFNOOONFFOOFFNFNNNNN	NNNN4NNNNNNNNN	J,T	147	499	06.02.15	7676	000000	92962
529.367-010	CIGARETTE-AND-FILTER CHIEF INSPECTOR (tobacco)	3225	34333344455	LNNNNNNFFFOOFFNFNNN	NNNN4NNNNNNNNN	J,T	212	401	06.03.01	7820	000000	83005
529.367-014	HOGSHEAD INSPECTOR (tobacco)	3224	34444344353	LNNNNNNFFFNNFNFNFNN	NNNN4NNNNNNNNN	J,T	212	404	06.03.01	7820	000000	83005
529.367-018	QUALITY-CONTROL INSPECTOR (bakery products)	3224	34444344353	LNNNNNNFFFNOONFNFFFN	NNNN3NNNNNNNNN	J,T	212	384	06.03.01	7840	000000	83005
529.367-022	QUALITY-CONTROL TECHNICIAN (beverage)	3325	33333433355	LNNNNNNFFFNOONFNFFN	NNNN3NNNNNNNNN	V,T	211	395	05.09.02	7830	000000	83005
529.367-026	ROUGH-RICE GRADER (grain-feed mills)	3225	34333333453	LNNOOOFFFFOONFFFFN	NNNN4NOONNNNNN	P,J,T	212	301	06.03.01	7850	010401	83005
529.367-030	YIELD-LOSS INSPECTOR (grain-feed mills)	4335	33433344354	LOOOOOOFFFNOONFNFNON	ONNN4NNNNNNNNN	J	211	389	06.03.01	7820	000000	92998
529.367-034	QUALITY CONTROL INSPECTOR (sugar & conf.)	3227	32443344455	HFNFFFNFFFNOONFNNNNN	NNON3NFNNNNNNNN	V,T,J	211	392	06.03.01	7820	020301	92932
529.381-010	COMPOUNDER, FLAVORINGS (beverage)	4236	33343334354	MNNONNNFFNNNNFFNNNON	NNNN4NONNNNNNNN	J,T	146	394	06.02.28	6869	000000	89808
529.382-010	BUTTERMAKER, CONTINUOUS CHURN (dairy products)	3233	34334444354	MNNONNNFFFOFNFNNNFN	NNOO4NOONNNNNN	J,T	147	385	06.02.15	7664	000000	92998
529.382-014	CHOCOLATE-PRODUCTION-MACHINE OPERATOR (sugar & conf.)	4336	33344334354	HNNONONFFNNNNNONNOON	NNON4NNNNNNNNN	T,V	146	393	06.02.15	7679	000000	92962
529.382-018	DAIRY-PROCESSING-EQUIPMENT OPERATOR (dairy products)	4235	33433443354	HOOONONFFNNNNNNNNN	NNON4NOONNNNNN	J,T	146	383	06.03.01	7476	020301	92932
529.382-022	GELATIN MAKER, UTILITY (chemical)	4236	33343334354	MNNONNNFFNNNNFFNNNON	NNOO4NONNNNNNNN	V,T	147	499	06.02.18	7679	000000	89808
529.382-026	HYDROGENATION OPERATOR (oils & grease)	3224	34444344354	MNNNNNNFFFNNNNFFFFN	NNOO4NOONNNNNN	J,T	147	385	06.02.15	7679	000000	92998
529.382-030	IRISH-MOSS OPERATOR (chemical)	3215	34434343354	MNNNNNNFFFNNNNFNFFFN	NNNN4NNNNNNNNN	R,T	146	399	06.02.11	7676	000000	92962
529.385-010	NOODLE MAKER (food prep., nec)	2123	44443434355	HNNFNNNCCOONNNFNNNNN	NNNN4NONNNNNNNN	R,T	146	397	06.04.15	7679	200409	92998
529.387-010	CHEESE GRADER (dairy products)	3225	34432443453	LNNNNNNFFFFNFNNFFFN	NNNN4NNONNNNNN	J	212	383	06.03.01	7850	020301	83005
529.387-014	CIGARETTE TESTER (tobacco)	3335	33344434355	LNNNNNNFFFNNFNFFNN	NNNN4NNONNNNNN	J,T	212	401	06.03.01	7850	010401	83005
529.387-018	FRUIT-BUYING GRADER (can. & preserv.; wholesale tr.)	3323	33343334354	MNNNNNNFFFONNNFNNNNN	ONNN4NNNNNNNNN	J	212	305	06.03.01	7830	010401	83005
529.387-022	GAUGER (beverage)	3225	33343333453	LNNNNNNFFFNNNNFNNNN	NNNN3NNNNNNNNN	J	212	395	06.03.01	7830	000000	83005
529.387-026	INSPECTOR, GRAIN MILL PRODUCTS (grain-feed mills)	3223	33344344355	MNNNNNNFFFNNNNFFFFN	NNNN3NNNNNNNNN	J,T	212	381	06.03.01	7820	000000	83005
529.387-030	QUALITY-CONTROL TECHNICIAN (can. & preserv.; food prep., nec)	3234	33443433354	LNNNNNNFFFNNNFFFFN	NNNN3NONNNNNNNN	R,T,J	212	380	06.03.01	7830	000000	83005
529.387-034	SAMPLER (oils & grease)	3224	33444444454	LNNNNNNFFFNNNNONOOONN	NNNN4NNNNNNNNN	J,T	212	300	06.03.01	7840	000000	83005
529.462-010	SYRUP MIXER (grain-feed mills)	3235	33343344354	MONNNNNFFFNOONFNFFON	NNNN5NNNNNNNNN	J,T	146	392	06.02.15	7664	200409	92965
529.467-010	TIP-LENGTH CHECKER (tobacco)	3323	34344344455	LNNNNNNFFFNOONFNFFNN	NNNN4NNNNNNNNN	R,T	212	404	06.03.01	7820	000000	83005
529.482-010	FREEZER OPERATOR (dairy products)	3225	34444444345	LNNNNNNFFFONNNNFNNNNN	NONN3NNNNNNNNN	J,T	146	383	06.02.15	7665	000000	92928
529.482-014	NOVELTY MAKER I (dairy products)	3224	33344444345	LNNNNNNNFFFNNNNFNFFNN	NONO4NNNNNNNNN	J,T	146	383	06.02.15	7665	000000	92928

DOT #	DOT Title & Industry	Trng	Aptitude	Physical	Enviroment	Tempra	WkF	MPSMS	GOE	SOC	CIP	OES
529.482-018	NOVELTY MAKER II (dairy products)	3225	33344444345	LNNNNNNFFNNNNONNNNN	NONO4NNONNNNNN	J,T	146	383	06.02.15	7665	000000	92928
529.482-022	SYRUP MAKER (sugar & conf.)	3225	33333333455	LNNNNNNNCCONNNNFNNNNN	NNNN3NNNNNNNN	J,T	146	393	06.02.15	7679	200409	92998
529.484-010	STEAK SAUCE MAKER (can. & preserv.)	3233	44444443354	MNNNNNNNCCNNNNNFNNNNN	NNNN3NNNNNNNN	V,T	146	387	06.02.28	7759	200409	93999
529.485-010	BARREL FILLER (grain-feed mills)	2212	44344343345	HOONNNNFFONNNNNONOONN	ONNN3NNNNNNNN	R,T	041	392	06.04.15	7665	000000	92928
529.485-014	BLOW-UP OPERATOR (sugar & conf.)	3233	33344444355	MNNNNNNFFNNNNNFFNN	NNNO4NNNNNNNN	J,T	143	392	06.04.15	7664	000000	92965
529.485-018	DRIER, BELT CONVEYOR (food prep., nec)	3123	44434444455	MNNNNNNNFFNNNNNFNNNNN	NNNN4NNNNNNNN	J,T	146	399	06.04.15	7679	000000	92998
529.485-022	MATURITY CHECKER (can. & preserv.)	3322	34343443355	LNNNONFFNNNNNFNNNNN	NNNN4NNNNNNNN	J,T	212	303	06.03.01	7679	000000	92998
529.485-026	WEIGH-TANK OPERATOR (oils & grease)	3223	34343434355	LNNNNNNFFONNNNFNNNN	NNNN4NNNNNNNN	R,T	212	385	06.03.02	7840	000000	83005
529.486-010	NUT-PROCESS HELPER (can. & preserv.)	1112	44444434355	HNNFNFFNNNNNONONN	NNNO4NNNNNNNN	R	146	393	06.04.15	8618	000000	98999
529.487-010	SPECIAL TESTER (tobacco)	3333	33344344354	LNNNNNNFFONNNNNNNNON	NNNN3NNNNNNNN	J,T	212	403	06.03.01	7830	000000	83005
529.565-010	SUGAR CONTROLLER (sugar & conf.)	2223	33344344354	LNNNNNNMFFNNOONFNNFON	NNNN4NNNNNNNN	J	011	392	06.04.15	7679	000000	92998
529.567-010	CIGARETTE INSPECTOR (tobacco)	2123	34443444355	LNNNNNNNFFNNOONFNNNNN	NNNN4NNNNNNNN	R,T	041	401	06.03.02	7820	000000	83005
529.567-014	MARKER, COMPANY (tobacco)	2113	34444444453	LNNNNNNNFFNFFNFFFN	NNNN3NONNNNNNN	J,T	212	403	05.09.03	7820	000000	83005
529.582-010	CARBONATION EQUIPMENT OPERATOR (sugar & conf.)	4336	33433444453	LNNNNNNFFNNNNNFNFFN	NNNN4NNNNNNNN	J,T	147	392	06.02.15	7676	000000	92962
529.582-014	FLASH-DRIER OPERATOR (grain-feed mills)	4237	34433334355	LOOONNOOOONFNFNNNNN	ONNN4NOONNNNNN	J,T	146	381	06.02.15	7676	000000	92962
529.585-010	CHEESE CUTTER (dairy products)	2112	44443434353	MNNONNNCCFNNNNNFFON	NNNN4NNNNNNNN	R,J,T	054	383	06.04.15	7678	000000	92944
529.585-014	TANK TENDER (sugar & conf.)	3223	33444344355	MNNNNNNNFFNNFFNN	NNNO4NNNNNNNN	R,T	014	392	06.04.15	7679	000000	92998
529.587-010	BOTTLE GAUGER (beverage)	3223	34343333355	LNNNNNNFFNNNNNFNFNNN	NNNN4NNNNNNNN	R,T	212	395	06.03.02	7830	000000	83005
529.587-014	SAUSAGE INSPECTOR (meat products)	1112	44443444455	LNNNNNNFFNNNNNFNNNN	NONN4NNNNNNNN	R,T	212	382	06.03.02	7820	120506	83005
529.587-018	SCRAP SEPARATOR (food prep., nec)	1112	44454434354	LNNFFFNFFNNNNNONFNON	NNNN3NNNNNNNN	R	221	397	06.03.02	7850	000000	83005
529.587-022	TOBACCO-SAMPLE PULLER (tobacco)	2112	44444444455	LNNNNNNNFFONNNNNNNNN	NNNN4NONNNNNNN	R,T	142	404	06.04.28	7840	000000	83005
529.665-010	FRUIT-GRADER OPERATOR (agriculture; wholesale tr.)	2112	44543544355	LNNFFFNFFONOONOONFFOONO	NNNN4NNNNNNNN	R,T	212	305	06.04.15	7662	000000	92974
529.665-014	WASHROOM OPERATOR (sugar & conf.)	2112	44544534355	SNNNNNNFFNNOONNNNNNN	NNNO4NNNNNNNN	R	031	309	06.04.15	7673	000000	92958
529.665-018	WET-AND-DRY-SUGAR-BIN OPERATOR (sugar & conf.)	2113	44443444355	MNNNNNNNFFNOONNNNNNN	NNNO4NNNNNNNN	R	031	392	06.04.15	7679	000000	92998
529.665-022	YEAST-CUTTING-AND-WRAPPING-MACHINE OPERATOR (food prep., nec)	2112	44444534355	LNNNNNNFFNNNNNFNNNNN	NNNN4NNNNNNNN	R,T	146	399	06.04.15	7679	000000	92974
529.666-010	CATCHER, FILTER TIP (tobacco)	2222	44443434355	MNNNNNNCCFNNNNNFNNNN	NNNN4NNNNNNNN	R,T	041	401	06.04.15	7820	000000	83005
529.666-014	CIGARETTE-MAKING-MACHINE CATCHER (tobacco)	2122	44443434355	SNNNNNNCCFNOONFNNNNN	NNNN4NNNNNNNN	R,T	041	401	06.04.15	7820	000000	83005
529.667-010	INSPECTOR, FILTER TIP (tobacco)	2223	44444444355	LNNNNNNFFONNNFNFNN	NNNN4NNNNNNNN	J,T	212	401	06.03.02	7820	000000	83005
529.667-014	MASH-FILTER-CLOTH CHANGER (beverage)	1112	44443534355	MNNONNNFFONNNNNNNNN	NNOO3NNNNNNNN	R	062	567	06.04.15	8769	000000	98999
529.682-010	CENTRIFUGE OPERATOR (sugar & conf.)	3224	34443434355	LNNNNNNFFONNNNNFNNNNN	NNNN4NNNNNNNN	V,T	146	393	06.02.15	7666	000000	92962
529.682-014	CHEESEMAKER HELPER (dairy products)	3226	34343444354	MNNNNNNNFFOONNNNFNNNN	NNNO4NNNNNNNN	J,T	146	383	06.02.15	7664	000000	92965
529.682-018	DEPOSITING-MACHINE OPERATOR (sugar & conf.)	3225	33444444355	LNNNNNNFFNNNNNFNNNNN	NNNN3NNNNNNNN	J,T	132	393	06.02.15	7679	000000	92971
529.682-022	DRIER OPERATOR (sugar & conf.)	4235	34444434354	MNNNNNNNFFONNNNNFNNNNN	NNON4NNNNNNNN	V,T	146	393	06.02.15	7676	000000	92962
529.682-026	LOZENGE MAKER (sugar & conf.)	3125	33433334355	HNNNNNNNFFFNNNNFNNNNN	NNNN4NNNNNNNN	J,T	135	393	06.02.15	7479	000000	92997
529.682-030	SILO OPERATOR (tobacco)	3224	34343444454	LNNNNNNNFFONNNNFNNNON	NNNN3NNNNNNNN	J,T	011	404	06.02.15	8319	000000	97989
529.682-034	WHIPPED-TOPPING FINISHER (oils & grease)	3225	33344444355	LNNONONFFNNNNNFNNNNN	NNNF4NNNNNNNN	J,T	146	385	06.02.15	7664	000000	92965
529.682-038	EGG PASTEURIZER (agriculture)	3234	33344444355	MNNONNNFFONNNNFNFNNN	NNNN4NNNNNNNN	T,J	145	382	06.02.15	7676	010401	92962
529.684-010	FROZEN PIE MAKER (can. & preserv.)	2112	34443434354	MNNNNNNCCNNNNNFNNFFON	NONO4NONNNNNNN	R,T	146	382	06.04.28	7759	200409	93999
529.684-014	INGREDIENT SCALER (bakery products; dairy products)	3232	34444444355	MNOONNNFFONNNNNFNFNN	NNNO4NONNNNNNN	J,T	212	384	06.04.28	7840	200409	83005
529.684-018	SIEVE MAKER (grain-feed mills)	2112	44434444355	MOOONNNFFONNNNNNFONN	NNNN4NONNNNNNN	R	102	567	06.04.25	7740	470303	93999
529.685-010	AUTO ROLLER (tobacco)	1112	44444444455	LNNNNNNFFNNNNNNFONN	NNNO4NNNNNNNN	R,T	041	402	06.04.15	7663	000000	92971
529.685-014	AUTOMATIC LUMP MAKING MACHINE TENDER (tobacco)	2122	44543533355	LONNNNNNFFONNNNFONNN	NNNN4NNNNNNNN	R,J,T	054	403	06.04.15	7678	000000	92974
529.685-018	BINDER LAYER (tobacco)	2112	44543533345	LNNNNNNNCCNNNNNFNFNN	NNNN4NNNNNNNN	R,T	054	402	06.04.15	7679	000000	92944
529.685-022	BLENDER-CONVEYOR OPERATOR (dairy products)	2122	44444444455	HONONNNFFOONNNNFNFNN	NNNN4NNNNNNNN	R,T	145	383	06.04.15	7662	000000	92998
529.685-026	BOTTLED-BEVERAGE INSPECTOR (beverage)	2123	44543534355	LNNNNNNNCCNNNNNFNFNN	NNNN4NNNNNNNN	R,T	212	400	06.03.02	7679	000000	83005
529.685-030	BRINE-TANK TENDER (dairy products)	2112	44444534344	MNNNNNNFFONNNNNNNFNON	NNNO4NNNNNNNN	R,T	146	387	06.04.15	7662	000000	92998
529.685-034	BULKER, CUT TOBACCO (tobacco)	1112	44444444455	LNNNNNNFFNNNNNNFNNNN	NNNN4NNNNNNNN	R	041	403	06.04.15	7679	000000	92998
529.685-038	BUNCH MAKER, MACHINE (tobacco)	2112	44444544445	LNNNNNNNFFNNNNNNFNNNN	NNNN4NNNNNNNN	R,T	132	403	06.04.15	7662	000000	92974
529.685-042	BUTT MAKER (tobacco)	2112	44445453455	LNNNNNNNFFNNNNNFNNNNN	NNNN4NNNNNNNN	R,T	041	403	06.04.15	7663	000000	92971
529.685-046	CAN-CONVEYOR FEEDER (food prep., nec)	2112	44544544455	LNNNNNNFFNNNNNFNFNNN	NNNN4NNNNNNNN	R	011	551	06.04.40	7679	000000	92998
529.685-050	CHAR-CONVEYOR TENDER (sugar & conf.)	2112	44444544355	MNNNNNNNFFNNNNNFNFNNN	NNOO4NOONNNNNN	R,T	011	499	06.04.40	7679	000000	97951

DOT #	DOT Title & Industry	Trng	Aptitude	Physical	Environment	Tempra	WkF	MPSMS	GOE	SOC	CIP	OES
529.685-054	CHOCOLATE MOLDER, MACHINE (sugar & conf.)	3224	34444444354	LNNNNNNNCCNNNNNFNNNON	NNNN4NNNNNNNNNN	J,T	132	393	06.04.15	7663	000000	92971
529.685-058	CIGAR-HEAD PIERCER (tobacco)	2112	44444454455	SNNONONFFNNNNNFNNNNN	NNNN4NNNNNNNNNN	R,T	053	402	06.04.28	7679	000000	92998
529.685-062	CIGARETTE-FILTER-MAKING-MACHINE OPERATOR (tobacco)	2113	33433444455	LNNNNNNNFFNNNNNFNFNN	NNNN4NNNNNNNNNN	R,T	041	401	06.04.15	7679	000000	92998
529.685-066	CIGARETTE-MAKING-MACHINE OPERATOR (tobacco)	3113	44434444345	MNNNNNNNCCFNNNNNONNN	NNNN4NNNNNNNNNN	R,T	041	401	06.04.15	7679	000000	92998
529.685-070	COLORER, CITRUS FRUIT (wholesale tr.)	2112	33344444354	LNNNNNNNFFNNNNNFNNNON	NNON4NONNNNNNNN	R,T	152	304	06.04.15	7679	000000	92958
529.685-074	CONTAINER WASHER, MACHINE (any industry)	2112	44545544355	MONONNNFFNNNNNNFNFFNN	NNNO4NNNNNNNNNN	R,T	031	380	06.04.39	7673	000000	92958
529.685-078	CORN-PRESS OPERATOR (food prep., nec)	2113	44434544354	MNNONONFFOONNNONNNON	NNNN4NNNNNNNNNN	J,T	146	384	06.04.15	7673	000000	92971
529.685-082	CUTTER (food prep., nec)	1112	44445433355	LNNNNNNNFFNNNNNNNNNN	NNNN4NONNNNNNNN	R,T	056	397	06.04.15	7678	000000	92944
529.685-086	DECAY-CONTROL OPERATOR (wholesale tr.)	2112	34444444355	LNNNNNNNFONNNNONNNNN	NNNN4NNNNNNNNNN	R,T	152	300	06.04.15	7679	000000	92998
529.685-090	DEFECTIVE-CIGARETTE SLITTER (tobacco)	2112	44545544455	MNNNNNNNFFONNNNNNNNN	NNNN4NNNNNNNNNN	R	054	401	06.04.15	7678	000000	92944
529.685-094	DEOILING-MACHINE AND PASTEURIZING-MACHINE OPERATOR (beverage)	1112	34433454355	LONOOONFFONNNNNOOONN	NNNO4NNNNNNNNNN	R,T	145	387	06.04.15	7676	000000	92962
529.685-098	DRIER OPERATOR, DRUM (food prep., nec)	2122	44434454454	LNNNNNNNFFNNNNNFNFNON	NNNN4NNNNNNNNNN	J,T	146	399	06.04.15	7679	000000	92998
529.685-102	DUMPING-MACHINE OPERATOR (can. & preserv.; wholesale tr.)	1112	44434434455	LNNNNNNNFFNNNNNCNNNN	NNNN4NNNNNNNNNN	R	011	300	06.04.40	8319	490299	97989
529.685-106	EXPELLER OPERATOR (grain-feed mills; oils & grease)	2114	44444444355	MONNNNNNFFOONNNNFNNNN	NNNN4NONNNNNNNN	J,T	141	380	06.04.15	7679	000000	92998
529.685-110	FILLER SHREDDER, MACHINE (tobacco)	2113	44444444355	MNNNNNNNFFNNNNNNNNNN	NNNN4NNNNNNNNNN	R	054	403	06.04.15	7678	000000	92944
529.685-114	FILTER TENDER, JELLY (can. & preserv.)	3213	44444444455	LNNNNNNNFFNNNNNNNNNN	NNNN3NNNNNNNNNN	R,T	145	387	06.04.15	7666	000000	92962
529.685-118	FISH CLEANER MACHINE TENDER (can. & preserv.)	2112	34555534355	MNNOOONFFNNNNNNNFNNN	NNNO4NONNNNNNNN	R,T	034	386	06.04.15	7678	000000	92944
529.685-122	FISH-CAKE MAKER (food prep., nec)	2114	34443444354	LNNNNNNNFFNNNNNNNNNN	NNNO4NONNNNNNNN	R	146	386	06.04.15	7679	000000	92998
529.685-126	FLAVOR EXTRACTOR (grain-feed mills)	2113	44444444354	MNNNNNNNFFNNNNNOOOON	NNNN4NNNNNNNNNN	R,T	143	394	06.04.15	7664	000000	92965
529.685-130	FLAVOR ROOM WORKER (dairy products)	3234	34343444354	LNNNONNNFFNNNNNFNFNON	NNOO4NOONNNNNNN	R,T	146	390	06.04.15	7679	000000	92965
529.685-134	FRUIT-BAR MAKER (sugar & conf.)	2112	44444433455	LNNNNNNNFFNNNNNNNNNN	NNNN3NNNNNNNNNN	R	142	393	06.04.15	7677	000000	92965
529.685-138	HAM-ROLLING-MACHINE OPERATOR (meat products)	1112	45544534345	LNNNNNNNFFNNNNNNFNFNN	NNNO4NNNNNNNNNN	R	163	382	06.04.15	7662	120506	92974
529.685-142	HORSERADISH MAKER (can. & preserv.)	2112	44544544355	LNNONONFFONNNNNFNFNN	NNNO4NOONNNNNNN	R,T	146	386	06.04.15	7679	000000	92998
529.685-146	ICE CREAM FREEZER ASSISTANT (dairy products)	2112	44444444344	MNNNNNNNFFNNNNNONNNON	NONO4NOONNNNNNN	R,J,T	146	383	06.04.15	8618	000000	99899
529.685-150	ICE CUTTER (food prep., nec)	1112	44434544355	HNNFNNNFFONNNNNFNFNN	NOOO4NNNNNNNNNN	R	054	399	06.04.15	7678	000000	92944
529.685-154	LABORER, STARCH FACTORY (grain-feed mills)	2113	44444434355	HNNONNNNCCNNNNNNNNNN	NNNO4NNNNNNNNNN	R,T	146	387	06.04.15	7666	000000	92962
529.685-158	LARD REFINER (meat products; oils & grease)	2113	44444544354	MONNNNNNCCNNNNNNNNNON	NNON4NCNNNNNNNN	R,T	146	385	06.04.15	7679	000000	92998
529.685-162	LINKING-MACHINE OPERATOR (meat products)	2123	44544534355	LNNNNNNNFFNNNNNNNNNN	NNNN4NNNNNNNNNN	R,T	146	382	06.04.15	7662	120506	92974
529.685-166	MEAT BLENDER (can. & preserv.)	2222	44444444355	HNNNNNNNCCONNNNNONONNN	NNNN3NNNNNNNNNN	R,T	146	382	06.04.15	7679	000000	92998
529.685-170	MOISTURE-MACHINE TENDER (tobacco)	2112	44444444455	LNNNNNNNFFONOONFNNNNN	NNNN3NNNNNNNNNN	R,T	152	404	06.04.15	7679	000000	92998
529.685-174	NUT ROASTER (can. & preserv.)	2223	34444444353	HNNONNNFFNNNNNNNNFN	NNFF4NFNNNNNNNN	J	146	393	06.04.15	7672	000000	92921
529.685-178	PEANUT-BUTTER MAKER (can. & preserv.; food prep., nec)	2114	44444444355	MNNONNNFFONNNNNFNNNNN	NNNN4NNNNNNNNNN	R,T	146	393	06.04.15	7679	000000	92998
529.685-182	PLUG-CUTTING-MACHINE OPERATOR (tobacco)	1112	44544544355	LNNNNNNNFFONNNNOONNNN	NNNN4NNONNNNNNN	R	054	403	06.04.15	7678	000000	92944
529.685-186	PLUG-OVERWRAP-MACHINE TENDER (tobacco)	2123	44544544355	MNNNNNNNFFONNNNFONNNN	NNNN4NFNNNNNNNN	R,T	041	403	06.04.15	7662	000000	92974
529.685-190	PRESERVATIVE FILLER, MACHINE (can. & preserv.)	2123	44444444355	LNNONNNFFONNNNNONONNN	NNNN4NNNNNNNNNN	R	041	391	06.04.15	7679	120506	92974
529.685-194	RAW-JUICE WEIGHER (sugar & conf.)	1112	44444455455	LONFNNNFFNNNNNNNNNNN	NNNN4NONNNNNNNN	R	011	403	06.04.40	7840	000000	83005
529.685-198	REFINING-MACHINE OPERATOR (oils & grease)	3223	34434444354	LNNNNNNNFFNNNNNFNFNN	NNNN4NNNNNNNNNN	J,T	147	385	06.04.39	7673	000000	92958
529.685-202	RENDERING-EQUIPMENT TENDER (meat products)	3223	44454444355	MFNFNFNFFNFFNNNNNNNN	NNFF4NNNNNNNNNN	T	146	382	06.04.15	7679	120506	92998
529.685-206	RESERVE OPERATOR (tobacco)	2113	44433433355	LNNNNNNNFFONNNNFNFNN	NNNN4NNNNNNNNNN	J,T	136	403	06.04.15	7679	000000	92998
529.685-210	SANDWICH-MACHINE OPERATOR (dairy products)	2122	44445544455	LNNNNNNNFFNNNNNFNFNN	NFNN4NNNNNNNNNN	R	041	383	06.04.15	7663	000000	92971
529.685-214	SHELLFISH-PROCESSING-MACHINE TENDER (can. & preserv.)	2112	44454544355	HONFNONFFONNNNNFNFNF	NNOO4NOONNNNNNO	R,T	146	386	06.04.15	7679	000000	92998
529.685-218	SPICE FUMIGATOR (food prep., nec)	3222	32445444455	HNNFNFNFFNNNNNFNNNNN	NNNN4NFNNNNNNNN	R,T	293	391	06.04.15	7679	000000	92998
529.685-222	SPREADER OPERATOR, AUTOMATIC (tobacco)	1112	44544444355	MNNNNNNNFFNNNNNNNNNN	NNNN4NONNNNNNNN	R	011	403	06.04.40	7679	000000	92998
529.685-226	STEAMER (beverage)	2112	44444444455	LONFNNFNNFFNNNNNFNFNN	NNNN4NNNNNNNNNN	R	014	491	06.04.39	7673	000000	92958
529.685-230	STEM-DRYER MAINTAINER (tobacco)	1112	44544444455	MNNNNNNNFFNNNNNNNNNN	NNNN3NFNNNNNNNN	R	011	404	06.04.15	6140	000000	85128
529.685-234	SUCKER-MACHINE OPERATOR (sugar & conf.)	1113	44444534355	MNNOOONFFNNNNNNFNNNN	NNNN4NNNNNNNNNN	R	132	393	06.04.15	7663	000000	92971
529.685-238	TABLET-MACHINE OPERATOR (dairy products)	2112	44344543455	LNNNNNNNFFNNNNNNFFNN	NNNN4NNNNNNNNNN	J,T	134	383	06.04.15	7667	000000	92971
529.685-242	TANK PUMPER, PANELBOARD (beverage)	2113	34434443345	MNNOOONFFNNNNNNFNNNN	NNNN3NNNNNNNNNN	J,T	014	395	06.04.15	7679	000000	97953
529.685-246	TAPPER (beverage)	2212	34443444355	LNNONONFFNNNNNNFNNNN	NNNN4NNNNNNNNNN	J,T	014	395	06.04.15	7679	000000	97953
529.685-250	VOTATOR-MACHINE OPERATOR (meat products; oils & grease)	2113	44443444355	LNNNONONFFNNNNNFNFNN	NNNN4NNNNNNNNNN	J	133	385	06.04.39	7665	120506	92928
529.685-254	WASH-HOUSE WORKER (beverage)	2112	44444535355	MONONONFFNNNNNFNFNN	NNOO4NNNNNNNNNN	R	031	551	06.04.15	7673	000000	92958

DOT #	DOT Title & Industry	Trng	Aptitude	Physical	Environment	Tempra	WkF	MPSMS	GOE	SOC	CIP	OES
529.685-258	WASHER, AGRICULTURAL PRODUCE (agriculture; can. & preserv.; sugar & conf.;)	1112	44444534344	LONONNNFFNNNNNNNNON	NNNON4NNNNNNNNNNN	R	031	300	06.04.39	7673	000000	92958
529.685-262	WHEAT CLEANER (grain-feed mills)	2113	44444444355	LONNNNNFFNNNNNNFNNN	NNNNN3NONNONNNNNN	R,T	146	381	06.04.15	7673	000000	92958
529.685-266	WRAPPER LAYER (tobacco)	2123	44543533345	LNNNNNNNCCFNNNCNCNNN	NNNNN4NNNNNNNNNNN	R,T	054	403	06.04.15	7662	000000	92974
529.685-270	WRAPPER-LAYER-AND-EXAMINER, SOFT WORK (tobacco)	1112	44555433345	LNNNNNNNFFONNNNFNNFNN	NNNNN4NNNNNNNNNNN	R	041	402	06.04.15	7662	000000	92974
529.685-274	X-RAY INSPECTOR (can. & preserv.; tobacco)	2112	44543444455	LNNNNNNNFFONNNNFNNFNN	NNNNN4NNNNNNNNNNN	R,T	212	403	06.03.02	7820	000000	83005
529.685-278	YEAST WASHER (food prep., nec)	3232	33444444355	LNNNNNNNFFNNNNFNNONN	NNNON4NNNNNNNNNNN	J,T	146	399	06.04.15	7673	000000	92958
529.685-282	CAN-FILLING-AND-CLOSING-MACHINE TENDER (can. & preserv.)	2112	44434434355	LNNNNNNNFFFNNNNFNNNN	NNNON4NNNNNNNNNNN	R	041	387	06.04.15	7662	000000	92974
529.685-286	CIGAR-WRAPPER TENDER, AUTOMATIC (tobacco)	2122	44434444355	LNNNNNNNFFONNNNFNNNNN	NNNNN4NNNNNNNNNNN	R,T	041	402	06.04.15	7662	000000	92974
529.685-290	COOK, SOYBEAN SPECIALTIES (food prep., nec)	2122	44444443354	MFNFNNNNFFONNNNFNNNNN	NNOO3NNNNNNNNNNN	R,T	146	399	06.04.15	7679	010401	92917
529.686-010	BUNDLES HANGER (tobacco)	1111	44544534353	LNNNNNNNCCNNNNNFNNNCN	NNNN4NONNNNNNNNN	R	011	404	06.04.40	8725	000000	98502
529.686-014	CANNERY WORKER (can. & preserv.)	2222	44444433354	LNNONNNCCCNNNNFNFFON	NNNO4NNNNNNNNNNN	R,T	146	380	06.04.15	7759	000000	93935
529.686-018	CIGARETTE-MAKING-MACHINE-HOPPER FEEDER (tobacco)	1112	44444434355	MNNNNNNNFFFNNNNFNNNNN	NNNNN4NNNNNNNNNNN	R	041	401	06.04.15	8725	000000	98502
529.686-022	CUTLET MAKER, PORK (meat products)	1112	44544434355	LNNNNNNNFFNNNNFNNFNNN	NNNNN4NNNNNNNNNNN	R,T	146	382	06.04.15	8725	120506	98502
529.686-026	DAIRY HELPER (dairy products)	2112	44544544355	HNNONONFFNNNNOONONNN	NONO4NONNNNNNNNN	R,T	011	383	06.04.39	8618	000000	79999
529.686-030	EGG WASHER, MACHINE (agriculture; wholesale tr.)	1111	44544434354	LNNONONFFFNNNNNFNNNN	NNNN3NNNNNNNNNNN	R	031	382	06.04.39	5617	000000	79999
529.686-034	FACTORY HELPER (sugar & conf.)	1112	44545444355	MNNONONFFOONNNFNFNON	NNNN4NNNNNNNNNNN	R	146	393	06.04.15	8618	000000	98999
529.686-038	FEEDER-CATCHER, TOBACCO (tobacco)	1112	44444443355	HNNONNNFFONNNNFNNNNN	NNNN4NONNNNNNNNN	R	011	403	06.04.40	8725	000000	98502
529.686-042	FILLER FEEDER (tobacco)	1112	44444443355	LNNNNNNNFCCFNNNNNNNN	NNNN4NNNNNNNNNNN	R,T	041	403	06.04.15	8725	000000	98502
529.686-046	GENERAL HELPER (sugar & conf.)	1112	44444444355	HONONONFFNNNNNNNNNNN	NNNN4NNNNNNNNNNN	R	011	393	06.04.40	8618	000000	98999
529.686-050	LABORER, CHEESEMAKING (dairy products)	2112	44444444355	MNNONNNFFOONNNNONNNNN	NNNO4ONNNNNNNNNN	R,T	146	383	06.04.28	8769	000000	98502
529.686-054	LABORER, PIE BAKERY (bakery products)	2112	44544544344	MNNNNNNNFFFNNNNNFNON	NNNNN4NNNNNNNNNN	R	146	384	06.04.15	8725	000000	98999
529.686-062	LONG-GOODS HELPER, MACHINE (food prep., nec)	2112	44544534355	MNNIFNNNCCNNNNNNNNNN	NNNN4NNNNNNNNNNN	R	011	397	06.04.15	8725	000000	98502
529.686-066	PRESS MACHINE FEEDER (tobacco)	2112	44454544455	LNNNNNNNCCNNNNNNNNNN	NNNN4NNNNNNNNNNN	R	134	402	06.04.15	7667	000000	92971
529.686-070	PRODUCTION HELPER (can. & preserv.; food prep., nec)	2112	44444444355	MNNFNNNFFNNNNNNNNNN	NNNNN4NNNNNNNNNN	R,T	146	380	06.04.15	8725	000000	98502
529.686-074	RACK LOADER I (tobacco)	1112	44544544355	MNNNNNNNFFOONNNNNNNN	NNNNN4NNNNNNNNNN	R	011	404	06.04.40	8725	000000	98502
529.686-078	RAW-CHEESE WORKER (dairy products)	2112	44444444355	HNNONNNNFFONNNNONONNN	NNNNN4NOONNNNNNN	R	146	383	06.04.28	8769	000000	98999
529.686-082	STEAK TENDERIZER, MACHINE (meat products)	1112	44554544455	LNNNNNNNFFNNNNNFNNN	NNNNN4NNNNNNNNNN	R	146	382	06.04.15	8725	120506	98502
529.686-086	UTILITY WORKER (sugar & conf.)	2112	44544544455	LNNONNNCCNNNNNFNFNNN	NNNNN4NONNNNNNNN	R	011	393	06.04.15	8725	000000	98502
529.687-010	BASKET FILLER (can. & preserv.)	1111	44544544355	LNNNNNNNFFNNNNNNNNNN	NNNNN4NNNNNNNNNN	R	011	380	06.04.40	8769	000000	98999
529.687-014	BIN CLEANER (beverage; grain-feed mills)	1112	44443434354	MFFFFNFFNNNNNNNNNN	NNNNN4NONNNNNNON	R	031	381	06.04.39	8750	000000	98905
529.687-018	BOX-TRUCK WASHER (meat products)	1111	44455444355	MNNONONCCNNNNNNNNNN	NNNO4NONNNNNNNN	R	031	565	06.04.39	8750	000000	98905
529.687-022	BULK FILLER (can. & preserv.)	2123	44444444355	HNNNNNNNFFNNNNNONNNNN	NNNF4NNNNNNNNNNN	R,T	041	380	06.04.28	8761	000000	98902
529.687-026	CASING GRADER (meat products)	2112	44444443355	LNNNNNNNCCNNNNFNFNNN	NNNO4NNNNNNNNNNN	R,T	212	382	06.03.02	7850	120506	83005
529.687-030	CASING SEWER (meat products)	2112	44444434345	LNNNNNNNFFFNNNNFNFNN	NNNN3NNNNNNNNNNN	R	171	382	06.04.28	7752	120506	93923
529.687-034	CASING TIER (meat products)	1111	44544543355	LNNNNNNNFFONNNNNFNNN	NNNN3NNNNNNNNNNN	R	041	382	06.04.28	7740	000000	93999
529.687-038	CHAR-DUST CLEANER AND SALVAGER (sugar & conf.)	2112	44445445455	HNNNNNNNFFONNNNNNNNN	NONN3NFNNNNNNNNN	R,T	011	380	06.04.40	8769	000000	98999
529.687-042	CIGAR INSPECTOR (tobacco)	1112	44443444355	LNNNNNNNFFFNNNNFNFNN	NNNNN4NNNNNNNNNN	J,T	212	402	06.03.02	7820	000000	83005
529.687-046	COFFEE WEIGHER (food prep., nec)	1111	44444444345	HNNNNNNNFFONNNNNFNNN	NNNN3NNNNNNNNNN	R,T	212	391	06.03.02	7840	000000	83005
529.687-050	COOK HELPER (can. & preserv.)	2223	44444444355	MNNNONONFFONNNNNNNNN	NNNO3ONNNNNNNNN	R,T	146	380	06.04.28	8618	200409	98999
529.687-054	COOKER CLEANER (can. & preserv.)	1112	44444534355	MNNFFFNFFNNNNNNNNNNN	NNNF4NNNNNNNNNN	R	031	567	06.04.39	8750	000000	98905
529.687-058	DEFLECTOR OPERATOR (beverage)	2112	44444443355	LNNNNNNNFFNNNNNFNFFNN	NNNNN4NNNNNNNNNN	R,T	212	382	06.03.02	7820	000000	83005
529.687-062	DIE CLEANER (food prep., nec)	2123	44444434354	HNNONNNFFONNNNFNOOON	NNNF3NNNNNNNNNN	R	031	395	06.03.02	7820	000000	98905
529.687-066	DISTILLERY WORKER, GENERAL (beverage)	2112	44544543355	HNNOOOFFNNNNNNNNNN	NNNO4NNNNNNNNNN	R	011	567	06.04.40	8750	000000	98999
529.687-070	DISTRIBUTOR-CLEANER (tobacco)	1111	44454444345	HNNONNNCCONNNNNNFNNFN	NNNN3NNNNNNNNNN	R	031	454	06.04.40	8769	000000	98999
529.687-074	EGG CANDLER (any industry)	2112	44443444353	LNNNNNNNCCCCNNFNNFFN	NNNNN4NNNNNNNNNN	J,T	212	382	06.03.01	7820	000000	79011
529.687-078	FILLER-SHREDDER HELPER (tobacco)	2112	45444444355	MMNONNNFFNNNNNNNNON	NNNNN3NNNNNNNNNN	R	054	402	06.04.28	8618	000000	98999
529.687-082	FISH-BIN TENDER (can. & preserv.)	2112	44454444444	MOOONNNFFONNNNNNNNNN	NFNC3NNNNNNNNNN	R,T	041	386	06.04.28	7850	000000	83005
529.687-086	FISH-EGG PACKER (can. & preserv.)	1112	44544543354	MNNFNNNFFNNNNFNNNN	NNNO3NCNNNNNNNN	R	031	386	06.04.28	8761	000000	98902
529.687-090	FRESH-WORK INSPECTOR (tobacco)	2223	44444444354	LNNNNNNNFFFNNNNFNNNN	NNNNN4NNNNNNNNNN	J,T	212	401	06.03.02	7820	000000	83005
529.687-094	GENERAL HELPER (oils & grease)	1112	44545454355	MNNNNNNNFFONNNNNNNNN	NNNO3NNNNNNNNNN	R	011	475	06.04.40	8769	000000	98999
529.687-098	GRADER (can. & preserv.)	2123	44443444353	LNNNNNNNCCCCNNFFNNFFN	NONO4NOONNNNNNN	J,R,T	212	386	06.03.02	7850	000000	83005

DOT #	DOT Title & Industry	Trng	Aptitude	Physical	Environment	Tempra	WkF	MPSMS	GOE	SOC	CIP	OES
529.687-102	GRADER, DRESSED POULTRY (meat products)	2123	44444443353	LNNNNNNFFOFNNNFNNFFN	NONO4NOONNNNNNN	J,T	212	382	06.03.02	7850	120506	83005
529.687-106	GRADER, GREEN MEAT (meat products)	2123	34443444355	LNNNNNNCCFFNNNFFFNNN	NNNO4NNNNNNNNNN	J,T	212	382	06.03.02	7850	120506	83005
529.687-110	GRAIN PICKER (grain-feed mills)	2222	44444444355	LNNNNNNFFNNNNFFNNFNN	NNNN3NNNNNNNNNN	J,T	145	301	06.03.02	7840	000000	79011
529.687-114	INSPECTOR (sugar & conf.)	2122	44444443355	LNNNNNNFFFNNNNFNNONN	NNNN3NNNNNNNNNN	R,T	212	367	06.03.02	7820	000000	83005
529.687-118	INSPECTOR, CANNED FOOD RECONDITIONING (can. & preserv.)	2124	44444444355	LNNNNNNFFNNNNFNNNNNN	NNNN3NNNNNNNNNN	R	212	387	06.03.02	7820	000000	83005
529.687-122	KISS SETTER, HAND (sugar & conf.)	1114	44533433355	LNNNNNNCCONNNNFNNNNN	NNNN3NNNNNNNNNN	R	136	393	06.04.28	7740	200409	93999
529.687-126	KOSHER INSPECTOR (dairy products)	3112	43444444454	LNNNNNNNNNNNNOFNNNFN	ONNN3NNNNNNNNNN	R,T	212	383	06.03.02	7820	000000	98999
529.687-130	LABORER (meat products)	2112	34443444355	HNNFNFNFFONNNNNNNNNN	NONF3NNNNNNNNNN	R	011	382	06.04.40	8769	000000	98999
529.687-134	LEAF SORTER (tobacco)	2112	34443444453	LNNNNNNCCCNNNFNNNFN	NNNN3NNNNNNNNNN	R,T	212	382	06.03.02	7850	000000	83005
529.687-138	LEAF TIER (tobacco)	1111	44544544455	SNNNNNFFNNNNNNNNNNN	NNNN3NNNNNNNNNN	R	041	404	06.04.28	8726	000000	98799
529.687-142	LEAF-SIZE PICKER (tobacco)	1112	44444444455	LNNNNNNFFNNNNFNNNNN	NNNN3NNNNNNNNNN	R	212	403	06.03.02	7850	000000	83005
529.687-146	LIGHTOUT EXAMINER (beverage)	2123	44454444355	LNNFNNFCCCNNNNFNNNNN	NNOO3NONNNNNNNN	R	212	454	06.03.02	7820	000000	83005
529.687-150	LINKER (meat products)	2113	44435343355	MNNNNNNFFONNNNNNNNNN	NNNN3NNNNNNNNNN	R	041	382	06.04.28	8761	120506	98902
529.687-154	MAT SEWER (oils & grease)	2112	44544544455	LNNNNNNFFNNNNFNNNNN	NNNN3NNNNNNNNNN	R	171	429	06.04.27	7740	000000	93999
529.687-158	MELT-HOUSE DRAG OPERATOR (sugar & conf.)	2113	44444544455	MNNNNNNFFONNNNNNNNNN	NNNN3NNNNNNNNNN	R	011	392	06.04.40	7679	000000	92998
529.687-162	MOISTURE-METER OPERATOR (tobacco)	2222	33344344355	LNNNNNNFFNNNNFNFNNN	NNNN3NNNNNNNNNN	R,T	212	404	06.03.02	7830	000000	83005
529.687-166	ODD BUNDLE WORKER (tobacco)	1112	44544544455	LNNNNNNFFNNNNNNNNNN	NNNN4NNNNNNNNNN	R	061	403	06.04.15	8769	000000	98999
529.687-170	PRESS PULLER (grain-feed mills)	1112	44544544455	HONNNNNFFONNNNFNNNNN	NNNN3NONNNNNNNN	R	145	381	06.04.15	7666	000000	92962
529.687-174	SALVAGE INSPECTOR (can. & preserv.)	2113	44444443355	LNNNNNNFFONNNNFNNFNN	NNNN3NNNNNNNNNN	R	212	387	06.03.02	7820	000000	83005
529.687-178	SAMPLER (beverage)	2222	44454444455	LNNNNNNFFNNNNFNFNNN	NNNN3NNNNNNNNNN	R	011	395	06.04.40	7840	000000	83005
529.687-182	SHREDDED-FILLER HOPPER-FEEDER (tobacco)	2112	45544544455	MNNNNNOCNNNNCNNNCN	NNNN3NNNNNNNNNN	R	041	402	06.04.28	8725	000000	98502
529.687-186	SORTER, AGRICULTURAL PRODUCE (agriculture; can. & preserv.; wholesale tr.)	1112	44544544354	LNNNNNNOCNNNNCNNNCN	NNNN4NNNNNNNNNN	R	212	300	03.04.01	5625	010401	79011
529.687-190	STONE CLEANER (beverage)	2112	44544543355	LONOOONFFNNNNNNNNNN	NNNF3NNNNNNNNNN	R	031	539	06.04.39	8750	000000	98905
529.687-194	SUCTION-PLATE-CARRIER CLEANER (tobacco)	2112	44544544455	LNNNNNNFFNNNNFNFNN	NNNF3NNNNNNNNNN	R	031	568	06.04.39	8750	000000	98905
529.687-198	SUMATRA OPENER (tobacco)	1112	44444443355	LNNNNNNFFNNNNFNNNNN	NNNN3NNNNNNNNNN	R	041	404	06.04.28	7850	000000	83005
529.687-202	TEMPERATURE INSPECTOR (meat products)	2123	34454444355	MNNONONFFNNNNNNFFNN	ONNN4NNNNNNNNNN	R,T	212	573	06.03.02	8769	000000	98502
529.687-206	TROLLEY CLEANER (meat products)	1112	45544544355	MNNONONFFNNNNNNNNNN	NNNF3NNNNNNNNNON	R	031	565	06.04.39	8750	000000	98905
529.687-210	WASHER (grain-feed mills)	2112	44544544455	MNNNNNNFFNNNNNNNNNN	NNNF3NNNNNNNNNN	R	031	389	06.04.39	8750	000000	98905
529.687-214	WASHROOM CLEANER (sugar & conf.)	1112	44555443355	MNNNNNOCNNNNCNNNCN	ONNF3NNNNNNNNNN	R	031	303	06.04.39	8750	000000	98905
529.687-218	WRAPPER SELECTOR (tobacco)	2113	34343443353	HONNNNNFFNNNNFNONON	NNNF3NFNNNNNNNN	R,T	212	403	06.03.02	7850	000000	83005
529.687-222	WRAPPING MACHINE HELPER (tobacco)	1112	44544544455	MNNNNNNCCNNNNFNNNNN	NNNN4NNNNNNNNNN	R	041	403	06.04.28	8618	000000	98999
529.687-226	INSPECTOR, PROCESSING (sugar & conf.)	3224	33343344455	LNNNNNNFFNNNNFNNFNN	NNNF3NNNNNNNNNN	T	212	393	06.03.02	7820	150702	83005
529.687-230	LABORER, SHELLFISH PROCESSING (can. & preserv.)	2112	44444444455	HNNONNNCCCNNNNFNNNNN	NONO4NONNNNNNNN	R,T	212	386	06.04.40	8725	000000	98502
530.132-010	COATING-MIXER SUPERVISOR (paper & pulp)	4347	33333343354	LNNOONNFFNFFNNFNONON	NNNN4NNNNNNNNNN	D,J,T	143	590	06.04.01	7100	000000	81008
530.132-014	SUPERVISOR, BEATER ROOM (paper & pulp)	4447	33344344454	LNNNNNNFFONFFNFNNOON	NNNN3NNNNNNNNNN	V,D,P,J	147	471	06.02.01	7100	000000	81008
530.132-018	SUPERVISOR, WOOD ROOM (paper & pulp)	4347	33343344454	LONONONFFONFFNFNNFON	NNNN4NNONNNNNNN	V,D,P,J	142	451	06.02.01	7100	000000	81008
530.132-022	WOOD GRINDER, HEAD (paper & pulp)	4236	33433443354	LONONONFFONFFNFNNFON	NNOO4NNONNNNNNN	V,D,P,J	142	451	06.02.01	7100	000000	81008
530.261-010	COLOR DEVELOPER (paper & pulp)	4447	22333333342	MNNFNFNFFONONONONNNN	NNNN4NNNNNNNNNN	J,T	147	471	02.04.01	6869	000000	89999
530.382-010	PULP-REFINER OPERATOR (paper & pulp)	3324	34343443355	MNNNNNNFFONNNNONNNNN	NNNN4NNNNNNNNNN	J,T	147	471	06.02.14	7677	000000	92965
530.384-010	MIXER HELPER (concrete prod.)	2112	34434444355	LNNNNNNFFONNNNONNNNN	NNFN4NNNNNNNNNN	R	143	536	06.04.34	8618	000000	98999
530.582-010	PULPER, SYNTHETIC SOIL BLOCKS (paper & pulp)	3324	34343434354	HONNNNNFFNNNNFNONON	NNNF3NFNNNNNNNN	J,T	143	471	06.02.14	7664	000000	92965
530.662-010	BEATER ENGINEER (paper & pulp; tex. prod., nec)	3325	34344343354	MONONONFFONFFNFNNFON	NNNN4NNNNNNNNNN	R,T	147	471	06.02.18	7677	000000	92965
530.662-014	WOOD GRINDER OPERATOR (paper & pulp)	3225	34344343343	MNNNNNNFFONOONFNNFON	NNNF4NNNNNNNNNN	J,T	142	451	06.02.14	7677	000000	92965
530.665-010	BEATER-ENGINEER HELPER (paper & pulp; tex. prod., nec)	2222	44454444355	MNNOOONFFONOONFNNNNN	NNNO4NNNNNNNNNN	R,T	147	471	06.04.19	7664	000000	92944
530.665-014	RAG-CUTTING-MACHINE TENDER (paper & pulp; tex. prod., nec)	2212	44444434355	MNNFNFNFFNNOONONONNNO	NNNN4NNNNNNNNNNO	R	054	429	06.04.05	7678	000000	92944
530.666-010	RAG-CUTTING-MACHINE FEEDER (paper & pulp; tex. prod., nec)	2112	44444434455	MNNFNFNFFNNOONONONNNN	NNNN4NNNNNNNNNN	R	054	429	06.04.05	8725	000000	98502
530.682-010	PULP GRINDER AND BLENDER (paper & pulp; wood prod., nec)	3226	33333343354	LNNNNNNFFONNNNFNNFON	NNNN4NNONNNNNNN	J,T	147	456	06.02.14	7677	000000	92965
530.685-010	COATING-MIXER TENDER (paper & pulp)	2222	34344344355	HNNNNNNFFONNNNFNNFNN	NNFN3NNNNNNNNNN	T	143	471	06.04.14	7664	000000	92965
530.685-014	PULPER (paper & pulp; tex. prod., nec)	2212	44444544355	MOOONNNFFONCOONONONNN	NNNF4NNNNNNNNNO	R,T	142	471	06.04.14	7677	000000	92965
530.686-010	BEATER-AND-PULPER FEEDER (paper & pulp; tex. prod., nec)	2112	44454544354	MNNFNFNFFNNNNNNNNNN	NNNN4NNNNNNNNNN	R	142	471	06.04.14	8725	000000	98502
530.686-014	LOADER, MAGAZINE GRINDER (paper & pulp)	2112	44444443345	HNNFNNNFFNNNNNNNNNN	NNNN3NNNNNNNNNN	R	142	451	06.04.14	8725	000000	98502

DOT #	DOT Title & Industry	Trng	Aptitude	Physical	Environment	Tempra	WkF	MPSMS	GOE	SOC	CIP	OES
530.686-018	WASTE-PAPER-HAMMERMILL OPERATOR (paper & pulp)	1111	44554534355	LNNNNNNFFONNNNNNNNNN	NNNN3NNNNNNNNNN	R	054	473	06.04.14	8725	000000	98502
530.687-010	RAG INSPECTOR (paper & pulp)	2212	44443444354	LNNNNNNFFONNNNFNNNFN	NNNN3NNNNNNNNNN	R	212	429	06.03.02	7820	000000	83005
532.362-010	DIGESTER OPERATOR (paper & pulp; paper goods)	3336	33433444354	LONOOONFFONNNONNONNN	NNFF3NNNNNNNNNN	J,T	147	471	06.02.14	7679	000000	92998
532.585-010	MATRIX-DRIER TENDER (paper & pulp)	2223	44444444355	MNNNNNNFFOONNNONNONN	NNNN3NNNNNNNNNN	R,T	141	473	06.02.14	7675	000000	92923
532.685-010	BACK TENDER, INSULATION BOARD (wood prod., nec)	2112	44444444455	LOOFNNNFFNNNNNONNONN	NNNN3NFNNNNNNNN	R,T	141	473	06.04.14	7675	000000	92923
532.685-014	COOKER TENDER (paper & pulp)	2113	44444434355	MNNNNNNFFNNNNNNNNNNN	NNNN3NNNNNNNNNN	R,T	147	451	06.04.11	7679	000000	92962
532.685-018	EVAPORATOR OPERATOR (paper & pulp)	2212	44444444355	LNNNNNNFFONNNNNONNONN	NNNN3NFNNNNNNNN	R,T	144	499	06.04.14	7676	000000	92962
532.685-022	MOISTURE-CONDITIONER OPERATOR (paper & pulp)	2214	44444434355	MNNONNNFFONNNNNNNNNN	NNNN4NNNNNNNNNN	R,T	147	470	06.04.14	7679	000000	92998
532.685-026	PULP-PRESS TENDER (paper & pulp)	2123	44544544355	LNNNNNNFFNNNNNNNNNNN	NNNF3NNONNNNNNO	R	145	471	06.04.14	7667	000000	92971
532.686-010	DIGESTER-OPERATOR HELPER (paper & pulp; paper goods)	2212	44444544355	LOOOONFFONNNNNNFNNN	NNNN3NFNNNNNNNN	R	147	471	06.04.18	8725	000000	98502
532.686-014	PAPER-CONE-DRYING-MACHINE OPERATOR (paper goods)	1111	44544544455	LNNNNNNFFNNNNNNNNNNN	NNNN3NNNNNNNNNN	R	141	474	06.04.18	7675	000000	92923
532.687-010	LABEL DRIER (recording)	2112	44444444454	LNNNNNNFFONNNNFNNNON	NNNN4NNNNNNNNNN	R	141	474	06.04.34	7675	000000	92923
533.362-010	BLEACHER, PULP (paper & pulp)	3335	34434434354	MNONNNNFFONNNNFNNNON	NNNN3NFNNNNNNNN	J,T	147	471	06.02.14	7673	000000	92958
533.665-010	BLOW-PIT OPERATOR (paper & pulp)	2113	44444544355	MOONNNNFFNOONNNNNNNN	NNNO3NOONNNNNNN	R	145	471	06.04.14	7673	000000	92958
533.682-010	DECKER OPERATOR (paper & pulp)	3224	34434444355	LNNNNNNFFONNNNFNNNNN	NNNF3NNNNNNNNNN	R,T	145	471	06.02.14	7666	000000	92962
533.685-010	BLEACH-BOILER FILLER (paper & pulp)	2212	44544444454	LNNNNNNFFONNNNNNNNNN	NNNF3NONNNNNNNN	R	147	429	06.04.14	7673	000000	92958
533.685-014	BROWN-STOCK WASHER (paper & pulp)	2212	44544444354	NNNF3NONNNNNNNN	NNNF3NONNNNNNN	R,T	145	471	06.04.14	7673	000000	92958
533.685-018	SAVE-ALL OPERATOR (paper & pulp)	2112	44444434355	LNNNNNNFFONNNNNNNNNN	NNNO4NNNNNNNNNN	R,T	145	471	06.04.14	7676	000000	92962
533.685-022	SCREEN TENDER (paper & pulp)	3214	44444444354	MNNFNFNFFONNNFNNNON	NNNC4NNONNNNNNF	R,T	145	471	06.04.18	7666	000000	92962
533.685-026	SCREEN TENDER, CHIPS (paper & pulp)	2113	44544544355	MNNNNNNFFONNNNNNNNNN	ONNN4NNNNNNNNNN	R	145	471	06.04.03	7666	000000	92962
533.685-030	THRASHER FEEDER (paper & pulp)	2112	44544544355	LNNNNNNFFONNNNNNNNNN	NNNN3NONNNNNNNN	R	145	429	06.04.05	7679	000000	92998
533.685-034	WASHER ENGINEER (paper & pulp)	2213	44444444355	LNNONONFFONNNNONNNNN	NNNO3NNNNNNNNNN	R,T	147	429	06.04.14	7673	000000	92958
533.686-010	BLOW-PIT HELPER (paper & pulp)	2112	44544544455	MNNNONNFFNNNNNNNNNNN	NNNF4NONNNNNNNN	R	145	471	06.04.14	8618	000000	98999
533.686-014	WASHER-ENGINEER HELPER (paper & pulp)	2112	44544444345	MNNONONFFNNNNONONNNN	NNNN4NNNNNNNNNN	R	147	429	06.04.14	8618	000000	98999
533.687-010	SCREEN-TENDER HELPER (paper & pulp)	2112	44564534455	MONONNNFFONNNNNNNNNN	NNNF3NNNNNNNNNN	R	145	471	06.04.14	8618	000000	98999
534.130-010	SUPERVISOR, COATING (photo. appar.)	4337	33343333355	LNNNNNNFFONFFNFNNNN	NNNN3NNNNNNNNNN	V,D,P,J	151	606	06.02.01	7100	000000	81008
534.132-010	SUPERVISOR, CALENDERING (paper & pulp)	4348	33333334344	LNNNNNNFFOFFNFNOOON	NNNN4NNNNNNNNNN	D,P,T,V	032	470	06.02.04	7100	000000	81008
534.132-014	SUPERVISOR, PAPER COATING (paper & pulp; paper goods)	4348	33333334344	LNNONONFFNFFNFNOOON	NNNN4NNNNNNNNNNO	V,D,P,T	153	470	06.02.01	7100	000000	81008
534.137-010	SUPERVISOR, CARBON-PAPER-COATING (pen & pencil)	4347	33333344455	LNNNNNNFFNFFNFNNNNN	NNNN4NNNNNNNNNN	D,P,V,J	147	474	06.02.01	7100	000000	81008
534.380-010	CARBON-PAPER-COATING-MACHINE SETTER (pen & pencil)	3335	33433334355	HNNFFNFFONNNNFNNONN	NNNN3NNONNNNNNN	J,T	153	617	06.01.02	7343	000000	91923
534.482-010	WAXING-MACHINE OPERATOR (paper goods)	3225	34433434354	HNNNONNFFOONNFNNNON	NNNN3NNONNNNNNN	J,T	153	470	06.02.14	7669	000000	92953
534.565-010	OVEN TENDER (ordnance)	2212	44444444355	HNNONONFFOONNNFNNNON	NNCN3NFNNNNNNNN	R,T	147	475	06.04.14	7675	000000	92923
534.582-010	PAPER-COATING-MACHINE OPERATOR (photo. appar.)	3325	34343334355	MONONONFFONNNNONNOON	NNOF4NNNNNNNNNO	J,T	151	606	06.02.14	7669	000000	92953
534.662-010	BACK TENDER, PAPER MACHINE (paper & pulp)	3336	34433433354	MNNOOONFFOOOONFNOFON	NNNF4NONNNNNNNN	J,T,V	141	470	06.02.14	7679	000000	92998
534.665-010	SCREEN TENDER (paper & pulp; wood prod., nec)	2123	44435444344	LONONONFFONOONFNOON	NNNF4NNNNNNNNNN	R,T	145	471	06.04.14	7679	000000	92998
534.682-010	AIR-DRIER-MACHINE OPERATOR (paper & pulp)	3225	34443434354	MNNFFNFFONNNNFNNONN	NNFN4NNNNNNNNNN	J,T	151	474	06.02.14	7669	000000	92953
534.682-014	CARBON-COATER-MACHINE OPERATOR (pen & pencil)	3223	34343444355	HNNNNONFFOONNFNNNON	NNNN3NNNNNNNNNN	J,T	151	617	06.02.21	7669	000000	92953
534.682-018	COATING-MACHINE OPERATOR (paper & pulp; paper goods)	3224	34433434354	MONONONFFONNNNONNOON	NNNN4NNNNNNNNNN	J,T	151	470	06.02.14	7669	000000	92953
534.682-022	COATING-MACHINE OPERATOR, HARDBOARD (paper goods; wood prod., nec)	3224	34433444354	MNNFNFNFFONNNNONNOON	NNNN3NFNNNNNNNN	J,T	153	473	06.02.14	7669	000000	92953
534.682-026	COMBINER OPERATOR (paper & pulp; paper goods)	3224	34433444354	MONONNNFFONNNNONNOOON	NNNN4NNNNNNNNNN	J,T	063	473	06.02.09	7479	000000	92997
534.682-030	CREPING-MACHINE OPERATOR (paper goods)	3223	34433444355	LONONONFFONNNNFFNONN	NNNN3NNNNNNNNNN	R,T	147	474	06.02.14	7679	000000	92998
534.682-034	STRAP-MACHINE OPERATOR (paper goods)	3224	34433444343	LOOOOONFFONNNNFFNOON	NNNN3NNNNNNNNNN	R,T	063	474	06.02.05	7669	000000	92953
534.682-038	SUPERCALENDER OPERATOR (paper & pulp)	3225	34433444343	MNNOONFFONNNNFFNOON	NNNC4NNNNNNNNNN	J,T	032	470	06.02.04	7667	000000	92953
534.685-010	DAMPENER OPERATOR (paper & pulp)	2212	44543534355	HNNONNNFFONNNNFFNOON	NNON4NNNNNNNNNN	R,T	152	470	06.04.21	7679	000000	92971
534.685-014	FRICTION-PAINT-MACHINE TENDER (fabrication, nec)	2112	44444433344	HNNONNNFFONNNFNNONN	NNON4NONNNNNNNN	R,T	153	619	06.04.21	7679	000000	92998
534.685-018	OILING-MACHINE OPERATOR (paper & pulp; paper goods)	2113	44443444354	LNNNNNNFFONNNNNFNONN	NNNN3NNNNNNNNNN	R,T	151	473	06.04.14	7669	000000	92953
534.685-022	PAPER COATER (paper & pulp; paper goods)	2112	44544544455	LNNNNNNFFONNNNFNNONN	NNNN3NNONNNNNNN	R,T	152	470	06.04.14	7669	000000	92953
534.685-026	PARAFFIN-MACHINE OPERATOR (paper goods)	2112	44444544355	LNNNNNNNFFONNNNFNNNON	NNNN3NNNNNNNNNN	R	153	475	06.04.21	7669	000000	92953
534.685-030	VARNISHING-MACHINE OPERATOR (print. & pub.)	2212	44443543355	LNNNNNNFFONNNNFNNNNN	NNNN3NNNNNNNNNN	R	153	474	06.04.14	7669	000000	92953
534.685-034	WET-END HELPER (wood prod., nec)	2222	44443444344	LFNFNNNFFONNNNNFNFON	NNNN4NNONNNNNNN	R,T	153	473	06.04.14	7679	000000	92998
534.686-010	PAPER-PROCESSING-MACHINE HELPER (paper & pulp; paper goods)	2112	44544544355	HNNOOONFFONONONONNNN	NNNO4NNNNNNNNNN	R	151	470	06.04.14	8618	000000	98899

DOT #	DOT Title & Industry	Trng	Aptitude	Physical	Environment	Tempra	WkF	MPSMS	GOE	SOC	CIP	OES
534.687-010	CONE TREATER (paper goods)	2112	44544544455	MNNNNNNFFONNNNNNNNNN	NNNN3NNNNNNNN	R	152	475	06.04.14	8769	000000	98999
534.687-014	CREPING-MACHINE-OPERATOR HELPER (paper goods)	2212	44443444355	HNNNNNNFFONNNNNNNNNN	NNNN4NNNNNNNN	R	147	474	06.04.40	8618	000000	98999
535.482-010	WAD-COMPRESSOR OPERATOR-ADJUSTER (ordnance)	3324	34333344335	LNNOOONFFONNNNFNNONN	NNNC4NNNNNNNN	J,T	134	474	06.02.18	7663	000000	92971
535.685-010	PLATE WORKER (paper & pulp)	2222	44544444355	MNNNNNNFFONNNNNNNNNN	NNFF3NONNNNNNN	R	134	473	06.04.04	7667	000000	92971
539.130-010	SUPERVISOR, HARDBOARD (wood prod., nec)	4347	33333334354	LFNNNNNFFFFFNFNNFON	NNCN4NNNNNNNNN	V,D,P,J	142	471	06.02.01	7100	000000	81008
539.130-014	SUPERVISOR, WET ROOM (paper & pulp)	4438	33333333455	LFNNNNNFFONFFNFNNNN	NNNF4NNNNNNNNN	V,D,P,J	145	471	06.02.01	7100	000000	81008
539.131-010	SUPERVISOR, WET END (wood prod., nec)	4337	33333433354	LNNONONFFONFFNOONNOO	NNNN3NNNNNNNNN	V,D,P,J	147	471	06.02.01	7100	000000	81008
539.132-010	SUPERVISOR, PAPER MACHINE (paper & pulp)	4337	33333433354	LOOOOONFFONFFNFNNON	NNOO4NNNNNNNNN	V,D,P,J	163	470	06.02.01	7100	000000	81008
539.132-014	SUPERVISOR, PULP PLANT (paper & pulp)	4448	33343343354	LOOOOONFFOOFFNFNNON	NNNN4NNNNNNNNN	V,D,P,J	147	471	06.01.01	7100	000000	81008
539.132-018	SUPERVISOR, REPULPING (paper & pulp)	4348	33333344454	LNNNNNNFFNFFNFNOOON	NNNN4NNNNNNNNN	D,P,T,J	147	471	06.02.01	7100	000000	81008
539.134-010	SUPERVISOR, PAPER TESTING (paper & pulp; paper goods)	4448	23343344454	LNNNNNNFFNFFNFNNFON	NNNN4NNNNNNNNN	D,P,T,V	212	470	06.02.01	7100	000000	81008
539.137-010	SUPERVISOR, RAG ROOM (paper & pulp)	3335	34343344454	LNNNNNOOONFFNONNNNN	NNNN3NNNNNNNNN	V,D,P,J	054	429	06.04.01	7100	000000	81008
539.137-014	PRODUCTION SUPERVISOR (nonmet. min.)	4346	33333344455	LNNNNNOOONFFNOONNNN	NNNN3NNNNNNNNN	D,V,P,J	142	473	06.02.01	7100	490299	81008
539.362-010	CYLINDER-MACHINE OPERATOR (paper & pulp; wood prod., nec)	3236	33433434344	LONNNNNNFFOOFFNFOOON	NNNF3NNNNNNNNN	J,T	147	473	06.02.18	7679	000000	92998
539.362-014	FOURDRINIER-MACHINE OPERATOR (paper & pulp; paper goods)	3236	33433434354	MONONNNFFOOFFNFOOON	NNFF4NNNNNNNNN	J,T	147	472	06.02.14	7679	000000	92998
539.362-018	SLURRY MIXER (ordnance)	3224	34444434344	MNNONONFFONOONFNNNON	NNNN4NFNNNNNNN	J,T	142	456	06.02.18	7679	000000	92998
539.364-010	PULP-AND-PAPER TESTER (paper & pulp)	3335	33332343353	LNNNNNNFFNOONFNNFFN	NNNN3NNNNNNNNN	J,T	212	471	06.03.01	7830	000000	83005
539.367-010	FINAL INSPECTOR, PAPER (paper & pulp)	3335	34444344454	LNNNNNNFFONFFNFNNFON	NNNN3NNNNNNNNN	V,J,T	212	470	06.03.01	7820	000000	83005
539.367-014	WATER-QUALITY TESTER (paper & pulp)	3335	33332343353	LNNOOONFFNOONFNFFON	NNNN4NNNNNNNNN	J,T	212	874	05.07.04	7820	000000	83005
539.387-010	CHIP TESTER (paper & pulp)	3323	34444344455	LFNFFFNFFNNNNFNOONN	NNNN4NNNNNNNNN	J,T	212	459	06.03.01	7840	000000	83005
539.482-010	CALENDER OPERATOR, INSULATION BOARD (wood prod., nec)	3214	33333344353	LFNONNNFFONNNNONNOON	NNNN3NNNNNNNNN	J,T	032	473	06.02.09	7669	000000	92953
539.485-010	WEIGHT TESTER (paper & pulp)	3332	34354344455	SNNNNNNFFONNNNNNNNN	NNNN3NNNNNNNNN	R,T	231	470	06.03.01	7840	000000	83005
539.487-010	INSPECTOR, FIBROUS WALLBOARD (wood prod., nec)	3324	33333443354	LOONNNNNFFONNNFNNFON	NNNN3NNNNNNNNN	J,T	212	473	06.03.01	7820	000000	83005
539.565-010	HIGH-DENSITY FINISHING OPERATOR (wood prod., nec)	3223	34433434354	MNNNNNNFFNNNNFFOOOF	NNNN3NFNNNNNNN	J,T	153	473	06.02.18	7479	000000	92997
539.565-010	VULCANIZED-FIBER-UNIT OPERATOR (paper goods)	3335	34433434344	MNNFNNNFFNOONFNFNON	NNNF4NNNNNNNNNF	J,T	136	472	06.02.04	7667	000000	92971
539.587-010	LABORER, RAGS (paper & pulp)	2112	44444444355	LNNNNNNFFONNNNONFNNN	NNNN4NNNNNNNNN	R	011	470	06.04.40	8769	000000	98999
539.667-010	CONTROL INSPECTOR (paper & pulp; wood prod., nec)	3224	34332344453	LNNNNNNFFONONOONFNNFON	NNNN3NNNNNNNNN	R,T	212	473	06.03.02	7820	000000	83005
539.685-010	COATER OPERATOR, INSULATION BOARD (wood prod., nec)	2212	44354344455	LNNNNNNFFONNNNFNNNNN	NNNN4NNNNNNNNN	R,T	153	473	06.04.21	7667	000000	92971
539.685-014	IMPREGNATION OPERATOR (paper goods)	2123	44444434354	LNNNNNNFFNNNNFNFNON	NNNN3NNNNNNNNN	R,T	152	470	06.04.09	7663	000000	92953
539.685-018	MOLDING-MACHINE TENDER (paper & pulp)	2213	44443443344	MNNNNNNFFNNNNNNFNNN	NNNO4NFNNNNNNN	R,T	132	470	06.04.09	7663	000000	92971
539.685-022	PUMP-PRESS OPERATOR (paper & pulp)	3224	44544434345	LONOONFFONNNNFNNONN	NNON3NNNNNNNNN	J,T	147	471	06.04.14	7663	000000	92971
539.685-026	SCREEN HANDLER (paper & pulp)	2112	44544444345	HOOOOONFFONNNNFNNNNN	NNFN4NNNNNNNNN	R	134	473	06.04.14	7663	000000	92965
539.685-030	WET-MACHINE TENDER (paper & pulp)	2223	44444434355	LONONONFFNFFNFNFFON	NNNC4NNNNNNNNN	R,T	135	471	06.04.14	7663	000000	92971
539.686-010	CUTTER, WET MACHINE (paper & pulp)	2112	44454434355	MFFNNNNFFNNNNNNNNNN	NNNN4NNONNNNNO	R	135	471	06.04.14	8725	000000	98502
539.687-010	WINDER HELPER (paper & pulp)	2213	44545544355	LNNFNNNFFONNNNFNFFON	NNNO4NNONNNNNO	R	163	470	06.04.14	7679	000000	92998
540.382-010	COMPOUNDER (petrol. refin.)	3337	44544544355	LONOONFFNFFNFNFFON	NNON3NNNNNNNNN	J,T	147	501	06.02.12	7664	000000	92965
540.462-010	BLENDER (petrol. refin.)	3326	33334433354	LONONONFFNFFNFNNFON	FNNN4NOONNNNNN	J,T	143	500	06.02.12	7664	000000	92965
540.585-010	MIXER OPERATOR, CARBON PASTE (elec. equip.; smelt. & refin.)	2224	33334444344	LNNNNNNFFONNNNONNNN	NNNN4NOONNNNNN	R,T	143	340	06.04.19	7664	000000	92965
540.686-010	COMPOUNDER HELPER (petrol. refin.)	2222	44444444355	MFFNNNNFFONNNNONNNN	ONNN4NOONNNNNO	R	147	501	06.04.12	8618	000000	98999
540.687-010	SEAL MIXER (elec. equip.)	2222	44454444454	LNNFNNNFFONNNNFNFFON	NNNO4NNNNNNNNN	R,T	143	499	06.04.34	8769	000000	98999
541.362-010	DESULFURIZER OPERATOR (steel & rel.)	4326	33433433354	MFNNNNNFFONOONFNOOFN	FNNN4NONNNNNNN	J,T	147	509	06.02.11	7666	000000	92962
541.362-014	PUMP OPERATOR, BYPRODUCTS (steel & rel.)	3225	33434334355	LONNNNNFFONOONFNOONN	NNNO4NONNNNNNN	J,T	147	509	06.02.17	7666	000000	92962
541.382-010	COAL WASHER (mine & quarry)	3225	34434334354	LNNOOONCCCONNNNCCCOC	NNNN4NONNNNNNN	R,T	145	341	06.02.18	7666	000000	92962
541.382-014	CRUDE-OIL TREATER (petrol. & gas)	3335	33333333354	LOOOOONFFNNNFNFNFON	NNNN4NONNNNNNN	J,T	145	342	06.02.12	7666	000000	92962
541.585-010	CENTRIFUGE-SEPARATOR TENDER (nonfer. metal)	2224	44445434355	LNNNNNNCCCONNNNONNONN	NNNN4NONNNNNNN	R,T	145	568	06.04.12	7666	000000	92962
541.665-010	SHAKER TENDER (steel & rel.)	2213	44454544355	LFNNNNNFFNNFFNFNNFON	NNNN4NNNNNNNNN	R	145	505	06.04.12	7666	000000	92962
541.682-010	PARAFFIN-PLANT OPERATOR (petrol. refin.)	3225	34443444354	LOONNNNNFONNNNNNNNNN	NNNN4NNNNNNNNN	J,T	145	501	06.02.12	7666	000000	92962
541.685-010	HEAVY-MEDIA OPERATOR (mine & quarry)	2113	44543544355	MNNNNNNFFONNNNNNNNN	NNNN4NNNNNNNNN	R,T	145	341	06.04.08	7666	000000	92962
541.685-014	LEAD RECOVERER, CONTINUOUS-NAPHTHA-TREATING PLANT (petrol. refin.)	3224	34434444355	MOONNNNNFFNNNNNNNNNN	ONNN4NNNNNNNNN	R,T	145	499	06.04.12	7666	000000	92962
542.130-010	SUPERVISOR, NATURAL-GAS PLANT (petrol. refin.)	4348	23333333354	LOOOOOOOOONFFNONFONN	NNNO4NNONNNNNO	V,D,P,J	144	501	05.06.04	6700	520205	81008
542.130-014	SUPERVISOR, TAR DISTILLATION (chemical)	4347	23333333354	LONNNNNFFONOONFNOOON	ONON4NONNNNNNN	V,D,P,J	144	509	06.01.01	7100	000000	81008

DOT #	DOT Title & Industry	Trng	Aptitude	Physical	Environment	Tempra	WkF	MPSMS	GOE	SOC	CIP	OES
542.132-010	SUPERVISOR, BYPRODUCTS (steel & rel.)	4347	33334333355	LONNNNNFFONOONFNFNFN	NNON4NOONNNNNON	V,D,P,J	147	499	06.04.01	7100	000000	81008
542.132-014	SUPERVISOR, OVENS (steel & rel.)	4348	33333333353	LONNNNNOOONFFNFONFON	ONNN4NOONNNNNNN	V,D,P,J	147	505	06.04.01	7100	000000	81008
542.362-010	HEATER II (steel & rel.)	3226	33333444453	LFFFNFFNOONNNNNFON	FNON4NOONNNNNON	J,T	147	505	06.02.17	7675	000000	92923
542.362-014	REFINERY OPERATOR HELPER (petrol. refin.)	3226	34343444344	LFFFNFFNOONNNFFFN	FNON4NOONNNNNON	J,T	147	501	06.02.12	8619	000000	98999
542.562-010	FURNACE OPERATOR (petrol. refin.)	3226	33434444354	MFFFFFNFFNOONFNFOF	ONFN4NOONNNNNON	J,T	144	501	06.02.12	7675	000000	92923
542.567-010	COKE INSPECTOR (steel & rel.)	3224	33432434443	LONONNNFFONOONFFFON	NNON4NOONNNNNON	R,T	212	505	06.03.02	7820	000000	83005
542.665-010	OVEN-HEATER HELPER (steel & rel.)	2223	44444444353	MONNNNNFFNNOONFNFON	NNON4NOONNNNNON	R,T	147	505	06.04.12	8618	000000	98999
542.667-010	WHARF TENDER (steel & rel.)	1112	44444544355	HNNONNNFFNNOONNFNNN	FNNO4NOONNNNNON	R	011	505	06.04.12	8726	000000	98799
542.685-010	PLANT OPERATOR, CHANNEL PROCESS (chemical)	3222	34433444453	LNNNNNFFNNNNNNNFNON	ONNN4NNNNNNNNNN	R,T	147	499	06.04.19	7675	000000	92923
542.685-014	SUBLIMER (chemical)	2213	44444444455	LNNNNNFFONNNNNOOONN	NNNN4NNNNNNNNNN	R,T	144	496	06.04.11	7676	000000	92962
542.685-018	UNIT OPERATOR (chemical)	3213	34444434355	LONNNNNFFOONNNONNNN	NNFN4NNNNNNNNNN	R,T	147	499	06.04.19	7675	000000	92923
543.362-010	OIL BOILER (tex. prod., nec)	3325	33333344345	HNNNNNFFOONNNONOONN	ONNN4NOONNNNNON	J,T	133	509	06.02.18	7675	000000	92923
543.382-010	DRIER OPERATOR (utilities)	3224	34434444355	MNNNNNFFONNNNNONONN	NNNN4NNNNNNNNNN	R,T	141	341	06.02.08	7675	000000	92923
543.562-010	CARBON-FURNACE OPERATOR (smelt. & refin.)	3225	33334434344	LFNFNNNFFNNOONFNFNFN	NNON4NOONNNNNON	J,T	141	355	06.02.18	7675	000000	98999
543.664-010	CARBON-FURNACE-OPERATOR HELPER (smelt. & refin.)	3223	44434544345	MFNFNNNFFNNNNNNNFFN	NNON4NOONNNNNON	R,T	141	355	06.04.19	8618	000000	93999
543.666-010	FURNACE WORKER (elec. equip.)	2222	44443534354	MNNNNNFFNNNNNNNFFON	ONON4NNNNNNNNNN	R,T	141	582	06.04.19	7759	000000	92923
543.682-014	COKE BURNER (steel & rel.)	3325	33433433353	MNNNNNFFONNNNNONFNN	NNNN4NNNNNNNNNN	J,T	147	505	06.02.17	7675	000000	92923
543.682-014	DRIER OPERATOR (mine & quarry)	3224	34443434354	LNNNNNNNFFNNNNNNFNFN	ONON4NONNNNNNNN	J,T	141	340	06.04.10	7675	000000	92923
543.682-018	FURNACE OPERATOR (elec. equip.)	3223	34444434355	LOONNNNFONNNNONNNN	NNNN4NNNNNNNNNN	J,T	131	582	06.04.10	7666	000000	92962
543.682-022	PARAFFIN-PLANT-SWEATER OPERATOR (petrol. refin.)	3224	34444434354	LONONNNFFONNNNNONFNN	NNNN4NNNNNNNNNN	J,T	131	501	06.02.12	7676	000000	92962
543.682-026	STILL OPERATOR (build. mat., nec)	3225	33233434355	LNNNNNFFONNNNNNFNFN	NNON3NOONNNNNNO	J,T	131	503	06.03.02	7830	150702	83005
543.684-010	QUALITY-CONTROL TESTER (fabrication, nec)	3233	44444344454	LNNNNNFFOONNNFNFNN	NNNN3NNNNNNNNNN	T	211	504	06.04.19	7679	000000	92965
543.685-010	BULLET-LUBRICANT MIXER (ordnance)	2212	44544544455	MMNFNONFFNNNNNONONNN	NNON4NNNNNNNNNN	R,T	131	499	06.04.19	7675	000000	92923
543.685-014	DRIER TENDER (fabrication, nec)	2223	44434443355	LNNNNNFFOONNNFNFNN	NNNN4NNNNNNNNNN	R,T	133	504	06.04.12	7675	000000	92923
543.685-018	OVEN TENDER (elec. equip.)	2223	44544544355	MMNONNNFFNNNNNNNNNN	NNFN3NONNNNNNNN	R,T	133	582	06.04.19	7675	000000	92965
543.685-022	THAW-SHED HEATER TENDER (steel & rel.)	2214	44544544455	MMNONNNFFNNNNNNNNNN	ONNN4NONNNNNNNN	R,T	141	341	06.04.12	7675	000000	92923
543.687-010	COKE DRAWER, HAND (steel & rel.)	1112	44544544455	MONNNNNFFNNNNNNNNNN	NNNN4NNNNNNNNNN	U	011	505	05.12.03	8769	000000	98999
543.687-014	OVEN DAUBER (steel & rel.)	2112	44344443355	MMNONNNCCONNNNONONNN	ONON4NONNNNNNNN	R	094	568	06.04.30	8769	000000	98999
544.565-010	GRINDER, CARBON PLANT (smelt. & refin.)	3214	34443434355	MNOOONCFONNNNNONONNN	NNNN4NOONNNNNNN	R,T	142	505	06.04.12	7677	000000	92965
544.582-010	CRUSHER-AND-BLENDER OPERATOR (steel & rel.)	3224	34443444355	MOOOONFFONNNNNONONNN	NNNN4OOONNNNOON	R,T	142	341	06.02.08	7677	000000	92965
544.585-010	MIX-CRUSHER OPERATOR (elec. equip.)	2112	44544444355	MMNFNNNFFONNNNONFNNN	NNNN4NANNNNNNNN	R	142	584	06.04.09	7677	000000	92965
544.662-010	COKE-CRUSHER OPERATOR (steel & rel.)	3214	33433434355	MMNNNNNFFNNOONFNNNNN	FNNN4NOONNNNNNN	R,T	142	505	06.02.08	7677	000000	92965
544.665-010	MILL-AND-COAL-TRANSPORT OPERATOR (utilities)	2223	44444444445	LFNNNNNFFNNNNNNNNNNN	NNNN4NFNNNNNNNN	R,T	142	341	06.04.08	7677	000000	92965
544.685-010	BREAKER TENDER (steel & rel.)	2113	44544534455	LFNNNNNFFNNNNNNNNNNN	NNNN4NONNNNNNNN	R	142	505	06.04.12	7677	000000	92965
546.382-010	CONTROL-PANEL OPERATOR (petrol. refin.)	3327	33433334354	LNNNNNNFFNFFNFNNOFN	NNNN3NONNNNNOFN	J,T	147	500	06.02.01	6950	000000	95014
546.385-010	GAS TREATER (any industry)	3324	34434344344	LNNOOONFFNNNNNOONOON	ONNN4NOONNNNNNO	J,T	147	501	06.02.12	7676	000000	92938
549.130-010	SUPERVISOR, TOWER (petrol. refin.)	4347	33324344343	LOOONONOOQFNFNFFFFFF	NNON4NOONNNNNON	V,D,P,J	147	501	06.01.01	6700	520205	81008
549.131-010	SUPERVISOR, NATURAL-GAS-FIELD PROCESSING (petrol. & gas; pipe lines)	4337	23333344355	LOOOOONFFONFFNFOOONN	FNNN4NNNNNNNNNF	D,J,P	147	501	06.01.01	7100	520205	81008
549.132-010	SUPERVISOR, GREASE MAKER, HEAD (petrol. refin.)	4448	33334444455	LNNNNNNFFONFFNFNNNNN	NNNN4NNNNNNNNNN	V,D,P,J	147	501	06.04.01	7100	520205	81008
549.132-014	SUPERVISOR III (fabrication, nec)	4337	33333333355	LONNNNNFFFFFNFNONNN	LONNN4NFNNNNNNN	V,D,P,J	147	504	06.04.01	7100	000000	81008
549.132-018	SUPERVISOR, COAL HANDLING (steel & rel.)	4338	33333343354	LONONONFFONFFNFOONON	FNNN4NFNNNNNNNN	V,D,P,J	147	341	06.04.01	7100	000000	81008
549.132-022	SUPERVISOR, COKE HANDLING (steel & rel.)	4347	33433344444	LFNOOOOFFONFFNFNNNNN	FNNN4NFFNNNNNNN	V,D,P,J	147	505	06.02.01	7100	000000	81008
549.132-026	SUPERVISOR, PASTE PLANT (steel & rel.)	4447	33433344354	LONONONFFNFNFNNOFON	ONON4NFNNNNNFON	V,D,P,J	147	500	06.01.01	7100	520205	81008
549.132-030	SUPERVISOR, PURIFICATION (petrol. refin.)	4348	23333334354	LONNNNNFFNFFNFNNOON	FNNN4NFFNNNNNNF	V,D,P,J	147	501	06.01.01	7100	000000	81008
549.132-034	SUPERVISOR, TREATING AND PUMPING (petrol. refin.)	4346	33333334355	LNNNNNNOOONFFNFNOONN	ONON4NONNNNNNNN	V,D,P,J	147	589	06.02.01	7100	520205	81008
549.137-010	SUPERVISOR, CARBON ELECTRODES (steel & rel.)	4337	33323344344	LONOOONFFNFFNFNOOON	FNON4NFNNNNNNNN	D,J,P	147	501	06.01.01	7100	150901	81008
549.137-014	SUPERVISOR, PREPARATION PLANT (mine & quarry)	4447	33333344445	LNNNNNNFFNFNFNFNONN	ONNN4NFNNNNNNNF	V,D,P	041	340	06.01.01	7100	520205	81008
549.137-018	SUPERVISOR, SPECIALTY PLANT (petrol. refin.)	4338	23333444354	LOOONONOOQFNFFFFFNN	FNON4NNNNNNNNNF	S,J,T,V	147	500	06.01.03	6950	150903	95014
549.260-010	REFINERY OPERATOR (petrol. refin.)	4337	33332344344	LONOONNFFONNNNFNNOON	FNNN4NNNNNNNONO	V,J,T	121	568	05.07.01	6881	470303	83002
549.261-010	MECHANICAL INSPECTOR (petrol. refin.)	4336	33334344354	MONONNNFFNOONFNNNON	NNNN4NFNNNNNNNF	J,T	014	501	06.02.12	6950	470501	95011

DOT #	DOT Title & Industry	Trng	Aptitude	Physical	Environment	Tempra	WkF	MPSMS	GOE	SOC	CIP	OES
549.362-010	STILL-PUMP OPERATOR (petrol. refin.)	3325	44444444355	MFOFONNFFNNOONNOONNN	FNNN4NFNNNNNNNF	R,T	014	501	06.02.12	7679	470501	97953
549.362-014	TREATER (petrol. refin.)	4337	33323344344	LONOOONFFNNNNFFNONON	FNNN4NFNNNNNNNF	J,T	147	500	06.02.12	7676	150903	92935
549.364-010	TESTER, COMPRESSED GASES (chemical)	3323	33333333343	MNNNNNNNFFNOONFNFFFN	NNNN3NNNNNNNNNN	J,T	212	491	06.03.01	7830	000000	83005
549.367-010	INSPECTOR (build. mat., nec)	3225	34443344343	MNNFNNNFFFOONFNNNFN	NNNN4NNNNNNNNNN	J,T	212	503	06.03.01	7820	000000	83005
549.382-010	NATURAL-GAS-TREATING-UNIT OPERATOR (petrol. & gas)	3326	33334344355	LONOOONFFONNNNFNNONN	FNNN4NCNNNNNNNC	J,T	147	500	06.02.12	7679	000000	92998
549.382-014	OIL-RECOVERY-UNIT OPERATOR (petrol. refin.)	3323	33334334345	HFNFFFNFFNNNNFNNNN	CNNN4NNNNNNNNNN	J,T	147	501	06.02.12	7676	000000	92962
549.382-018	WASH-OIL-PUMP OPERATOR (steel & rel.)	3325	33334344345	LONONONFFONNNNFNNNNN	NNFN4NFNNNNNNNF	J,T	147	509	06.02.17	7676	000000	97953
549.387-010	CARGO INSPECTOR (petrol. refin.; pipe lines)	3325	33334344344	LONONNNFFONNNNONOOON	FNNN3NFNNNNNNNF	J,T	212	501	05.07.05	7820	470501	83005
549.585-010	ACETYLENE-PLANT OPERATOR (chemical)	2223	44444434344	HNNFNFNNFFFNNNFNNNON	NNNN3NNNNNNNNNN	R,T	147	491	06.04.11	7676	000000	92962
549.587-010	COMPRESSED-GAS-PLANT WORKER (chemical)	2222	44444334345	MNNONONFFFNNNNFNNNNN	NNNN4NFNNNNNNNF	R	011	551	06.04.40	7840	000000	83005
549.587-014	SAMPLER (petrol. refin.)	2213	44444444444	LFNNNNNFFNNNNFNNNNON	NNNN4NFNNNNNNNN	R	011	500	06.04.40	7840	000000	83005
549.587-018	SAMPLER (elec. equip.)	2212	44444444354	LNNONONFFNNNNFNNNNON	NNNN3NNNNNNNNNN	R	011	341	05.12.07	7840	000000	92965
549.662-010	BRIQUETTE-MACHINE OPERATOR (fabrication, nec)	3224	34444444355	MONFNFNNFFFNNNFNNNNN	NNNN4NFNNNNNNNF	R,T	147	504	06.02.17	7679	000000	92998
549.665-010	ACETYLENE-CYLINDER-PACKING MIXER (chemical)	2222	44444434355	MNNNNNNFFONNNFNNNNNN	NNON3NNNNNNNNNN	R,T	147	491	06.04.19	7664	000000	92965
549.682-010	GREASE MAKER (petrol. refin.)	3235	33333444454	MNNOONNFFNNNNNONFNON	NNNN4NNNNNNNNNN	J,T	147	501	06.04.12	7664	000000	92965
549.684-010	PUMPER HELPER (petrol. refin.)	2223	44444444455	MFOFNFNFFNNNNNFNNNNF	FNNN4NFNNNNNNNF	R,T	014	501	06.04.12	8619	470501	98999
549.685-010	AIR-TABLE OPERATOR (mine & quarry)	2112	44444544355	LNNNNNNNFFNNNNNNNNNN	NNNN4NCNNNNNNNN	R	031	341	06.04.08	7673	000000	92958
549.685-014	GRAPHITE PAN-DRIER TENDER (nonmet. min.)	2214	34443544443	LNNNNNNFFNNNNNNONONN	NNON4NONNNNNNNN	J,T	141	349	06.04.19	7679	470501	92998
549.685-018	MOLDER, WAX (petrol. refin.)	2214	44444444355	MNNNNNNFFNNNNNNNONNN	NNNN4NNNNNNNNNN	R,T	132	509	06.04.12	7663	000000	92971
549.685-022	REELER (build. mat., nec)	2213	44554534345	HNNNNNNFFNNNNNNNONNN	NNNN4NNNNNNNNNN	R	163	503	06.04.09	7679	000000	92998
549.685-026	SCREENER-AND-BLENDER OPERATOR (steel & rel.)	2222	44444544455	HNNNNNNNFFNNNNNNNNNN	ONNN4NONNNNNNNN	R	147	505	06.04.12	7664	000000	98999
549.685-030	TREATER HELPER (petrol. refin.)	2224	44444444355	MF-OOOONNFFNNNNNNNNNN	FNNN4NNNNNNNNNF	R,T	147	500	06.04.12	8618	470501	98999
549.685-034	WASH-OIL-PUMP OPERATOR HELPER (steel & rel.)	2223	44544544455	LONONNNFFONNNNONOCONN	NNNO4NOONNNNNNN	R,T	144	509	06.04.12	8618	470501	98999
549.685-038	WAX MOLDER (foundry; jewelry-silver.)	2122	44443344355	LNNNNNNNFFNNNNNFNNNNN	NNNN3NNNNNNNNNN	R,T	132	568	06.04.09	7663	470408	92971
549.685-042	UTILITY OPERATOR III (chemical)	2113	44444433455	MFNONNNFOONNNNFNNONN	ONNN4NNNNNNNNNN	R,T	145	491	06.04.11	7666	470501	85128
549.686-010	BRIQUETTE-MACHINE-OPERATOR HELPER (fabrication, nec)	2112	44544544455	HNNNNNNNFFNNNNNNNNNN	NNNN4NNNNNNNNNN	V	147	504	06.04.12	8618	000000	98999
549.686-014	FELT HANGER (build. mat., nec)	2222	44444534355	LNNNNNNNFONFFFNNOOFN	NNNN3NNNNNNNNNN	R	152	503	06.04.19	8725	000000	98502
549.687-010	CHASER, TAR (steel & rel.)	1112	44544544355	MFNNNNNFFNNNNNNNNNNN	FNFN4NFNNNNNNNF	R	031	568	06.04.39	8769	000000	98999
549.687-014	HOTHOUSE WORKER (chemical)	2222	44534534345	MNNOOONFFNNNNNNNNNN	NNNN3NFNNNNNNNN	R	121	568	06.04.34	7740	000000	93999
549.687-018	LABORER, PETROLEUM REFINERY (petrol. refin.)	2113	44444544355	HFFFFNFNNNNNNNNNNNNN	CNNN4NFNNNNNNNF	R	031	501	05.12.03	8769	000000	98999
549.687-022	MUD-MIXER HELPER (steel & rel.)	1112	44544544355	HNNFNFNFFNNNNNNNNNNN	ONFN4NFNNNNNNNF	R	011	346	06.04.30	8618	000000	98999
550.131-010	COSMETICS SUPERVISOR (pharmaceut.)	4337	33333333352	LNNNNNNNFFFFFNNNOFN	NNNN3NNNNNNNNNN	V,D,P,J	147	494	06.01.01	7100	410301	81008
550.132-010	SUPERVISOR II (chemical)	4236	33444444455	LNNNNNNNFFNNFNFNFONN	NNNN4NCNNNNNNCN	D,P,V	143	497	06.01.01	7100	410301	81008
550.132-014	SUPERVISOR, FISH BAIT PROCESSING (toy-sport equip.)	4237	33443344454	LNNNNNNNFONFFFNNOOFN	NNNN4NNNNNNNNNN	D,J,P	147	616	06.02.01	6869	000000	89999
550.135-010	SUPERVISOR, COLOR-PASTE MIXING (textile)	4337	33343344451	LNNNNNNNFFNFNFNNNN	NNNN4NNNNNNNNNN	D,J	143	491	06.02.01	6869	000000	89999
550.135-014	MIXING SUPERVISOR (plastic prod.)	4335	33443344452	LNNNNNNNOOONFFNFNFFN	NNNN4NFNNNNNNNN	D,P,J	143	490	06.02.01	7100	150607	92965
550.137-010	SUPERVISOR, COMPOUNDING-AND-FINISHING (chemical)	4338	33343333353	LNNNNNNNFFFFFNNFFN	NNNN4NFNNNNNNNN	D,P,J,T	147	494	06.01.01	7100	410301	81008
550.137-014	SUPERVISOR, PASTE MIXING (chemical)	4336	33444444455	HNNFNNNFFNNNNNNNNN	NNNN4NNNNNNNNNN	V,D,P	143	490	06.04.01	7100	000000	81008
550.137-018	SUPERVISOR, SHIPPING (chemical)	4237	33344344455	LNNNNNNNFFFFNNNNNN	NNNN4NFNNNNNNNN	V,D,P,J	143	499	06.04.01	7100	000000	81008
550.362-010	FROTHING-MACHINE OPERATOR (rubber goods)	3225	33444334355	LNNNNNNNFFNNOONFNNNN	NNNN4NCNNNNNNNN	J,T	143	519	06.02.13	7664	000000	92965
550.381-010	COLOR MATCHER (leather mfg.; plastic-synth.; tex. prod., nec)	3235	33343433352	MNNONONFFFNNNNFNNFFN	NNNN4NONNNNNNNN	J	143	490	06.02.32	6869	150607	89999
550.381-014	TINTER (paint & varnish)	3236	33344344353	MNNNNNONFFFNNNNFNNNFN	NNNN4NFNNNNNNNF	J,T	143	495	06.02.11	6869	000000	89999
550.382-010	COLOR MAKER (chemical)	3225	33344334353	MMNNONONFFFNNNNONNNFN	NNNN3NNNNNNNNNN	J,T	147	496	06.02.11	7664	000000	92965
550.382-014	COLOR MAKER (tex. prod., nec)	3235	34443433353	MNNONONFFFNNNNONNNFN	NNNN4NFNNNNNNNN	J,T	143	491	06.02.11	7664	000000	92965
550.382-018	MIXER OPERATOR I (chemical)	3224	34433534354	MNNONONFFNNNNNFNNNNF	NNNN4NNNNNNNNNN	R,J,T	143	499	06.02.18	7664	000000	92965
550.382-022	MIXING-MACHINE OPERATOR (any industry)	3224	33444344355	HNNNNNNNFFONNONONNNN	NNNN4NFNNNNNNNN	J	143	492	06.02.13	7664	000000	92965
550.382-026	OPERATOR, CATALYST CONCENTRATION (plastic-synth.)	3225	34333344344	HONNNNNFFNNNFNNNNON	ONNN4NFNNNNNNNN	V,J,T	147	492	06.02.13	7664	000000	92965
550.382-030	ROOF-CEMENT-AND-PAINT MAKER (build. mat., nec; nonmet. min.)	3225	34443434354	HNNFNFNFFNNNNNFNNNNO	NNNN4NFNNNNNNNO	J,T	143	503	06.02.18	7664	000000	92965
550.382-034	SOLUTIONS OPERATOR (plastic-synth.)	3225	33343434454	LONNNNNFFNNNNFONNNON	NNNN4NNNNNNNNNN	J,T	143	492	06.02.13	7664	150607	92965
550.485-010	CHEMICAL MIXER (photofinishing)	3226	34333333354	HFNNNNNFFOONNFNFNFN	NNNN4NFNNNNNNNN	J,T	143	491	06.02.11	7664	000000	92965
550.485-018	PAINT MIXER, MACHINE (any industry)	2113	34444434353	HNNFNNNFFFONNNFNFNFN	NNNN4NFNNNNNNNN	R,T	143	495	06.04.11	7664	000000	92965

DOT #	DOT Title & Industry	Trng	Aptitude	Physical	Environment	Tempra	WKF	MPSMS	GOE	SOC	CIP	OES
550.485-022	POWDER BLENDER AND POURER (chemical)	2223	34343434344	MNNNNNNFFNNNFNFNON	NNNN4NFNNNNNNF	J,T	143	499	06.04.11	7664	000000	92965
550.485-026	PULVERIZING-AND-SIFTING OPERATOR (chemical)	3224	34444444455	HNNNONFFONNNNONNNNN	NNFN4NNNNNNNNF	R,T	142	499	06.02.18	7664	000000	92965
550.564-010	METAL-BONDING CRIB ATTENDANT (chemical)	3224	34344344455	MMNNONONFFONNNNNNNNN	NNNN4NNNNNNNNNF	J,T	143	499	06.02.32	7664	000000	92965
550.565-010	PRIMER-POWDER BLENDER, DRY (ordnance)	2123	44443433355	LNNNNNNFFFFNNNFNNNNN	NNNN4NNNNNNNNC	R,S	143	374	06.04.13	7664	000000	92965
550.582-010	PRIMER-POWDER BLENDER, WET (chemical)	3224	34343434355	LNNNNNNNFFOFNNNFNNNNN	NNNN4NFNNNNNNF	J,T	143	499	06.02.18	7664	000000	92965
550.582-014	WEIGHER-BULKER (chemical)	3225	34343434354	HONNNNNFFFNNNNFNNNFN	NFFN4NNNNNNNNN	J,T	143	494	06.02.11	7664	000000	92965
550.584-010	FLUX MIXER (chemical)	3114	34443444355	MMNFNFNFFONNNNONNNNN	NNNN4NNNNNNNNN	R,T	143	499	06.04.34	7759	000000	93999
550.584-014	SAMPLE-COLOR MAKER (paint & varnish)	2112	44444444453	LNNNNNNNFFFNNNNFNNNFN	NNNN3NNNNNNNNN	R	143	495	06.04.34	7840	000000	83005
550.585-010	BINDER TECHNICIAN (glass mfg.)	3223	44444444354	LNNNNNNNFFNNNNFNNNNN	NNNN4NNNNNNNNN	R	143	499	06.04.11	7664	000000	92965
550.585-014	CELLOPHANE-BATH MIXER (plastic-synth.)	3223	34444444355	LFNNNNNFFFNNNNFNNNNNN	NNNN4NNNNNNNNN	J,T	143	491	06.04.13	7664	150607	92965
550.585-018	CHEMICAL MIXER (textile)	3224	34444444354	MNNNNNNFFFNNNNFNNNNN	NNNF4NNNNNNNON	R,T	143	490	06.04.11	7664	000000	92965
550.585-022	COATING OPERATOR (chemical)	3124	44443434345	LNNNNNNNFFNNNFNNNNN	NNNN3NNNNNNNNN	R,T	147	490	06.04.11	7664	000000	92965
550.585-026	LIME-SLUDGE MIXER (paper & pulp)	2113	34444434354	MMNONNNFFFNNNONNOON	NNNN4NNNNNNNNN	J,T	143	499	06.04.11	7664	000000	92965
550.585-030	NITRATING-ACID MIXER (chemical)	3225	34444444445	LFNNNNNFFNNNNNFNNNNN	NNNF4NFNNNNNNF	R,T	143	499	06.04.11	7664	000000	92965
550.585-034	PASTE MIXER (chemical)	2113	44444444355	MMNONONFFFNNNNFNNNNN	NNNN4NFNNNNNNN	R,T	143	491	06.04.11	7664	000000	92965
550.585-038	THINNER (paint & varnish)	3223	34444434354	HNNNNNNFFFNNNFNONON	NNNN4NFNNNNNNF	J,T	143	495	06.04.11	7664	000000	92965
550.585-042	TRACER-POWDER BLENDER (chemical)	3223	34444434355	NNNNNNNFFFNNNNFNNNNN	NNNO3NCNNNNNNC	J,T	143	499	06.04.11	7664	000000	92965
550.585-046	WAX BLENDER (fabrication, nec)	3123	34444334353	HNNFNNNFFFNNNNFNFNFN	NNNN3NNNNNNNNN	R,T	152	619	06.04.19	7664	000000	92965
550.586-010	BLENDER HELPER (plastic prod.; plastic-synth.)	2112	44444444355	HFNFFFNFFFNNNNFNNNNN	NNNN3NNNNNNNNN	R,T	143	492	06.04.40	8618	000000	98999
550.587-010	MAKE-UP OPERATOR HELPER (chemical)	2123	44444444355	LNNFNFNFFFNNNNFNNNNN	NNNN4NFNNNNNNN	R	212	490	06.03.02	8618	000000	98999
550.587-014	SAMPLE COLLECTOR (chemical)	2112	44444444355	LNNONONFFFNNNNFNNNNN	NNNN4NFNNNNNNN	R	143	497	06.04.17	7840	000000	83005
550.662-010	BLEACH-LIQUOR MAKER (paper & pulp)	3225	34443434354	LNNNNNNFFONNNNONNNOON	NNNN4NFNNNNNNN	J,T	147	490	06.02.14	7664	000000	92965
550.663-010	FORMULA WEIGHER (rubber goods)	2123	44435344355	LNNNNNNFFNNOONOONFNNN	NNNN4NNNNNNNNN	R,T	212	499	06.04.11	7679	000000	92998
550.665-010	BLENDER II (chemical)	3224	34434434354	LNNNNNNNFFFNNNNFNNNNN	NNNN4NFNNNNNNN	R,T	143	499	06.04.11	7664	000000	92965
550.665-014	COMPOSITION MIXER (fabrication, nec)	3124	34434434353	MFNFNFNFFOOONNFNNNNN	NFFN4NNNNNNNNF	J,T	143	619	06.04.19	7664	000000	92965
550.665-018	FERTILIZER MIXER (chemical)	2112	44444444355	LNNNNNNNFFFNNNNFNNNNN	NNNN4NFNNNNNNN	R,T	143	497	06.04.11	7664	000000	92965
550.665-022	MOTTLER OPERATOR (fabrication, nec)	2113	44435434353	HNNFNFNFFOONNNONNNFN	NNNN4NFNNNNNNN	R,T	143	619	06.04.11	7664	000000	92965
550.682-010	SIZE MAKER (paper & pulp)	3225	34443434355	HFNOOONFFONNNNFNNNNN	NNNF4NNNNNNNNF	J,T	147	499	06.04.14	7664	000000	92965
550.682-014	TANNING-SOLUTION MAKER (chemical)	3125	34344444355	MMNONONFFNNNNNONNNNN	NNNN4NNNNNNNNN	J,T	143	499	06.04.11	7664	000000	92965
550.684-010	COAGULATING-BATH MIXER (plastic-synth.)	3224	34444444354	MNNNNNNCCFNNNNOFNFNN	NNNN4NNNNNNNON	J,T	143	490	06.04.11	7759	000000	93999
550.684-014	DYE WEIGHER (any industry)	3223	34444444354	HNNFNNNFFONOOONFNNNN	NNNF-4NNNNNNNNN	R,T	143	491	06.04.34	7759	000000	93999
550.684-018	PAINT MIXER, HAND (any industry)	2113	44444444355	LNNNNNNNFFFNNNNFNNNFN	NNNN4NFNNNNNNN	R,J	143	495	06.04.11	7759	000000	93999
550.684-022	PRIMING-POWDER-PREMIX BLENDER (chemical)	2123	44444444353	LNNNNNNNFFFNNNNFNNNNN	NNFN4NFNNNNNNF	R,T	143	499	06.04.34	7759	000000	93999
550.684-026	SILVER-SOLUTION MIXER (chemical)	3223	34343434355	LNNNNNNNFFFNNNNFNNNFN	NNNN3NNNNNNNNN	J,T	143	491	06.04.13	7664	000000	92965
550.685-010	BATCH MIXER (soap & rel.)	2113	44444434354	MNNNNNNNFFFNNNNFNNNFN	NNNN4NNNNNNNNN	R,T	143	494	06.04.11	7664	000000	92965
550.685-014	BLENDER I (chemical)	2112	44445434355	MNNNNNNNFFNNNNONFNNN	NNNN4NNNNNNNNN	R,T	143	496	06.04.19	7664	000000	92965
550.685-018	BRINE MAKER I (chemical)	3223	34344434355	MMNNNNNFFONNNONNNNN	NNNN4NFNNNNNNN	J,T	143	490	06.04.11	7664	000000	92965
550.685-022	CD-MIXER (rubber reclaim.)	2113	34454344345	MMNONONFFONNNNONNNNN	ONNN4NFNNNNNNON	J,T	143	513	06.04.13	7664	000000	92965
550.685-026	CEMENT MIXER (rubber goods; rubber tire)	2123	34394344344	MNNONONFFONNNNONNNNN	NNNN4NFNNNNNNN	R,T	143	519	06.04.13	7664	000000	92965
550.685-030	CHEMICAL PREPARER (chemical; electron. comp.)	3334	33343333354	HFNONNNNFFONNNNONNOON	NNNN3NFNNNNNNFN	T,U	143	490	06.04.11	7664	000000	92965
550.685-034	CHURN TENDER (plastic-synth.)	3223	34444444355	LNNNNNNNFFFNNNNFNNNNN	NNNN4NNNNNNNNN	R,T	143	490	06.04.13	7664	150607	92965
550.685-038	COLOR-PASTE MIXER (textile)	3223	34344434354	MNNNNNNNFFFNNNNFNNNFN	NNNN4NNNNNNNNN	J,T	143	491	06.04.11	7664	000000	92965
550.685-042	COMPOUND FINISHER (chemical)	2113	34444434354	MMNNNNNNFFFNNNNFNNFNON	NNNN4NNNNNNNNF	R,T	143	490	06.04.11	7664	000000	92965
550.685-046	COMPOUNDER (pharmaceut.; soap & rel.)	3224	34444434354	HNNNNNNFFFNNNNFNNNNN	NNNN4NFNNNNNNN	J,T	147	494	06.04.11	7664	000000	92965
550.685-050	COMPOUNDER (chemical)	2113	44444434354	HNNNNNNNFFFNNNNFNNNNN	NNNN4NNNNNNNNF	R,T	143	490	06.04.11	7664	000000	92965
550.685-054	CRUTCHER (soap & rel.)	3224	34444434354	MMNNONONFFFNNNNFNNNNN	NNNN4NNNNNNNNN	R,T	143	494	06.04.19	7664	000000	92965
550.685-058	DUSTLESS OPERATOR (chemical)	3123	34343434354	LNNNNNNNFFFNNNNFNNNNN	NNNN4NNNNNNNNN	R,T	143	499	06.04.19	7664	000000	92965
550.685-062	GLUE MIXER (any industry)	3223	44444444454	HOOONNNNFFONNNNNONNNN	NNNN4NFNNONNFO	R,T	143	499	06.04.19	7664	000000	92965
550.685-066	GROUND MIXER (chemical)	2112	44444444454	HNNONNNFFFNNNNONNONNN	NNNN4NNNNNNNNN	R	143	490	06.04.11	7664	000000	92965
550.685-070	INSECTICIDE MIXER (chemical)	2112	44444444455	HNNONNNFFFNNNNFNNNNN	NNNN4NFNNNNNNF	R,T	143	497	06.04.11	7664	000000	92965
550.685-074	MIXER I (tex. prod., nec)	3213	34444434354	HNNONONFFFNNNNFNFNONON	NNNN4NFNNNNNNN	J,T	143	499	06.04.11	7664	000000	92965

DOT #	DOT Title & Industry	Trng	Aptitude	Physical	Environment	Tempra	WkF	MPSMS	GOE	SOC	CIP	OES
550.685-078	MIXER (paint & varnish)	3123	4444434354	HNNNNNNFFFNNNNFNFFFN	NNNN4NFNNNNNNN	R,J,T	143	495	06.04.11	7664	000000	92965
550.685-082	MIXER OPERATOR (chemical; electron. comp.)	2223	4444344355	HNNNNNNFFOONNFNONNNN	NNNN3NCNNNNNNON	T,U	143	490	06.04.11	7664	000000	92965
550.685-086	MIXER, FOAM RUBBER (rubber goods)	2112	3434344354	MNNFNFNFFNNNNFNNNNNN	NNNN4NNNNNNNNN	R,T	143	519	06.04.13	7664	000000	92965
550.685-090	MIXING-MACHINE TENDER (chemical; pharmaceut.)	3224	4444434354	HNNOOONFFONNNNFNNNON	NNNN4NFNNNNNNF	J,T	147	490	06.04.11	7664	000000	92965
550.685-094	PEARL-GLUE OPERATOR (chemical)	2113	4444544355	LNNNNNNFFNNNNNNNNNNN	NNNN4NNNNNNNN	R	133	499	06.04.19	7664	000000	92965
550.685-098	POWERHOUSE HELPER (chemical)	2113	4443343355	MNNNNNNFFFNNNNFNNNNN	ONNN4NNNNNNNN	J,T	147	492	06.04.19	7664	000000	92965
550.685-102	RUBBER-MILL TENDER (plastic-synth.; rubber goods; rubber reclaim.; rubber)	2223	4443344345	HNNFNFNFFONNNNNONNNN	NNNN4NFNNNNNNF	J,T	147	490	06.04.13	7664	000000	92965
550.685-106	SEASONING MIXER (chemical)	2223	4444344355	LNNNNNNNFFNNNNNNNNON	NNNN4NNNNNNNN	R,T	143	494	06.04.11	7664	000000	92965
550.685-110	SWEEPING-COMPOUND BLENDER (chemical)	2123	4444344345	HNNONONFFNNNNONNNNNN	NNNN3NNNNNNNNO	R,T	143	499	06.04.11	7664	000000	92965
550.685-114	TETRYL-DISSOLVER OPERATOR (chemical)	3123	4444434355	LNNNNNNFFFNNNNFNNNNN	NNNN3NNNNNNNC	R,T	147	499	06.04.11	7664	000000	92965
550.685-118	TUMBLER OPERATOR (chemical)	2112	4454444345	MNNNNNNFFFNNNNNNNNNNN	NNNF4NNNNNNNF	R	143	499	06.04.11	7664	000000	92965
550.685-122	WEIGHER AND MIXER (chemical)	2114	4444434353	HNNFNFNFFNNNNNFNNNNN	NNNN4NNNNNNNF	R,T	143	497	06.04.11	7664	000000	92965
550.685-126	WET MIXER (chemical)	2112	4444444355	LNNNNNNNFFNNNNFNNNNN	NNNN4NFNNNNNNN	R,T	143	490	06.04.11	7664	000000	92965
550.685-130	MATERIAL MIXER (plastic prod.)	2222	2222434344	VNNONNNFFFNNNNFNNNNN	NNNN4NFNNNNNNN	R,T	143	492	06.04.13	7664	150607	92965
550.685-134	MIXING-MACHINE OPERATOR (plastic prod.; plastic-synth.)	3224	3444434344	MNNFOONFFOONNFNNNNON	NNNN4NNNNNNNNO	R,T	143	492	06.04.13	7664	000000	92965
550.686-010	BATCH TRUCKER (rubber reclaim.)	1112	4445444445	MNNFNFNFFNNNNFNNNNNN	NNNN2NFNNNNNNN	R	041	513	06.04.11	8725	000000	98502
550.686-014	COMPOUND FILLER (chemical)	1112	4454544355	HNNNNNNFFNNNNNONNNNN	NNNO4NONNNNNON	R	143	490	06.04.11	8725	000000	98502
550.686-018	CRUTCHER HELPER (soap & rel.)	2112	4454544355	HNNONONFFNNNNONNNNNN	NNNN3NFNNNNNNN	R	143	494	06.04.19	8618	000000	98999
550.686-022	GLAZING OPERATOR, BLACK POWDER (chemical)	3114	3444434355	HNNNNNNFFONNNNNNNNNN	NNNN4NNNNNNNNF	R,T	147	499	06.04.19	8725	000000	98502
550.686-026	MIXER HELPER (build. mat., nec)	1112	4454544355	LNNFNNNCCNNNNNNNNNNN	NNNN4NCNNNNNNN	R	011	503	06.04.19	8618	000000	98999
550.686-030	MIXING-MACHINE FEEDER (chemical)	1112	4444434355	HNNONNNFFNNNNNFNNFNF	NNNN4NCNNNNNNN	R	041	497	06.04.11	8725	000000	98502
550.686-034	MOTTLER-MACHINE FEEDER (fabrication, nec)	2112	4454544354	HNNFNFNFFOONNNNNNNON	NNNN3NNNNNNNN	R	041	495	06.04.19	8618	000000	98999
550.686-038	ROOF-CEMENT-AND-PAINT-MAKER HELPER (build. mat., nec; nonmet. min.)	1112	4444444454	HNNFNFNFFNNNNFNNNNON	NNNN3NNNNNNNN	R	143	490	06.04.11	8618	000000	98999
550.687-010	CHEMICAL-COMPOUNDER HELPER (chemical)	2112	4454544355	MNNFNFNFFNNNNFNNNNNN	NNNN3NNNNNNNN	R	143	491	06.04.11	8769	000000	98999
550.687-014	COLOR STRAINER (textile)	1112	4444444454	HNNFNFNFFNNNNFNNNNNN	NNNO4NNNNNNNN	R,T	143	491	06.04.16	8769	000000	98999
550.687-018	DYE-WEIGHER HELPER (any industry)	2112	4444444454	MNNFNNNFFNNNNNNNNNON	NNNF4NNNNNNNN	R,T	143	499	06.04.34	8618	000000	98999
551.130-010	SUPERVISOR, PROCESSING (chemical)	4337	3334334355	LNNNNNNFFNFFNFNNNNNN	ONNN4NNNNNNNN	V,D,P,J	145	499	06.04.01	7100	000000	81008
551.362-010	PURIFICATION OPERATOR II (chemical)	4237	3444434343	LFNONONFFNOONFNNNFN	NNNN3NFNNNNNNN	J,T	145	490	06.02.11	7676	000000	92962
551.365-010	STRAINER TENDER (rubber reclaim.)	2124	3444434354	LNNNNNNFFFOONFNFNFN	NNNN4NFNNNNNNN	R,T	145	513	06.02.07	7666	000000	92962
551.382-010	ABSORPTION OPERATOR (chemical)	3225	3334334354	LONONONFFNOONFNNNNN	NNNN4NCNNNNNNNC	J,T	147	490	06.02.11	7666	000000	92962
551.465-010	PURIFICATION-OPERATOR HELPER (chemical)	3224	3434334355	LONONONFFNOOONFNNNNN	ONNN3NFNNNNNNN	R,T	147	490	06.02.11	7664	000000	92938
551.485-010	WATER-TREATMENT-PLANT OPERATOR (chemical)	3224	3434344345	LONFNFNFFNNNNFNFNNN	NNNO4NNNNNNNN	J,T	145	490	06.02.11	7676	000000	92962
551.562-010	FILTRATION OPERATOR, POLYETHYLENE CATALYST (chemical)	3225	3443444344	LONNNNNFFNOONFNONON	NNNN4NFNNNNNNN	J,T	145	492	06.02.11	7666	000000	92962
551.582-010	HYDRAULIC-STRAINER OPERATOR (plastic-synth.)	3125	3444434355	MNNONONFFNNNNFNNNNN	NNNN3NNNNNNNN	R,T	145	490	06.02.13	7529	150607	92198
551.585-010	FILTER-TANK OPERATOR (chemical)	2112	4444444455	MFNONOFFNNNNNFNNNNN	NNNN4NNNNNNNN	R,T	145	494	06.04.11	7666	000000	92962
551.585-014	MERCURY PURIFIER (chemical)	2214	4444434355	MFNNNNNNFFNNNNNFNNNN	NNNN4NFNNNNNNN	R,T	147	490	06.04.11	7676	000000	92962
551.585-018	PAN HELPER (chemical)	3124	3444434354	HNNNNNNFFNFFNNFNNNNN	NNNN4NFNNNNNNN	R,T	147	499	06.04.11	7654	000000	92705
551.585-022	ROTARY-CUTTER OPERATOR (rubber goods)	1112	4444444454	HNNNNNNFFNOOFNONON	NNNF3NONNNNNNN	R	142	510	06.04.05	7654	000000	92962
551.665-010	NAPHTHALENE OPERATOR (steel & rel.)	2113	4444444355	MNNFNFNFFNNOONONNNNN	NNNN3NFNNNNNNN	R,T	145	490	06.04.11	7676	000000	92962
551.666-010	PITCH WORKER (optical goods)	1112	4444444455	LNNNNNNFFNNNNFNNNNNN	NNNN4NNNNNNNN	R	145	500	06.04.19	8725	000000	98502
551.682-010	BENZENE-WASHER OPERATOR (chemical; steel & rel.)	3235	3343343454	LNNNNNNFFONNNFNFNON	NNNN3NFNNNNNON	J,T	145	490	06.02.11	7673	000000	92965
551.685-010	BAND TUMBLER (rubber goods)	1112	4444544355	MNNNNNNFFNNNNFNNNNNN	NNNN3NNNNNNNN	R	145	519	06.04.07	7679	000000	92998
551.685-014	BOILING-TUB OPERATOR (chemical)	2112	4444444354	LNNNNNNFFONNNNFONNNN	NNCC4NNNNNNNN	R,T	147	499	06.04.11	7676	000000	92962
551.685-018	BONE-COOKING OPERATOR (chemical)	3123	3444444354	HNNNNNNNFFNNNNNNNNNN	NNNF3NONNNNNNN	R,T	145	490	06.04.11	7666	000000	92962
551.685-022	CATALYST-RECOVERY OPERATOR (chemical)	3223	3443444355	HNNFNNNFFFNNNNFNNNNN	NNNN3NONNNNNNF	J,T	147	385	06.04.11	7676	000000	92923
551.685-026	CENTRIFUGAL-DRIER OPERATOR (chemical)	3114	3444534355	MNNNNNNFFNNNNNFFNNNN	NNNO4NNNNNNNN	R,T	145	490	06.04.11	7675	000000	92962
551.685-030	CENTRIFUGE OPERATOR (soap & rel.)	2112	4454544355	HNNNNNNFFNNNNFNNNNNN	NNFN4NNNNNNNN	R,T	145	494	06.04.19	7676	000000	92962
551.685-034	CENTRIFUGE OPERATOR (paint & varnish)	2112	4544454355	LNNNNNNFFNNNNNNNNNNN	NNNN4NNNNNNNN	R	145	495	06.04.11	7666	000000	92962
551.685-038	CENTRIFUGE-SEPARATOR OPERATOR (chemical)	2112	4455544455	LNNNNNNFFNNNNFNNNNNN	NNNN3NNNNNNNN	R	145	499	06.04.11	7676	000000	92962
551.685-042	CHILLER OPERATOR (chemical)	2123	4444443455	LNNNNNNFFONNNNNONNNN	NNNN3NNNNNNNN	R,T	147	490	06.04.11	7665	150607	92928
551.685-046	DEHYDRATING-PRESS OPERATOR (chemical; plastic-synth.)	2122	4444444355	MNNNNNNFFFNNNNNNNNNN	NNNN4NNNNNNNNF	R	145	499	06.04.11	7667	150607	92971

DOT #	DOT Title & Industry	Trng	Aptitude	Physical	Environment	Tempra	WkF	MPSMS	GOE	SOC	CIP	OES
551.685-050	DUST-COLLECTOR OPERATOR (soap & rel.)	2113	44444444455	LNNNNNNFFFNNNFNNNNN	NNNN4NNNNNNNNNNN	R,T	145	494	06.04.19	7676	000000	92962
551.685-054	EXTRACTOR OPERATOR (chemical; oils & grease)	2112	44445544355	HNNNNNNFFFNNNONNNNN	NNNN4NNNNNNNNNNN	R	145	499	06.04.19	7676	000000	92962
551.685-058	EXTRACTOR OPERATOR (pharmaceut.)	2223	44444434355	MNNNNNNFFNNNNFNNNNN	NNNN3NNNNNNNNNNN	R,T	145	493	06.04.11	7676	000000	92962
551.685-062	EXTRACTOR OPERATOR, SOLVENT PROCESS (chemical)	2112	34444444455	LNNNONNFFFNNNFNNNNN	NNNN4NNNNNNNNNNN	R,T	145	385	06.04.11	7676	000000	92962
551.685-066	EXTRACTOR-AND-WRINGER OPERATOR (chemical)	2112	44444434355	LNNNNNNFFNNNNNNNNNN	NNNN3NNNNNNNNNNN	R,T	147	490	06.04.11	7676	000000	92962
551.685-070	FAT-PURIFICATION WORKER (oils & grease)	3123	34444444454	LNNNNNNFFONNNNNNNON	NNNN4NNNNNNNNNNN	R,T	145	499	06.04.11	7676	000000	92962
551.685-074	FILTER HELPER (chemical)	2112	44444444354	MNNFNFFNNNNNNFNNNNN	NNNF3NNNNNNNNNNN	R,T	145	499	06.04.19	7666	000000	92962
551.685-078	FILTER OPERATOR (any industry)	2112	44444444354	MCNOOONFFNNNNNFNNNON	NNNN4NNNNNNNNNNON	R,T	145	490	06.04.19	7666	000000	92962
551.685-082	FILTER-PRESS OPERATOR (any industry)	2113	44444444355	HNNNNNNFFNOONNNNNNNN	NNOO4NNNNNNNNNNN	R,T	145	490	06.04.11	7666	000000	92962
551.685-086	GREASE-REFINER OPERATOR (oils & grease)	2113	44544544455	LFNNNNNFFONNNNFNNNNN	NNFF3NNNNNNNNNNN	R,T	147	499	06.04.19	7676	000000	92938
551.685-090	LEACHER (paper & pulp)	2113	44444444355	LFNNNNNFFONNNFNNNNN	NNNN4NFNNNNNNNNN	R,T	145	499	06.04.11	7676	000000	92938
551.685-094	LYE TREATER (chemical; soap & rel.)	3223	34444434355	MNNNNNNFFFNNNFNNNNN	NNNO4NFNNNNNNNNN	J,T	147	490	06.04.11	7676	000000	92962
551.685-098	MERCURY WASHER (chemical)	2113	44444444355	HNNFNFNFFONNNNNNNNN	NNNO3NFNNNNNNNNN	R	147	490	06.04.11	7676	000000	92962
551.685-102	NITROGLYCERIN-SEPARATOR OPERATOR (chemical)	3114	34344344353	LNNNNNNFFFNNNNFNNFN	NNNN4NCNNNNNNNNC	R,S,T	145	499	06.02.18	7676	000000	92962
551.685-106	POACHER OPERATOR (chemical)	3124	34433444355	LNNNNNNFFFNNNNFNNNN	NNNC4NNNNNNNNNNN	R,T	145	499	06.02.18	7666	000000	92962
551.685-110	PRECIPITATE WASHER (chemical)	3113	34444434354	MNNNNNNFFFNNNNFNNNON	NNNN3NNNNNNNNNNN	J,T	145	490	06.04.11	7673	000000	92958
551.685-114	PRESS OPERATOR (oils & grease)	2112	44544544355	HNNFNFNFFONNNNNNNNN	NNNN3NNNNNNNNNNN	R	145	499	06.04.19	7667	000000	92962
551.685-118	PRESS OPERATOR II (chemical)	2112	44444544355	MNNFNNNNFFONNNNNNNNN	NNNN4NNNNNNNNNNN	R	145	499	06.04.11	7667	000000	92971
551.685-122	PURIFICATION OPERATOR I (chemical)	3222	34344434355	MNNNNNNFFONNNNNONNNNN	NNNN5NFNNNNNNNNN	R,T	145	496	06.04.12	7676	000000	92962
551.685-126	SALT WASHER (chemical)	3124	34444444355	LNNNNNNFFNNNNFNNNNN	NNNF4NNNNNNNNNNN	R,T	145	499	06.04.11	7676	000000	92962
551.685-130	SCREEN OPERATOR (chemical)	2113	44444444355	LNNNNNNFFFNNNFNNNNN	NNNN4NNNNNNNNNNN	R	145	490	06.04.11	7666	000000	92962
551.685-134	SODA DIALYZER (plastic-synth.)	3124	34444444355	LNNNNNNFFNNNONNNNNN	NNNN4NNNNNNNNNNN	R	145	490	06.04.13	7676	000000	92962
551.685-138	STEEPING-PRESS TENDER (plastic-synth.)	2123	44544544444	LNWFNFNCCONNNNOFNFNN	NNNN4NNNNNNNNNNFN	R	147	490	06.04.18	7667	000000	92971
551.685-142	SULFATE DRIER-MACHINE OPERATOR (steel & rel.)	2114	44454544455	MFNFNFNFFNNNNNNNNNN	NNNO3NONNNNNNNON	R	147	347	06.04.19	7679	000000	92998
551.685-146	TETRYL-SCREEN OPERATOR (chemical)	2122	44444544355	MNNNNNNFFFNNNONNNNN	NNNN4NFNNNNNNNNF	R	145	499	06.04.11	7666	000000	92962
551.685-150	VACUUM-PAN OPERATOR I (chemical)	2122	44454544355	MNNFNFNFFNNNNNNNNNN	NNNO3NNNNNNNNNNN	R	145	499	06.04.11	7676	000000	93999
551.685-154	VACUUM-PAN OPERATOR II (chemical)	2123	44444534355	LNNFNFNFFNNNNNNNNNN	NNNO3NNNNNNNNNNF	R	145	499	06.04.11	7676	000000	92962
551.685-158	WAX BLEACHER (chemical)	3123	34444444354	HNNFNNNNFFNNNNFNNNON	NNNN4NNNNNNNNNNN	R,T	145	499	06.04.11	7666	000000	92962
551.685-162	WRINGER OPERATOR (chemical)	2112	44444544355	MNNNNNNNFFNNNNNNNNNN	NNNN4NFNNNNNNNNN	R	145	499	06.04.11	7679	000000	92962
551.686-010	BEAD PICKER (rubber reclaim.)	1111	44555534455	LNNNNNNFFNNNNNFNNN	NNNN4NNNNNNNNNNN	R	145	513	06.04.29	8725	000000	98502
551.686-014	EXTRACTOR LOADER AND UNLOADER (chemical)	2112	45544544444	LNWFNFNCCONNNNOFNNN	NNNN4NNNNNNNNNON	R	145	499	06.04.19	8725	000000	98502
551.686-018	HOPPER FEEDER (oils & grease)	1112	44554544455	MFNFNFNFNNNNNNNNNN	NNFF3NNNNNNNNNNN	R	145	499	06.04.19	8725	000000	98502
551.687-010	BONE PICKER (chemical)	1111	44454544355	LONONNNFFONFFNFNFNN	NNNN3NNNNNNNNNNN	R	145	499	06.04.11	8769	000000	98999
551.687-014	BRINE MAKER II (chemical)	2113	44444534355	LFNNNNNNFFONNNNONNNN	ONNF3NNNNNNNNNNN	R	145	499	06.04.11	7759	000000	93999
551.687-018	DYNAMITE RECLAIMER (chemical)	2112	44444544455	HNNFNFNFFONNNNONONNN	NNNN3NCNNNNNFNN	R	145	499	06.02.11	8769	000000	98999
551.687-022	LABORER, COOK HOUSE (chemical)	1112	44544544455	HFNFNFNFFNNNNNNNNNN	NNFF4NNNNNNNNNNN	R,S	147	499	06.04.34	8769	000000	98999
551.687-026	NAPHTHALENE-OPERATOR HELPER (steel & rel.)	1112	44544544455	HNNFNFNFFNNNNNNNNNN	NNNF3NFNNNNNNNN	R	145	499	06.04.34	8618	000000	98999
551.687-030	SIFTER (pharmaceut.)	2112	44443434455	LNNONNNFFOONNNFNOFNN	NNNN4NFNNNNNNNNN	R	145	491	06.04.34	8769	000000	98999
551.687-034	SODA-ROOM OPERATOR (plastic-synth.)	1112	44544544355	MNNFNFNCCFNNNNOFNFNN	NNNN4NOONNNNNON	R	152	471	06.04.19	8769	000000	98999
552.132-010	SHIFT SUPERINTENDENT, CAUSTIC CRESYLATE (chemical)	4338	33333333355	LONONNNFFONFFNFFNN	ONNO4NOONNNNOON	V,D,P,J	147	491	06.02.11	7100	410301	81008
552.362-010	MONOMER-PURIFICATION OPERATOR (chemical)	3225	34343434354	LNNNNNNFFONNNNFNNNNN	NNNN4NNONNNNNNN	R	144	492	06.02.11	7676	000000	92962
552.362-014	OXYGEN-PLANT OPERATOR (chemical)	3334	33333433355	LNNNNNNFFONNNNFFNN	NNNN4NONNNNNNNN	J,T	147	490	06.02.11	6920	000000	95008
552.362-018	RECOVERY OPERATOR (paper & pulp)	4335	33333433454	LONOOONFFNNOONFNFFN	NNOA2NONNNNNNNN	D,J,T	147	491	06.02.11	6960	000000	95099
552.362-022	STILL OPERATOR, BATCH OR CONTINUOUS (chemical)	4336	33343334353	LONNNNNFFONOONFNFON	NNNN4NONNNNNNN	J,T	144	490	06.02.11	7676	410301	95099
552.382-010	PYRIDINE OPERATOR (steel & rel.)	3336	33333433354	MNNNNNNFFONNNNFNFFON	ONNN4NNNNNNNNNN	J,T	144	490	06.02.11	7676	000000	92962
552.462-010	DISTILLATION OPERATOR (chemical)	4336	33334434354	MNNNNNNFFNNOONFNFFN	ONNN4NOONNNOON	J,T	144	496	06.02.18	7676	000000	92962
552.682-010	DISTILLER I (chemical)	3225	34433544355	LFNNNNNFFONNNNFNNNN	NNNN4NNONNNNNN	R,T	144	496	06.04.11	7676	000000	92962
552.682-014	DISTILLER II (chemical)	3224	34433444454	LONONNNFFONNNNFNNNFN	NNNN4NNNNNNNNNN	J,T	144	496	06.02.11	7676	000000	95099
552.682-018	EXTRACTOR OPERATOR (chemical)	3225	34435544355	LFOFNONOONNNNNFFNNNN	NNNN4NNNNNNNNNN	R,T	144	496	06.04.18	7676	000000	92962
552.685-010	ACETONE-RECOVERY WORKER (plastic-synth.)	2123	44444444355	LNNNNNNFFNNNNNNNNNN	NNNN4NONNNNNNNN	R,T	144	491	06.04.11	7676	000000	92962
552.685-014	BATCH-STILL OPERATOR I (chemical)	3224	34444444354	LNNNNNNFFONNNNFFON	NNNN4NNNNNNNNNN	J,T	144	490	06.04.11	7676	000000	92962

DOT #	DOT Title & Industry	Trng	Aptitude	Physical	Environment	Tempra	WkF	MPSMS	GOE	SOC	CIP	OES
552.685-018	BATH-MIX OPERATOR (plastic-synth.)	2112	44544534455	HNNNONNNFFNNNNNNNNNNN	NNNN4NONNNNNNNN	R	144	499	06.04.11	7676	150607	92962
552.685-022	RETORT-CONDENSER ATTENDANT (chemical)	3223	34443444455	LNNNNNNFFNNNNNNNNNNN	NNNN4NNNNNNNNNN	R,T	144	496	06.04.19	7639	000000	92998
552.685-026	STILL TENDER (any industry)	3223	44444444355	LNNNNNNFFONNNNNOFNFNN	NNNN4NNNNNNNNNN	J,T	144	490	06.04.19	7676	000000	92962
552.685-030	STILL-OPERATOR HELPER (chemical)	3223	34444434355	HNNNNNNNFFONNNNONNNNNN	NNNN4NONNNNNNNN	R,T	144	490	06.04.11	7666	000000	92962
552.686-010	EXTRACTOR-OPERATOR HELPER (chemical)	2112	44544544355	MNNFNNNCCNNNNNNNNNNNN	NNNN4NNNNNNNNN	R	144	496	06.04.18	8725	000000	98502
552.687-010	DISTILLATION-OPERATOR HELPER (chemical)	2112	44444444355	MNNNNNNFFNNNNNNNNNNNN	NNNN4NONNNNNNN	R	144	496	06.04.40	8618	000000	98999
553.132-010	SUPERVISOR, GREASE REFINING (oils & grease)	4337	33343333355	LONONNNFFONFNFNNNNN	NNNO4NNNNNNNNNN	V,D,P,J	145	499	06.02.01	7100	000000	81008
553.362-010	BELT-PRESS OPERATOR I (rubber goods)	3225	33343434345	HNNNNNNNFFNNNNNNFNFNN	NNNO4NNNNNNNNNN	R,J,T	141	514	06.02.13	7479	000000	92997
553.362-014	AUTOCLAVE OPERATOR (aircraft mfg.)	4336	33333334444	MONOOONFOFOOFOFNOFON	NNNN3NNONNNNNNO	T,J	063	592	06.02.18	7830	000000	92923
553.364-010	SAMPLE TESTER (chemical)	3235	33334343354	LNNNNNNNCCFNOONFNFNFN	NNNN4NNNNNNNNFN	J,T	212	347	02.04.01	7830	000000	83005
553.382-010	AUTOCLAVE OPERATOR I (chemical)	3225	33334434345	HNNONNNNFFNNNNNNNNNNNN	NNNN4NONNNNNNNN	J,T	147	491	06.02.11	7675	000000	92962
553.382-018	EVAPORATOR OPERATOR I (chemical)	4336	33334434454	LONONONFFONNNNNFCFFON	NNNO4ONNNNNNNON	J,T	144	347	06.02.11	7666	410301	92923
553.382-022	VARNISH MAKER (paint & varnish)	4337	33334444355	LNNONNNFFNNNNNNFNFNN	NNNN4NNNNNNNNNN	J,T	147	495	06.02.11	7675	000000	92923
553.382-026	METAL-BONDING PRESS OPERATOR (aircraft mfg.)	3225	33334444355	MNNNONNNFFNNNNNFNFNNN	NNNN4NNNNNNNNNN	T	063	592	06.02.02	7339	480501	92197
553.385-014	PRIMER EXPEDITOR AND DRIER (chemical)	2123	44444444355	LNNONNNFFNNNNNFNNNNNN	ONNO4NNNNNNNNON	R,T	141	374	06.04.11	7675	000000	92923
553.462-010	FLASH-DRIER OPERATOR (chemical)	3224	34344444355	MNNNNNNNFFONFFNFNFNN	NNON4NONNNNNON	J,T	141	499	06.02.18	7675	000000	92923
553.482-010	AGER OPERATOR (plastic-synth.)	3225	34343434355	LNNNNNNFFONNNNFNFNN	NNNN4NNNNNNNNNN	J,T	147	492	06.02.13	7675	150607	92923
553.486-010	CALCINE FURNACE LOADER (paint & varnish)	1112	45454544354	HNNNNNNNFFONNNNNONFNON	NNNN4NNNNNNNNNN	R	141	499	06.04.11	8725	000000	98502
553.582-010	DRIER OPERATOR II (chemical)	3224	34434444355	LNNNNNNNFFOONNNFFFNN	NNNO4NNNNNNNNNN	J,T	141	490	06.02.11	7675	000000	92923
553.582-014	POT FIRER (chemical)	3225	34434434354	LNNONNNNFFOONNNFNFNN	NNFN4NONNNNNNNN	J,T	144	875	06.02.11	7675	150607	92923
553.585-010	DEBUBBLIZER (plastic-synth.)	2113	44444444355	MNNONNNFFONNNNNOFNFNN	NNNO4NNNNNNNNON	R,T	147	492	06.04.11	7675	000000	92998
553.585-014	DRY-HOUSE ATTENDANT (chemical)	2113	44444444355	MNNNNNNFFNNNNNFNFNN	NNNN4NONNNNNNNN	R,T	141	499	06.04.11	7679	000000	92998
553.585-018	DRYING-ROOM ATTENDANT (soap & rel.)	1112	45454444455	MNNNNNNNFFONNNNONFNNN	NNNN4NNNNNNNNNN	R	141	494	06.04.19	7679	000000	92998
553.585-022	THERMAL MOLDER (rubber goods)	2123	44433444355	MNNONNNFFONNNNNFNFNNN	NNNO4NNNNNNNNNN	R	141	519	06.04.13	7679	000000	92998
553.585-026	TUMBLER OPERATOR (rubber goods)	2112	44444444355	MNNNNNNFFONNNNNONNNNN	NNNN4NNNNNNNNNN	R	141	519	06.04.13	7679	000000	92998
553.665-010	BELT-PRESS OPERATOR II (rubber goods)	2113	44434434355	HNNNNNNFFNNNNNNFNFNN	NNNN4NNNNNNNNNN	R,T	141	514	06.04.13	7667	000000	92971
553.665-014	BLACK-MILL OPERATOR (chemical)	3224	34343434345	LONONNNFFNNNFFNFNNNN	NNFN4NONNNNNNNN	R,T	147	499	06.04.19	7675	000000	92923
553.665-018	COOK (chemical)	3223	34344444355	LONONNNFFNNOONNNNNNN	NNNO4NNNNNNNNNN	R,T	147	499	06.04.19	7679	000000	92998
553.665-022	COOKER TENDER (oils & grease)	2112	44554544355	HONFNNNFFNNOONNNNNNN	NNNO4NONNNNNNNN	R	131	499	06.04.11	7675	000000	92998
553.665-026	DRIER OPERATOR I (chemical)	2113	44444453355	MNNNNNNNFFNNOONOFNINN	NNOO4NNNNNNONFNNN	R,T	141	490	06.04.11	7675	000000	92923
553.665-030	DRUM-DRIER OPERATOR (chemical)	2113	44444444355	LNNNNNNNFFNNNNNFNFNN	NNON4NONNNNNNNN	R,T	141	499	06.04.19	7675	000000	92923
553.665-034	FIRER HELPER (paper & pulp)	2112	44444534355	LFNONONFFNNOONFNNNNN	NNFO4OONNNNNNON	R,T	147	491	06.04.14	7675	000000	92923
553.665-038	HEATER TENDER (rubber goods; rubber reclaim.; rubber tire)	2122	44444444355	MNNNNNNFFNNOONNNFNNN	NNNO4NNNNNNNNN	R,T	141	510	06.04.13	7675	000000	92965
553.665-042	PLASTICS-SEASONER OPERATOR (plastic-synth.)	2112	44444444355	MNNNNNNFFNNOONNNNNNN	NNON4NNNNNNNNNN	R,T	141	492	06.04.13	7675	150607	92923
553.665-046	STEAM-PRESS TENDER I (rubber goods)	2114	44545544355	HNNONNNFFNNOONNNNNN	NNNO4NNNNNNNNN	R	141	514	06.04.13	7667	000000	92971
553.665-050	STEAM-PRESS TENDER II (rubber goods)	2113	44444444355	MNNNNNNNFFONNNNONNNNON	NNNO4NNNNNNNNNN	R,T	141	496	06.04.11	7675	000000	92962
553.665-054	TRAY-DRIER OPERATOR (chemical)	2113	44444444355	HNNNNNNNCCFFNNNFNNNNN	NNQN4NNNNNNNNNN	R,T	141	499	06.04.19	7675	000000	92923
553.682-010	BLACK-ASH-BURNER OPERATOR (paper & pulp)	3224	34444434355	LNNNNNNNFFNNNNONNNNNN	NNFO4NONNNNNNNN	J,T	141	499	06.02.14	7675	000000	92923
553.682-014	CURER, FOAM RUBBER (rubber goods)	3224	33343434455	LNNNNNNFFONNNNFNFNNN	NNNN4NONNNNNNNN	J,T	147	519	06.02.13	7664	000000	92965
553.682-018	EVAPORATOR OPERATOR II (chemical)	3124	34344344355	MONNNNNNFFOONNNNNNNN	NNNN4NNNNNNNNNN	R,T	144	496	06.02.18	7666	000000	92962
553.682-022	REDUCTION-FURNACE OPERATOR (chemical)	3224	33444444354	LONONONFFONNNNONNNNON	NNFN4NNNNNNNNN	R,T	147	491	06.02.15	7675	000000	92923
553.682-026	V-BELT CURER (rubber goods)	3224	34433333355	MNNNNNNFFNNNNNNFFNNN	NNON3NNONNNNNNON	J,T	141	514	06.02.13	7667	000000	92971
553.684-010	HEAT WELDER, PLASTICS (plastic prod.)	2213	34433434355	MNNNNNNNFFOONNNNONOCONN	NNON4NNNNNNNNNN	R,J	081	519	06.04.31	7714	000000	93914
553.684-014	NITROCELLULOSE OPERATOR (chemical)	3114	34433444355	HNNNNNNCCFFNNNFNNNNN	NNNO4NNNNNNNOON	R,S,T	147	499	06.04.34	7675	000000	92923
553.685-010	AMMONIUM-NITRATE CRYSTALLIZER (chemical)	3224	34443434355	LNNNNNNNFFNFNNFNNNN	NNNN4NFNNNNNNN	R,T	141	499	06.02.18	7676	000000	92962
553.685-014	BAGGER (plastic prod.)	2113	44443344355	HNNNNNNNFFOONNNNNNNNN	NNNN4NONNNNNNNN	R,T	141	510	06.04.13	7544	000000	91938
553.685-018	BONE-CHAR KILN TENDER (chemical)	2112	44544544355	MONNNNNNFFNNNNNNNNNNN	NNNN4NNNNNNNNNN	R,T	141	496	06.04.19	7675	000000	92923
553.685-022	BONE-DRIER OPERATOR (chemical)	2112	44544544355	MNNNNNNFFNNNNNNNNNNN	NNNN4NONNNNNNNN	R,T	141	499	06.04.19	7675	000000	92923
553.685-026	CADMIUM-LIQUOR MAKER (paint & varnish)	2112	44544544355	HNNNNNNFFNNNNNNNNNNNN	NNNN4NNNNNNNNNN	R,T	147	496	06.04.11	7676	000000	92938
553.685-030	CALCINE-FURNACE TENDER (paint & varnish)	2113	34443344354	HNNNNNNFFNNNNNNNNNNFN	NNNN4NNNNNNNNNN	J,T	141	495	06.04.11	7675	000000	92923

DOT #	DOT Title & Industry	Trng	Aptitude	Physical	Environment	Tempra	WkF	MPSMS	GOE	SOC	CIP	OES
553.685-034	CONTINUOUS-LINTER-DRIER OPERATOR (chemical)	2112	4444354355	MNNFNNNFFNNNNNNNNNNN	NNNN4NONNNNNNN	R	141	471	06.04.19	7675	000000	92923
553.685-038	CURING-OVEN TENDER (chemical)	3114	3444334344	LNNNNNNFFNNNNNFFFON	NNNN4NNNNNNNNO	R,T	141	499	06.04.11	7675	000000	92923
553.685-042	DRIER OPERATOR (chemical; pharmaceut.)	3223	3444433455	MNNONONFFOFNNNONONNN	NNON4NONNNNNNN	J,T	141	490	06.04.11	7675	000000	92923
553.685-046	DRIER OPERATOR II (plastic-synth.)	2112	4444444345	MNNNNNNFFNNNNFNFNNN	FNNN4NONNNNNNN	R,T	141	492	06.04.13	7675	150607	92923
553.685-050	DRIER OPERATOR III (chemical)	3225	3444344355	MNNNNNNFFONNNNFNFNNN	NNNO4NONNNNNNN	R,T	141	490	06.04.11	7675	000000	92923
553.685-054	DRIER OPERATOR IV (chemical)	3224	3434434355	MNNNNNNFFNNNNNOOONNN	NNNN4NONNNNNNN	J,T	141	490	06.04.11	7675	000000	92923
553.685-058	DRIER-OPERATOR HELPER (chemical)	1112	4554544355	MNNONNNFFNNNNNNNNNNF	NNNN4NNNNNNNNN	R	141	499	06.04.19	8618	000000	98999
553.685-062	FIRE-HOSE CURER (rubber goods)	2112	4454453455	HNNNNNNFFNNNNNFNFNNN	NNNO4NNNNNNNNN	R,T	141	514	06.04.13	7679	000000	92998
553.685-066	FIRER, RETORT (chemical)	2113	4444544355	LNNNNNNFFNNNNNNNNNNN	NNON4NNNNNNNNN	R,T	021	490	06.04.11	7668	000000	92926
553.685-070	KETTLE WORKER (soap & rel.)	3224	3444444355	MNNFNNNFFNNNNNFNFNN	NNNO4NONNNNNNN	J	147	494	06.02.18	7679	000000	92923
553.685-074	LIME-SLUDGE KILN OPERATOR (paper & pulp)	2112	4444444455	LONNNNNNFFNNNNNFOONNN	NNNO4NONNNNNNN	R,T	141	491	06.04.11	7675	000000	92923
553.685-078	MILLED-RUBBER TENDER (rubber goods; rubber tire)	2112	4454544355	MNNNONNFFNNNNNNNNNNN	NNNO4NONNNNNNN	R	147	492	06.04.13	7675	000000	92998
553.685-082	OVEN TENDER (paint & varnish)	3113	3444454355	MNNNNNNFFNNNNNNNNNNN	NNNN4NNNNNNNNN	R	133	460	06.04.21	7675	000000	92923
553.685-086	PIGMENT FURNACE TENDER (chemical)	3223	3444343453	HNNNNNNFFNNNNNONNNON	NNON4NNNNNNNNN	J,T	141	490	06.04.11	7675	000000	92923
553.685-090	RABBLE-FURNACE TENDER (chemical)	3113	3444444355	LNNNNNNFFNNNNNNNNNNN	NNFN4NONNNNNNN	R,T	147	499	06.04.19	7675	000000	92923
553.685-094	ROTARY-FURNACE TENDER (chemical)	2113	4444434355	HNNNNNNFFNNNNNONONNN	NNON4NONNNNNNN	R,T	141	490	06.04.11	7675	000000	92923
553.685-098	SOAP-DRIER OPERATOR (soap & rel.)	2112	4444443355	HNNNNNNFFONNNNONONNN	NNNN4NNNNNNNNN	R,T	147	494	06.04.19	7675	000000	92923
553.685-102	TIRE MOLDER (rubber tire)	2113	4544544355	HNNNNNNFFONNNNFNFNNN	NNON4NNNNNNNNN	R,T	132	511	06.04.13	7679	000000	92998
553.685-106	VACUUM-DRIER TENDER (chemical)	3114	3444444455	LNNNNNNFFONNNNFNFNNN	NNNN4NNNNNNNNN	J,T	141	490	06.04.11	7675	000000	92923
553.685-110	WAX-POT TENDER (foundry)	2212	4444544355	MNNNNNNFFFNNNNONONNN	NNNN4NNNNNNNNO	R,T	131	499	06.04.32	7679	480599	91935
553.685-114	CADMIUM BURNER (chemical)	2122	4444444355	HFNONNNFFNNNNNNNNNNN	NNON3NNNNNNNNN	R	147	491	06.04.11	7675	000000	92923
553.685-118	DRIER OPERATOR VI (chemical)	3114	3453454355	MONNNNNFFOONNNNFNNNF	NNOO4NONNNNNNN	R,T	141	499	06.04.19	7675	000000	92923
553.686-010	BONE-CHAR OPERATOR (chemical)	1112	4544544345	MONNNNNFFNNNNNNFNNN	NNNN4NNNNNNNNN	R	141	499	06.04.19	8725	000000	98502
553.686-014	CD-MIXER HELPER (rubber reclaim.)	1112	4444544355	HNNNNNNCCFNNNNNONFNNN	NNNO4NOONNNNNN	R,T	147	513	06.04.11	8618	000000	98999
553.686-018	CURING-PRESS OPERATOR (rubber tire)	1112	4443444345	HNNFFNNFFNNNNNNNNNN	NNNO4NONNNNNNN	R,T	136	511	06.04.13	8725	000000	98502
553.687-010	DRIER HELPER (chemical)	1112	4454544355	HNNNNNNFFONNNNFFNN	NNNN4NONNNNNNN	R	131	319	06.04.11	8725	000000	98502
553.687-014	FURNACE HELPER (chemical)	2112	4444444355	HNNNNNNFFNNOONNNNNNF	NNNN4NONNNNNNN	R	141	499	06.04.34	8618	000000	98999
554.137-010	FINISHING SUPERVISOR, PLASTIC SHEETS (plastic-synth.)	3226	3333334455	LNNNNNNFFONONONOONN	NNNN4NNNNNNNNN	V,D,P,J	051	492	06.04.01	7100	000000	81008
554.137-014	SUPERVISOR, COATING (plastic-synth.)	4337	3334434455	LNNNNNNOOFFNONFONN	NNNN4NNNNNNNNN	D,P,T	151	492	06.02.01	7100	000000	81008
554.362-010	CALENDER OPERATOR (rubber goods; rubber tire)	3224	3434434355	MNNNNNNFFOOONONFNNN	NNNN4NNNNNNNNN	J,T	134	519	06.04.34	7669	000000	92953
554.382-010	COATER (pharmaceut.)	3225	3434343353	MNNONNNFFOONNNNFFFF	NNNN4NNNNNNNNN	J,T	151	493	06.02.21	7669	000000	92953
554.382-014	PLASTICS-SPREADING-MACHINE OPERATOR (plastic-synth.)	3224	3433434344	LNNNNNNFFNNNNNFFFON	NNNN4NONNNNNNN	J,T	151	492	06.02.13	7543	150607	91926
554.384-010	DYER (chemical)	3223	3434434352	LNNFNNNCCONNNNFNNOFN	NNNF4NNNNNNNNN	J,T	151	618	06.02.32	7669	000000	92953
554.485-010	BUCKLE-STRAP-DRUM OPERATOR (rubber goods)	2113	4443434355	LNNNNNNFFONNNONFNNN	NNNN4NNNNNNNNN	R,T	151	512	06.04.13	7669	000000	92953
554.485-014	STRAP-FOLDING-MACHINE OPERATOR (rubber goods)	3222	4444444455	MNNNNNNFFONOONFNFNNN	NNNN4NNNNNNNNN	R	062	512	06.04.07	7674	000000	92998
554.585-010	CATHODE MAKER (chemical)	3224	3433443355	HNNNNNNFFONNNNFFFNN	NNON4NONNNNNNON	J,T	151	589	06.04.21	7669	000000	92953
554.585-014	COATER OPERATOR (plastic-synth.)	3123	3434443354	MONOOONFFNNNNNFNNNN	NNNN4NONNNNNNN	R,T	151	492	06.04.21	7543	150607	91926
554.586-010	FINISHER (plastic-synth.)	2112	4444444355	MNNNNNNFFONNNNONOONN	NNNN4NNONNNNON	R	011	492	06.04.40	8769	150607	98999
554.587-010	ROLL INSPECTOR (plastic-synth.)	2223	3443334354	LNNNNNNCCFCNNNFNOOON	NNNN4NNNNNNNNN	R,J,T	212	492	06.03.02	7820	150607	83005
554.662-010	CALENDER OPERATOR, FOUR-ROLL (plastic prod.; rubber goods; rubber tire)	3225	3343434355	LONONONFFNNOOFNNNNN	NNNN4NNONNNNNNN	J,T	135	510	06.02.13	7669	000000	92953
554.665-010	CALENDER-WIND-UP TENDER (rubber goods; rubber tire)	2112	4444444355	MNNNNNNFFNOONFNFNNN	NNNN4NNONNNNNNN	R,T	163	519	06.04.07	7651	000000	92705
554.665-014	LAMINATING-MACHINE TENDER (rubber goods)	2122	4443444355	MNNNNNNFFONOONFNFONO	NNON4NNONNNNNNN	R,T	063	519	06.04.09	7667	000000	92971
554.682-010	CALENDER-LET-OFF OPERATOR (rubber goods; rubber tire)	3214	3444434354	MNNNNNNFFONNNNFNNN	NNNN4NNNNNNNNN	R,T	141	519	06.02.13	7679	150607	92998
554.682-014	MASKING-MACHINE OPERATOR (plastic-synth.)	3224	3433334354	MNNNNNNFFONNNFNFNON	NNNN4NNNNNNNNN	R,T	063	492	06.04.38	7662	150607	92974
554.682-018	ROLL OPERATOR (plastic-synth.)	3115	3443434354	MNNNNNNFFONNNNONFOON	NNNN4NNNNNNNNN	J,T	135	492	06.02.13	7549	150607	92198

DOT #	DOT Title & Industry	Trng	Aptitude	Physical	Environment	Tempra	WkF	MPSMS	GOE	SOC	CIP	OES
554.682-022	ROOFING-MACHINE OPERATOR (build. mat., nec)	3124	34433434355	LNNNFNNNFOONNNNONFONNN	NNNN4NONNNNNNON	J,T	151	503	06.02.18	7669	000000	92953
554.684-010	CAUSTIC OPERATOR (plastic-synth.)	2113	44443434354	MNNNNNNNFFNNNNNRNONONON	NNNNO4NNNNNNNON	R,T	151	492	06.04.13	7756	150607	93947
554.684-014	FOAM DISPENSER (rubber goods)	2113	44433433344	MNNNNNNNFFONNNNNNNNNNN	NNNN4NNNNNNNNN	R,T	153	519	06.04.32	7662	000000	92974
554.685-010	BULK-SEALER OPERATOR (plastic-synth.)	2112	44444544455	LNNNNNNFFNNNNNFNFNNN	NNNN4NNNNNNNNN	R	133	510	06.04.02	7549	150607	92198
554.685-014	COATING-AND-BAKING OPERATOR (any industry)	3123	44443444354	LNNNNNNFFNNNNNNFNNNON	NNON4NONNNNNNN	R,T	153	495	06.04.21	7543	000000	91926
554.685-018	COMBINING-MACHINE OPERATOR (plastic-synth.)	3114	34443444355	LNNNNNNFFNNNNNFNONNN	NNNN4NONNNNNNN	R,T	135	492	06.04.20	7667	150607	92971
554.685-022	LINER REROLL TENDER (rubber goods; rubber tire)	2113	44443443345	HNNNNNNCCNNNNCNCCNN	NNNN4NNONNNNNN	R	163	519	06.04.07	7679	000000	92998
554.685-026	SIZING-MACHINE OPERATOR (nonmet. min.)	2113	44444444354	MNNNNNNNFFNNNNNNNNN	NNNN4NNNNNNNNN	R,T	153	538	06.04.21	7669	000000	92953
554.685-030	LAMINATOR (wood prod., nec)	3123	44444444355	LONONONFFONNNNFNNONN	NNNN4NNNNNNNNN	T	063	456	06.04.34	7661	030404	92956
554.685-034	PHOTORESIST LAMINATOR, PRINTED CIRCUIT BOARD (electron. comp.)	2122	44444444455	MNNNNNNCCFNNNNFNONNN	NNNN3NONNNNNNN	R,U	063	587	06.04.09	7679	000000	92998
554.686-010	CALENDER FEEDER (rubber goods)	1112	44544544455	HNNNNNNCCNNNNNNNFNNN	NNNN4NNONNNNNN	R	134	492	06.04.13	8725	000000	98502
554.686-014	CALENDER-LET-OFF HELPER (rubber goods; rubber tire)	2112	44444544445	HNNNNNNFFFNNNNNNFNN	NNNN4NOONNNNNN	R	011	519	06.04.40	8618	000000	98999
554.686-018	CALENDER-OPERATOR HELPER (rubber goods; rubber tire)	2112	44444443345	HNNFNNNFFONNNNNONFNNN	NNNN4NNONNNNNN	R	163	519	06.04.13	8618	000000	98999
554.686-022	CALENDER-WIND-UP HELPER (rubber goods; rubber tire)	1112	44544544455	MNNNNNNNFFNNNNNNNNNN	NNNN4NNNNNNNNN	R	163	519	06.04.29	8617	000000	98999
554.687-010	SPREADER (plastic-synth.)	2112	45544534355	MNNNNNNFFNNNNNNNNNNN	NNNN4NONNNNNNN	R	152	492	06.04.27	8769	000000	98999
555.382-010	PULVERIZER-MILL OPERATOR (rubber goods; rubber reclaim.)	3224	33343444344	MNNNNNNNFFNNNNNNOFOON	NNNN4NONNNNNNN	R,J,T	142	510	06.02.13	7677	000000	92965
555.565-010	MILL ATTENDANT I (chemical)	3113	34443434355	MNNNNNNNFFONOONONFNNN	NNNN4NONNNNNNN	R,T	142	499	05.12.07	7677	000000	92965
555.585-010	CUTTER OPERATOR (plastic-synth.)	3113	34444444355	MNNNNNNNFFONNNNNONFNNN	NNNN4NNNNNNNNN	R,T	054	450	06.04.03	7678	150607	92944
555.665-010	SHREDDER TENDER (chemical)	2112	44544534355	LNNONNNFFONNNNFNNNNN	NNNN4NONNNNNNN	R	142	320	06.04.19	7678	000000	92944
555.682-010	MILLER II (chemical)	3117	34443434355	HNNNNNNOOONOONFNFFNN	NNNN4NNNNNNNNN	J,T	142	499	06.02.11	7677	000000	92965
555.682-014	ROLLER-MILL OPERATOR (paint & varnish)	3225	34443444354	MNNONNNFFNNNNNONFOON	NNNN4NNNNNNNNN	R,T	142	495	06.02.11	7677	000000	92965
555.682-018	SAND-MILL GRINDER (paint & varnish)	3123	34444444455	MNNONONFFONNNNNONONN	NNNN4NNNNNNNNN	J,T	142	495	06.02.11	7677	000000	92965
555.682-022	STONE-MILL OPERATOR (paint & varnish)	3123	44443444355	HNNNNNNNFFNNNNNFNNNN	NNNO4NNNNNNNNN	J,R,T	142	495	06.02.11	7678	000000	92944
555.685-010	BEATER OPERATOR (chemical)	2113	44444434355	LNNNNNNNFFNNNNNNNNNNN	NNNN4NNNNNNNNN	R,T	142	499	06.04.11	7677	000000	92965
555.685-014	BONE CRUSHER (chemical)	2112	44544544455	LNNNNNNNFFONNNFNNNN	NNNN4NNNNNNNNN	R	142	499	06.04.19	7677	000000	92965
555.685-018	COPRA PROCESSOR (soap & rel.)	3123	44544544455	LNNNNNNFFONNNNFNNNNN	NNNN4NNNNNNNNN	J,T	142	385	06.04.19	7677	000000	92965
555.685-022	CRUSHER TENDER (fabrication, nec)	2112	44444544455	HONFNFFOONNNOFNFFF	NNNN4NONNNNNNN	R	142	619	06.04.09	7677	000000	92965
555.685-026	GRINDER (plastic prod., plastic-synth.)	2112	44543544354	HNNFNNNFFONNNNNONNN	NNNN4NONNNNNNN	R	142	492	06.04.02	7677	000000	92965
555.685-030	GRINDER (rubber goods; rubber reclaim.)	2122	44544544455	HNNNNNNFFONNNNNFNNN	NNNN4NNONNNNNN	R,T	142	513	06.04.07	7677	000000	92965
555.685-034	GRINDER OPERATOR (chemical)	2123	44444444345	LNNNNNNCCNNNNNOFNFNN	NNON4NNNNNNNNN	R,T	142	490	06.04.11	7677	000000	92965
555.685-038	MILL ATTENDANT II (chemical)	2112	44444544355	MNNNNONNNNOONNNNCCNNON	NNNN4NNNNNNNNN	R,T	142	494	06.04.11	7677	000000	92965
555.685-042	PELLET-PRESS OPERATOR (chemical)	3213	34433434355	MNNONONFFNNNNNFNNN	NNNN4NNONNNNNN	J,T	134	490	06.04.11	7663	000000	92971
555.685-046	PULVERIZER (chemical)	2112	44444444355	MMOOOONFFNNONNNFOOON	NONN4NOONNNNNN	R	142	499	06.04.11	7677	000000	92965
555.685-050	SCRATCHER TENDER (fabrication, nec)	2113	44444434354	HNNNONONFFNNNNNNNNNNN	NNNN4NONNNNNNN	R	142	496	06.04.09	7677	000000	92965
555.685-054	SECOND OPERATOR, MILL TENDER (chemical)	3113	34443344355	HONONONFFNNNNFOOFFF	NNNN4NONNNNNNN	J,T	142	619	06.04.11	7679	000000	92998
555.685-058	SHREDDER OPERATOR (plastic-synth.)	2123	44444444355	LNNNNNNCCNNNNNOFNFNN	NNNN4NONNNNNNN	R,T	142	347	06.04.09	7677	000000	92965
555.685-062	SOAP GRINDER (soap & rel.)	2112	44545544354	HNNNNNNNFFONFNFNFFNN	NNNN4NNONNNNNN	R	142	490	06.04.19	7677	000000	92965
555.685-066	WHEEL-MILL OPERATOR (chemical)	2112	44444444355	HNNFNFNFFNNNNNNNNNNN	NNNN4NNONONNNNN	R,T	142	494	06.04.11	8725	000000	92965
555.686-010	BLOCK-BREAKER OPERATOR (chemical)	2112	44444444355	MMNFNFNFFNNNNNNNNNN	NONN4NOONNNNNNN	R	142	499	06.04.11	8725	000000	98502
555.686-014	SOAP CHIPPER (soap & rel.)	1112	44544544354	LNNNNNNNFFONNNFNNNN	NNNN4NNNNNNNNN	R	142	494	06.04.09	8725	000000	98502
555.687-010	SCALE OPERATOR (chemical)	2122	44444444455	LNNNNNNNFFNNNNNNNNNN	NNNN4NNNNNNNNN	R	212	499	06.03.02	7840	000000	83005
556.130-010	SUPERVISOR, PLASTICS FABRICATION (boot & shoe; inst. & app.; plastic prod.;)	4347	33332333354	LOOOONFFFOFFNFNOOOO	NNNN4OOONNNNON	D,V,T,P,J	102	510	06.01.01	7100	150607	81008
556.130-014	SUPERVISOR, PLASTICS (toy-sport equip.)	4337	33333433354	LNNNNNNNOOONFFNONOOON	NNNN4NNNNNNNNN	V,D,P,J	132	615	06.02.01	7100	000000	81008
556.130-018	MOLDING SUPERVISOR (plastic prod.)	4336	32343344453	LNNOOONFFOOFFNFOOOON	NNNN4NOONNNNNON	D,J,P	132	510	06.02.01	7100	150607	81008
556.362-010	ARCH-CUSHION-PRESS OPERATOR (rubber goods)	3224	44445444355	MNNNNNNNFFONFNFNFFNN	NNNN4NNNNNNNNN	J,T	132	512	06.02.13	7679	000000	92998
556.380-010	MOLD SETTER (inst. & app.; office machines; plastic prod.; recording)	3236	33333434344	MOOOOONFFFNONNNFOOON	NNNN4NNONONNNN	T,J	132	510	06.01.02	7349	000000	91902
556.380-014	PREFORM-MACHINE OPERATOR (button & notion)	3124	34433444355	LNNNNNNNFFONFNFFNN	NNNN4NNNNNNNNN	J,T	135	519	06.01.02	7100	000000	92197
556.382-010	INJECTION-MOLDING-MACHINE OPERATOR (plastic prod.)	3225	34433433355	MNNNNNNNFFNNNNNFONNNN	NNNN4NNNNNNNNN	J,T	132	510	06.02.13	7342	000000	91902
556.382-018	POLYSTYRENE-BEAD MOLDER (plastic prod.)	3224	34333444355	MONONONFFONNNNNFNNNNN	NNNN3NNNNNNNNN	J,T	132	519	06.02.13	7663	000000	92971
556.385-010	CENTRIFUGAL-CASTING-MACHINE TENDER (button & notion)	3223	34443434355	MNNNNNNFFONNNNNFNNNNN	NNNN4NNNNNNNNN	R,T	132	618	06.04.19	7542	000000	91905
556.484-010	SCAGLIOLA MECHANIC (nonmet. min.)	2215	34444444354	HNNNNNNNFFFNNNNFNFFON	NNNN4NNNNNNNNN	R,T	132	539	06.02.30	7754	489999	93944

DOT #	DOT Title & Industry	Trng	Aptitude	Physical	Environment	Tempra	WkF	MPSMS	GOE	SOC	CIP	OES
556.582-010	PLATE MOLDER (pen & pencil; print. & pub.)	3224	34343443355	MNNNNNNFFNNNNNNFNNFNN	NNFN4NNONNNNNNN	T	132	567	06.02.18	7667	000000	92971
556.585-010	CASTING-ROOM OPERATOR (plastic-synth.)	3224	34423444354	LNNNONNFFONNNNFNNNFON	NNNN4NNNNNNNNNN	J,T	135	492	06.04.13	7542	150607	91321
556.585-014	POLYMERIZATION-OVEN OPERATOR (plastic-synth.)	2113	44443444355	MNNNNNNNFFFNNNNFNNFON	NNNN3NNNNNNNNNN	J,T	132	492	06.04.13	7675	150607	92923
556.587-010	MOLD PARTER (plastic-synth.)	2112	44444444354	MNNNNNNNFFNNNNFNNFFON	NNNN4NNNNNNNNNN	R	011	492	06.04.40	8769	150607	98999
556.665-010	CAKE-PRESS OPERATOR (plastic-synth.)	3214	34433444344	HNNONNNFFNOONFNNNON	NNNN4NONNNNNNN	R,T	132	492	06.04.13	7542	150607	91905
556.665-014	CORRUGATOR OPERATOR (plastic-synth.)	3224	34433443354	LNNNNNNFFFOONFNFFON	NNNN4NONNNNNNN	J,T	132	492	06.04.13	7542	150607	91905
556.665-018	MOLDER, PIPE COVERING (plastic prod.)	2113	34343433355	MNNNNNNFFNNNNFNFFNN	NNNN4NNNNNNNNNN	T	132	519	06.04.13	7542	000000	91905
556.682-010	BLOW-MOLDING-MACHINE OPERATOR (plastic prod.)	3223	34343434355	MNNNNNNFFONNNNFNNNNN	NNNN3NNNNNNNNNN	J,T	132	519	06.02.13	7663	000000	92971
556.682-014	COMPRESSION-MOLDING-MACHINE OPERATOR (elec. equip.; plastic prod.)	3225	34433434344	HONONNNFFONNNFNNNON	NNNN4NOONNNNNNN	R,T	132	510	06.02.13	7342	000000	91902
556.682-018	PLODDER OPERATOR (soap & rel.)	3124	34343343353	LNNONONFFFFNNNFNNNFF	NNNN4NNNNNNNNNN	J,T	132	494	06.02.18	7467	000000	92968
556.682-022	COMPRESSOR (elec. equip.; pharmaceut.)	3224	34443433355	MONONONFFFOONFNFFFN	NNNN4NOONNNNNNON	R,T	134	493	06.02.11	7467	000000	92968
556.684-010	CELL INSPECTOR (plastic-synth.)	2114	34443443355	LNNNNNNFFFNNNNFNFNNN	NNNN4NNNNNNNNNN	R,T	212	492	06.03.02	7820	150607	83005
556.684-014	ENCAPSULATOR (aircraft mfg.)	3224	34443433355	MNNONNNFFOONNNONFNNN	NNNN3NONNNNNNN	T	132	592	06.04.34	7754	000000	93944
556.684-018	MOLD-FILLING OPERATOR (plastic-synth.)	2114	34443434355	MNNNNNNFFONNNNFNFFNN	NNNN4NNNNNNNNNN	R,T	132	492	06.04.32	7754	150607	93944
556.684-022	NEEDLE-BAR MOLDER (carpet & rug)	2112	44444443455	LNNNNNNFFNNNNNFNOONN	NNNN3NNNNNNNNNN	R,T	132	567	06.04.32	7663	000000	92971
556.684-026	RUBBER MOLDER (fabrication, nec)	2114	34453444355	LNNNNNNCCNNNNNNNNNNN	NNNN4NONNNNNNN	R,T	132	519	06.02.29	7754	000000	93944
556.684-030	LOADER-DEMOLDER (furniture)	2113	34343434355	MNNNNNNFFNNNNNNNFNNN	NNNN3NNNNNNNNNN	R	011	519	06.04.32	8725	150607	98502
556.685-010	AIR-BAG CURER (rubber tire)	2112	44444444355	MNNNNNNFFNNNNNNNFNNN	NNNN4NNNNNNNNNN	R,T	132	511	06.04.13	7667	000000	92971
556.685-014	BLOCK-PRESS OPERATOR (chemical)	2112	44444454355	MNNNONONFFNNNNNFNNNNN	NNNN4NNONNNNNNN	R	134	499	06.04.11	7667	000000	92971
556.685-018	BOWLING-BALL MOLDER (toy-sport equip.)	2113	44444534355	MNNNNNNNFFNNNNFNNNNN	NNNN4NNNNNNNNNN	R	132	616	06.04.13	7667	000000	92971
556.685-022	COMPRESSION-MOLDING-MACHINE TENDER (plastic prod.)	2112	44544534355	LNNNNNNFFNNNFNFNNN	NNNN4NNNNNNNNNN	R,T	132	519	06.04.13	7542	000000	91905
556.685-026	COSMETICS PRESSER (pharmaceut.)	2113	44443544355	LNNONONFFNNNNNNFNNNN	NNNN4NNNNNNNNNN	R	132	494	06.04.09	7667	000000	92971
556.685-030	DIPPER (rubber goods)	2112	44454544355	MNNNNNNFFNNNNNFNNN	NNNN4NNNNNNNNNN	R,T	151	519	06.04.13	7663	000000	92971
556.685-034	DIPPING-MACHINE OPERATOR (rubber goods)	2113	34343443355	MNNNNNNFFNNNNNONFONN	NNON4NONNNNNNN	J,T	132	519	06.04.13	7663	000000	92971
556.685-038	INJECTION-MOLDING-MACHINE TENDER (plastic prod.; recording; rubber goods)	2112	44444544355	LNNNNNNFFFOONFNNNNN	NNNN4NNNNNNNNNN	T,R	132	519	06.04.10	7542	000000	91905
556.685-042	MATTING-PRESS TENDER (rubber goods)	2112	44443445355	MNNNNNNFFNNNNONONNN	NNNO4NONNNNNNN	R	132	519	06.04.13	7667	000000	92971
556.685-046	MOLDER, FOAM RUBBER (rubber goods)	2113	44454544455	MNNNNNNFFNNNNNNFNNN	NNNN4NNNNNNNNNN	R	132	519	06.04.13	7667	000000	92971
556.685-050	MOLDER, MACHINE (pharmaceut.)	3214	34343433355	MNNNNNNFFNNNNNNNNNNN	NNNN4NNNNNNNNNN	R,T	132	493	06.04.11	7663	000000	92928
556.685-054	PARADICHLOROBENZENE TENDER (chemical)	2112	44444443355	LNNNNNNFFFOONFNNNNN	NNNN4NNNNNNNNNN	R,T	133	496	06.04.11	7665	000000	92198
556.685-058	PILLING-MACHINE OPERATOR (plastic prod.; plastic-synth.)	2114	44444544355	MNNNNNOOONNNNONONNN	NNNN4NONNNNNNN	R,T	132	492	06.04.13	7542	150607	91905
556.685-062	POLYSTYRENE-MOLDING-MACHINE TENDER (plastic prod.)	2112	44445534355	LNNOOONFFNNNNNFNNNN	NNNN3NNNNNNNNNF	R,T	132	519	06.04.13	7663	000000	91905
556.685-066	PRESS TENDER (rubber goods; rubber tire; toy-sport equip.)	2112	44443433355	HNNFNNNNFFNNNNNFNNN	NNNN4NNNNNNNNNN	R	132	519	06.04.13	7663	000000	92971
556.685-070	RECORD-PRESS TENDER (recording)	2113	44443444354	LNNOONNFFNNNNNNNNNNN	NNNN4NNNNNNNNNN	R,T	132	585	06.04.20	8614	000000	98502
556.685-074	SLUG-PRESS OPERATOR (elec. equip.)	2112	44544544355	MNNNNNNCCNNNNNNNNNNN	NNNN4NNNNNNNNNN	R	132	491	06.04.19	7667	000000	92971
556.685-078	STAMPER (chemical)	2112	44544544355	MNNNNNNFFNNNNNNNNNNN	NNNN4NNNNNNNNNN	R	132	499	06.04.11	7667	000000	92971
556.685-082	VACUUM PLASTIC-FORMING-MACHINE OPERATOR (plastic prod.)	2112	44444544355	LNNNNNNFFNNNNFNFNNN	NNNN4NNNNNNNNNN	R,T	132	519	06.04.13	7542	000000	91905
556.685-086	BLOW-MOLDING-MACHINE TENDER (toy-sport equip.)	2112	45444455455	LNNNNNNNFFONNNFNNNN	NNNN4NNNNNNNNNN	R	132	615	06.04.13	7542	150607	91905
556.685-090	CENTRIFUGAL-CASTING-MACHINE TENDER (plastic prod.)	1112	44445535354	HNNONNNFFNFFNFNNON	NNON4NNNNNNNNN	R,U	132	519	06.04.19	7542	150607	91905
556.686-010	CAKE-PRESS-OPERATOR HELPER (plastic-synth.)	2112	45444544444	HNNFNNNNNFFNNNNFNNN	NNNN4NNNNNNNNNN	R	132	519	06.04.13	7663	000000	92971
556.686-014	CELL STRIPPER (plastic-synth.)	2112	45444544355	LNNOONNFFNNNNNNNONNN	NNNO4NOONNNNNNN	R	134	492	06.04.13	8725	000000	98502
556.686-018	STRIPPER (plastic prod.; rubber goods)	2112	45444544355	MNNNNNNFFNNNNNNNNNNN	NNNN4NNNNNNNNNN	R	132	519	06.04.13	8725	000000	98502
556.686-022	SUPPOSITORY-MOLDING-MACHINE OPERATOR (pharmaceut.)	1112	45444544455	MNNNNNNCCNNNNNNNNNNN	NNNN4NNNNNNNNNN	R	132	519	06.04.13	8725	000000	98502
556.687-010	BOWLING-BALL-MOLD ASSEMBLER (toy-sport equip.)	1112	45444544355	LNNNNNNFFNONNNNNNNN	NNNN4NNNNNNNNNN	R	041	493	06.04.11	8725	000000	98999
556.687-014	CELL PREPARER (plastic-synth.)	2112	45443534355	MNNNNNNFFNNNNFNNNNN	NNNN4NNNNNNNNNN	R	102	616	06.04.32	7720	000000	93999
556.687-018	MOLD CLEANER (rubber goods)	2112	44444443355	HNNNNNNFFNNNNNFNNNN	NNNO4NNNNNNNNNN	R	132	492	06.04.24	8769	150607	98999
556.687-022	MOLDER, TOILET PRODUCTS (pharmaceut.)	2113	44444434355	LNNOONNFFNNNNNNFNNN	NNNN4NNNNNNNNNN	R	031	566	06.04.39	8769	000000	98999
556.687-026	POURER (rubber goods)	1112	45444544355	MNNNNNNFFNONNNNNNNN	NNNN4NNONNNNNNN	R	132	493	06.04.11	7740	000000	93999
556.687-030	MOLD FILLER (toy-sport equip.)	1111	45444544455	MNNNONONFFNNNNNONONNN	NNNN4NNONNNNNNN	R	132	519	06.04.32	8769	000000	98999
557.130-010	SUPERVISOR, EXTRUDING DEPARTMENT (plastic prod.)	4338	33333343353	MNNONONFFFNNNFNFFN	NNNN4NFNNNNNNN	R	132	616	06.02.01	7754	000000	93944
557.130-014	SUPERVISOR, PLASTIC SHEETS (plastic prod.)	4337	33333333355	MNNNNNNFFFNNNNONNN	NNNN4NNNNNNNNNO	D,J,P	135	492	06.02.01	7100	000000	81008
557.382-010	EXTRUDER OPERATOR (plastic prod.; plastic-synth.)	3225	34433433354	MNNNNNNNFFOONNNNFNNNON	NNOO4NNNNNNNNNN	J,T	135	492	06.02.13	7315	150607	91311

DOT #	DOT Title & Industry	Trng	Aptitude	Physical	Environment	Tempra	WkF	MPSMS	GOE	SOC	CIP	OES
557.382-014	WINK-CUTTER OPERATOR (rubber goods)	3224	34444434355	LNNONNNNFFNNNNFNOONN	NNNNN4NNNNNNNNN	J,T	135	512	06.02.07	7463	000000	92968
557.564-010	EXTRUDER-OPERATOR HELPER (plastic prod.; plastic-synth.)	2212	44444433355	HNNOOONFFNOONFNNFNN	NNNNN4NOONNNNNNN	R,T	135	492	06.04.13	8619	150607	98999
557.564-014	PUMP TESTER (plastic-synth.)	3224	34444344355	LNNNNNNCCFNNNNOFNFNN	NNNNN4NNNNNNNNN	J,T	212	567	06.03.02	7830	000000	83005
557.565-010	EXTRUDING-MACHINE OPERATOR (tex. prod., nec)	2113	44444433354	HONNNNNFFNOONFNNNON	NNNNN4NNNNNNNNN	R,T	135	492	06.04.13	7663	000000	92971
557.565-014	SYNTHETIC-FILAMENT EXTRUDER (plastic-synth.)	2113	44433443355	MFNOONNFFONOONFONNNN	NNNF4NNNNNNNNNF	V,T	135	492	06.04.13	7663	000000	92708
557.665-010	SYNTHETIC-STAPLE EXTRUDER (plastic-synth.)	3124	34433433254	MONOONNFFNOONFFNFF	NNNNN4NNNNNNNNN	R,T	135	492	06.04.13	7659	000000	92708
557.682-010	GRAINING-PRESS OPERATOR (chemical)	2113	44434533355	HNNNNNNNFFNNNNFNFFN	NNNNN4NNNNNNNON	J,T	135	499	06.02.18	7463	000000	92968
557.684-010	JET HANDLER (plastic-synth.)	2114	44434433355	HNNNNNNNFFNNNNFFFN	NNOO4NOONNNNNON	R,T	031	567	06.04.39	6179	000000	85999
557.684-014	JET WIPER (plastic-synth.)	2112	44444443355	LNNNNNNNCCONNNNOFNFNN	NNNNN4NNNNNNNNN	R,T	135	492	06.04.27	7759	000000	93999
557.685-010	CORE EXTRUDER (elec. equip.)	2112	45454544355	LNNNNNNFFNNNNNNNNN	NNNNN4NNNNNNNNN	R,T	135	589	06.04.10	7759	000000	92971
557.685-014	EXTRUDER TENDER (rubber goods)	2113	44445343355	LNNNNNNFFNNNNNNNNN	NNNNN3NNNNNNNNN	R,T	135	519	06.04.13	7663	000000	92971
557.685-018	PROCESSOR (plastic-synth.)	2113	44443433355	LNNNNNNFFNNNNFFNNF	NNNNN4NNNNNNNNN	R,T	147	492	06.04.13	7659	000000	92998
557.685-022	SECOND-FLOOR OPERATOR (plastic-synth.)	2113	44444344355	MNNONNNFFNNNNFNONNN	NNNF4NNNNNNNNN	R	135	492	06.04.13	7659	000000	92708
557.685-026	SPINNER (plastic-synth.)	2113	44434433355	LNNNNNNNCCFNNNNNOFNNNN	NNNNN4NNNNNNNNN	R	135	492	06.04.13	7659	000000	92708
557.685-030	SPINNING-BATH PATROLLER (plastic-synth.)	2124	44444433355	LNNNNNNNCCNNNNOFNFNN	NNNNN4NNNNNNNNN	R,T	014	492	06.04.11	7659	000000	92998
557.685-034	TAKE-UP OPERATOR (plastic-synth.)	2113	44444433354	MNNFNNNFFCNNNNCNCNOF	NNNNN5NNNNNNNNN	R	163	414	06.04.13	7651	150699	92705
558.130-010	SUPERVISOR, PHOSPHATIC FERTILIZER (chemical)	4338	23344444454	LONNNNNNOOONFFNFNNONN	NNNNN3NNNNNNNNN	D,J,T	147	347	06.01.01	7100	000000	81008
558.132-010	SUPERVISOR, CHEMICAL (plastic-synth.)	4337	33333334355	LNNNNNNFFNFFNNNNON	NNNNN4NNNNNNNNN	D,P	147	492	06.01.01	7100	000000	81008
558.132-014	SUPERVISOR, PHOSPHORIC ACID (chemical)	4348	33344344354	LONNNNNOOONFFNNNNON	NNNNN3NNNNNNNNN	D,J,P	147	347	06.04.01	7100	000000	81008
558.132-018	SUPERVISOR, SULFURIC-ACID PLANT (chemical)	4348	33334433454	LNNNNNNFFNFNFONNON	NNNNN4NNNNNNNNN	D,P,J,T	147	347	06.01.01	6700	000000	81008
558.134-010	SUPERVISOR, BRINE (chemical)	4337	33333434355	MNNNNNNFFNFFNFNNNNN	NNNNN3NNNNNNNNN	V,D,P,J	147	491	06.02.01	7100	000000	81008
558.134-014	SUPERVISOR, CELL ROOM (chemical)	4337	33333334355	MNNNNNNFFNFFNFNNNNN	NNNNN3NNNNNNNNN	V,D,P,J	147	491	06.02.01	7100	000000	81008
558.134-018	SUPERVISOR, CELL-EFFICIENCY (chemical)	4347	33333334355	MNNNNNNFFNFFNFNNNNN	NNNNN3NNNNNNNNN	V,D,P,J	147	491	06.02.01	7100	000000	81008
558.134-022	SUPERVISOR, HYDROCHLORIC AREA (chemical)	4337	33333344355	MNNNNNNFFNFFNFNNNNN	NNFN3NONNNNNNNN	V,D,P,J	147	491	06.02.01	7100	000000	81008
558.260-010	CHIEF OPERATOR (chemical)	4347	33333344354	LNNNNNNFFNFFNFONOFF	NNNN4NONNNNNNNN	J,T	147	490	06.01.03	6940	410301	95008
558.362-010	CATALYTIC-CONVERTER OPERATOR (chemical)	3227	34443444355	LFNONNNNFFNOONFNNNN	NNNN4NFNNNNNNNN	J,T	147	490	06.02.11	7676	000000	92935
558.362-014	CD-REACTOR OPERATOR, HEAD (chemical)	3337	33344443353	MNNNNNNFFNOONFNNNFN	NNNO4NNNNNNNNN	J	147	492	06.02.11	7676	000000	92935
558.362-018	SATURATOR OPERATOR (chemical; steel & rel.)	3225	33443434353	LNNNNNNFFNOONFNNFFN	NNNN4NFNNNNNNNN	J,T	147	491	06.02.11	7676	000000	92935
558.382-010	ACID EXTRACTOR (steel & rel.)	3235	33433434353	LNNNNNNFFNOONFNNFN	NNNF4NNNNNNNNN	J,T	147	499	06.02.11	7676	000000	92962
558.382-014	BURNER OPERATOR (chemical)	3335	33344434355	MFNNNNNFFNNNNNFNNNN	NNNNN4NNNNNNNNN	J,T	147	491	06.02.11	7676	000000	92935
558.382-018	CAUSTICISER (paper & pulp)	3214	34434434354	LFNOOONFFFNNNNFNNNN	NNNO3NFNNNNNNNN	J,S,T	147	499	06.02.11	7664	000000	92935
558.382-022	CAUSTICISER (chemical)	3225	34434433355	MNNONONFFFNNNNNFNNNFN	NNNNN4NNNNNNNNN	J,T	147	492	06.02.13	7676	150607	92935
558.382-026	CELL TENDER (chemical)	3235	33333334354	LNNFNFNFFNNNNNFNNNNN	NNNNN4NFNNNNNNN	J,T	147	496	06.02.11	7676	000000	92935
558.382-030	CHLORINATOR OPERATOR (chemical)	3225	34444434353	LNNNNNNFFNNNNNFNNNFN	NNFN3NONNNNNNNN	J,T	147	491	06.02.11	7676	000000	92935
558.382-034	CUPROUS-CHLORIDE OPERATOR (chemical)	3224	34334334355	MFNNNNNFFNNNNNFNNNFN	NNNNN4NFNNNNNNNN	R,T	147	492	06.02.11	7676	000000	92938
558.382-038	KETTLE OPERATOR I (chemical)	3225	34444434354	MNNFNFNFFNNNNNFNNNON	NNNNN4NFNNNNNNNN	J,T	147	490	06.02.11	7676	000000	92962
558.382-042	KETTLE OPERATOR (plastic-synth.)	3225	33343434354	LNNNNNNFFFNNNNFNNNNN	NNNO4NFNNNNNNNN	J,T	147	492	06.02.13	7676	150607	92962
558.382-046	NITRATOR OPERATOR (chemical)	3226	34443434353	MNNONONFFFNNNNNFNNNNN	NNNN4NFNNNNNNNN	J,S,T	147	499	06.02.11	7664	150607	92935
558.382-050	POLYMERIZATION-KETTLE OPERATOR (plastic-synth.)	4337	34434444354	MNNONONFFFNNNNFNNNNFN	NNNNN4NNNNNNNNN	J,T	147	492	06.02.13	7676	000000	92935
558.382-054	SODA-COLUMN OPERATOR (chemical)	3224	34344434355	LNNNNNNFFFNNNNFNNNNN	NNNNN3NFNNNNNNN	J,T	147	496	06.02.11	7676	000000	92935
558.382-058	WET-MIX OPERATOR (chemical)	3224	34434344354	MFNNNNNFFFNNNNFNNNNN	NNNNN4NFNNNNNNN	R,T	147	492	06.02.11	7676	000000	92938
558.385-010	CD-REACTOR OPERATOR (chemical)	3224	34344434354	MNNNNNNFFFNNNNFNNNON	NNNNN3NNNNNNNNN	J,T	147	491	06.04.11	7676	000000	92938
558.385-014	TOWER HELPER (chemical)	3223	34434334354	MNNNFNFNFFNNNNNFNNNNN	NNNNN3NNNNNNNNN	J,T	147	491	06.02.11	7675	000000	92923
558.482-010	FURNACE OPERATOR (chemical)	3324	34344334355	MNNNNNNFFFNNNNFNNNNN	NNNO3NNNNNNNNN	J,T	147	491	06.02.11	7676	000000	92938
558.485-010	CAUSTIC OPERATOR (paper & pulp)	3324	34443344354	LONONONFFFNNNNNNFNNNN	NNNO4NFNNNNNNNN	J,T	147	491	06.04.11	7676	000000	92962
558.565-010	ACID-PLANT HELPER (chemical)	3124	44443344455	LFNNNNNNFFFNNNNFNNNNN	ONNO4NFNNNNNNN	R,T	147	491	06.04.11	7676	000000	92938
558.565-014	ELECTRIC-CELL TENDER (chemical)	3224	34434444355	MNNNNNNFFFNOONFNNNNN	NNNN3NNNNNNNNN	J,T	147	491	06.04.11	7676	000000	92938
558.582-010	PHOSPHORIC-ACID OPERATOR (chemical)	4337	34333434354	LONNNNNNFFNNOONFFNNON	NNFN3NFNNNNNNN	J,T	147	347	06.02.11	7676	000000	92962
558.584-010	CELL TESTER (chemical)	2115	34444433355	LNNNNNNFFFNNNNNFNNNNN	NNFN3NFNNNNNNNN	J,T	111	589	06.03.02	7820	410301	83005
558.585-010	CATALYTIC-CONVERTER-OPERATOR HELPER (chemical)	3224	44444434355	LNNNNNNFFFNNNNFNNNNN	ONNN3NNNNNNNNN	R,T	147	490	06.04.11	7679	000000	92938
558.585-018	CONTACT-ACID-PLANT OPERATOR (chemical)	3225	34344434454	LNNNNNNFFFNNNNNFOOOOO	NNNNN4NNNNNNNNN	J,T	147	491	06.02.11	7676	000000	92938

DOT #	DOT Title & Industry	Trng	Aptitude	Physical	Environment	Tempra	WkF	MPSMS	GOE	SOC	CIP	OES
558.585-022	CUPROUS-CHLORIDE HELPER (chemical)	2122	4444443455	MFNNNNNFFNNNFNNNNN	NNNNN3NFNNNNNNNN	R	147	491	06.04.11	7679	000000	92938
558.585-026	DEVULCANIZER TENDER (rubber reclaim.)	2223	4444443455	MNNNNNNNFFONNNNFNNNNN	NNNN4NCNNNNNNNN	R,T	147	513	06.04.13	7676	000000	92938
558.585-030	LEAD-NITRATE PROCESSOR (chemical)	2123	4444443454	HNNFNFNFFFNNNNFNFNFN	NNFN4NFNNNNNNNN	J,T	147	490	06.04.11	7675	000000	92938
558.585-034	NEUTRALIZER (soap & rel.)	2223	4444444455	LFNNNNNFFNNNNFNNNNN	NNNF4NFNNNNNNNF	R,T	147	494	06.04.19	7675	000000	92938
558.585-038	POLYMERIZATION HELPER (plastic-synth.)	3224	3444443455	MONFNFNFFNNNNNNFNNN	NNNN4NFNNNNNNNN	R,T	147	492	06.04.13	8618	150607	98999
558.585-042	TWITCHELL OPERATOR (chemical)	2223	4444443454	LNNNNNNFFFNNNNNFNNNFN	NNNN4NFNNNNNNNN	R,T	147	499	06.04.11	7679	000000	92938
558.666-010	DEVULCANIZER CHARGER (rubber reclaim.)	2112	4444444355	HNNONONFFNNOONFNNNNN	NNNN4NFNNNNNNNN	R,T	147	513	06.04.13	8725	000000	98502
558.682-010	CRACKING-UNIT OPERATOR (plastic-synth.)	3225	3434444354	MNNFNFNFFNNNNNNNNNN	NNNN4NNNNNNNNN	R,T	144	492	06.02.13	7676	150607	92935
558.682-014	DISSOLVER OPERATOR (chemical)	3224	3434443454	LNNNNNNFFNNNNNNNNN	NNNN4NNNNNNNNN	J,T	147	491	06.02.11	7676	000000	92935
558.682-018	FERMENTATION OPERATOR (chemical)	3225	4444444355	MNNNNNNFFFNFNNFFNFN	NNNF3NNNNNNNNN	J,T	147	496	06.04.11	7676	000000	92962
558.682-022	RECOVERY OPERATOR (chemical)	3124	3444444455	LNNNNNNFFNNNNNNNNN	NNNN4NNNNNNNNF	J,T	147	491	06.04.11	7676	000000	92962
558.685-010	ACID-POLYMERIZATION OPERATOR (chemical)	3213	3444434455	MNNNNNNFFNNNNNNNNN	NNNN3NFNNNNNNN	R,T	147	491	06.04.11	7676	000000	92938
558.685-014	BALL-MILL OPERATOR (chemical)	3223	3444444455	LNNNNNNFFFNNNNNNNNN	NNNN3NNNNNNNNN	R,T	147	491	06.04.11	7676	000000	92938
558.685-018	BLEACHER OPERATOR (chemical; soap & rel.)	2113	4444444455	MNNNNNNFFFNNNONNNNN	NNNN4NNNNNNNNN	R,T	147	490	06.04.19	7673	000000	92958
558.685-022	CELL-TENDER HELPER (chemical)	2224	4443344455	LNNFNFNFFFNNNNNFNNN	NNFO3NONNNNNNN	T	147	491	06.04.11	7679	000000	92998
558.685-026	DE-IONIZER OPERATOR (chemical)	3224	4444444355	LNNNNNNFFONNNNONNNNN	NNNN4NNNNNNNNN	R,T	147	499	06.04.11	7676	000000	92962
558.685-030	ION-EXCHANGE OPERATOR (smelt. & refin.)	3124	4444444355	LNNNNNNNFFNNNNNNNNN	NNNN4NNNNNNNNN	R,T	147	358	06.04.10	7676	000000	92938
558.685-034	ION-EXCHANGE OPERATOR (chemical)	3223	3434444455	LNNNNNNNFFNNNNNFNNN	NNNF3NNNNNNNNN	T	147	499	06.04.19	7676	000000	92938
558.685-038	ION-EXCHANGE OPERATOR (pharmaceut.)	3225	3444444454	MNNNNNNFFONNNNNFNNN	NNNN3NNNNNNNNO	R,T	147	499	06.04.11	7676	000000	92938
558.685-042	LEAD-OXIDE-MILL TENDER (elec. equip.)	2213	4444434455	MNNNNNNFFONNNNFNNNN	NNCN3NNNNNNNNF	R,T	147	491	06.04.10	7679	000000	92998
558.685-046	MVA-REACTOR OPERATOR (chemical)	3224	4444434354	MNNNNNNFFNNNNFNNNN	NNNO4NNNNNNNNN	J,T	147	492	06.04.11	7676	000000	92938
558.685-050	NITROGLYCERIN NEUTRALIZER (chemical)	3125	3444444353	LNNFNNNFFONNNNNFNNFN	NNNN4NFNNNNNNN	J,T	147	499	06.04.11	7673	000000	92938
558.685-054	RED-LEAD BURNER (paint & varnish)	2112	4455444455	MNNNNNNCCFNNNNONNNNN	NNFN4NFNNNNNNN	R,T	147	495	06.04.11	7675	000000	92923
558.685-058	CHEMICAL RECLAMATION EQUIPMENT OPERATOR (electron. comp.)	2123	4444444455	HNNNNNNCCFNNNNONNNNN	NNNN3NNNNNNNNN	R,U	147	490	06.04.11	7676	000000	92962
558.685-062	CHEMICAL OPERATOR II (chemical)	3224	3434444454	MONONONFFNNONFNONON	NNNN4NNNNNNNNN	J,T	147	490	06.04.11	7676	000000	92938
558.686-010	FURNACE HELPER (chemical)	1112	4444544355	HNNFNFNFFNNNNNNNNN	NNON3NFNNNNNNN	R	147	490	06.04.11	8618	000000	98999
558.687-010	BLEACH PACKER (chemical)	1111	4444544455	MNNFNFNFFNFNFNNNNN	NNNN3NFNNNNNNN	R	011	491	06.04.11	8769	000000	98999
559.130-010	CHEMICAL-PROCESSING SUPERVISOR (pharmaceut.)	4338	3333334354	MNNONONFFNFNFNOOON	NNNN4NNNNNNNNN	V,D,P,J	147	493	06.01.01	7100	000000	81008
559.130-014	SUPERVISOR, FERTILIZER PROCESSING (chemical)	4337	3333334355	LNNNNNNFONFFNFNNONN	NNNN4NNNNNNNNN	V,D,P,J	147	497	06.02.01	7100	000000	81008
559.130-018	SUPERVISOR, RECORD PRESS (recording)	4337	3333333355	LNNNNNNFFOFFNFNNONN	NNNN4NNNNNNNNN	D,P,J	212	585	06.02.01	7100	000000	81008
559.130-022	SUPERVISOR, TILE-AND-MOTTLE (fabrication, nec)	4336	3333334354	MONONONFFONFNFNNOON	NNNN4NCNNNNNNN	D,P,J	147	619	06.02.01	7100	000000	81008
559.131-010	PHARMACEUTICAL-COMPOUNDING SUPERVISOR (pharmaceut.)	4337	3333334353	LNNNNNNFFFNFNNFNN	NNNN4NNNNNNNNN	V,D,P,T,J	212	493	06.01.01	7100	000000	81008
559.131-014	QUALITY-CONTROL SUPERVISOR (plastic-synth.)	4337	3333333354	LNNNNNNFFFNFNNNON	NNNN4NNNNNNNNN	D,P,J,T	212	519	06.02.01	7100	000000	81008
559.131-018	TNT-LINE SUPERVISOR (chemical)	4238	3334333333	LONNNNNFFOFFNFNNOON	NNFN4NFNNNNNNN	V,D,P,J	147	494	06.04.01	7100	000000	81008
559.132-010	ACID SUPERVISOR (chemical)	4337	3334333344	LONNNNNFFFNFNNNON	NNNN4NFNNNNNNN	V,D,P,S,T	147	499	06.04.01	7100	000000	81008
559.132-014	CALENDER SUPERVISOR (plastic-synth.)	4337	3333333455	LNNOOONFFFNFNNNON	NNNN4NFNNNNNNN	D,P,S,T	147	499	06.02.01	7100	000000	81008
559.132-018	CATALYST OPERATOR, CHIEF (chemical)	4337	3333333354	LONNNNNFFOFFNNOOFN	NNNN4NNNNNNNNN	V,D,P,J	135	492	06.02.01	7100	150607	81008
559.132-022	FINISHING-AREA SUPERVISOR (plastic-synth.)	4338	3334343354	LONNNNNFFNFNNOOON	NNNN4NFNNNNNNF	V,D,P,J	147	491	06.01.01	6700	410301	81008
559.132-026	HEAD OPERATOR, SULFIDE (chemical)	4338	3333333344	LONNNNNFFOFFNNNOON	NNNF4NNNNNNNNN	V,D,P,J	147	492	06.01.01	7100	150607	81008
559.132-030	HEATING-AND-BLENDING SUPERVISOR (chemical)	4338	3333333355	LONNNNNFFOFFNFNNOON	ONNN4NFNNNNNNN	V,D,P,J	147	568	06.01.01	6700	000000	81008
559.132-034	MILL SUPERVISOR (nonmet. min.)	4238	3334333333	LONNNNNFFOFFNFNNOON	NNFN4NFNNNNNNN	V,D,P,J	147	494	06.02.01	7100	000000	81008
559.132-038	NITROGLYCERIN SUPERVISOR (chemical)	4337	3334333344	LNNOONFFNFNFNNNON	NNNN4NFNNNNNNN	V,D,P,J	147	349	06.04.01	7100	000000	81008
559.132-042	PROCESS-AREA SUPERVISOR (plastic-synth.)	4337	3333333354	LNNOOONFFFNFNNOOON	NNNN4NFNNNNNNN	D,P,J,T	147	499	06.01.01	7100	000000	81008
559.132-046	PRODUCTION SUPERVISOR, ANHYDROUS AMMONIA (chemical)	4338	3333333354	LONONONFFFNFNNOOON	NNNN4NNNNNNNNO	V,D,P,J	147	491	06.01.01	7100	000000	81008
559.132-050	PRODUCTION SUPERVISOR, DEFLUORINATED PHOSPHATE (chemical)	4337	3333343355	LONNNNNFFFNFNNOOFN	ONFN4NNNNNNNNN	V,D,P,J	147	491	06.02.01	7100	000000	81008
559.132-054	SUPERVISOR I (chemical)	4337	2334433355	MNNNNNNFFNFNNOON	ONFN4NNNNNNNNF	V,D,P,J	147	496	06.01.01	7100	000000	81008
559.132-058	SUPERVISOR (rubber reclaim.)	4336	3333333353	LFNNNNNFFFNFNNNON	NNNN4NNNNNNNNN	V,D,P,J	147	513	06.02.01	7100	000000	81008
559.132-062	SUPERVISOR, ALUM PLANT (chemical)	4337	3333333355	LNNNNNNFFFNFNNOON	NNNN3NNNNNNNNN	V,D,P,J	147	491	06.02.01	7100	000000	81008
559.132-066	SUPERVISOR, BONE PLANT (chemical)	4338	3333333355	LNNNNNNFFFNFNNOON	NNNN4NFNNNNNNN	V,D,P,J	147	499	06.02.01	6700	000000	81008
559.132-070	SUPERVISOR, CD-AREA (chemical)	4347	3333344355	MNNNNNNFFNFNNNON	NNNN3NNNNNNNNN	V,D,P,J	147	491	06.02.01	7100	000000	81008
559.132-074	SUPERVISOR, COOK HOUSE (chemical)	4337	3334344455	LONFNFNFFNFNFNNNNN	NNNN4NNNNNNNNN	V,D,P,J	147	499	06.02.01	7100	000000	81008

DOT #	DOT Title & Industry	Trng	Aptitude	Physical	Environment	Tempra	WkF	MPSMS	GOE	SOC	CIP	OES
559.132-078	SUPERVISOR, DEHYDROGENATION (chemical; petrol. refin.)	4338	33333333355	LONONONFFFNFFNFNOONN	ONON4NFNNNNNNNN	V,D,P,J	147	491	06.01.01	7100	520205	81008
559.132-082	SUPERVISOR, DRY PASTE (chemical)	4237	33344344455	LONNNNNFFFFFNNNNN	NNFN3NNNNNNNNNN	V,D,P,J	147	499	06.02.01	7100	000000	81008
559.132-086	SUPERVISOR, ESTERS-AND-EMULSIFIERS (chemical)	4337	33333333355	LNNNNNNFFNFFFNNNNN	NNNN4NNNNNNNNNN	D,P,J,T	147	499	06.02.01	7100	000000	81008
559.132-090	SUPERVISOR, FERTILIZER (chemical)	4336	33333334355	LNNNNNNFFOFFNFNNNN	NNNN4NNNNNNNNNN	V,D,P	143	497	06.04.01	7100	000000	81008
559.132-094	SUPERVISOR, FURNACE PROCESS (chemical)	4337	33333333355	LNNNNNNFFFNFFFNNNN	ONON3NNNNNNNNNN	V,D,P,J	147	499	06.02.01	7100	000000	81008
559.132-098	SUPERVISOR, GLYCERIN (soap & rel.)	4347	33344344454	LNNNNNNFFNFFFNNNNN	NNNN4NNNNNNNNNN	D,P,J,T	147	499	06.02.01	7100	000000	81008
559.132-102	SUPERVISOR, INSECTICIDE (chemical)	4337	33333333355	LNNNNNNFFNFFFNNNNN	NNNN4NNNNNNNNNN	V,D,P	147	497	06.02.01	7100	000000	81008
559.132-106	SUPERVISOR, LIQUEFACTION (chemical)	4337	33333333355	LNNNNNNFFNFFFNNNNN	ONNN4NNNNNNNNNF	V,D,P,J	147	491	06.02.01	7100	000000	81008
559.132-110	SUPERVISOR, LITHARGE (paint & varnish)	4337	33333333354	LNNNNNNFFFNFFNNNNN	NNNN4NNNNNNNNNN	V,D,J,T	147	495	06.01.01	7100	000000	81008
559.132-114	SUPERVISOR, PAINT (paint & varnish)	4337	33334344453	LFNNNNNNFFFNFFNNNOFN	NNNN4NFNNNNNNNN	V,D,P,J,T	147	495	06.01.01	7100	000000	81008
559.132-118	SUPERVISOR, PHOSPHORUS PROCESSING (chemical)	4338	33333333355	LFNNNNNNFFFNFFNNNON	ONNN3NNNNNNNNNN	V,D,P,J	147	491	06.02.01	7100	000000	81008
559.132-122	SUPERVISOR, PIGMENT MAKING (chemical)	4337	33344344454	LNNNNNNFFFNFFFNNNNN	NNNN4NFNNNNNNNN	V,D,P,J	147	491	06.02.01	7100	000000	81008
559.132-126	SUPERVISOR, REFINING (chemical)	4337	33333333354	LNNNNNNNFFNFFFNNNON	NNNN4NNNNNNNNNN	V,D,P,J	147	389	06.01.01	7100	000000	81008
559.132-130	SUPERVISOR, TOILET-AND-LAUNDRY SOAP (soap & rel.)	4337	33333333354	LNNNNNNFFFNFNFFFN	NNNN4NNNNNNNNNN	V,D,P,J	147	494	06.01.01	7100	000000	81008
559.132-134	SUPERVISOR, VARNISH (paint & varnish)	4338	33333344354	LNNNNNNFFFNFNFFFN	NNNN4NFNNNNNNNN	V,D,P,J	147	495	06.02.01	7100	000000	81008
559.132-138	TRANSFER-AND-PUMPHOUSE OPERATOR, CHIEF (chemical)	4337	33333334355	LOONNNNNFFFOFFNFNONNN	FNNN4NNNNNNNNNN	V,D,P,J	014	490	06.04.01	7100	000000	81008
559.134-010	QUALITY-CONTROL SUPERVISOR (plastic prod.)	4244	22433444453	SNNONNNOOONFFNFNFFN	NNNN4NNNNNNNNNN	D,P,J	211	510	06.02.01	7100	150702	81005
559.134-014	SUPERVISOR, DRYING AND WINDING (plastic-synth.)	3226	33344344434	MFNONNNNOOOFFNFNONOF	NNNN4NNNNNNNNNO	D,P,J	163	414	06.02.01	7100	150699	81008
559.137-010	SALVAGE SUPERVISOR (paint & varnish)	4337	33344344455	LNNNNNNFFFNFFFNNNNN	NNNN3NNNNNNNNNN	V,D,P,J	212	495	06.01.01	7100	000000	81008
559.137-014	SUPERVISOR II (rubber goods)	4337	33333333355	LNNNNNNNFFNFFFNNNON	NNNN4NNNNNNNNNN	V,D,P,J	147	510	06.02.01	7100	000000	81008
559.137-018	SUPERVISOR, BLEACH (chemical)	4337	33333344455	MNNNNNNNFFFNFFFNNNNN	NNNN4NNNNNNNNNN	V,D,P,J	147	491	06.02.01	7100	000000	81008
559.137-022	SUPERVISOR, CHANNEL PROCESS (chemical)	4337	33334344344	LNNNNNNFFFNFFFNNNON	ONNN3FNNNNNNNN	V,D,P,J	147	499	06.02.01	7100	000000	81008
559.137-026	SUPERVISOR, EVAPORATOR (chemical)	4347	33333344455	MNNNNNNNFFFNFFFNNNNN	NNNN3NNNNNNNNNN	V,D,P,J	147	491	06.04.01	7100	000000	81008
559.137-030	SUPERVISOR, GELATIN PLANT (chemical)	4338	33333344454	LOONNNNNFFFNFNFOOON	NNNN4NNNNNNNNNN	V,D,P,J	147	499	06.02.01	7100	000000	81008
559.137-034	SUPERVISOR, GLUE SPECIALTY (chemical)	4337	33344344455	LNNNNNNFFFNFFFNNNNN	NNNN3NNNNNNNNNN	V,D,P,J	147	499	06.02.01	7100	000000	81008
559.137-038	SUPERVISOR, INSPECTION (plastic-synth.)	4337	33333333355	LNNNNNNFFFNFFFNNNNN	NNNN4NNNNNNNNNN	V,D,P,J	212	492	06.02.01	7100	150607	81008
559.137-042	SUPERVISOR, PUTTY AND CAULKING (paint & varnish)	4227	33344344355	LNNNNNNFFFNFFFNNNNN	NNNN4NNNNNNNNNN	V,D,P,J	147	495	06.02.01	7100	000000	81008
559.137-046	SUPERVISOR, ROCKET PROPELLANT PLANT (ordnance)	4336	33333344455	LNNNNNNFFFNFFFNNNNN	NNNN4NNNNNNNNNO	V,D,P	147	490	06.02.01	7100	000000	81008
559.137-050	SUPERVISOR, TANK CLEANING (paint & varnish)	4236	33444344444	LFNFNFNFFFNFNFNFNON	NNNN3NNNNNNNNNN	V,D,P,J	031	568	06.04.01	7100	000000	81008
559.165-010	CHECKER (chemical)	3225	34444343354	LNNNNNNFFNOONFNNNFN	NNNN4NNNNNNNNNN	D,T	147	499	06.02.11	7820	000000	83005
559.167-010	CD-STORAGE-AND-MATERIALS-MAKE-UP OPERATOR, HEAD (chemical)	4337	33344344454	MNNNNNNNFFFNFFNNNON	NNNN4NFNNNNNNNN	D,P,T	147	492	06.02.11	7100	000000	81008
559.361-010	LABORATORY TECHNICIAN, PHARMACEUTICAL (pharmaceut.)	5446	33333432354	LNNNNNNNFFONNNFNFFON	NNNN2NNNNNNNNNN	V,J,T	147	493	02.04.02	3690	000000	32905
559.362-010	ALUM-PLANT OPERATOR (chemical)	3224	34433434355	LNNNNNNFFOONFNNNNN	NNNN4NFNNNNNNNN	J,T	147	491	06.02.11	7676	000000	95099
559.362-014	FINISHING-AREA OPERATOR (plastic-synth.)	3226	34444334355	LOOONNNFFFNFFNNNNN	NNNN4NFNNNNNNNN	V,J,T	147	492	06.02.13	6960	150607	95099
559.362-018	LIQUEFACTION-PLANT OPERATOR (chemical)	3324	33344434355	LNNNNNNFFFNFFNNNNN	NNNN4NNNNNNNNNN	J,T	147	491	06.02.12	6920	470501	95005
559.362-022	MVA-REACTOR OPERATOR, HEAD (chemical)	3336	33344433455	LNNNNNNFFFNOONFNNNNN	NNNN4NNNNNNNNNN	J,T	147	492	06.02.11	7676	000000	92935
559.362-026	PLANT OPERATOR, FURNACE PROCESS (chemical)	3235	33344344355	LNNNNNNNFFOONFNONNN	NNON4NONNNNNNNN	V,D,P	147	499	06.02.18	6960	000000	95099
559.362-030	ROLL TENDER (chemical)	3225	34444434355	LNNNNNNFFFOONFNNNNN	NNFF4NNNNNNNNNF	J	147	499	06.02.18	7679	000000	92998
559.362-034	TOWER OPERATOR (soap & rel.)	3334	33344334355	LONNNNNFFNOONFNNNNN	NNFN4NNNNNNNNNN	J,T	212	589	06.03.01	6960	000000	83005
559.364-010	FURNACE-STOCK INSPECTOR (elec. equip.)	3324	34343343355	LNNNNNNFFFONNNFNFFN	NNFN4NNNNNNNNNN	J,T	212	492	06.03.01	7830	150607	83005
559.367-010	QUALITY-CONTROL TESTER (paper goods; plastic-synth.)	3234	33333343353	LNNNNNNNFFOOONFNNNFN	NNFF3NFNNNNNNNN	J,T	212	510	06.03.01	6881	150607	83002
559.381-010	INSPECTOR (plastic prod.; plastic-synth.)	3335	33333334354	LNNNNNNNFFNNNNFNON	NNNN3NNNNNNNNNN	J,T	212	519	06.01.05	6881	000000	83002
559.381-014	RUBBER TESTER (rubber goods; rubber tire)	3226	33344333354	LFNFNFNFFFNNNNNFFON	NNNN4NFNNNNNNNN	J,T	147	491	06.02.17	6940	000000	95099
559.382-010	AMMONIA-STILL OPERATOR (steel & rel.)	3325	34344444454	HONNNNNFFFNNNNNNON	NNNN4NNNNNNNNON	J,T	147	491	06.02.11	7664	000000	92965
559.382-014	CATALYST OPERATOR, GASOLINE (chemical)	3325	33333334354	MFNONONFONNNONFFOFFN	NNNN4NNNNNNNNNN	J,T	147	490	06.01.03	7676	000000	92935
559.382-018	CHEMICAL OPERATOR III (chemical)	3327	33333334354	MNNNNNNFFNNNNFNNN	NNNF3NFNNNNNNNN	J	147	499	06.02.18	7666	000000	92962
559.382-022	GLUE MAKER, BONE (chemical)	3225	34444444454	MNNNNNNNFFNNNNFNON	NNNO4FNNNNNNNN	J	147	493	06.02.11	7666	000000	92965
559.382-026	GRANULATOR-MACHINE OPERATOR (pharmaceut.)	3224	34444444353	MNNNNNNFONNNNONONNFN	NNNO4NNNNNNNNNF	J,T	147	499	06.02.11	7666	000000	92935
559.382-030	LINSEED-OIL REFINER (oils & grease)	3224	34434334354	MNNNNNNFFNNNNNFNON	NNNN3NFNNNNNNNN	J,T	147	491	06.02.11	7664	000000	92935
559.382-034	MAKE-UP OPERATOR (chemical)	3225	34334434334	LONNNNNFFFNNNFNNNON	ONNF4NNNNNNNNNF	R,T	031	568	06.02.13	6940	000000	95099

DOT #	DOT Title & Industry	Trmg	Aptitude	Physical	Environment	Tempra	WkF	MPSMS	GOE	SOC	CIP	OES
559.382-042	PHARMACEUTICAL OPERATOR (pharmaceut.)	3225	33333433354	MNNOONOFFONNNFNNNON	NNNN4NFNNNNNNNN	T,J	147	493	06.02.11	6940	000000	95099
559.382-046	PILOT-CONTROL OPERATOR (chemical; plastic-synth.)	4337	22223333353	LNNNNNNFFNNNNFNNNN	NNNN3NFNNNNNNNN	V,J,T	211	568	02.04.01	7476	410301	92997
559.382-050	SHREDDING-FLOOR-EQUIPMENT OPERATOR (plastic-synth.)	3225	34444444355	MNNNNNNFFNNNNFNNNN	NNNN4NNNNNNNNNN	J,T	142	471	06.02.13	7549	150607	92198
559.382-054	SOAP MAKER (soap & rel.)	3237	33443444353	LNNNNNNFFNNNNFNNNFN	NNNO4NFNNNNNNON	J,T	147	494	06.02.18	7664	000000	92965
559.384-010	LABORATORY ASSISTANT, CULTURE MEDIA (pharmaceut.)	3335	33333333354	LNNONNNFFNOONFNNNNN	NNNN4NNNNNNNNFN	V,J,T	147	493	02.04.02	3820	410101	24502
559.387-010	INSPECTOR IV (ordnance)	3225	33333344454	LNNONONFFONNNFONNFO	NNNN4NCNNNNNCNN	S,J,T	212	499	06.03.01	7820	000000	83005
559.387-014	INSPECTOR (pharmaceut.)	3234	34443344454	LNNONONFFONNNNFONNFO	NNNN3NFNNNNNNNN	T	211	493	06.03.02	7830	150702	83005
559.467-010	TEMPERATURE-CONTROL INSPECTOR (plastic-synth.)	3224	34443344454	LFFFNFNFFOOONFFFFN	NNNF4NFNNNNNNNF	J,T	212	492	06.03.01	7820	200306	83005
559.482-010	COMPOSITION-ROLL MAKER AND CUTTER (rubber goods)	3224	34433433355	MNNOONNFFFNNNNFNNNN	NNNN4NNNNNNNNNN	J,T	132	519	06.02.07	7679	000000	92998
559.482-014	PUTTY TINTER-MAKER (paint & varnish)	3225	34444444353	MNNNNNNFFNNNNFNNNFN	NNNN4NNNNNNNNNN	J,T	143	495	06.02.18	7479	000000	92997
559.485-010	WASH-MILL OPERATOR (chemical)	2213	34343444455	MONONNNFFNNNNNONNNNN	NNNO4QNNNNNNNN	R,T	031	320	06.04.19	7673	000000	92958
559.562-010	DRIER OPERATOR I (plastic-synth.)	3236	34333334355	LONOOONFFNOONFNNNNN	NNNN4NNNNNNNNFN	V,J,T	141	492	06.02.13	7529	150607	92198
559.565-010	CYLINDER FILLER (chemical)	3223	44443434355	HNNFNFNFFNNNONFNNNN	NNNN3NFNNNNNNNF	T	014	491	06.04.12	7662	000000	92974
559.567-014	WEIGHER AND GRADER (chemical)	2223	44444444453	LNNNNNNFFFFFFNFNFN	NNNN4NNNNNNNNNN	J	212	319	06.03.02	7850	000000	83005
559.582-010	COAGULATION OPERATOR (plastic-synth.)	3225	33334333344	LONFNFNFFOOONFFFFN	NNNF4NNNNNNNNN	V,J,T	147	492	06.02.13	7676	150607	92962
559.582-014	SPECIALTIES OPERATOR (chemical)	3325	33334333355	LONNNNNFFNNNNNFNNNN	NNNF4NFNNNNNNNN	J,T	147	490	06.02.11	7664	150607	92935
559.584-010	ROLL-TENSION TESTER (plastic-synth.)	2123	44443433354	LNNNNNNFFNNNNNFNFN	NNNN4NNNNNNNNNN	J,T	212	492	06.03.02	7830	150607	83005
559.584-014	VARNISH INSPECTOR (paint & varnish)	2213	44443444454	LNNNNNNFFFONNNFNNOFN	NNNN3NNNNNNNNNN	J,T	212	495	06.04.09	7820	000000	92998
559.585-010	DRY-HOUSE TENDER (ordnance)	2222	44444444455	LNNONONFFFNNNNFNNNN	NNCC3NNNNNNNNOC	J,T	147	499	06.04.11	7679	000000	92998
559.585-014	GREASE-AND-TALLOW PUMPER (oils & grease)	2112	44444444455	LNNNNNNFFNNNNFNNNNN	ONNN3NNNNNNNNN	R	014	499	06.04.19	7679	000000	97953
559.585-018	TANKROOM TENDER (plastic-synth.)	2123	44444444355	LNNNNNNFFNNNNFNNNN	NNNN4NNNNNNNNNN	R	147	492	06.04.13	7679	150607	92998
559.585-022	VACUUM-PAN OPERATOR III (chemical)	3223	44444444355	LNNNNNNOOONOOONFOFFOO	NNNO4NOONNNNNON	R,T	145	499	06.04.11	7679	000000	92962
559.587-010	ROD-AND-TUBE STRAIGHTENER (plastic-synth.)	2112	44444444345	MNNNNNNFFONNNNONONNN	NNNO4NNNNNNNNN	R	133	492	06.04.24	8769	150607	98999
559.662-010	ACID MAKER (paper & pulp)	3225	34444444354	LNNNNNNFFNNNNFNNNNN	NNON4NFNNNNNNNN	J,T	147	491	06.04.11	7675	000000	92923
559.662-014	WASH OPERATOR (chemical)	3325	33333433354	LNNNNNNFFNOONFNFN	NNNN3NNNNNNNNN	J,T	147	499	06.02.18	6940	000000	95008
559.664-010	NITROGLYCERIN DISTRIBUTOR (chemical)	2112	44443434354	HNNNNNNFFNNFFNFNNNN	NNNN4NFNNNNNNNF	S,T	011	499	06.04.40	7664	000000	92965
559.664-014	PILOT-CONTROL-OPERATOR HELPER (chemical; plastic-synth.)	2225	34343444344	MFNNNNNNFFNOONFNNNFN	ONNN3NFNNNNNNNF	R,T	212	490	06.04.11	8619	150607	98999
559.665-010	BONE-PROCESS OPERATOR (chemical)	2224	44434444355	LNNNNNNFFNNNNNONNNNN	NNNN4NNNNNNNNN	R,T	142	499	06.04.09	7679	000000	92998
559.665-014	DRY-END OPERATOR (plastic-synth.)	3223	34343434355	MNNFNFNFFNNNNFNNNNN	NNOO4NNNNNNNNN	R,T	141	492	06.04.13	7679	150607	92998
559.665-018	EXTRACTOR-PLANT OPERATOR (chemical; oils & grease)	3224	34434434353	LNNNNNNFFNNOONFNNNFN	NNNN3NNNNNNNNN	J,T	144	499	06.02.18	7676	000000	92962
559.665-022	FORMING-MACHINE OPERATOR (button & notion)	3225	34434494355	LNNNNNNFFOONFNFFNN	NNNN3NNNNNNNNN	J,T	135	618	06.02.02	7663	000000	92971
559.665-026	MIXER I (chemical)	2224	44444444354	MNNFNFNFFNNNNONNNON	NNFF3NONNNNNNNF	T	143	494	06.04.11	7664	000000	92965
559.665-030	PRESS OPERATOR I (chemical)	2213	44444444445	LNNNNNNFFNNNNNNNNN	NCNN3NNNNNNNNN	T	135	491	06.04.19	7667	000000	92971
559.665-034	SPLASH-LINE OPERATOR (fabrication, nec)	2224	44444444344	MFNNNNNNFFNNNFNFNFN	NNFF4NFNNNNNNNN	T	143	619	06.04.19	7679	000000	92998
559.665-038	TANK-FARM ATTENDANT (chemical)	3324	34343444344	MFNFOFNFFONFFNFFFON	FNNN4NNNNNNNNN	T	014	490	06.04.11	8769	000000	92998
559.665-042	WASH HELPER (chemical)	3224	34343444354	MNNNNNNFFONNNNFNNNNN	NNNF4NONNNNNNNN	J,T	147	499	06.04.19	7673	000000	92958
559.666-010	TOWER ATTENDANT (paper & pulp)	2112	44444444455	HNNNONONFFNNNNNFNNNON	NNNN3NONNNNNNN	R	147	496	06.04.14	7679	000000	83005
559.667-010	TABLET TESTER (pharmaceut.)	2223	34434434354	SNNNNNNFFFOONFNFFNN	NNNN3NNNNNNNNN	T	212	493	06.03.02	7830	000000	83005
559.667-014	LABORER, GENERAL (plastic-synth.)	2112	44444444355	MONONNNFFONOONNNOONN	NNOO4NONNNNNNN	R	011	492	06.04.40	8769	000000	98999
559.682-010	CAPSULE-FILLING-MACHINE OPERATOR (pharmaceut.)	3224	33433433343	MMNONNNFFFNNNNFNNONF	NNNN3NNNNNNNNN	J,T	041	493	06.02.18	7662	000000	92974
559.682-014	CASTING-AND-CURING OPERATOR (chemical)	3225	34433433355	LNNNNNNFFNNNNFNNNN	NNNN4NNNNNNNNN	J,T	041	501	06.02.13	7679	000000	92998
559.682-018	CHEMICAL COMPOUNDER (chemical)	3224	34444444354	MNNNNNNFFONNNNFNNNNN	NNNN3NFNNNNNNNN	J,T	147	496	06.02.18	7676	000000	92962
559.682-022	FILM-CASTING OPERATOR (plastic-synth.)	3214	33444344354	MNNNNNNFFNNNNNNNNON	NNNN4NNNNNNNNN	J,T	147	492	06.02.13	7529	150607	92198
559.682-026	FLUSHER (chemical)	3225	34444444354	MMNNONONFFFNNNNFNNNNN	NNNN4NNNNNNNNN	T	147	496	06.04.12	7666	000000	92962
559.682-030	LACQUER MAKER (paint & varnish)	3225	44444444354	MMNNONNNFFFNNNNNFNNNNN	NNNF3NNNNNNNNN	T	143	495	06.04.11	7679	000000	92965
559.682-034	LATEX-RIBBON-MACHINE OPERATOR (rubber goods)	3226	33433433344	MNNNNNNFFNNNFNFNFON	NNNN3NNNNNNNNN	T	147	519	06.02.13	7679	000000	92998
559.682-038	RIPENING-ROOM ATTENDANT (plastic-synth.)	3224	34444444355	LNNONNNCCNNNNNOFNFNN	NNNN4NNNNNNNNN	J,T	147	492	06.02.13	7666	000000	92962
559.682-042	RUBBER-MILL OPERATOR (plastic-synth.)	3125	34443433343	LONNNNNFFNNNNNNNNFN	NNNO3NNNNNNNNN	J,T	145	492	06.02.13	7679	000000	92998
559.682-046	SODA-ROOM OPERATOR (beverage)	3224	44443343354	MONFFNFNFFNNNNNFNNNON	NNFF3NFNNNNNNNN	T	147	494	06.04.11	7673	000000	92958
559.682-050	SPONGE-PRESS OPERATOR (rubber goods)	3224	34434434355	MONFNFNFFNNNNFNNFNN	NNNN4NNNNNNNNNF	J,T	141	519	06.02.13	7663	000000	92971
559.682-054	STERILE-PRODUCTS PROCESSOR (pharmaceut.)	3225	33343343354	HNNONONFFNNNNFNNFNN	NNNO4NNNNNNNNO	T	147	493	06.02.18	7676	000000	92962

DOT #	DOT Title & Industry	Trng	Aptitude	Physical	Environment	Tempra	WkF	MPSMS	GOE	SOC	CIP	OES
559.682-058	STRETCH-MACHINE OPERATOR (plastic prod.)	3225	34343443355	HNNNNNFFNNNNNNFNNNNN	NNNNN4NNNNNNNNNN	T	032	519	06.02.02	7549	000000	92198
559.682-062	STRONG-NITRIC OPERATOR (chemical)	3224	34434434355	LNNNNNNFFFNNNNNFNNNN	NNNN4NFNNNNNNNNN	T	147	491	06.02.18	7676	000000	92962
559.682-066	UTILITY OPERATOR I (chemical)	3225	33434434355	MONNNNNNFFNNNNNFNNNN	NNNN4NNNNNNNNNNN	J,T	147	490	06.02.11	7676	000000	92962
559.682-070	SCREEN-MACHINE OPERATOR (tex. prod., nec)	3125	34433434354	HNNONNNFFONNNNCNFNNN	NNNNO3NNNNNNNNNN	J,T	063	510	06.02.13	7549	150607	92198
559.684-010	PACK-ROOM OPERATOR (plastic-synth.)	3214	34333434355	HNNNNNNCCONNNNCNFNNN	NNNNO3NNNNNNNNNN	J,T	041	567	06.04.30	7740	000000	93999
559.684-018	RUBBER-MOLD MAKER (jewelry-silver.)	2113	44433443355	LNNNNNNFFFNNNNFNFNNN	NNNN3NNNNNNNNNN	R,T	136	519	06.04.32	7663	000000	92971
559.684-022	TANK CLEANER (paint & varnish)	2113	44444534355	HFNFFFOFFNNNNNNNNNNN	ONNF4NFNNNNNNNF	R,T	031	568	06.04.39	8750	000000	98905
559.684-026	UTILITY WORKER, MOLDING (plastic prod.)	3123	34443443353	LNNNNNNNFFNNNNFNNFFN	NNNNN4NNNNNNNNNN	V	041	510	06.04.24	8769	000000	98999
559.684-030	HAT-FINISHING-MATERIALS PREPARER (hat & cap)	3225	34443334353	MNNNNNNFFONNNNFNNNON	NNON3NNNNNNNNNN	T	143	490	06.04.34	7759	200303	93999
559.684-034	UTILITY WORKER, PRODUCTION (pharmaceut.)	3234	33443333355	MNNONONFFFNNNNFNNNNN	NONO3NNNNNNNNNN	R,U	014	493	06.04.19	8319	410301	97989
559.685-010	ACID PURIFIER (chemical)	2113	44444444355	LNNNNNNFFNNNNNFNNNNN	NNNNN3NFNNNNNNN	R,T	147	491	06.04.11	7676	000000	92962
559.685-014	ALUMINUM-HYDROXIDE-PROCESS OPERATOR (chemical; pharmaceut.)	3224	34434444353	MNNFNFNFFNNNNNONNNFN	NNNN3NFNNNNNNNN	J,T	147	491	06.04.11	7676	000000	92938
559.685-018	AMPOULE FILLER (pharmaceut.)	2112	44443444355	LNNNNNNNFFNNNNNFNFNN	NNNN3NNNNNNNNNN	R	041	531	06.04.19	7662	000000	92974
559.685-022	AMPOULE-WASHING-MACHINE OPERATOR (pharmaceut.)	2112	44543533345	LNNNNNNNFFNNNNNFNNNN	NNNF3NNNNNNNNNN	R	031	531	06.04.39	7673	000000	92958
559.685-026	BRINE-WELL OPERATOR (chemical)	3224	44434444355	LNNNNNNNFFNNNNFNNNNN	NNNNN4NNNNNNNNNN	J,T	014	490	06.04.11	7679	000000	97953
559.685-030	BRIQUETTER OPERATOR (chemical)	3223	44444434355	MNNFNFNFFNNNNFNNNNNN	NNNN4NNNNNNNNNN	J,T	132	490	06.04.11	7663	000000	92971
559.685-034	CD-STORAGE-AND-MATERIALS MAKE-UP HELPER (chemical)	2224	34344434355	MNNNNNNNFFNNNNNFNNNN	NNNO4NNNNNNNNNN	R,T	147	491	06.04.11	7664	000000	92965
559.685-038	COMPRESSOR OPERATOR II (chemical)	2112	44444544355	HNNFNFNFFONNNNNFNNNN	NNNN4NNNNNNNNNN	R	134	499	06.04.11	7667	000000	92971
559.685-042	CRYSTALLIZER OPERATOR I (chemical)	3224	44444444355	HONNNNNFFFNNNNFNNNNN	NNNN4NFNNNNNNNN	R,T	147	496	06.04.11	7676	000000	92962
559.685-046	DOPE-DRY-HOUSE OPERATOR (chemical)	2112	44444444355	MNNFNFNFFNNNNFNNNNNN	NNNN4NFNNNNNNNN	R	147	499	06.04.19	7679	000000	92998
559.685-050	DRIER-AND-PULVERIZER TENDER (chemical)	2112	44444544345	HNNNNNNNFFNNNNFNNNNN	NNNN4NFNNNNNNNN	R,T	141	490	06.04.11	7679	000000	92998
559.685-054	DUSTING-AND-BRUSHING-MACHINE OPERATOR (rubber goods)	2112	44545544455	MNNFNFNFFNNNNFNNNNNN	NNNN3NFNNNNNNNF	R	031	519	06.04.21	7679	000000	92998
559.685-058	EFFERVESCENT-SALTS COMPOUNDER (pharmaceut.)	3224	34344444355	HNNONONFFFNNNNNNNNNN	NNNN3NNNNNNNNNN	R,T	147	519	06.04.11	7679	000000	92998
559.685-062	ELECTRODE-CLEANING-MACHINE OPERATOR (elec. equip.)	2112	44545544455	HNNONONFFFNNNNNFNNNN	ONNN4NFNNNNNNNN	R,T	031	589	06.04.09	7673	000000	92958
559.685-066	FABRIC NORMALIZER (rubber goods)	2113	44544534355	MNNFNFNFFNNNNNNNNNNN	NNNF3NNNNNNNNNN	R	152	519	06.04.16	7679	000000	92998
559.685-070	FERMENTER OPERATOR (pharmaceut.)	3224	34444444355	LNNONONFFFNNNNFNNNNN	NNNN3NFNNNNNNNN	J,T	147	493	06.04.11	7676	000000	92938
559.685-074	FLAKER OPERATOR (chemical; smelt. & refin.)	2223	44443544355	MNNNNNNNFFNNNNONFNNON	NNNN3NFNNNNNNNN	R,T	147	496	06.04.11	7676	000000	92962
559.685-078	FOAM-MACHINE OPERATOR (plastic prod.; plastic-synth)	2112	44444534355	MNNNNNNNFFNNNNFNNNNN	NNNN3NFNNNNNNNN	R	147	519	06.04.13	7549	000000	92198
559.685-082	FORMULA WEIGHER (pen & pencil)	3224	44444444355	MONONONFFONNNNONNNNN	NNNN4NNNNNNNNNN	J,T	147	499	06.02.18	7679	000000	92965
559.685-086	FRAME STRIPPER (soap & rel.)	2112	44444544355	MNNFNFNFFNNNNFNNNNNN	NNNN4NFNNNNNNNN	R	054	494	06.04.19	7679	000000	92998
559.685-090	FREEZING-MACHINE OPERATOR (pharmaceut.)	3223	34432433355	MNNFNFNFFNNNNNFNFNNN	NONF3NONNNNNNNO	T	133	493	06.04.11	7665	000000	92928
559.685-094	FUSE MAKER (chemical)	2123	44444444354	MNNNNNNFFONNNNNONFNON	NNNN4NFNNNNNNNF	R	162	499	06.04.19	7679	000000	92998
559.685-098	GLUE-MILL OPERATOR (chemical)	2213	44444534355	HNNFNNNNFFNNNNFNNNNN	NNNN4NNNNNNNNNN	R,T	145	499	06.04.19	7679	000000	92998
559.685-102	GOLF-BALL-COVER TREATER (toy-sport equip.)	2222	44445444354	HNNFNNNFFNNNNONFNNON	NNNN3NFNNNNNNNN	R,T	147	616	06.04.11	7676	000000	92998
559.685-106	IMPREGNATOR OPERATOR (chemical)	2224	34444444355	MNNNNNNFFFNNNNFNNNNN	NNNN3NNNNNNNNNN	R	147	492	06.04.11	7679	000000	92938
559.685-110	LABORER, GENERAL (paint & varnish)	2112	44444434344	HNNFNFNFFNNNNFNNNNNN	NNNO4NFNNNNNNNN	R	142	495	06.04.11	8769	000000	98999
559.685-114	LATEX SPOOLER (rubber goods)	2114	44444432355	MNNFNFNFFONNNNNNNNNNN	NNNN4NNNNNNNNNN	R	163	519	06.04.07	7679	000000	92998
559.685-118	LIME-KILN OPERATOR (paper & pulp)	3224	44444444344	LNNONNNOOONNNNNONNON	NNNCN3NFNNNNNNN	J,T	147	496	06.02.18	7676	000000	92962
559.685-122	LINSEED-OIL-PRESS TENDER (oils & grease)	2213	44444534355	MNNNNNNNFFNNNNNNNNNNN	NNNN4NNNNNNNNNN	R	142	499	06.04.19	7673	000000	92958
559.685-126	NOODLE-CATALYST MAKER (chemical)	2112	44434344354	MNNFNFNFFNNNNFNNNNNN	NNNN3NNNNNNNNNN	R	143	499	06.04.11	7663	000000	92944
559.685-130	PIGMENT PROCESSOR (chemical; paint & varnish)	3223	34344344454	MONNNNNFFNNNNNONNNNN	NNON4NNNNNNNNNN	J,T	147	495	06.04.07	7678	000000	92938
559.685-134	POWDER-CUTTING OPERATOR (chemical)	2112	44544534355	MNNNNNNNFFONNNNNFNNNN	NNNN4NNNNNNNNNN	R	054	499	06.04.11	7676	000000	92958
559.685-138	PRESS OPERATOR (rubber reclaim,)	2113	44434444354	LONNNNNFFFNNNNNNNNNN	NNNF3NNNNNNNNNN	R	031	513	06.04.13	7673	000000	92944
559.685-142	PRESSER (soap & rel.)	2112	44443444354	LNNNNNNFFFNNNNNFNNFN	NNNN4NNNNNNNNNN	R,T	054	494	06.04.09	7678	000000	92958
559.685-146	PRESSROOM WORKER, FAT (oils & grease)	2112	44445444443	LNNNNNNFFFNNNNNFNNNFN	NNNN3NNNNNNNNNN	R,T	147	499	06.04.19	7673	000000	92958
559.685-150	REBRANDER (rubber goods)	2112	44434434335	LNNNNNNFFFNNNNFNNNNN	NNNN3NNNNNNNNNC	R,T	051	512	06.04.07	7679	000000	92998
559.685-154	RESTRICTIVE-PREPARATION OPERATOR (ordnance)	2213	44433434355	MNNNNNNFFFNNNFNFNNNN	NNNN4NNNNNNNNNN	J,T	143	499	06.04.11	7664	000000	92965
559.685-158	RUBBER CUTTER (rubber goods; rubber tire)	1112	44544544355	HNNFNNNNFFFNNNNNNNNNN	NNNNN4NFNNNNNNN	R	054	519	06.04.07	7678	000000	92944
559.685-162	SCREENER-PERFUMER (soap & rel.)	2113	44444444355	MNNNNNNFFNNNNFNNNNN	NNNN4NNNNNNNNNN	R,T	152	494	06.04.19	7679	000000	92998
559.685-166	SEPARATOR OPERATOR (chemical)	2212	44444444445	LNNNNNNFFFNNNNNFNFNNN	NNNN4NNNNNNNNNN	R	145	499	06.04.19	7666	000000	92962
559.685-170	SPREADING-MACHINE OPERATOR (chemical)	2113	44443544355	LNNNNNNFFNNNNNNNNNNN	NNNN3NNNNNNNNNN	R,T	147	499	06.04.19	7669	000000	92953

DOT #	DOT Title & Industry	Trng	Aptitude	Physical	Environment	Tempra	WkF	MPSMS	GOE	SOC	CIP	OES
559.685-174	TUBE-BUILDING-MACHINE OPERATOR (rubber goods)	2113	44543533355	LNNFNNNFFNNNNFNNNNN	NNNN3NNNNNNNNNNN	J,T	134	514	06.04.05	7663	000000	92971
559.685-178	TUMBLER-MACHINE OPERATOR (rubber goods)	2112	44454433345	MNNFNFNFFOONNNONONNN	NNNN4NNNNNNNNNNN	R	051	519	06.04.07	7679	000000	92998
559.685-182	WASH-TANK TENDER (chemical)	2223	34343434354	LNNNNNNNNFFNNNNNNNNN	NNNN4NNNNNNNNNNN	R,T	147	499	06.04.11	7673	000000	92958
559.685-186	WET-END OPERATOR I (plastic-synth.)	3224	44444444354	MNNONNNNOOOONNFONNON	NNNN4NNNNNNNNNNN	R,T	147	492	06.04.13	7515	000000	91321
559.685-190	WET-END OPERATOR II (plastic-synth.)	2213	34344433353	LNNNNNNNFFNNNNNNNNN	NNOO4NONNNNNNNN	R,T	147	492	06.04.13	7676	000000	92962
559.686-010	COMPOUND WORKER (recording)	1112	44444444455	MNNNNNNNFFNNNNNONNNNN	NNON4NOONNNNNNN	R	212	492	06.04.13	8725	000000	98502
559.686-014	DRIER FEEDER (rubber reclaim.)	1112	44545535345	MNNFNFNFFNNNNNNNNNN	NNNF3NNNNNNNNNN	R	031	513	06.04.07	8725	000000	98502
559.686-018	HOSE-TUBING BACKER (rubber goods)	2112	44544544455	MNNNNNNCCNNNNNNNNNN	NNNN4NNNNNNNNNN	R	063	519	06.04.07	8725	000000	98502
559.686-022	LABORER (pharmaceut.)	2122	44444444355	HNNFNFNFFNNNNNNNNNN	NNNN3NNNNNNNNNN	R	147	493	06.04.19	8725	000000	98502
559.686-026	LABORER, GENERAL (rubber goods; rubber reclaim.; rubber tire)	1112	44444444354	MNNFOFNFFONNNNONONON	NNNN4NNNNNNNNNN	R,T	011	510	06.04.13	7679	000000	92998
559.686-030	LABORER, VAT HOUSE (chemical)	1112	44544544445	HONNNNNNFFNNNNNNNNNN	NNNN4NNNNNNNNNN	R,T	147	499	06.04.19	8725	000000	98502
559.686-034	OPENER (rubber goods)	1112	44544534355	LNNNNNNNFFNNNNNNNNN	NNNN3NNNNNNNNNN	R	135	519	06.04.07	7666	000000	92962
559.686-038	REDUCTION-FURNACE-OPERATOR HELPER (chemical; oils & grease)	2112	44445444355	HNNNNNNNFFNNNNNNNNN	NNNN4NNNNNNNNNN	R	147	491	06.04.11	8618	000000	98999
559.686-042	SLABBER (soap & rel.)	1112	44544544455	MNNONNNNFFNNNNNNNNNN	NNNN4NOONNNNNNN	R	054	494	06.04.09	8725	000000	98502
559.687-010	AMPOULE EXAMINER (pharmaceut.)	2123	44343443454	SNNNNNNFFNNNNFNNNFN	NNNN3NNNNNNNNNN	R,T	212	493	06.03.02	7820	000000	83005
559.687-014	AMPOULE SEALER (pharmaceut.)	2112	44544533455	SNNNNNFFNNNNFNNOONN	NNNN4NNNNNNNNNN	R	131	531	06.04.34	7740	000000	98902
559.687-018	CASTING-MACHINE-SERVICE OPERATOR (plastic-synth.)	2113	44454534355	MNNFNFNCCFNNNNNNNNNN	NNNO4NNNNNNNNNN	R	014	492	06.04.39	8750	000000	98905
559.687-022	CELL CLEANER (chemical)	2112	44544544355	HNNONNNNFFNNNNNNNONNN	NNNO4NNNNNNNNNN	R	031	589	06.04.39	8750	000000	98999
559.687-026	CONTACT-ACID-PLANT-OPERATOR HELPER (chemical)	2112	44444444355	MNNOONNOOONNNNONNNNN	ONNO3NNNNNNNNNN	R	147	491	06.04.11	8618	000000	98999
559.687-030	COTTON WASHER (plastic-synth.)	1111	44544544355	HNNNNNNNFFNNNNNNNNN	NNNN4NONNNNNNNN	R	152	302	06.04.39	8769	000000	98999
559.687-034	EGG PROCESSOR (pharmaceut.)	2112	44544433355	SNNNNNNFFNNNNFNFFNN	NNNN3NNNNNNNNNN	R	147	493	06.04.34	7759	000000	93999
559.687-038	FILTER CLEANER (plastic-synth.)	2112	44544543355	MNNONNNCCFNNNNNNNNNN	NNNN4NONNNNNNNN	R	031	568	06.04.39	8750	000000	98905
559.687-042	FILTER WASHER (chemical)	2112	44544544355	MNNNNNNNFFNNNNNNNNN	NNNO4NNNNNNNNNN	R	031	568	06.04.39	8750	000000	98905
559.687-046	FRAME STRIPPER (chemical)	1111	44444544455	MNNNFNNNFFNNNNNNNNNN	NNON4NNNNNNNNON	R	142	499	06.04.19	8769	000000	98999
559.687-050	LABORER, CHEMICAL PROCESSING (chemical)	2113	44444444355	HFFFNNNFFNNNNNNNOONN	NNNO4NNNNNNNNOO	R	031	490	06.04.40	8769	000000	98999
559.687-054	SKEIN-WINDING OPERATOR (any industry)	1111	44444444355	LNNNNNNNFFNNNNNONNNNN	NNNN4NNNNNNNNNN	R,T	163	412	06.04.27	8769	000000	98999
559.687-058	SOAP INSPECTOR (soap & rel.)	2112	44433444353	LNNNNNNNFFOONNFNNOFN	NNNN3NNNNNNNNNN	J	212	494	06.03.02	7820	000000	83005
559.687-062	TANK CLEANER (chemical; plastic-synth.)	2112	44544544355	MNNFFNNFFNNNNNNNNNN	ONNO4NNNNNNNNOON	R	031	568	06.04.39	8750	000000	98905
559.687-066	TUBE SORTER (rubber reclaim.)	2123	44443433354	LNNFNNNNFFFNNNFNNNON	NNNN3NNNNNNNNNN	R	221	511	06.03.02	7850	000000	83005
559.687-070	WEIGHER OPERATOR (chemical)	2123	44444444355	LNNONNNNFFNNNNFNNNON	NNNN4NNNNNNNNNN	R	212	499	06.03.02	7840	000000	83005
559.687-074	INSPECTOR AND HAND PACKAGER (plastic prod.)	2122	44443443353	LNNONNNNFFNNNNFNNFFN	NNNN4NNNNNNNNNN	R	212	510	06.03.02	7820	150607	83005
560.465-010	CHIP-MIXING-MACHINE OPERATOR (wood prod., nec)	3323	34444443355	LNNNNNNNFFOOOONONOONN	NNNO4NNNNNNNNNN	R,T	143	456	06.04.14	7639	000000	92965
560.585-010	MIXING-MACHINE TENDER (wood prod., nec)	2223	44444434355	MNNNNNNNFFNNNNNFNNNN	NNNN4NNNNNNNNNN	R,T	147	459	06.04.14	7639	000000	92965
560.587-010	COMPOUNDER, CORK (wood prod., nec)	2222	44444434345	MNNNNNNFFNNNNFNOONN	NNNN4NNNNNNNNNN	R	212	459	06.04.14	7840	000000	83005
561.131-010	TREATING-PLANT SUPERVISOR (wood prod., nec)	4337	23333333343	LNNONONOOONFFNOFFOFC	FNNN4NOONNNNNNO	V,D,P,J	152	452	06.02.01	7100	000000	81008
561.362-010	TREATING ENGINEER (wood prod., nec)	3336	33334434354	MOOONONOOONOONONNON	ONNN4NOONNNNNNN	J,T	152	452	06.02.18	7639	000000	92923
561.585-010	STAIN APPLICATOR (wood prod., nec)	2222	44444444345	HONNNNNNFFONNNNFNNNNN	NNNO3NCNNNNNNNN	R,T	152	452	06.04.21	7669	000000	92953
561.587-010	POLE INSPECTOR (wood prod., nec)	2223	34443444455	LNNONNNOOONNNNNONNNN	NNNN4NNNNNNNNNN	R,T	212	450	06.03.02	7820	000000	83005
561.665-010	TANKER (wood prod., nec)	2113	44444444345	HNNNNNNNFFNNNNFNOONN	ONNO4NNNNNNNNNN	R,T	152	452	06.04.18	7639	000000	92998
561.685-010	TREATING-ENGINEER HELPER (wood prod., nec)	2112	44444544355	MNNFNNNFFNNNNNFNNNN	FNNO4NONNNNNNNN	R,T	152	452	06.04.18	8615	000000	98999
561.686-010	LABORER, WOOD-PRESERVING PLANT (wood prod., nec)	2112	44434534335	VOFFNNFFNNNNFNNNN	ONNNN4NNNNNNNOO	R	011	452	06.04.25	8769	000000	98999
561.687-010	WOOD-POLE TREATER (wood prod., nec)	1111	44544544345	HNNFOONNFFNNNNNNNNNN	FNNN4NNNNNNNNNN	R	153	452	06.04.18	8769	000000	98999
562.485-010	WHITING-MACHINE OPERATOR (wood prod., nec)	2224	44444434355	MNNNNNNNFFNNNFNNFNN	NNNN4NNNNNNNNNN	R,T	151	457	06.04.21	7639	000000	92953
562.665-010	LOG COOKER (wood. container)	2112	44444444345	HNNFOONFFNNNNNNFNNN	FNNO4NNNNNNNNNN	R,T	152	451	06.04.18	7639	000000	92923
562.665-014	STEAM-BOX OPERATOR (woodworking)	2222	44444444455	MONNNNNFFNNOONONNNNN	NNNO4NNNNNNNNNN	R,T	152	450	06.04.18	7639	000000	92923
562.682-010	HUMIDIFIER OPERATOR (wood prod., nec)	3224	34333434354	MONNNNNNFFONNNNFNNOON	NNNF4NNNNNNNNNN	J,T	152	456	06.02.18	7679	000000	92998
562.685-010	GLUE-SIZE-MACHINE OPERATOR (furniture)	2222	44444444355	MONNNNNFFONNNNFNNNNN	NNNN4NNNNNNNNNN	R,T	153	460	06.04.21	7820	480702	92956
562.685-014	IMPREGNATOR (pen & pencil)	2222	44444444355	HNNNNNNNFFNNNNNNNNN	NNNN4NNNNNNNNNN	R,T	152	617	06.04.18	7639	000000	92953
562.685-018	OPERATOR, PREFINISH (millwork-plywood)	3225	34443444354	MNNNNNNNFFOONNNFNNNNN	NNNN4NFNNNNNNNN	R,T	153	453	06.02.21	8769	000000	98999
562.685-022	COATER, SMOKING PIPE (fabrication, nec)	2223	44444444345	MNNNNNNCCNNNNNNONNNN	NNNN3NNNNNNNNNN	R,T	153	619	06.04.21	7669	000000	92953
562.686-010	STEAM-TUNNEL FEEDER (saw. & plan.)	1111	44544544455	MNNNNNNNFFNNNNNNNNN	NNNO4NNNNNNNNNN	R	152	452	06.04.18	8725	000000	98502

DOT #	DOT Title & Industry	Trng	Aptitude	Physical	Environment	Tempra	WkF	MPSMS	GOE	SOC	CIP	OES
562.687-010	DYER (woodworking)	2112	44444444454	MNNNNNNNFFNNNNNNNNNON	NNFN4NONNNNNNNN	R	151	457	06.04.33	7639	000000	92953
562.687-014	RESIN COATER (wood prod., nec)	2222	44444444355	LNNNNNNNFFNNNNNNNNNNN	NNNO4NNNNNNNN	R	151	459	06.04.33	7756	000000	93947
563.135-010	SUPERVISOR, DRYING (millwork-plywood)	4336	33333444355	MONONNNFFONFFNFNNNNNN	NNFN3NNNNNNNNNO	V,D,P	141	453	06.02.01	7100	000000	81008
563.137-010	SUPERVISOR, BEEHIVE KILN (chemical)	3336	33343343454	LNNNNNNOOOFFNNNOOF	CFFF3NCNNNNNCF	D,P,V,J	141	496	06.02.01	7100	000000	81008
563.382-010	KILN OPERATOR (woodworking)	3326	34343343444	LNNNNNNNFFONNNNFNNNON	FNON4NNONNNNNNN	J,T	141	451	06.02.18	7675	000000	92923
563.585-010	DRIER TENDER (wood prod., nec)	3224	34444443355	LONONONFFONNNNOONONN	NNNN4NNNNNNNNN	R,T	141	456	06.02.18	7639	000000	92923
563.662-010	TREATING-PLANT OPERATOR (wood prod., nec)	3224	34334434344	MONNNNNFFONOONFNNNON	NNFN3NNNNNNNNN	J,T	147	456	06.02.18	7639	000000	92998
563.682-010	CHARCOAL BURNER, BEEHIVE KILN (chemical)	3224	34534544454	HNNONNNNFFONOONFNNNNN	FNNNN4NNNNNNNFN	J,T	141	496	06.02.18	7675	000000	92923
563.685-010	BARK-PRESS OPERATOR (paper & pulp)	2112	44544544345	LNNONNNFFNNNNNNNNNNN	NNNN4NNNNNNNNN	R	145	459	06.04.14	7667	000000	92971
563.685-014	CLOTHESPIN-DRIER OPERATOR (woodworking)	1112	44444444345	MNNNNNNFFNNNNNNNNNNN	NNNN4NNNNNNNNN	R	141	457	06.04.21	7639	000000	92923
563.685-018	DRY-HOUSE ATTENDANT (woodworking)	2113	44444434354	MNNNNNNFFONNNNNNNON	NNNN4NNNNNNNNN	R,T	141	457	06.04.18	7639	000000	92923
563.685-022	VENEER DRIER (millwork-plywood)	2112	44444444354	MNNONNNCCNNNNNONNNON	NNON4NNNNNNNNN	R,T	141	453	06.04.18	7639	000000	92923
563.685-026	VENEER REDRIER (millwork-plywood)	2112	44444444355	MNNFNNNFFNNNNNNNNNN	NNNO4NNNNNNNNN	R,T	141	453	06.04.18	7639	000000	92923
563.686-010	STICKER (saw. & plan.)	2112	44544533345	MNNONNNCCNNNNNNFNNN	NNNN4NNNNNNNNN	R	141	450	06.04.03	8725	000000	98502
563.686-014	VENEER-DRIER FEEDER (millwork-plywood)	1111	44544544355	MNNFNNNFFNNNNNNNNNN	NNNN3NNNNNNNNN	R	141	453	06.04.18	8725	000000	98502
563.686-018	OFFBEARER, PIPE SMOKING MACHINE (fabrication, nec)	2111	44443534455	MNNNNNFFONNNNNNNNNN	NNNN3NNNNNNNNN	R	141	619	06.04.03	8725	000000	98502
563.687-010	ANTICHECKING-IRON WORKER (wood prod., nec)	1112	44544544455	LNFNNNNFFNNNNNNNNNN	ONNN4NNNNNNNNN	R	072	452	06.04.25	7740	000000	93999
563.687-014	MOISTURE TESTER (woodworking)	2212	44454444455	LNNNNNNNFFNNNNNFNNNN	NNNO4NNNNNNNNN	R,T	212	450	06.03.02	7830	000000	83005
564.132-010	WOOD-CREW SUPERVISOR (chemical; saw. & plan.)	4337	33333433355	MONNNNNFFNNFNFNNONN	ONNN4NONNNNNNNN	V,D,P	142	452	06.02.03	7100	000000	81008
564.662-010	LOG-CHIPPER OPERATOR (logging)	3124	34434433345	MNNOONFFONNNNNFNNNNN	NNNN4NNNNNNNNN	R,T	142	459	06.02.03	7677	030404	92965
564.682-010	CHIPPING-MACHINE OPERATOR (wood prod., nec)	3115	34434433355	MNNONONFFFNNNNONOONN	ONNN4NNNNNNNNN	R,T	142	456	06.02.03	7639	000000	92998
564.682-014	FLAKE-CUTTER OPERATOR (wood prod., nec)	3224	34444434355	MNNNNNNFFNNNNNONNNN	ONNN4NNONNNNNNN	R,T	142	459	06.02.03	7639	000000	92944
564.682-018	MILLER, WOOD FLOUR (woodworking)	3226	34433434355	LNNNNNNNFFNNNNNFNNNN	NNNN4NONNNNNNNN	J,T	142	459	06.02.03	7639	000000	92965
564.684-010	KNIFE SETTER, GRINDER MACHINE (paper & pulp)	2113	44433534355	MNNNNNFFONNNNNFNNNN	NNNN4NNNNNNNNN	R,T	121	567	05.10.02	6140	000000	85128
564.685-010	BREAKER-MACHINE OPERATOR (saw. & plan.; wood prod., nec)	2114	44444534355	LOOONNNCCCNNNNNNNNN	NNNN4NONNNNNNNN	R,T	142	459	06.04.14	7677	000000	92965
564.685-014	CHIPPER (chemical; paper & pulp; saw. & plan.)	2112	44454534355	MNNONONFFNNNONONFNNF	NNNN4FONNNNNNN	R	142	451	06.04.03	7639	000000	92944
564.685-018	HOG TENDER (woodworking)	2112	44454544445	MONFNNNFFNNNNNNNNNN	NNNN4NNNNNNNNN	R	142	451	06.04.03	7677	000000	92965
564.686-010	WOOD SCRAP HANDLER (millwork-plywood)	1112	44544544355	HNNFNNNFFNNNNNNNNNN	NNNN4NNNNNNNNNO	R,U	142	452	06.04.03	8725	000000	98502
564.687-010	CHOPPER (chemical)	1111	44544544455	HNNNNNNCCNNNNNNNNNN	CNNN4NNNNNNNNN	R	056	451	06.01.01	8769	000000	98999
569.130-010	GASKET SUPERVISOR (wood prod., nec)	4336	33323344355	LNNNNNFFONNOONONOONN	ONNN4NFNNNNNNN	V,D,P,J	102	459	06.01.01	7100	000000	81008
569.132-010	SUPERVISOR, PARTICLEBOARD (wood prod., nec)	4336	33333444455	LNNNNNNFFOONFNNFNN	ONNN4NFNNNNNNN	V,D,P,J	147	456	06.02.01	7100	000000	81008
569.135-010	SUPERVISOR, VENEER (millwork-plywood)	4336	33334444344	LNNNNNNNFFOFFNFNON	NNNN4NNNNNNNN	V,D,P,J	102	453	06.02.01	7100	000000	81008
569.367-010	TREATING INSPECTOR (wood prod., nec)	3333	33343444445	LNNNNNNNFFNNOONFNOONN	ONNN4NNNNNNNNN	J,T	212	451	05.07.06	7820	000000	83005
569.382-010	LINE TENDER, FLAKEBOARD (wood prod., nec)	3225	33433443355	LOONNNNFFONNNNFNNNNN	NNNF3NFNNNNNNN	J,T	147	474	06.02.18	7639	000000	92998
569.384-010	QUALITY-CONTROL TESTER (wood prod., nec)	4336	33344444455	LNNNNNNNFFONNNNONONN	NNNN3NNNNNNNNN	R,T	212	456	06.03.01	7830	030404	83005
569.565-010	CREW LEADER, GLUING (millwork-plywood)	3334	34434434354	MONONONFFONOONONNNON	NNNN4NNNNNNNNN	J,P	063	453	06.04.03	7661	030404	92956
569.662-010	INCISING-MACHINE OPERATOR (wood prod., nec)	3224	34434434345	LFNNONFFNNNONONONN	ONNN4NNONONONNNN	R,T	134	450	06.02.18	7639	000000	92998
569.682-010	GRINDER, HARDBOARD (wood prod., nec)	3326	33333444454	MFNFOONFFNNNNNFFON	NNNN4NFNNNNNNN	J,T	147	459	06.02.18	7639	000000	92965
569.682-014	PRESS OPERATOR, HARDBOARD (wood prod., nec)	3225	33443443334	MONONNNFFNNOONFNOONN	NNNN4NCONNNNNNN	J,T	134	473	06.02.18	7663	000000	92971
569.683-010	KILN-TRANSFER OPERATOR (woodworking)	2113	44434534335	MNNNNNNCCNNNNNNCNOONN	FNNN4NNNNNNNNN	R	011	450	05.11.04	8319	490299	97989
569.684-010	LOG PEELER (saw. & plan.)	2112	44544544345	VNNFNNNFFONNNNNFNNNN	FNNN3NNNNNNNNN	R,T	054	451	06.04.25	7753	030404	93999
569.685-010	ARTIFICIAL-LOG-MACHINE OPERATOR (fabrication, nec; saw. & plan.)	2214	34443444344	LNNOOOOFFNNNNNNNNNOC	NNNN4NONNNNNNN	R,T	135	459	06.04.03	7635	000000	92314
569.685-014	BENDER, MACHINE (woodworking)	2113	44444443355	MNNNNNNFFNNNNNNNNNN	NNNO4NNNNNNNNN	R,T	134	450	06.04.03	7635	000000	92314
569.685-018	CORE FEEDER, PLYWOOD LAYUP LINE (millwork-plywood)	2113	44444544345	MONFNNNFFNNNNNNNNNN	NNNN4NNNNNNNNN	R,T	063	453	06.04.03	7661	000000	92956
569.685-022	CORE-COMPOSER-MACHINE TENDER (millwork-plywood)	2113	44443443455	MONONNNFFNNONFNNONNN	NNNN3NNNNNNNNN	R,T	063	453	06.04.03	7661	000000	92956
569.685-026	CORE-LAYING-MACHINE OPERATOR (millwork-plywood)	2214	44444433345	MNNONNNFFNNNNNNNNNN	NNNN3NNNNNNNNN	R,T	063	453	06.04.03	7661	000000	92956
569.685-030	CORK MOLDER (wood prod., nec)	2213	44434343345	HNNFNNNFFNNNNNNFNNNN	NNON4NONNNNNNN	R,T	132	459	06.04.09	7635	000000	92314
569.685-034	EDGE-GLUE-MACHINE TENDER (millwork-plywood)	2112	44444443355	MMNNNNNFFONNNNNNNNN	NNNN4NNNNNNNNN	R,T	063	453	06.04.03	7661	000000	92956
569.685-038	EXTRUDER OPERATOR (wood prod., nec)	2222	44444444355	LNNNNNNNFFNNNNNNNNNN	NNNN4NNNNNNNNN	R,T	135	456	06.04.19	7663	000000	92971
569.685-042	GLUE SPREADER, VENEER (millwork-plywood; wood prod., nec)	2113	44434534345	LNNNNNNCCNONNNCNOOIN	NNNO4NNONNNNNNN	R,T	063	453	06.04.03	7661	000000	92956
569.685-046	GLUING-MACHINE OPERATOR (woodworking)	2223	44434534345	HNNFNNNFFONNNNNNNOON	NNNN4NNNNNNNNN	R,T	063	451	06.04.03	7661	000000	92971

DOT #	DOT Title & Industry	Trng	Aptitude	Physical	Environment	Tempra	WkF	MPSMS	GOE	SOC	CIP	OES
569.685-050	GLUING-MACHINE OPERATOR, ELECTRONIC (woodworking)	2214	44444434355	MNNNNNNFFNNNNONOONN	NNNNN4NNNNNNNNN	R,T	063	451	06.04.03	7661	000000	92971
569.685-054	HOT-PLATE-PLYWOOD-PRESS OPERATOR (millwork-plywood)	2113	44444434355	HNNNNNNFFNNNNNNNNNN	NNFF4NNONNNNNNN	R,T	063	453	06.04.03	7639	000000	92971
569.685-058	HYDRAULIC-PRESS OPERATOR (millwork-plywood)	2123	44444434335	HNNNNNNNFFNNNNNONONN	NNNN4NNNNNNNNNN	R,T	063	450	06.04.03	7639	000000	92971
569.685-062	SPLICER OPERATOR (millwork-plywood)	2114	44433434355	MNNONNNCCONNNNCNCCNN	NNNN4NNNNNNNNNN	R,T	063	453	06.04.03	7639	000000	92971
569.685-066	STACKER MACHINE (woodworking)	2112	44444544345	MNNNNNNFFONNNNNFNNN	NNNN4NNNNNNNNNN	R	011	451	06.04.03	8319	490299	97989
569.685-070	VARNISHER (fabrication, nec)	1112	44544544455	LNNNNNNFFNNNNFNFNNN	NNNN4NNNNNNNNNN	R	151	619	06.04.21	7639	000000	92953
569.685-074	VENEER TAPER (millwork-plywood)	2113	44434434355	LNNNNNNFFONNNNFNFNNN	NNNN4NNNNNNNNNN	R,T	063	453	06.04.03	7639	000000	92998
569.685-078	WOOD-FUEL PELLETIZER (fabrication, nec)	3224	34434444354	MNNNNNNFFONNFNNNNFN	NNNN3NNNNNNNNNN	T,J	147	459	06.04.03	7663	030404	92314
569.686-010	BACK FEEDER, PLYWOOD LAYUP LINE (millwork-plywood)	1112	44544544445	MNNNNNNFFONNNNNNNNNN	NNNN4NNNNNNNNNNF	R,T	063	453	06.04.40	8725	000000	98502
569.686-014	CORE LAYER, PLYWOOD LAYUP LINE (millwork-plywood)	2112	44444544445	MONNNNNFFONNNNNNNNNN	NNNN4NNNNNNNNNN	R,T	063	453	06.04.40	8725	000000	98502
569.686-018	CORK-PRESSING-MACHINE OPERATOR (wood prod., nec)	1112	44544534355	LNNNNNNFFNNNNNNNNNN	NNNN4NNNNNNNNNN	R	134	459	06.04.09	8725	000000	98502
569.686-022	GLUING-MACHINE OFFBEARER (woodworking)	2112	44544544355	HNNONNNCCNNNNNNNNNN	NNCN4NFNNNNNNNN	R	063	452	06.04.03	8725	000000	98502
569.686-026	LABORER, HOT-PLATE PLYWOOD PRESS (millwork-plywood)	2112	44444444355	HNNFNNNCCONNNNNNFONN	NNON4NONNNNNNNN	R	063	453	06.04.03	8725	000000	98502
569.686-030	PAD-MACHINE OFFBEARER (saw. & plan.)	1111	44544544455	LNNNNNNFFNNNNNNNNNN	NNNN4NONNNNNNNN	R	041	459	06.04.09	8725	000000	98502
569.686-034	RETORT UNLOADER (chemical)	1112	44544544355	HNNFNFNFFNNNNNNNNNN	ONNN4NFNNNNNNNN	R	011	496	06.04.40	8725	000000	98502
569.686-038	GLUING-MACHINE FEEDER (woodworking)	2112	44444444355	MNNNNNNCCNNNNNNNNNN	NNNN4NNNNNNNNNN	R,U	063	450	06.04.03	8725	030404	98502
569.686-042	LAMINATING-MACHINE FEEDER (wood prod., nec)	1111	44544545455	MNNNNNNFFNNNNNONNNN	NNNN3NNNNNNNNNN	R,U	063	456	06.04.09	8725	030404	98502
569.686-046	LAMINATING-MACHINE OFFBEARER (wood prod., nec)	2122	44543444454	LNNONNNOOONNNNFNONNN	NNNN4NNNNNNNNNN	R,T,U	063	456	06.03.02	7820	030404	83005
569.686-050	PRESS BREAKER (wood prod., nec)	2112	44433434335	VFFFFFFNFFONNNNFNFNF	NNNN4NFFNNNNNNN	R,U	134	456	06.04.40	8725	490299	98502
569.686-054	VENEER-TAPING-MACHINE OFFBEARER (millwork-plywood)	2112	44544444355	MNNONNNCCNNNNNNNNNN	NNNN4NNNNNNNNNN	R	063	453	06.04.03	8725	030404	98502
569.687-010	CLAMP REMOVER (millwork-plywood)	1112	44544544355	MNNFNNNCCONNNNNNFONN	NNNN4NONNNNNNNN	R	063	453	06.04.03	8725	000000	98999
569.687-014	LOG WASHER (saw. & plan.)	1112	44544544444	LNNNNNNFFNNNNNNNNNN	ONNN4NNNNNNNNNN	R	031	451	06.04.39	8769	000000	98999
569.687-018	SCREEN CLEANER (wood prod., nec)	1112	44544544355	MNNFNFNFFNNNNNNNNFNN	NNNN4NONNNNNNFNN	R	031	568	06.04.39	8750	000000	98999
569.687-022	SORTER I (wood prod., nec)	1112	44544544455	LNNNNNNFFNNNNFNNNNNN	NNNN4NNNNNNNNNN	R	212	459	06.03.02	7850	000000	93926
569.687-026	WOOD HACKER (fabrication, nec; paper & pulp)	2113	44444434344	MNNNNNNFFNNNNNNNNNON	NNNN4NNNNNNNNNN	R	052	451	06.04.25	7753	000000	83005
569.687-030	QUALITY CONTROL INSPECTOR (furniture; millwork-plywood)	3223	33333344354	LNNNNNNFFFOONFNFFON	NNON4NONNNNNNNN	D,P,T	143	346	06.03.02	7850	030404	83005
570.130-010	SUPERVISOR, CLAY PREPARATION (pottery & porc.)	4338	33334334345	LNNNNNOOONOONFNOONN	NNON4NONNNNNNNN	D,P,T	143	346	06.02.01	7100	520205	81008
570.132-010	CONCRETE-BATCHING AND MIXING-PLANT SUPERVISOR (construction)	4327	33343344454	LFNNNNNFFNFFNFNFF	ONNN4NOONNNNNNN	D,P	143	536	05.11.01	7100	469999	81008
570.132-014	MILLING SUPERVISOR (brick & tile)	4327	33443434453	HFNONONFFNNNNONNNNN	NNNN4NNNNNNNNNN	D,P	142	346	06.04.01	7100	520205	81008
570.132-018	WASHING-AND-SCREENING PLANT SUPERVISOR (construction)	4337	44444444445	HONFNNNFFONFNFNNNN	NNNN4NOONNNNNNN	D,P,V	007	536	06.02.17	7100	000000	81008
570.132-022	SUPERVISOR (brick & tile)	4236	33344344453	HONFNNNFFOONFNFNNNN	ONNN4NONNNNNNNN	D,P	142	349	06.02.18	7100	000000	81008
570.137-010	SUPERVISOR (mine & quarry)	3225	33344344344	LNNNNNOOONFNFNFNNF	NNNN4NFNNNNNFN	D,P	143	349	06.04.01	7100	000000	81017
570.362-010	BULK-STATION OPERATOR (petrol. & gas)	3215	34344333355	HOOFFNFFONOONFNOOON	ONNN4NNNNNNNNNN	J,T	143	533	06.02.01	7759	000000	93999
570.382-010	MILL OPERATOR (brick & tile; pottery & porc.)	3215	34344333355	MNNNNNNFFNNNNONONNN	NNNN4NOONNNNNNN	J,T	142	346	06.04.34	7664	489999	92965
570.382-014	PLASTER MIXER, MACHINE (concrete prod.)	4224	34334334355	HONONONFFOONNNONOON	NNNN4NONONNNNNN	J,T	143	536	06.04.12	7664	000000	92965
570.382-018	SUPPLY CONTROLLER (concrete prod.)	3225	34444444445	MONONNNFFOONNNONOONN	NNNN4NNNNNNNNNN	J,T	143	536	06.04.19	7664	000000	92965
570.482-010	CLAY MAKER (brick & tile; pottery & porc.)	2224	34344434355	MONNNNNFFOONNNNOONN	ONNN4NONNNNNNNN	R,J,T	014	346	06.04.17	7664	480599	92965
570.484-010	MIXER, DIAMOND POWDER (nonmet. min.)	3214	34344434344	MONOOONFFONNNNONONON	NNNO3NONNNNNNNN	R	143	349	06.04.40	7759	480599	93999
570.485-010	ABRASIVE MIXER (nonmet. min.)	2214	34444244354	HNNONNNFFONNNNOOONOO	ONNN4NNNNNNNNNN	R,T	143	538	05.11.02	7850	489999	92965
570.665-010	DRY-PAN OPERATOR (brick & tile)	3224	34443444345	MNNNNNNFFONNONNNFNNN	NNNN4NONNNNNNN	J	142	346	06.02.09	6960	000000	83005
570.682-010	ABRASIVE GRADER (optical goods)	3224	34443444345	MONONNNFFNNOONFNOON	FNNN4NFNNNNNNNN	J,T	143	340	06.04.17	7664	000000	95099
570.682-014	PLANT OPERATOR (concrete prod.; construction)	3114	34443434355	MMNFNNNFFNNOONFNNOON	NNNN4NNNNNNNNNN	T,J	143	345	06.02.10	7759	000000	93999
570.682-018	SAND MIXER, MACHINE (foundry)	3225	34344434335	MNNONNNFFOONNNONONNN	ONNN4NONNNNNNNN	R	011	346	06.04.40	7664	489999	92965
570.683-010	DRY-PAN CHARGER (brick & tile)	2114	44445434345	LNNNNNNFFOONNNNNNNN	NNNO3NONNNNNNNN	J,T	143	345	06.04.08	7664	480599	92965
570.683-014	SAND-CUTTER OPERATOR (foundry)	2213	44444434355	HNNONNNFFONNNNNFNNNN	ONNN4NONNNNNNNN	R,T	143	533	06.04.17	7664	489999	92965
570.685-010	AUXILIARY-EQUIPMENT TENDER (cement)	2112	44444444444	HONONNNFFONNNNOOONOO	NNNN4NNONNNNNNN	R,T	143	340	06.04.17	7664	489999	92965
570.685-014	CLAY MIXER (brick & tile)	3112	44444435355	HONNNNNFFONNNNNNONNN	ONNO4NNONNNNNNN	R	142	349	06.04.08	7677	000000	92965
570.685-018	CRUSHER OPERATOR (concrete prod.)	2213	44445434354	MONOOONFFONNNNNONONON	NNNN4NFONNNNNNN	R	142	340	06.04.08	7677	000000	92965
570.685-026	CULLET CRUSHER-AND-WASHER (glass mfg.)	2212	44445444454	MNNNNNNFFNNNNNNNNNN	ONNN4NOONNNNNNN	J,R	142	539	06.04.08	7677	489999	92965

DOT #	DOT Title & Industry	Trng	Aptitude	Physical	Environment	Tempra	WkF	MPSMS	GOE	SOC	CIP	OES
570.685-030	HAMMER-MILL OPERATOR (nonmet. min.)	2113	44444444455	LNNNNNNNFFNNNNNNNNNN	NNNN4NNNNNNNNNN	R	142	344	06.04.08	7677	000000	92965
570.685-034	LIME SLAKER (concrete prod.)	2214	44444444355	LNNNNNNNFFNNNNNONNNN	NNNO4NNNNNNNNNN	J,T	143	349	06.04.11	7664	000000	92965
570.685-038	MILLER (mine & quarry)	2112	44444434345	MNNNNNNNFFOONNNONNNNN	ONNN4NOONNNNNON	J,T	142	349	06.04.17	7677	000000	92965
570.685-042	MILLER I (chemical)	2112	44544544355	LONNNNNNFFOOONOOONNN	ONNN4NONNNNNNNN	R	142	347	06.04.11	7677	000000	92965
570.685-046	MILLER (cement)	2113	44544444354	MNNNNNNNFFNNONNNONNN	NNNN4NOONNNNNNN	T,R	142	533	06.04.08	7677	469999	92965
570.685-050	MIXER (nonmet. min.)	2112	44444444355	HNNONNNNFFONNNNONONN	NNNO4NONNNNNNNN	R,T	143	538	06.04.19	7664	000000	92965
570.685-054	MIXER (glass mfg.)	2113	44444443454	LNNNNNNNFFONNNNNFOOOON	NNNN4NONNNNNNNN	R,T	143	340	06.04.13	7664	000000	92965
570.685-058	MIXER OPERATOR (concrete prod.)	1112	44444444455	LNNNNNNNFFNNNNNNNNNN	NNNN4NNNNNNNNNN	R	143	349	06.04.11	7664	000000	92965
570.685-062	MIXER TENDER, BOARD (concrete prod.)	3214	34434434355	LNNNNNNNFFNNNNNNNNNN	NNNN4NNNNNNNNNN	J,T	143	536	06.04.19	7664	000000	92965
570.685-066	MOLDING-MACHINE TENDER (pen & pencil)	2112	44544544444	MNNNNNNNFFNNNNNNOOON	NNNN4NNNNNNNNNN	R	132	617	06.04.17	7664	000000	92965
570.685-070	MUD-MIXER OPERATOR (smelt. & refin.; steel & rel.)	2112	44455444355	HNNNNNNNFFNNNNNNNNNN	NNNO4NNNNNNNNNN	R,T	143	534	06.04.17	7664	000000	92965
570.685-074	PUG-MILL-OPERATOR HELPER (brick & tile; pottery & porc.)	2112	44444544355	VNNNNNNNFFNNNNNNNNNN	NNNO3NNNNNNNNNN	R	143	346	06.04.17	7664	489999	92965
570.685-078	REFRACTORY MIXER (steel & rel.)	2113	44443434355	HNNNNNNNFFOONNNNNNNN	NNNO4NNNNNNNNNN	R,T	142	349	06.04.08	7664	000000	92965
570.685-082	ROUGE MIXER (optical goods)	1112	44444444455	MNNNNNNNFFNNNNNNNNNN	NNNN4NONNNNNNNN	R	143	538	06.04.19	7664	489999	92965
570.685-086	SAGGER PREPARER (pottery & porc.)	2113	44444444355	MNNNNNNNFFNNNNNNNNNN	NNNN4NNNNNNNNNN	R	143	535	06.04.17	7677	000000	92965
570.685-090	SILICA-SPRAY MIXER (smelt. & refin.)	2113	44444444355	MNNNNNNNFFNNNNNNNNNN	NNNO4NOONNNNNNN	R,T	143	539	06.04.17	7664	489999	92965
570.685-094	SLATE MIXER (build. mat., nec)	2112	44444434354	LNNNNNNNFFNNNNNNNNNO	NNNN4NNNNNNNNNN	R,T	143	503	06.04.08	7664	000000	92965
570.685-098	GLAZE MAKER (brick & tile; pottery & porc.)	3213	34444344443	HNNNNNNNFFONNNNFNONON	NNON3NONNNNNNNN	R,T	142	340	06.04.09	7664	489999	92965
570.686-010	ABRASIVE-GRADER HELPER (optical goods)	1112	44544444354	MNNNFNNNFFNNNNNNNNNN	NNNN4NANNNNNNNN	R	142	538	06.04.19	8725	000000	98502
570.686-014	ABRASIVE-MIXER HELPER (nonmet. min.)	2112	44455444455	MNNNNNNNFFFNNNNNNNNN	NNNN4NNNNNNNNNN	R	143	538	06.04.19	8618	000000	98999
570.686-018	PREPARATION-ROOM WORKER (nonmet. min.)	1112	44444444355	MNNNNNNNCCONNNNNNNNN	NNNN4NONNNNNNNN	R	143	349	06.04.19	8725	000000	98502
570.687-010	BATCH MIXER (brick & tile)	2112	44444444355	HNNNNNNNFFNNNNNNNNNN	NNNN4NONNNNNNNN	R,T	143	340	06.04.17	8725	489999	98502
571.685-010	BURNER TENDER (mine & quarry)	2114	44444544345	LNNNNNNNFFNNFNFNFNFF	NNNN4NNNNNNNNNN	R	141	349	06.04.19	7666	489999	92923
571.685-014	GLAZE HANDLER (brick & tile)	2114	44444544354	MONOONNNFFONNNNNFOONN	NNNN4NNNNNNNNNN	R	145	346	06.04.17	6881	489999	92962
572.360-010	FURNACE-COMBUSTION ANALYST (glass mfg.)	4336	33343434435	LNNNNNNNFFONONONOOON	NNON4NNNNNNNNNN	J,T	131	340	06.01.05	6960	489999	83002
572.382-010	BATCH-AND-FURNACE OPERATOR (glass mfg.)	4337	33343434353	LNNNNNNNFFONNNNOONNON	NNON4NNNNNNNNNN	J,T	131	340	06.02.13	6960	489999	95099
572.382-014	GLASS-FURNACE TENDER (paint & varnish)	2112	44444544355	HNNNNNNNFFNNNNNNONNNN	NNFN4NNNNNNNNNN	R,T	131	539	06.04.13	7675	489999	92923
572.686-010	CUPOLA CHARGER, INSULATION (nonmet. min.)	2113	44444444355	MONOONNNFFNNNNONONNNN	NNNN4NONNNNNNNN	R,T	131	340	06.04.19	8725	000000	98502
573.132-010	BURNING SUPERVISOR (brick & tile)	4327	33433333344	LNNNNNNNFFNFNFNFNFF	ONON4NNNNNNNNNN	D,P	141	534	06.02.01	7100	520205	81008
573.362-010	DRY-KILN OPERATOR (brick & tile)	3215	34333444345	MONOONNNFFONNNNNFOON	NNNN4NNNNNNNNNN	R,T	141	534	06.04.19	7675	489999	92923
573.382-010	ROTARY-KILN OPERATOR (cement; chemical; mine & quarry)	3224	34333444454	LNNNNNNNFFNNNNONFFON	ONON4NNNNNNNNNN	J,T	141	530	06.02.17	7675	489999	92923
573.382-014	SPRAY-DRIER OPERATOR (brick & tile)	3214	34443344455	LNNNNNNNFFNNNNNNFNNNN	NNNN4NNNNNNNNNN	J,T	141	346	06.02.17	7675	489999	92923
573.382-018	TUNNEL-KILN OPERATOR (brick & tile)	3225	34344344343	MONOONNFFNNNNONOOOON	NNON4NNNNNNNNNN	J,T	141	534	06.02.17	7675	489999	92923
573.462-010	LIME-KILN OPERATOR (concrete prod.)	3215	34343434344	LNNNNNNNFFONNNNONOONN	NNON4NNNNNNNNNN	J,T	141	536	06.02.18	6960	000000	95099
573.684-010	KILN-DOOR BUILDER (brick & tile)	2222	44444444354	MNNNNNNNFFNNNNNFNFON	NNNN4NNNNNNNNNN	R,T	141	419	06.04.13	6479	000000	87302
573.684-014	SETTER (brick & tile)	4325	33344444443	HONFNONFNNNNNNNNNN	NNNN3NNNNNNNNNN	R,T	011	534	06.04.40	7759	489999	93999
573.685-010	ANNEALER (glass products)	3113	44434544344	LNNOONNFFONNNNONFNON	NNON4NNNNNNNNNN	R,T	133	532	06.04.13	7675	489999	92923
573.685-014	CLAY ROASTER (petrol. refin.)	3224	44433444355	MNNNNNNNFFNNNNNNNNON	NNON4NONNNNNNNO	R,T	147	539	06.04.17	7675	489999	92923
573.685-018	GLAZING-MACHINE OPERATOR (glass mfg.)	2112	44444453354	LNNNNNNNCCNNNNNNNNN	NNON3NNNNNNNNNN	R,T	133	531	06.04.13	7669	489999	92953
573.685-022	KILN-OPERATOR HELPER (concrete prod.)	2112	44544544345	MNNNNNNNFFNNNNNNNNNN	NNON4NNNNNNNNNN	R	141	344	06.04.11	8618	000000	98999
573.685-026	LEHR TENDER (glass mfg.)	2113	44435534345	MNNNNNNNFFONNNNFNFNON	NNON4NONNNNNNNN	R,T	133	531	05.10.01	7675	489999	98999
573.685-030	LENS HARDENER (optical goods)	2212	44344444454	LNNNNNNNFFNNNNNFNFFN	NNNN4NNNNNNNNNN	R,T	133	605	06.04.13	7675	000000	92923
573.685-034	REGENERATOR OPERATOR (sugar & conf.)	2224	44433444344	LNNNNNNNFFOONNNNNNNN	NNFN4NNNNNNNNNN	R,T	141	349	06.04.17	7675	000000	92923
573.685-038	BURNER (brick & tile)	2112	44444344344	LFNNNNNNOOONNNNNNNN	NNFN4NNNNNNNNNN	R	141	539	06.04.17	7675	489999	92923
573.685-042	OVEN-PRESS TENDER I (nonmet. min.)	2114	44444453355	MNNNNNNNFFNNNNNNNNNN	NNNN4NONNNNNNNN	R,U	133	538	06.04.19	7675	000000	92923
573.685-046	OVEN-PRESS TENDER II (nonmet. min.)	2114	44444534355	MNNNNNNNFFONNNNFNNNN	NNNN4NONNNNNNNN	R,U	133	538	06.04.19	7675	000000	92923

DOT #	DOT Title & Industry	Trng	Aptitude	Physical	Environment	Tempra	WkF	MPSMS	GOE	SOC	CIP	OES
573.686-010	BRAKE-LINING CURER (nonmet. min.)	1112	4444444355	LNNNNNNCCONOONFNFNNN	NNNN3NNNNNNNNNN	R	133	538	06.04.19	8725	000000	98502
573.686-014	FUSING-FURNACE LOADER (optical goods)	2112	4444443355	LNNNNNNNFFONNNNONNNNN	NNON4NONNNNNNNN	R	131	605	06.04.13	8725	000000	98502
573.686-018	GLASS-VIAL-BENDING-CONVEYOR FEEDER (cutlery-hrdwr.)	2112	4444443355	LNNNNNNNFFONNNNNNFNNN	NNNN4NNNNNNNNNN	R	011	531	06.04.13	8725	489999	98502
573.686-022	HACKER (brick & tile)	1112	4444544355	MNNFNNNCCNNNNNNNNNNN	NNNN4NNNNNNNNNN	R	011	534	06.04.40	8725	489999	98502
573.686-026	KILN PLACER (pottery & porc.)	2112	4444444355	MONNNNNFFONNONNNOONN	NNON3NONNNNNNNN	R	041	535	06.04.17	8725	489999	98502
573.687-010	BEDDER (pottery & porc.)	2113	45444544354	MNNNNNNFFNNNNNFNNNNN	NNNN4NNNNNNNNNN	R,J	141	535	06.04.30	8769	489999	98999
573.687-014	DRY-KILN OPERATOR HELPER (brick & tile)	2112	4444454354	MNNNNNNFFNNNNNONNNNN	NNOO4NNNNNNNNNN	R	141	534	06.04.17	8618	000000	98999
573.687-018	KILN CLEANER (concrete prod.)	2112	4444444354	MNNFNNNNFFNNNNNNNNNN	NNNN3NONNNNNNNN	R	031	568	06.04.39	8750	000000	98905
573.687-022	KILN WORKER (pottery & porc.)	1112	44543544345	MNNNNNNCCNNNNNNNNNNN	NNNN4NNNNNNNNNN	R	102	568	06.04.17	8769	489999	98999
573.687-026	KILN-BURNER HELPER (brick & tile)	2113	44434534344	MNNOONNFFONNNNOONNFN	NNFN3NONNNNNNNN	R	141	534	06.04.17	8618	489999	98999
573.687-030	SETTER HELPER (brick & tile)	1112	4444544355	HNNNNNNFFNNNNNNNNNNN	NNNN4NNNNNNNNNN	R	011	534	06.04.40	8726	489999	98799
573.687-034	SORTER (brick & tile)	2222	44433535343	LNNOONNFFNNNNONOOON	NNNN3NNNNNNNNNN	R,J	212	534	06.03.02	7850	489999	83005
573.687-038	TILE SORTER (brick & tile)	2123	34433634353	LNNNNNNFFONNNNFNFFN	NNNN4NNNNNNNNNN	J,T	212	534	06.03.02	7850	489999	83005
574.130-010	GLAZE SUPERVISOR (brick & tile)	4227	33333333343	MNNNNNNFFONFFNFNOOFN	NNOO4NNNNNNNNNN	D,P	131	534	06.02.01	7100	520205	81008
574.132-010	GLAZE SUPERVISOR (pottery & porc.)	4327	33333433354	LNNONONFFFFNFNFNFN	NNNN3NNNNNNNNNN	D,J,P	153	535	06.02.01	7100	520205	81008
574.132-014	SUPERVISOR, SILVERING DEPARTMENT (glass products)	4227	33344333354	LNNNNNNFFNFNFNFFFN	NNNN4NNNNNNNNNN	D,P	153	532	06.02.01	7100	520205	81008
574.134-010	SUPERVISOR, HAND SILVERING (glass products)	4347	33443333354	MNNNNNNFFFFFFNFOOOOO	NNNN4NNNNNNNNNN	D,P,J,T	147	531	06.02.01	7100	520205	81008
574.367-010	TILE SHADER (brick & tile)	3225	33443344342	LNNNNNNCCONOONFNOOCN	NNNN4NNNNNNNNNN	J,T	212	534	06.03.01	7850	489999	83005
574.462-010	ABRASIVE-COATING-MACHINE OPERATOR (nonmet. min.)	3214	34434444355	LNNNNNNFFONNNNFNNNNN	NNNN4NONNNNNNNN	T	153	538	06.02.21	7479	000000	92951
574.484-010	OPTICAL-GLASS SILVERER (optical goods)	3114	34343434355	LNNNNNNFFONNNNFNNNN	NNNN3NNNNNNNNNN	J,T	154	603	06.04.33	7669	000000	92953
574.582-010	SILVERING APPLICATOR (glass products)	3225	34433434354	MNNNNNNFFNNNNFNNNFN	NNNN4NNNNNNNNNNF	J,T	143	532	06.02.21	7479	489999	92951
574.585-010	PAPERHANGER (concrete prod.)	2212	44434444344	MNNNONNFFOONNNONONON	NNNN4NNNNNNNNNN	R,T	135	536	06.04.19	7679	000000	92998
574.665-010	FIBERGLASS-BONDING-MACHINE TENDER (glass mfg.)	2222	44444534354	LONONNNFFOONNNNFNFNN	NNNN3NNNNNNNNNN	R,T	152	419	06.04.16	7679	000000	92998
574.667-010	DUST BOX WORKER (build. mat., nec)	2112	44445434344	LONONNNNFFNNOONONON	NNFN4NONNNNNNNN	R	153	503	06.04.34	8769	489999	98999
574.682-010	FIBERGLASS-MACHINE OPERATOR (glass products)	3214	44434333354	MNNNNNNNFFFFNFNNNNNN	NNNN4NNNNNNNNNN	R,T	153	531	06.02.13	7669	520205	81008
574.682-014	SPRAY-MACHINE OPERATOR (brick & tile; pottery & porc.)	3213	33333333354	MNNNNNNFFONNNNNOONON	NNON4NONNNNNNNN	J,T	153	535	06.02.21	7479	489999	92951
574.684-010	GROUND LAYER (pottery & porc.)	2113	44454344355	LNNNNNNFFONNNNNNNNN	NNNN4NNNNNNNNNN	R	153	535	06.04.33	7756	000000	93947
574.684-014	SILVERER (glass products)	3113	34443434354	MNNNNNNFFONNNNFNNNNN	NNNN3NNNNNNNNNN	R,T	153	532	06.04.33	7669	000000	92953
574.685-010	COATER, BRAKE LININGS (nonmet. min.)	2122	44444444355	SNNNNNNCCNNNNNCNNNNN	NNNN3NNNNNNNNNN	R	151	538	06.04.21	7669	489999	92953
574.685-014	PAINT-SPRAY TENDER (glass products)	3214	44444443354	MNNNONONOOFNNNNFNONON	NNNN4NNNNNNNNNN	R,T	153	532	06.04.21	7669	000000	92953
574.686-010	SPRAY-MACHINE LOADER (brick & tile; pottery & porc.)	2112	44445434354	LNNNNNNFFONFFNFNFFNN	ONNN3NNNNNNNNNN	R	102	536	06.04.21	8725	000000	98502
575.130-010	PRESS SUPERVISOR (brick & tile)	4327	33333333255	LNNNNNNFFONFFNFNNNN	NNFN4NNNNNNNNNN	D,P	131	531	06.02.01	7100	520205	81008
575.130-014	SUPERVISOR III (nonmet. min.)	3225	33333434354	MMNONONNFFNFNFFNFNNN	NNCN3NNNNNNNNNC	D,P	136	538	06.02.01	7100	000000	89905
575.130-018	SUPERVISOR, FORMING DEPARTMENT I (glass mfg.)	4337	33333334354	MNNONONFFFFNFFNFNFON	NNNN4NNNNNNNNNN	D,J,P	212	531	06.02.01	7100	520205	81008
575.131-010	SUPERVISOR, CONCRETE-STONE FABRICATING (concrete prod.)	4327	33333434444	MNNNNNNCCNNNNNNNNNNN	NNCN4NNNNNNNNNN	D,P	132	536	06.02.01	7100	520205	81008
575.131-014	SUPERVISOR, PRECAST AND PRESTRESSED CONCRETE (concrete prod.)	4337	33333434455	MNNNNNNFFONFFNFNONON	FNNN4NNNNNNNNNN	D,P	102	536	05.05.01	7100	520205	81008
575.137-010	DRAWING-KILN SUPERVISOR (glass mfg.)	4335	33333434455	LNNNNNNFFONFFNFFNN	NNFN4NNNNNNNNNN	V,D,P,J	131	531	06.02.01	7100	520205	81008
575.137-014	SUPERVISOR, WET POUR (concrete prod.)	4227	33343344455	MNNNONNFFONFFNFNNNN	FNNN3NNNNNNNNNN	D,P	132	536	06.02.01	7100	520205	81008
575.360-010	GLASS-BULB-MACHINE ADJUSTER (glass mfg.)	4336	34434344345	MNNNNNNFFONFFNFFNNON	NNFN3NNNNNNNNNN	J	132	531	06.01.02	7663	000000	92971
575.362-010	DRAWING-KILN OPERATOR (glass mfg.)	3223	34433344354	LNNNNNNFFONFFNFONOON	NNNN3NNNNNNNNNN	J,T	135	531	06.02.13	7663	489999	92971
575.362-014	GLASS-RIBBON-MACHINE OPERATOR (glass mfg.)	3223	34333434354	LNNNNNNFFFONFFNFONON	NNFN3NNNNNNNNNN	J	132	531	06.02.13	7663	489999	92971
575.365-010	GLASS-RIBBON-MACHINE-OPERATOR ASSISTANT (glass mfg.)	4337	34444443354	MNNNNNNFFONFFNFONOON	NNFN3NNNNNNNNNN	J	132	531	06.02.13	7663	489999	92971
575.380-010	FORMING-MACHINE UPKEEP MECHANIC (glass mfg.)	3236	33323434355	LONONNNFFONOONFONOON	NNOO3NNNNNNNNNN	J	132	531	06.02.13	8725	489999	92968
575.381-010	MOLDER (optical goods)	4337	34433534344	MONOOONFFOONNFNNNN	NNON4NNONNNNNNN	V,J,T	121	531	06.01.02	7463	489999	89905
575.382-010	BRICK-AND-TILE-MAKING-MACHINE OPERATOR (brick & tile)	3226	34335344344	MNNNNNNFFNNNNFNNFON	NNCN3NNNNNNNNNC	J,T	136	603	06.02.30	6861	000000	89905
575.382-014	FORMING-MACHINE OPERATOR (glass mfg.)	3225	34344444345	MNNNNNNFFONFFNFNFFN	NNNN4NNNNNNNNNN	V,J,T	143	534	06.02.17	7463	489999	92968
575.382-018	GLASS-BULB-MACHINE FORMER, TUBULAR STOCK (glass mfg.)	3327	34333434354	MNNNNNNFFNNNNFONOON	NNFN4NNNNNNNNNN	V,J,T	132	531	06.02.13	7463	489999	92968
575.382-022	GLASS-ROLLING-MACHINE OPERATOR (glass mfg.)	3235	34433434354	LNNNNNNNFFONNNNFNNNN	NNFN3NNNNNNNNNN	J,T	132	531	06.02.13	7663	489999	92971
575.382-026	RETORT-OR-CONDENSER PRESS OPERATOR (brick & tile)	3236	34334343354	LNNNNNNFFONNNNFNNNN	NNNN3NNNNNNNNNN	J,T	135	531	06.02.13	7463	489999	92968
575.461-010	CONCRETE-STONE FABRICATOR (concrete prod.)	3114	34434334355	HNNONNNFFNNNNNNNNNN	NNNN4NNNNNNNNNN	R	134	534	06.02.17	7663	489999	92971
575.462-010	AUGER PRESS OPERATOR, MANUAL CONTROL (brick & tile)	3227	34333433344	LNNNNNNNFFNNNNONNNNN	NNNN3NNNNNNNNNN	J,T	132	536	06.02.30	6861	469999	89905
575.462-010	AUGER PRESS OPERATOR, MANUAL CONTROL (brick & tile)	3226	34334434355	LNNNNNNFFONNNNOONNNNN	NNNN3NNNNNNNNNN	J,T	135	534	06.02.08	7663	489999	92971

DOT #	DOT Title & Industry	Trng	Aptitude	Physical	Environment	Tempra	WkF	MPSMS	GOE	SOC	CIP	OES
575.565-010	LINING-MACHINE OPERATOR (concrete prod.)	2112	44444444355	LNNNNNFFNNOONFNNNNN	FNNN4NNNNNNNNN	R,T	132	536	06.04.21	7679	469999	92971
575.662-010	DRY-PRESS OPERATOR (brick & tile)	3225	34343434344	MNNNONFFONOONFONNON	NNNN4NONNNNNNNN	J,T	134	534	06.02.17	7663	489999	92971
575.662-014	YARDAGE-CONTROL OPERATOR, FORMING (glass mfg.)	3335	34443443345	LNNNNNNFFONNNNFNFNN	NNON4NNNNNNNNN	J,T	135	419	06.02.13	7663	489999	92971
575.664-010	CENTRIFUGAL SPINNER (concrete prod.)	2112	44444444355	MNNONONFFNNOONFNFNNN	FNNF4NNNNNNNNN	R,T	132	536	06.04.21	7679	469999	92971
575.665-010	CONCRETE-PIPE-MAKING-MACHINE OPERATOR (concrete prod.)	2112	44444534355	MNNNNNNFFOOONFFNNO	NNNN4NNNNNNNNN	R,T	132	536	06.04.19	7663	469999	92971
575.665-014	DIE TRIPPER (brick & tile)	2212	44454544355	MNNNNNNFFONNNNNNNNN	NNNN3NNNNNNNNN	R	054	534	06.04.17	7663	489999	92953
575.665-018	SHOT-COAT TENDER (concrete prod.)	2112	44545534355	LNNNNNNFFNNOONONNNN	NNNN4NNNNNNNNN	R	132	536	06.04.21	7669	469999	92953
575.682-010	FIBERGLASS-DOWEL-DRAWING-MACHINE OPERATOR (plastic prod.)	3214	34343434344	LNNNNNNFFONNNNFNNNN	NNNN3NONNNNNNN	R,T	152	492	06.04.13	7463	000000	92968
575.682-014	MOLDING-MACHINE OPERATOR (toy-sport equip.)	3114	34434343355	MNNNNNNFFONNNNFNNON	NNNN3NNNNNNNNN	R,T	132	616	06.02.18	7663	489999	92971
575.682-018	PRESS OPERATOR (brick & tile)	2113	44444434344	MNNNNNNNFFOONNNFNNNON	NNNN4NNNNNNNNN	J,T	134	534	06.02.08	7663	489999	92971
575.682-022	RAM-PRESS OPERATOR (pottery & porc.)	3215	34333433335	MNNNNNNFFONNNNFNFNN	NNNN3NNNNNNNNN	R,T	134	535	06.04.40	7463	490299	92968
575.683-010	BUCKET OPERATOR (concrete prod.)	2113	44444534355	LNNNNNNFFNNNNNNNNNN	FNNO4NNNNNNNNN	R,T	132	536	06.04.30	8319	489999	92998
575.684-010	BATTER-OUT (pottery & porc.)	2124	44433433345	MNNNNNNCCNNNNNNNNNN	NNNC4NNNNNNNNN	R	136	535	06.02.30	7755	489999	93944
575.684-014	CASTER (pottery & porc.)	2112	44533533355	MNNNONNFFNNNNFNNNNN	NNNF3NNNNNNNNN	R	132	535	06.02.30	7754	489999	93944
575.684-018	CASTER (nonmet. min.)	2114	34433543354	MNNNONNFFNNNFNNNNN	NNNF3NNNNNNNNN	J,T	054	530	06.02.30	7755	489999	93944
575.684-022	CROSSCUTTER, ROLLED GLASS (glass mfg.)	2122	44444433355	LNNNNNNNFFNNNNFNNNN	NNNN4NNNNNNNNO	R,T	136	531	06.04.30	7753	489999	93926
575.684-026	GATHERER (glass mfg.)	2125	34543533354	MNNNONNFFONNNNFNNNON	NNFN4NNNNNNNNN	J,T	136	531	06.04.30	7755	489999	93999
575.684-030	HANDLE MAKER (pottery & porc.)	2113	44443433355	MNNNNNNFFNNNFNNNNN	NNNF3NNNNNNNNN	R	136	535	06.04.30	7754	489999	93944
575.684-034	LAUNDRY-TUB MAKER (concrete prod.)	3224	44544434355	HNNNONONFFNNNNFNNNNNO	NNNN4NNNNNNNNNO	R,T	132	536	06.02.30	7754	469999	93944
575.684-038	MOLD MAKER, TERRA COTTA (brick & tile)	2113	34433444345	MMNNNNNNFFNNNNONNON	NNNN3NNNNNNNNN	R,T	136	530	06.04.32	7754	489999	93944
575.684-042	MOLDER, HAND (brick & tile; elec. equip.)	3113	34433443355	HNNONNNFFNNNNFNNNNN	NNNF3NNNNNNNNN	R,T	136	534	06.02.30	7754	489999	93944
575.684-046	TERRAZZO-TILE MAKER (brick & tile)	2113	34433543353	MNNNNNNFFONNNFNNNON	NNNC3NNNNNNNNN	R,T	136	534	06.04.32	7754	489999	93944
575.684-050	CULTURED-MARBLE-PRODUCTS MAKER (stonework)	3235	34443434354	HNNONNNFFONNNNFNON	NNNN3NONNNNNNN	T	132	539	06.02.30	7754	489999	93944
575.685-010	ABRASIVE-WHEEL MOLDER (nonmet. min.)	3214	34433433355	LNNNNNNFFONNNNNNNNN	NNNN3NNNNNNNNN	R,T	132	538	06.02.18	7667	000000	92971
575.685-014	BLOCK-MAKING-MACHINE OPERATOR (concrete prod.)	2214	44435434355	MONNNNNNFFONNNNONONO	NNNN5NNNNNNNNN	R	132	536	06.04.09	7663	469999	92971
575.685-018	CHALK-EXTRUDING-MACHINE OPERATOR (pen & pencil)	2113	44444444345	LNNNNNNFFNNNNFNNNNN	NNNN3NNNNNNNNN	R	135	617	06.04.19	7663	000000	92971
575.685-022	CHALK-MOLDING-MACHINE OPERATOR (pen & pencil)	2113	44444344345	LNNNNNNFFONNNNONNNNN	NNNN3NNNNNNNNN	R,T	143	617	06.04.08	7663	000000	92971
575.685-026	DIE PRESSER (pottery & porc.)	3213	44434434355	LNNNNNNFFONNNNONNNNN	NNNN3NNNNNNNNN	R,T	132	535	06.04.13	7663	489999	92971
575.685-030	FIBER-MACHINE TENDER (glass mfg.)	3113	44434343344	LNNNNNNFFNNFFNNNNOON	NNON4NNNNNNNNN	R	135	419	06.04.17	7663	489999	92708
575.685-034	FLOWER-POT-PRESS OPERATOR (pottery & porc.)	2112	44444544355	LNNNNNNNCCONNNFNNNNN	NNNN3NNNNNNNNN	R	132	535	06.02.08	7667	489999	92971
575.685-038	FORMING-MACHINE TENDER (glass mfg.)	3224	34433444445	MNFNFNFFOONNNFNFNN	NNON4NNNNNNNNN	J,T	132	531	06.02.08	7663	489999	92971
575.685-042	HOT-PRESS OPERATOR (nonmet. min.)	2113	34544544355	LNNNNNNNFFNNNONNNNN	NNNN4NONNNNNNN	R,T	134	538	06.04.08	7663	000000	92971
575.685-046	HYDRAULIC-BILLET MAKER (pen & pencil)	2113	44444444345	LNNNNNNFFNNNNFNNNNN	NNNN3NNNNNNNNN	R,T	132	349	06.04.19	7663	000000	92971
575.685-050	LEAD FORMER (pen & pencil)	1112	44444534355	MMNNNNNFFNNNNNNNNNN	NNFN3NNNNNNNNN	R	135	349	06.04.19	7663	000000	92971
575.685-054	LENS-MOLDING-EQUIPMENT OPERATOR (glass mfg.)	2113	44434534354	LNNNNNNFFONNNNONONNN	NNON4NNONNNNNN	R	132	539	06.04.13	7663	489999	92971
575.685-058	MARBLE-MACHINE TENDER (glass mfg.)	2223	44444443345	LNNNNNNFFNNNNNNNNNN	NNCN4NNNNNNNNN	R,T	135	539	06.04.13	7663	489999	92971
575.685-062	MOLDER-MACHINE TENDER (nonmet. min.)	2112	44444433345	HNNONNNFFNNNNFNNNN	NNNF4NNNNNNNNN	R,T	132	538	06.04.17	7663	489999	92971
575.685-066	MOLDER, FIBERGLASS LUGGAGE (leather prod.)	2113	44444544355	LNNNNNNFFONNNNONNNN	NNCN4NONNNNNNN	R,T	136	524	06.04.13	7667	000000	92971
575.685-070	PRESS OPERATOR (mine & quarry)	2113	34444544355	LNNNNNNFFONNNNNNNNNN	NNNN3NNNNNNNNN	R,T	134	349	06.04.08	7663	489999	92971
575.685-074	PRESSER (glass mfg.)	2113	44444534345	MMNNNNNFFNNNNFNNNNN	NNCN4NNNNNNNNN	R,T	132	531	06.04.30	7663	489999	92971
575.685-078	SYNTHETIC-GEM-PRESS OPERATOR (jewelry-silver.)	2112	44545544345	LNNNNNNFFONNNNFNNNNN	NNNN3NNNNNNNNN	R,T	136	611	06.04.02	7663	470408	92708
575.685-082	TEST-SKEIN WINDER (glass mfg.)	3233	44444443345	MNNNNNNFFFNNNNFNNFNN	NNCN4NNONNNNNN	R,T	033	419	06.04.16	7679	000000	92971
575.686-010	DRY-PRESS-OPERATOR HELPER (brick & tile)	1112	44444434355	HONONONFFONNNNNNNNNN	NNNN3NNNNNNNNN	R	134	534	06.04.17	7663	489999	98999
575.686-014	MOLDER HELPER (optical goods)	1112	44444443355	LNNNNNNFFONNNNFNNNN	NNFN3NNNNNNNNN	R	133	603	06.04.13	8618	489999	98502
575.686-018	PIN MAKER (pottery & porc.)	2112	44445534345	MNNNNNNFFNNNNFNNNNN	NNNN3NNNNNNNNN	R	135	535	06.04.17	8725	489999	98502
575.687-010	BALCONY WORKER (glass mfg.)	2112	44543544354	LNNNNNNNFOFNNNFNNFNN	NNFN3NNNNNNNNN	R,T	135	531	06.04.13	8725	489999	92971
575.687-014	FORMING-MACHINE UPKEEP-MECHANIC HELPER (glass mfg.)	3223	44444444355	MNNNNNNFFFNNNNFNNFNN	NNON4NNONNNNNN	R	033	567	06.04.13	8619	489999	98999
575.687-018	LABORER, PRESTRESSED CONCRETE (concrete prod.)	1112	44444444345	HONONONNFFONNNNNNNNN	ONNN4NNNNNNNNN	R	132	536	06.04.34	8769	489999	98999
575.687-022	MAT INSPECTOR (concrete prod.)	3223	34433344455	LNNNNNNFFONNNNFNNFNN	NNNN4NNNNNNNNN	J,T	212	538	06.03.02	7820	000000	83005
575.687-026	PIPE STRIPPER (concrete prod.)	1112	44554544345	MNNNNNNFFNNNNNONNNN	NNNN4NONNNNNNN	R	011	536	06.04.40	8726	000000	98799
575.687-030	PRESS-PIPE INSPECTOR (brick & tile)	3222	44444444355	LNNNNNNFFOFNNNFNNFNN	NNNN3NNNNNNNNN	R,T	212	534	06.03.02	7820	489999	83005

DOT #	DOT Title & Industry	Trmg	Aptitude	Physical	Environment	Tempra	WkF	MPSMS	GOE	SOC	CIP	OES
575.687-034	INSPECTOR I (pottery & porc.)	2112	44443444355	HNNONNNFFONNNFNFNN	NNNO4NNNNNNNNNN	R,T	212	535	06.03.02	7820	489999	83005
575.687-038	TIP-OUT WORKER (concrete prod.)	1112	44444534355	VNNNNNNFFONNNNNNNN	NNNN4NNNNNNNNNN	R	011	536	05.12.04	8726	490299	97951
579.130-010	SUPERVISOR, BOARD MILL (concrete prod.)	4338	33343334355	LNNNNNNOONNFFNONNNN	NNNN4NNNNNNNNNN	V,D,P	147	536	06.02.01	7100	000000	81008
579.130-014	SUPERVISOR, CONCRETE BLOCK PLANT (concrete prod.)	4337	33343344455	LNNNNNNFFONFFNONNNN	NNNN4NNNNNNNNNN	V,D,P	132	536	06.02.01	7100	520205	81008
579.130-018	SUPERVISOR, CONCRETE PIPE PLANT (concrete prod.)	4337	33343344455	LNNNNNNFFFNFFNFNNNN	NNNN4NNNNNNNNNN	D,P	143	536	06.02.01	7100	520205	81008
579.130-022	SUPERVISOR, FORMING DEPARTMENT II (glass mfg.)	4336	33433444354	LNNNNNNFFONFFNFONONN	NNNN4NNNNNNNNNN	D,P	147	539	06.02.01	7100	520205	81008
579.131-010	SUPERVISOR, MIRROR MANUFACTURING DEPARTMENT (glass products)	4327	33333343354	LNNNNNNFFOOFFNFNNFON	NNNN3NNNNNNNNNN	V,D,P	054	532	06.02.01	7100	000000	81008
579.132-010	SUPERVISOR II (nonmet. min.)	4337	33333333245	LNNNNNNNFFNFNFFNNN	NNNN4NNNNNNNNNN	D,P,J	147	538	06.01.01	7100	000000	81008
579.132-014	SUPERVISOR, LIME (concrete prod.)	4328	33333333354	LONNNNNNFFONFFNNONNN	ONNN3NNNNNNNNNN	D,P	141	344	06.02.01	7100	000000	81008
579.134-010	SUPERVISOR, INSPECTION (glass mfg.)	4336	33343343454	LNNNNNNNFFNFNFNNOON	NNNN4NNNNNNNNNN	V,D,P,J	212	530	06.02.01	7100	520205	81008
579.134-014	SUPERVISOR, EPOXY FABRICATION (brick & tile)	3226	33433434335	MNNNNNNNFFOOFFNFFNOO	NNNN4NNNNNNNNNN	D,V,P	063	534	06.02.01	7100	520205	81008
579.134-018	SUPERVISOR, REFRACTORY PRODUCTS (brick & tile)	3236	33434444455	MNNOOONCCONFFNOOOONO	NNON4NNNNNNNNNN	D,P	147	534	06.04.01	7100	489999	81008
579.137-010	SUPERVISOR (cement)	4227	33333344444	LONNNNNOOONFFNONNNON	NNNN4NONNNNNNNN	V,D,P	147	533	06.04.01	7100	520205	81008
579.137-014	SUPERVISOR, ASBESTOS TEXTILE (nonmet. min.)	4327	33344344454	LNNNNNNFFONFFNONNNON	NNNN3NNNNNNNNNN	V,D,P	162	538	06.02.01	7100	000000	81008
579.137-018	SUPERVISOR, MOLD CLEANING AND STORAGE (glass mfg.)	3336	33432344455	MNNNNNNFFOOFFNFNONNN	NNNN3NNNNNNNNNN	V,D,P,J	212	542	06.04.01	7100	000000	81008
579.137-022	SUPERVISOR, MOLD-MAKING PLASTICS SHEETS (plastic-synth.)	3226	33333344455	LNNNNNNNFFONFFNFNONN	NNNN3NNNNNNNNNN	D,P	031	566	06.04.01	7100	000000	81008
579.137-026	SUPERVISOR, RECEIVING AND PROCESSING (glass mfg.)	4337	33333344454	LNNNNNNNFFONFFNFNFON	ONFN4NNNNNNNNNN	V,D,P,J	131	898	06.02.01	7100	520205	81008
579.137-030	DISPATCHER, CONCRETE PRODUCTS (concrete prod.; construction)	4335	33344343455	LNNNNNNNFFNFNFNNNON	NNNN3NNNNNNNNNN	D,V,P,T	013	536	07.05.01	7100	520499	55347
579.364-010	QUALITY CONTROL TECHNICIAN (concrete prod.)	3336	33343343455	MOONNNNNFFOOONFNONNN	NNNN4NONNNNNNNN	V,T,J	212	349	06.03.01	7830	030404	83005
579.367-010	QUALITY-CONTROL INSPECTOR (glass mfg.)	3233	33443444355	LNNNNNNNFFNOONFNNFNN	NNNN3NNNNNNNNNN	J,J	212	531	06.03.01	7820	489999	83005
579.367-014	QUALITY-CONTROL TECHNICIAN (glass mfg.)	3334	23243244455	LNNNNNNNFFNNNNNFNNFN	NNNN3NNNNNNNNNN	R,J,T	212	531	06.03.01	7830	489999	83005
579.380-010	BOARD-MACHINE SET-UP OPERATOR (concrete prod.)	3226	33333333355	LONOOONFFONNNNFNNNNN	NNNN4NNNNNNNNNO	V,J,T	102	536	06.01.03	7479	000000	92997
579.382-010	CALCINER, GYPSUM (concrete prod.)	3224	34434434355	LNNNNNNFFFNNNNNFFNNN	NNFN4NNNNNNNNNN	J,T	141	538	06.02.18	7677	000000	92965
579.382-014	CUPOLA OPERATOR, INSULATION (nonmet. min.) –	3226	34444444352	HNNNNNNNFFONNNNFNFON	NNCN4NNONNNNNNN	J,T	147	538	06.02.09	7675	000000	92923
579.382-018	KNIFE OPERATOR (concrete prod.)	3225	34334443355	MNNNNNNNFFONNNNFFNONN	NNNN4NNNNNNNNNN	R,T	054	536	06.02.09	7478	000000	92941
579.382-022	BLANKMAKER (glass mfg.)	3336	33332234453	LNNONNNNOOONNNNFNNOON	NNNN4NNNNNNNNNN	T	147	532	06.02.13	7679	489999	92998
579.384-010	BRICK TESTER (brick & tile)	2214	33333434353	LNNNNNNNFFNNNNNFNNFFN	NNNN3NNNNNNNNNN	J,T	136	534	06.02.30	7830	489999	83005
579.384-014	QUALITY TECHNICIAN, FIBERGLASS (glass mfg.)	3334	33332443354	LNNNNNNFFNNNNNFNNFON	NNNN3NNNNNNNNNN	J,T	212	410	06.03.01	7830	489999	83005
579.384-018	WARE TESTER (glass mfg.)	3335	33343433354	LNNNNNNNFFONNNNNFNFON	NNNN3NNNNNNNNNN	J,T	212	531	06.03.01	7830	489999	83005
579.387-010	MAT TESTER (nonmet. min.)	3223	33443344455	LNNNNNNNFFNNNNFNNNNN	NNNN4NNNNNNNNNN	J,T	212	538	06.03.01	7830	000000	83005
579.484-010	SAMPLER (mine & quarry)	3214	34344333444	MONNNNNNFFONNNNFNOOON	ONNN4NNNNNNNNNN	J,T	212	340	02.04.01	7840	000000	83005
579.584-010	FIBERGLASS-CONTAINER-WINDING OPERATOR (glass products)	2224	33333333355	MNNNNNNFFONNNNFNNNNN	NNOO4NNNNNNNNNN	R,T	102	539	06.04.13	7720	000000	93999
579.585-010	SAMPLER-TESTER (nonmet. min.)	2223	34344444355	LNNNNNNNFFONNNNNNNNN	NNNN4NNNNNNNNNN	J,T	212	538	06.03.02	7840	000000	83005
579.587-010	ROUND-UP-RING HAND (concrete prod.)	2123	34434444355	MNNFNNNNFFNNNNNNNNNN	FNNN4NNNNNNNNNN	R	071	536	06.04.22	7740	469999	93999
579.662-010	MAT-MACHINE OPERATOR (nonmet. min.)	3214	34344344355	LNNNNNNNFFOQOONONNN	NNNN4NNONNNNNNN	J,T	054	419	06.02.09	7675	000000	92923
579.664-010	CLAY-STRUCTURE BUILDER AND SERVICER (glass mfg.)	3224	34433444454	MNNFFNNCCONONONOONN	NNON4NNNNNNNNNN	J,T	102	534	05.10.01	6479	489999	85126
579.664-014	INSPECTOR II (concrete prod.)	3234	34333444454	LNNNNNNNFFNNNNFFNNFON	NNNN3NNNNNNNNNN	J,T	212	536	06.03.02	7820	469999	93999
579.665-010	BRAKE-LINING FINISHER, ASBESTOS (nonmet. min.)	3113	34444444355	SNNNNNNNFFFNNNNNONNN	NNNN3NNNNNNNNNN	R,T	152	538	06.04.19	7679	489999	93999
579.665-014	LABORER, CONCRETE-MIXING PLANT (construction)	2112	44544544445	HFFOONNFFFNOONNNNNNN	FNNN4NNNNNNNNNN	R,T	011	536	05.12.04	8726	469999	98799
579.665-018	WIRE SETTER (glass mfg.)	2112	44454444455	LNNNNNNNFFNFNFNNNNN	NNNN4NNNNNNNNNN	R	163	531	06.04.02	7679	000000	92998
579.667-010	LABORER, GENERAL (brick & tile)	1111	44444444345	HNNNNNNNFFONNNNNNNN	ONNN3NNONNNNNNN	R	011	534	06.04.30	8769	000000	98899
579.682-010	MIXER, WET POUR (concrete prod.)	3214	44444444355	VONONNNFFNNNNNONNNNO	NNNN4NOONNNNNNO	J,T	143	536	06.04.17	7664	469999	92965
579.684-010	CONCRETE-VAULT MAKER (concrete prod.)	2112	44544544455	HNNONONFFFNNNNNNNNN	NNNN4NNNNNNNNNN	R,T	132	619	06.04.32	7754	469999	93944
579.684-014	CRAYON GRADER (mine & quarry)	2123	44443433355	SNNNNNNCCCSNNNNCNNCNN	NNNN3NCNNNNNNNN	J,T	212	617	06.03.02	7850	000000	83005
579.684-018	KILN-FURNITURE CASTER (pottery & porc.)	2114	34443434344	MNNNNNNFFFFNNNONNON	NNNN4NNNNNNNNNN	J,T	132	535	06.04.17	7754	489999	93944
579.684-022	MICA-PLATE LAYER, HAND (mine & quarry)	2112	44443434355	SNNNNNNFFFNNNNNNNON	NNNN3NNNNNNNNNN	R	153	349	06.04.33	7740	489999	93999
579.684-026	CASTER (brick & tile)	2123	44453434355	HNNONNNFFONOONFNNNNN	NNNN4NNNNNNNNNN	R,T	132	539	06.04.32	7679	489999	93944
579.684-030	CUTTER (brick & tile)	2112	44444544355	MNNFNNNCCONNNFNNNNN	NNNN4NNNNNNNNNN	R,T	056	534	06.04.30	7753	489999	93926
579.685-010	DRIER-AND-GRINDER TENDER (mine & quarry)	3114	44444444454	LONNNNNFFFNNFNNNNN	NNNN4NOONNNNNNN	R,T	141	349	06.04.08	7754	489999	92998
579.685-014	FRIT-MIXER-AND-BURNER (brick & tile; pottery & porc.)	2214	44444444343	HNNFNNNFFNNNNONNNFN	NNNN4NONNNNNNO	R,T	131	340	06.04.17	7664	489999	92965
579.685-018	GLASS-CLEANING-MACHINE TENDER (glass products)	2113	44444444355	LNNNNNNNFFNNNNNNNNN	NNNN3NNNNNNNNNN	R	031	531	06.04.08	7673	489999	92958

DOT #	DOT Title & Industry	Trng	Aptitude	Physical	Environment	Tempra	WkF	MPSMS	GOE	SOC	CIP	OES
579.685-022	GLASS-WOOL-BLANKET-MACHINE FEEDER (glass products)	2113	44434444355	LNNNNNNFFNNNNNNNNNN	NNNN4NNONNNNNNNN	R	063	538	06.04.09	7661	000000	92956
579.685-026	MICA-PLATE LAYER (mine & quarry)	2112	44444544355	MNNNNNNFFONNNNNNNNN	NNNN4NONNNNNNNN	R,T	063	349	06.04.08	7663	000000	92971
579.685-030	MOLD POLISHER (glass mfg.)	2223	44444444345	HNNONNNFFNNNNNNFNNNN	NNNN4NNNNNNNNNN	R,J,T	031	566	06.04.39	7673	000000	92965
579.685-034	NODULIZER (cement)	3223	44443434344	LNNNNNNOONNNNONNNNON	NNNN4NONNNNNNNN	R,T	147	533	06.04.19	7675	000000	92923
579.685-038	PACKER, INSULATION (nonmet. min.)	2112	44544544355	MNNFNNNFFONNNNNNNNN	NNNF4NNNNNNNNNN	R	041	538	06.04.09	7662	000000	92974
579.685-042	PRECAST MOLDER (concrete prod.)	2123	44444444344	HNNFOONFFNNNNNFNFON	NNNF4NNNNNNNNNN	R,T	132	536	06.04.19	7663	469999	92971
579.685-046	ROUGE SIFTER AND MILLER (optical goods)	1112	44444444354	LNNNNNNFFNNNNNNNNNN	NNNN4NNONNNNNNNN	R	142	538	06.04.09	7666	000000	92962
579.685-050	SILO TENDER (cement)	2213	44444444345	MNOOOONFFFNNNNNNNNNN	ONNO4NNNNNNNNNN	R,T	014	533	06.04.40	8319	490299	97951
579.685-054	SILVER STRIPPER, MACHINE (glass products)	2212	44444443355	HNNNNNNNFFNFNNFNFNN	NNNO3NONNNNNNOO	R,T	031	532	06.04.39	7673	000000	92958
579.685-058	BRICK SETTER OPERATOR (brick & tile)	3123	34444434345	MONONNNFFONNNNFONNNN	NNNN4NNNNNNNNNN	R,T	054	534	06.04.08	7678	489999	92944
579.685-062	BRICK UNLOADER TENDER (brick & tile)	2223	44433444455	LONNNNNFFONNNNNNNNNN	NNNN3NNNNNNNNNN	R	011	534	06.04.40	8319	490299	97951
579.685-066	BRIQUETTE OPERATOR (brick & tile)	3112	34444444455	LFNONNNCCONNNNFNNNNN	NNON4NNNNNNNNNN	R,T	141	530	06.04.19	7663	489999	92971
579.685-070	MARKER MACHINE ATTENDANT (glass mfg.)	2113	44544544355	LNNNNNNFFONNNNFFNNNN	NNNN4NNNNNNNNNN	R,U	212	531	06.04.08	7679	000000	92998
579.685-074	MIXER (brick & tile)	2112	44444444355	HNNNNNNNFFNNNNNFNFNN	NNNN4NNNNNNNNNN	R,T	141	340	06.04.17	7664	489999	92965
579.686-014	MAT PACKER (nonmet. min.)	2112	44444444355	MNNNNNNFFFNNNNFNNNNN	NNNN3NNNNNNNNNN	R,T	041	538	06.04.38	8725	000000	98502
579.686-018	MICA-LAMINATING-MACHINE FEEDER (mine & quarry)	2112	44444343455	LNNNNNNFFNNNNFNNNNN	NNNN3NNNNNNNNNN	R	063	349	06.04.19	8725	000000	98502
579.686-022	MIRROR-MACHINE FEEDER (glass products)	1112	44544544355	HNNFONNFFONNNNNNNNNN	NNNN4NNNNNNNNNO	R	031	532	06.04.21	8725	000000	98502
579.686-026	OFFBEARER, SEWER PIPE (brick & tile)	1112	44444444355	HNNONONFFNNNNNNNNNNN	NNNN4NNNNNNNNNN	R	135	534	06.04.17	8725	489999	98502
579.686-030	PRESS OFFBEARER (brick & tile)	1111	44444444455	HNNFNNNFFONNNNFNNNNN	NNNN4NNNNNNNNNNO	R,U	136	534	06.04.30	8725	490299	98502
579.687-010	BRAKE-LINING-FINISHER HELPER, ASBESTOS (nonmet. min.)	2112	44544544355	MNNNNNNCCNNNNNCNNNNN	NNNN4NONNNNNNNNO	V	011	538	06.04.19	8618	000000	98999
579.687-014	DECORATING INSPECTOR (glass mfg.)	2212	44443444454	LNNNNNNFFFONNNFNFOFN	NNNN3NNNNNNNNNN	R,T	212	532	06.03.02	7820	000000	83005
579.687-018	FLOOR ATTENDANT (glass mfg.)	2112	44444444354	MNNONNNFFNNNNNNFNFON	NNON4NONNNNNNNN	V	011	531	06.04.40	8726	000000	98799
579.687-022	GLASS INSPECTOR (any industry)	2123	44443444354	LNNNNNNFFFNNNNCNCCCN	NNNN3NNNNNNNNNN	R,T	212	531	06.03.02	7820	489999	83005
579.687-026	MICA PATCHER (mine & quarry)	2112	44544534355	LNNNNNNFFNFNNNFNFNN	NNNN3NNNNNNNNNN	R,T	212	349	06.03.02	7820	000000	83005
579.687-030	SELECTOR (glass mfg.)	2213	44443433354	LNNNNNNFFONNNNFNNFON	NNNN3NNNNNNNNNN	R,J,T	212	531	06.03.02	7820	489999	83005
579.687-034	DISC-PAD KNOCKOUT WORKER (nonmet. min.)	2113	44544534355	MNNNNNNFFONNNNFNNNNN	NNNN4NNNNNNNNNN	R,U	011	538	06.04.34	8769	000000	98999
579.687-038	DISC-PAD-PLATE FILLER (nonmet. min.)	2113	44534534355	MNNNNNNFFONNNNFNNNNN	NNNN4NNNNNNNNNON	R,U	011	538	06.04.34	8769	000000	98999
579.687-042	LABORER, CONCRETE PLANT (concrete prod.)	2112	44544544355	HNNFNNNCCONNNNNNOONN	ONNO4NONNNNNNNN	R	011	536	06.04.40	8769	000000	98999
580.380-010	FIXER, BOARDING ROOM (knitting)	4237	34433333355	MNNOONNFFONNNNONNONN	NNNN4NNNNNNNNNN	J,T	121	567	06.01.02	7459	470303	92702
580.485-010	CALENDERING-MACHINE OPERATOR (knitting)	2123	34343434354	HNNNONNFFNNNNNFNOOFN	NNNN4NOONNNNNNN	R,T	032	424	06.04.05	7659	000000	92998
580.682-010	WEFT STRAIGHTENER (textile)	3124	33433343455	MNNNNNNFFONNNNFNNNNN	NNNN4NNNNNNNNNN	R,T	032	420	06.04.16	7659	000000	92998
580.684-010	BLOCKER, HAND I (hat & cap)	2123	44433444355	LNNNNNNFFNNNNNFNFNNN	NNOO4NNNNNNNNNN	R,T	032	445	06.02.27	7755	200303	93956
580.684-014	BLOCKER, HAND II (hat & cap)	2112	44444444354	LNNNNNNCCCCNNONFNFFN	NNNO4NNNNNNNNNN	R,T	032	445	06.04.27	7755	200303	93956
580.685-010	BRIM-STRETCHING-MACHINE OPERATOR (hat & cap)	2113	44433434445	LNNNNNNFFONNONNNNNNN	NNNO4NNNNNNNNNN	R,T	032	445	06.04.05	7659	200303	92998
580.685-014	CLOTH DRIER (knitting)	2122	44243434355	MNNNNNNFFONNNNFNNNNN	NNON4NNNNNNNNNN	R,T	032	424	06.04.05	7659	000000	92923
580.685-018	COLLAR-TURNER OPERATOR (garment)	2122	44243434345	LNNNNNNCCNNNNNNNNNNN	NNNN4NNNNNNNNNN	R	062	443	06.04.05	7659	200303	92998
580.685-022	COTTON-BALL-MACHINE TENDER (protective dev.)	3224	34444434355	LNNNNNNCCFFNONONOONN	NNNN4NOONNNNNNN	R,T	161	414	06.02.06	7659	000000	92702
580.685-026	HAT-BLOCKING-MACHINE OPERATOR I (hat & cap)	2114	44444434345	LNNNNNNCCFFNONOOOONN	NNOO4NNNNNNNNNN	R	152	445	06.04.05	7659	200303	92998
580.685-030	HAT-BLOCKING-MACHINE OPERATOR II (hat & cap)	1112	44444434355	MNNNNNNFFNNNNNNNNNNN	NNNN4NNNNNNNNNN	R	032	445	06.04.05	7659	200303	92998
580.685-034	HOOKING-MACHINE OPERATOR (textile)	2123	44443433345	MNNNNNNFFFNNNONNOONN	NNOO4NONNNNNNNN	R	032	412	06.04.05	7651	000000	92705
580.685-038	HYDRAULIC BLOCKER (hat & cap)	2123	44444444355	LNNNNNNCCFFNONONOONN	NNON4NNNNNNNNNN	R	032	445	06.04.09	7659	200303	92998
580.685-042	MOLDER (hat & cap)	2114	44434534345	LNNNNNNFFNNNNNFNNNNN	NNNN3NNNNNNNNNN	R,T	134	445	06.04.05	7659	200303	92998
580.685-046	ROLLER OPERATOR (hat & cap)	2122	44434344355	LNNNNNNFFONNNNNNNNNN	NNNN3NNNNNNNNNN	R	163	445	06.04.05	7659	200303	92998
580.685-050	STAKER, MACHINE (leather mfg.)	2112	44543534355	LNNNNNNFFNNNNNNFNNNN	NNNN4NNNNNNNNNN	R,T	032	520	06.04.16	7659	200303	92998
580.685-054	STRETCHER (hat & cap)	2112	44434434355	MNNONNNFFNCNNCNCNONN	NNNN4NNONNNNNNN	R	032	521	06.04.16	7659	200309	98999
580.685-058	STRETCHING-MACHINE OPERATOR (tex. prod., nec)	2123	44443434355	MNNNONNFFNNNNNNNNNNN	NNNN4NNNNNNNNNN	R,T	032	439	06.04.05	7659	200303	92998
580.685-062	TIP STRETCHER (hat & cap)	2112	44444444355	LNNNNNNCCCONNNNNNOONN	NNOO4NNNNNNNNNN	R	032	445	06.04.05	7659	000000	92705
580.685-066	TENTER-FRAME OPERATOR (textile)	2123	34444444344	MNNNNNNFFFNNNNNOFFON	NNNN4NNNNNNNNNN	J,T	032	420	06.04.16	7659	000000	92705
580.687-010	ORIENTAL-RUG STRETCHER (any industry)	2122	44444444355	MNNONNNFFNNNNNNNNNNN	NNNN4NNNNNNNNNN	R	032	431	06.04.27	8769	200309	98999
580.687-014	HIDE STRETCHER, HAND (leather mfg.)	1111	44544444455	LNNNNNNFFONNNNNNNNNN	NNNO3NNNNNNNNNN	R	032	521	06.04.27	7759	000000	93999
581.585-010	CARBONIZER (textile)	2123	34444444345	MNNNNNNFFFNNNNNOFOFNN	NNNN4NNNNNNNNNN	J,T	147	422	06.04.16	7659	000000	92998

DOT #	DOT Title & Industry	Trng	Aptitude	Physical	Environment	Tempra	WkF	MPSMS	GOE	SOC	CIP	OES
581.586-010	HEAT CURER (textile)	2112	4444444455	LNNNNNNFFONNNNONNNN	NNNN3NNNNNNNNNN	R	141	420	06.04.16	8725	000000	98502
581.685-010	CLOTH SANDER (textile)	1112	44544544345	MNNNNNNNNFFNNNNONNNN	NNNNNNNNNNNNNN	R	031	421	06.04.16	7659	000000	92998
581.685-014	DRIER (garment)	2123	44444444355	LNNNNNNNFFONNNFNNNNN	NNNN3NNNNNNNNN	R,T	141	440	06.04.16	7675	200303	92923
581.685-018	DRIER OPERATOR III (plastic-synth.)	2113	44444444355	LNNNNNNCCONONNNOONN	NNNO4NNNNNNNNN	R,T	141	414	06.04.16	7659	000000	92923
581.685-022	DRY-CANS OPERATOR (textile)	2122	44544544455	MNNNNNNNFFOONNNONNNN	NNNN4NNNNNNNNN	R	141	420	06.04.16	7659	000000	92923
581.685-026	DRYING-MACHINE OPERATOR, PACKAGE YARNS (textile)	2112	44443344354	MNNONNNCCFCNNNONNOFN	NNNO4NNNNNNNNN	R,T	141	411	06.04.16	7659	000000	92923
581.685-030	DRYING-MACHINE TENDER (textile)	2124	44444444455	MNNNNNNNFCONNNNFNNNNN	NNNN3NNNNNNNNN	R,T	141	420	06.04.16	7659	000000	92923
581.685-034	DRYING-UNIT-FELTING-MACHINE OPERATOR (tex. prod., nec)	2124	44444444455	LNNNNNNNFFNNNNNNNNNN	NNNN4NNNNNNNNN	R,T	141	439	06.04.16	7659	000000	92923
581.685-038	EXTRACTOR OPERATOR (any industry)	2112	44544544455	MNNNONNNFFFNNNNNNFNNN	NNNO4NNNNNNNNN	R	145	440	06.04.16	7659	000000	92998
581.685-042	EXTRACTOR OPERATOR (textile)	2122	44444444455	MNNFNNNNFFNNNNNNNONNO	NNNN4NNNNNNNNN	R	145	420	06.04.16	7659	200309	92998
581.685-046	RAW-STOCK-DRIER TENDER (textile)	2112	44544544455	LOOONONOFFOONNNNNNNNN	NNNN4NNNNNNNNN	R,T	141	414	06.04.16	7659	000000	92923
581.685-050	RUG-DRYING-MACHINE OPERATOR (carpet & rug)	2123	44444433354	LNNNNNNNFFOONNNFNNFOF	NNNN4NNNNNNNNN	R,T	141	420	06.04.16	7659	000000	92923
581.685-054	SKEIN-YARN DRIER (textile)	1112	44444444455	MNNNNNNNCCOONNNONOONN	NNNO4NNNNNNNNN	R	141	411	06.04.16	7659	000000	92923
581.685-058	STEAM-DRIER TENDER (carpet & rug)	3235	34434444355	HNNONNNFFNNNNNNNNNNN	NNNO4NNNNNNNNN	R,T	141	431	06.04.16	7659	000000	92998
581.685-062	TUMBLER TENDER (knitting)	2114	44444444454	MNNFNFNFFNNNNNFNNNFN	NNNO4NNNNNNNNN	R	141	424	06.04.16	7659	000000	92923
581.685-066	VACUUM-DRIER OPERATOR (tex. prod., nec)	2114	44444444455	MNNNNNNNFFOONNNNNNNN	NNNN4NNNNNNNNN	R,T	141	439	06.04.16	7659	000000	92923
581.685-070	WHIZZER (hat & cap)	2112	44444444355	MNNNNNNNFFNNNNNNNNNN	NNNN4NNNNNNNNN	R,T	145	445	06.04.16	7659	000000	92998
581.685-074	WINDING-RACK OPERATOR (tex. prod., nec)	2123	44443344344	MNNONNNFFNNNNNONONON	NNNN4NNNNNNNNN	R	141	434	06.04.16	7651	000000	92705
581.685-078	FLAT DRIER (tex. prod. nec)	3124	34444444355	MNNNNNNNFFOONNNONNNN	NNON3NNNNNNNNN	R	141	439	06.04.16	7659	150699	92923
581.685-082	DRUM-DRIER OPERATOR (plastic-synth.)	2113	44444443345	VFNFNNNFCCNNNNOFFNNF	NNNN4NNNNNNNNNO	R,T	141	492	06.04.16	7659	150699	92923
581.686-010	BLOWER FEEDER, DYED RAW STOCK (textile)	1112	44544544455	HNNNNNNNFFNNNNNNNNNN	NNNN4NNNNNNNNN	R	014	410	06.04.40	8725	000000	98502
581.686-014	DRIER (knitting)	2112	44444444355	LNNONNNCCONNNNNNNNNN	NNNN3NNNNNNNNN	R	141	420	06.04.16	8725	000000	98502
581.686-018	DRIER ATTENDANT (garment)	1111	44444444355	MNNNNNNNCCNNNNNNNNNN	NNNN4NNNNNNNNN	R	011	440	06.04.40	8725	000000	98502
581.686-022	DRYING-OVEN ATTENDANT (hat & cap)	1111	44544544455	MNNNNNNNNCCNNNNNNNNNNN	NNNO4NNOONNNNON	R	141	521	06.04.16	8725	000000	98502
581.686-026	DRYING-RACK CHANGER (boot & shoe)	2112	45455444455	LNNNNNNNFFNNNNNNNNNN	NNNN4NNNNNNNNN	R	141	522	06.04.05	8725	480304	98502
581.686-030	DUST-MILL OPERATOR (tex. prod. nec)	1111	44444534355	MNNNNNNNFFNNNNNNNNNN	NNNN3NONNNNNNN	R	031	618	06.04.39	8725	000000	98502
581.686-034	FEATHER-DRYING-MACHINE OPERATOR (tex. prod., nec)	1112	44445434355	MNNNNNNNFFNNNNNNNNNN	NNNN4NNNNNNNNN	R	141	618	06.04.09	8725	000000	98502
581.686-038	TRAY DRIER (knitting)	1112	44444444355	MNNONNNCCONNNNNNNNNN	NNNN3NNNNNNNNN	R	141	446	06.04.16	7659	000000	92923
581.686-042	WET-COTTON FEEDER (textile)	1112	44544544355	MFNONNNFFNNNNNNNNNN	NNNO4NNNNNNNNN	R	145	410	06.04.16	8725	000000	98502
581.687-010	BURLAP SPREADER (tex. prod., nec)	1111	44544444455	LNNONNNFFNNNNNNNNNN	NNNO4NNNNNNNNN	R	011	439	06.04.27	8769	000000	98999
581.687-014	DRYING-ROOM ATTENDANT (hat & cap)	1111	44544544355	LNNOONNNFFNNNNNNNNNN	NNNN4NNNNNNNNN	R	141	445	06.04.27	8769	000000	98999
581.687-018	DRYING-UNIT-FELTING-MACHINE-OPERATOR HELPER (tex. prod., nec)	1112	44544544455	HNNFNFNFFNNNNNNNNNN	NNNN4NNNNNNNNN	R	141	439	06.04.16	8617	000000	98999
581.687-022	SPREADER (hat & cap)	1111	44444444455	MNNNNNNNFFNNNNNNNNNN	NNNO3NONNNNNNN	R	141	521	06.04.27	8769	000000	98999
582.130-010	SUPERVISOR, GLAZING DEPARTMENT (textile)	4337	33343343354	MNNONONFFFFFNFNNNON	NNNN4NNNNNNNNN	V,D,P	151	412	06.02.01	7100	000000	81008
582.131-010	DYE-HOUSE SUPERVISOR (leather mfg.)	4337	33333344352	LNNNNNNNFFONOONFNNNFN	NNNO3NNNNNNNNN	D,P,J,T	152	521	06.02.01	7100	000000	81008
582.131-014	DYER, SUPERVISOR (knitting; tex. prod., nec; textile)	4347	33333344452	LNNNNNNNFFOOOONFNNNFN	NNNO4NNNNNNNNN	D,P,J	152	420	05.10.07	7100	150699	81008
582.132-010	AGING-DEPARTMENT SUPERVISOR (textile)	4336	33443344454	MNNFNNNNFFFFFNNNNFN	NNNN4NNNNNNNNN	D,P,J,T	147	420	06.02.01	7100	000000	81008
582.132-014	SOAPING-DEPARTMENT SUPERVISOR (textile)	4336	33443344454	LNNNNNNNFFOOOONFNONFN	NNNN4NNNNNNNNN	D,P,J,T	152	420	06.02.01	7100	000000	81008
582.132-018	SUPERVISOR, TAN ROOM (leather mfg.)	4337	33343333344	HNNONNNFFNNNNNNNOOON	NNNO4NONNNNNNN	D,P,J	152	521	06.02.01	7100	000000	81008
582.132-022	SUPERVISOR, VAT HOUSE (chemical; leather mfg.)	4337	33343333455	LONONNNFFFNFFNFNNNNN	NNNF4NFNNNNNNNF	V,D,P,J	152	499	06.02.01	7100	000000	81008
582.261-010	COLOR MATCHER (knitting)	3236	34344444452	LNNNNNNNFFOONNNFNNFFN	NNNN3NNNNNNNNN	R,J,T	152	446	06.01.05	6855	000000	89521
582.362-010	PANELBOARD OPERATOR (textile)	3124	33443444454	LNNNNNNNFFNOONFONFON	NNNN3NNNNNNNNN	J,T	152	420	06.04.16	7659	000000	92998
582.362-014	DYE AUTOMATION OPERATOR (textile)	3335	33344333355	LNNNNNNNCCNNFFNCCNCNN	NNNN3NNNNNNNNN	J,T	152	412	06.02.16	7659	150699	92714
582.384-010	DYE-LAB TECHNICIAN (knitting)	3325	34344333353	MNNFNNNNFCCNNNNCNNNFN	NNNN4NNNNNNNNNF	T,J	152	424	02.04.01	7659	150699	92714
582.387-010	COLOR CHECKER, ROVING OR YARN (textile)	3233	34444434453	LNNNNNNNFFNNNNNOFNFFN	NNNN3NNNNNNNNN	R,J	152	410	06.03.01	7830	000000	83005
582.482-010	COLORER, HIDES AND SKINS (leather mfg.)	3224	34343444354	HNNONNNFFNNNNNNOOOON	NNNO4NONNNNNNN	R,T	152	521	06.02.16	7679	000000	92998
582.482-014	TANNER, ROTARY DRUM, CONTINUOUS PROCESS (leather mfg.)	3335	33433433354	MNNNNNNNFFNNNNNFNNNON	NNNO3NNNNNNNNN	R,J,T	152	521	06.02.16	7659	000000	92998
582.482-018	TANNING-DRUM OPERATOR (leather mfg.)	3224	34443444354	MNNNNNNNFFNNNNFNNNON	NNNO3NNNNNNNNN	R,T	152	521	06.04.16	7659	000000	92998
582.562-010	SLASHER TENDER (textile)	3236	34433433354	HNNFNFNFFFOOONFFFNFN	NNFF4NNNNNNNNN	R,T	152	411	06.04.16	7659	000000	92998
582.582-010	DYE-RANGE OPERATOR, CLOTH (textile)	3224	34444444444	MNNONONCCFNNNNOFNNON	NNNF4NNNNNNNNN	J,T	152	420	06.02.16	7659	000000	92714
582.585-010	AGER OPERATOR (textile)	2122	44444444444	MOOOONFFFONNNFNNNFN	NNNO4NFNNNNNNN	R,T	147	420	06.04.16	7659	000000	92998

DOT #	DOT Title & Industry	Trng	Aptitude	Physical	Environment	Tempra	WkF	MPSMS	GOE	SOC	CIP	OES
582.587-010	CHEMICAL-STRENGTH TESTER (textile)	3222	344543444454	LNNONONCCNNNNFFNFFN	NNNO4NNNNNNNNNN	R,J,T	212	491	06.03.02	7830	000000	83005
582.665-010	CYLINDER BATCHER (textile)	2123	44543543345	MNNNONNNFFNNNNNFNNNN	NNNN4NNNNNNNNNN	R	152	420	06.04.16	7659	000000	92998
582.665-014	DYE-REEL OPERATOR (textile)	2123	34444444344	MNNFNFNCCFNOONONONON	NNFF4NONNNNNNNNO	R,T	152	420	06.04.16	7659	000000	92714
582.665-018	JIGGER (textile)	2123	44444444354	LNNONNNNCCFNOONOFONON	NNFO4NNNNNNNNNN	R,T	152	421	06.04.19	7659	000000	92998
582.665-022	SATURATION-EQUIPMENT OPERATOR (fabrication, nec)	3224	33334434354	NNNNNNNFFFNNNNNFNNNON	NNFN3NFNNNNNNNF	J,T	151	619	06.04.19	7659	000000	92953
582.665-026	SIZING-MACHINE-AND-DRIER OPERATOR (tex. prod., nec)	3124	44444544455	MONONNNNFFNNNNNFNNNON	NNNNF4NNNNNNNNN	R,T	152	422	06.04.16	7659	000000	92998
582.682-010	FINISHING-MACHINE OPERATOR (narrow fabrics)	3224	44444444354	MNNNNNNNFFFNNNNNONONON	NNNN4NNNNNNNNNN	R,T	152	423	06.02.16	7659	000000	92998
582.684-010	PATCH FINISHER (textile)	2122	44444444355	LNNNNNNNNNFFONNNNNNNNN	NNFF4NNNNNNNNNN	R	152	420	06.04.27	7840	000000	83005
582.684-014	SPOT CLEANER (garment; knitting)	2123	44443443343	LNNONNNFFNNNNFNNNFN	NNNF4NCNNNNNNNC	R,T	031	424	06.04.27	7759	200301	93999
582.685-010	BACK WASHER (textile)	2122	44444434354	HNNNNNFFFNNNNNFNFNON	NNNO3NNNNNNNNNN	R	152	414	06.04.16	7659	000000	92998
582.685-014	BEAM-DYER OPERATOR (textile)	3223	34444444344	MNNNONONFFONNNNFNNNON	NNNC4NNNNNNNNNN	R,T	152	420	06.04.16	7659	000000	92714
582.685-018	BLEACH-RANGE OPERATOR (textile)	2123	44444444345	MNNNONONFFONNNNFNNNON	NNNF4NNNNNNNNNN	R	152	420	06.04.16	7659	000000	92714
582.685-022	BOIL-OFF-MACHINE OPERATOR, CLOTH (textile)	2122	34444444445	MNNFNFNFFNNNNNFFNNNN	NNFF4NNNNNNNNNN	R	152	420	06.04.16	7659	200309	92714
582.685-026	CLOTH SHADER (garment; textile)	2124	44243434452	LNNNNNNCCNNNNCNNCCN	NNNN3NNNNNNNNNN	R,J	212	420	06.03.02	7820	200309	83005
582.685-030	DYED-YARN OPERATOR (textile)	2122	44444444354	MNNONONFFNNNNNFNFNON	NNNC4NNNNNNNNNN	R,T	152	420	06.04.16	7659	200309	92998
582.685-034	COLORING-MACHINE OPERATOR (hat & cap)	3223	34444434354	LNNNNNNFFONNNNNFNFNNN	NNNF4NNNNNNNNNN	R	152	445	06.04.16	7659	200303	92998
582.685-038	CRABBER (textile)	3122	44444434445	MNNNNNNFFNNNNONONON	NNNF3NNNNNNNNNN	R,T	152	422	06.04.16	7659	000000	92998
582.685-042	DECATING-MACHINE OPERATOR (textile)	2122	34444444344	MNNNNNNNCCOONNNNNFNON	NNNF4NNNNNNNNNN	R,T	152	420	06.04.16	7659	000000	92998
582.685-046	DESIZING-MACHINE OPERATOR, HEAD-END (textile)	2123	34444444345	HNNFNONCCONNNNFNONNN	NNNF4NNNNNNNNNN	R,T	152	420	06.04.16	7659	200309	92998
582.685-050	DRUM ATTENDANT (leather mfg.; tex. prod., nec)	1112	44544544355	MNNFNNNFFNNNNNONFNNN	NNNC4NFNNNNNNNN	R	031	521	06.04.16	7659	200309	92998
582.685-054	DYE-TANK TENDER (tex. prod., nec)	2123	34344434354	MNNFNFNFFNNNNNFNFN	NNNF3NNNNNNNNNN	R,T	152	439	06.04.16	7659	000000	92714
582.685-058	DYED-YARN OPERATOR (textile)	2122	44444444354	LNNNNNNNFFNNNNFNNFON	NNNN3NNNNNNNNNN	R,T	151	419	06.04.16	7659	000000	92714
582.685-062	EXTRACTOR OPERATOR (tex. prod., nec)	2123	44444444355	NNNNNNNNFFNNNNNNNNNN	NNNF3NNNNNNNNNN	R	147	439	06.04.16	7659	000000	92998
582.685-066	FEATHER WASHER (tex. prod., nec)	2112	44444534355	LONONNNNFFONNNNNNNNNN	NNNO3NNNNNNNNNN	R	152	618	06.04.19	7659	000000	92998
582.685-070	FELT-WASHING-MACHINE TENDER (tex. prod., nec)	2123	44444443354	MNNNNNNNNFFONONFNNOFN	NNNO3NCNNNNNNCN	R	152	439	06.04.16	7659	200309	92998
582.685-074	FUMIGATOR AND STERILIZER (furniture)	2122	44444433355	HNNNNNNNFFNNNNNNONNNN	NNNN3NFNNNNNNNF	R,T	031	464	06.04.19	7659	000000	92998
582.685-078	GARMENT STEAMER (knitting)	2112	44445434355	LNNNNNNNFFNNNNNNNNNN	NNNO3NNNNNNNNNN	R	032	424	06.04.16	7659	200303	92998
582.685-082	GREASER OPERATOR (hat & cap)	2113	44444444355	LNNNNNNNNFFNNNNFNNFON	NNNN4NNNNNNNNNN	R	152	445	06.04.19	7659	200303	92998
582.685-086	HAIR-BOILER OPERATOR (leather mfg.)	2122	44444444455	MNNNNNNNFFNNNNNNNNNN	NNNO3NNNNNNNNNN	R	152	529	06.04.19	7659	000000	92714
582.685-090	JET-DYEING-MACHINE TENDER (textile)	2123	44444433354	MNNNNNNNFFNNNNNFNNNN	NNNN4NNNNNNNNNN	R	152	420	06.04.16	7659	000000	92998
582.685-094	KNIT-GOODS WASHER (knitting)	3124	34444344345	HNNONONFFONNNNFNNNON	NNNN4NNNNNNNNNN	R,T	152	424	06.04.16	7659	200309	92998
582.685-098	OPEN-DEVELOPER OPERATOR (textile)	3224	34444544455	LNNNNNNCCFNNNNNNNNNNN	NNNO4NNNNNNNNNN	R,T	147	420	06.04.16	7659	000000	92998
582.685-102	PACKAGE-DYEING-MACHINE OPERATOR (textile)	3124	33444434353	MMNFNNNCCFNNNNFOFNFN	NNFF4NFNNNNNNNF	R,T	152	410	06.02.16	7659	000000	92714
582.685-106	PADDING-MACHINE OPERATOR (textile)	2112	44444444344	MONFNNNCCONNNNONFNON	NNFF4NNNNNNNNNO	R	152	420	06.04.16	7659	000000	92998
582.685-110	PATCH WASHER (textile)	2112	44444444455	LNNNNNNNNFFNNNNONFNNN	NNOO3NNNNNNNNNN	R	152	420	06.04.16	7659	000000	92998
582.685-114	ROPE-SILICA-MACHINE OPERATOR (textile)	2123	44444434355	LNNNNNNFFNNNNNFNON	NNNN3NNNNNNNNNN	R,T	153	413	06.04.16	7659	000000	92953
582.685-118	SATURATOR TENDER (build. mat., nec)	3123	34434434355	LONONONFFNNNNONFNNN	NNCC4NCNNNNNNNC	R,T	152	503	06.04.19	7659	000000	92953
582.685-122	SCRUBBING-MACHINE OPERATOR (tex. prod., nec)	2112	44454544455	LNNNNNNNFFONNNNNFNNNNC	NNNN3NNNNNNNNNN	R,T	031	413	06.04.16	7659	000000	92998
582.685-126	SHEEPSKIN PICKLER (meat products)	2122	44444443345	MONFNFNFFONNNNNNNNNN	NNNF3NNNNNNNNNN	R,T	152	521	06.04.16	7659	000000	92998
582.685-130	SKEIN-YARN DYER (textile)	2113	44444434354	MMNONNNFFNNNNNONOOON	NNNO4NNNNNNONON	R,T	152	411	06.04.16	7659	000000	92714
582.685-134	SOAKER, HIDES (meat products)	2122	44444434344	MONFNFNFFNNNNNNNNON	NNNF3NFNNNNNNNN	R	031	521	06.04.16	7659	000000	92998
582.685-138	SPRAY-MACHINE OPERATOR (textile)	2122	44443444355	LNNNNNNNNONFNNN	NNNN3NNNNNNNNNN	R,J,T	153	420	06.04.16	7659	000000	92953
582.685-142	STAINING-MACHINE OPERATOR (tex. prod., nec)	2123	44444544354	LNNNNNNNFFNNNNFNON	NNNN3NNNNNNONON	R	152	413	06.04.16	7659	000000	92998
582.685-146	STEAMER TENDER (textile)	2122	44444444455	MNNFNNNFFFNNNONONNNN	NNFF3NNNNNNNNNN	R,T	152	420	06.04.16	7659	000000	92998
582.685-150	STEAMING-CABINET TENDER (garment)	2112	44444444355	LNNNNNNNFFONNNNFNNNNC	NNNN3NNNNNNNNNN	R,T	152	444	06.04.16	7659	000000	92998
582.685-154	TIN-WHIZ-MACHINE OPERATOR (textile)	3224	34444443355	MNNNNNNNFFONNNNNNNNNN	NNNF3NNNNNNNNNN	R,J,T	152	420	06.04.16	7659	000000	92998
582.685-158	WARP-DYEING-VAT TENDER (textile)	2124	33444344454	MONONNNFFOONNNONONOFN	NNFF4NNNNNNONON	R,T	152	411	06.04.16	7659	000000	92714
582.685-162	WASHER (plastic-synth.)	2123	44444434344	MMNFNFNCCFNNNNNFFNON	NNNO4NFNNNNNNNN	R	152	492	06.04.16	7659	200309	92714
582.685-166	WOOL-WASHING-MACHINE OPERATOR (textile)	2112	44444544354	LNNNNNNFFONNNNONONON	NNNN3NNNNNNNNNN	R,T	031	422	06.04.05	7659	200309	92998
582.685-170	DYE-TUB OPERATOR (knitting)	2113	44444444354	MMNFNNNFFNNNNNONNNFN	NNNC4NNNNNONONFN	R,T	152	446	06.04.16	7659	200303	92714
582.686-010	DYE-HOUSE WORKER (leather mfg.)	1112	45555545455	HNNFNNNFFNNNNNNNNNN	NNNF3NNNNNNNNNN	R	152	521	06.04.16	8725	000000	98502

DOT #	DOT Title & Industry	Trng	Aptitude	Physical	Environment	Tempra	WKF	MPSMS	GOE	SOC	CIP	OES
582.686-014	DYE-REEL-OPERATOR HELPER (textile)	2122	44444443345	HONONONFFONNNNNFNNNNN	NNFC3NNNNNNNNNO	R	152	420	06.04.16	8617	000000	98999
582.686-018	RAW-STOCK-MACHINE LOADER (textile)	1112	44444444454	HOOONNOFFONNNNNONNNON	NNNC3NNNNNNNNNN	R	152	410	06.04.16	8725	000000	98502
582.686-022	SKEIN-YARN-DYER HELPER (textile)	2112	44444433355	MNNNNNNNCCFNNNNNFNNNNN	NNNC3NNNNNNNNNN	R	152	411	06.04.16	8617	000000	98999
582.686-026	SLASHER-TENDER HELPER (textile)	2122	44444544354	HOOONONFFNNNNNFFNNFF	NNFF3NNNNNNNNNN	R	151	411	06.04.16	8617	000000	98999
582.686-030	TOP-DYEING-MACHINE LOADER (tex. prod., nec; textile)	2112	44544544455	MOOONNNFFNNNNNNNNNNN	NNCC3NNNNNNNNNN	R	152	410	06.04.16	8725	000000	98502
582.686-034	TUBE HANDLER (textile)	1112	44454544455	LNNNNNNFFNNNNNNNNNNN	NNNN3NNNNNNNNNN	R	152	420	06.04.27	8725	000000	98502
582.686-038	WARP COILER (knitting)	2112	44444544445	MOOONONFFONNNFFNONN	NNNO4NNNNNNNNNN	R	152	411	06.04.16	8725	000000	98502
582.687-010	BAGGER (button & notion)	1112	44444444354	LNNONNNCCFNNNNNNNNON	NNNN3NNNNNNNNNN	R	041	446	06.04.38	7850	000000	83005
582.687-014	DYER (button & notion)	1112	44544544454	LNNNNNNNFFNNNNNNNNFN	NNNN4NNNNNNNNNN	R	152	618	06.04.19	8769	000000	98999
582.687-018	FELT-HAT STEAMER (hat & cap)	1111	44544544455	LNNNNNNNFFFNNFNNNNON	NNNN3NNNNNNNNNN	R	152	445	06.04.27	7659	000000	92998
582.687-022	SHADE MATCHER (textile)	2123	34424343352	LNNNNNNNFFFNNNNNNNFN	NNNN3NNNNNNNNNN	R,J,T	212	420	06.03.02	7820	000000	83005
582.687-026	SIZER (textile)	2113	44444544455	MNNONNNCCNNNNNNNNNNN	NNNN3NNNNNNNNNN	R	152	411	06.03.02	8769	000000	98999
582.687-030	TREATER (any industry)	1112	44544444355	MFFONNNFFONNNNONNNNN	NNNO3NNNNNNNNNN	R	153	969	06.04.33	8769	000000	98999
583.132-010	SUPERVISOR, PRESSING DEPARTMENT (garment)	4337	33333333344	LNNNNNNNOOONFNFNNOON	NNNN3NNNNNNNNNN	V,D,P	032	440	06.02.01	7100	200309	81008
583.137-010	SUPERVISOR, PLEATING (tex. prod, nec)	4338	34333343355	LNNNNNNNFFONFFNFNNONN	NNNN3NNNNNNNNNN	D,J,T	062	420	06.04.01	7100	200303	81008
583.585-010	CALENDER-MACHINE OPERATOR (nonmet. min.)	2223	34343434354	MNNNNNNNFFNNNNNFNNNON	NNNN4NNNNNNNNNN	J,T	032	538	06.04.05	7659	000000	92998
583.682-010	COATING-AND-EMBOSSING-UNIT OPERATOR (tex. prod., nec; textile)	3226	34343444353	MNNONNNFFNNNNNFNFNN	NNNN3NNNNNNNNNN	V,J,T	153	430	06.02.16	7659	000000	92953
583.684-010	PLEATER, HAND (tex. prod., nec)	2123	34443333355	LNNNNNNCCCNNNNCNNNNN	NNNN3NNNNNNNNNN	R,T	062	420	06.04.27	7755	200303	93999
583.684-014	WAIST PLEATER (tex. prod., nec)	2124	34443434455	LNNNNNNNFFFNNNNNFNNN	NNNF3NNNNNNNNNN	R,T	062	420	06.04.27	7755	200303	93999
583.685-010	BREAKER-MACHINE TENDER (textile)	2122	44444444355	MNNNNNNFFONNNNFNNNNN	NNNN4NNNNNNNNNN	R,T	032	420	06.04.16	7659	000000	92998
583.685-014	BRIM CURLER (hat & cap)	2112	44444444455	LNNNNNNCCNNNNNCNNNNN	NNNN3NNNNNNNNNN	R	134	445	06.04.05	7659	200303	92728
583.685-018	BRIM PRESSER I (hat & cap)	2112	44444444455	LNNNNNNNFFNNNNNFNNNN	NNNN3NNNNNNNNNN	R	032	445	06.04.05	7657	200303	92728
583.685-022	BRIM-AND-CROWN PRESSER (hat & cap)	2112	34443444344	MNNNNNNFFOONNNONFNON	NNFN4NNNNNNNNNN	R,T	032	445	06.04.05	7657	200303	92728
583.685-026	CALENDER OPERATOR (tex. prod., nec; textile)	2123	34443444344	MNNNNNNFFOONNNONFNON	NNFN4NNNNNNNNNN	R,T	032	420	06.04.16	7659	000000	92998
583.685-030	EMBOSSER (any industry)	2123	44444444345	MNNNNNNNFFOONNFFONNF	NNNN4NNNNNNNNNN	R,T	192	420	06.04.02	7659	000000	92998
583.685-034	EMBOSSING-MACHINE OPERATOR (tex. prod., nec)	3224	34343434354	MNNNONOOFFONNNNFNONON	NNNN4NNNNNNNNNF	R	192	434	06.04.02	7659	000000	92998
583.685-038	EMBOSSING-MACHINE-OPERATOR HELPER (plastic-synth.)	2122	44444444354	MNNFNFNFFNNNNNNFNNNN	NNNN4NNNNNNNNNO	R	192	519	06.04.02	7659	000000	92998
583.685-042	FOLDING-MACHINE OPERATOR (garment)	2112	44444533345	LNNNNNNNCCCNNNNNNNNN	NNNN3NNNNNNNNNN	R	032	424	06.04.05	7659	200303	92998
583.685-046	FUSING-MACHINE TENDER (garment; knitting)	1112	44444444344	LNNNNNNNFFNNNNFNNNON	NNNN4NNNNNNNNNN	R	032	446	06.04.16	7659	200303	92998
583.685-050	HAT-LINING BLOCKER (hat & cap)	2112	44444444345	LNNNNNNNFFNNNNNFNNNN	NNNF3NNNNNNNNNN	R	032	445	06.04.05	7657	200303	92728
583.685-054	HYDRAULIC-PRESS OPERATOR (any industry)	2112	44444534355	LNNFNNNNCCNNNNNFNNNN	NNNF3NNNNNNNNNN	R	032	424	06.04.05	7659	000000	92998
583.685-058	HYDRAULIC-PRESS OPERATOR (tex. prod., nec)	2122	44444433355	LNNONONFFNNNNNONFNNN	NNNO3NNNNNNNNNN	R,T	134	439	06.04.05	7657	000000	92728
583.685-062	JACQUARD-TWINE-POLISHER OPERATOR (tex. prod., nec)	2123	44443433355	LNNONONFFNNNNNNNNNNN	NNNN3NNNNNNNNNN	R,T	032	410	06.04.16	7659	000000	92998
583.685-066	LEATHER ETCHER (garment)	3233	44443434355	LNNNNNNNFFNNNNONFNNN	NNNN3NNNNNNNNNN	R,T	192	440	06.04.16	7659	200303	92998
583.685-070	MANGLER (knitting)	2122	44443434355	LNNNNNNNFFFNNNNFNNNN	NNNN3NNNNNNNNNN	R	032	424	06.04.05	7657	200303	92728
583.685-074	NARROW-FABRIC CALENDERER (narrow fabrics)	2112	44444444355	MNNNNNNNFFONNNNFNFNNN	NNNC4NNNNNNNNNN	R,T	032	423	06.04.16	7659	000000	92998
583.685-078	PILLOWCASE TURNER (tex. prod., nec)	2113	44444434345	LNNNNNNNCCNNNNNNFNNN	NNNN4NNNNNNNNNN	R	032	435	06.04.05	7659	000000	92998
583.685-082	PLEATING-MACHINE OPERATOR (any industry)	3234	44443434355	LNNONNNFFONNNNNFNNNN	NNNF4NNNNNNNNNN	R	062	420	06.04.09	7674	000000	92998
583.685-086	PRESS OPERATOR (textile)	2114	44434544355	MNNNNNNNFFNNNNNFNNNN	NNNF3NNNNNNNNNN	R,T	032	420	06.04.05	7657	200303	92728
583.685-090	PRESSER, BUFFING WHEEL (tex. prod., nec)	1112	44444444345	LNNNNNNNFFFNNNNNONFFN	NNNN4NNNNNNNNNN	R	032	538	06.04.05	7657	000000	92728
583.685-094	ROLLER-MACHINE OPERATOR (leather mfg.)	2122	44444343345	LNNNNNNNCCCNNNNNNNNN	NNNO3NNNNNNNNNN	R	032	521	06.04.16	7651	200303	92705
583.685-098	SEAM PRESSER (hat & cap)	2113	44443443345	LNNNNNNNFFOONNNNFNNN	NNNN4NNNNNNNNNN	R,T	032	445	06.04.05	7657	200303	92728
583.685-102	SHAPER AND PRESSER (garment)	2112	44444344445	MNNNNNNNFFOONNNNFNNN	NNNN4NNNNNNNNNN	R,T	032	440	06.04.05	7657	200303	92728
583.685-106	STEAM-PRESS TENDER (textile)	2123	34444444345	MNNNNNNNFFFFNNNNFNNN	NNNF4NNNNNNNNNN	R,T	032	420	06.04.09	7657	000000	92728
583.685-110	STRAW HAT PRESSER, MACHINE (hat & cap)	2122	44444434355	LNNNNNNNFFFNNNNNFNNN	NNNN4NNNNNNNNNN	R	032	445	06.04.05	7657	200303	92728
583.685-114	STRAW-HAT-PLUNGER OPERATOR (hat & cap)	2122	44444444355	LNNNNNNNFFFNNNNNFNNN	NNNN4NNNNNNNNNN	R	032	445	06.04.05	7657	000000	92728
583.685-118	STRIP PRESSER (boot & shoe)	1112	44434544354	LNNNNNNNFFFNNNNONFFN	NNNN4NNNNNNNNNN	R	032	522	06.04.05	7657	000000	92998
583.685-122	TRIMMING-MACHINE OPERATOR (garment; knitting)	2112	44444443345	LNNNNNNNFFNNNNNNFNFN	NNNO3NNNNNNNNNN	R	032	432	06.04.05	7651	200303	92705
583.685-126	YARN-POLISHING-MACHINE OPERATOR (textile)	2112	44444443354	MNNFNFNCCFONNNFNNNNFN	NNCN4NNNNNNNNNN	R,T	151	410	06.04.16	7659	200303	92998
583.686-010	BEAD-MACHINE OPERATOR (hat & cap)	2122	44444443355	LNNNNNNNFFONNNNNNNNN	NNNN3NNNNNNNNNN	R	192	529	06.04.05	7659	200303	92998
583.686-014	FUSING-MACHINE FEEDER (garment)	1111	44544444355	LNNNNNNNFFONNNNNFNNN	NNNN3NNNNNNNNNN	R	032	440	06.04.05	8725	000000	98502

DOT #	DOT Title & Industry	Trng	Aptitude	Physical	Environment	Tempra	WkF	MPSMS	GOE	SOC	CIP	OES
583.686-018	GLOVE TURNER AND FORMER, AUTOMATIC (glove & mit.)	1112	44444423255	LNNNNNNFFNNNFONNNN	NNNN4NNNNNNNNNNN	R	032	449	06.04.05	8725	000000	98502
583.686-022	MANGLE-PRESS CATCHER (textile)	1112	44454534455	LNNFNNNCNNNNNNNNNN	NNNN3NNNNNNNNNNN	R	032	420	06.04.05	8725	000000	98502
583.686-026	OUTSOLE FLEXER (boot & shoe)	1112	44444434355	LNNFNNNCCNNNNNNNNN	NNNN4NNNNNNNNNNN	R	134	522	06.04.05	8725	480304	98502
583.686-030	PRESS FEEDER (knitting; textile)	1112	44444534355	LNNFNNNFFNNNNNNNNN	NNNN3NNNNNNNNNNN	R	032	420	06.04.16	8725	000000	98502
583.687-010	PRESS HAND (knitting)	1112	44444534355	LNNNNNNCCNNNNNNNNN	NNNN3NNNNNNNNNNN	R	032	424	06.04.27	8769	000000	98999
584.382-010	COATING-MACHINE OPERATOR I (tex. prod., nec)	3225	34343434344	MNNNNNNFFFNNNFNONON	NNNN3NFNNNNNNNNN	J,T	153	434	06.02.21	7659	000000	92953
584.382-014	QUILTING-MACHINE OPERATOR (tex. prod., nec)	3225	34422434353	HNNONONFFONOONFNNNFN	NNNN3NNNNNNNNNNN	J,T	063	434	06.02.09	7679	150699	92998
584.562-010	COATING-MACHINE OPERATOR (carpet & rug; tex. prod., nec)	3225	33433434355	LNNFNNNFFNNNNNNFNNN	NNNN4NNNNNNNNNNN	R,T	151	430	06.02.21	7659	000000	92953
584.665-010	COATER HELPER (textile)	2123	44434444354	MNNFOONFFONNNNFNNNON	NNON4NNNNNNNNNNN	R,T	153	420	06.04.16	7659	000000	92998
584.665-014	GLUE-SPREADING-MACHINE OPERATOR (leather prod.)	2112	44444434355	LNNNNNNCCNNNNCNNNNN	NNNN4NNNNNNNNNNN	R	063	520	06.04.05	7659	000000	92956
584.665-018	SIZING-MACHINE TENDER (textile)	2223	34444443354	LNNFNFNFFNOONFNFNNN	NNNN4NNNNNNNNNNN	R,T	151	411	06.04.16	7659	000000	92998
584.682-010	COATER (textile)	3224	34443444344	MNNONONFFOONNNFFNNOC	NNNN4NNNNNNNNNNN	J,T	153	420	06.02.21	7659	000000	92998
584.682-014	LAMINATING-MACHINE OPERATOR (knitting; textile)	3235	34433433345	MNNFNNNFFNNNNFNFNNN	NNNN4NNNNNNNNNNN	R	147	431	06.02.09	7756	000000	93947
584.684-010	LATEXER (carpet & rug)	2123	44434434355	MNONONONFFONNNNFONNON	NNNN4NFNNNNNNNNN	R	153	434	06.04.33	7756	000000	92998
584.685-010	CALENDER OPERATOR, ARTIFICIAL LEATHER (tex. prod., nec)	2223	44444343344	MONONONFFONNNNFONNON	NNNN4NNNNNNNNNNN	R,T	134	420	06.04.16	7659	000000	92998
584.685-014	CLOTH-MERCERIZER OPERATOR (textile)	3223	34443444345	MNNNNNNCCFNNNNOFNNNN	NNNN4NNNNNNNNNNN	R,T	152	439	06.04.16	7659	000000	92953
584.685-018	COATING-MACHINE OPERATOR II (tex. prod., nec)	2122	44444444355	MNNNNNNFFONNNNNNNNN	NNNN3NNNNNNNNNNN	R	153	512	06.04.16	7659	000000	92953
584.685-022	FOXING PAINTER (rubber goods)	2222	44443423354	LNNNNNNFFNNNFNNNON	NNNN3NNNNNNNNNNN	R	262	420	06.04.21	7659	000000	92998
584.685-026	HAT-STOCK-LAMINATING-MACHINE OPERATOR (hat & cap)	2124	44434434355	HNNNNNNFFOONNNFNNNNN	NNNN4NNNNNNNNNNN	R,T	063	420	06.04.05	7659	000000	92953
584.685-030	KNIFE-MACHINE OPERATOR (textile)	2124	34443434355	MNNNNNNCCNNNNNFNONNN	NNCN4NNNNNNNNNNN	R,T	141	435	06.04.16	7659	000000	92953
584.685-034	LAMINATOR (tex. prod., nec)	2113	44444433355	LNNNNNNFFNNNNFNNNN	NNNN3NNNNNNNNNNN	R	063	604	06.04.05	7659	000000	92998
584.685-038	LATEXER I (protective dev.)	2122	44444444445	LNNOONFFNNNNNNNNNN	NNNN4NNNNNNNNNNN	R	153	420	06.04.16	7659	000000	92953
584.685-042	MANGLE TENDER (textile)	2113	44454544455	LNNNNNNFFNNNNNNNNN	NNNN4NNNNNNNNNNN	R,T	152	413	06.04.16	7659	000000	92998
584.685-046	TARRING-MACHINE OPERATOR (tex. prod., nec)	2123	44444444455	LNNNNNNFFNNNNNFNFNN	NNNN3NNNNNNNNNNN	R,T	151	411	06.04.16	7659	000000	92998
584.685-050	WAX-MACHINE OPERATOR (textile)	2123	44444433354	MNNNNNCCONNNONONNNON	NNNO4NNNNNNNNNNN	R,T	151	411	06.04.16	7669	000000	92998
584.685-054	YARN-MERCERIZER OPERATOR I (textile)	2112	34443434344	MNNFNFNCCFNNNNFFONFN	NNNO3NNNNNNNNNNN	R,T	152	411	06.04.16	7659	000000	92998
584.685-058	YARN-MERCERIZER OPERATOR II (textile)	2123	44544544445	MMNNNNNFFNNNNNNFNNN	NNNO4NNONNNNNOO	R,T	152	411	06.04.16	7659	000000	92998
584.686-010	YARN-MERCERIZER-OPERATOR HELPER (textile)	1112	44544534355	MNNNNNNFFNNNNNNNNNON	NNFF4NNNNNNNNNNN	R	153	411	06.04.16	8617	000000	98999
584.687-010	LEATHER COATER (leather mfg.)	1111	44544544354	LNNNNNNFFNNNNNNNNNN	NNNN3NNNNNNNNNNN	R	153	521	06.04.27	8769	000000	98999
584.687-014	SPRAYER, HAND (leather mfg.)	1112	33333444354	LNNNNNNFFNNNNFNNNON	NNNN3NNNNNNNNNNN	R,T	153	521	06.04.27	8769	000000	98999
585.130-010	SUPERVISOR, CORDUROY CUTTING (textile)	4236	33333444354	MNNNNNNFFONFFNFNNNON	NNNN4NNNNNNNNNNN	D,P,T	054	420	06.01.01	7100	000000	81008
585.380-010	CUTTING-MACHINE FIXER (textile)	4336	34443433345	MNNONONFFOONNNOFNNNN	NNNN4NFNNNNNNNNN	J,T	054	420	06.01.02	7459	470303	92702
585.565-010	CORDUROY-CUTTER OPERATOR (textile)	2123	44444444355	SNNNNNNCCNOONFNNNNN	NNNO3NNNNNNNNNNN	R,T	054	420	06.04.05	7659	200303	92944
585.665-010	NAPPER TENDER (knitting)	2112	44443423355	LNNNNNCCNCONNCNFNNN	NNNN4NNNNNNNNNNN	R	161	446	06.04.05	7659	000000	92998
585.681-010	FLESHER (leather mfg.)	3126	44443423355	LNNONNNFFNNNNNNNNNN	NNNN5NNNNNNNNNNN	R,J,T	054	521	06.01.04	7753	000000	93926
585.681-014	FUR PLUCKER (leather mfg.)	3126	44443444454	LNNNNNNFFNNNNNNNNNN	NNNN4NNNNNNNNNNN	R,J,T	054	521	06.02.27	7753	000000	93926
585.684-010	TRIMMER, HAND (leather mfg.)	1112	44444444345	LNNNNNNFFONNNNFNNNN	NNNF3NFNNNNNNNNO	R,T	054	521	06.04.27	7753	000000	92944
585.685-014	BUFFER (hat & cap)	2112	44443444345	LNNNNNNFFONNNFNNNNN	NNNN4NNNNNNNNNNN	R,T	051	420	06.04.05	7659	000000	92998
585.685-018	BUFFER, MACHINE (leather mfg.)	2113	44443444444	LNNNNNNFFNNNNNONNNN	NNNN3NNNNNNNNNNN	R	051	521	06.04.16	7659	000000	92965
585.685-022	CHINCHILLA-MACHINE OPERATOR (textile)	2122	44444444445	MNNNNNNCCFONNNOFNNNN	NNNN4NNNNNNNNNNN	R,T	161	420	06.04.16	7659	000000	92998
585.685-026	CLOTH TRIMMER, MACHINE (textile)	2123	44444444445	MNNNNNNCCFONNNOFNNON	NNNN4NNNNNNNNNNN	R,T	054	420	06.04.05	7654	200303	92705
585.685-030	CONCAVING-MACHINE OPERATOR (boot & shoe)	2122	44443444344	MMNNFNNNFFNNNNNNNNNN	NNNN4NNNNNNNNNNN	R	054	522	06.04.05	7659	480304	92944
585.685-034	CORDUROY-BRUSHER OPERATOR (textile)	2122	44443444445	MNNONONCCFONNNOFNNON	NNNN4NNNNNNNNNNN	R	161	420	06.04.16	7659	000000	92998
585.685-038	CUT-LACE-MACHINE OPERATOR (leather prod.)	2123	44443434344	MNNONONCCFONNOFNNNN	NNNN4NNNNNNNNNNN	R,T	054	529	06.04.05	7654	000000	92944
585.685-042	ELECTRIFIER OPERATOR (textile)	2123	44443433345	LNNNNNNFFNNNNONNNON	NNNN4NNNNNNNNNNN	R,T	161	420	06.04.16	7659	000000	92998
585.685-046	FUR-CUTTING-MACHINE OPERATOR (hat & cap)	2122	44444444455	LNNNNNNFFONNNFNNNNNF	NNNN4NFNNNNNNNNN	R,T	054	521	06.04.05	7654	200303	92705
585.685-050	GASSER (textile)	2122	44544444445	LNNNNNNFFNNNNNNNNNN	NNNN3NNNNNNNNNNN	R,T	031	412	06.04.16	7659	000000	92998
585.685-054	GIG TENDER (textile)	2122	44544434355	LNNNNNNFFOONNNNNNNN	NNNN3NNNNNNNNNNN	R,T	161	422	06.04.16	7659	000000	92998
585.685-058	JIGGER-CROWN-POUNCING-MACHINE OPERATOR (hat & cap)	2113	44544434355	LNNNNNNFFOONNNNNNNN	NNNN4NNNNNNNNNNN	R,T	051	445	06.04.16	7659	200303	92998
585.685-062	LABEL PINKER (narrow fabrics)	2112	44444434355	SNNNNNNFFNNNNFNONON	NNNN3NNNNNNNNNNN	R,T	054	423	06.04.05	7654	200303	92705

DOT #	DOT Title & Industry	Trng	Aptitude	Physical	Environment	Tempra	WkF	MPSMS	GOE	SOC	CIP	OES
585.685-066	MELLOWING-MACHINE OPERATOR (hat & cap)	2112	44444434345	LNNNNNNFFNNNNFNNNNN	NNNN4NNNNNNNNNN	R	032	445	06.04.16	7659	200303	92998
585.685-070	NAPPER TENDER (tex. prod., nec; textile)	2123	34444444444	LMNNONOFFFNNNFFNNON	NNNN4NFNNNNNNNNN	R,T	161	420	06.04.16	7659	000000	92998
585.685-074	POUNCING-LATHE OPERATOR (hat & cap)	2122	44443444455	LMNNNNNNFFNNNNNNNNN	NNNN4NNNNNNNNNN	R,T	051	445	06.04.16	7659	200303	92998
585.685-078	ROLLING-MACHINE OPERATOR (textile)	2112	44443433355	MNNNNNNCCNNNNNONNNN	NNNN4NNNNNNNNNN	R	161	410	06.04.16	7659	200303	92998
585.685-082	ROTARY CUTTER (boot & shoe)	2123	44443444344	MNNNNNNFFONNNNFNNNO	NNNN4NNNNNNNNNN	R,T	054	529	06.04.05	7654	480304	92944
585.685-086	ROUNDING-MACHINE OPERATOR (hat & cap; tex. prod., nec)	2112	44443444445	LNNFNNNNFFNNNNFNFONN	NNNN4NNNNNNNNNN	R,T	054	445	06.04.05	7659	200303	92944
585.685-090	RUG INSPECTOR (tex. prod., nec)	2114	44443433355	LNNNNNNFFNNNNFNNFNN	NNNN4NNNNNNNNNN	R	054	422	06.03.02	7820	000000	83005
585.685-094	SHAVING-MACHINE OPERATOR (leather mfg.)	2123	44443433344	MNNNFNNNFFNNNNFNNON	NNNN4NFNNNNNNNNF	R,T	054	520	06.04.16	7659	000000	92944
585.685-098	SHEARING-MACHINE FEEDER (leather mfg.)	2123	44443444345	MNNNNNNFFONNNNNONNNN	NNNN4NNNNNNNNNN	R,T	054	521	06.04.16	7659	000000	92944
585.685-102	SHEARING-MACHINE OPERATOR (carpet & rug; textile)	2122	44433433344	HNNFNFNFFONNNOFFOOO	NNNN4NCNNNNNNNN	R,T	054	420	06.04.06	7654	000000	92705
585.685-106	SINGER (textile)	2123	44443443344	LNNNNNNNFFNNNNNFNNNN	NNNN4NCNNNNNNNN	R	031	420	06.04.16	7659	000000	92998
585.685-110	SKIVER, BLOCKERS (boot & shoe)	2122	44443444344	LNNNNNNNFFNNNNFNNNFN	NNNN4NNNNNNNNNN	R	054	529	06.04.05	7659	480304	92944
585.685-114	SPLITTER, MACHINE (boot & shoe; leather prod.)	2123	44444444445	LNNNNNNNFFNNNNNNNNNN	NNNN4NNNNNNNNNN	R	054	520	06.04.05	7659	480304	92998
585.685-118	STRIPPING CUTTER AND WINDER (boot & shoe)	2123	44443444345	MNNNNNNFFNNNNFNONNN	NNNN4NNNNNNNNNN	R,T	054	420	06.04.05	7654	480304	92705
585.685-122	SWEATBAND SEPARATOR (hat & cap)	2112	44444444355	LNNNNNNNFFNNNNNFNNNNN	NNNN4NNNNNNNNNN	R	054	439	06.04.05	7654	200303	92944
585.685-126	TRIMMER, MACHINE (leather mfg.)	2122	44544544355	HNNNNNNNFFNNNNFNFNNN	NNNN3NFNNNNNNNN	R,T	054	521	06.04.16	7654	000000	92944
585.686-010	FEATHER-CUTTING-MACHINE FEEDER (tex. prod., nec)	1111	44544544355	LNNNNNNNFFNNNNNNNNNN	NNNN4NCNNNNNNNN	R	054	618	06.04.09	8725	000000	98502
585.687-010	BEAMING INSPECTOR (leather mfg.)	2123	44443444355	LNNNNNNFFFNNNFNNNN	NNNF4NFNNNNNNNN	R,T	212	521	06.03.02	7820	000000	83005
585.687-014	CARPET CUTTER II (carpet & rug)	2113	44444444355	LNNFFNNNFFNNNNNFNFNNN	NNNN3NNNNNNNNNN	R	054	430	06.04.27	8769	000000	98999
585.687-018	CLOTH-EDGE SINGER (textile)	2112	44444544455	LNNFNNNNFFNNNNFNNNNN	NNNN3NNNNNNNNNN	R	032	420	06.04.16	8769	000000	98999
585.687-022	PATCHER (leather mfg.)	2122	34433433353	LLNNFNNNFFFNNNFNFFFN	NNNN3NNNNNNNNNN	R,J,T	212	521	06.04.27	7820	000000	93956
585.687-026	SHADE-CLOTH FINISHER (furniture)	2122	44444444444	LNNONONCCNNNNNCCNNFN	NNNN3NNNNNNNNNN	R,T	161	439	06.04.33	8769	000000	98999
585.687-030	SINGER (narrow fabrics)	1112	44444544355	LNNNNNNNFFNNNNNNNNNN	NNNN3NNNNNNNNNN	R	032	423	06.04.27	8761	000000	98902
586.130-010	SUPERVISOR V (tex. prod., nec)	3226	33433344355	MNNOONOONOOONONNNNNN	NNNN4NNNNNNNNNN	D,J,P,T	032	439	06.04.01	7100	150699	81008
586.382-010	FULLING-MACHINE OPERATOR (tex. prod., nec)	3224	34333434355	LNNNNNNNFFFFNNFNNNNN	NNNN4NNNNNNNNNN	R,T	134	422	06.02.16	7659	000000	92998
586.662-010	FELTING-MACHINE OPERATOR (tex. prod., nec)	3234	34444344355	MNNNNNNNFFOONNNFNFNNN	NNNO4NNNNNNNNNN	R,T	134	432	06.02.05	7659	000000	92998
586.682-010	FULLER (textile)	3234	34444444354	MNNNNNNNFFNNNNNOFNNON	NNNN3NNNNNNNNNN	R,T	152	422	06.02.16	7659	000000	92998
586.685-010	CARROTING-MACHINE OPERATOR (hat & cap)	2112	44444434355	LNNNNNNNFFNNNNNNNNNN	NNNN4NCNNNNNNNC	R	153	521	06.04.16	7659	000000	92998
586.685-014	CONTINUOUS-CRUSHER OPERATOR (textile)	2112	44444444455	MNNNNNNNFFNNNNNOFNNNN	NNNN4NNNNNNNNNN	R,T	031	422	06.04.16	7677	000000	92965
586.685-018	FELT-STRIP FINISHER (tex. prod., nec)	2123	44443444354	HNNNNNNNFFNNNNNNNNNN	NNNN4NNNNNNNNNN	R,T	051	422	06.04.16	7659	000000	92998
586.686-022	FELTMAKER AND WEIGHER (tex. prod., nec)	2223	44444444454	LNNNNNNNFFFFNNNFNNNFN	NNNN4NNNNNNNNNN	R,J,T	143	422	06.04.16	7659	000000	92998
586.685-026	HARDENING-MACHINE OPERATOR (hat & cap)	2123	44443433355	LNNNNNNNFFFFNNFNNNNN	NNNF4NNNNNNNNNN	R	134	529	06.04.16	7659	000000	92998
586.685-030	HAT-FORMING-MACHINE OPERATOR (hat & cap)	3223	44443434345	MNNNNNNNCCCNONONNONN	NNNN4NNNNNNNNNN	R	152	445	06.04.16	7659	000000	92998
586.685-034	SHRINKING-MACHINE OPERATOR (hat & cap)	2123	44443444355	LNNNNNNNCCONNNNCNNNN	NNOO4NNNNNNNNNO	R	152	445	06.04.16	7659	000000	92998
586.685-038	TESTING-MACHINE OPERATOR (tex. prod., nec)	3234	34443433344	LNNNNNNNFFNNNNNFNFON	NNNN4NNNNNNNNNN	R,T	212	439	06.03.02	7830	000000	83005
586.686-010	CARROTING-MACHINE OFFBEARER (hat & cap)	1111	44544534355	LNNNNNNNFFONNNNNNNNNN	NNNN3NNNNNNNNNN	R	153	521	06.04.16	8725	000000	98502
586.686-014	FELTING-MACHINE-OPERATOR HELPER (tex. prod., nec)	1112	44444444355	MNNNNNNNFFNNNNNONNNN	NNNN4NNNNNNNNNN	R	134	422	06.04.05	8617	000000	98999
586.686-018	HAT-FORMING-MACHINE FEEDER (hat & cap)	2112	44443434355	LNNNNNNNFFFNNNNFNFNNN	NNFF3NNNNNNNNNN	R,T	152	432	06.04.16	8725	000000	98502
586.686-022	MACHINE HELPER (tex. prod., nec)	2112	44444444455	MNNNNNNNFFONOONNNOONN	NNNN4NONNNNNNNN	R	011	439	06.04.05	8617	000000	98999
586.687-010	FELT CARBONIZER (tex. prod., nec)	2123	44444444355	LNNNNNNNFFNNNNNONNNON	NNNO4NONNNNNNON	R	031	439	06.04.16	7659	000000	92998
587.384-010	CLOTH-SHRINKING TESTER (textile)	3233	34343444455	LNNNNNNNFFONNNNNONONNN	NNNN4NNNNNNNNNN	V,J	152	420	06.03.01	7830	000000	83005
587.585-010	AUTOCLAVE OPERATOR (knitting)	2122	44443344355	MNNNFNNNFFNNNNNFNFNNN	NNNN4NONNNNNNNN	R,T	152	424	06.04.05	7659	000000	92923
587.682-010	AUTOCLAVE OPERATOR (textile)	3224	34444444354	HNNNONNFFONNNNNONNNN	NNNN4NNNNNNNNNN	R	152	411	06.04.16	7659	000000	92998
587.685-010	BRUSH OPERATOR (textile)	2112	44444444354	LNNOONONFFFNNNNONNNON	NNNO4NONNNNNNNN	R	031	420	06.04.05	7659	000000	92998
587.685-014	BRUSHER, MACHINE (hat & cap)	2123	34343444345	MNNNNNNNFFONNNNNNONNN	NNNN4NNNNNNNNNN	R,T	161	521	06.04.16	7659	000000	92998
587.685-018	CLOTH-SHRINKING-MACHINE OPERATOR (textile)	2123	44443443355	MNNONNNCFONNNNNNONNN	NNNO3NNNNNNNNNN	R,T	152	420	06.04.16	7659	000000	92998
587.685-022	CONDITIONER TENDER (textile)	2113	44443444354	MNNFNFNFFONNNNNONNNN	NNNO4NONNNNNNNN	R	152	411	06.04.16	7659	000000	92998
587.685-026	DUSTER (hat & cap)	2112	44443444345	LNNNNNNNFFOONONFNNNNN	NNNN4NNNNNNNNNN	R	031	445	06.04.05	7659	200303	92998
587.685-030	STRIKE-OUT-MACHINE OPERATOR (textile)	2122	44444444455	LNNNNNNNFFNNNNNNNNNN	NNNN4NNNNNNNNNN	R,T	161	420	06.04.16	7659	000000	92998
587.686-010	CLOTH-SHRINKING-MACHINE-OPERATOR HELPER (textile)	1112	44445544344.	LNNFFFNFFNNNNNFNNNN	NNNO4NNNNNNNNNO	R	152	420	06.04.16	8617	000000	98999
587.687-010	CANVAS SHRINKER (textile)	1112	44444444355	HNNNNNNNFFNNNNNNNNNN	NNNO4NNNNNNNNNN	R	152	431	06.04.27	8769	000000	98999

DOT #	DOT Title & Industry	Trng	Aptitude	Physical	Environment	Tempra	WkF	MPSMS	GOE	SOC	CIP	OES
589.130-010	CLOTH FINISHER (carpet & rug; textile)	4347	22243344452	LNNNNNNFONFFNFFNNFF	NNNNN4NONNNNNNON	V,D,P,J	152	420	05.09.02	7100	150699	81008
589.130-014	FABRIC-COATING SUPERVISOR (tex. prod., nec)	4338	33332344352	LNNNOOONFFFOFFNFNOOON	NNNNN3NONNNNNNNN	V,D,P,J,T	153	434	06.01.01	7100	200303	81008
589.130-018	SUPERVISOR, FINISHING ROOM (leather mfg.)	4337	33343333333	LNNNNNNOOONFFNONOOON	NNNN3NNNNNNNNN	V,D,P,J	134	521	06.02.01	7100	000000	81008
589.130-022	SUPERVISOR, FUR DRESSING (leather mfg.)	4337	33343343454	LNNNNNNNFFFFNFNNFFN	NNNN4NNNNNNNNN	V,D,P,J	031	521	06.01.01	7100	000000	81008
589.130-026	SUPERVISOR, MILL (tex. prod., nec)	4237	33333344445	LNNNNNNNFFNFNFNNONN	NNNNN4NNNNNNNNN	V,P,J	031	413	06.04.01	7100	000000	81008
589.130-030	SUPERVISOR, SPLIT LEATHER DEPARTMENT (leather mfg.)	3236	33343334444	LNNNNNNNNFFONFFNFNOOON	NNNO3NONNNNNNNN	V,D,P,J	054	521	06.02.01	7100	000000	81008
589.132-010	SUPERVISOR VI (tex. prod., nec)	4337	33333334444	MNNNNNNNFFNNFFNNNOOON	NNNN4NNNNNNNNN	V,D,P,J,T	031	419	06.02.01	7100	000000	81008
589.132-014	SUPERVISOR, SPLIT AND DRUM ROOM (leather mfg.)	4337	33343333343	LNNNNNNFFFNFFNFFFF	NNNN4NNNNNNNNN	V,D,P,J	063	521	06.02.01	7100	000000	81008
589.134-010	SUPERVISOR, BEAM DEPARTMENT (leather mfg.)	4337	33343344444	LNNNONNNFFNFNFNFFFFF	NNNO3NONNNNNNNN	V,D,P,J	031	521	06.04.01	7100	000000	81008
589.135-010	SUPERVISOR, PRODUCTION (tex. prod., nec)	4337	33334334354	LONNNNNNFONFFNFNNNNN	NNNN4NFNNNNNNNN	D,P	147	618	06.04.01	7100	000000	81008
589.137-010	SUPERVISOR, PACKING ROOM (leather mfg.)	4237	33343344444	LNNNNNNOOOOFFNFOOOOO	NNNN3NONNNNNNNN	V,D,P,J	041	521	06.02.01	7100	000000	81008
589.137-014	SUPERVISOR, BONDING (textile)	4237	33343344454	LNNNNNNFFOOFFNFFNFON	NNNON4NNNNNNNNN	D,P,V	133	412	06.01.01	7100	150699	81008
589.360-010	BONDING-MACHINE SETTER (textile)	3235	33333433354	MONFNFNFNNNNFNNNNN	NNNNN4NNNNNNNNN	V,J,T	147	412	06.01.02	7459	000000	92702
589.361-010	FUR DRESSER (leather mfg.)	3237	33342433354	MNNFNNNFFFOONFNOOON	NNNNN4NOONNNNNN	V,J,T	054	521	06.01.04	6859	000000	89599
589.384-010	PRODUCT TESTER, FIBERGLASS (textile)	3235	33343344454	LNNNNNNFFONNNNFNNFON	NNNO3NNNNNNNNNN	V,J,T	212	419	06.03.01	7830	000000	83005
589.387-010	INSPECTOR AND SORTER (leather mfg.)	3234	34444344453	LNNONNNFFFNNNFNNOFN	NNNO3NNNNNNNNN	J,T	212	521	06.03.01	7820	000000	83005
589.387-014	WOOL SORTER (textile)	4236	33343433353	LNNOONONFFFONNNFNFNN	NNNN4NONNNNNNNN	R,J,T	212	414	06.03.01	5625	000000	79011
589.387-018	WOOL-AND-PELT GRADER (meat products)	3224	33443434354	MNNONNNFFFNNNFNNFFN	NNNN3NONNNNNNNN	R,J,T	212	521	06.03.01	7850	000000	83005
589.387-022	INSPECTOR, FINISHING (tex. prod., nec)	3225	34443434353	MOONNNNFFOOOONFNOFOO	NNNO4NNNNNNNNNN	T	211	422	06.03.02	7830	150699	95099
589.464-010	COLOR MIXER (furniture)	2223	34344444442	LNNONONFFONOONFNNFFN	NNNF3NNNNNNNNN	R,T	143	495	06.04.34	7664	000000	92965
589.485-010	PAD-EXTRACTOR TENDER (knitting)	2123	44444434455	LNNNNNNCCONNNONNNNNF	NNNF4NNNNNNNNN	R,J,T	152	424	06.04.16	7659	000000	92923
589.487-010	WEIGHT-YARDAGE CHECKER (textile)	3333	34355434455	LNNNNNNCCFNNNNCNNCNN	NNNN4NNNNNNNNN	R,T	212	420	06.03.01	7820	000000	83005
589.562-010	CLOTH-FINISHING-RANGE OPERATOR, CHIEF (textile)	3235	33443434354	MOONNNNFFOOOONFNOFOO	NNNO4NNNNNNNON	D,J	152	420	06.04.16	7659	000000	95099
589.662-010	SCOURING-TRAIN OPERATOR (carpet & rug; textile)	3234	33444434354	MFNNNNNFFOOOONFNOOON	NNNF3NONNNNNNNN	J,T	031	414	06.02.18	7659	000000	92998
589.662-014	TIRE-FABRIC-IMPREGNATING-RANGE OPERATOR, CHIEF (tex. prod., nec)	3225	34433433354	MONOONNFFNFFNFNNNON	NNNN4NNNNNNNNN	J,T	152	430	06.02.16	7659	000000	92998
589.665-010	BONDING-MACHINE TENDER (textile)	3224	44443433354	MONONONFFFNNNNFNNOON	NNNN4NNNNNNNNN	J,T	147	412	06.04.16	7659	000000	92998
589.665-014	CLOTH-FINISHING-RANGE OPERATOR (textile)	2222	44443434344	MNNNONONFFOOOONFNONFN	NNFF4NNNNNNNNF	R,T	152	420	06.04.16	7659	000000	92998
589.684-010	RAKER, BUFFING WHEEL (tex. prod., nec)	2112	44544444355	LNNFNNNFFNNNNNFNNNNN	NNNNN4NONNNNNNN	R	212	538	06.03.02	7830	000000	83005
589.685-010	BOARDING-MACHINE OPERATOR (knitting)	2123	44444433344	LNNNNNNCCCONNNCNFNFN	NNNF3NONNNNNNNN	R	032	446	06.04.16	7659	000000	92998
589.685-014	BREAKER-UP-MACHINE OPERATOR (hat & cap)	1112	44544544455	LNNNNNNFFNNNNNNNNNNN	NNNN4NNNNNNNNN	R	032	445	06.04.16	7659	000000	92998
589.685-018	BURN-OUT TENDER, LACE (tex. prod., nec)	2123	44443434354	MNNNNNNFFNNNNNFNNNON	NNNN4NNNNNNNNN	R	031	432	06.04.21	7659	000000	92998
589.685-022	CLOTH MEASURER, MACHINE (garment; textile)	2123	44443444344	LNNONNNFFNNNNNNNNNN	NNNN3NNNNNNNNN	R,J	221	420	06.03.02	7659	000000	92998
589.685-026	CLOTH-FINISHING-RANGE TENDER (textile)	3123	34443444344	HNNONONFFNNNNOFNNON	NNNF4NNNNNNNNN	R,T	152	420	06.04.16	7659	000000	92714
589.685-030	DETACKER (knitting; textile)	1112	44544544455	MNNONNNFFNNNNFNNNNN	NNNN3NNNNNNNNN	R	062	420	06.04.05	7659	000000	92998
589.685-034	DRUMMER (hat & cap)	2122	44433433344	LNNNNNNFFONNNNFNNNNN	NNOO4NNNNNNNNN	R,T	032	445	06.04.16	7659	000000	92998
589.685-038	DRY CLEANER (knitting)	2112	44544544354	HNNNNNNFFNNNNNNNNNNN	NNNO4NONNNNNNNN	R,T	031	424	06.04.16	7658	200301	92726
589.685-042	DYER HELPER (hat & cap)	2222	44444444454	LNNNNNNFFNNNNNNNNON	NNNO4NNNNNNNNN	R,T	147	445	06.04.16	7659	000000	92998
589.685-046	EDGE STAINER I (leather prod.)	2113	44444443354	LNNNNNNFFNNNNNFNNNON	NNNN4NNNNNNNNN	R,T	153	529	06.04.21	7659	000000	92998
589.685-050	FEATHER MIXER (tex. prod., nec)	2112	44444434355	MNNNNNNFFNNNNNONNNN	NNNN4NONNNNNNNN	R	212	618	06.04.09	7664	000000	92965
589.685-054	FEATHER SEPARATOR (tex. prod., nec)	2113	44444434344	LNNNNNNFFNNNNNNNNON	NNNN4NONNNNNNNN	R	145	433	06.04.09	7666	000000	92962
589.685-058	FOLDING-MACHINE OPERATOR (knitting; textile)	2122	44444434355	MNNONNNFFONNNNFNNNON	NNNN3NNNNNNNNN	R,T	032	424	06.04.05	7659	000000	92998
589.685-062	HAT FINISHER (hat & cap)	2224	44433433344	LNNNNNNFFNNNNNFNNNNN	NNOO4NNNNNNNNN	R,T	032	445	06.04.16	7659	200303	92998
589.685-066	LAUNDRY-MACHINE TENDER (tex. prod., nec)	2113	44443434344	MNNONNNFFONNNNFNNNON	NNNO4NNNNNNNNON	R,T	152	435	06.04.16	7659	200309	92998
589.685-070	MEASURING-MACHINE OPERATOR (leather mfg.)	2113	44444444455	LNNNONNFFNNNNFNNNON	NNNN3NNNNNNNNN	R,T	231	521	06.03.02	7659	000000	92998
589.685-074	PLEATER (textile)	1112	44544544445	MNNNNNNCCONNNNONNNNN	NNNN3NNNNNNNNN	R	041	420	06.04.16	7659	000000	92998
589.685-078	PULLER, MACHINE (leather mfg.)	1112	44444443345	LNNNNNNFFNNNNNFNNNON	NNNN4NNNNNNNNN	R,T	031	521	06.04.16	7659	000000	92998
589.685-082	RENOVATOR-MACHINE OPERATOR (tex. prod., nec)	1112	45454544355	HNNNNNNFFNNNNNNNNNN	NNNN4NONNNNNNNN	R	031	618	06.04.19	7659	000000	92998
589.685-086	ROLLING-DOWN-MACHINE OPERATOR (knitting; textile)	2122	44443443345	HNNFNFNCCFNNNNNOFNNN	NNNN4NNNNNNNNN	R	163	420	06.04.05	7651	000000	92705
589.685-090	SCUTCHER TENDER (textile)	2112	44444444444	MNNNNNNFFNNNNNOFNNON	NNNO4NNNNNNNNN	R	032	420	06.04.16	7659	000000	92998
589.685-094	SHAKER (hat & cap)	1112	44444444455	MNNNNNNFFNNNNNNNNNNN	NNNNN4NNNNNNNNN	R	031	521	06.04.16	7659	000000	92998
589.685-098	WRINGER-MACHINE OPERATOR (leather mfg.; tex. prod., nec)	1112	44544544345	MNNONNNFFNNNNNNNNNN	NNNO4NOONNNNNN	R	032	521	06.04.16	7659	000000	92998

DOT #	DOT Title & Industry	Trng	Aptitude	Physical	Environment	Tempra	WkF	MPSMS	GOE	SOC	CIP	OES
589.685-102	YARN-TEXTURING-MACHINE OPERATOR (plastic-synth.)	2123	4444443344	LNNNNNNFFFNNNNNFFNNNN	NNNN4NNNNNNNNNN	R,T	134	411	06.04.16	7659	000000	92998
589.686-010	BACK TENDER (textile)	2122	4444444354	MOOONONFFFOONOFONON	NNNO4NNNNNNNNNNO	R,T	152	420	06.04.16	8725	000000	98502
589.686-014	CLOTH FEEDER (textile)	1112	4444444344	HNNONNNCCNNNNNFFNNOF	NNNN4NNNNNNNNNNN	R	147	420	06.04.16	8725	000000	98502
589.686-018	FEATHER-CURLING-MACHINE OPERATOR (tex. prod., nec)	1111	44444534355	MNNNNNNFFNNNNNNNNNN	NNNN3NNNNNNNNNN	R	142	618	06.04.09	8725	000000	98502
589.686-022	FUR-FLOOR WORKER (leather mfg.)	1112	4444444344	MMNFNNNFFOONNFNNOON	NNON4NONNNNNNNNN	R	031	521	06.04.16	7659	000000	92998
589.686-026	LABORER, GENERAL (leather mfg.)	2112	4444444355	MMNNNNNFFFNNNNFNFNNN	ONNC3NNNNNNNNNN	R	011	521	06.04.27	8769	000000	98999
589.686-030	OPENER II (hat & cap)	1112	44544534455	LNNNNNNCCCNNNNCNNNNN	NNNN4NNNNNNNNNN	R	054	521	06.04.16	8725	000000	98502
589.686-034	PACKAGE CRIMPER (textile)	1112	44544444445	MMNFNNNCCNNNNNNNNNNN	NNNN3NNNNNNNNNN	R	134	410	06.04.16	8725	000000	98502
589.686-038	RUG-INSPECTOR HELPER (tex. prod., nec)	1112	44444444455	MMNNNNNFFNNNNNFNNNNN	NNNN4NNNNNNNNNN	R	212	439	06.03.02	8620	000000	98999
589.686-042	SOCK BOARDER (knitting)	2112	4444433355	LNNONNNCCONNNNNNNNNN	NNNF3NNNNNNNNNN	R	032	446	06.04.16	8725	000000	98502
589.686-046	TAKER-OFF, HEMP FIBER (tex. prod., nec)	1111	44544544455	MMNNONNNFFFNNNNNNNNN	NNNN4NONNNNNNNN	R	161	413	06.04.16	8725	000000	98502
589.686-050	TOBACCO-CLOTH RECLAIMER (tex. prod., nec)	2112	44544544455	MMNNONNNFFFNNNNNNNNN	NNNN4NONNNNNNNN	R	031	419	06.04.05	8725	000000	98502
589.687-010	CAKE WRAPPER (plastic-synth.)	1112	44544533355	MMNFNFNFCCONNNNOFNFNN	NNNN4NNNNNNNNNN	R	041	492	06.04.38	8769	000000	98999
589.687-014	CLOTH FOLDER, HAND (tex. prod., nec; textile)	2122	4444443454	LNNNNNNCCFNNNNFNNFON	NNNN4NNNNNNNNNN	R	062	420	06.04.27	7759	000000	98999
589.687-018	DIPPER (knitting; textile)	1112	44544544455	MMNNONNNFFNNNNNNNNNN	NNNN4NNNNNNNNNN	R	063	420	06.04.27	8769	000000	98999
589.687-022	FABRIC-LAY-OUT WORKER (textile)	2122	4444444354	LNNNNNNFFFNNNNFNNFFN	NNNN4NNNNNNNNFFN	R	062	420	06.04.27	8769	000000	98999
589.687-026	LABORER, GENERAL (tex. prod., nec)	1112	4444444334	MMNNONONFFFNNNNONONON	NNNN4NONNNNNNNO	R	011	434	06.04.05	8769	000000	98999
589.687-030	PAD MAKER (textile)	2123	44443443353	MNNNNNNCCONNNNNNFNNNN	NNNO3NNNNNNNNNN	J,T	136	419	06.04.27	7740	000000	93999
589.687-034	STAINER (leather prod.)	2112	4444444354	MMNNNNNFFNNNNNNNNNN	NNNN4NNNNNNNNNN	R	153	529	06.04.27	8769	000000	98999
589.687-038	STIFFENER (hat & cap)	2113	44443444355	LNNNNNNCCFNNNNFNFNNN	NNNO4NFNNNNNNNN	R	152	445	06.04.27	8769	200303	98999
589.687-042	TUBE CLEANER (textile)	1112	44544533355	LNNFNFNCCFNNNNNNNNNN	NNNN4NNNNNNNNNN	R	031	559	06.04.27	8769	000000	98999
589.687-046	TUBE COVERER (textile)	1112	44544534355	LNNNONNFFNNNNNFNNNNN	NNNN4NNNNNNNNNN	R	041	559	06.04.27	7759	000000	93999
589.687-050	WOOL PULLER (leather mfg.; meat products)	2123	44443443353	LNNONONCCFNNNFNNNFN	NNNN4NNNNNNNNNN	R,T	212	414	06.03.02	7850	000000	83005
589.687-054	WOOL-FLEECE GRADER (agriculture)	3334	33442434453	MNNNNNNFFFNNNNNNNFN	NNNN3NNNNNNNNNN	J,T	212	414	06.03.02	5625	000000	79011
589.687-058	SHAKER (knitting)	2112	4444434344	LNNNNNNCCFONNNNNNNNON	NNNO3NNNNNNNNNN	R	061	604	06.04.35	8769	200303	98999
589.687-062	DYE-STAND LOADER (textile)	1112	4444444355	MMNFNONFFNNNNNFNONNN	NNNN4NNNNNNNNNN	R	011	411	06.04.16	8725	000000	98502
590.130-010	SUPERVISOR, ELECTRONICS PROCESSING (electron. comp.)	4337	23333333354	LNNNNNNOOONFFNONOOON	NNNN3NNNNNNNNNN	D,V,T,P,J	147	587	06.01.01	7100	520205	81008
590.130-014	SUPERVISOR, INSULATION (nonmet. min.)	4348	33333334355	LNNOOONFFFOOOONFNNNN	NNON4NOOONNNNNN	V,D,P,J	131	538	06.02.01	7100	000000	81008
590.130-018	SUPERVISOR, ROOFING PLANT (build. mat., nec)	4347	23334333343	MMNNNNNFFONFFNFNNNN	NNNN4NNNNNNNNNN	V,D,P,J	147	503	06.02.01	7100	000000	81008
590.131-010	PORCELAIN-ENAMELING SUPERVISOR (any industry)	4337	33343334353	LONNNNNOOOOOONFNNOFN	NNNO4NONNNNNNNN	V,D,P,J	151	550	06.02.01	7100	000000	81008
590.132-010	SUPERVISOR, CANDLE MAKING (fabrication, nec)	4337	33343333353	LNNNNNNFFONFFNFNNNN	NNNN4NNNNNNNNNN	V,D,P,J	147	619	06.02.01	7100	000000	81008
590.134-010	SUPERVISOR, PIPE JOINTS (brick & tile)	4347	33333333355	LNNNNNNFFNNFFNFNOONN	NNNN4NNNNNNNNNN	D,J,T	132	492	06.02.02	7100	000000	81008
590.262-010	CRYSTAL GROWING TECHNICIAN (electron. comp.)	4336	23222233353	MONNNNNOOONFFNFNFFN	NNNN4NNNNNNNNNN	T,J	147	587	06.02.18	7479	470105	92902
590.262-014	TEST TECHNICIAN, SEMICONDUCTOR PROCESSING EQUIPMENT (electron. comp.)	4347	22333223355	LNNNNNNNFFNOONFNOONN	NNON4NNNNNNNNNN	V,T,J	212	587	06.01.05	6881	470105	92902
590.282-010	EPITAXIAL REACTOR TECHNICIAN (electron. comp.)	4446	23322232354	MONNNNNNFFFNNNNNNFN	NNNN4NNNNNNNNNN	V,T,J	147	587	06.01.03	3711	150303	92923
590.362-010	FORMING-PROCESS WORKER (elec. equip.)	3335	34423433355	LNNNNNNFFONFFNFNOONN	NNNN4NNNNNNNNNN	P,J,T	154	589	06.02.11	6960	000000	95099
590.362-014	IMPREGNATING-MACHINE OPERATOR (metal prod., nec)	3224	34343443355	MMNNNNNFFFNNFFNFNNN	NNON4NNONNNNNN	V,J	152	557	06.02.18	7479	000000	92997
590.362-018	GROUP LEADER, SEMICONDUCTOR PROCESSING (electron. comp.)	3227	23343333355	LNNNNNNFFNFFNFNFNNN	NNNN3NNNNNNNNNN	V,P,J	147	587	06.02.18	7679	470105	92902
590.362-022	MICROELECTRONICS TECHNICIAN (electron. comp.)	4436	33333433344	LNNNNNNFFFNOONFFFON	NNON3NNNNNNNNNN	J,V,T	147	587	06.01.03	7675	000000	92902
590.364-010	LEAD WORKER, WAFER PRODUCTION (electron. comp.)	3236	34443444455	MNNNNNNFFONFFNONNNNNN	NNNN4NNONNNNNN	D,P,J,T	051	587	06.02.01	7679	470105	92902
590.365-010	IRON-PLASTIC BULLET MAKER (ordnance)	3233	34434344345	HFNFNQNFFONFFNFNONNN	NNFN4NNNNNNNNNN	J,T	143	374	06.04.10	7820	000000	92998
590.367-010	INSPECTOR II (fabrication, nec)	3225	33443434353	LNNNNNNFFFOONCCCCCC	NNNN4NNOONNNNNN	J,T	212	619	06.03.01	7675	000000	83005
590.382-010	OPERATOR, AUTOMATED PROCESS (electron. comp.)	3334	33322433255	MMNNONNNFFFNNNNNNFN	NNON3NNNNNNNNNN	V,T	111	587	06.02.18	7675	000000	92923
590.382-014	CRYSTAL GROWER (comm. equip.; electron. comp.)	3235	33322333353	MMNNONNNFFFNNONFNFN	NNFN4NNNNNNNNNN	T,J	147	586	06.02.18	7675	000000	92902
590.382-018	EPITAXIAL REACTOR OPERATOR (electron. comp.)	3334	33344343455	LNNNNNNFFFNNNONFNFFN	NNON4NNNNNNNNNN	J,T	147	587	06.02.18	7679	000000	92902
590.382-022	ION IMPLANT MACHINE OPERATOR (electron. comp.)	3334	33334343455	LNNNNNNFFFNNNNONNN	NNNN3NNNNNNONNN	T,J	147	587	06.02.18	7679	000000	92902
590.384-010	CHARGE PREPARATION TECHNICIAN (electron. comp.)	2224	34433333355	LNNNNNNFFONNNNONONN	NNNN4NNNNNNNNFN	T,R	147	587	06.02.32	7759	000000	92902
590.384-014	PRODUCTION TECHNICIAN, SEMICONDUCTOR PROCESSING EQUIPMENT (electron. comp.)	3225	33343334355	VONONNNFFFNNNNOFNOONN	NNON4NNNNNNNNNN	V,T	031	567	05.09.01	6140	470105	85128
590.464-010	PROCESSOR, SOLID PROPELLANT (chemical)	3334	32223333355	MMNNNNNFFFNNNNFFNNNN	NNON4NNNNNNNNNN	S,J,T	147	379	06.02.32	7759	000000	93999
590.487-010	COLOR WEIGHER (fabrication, nec)	3234	34344334354	LNNFNFNFNFNNNNFNNNON	NNNN4NONNNNNNNN	J,T	212	619	06.03.02	7840	000000	83005

DOT #	DOT Title & Industry	Trmg	Aptitude	Physical	Environment	Tempra	WkF	MPSMS	GOE	SOC	CIP	OES
590.662-010	CONTROLS OPERATOR, MOLDED GOODS (fabrication, nec)	3235	33343444454	LNNNNNNFFNNOONFNNNON	NNNN4NNNNNNNNN	D,J,T	136	619	06.02.18	7679	000000	92998
590.662-014	MECHANICAL OXIDIZER (fabrication, nec)	3335	34344444453	MNNNNNNFFONNNNFNNOFN	NNON4NOONNNNNNN	J	147	619	06.02.18	7679	000000	92998
590.662-018	MIXING-ROLL OPERATOR (fabrication, nec)	3234	34444444353	MNNNNNNNFFONNNNFNNNFN	NNFN4NNNNNNNNN	R,T	143	509	06.04.19	7664	000000	92965
590.662-022	STOVE-CARRIAGE OPERATOR (fabrication, nec)	3224	33433343355	MNNNNNNNFFONNNFNNNNN	NNON4NOONNNNNNN	R,J	141	619	06.02.18	7675	000000	92923
590.665-010	OVEN OPERATOR (fabrication, nec)	2123	44434433354	LNNNNNNNFFNNNNFNNOON	NNON3NONNNNNNN	J,T	141	619	06.04.14	7675	000000	92923
590.665-014	PRESS-MACHINE OPERATOR (fabrication, nec)	2222	44443444353	MNNNNNNNFFNNNNFNNNON	NNON4NOONNNNNNN	R	134	619	06.04.19	7667	000000	92971
590.665-018	WINDER OPERATOR (fabrication, nec)	2112	44434444354	HNNNNNNNFFONNNNFNNFON	NNNN4NNNNNNNNN	R,T	163	619	06.04.09	7679	000000	92998
590.667-010	STOVE-BOTTOM WORKER (fabrication, nec)	2122	44443434454	LNNNNNNNFFONNNNNNNNN	NNNO4NNNNNNNNN	R	141	619	06.04.09	8769	000000	98999
590.682-010	CALENDER OPERATOR (fabrication, nec)	3234	33434343454	LNNNNNNNFFNNNNNNNOON	NNON4NONNNNNNN	J,T	136	619	06.02.18	7663	000000	92971
590.684-010	CERAMIC CAPACITOR PROCESSOR (electron. comp.)	2223	44443433354	LNNNNNNNCCNNNNCNONON	NNON3NNONNNNNNN	T	147	587	06.04.08	7679	470105	92998
590.684-014	ELECTRONIC-COMPONENT PROCESSOR (electron. comp.)	2223	44443433354	LNNNNNNNFFONNNNNONFOON	NNNN3NNNNNNNNN	R,U	147	587	06.04.19	7679	470105	92902
590.684-018	ETCHED-CIRCUIT PROCESSOR (electron. comp.)	3334	34432543354	LNNNNNNNFFNNNNFNCOON	NNNN4NONNNNNNN	T	111	587	06.02.32	7757	470105	93951
590.684-022	SEMICONDUCTOR PROCESSOR (electron. comp.)	2223	34443444355	MNNNNNNNFFNNONFNFNNN	NNNN3NNONNNNNNN	R,T,U	147	587	06.04.32	7679	470105	92902
590.684-026	ETCHER-STRIPPER, SEMICONDUCTOR WAFERS (electron. comp.)	2122	44543434454	MNNNNNNOOFNNNNFNOOON	NNNN3NONNNNNNON	R,U	182	587	06.04.19	7679	000000	92902
590.684-030	MATERIAL PREPARATION WORKER (electron. comp.)	2224	34444444355	MNNNNNNFFONNNNFNNNNN	NNNN4NONNNNNNNOO	R,T	212	587	06.03.02	7759	000000	93999
590.684-034	PHOTO MASK CLEANER (electron. comp.)	2122	44544444455	LNNNNNNNFFONNNNONNNNN	NNNN3NNNNNNNNN	T,U	182	587	06.04.34	7759	000000	98905
590.684-038	POLYSILICON PREPARATION WORKER (electron. comp.)	2222	44433434344	VNNNNNNNFFNNONFNFN	NNNN4NNONNNNNNN	R,U	057	349	06.04.19	7679	000000	92998
590.684-042	INTEGRATED CIRCUIT FABRICATOR (electron. comp.)	3223	44433443354	LNNNNNNNFFNNNNNFNOOON	NNNN3NNNNONNNNON	R,T,U	147	587	06.04.34	7740	000000	92902
590.685-010	BACKING-IN-MACHINE TENDER (fabrication, nec)	2112	44544544345	HNNNNNNNFFNNNNNNFNNN	NNNN4NNNNNNNNN	R	133	619	06.04.19	7675	000000	92923
590.685-014	COATING-MACHINE OPERATOR (fabrication, nec)	3234	33444434354	MNNNNNNNFFONNNNFNNNON	NNOO4NONNNNNNN	R,T	151	619	06.04.21	7669	000000	92953
590.685-018	DIAMOND BLENDER (cutlery-hrdwr.)	2224	34444344355	MNNNNNNNFFNNNNFNNNNN	NNNN4NNNNNNNNN	R,T	143	549	06.04.19	7542	000000	91911
590.685-022	DIPPER (fabrication, nec)	2123	44444433344	MNNNNNNNFFNNNNONNNNN	NNNF4NNNNNNNNN	R,T	151	619	06.04.21	7669	000000	92953
590.685-026	DRY-CHARGE-PROCESS ATTENDANT (elec. equip.)	3224	34434433344	MNNNONONFFFFNNNNFNNONN	NNNO4NFNNNNNNN	R,J,T	031	589	06.04.19	7673	000000	92958
590.685-034	FIRER (jewelry-silver.)	2123	44444433454	LNNNNNNNFFONNNNONOOFN	NNON3NNNNNNNNN	R,T	141	611	06.04.21	7675	470408	92923
590.685-038	HEEL SPRAYER, MACHINE (boot & shoe)	2123	44433444344	LNNNNNNNFFONNNNFNNNON	NNNN3NNNNNNNNN	R,J,T	153	522	06.04.21	7669	480304	92953
590.685-042	IRONER (button & notion)	2112	44434444455	LNNONNNOOONNNNNONNNNN	NNNN3NNNNNNNNN	R	032	618	06.04.02	7679	000000	92998
590.685-046	JEWELRY COATER (jewelry-silver.)	2122	44444444454	LNNNNNNNFFONNNNFNNNNN	NNNN3NNNNNNNNN	R,T	153	611	06.04.21	7543	470408	91926
590.685-050	ROLL-UP-GUIDER OPERATOR (fabrication, nec)	2114	34443434344	MNNNNNNNFFONNNNFNFOON	NNNN4NNONNNNNNON	R,T	163	619	06.04.09	7678	000000	92944
590.685-054	WAD IMPREGNATOR (ordnance)	2122	34443444454	MNNNNNNNFFONNNNFNNNON	NNNN4NNONNNNNNN	R,J,T	152	587	06.04.14	7669	000000	92953
590.685-058	WAD LUBRICATOR (ordnance)	2122	44444444445	MNNNNNNNFFONNNNFNNNON	NNNN4NNNNNNNNN	R,T	033	374	06.04.14	7679	000000	92998
590.685-062	CLEANING MACHINE TENDER, SEMICONDUCTOR WAFERS (electron. comp.)	2222	44444433355	LNNNNNNNFFNNNNFNNCNNONN	NNNN4NNNNNNNNN	R,U,T	031	587	06.04.39	7673	000000	92958
590.685-066	COATING EQUIPMENT OPERATOR, PRINTED CIRCUIT BOARDS (electron. comp.)	2223	34444434355	MNNNONNCCFNNNNFNONNN	NNON3NNNNNNNNN	R,U	151	587	06.04.19	7669	000000	92953
590.685-070	DIFFUSION FURNACE OPERATOR, SEMICONDUCTOR WAFERS (electron. comp.)	2224	34434434355	LNNNNNNNFFNNNNFNFFNN	NNON3NNNNNNNNN	R,T,U	133	587	06.04.19	7675	000000	92902
590.685-074	ETCH OPERATOR, SEMICONDUCTOR WAFERS (electron. comp.)	2122	44443343454	LNNNNNNNFFNNNNFNFOON	NNNN3NNNNNNNNN	R,U	182	587	06.04.19	7549	000000	92198
590.685-078	ETCHER (electron. comp.)	2222	44444444455	MNNNNNNNCCFNNNONFNNNN	NNNN4NNNNNNNNN	R,U	182	587	06.04.19	7679	000000	92902
590.685-082	STRIPPER-ETCHER, PRINTED CIRCUIT BOARDS (electron. comp.)	2223	34444434354	MNNNNNNNNFFONNNNFNNFNN	NNNN4NFNNNNNNN	R,T,U	182	587	06.04.19	7549	000000	92958
590.685-086	METALLIZATION EQUIPMENT TENDER, SEMICONDUCTORS (comm. equip.; electron. com)	3223	34444434354	MNNNNNNNFFONNNNFNONFNN	NNNN4NFNNNNNNN	R,T,U	147	587	06.04.19	7675	000000	98999
590.685-090	CURING OVEN ATTENDANT (aircraft mfg.; electron. comp.)	3224	44434444455	MNNNNNNNFFONNNFNFNN	NNON3NNNNNNNOO	R,U	141	587	06.04.19	7549	000000	92923
590.685-094	PLASMA ETCHER, PRINTED CIRCUIT BOARDS (electron. comp.)	2113	34443443454	LNNNNNNNFFONNNNFNFNFNN	NNON4NNNNNNNNN	R,T,U	182	587	06.04.19	7549	000000	92198
590.685-098	ROOFING-MACHINE TENDER (nonmet. min.)	2222	44444444455	LOONNNNNFFONNNNFFONON	NNNN4NNNNNNNNN	R,T	133	503	06.04.09	7679	000000	92998
590.685-102	WAFER CLEANER (electron. comp.)	2112	44444444445	LNNNNNNNFFNNNNFNNNNN	NNNN4NNNNNNNNN	R,U	031	587	06.04.19	7673	000000	92958
590.686-010	COATING-MACHINE-OPERATOR HELPER (fabrication, nec)	1112	44444433354	MNNNNNNNFFONNNFNFFNN	NNON4NOONNNNNNN	R,T	151	619	06.04.21	8618	000000	98999
590.686-014	GUIDER (fabrication, nec)	2112	44434433354	MNNNNNNNFFFNNNNNNNNN	NNNN4NNNNNNNNN	R	011	619	06.04.40	8725	000000	98502
590.687-010	LABORER (fabrication, nec)	2112	44444444444	HNNFNNNFFONNNNNONNNNN	NNNN4NNNNNNNNN	R	143	619	06.04.34	8769	000000	98999
590.687-014	PLASTIC-JOINT MAKER (brick & tile)	2113	44444444355	HNNNNNNNFFONNNNNNONNNN	NNNN3NNNNNNNNN	R	132	492	06.04.32	7740	000000	93999
590.687-018	RACK LOADER (fabrication, nec)	1111	44444444445	MNNNNNNNFFONNNNNONNNN	NNNN4NNNNNNNNN	R	011	619	06.04.40	8725	000000	98502
590.687-022	RUG CUTTER (fabrication, nec)	1111	44444444355	MNNNNNNNFFONNNNNNNON	NNNN3NNNNNNNNN	R	054	619	06.04.24	7753	000000	93926
599.132-010	SUPERVISOR, TUMBLERS (ordnance)	4337	33343333454	LNNNNNNNFFONFFNONNNNN	NNNN4NONNNNNNNNO	D,J,P	031	370	06.02.01	7100	520205	81008
599.137-010	SUPERINTENDENT, SEED MILL (agriculture)	3236	33334334354	MONONONFFFFFNNFFOFN	NNNN4NNONNNNNNN	D,V,P,J	145	311	06.02.01	7100	010501	81008
599.382-010	PAINT-SPRAYER OPERATOR, AUTOMATIC (any industry)	3235	34343434354	MNNNNNNNFFONNNNONNNON	NNNN4NONNNNNNN	J,T	153	495	06.02.21	7479	000000	92951
599.382-014	EXHAUST EQUIPMENT OPERATOR (electron. comp.)	4446	33333444354	MNNNNNNNFFONNNONFNONON	NNNN3NNNNNNNNN	T	111	586	06.01.03	7479	000000	92997

DOT #	DOT Title & Industry	Trng	Aptitude	Physical	Environment	Tempra	WkF	MPSMS	GOE	SOC	CIP	OES
599.585-010	STERILIZER (medical ser.; pharmaceut.; protective dev.)	3233	33444444355	LNNNNNNFFONNNNFNNNNN	NNNN4NNNNNNNNNNN	R,T	141	493	06.04.19	7679	510799	92998
599.665-010	SEED-CLEANER OPERATOR (agriculture; oils & grease)	2112	44444434355	LNNNONNFFONNNNNONNNNN	NNNN4NCNNNNNNNNN	R	145	311	06.04.09	7666	000000	92962
599.682-010	PAINTER, ELECTROSTATIC (any industry)	3234	33344434353	LNNNONNFFNNNNFOONOF	NNNN4NFNNNNNNNNN	R,J,T	153	495	06.02.21	7756	460408	93947
599.682-014	IMPREGNATOR AND DRIER (elec. equip.; electron. comp.)	3235	33344333454	LNNONNNFFNNNNFOONOF	NNNF4NONNNNNNNOF	T	141	580	06.02.18	7675	470105	92923
599.684-010	EQUIPMENT CLEANER (any industry)	2122	44443434344	HOOOONFFONNONFOOONON	NNNF4NOONNNNNNN	R	031	550	06.04.39	8750	000000	98905
599.684-014	SAMPLER (steel & rel.)	2223	33443344455	LNNONNNFFONNNNNNNNNN	ONNN4NONNNNNNNN	R,J,T	142	505	06.03.02	7840	000000	83005
599.685-014	BRAN MIXER (grain-feed mills)	2112	44444434355	HNNNNNNFFONNNNNNNNNN	NNNN4NONNNNNNNN	R,T	143	301	06.04.19	7664	000000	92965
599.685-018	CENTRIFUGE OPERATOR, PLASMA PROCESSING (medical ser.; pharmaceut.)	2222	33344333353	LNNONONFFFNNNNFNNFFN	NONN3NNNNNNNNNN	R,J,T	212	493	06.04.11	7666	200303	92962
599.685-022	DEFINER (button & notion)	2112	44444444355	MNNFNFNFONNNNNONNN	NONN4NNNNNNNNNN	R	051	618	06.04.10	7673	000000	92958
599.685-026	DIPPER (any industry)	2112	44444444454	MNNFNFNFONNNNNONNN	NNNN4NNNNNNNNNN	R	151	460	06.04.10	7669	000000	92953
599.685-030	DIPPER AND BAKER (any industry)	2112	44444444344	MNNNNNNFFONNNNFNNNON	NNON4NONNNNNNNN	R,T	151	582	06.04.21	7669	000000	92953
599.685-034	DYER (fabrication, nec)	2222	44444444354	MNNNNNNFFONNNNFNNNON	NNNN4NONNNNNNNN	R,T	152	309	06.04.19	7639	000000	92953
599.685-038	FILTER WASHER AND PRESSER (beverage; chemical)	2122	44444434345	LNNFFNCCCNNNNNNNNN	NNNO4NNNNNNNNNN	R,T	031	499	06.04.19	7673	000000	92958
599.685-042	FILTER-PRESS TENDER (beverage; chemical)	2123	44444444454	LONONONFFONNNNFNNNON	NFNO3NNNNNNNNNN	R,T	145	395	06.04.19	7666	000000	92962
599.685-046	IMPREGNATING-TANK OPERATOR (any industry)	3224	34343334353	MFNONOOOCFNIFFNNNNCOC	NNNN4NNONNNNNNN	R,J,T	151	430	06.04.21	7669	000000	92953
599.685-050	IMPREGNATOR-AND-DRIER HELPER (elec. equip.; light. fix.)	2123	44444444455	MNNNNNNFFONNNNNONNNN	NNON3NONNNNNNNN	R,T	141	580	06.04.19	7669	000000	92953
599.685-054	LACQUERER (plastic prod.)	2113	44444434354	MNNNNNNFFONNNNFNNFN	NNNN4NONNNNNNNN	R,T	153	519	06.04.21	7677	000000	91926
599.685-058	MILL OPERATOR (any industry)	2123	44444434355	MONONNNOOONNNNNNNNN	NNNO4NONNNNNNNN	R,T	142	344	06.04.10	7543	000000	92965
599.685-062	OXIDIZED-FINISH PLATER (any industry)	2122	44444434354	MOOOOONFFFNNNNNNON	NNNN4NNNNNNNNNN	R,T	151	373	06.04.10	7543	000000	91926
599.685-066	PAINT-LINE OPERATOR (toy-sport equip.)	2123	44443434354	MOOOOONFFNNNNFNNNON	NNNN4NNNNNNNNNN	R,T	031	615	06.04.21	7669	460408	92953
599.685-070	PAINTER, TUMBLING BARREL (any industry)	3223	44443434354	MNNNNNNCCCNNNNFNNNON	NNNN4NNNNNNNNNN	J	151	495	06.04.21	7669	460408	92953
599.685-074	PAINTING-MACHINE OPERATOR (any industry)	2123	44444444454	MNNONONFFONNNNFNNNFN	NNNN3NONNNNNNNN	R,T	153	473	06.04.21	7669	460408	92953
599.685-078	POLISHER (button & notion)	2122	44444444354	MNNONNNCCFFNNNFNNNON	NNNO4NNNNNNNNNN	R	031	618	06.04.09	7679	000000	92998
599.685-082	SCREENER OPERATOR (any industry)	2122	44444444455	MNNNNNNFFONNNNNNNNN	NNNN4NNNNNNNNNN	R	145	340	06.04.09	7666	000000	92962
599.685-086	SHREDDER TENDER, PEAT (agriculture)	2222	34544533345	HNNFNFNFFNNNONFNNN	FNON4NFNNNNNNNN	R,T	147	319	03.04.01	7679	000000	92998
599.685-090	SPRAY-MACHINE TENDER (tinware)	3224	34443434344	LNNNNNNFFONNNNFNNNON	NNNN4NNNNNNNNNN	R,T	153	551	06.04.10	7543	000000	91926
599.685-094	SPRAYER, MACHINE (leather mfg.)	2122	44444444344	MNNNNNNFFONNNNFNNNON	NNNN3NONNNNNNNN	R	153	520	06.04.21	7669	460408	92953
599.685-098	TUBBER (jewelry-silver.)	2122	44444444355	LNNNNNNFFONNNNFNNNNN	NNNO4NNNNNNNNNN	R,T	051	611	06.04.02	7673	470408	92958
599.685-102	TUBE COATER (metal prod., nec)	2112	44434533345	LNNNNNNFFNNNNNNNNN	NNNN4NONNNNNNNN	R	153	559	06.04.21	7543	460408	91926
599.685-106	TUMBLER (clock & watch)	2122	44444433355	LNNOONFFNNNNNONNNN	NNNN4NNNNNNNNNN	R	051	607	06.04.02	7673	470408	92958
599.685-110	TUMBLER OPERATOR (any industry)	2112	44444444355	MNNNNNNFFONNNNFNNNNN	NNNN4NNNNNNNNNN	R	051	550	06.04.09	7677	470408	92965
599.685-114	WASHER, MACHINE (any industry)	2112	44444444454	MNNNNNNFFONNNNFNNNNN	NNNF4NNNNNNNNNN	R	031	492	06.04.09	7673	000000	92958
599.685-118	WASHING-MACHINE OPERATOR (any industry)	2122	44444444355	MNNNNNNFFONNNNFNNNNN	NNNO4NONNNNNNNN	R	031	519	06.04.39	7673	000000	92958
599.685-122	WATER TENDER (any industry)	2224	44444444355	LOOOONFFNNNNNNNNNN	NNNO4NONNNNNNNN	R	014	875	05.12.06	7679	000000	99999
599.685-126	SEED PELLETER (agriculture)	2122	44443344355	LNNNNNNFFNNNNNNNNN	ONON4NNNNNNNNNN	R	151	311	06.04.21	7669	000000	92953
599.685-130	PAINT STRIPPER (petrol. refin.)	3115	34443534355	HNNFNNNCCONNNNNNNNN	ONON4NNNNNNNNNN	R	013	541	06.04.40	7820	490299	98999
599.685-134	SCRUBBER MACHINE TENDER (electron. comp.)	2122	44544544455	MNNONNNCCONNNNFNNNNN	NNNN4NNNNNNNNNN	R	031	551	06.04.39	7673	000000	92958
599.686-010	MILL-OPERATOR HELPER (any industry)	1112	44444444345	MNNNNNNFFOFFNFNNNON	NNNN4NONNNNNNNN	R,U	142	587	06.04.19	7673	000000	98502
599.686-014	SPRAY-UNIT FEEDER (any industry)	2112	44444444355	LNNOOONFFONNNNFNNFON	NNNO4NONNNNNNNN	R	153	344	06.04.21	8725	000000	98502
599.687-010	BALLOON DIPPER (rubber goods)	2112	44444444355	MNNNNNNFFONNNNFNNNNN	NNNF3NNNNNNNNNN	R	153	495	06.04.21	8725	000000	98502
599.687-014	BOOKER (rubber goods; rubber tire)	1111	44444444355	LNNNNNNFFNNNNNNNNN	NNNF3NNNNNNNNNN	R	151	519	06.04.27	7756	000000	93947
599.687-018	LEAD HANDLER (ordnance)	2113	44444444355	HNNFNNNCCONNNNNNNNN	NNNN4NNNNNNNNNN	R	011	510	06.04.40	8769	000000	99999
599.687-022	NET WASHER (rubber goods)	1112	44544433355	LNNNNNNFFONNNNNNNNN	NNNF4NNNNNNNNNN	R	031	550	06.04.39	8750	490299	98905
599.687-026	SIPHON OPERATOR (medical ser.; pharmaceut.)	2112	44444444355	LNNNNNNFFONNNNNNNNN	NNNN3NNNNNNNNNN	R	031	568	06.03.02	7759	000000	93999
599.687-030	WASHER (any industry)	2112	44444444454	MNNNNNNFFONNNNONFNON	NNNF3NNNNNNNNNN	R	014	493	02.04.02	7820	000000	98999
599.687-034	DRUM CLEANER (petrol. refin.)	2112	44543434355	HNNFNNNFFONNNNNNNNN	NNNN4NNNNNNNNNN	R,U	031	530	06.04.39	8769	000000	98905
599.687-038	DRUM TESTER (petrol. refin.)	2112	44544533335	MNNNNNNFFONNNNNFNNNN	NNNN4NNONNNNNNN	R,U	212	559	06.03.02	8750	000000	83005
600.130-010	MACHINE-SHOP SUPERVISOR, TOOL (machine shop)	4448	23322333345	MNNNNNNFFOFFNFFNFON	NNNN4NNONNNNNNN	D,V,T,P,J	057	540	05.05.07	7100	480503	81008
600.131-014	SALVAGE ENGINEER (machinery mfg.)	4437	33333433354	MNNNNNNFFNFNFFFON	NNNN3NNNNNNNNNN	D,P,J,T	212	568	06.01.01	7100	480503	81008
600.260-014	EXPERIMENTAL MECHANIC (motor-bicycles)	4438	33323433244	MNNNNNNFFNFNFFFN	NNNN4NNONNNNNNN	V,J,T	121	595	05.05.09	7329	480503	92197
600.260-018	MODEL MAKER, FIREARMS (ordnance)	4438	33322433254	MNNNNNNFFFNNNFNFNN	NNNN4NNNNNNNNNN	V,J,T	121	373	05.05.07	6817	480501	89108

DOT #	DOT Title & Industry	Trng	Aptitude	Physical	Environment	Tempra	WkF	MPSMS	GOE	SOC	CIP	OES
600.260-022	MACHINIST, EXPERIMENTAL (machine shop)	4438	23322333254	HNNOOONFFFOOONFNFOON	NNNN4NNOONNNNNN	V,T,J	057	566	05.05.07	6813	480503	89108
600.261-010	ASSEMBLER, STEAM-AND-GAS TURBINE (engine-turbine)	4338	33322432245	MOOOOOOFFNNNNFNFONONN	NNNN3NNNNNNNNNN	J	057	561	05.05.07	6812	480503	93105
600.280-010	INSTRUMENT MAKER (any industry)	4437	33322433255	MNNNNNNFFNNNNFNFNOONN	NNNN3NNNNNNNNNN	V,J,T	121	580	05.05.11	6813	480503	89105
600.280-014	INSTRUMENT-MAKER AND REPAIRER (petrol. & gas)	4427	33234432355	LNNOOONCCCNNNNFNFFNN	NNNN3NNNNNNNNNN	V,J,T	111	580	05.05.10	6813	480503	89105
600.280-018	INSTRUMENT-MAKER APPRENTICE (any industry)	4437	33322433255	MNNNNNNFFFONONNFNOONN	NNNN3NNNNNNNNNN	V,J,T	121	580	05.05.11	6813	480503	89105
600.280-022	MACHINIST (machine shop)	4447	23322432254	MNNNOONFFFONONFNFOON	NNNN4NOFNNNNNNN	J,T,V	057	550	05.05.07	6813	480503	89108
600.280-026	MACHINIST APPRENTICE (machine shop)	4447	23322432254	MNNOOONFFFONONFNFOON	NNNN4NOFNNNNNNN	J,T,V	057	550	05.05.07	6813	480503	89108
600.280-030	MACHINIST APPRENTICE, AUTOMOTIVE (automotive ser.)	4337	33223433355	MNNNONNNFFNNNNFNNOONN	NNNN4NNOONNNNNN	V,J,T	057	591	05.05.07	6813	480503	89108
600.280-034	MACHINIST, AUTOMOTIVE (automotive ser.)	4337	33323433355	MNNONNNFFNNNNNFNNOONN	NNNN4NNONNNNNNN	V,J,T	057	591	05.05.07	6813	480503	89108
600.280-042	MAINTENANCE MACHINIST (machine shop)	4437	33323333344	MOOOOOOFFFONONFNFOON	NNNN4NNONNNNNNN	V,T,J	057	560	05.05.07	6813	480503	89108
600.280-046	PATTERNMAKER APPRENTICE, METAL (foundry)	4438	33322433354	MNNNNNNFFFONNNFNFONN	NNNN4NNNNNNNNNN	V,J,T	057	540	05.05.07	6817	480501	89114
600.280-050	PATTERNMAKER, METAL (foundry)	4438	33322433354	MNNNNNNFFFONNNFNOFON	NNNN4NNNNNNNNNN	V,J,T	057	540	05.05.07	6817	480501	89114
600.280-054	SAMPLE MAKER, APPLIANCES (house. appl.; light. fix.)	4438	33322433244	LNNONNNFFFONONFNFOON	NNNN4NNNNNNNNNO	V,J,T	057	583	05.05.07	6817	480501	89114
600.281-010	FLUID-POWER MECHANIC (any industry)	4437	23222333333	LNNONNNFFFOONNFNOFN	NNNN3NNNNNNNNNN	J,T	057	568	05.05.07	6130	480503	89108
600.281-014	LAY-OUT INSPECTOR (machine shop)	4436	33223433355	MNNOOONFFOONNFNONNN	NNNN3NNNNNNNNNN	J,T	241	542	06.01.05	6881	480503	83002
600.281-018	LAY-OUT WORKER (machine shop)	4437	23322433355	MNNNNNNFFNOONFNFFNN	NNNN4NNNNNNNNNN	J,T	241	540	05.05.07	6821	480503	89117
600.281-022	MACHINE BUILDER (machinery mfg.; machine tools)	4437	33322433355	MNNOOONFFNNNNFNNOONN	NNNN4NNNNNNNNNN	V,J,T	121	566	05.05.09	6812	480503	93105
600.360-010	MACHINE TRY-OUT SETTER (machine tools)	4437	33234433355	MNNNNNNFFNNNNFNFFNN	NNNN4NNNNNNNNNN	V,T,J	057	566	06.01.05	7329	480503	91505
600.360-014	MACHINE SETTER (machine shop)	4437	33322333355	MNNNNNNFFFOOONFNFFNN	NNNN4NNONNNNNNN	V,T,J	057	560	06.01.02	7329	000000	91505
600.380-010	FIXTURE MAKER (light. fix.)	4337	33323433255	LNNNNNNFFNNNNFNFONN	NNNN4NNFNNNNNNN	V,J,T	057	584	05.05.07	7329	480503	89108
600.380-014	MACHINE SET-UP OPERATOR (machine shop)	4436	33333333354	MNNOOONFFFOOFNFFOON	NNNN4NNNNNNNNNN	T,J	057	540	06.01.03	7329	480503	91505
600.380-018	MACHINE SETTER (clock & watch)	4437	33322432255	MNNNNNNFFFOOONFNFFNN	NNNN4NNNNNNNNNN	V,J,T	057	540	06.01.02	7329	470408	91505
600.380-022	MACHINE SETTER (clock & watch)	4336	33333433345	MNNNNNNFFNNNNFNFNNN	NNNN4NNNNNNNNNF	V,T	102	561	06.01.03	6812	480503	93105
600.380-026	TURBINE-BLADE ASSEMBLER (engine-turbine)	4448	23323333355	LNNNNNNFFFFFNFOOFNN	NNNN4NNNNNNNNNN	V,D,P,J	057	566	05.05.07	7100	150603	81008
601.130-010	TOOL-AND-DIE SUPERVISOR (machine shop)	4448	23222332254	MNNOOONFFFOONONFNFOON	NNNN4NOFNNNNNNN	J,T,V	057	566	05.05.07	6811	480507	89102
601.260-010	TOOL-AND-DIE MAKER (machine shop)	4448	23222332254	MNNOOONFFFONONFNFOON	NNNN4NOFNNNNNNN	J,T,V	057	566	05.05.07	6811	480507	89102
601.260-014	TOOL-AND-DIE-MAKER APPRENTICE (machine shop)	4448	23222332354	LNNNNNNCCONNNFNFCNN	NNNN4NOFNNNNNNN	V,J,T	241	566	05.05.07	6811	480507	89102
601.261-010	INSPECTOR, SET-UP AND LAY-OUT (machine shop)	4437	33322333354	MNNOOONFFONNNFNFFNN	NNNN4NNNNNNNNNN	J,T	057	566	05.05.07	6881	150603	83002
601.280-010	DIE MAKER, STAMPING (machine shop)	4437	33322433355	MNNNOONFFFONNNFNFNN	NNNN4NNNNNNNNNN	J,T	057	566	05.05.07	6811	480507	89102
601.280-014	DIE MAKER, TRIM (machine shop)	4437	33322433355	MNNOOONFFONNNFNFNNN	NNNN4NNNNNNNNNN	J,T	057	566	05.05.07	6811	480507	89102
601.280-018	DIE MAKER, WIRE DRAWING (machine shop)	4337	33322433355	MNNNOONFFFONNNFNFFNN	NNNN4NNNNNNNNNN	J,T	057	566	05.05.07	6811	480507	89102
601.280-022	DIE SINKER (machine shop)	4338	33322433355	MNNNOONFFFONNNFNFFNN	NNNN4NNNNNNNNNN	J,T	057	566	05.05.07	6811	480507	89102
601.280-030	MOLD MAKER, DIE-CASTING AND PLASTIC MOLDING (machine shop)	4447	23323433355	HOOOOONFFFOOONFNFONN	NNNN4NNNNNNNNNO	J	057	566	05.05.07	6811	480507	89102
601.280-034	TAP-AND-DIE-MAKER TECHNICIAN (clock & watch)	4437	33322443354	LNNNNNNFFFONNNFNNFNN	NNNN4NNNNNNNNNN	J,T	057	566	05.05.07	6817	480507	89114
601.280-038	TEMPLATE MAKER, EXTRUSION DIE (machine shop)	4448	23222333354	MNNOOONFFFONONFNFOON	NNNN4NNNNNNNNNN	V,T,J	241	566	05.05.07	6881	480507	89102
601.280-042	TOOL MAKER (machine shop)	4337	33322432255	MNNNOONFFFOONONFNFNN	NNNN4NOFNNNNNNN	J,T	121	550	05.07.01	6881	480507	91505
601.280-054	TOOL-MACHINE SET-UP OPERATOR (machine shop)	4437	33322433355	MNNOOONFFOONONFNFNN	NNNN4NOFNNNNNNN	J,T	057	550	05.05.07	7329	480503	89102
601.280-058	TOOL-MAKER APPRENTICE (machine shop)	4447	23333333354	MNNNNNNFFFONNNFNOFFNN	NNNN4NNNNNNNNNN	J,T	121	566	05.05.07	6811	480507	89102
601.281-010	DIE MAKER, BENCH, STAMPING (machine shop)	4437	33322432254	MNNNNNNFFFONONFNFNF	NNNN4NNNNNNNNNN	J,T	057	566	05.05.09	6811	480507	89102
601.281-014	DIE-TRY-OUT WORKER, STAMPING (machine shop)	4337	23323433354	MNNOOONFFOOONFNFNFO	NNNN4NNNNNNNNNN	J,T	121	566	06.01.05	6881	480503	89102
601.281-018	INSPECTOR, GAUGE AND INSTRUMENT (machine shop)	4448	23222433354	MNNNNNCCONNNFNFCON	NNNN3NNNNNNNNNN	V,T,J	212	566	05.07.01	6881	480503	83002
601.281-022	INSPECTOR, TOOL (machine shop)	4337	33322432255	MNNNNNNFFOONNNFNFFON	NNNN3NNNNNNNNNN	J,T	211	566	05.05.07	6881	480507	83002
601.281-026	TOOL MAKER, BENCH (machine shop)	4447	33322433355	MNNOOONFFFONNNFNFFNN	NNNN4NNNNNNNNNN	T,J	121	566	05.05.09	6811	480507	89102
601.281-030	TOOL AND FIXTURE REPAIRER (auto. mfg.)	4436	33333433344	MNNNNNNFFNNNNFNFFNN	NNNN4NNNNNNNNNN	V,J,T	057	566	05.05.07	6829	470303	85119
601.380-010	CARBIDE OPERATOR (machine shop)	4337	33432432254	MNNNNNNFFFONNNFNFOON	NNNN4NNNNNNNNNN	J	057	566	05.05.07	6130	480503	89102
601.381-010	DIE FINISHER (machine shop)	4337	33322432255	MNNNNNNFFFONNNFNFFNN	NNNN3NNNNNNNNNN	V,J,T	057	566	05.05.07	6811	480507	89111
601.381-014	DIE MAKER (jewelry-silver.)	3326	34333433355	LNNNNNNCCCNNNNCNCFNN	NNNN4NNNNNNNNNN	J,T	051	566	05.05.07	6816	480507	89102
601.381-018	DIE POLISHER (nonfer. metal)	4337	33322432255	MNNNNNFFFONNNNFNFNN	NNNN3NNNNNNNNNN	V,J,T	057	566	05.05.07	6811	480507	89102
601.381-022	DIE-MAKER APPRENTICE (jewelry-silver.)	4337	33322433355	MNNNNNNCCCNNNFNFFNN	NNNN3NNNNNNNNNN	J,T	136	568	06.01.04	6811	480507	89102
601.381-026	PLASTIC TOOL MAKER (machine shop)	4337	33322432254	MNNNNNNCCCNNNNFNFCNN	NNNN3NONNNNNNNN	V,J,T	132	566	05.05.07	6130	480503	89102
601.381-030	PLASTIC-FIXTURE BUILDER (machine shop)	4337	34333433354	MNNNNNNCCCNNNNFNFFON	NNNN4NNONNNNNNN	J,T	132	566	05.05.07	6811	480503	89102
601.381-034	SAW MAKER (cutlery-hrdwr.)	4436	34332433354	LNNNNNNFFFNNNNFNFFNN	NNNN4NNONNNNNNN	J,T	102	552	05.05.07	6811	480501	89102

DOT #	DOT Title & Industry	Trng	Aptitude	Physical	Environment	Tempra	WkF	MPSMS	GOE	SOC	CIP	OES
601.381-038	TEMPLATE MAKER (any industry)	4437	33323433345	MNNONONFFFONNFNFFNN	NNNN4NNONNNNON	T,J	102	566	06.01.04	6817	480501	89114
601.381-042	DIE MAKER, ELECTRONIC (machine shop)	4327	34333333355	MNNNNNNFFNOONFNFNNN	NNNN4NNNNNNNNNN	T,J	057	566	05.05.07	6811	480507	89102
601.482-010	PROFILE-GRINDER TECHNICIAN (clock & watch)	3336	34322432255	LNNNNNNFFFNNNNNFFNN	NNNN4NNNNNNNNNO	J,T	051	566	05.05.07	7322	480503	91114
601.682-010	TOOL DRESSER (any industry)	3225	34443434354	MNNNNNNFFFNNNNNFFNN	NNNN4NNNNNNNNNO	J,T	134	552	06.04.02	7529	480503	92198
602.280-010	GEAR-CUTTING-MACHINE SET-UP OPERATOR, TOOL (machine shop)	4437	33322433355	MNNNNNNCCFNNNFNFNNN	NNNN4NNNNNNNNNN	J	055	568	06.01.03	7529	480503	91505
602.360-010	GRINDER SET-UP OPERATOR, GEAR, TOOL (machine shop)	4337	33322333355	LNNONNNFFFNNNNFNFFNN	NNNN4NNNNNNNNNN	J	051	540	06.01.03	7329	480503	91114
602.362-010	GEAR INSPECTOR (machine shop)	4336	33332433354	MNNNNNNFFFONNNFNFFNN	NNNN3NNNNNNNNNN	J,T	212	595	06.03.01	7820	480503	83005
602.362-014	GEAR-SORTING-AND-INSPECTING MACHINE OPERATOR (machine shop)	3324	34433433454	LNNNNNNCCONNNCNCCON	NNNN4NNNNNNNNNN	J,T	121	595	06.03.01	7529	480503	83005
602.380-010	GEAR-CUTTING-MACHINE SET-UP OPERATOR (machine shop)	4336	33333433345	MNNNNNNCCFNNNFNFFNN	NNNN4NNNNNNNNNN	J,T	055	568	06.01.03	7329	480503	91505
602.382-010	GEAR HOBBER SET-UP OPERATOR (machine shop)	3335	33333433355	MNNNNNNFFFNNNFNFFNN	NNNN4NNNNNNNNNN	J,T	055	568	06.03.01	7329	480503	91505
602.382-014	GEAR-GENERATOR SET-UP OPERATOR, SPIRAL BEVEL (machine shop)	3335	33333433355	MNNNOONFFFNNNNFNFFNN	NNNN4NNNNNNNNNN	J,T	055	568	06.02.02	7329	480503	91505
602.382-018	GEAR-GENERATOR SET-UP OPERATOR, STRAIGHT BEVEL (machine shop)	3335	33333433355	MNNOOONFFFNNNNFNFFNN	NNNN4NNNNNNNNNN	J,T	055	568	06.02.02	7329	480503	91505
602.382-022	GEAR-MILLING-MACHINE SET-UP OPERATOR (machine shop)	3335	33333433355	MNNNOONFFFNNNNFNFFNN	NNNN4NNNNNNNNNN	J,T	055	568	06.02.02	7329	480503	91505
602.382-026	GEAR-SHAPER SET-UP OPERATOR (machine shop)	3335	33333433355	MNNONNNFFFNNNNFNFFNN	NNNN4NNNNNNNNNN	J,T	055	568	06.02.02	7329	480503	91505
602.382-030	GEAR-SHAVER SET-UP OPERATOR (machine shop)	3336	33333433355	MNNONNNFFFNNNNFNFFNN	NNNN4NNNNNNNNNN	J,T	055	568	06.01.03	7329	480503	91505
602.382-034	GRINDER, GEAR (machine shop)	3335	34333433355	MNNONNNFFFNNNNFNFFNN	NNNN4NNNNNNNNNN	J,T	051	568	06.02.02	7322	480503	91114
602.482-010	GEAR-LAPPING-MACHINE OPERATOR (machine shop)	3335	33333433355	MNNNNNNFFFNNNFNFFNN	NNNN4NNNNNNNNNN	J,T	051	568	06.02.02	7324	480503	91114
602.685-010	GEAR-CUTTING-MACHINE OPERATOR, PRODUCTION (machine shop)	2223	44433433355	MNNNNNNFFFNFNNNNNN	NNNN4NNNNNNNNNN	R,T	057	568	06.04.02	7529	480503	91508
603.130-010	SUPERVISOR, GRINDING (any industry)	4337	33333444355	MNNNNOONFFNFFNFNNNNN	NNNN4NNNNNNNNNN	D,J,P	051	540	06.02.01	7100	520205	81008
603.137-010	FILING-AND-POLISHING SUPERVISOR (ordnance)	4447	33333444355	MNNNNNNFFNFFNFNOONN	NNNN3NNNNNNNNNN	V,D,P,J	373	373	06.02.01	7100	520205	81008
603.260-010	GRINDER SET-UP OPERATOR, THREAD TOOL (machine shop)	4437	33322433355	MNNOOONFFFOONFNFNNN	NNNN4NNNNNNNNNN	J,T	051	540	06.01.03	7322	480503	91114
603.280-010	GRINDER OPERATOR, EXTERNAL, TOOL (machine shop)	4337	33322433355	MNNNNNNFFFNNNNFNFFNN	NNNN3NNNNNNNNNN	J,T	051	540	06.01.03	6816	480503	89111
603.280-014	GRINDER OPERATOR, SURFACE, TOOL (machine shop)	4337	33322433355	MNNNNNFFFNNNNFNFFNN	NNNN3NNNNNNNNNN	J,T	051	540	06.01.03	6816	480503	89111
603.280-018	GRINDER SET-UP OPERATOR, TOOL (machine shop)	4437	33322433355	MNNONNNFFFNNNNFNFFNN	NNNN4NNNNNNNNNN	J,T	051	540	06.01.03	6816	480503	89111
603.280-022	GRINDER SET-UP OPERATOR, INTERNAL (machine shop)	4337	33322433355	MNNOOONFFONONFNFFNN	NNNN4NNNNNNNNNN	J,T	051	541	06.01.03	6816	480503	89111
603.280-026	GRINDER SET-UP OPERATOR, JIG (machine shop)	4437	33322433355	LNNOONNFFFNNNNFNFFNN	NNNN4NNNNNNNNNN	J,T	051	540	06.01.03	6816	480503	89111
603.280-030	GRINDER SET-UP OPERATOR, UNIVERSAL (machine shop)	4437	33322433355	MNNOOONFFFNNNNFNFFNN	NNNN4NNNNNNNNNN	J,T	051	540	06.01.03	6816	480503	89111
603.280-034	JOB SETTER, HONING (machine shop)	4336	33333433355	MNNOOONFFFNNNNFNFFNN	NNNN4NNNNNNNNNN	J,T	051	540	06.01.02	7324	480503	91114
603.280-038	TOOL-GRINDER OPERATOR (machine shop)	4337	33322433355	MNNNNNNFFFONNNFNFFNN	NNNN4NNNNNNNNNN	J,T	051	566	06.01.03	6816	480503	89111
603.360-010	BUFFING-LINE SET-UP WORKER (any industry)	3225	33333433355	MNNFFNFFFNNOONFNFNNN	NNNN4NNNNNNNNNN	J,T	051	550	06.01.02	7322	480503	91114
603.380-010	GRINDER MACHINE SETTER (machine shop)	4336	33332433355	MNNOOONFFFNNNNFNFNNN	NNNN4NNNNNNNNNN	J,T	051	540	06.01.02	7322	480503	91114
603.382-010	BUFFING-MACHINE OPERATOR (any industry)	3224	33333434354	LNNNNNNFFFNNNNNFONN	NNNN4NNNNNNNNNN	J,T	051	540	06.02.02	7322	480503	91114
603.382-014	GRINDER SET-UP OPERATOR, CENTERLESS (machine shop)	3335	34433444355	MNNNONONFFFNNNNNFFNN	NNNN4NNNNNNNNNN	J,T	051	540	06.02.02	7322	480503	91114
603.382-018	HONING-MACHINE SET-UP OPERATOR (machine shop)	3225	34333444355	MNNNNNONFFFNNNNFNFNNN	NNNN4NNNNNNNNNN	J,T	051	552	06.02.02	7324	480503	91114
603.382-022	HONING-MACHINE SET-UP OPERATOR, TOOL (machine shop)	4336	34333444355	MNNONONFFFONNNFNFNNN	NNNN4NNNNNNNNNN	J,T	051	550	06.02.02	7322	480503	91114
603.382-026	LAPPING-MACHINE SET-UP OPERATOR (machine shop)	3226	34333433355	MNNONONFFFONNNFNFNNN	NNNN4NNNNNNNNNN	J,T	051	540	06.02.02	7324	480503	91114
603.382-030	PRINTING-ROLLER POLISHER (machine shop)	3226	34433533345	HNNNNNNFFFNNNNNFNOONN	NNNO4NNNNNNNNNN	J,T	055	567	06.02.09	7522	480503	91117
603.382-034	GRINDER SET-UP OPERATOR (machine shop)	3336	33333533355	MNNNNNNFFFONNNFNFFNN	NNNN4NNONNNNNNN	T	051	540	06.02.02	7322	000000	91114
603.382-038	KNIFE GRINDER (machine shop)	3235	34433433355	MNNONNNFFFONNNFNFNNN	NNNN4NNNNNNNNNN	T	051	552	06.02.02	7322	480503	91114
603.482-010	DEBURRER, STRIP (clock & watch)	3226	33332433355	MNNNNNFFFONNNFNFFNN	NNNN4NNNNNNNNNN	J,T	051	607	06.02.02	7322	480503	91114
603.482-030	GRINDER I (clock & watch)	3225	34433434355	LNNNNNNFFFONNNNFFNN	NNNN4NNNNNNNNNN	R,T	051	607	06.02.02	7522	470408	91114
603.482-034	HONING-MACHINE OPERATOR, PRODUCTION (machine shop)	3224	34433434355	MNNNONFFFNNNNFNFNNN	NNNN4NNNNNNNNNN	J,T	051	540	06.02.02	7322	480503	91114
603.664-010	TOOL GRINDER II (any industry)	2112	44543544355	MNNNNNNFFFNNNFNFNONN	NNNN4NNNNNNNNNN	R,T	051	552	06.02.01	7522	480503	91117
603.665-010	BUFFING-MACHINE TENDER (any industry)	3224	33443444355	MNNONONFFFONNNFNFNNN	NNNN4NNNNNNNNNN	R,T	051	550	06.04.02	7522	480503	91114
603.682-010	BUFFING-MACHINE OPERATOR, SILVERWARE (jewelry-silver.)	3324	34333433355	MNNONONFFFONNNFNFONN	NNNN4NNNNNNNNNN	J,T	055	612	06.02.02	7522	480503	91114
603.682-018	LINTER-SAW SHARPENER (oils & grease)	3324	34333433355	LNNOONNFFFONNNFNFONN	NNNN4NNNNNNNNNN	J,T	051	552	06.02.02	7322	480503	91117
603.682-022	MIRROR-FINISHING-MACHINE OPERATOR (jewelry-silver.)	3224	34433433355	MNNNONONFFFOONNFNFNNN	NNNN4NNNNNNNNNN	J,T	051	612	06.02.02	7322	480503	91114
603.682-026	POLISHING-MACHINE OPERATOR (any industry)	3224	34433544355	LNNNNNNFFFOONNNONONNN	NNNN4NNNNNNNNNN	R,T	051	373	06.02.02	7322	480503	91114
603.682-030	DRILL-BIT SHARPENER (electron. comp.)	3223	45433534355	LNNNNNNFFFONNNNFFNN	NNNN3NNNNNNNNNN	R,T	051	552	06.04.02	7322	470105	91108
603.685-010	BAND-REAMER-MACHINE OPERATOR (nonfer. metal)	2113	44445444355	MNNNNNNFFFNNNNFNFNNN	NNNN4NNNNNNNNNN	R,T	054	549	06.04.02	7522	480503	91117
603.685-014	BARREL POLISHER, INSIDE (ordnance)	2113	44443434355	LNNNNNNFFOONNNFNOONN	NNNN4NNNNNNNNNN	R,T	051	373	06.04.02	7522	480503	91117

DOT #	DOT Title & Industry	Trng	Aptitude	Physical	Environment	Tempra	WkF	MPSMS	GOE	SOC	CIP	OES
603.685-022	BEVEL POLISHER (clock & watch)	2223	4444444355	LNNNNNNFFFNNNFNNONN	NNNN4NNNNNNNNNN	R,T	051	607	06.02.02	7522	470408	91117
603.685-026	BIT-SHARPENER (any industry)	2113	44433433343	MNNNNNNNFFONNNFNFFNN	NNNN4NNNNNNNNNNO	R,T	051	567	06.04.02	7522	480503	91117
603.685-030	BIT-SHARPENER OPERATOR (mine & quarry)	2112	4444444455	MNNNNNNNFFONNNFNNONN	NNNN4NNNNNNNNNNN	R,T	051	564	05.12.02	7522	480503	91117
603.685-034	BOTTOM POLISHER (elec. equip.)	2112	4544544455	LNNONNNFFONNNNFNFFNN	NNNN4NNNNNNNNNNN	R,T	051	589	06.04.02	7522	480503	91117
603.685-038	BRUSH POLISHER (clock & watch)	2113	4444444355	SNNNNNNFFNNNNFNNNNN	NNNN3NNNNNNNNNN	R,T	051	607	06.04.02	7522	480503	91117
603.685-042	BURNISHER (clock & watch)	2112	4544543345	LNNNNNNCCFNNNNFNNNNN	NNNN3NNNNNNNNNN	R,T	051	607	06.04.02	7522	480503	91117
603.685-046	BURRER, MACHINE (clock & watch)	2112	4444544345	LNNNNNNFFNNNNFNNFFNN	NNNN4NNNNNNNNNN	R,T	051	607	06.04.02	7522	480503	91117
603.685-050	DEBURRER (button & notion)	2112	4443544355	LNNNNNNFFFONNNFNNONN	NNNN3NNNNNNNNNN	R,T	051	618	06.04.02	7522	480503	91117
603.685-054	FLAT POLISHER (clock & watch)	2114	4443433355	LNNNNNNCCFNNNNFNNONN	NNNN3NNNNNNNNNN	R,T	051	607	06.02.02	7522	480503	91117
603.685-058	GRINDER OPERATOR, AUTOMATIC (cutlery-hrdwr.)	2112	4543543335	LNNNNNNNFFONNNFNNOONN	NNNN4NNNNNNNNNN	R,T	051	550	06.04.02	7522	480503	91117
603.685-062	GRINDING MACHINE TENDER (machine shop)	3223	4444443355	MNNONNNFFONNNNFNFONN	NNNN4NOONNNNNN	T,U	051	540	06.04.02	7522	480503	91117
603.685-066	GRINDER, LAP (clock & watch)	2113	4444444355	LNNONONCCCNNNNFNNNNNN	NNNN3NNNNNNNNNN	R,T	051	607	06.04.02	7522	480503	91117
603.685-070	LAPPING-MACHINE OPERATOR, PRODUCTION (machine shop)	2223	4443433355	MNNONONFFNNNNFNNONN	NNNN4NNNNNNNNNN	R,T	051	540	06.04.02	7522	480503	91117
603.685-074	SHOT-GRINDER OPERATOR (ordnance)	2122	3343433355	MNNONNNFFONNNNFNNOONN	NNNN3NNNNNNNNNN	R,T	051	374	06.04.02	7522	480503	91117
603.685-078	SNAILER (clock & watch)	2112	4544543355	LNNNNNNFFNNNNFNNNNN	NNNN4NNNNNNNNNN	R	051	607	06.04.02	7522	000000	91117
603.685-082	STONER AND POLISHER, BEVEL FACE (clock & watch)	2113	4544534355	LNNNNNNFFFNNNONNNNN	NNNN3NNNNNNNNNN	R,T	051	607	06.04.02	7522	480503	91117
603.686-010	POLISHING-MACHINE-OPERATOR HELPER (any industry)	2112	4444544355	MNNNNNNFFONNNNONNNNN	NNNF4NNONNNNNN	R	051	373	06.04.02	8725	480503	98502
603.686-014	DEBURRER, PRINTED CIRCUIT BOARD PANELS (electron. comp.)	1112	4444444455	HNNNNNNCCFNNNNFNNNNN	NNNN4NNNNNNNNNN	R,U	051	587	06.04.09	8725	000000	98502
604.130-010	SUPERVISOR, ROLL SHOP (steel & rel.)	4337	3333333355	LNNNNNNNFONFFNNNNONN	NNNN4NFNNNNNNNN	V,D,P,J	057	568	06.02.01	7100	520205	81008
604.260-010	SCREW-MACHINE SET-UP OPERATOR, SWISS-TYPE (clock & watch)	4337	3332433255	MNNNNNNNFFONNNNFNFFNN	NNNN4NNNNNNNNNN	J,T	053	607	06.01.03	7312	480503	91105
604.280-010	ENGINE-LATHE SET-UP OPERATOR, TOOL (machine shop)	4447	3322433355	MNNONONFFFNNNNFNNOONN	NNNN4NNNNNNNNNN	J,T	053	540	06.01.03	7312	480503	91105
604.280-014	SCREW-MACHINE SET-UP OPERATOR, MULTIPLE SPINDLE (machine shop)	4338	3333433355	MNNNNNNFFNNNNFNNFFNN	NNNN4NNNNNNNNNN	J	057	541	06.01.03	7312	480503	91105
604.280-018	SCREW-MACHINE SET-UP OPERATOR, SINGLE SPINDLE (machine shop)	4337	3333433355	MNNNNNNFFNNNNFNNFFNN	NNNN4NNNNNNNNNN	J	055	566	06.01.03	7312	480503	91105
604.280-022	TURRET-LATHE SET-UP OPERATOR, TOOL (machine shop)	4447	3322433355	MNNONONFFFNNNNFNNNNN	NNNN4NNNNNNNNNN	J	053	540	06.01.03	7312	480503	91105
604.360-010	SETTER, AUTOMATIC-SPINNING LATHE (any industry)	4336	3322433355	MNNNNNNFFFNNNNFNNFFNN	NNNN4NNNNNNNNNN	J,T	055	550	06.01.03	7326	480503	91502
604.362-010	LATHE OPERATOR, NUMERICAL CONTROL (machine shop)	4336	3322433355	MNNNNNNFFFNNNNFNNFFNN	NNNN4NNNNNNNNNN	J,T	055	540	06.01.03	7312	480503	91105
604.380-010	CHUCKING-MACHINE SET-UP OPERATOR (machine shop)	4446	3322433355	MNNNFFFNNNNNFNFFNN	NNNN4NNNNNNNNNN	J,T	055	540	06.01.03	7312	480503	91105
604.380-014	CHUCKING-MACHINE SET-UP OPERATOR, MULTIPLE SPINDLE, VERTICAL (machine shop)	4446	3322433355	MNNNNNNFFNNNNFNNFNN	NNNN4NNNNNNNNNN	J,T	055	566	06.01.03	7312	480503	91105
604.380-018	ENGINE-LATHE SET-UP OPERATOR (machine shop)	4436	3333333345	MNNNNNNFFNNNNNFNFFNN	NNNN4NOFNNNNNN	T,J	055	541	06.01.03	7312	480503	91105
604.380-022	SCREW-MACHINE SET-UP OPERATOR (machine shop)	3336	3333433355	MNNOOONFFONNNFNFONN	NNNN4NCFNNNNON	T,J	053	540	06.01.03	7312	480503	91105
604.380-026	TURRET-LATHE SET-UP OPERATOR (ordnance)	4446	3322433345	MNNNNNNCCNNNNNFNNNNNN	NNNN4NNNNNNNNNN	J,T	053	540	06.04.02	7312	480503	91105
604.382-010	SCREW-MACHINE OPERATOR, MULTIPLE SPINDLE (machine shop)	3226	3433433355	MNNONONFFFONNNNFNNFFNN	NNNN3NNNNNNNNNN	J,T	057	541	06.02.02	7512	480503	91117
604.382-014	SCREW-MACHINE OPERATOR, SINGLE SPINDLE (machine shop)	3225	3433433355	MMNOOONFFFNNNNFNNNNNN	NNNN4NNNNNNNNNN	J,T	057	541	06.02.02	7512	480503	91117
604.666-010	THREADING-MACHINE FEEDER, AUTOMATIC I (machine shop)	2112	4444444455	HNNNOONFFNNNNONFNNNNN	NNNN4NNNNNNNNNN	R	055	555	06.04.02	8725	480503	98502
604.682-010	SCREW-MACHINE OPERATOR, SWISS-TYPE (clock & watch)	3326	3333433355	LNNONONFFFNNNNFNNFFNN	NNNN4NNNNNNNNNN	J,T	057	607	06.02.02	7512	470408	91117
604.682-014	THREADING-MACHINE OPERATOR (machine shop)	3335	3433433355	MNNOOONFFNNNNFNNFFNN	NNNN4NNONNNNNN	T,U	055	540	06.02.02	7512	480503	91117
604.685-010	BALANCE RECESSER (clock & watch)	2113	4443434345	LNNONONFFFNNNNFNNFFNN	NNNN3NNNNNNNNNN	R,T	055	607	06.04.02	7512	480503	91117
604.685-014	FACING-MACHINE OPERATOR (clock & watch)	2113	3333433345	LNNONONFFFNNNNNFNFFNN	NNNN4NNNNNNNNNN	R,T	055	607	06.04.02	7512	480503	91117
604.685-018	KNURLING-MACHINE OPERATOR (ordnance)	2223	4433433345	MNNONNNCCNNNNNFNNNNNN	NNNN4NNNNNNNNNN	R,T	055	370	06.04.02	7512	480503	91117
604.685-022	LAP CUTTER-TRUER OPERATOR (optical goods)	2112	4444444455	LNNONNNFFFNNNNFNNNNN	NNNN4NNNNNNNNNN	R,T	055	566	06.04.02	7512	480503	91117
604.685-026	LATHE TENDER (machine shop)	2223	4444443355	MNNNNNNFFFONNONFNNNNN	NNNN3NNNNNNNNNN	T,U	055	541	06.02.02	7512	480503	91117
604.685-030	RIM-TURNING FINISHER (clock & watch)	2113	2332433355	LNNONONFFFNNNNFNNFFNN	NNNN4NNNNNNNNNN	R,T	055	607	06.04.02	7512	470408	91117
604.685-034	SCREW-MACHINE TENDER (machine shop)	2223	4444443356	MMNNONNFFONNNNFNNNNNN	NNNN4NONNNNNNNN	T,U	057	541	06.04.02	7512	480503	91117
604.685-038	THREADING-MACHINE OPERATOR (ordnance)	2124	3443533355	LNNONNNFFFNNNNFNNFFNN	NNNN4NNNNNNNNNN	R,T	055	372	06.04.02	7512	480503	91117
604.685-042	TURRET-LATHE OPERATOR, TUMBLE TAILSTOCK (clock & watch)	2113	4444434345	LNNONNNFFFNNNNFNNFFNN	NNNN3NNNNNNNNNN	R,T	055	607	06.04.02	7512	480503	91117
604.686-010	WIRE THREADER (clock & watch)	2112	4454453355	LNNNNNNCCNNNNNNNNNNN	NNNN3NNNNNNNNNN	R	055	555	06.02.02	7512	470408	83005
605.280-010	MILLING-MACHINE SET-UP OPERATOR I (machine shop)	4437	23323433355	MNNNONNFFFNNNNFNNOONN	NNNN4NNNNNNNNNN	J,T	055	540	06.01.03	7313	480503	91111
605.280-014	PROFILING-MACHINE SET-UP OPERATOR I (machine shop)	4437	33323433355	MNNNONNFFOONNNFNNOFNN	NNNN4NNNNNNNNNN	J,T	055	540	06.01.03	7313	480503	91111
605.280-018	PROFILING-MACHINE SET-UP OPERATOR, TOOL (machine shop)	4437	33323433355	MMNNNONNFFFNNNNFNNFFNN	NNNN4NNNNNNNNNN	J,T	055	540	06.01.03	7313	480503	91111
605.282-010	MILLING-MACHINE SET-UP OPERATOR II (machine shop)	4437	33323433355	MNNONONFFFNNNNFNONNN	NNNN4NNNNNNNNNNO	J,T	055	540	06.02.02	7313	480503	91111
605.282-014	PLANER SET-UP OPERATOR, TOOL (machine shop)	4337	33323433355	HNNOOONFFFONNNNFNFFNN	NNNN4NNNNNNNNNN	J,T	055	540	06.02.02	7313	480503	91111

DOT #	DOT Title & Industry	Trng	Aptitude	Physical	Environment	Tempra	WkF	MPSMS	GOE	SOC	CIP	OES
605.282-018	PLANER-TYPE-MILLING-MACHINE SET-UP OPERATOR (machine shop)	4337	33323434355	MNNNONONFFONNNMNFNFFNN	NNNN4NNNNNNNNN	J,T	055	540	06.02.02	7313	480503	91111
605.360-010	ROUTER SET-UP OPERATOR, NUMERICAL CONTROL (machine shop)	4336	33323433355	MNNNONONFFNOONFNONNN	NNNN4NNNNNNNNN	J,T	055	560	06.01.03	7326	480503	91502
605.380-010	MILLING-MACHINE SET-UP OPERATOR, NUMERICAL CONTROL (machine shop)	3336	33333333355	MOOOONFFONNNNFNFONN	NNNN4NNNNNNNNN	T,J	055	560	06.01.03	7326	480503	91502
605.382-010	BROACHING-MACHINE SET-UP OPERATOR (machine shop)	3324	34433434355	MNNNONONFFONNNMNFNFFNN	NNNN4NNNNNNNNN	J,T	055	540	06.02.02	7313	480503	91111
605.382-014	ENGRAVER, TIRE MOLD (machine shop)	3325	34433433355	MNNNONNFFNNNMNFFNN	NNNN4NNNNNNNNN	J,T	055	566	06.02.02	7313	480503	91111
605.382-018	KEYSEATING-MACHINE SET-UP OPERATOR (machine shop)	3324	34433433355	MNNONONFFNNNMNFNFNN	NNNN4NNNNNNNNN	J,T	055	540	06.02.02	7313	480503	91111
605.382-022	PANTOGRAPH-MACHINE SET-UP OPERATOR (machine shop)	3337	34433433355	MNNNONFFNNNMNFNFNN	NNNN4NNNNNNNNN	J,T	055	540	06.02.02	7313	480503	91111
605.382-026	PROFILING-MACHINE SET-UP OPERATOR II (machine shop)	3225	34433434355	MNNNONNFFNNNMNFNFNN	NNNN4NNNNNNNNN	J,T	055	540	06.02.02	7313	480503	91111
605.382-030	ROTARY-HEAD-MILLING-MACHINE SET-UP OPERATOR (machine shop)	4337	33323433355	MNNNONONFFNNNFNOONN	NNNN4NNNNNNNNN	J,T	055	540	06.02.02	7313	480503	91111
605.382-034	ROUTER OPERATOR (any industry)	3336	33333434345	MNNNONONNNCCOONNNFNFONN	NNNN4FOFNNNNNNN	T	055	540	06.02.02	7313	480503	91111
605.382-038	SHAPER SET-UP OPERATOR, TOOL (machine shop)	4336	33322433355	MNNNONONFFONNNFNFFNN	NNNN3NNNNNNNNN	J,T	055	540	06.02.02	7313	480503	91111
605.382-042	THREAD-MILLING-MACHINE SET-UP OPERATOR (machine shop)	3326	34433433355	MNNNONONFFNNNMNFNFNN	NNNN3NNONNNNNN	J,T	055	540	06.02.02	7313	480503	91111
605.382-046	NUMERICAL-CONTROL ROUTER OPERATOR (aircraft mfg.; electron. comp.)	3224	33434443455	MNNNNNFFNNNNNFNFONN	NNNN4NNNNNNNNN	T,J	055	587	06.02.09	7326	470105	91502
605.482-010	STEEL-WOOL-MACHINE OPERATOR (nonmet. min.)	3335	34433434355	LNNOOONFFNNNNNFNNNNN	NNNN3NNNNNNNNN	R,T	054	557	06.02.02	7313	480503	91111
605.682-010	BARREL-RIB MATTING-MACHINE OPERATOR (ordnance)	3224	44433434355	MNNNNNFFONNNNFNOONN	NNNN3NNNNNNNNN	J,T	055	373	06.02.02	7313	480503	91117
605.682-014	BROACHING-MACHINE OPERATOR, PRODUCTION (machine shop)	3224	44433434355	MNNONOONFFONNNNFNOONN	NNNN4NNNNNNNNNO	J,T	055	540	06.02.02	7313	480503	91111
605.682-022	SCALPER OPERATOR (nonfer. metal)	3224	34433434355	LNNNNNFFNNNNNFNOFNN	NNNN3NNNNNNNNN	J,T	055	541	06.02.02	7313	480503	91111
605.682-026	TOOTH CUTTER, ESCAPE WHEEL (clock & watch)	3224	34433433355	LNNNNNFFFONNNNFNOFNN	NNNN3NNNNNNNNN	J,T	055	607	06.02.02	7513	480503	91117
605.682-030	WHEEL CUTTER (clock & watch)	3225	34433434355	LNNNNNFFFONNNNFNOFNN	NNNN4NNFNNNNNNN	R,T	055	587	06.02.02	7513	480503	91117
605.682-034	ROUTER, PRINTED CIRCUIT BOARDS (electron. comp.)	3124	34433434355	LNNNNNFFOONNNNFNOFNN	NNNN4NNFNNNNNNN	R,T	055	587	06.04.02	7513	470105	91117
605.685-010	BARREL RIFLER (ordnance)	2123	44434443355	LNNNNNFFNNNNNFNOFNN	NNNN3NNNNNNNNN	R,T	055	373	06.04.02	7513	480503	91117
605.685-014	FILE CUTTER (cutlery-hrdwr.)	3224	44434443355	LNNNNNFFNNNNNFNOFNN	NNNN4NNNNNNNNN	R,T	055	552	06.04.02	7513	480503	91117
605.685-018	HOOKING-MACHINE OPERATOR (clock & watch)	2113	44444443355	LNNNNNFFFONNNNFNOONN	NNNN4NNNNNNNNNO	R,T	055	607	06.04.02	7513	470408	91117
605.685-022	JEWEL STRIPPER (clock & watch)	2122	44444544355	LNNNNNFFNNNNNNFNNNN	NNNN3NNNNNNNNN	R,T	055	607	06.04.02	7513	470408	91117
605.685-026	LEVER MILLER (clock & watch)	2122	44443443355	LNNNNNNFFONNNNFNOONN	NNNN3NNNNNNNNN	R,T	055	607	06.04.02	7513	470408	91117
605.685-030	MILLING-MACHINE TENDER (machine shop)	2223	44443433345	MNNNONNFFONNNNFNONN	NNNN4NOFNNNNNNN	T,U	055	540	06.04.02	7513	480503	91117
605.685-034	PLANING-MACHINE OPERATOR (clock & watch)	2113	44444434345	LNNNNNFFFONNNNFNOFNN	NNNN3NNNNNNNNN	R,T	055	607	06.04.02	7513	470408	91117
605.685-038	PROFILING-MACHINE OPERATOR (clock & watch)	2112	44444433345	LNNNNNFFFNNNNNFNNFNN	NNNN3NNNNNNNNNO	R,T	055	607	06.04.02	7513	470408	91117
605.685-042	SCRIBING-MACHINE OPERATOR (cutlery-hrdwr.)	2222	44444544355	LNNNNNFFNNNNNFNOONN	NNNN3NNNNNNNNN	R,T	183	552	06.04.02	7513	470408	91117
605.685-046	SQUARING-MACHINE OPERATOR (clock & watch)	2112	44443443355	LNNNNNNFFOONNNNFNONN	NNNN3NNNNNNNNN	R,T	055	607	06.04.02	7513	480503	91117
605.685-050	TOOTH CUTTER (clock & watch)	2223	44443433345	LNNNNNNFFONNNNFNFONN	NNNN4NOFNNNNNNN	R,T	055	607	06.04.02	7513	470408	91117
605.685-054	ROUTER MACHINE OPERATOR (plastic prod.)	2112	44444444455	LNNNNNFFFONNNNFNOFNN	NNNN4NNNNNNNNN	R,U	055	519	06.04.02	7513	480503	91117
606.280-010	BORING-MACHINE SET-UP OPERATOR, JIG (machine shop)	4437	33323443355	MNNNONFFNNNNNFNFNN	NNNN4NNNNNNNNN	J,T	053	566	06.01.03	7318	480503	91108
606.280-014	BORING-MILL SET-UP OPERATOR, HORIZONTAL (machine shop)	4437	33323433355	MNNNONFFNNNNNFNFFNN	NNNN4NNNNNNNNN	J,T	053	540	06.01.03	7318	480503	91108
606.362-010	DRILL-PRESS OPERATOR, NUMERICAL CONTROL (machine shop)	3336	33333433355	MNNONONFFONNNNFNFNN	NNNN4NNNNNNNNN	J,T	053	540	06.02.02	7326	480503	91502
606.380-010	DRILL-PRESS SET-UP OPERATOR, MULTIPLE SPINDLE (machine shop)	4436	33333433355	MNNONONFFONNNNFNFFNN	NNNN4NNNNNNNNNO	J,T	053	540	06.02.02	7318	480503	91108
606.380-018	DRILL-PRESS SET-UP OPERATOR, RADIAL (machine shop)	4436	33332453355	MNNONONFFNNNNNFNFFNN	NNNN4NNNNNNNNN	J,T	053	540	06.01.03	7318	480503	91108
606.382-010	DRILL-PRESS SET-UP OPERATOR, RADIAL, TOOL (machine shop)	3224	33434434355	LNNNNNFFONNNNNFNFFNN	NNNN4NNNNNNNNNO	J,T	053	540	06.01.03	7318	480503	91108
606.382-014	DRILLER-AND-REAMER, AUTOMATIC (musical inst.)	4437	33322443355	MNNOOOOFFONNNNFNOONN	NNNN4NNNNNNNNN	J,T	053	614	06.02.02	7518	480503	91117
606.382-018	JIG-BORING MACHINE OPERATOR, NUMERICAL CONTROL, PRINTED CIRCUIT BOARDS (electron. comp.)	3334	33333443355	LNNNNNFFONNNNNFNOONN	NNNN4NNNNNNNNN	J,T	053	540	06.02.02	7326	470105	91502
606.382-022	BORING MACHINE OPERATOR (machine shop)	3336	33333433355	MNNONONFFONNNNFNOFNN	NNNN4NNFNNNNNNN	T,J	053	587	06.02.02	7318	480503	91108
606.382-026	ROBOTIC MACHINE OPERATOR (aircraft mfg.)	3235	33433443355	MONONONFFOONONFNNNN	NNNN4NOONNNNNON	T	053	592	06.02.09	7326	000000	91502
606.682-014	DRILL-PRESS OPERATOR (machine shop)	3223	44433433355	MNNONONFFONNNNFNFNN	NNNN4NNNNNNNNN	R,T	053	540	06.02.02	7518	480503	91117
606.682-018	DRILL-PRESS SET-UP OPERATOR, SINGLE SPINDLE (machine shop)	3324	44433433355	MNNONONFFONNNNFNFFNN	NNNN4NNNNNNNNNO	J,T	053	540	06.02.02	7318	480503	91108
606.682-022	TAPPER OPERATOR (nut & bolt)	3334	33433433355	MNNNNNFFFONNNNFNNNNN	NNNN4NNNNNNNNN	J,T	053	555	06.02.02	7318	480503	91108
606.685-010	BORING-MACHINE OPERATOR, PRODUCTION (machine shop)	2223	44433433355	MNNNNNNFFONNNNFNOONN	NNNN4NNNNNNNNNO	J,T	053	540	06.04.02	7518	480503	91117
606.685-014	CHAMFERING-MACHINE OPERATOR I (ordnance)	3223	33433433355	LNNNNNFFFONNNNFNFNN	NNNN4NNNNNNNNN	J,T	053	372	06.04.02	7518	480503	91117
606.685-018	CHAMFERING-MACHINE OPERATOR II (ordnance)	2112	34443544455	LNNNNNFFONNNNNFNNNNN	NNNN4NNNNNNNNN	R	055	374	06.04.02	7518	480503	91117
606.685-022	CHOKE REAMER (ordnance)	2113	44443444355	LNNNNNFFONNNNNFNNFNN	NNNN4NNNNNNNNN	R,T	053	373	06.04.02	7518	000000	91117
606.685-026	DRILL PRESS TENDER (machine shop)	2223	44444444455	MNNNONNNCCCONNNCNFONN	NNNN4NOCNNNNNN	T,U	053	540	06.04.02	7518	480503	91117

DOT #	DOT Title & Industry	Trng	Aptitude	Physical	Environment	Tempra	WkF	MPSMS	GOE	SOC	CIP	OES
606.685-030	DRILLING-MACHINE OPERATOR, AUTOMATIC (clock & watch)	2113	44443433345	LNNNNNNFFONOONFNNNNN	NNNN4NNNNNNNNNN	R,T	053	607	06.04.02	7518	470408	91117
606.685-034	REAMING-MACHINE TENDER (nonfer. metal)	2112	44444544355	MNNNNNNFFONNNNONNNN	NNNN4NNNNNNNNNN	R	053	541	06.04.02	7518	480503	91117
607.382-010	CONTOUR-BAND-SAW OPERATOR, VERTICAL (machine shop)	3324	34333433345	MNNONONFFNNNNNFNOONN	NNNN4NNNNNNNNNNO	J,T	056	540	06.02.02	7329	480503	91102
607.382-014	SAW OPERATOR (aircraft mfg.)	3224	34433444355	MNNNNNNFFONNNNFNNNNN	NNNN4NNFNNNNNNN	T	056	592	06.02.02	7329	480503	91102
607.682-010	CUT-OFF-SAW OPERATOR, METAL (machine shop)	3224	34433434355	LNNNNNNFFONNNNFNOONN	NNNN4NONNNNNNN	J,T	056	540	06.02.02	7329	480503	91102
607.682-014	PROFILE TRIMMER (jewelry-silver.)	2222	34433434245	MNNNFNNNFFONNNNFNOONN	NNNN4NNNNNNNNN	R,T	056	612	06.02.02	7529	480503	91117
607.685-010	CUT-OFF SAW TENDER, METAL (machine shop)	2222	44445444345	LNNNFNNNFFONNNNFNNNN	NNNN4NNNNNNNNN	R,J	056	540	06.04.02	7529	480503	91117
607.685-014	DEBRIDGING-MACHINE OPERATOR (nonfer. metal)	2123	44444444454	MNNNFNNNNFFNNNNFNFON	NNNN4NNNNNNNNN	R,T	056	554	06.04.02	7529	480501	91117
607.686-010	MAGNESIUM-MILL OPERATOR (nonfer. metal)	2112	44444454455	MNNNNNNFFNNNNNNNNNN	NNNN4NNNNNNNNNO	R	054	541	06.04.02	7513	480503	91117
609.130-010	MACHINE-SHOP SUPERVISOR, PRODUCTION (machine shop)	4438	33333333355	LNNNNNNOOONFNFOFFNO	NNNN4NONNNNNNN	D,J,P,T	057	540	06.01.01	7100	520205	81008
609.130-014	SCREW SUPERVISOR (clock & watch)	4337	33333444355	LNNNNNNFFONFFNFNFONN	NNNN4NNNNNNNNN	D,J,P	121	607	06.02.01	7100	520205	81008
609.130-018	SUPERVISOR (plumbing-heat.)	4447	33322333355	LNNNNNNFFNFFNFNFONN	NNNN3NNNNNNNNN	V,D,P,J	121	553	06.01.01	7100	520205	81008
609.130-022	SUPERVISOR, AUTOMATIC MACHINES (clock & watch)	4447	34433444355	LNNNONONFFOOFFNFNNNN	NNNN4NNNNNNNNN	V,D,P,J	057	607	06.01.01	7100	520205	81008
609.130-026	WATCH MANUFACTURING SUPERVISOR (clock & watch)	4337	33333333354	LNNNONONFFOOFFNFNOONN	NNNN4NNNNNNNNN	D,J,P	057	607	06.01.01	7100	520205	81008
609.131-010	INSPECTION SUPERVISOR (machine shop)	4337	33333333455	LNNNNNNFFOFFNFNOONN	NNNN3NNNNNNNNN	D,J	121	550	06.01.01	7100	150702	81008
609.131-014	SUPERVISOR, MOLD MAKING (glass mfg.)	4448	33333433354	LNNNNNNFFOFFNFNOONN	NNNN3NNNNNNNNN	V,D,P,J	057	566	05.05.07	7100	520205	81008
609.131-018	SUPERVISOR, MOLD SHOP (glass mfg.)	4448	22222233355	LNNNNNNFFONFNFNOOONN	NNNN4NFNNNNNNN	V,D,P,J	057	542	06.02.01	7100	520205	81008
609.132-010	SLAB-CONDITIONER SUPERVISOR (nonfer. metal)	4448	23312333344	LNNNNNNFFONFNFNOOONN	NMON4NFNNNNNNN	T,J,V,P	057	541	05.05.07	7100	520205	81008
609.260-010	GUNSMITH, BALLISTICS LABORATORY (ordnance)	3326	33333333355	SNNNNNNFCCNOONFNNNFN	NNNN3NNNNNNNNN	T,J,V,P	244	373	05.01.06	7329	110201	92197
609.262-010	TOOL PROGRAMMER, NUMERICAL CONTROL (electron. comp.)	4448	33322223344	MNNNFNNNFFCNOONFNNNN	NNNN3NNNNNNNNN	V,T,J	233	706	05.05.07	3974	000000	25111
609.280-010	TRIM-MACHINE ADJUSTER (ordnance)	3335	34433533355	MNNNNNFFNNNNFNNOONN	NNNN4NOONNNNNNN	J,T	054	372	06.01.02	7329	480503	91102
609.360-010	NUMERICAL CONTROL MACHINE SET-UP OPERATOR (machine shop)	3235	33333433355	MNNOOONFFOOOONFNONNN	NNNN4NOONNNNNNN	T,J	057	540	06.01.03	7326	480503	91502
609.361-010	INSPECTOR, FLOOR (machine shop)	4436	33333333354	MNNONONFFONNNNNONNNF	NNNN4NNONNNNNN	J	212	550	05.07.01	6881	480503	83002
609.362-010	NUMERICAL CONTROL MACHINE OPERATOR (machine shop)	3336	33333433455	MNNNNNNFFOOOONFNFNNN	NNNN4NNNNNNNNN	T	057	540	06.02.02	7326	480503	91502
609.380-010	ELECTRICAL-DISCHARGE-MACHINE SET-UP OPERATOR (machine shop)	3335	23323333355	LNNOOONFFONNNFNFONN	NNNN4NNNNNNNNN	J,T	054	540	06.01.03	7329	480503	92197
609.380-014	THREADING-MACHINE SETTER (machine shop)	4447	34333433345	MNNOOONFFONNNFNNNNN	NNNN4NNNNNNNNN	J,T	057	550	06.01.02	7312	480503	91105
609.462-010	BALANCING-MACHINE OPERATOR (any industry)	4336	34334433355	MNNNNNFFNNNNFNNNNN	NNNN4NNNNNNNNN	R,J,T	121	560	06.02.02	7529	480503	92198
609.482-010	ELECTRICAL-DISCHARGE-MACHINE OPERATOR, PRODUCTION (machine shop)	3226	34433433355	HNNOOONFFONNNNFNONN	NNNN4NNNNNNNNN	R,T	057	540	06.02.02	7329	480503	92197
609.482-014	STRAIGHT-PIN-MAKING-MACHINE OPERATOR (button & notion)	3224	33334433355	MNNNNNNFFNNONFFFONN	NNNN4NNNNNNNNN	R,J,T	057	618	06.02.02	7529	480503	92198
609.682-010	AUTOMATIC-WHEEL-LINE OPERATOR (machine shop)	3335	34444434455	LNNNNNNFFNNNNFFFNNN	NNNN4NNNNNNNNN	J,T	057	594	06.02.02	7529	480503	92198
609.682-014	COLLET MAKER (clock & watch)	3336	33433533335	LNNONONFFONNNONFNNN	NNNN4NNNNNNNNN	T	055	607	06.02.02	7529	470408	92198
609.682-018	CROOK OPERATOR (musical inst.)	3225	34444534355	LNNONONFFONNNNFNFONN	NNNN4NNNNNNNNN	T	051	614	06.02.02	7529	480503	92198
609.682-022	MACHINE OPERATOR, CENTRIFUGAL-CONTROL SWITCHES (elec. equip.)	3234	44443433355	LNNNNNNFFNFFNNFNFONN	NNNN4NNNNNNNNNO	J,T	057	582	06.02.02	7529	480503	91508
609.682-026	NICKING-MACHINE OPERATOR (cutlery-hrdwr.)	3226	34443433355	MNNFFNNNFFONNNNFNNNN	NNNN4NNNNNNNNN	J,T	192	566	06.02.02	7322	480503	91114
609.685-018	PRODUCTION MACHINE TENDER (machine shop)	3225	44443434355	MNNNNNNFFONNNNFNNNNN	NNNN4NNNNNNNNN	R,T	055	555	06.04.02	7529	480503	92198
609.685-022	TRANSFER-MACHINE OPERATOR (machine shop)	3225	34433433355	MNNFFNNNFFONNNFNNFNN	NNNN4NNNNNNNNN	R,T	212	540	06.03.02	7820	480503	83005
609.685-026	SCREWMAKER, AUTOMATIC (clock & watch)	3224	44435444455	MNNNNNNFFONNNFNFFNN	NNNN3NNNNNNNNN	R	054	372	06.02.02	7319	480503	91317
609.684-010	INSPECTOR, GENERAL (any industry)	2112	33433433345	LNNOONFFFONNNONONN	NNNN4NNNNNNNNN	R	031	550	06.04.39	6179	000000	85999
609.684-014	LABORER, GENERAL (machine shop)	2112	44444444455	HNNFFFNFFONNNFNONN	NNNN4NNNNNNNNN	R,T	212	540	06.04.02	6179	470408	85999
610.362-010	TRIM-MACHINE OPERATOR (ordnance)	3336	33333333343	LNNNNNNFFNNNNFNFNFN	NNFN5FNCNNNNNN	R,T	183	568	06.04.02	7679	480503	98102
610.362-010	DROPHAMMER OPERATOR (aircraft mfg.; forging)	4327	33323433343	LNNNNNNFFONNNNFNFNFN	NNFN5NNNNNNNNN	R,T	057	607	06.04.02	7529	480503	92998
610.381-010	BLACKSMITH (forging)	4327	33323433343	MNNNNNNFFONNNNFFONN	NNFN5NNNNNNNNF	R,T	057	555	06.04.02	7529	480503	92198
610.381-014	BLACKSMITH APPRENTICE (forging)	2114	44444534354	MNNVFNFNNNNNNFNFNON	NNFN4NNNNNNNNN	R	054	540	06.04.02	7519	000000	91508
610.684-010	BLACKSMITH HELPER (forging)	2114	44443433354	MNNNNNNFFNNNNFNFFN	NNFN5NNNNNNNNF	R	134	372	05.12.10	8637	000000	91508
610.684-014	SPRING SALVAGE WORKER (metal prod., nec)	3225	44433433334	HNNNNNNNFFNNNNFNFNFN	NNFN5NNONNNNNN	R	134	559	06.04.02	7519	000000	98102
611.482-010	FORGING-PRESS OPERATOR I (forging)	3214	34334433333	MNNNNNNFFONNNNFNFNFN	NNFN4NNONNNNNN	J,T	134	541	06.02.02	7319	480503	91321
611.482-014	ROLLER-MACHINE OPERATOR (metal prod., nec)	3225	34333443355	HNNOOONFFNNNNFNFNFN	NNFN5NNONNNNNN	R,J,T	135	559	06.02.02	7519	480503	91317
611.662-010	UPSETTER (forging)	3225	34333443344	HNNOOONFFNNNNNFNFNFN	NNFN4FNCNNNNNN	T,J	134	541	06.02.02	7319	480503	91317
611.682-010	STEEL-SHOT-HEADER OPERATOR (ordnance)	3124	34433433355	MNNNNNNFFNNNNFNFONN	NNNN4NNNNNNNNN	R,T	134	374	06.02.02	7319	480503	91317

DOT #	DOT Title & Industry	Trng	Aptitude	Physical	Environment	Tempra	WkF	MPSMS	GOE	SOC	CIP	OES
611.682-014	AUTOMATIC CASTING-FORGING MACHINE OPERATOR (forging)	4235	33433444353	LNNNNNNOOFNNNNFNOOON	NNNNN4NNONNNNNNN	J,T	134	556	06.02.10	7519	480599	91321
611.685-010	FORGING-PRESS OPERATOR II (forging)	2222	44444534343	HNNNNNNFFONNNNFNFNFN	NNFN4NNONNNNNNNF	R,T	134	556	06.04.02	7519	480503	91321
611.685-014	HYDRAULIC OPERATOR (nonfer. metal)	2113	44444544355	MNNNNNNNFFNNNNONNNNN	NNON4NNNNNNNNNN	R,T	134	544	06.04.02	7519	480503	91321
612.130-010	SPIKEMAKING SUPERVISOR (steel & rel.)	3217	33333333353	MMNOOONFFOFFNFNFOFN	NNON4NNNNNNNNNN	V,D,P,J	133	557	06.01.01	7100	000000	81008
612.131-010	FORGE-SHOP SUPERVISOR (forging)	4338	33323444454	MMNONONFFNFNNNNFOON	NNNN4NFNNNNNNO	V,D,P,J	134	540	06.01.01	7100	000000	81008
612.260-010	FASTENER TECHNOLOGIST (nut & bolt)	4337	22222223234	HONFNNNFFNNNNNFNFOON	NNNN5NNNNNNNNNN	J,T,V	135	555	06.02.02	7319	480503	91317
612.261-010	INSPECTOR (forging)	4336	33323433354	MNNONNNFFOFFNFNFOFN	NNFN4NNNNNNNNNF	J,T	212	556	06.01.05	6881	000000	83002
612.360-010	DIE SETTER (forging)	4337	33322433255	MMNOOONFFNNNNNFNFONN	NNFN4NNNNNNNNNF	J,T	134	556	06.01.02	7319	480507	91317
612.361-010	HEAVY FORGER (forging)	4438	33332433353	MMNOONNFFNNOONFNFOON	NNCN5NNNNNNNNNN	J	134	556	06.02.02	6829	000000	89199
612.384-010	INSPECTOR, COLD WORKING (ordnance)	3334	33333433355	LNNOOONFFFNNNNFNOONN	NNNN3NNNNNNNNNN	J,T	212	371	06.03.01	7820	470402	83005
612.462-010	MULTI-OPERATION-MACHINE OPERATOR (any industry)	3326	34433443354	MMNOOONFFFNNNNNFOONN	NNON4NNNNNNNNNN	J,T	134	555	06.01.03	7319	480503	91317
612.462-014	NUT FORMER (nut & bolt)	3325	34444434354	MMNOOONFFNNNNNFOON	NNNN5NNNNNNNNNN	J,T	134	555	06.02.02	7319	480503	91317
612.662-010	SPIKE-MACHINE OPERATOR (steel & rel.)	3217	33443434343	MMNFNFNFFONOONFNOOFN	NNFN5NNNNNNNNNN	R,T	134	557	06.02.02	7319	480503	91317
612.666-010	SPIKE-MACHINE FEEDER (steel & rel.)	2112	44444544454	MMNFNFNNFFNNNNNONNNN	NNFN4NNNNNNNNNN	R,T	134	557	06.04.02	8725	000000	98502
612.682-014	BUCKSHOT-SWAGE OPERATOR (ordnance)	3224	34434444344	HNNFNONFFNNNNFNFONN	NNNN4NNNNNNNNNN	J,T	134	557	06.02.02	7319	480503	91317
612.683-010	FORGING-ROLL OPERATOR (forging)	2225	34434534334	LNNNNNNFFONNNNFNOOON	NNFN4NNNNNNNNNN	R,T	134	374	06.02.02	7319	480503	91317
612.684-010	MANIPULATOR OPERATOR (forging)	2112	44534534345	MNNFNNNFFONNNNFNOONN	NNCN4FNNNNNNNNNF	R,T	134	541	06.04.02	8319	000000	97989
612.684-010	UTILITY WORKER, FORGE (forging)	2114	44444434344	MMNNNFFNNNNNNFNFNON	NNFN5NNNNNNNNNN	R	011	556	05.12.10	8611	000000	98999
612.685-010	LEVER TENDER (forging)	3224	44444434355	LNNNNNFFNNNNNFNNNNF	NNFN4NNNNNNNNNN	R,T	134	556	06.04.02	7519	000000	91321
612.685-014	SPRING TESTER I (metal prod., nec)	2223	44444444453	LNNNNNNCCNNNNNNCNNNCN	NOCN4NNNNNNNNNN	R,J,T	212	557	06.03.02	7517	000000	83005
612.687-010	HEAT READER (forging)	2113	44434534344	HNNNNNNNFFNNNNNFNNNNO	NNFN5NNNNNNNNNF	J,T	134	540	05.12.10	8611	000000	98999
612.687-014	HEAVY-FORGER HELPER (forging)	4437	33333333354	MNNOOONFFNFFNNOOON	NNON4NNNNNNNNNO	R	134	541	06.02.01	7100	000000	81008
613.130-014	SUPERVISOR, BLOOMING MILL (steel & rel.)	4337	33333333355	MNNNNNNNFFFNFFNFNNN	NNON4NNNNNNNNNN	V,D,P,J	135	541	06.02.01	7100	000000	81008
613.130-014	SUPERVISOR, MERCHANT-MILL ROLLING AND FINISHING (steel & rel.)	4348	33333433355	MNNNNNNFFNFFNFNFNN	NNFN4NFNNNNNNN	V,D,P,J	135	541	06.02.01	7100	000000	81008
613.130-018	SUPERVISOR, STRUCTURAL ROLLING-AND-FINISHING (steel & rel.)	4337	33333433355	LNNNNNNNFFNFFNFNOONN	NNOO4NNNNNNNNNO	V,D,P,T,J	135	541	06.02.01	7100	000000	81008
613.132-010	SUPERVISOR, HOT-STRIP MILL (steel & rel.)	4326	34323433255	MMNOOONFFNNNNFNFNNN	NNNN4NNNNNNNNNN	J,T	135	554	06.01.02	7316	480503	91314
613.360-010	ROLL-FORMING-MACHINE SET-UP MECHANIC (any industry)	3216	34434433355	MMNNNFFONFFNNNNFNNN	NNFN4NNNNNNNNNN	J,T	121	568	06.01.02	7316	480599	91314
613.360-014	ROLL-TUBE SETTER (steel & rel.)	4337	33334444454	MNNNNNNFFNOONFNFNNN	NNFN4NFNNNNNNNF	J,T	135	541	06.01.03	7316	480503	91314
613.360-018	TIN ROLLER, HOT MILL (steel & rel.)	3226	34343434355	MNNNNNNFFONNNNFNFNN	NNNN4NNNNNNNNNN	J,T	121	568	06.01.02	7316	480599	91314
613.361-010	GUIDE SETTER (steel & rel.)	3226	34333444343	LNNNNNNNFONFFNFNFN	NNFN4NNNNNNNNNN	J,T	133	541	06.02.10	7544	000000	91938
613.362-014	HEATER I (steel & rel.)	4347	33333434343	LNNNNNNNFFONFFNFNFN	NNFF4NNNNNNNNNF	J,T	135	541	06.02.02	7516	000000	91321
613.362-014	ROLLER, PRIMARY MILL (steel & rel.)	3337	33333343355	LNNNNNNNFFONFFNNNFN	NNNN4NNNNNNNNNN	T,J	135	541	06.02.02	7516	000000	91321
613.362-018	ROUGHER (steel & rel.)	3326	34344444355	LNNNNNNNFFNNNNNFNNN	NNNN4NNNNNNNNNN	J,T	135	541	06.02.10	7516	000000	91321
613.362-022	SPEED OPERATOR (steel & rel.)	3116	34434444355	LNNNNNNFFNNONFNFNNN	NNON4NONNNNNNNN	R,T	163	541	06.01.03	7529	000000	92198
613.382-010	COILER OPERATOR (steel & rel.)	3226	34333433355	MNNNOOONFFFNNNNNFNOONN	NNNN4NNNNNNNNNN	J,T	135	541	06.02.02	7316	480599	91314
613.382-014	FINISHER (steel & rel.)	3225	34334433355	MNNNNNNNFFNNNNNFNNNN	NNFN4NNNNNNNNNN	J,T	135	541	06.02.02	7516	000000	91321
613.382-018	SCREWDOWN OPERATOR (steel & rel.)	3216	34344444355	LONOONNFFFNNNNNFNNN	NNFN4NNNNNNNNNN	J,T	133	541	06.02.10	7544	000000	91938
613.462-014	FURNACE OPERATOR (nonfer. metal)	3225	34433433355	LNNNONONFFNOONFNFNN	NNON4NNNNNNNNNN	J,T	135	540	06.02.02	7316	480503	91314
613.462-018	ROLLING-MILL OPERATOR (nonfer. metal)	3216	34343444354	MNNNNNNFFNNNNNFNNNN	NNFN4NNNNNNNNNN	J,T	134	541	06.02.02	7316	480503	91314
613.482-014	PIERCING-MACHINE OPERATOR (nonfer. metal)	3225	34433433355	LNNNNNNNFFNNNNNFFNON	NNFN4NNNNNNNNNN	V,J,T	135	541	06.01.03	6960	000000	95099
613.662-010	ROLLING ATTENDANT (steel & rel.)	4336	33333322344	MNNNNNNFFNONOONFNONN	NNFN4NNNNNNNNNN	R,T	135	541	06.02.02	7316	480503	91314
613.662-014	ROUGHER OPERATOR (steel & rel.)	3225	34344434355	MMNFONNFFNNOONFONN	NNNF4NNNNNNNNNN	J,T	135	541	06.02.10	7316	000000	91321
613.662-018	COLD-MILL OPERATOR (steel & rel.)	4337	33333433355	MMNFONNNFFNONNNFFFNN	NNFN4NNNNNNNNNN	J,T	135	541	06.02.02	7516	480503	91314
613.662-022	STRAIGHTENING-ROLL OPERATOR (any industry)	3114	34333433345	MMNFONNFFONNNNFFFNN	NNFN4NFNNNNNNNF	T,J	135	554	06.02.10	7516	000000	91321
613.667-010	LINER ASSEMBLER (nonfer. metal)	2113	44443444355	MNNNNNNFFNNNNNFNFNN	NNNN4NFNNNNNNN	R,T	081	541	06.04.31	7714	000000	93914
613.682-010	MILL HAND, PLATE MILL (steel & rel.)	2114	44443444355	LNNNNNNFFNNONONFFNN	NNNN4NNONNNNNN	R	212	541	06.04.10	7820	000000	83005
613.682-014	MANIPULATOR (steel & rel.)	3225	34434434355	LNNNNNNNFFONNONFFNNN	NNON4NNONNNNNNF	J,T	135	541	06.02.10	7516	000000	91321
613.682-014	REELING-MACHINE OPERATOR (steel & rel.)	3215	34433434355	LNNNNNNNFFNNNNNFNNNN	NNNN4NNNNNNNNNN	R,T	135	541	06.02.02	7316	480503	91314
613.682-018	ROLLER (jewelry-silver-)	3324	34343444344	MNNNNNNNFFNNNNNFNNN	NNNN4NNNNNNNNNN	R,T	135	611	06.02.02	7316	470408	91321
613.682-022	STRIP ROLLER (metal prod., nec)	3324	34344433355	MNNNNNNNFONNONFFNNO	NNNN3NNNNNNNNNN	J,T	135	559	06.02.02	7516	480599	91321
613.682-026	TABLE OPERATOR (nonfer. metal; steel & rel.)	3215	34433524355	LNNNNNNNFONNONFFFNNO	NNON4NNNNNNNNNF	T,J	135	541	06.04.02	7516	000000	91321

DOT #	DOT Title & Industry	Trng	Aptitude	Physical	Environment	Tempra	WkF	MPSMS	GOE	SOC	CIP	OES
613.682-030	MILL OPERATOR, ROLLS (any industry)	3324	34333242355	MNNFNFNFFNNNNFFFNN	NNNO4NNNNNNNNF	T,J	135	541	06.02.02	7316	480503	91314
613.685-010	COILER (nonfer. metal; steel & rel.)	2114	44433353355	LNNNNNFFNNNNFNFFNN	NFFN4NFFNNNNON	R,T	163	540	06.04.02	7529	000000	92198
613.685-014	HEATER HELPER (steel & rel.)	2224	34443444353	MNNNNNNFFONNONFNNNON	NNON4NNNNNNNNNNO	R	133	541	05.12.10	8614	000000	98999
613.685-018	PIERCING-MILL OPERATOR (steel & rel.)	2223	44443444355	MNNNNNNNNFFONNNNNNNNN	NNNN4NNNNNNNNN	R,T	135	549	06.04.02	7516	000000	91321
613.685-022	ROLLER-LEVELER OPERATOR (steel & rel.)	2112	44443544355	MNNNNNNFFONNNNNNNN	NNNN4NNNNNNNN	R	135	541	06.04.02	7516	000000	91321
613.685-026	ROLLING-MILL-OPERATOR HELPER (nonfer. metal)	2113	44443534345	MNNNONONFFONNNNONONNN	NNNNO4NNFNNNNNO	R,T	135	541	06.04.10	8619	000000	98999
613.685-030	TUBING-MACHINE OPERATOR (nonfer. metal; steel & rel.)	2114	44444444355	MNNNNNNNFFONNNNNNNN	NNNN4NNNNNNNNN	R	083	559	06.04.02	7516	000000	91321
613.685-034	BED OPERATOR (steel & rel.)	3214	34434433355	LNNNNNNNFFNNNNFNFNN	NNFN4NNNNNNNNNN	R,T	011	541	06.02.10	7516	000000	97951
613.686-010	CATCHER (steel & rel.)	2113	44434534355	MNNNNNNNFFNNNNNNNNN	NNFN4NNNNNNNNNF	R,T	135	541	06.04.02	8725	000000	98502
613.687-010	PLUGGER (steel & rel.)	2222	44434544355	MNNNNNNNFFNNNNNNNNN	NNFN4NNNNNNNNNN	R	061	559	06.04.02	8611	000000	98999
614.132-010	SUPERVISOR, DRAWING (nonfer. metal; steel & rel.)	4337	33333334355	LNNNNNNNFFNFFNFONN	NNNN4NNNNNNNNNN	V,D,J	135	541	06.04.01	7100	000000	81008
614.132-014	SUPERVISOR, EXTRUSION (forging)	4337	33333344354	LNNNNNNFFNFFNFNFOON	NNNN4NNNNNNNNNN	V,D,P,J	135	540	06.02.02	7100	000000	81008
614.380-010	EXTRUSION-PRESS ADJUSTER (elec. equip.)	3325	33333433355	MNNNNNFFNNNFNFFNN	NNNN4NNNNNNNNN	J,T	135	557	06.01.02	7315	480503	91311
614.382-010	WIRE DRAWER (nonfer. metal)	3214	34333433355	HNNNNNNFFNNNNFNFONN	NNNN4NNNNNNNNN	J,T	135	541	06.02.02	7315	480503	91311
614.382-014	WIRE DRAWER (clock & watch)	3224	34443433355	LNNNNNNNFFNNNNNNNNN	NNNN3NNNNNNNNN	J,T	135	607	06.02.02	7515	480503	91321
614.382-018	WIRE DRAWING MACHINE OPERATOR (inst. & app.; jewelry-silver.)	3224	34443444355	MNNNNNNNFFFNNNFNNONN	NNNN4NNNNNNNNN	J,T	135	544	06.02.02	7515	000000	91321
614.482-010	DRAW-BENCH OPERATOR (nonfer. metal; steel & rel.)	3124	34443434344	HNNNNNNNFFNNNNFNFFON	NNNN4NNNNNNNNN	J	135	540	06.02.02	7315	480503	91311
614.482-014	EXTRUDER OPERATOR (forging)	3225	33443434354	MNNNONONFFONNNNOFNNON	NNCN5NNNNNNNNNO	J,T	135	541	06.02.02	7315	480503	91311
614.482-018	EXTRUSION-PRESS OPERATOR I (elec. equip.)	3325	34343433355	LNNNNNNFFONNNFNFNNN	NNNN4NNNNNNNNN	J,T	135	580	06.02.18	7315	480503	91311
614.586-010	WIRE CHARGER (elec. equip.)	2222	44444444355	HNNNNNNNNFFONNNONNNNN	NNON4NNNNNNNNN	R	135	582	06.04.21	8725	000000	98502
614.682-010	DRAW-BENCH OPERATOR (any industry)	4335	34422433354	MNNNNNFFNNNNNFNONON	NNNN4NNNNNNNN	J,T	135	566	06.02.02	7515	000000	91321
614.684-010	BILLET ASSEMBLER (chemical)	3224	34444433355	MNNNNNNNFFNNNNFNFNN	NNNN3NNNNNNNNN	R,T	102	543	06.02.22	7532	000000	91705
614.684-014	TESTER OPERATOR (nonfer. metal)	2223	34443433344	MNNFNFNFFONNNNNNNN	NNNN4NNNNNNNNN	R,J,T	054	540	06.03.02	7830	000000	83005
614.685-010	EXTRUDING-PRESS OPERATOR (ordnance)	2224	44444544355	HNNFNFNFFONNNNNNNN	NNFN4NNNNNNNNN	R,T	135	541	06.04.02	7515	000000	91321
614.685-014	EXTRUSION-PRESS OPERATOR II (elec. equip.)	2222	44349534355	LNNNNNNNFFONNNNFNNN	NNNN4NNNNNNNN	J,T	135	582	06.04.21	7515	000000	91321
614.685-018	REDUCING-MACHINE OPERATOR (optical goods)	1112	44444434355	LNNNNNNNFFONNNNONNNNN	NNNN4NNNNNNNNN	R	134	605	06.04.02	7515	000000	91321
614.685-022	TUBE DRAWER (nonfer. metal; steel & rel.)	2113	44444344355	MNNOOONFFFONNNNFNFFNN	NNNN4NNNNNNNNN	J	135	540	06.04.02	7515	480503	91321
614.685-026	WIRE-DRAWING-MACHINE TENDER (nonfer. metal)	2123	44443444355	MNNNNNNFFONNNNONNNNN	NNNF4NNNNNNNNN	R	081	541	06.04.02	7532	000000	98999
614.686-010	DRAW-BENCH-OPERATOR HELPER (nonfer. metal; steel & rel.)	2112	44544534345	HNNNONOFFONNNNNONNNNN	NNNN3NNNNNNNNN	R	135	540	06.04.40	8611	000000	98502
614.686-014	TESTER-OPERATOR HELPER (nonfer. metal)	2112	44543544355	HNNNNNNFFONNNNONNONNN	NNNN3NNNNNNNONN	R	056	540	06.04.02	8725	000000	98502
615.130-010	PRESS-HAND SUPERVISOR (jewelry-silver.)	4337	33333433355	LNNONONFFOFFNFNFONN	NNNN4NNNNNNNNN	V,D,P,J	057	611	06.02.02	7100	520205	81008
615.132-010	SUPERVISOR (cutlery-hrdwr.)	4337	33333433255	HNNNONONFFFNFNFNOONN	NNNN4NONNNNNNN	V,D,P,J	057	552	06.02.01	7100	000000	81008
615.132-014	SUPERVISOR, SHEARING (any industry)	4337	32333433355	MNNNNNNFFOFFNFNFNNN	NNNN4NNFNNNNNNN	V,J,T	054	540	06.01.01	7100	000000	81008
615.280-010	SLITTER SERVICE AND SETTER (tinware)	4336	34333442355	MNNONNNFFNNNNFNFFNN	NNNN4NNFNNNNNNN	V,J,T	121	566	06.01.02	7314	480501	91308
615.380-010	SHEAR SETTER (any industry)	4346	34344433345	MMNFNNNFFNNNNFNFNN	NNNN4NNNNNNNNF	J,T	054	541	06.01.02	7314	480506	91308
615.382-010	PUNCH-PRESS OPERATOR I (any industry)	3225	34334434345	MNNNNNNFFONNNFNFONN	NNNN4FNFNNNNNNN	R,T	134	540	06.04.02	7314	480501	91302
615.482-014	ANGLE SHEAR OPERATOR (any industry)	3223	34333433355	HNNNONOFFFNNNNFNFNNN	NNNN4NFNNNNNNNN	R,J,T	054	554	06.02.02	7314	480501	91308
615.482-014	DUPLICATOR-PUNCH OPERATOR (any industry)	4335	34333433355	HNNONONFFFNNNNFNFNNN	NNNN4NNNNNNNNN	J,T	134	554	06.02.02	7314	480506	91302
615.482-018	IRONWORKER-MACHINE OPERATOR (any industry)	3224	34434434345	HHNFNNNFFONNNNFNFFNN	NNNN4NNNNNNNNF	R,T	134	554	06.02.02	7314	480501	91302
615.482-026	PUNCH-PRESS OPERATOR, AUTOMATIC (any industry)	3325	34434434345	MNNNNNNFFONNNNFNFNNN	NNNN4NNNNNNNNNF	J	134	541	06.02.02	7314	480506	91302
615.482-026	PUNCH-PRESS OPERATOR I (any industry)	3224	34433444345	HNNOONOFFONNNNFNFNNN	NNNN4NNNNNNNNF	J,T	054	554	06.02.02	7514	480506	91321
615.482-030	ROTARY-SHEAR OPERATOR (any industry)	3224	34433444345	HNNNONOFFONNNNFNFNNN	NNNN4NNNNNNNNF	J,T	054	554	06.02.02	7514	480506	91321
615.482-038	TURRET-PUNCH-PRESS OPERATOR (any industry)	4335	34333433335	HHNFNNNFFNNNNFNFNNN	NNNN5NNNNNNNNN	J,T	134	554	06.02.02	7514	480506	91308
615.662-010	SLITTING-MACHINE OPERATOR II (any industry)	3225	33343322355	MMNNNONFFOOONFNFFNN	NNNN5NNFNNNNNNF	J,T	054	541	06.02.02	7314	480506	91308
615.682-010	FLYING-SHEAR OPERATOR (steel & rel.)	3325	34434433355	MNNNNNNFFNNONFNFFNN	NNFN4NNFNNNNNNF	R,T	054	541	06.02.02	7514	480506	91321
615.682-018	PUNCH-PRESS OPERATOR III (any industry)	3224	34433444345	HNNONONFFONNNNFNFFNN	NNNN4NNNNNNNNN	R,T,J	134	541	06.02.02	7514	480506	91321
615.682-018	SHEAR OPERATOR I (any industry)	3224	34433443345	HNNNNNNNFFNNNNFNFFNN	NNFN4NFFNNNNNNF	R,T	054	554	06.02.02	7514	480506	91321
615.685-010	BURRING-MACHINE OPERATOR (nut & bolt)	2122	44444533455	MMNFONNFFNNNNFNFNNN	NNNN4NNNNNNNNN	R,T	054	555	06.04.02	7514	000000	92198
615.685-014	CLEARANCE CUTTER (clock & watch)	2112	44544533455	SNNNNNNFFOONNNNNNNN	NNNN4NNNNNNNNN	R	134	607	06.04.02	7678	470408	91321
615.685-018	CUP-TRIMMING-MACHINE OPERATOR (ordnance)	2112	44445544345	LNNNNNNNFFONNNNNNNN	NNNN4NNNNNNNNN	R,T	054	541	06.04.02	7512	480503	91117
615.685-022	CUT-OFF-MACHINE OPERATOR (ordnance)	2112	44444444355	MNNNNNNNFFONNNNONNNNN	NNNN4NNNNNNNNN	R,T	054	541	06.04.02	7514	480503	91321
615.685-026	NIBBLER OPERATOR (any industry)	2223	34434544345	MNNNFNNNFFONNNNFNONNN	NNNN5NFNNNNNNNF	R,T	054	554	06.04.02	7514	480506	91321

DOT #	DOT Title & Industry	Trng	Aptitude	Physical	Environment	Tempra	WkF	MPSMS	GOE	SOC	CIP	OES
615.685-030	PUNCH-PRESS OPERATOR II (any industry)	2123	44454544345	MNNNNNNFFNNONFNFNNN	NNNN4NNFNNNNNN	R,U,T	134	540	06.04.02	7514	480501	91321
615.685-034	SHEAR OPERATOR II (any industry)	2224	34433534345	HNNFNFFONNNNFOFFNO	NNFN4NCFNNNNNNC	R,T	054	550	06.04.02	7514	480506	91321
615.685-038	STRIP-METAL-PUNCH-AND-STRAIGHTENER OPERATOR (wood. container)	2113	44543534355	NNNN4NNNNNONONNN	NNNN4NNNNNNNN	R,T	054	541	06.04.02	7514	480501	91321
615.685-042	TURRET-PUNCH-PRESS OPERATOR, TAPE-CONTROL (any industry)	2223	44444543455	HNNFNNNFFFNNNNFNOONN	NNNN4NNNNNNNNF	R,T	134	554	06.04.02	7514	480506	91321
615.685-046	CUTTER-MACHINE TENDER (electron. comp.)	2222	44444444445	MNNNNNNFFNNNNONONNN	NNNN3NNONNNNNN	R,U	054	587	06.04.09	7678	470105	92944
615.687-010	HELPER, SHEAR OPERATOR (steel & rel.)	2113	44444433355	HNNNNNNFFNFFNFNFNNN	NNON3NNNNNNNN	R,U	054	541	06.04.24	8611	000000	98999
616.130-010	SUPERVISOR (nut & bolt)	4337	33333333354	LNNONONFFNFFNFNFNOON	NNNN4NNNNNNNNN	V,D,P,J	057	555	06.02.01	7100	520205	81008
616.130-014	SUPERVISOR, SPECIALTY MANUFACTURING (steel & rel.)	4337	33333334355	MNNONONFFNFFNFNFNNN	ONNN4NFNNNNNNN	V,D,P,J	134	541	06.02.01	7100	520205	81008
616.130-018	SUPERVISOR, SPRING PRODUCTION (metal prod., nec)	4338	33333333355	LNNONONFFFOFFNFNFONN	NNNN4NNNNNNNNO	V,D,P,J	102	559	06.02.01	7100	520205	81008
616.130-022	SUPERVISOR, STEEL DIVISION (furniture)	4337	33343333355	LNNONNNFFNFFNFNFNOON	NNNN5NNNNNNNNN	V,D,P,J	102	464	06.02.01	7100	520205	81008
616.260-010	EMBOSSING TOOLSETTER (ordnance)	4326	33343433355	LNNONNNFFFNNNNFNNNNN	NNNN5NNNNNNNNN	J,T	121	566	06.01.02	7329	480501	92197
616.260-014	MULTI-OPERATION-FORMING-MACHINE SETTER (any industry)	4337	33323433245	MNNONONFFFNNNNFNNNNN	NNNN4NNONNNNNN	V,J,T	102	554	06.01.02	7339	480501	91714
616.260-018	SPRING COILING MACHINE SETTER (metal prod., nec)	4437	33322444355	LNNONONFFFONNNNFNFONN	NNNN4NNNNNNNNO	J,T	134	557	06.01.02	7339	480501	92197
616.260-022	TORSION SPRING COILING MACHINE SETTER (metal prod., nec)	4437	33322444355	LNNONNNFFNOONFNFONN	NNNN4NNNNNNNNN	J,T	134	557	06.01.02	7339	480501	92197
616.280-010	SPRING MAKER (metal prod., nec)	4337	33333433354	MNNFNONFFONNNNFNFONN	NNNN4NNNNNNNNO	V,J,T	134	559	06.01.02	7339	480501	92197
616.360-010	BODY-MAKER-MACHINE SETTER (tinware)	3226	34433533354	LONOOONFFFOOONFNFFIN	NNFN4NNNNNNNNN	J,T	102	551	06.01.02	7339	480501	92197
616.360-014	LOOM SETTER, WIRE WEAVING (metal prod., nec)	4337	34335443345	MNNNOOONFFFOOONFNFFIN	NNNN4NNNNNNNNN	J,T	164	557	06.01.02	7339	480501	92197
616.360-018	MACHINE SETTER (any industry)	4336	33323433245	MNNFOONFFFNOONFNFONN	NNNN4NNFNNNNNNF	V,J,T	054	554	06.01.02	7329	480501	91505
616.360-022	MULTI-OPERATION-FORMING-MACHINE OPERATOR I (any industry)	4336	34433433345	MNNFOONFFNNNNNFNFONN	NNNN5NNNNNNNNN	J,T	102	554	06.01.02	7339	480501	92197
616.360-026	SHOTGUN-SHELL-ASSEMBLY-MACHINE ADJUSTER (ordnance)	3224	33333443355	LNNOONFFNOONFNFNNN	NNNN5NNNNNNNNF	J,T	134	374	06.01.02	7339	480501	92197
616.360-030	STRAIGHT-LINE-PRESS SETTER (ordnance)	3224	34433433355	MNNFNONFFNNNNNONNNNN	NNFN4NNNNNNNNN	V,J,T	134	374	06.01.02	7339	480501	92197
616.361-010	SPRING INSPECTOR I (metal prod., nec)	4337	33333433355	LNNNNNNFFNOONFNFONN	NNNN4NNNNNNNNN	V,J,T	212	374	06.01.05	6881	000000	83002
616.362-010	FABRIC-MACHINE OPERATOR I (furniture)	3336	33333433355	MNNOOONFFNNNNNFNFONN	NNNN4NNNNNNNNN	J,T	134	559	06.02.02	7339	480501	92197
616.380-010	FOUR-SLIDE-MACHINE SETTER (any industry)	3336	33322433355	LNNNNNNFFNNNNNFNFONN	NNNN4NNNNNNNNO	J,T	134	557	06.01.02	7339	480501	92197
616.380-014	JOB SETTER (electron. comp.)	3335	33333443355	LNNNNNNNFFNNNNNFNFONN	NNNN3NNNNNNNNN	J,T	102	540	06.01.02	7339	480501	92197
616.380-018	MACHINE OPERATOR I (any industry)	3336	34433433345	MNNNNNNFFONNNNFNFNNN	NNNN4NQONNNNNNN	T,J	111	587	06.01.03	7329	480501	91505
616.382-010	BARBED-WIRE-MACHINE OPERATOR (metal prod., nec)	3115	34434433344	LNNNNNNFFONNNNNFNFNNN	NNNN5NNNNNNNNF	R,T	057	550	06.01.03	6881	000000	83002
616.382-014	WIRE WEAVER, CLOTH (metal prod., nec)	3227	33343433355	MNNONONFFFONNNNFNFONN	NNNN4NNNNNNNNN	R,T	162	559	06.04.02	7539	480501	92198
616.382-018	TYPING-ELEMENT-MACHINE OPERATOR (office machines)	3336	33334433355	MNNOONOFFFONNNNFNFONN	NNNN4NNNNNNNNN	J,T	164	557	06.02.02	7339	480501	92998
616.460-010	NAIL-MAKING-MACHINE SETTER (steel & rel.)	3114	33333433355	MNNNNNNFFNNNNNFNOOONN	NNNN3NNNNNNNNN	T,J	061	519	06.01.03	7679	000000	92197
616.482-010	SAFETY-PIN-ASSEMBLING-MACHINE OPERATOR (button & notion)	3236	33333433355	MNNFOONFFONNNNFNFNNN	NNNN4NNNNNNNNF	J,T	135	563	06.01.02	7339	480501	92198
616.484-010	TRUER (metal prod., nec)	2224	34443433355	HNNONOOFFFNNNNNFNNNON	NNNN4NNNNNNNNF	R,T	163	618	06.02.02	7539	480501	92197
616.485-010	BENCH WORKER (metal prod., nec)	2223	34434534345	MNNNNNNFFNNNNNFNFFNN	NNNN4NNNNNNNNN	R,T	134	559	06.03.02	7820	000000	83005
616.485-014	SPRING COILER (metal prod., nec)	2114	44443443355	LNNNNNNNFFNNNNNFNFNNN	NNNN4NNNNNNNNN	R,T	102	551	06.04.02	7539	480501	92198
616.582-010	FENCE-MAKING MACHINE OPERATOR (metal prod., nec)	3116	34444533345	MNNONONFFONOONFNOFNN	NNNN4NNNNNNNNN	R,T	134	557	06.04.02	7539	480501	92198
616.662-010	HYDRAULIC PRESS OPERATOR (construction)	3214	34433433345	LNNFNONFFNNNNFNFNNN	NNNN5NONNNNNNN	J,T	135	557	06.02.02	7539	480501	92198
616.665-010	TENSIONING-MACHINE OPERATOR (concrete prod.)	3114	34434343455	MNNNNNNFFNNOONFNFNON	NNNN5NNNNNNNNN	R,T	061	563	06.04.02	7539	480501	92198
616.682-010	WEAVER, BENCH LOOM (metal prod., nec)	3225	34433433334	LNNNNNNNFFNNNNNNNNNN	FNNN3NNNNNNNNN	J,T	162	557	06.02.02	7539	480501	92197
616.682-010	ARBOR-PRESS OPERATOR I (any industry)	2112	44444534345	LNNNNNNFFONNNNONNNNN	NNNN3NNNNNNNNF	R,T	134	556	06.04.20	7830	000000	83005
616.682-014	BALE-TIE-MACHINE OPERATOR (metal prod., nec)	2114	44443443355	MNNNFNNNFFONNNNNONNNN	NNNN4NNNNNNNNN	R	134	580	06.04.20	7539	480501	92198
616.682-018	CAGE MAKER, MACHINE (concrete prod.)	3116	34444533345	LNNFNONFFFNNNNNFNFNNN	ONNN4NNNNNNNNNO	R,T	102	559	06.02.02	7339	480501	92197
616.682-022	CRIMPING-MACHINE OPERATOR (any industry)	3225	34433434355	LNNONNNFFNNNNNFNFNNN	NNNN5NNNNNNNNN	J,T	134	536	06.02.02	7539	480501	92198
616.682-026	KICK-PRESS OPERATOR I (any industry)	3224	34433433345	MNNNNNNNFFNNNNNFNFNNN	NNNN5NNNNNNNNO	J,T	134	610	06.02.02	7339	480501	92197
616.682-030	NAIL-ASSEMBLY-MACHINE OPERATOR (steel & rel.)	3224	34444544355	MNNNNNNNFFNNNNNFNONNN	NNNN4NNNNNNNNN	R,T	102	557	06.04.02	7539	480501	92198
616.682-034	STRANDING-MACHINE OPERATOR (elec. equip.; light. fix.; metal prod., nec; nofer. metal)	3224	34433433354	MNNNNNNFNONFFNNNNNFNON	NNNN4NNNNNNNNN	J,T	162	557	06.03.02	7830	480501	83005
616.685-010	CHAIN-TESTING-MACHINE OPERATOR (forging)	2124	44444444355	LNNNNNNFFNNNNNNNNNNN	NNNN3NNNNNNNNF	R,T	134	556	06.04.20	7539	480501	92198
616.685-014	CLINCHING-MACHINE OPERATOR (elec. equip.)	2112	44444534345	LNNNNNNFFONNNNNNONNNN	NNNN4NNNNNNNNN	R	134	580	06.04.20	7539	480501	92198
616.685-018	COIL ASSEMBLER, MACHINE (furniture)	2114	44443433355	MNNNNNNFFNNNNNNNNNNN	NNNN4NNNNNNNNN	R	061	559	06.04.02	7539	480501	92198
616.685-022	FABRIC-MACHINE OPERATOR II (furniture)	2113	44443543355	MNNNNNNFFONNNNNNNONNN	NNNN4NNNNNNNNN	R,T	102	557	06.04.02	7539	480501	92198
616.685-026	HEDDLE-MACHINE OPERATOR (machinery mfg.)	2113	44443544355	MNNNNNNFFONNNNNNNNNN	NNNN3NNNNNNNNN	R,T	054	567	06.04.02	7539	480501	92198
616.685-030	KNITTER, WIRE MESH (metal prod., nec)	2222	44443433355	MNNNONONFFFNNNNFNNONN	NNNN4NNNNNNNNN	R,T	165	557	06.04.02	7539	480501	92198

DOT #	DOT Title & Industry	Trng	Aptitude	Physical	Environment	Tempra	WkF	MPSMS	GOE	SOC	CIP	OES
616.685-034	LOAD TESTER (metal prod., nec)	2223	34433345355	LNNNNNNFFNNNNFNFNNN	NNNN4NNNNNNNNNNN	R,T	212	559	06.03.02	7830	000000	83005
616.685-038	METAL-SPONGE-MAKING-MACHINE OPERATOR (nonfer. metal)	2113	44443444355	MNNNNNNNFFNNNNFNNONN	NNNN3NNNNNNNNNNN	R,T	163	541	06.04.02	7539	480501	92198
616.685-042	MULTI-OPERATION-FORMING-MACHINE OPERATOR II (any industry)	2112	44444544355	MNNNNNNNFFNNNNFNNOONN	NNNN4NNNNNNNNNNN	R,T	102	554	06.04.02	7539	480501	92198
616.685-046	PAPERBACK-MACHINE OPERATOR (metal prod., nec)	2113	34433433355	LNNNNNNNFFNNNNFNNONN	NNNN4NNNNNNNNNNN	R,T	171	557	06.04.09	7539	000000	92198
616.685-050	POCKET-MACHINE OPERATOR (furniture)	2113	44444434355	LNNNNNNNFFNNNNFNNNNN	NNNN3NNNNNNNNNNN	R,T	162	464	06.04.20	7539	000000	92198
616.685-054	RIVETER (light. fix.)	2112	44444444345	LNNNNNNNFFONNNNNNNNNN	NNNN4NNNNNNNNNNN	R	061	584	06.04.20	7539	480501	92198
616.685-058	RIVETING-MACHINE OPERATOR (furniture)	2112	44444534345	MNNNNNNNFFONNNNFNNNNN	NNNN4NNNNNNNNNNN	R	073	463	06.04.02	7539	480501	92198
616.685-062	SCROLL-MACHINE OPERATOR (struct. metal)	2112	44445544455	MNNNOOONFFONNNNNNNNNN	NNNN4NNNNNNNNNNN	R,T	135	554	06.04.02	7539	480501	92198
616.685-066	SLAT TWISTER (furniture)	1112	44544544355	MNNNNNNNFFONNNNNNNNNN	NNNN4NNNNNNNNNNN	R	134	463	06.04.02	7539	000000	91321
616.685-070	SPIRAL SPRING WINDER (metal prod., nec)	2113	44443433355	LNNNNNNNFFONNNNFNNONN	NNNN3NNNNNNNNNNN	R	163	557	06.04.02	7539	480501	92198
616.685-074	SPIRAL WEAVER (metal prod., nec)	2223	44443433355	LNNONONFFNNNNNNNNNNN	NNNN4NNNNNNNNNNN	R,T	164	557	06.04.02	7539	480501	92198
616.685-078	SWAGER OPERATOR (pen & pencil)	2112	44444534355	LNNNNNNNFFONNNNNNNNNN	NNNN3NNNNNNNNNNN	R,T	134	617	06.04.02	7539	480501	92198
616.685-082	SWEEP-PRESS OPERATOR (clock & watch)	2112	44544544355	LNNNNNNNFFONNNNNNNNNN	NNNN3NNNNNNNNNNN	R	055	607	06.04.02	7517	000000	91321
616.685-086	WIRE COINER (button & notion)	2113	44443433355	MNNNNNNFFNNNNFNFNNN	NNNN3NNNNNNNNNNN	R,T	134	618	06.04.02	7539	000000	92198
616.685-090	ZIPPER CUTTER (button & notion)	2112	44435343345	LNNNNNNFFNNNNFNFNNN	NNNN3NNNNNNNNNNN	R	054	618	06.04.02	7539	000000	92198
616.687-010	STRANDING-MACHINE-OPERATOR HELPER (nonfer. metal)	2112	44444444455	HNNFNFNNFFNNONFNFNNN	NNNN4NNNNNNNNNNN	R	162	557	06.04.02	8619	480501	98999
616.687-014	WIRE-WEAVER HELPER (metal prod., nec)	2113	44435333355	LNNNNNNFFNNNNFNFNNN	NNNN4NNNNNNNNNNN	R	164	557	06.04.02	8619	480501	98999
617.130-010	SUPERVISOR (struct. metal)	4346	23322434354	LNNNNNNNFOFFFNFNNOOFN	NNNN4NNFNNNNNNNN	V,D,J	135	554	06.02.01	7100	000000	81008
617.130-014	SUPERVISOR, FENCE MANUFACTURE (metal prod., nec)	4226	34333433355	LNNNNNNNFFNFNFNFONN	NNNN4NCNNNNNNNNN	D,J,P	102	557	06.01.01	7100	000000	81008
617.260-010	PRESS OPERATOR, HEAVY DUTY (any industry)	3227	34334344343	HNNONONFFNNNNNFOOFON	NNON4NNNNNNNNNNC	J,T	134	554	06.02.02	7317	480501	91305
617.280-010	SHOT-PEENING OPERATOR (aircraft mfg.)	4346	33322433255	MONOONCCOONNNONFNNN	NNNN4NNONNNNNON	T	134	592	06.02.02	7326	480501	91502
617.360-010	BRAKE OPERATOR I (any industry)	3336	34333434335	HNNONNNFFNNNNNFNFFN	NNNN4NNONNNNNNN	J,T	134	554	06.02.02	7317	480506	91305
617.360-014	SWAGING-MACHINE ADJUSTER (ordnance)	3236	33433433355	MNNONONFFNOONFNOFNN	NNNN5NNONNNNNNN	V,J,T	134	374	06.01.02	7317	480501	91305
617.380-010	KICK PRESS SETTER (button & notion)	3235	34433534345	LNNNNNNNFFONNNFNFNN	NNFN4NNNNNNNNNN	R,J,T	134	618	06.01.02	7339	480501	92197
617.382-010	STRAIGHTENING-PRESS OPERATOR II (any industry)	3224	34433533345	LNNNNNNNFFONNNFNFNN	NNNN4NNNNNNNNNN	R,T	134	554	06.02.02	7517	480501	91321
617.382-014	TUBE BENDER, BRASS-WIND INSTRUMENTS (musical inst.)	3215	34433533355	LNNNNNNNFFONNNFNFNNN	NNNN4NNNNNNNNNN	R,T	134	614	06.02.02	7529	000000	92198
617.382-018	HAMMER OPERATOR (aircraft mfg.)	3225	34433533355	MNNNONNNCCOFNNNFNFNNN	NNNN5FNFNNNNNNN	T	134	592	06.02.02	7529	000000	92198
617.480-010	JOB SETTER, SPLINE-ROLLING MACHINE (machine shop)	3235	34333433354	MONFNNNCCONNNNCNCCON	NNNN4NNNNNNNNNNN	J,T	135	568	06.01.02	7316	480501	91314
617.480-014	PRESS SETTER (nonfer. metal; steel & rel.)	3225	33333433355	MNNNNNNNFFNNNNFNFONN	NNNN4NNNNNNNNNNN	V,J,T	134	549	06.01.02	7317	480501	91305
617.482-010	BENDING-MACHINE OPERATOR I (any industry)	3225	34434444345	MNNFNNNFFONNNNFNFNN	NNNN4NNNNNNNNNNN	R,T	134	554	06.02.02	7317	480501	91314
617.482-014	FORMING-ROLL OPERATOR I (any industry)	3224	34433444345	HNNNONNNFFNNNNNFNFFN	NNNN4NNNNNNNNNNN	J,T	134	554	06.02.02	7316	480506	91314
617.482-018	ROLL-FORMING-MACHINE OPERATOR I (any industry)	3335	34333433355	MNNNNNNNFFNNNNFNFFN	NNNN5NNONNNNNNNN	R,J,T	134	559	06.02.02	7339	480501	92197
617.482-022	ROLL-FORMING-MACHINE OPERATOR II (any industry)	3214	34433534345	NNFNONNNFFONNNNNNNNN	NNFN4NNNNNNNNNNN	R,J	134	559	06.02.02	7517	480501	91321
617.482-026	STRAIGHTENING-PRESS OPERATOR II (any industry)	3215	34433533345	MMNFNNNNFFONNNFNFFN	NNNN4NNNNNNNNNN	J,T	134	554	06.04.02	7539	480501	92198
617.585-010	SWAGING-MACHINE OPERATOR (ordnance)	2112	44443433345	MNNNONNNFFONNNNFNNNNN	NNNN4NNNNNNNNNN	R,T	134	373	06.04.02	7539	480501	92198
617.665-010	NAIL-MAKING-MACHINE TENDER (steel & rel.)	2112	44443433355	MNNNONNFFONNNNFNFNN	NNNN5NNONNNNNNN	R,U	132	557	06.04.02	7529	480501	92198
617.682-010	BARREL-DEDENTING-MACHINE OPERATOR (beverage)	2114	34433544355	MNNNNNNFFNNNNFNFNNN	NNNN3NNNNNNNNNNN	R,T	054	551	06.04.02	7539	480503	92198
617.682-018	HOBBING-PRESS OPERATOR (any industry)	3114	33333433355	LNNNNNNNFFONNNNFNNONN	NNNN4NNNNNNNNNNN	R,T	135	566	06.02.02	7516	480501	92198
617.682-022	SETTER, COLD-ROLLING MACHINE (machine shop)	4337	34323433355	MNNNNNNCCONNNNCNCNCNN	NNNN4NNNNNNNNNNN	J	135	591	06.02.02	7516	480501	91314
617.685-010	BENDING-MACHINE OPERATOR II (any industry)	2113	44445534345	LNNNNNNNFFONNNNFNNONN	NNNN4NNNNNNNNNNN	R,T	134	554	06.04.02	7517	480501	91321
617.685-014	CORNER FORMER (wood. container)	2113	44544534355	LNNNNNNNFFONNNNNNNNN	NNNN3NNNNNNNNNNN	R	134	551	06.04.02	7517	480501	91321
617.685-018	EMBOSSING-MACHINE OPERATOR (nonfer. metal)	2224	44444443355	MMNNNNNNFFONNNNFNNOONN	NNNN3NNNNNNNNNNN	R,T	192	540	06.02.02	7539	480501	92198
617.685-022	EXPANDING MACHINE OPERATOR (steel & rel.)	2223	44444444355	MMNNNNNNFFONNNNFNNONN	NNNN3NNNNNNNNNNN	R,T	134	544	06.04.02	7529	480501	92198
617.685-026	POWER-PRESS TENDER (any industry)	2123	44444434345	MMNONONFFNNNNNNONNNNN	NNNN5NNONNNNNNNN	R,U	134	556	06.04.02	7517	480501	91321
617.685-030	RIPPER (furniture)	2112	44544544345	LNNNNNNNFFONNNNONNNNN	NNNN3NNNNNNNNNNN	R	134	460	06.04.20	7539	480501	92198
617.685-034	ROLL-FORMING-MACHINE OPERATOR II (any industry)	2112	44544444355	MNNNNNNNFFONNNNFNONN	NNNN4NNNNNNNNNNO	R,T	134	554	06.04.02	7516	480501	91321
617.685-038	SINTERING-PRESS OPERATOR (nonfer. metal; steel & rel.)	2222	44343433355	LNNNNNNNFFNNOONFNOFNN	NNNN4NNNNNNNNNNN	R,J,T	134	549	06.04.10	7517	480501	91321
617.685-042	SWAGE TENDER (ordnance)	2112	44444444355	LNNNNNNNFFONNNNNNNNN	NNNN4NNNNNNNNNNN	R,T	134	373	06.04.02	7517	000000	91321
617.686-010	HOOP COILER (wood. container)	1112	44544544355	MNNNNNNNFFONNNNNNNNN	NNNN3NNNNNNNNNNN	R	134	551	06.04.02	8725	000000	98502
619.130-010	HYDRAULIC-PRESSURE-AUTO-FRETTAGE-MACHINE-OPERATOR SUPERVISOR (ordnance)	4347	33344334345	LNNNNNNFFONFFNFONNNNN	NNNN3NNNNNNNNNNN	V,D,P,J	102	371	06.02.02	7100	000000	81008
619.130-014	SUPERVISOR, ALUMINUM FABRICATION (ship-boat mfg.)	4338	33333433344	MNNOONNFFNFNFNNNOON	NNNN4NNNNNNNNNNN	D,P,J,T	057	593	06.02.01	7100	000000	81008
619.130-018	SUPERVISOR, COLD ROLLING (steel & rel.)	4336	33333333355	LNNNNNNFFONFNFFNFNN	NNON4NFNNNNNNNFN	V,D,P,J	135	541	06.02.01	7100	000000	81008

DOT #	DOT Title & Industry	Trng	Aptitude	Physical	Environment	Tempra	WKF	MPSMS	GOE	SOC	CIP	OES
619.130-022	SUPERVISOR, CONTINUOUS-WELD-PIPE MILL (steel & rel.)	4338	33333333354	MNNNNNNNFFONFFNFNNFNN	NNFN4NNNNNNNNF	V,D,P,J	135	544	06.02.01	7100	000000	81008
619.130-026	SUPERVISOR, HOT-WOUND SPRING PRODUCTION (metal prod., nec)	4338	23333334355	LNNNNNNFFONFFNFNFNN	NNONN4NNNNNNNNO	V,D,P,J	102	559	06.02.01	7100	000000	81008
619.130-030	SUPERVISOR, LINE (any industry)	4238	33333433353	LNNNNNNNFFONFFNFONONN	NNNNN4NNNNNNNNO	D,P,J	102	554	06.02.01	7100	520205	81008
619.130-034	SUPERVISOR, MACHINE SETTER (any industry)	4348	33322233355	LNNNNNNNFFONFNFNFOOFNN	NNNNN4NNNNNNNNO	V,D,P	134	554	05.05.06	7100	520205	81008
619.130-038	SUPERVISOR, PIPE FINISHING (steel & rel.)	4337	33344434455	MNNNNNNNFFONFFNFONONN	NNNNN4NONNNNNNO	V,D,P,J	212	541	06.01.01	7100	520205	81008
619.130-042	SUPERVISOR, PUNCH-AND-ASSEMBLY DEPARTMENT (elec. equip.)	4347	33333333354	LNNNNNNNFFONFFNFFOONN	NNNN4NNNNNNNNN	V,D,P,J	134	582	06.02.01	7100	520205	81008
619.130-046	SUPERVISOR (comm. equip.)	4337	33333333355	MNNNONFFNFNFFNFNNOONN	NNNN4NNNNNNNNN	D,T,P,J	102	556	06.02.01	7100	480501	81008
619.131-010	MACHINING-AND-ASSEMBLY SUPERVISOR (elec. equip.)	4235	33323334354	MNNNONFFNFNFFNFNFNN	NNNN4NNNNNNNNN	V,D,P,J	057	582	06.01.01	7100	520205	81008
619.131-014	SHOP SUPERVISOR (struct. metal)	4337	33333433345	MNNNONONFFNFFNFNFONONN	ONNN3NNNNNNNNN	V,D,J,T	102	544	05.10.01	7100	520205	81008
619.131-018	SHRINK-PIT SUPERVISOR (ordnance)	4437	33333434355	LNNNNNNNFFONFFNONONN	NNNN4NNNNNNNNN	J	102	371	06.02.01	7100	000000	81008
619.132-010	LEAD-SECTION SUPERVISOR (ordnance)	4338	33333334355	LNNNNNNFFNNFFNOONNNN	NNNNN4NNNNNNNNN	V,D,P,J	135	541	06.02.10	7100	000000	81008
619.132-014	SHEET-MILL SUPERVISOR (nonfer. metal)	3227	33333433344	LNNNNNNNFNNFFNFONONN	NNON4NNNNNNNNO	V,D,P,T	135	540	06.02.01	7100	520205	81008
619.132-018	SHELL-SHOP SUPERVISOR (ordnance)	4328	33334434355	LNNNNNNNFFNNFFNFONONN	NNNN3NNNNNNNNN	V,D,P,J	057	370	06.02.01	7100	000000	81008
619.132-022	STRUCTURAL-MILL SUPERVISOR (nonfer. metal)	4236	33444344355	LNNNNNNNFFONFFNFNNNNN	NNNN3NNNNNNNNN	D,J,P	056	543	06.02.01	7100	520205	81008
619.132-026	SUPERVISOR, FINISHING-AND-SHIPPING (steel & rel.)	4336	33333443355	MNNNNNNNFFNFNFNFNOFNN	NNON4NONNNNNNO	V,D,P,J	054	541	06.01.01	7100	520205	81008
619.132-030	SUPERVISOR, PLATE HEATING, ROLLING, AND FINISHING (steel & rel.)	4338	33333333353	MNNNNNNOONNFFNNONNNNO	NNON4NNNNNNNNO	V,D,P,J	135	541	06.04.01	7100	520205	81008
619.134-010	SUPERVISOR, CONDITIONING YARD (steel & rel.)	3228	33333333355	MNNNNNNOONNFFNNONNNNO	FNNN3NNONNNNNO	V,D,P,J	082	541	06.04.01	7100	000000	81008
619.137-010	MACHINE-ADJUSTER LEADER (ordnance)	4338	33333433355	LNNNNNNNFFNNFFNFNNFNF	NNNN4NNNNNNNNN	D,P,J	121	374	06.02.01	7100	000000	81008
619.260-010	ORNAMENTAL-METAL-WORKER APPRENTICE (metal prod., nec)	4338	33322432254	MNONNONFFONNNNFNNONN	NNNN4NNNNNNNNO	V,J,T	102	554	05.05.06	7339	480501	89199
619.260-014	ORNAMENTAL-METAL WORKER (metal prod., nec)	4338	33322432254	MNONNONFFONNNFNNONN	NNNN4NNNNNNNNN	V,J,T	102	554	05.05.06	7339	480501	89199
619.261-010	INSPECTOR, METAL FABRICATING (any industry)	4447	33333333345	LFFFNNNCCFNOONCNNFNN	NNNN4NFNNNNNNO	V,J,T	057	550	06.01.05	6881	480501	83002
619.280-010	NEEDLEMAKER (button & notion)	4436	33222332244	MNONNONFFNNNNFNNONN	NNNN4NONNCNNFNN	V,J,T	102	618	06.01.03	7339	480501	92197
619.281-010	CASTING REPAIRER (any industry)	4447	33333343255	LNNNNNNFFNNNNFNNFFN	NNFN3NNNNNNNNN	V,J,T	057	607	06.01.03	6179	480501	85999
619.361-010	FORMER, HAND (any industry)	3336	34333444355	MNONONFFNNNNNFNNOONN	NNNN3NNNNNNNNN	V,J,T	102	542	05.10.01	6829	000000	89199
619.361-014	METAL FABRICATOR (any industry)	4337	33323432244	HNONNONFFNOONFNOFON	NNOO4NONNNNNNN	V,J,T	134	554	05.05.06	7339	480501	91714
619.361-018	METAL-FABRICATOR APPRENTICE (any industry)	4437	33323432244	HNONNONFFNOONFNOFON	NNNN4NNNNNNNNO	V,J,T	102	554	06.02.02	7529	480501	92198
619.362-014	FLANGING-ROLL OPERATOR (any industry)	3226	34334444355	MNONONFFONNNNONOONN	NNNN4NNNNNNNNO	J,T	134	554	05.05.06	7516	480501	91321
619.362-018	ROLL OPERATOR I (any industry)	4337	34333444355	MNONNONFFONNNNFNOFN	NNNN4NNNNNNNNN	J,T	134	554	06.02.02	7312	480501	91105
619.362-022	SPINNER, HAND (any industry)	4337	33322434344	MNONONFFONNNNFNOFON	NNNN4NNNNNNNNN	J,T	134	550	06.02.02	7312	000000	91105
619.364-010	SPINNER, HYDRAULIC (any industry)	4336	33333434344	HNONNNNFFONNNNFNNOON	NNNN4NNNNNNNNN	J,T	134	550	06.02.02	7820	480501	91105
619.365-010	INSPECTOR I (nonfer. metal)	3336	33333434454	LNONONFFNQONFNOFON	NNNN4NNNNNNNNN	J	212	540	06.03.01	6881	000000	83005
619.380-010	PRODUCTION-MACHINE TENDER (nut & bolt)	2222	44444444355	MNONONFFNNNNNFNNFNN	NNNN4NNNNNNNNN	J	134	540	06.04.02	7529	480501	83002
619.380-014	HIGH-ENERGY-FORMING EQUIPMENT OPERATOR (aircraft mfg.)	4336	33323443355	MNONONFFONNNNNOFNN	NNNN4NNONNNFNN	R,T	134	540	06.04.02	7529	480501	92198
619.382-010	PUNCH-PRESS SETTER (any industry)	3236	34323433445	MNNONONFFONNNNONONN	NNNN3NNNNNNNNN	T	134	592	06.01.03	7339	480501	92197
619.382-014	FITTINGS FINISHER (plumbing-heat)	3236	34323432355	MNONONFFONNNNNFFNN	NNNN4NNFFNNNNFN	J,T	134	541	06.01.02	7314	480501	91302
619.382-018	FOUR-SLIDE-MACHINE OPERATOR I (any industry)	4335	33333433343	MNONONFFONNNNFNOFON	NNON4NNNNNNNNN	J,T	134	559	06.02.02	7529	480501	92198
619.382-022	TYPE-ROLLING-MACHINE OPERATOR (office machines)	3214	34333433355	LNONONNFFNNONFNNOFON	NNNN4NNNNNNNNN	J,T	102	540	06.02.02	7329	480501	92197
619.387-010	SALVAGE WORKER (nonfer. metal)	3224	34443334345	MNONNNNFFONFFNFNNFNN	NNFN4NOFNNNNNF	V,T,J	212	571	05.05.06	7339	000000	92197
619.462-010	ROLL-THREADER OPERATOR (nut & bolt)	3224	34343443355	MNONONFFNQONFNOONNN	NNNN4NNNNNNNNN	R,T	212	540	06.03.01	7850	480501	83005
619.462-014	TRIMMER OPERATOR (nut & bolt)	3225	34443443355	HNONNNNFFNQONFNOFNN	NNNN4NNNNNNNNN	J,T	134	555	06.02.02	7329	480501	92197
619.482-010	LATHE WINDER (metal prod., nec)	3324	34432433255	LNNNNNNNFNNNNNFNNOFNN	NNNN4NNONNNNNNN	R,J,T	134	557	06.02.02	7512	480501	92197
619.484-010	ORNAMENTAL-METAL-WORKER HELPER (metal prod., nec)	2115	44433534344	MNNONONFFONNNNFNONON	NNFN4NNNNNNNNO	J,T	102	554	05.12.12	8619	480501	98999
619.485-010	SPOOL WINDER (nonfer. metal)	2112	44444544345	MOONNONFFNNNNNNNNNN	NNNN3NNNNNNNNN	J	163	557	06.04.02	7529	480501	92198
619.485-014	TWISTING-MACHINE OPERATOR (any industry)	2112	44445544355	MNNNNNNFFNNNNONOONN	NNNN4NNNNNNNNN	J,T	102	554	06.04.02	7529	480501	91321
619.582-010	STRETCHER-LEVELER OPERATOR (nonfer. metal)	3225	34333444355	MNNNNNNFFONNNNFNNOONN	NNNN4NNONNNNNNN	J,T	134	541	06.02.02	7529	480506	92198
619.662-010	SHRINK-PIT OPERATOR (ordnance)	3225	34434434355	MNNNNJNNFFONNNNFNOONN	NNFN3NNNNNNNNN	J,T	102	371	06.02.10	7675	000000	92923

DOT #	DOT Title & Industry	Trng	Aptitude	Physical	Environment	Tempra	WkF	MPSMS	GOE	SOC	CIP	OES
619.662-014	SKELP PROCESSOR (steel & rel.)	3224	33334334355	LONONONCCONOONFCFFNC	NNNN4NNONNNNNNN	T	135	544	06.02.10	7529	000000	91321
619.665-010	WINDING-MACHINE OPERATOR (concrete prod.)	2112	44544544345	LNNNNNNFFONNNNNNN	ONNN3NNNNNNNNNN	R	163	557	06.04.02	7529	480501	92198
619.682-010	BELL SPINNER (musical inst.)	3237	34434434355	HNNNNNNCCOONNFNOFNN	NNNN3NOONNNNNNN	R,T	055	614	06.02.02	7512	000000	91117
619.682-014	COUPLING-MACHINE OPERATOR (steel & rel.)	3224	34444444355	MNNNNNNFFNNNNNNNN	NNNN4NNNNNNNNNN	R,T	061	559	06.04.20	7529	000000	92198
619.682-018	FISHING ACCESSORIES MAKER (toy-sport equip.)	3224	34444444445	LNNNNNNFFNNNNNNNN	NNNN4NNNNNNNNNN	R,T	102	616	06.02.02	7329	480501	92197
619.682-022	HEATER (forging)	3224	34434434354	HNNNONONFFONNNNCOOCFF	NNFF4NOFNNNNNNO	J,T	133	556	06.02.02	7544	000000	91938
619.682-026	HOOP BENDER, TANK (wood. container)	3223	34443434354	MNNNNNNFFONNNNNNN	NNNN4NNNNNNNNNN	R,T	134	559	06.02.02	7529	480503	92198
619.682-030	HOOP MAKER, MACHINE (wood. container)	3224	34432434355	MNNNNNONFFONNNNFNOONN	NNNN4NNFNNNNNNO	R	134	559	06.02.02	7529	480501	92198
619.682-034	HOOP-FLARING-AND-COILING-MACHINE OPERATOR (wood. container)	3224	34344544355	LNNNNNNFFONNNNNFNNNN	NNNN4NNNNNNNNNN	R	134	551	06.02.02	7529	000000	92198
619.682-038	SAMPLER, FIRST (smelt. & refin.)	4235	33433433354	MNNNNNNFFNNNNONNNNN	NNFN3NNNNNNNNNN	V,T	135	541	06.02.02	7529	000000	83005
619.682-042	SEAMLESS-TUBE ROLLER (steel & rel.)	3225	34434434355	MNNOONFFONNNNNNNNN	NNNN3NNNNNNNNNN	R,T	135	541	06.02.02	7329	480501	92197
619.684-010	FORMER HELPER, HAND (any industry)	2113	44443444343	HNNONONFFONNNNFNOFON	NNON4NNNNNNNNNN	R,T	134	554	06.04.24	8619	480501	92198
619.685-010	BAND MAKER (agriculture)	2112	45445444355	LNNNNNNNFFONNNNNNN	NNNN4NNNNNNNNNN	R	062	302	06.04.20	7517	480501	91321
619.685-014	BANDING-MACHINE OPERATOR (furniture)	2112	44445444355	MNNNNNNFFONNNNFNNNN	NNNN3NNNNNNNNNN	R	061	463	06.04.02	7517	480501	91321
619.685-018	BANDING-MACHINE OPERATOR (ordnance)	2113	44443544355	MNONNNNFFONNNNNNNNN	NNNN4NNNNNNNNNN	R	121	370	06.04.02	7517	480501	91321
619.685-022	BOBBIN-WINDER TENDER (glass mfg.)	1112	44444433355	LNNNNNNNFFNNNNNNNN	NNNN4NNNNNNNNNN	R	163	557	06.04.02	7529	480501	92198
619.685-026	BRAKE OPERATOR II (any industry)	3224	34434534345	MNNNNNNFFONNNFNOFNN	NNNN4NNNNNNNNNN	R,T	134	554	06.02.02	7517	480506	91321
619.685-030	COIL-REWIND-MACHINE OPERATOR (nonfer. metal)	2112	44444544355	MNNNNNNFFONNNNNNNNN	NNNN3NNNNNNNNNN	R,J	163	541	06.04.02	7529	480506	92198
619.685-034	DRUM STRAIGHTENER I (any industry)	2112	44544544355	HNNONNNFFONNNNFNNNF	NNFF4NNNNNNNNNN	R,T	134	551	06.04.02	7516	480501	91321
619.685-038	EMBOSSING-MACHINE OPERATOR (ordnance)	2222	44443434355	LNNNNNNFFNNNNNFNNNN	NNNN4NNNNNNNNNN	R,T	134	374	06.04.02	7529	480501	92198
619.685-042	ETCHER, MACHINE (cutlery-hrdwr.)	2224	44434544355	MNNONNNFFONNNNFNNNN	NNNN3NNNNNNNNNN	R,T	182	552	06.04.02	7529	480501	92198
619.685-046	FORMING-ROLL OPERATOR II (any industry)	2113	44544544355	HNONNNNFFNNNNFNFNNN	NNNN4NNNNNNNNNN	R	134	559	06.04.02	7516	480506	91321
619.685-050	FOUR-SLIDE-MACHINE OPERATOR II (any industry)	2223	44443543455	MNNNNNNFFNNNNFNFNNN	NNNN4NNNNNNNNNN	J	134	540	06.04.02	7529	480501	92198
619.685-054	HEAD-GAUGE-UNIT OPERATOR (ordnance)	1112	34434534345	MNNNNNNFFONNNNNNNNN	NNNN3NNNNNNNNNN	R,T	212	374	06.04.20	7517	480501	91321
619.685-058	HEEL-WASHER-STRINGING-MACHINE OPERATOR (rubber goods)	2112	44444544355	LNNNNNNNFFONNNNNNN	NNNN4NNNNNNNNNN	R	061	555	06.04.02	7529	480501	92198
619.685-062	MACHINE OPERATOR II (any industry)	2123	44434444345	MNNONNNCCFNNNNFNFNNN	NNNN4NNONNNNNNN	R	054	554	06.04.02	7539	480501	91714
619.685-066	METAL FABRICATOR HELPER (any industry)	2114	34443534355	HOOOOOOFFONNNNNNNNN	NNNN4NNNNNNNNNN	R,T	102	554	06.04.02	7529	480501	92198
619.685-070	METALLIC-YARN-SLITTING-MACHINE OPERATOR (nonfer. metal)	2113	44444534345	LNNNNNNFFONNNNFNNNNN	NNNN3NNNNNNNNNN	R,T	054	559	06.04.02	7529	480501	92198
619.685-074	REPAIRER, SHOE STICKS (rubber goods)	1112	44444534345	MNNNNNNFFONNNNONNNN	NNFN3NNNNNNNNNN	R	134	550	06.04.02	7529	480501	98502
619.685-078	ROD-PULLER AND COILER (nonfer. metal)	2112	44433434345	LNFNNNNFFNNOONFNNFNN	NNFN4NNNNNNNNNN	R,T	163	541	06.04.02	8611	480501	98999
619.685-082	SPINNING-LATHE OPERATOR, AUTOMATIC (any industry)	2112	44444444455	LNFNNNFFNNOONFFNNNN	NNFN4NNNNNNNNNN	R	134	550	06.04.02	7512	480506	98502
619.685-086	WINDING-LATHE OPERATOR (ordnance)	2113	44444544345	MNNNNNNFFNNNNNNNNNN	NNCN3NNNNNNNNNN	R	134	372	06.04.02	7512	480501	91117
619.685-090	WIRE-WINDING-MACHINE OPERATOR (wood. container)	2112	45544534355	MNNNNNNFFONNNNNNNNN	NNCN3NNNNNNNNNNO	R	163	557	06.04.02	7529	480501	92198
619.685-094	CUT-OFF-MACHINE OPERATOR (steel & rel.)	2223	44434444345	HNNNNNNFFONNNNFNNNN	NNNN3NNNNNNNNNN	R,T	163	557	06.04.02	7529	480503	91117
619.686-010	AUTOMATIC STACKER (tinware)	1112	45554544455	LNNNNNNFFONNNNNNNNN	NNFO4NNFNNNNNNF	R	056	541	06.04.40	8725	000000	98999
619.686-014	HOOP-MAKER HELPER, MACHINE (wood. container)	2112	44443544355	MNNNNNNFFONNNNNONNN	NNNN4NNNNNNNNNN	R	134	551	06.04.02	8611	000000	98502
619.686-018	HOPPER FEEDER (ordnance)	1112	45444534455	HFNFNNNFFONNNNNNNN	NNNN4NNNNNNNNNN	R	011	374	06.04.02	8725	000000	98502
619.686-022	METAL-FABRICATING-SHOP HELPER (any industry)	2112	44444544345	HONOOONFFONONFFNNN	NNNN4NOFNNNNNNN	R	102	554	06.04.02	8611	480501	98999
619.686-026	SPIKE-MACHINE HEATER (steel & rel.)	2112	45544545355	LNNOOONFFNNFNFNNNNN	NNFN4NNNNNNNNNN	R	133	557	06.04.02	8725	000000	98502
619.686-030	STRETCHER-LEVELER-OPERATOR HELPER (nonfer. metal)	2112	44544544355	MNNNNNNFFNNNNNNNNNN	NNNN3NNNNNNNNNN	R,T	134	541	06.04.02	8611	480501	98999
619.686-034	FORGE HELPER (forging)	2112	45544544444	HNNFNFNFFONNNNNNNNN	NNFO4NFNNNNNNNF	R	011	556	06.04.40	8611	480501	98999
619.687-010	COIL BINDER (nonfer. metal)	2112	44544534355	LNNNNNNFFONNNNNNNNON	NNNN4NNNNNNNNNN	R	041	541	06.04.38	7740	000000	93999
619.687-014	MACHINE HELPER (any industry)	2113	44444444344	HNNONNNFFONNNNNFOOON	NNNN4NNNNNNNNNN	R	134	540	06.04.24	8611	480506	98999
619.687-018	PITCH FILLER (any industry)	2112	45544544355	MNNNNNNFFONNNNFNNNN	NNFN3NNNNNNNNNN	R	131	500	05.12.10	7740	000000	93999
620.131-010	SUPERVISOR, ENDLESS TRACK VEHICLE (automotive ser.)	4447	33323344355	LNNONNNFFONFFNFNOFNN	NNNN4NNNNNNNNNN	V,P,J	121	590	05.05.09	7100	520205	81008
620.131-014	SUPERVISOR, GARAGE (automotive ser.)	4347	33333333334	LNNOOONFFFNFFNFNFNON	NNNN4NNNNNNNNNN	V,D,P,J,T	121	590	05.05.09	7100	520205	81002
620.131-018	SUPERVISOR, MOTORCYCLE REPAIR SHOP (automotive ser.)	4348	33333333334	LNNOOONFFNFFNFNNNNN	NNFN4NNNNNNNNNN	V,D,P,J	121	595	05.05.09	7100	520205	81002
620.137-010	TANK AND AMPHIBIAN TRACTOR OPERATIONS CHIEF (military ser.)	3227	33333333335	LNNNNNNFFNFNFNFNOONO	FNNN4NNNNNNNNNO	D,P	121	598	05.10.02	6000	000000	81002
620.261-010	AUTOMOBILE MECHANIC (automotive ser.)	4337	33423433244	MNNOOOOFFNOONFFOON	NNNN4NFNNNNNNNN	V,J,T	111	591	05.05.09	6111	470604	85302
620.261-012	AUTOMOBILE-MECHANIC APPRENTICE (automotive ser.)	4337	33423433244	MNNOOOOFFNOONFFOON	NNNN4NFNNNNNNNN	V,J,T	111	591	05.05.09	6111	470604	85302
620.261-014	AUTOMOBILE TESTER (automotive ser.)	4337	33433443334	LNNOOONFFONFNFNNQON	NNNN3NNNNNNNNNN	V,J	121	591	05.07.02	6881	470604	83002

DOT #	DOT Title & Industry	Trng	Aptitude	Physical	Environment	Tempra	WkF	MPSMS	GOE	SOC	CIP	OES
620.261-018	AUTOMOBILE-REPAIR-SERVICE ESTIMATOR (automotive ser.)	4337	33334344345	LNNOOONFFONFFNOFFNN	ONNN3NOONNNNNNN	V,J	211	591	05.07.02	6881	470603	83002
620.261-022	CONSTRUCTION-EQUIPMENT MECHANIC (construction)	3237	33333343345	MNNFFFNFFNFFFNN	CNNN4NFFNNNNNN	V,J,T	111	563	05.05.09	6117	470302	85314
620.261-026	ELECTRIC-GOLF-CART REPAIRER (amuse. & rec.; automotive ser.)	3235	33332433254	MNNOOONFFFNNNFNOOON	NNNN3NNNNNNNN	V,J,T	111	582	05.10.03	6152	470106	85714
620.261-030	AUTOMOBILE-SERVICE-STATION MECHANIC (automotive ser.)	3235	33332493355	MNNFFFNFFNFNFNN	NNNN3NNNNNNNN	T,J	121	591	05.05.09	6111	470604	85302
620.261-034	AUTOMOTIVE-COOLING-SYSTEM DIAGNOSTIC TECHNICIAN (automotive ser.)	4337	23333334354	MNNONONFFFOOONFNOFON	NNNN3NNNNNNNN	T,J	121	591	05.05.09	6111	150803	85302
620.281-010	AIR-CONDITIONING MECHANIC (automotive ser.)	3236	33323433355	MNNOOONFFFNNNNFNONN	NNNN3NNNNNNNN	V,J,T	121	591	05.05.09	6111	470604	85302
620.281-014	AUTOMOTIVE TECHNICIAN, EXHAUST EMISSIONS (government ser.)	4237	34333322234	LNNONNNFFFOOONFOOOON	NNNN4NNNNNNNN	J	212	591	05.05.09	6881	470604	83002
620.281-018	AUTOMOTIVE-MAINTENANCE-EQUIPMENT SERVICER (any industry)	4337	33323433254	MNNFFFNFFOONNFNOONN	NNNN4NNNNNNNN	V,J,T	121	568	05.05.09	6130	470303	85119
620.281-026	BRAKE REPAIRER (automotive ser.)	3336	33333433355	MNNOOONFFFONNFNNOON	NNNN4NNNNNNNN	V,J,T	121	591	05.10.02	6111	470604	83002
620.281-030	BUS INSPECTOR (automotive ser.)	4447	33332333344	MNNOOONFFNFFNFNOOON	ONNN4NNONNNNNN	V,J,T	121	591	05.05.09	6881	470604	83002
620.281-034	CARBURETOR MECHANIC (automotive ser.)	3237	34432443355	LNNNNNNFFFNNNFNNONN	NNNN3NNNNNNNN	J,T	121	591	05.10.02	6111	470604	85302
620.281-038	FRONT-END MECHANIC (automotive ser.)	3336	34433433345	MNNFFFNFFONNNFNFNN	NNNN3NFFNNNNNN	V,J,T	121	591	05.10.01	6111	470604	85302
620.281-042	LOGGING-EQUIPMENT MECHANIC (logging)	4337	33333433335	VFFFFFFFFFOONFNOOON	FNNN4NONNNNNNN	V,J,T	121	563	05.05.09	6117	470302	85314
620.281-046	MAINTENANCE MECHANIC (construction; petrol. & gas; pipe lines)	4337	33333433244	MNNOOONFFFNNNNFNOONN	NNNN4NNNNNNNN	V,J,T	121	568	05.05.09	6111	470302	85302
620.281-050	MECHANIC, INDUSTRIAL TRUCK (any industry)	3336	33342433244	MNNOOONFFFNNONFNOON	ONNN4NFFNNNNFF	J,T	121	565	05.05.09	6112	470302	85311
620.281-054	MOTORCYCLE REPAIRER (automotive ser.)	4337	33342433244	MNNOOONFFFNNNFNOOON	NNNN4NNNNNNNN	V,T,J	121	595	05.05.09	6114	470606	85308
620.281-058	TRACTOR MECHANIC (automotive ser.)	4337	33323433244	MONFFFFFOOFNFNOOON	NNNN3NNNNNNNN	V,J,T	121	565	05.05.09	6112	470302	85302
620.281-062	TRANSMISSION MECHANIC (automotive ser.)	3337	34423433244	MNNOOONFFFOOFNFNONN	NNNN4NNNNNNNN	V,J,T	121	591	05.10.02	6111	470604	85311
620.281-066	TUNE-UP MECHANIC (automotive ser.)	4337	33322432354	LNNONONFFFNOFNFNOOON	NNNN4NNNNNNNN	J,T	121	591	05.10.02	6111	470604	85302
620.364-010	VEHICLE-FUEL-SYSTEMS CONVERTER (automotive ser.)	3236	33332433344	LNNNNNNFFFNNNNFNFNON	NNNN3NNNNNNNN	J	121	591	05.10.02	6111	470604	85302
620.384-010	SQUEAK, RATTLE, AND LEAK REPAIRER (automotive ser.)	2224	34433444355	MNNONONFONFFNONONNO	NNNN3NNNNNNNN	V,J	121	591	05.12.15	6115	470603	85305
620.381-010	AUTOMOBILE-RADIATOR MECHANIC (automotive ser.)	3236	44423433355	MNNOOONFFFOOONFNONN	NNNO3NNNNNNNN	V,J,T	121	591	05.10.02	6111	470604	85302
620.381-014	MECHANIC, ENDLESS TRACK VEHICLE (automotive ser.)	4337	34423433255	MNNONONFFFNNNNFNOONN	NNNN3NNNNNNNN	V,J,T	121	590	05.05.09	6117	470604	85314
620.381-018	MECHANICAL-UNIT REPAIRER (automotive ser.; railroad equip.)	4337	33333432255	MNNONONFFFNOONFNFONN	ONNN3NNNNNNNN	V,J,T	121	594	05.05.09	6117	470302	85317
620.381-022	REPAIRER, HEAVY (auto. mfg.)	3236	34433432255	HNNONONFFFNNNNFNFFNN	NNNN4NNNNNNNN	J,T	121	591	05.05.09	6112	470302	85302
620.384-010	MOTORCYCLE TESTER (motor-bicycles)	3335	33333433344	MNNONONFFFNNOFNFNFON	NNNN3NNNNNNNFN	R,T	121	591	06.03.01	7830	470606	83005
620.584-010	SPRING-REPAIRER HELPER, HAND (automotive ser.)	2124	44444444345	HNNOOONFFONNNFNONNN	NNNN4NNNNNNNN	R	102	591	05.12.12	8619	470604	98999
620.664-010	CONSTRUCTION-EQUIPMENT-MECHANIC HELPER (construction)	2123	34444433355	MOOFFFNFFONNNFNNNNN	FNNO4NONNNNNNN	V	121	563	05.12.15	8632	470302	98102
620.664-014	MAINTENANCE MECHANIC HELPER (construction; petrol. & gas; pipe lines)	3225	34433434355	HNNOOONFFONNNFNONNN	NNNN3NNNNNNNN	R,T	121	560	05.10.02	8632	010204	98102
620.682-010	BRAKE-DRUM-LATHE OPERATOR (automotive ser.)	3225	34332432355	MNNFFFNFFNNNFNFNN	NNNN3NONNNNNNN	R,J,T	051	591	06.02.02	7312	480503	91105
620.684-010	AUTOMOBILE WRECKER (wholesale tr.)	3224	44444433355	HONOOONFFFNNNNFNNOON	FNNN3NNNNNNNN	V	121	591	05.10.04	6179	470603	85999
620.684-014	AUTOMOBILE-MECHANIC HELPER (automotive ser.)	2123	44433444355	HNNFFFNFFOONNFNNNNN	ONNO3NFFNNNNFN	R	121	591	05.12.10	8632	470604	98102
620.684-018	BRAKE ADJUSTER (automotive ser.)	2222	34444444345	LNOOOONFFONNNNFNONON	ONNN3NNNNNNNN	R	121	591	05.05.09	7661	470604	98102
620.684-022	CLUTCH REBUILDER (automotive ser.)	3234	34433434355	MNNFFFNFFONOFNFOOON	ONNN3NNNNNNNN	R,T	121	591	05.07.02	6881	470604	83002
620.684-026	MOTORCYCLE SUBASSEMBLY REPAIRER (motor-bicycles)	3225	34433334354	HNNOOONFFONOFNNONNN	NNNN4NOOOONNNN	R,T	102	595	05.10.02	6114	470606	85308
620.684-030	TRACTOR-MECHANIC HELPER (automotive ser.)	2124	34433444345	HNNOOONFFOOFFNNFFF	NNNN5NNONONNNN	R,T	102	565	05.12.15	8632	470606	98102
620.684-034	USED-CAR RENOVATOR (retail trade)	3224	34434443344	MNNONONFFFOONNFNNON	FNNN3NONNNNNNN	V,J,T	121	591	05.10.04	6115	010204	85305
620.685-010	BONDER, AUTOMOBILE BRAKES (automotive ser.)	2123	44434444355	LNNNNNNFFNFFNFNFFNN	NNON3NNNNNNNN	R,T	063	591	05.12.10	7661	000000	92956
621.131-010	SUPERCHARGER-REPAIR SUPERVISOR (air trans.)	4447	33333433355	LNNNNNNFFNFFNFNFFNN	NNNN5NNNNNNNN	D,P,J,T	121	592	05.05.09	7100	520205	81002
621.131-014	SUPERVISOR, AIRCRAFT MAINTENANCE (air trans.)	4448	33333433344	LOOONFFOOFNFFNFF	NNNN5NNNNNNNN	D,P,J,T	121	592	05.05.09	7100	520205	81002
621.137-010	SUPERVISOR, RECLAMATION (wholesale tr.)	4336	33333444455	LNNNNNNFFNFFNFNFFNN	ONNN5NONONNNNN	D,P	102	592	05.05.09	7100	520205	81008
621.221-010	FIELD-SERVICE REPRESENTATIVE (aircraft mfg.)	5447	22322433344	LONOOOFFFNFNNFNNNON	NNNN4NNONONNON	V,D,J,P	296	592	05.05.09	2390	470608	31314
621.261-010	AIRPLANE INSPECTOR (air trans.)	4448	23322433344	LFFOOOOFFFNNNNFNFFNN	ONNN5NNONONNON	J	121	592	05.07.02	6881	470608	83002
621.261-014	ENGINE TESTER (aircraft mfg.; air trans.)	4447	22333343355	MOOOOONFFFONFNNFNNNN	NNNN4NOOOONNNN	V,T,J	121	592	06.01.05	6881	150801	83002
621.261-018	FLIGHT ENGINEER (air trans.)	4447	22233233344	MNNNNNFFNFNFNNFFN	ONNN5NNONNNNNN	V,S,J,T	111	592	05.03.06	8250	490102	97702
621.261-022	EXPERIMENTAL AIRCRAFT MECHANIC (aircraft mfg.)	4347	33322333344	MOOOOONFFOOOOFFOON	ONNN5NOOOOONNN	V,T,J	111	592	05.05.09	6116	150801	85323
621.281-014	AIRFRAME-AND-POWER-PLANT MECHANIC (aircraft mfg.; air trans.)	4447	33322433244	MOOOOOOFFOONOONFOON	ONNN4NOOOONNOO	J,T,V	102	592	05.05.09	6116	470608	85323
621.281-018	AIRFRAME-AND-POWER-PLANT-MECHANIC APPRENTICE (air trans.)	4447	33322433244	MOOOOOOFFFONOOONFOON	ONNN4NOOONNOO	J,T,V	102	592	05.05.09	6116	470608	85323
621.281-030	ROCKET-ENGINE-COMPONENT MECHANIC (aircraft mfg.)	4447	33322433354	MONONONFFOONNNFNFNON	NNNN4NNONONNON	T,J	121	592	05.05.09	6175	000000	85928
621.684-010	AIRFRAME-AND-POWER-PLANT-MECHANIC HELPER (aircraft mfg.; air trans.)	4448	23322433344	MOOOOOONFFONONFNOON	ONNN4NOOONNON	V,T	102	592	05.10.02	8632	470608	98102
621.684-014	RECLAMATION WORKER (wholesale tr.)	3224	34434344355	MNNNNNFFNNNNNNNN	FNNN4NONNNNNNN	R	102	592	05.12.12	6179	470608	85323

DOT #	DOT Title & Industry	Trng	Aptitude	Physical	Environment	Tempra	WkF	MPSMS	GOE	SOC	CIP	OES
622.131-010	SUPERVISOR, RAILROAD CAR REPAIR (railroad equip.)	4348	33333333354	LONFOONFFFOFFNFFOFON	FNNN4NNNNNNNNNN	V,D,P,J	102	594	05.05.06	7100	000000	81002
622.131-014	SUPERVISOR, ROUNDHOUSE (railroad equip.)	4348	33333333344	LNNOOONFFFNFNONONON	NNNN4NNNNNNNNNN	V,D,P,J	121	594	05.05.09	7100	000000	81008
622.131-018	SUPERVISOR, WHEEL SHOP (railroad equip.)	4348	33333433354	MFOFNNFFFNFFNFFNFNN	NNNN4NNNNNNNNNN	V,D,P,J	057	594	05.05.07	7100	000000	81002
622.137-010	SUPERVISOR, BRAKE REPAIR (r.r. trans.)	3227	33433445455	LNNFNNNOOONFFNFFNNN	FNNN4NNNNNNNNNN	D,V,P	121	367	05.02.02	6000	470302	81002
622.137-014	SUPERVISOR, CAR AND YARD (r.r. trans.)	3226	33433444455	LNNNNNNFFONOONOFNNNN	NNNN4NNNNNNNNNN	D,P,J	102	594	05.05.06	6000	470302	81002
622.261-010	BRAKE REPAIRER, RAILROAD (r.r. trans.)	3226	34434434345	VONONONFCFNFFNFNNO	FNNN4NNNNNNNNNNO	T	121	367	05.05.09	6175	470302	87714
622.281-010	LOCOMOTIVE INSPECTOR (railroad equip.)	4337	33333443344	LFNFFFNFFONNNNFFFON	ONNN4NNNNNNNNNN	J,T	102	594	05.07.01	6881	000000	83002
622.381-010	AIR-VALVE REPAIRER (railroad equip.)	3226	34434444354	LNNNNNNFFONNNFNFFN	NNNN4NNNNNNNNNN	R,T	121	594	05.10.02	6175	470401	85928
622.381-014	CAR REPAIRER (railroad equip.)	4337	34434444355	HOOOOOOFFONOONFFFNN	ONNN4NNNNNNNNNN	J,T	102	594	05.05.06	6117	470302	85317
622.381-018	CAR REPAIRER, PULLMAN (r.r. trans.)	4337	33334434355	MOOOOOOFFOOOOOOOFFNO	ONNN4NNONNNNNNO	V,J,T	121	594	05.10.01	6117	469999	85317
622.381-022	CAR-REPAIRER APPRENTICE (railroad equip.)	4337	33333434355	MFNFFFFFONNNFFFNN	NNNN4NNNNNNNNNN	J,T	102	594	05.10.01	6462	470399	87605
622.381-026	FLOOR-COVERING LAYER (railroad equip.)	4337	33333433244	HNNONONFFFNNNNFNFFON	ONNN4NNNNNNNNNN	V,J,T	092	564	05.05.06	6117	470302	85117
622.381-030	MINE-CAR REPAIRER (mine & quarry)	4336	33333444355	LNNFNNNFFNOCFNNNNNN	NNNN4NNNNNNNNNN	J	102	594	06.01.05	6881	000000	83002
622.381-034	RAILROAD WHEELS AND AXLE INSPECTOR (railroad equip.)	4336	33333434355	MNNNNNNFFONNNNFNFFNN	NNNN4NNNNNNNNNN	J	212	556	06.01.05	6881	000000	83005
622.381-038	SALVAGE INSPECTOR (railroad equip.)	3337	34434444355	MNNNNNFFONNNNFNOONN	NNNN4NNNNNNNNNN	R,T	212	594	05.07.02	7830	470401	85317
622.382-010	TRIPLE-AIR-VALVE TESTER (railroad equip.)	3336	33433444354	MFOFFFFFONNNNFFFFNN	NNNN4NNNNNNNNNN	R,T	212	594	05.10.02	6117	470302	85317
622.684-010	AIR-COMPRESSOR MECHANIC (railroad equip.)	2124	24434434345	LNNOOONFFONNNNONOONN	ONNN4NONNNNNNNN	R,T	121	594	05.12.12	8632	000000	98102
622.684-014	CAR-REPAIRER HELPER (railroad equip.)	3225	33334434355	MNNFOONFFONNNNFNFNNN	FNNN4NNNNNNNNNN	R,T	102	367	05.10.02	6179	000000	85999
622.684-018	SWITCH REPAIRER (r.r. trans.)	2124	34434434355	MOOFFFNFFONFFNONONN	ONNO4NNNNNNNNNF	V,J,T	121	594	05.12.12	7820	000000	83005
622.684-022	TANK-CAR INSPECTOR (chemical)	4338	34444434345	LNNNNNNNFFONFNFNOONN	ONNO4NNONNNNNNN	V,D,P,J	121	593	05.05.09	6700	490306	81008
623.131-010	MACHINIST SUPERVISOR, OUTSIDE (ship-boat mfg.)	4337	33333334355	MNOOONNFFONFFNFNFFON	OOON4NNONNNNNNN	V,D,P,J	121	565	05.10.02	6000	490306	81002
623.131-014	SUPERVISOR, GEAR REPAIR (water trans.)	4447	33322433345	LNNNNNNNFFONFNFNOONN	FNNN4NNNNNNNNNN	D,P,V	121	561	05.05.09	6114	490306	85328
623.261-010	EXPERIMENTAL MECHANIC, OUTBOARD MOTORS (engine-turbine)	4336	33324232354	MNOOONNFFNOONFNOONN	FNNN4NNNNNNNNNN	V,T	121	561	06.01.05	6114	490306	85328
623.261-014	OUTBOARD-MOTOR TESTER (engine-turbine)	4337	33333433354	MNNNNNNFFNOONFNOONN	NNNN4NNNNNNNNNN	J	121	565	05.05.09	6130	490306	85116
623.281-010	DECK ENGINEER (water trans.)	4335	33323433235	MMNFFFOFFNNNNFNNFNN	ONNN4NNNNNNNNNN	V,J,T	121	565	05.05.09	6179	000000	85999
623.281-014	DEEP SUBMERGENCE VEHICLE CREWMEMBER (military ser.)	4337	33333443434	MNNFFFOFFNNNNNFNNNON	NNNF3NNNNNNNNNF	J,S	121	593	05.10.02	6112	490306	85116
623.281-018	MACHINIST APPRENTICE, MARINE ENGINE (ship-boat mfg.)	4337	33333433355	MONOONFFFNNNNFNFOFON	ONNN4NNNNNNNNNN	V,J,T	121	593	05.05.09	6130	490306	85116
623.281-022	MACHINIST APPRENTICE, OUTSIDE (ship-boat mfg.)	4337	33322433235	MOOFOONFFNNNONONFFNN	ONNN4NNNNNNNNNN	V,T,J	121	593	05.05.09	6112	490306	85116
623.281-026	MACHINIST, MARINE ENGINE (ship-boat mfg.)	4337	33323433235	MOOOOOONFFONNNNFNFOFNN	NNNN4NNNNNNNNNN	V,J,T	121	593	05.05.09	6130	490306	85116
623.281-030	MACHINIST, OUTSIDE (ship-boat mfg.)	3337	33333443344	MOOFOONFFNNNNFNOONN	ONNN4NNNNNNNNNN	V,T,J	121	593	05.05.09	6179	490306	85116
623.281-034	MAINTENANCE MECHANIC, ENGINE (water trans.)	4337	33333433344	MOOFNFNFFNNNNFNOONN	NNNN4NNNNNNNNNN	V,J,T	111	593	05.05.09	6114	490306	85328
623.281-038	MOTORBOAT MECHANIC (engine-turbine; ship-boat mfg.)	4337	33323433255	MONOOOOFFFONNNNOONN	NNNN4NNNNNNNNNN	V,J,T	121	593	05.05.09	6130	490306	85328
623.281-042	OUTBOARD-MOTOR MECHANIC (engine-turbine; ship-boat mfg.)	4337	33322433345	HONOOONFFONNNNNNNNN	FNNN4NNNNNNNNNN	J,T	121	565	05.10.02	6179	490306	85999
623.381-010	GEAR REPAIRER (water trans.)	3236	33433443345	HNNFFONFFONNNONONNN	ONNN4NNNNNNNNNN	V,J,T	121	593	05.12.08	6179	490306	98102
623.684-010	MOTORBOAT-MECHANIC HELPER (engine-turbine; ship-boat mfg.)	2123	44444443345	MNNNNNNFFFNNNNNFNNN	ONNN4NNONNNNNNO	V,J,T	071	593	05.12.15	8632	490306	98102
623.687-010	MOTORBOAT HELPER, OUTSIDE (ship-boat mfg.)	2123	44444443345	HOOFFFNFFFNFNNNFNN	ONNN4NNONNNNNNN	R,T	121	593	05.12.15	8633	490306	81002
624.131-010	SUPERVISOR, FARM-EQUIPMENT MAINTENANCE (agric. equip.)	4347	33333334345	MNNFFFNFFNFFNFNFNN	FNNN4NNNNNNNNNN	V,D,P,J	121	562	05.05.09	6000	490306	81002
624.281-010	FARM-EQUIPMENT MECHANIC I (agric. equip.)	4337	33323433244	MONOOOOFFFNNONFNOOON	ONNN4NNONNNNNNN	V,J,T	121	562	05.05.09	6118	010204	85321
624.281-014	FARM-EQUIPMENT-MECHANIC APPRENTICE (agric. equip.)	4336	34433433344	MNOOOOFFFONNNNONOOON	NNNN4NNONNNNNNN	V,J,T	121	562	06.01.05	6881	010204	83002
624.361-010	INSPECTOR AND TESTER (agric. equip.)	4236	34433433344	MNNONNNFFONOONONONN	CNNF4NNNNNNNNNN	J,T	102	562	05.10.01	6118	010299	85321
624.361-014	SPRINKLER-IRRIGATION-EQUIPMENT MECHANIC (agric. equip.)	3335	34433433355	HFFOOONFFNFFNFFOFF	NNNN4NNNNNNNNNN	J,T	121	562	06.02.24	6118	010204	85321
624.381-010	ASSEMBLY REPAIRER (agric. equip.)	3236	44444443344	MNNFOFNFFONNNNFNOONN	ONNN4NNOONNNNNO	J,T	121	562	05.10.02	6118	010204	85321
624.381-014	FARM-EQUIPMENT MECHANIC II (agric. equip.)	4446	44434434345	MONOOOOFFONNNNNNNOONN	ONNN4NONNNNNNNN	V,J,T	121	562	05.10.02	6812	010204	93105
624.381-018	FARM-MACHINERY SET-UP MECHANIC (agric. equip.)	2124	44444444345	HNNFFONFFONNNONONNN	FNNN4NNNNNNNNNN	R,T	033	562	05.12.08	6118	010204	85321
624.684-010	GREASER (agric. equip.)	4448	33332344445	LNNOOONFFOFFNFNOONN	NNNN4NNONNNNNNN	V,D,P,J	121	561	06.01.01	6000	520205	81002
625.131-010	ENGINE-TESTING SUPERVISOR (engine-turbine)	4448	33334333355	LNNNNNNOOONFFNNNNNN	NNNN4NNONNNNNNN	V,D,P,J	121	561	05.05.09	6000	520205	81002
625.131-014	SUPERVISOR, ENGINE-REPAIR (engine-turbine)	4447	34433444455	LNNNNNNFFFONNNNNNNN	NNNN4NNONNNNNNN	D,J,P	121	594	05.05.09	6000	470302	81002
625.137-010	SUPERVISOR, LOCOMOTIVE (r.r. trans.)	4337	33334433344	MONNNNNNFFONNNONOOONN	NNNN4NNONNNNNNN	J	121	561	06.01.05	6881	470605	83002
625.261-010	DIESEL-ENGINE TESTER (engine-turbine)	4337	33333433244	HONFFFNFFONNONFFFON	ONON4NONNNNNNOO	J,T,V	121	560	05.05.09	6112	470605	85311
625.281-010	DIESEL MECHANIC (any industry)	4337	33333433244	HONFFNFFONNONFFFON	ONON4NONNNNNNNO	J,T,V	121	560	05.05.09	6112	470605	85311

DOT #	DOT Title & Industry	Trng	Aptitude	Physical	Environment	Tempra	WkF	MPSMS	GOE	SOC	CIP	OES
625.281-018	ENGINE REPAIRER, SERVICE (engine-turbine)	4337	33333433244	MNNNNNFFNNNNFNOOON	NNNN4NNNNNNNNNN	J,T	121	561	05.05.09	6114	470606	85328
625.281-022	FUEL-INJECTION SERVICER (any industry)	4446	34443443355	MNNONNNFFNOONFNNNN	NNNN4NNNNNNNNNNN	J	121	567	05.05.09	6111	470604	85302
625.281-026	GAS-ENGINE REPAIRER (any industry)	3336	33333433255	MNNNNNNFFNNNNFNOONN	NNNN4NNNNNNNNNN	J,T	121	561	05.05.09	6114	470606	85328
625.281-030	POWER-SAW MECHANIC (any industry)	3336	33433434255	MNNNNNNFFNNNNFNOONN	NNNN4NNONNNNNNN	J,T	121	567	05.05.09	6114	010201	85328
625.281-034	SMALL-ENGINE MECHANIC (any industry)	3336	33322432235	MNNOONNFFONOFNFNFNN	ONNN4NNNNNNNNNN	R,J,T	121	561	05.05.09	6114	010204	85328
625.361-010	DIESEL-ENGINE ERECTOR (engine-turbine)	4337	33322432235	MONONNNFFNOONFNOONN	NNNN4NNONNNNNNN	V,J,T	121	561	05.05.09	6112	470606	85311
625.381-010	ENGINE REPAIRER, PRODUCTION (engine-turbine)	4336	33333433254	MNNNNNFFNNOONFNOONN	NNNN4NNNNNNNNN	J,T	121	561	06.01.04	6114	470606	85328
625.684-010	DIESEL-MECHANIC HELPER (any industry)	2224	44444444355	MFNFFNFFONOONFNOONN	NNNN4NNNNNNNNNN	R,T	121	561	05.12.15	8632	470605	98102
626.137-010	SUPERVISOR, WELDING EQUIPMENT REPAIRER (welding)	4448	23222233344	LONOOOOOOOOFNFFOOF	NNNN4NNNNNNNNNN	D,P,J	111	580	05.05.10	6000	150603	81002
626.261-010	FORGE-SHOP-MACHINE REPAIRER (forging)	4337	33344434344	MNNNOOONFFONFNFNFNN	NNNN4NNNNNNNNNN	J	121	566	05.05.09	6130	470303	85119
626.261-014	REPAIRER, WELDING SYSTEMS AND EQUIPMENT (welding)	4447	23222333254	MOOOOONFFOOONOOOOOO	NNNN4NNNNNNNNNN	T,J	111	566	05.05.09	6130	480508	85119
626.361-010	REPAIRER, WELDING, BRAZING, AND BURNING MACHINES (welding)	4337	34332443343	MNNNNNNFFNNNNFNNFFON	NNNN4NOOONNNNNN	V,J,T	121	566	06.01.04	6130	470303	85119
626.381-010	CASE-FINISHING-MACHINE ADJUSTER (ordnance)	3335	34434433355	LNNNNNNFFONNNFNFNN	NNNN4NNNNNNNNNN	V,J,T	121	566	05.05.09	6130	470303	85119
626.381-014	GAS-WELDING-EQUIPMENT MECHANIC (any industry)	3337	33343443255	LNNNNNNFFONNNFNOONN	NNNN4NNNNNNNNNN	J,T	121	566	05.05.09	6130	480508	85119
626.381-018	HYDRAULIC-PRESS SERVICER (ordnance)	3236	33433533355	LNNONNNFFFONNNFNOOON	NNNN4NNNNNNNNN	J,T	121	566	05.05.09	6130	470303	85119
626.384-010	REPAIRER, WELDING EQUIPMENT (welding)	3224	34443443355	MNNOOONFFFNNOONFNOONN	NNNN4NNNNNNNNNN	T,R	121	582	05.10.02	6130	000000	85119
627.261-010	COMPOSING-ROOM MACHINIST (print. & pub.)	4338	33323433354	HNNFNONFFNNOONFNFON	NNNN4NNNNNNNNN	J,T	111	567	05.05.09	6130	470303	85119
627.261-014	MACHINIST APPRENTICE, COMPOSING ROOM (print. & pub.)	4338	33323433354	HNNFNONFFNOONFNFON	NNNN4NNNNNNNNNN	J,T	111	567	05.05.09	6130	470303	85119
627.261-018	MACHINIST APPRENTICE, LINOTYPE (print. & pub.)	4337	33323433355	HNNOOONFFNOONFNFNN	NNNN4NNNNNNNNNN	J,T	121	567	05.05.09	6130	470303	85119
627.261-022	MACHINIST, LINOTYPE (print. & pub.)	4337	33323433355	HNNOONNFFNOONFNFNN	NNNN4NNNNNNNNNN	J,T	121	567	05.05.09	6130	470303	85119
628.261-010	OVERHAULER (textile)	4346	33333433255	HNNOONNFFONOOONFNFNN	NNNN3NFFNNNNFN	T,J	121	567	05.05.09	6130	470303	85112
628.684-042	SPINDLE REPAIRER (textile)	2112	44543533355	LONNNNNFFONNNNNNNNN	NNNN4NNNNNNNNNN	R	102	567	05.12.15	6140	470303	85128
628.684-046	TEXTURING-MACHINE FIXER (textile)	3124	34434433355	MNNFNFNFFOFNNNNNNNN	NNNN4NNNNNNNNNN	R,T	121	567	05.10.02	7753	470303	93926
628.687-010	FLYER REPAIRER (textile)	2123	44444544455	LNNNNNNCCFNNNNCNNNN	NNNN3NNNNNNNNN	R	031	567	06.04.06	6000	470303	81002
628.687-014	SHEAR-GRINDER-OPERATOR HELPER (textile)	2112	44444544455	HNNONONFFONNNNNONNONN	NNNN4NNNNNNNNNN	R	051	566	06.04.02	7100	470303	98999
629.261-030	MAINTENANCE MECHANIC (grain-feed mills)	4336	34433433354	MONOOONFFONNNFNOONN	NNNN4NOONNNNNNN	V,J,T	121	567	05.05.09	6130	010204	85119
629.281-034	PUMP MECHANIC (paper & pulp)	4337	34433433345	MONOOONFFONNNNFNNNN	NNNN4NNNNNNNNNN	V,J	121	568	05.05.09	6130	470303	85119
629.361-010	MACHINE-CLOTHING REPLACER (paper & pulp)	4337	34433433345	MONOOONFFONNNNFNNNN	NNNN4NNNNNNNNNN	J,T	121	567	05.10.02	6130	470303	85119
629.381-010	FOILING-MACHINE ADJUSTER (ordnance)	3235	34433433355	LNNNONNNFFFNNNNFNOONN	NNNN4NNNNNNNNN	R,J,T	121	567	06.01.04	6130	470303	85119
629.381-014	OIL-FIELD EQUIPMENT MECHANIC (petrol. & gas)	4336	33333433355	MNNNNNNFFNNNNNFNOONN	NNNN4NNNNNNNONO	R,J,T	121	567	06.03.01	7830	470303	83005
629.382-010	MACHINE TESTER (machinery mfg.)	3334	34433433355	MNNOOONFFFNNNNNFNNNN	ONNN4NNNNNNNNNN	J,T	142	567	06.02.02	7322	480503	91114
629.682-010	ROLL GRINDER (rubber reclaim.)	3235	34433433355	MNNNNNNFFONNNNFNNNN	NNNN4NOONNNNNN	V,J,T	051	567	06.02.02	6140	470399	85119
629.684-010	CURING-PRESS MAINTAINER (rubber tire)	2222	44444433344	MFNFFNFFNNNNNFNNNON	NNON3NNNNNNNNNN	R,T	121	568	05.12.15	6140	470303	85128
629.684-014	MILLER, HEAD, ASSISTANT, WET PROCESS (grain-feed mills)	2125	34433544355	HONNNNFFOONNNFNFNN	NNNN4NNNNNNNNNO	R,T	052	568	06.04.30	7753	470303	93926
630.131-010	PUMP-SERVICER SUPERVISOR (any industry)	4337	33333333245	LNNNOONFFNFFNNNNN	NNNN4NNNNNNNNNN	V,D,P,J	121	537	05.10.02	6000	520205	81002
630.134-010	ANODE-CREW SUPERVISOR (smelt. & refin.)	4337	33333333245	LNNNNNNFFFOONFNNONN	ONNN4NNNNNNNNNN	V,D,P,J	121	568	05.10.02	7100	520205	81008
630.261-010	MAINTENANCE MECHANIC, COMPRESSED-GAS PLANT (chemical)	4337	33322433233	MONOOONFFNNONFNNNNN	FNNN4NNNNNNNNNN	V,J,T	121	568	05.05.09	6130	470303	85119
630.261-014	OVEN-EQUIPMENT REPAIRER (steel & rel.)	4336	33422433244	MOOFFFNFFNNONNONFFON	NNNN4NOONNNNNON	V,J,T	111	568	05.10.01	6130	470303	85119
630.261-018	REPAIRER I (chemical)	3337	33425533355	MFFNNNNFFNNNNFNNFFON	FNFN4NFNNNNNNNN	J	121	568	05.10.02	6130	470303	85119
630.281-010	PNEUMATIC-TOOL REPAIRER (any industry)	4337	34323343344	HOOOOONFFONNNNFNOOON	ONNN4NNNNNNNNNN	V,J,T	102	568	05.05.09	6130	470303	85119
630.281-014	PNEUMATIC-TUBE REPAIRER (any industry)	4337	33333433245	MNNFFNFFNNNFNFNNN	NNNN4NNONNNNNNN	J,T	121	566	05.05.09	6130	470303	85119
630.281-018	PUMP SERVICER (any industry)	3336	33333433255	MOOFFFFFFOONFNNONN	NNNN3NNNNNNNNNN	J,T	121	565	05.10.02	6130	470303	85119
630.281-022	REPAIRER (mine & quarry)	3337	33333433254	MNNNOOOFFNNNNNONON	FNNN4NNONNNNNNN	J,T	121	568	05.05.09	6130	010204	85119
630.281-026	REPAIRER (smelt. & refin.)	4336	33333443344	MOOFFFNFFONNNONFFNON	ONNN4OONNNNNNON	V,T	121	565	05.05.09	6130	470399	85119
630.281-030	RUBBERIZING MECHANIC (any industry)	4337	33322433244	MNNNNNNFFNNNNFNNFFON	NNNN4NNNNNNNNN	V,J,T	121	560	05.10.02	6130	470303	85119
630.281-034	SERVICE MECHANIC, COMPRESSED-GAS EQUIPMENT (chemical)	4337	33333433355	MONOOONFFNNNNFNFFON	ONNO4NNNNNNNNNN	J,T	121	567	05.10.02	6130	470303	85119
630.281-038	TREATMENT-PLANT MECHANIC (waterworks)	4337	33333433355	MNNNNNNFFNNNNNFNFFON	NNNN4NNNNNNNNN	V,J	121	568	05.05.09	6130	470303	85119
630.381-010	CONVEYOR-MAINTENANCE MECHANIC (any industry)	4336	34435444245	MOOOOONFFONNNNFOOONN	NNNO4NNNNNNNNN	V,J,T	121	565	05.10.02	6130	470303	85118
630.381-014	DOOR-CLOSER MECHANIC (any industry)	3336	33334433344	LNNNNNNFFONNNNNFNNNN	NNNO4NNNNNNNNNN	V,J,T	121	560	05.10.02	6130	470303	85119
630.381-018	LEAD OPERATOR (smelt. & refin.)	4336	34334343335	LFNNNNNFFONNNNNFNNNN	NNNN4NNNNNNNNNN	V,J	121	559	05.05.09	6175	470303	85928
630.381-022	LUBRICATION-EQUIPMENT SERVICER (any industry)	3226	34433434345	MNNNNNNFFFNNNNFNNNN	NNNN3NNNNNNNNNN	J,T	121	568	05.10.02	6130	470303	85119

DOT #	DOT Title & Industry	Trng	Aptitude	Physical	Environment	Tempra	WkF	MPSMS	GOE	SOC	CIP	OES
630.381-026	SPRAY-GUN REPAIRER (any industry)	3337	33423433254	LNNONONFFFNNNNFNOONN	NNNN3NNNNNNNNNN	J,T	121	568	05.10.02	6130	470303	85119
630.381-030	VALVE REPAIRER (chemical)	3336	34433433355	MNNNNNNFFNFNFNONNN	NNNN4NNNNNNNNNN	R,T	121	559	05.10.02	6175	470401	85928
630.384-010	FIXTURE REPAIRER-FABRICATOR (any industry)	3225	33433443355	MNNNONNFFNOONFNONNN	NNON4NONNNNNNNN	J,T	102	550	05.10.01	6130	480501	85119
630.384-010	EQUIPMENT CLEANER-AND-TESTER (smelt. & refin.)	3224	34444344334	MONONONFFONNNNFNNNON	NNNO4NOONNNNNON	V,T	031	560	06.04.39	6140	470303	85128
630.664-010	REPAIRER HELPER (smelt. & refin.)	2223	34433434334	HONONONFFNNNNNONOONN	ONNN4NNONNNNNNN	V	121	560	05.12.15	8633	470303	98102
630.664-014	SCREEN-AND-CYCLONE REPAIRER (mine & quarry)	3224	34433434355	MNNNNNNFFONNNNNNNNNN	NNON4OONNNNNNNN	J,T	102	568	05.10.01	6130	470399	85119
630.664-018	SERVICE-MECHANIC HELPER, COMPRESSED-GAS EQUIPMENT (chemical)	2124	44443443355	MNNNOOONFFNOONONFNNN	NNNN4NONNNNNNNN	R	121	568	05.12.15	8633	470303	98102
630.684-010	ANODE REBUILDER (smelt. & refin.)	3225	44444444355	MNNNNNNFFONNNNFNNNNN	NNNN4NONNNNNNNN	V,T	121	568	05.10.01	6130	470303	85119
630.684-014	BELT REPAIRER (any industry)	2114	44444444355	LNNNNNNFFONNNNFNNNNN	NNNN4NNNNNNNNNN	R,T	121	560	05.12.15	6140	470303	85128
630.684-018	PUMP INSTALLER (any industry)	3235	33433443355	HNNFNFNFFNNNNFNNNNN	ONNN3NNNNNNNNNN	R,T	121	568	05.10.01	6179	010204	85999
630.684-022	PUMP-SERVICER HELPER (any industry)	2125	34434434355	MNNNONNFFFNNNNFNNNNN	FNNN3NNNNNNNNNN	R,T	121	568	05.12.15	8633	470303	98102
630.684-026	REPAIRER II (chemical)	3224	34433434344	HOOOOOOFFFNNONFNONON	NNOO4NONNNNNNNN	R,T	102	565	05.12.12	6130	470303	85119
630.684-030	SCREEN REPAIRER, CRUSHER (mine & quarry)	3224	34434434355	MNNNNNNFFONNNNFNNNNN	NNNN4NNNNNNNNNN	R	121	568	05.12.15	8637	470399	98102
630.684-034	SPRAY-GUN-REPAIRER HELPER (any industry)	2123	44444443355	MNNNNNNFFONNNNNFNNNNN	NNNN4NFNNNNNNNN	R	121	565	05.12.15	6179	470303	85999
630.684-038	WHEEL-AND-CASTER REPAIRER (any industry)	2122	44444444455	MNNFNNNFFONNNNNNNNNN	NNNN3NNNNNNNNNN	R	121	565	05.12.15	6179	470303	85999
630.687-010	PULLEY MAINTAINER (mine & quarry)	1113	44444444345	MONONONFFONNNNNNNNNNN	NNNN4NOONNNNNNN	R,T	033	564	05.12.08	7740	470399	93999
631.131-010	POWERHOUSE-MECHANIC SUPERVISOR (utilities)	4448	23332333244	LONONONFFFNOONFNNNON	ONNN4NNONNNNNNN	V,D,P,J	121	560	05.05.05	6000	520205	81002
631.261-010	HYDROELECTRIC-MACHINERY MECHANIC (utilities)	4337	33332433344	HONONONFFFNNNNFNOOON	NNNN4NNONNNNNNN	V,J,T	121	560	05.10.02	6130	470303	85118
631.261-014	POWERHOUSE MECHANIC (utilities)	4338	23322333334	HOOFOOOFFFNFNFFNNNN	ONNN4OFFFFNNNN	V,J,T	121	560	05.05.09	6130	470303	85118
631.261-018	POWERHOUSE-MECHANIC APPRENTICE (utilities)	4338	23322333334	HOOFOOOFFFNFNFNFFON	ONNN4OFFFFNNNN	V,J,T	121	560	05.05.09	6130	470501	85118
631.364-010	HYDROELECTRIC-MACHINERY-MECHANIC HELPER (utilities)	3293	33332433344	HONONONFFFNNNNNONNNNN	NNNN4NNONNNNNNN	R	121	560	05.10.02	8633	470303	98102
631.684-010	POWERHOUSE-MECHANIC HELPER (utilities)	3235	34434434335	MONONONFFFNNNNNONNNN	NNNN4NNNNNNNNNN	R,T	121	561	05.12.15	8633	470303	98102
632.131-010	ARTILLERY-MAINTENANCE SUPERVISOR (ordnance)	4447	33333444355	LNNNNNNQOONFFNFNONNN	NNNN4NNNNNNNNNN	V,D,P,J	121	371	05.10.02	6000	000000	81002
632.261-010	AIRCRAFT-ARMAMENT MECHANIC (government ser.)	4336	23222432344	MONONONFFFNOOFNOFON	ONON4NNNNNNNNNN	J	111	370	05.05.10	6179	000000	85999
632.261-014	FIRE-CONTROL MECHANIC (government ser.)	4336	23222432344	MONONONFFFNNNNFNOOON	ONNN3NNNNNNNNNN	J	111	370	05.05.11	6179	000000	85999
632.261-018	ORDNANCE ARTIFICER (government ser.)	4446	23222432345	MONONONFFFNNNNFNOONN	ONNN4NNNNNNNNNO	S,J,T	111	370	05.10.02	6179	470402	85999
632.281-010	GUNSMITH (any industry)	4338	23322432253	LNNNNNNFFFNNNNFNFFON	NNNN4NNNNNNNNNN	V,J,T	121	373	05.05.07	7479	470303	92997
632.360-010	GAUGE-AND-WEIGH-MACHINE ADJUSTER (ordnance)	3235	34433433355	LONFFFNFFFNNNNFNFFNN	NNNN4NNNNNNNNNN	J,T	121	374	06.01.02	7479	470303	92997
632.360-014	LOADING-MACHINE ADJUSTER (ordnance)	3234	44433433355	LONONONFFONNNFNONNN	NNNN4OONNNNNNNN	J,T	121	374	06.01.02	7462	470303	92997
632.360-018	PRIMER-INSERTING-MACHINE ADJUSTER (ordnance)	3235	34433433355	LNNNNNNFFONNNNFNNNNN	NNNN4NNNNNNNNNN	J,T	121	374	06.01.02	7462	470303	92997
632.380-010	INSPECTING-MACHINE ADJUSTER (ordnance)	3234	34433433345	MNNNNNNFFFNNNNFNOFON	NNNN3NNNNNNNNNN	J,T	121	374	06.01.02	6130	470303	85119
632.380-014	LOADING-UNIT TOOL-SETTER (ordnance)	3235	34433433354	LNNNONONFFFONNNFNOONN	NNNN4NNNNNNNNNN	J,T	121	374	06.01.02	7462	470303	92997
632.380-018	PRIMER-WATERPROOFING-MACHINE ADJUSTER (ordnance)	3235	34433433354	LNNNNNNFFFONNNNFNONON	NNNN4NNNNNNNNNN	R,J,T	153	374	06.01.02	7462	470303	92997
632.380-022	RIM-FIRE-PRIMING TOOL SETTER (ordnance)	3334	34433443354	MNNONONFFONNNNFNOONN	NNNN3NNNNNNNNNN	J,T	121	374	06.01.02	7462	470303	92997
632.380-026	VARNISHING-UNIT TOOL SETTER (ordnance)	3233	34433443355	LNNNNNNFFFNNNNFNNNNN	NNNN4NNNNNNNNNN	R,J,T	151	374	06.01.02	7479	470303	92997
632.381-010	GUN SYNCHRONIZER (ordnance)	3335	44444444355	MNNNNNNFFONNNNNFNOONN	NNNN4NNNNNNNNNN	R,T	121	370	06.01.04	6179	470402	85999
632.381-014	INSPECTOR, FIREARMS (ordnance)	4336	33333543354	LNNNNNNCCONNNNCNCCCN	NNNN3NNNNNNNNNN	R,J,T	121	370	06.01.05	6881	470402	83002
632.684-010	ORDNANCE-ARTIFICER HELPER (government ser.)	2224	44443434355	LNNNNNNFFONNNNFNFNN	NNNN4NNNNNNNNFNN	R,T	111	370	05.12.16	8637	470303	98102
633.131-010	OFFICE-MACHINE-SERVICE SUPERVISOR (any industry)	4337	33322333354	LNNNNNNFFNFFNNNNFON	NNNN4NNNNNNNNNN	V,D,P,J,T	111	571	05.05.09	6000	520205	81002
633.131-014	ASSEMBLY TECHNICIAN (office machines)	4336	23322433354	LNNOOONFFCNNNFNOFON	NNNN3NNNNNNNNNN	J,T	111	571	06.01.04	6154	470102	85705
633.261-014	MAIL-PROCESSING-EQUIPMENT MECHANIC (government ser.)	4336	33333433255	MNNNNNNFFFNNNNFNOONN	NNNN4NNNNNNNNNN	V,J,T	111	565	05.05.09	6174	470102	85926
633.281-010	CASH-REGISTER SERVICER (any industry)	4337	33332433253	MNNNNNNFFFNNNNFNNNNN	NNNN4NNNNNNNNNN	V,J,T	111	571	05.05.09	6174	470102	85926
633.281-014	DICTATING-TRANSCRIBING-MACHINE SERVICER (any industry)	4337	33333333255	LNNNNNNFFFNNNFNOONN	NNNN3NNNNNNNNNN	V,J,T	121	571	05.05.09	6174	470102	85926
633.281-018	OFFICE-MACHINE SERVICER (any industry)	4337	33323433255	LNNNNNNFFFNFNFNOONN	NNNN3NNNNNNNNNN	J,T	121	571	05.05.09	6171	470102	85926
633.281-022	OFFICE-MACHINE-SERVICER APPRENTICE (any industry)	4337	33333333254	MNNOOONFFFNNNNFNNFNN	NNNN3NNNNNNNNNN	V,J,T	121	571	05.05.09	6174	470401	89999
633.281-026	SCALE MECHANIC (any industry)	4337	33323333254	LNNINNNNFFNFNFNFFON	NNNN3NNNNNNNNNN	V,J,T	121	571	05.05.09	6171	470102	85926
633.281-030	STATISTICAL-MACHINE SERVICER (any industry)	4337	33323333244	LNNINNNNFONFNKONNN	NNNN3NNNNNNNNNN	V,J,T	111	573	05.10.03	6000	520205	81002
637.131-010	SUPERVISOR, COOLER SERVICE (svc. ind. mach.)	4337	33334344355	LNNNNNNFFONFFNONNN	ONNN3NNNNNNNNNN	V,D,P,J	111	573	05.05.09	6156	470201	85711
637.261-010	AIR-CONDITIONING INSTALLER-SERVICER, WINDOW UNIT (construction)	4338	33323433345	HONOOONFFFNNNNFNFFON	ONNN4NONNNNNNNN	J,T	111	573	05.05.09	6160	470201	85902
637.261-014	HEATING-AND-AIR-CONDITIONING INSTALLER-SERVICER (construction)	4337	33323433345	MONOONOOONOONONNFFNN	ONNN4NONNNNNNNN	V,J,T	111	573	05.05.09	6160	470201	85902
637.261-018	GAS-APPLIANCE SERVICER (any industry)	4337	33333443344	MONOOONFFFOONNFNOOON	ONNN3NNNNNNNNNN	V,J,T	121	553	05.10.02	6179	470106	85944

DOT #	DOT Title & Industry	Trng	Aptitude	Physical	Environment	Tempra	WkF	MPSMS	GOE	SOC	CIP	OES
637.261-010	INDUSTRIAL-GAS SERVICER (utilities)	4337	33333343343	MNNOOONFFNOONFNOOON	ONNN3NNNNNNNNNN	J,T	121	602	05.05.11	6175	470303	85928
637.261-026	REFRIGERATION MECHANIC (any industry)	4338	33323433344	HONOONFFNNNNNFFNN	FFNF4NFNNNNNNNN	J,T	102	573	05.05.09	6160	470201	85902
637.261-030	SOLAR-ENERGY-SYSTEM INSTALLER (any industry)	4447	34322333345	HOOOFONFFNNNNFNOON	FNNN4NNOONNNNNN	J,T	102	364	05.05.09	6160	150505	85902
637.261-034	AIR AND HYDRONIC BALANCING TECHNICIAN (any industry)	4337	33333244335	MFFOOOFFONOONFNOFNN	NNNN4NNNNNNNNNN	T,J	211	573	05.05.09	6160	150501	85902
637.281-010	PUMP ERECTOR (construction)	4336	33333433245	HNOOONFFNNNNONOOONN	CNNN3NNNNNNNNNNO	V,D,J,T	121	568	05.05.09	6179	470501	85999
637.281-014	STOKER ERECTOR-AND-SERVICER (any industry)	4337	33433433254	HNNFNFFNNNNFFNN	NNNN3NONNNNNNN	J,T	111	568	05.05.09	6130	470201	85902
637.381-010	EVAPORATIVE-COOLER INSTALLER (any industry)	3336	33433433235	MONNNNFFNNNNFNNN	ONNN3NNNNNNNNNN	R,T	111	568	05.10.04	6160	470201	85902
637.381-014	REFRIGERATION UNIT REPAIRER (svc. ind. mach.)	3236	34343434353	MNNNNNFFONNNNFNON	ONNN3NNNNNNNNNN	J,T	102	583	05.10.02	6160	470201	85902
637.384-010	INDUSTRIAL-GAS-SERVICER HELPER (utilities)	3224	34433444344	MNNFFNFFNNNNONFNFNNN	FNNN3NNNNNNNNNN	R	121	553	05.10.02	8637	470303	98102
637.664-010	HEATING-AND-AIR-CONDITIONING INSTALLER-SERVICER HELPER (construction)	3226	33332433334	HONOONFFNNNNNFNFNNN	ONNN4NNONNNNNNN	J,T	111	573	05.10.01	8637	470201	98102
637.684-010	GAS-APPLIANCE-SERVICER HELPER (any industry)	2224	34433434354	HONOONFFONNNNFNNON	ONNN3NNNNNNNNNN	V,J	121	553	05.12.15	8635	470106	83005
637.684-014	QUALITY-CONTROL TECHNICIAN (svc. ind. mach.)	3333	34333433454	LNNNNNFFNNNNNFFNN	NNNN3NNNNNNNNNN	J,T	111	572	06.03.02	7830	470199	98102
637.687-010	AIR-CONDITIONING INSTALLER-SERVICER HELPER, WINDOW UNIT (construction)	2123	44444444455	HONOOONFFONNNNFNONNN	FNNN3NNNNNNNNNN	J,T	102	573	05.12.12	8635	470201	98102
637.687-014	REFRIGERATION-MECHANIC HELPER (any industry)	2122	44444544455	HNNONONFFONNNNNNNNNN	NNNN4NNNNNNNNNN	R	102	573	05.12.12	8637	470201	98102
637.687-018	SOLAR-ENERGY-SYSTEM-INSTALLER HELPER (any industry)	2224	44333433355	HFFFFNFFNNNNNFNNN	FNNN4NNONONNNNN	J	102	364	05.10.01	6160	150505	98102
638.131-010	FUEL-SYSTEM-MAINTENANCE SUPERVISOR (any industry)	4447	33332433334	LNNOOONFFFNFFNNNNN	ONNN4NNONONNNNN	V,D,J,T	121	568	05.06.03	6000	150701	81002
638.131-014	MACHINE-ASSEMBLER SUPERVISOR (machinery mfg.)	4448	23223333355	LOOOOONFFNFFNFFFFNN	NNNN3NNNNNNNNNN	D,P,V	.121	567	06.01.01	7100	520205	81008
638.131-018	MAINTENANCE SUPERVISOR, FIRE-FIGHTING-EQUIPMENT (government ser.)	4348	33333334345	MONOOONFFONOONFNFFNN	ONNF4FOONNNNNNO	D,P,J	102	361	05.05.09	6000	000000	81002
638.131-022	MAINTENANCE-MECHANIC SUPERVISOR (any industry)	4448	22222233345	MOOOONFFNFFNOONNN	NNNN4NNNNNNNNNN	D,V,T,P,J	102	550	05.05.09	6000	520205	81002
638.131-026	MECHANICAL-MAINTENANCE SUPERVISOR (any industry)	4337	33323333255	MOOOONFFONOONFFFNN	ONNN4NNNNNNNNNN	V,D,P,J,T	121	590	05.05.09	6000	520205	81002
638.131-030	MILLWRIGHT SUPERVISOR (any industry)	4448	23223333245	LOOOOOFFNFFNFNOONN	ONNN4NNONONNNNN	V,D,P,J	102	567	05.05.06	7100	520205	81002
638.131-034	MAINTENANCE SUPERVISOR, MOBILE BATTERY EQUIPMENT (mine & quarry)	3337	33433443344	MONOOOOFFOFOOFNFFN	NNNN4NNNNNNNNNNO	D,P,T,J	121	589	05.05.09	6000	470399	81005
638.261-010	AUTOMATED EQUIPMENT ENGINEER-TECHNICIAN (machinery mfg.)	4447	23232322343	HOOOOONFFNNOONFNFN	NNNN3NNNNNNNNNN	V,P,J,T	111	567	05.05.05	6178	470399	85123
638.261-014	MACHINERY ERECTOR (engine-turbine; machinery mfg.)	4448	33332422244	HOOFFNCCNOONONOONN	NNNN4NNNNNNNNNN	V,D,J,T	121	561	05.05.09	6178	470303	85123
638.261-018	MANUFACTURER'S SERVICE REPRESENTATIVE (machinery mfg.; machine tools)	4338	33323332255	MNNNNNNFFNNFNFFNN	NNNN4NNNOONNNNN	V,D,P,J	121	567	05.05.09	6178	470303	85123
638.261-022	PINSETTER MECHANIC, AUTOMATIC (any industry)	3224	33433433344	MFFFFFNFFNNOONOONNON	NNNN3NNNNNNNNNN	V,J,T	111	616	05.10.04	6179	470199	85999
638.261-026	FIELD SERVICE TECHNICIAN (machinery mfg.)	4447	22222233254	HOOOOONFFOOFOFOFFFF	NNON4NNONNNNNNN	T,P,J	111	560	05.05.09	6178	470401	85123
638.261-030	MACHINE REPAIRER, MAINTENANCE (any industry)	4447	23222433254	HONFFNFFNOONFNOFON	NNNN4NNONONNNNN	T,J	121	560	05.05.09	6130	470303	85119
638.281-010	FIRE-FIGHTING-EQUIPMENT SPECIALIST (government ser.)	4347	33343333344	HOOOONNFFONNNNFNONON	ONNN4NNNNNNNNNN	T,J	121	361	05.05.09	6179	430203	85132
638.281-014	MAINTENANCE MECHANIC (any industry)	4437	33324423244	HOOOOONFFOOONFNOON	ONNF4NFONNNNNNN	V,T,J	121	567	05.05.09	6130	470303	85119
638.281-018	MILLWRIGHT (any industry)	4337	23323433235	HONOOFNFFNOONFNOONN	NNNN4NNNNNNNNNN	J,T,V	102	550	05.05.06	6178	470303	85123
638.281-022	MILLWRIGHT APPRENTICE (any industry)	4337	23323433235	HONOOFNFFNOONFNOONN	NNNN4NNNNNNNNNN	J,T,V	102	550	05.05.09	6178	470303	85123
638.281-026	PARTS SALVAGER (any industry)	4337	33333433255	MNNNNNNFFNNNNNFFNN	NNNN4NNNNNNNNNN	V,J,T	121	567	05.05.09	6179	470106	85999
638.281-030	HYDRAULIC-RUBBISH-COMPACTOR MECHANIC (sanitary ser.)	4338	33324333243	MNNNNOOFFFNNONNFNNON	ONNN4NNNNNNNNNN	T,J	111	568	05.05.09	6130	470106	85999
638.281-034	HYDRAULIC REPAIRER (any industry)	3337	33344433355	HOOOONFFFNONONFONN	NNNN4NNOONNNNNN	T,J	121	560	05.05.09	6812	470401	85119
638.361-010	FUEL-SYSTEM-MAINTENANCE WORKER (any industry)	3336	34332433255	MONOONFFNNNNFNNNN	NNNN4NNNONNNNNN	J,T	121	567	06.02.22	6179	470303	93105
638.484-010	MILLWRIGHT HELPER (any industry)	2223	34434433335	HONNNFFFNNNNNFNNON	FNNO4NONNNNNNNN	J,T	121	568	05.05.09	6179	470401	85999
638.684-010	KNIFE CHANGER (tobacco)	1112	44444434355	LNNNNNNFFNNNNNOFNNN	NNNN4NNNNNNNNNN	R	121	560	05.12.12	8637	010201	98102
638.684-014	KNIFE SETTER (sugar & conf.)	3224	34333433355	MNNNNNNFFNNNNNFNNN	NNNN4NNNNNNNNNN	R	121	403	06.04.15	6140	470303	85128
638.684-018	MAINTENANCE-MECHANIC HELPER (any industry)	2124	44444433345	MNNONONFFONNNNNFNNN	NNNN4NNNNNNNNNN	R,T	121	567	06.01.02	6140	470303	85128
639.281-010	AVIATION SUPPORT EQUIPMENT REPAIRER (military ser.)	4337	33325323224	HONOOONFFONNNNFNONON	ONNN4NOONNNNNNN	R	121	560	05.12.15	8637	470303	98102
639.281-014	COIN-MACHINE-SERVICE REPAIRER (any industry)	3335	34322323354	LNNNNNNFFONNNNFNNON	NNNN3NNNNNNNNNN	V,J,T	121	566	05.10.02	6179	470303	85999
639.281-018	SEWING-MACHINE REPAIRER (any industry)	3337	34322323354	MNNFFFNFFNNNONFNFFN	NNOO3NOOONNNNNN	V,T,J	111	572	05.10.02	6179	470199	85947
639.281-022	MEDICAL-EQUIPMENT REPAIRER (protective dev.; retail trade)	3235	34434433254	MNNNOOONFFONFFNFOOO	NNNA4NONNNNNNNN	J,T	121	583	05.10.02	6130	470199	85113
639.681-010	BICYCLE REPAIRER (any industry)	3234	34433433353	HNNNNONFFNNNNFNNFN	NNNN3NNNNNNNNNN	T,J	121	604	05.10.02	6179	150401	85999
639.684-010	SEWING-MACHINE-REPAIRER HELPER (any industry)	2224	44433444355	MNNNONOFFFNNNNFNNON	NNNN3NNNNNNNNNN	R,T	121	595	05.10.02	8633	470499	85951
640.132-010	SUPERVISOR, COREMAKER (paper & pulp)	4337	33333444445	MNNNONNFFONFFNONNONO	NNNN4NNOONNNNNN	R,T	121	583	05.12.15	6179	470199	98102
640.360-010	PANEL-MACHINE SETTER (paper goods)	3236	33433444345	LNNNNNFFONNNNFNONN	NNNN4NFNNNNNNNN	V,D,P,J	163	474	06.02.04	7100	000000	81008
640.385-010	RIBBON-HANKING-MACHINE OPERATOR (paper goods)	2112	44545434355	LNNNNNNFFONNNNFNNNN	NNNN3NNNNNNNNNN	R,T	054	474	06.04.04	7679	000000	92998
640.565-010	PAPER CUTTER (beverage)	2112	44454433355	LNNNNNNFFNNNNFNNNNN	NNNN3NNNNNNNNNN	R,T	054	898	06.04.04	7678	000000	92944

DOT #	DOT Title & Industry	Trng	Aptitude	Physical	Environment	Tempra	WkF	MPSMS	GOE	SOC	CIP	OES
640.682-010	CONVOLUTE-TUBE WINDER (paper goods)	3224	34433433355	MNNNNNNFFNNNNFNNNNN	NNNN4NNONNNNNN	J,T	163	475	06.02.04	7479	000000	92914
640.682-014	CORE WINDING OPERATOR (paper & pulp)	3335	34433434354	MNNNNNNOOOONNNONOOFO	NNNN4NNONNNNNNN	T,J	163	470	06.02.04	7679	000000	92998
640.682-018	CUTTING-MACHINE OPERATOR (print. & pub.)	3224	34433434355	HNNNNNNCCFNNONCNCONN	NNNN5FFNNNNNN	R,T	054	470	06.02.04	7478	000000	92941
640.682-022	SPIRAL-TUBE WINDER (paper goods)	3224	34444434355	MNNNNNNFFOONNNFNOONN	NNNN4NCONNNNNNN	T,J	163	474	06.02.04	7479	480299	92914
640.685-010	BOOK TRIMMER (print. & pub.)	2113	44444443344	MNNONNNFFONNONFNONON	NNNN4FNFNNNNNN	R,T	054	480	06.04.04	7678	000000	92944
640.685-014	BOOK-JACKET-COVER-MACHINE OPERATOR (paper goods)	3223	44443434355	LNNNNNNFFONNNNFNNNNN	NNNN3NNNNNNNNN	R,T	063	486	06.04.09	7661	000000	92956
640.685-018	CARBON-PAPER INTERLEAFER (pen & pencil)	2212	44444434355	MNNNNNNFFNNNNFNNNNN	NNNN4NNNNNNNNN	R,T	163	617	06.04.04	7679	000000	92998
640.685-022	COMB-MACHINE OPERATOR (fabrication, nec)	2113	44444433354	HNNONNNFFNNNNFNNOON	NNNN4NNNNNNNNN	R,T	054	619	06.04.04	7678	000000	92944
640.685-026	COMPENSATOR (paper goods)	1112	45543534455	LNNNNNNFFNNNNFNNNNN	NNNN4NNNNNNNNN	R	054	474	06.04.04	7678	000000	92944
640.685-030	CORNER CUTTER (paper goods)	2112	44445434345	LNNNONNNFFNNNNFNFNNN	NNNN4NFONNNNNN	R	054	475	06.04.04	7678	000000	92944
640.685-034	CUT-OFF-MACHINE OPERATOR (paper goods)	2112	44444444345	MNNNONNNFFONNNNFONN	NNNN4NOFNNNNNN	R,T	054	470	06.04.04	7678	000000	92944
640.685-038	PANEL-MACHINE OPERATOR (paper goods)	2112	44444444345	LNNONONFFNNNNFNNNNN	NNNN4NNNNNNNNN	R	054	474	06.04.04	7679	000000	92998
640.685-042	PAPER-CORE-MACHINE OPERATOR (paper goods)	2112	44433434355	LNNNNNNFFNNNNNONNNN	NNNN3NNNNNNNNN	R	063	479	06.04.04	7679	000000	92998
640.685-046	PAPER-REEL OPERATOR (paper goods)	2213	44444434355	MNNONNNFFOONNNNONNN	NNNN4NNNNNNNNN	R,T	163	474	06.04.04	7679	000000	92944
640.685-050	PROCESS-MACHINE OPERATOR (paper goods)	2113	44443443355	MNNONONFFFNNNNFNNNNN	NNNN4NNNNNNNNN	R	163	474	06.04.04	7679	000000	92998
640.685-054	REELER (paper goods)	2112	44554534355	MNNNNNNFFONNNNNNNNNN	NNNN4NNNNNNNNN	R	163	474	06.04.04	7679	000000	92998
640.685-058	REWINDER OPERATOR (paper goods)	2223	34444434345	MNNNONONFFFNNONFNFNNN	NNNN4NNOONNNNNN	T	163	470	06.04.04	7679	000000	92998
640.685-062	ROLL RECLAIMER (paper goods)	2112	44444443355	LNNNNNNFFNNNNONNNNN	NNNN3NNNNNNNNN	R	163	474	06.04.04	7678	000000	92944
640.685-066	ROLL-SLICING-MACHINE TENDER (pen & pencil)	2112	44444544355	LNNNNNNFFONNNNFNNONN	NNNN3NNNNNNNNN	R,J,T	054	617	06.04.04	7679	000000	92998
640.685-070	ROLLING-MACHINE OPERATOR (paper goods)	2112	44444544355	MNNNNNNFFONNNNONONNN	NNNN3NNNNNNNNN	R	163	474	06.04.04	7678	000000	92944
640.685-074	ROUND-CORNER-CUTTER OPERATOR (paper goods; print. & pub.)	2212	44444434345	MNNONNNFFONNNONFNNNNN	NNNN4NNONNNNNN	R	054	475	06.04.04	7678	000000	92998
640.685-078	SLOTTER OPERATOR (paper goods)	2213	44444444345	HNNNFNNNFFNNOONFNNNNN	NNNN3NNNNNNNNN	R,T	054	475	06.04.04	7678	000000	92944
640.685-082	TIGHTENING-MACHINE OPERATOR (paper goods)	1112	44544534355	MNNOOONFFFNNNNNFNNNNN	NNNN4NNNNNNNNN	R	163	479	06.04.04	7679	000000	92998
640.685-086	TUBE SIZER-AND-CUTTER OPERATOR (ordnance)	2213	33443433355	MONFNONFFFNNNNFONNNNN	NNNN3NNNNNNNNNF	R,T	163	475	06.04.04	7678	030404	92944
640.685-090	BAND-SAW OPERATOR (paper goods)	2224	44444434355	HNNONNNFFOONNNNFNFNNN	NNON4NNNNNNNNN	R,T	056	472	06.04.04	7678	000000	92944
640.686-010	ROTARY-CUTTER FEEDER (paper & pulp)	2112	44444434355	MONFNONFFNNNNNNNNNNN	NNNN4NNNNNNNNN	R	054	474	06.04.04	8725	000000	98502
640.686-014	SLOTTER-OPERATOR HELPER (paper goods)	1112	44544544455	MNNNNNNFFNNNNNNNNNN	NNNN4NNNNNNNNN	R,T	011	475	06.04.26	8618	000000	98999
640.687-010	ROLL EXAMINER (paper & pulp)	2122	44445534454	LNNNNNNFFONNNNFNNOON	NNON3NNNNNNNNN	R,T	212	470	06.03.02	7820	000000	83005
640.687-014	SPIRAL-TUBE-WINDER HELPER (paper goods)	2112	44544544355	MONONNNFFONNNNNFNNNNN	NNNN4NFONONNNNN	R	163	474	06.04.26	8619	000000	98999
641.380-010	ENVELOPE-FOLDING-MACHINE ADJUSTER (paper goods)	3227	33433433354	MNNFNONFFNNONFNFNOO	NNNN4NNONNNNNN	T,J	063	474	06.01.02	7474	000000	92956
641.562-010	CORRUGATOR OPERATOR (paper goods)	3225	34434434355	MNNNONNNFFNNNNFNOONN	NNNN4NNNNNNNNN	J,T	102	475	06.02.04	7661	000000	92997
641.662-010	BOX-SEALING-MACHINE OPERATOR (paper goods)	3224	44434434355	HNNFNNNNFFNNOONFNNNNN	NNNN3NNNNNNNNNF	J,T	063	475	06.02.04	7679	000000	92956
641.662-014	TUBE-MACHINE OPERATOR (paper goods)	3225	34433433355	MNNOOONFFFNNNNFNNNNN	NNNN4NNNNNNNNN	J,T	102	474	06.02.04	7661	000000	92998
641.682-010	BLANKET-WINDER OPERATOR (paper goods)	3224	34434434355	MMNFNONFFFONNNNFNFNNN	NNNN4NANONNNNNN	J,T	063	474	06.02.20	7661	000000	92956
641.682-014	GLUING-MACHINE OPERATOR, AUTOMATIC (print. & pub.)	3224	33434434355	LNNNONNFFONNNNFNNNNN	NNNN4NNONNNNNN	R,T	063	474	06.02.20	7474	480299	92997
641.685-010	BENDER, MACHINE (paper goods)	2213	44444534355	LNNNNNNFFNNNNNNNNNN	NNNN4NNONNNNNNO	R	062	474	06.04.04	7674	000000	92998
641.685-014	BOARD-LINER OPERATOR (wood. container)	2113	44444534355	MNNNNNNFFNNNNNNNNNN	NNNN3NNNNNNNNN	R	063	474	06.04.20	7661	000000	92956
641.685-018	BOX-LINING-MACHINE FEEDER (paper goods)	2113	44434434345	LNNNNNNFFNNNNNONNNNN	NNNN4NNNNNNNNN	R	063	474	06.04.04	7661	000000	92956
641.685-022	CARTON-FORMING-MACHINE OPERATOR (any industry)	2112	44444434455	LNNNNNNFFONNNNNFONN	NNNN4NNNNNNNNNO	R,T	062	474	06.04.04	7674	000000	92998
641.685-026	CARTON-FORMING-MACHINE TENDER (paper goods)	2113	44444434355	HNNONNNFFONNNNFNNNNN	NNNN4NNNNNNNNN	R	102	474	06.04.04	7679	000000	92956
641.685-030	CHIP-APPLYING-MACHINE TENDER (paint & varnish; print. & pub.)	2113	34433433355	MNNOOONFFFNNNNFNNNNN	NNNN4NNONONNNNN	R	063	479	06.04.04	7661	000000	92956
641.685-034	COVER STRIPPER (paper goods)	2112	44443533345	MNNFNONFFFONNNNFNNNNN	NNNN4NNONONNNNN	R	063	475	06.04.04	7661	000000	92956
641.685-038	DOMER (paper goods)	2112	44544534455	LNNNONNFFONNNNFNNNNN	NNNN4NNONONNNNN	R	134	475	06.04.04	7663	000000	92971
641.685-042	ENDING-MACHINE OPERATOR (paper goods)	2113	44544543345	LNNNNNNFFNNNNNNNNNN	NNNN3NNNNNNNNN	R,T	063	475	06.04.04	7661	000000	92956
641.685-046	EXTENSION EDGER (paper goods)	2112	44445433345	LNNNNNNFFNNNNNNNNNN	NNNN4NNNNNNNNN	R	063	475	06.04.04	7661	000000	92956
641.685-050	FOLDING-MACHINE FEEDER (paper goods)	2112	44444434345	MNNONNNFFONNNNONONNN	NNNN4NNNNNONONNN	R	062	474	06.04.04	7674	000000	92998
641.685-054	FOUR-CORNER-STAYER-MACHINE OPERATOR (paper goods)	2112	44444434345	MNNONNNFFONNNNFNFONN	NNNN4NNNNNONNNN	R,T	062	475	06.04.04	7674	000000	92998
641.685-058	LINER-MACHINE OPERATOR (paper goods)	2113	44434534355	LNNNNNNFFONNNNFNNNNN	NNNN4NNNNNNNNN	R	063	475	06.04.04	7663	000000	92971
641.685-062	PAPER-CONE-MACHINE TENDER (paper goods)	2112	44544544455	LNNNNNNFFONNNNFNFNNN	NNNN4NNONNNNNN	R	102	474	06.04.04	7661	000000	92956
641.685-066	PATCH-MACHINE OPERATOR (paper goods)	2112	44444544355	LNNNNNNFFONNNNNNNNNN	NNNN4NNNNNNNNN	R	063	474	06.04.04	7661	000000	92956
641.685-070	SCORER (paper goods)	2112	44444444355	MNNNONONFFONNNNONONNN	NNNN4NNNNNONONNN	R,T	062	475	06.04.04	7679	000000	92998

DOT #	DOT Title & Industry	Trng	Aptitude	Physical	Environment	Tempra	WkF	MPSMS	GOE	SOC	CIP	OES
641.685-074	SEALING-MACHINE OPERATOR (paper goods)	2112	44444544355	LNNNNFNNNFONNNNONNNNN	NNNN4NNNNNNNNN	R	063	474	06.04.21	7661	000000	92956
641.685-078	SLIDE-MACHINE TENDER (fabrication, nec)	2112	4444343434	LNNNNNNFFNNNNNNNNNN	NNNN3NNNNNNNNN	R	102	475	06.04.04	7674	000000	92998
641.685-082	SPOOL MAKER (paper goods)	1112	4554453345	LNNNNNFFNNNNNNNNNN	NNNN3NNNNNNNNN	R	063	474	06.04.04	7661	000000	92956
641.685-086	STRING-TOP SEALER (paper goods)	2112	44544533345	LNNNNNNFFNNNNNNNNN	NNNN3NNNNNNNNN	R,T	062	474	06.04.02	7674	000000	92998
641.685-090	STRIPPING-MACHINE OPERATOR (paper goods)	2112	44444434355	LNNOOONFFONNNNNONNNNN	NNNN3NNNNNNNNN	R,T	063	474	06.04.04	7661	000000	92956
641.685-094	VALVING-MACHINE OPERATOR (paper goods)	2112	44444434355	LNNONNNFFFNNNFNFNNN	NNNN4NNNNNNNNN	R	062	474	06.04.04	7674	000000	92998
641.685-098	WRAPPING-MACHINE OPERATOR (paper goods)	2112	44544534345	MNNOOONFFONNNNNNNNN	NNNN4NNNNNNNNN	R	063	475	06.04.04	7661	000000	92956
641.686-010	BLANKET-WINDER HELPER (paper goods)	2112	44544544355	MNNFNNNFFNNNNNFNNN	NNNN4NNNNNNNNN	R	063	474	06.04.04	8618	000000	98999
641.686-014	CARTON-FORMING-MACHINE HELPER (any industry)	2112	44444544355	MNNNNNNFFNNNNNONONNN	NNNN4NNNNNNNNN	R	062	475	06.04.04	8618	000000	98999
641.686-018	CORRUGATOR-OPERATOR HELPER (paper goods)	2212	44444534355	HNNFOONFFNNNNNNNNNN	NNNN4NNNNNNNNN	R	102	475	06.04.26	8618	000000	98999
641.686-022	LINER-MACHINE-OPERATOR HELPER (paper goods)	2112	44444544455	MNNONNNFFNNNNNNNNNN	NNNN4NNNNNNNNN	R	063	474	06.04.04	8618	000000	98999
641.686-026	PAPER-BAG-PRESS OPERATOR (paper goods)	1112	44445534455	LNNNNNNCCNNNNNNNNN	NNNN3NNNNNNNNN	R	063	474	06.04.04	8618	000000	98502
641.686-030	SCORER HELPER (paper goods)	2112	44444544355	MNNFNNNFFFNNNNNNNN	NNNN4NNNNNNNNN	R	062	475	06.04.04	8725	000000	98502
641.686-034	SLEEVER (paper goods)	1112	45544533355	LNNNNNFFNNNNNNNNN	NNNN4NNNNNNNNN	R	102	474	06.04.04	8725	000000	92998
641.686-038	TUBE-MACHINE-OPERATOR HELPER (paper goods)	2112	44444444355	MONFOONFFNNNNONONNN	NNNN4NNNNNNNNN	R	102	474	06.04.04	8618	000000	98999
641.687-010	BOX BENDER (paper goods)	1111	45454544355	MNNONNNCNNNNNNNNNN	NNNN4NNNNNNNNN	R	062	475	06.04.04	7740	000000	93999
641.687-014	BOX-SEALING INSPECTOR (paper goods)	2112	44443433355	LNNNNNFFFNNNFNFNNN	NNNN4NNNNNNNNN	J,T	212	475	06.03.02	7820	000000	83005
649.130-010	SUPERVISOR, PAPER PRODUCTS (paper goods)	4338	33323333344	LNNONONOOOFFNFFOOON	NNNN4NFNNNNNNO	V,D,P,J	102	470	06.02.01	7100	000000	81008
649.361-010	PATTERNMAKER, ENVELOPE (paper goods)	4437	23222343354	LNNNNNFFFNNNNFNOOON	NNNN3NNNNNNNNN	J,T	242	474	05.03.02	6862	000000	89908
649.367-010	INSPECTOR, PAPER PRODUCTS (paper goods)	3225	34434444453	LNNNNNFFFOOONFNOOFN	NNNN4NNNNNNNNN	T,J	212	470	06.03.01	7820	000000	83005
649.380-010	MACHINE SET-UP OPERATOR, PAPER GOODS (paper goods)	3227	33433433344	MONFOONFFONNONFOOOON	NNOO4NOONNNNNNO	T,J	121	474	06.01.02	7479	000000	92914
649.487-010	INSPECTOR (paper & pulp)	3223	34443443453	LNNONNFFFNNNFNNFFN	NNNN4NNNNNNNNN	T,J	212	470	06.03.01	7820	000000	83005
649.582-010	PARTITION-ASSEMBLY-MACHINE OPERATOR (any industry)	3225	34443434355	HNNOONFFFNNNNONONNN	NNNN4NNNNNNNNF	T,J	212	475	06.02.20	7679	000000	92998
649.582-014	SIZING-MACHINE OPERATOR (ordnance)	3224	44433434345	LFNONONFFNOONFNNNN	NNNN4NNNNNNNNO	J,T	135	475	06.02.18	7467	000000	92968
649.665-010	SORTING-MACHINE OPERATOR (paper goods)	2112	44443433355	LFNONONFFNOONFNFNNN	NNNN4NFNNNNNNO	R	212	474	06.03.02	7850	000000	83005
649.682-010	BOX-FOLDING-MACHINE OPERATOR (paper goods)	3224	34433434355	HNNFOONFFONNONFFNNN	NNNN4NNONNNNNN	T,J	062	474	06.02.04	7474	000000	92997
649.682-014	CYLINDER-DIE-MACHINE OPERATOR (paper goods)	3225	34433433353	HONOOONFFOONONONOOON	NNNN4NNONNNNNN	T,J	134	475	06.02.04	7678	000000	92944
649.682-018	DRILL-PRESS OPERATOR, ACOUSTICAL TILE (wood prod., nec)	3225	34433433355	LONOOONFFNNNNNFNFNNN	NNNN4NNNNNNNNN	J,T	053	473	06.02.09	7479	000000	92997
649.682-022	EMBOSSER OPERATOR (paper goods)	3225	34433444355	MNNONNNFFONNNFNFNNN	NNNN4NNNNNNNNN	J,T	054	474	06.02.09	7479	000000	92997
649.682-026	PLATEN-PRESS OPERATOR (paper goods)	3225	34433433355	MNNNNNNFFNNNNNFONN	NNNN4NNNNNNNNN	J,T	135	475	06.02.04	7474	000000	92997
649.682-030	SHELL-MACHINE OPERATOR (chemical)	3214	34434343355	MNNNNNNFFONNNNFNONN	NNNN4NONNNNNNN	J,T	054	474	06.02.04	7474	000000	92997
649.682-034	SLITTER-CREASER-SLOTTER OPERATOR (paper goods)	2224	34434434355	MNNNNNNFFONNNNFNFNNN	NNNN5NNNNNNNNF	J,T	054	475	06.02.04	7474	000000	92997
649.682-038	SLITTER-SCORER-CUT-OFF OPERATOR (paper goods)	3225	34433434355	HNNOONFFNNNNNFNFNNN	NNNN4NNONNNNNN	T,J	054	475	06.02.09	7474	000000	92944
649.682-042	TABLET-MAKING-MACHINE OPERATOR (paper goods)	3224	34433434355	MNNONNNFFNNNNNFNNN	NNNN4NNNNNNNNN	T,J	102	474	06.02.04	7478	000000	92941
649.682-046	TAG-PRESS OPERATOR (paper goods)	3216	34433433354	MNNFNONFFNNNNNFNON	NNNN4NNNNNNNNN	J,T	054	474	06.02.04	7449	000000	92529
649.685-010	AUTOMATIC-MACHINE ATTENDANT (paper goods)	2113	44444444345	MNNONNNFFONNNNFNFNON	NNNN4NFFNNNNNFO	R	062	474	06.04.04	7679	000000	92998
649.685-014	BAG-MACHINE OPERATOR (paper goods)	2113	34434344354	MNNONNNFFNNNNNFONN	NNNN4NNNNNNNNN	J,T	102	474	06.04.04	7679	000000	92998
649.685-018	BINDERY WORKER (paper goods)	2113	34434343345	MNNNNNNFFONNNNNFNON	NNNN4NNNNNNNNN	J,T	102	474	06.04.04	7679	000000	92998
649.685-022	BOTTOMING-MACHINE OPERATOR (paper goods)	2113	44444544355	MNNNONNNFFONNNNFNNNN	NNNN4NNNNNNNNN	R,T	102	474	06.04.04	7679	000000	92998
649.685-026	CORE-CUTTER AND REAMER (paper goods)	3224	44444434345	MNNNNNNFFNNNNNFNNN	NNNN4NNNNNNNNN	J,T	057	474	06.04.09	7678	000000	92944
649.685-030	COUNTING-MACHINE OPERATOR (paper goods)	2113	44444444355	HNNFNFNFFONNNNFNNN	NNNN4NNNNNNNNN	R,T	221	474	06.04.04	7679	000000	92998
649.685-034	DRILL-PUNCH OPERATOR (paper goods; print. & pub.)	2112	44443434345	MNNONNNFFONNONFNONN	NNNN4NNONNNNNN	R	053	470	06.04.04	7649	000000	92543
649.685-038	EMBOSSING-MACHINE TENDER (paper goods)	2124	44443434355	MNNONNNFFFNNNNNFONN	NNNN4NNONNNNNN	J,T	192	485	06.04.04	7674	000000	92998
649.685-042	ENVELOPE-MACHINE OPERATOR (paper goods)	3223	44444444445	MNNOOONFFFNNNNNFONN	NNNN4NNONNNNNN	R,T	062	474	06.04.04	7674	000000	92998
649.685-046	FOLDING-MACHINE OPERATOR (paper goods)	2113	44444444355	MNNONONFFNNNNNFNNN	NNNN4NNONNNNNN	T	061	474	06.04.04	7661	000000	92956
649.685-050	HANDLE-MACHINE OPERATOR (paper goods)	2113	44444444455	LNNONNNFFONNNNNNNNN	NNNN4NNNNNNNNN	R	054	474	06.04.04	7679	000000	92998
649.685-054	KNOTTING-MACHINE OPERATOR (paper goods)	2112	44444544455	LNNONNNFFONNNNNNNNN	NNNN4NNNNNNNNN	R	062	474	06.04.04	7679	000000	92956
649.685-058	LACE-PAPER-MACHINE OPERATOR (paper goods)	2113	44435444455	MNNNNNNFFONNNNNNNNN	NNNN4NNNNNNNNN	J,T	192	474	06.04.04	7679	000000	92998
649.685-062	LAUNDRY-BAG-PUNCH OPERATOR (paper goods)	1112	44544534355	LNNFNFFNNNNNNNNNN	NNNN3NNNNNNNNN	R	062	474	06.04.04	7679	000000	92998
649.685-066	LAYBOY TENDER (paper & pulp; paper goods; print. & pub.)	2112	44443433354	LNNFNFNFFNNNNNFNNNON	NNNN4NNNNNNNNN	R,T	212	474	06.04.04	7679	000000	92998
649.685-070	MACHINE OPERATOR, GENERAL (paper goods)	2113	44444433345	MNNONNNFFFNNNNFNOONN	NNNN4NNNNNNNNNO	R,T	062	474	06.04.04	7679	000000	92998

DOT #	DOT Title & Industry	Trng	Aptitude	Physical	Environment	Tempra	WkF	MPSMS	GOE	SOC	CIP	OES
649.685-074	MATCHBOOK ASSEMBLER (fabrication, nec)	2113	44444433355	MNNNNNCCCNNNNFNFNNN	NNNN4NNNNNNNNNN	R	102	619	06.04.04	7679	000000	92998
649.685-078	PAPER-CUP-MACHINE OPERATOR (paper goods)	2113	44444544455	MNNNNNNFFNNNNNONFNNN	NNNN4NNNNNNNNNN	R	102	474	06.04.04	7663	000000	92971
649.685-082	PARTITION-MAKING-MACHINE OPERATOR (paper goods)	2112	44444544355	LNNFNNNFFFNNNNFNFNNN	NNNN4NNNNNNNNNNO	J,T	054	475	06.04.04	7678	000000	92944
649.685-086	PATTERNMAKER, ACOUSTICAL TILE (wood prod., nec)	3214	33433443355	MNNONNNFFOONNNNNFNNN	NNNN3NNNNNNNNNN	R,T	134	473	06.04.09	7663	000000	92971
649.685-090	PERFORATING-MACHINE OPERATOR (print. & pub.)	2114	44443443355	LNNNNNNNFFOONNNNNFNNN	NNNN4NNNNNNNNNN	R	134	567	06.04.04	7679	480299	92998
649.685-094	PUNCHBOARD-FILLING-MACHINE OPERATOR (paper goods)	2112	44545434345	LNNNNNNNFFFNNNNNNNNN	NNNN3NNNNNNNNNN	R	102	474	06.04.20	7662	000000	92974
649.685-098	RING-MAKING-MACHINE OPERATOR (paper goods)	2112	44544544455	LNNNNNNNFFONNNNNNNNN	NNNN4NNNNNNNNNN	R	102	474	06.04.04	7663	000000	92971
649.685-102	SALVAGE WINDER AND INSPECTOR (paper goods)	2223	44443534334	LNNNNNNNFONNNNNFNNON	NNNN4NNNNNNNNNNO	R,T	163	474	06.03.02	7679	000000	92998
649.685-106	SHOT-TUBE-MACHINE TENDER (paper goods)	2112	44443534335	LNNONNNFFNNNNNNNNN	NNNN4NNNNNNNNNN	R	134	475	06.04.04	7674	000000	92998
649.685-110	STEEL-TIE ADJUSTER, AUTOMATIC (paper goods)	2112	44544544455	LNNNNNNNFFNNNNNNNNN	NNNN4NNNNNNNNNN	R	102	474	06.04.09	7678	000000	92944
649.685-114	STITCHER OPERATOR (paper goods)	2114	44443444355	HNNONNNFFFNNNNFNFNNN	NNNN4NNONNNNNNN	R	062	475	06.04.04	7679	000000	92998
649.685-118	TAG-MACHINE OPERATOR (paper goods)	2112	44443444355	LNNONNNFFONNNNFNNOON	NNNN4NNNNNNNNNN	R	054	474	06.04.37	7679	000000	92998
649.685-122	TAPE-FASTENER-MACHINE OPERATOR (paper goods)	2112	44444534345	LNNNNNNNFFNNNNNONNNN	NNNN3NNNNNNNNNN	R,T	062	474	06.04.04	7662	000000	92974
649.685-126	TAPER OPERATOR (paper goods)	2113	44444434345	HNNNNNNFFNNNNNFNFNNN	NNNN4NNONNNNNNNO	R,T	062	475	06.04.04	7661	000000	92956
649.685-130	TABLET-MAKING-MACHINE-OPERATOR HELPER (paper goods)	3223	34433333354	MNNFONNNFFNNNNFNFFON	NNNN4NNNNNNNNNN	R	054	474	06.04.04	8619	030404	98999
649.686-010	BAG-MACHINE-OPERATOR HELPER (paper goods)	2112	44444543344	MNNFNNNFFFNNNNFNNNON	NNNN4NFNNNNNNNO	R	102	474	06.04.04	8618	000000	98999
649.686-014	CARD DECORATOR (print. & pub.)	2112	45544544455	LNNNNNNNFFNNNNNNNNN	NNNN3NNNNNNNNNN	R	063	485	06.04.04	7661	000000	92956
649.686-018	CYLINDER-DIE-MACHINE HELPER (paper goods)	2112	44444434355	HNNFNFNFFNNNNNFNFNNN	NNNN4NNNNNNNNNN	R	134	475	06.04.04	8618	000000	98999
649.686-022	FINISHING-MACHINE OPERATOR (paper goods)	1111	44554533355	LNNNNNNNFFFNNNNNNNNN	NNNN3NNNNNNNNNN	R	062	474	06.04.04	8725	000000	98502
649.686-026	PLATING-MACHINE OPERATOR (paper & pulp)	2112	44444534455	LNNNNNNNFFNNNNNFNNNN	NNNN4NNNNNNNNNN	R	192	474	06.04.04	8725	000000	98502
649.686-030	SLITTER-CREASER-SLOTTER HELPER (paper goods)	2112	44544544355	HNNFNONCNNNNNNNNNNN	NNNN4NNNNNNNNNN	R	054	475	06.04.04	8725	000000	98502
649.687-010	PAPER SORTER AND COUNTER (paper & pulp)	2212	44434433354	LNNONNNFFFNNNFNNFFN	NNNN3NNNNNNNNNN	R,T	212	474	06.03.02	7850	000000	83005
649.687-014	PAPER-PATTERN INSPECTOR (paper goods)	2112	44554534355	LNNNNNNNFFNNNNNNFFNN	NNNN3NNNNNNNNNN	R,T	212	474	06.03.02	7850	000000	83005
649.687-018	PAPER-CONE GRADER (paper goods)	2112	44443444455	LNNNNNNNFFONNNNFNFNN	NNNN3NNNNNNNNNN	R,T	212	479	06.03.02	7820	000000	83005
650.132-010	SUPERVISOR, TYPESETTING (print. & pub.)	4338	23333333455	LNNNNNNNFFNFFNFNFFNN	NNNN4NNFNNNNNNN	D,J,P	191	567	07.06.02	7100	520205	81008
650.582-010	LINOTYPE OPERATOR (print. & pub.)	4237	33333233355	MNNNNNNNFFNNNNFNFNNN	NNNN4NNFNNNNNNNO	J,T	191	567	07.06.02	7642	480205	92541
650.582-014	MONOTYPE-KEYBOARD OPERATOR (machinery mfg.; print. & pub.)	4236	33333233355	LNNNNNNNCCNOOONCNOCNN	NNNN4NNNNNNNNNN	R,T	191	567	07.06.02	7642	480205	92541
650.582-018	PHOTOCOMPOSING-MACHINE OPERATOR (print. & pub.)	3116	33433334354	LNNNNNNNFFNNNNNFNON	NNNN3NNNNNNNNNN	R,T	191	897	05.10.05	7642	480205	92541
650.582-022	PHOTOTYPESETTER OPERATOR (print. & pub.)	4235	33333233354	LNNOONNNFFNNOONFNNON	NNNN4NNNNNNNNNN	J,T	191	567	07.06.02	7642	480205	92541
650.682-010	EQUIPMENT MONITOR, PHOTOTYPESETTING (print. & pub.)	3124	44444333455	LNNNNNNNFFFONNNNFNNNN	NNNN3NNNNNNNNNN	J,T	191	567	05.10.05	7642	480205	92541
650.685-010	TYPESETTING-MACHINE TENDER (print. & pub.)	3124	34433444355	LNNNNNNNFFNNNNFNNNNN	NNNN4NNNNNNNNNN	R,T	191	567	05.10.05	7642	480205	92541
651.130-010	SUPERVISOR, PRESS ROOM (print. & pub.)	4348	33322333352	LNNONNNFFFNNFNFFOON	NNNN5OOONNNNNNN	V,D,P,T,J	191	480	05.05.13	7100	520205	81008
651.362-010	CYLINDER-PRESS OPERATOR (print. & pub.)	4337	33332333353	MNNNOONFFFNNNNFNOOFN	NNNN4NNNNNNNNNN	J,T	191	567	05.05.13	7443	480208	92515
651.362-014	CYLINDER-PRESS-OPERATOR APPRENTICE (print. & pub.)	4337	33332433353	MNNOOONFFFNNNNFNOOFN	NNNN4NNNNNNNNNN	J,T	191	567	05.05.13	7443	480208	92515
651.362-018	PLATEN-PRESS OPERATOR (print. & pub.)	4227	33332333353	LNNNONNFFFNNOONFNOOON	NNNN4NNOONFNOOON	V,J,T	191	567	05.05.13	7443	480208	92515
651.362-022	PLATEN-PRESS-OPERATOR APPRENTICE (print. & pub.)	4227	33332433353	LNNOONNNFFFNNOONFNOOON	NNNN4NNOONFNOOON	V,J,T	191	567	05.05.13	7443	480208	92515
651.362-026	ROTOGRAVURE-PRESS OPERATOR (print. & pub.)	3227	34443333355	LNNFNNNFFONNNNFNOFN	NNNN3NNNNNNNNNN	V,J,T	191	567	05.10.05	7443	480208	92519
651.362-030	WEB-PRESS OPERATOR (print. & pub.)	4337	33333443344	MNNOOONFFFNNOONFNOON	NNNN4NNNNNNNNNN	J,T	191	567	05.10.05	7443	480208	92515
651.362-034	WEB-PRESS-OPERATOR APPRENTICE (print. & pub.)	4337	33333444344	MNNOOONFFFNNOONFNFOON	NNNN4NNNNNNNNNN	J,T	191	567	05.05.13	7443	480208	92519
651.382-010	ENGRAVING-PRESS OPERATOR (print. & pub.)	4237	33433333343	LNNNONNNFFNNNNFNOOFN	NNNN3NNNNNNNNNNO	R,J,T	192	567	05.10.05	7444	480208	92522
651.382-014	LITHOGRAPH-PRESS OPERATOR, TINWARE (tinware)	3227	33332433343	LONOOONFFONNNFNFFFN	NNNN4NCNNNNNNNF	J,T	191	551	06.02.02	7444	480208	92522
651.382-026	PRINTER, PLASTIC (plastic prod.; tex. prod., nec)	3125	33433443353	MNNONNNFFONNNNFNONFN	NNNN4NCNNNNNNNN	J,T	191	519	06.02.09	7444	480208	92522
651.382-030	STEEL-DIE PRINTER (print. & pub.)	3227	34433433354	LNNFNNNFFONNNNFNFNNN	NNNN4NNNNNNNNNN	J,T	191	567	05.10.05	7443	480208	92519
651.382-034	TAB-CARD-PRESS OPERATOR (print. & pub.)	3235	34432343354	LNNFNNNFFONNNNFNOOON	NNNN4NNNNNNNNNN	J,T	191	567	05.10.05	7443	480208	92515
651.382-038	TRANSFER OPERATOR (print. & pub.)	3224	33433444354	LNNNNNNFFFNNNNFNOOON	NNNN3NNNNNNNNNN	R,J,T	191	567	05.10.05	7443	480208	92519
651.382-042	OFFSET-PRESS OPERATOR I (print. & pub.)	4238	33332333353	LNNNONNNFFFNNNOFFFOON	NNNO5OFFNNNNNNN	V,T	191	480	05.05.13	7443	480208	92512
651.382-046	OFFSET-PRESS-OPERATOR APPRENTICE (print. & pub.)	4238	33332333353	LNNOONNNFFNNONFFFOON	NNNO5OFFNNNNNNN	V,T	191	480	05.05.13	7443	480208	92512
651.384-010	PLATEN BUILDER-UP (print. & pub.)	2124	34432433355	LNNNNNNNFFNNNNFNFNNN	NNNN4NNNNNNNNNN	J,T	102	567	05.10.05	7444	480208	92519
651.582-010	PROOF-PRESS OPERATOR (print. & pub.)	3225	33444344355	MNNNNNNFFFNNNNFNONNN	NNNN3NNNNNNNNNN	J,T	191	567	05.05.13	7643	480208	92543
651.582-014	LITHOGRAPHIC-PROOFER APPRENTICE (print. & pub.)	3225	33444344355	MNNONNNFFFNNNNFNONNN	NNNN4NNNNNNNNNN	J,T	191	567	05.05.13	7643	480208	92543
651.585-010	ASSISTANT-PRESS OPERATOR (print. & pub.)	3226	34333433354	MNNFOONFFFNNNNFNFNON	NNNN4NOFNNNNNNN	J,T	191	567	05.05.13	7643	480208	92543

DOT #	DOT Title & Industry	Trng	Aptitude	Physical	Environment	Tempra	WkF	MPSMS	GOE	SOC	CIP	OES
651.586-010	PRESS HELPER (plastic prod.)	2112	44443434355	HNNFNONFFNNNNFNOONN	NNNN3NNNNNNNNNNN	R	191	519	06.04.02	8616	480208	98999
651.682-010	FLEXOGRAPHIC-PRESS OPERATOR (paper goods; print. & pub.)	3234	44433433354	MNNOOONFFOONNNFNFNFN	NNNN4NFNNNNNNNO	J,T	191	567	06.02.09	7443	480208	92519
651.682-014	OFFSET-DUPLICATING-MACHINE OPERATOR (print. & pub.)	3224	34433444354	LNNONONFFFNNNONFNFOFN	NNNN4NNONNNNNNN	T,J	191	480	05.10.05	7643	480299	92543
651.682-018	STRIPER (paper goods)	3115	34433434344	LNNONONFFFNNNNNFNFNFN	NNNN4NNNNNNNNNO	R,T	191	474	06.04.37	7643	480208	92522
651.682-022	TIP PRINTER (hat & cap)	3223	33433333354	LNNNNNNFFNNNNNFNFNFN	NNNN4NNNNNNNNNO	R,T	191	445	06.04.04	7444	480208	92543
651.685-010	BAG PRINTER (print. & pub.)	2224	44444444344	MNNONNNFFONNNNNFNFNON	NNNN4NNNNNNNNNN	R,T	191	567	06.04.04	7643	480208	92543
651.685-014	DESIGN PRINTER, BALLOON (rubber goods)	2112	44443433354	LNNNNNNFFFNNNNNONNNON	NNNN3NNNNNNNNNN	R	191	519	06.04.07	7643	480208	92543
651.685-018	OFFSET-PRESS OPERATOR II (print. & pub.)	2113	44443434354	LNNNNNNFFONNNNNFNONON	NNNN3NNNNNNNNNN	R	191	567	06.04.09	7643	480208	92543
651.685-022	PLATEN-PRESS FEEDER (print. & pub.)	2113	44445533344	LNNONNNFFONNNNNONONON	NNNN4NNNNNNNNNO	R,T	191	567	06.04.09	7643	480208	92543
651.685-026	ASSISTANT PRESS OPERATOR, OFFSET (print. & pub.)	3237	33333333353	NNNONNNFFONNNNONFFOON	NNNO5OOFNNNNNNN	V,T	191	480	05.05.13	7643	000000	92543
651.686-010	CYLINDER-PRESS FEEDER (print. & pub.)	2113	44443433344	HHNFNNNFFONNNNONONON	NNNN4NNNNNNNNNO	R	191	474	05.12.19	8725	480208	98502
651.686-014	FEEDER (print. & pub.)	2113	44434433344	HHNFNNNCCFNNONCNCNNN	NNNN5FCFNNNNNNN	R,U	191	472	05.12.19	8725	480208	98502
651.686-018	JOGGER (print. & pub.)	2112	44434433355	HNNONNNCCNOONCNCNNNO	NNNN5CFONNNNNNN	R	191	480	06.04.26	8725	480208	98502
651.686-022	ROLL TENDER (print. & pub.)	2115	44444544355	VNNFNNNCCFNNONCOOONO	NNNN5FCFNNNNNNN	R,U	191	472	05.12.19	8725	480208	98502
651.687-010	LITHOGRAPHED-PLATE INSPECTOR (tinware)	1112	44445544455	MNNONNNFFONNNNFNFNN	NNNN3NNNNNNNNNN	R	212	551	06.03.02	7820	000000	83005
652.130-010	SUPERVISOR, DECORATING (glass mfg.)	4336	33333343344	LNNNNNNFFFNNNNFNNON	NNNN3NNNNNNNNNN	V,D,P,J	191	531	01.06.03	7100	520205	81008
652.130-014	SUPERVISOR, PRINTING AND STAMPING (jewelry-silver.; leather prod.)	4238	33343433344	MNNNNNNFFNFFNNNNNON	NNNN4NNNNNNNNNN	V,D,P,J	191	529	06.02.01	7100	480208	81008
652.130-018	SUPERVISOR, ROLLER PRINTING (textile)	4237	33332344352	LNNNNNNFFOFFNFNFFF	NNFN4NNNNNNNNNN	D,P,V	191	420	06.02.01	7100	520205	81008
652.132-010	SUPERVISOR, PRINT LINE (furniture)	4337	33333344354	MNNNNNNFFOOFFNFOOOON	NNNN3NONNNNNNNN	D,T,P	191	461	06.02.01	7100	480208	81008
652.137-010	PRODUCTION MANAGER, REPRODUCTION (print. & pub.)	4237	33333344355	LNNNNNNFFONFFNFNOOONN	NNNN3NNNNNNNNNN	D,T,P	191	567	05.10.05	7100	480208	92543
652.137-014	SUPERVISOR, SCREEN PRINTING (textile)	4238	22333444452	LNNNNNNFFOFFNFNFOFN	NNNN4NNNNNNNNNN	D,J,P,V	191	435	06.02.01	7100	520205	92524
652.260-010	SECTION LEADER, SCREEN PRINTING (textile)	4237	33333443353	MNNFFFFFFOFFNFFON	NNNN4NNNNNNNNNN	D,J,P,V	191	435	06.01.02	7449	480299	92524
652.380-010	DECORATING-EQUIPMENT SETTER (glass mfg.: glass products)	3225	34433434344	MNNOOONFFONNNFNFNON	NNNN4NNNNNNNNNN	J,T	191	531	06.01.02	7449	480208	92524
652.382-010	CLOTH PRINTER (any industry)	4137	34432433352	MNNOOONFFONONFFOOFN	NNFN4NFNNNNNNNN	J,T	191	420	06.02.09	7444	480208	92522
652.385-010	PRINTING-ROLLER HANDLER (textile)	2112	34433444444	HNNOOONFFONNNNNNNN	NNNN4NNNNNNNNNN	R	061	567	06.04.05	6140	480208	85128
652.462-010	RUBBER-PRINTING-MACHINE OPERATOR (rubber goods)	3214	33343444454	MNNNNNNFFNFFNNNNNFNON	NNNN3NNNNNNNNNN	R,J,T	191	512	06.02.09	7444	480208	92543
652.567-010	CLOTH-PRINTING INSPECTOR (textile)	3114	34442444453	LNNNNNNFFONOONFNNOFN	NNNN3NNNNNNNNNN	J,T	212	420	06.03.02	7820	480208	83005
652.582-010	MARKER (ordnance)	3114	34443433355	MNNNNNNFFNNNNNFNFFN	NNNN4NNNNNNNNNN	R,T	192	373	06.02.02	7643	480208	92543
652.582-014	ROTARY-SCREEN-PRINTING-MACHINE OPERATOR (textile)	3114	34432433352	MNNNNNNFFNNNNNFFOFFF	NNNN4NNNNNNNNNN	J,T	191	420	06.02.06	7643	480208	92543
652.585-010	PHOTOLETTERING-MACHINE OPERATOR (print. & pub.)	2124	43443434354	LNNNNNNFFNNNFNFNON	NNNN3NNNNNNNNNN	R,T	191	606	05.12.19	7642	480205	92541
652.586-010	UTILITY WORKER, CLOTH PRINTING (textile)	2112	44444444355	HNNOOONFFONNONONNNNN	NNFO4NFNNNNNNNN	R	191	420	06.04.05	8725	480208	98502
652.662-010	PRINTING-MACHINE OPERATOR, TAPE RULES (cutlery-hrdwr.)	3215	33443444355	LNNNNNNFFOONNNFNFN	NNNN3NNNNNNNNNN	R,T	191	552	06.02.09	7444	480208	92522
652.662-014	WALLPAPER PRINTER I (paper goods)	3116	33442434354	MNNNNNNFFONNNNNFNONON	NNNN3NNNNNNNNNN	J,T	191	474	06.02.04	7479	480208	92997
652.662-018	PRINT-LINE OPERATOR (furniture; wood prod., nec)	3225	34344444454	MNNONNNFFOFFNFNFN	NNNN3NNNNNNNNNN	R,T	191	541	06.02.09	7444	480208	92522
652.665-014	STRICKLER ATTENDANT (fabrication, nec)	3114	44433433344	LNNONONFFNOONFFFFN	NNNN4NFNNNNNNNN	J,T	191	567	06.02.18	7643	480208	92543
652.682-010	BOX PRINTER (any industry)	2113	44433433344	LNNONONFFNOONFNNON	NNON4ONFNNNNNNN	R,T,U	191	470	06.04.09	7644	480299	92545
652.685-010	BACK TENDER, CLOTH PRINTING (textile)	2112	44445454354	HNNOOONFFOONNFNONON	NNFO4NFNNNNNNNN	R,T	191	420	06.04.05	7643	480208	92543
652.685-014	BINDING PRINTER (textile)	2112	44444444355	MNNNNNNFFNNNNFNNONN	NNNN3NNNNNNNNNN	R,T	191	421	06.04.05	7643	480208	92549
652.685-018	CARTON MARKER, MACHINE (boot & shoe; garment)	2112	44444433345	MNNONNNFFONNNNFNNNN	NNNN4NNNNNNNNNN	R	191	522	06.04.37	7644	480208	92545
652.685-022	CUTTING-AND-PRINTING-MACHINE OPERATOR (tex. prod., nec)	3213	44443444444	HONONNNFFONNNNFNNOON	NNNN4NNNNNNNNNN	R	191	436	06.04.05	7644	480299	92543
652.685-026	DECORATING-MACHINE OPERATOR (glass products)	3113	34434444444	LNNNNNNFFONNNNNFNNON	NNNN4NNNNNNNNNN	R,T	191	531	06.04.09	7643	480208	92543
652.685-034	GLOVE PRINTER (glove & mit.)	2113	44434434345	LNNNNNNFFONNNNFNFNN	NNNN4NNNNNNNNNN	R	191	449	06.04.37	7643	480208	92549
652.685-038	INK PRINTER (jewelry-silver.; leather prod.; plastic prod.)	2122	44544534354	SNNNNNNFFFONNNNFNNNN	NNNN3NNNNNNNNNN	R	191	529	06.04.37	7643	000000	92543
652.685-042	KEYING-MACHINE OPERATOR (print. & pub.)	2112	44444444355	LNNNNNNFFONNNNFNNNN	NNNN3NNNNNNNNNN	R	191	474	06.04.37	7643	480208	92549
652.685-046	MARKING-MACHINE OPERATOR (textile)	2122	44434444350	LNNNNNNFFONNNNFNNNON	NNNN4NNNNNNNNNN	R,T	191	420	06.04.05	7643	480208	92543
652.685-050	MARKING-MACHINE OPERATOR (knitting; tex. prod., nec)	2112	44443434344	LNNNNNNFFONNNNFNNNON	NNNN4NNNNNNNNNN	R	191	420	06.04.37	7643	480208	92543

DOT #	DOT Title & Industry	Trng	Aptitude	Physical	Environment	Tempra	WKF	MPSMS	GOE	SOC	CIP	OES
652.685-054	NAME-PLATE STAMPER (any industry)	2112	44444344445	LNNNNNNNCNNNNNNNFNNNN	NNNN3NNNNNNNNNN	R	192	567	06.04.37	7643	480208	92543
652.685-058	PRESS FEEDER (tinware)	2113	44444444354	MNNOOONFFONNNNFNONON	NNNN3NFNNNNNNNN	R,T	191	541	06.04.02	7643	480208	92543
652.685-062	PRINTER (pen & pencil)	2113	34443434344	LNNNNNNNFFONNNNFNONON	NNNN4NNNNNNNNNN	R,T	191	617	06.04.37	7643	480208	92543
652.685-066	PRINTER, FLOOR COVERING (fabrication, nec)	2113	34443544354	LNNONNNNFFONNNNFNONON	NNNN3NNNNNNNNNN	R	191	619	06.04.04	7643	480208	92549
652.685-070	PRINTER, MACHINE (hat & cap)	2113	44444444443	LNNNNNNNFFNNNNNFNNON	NNNN4NNNNNNNNNN	R,T	191	445	06.04.09	7643	480208	92549
652.685-074	PRINTING-MACHINE OPERATOR, FOLDING RULES (cutlery-hrdwr.)	2112	44443443455	LNNNNNNNFFNNNNNFNOONN	NNNN3NNNNNNNNNN	R,T	191	552	06.04.03	7643	480208	92543
652.685-078	ROLLER OPERATOR (toy-sport equip.)	2112	45454543354	LNNNNNNNNFFNNNNNNNNNN	NNNN3NNNNNNNNNN	R	191	615	06.04.21	7643	480208	92543
652.685-082	STAMPER II (tex. prod., nec)	2112	44443444343	MNNONONFFFNNNNFNONNN	NNNN4NNNNNNNNNN	R,T	191	420	06.04.06	7644	480208	92545
652.685-086	STENCIL-MACHINE OPERATOR (textile)	2113	44444544355	MNNNNNNNFFNNNNNFNNNN	NNNN4NNNNNNNNNN	R,T	191	420	06.04.05	7643	480208	92543
652.685-090	STRIKE-OFF-MACHINE OPERATOR (textile)	2113	44444444343	LNNNNNNNFFONNNNFNNFN	NNNN4NNNNNNNNNN	R	191	420	06.04.05	7643	480208	92549
652.685-094	TICKET PRINTER AND TAGGER (garment)	2112	44444433355	LNNNNNNNFFNNNNNFNOONN	NNNN3NNNNNNNNNN	R	191	440	06.04.37	7643	480208	92543
652.685-098	TICKETER (any industry)	2123	44444443344	LNNONNNFFFNNNNFNNOON	NNNN4NNNNNNNNNN	R	191	479	06.04.37	7643	480208	92543
652.685-102	WAD-PRINTING-MACHINE OPERATOR (ordnance)	2112	44444443355	LNNNNNNNFFNOONFNNFNN	NNNN3NNNNNNNNNN	R	191	374	05.10.05	7642	480205	92541
652.685-106	TYPE-PROOF REPRODUCER (machinery mfg.)	2112	33443434355	LNNNNNNNNFFNNNNNFNNNN	NNNN3NNNNNNNNNN	R	191	567	06.04.09	7643	000000	92543
652.685-110	SYMBOL STAMPER, SEMICONDUCTOR PACKAGES (electron. comp.)	2122	45454444445	LNNNNNNNFFONNNNNONNNNN	NNNN4NNNNNNNNNN	R,U	191	587	06.04.09	7643	000000	92543
652.686-010	CLOTH-PRINTER HELPER (any industry)	2112	45454544345	MNNONONFFONNNNONNNNNN	NNNN4NNNNNNNNNN	R	191	435	06.04.05	8725	480208	98502
652.686-014	GRAINER, MACHINE (any industry)	2112	34433533354	MNNONNNFFFNNNNNFNFNON	NNNN3NNNNNNNNNN	R	191	456	06.04.02	8725	480208	98502
652.686-018	GRAY-CLOTH TENDER, PRINTING (textile)	2112	44443444343	HNNOOONFFNOONFNNFNFN	NNFN4NFNNNNNNNN	R,T	191	420	06.04.05	8725	480208	98502
652.686-022	LOADER-UNLOADER, SCREEN-PRINTING MACHINE (textile)	2112	45454534455	LNNNNNNNCCNNNNNNNNNNN	NNNN4NNNNNNNNNN	R	191	420	06.04.05	8725	480299	98502
652.686-026	PRINT-LINE FEEDER (furniture)	1111	45544544455	MNNONNNFFNNNNNNNNNNN	NNNN4NNNNNNNNNN	R	191	567	06.04.03	8725	000000	98502
652.686-030	PRINT-LINE TAILER (furniture)	1111	45544544455	MNNFNNNFFNNNNNNNNNNN	NNNN4NNNNNNNNNN	R	191	461	06.04.03	8725	000000	98502
652.686-034	RAISED PRINTER (print. & pub.)	1112	44443443344	LNNNNNNNCCNNNNNONFNON	NNNN3NNNNNNNNNN	R	141	567	06.04.21	8725	480208	98502
652.686-038	SCREEN-PRINTING-MACHINE-OPERATOR HELPER (textile)	2112	44444444454	MNNFFFFFOONONNNNNNNN	NNNN4NNNNNNNNNN	R	191	420	06.02.06	8616	480299	98999
652.686-042	TOWEL SERVER (textile)	2123	44444334353	LNNFNNNNFFNNNNFNNFFN	NNNN3NNNNNNNNNN	J	212	435	06.03.02	7820	480299	83005
652.686-046	WARE SERVER (glass mfg.)	1112	44544544355	MNNFNNNCCNNNNNNNNNNN	NNNN3NNNNNNNNNN	R	191	531	06.04.37	8725	000000	98502
652.687-010	CLOTH SPREADER, SCREEN PRINTING (textile)	2113	44544544455	MNNNNNNNCCONNNNNNNNNN	NNNN4NNNNNNNNNN	R,T	191	420	06.04.27	8769	000000	98999
652.687-014	COLOR DIPPER (textile)	2112	45454544353	MNNONONCCNNNNNNFNNNCN	NNNN4NNNNNNNNNN	R	041	491	06.04.16	8769	000000	98999
652.687-018	FILLER-BLOCK INSERTER-REMOVER (furniture)	1111	44544544455	MNNONNNFFNNNNNNNNNNN	NNNN4NNNNNNNNNN	R	061	461	06.04.25	8769	000000	98999
652.687-022	PAINT POURER (fabrication, nec)	1111	44444544353	MNNNNNNNCCNNNNNONNNFN	NNNN4NFNNNNNNNN	R	041	619	06.04.34	8769	000000	98999
652.687-026	PASTER, SCREEN PRINTING (textile)	1112	45454544355	LNNNNNNNCCNNNNNNNNNNN	NNNN3NNNNNNNNNN	R	191	420	06.04.27	8769	000000	98999
652.687-030	PATTERN HAND (woodworking)	2113	44443434355	LNNNNNNNFFNNNNNFNNNN	NNNN3NNNNNNNNNN	R,T	191	519	06.04.27	7759	480208	93999
652.687-034	PRINT-LINE INSPECTOR (furniture)	2112	44543544454	LNNFNNNFFFNNNNFNNNFN	NNNN4NNNNNNNNNN	J,T	212	461	06.03.02	7820	480208	83005
652.687-038	PRINTER, FLOOR COVERING, ASSISTANT (fabrication, nec)	2112	44454544354	LNNNNNNNFFNNNNNFNONON	NNNN3NNNNNNNNNN	R	191	619	06.04.09	8725	480208	98502
652.687-042	WALLPAPER INSPECTOR (paper goods)	2114	34422444452	LNNNNNNNFFONNNNFNNFFN	NNNN4NNNNNNNNNN	J,T	212	474	06.03.02	7820	480208	83005
652.687-046	WALLPAPER INSPECTOR AND SHIPPER (paper goods)	2123	44443444344	LNNNNNNNFFONNNNNFNNFFN	NNNN3NNNNNNNNNN	R,J,T	212	474	06.03.02	7820	480208	83005
652.687-050	WALLPAPER-PRINTER HELPER (paper goods)	2112	45454544354	MNNFNONFFNNNNNNONNNON	NNNO3NNNNNNNNNN	R	191	474	06.04.26	8619	480208	98999
653.131-010	SUPERVISOR, BINDERY (print. & pub.)	4338	33333333355	LNNONOOOONFFNFOOONN	NNNO4OFONNNNNNN	D,V,T,P,J	054	480	06.02.01	7100	520205	81008
653.360-010	CASING-IN-LINE SETTER (print. & pub.)	3238	33333433254	LNNNNNNNFFONNNNFNNNN	NNNN4NNNNNNNNNN	J,T	102	480	06.01.02	7449	480299	92525
653.360-018	BINDERY-MACHINE SETTER (print. & pub.)	3228	33333433355	LNNNNNNNFFNOONFNNFFN	NNNN4NNFNNNNNNN	T,J	054	480	06.01.02	7449	480299	92525
653.382-010	FOLDING-MACHINE OPERATOR (print. & pub.)	3225	34433443355	LNNNNNNNFFNNNONFNONF	NNNN4CNFNNNNNNN	J,T	061	480	06.02.04	7649	480299	92546
653.382-014	COLLATING-MACHINE OPERATOR (print. & pub.)	3234	33333433354	LNNNNNNNFFNOONFFFON	NNNN4FNNNNNNNNN	T,R	062	480	06.02.04	7649	480299	92546
653.662-010	STITCHING-MACHINE OPERATOR (print. & pub.)	3126	33433344355	LNNONNNFFNOONFNFFNN	NNNN4FCCNNNNNNN	T	054	480	06.02.04	7449	480299	92525
653.667-010	INSPECTOR, PUBLICATIONS (print. & pub.)	3125	34433443354	LNNNNNNNFFNOONFNOFFN	NNNN4NFFNNNNNNN	R,T	212	480	06.03.02	7820	480299	83005
653.682-010	BOOK-SEWING-MACHINE OPERATOR II (print. & pub.)	2114	34443433345	LNNNNNNNFFNNNONFNNNN	NNNO4FOONNNNNNN	R,T	171	480	06.02.04	7449	480299	92525
653.682-014	COVERING-MACHINE OPERATOR (print. & pub.)	3215	34444444355	LNNOOOOFFONNNNNFNNNN	NNNN4NNNNNNNNNN	R,J,T	063	486	06.02.20	7449	480299	92546
653.682-018	HEAD-BANDER-AND-LINER OPERATOR (print. & pub.)	3223	34433433355	LNNNNNNNFFNNONFNNONN	NNNN4NNNNNNNNNN	T	063	480	06.02.20	7449	480299	92525
653.682-022	TINNING-MACHINE SET-UP OPERATOR (print. & pub.)	3125	34344444455	MNNNNNNFFONNNNFNNNNN	NNNN4NNFNNNNNNN	J,T	062	474	06.02.09	7449	480299	92546
653.685-010	BINDERY WORKER (print. & pub.)	2224	44443433344	LNNNNNNNFFNNNNNNNNNN	NNNN4NNFNNNNNNN	R,T	062	480	06.04.04	7649	480299	92546
653.685-014	BOOK-SEWING-MACHINE OPERATOR I (print. & pub.)	2114	44444433335	LNNNNNNNFFNONFNNNNN	NNNN4FOFNNNNNNN	R	171	480	06.02.04	7649	480299	92546
653.685-018	CASE-MAKING-MACHINE OPERATOR (print. & pub.)	2114	44444443354	LNNNNNNNFFFNNONCNOOON	NNNN4NNONNNNNNN	R,T	054	480	06.04.09	7661	480299	92956
653.685-022	MAGAZINE REPAIRER (print. & pub.)	2123	44444444345	LNNNNNNNFFNNNNNFNFNNN	NNNN4NNNNNNNNNN	J,T	062	486	06.04.04	7649	480299	92546

DOT #	DOT Title & Industry	Trng	Aptitude	Physical	Environment	Tempra	WkF	MPSMS	GOE	SOC	CIP	OES
653.685-026	ROUNDING-AND-BACKING-MACHINE OPERATOR (print. & pub.)	3224	4444443355	LNNNNNNFFONNONFNNNNN	NNNN4NNNNNNNNNN	R,T	134	480	06.02.09	7649	480299	92546
653.685-030	SPIRAL BINDER (paper goods; print. & pub.)	1112	4444444345	MMNNONNFFONNONFNNNNN	NNNN4NNFNNNNNN	U,R	062	474	06.04.09	7649	480299	92546
653.686-010	CASING-IN-LINE FEEDER (print. & pub.)	1112	44544543354	LNNFNNNFFNNNNNNNNNN	NNNN3NNNNNNNNNN	R	062	486	06.04.04	8725	480299	98502
653.686-026	BINDERY-MACHINE FEEDER-OFFBEARER (print. & pub.)	1112	4444444354	LNNONNNFFNNONFNNNNN	NNNN4FNNNNNNNNN	R	011	480	06.04.04	8725	480299	98502
653.687-010	COLLATOR (print. & pub.)	2212	44443333355	LNNONNNFFFNNNNFNNNNN	NNNN3NNNNNNNNNN	R,T	212	486	07.07.03	7820	480299	83005
654.382-010	CASTING-MACHINE OPERATOR (machinery mfg.; print. & pub.)	3226	33443333355	MNNNNNNFFNNNNNFNNNNN	NNNN4NNNNNNNNNN	J,T	191	567	05.10.05	7449	480205	92529
654.582-010	TYPE-CASTING MACHINE OPERATOR (print. & pub.)	3226	33432333355	LNNNNNNFFNNNNFNNNNN	NNON3NONNNNNNNN	J,T	191	567	05.10.05	7449	480205	92529
654.687-014	MATRIX INSPECTOR (machinery mfg.)	2123	4442555554	SNNNNNNOONNNNNFNNNNN	NNNN4NNNNNNNNNN	R,J	212	567	06.03.02	7820	480205	83005
654.687-010	PAGER (machinery mfg.)	2112	44443533355	SNNNNNNFFNNNNNNNNNN	NNNN4NNNNNNNNNN	R	031	567	06.04.37	7740	480206	93999
659.360-010	PLATE FINISHER (print. & pub.)	4228	33332433254	MNNNNNNFFNNNNNNNFFN	NNNN4NNNNNNNNNN	J,T	191	567	05.05.07	7449	480206	92529
659.381-010	PLATE SETTER, FLEXOGRAPHIC PRESS (print. & pub.)	3336	34432433345	MNNONONFFFNNNNNFFNN	NNNN4NFNNNNNNNN	J	192	474	06.01.02	7443	480208	92519
659.382-010	EMBOSSER (print. & pub.)	4226	34432344455	LNNNNNNFFNNNNNFNNNN	NNNN4NNNNNNNNNN	J,T	191	567	05.10.05	7449	480205	92529
659.462-010	ELECTROTYPE SERVICER (print. & pub.)	3233	33432344455	LNNNNNNFFONFFNFNNNNN	NNNN4NNNNNNNNNN	P,J,T	191	752	05.10.05	4664	000000	55323
659.662-010	PRINTER-SLOTTER OPERATOR (paper goods)	3225	34333433353	HNNFNNNFFOOOONFNOOON	NNNN4NNNNNNNNNO	J,T	054	475	06.02.04	7643	000000	92543
659.667-010	INKER (print. & pub.)	3224	34343344452	LONONNNFFONNNNFNNNFN	NNNN4NNNNNNNNNN	R,J,T	191	499	06.03.02	7820	480208	83005
659.682-010	CUT-AND-PRINT-MACHINE OPERATOR (ordnance)	3224	34433433353	HNNFFFNFFOONNNNFNOONN	NNNN4NNNNNNNNNN	J,T	191	567	06.02.09	7449	480205	92529
659.682-014	EMBOSSING-PRESS OPERATOR (print. & pub.)	3227	34433433355	LNNNNNNFFFNNNFNOONN	NNNN4NNNNNNNNNN	J,T	192	567	06.02.04	7449	480205	92529
659.682-018	EMBOSSING-PRESS-OPERATOR APPRENTICE (print. & pub.)	3227	34433433343	LNNNNNNFFFNNNFNOONN	NNNN4NNNNNNNNNN	J,T	192	567	06.02.04	7449	480205	92529
659.682-022	RULING-MACHINE SET-UP OPERATOR (paper goods; print. & pub.)	3224	34333433343	MNNOONNFFONNONFNFFON	NNNN4NNONNNNNNN	T,J	191	474	06.02.04	7449	480208	92529
659.682-026	SIGN WRITER, MACHINE (any industry)	3124	33432323242	LNNNNNNFFFNNNFNFNFN	NNNN4NNNNNNNNNN	R	191	619	06.02.09	7449	480205	92529
659.684-010	DIE MOUNTER (paper goods)	3225	34433433353	MNNOONNFFNNNONFNFOON	NNNN4NOONNNNNNN	J,T	102	567	06.02.31	7759	480299	93999
659.685-014	SAMPLE-BOOK MAKER (paper goods)	2115	44444553355	MMNONONFFFNNNONNNNNN	NNNN4NNNNNNNNNN	R,T	062	474	06.04.04	7678	480299	92944
659.685-018	SHOTGUN-SHELL-REPRINTING-UNIT OPERATOR (ordnance)	2122	44444443345	MONONONFFFNNNNONNNNN	NNNN4NNNNNNNNNN	R,T	031	374	06.04.37	7649	480208	92549
659.685-022	TRANSFER-MACHINE OPERATOR (knitting; tex. prod., nec)	2122	44444444344	LNNNNNNCCFNNONFNONNN	NNON3NNNNNNNNNN	R	191	421	06.04.37	7649	480208	92549
659.685-026	MILL STENCILER (steel & rel.)	2112	44444444445	LNNNNOOONNNNNOFONNN	NNNN4NNONNNNNNN	R	191	541	06.04.10	7649	000000	92549
659.686-014	PRINTER-SLOTTER HELPER (paper goods)	2112	44544444354	HNNFONNFFONONONONON	NNNN4NFNNNNNNNN	R	054	475	06.04.04	8725	480208	98502
659.687-010	RACKER (paper goods)	1112	44544444455	LNNFNNNFFNNNNNFNNNNN	NNNN4NNNNNNNNNN	R	011	474	06.04.26	8725	480299	98502
659.687-014	RACKER, SILK-SCREEN PRINTING (any industry)	1112	44443544353	LNNONNNFFFNNNNFNNNNN	NNNN4NNNNNNNNNN	R,T	212	486	06.03.02	7820	480299	83005
660.130-010	CABINETMAKER, SUPERVISOR (woodworking)	4448	33333333344	MNNONONOOONFFNNNNON	NNNN4NOONNNNNNN	V,D,P,J	102	467	05.05.08	6700	520205	81008
660.280-010	CABINETMAKER (woodworking)	4436	33333333344	MNNNNNNFFNNNNNFNFOON	NNNN4NNNNNNNNNN	V,J,T	102	450	05.05.08	6832	480703	89311
660.280-014	CABINETMAKER APPRENTICE (woodworking)	4436	33333333344	MMNNNNNFFNNNNNNNOON	NNNN4NNNNNNNNNN	V,J,T	102	450	05.05.08	6832	480703	89311
661.131-010	LOFT WORKER, HEAD (ship-boat mfg.)	4438	33323333355	LNNONONFFFNNONONONN	NNNN4NNNNNNNNNN	V,D,P,J	057	593	05.05.06	7100	490306	89302
661.137-010	SUPERVISOR, FRAME SAMPLE AND PATTERN (furniture)	4448	22233343455	LNNNNNNFFNNFNFNOONN	NNNN4NNNNNNNNNN	D,P,J	102	460	06.02.01	7100	480702	81008
661.280-010	PATTERNMAKER (furniture)	4447	23322433255	MMNFNNNFFNNFFNFNNON	NNNN4NNNNNNNNNN	J,T,V	241	460	05.05.08	6831	480703	89302
661.281-010	LOFT WORKER (ship-boat mfg.)	4437	33323433355	LNNONONFFFNNNNFNCONN	NNNN3NNNNNNNNNN	J,T	241	593	06.01.04	6639	490306	89302
661.281-014	LOFT WORKER APPRENTICE (ship-boat mfg.)	4437	33323423355	LNNONONFFFNNNNFNCONN	NNNN3NNNNNNNNNN	J,T	241	593	06.02.03	7434	490306	89302
661.281-018	PATTERNMAKER APPRENTICE, WOOD (foundry)	4438	23322422254	MMNNFONNCCOONONONONN	NNNN4NOONNNNNON	J,T	102	560	06.02.03	7434	480703	89302
661.281-022	PATTERNMAKER, WOOD (foundry)	4438	23322422254	MMNNFONNCCCFNNNCNCNN	NNNN4NOONNNNNON	J,T	102	560	06.02.03	7634	480703	89302
661.380-010	MODEL MAKER, WOOD (any industry)	4437	33322432254	MMNFOONFFFOONFNFNNN	NNNN4NNNNNNNNNN	J,T	102	566	05.05.08	6831	480703	89302
661.381-010	HAT-BLOCK MAKER (woodworking)	3326	34333534355	LNNNNNNFFOOONFNNNNN	NNNN3NNNNNNNNNN	R	051	450	06.04.03	7634	000000	89399
662.132-010	SUPERVISOR, SANDING (woodworking)	4437	33323433355	LNNNNNNFFOOONFOONNN	NNNN4NNNNNNNNNN	V,J,T	055	457	06.04.25	7634	520205	81008
662.682-010	MOLDING SANDER (woodworking)	3214	34433434355	MMNFNNNFFFFNONFNNNN	NNNN4NOONNNNNON	V,D,P	051	461	06.02.03	7434	480703	92311
662.682-014	MULTIPLE-DRUM SANDER (woodworking)	3224	34433434345	MMNNFONNCCOONONONNON	NNNN4NOONNNNNON	J,T	051	450	06.02.03	7634	480703	92311
662.682-018	STROKE-BELT-SANDER OPERATOR (woodworking)	2112	44444534455	LNNONONFFONNNNNNNNN	NNNN4NNNNNNNNNN	J,T	051	450	06.04.09	7634	480703	92314
662.685-010	CORK GRINDER (toy-sport equip.)	2114	44444534455	LNNONONFFONNNNFNNNNN	NNNN4NNNNNNNNNN	R	051	616	06.04.03	7634	000000	92314
662.685-014	CYLINDER-SANDER OPERATOR (woodworking)	2112	44433434355	MONOOONFFOOOONFNOONN	NNNN4NNNNNNNNNN	R	051	450	06.04.03	7634	480703	92314
662.685-018	LAST SCOURER (wood prod., nec)	2114	44433434355	LNNNNNNFFOOONFNNNNN	NNNN4NNNNNNNNNN	R,J,T	051	450	06.04.03	7634	480703	92314
662.685-022	SANDING-MACHINE BUFFER (wood prod., nec)	2112	44435534355	LNNNNNNFFOOONONONONN	NNNN3NNNNNNNNNN	R,T	051	522	06.04.05	7634	480703	92314
662.685-026	SANDING-MACHINE TENDER (wood prod., nec)	2112	44444443345	LNNONNNFFOONNNONONNN	NNNN3NONNNNNNNN	R,T	051	459	06.04.09	7634	000000	92314
662.685-030	SIZING-MACHINE TENDER (pen & pencil)	2112	45454544455	LNNNNONFFONNNNNNNNN	NNNN4NNNNNNNNNN	R	051	617	06.04.03	7634	000000	92314
662.685-034	SPEED-BELT-SANDER TENDER (woodworking)	2112	44434434355	MNNONNNCCOONNNFNONNN	NNNN4NFNNNNNNNN	R,T	051	460	06.04.03	7634	480703	92314

DOT #	DOT Title & Industry	Trng	Aptitude	Physical	Environment	Tempra	WkF	MPSMS	GOE	SOC	CIP	OES
662.685-038	TURNING-SANDER TENDER (woodworking)	2113	44433544355	LNNFNNNCCFFNONFNONNN	NNNN4NOONNNNON	R,T	051	461	06.04.03	7634	480703	92314
662.685-042	WOOD-HEEL BACK-LINER (boot & shoe)	2112	44544544455	LNNNNNNNFFNNNNONNNNN	NNNN4NNNNNNNNNN	R	051	522	06.04.03	7634	480304	92314
662.686-010	END-TOUCHING-MACHINE OPERATOR (wood prod., nec)	1111	44544544455	LNNNNNNNFFNNNNNNNNNN	NNNN3NNNNNNNNNN	R	051	459	06.04.09	8725	000000	98502
662.686-014	MULTIPLE-DRUM-SANDER HELPER (woodworking)	2122	44544544455	MNNONNNFFOONNNONNOONN	NNNN4NONNNNNNN	R	051	452	06.04.03	8725	480703	98502
663.132-010	SUPERVISOR, GREEN END DEPARTMENT (millwork-plywood)	4337	33333433354	LNNONNNFFNFFNFNFNON	NNNN4NNNNNNNNNN	V,D,P,J	054	453	06.02.01	7100	000000	81008
663.380-010	KNIFE SETTER (saw. & plan.)	3124	33433433355	LNNNNNNNFFNNNNNNNNNN	NNNN4NNNNNNNNNN	R,T	054	459	06.01.02	7439	000000	92311
663.585-010	CLIPPER, AUTOMATIC (millwork-plywood)	2114	44444444355	LONNNNNNFFCNOOONFNOCCC	NNNN4NOONONNNNN	R,T	054	453	06.04.03	7635	000000	92314
663.682-010	BARKER OPERATOR (millwork-plywood)	2113	44434534355	MNNNNNNFFONNNNNNNNNN	NNNN4NNNNNNNNNN	R,T	054	451	06.04.03	7631	000000	92314
663.682-014	POLE-PEELING-MACHINE OPERATOR (saw. & plan.; wood prod., nec)	3113	34434534355	LNNNNNNNFFONNNNFNNNNN	NNNN4NNONNNNNNN	J,T	054	451	06.04.03	7678	030404	92944
663.682-018	VENEER-SLICING-MACHINE OPERATOR (millwork-plywood)	3113	34434434355	MNNOONNFFONNNNFNNNNN	NNNN4NNNNNNNNNN	R,T	054	453	06.02.03	7639	000000	92944
663.685-010	BLOCK-SPLITTER OPERATOR (paper & pulp)	2113	44544544345	MNNNNNNNFFONNNNNNNNNN	NNNN4NNNNNNNNNN	R	054	451	06.04.03	7678	480703	92944
663.685-014	EXCELSIOR-MACHINE TENDER (saw. & plan.)	2112	44335544345	MNNNNNNNFFONNNNNNNNNN	NNNN4NNONNNNNNN	R	054	459	06.04.03	7639	000000	92944
663.685-018	MOLDING CUTTER (woodworking)	2112	44433434345	LNNNNNNNFFNNNNNNNNNN	NNNN4NNNNNNNNNN	R,T	054	457	06.04.03	7635	480703	92314
663.685-022	PUNCHER (woodworking)	2112	44544534355	LNNNNNNFFONNNNNNNNNN	NNNN3NNNNNNNNNN	R	054	457	06.04.03	7635	000000	92314
663.685-026	ROUNDING-MACHINE TENDER (pen & pencil)	2112	44444434444	MNNONNNFFONNNNNFNOONN	NNNN4NNNNNNNNNN	R	054	617	06.04.03	7635	000000	92314
663.685-030	SHAKE BACKBOARD NOTCHER (saw. & plan.)	2112	44545544345	LNNNNNNNFFONNNNFNNNNN	NNNN3NNNNNNNNNN	R	054	452	06.04.03	7635	000000	92314
663.685-034	SLICING-MACHINE TENDER (furniture)	2113	44444434355	MNNOONNFFONNNNNNNNNN	NNNN4NONNNNNNNN	R	054	467	06.04.03	7635	000000	92314
663.685-038	SPLITTER TENDER (saw. & plan.)	2112	44444534355	HNNNNNNNFFONNNNNNCNNN	NNNN3NNNNNNNNNN	R	054	452	06.04.09	7635	000000	92314
663.685-042	SPLITTING-MACHINE TENDER (wood prod., nec)	2113	34434434355	HNNNNNNNFFONNNNFNOONN	NNNN3NNNNNNNNNN	R,T	054	456	06.04.09	7635	000000	92314
663.685-046	STAVE-MACHINE TENDER (wood. container)	2112	44444544355	LNNONONFFONNNNNNNNNN	NNNN4NNNNNNNNNN	R,T	054	452	06.04.03	7635	000000	92314
663.685-050	VENEER CLIPPER (millwork-plywood)	2114	44444434344	MNNFNFNCCFNNONFNNNFN	NNNN4NNONNNNNNN	R,T	054	453	06.04.03	7635	000000	92314
663.686-010	BLOCK FEEDER (fabrication, nec)	2112	44444433444	LNNONNNFFFNNNNNNNNNN	NNNN4NNNNNNNNNN	R	054	619	06.04.03	8725	000000	98502
663.686-014	BREAK-OFF WORKER (millwork-plywood)	2112	44544534355	MNNFNNNFFNNNNNNNNNN	NNNN4NNNNNNNNNN	R	054	453	06.04.03	8725	000000	98502
663.686-018	GREEN-CHAIN OFFBEARER (millwork-plywood)	2112	44444534344	MNNNNNNCCNNNNNFNNNON	NNNN4NNNNNNNNNN	R	054	453	06.04.40	8725	000000	98502
663.686-022	LATHE SPOTTER (millwork-plywood)	2113	34434434355	HNNONNNFFONNNNNONNNN	NNNN3NNNNNNNNNN	R	054	453	06.04.03	8615	000000	99999
663.686-026	SLICING-MACHINE TENDER (wood prod., nec)	1111	44444544355	LNNNNNNFFONNNNNNNNNN	NNNN4NNNNNNNNNN	R	054	459	06.04.09	8725	000000	98502
663.686-030	VENEER-CLIPPER HELPER (millwork-plywood)	1112	44444544355	HNNFNNNCCNNNNNFNNNNN	NNNN4NNNNNNNNNN	R	054	453	06.04.03	8615	000000	99999
663.687-010	WOOD INSPECTOR (paper & pulp)	2222	44543534344	LNNONNNFFNNNNNONNNON	NNNN4NNNNNNNNNN	R,T	212	471	06.03.02	7820	000000	83005
664.382-010	SWING-TYPE-LATHE OPERATOR (woodworking)	3324	34333434355	MNNONNNFFFONONFNFONN	NNNN4NFONNNNNOO	J,T	055	450	06.02.03	7431	480703	92311
664.382-014	WOOD-TURNING-LATHE OPERATOR (woodworking)	4215	44434524355	MNNNNNNFFFNNNNNFNOONN	NNNN3NNONNNNNNN	J,T	055	450	06.02.03	7631	480703	92314
664.382-018	TRIMMING MACHINE SET-UP OPERATOR (fabrication, nec)	3224	34434534355	MNNNNNCCONNNFNONNNN	NNNN4NFNNNNNNN	J,T	055	619	06.02.03	7431	000000	92311
664.662-010	VENEER-LATHE OPERATOR (millwork-plywood)	3114	34434434355	MNNNNNFFONNNNNNNNNN	NNNN4NOONNNNON	J,T	055	453	06.02.03	7631	480703	92314
664.682-010	BARREL-LATHE OPERATOR, INSIDE (wood. container)	3114	34433533355	MNNNNNNFFONNNNNNONNN	NNNN4NNNNNNNNNN	R,T	055	454	06.02.03	7631	480703	92314
664.682-014	BARREL-LATHE OPERATOR, OUTSIDE (wood. container)	2114	44443544355	MNNNNNFFNNNNNFNNNNN	NNNN3NNNNNNNNNN	R	055	454	06.04.03	7631	480703	92314
664.682-018	SKIVING-MACHINE OPERATOR (ordnance)	2114	44443434345	MNNNNNNFFNNNNFNNOONN	NNNN4NNNNNNNNNN	R,J	055	373	06.02.03	7631	000000	92314
664.682-022	SPAR-MACHINE OPERATOR (wood prod., nec)	3225	34433544355	LNNOOONFFONNNNFNOONN	FNNN4NNONNNNNNN	J,T	055	452	06.04.03	7631	480703	92314
664.684-010	BOWL TURNER (fabrication, nec)	2112	44434524355	LNNNNNNCCNNNNCNCNNN	NNNN3NONNNNNNN	R	055	619	06.04.23	7631	480703	92314
664.685-010	BRIAR CUTTER (fabrication, nec)	2112	44444434455	LNNNNNNFFONNNNNNNNNN	NNNN3NNNNNNNNNN	R	055	619	06.04.03	7631	480703	92314
664.685-014	BUCKET CHUCKER (wood. container)	2113	34434534345	MNNNNNNFFNNNNNNNNNN	NNNN3NNNNNNNNNN	R	055	454	06.04.03	7634	480703	92314
664.685-018	COPY-LATHE TENDER (woodworking)	2113	44433534355	MNNNNNNFFONNNONNNNN	NNNN4NNNNNNNNNN	R,T	055	457	06.04.03	7631	480703	92314
664.685-022	FRAZER (fabrication, nec)	2112	44454534355	MNNNNNNNFFNNNNFNFFNN	NNNN4NNONNNNNNN	R	055	619	06.04.03	7634	480703	92314
664.685-026	SHUTTLE SPOTTER (woodworking)	2112	44443434345	MNNNNNNFFNNNNFNONNNN	NNNN3NNNNNNNNNN	R	055	457	06.04.03	7631	480703	92311
664.685-030	SPAR-MACHINE-OPERATOR HELPER (wood prod., nec)	2223	44443534355	HNNONNNFFONNNNONOONN	FNNN4NNONNNNNNN	R	053	450	06.04.03	8615	480703	98999
664.685-034	TURNING LATHE TENDER (furniture)	2112	44434524355	MNNFNNNCCOONCNCNCCNN	NNNN4NNCNNNNNNN	R,T,U	055	461	06.04.23	7631	480703	92314
665.382-010	CHUCKING-MACHINE OPERATOR (woodworking)	3215	44344534355	MNNNNNNFFONNNNFNOONN	NNNN4NOONNNNNNN	J,T	055	450	06.02.03	7432	480703	92311
665.382-014	LOCK-CORNER-MACHINE OPERATOR (woodworking)	3224	34433434345	MNNONNNCCONNONCNFNNN	NNNN4NFONNNNNNN	J,T	055	452	06.02.03	7632	480703	92314
665.382-018	WOOD-CARVING-MACHINE OPERATOR (woodworking)	3324	34333433355	MNNNNNNNFFONNNFNFFNN	NNNN4NOONNNNON	J,T	055	462	06.02.03	7431	480703	92311
665.482-014	MORTISING-MACHINE OPERATOR (woodworking)	3324	34333433345	MNNNNNNFFNNNNNONNNN	NNNN3NNNNNNNNNN	J,T	055	452	06.02.03	7432	480703	92314
665.482-018	TIMBER-SIZER OPERATOR (saw. & plan.)	3214	34333434345	MNNONONFFONNOOFNNNNN	ONNN4NOONNNNNNN	J,T	055	452	06.02.03	7632	480703	98999
665.665-010	ROUGH PLANER TENDER (woodworking)	3323	44433534345	HNNNNNNCCONNNNONONNO	NNNN4NNNNNNNNNN	R,T	055	452	06.04.03	7632	030404	92314
665.682-010	DOWEL-MACHINE OPERATOR (woodworking)	3215	34333434345	MNNONONFFONNNNNFNOONN	NNNN4NNONNNNNNN	J,T	055	459	06.02.03	7431	480703	92311

DOT #	DOT Title & Industry	Trng	Aptitude	Physical	Environment	Tempra	WkF	MPSMS	GOE	SOC	CIP	OES
665.682-014	HEADER (wood prod., nec)	3324	34333434345	MNNNNNNFFONNNNFNOONN	NNNN4NOONNNNNN	R,T	055	459	06.02.03	7635	000000	92314
665.682-018	MOLDER OPERATOR (woodworking)	3325	33433433355	MNNONNNCCOONONFNFONN	NNNN4NFFNNNNNN	R,T	055	450	06.02.03	7435	480703	92311
665.682-022	PLANER OPERATOR (woodworking)	3224	34433434355	MNNNNNNCCOONONCNONNN	NNNN4NCCNNNNCN	J,T	055	451	06.02.03	7432	480703	92311
665.682-026	PROFILE-SHAPER OPERATOR, AUTOMATIC (woodworking)	3214	34433434345	MNNNFNONCCOONONFNFONN	NNNN4NCNNNNNCN	J,T	055	450	06.02.03	7439	480703	92311
665.682-030	ROUTER OPERATOR (woodworking)	3224	34433434345	MNNNFNNNCCONNONFNFFNN	NNNN4NOONNNNNN	J,T	055	452	06.02.03	7432	480703	92314
665.682-034	SHAPER OPERATOR (woodworking)	3225	34433434345	MNNFNNNNCCFFNNNFNONN	NNON4NFONNNNOO	R,T	055	450	05.05.08	7432	480703	92311
665.682-038	VENEER-JOINTER (millwork-plywood)	3224	34444434345	MMNFNNNNCCNNNONFNONNN	NNNN4NOONNNNON	J,T	055	453	06.02.03	7432	000000	92311
665.682-042	JOINTER OPERATOR (woodworking)	3234	34433444344	MMNFNNNFFONONFOFNFN	NNNN4NCNNNNNNF	J,T	055	450	05.05.08	7435	480703	92311
665.685-010	BOTTOM-TURNING-LATHE TENDER (wood. container)	2113	44443544355	LNNNNNNNFFONNNNNNNNN	NNNN3NNNNNNNNN	R,T	055	454	06.04.03	7631	480703	92314
665.685-014	END FRAZER (fabrication, nec)	2213	34434444355	LNNNNNNNFFONNNNNNONN	NNNN4NNNNNNNNN	J,T	055	619	06.04.03	7632	480703	92314
665.685-018	PLOW-AND-BORING-MACHINE TENDER (woodworking)	2112	44444534455	MNNNNNNNFFNNNNNNNNN	NNNN4NNNNNNNNN	R	057	452	06.04.03	7639	480703	92998
665.685-022	PLYWOOD-SCARFER TENDER (millwork-plywood)	2114	44444534345	MNNNFNNNFFNNNNONONNN	NNNN4NNNNNNNNN	R,T	055	453	06.04.03	7632	000000	92314
665.685-026	SCOOPING-MACHINE TENDER (furniture)	3224	34434444355	MNNNNNNFFNNOONFNNONN	NNNN4NONNNNNNN	R,T	055	461	06.04.03	7632	480703	92314
665.685-030	STAVE JOINTER (wood. container)	2113	44434534345	LNNNNNNNFFONNNNNNONN	NNNN4NNNNNNNNN	R	055	452	06.04.03	7635	480703	92314
665.685-034	STOCK CHECKERER II (ordnance)	2112	44443534355	LNNNNNFFONNNNONNONN	NNNN4NNNNNNNNN	R	055	373	06.04.03	7639	470402	92998
665.685-038	RODDING MACHINE TENDER (furniture)	2112	44533534355	MNNNNNNFFFNNNNNNNNN	NNNN4NNNNNNNNN	R	055	457	06.04.03	7639	480703	92314
665.685-042	ROUTER TENDER (furniture)	2112	44444544455	HNNNNNNNCCNNNNNNNNN	NNNN4NNONNNNNN	R	055	452	06.04.03	7639	480703	92314
665.685-046	SHAPING MACHINE TENDER (furniture)	3123	44433444455	HNNONNNFFNNNNNFFNN	NNNN4NNNNNNNNN	R,T	055	453	06.04.03	7633	030404	92308
665.686-010	POLE-PEELING-MACHINE-OPERATOR HELPER (wood prod., nec)	1112	44544535345	HFONNNNNFFNNNNNNNNN	FNNN3NNONNNNNN	R	055	451	06.04.03	8725	030404	98502
665.686-014	STAVE-PLANER TENDER (saw. & plan.)	2112	44544544355	LNNNNNNNFFONNNNNNNN	NNNN4NNNNNNNNN	R	055	454	06.04.03	8725	480703	98502
665.686-018	VENEER-JOINTER HELPER (millwork-plywood)	1112	44544544355	LNNNNNNNFFNNNNNNNNN	NNNN3NNNNNNNNN	R,T	055	453	06.04.03	8615	000000	98999
665.686-022	VENEER-JOINTER OFFBEARER (millwork-plywood)	2112	44544544355	MNNONNNCCONNNNFNNNNN	NNNN4NNNNNNNNN	R	055	453	06.04.03	8725	000000	98502
666.382-010	BORING-MACHINE OPERATOR (woodworking)	3324	34434434345	MNNNFONNCCONNONFNFONN	NNNN4NOONNFNONN	J,T	053	450	06.02.03	7439	480703	92311
666.482-010	PULLEY-MORTISER OPERATOR (woodworking)	3224	34434444355	MNNNNNNNFFONNNFNFNNN	NNNN4NNNNNNNNN	J,T	053	452	06.02.03	7639	480703	92314
666.582-010	PREFITTER, DOORS (woodworking)	3224	34434433355	HNNONONFFNNNNFNNNN	NNNN4NNNNNNNNN	J,T	053	450	06.02.03	7639	480703	92314
666.684-010	FRAMER (wood prod., nec)	2123	44434534335	MNNFOONFFNNNNNNOOFNNF	FNNN4NNNNNNNNNO	J,T	053	450	06.04.25	7639	000000	92314
666.685-010	STEMHOLE BORER (fabrication, nec)	2112	44434544445	LNNNNNNCCFFNONFNFNNN	NNNN4NONNNNNNN	R,T	053	619	06.04.03	7639	480703	92314
666.685-014	BORING-MACHINE OPERATOR (furniture)	2222	34434434355	MNNFNNNCCONNNNCNNNNN	NNNN4NNNNNNNNN	R,U	053	460	06.04.03	7639	480703	92314
667.137-010	SUPERVISOR, STAVE CUTTING (wood. container)	3227	33333434454	MNNNNNNFFNFNFNFNFFN	NNNN4NNNNNNNNN	D,J,T	056	452	06.02.01	7100	520205	81008
667.382-010	STOCK GRADER (woodworking)	3225	34433534334	MONFNNNCCONNNNNCNCCON	NNNN4NOONNNNNN	J	212	450	06.02.03	7633	480703	92308
667.482-014	POCKET CUTTER (woodworking)	3224	34434334345	MNNNNNNFFONNNONFNFONN	NNNN4NNNNNNNNN	J,T	056	452	06.02.03	7633	480703	92308
667.482-018	STOCK CUTTER (saw. & plan.)	3224	34343334355	MNNNNNNNFFNNNNNNNNN	NNNN4NNNNNNNNN	J,T	056	452	06.02.03	7633	480703	92308
667.485-010	SHINGLE SAWYER (saw. & plan.)	3114	44433533344	MNNNNNNFFONNNFNNOON	NNNN4NNNNNNNNN	R,T	056	452	06.02.03	7633	480703	92308
667.662-010	HEAD SAWYER (saw. & plan.)	3217	34433523333	LNNOONNFFNNNNFNNNNN	NNNN4NNNNNNNNN	J	056	452	06.02.03	7633	000000	92305
667.662-014	MACHINE-TANK OPERATOR (wood. container)	3225	34433434355	MNNNNNNNFFONOONFNOONN	NNNN4NNNNNNNNN	V,T	056	454	06.02.03	7633	480703	92308
667.662-018	BAND-SCROLL-SAW OPERATOR (woodworking)	3225	34433433355	LNNONNNFFOOONONFNFNNN	NNNN4NFFNNNNNN	R,T	056	450	06.02.03	7633	480703	92308
667.682-014	BOTTOM-SAW OPERATOR (saw. & plan.)	3114	34434434355	MNNNNNNFFNNNNONONNNN	NNNN4NNNNNNNNN	R,T	056	452	06.02.03	7633	480703	92308
667.682-018	CORNER-TRIMMER OPERATOR (wood. container)	3115	34345434355	MNNNNNNFFNNNNNNNNN	NNNN4NNNNNNNNN	R,T	056	454	06.04.03	7633	480703	92308
667.682-022	CUT-OFF-SAW OPERATOR I (woodworking)	3224	34434434345	MNNNONONFFONNNONFNFONN	NNNN4FFNNNNNNN	R,T	056	450	06.02.03	7633	480703	92308
667.682-026	EDGER, AUTOMATIC (saw. & plan.)	3215	34343523345	MNNNONNNFFFONNNFNFFNN	NNNN4NNNNNNNNN	J,T	056	452	06.02.03	7633	480703	92308
667.682-030	GANG SAWYER (saw. & plan.)	3215	34443434345	LNNNNNNFFONNNNFNNNNN	NNNN4NOFNNNNNN	R,T	056	452	06.02.03	7633	000000	92308
667.682-034	HEAD SAWYER, AUTOMATIC (paper & pulp; saw. & plan.)	3216	34343533345	LONNNNNNFFONNNNFNNONN	NNNN4NONNNNNNN	J	056	452	06.02.03	7633	000000	92305
667.682-038	HEADING-SAW OPERATOR (saw. & plan.)	3114	34434544355	MNNNNNNNFFONNNNFNONN	NNNN4NFFNNNNNN	R,T	056	452	06.02.03	7633	480703	92308
667.682-042	JIGSAW OPERATOR (woodworking)	3114	34433444455	MNNNNNNFFNNNNNFFNN	NNNN4NOONNNNNN	R,T	056	450	06.02.03	7633	480703	92308
667.682-046	PACKAGER, HEAD (saw. & plan.)	2114	44434544355	LNNNNNNFFFNNNNNNNNN	ONNN3NNNNNNNNN	R,T	056	452	06.04.03	7633	000000	92308
667.682-050	PONY EDGER (saw. & plan.)	3216	34434534345	MNNNNNNFFONNCNFNNNN	NNNN4NNONNNNNN	J,T	056	452	06.02.03	7633	480703	92308
667.682-054	RADIAL-ARM-SAW OPERATOR (woodworking)	3124	44433434355	MNNONNNFFFONNNFNFFNN	NNNN4NOFNNNNNN	R,T	056	450	06.02.03	7633	000000	92308
667.682-058	RESAW OPERATOR (woodworking)	3216	34433434335	HNNFNFNFFONNNNFNFNNN	NNNN4NOONNNNNNO	J,T	056	452	06.02.03	7633	480703	92308
667.682-062	RIP-AND-GROOVE-MACHINE OPERATOR (furniture)	3214	34334433355	LNNNNNNNFFFONNNNNNNN	NNNN4NNNNNNNNN	R,T	056	460	06.02.03	7633	480703	92308
667.682-066	RIPSAW OPERATOR (woodworking)	3224	34433434355	MNNIONONCCOONONFNFNNN	NNNN4NFFNNNNNN	R,T	056	450	06.02.03	7633	480703	92308
667.682-070	SHAKE SAWYER (saw. & plan.)	3214	34443534354	MNNNNNNFFONNNNFNNNNN	NNNN4NNONNNNNN	R,T	056	452	06.02.03	7633	000000	92308

DOT #	DOT Title & Industry	Trng	Aptitude	Physical	Environment	Tempra	WkF	MPSMS	GOE	SOC	CIP	OES
667.682-074	STAVE-BOLT EQUALIZER (saw. & plan.)	2114	34443544355	MNNNNNNFFONNNNNNNNNN	NNNN3NNNNNNNNNN	R,T	056	452	06.04.03	7633	000000	92308
667.682-078	STAVE-LOG-CUT-OFF SAW OPERATOR (saw. & plan.)	3214	34443444355	HNNNNNNFFONNNNNNNNNN	FNNN3NNNNNNNNNN	R,T	056	452	06.02.03	7633	000000	92308
667.682-082	STOCK-PATCH SAWYER (woodworking)	3214	34443534345	MNNNNNNFFONNNNFNNONN	NNNN3NNNNNNNNNN	J	056	452	06.02.03	7633	000000	92308
667.682-086	VARIETY-SAW OPERATOR (woodworking)	3225	34433434355	MNNFNFNFFONNONFNONNN	NNNN4FONNNNNNNN	T,J	056	450	05.05.08	7633	480703	92308
667.682-090	LOG-CUT-OFF SAWYER, AUTOMATIC (saw. & plan.)	3225	34433434345	MNNNNNNCCONNFNFFNNN	NNNN4NOONNNNNNN	J,T	056	451	06.02.03	7633	000000	92308
667.682-094	TRIMMER SAWYER (saw. & plan.)	3214	34333434344	MNNNNNNCCNNNNCCNNON	NNNN4NOONNNNNNN	J,T	056	452	06.02.03	7633	000000	92308
667.685-010	BAND-SAW OPERATOR (wood. container)	2112	44443434344	HNNONONFFONNNNFNNNN	NNNN4NNONNNNNNN	R	056	454	06.04.03	7633	480703	92308
667.685-014	BAND-SAW OPERATOR (woodworking)	1112	44444544455	LNNNNNNFFONNNNFNNNN	NNNN4NNNNNNNNNN	R,T	056	459	06.04.03	7633	480703	92308
667.685-018	BEADING SAWYER (fabrication, nec)	2112	44443534445	LNNNNNNFFONNNNFNOONN	NNNN4NNNNNNNNNN	R,T	056	619	06.04.03	7633	480703	92308
667.685-022	BOLTER (saw. & plan.)	2113	44444534345	MNNNNNNCCONNNNONONNN	NNNN4NOONNNNNNN	R,T	056	451	06.04.03	7633	000000	92308
667.685-026	BUZZSAW OPERATOR (any industry)	2113	44544544445	HNNNNNNFFONNNNNONNNN	FNNN4NNNNNNNNNN	R,T	056	619	06.04.09	7633	480703	92308
667.685-030	COB SAWYER (fabrication, nec)	1112	44453535335	HOOONNNFFNNNNNNNNNN	ONNN4NNNNNNNNNN	R	056	452	03.04.02	7633	030404	92308
667.685-034	CUT-OFF SAWYER, LOG (paper & pulp; saw. & plan.)	2112	45454434355	LNNONONFFONNNNFNOONN	NNNN4NOONNNNNNN	R,T	056	450	06.04.03	7633	480703	92308
667.685-038	DOWEL POINTER (woodworking)	2113	44335443444	LNNNNNNFFNNNNNFNONON	NNNN4NNNNNNNNNN	R,T	056	460	06.04.03	7633	480703	92308
667.685-042	KERFER-MACHINE OPERATOR (furniture)	1112	44444544355	LNNNNNNFFONNNNNNNNNN	NNNN4NNNNNNNNNN	R,T	056	459	06.04.09	7633	000000	92308
667.685-046	SAWYER, CORK SLABS (wood prod., nec)	3114	34443534355	LNNNNNNFFONNNNFNNNN	NNNN4NNNNNNNNNN	R,T	056	452	06.02.02	7633	000000	92308
667.685-050	SHINGLE TRIMMER (saw. & plan.)	2112	44544534345	MNNNNNNFFONNNNNNNNN	NNNN4NNNNNNNNNN	R,T	056	451	06.04.03	7633	000000	92308
667.685-054	SLASHER OPERATOR (paper & pulp; saw. & plan.)	2114	34443434355	MNNNNNNFFONNNNNNNNNN	NNNN3NONNNNNNNN	R	056	452	06.04.03	7633	480703	92308
667.685-058	STAVE-LOG-RIPSAW OPERATOR (saw. & plan.)	3114	34434434345	MNNNNNFFNNNNNONOONN	NNNN4NONNNNNNNN	R,T	056	452	06.04.03	7633	480703	92308
667.685-062	STAVE-SAW OPERATOR (wood. container)	2112	44434534355	LNNNONNFFONNNNFNOONN	NNNN4NFNNNNNNNN	R,T	056	452	06.04.03	7633	480703	92308
667.685-066	TURNING-MACHINE OPERATOR (wood. container)	3224	44444433355	MONNNNNCCCNNNNCNCCNIN	NNNN4NFNNNNNNNN	R	056	452	06.04.03	7633	480703	92308
667.685-070	AUTOMATIC BANDSAW TENDER (furniture)	2112	44433544445	MNNFNNNCCNNNNNCNCNNN	NNNN4NOONNNNNNN	R,T	056	450	06.04.03	7633	480703	92308
667.685-074	CUT-OFF-SAW OPERATOR II (woodworking)	1112	44545544445	MNNNNNNFFONNNNNNNNNN	NNNN3NNNNNNNNNN	R	056	457	06.04.03	8725	000000	98502
667.686-010	CLOTHESPIN-MACHINE OPERATOR (woodworking)	2112	44544444345	MCNNNNNFFNNNNNNNNNN	ONNN4NNNNNNNNNN	R,T	056	450	06.04.03	8725	000000	98502
667.686-018	TRIMMER HELPER (saw. & plan.)	2112	44544544355	MNNNNNNFFNNNNNNNNNN	NNNN3NNNNNNNNNN	R,T	056	454	06.04.03	8615	480703	98999
667.686-022	TURNING-MACHINE-OPERATOR HELPER (wood. container)	1111	44544544455	HNNFNNNNFFNNNNNNNNNN	FNNN4NNNNNNNNNN	R	056	452	06.04.03	8615	030405	98999
667.687-010	BUZZSAW-OPERATOR HELPER (any industry)	2113	44443534345	MNNNNNFFNNNNFNFNN	ONNN4NNNNNNNNNN	R	212	452	03.04.02	7820	030404	83005
667.687-014	LOG INSPECTOR (saw. & plan.)	3113	34434534345	MFFFNNNNFFONFFNFNOON	NNNN4NNNNNNNNNO	R,T	056	451	06.04.40	7633	030404	92308
667.687-018	SAWMILL WORKER (saw. & plan.)	4337	33322334254	LNNNNNNFFONFFNFNOOON	NNNN4NNNNNNNNNN	V,D,P,J	102	467	06.02.01	7100	520205	81008
669.130-010	SUPERVISOR, ASSEMBLY ROOM (furniture)	4237	33443444455	LNNNNNNOOONFFNNNONN	NNNN4NNNNNNNNNN	V,D,P,T	102	617	06.01.01	7100	520205	81008
669.130-014	SUPERVISOR, CUTTING DEPARTMENT (pen & pencil)	4228	33343334344	LONONONFNNFNFNNNON	ONNN4NNONNNNNN	V,D,P,J	057	450	06.02.01	7100	520205	81008
669.130-018	SUPERVISOR, FRAMING MILL (wood prod., nec)	4337	33333334355	LNNOONNFFOFFNFNFONN	NNNN4NOONNNNNN	D,V,P,J	057	450	05.05.08	6832	520205	81008
669.130-022	SUPERVISOR, MACHINING (woodworking)	4337	33333334354	MNNONNNFFOFFNFNFNFN	FNNN4NNNNNNNNF	D,V,P,J,T	057	451	06.01.01	7100	520205	81008
669.130-026	SUPERVISOR, SAWMILL (saw. & plan.)	4227	33323433355	LNNNNNNFFNFFNFNNNNN	NNNN3NNNNNNNNN	V,D,P,J	057	450	06.02.01	7100	520205	81008
669.130-030	SUPERVISOR, SHUTTLE FITTING (woodworking)	4227	33323433355	LNNNNNNFFFNFFNFNNNN	NNNN3NNNNNNNNN	V,D,P,J	057	457	06.02.01	7100	520205	81008
669.130-034	SUPERVISOR, SHUTTLE PREPARATION (woodworking)	4337	33322433355	LNNNNNNFFFNFFNFNNNN	NNNN3NNNNNNNNN	V,D,P,J	063	457	06.02.01	7100	520205	81008
669.130-038	SUPERVISOR, SHUTTLE VENEERING (woodworking)	4337	33333323355	MNNFNNNCCFOFFNFNFFNN	NNNN4NOONNNNNN	D,V,T,P	057	461	06.02.01	7100	520205	81008
669.132-010	SUPERVISOR, SAWING AND ASSEMBLY (furniture)	3226	33444434355	LNNNNNNFFNFNFNNNN	FNNN3NNNNNNNNN	V,D,P,J	056	450	03.02.02	7100	030405	81008
669.137-010	SUPERVISOR, WOOD-CREW (saw. & plan.)	3337	33333433355	MNNNFNONFFOONOONFNONFON	NNNN4NFFNNNNNN	J,V,T	057	450	06.01.02	7439	480703	92311
669.280-010	MACHINE SETTER (woodworking)	3217	33324433255	MNNONNNFFONNNNFNNOONN	NNNN3NNNNNNNNN	V,J,T	055	373	06.01.02	7720	470402	92311
669.360-010	CHECKERING-MACHINE ADJUSTER (ordnance)	3226	33333434355	LNNNNNNCCCOFFNCNFFNN	NNNN4NNNNNNNNN	J,T,V	102	461	06.02.22	7720	150702	93956
669.364-010	INSPECTOR, ASSEMBLY (furniture)	3336	34333433344	MNNFOFNFFFONONFNOOON	NNNN4NFFNNNNOO	J,T,V	057	450	05.05.08	6832	480703	89308
669.380-010	MACHINIST APPRENTICE, WOOD (woodworking)	3336	34333433344	MNNFOFNFFONONFNOOON	NNNN4NFFNNNNOO	J,T,V	057	450	05.05.08	6832	480703	89308
669.380-014	MACHINIST, WOOD (woodworking)	3227	34433433345	MNNNNNNFFONNNNFNFNN	NNNN4NNONNNNNN	V,J,T	102	454	05.10.01	7439	480703	92311
669.380-018	PIPE-AND-TANK FABRICATOR (wood. container)	3215	34434434345	MNNFNNNFFONNNONFNONN	NNNN4NOONNNNNON	J,T	057	452	05.05.08	7432	480703	92311
669.382-010	DADO OPERATOR (woodworking)	3324	34333434345	HONFNFNFONNNNNFNNNN	NNNN4NOONNNNNON	J,T	057	455	06.02.03	7432	480703	92311
669.382-014	RAFTER-CUTTING-MACHINE OPERATOR (mfd. bldgs.)	4335	34433434455	MNNONNNCCCONNNNFNNONN	NNNN4NONNNNNON	J,T	057	450	05.05.08	7439	480703	92311
669.382-018	TENONER OPERATOR (woodworking)	3336	34423433355	MNNNONNFFONNNNFFONF	NNNN4NONNNNNNN	T	057	461	06.02.03	7439	480703	92311
669.382-022	MULTI-PURPOSE MACHINE OPERATOR (furniture)	3224	34334433355	MNNNNNNFFONNNCNFNNN	NNNN4NONNNNNNN	J,T	055	619	06.02.03	7431	000000	92311
669.382-026	TURNING MACHINE SET-UP OPERATOR (fabrication, nec)	3223	34434534345	LNNNNNNFFONNNNFNNNN	ONNF4NNONNNNNN	R,T	031	451	06.04.03	7639	480703	92998
669.485-010	POWER-BARKER OPERATOR (paper & pulp; saw. & plan.)											

DOT #	DOT Title & Industry	Trng	Aptitude	Physical	Environment	Tempra	WkF	MPSMS	GOE	SOC	CIP	OES
669.662-010	BOX-BLANK-MACHINE OPERATOR (wood. container)	3224	33444444455	LNNOOONFFONNNNFNNNNN	NNNNN4NNNNNNNNN	J,T	102	454	06.02.20	7439	480703	92311
669.662-014	FRAME-TABLE OPERATOR (wood prod., nec)	3225	34433334345	MNNFNNNFFONNNNFNFNNN	FNNN4NNONNNNNNN	R,J,T	056	450	06.02.03	7639	480703	92998
669.662-018	TONGUE-AND-GROOVE-MACHINE OPERATOR (woodworking)	3235	34433444355	MNNNNNNFFONNNNFNONNN	NNNN4NNNNNNNNN	J,T	055	450	06.02.03	7635	480703	92314
669.682-010	ADZING-AND-BORING-MACHINE OPERATOR (wood prod., nec)	3235	34434544345	LONOOONFFONNNNNONNNN	NNNN4NNONNNNNNN	R,J,T	057	450	06.02.03	7632	480703	92314
669.682-014	BARREL ASSEMBLER (wood. container)	3224	34434534345	MNNNFNNNCCONNNNCNFNNN	NNNN4NOONNNNNNN	R,T	102	454	06.02.20	7720	480703	93956
669.682-018	BUCKET TURNER (wood. container)	2114	44533544355	MNNNNNNFFONNNNNONNN	NNNN3NOONNNNNNN	R,T	055	454	06.04.03	7631	480703	92314
669.682-022	CHUCKING-AND-BORING-MACHINE OPERATOR (furniture)	3224	34434444345	MNNNNNNFFONNNNFNONNN	NNNN4NOONNNNNNN	R,T	057	460	06.02.03	7632	480703	92314
669.682-026	CHUCKING-AND-SAWING-MACHINE OPERATOR (woodworking)	3214	34433433345	LNNNNNNFFFNNNNFNONNN	NNNN4NNNNNNNNN	R,T	057	450	06.02.03	7433	480703	92302
669.682-030	CORNER-BRACE-BLOCK-MACHINE OPERATOR (furniture)	3224	34434444355	MNNONNNFFONNNNFNONNN	NNNN4NOONNNNNON	R,T	057	460	06.02.03	7433	480703	92302
669.682-034	CROZE-MACHINE OPERATOR (wood. container)	3114	34434534345	LNNNNNNFFONNNNNONNN	NNNN4NONNNNNNN	R,T	057	454	06.02.03	7633	480703	92308
669.682-038	DOUBLE-END-TRIMMER-AND-BORING-MACHINE OPERATOR (furniture)	3234	34434334345	MMNFNNNCCCNNONFNOFNN	NNNN4NOONNNNNOFNN	J,T	056	460	06.02.03	7439	480702	92311
669.682-042	DOWEL-INSERTING-MACHINE OPERATOR (woodworking)	2114	34444534455	MNNNNNNFFONNNNNONNN	NNNN4NNNNNNNNN	R,T	053	452	06.02.03	7499	480703	92311
669.682-046	EMBOSSING-MACHINE OPERATOR (wood prod., nec)	3224	34433433355	LNNNNNNFFFNNNNFNONNN	NNNN3NNNNNNNNN	R,J,T	192	457	06.02.03	7499	480703	92998
669.682-050	INLETTER (ordnance)	3124	34433434355	LNNNNNNFFNNNNFNONONN	NNNN4NNNNNNNNN	R,T	055	373	06.02.03	7632	470402	92314
669.682-054	LAST TRIMMER (wood prod., nec)	3223	34444533355	MNNNNNNFFNNNNNFNOONN	NNNN4NNNNNNNNN	J,T	051	457	06.02.03	7639	000000	92314
669.682-058	NAILING-MACHINE OPERATOR (any industry)	2114	44443534345	MNNNNNNFFONNNNNNNNN	NNNN4NNONNNNNNN	R,T	072	450	06.02.03	7499	480702	92311
669.682-062	PLUGGING-MACHINE OPERATOR (woodworking)	3114	34433534355	MNNNNNNFFONNNNNONNNN	NNNN3NNNNNNNNN	R,J	057	450	06.02.03	7632	000000	92314
669.682-066	TIP INSERTER (woodworking)	3114	34433534355	MNNNNNFFONNNNFNONNN	NNNN4NNNNNNNNN	R,J,T	057	457	06.02.09	7639	000000	92314
669.682-070	UTILITY OPERATOR (saw. & plan.)	4226	33333434334	MNNNNNNCCOONFNFFFON	NNNN4NFONNNNNNN	V,J,T	056	452	06.02.03	7633	030404	92308
669.685-010	BARREL-ASSEMBLER HELPER (wood. container)	2122	44543544355	MMNONONFFONNNNNNNN	NNNN4NNNNNNNNN	R	102	454	06.04.03	8615	480703	98999
669.685-014	BASKET ASSEMBLER I (wood. container)	2112	44345533345	LNNNNNNNCCONNNNONONN	NNNN4NOONNNNNNN	R,T	102	454	06.04.20	7635	000000	92314
669.685-018	BLIND-SLAT-STAPLING-MACHINE OPERATOR (woodworking)	2112	44544544445	LNNNNNNNFFONNNNNONNN	NNNN3NNNNNNNNN	U	072	452	06.04.20	7636	000000	92314
669.685-022	BOTTOM-HOOP DRIVER (wood. container)	2113	44543544335	MNNNNNNFFNNNNNONNNN	NNNN3NNNNNNNNN	R	061	454	06.04.20	7635	480703	92314
669.685-026	CIRCLE-CUTTING-SAW OPERATOR (wood. container)	1112	44544544355	LNNNNNNFFONNNNNONNN	NNNN4NNNNNNNNN	R,T	057	454	06.04.03	7633	000000	92308
669.685-030	CLAMPER (woodworking)	2113	44544444345	HNNONNNFFNNNNFNFNNF	NNNN4NFONNNNNNN	R,T	063	450	06.04.20	7720	480703	93999
669.685-034	COAT-HANGER-SHAPER-MACHINE OPERATOR (woodworking)	2113	44543544355	MNNNNNNNCCONNNNOONNNN	NNNN4NNONNNNNNN	R,T	051	457	06.04.03	7635	480703	92314
669.685-038	CORE-COMPOSER FEEDER (millwork-plywood)	2113	44444534345	MNNNNNNFFONNNNNONNNN	NNNN4NNNNNNNNN	R,T	057	453	06.04.20	7639	000000	92998
669.685-042	CORRUGATED-FASTENER DRIVER (woodworking)	2112	44544534345	MMNONONFFONNNNNONNN	NNNN4NNNNNNNNN	R	072	450	06.04.20	7636	480703	92314
669.685-046	DOVETAIL-MACHINE OPERATOR (wood. container)	2112	44443554435	MNNNNNNNFFONNNNONNNN	NNNN4NNNNNNNNN	R,T	061	454	06.04.20	7635	480703	92314
669.685-050	DOWELING-MACHINE OPERATOR (woodworking)	2113	44444434345	MMNFNNNFFNNNNFNFNNN	NNNN4NNNNNNNNN	R,T	072	454	06.04.20	7636	480703	92314
669.685-054	END STAPLER (wood. container)	2113	44443534335	LNNNNNNFFONNNNNFNONO	NNNN4NNNNNNNNO	R,U	063	461	06.04.20	7639	480703	92998
669.685-058	FRAME-TABLE-OPERATOR HELPER (wood prod., nec)	2212	44444534345	MNNNONFFONNNNNNNNN	NNNN4NNNNNNNNN	R	072	454	06.04.20	7635	480703	92314
669.685-062	HEADING-MACHINE OPERATOR (pen & pencil)	2112	44554544454	MMNONONFFONNNNFNNNNN	FNNN4NNONNNNNNN	R	011	452	06.04.18	8615	480703	98999
669.685-066	NAILING-MACHINE OPERATOR, AUTOMATIC (any industry)	2212	44444434345	MNNNNNNNFFONNNNFNONON	NNNN4NONNNNNNN	R,T	051	617	06.04.03	7634	480703	92314
669.685-070	ROOF-TRUSS-MACHINE TENDER (mfd. bldgs.)	2112	44434444354	LNNFNNNFFNNNNNONNNN	NNNN4NNOONNNNNNN	R,U	056	450	06.04.20	7636	000000	92314
669.685-074	SLAT-BASKET MAKER, MACHINE (wood. container)	2112	44434444355	LNNNNNNFFONNNNNONNN	NNNN4NNNNNNNNN	R,T	102	456	06.04.03	7635	030404	92314
669.686-010	AUTOMATIC-NAILING-MACHINE FEEDER (woodworking)	1112	45544534355	LNNNNNNNFFNNNNNONNN	NNNN4NNNNNNNNN	R	134	456	06.04.03	7639	030404	98502
669.686-014	BOX-BLANK-MACHINE-OPERATOR HELPER (wood. container)	2112	44444534355	MNNOOONFFNOOINFNNNNN	NNNN4NNNNNNNNN	R	072	452	06.04.03	8725	000000	98502
669.686-018	CHAIN OFFBEARER (saw. & plan.)	2112	44534534355	MNNNNNNNCCONNNNNCNNN	ONNN4NNONNNNNNN	R	011	452	06.04.03	8615	480703	98999
669.686-022	REED-PRESS FEEDER (wood prod., nec)	2112	44544534355	HNNNNNNNFFNNNNNONNN	NNNN3NNNNNNNNN	R,T	072	459	06.04.03	8725	000000	98502
669.686-026	SLAT-BASKET MAKER HELPER, MACHINE (wood. container)	1112	44544544355	LNNNNNNFFFNNNNNNNNN	NNNN4NNNNNNNNN	R	072	454	06.04.20	8725	480703	98502
669.686-030	WOODWORKING-MACHINE FEEDER (woodworking)	2112	44444534345	MMNFNONCCNNONONNNNN	NNNN4NNNNNNNNN	R	057	450	06.04.03	8725	000000	98502
669.686-034	WOODWORKING-MACHINE OFFBEARER (woodworking)	2112	44444434345	MNNFNONCCONNONONNNNN	NNNN4NNNNNNNNN	R	057	450	06.04.03	8725	480703	98502

DOT #	DOT Title & Industry	Trng	Aptitude	Physical	Environment	Tempra	WkF	MPSMS	GOE	SOC	CIP	OES
669.687-010	CLEAT FEEDER (wood. container)	1112	4444534355	LNNONNNCCNNNNNNNCNNN	NNNN3NNNNNNNNN	R	072	454	06.04.40	8725	000000	98502
669.687-014	DOWEL INSPECTOR (woodworking)	1112	45543543355	SNNNNNNFFONNNNFNFNNN	NNNN3NNNNNNNNN	R,J	212	457	06.03.02	7820	000000	83005
669.687-018	LUMBER STRAIGHTENER (saw. & plan.)	2112	4444534345	MNONNNNCCONNNNNNNONNN	ONNN4NNONNNNNNN	R	056	452	06.04.40	8726	480703	98799
669.687-022	PICKER (saw. & plan.)	2122	4444354345	HNNNNNNNFFNNNNNFNFNNN	CNNN4NNNNNNNNN	R,J	212	451	03.04.02	5790	000000	98502
669.687-026	TIE INSPECTOR (saw. & plan.)	2122	4444544455	HNNOONFFFNNNNNFNNN	FNNN4NNNNNNNNN	R	212	451	03.04.02	5790	000000	83005
669.687-030	GRADER (woodworking)	3224	34333434344	LNNNNNNCCFNNONCCFCFN	NNNN4NOONNNNNN	J,T	212	450	06.03.02	7850	030404	83005
670.362-010	GANG SAWYER, STONE (stonework)	3215	34434444345	MOONNNNFFNNNNNNFFNNN	NNOO4NOONNNNNN	R,T	056	343	06.02.08	7478	490299	92941
670.384-010	STONE GRADER (stonework)	3226	34433444443	HNNNNNNFFONNNNFNNFON	NNNN3NNNNNNNNN	J,T	212	537	05.07.01	7820	460101	83005
670.587-010	STONE LAYOUT MARKER (stonework)	3213	34433333354	MNNNNNNFFFNNNNNFNNNN	NNNN4NCNNNNNNNC	R,J	241	537	06.02.31	7759	460101	93999
670.685-010	STONE TRIMMER (stonework)	2113	34434534355	MNNNNNNFFONNNNFNNNNN	NNNN4NNONNNNNN	R,T	054	537	06.04.08	7678	460101	92944
673.130-010	SUPERVISOR, EDGING (glass products)	3226	33444344455	MNNONNNFFFOFFNFFNN	NNNN4NNNNNNNNN	D,P,V	051	531	06.02.01	7100	520205	81008
673.364-010	LEAD WORKER, WAFER POLISHING (electron. comp.)	3336	33343343355	MNNNNNNFFNFFNONNNNN	NNNF4NNNNNNNNN	T,J,P	051	587	06.02.09	7677	470105	92965
673.380-010	EDGING-MACHINE SETTER (glass products)	3225	34433433355	MNNOOONFFFONONFNFNNN	NNNF4NNNNNNNNN	J,T	051	532	06.01.02	7477	489999	92997
673.382-010	SANDBLASTER, STONE (stonework)	3116	34422433355	MNNNNNNFFNNNNNFONNN	NNNN4NFNNNNNNN	J	051	537	05.10.01	7677	460101	92965
673.382-014	SANDBLASTER, STONE APPRENTICE (stonework)	3116	34422433355	MNNNNNNFFNNNNNNFNNN	NNNN4NFNNNNNNN	J	051	537	05.10.01	7677	460101	92965
673.382-018	STONE POLISHER, MACHINE (stonework)	3116	34433434355	MNNNNNNFFOONNNFNFNNN	NNNF4NNNNNNNNN	J,T	051	537	06.02.08	7477	460101	92997
673.382-022	STONE POLISHER, MACHINE APPRENTICE (stonework)	3116	34433434355	HNNNNNNFFNNFNFNFNNN	NNNN4NNONNNNNNN	T	051	587	06.02.02	7677	470105	92965
673.382-026	CRYSTAL GRINDER (electron. comp.)	3225	34433444355	MNNNNNNFFOOONFNFNNN	NNNC4NCNNNNNNN	J,T	051	537	06.02.08	7677	460101	92965
673.662-010	TOP POLISHER (stonework)	3216	34434333355	MNNNNNNFFFOOONFNFNNF	NNNC4NCNNNNNNN	J,T	051	537	06.02.08	7677	460101	92965
673.666-010	BELT SANDER, STONE (stonework)	2112	44344344355	VNNNNNNCCOOONONNNNN	NNNN4NCNNNNNNN	R	051	537	06.04.08	8725	460101	98502
673.666-014	STRIPPER (glass mfg.)	2112	44544534355	LNNNNNNFFONNNNNNNNN	NNNN4NNNNNNNNN	R,T	051	531	06.04.08	7679	489999	92998
673.682-010	AUTOMATIC PATTERN EDGER (glass products)	3113	34434534345	HNNFNONCCOONNNCNCNNN	NNNC4NNNNNNNNNF	J,T	051	531	06.02.08	7477	489999	92997
673.682-014	BEVELING-AND-EDGING-MACHINE OPERATOR (glass mfg.; glass products)	3234	34433444355	MNNNNNNFFNNNNNNFNONNN	NNNN4NNNNNNNNN	R,J,T	051	532	06.02.08	7477	489999	92997
673.682-018	EDGER-MACHINE OPERATOR (stonework)	2113	34433434355	HNNNNNNFFOONNNFNFNO	NNNC4NCNNNNNNN	R,J,T	051	537	06.02.08	7477	460101	92965
673.682-022	FINISH OPENER, JEWEL HOLE (clock & watch)	3215	34333432355	LNNNNNNFFOONNNFNNNN	NNNO4NNNNNNNNN	J,T	051	607	06.02.08	7677	470408	92965
673.682-026	MITER GRINDER OPERATOR (glass mfg.; glass products)	3234	34433434345	MNNONNNFFOONNNFNNNNN	NNNN4NNNNNNNNN	R,J,T	051	531	06.02.08	7477	489999	92997
673.682-030	SLAB GRINDER (stonework)	3115	34433434355	LNNNNNNFFONNNNNNNNN	NNNN3NNNNNNNNN	R,T	051	537	06.02.08	7677	460101	92965
673.685-010	ABRASIVE GRINDER (nonmet. min.)	3113	34344533355	LNNNNNNFFNNNNNNNNN	NNNN3NNNNNNNNN	R,T	051	538	06.04.09	7677	000000	92965
673.685-014	BED RUBBER (stonework)	3214	34434533355	HNNNNNNFFNFNFNNNN	NNNO4NNNNNNNNN	J,T	051	537	06.02.08	7677	460101	92965
673.685-018	BEVELER (glass products)	2113	44434434355	MNNNNNNFFONNNNFNNNNN	NNNN3NONONNNNNN	R,T	051	531	06.04.08	7677	489999	92965
673.685-022	BEVELER (nonmet. min.)	2112	34433444355	MNNNNNNNFFFNNNNFNFNNN	NNNN4NCNNNNNNN	R,J	051	538	06.04.08	7677	000000	92965
673.685-026	BLOCKER (glass mfg.; glass products)	2222	44444444355	MNNNNNNFFONNNNFNNNNN	NNNN4NNNNNNNNN	R	051	531	06.04.08	7677	489999	92965
673.685-030	BLOCKER, AUTOMATIC (glass mfg.; glass products)	2112	44444444355	HNNONONFFONNNNNNNNN	NNNN4NNNNNNNNN	R,T	051	531	06.04.08	7677	489999	92965
673.685-034	CIRCLE BEVELER (glass products)	2113	34434344345	MNNONNNOOOONNNONOONN	NNNN4NNNNNNNNNO	R,T	051	532	06.04.08	7677	489999	92965
673.685-038	CIRCLE EDGER (glass products)	2112	44545544345	MNNONNNFFOONNNFNFNNN	NNNC4NNNNNNNNN	R,T	051	532	06.04.08	7677	489999	92965
673.685-042	CONVEX-GRINDER OPERATOR (button & notion)	2112	44544543354	SNNNNNNFFNNNNNNFNNN	NNNN3NNNNNNNNN	R	051	618	06.04.08	7677	000000	91117
673.685-046	DIAMOND-POWDER TECHNICIAN (nonmet. min.)	2113	44444444355	HNNNNNNFFONNNNNNNNN	NNNN4NNNNNNNNN	R,T	142	349	06.02.08	7677	000000	92965
673.685-050	ENGRAVER TENDER (glass products)	2113	44543343355	LNNNNNNFFNNNNNFNFNNN	NNNF4NNNNNNNNN	R,T	051	531	06.04.08	7677	489999	92965
673.685-054	FINGER-GRIP-MACHINE OPERATOR (glass products)	3213	34434344355	MNNNNNNNFFONNNONONNN	NNNO3NNNNNNNNN	R,T	051	531	06.04.08	7477	489999	92997
673.685-058	FINISH-MACHINE TENDER (pottery & porc.)	3115	34434344355	HNNNNNNFFNNNNNFNFNNN	NNNN4NNNNNNNNN	R,T	051	535	06.02.09	7677	000000	92965
673.685-062	GROOVER (nonmet. min.)	2112	44444444355	LNNNNNNFFFNNNNNFNFNNN	NNNN4NNNNNNNNN	R,T	051	538	06.04.08	7677	489999	92965
673.685-066	LEVEL-VIAL INSIDE GRINDER (cutlery-hrdwr.)	2123	34433333355	SNNNNNNFFNNNNFNNNN	NNNO3NNNNNNNN	R	051	552	06.04.08	7677	489999	92965
673.685-070	NOTCH GRINDER (glass products)	3112	34433433355	LNNNNNNFFNNNNNFFNONN	NNNO4NNNNNNNNN	R,J	051	605	06.04.08	7677	000000	92965
673.685-074	STONE ROUGHER (optical goods)	2223	44354544355	LNNNNNNFFONNNNNNNNN	NNNN4NNNNNNNNN	R,T	051	531	06.04.08	7677	489999	92965
673.685-078	STRAIGHT-LINE EDGER (glass mfg.; glass products)	2112	44445433355	MNNONNNFFONNNNNONNNNN	NNNO4NNNNNNNNN	R,T	051	537	06.04.08	7677	460101	92965
673.685-082	STRIP POLISHER (stonework)	2114	44443434355	LNNNNNNFFONNNNFNNNN	NNNN4NNNNNNNNON	R,U	051	538	06.04.08	7677	000000	92965
673.685-086	DISC-PAD GRINDER (nonmet. min.)	3223	34433343355	MNNNNNNFFNNFNFNFNNN	NNNN3NONNNNNNNON	T	051	587	06.04.09	7677	470105	92965
673.685-094	POLISHING MACHINE TENDER (electron. comp.)	3223	34433343355	HNNONNNFFOONNNNONONN	NNNO4NNNNNNNNN	R	051	531	06.04.08	7677	489999	92965
673.685-098	RADIUS CORNER MACHINE OPERATOR (glass products)	2112	44444443355	HNNNNNNFFOONNNONONNN	NNNO4NNNNNNNNN	R	051	531	06.04.08	7677	489999	92965
673.685-102	WAFER ABRADING MACHINE TENDER (electron. comp.)	2223	44445544455	LNNNNNNFFNNNONCONNN	NNNN4NNNNNNNNN	R,U	051	587	06.04.09	7677	000000	92965
673.686-010	BEVELING-AND-EDGING-MACHINE-OPERATOR HELPER (glass mfg.; glass products)	2112	44444434355	HNNNONNNCCFFNONFNONNN	NNNN4NNNNNNNNN	R	051	531	06.04.08	8725	489999	98502

DOT #	DOT Title & Industry	Trng	Aptitude	Physical	Environment	Tempra	WkF	MPSMS	GOE	SOC	CIP	OES
673.686-014	BURR GRINDER (optical goods)	1111	4444444455	LNNNNNNFFONNNNNNNNNN	NNNN3NNNNNNNNNN	R	051	605	06.04.08	8725	000000	98502
673.686-018	EDGER-MACHINE HELPER (stonework)	2112	44444544355	HNNNNNNNCCNFNNNNNNNN	NNNN4NFNNNNNNNF	R,T	051	537	06.04.08	8725	460101	98502
673.686-022	EDGING-MACHINE FEEDER (glass mfg.)	1112	4444444455	NNNNNNNNFFONNNNNNNNN	NNNN4NNNNNNNNNN	R	051	531	06.04.08	8725	489999	98502
673.686-026	LAYER (glass mfg.)	2112	34444534354	LONONONFFONNNNNNNNNN	NNNN4NNNNNNNNNN	R,T	051	531	06.04.08	8725	000000	98502
673.686-030	DISC-PAD GRINDING MACHINE FEEDER (nonmet. min.)	1112	44544544455	LNNNNNNNFFNNNNNNNNNN	NNNN4NONNNNNNNN	R,U	051	538	06.04.09	8725	000000	98502
673.687-010	JOINER (glass mfg.)	2112	44444534355	LNNNNNNNFFONNNNNFNNN	NNNN3NNNNNNNNNN	R,T	051	531	06.04.30	7740	489999	93999
674.382-010	GLASS-LATHE OPERATOR (electron. comp.)	3234	34443333344	MNNONNNFCOONNNFNFOFN	NNON4NNFNNNNNNO	T	081	587	06.02.08	7679	489999	92998
674.662-010	STONE-LATHE OPERATOR (stonework)	4227	34334334354	HNNNNNNNFFFOOONFNFFON	NNNN4NOONNNNNON	J,T	057	537	06.02.08	7477	460101	92997
674.682-010	FINISHING-MACHINE OPERATOR (nonmet. min.)	3215	34433433355	LNNFNNNNFFNNNNNNNNNN	NNNN3NNNNNNNNNN	J,T	057	538	06.02.02	7477	000000	92997
675.682-010	CONTOUR GRINDER (stonework)	3225	34433433355	MNNNNNNNFFNOONFNOONN	NNNN4NNONNNNNNN	J,T	051	537	06.02.08	7477	460101	92997
675.682-014	PLANER OPERATOR (elec. equip.)	3225	34433433254	LNNNNNNNFFNNNNNFNNNN	NNNN4NONNNNNNNN	J,T	055	582	06.02.09	7677	000000	92965
675.682-018	PLANER, STONE (stonework)	3225	34333433355	HNNNNNNNFFNNNNNFNNNN	NNNN3NNNNNNNNNN	J,T	054	343	06.02.08	7477	460101	92997
676.382-010	DRILL-PRESS OPERATOR, PRINTED CIRCUIT BOARDS (electron. comp.)	3223	34333433344	LNNNNNNNFFNNNNNFFON	NNNN4NNNNNNNNNN	T,J	053	587	06.02.02	7318	470105	91108
676.462-010	ROUTER OPERATOR (stonework)	3333	34333333355	HNNNNNNNCCFNNNNFFFFN	NNNN4NCFNNNNNNN	J,T	055	537	06.02.08	7479	460101	92997
676.682-010	DRILL OPERATOR, AUTOMATIC (glass products)	3214	34433434345	HNNFNNNNFFONNNNFNNONN	NNNO4NNNNNNNNNN	J,T	053	531	06.02.08	7479	489999	92997
676.682-014	STONE DRILLER (stonework)	3224	34433443355	HNNNNNNNFFONNNNNFNNNN	NNNC4NNNNNNNNNN	J,T	053	537	06.02.08	7679	460101	92998
676.685-010	DRILLER, BRAKE LINING (nonmet. min.)	2112	44443444345	LNNNNNNCCONNNNCNCNNN	NNNN4NNNNNNNNNN	R,T	053	538	06.04.08	7679	000000	92998
676.685-014	DRILLER, MACHINE (glass products)	2112	34433434355	HNNNNNNNFFNNNNNNFNNN	NNNN3NNNNNNNNNN	R,T	053	531	06.04.08	7663	489999	92971
676.686-010	STONE-DRILLER HELPER (stonework)	1112	44445434355	HNNNNNNNFFNNNNNONFNNN	NNNC4NCNNNNNNNN	R	053	537	06.04.08	8725	460101	98502
676.686-014	DRILLER AND DEBURRER, REFLECTOR (light. fix.)	2112	44544544455	LNNNNNNNFFNNNNNFNFNNN	NNNN4NNNNNNNNNO	U	053	584	06.02.08	8725	000000	98502
677.131-010	GLASS-CUT-OFF SUPERVISOR (glass mfg.)	4337	23333334455	LNNNNNNNFFONFFNFNFNFN	NNNN3NNONNNNNNN	V,D,P,J	054	531	06.02.01	7100	520205	81008
677.382-010	BATTING-MACHINE OPERATOR, INSULATION (nonmet. min.)	3235	33433443335	MONONONFFFNNNNNNNNNN	NNNN3NNONNNNNNN	J,T	054	538	06.02.09	7478	000000	92941
677.382-014	SAWYER, OPTICAL GLASS (optical goods)	3227	34433443355	LNNNNNNNFFONNNNNFNOONN	NNNN4NNNNNNNNNN	T,J	056	603	06.02.08	7678	000000	92944
677.382-018	CRYSTAL SLICER (electron. comp.)	3224	34433443355	MNNNNNNNFFNNNNNCNCNNN	NNNN4NNONNNNNNN	T,J	056	587	06.02.09	7678	000000	92902
677.462-010	CIRCULAR SAWYER, STONE (stonework)	3214	34433434355	LNNNNNNCCONNNNCNCNNN	NNNN4NNNNNNNNNN	R,T	053	343	06.02.08	7478	490299	92941
677.462-014	WIRE SAWYER (stonework)	3215	34433434355	HNNNNNNNFFNNNNNONFNNN	NNNN4NNNNNNNNNO	J,T	056	537	06.02.08	7663	490299	92971
677.486-010	CIRCULAR-SAWYER HELPER (stonework)	2113	44444434355	HNNNNNNNFFONNNONFNCNNN	NNNC4NNNNNNNNNN	R,J	056	537	06.04.08	8619	490299	98999
677.562-010	GLASS-CUTTING-MACHINE OPERATOR, AUTOMATIC (glass mfg.)	3223	34443434354	LONONONFFNNNNNFNNOOON	NNNN3NNNNNNNNNN	R,J,T	054	531	06.02.08	7478	489999	92941
677.665-010	GLASS-UNLOADING-EQUIPMENT TENDER (glass mfg.)	2112	44444444354	LNNNNNNNFFNNNNNONONNN	NNNN3NNNNNNNNNO	R,J	011	531	06.04.08	7679	489999	92998
677.666-010	SPLITTING-MACHINE-OPERATOR HELPER (stonework)	1112	44543544455	HNNNNNNNCCNNNNNCNCNNN	NNNN4NCFNNNNNNCF	R	054	537	06.04.08	8618	490299	98999
677.682-010	HEAD-SAW OPERATOR, INSULATION BOARD (wood prod., nec)	3216	34343444355	LOOONNNFFNNNNFNNONN	NNNN3NNNNNNNNNN	V,J,T	056	459	06.02.03	7678	480703	92944
677.682-014	REFRACTORY-GRINDER OPERATOR (brick & tile)	2216	34433433355	MNNNNNNNFFNNNNNNFNNNN	NNNN4NNONNNNNNN	R,T	051	534	06.02.08	7678	489999	92944
677.682-018	SINK CUTTER (stonework)	2123	34433433355	VNNNNNNNCCFONNNFNFNNN	NNNN4NCCFONNNNNN	R,T	056	537	06.04.08	7678	460101	92944
677.682-022	STONECUTTER, MACHINE (stonework)	3216	34433434355	MNNNNNNNFFNNNNNFNFNNN	NNNN4NNNNNNNNNN	R,T	052	537	06.02.08	7678	000000	92944
677.682-026	TENONER OPERATOR (wood prod., nec)	3214	33433434355	LNNNNNNNFFNNNNNFNNONN	NNNN4NNONNNNNNN	R,J,T	055	459	06.02.09	7478	000000	92941
677.685-010	ABRASIVE SAWYER (nonmet. min.)	2212	44444434354	LNNNNNNNCCNNNNNCNNNNN	NNNN4NNNNNNNNNN	J,T	056	538	06.04.08	7678	000000	92944
677.685-014	ASSEMBLER, LAY-UPS (toy-sport equip.)	2112	44444444454	HNNOONNNFFNNNNNFNNONON	NNNN4NCNNNNNNNN	R,T	054	419	06.04.08	7678	489999	92944
677.685-018	CARBON CUTTER (elec. equip.)	3214	34333343355	LNNNNNNNFFNNNNNFNNONN	NNNN4NNNNNNNNNN	R	056	582	06.02.08	7678	000000	92944
677.685-022	CRAYON SAWYER (mine & quarry)	1112	44444443355	LNNNNNNCCCNNNNNCNNCNN	NNNN4NCFNNNNNNC	R,T	056	399	06.04.08	7678	000000	92944
677.685-026	CUT-OFF-SAW OPERATOR, PIPE BLANKS (nonmet. min.)	2113	34433444355	MNNNNNNNCCONNNNCNNNNN	NNNN4NCNNNNNNNN	R,T	056	538	06.04.08	7678	000000	92944
677.685-030	GLASS CUT-OFF TENDER (glass mfg.)	2222	44443444345	HNNFNNNNFFONNNNFNNNNN	NNNN3NNNNNNNNNO	R,T	054	531	06.04.08	7678	489999	92944
677.685-034	SAMPLE SAWYER (brick & tile)	1112	44444444345	LNNNNNNNFFONNNNFNCNNN	NNNN4NCNNNNNNNN	R,T	056	534	06.04.08	7678	000000	92944
677.685-038	SAWYER II (nonmet. min.)	2112	44443434355	MNNNNNNNFFNOONFNCNNN	NNNN4NCCNNNNNCN	R,T	056	538	06.04.08	7678	000000	92944
677.685-042	SPLITTER OPERATOR (stonework)	2112	44445434345	HNNNNNNNFFONNNNFNNNN	CNNN4NNNNNNNNNN	R,J	052	537	05.12.13	7679	460101	92944
677.685-046	SPLITTING-MACHINE OPERATOR (stonework)	3213	34433434345	LNNNNNNNFFONNNNFNNONN	ONNN4NNONNNNNNN	R,J,T	054	537	06.04.08	7678	460101	92944
677.685-050	STONE SPLITTER (concrete prod.)	2212	44444434335	LNNNNNNNFFONNNNFNNNNN	NNNN3NNNNNNNNNN	R,J	054	536	06.04.08	7678	460101	92944
677.685-054	SAW OPERATOR (brick & tile)	2112	44444544355	MNNNNNNNCCFNNNNFNNNN	NNNN4NFFNNNNNNN	R	056	534	06.04.08	7678	489999	92944
677.686-010	SAWYER I (nonmet. min.)	2112	44544544355	MNNNNNNNOCNNONONONNN	NNNN4NOONNNNNNN	R,U	056	538	06.04.09	8725	000000	98502
677.686-014	GLASS-CUTTING-MACHINE FEEDER (glass products)	1112	44544544355	MNNNNNNNFFNNNNNFNFNNN	NNNN4NNNNNNNNNN	R,U	054	531	06.04.08	8725	489999	98502
677.687-010	LOG ROLLER (saw. & plan.)	2112	44533534354	MNNNNNNNFFNNNNNNFNNNN	CONN3NNNNNNNNNN	R,T	011	452	06.04.40	8726	000000	98799
677.687-014	CRYSTAL MOUNTER (electron. comp.)	2212	44444444455	HNNONNNFFONNNNFNONNN	NNNN3NNNNNNNNNN	R,U	063	587	06.04.34	7740	000000	92902

DOT #	DOT Title & Industry	Trng	Aptitude	Physical	Environment	Tempra	WkF	MPSMS	GOE	SOC	CIP	OES
679.130-010	SUPERVISOR (stonework)	4347	33333334355	MNNONONFFONFFNFNNNNN	NNNN4NOONNNNNN	V,D,P,J	102	537	05.05.01	7100	520205	81008
679.130-014	SUPERVISOR, ASBESTOS PIPE (nonmet. min.)	4327	33323334355	LNNNNNNFFONFFNFNFONN	NNNN4NNNNNNNNNN	V,P,T	057	538	06.02.01	7100	000000	81008
679.130-018	SUPERVISOR, ASBESTOS-CEMENT SHEET (nonmet. min.)	4337	33323332345	MNNNNNNFFOFFNFNFNNN	NNNN4NCNNNNNNNN	D,P,J,T	102	538	06.02.01	7100	000000	81008
679.137-010	SUPERVISOR, FINISHING DEPARTMENT (nonmet. min.)	3224	33344434355	HNNONNNFFONFFNFNFNNN	NNNN4NCNNNNNNN	D,J	056	538	06.02.01	7100	000000	81008
679.137-014	SUPERVISOR, MIRROR FABRICATION (glass products)	4227	33333334355	MNNONNNNFFNFFNFNNN	NNNN4NNNNNNNN	V,D,P,J	057	531	06.02.01	7100	520205	81008
679.362-010	CRYSTAL MACHINING COORDINATOR (electron. comp.)	3336	33333344455	HNNNNNNFFNFFNFNONNN	NNNN4NNONONNNNN	T,J,P	057	587	06.02.09	7679	520205	92902
679.384-010	SEED CORE OPERATOR (electron. comp.)	3325	34433434355	MNNNNNNCCFNNNNFNONNN	NNNN4NNONNNNNN	T,J	057	587	06.02.09	7679	000000	92902
679.567-010	STONE GRADER (mine & quarry)	2224	34333444454	LNNONONFFONNNNFNNFON	ONNN3NNNNNNNNN	J,T	212	343	06.03.02	7850	000000	83005
679.664-010	BED SETTER (stonework)	2113	44434434345	HNNNNNNFFONNNNFNNNNN	NNNO4NOONNNNNO	R,T	102	537	05.12.12	7759	460101	93999
679.665-010	LEVEL-GLASS-FORMING-MACHINE OPERATOR (cutlery-hrdwr.)	2112	44443433355	LNNNNNNFFNNNNFNNONN	NNNN3NNNNNNNNN	R,T	082	531	06.04.08	7679	489999	92998
679.682-010	BANDING-MACHINE OPERATOR (pottery & porc.)	3114	44443453344	LNNNNNNFFNNNNFNNNNN	NNNN3NNNNNNNNN	R,T	153	535	06.02.08	7479	489999	92951
679.685-010	MACHINE OPERATOR, CERAMICS (pottery & porc.)	2113	44444444355	LNNNNNNFFONNNNFNFFNN	NNNN3NNNNNNNNN	R,T	057	539	06.04.08	7679	489999	92998
679.685-014	PRODUCTION-MACHINE TENDER, GLASS CUTTING-OR-GRINDING (electron. comp.; glas)	2122	44444443355	MNNONONFFOONNINONONNN	NNNN4NNNNNNNNN	R,U	051	531	06.04.08	7679	489999	92998
679.685-018	THERMAL-SURFACING-MACHINE OPERATOR (stonework)	2112	44444444455	LNNNNNNOOONCNFNFNNNN	NNNN4NCNNNNNNNO	R,T	133	537	05.12.10	7679	460101	92998
679.685-022	TILE GRINDER (brick & tile)	2112	44444444355	LNNNNNNFFNNNNFNNNNN	NNNN4NNNNNNNNN	R,T	051	534	06.04.08	7677	489999	92965
679.685-026	TURNING-AND-BEADING-MACHINE OPERATOR (button & notion)	2123	44444443355	LNNONNNFFNNNNNNNNN	NNNN3NNNNNNNNN	R,T	055	618	06.04.09	7663	000000	92971
679.686-010	ASBESTOS-SHINGLE SHEARING-MACHINE OPERATOR (nonmet. min.)	1112	44544544355	MNNNNNNFFONNNNNNNNN	NNNN3NNNNNNNNN	R	054	538	06.04.08	8725	000000	98502
679.687-010	ASBESTOS-SHINGLE INSPECTOR (nonmet. min.)	2123	44443444355	SNNNNNNFFONNNNFNNFNN	NNNN3NNNNNNNNN	R,T	212	538	06.03.02	7820	000000	83005
680.130-010	SUPERVISOR, CARDING (textile)	4347	33333333354	MNNOOONFFFOFFNFFOOON	NNNN4NNNNNNNNN	D,J,P,V	161	414	06.02.01	7100	000000	81008
680.135-010	SUPERVISOR, MIXING (textile)	4337	33343444354	MOOFNFNCCFOOONOFONFO	NNNN4NNNNNNNN	D,P	143	410	06.02.01	7100	000000	81008
680.135-014	SUPERVISOR, MIXING (tex. prod, nec)	4235	33333333344	HNNONNNFFNOONFNOOON	NNNN3NNNNNNNNN	V,D,P	143	414	06.04.01	7679	000000	92965
680.367-010	ROVING SIZER (textile)	3234	33434444454	LNNNNNNFFONNNNFNNNNN	NNNN3NNNNNNNNN	J,T	212	414	06.03.01	7840	000000	83005
680.380-010	CARD GRINDER (nonmet. min.; textile)	4337	33433443354	MNNFFFNFFFNONFFFFON	NNNN4NOONNNNNN	J,T,V	051	567	06.01.02	6816	480503	89111
680.585-010	BATTING-MACHINE OPERATOR (tex. prod., nec; textile)	2112	44444444455	MNNONNNFFONNNNNNNNN	NNNN3NFNNNNNNN	R,T	161	414	06.04.06	7651	000000	92705
680.585-014	STAPLE-PROCESSING-MACHINE OPERATOR (textile)	2123	44444444355	MNNNNNNFFONNNNOFNFN	NNNN4NNNNNNNNN	R	152	414	06.04.06	7659	000000	92998
680.665-014	DRAW-MACHINE OPERATOR (plastic-synth.)	2113	44344434355	MNNNNNNFFNOONFONONN	NNNN4NONNNNNNN	R	134	414	06.04.06	7659	000000	92711
680.665-018	MIDDLE-CARD TENDER (nonmet. min.; textile)	2112	44544544455	LONFNFNFONNNNNFNNONN	NNNN4NONNNNNNN	R	161	410	06.04.06	7659	000000	92998
680.684-010	CARD GRINDER HELPER (textile)	2223	34434433354	VNNFFFNFFFFNFNFOFFNN	NNNN4NNNNNNNNN	T,U	121	414	06.01.02	6140	200303	85128
680.685-010	BLENDING-MACHINE OPERATOR (textile)	2123	44444434354	MFFNNONCCFNNONNNOOON	NNNN4NNNNNNNNN	R,T	143	414	06.04.06	7659	000000	92965
680.685-014	CARD STRIPPER (textile)	2113	44544534355	MNNONONNFFOONNFNOOON	NNON4NONNNNNNN	R,T	031	567	06.04.06	7659	000000	92998
680.685-018	CARD TENDER (nonmet. min.; textile)	2123	44545534355	MNNONONFFFNNONFFOFNN	NNNN4NOONNNNNN	R,T	161	414	06.04.09	7659	000000	92998
680.685-022	CHOPPED-STRAND OPERATOR (textile)	2122	44444444455	LNNNNNNFFONNNNNNFFNN	NNNN4NNNNNNNN	R,T	054	419	06.04.08	7654	000000	92705
680.685-026	CRIMP SETTER (textile)	2113	44444443355	MNNNNNNFFOONNNOFNFNN	NNNN4NNNNNNNN	R	152	414	06.04.06	7659	000000	92998
680.685-030	CRIMPING-MACHINE OPERATOR (textile)	2113	44344434355	MNNNNNNCCCNNNNFNFNN	NNNN4NNNNNNNN	R	134	414	06.04.06	7659	000000	92998
680.685-034	DRAW-FRAME TENDER (tex. prod., nec)	2123	44434434355	MNNONONFFONNNNFNNONN	NNNN4NOONNNNNN	R	161	414	06.04.06	7659	000000	92711
680.685-038	DRAWING-FRAME TENDER (textile)	2123	44544443354	MNNONONFFNNONFFOFFN	NNNN4NONNNNNNN	R	162	410	06.04.06	7659	000000	92711
680.685-042	FINISHER-CARD TENDER (nonmet. min.; textile)	2112	44444434354	MNNONONCCFNNONNNNNN	NNNN4NNNNNNNN	R,T	161	410	06.04.06	7651	000000	92705
680.685-046	FUR-BLOWER OPERATOR (hat & cap)	2114	44433444454	LNNNNNNFFOONNNFONNNN	NNNN4NNNNNNNN	R,T	031	432	06.04.06	7659	000000	92998
680.685-050	GARNETT-MACHINE OPERATOR (textile)	2113	44444444355	MNNNNNNFFONNNNNNNNNN	NNNN3NNNNNNNN	R,T	161	419	06.04.06	7659	000000	92998
680.685-054	GARNETTER (furniture; tex. prod., nec)	3123	44444444355	MNNONONFFONNNNNNNNN	NNNN4NONNNNNNN	R,T	161	419	06.04.06	7659	000000	92711
680.685-058	GILL-BOX TENDER (textile)	2113	44444444355	HNNNNNNFFNOOONFNNNNN	NNNN4NNNNNNNN	R,T	161	414	06.04.06	7659	000000	92998
680.685-062	MIXER (hat & cap)	2112	44443444354	LNNNNNNFFONNNNFNNONN	NNNN4NONNNNNNN	R	161	422	06.04.09	7659	000000	92965
680.685-066	MIXING-MACHINE OPERATOR (fabrication, nec)	2113	44493444353	MNNONONFFONNNNNFONNN	NNNN4NONNNNNNN	R	161	619	06.04.06	7659	000000	92965
680.685-070	OPENER TENDER (textile)	2112	44444444454	MNNONONFFONNNNFNNNON	NNNN4NONNNNNNN	R	161	410	06.04.06	7659	000000	92998
680.685-074	PICKER TENDER (textile)	2123	44443444355	HNNONONFFFNNONFFOFNN	NNNN4NNNNNNNN	R,T	161	414	06.04.06	7659	000000	92998
680.685-078	PICKER-MACHINE OPERATOR (furniture)	2123	44544443355	MNNNNNNFFONNNNONNNNN	NNNN4NONNNNNNN	R	031	433	06.04.06	7659	000000	92998
680.685-082	PICKING-MACHINE OPERATOR (any industry)	2112	44545444455	MNNNNNNFFONNNNONFONN	NNNN4NNNNNNNN	R	161	410	06.04.06	7659	000000	92998
680.685-086	RIBBON-LAP-MACHINE TENDER (textile)	2112	44444443455	MNNNNNFFNNNFFNFONNNN	NNNN4NNNNNNNN	R	161	414	06.04.06	7659	000000	92998
680.685-090	SILK SPREADER (textile)	2113	44443433355	LNNNNNNFFNNNNFNNNNN	NNNN3NNNNNNNN	R	161	414	06.04.06	7659	000000	92998
680.685-094	SLIVER-LAP-MACHINE TENDER (textile)	2112	44444433444	MNNFNONFFNNONFOFFON	NNNN4NOONNNNNN	R,T	161	414	06.04.06	7651	000000	92965
680.685-098	SLUBBER TENDER (textile)	2123	44444444354	MNNFOFNFFONONFFNNON	NNNN4NNONNNNNN	R,T	162	410	06.04.06	7659	000000	92711

DOT #	DOT Title & Industry	Trng	Aptitude	Physical	Environment	Tempra	WkF	MPSMS	GOE	SOC	CIP	OES
680.685-102	STAPLE CUTTER (textile)	2112	4444443455	MNNFNNNFFNOONFNNNNN	NNNN4NONNNNNNN	R,T	054	410	06.04.06	7654	000000	92705
680.685-106	STRAND-AND-BINDER CONTROLLER (nonmet. min.)	2112	44454544455	LNNNNNNNFFONNNNOONNNN	NNNO4NNNNNNNN	R	054	538	06.04.06	7659	000000	92998
680.685-110	STRETCH-BOX TENDER (textile)	2112	44454544355	MNNNNNNNFFONNNNNONNNNN	NNNN3NNNNNNNNNN	R,T	032	414	06.04.06	7659	000000	92998
680.685-114	WASTE-MACHINE TENDER (tex. prod., nec; textile)	1112	44454544455	MNNFNFNFFNONNNNFONNN	NNNN4NNNNNNNNNN	R,T	161	410	06.04.06	7659	000000	92998
680.685-118	COMBER TENDER (textile)	2113	44544544454	MNNFNFNFFONNNOFOFFN	NNNN4NNNNNNNNNN	R,T	161	414	06.04.40	7659	000000	92998
680.686-010	CAN DOFFER (textile)	1112	44544544455	MNNFNFNFFONNNNOONNNN	NNNN4NAONNNNNNN	R	011	410	06.04.40	8725	000000	98502
680.686-014	FIRST-BREAKER FEEDER (tex. prod., nec)	1112	44544544445	MNNNONNNFFONNNNNONNNN	NNNN3NNNNNNNNNN	R	161	414	06.04.16	8725	000000	98502
680.686-018	MACHINE FEEDER, RAW STOCK (tex. prod., nec; textile)	1112	44444444455	HNNFNFNCCONNONONONNNN	NNNN4NONNNNNNN	R	161	410	06.04.16	8725	000000	98502
680.686-022	WASTE-MACHINE OFFBEARER (tex. prod., nec)	2112	44544543345	MNNNNNNNFFONNNNNNNNNN	NNNN4NNNNNNNNNN	R	161	419	06.04.16	8725	000000	98502
680.687-010	APRON CLEANER (nonmet. min.)	1112	44554534355	MNNNNNNNFFONNNNNNNNN	NNNN3NONNNNNNN	R	161	419	06.04.34	8769	000000	98999
680.687-014	ROLLER CLEANER (textile)	2122	44544534455	LNNFNFNFFONONFFONNN	NNNN4NNNNNNNNNN	R	031	567	06.04.39	8750	000000	98905
680.687-018	ROVING-WEIGHT GAUGER (textile)	2124	4444444455	MNNNNNNNFFONNNNOONFNN	NNNN4NNNNNNNNNN	R,T	161	414	06.03.02	7840	000000	83005
681.130-010	SUPERVISOR, PREPARATION DEPARTMENT (textile)	4337	23333444454	LNNOOONFFONFFNFONOON	NNNN4NNNNNNNNNN	D,P,J	163	411	06.02.01	7100	000000	81008
681.130-014	SUPERVISOR, WINDING AND TWISTING DEPARTMENT (textile)	4337	33333443355	LNNNNNNCCFNFFNFCNOFN	NNNN4NNNNNNNNNN	D,P,J,V	162	411	06.01.01	7100	000000	81008
681.380-010	ROPE-MACHINE SETTER (tex. prod., nec)	3236	34333443355	MNNONONFFFNNNNONNNNN	NNNN4NOONNNNNNN	V,J,T	162	413	06.01.02	7451	000000	92702
681.387-010	QUALITY CONTROL CHECKER, TEXTURING PROCESS (textile)	3227	34443232354	LNNNNNNFFNNNNNFNNOON	NNNN4NNNNNNNNNN	T,J	211	411	06.03.01	7820	150702	83005
681.485-010	ROVING WINDER, FIBERGLASS (textile)	2123	44434344455	HNNNNNNNFFNNOONFNNFNN	NNNN3NNNNNNNNNN	R,T	163	419	06.04.06	7651	000000	92705
681.585-010	BEAMER (textile)	2113	44433433355	MNNNNNNNFFNNOOFONNNN	NNNN4NNNNNNNNNN	R,T	163	411	06.04.06	7651	000000	92705
681.585-014	BOBBIN WINDER, MACHINE (tex. prod., nec; textile)	2112	44544533355	LNNNNNNNFFNNNNNFNNNON	NNNN4NNNNNNNNNN	R,T	163	410	06.04.06	7651	000000	92705
681.585-018	SINGE WINDER (textile)	2113	44444433454	LNNONOFFFNNNNNOONNON	NNNN4NNNNNNNNNN	R	163	411	06.04.06	7651	000000	92705
681.682-010	DRESSER TENDER (textile)	3124	34443433344	HNNNNNNNFFNNNNFNOOON	NNNN4NNNNNNNNNN	R,T	163	411	06.02.06	7651	000000	92705
681.682-014	ROPE-MAKER, ROPEWALK (tex. prod., nec)	3124	34434433355	HNNNNNNNFFNNNNNNNNNN	NNNN4NNNNNNNNNN	J	162	413	06.02.09	7651	000000	92705
681.682-018	RUG SETTER, AXMINSTER (carpet & rug)	3125	34433533354	MNNOOOOFFFNNNNFNNOON	NNNN4NNNNNNNNNN	J,T	163	411	06.02.06	7651	000000	92705
681.685-010	BALL-WARPER TENDER (textile)	2113	44435433345	MNNFNFNFFNNNNFONONN	NNNN4NNNNNNNNNN	R,T	163	411	06.04.06	7651	000000	92705
681.685-014	BALLING-MACHINE OPERATOR (textile)	2113	45454533355	LNNFNFNFFNNNNFNNNNN	NNNN4NNNNNNNNNN	R	163	410	06.04.06	7651	000000	92705
681.685-018	BEAM-WARPER TENDER, AUTOMATIC (knitting; narrow fabrics; nonmet. min.; textile)	2114	44443433354	LNNNNNNNFFNNNNOFFNOO	NNNN4NNNNNNNNNN	R,T	163	411	06.04.06	7651	000000	92705
681.685-022	BOBBIN WINDER, MACHINE (boot & shoe)	1112	44544533355	LNNNNNNNFFNNNNNNFNNN	NNNN4NNNNNNNNNN	R	163	412	06.04.05	7651	480304	92705
681.685-026	BOBBIN WINDER, SEWING MACHINE (textile)	2113	44444433254	LNNONONCCFNNNNFNNFON	NNNN4NNNNNNNNNN	R,T	163	412	06.04.05	7651	000000	92705
681.685-030	CARDING-MACHINE OPERATOR (tex. prod., nec)	1112	45454544455	SNNNNNNFFONNNNNNNNNN	NNNN4NNNNNNNNNN	R	163	432	06.04.38	7651	000000	92705
681.685-034	COILER (tex. prod., nec)	2112	44444433355	VNNNNNNFFNNNNNNNNNN	NNNN4NNNNNNNNNN	R	163	413	06.04.06	7651	000000	92705
681.685-038	COVERING-MACHINE OPERATOR (textile)	2113	44443433354	MNNNNNNFFFNNNNFONNON	NNNN4NNNNNNNNNN	R	162	411	06.04.09	7651	000000	92705
681.685-042	COVERING-MACHINE-OPERATOR HELPER (textile)	2123	44443434354	LNNNNNNNFFNNNNFNNON	NNNN4NNNNNNNNNN	R	212	567	06.03.02	8617	000000	98999
681.685-046	DOUBLING-MACHINE OPERATOR (textile)	2112	44444544354	LNNFNFNFFNNNNFNNOON	NNNN4NNNNNNNNNN	R,T	163	411	06.04.06	7651	000000	92705
681.685-050	FLOOR WINDER (textile)	3124	34444344455	LNNNNNNNFFNNOONFNNNN	NNNN4NNNNNNNNNN	R	163	419	06.04.06	7679	000000	92705
681.685-054	LEASING-MACHINE TENDER (textile)	2112	44444444354	MNNNNNNNFFONNNNFNONNN	NNNN4NNNNNNNNNN	R	161	411	06.04.07	7651	000000	92705
681.685-058	LONG-CHAIN BEAMER (textile)	2113	44443433344	LNNNNNNNCCFNOONCNNNON	NNNN3NNNNNNNNNN	R,T	163	410	06.04.06	7651	000000	92705
681.685-062	LOOM-WINDER TENDER (textile)	2112	44454534354	LNNFNFNFFONNNNONNFON	NNNN4NNNNNNNNNN	R	163	411	06.04.06	7651	000000	92705
681.685-066	PRECISE WINDER (textile)	2112	44443433354	LNNFNFNFFONONFOOON	NNNN4NNNNNNNNNN	R	163	411	06.04.06	7651	000000	92705
681.685-070	QUILLER OPERATOR (textile)	2114	44444433344	LFFFNFNFFONNNFNNNN	NNNN4NNNNNNNNNN	R	163	410	06.04.06	7651	000000	92705
681.685-074	QUILLING-MACHINE OPERATOR, AUTOMATIC (textile)	2123	44444443454	LNNONONFFFNNOOOOOO	NNNN4NOONNNNNNN	R	163	411	06.04.06	7651	000000	92705
681.685-078	REELING-MACHINE OPERATOR (textile)	2113	44444433355	LNNFNFNFFNNOONFNNNN	NNNN4NNNNNNNNNN	R	163	411	06.04.06	7651	000000	92705
681.685-082	ROPE MAKER, MACHINE (nonmet. min.)	2113	44444533345	LNNNNNNNFFNNNNFNNON	NNNN3NNNNNNNNNN	R	162	538	06.04.06	7651	000000	92705
681.685-086	ROPE-LAYING-MACHINE OPERATOR (tex. prod., nec)	2113	44444433354	MOOONONFFFNOONFOONON	NNNN4NOONNNNNNN	R	162	413	06.04.06	7651	000000	92705
681.685-090	RUBBER-THREAD SPOOLER (toy-sport equip.)	2112	44444433345	LNNNNNNNFFNNNNFNNNN	NNNN3NNNNNNNNNN	R	163	510	06.04.07	7651	000000	92705
681.685-094	SELVAGE-MACHINE OPERATOR (textile)	2113	44443433355	LNNNNNNNCCFNOONCNNNON	NNNN4NNNNNNNNNN	R	163	411	06.04.06	7651	000000	92705
681.685-098	SKEIN WINDER (textile)	2112	45435533344	LNNFNNNCCFNOONCNNNON	NNNN4NNNNNNNNNN	R	163	410	06.04.06	7651	000000	92705
681.685-102	SKEINER (narrow fabrics)	2112	4444444444	LNNFNNNNCFNNNNFNNNNN	NNNN4NNNNNNNNNN	R	163	423	06.04.06	7651	000000	92705
681.685-106	SPEEDER TENDER (textile)	2112	44444433354	MNNFNNNFFNNNNNNNNNN	NNNN4NNNNNNNNNN	R	162	414	06.04.16	7651	000000	92705
681.685-110	SPINNING-MACHINE TENDER (tex. prod., nec)	2112	44544543354	HNNNNNNNFFNNNNFNNNNN	NNNN4NOONNNNNNN	R	162	413	06.04.16	7651	000000	92705
681.685-114	SPOOLING-MACHINE OPERATOR (tex. prod., nec)	1112	44544544455	LNNNNNNNFFONNNNNNNNN	NNNN4NNNNNNNNNN	R,T	163	432	06.04.38	7651	000000	92705
681.685-118	STRAND-FORMING-MACHINE OPERATOR (tex. prod., nec)	2113	44444443355	HNNFNFNFFNNNNONNONN	NNNN4NNNNNNNNNN	R,T	162	413	06.04.06	7651	000000	92705

DOT #	DOT Title & Industry	Trng	Aptitude	Physical	Environment	Tempra	WkF	MPSMS	GOE	SOC	CIP	OES
681.685-122	THREAD WINDER, AUTOMATIC (textile)	2112	44543533353	LNNONONFFFNNNNFNNFFN	NNNN4NNNNNNNNNNN	R,T	163	412	06.04.06	7651	000000	92705
681.685-126	TWISTER (tex. prod., nec)	2113	44443433344	LNNONONFFFNNNNFNNNON	NNNN4NNNNNNNNNNN	R,T	162	413	06.04.06	7651	000000	92705
681.685-130	TWISTER TENDER (glass mfg.; nonmet. min.; plastic-synth.; textile)	2123	44444433344	MNNNFNONCCFNNONCCONOC	NNNN4NNNNNNNNNNN	R,T	162	411	06.04.06	7651	000000	92705
681.685-134	TWISTER TENDER, PAPER (tex. prod., nec)	2114	44443433354	MNNNNNNFFNNNNNFFNOON	NNNN4NONNNNNNNN	R,T	162	413	06.04.04	7651	000000	92705
681.685-138	UPTWISTER TENDER (textile)	2113	44443433354	MONFNFNFFFNNNNNOFNNON	NNNN4NONNNNNNNN	R,T	163	411	06.04.06	7651	000000	92705
681.685-142	WARP SPOOLER (narrow fabrics; textile)	2113	44543533354	MONFNFNFFFNNNNNOFNOON	NNNN3NNNNNNNNNNN	R,T	163	411	06.04.06	7659	000000	92998
681.685-146	WARPER (narrow fabrics)	2114	44444433355	MNNNNNNFFFNNNNNFNFNN	NNNN4NONNNNNNNN	R,T	163	411	06.04.06	7651	000000	92705
681.685-150	WINDER OPERATOR, AUTOMATIC (textile)	2113	44444433344	LNNONNNFFFNNONFNONON	NNNN4NNNNNNNNNNN	R	163	411	06.04.06	7651	000000	92705
681.685-154	YARN WINDER (tex. prod., nec; textile)	2123	44444433354	MNNONONFFFONONFOFOON	NNNN4NNNNNNNNNNN	R,T	163	411	06.04.06	7651	000000	92705
681.685-158	YARN-TEXTURING-MACHINE OPERATOR I (textile)	2113	44443433354	LOOFNFNFFFONONFFNOON	NNNN4NNNNNNNNNNN	R,T	162	411	06.04.16	7651	000000	92705
681.686-010	BEAM RACKER (textile)	2112	44544544444	HNNFFFNFFONNNNFNNNON	NNNN4NNNNNNNNNNN	R	163	411	06.04.05	8725	000000	98502
681.686-014	BEAMER HELPER (textile)	2112	44544543345	MNNNNNNFFNNNNNFONNNN	NNNN3NNNNNNNNNNN	R	163	411	06.04.06	8617	000000	98999
681.686-018	SPOOLER OPERATOR, AUTOMATIC (textile)	2112	44444433355	LNNFNNNCCFFNONFFFNNN	NNNN4NNNNNNNNNNN	R	163	411	06.04.06	8725	000000	98502
681.687-010	END FINDER, FORMING DEPARTMENT (textile)	2122	44444443355	LNNNNNNFFFNNNNNFNNNNN	NNNN3NNNNNNNNNNN	R,T	212	419	06.03.02	7820	000000	83005
681.687-014	LOOSE-END FINDER, BOBBIN (knitting)	1112	44545533355	LNNNNNNFFFNNNNNNNNNNN	NNNN3NNNNNNNNNNN	R	163	410	06.04.27	8769	000000	98999
681.687-018	THREAD INSPECTOR (plastic-synth.)	3113	44533544453	LNNNNNNFFONNNNNFNFFON	NNNN3NNNNNNNNNNN	R,T	212	414	06.03.02	7820	000000	83005
681.687-022	WARP-YARN SORTER (textile)	2122	44444444454	LNNNNNNCCONNNNONNNNON	NNNN3NNNNNNNNON	R	221	411	06.03.02	7850	000000	83005
681.687-026	YARN CLEANER (tex. prod., nec; textile)	2112	44443444454	LNNFNONCCFONOFONONON	NNNN4NNNNNNNNNO	R	163	411	06.03.02	8769	000000	98999
681.687-030	YARN EXAMINER (glass mfg.; plastic-synth.; textile)	2123	44443433354	MNNFNNNCCFFNONFNFFFN	NNNN4NNNNNNNNNNN	R,T	212	411	06.03.02	7820	000000	83005
682.130-010	SUPERVISOR, SPINNING (textile)	4347	33333433354	LONONONFFFOFFNNFOOON	NNNN4NOONNNNNNN	D,P,J,V	162	411	06.01.01	7100	000000	81008
682.684-010	ROLLER CHECKER (textile)	2113	44444433354	LNNNNNNCCFONNNNNFFNFN	NNNN4NNNNNNNNNNN	R,T	162	411	06.03.02	6140	000000	85128
682.685-010	SPINNER, FRAME (nonmet. min.; textile)	2123	44444433354	MNNFNFNFFFNNONFFFNON	NNNN4NOONNNNNNN	R,T	162	411	06.04.06	7651	000000	92705
682.685-014	SPINNER, MULE (nonmet. min.; textile)	2114	34444433355	LNNNNNNFFFNNNNNCNCNO	NNNN4NONNNNNNNN	R,T	162	411	06.04.06	7651	000000	92705
682.687-010	TRAVELER CHANGER (textile)	2112	44444443355	LNNNONONFFFONONONONNN	NNNN4NCNNNNNNNN	R	162	411	06.04.06	7740	000000	93999
683.130-010	FLOOR SUPERVISOR, ENDLESS-BELT-WEAVING DEPARTMENT (narrow fabrics)	4337	23333444454	LNNNNNNFFONFFNFNNFON	NNNN3NNNNNNNNNNN	D,P,J,T	164	423	06.04.01	7100	000000	81008
683.130-014	LOOM-FIXER SUPERVISOR (narrow fabrics)	4347	33332333354	MNNONONFFFNFFNFOOOOO	NNNN4NNNNNNNNNNN	D,P,J,T	164	423	06.01.01	7100	000000	81008
683.130-018	WEAVE-ROOM SUPERVISOR (carpet & rug)	4347	33333444453	LNNNNNNCCFFNONFNFNNON	NNNN4NNNNNNNNNNN	D,P,J	164	431	06.02.01	7100	000000	81008
683.130-022	WEAVING SUPERVISOR (nonmet. min.; textile)	4347	33333433354	LONOOONFFOOFFNFOOFON	NNNN4NNNNNNNNNNN	D,P,J,T	164	420	06.01.01	7100	200303	81008
683.132-010	PATTERN-CHAIN MAKER SUPERVISOR (textile)	4237	23332343344	MNNFNFNFFFONONFFFNN	NNNN4NNNNNNNNNNN	D,P,J	192	489	06.02.01	7100	000000	83002
683.222-010	INSTRUCTOR, WEAVING (textile)	3237	33433433354	LNNONNNFFFFNFFNFOFON	NNNN4NNNNNNNNNNN	D,P	164	420	06.02.01	2390	000000	31314
683.260-010	BRAID-PATTERN SETTER (narrow fabrics)	4347	33333433354	LNNOOONFFFNNNNFNOOON	NNNN4NNNNNNNNNNN	J,T	164	423	06.01.02	7452	000000	92702
683.260-014	CARPET-LOOM FIXER (carpet & rug)	4337	34432433354	MNNFFNFFFNNNNNFNOOON	NNNN4NNNNNNNNNNN	J	121	431	06.01.02	7452	000000	92702
683.260-018	LOOM FIXER (narrow fabrics; nonmet. min.; textile)	4337	34433433354	MONFFFOFFFOQOONFFFON	NNNN4NOONNNNNNN	J,T	121	567	06.01.02	7452	000000	83002
683.260-022	SWATCH CHECKER (textile)	4337	33432333352	LOONNNNFFFNOONFNNFON	NNNN4NONNNNNNNN	J	164	420	06.01.02	6881	000000	92705
683.360-010	LOOM CHANGER (textile)	3227	33333433354	MONFFNFFFFOONFNFOON	NNNN3NNFFNNNNNNN	J,T	121	567	06.01.02	7452	000000	92702
683.360-014	LOOM STARTER (textile)	4237	34432433353	LNNFFFNNFFNNNNNFNNFON	NNNN4NFNNNNNNNN	J	164	410	06.01.02	6881	000000	83002
683.380-010	HARNESS BUILDER (textile)	4236	44444433355	LNNONNNFFFNNNNFNNNFFN	NNNN4NNNNNNNNNNN	J,T	121	420	06.01.02	6130	000000	85119
683.381-010	CHAIN BUILDER, LOOM CONTROL (textile)	3125	34443433354	LNNONONFFFNNNNFNONNN	NNNN3NNNNNNNNNNN	R,T	121	567	06.01.04	7452	000000	92702
683.384-010	PATTERN-LEASE INSPECTOR (textile)	3114	34432433354	LNNNNNNFFFNNOONFNNFON	NNNN4NNNNNNNNNNN	J,T	164	420	06.03.01	7820	000000	83005
683.487-010	BELTING-AND-WEBBING INSPECTOR (narrow fabrics)	2112	44443444454	LNNNNNNFFONNNNFNNNFON	NNNN3NNNNNNNNNNN	J,T	212	423	06.03.01	7820	000000	83005
683.582-010	CARD CUTTER, JACQUARD (narrow fabrics; textile)	3125	34433433445	LNNNNNNFFFNNNNFNNNNN	NNNN4NNNNNNNNNNN	R,T	192	479	06.02.04	7652	000000	92705
683.662-010	JACQUARD-LOOM WEAVER (textile)	3115	34443443354	LNNFFFNCCFNOONOFNFON	NNCO4NCNNNNNNNN	R,T	164	420	06.02.06	7652	000000	92705
683.665-010	WEAVER, NEEDLE LOOM (narrow fabrics)	3124	34443443354	LOOONONCCCNNNNFNNFFN	NNNN4NNNNNNNNNNN	R,T	164	423	06.02.06	7652	000000	92705
683.680-010	HARNESS PLACER (textile)	3124	34433433354	MNNFFNFFNNNNNONNOON	NNNN4NFNNNNNNNN	R,T	164	420	06.01.02	7452	000000	92702
683.680-014	HEDDLES TIER, JACQUARD LOOM (narrow fabrics; textile)	3115	34443443355	LOOFFNFFFNNNNNFNOOON	NNNN4NONNNNNNNN	R,J,T	164	420	06.01.02	7452	000000	92702
683.682-010	CARPET WEAVER (carpet & rug)	3124	34433433354	LNNONONFFFNNNNFONNNON	NNNN4NNNNNNNNNNN	R,T	164	431	06.02.06	7652	000000	92705
683.682-014	CARPET WEAVER, JACQUARD LOOM (carpet & rug)	3124	34443443354	LNNFNFFFFOONFONONOOO	NNNN4NNNNNNNNNNN	R,T	164	431	06.02.06	7652	000000	92705
683.682-018	DRAWING-IN-MACHINE TENDER (textile)	3125	34443433344	HNNONONFFFNNNNFONOON	NNNN3NNNNNNNNNNN	R,T	164	420	06.02.06	7452	000000	92702
683.682-022	JACQUARD-LOOM WEAVER (narrow fabrics)	3125	34443433354	LNNFNFNCCFFOONONFFOF	NNNN4NNNNNNNNNNN	R,T	164	420	06.02.06	7652	000000	92705
683.682-026	LEVERS-LACE MACHINE OPERATOR (tex. prod., nec)	3126	34433432354	MNNONONCCFNOONCNNFFN	NNNN4NNNNNNNNNNN	R,T	164	432	06.02.06	7652	000000	92705
683.682-030	PLUSH WEAVER (textile)	3124	34433433354	LNNFOONFFFNONFNFFFO	NNNN4NNNNNNNNNNN	R,T	164	420	06.02.06	7652	000000	92705

DOT #	DOT Title & Industry	Trng	Aptitude	Physical	Environment	Tempra	WkF	MPSMS	GOE	SOC	CIP	OES
683.682-034	WEAVER (carpet & rug)	3125	34433433354	MONONONCCFNOONCNNNCCN	NNNN4NNNNNNNNNN	R,T	164	431	06.02.06	7652	000000	92705
683.682-038	WEAVER (nonmet. min.; textile)	3124	34433433354	LNNOOONCCCONONFNNOON	NNNN4NCNNNNNNNN	R,T	164	420	06.02.06	7652	000000	92705
683.682-042	WEAVER APPRENTICE (nonmet. min.; textile)	3124	34433433354	LNNOOONCCCONONFNNOON	NNNN4NCNNNNNNNN	R,T	164	420	06.02.06	7652	000000	92705
683.682-046	WEAVER, NARROW FABRICS (narrow fabrics; nonmet. min.)	3125	34433433354	LNNNOONCCCNNNNFNNOON	NNNN4NNNNNNNNNN	R,T	164	423	06.02.06	7652	000000	92705
683.682-050	WEAVER, TIRE CORD (tex. prod., nec)	3114	34443443355	LNNFNNNFFFNNNNCCNNNC	NNNN4NNNNNNNNNN	R,T	164	439	06.02.06	7652	000000	92998
683.684-010	CHAIN REPAIRER (carpet & rug)	3125	34433433345	MONONONFFFNNNNFFNO	NNNN4NNNNNNNNNN	T	121	567	06.02.24	6130	470303	85112
683.684-014	DRAWER-IN, HAND (textile)	3124	34433433354	LNNFNFNFFFONONFNFFON	NNNN4NNNNNNNNNN	R,T	164	420	06.02.06	7759	000000	93999
683.684-018	HARNESS PULLER (textile)	3124	33433333453	LNNNNNNNNFFNNNNFNFON	NNNN4NNNNNNNNNN	J,T	164	420	06.03.02	7820	000000	83005
683.684-022	LEASE-OUT WORKER (textile)	2123	44543533344	HNNFFFNCCCNNNNFNFNON	NNON4NONNNNNNNN	R,T	164	420	06.04.27	6140	000000	85128
683.684-026	SMASH HAND (narrow fabrics; textile)	3123	34443433354	LNNNONNFFFNNNNNFNFNFN	NNNF4NONNNNNNNN	R,T	164	420	06.04.27	7759	470303	93999
683.684-030	WEAVER, HAND LOOM (carpet & rug; textile)	4126	34433433323	MNNOOONFFFNNNNFNFNFN	NNNN3NNNNNNNNNN	R,T	164	422	06.02.27	7759	000000	93999
683.684-034	WEAVING INSPECTOR (carpet & rug; textile)	2123	34433433454	LNNFNFNFFFNNNNFNFON	NNNN4NNNNNNNNNN	R,T	212	420	06.02.06	7820	000000	83005
683.685-010	BRAIDING-MACHINE OPERATOR (narrow fabrics; nonmet. min.)	2113	44444443355	MNNONONFFFNNNNFNOONN	NNNN4NNNNNNNNNN	R,T	164	423	06.04.27	7659	000000	92998
683.685-014	CARD CHANGER, JACQUARD LOOM (textile)	2124	34444444445	MFFNNNNFFONNNNNFNONN	NNNF4NCNNNNNNNN	R,T	164	420	06.04.27	6140	470303	85128
683.685-018	CARD LACER, JACQUARD (narrow fabrics; textile)	2112	44444444455	LNNFNFNFFFNNNNFONNNN	NNNN4NNNNNNNNNN	R,T	062	479	06.04.06	7659	000000	92998
683.685-022	DRAWING-IN-MACHINE-TENDER HELPER (textile)	2114	44444433344	HNNFNFNNCCFNNNNFNNOON	NNNN3NNNNNNNNNN	R,T	164	420	06.04.05	8619	000000	98999
683.685-026	PATTERN DUPLICATOR (textile)	2122	44444544455	LNNFFFNFFONNNNNFNOFNN	NNNN4NNNNNNNNNN	R,T	192	479	06.04.06	7679	000000	92998
683.685-030	THREADING-MACHINE TENDER (carpet & rug)	2113	44444444345	LNNNNNNNFFFNNNNFNNNNN	NNNN4NNNNNNNNNN	R,T	164	411	06.04.06	7652	000000	92705
683.685-034	WARP-TYING-MACHINE TENDER (narrow fabrics; textile)	3124	34443433354	MNNFOONFFFONNNFNNFON	NNNN4NOONNNNNON	R,T	164	411	06.04.06	7659	000000	92998
683.685-038	WEAVER, AXMINSTER (carpet & rug)	2114	44443533354	MNNNNNNNFFFNNNNFOONOF	NNNN4NNNNNNNNNN	R,T	164	431	06.04.06	7652	000000	92705
683.686-010	BATTERY LOADER (textile)	1112	44544544354	LNNONNNCCCNNNNCNNCON	NNNN4NONNNNNNNN	R	164	420	06.04.06	8725	000000	98502
683.687-010	DRAWER-IN HELPER, HAND (textile)	2112	44444433354	MNNFNFNFFFNNNNNFNNNN	NNNN4NNNNNNNNNN	R	164	411	06.04.05	8617	000000	98999
683.687-014	DROP-WIRE HANGER (textile)	1112	44443432354	LNNFNFNFFFNNNNOFNNNN	NNNN4NNNNNNNNNN	R	061	411	06.04.06	8769	000000	98999
683.687-018	HANDER-IN (narrow fabrics; textile)	2112	44445543454	SNNNNNNFFFNNNNNNFNFON	NNNN4NNNNNNNNNN	R	164	420	06.04.05	8769	000000	98999
683.687-022	HOOK PULLER (narrow fabrics)	1111	44454544455	LNNNNNNNFFONNNNNNNNNN	NNNN3NNNNNNNNNN	R	011	567	06.04.40	8769	000000	98999
683.687-026	LINGO CLEANER (textile)	2112	44444444355	LNNNNNNNFFONNNNNNNNNN	NNNN4NNNNNNNNNN	R	031	567	06.04.39	8750	000000	98905
683.687-030	LOOM CHANGEOVER OPERATOR (carpet & rug)	2113	44444444453	LNNONONFFFNNNNFNNNFN	NNNN4NNNNNNNNNN	R	164	431	06.04.05	8617	000000	98999
683.687-034	WARP-TENSION TESTER (textile)	2122	44444444454	LNNFNNNFFFNNNNFNNNNN	NNNN4NNNNNNNNNN	R,J	164	411	06.03.02	6140	000000	85128
684.137-010	SUPERVISOR (knitting)	4337	33334444454	LNNONONFFOOFFNFNNNON	NNNN3NNNNNNNNNN	D,P	165	446	06.02.01	7100	200303	81008
684.384-010	QUALITY-CONTROL TESTER (knitting)	3224	33333433354	LNNNNNNCCFNNNNCNNFON	NNNN3NNNNNNNNNN	R,T	212	446	06.03.01	7830	000000	83005
684.682-010	KNITTING-MACHINE OPERATOR, FULL-FASHIONED HOSIERY, AUTOMATIC (knitting)	3215	33422433354	LNNNNNNNCCFNNNNFONOON	NNNN4NNNNNNNNNN	R,T	165	446	06.02.06	7652	000000	92705
684.662-014	SEWER AND INSPECTOR (knitting)	3113	34443433345	LNNNNNNNCCFNNNNFFNN	NNNN3NNNNNNNNNN	R,T	171	446	06.01.02	7655	000000	92717
684.684-010	STOCKING INSPECTOR (knitting)	2113	44443433354	LNNNNNNNCCCONONCNNFFN	NNNN3NNNNNNNNNN	R,T	212	446	06.03.02	7452	000000	83005
684.684-014	SIZER (knitting)	3224	44444444354	LNNNNNNNCCFNNNONFNNNN	NNNN4NNNNNNNNNN	R,T	212	446	06.03.02	7820	000000	83005
684.685-010	SEAMLESS-HOSIERY KNITTER (knitting)	2113	44434433354	LNNFNNNCCFNNONFNNNON	NNNN4NNNNNNNNNN	R,T	165	446	06.04.06	7652	000000	92705
684.686-010	CLIPPER, MACHINE (knitting)	1112	44544544355	LNNNNNNCCONNNNNNNNN	NNNN4NNNNNNNNNN	R	054	446	06.04.06	8725	000000	98502
684.687-010	PAIRER (knitting)	2213	44443422354	LNNNNNNNCCFFNONCNNCCN	NNNN3NNNNNNNNNN	R,T	212	446	06.03.02	7850	200303	83005
684.687-014	REINSPECTOR (knitting)	3213	44443434454	LNNNNNNNCCFNNONCNNCCN	NNNN3NNNNNNNNNN	R,T	212	446	06.03.02	7820	200303	83005
684.687-022	COLLECTOR (knitting)	2112	44444444445	MNNFNNNNCCFNNNNFNNNN	NNNN4NNNNNNNNNN	R	011	446	06.04.40	8726	000000	98799
685.130-010	SUPERVISOR, KNITTING II (knitting)	4337	33333444354	MNNOOONFFFOFFNFNOFFN	NNNN4NNNNNNNNNN	D,J,P	165	424	06.01.01	7100	200303	81008
685.360-010	KNITTER MECHANIC (knitting)	4337	33322433254	MNNNNNNFFFNNNNFNNOON	NNNN3NNNNNNNNNN	J,T	165	424	06.01.02	7452	470303	92702
685.380-010	LINK-AND-LINK-KNITTING-MACHINE OPERATOR (knitting)	3236	33333433254	LNNNNNNNFFFNNNNFNNONN	NNNN3NNNNNNNNNN	J,T	165	424	06.01.03	7452	000000	92702
685.381-010	JACQUARD-PLATE MAKER (knitting)	3325	34433433334	LNNNNNNNFFFNNNNFFNNN	NNNN4NNNNNNNNNN	J,T	061	424	06.02.23	7452	000000	92702
685.382-010	SURGICAL-ELASTIC KNITTER, HAND FRAME (protective dev.)	4215	44444444354	LNNNNNNNFFFNNNNFNNFON	NNNN3NNNNNNNNNN	R,J,T	165	604	06.02.06	7652	000000	92705
685.665-010	KNITTER, FULL-FASHIONED GARMENT (knitting)	2114	44444433355	LNNNNNNNFFNNNNFNNFON	NNNN4NNNNNNNNNN	R,J,T	165	424	06.04.06	7652	000000	92705
685.665-014	KNITTING-MACHINE OPERATOR (knitting)	3113	44444433354	MNNONONFFFONONFNNFOF	NNNN4NNNNNNNNNN	R,J,T	165	424	06.04.06	7652	000000	92705
685.665-018	WARP-KNITTING-MACHINE OPERATOR (knitting)	3224	34432433354	MNNNONONFFFNNNNFNOFON	NNNN4NNNNNNNNNN	R,T	165	420	06.02.06	7652	000000	92705
685.680-010	THREADER (knitting)	3225	44432433354	LNNNNNNNCCNNNNNCCFN	NNNN4NNNNNNNNNN	R,J,T	165	420	06.02.27	7452	000000	92702
685.682-010	CROCHET-MACHINE OPERATOR (knitting)	3224	44433433344	LNNNNNNNFFFNNNNFNNOON	NNNN4NNNNNNNNNN	R,T	171	424	06.02.06	7652	200303	92705
685.684-010	PATTERN WHEEL MAKER (knitting)	3225	44433433355	LNNNNNNNCCCNNNNNCCONN	NNNN3NNNNNNNNNN	R,T	061	424	06.02.27	7652	000000	92705
685.685-010	KNITTING-MACHINE OPERATOR (tex. prod., nec)	2124	44444432344	LNNNONONFFFNNNNFNNFON	NNNN3NNNNNNNNNN	R,T	165	439	06.04.06	7652	000000	92705

DOT #	DOT Title & Industry	Trng	Aptitude	Physical	Environment	Tempra	WkF	MPSMS	GOE	SOC	CIP	OES
685.685-014	PATTERN ASSEMBLER (knitting)	2223	44443433354	LNNNNNNFFNNNNFNNFNN	NNNN3NNNNNNNNNN	R,T	051	567	06.04.06	6140	000000	85128
685.686-010	FRINGING-MACHINE OPERATOR (knitting)	2112	44444534355	LNNNNNNCCFNNNNNNNNNN	NNNN3NNNNNNNNNN	R	171	424	06.04.06	8725	000000	98502
685.686-014	KNITTING-MACHINE OPERATOR HELPER (knitting)	2122	44445533355	MNNONONFFFNNNONNNNN	NNNN4NNNNNNNNNN	R	165	424	06.04.06	8617	000000	83005
685.687-010	CLOTH INSPECTOR (knitting)	2124	34443433354	LNNNNNNFFNNNNFNNFON	NNNN3NNNNNNNNNN	R,J	212	424	06.03.02	7820	000000	83005
685.687-014	CUFF FOLDER (knitting)	1112	44545454455	SNNNNNNNFFNNNNNNNNNN	NNNN3NNNNNNNNNN	R	062	424	06.04.27	8769	200303	92705
685.687-018	LACE WINDER (tex. prod., nec)	2112	44544544355	LNNNNNNNFFONNNNNNNNN	NNNN3NNNNNNNNNN	R	163	432	06.04.05	7651	000000	92705
685.687-022	PATROLLER (knitting)	2122	44543544453	LNFFFNNFFNNNNCNNFON	NNNN4NNNNNNNNNN	R,J,T	212	424	06.03.02	7820	000000	83005
685.687-026	TOPPER (knitting)	1112	44444533354	SNNNNNNNFFNNNNFNNNON	NNNN4NNNNNNNNNN	R	165	424	06.04.27	7740	000000	93999
686.462-010	DIE-CUTTING-MACHINE OPERATOR, AUTOMATIC (tex. prod., nec; textile)	3124	44443444355	LNNNNNNNFFONNNFNNONN	NNNN3NNNNNNNNNN	J,T	134	430	06.02.05	7654	200303	92705
686.585-010	CUTTING-MACHINE OPERATOR (tex. prod., nec)	2122	44443444345	HNNONONFFONNONONONNN	NNNN3NNNNNNNNNN	R,T	054	436	06.04.05	7654	200303	92705
686.662-010	RUG CUTTER (carpet & rug)	3124	34433443354	MNNNNNNFFONNNNFNNOON	NNNN3NNNNNNNNNN	R,T	054	431	06.02.05	7654	000000	92705
686.682-010	BAND-SAW OPERATOR (tex. prod., nec)	3124	44444433355	MNNONNNFFNNNNFNNNNNN	NNNN4NNONNNNNNN	R,T	056	439	06.02.05	7654	200303	92705
686.682-014	BIAS-CUTTING-MACHINE OPERATOR (tex. prod., nec)	3124	44443434345	MNNONNNNFFONNNNFNNNNN	NNNN4NNNNNNNNNN	R,T	054	424	06.02.05	7654	200303	92705
686.682-018	FELT-CUTTING-MACHINE OPERATOR (tex. prod., nec)	3224	34343434335	MNNNNNNFFONNNNFNNNNN	NNNN3NNNNNNNNNN	R,T	054	422	06.02.05	7654	200303	92705
686.685-010	CHIN-STRAP CUTTER (hat & cap)	2112	44345533355	LNNNNNNFFNNNONNNNNN	NNNN4NNNNNNNNNN	R,T	054	425	06.04.05	7654	200303	92705
686.685-014	CONTINUOUS PILLOWCASE CUTTER (tex. prod., nec)	2123	44443433354	MNNFNFNFFNNNNFNNNNON	NNNN3NNNNNNNNNN	R,T	062	435	06.04.05	7654	000000	92705
686.685-018	CUFF CUTTER (glove & mit.)	2123	44444444354	MNNONONFFONNNNFNNNNON	NNNN4NNNNNNNNNN	R,T	054	424	06.04.05	7654	200303	92705
686.685-022	CUTTER (tex. prod., nec)	2122	44444433445	MNNNNNNFFFNNNNNNNNNN	NNNN3NNNNNNNNNN	R,T	054	411	06.04.05	7654	000000	92705
686.685-026	FELT CUTTER (ordnance)	2122	44434444355	LNNONONFFONNNFNNOONN	NNNN3NNNNNNNNNN	R,J	054	439	06.04.05	7654	200303	92705
686.685-030	FOLDER (narrow fabrics)	2122	44434444355	LNNNNNNFFFNNNNFNNONN	NNNN3NNNNNNNNNN	R,T	054	423	06.04.05	7659	200303	92998
686.685-034	HANDLE-AND-VENT-MACHINE OPERATOR (furniture)	2112	44443544345	HNNONONFFONNNNFNNFON	NNNN3NNNNNNNNNN	R	062	464	06.04.20	7659	000000	92998
686.685-038	PERFORATING-MACHINE OPERATOR (hat & cap)	2122	44344434345	LNNNNNNNFFONNNNFNNOONN	NNNN4NNNNNNNNNN	R,T	134	445	06.04.05	7659	200303	92944
686.685-042	PINKING-MACHINE OPERATOR (boot & shoe; garment)	2123	44444433345	LNNNNNNNFFNNNNFNNOON	NNNN3NNNNNNNNNN	R,T	054	440	06.04.05	7654	200303	92705
686.685-046	PREP.-EATER (tex. prod., nec)	3123	34434434345	LNNNNNNCCONNNNNNNNNN	NNNN4NNNNNNNNNN	R,T	062	435	06.04.05	7659	200502	92998
686.685-050	PRESS OPERATOR (protective dev.)	2113	44544544445	LNNNNNNFFONNNNNNNNNN	NNNN3NNNNNNNNNN	R,T	063	604	06.04.05	7657	000000	92728
686.685-054	RIVET-HOLE PUNCHER (garment)	2112	44445534345	LNNNNNNNFFONNNNFNNNNN	NNNN3NNNNNNNNNN	R,T	134	440	06.04.05	7659	200303	92998
686.685-058	SCALLOP CUTTER, MACHINE (tex. prod., nec)	2112	44434434355	LNOONNFFONNNNFNOFNN	NNNN4NNONNNNNNN	R,T	054	432	06.04.05	7654	200303	92705
686.685-062	SHOE-LACE-TIPPING-MACHINE OPERATOR (narrow fabrics)	2112	44444444354	HNNONONFFONNNNFNNFON	NNNN3NNNNNNNNNN	R,T	054	423	06.04.20	7659	000000	92998
686.685-066	STRIP-CUTTING-MACHINE OPERATOR (textile)	2112	44444434354	HNNONONFFONNNNFNFON	NNNN4NNNNNNNNNN	R,T	054	420	06.04.05	7659	200303	92705
686.685-070	TUBULAR-SPLITTING-MACHINE TENDER (textile)	2122	44444434355	MNNNNNCCONNNNCNCNCNN	NNNN3NNNNNNNNNN	R	054	424	06.04.05	7659	000000	92998
686.685-074	WELT-TRIMMING-MACHINE OPERATOR (hat & cap)	3123	44435033345	LNNNNNNFFNNNNCNNCFN	NNNN4NNNNNNNNNN	R,T	054	445	06.04.05	7654	200303	92705
686.686-010	FELT-TIPPING-MACHINE TENDER (pen & pencil)	1111	44554544455	LNNNNNNFFONNNNNFNFNN	NNNN3NNNNNNNNNN	R	051	617	06.04.09	8725	000000	98502
686.686-014	RUG-CUTTER HELPER (carpet & rug)	2122	44444444455	MNNFNFNFFNNNNNNNNNN	NNNN3NNNNNNNNNN	R	054	431	06.04.05	8617	000000	98999
687.132-010	SUPERVISOR, TUFTING (carpet & rug)	4346	33333444354	LNNNNNNOOONFFNFONNNN	NNNN3NNNNNNNNNN	D,P,V	166	431	06.02.01	7100	000000	81008
687.464-010	RUG-FRAME MOUNTER (carpet & rug)	2123	44343433354	HNONNNNFFONNNNFNONN	NNNN3NNNNNNNNNN	R	166	431	06.04.27	7759	000000	93999
687.682-010	FLOWER-MACHINE OPERATOR (tex. prod., nec)	3124	44443433344	LNNNNNNCCFNNNNCNFFFN	NNNN4NNNNNNNNNN	R,T	166	420	06.02.05	7659	000000	92998
687.682-014	TUFT-MACHINE OPERATOR (carpet & rug; tex. prod., nec)	3124	44443433344	LNNNNNNCCNNNNNCNFCFN	NNNN4NNNNNNNNNN	R,T	166	420	06.02.05	7659	000000	92998
687.684-010	RUG HOOKER (carpet & rug)	3125	44433433354	LNNNNNNCCONNNNCNOCFN	NNNN3NNNNNNNNNN	R,T	166	431	06.02.27	7759	000000	93999
687.684-014	TUFTER (furniture)	2114	44444543355	MNNFNONFFNNNNNFNFNN	NNNN4NNNNNNNNNN	R	166	464	06.04.05	7759	000000	93999
687.685-010	NEEDLE-CONTROL CHENILLER (tex. prod., nec)	3223	34443433354	MNNNNNNFFNNNNCNCCON	NNNN4NNNNNNNNNN	R,T	166	420	06.04.05	7659	000000	92998
687.685-014	TUFTING-MACHINE OPERATOR (furniture)	2123	44434434354	MNNNNNNFFNNNNFNFOON	NNNN4NNNNNNNNNN	R,T	166	464	06.04.05	7659	000000	92998
687.685-018	TUFTING-MACHINE OPERATOR (carpet & rug; textile)	3233	34443433354	MNNOONCCFNNNNCNFFFN	NNNN4NNNNNNNNNN	R,T	166	420	06.04.05	7659	000000	92998
687.685-022	TUFTING-MACHINE OPERATOR, SINGLE-NEEDLE (carpet & rug)	2123	44444433344	LNNNONCCCNNNNOCOFON	NNNN3NNNNNNNNNN	R,T	166	431	06.04.05	7659	000000	92998
689.130-010	EMBROIDERY SUPERVISOR (tex. prod., nec)	4347	33332333343	LNNOOONFFFNFONOONN	NNNN4NNNNNNNNNN	V,D,P,J	171	432	06.02.01	6700	200303	81008
689.130-014	FELT-GOODS SUPERVISOR, NEEDLE PROCESS (tex. prod., nec)	4338	33323343355	LNNNNNNFFOOFFNFONNNN	NNNN3NONNNNNNNN	D,P,J	171	422	06.02.01	7100	000000	81008
689.130-018	KNITTING-MACHINE FIXER, HEAD (knitting)	4347	33333344454	LNNONONFFONFNFNNFON	NNNN4NNNNNNNNNN	D,P,J,T	165	424	06.01.01	7100	520205	81008
689.130-022	SUPERVISOR, CLOTH WINDING (tex. prod., nec)	4336	33444444454	LNNONONFFONOONFNOOON	NNNN4NNNNNNNNNN	D,P,J	163	436	06.02.01	7100	000000	81008
689.130-026	SUPERVISOR, ROVING DEPARTMENT (textile)	4337	33333333355	LNNNNNNFFNFNFONFNN	NNNN4NNNNNNNNNN	V,D,P,J	054	419	06.01.01	7100	000000	81008
689.130-030	SUPERVISOR, WEAVING (carpet & rug)	4336	33333334454	LNNNNNNFFONFFNFONOON	NNNN4NNNNNNNNNN	D,P,J,T	164	431	06.02.01	7100	000000	81008
689.130-034	SUPERVISOR, YARN PREPARATION (textile)	4347	33333343355	LNNFFFNFFFFNFFOFNN	NNNN4NNNNNNNNNN	D,P,V	161	411	06.01.01	7100	520205	81008
689.130-038	SUPERVISOR, SPINNING AND WINDING (plastic-synth.)	4237	23344334334	MFNOONNFFOOFFNFFONOO	NNNN4NNNNNNNNNO	V,T,P,J	163	414	06.02.01	7100	520205	81008

DOT #	DOT Title & Industry	Trmg	Aptitude	Physical	Environment	Tempra	WkF	MPSMS	GOE	SOC	CIP	OES
689.132-010	SUPERVISOR, BURLING AND JOINING (textile)	4346	33333333355	MNNFFFNFFNFFNFNFNNFNN	NNNN3NNNNNNNNNNN	D,V,P,T	164	420	06.02.01	7100	150699	81008
689.132-014	SUPERVISOR, FIBER-LOCKING (textile)	4346	33333333355	LNNFNNNNFFNFFNFFFONN	NNNN4NNNNNNNNNNN	D,V,P	161	414	06.02.01	7100	150699	81008
689.134-010	CLOTH-GRADER SUPERVISOR (textile)	4337	32433444454	LNNONNNFFONFFNFNNOON	NNNN4NNNNNNNNNNN	D,P,J,T	212	420	06.01.01	7100	000000	81008
689.134-014	SUPERVISOR, LACE TEARING (tex. prod., nec)	4337	33333344454	LNNNNNNNFFFFFFNFOFN	NNNN4NNNNNNNNNNN	D,P,J,T	163	432	06.02.01	7100	000000	81008
689.134-018	SUPERVISOR, PRODUCT INSPECTION (textile)	4236	33343443453	LNNNNNNNFFFFFFNFOFN	NNNN4NNNNNNNNNNN	D,P	212	420	06.02.01	7100	000000	81008
689.134-022	SUPERVISOR, QUILTING (textile)	4236	33343433344	MNNNNNNNFFNFFNFNFNFON	NNNN4NNNNNNNNNNN	D,P,J,T	171	435	06.02.01	7100	000000	81008
689.134-026	SUPERVISOR, LABORATORY (textile)	4346	22232334355	MNNNNNNNFFNFFNFNFNFNN	NNNN4NNNNNNNNNNN	D,V,P,T	211	410	02.04.01	1845	520205	24105
689.137-010	SUPERVISOR, SEWING DEPARTMENT (carpet & rug)	4336	33343344453	LNNNNNNNFFFNFNFNOOON	NNNN4NNNNNNNNNNN	D,P,J	171	431	06.02.01	7100	000000	81008
689.137-014	SUPERVISOR, TUBING (textile)	3226	34343344453	HNNONNNFFOOFFNFNNOOFN	NNNN3NNNNNNNNNNN	D,T,P	212	420	06.02.01	7100	520205	81008
689.260-010	MACHINE FIXER (textile)	4236	33433433354	MNNFFNFFFFFFFNFOFOON	NNNN4NOONNNNNNNNN	V,J,T	212	411	06.01.02	7451	470303	92702
689.260-014	QUILTER FIXER (tex. prod., nec)	4336	33433433354	LNNFNFNFFFOOONFNFOON	NNNN4NNNNNNNNNNN	J,T	171	420	06.01.02	7459	470303	92702
689.260-018	SECTION LEADER AND MACHINE SETTER (textile)	4246	33323333354	MOOFFFNFFFFFFFFFFON	NNNN4NNNNNNNNNNN	D,T,V	161	411	06.01.02	7459	470303	92702
689.260-022	SECTION LEADER AND MACHINE SETTER, POLISHING (textile)	3335	33333334355	MNNFNFNCCCFOONFNNFFN	NNNN4NNNNNNNNNNN	V,J,T	151	412	06.01.02	7459	470303	92702
689.260-026	KNITTING-MACHINE FIXER (knitting)	4337	33422833354	LNFOONFFFOOONFNFFON	NNNN4NNNNNNNNNNN	V,T,J	121	420	06.01.02	7452	470303	92702
689.280-010	BOX TENDER (plastic-synth.)	4336	33333432255	MNNFNFNFFFOONFFNFNN	NNNN4NNNNNNNNNNN	V,J,T	162	492	06.01.02	7451	470303	92702
689.324-010	INSTRUCTOR (textile)	3226	33333333354	MONFNNNFFFFCCNFNFOON	NNNN4NNONNNNNNNN	V,D,P,T	296	420	06.02.01	2390	000000	31314
689.360-010	NEEDLE-LOOM SETTER (tex. prod., nec)	3236	34333444355	LNNONONFFONNNNFNNONN	NNNN4NNONNNNNNNN	J,T	171	422	06.01.02	7459	470303	92702
689.362-010	NEEDLE-FELT-MAKING-MACHINE OPERATOR (tex. prod., nec)	3235	34433444355	LNNONONFFONNNNFOOONN	NNNN3NNONNNNNNNN	V,J,T	161	439	06.02.06	7459	000000	92702
689.364-010	STROBOSCOPE OPERATOR (textile)	3235	34442443355	LNNONONFFNOONFONFNN	NNNN3NNNNNNNNNNN	J,T	212	410	06.03.01	6140	470303	85128
689.364-014	PROCESS CONTROLLER (textile)	3334	33342334354	LONNNFNFFNOONFNNFFON	NNNN3NNNNNNNNNNN	T,J	211	567	06.03.01	7830	470303	83005
689.366-010	HEAD DOFFER (textile)	3234	34343333355	LNNONONFFFNFNFNFNN	NNNN4NNNNNNNNNNN	D,V,P	162	411	06.01.01	7850	000000	83005
689.380-010	EMBLEM DRAWER-IN (tex. prod., nec)	3233	34433443354	LNNOONFFNOONFNNOON	NNNN3NNNNNNNNNNN	R	165	432	06.01.02	4752	200303	92998
689.382-010	AUTOMATIC-PAD-MAKING-MACHINE OPERATOR (tex. prod., nec)	3234	34333443355	MNNONNNFFNNNNNFNNFNN	NNNN4NNONNNNNNNN	J,T	054	433	06.02.18	7459	000000	92702
689.384-010	CLOTH TESTER, QUALITY (textile)	3334	34434434345	LNIFNNNFFNOONFNNFFN	NNNN3NNONNNNNNNN	V,J,T	212	420	06.03.01	7830	000000	83005
689.387-010	LABORATORY TESTER (textile)	3334	33333333354	LNNONONFFONONFOFFN	NNNN3NNNNNNNNNNN	V,J,T	212	410	06.03.01	7830	470303	83005
689.564-010	NUMBERER AND WIRER (textile)	3125	34443444352	LNNONONFFONNNNCNNCCN	NNNN4NNCNNNNNNN	R	062	567	06.04.06	7759	000000	93999
689.662-010	NEEDLE-LOOM OPERATOR (tex. prod., nec)	3235	34433343355	MNNONNNFFOOOONFNOONN	NNNN4NNCNNNNNNN	J,T	171	422	06.02.06	7652	200303	92998
689.662-014	STRIPE MATCHER (knitting)	3223	34433433344	LNNOOOOFOOFFNFNNFFN	NNNN4NNCNNNNNNN	R,T	054	424	06.02.05	7655	200303	92721
689.665-010	STRAP BUCKLER, MACHINE (garment)	2123	44443443335	SNNNNNNNFFNNNNNNFNNON	NNNN4NNCNNNNNNN	R	062	440	06.04.05	7659	200303	92998
689.665-014	THREAD-CUTTER TENDER (tex. prod., nec)	3122	44444434235	LNNONNNFFONNNNFNNONN	NNNN4OONNNNNNNN	R,T	054	432	06.04.05	7654	200303	92705
689.665-018	VACUUM-TANK TENDER (textile)	2112	44544445355	MNNFNNNFFONONONNNNNN	NNNN4NNNNNNNNNNN	R	031	419	06.04.16	7659	000000	92998
689.667-010	RUG INSPECTOR I (carpet & rug)	2123	44443444453	LNNONONFFOONINNCNNOON	NNNN3NNNNNNNNNNN	R,T	212	431	06.03.02	7820	000000	83005
689.682-010	LOOPER (knitting)	3124	44432424444	LNNONNNNCCNNNNCNNCON	NNNN4NNCNNNNNNN	J,T	165	424	06.02.06	7820	000000	93999
689.682-014	NEEDLE-PUNCH-MACHINE OPERATOR (textile)	2123	34443443354	LNNONNNCCNNNNNFNFON	NNNN4NNNNNNNNNNN	R,T	165	425	06.04.05	7659	200303	92998
689.682-018	SPLICING-MACHINE OPERATOR (tex. prod., nec)	2114	44443433344	LNNNNNNFFONNNNFFON	NNNN4NNNNNNNNNNN	R	171	413	06.02.05	7655	000000	92721
689.682-022	STITCHER (tex. prod., nec)	3224	34434433345	LNNNNNNCCNNNNNCNNNNNN	NNNN4OONNNNNNNN	R,T	171	432	06.04.05	7659	200303	83005
689.684-010	BURLER (carpet & rug; textile)	3123	34443443344	LNNONONFFFNNNNFNNNNN	NNNN3NNNNNNNNNNN	R,T	212	420	06.03.02	7820	000000	83005
689.684-014	DRAWER-IN, STITCH-BONDING MACHINE (textile)	2112	44444443354	LNNNNNNCCNNNNFFNNNNN	NNNN4NNNNNNNNNNN	R	165	425	06.04.05	7759	000000	93999
689.684-018	LEASE PICKER (textile)	3123	34433433355	MNNNNNNNFFNNNNFNFNNN	NNNN4NNNNNNNNNNN	R	164	411	06.04.27	7759	150699	93999
689.685-010	BALL-FRINGE-MACHINE OPERATOR (tex. prod., nec)	2113	34545445355	LNNNONNFFONNNNNNNNNN	NNNN4NNNNNNNNNNN	R	163	432	06.04.05	7659	000000	92998
689.685-014	BLOCKER (narrow fabrics; nonmet. min.)	2122	44443444344	LNNNNNNFFONNNNNNNONO	NNNN4NNNNNNNNNNN	R	163	423	06.04.19	7651	000000	92705
689.685-018	BOBBIN PRESSER (tex. prod., nec)	2112	44445533355	MNNFNNNFFONNNFFNNNN	NNNN4ONNNNNNNNNN	R,T	134	559	06.04.19	7657	000000	92728
689.685-022	BOBBIN STRIPPER (tex. prod., nec)	2112	44545533355	LNNNNNNCCNNNNNCNNNNNN	NNNN4NNNNNNNNNNN	R	163	559	06.04.05	7659	000000	92998
689.685-026	BOUFFANT-CURTAIN-MACHINE TENDER (tex. prod., nec)	3124	34443434344	LNNNNNNCCFNNNNCNNNFN	NNNN4NNNNNNNNNNN	R,T	171	435	06.04.05	7655	200502	92721
689.685-030	BOW-MAKER-MACHINE TENDER, AUTOMATIC (tex. prod., nec)	2113	44444443354	LNNNNNNFFFNNNFNFNON	NNNN4NNNNNNNNNNN	R	062	423	06.04.05	7659	000000	92998

DOT #	DOT Title & Industry	Trng	Aptitude	Physical	Environment	Tempra	WkF	MPSMS	GOE	SOC	CIP	OES
689.685-034	BUFFING-WHEEL FORMER, AUTOMATIC (tex. prod., nec)	2122	44443434355	MNNNNNNFFONNNNFNNNNN	NNNN4NNNNNNNNNN	R,T	062	538	06.04.16	7659	000000	92998
689.685-038	CLOTH EXAMINER, MACHINE (textile)	3223	34443443344	MNNFNNCCOONFNFNNOFN	NNNN4NNNNNNNNNN	J,T	212	420	06.03.02	7820	000000	83005
689.685-042	CLOTH REELER (textile)	2112	44544444455	MNNNNNNNFFONNNNNNNNNN	NNNN3NNNNNNNNNN	R	032	420	06.04.06	7659	000000	92705
689.685-046	CLOTH WINDER (textile)	2112	44443444344	MNNONONFFONNNNNFNNON	NNNN4NNNNNNNNNN	R	163	420	06.04.06	7651	000000	92705
689.685-050	CLOTH-DOUBLING-AND-WINDING-MACHINE OPERATOR (textile)	2113	44443444344	MNNNNNNNFFONNNNNONNON	NNNN4NNNNNNNNNN	R,T	163	420	06.04.06	7651	000000	92705
689.685-054	CRUSHER-AND-BINDER OPERATOR (tex. prod., nec)	2112	44544544355	LNNNNNNFFFNNNNNNNNNN	NNNN3NNNNNNNNNN	R	062	413	06.04.06	7659	000000	92998
689.685-058	DRAWSTRING KNOTTER (tex. prod., nec)	2112	44444444455	LNNNNNNFFONNNNONONNN	NNNN4NNNNNNNNNN	R	062	439	06.04.05	7659	000000	92998
689.685-062	DROP-WIRE ALIGNER (textile)	1112	44443443355	LNNNNNNCCCNNNNCNNNNN	NNNN3NNNNNNNNNN	R	061	557	06.04.06	7659	000000	92998
689.685-066	FISHING-LINE-WINDING-MACHINE OPERATOR (tex. prod., nec)	2112	44455533355	LNNNNNNNFFNNNNNNNNNN	NNNN3NNNNNNNNNN	R	163	616	06.04.39	7651	000000	92998
689.685-070	HEDDLE CLEANER, MACHINE (textile)	2112	44444443455	HNNFNNCCFNNNNFNFNNN	NNNN4NNNNNNNNNN	R	031	567	06.04.39	7659	000000	92998
689.685-074	HELMET COVERER (hat & cap)	2113	44444434345	LNNNNNNNFFONNNNONNNN	NNNN4NNNNNNNNNN	R,T	032	445	06.04.20	7659	000000	92998
689.685-078	HOOKER INSPECTOR (textile)	3123	34443434344	MNNNNNNNFFOFNNNFNNFON	NNNN3NNNNNNNNNN	J,T	212	420	06.03.02	7820	000000	83005
689.685-082	KAPOK-AND-COTTON-MACHINE OPERATOR (tex. prod., nec)	2112	44444444345	MNNNNNNNFFONNNNNNNNNN	NNNN4NONNNNNNNNN	R	031	419	06.04.16	7659	000000	92998
689.685-086	LABEL-CUTTING-AND-FOLDING-MACHINE OPERATOR, AUTOMATIC (narrow fabrics)	2112	44443434455	LNNNNNNNFFONNNNNONNNON	NNNN4NNNNNNNNNN	R,T	054	423	06.04.05	7659	200303	92944
689.685-090	NEEDLE-LOOM TENDER (tex. prod., nec)	3123	44444544355	LNNFNFNFFNNNNNNNNNNN	NNNN4NFONNNNNNNN	R,T	171	422	06.04.06	7659	000000	92998
689.685-094	PICK-PULLING-MACHINE OPERATOR (textile)	2112	44544544445	MNNNNNNNFFNNNNNONONN	NNNN3NNNNNNNNNN	R	164	420	06.04.06	7659	000000	92998
689.685-098	PICK-UP OPERATOR (textile)	2122	34443433345	LNNNNNNNFFNNNNNFNNNN	NNNN4NNNNNNNNNN	R,T	212	421	06.03.02	7820	000000	83005
689.685-102	QUILT STUFFER, MACHINE (tex. prod., nec)	2122	44443443344	LNNONNNFFONNNNONONON	NNNN4NNNNNNNNNN	R	041	439	06.04.05	7659	000000	92998
689.685-106	QUILTING-MACHINE OPERATOR (glove & mit., tex. prod., nec)	3124	44443443455	MNNNNNFFFNNNNFNFFNN	NNNN4NNNNNNNNNN	R,T	171	420	06.04.05	7655	000000	92721
689.685-110	ROLL TURNER (knitting)	1112	44444443354	MNNNNNNCCFNNNONNNNNN	NNNN3NNNNNNNNNN	R	062	424	06.04.06	7659	000000	92998
689.685-114	ROLLING-MACHINE TENDER (knitting)	1112	44444444355	MNNONNNFFONNNNFNNNNN	NNNN4NNNNNNNNNN	R	163	424	06.04.16	7651	000000	92705
689.685-118	SEWING-MACHINE OPERATOR, SPECIAL EQUIPMENT (furniture)	2122	44443544354	LNNNNNNFFONNNNFNOOON	NNNN4NNNNNNNNNN	R,T	171	464	06.04.05	7655	000000	92721
689.685-122	SPLICING-MACHINE OPERATOR, AUTOMATIC (tex. prod., nec)	2112	34444433344	LNNFNNNFFNNNNFNNNNN	NNNN4NNNNNNNNNN	R	171	439	06.04.05	7659	000000	92998
689.685-126	STITCH-BONDING-MACHINE TENDER (textile)	2113	44443443354	MNNNNNNCCFNNNNFNFON	NNNN4NNNNNNNNNN	R	165	425	06.04.05	7655	000000	92721
689.685-130	SURGICAL-DRESSING MAKER (protective dev.)	2112	44444444444	LNNNNNNNFFONNNNNOONN	NNNN3NNNNNNNNNN	R,T	054	604	06.04.05	7659	000000	92998
689.685-134	TAPE-FOLDING-MACHINE OPERATOR (rubber goods; tex. prod., nec)	2123	44544544455	LNNNNNNNFFONNNNONNNNN	NNNN4NNNNNNNNNN	R,T	062	432	06.04.05	7659	000000	92998
689.685-138	TAPE-MAKING-MACHINE OPERATOR (tex. prod., nec)	2123	34444433355	LNNNNNNNFFNNNNNONNNN	NNNN3NNNNNNNNNN	R,T	063	413	06.04.04	7861	000000	92956
689.685-142	TASSEL-MAKING-MACHINE OPERATOR (tex. prod., nec)	2112	44544544445	LNNNNNNNFFNNNNNONNNN	NNNN4NNNNNNNNNN	R	162	439	06.04.06	7659	000000	92998
689.685-146	TURNING-MACHINE OPERATOR (tex. prod., nec)	2112	44444434345	LNNFNNNFFNNNNFNNNNN	NNNN4NNNNNNNNNN	R	062	436	06.04.05	7659	000000	92998
689.685-150	WATCHER, AUTOMAT (tex. prod., nec)	2124	44443533444	LNNNNNNNFFNNNNFNNCON	NNNN3NNNNNNNNNN	R,T	171	432	06.04.05	7655	000000	92717
689.685-154	WATCHER, PANTOGRAPH (tex. prod., nec)	2124	44543533444	LNNNNNNNFFNNNNFNNOON	NNNN4NNNNNNNNNN	R,T	171	432	06.04.05	7655	000000	92717
689.685-158	YARN-TEXTURING-MACHINE OPERATOR II (textile)	2113	44443433354	LNNONNNCCFNNNNFFNFON	NNNN4NNNNNNNNNN	R,T	161	411	06.04.16	7659	000000	92998
689.685-162	TOE PUNCHER (knitting)	2112	44444433355	LNNNNNNNCCCNNNNNNNNNN	NNNN3NNNNNNNNNN	R	032	425	06.04.06	7659	200303	92998
689.685-166	UTILITY TENDER, CARDING (textile)	2123	34444433354	MNNNNNNNFFNNNNFFNFNN	NNNN4NNNNNNNNNN	R	161	414	06.04.06	7659	200303	92711
689.686-010	AUTOMATIC-PAD-MAKING-MACHINE OPERATOR HELPER (tex. prod., nec)	2112	44544544455	MNNNNNNNCCONNNNFFNFON	NNNN4NNNNNNNNNN	R	171	433	06.04.05	8617	000000	98502
689.686-014	BOBBIN-CLEANING-MACHINE OPERATOR (textile)	1112	44444444354	MNNFNNNFFNNNNNONONNN	NNNN4NNNNNNNNNN	R	031	410	06.04.05	8725	000000	98502
689.686-018	CUTTING-MACHINE OFFBEARER (tex. prod., nec)	2112	44444433345	HNFNNNNFFONNNNFNNNNN	NNNF4NNNNNNNNNN	R	011	410	06.04.40	8769	000000	98999
689.686-022	DOFFER (textile)	2122	44444443344	MNNFNNNFFNNONFFFFON	NNNN4NFNNNNNNNN	R	162	410	06.04.06	8725	000000	98502
689.686-026	FRAME CHANGER (textile)	2112	44454444454	LNNONNNFFNNNNNNNNNNN	NNNN4NNNNNNNNNN	R	162	412	06.04.06	6140	000000	85128
689.686-030	HAIR-SPINNING-MACHINE OPERATOR (leather mfg.)	1111	44444533355	HNNNNNNFFFNNNNNNONNNN	NNNO3NONNNNNNNNN	R	162	529	06.04.05	8725	000000	98502
689.686-034	NEEDLE-PUNCH-MACHINE-OPERATOR HELPER (textile)	1112	44444543354	LNNNNNNFFNNNNFNFON	NNNN4NNNNNNNNNN	R	165	425	06.04.05	8617	000000	98999
689.686-038	SHUTTLE HAND (textile)	2112	44544533454	LNNCNNNFFNNNNNONNOON	NNNN4NONNNNNNNN	R	164	420	06.04.06	8725	000000	98502
689.686-042	STITCH-BONDING-MACHINE-TENDER HELPER (textile)	1112	44444444354	MNNNNNNCCONNNNFFNFON	NNNN4NNNNNNNNNN	R	165	425	06.04.05	8617	000000	98999
689.686-046	THREAD-PULLING-MACHINE ATTENDANT (garment)	1111	44444434355	LNNNNNNCCNNNNNNFNNNN	NNNN3NNNNNNNNNN	R	031	442	06.04.05	8725	000000	98502
689.686-050	UTILITY WORKER, WOOLEN MILL (textile)	2112	44454434345	HNFNNNNFFONNNNFNNNNN	NNNF4NNNNNNNNNN	R	011	410	06.04.40	8769	000000	98999
689.686-054	WASTE CHOPPER (tex. prod., nec)	2112	44454444454	LNNNNNNNFFONNNNONNNON	NNNN4NNNNNNNNNN	R	054	412	06.04.16	8725	000000	98502
689.686-058	CLOTH DOFFER (textile)	2122	44444444344	HNNFFFNFFFNNNNONNNNNN	NNNN4NCNNNNNNNNN	R	011	420	06.04.06	8725	000000	98502
689.687-010	BAGGING SALVAGER (textile)	1111	44544543455	LNFNFNFFFNNNNNNNNNNN	NNNN4NNNNNNNNNN	R	031	436	06.04.38	8769	000000	98999
689.687-014	BOBBIN CLEANER, HAND (textile)	1112	44544543354	HONONONCCFNNNNONNNNON	NNNN5NNNNNNNNNN	R	031	410	06.04.39	8769	000000	98999
689.687-018	BUNDLE BREAKER (tex. prod., nec)	1112	44443434355	LNNOONNNFFNNNNONNNNNN	NNNN4NONNNNNNNN	R	011	414	06.04.40	8769	000000	98999
689.687-022	CLOTH EXAMINER, HAND (narrow fabrics)	2112	44443434354	LNNNNNNFFONNNNNFNNFON	NNNN4NNNNNNNNNN	R,T	212	423	06.03.02	7820	000000	83005

DOT #	DOT Title & Industry	Trng	Aptitude	Physical	Environment	Tempra	WkF	MPSMS	GOE	SOC	CIP	OES
689.687-026	CLOTH FRAMER (textile)	2112	44544544455	MNNFNFFONNNNONNONN	NNNN4NNNNNNNNN	R	163	420	06.04.38	7740	000000	93999
689.687-030	CREELER (textile)	2112	44444443454	MONFNFNCCFNNONOFOOON	NNNN4NNNNNNNNN	R	163	411	06.04.05	8769	000000	98999
689.687-034	DROP-WIRE BUILDER (textile)	2112	44444443355	LNNNONONFFNNNNNNNNN	NNNN4NNNNNNNNN	R	031	567	06.01.02	7740	000000	93999
689.687-038	END FINDER, ROVING DEPARTMENT (glass mfg.)	2122	44444443355	LNNNNNFFFNNNFNFNNN	NNNN4NNNNNNNNN	R	163	411	06.04.27	8769	000000	98999
689.687-042	END FINDER, TWISTING DEPARTMENT (textile)	2122	44444443355	MNNNNNNFFONNNNNNNNN	NNNN4NNNNNNNNN	R	163	419	06.04.27	8769	000000	98999
689.687-046	FRAME HAND (tex. prod., nec)	1112	44544544344	LNNNNNNFFFNNNNOFNFFN	NNNN4NNNNNNNNN	R	171	432	06.04.27	8769	000000	98999
689.687-050	OIL-SPOT WASHER (tex. prod., nec; textile)	2112	44544544454	LNNNNNNFFNNNNOFNFFN	NNNN3NNNNNNNNN	R	031	420	06.04.39	8769	200309	98999
689.687-054	PEGGER, DOBBY LOOMS (narrow fabrics; textile)	2122	44444443355	LNNNNNNFFFNNNNONNONN	NNNN3NNNNNNNNN	R	164	420	06.04.06	7740	000000	93999
689.687-058	PICK REMOVER (textile)	1112	44544544455	MNNNNNNNFFONNNNONNNN	NNNN3NNNNNNNNN	R	054	420	06.04.27	8769	000000	98999
689.687-062	RAW-SILK GRADER (textile)	3224	33442434453	SNNNNNFFFNNNFNNOFN	NNNN4NNNNNNNNN	J,T	212	414	06.03.02	7850	000000	83005
689.687-066	RUG CLEANER (carpet & rug)	2112	44443554354	LNNNNNNFFFNNNNNNNNN	NNNN4NNNNNNNNN	R	031	431	06.02.16	8769	200309	98999
689.687-070	SHUTTLER (tex. prod., nec)	2112	44544544455	LNNNNNNFFFNNNNFNNONN	NNNN4NNNNNNNNN	R	061	432	06.04.06	6140	000000	85128
689.687-074	SPANNER (tex. prod., nec)	1112	44544544355	LNNNNNNFFONNNNNNNNN	NNNN3NNNNNNNNN	R	062	432	06.04.06	7659	000000	92998
689.687-078	THREADER (tex. prod., nec)	2112	44444544355	LNNNNNNFFFNNNNNNNNN	NNNN4NNNNNNNNN	R	061	411	06.04.06	7740	000000	93999
689.687-082	YARN EXAMINER, SKEINS (textile)	2113	34443433353	LNNFNNNFFFNNNNFNNFON	NNNN4NNNNNNNNNN	R,J,T	212	411	06.03.02	7820	000000	83005
689.687-086	YARN SORTER (textile)	2122	44444444454	LNNOONNFFFONNNFNNFN	NNNN4NNNNNNNNN	R	221	410	06.03.02	7850	000000	83005
689.687-090	LAPPER (textile)	2112	44434534354	MNNONONFFFNNFFNFNNNON	NNNN4NNNNNNNNN	R	162	411	06.04.16	7753	200303	93926
690.130-010	SUPERVISOR III (button & notion)	3236	33333332255	MNNNNNNNFFNFFNFNNNN	NNNN4NNNNNNNNN	V,D,P	057	618	06.02.01	7100	000000	81008
690.130-014	SUPERVISOR, SLITTING-AND-SHIPPING (plastic-synth.)	4337	33333333344	MNNONONFFFNNFNNNON	NNNN3NNNNNNNNN	V,D,P,J	054	492	06.02.01	7100	000000	81008
690.130-018	SUPERVISOR (plastic prod.)	4346	33333333344	LNNONNNFFFNFNFFFN	NNNN4NNOONNNNNN	T,P,J,D	134	519	06.02.01	7100	150607	81008
690.130-022	SUPERVISOR, FOAM CUTTING (tex. prod., nec)	3226	34434344355	HNNFNNNFFONOONFNFNNN	NNNN4NNNNNNNNN	D,T,P	054	519	06.02.01	7100	520205	81008
690.280-010	DEBURRING-AND-TOOLING-MACHINE OPERATOR (office machines)	4438	33333344355	MNNNNNNFFONNNNFFFONN	NNNN3NNNNNNNNN	T,J	057	519	06.01.03	7329	480503	91114
690.360-010	WAD-BLANKING-PRESS ADJUSTER (ordnance)	3224	33333443355	LNNONONFFFNOOONFNONN	NNNN4NNNNNNNNN	V,J,T	134	422	06.01.02	7479	000000	92997
690.362-010	LEAD OPERATOR, AUTOMATIC VULCANIZING (rubber goods)	3225	33324443354	MNNNONFFFNNONFNOOONN	NNNN3NNNNNNNNN	V,J,T	133	514	06.02.07	7479	000000	92997
690.380-010	MACHINE SETTER (button & notion)	3235	33333433344	MNNFNFNFFFNNNFFNNNNN	NNNN4NNNNNNNNN	J,T	057	618	06.01.02	7479	000000	92997
690.380-014	MACHINE SETTER-AND-REPAIRER (plastic prod.)	3224	34423422343	HNNNNNNFFNNOOFNGOONN	NNNN4NNNNNNNNN	T,J	081	509	06.01.02	7329	150607	92197
690.382-010	SHEETER OPERATOR (plastic-synth.)	3224	34333334344	LNNNNNNFFONNNNFNOOON	NNNN4NNONNNNNNF	R,T	054	492	06.02.02	7549	000000	92198
690.382-014	WEATHERSTRIP-MACHINE OPERATOR (rubber goods)	3234	33343444355	MNNNNNNFFFNNNNFNONNN	NNNN3NNNNNNNNN	R,J,T	136	519	06.02.09	7479	000000	92997
690.385-010	PLATEN GRINDER (office machines)	3123	34443434355	LNNNNNNFFONNNFNNNNN	NNNN3NNNNNNNNN	R,J,T	051	519	06.04.07	7677	000000	92965
690.462-010	OUTSOLE CUTTER, AUTOMATIC (rubber goods)	3224	33344444355	MNNONONFFONOOFNNNNN	NNNN4NNNNNNNNN	R,T	054	512	06.02.09	7478	480304	92941
690.482-010	SAWYER (plastic prod.; plastic-synth.)	3225	44443434355	MNNONONFFFONONNNFNN	NNNN4NFNNNNNNN	R,T	056	510	06.02.07	7463	000000	92968
690.482-014	TRIMMER (plastic prod.)	3224	44443434345	LNNNONFFFNNNFFNNNNN	NNNN4NFNNNNNNN	R,T	057	519	06.04.02	7514	000000	92198
690.485-010	BAND-SAWING-MACHINE OPERATOR (fabrication, nec)	2123	44444534355	MNNONONFFNONNNFNFNN	NNNN4NONNNNNNNF	R,T	056	619	06.04.09	7678	000000	92944
690.580-010	HIDE SPLITTER (leather mfg.)	3224	34434444355	LNNNNNNFFFNNNNONNNN	NNNO4NNONNNNNNN	D,T	054	521	06.02.05	7479	000000	92997
690.585-010	MILL-ROLL REWINDER (plastic-synth.)	2124	44434434355	MNNNNNNFFFNNFNFFNN	NNNN4NNNNNNNNNF	R,T	163	492	06.04.02	7679	000000	92998
690.585-014	MOTTLE-LAY-UP OPERATOR (plastic-synth.)	2224	34334434343	LNNNONNFFFNNNNFNONON	NNNN4NNNNNNNNNO	R,T	054	492	06.04.02	7514	000000	91321
690.662-010	TIRE-REGROOVING-MACHINE OPERATOR (automotive ser.)	3234	44433333344	MNNOOONFFONNNNFNONON	ONNN3NNNNNNNNNO	J	054	511	05.12.13	7479	000000	92997
690.662-014	TUBER-MACHINE OPERATOR (rubber goods; rubber tire)	3224	33433434355	MNNONONFFFONNNNNNNN	NNNN4NNNNNNNNN	R,J,T	135	510	06.02.07	7463	000000	92968
690.665-010	SLASHER (plastic-synth.)	2113	34443434355	LNNNONNFFFNNNNNNNNN	NNNN3NNNNNNNNN	R,T	054	492	06.04.02	7514	000000	92198
690.680-010	RUBBER-GOODS CUTTER-FINISHER (rubber goods)	3234	33433433355	MNNNNNNFFONNNNFFNN	NNNN3NNNNNNNNN	R,J,T	054	519	06.01.03	7479	000000	92997
690.682-010	ARCH-CUSHION-SKIVING-MACHINE OPERATOR (rubber goods)	3224	34334434345	MNNONONFFFNNNNFOOONN	NNNN3NNNNNNNNN	J,R	054	512	06.02.07	7478	480304	92941
690.682-014	BALL-TRUING-MACHINE OPERATOR (toy-sport equip.)	3225	33433534344	MNNONONFFONNNFNOOON	NNNF4NNONNNNNNN	R,J,T	051	616	06.02.09	7477	000000	92998
690.682-018	BED LASTER (boot & shoe)	3225	34433433334	LNNNONNCCFNNNNFNFON	NNNN4NNNNNNNNN	R,J,T	061	522	06.02.05	7679	480304	92944
690.682-022	BIAS-MACHINE OPERATOR (rubber tire)	3224	33433433355	MNNNNNNFFNNNNNNNNN	NNNN3NNNNNNNNN	R,J,T	054	519	06.02.09	7678	000000	92997
690.682-026	CUTTER, BARREL DRUM (tex. prod., nec)	3124	34444434344	MNNONONFFONNNNNNNNN	NNNN3NNNNNNNNN	R,T	054	435	06.02.02	7651	000000	92705
690.682-030	EMBOSSER (leather mfg.; leather prod.)	3234	44443443344	LNNNONNFFFNNNNFNONON	NNNF4NFNNNNNNNN	R,J	192	520	06.02.05	7679	000000	92998
690.682-034	EMBOSSING-PRESS OPERATOR, MOLDED GOODS (fabrication, nec)	3225	34343434355	LONNNNNFFFNNNNFNONON	LNNNN4NFNNNNNNN	J,T	192	619	06.02.09	7479	000000	92997
690.682-038	FOXING-CUTTING-MACHINE OPERATOR, AUTOMATIC (boot & shoe)	3224	44434434355	LNNONONFFONNNNONONNN	NNNN4NNONNNNNNNF	R,J	054	512	06.02.05	7478	480304	92941
690.682-042	HEEL BREASTER, LEATHER (boot & shoe)	3224	44444434345	LNNNONNFFFONNNNNONNN	NNNN3NONNNNNNNN	R,J,T	054	522	06.02.05	7478	480304	92941
690.682-046	HEEL-SEAT FITTER, MACHINE (boot & shoe)	3224	44443444345	LNNNNNNFFONNNNONNNNN	NNNN3NNONNNNNNN	R,T	054	522	06.02.05	7478	480304	92941
690.682-050	HOT-DIE-PRESS OPERATOR (boot & shoe)	3224	44444444455	LNNNNNNNFFONNNNNONNNNN	NNON4NNNNNNNNN	R,T	134	512	06.02.09	7478	480304	92941

DOT #	DOT Title & Industry	Trng	Aptitude	Physical	Environment	Tempra	WkF	MPSMS	GOE	SOC	CIP	OES
690.682-054	ORNAMENTAL-MACHINE OPERATOR (wood prod., nec)	3224	34433433354	LNNNNNNFFNNNNFNNNON	NNNN4NNNNNNNNNN	R,T	132	457	06.02.09	7669	000000	92953
690.682-058	PLANISHING-PRESS OPERATOR (plastic-synth.)	3225	34444433344	HNNNONONFFONNNFNNONN	NNNN4NNONNNNNNO	R,T	134	492	06.02.02	7549	000000	92198
690.682-062	PRESS OPERATOR (plastic prod.)	3224	44443434355	HNNONNNFFONNNNFNNNN	NNFN3NNNNNNNNN	R,T	134	519	06.02.02	7549	000000	92198
690.682-066	RING-ROLLING-MACHINE OPERATOR (rubber goods)	3234	44443533355	LNNNNNNFFNNNNNNNNN	NNNN3NNNNNNNNN	R,T	062	519	06.02.07	7679	000000	92998
690.682-070	SOLE-CONFORMING-MACHINE OPERATOR (boot & shoe)	3224	44434434345	LNNONONCCONNNNNFNFNNN	NNNN3NNNNNNNNN	R,T	134	522	06.02.05	7663	480304	92971
690.682-074	SPAGHETTI-MACHINE OPERATOR (plastic prod.)	3234	34444444345	MNNNNNNFFNNNNNONONNN	NNNN3NNNNNNNNN	R,T	061	519	06.02.20	7529	000000	92198
690.682-078	STITCHER, SPECIAL MACHINE (boot & shoe)	3224	44443444344	LNNONNNFFNNNNFNONON	NNNN4NNNNNNNNN	R,T	171	522	06.02.05	7656	480304	92723
690.682-082	STITCHER, STANDARD MACHINE (boot & shoe)	3224	44433433344	LNNNNNNNCCFNNONCNOCON	NNNN4NNNNNNNNN	R,T	171	522	06.02.05	7656	480304	92723
690.682-086	TRIMMER, MACHINE II (boot & shoe)	3224	44443434344	LNNNNNNNFFNNNNNFNONON	NNNN3NNNNNNNNN	R,T	054	512	06.02.07	7678	480304	92944
690.682-090	TRIMMING-MACHINE OPERATOR (button & notion)	3224	44443434355	MNNNONONFFONNNNONOONN	NNNN3NNNNNNNNN	R,T	134	618	06.02.02	7479	000000	92997
690.685-010	ASSEMBLER FOR PULLER-OVER, MACHINE (boot & shoe)	2123	44443533355	MNNONNNFFFNNNNFNFNN	NNNN4NFCNNNNNNN	R,T,U	063	550	06.04.20	7679	000000	92998
690.685-014	ASSEMBLY-PRESS OPERATOR (any industry)	2122	44444434345	LNNNNNNFFNNNNNFNFNNN	NNNN4NFCNNNNNN	R,J	054	512	06.04.07	7679	480304	92998
690.685-018	BACK-STRIP-MACHINE OPERATOR (boot & shoe)	1112	44444434345	LNNNNNNFFONNNNFNFNN	NNNN4NNNNNNNNN	R,J	041	492	06.04.07	7662	000000	92974
690.685-022	BALER (plastic-synth.)	2112	44443444355	LNNNNNNNFFONNNNNFNOONN	NNNO3NNNNNNNNN	R	054	519	06.04.07	7678	000000	92944
690.685-026	BAND CUTTER (rubber goods)	2113	44443433355	MNNNNNNNFFONNNNNNONNNN	NNNN3NFNNNNNNN	R,T	054	519	06.04.07	7679	000000	92998
690.685-030	BAND-MACHINE OPERATOR (rubber goods)	2224	44443434345	HNNONONFFFNNNNONNNNN	NNNN4NNNNNNNNN	R	032	522	06.04.05	7679	480304	92998
690.685-034	BOTTOM PRESSER (boot & shoe)	2122	44543543345	MNNONNNCCFNNNNFNFNNN	NNNN4NNNNNNNNN	R	051	616	06.04.09	7677	000000	92965
690.685-038	BOWLING-BALL FINISHER (toy-sport equip.)	2122	44444434355	MNNNNNNNFFONNONFNFNNN	NNNN3NNNNNNNNF	R,T	191	514	06.04.07	7679	480304	92998
690.685-042	BRANDING-MACHINE TENDER (rubber goods)	2113	44434434454	MNNONONFFNNNNNNNNON	NNNN3NNNNNNNNN	R,T	051	522	06.04.05	7677	480304	92965
690.685-046	BUFFER (boot & shoe)	1112	44444434335	LNNONNNCCOONONFNFNNN	NNNN4NNNNNNNNN	R	051	512	06.04.05	7677	480304	92965
690.685-050	BUFFER, AUTOMATIC (boot & shoe)	2113	44444433344	LNNFNNNFFNNNNONNNNN	NNNN3NNNNNNNNN	R	051	522	06.04.05	7677	480304	92965
690.685-054	BUFFER, INFLATED-PAD (boot & shoe)	1113	44443434344	LNNNNNNFFONNNNNFNNON	NNNN4NNNNNNNNO	R,T	153	522	06.04.05	7679	480304	92998
690.685-058	BURNISHER (boot & shoe)	2122	44444443355	LNNNNNNNFFNNNNONONNN	NNNN4NNNNNNNNN	R	057	618	06.04.09	7678	000000	91905
690.685-062	BUTTON-DECORATING-MACHINE OPERATOR (button & notion)	2122	44443544355	MNNNNNNNFFONNNNNNNNN	NNNN4NNNNNNNNN	R	057	618	06.04.09	7654	480304	92944
690.685-066	BUTTON-FACING-MACHINE OPERATOR (button & notion)	2123	44443433344	LNNONNNFFFNNNNNNNON	NNNN4NNNNNNNNN	R,T	063	522	06.04.05	7659	480304	92998
690.685-070	CEMENTER AND FOLDER, MACHINE (boot & shoe)	2122	44443434345	LNNNNNNFFFONNNNFNNNON	NNNN4NNNNNNNNN	R,T	063	522	06.04.05	7679	480304	92956
690.685-074	CEMENTER, MACHINE JOINER (boot & shoe)	1112	44444433455	LNNNNNNFFNNNNFNONNN	NNNN3NNNNNNNNNF	R,T	134	556	06.04.02	7514	000000	92956
690.685-078	CENTER-PUNCH OPERATOR (recording)	1112	44444544355	LNNONNNFFNNNNNONNNN	NNNN4NNNNNNNNN	R	134	522	06.04.05	7679	480304	91321
690.685-082	CHANNEL OPENER, OUTSOLES (boot & shoe)	2123	44443434345	LNNNNNNNCCNNNNONNNNN	NNNN4NNNNNNNNN	R,T	054	522	06.04.05	7659	480304	92998
690.685-086	CHANNELER, INSOLE (boot & shoe)	2123	44443434345	LNNNNNNFFNNNNNONNNON	NNNN4NNNNNNNNN	R,T	054	522	06.04.05	7679	480304	92998
690.685-090	CONTACT-LENS MOLDER (optical goods)	2223	34432433354	LNNNNNNFFNNNNNFNOOON	NNNN3NNNNNNNNN	R,J,T	132	605	06.04.13	7542	000000	91905
690.685-094	COUNTER CUTTER (boot & shoe)	2123	44443444345	MNNNONONFFONNONFFNN	NNNN4NNNNNNNNN	R,T	054	522	06.04.09	7654	480304	92944
690.685-098	COUNTER FORMER (boot & shoe)	2122	44444444445	LNNONNNFFONNNNNNNNN	NNNN4NNNNNNNNN	R,T	032	522	06.04.05	7659	480304	92998
690.685-102	COUNTER MOLDER (boot & shoe)	3123	44434434454	LNNFNNNNFFNNNNNNNON	NNNN4NNNNNNNNN	R,T	136	522	06.04.05	7679	480304	92998
690.685-106	COUNTER ROLLER (boot & shoe)	2112	44444434355	LNNNNNNFFFONNNNNNNNN	NNNN4NNNNNNNNN	R	054	522	06.04.05	7679	480304	92998
690.685-110	CUT-OUT-AND-MARKING-MACHINE OPERATOR (boot & shoe)	2113	44443434355	LNNNNNNFFNNNNCNNNNNN	NNNN4NNNNNNNNN	R,T	054	522	06.04.05	7679	480304	92998
690.685-114	CUT-OUT-MACHINE OPERATOR (boot & shoe)	2112	44443434345	LNNNNNNFFNNNNNONNNON	NNNN4NNNNNNNNN	R	054	522	06.04.05	7654	480304	92998
690.685-118	CUTTER I (fabrication, nec)	2122	44444444344	MNNNNNNFFONNNNONONON	NNNN4NNNNNNNNN	R	054	510	06.04.09	7678	000000	92944
690.685-122	CUTTING-MACHINE TENDER (any industry)	3223	44444433345	MNNONONFFONNNNONOFFNN	NNNN4NNNNNNNNN	R,T	054	512	06.04.09	7678	000000	92944
690.685-126	DESKIDDING-MACHINE OPERATOR (boot & shoe)	2122	44443434345	LNNONNNFFONNNFNNNNON	NNNN3NNNNNNNNN	R,T	063	492	06.04.07	7529	480304	92998
690.685-130	DICER OPERATOR (plastic-synth.)	2112	44444444354	LNNFNNNNFFONNNNFNNNNN	NNNN4NFNNNNNNN	R	054	514	06.04.02	7661	000000	92198
690.685-134	DUAL-HOSE CEMENTER (rubber goods)	2122	44434434455	LNNNNNNFFFONNNNFNNNON	NNNN3NNNNNNNNN	R	063	522	06.04.07	7659	000000	92956
690.685-138	EDGE BURNISHER, UPPERS (boot & shoe)	2113	44444434355	LNNNNNNFFFONNNNCNNNNN	NNNN4NNNNNNNNN	R,T	032	519	06.04.05	7522	480304	92998
690.685-142	EDGE GRINDER (plastic prod.)	2113	34443444344	LNNONNNFFNNNNNNNNON	NNNN4NFNNNNNNN	R	051	522	06.04.02	7679	000000	92998
690.685-146	EDGE SETTER (boot & shoe)	2123	44443434354	MNNNNNNFFONNNNNONONON	NNNN4NNNNNNNNN	R	032	522	06.04.05	7679	480304	92944
690.685-150	EDGE TRIMMER (boot & shoe)	2114	44443434355	LNNNNNNNCCNNNNNFNNNNF	NNNN4NNNNNNNNNF	R,T	054	522	06.04.02	7539	480304	92998
690.685-154	ELECTRIC-SEALING-MACHINE OPERATOR (any industry)	2122	44444444345	LNNONNNFFONNNNFNNNNN	NNNN4NNNNNNNNN	R,T	063	492	06.04.02	7679	150607	92198
690.685-158	EMBOSSER (boot & shoe)	2122	44443434344	LNNONNNFFONNNNFNNNNN	NNNN3NNNNNNNNN	R	192	522	06.04.05	7679	480304	92998
690.685-162	FASTENER, MACHINE (boot & shoe)	2112	44444444345	LNNNNNNFFFONNNNFNNNNN	NNNN4NNNNNNNNN	R	062	522	06.04.05	7678	480304	92998
690.685-166	FEATHEREDGER AND REDUCER, MACHINE (boot & shoe)	2122	44443434345	LNNONNNFFONNNNFNNNNN	NNNN4NNNNNNNNN	R	054	522	06.04.05	7678	480304	92944
690.685-170	FINISHER, MACHINE (plastic prod.)	2222	44443434355	MNNONONNFFONNNNFNNNON	NNNN3NNNNNNNNN	R,T	051	519	06.04.02	7522	000000	91117

DOT #	DOT Title & Industry	Trng	Aptitude	Physical	Environment	Tempra	WkF	MPSMS	GOE	SOC	CIP	OES
690.685-174	FOLDER, MACHINE (boot & shoe)	2123	44444434345	LNNNNNNFFONNNNNFNNNNNO	NNNN3NNNNNNNNNNO	R	063	522	06.04.05	7659	480304	92998
690.685-178	FOLDING-MACHINE OPERATOR (leather prod.)	2112	44443433345	LNNNNNNFFNNNNNNFNNNNNN	NNNN4NNNNNNNNNNN	R,T	062	520	06.04.05	7659	000000	92998
690.685-182	FORCE-VARIATION EQUIPMENT TENDER (rubber tire)	2122	44444444445	MNNNNNNCCFNOONFNFNNNN	NNNN3NNNNNNNNNNO	R	051	511	06.03.01	7830	000000	83005
690.685-186	FOREPART LASTER (boot & shoe)	2122	44444434355	LNNNNNNNFFNNOONONONON	NNNN4NNNNNNNNNNN	R	063	522	06.04.05	7679	480304	92998
690.685-190	FOUNTAIN PEN TURNER (pen & pencil)	2123	44444433354	SNNNNNNNFFNNNNNNNNNNN	NNNN3NNNNNNNNNNN	R,T	055	617	06.04.09	7512	000000	92198
690.685-194	GRINDING-MACHINE OPERATOR, AUTOMATIC (button & notion)	2122	44433544455	LNNNNNNNFFNNNNNFNNNNNN	NNNN4NNNNNNNNNNN	R	051	618	06.04.08	7522	000000	91117
690.685-198	GROOVER AND TURNER (boot & shoe)	2122	44443434345	LNNNNNNFFONNNNNFNNNNNN	NNNN4NNNNNNNNNNN	R,T	054	522	06.04.09	7678	480304	92944
690.685-202	GROOVING-LATHE TENDER (plastic prod.)	2122	44443434355	LNNNNNNFFNNNNNNFNNNNNN	NNNN4NNNNNNNNNNN	R	054	519	06.04.02	7512	000000	91117
690.685-206	HEEL BUILDER, MACHINE (boot & shoe)	2113	44444434345	LNNNNNNNFFONNNNNFNNNNN	NNNN4NNNNNNNNNNN	R,T	063	522	06.04.09	7659	480304	92998
690.685-210	HEEL COMPRESSOR (boot & shoe)	1112	44444434345	LNNNNNNNNFFFONNNNNNNNF	NNNN4NNNNNNNNNNN	R	134	522	06.04.05	7659	480304	92998
690.685-214	HEEL GOUGER (boot & shoe)	2123	44444434345	LNNNNNNNFFNNNNNONNNNNN	NNNN3NNNNNNNNNNN	R,T	054	522	06.04.05	7678	480304	92944
690.685-218	HEEL PRICKER (boot & shoe)	2123	44444434345	LNNNNNNNFFNNNNNNONNNNN	NNNN4NNNNNNNNNNN	R,T	134	522	06.04.05	7659	480304	92998
690.685-222	HEEL SCORER (boot & shoe)	2122	44444434345	LNNNNNNNFFONNNNNFNNNNN	NNNN3NNNNNNNNNNN	R,T	061	522	06.04.05	7679	480304	92998
690.685-226	HEEL-NAILING-MACHINE OPERATOR (boot & shoe)	2122	44444433345	LNNNNNNNFFONNNNNONNNNN	NNNN4NNNNNNNNNNN	R,T	072	512	06.04.09	7636	000000	92998
690.685-230	HEEL-SEAT LASTER, MACHINE (boot & shoe)	2123	44444434345	LNNNNNNNFFONNNNNFNNNNN	NNNN4NNNNNNNNNNN	R,T	072	522	06.04.05	7679	480304	92998
690.685-234	INKER, MACHINE (boot & shoe)	2122	44434434344	LNNONNNNFFONNNNNFNONON	NNNN4NNNNNNNNNNN	R,T	153	522	06.04.21	7679	480304	92998
690.685-238	INSEAM TRIMMER (boot & shoe)	2122	44444444345	LNNNNNNNFFFNNNNNNNNNNN	NNNN4NNNNNNNNNNN	R,T	054	522	06.04.05	7679	480304	92944
690.685-242	INSOLE BEVELER (boot & shoe)	2112	44444444445	LNNNNNNNNFFONNNNNNNNNN	NNNN4NNNNNNNNNNN	R,T	054	522	06.04.05	7659	480304	92998
690.685-246	INSOLE REINFORCER (boot & shoe)	2113	44444443345	LNNNNNNNFFFNNNNNNNNNNN	NNNN4NNNNNNNNNNN	R	054	522	06.04.05	7659	480304	92998
690.685-250	JOINT CUTTER, MACHINE (boot & shoe)	2112	44443434355	LNNONONNFFONNNNNFNNNNN	NNNN4NNNNNNNNNNN	R,T	054	522	06.04.05	7679	480304	92998
690.685-254	LACER II (boot & shoe)	2122	44443433345	SNNNNNNNNCCFNNNNFNFNNN	NNNN4NNNNNNNNNNO	R,T	062	522	06.04.05	7679	480304	92998
690.685-258	LAMINATOR I (leather prod.)	2112	44443434355	MNNNNNNNFFNNNONFNNNNN	NNNN4NNNNNNNNNNN	R	063	529	06.04.05	7667	000000	92971
690.685-262	LAST SAWYER (wood prod., nec)	2112	44443533355	LNNNNNNNFFNNNNNFNNONON	NNNN4NNNNNNNNNNN	R,T	056	519	06.04.02	7529	000000	91117
690.685-266	LEATHER-BELT MAKER (leather prod.)	2123	44443434344	LNNNNNNNNFFNNNNNFNNNNN	NNNN3NNNNNNNNNNN	R,T	054	529	06.04.05	7659	480304	92998
690.685-270	LIP CUTTER AND SCORER (boot & shoe)	2122	44444444344	LNNNNNNNNFFONNNNFNONON	NNNN4NNNNNNNNNNN	R,T	192	522	06.04.05	7679	480304	92944
690.685-274	LIP-OF-SHANK CUTTER (boot & shoe)	2112	44444444345	LNNNNNNNFFONNNNNONNNNN	NNNN4NNNNNNNNNNN	R,T	054	522	06.04.05	7659	480304	92944
690.685-278	LUMITE INJECTOR (boot & shoe)	2222	44444443345	LNNONNNNFFONNNNFNNNNNN	NNNN3NNNNNNNNNNN	R	132	522	06.04.05	7659	480304	92998
690.685-282	MARKER, MACHINE (boot & shoe)	2123	44444434345	MNNONONNFFNNNNONONNNNN	NNNN4NNNNNNNNNNO	R,T	191	522	06.04.05	7679	480304	92944
690.685-286	MAT PUNCHER (rubber goods)	2122	44443434355	MNNNNNNNFFFNNNONONNNNN	NNNN3NNNNNNNNNNN	R	134	519	06.04.07	7667	000000	92944
690.685-290	MOLDED-RUBBER-GOODS CUTTER (rubber goods)	2112	44443433355	MNNNNNNNFFFNNNNFNONON	NNNN3NNNNNNNNNNN	R	134	519	06.04.07	7678	000000	92944
690.685-294	MOLDER, LABELS (boot & shoe)	2112	44443434355	LNNNNNNNCCNNNNNNFNFNNN	NNNN3NNNNNNNNNNN	R,T	192	512	06.04.07	7667	480304	92998
690.685-298	NICKER (boot & shoe)	2122	44444444345	LNNNNNNNNFFNNNNCNNNNNN	NNNN4NNNNNNNNNNN	R,T	054	522	06.04.05	7659	480304	92944
690.685-302	PAD CUTTER (plastic prod.)	2123	44443434355	LNNNNNNNFFNNNNCNNNNNNN	NNNN4NNNNNNNNNNN	R,T	054	519	06.04.07	7678	000000	92944
690.685-306	PLUG CUTTER (pen & pencil)	2122	44443434354	MNNONONNFFNNNNONNNNNN	NNNN4NNNNNNNNNNN	R,T	054	519	06.04.07	7678	480304	92198
690.685-310	POINTING-MACHINE OPERATOR (plastic prod.; rubber goods)	1112	44444444455	LNNONONFFONNNNFNNNNN	NNNN3NNNNNNNNNNO	R,T	055	605	06.04.02	7529	000000	92198
690.685-314	POUNDER (boot & shoe)	2113	44454434355	LNNNNONFFONNNNFONNN	NNNN4NNNNNNNNNNN	R	054	616	06.04.07	7678	480304	92944
690.685-318	PRESSER (rubber goods)	2112	44443434345	LNNNONNNNCNNNNNNFNONN	NNNN4NNNNNNNNNNN	R,T	134	522	06.04.05	7679	000000	92998
690.685-322	ROLL CUTTER (rubber goods)	2112	44444444345	LNNNNNNNCCNNNNNNFNFNNN	NNNN4NNNNNNNNNNN	R,T	134	519	06.04.07	7667	000000	92971
690.685-326	ROLL-OVER-PRESS OPERATOR (optical goods)	1112	44444444355	LNNONONFFNNNNNONNNNN	NNNN3NNNNNNNNNNO	R,T	054	512	06.04.07	7678	000000	92944
690.685-330	ROUGH-AND-TRUEING-MACHINE OPERATOR (toy-sport equip.)	2113	34444444355	LNNNNONFFNNNNNNNONN	NNNN4NNNNNNNNNNN	R	134	605	06.04.02	7539	000000	92198
690.685-334	ROUGH-ROUNDER, MACHINE (boot & shoe)	2113	34444434355	LNNNNNNNCCNNNNNNCNNNNN	NNNN4NNNNNNNNNNN	R,T	051	616	06.04.09	7677	000000	92965
690.685-338	ROUNDER (boot & shoe)	2123	44443434345	LNNNNNNNNCNNNNNCNNNNNN	NNNN4NNNNNNNNNNN	R,T	054	522	06.04.05	7678	480304	92944
690.685-342	RUBBER-CUTTING-MACHINE TENDER (rubber goods)	2112	44444444455	HNNONONFFNNNNNONNNNN	NNNN3NNNNNNNNNNN	R,T	054	522	06.04.07	7678	000000	92944
690.685-346	SANDER (toy-sport equip.)	2112	44443434345	LNNNNNNNCNNNNNNFONN	NNNN4NNNNNNNNNNN	R	054	519	06.04.09	7677	470499	92965
690.685-350	SEAM-RUBBING-MACHINE OPERATOR (boot & shoe)	2112	44444443345	LNNNONNNFFNNNNNFNONN	NNNN4NNNNNNNNNNN	R,T	051	616	06.04.05	7679	480304	92998
690.685-354	SHAPING-MACHINE OPERATOR (plastic prod.)	1112	44444434345	LNNNNNNNFFNNNNNFNFNNN	NNNN4NNNNNNNNNNN	R	032	522	06.04.02	7678	000000	92944
690.685-358	SIDE LASTER, CEMENT (boot & shoe)	2113	44443434355	LNNNNNNCNNNNNFNFON	NNNN4NNNNNNNNNNN	R	055	519	06.04.05	7659	480304	92998
690.685-362	SIDE LASTER, STAPLE (boot & shoe)	2123	44444434345	LNNNNNNFFNNNNNFNFNNN	NNNN4NNNNNNNNNNN	R,T	063	522	06.04.05	7659	480304	92998
690.685-366	SIZING-MACHINE TENDER (clock & watch)	2112	44443433335	LNNNNNNNNFFNNNNNNNNNNN	NNNN3NNNNNNNNNNN	R,T	062	522	06.04.02	7679	470408	92944
690.685-370	SKI-TOP TRIMMER (plastic prod.)	2112	44443434344	LNNNNNNNNFFNNNNNNFFON	NNNN4NNNNNNNNNNN	R,J	055	607	06.04.02	7678	470499	92944
690.685-374	SKIVER (leather prod.)	2124	44443434345	LNNNNNNCCFNNNNNFNOONN	NNNN4NNNNNNNNNNN	R,T	054	525	06.04.05	7659	000000	92944

DOT #	DOT Title & Industry	Trng	Aptitude	Physical	Environment	Tempra	WkF	MPSMS	GOE	SOC	CIP	OES
690.685-378	SKIVER, MACHINE (boot & shoe; rubber goods)	2123	44443433345	LNNONNNCCFNNNNFNOONN	NNNN4NNNNNNNNNN	R,T	054	522	06.04.05	7679	480304	92944
690.685-382	SOLE LEVELER, MACHINE (boot & shoe)	2122	44444434345	LNNONNNCCNNNNNFNONNN	NNNN4NNNNNNNNNN	R,T	134	522	06.04.05	7679	480304	92998
690.685-386	SPLITTING-MACHINE OPERATOR (rubber goods; rubber reclaim.)	2122	44444434345	HNHFNFNFNNNNNFNONNN	NNNN4NNNNNNNNNF	R	054	510	06.04.07	7678	000000	92944
690.685-390	SPONGE BUFFER (plastic prod.)	2113	44443434345	LNNNNNNCCNNNNNCNNNNN	NNNN4NCNNNNNNNN	R	051	519	06.04.02	7677	000000	92965
690.685-394	SPORT-SHOE-SPIKE ASSEMBLER (boot & shoe)	2123	44444443455	LNNNNNFFNNNNNFNNNN	NNNN4NNNNNNNNNN	R	071	522	06.04.05	7679	480304	92998
690.685-398	STAMPING-MACHINE OPERATOR (boot & shoe)	2124	44434434344	LNNONNNCCNNNNNFNNNON	NNNN4NNNNNNNNNN	R,T	192	522	06.04.05	7679	480304	92998
690.685-402	STRAP-CUTTING-MACHINE OPERATOR (rubber goods)	2122	44343444454	LNNONNNFFONNNNFNONON	NNNN4NNNNNNNNNN	R,T	054	512	06.04.07	7678	000000	92944
690.685-406	STRING LASTER (boot & shoe)	2122	44433334345	MNNNNNNFFNNNNNFNFNNN	NNFN3NNNNNNNNNF	R,J	062	512	06.04.09	7679	480304	92998
690.685-410	TACK PULLER, MACHINE (boot & shoe)	1112	44544444455	LNNONNNFFNNNNNFNNNNN	NNNN4NNNNNNNNNN	R	072	522	06.04.05	7679	480304	92998
690.685-414	TAPER, MACHINE (boot & shoe)	2123	44444434345	LNNONNNFFONNNNFNNNNN	NNNN4NNNNNNNNNO	R,T	063	522	06.04.05	7659	480304	92998
690.685-418	TIP FINISHER (boot & shoe)	2122	44444444345	LNNNNNNFFNNNNNFNNNNN	NNNN4:NNNNNNNNN	R,T	054	522	06.04.05	7679	480304	92998
690.685-422	TIRE BUFFER (automotive ser.)	3223	44443544455	LNNONONFFNNNNNFNONNN	NNNN4NFNNNNNNNF	R	051	511	05.12.13	7679	000000	92944
690.685-426	TOE FORMER, STITCHDOWNS (boot & shoe)	2113	44444434345	LNNNNNNCCNNNNNFNNNNN	NNNN4NNNNNNNNNN	R,T	134	522	06.04.05	7679	480304	92998
690.685-430	TOE LASTER, AUTOMATIC (boot & shoe)	2123	44434434345	LNNONNNCCNNNNNFNONNN	NNNN4NNNNNNNNNN	R,T	062	522	06.04.05	7659	480304	92998
690.685-434	TRIMMER, MACHINE I (boot & shoe)	2113	44444434345	LNNONNNCCNNNNNFNONNN	NNNN4NNNNNNNNNO	R,T	054	522	06.04.05	7678	480304	92944
690.685-438	TUBE MOLDER, FIBERGLASS (plastic prod.)	2122	44444434345	MNNNNNNFFNNNNONONNN	NNNN3NNNNNNNNNN	R,T	147	519	06.04.09	7679	000000	92998
690.685-442	TUBE SPLICER (rubber tire)	2113	44444434345	MNNNNNNFFNNNNNFNNNNN	NNNN3NNNNNNNNNN	R,J,T	063	511	06.04.07	7679	000000	92998
690.685-446	TUBER-MACHINE CUTTER (rubber goods; rubber tire)	2122	44434434345	LNNOONNFFONNNNNFNFNNN	NNNN4NNNNNNNNNO	R,T	054	510	06.04.07	7678	000000	92944
690.685-450	V-BELT COVERER (rubber goods)	2112	44444433245	LNNNNNNFFNNNNNFNNNN	NNNN3NNNNNNNNNN	R	061	514	06.04.05	7679	000000	92998
690.685-454	V-BELT FINISHER (rubber goods)	2113	44443433245	LNNNNNNFFNNNNNFNNNN	NNNN3NNNNNNNNNN	R	191	514	06.04.07	7678	000000	92944
690.685-458	V-BELT SKIVER (rubber goods)	2113	44443434345	LNNONNNFFONNNNFNONNN	NNNN3NNNNNNNNNN	R	054	514	06.04.07	7659	480304	92998
690.685-462	VULCANIZER (boot & shoe)	2112	44444434355	LNNONONFFNNNNNNNNNN	NNNN3NNNNNNNNNN	R	136	522	06.04.13	7659	480304	92998
690.685-466	VULCANIZING-PRESS OPERATOR (boot & shoe)	2113	44444434355	LNNONONFFONNNNNNNNNN	NNNN3NNNNNNNNNO	R	136	522	06.04.07	7667	480304	92971
690.685-470	WELT BEATER (boot & shoe)	2123	44444434345	LNNONNNFFONNNNFNNNN	NNNN4NNNNNNNNNN	R,T	134	522	06.04.05	7679	480304	92998
690.685-474	WELT BUTTER, MACHINE (boot & shoe)	2122	44444434345	LNNOONNFFONNNNNONONNN	NNNN4NNNNNNNNNN	R,T	054	522	06.04.05	7659	480304	92998
690.685-478	WELT CUTTER (boot & shoe)	2124	44443444345	LNNONNNFFNNNNNFNONNN	NNNN3NNNNNNNNNN	R,T	054	522	06.04.05	7654	480304	92944
690.685-482	WELT WHEELER (boot & shoe)	2122	44443434345	LNNONNNCCNNNNNFNONNN	NNNN4NNNNNNNNNN	R	192	522	06.04.05	7679	480304	92998
690.685-486	WIDTH STRIPPER (boot & shoe)	2113	44443434345	LNNNNNNFFNNNNNFNONNN	NNNN4NNNNNNNNNN	R,T	054	529	06.04.05	7659	480304	92944
690.685-490	WIRE-WINDING-MACHINE TENDER (rubber goods)	2112	44443433355	HNHFNFNFFNNNNNFNNNN	NNNN4NNNNNNNNNN	R	163	514	06.04.09	7539	000000	92198
690.685-494	STITCHER, TAPE-CONTROLLED MACHINE (boot & shoe)	2112	44433433354	LNNONNNFFNNNNNFNNFON	NNNN4NNNNNNNNNN	R,T	171	522	06.04.05	7656	480304	92723
690.685-498	PLASTIC ROLLER (plastic prod.)	2111	44444434345	LNNNNNNFFNNNNNNNNN	NNNN4NNNNNNNNNN	R	163	519	06.04.02	7679	000000	92998
690.685-502	ROLLER MAKER (rubber goods)	3223	34443444245	MNNONNNFFONNNNFNNONN	NNNN4NNNNNNNNNN	U	092	510	06.04.07	7679	000000	92944
690.685-506	SAMPLE MAKER (boot & shoe)	3224	44444433344	LNNNNNNFFOONOOFNFFON	NNNN3NNNNNNNNNN	R,U	102	522	06.04.05	7656	480304	92998
690.685-510	TRADE MARKER (fabrication, nec)	3123	44433433334	MNNNNNNCCCNNNNCNNNFN	NNNN4NNNNNNNNNN	R,T	134	510	06.04.02	7518	000000	91117
690.686-010	BEVELING-MACHINE OPERATOR (hat & cap)	1112	44444434355	LNNNNNNFFONNNNNNNNN	NNNN3NNNNNNNNNN	R	054	420	06.04.05	8725	000000	98502
690.686-014	BIAS-MACHINE-OPERATOR HELPER (rubber tire)	1112	44444434335	HONFNFFONNNNNNNNN	NNNN4NNNNNNNNNN	R	054	511	06.04.07	8618	000000	98999
690.686-018	CEMENTER, MACHINE APPLICATOR (boot & shoe)	1112	44544544345	LNNNNNNCNNNNNNNNN	NNNN4NOONNNNNN	R	063	522	06.04.05	8725	480304	98502
690.686-022	COATING-MACHINE FEEDER (leather prod.)	1112	44544544355	LNNNNNNFFNNNNNNFNNN	NNNN4NNNNNNNNNN	R	153	520	06.04.16	8725	000000	98502
690.686-026	CRIMPER (rubber goods)	1112	44545544355	LNNNNNNFFNNNNNNNNN	NNNN3NNNNNNNNNN	R	062	519	06.04.07	8725	000000	98502
690.686-030	CUTTING-MACHINE-TENDER HELPER (any industry)	2112	44444434344	MNNONONFFONNNNNONNNON	NNNN4NNNNNNNNNN	R	054	470	06.04.09	8618	000000	98999
690.686-034	FOLDING-MACHINE OPERATOR (hat & cap)	1112	44444434355	LNNNNNNFFONNNNFNNNN	NNNN3NNNNNNNNNN	R	062	445	06.04.05	8725	200303	98502
690.686-038	INJECTION-MOLDING-MACHINE OFFBEARER (pen & pencil)	2112	44433443355	LNNNNNNFFNNNNNNOONN	NNNN3NNNNNNNNNF	R	132	617	06.04.02	8725	000000	98502
690.686-042	INJECTION-MOLDING-MACHINE OFFBEARER (musical inst.)	1112	44444444455	MNNFNNNCCNNNNNNFNNN	NNNC4NNNNNNNNN	R	132	614	06.04.02	8725	000000	98502
690.686-046	PLASTIC-DESIGN APPLIER (boot & shoe)	1111	44544544355	SNNNNNNCCNNNNNNNNN	NNNN3NNNNNNNNNN	R	081	522	06.04.05	8725	000000	98502
690.686-050	RUBBER-ROLLER GRINDER (pen & pencil)	1111	44444444455	LNNNNNNFFONNNNNNNNN	NNNN3NNNNNNNNNN	R	051	617	06.04.07	8725	000000	98502
690.686-054	SPLITTING-MACHINE FEEDER (leather mfg.)	1112	44444444355	LNNONNNFFNNNNNNNNN	NNNN3NNNNNNNNNO	R	054	521	06.04.05	8725	000000	98502
690.686-058	SWEATBAND FLANGER (hat & cap)	1112	44444434345	LNNNNNNFFFNNNNNNNNN	NNNN4NNNNNNNNNN	R	032	420	06.04.05	8725	000000	98502
690.686-062	SWEATBAND-CUTTING-MACHINE OPERATOR (hat & cap)	2112	44444433345	LNNNNNNFFNNNNNNNNN	NNNN4NNNNNNNNNN	R	054	529	06.04.05	8725	200303	98502
690.686-066	TOGGLE-PRESS FOLDER-AND-FEEDER (boot & shoe)	1112	44444434355	SNNNNNNCCNNNNNNNNN	NNNC4NNNNNNNNNF	R	062	512	06.04.05	7659	480304	92998
690.686-070	TUBER-MACHINE-OPERATOR HELPER (rubber goods; rubber tire)	1112	44544544355	MNNONNNFFNFNFNFNOONN	NNNN4NNNNNNNNNO	R	135	511	06.04.07	8618	000000	98999
691.130-010	SUPERVISOR (nonfer. metal)	4337	33333333355	LNNONNNFFNFNFNOONN	NNNN4NNNNNNNNNO	V,D,P,J	163	541	06.01.01	7100	000000	81008

DOT #	DOT Title & Industry	Trng	Aptitude	Physical	Environment	Tempra	WkF	MPSMS	GOE	SOC	CIP	OES
691.130-014	SUPERVISOR, WIRE-ROPE FABRICATION (metal prod., nec)	4337	33333333355	LNNNONONFFONFFNFNNONN	NNNN4NNNNNNNNNNN	V,D,P,J	102	541	06.02.01	7100	000000	81008
691.367-010	INSPECTOR, WIRE (metal prod., nec; nonfer. metal)	3335	33332332354	LNNNNNNNFFONNNFFONONN	NNNN3NNNNNNNNNNN	J,T	212	541	06.03.01	7820	000000	83005
691.382-010	EXTRUDING-MACHINE OPERATOR (nonfer. metal)	3224	34443443454	MNNNNNFFNNNNFNNNON	NNNN4NFNNNNNNNNO	R,J,T	135	541	06.02.09	7663	000000	92971
691.382-014	LEAD-PRESS OPERATOR (nonfer. metal)	3224	44444444455	LNNNNNNFFONNNNNNNON	NNNN3NNNNNNNNNNN	R,J,T	135	541	06.02.02	7663	000000	92971
691.387-010	INSPECTOR, INSULATION (nonfer. metal)	3335	33342343355	LNNNNNNFFONNNFNFONN	NNNN3NNNNNNNNNNO	V,J,T	212	541	06.03.01	7820	000000	83005
691.667-010	PNEUMATIC JACKETER (nonfer. metal)	1112	44544534355	MNNNNNNFFNNNNNNNNN	FNNN3NNNNNNNNNN	R	061	541	06.04.34	7759	000000	93399
691.682-010	ASBESTOS-WIRE FINISHER (nonfer. metal)	3224	33444444455	MNNNNNNFFNNNNNONONN	NNNN3NNNNNNNNNNN	R	163	541	06.02.09	7479	000000	92997
691.682-014	BRAIDER OPERATOR (nonfer. metal)	3225	34433433355	LNNNONNNFFNNNFFNFNNN	NNNN4NNNNNNNNNNN	J,T	164	541	06.02.09	7479	000000	92997
691.682-018	INSULATING-MACHINE OPERATOR (nonfer. metal)	3224	44444434355	MNNNNNFFNNNNFONNNNN	NNNN4NNNNNNNNNNN	R,J,T	163	541	06.02.09	7679	000000	92998
691.685-010	ARMORING-MACHINE OPERATOR (nonfer. metal)	2122	44443434355	MNNNNNNFFNNNNFNFONN	NNNN3NNNNNNNNNNN	R,T	163	541	06.04.09	7679	000000	92998
691.685-014	LAGGING-MACHINE OPERATOR (nonfer. metal)	2112	44444444445	MNNNNNNFFNNNNNNNNN	NNNN3NNNNNNNNNNN	R	061	584	06.04.38	7679	000000	92998
691.685-018	LEAD FORMER (elec. equip.)	2112	44443433344	LNNNNNNNFFNFFNNNFFFN	NNNN4NNNNNNNNNNN	R,T	111	580	06.04.34	7539	000000	92198
691.685-022	PAIRING-MACHINE OPERATOR (nonfer. metal)	2123	44443434344	MNNNONNFFNNNONONON	NNNN4NNNNNNNNNNN	R,T	162	541	06.04.09	7539	000000	92198
691.685-026	SPOOLING-MACHINE OPERATOR (metal prod., nec; nonfer. metal)	2123	44444444344	HNNNONFFFNNNNFONNON	NNNN4NNNNNNNNNNN	R,T	163	541	06.04.02	7679	000000	92998
691.685-030	UTILITY WORKER, EXTRUSION (nonfer. metal)	2223	44434434355	HNNNNNFFNNNNFNNNNN	NNNN4NNNNNNNNNNN	R	133	541	06.04.09	8725	000000	98502
691.686-010	TWISTING-MACHINE OPERATOR (comm. equip.; elec. equip.)	1112	44444444455	LNNNNNNCCNNNNNNNNNN	NNNN3NNNNNNNNNNN	R	162	584	06.04.09	8725	000000	98502
691.687-010	PRODUCTION HELPER (nonfer. metal)	1111	44444444355	MNNNNNNFFNNNNONNNNN	NNNN4NNNNNNNNNNN	R	011	541	06.04.40	8611	000000	92198
692.130-010	BRUSH-FABRICATION SUPERVISOR (fabrication, nec)	4337	33333334344	MNNNONNFFNFFNONONN	NNNN4NNNNNNNNNNN	V,D,P,J,T	102	619	06.02.01	7100	000000	81008
692.130-014	FINISHING SUPERVISOR (elec. equip.)	4337	33323433355	MNNNNNFFFNFFNNONONN	NNNN4NNNNNNNNNNN	V,D,P,J	057	582	06.02.01	7100	000000	81008
692.130-018	SUPERVISOR I (button & notion)	4337	33333333343	MNNNONFFFOFFNFNOOON	NNNN4NNNNNNNNNNO	V,D,P,J	121	618	06.02.01	7100	000000	81008
692.130-022	SUPERVISOR VI (nonmet. min.)	4336	33333433355	MNNNNNONFFNFNFONN	NNNN4NFNNNNNNNNN	V,D,T	134	538	06.01.01	7100	000000	81008
692.130-026	SUPERVISOR, BROOMMAKING (fabrication, nec)	4336	33333433345	MNNOOONFFOFFNFNNONN	NNNN3NNNNNNNNNNN	D,P,V	102	619	06.02.01	7100	000000	81008
692.130-030	SUPERVISOR, PAINT ROLLER COVERS (fabrication, nec)	4337	33343434355	LNNONONFFFNFFNNNNN	NNNN4NNNNNNNNNNN	V,D,P,J	054	619	06.02.01	7100	000000	81008
692.130-034	SUPERVISOR, TOY PARTS FORMER (toy-sport equip.)	4347	33323334355	LNNNNNFFNFFNFNFNN	NNNN4NNNNNNNNNNN	D,P,V	134	615	06.01.01	7100	000000	81008
692.130-038	SUPERVISOR, KEYMODULE ASSEMBLY (office machines)	4337	23332444455	LNNNNNOOONFFNONNNNN	NNNN4NNNNNNNNNNN	D,J,P	121	571	06.02.01	7100	520205	81008
692.130-042	SUPERVISOR, SHOP (fabrication, nec)	3335	33334433345	MNNNONFFFOOONFNNONN	NNNN4NNNNNNNNNNN	D,V,P	102	559	06.02.01	7100	480501	81008
692.132-010	SUPERVISOR IV (nonmet. min.)	4336	33334434345	LNNNONFFFNFFNFFOFN	NNFN3NNONNNNNNN	T,J	111	587	06.01.02	7479	470105	92941
692.132-014	SUPERVISOR V (nonmet. min.)	4336	29344344454	LNNOOONFFFFFFNNONN	NNNN4NNNNNNNNNNN	D,J,T	102	538	06.02.01	7100	000000	81008
692.132-018	SUPERVISOR, SKI PRODUCTION (toy-sport equip.)	3236	33443433354	LNNNNNNFFNFNFNFOFN	NNNN4NNNNNNNNNNN	D,P,V	102	616	06.02.09	7100	000000	81008
692.137-010	SUPERVISOR, PAINTING DEPARTMENT (pen & pencil)	4337	33433433354	LNNNNNNNFFOOOONFOON	NNNN4NNNNNNNNNNN	D,P,J	151	617	06.02.01	7439	470303	81008
692.137-014	SUPERVISOR I (protective dev.)	4347	33333334455	LNNNNNNFFNFNFNNNNN	NNNN3NNNNNNNNNNN	D,T,P,V	102	449	06.04.01	7100	520205	81008
692.260-010	MACHINE SETTER (nonmet. min.)	3336	33333333344	LNNNOONFFFOOONFOON	NNNN3NNNNNNNNNNN	V,J,T	102	538	06.01.02	7479	480503	92997
692.360-010	ASSEMBLY-MACHINE-SET-UP MECHANIC (elec. equip.)	3335	33332334345	MNNNONNFFFOOONFNFON	NNNN3NNNNNNNNNNO	V,J,T	111	581	06.01.02	7479	470303	92997
692.360-014	BRUSH-MACHINE SETTER (fabrication, nec)	3235	34333434355	MNNNONNFFNFFNNNNNN	NNNN4NNNNNNNNNNN	J,T	102	619	06.01.02	7478	470303	92941
692.360-018	FIRESETTER (elec. equip.; electron. comp.; inst. & app.)	4336	33333433354	MNNNNNNFFNNNNFOFFN	NNFN3NNONNNNNNN	T,J	111	587	06.01.03	7479	470105	92941
692.362-010	SET-UP MECHANIC, CROWN ASSEMBLY MACHINE (any industry)	3225	33334443355	LNNNONONFFNOONFNONN	NNNN4NNNNNNNNNNN	R,T	063	556	06.02.20	7467	470303	92968
692.380-010	SET-UP MECHANIC (pen & pencil)	4336	33433433244	MNNNOOONFFNNNNNFOON	NNNN4NNNNNNNNNNO	V,J,T	102	617	06.01.02	7439	470303	92311
692.380-014	SET-UP MECHANIC, AUTOMATIC LINE (pen & pencil)	4336	33332433254	MNNNONOOONFFONNNNN	NNNN4NNNNNNNNNNN	V,J,T	102	617	06.01.02	7479	470303	92997
692.382-010	BALLPOINT-PEN-ASSEMBLY-MACHINE OPERATOR (pen & pencil)	4336	34333433354	LNNNONNNFFONNNFNNON	NNNN4NNNNNNNNNNN	V,J,T	102	617	06.02.20	7479	470303	92997
692.382-014	PLATE STACKER, MACHINE (elec. equip.)	3224	34434343355	LNNONONFFNNNNFNNNNN	NNNN4NFNNNNNNNNN	R,J,T	061	589	06.02.09	7479	000000	92997
692.462-010	CALENDER-ROLL PRESS OPERATOR (machinery mfg.)	3324	34344433355	MONONONFFNNOONOFFON	NNNN3NFFNNNNNNN	R,T	136	567	06.02.09	7517	000000	91321
692.482-010	CARBON-AND-GRAPHITE-BRUSH-MACHINE OPERATOR (elec. equip.)	3334	34433434354	MNNNNNNFFONNNFNFFON	NNNN3NFFNNNNNNN	R	163	582	06.04.09	7479	470105	92997
692.485-010	STRINGER-MACHINE TENDER (protective dev.)	2122	44444433355	LNNNNNNFFNFNFNNNNN	NNNN4NNNNNNNNNNN	R	163	604	06.04.09	7663	000000	92997
692.662-010	DYNAMITE-PACKING-MACHINE OPERATOR (chemical)	3235	34343434354	MNNFNFNFFFFOONOFFON	NNNN4NOONNNNNON	J,S,T	041	499	06.02.09	7462	000000	92997
692.662-014	GELATIN-DYNAMITE-PACKING OPERATOR (chemical)	3235	34433434354	MNNFNFNFFFOONOFFON	NNNN4NOONNNNNON	S,T	041	499	06.02.09	7662	000000	92974
692.662-018	WAFER-MACHINE OPERATOR (elec. equip.)	3224	34433443355	LNNNNNONFFNOONFNNON	NNNN4NNNNNNNNNNN	R,T	102	589	06.02.09	7679	000000	92998
692.662-022	WIRE-WRAPPING-MACHINE OPERATOR (office machines)	3234	34423433354	LNNNNNONFFFNNOONFNNON	NNNN4NNNNNNNNNNN	J,T	111	571	06.02.09	7679	470102	92998
692.665-010	BRAIDING-MACHINE TENDER (rubber goods)	2123	44443433345	MNNNNNNFFOOOONFONNON	NNNN4NNNNNNNNNNN	R	162	514	06.04.09	7679	000000	92998
692.665-014	PUNCH-PRESS OPERATOR (fabrication, nec)	2122	44444444454	MNNNNNNNFFOOOONFONNNN	NNCN4NFNNNNNNN	R,T	054	619	06.04.09	7679	000000	91321
692.665-018	DRY-CELL-ASSEMBLY-MACHINE TENDER (elec. equip.)	3234	44433443354	HONONONFFONNNNNNNN	NNNN4NNNNNNNNNNN	R,T	061	589	06.04.20	7679	000000	92998
692.682-010	ANKLE-PATCH MOLDER (boot & shoe)	3234	44433444354	LNNNNNNFFFNNNNONONN	NNNN3NNNNNNNNNNF	J,T	132	512	06.02.02	7679	480304	92998

DOT #	DOT Title & Industry	Trng	Aptitude	Physical	Environment	Tempra	WkF	MPSMS	GOE	SOC	CIP	OES
692.682-014	BEAD-FORMING-MACHINE OPERATOR (rubber tire)	3224	34443433345	MNNNNNNFNFFNNNNN	NNNN4NNNNNNNNN	R,T	135	511	06.02.09	7479	480501	92951
692.682-018	BORING-AND-FILLING-MACHINE OPERATOR (fabrication, nec)	3225	33334433335	MNNNNNNNFFNNNNNNN	NNNN4NNNNNNNNNO	R,T	053	619	06.02.09	7462	000000	92997
692.682-022	BROOM STITCHER (fabrication, nec)	3224	34433433344	MNNONNNCCNNNNNN	NNNN4NNNNNNNNN	R,T	102	619	06.02.09	7679	000000	92998
692.682-026	CANDLE-EXTRUSION-MACHINE OPERATOR (fabrication, nec)	3234	34443434354	LNNNNNNFFONNNFNFNON	NNNN3NNNNNNNNN	R,T	135	619	06.02.18	7663	000000	92971
692.682-030	COREMAKING-MACHINE OPERATOR (elec. equip.)	3224	34434434355	LNNONNNFFNNNNFNNNN	NNNN4NNNNNNNNN	R,T	061	589	06.02.20	7679	000000	92998
692.682-034	ELECTRODE TURNER-AND-FINISHER (elec. equip.)	3224	33343434355	MNNNNNNFFNNNNFNNNN	NNNN4NNNNNNNNN	R,J,T	057	582	06.02.09	7478	000000	92941
692.682-038	FILLING-AND-STAPLING-MACHINE OPERATOR (fabrication, nec)	3224	44444544445	MNNNNNNFFNNNNNFNNNN	NNNN4NNNNNNNNN	R,T	062	619	06.02.09	7679	000000	92998
692.682-042	GAUGE OPERATOR (fabrication, nec)	3124	44444444355	LNNONNNFFNNNNNONONNN	NNNN4NNNNNNNNN	R,T	054	619	06.02.09	7678	000000	92944
692.682-046	PAINT-ROLLER-COVER-MACHINE SETTER (fabrication, nec)	3235	33334433333	LNNNNNNFFNNNNNFNNNN	NNNN4NNNNNNNNN	V,J	102	619	06.02.09	7478	470303	92941
692.682-050	POWER-DRIVEN-BRUSH MAKER (fabrication, nec)	3225	33334444355	MNNONNNFFNNNNNFNOONN	NNNN4NNNNNNNNNO	R,T	102	619	06.02.02	7462	000000	92997
692.682-054	STACKING-MACHINE OPERATOR I (any industry)	3234	34434434455	LNNFNFNFFNNNNFNONNN	NNNN4NNNNNNNNN	R,J,T	061	554	06.02.20	8319	490299	97989
692.682-058	STRAPPING-MACHINE OPERATOR (wood. container)	3124	34443434355	HNNFNNNFFNNNNFNNNNN	NNNN3NNNNNNNNN	R	102	454	06.04.38	7662	000000	92974
692.682-062	STRING-WINDING-MACHINE OPERATOR (musical inst.)	3225	34434423343	LNNNNNNFFNNNNNFNNNN	NNNN3NNNNNNNNN	R,T	163	614	06.02.09	7679	480501	92998
692.682-066	SWEEPER-BRUSH MAKER, MACHINE (fabrication, nec)	3224	34443433345	HNNONNNFFNNNNFNNNON	NNNN4NNNNNNNNNO	R,T	163	619	06.02.09	7679	000000	92998
692.682-070	TWISTING-MACHINE OPERATOR (fabrication, nec)	3225	33434444345	LNNNNNNFFNNNNNFNNNN	NNNN4NNNNNNNNN	R,T	061	619	06.02.20	7479	000000	92997
692.685-010	ABRASIVE-BAND WINDER (nonmet. min.)	2112	44443433335	LNNNNNNCCNNNNNCNCNNN	NNNN4NNNNNNNNN	R,T	063	538	06.04.20	7679	000000	92998
692.685-014	ADHESIVE-BANDAGE-MACHINE OPERATOR (protective dev.)	2123	34433433353	LNNNNNNFFNNNNFNNOON	NNNN3NNNNNNNNN	R,T	062	604	06.04.05	7679	000000	92998
692.685-018	AIR-HOLE DRILLER (fabrication, nec)	2112	44444433355	LNNNNNNFFNNNNFNONNN	NNNN3NNNNNNNNN	R	053	619	06.04.03	7679	000000	92956
692.685-022	BEAD PREPARER (rubber goods)	2113	44444443355	HNNNNNNFFONNNNFNFNNN	NNNN3NNNNNNNNN	R	063	519	06.04.07	7661	000000	92998
692.685-026	BRASSIERE-SLIDE-MAKING-MACHINE TENDER, AUTOMATIC (garment)	1112	44444434455	LNNNNNNFFONNNFNFNNN	NNNN3NNNNNNNNN	R	063	618	06.04.05	7659	000000	92998
692.685-030	BROOM BUNDLER (fabrication, nec)	2122	44444444345	MNNNNNNNFFNNNNONONNN	NNNN3NNNNNNNNN	R	041	619	06.04.38	7667	000000	92971
692.685-034	BUCKLE-FRAME SHAPER (button & notion)	2123	44444443345	LNNONNNFFONNNNFNONN	NNNN4NNNNNNNNN	R	134	618	06.04.09	7663	480501	92971
692.685-038	CANDLE MOLDER, MACHINE (fabrication, nec)	2124	44444444344	MNNNNNNNFFNNNNNFNNNN	NNNN3NNNNNNNNN	R	132	619	06.04.19	7663	000000	92971
692.685-042	CAPPING-MACHINE OPERATOR (elec. equip.)	2123	44444444355	LNNNNNNFFNNNNNFNNNNN	NNNN4NNNNNNNNN	R,T	061	589	06.04.20	7679	000000	92998
692.685-046	CELL TUBER, MACHINE (elec. equip.)	2112	44444444455	LNNNNNNFFNNNNNFNONN	NNNN4NNNNNNNNN	R,U	041	589	06.04.05	7679	000000	92998
692.685-050	CEMENTER, MACHINE (boot & shoe)	1112	44443433335	LNNONNNCCNNNNNCNCNNN	NNNN3NNNNNNNNN	R,U	153	512	06.04.05	7661	480304	92956
692.685-054	COATING-MACHINE OPERATOR (pen & pencil)	2122	44444444454	MNNNNNNFFONNNNFNNNON	NNNN4NNNNNNNNN	R	151	617	06.04.21	7669	000000	92953
692.685-058	CORE SHAPER (toy-sport equip.)	2122	44434534355	MNNONNNFFOONNNFNFNNN	NNNN4NNNNNNNNN	R,T	055	519	06.04.09	7663	000000	92971
692.685-062	CROWN-ASSEMBLY-MACHINE OPERATOR (any industry)	2112	44434434355	LNNNNNNFFONNNNFNNNN	NNNN4NNNNNNNNN	R	063	556	06.04.09	7661	000000	92956
692.685-066	DEICER-ELEMENT WINDER, MACHINE (rubber goods)	2224	44443433355	LNNONONFFNNNNNNNNNNN	NNNN3NNNNNNNNN	J,T	163	519	06.04.20	7679	000000	92998
692.685-070	DESIGN INSERTER (plastic prod.)	2123	44434443344	LNNNNNNFFNNNNNFNNNN	NNFN4NNNNNNNNN	R,T	192	619	06.04.02	7539	000000	92198
692.685-074	DIELECTRIC-PRESS OPERATOR (auto. mfg.)	2122	44444443354	LNNNNNNFFNNNNNFNNNON	NNNN3NNNNNNNNN	R	063	492	06.04.05	7659	000000	92998
692.685-078	DYNAMITE-CARTRIDGE CRIMPER (chemical)	3224	34434434345	MNNNNNFFFNNNNNFNNNNN	NNNN4NCNNNNNNNN	R,S	062	499	06.02.04	7539	000000	92198
692.685-082	FILM SPOOLER (photo. appar.)	2112	44444434344	LNNFNFNFFONNNNNFNNNON	NNNN4NNNNNNNNN	R	163	606	06.04.04	7679	000000	92998
692.685-086	FOILING-MACHINE OPERATOR (ordnance)	1112	44443434355	LNNNNNNFFONNNNNNNNNN	NNNN4NNNNNNNNN	R	134	374	06.04.09	7667	000000	92974
692.685-090	GARLAND-MACHINE OPERATOR (fabrication, nec)	2112	44434534344	LNNFNNNFFFNNNNNNNNON	NNNN4NNNNNNNNNN	R,T	062	619	06.04.36	7662	000000	92998
692.685-094	GLUE-MACHINE OPERATOR (pen & pencil)	2112	44444444455	LNNONNNFFFOOONFNFNON	NNNN4NNNNNNNNNF	R,U	111	584	06.04.20	7720	000000	93956
692.685-098	GLUING-MACHINE OPERATOR (rubber goods)	1112	44444434345	LNNNNNNCCNNNNNNNNNNN	NNNN3NNNNNNNNN	R,T	153	519	06.04.09	7679	000000	92956
692.685-102	KICK-PRESS OPERATOR (protective dev.)	2112	34444443354	LNNNNNNFFNNNNFNNNON	NNNN3NNNNNNNNN	R,T	134	439	06.04.20	7679	000000	92998
692.685-106	LAMINATING-MACHINE OPERATOR (furniture)	3123	34434434355	MNNONNNFFFNNNNFNNNNN	NNNN4NCNNNNNNNN	R,T	063	460	06.04.09	7539	480702	92956
692.685-110	LAMP-SHADE JOINER (fabrication, nec)	1112	44444444344	LNNFNFNFFONNNNNFNNNON	NNNN3NNNNNNNNN	R	063	619	06.04.04	7659	000000	92998
692.685-114	LEVEL-GLASS-VIAL FILLER (cutlery-hrdwr.)	1112	44443444455	LNNNNNNFFONNNNNNNNNN	NNNN3NNNNNNNNN	R,T	041	552	06.04.09	7662	000000	92944
692.685-118	LIGHT-BULB ASSEMBLER (light. fix.)	2112	44444444355	LNNONNNFFFOOONFNFNON	NNNN4NNNNNNNNNF	R,U	111	584	06.04.20	7720	000000	92998
692.685-122	MAT-MAKING MACHINE TENDER (furniture)	2222	44444444355	LNNNNNNFFNNNNFNNONNNNN	NNNN4NNNNNNNNNF	R	061	460	06.04.09	7539	000000	92198
692.685-126	MOUNTER II (light. fix.)	1113	44444433355	SNNNNNNFFONNNONFNONNN	NNNN3NNNNNNNNN	R	061	584	06.04.16	7678	000000	92944
692.685-130	PINKING-MACHINE OPERATOR (button & notion)	2122	44443444344	LNNNNNNFFNNNNNNNONNN	NNNN3NNNNNNNNN	R,T	054	618	06.04.09	7678	000000	92944
692.685-134	POULTICE-MACHINE OPERATOR (pharmaceut.)	2124	44433444345	LNNNNNNFFONNNNFNONNN	NNNN3NNNNNNNNN	R,T	041	493	06.04.09	7679	000000	92998
692.685-138	PROTECTOR-PLATE ATTACHER (cutlery-hrdwr.)	1112	44444444445	LNNONNNFFNNNNNONONNN	NNNN3NNNNNNNNN	R,T	062	552	06.04.09	7539	000000	92953
692.685-142	RIBBON INKER (pen & pencil)	2122	44444443354	LNNFNNNFFNNNNNFNNNOON	NNNN3NNNNNNNNN	R,T	152	617	06.04.16	7661	000000	92198
692.685-146	SADDLE-AND-SIDE WIRE STITCHER (print. & pub.)	2112	44443433345	LNNNNNNFFNNNNNFNNNNN	NNNN4NNNNNNNNNNF	R	062	474	06.04.04	7679	480299	92546
692.685-150	SANITARY-NAPKIN-MACHINE TENDER (protective dev.)	2122	44443443355	LNNNNNNFFNNNNNFNNNNN	NNNN4NNNONNNNNN	R,T	062	604	06.04.09	7659	000000	92998

DOT #	DOT Title & Industry	Trng	Aptitude	Physical	Environment	Tempra	WkF	MPSMS	GOE	SOC	CIP	OES
692.685-154	SEAL-EXTRUSION OPERATOR (elec. equip.)	2112	4444443434345	LNNNONNFFNNNNNFNNNNNN	NNNN3NNNNNNNNNN	R,T	063	589	06.04.36	7662	000000	92974
692.685-158	SEALER, DRY CELL (elec. equip.)	2113	4444443433355	LNNNONFFNNNNNONNNNNN	NNNN3NNNNNNNNNO	R,T	094	589	06.04.09	7679	000000	92998
692.685-162	SEALING-MACHINE OPERATOR (light. fix.)	2123	4444443334355	LMNNONNFFONNNNNNNNNN	NNNN3NNNNNNNNNF	R	081	584	06.04.19	7669	000000	92953
692.685-166	SEPARATOR OPERATOR (button & notion)	2112	4443343434344	LMNNONNFFONNNNNNNNNN	NNNN4NNNNNNNNNN	R	145	618	06.04.09	7666	000000	92962
692.685-170	SKI TOPPER (toy-sport equip.)	2112	4443343453455	LNNNNNNFFNNNNNFNNFFON	NNNN3NNNNNNNNNN	R	136	616	06.04.20	7661	470499	92956
692.685-174	SLICING-MACHINE OPERATOR (button & notion)	2112	4443343453453	LNNNNNNFFFNNNNFONNNNN	NNNN3NNNNNNNNNN	R	056	618	06.04.08	7678	000000	92944
692.685-178	SLINGER, SEQUINS (plastic prod.)	2122	4444444444455	LNNNNNNFFNNNNNFNNOFN	NNNN3NNNNNNNNNN	R	171	510	06.04.09	7679	000000	92998
692.685-182	SORTER, MACHINE (button & notion)	2112	4443343334355	LNNONONFFONNNNNNNNNN	NNNN3NNNNNNNNNN	R	145	618	06.04.09	7679	000000	92998
692.685-186	SPIRAL-MACHINE OPERATOR (paper goods)	1112	4444443434345	LNNNNNNFFONNNNNNNNNN	NNNN3NNNNNNNNNN	R	163	474	06.04.09	7679	000000	92998
692.685-190	SPUN-PASTE-MACHINE OPERATOR (elec. equip.)	2122	4444434434345	LNNNNNNFFNNNNNFNFNNN	NNNN4NNNNNNNNNN	R,T	153	589	06.04.21	7679	000000	92998
692.685-194	STAMPING-MACHINE OPERATOR (pen & pencil)	2112	4544544444454	LNNNNNNFFONNNNONNNON	NNNN4NNNNNNNNNN	R	192	617	06.04.09	7679	480702	92998
692.685-198	STAPLER, MACHINE (furniture)	2113	4454453434355	MNNONNNCCFNNNNNNNNNN	NNNN3NNNNNNNNNN	R,T	062	464	06.04.20	7539	480501	92198
692.685-202	STAPLING-MACHINE OPERATOR (any industry)	2122	4444443333355	MNNONNNFFNNNNNFNNNNN	NNNN3NNNNNNNNNN	R	062	610	06.04.20	7679	000000	92998
692.685-206	STOP ATTACHER (button & notion)	2122	4443343434355	SNNNNNNFFNNNNNFNNNNN	NNNN3NNNNNNNNNN	R,T	062	618	06.04.20	7539	000000	92198
692.685-210	TAPE COATER (nonmet. min.)	1112	4444443434355	LNNNNNNFFNNNNNFNNNNN	NNNN3NNNNNNNNNN	R	151	538	06.04.21	7669	000000	92953
692.685-214	TAPER, MACHINE (fabrication, nec)	2122	4444443434345	LNNNNNNFFNNNNNFNFNNN	NNNN4NNNNNNNNNN	R	063	619	06.04.09	7679	000000	92998
692.685-218	THERMOSTAT-ASSEMBLY-MACHINE-TENDER, AUTOMATIC (inst. & app.)	2123	4444433433355	LNNNNNNFFONNNNNNNNNN	NNNN4NNNNNNNNNN	U	121	602	06.04.20	7720	470401	93956
692.685-222	TILE-POWER-SHEAR OPERATOR (fabrication, nec)	2112	4444343434345	LNNNNNNFFONNNNONNNON	NNNN3NNNNNNNNNN	R	054	619	06.04.09	7678	000000	92944
692.685-226	TINSEL-MACHINE OPERATOR (fabrication, nec)	2112	4444343434355	LNNNNNNFFONNNNNFNNNN	NNNN3NNNNNNNNNN	R	162	619	06.04.09	7679	000000	92998
692.685-230	TRIM ATTACHER (cutlery-hrdwr.)	2122	4444443434354	MNNONONFFONNNNONONON	NNNN4NNNNNNNNNN	R,T	061	552	06.04.20	7539	000000	92198
692.685-234	TUBE WINDER, HAND (nonmet. min.)	2122	4444443434354	MNNNNNNFFNNNNNFNNNNN	NNNN3NNNNNNNNNN	R,T	163	538	06.04.09	7679	000000	92998
692.685-238	VACUUM-APPLICATOR OPERATOR (fabrication, nec)	2112	4444434344345	MNNNNNNFFNNNNNNNNNN	NNNN3NNNNNNNNNN	R,T	063	619	06.04.21	7543	000000	91926
692.685-242	WICKER, MOLDED CANDLES (fabrication, nec)	2123	4444343333355	LNNNONFFONNNNFNNONN	NNNN3NNNNNNNNNN	R	061	619	06.04.09	7679	000000	92998
692.685-246	WINDER (toy-sport equip.)	2122	4444343433355	LNNNNNNFCONNNNNNNNNN	NNNN4NNNNNNNNNN	R,T	163	616	06.04.09	7679	000000	92998
692.685-250	WINDOW-SHADE CUTTER AND MOUNTER (furniture)	2113	4444433434335	SNNNNNNFFNNNNNFNNNNN	NNNN3NNNNNNNNNN	R,T	102	467	06.04.09	7654	200502	92705
692.685-254	WINDOW-SHADE-RING SEWER (furniture)	2112	4444444444444	LNNONONFFONNNNNNNNNN	NNNN3NNONNNNNNN	R,T	165	467	06.04.09	7655	200502	92721
692.685-258	WIRE-TURNING-MACHINE OPERATOR (wood. container)	1112	4444444444455	MNNNNNNFFONNNNNNNNNN	NNNN4NNNNNNNNNN	R	054	454	06.04.09	7678	000000	92998
692.685-262	WOOD-WEB-WEAVING-MACHINE OPERATOR (furniture)	2123	4443343434345	SNNNNNNFFNNNNNFNNFNN	NNNN4NNNNNNNNNN	R	061	467	06.04.09	7639	200502	92944
692.685-266	ZIPPER TRIMMER, MACHINE (button & notion)	2112	4443343433335	LNNNNNNFFNNNNNFNNFNN	NNNN3NNNNNNNNNN	R,T	054	618	06.04.34	7678	000000	92198
692.685-270	ZIPPER-MACHINE OPERATOR (button & notion)	2222	3344343434355	LNNONONFFONNNNFONNNN	NNNN4NNNNNNNNNN	R,J,T	134	618	06.04.02	7539	000000	92998
692.685-274	KEYMODULE-ASSEMBLY-MACHINE TENDER (office machines)	2222	4444343434355	LNNNONFFONNNNNNNNNN	NNNN3NNNNNNNNNN	R,T	121	601	06.04.09	7679	000000	92998
692.685-278	DIAPER MACHINE TENDER (protective dev.)	3234	3443343433345	MNNNNNNFFNNONONOONN	NNNN4NNNNNNNNNN	R,T	102	449	06.04.09	7659	000000	92971
692.685-282	LAMINATOR, PRINTED CIRCUIT BOARDS (electron. comp.)	2123	4454343334355	LNNNNNNFFNNNNNNNNNN	NNON3NNNNNNNNNO	R,U	063	587	06.04.09	7667	000000	92998
692.685-286	MOLDER, AUTOMOBILE CARPETS (tex. prod., nec)	2113	4453353533255	MNNNNNNFFFNNNNONOONN	NNNN4NNNNNNNNNN	R,U	132	431	06.04.09	7659	000000	92998
692.685-290	TRACK LAMINATING MACHINE TENDER (inst. & app.)	1112	4444443434354	MNNONNNFFFNNNNFNNNNN	NNNN3NOONNNNNON	R,U	054	601	06.04.09	7679	000000	92998
692.686-010	ASSEMBLY-MACHINE OPERATOR (pen & pencil)	2112	4444444444455	LNNNNNNFFFNNNNFNNNN	NNNN3NNNNNNNNNN	R	061	617	06.04.20	8725	000000	98502
692.686-014	BASE REMOVER (light. fix.)	1112	4454434434355	MNNNNNNFFONNNNNNNNNN	NNNN3NNNNNNNNNN	R	063	584	06.04.09	8725	000000	98502
692.686-018	BROOMCORN SEEDER (fabrication, nec)	1112	4544544434355	MNNONNNFFONNNNNNNNNN	NNNN3NONNNNNNNN	R	031	619	06.04.09	8725	000000	98502
692.686-022	BULB FILLER (light. fix.)	1111	4444444444455	LNNNNNNFFONNNNFNNNN	NNNN4NNNNNNNNNN	R	054	589	06.04.09	8725	000000	98502
692.686-026	CARBON ROD INSERTER (elec. equip.)	1112	4544544444455	LNNNNNNFFNNNNNFNNNNN	NNNN3NNNNNNNNNN	R	061	589	06.04.20	8725	000000	98502
692.686-030	CUTTER II (fabrication, nec)	1112	4444344434354	LNNNNNNFFNNNNNFNNNNN	NNNN3NNNNNNNNNN	R	054	619	06.04.09	8725	000000	98502
692.686-034	DESIGN ASSEMBLER (fabrication, nec)	1112	4444344434345	LNNNNNNFFNNNNNFNNNNN	NNNN3NNNNNNNNNN	R	061	619	06.04.09	8725	000000	98502
692.686-038	DYNAMITE-PACKING-MACHINE FEEDER (chemical)	2112	4444444444345	HNNFNNNFFNNNNNFNNNNN	NNNN4NONNNNNOOO	R,S	041	499	06.04.09	8725	000000	98502
692.686-042	GROOVER (any industry)	1112	4544544355	LNNONNNCCNNNNNNNNNN	NNNN4NONNNNNNNO	R	055	450	06.04.20	8725	000000	98502
692.686-046	LAMINATED-PLASTIC-TABLETOP-MOLDING WRAPPER (furniture)	1112	4444544345	MNNNNNNFFONNNNNNNNNN	NNNN3NNNNNNNNNN	R,T	061	460	06.04.20	8725	000000	98502
692.686-050	MOUNTER I (light. fix.)	1112	4544544455	LNNNNNNFFONNNNFNFNNN	NNNN4NNNNNNNNNN	R	061	584	06.04.09	8725	000000	98502
692.686-054	NAIL-POLISH-BRUSH-MACHINE FEEDER, AUTOMATIC (fabrication, nec)	2112	4444443355	MNNNNNNFFNNNNNNNNNN	NNNN3NNNNNNNNNN	R	102	619	06.04.20	8725	000000	98502
692.686-058	NECKER (jewelry-silver.)	1112	4544544455	LNNNNNNFFNNNNNNNNNN	NNNN4NNNNNNNNNN	R	062	472	06.04.09	8725	000000	98502
692.686-062	STEM SIZER (fabrication, nec)	1112	4444544455	MNNNNNNFFNNNNNNNNNN	NNNN3NNNNNNNNNN	R	145	309	06.04.20	8725	000000	98502
692.686-066	THIRD DRY-CELL-ASSEMBLING-MACHINE TENDER (elec. equip.)	1111	4444544455	LNNNNNNFFNNNNNNNNNN	NNNN3NNNNNNNNNN	R	041	589	06.04.20	8725	000000	98502
692.686-070	PASTER, HAT LINING (hat & cap)	1113	4444544455	LNNNNNNFFNNNNNNNNNN	NNNN4NNNNNNNNNN	R,U	063	445	06.02.27	7661	200303	92956

DOT #	DOT Title & Industry	Trng	Aptitude	Physical	Environment	Tempra	WkF	MPSMS	GOE	SOC	CIP	OES
692.687-010	SPLICER (fabrication, nec)	1112	44544433355	MNNNNNNFFNNNNFNOONN	NNNN4NONNNNNNN	R	063	619	06.04.34	7679	000000	92998
693.130-010	SUPERVISOR, MODEL MAKING (clock & watch)	4347	33322333245	LNNONONFFNFFNFNFFNN	NNNN4NNNNNNNNN	D,P,J	057	607	05.05.07	7100	520205	81008
693.131-010	PATTERN-SHOP SUPERVISOR (foundry)	4338	33322344344	LNNNNNNNFFNFNFNNNON	NNNN4NNNNNNNNN	V,D,P,J,T	057	566	05.05.07	6700	520205	81008
693.132-010	PATTERN-GRADER SUPERVISOR (wood prod., nec)	4337	33322333355	LNNNNNNNFFNFNFNFONN	NNNN3NNNNNNNNN	D,P,J,T	054	489	06.02.04	7100	520205	81008
693.260-018	ENGINEERING MODEL MAKER (inst. & app.; office machines)	4448	29222323244	MNNNNNNFFFOOONFNFOON	NNNN4NNFNNNNNNO	V,T,J	111	540	05.05.07	6817	480501	89908
693.261-010	DEVELOPER PROVER, INTERIOR ASSEMBLIES (aircraft mfg.)	4446	33324433344	MOOOOOFFOOOONFNOOON	NNNN4NNONONNNNN	V,T,J	101	592	05.05.15	6862	000000	89908
693.261-014	DEVELOPMENT MECHANIC (aircraft mfg.)	4447	23222433344	MOOOOONFFOOONFNOON	NNNN4NNFNONNNNN	T,J	102	592	06.01.04	6817	000000	89114
693.261-018	MODEL MAKER (aircraft mfg.)	4447	33223433344	MOOOOONFFOOOONFOOON	NNON4NOONONONON	V,J,T	102	592	06.01.04	6813	480501	89908
693.261-022	ROCKET-MOTOR MECHANIC (aircraft mfg.)	4447	33293433355	MONONNNFFNNNNFNFON	NNNN4NNONONONON	T,J	121	596	05.05.07	6862	000000	89108
693.280-014	PATTERNMAKER, ALL-AROUND (foundry; plastic prod.)	4438	23232433254	MNNNNNNFFNNNNFFON	NNNN4NNNNNNNNN	J,T,V	102	567	05.05.07	6862	480501	89908
693.281-014	PATTERNMAKER (metal prod., nec)	4337	33333433355	MNNNNNNFFONNNNFNNNN	NNON4NNNNNNNNN	V,T	102	559	05.05.06	6817	480501	89114
693.281-018	PATTERNMAKER, METAL, BENCH (foundry)	4348	33322432254	MNNNNNNFFNNNNFNFFON	NNNN4NNNNNNNNN	J,T	102	566	05.05.06	6817	480501	89114
693.281-022	PATTERNMAKER, SAMPLE (cutlery-hrdwr.)	4447	33323433345	LNNNNNNNFFNNNNFNFNN	NNNN3NNNNNNNNN	V,J,T	102	552	05.05.06	6817	480501	89114
693.281-030	TOOL BUILDER (aircraft mfg.)	4447	23322333254	MOOOOONFFONNNFNFOON	NNNN4NOONNNNNN	T	102	566	06.01.04	6862	000000	89908
693.361-014	MOCK-UP BUILDER (aircraft mfg.)	4447	33322433344	MONOOONFFONNNFNFOON	NNNN4NNFNNNNNNN	T,V	102	592	05.05.07	6817	480501	89114
693.380-010	MODEL MAKER (clock & watch)	4347	33332433355	LNNNNNNNFFNNNNFNONN	NNON4NOONNNNNN	J,T	057	592	05.05.07	6817	470408	89114
693.380-014	MODEL MAKER (auto. mfg.)	4338	34322433254	LNNNNNNNFFNNNNFNONN	NNNN4NNNNNNNNN	V,J,T	061	591	05.05.07	6862	480503	89908
693.381-018	MOCK-UP BUILDER (vehicles, nec)	4347	33322433345	LNNOOONFFFNNNNFNOONN	NNNN4NNNNNNNNNF	V,J,T	102	599	05.05.07	6862	480501	89908
693.381-022	MOLDER, PATTERN (foundry)	4337	33432433255	MNNNNNNCCNOONFNONNN	NNNN4NNNNNNNNNF	J,T	132	542	06.02.24	6861	480501	89905
693.381-026	ELECTRICAL AND RADIO MOCK-UP MECHANIC (aircraft mfg.)	4337	33334333344	LONOOONFFNNNNFNFNON	NNNN4NNOOONNNNN	T,V	102	568	06.01.04	6862	460302	89908
693.382-010	LAST-PATTERN GRADER (wood prod., nec)	4337	34433242255	MNNNNNNFFFOONFNFFNN	NNNN3NNNNNNNNN	J,T	054	479	06.02.04	7678	480501	89114
694.131-010	TRACER-BULLET-SECTION SUPERVISOR (ordnance)	4338	33344334354	LNNNNNNNFFNFNFNNNON	NNNN3NNNNNNNNN	V,D,P,J	041	370	06.01.01	7100	000000	81008
694.132-010	EXPLOSIVE-OPERATOR SUPERVISOR (ordnance)	4348	33433334354	MNNNNNNFFOOOONFNFOON	NNNN3NNNNNNNNN	V,D,P,J	102	370	06.02.01	7100	000000	81008
694.260-010	LOADING-MACHINE TOOL-SETTER (ordnance)	4336	33433443355	LFFOONNFFONNNNFNNNN	NNNN4NNNNNNNNN	V,J,T	061	374	06.01.02	7339	480503	92197
694.360-010	PRIMER-CHARGING TOOL SETTER (ordnance)	4336	34433433355	LNNNNNNNFFNNNNFNONN	NNNN4NNONNNNON	J,T	061	374	06.01.02	7339	480503	92198
694.362-010	CLIP-LOADING-MACHINE ADJUSTER (ordnance)	3234	34433433355	LNNNONNFFNNNNFNONN	NNNN3NNNNNNNNN	V,J,T	061	374	06.02.20	7479	000000	92997
694.382-010	SALVAGE-MACHINE OPERATOR (ordnance)	3224	34344433355	MNNNNNNFFNNNNFNONN	NNNN3NNNNNNNNNF	R,J,T	134	374	06.02.20	7479	000000	92997
694.382-014	TRACER-BULLET-CHARGING-MACHINE OPERATOR (ordnance)	3234	34433433355	HNNNNNNFFONNNFNFONN	NNNO3NFNNNNNONN	V,J,T	041	374	06.02.09	7662	000000	92974
694.385-010	SHOTGUN-SHELL-ASSEMBLY-MACHINE OPERATOR (ordnance)	2123	44443444355	MNNONONFFNNNNFONOONN	NNNN5NNNNNNNNNF	R,T	134	374	06.04.20	7539	000000	92198
694.585-010	SHELL-SIEVE OPERATOR (ordnance)	1112	44444444455	HNNNONONFFNNNNNNNNNN	NNNN3NNNNNNNON	R,S	145	374	06.04.09	7529	000000	92198
694.665-010	SHOTGUN-SHELL-LOADING-MACHINE OPERATOR (ordnance)	2223	34433443343	LONNNNNFFNNOOONFONOFN	NNNN4NNNNNNNNNC	R,J,T	041	374	06.04.09	7679	000000	92998
694.682-010	BULLET-ASSEMBLY-PRESS SETTER-OPERATOR (ordnance)	3234	34433433255	LNNNNNNNFFFNNNFNFNN	NNNN4NNNNNNNNN	J,T	134	374	06.02.02	7349	480503	92197
694.682-014	HYDRAULIC-PRESSURE-AUTO-FRETTAGE-MACHINE OPERATOR (ordnance)	3225	34444434455	MNNNNNNNFFONNNFNNONN	NNNN3NNNNNNNNN	J,T	134	371	06.02.02	7549	000000	92198
694.685-010	ANVIL-SEATING-PRESS OPERATOR (ordnance)	2123	44443443354	LNNNONNFFNNNNFNOON	NNNN4NNNNNNNNN	R	061	374	06.04.20	7539	000000	92198
694.685-014	BULLET-ASSEMBLY-PRESS OPERATOR (ordnance)	2123	44444444345	HFNFNNNFFONNNNFNOONN	NNNN4NNONNNNNN	R	134	370	06.04.02	7539	000000	92198
694.685-018	BULLET-LUBRICATING-MACHINE OPERATOR (ordnance)	1112	44444444355	LNNNNNNFFNNNNNNNNNN	NNON3NNONNNNNN	R	033	374	06.04.21	7543	000000	91926
694.685-022	FUSE-CUP EXPANDER (ordnance)	1112	44444444355	LNNNNNNFFNNNNNNNNNN	NNNN3NNONNNNNN	R	061	370	06.04.02	7529	000000	92198
694.685-026	LOADING-MACHINE OPERATOR (ordnance)	2113	44444433335	LNNNNNCCFNNNNFNNNNN	NNNN4NNNNNNNNNC	R,T	061	374	06.04.20	7662	000000	92998
694.685-030	LOADING-UNIT OPERATOR (ordnance)	2122	44444433355	LNNNNNNCCFNNNNFNNNNN	NNNN4NNNNNNNNNC	R,T	041	374	05.04.09	7662	000000	92974
694.685-034	PELLET-PRESS OPERATOR (ordnance)	2123	44443434344	LNNNNNNFFONOONFNNNN	NNNN4NNNNNNNNON	R,T	134	370	06.04.09	7663	000000	92971
694.685-038	PRESS TENDER, PYROTECHNICS (chemical)	2122	34433443355	MNNNNNNFFNOONFNNNNN	NNNN4NFNNNNNNN	R,T	134	499	06.04.09	7667	000000	98502
694.685-042	PRIMER-INSERTING-MACHINE OPERATOR (ordnance)	2122	44444433355	LNNNNNNFFNOONFNNONN	NNNN4NNNNNNNNNC	R	061	374	06.04.20	7679	000000	92998
694.685-046	PRIMER-WATERPROOFING-MACHINE OPERATOR (ordnance)	2122	44444443455	LNNNNNNFFNOONFNNONN	NNNN4NNNNNNNNN	R	153	374	06.04.21	7543	000000	91926
694.685-050	RIM-FIRE-PRIMING OPERATOR (ordnance)	2123	44444434355	MNNNNNNFFNOONFNONNN	NNNN3NNNNNNNNN	R	041	370	06.04.09	7662	000000	92974
694.686-010	CLIP-LOADING-MACHINE FEEDER (ordnance)	1112	34433443355	SNNNNNNCCCNNNNNNNNN	NNNN4NFNNNNNNN	R	061	374	06.04.20	8725	000000	92502
699.130-010	PRODUCTION SUPERVISOR (any industry)	4347	33333344455	LNNNNONFFNFFNFNNFNN	NNNN4NNNNNNNNN	V,D,P,J	057	560	06.02.01	7100	150603	81008
699.131-010	SUPERVISOR, LUBRICATION (any industry)	4337	33333344355	LNNNNNNFFNNNFNFNNN	ONNNNANNONNNNNN	V,D,P,J	033	560	06.04.01	7100	520205	81008
699.137-010	SUPERVISOR, CLEANING (beverage; can. & preserv.; dairy products; food prep.)	4237	33343333354	LNNOOONFFONFFNONNNON	NNNO3NNNNNNNNON	V,D,P,J	031	383	06.04.01	8500	200604	81017
699.362-010	AUTOMATED CUTTING MACHINE OPERATOR (aircraft mfg.)	3234	33433444455	LNNNNNNFFONOONFNNNN	NNNN3NNNNNNNNN	T	054	592	06.02.09	7326	000000	91502
699.380-010	DIE SET-UP OPERATOR, PRINTED CIRCUIT BOARDS (electron. comp.)	3223	34433444355	HNNNNNNFFOONNFNFNNN	NNNN4NNONNNNNN	J,T	121	587	06.01.02	7314	470105	91302
699.382-010	FLUID JET CUTTER OPERATOR (aircraft mfg.)	3235	33433433345	MNNNONNFFFONONFNFONN	NNNN4NNFNNNNNNN	T	051	592	06.02.09	7678	000000	92941

DOT #	DOT Title & Industry	Trng	Aptitude	Physical	Environment	Tempra	WkF	MPSMS	GOE	SOC	CIP	OES
699.384-010	COMPARATOR OPERATOR (any industry)	3334	33432333455	LNNNNNNFFFNNNNNFNFFNN	NNNN3NNNNNNNNNN	J,T	121	587	06.03.01	7820	000000	83005
699.482-010	RIVETING-MACHINE OPERATOR I (any industry)	3235	33333443345	MNNONONFFFNNNNFNFNNN	NNNN3NNNNNNNNNN	R,J,T	073	580	06.02.02	7339	480501	92197
699.587-010	SLITTING-MACHINE-OPERATOR HELPER I (any industry)	2112	44444434354	HNNOOONFFONOONONNNON	NNNN4NNNNNNNNNN	R,T	054	470	06.04.09	8618	000000	98999
699.682-010	BINDING CUTTER, SYNTHETIC CLOTH (tex. prod., nec)	3224	34433434354	MMNFNFNFFONNNNNFOONON	NNNN4NNNNNNNNNN	R,T	054	421	06.02.05	7654	000000	92705
699.682-014	CUTTER (glove & mit.; tex. prod., nec)	3224	34433434345	MNNNNNNFFONNNNFNNNNN	NNNN4NNNNNNNNNN	R,T	134	420	06.02.05	7654	200303	92705
699.682-018	CUTTER OPERATOR (any industry)	3225	34444444345	MNNONNNFFFNNNNNFFNN	NNNN4NFNNNNNNNN	T	054	420	06.02.09	7678	000000	92944
699.682-022	DIE CUTTER (any industry)	3234	34443434344	MNNNNNONFFFONNNNFNFNN	NNNN4NNNNNNNNNN	R,T	134	420	06.02.09	7678	480304	92944
699.682-026	ROLL-SHEETING CUTTER (tex. prod., nec)	3224	33442433344	MNNONONFFFNNQONFOONON	NNNN3NNONNNNNNN	R,J,T	054	519	06.02.09	7678	000000	92944
699.682-030	SLITTING-MACHINE OPERATOR I (any industry)	3234	34443434354	MNNNONNFFONNNNFOONON	NNNN3NNONNNNNNN	J,T	054	420	06.02.09	7678	000000	92944
699.682-034	BEVELER, PRINTED CIRCUIT BOARDS (electron. comp.)	2122	44443443344	LNNNNNNNFOFFNNNFNFNN	NNNN4NNNNNNNNNN	R,U	054	587	06.04.09	7322	470105	91114
699.685-010	BUTTON-ATTACHING-MACHINE OPERATOR (garment; hat & cap)	2112	44443443344	LNNNNNNFFFOOONFNNNON	NNNN4NNNNNNNNNN	R	072	445	06.04.05	7322	470105	92998
699.685-014	CUTTER, MACHINE II (any industry)	2122	44443444344	LNNNNNNNFFONNNNFNFNON	NNNN3NNNNNNNNNN	R,T	054	420	06.04.09	7678	480304	92944
699.685-018	EYELET-MACHINE OPERATOR (any industry)	2112	44444433345	LNNNNNNNFFNOONFNFFNN	NNNN3NNNNNNNNNN	R	062	430	06.04.05	7659	480304	92998
699.685-022	EYELET-PUNCH OPERATOR (furniture)	2112	44444433355	LNNNNNNNFFFNNNNFNNNNN	NNNN3NNNNNNNNNN	R,T	062	464	06.04.20	7659	000000	92998
699.685-026	POWER-SCREWDRIVER OPERATOR (any industry)	1112	44444444445	LNNNNNNFFONNNNFNNNNN	NNNN4NNONNNNNNN	R	071	450	06.04.20	7539	000000	92198
699.685-030	RIVETING-MACHINE OPERATOR II (any industry)	1112	44444443345	LNNNNNNNFFFNNNNFNNNNN	NNNN4NNNNNNNNNN	R	073	430	06.04.20	7539	000000	92198
699.685-038	FILLING-MACHINE OPERATOR (nonfer. metal)	2123	44444444355	LNNNNNNNFFONNNNNFNNNNN	NNNN4NNNNNNNNNN	R	041	554	06.04.36	7667	000000	92974
699.685-046	PINNER, PRINTED CIRCUIT BOARDS (electron. comp.)	2212	44444444455	MNNNNNNNCCNNNNFNFFNN	NNNN4NNNNNNNNNN	R	053	587	06.04.09	7518	470105	91117
699.685-050	PRODUCTION-MACHINE TENDER (auto. mfg.)	2123	34433334455	MMNNNNNFFNOONFNFFNN	NNNN3NNNNNNNNNC	R,U	102	591	06.04.02	7529	480503	92198
699.685-054	TRIMMER, PRINTED CIRCUIT BOARD PANELS (electron. comp.)	2112	44444444455	MNNNNNNNCCFNNNNFNFNN	NNNN4ONNNNNNNNN	R,U	054	587	06.04.09	7514	470105	91117
699.686-010	MACHINE FEEDER (any industry)	1112	44544544455	MNNNNNNNCCNNNNNNNNNN	NNNN4NNNNNNNNNN	R	054	492	06.04.09	8725	000000	98502
699.687-010	HARNESS CLEANER (textile)	1112	44544543355	MNNFNFNFFNNNNNNNNNN	NNNN4NNNNNNNNNN	R,T	031	567	06.04.39	8750	000000	98905
699.687-014	MACHINE CLEANER (any industry)	2112	44544544355	MONOOOOFFONNNNNFNNNNN	NNNO4NNNNNNNNNN	R,U	031	568	06.04.39	8750	470303	98905
699.687-018	OILER (any industry)	2113	44544543355	MNNOOONFFNOOFNNNNNN	NNNN3NNNNNNNNNN	R	033	560	05.12.08	6140	470303	85128
699.687-022	ROPE CLEANER (textile)	1112	44544544455	MNNOOONFFNOOFNNNNNN	NNNN3NNNNNNNNNN	R	031	567	06.04.27	8769	000000	89999
700.130-010	SUPERVISOR (jewelry-silver.)	4337	33332333355	LNNNNNNNFFNFFNNFNNNN	NNNN4NNNNNNNNNN	V,D,P,J	102	612	06.01.01	7100	000000	81008
700.131-010	SUPERVISOR (jewelry-silver.; plastic prod.)	4337	33344344454	LNNNNNNNFFNNFFNONNNON	NNNN3NNNNNNNNNN	V,D,P,J	102	612	06.02.01	7100	520205	81008
700.131-014	SUPERVISOR (metal prod., nec)	4338	33332333344	LNNNNNNNFFNFFNFNNONN	NNNN3NNNNNNNNNN	V,D,P,J	134	529	06.02.01	7100	520205	81008
700.131-018	SUPERVISOR, JEWELRY DEPARTMENT (jewelry-silver.)	4437	33344333355	LNNNNNNNFFONFNFNNNN	NNNN4NNNNNNNNNN	V,D,P,J	102	611	06.02.01	6700	000000	81008
700.261-010	PEWTERER (jewelry-silver.)	3338	22332332254	LNNNNNNNFFONFNFNNFNN	NNNN4NNNNNNNNNN	V,E,T,J	241	612	01.06.02	6861	480501	89905
700.281-010	JEWELER (jewelry-silver.)	4337	33322432355	SNNNNNNNCCFFNNNCNCCNN	NNON3NNNNNNNNNN	V,J,T	057	611	01.06.02	6822	470408	89123
700.281-014	JEWELER APPRENTICE (jewelry-silver.)	4337	33322432355	SNNNNNNNCCFFNNNCNCCNN	NNON3NNNNNNNNNN	V,J,T	057	611	01.06.02	6822	470408	89123
700.281-018	MODEL MAKER I (jewelry-silver.)	4337	23322322254	LNNNNNNNFCFFOONCNFFON	NNNN3NNNNNNNNNN	J,T	136	610	01.06.02	6822	000000	89123
700.281-022	SILVERSMITH II (jewelry-silver.)	4237	34422432255	LNNNNNNNFFNNFNNONN	NNON3NNNNNNNNNN	V,J,T	102	612	01.06.02	6822	000000	89126
700.281-026	PEWTER FINISHER (jewelry-silver.)	3227	34433433354	MNNONNNFFFNNNNFNOOON	NNNN4NNNNNNNNNN	V,T,J	055	612	01.06.02	6861	480501	89905
700.381-014	CHAIN MAKER, HAND (jewelry-silver.)	4236	33322432355	LNNNNNNNFFONNNCNONFN	NNNN3NNNNNNNNNN	V,T,J	102	611	01.06.02	6822	470408	89123
700.381-018	FANCY-WIRE DRAWER (jewelry-silver.)	4337	33323432355	SNNNNNNNFFCONNNFFNN	NNNN4NNNNNNNNNN	V,J,T	135	611	06.01.04	6822	470408	89126
700.381-022	GOLDBEATER (metal prod., nec)	3226	34433434355	LNNNNNNNFFCONNNFNFNN	NNNN3NNNNNNNNNN	J,T	134	559	06.01.04	6822	470408	89126
700.381-026	HAMMERSMITH (jewelry-silver.)	3126	33432433355	LNNNNNNNFFFNNNNFNFNN	NNNN3NNNNNNNNNN	J,T	134	612	06.01.04	6822	000000	89126
700.381-030	LAY-OUT WORKER (jewelry-silver.)	4237	33322433353	SNNNNNNNFFNNNNFNOONN	NNNN3NNNNNNNNNN	J,T	241	611	01.06.02	6822	470408	89123
700.381-034	MOLD MAKER I (jewelry-silver.)	3227	34433433354	LNNNNNNFFFNNNNFNNFON	NNNN3NNNNNNNNNN	V,J,T	057	611	06.01.04	6822	470408	89126
700.381-038	MOLD-MAKER APPRENTICE (jewelry-silver.)	4338	33334433355	LNNNNNNNFFNNNNFNOONN	NNNN3NNNNNNNNNN	V,J,T	183	611	01.06.02	6822	470408	89126
700.381-042	RING MAKER (jewelry-silver.)	3227	33433433354	LNNNNNNNCCONNNNFNNNN	NNNN3NNNNNNNNNN	V,J,T	183	611	06.01.04	6822	470408	89123
700.381-046	SAMPLE MAKER I (jewelry-silver.)	3227	33422422353	LNNNNNNNCCFNNNNCNONFN	NNNN3NNNNNNNNNN	V,J,T	132	611	01.06.02	6822	470408	89126
700.381-050	SOLDERER (jewelry-silver.)	3235	34433433354	SNNNNNNNFFFNNNNFNNNN	NNNN3NONNNNNNNN	V,J,T	102	611	06.01.04	6822	470408	89126
700.381-054	STONE SETTER (jewelry-silver.; optical goods)	3227	33322422355	LNNNNNNNCCOONNNCNCCNN	NNNN3NNNNNNNNNN	V,J,T	083	611	06.01.04	6822	000000	89126
700.381-058	STONE-SETTER APPRENTICE (jewelry-silver.; optical goods)	3227	33322422355	LNNNNNNNCCOONNNCNCCNN	NNNN3NNNNNNNNNN	V,J,T	061	605	05.05.14	6822	000000	89126
700.682-010	FLATWARE MAKER (jewelry-silver.)	3227	33432433344	LNNNNNNNFFFNNNNFNNNON	NNNN3NNNNNNNNNN	V,J,T	061	605	05.05.14	6822	470408	89126
700.682-014	LATHE HAND (jewelry-silver.)	3227	33433433355	LNNNNNNFFONNNNFNNNNN	NNNN4NNONONNNNN	J,T	134	612	06.02.02	7663	000000	92971
700.682-018	PROFILE-SAW OPERATOR (jewelry-silver.)	3223	33433434255	LNNNNNNNFFONNNNFNFFNN	NNNN4NNONNNNNNN	R,T	056	612	06.02.02	7329	480503	91102

DOT #	DOT Title & Industry	Trng	Aptitude	Physical	Environment	Tempra	WkF	MPSMS	GOE	SOC	CIP	OES
700.684-010	ARBORER (jewelry-silver.)	2112	44544543355	LNNNNNNFFNNNNFNNNN	NNNNN3NNNNNNNNNN	R,T	134	611	06.04.24	7720	470408	93999
700.684-014	ASSEMBLER (jewelry-silver.)	2113	34443533355	SNNNNNNCCFNNNNFNNNNO	NNNNN3NNNNNNNNNNO	R,T	061	611	06.04.23	7720	470408	93956
700.684-018	BRIGHT CUTTER (jewelry-silver.)	3223	34443534354	SNNNNNNCCFNNNNFNNNFON	NNNNN3NNNNNNNNNN	R,T	054	611	06.02.24	7753	470408	93926
700.684-022	CHAIN MAKER, MACHINE (jewelry-silver.)	3223	34444544345	LNNNNNFFNNNNNFNNNN	NNNNN3NNNNNNNNNN	R,T	102	611	06.02.23	7720	470408	93999
700.684-026	DRILLER (jewelry-silver.)	2123	34444534345	SNNNNNNFFONNNNFNNNON	NNNNN3NNNNNNNNNN	R,T	053	611	06.04.24	7518	470408	91117
700.684-030	EARRING MAKER (jewelry-silver.)	3223	34443534454	SNNNNNNFFNNNNFNNNON	NNNNN3NNNNNNNNNNO	R,T	061	611	06.04.24	7720	470408	93999
700.684-034	FILER (jewelry-silver.)	3123	34533533354	LNNNNNNFFNNNNFNNNON	NNNNN3NNNNNNNNNN	R,T	051	611	06.04.24	7758	470408	93953
700.684-038	GOLD CUTTER (metal prod., nec)	3124	34443433355	LNNNNNNFFFNNNFNNFNN	NNNNN3NNNNNNNNNN	R,T	054	559	06.02.24	7753	000000	93926
700.684-042	HOLLOW-HANDLE-KNIFE ASSEMBLER (jewelry-silver.)	2112	44443434345	LNNNNNNFFFNNNFNOONN	NNNNN3NNNNNNNNNN	R,J,T	102	612	06.04.23	7720	000000	93956
700.684-046	JIGSAWYER (jewelry-silver.)	2114	34443533355	LNNNNNNFFNNNNFNNNNN	NNNNN3NNNNNNNNNN	R,T	056	611	06.04.24	7529	470408	91117
700.684-050	MESH CUTTER (jewelry-silver.)	3123	34433533355	SNNNNNNFFNNNNFNNNNN	NNNNN3NNNNNNNNNN	R,T	054	611	06.02.24	7753	470408	93926
700.684-054	OXIDIZER (jewelry-silver.)	2122	44443534355	LNNONONFFONNNNONNNNN	NNNNN3NONNNNNNNNN	R,T	151	612	06.04.24	7756	000000	93947
700.684-058	PREPARER, MAKING DEPARTMENT (jewelry-silver.)	3226	34443533345	LNNNNNNFFFNNNFNOONN	NNNNN3NNNNNNNNNN	R,T	057	611	06.02.24	7720	470408	93999
700.684-062	PREPARER, SAMPLES AND REPAIRS (jewelry-silver.)	3224	34443534345	LNNNNNNFFFNNNFNOONN	NNON4NNONNNNNNNN	R,J,T	134	611	06.02.24	7720	470408	92198
700.684-066	RING STAMPER (jewelry-silver.)	2115	34533534354	LNNNNNNFFFNNNFNOOON	NNNNN4NNNNNNNNNN	R,T	102	612	06.04.23	7720	000000	93956
700.684-070	SILVERWARE ASSEMBLER (jewelry-silver.)	2123	34433433355	LNNNNNNFFNNNNFNNNNN	NNNNN3NNNNNNNNNN	R,T	134	611	06.02.24	7755	470408	93999
700.684-074	SPINNER (jewelry-silver.)	3225	34433433355	SNNNNNNNFFONNNNONNNNN	NNNNN3NNNNNNNNNN	J,T	134	611	06.04.24	7755	470408	93999
700.684-078	STRETCHER (jewelry-silver.)	2123	44443433355	LNNNNNNFFNNNNFNNNNN	NNNNN3NNNNNNNNNN	R,T	134	611	06.04.23	7720	470408	93956
700.684-082	WATCH-BAND ASSEMBLER (jewelry-silver.)	2113	44443533355	LNNNNNNFFFNNNNFNNNNN	NNNNN3NNNNNNNNNN	R,T	061	607	06.04.23	7720	470408	93956
700.687-010	BENCH WORKER, HOLLOW HANDLE (jewelry-silver.)	2112	44544544355	LNNNNNNFFONNNNONNNNN	NNNNN3NNNNNNNNNN	R	083	612	06.04.23	7720	470408	93956
700.687-014	BOILER-OUT (jewelry-silver.)	2112	44544544455	LNNNNNNFFONNNNONNNNN	NNNNN3NNNNNNNNNN	R	151	611	06.04.33	7756	470408	93947
700.687-018	BRIMER (metal prod., nec)	1112	44444534355	SNNNNNNNFFONNNNFNNNNN	NNNNN3NNNNNNNNNN	R	153	559	06.04.33	7759	000000	93999
700.687-022	CASTER HELPER (jewelry-silver.)	2113	45444544355	LNNNNNNNFFONNNNFNNNNN	NNNNN3NNNNNNNNNN	J,T	132	611	05.12.10	7754	489999	93944
700.687-026	CHARGER II (jewelry-silver.)	2113	44544543355	SNNNNNNNFFNNNNFNNNNN	NNNNN3NNNNNNNNNN	R	083	611	06.04.23	7720	470408	93956
700.687-030	CUTCH CLEANER (metal prod., nec)	2112	44444544355	LNNNNNNFFFNNNNFNNNNN	NNNF3NNNNNNNNNN	R	031	559	06.04.27	8750	000000	98905
700.687-034	INSPECTOR (jewelry-silver.)	3224	34443443454	SNNNNNNNFFFNNNNFNNOON	NNNNN3NNNNNNNNNN	R,T	212	611	06.03.02	7820	470408	83005
700.687-038	LABORER, GOLD LEAF (metal prod., nec)	2112	44544544355	LNNNNNNFFONNNNFNNNNN	NNNNN4NNNNNNNNNN	R	061	559	06.04.24	8761	000000	98902
700.687-042	MELTER (jewelry-silver.)	2122	44444544454	MNNNNNNFFONNNNFNNNFN	NNFN3NNONNNNNNNN	R,J,T	131	541	05.04.24	7549	470408	92198
701.137-010	SUPERVISOR, ASSEMBLY-AND-PACKING (cutlery-hrdwr.)	4337	33343334455	LNNNNNNFFONFFNFNNNNN	NNNNN3NNONNNNNNN	V,D,P,J	102	552	06.04.01	7100	000000	81008
701.261-010	QUALITY-CONTROL INSPECTOR (cutlery-hrdwr.)	4336	33343334454	LNNNNNNFFONNFNFNNFON	NNNNN3NNONNNNNNN	V,P,J,T	121	552	06.01.05	6881	000000	83002
701.381-010	REPAIRER, HANDTOOLS (cutlery-hrdwr.)	3225	33433333355	LNNNNNNFFFNNNNFNOFNN	NNNNN3NNNNNNNNNN	J,T	121	552	05.10.02	6179	470303	85999
701.381-014	SAW FILER (any industry)	3336	33333433345	MNNONNNFFNNNNNFNNNN	NNNN4NOONNNNNNNN	J,T	121	552	05.05.07	6816	010201	89111
701.381-018	TOOL GRINDER I (any industry)	3226	44442533354	SNNNNNNNFFNNNNFNNNON	NNNNN3NNNNNNNNNN	J,T	051	552	05.05.07	6816	010201	89111
701.384-010	TOOL-MAINTENANCE WORKER (office machines)	2113	33433333355	LNNNNNNFFFNNNNFNNNNN	NNNNN3NNNNNNNNNN	R,J	121	566	06.02.24	7758	470408	93953
701.684-010	CALIBRATOR (cutlery-hrdwr.)	2124	34444444355	LNNNNNNFFFNNNNFNNNNN	NNNNN3NNNNNNNNNN	R,T	121	552	06.04.24	6140	470401	85999
701.684-014	INSPECTOR, OPEN DIE (cutlery-hrdwr.)	3224	33433433345	LNNNNNNNFFONNNNFNNNNN	NNNNN4NNNNNNNNNN	V,J,T	212	566	06.03.02	7820	480507	83005
701.684-018	LEVEL-VIAL SETTER (cutlery-hrdwr.)	2113	33433433355	LNNNNNNNFFNNNNFNNFNN	NNNNN3NNNNNNNNNN	R,T	061	552	06.04.23	7720	000000	93956
701.684-022	SAW SETTER (stonework)	3125	34433544345	LNNOOONFFNNNNNONNNNN	ONNNN4NNNNNNNNNN	J,T	102	566	05.10.01	6140	470303	85128
701.684-026	SAW-EDGE FUSER, CIRCULAR (cutlery-hrdwr.)	2223	34444444355	MNNNNNNFFONNNNFNNNNN	NNNNN3NNNNNNNNNN	R,T	081	552	06.04.32	7539	480503	92198
701.684-030	TOOL FILER (pottery & porc.)	3125	34433433355	LNNNNNNFFFNNNNFNNONN	NNNNN3NNNNNNNNNN	R,T	051	566	05.12.13	6140	470303	85128
701.687-010	ASSEMBLER (cutlery-hrdwr.)	2122	44444433355	LNNNNNNFFONNNFNNNNN	NNNNN4NNNNNNNNNN	R	102	552	06.04.23	7840	000000	93956
701.687-014	BLADE BALANCER (agric. equip.)	1112	44444444455	LNNOOONFFNNNNNONNNNN	NNNNN3NNNNNNNNNN	R	212	562	06.03.02	7840	000000	83005
701.687-018	COLD-PRESS LOADER (cutlery-hrdwr.)	2123	44544534355	LNNNNNNFFFNNNNFNNNNN	NNNNN3NNNNNNNNNN	R	083	552	06.04.32	7740	480503	99999
701.687-022	LEVEL-VIAL CURVATURE GAUGER (cutlery-hrdwr.)	2123	34443432355	LNNNNNNFFONNNNFNNFNN	NNNNN3NNNNNNNNNN	R,T	212	552	06.03.02	7820	489999	83005
701.687-026	LEVEL-VIAL INSPECTOR-AND-TESTER (cutlery-hrdwr.)	2123	44444344355	LNNNNNNFFONNNNFNNFNN	NNNNN3NNNNNNNNNN	R,J	212	552	06.03.02	7820	489999	83005

DOT #	DOT Title & Industry	Trng	Aptitude	Physical	Environment	Tempra	WKF	MPSMS	GOE	SOC	CIP	OES
701.687-030	POWER-CHISEL OPERATOR (cutlery-hrdwr.)	2112	44544545455	LNNNNNNNFFNNNNFNFNNNNN	NNNN4NNNNNNNNN	R	052	552	06.04.25	7740	000000	93999
701.687-034	WEDGER, MACHINE (cutlery-hrdwr.)	2112	44444454335	MNNNNNNNFFNNNNNFNNNNNN	NNNN4NNNNNNNNN	R,T	061	552	06.04.23	7740	000000	93999
703.132-010	SUPERVISOR, METAL CANS (tinware)	4337	33333343355	LNNNNNNNFFNFFONONNNNNN	NNNN4NNNNNNNNN	V,D,P	102	551	06.02.01	7100	520205	81008
703.381-010	PATTERNMAKER (stonework)	4337	33323333355	LNNNNNNNFFNOONFNNFNN	NNNN3NNNNNNNNN	J,T	241	537	05.05.06	6862	480501	89114
703.684-010	BENCH-SHEAR OPERATOR (furniture)	3125	33434444344	MNNNNNNFONNNNFNNNNN	NNNN3NNNNNNNNN	R,T	054	460	06.02.25	7529	480506	92198
703.684-014	CUPBOARD BUILDER (furniture)	3124	34334444344	LNNNNNNNFFONNNNFNNNNN	NNNN3NNNNNNNNN	R,T	102	460	06.02.22	7720	480501	93956
703.684-018	TEMPLATE CUTTER (cutlery-hrdwr.)	2222	34334443345	LNNNNNNNFFNNNNFNNONN	NNNN3NNNNNNNNN	R,T	054	566	06.04.24	7753	480506	93926
703.685-010	PAIL BAILER (tinware)	3123	34434434345	LNNNNNNNNFFNNNNFNNFNN	NNNN4NNNNNNNNN	R,T	061	559	06.04.02	7740	480506	93956
703.685-014	TESTING-MACHINE OPERATOR (tinware)	2112	44444494355	LNNFNFNFFONONONNNNN	NNNN4NNNNNNNNN	R	212	551	06.03.02	7830	480506	83005
703.687-010	ASSORTER (steel & rel.)	3224	34443434355	LNNNNNNNFONNNNFNFNN	NNNN3NNNNNNNNN	R,T	212	541	06.03.02	7820	480506	83005
703.687-014	METAL-FINISH INSPECTOR (any industry)	3225	33443444355	LNNONNNFONNNNFNNFNN	NNNN3NNNNNNNNN	R,T	212	556	06.03.02	7820	480506	83005
703.687-018	METAL-FINISH INSPECTOR (furniture)	3124	33444444344	LNNNNNNNFFOONNFNNFON	NNNN3NNNNNNNNN	R,J	212	460	06.03.02	7820	480501	83005
703.687-022	STEEL-BARREL REAMER (wood. container)	1112	44534544355	LNNNNNNNFFNNNNNNNNN	NNNN3NNNNNNNNN	R	053	559	06.04.24	7758	000000	93953
704.131-010	ENGRAVING SUPERVISOR (engraving)	4338	33322333355	LNNNNNNFFOFNFFOONN	NNNN4NONNNNNON	V,D,P,J,T	183	556	01.06.01	6700	520205	81008
704.131-014	SUPERVISOR, ENGRAVING (pen & pencil)	4338	33333433355	LNNNNNNFFNFFNFNNNN	NNNN3NNNNNNNNN	D,P,J,T	183	617	01.06.01	6700	000000	81008
704.381-010	CHASER (jewelry-silver.)	4236	33333432354	LNNNNNNNFFNNNNFFON	NNNN4NNNNNNNNN	J	134	611	01.06.02	6822	470408	89126
704.381-014	CHEMICAL-ETCHING PROCESSOR (aircraft mfg.)	3236	33333433355	MNNONNNFFOONNNFNFONN	NNNN4NFNNNNNNON	T	182	592	06.01.04	6829	000000	89199
704.381-018	ENGINE TURNER (jewelry-silver.)	3226	34432433354	SNNNNNNNFFONNNNFNNN	NNNN3NNNNNNNNN	J,T	183	611	01.06.01	6822	470408	89126
704.381-022	ENGRAVER APPRENTICE, DECORATIVE (engraving)	3227	33422432255	SNNNNNNCCFNNNNFNFFNN	NNNN3NNNNNNNNN	J,T	183	605	01.06.01	6823	000000	89128
704.381-026	ENGRAVER, HAND, HARD METALS (engraving)	4338	33322432255	MNNNNNNCCONNNFNFFNN	NNNN3NNNNNNNNN	J	183	617	01.06.01	6823	000000	89128
704.381-030	ENGRAVER, HAND, SOFT METALS (engraving)	3227	33422432255	SNNNNNNCFNNNNFNFFNN	NNNN3NNNNNNNNN	J,T	183	605	01.06.01	6823	470408	89128
704.381-034	ENGRAVER, SEALS (pen & pencil)	4236	33333433355	SNNNNNNNFFNNNNFNFFNN	NNNN3NNNNNNNNN	J,T	132	617	01.06.01	6823	000000	89128
704.382-010	ENGRAVER, PANTOGRAPH I (engraving)	3226	33333433355	SNNNNNNNFFNNNNFNNNNN	NNNN3NNNNNNNNN	J,T	183	556	05.10.05	7757	000000	93951
704.582-010	ENGRAVER, MACHINE II (engraving)	3223	44444433355	LNNNNNNNFFNNNNFNNONN	NNNN3NNNNNNNNN	J,T	183	610	05.10.05	7757	000000	93951
704.682-010	ENGRAVER, MACHINE I (engraving)	3223	44443433355	SNNNNNNNFFNOONFNNONN	NNNN3NNNNNNNNN	R	183	610	05.10.05	7757	000000	93951
704.682-014	ENGRAVER, PANTOGRAPH II (engraving)	3223	34433433345	LNNNNNNNFFNNNNFNNNNN	NNNN4NNNNNNNNN	R,T	183	556	05.10.05	7757	000000	93951
704.684-010	ETCHER (engraving)	3226	34432544355	LNNNNNNFFONNNNFNNOONN	NNNN3NNNNNNNNN	J,T	182	556	01.06.01	7757	000000	93951
704.684-014	SILK-SCREEN ETCHER (engraving)	2113	44443544355	LNNNNNNNFFNNNNFNNNNN	NNNN3NONNNNNNNN	R,T	182	550	06.04.24	7757	480299	93951
704.687-010	CLEANER (engraving)	1112	44443544355	LNNNNNNNFFNNNNFNNNNN	NNNN3NNNNNNNNN	R	031	556	06.04.24	8750	000000	98905
704.687-014	ETCHER, HAND (cutlery-hrdwr.)	2113	44443443455	LNNNNNNNFFONNNNFNNNNN	NNNN3NNNNNNNNN	R,T	182	552	06.04.24	7757	000000	93951
705.381-010	DIE BARBER (machine shop)	3127	33432433254	MNNNNNNNFFNNNFNFNN	NNNN3NNNNNNNNN	J,T	051	566	05.05.06	6816	480503	89111
705.381-014	EXTRUSION-DIE REPAIRER (nonfer. metal)	3336	33332323354	LNNNNNNNFFNNNNFFON	NNNN4NNNNNNNNN	J,T	051	566	05.05.06	6829	480507	89199
705.384-010	SCRAPER, HAND (machine shop)	3126	34343433354	MNNOOONFFNNNNFNNNNN	NNNN3NNNNNNNNN	J,T	051	540	06.04.02	7758	480503	93953
705.481-010	FILER, FINISH (ordnance)	3225	34323433355	MNNNNNNFFNNNNFNFNN	NNNN3NNNNNNNNN	R,J,T	057	373	06.01.04	6816	480503	89111
705.481-014	LAPPER, HAND, TOOL (machine shop)	3325	34433432354	LNNOONNFFFONNNFNOOON	NNNN4NOONNNNNNN	J	051	540	05.05.07	6816	480503	89111
705.484-010	FILER, HAND, TOOL (machine shop)	3226	34422423355	MNNNNNNFFONNNFNFFNN	NNNN4NNOONNNNNN	J,T	051	540	05.05.07	7758	480503	93953
705.484-014	FINAL FINISHER, FORGING DIES (machine shop)	3226	34333433355	MNNOOONFFONNNFNONNN	NNNN3NNNNNNNNNO	J,T	051	540	06.04.24	7758	480503	93953
705.582-010	BLADE GROOVER (cutlery-hrdwr.)	2112	44443544355	LNNNNNNNFFONNNNFNNNNN	NNNN4NOONNNNNNN	R,T	051	552	06.04.24	7522	000000	91117
705.682-010	GOLD-NIB GRINDER (pen & pencil)	2122	44443443455	LNNNNNNNFFONONFNNONN	NNNN4NOONNNNNNO	R,T	051	617	06.04.02	7522	000000	91117
705.682-014	TRIMMER (jewelry-silver.)	3124	34542534254	MNNONONFFOOONFNNNNN	NNNN4NOONNNNNNN	J,T	051	612	06.02.02	7522	000000	91117
705.684-010	BENCH GRINDER (any industry)	2113	44443434355	LNNNNNNNFFONNNNFNNOONN	NNNO4NNONNNNNNN	R,J,T	051	550	06.02.24	7758	480503	93953
705.684-014	BUFFER I (any industry)	2124	34443433355	LNNNNNNNFFOONNNFNNONN	NNNN3NNNNNNNNNO	R,J,T	051	556	06.04.24	7529	470603	92198
705.684-018	FILER AND SANDER (woodworking)	2113	44543534355	MNNONONFFNNNNONNNNN	NNNN3NNNNNNNNN	J,T	051	542	06.04.24	7755	480503	91117
705.684-022	GREASE BUFFER (jewelry-silver.)	3124	34443443354	LNNNNNNNFFNNNNFFNN	NNNN4NOONNNNNNN	R,J,T	051	612	06.02.24	7758	000000	93953
705.684-026	GRINDER I (any industry)	2123	44443434355	MNNONONFFOOONFNNNNN	NNNN4NOONNNNNNN	J,T	051	540	06.04.24	7758	480503	93953
705.684-030	GRINDER-CHIPPER I (any industry)	3224	34443433355	LNNNNNNNFFOONNNFNNONN	NNNN4NNNNNNNNN	J,T	051	550	06.02.24	7758	480503	93953
705.684-034	METAL FINISHER (any industry)	2124	44434433355	LNNNNNNNFFOONNNFNNONN	NNNN4NNONNNNNNN	R,T	051	556	06.04.24	7529	470603	92198
705.684-038	MOLD FINISHER (machine shop)	3225	34335343355	MNNONONFFNNNNFNFOON	NNNN3NNNNNNNNN	T	051	542	06.02.24	7755	480503	91117
705.684-042	MOTHER REPAIRER (recording)	3224	34433443455	LNNNNNNNFFFNNNNFNNNN	NNNN3NNNNNNNNN	R,T	051	585	06.02.24	6179	000000	85999
705.684-046	NEEDLE POLISHER (button & notion)	2113	44443434355	MNNNNNNFNFOFNNNCNCNIN	NNNN3NNNNNNNNN	R,T	051	618	06.04.24	7758	480501	93953
705.684-050	NIB FINISHER (pen & pencil)	2124	34433432354	LNNNNNNNFFONNNNFNNOON	NNNN3NNNNNNNNN	R,T	051	617	06.04.24	7758	000000	93953

DOT #	DOT Title & Industry	Trng	Aptitude	Physical	Environment	Tempra	WkF	MPSMS	GOE	SOC	CIP	OES
705.684-054	PIPE BUFFER (construction)	2112	44543544345	MNNFFNNFFNNNNFNFNNN	CNNN4NNNNNNNNF	R	051	541	05.12.18	7758	480503	93953
705.684-058	POLISHER (any industry)	3226	34333433355	MNNNNNNFFNNNNFNNNN	NNNN4NONNNNNNNN	R,T	051	550	06.04.24	7522	470603	91117
705.684-062	POLISHER AND BUFFER II (any industry)	2122	44443434355	MNNNNNNFFNNNNFNNNN	NNNN3NNNNNNNNN	R,T	051	550	06.04.24	7758	480503	93953
705.684-066	POLISHER APPRENTICE (any industry)	3226	34433433355	MNNNNNNFFNNNNFNNONN	NNNN4NONNNNNNNN	R,T	051	550	06.04.24	7522	470603	91117
705.684-070	POLISHER, SAND (jewelry-silver.)	3126	34443433354	LNNNNNNFFFNNNNFNNNNN	NNNN4NONNNNNNNN	R,J,T	051	612	06.02.24	7522	000000	91117
705.684-074	SNAG GRINDER (foundry)	2123	44443544355	MNNONNNFFONNNNFNNNNN	NNNN4NONNNNNNN	R,J	051	542	06.04.24	7522	480599	91117
705.687-010	JIGGER (jewelry-silver.)	1112	44544544455	LNNNNNNFFONNNNFNNNN	NNNN4NONNNNNNNN	R	061	611	06.04.34	8769	470408	98999
705.687-014	LABORER, GRINDING AND POLISHING (any industry)	2222	44443433355	MNNONNNFFFNNNNFNFNN	NNNN4NONNNNNNNN	R,T	051	540	06.04.34	8769	480503	98999
705.687-018	METAL SANDER AND FINISHER (furniture)	2113	44543533355	MNNNNNNFFNNNNONNNNN	NNNN3NNNNNNNNN	R,T	051	466	06.04.24	7758	480501	93953
706.130-010	SUPERVISOR, COIN-MACHINE (svc. ind. mach.)	4337	33333433355	LNNNNNNFFONFFNFONNNN	NNNN3NNNNNNNNN	D,P,T	121	572	06.01.01	7100	520205	81008
706.131-010	LABORATORY SUPERVISOR (machine shop)	4338	33332332355	MNNNNNNFFNFFNNNFFNN	NNNN3NNNNNNNNN	D,P,J,T	212	559	06.01.01	6700	520205	81008
706.131-014	SUPERVISOR (office machines)	4347	33322332355	LNNNNNNFFFOFFNFFNNNN	NNNN4NNONNNNNNN	V,D,P,J,T	121	571	06.02.01	7100	000000	81008
706.131-018	CHIEF INSPECTOR (office machines)	3337	33322332354	MNNFONNNFFFOFFNFNOFON	NNNN3NNNNNNNNN	D,J,T	121	571	06.03.02	6700	150702	83005
706.361-010	ASSEMBLER (machinery mfg.)	3235	33434443355	MONOOONFFNOONFNFONNN	NNNN4NNNNNNNNO	R	211	571	06.02.22	6812	490299	93105
706.361-014	ASSEMBLY INSPECTOR (agric. equip.)	3215	33434433354	LNNONONFFFNNFNFONNN	NNNN4NNNNNNNNO	J,T	212	567	06.01.05	6881	010204	83002
706.381-010	ALIGNER, TYPEWRITER (office machines)	3224	34432433355	LNNNNNNFFFNNNNFNFFNN	NNNN3NNNNNNNNN	R,T	121	562	06.02.24	6174	470102	85926
706.381-014	BENCH HAND (furniture)	3236	33333432355	MNNNNNNFFFNNNNFNFNNN	NNNN3NNNNNNNNN	J,T	121	571	06.02.24	6829	480501	89199
706.381-018	FINAL ASSEMBLER (office machines)	3236	33333433354	MNNOOONFFONNNFNFNON	NNNN3NNNNNNNNN	J,T	102	571	06.01.04	6812	470102	93111
706.381-022	INSPECTOR, TYPEWRITER ASSEMBLY AND PARTS (office machines)	3336	33333333354	MNNNNNNFFNNNNFNNFFON	NNNN4NNNNNNNNN	J,T	212	550	06.01.05	6881	470102	83002
706.381-026	OPERATING-TABLE ASSEMBLER (furniture)	4336	33333432255	MNNNNNNFFNNNNFNFNNN	NNNN3NNNNNNNNN	J,T	121	466	06.01.04	6812	480501	93197
706.381-030	REPAIRER, TYPEWRITER (office machines)	3236	33333433355	MNNNNNNFFONNNFNFONN	NNNN3NNNNNNNNN	J,T	121	571	06.02.24	6174	470102	85926
706.381-034	SEWING-MACHINE ASSEMBLER (machinery mfg.)	3226	34344444355	MNNNNNNFFNNNNNNNNN	NNNN3NNNNNNNNN	J,T	121	583	06.02.23	6812	470199	93105
706.381-038	SUBASSEMBLER (machinery mfg.)	3326	34322444355	MNNNNNNFFONNNFNFNNN	NNNN3NNNNNNNNN	J,T	121	567	06.02.24	6812	000000	93105
706.381-042	TURBINE SUBASSEMBLER (engine-turbine)	3236	34333533255	MNNOOONFFFONNNFOFONN	NNNN4NNNNNNNNO	J,T	121	561	06.02.22	6812	000000	93105
706.381-046	WHEELWRIGHT (automotive ser.)	3125	34433433355	MOOOONFFFONNNFNFNNN	NNNN4NNNNNNNN	V,T	134	591	05.10.01	6111	470603	85302
706.381-050	PRECISION ASSEMBLER, BENCH (aircraft mfg.)	3226	34332433344	HNNONNNFFONNNNFNFNNN	NNNN4NOONNNNNN	T	121	592	06.02.23	6812	000000	93111
706.382-010	FUNCTIONAL TESTER, TYPEWRITERS (office machines)	3224	34443433354	MNNOOONFFFONNNFNFOON	NNNN3NNNNNNNNN	R,J,T	212	571	06.03.01	7830	470102	83005
706.382-014	TESTER, SOUND (machinery mfg.)	3224	33434433355	LNNNNNNFFNNNFNFNNN	NNNN3NNNNNNNNN	R,T	212	591	06.03.01	7830	480503	83002
706.384-010	INSPECTOR-ADJUSTER, OFFICE-MACHINE COMPONENTS (office machines)	3233	33333432233	LNNNNNNFFNNNNFNFFN	NNNN3NNNNNNNNN	R,T	211	571	06.01.05	7820	150301	83002
706.387-010	INSPECTOR, AUTOMATIC TYPEWRITER (office machines)	3224	33433443355	MNNNNNNFFFOFNFFNNN	NNNN3NNNNNNNNN	J	212	560	06.03.01	7820	470102	83005
706.387-014	MACHINE TESTER (office machines)	3224	33443333355	LNNNNNNFFNNONFNFNNN	NNNN4NNNNNNNNN	R,J,T	212	611	06.03.01	7830	470102	83005
706.481-010	INTERNAL-COMBUSTION-ENGINE SUBASSEMBLER (engine-turbine)	3225	33434433255	MNNONNNFFFNNNNFNFNNN	NNNN3NNNNNNNNN	R,J,T	121	571	06.02.22	6812	000000	93105
706.484-010	DRAPERY-ROD ASSEMBLER (retail trade)	2123	44433433355	MONOONFFFNNNNNNNNN	NNNN3NNNNNNNNN	R,J	102	469	05.12.12	7720	200502	93956
706.587-010	CLEANER-TOUCH-UP WORKER (office machines)	2123	44444444354	LNNNNNNFFNOONFNNNNN	NNNN3NNNNNNNNN	R,J	031	571	06.03.02	8769	470102	98999
706.587-014	SORTER (office machines)	2223	44444343353	LNNNNNNFFNOONFNNNFN	NNNN3NNNNNNNN	R,T	221	571	06.03.02	7850	470102	83005
706.684-010	AIR-CONDITIONING-COIL ASSEMBLER (svc. ind. mach.)	3223	34443533355	MNNNNNNFFNNNNFNONNN	NNNN4NNNNNNNNN	R,T	102	573	06.02.23	7720	470102	93902
706.684-014	ASSEMBLER I (office machines)	3224	33333433355	MNNOOONFFNNNNNFNNNN	NNNN4NNNNNNNNN	J,T	121	571	06.02.23	7720	470102	93902
706.684-018	ASSEMBLER, PRODUCT (machine shop)	3223	34433433354	MNNOOONFFOOONFNONON	NNNN3NNNNNNNNO	R,J,T	121	560	06.02.23	7720	000000	93956
706.684-022	ASSEMBLER, SMALL PRODUCTS I (any industry)	2112	44543433355	LNNNNNNFFNNNNNFNNNN	NNNN4NNNNNNNNN	R,U	061	611	06.04.23	7720	000000	93956
706.684-026	ASSEMBLER, TYPE-BAR-AND-SEGMENT (office machines)	3223	34433433355	LNNNNNNFCFNNNNFNFNNN	NNNN3NNNNNNNNN	J,T	121	571	06.02.23	7720	470102	93902
706.684-030	ATOMIZER ASSEMBLER (fabrication, nec)	2112	44434433455	SNNNNNNNFFNNNNNNNNN	NNNN3NNNNNNNNN	R	121	559	06.04.23	7720	000000	93956
706.684-034	BAR AND FILLER ASSEMBLER (furniture)	2122	44544544355	LNNNNNNFFONNNNNNNNN	NNNN3NNNNNNNNN	R	061	463	06.04.22	7720	480501	93956
706.684-038	BEARING-RING ASSEMBLER (machinery mfg.)	2223	44433433355	LNNONONFFFNNNNNONNN	NNNN3NNNNNNNNN	R,T	061	568	06.04.23	7720	480503	93902
706.684-042	BENCH ASSEMBLER (agric. equip.)	2122	44344433355	LNNNNNNFFFNNNNNNNNN	NNNN3NNNNNNNNN	R,T	121	562	06.04.23	7720	010204	93956
706.684-046	BENCH HAND (motor-bicycles)	2223	44444544345	LNNNNNNFFNNNNFNNNNN	NNNN3NNNNNNNNN	R,T	121	595	06.04.22	7720	470499	93902
706.684-050	DRAWER UPFITTER (furniture)	2114	34334444345	MNNNNNNNFFONNNNNNNNNN	NNNN3NNNNNNNNN	R,T	102	466	06.04.23	7720	480501	93956
706.684-054	FITTER II (any industry)	2125	34433433345	HNNFNNNFFNNNNFNFNNN	NNNN4NNNNNNNNF	R,J,T	102	554	06.02.22	7529	480501	92198
706.684-058	HYDRAULIC-CHAIR ASSEMBLER (furniture)	3225	44334444344	LNNNNNNFFONNNNFNFNON	NNNN3NNNNNNNNN	R,T	102	466	06.02.22	7720	480501	93956
706.684-062	INJECTOR ASSEMBLER (engine-turbine)	3225	33332432455	LNNNNNNFFNNNNFNFFNN	NNNN3NNNNNNNNN	R,T	121	561	06.02.23	7720	470605	93902
706.684-070	LOCK ASSEMBLER (furniture)	3226	33333344344	MNNNNNNFFONNNFNNNNON	NNNN3NNNNNNNNN	V,T	061	466	06.02.22	7720	480501	93956
706.684-074	LOCK ASSEMBLER (cutlery-hrdwr.)	2123	44534543445	SNNNNNNNFFNNNNFNFNNN	NNNN4NNNNNNNNN	R,T	073	552	06.04.23	7720	470403	93956

DOT #	DOT Title & Industry	Trng	Aptitude	Physical	Environment	Tempra	WkF	MPSMS	GOE	SOC	CIP	OES
706.684-078	LOCK INSTALLER (furniture)	2113	34334544345	LNNNNNFFONNNNNNNNNN	NNNNN3NNNNNNNNNN	T	053	466	06.04.24	7720	470403	93956
706.684-082	METAL-BED ASSEMBLER (furniture)	2123	34334434344	MNNNONNNFFNNNNNONONN	NNNNN3NNNNNNNNNN	R	061	463	06.02.22	7720	480501	93956
706.684-086	PLUMBING-HARDWARE ASSEMBLER (plumbing-heat.)	2122	44444533355	LNNNONNNFFNNNNNFNNNN	NNNNN4NNNNNNNNNN	R,T	102	553	06.04.23	7720	000000	93956
706.684-090	SPRING ASSEMBLER (metal prod., nec)	2114	34533534455	HNNNNNNNFFFNONFNNNN	NNNNN3NNNNNNNNNN	R,T	071	559	06.04.22	7720	480501	93956
706.684-094	SUBASSEMBLER (office machines)	3234	34433433354	LNNNNNNFFFNONFFOON	NNNNN3NNNNNNNNNN	R,T	121	571	06.02.23	7720	470102	93902
706.684-098	VALVE GRINDER (machine shop)	3225	33433433355	MNNOOONFFNNNNFNFNNN	NNNNN3NNNNNNNNNN	J,T	051	591	06.02.24	7758	480503	93953
706.684-102	VENDING-MACHINE ASSEMBLER (svc. ind. mach.)	2122	34434434355	MNNNONNFFNNNNFNFNNN	NNNNN4NNNNNNNNNN	R,T	121	572	06.02.23	7720	480501	93956
706.684-106	WHEEL LACER AND TRUER (motor-bicycles)	2124	44443443355	MNNOOONFFFNNNNFNNNN	NNNNN3NNNNNNNNNN	R,J,T	061	595	06.02.23	7720	000000	93956
706.684-110	WRAPPER OPERATOR (metal prod., nec)	2222	44544545355	MNNFNFNFFONNNNNNNNN	NNFN4NNNNNNNNNN	R	061	559	06.04.22	7755	480501	93999
706.685-010	TYPE-SOLDERING-MACHINE TENDER (office machines)	2123	44444533345	SNNNNNNFFNNNNFNNNN	NNNNN4NNNNNNNNNN	R,T	083	571	06.04.20	7533	470102	91711
706.685-014	WHEEL-TRUING MACHINE TENDER (motor-bicycles)	2222	44443434355	MNNNONNFFNNNNNFNOONN	NNNNN3NNNNNNNNNN	R,T	121	595	06.04.24	7720	000000	93956
706.687-010	ASSEMBLER, PRODUCTION (any industry)	2112	44444444355	LNNNONFFFNNNNNFNNNN	NNNNN4NNNNNNNNNN	R,U	102	550	06.04.22	7720	000000	93999
706.687-018	FAN-BLADE ALIGNER (elec. equip.)	2122	44443444355	LNNNNNNFFONNNNFNFNN	NNNNN3NNNNNNNNNN	R,T	061	583	06.04.24	7740	000000	93956
706.687-022	INSPECTOR, ALIGNING (office machines)	3224	34432493354	LNNNNNNFFNNNNNFFON	NNNNN3NNNNNNNNNN	R,J,T	212	571	06.03.02	7820	470102	83005
706.687-026	INSPECTOR, TYPE (office machines)	2123	44544533355	SNNNNNNFFFNNONFNFNN	NNNNN3NNNNNNNNNN	R,J,T	212	571	06.03.02	7820	470102	83005
706.687-030	PUSH-CONNECTOR ASSEMBLER (house. appl.)	2112	44544533355	LNNNNNNFFFNNNNONOONN	NNNNN3NNNNNNNNNN	R	061	583	06.04.23	7720	470199	93956
706.687-034	ROLLER-BEARING INSPECTOR (machinery mfg.; motor-bicycles)	2123	34343443455	LNNONONFFFNNNNFNOONN	NNNNN3NNNNNNNNNN	R,J,T	212	568	06.03.02	7820	000000	83005
709.134-010	SUPERVISOR, METAL FURNITURE ASSEMBLY (furniture)	4337	33332443354	LNNONONFFFNFNFNONON	NNNNN3NNNNNNNNNN	V,D,T	102	463	06.02.01	6700	520205	81008
709.137-010	INSPECTION SUPERVISOR (chemical; nonfer. metal)	4338	22322333354	MNNNNNNFFFNFNFNNOON	NNNNN3NNNNONONON	D,J,T	212	559	06.01.01	6700	410205	81008
709.281-010	LOCKSMITH (any industry)	4336	33332433255	LNNNNOONFFFNONFNFNNN	NNNNN3NNNNNNNNNN	J,T	121	552	05.05.09	6173	470403	85923
709.281-014	LOCKSMITH APPRENTICE (any industry)	4336	33332433255	LNNNOONFFFNNONFNFNNN	NNNNN3NNNNNNNNNN	J,T	121	552	05.05.09	6173	470403	85923
709.364-010	INSPECTOR, MAGNETIC PARTICLE AND PENETRANT (any industry)	3335	33343434353	MNNONNNFFFNOONFNFNN	NNNO4NFNNNNNNFN	T	212	540	06.03.01	7820	000000	83005
709.364-014	TOWEL-CABINET REPAIRER (business ser.)	2123	34433443455	MNNNNNNFFNNNNFNNNNN	NNNNN3NNNNNNNNNN	R,T	121	568	05.10.01	6179	470199	85999
709.367-010	INSPECTOR, METAL CAN (tinware)	4335	33333333344	LNNFNONFFFNNNNFNNFON	NNNNN4NNNNNNNNNN	V,J,T	212	551	06.03.01	7820	000000	83005
709.381-010	ATOMIC-FUEL ASSEMBLER (chemical)	4224	34433433355	LNNNNNNFFFNNNNNFNONN	NNNNN3NNNNNONNF	J,T	102	499	06.01.04	6869	410205	89999
709.381-014	MODEL BUILDER (furniture)	3237	33322432355	MNNNNNNFFFNOONFNFONN	NNNNN3NNNNNNNNNN	V,J,T	102	466	05.05.06	6817	000000	89114
709.381-018	MODEL MAKER II (jewelry-silver.)	4337	33322432255	LNNNNNNFFFNNNNFNNFNN	NNNNN3NNNNNNNNNN	V,J,T	241	611	01.06.02	6822	470408	89126
709.381-022	MODEL-MAKER APPRENTICE (jewelry-silver.)	4337	33322432255	LNNNNNNFFFNNNNNFNONN	NNNNN3NNNNNNNNNN	V,J,T	241	611	01.06.02	6822	480501	89126
709.381-026	MOLD STAMPER AND REPAIRER (rubber tire)	3226	33434333244	HNNNONONFFFONNNFNNON	NNNNN3NNNNNNNNNN	V,T	102	511	05.10.01	6861	480501	85999
709.381-030	ORGAN-PIPE MAKER, METAL (musical inst.)	3227	33433433355	MNNONONFFONNNFNNNN	NNNN4NNNNNNNNNN	V,T	132	614	05.05.06	6812	000000	93197
709.381-034	PATTERNMAKER (furniture)	4337	23222433355	LNNNNNNFFFNNNNFNFONN	NNNNN3NONNNNNNNO	V,J,T	241	466	05.05.07	6817	480501	89114
709.381-038	REED MAKER (machinery mfg.)	3226	34334444355	MNNNNNNFFNOONFNFONN	NNNNN3NNNNNNNNNN	V,T	102	567	06.01.04	6812	480501	93197
709.381-042	SPRING FORMER, HAND (metal prod., nec)	3227	34433433355	LNNNNNNFFFNNNNFNFONN	NNFN4NNNNNNNNNNF	J,T	134	559	06.02.24	6829	480501	93197
709.381-046	WIRE-MESH-FILTER FABRICATOR (metal prod., nec)	4336	33333433355	LNNNNNNFFFONNNNNNNNN	NNON3NNNNNNNNNN	J,T	102	557	06.02.24	6829	480501	89199
709.382-010	SEWING-MACHINE TESTER (machinery mfg.)	3225	33234344355	LNNNNNNFFFNNNNFNNONN	NNNNN3NNNNNNNNNN	J	111	567	06.03.01	7830	470199	83005
709.384-010	FIRE-EXTINGUISHER REPAIRER (any industry)	3223	33433433355	MNNONONFFONNNFNNNNN	NNNNN3NONNNNNNO	T	121	969	05.10.04	6179	480501	85999
709.484-010	SILK-SCREEN-FRAME ASSEMBLER (any industry)	3223	33333433354	LNNNNNNFFFNNNNFNFONN	NNNNN4NNNNNNNNNN	R,T	102	567	06.04.23	7720	480299	93956
709.484-014	STRAIGHTENER, HAND (any industry)	3225	33333433354	LNNNNNNFFFNNNNNNNNN	NNNNN3NNNNNNNNNN	R,T	134	540	06.04.23	7720	480501	93999
709.587-010	INSPECTOR (cutlery-hrdwr.)	2223	44443434454	MNNFNFNFFONNNNFNNNN	NNNNN4NNNNNNNNNN	R,T	212	552	06.03.02	7820	000000	83005
709.587-014	SPOILAGE WORKER (tinware)	2124	44443444354	LNNNNNNFFFONNNFNFON	NNNNN3NNNNNNNNNN	R,T	102	551	06.03.02	7820	480506	83005
709.667-010	FABRIC STRETCHER (furniture)	2113	44445533355	LNNNNNNFFFONNNNNNNNN	NNNNN3NNNNNNNNNN	R	061	464	06.04.22	7720	480501	93956
709.682-010	AUTOCLAVE OPERATOR II (chemical)	3236	34434344345	LNNNNNNFFONNNNFNNNN	NNNNN3NNNNNONNO	R,T	212	559	06.03.01	7675	000000	92923
709.684-014	ASSEMBLER, METAL FURNITURE (furniture)	2222	44444433355	MNNNNNNFFONNNNNONNON	NNNNN4NNNNNNNNNN	R,T	134	460	05.10.01	7755	480501	93999
709.684-018	ASSEMBLY-LINE INSPECTOR (furniture)	3224	33443444355	LNNNNNNFFFNNNNFNNNN	NNNNN4NNNNNNNNNN	R,T	102	460	06.04.22	7720	480501	93956
709.684-022	BABBITTER (machine shop)	3216	34433433355	LNNNNNNFFNNNNNFNNNN	NNNNN3NNNNNNNNNN	J,T	212	460	06.03.02	7820	480501	83005
709.684-026	BIRD-CAGE ASSEMBLER (metal prod., nec)	2114	44444433355	LNNNNNNFFFNNNNNNNNN	NNNNN3NFNNNNNNNN	J,T	136	540	06.02.24	7756	480503	93947
709.684-030	CAGE MAKER (concrete prod.)	3125	33433433354	LNNNNNNFFNNNNNNNNNN	NNNNN4NNNNNNNNNN	R,T	102	557	06.04.23	7720	480501	93956
709.684-034	CIGARETTE-LIGHTER REPAIRER (any industry)	2123	44443443355	MNNFNFNFFONNNNFNNNN	NNNNN3NNNNNNNNNN	V,T	102	557	06.02.24	7539	480501	92198
709.684-038	CLIP-BOLTER AND WRAPPER (metal prod., nec)	2213	44444433345	MNNNNNNFFFNNNNFNNNN	NNNNN4NNNNNNNNNN	R,T	121	619	05.12.15	6179	000000	85999
709.684-042	HAND STAMPER (any industry)	2123	34443434355	MNNNNNNFFFNNNNFNNNN	NNNNN4NNNNNNNNNN	R,T	192	540	06.04.24	7759	480501	93999

DOT #	DOT Title & Industry	Trng	Aptitude	Physical	Environment	Tempra	WkF	MPSMS	GOE	SOC	CIP	OES
709.684-046	HOT-TOP LINER (steel & rel.)	2113	44454354355	HNNONNNFFNNNNNNNNNN	ONCN4NCNNNNNNNN	R,T	092	534	05.12.09	6412	460101	87302
709.684-050	KEY CUTTER (any industry)	2222	44433434355	LNNNNNNFFONNNNNNNNNN	NNNN4NNNNNNNNNN	R,T	055	552	05.12.13	7529	470403	92198
709.684-054	MOLD STAMPER (machine shop)	3336	34433434355	MNNOOONFFNNNNNNNNNN	NNNN3NNNNNNNNNN	J,T	192	566	06.02.31	7757	000000	93951
709.684-058	REAMER, HAND (machine shop)	3125	34433433355	MNNOOONFFNNNNNFNNOONN	NNNN3NNNNNNNNNN	R,T	053	540	06.02.24	7758	000000	93953
709.684-062	REPAIRER (furniture)	3125	34433533355	LNNNNNNFFNNNNNNNNNN	NNNN3NNNNNNNNNO	R,T	102	466	05.10.01	6179	480501	85999
709.684-066	RIVETER, HAND (any industry)	2112	44454543355	MNNNNNNFFFNNNNFNNNNN	NNNN4NNNNNNNNNN	R,T	073	463	06.04.22	7720	480501	93956
709.684-070	SALVAGER (petrol. refin.)	3225	34433433355	HNNFFNNFFNNNNNFNNONN	FNNN4NFNNNNNNNF	R,T	121	559	05.10.02	6175	000000	85928
709.684-074	SHEARER AND TRIMMER, WIRE SCREEN AND FABRIC (metal prod., nec)	2123	44454543355	MNNNONONFFNNNNNFNNONN	NNNN3NNNNNNNNNN	R,T	054	557	06.04.24	7529	480501	92198
709.684-078	SPRING FITTER (metal prod., nec)	3225	44322335345	MNNFNNNFFNNNNNFNNONN	NNNN4NNNNNNNNNN	J,T	061	559	06.02.24	7720	480501	93956
709.684-082	STAB SETTER AND DRILLER (cutlery-hrdwr.)	2223	44434444445	LNNNNNNFFNNNNNFNNNNN	NNNN3NNNNNNNNNN	R,T	054	566	06.02.02	7518	480503	91117
709.684-086	TORCH-STRAIGHTENER-AND HEATER (any industry)	3224	44435444355	HONOOONFFONNNNFNNOOFN	NNON4NONNNNNNNO	J,T	102	540	05.10.01	7714	480508	93914
709.684-090	TUBE BENDER, HAND I (any industry)	3114	44434434345	LNNNNNNFFONNNNNONNNNN	NNNN3NNNNNNNNNN	T	134	592	06.02.24	7755	460302	93999
709.684-094	UTILITY OPERATOR II (chemical)	3223	34434434345	MONONONFFOONNNFFNNNN	NNNN3NNNNNONNNN	R,T	102	559	05.12.12	7679	000000	92998
709.684-098	WIRE-FRAME-LAMP-SHADE MAKER (fabrication, nec)	3235	33333433355	LNNNNNNFFNNNNNFNONNN	NNNN3NNNNNNNNNN	J,T	102	619	06.02.24	7529	480501	92198
709.684-102	WIRE-ROPE-SLING MAKER (metal prod., nec)	3125	34433433355	MNNNONONFFNNONFNFNNN	NNNN4NNNNNNNNNN	V,T	134	557	06.02.24	7529	480501	92198
709.685-010	GOLD RECLAIMER (metal prod., nec)	2123	44444444355	MNNNNNNFFONNNNFNNNNN	NNNN3NNNNNNNNNN	R,T	142	559	06.04.02	7679	000000	92998
709.685-014	HOT BOX OPERATOR (metal prod., nec)	2122	44444444355	LNNNNNNFFONNNNNFNNNNN	NNNN3NNNNNNNNNN	R,T	032	559	06.04.02	7667	000000	92971
709.685-018	ROLLER, GOLD LEAF (metal prod., nec)	2123	44454534355	LNNNNNNFFONNNNNFNNNNN	NNNN3NNNNNNNNNN	R,T	163	559	06.04.34	7667	000000	92971
709.686-010	LABORER, TIN CAN (tinware)	2112	44544544354	HOOF-OFOFFONNNNNNNNN	NNNN3NNNNNNNNNN	R	041	551	06.04.24	8769	480506	98999
709.687-010	CLEANER AND POLISHER (any industry)	1112	44544543354	LNNNNNCCONNNNCNNNON	NNNN3NNNNNNNNNN	R	031	550	06.04.39	8769	000000	98999
709.687-014	CLEANER, FURNITURE (furniture)	1112	44543544354	MNNNOOOFFNONNNFNONON	NNNN4NNNNNNNNNN	R	031	466	06.04.39	8769	000000	98999
709.687-018	HOT-TOP-LINER HELPER (steel & rel.)	1113	44433544355	HNNNNNNFFNNNNNNFNNNN	ONFN4NFNNNNNNNN	R	092	534	05.12.09	8641	460101	98311
709.687-022	INSPECTOR (chemical)	3224	34433434354	LNNNNNNFFNNNNNFNNFON	NNNN3NNNNNNNNNN	J,T	212	559	06.03.02	7820	000000	83005
709.687-026	INSPECTOR, WIRE PRODUCTS (metal prod., nec)	2123	44434443355	LNNONONFFNNNFNFNNNN	NNNN4NNNNNNNNNN	R,T	212	557	06.03.02	7820	480501	83005
709.687-030	PROOF-COIN COLLECTOR (government ser.)	3224	34422332354	HNNFFONFFNNNNNNNNNNN	NNNN4NNNNNNNNNN	R,T	212	556	06.03.02	7820	000000	83005
709.687-034	SALVAGER HELPER (petrol. refin.)	2114	44434434355	HNNFONFFNNNNNNNNNNN	FNNO3NONNNNNNNO	R	121	559	05.12.15	8637	000000	98102
709.687-038	SPRING INSPECTOR II (metal prod., nec)	2222	44444444455	LNNNNNNFFNNNNFNFNN	NNNN4NNNNNNNNNN	R,T	212	559	06.03.02	7820	480501	83005
709.687-042	SPRING TESTER II (metal prod., nec)	2122	44444444455	LNNNNNNFFNNNNFNFNN	NNNN3NNNNNNNNNN	R,T	212	557	06.03.02	7830	480501	83005
709.687-046	TIN-CONTAINER STRAIGHTENER (tobacco)	1111	44544544455	LNNNNNNFFNNNNNNNNN	NNNN3NNNNNNNNNN	R	134	551	06.04.24	8769	000000	98999
709.687-050	TUBE BENDER, HAND II (any industry)	2112	44443444355	LNNNNNNFFNNNNNNNNNN	NNNN3NNNNNNNNNN	R	134	550	06.04.24	7740	470105	93999
709.687-054	ULTRASONIC TESTER (chemical)	3223	34433434345	MNNONONFFNNOONFNFNN	NNNN3NNNNNONNNN	R,T	212	559	06.03.01	7830	000000	83005
709.687-058	WIRE BENDER (furniture)	1113	44444444345	MNNNNNNFFNNNNNFNFNNN	NNNN4NNNNNNNNNN	R,T	134	557	06.04.24	7529	000000	92198
709.687-062	WIRE-BASKET MAKER (metal prod., nec)	2112	44444434355	LNNNNNNFFNNFNNNNNNN	NNNN3NNNNNNNNNN	R,T	102	557	06.04.24	7740	480501	93999
710.131-010	SUPERVISOR, GAS METER REPAIR (utilities)	4338	33333333344	LNNNNNNFFNFFNFNNNN	NNNN3NNNNNNNNNN	D,P,J,T	121	602	05.10.02	6000	520205	81002
710.131-014	SUPERVISOR, INSTRUMENT MAINTENANCE (any industry)	4448	33233333344	LNNNNNNFFFOFFNFNNOOON	NNNN4NNNNNNNNNO	D,T,P,J	111	602	05.05.11	6700	520205	81008
710.131-018	SUPERVISOR, INSTRUMENT MECHANICS (utilities)	4448	23332333243	LONONONFFNNNNNFNNOON	NNON4NNNNNNNNNO	D,P,J,T	111	602	05.05.10	6000	150403	81002
710.131-022	SUPERVISOR, INSTRUMENT REPAIR (any industry)	4337	33332333244	LONOOONFFNFFNFNOOON	ONNN4NNNNNNNNN	D,P,J,T	111	602	05.05.10	6000	520205	81002
710.131-026	SUPERVISOR, METER REPAIR SHOP (utilities)	4348	33333333354	LNNNNNNFFNFFNFNNNON	NNNN3NNNNNNNNNN	D,P,J,T	111	581	05.05.10	6000	150403	81002
710.131-030	SUPERVISOR, METER SHOP (waterworks)	4337	33333334355	MONOOONFFNFFNFNNNNN	NNNN3NNNNNNNNNN	D,P,J,T	121	600	05.10.02	6000	520205	81008
710.131-034	SUPERVISOR, SHOP (petrol. & gas)	4338	33333333355	LNNOOONFFNFFNFNNONN	NNNN3NNNNNNNNNN	D,P,J,T	121	601	05.05.10	7100	520205	81008
710.131-038	SUPERVISOR, INSTRUMENT ASSEMBLY (electron. comp.; inst. & app.)	4338	33322333354	LNNOOONFFNFFNFNNONN	NNNN3NNNNNNNNNN	D,P,J,T	111	600	06.01.01	7100	150404	81008
710.131-042	SUPERVISOR, INSTRUMENT CONTROLS (inst. & app.)	4337	33333343354	LNNNNNNFFONFFNFNOOON	NNNN4NNOONNNNNN	D,V,T,P,J	111	602	06.01.01	7100	520205	81008
710.137-010	SUPERVISOR, THERMOSTATIC CONTROLS (inst. & app.)	4337	33334343354	LNNNNNNFFONFFNFNOOON	NNNN3NNNNNNNNNN	D,V,T,P	111	602	06.02.01	6700	520205	81008
710.137-014	SUPERVISOR, ASSEMBLY I (office machines)	4337	33333344455	LNNNNNNNOFFONNNFNNN	NNNN3NNNNNNNNNN	D,P,J,T	121	571	06.02.01	6000	150404	81002
710.137-018	SUPERVISOR, METER-AND-REGULATOR SHOP (petrol. refin.; utilities)	4348	33333344454	LNNNNNNFFNFFNFNOOON	ONNN3NNNNNNNNNN	D,P,J,T	121	602	05.05.11	6171	470604	85905
710.261-010	INSTRUMENT REPAIRER (any industry)	4348	33322332254	LNNOOOOFFNOONFNOOON	ONNN3NNNNNNNNNN	J	121	602	05.05.11	6171	470604	85905
710.281-010	ASSEMBLER AND TESTER, ELECTRONICS (office machines)	4336	33333332343	LNNNNNNFFNNNNFNNNNN	NNNN3NNNNNNNNNN	J,T	111	571	06.01.04	6867	470401	93956
710.281-018	ELECTROMECHANICAL TECHNICIAN (inst. & app.)	4447	23223333254	LNNNNNNFFONONFFON	NNNN4NNOONNNNNN	V,T,J	111	589	05.05.11	6867	150403	93111
710.281-022	GAS-METER PROVER (utilities)	3337	33344443344	MNNNNNNFFNNNNNFNNOOON	NNNN3NNNNNNNNNN	J,T	212	602	06.01.05	6175	470401	85928
710.281-026	INSTRUMENT MECHANIC (any industry)	4347	33333332254	MNNOOONFFONNNFNFFON	NNNN3NNNNNNNNNN	T,J	111	602	05.05.10	6171	470501	85905
710.281-030	INSTRUMENT TECHNICIAN (utilities)	4338	33332422253	LONFFFOFFNNNNFNOOFN	NNNN4NNNNNONNNF	J,T	121	602	05.05.11	6171	150403	85905
710.281-034	METER REPAIRER (any industry)	4235	33333433355	MNNOOONFFNNNFNNOONN	ONNO4NNNNNNNNNO	J,T	121	602	05.10.02	6175	470401	85928

DOT #	DOT Title & Industry	Trng	Aptitude	Physical	Environment	Tempra	WkF	MPSMS	GOE	SOC	CIP	OES
710.281-038	TAXIMETER REPAIRER (automotive ser.)	4336	33333433355	LNNONONFFNNNNNNNNN	NNNN3NNNNNNNNNNN	J,T	121	602	05.05.11	6171	470401	85905
710.281-042	INSTRUMENT-TECHNICIAN APPRENTICE (utilities)	4338	33332422253	LONFFFOFFFNNNNNNNNNF	NNNN4NNNNNNONNF	J,T	121	602	05.05.11	6171	470401	85905
710.360-010	SCALE ASSEMBLY SET-UP WORKER (office machines)	4437	33322323245	LNNNNNNFFNOONFNFFNN	NNNN3NNNNNNNNNN	J,T	121	571	06.01.02	7329	470401	92197
710.361-010	MODEL MAKER, SCALE (office machines)	4337	33322433344	LNNNNNNFFNNNNFNNNON	NNNN3NNNNNNNNNNN	J,T	111	571	05.05.11	6817	480501	89114
710.361-014	TEST EQUIPMENT MECHANIC (aircraft mfg.)	4447	33323433344	MOOOOOOFFOOONFOOOO	NNNN4NNOOONNNNN	V,T,J	102	601	06.01.04	6862	000000	89908
710.381-010	ASSEMBLER II (office machines)	3225	33433433354	LNNONNNFFFNNNNFNFOON	NNNN3NNNNNNNNN	J,T	121	571	06.02.23	7720	470401	93956
710.381-014	BALANCER, SCALE (office machines)	4226	33333433354	LNNNNNNFFNNNNNFNNON	NNNN3NNNNNNNNNN	J	121	571	06.01.05	6882	470401	93117
710.381-022	GAS-METER MECHANIC I (utilities)	3335	33323333355	LNNNNNNFFNNNNNNNNNN	NNNN3NNNNNNNNNN	J,T	121	602	05.10.02	6175	470401	85928
710.381-026	GAS-REGULATOR REPAIRER (petrol. refin.; pipe lines; utilities)	4337	33333433334	MONOOONFFFNNNNFNOOON	NNNN3NNNNNNNNNN	J,T	121	602	05.05.09	6175	470401	85928
710.381-030	HYDROMETER CALIBRATOR (inst. & app.)	3226	34344434355	LNNNNNNFFONNNNFNOONN	NNNN3NNNNNNNNNN	T,J	051	602	06.01.04	6882	470401	89999
710.381-034	CALIBRATOR (inst. & app.)	4336	33333332254	LNNNNNNFFNNNNFNFFON	NNNN3NNNNNNNNNN	T,J	111	600	06.01.04	6881	470401	83002
710.381-042	CALIBRATOR, BAROMETERS (inst. & app.)	4336	33333433354	LNNNNNNFFONNFNFFON	NNNN3NNNNNNNNNN	T,J	111	602	06.03.01	7820	470401	83005
710.381-046	TESTER, ELECTRONIC SCALE (office machines)	3226	34333433354	LNNNNNNFFNNNNFNNNON	NNNN3NNNNNNNNNN	J,T	212	571	05.10.03	8632	470401	98102
710.381-050	THERMOSTAT REPAIRER (inst. & app.)	3335	33433333355	LNNNNNNFFONNNNFNNNN	NNNN3NNNNNNNNNN	T	121	602	05.10.02	7820	470401	83005
710.381-054	REPAIRER, GYROSCOPE (inst. & app.)	3336	33333433354	MNNNNNNFFFNNNFNNNN	NNNN4NNOONNNNN	T	111	601	05.05.10	6171	470401	85905
710.384-010	GAS-REGULATOR-REPAIRER HELPER (petrol. refin.; pipe lines; utilities)	3225	34433433344	MFOFFFNFFNNNNNFNOON	FNNN3NFNNNNNNO	R	121	602	05.10.02	8637	470401	98102
710.384-014	INSPECTOR (office machines)	4337	33333333355	LNNNNNNFFNNNNFNFNN	NNNN3NNNNNNNFN	J	212	571	06.03.01	7820	470401	83005
710.384-018	INSTRUMENT-REPAIRER HELPER (any industry)	3225	33333433334	MOOOOONFFOONFNOOON	ONNO4NNNNNNNNNO	J,T	121	602	05.12.15	8632	470401	98102
710.384-022	METER INSPECTOR (utilities)	3334	33344344344	LNNNONFFFNNNNFNNNON	ONNN3NNNNNNNNN	J,T	212	602	06.03.01	7820	470401	83005
710.384-026	PARKING-METER SERVICER (government ser.)	3224	34433433355	MNNFNONFFFNNNNFNNONN	ONNN3NNNNNNNNN	J,T	121	602	05.10.02	6179	470401	85999
710.384-030	THERMOMETER TESTER (inst. & app.)	3225	34433443354	LNNNNNNFFNNNNNNOONN	NNNN3NNNNNNNNN	T	212	602	06.03.01	7830	470401	83005
710.387-010	TESTER, REGULATOR (protective dev.; toy-sport equip.)	3224	34433533355	LNNNNNNFFNNNNFNFNN	NNNN4NNNNNFNFN	J,T	212	602	06.03.01	7830	470401	83005
710.584-010	SCROLL ASSEMBLER (office machines)	2113	44434434354	LNNNNNNFFNNNNNFNNNN	NNNN3NNNNNNNNN	R,T	102	571	06.04.23	7720	470401	93956
710.681-018	REGISTER REPAIRER (r.r. trans.)	3226	34333433355	LNNNNNNFFNNNNFNNNN	NNNO3NNNNNNNNN	J,T	121	571	05.10.02	6179	470401	85999
710.681-026	THERMOMETER MAKER (inst. & app.)	3224	34433433354	SNNNNNNFFONNNNFNOON	NONN3NNNNNNNNN	T	102	602	06.02.30	6869	470401	89999
710.684-010	AGATE SETTER (office machines)	3124	34433433355	LNNNNNNFFNNNNFNFNNN	NNNN4NNNNNNNNN	J,T	061	571	06.02.32	7720	000000	93956
710.684-014	BELLOWS FILLER (inst. & app.)	3224	34433433354	MNNNNNNFFNNNNFNFNNN	NNNN3NNNNNNNNN	T,U	041	602	06.04.36	7720	000000	93999
710.684-018	DIAL MAKER (office machines)	3224	34433433354	LNNNNNNFFNNNNFNNNON	NNNN3NNNNNNNNN	J,T	262	571	06.02.31	7757	480299	93951
710.684-026	GAS-METER MECHANIC II (utilities)	2113	44433533355	LNNNNNNFFNNNNNNNON	NNNN3NNNNNNNNN	R,T	121	602	05.10.02	6175	470501	85928
710.684-030	INSTRUMENT-TECHNICIAN HELPER (utilities)	3224	34433343343	LOOFFNNNFFNNNNFNNOOON	NNON4NNNNNNNNN	J,T	121	602	05.10.02	8637	470401	98102
710.684-034	METER-REPAIRER HELPER (any industry)	3114	34434443355	LNNNONFFFNNNNNFNNNNN	NNNN3NNONNNNNN	R,T	121	602	05.12.15	8637	470401	98102
710.684-038	SEALER (office machines)	3225	34434433354	MNNONNNFFFNNNNFNFNON	NNNN3NNNNNNNNN	J,T	102	571	06.02.24	7720	000000	93956
710.684-042	BELLOWS ASSEMBLER (inst. & app.)	2123	44434433354	LNNNNNNFFONNNFNNNFN	NNNN4NNNNNNNNN	T,U	102	602	06.04.23	7720	000000	93956
710.684-046	INSTRUMENT ASSEMBLER (inst. & app.)	3224	34433433354	LNNNNNNFFONNNFNFOON	NNNN3NNNNNNNNN	T,U	111	600	06.02.23	7720	000000	93956
710.684-050	INSTRUMENT INSPECTOR (inst. & app.)	3224	34433433355	LNNNNNNFFONNNFNNFNN	NNNN3NNNNNNNNN	T	212	602	06.03.02	7820	000000	83005
710.685-014	THERMOMETER PRODUCTION WORKER (inst. & app.)	2112	44444443454	LNNNNNNFFNNNNFNNNN	NNNN4NNONNNNNN	R,U	133	609	06.04.19	7679	000000	92998
710.687-014	BELLOWS TESTER (inst. & app.)	3223	33444344355	LNNNNNNFFNNNNFNNNNN	NNNN3NNNNNNNNN	T,U	212	602	06.03.02	7830	000000	83005
710.687-034	TIE-UP WORKER (office machines)	2113	44444443355	LNNNNNNFFNNNNFNNNN	NNNN3NNONNNNNN	R	071	571	06.04.38	8761	000000	98902
711.137-010	SUPERVISOR, OPTICAL INSTRUMENTS (inst. & app.)	4337	33333344455	LNNNNNNFFNFFNFNNONN	NNNN3NNNNNNNNN	D,T,P	121	603	06.02.01	7100	520205	81008
711.281-010	INSPECTOR, OPTICAL INSTRUMENT (optical goods)	4447	23232432355	LNNNNNNFFNNNNFNNNN	NNNN3NNNNNNNNN	J	212	603	06.01.05	6881	000000	83002
711.281-014	INSTRUMENT MECHANIC, WEAPONS SYSTEM (inst. & app.)	4338	33322433355	MNNNNNNFFOFFNNOOONN	NNNN4NNNNNNNNN	J	102	604	06.02.01	7100	000000	83002
711.381-010	OPTICAL-INSTRUMENT ASSEMBLER (optical goods)	4346	23322432355	LNNNNNNFFONNNFOFFNN	NNNN3NNONNNNNN	T,J	121	603	05.05.11	6171	470401	85905
711.684-010	ASSEMBLY LOADER (inst. & app.)	2113	44444433355	LNNNNNNFFNFNFNNNNN	NNNN3NNNNNNNNN	R,U	221	601	06.01.04	6864	000000	89917
711.684-014	CEMENTER (optical goods)	2225	34433443454	SNNNNNNFFONNNNFNNNNN	NNNN3NNNNNNNNN	R,T	063	603	06.04.34	7720	000000	93999
712.131-010	SUPERVISOR, DENTAL LABORATORY (protective dev.)	4347	33333333354	LNNNNNNFFNFNFNNOFN	NNNN3NNNNNNNNN	D,J,P,T	102	603	06.02.30	7720	000000	93956
712.132-010	SUPERVISOR, SURGICAL GARMENT ASSEMBLY (protective dev.)	4347	33333443445	LNNNNNNFFNNNNFNNNN	NNNN3NNNNNNNNN	D,J,P,T	102	604	05.05.11	6700	510603	81008
712.134-010	SUPERVISOR, ARTIFICIAL BREAST FABRICATION (protective dev.)	4226	33343343355	MNNNNNNNFFOFFNFNOONN	NNNN4NNNNNNNNN	V,P,D,T	102	604	06.02.01	7100	000000	81008
712.137-010	SUPERVISOR, FACEPIECE LINE (protective dev.)	4337	33333344455	LNNNNNNFFONFNFNNNNN	NNNN3NNNNNNNNN	D,V,P	102	604	06.02.01	7100	150607	81008
712.137-014	SUPERVISOR, FINAL ASSEMBLY AND PACKING (protective dev.)	4337	33333344455	LNNNNNNFFNFNFNNNNN	NNNN3NNNNNNNNN	V,D,P,J	102	604	06.02.01	7100	000000	81008
712.281-014	DESIGNER (protective dev.)	4236	22423422345	LNNONONFFFNNNNFNNNN	NNNN3NNNNNNNNN	J,V	264	604	05.05.11	6859	200303	89599
712.381-010	ARCH-SUPPORT TECHNICIAN (protective dev.)	3225	34433433355	LNNNNNNFFNNNNFNNONNN	NNNN3NNNNNNNNN	J,T	102	604	05.10.01	6869	000000	89923

DOT #	DOT Title & Industry	Trng	Aptitude	Physical	Environment	Tempra	WkF	MPSMS	GOE	SOC	CIP	OES
712.381-014	CONTOUR WIRE SPECIALIST, DENTURE (protective dev.)	4337	33322422352	SNNNNNNFFNNNNNNFNN	NNNNN3NNNNNNNNNN	J,T	102	925	05.05.11	6865	510603	89921
712.381-018	DENTAL-LABORATORY TECHNICIAN (protective dev.)	4347	33322432343	LNNNNNNNFFFONNNFNFOFN	NNNN3NNNNNNNNNN	J,T	102	604	05.05.11	6865	510603	89921
712.381-022	DENTAL-LABORATORY-TECHNICIAN APPRENTICE (protective dev.)	4347	33322432343	LNNNNNNNFFFONNNFNFOFN	NNNN3NNNNNNNNNN	J,T	102	604	05.05.11	6865	510603	89921
712.381-026	ORTHODONTIC BAND MAKER (protective dev.)	4347	33333432354	LNNNNNNNFFFNNNNNNNON	NNNN3NNNNNNNNNN	V,J,T	102	604	05.05.11	6865	510603	89921
712.381-030	ORTHODONTIC TECHNICIAN (protective dev.)	4346	33322432354	SNNNNNNNFFFNNNNFNFNON	NNNN3NNNNNNNNNN	J,T	102	925	05.05.11	6865	510603	89921
712.381-034	ORTHOTICS TECHNICIAN (protective dev.)	4446	33333332244	MNNNNNNNFFNNNNNFFFON	NNNN4NOONNNNNN	V,J,T	121	604	05.05.11	6869	000000	89923
712.381-038	PROSTHETICS TECHNICIAN (protective dev.)	4446	23322432243	MNNNNNNNCCFNNNCNCOCON	NNNN3NNNNNNNNNN	V,J,T	121	604	05.05.11	6869	000000	89923
712.381-042	DENTAL CERAMIST (protective dev.)	4347	33323332343	SNNNNNNNFFNNNNFNFN	NNNN3NNNNNNNNNN	J,T	136	604	05.05.11	6865	510603	89921
712.381-046	DENTURE WAXER (protective dev.)	3336	33333433355	SNNNNNNNFFFONNNFNFNON	NNNN3NNNNNNNNNN	T,J	136	925	06.02.32	6865	510603	89921
712.381-050	FINISHER, DENTURE (protective dev.)	3235	33333433355	LNNNNNNNFFFONNNFNNNNN	NNNN3NNNNNNNNNN	J,T	102	604	05.05.11	6865	510603	89921
712.487-010	INSPECTOR, SURGICAL GARMENT (protective dev.)	3323	34333344454	LNNNNNNNFFFNNNNFNNFON	NNNN3NNNNNNNNNN	J,T	212	604	06.03.01	7820	000000	83005
712.664-010	DENTAL CERAMIST ASSISTANT (protective dev.)	3236	33433433352	SNNNNNNNFFFOOONFNFFON	NNNN3NNNNNNNNNN	T	102	925	05.05.11	8619	510603	98999
712.684-010	ASSEMBLER, SURGICAL GARMENT (protective dev.)	2223	34434433345	LNNNNNNNFFONNNNFNNNNN	NNNN3NNONNNNNN	T	102	604	06.02.23	7720	510603	93956
712.684-014	BITE-BLOCK MAKER (protective dev.)	3114	34433433454	SNNNNNNNFFFNNNFNFNON	NNNO3NNNNNNNNN	J,T	136	604	06.02.23	7720	510603	93956
712.684-018	FLANGER (inst. & app.)	2113	34433443354	LNNNNNNNCCNNNNCNCNCN	NNFN3NNNNNNNNO	R,T	133	601	06.04.30	7759	489999	93999
712.684-022	GAS-MASK ASSEMBLER (protective dev.)	2114	34443533445	MNNNNNNNFFONNNNFNNNNN	NNNN3NNNNNNNNNN	R,T	102	604	06.04.23	7720	000000	93956
712.684-026	GLAZIER (inst. & app.)	2112	44434443354	LNNNNNNNCCCNNNNCNCNCN	NNFN3NONNNNNNNO	R,T	133	601	06.04.30	7759	489999	93999
712.684-030	OPAQUER (protective dev.)	3224	34443433353	SNNNNNNNFFFOONFNFNFN	NNNN3NNNNNNNNNN	J,T	153	925	06.02.32	7756	510603	93947
712.684-034	PACKER, DENTURE (protective dev.)	3235	34433543354	LNNNNNNNFFFNNNNFNFNFN	NNNN3NNNNNNNNNN	J,T	132	925	05.05.11	7754	510603	93944
712.684-038	REFINER (protective dev.)	3224	34444344355	LNNNNNNNFFONNNNFNFNNN	NNOF3NFNNNNNNNN	J,T	145	549	06.04.24	7759	000000	93999
712.684-042	FABRICATOR, ARTIFICIAL BREAST (protective dev.)	2112	44444444355	LNNNNNNNFFFONNNNNNNNN	NNNN4NNNNNNNNNN	R,U	132	604	06.04.02	7740	150607	93956
712.684-046	DENTURE-MODEL MAKER (protective dev.)	3235	33433433354	LNNNNNNNFFONNNNFNFNON	NNNO3NNNNNNNNN	J,T	132	925	05.05.11	7754	510603	93944
712.684-050	INSPECTOR, SURGICAL INSTRUMENTS (inst. & app.)	2212	44433433455	LNNNNNNNOCCONNCNCOONN	NNNN3NNNNNNNNNN	T	212	604	06.03.02	7820	000000	83005
712.684-054	SURGICAL-FORCEPS FABRICATOR (inst. & app.)	3224	33433432255	LNNNNNNNFFNNNNFNNFNN	NNNN3NNNNNNNNNN	T	111	604	06.04.24	7720	000000	93956
712.687-010	ASSEMBLER, PLASTIC HOSPITAL PRODUCTS (inst. & app.)	2112	44544433454	LNNNNNNNFFFNNNFNFNNN	NNNN3NONNNNNNN	R,U	041	604	06.04.24	7720	000000	93956
712.687-014	COILER (protective dev.)	2112	44434533455	LNNNNNNNFFNNNNFNNNNN	NNNN3NNNNNNNNNN	R	061	604	06.04.23	7759	000000	93999
712.687-018	GAUGER (protective dev.)	2122	44443534354	SNNNNNNNFFNNNNFNFON	NNNN3NNNNNNNNNN	R,T	212	604	06.03.02	7850	000000	83005
712.687-022	GAS-MASK INSPECTOR (protective dev.)	3224	34443444454	LNNNNNNNFFONNNNFNNNNN	NNNN3NNNNNNNNNN	J,T	212	604	06.03.02	7820	000000	83005
712.687-030	SUTURE POLISHER (protective dev.)	2112	44544544355	LNNNNNNNFFONNNNNNNNNN	NNNN3NNNNNNNNNN	R	051	604	06.04.34	8769	000000	98999
712.687-034	SUTURE WINDER, HAND (protective dev.)	2112	45444533444	SNNNNNNNFFFNNNNFNNNNN	NNNO3NNNNNNNNN	R,T	163	604	06.04.23	8769	000000	98999
712.687-038	TOOTH INSPECTOR (protective dev.)	2112	44543444453	LNNNNNNNFFFNNNNFNNFFN	NNNN3NNNNNNNNNN	R,T	212	925	06.03.02	7820	510603	83005
713.261-010	ARTIFICIAL-GLASS-EYE MAKER (optical goods)	4248	33322432352	LNNNNNNNFFFOOONCNOCFN	NNNN3NNNNNNNNNN	J	102	604	05.05.11	6864	000000	89917
713.261-014	ARTIFICIAL-PLASTIC-EYE MAKER (optical goods)	4348	33322422352	LNNNNNNNFFOFFNNFNFFN	NNNN3NNNNNNNNNN	J	102	604	05.05.11	6864	000000	89917
713.381-010	LENS-MOLD SETTER (optical goods)	3325	33333433354	LNNNNNNNFFNNNNNFNFFON	NNNN3NNNNNNNNNN	R	061	605	06.02.23	6864	000000	89917
713.384-010	ASSEMBLER, GOLD FRAME (optical goods)	2122	44534533355	LNNNNNNNFFNOONFNOONN	NNNN3NNNNNNNNNN	R	102	605	06.01.04	7720	000000	93956
713.384-014	INSPECTOR, EYEGLASS (optical goods)	3325	33333243353	SNNNNNNNCCCNNNNCNOCFN	NNNN3NNNNNNNNNN	J,T	212	605	06.01.04	7820	000000	83005
713.667-010	INSPECTOR, CLIP-ON SUNGLASSES (optical goods)	2123	44443433353	LNNNNNNNFFFNNNNNNNFFN	NNNN3NNNNNNNNNN	J,T	212	605	06.03.02	7820	000000	83005
713.681-010	LENS MOUNTER II (optical goods)	3236	34433433354	MNNNNNNNCCCONNNCNFFON	NNNN3NNNNNNNNNN	J,T	102	605	05.05.11	6864	000000	89917
713.684-010	ASSEMBLER, CLIP-ON SUNGLASSES (optical goods)	2113	34433433354	LNNNNNNNFFFNNNNFNNNNN	NNNN3NNNNNNNNNN	R	062	605	06.04.23	7720	000000	93956
713.684-014	ASSEMBLER, MOLDED FRAMES (optical goods)	2112	44444443445	LNNNNNNNFFNNNFNNNNNNN	NNNN3NNNNNNNNNN	R	073	605	06.04.23	7720	000000	93956
713.684-018	BENCH WORKER (optical goods)	2113	44435334445	LNNNNNNNFFFNNNNFNNOONN	NNNN3NNNNNNNNNN	R	102	605	06.04.24	7759	000000	93999
713.684-022	EMBOSSER (optical goods)	2113	34434433355	LNNNNNNNFFFNNNNFNNNNNN	NNNN3NNNNNNNNNN	R,T	192	605	06.04.37	7757	000000	93951
713.684-026	EYEGLASS-FRAME TRUER (optical goods)	2123	44435333354	LNNNNNNNFFONNNNFNNNNN	NNNN3NNNNNNNNNN	R,T	102	605	06.04.02	7759	000000	93999
713.684-030	FRAME CARVER, SPINDLE (optical goods)	2223	44435333355	SNNNNNNNFFFNNNNNFNOONN	NNNN3NNNNNNNNNN	R,T	055	605	06.04.24	7529	000000	92198
713.684-034	MULTIFOCAL-LENS ASSEMBLER (optical goods)	2123	44435533454	SNNNNNNNFFFNNNNFNNFFON	NNNN3NNNNNNNNNN	R,T	061	605	06.04.23	7522	000000	93956
713.684-038	POLISHER, EYEGLASS FRAMES (optical goods)	2113	34543543455	SNNNNNNNFFFNNFFNNNNN	NNNN3NNNNNNNNNN	R	051	605	06.04.24	7522	000000	91117
713.684-042	WASHER (optical goods)	2113	44435443354	LNNNNNNNFFFNNNNFNNFON	NNNN3NNNNNNNNNN	R,T	031	605	06.04.39	7756	000000	93947
713.687-010	CLIP COATER (optical goods)	2112	44444443354	LNNNNNNNFFFNNNNFNNNNN	NNNN3NNNNNNNNNN	R	151	605	06.04.33	7740	000000	93999
713.687-014	CONTACT-LENS-FLASHING PUNCHER (optical goods)	2112	44444444455	LNNNNNNNFFONNNNNONNNNN	NNNN3NNNNNNNNNN	R	054	605	06.04.24	7740	000000	93999
713.687-018	FINAL ASSEMBLER (optical goods)	1112	44544533355	SNNNNNNNFFFNNNNFNFNN	NNNN3NNNNNNNNNN	R	071	605	06.04.23	7720	000000	93956
713.687-022	INSPECTOR, EYEGLASS FRAMES (optical goods)	2123	44443354454	SNNNNNNNFFFNNNNFNNFON	NNNN3NNNNNNNNNN	J,T	212	605	06.03.02	7820	000000	83005

DOT #	DOT Title & Industry	Trng	Aptitude	Physical	Environment	Tempra	WkF	MPSMS	GOE	SOC	CIP	OES
713.687-026	LENS INSERTER (optical goods)	1112	4444443455	SNNNNNFFNNNNFNNNNN	NNNNN3NNNNNNNNNNNN	R	061	605	06.04.23	7740	000000	93956
713.687-030	LENS MATCHER (optical goods)	2122	4444444453	LNNNNNNFFONNNNFNNOFN	NNNNN3NNNNNNNNNNNN	R	212	605	06.03.02	7820	000000	83005
713.687-034	POLISHER, IMPLANT (optical goods)	2112	44443443354	SNNNNNNFFFONNNFNOFON	NNNNN3NNNNNNNNNNNN	R	051	604	06.04.24	7758	000000	93953
713.687-038	SALVAGER (optical goods)	2112	44433544454	LNNNNNNFFNNNNFNNOON	NNNNN3NNNNNNNNNNNN	R	061	605	06.04.34	7740	000000	93999
713.687-042	SUNGLASS-CLIP ATTACHER (optical goods)	2112	44434444354	LNNNNNNFFONNNNNNNNN	NNNNN3NNNNNNNNNNNN	R	131	605	06.04.23	7720	000000	93956
714.131-010	SUPERVISOR, MOTION-PICTURE EQUIPMENT (motion picture; photo. appar.)	4448	3333333344	LNNNNNNFFNFFFNNNOON	NNNNN3NNNNNNNNNNNN	V,D,P,J	121	606	05.05.11	7100	500602	81008
714.281-010	AIRCRAFT-PHOTOGRAPHIC-EQUIPMENT MECHANIC (photo. appar.)	4448	23333222244	LNNNNNNFFFNNNNFNFFON	ONNNN3NNNNNNNNNNNN	V,J,T	121	606	05.05.09	6171	470499	85914
714.281-014	CAMERA REPAIRER (photo. appar)	4448	33322332255	SNNNNNNFFNNNNFNFFNN	NNNNN3NNNNNNNNNNNN	V,J,T	121	606	05.05.11	6171	470499	85914
714.281-018	MACHINIST, MOTION-PICTURE EQUIPMENT (motion picture; photo. appar.)	4448	33322422254	MNNNNNNFFFONNNNFNOON	NNNNN3NNNNNNNNNNNN	V,J,T	121	606	05.05.09	6813	470499	89108
714.281-022	PHOTOGRAPHIC EQUIPMENT TECHNICIAN (photo. appar.)	4448	33322422245	LNNNNNNNCCGNNNFNNNNO	NNNNN3NNNNNNNNNNNN	J,T	121	606	05.05.11	6171	470499	85914
714.281-026	PHOTOGRAPHIC-EQUIPMENT-MAINTENANCE TECHNICIAN (photo. appar.)	4347	33333443353	LNNNNNNFFNNNNFNNOOFN	NNNNN3NNNNNNNNNNNN	V,J,T	121	606	05.05.09	6171	470499	85914
714.281-030	SERVICE TECHNICIAN, COMPUTERIZED-PHOTOFINISHING EQUIPMENT (photofinishing)	4346	33333333354	MNNOONNFFNNNNFNNFFON	NNNNN3NNNNNNNNNNNN	T,J	121	606	05.05.09	6171	150402	85119
714.381-010	ASSEMBLER, PHOTOGRAPHIC EQUIPMENT (photo. appar.)	4336	33324432254	LNNNNNNFFNNONFNFFON	NNNNN3NNNNNNNNNNNN	T,J	121	606	06.01.04	6869	470105	89999
714.381-014	INSPECTOR, PHOTOGRAPHIC EQUIPMENT (photo. appar.)	4336	33322433354	LNNNNNNFFNNNNFNNFFFN	NNNNN3NNNNNNNNNNNN	J	121	606	06.01.05	6881	470499	83002
714.381-018	PHOTOGRAPHIC-PLATE MAKER (electron. comp.)	4336	33332543354	LNNNNNNFFNNNNFNOFON	NNNNN3NNNNNNNNNNNN	J,T	212	567	05.10.05	6869	000000	89718
714.667-010	SENSITIZED-PAPER TESTER (photo. appar.)	2113	44443444353	LNNNNNNFFNNNNFNNFN	NNNNN3NNNNNNNNNNNN	J,T	202	606	06.03.02	7830	000000	83005
714.684-010	ASSEMBLER, PRODUCTION LINE (photo. appar.)	3224	34433433355	LNNNNNNFFNNNNFNNNNN	NNNNN3NNNNNNNNNNNN	J,T	212	606	06.02.23	7720	470499	93956
714.684-014	BELLOWS MAKER (photo. appar.)	3224	34443344454	LNNNNNNFFOONNFNNNOON	NNNNN3NNNNNNNNNNNN	J,T	102	606	06.02.32	7720	100103	83005
714.687-010	CHECKER, FILM TESTS (photo. appar.)	3124	33333444355	LNNNNNNFFOOFFFNFNFN	NNNNN3NNNNNNNNNNNN	R,T	041	606	06.03.02	7840	100103	81008
715.131-010	SUPERVISOR, DIALS (clock & watch)	4337	33333333355	LNNNNNNFFONFFNFNNONN	NNNNN3NNNNNNNNNNNN	V,D,P,J	121	607	06.01.01	7100	520205	81008
715.131-014	SUPERVISOR, HAIRSPRING FABRICATION (clock & watch)	4337	33333333355	LNNNNNNFFONFFNFNFNNN	NNNNN3NNNNNNNNNNNN	V,D,P,J	121	607	06.02.01	7100	520205	81008
715.131-018	SUPERVISOR, INSPECTION (clock & watch)	4337	33333333355	LNNNNNNFFNFFFNFNNNN	NNNNN3NNNNNNNNNNNN	D,P,J,T	121	607	06.01.01	7100	000000	81008
715.131-022	SUPERVISOR, MAINSPRING FABRICATION (clock & watch)	4337	33333333355	LNNNNNNFFOOFFNNOONN	NNNNN3NNNNNNNNNNNN	D,P,J,T	212	607	06.01.01	7100	520205	81008
715.131-026	SUPERVISOR, TUMBLING AND ROLLING (clock & watch)	4347	33333444355	LNNNNNNOOONFFNONNNNN	NNNNN3NNNNNNNNNNNN	D,P,J,T	121	607	06.02.01	7100	520205	81008
715.221-010	INSTRUCTOR, WATCH ASSEMBLY (clock & watch)	4447	22333333355	LNNNNNNFFOFFFNFNFN	NNNNN3NNNNNNNNNNNN	P,J	296	607	06.02.01	2390	470408	31314
715.261-010	MECHANICAL TECHNICIAN, LABORATORY (clock & watch)	4338	33424343355	LNNNNNNFFNNNNNCOONN	NNNNN3NNNNNNNNNNNN	J,T	057	607	02.04.01		480503	83002
715.281-010	WATCH REPAIRER (clock & watch)	4338	33322432345	LNNNNNNCCCONNNCNOCNN	NNNNN3NNONNNNNNNNNN	J,T	121	607	05.05.11	6171	470408	85917
715.281-014	WATCH REPAIRER APPRENTICE (clock & watch)	4237	33322432345	LNNNNNNCCCONNNCNOCNN	NNNNN3NNONNNNNNNNNN	J,T	121	607	05.05.11	6171	470408	85917
715.381-010	ASSEMBLER (clock & watch)	4237	34433433355	LNNNNNNFFONNNFNNFNN	NNNNN3NNNNNNNNNNNN	J,T	121	607	06.01.04	6882	470408	89999
715.381-014	ASSEMBLER, WATCH TRAIN (clock & watch)	4226	34432432355	SNNNNNNNCCONNNCNNCNN	NNNNN3NNNNNNNNNNNN	J	121	607	06.01.04	6882	470408	93117
715.381-018	BANKING PIN ADJUSTER (clock & watch)	3225	34432432355	LNNNNNNFFONNNFNNFCNN	NNNNN3NNNNNNNNNNNN	J,T	121	607	06.01.04	6882	470408	89999
715.381-022	BARREL ASSEMBLER (clock & watch)	3226	34432432355	SNNNNNNNCCFFNNCNOONN	NNNNN3NNNNNNNNNNNN	J	121	607	06.01.04	6882	470408	93117
715.381-026	BARREL-BRIDGE ASSEMBLER (clock & watch)	3225	34432432355	SNNNNNNNCCFFNNCNOONN	NNNNN3NNNNNNNNNNNN	J	121	607	06.01.04	6882	470408	83002
715.381-030	BARREL-ENDSHAKE ADJUSTER (clock & watch)	3226	34433433355	LNNNNNNNCCONNNCNNCNN	NNNNN3NNNNNNNNNNNN	J	121	607	06.01.04	6882	470408	83002
715.381-034	BLOCKER AND POLISHER, GOLD WHEEL (clock & watch)	3225	34432532355	SNNNNNNFFNNNNFNNNNN	NNNNN3NNNNNNNNNNNN	J	212	607	06.01.04	6882	470408	89999
715.381-038	CHRONOMETER ASSEMBLER AND ADJUSTER (clock & watch)	4337	33324432355	LNNNNNNCCCONNNCNOCNN	NNNNN3NNNNNNNNNNNN	J,T	121	607	06.01.04	7522	470408	91117
715.381-042	CHRONOMETER-BALANCE-AND-HAIRSPRING ASSEMBLER (clock & watch)	3226	33332432355	LNNNNNNCCCONNNCNNCNN	NNNNN3NNNNNNNNNNNN	J	121	607	06.01.04	6882	470408	93117
715.381-046	DIAL MAKER (clock & watch)	3226	33333433355	LNNNNNNFFNNNNFNNONN	NNNNN3NNNNNNNNNNNN	J,T	102	607	06.01.04	6869	470408	89999
715.381-050	FINAL INSPECTOR (clock & watch)	4337	33332432355	LNNNNNNNFFONFNOFNN	NNNNN3NNNNNNNNNNNN	J,T	212	607	06.01.05	6881	470408	83002
715.381-054	HAIRSPRING ASSEMBLER (clock & watch)	3125	34433533355	LNNNNNNCCFNNNCNNCNN	NNNNN3NNNNNNNNNNNN	V,J,T	121	607	06.01.04	6882	470408	93117
715.381-058	HAIRSPRING TRUER (clock & watch)	3226	34324422355	SNNNNNNFFONNNFNNFCNN	NNNNN3NNNNNNNNNNNN	J	121	607	06.01.04	7820	470408	83005
715.381-062	HAIRSPRING VIBRATOR (clock & watch)	3226	34432432355	LNNNNNNCCFNNNCNNCNN	NNNNN3NNNNNNNNNNNN	J,T	212	607	06.01.04	6882	470408	93117
715.381-066	INSPECTOR, HAIRSPRING I (clock & watch)	3226	34432432355	SNNNNNNNCCNNNNCNNCNN	NNNNN3NNNNNNNNNNNN	J,T	212	607	06.01.05	6881	470408	83002
715.381-070	INSPECTOR, WATCH ASSEMBLY (clock & watch)	3226	34432432355	LNNNNNNNCCFNNNCNNCNN	NNNNN3NNNNNNNNNNNN	J	212	607	06.01.05	6881	470408	83002
715.381-074	INSPECTOR, WATCH TRAIN (clock & watch)	4237	34324432355	SNNNNNNNCCFNNNNCNCNN	NNNNN3NNNNNNNNNNNN	J	212	607	06.01.05	6881	470408	83002
715.381-078	LOCATION-AND-MEASUREMENT TECHNICIAN (clock & watch)	4336	33333433355	LNNNNNNCCCNOONCNCNN	NNNNN3NNNNNNNNNNNN	J	212	607	06.01.05	6881	470408	83002
715.381-082	PALLET-STONE INSERTER (clock & watch)	3226	34324422355	LNNNNNNCCCNNNNCNCNN	NNNNN3NNNNNNNNNNNN	J,T	212	607	06.01.04	6822	470408	93117
715.381-086	PALLET-STONE POSITIONER (clock & watch)	3226	34324422355	SNNNNNNCCNNNNNCNCNN	NNNNN3NNNNNNNNNNNN	J	061	607	06.02.32	6822	470408	93117
715.381-090	SCREWHEAD POLISHER (clock & watch)	3225	34433432355	SNNNNNNCCNNNNNFFNN	NNNNN3NNNNNNNNNNNN	J	051	607	06.01.04	7522	470408	91117
715.381-094	WATCH ASSEMBLER (clock & watch)	4336	34324432355	LNNNNNNNCCCNNNNCNCNN	NNNNN3NNNNNNNNNNNN	J,T	121	607	06.01.04	6882	470408	93117

DOT #	DOT Title & Industry	Trng	Aptitude	Physical	Environment	Tempra	WkF	MPSMS	GOE	SOC	CIP	OES
715.384-010	BALANCE ASSEMBLER (clock & watch)	3223	34432432355	SNNNNNNCCCONNNCNNCNN	NNNNN3NNNNNNNNNN	J,R,T	071	607	06.02.23	7720	470408	93117
715.384-014	INSPECTOR, MECHANISM (clock & watch)	3224	34432422355	SNNNNNNNCCNNNNCNNCNN	NNNNN3NNNNNNNNNN	J,T	212	607	06.03.01	7820	470408	83005
715.384-018	INSPECTOR, POISING (clock & watch)	3224	34432532355	SNNNNNNNCCNNNNCNNCNN	NNNNN3NNNNNNNNNN	J,T	212	607	06.01.05	7820	470408	83005
715.384-022	INSPECTOR, WATCH PARTS (clock & watch)	3236	33332332355	SNNNNNNNFFOONNNFNOONN	NNNNN3NNNNNNNNNN	J,T	212	607	06.01.04	7820	470408	83005
715.584-010	DIAL REFINISHER (clock & watch)	2125	44443434354	SNNNNNNNFFONNNNFNNFON	NNNNN3NNNNNNNNNN	R,T	192	607	06.04.33	7756	470408	93947
715.584-014	REPAIRER, AUTO CLOCKS (clock & watch)	2113	44443433355	LNNNNNNFFNNNNFNNNNN	NNNNN3NNNNNNNNNN	R,T	121	607	06.04.34	6171	470408	85917
715.584-018	STONER, HAND (clock & watch)	2113	34443433355	LNNNNNNNCCFFNNFNNFNN	NNNNN4NNNNNNNNNN	J,T	051	607	06.02.24	7758	470408	93953
715.660-010	SET-UP WORKER (clock & watch)	3235	34433433345	LNNNONNNFFNFFNFNOFNN	NNNN4NNNNNNNNNN	J,T	121	607	06.01.02	7339	480503	92197
715.681-010	TIMING ADJUSTER (clock & watch)	3226	34433532355	LNNNNNNNCGFNNNNCNOCNN	NNNNN3NNNNNNNNNN	J,T	121	607	06.02.24	6882	470408	93117
715.682-010	BARREL FINISHER (clock & watch)	2123	44444443355	SNNNNNNCCNNNNNNNNN	NNNNN3NNNNNNNNNN	R	055	607	06.02.02	7512	470408	91117
715.682-014	COUNTERSINKER (clock & watch)	2213	44433433355	LNNNNNNNCCNNNCNCNNN	NNNNN3NNNNNNNNNN	J,T	053	607	06.02.02	7518	470408	91117
715.682-018	POLISHER (clock & watch)	3225	34433433355	LNNNNNNNFFONNNNFNOONN	NNNNN3NNNNNNNNNN	J,T	051	607	06.02.02	7522	470408	91117
715.682-022	TAPPER, BALANCE-WHEEL SCREW HOLE (clock & watch)	3223	34433433355	LNNNNNNNCCFNNNNCNNCNN	NNNNN4NNNNNNNNNN	J,T	053	607	06.02.02	7679	470408	92998
715.682-026	TOOTH POLISHER (clock & watch)	3225	34433433345	LNNNNNNNCCFNNNNCNFFNN	NNNNN3NNNNNNNNNN	J,T	051	607	06.02.02	7522	470408	91117
715.684-010	ADJUSTER, ALARM MECHANISM (clock & watch)	2122	44433443355	SNNNNNNNFFNNNNFNNNNN	NNNNN3NNNNNNNNNN	R,T	121	607	06.04.34	7759	470408	93999
715.684-014	ASSEMBLER, MOVEMENT (clock & watch)	2113	44434433355	LNNNNNNNCCFNNNNFNOFNN	NNNNN3NNNNNNNNNN	R,T	121	607	06.04.23	7720	470408	93117
715.684-018	BALANCE TRUER (clock & watch)	3224	34432432355	LNNNNNNNCCCONNNCNNCNN	NNNNN3NNNNNNNNNN	R,J,T	061	607	06.01.04	7830	470408	83005
715.684-022	BALANCE-BRIDGE ASSEMBLER (clock & watch)	3223	34433433355	LNNNNNNNCCCONNNCNNCNN	NNNNN3NNNNNNNNNN	R,J	071	607	06.02.23	7720	470408	93117
715.684-026	BENCH HAND (clock & watch)	1112	44533532355	SNNNNNNNCCNNNCNNCNNN	NNNNN3NNNNNNNNNN	R	071	607	06.04.23	7759	470408	93999
715.684-030	BEVELER (clock & watch)	2113	44544543455	SNNNNNNCCCNNNCNNNNN	NNNNN3NNNNNNNNNN	R	134	607	06.02.24	7517	470408	91321
715.684-034	BLOCKER (clock & watch)	2114	34433533355	LNNNNNNNCCCNNNFNNFNN	NNNNN3NNNNNNNNNN	R	063	607	06.02.24	7759	470408	93999
715.684-038	BURNISHER, BALANCE WHEEL ARM (clock & watch)	2113	34533533355	LNNNNNNNCCCNNNNFNNFNN	NNNNN3NNNNNNNNNN	R,T	051	607	06.02.24	7758	470408	93953
715.684-042	BURRER (clock & watch)	2113	34433433355	LNNNNNNNCCCNNNNCNNONN	NNNNN3NNNNNNNNNN	R,T	051	607	06.02.24	7529	470408	92198
715.684-046	CANNON-PINION ADJUSTER (clock & watch)	3223	34433532355	SNNNNNNFFNNNNFNNFFNN	NNNNN3NNNNNNNNNN	R,T	061	607	06.04.23	7720	470408	93999
715.684-050	CAP-JEWEL PLATE ASSEMBLER (clock & watch)	3223	34432432355	LNNNNNNNCCFNNNNFNOFNN	NNNNN3NNNNNNNNNN	R	071	607	06.04.30	7677	470408	92965
715.684-054	CASER (clock & watch)	2123	34433432355	LNNNNNNNCCFNNNNFNOFNN	NNNNN3NNNNNNNNNN	R,T	071	607	06.04.23	7720	470408	93117
715.684-058	CLOCK ASSEMBLER (clock & watch)	2123	44434533355	LNNNNNNNFFFNNNNFNFNN	NNNNN3NNNNNNNNNN	R	071	607	06.02.23	7720	470408	93117
715.684-062	COLLET DRILLER (clock & watch)	2112	44434543355	LNNNNNNNCCFNNNNFNNONN	NNNNN3NNNNNNNNNN	R	053	607	06.02.02	7518	470408	91117
715.684-066	COLLETER (clock & watch)	2123	34433532355	SNNNNNNNCCCNNNCNNCNN	NNNNN3NNNNNNNNNN	T	061	607	06.04.23	7720	470408	93999
715.684-070	CROWN ATTACHER (clock & watch)	2122	44444333455	LNNNNNNNCGFNNNFNNFNN	NNNNN3NNNNNNNNNN	R	071	607	06.04.23	7720	470408	93956
715.684-074	CROWN-WHEEL ASSEMBLER (clock & watch)	3223	34433532355	SNNNNNNFFFNNNNFNFFNN	NNNNN3NNNNNNNNNN	R,T	071	607	06.01.04	7820	470408	83005
715.684-078	CRYSTAL CUTTER (clock & watch)	2223	44443434355	SNNNNNNNFFOONNNFNOONN	NNNNN3NNNNNNNNNN	R,T	061	607	06.04.30	7677	470408	92965
715.684-082	DIAL-SCREW ASSEMBLER (clock & watch)	2122	44443432355	LNNNNNNNCCFNNNNFNOFNN	NNNNN3NNNNNNNNNN	R	071	607	06.02.24	7720	470408	93956
715.684-086	DIALER (clock & watch)	3223	44533533355	SNNNNNNNCCCNNNNFNNFNN	NNNNN4NNNNNNNNNN	R,T	071	607	06.02.23	7720	470408	93117
715.684-090	DISASSEMBLER (clock & watch)	2113	34433433355	LNNNONNNFFNFFNFNOFNN	NNNNN4NNNNNNNNNN	R,T	121	607	06.02.24	7720	470408	93999
715.684-094	FINAL INSPECTOR, MOVEMENT ASSEMBLY (clock & watch)	3224	34432443355	SNNNNNNNFFFNNNFNNFNN	NNNNN3NNNNNNNNNN	J,T	212	607	06.01.05	7820	470408	83005
715.684-098	FINER (clock & watch)	2223	34433533355	LNNNNNNNCCONNNCNNCNN	NNNNN3NNNNNNNNNN	R,T	061	607	06.04.23	7720	470408	93117
715.684-102	HAIRSPRING ADJUSTER (clock & watch)	3124	34433533355	LNNNNNNNCCFNNNCNCNCN	NNNNN3NNNNNNNNNN	R,T	121	607	06.01.04	7820	470408	83005
715.684-106	HAND FILER, BALANCE WHEEL (clock & watch)	2113	34434433355	SNNNNNNNFFNNNFNNFNN	NNNNN3NNNNNNNNNN	R,T	051	607	06.02.24	7758	470408	93953
715.684-110	HANDS ASSEMBLER (clock & watch)	2223	34433433355	LNNNNNNNCCFFNNFNOFNN	NNNNN3NNNNNNNNNN	R,T	061	607	06.04.23	7720	470408	93956
715.584-018	STONER, HAND (clock & watch)	2113	34443433355	LNNNNNNNCCFFNNFNNFNN	NNNNN4NNNNNNNNNN	J,T	051	607	06.02.24	7758	470408	93953
715.660-010	SET-UP WORKER (clock & watch)	3235	34433433345	LNNNONNNFFNFFNFNOFNN	NNNNN4NNNNNNNNNN	J,T	121	607	06.01.02	7339	480503	92197
715.681-010	TIMING ADJUSTER (clock & watch)	3226	34433532355	LNNNNNNNCCFNNNNCNOCNN	NNNNN3NNNNNNNNNN	J,T	121	607	06.02.02	7512	470408	93117
715.682-010	BARREL FINISHER (clock & watch)	2123	44444443355	SNNNNNNCCNNNNNNNNN	NNNNN3NNNNNNNNNN	R	055	607	06.02.02	7518	470408	91117
715.682-014	COUNTERSINKER (clock & watch)	2213	44433433355	LNNNNNNNCCNNNCNCNNN	NNNNN3NNNNNNNNNN	J,T	053	607	06.02.02	7522	470408	91117
715.682-018	POLISHER (clock & watch)	3225	34433433355	LNNNNNNNFFONNNNFNOONN	NNNNN3NNNNNNNNNN	J,T	051	607	06.02.02	7522	470408	91117
715.682-022	TAPPER, BALANCE-WHEEL SCREW HOLE (clock & watch)	3223	34433433355	LNNNNNNNCCFNNNNCNNCNN	NNNNN4NNNNNNNNNN	J,T	053	607	06.02.02	7679	470408	92998
715.682-026	TOOTH POLISHER (clock & watch)	3225	34433433345	LNNNNNNNCCFNNNNCNFFNN	NNNNN3NNNNNNNNNN	J,T	051	607	06.02.02	7522	470408	93999
715.684-010	ADJUSTER, ALARM MECHANISM (clock & watch)	2122	44433443355	SNNNNNNNFFNNNNFNNNNN	NNNNN3NNNNNNNNNN	R,T	121	607	06.04.34	7759	470408	93999
715.684-014	ASSEMBLER, MOVEMENT (clock & watch)	2113	44434433355	LNNNNNNNCCFNNNNFNOFNN	NNNNN3NNNNNNNNNN	R,T	121	607	06.04.23	7720	470408	93117
715.684-018	BALANCE TRUER (clock & watch)	3224	34432432355	LNNNNNNNCCCONNNCNNCNN	NNNNN3NNNNNNNNNN	R,J,T	061	607	06.01.04	7830	470408	83005

DOT #	DOT Title & Industry	Trng	Aptitude	Physical	Environment	Tempra	WkF	MPSMS	GOE	SOC	CIP	OES
715.684-022	BALANCE-BRIDGE ASSEMBLER (clock & watch)	3223	34433343355	LNNNNNNCCCONNNCNNCNN	NNNN3NNNNNNNNNN	R,J	071	607	06.02.23	7720	470408	93117
715.684-026	BENCH HAND (clock & watch)	1112	44533532355	SNNNNNNCCFNNNNCNNNN	NNNN3NNNNNNNNNN	R	071	607	06.04.23	7759	470408	93999
715.684-030	BEVELER (clock & watch)	2113	44544543455	SNNNNNNCCCNNNNCNNNNN	NNNN3NNNNNNNNNN	R	134	607	06.02.24	7517	470408	91321
715.684-034	BLOCKER (clock & watch)	2114	34433433355	LNNNNNNCCCNNNNFNNFNN	NNNN3NNNNNNNNNN	R	063	607	06.02.24	7759	470408	93999
715.684-038	BURNISHER, BALANCE WHEEL ARM (clock & watch)	2113	34533533355	LNNNNNNCCNNNNFNNFNN	NNNN3NNNNNNNNNN	R	051	607	06.02.24	7758	470408	93953
715.684-042	BURRER (clock & watch)	2113	34433433355	LNNNNNNCCNNNNCNNONN	NNNN3NNNNNNNNNN	R,T	051	607	06.02.24	7529	470408	92198
715.684-046	CANNON-PINION ADJUSTER (clock & watch)	3223	34433343355	LNNNNNNCCFNNNNCNNCNN	NNNN3NNNNNNNNNN	R,T	061	607	06.04.23	7720	470408	93999
715.684-050	CAP-JEWEL PLATE ASSEMBLER (clock & watch)	3223	34433532355	LNNNNNNCCFNNNNCNNCNN	NNNN3NNNNNNNNNN	R,T	071	607	06.02.23	7720	470408	93117
715.684-054	CASER (clock & watch)	2123	34433432355	LNNNNNNCCFNNNNFNOFNN	NNNN3NNNNNNNNNN	R,T	071	607	06.04.23	7720	470408	93117
715.684-058	CLOCK ASSEMBLER (clock & watch)	2123	44434543355	LNNNNNNFFFNNNNFNNFNN	NNNN3NNNNNNNNNN	R	071	607	06.04.23	7720	470408	93956
715.684-062	COLLET DRILLER (clock & watch)	2112	44434543355	LNNNNNNFFFNNNNFNNONN	NNNN3NNNNNNNNNN	R	053	607	06.02.02	7518	470408	91117
715.684-066	COLLETER (clock & watch)	2123	34433533355	SNNNNNNCCCNNNNCNOCNN	NNNN3NNNNNNNNNN	T	061	607	06.04.23	7720	470408	93999
715.684-070	CROWN ATTACHER (clock & watch)	2122	44444533455	LNNNNNNCCFNNNNFNNFNN	NNNN3NNNNNNNNNN	R	071	607	06.04.23	7720	470408	93956
715.684-074	CROWN-WHEEL ASSEMBLER (clock & watch)	3223	34433532355	SNNNNNNFFFNNNNFNNFNN	NNNN3NNNNNNNNNN	R,T	071	607	06.02.23	7720	470408	93117
715.684-078	CRYSTAL CUTTER (clock & watch)	2223	44443434355	LNNNNNNFFOONNNNFNFNN	NNNN3NNNNNNNNNN	J,T	051	607	06.04.30	7677	470408	92965
715.684-082	DIAL-SCREW ASSEMBLER (clock & watch)	2122	44433432355	SNNNNNNCCCNNNNFNFNN	NNNN3NNNNNNNNNN	R	071	607	06.02.23	7720	470408	93956
715.684-086	DIALER (clock & watch)	3223	44533533355	LNNNNNNFFNNNNFNFNN	NNNN3NNNNNNNNNN	R,T	071	607	06.02.23	7720	470408	93117
715.684-090	DISASSEMBLER (clock & watch)	2113	34433433355	LNNNNNNFFFNNNNFNFNN	NNNN3NNNNNNNNNN	R,T	121	607	06.02.24	7720	470408	93999
715.684-094	FINAL INSPECTOR, MOVEMENT ASSEMBLY (clock & watch)	3224	34432443355	SNNNNNNFFFNNNFNFNN	NNNN3NNNNNNNNNN	J,T	212	607	06.01.05	7820	470408	83005
715.684-098	FINER (clock & watch)	2223	34433433355	LNNNNNNCCCONNNCNNCNN	NNNN3NNNNNNNNNN	R,T	061	607	06.04.23	7720	470408	93117
715.684-102	HAIRSPRING ADJUSTER (clock & watch)	3124	34433533355	LNNNNNNCCFNNNNCNNCNN	NNNN3NNNNNNNNNN	R,T	121	607	06.01.04	7820	470408	83005
715.684-106	HAND FILER, BALANCE WHEEL (clock & watch)	2113	34433433355	SNNNNNNCCFFNNNNCNNCNN	NNNN3NNNNNNNNNN	R,T	051	607	06.02.24	7758	470408	93953
715.684-110	HANDS ASSEMBLER (clock & watch)	2223	34433433355	LNNNNNNCCNNNNCNNCNN	NNNN3NNNNNNNNNN	R,T	061	607	06.04.23	7720	470408	93956
715.684-114	INSPECTOR, BARREL ASSEMBLY (clock & watch)	3226	34433433355	SNNNNNNCCFNNNNCNNCNN	NNNN3NNNNNNNNNN	R,T	212	607	06.01.05	7820	470408	83005
715.684-118	INSPECTOR, HAIRSPRING TRUING (clock & watch)	3224	34533533355	SNNNNNNCCFNNNNCNNCNN	NNNN3NNNNNNNNNN	R,J,T	212	607	06.03.02	7820	470408	83005
715.684-122	INSPECTOR, HAIRSPRING II (clock & watch)	2123	34532532355	SNNNNNNCCFNNNNCNNCNN	NNNN3NNNNNNNNNN	R,T	212	607	06.01.05	7820	470408	83005
715.684-126	INSPECTOR, WHEEL AND PINION (clock & watch)	3224	34433433355	SNNNNNNCCCNNNNCNNCNN	NNNN3NNNNNNNNNN	R,T	212	607	06.01.05	7820	470408	83005
715.684-130	JEWEL INSERTER (clock & watch)	2223	34433433355	LNNNNNNCCFONNNCNNNNN	NNNN3NNNNNNNNNN	R,T	061	607	06.04.23	7720	470408	93117
715.684-134	JEWEL STAKER (clock & watch)	2223	34433544355	LNNNNNNFFOONNNFNFNN	NNNN3NNNNNNNNNN	R	061	607	06.04.23	7756	470408	93947
715.684-138	LACQUERER (clock & watch)	1112	44543544355	SNNNNNNFFONNNNFNOFNN	NNNN3NNNNNNNNNN	R	153	607	06.04.33	7720	470408	93117
715.684-142	MECHANISM ASSEMBLER (clock & watch)	2123	34433433355	SNNNNNNCCFNNNNFNOFNN	NNNN3NNNNNNNNNN	R,T	061	607	06.04.23	7820	470408	93117
715.684-146	OILER (clock & watch)	2112	44543533355	SNNNNNNCCCONNNNFNOFNN	NNNN3NNNNNNNNNN	R	033	607	06.04.33	7759	470408	93999
715.684-150	OVERCOILER (clock & watch)	2123	34433433355	SNNNNNNCCFNNNNCNNCNN	NNNN3NNNNNNNNNN	R,T	062	607	06.04.23	7720	470408	93999
715.684-154	PALLET ASSEMBLER (clock & watch)	2123	34433433355	SNNNNNNCCCNNNNCNNCNN	NNNN3NNNNNNNNNN	R,J	061	607	06.02.24	7720	470408	93117
715.684-158	PALLET RECTIFIER (clock & watch)	2224	34433423355	SNNNNNNCCCONNNFNFFNN	NNNN3NNNNNNNNNN	R,T	051	607	06.04.23	7522	470408	91117
715.684-162	PEARLER (clock & watch)	2112	44433444355	LNNNNNNCCCNNNNFNFNN	NNNN3NNNNNNNNNN	R	134	607	06.02.24	7720	470408	93926
715.684-166	PIN INSERTER, REGULATOR (clock & watch)	2123	34433433355	LNNNNNNCCFNNNNCNNCNN	NNNN3NNNNNNNNNN	R	054	607	06.04.23	7753	470408	93117
715.684-170	POLISHER, DIAL (clock & watch)	2113	34433433355	SNNNNNNCCCNNNNFNOCNN	NNNN3NNNNNNNNNN	R	051	607	06.02.24	7720	470408	93953
715.684-174	PUT-IN-BEAT ADJUSTER (clock & watch)	3223	34433432355	SNNNNNNCCFONNNCNCNN	NNNN3NNNNNNNNNN	R,T	061	607	06.02.23	7758	470408	93117
715.684-178	SET-STAFF FITTER (clock & watch)	2112	44543533355	SNNNNNNCCFFNNNNCNNCNN	NNNN3NNNNNNNNNN	R,T	061	607	06.04.23	7759	470408	93956
715.684-182	STAKER (clock & watch)	2223	34433433355	LNNNNNNFFONNNNFNNNNN	NNNN3NNNNNNNNNN	R,T	061	607	06.04.23	7720	470408	93117
715.684-186	STUDDER, HAIRSPRING (clock & watch)	2113	44543533355	LNNNNNNCCCNNNNCNNCNN	NNNN3NNNNNNNNNN	R,T	061	607	06.04.23	7720	470408	93117
715.684-190	TRANSFERRER (clock & watch)	3113	34433533355	SNNNNNNFFFNNNNCNNFNN	NNNN3NNNNNNNNNN	J,T	051	607	06.01.04	7512	470408	93951
715.684-194	TRUER, PINION AND WHEEL (clock & watch)	2113	34432433355	SNNNNNNCCFNNNNCNNCNN	NNNN3NNNNNNNNNN	R,T	121	607	06.02.02	7518	470408	83005
715.685-010	COLLET GLUER (clock & watch)	2112	44444433455	LNNNNNNFFONNNNFNNNNN	NNNN3NNNNNNNNNN	R	063	607	06.04.24	7661	470408	92956
715.685-014	CUTTER, V-GROOVE (clock & watch)	2223	44433534345	LNNNNNNCCCNNNNCNNCNN	NNNN3NNNNNNNNNN	R,T	055	607	06.04.02	7512	470408	93117
715.685-018	DEBURRER, MACHINE (clock & watch)	2113	34433532355	LNNNNNNCCCNNNNCNNCNN	NNNN3NNNNNNNNNN	J,T	051	607	06.04.02	7512	470408	91117
715.685-022	DRILLER AND BROACHER (clock & watch)	3225	34432432355	LNNNNNNCCCNNNNCNNCNN	NNNN3NNNNNNNNNN	R,T	053	607	06.02.02	7518	470408	91117
715.685-026	END POLISHER (clock & watch)	2224	44433433345	LNNNNNNCCCNNNFNOONN	NNNN3NNNNNNNNNN	R,T	051	607	06.02.02	7522	470408	91117
715.685-030	GRINDER II (clock & watch)	2113	34433433345	LNNNNNNCCFNNNNCNNCNN	NNNN4NNNNNNNNNN	R,T	051	607	06.04.02	7529	470408	92198
715.685-034	INSPECTOR, TIMING (clock & watch)	3225	34433333355	LNNNNNNCCFNNNNCNNCNN	NNNN3NNNNNNNNNN	J,T	212	607	06.01.05	7830	470408	83005

DOT #	DOT Title & Industry	Trng	Aptitude	Physical	Environment	Tempra	WkF	MPSMS	GOE	SOC	CIP	OES
715.685-038	MAINSPRING WINDER AND OILER (clock & watch)	2112	44544544355	SNNNNNNCCONNNNNNNNNN	NNNN3NNNNNNNNNN	R	163	607	06.04.02	7720	470408	93999
715.685-042	PINION POLISHER (clock & watch)	2113	44533433355	LNNNNNNCCCNNNNCNNCNN	NNNN3NNNNNNNNNN	R,T	051	607	06.04.02	7522	470408	91117
715.685-046	POLISHER, BALANCE SCREWHEAD (clock & watch)	2113	44433433345	SNNNNNNCCONNNNNFNNNNN	NNNN4NNNNNNNNNN	R,T	055	607	06.04.02	7522	470408	91117
715.685-050	PRESS OPERATOR, PIERCE AND SHAVE (clock & watch)	2112	44433434355	SNNNNNNCCFNNNNFNONNN	NNNN4NNNNNNNNNN	R,J	054	607	06.04.02	7529	470408	92198
715.685-054	PROFILER, HAND (clock & watch)	3224	34432433355	LNNNNNNCCFONNNCNFFNN	NNNN4NNNNNNNNNN	J,T	055	607	06.02.02	7529	470408	92198
715.685-058	SOLDERER (clock & watch)	2112	44543533355	LNNNNNNCCFFNNNNCNCNN	NNNN4NNNNNNNNNN	R,T	083	607	06.04.02	7533	470408	91711
715.685-062	TAPPER II (clock & watch)	2113	44443433355	LNNNNNNCCFFNNNFNFFNN	NNNN4NNNNNNNNNN	J,T	053	607	06.04.02	7512	470408	91117
715.685-066	TORQUE TESTER (clock & watch)	2123	44444433355	LNNNNNNNFFFNNNNFNNONN	NNNN3NNNNNNNNNN	R	212	607	06.03.02	7830	470408	83005
715.685-070	TUBING-MACHINE TENDER (clock & watch)	2113	44444433355	SNNNNNNCCFNNNNNFNFNNN	NNNN4NNNNNNNNNN	R	134	607	06.04.24	7514	470408	91321
715.686-010	DESTATICIZER FEEDER (clock & watch)	2112	44444434355	LNNNNNNFFONNNNFNNONN	NNNN3NNNNNNNNNN	R	153	607	06.04.21	8725	470408	98502
715.686-014	MACHINE FEEDER (clock & watch)	1111	44554533455	LNNNNNNFFFNNNNFNONNN	NNNN3NNNNNNNNNN	R	011	607	06.04.09	8725	470408	98502
715.687-010	BAND ATTACHER (clock & watch)	1112	44544543355	SNNNNNNCCCNNNNFNONNN	NNNN3NNNNNNNNNN	R	061	607	06.04.23	7740	470408	93956
715.687-014	BARREL-CAP SETTER (clock & watch)	2113	44544543355	LNNNNNNCCFNNNNFNNFNN	NNNN3NNNNNNNNNN	R	061	607	06.04.23	7720	470408	93956
715.687-018	CRYSTAL ATTACHER (clock & watch)	1112	44544533355	SNNNNNNCCCNNNNONONNN	NNNN3NNNNNNNNNN	R	061	607	06.04.33	7720	470408	98999
715.687-022	DIAL BRUSHER (clock & watch)	1112	44543533355	SNNNNNNCCCNNNNFFFNN	NNNNO4NNNNNNNNNN	R,T	031	607	06.04.33	8769	470408	98999
715.687-026	DIPPER, CLOCK AND WATCH HANDS (clock & watch)	1112	44554544455	SNNNNNNCCNNNNNFNONNN	NNNN3NNNNNNNNNN	R	151	607	06.04.33	8769	470408	98999
715.687-030	FOOT STRAIGHTENER (clock & watch)	2112	44544533455	LNNNNNNCCFNNNNFNFNNN	NNNN3NNNNNNNNNN	R	062	607	06.02.24	7740	470408	98999
715.687-034	GAUGER (clock & watch)	3224	34433432355	LNNNNNNCCCNNNNCNNCNN	NNNN3NNNNNNNNNN	R,T	212	607	06.01.05	7830	470408	83005
715.687-038	HAIRSPRING CUTTER I (clock & watch)	2112	44453433455	LNNNNNNCCCONNNNCNNNNN	NNNN3NNNNNNNNNN	R,T	054	607	06.02.24	8769	470408	98999
715.687-042	HAIRSPRING CUTTER II (clock & watch)	2122	44444433455	LNNNNNNCCCONNNCNNNNN	NNNN3NNNNNNNNNN	R	054	607	06.02.24	8769	470408	98999
715.687-046	HAMMER ADJUSTER (clock & watch)	1111	44544534355	LNNNNNNCCNNNNNCNNNNN	NNNN3NNNNNNNNNN	R	134	607	06.02.24	7740	470408	98999
715.687-050	INSPECTOR, BALANCE TRUING (clock & watch)	3223	34432433355	SNNNNNNCCCNNNNCNNCNN	NNNN3NNNNNNNNNN	J,T	212	607	06.01.05	7820	470408	83005
715.687-054	INSPECTOR, BALANCE WHEEL MOTION (clock & watch)	2223	44443433455	SNNNNNNCCCNNNNCNNCNN	NNNN3NNNNNNNNNN	R,T	212	607	06.03.02	7820	470408	83005
715.687-058	INSPECTOR, BALANCE-BRIDGE (clock & watch)	2123	34433432355	SNNNNNNCCCNNNNCNCNCNN	NNNN3NNNNNNNNNN	R,T	212	607	06.03.02	7820	470408	83005
715.687-062	INSPECTOR, CASING (clock & watch)	2223	34443443355	LNNNNNNFFONNNNFNNONN	NNNN3NNNNNNNNNN	R,T	212	607	06.03.02	7820	470408	83005
715.687-066	INSPECTOR, DIALS (clock & watch)	3234	34433333355	SNNNNNNFFONNNNFNNONN	NNNN3NNNNNNNNNN	J,T	212	607	06.03.02	7820	470408	83005
715.687-070	INSPECTOR, SOLDERING (clock & watch)	2123	44443433355	LNNNNNNNFFFNNNNFNFNN	NNNN3NNNNNNNNNN	J,T	212	607	06.03.02	7820	470408	83005
715.687-074	INSPECTOR, TIMERS (clock & watch)	2123	44434444355	LNNNNNNFFONNNNFNNFNN	NNNN3NNNNNNNNNN	R	212	607	06.02.24	7740	470408	93999
715.687-078	MAINSPRING FORMER, ARBOR END (clock & watch)	2122	44544543355	SNNNNNNCCFNNNNFNNNNN	NNNN3NNNNNNNNNN	R	062	607	06.02.24	7740	470408	98999
715.687-082	MAINSPRING FORMER, BRACE END (clock & watch)	2112	44544544455	SNNNNNNCCFNNNNFNNONN	NNNN3NNNNNNNNNN	R	153	607	06.04.33	8769	470408	98999
715.687-086	MASKER (clock & watch)	1112	44444434455	SNNNNNNFFONNNNNNNNNN	NNNN3NNNNNNNNNN	R	111	607	06.04.23	8769	470408	98999
715.687-090	MOTOR POLARIZER (clock & watch)	1112	44444434355	SNNNNNNCCCNNNNFNFNNN	NNNN3NNNNNNNNNN	R	063	607	06.04.23	7740	470408	93999
715.687-094	MOUNTER, CLOCK AND WATCH HANDS (clock & watch)	1112	44544533455	SNNNNNNCCCNNNNCNNNNN	NNNN3NNNNNNNNNN	R	153	607	06.04.33	7756	470408	93947
715.687-098	PAINTER, CLOCK AND WATCH HANDS (clock & watch)	1112	44544544355	LNNNNNNFFNNNNONONNN	NNNN3NNNNNNNNNN	R	131	607	06.04.34	8769	470408	98999
715.687-102	PARTS REMOVER (clock & watch)	1112	44444434355	LNNNNNNFFONNNNNNNNNN	NNNN3NNNNNNNNNN	R	011	607	06.04.34	8769	470408	98999
715.687-106	RACKER (clock & watch)	2112	44543533355	LNNNNNNCCFNNNNCNCNN	NNNN3NNNNNNNNNN	R	053	607	06.02.24	7758	470408	93953
715.687-110	REAMER, CENTER HOLE (clock & watch)	2122	44544543355	SNNNNNNCCNNNNNFNONNN	NNNN3NNNNNNNNNN	R	061	607	06.04.23	7720	470408	93956
715.687-114	ROTOR ASSEMBLER (clock & watch)	1112	44544533455	LNNNNNNCCFNNNNFNFNNN	NNNN3NNNNNNNNNN	R	061	607	06.04.23	7720	470408	93956
715.687-118	SET-KEY DRIVER (clock & watch)	2112	44544544355	LNNNNNNCCNNNNNFNFNNN	NNNN3NNNNNNNNNN	R,T	163	607	06.02.24	7740	470408	93999
715.687-122	SPRING LAYER (clock & watch)	2112	44544534355	LNNNNNNCCFNNNNNFNFNON	NNNNF3NNNNNNNNNN	R	031	607	06.04.39	8769	470408	98999
715.687-126	WASHER (clock & watch)	2123	44444444455	SNNNNNNCCFNNNNONNNNN	NNNN3NNNNNNNNNN	R	163	607	06.03.02	7830	470408	83005
715.687-130	WINDER (clock & watch)	2123	44444444455	SNNNNNNCCFNNNNONNNNN	NNNN3NNNNNNNNNN	R	163	607	06.03.02	7830	470408	83005
716.130-010	SUPERVISOR (optical goods)	4347	22322342244	LNNNNNNFFFNFFNNFNFON	NNNN3NNNNNNNNNN	D,P,T,V	102	605	06.01.01	7100	150699	81008
716.280-010	OPTICIAN APPRENTICE (optical goods; retail trade)	4448	33322433254	LNNNNNNFFFONNNFNOOON	NNNN3NNNNNNNNNN	J,T,V	102	605	05.05.11	6864	150699	89917
716.280-014	OPTICIAN (optical goods; retail trade)	4448	33322433254	LNNNNNNFFFONNNFNOON	NNNN3NNNNNNNNNN	J,T,V	102	603	05.05.11	6864	150699	89917
716.280-018	OPTICIAN (optical goods)	3337	34333433354	LNNNNNNFFFNNNNFNOON	NNNN3NNNNNNNNNN	J,T	051	603	06.01.02	7322	000000	91114
716.360-010	SIZER, MACHINE (optical goods)	4347	33322433353	SNNNNNNFCCNNNONCNNCON	NNNN3NNNNNNNNNN	J,T	212	605	06.01.05	6881	150699	83002
716.381-010	INSPECTOR, PRECISION (optical goods)	3336	33333433354	SNNNNNNFFFNNNNONNN	NNNN3NNNNNNNNNN	J,T	241	605	06.01.04	6864	000000	89917
716.381-014	LAY-OUT TECHNICIAN (optical goods)	3335	33333433354	LNNNNNNFFFONNNFNFOON	NNNN3NNNNNNNNNN	J,T	055	605	06.02.08	6864	000000	89917
716.382-010	LATHE OPERATOR, CONTACT LENS (optical goods)	3225	33443344353	LNNNNNNFFFNNNNFNNOON	NNNN3NNNNNNNNNN	J,T	151	603	06.02.21	6864	000000	89917
716.382-014	OPTICAL-ELEMENT COATER (optical goods)	3225	33443344353	LNNNNNNFFFNNNNFNNOON	NNNN3NNNNNNNNNN	J,T	151	603	06.02.21	6864	000000	89917

DOT #	DOT Title & Industry	Trng	Aptitude	Physical	Environment	Tempra	WkF	MPSMS	GOE	SOC	CIP	OES
716.382-018	PRECISION-LENS GRINDER (optical goods)	4347	33323423355	LNNNNNOCCNNNNFNFNNN	NNNN3NNNNNNNNNN	J,T	051	603	06.02.08	6864	150699	89917
716.382-022	PRECISION-LENS-GRINDER APPRENTICE (optical goods)	4347	33323423355	LNNNNNOCCNNNNFNFNNN	NNNN3NNNNNNNNNN	J,T	051	603	06.02.08	6864	150699	89917
716.462-010	PRECISION-LENS CENTERER AND EDGER (optical goods)	3326	33322433355	LNNNNNNFFFNNNNFFNN	NNNN3NNNNNNNNNN	J,T	051	603	06.02.08	6864	000000	89917
716.681-010	BLOCKER AND CUTTER, CONTACT LENS (optical goods)	3235	34433522355	LNNNNNNFFNOONFNFNN	NNNN3NNNNNNNNNN	J,T	055	605	06.01.04	6864	000000	89926
716.681-014	GLASS CUTTER, HAND (optical goods)	3224	34333422355	LNNNNNNFFNNNNFNFNN	NNNN3NNNNNNNNNN	J,T	056	603	06.01.04	6864	000000	93926
716.681-018	LENS POLISHER, HAND (optical goods)	3225	33332433354	LNNNNNNFFFNNNNFNFNN	NNNN3NNNNNNNNNN	J	051	603	06.01.04	6864	000000	89917
716.681-022	OPTICAL-GLASS ETCHER (optical goods)	3224	34433443354	SNNNNNNFFNNNNCNFOFON	NNNO3NFNNNNNNN	J,T	182	603	06.02.30	7757	000000	93951
716.682-014	EYEGLASS-LENS CUTTER (optical goods)	3223	34433533355	LNNNNNNFFNNNNFNOONN	NNNN3NNNNNNNNNN	R,T	054	605	06.02.08	7478	000000	92941
716.682-014	PRECISION-LENS GENERATOR (optical goods)	3336	33333433354	LNNNNNNFFNNNNFNNFFNN	NNNN3NNNNNNNNNN	J,T	051	603	06.02.08	6864	000000	92965
716.682-018	PRECISION-LENS POLISHER (optical goods)	3227	33332433353	LNNNNNNFFNNNNFNOON	NNNN3NNNNNNNNNN	T,J	051	605	06.02.08	6864	000000	89917
716.684-010	BLOCKER, HAND (optical goods)	3113	34433543355	LNNNNNNFFFNNNFNNNNN	NNNN3NNNNNNNNNN	J,T	063	603	06.02.30	7759	000000	93999
716.685-010	BLOCKING-MACHINE TENDER (optical goods)	2123	44544544355	LNNNNNNFFFNNNNFNOONN	NNNN3NNNNNNNNNN	R	063	605	06.04.08	7679	000000	92998
716.685-014	DRILLER (optical goods)	2113	44544533455	SNNNNNNFFFNNNNFNONNN	NNNN3NNNNNNNNNN	R	053	605	06.04.08	7663	000000	92971
716.685-018	GRINDER, HAND (optical goods)	2112	34443433355	LNNNNNNFFFNNNNFNOONN	NNNF3NNNNNNNNN	R,T	051	605	06.04.08	7677	000000	92965
716.685-022	LENS-FABRICATING-MACHINE TENDER (optical goods)	2224	44443444355	LNNNNNNFFONNNNFNONN	NNNN3NNNNNNNNNN	R,T	051	603	06.04.08	7677	000000	92965
716.687-010	DEBLOCKER (optical goods)	2113	44444444453	LNNNNNNFFFNNNNFNNFFN	NNNN3NNNNNNNNNN	R	031	603	06.04.39	8769	000000	98999
716.687-014	GLASS CHECKER (optical goods)	2112	44444444453	LNNNNNNFFFNNNNFNNFFN	NNNN3NNNNNNNNNN	R	212	605	06.03.02	7820	000000	83005
716.687-018	INSPECTOR, MULTIFOCAL LENS (optical goods)	3223	34433443354	LNNNNNNFFNNNNCNNCON	NNNN3NNNNNNNNNN	J,T	212	605	06.03.02	7820	000000	83005
716.687-022	LENS EXAMINER (optical goods)	2124	34543544554	LNNNNNNFFONNNNCNNCON	NNNN3NNNNNNNNNN	J,T	212	603	06.03.02	7820	000000	83005
716.687-026	LENS-BLANK GAUGER (optical goods)	3223	34433443355	LNNNNNNFFNNNNFNFNNN	NNNN3NNNNNNNNNN	J,T	212	605	06.03.02	7850	000000	83005
716.687-030	LENS-BLOCK GAUGER (optical goods)	2122	44544444455	SNNNNNNFFNNNNFNNFNN	NNNN3NNNNNNNNNN	R	212	605	06.03.02	7820	000000	83005
716.687-034	WET INSPECTOR, OPTICAL GLASS (optical goods)	2223	34443444454	LNNNNNNFFFNNNNFNFNN	NNNN3NNNNNNNNNN	J,T	212	603	06.03.02	7820	000000	83005
719.261-014	RADIOLOGICAL-EQUIPMENT SPECIALIST (inst. & app.)	5557	22222322233	MOOFONCCCFFFOCNOFFN	NNNN3NNNFNFNNN	J,P,S,T	111	589	05.05.11	6179	150401	85908
719.381-014	HEARING-AID REPAIRER (inst. & app.)	4346	33333432253	SNNNNNCCCNNONCNCON	NNNN2NNNNNNNNN	J,T	111	589	05.10.03	6171	000000	85905
719.381-018	BLOCK MAKER (protective dev.)	3333	33333432355	MNNONNNFFNNNNFNFNN	NNNN2NNNNNNNNN	T,J	241	604	05.12.13	7754	000000	93944
720.281-010	RADIO REPAIRER (any industry)	4226	33332433254	LNNFFNFFNNNNFNNFON	NNNN4NNNNNNNNNN	V,J,T	111	585	05.10.03	6155	470103	85708
720.281-014	TAPE-RECORDER REPAIRER (any industry)	4327	33322433253	MNNNNNNFFFNFNFNFOFN	NNNN3NNNNNNNNNN	J,T	111	585	05.10.03	6155	470103	85708
720.281-018	TELEVISION-AND-RADIO REPAIRER (any industry)	4327	33322433254	MNNNNNNCCFNNNNFNNFON	NNNN3NNNONNNNNN	V,J,T	111	585	05.10.03	6155	470103	85708
720.684-010	ASSEMBLY ADJUSTER (comm. equip.)	2213	33444443355	LNNNNNNFFNFNFNOFON	NNNN4NNNNNNNNN	J,T	121	585	06.04.34	7830	470103	83005
720.684-014	PHONOGRAPH-CARTRIDGE ASSEMBLER (comm. equip.)	2225	33443433355	SNNNNNNFFNNNNFNFNN	NNNN4NNNNNNNNN	J,T	121	585	06.04.23	7720	470103	93905
720.687-010	RECORD-CHANGER ASSEMBLER (comm. equip.)	2112	44544533355	LNNNNNNFFNNNNFNFNN	NNNN4NNNNNNNNN	R	121	585	06.04.23	7720	470103	93905
720.687-014	RECORD-CHANGER TESTER (comm. equip.)	2112	44545544355	LNNNNNNFFONNNNNNNNNN	NNNN4NNNNNNNNN	J,T	212	585	06.03.02	7830	470103	83005
721.131-010	ELECTRIC MOTOR REPAIRING SUPERVISOR (any industry)	4337	33333333354	LNNNNNNFFFFNFNOOON	NNNN3NNNNNNNNNN	D,P	111	582	06.03.02	6000	520205	81002
721.131-014	SUPERVISOR, INSPECTION AND TESTING (elec. equip.)	4337	23322344454	LNNNNNNFFONNNNFNNNN	NNNN3NNNNNNNNNN	D,P,J	111	582	06.02.01	7100	520205	81008
721.261-010	ELECTRIC-MOTOR ANALYST (any industry)	4327	33332443253	LNNNNNNFFFONNNFNFNN	NNNN4NNNNONNNNN	V,J,T	212	582	05.07.02	6152	470199	83002
721.261-014	FINAL TESTER (elec. equip.)	4337	33332333354	MNNONONFFFNOONFNNOON	NNNN3NNNNONNNNN	J,T	111	582	06.01.05	6881	470199	83002
721.281-010	AUTOMOTIVE-GENERATOR-AND-STARTER REPAIRER (automotive ser.)	4326	33335443254	MNNNNNNFFONNNFNOON	NNNN3NNNONNNNNN	V,J,T	111	589	05.05.05	6152	470199	85714
721.281-014	ELECTRIC-MOTOR ASSEMBLER AND TESTER (any industry)	4327	33333433254	LNNNNNNFFONNNNFNFNN	NNNN3NNNNNNNNNN	J,T	111	582	06.02.23	6152	470199	85714
721.281-018	ELECTRIC-MOTOR REPAIRER (any industry)	4337	33332433254	MNNNNNNFFONNNNFNFFON	NNNN3NNNNNNNNNN	J,T	111	582	05.05.10	6152	470199	85714
721.281-022	MAGNETO REPAIRER (any industry)	4226	33333433255	LNNNNNNFFFNNNNFNFON	NNNN3NNNNNNNNNN	J,T	111	582	06.01.04	6867	470199	85328
721.281-026	PROPULSION-MOTOR-AND-GENERATOR REPAIRER (automotive ser.)	4327	33333433354	MNNONONFFNNNNFNFNON	NNNN4NNNNNNNNNN	V,J,T	111	582	06.01.04	6869	470199	85714
721.281-030	TESTER, MOTORS AND CONTROLS (elec. equip.)	4336	33333433354	MNNNFNONFFNNNNFNNFON	NNNN3NNNNNNNNNN	V,J,T	111	582	06.01.05	6881	470199	83002
721.361-010	INSPECTOR, MOTORS AND GENERATORS (elec. equip.)	4337	33332433354	MNNNNNFFFOONFNOOON	NNNN3NNNNONNNNN	J,T	212	582	06.02.32	6152	470199	83002
721.381-010	ELECTRIC-MOTOR FITTER (railroad equip.)	4237	33334433354	LNNNONFFOONNNFNONNN	NNNN4NNNNNNNNNN	R,T	057	582	05.05.05	7678	470199	92944
721.381-014	ELECTRIC-MOTOR-CONTROL ASSEMBLER (elec. equip.)	4326	34332433344	MOOOOONFFNNNNFNOOFN	NNNN4NNNNNNNNNN	J,T	111	581	06.01.04	6867	470199	93114
721.381-018	GOVERNOR ASSEMBLER, HYDRAULIC (elec. equip.)	4327	33333433245	MNNNNNNFFFNNNNFNFONN	NNNN4NNNNNNNNNN	V,J,T	111	582	06.01.04	6869	470199	83911
721.484-010	ELECTRIC-MOTOR WINDER (elec. equip.)	3226	34333433354	MNNNNNNFFFNNNNFNOOON	NNNN3NNNNNNNNNN	R,T	111	582	06.02.23	7720	470199	93905
721.484-014	FIELD-RING ASSEMBLER (elec. equip.)	3226	34333443354	MNNNNNNFFOONFNOOON	NNNN3NNNNONNNNN	R,T	111	582	06.02.32	7720	470199	93905
721.484-018	INSULATION CUTTER AND FORMER (elec. equip.)	3223	34344434345	LNNONONFFONNNNFNONNN	NNNN3NNNNNNNNNN	R,T	212	582	06.02.32	7678	470199	92944
721.484-022	SKEIN WINDER (elec. equip.)	3225	34333432354	LNNNNNNFFNNNNFNFFON	NNNN4NNNNNNNNNN	R,T	111	582	06.02.32	7720	470199	93905
721.684-010	ARMATURE-WINDER HELPER, REPAIR (any industry)	2113	44443542445	MNNONNNFFFNNNNFNONNN	NNNN3NNNNNNNNNN	R	111	582	05.12.16	8635	470199	98102

DOT #	DOT Title & Industry	Trng	Aptitude	Physical	Environment	Tempra	WkF	MPSMS	GOE	SOC	CIP	OES
721.684-014	ASSEMBLER, CARBON BRUSHES (elec. equip.)	3124	34444333355	LNNNNNNFFFNNNNFNFNNN	NNNN3NONNNNNNNN	R,T	111	582	06.02.23	7720	470105	93905
721.684-018	COIL CONNECTOR (elec. equip.)	3225	34332433254	MNNNNNNFFFNNNNFNFNON	NNNN3NNNNNNNN	R,T	111	582	06.02.32	7720	470105	93999
721.684-022	ELECTRIC-MOTOR ASSEMBLER (elec. equip.)	2123	44444532354	LNNONONFFFONNNFNOOON	NNNN4NNNNNNNN	R,T	111	582	06.04.23	7720	470199	93905
721.684-026	SPIDER ASSEMBLER (elec. equip.)	4226	34333434344	MNNNNNNFFONNNNONONNN	NNNN3NNNNNNNN	R,T	111	582	06.02.23	7720	470105	93947
721.687-010	CLEANER AND PREPARER (elec. equip.)	1112	44444544355	MNNFFNFFOONNNONNNNN	NNNN4NNNNNNNN	R	153	582	06.04.33	7756	470105	93947
722.131-010	INSTRUMENT-SHOP SUPERVISOR (tel. & tel.)	4237	33332443343	LNNNNNNFFNFFNFNNNOFN	NNNN3NNNNNNNN	D,P,T	111	586	05.05.10	7100	520205	81008
722.281-010	INSTRUMENT REPAIRER (tel. & tel.)	4337	33333333354	MNNNNNNFFFNNNNNFOFN	NNNN3NNNNNNNN	J,T	111	586	05.05.10	6151	470103	85599
722.381-010	ASSEMBLER (tel. & tel.)	4337	33333433354	LNNONNNFFFNNNNNFFON	NNNN3NNNNNNNN	J,T	111	586	06.01.04	6867	470103	93114
722.381-014	INSTRUMENT INSPECTOR (aircraft mfg.; air trans.)	4437	33233433354	MONOOONFFFONNNFNOOON	ONNN3NNNONNNNN	T,J	111	600	06.01.05	6881	470608	83002
722.687-010	SWITCHBOX ASSEMBLER I (comm. equip.)	1112	44544544455	LNNNNNNFFFNNNNFNFNNN	NNNN3NNNNNNNN	R	061	581	06.04.23	7720	470105	93956
723.131-010	SUPERVISOR, SMALL APPLIANCE ASSEMBLY (house. appl.)	4337	33333344454	LNNNNNNFFEFFNFNNNNN	NNNN3NNNNNNNN	V,D,P	111	583	06.02.01	7100	520205	81008
723.132-010	SUPERVISOR, FABRICATION DEPARTMENT (light. fix.)	4338	33322334345	LNNNNNNFFFNFNFNNNNN	NNNN3NNNNNNNN	D,P	111	584	06.02.01	7100	000000	89114
723.361-010	MODEL MAKER, FLUORESCENT LIGHTING (light. fix.)	4337	33333433345	LNNNNNNFFFONNNFNFNN	NNNN3NNNNNNNN	J,T	241	584	05.05.06	6817	000000	89114
723.381-010	ELECTRICAL-APPLIANCE REPAIRER (any industry)	4236	34433433354	LNNNNNNFFFNNNNNOOFN	NNNN3NNNNNNNN	J,T	111	583	05.10.03	6156	470199	85711
723.381-014	VACUUM CLEANER REPAIRER (any industry)	3226	33333433254	MNNONNNFFFONNNFNOOFN	NNNN3NNNNNNNN	J	111	583	05.10.03	6156	470199	85711
723.584-010	APPLIANCE REPAIRER (house. appl.)	3223	34433434344	MNNNNNNFFONNNFNOOFN	NNNN3NNNNNNNN	J	111	583	05.10.03	6156	470199	85711
723.684-010	ASSEMBLER (house. appl.)	2223	44443533354	LNNNNNNFFFNNNNFNNNN	NNNN3NNNNNNNN	R,T	111	583	06.04.23	7720	470105	93905
723.684-014	ASSEMBLER I (light. fix.)	3223	34443543355	LNNNNNNCFNNNNFNNNN	NNNN4NNNNNNNN	R,T	111	584	06.02.23	7720	000000	93905
723.684-018	ASSEMBLER II (light. fix.)	2122	44444433355	LNNNNNNNFFFNNNNFNNNN	NNNN4NNNNNNNN	R	061	584	06.04.23	7720	000000	93956
723.684-022	FLASHER ADJUSTER (light. fix.)	2112	44544545455	LNNNNNNNFFNNNNFNNNNN	NNNN3NNNNNNNN	R,T	212	583	06.03.02	7830	470199	92198
723.685-010	HEATING-ELEMENT WINDER (elec. equip.; house. appl.)	2113	44435433345	LNNNNNNFFNNNNCNNNNN	NNNN3NNNNNNNN	R	163	583	06.04.20	7529	470199	92997
723.687-010	PATCHER (house. appl.)	2112	44544543355	SNNNNNNFFFNNNNFNNNN	NNNN3NNNNNNNN	R	062	583	06.04.34	7720	470105	93999
723.687-014	TESTER AND INSPECTOR, LAMPS (light. fix.)	2122	44544534455	LNNNNNNNFFNNNNFNNNN	NNNN3NNNNNNNN	R,T	212	584	06.03.02	7820	000000	83005
723.687-018	TESTER, WASTE DISPOSAL LEAKAGE (house. appl.)	2223	44444534345	LNNNNNNFFNNNNONONNN	NNNN3NNNNNNNN	R,T	212	583	06.03.02	7830	470199	83005
723.687-022	WIPER (light. fix.)	2112	44544544455	LNNNNNNCCNNNNNNNNN	NNNN4NNNNNNNN	R	031	584	06.04.39	8769	000000	98999
724.130-010	SUPERVISOR, ELECTRONIC COILS (elec. equip.; electron. comp.)	4348	33333344454	LNNNNNNOOONFNFNONON	NNNN3NNNNNNNNN	D,P,T,V,J	111	580	06.01.01	7100	520205	81008
724.131-010	SUPERVISOR, COIL WINDING (elec. equip.)	4337	33333433355	LNNNNNNFFONFFNFNOONN	NNNN3NNNNNNNN	D,P	111	582	06.02.01	7100	520205	81008
724.131-014	TRANSFORMER SHOP SUPERVISOR (any industry)	4337	33332333254	LNNNNNNNFFNOONFNFNON	NNNN3NNNNNNNN	V,D,P	111	581	05.05.10	7100	520205	81008
724.281-010	TRANSFORMER TESTER (utilities)	4337	23333344354	MNNNNNNFFONNNFNNNNN	NNNN3NNNNNNNN	J,T	111	581	06.01.05	6881	470199	83002
724.360-010	SET-UP MECHANIC, COIL-WINDING MACHINES (elec. equip.)	4346	33333333355	MNNOOONFFFOOONFOFONO	NNNN4NONNNNNNNO	V,T,J	111	580	06.01.02	7479	470199	92997
724.362-010	WIRE COILER (house. appl.)	4235	34433443345	LNNNNNNFFFNNNFNNNNN	NNNN4NFNNNNNN	V,J,T	163	583	06.02.02	6867	470199	93908
724.364-010	WINDING INSPECTOR AND TESTER (elec. equip.)	3224	33442433354	LNNNNNNFFONOOONFFFON	NNNN3NNNONNNNN	R,T	111	582	06.03.01	7820	470199	83005
724.381-010	ADJUSTER, ELECTRICAL CONTACTS (elec. equip.)	3226	34432432354	LNNNNNNFFFNNNNFNFNON	NNNN4NNNNNNNN	R,J,T	111	580	05.10.03	6882	470105	89999
724.381-014	COIL WINDER, REPAIR (any industry)	3225	34333433344	LNNNNNNFFFNNNNFNNFON	NNNN4NNNNNNNN	R,T	163	582	06.02.32	6867	470105	89999
724.381-018	TRANSFORMER REPAIRER (any industry)	3227	33333433354	MNNNNNNFFONNNFNONON	NNNN3NNNNNNNN	J,T	111	581	05.10.03	6152	470105	85714
724.384-010	ARMATURE TESTER I (elec. equip.)	3224	34432443355	MNNNNNNFFOONNFNNFNN	NNNN3NNNNNNNN	R,T	111	582	05.10.03	7830	470199	83005
724.384-014	STATIC BALANCER (any industry)	3225	34443433355	LNNNNNNNFFFONNNFNNNN	NNNN4NNFNNNNNN	J,T	163	582	06.03.01	7830	470105	83005
724.684-010	ARMATURE BANDER (any industry)	3225	34433433345	MNNNNNNNFFFNNNNFNNON	NNNN4NNFNNNNNN	R,T	111	582	06.02.24	7720	470199	93908
724.684-014	ARMATURE CONNECTOR II (elec. equip.)	2223	44432433354	MNNNNNNFFFNNNNFNNNN	NNNN3NNNNNNNN	R,T	111	582	06.04.23	7720	470105	93908
724.684-018	ARMATURE WINDER, REPAIR (any industry)	3224	34432433354	LNNNNNNFFONOONFNFFON	NNNN4NNNONNNNN	R,T	163	591	06.02.24	6152	470199	85714
724.684-022	COIL SHAPER (any industry)	3225	34333433345	LNNNNNNFFFONNNFNFNON	NNNN3NNNNNNNN	R,T	111	582	06.02.24	7517	470105	91321
724.684-026	COIL WINDER (elec. equip.; electron. comp.)	2224	44443433344	LNNNNNNFFNOONFNFFON	NNNN3NNNNNNNN	R,T,U	163	580	06.04.23	7720	470105	93908
724.684-030	COMMUTATOR ASSEMBLER (elec. equip.)	2125	34333443355	MNNNNNNFFOONNNFNNFNN	NNNN4NNNNNNNN	V,T	111	582	06.04.24	7830	470105	93999
724.684-034	MAGNET-VALVE ASSEMBLER (elec. equip.)	2123	44435532355	LNNNNNNFFONNNFNNNNN	NNNN4NNNNNNNN	V,T	111	589	06.04.23	7720	470105	93902
724.684-038	MOTOR-AND-GENERATOR-BRUSH MAKER (elec. equip.)	3214	34433433345	LNNNNNNNFFFONNNFNNNN	NNNN4NNFNNNNNN	R,T	111	582	06.04.24	7720	470105	93905
724.685-010	ELEMENT WINDING MACHINE TENDER (elec. equip.; inst. & app.)	3223	34443443344	LNNONNNFFFONNNFNFOON	NNNN3NNFNNNNNN	R,T	163	567	06.04.09	7720	470105	93908
724.685-014	WELD INSPECTOR (elec. equip.)	2112	44444434455	LNNNNNNFFFNNNNFNNNN	NNNN4NNNNNNNN	R	212	589	06.03.02	7820	470105	83005
724.687-010	LACER AND TIER (elec. equip.)	1112	44444433355	MNNNNNNCCNNNNNFNFNNN	NNNN3NNNNNNNN	R	163	582	06.04.23	7720	470103	93999
725.381-010	TUBE REBUILDER (electron. comp.)	4346	33223333353	MNNNNNNFFONNNNONONON	NNNN3NNNNNNNN	T,J	111	587	05.05.10	6869	470105	89999
725.384-010	TUBE ASSEMBLER, ELECTRON (electron. comp.)	2222	44444433354	LNNNNNFFFNNNNFNNNNN	NNNN3NNNNNNNN	J,T	111	587	06.02.23	7720	470105	93956
725.684-010	COILED-COIL INSPECTOR (light. fix.)	3223	34433333355	SNNNNNNFFFNNNFNNFNN	NNNN3NNNNNNNN	R,J,T	212	584	06.03.01	7820	470105	83005

DOT #	DOT Title & Industry	Trng	Aptitude	Physical	Environment	Tempra	WkF	MPSMS	GOE	SOC	CIP	OES
725.684-014	MOUNTER, HAND (light. fix.)	2223	44444532355	LNNNNNFFNNNNFNFNNN	NNNN3NNNNNNNNNN	R	111	584	06.04.23	7720	470105	93999
725.684-018	STEM MOUNTER (light. fix.)	2112	44433453355	MNNNNNNNCCNNNNNCNNNN	NNNN4NNNNNNNNNN	R	061	584	06.04.23	7720	470105	93999
725.684-022	TUBE ASSEMBLER, CATHODE RAY (electron. comp.)	2113	34443343354	MNNNNNNNFFONNNNNONOOON	NNNN3NNNNNNNNNN	U,R	111	587	06.02.23	7720	470103	93956
725.684-026	CATHODE RAY TUBE SALVAGE PROCESSOR (electron. comp.)	2113	44444443355	HNNNNNNNFFONNNNONONNN	NNNN4NONNNNONNN	U	111	587	06.02.32	7720	000000	93956
725.685-010	DISPLAY-SCREEN FABRICATOR (electron. comp.)	2222	44444543355	MNNNNNNNFFNNNNONONNN	NNON3NONNNNNNNN	U,T	134	587	06.04.19	7549	470105	92198
725.687-010	BEAD INSPECTOR (light. fix.)	2223	44443433354	SNNNNNNNFFNNNNNFFNNNN	NNNN3NNNNNNNNNN	R,T	212	584	06.03.02	7820	470105	83005
725.687-014	COILER (light. fix.)	2223	44544544353	LNNNNNNNFFONNNNFNONFN	NNNN3NNNNNNNNNN	R,T	111	584	06.03.02	7830	470105	83005
725.687-018	FOCUSER (light. fix.)	2123	44443433354	SNNNNNNNFFNNNNFNNNON	NNNN4NNNNNNNNNN	R,T	212	584	06.03.02	7820	470105	83005
725.687-022	GETTERER (light. fix.)	1112	44444533355	SNNNNNNNFFNNNNNFNNNNN	NNNN4NNNNNNNNNN	R	153	584	06.04.33	7740	000000	93999
725.687-026	QUALITY-CONTROL INSPECTOR (light. fix.)	3223	34333433354	LNNNNNNNFFNNNNNFNNNNN	NNNN3NNNNNNNNNN	R,T	212	584	06.03.02	7820	470105	83005
726.130-010	SUPERVISOR, ELECTRONICS PRODUCTION (comm. equip.; electron. comp.; office machines)	4337	33333344354	LNNNNNNNFFONFFNFNFOFN	NNNN3NNNNNNNNNN	D,V,T,P,J	111	580	06.01.01	7100	150303	81008
726.131-014	SUPERVISOR, HEARING-AID ASSEMBLY (protective dev.)	3337	33333333353	LNNNNNNNFFNNFFNCNCCON	NNNN3NNNNNNNNNN	D,P,J,T	111	604	06.01.01	7100	470105	81008
726.131-018	SUPERVISOR, PRINTED CIRCUIT BOARD TESTING (electron. comp.)	4348	33333333353	LNNNNNNNFFNNFFNFNNFFN	NNNN3NNNNNNNNNN	D,T,P,J	212	587	06.01.01	7100	520205	81008
726.134-010	SUPERVISOR, PRINTED CIRCUIT BOARD ASSEMBLY (electron. comp.)	4347	33333333354	LNNNNNNNFFNNFFNFNNOON	NNNN3NNNNNNNNNN	D,T,P,J	111	587	06.01.01	7100	470105	81008
726.261-010	ELECTRONICS ASSEMBLER, DEVELOPMENTAL (any industry)	4447	23322322253	LNNNNNNNFFNOONFNFOFN	NNNN3NNNNNNNNNN	T,J	111	580	05.05.05	3711	470103	22505
726.261-014	ELECTRICIAN, RESEARCH (aircraft mfg)	4437	23323333354	MOOOOOOFFOOOOFOOOON	NNNN3NNOONNNNNN	T,J	111	581	05.03.05	3711	150303	22505
726.261-018	ELECTRONICS TESTER (any industry)	4437	23323333354	MNNNNNNNFFNNFFNFOFON	NNNN3NNNNNNNNNN	T,J	211	580	06.01.05	6881	470104	83002
726.361-014	GROUP LEADER, PRINTED CIRCUIT BOARD ASSEMBLY (electron. comp.)	3235	33333333354	LNNNNNNNFFNNFFNFOFOON	NNNN3NNNNNNNNNN	J,P,V	111	586	06.02.23	6867	470105	93114
726.361-018	GROUP LEADER, PRINTED CIRCUIT BOARD QUALITY CONTROL (electron. comp.)	3336	33333333354	LNNNNNNNFFNNFFNFNOOON	NNNN3NNNNNNNNNN	J,P,T,V	211	587	06.03.01	6881	150702	83002
726.361-022	REPAIRER, PROBE TEST CARD, SEMICONDUCTOR WAFERS (electron. comp.)	3224	33322322254	LNNNNNNNCCNOONCNCFFN	NNNN3NNNNNNNNNN	T,J	111	587	06.01.04	6867	150303	85717
726.362-010	GROUP LEADER, SEMICONDUCTOR TESTING (electron. comp.)	3227	23323333345	SNNNNNNOOONCCNFNOONN	NNON4NNNNNNNNNN	D,V,P,J	212	587	06.01.05	7830	150303	83002
726.362-014	WAVE-SOLDERING MACHINE OPERATOR (comm. equip.; electron. comp.; inst. & app.; office machines)	3234	34433343353	MNNNNNNNFFNOONFNFFON	NNNN3NNNNNNNNNN	T,J	083	587	06.02.19	7533	470105	91711
726.364-010	LEAD HAND, INSPECTING AND TESTING (electron. comp.)	3236	33322233354	MNNOOONFFNFFNFNFNFN	NNNN3NNNNNNNNNN	D,T,P,J	212	587	06.03.02	7820	150303	83005
726.364-014	TEST FIXTURE DESIGNER (electron. comp.)	4337	33334344355	SNNNNNNNFFONOONFNNNNN	NNNN3NNNNNNNNNN	T,J	241	703	05.03.02	3720	480104	22514
726.364-018	ELECTRONICS UTILITY WORKER (comm. equip.; electron. comp.)	3235	33343343354	LNNNNNNNFFONOONFNFNON	NNNN3NNNNNNNNNN	T	111	587	06.04.34	7870	470104	93905
726.367-010	GREEN INSPECTOR (elec. equip.)	3224	33343343354	LNNNNNNNFFNFFNFNNNON	NNNN4NONNNNNNNN	J,T	212	589	06.03.01	7820	470105	83005
726.380-010	ELECTRONIC EQUIPMENT SET-UP OPERATOR (electron. comp.)	4436	33322322255	LNNNNNNNFFFNNNNFNOFNN	NNNN3NOONNNNNON	V,T,J	102	587	06.01.03	7329	470105	92197
726.381-010	ELECTRONICS INSPECTOR (comm. equip.; electron. comp.; inst. & app.)	4446	33333332254	LNNNNNNNFFONNNFFNNFFN	NNNN3NNNNNNNNNN	T,J	211	580	06.01.05	6881	470103	83002
726.381-014	ELECTRONIC EQUIPMENT REPAIRER (comm. equip.; electron. comp.)	3336	33333333353	HNNNNNNNFFONNNNFNFOFN	NNNN3NNNONNNNNN	T,J	111	585	05.10.03	6151	470105	85514
726.382-010	SEQUENCING-MACHINE OPERATOR (electron. comp.)	3235	44433343354	LNNNNNNNFFNNNNNFNNNNN	NNNN3NNNNNNNNNN	R,T	061	587	06.02.20	7479	470105	92997
726.384-014	INSPECTOR, CIRCUITRY NEGATIVE (electron. comp.)	3335	34432343354	LNNONNNNCCFNNNNCNFFON	NNNN3NNNNNNNNNN	T	212	587	06.03.01	7820	150303	83005
726.384-018	INSPECTOR, SEMICONDUCTOR WAFER PROCESSING (electron. comp.)	3224	34432343355	SNNNNNNNFFONNNNNCONN	NNNN3NNNNNNNNNN	R,T,J	212	587	06.03.01	7820	150702	83005
726.384-022	PHOTO MASK INSPECTOR (electron. comp.)	4346	33322223353	LNNNNNNNFFONNNNFNNFFN	NNNN4NNNNNNNNNN	T,J	212	587	06.01.05	7820	150304	83005
726.682-010	LASER-BEAM-TRIM OPERATOR (electron. comp.)	3334	33434432244	LNNNNNNNFFNNNNFNFFON	NNNN3NNNNNNONNN	T,J	082	587	06.02.02	7532	150304	92944
726.682-014	WIRE-WRAPPING-MACHINE OPERATOR (electron. comp.)	3332	44534442355	LNNNNNNNFFNNNNFNFNN	NNNN3NNNNNNNNNN	R,T	163	587	06.02.09	7679	470105	93908
726.682-022	COORDINATE MEASURING EQUIPMENT OPERATOR (electron. comp.)	3323	33333333355	LCNNNNNNFCCNNNNFNONNN	NNNN4NONNNNNNNN	R,T,U	212	587	06.03.02	7820	150702	83005
726.682-026	SAW OPERATOR (electron. comp.)	3214	44444433355	MNNONONFFFNNNNFFOFON	NNNN4NONNNNNNNN	R,T,U	056	587	06.02.09	7529	470105	91117
726.684-010	CAPACITOR-PACK-PRESS OPERATOR (elec. equip.)	2114	44444444355	MNNNONONFFONNNNFNNNON	NNNN4NONNNNNNNN	R	134	587	06.04.34	7720	470105	99999
726.684-014	ELECTRONIC-SCALE SUBASSEMBLER (office machines)	3113	44433433354	LNNNNNNNFFONNNNFNFNNN	NNNN3NNNNNNNNNN	R,T	111	587	06.03.02	7720	470105	93905
726.684-018	ELECTRONICS ASSEMBLER (comm. equip.; electron. comp.; inst. & app.)	2124	44433442254	LNNNNNNNCCFNNNNCNNNNFN	NNNN3NNNNNNNNNN	R,U	102	580	06.02.23	7720	470105	93905
726.684-022	ELECTRONICS INSPECTOR (electron. comp.)	3223	34443443354	LNNNNNNNFFNNNNFNFOON	NNNN3NNNNNNNNNN	R,T,U	212	587	06.03.02	7820	470103	83005
726.684-026	ELECTRONICS TESTER (comm. equip.; electron. comp.; inst. & app.; office machines)	3333	34444444454	LNNNNNNNFFNNNNFNFFON	NNNN3NNNNNNNNNN	R,T	212	580	06.03.02	7830	470104	83005
726.684-034	ASSEMBLER, SEMICONDUCTOR (electron. comp.)	3223	33432332344	SNNNNNNNFFNNNNFFOFON	NNNN3NNNNNNNNNN	J,R,T	111	587	06.02.23	7720	470105	83005
726.684-042	DIE ATTACHER (electron. comp.)	2122	44444443355	LNNNNNNNFFNNNCNCCONN	NNNN3NNNNNNNNNN	R,U	063	587	06.04.23	7720	470105	93956
726.684-050	FILM TOUCH-UP INSPECTOR (electron. comp.)	2112	44444433355	SNNONNNCCCNNNNCNNNNFN	NNNN3NNNNNNNNNN	R,U,T	212	587	06.03.02	7820	150303	83005
726.684-054	INSPECTOR, CRYSTAL (electron. comp.)	3224	34343334455	HNNNNNNNFFONNNNFNONNN	NNNN3NNNNNNNNNN	T	212	587	06.03.02	7820	150303	83005
726.684-058	INSPECTOR, INTEGRATED CIRCUITS (electron. comp.)	2223	44433443455	LNNNNNNNFCCNNNNNCNCNN	NNNN3NNNNNNNNNN	R,T	212	587	06.03.02	7820	150702	83005
726.684-062	INSPECTOR, PRINTED CIRCUIT BOARDS (electron. comp.)	3223	33443433355	LNNNNNNNFFNNNNFNFON	NNNN3NNNNNNNNNN	T,U	212	587	06.03.01	7820	150303	83005
726.684-066	INSPECTOR, SEMICONDUCTOR WAFER (electron. comp.)	3223	34443433455	LNNNNNNNFCFNNNNFNFNNN	NNNN3NNNNNNNNNN	T,U	212	587	06.03.02	7820	470105	83005
726.684-070	PRINTED CIRCUIT BOARD ASSEMBLER, HAND (comm. equip.; electron. comp.; inst.)	3124	44433432354	LNNNNNNNFFNNNNFNFFFN	NNNN3NNNNNNNNNN	R,T	111	587	06.02.23	7720	470105	93905

DOT #	DOT Title & Industry	Trng	Aptitude	Physical	Environment	Tempra	WkF	MPSMS	GOE	SOC	CIP	OES
726.684-074	PRINTED CIRCUIT BOARD COMPONENT TESTER, CHEMICAL (electron. comp.)	3225	33333343354	MNNFNNNFFNNNNFNFNN	NNNN3NNNNNNNNON	R,T	212	587	06.03.02	7820	150702	83005
726.684-078	PRINTED CIRCUIT BOARD COMPONENT TESTER, PRE-ASSEMBLY (electron. comp.)	3225	33333343354	LNNONNNFFNNNNFNFFN	NNNN3NNNNNNNNNN	R,T	212	587	06.03.02	7830	150303	83005
726.684-082	PRINTED CIRCUIT BOARD INSPECTOR, PRE-ASSEMBLY (electron. comp.)	3226	33333333354	LNNNNNNNFFCNNNNCNCFFN	NNNN3NNNNNNNNNN	R,T	212	587	06.03.02	7820	150303	83005
726.684-086	PRINTED CIRCUIT BOARD ASSEMBLY REPAIRER (electron. comp.)	3134	34443433344	LNNNNNNNFFNNNNFNFOON	NNNN3NNNNNNNNNN	R,T	111	587	06.02.23	7720	470105	93905
726.684-090	REWORKER, PRINTED CIRCUIT BOARD (electron. comp.)	2223	34443443355	LNNNNNNNFFNNNNFNFFNN	NNNN3NNNNNNNNN	R,T	111	587	06.02.23	7720	470105	85717
726.684-094	SOLDER DEPOSIT OPERATOR (electron. comp.)	2223	34443433355	MNNNNNNNCFNNNNONFNNN	NNOO4NONNNNNNON	R	083	587	06.04.10	7533	470105	91711
726.684-098	TEST FIXTURE ASSEMBLER (electron. comp.)	3223	34433433355	MNNNNNNNCCFNNNNCNCNNNN	NNNN3NNNNNNNNN	R,T	111	584	06.04.23	7720	470105	93956
726.684-102	TESTER, SEMICONDUCTOR WAFERS (electron. comp.)	2223	34433433355	SNNNNNNNFFNNNNFNFFNN	NNNN3NNNNNNNNN	R,T,U	212	587	06.03.02	7830	150303	83005
726.684-106	TESTER, WAFER SUBSTRATE (electron. comp.)	3234	33444443455	LNNNNNNNFFNNNNFNFNN	NNNN3NNNNNNNON	R,T,U	212	587	06.03.02	7830	150303	83005
726.684-110	TOUCH-UP SCREENER, PRINTED CIRCUIT BOARD ASSEMBLY (electron. comp.)	2122	44443343355	SNNNNNNNFFNNNNCNNNNN	NNNN3NNNNNNNNN	R,T	212	587	06.03.02	7820	470105	83005
726.685-010	MAGNETIC-TAPE WINDER (recording)	2112	44444333345	LNNNNNNNCCCNNNFNNONN	NNNN3NNNNNNNNN	R,T	163	589	06.04.02	7679	470105	92998
726.685-014	INSERTION MACHINE TENDER, ELECTRONIC COMPONENTS (comm. equip.; electron. comp.; office machines)	3234	34443433354	LNNNNNNNFFNNNNNFNFOON	NNNN4NNNNNNNNN	R,T	061	587	06.04.09	7679	470105	92998
726.685-018	BREAK-AND-LOAD OPERATOR (electron. comp.)	2113	44444433355	LNNNNNNNFFFNNNNFNNNN	NNNN4NNNNNNNNN	R,U	054	587	06.04.19	7679	470105	92998
726.685-022	DEFLASH AND WASH OPERATOR (electron. comp.)	2113	44543455555	MNNNNNNNFFONOONFNNNNN	NNNN4NNNNNNNNN	R,U	051	587	06.04.19	7679	000000	92958
726.685-026	DIE ATTACHING MACHINE TENDER (electron. comp.)	2122	44544444455	LNNNNNNNFFONNNNCNFNNN	NNNN4NNNNNNNNN	R,U	081	587	06.04.09	7539	000000	92198
726.685-030	DIE TESTER (electron. comp.)	2223	44444333355	LNNNNNNNFFFNNNNFNFNNN	NNNN4NNNNNNNNN	R,U	212	587	06.03.02	7830	150303	83005
726.685-034	LEAK TESTER, SEMICONDUCTOR PACKAGES (electron. comp.)	2122	44543443455	MNNFNNNNFFFNNNNFNFNNN	NNNN4NNNNNONNN	R,T,U	212	587	06.03.02	6881	150303	83002
726.685-038	REFLOW OPERATOR (electron. comp.)	2222	44444444355	MNNNNNNNFFOONNNNFNFFNN	NNON4NNNNNNNCN	R,U	083	587	06.04.19	7533	470105	91711
726.685-042	ROD TAPE OPERATOR (electron. comp.)	2113	44434433355	MNNONONFFOONNNNNONNNNN	NNNN4NNNNNNNNN	R,U	163	587	06.04.19	7679	470105	92998
726.685-046	SAW OPERATOR, SEMICONDUCTOR WAFERS (electron. comp.)	2123	44443433355	LNNNNNNNOOFNNNNNFNNNNN	NNNN3NNNNNNNNN	R,U,T	056	587	06.04.09	7678	470105	92902
726.685-050	SOLDER-LEVELER, PRINTED CIRCUIT BOARDS (electron. comp.)	2223	34443444354	LNNNNNNNFFCFNNNNFNNOOON	NNNN3NNNNNNNON	R,T,U	083	587	06.04.21	7543	470105	91926
726.685-054	TESTER, SEMICONDUCTOR PACKAGES (electron. comp.)	2223	44444433355	LNNNNNNNFFFNNNNFNFNNN	NNNN4NNNNNNNNN	R,U	212	587	06.03.02	7830	150303	83005
726.685-058	WAFER MOUNTER (electron. comp.)	2122	44444444455	MNNNNNNNFFOONNNFNFNNN	NNNN4NNNNNNNNN	R,U	061	587	06.04.09	7679	470105	92998
726.685-062	PROGRAMMING EQUIPMENT OPERATOR (electron. comp.)	3233	33443334355	SNNNNNNNFFNNONCNFNNN	NNNN3NNNNNNNNN	R,T	233	587	06.04.19	7679	470105	92998
726.685-066	BONDER, SEMICONDUCTOR (electron. comp.)	2122	44444433455	SNNNNNNOFFNNNNFNFFNN	NNNN3NNNNNNNNN	R,U,T	081	587	06.04.09	7539	000000	92198
726.686-010	WAVE-SOLDER OFFBEARER (electron. comp.)	2122	44444433355	LNNNNNNNFFNNNNFNFNNN	NNNN4NNNNNNNNN	R,U	083	587	06.04.40	8725	000000	98502
726.687-010	ELECTRONICS WORKER (electron. comp.)	2122	44444443354	MNNNNNNNFFOONNFNOOON	NNNN3NNNNNNNNN	R,U	111	580	06.04.34	7740	470103	93999
726.687-014	PLUG WIRER (elec. equip.)	2113	45454543345	LNNNNNNNFFFNNNNFNFNNN	NNNN3NNNNNNNNN	R	061	589	06.04.23	7720	470105	93905
726.687-022	ENCAPSULATOR (elec. equip.; electron. comp.)	2122	44444433344	LNNNNNNNFFFNNNNFNFOFON	NNON3NNNNNNNNN	R,U	151	587	06.04.24	7740	470105	93956
726.687-026	LAMINATION ASSEMBLER, PRINTED CIRCUIT BOARDS (electron. comp.)	2222	44443433355	MNNNNNNNFFNNNNFNONNN	NNNN3NNNNNNNNN	R,U	061	587	06.04.34	7720	470105	93999
726.687-030	LOADER, SEMICONDUCTOR DIES (electron. comp.)	2122	44544443455	SNNNNNNNCCNNNNCNCNNNN	NNNN3NNNNNNNNN	R,U	041	587	06.04.40	7759	470105	92902
726.687-034	MASKER (electron. comp.)	4336	44555544455	LNNNNNNNFFNNNNFNNNNN	NNNN3NNNNNNNNN	R,U	153	587	06.04.23	7720	470105	93999
726.687-038	PREASSEMBLER, PRINTED CIRCUIT BOARD (electron. comp.)	2122	44444334355	LNNNNNNNFCFNNNNFNNNNN	NNNO3NNNNNNNNN	R,U	061	587	06.04.34	7740	470105	93999
726.687-042	SEALER, SEMICONDUCTOR PACKAGES (electron. comp.)	2112	44444444455	LNNNNNNNFFNNNNFNFNNN	NNON3NNNNNNNNN	R,U	083	587	06.04.23	7720	470105	92902
726.687-046	WAFER BREAKER, SEMICONDUCTORS (electron. comp.)	2122	44544443355	SNNNNNNNCCFNNNNCNCNNNN	NNNN4NNONNNNNO	R,U	134	587	06.04.34	7759	470105	92902
727.130-010	SUPERVISOR, BURNING, FORMING, AND ASSEMBLY (elec. equip.)	4337	33333333354	LNNONONFFNFFNNFNNON	NNNN4NNNNNNNNN	D,P,J,T	094	589	06.02.01	7100	000000	81008
727.137-010	SUPERVISOR, DRY-CELL ASSEMBLY (elec. equip.)	4337	33333333354	LNNNNNNNFFONFFNFNNOON	NNNN3NNNNNNNNN	D,P	111	589	06.02.01	7100	000000	81008
727.381-010	BATTERY RECHARGER (elec. equip.)	3225	34433433454	MNNNNNNNFFONFFNFNNOON	NNNN3NNNNNNNNN	J,T	111	589	06.02.32	6881	000000	83002
727.381-014	BATTERY REPAIRER (any industry)	3226	34432433354	MNNNNNNNFFNNNNFNNNOO	NNNN3NNNNNNNNN	J,T	111	589	05.10.03	6152	000000	85714
727.381-018	DRY-CELL TESTER (elec. equip.)	4336	33343343354	LNNNNNNNFFNNNNNFNNON	NNNN3NNNNNNNNN	J,T	111	589	06.03.01	6881	000000	83002
727.381-022	STORAGE BATTERY INSPECTOR AND TESTER (elec. equip.)	4247	33333333354	LNNNNNNNFCFNNNNFNNNNN	NNNO3NNNNNNNNN	J,T	212	589	06.01.05	6881	000000	83005
727.384-010	BATTERY TESTER (elec. equip.)	3323	33433434355	LNNNNNNNFFNNNNFNNNNN	NNNN3NNNNNNNNN	J,T	212	589	06.03.01	7830	000000	83005
727.484-010	ACID ADJUSTER (elec. equip.)	2222	34344444355	LNNNNNNNFFNNNNONNNNN	NNNN3NNNNNNNNN	R,T	143	589	06.04.34	7664	000000	92965
727.587-010	BATTERY CHARGER (elec. equip.)	2213	44444444355	LNNNNNNNFFNNNNONNNNN	NNNN3NNNNNNNNN	R,T	111	589	06.04.34	8769	000000	98999
727.662-010	LEAD BURNER, MACHINE (elec. equip.)	3225	34433433353	MNNNNNNFFNFNFNFNFNF	NNNN4NNNNNNNNF	J,T	081	589	06.02.19	7332	000000	91702
727.664-010	BATTERY ASSEMBLER, DRY CELL (elec. equip.)	3224	34433433345	MNNONNNNCCCNOONCNCNNN	NNNN4NNONNNNNON	R,T	061	589	06.04.23	7720	000000	93956
727.684-010	BATTERY ASSEMBLER (elec. equip.)	3224	34433433354	LNNNNNNNFFNNNNFNNOON	NNNN3NNNNNNNNN	R,T	111	589	06.02.23	7720	000000	93905
727.684-014	BATTERY ASSEMBLER, PLASTIC (elec. equip.)	2222	34434433355	LNNNNNNNFFNNNNNFNNNON	NNNN3NNNNNNNNN	R,T	111	589	06.04.23	7720	000000	93956
727.684-018	CELL REPAIRER (elec. equip.)	2223	34443553354	LNNNNNNNFFOONNFNNNON	NNNN3NNNNNNNNN	R,T	111	589	06.04.34	6152	000000	85714
727.684-022	LEAD BURNER (elec. equip.)	2123	34443433354	LNNNNNNNFFNNNNFNNNON	NNNN3NNNNNNNNNC	R,T	081	589	06.04.31	7714	480508	93914

DOT #	DOT Title & Industry	Trng	Aptitude	Physical	Environment	Tempra	WkF	MPSMS	GOE	SOC	CIP	OES
727.684-026	PLATE ASSEMBLER, SMALL BATTERY (elec. equip.)	3223	34444544345	LNNNNNNCCFNNNNNNNNNN	NNNN3NNNNNNNNNNN	R,T	111	589	06.02.23	7720	000000	93905
727.684-030	SEALER (elec. equip.)	2123	44544544355	LNNNNNNNFFONNNNFNNNNN	NNNN3NNNNNNNNNNN	R,T	153	589	06.04.34	7720	000000	93999
727.685-010	PLATE SLITTER-AND-INSPECTOR (elec. equip.)	2222	44444344355	LNNNNNNNFFONNNNFNNNNN	NNNN3NNNNNNNNNNN	R,T	054	589	06.04.24	7514	000000	91321
727.687-010	ACID DUMPER (elec. equip.)	2112	44544544355	MNNNNNNNFFONNNNNNNNNN	NNNN3NNNNNNNNNNN	R	041	589	06.04.24	8725	000000	98502
727.687-014	ACID FILLER (elec. equip.)	2112	44444534345	LNNNNNNNFFNNNNNNNNNN	NNNN3NNNNNNNNNNN	R,T	041	589	06.04.36	8769	000000	98999
727.687-018	ALUMINUM-CONTAINER TESTER (elec. equip.)	2223	44444344354	LNNNNNNNFFNNNNNFNNNNN	NNNN3NNNNNNNNNNN	R,T	212	589	06.03.02	7830	000000	83005
727.687-022	ASSEMBLER, DRY CELL AND BATTERY (elec. equip.)	1112	44544533355	LNNNNNNNFFNNNNNFNNNNN	NNNN3NNNNNNNNNNN	R	111	589	06.04.23	7720	000000	93956
727.687-026	BATTERY CHARGER, CONVEYOR LINE (elec. equip.)	2112	44544444455	LNNNNNNNFFONNNNFNNNNN	NNNN3NNNNNNNNNNN	R	011	589	06.04.34	8769	000000	98999
727.687-030	BATTERY STACKER (elec. equip.)	1112	44544544355	MNNNNNNNFFNNNNNNNNNN	NNNN3NNNNNNNNNNN	R	011	589	06.04.40	8726	000000	98799
727.687-034	BATTERY-CONTAINER-FINISHING HAND (elec. equip.)	1112	44543544354	LNNNNNNNFFONNNNFFON	NNNN3NNNNNNNNNNN	R	051	589	06.04.33	7756	000000	93947
727.687-038	BATTERY-PARTS ASSEMBLER (elec. equip.)	2123	44444433354	LNNNNNNNFFONNNNFNNNNN	NNNN3NNNNNNNNNNFN	R	111	589	06.04.23	7720	000000	93905
727.687-042	CELL COVERER (elec. equip.)	2112	44544544355	LNNNNNNNFFONNNNNNNNNN	NNNN3NNNNNNNNNNN	R	061	589	06.04.23	7720	000000	93999
727.687-046	CELL TUBER, HAND (elec. equip.)	1112	44544444454	LNNNNNNNFFONNNNONNNNN	NNNN3NNNNNNNNNNN	R	061	589	06.04.23	7740	000000	93956
727.687-050	ELECTRIC-CONTAINER TESTER (elec. equip.)	2223	44444444354	LNNNNNNNFFNNNNNFNNNNN	NNNN3NNNNNNNNNNN	R,T	212	589	06.03.02	7830	000000	83005
727.687-054	FINAL INSPECTOR (elec. equip.)	2112	44543544355	LNNNNNNNFFOONNNFNFNNN	NNNN3NNNNNNNNNNN	R,T	212	589	06.03.02	7820	000000	83005
727.687-058	FORMING-PROCESS-LINE WORKER (elec. equip.)	2112	44544543355	MNNONNNFFNNNNNFNNNNN	NNNO3NNNNNNNNNNN	R	111	589	06.04.24	7759	000000	93999
727.687-062	INSPECTOR (elec. equip.)	2112	44444444354	LNNNNNNNFFNNNNNFNNNNN	NNNN3NNNNNNNNNNN	J,T	212	589	06.03.02	7820	000000	83005
727.687-066	INSPECTOR, CONTAINER FINISHING (elec. equip.)	2222	44443434355	LNNNNNNNFFNNNNNFNNNNN	NNNN3NNNNNNNNNNN	R,T	212	589	06.03.02	7820	000000	83005
727.687-070	LEAD-BURNER HELPER (elec. equip.)	2122	44444444455	MNNNNNNNFFNNNNFNNOFNN	NNNN3NNNNNNNNNNN	R	061	589	06.04.23	8614	480508	98999
727.687-074	MOLDED-PARTS INSPECTOR (elec. equip.)	3223	44443443355	LNNNNNNNFFONNNNFNNOON	NNNN3NNNNNNNNNNN	J,T	212	589	06.03.02	7820	000000	83005
727.687-078	SPARK TESTER (elec. equip.)	2222	44443444354	LNNNNNNNFFONNNNFNNNNN	NNNN3NNNNNNNNNNN	R,T	212	589	06.04.23	7830	000000	83005
727.687-082	WAFER-LINE WORKER (elec. equip.)	2112	44544544355	LNNNNNNNFFONNNNFNNNNN	NNNN3NNNNNNNNNNN	R	111	589	06.03.02	7720	000000	93956
728.684-010	WIRE HARNESS ASSEMBLER (elec. equip.; electron. comp.; office machines)	2113	34433433343	LNNNNNNNCCCNNNNCNFFFN	NNNN3NNNNNNNNNNN	R,T	111	589	06.02.32	7720	470105	93999
728.684-014	ELECTRICAL-LINE SPLICER (petrol. & gas)	3225	34443443354	MNNNNNNNFFONNNNFNNNNN	NNNN3NNNNNNNNNNN	R,T	111	580	05.10.03	7720	470105	93999
728.684-018	SPARK TESTER (elec. equip.; nonfer. metal)	2224	34443443355	LNNNNNNNFFONNNFFNNNNN	NNNN3NNNNNNNNNNN	R,T	111	557	05.05.10	7720	470499	85708
728.684-022	WIREWORKER (elec. equip.; electron. comp.)	2122	44443433354	LNNNNNNNFFNNNNFFON	NNNN3NNNNNNNNNNN	R,T	111	584	06.03.02	7830	470401	85911
728.685-010	WIRE PREPARATION MACHINE TENDER (any industry)	2122	44444433344	LNNNNNNNFOFNNNNFNFNON	NNNN3NNNNNNNNNNN	R,T	054	587	06.04.34	7740	470105	83005
729.130-010	SUPERVISOR, ELECTRICAL ASSEMBLY (elec. equip.)	4336	33333433354	LNNNNNNNFFNFNNNFNON	NNNN3NNNNNNNNNNN	V,D,P	111	582	06.01.01	6700	520205	81008
729.131-010	INSPECTOR, CHIEF (elec. equip.)	4336	33333333345	LNNNNNNNFONFFNFNNNNN	NNNN3NNNNNNNNNNN	D,P,T	212	580	06.01.01	6700	470105	81008
729.131-014	RELAY-SHOP SUPERVISOR (utilities)	4337	23322923244	LNNNNNNNFFNFNFNOOON	NNNN3NNNNNNNNNNN	D,P,T	111	581	05.05.10	7100	520205	81008
729.281-010	AUDIO-VIDEO REPAIRER (any industry)	4336	34433443354	LNNNNNNNFFNNNNNFFN	NNNN3NNNNNNNNNNN	R,T	111	585	05.05.10	6155	470499	85708
729.281-014	ELECTRIC-METER REPAIRER (utilities)	4237	33332432354	LNNNNNNNFFONNNFFON	NNNN3NNNNNNNNNNN	J,T	111	581	05.05.10	6171	470401	85911
729.281-018	ELECTRIC-METER-REPAIRER APPRENTICE (utilities)	4237	33332432354	LNNNNNNNFFONNNFFON	NNNN3NNNNNNNNNNN	J,T	111	581	05.05.10	6171	470401	85911
729.281-022	ELECTRIC-TOOL REPAIRER (any industry)	4336	33333433254	LNNNNNNNFFNNNNFFON	NNNN3NNNNNNNNNNN	J,T	111	566	05.10.03	6867	470199	85711
729.281-026	ELECTRICAL-INSTRUMENT REPAIRER (any industry)	4336	23222333253	LNNNNNNNFFOONNNFNNNNN	NNNN3NNNNNNNNNNN	J,T	111	581	05.05.10	6171	470401	85905
729.281-030	ELECTROMEDICAL-EQUIPMENT REPAIRER (any industry)	4336	33332433253	MNNNNNNNFFONNNFNOOON	NNNN3NNNNNNNNNNN	V,J,T	111	589	05.05.11	6171	150401	85908
729.281-034	INSIDE-METER TESTER (utilities)	4337	33322333343	LNNNNNNNFFONNNFFON	NNNN3NNNNNNNNNNN	J,T	111	581	05.05.11	6171	470401	85911
729.281-038	RELAY TESTER (utilities)	4347	34424432353	LNNNNNNNFFONNNNFFON	NNNN3NNNNNNNNNNN	J,T	111	581	05.05.05	6881	470501	83002
729.281-042	WIRER (office machines)	3326	34423343354	LNNNNNNNFFONNNNFFN	NNNN3NNNNNNNNNNN	J,T	111	571	06.02.32	6154	470102	93114
729.281-046	X-RAY-EQUIPMENT TESTER (any industry)	4336	23232343354	LNNNNNNNFCCNFNFNCNNN	NNNN4NNNNNNNNNNN	V,J	212	589	06.01.05	6881	150401	83002
729.360-010	PROBE TEST EQUIPMENT TECHNICIAN, SEMICONDUCTOR WAFERS (electron. comp.)	3235	33433322255	LNNNNNNNFCCNFNFNCNNN	NNNN4NNNNNNNNNNON	T,J	212	587	06.01.02	7479	150303	92997
729.361-010	INSPECTOR, ELECTROMECHANICAL (inst. & app.)	4347	33322333354	MNNNNNNNFFOOONFNOOON	NNNN3NNNNNNNNNNN	T,J	111	587	06.01.02	6881	470105	83002
729.381-010	ELECTRICAL-EQUIPMENT TESTER (aircraft mfg.)	3336	33343443354	LNNONONFFOONNOFNNOON	NNNN3NNNNNNNNNNN	T	111	589	06.01.05	6881	150303	83002
729.381-014	PIN-GAME-MACHINE INSPECTOR (svc. ind. mach.)	4235	33333443344	LNNNNNNNFFNNNNNFNNNNN	NNNN3NNNNNNNNNNN	T	111	572	05.10.03	6179	470199	85999
729.381-018	STREET-LIGHT REPAIRER (utilities)	4237	33333433344	LNNNNNNNFFNNNFNNNNON	NNNN3NNNNNNNNNNN	J,T	111	584	05.05.05	6159	470105	87202
729.381-022	WIRER, CABLE (comm. equip.; elec. equip.)	3226	34533433354	MNNNNNNNFFONNNFNFON	NNNN3NNNNNNNNNNN	J,T	111	586	05.10.03	6867	470103	93114
729.384-010	ASSEMBLER, ELECTRICAL ACCESSORIES II (elec. equip.)	3223	34443543354	LNNNNNNNFFNNNNFNOFON	NNNN3NNNNNNNNNNN	R,T	111	581	06.02.23	7720	470105	93905
729.384-014	FARE-REGISTER REPAIRER (motor trans.)	3226	34334432355	LNNNNNNNFFNNNNNFNNNNN	NNNN3NNNNNNNNNNN	T,J	111	571	05.10.03	6179	470401	85999
729.384-018	SALVAGE REPAIRER II (utilities)	3125	34433443344	MNNFFNNNFFNNNNNFNNNNN	NNNN3NNNNNNNNNNN	R,T	111	581	05.10.03	6152	470501	85714
729.384-022	WINDING INSPECTOR (house. appl.)	3234	34333443354	LNNNNNNNFFNNNNNFNNNNN	NNNN3NNNNNNNNNNN	J,T	111	582	06.03.01	7820	470199	83005
729.384-026	ELECTRICAL ASSEMBLER (aircraft mfg.)	3233	33433433354	LNNONNNNFFNNNNNFFOON	NNNN3NNNNNNNNNNN	T	111	592	06.02.23	7720	000000	93905

DOT #	DOT Title & Industry	Trng	Aptitude	Physical	Environment	Tempra	WkF	MPSMS	GOE	SOC	CIP	OES
729.387-010	DEICER INSPECTOR, ELECTRIC (rubber goods)	3224	33333444455	LNNNNNNFFNNNNFNFNN	NNNN3NNNNNNNNN	R,J,T	212	580	06.03.01	7820	470105	83005
729.387-014	DEICER TESTER (rubber goods)	3224	33343444455	LNNNNNNFFNNNNFNFNN	NNNF3NNNNNNNNNF	R,J,T	212	580	06.03.01	7830	470105	83005
729.387-018	FINISHING INSPECTOR (elec. equip.)	3235	33332493355	LNNNNNNFFNNNNFNFNN	NNNN3NNNNNNNNN	J	111	582	06.03.01	7820	470105	83005
729.387-022	INSPECTOR (house. appl.)	3224	34433444354	LNNNNNNFONNNNFNNFON	NNNN3NNNNNNNNN	R,T	111	583	06.03.01	7820	470199	83005
729.387-026	INSULATOR TESTER (utilities)	3224	34433444354	LNNNNNNFONNNNFNNNON	NNNN3NNNNNNNNN	R,T	212	535	06.03.01	7830	470105	83005
729.664-010	TEST-DEPARTMENT HELPER (comm. equip.; elec. equip.)	2223	34434544354	HNNFNFFONOONFONNFO	NNNN3NNNNNNNNN	R,T	111	580	05.12.16	8620	470105	98999
729.682-010	OPERATOR, CAVITY PUMP (elec. equip.)	3234	33434443454	LNNNNNNFFNNNNFNNNON	NNNN3NNNNNNNNN	J,T	014	580	06.02.18	7679	470105	92998
729.684-010	BATTERY-CHARGER TESTER (elec. equip.)	3223	34434443454	LNNNNNNFFNNNNFNFNN	NNNN3NNNNNNNNN	R,T	111	589	06.03.02	7830	000000	83005
729.684-014	CAPACITOR ASSEMBLER (elec. equip.)	3224	34443433355	MNNNNNNFFNNNNFNFNN	NNNN3NNNNNNNNN	R,T	111	581	06.02.23	7720	470105	93905
729.684-018	DIAL MARKER (elec. equip.)	2222	34342532354	SNNNNNNFFNNNNFNFON	NNNN3NNNNNNNNN	J	262	581	01.06.03	7756	000000	93947
729.684-022	ELECTRIC-SIGN ASSEMBLER (fabrication, nec)	3223	34433433354	MNNNNNNFFNNNNFNNNON	NNNN3NNNNNNNNN	R,T	111	584	06.02.22	7720	000000	93905
729.684-026	ELECTRICAL-CONTROL ASSEMBLER (comm. equip.; elec. equip.)	3224	34332433344	LNNNNNNFFNNNNFNFFN	NNNN3NNNNNNNNN	R,T	111	580	06.02.23	7720	470105	93905
729.684-030	MOLD OPERATOR (elec. equip.)	3224	34344444354	LNNNNNNFFNNNNFNNNON	NNNN3NNNNNNNNN	R,T	132	584	06.02.32	7720	470105	93999
729.684-034	MOTOR-VEHICLE-LIGHT ASSEMBLER (light. fix.)	2113	44435543354	LNNNNNNCCFNNNNCNFNON	NNNN4NNNNNNNNN	R,T	061	584	06.04.23	7720	000000	93956
729.684-038	REPAIRER, SWITCHGEAR (comm. equip.; elec. equip.)	3225	33433433355	LNNNNNNFFNNNNFNNON	NNNN3NNNNNNNNN	J,T	111	582	05.10.03	6152	460302	85714
729.684-042	SAFETY-LAMP KEEPER (mine & quarry)	3214	33443343354	LNNNNNNFFONNNFNFFN	NNNN3NNNNNNNNN	R,J,T	221	584	05.09.01	6560	470399	87999
729.684-046	SPARK-PLUG ASSEMBLER (elec. equip.)	2112	44444544355	LNNNNNNFFNNNNFNNFFN	NNNN3NNNNNNNNN	R	111	589	06.04.23	7720	000000	93956
729.684-050	STREET-LIGHT-REPAIRER HELPER (utilities)	2223	44543534344	MOONNNNFFNNNNFNFNON	FNNN3NNNNNNNNN	R,T	111	584	05.12.16	8637	000000	98102
729.684-054	SUBASSEMBLER (elec. equip.)	2122	34433433354	LNNNNNNFFNNNNCNNNON	NNNN3NNNNNNNNN	R,T	111	582	06.04.23	7720	470199	93956
729.684-058	TESTER, ELECTRICAL CONTINUITY (elec. equip.; house. appl.; light. fix.)	3223	44443433354	LNNNNNNFFNNONFNOOFN	NNNN3NNNNNNNNN	R,T	212	580	06.03.02	7830	470199	83005
729.684-062	WIRER, SUBASSEMBLIES (office machines)	3214	34433433354	LNNNNNNCCFONNNCNFON	NNNN4NNNNNNNNN	R,T	111	571	06.02.23	7720	470102	93956
729.684-066	LAMINATION ASSEMBLER (elec. equip.; electron. comp.)	2123	44444434355	LNNNNNNFFNNNNFNFNN	NNNN3NNNNNNNNN	R,T	063	580	06.02.23	7720	470105	93956
729.687-010	ASSEMBLER, ELECTRICAL ACCESSORIES I (elec. equip.; light. fix.)	2122	44444433344	LNNNNNNFFNNONFNFNON	NNNN3NNNNNNNNN	R	111	584	06.04.23	7720	470105	93956
729.687-014	ELECTRODE CLEANER (elec. equip.)	1111	45554544355	LNNNNNNNFFNNNNNNNNN	NNNN3NNNNNNNNN	R	031	582	06.04.39	8769	000000	98999
729.687-018	LAMINATION SPINNER (elec. equip.)	2112	45443434355	LNNNNNNFFNNNONNNNNN	NNNN3NNNNNNNNN	R	061	582	06.04.34	8769	000000	98999
729.687-022	MICA-WASHER GLUER (mine & quarry)	2222	44444433354	MNNNNNNFFONNNNNNNNN	NNNN3NNNNNNNNN	R,T	063	584	06.04.33	7740	000000	93999
729.687-026	PLATE STACKER, HAND (elec. equip.)	1112	44444544355	LNNNNNNCCFNNNNFNNNNN	NNNN3NNNNNNNNN	R	011	589	06.04.40	8769	000000	98999
729.687-030	SALVAGER (utilities)	2113	44544544355	MNNNNNNFFNNNNNNNNN	ONNN3NNNNNNNNN	R	031	580	05.12.18	6140	470501	85128
730.131-010	SUPERVISOR (musical inst.)	4337	33333334454	LNNNNNOOONFFNFNOOON	NNNN3NNNNNNNNN	V,D,J,T	102	614	06.02.01	7100	520205	81008
730.281-010	ACCORDION MAKER (musical inst.)	4338	33322443253	MNNNONNFFOONONFNFNON	NNNN3NNNNNNNNN	J	121	614	05.05.12	6869	000000	89399
730.281-014	ACCORDION REPAIRER (any industry)	4337	33423533254	LNNNNNNFFNNNNFNFON	NNNN3NNNNNNNNN	J	121	614	05.05.12	6172	470404	85921
730.281-018	ELECTRIC-ORGAN INSPECTOR AND REPAIRER (musical inst.)	4346	34344443334	LNNOOONFFNNONFNNOON	NNNN3NNNNNNNNN	J,T	212	614	05.05.12	6155	470404	85708
730.281-022	FRETTED-INSTRUMENT MAKER, HAND (musical inst.)	4348	33322432254	LNNNNNNFFONONFNNOON	NNNN3NNNNNNNNN	J	102	614	05.05.12	6861	470404	89999
730.281-026	FRETTED-INSTRUMENT REPAIRER (any industry)	4336	33322432354	MNNONNNFFONFNNFFON	NNNN3NNNNNNNNN	J	102	614	05.05.12	6172	470404	85921
730.281-030	HARP MAKER (musical inst.)	4438	33333443355	HNNFFNNFFNNNNFNFFNN	NNNN3NNNNNNNNN	J	102	614	05.05.12	6861	470404	89999
730.281-034	HARPSICHORD MAKER (musical inst.)	4336	23323433243	HNNOOONFFOONONFNNFFON	NNNN3NNNNNNNNN	J	121	614	05.05.12	6861	470404	89999
730.281-038	PIANO TECHNICIAN (any industry)	3227	32333433245	LNNOOONFFNNCNFNNNNN	NNNN4NNNNNNNNN	V,J,T	121	614	05.05.12	6869	470404	85921
730.281-042	PIPE-ORGAN BUILDER (musical inst.)	4338	33323433335	HOOOONNFFONONFNNOONO	NNNN3NNNNNNNNNO	V,J,T	102	614	05.05.12	6839	470404	89399
730.281-046	VIOLIN MAKER, HAND (musical inst.)	4338	33322432253	LNNNNNNFFCCNFNFNNOON	NNNN3NNNNNNNNN	J	102	614	05.05.12	6861	470404	89999
730.281-050	VIOLIN REPAIRER (any industry)	4227	33423532253	LNNONNNFFONFNFNFFON	NNNN3NNNNNNNNN	J,T	102	614	05.05.12	6172	470404	85921
730.281-054	WIND-INSTRUMENT REPAIRER (any industry)	4227	33433432255	MNNNNNNFFONFFNFNFON	NNNN3NNNNNNNNN	V,J,T	121	614	05.05.12	6172	470404	85921
730.281-058	BOW MAKER (musical inst.)	3236	33323432253	LNNNNNNFFNNNNFNNOON	NNNN3NNNNNNNNN	J	102	614	05.05.12	6861	470404	89399
730.361-010	PIANO TUNER (any industry)	3235	33333433355	LNNOOONFFONCNFNNNNN	NNNN3NNNNNNNNN	J,T	121	614	05.05.12	6172	470404	85921
730.361-014	PIPE-ORGAN TUNER AND REPAIRER (any industry)	4338	34433443345	MFFFFNNFFNFNFFNFNN	NNNN4NNNNNNNNN	J	111	614	05.05.12	6172	470404	85921
730.367-010	FINAL INSPECTOR (musical inst.)	3235	34433533353	LNNNNNNFFFOFONONNNN	NNNN3NNNNNNNNN	J,T	212	614	06.03.01	7820	470404	83005
730.381-010	ACCORDION TUNER (any industry)	3226	34444443445	LNNNNNNFFNNFNONNNNN	NNNN3NNNNNNNNN	J,T	121	614	05.05.12	6172	470404	85921
730.381-014	BELL MAKER (musical inst.)	3127	33333534355	MNNNNNNFFOONNFNNONN	NNNN3NNNNNNNNN	V,T	102	614	05.05.12	6822	470404	93197
730.381-018	BRASS-WIND-INSTRUMENT MAKER (musical inst.)	4447	33333443355	MNNNNNNFFONNNFNNOONO	NNNN4NNNNNNNNNO	V,J,T	121	614	05.05.12	6812	470404	93197
730.381-022	ELECTRIC-ORGAN ASSEMBLER AND CHECKER (musical inst.)	3226	34444344354	LNNNNNNFFOONONONONO	NNNN3NNNNNNNNN	V,T	111	614	06.02.23	6867	470404	93114
730.381-026	HARP REGULATOR (musical inst.)	3216	34454433355	MNNNNNNCCFNNNNFNONNN	NNNN3NNNNNNNNN	J,T	102	614	06.02.23	6172	470404	85921
730.381-030	HARP-ACTION ASSEMBLER (musical inst.)	4226	33333433345	MNNNNNNCCFNNNFNOONN	NNNN3NNNNNNNNN	J,T	121	614	05.05.12	6812	470404	93197

DOT #	DOT Title & Industry	Trng	Aptitude	Physical	Environment	Tempra	WkF	MPSMS	GOE	SOC	CIP	OES
730.381-034	METAL-REED TUNER (any industry)	3227	34444433345	LNNFFNFFNNFNONONN	NNNN3NNNNNNNNNNN	J,T	121	614	05.05.12	6172	470404	85921
730.381-038	ORGAN-PIPE VOICER (musical inst.)	4227	33344443455	MFFOOONFFFONFNNNNN	NNNN4NNNNNNNNNNN	J	102	614	05.05.12	6172	470404	85921
730.381-042	PERCUSSION-INSTRUMENT REPAIRER (any industry)	3226	34433432335	MNNONNNFFFONONFNFFNN	NNNO4NNNNNNNNNNN	V,J,T	102	614	05.05.12	6172	470404	85921
730.381-046	PIPE-ORGAN INSTALLER (musical inst.)	4337	33323433355	MOOFFNFFFOONONFOFFNN	NNNN4NNNNNNNNNNN	V,J,T	111	587	05.05.12	6812	470404	93197
730.381-050	PLAYER-PIANO TECHNICIAN (musical inst.)	3334	34332433355	HNNFFNCCFNNONFNFFNN	NNNN4NNNNNNNNNNN	J	102	614	05.05.12	6869	470404	89999
730.381-054	TROMBONE-SLIDE ASSEMBLER (musical inst.)	3227	33432444355	LNNNNNNFFFNNNFNFFNN	NNNN3NNNNNNNNNNN	R,T	102	614	06.01.04	6812	470404	93197
730.381-058	TUNER, PERCUSSION (musical inst.)	3226	33444534355	MNNONNNFFNNNONONNONN	NNNN3NNNNNNNNNNN	J	102	614	05.05.12	6172	470404	85921
730.384-010	ASSEMBLER, PIANO (musical inst.)	3224	34434533354	LNNNNNNFFFNNNFNFFNN	NNNN3NNNNNNNNNNN	R,T	121	614	06.02.22	7720	470404	93956
730.681-010	PIANO REGULATOR-INSPECTOR (musical inst.)	3225	34433433355	LNNNNNNFFFONNNFNNFNN	NNNN3NNNNNNNNNNN	J	121	614	06.01.04	6172	470404	85921
730.681-014	PISTON MAKER (musical inst.)	3226	33433433345	LNNNNNNFFFONNNFNFFNN	NNNN4NNNNNNNNNNN	R,T	102	614	06.01.04	6869	470404	89999
730.681-018	VALVE MAKER II (musical inst.)	3226	33433433355	LNNNNNNCCCONNNNFNFNN	NNNN3NNNNNNNNNNN	J,T	121	614	06.02.24	7529	470404	92198
730.682-010	SOCKET PULLER (musical inst.)	3114	34433433355	MNNNNNNNFFFNNNFNNNNN	NNNN3NNNNNNNNNNN	R,T	134	614	06.02.02	7529	470404	92198
730.684-010	ASSEMBLER, MUSICAL INSTRUMENTS (musical inst.)	3223	34433433355	MNNNNNNFFFNNNFNOONN	NNNN3NNNNNNNNNNN	R,T	102	614	06.02.02	7720	470404	93956
730.684-014	BELL-NECK HAMMERER (musical inst.)	2112	44534534355	MNNNNNNFFFNNNNFNNNNN	NNNN3NNNNNNNNNNN	R,T	134	614	06.04.24	7740	470404	93999
730.684-018	BELLY BUILDER (musical inst.)	3333	34444433355	HNNONNNFFONNNNFNFNNN	NNNN3NNNNNNNNNNN	J,T	102	614	06.02.32	7720	470404	93956
730.684-022	BOW REHAIRER (any industry)	3116	34444433353	SNNNNNNFFFNNNNFNFFON	NNNN3NNNNNNNNNNN	J,T	102	614	05.05.12	6172	470404	85921
730.684-026	CHIP TUNER (musical inst.)	3233	44445444355	MNNNOONNFFOONFNNNNNN	NNNN3NNNNNNNNNNN	J,T	121	614	06.02.32	6172	470404	85921
730.684-030	CONSOLE ASSEMBLER (musical inst.)	3224	34433533344	MNNOONNFFOONNNONONNN	NNNN3NNNNNNNNNNN	R,J	111	614	06.02.23	7720	470404	93956
730.684-034	FRETTED-INSTRUMENT INSPECTOR (musical inst.)	3224	34433542254	LNNNNNNFFFONFNONNOON	NNNN3NNNNNNNNNNN	J	102	614	06.01.04	7820	470404	83005
730.684-038	INSPECTOR, WOODWIND INSTRUMENTS (musical inst.)	3224	34433432355	LNNNNNNFFFNNNNFNFNN	NNNN3NNNNNNNNNNN	J,T	121	614	06.03.02	7820	470404	83005
730.684-042	KEYBOARD-ACTION ASSEMBLER (musical inst.)	3224	34334533355	LNNNNNNCCFNNNNFNNNNN	NNNN3NNNNNNNNNNN	V	121	614	06.02.23	7720	470404	93956
730.684-046	MANUAL WINDER (musical inst.)	3223	34433433345	LNNNNNNFFFNNNONONNNN	NNNN3NNNNNNNNNNN	R,T	111	614	06.02.23	7720	470404	93956
730.684-050	MUSICAL-STRING MAKER (musical inst.)	3114	34444533355	LNNNNNNFFFNNNFNFFNN	NNNN3NNNNNNNNNNN	J,T	102	614	06.02.32	7720	470404	93999
730.684-054	PIANO STRINGER (musical inst.)	2124	34433544355	MNNFNNNFFONNNFNONNNN	NNNN3NNNNNNNNNNN	R,T	102	614	06.04.24	7720	470404	93956
730.684-058	PREASSEMBLER AND INSPECTOR (musical inst.)	2114	44543544355	LNNNNNNFFFNNNFNNNNN	NNNN3NNNNNNNNNNN	R,T	051	614	06.04.23	7720	470404	93956
730.684-062	RACKER, OCTAVE BOARD (musical inst.)	3223	34434433355	LNNNNNNFFFNNNFNFFNN	NNNN3NNNNNNNNNNN	R,T	111	614	06.02.23	7720	470404	93956
730.684-066	SANDER-AND-BUFFER (musical inst.)	2123	44543544354	LNNNNNNCCFFNNNFNNOON	NNNN3NCNNNNNNNNNN	R	051	614	06.04.25	7758	470404	93953
730.684-070	SEAM HAMMERER (musical inst.)	3113	44544534345	LNNNNNNCCFFNNNFNNOON	NNNN4NNNNNNNNNNN	R,T	134	614	06.02.24	7529	470404	92198
730.684-074	SHEET-METAL-PATTERN CUTTER (musical inst.)	2213	44433444355	LNNNNNNCCFNNNNFNFFNN	NNNN3NNNNNNNNNNN	R,T	241	614	06.02.24	7529	470404	92198
730.684-078	SLIDING-JOINT MAKER (musical inst.)	3223	34443433355	SNNNNNNFFFNNNNFNNNNN	NNNN3NNNNNNNNNNN	R	102	614	06.02.24	7720	470404	93999
730.684-082	STOPBOARD ASSEMBLER (musical inst.)	3334	33445533345	LNNNNNNCCFFNNNFNNNNN	NNNN3NNNNNNNNNNN	R	111	614	06.02.23	7720	470404	93956
730.684-086	TESTER (musical inst.)	3226	34444443355	LNNNNNNCCFONFNONONNN	NNNN3NNNNNNNNNNN	R	211	614	06.03.02	7830	470404	83005
730.684-090	TONE CABINET ASSEMBLER (musical inst.)	3223	34333433354	MNNFFNFFNNNNNCNCNNN	NNNN4NNNNNNNNNNN	J,T	111	614	06.02.01	7100	000000	81008
730.684-094	TONE REGULATOR (musical inst.)	2114	44544544355	LNNNNNNFFFNNNFNNNNN	NNNN3NNNNNNNNNNN	J,T	102	614	06.02.23	7720	470404	93956
730.685-010	LOOPER (musical inst.)	2123	44444422245	LNNNNNNFFFNNNNCNNNN	NNNN3NNNNNNNNNNN	R	061	614	06.04.34	6172	470404	85921
730.685-014	MOUTHPIECE MAKER (musical inst.)	3223	44444434345	LNNNNNNFFONNNFNNFNN	NNNN3NNNNNNNNNNN	J,T	057	614	06.04.09	7679	470404	92998
730.686-010	CUTTER, WOODWIND REEDS (musical inst.)	2112	44543532455	LNNNNNNCCFFNONNNNNNN	NNNN3NNNNNNNNNNN	R	102	614	06.04.25	7678	470404	92944
731.131-010	SUPERVISOR, TOY ASSEMBLY (toy-sport equip.)	4347	33333432253	LNNNNNNFFNFFNNNNOFN	NNNN3NNNNNNNNNNN	V,D,P,J	121	615	06.02.01	7820	000000	89908
731.280-010	MODEL MAKER (toy-sport equip.)	4447	34322333255	MNNFFNFFNNNCNCNNN	NNNN4NNNNNNNNNNN	V,T	121	615	01.06.02	6862	000000	89908
731.381-010	DICE MAKER (toy-sport equip.)	3226	33333333355	LNNNNNNFFFOONNFNFNN	NNNN3NNNNNNNNNNN	V,T	102	615	06.02.24	6869	000000	89999
731.587-010	FINISHER, HAND (toy-sport equip.)	2112	44444443355	LNNNNNNFFFNNNNONNNNN	NNNN3NNNNNNNNNNN	J,T	102	615	06.04.23	6869	000000	98999
731.684-010	COIN-MACHINE ASSEMBLER (svc. ind. mach.)	2123	44444422245	SNNNNNNFFCNNNCNNNNN	NNNN3NNNNNNNNNNN	R	062	572	06.04.23	8769	470199	93956
731.684-014	DOLL REPAIRER (any industry)	2113	44433443353	LNNNNNNFFFNNNFNFFN	NNNN3NNNNNNNNNNN	R,T	083	615	05.10.04	6179	000000	85999
731.684-018	TOY ASSEMBLER (retail trade)	2223	44434444355	LNFFFNFFNNNNNNFNNN	NNNN4NNNNNNNNNNN	R,T	102	615	05.12.15	6179	000000	93956
731.684-022	TOY-ELECTRIC-TRAIN REPAIRER (retail trade)	3223	34422432353	LNNNNNNFFFNNNNFNOON	NNNN3NNNNNNNNNNN	J	111	615	05.10.03	6179	470199	85999
731.685-010	ROOTER OPERATOR (fabrication, nec)	2123	34434533335	SNNNNNNFFONNNNFNNFN	NNNN3NNNNNNNNNNN	R,T	171	619	06.04.09	7655	000000	92721
731.685-014	STUFFER (toy-sport equip.)	2112	44444444345	LNNNNNNOFFNNNNNFNNNN	NNNN4NNNNNNNNNNN	R	102	615	06.04.34	7662	000000	92974
731.685-018	TIRE SETTER (toy-sport equip.)	2112	44545534355	LNNFFNFFNNNNNFNNNN	NNNN3NNNNNNNNNNN	R	061	615	06.04.34	7679	470499	92998
731.687-010	ASSEMBLER (svc. ind. mach.)	1112	44545534355	LNNNNNNFFFNNNNONNNNN	NNNN3NNNNNNNNNNN	R	071	572	06.04.23	7720	470199	93956
731.687-014	FINISHER (fabrication, nec)	2112	34434533344	SNNNNNNFFFNNNFNNNNNN	NNNN3NNNNNNNNNNN	R,T	054	619	06.04.34	7740	000000	93999
731.687-018	HACKLER, DOLL WIGS (toy-sport equip.)	2112	44544533345	LNNNNNNFFFNNNNNNNNNN	NNNN3NNNNNNNNNNN	R	161	619	06.04.34	8769	000000	98999

DOT #	DOT Title & Industry	Trng	Aptitude	Physical	Environment	Tempra	WkF	MPSMS	GOE	SOC	CIP	OES
731.687-022	INSPECTOR, TOYS (toy-sport equip.)	3224	34443444353	LNNNNNNFFNNNNFNFFN	NNNN3NNNNNNNNNNN	J,T	212	615	06.03.02	7820	000000	83005
731.687-026	MOLD FILLER, PLASTIC DOLLS (toy-sport equip.)	2113	44443544355	HNNNNNNFFONNNNNNNNN	NNNN4NNNNNNNNNNN	R	132	492	06.04.32	7740	000000	93956
731.687-030	PUZZLE ASSEMBLER (toy-sport equip.)	2112	44443443354	LNNNNNNFFNNNNFNNNON	NNNN3NNNNNNNNNNN	R,T	061	615	06.04.23	7720	000000	93956
731.687-034	TOY ASSEMBLER (toy-sport equip.)	2112	45445453344	LNNNNNNFFNNNNNFNOFON	NNNN3NNNNNNNNNNN	R,T	102	615	06.04.23	7720	000000	99999
731.687-038	WIRE CUTTER (svc. ind. mach.)	1111	45554544455	LNNNNNNFFOFFNFNOONN	NNNN3NNNNNNNNNNN	R	054	557	06.04.24	8769	000000	98999
732.130-010	SUPERVISOR (toy-sport equip.)	4336	33333443355	LNNNNNNNFFOFFNFNOONN	NNNN4NFONNNNNFN	D,J,P	102	616	06.02.01	7100	520205	81008
732.281-010	CUSTOM SKI MAKER (toy-sport equip.)	4447	23322323244	LNNNNNNNNCFONNNNNFFOON	NNNN4NNNNNNNNNNN	J	102	612	05.10.01	6862	470499	88908
732.364-014	SKI-BINDING FITTER-AND-REPAIRER (toy-sport equip.)	4335	33333333355	LNNNNNNNFFNFNFNNNN	NNNN3NNNNNNNNNNN	T,P	102	616	06.02.24	7755	470499	85999
732.381-010	BOW MAKER, CUSTOM (toy-sport equip.)	4227	34322403344	LNNNNNNNFFONNNNNNON	NNON4NONNNNNNNNN	J,T	102	616	01.06.02	6861	470499	89999
732.381-014	BOWLING-BALL GRADER AND MARKER (toy-sport equip.)	3226	33333433354	LNNNNNNNFFNNNNFNFFN	NNNN3NNNNNNNNNNN	J,T	212	616	06.02.24	6881	470499	83002
732.381-018	GOLF-CLUB HEAD FORMER (toy-sport equip.)	3226	33433433354	LNNNNNNNCCONNNNFNNNNN	NNNN3NNNNNNNNNNN	J,T	134	616	06.02.24	6816	470499	89111
732.381-022	GOLF-CLUB REPAIRER (toy-sport equip.)	3226	33433433354	MNNNNNNFFONNNNFNNNON	NNNN3NNNNNNNNNNN	J,T	051	616	05.10.01	6179	470499	85999
732.384-010	ASSEMBLER, BILLIARD-TABLE (toy-sport equip.)	3223	34433433334	LNNNNNNNFFOFFNFNOONN	NNNN3NNNNNNNNNNN	R,T	102	616	05.10.01	7720	470499	93956
732.384-014	INSPECTOR AND ADJUSTER, GOLF CLUB HEAD (toy-sport equip.)	3334	34344443355	LNNNNNNNCFONNNNFNFNN	NNNN3NNNNNNNNNNN	J,T	102	616	06.03.02	7820	470499	83005
732.487-010	BOWLING-BALL WEIGHER AND PACKER (toy-sport equip.)	2214	44344344355	LNNNNNNNNFFNNNNFNNNNN	NNNN3NNNNNNNNNNN	R,T	041	616	06.04.38	7840	470499	83005
732.567-010	INSPECTOR, GOLF BALL (toy-sport equip.)	3223	34443444344	LNNNNNNNFFONOONFNNFON	NNNN3NNNNNNNNNNN	J,T	212	616	06.03.02	7820	470499	83005
732.584-010	BOWLING-BALL ENGRAVER (toy-sport equip.)	2123	34433433355	LNNNNNNNFFONNNFNNNNN	NNNN3NNNNNNNNNNN	J,T	183	616	06.04.24	7757	470499	93951
732.584-014	FINISHER (toy-sport equip.)	2124	44443433445	SNNNONNFFNNNNFNFNNN	NNNN3NONNNNNNNNN	R,T	051	616	06.04.25	7759	470499	93999
732.587-010	GOLF-BALL TRIMMER (toy-sport equip.)	2112	44444434455	LNNNNNNNFFONNNFNNNNN	NNNN4NNNNNNNNNNN	R	054	616	06.04.34	7740	470499	93999
732.587-014	GOLF-CLUB WEIGHER (toy-sport equip.)	2122	44444444455	LNNNNNNNFFNNNNFNNNNN	NNNN3NNNNNNNNNNN	R	212	616	06.03.02	7840	470499	83005
732.684-010	ARROWSMITH (toy-sport equip.)	2222	44443544354	LNNNNNNNFFONOONFNNFON	NNNN3NNNNNNNNNNN	R	063	616	06.04.34	7755	470499	93999
732.684-014	ASSEMBLER (toy-sport equip.)	2223	34433433355	LNNNNNNNFFONNNNFNFNNN	NNNN4NNNNNNNNNNN	R,T	102	616	06.04.23	7720	470499	93956
732.684-018	ASSEMBLER, LIQUID CENTER (toy-sport equip.)	2112	44444434355	MNNNNNNNFFNNNNNNNNN	NNNN3NNNNNNNNNNN	R,T	132	616	06.04.32	7720	470499	93956
732.684-022	ASSEMBLER, PING-PONG TABLE (toy-sport equip.)	2112	44434534355	LNNNNNNNFFNNNNFNFNNN	NNNN4NNNNNNNNNNN	R,T	102	616	06.04.22	7720	470499	93956
732.684-026	BALL ASSEMBLER (toy-sport equip.)	2223	44453533355	LNNNNNNNFFONNNNFNNNNN	NNNN3NNNNNNNNNNN	R,T	063	616	06.04.23	7720	470499	93956
732.684-030	BASEBALL INSPECTOR AND REPAIRER (toy-sport equip.)	3223	34433433355	LNNNNNNNFFONNNFNNNNN	NNNN3NNNNNNNNNNN	J,T	102	616	06.03.02	7820	470499	83005
732.684-034	BASEBALL SEWER, HAND (toy-sport equip.)	2113	45435223355	LNNNNNNNNCCCNNNFNNNN	NNNN3NNNNNNNNNNN	R,T	171	616	06.04.27	7752	470499	93923
732.684-038	BOW MAKER, PRODUCTION (toy-sport equip.)	3325	34343433344	LNNNNNNNNCCCNNNNFFON	NNNN4NNNNNNNNNNN	T	102	616	06.02.32	7755	470499	93999
732.684-042	BOW-STRING MAKER (toy-sport equip.)	2113	44544543455	LNNNNNNNNFFONNNNNNNNN	NNNN3NNNNNNNNNNN	R,T	162	616	06.04.34	7720	470499	93999
732.684-046	CELLULOID TRIMMER (toy-sport equip.)	2112	44544533355	LNNNNNNNFFONNNNNNNNN	NNNN3NNNNNNNNNNN	R,T	102	616	06.04.34	7720	470499	93999
732.684-050	FEATHER STITCHER (toy-sport equip.)	2113	44444433455	LNNNNNNNFFNNNNFNNNN	NNNN3NNNNNNNNNNN	R,T	171	616	06.04.34	7752	470499	93923
732.684-054	FISH-STRINGER ASSEMBLER (toy-sport equip.)	2212	44444433355	LNNNNNNNFFONNNNCNCNN	NNNN3NNNNNNNNNNN	R,T	061	616	06.04.23	7720	470499	93956
732.684-058	FISHING-LURE ASSEMBLER (toy-sport equip.)	3223	34434433344	LNNNNNNNNCCONNNFNNNON	NNNN3NNNNNNNNNNN	R	102	529	06.02.24	7720	470499	93956
732.684-062	FISHING-REEL ASSEMBLER (toy-sport equip.)	2112	44444433355	SNNNNNNFFONNNNNNNNN	NNNN3NNNNNNNNNNN	R,T	121	616	06.04.23	7720	470499	93956
732.684-066	FISHING-ROD ASSEMBLER (toy-sport equip.)	2122	44544532354	LNNNNNNNFFNNNNFNNON	NNNN3NNNNNNNNNNN	R,T	102	616	06.04.23	7720	470499	93956
732.684-070	FISHING-ROD MARKER (toy-sport equip.)	2123	34343433454	LNNNNNNNNCCCNNNFNFON	NNNN4NNNNNNNNNNN	R,T	241	616	06.02.31	7755	470499	93999
732.684-074	FLY TIER (toy-sport equip.)	2124	44442532354	LNNNNNNNNCCCONNNNCNON	NNNN3NNNNNNNNNNN	R,T	062	616	06.04.23	7720	470499	93999
732.684-078	GOLF-CLUB ASSEMBLER (toy-sport equip.)	2113	44444434355	LNNONONFFFNNNNFNFONN	NNNN4NNNNNNNNNNN	R,T	102	616	06.04.23	7720	470499	93956
732.684-082	GRIP WRAPPER (toy-sport equip.)	2113	44444433355	LNNNNNNNCCNNNNCNCNN	NNNN3NNNNNNNNNNN	R	063	529	06.04.27	7720	470499	93956
732.684-086	GUIDE WINDER (toy-sport equip.)	2223	44443423244	SNNNNNNNCCONNNFNNNON	NNNN3NNNNNNNNNNN	R,T	163	616	06.04.34	7752	470499	93923
732.684-090	PELOTA MAKER (toy-sport equip.)	2114	44435433455	LNNNNNNNFFNNNNNNNNN	NNNN3NNNNNNNNNNN	R,T	171	616	06.04.34	7752	470499	93956
732.684-094	RACKET STRINGER (toy-sport equip.)	3225	34433433334	LNNNNNNNNCCCNNNNFNON	NNNN3NNNNNNNNNNN	R,T	164	616	06.02.32	7720	470499	93956
732.684-098	ROLLER-SKATE ASSEMBLER (toy-sport equip.)	2112	44544533355	LNNNNNNNFFNNNNNNNNN	NNNN3NNNNNNNNNNN	R	121	616	06.04.23	7720	470499	93956
732.684-102	ROLLER-SKATE REPAIRER (any industry)	2214	44444443355	LNNNNNNNFFNNNNNNNNN	NNNN3NNNNNNNNNNN	R,T	121	616	05.12.15	6179	470499	85999
732.684-106	SHAPER, BASEBALL GLOVE (toy-sport equip.)	2112	44544534355	MNNNNNNNCCCNNNFNFFN	NNNN4NNNNNNNNNNN	R	134	616	06.04.27	7755	470499	93999
732.684-110	SKI BASE TRIMMER (toy-sport equip.)	2112	44443434345	MNNNNNNFFFNNNNFNFONN	NNNN4NNNNNNNNNNN	R,T	102	616	06.04.34	7755	470499	93999
732.684-114	SKI MOLDER (toy-sport equip.)	3123	44435343345	LNNNNNNNFFFNNNNFNFONN	NNNN4NNNNNNNNNNN	J,T	102	616	06.02.32	7755	470499	93999
732.684-118	SKI REPAIRER, PRODUCTION (toy-sport equip.)	2115	44444343354	LNNNNNNNNFFOONNNFNOOON	NNNN3NNNNNNNNNNN	J,T	102	616	06.02.24	7755	470499	85999
732.684-122	SPORTS-EQUIPMENT REPAIRER (any industry)	3224	44433433355	LNNNNNNNNOFFONNNFNFFN	NNNN3NNNNNNNNNNN	R,T	102	616	05.10.04	6179	470499	93999
732.684-126	SURFBOARD MAKER (toy-sport equip.)	2223	34434533355	MNNNNNNNFFONNNNNNNNN	NNNN3NNNNNNNNNNN	R,T	054	616	06.04.24	7720	470499	93999
732.684-130	INSPECTOR (toy-sport equip.)	3233	33442444454	LNNNNNNNFFONONFNNFON	NNNN3NNNNNNNNNNN	J,T	212	616	06.03.01	7820	470499	83005

DOT #	DOT Title & Industry	Trng	Aptitude	Physical	Environment	Tempra	WkF	MPSMS	GOE	SOC	CIP	OES
732.685-010	BASE-FILLER OPERATOR (toy-sport equip.)	2112	44444533345	LNNNNNNFFONNNNONNONN	NNNN3NNNNNNNNNN	R	102	616	06.04.36	7662	470499	92974
732.685-014	FEATHER SAWYER (toy-sport equip.)	2112	44543533354	LNNNNNNFFONNNNFNNON	NNNN3NNNNNNNNNN	R	054	616	06.04.09	7678	470499	92944
732.685-018	FIXING-MACHINE OPERATOR (toy-sport equip.)	2113	44444443345	MNNNNNNFFONNNNNNNNNN	NNNN3NNNNNNNNNN	R	061	616	06.04.20	7720	470499	93956
732.685-022	GUIDE-BASE WINDER, MACHINE (toy-sport equip.)	2112	44443433354	LNNNNNNFFONNNNNFNFON	NNNN3NNNNNNNNNN	R,T	163	616	06.04.09	7679	470499	92998
732.685-026	MACHINE SNELLER (toy-sport equip.)	2112	44433532245	LNNNNNNFFFNNNNFNFNN	NNNN3NNNNNNNNNN	R	062	616	06.04.34	7740	470499	93999
732.685-030	SINKER WINDER (toy-sport equip.)	2112	44444434455	LNNNNNNFFNNNNFNFNNN	NNNN4NNNNNNNNNN	R	135	616	06.04.20	7679	000000	92998
732.685-034	STUFFING-MACHINE OPERATOR (toy-sport equip.)	2112	44445334345	LNNNNNNNFFNNNNONONNN	NNNN4NNNNNNNNNN	R	041	616	06.04.05	7662	470499	92974
732.685-038	TRIMMING-MACHINE OPERATOR (toy-sport equip.)	1112	44544544445	LNNNNNNFFNNNNNNNNNN	NNNN3NNNNNNNNNN	R	054	616	06.04.05	7678	470499	92944
732.686-010	HAY SORTER (toy-sport equip.)	1111	44544544455	MNNNNNNFFNNNNNNNNNN	NNNN3NNNNNNNNNN	R	041	616	06.04.34	8725	470499	98502
732.687-010	ADHESIVE PRIMER (toy-sport equip.)	1112	44544533355	MNNNNNNFFFNNNFNOFNN	NNNN4NNNNNNNNNN	R,T	051	616	06.04.33	7755	470499	93999
732.687-014	ASSEMBLER, FISHING FLOATS (toy-sport equip.)	1112	44544533345	LNNNNNNFFONNNNNNNNNN	NNNN3NNNNNNNNNN	R	061	616	06.04.23	7720	470499	93956
732.687-018	BASE FILLER (toy-sport equip.)	1111	44544533355	LNNNNNNNFFNNNNNNNNNN	NNNN3NNNNNNNNNN	R	041	616	06.04.23	7740	470499	93999
732.687-022	CASTING-PLUG ASSEMBLER (toy-sport equip.)	1112	44544534455	LNNNNNNFFONNNNNNNNN	NNNN3NNNNNNNNNN	R	071	616	06.04.23	7740	470499	93956
732.687-026	GOLF-CLUB WEIGHTER (toy-sport equip.)	2112	44444433355	LNNONONCCFNNNNFNNNF	NNNN4NNNNNNNNNN	R,T	053	616	06.04.34	7740	470499	93999
732.687-030	LABORER (toy-sport equip.)	1112	44444534354	MNNONONFFFONNNFNFOON	NNNN4NNNNNNNNNN	R	011	616	06.04.34	8769	470499	98999
732.687-034	LACER (toy-sport equip.)	2113	44444533355	LNNNNNNFFNNNNNFNFNNN	NNNN3NNNNNNNNNN	R	062	616	06.04.34	7740	470499	93999
732.687-038	LEADER TIER (toy-sport equip.)	2112	44434532255	LNNNNNNFFNNNNFNFNNN	NNNN3NNNNNNNNNN	R	062	616	06.04.34	7720	470499	93956
732.687-042	LINING INSERTER (toy-sport equip.)	2112	44544544355	LNNNNNNFFONNNNNNNNNN	NNNN4NNNNNNNNNN	R	061	616	06.04.23	7740	470499	93999
732.687-046	MOLD CLEANER (toy-sport equip.)	1112	44544534455	LNNNNNNFFFONNNFNNNN	NNNN4NNNNNNNNNN	R	051	616	06.04.39	8750	470499	98905
732.687-050	MOLD STRIPPER (toy-sport equip.)	1112	44544534345	LNNNNNNFFNNNNNNNNNN	NNNN4NNNNNNNNNN	R	071	616	06.04.24	7740	470499	93999
732.687-054	MOLDER, INFLATED BALL (toy-sport equip.)	2112	44444534355	MNNNNNNFFONNNNFNNNN	NNNN4NNNNNNNNNN	R	132	616	06.04.32	7663	470499	92971
732.687-058	MOLDER, WAX BALL (toy-sport equip.)	2112	44444434355	MNNNNNNFFFNNNNFNNNN	NNFN3NNNNNNNNNN	R	132	566	06.04.32	7740	470499	93999
732.687-062	PAINTER AND GRADER, CORK (toy-sport equip.)	2112	44434443454	LNNNNNNFFNNNNFNFNON	NNNN3NNNNNNNNNN	R,T	153	616	06.04.33	7756	470499	93947
732.687-066	REVERSER (toy-sport equip.)	2112	44544534355	MNNNNNNFFNNNNONNNNN	NNNN3NNNNNNNNNN	R	062	616	06.04.34	8769	470499	98999
732.687-070	SOFTBALL CORE MOLDER (toy-sport equip.)	2112	44444534355	MNNNNNNNFFNNNNFNONNN	NNCN4NNNNNNNNNN	R	132	616	06.04.32	7667	470499	92971
732.687-074	SPIN-TABLE OPERATOR (toy-sport equip.)	2113	44544534355	MNNNNNNFFONNNNFNNNN	NNNO3NNNNNNNNNN	R	051	616	06.04.24	7677	470499	92965
732.687-078	TARGET TRIMMER (toy-sport equip.)	2112	44544544355	MNNNNNNFFONNNNNNNNNN	NNNN3NNNNNNNNNN	R	054	616	06.04.34	7753	470499	93926
732.687-082	WAX-BALL KNOCK-OUT WORKER (toy-sport equip.)	1112	44544544355	MNNNNNNFFONNNNNNNNNN	NNNN3NNNNNNNNNN	R	142	616	06.04.39	8769	000000	98999
732.687-086	WEIGHER (toy-sport equip.)	2212	44444433355	LNNNNNNFFONNNNFNNNN	NNNN3NNNNNNNNNN	R,T	212	616	06.04.34	7840	470499	83005
733.130-010	SUPERVISOR, PLATING AND POINT ASSEMBLY (pen & pencil)	4337	33333443454	LNNNNNNFFFFFNFFFON	NNNF4NNNNNNNNNO	D,P,J,T	121	617	06.01.01	7100	000000	81008
733.131-010	SUPERVISOR, RUBBER STAMPS AND DIES (pen & pencil)	4347	33333443344	LNNNNNNFFNFFNFNOOON	NNNN3NNNNNNNNNN	D,P,T,V	136	617	06.02.01	7100	000000	81008
733.137-010	SUPERVISOR, ASSEMBLY (pen & pencil)	4347	33333443344	LNNNNNNFFFFFNFOFON	NNNN4NNNNNNNNNN	D,J,T	061	617	06.02.01	7100	000000	81008
733.137-014	SUPERVISOR, FINISHING DEPARTMENT (pen & pencil)	4337	33333433354	LNNOONNFFOFFNFFOON	NNNN4NNNNNNNNNN	V,D,P,J	041	617	06.02.01	7100	000000	81008
733.137-018	SUPERVISOR, INSPECTION (pen & pencil)	4347	33333444454	LNNNONNFFFOFFNFOOON	NNNN4NNNNNNNNNN	V,D,J,T	041	617	06.02.01	7100	000000	81008
733.281-010	BALLPOINT PEN CARTRIDGE TESTER (pen & pencil)	3225	33323433355	LNNNNNNFFNNNNFNFNNN	NNNN4NNNNNNNNNN	J,T	212	617	06.03.01	6881	000000	83002
733.364-010	QUALITY-CONTROL TECHNICIAN, INKED RIBBONS (pen & pencil)	3335	33333333334	LNNNNNNFFNNOOFNFON	NNNN3NNNNNNNNNN	J,T	212	617	06.03.02	7820	150702	83005
733.381-010	ENGRAVER, RUBBER (pen & pencil)	4327	33423433355	LNNNNNNCCFNNNCNCFNN	NNNN4NNNNNNNNNN	J,T	183	617	05.10.05	6863	000000	89911
733.381-014	RUBBER-STAMP MAKER (pen & pencil)	4336	34433333355	LNNNNNNFFONNNFNFFNN	NNNN3NNNNNNNNNN	J,T	102	617	06.01.04	6869	000000	89999
733.384-010	REPAIRER, PENS AND PENCILS (pen & pencil)	3233	44544533355	LNNNNNNFFFONNNFONN	NNNN4NNNNNNNNNN	J	121	617	06.02.32	6179	000000	85999
733.684-010	PAINT-BRUSH MAKER (fabrication, nec)	2224	44433444355	LNNIONNFFNNNNFNNNN	NNNN4NNNNNNNNNN	R	061	619	06.04.34	6179	000000	85999
733.684-014	PEN-AND-PENCIL REPAIRER (any industry)	3124	33443433355	LNNNNNNFFNNNNFNNNN	NNNN4NNNNNNNNNN	V,T	121	617	05.12.15	6179	000000	85999
733.684-018	STAMP MOUNTER (pen & pencil)	2212	44444533355	LNNNNNNFFNNNNNFFON	NNNN4NNNNNNNNNN	R	102	617	06.04.34	7720	000000	93956
733.685-010	ASSEMBLER (pen & pencil)	2222	45444544354	SNNNNNNCCCFNNNFNNNN	NNNN4NNNNNNNNNN	R	061	617	06.04.24	7522	000000	93956
733.685-014	FILLING-MACHINE OPERATOR (pen & pencil)	2222	44444544355	LNNNNNNFFNNNNFNNNN	NNNN4NNNNNNNNNN	R,T	061	617	06.04.36	7669	000000	92953
733.685-018	GROOVING-MACHINE OPERATOR (pen & pencil)	2112	44445334355	MNNNNNNFFOONNNFNFNN	NNNN3NNNNNNNNNN	R,T	041	617	06.04.20	7679	000000	92998
733.685-022	RIBBON WINDER (pen & pencil)	2223	44443533344	LNNNNNNFFFNNNNFNNNN	NNNN3NNNNNNNNNN	R,T	053	617	06.04.09	7740	000000	93999
733.685-026	SMOOTHER (pen & pencil)	2112	44444433355	LNNNNNNFFFNNNNNFFON	NNNN3NNNNNNNNNN	R,T	163	617	06.04.09	7679	000000	93956
733.685-030	TIP BANDER (pen & pencil)	2112	45444544455	LNNNNNNFFFONNNFNFNN	NNNN4NNNNNNNNNN	R	051	617	06.04.24	7522	000000	92998
733.685-034	TIPPING-MACHINE OPERATOR (pen & pencil)	2222	44454544355	LNNNNNNFFOONNNFFNNN	NNNN4NNNNNNNNNN	R,T	153	617	06.04.21	7669	000000	92953
733.687-010	ASSEMBLER, MARKING DEVICES (pen & pencil)	2222	44454544355	LNNNNNNFFNNNNNFNFNN	NNNN4NNNNNNNNNN	R,T	041	617	06.04.20	7679	000000	92998
733.687-014	ASSEMBLER, MECHANICAL PENCILS AND BALLPOINT PENS (pen & pencil)	2222	44444443344	LNNNNNNFFONNNFNFOON	NNNN4NNNNNNNNNN	J,R	061	617	06.04.23	7720	000000	93956

DOT #	DOT Title & Industry	Trng	Aptitude	Physical	Environment	Tempra	WkF	MPSMS	GOE	SOC	CIP	OES
733.687-018	BANDER (pen & pencil)	2112	44544544455	LNNNNNNFFNNNNNNNNNN	NNNNN4NNNNNNNNNNN	R	061	617	06.04.23	7740	000000	93956
733.687-022	CHALK CUTTER (pen & pencil)	1112	44444443455	MNNNNNNNFFNNNNNNNNNN	NNNN3NNNNNNNNNNN	R	054	617	06.04.34	8769	000000	98999
733.687-026	CLAMPER (pen & pencil)	1112	44545443345	MNNNNNNNFFNNNNNNNNNN	NNNN4NNNNNNNNNNNF	R	063	617	06.04.25	8769	000000	98999
733.687-030	DATER ASSEMBLER (pen & pencil)	2112	44444443354	LNNNNNNFFONNNFNFOON	NNNN3NNNNNNNNNNN	R	102	617	06.04.23	7720	000000	93956
733.687-034	DESK-PEN-SET ASSEMBLER (pen & pencil)	2112	44444544355	LNNNNNNNFFNNNNFNFNNN	NNNN4NNNNNNNNNNN	R	061	617	06.04.23	7720	000000	93956
733.687-038	DIPPER (pen & pencil)	1112	44544544355	MNNNONONFFNNNNONONNN	NNNN4NNNNNNNNNNN	R	151	617	06.04.33	8769	000000	98999
733.687-042	INSPECTOR (pen & pencil)	2123	44443443355	LNNNNNNFFONNNFNFONN	NNNN3NNNNNNNNNNN	R,T	212	617	06.03.02	7820	000000	83005
733.687-046	INSPECTOR, BALL POINTS (nonfer. metal)	2223	44443443454	LNNNNNNCCFNNNNFNFFFN	NNNN3NNNNNNNNNNN	R,T	212	617	06.03.02	7820	000000	83005
733.687-050	INSPECTOR, FINAL ASSEMBLY (pen & pencil)	2223	44443433354	LNNONNNFFONNNNFNFFFN	NNNN4NNNNNNNNNNN	J	212	617	06.03.02	7820	000000	83005
733.687-054	INSPECTOR, RUBBER-STAMP DIE (pen & pencil)	3114	34434444444	LNNNNNNNFFOONNNFNFNFON	NNNN3NNNNNNNNNNN	R,T	212	617	06.03.02	7820	000000	83005
733.687-058	NIB INSPECTOR (pen & pencil)	3223	34434334354	LNNNNNNNFFFNNNNFNFON	NNNN4NNNNNNNNNNN	R,T	212	617	06.03.02	7820	000000	83005
733.687-062	PENCIL INSPECTOR (pen & pencil)	2112	44443533354	LNNONNNFFFNNNNFNFFFN	NNNN4NNNNNNNNNNN	R,T	212	617	06.03.02	7820	000000	83005
733.687-066	STAMP-PAD FINISHER (pen & pencil)	1111	44555544455	LNNNNNNNFFNNNNNNFNNNN	NNNN3NNNNNNNNNNN	R	061	617	06.04.23	7740	000000	93999
733.687-070	STAMP-PAD MAKER (pen & pencil)	2112	44544544355	LNNNNNNNFFNNNNFNFNNNN	NNNN3NNNNNNNNNNN	R	063	617	06.04.23	7720	000000	93956
733.687-074	STENCIL INSPECTOR (pen & pencil)	2112	44443444355	LNNNNNNNFFNNFNFNNNN	NNNN3NNNNNNNNNNN	R,T	212	617	06.03.02	7820	000000	83005
733.687-078	WASHER (pen & pencil)	1111	44544544455	HNNNNNNNCCNNNNNNNNNNN	NNNO4NNNNNNNNNNN	R	031	617	06.04.01	7100	000000	81008
734.131-010	SUPERVISOR II (button & notion)	4235	33433433353	LNNNNNNNFFNFFNFNFNFN	NNNN3NNNNNNNNNNN	D,J,T	102	618	06.04.39	8769	000000	93926
734.384-010	BUTTON-CUTTING-MACHINE OPERATOR (button & notion)	2113	44433534445	LNNNNNNNFFNNNNNFNFONN	NNNN4NNNNNNNNNNN	R,T	056	618	06.02.30	7753	480501	93926
734.481-010	WIRE-FRAME MAKER (button & notion)	2223	34433422455	LNNNNNNNFFONNNNFNNONN	NNNN3NNNNNNNNNNN	J,T	083	618	06.04.24	6829	480501	99199
734.584-010	NEEDLE GRINDER (button & notion)	2122	44432433355	LNNNNNNFFONNNFNNONN	NNNN3NNNNNNNNNNN	R,T	051	618	06.04.24	7522	480503	91117
734.684-010	FEATHER SHAPER (button & notion)	2113	44443343355	SNNNNNNNFFNNNNFNFNNN	NNNN3NNNNNNNNNNN	R	054	619	06.04.34	7720	000000	93999
734.684-014	FEATHER-DUSTER WINDER (tex. prod., nec)	3224	44443433354	LNNNNNNFFNNNNNNFNFNNN	NNNN3NNNNNNNNNNN	R,T	102	618	06.04.23	7720	000000	93999
734.684-018	INSPECTOR-REPAIRER (button & notion)	2222	34433422453	LNNNNNNCCNNNNCNNCNCN	NNNN3NNNNNNNNNNN	V,J,T	083	618	06.03.02	7820	000000	83005
734.684-022	SLIDE-FASTENER REPAIRER (button & notion)	2112	44444433355	LNNNNNNFFNNNNNFNNOONN	NNNN3NNNNNNNNNNN	R,T	102	618	06.04.24	7740	000000	93999
734.684-026	WIRE-FRAME DIPPER (button & notion)	2112	44433433454	LNNNNNNCCNOONCNFNON	NNNN3NNNNNNNNNNN	J,T	151	618	06.04.33	7759	000000	93999
734.685-010	STAMPER (button & notion)	2112	44544533355	MNNNNNNCCNNNNFNFNNN	NNNN4NNNNNNNNNNN	R	192	618	06.04.25	7679	000000	92998
734.685-014	BUTTON MAKER AND INSTALLER (tex. prod., nec)	2112	44434434344	MNNONNNCCNNNNNFNFN	NNNN4NNNNNNNNNNN	R	062	618	06.04.09	7659	480303	98999
734.687-010	ACETONE-BUTTON PASTER (button & notion)	1112	44544532355	SNNNNNNCCNNNNCNNNN	NNNN3NNNNNNNNNNN	R	063	618	06.04.24	7740	000000	93956
734.687-014	ASSEMBLER (button & notion)	2112	44544533454	LNNNNNNCCCNNNNCNNN	NNNN3NNNNNNNNNNN	R	061	618	06.04.23	7720	000000	93956
734.687-018	ASSEMBLER (button & notion)	2112	44544533355	SNNNNNNCCCNNNNCNNNN	NNNN4NNNNNNNNNNN	R	061	411	06.04.23	7720	000000	98999
734.687-022	BOBBIN DISKER (glass mfg.)	2124	44444543455	LNNNNNNFFNNNNNCNNNN	NNNN3NNNNNNNNNNN	R,J	212	618	06.04.23	8769	000000	98999
734.687-026	BUCKLE INSPECTOR (button & notion)	1112	44444443355	LNNNNNNFFNNNNFNFNN	NNNN3NNNNNNNNNNN	R,T	212	618	06.03.02	7820	470408	83005
734.687-030	BUCKLE SORTER (button & notion)	2123	44444544355	LNNNNNNFFNNNFNFNNN	NNNN3NNNNNNNNNNN	R	221	618	06.03.02	7850	470408	83005
734.687-034	BUCKLE-WIRE INSERTER (button & notion)	3124	34544533355	SNNNNNNCCNNNNCNNNN	NNNN3NNNNNNNNNNN	R	061	618	06.04.23	7740	000000	93999
734.687-038	BUTTON GRADER (button & notion)	2112	44443533352	SNNNONFFFNNNNFNFOFN	NNNN3NNNNNNNNNNN	R,T	212	618	06.03.02	7820	000000	83005
734.687-042	BUTTON RECLAIMER (knitting)	2122	44544544455	LNNNNNNFFONNNFNFONN	NNNN3NNNNNNNNNNN	R,T	212	618	06.03.02	7850	000000	83005
734.687-046	BUTTON-AND-BUCKLE MAKER (any industry)	2113	44434533344	LNNNNNNFFONNNFNFNFN	NNNN3NNNNNNNNNNN	R	061	618	06.04.27	7820	470408	93956
734.687-050	COVERED-BUCKLE ASSEMBLER (button & notion)	1113	44544532354	LNNNNNNFFNNNNNNNON	NNNN3NNNNNNNNNNN	R	063	618	06.04.27	7720	470408	83005
734.687-054	GRINDER, HAND (button & notion)	1112	44544532355	LNNNNNNFFNNNNFNFNN	NNNN4NNNNNNNNNNN	R	051	618	06.04.34	7758	470408	93953
734.687-058	HOT-STONE SETTER (button & notion)	1112	44544543455	SNNNNNNFFNNNNCNNNN	NNNN3NNNNNNNNNNN	R	061	618	06.04.23	7740	470408	93956
734.687-062	INSPECTOR, SLIDE FASTENERS (button & notion)	3224	34443343455	LNNNNNNFFNCNNFNFNNN	NNNN3NNNNNNNNNNN	R,J,T	212	618	06.03.02	7820	480501	83005
734.687-066	QUILL-BUNCHER-AND-SORTER (tex. prod., nec)	2123	44443433354	SNNNNNNFFNNNNNCNNNN	NNNN3NNNNNNNNNNN	R,T	212	618	06.03.02	7850	000000	83005
734.687-070	SHELL-GRADER (button & notion)	3124	34433544355	SNNNNNNFFNNNNFNFONN	NNNO3NNNNNNNNNNN	R,T	212	618	06.03.02	7820	000000	83005
734.687-074	SLIDE-FASTENER-CHAIN ASSEMBLER (button & notion)	2112	44443543355	SNNNNNNFFNNNFNFONN	NNNN3NNNNNNNNNNN	R,T	061	618	06.04.23	7720	470408	93956
734.687-078	SLIDER ASSEMBLER (button & notion; garment)	2122	44534533345	LNNNNNNFFNNNNFNFNNN	NNNN4NNNNNNNNNNN	R	061	618	06.04.23	7720	470408	93956
734.687-082	SORTER (button & notion)	2123	44544543355	SNNNNNNCCCNNNNCNNNN	NNNN3NNNNNNNNNNN	R	212	618	06.03.02	7850	000000	83005
734.687-086	SPLITTER, HAND (button & notion)	1112	45435533355	SNNNNNNFFNNNNFNFNNN	NNNN4NNNNNNNNNNN	R	054	618	06.04.34	8769	000000	98999
734.687-090	STICKER (button & notion)	1111	44544533455	SNNNNNNCCNNNNCNNNN	NNNN3NNNNNNNNNNN	R	063	618	06.04.23	7720	000000	93956
734.687-094	ZIPPER TRIMMER, HAND (button & notion)	2222	44433424255	LNNNNNNFFONNNFNFNNN	NNNN3NNNNNNNNNNN	R,T	212	618	06.04.24	7850	200303	83005
735.381-010	BENCH HAND (jewelry-silver.)	3216	33433243355	LNNNNNNFFONNNFNFNNN	NNNN3NNNNNNNNNNN	V,J,T	102	611	06.01.04	6822	470408	89126
735.381-014	PEARL RESTORER (jewelry-silver.)	3226	34422533354	LNNNNNNFFNNNNFNFNNFN	NNNN3NNNNNNNNNNN	V,J,T	051	611	05.05.14	6822	470408	89126

DOT #	DOT Title & Industry	Trng	Aptitude	Physical	Environment	Tempra	WKF	MPSMS	GOE	SOC	CIP	OES
735.381-018	SAMPLE MAKER II (jewelry-silver.)	4226	32222332354	SNNNNNNFFFNNNNFNNNNN	NNNNN2NNNNNNNNNN	J	264	611	05.03.02	6822	470408	89126
735.587-010	COLORING CHECKER (jewelry-silver.)	3114	33343334453	LNNNNNNFFFNNNNFNNNFN	NNNNN3NNNNNNNNNN	R,J	212	611	06.03.02	7820	470408	83005
735.681-010	BRACELET AND BROOCH MAKER (jewelry-silver.)	3217	33433532354	LNNNNNNFFFNNNNFNNFON	NNNNN4NNNNNNNNNN	R,T	061	611	06.02.23	6822	470408	89126
735.684-010	BEAD STRINGER (jewelry-silver.)	2123	34443533453	SNNNNNNFFFNNNNFNFOFN	NNNNNO3NNNNNNNNNN	R,T	061	611	06.04.34	7720	470408	93956
735.684-014	STONER (jewelry-silver.)	2124	44543533355	SNNNNNNNFFFNNNNFNNNNN	NNNNN3NNNNNNNNNN	R,T	051	611	06.04.24	7758	470408	93953
735.684-018	TROPHY ASSEMBLER (jewelry-silver.)	3225	34433433354	LNNNNNNNFFONNNFNNNNN	NNNNN3NNNNNNNNNN	R,T	102	612	06.02.24	7720	470408	93956
735.687-010	DIPPER (jewelry-silver.)	2112	44555544455	LNNNNNNNFFONNNNNNNNN	NNFO3NNNNNNNNNN	R	031	611	06.04.39	8769	470408	98999
735.687-014	LINKER (jewelry-silver.)	2123	44444432355	SNNNNNNNFFFNNNNCNFNNN	NNNNN3NNNNNNNNNN	R	061	611	06.04.23	7720	470408	93956
735.687-018	PAINTER (jewelry-silver.)	2122	44443433354	SNNNNNNNFFFNNNNFNNNON	NNNNN3NNNNNNNNNN	R,T	153	611	06.04.33	7756	470408	93947
735.687-022	PIN-OR-CLIP FASTENER (jewelry-silver.)	2112	44544533445	SNNNNNNNFFFNNNNFNFNNN	NNNNN3NNNNNNNNNN	R	061	611	06.04.23	7720	470408	93956
735.687-026	RACKER (jewelry-silver.)	1112	44544533355	LNNNNNNNOFFNNNNCNNNNN	NNNNN3NNNNNNNNNN	R	061	611	06.04.34	8769	470408	98999
735.687-030	SORTER (jewelry-silver.)	2223	44444444355	SNNNNNNNFFFNNNNFNNNNN	NNNNN3NNNNNNNNNN	R	221	611	06.03.02	7850	470408	83005
735.687-034	STONE SETTER (jewelry-silver.)	1112	44443533355	SNNNNNNNFFFONNNFNFNNN	NNNNN3NNNNNNNNNN	R,T	063	611	06.04.30	7740	470408	93956
735.687-038	SWEDGER (jewelry-silver.)	2112	44544534345	LNNNNNNNFFFNNNNFNFNNN	NNNNN3NNNNNNNNNN	R	061	611	06.04.23	7720	470408	93956
735.687-042	WIRE DRAWER (jewelry-silver.)	2112	34444534355	LNNNNNNNFFFNNNNNNNNNN	NNNNN4NNNNNNNNNN	R	135	541	06.04.24	7740	470408	93956
736.131-010	AUTOMOTIVE-TIRE-TESTING SUPERVISOR (ordnance)	4338	33333333355	LNNNNNNNFNFFNNNNNNNNN	NNNNN4NNNNNNNNNN	V,D,P,J	212	511	06.01.01	7100	000000	81008
736.131-014	FIREARMS-ASSEMBLY SUPERVISOR (ordnance)	4337	33333433355	LNNNNNNNFFNFFNNNNNNNN	NNNNN3NNNNNNNNNN	V,D,P	121	373	06.04.01	7100	520205	81008
736.131-018	INSPECTION SUPERVISOR I (ordnance)	4337	33333433355	LNNNNNNNFFOFFNNNNNNNN	NNNNN4NNNNNNNNNN	V,D,P,J	212	373	06.01.01	7100	520205	81008
736.281-010	GUN EXAMINER (ordnance)	4336	33432333355	MNNNNNNNNFFNNNNFOFONN	NNNNN4NNNNNNNNNO	J	121	373	06.01.05	6881	470402	83002
736.367-010	AUTOMOTIVE-TIRE TESTER (ordnance)	4347	33333334355	SNNNNNNNNFFONNNFNNNNN	ONNNN4NNNNNNNNNO	V,J,T	212	591	06.03.01	7820	470402	83005
736.381-010	ASSEMBLER I (ordnance)	3325	34432433355	LNNNNNNNFFFONNNNFNNNN	NNNNN4NNNNNNNNNNO	J	121	373	06.03.01	7830	000000	83005
736.381-014	FITTER, VENTILATED RIB (ordnance)	3225	34422433355	MNNNNNNNFFONNNNNFNNNN	NNNNN4NNNNNNNNNN	J	121	373	06.02.23	6812	470402	93197
736.381-018	PROCESS INSPECTOR (ordnance)	3236	34432344444	LNNNNNNNOFFNNNNNNFOON	NNNNN4NNNNNNNNNN	J,T	061	373	06.02.23	6882	470402	89999
736.384-010	PROOF INSPECTOR (ordnance)	3223	34444344355	LNNNNNNNNFFFNNNFFNNNN	NNNNN4NNNNNNNNNC	V,J,T	147	372	06.01.05	6881	470402	83002
736.387-010	INSPECTOR, ASSEMBLY (ordnance)	3224	34443433355	LNNNNNNNFFONNNFNFONN	NNNNN5NNNNNNNNNF	J	121	373	06.03.01	7820	470402	83005
736.387-014	PROOF-TECHNICIAN HELPER (ordnance)	3234	34434434355	HNNNNNNNNFFFNNNFFFNNN	ONNNN5NNNNNNNNNF	J	212	370	06.03.01	7830	470402	83005
736.481-010	SIGHT MOUNTER (ordnance)	3325	34433443355	LNNNNNNNNFFFONNNFNFONN	NNNNN4NNNNNNNNNN	J,T	121	373	06.02.24	6882	470402	89999
736.587-010	BARREL LOADER AND CLEANER (ordnance)	2112	44445543355	MNNNNNNNNFFNNNNFNNNNN	NNNNN4NNNNNNNNNF	R	061	373	06.04.34	8769	470402	98999
736.684-010	ALIGNER, BARREL AND RECEIVER (ordnance)	3213	34433433355	LNNNNNNNFFONNNNNFONN	NNNNN4NNNNNNNNNN	J,T	121	373	06.02.23	7720	470402	93956
736.684-014	ASSEMBLER II (ordnance)	2113	44444433355	LNNNNNNNFFONNNFNFONN	NNNNN3NNNNNNNNNN	R,T	121	373	06.04.23	7720	470402	93956
736.684-018	BARREL FINISHER (ordnance)	2124	34443444355	MNNNNNNNNFFONNNFNFNNN	NNNNN3NNNNNNNNNN	R,T	051	373	06.04.24	7758	470402	93953
736.684-022	BARREL REPAIRER (ordnance)	2115	34433434355	MNNNNNNNNFFONNNNFNFONN	NNNNN4NNNNNNNNNN	R,T	102	373	05.10.01	6179	470402	85999
736.684-026	BARREL STRAIGHTENER I (ordnance)	3124	34432434355	LNNNNNNNFFONNNNFNFONN	NNNNN3NNNNNNNNFNN	J,T	134	373	06.02.24	7720	470402	93999
736.684-030	FRONT-SIGHT ATTACHER (ordnance)	2112	44444543355	LNNNNNNNFFONNNFNFNNN	NNNNN4NNNNNNNNNN	R,T	102	373	06.04.23	7740	470402	93956
736.684-034	GAS-CHECK-PAD MAKER (ordnance)	3224	34434444355	LNNNNNNNFFFNNNFNFNNN	NNNNN3NNNNNNNNNN	R,T	143	371	06.02.32	7720	470402	93956
736.684-038	SOLDERER, BARREL RIBS (ordnance)	2113	44443444355	LNNNNNNNFFFNNNNFNFONN	NNNNN4NNNNNNNNNN	R	083	373	06.04.31	7717	480508	93917
736.684-042	TARGETEER (ordnance)	3113	34433433355	LNNNNNNNNFFFNNNNFFONN	NNNNN5NNNNNNNNNF	J,T	121	373	06.03.02	7830	470402	83005
736.687-010	GREASER (ordnance)	1112	45454544455	MNNNNNNNNFFONNNNNNNNN	NNNNN3NNNNNNNNNN	R	033	370	05.12.08	8769	000000	98999
736.687-014	INSPECTOR, BARREL (ordnance)	2123	44444444355	LNNNNNNNFFNNNNFNFNNN	NNNNN3NNNNNNNNNN	R,T	212	373	06.03.02	7720	470402	83005
736.687-018	INSPECTOR, LIVE AMMUNITION (ordnance)	1112	44444444455	LNNNNNNNFFNFFNFNNNNN	NNNNN3NNNNNNNNNN	R,T	212	373	06.03.02	7820	470402	83005
737.131-010	SUPERVISOR, FIREWORKS ASSEMBLY (chemical)	4237	33343434355	LNNONONFFOFFNFNNNNONN	NNNNN4NNNNNNNNNF	V,D,P,J	061	499	06.02.01	7100	000000	81008
737.132-010	PRIMER SUPERVISOR (ordnance)	4238	33343434454	LNNNNNNFFOFFNFNNNNNN	NNNNN4NNNNNNNNNF	V,D,P,J	121	370	06.02.01	7100	000000	81008
737.134-010	INSPECTION SUPERVISOR II (ordnance)	4337	33333344455	LNNNNNNNFFFNNNFNNNNN	NNNNN4NNNNNNNNFNN	V,D,P,J	212	370	06.01.01	7100	000000	81008
737.137-010	INSPECTOR, CHIEF (ordnance)	4338	33343444454	LNNNNNNNFFFNFFNNNNON	NNNNN4NCNNNNNCNN	D,P,J	221	370	06.01.01	7100	000000	81008
737.137-014	POWDER-AND-PRIMER-CANNING LEADER (ordnance)	4498	33343444454	LNNNNNNNFFNNNNNCNN	NNNNN4NCNNNNNCNN	V,D,P,J	041	370	06.01.01	7100	000000	81008
737.137-018	SUPERVISOR (ordnance)	4338	33343334354	LNNNNNNNFFFNNNNNNON	NNNNN3NNNNNNNNNN	V,D,P,J	061	374	06.02.01	7100	000000	81008
737.137-022	SUPERVISOR, BELT-AND-LINK ASSEMBLY (ordnance)	4338	33343343354	LNNNNNNNFFNFNFNNNON	NNNNN4NNNNNNNNNN	V,D,P,J	212	374	06.02.01	7820	000000	83005
737.364-010	PROCESS CHECKER (ordnance)	3323	33333344455	LNNONONFFOFFNFNOOONN	ONNNN4NNNNNNNONN	J,T	212	370	06.03.01	7820	000000	83005
737.367-010	INSPECTOR III (ordnance)	4336	33333444455	LNNNNNNFFOFFNFNNNNNN	NNNNN4NNNNNNNONN	R,T	061	374	06.03.01	7100	000000	81008
737.381-010	ASSEMBLER, IGNITER (ordnance)	3336	34333433355	LNNNNNNNFFFNNNNNNCNN	NNNNN3NNNNNNNNNN	R,T	102	372	06.02.23	6869	000000	89999
737.387-010	DROP TESTER (ordnance)	3323	34343343355	LNNNNNNNRFFNNNNFNNNNN	NNNNN4NNNNNNNNNN	R,J,T	212	374	06.03.01	7830	000000	83005

DOT #	DOT Title & Industry	Trng	Aptitude	Physical	Environment	Tempra	WkF	MPSMS	GOE	SOC	CIP	OES
737.387-014	INSPECTOR I (ordnance)	3225	34444444455	MNNNNNNFFNNNNFNOONN	NNNN3NNNNNNNNNN	J,T	212	372	06.03.01	7820	000000	83005
737.387-018	PRESSURE-TEST OPERATOR (ordnance)	3324	34333433355	LNNNNNNFFNNNNFNOONN	NNNN4NNNNNNNONO	J,T	212	374	06.03.01	7830	000000	83005
737.487-010	PROPELLANT-CHARGE LOADER (ordnance)	2222	34433444355	MNNNNNNFFNNNNFNNNNN	NNNN3NNNNNNNNNC	R,T	212	499	06.04.34	7840	000000	93956
737.587-010	BANDOLEER STRAIGHTENER-STAMPER (ordnance)	1112	44453444455	SNNONNNFFNNNNFNNNNN	NNNN4NNNNNNNNNN	R	221	436	06.04.37	8769	000000	98999
737.587-014	FIREWORKS ASSEMBLER (chemical)	2112	44444533345	LNNNNNNFFONNNNFNONN	NNNN4NNNNNNNNN	J	041	499	06.04.23	7720	000000	93956
737.587-018	PRIMER BOXER (ordnance)	2122	44444444355	LNNNNNNFFFNNNNNFNNN	NNNO3NNNNNNCNN	R	041	499	06.04.38	8761	000000	98902
737.684-010	ASSEMBLER, MECHANICAL ORDNANCE (ordnance)	3333	34333433344	LNNNNNNFFNNNNNFFON	NNNN4NNNNNNNNNN	R,T	121	372	06.02.22	7720	000000	93956
737.684-014	BOMB LOADER (ordnance)	3223	34443433354	MNNFNFNFFNNNNFNNNON	NNNN4NNNNNNNNNC	V,T	041	499	06.02.32	7720	000000	93999
737.684-018	FIREWORKS MAKER (chemical)	3126	34433433355	MNNONNNFFFNNNNFNNOFN	NNNN4NFNNNNNFNN	J	061	499	06.02.32	7720	000000	93956
737.684-022	FUSE ASSEMBLER (ordnance)	3223	34433433355	LNNNNNNFFNNNNFNFNN	NNNN3NNNNNNNNNC	R,S,T	102	499	06.02.23	7720	000000	93956
737.684-026	INSPECTOR, SALVAGE (ordnance)	2212	34444433344	MNNNNNNFFNNNNFNFFNN	NNNN4NNONNNNNN	R,T	134	374	06.04.34	7820	000000	83005
737.684-030	POWDER WORKER, TNT (ordnance)	3224	34444433344	MNNNNNNFFFNNNNFNON	NNFN4NNNNNNNCNN	J,T	147	499	06.02.32	7720	000000	93999
737.684-034	PRODUCTION ASSEMBLER (ordnance)	2223	34443433355	LNNONONFFFNNONFNNNN	NNNN4NNNNNNNNNN	R,T	121	370	06.04.23	7720	000000	93956
737.684-038	SHELL ASSEMBLER (ordnance)	2125	34433533355	MNNFNNNFFNNNNNNNNN	NNNN3NNNNNNNNNN	R,T	061	372	06.04.23	7720	000000	93956
737.685-010	GAUGE-AND-WEIGH-MACHINE OPERATOR (ordnance)	2123	44443533355	LNNNNNNFFNNNNFONN	NNNN4NNNNNNNNNN	R,T	212	374	06.03.02	7840	000000	83005
737.685-014	SHAKER-PLATE OPERATOR (ordnance)	2122	44442433355	MOOONNNFFNNNNFNFNNN	NNNN3NNNNONNNO	J,T	212	374	06.03.02	7820	000000	83005
737.685-018	WAX POURER (chemical)	2112	44444443445	LNNNNNNFFNNNNNFNNNN	NNNN3NNNNNNNNNN	R,T	131	499	06.04.19	7679	000000	92998
737.687-010	ASSEMBLER (ordnance)	2112	44433433355	LNNNNNNFFNNNNONNNNN	NNNN3NNNNONNN	R,T	061	372	06.04.23	7720	000000	93956
737.687-014	BAG LOADER (ordnance)	1111	45454544455	MNNNNNNCCNNNNNNNNNN	NNNN3NFNNNNNNN	R	041	499	06.04.36	8761	000000	98902
737.687-018	BLASTING-CAP ASSEMBLER (ordnance)	2112	44444433355	LNNONONFFNNNNNFNNNN	NNNN3NNNNNNNNNN	R	061	499	06.04.23	7720	000000	93956
737.687-022	BOOSTER ASSEMBLER (ordnance)	2212	44444433355	LNNNNNNFFFNNNNFNNNN	NNNN3NNNNNNNNNN	R	061	372	06.04.23	7720	000000	93956
737.687-026	CHECK WEIGHER (ordnance)	1112	44444433355	SNNNNNNCCFNNNNCNNNNN	NNNN3NCNNNNNNNC	R,T	212	499	06.03.02	7840	000000	83005
737.687-030	CORE LOADER (ordnance)	1111	44544544455	LNNNNNNFFNNNNNNNNN	NNNN4NCNNNNNNN	R	041	499	06.04.36	8761	000000	98999
737.687-034	DEMOLITION SPECIALIST (ordnance)	2114	44544544355	HNNNNNNFFNNNNFNFNNN	NNNN4NFNNNNNNNF	R	011	370	05.12.03	8710	000000	98999
737.687-038	DETONATOR ASSEMBLER (ordnance)	2112	44443433355	LNNNNNNFFNNNNNFNNNN	NNNN3NNNNNCNN	R,T	061	372	06.04.23	7720	000000	93956
737.687-042	EXPLOSIVE OPERATOR I (ordnance)	2223	34443433354	LNNNNNNCCFONNNCNNNNN	NNNN4NNNNNNCNN	R,S,T	031	372	06.04.34	7720	000000	93999
737.687-046	EXPLOSIVE OPERATOR II (ordnance)	2222	44444534355	LNNNNNNFFNNNNFNFNN	NNNN3NNNNNCNN	R,T	041	499	06.04.34	7720	000000	93999
737.687-050	IGNITER CAPPER (ordnance)	1111	44544543455	LNNNNNNFFNNNNNNNNN	NNNN3NNNNNNNNN	R	041	499	06.04.34	8769	000000	98999
737.687-054	INSPECTOR II (ordnance)	3224	33433433355	LNNNNNNFFNNNNFNFONN	NNNN3NNNNNNFNN	R,J,T	212	499	06.03.02	7820	000000	83005
737.687-058	INSPECTOR, BULLET SLUGS (ordnance)	2123	44543543455	LNNNNNNCCFONNNCNNNNN	NNNN4NNNNNNNNNN	R,T	212	374	06.03.02	7820	000000	83005
737.687-062	INSPECTOR, FIREWORKS (chemical)	2123	44444453355	LNNNNNNFFFNNNNFNNN	NNNN4NNNNNNNNNN	J	212	499	06.03.02	7820	000000	93956
737.687-066	INSPECTOR, SHELLS (ordnance)	2212	34433533344	LNNNNNNFFFNNNFNOFN	NNNN3NNNNNNCNN	R,J	212	374	06.03.02	7820	000000	83005
737.687-070	LABORER, AMMUNITION ASSEMBLY I (ordnance)	2113	44444544355	MNNNNNNFFFNNNNFNNNN	NNNN3NNNNNNCNN	R	061	370	06.04.23	7720	000000	93956
737.687-074	LABORER, AMMUNITION ASSEMBLY II (ordnance)	2112	44444444355	MNNNNNNFFFNNNNFNNNN	NNNN4NNNNNNNCNN	R	041	370	06.04.34	7720	000000	93999
737.687-078	LACQUER-PIN-PRESS OPERATOR (ordnance)	1111	44544444455	LNNNNNNFFNNNNFNFNN	NNNN3NNNNNNNNN	R	151	374	06.04.33	7740	000000	93999
737.687-082	MANUAL-PLATE FILLER (ordnance)	1112	44544543355	LNNONNNCCCNNNNNNNNN	NNNN4NNNNNNNNN	R	061	374	06.04.24	8769	000000	98999
737.687-086	MERCURY-CRACKING TESTER (ordnance)	1112	44543543354	LNNNNNNCCNNNNFNNNN	NNNN3NNNNNNFFN	R,J	212	374	06.03.02	7830	000000	83005
737.687-090	MIXER II (chemical)	2222	44443434454	HNNONNNFFFOONFNNOFN	NNNN4NFNNNNNNNF	R,J,T	143	499	06.04.38	7759	000000	98902
737.687-094	PACKER-FUSER (chemical)	1111	44444533454	LNNNNNNCCCNNNNNCNCON	NNNN3NNNNNNNNNC	R	061	499	06.04.23	8761	000000	98902
737.687-098	PRIMER ASSEMBLER (ordnance)	2122	44444443344	MNNNNNNFFNNNNNFNON	NNNN4NNNNNNCNN	R	061	372	06.03.02	7720	000000	93956
737.687-102	PRIMER CHARGER (ordnance)	2113	44543534353	MNNNNNNFFNNNNFNNNN	NNNN4NNNNNNNNNN	R,T	041	374	06.04.34	7720	000000	93999
737.687-106	PRIMER INSPECTOR (ordnance)	2123	44443333355	LNNNNNNCCNNNNCNNCNN	NNNN3NNNNNNNNN	R,T	212	374	06.03.02	7820	000000	83005
737.687-110	PROPELLANT-CHARGE-ZONE ASSEMBLER (ordnance)	2113	44444443355	MNNFNFNFFNNNNFNNNN	NNNN3NNNNNNCNN	R	061	499	06.04.23	7720	000000	93956
737.687-114	SALVAGER I (ordnance)	3124	34333433355	LNNNNNNFFNNNNNFFNN	NNNN3NNNNNNNNN	R,T	212	370	06.03.02	7820	000000	83005
737.687-118	SALVAGER II (ordnance)	3223	34444443355	LNNNNNNFFNNNNFNONN	NNNN3NNNNNCNN	J,T	212	372	06.03.02	7820	000000	83005
737.687-122	SCREW-EYE ASSEMBLER (ordnance)	1111	44543543455	LNNNNNNFFNNNNNNNNN	NNNN3NNNNNNNNN	R	061	372	06.04.23	7720	000000	93956
737.687-126	SHADOWGRAPH-SCALE OPERATOR (ordnance)	2122	44444433344	SNNNNNNFFNNNNFNNNN	NNNN3NCNNNNNNN	R,T	212	499	06.03.02	7840	000000	93956
737.687-130	SHELLACKER (ordnance)	2113	44544544354	LNNNNNNFFNNNNNFNON	NNNN3NNNNNNNNN	R	153	370	06.04.33	7756	000000	93947
737.687-134	TAPPER, HAND (ordnance)	1111	45544544455	MNNNNNNFFNNNNFNFNNN	NNNN3NNNNNNNNN	R	053	372	06.04.24	7740	000000	93999
737.687-138	VARNISHING-UNIT OPERATOR (ordnance)	2112	44543433355	LNNNNNNFFNNNNFNFNN	NNNN3NNNNNNNNN	R,T	061	374	06.04.33	7740	000000	93956
739.130-010	SUPERVISOR, BIT AND SHANK DEPARTMENT (fabrication, nec)	4337	33334333355	LNNNNNNFFFFFNFNQOONN	NNNN4NNNNNNNNNN	V,D,J,T	102	619	06.02.01	7100	000000	81008

DOT #	DOT Title & Industry	Trng	Aptitude	Physical	Environment	Tempra	WkF	MPSMS	GOE	SOC	CIP	OES
739.131-010	SUPERVISOR I (fabrication, nec)	4237	33333333353	LNNONNNFFFFFNFNFOFN	NNNN4NNNNNNNNNN	V,D,P,J	171	619	06.02.01	7100	000000	81008
739.131-014	SUPERVISOR II (fabrication, nec)	4237	33342344454	LNNNNNFFNFFNFNFFN	NNNN4NNNNNNNNNN	V,D,P,J	102	619	01.06.02	7100	000000	81008
739.132-010	SUPERVISOR, CORNCOB PIPE MANUFACTURING (fabrication, nec)	3236	33433444354	LNNOOONFFFOFFNFNONON	NNNN4NNNNNNNNNN	V,D,T,J	102	619	06.02.01	7100	000000	81008
739.134-010	SUPERVISOR, ASSEMBLY ROOM (fabrication, nec)	4337	33333443354	LNNOOONFFFOFFNFNONON	NNNN4NNNNNNNNNN	V,D,P,J	102	619	06.04.01	7100	000000	81008
739.134-014	SUPERVISOR, DISPLAY FABRICATION (fabrication, any industry)	4337	33333343454	MNNFNNNFFFFFNFNNFFN	NNNN4NONNNNNNNNN	D,P,V	102	619	06.04.01	7100	000000	81008
739.137-010	ASSEMBLY SUPERVISOR (any industry)	4227	33333434454	LNNNNNNFFNFFNFNOOON	NNNN4NNNNNNNNNN	D,P,J	111	589	06.02.01	7100	520205	81008
739.137-014	SUPERVISOR, LAMP SHADES (fabrication, nec)	4337	33333444454	LNNNNNNFFNFNFNOOON	NNNN3NNNNNNNNNN	V,D,P,J	041	619	06.02.01	7100	000000	81008
739.137-018	SUPERVISOR, PIPE MANUFACTURE (fabrication, nec)	4337	34434444455	LNNNNNNFFOFFNFNOOON	NNNN4NCNNNNNNNNN	D,J,T	051	619	06.04.01	7100	000000	81008
739.137-022	SUPERVISOR, WALL MIRROR DEPARTMENT (glass products)	3335	33244443355	LNNNNNNFFNFFNFNOONN	NNNN4NNNNNNNNNN	D,P,V	102	532	06.02.01	7100	000000	81008
739.261-010	EXHIBIT BUILDER (museums)	4447	33322433254	MOOONOOFFFOOONFOFFON	NNNN4NNNNNNNNNN	J,T,V	102	360	01.06.02	6862	460201	89908
739.281-010	PACKAGING TECHNICIAN (paper goods)	4336	34334433355	MNNNNNNFFNNNNFNNN	NNNN3NNNNNNNNNN	J,T	241	475	06.01.04	6862	000000	89908
739.281-014	ULTRASONIC TESTER (any industry)	4336	33333333355	MNNNNNNFFFNNFNNNONN	NNNN4NNNNNNNNNN	T,J	211	560	05.07.01	6881	150702	83002
739.361-010	DISPLAY MAKER (fabrication, nec)	4437	33432433353	MOOOOOOFFOOONFFFFF	NNNN4NNNNNNNNNN	J	102	896	01.06.02	6862	080299	89908
739.381-010	CANVAS WORKER (ship-boat mfg.; tex. prod., nec)	4327	34334433355	MOOOOONFFFONOFONO	ONNN4NNNNNNNNNO	V,J,T	171	436	06.01.04	6859	490306	89599
739.381-014	CANVAS-WORKER APPRENTICE (ship-boat mfg.; tex. prod., nec)	4327	34333433355	MOOOOONFFFONNNFOFONO	ONNN4NNNNNNNNNO	V,J,T	171	436	06.01.04	6859	490306	89599
739.381-018	DIE MAKER (paper goods)	4338	33322433354	MNNONNNFFOONNNFNFOON	NNNN4NNNNNNNNNN	J,T	057	566	05.05.06	6811	480507	89102
739.381-022	DIE-MAKER APPRENTICE (paper goods)	4338	33322433354	MNNONNNFFOONNNFNFOON	NNNN4NNNNNNNNNN	J,T	057	566	05.05.06	6811	480507	89102
739.381-026	EXPERIMENTAL ASSEMBLER (any industry)	4446	33332433344	MNNNNNNFFONNNFNFOON	NNNN4NNNNNNNNNN	V,J,T	111	600	05.05.11	6869	000000	89999
739.381-030	FABRICATOR, SHOWER DOORS AND PANELS (struct. metal)	3325	34434433344	MNNOOONFFFNNNNFNNON	NNNN4NNNNNNNNNN	J,T	102	554	06.02.22	6869	000000	89999
739.381-034	FIGURE REFINISHER AND REPAIRER (retail trade)	3225	23332433352	LNNONONFFFNNNNFNFFN	NNNN3NNNNNNNNNN	V,J,T	102	889	01.06.02	6179	000000	85999
739.381-038	INSET CUTTER (fabrication, nec)	4336	33332424253	LNNONNNFFFOONNNFNFOFN	NNFN3NNNNNNNNNN	V,J,T	241	619	01.06.02	6862	000000	89908
739.381-042	MANNEQUIN WIG MAKER (fabrication, nec)	3226	34433432352	SNNNNNNFFFFFNNNNFN	NNNN3NNNNNNNNNN	J,T	161	619	06.01.04	6869	000000	89999
739.381-046	MANNEQUIN-MOLD MAKER (fabrication, nec)	4227	34433533355	MNNNNNNFFNNNNFNNNN	NNNN3NNNNNNNNNN	R,T	136	538	06.01.04	6861	000000	89905
739.381-050	SOUVENIR AND NOVELTY MAKER (metal prod., nec)	3335	34334433353	LNNNNNNFFONNNFNNON	NNNN3NNNNNNNNNN	J,T	102	619	01.06.02	6869	000000	89999
739.381-054	SURVIVAL-EQUIPMENT REPAIRER (government ser.)	3226	34234443454	MNNOOONFFONNNFNNNON	NNNN2NNNNNNNNNN	R,J	102	519	05.10.01	6179	470499	85999
739.381-058	WIG MAKER (fabrication, nec)	3237	34433422353	LNNNNNNFFFFFNNNNNNFFN	NNNN5NNNNNNNNNF	J,T	062	619	05.05.15	6869	000000	89999
739.384-010	DIAMOND MOUNTER (machine tools)	3334	34432432354	LNNNNNNFFFFNNNNFNFNON	ONNN3NONNNNNNNN	J,T	061	566	06.02.32	7529	000000	92198
739.384-014	FOUNDATION MAKER (fabrication, nec)	3215	34333433353	LNNNNNNFFFFNNNFNNON	NNNN4NNNNNNNNNN	J,T	171	619	06.02.27	7752	000000	93923
739.384-018	HAIR PREPARER (fabrication, nec)	3117	34433433352	LNNNNNNNFFNNNNNFNFN	NNNF3NNNNNNNNNN	J	152	619	06.02.32	7756	000000	93947
739.384-022	VENTILATOR (fabrication, nec)	3115	34433432353	SNNNNNNFFFNNNFNFON	NNNN3NNNNNNNNNN	J,T	062	619	06.02.32	7720	000000	93999
739.387-010	CASKET INSPECTOR (fabrication, nec)	3115	34443443454	SNNNNNNFFFFNNNNNON	NNNN4NNNNNNNNNN	J,T	212	619	06.03.01	7820	000000	83005
739.387-014	HAIR-SAMPLE MATCHER (fabrication, nec)	3215	34433443452	SNNNNNNNFFFNNNFNFFN	NNNN2NNNNNNNNNN	J,T	211	619	05.05.15	7830	000000	83005
739.484-010	CHRONOGRAPH OPERATOR (ordnance)	3333	33333333355	LNNNONNNFFFONNNFNNNN	NNNN5NNNNNNNNNN	R,T	231	370	06.03.01	7820	000000	83005
739.484-014	FIRE-EQUIPMENT INSPECTOR (any industry)	3234	34434444344	LONONONFFNNNFNNNFN	ONNN3NGNNNNNNN	V,J,T	212	568	05.07.01	6179	480703	85999
739.484-018	SMOKING-PIPE REPAIRER (any industry)	3225	33333432354	LNNNNNNNFFONNNFNFOON	NNNN4NNNNNNNNNN	V,T	102	619	05.10.01	6179	000000	85999
739.587-010	INSPECTION CLERK (fabrication, nec)	3324	34344433454	HNNNNNNFFONNNFNFOON	NNFF4NNNNNNNNNN	V,T	221	619	06.04.37	7820	000000	83005
739.664-010	CANDLEMAKER (fabrication, nec)	2114	34444433353	MNNNNNNNFFONNNFNFNFN	NNNN3NCNNNNNNNN	R,T	136	619	06.04.32	7679	000000	92998
739.667-010	SPOT PICKER, MOLDED GOODS (fabrication, nec)	2113	34543533353	LNNOOONFFONNNFNFFN	NNNN3NNNNNNNNNN	J,T	212	619	06.03.02	7820	000000	83005
739.684-010	ARTIFICIAL-CANDY MAKER (fabrication, nec)	3225	34433533354	LNNNNNNFFFNNFNNNN	NNNN4NNNNNNNNNN	R,T	132	619	06.02.32	7754	000000	93944
739.684-014	ARTIFICIAL-FLOWER MAKER (button & notion)	2113	44443443354	LNNNNNNNFFNNFNNNN	NNNN4NNNNNNNNNN	R,T	102	618	06.04.23	7720	200501	93956
739.684-018	BROOMMAKER (fabrication, nec)	2114	44434434345	LNNONNNFFONNNFNNOON	NNNN3NNNNNNNNNN	R,T	063	619	06.04.34	7755	000000	93956
739.684-022	BRUSH MATERIAL PREPARER (fabrication, nec)	2115	44444443354	LNNNNNNNFFNNNFNNNN	NNFF4NNNNNNNNNN	R,T	102	619	06.02.32	7759	000000	93999
739.684-026	BUFFER (fabrication, nec)	2113	44434343455	LNNNNNNFFONNNFNFNON	NNNN3NCNNNNNNNN	R,T	051	619	06.04.34	7758	000000	93953
739.684-030	BUFFING-AND-POLISHING-WHEEL REPAIRER (any industry)	2113	34343434354	LNNNNNNNFFONNNFNFNON	NNNN3NNNNNNNNNN	R,T	102	538	06.04.34	6179	000000	85999
739.684-034	CASE FINISHER (leather prod.)	3222	44444443333	MNNNNNNNFFFONNNNFOON	NNNN4NNNNNNNNNO	R,T	102	520	06.04.27	7720	000000	93956
739.684-038	CLIP-AND-HANGER ATTACHER (glass products)	2224	43444433345	LNNNNNNFFCFNNNNFNNNN	NNNN4NNNNNNNNNN	R,T	102	457	06.04.34	7720	000000	93956
739.684-042	CURTAIN-ROLLER ASSEMBLER (furniture)	2113	34444433345	LNNNNNNNFFFNNNNFNNNN	NNNN3NNNNNNNNNN	R,T	121	467	06.04.23	7720	000000	93944
739.684-046	DECORATOR (leather prod.)	2212	44444534354	LNNNNNNNFFNNNNFNNNN	NNNN4NNNNNNNNNN	R,T	063	529	06.04.27	7720	000000	93956
739.684-050	DEICER ASSEMBLER, ELECTRIC (rubber goods)	3225	33332433255	MNNONONFFFNNNNFNFNNN	NNNN3NNNNNNNNNN	R,T	111	519	06.02.22	7720	000000	93905
739.684-054	DEICER FINISHER (rubber goods)	2224	44443433355	LNNNNNNNFFNNNFNFNNN	NNNN4NNNNNNNNNN	R,T	083	589	06.04.34	7759	000000	93999
739.684-058	DEICER-ELEMENT WINDER, HAND (rubber goods)	2114	44443433255	LNNNNNNFFFNNNNFNFNNN	NNNN3NNNNNNNNNN	R,T	111	589	06.02.32	7720	000000	93999

DOT #	DOT Title & Industry	Trng	Aptitude	Physical	Environment	Tempra	WkF	MPSMS	GOE	SOC	CIP	OES
739.684-062	FINISHER, BRUSH (fabrication, nec)	2123	44433433354	LNNNONNNFFONONFNFOON	NNNN4NFNNNNNNNO	V,J,T	054	619	06.04.34	7759	000000	93999
739.684-066	FOOT-MITER OPERATOR (wood prod., nec)	2212	44443544345	LNNNNNNNFFFNNNNFNNNN	NNNN4NNNNNNNNF	R,T	054	457	06.04.25	7639	000000	92314
739.684-070	FORM COVERER (fabrication, nec)	2113	44444433355	LNNNNNNNFFFNNNNFNNNN	NNNN3NNNNNNNNN	R,T	062	538	06.04.27	7759	000000	93999
739.684-074	FRAME REPAIRER (glass products)	2223	44443433355	LNNONNNNFFFNNNNFNNNN	NNNN3NNNNNNNNN	J,T	102	532	06.04.34	7758	000000	93953
739.684-078	FRAMER (glass products; wood prod., nec)	2223	44443433355	MNNFNNNNFFFNNNNFNNNN	NNNN3NNNNNNNNN	R,T	102	532	06.04.34	7720	000000	93956
739.684-082	FURNITURE ASSEMBLER-AND-INSTALLER (retail trade)	3214	34433434344	HNNNFNONFFFONNNFNFOON	NNNN3NNNNNNNNN	V,J,T	102	460	05.10.01	7759	000000	93999
739.684-086	HAIR WORKER (fabrication, nec)	2115	44443543454	LNNNNNNNFFFNNNNFNFN	NNNN3NNNNNNNNN	R,T	161	619	06.04.34	7720	000000	93956
739.684-090	HANDBAG FRAMER (leather prod.)	2112	44434433345	LNNNNNNNFFFNNNNFNNNN	NNNN4NNNNNNNNN	J,R	062	525	06.04.23	7720	000000	93956
739.684-094	LAMP-SHADE ASSEMBLER (fabrication, nec)	2112	44434533455	SNNNNNNNFFFNNNNFNNNN	NNNN4NNNNNNNNN	R,T	062	619	06.04.23	7720	000000	93999
739.684-098	LAST IRONER (wood prod., nec)	2113	44433533355	MNNNNNNNFFFNNNNFNNNN	NNNN4NNNNNNNNN	R,T	102	457	06.04.27	7759	000000	93999
739.684-102	LAST MARKER (wood prod., nec)	2112	44434533355	LNNNNNNNFFFNNNNFNNNN	NNNN3NNNNNNNNN	R,T	241	457	06.04.34	7759	000000	93999
739.684-106	LAST REMODELER-REPAIRER (boot & shoe; wood prod., nec)	3224	34432533354	MNNNNNNNFFFNNNNFNFNON	NNNN4NNNNNNNNN	R,J,T	102	457	05.10.01	6179	480304	85999
739.684-110	LAST REPAIRER (boot & shoe)	2113	44434534355	MNNNNNNNFFFNNNNFNNNN	NNNN4NNNNNNNNN	R,T	102	457	06.04.25	6179	480304	85999
739.684-114	LAST-REPAIRER HELPER (boot & shoe)	2112	44434533355	LNNNNNNNFFFNNNNFNNNN	NNNN3NNNNNNNNN	R,T	102	522	06.04.34	8637	480304	98102
739.684-118	MANNEQUIN MOUNTER (fabrication, nec)	3225	44433434355	LNNNNNNNFFFNNNNFNNNN	NNNN3NNNNNNNNN	R,T	061	619	06.02.22	7759	000000	93999
739.684-122	MANNEQUIN SANDER AND FINISHER (fabrication, nec)	3113	34433433353	LNNNNNNNFFONNNFNFNON	NNNN4NFNNNNNNNN	R,J,T	102	538	06.02.32	7759	000000	93926
739.684-126	MAT CUTTER (wood prod., nec)	2112	44433534445	LNNNNNNNFFONNNFNFNN	NNNN3NNNNNNNNN	R,T	054	457	06.04.34	7753	000000	93956
739.684-130	MOUNTER, SMOKING PIPE (fabrication, nec)	2112	44434534355	LNNNNNNNFFFNNNNFNFNN	NNNN3NNNNNNNNN	R,T	061	619	06.04.23	7720	000000	93956
739.684-134	NEEDLE-BOARD REPAIRER (tex. prod., nec)	2123	44434544355	LNNNNNNNFFFNNNNFNNNN	NNNN4NNNNNNNNN	R,T	061	567	06.04.34	6179	000000	85999
739.684-138	OIL-SEAL ASSEMBLER (leather prod.)	2223	44444433355	SNNNNNNNFFONNNFNFNNN	NNNN4NNNNNNNNN	R,T	061	529	06.04.23	7720	000000	93956
739.684-142	PAINT-ROLLER COVERMAKER (fabrication, nec)	2112	44444544355	LNNNNNNNFFFNNNNFNNNN	NNNN4NNNNNNNNN	R	054	619	06.02.32	7759	000000	93999
739.684-146	PICTURE FRAMER (retail trade; wood prod., nec)	3115	33434433355	LNNFNONFFFONNNFNFOONN	NNNN3NNNNNNNNN	V,T	102	457	01.06.02	7720	000000	93956
739.684-150	SCREEN MAKER (paper goods)	2113	44443444355	LNNNNNNNFFFNNNNFNNNN	NNNN3NNNNNNNNN	R,J	102	567	06.04.34	7720	480299	93956
739.684-154	TICKET-CHOPPER ASSEMBLER (furniture)	2125	34334444344	MNNNNNNNNFFNNNNFNFNON	NNNN4NNNNNNNNN	R,T	102	469	06.04.22	7720	480501	93956
739.684-158	TIRE MOUNTER (fabrication, nec)	2112	45454544345	LNNNNNNNFFFNNNNNNNNN	NNNN4NNNNNNNNN	R	061	551	06.04.23	7740	000000	93923
739.684-162	UMBRELLA TIPPER, HAND (fabrication, nec)	2112	44444433354	SNNNNNNNFFFNNNNFNNNN	NNNN3NNNNNNNNN	R	171	619	06.04.27	7752	000000	93999
739.684-166	VENETIAN-BLIND ASSEMBLER (furniture; retail trade)	2223	44444434344	MNNONONFFFNNNNFNNNN	NNNN4NCONNNNNNN	R,T	121	467	06.04.22	7720	000000	93956
739.684-170	WEAVER (fabrication, nec)	2114	34433432353	SNNNNNNNFFFNNNNFFNN	NNNN3NNNNNNNNN	R,T	164	619	06.02.32	7759	000000	93999
739.684-174	WOODEN-SHADE HARDWARE INSTALLER (furniture)	3223	44444433355	MNNFNNNCCFNNONFNONNN	NNNN3NNNNNNNNN	R,T	102	467	06.02.22	7720	000000	93956
739.684-178	WOVEN-WOOD SHADE ASSEMBLER (furniture)	2223	44443533355	MNNNFNNNCCFNNONFNONNN	NNNN3NNNNNNNNN	R,T	102	469	06.04.23	7759	000000	93956
739.684-182	WREATH AND GARLAND MAKER (fabrication, nec)	2122	34434533353	LNNFNNNFFFNNNNFNFN	NNNN4NNNNNNNNN	R	062	619	06.04.23	7759	200501	92944
739.684-186	PIPE STEM REPAIRER (fabrication, nec)	2116	44433443454	SNNNNNNCCCNNNNCNCNON	NNNN3NNNNNNNNN	R,T	102	619	06.04.34	6179	000000	85999
739.684-190	CASKET ASSEMBLER (fabrication, nec)	3223	34333433355	MNNFNNNNFFFNNNNFFNN	NNNN4NCONNNNNNN	T	102	619	06.04.20	7720	480703	92998
739.685-010	ASSEMBLER, FINGER BUFFS (tex. prod., nec)	2112	44443534345	LNNNNNNNFFNNNNFNNN	NNNN4NNNNNNNNN	R	061	538	06.04.20	7720	000000	92998
739.685-014	BRUSH MAKER, MACHINE (fabrication, nec)	2112	44543544355	LNNONNNCCFNNNNCNCNNNN	NNNN4NNNNNNNNN	R	061	619	06.04.34	7679	000000	92998
739.685-018	BRUSH-HEAD MAKER (fabrication, nec)	2112	44534544355	SNNNNNNNFFNNNNFNNN	NNNN3NNNNNNNNN	R	053	619	06.04.20	7529	000000	92198
739.685-022	CLIPPER (fabrication, nec)	2112	44534533345	SNNNNNNNFFFNNNNFNNN	NNNN4NNNNNNNNN	R	062	619	06.04.20	7529	000000	92198
739.685-026	MOP MAKER (tex. prod., nec)	2113	34433533345	LNNNNNNNFFFNNNNONONNN	NNNN4NNNNNNNNO	R	163	619	06.04.20	7679	000000	93999
739.685-030	PAINT-ROLLER WINDER (fabrication, nec)	2113	44443444345	LNNNNNNNFFFNNNNFNNNN	NNNN4NNNNNNNNN	R,T	063	619	06.04.05	7651	000000	92705
739.685-034	SHANK THREADER (fabrication, nec)	2112	44445433355	LNNNNNNNFFFNNNNFNFN	NNNN3NNNNNNNNN	R,T	055	619	06.04.03	7631	000000	92314
739.685-038	STACKING-MACHINE OPERATOR II (any industry)	2112	44454544355	MNNNNNNNCCCNNONCNCNNN	NNNN4NNNNNNNNN	R	061	580	06.04.02	7679	480703	92998
739.685-042	STEM-PROCESSING-MACHINE OPERATOR (fabrication, nec)	2112	44543443345	LNNNNNNNFFNNNNFNNNN	NNNN4NNNNNNNNN	R	102	619	06.04.03	7529	000000	92198
739.685-046	TAPPER, BIT (fabrication, nec)	2112	44534544355	LNNNNNNNFFFNNNNFNNNN	NNNN3NNNNNNNNN	R	102	619	06.04.34	7529	000000	92198
739.685-050	TAPPER, SHANK (fabrication, nec)	1112	44534544355	SNNNNNNNFFFNNNNFNNNN	NNNN3NNNNNNNNN	R	053	619	06.04.20	7740	000000	93999
739.685-054	UMBRELLA TIPPER, MACHINE (fabrication, nec)	2112	45445533345	SNNNNNNNFFFNNNNFNNNN	NNNN4NNNNNNNNN	R	062	619	06.04.09	7679	000000	92998
739.685-058	WREATH MACHINE TENDER (button & notion)	2112	44454544355	MNNONNNNFFFNNNNFNNNN	NNNN4NNNNNNNNN	R	041	619	06.04.09	7720	000000	92998
739.687-010	ASSEMBLER-ARRANGER (fabrication, nec)	2112	44445544354	LNNNNNNNFFFNNNNFNFN	NNNN3NNNNNNNNN	R,T	063	619	06.04.23	7720	200501	92198
739.687-014	ASSEMBLER, CORNCOB PIPES (fabrication, nec)	1112	44444444455	LNNNNNNNFFFNNNNFNNNN	NNNN4NNNNNNNNN	R	061	619	06.04.02	7679	000000	93999
739.687-018	ASSEMBLER, FILTERS (glass products)	2113	44453443354	LNNNNNNNFFFNNNNFNNNN	NNNN3NNNNNNNNN	R	062	539	06.04.23	7720	000000	93956
739.687-022	ASSEMBLER, GARMENT FORM (fabrication, nec)	2112	44453443454	LNNNNNNNFFFNNNNFNNON	NNNN3NNNNNNNNN	R	061	538	06.04.23	7720	000000	93956
739.687-026	ASSEMBLER, FILTERS (auto. mfg.)	2222	44444453355	LNNNNNNNFFFNNNNNOONN	NNNN3NNNNNNNNN	R,T	102	590	06.04.23	7720	000000	93956

DOT #	DOT Title & Industry	Trng	Aptitude	Physical	Environment	Tempra	WkF	MPSMS	GOE	SOC	CIP	OES
739.687-030	ASSEMBLER, SMALL PRODUCTS II (any industry)	2112	44444533355	LNNNNNNCCCNNNNCNCCNN	NNNN3NNNNNNNNNN	R,T	102	610	06.04.23	7720	000000	93956
739.687-034	BEADER (furniture)	1112	44444444355	MNNFNONFFNNNNFNFNNN	NNNN4NNNNNNNNNN	R	102	466	06.04.24	7720	480501	93999
739.687-038	BLOCK INSPECTOR (fabrication, nec)	1112	44534353343	LNNNNNNNFFNNNNNNNNFN	NNNN3NNNNNNNNNN	R	212	619	06.03.02	7820	000000	83005
739.687-042	BROOMCORN GRADER (fabrication, nec)	2123	44434343353	LNNNNNNNFFNNNNNNNNNN	NNNN3NNNNNNNNNN	R,T	212	619	06.03.02	7850	000000	93956
739.687-046	BRUSH FILLER, HAND (fabrication, nec)	2223	44454433354	SNNNNNFFFNNNNNFNFNON	NNNN4NNNNNNNNNN	R,T	061	619	06.04.23	7720	000000	93956
739.687-050	CANDLE CUTTER (fabrication, nec)	1112	44543543354	MNNNNNNCCCNNNNFNFNFON	NNNN3NNNNNNNNNN	R,T	054	619	06.04.34	8769	000000	98999
739.687-054	CANDLE MOLDER, HAND (fabrication, nec)	2113	44543543354	LNNNNNNFFOONNNFNFNON	NNNO3NNNNNNNNNN	R	132	619	06.04.32	7754	000000	93944
739.687-058	CLEANER (fabrication, nec)	2112	44554534355	LNNNNNNCCNNNNNNNNNNN	NNNN3NNNNNNNNNN	R	031	619	06.04.39	8769	000000	98999
739.687-062	CLEANER, SIGNS (fabrication, nec)	2112	44544544325	MFFFOFNFFNNNNNNNNNN	ONNN4NNNNNNNNNF	R	031	969	05.12.18	8750	000000	98905
739.687-066	COMPACT ASSEMBLER (jewelry-silver.)	2112	44544544355	SNNNNNNNFFFNNNFNFNNN	NNNN3NNNNNNNNNN	R	061	619	06.04.23	7720	000000	93956
739.687-070	DIGGER (fabrication, nec)	2123	34433533355	SNNNNNNNFFFNNNFNFNNN	NNNN3NNNNNNNNNN	J	054	619	06.04.25	7759	000000	93956
739.687-074	DUST-BRUSH ASSEMBLER (house. appl.)	1112	44544544455	LNNNNNNNCCNNNNNNNNNN	NNNF4NNNNNNNNNN	R	061	583	06.04.23	7720	000000	93956
739.687-078	DUST-MOP MAKER (tex. prod., nec)	1112	44544544455	LNNNNNNNCCNNNNNNNNNN	NNNN3NNNNNNNNNN	R	062	619	06.04.23	7740	000000	93999
739.687-082	EXAMINER (fabrication, nec)	2112	44443444353	LNNNNNNFFOONNNFNFNNFN	NNNN3NNNNNNNNNN	J	212	619	06.03.02	7820	000000	83005
739.687-086	EYE-DROPPER ASSEMBLER (glass products)	2112	44444543455	SNNNNNNNCCNNNNNNNNNN	NNNN3NNNNNNNNNN	R	061	531	06.04.23	7720	000000	93956
739.687-090	FILLER (fabrication, nec)	1111	44544544455	LNNNNNNNFFFNNNFNFNNN	NNNN4NNNNNNNNNN	R	136	619	06.04.34	7740	000000	93999
739.687-094	FIRE-EQUIPMENT-INSPECTOR HELPER (any industry)	2223	44434444353	MONONONFFFNNNNFNFNON	ONNN3NONNNNNNNO	R,T	212	568	05.07.01	8637	000000	98102
739.687-098	FLOOR WORKER (wood prod., nec)	1111	44544544455	LNNNNNNNFFNNNNFNFNNN	NNNN3NNNNNNNNNN	R	145	459	06.04.34	8769	000000	98999
739.687-102	GASKET INSPECTOR (nonmet. min.)	2112	44544544355	LNNNNNNNFFFNNNFNFNNN	NNNN3NNNNNNNNNN	J,T	212	538	06.03.02	7820	000000	83005
739.687-106	INSPECTOR I (fabrication, nec)	2123	44443433354	LNNNNNNNCCNNNNCNNCCN	NNNN4NNNNNNNNNN	R,J	212	619	06.03.02	7820	000000	83005
739.687-110	INSPECTOR III (furniture)	2113	44543444453	LNNONONCNCOONFNONFN	NNNN3NNNNNNNNNN	J,T	212	463	06.03.02	7820	000000	83005
739.687-118	INSPECTOR, WREATH (fabrication, nec)	2113	44535543353	LNNNNNFFNNFNFNFN	NNNN4NNNNNNNNNN	R	212	619	06.03.02	7820	010603	83005
739.687-122	MOP-HANDLE ASSEMBLER (tex. prod., nec)	1112	44445433345	LNNNNNNNCCCNNNNNNNNN	NNNN3NNNNNNNNNN	R	061	619	06.04.23	7720	000000	93956
739.687-126	NAILER (tinware)	1112	44544544355	LNNNNNNNFFFNNNFNFNNN	NNNN4NNNNNNNNNN	R,T	072	551	06.04.23	7740	000000	93999
739.687-130	ORNAMENT MAKER, HAND (fabrication, nec)	2113	44543543455	LNNNNNNNFFNNNFNONNNN	NNNN3NNNNNNNNNN	R,T	062	619	06.04.23	7720	000000	93956
739.687-134	PAINT-ROLLER ASSEMBLER (fabrication, nec)	2112	44444443345	LNNNNNNNFFONNNNONNNNN	NNNN3NNNNNNNNNN	R	061	619	06.04.23	7720	000000	93956
739.687-138	PART MAKER (jewelry-silver.)	2123	44544443354	LNNNNNNNFFFNNNFNFNNN	NNNN3NNNNNNNNNN	R,T	102	529	06.04.27	7740	000000	93999
739.687-142	PATCH DRILLER (fabrication, nec)	2113	44435333354	LNNNNNNNFFFNNNFNFNON	NNNN4NNNNNNNNNN	R,J	053	619	06.04.25	7820	000000	83005
739.687-146	PATCHER (fabrication, nec)	2113	44444543454	LNNNNNNNCCCNONONCNCNCN	NNNN4NNNNNNNNNN	R,T	212	619	06.04.34	7820	000000	83005
739.687-150	PIPE-SMOKER-MACHINE OPERATOR (fabrication, nec)	2112	34443533354	LNNNNNNCFFNNNNFNFNON	NNNN3NNNNNNNNNN	R	141	619	06.04.18	8769	000000	98999
739.687-154	POLISHING-PAD MOUNTER (optical goods)	2112	44444534355	LNNNNNNNFFONNNNNNNNN	NNNN3NNNNNNNNNN	R	063	567	06.04.34	7720	000000	93999
739.687-158	POURER (fabrication, nec)	1112	44444434354	LNNNNNNNFFFNNNFNFNNN	NNNN3NNNNNNNNNN	R	132	619	06.04.32	8769	000000	98999
739.687-162	PULL-OUT OPERATOR (fabrication, nec)	2113	44344444344	LNNNNNNNFFNNNNONNNON	NNNF3NNNNNNNNNN	R,T	011	619	06.04.40	7759	000000	93999
739.687-166	SELECTOR (fabrication, nec)	3123	44442533354	LNNNNNNNFFFFNNNNNNNN	NNNN3NNNNNNNNNN	J,T	212	619	06.03.02	7820	000000	83005
739.687-170	SMOKING-PIPE LINER (fabrication, nec)	1112	44545544355	LNNNNNNNCCCNNNFNONNN	NNNN3NNNNNNNNNN	R	153	619	06.04.33	8769	000000	98999
739.687-174	STAINER (fabrication, nec)	2112	44443534354	LNNNNNNNFFFNNNNNNNNN	NNNN3NNNNNNNNNN	R	151	619	06.04.33	7756	000000	93947
739.687-178	STARCHER (button & notion)	1112	44544544355	LNNNNNNNFFFNFNFNFNN	NNNN3NNNNNNNNNN	R	152	429	06.04.34	8769	000000	98999
739.687-182	TABLE WORKER (fabrication, nec)	1112	44545443455	SNNNNNNNFFFNFNFNNNNN	NNNN3NNNNNNNNNN	R	212	619	06.03.02	7820	000000	83005
739.687-186	TRAVERSE-ROD ASSEMBLER (furniture)	1112	44444443455	MNNNNNNNFFFNNNNNNNNN	NNNN3NNNNNNNNNN	R	061	467	06.04.23	7720	000000	93956
739.687-190	UMBRELLA FINISHER (fabrication, nec)	1112	44444534355	LNNNNNNNFFFFNNNFNNNN	NNNN3NNNNNNNNNN	R	063	619	06.04.34	7740	000000	93999
739.687-194	VACUUM-BOTTLE ASSEMBLER (glass products)	2111	44544443355	SNNNNNNCCCNNNNCNFCFCN	NNNN3NNNNNNNNNN	R	061	531	06.04.23	7720	000000	93956
739.687-198	VENETIAN-BLIND CLEANER AND REPAIRER (any industry)	2112	44444444455	MNNFNNNNFFFNNNNNNNNN	NNNF3NNNNNNNNNN	R	061	467	05.12.18	5244	000000	67005
739.687-202	WICK-AND-BASE ASSEMBLER (fabrication, nec)	2112	44434433355	LNNNNNNNFFFNNNFNFNNN	NNNN3NNNNNNNNNN	R	061	619	06.04.23	7720	000000	93956
739.687-206	BRUSH LOADER AND HANDLE ATTACHER (fabrication, nec)	2112	44434533355	LNNNNNNNFFFNNNNNNNNN	NNNN3NNNNNNNNNN	R	061	619	06.04.34	8725	000000	98502
739.687-210	PIPE STEM ALIGNER (fabrication, nec)	2111	44444544455	MNNNNNNNCCCNNNNCNNNNNN	NNNN4NNNNNNNNNN	R	061	619	06.04.34	7759	000000	93999
740.221-010	INSTRUCTOR, DECORATING (pottery & porc.)	4237	22332333353	LNNNNNNNFFFNFNFNFNFN	NNNN3NNNNNNNNNN	D,P,J	296	535	01.06.03	2390	000000	31314
740.381-010	DECORATOR (glass mfg.; glass products)	4236	33432423353	LNNNNNNNFFFNNNFNFFFN	NNNN3NNNNNNNNNN	J,T	262	531	01.06.03	6863	000000	89911
740.381-014	LUSTER APPLICATOR (glass mfg.; glass products)	3226	34432423353	LNNNNNNNFFFNNNFNFFFN	NNNN3NNNNNNNNNN	R,T	262	531	01.06.03	6863	000000	89911
740.381-018	PAINTER (button & notion)	3225	34433433452	SNNNNNNCCCNNNNCNCFCN	NNNN3NNNNNNNNNN	J,T	262	618	01.06.03	6863	000000	89911
740.484-010	STRIPER, HAND (any industry)	3226	34433433353	LNNNNNNNFFFNNNFNFNFN	NNNN3NNNNNNNNNN	R,T	262	595	01.06.03	7756	000000	93947
740.681-010	LINER (pottery & porc.)	3115	34433423354	SNNNNNNNFFFNNNNFFFN	NNNN3NNNNNNNNNN	R,T	262	535	01.06.03	6863	000000	89911

DOT #	DOT Title & Industry	Trng	Aptitude	Physical	Environment	Tempra	WkF	MPSMS	GOE	SOC	CIP	OES
740.684-010	CHARGER I (jewelry-silver.)	3113	34433433353	SNNNNNNFFNNNNNFFFN	NNNN3NNNNNNNNNN	R,T	262	611	01.06.03	7756	470408	93947
740.684-014	DECORATOR (pottery & porc.)	3115	34443433353	SNNNNNNFFNNNNNFFFN	NNNO3NFNNNNNNNN	R,T	262	535	01.06.03	7756	000000	93947
740.684-018	ENAMELER (jewelry-silver.)	3224	34443422354	SNNNNNNFFNNNNNFNFN	NNNO3NNNNNNNNNN	R,T	262	611	01.06.03	7756	470408	93947
740.684-022	PAINTER, BRUSH (any industry)	2112	44444544354	MNNFOONFFNNNNNFNON	NNNN4NNNNNNNNNN	R,T	153	495	06.04.33	7756	000000	93947
740.684-026	TOUCH-UP PAINTER, HAND (any industry)	2112	44543533454	LNNNNNNFFONNNFNFOFN	NNNN3NNNNNNNNNN	R,T	153	495	06.04.33	7756	000000	93947
740.687-010	BUTTON SPINDLER (button & notion)	1112	44555533345	SNNNNNNFFNNNNNFNNNN	NNNN3NNNNNNNNNN	R,T	262	618	06.04.33	7756	000000	93947
740.687-018	PAINTER, EMBOSSED OR IMPRESSED LETTERING (any industry)	2112	44543534353	LNNNNNNCCNNNNNNNNON	NNNN3NNNNNNNNNN	R	153	495	06.04.33	7756	000000	93947
740.687-022	PAINTER, PANEL EDGE (furniture)	1112	44544544354	LNNFNNNFFNNNNNNNON	NNNN4NNNNNNNNNN	R	153	469	06.04.33	7756	000000	93947
741.684-010	ARTIST, MANNEQUIN COLORING (fabrication, nec)	3124	34443544353	LNNNNNNFFNNNNFNFN	NNNN3NNNNNNNNNN	R,T	153	619	01.06.03	7756	000000	93947
741.684-014	FOAM-GUN OPERATOR (plastic prod.)	3223	34443533355	MNNFNNNFFNNNNNFNNN	NNNN4NFNNNNNNNN	R,T	153	492	06.02.24	7756	000000	93947
741.684-018	PAINTER, AIRBRUSH (any industry)	3115	34433433353	LNNNNNNFFNNNNNFFFN	NNNN3NNNNNNNNNN	J,T	262	610	01.06.03	7756	000000	93947
741.684-022	PAINTER, MIRROR (glass products)	3224	34443434354	MNNOONFFNNNNNFNFO	NNNN4NCNNNNNNNN	R,T	153	532	06.04.33	7756	000000	93947
741.684-026	PAINTER, SPRAY I (any industry)	3224	34443433354	MNNFNONFCFNNONFNFO	NNNN4NCNNNNNNNN	R,T	153	460	05.10.07	7756	470603	93947
741.684-030	PORCELAIN-ENAMEL REPAIRER (any industry)	3112	44443534353	HNNONNNFFNNNFNFN	NNNN3NNNNNNNNNN	R,T	051	495	06.04.33	6179	000000	93947
741.685-010	SPRAY-PAINTING-MACHINE OPERATOR (any industry)	2112	44444533344	MNNOOONFFNNNNNONFNON	NNNN4NCNNNNNNNN	R	262	617	06.04.09	7669	000000	92953
741.687-010	PAINT-SPRAY INSPECTOR (any industry)	2122	44443444353	LNNONNNFCFFNONCNFFF	NNNN4NCNNNNNNNN	R,T	212	535	06.03.02	7820	000000	83005
741.687-014	PAINTER HELPER, SPRAY (any industry)	2113	44444544354	MNNFOONFFFNONFNFFON	NNNN4NFNNNNONNNO	R	011	450	05.12.03	8620	000000	98999
741.687-018	PAINTER, SPRAY II (any industry)	2112	44444544354	MNNONONFFNNNONFOFNON	NNNN4NFNNNNNOO	R	153	522	06.04.33	7756	000000	93947
741.687-022	STRIPER, SPRAY GUN (any industry)	2112	44543533354	LNNNNNNFFNNNNNFNFN	NNNN3NNNNNNNNNN	R,T	153	495	06.04.33	7756	000000	93947
742.134-010	SUPERVISOR, FINISHING (furniture)	4337	33343444453	MNNONONFFOFFNFNNOFF	NNNN3NFNNNNNNNN	D,P,V	153	460	06.02.01	7100	520205	81008
742.684-010	RUBBER (furniture; wood prod., nec)	2113	44543544354	MNNFNONCCFONONCNFCF	NNNN4NNNNNNNNNN	R,T	051	460	06.04.25	7756	000000	93947
742.684-014	STAINER (furniture; wood prod., nec)	2113	44543434354	LNNNNNNFFNNNNNFCCN	NNNN4NCNNNNNNNCN	R,T	153	460	06.04.33	7756	000000	93947
742.687-010	WIPER (furniture)	2112	44544544354	MNNFNNNCCONNNNFNNOCN	NNNN4NCNNNNNNNCN	R	153	460	06.04.25	7756	480702	93947
749.131-010	SUPERVISOR, DECORATING (pottery & porc.)	4337	33333444343	LNNNNNNFFNFNFNFNON	NNNN3NNNNNNNNNN	V,D,P,J	262	535	01.06.03	7100	000000	81008
749.131-014	SUPERVISOR, PAINT DEPARTMENT (any industry)	4437	33333333352	LNNNNNNFFNFNNNNON	NNNN3NONNNNNNNNN	V,D,P,T,J	153	495	06.02.01	7100	000000	81008
749.134-010	SUPERVISOR, FINISHING (fabrication, nec)	4238	33333344454	LNNONONFFFOFFNFNONON	NNNN3NNNNNNNNNN	V,D,P,J	051	619	06.02.01	7100	000000	81008
749.137-010	CHEST-PAINTING AND SEALING SUPERVISOR (ordnance)	4338	33343444453	LNNNNNNFFNFNFNONFN	NNNN3NNNNNNNNNN	V,D,P,J	153	454	06.02.01	7100	000000	81008
749.381-010	GILDER (any industry)	3116	34432432252	LNNNNNNFFONNNFNFFFN	NNNN3NFNNNNNNNN	J,T	092	559	01.06.03	6863	000000	89911
749.587-010	RACKER (toy-sport equip.)	2122	44444444355	LNNNNNNFFNNNNONNNNN	NNNN3NNNNNNNNNN	R	061	616	06.04.34	8769	000000	98999
749.684-010	DECAL APPLIER (any industry)	2112	44543433353	LNNNNNNFFNNNNFNNNON	NNNF3NNNNNNNNNN	R,T	063	474	06.04.34	7756	000000	93947
749.684-014	DECORATOR (furniture; toy-sport equip.)	2114	44543543353	LNNFNNNCCNOONCNNNCN	NNNN3NNNNNNNNNN	R,T	262	460	01.06.03	7756	480702	93947
749.684-018	DECORATOR, LIGHTING FIXTURES (light. fix.)	3123	44543533353	LNNNNNNFFNNNNFFFN	NNNN3NNNNNNNNNN	R,T	262	584	01.06.03	7756	000000	93947
749.684-022	EDGE STAINER II (leather prod.)	2113	44443434353	LNNNNNNFFNNNNNFNFN	NNNN4NNNNNNNNNN	R,T	153	529	06.04.33	7756	000000	93947
749.684-026	FINISHER (wood. container)	2114	34443434353	MNNOOONCCCONNNCNCNCN	NNNN4NNNNNNNNNN	R	153	454	06.04.33	7756	460408	93947
749.684-030	FRAME TRIMMER I (wood prod., nec)	2112	44544544354	LNNFNNNFFNNNNFNFN	NNNN3NFNNNNNNNN	R,T	153	595	06.04.33	8725	000000	98502
749.684-034	LACQUERER (jewelry-silver.)	1112	44544544355	HONONONFFFNNNNNNNON	NNNN4NFNNNNNNNNON	R	151	457	06.04.33	7756	480299	93947
749.687-014	KEG VARNISHER (wood. container)	1112	44544544355	MNNFNFNFNNNNNNNNNN	NNNN3NFNNNNNNNN	R	151	454	06.04.33	7756	000000	93947
749.687-018	MASKER (any industry)	2113	44444544355	LNNNNNNCCNNNNNFNFNNN	NNNN4NNNNNNNNNN	R	062	495	06.04.34	7759	000000	93999
749.687-022	PAINTER, SKI EDGE (toy-sport equip.)	2112	44444434354	LNNNNNNFFNNNNNFOON	NNNN3NNNNNNNNNN	R,T	153	616	06.04.33	7756	000000	93947
749.687-026	PLASTERER (furniture)	2112	44544544355	LNNNNNNFFNNNNNFNNN	NNNN3NNNNNNNNNN	R	094	463	06.04.33	7756	000000	93947
749.687-030	STRIPPER (furniture)	2112	44544544355	MNNNFFNFFFNNNNNNNN	NNNN3NCNNNNNNNNC	R	031	460	06.04.39	7756	480702	93947
749.687-034	PIPE RACKER (fabrication, nec)	3223	44443333353	LNNNNNNCCNNNNFNNFN	NNNN3NNNNNNNNNN	R	061	619	06.04.34	8769	000000	98999
750.130-010	SUPERVISOR (rubber tire)	4247	33343334454	LNNOOOOFFFOFFNFNFNON	NNNN4NNNNNNNNNN	D,P,J,T	147	511	06.02.01	7100	000000	81008
750.132-010	RETREAD SUPERVISOR (rubber tire)	4235	33433433355	MNNNNNNFFNFFFNFNNNNN	NNNN4NFNNNNNNNN	D,P,J,T	102	511	06.02.01	7100	000000	81008

DOT #	DOT Title & Industry	Trng	Aptitude	Physical	Environment	Tempra	WkF	MPSMS	GOE	SOC	CIP	OES
750.367-010	QUALITY-CONTROL INSPECTOR (rubber tire)	3324	3333333354	LNNFNNNFFNOONFNNOON	NNNNN4NNNNNNNNNN	J,T	212	511	06.03.01	7820	000000	83005
750.382-010	TIRE TECHNICIAN (rubber tire)	3335	34333333344	MNNOOONFFFONNNFNFFON	NNCF4NNNNNNNNNF	J,T	212	511	06.03.01	7830	000000	83005
750.384-010	TIRE BUILDER, AUTOMOBILE (rubber tire)	3223	34333433345	MNNFNNNFFFONNNFNFNNN	NNNNN4NNNNNNNNNN	102	511	06.02.29	7679	000000	92911
750.384-014	TUBE BUILDER, AIRPLANE (rubber tire)	2114	44443432355	LNNFNNNFFFNNNNFNFNNN	NNNNN4NNNNNNNNNN	R,T	102	511	06.02.29	7720	000000	93999
750.387-010	TIRE CLASSIFIER (rubber tire)	3123	33433433355	LNNNNNNFFFNNNNFNFNNN	NNNNN4NNNNNNNNNN	J,T	102	511	06.03.01	7820	000000	83005
750.681-010	TIRE REPAIRER (rubber tire)	3123	34443433355	MNNNONNNFFFNNNFNFNNN	NNNNN4NNNNNNNNNN	R,J,T	102	511	06.02.29	6179	000000	85999
750.684-010	BAND BUILDER (rubber tire)	2223	44443433355	LNNNNNNNCCFNNNFNFNNN	NNNNN4NNNNNNNNNN	R,T	102	511	06.04.29	7661	000000	92956
750.684-014	BEAD BUILDER (rubber tire)	2123	44444433355	LNNNNNNNFFFNNNNFNFNNN	NNNNN4NNNNNNNNNN	R,T	041	511	06.04.07	7651	000000	92705
750.684-018	GREEN-TIRE INSPECTOR (rubber tire)	3224	34433433355	LNNFNNNFFFNNNFNFONN	NNNNN4NNNNNNNNNN	J,T	102	511	06.03.02	7820	000000	83005
750.684-022	TIRE BUILDER (automotive ser.)	2113	34445533355	HNNNNNNNFFONNNNFNONNN	NNNNN4NNNNNNNNNN	R,T	102	511	05.12.12	7759	000000	93999
750.684-026	TIRE GROOVER (automotive ser.)	2123	44443434355	MNNONNNFFFNNNNFNFNNN	NNNNN4NNNNNNNNNNF	R,T	054	511	05.12.13	7759	000000	92998
750.684-030	TIRE INSPECTOR (rubber tire)	3224	34433433355	LNNNNNNFFFFNNNNFNFONN	NNNNN4NNNNNNNNNN	J,T	102	511	06.03.02	7820	000000	83005
750.684-034	TIRE TRIMMER, HAND (rubber tire)	2122	44444443355	HNNONNNNFFFNNNNFNFNNN	NNNNN4NNNNNNNNNN	R,T	054	511	06.04.29	7753	000000	93926
750.684-038	TIRE VULCANIZER (automotive ser.)	2113	34443433355	HNNNNNNFFFONNNNFNFNNN	NNFN4NNNNNNNNNNN	R,T	102	511	05.12.12	7759	000000	93999
750.684-042	TIRE-BLADDER MAKER (rubber tire)	2222	44444434355	MNNNNNNFFFFNNNNFNFNNN	NNNNN4NNNNNNNNNN	R,T	102	519	06.04.29	7740	000000	93999
750.684-046	TUBE BALANCER (rubber tire)	2113	44444444355	MMNFNFNFFFNNNNNFNFNNN	NNNNN3NNNNNNNNNN	R,T	063	511	06.04.29	7759	000000	93999
750.684-050	TUBE REPAIRER (rubber tire)	2113	44443434355	MNNNNNNFFFNNNNFNFNNN	NNNNN4NNNNNNNNNN	R,T	102	511	06.04.29	6179	000000	85999
750.685-010	SQUEEGEE TENDER (rubber tire)	2113	34444344355	HNNFFFNFFNNNNNNONNN	NNNNN4NNNNNNNNNN	R	102	511	06.04.07	7679	000000	92998
750.685-014	TIRE RECAPPER (automotive ser.)	2114	34443534355	HNNNNNNNFFNNNNNNNNNN	NNNNN4NONNNNNNNN	V,T	102	511	05.12.12	7679	000000	92998
750.687-010	INNER-TUBE INSERTER (rubber tire)	1112	45544534355	HNNNNNNFFFNNNNNNNNNN	NNNNN4NNNNNNNNNN	R	061	511	06.04.29	7720	000000	93999
750.687-014	TIRE BALANCER (rubber tire)	2112	44444444455	MMNFNNNCCNNNNNFNFNNN	NNNNN3NNNNNNNNNN	R,T	212	511	06.04.29	7820	000000	83005
750.687-018	TIRE INSPECTOR (automotive ser.)	3224	34443434355	LNNOOONFFFNNNFNFNNN	NNNNN4NNNNNNNNNN	R,T	212	511	06.03.02	7820	000000	83005
750.687-022	TIRE SORTER (rubber tire)	2123	44444444355	LNNNNNNNCCNNNNNFNFNNN	NNNNN4NNNNNNNNNN	R	221	511	06.03.02	7850	000000	83005
751.381-010	PATTERNMAKER (engraving)	4337	33322422355	LNNNNNNNFFFNNNNFNFONN	NNNNN3NNNNNNNNNN	J,T	241	510	01.06.01	6821	000000	89114
751.387-010	STOCK PREPARER (plastic prod.)	2113	34444434355	LNNOOONFFFNNNNFNFNNN	NNNNN4NNNNNNNNNNC	R	136	519	06.02.31	7753	000000	93926
751.584-010	COLD-ROLL INSPECTOR (plastic-synth.)	2124	44444434355	LNNFNNNFFFNNNNFNFN	NNNNN3NNNNNNNNNN	R,T	212	492	06.03.02	7820	000000	98502
751.684-010	CUTTER-INSPECTOR (nonmet. min.)	2122	44444444455	LNNNNNNFFFNNNNNNFNNNN	NNNNN3NNNNNNNNNN	R,T	054	519	06.04.29	7720	000000	83005
751.684-014	CUTTER, HAND (rubber goods)	2112	44443434355	LNNNNNNNFFFNNNNNFNFNNN	NNNNN3NNNNNNNNNN	R	054	519	06.04.34	7753	000000	93926
751.684-018	CUTTER, HOT KNIFE (boot & shoe; rubber goods)	2123	44543534355	LNNNNNNNFFFNNNNNFNFNNN	NNNNN4NNNNNNNNNN	R,T	054	512	06.04.29	7753	480304	93926
751.684-022	FOXING CUTTER, HOT KNIFE (boot & shoe; rubber goods)	2112	44544544355	LNNNNNNNFFFNNNNFNFNNN	NNNNN4NNNNNNNNNN	R	054	512	06.04.29	7753	480304	93926
751.684-026	PREFORM PLATE MAKER (ship-boat mfg.)	3225	34433433355	MNNOONNFFFNNNNFNFNNN	NNNNN4NNNNNNNNNN	R,T	241	593	06.02.31	7753	000000	93926
751.686-010	HOSE CUTTER, MACHINE (rubber goods)	2113	44545544355	LNNNNNNNFFFNNNFNFNNN	NNNNN3NNNNNNNNNN	R	054	514	06.04.07	8725	000000	98502
751.687-010	HOSE CUTTER, HAND (rubber goods)	2113	44443434345	HNNONNNFFFNNNNFNFNNN	NNNNN3NNNNNNNNNN	R,T	054	514	06.04.23	7753	000000	93926
752.684-010	BALLOON MAKER (rubber goods)	3223	34333534355	LNNNNNNNFFFNNNFNFNNN	NNNNN4NNNNNNNNNN	R	054	519	06.04.29	7678	000000	92944
752.684-014	BELT BUILDER (rubber goods)	2222	44443433355	HNNFNONFFNNNNNFNFNNN	NNNNN3NNNNNNNNNN	R,T	102	514	06.02.29	7720	000000	93956
752.684-018	BIT BENDER (fabrication, nec)	2113	44443433355	LNNFNFNCCFNNNFNFNON	NNNNN3NNNNNNNNNN	R	136	519	06.04.29	7679	000000	93999
752.684-022	BUFFER (plastic prod.)	2112	33334344453	HNNNNNNFFFOOONFNFNFN	NNNNN3NFNFNNNNNN	R,T	051	619	06.04.24	7755	000000	93953
752.684-026	CATHETER BUILDER (rubber goods)	2114	44443433345	LNNNNNNNFFFNNNNFNFNNN	NNNNN3NNNNNNNNNN	R,T	102	514	06.04.29	7754	000000	93944
752.684-030	HOSE MAKER (rubber goods)	3223	34343433344	MNNONONFFFONNNFNFNNN	NNNNN3NNNNNNNNNN	J,T	102	514	06.02.27	7720	000000	93956
752.684-034	PADDED-PRODUCTS FINISHER (rubber goods)	2123	34433434343	MNNNNNNNCCFFNNNNNNNN	NNNNN3NNNNNNNNNN	R,T	102	519	06.04.27	7759	000000	93999
752.684-038	RUBBER-GOODS ASSEMBLER (rubber goods)	2112	45435543355	LNNNNNNNCCFFNNNNFNNNN	NNNNN4NNNNNNNNNN	R,T	061	519	06.04.23	7720	000000	93956
752.684-042	RUBBER-TUBING SPLICER (rubber goods)	2122	44444443355	HNNFNONFFFNNNNNFNFNNN	NNNNN3NNNNNNNNNN	R,T	063	519	06.04.29	7667	000000	92971
752.684-046	SELF-SEALING-FUEL-TANK BUILDER (rubber goods)	3224	34443433355	HNNFNONFFFNNNNFNFNNN	NNNNN3NNNNNNNNNN	R,T	102	510	06.02.29	7679	000000	93999
752.684-050	SKIN FORMER (rubber goods)	2113	44435422434	LNNFNFNCCFNNNFNFNON	NNNNN3NNNNNNNNNN	R	136	519	06.04.32	7679	000000	92998
752.685-010	SECTIONAL-BELT-MOLD ASSEMBLER (rubber goods)	2113	44443433345	HNNNNNNNFFFNNNNONFNNN	NNNNN3NNNNNNNNNN	R,T	134	514	06.04.07	7667	000000	92971
753.381-010	BOOTMAKER, HAND (rubber goods)	3224	33433422355	LNNNNNNNFFFOOONFNFNFN	NNNNN3NNNNNNNNNN	J,T	102	552	06.02.29	6869	480304	89999
753.467-010	CLASSIFIER (rubber goods)	3223	33333344453	LNNONNNFFNNNNFNFNON	NNNNN3NNNNNNNNNN	R,T	212	512	06.03.01	7820	000000	83005
753.584-010	MACHINE-MADE-SHOE UNIT WORKER (boot & shoe)	2122	44443344354	LNNNNNNNFFFNNNNFNFNON	NNNNN3NFNFNNNNNN	R,T	063	512	06.04.32	7754	480304	93944
753.587-010	SORTER (boot & shoe)	2112	44543344354	LNNNNNNNFFFNNNNFNFNNN	NNNNN3NNNNNNNNNN	R	221	512	06.03.02	7850	480304	83005
753.684-010	BUFFING-AND-SUEDING-MACHINE OPERATOR (boot & shoe)	2112	45444444355	LNNNNNNNFFFNNNNNFNFNNN	NNNNN3NNNNNNNNNN	R	051	512	06.04.05	7677	480304	92965
753.684-014	CUT-AND-COVER LINE WORKER (boot & shoe)	2112	44543533355	LNNNNNNCCCNNNNCNCNNN	NNNNN3NNNNNNNNNN	R,T	061	512	06.04.27	7720	480304	93956

DOT #	DOT Title & Industry	Trng	Aptitude	Physical	Environment	Tempra	WkF	MPSMS	GOE	SOC	CIP	OES
753.684-018	HOOKER-LASTER (boot & shoe)	2123	44543534355	LNNONONCCFONNNFNFNNN	NNNN4NONNNNNNO	R	062	512	06.04.27	7720	480304	93999
753.684-022	LASTER (boot & shoe)	2123	44543534355	LNNNNNFFNNNNNFNFNNN	NNNN3NNNNNNNNN	R	063	512	06.04.27	7720	480304	93999
753.684-026	REPAIRER (boot & shoe)	2114	44443443354	LNNNNNNCCFNNNNFNFN	NNNN3NNNNNNNNN	R,T	063	512	06.04.29	6179	480304	85999
753.684-030	ROLLER-STITCHER (boot & shoe)	2112	44543534355	LNNONONCCNNNNNNNNNN	NNNN4NNNNNNNNN	R,T	032	512	06.04.29	7740	480304	93999
753.687-010	CLIPPER (boot & shoe)	2112	44543534354	LNNNNNNFFNNNNNFNONN	NNNN3NNNNNNNNN	R	054	512	06.04.29	8769	480304	98999
753.687-014	DEBRANDER (boot & shoe)	1112	44543534355	LNNNNNNCCNNNNNCNCNNN	NNNN3NNNNNNNNN	R	131	512	05.12.10	8761	480304	93999
753.687-018	FINAL INSPECTOR (boot & shoe)	3223	33433444453	LNNNNNNCCCNNNNFNNNFN	NNNN4NNNNNNNNN	J	212	512	06.03.02	7820	480304	83005
753.687-022	FITTER-PLACER (rubber goods)	1112	44543533355	LNNNNNNCCCNNNNNCNNNN	NNNN3NNNNNNNNN	R,T	061	512	06.04.23	7740	000000	93956
753.687-026	MAKING-LINE WORKER (boot & shoe)	2123	44543522355	LNNONONCCCONNNCNCNNN	NNNN4NNNNNNNNN	R,T	061	512	06.04.27	7820	480304	93999
753.687-030	MOLD FILLER AND DRAINER (boot & shoe)	2112	44544544455	LNNNNNNCCNNNNNNNNNN	NNNN3NNNNNNNNN	R	132	512	06.04.32	7740	480304	93999
753.687-034	MOLD-INSERT CHANGER (boot & shoe)	2113	44443544355	MNNNNNNFFNNNNNONFNNN	NNFN4NNNNNNNNN	R	061	512	06.04.32	8769	480304	98999
753.687-038	PACKING-LINE WORKER (rubber goods)	2212	44444443354	LNNNNNNCCFNNNNFNFNON	NNNN3NNNNNNNNN	R	041	512	06.04.38	8761	000000	98902
753.687-042	STOCKLAYER (boot & shoe)	2112	44444444345	MNNNNNNFFNNNNNFNFNNO	NNNN4NNNNNNNNN	R,T	163	512	06.04.34	7678	000000	92944
754.130-010	DECORATING-AND-ASSEMBLY SUPERVISOR (plastic prod.)	4235	33433443453	LNNONNNFFNNFFNFNNNOFN	NNNN3NNNNNNNNN	D,P,T,J	081	519	06.04.01	7100	520205	81008
754.137-010	SUPERVISOR, SAMPLE (plastic-synth.)	4337	33333444453	LNNNNNNFFFOFFNFNNON	NNNN3NNNNNNNNN	V,D,P,J	054	492	06.04.01	7100	000000	81008
754.381-010	INTERNAL CARVER (plastic prod.)	4337	33332422355	LNNNNNNFFFNNNFNNNN	NNNN3NNNNNNNNN	J,T	183	619	06.01.04	6863	000000	89911
754.381-014	PATTERNMAKER, PLASTICS (plastic prod.)	4336	33323433355	LNNOOONFFFNNNNFNONN	NNNN4NNNNNNNNF	J,T	102	566	05.05.07	6817	000000	89908
754.381-018	PLASTICS FABRICATOR (aircraft mfg.; plastic prod.)	4447	33333433344	MNNOOONFFFONNMNFNFOON	NNNN4NAOONNNNON	T,J	102	510	06.01.04	6869	150607	89999
754.684-010	ASSEMBLER (plastic prod.)	2214	44433433355	MNNOONFFFONNNFNFNNN	NNNO4NNNNNNNNO	R,T	102	519	06.04.24	7720	000000	93956
754.684-014	ASSEMBLER-AND-GLUER, LAMINATED PLASTICS (plastic prod.)	2123	34444544355	MNNNNNNFFFNNNNFNFNNN	NNNN4NNNNNNNNN	R,T	102	519	06.04.24	7720	000000	93956
754.684-018	BIT SHAVER (fabrication, nec)	2112	44443533355	SNNNNNNFFFNNNFNFNNN	NNNN3NNNNNNNNN	R,T	051	619	06.04.34	7529	000000	92198
754.684-022	CASTER (plastic prod.)	2124	44443434354	MNNOOONFFOONNNONFNON	NNNN4NNNNNNNNN	R,T	132	519	06.02.24	7754	000000	93944
754.684-026	DRILLER, HAND (button & notion)	2112	44453533355	LNNNNNNFFFNNNNFNFNNN	NNNN4NNNNNNNNN	R,T	053	618	06.04.24	7759	000000	93999
754.684-030	FINISHER, HAND (plastic prod.)	2113	44434434355	MNNNNNNFFFFNNNNFNNN	NNNN3NNNNNNNNN	R,T	051	519	06.04.24	7758	000000	93999
754.684-034	KNOCK-OUT HAND (plastic prod.)	2113	44534544355	MNNNNNNFFNNNNNNNNNNN	NNNF4NNNNNNNNN	R,T	136	519	06.04.32	7720	000000	93999
754.684-038	PLASTIC DUPLICATOR (machine tools)	3225	34433432254	MNNNNNNFFFNNNFNFNON	NNNN3NFNNNNNNN	J,T	132	566	06.02.24	7754	000000	93944
754.684-042	PLASTICS WORKER (aircraft mfg.)	3225	34433433354	MNNNONFFFONNNFNONON	NNNN4NOONNNNON	T,U	102	592	06.02.24	7720	000000	93956
754.684-046	PLASTICS REPAIRER (plastic prod.)	2123	44443544344	LNNOOONFFFONNNFNONON	NNNN4NNNNNNNNN	R,T	102	492	06.04.24	6179	000000	85999
754.684-050	LAMINATOR, PREFORMS (plastic prod.)	2124	44443534354	MNNNNNNFFFNNNNFNFNON	NNNN3NFNNNNNNN	R,T	136	590	06.04.24	7740	000000	93956
754.685-010	TAB-MACHINE OPERATOR (nonmet. min.)	2112	44444433455	LNNNNNNFFNNNNNFNNNN	NNNN4NNNNNNNOO	R,T	133	519	06.04.02	7679	000000	92998
754.685-014	ASSEMBLY-MACHINE TENDER (plastic prod.)	2112	44533433244	MNNNNNNFFOONNNFNFFFN	NNNN4NOFNNNNNN	R	081	519	06.04.20	7549	150607	92198
754.687-010	LABORER, GENERAL (plastic prod.)	2112	44543544353	MNNNNNNFFFNNNFNFNFN	NNNN3NNNNNNNNN	R	011	519	06.04.39	7740	000000	93999
754.687-014	SEQUINS STRINGER (plastic prod.)	1112	44444543455	LNNNNNNFFFNNNNFNFNNN	NNNN3NNNNNNNNN	R	171	510	06.04.24	8769	000000	98999
759.135-010	SUPERVISOR, SCOURING PADS (nonmet. min.)	4337	33333333355	MNNNNNNFFNFFNFNFNNN	NNNN4NNNNNNNNN	V,D,P,J	102	519	06.02.01	7100	000000	81008
759.137-010	SUPERVISOR I (rubber goods)	4337	33343332244	LNNQNONFFFOFFNFNFONN	NNNN3NNNNNNNNN	V,D,P,J	191	510	06.02.01	7100	000000	81008
759.261-010	PROTOTYPE-DEICER ASSEMBLER (rubber goods)	4336	33332433355	MNNONONFFFOOONFNFONN	NNNN3NNNNNNNNN	J,T	111	519	06.01.05	6869	000000	89999
759.364-010	HOSE INSPECTOR AND PATCHER (rubber goods)	3224	34433434355	LNNNNNNFFFNNNNFNFNNN	NNNN3NFNNNNNNN	J,T	102	514	06.03.01	7820	000000	83005
759.381-010	RUBBER-GOODS TESTER (elec. equip.; utilities)	3236	33443433355	LNNNNNNFFOONNNNNNNNF	NNNN5NNNNNNNNF	J,T	212	510	06.01.05	6881	000000	83002
759.384-010	SELF-SEALING-FUEL-TANK REPAIRER (rubber goods)	2114	44443433355	MNNNNFFONNNNNFNONNN	NNNN4NNNNNNNNN	R,T	102	510	06.04.29	6179	000000	85999
759.484-010	ROLL BUILDER (rubber goods)	2123	44443433355	MNNONONFFFNNNNFNFNNN	NNNN4NONNNNNNN	R,T	136	519	06.04.29	7661	000000	92956
759.664-010	BRAIDER SETTER (rubber goods)	2112	44533433244	MNNNNNNFFFOONNNNNNNN	NNNN4NNNNNNNNN	R,T	164	519	06.04.06	6179	000000	85999
759.664-014	EXPANSION-JOINT BUILDER (rubber goods)	3224	34333434355	MNNNNNNFFOONNNNFNONNN	NNNN4NNNNNNNNN	J,T	102	514	06.02.29	7720	000000	93999
759.664-018	ROLLER MAKER (print. & pub.)	3114	34423444355	MNNONONFFONOONFNOONN	NNNN4NNNNNNNNN	J,T	121	567	06.02.32	7679	000000	92998
759.684-010	AIRPLANE-GAS-TANK-LINER ASSEMBLER (rubber goods)	2112	44444543355	LNNNNNNFFFNNNNFNFNNN	NNNN4NNNNNNNNN	R,T	054	519	06.04.29	7720	000000	93956
759.684-014	BASE-PLY HAND (rubber goods)	2113	44444444355	HNNNNNNFFOONNHFNFNNN	NNNN4NNNNNNNNN	R,T	241	519	06.02.29	7759	000000	93956
759.684-018	BELT-BUILDER HELPER (rubber goods)	2113	44443434345	HNNNNNNFFOONNNFNFNNN	NNNN4NNNNNNNNN	R	063	519	06.04.29	7679	000000	92998
759.684-022	BUFFER (rubber goods; rubber tire)	2112	44443534355	MNNONNNFFNNNNNCNFNNN	NNNN4NNNNNNNNN	R,T	051	510	06.04.29	7677	000000	92965
759.684-026	DEICER REPAIRER (rubber goods)	2124	34433433355	LNNNNNNFFONNNNFNFNNN	NNNN4NNNNNNNNN	R,T	102	519	06.04.34	6179	000000	85999
759.684-030	DEICER-KIT ASSEMBLER (rubber goods)	2113	44444444455	MNNNNNNFFONNNNFNFNNN	NNNN4NNNNNNNNN	R,T	221	519	06.04.34	7720	000000	93956
759.684-034	FOLDER-TIER (nonmet. min.)	2112	44444433455	LNNNNNNFFFNNNNFNFNNN	NNNN3NNNNNNNNN	R,T	062	519	06.04.24	7759	000000	93999
759.684-038	HOSE WRAPPER (rubber goods)	2122	44443544355	HNNNNNNFFFNNNNFNNNNN	NNNN4NNNNNNNNN	R,T	041	519	06.04.34	7720	000000	93956

DOT #	DOT Title & Industry	Trng	Aptitude	Physical	Environment	Tempra	WkF	MPSMS	GOE	SOC	CIP	OES
759.684-042	MAT REPAIRER (rubber goods)	2112	34433533355	LNNNNNNFFNNNNNNFNNN	NNNN3NNNNNNNNNN	R,T	063	519	06.04.29	6179	000000	85999
759.684-046	PATCHER, BOWLING BALL (toy-sport equip.)	2113	44433533355	LNNNNNNFFNNNNNONONN	NNNN4NNNNNNNNNN	R,T	053	616	06.04.02	7759	000000	93999
759.684-050	RUBBER LINER (machinery mfg.)	3124	34433434355	MOOOOONFFNNNFNONNN	NNN3NONNNNNNNNN	J,T	063	510	06.02.29	7720	000000	93956
759.684-054	RUBBER-GOODS REPAIRER (any industry)	3114	34443544355	LNNNNNNFFOONNNFNONNN	NNNF4NNONNNNNNN	R,T	063	519	06.02.29	6179	000000	85999
759.684-058	SPLICER (rubber tire)	2122	44443434345	LNNNNNNCCCONNNFNFNNN	NNNN4NNONNNNNNN	R,T	054	519	06.04.29	7759	000000	93999
759.684-062	TUBE-AND-MANIFOLD BUILDER (rubber goods)	2123	44444434355	MNNONNNFFONNNFNFONN	NNNN3NNNNNNNNN	R,T	063	519	06.02.29	7720	000000	93999
759.684-066	V-BELT BUILDER (rubber goods)	3124	34443434355	MNNNNNNFFONNNNFNONNN	NNNN3NNNNNNNON	R,T	063	514	06.02.29	7661	000000	92956
759.684-070	SPLICER (protective dev.)	2112	44444543355	LNNNNNCCNNNNFNFNNN	NNNN3NNNNNNNNN	R	102	604	06.04.34	7720	000000	93999
759.684-074	RUBBER-GOODS INSPECTOR-TESTER (rubber goods)	3234	34443433355	LNNFNNNCCFONONFNNNNN	NNNN4NNNNNNNNN	R,J,T	212	604	06.03.02	7820	000000	83005
759.687-010	DEICER INSPECTOR, PNEUMATIC (rubber goods)	3224	34443444355	LNNNNNNFFOONNNFNNNNN	NNNN3NNNNNNNNN	R,T	212	519	06.03.02	7820	000000	83005
759.687-014	HOSE-COUPLING JOINER (rubber goods)	2122	44444544355	HNNNNNNNCCCNNNNCNNNNN	NNNN3NNNNNNNNN	R	061	514	06.04.34	7720	000000	93956
760.684-010	BENCH CARPENTER (woodworking)	2223	44444543455	HNNNNNNFFNNNNNFNFONN	NNNN4NNNNNNNNN	R,T	102	460	06.04.25	7720	480703	93956
760.684-014	BOX MAKER, WOOD (wood. container)	3223	34434433355	MNNFOONFFNNNNNFNONNN	NNNN4NNNNNNNNN	R,T	102	454	06.04.25	7720	480703	93956
761.130-010	SUPERVISOR, BRIAR SHOP (fabrication, nec)	4337	33333333354	LNNNNNNFFNFFNFNOOON	NNNN3NONNNNNNN	V,D,P,J	102	619	06.02.01	7100	480304	81008
761.131-010	SUPERVISOR, LAST-MODEL DEPARTMENT (wood prod., nec)	4338	33322433355	LNNNNNNFFFFFNFFFNN	NNNN4NNONNNNNNN	D,J,P,T	102	457	06.01.01	7100	480703	81008
761.281-010	CARVER, HAND (woodworking)	4438	23322423254	LNNCNNNCCCNNNCNCCON	NNNN3NNNNNNNN	V,J,T	057	460	01.06.02	6839	480702	89399
761.281-014	EXPERIMENTAL-BOX TESTER (wood. container)	4347	23222323355	LNNFNNNFFONNNFNNNNN	NNNN2NNNNNNNNN	J,T	264	454	05.05.02	6839	000000	22599
761.281-018	MARQUETRY WORKER (furniture)	4437	23222422254	LNNFNNNFFOFNOONFFNNN	NNNNNNNNNNNN	J,T	264	461	05.05.08	6839	480702	89399
761.381-010	BOAT-OAR MAKER (woodworking)	3226	33333424355	MNNNNNNFFFNNNFNFNNN	NNNN4NNNNNNNN	J,T	055	457	06.02.25	6839	480703	89399
761.381-014	JIG BUILDER (wood. container)	3226	34433434355	MNNNNNNFFFNNNNFNNF	NNNN4NNNNNNNN	J,T	102	450	05.10.01	6831	480703	89302
761.381-018	LAST-MODEL MAKER (wood prod., nec)	4446	34323433355	MNNNNNNFFONNNFNFFNN	NNNN3NONNNNNNN	J	057	457	06.01.04	6839	480304	89399
761.381-022	PATTERN MARKER I (woodworking)	4437	33323344455	LNNFNFNFFNNNNNFNFONN	NNNN4NNNNNNNN	J,T	241	450	06.02.31	6839	480703	89305
761.381-026	SKI MAKER, WOOD (toy-sport equip.)	3325	34433433345	MNNNNNNFFOONNNFNFONN	NNNO4NNNNNNNN	V,T	102	616	06.02.25	6839	000000	89399
761.381-030	SMOKING-PIPE MAKER (fabrication, nec)	4227	33322422233	MNNNNNNCCNNNCNFNON	NNNN4NNNNNNNN	J,T	057	619	06.02.03	6839	480703	89399
761.381-034	STOCK CHECKERER I (ordnance)	3235	35433534353	LNNNNNNNNFFNNNNNFNNN	NNNN3NNNNNNNN	J,T	183	373	01.06.02	6839	470402	89399
761.381-038	STOCK MAKER, CUSTOM (ordnance)	4337	33323433254	LNNNNNNFFFNNNNNFFOON	NNNN4NNNNNNNN	V,J,T	102	459	01.06.02	6839	470402	89399
761.682-010	LATHE SANDER (woodworking)	2112	34433534345	MNNFNNNCCFFNNNFNFONN	NNNN4NOONNNNNN	R,T	051	450	06.04.25	7634	000000	92314
761.682-014	SANDER, MACHINE (woodworking)	2113	34423433355	MNNONNNCCOFNONONFONN	NNNN4NFFNNNNNNN	R,T	051	450	06.02.03	7634	480703	92314
761.682-018	SPINDLE CARVER (woodworking)	3225	34423433355	LNNONNNCCOONNONFFFNN	NNNN4NCCNNNNNON	J,T	055	450	06.02.03	7431	480703	92311
761.684-010	GOLF-CLUB FACER (toy-sport equip.)	3214	34433434355	LNNNNNNCCNNNNFNOONN	NNNN4NNNNNNNN	J,T	051	616	06.02.25	7758	000000	93956
761.684-014	JIG BUILDER (metal prod., nec)	2213	44443544445	MNNNNNNFFNNNNFNFONN	NNNN4NNNNNNNN	R,T	102	450	06.02.25	7720	000000	93999
761.684-018	PANEL-LAY-UP WORKER (woodworking)	3224	35433534353	LNNNNNNNCCNNNCNNOFN	NNNN4NNNNNNNN	J	212	452	06.03.02	7720	480703	93999
761.684-022	PATTERN MARKER II (woodworking)	2222	44444434355	MNNNNNNFFONNNNNFNNN	NNNN4NOONNNNNN	R,T	241	450	06.04.25	7759	480703	93999
761.684-026	POLISHER (woodworking)	2112	44443533255	MNNNNNNCCNNNONCNCNNN	NNNN4NNNNNNNN	R,U	055	467	06.04.25	7753	000000	92965
761.684-030	SANDER (fabrication, nec)	2112	34443434355	LNNFNFNNCCNNONCNCNNN	NNNN4NNNNNNNN	R,T	051	457	06.04.25	7677	480703	92314
761.684-034	SANDER, PORTABLE MACHINE (woodworking)	2112	44544534355	LNNFNONCCOFNONFNCCNN	NNNN4NOONNNNNN	R,U,T	055	619	06.04.34	7634	480703	92314
761.684-038	SHAPER, HAND (furniture)	3114	44434534355	LNNNNNNFFOONNNFNNNNN	NNNN4NFONNNNNNN	R,T	055	461	06.04.25	7634	480703	92314
761.684-042	STOCK PATCHER (ordnance)	3113	34433434353	LNNNNNNFFNNNNNNOON	NNNN4NNNNNNNN	R,T	055	460	06.02.25	7755	480702	93956
761.684-046	JIG BUILDER (ordnance)	2113	44444434355	LNNNNNNFFFNNNNNFONN	NNNN3NNNNNNNN	R,T	102	373	06.04.25	6179	470402	85999
761.684-050	PANEL CUTTER (furniture)	2222	44444434355	MNNNNNNFFOONNNFNFNNN	NNNN4NNNNNNNN	R,T	051	373	06.04.25	7720	470402	93999
761.684-054	TOUCH-UP CARVER (fabrication, nec)	3113	34433333455	LNNONNNCCNNNNNCNCNNN	NNNN4NOONNNNNN	R,U	055	467	06.04.25	7753	480703	93999
761.684-058	WIRE BRUSH OPERATOR (fabrication, nec)	2112	44434534355	MNNNNNNCCNNNNCNCNNN	NNNN4NNNNNNNN	R,U,T	055	619	06.04.25	7677	000000	92998
761.687-010	SANDER, HAND (woodworking)	2112	44544534355	MNNNNNNCCNNNCNNNNN	NNNN3NCNNNNNNN	R,U,T	055	619	06.04.25	7758	480703	93953
762.134-010	SUPERVISOR, COMPONENT ASSEMBLER (mfd. bldgs.)	4338	33333344454	LNNFNNNCCFNONCNFFN	NNNN3NCNNNNNNN	D,P,T,J	212	455	06.02.01	7830	030404	83005
762.384-010	GLUED WOOD TESTER (woodworking)	4347	33333444454	MNNNNNNFFOONNNFNNNN	NNNN4NNNNNNNN	R	102	450	06.03.01	7830	480703	93956
762.484-010	REEL ASSEMBLER (woodworking)	2223	34434444345	HNNNNNNFFOONNNFNFNNN	NNNN4NNNNNNNN	R	102	454	06.04.22	7720	480703	93956
762.684-014	ASSEMBLER, COMPONENT (mfd. bldgs.; vehicles, nec)	3223	34434534354	LNNNNNNFFOONNNFNNNN	NNNN4NNNNNNNN	R	102	450	06.04.22	7720	480703	93956
762.684-018	ASSEMBLY OPERATOR (woodworking)	2223	34533534355	LNNNNNNFFFNNNNNFNNN	NNNN3NNNNNNNN	R,T	102	457	06.02.22	7720	480703	93956
762.684-022	BASKET MENDER (wood. container)	2113	34433433354	LNNNNNNFFFNNNFNFNNN	NNNN3NNNNNNNN	R,T	102	454	06.04.34	6179	000000	93926
762.684-026	BOX MAKER (fabrication, nec)	2112	44444533355	MNNFNNNCCCNNNNFNFNNN	NNNN4NNNNNNNN	R,T	072	454	06.04.25	7720	000000	93956

DOT #	DOT Title & Industry	Trng	Aptitude	Physical	Environment	Tempra	WkF	MPSMS	GOE	SOC	CIP	OES
762.684-030	CURTAIN-STRETCHER ASSEMBLER (woodworking)	2212	44443534355	LNNNNNNFFNNNNNFNFNNN	NNNN3NNNNNNNNNNN	R	102	457	06.04.22	7720	480703	93956
762.684-034	DOOR ASSEMBLER I (woodworking)	2113	44444534355	MNNNNNNFFNNNNNFNFNNN	NNNN3NNNNNNNNNNN	R,T	063	452	06.04.22	7720	480703	93956
762.684-038	EDGE BANDER, HAND (furniture)	2112	44544544355	MNNONNNFFONNNNFNFNNN	NNNN4NNNNNNNNNNN	R,T	063	460	06.04.22	7720	480702	93999
762.684-042	GRIP ASSEMBLER (woodworking)	3224	34433434355	LNNNNNNFFNNNNNFNFNNN	NNNN3NNNNNNNNNNN	R,T	102	457	06.02.23	7720	000000	93956
762.684-046	HARDWARE ASSEMBLER (woodworking)	2112	44544533344	MNNNNNCCNNNNCNCNON	NNNN4NNNNNNNNNN	R	071	452	06.04.23	7720	480703	93956
762.684-050	NAILER, HAND (any industry)	2113	44534534355	MNNFNONFFONNONFNFFNN	NNNN4NNNNNNNNNNN	R,T	072	450	06.04.22	7720	480703	93956
762.684-054	SCARF GLUER (millwork-plywood)	2114	44443534355	HNNFNNNFFFNNNNFNNNNN	NNNN4NNNNNNNNNNN	R,T	063	453	06.04.25	7720	000000	93956
762.684-058	SIDING STAPLER (millwork-plywood)	2222	44444434344	HNNFNNNCCONNNNFNFNON	NNNN3NNFNNNNNNNN	R,T	063	453	06.04.25	7720	000000	93956
762.684-062	TRUSS ASSEMBLER (millwork-plywood)	3223	34434434355	MNNNNNNFFONNNNFNFONN	NNNN4NNNNNNNNNNN	R,T	102	455	05.10.01	8650	000000	93956
762.684-066	WOODEN-FRAME BUILDER (furniture)	2112	44444544355	MNNNNNNCCCNNNNONONNN	NNNN4NFNNNNNNNN	T	192	464	06.04.25	7720	480702	93956
762.685-010	EDGE BANDER, MACHINE (furniture; millwork-plywood)	2223	44544544455	MNNONNNFFNNNNNNNNNNN	NNNN4NNNNNNNNNN	R	063	453	06.04.03	7661	480702	92956
762.686-010	EDGE-BANDING-MACHINE OFFBEARER (furniture; millwork-plywood)	1112	44544544455	MNNONNNFFNNNNNNNNNNN	NNNN4NNNNNNNNNN	R	063	453	06.04.03	8725	000000	98502
762.687-010	BANDER (wood. container)	1112	44544544355	MNNOOONCCONNNNNNNNNN	NNNN4NNNNNNNNNN	R	041	454	06.04.25	7740	000000	83005
762.687-014	BOX INSPECTOR (wood. container)	2122	44544544355	LNNONNNCCONNNNCNFNNN	NNNN3NNNNNNNNNNN	R,T	102	454	06.03.02	7820	480703	83005
762.687-018	BOX REPAIRER II (wood. container)	2113	44543544354	LNNONNNFFNNNNNFNFON	NNNN3NNNNNNNNNNN	R	094	454	06.03.02	7820	000000	83005
762.687-022	CLAMP-JIG ASSEMBLER (woodworking)	2222	44444534355	MNNFNNNCCOONNNCNFFNN	NNNN3NOONNNNNNN	R	102	452	06.04.22	7720	480703	93956
762.687-026	CROSSBAND LAYER (millwork-plywood)	2112	44444534355	MMNFNNNCCONNONFNONNN	NNNN4NFNNNNNNNN	R	063	453	06.04.25	8769	000000	98999
762.687-030	DOOR CORE ASSEMBLER (woodworking)	2112	44544534345	MNNNNNNFFNNNONONNNNN	NNNN4NNNNNNNNNN	R	063	452	06.04.22	7720	480703	93956
762.687-034	GLUER (woodworking)	2223	44444534355	MMNFNNNCCFNNONFNONNN	NNNN4NONNNNNNN	R	102	450	06.04.22	7720	480703	93956
762.687-038	GLUER-AND-WEDGER (woodworking)	2112	44544544355	LNNNNNNFFNNNNNFNFNNN	NNNN4NNNNNNNNNN	R	063	457	06.04.25	7720	000000	93956
762.687-042	HANDLE ASSEMBLER (woodworking)	2112	44534534355	MNNFNNNFFNNNNNFNFNNN	NNNN3NNNNNNNNNNN	R	102	552	06.04.22	7720	000000	93956
762.687-046	HARDWARE ASSEMBLER (wood. container)	2112	44544533355	LNNONNNCCCNNONONONNN	NNNN4NNNNNNNNNN	R	072	454	06.04.23	7720	000000	93956
762.687-050	KNOCK-UP ASSEMBLER (woodworking)	2112	44544544355	MMNFNFNFNNNNNNNNNNNN	NNNN4NNNNNNNNNN	R	063	450	06.04.22	7720	480703	93956
762.687-054	PARTITION ASSEMBLER (wood. container)	1111	44444534355	LNNNNNNCCNNNNNFNFNNN	NNNN4NNNNNNNNNN	R	061	454	06.04.23	7720	000000	93956
762.687-058	SCREEN TACKER (woodworking)	2112	44544544455	LNNNNNNFFNNNNNFNFNNN	NNNN3NNNNNNNNNNN	R	102	452	06.04.34	7720	000000	93999
762.687-062	SHEET TURNER (millwork-plywood)	1112	44544544355	MMNFNNNCCNNNNNNNNNNN	NNNN4NNNNNNNNNN	R	011	453	06.04.40	8620	000000	98999
762.687-066	VENEER-STOCK LAYER (millwork-plywood)	2112	44444534355	MMNFNNNCCONNNNNNNNNN	NNNN4NNNNNNNNNN	R	063	453	06.04.25	7740	000000	93999
762.687-070	WOODENWARE ASSEMBLER (woodworking)	2123	44444534355	MNNONNNFFONNONFNFFNO	NNNN4NOFNNNNNNN	R	102	467	06.04.22	7720	480702	93956
763.134-010	SUPERVISOR, QUALITY CONTROL (furniture)	4436	33333444354	MNNONNNFFFOFFNNFNFFN	NNNN4NOFNNNFFN	D,P,J	102	461	06.02.01	7100	520205	81008
763.134-014	SUPERVISOR, FURNITURE ASSEMBLY (furniture)	3337	33333344455	LNNNNNNFFONFFNCNOOONN	NNNN3NNNNNNNNNNN	D,P,J	102	461	06.02.01	7100	480702	81008
763.380-010	FURNITURE RESTORER (museums)	4346	33333433253	LNNONONFFOONFNOOFFN	NNNN4NNNNNNNNNN	J,T,V	102	460	05.05.08	6835	200501	89314
763.381-010	FURNITURE FINISHER (woodworking)	4227	34442434353	LNNOONNFFOONNFNFFN	NNNN4NONNNNNNN	J,T	051	460	05.05.08	6835	480702	89314
763.381-014	FURNITURE-FINISHER APPRENTICE (woodworking)	4227	34442434353	LNNOONFFOONNFNFNFFN	NNNN4NONNNNNNN	J,T	051	460	05.05.08	6835	480702	89314
763.681-010	FRAME REPAIRER (furniture)	3326	34433433355	HNNFFNFFFNNNNFNNONF	NNNN3NNNNNNNNNNN	J,T	101	462	05.10.01	6179	480702	85999
763.684-010	ASSEMBLY INSPECTOR (furniture)	3125	34434444354	MMNFNNNFFOFNNNCNCCCN	NNNN4NONNNNNNN	R,T	212	461	06.03.02	7820	480703	83005
763.684-014	CABINET ASSEMBLER (furniture)	3233	34434433355	LNNNNNNFFFNNNNFNFNNN	NNNN4NNNNNNNNNN	R,T	102	461	06.02.22	7720	480702	93956
763.684-018	CANER I (furniture)	3113	44444533355	LNNONNNCCCONONFNNNCN	NNNO3NNNNNNNNNN	R,T	164	460	06.04.25	6179	480702	93999
763.684-022	CANER II (furniture)	3113	44444434355	MMNOONNCCFONNNFNFFN	NNNN4NNNNNNNNNN	R,T	102	461	05.10.01	7720	480703	93999
763.684-026	CASE FITTER (furniture)	2112	44544544355	LNNNNNNCCCCNNNNONONN	NNNN3NNNNNNNNNNN	R	063	460	06.04.27	7759	480702	93999
763.684-030	DRAWER LINER (furniture)	3124	34443443353	MMNONNNCCFFNOONNNNNN	NNNN3NFNNNNNNNN	R,T	102	460	05.10.01	6179	480702	93947
763.684-034	FINISH PATCHER (furniture)	3224	34444433355	MMFNNNFFFNNNFNNFFN	NNNN4NOONNNNNNN	R,T	102	460	06.02.22	7720	480702	93956
763.684-038	FURNITURE ASSEMBLER (furniture)	2113	44444444354	LNNFNNNFFONNNFNFFN	NNNN3NFNNNNNNNN	R,T	102	460	06.04.22	7720	480702	93999
763.684-042	HARDWARE ASSEMBLER (furniture)	2222	44444544355	LNNNNNNFFFNNNNONNNNN	NNNN4NONNNNNNN	R,T	071	460	06.04.22	7720	480702	93999
763.684-046	LAG SCREWER (furniture)	2113	34434544355	LNNFNNNFFNNNNFNNNNNN	NNNN4NNNNNNNNNN	T	063	460	06.04.22	7720	480702	93999
763.684-050	LAMINATOR, HAND (furniture)	3225	34433544355	LNNFNNNCCCCNNNNCNFFN	NNNN3NNNNNNNNNNN	R,T	061	461	06.02.27	7759	480702	93956
763.684-054	LEATHER TOOLER (furniture)	2222	44444444454	LNNFNNNFFONNNNFNNONON	NNNN3NNNNNNNNNNN	R,T	102	614	06.04.22	7720	480702	93999
763.684-058	PIANO CASE AND BENCH ASSEMBLER (musical inst.)	2112	44443444354	HNNFNNNFFFNNNNFNNNFN	NNNN4NNNNNNNNNN	R,T	063	460	06.04.22	7720	480702	93956
763.684-062	PLASTIC-TOP ASSEMBLER (furniture)	2222	44433443355	HNNFNFNFFONNNNFNNNNN	NNNN4NNNNNNNNNN	R,T	055	460	06.04.25	7753	480702	93926
763.684-066	SLOT ROUTER (furniture)	3224	34443443355	LNNONNNCCOFNONCNCCCN	NNNN4NONNNNNNN	J,T	102	460	06.03.02	7820	480702	83005
763.684-070	STOCK-PARTS INSPECTOR (furniture)	3224	44433443352	LNNONNNCCOFNONCNCCCN	NNNN4NONNNNNNN	J,T	102	460	06.03.02	7820	480702	83005
763.684-074	TABLE-TOP TILE SETTER (brick & tile)	2224	44433434352	LNNNNNNCCCNNNNFNNNNN	NNNN3NNNNNNNNNNN	T	092	534	06.04.30	7759	480702	93999

DOT #	DOT Title & Industry	Trng	Aptitude	Physical	Environment	Tempra	WkF	MPSMS	GOE	SOC	CIP	OES
763.684-078	WICKER WORKER (furniture)	3125	34434443355	MNNNNNCCCNNNNNNNN	NNNN4NNNNNNNNNN	T	102	468	06.04.25	7720	480702	93999
763.687-010	BLOW-OFF WORKER (furniture)	1112	44544544455	LNNNFFNCNNNNNNNNN	NNNN4NNNNNNNNNN	R	031	460	06.04.39	8769	000000	98999
763.687-014	CHAIR INSPECTOR AND LEVELER (furniture)	2123	44443444354	LNNFNNNFFFNNNCNFCCN	NNNN4NNONNNNNNN	R,T	212	461	06.03.02	7820	480702	83005
763.687-018	DISTRESSER (furniture)	2113	44544544354	LNNFNNNNCOFFNONCNFCCN	NNNN4NONNNNNNNN	R	134	460	06.04.25	8769	480702	98999
763.687-022	DRAWER WAXER (furniture)	1111	44544544355	LNNNNNNCCCNNNNNNNN	NNNN3NNNNNNNNNN	R	153	460	06.04.33	7756	000000	93947
763.687-026	FINISHED-STOCK INSPECTOR (furniture)	3224	34443444354	LNNFFFNCCCONONCNNNCN	NNNN3NNNNNNNNN	R,J,T	212	460	06.03.02	7820	480702	83005
763.687-030	CANE CUTTER (furniture)	2111	45544544455	MNNNNNNNCCCNNNNNNN	NNNN4NNONNNNNN	R	054	461	06.04.25	7753	000000	93956
764.134-010	SUPERVISOR, COOPERAGE SHOP (wood. container)	4237	33333344355	LNNOONNFFONFFNFNNONN	NNNN4NNNNNNNNN	D,J,P	102	454	06.02.01	7100	000000	81008
764.387-010	HEAD INSPECTOR (wood. container)	3234	33333344453	LNNFNNNCCONNNNFNNFFN	NNNN4NNNNNNNNN	J,T	212	452	06.03.01	7820	000000	83005
764.387-014	MATERIAL INSPECTOR (wood. container)	4335	34343344455	LNNOONNCNNNNNNNNNNN	ONNN4NNNNNNNNN	J,T	102	452	05.07.06	7820	000000	83005
764.684-010	BARREL BRANDER (wood. container)	2112	44444444355	MNNNNNNMFFNNNNNNNNNN	NNNN4NNNNNNNN	R,T	192	454	06.04.37	7679	000000	92998
764.684-014	BARREL CHARRER (wood. container)	2114	44444444455	MNNNNNNCNNNNNNNNNN	NNNN4NNNNNNNN	R,T	141	454	06.04.18	7639	000000	92998
764.684-018	BARREL RAISER (wood. container)	2114	44445434345	MNNONONCNNNNNONONNN	NNNN4NNNNNNNN	R,T	061	454	06.04.22	7720	000000	93956
764.684-022	COOPER (wood. container)	3115	34433544355	MNNFNNNCCONNONCNCFNN	NNON4NNNNNNNN	R,T	102	454	05.10.01	6179	000000	85999
764.684-026	HOGSHEAD COOPER I (wood. container)	2112	44544543355	HNINFNNNCCCNNNNFNNNN	NNNN4NNNNNNNN	R	102	454	06.04.22	6179	000000	85999
764.684-030	TANK ASSEMBLER (wood. container)	3224	34333433355	MNNNNNNFFFNNNONONNN	NNNN4NNNNNNNN	R,T	102	454	06.02.25	7720	000000	93956
764.687-010	AIR-AND-WATER FILLER (wood. container)	2112	44444444355	MNNNNNNFNNNNNNNNNNN	NNNN4NNNNNNNN	R	041	454	06.04.36	8769	000000	98999
764.687-014	ASSEMBLER, FAUCETS (wood. container)	2112	44544543355	LNNNNNNNFFNNFNFNNN	NNNN4NNNNNNNN	R	063	454	06.04.23	7720	000000	93956
764.687-018	BARREL DRAINER (wood. container)	1111	44544544455	HNINFNNNFFONNNNNNNNN	NNNN4NNNNNNNN	R	011	454	06.04.40	8769	000000	98999
764.687-022	BARREL INSPECTOR, TIGHT (wood. container)	2124	44443444455	LNNONNNCNNNNNFNNNNN	NNNN4NNNNNNNN	R,T	102	454	06.03.02	7820	000000	83005
764.687-026	BARREL LINER (wood. container)	2112	44544544355	MNNFNNNNFFOONNNFNFNNN	NNNN3NNNNNNNN	R	094	454	06.04.33	7756	000000	93947
764.687-030	BARREL MARKER (wood. container)	2112	44544544455	LNNNNNNFFOONNNNONFNNN	NNNN3NNNNNNNN	R	241	454	06.04.25	8769	000000	98999
764.687-034	BARREL-CHARRER HELPER (wood. container)	2112	44544543355	MNNNNNNFFNNNNNNNNNN	NNNN3NNNNNNNN	R	141	454	06.04.18	8615	000000	98999
764.687-038	BARREL-RAISER HELPER (wood. container)	2112	44544544355	MNNONONNFFNNNNNNONNN	NNNN3NNNNNNNN	R	061	454	06.04.22	8620	000000	98999
764.687-042	BUNG DRIVER (wood. container)	1111	44544544455	LNNNNNNNFFONNNNONONN	NNNN4NNNNNNNN	R	061	454	06.04.22	7740	000000	93999
764.687-046	CHANNEL INSTALLER (wood. container)	2112	44544544455	MNNONNNFFNNNNNNNONNN	NNNN4NNNNNNNN	R	061	454	06.04.22	7720	000000	93999
764.687-050	COOPER HELPER (wood. container)	2222	44434544355	MNNFNNNCCONNNNCNCNNN	NNNN4NNNNNNNN	R	102	454	05.12.12	8637	000000	98102
764.687-054	CULLER (wood. container)	2123	44443444355	LNNNNNNCCNNNNICNNNNN	NNNN4NNNNNNNN	R,T	102	454	06.03.02	7820	000000	83005
764.687-058	HEADER (wood. container)	2112	44434544355	MNNNNNNFFOONNNFNFNNN	NNNN4NNNNNNNN	R	061	454	06.04.22	7720	000000	93999
764.687-062	HEADING MATCHER AND ASSEMBLER (wood. container)	2223	44443543355	LNNONNNCCCNNNNCNCNNN	NNNN4NNNONNNN	R,T	061	454	06.04.22	7720	000000	93956
764.687-066	HEADING REPAIRER (wood. container)	2113	44435543455	LNNNNNNCCONNONFNFNNN	NNNN4NNNNNNNN	R,T	061	454	06.04.25	7720	000000	93999
764.687-070	HOGSHEAD COOPER II (wood. container)	2112	44544544455	LNNNNNNNFNNNNNNNNNNN	NNNN4NNNNNNNN	R	102	454	06.04.22	7720	000000	93956
764.687-074	HOGSHEAD COOPER III (wood. container)	2112	44544544455	HNNONNNFFOFFNFNFNON	NNNN4NNNNNNNN	R	102	454	06.04.22	7720	000000	93956
764.687-078	HOGSHEAD HOOPER (wood. container)	1112	44544544455	MNNFNNNFFONNNNFFFN	NNNN4NNNNNNNN	R	061	454	06.04.22	7720	000000	93999
764.687-082	HOGSHEAD MAT ASSEMBLER (wood. container)	2112	44544544455	MNNFNNNFFNNNNNNNONNN	NNNN4NNNNNNNN	R	061	454	06.04.22	7720	000000	93956
764.687-086	HOGSHEAD MAT INSPECTOR (wood. container)	2123	44543543455	LNNFNNNFFNNNNNFNNNNN	NNNN4NNNNNNNN	R,T	212	454	06.03.02	7820	000000	83005
764.687-090	LEAK HUNTER (beverage)	2112	44444444455	MNNOOONCCCNNNNFNFNNN	NNNN4NNNNNNNN	R,T	094	454	05.12.12	7740	000000	93999
764.687-094	LEVELER I (wood. container)	2112	44544544355	MNNFNNNNFNNNNNNNNNN	NNNN5NNNNNNNN	R,T	061	454	06.04.22	7740	000000	93999
764.687-098	PLUGGER (wood. container)	1111	44544544355	LNNNNNNFFFNFFNNONN	NNNN4NNNNNNNN	R	061	454	06.04.22	7740	000000	93999
769.130-010	SUPERVISOR, FABRICATION (wood prod., nec)	4237	33343433345	LNNONNNCCCNNNNCNNNN	NNNN4NNNNNNNN	V,D,P,J	102	457	06.02.01	7100	000000	81008
769.134-010	SUPERVISOR, DIMENSION WAREHOUSE (furniture)	4337	33333333354	MNNONNNFFNFFNFNNOON	NNNN3NNNNNNNN	V,D,P	102	450	06.02.01	7100	520205	81008
769.137-010	STOCKING-AND-BOX-SHOP SUPERVISOR (ordnance)	4337	33323444355	LNNNNNNFFONFFNFNNNNN	NNNN4NNNNNNNN	V,D,P,J	102	379	06.02.01	7100	520205	81008
769.137-014	SUPERVISOR, ASSEMBLY (woodworking)	3226	33333433354	LNNONNNFFOFFNFNFNON	NNNN4NNNNNNNN	V,D,P	102	460	06.02.01	7100	000000	93999
769.381-010	COMPO CASTER (wood prod., nec)	3224	34433433355	LNNNNNNFFNNNNNFNFFN	NNNN3NNNNNNNN	J,T	132	457	06.02.32	6861	000000	89905
769.387-010	WOODWORK-SALVAGE INSPECTOR (ordnance)	3224	33333344455	HONONNNFFNNNNNFNOONN	NNNN3NNNNNNNN	J,T	102	457	06.03.01	7820	000000	83005
769.664-010	SHAKER REPAIRER (grain-feed mills)	2112	44433443345	LNNNNNNFFFNNNNFNOONN	NNNN4NNONNNN	R,T	102	567	06.04.25	6130	470303	85119
769.684-010	BASKET ASSEMBLER II (wood. container)	2112	44434533345	LNNNNNNFFNNNNFNNNN	NNNN4NNNNNNNN	R,T	102	454	06.04.34	7720	000000	93956
769.684-014	BASKET PATCHER (wood. container)	2112	44444444355	LNNNNNNCCNNNNNNNNNN	NNNN4NNNNNNNN	R,T	057	454	06.04.34	7759	000000	93999
769.684-018	BENDER, HAND (woodworking)	2112	44544544355	LNNNNNNFFNFFNNNNNNN	NNNN3NNNNNNNN	R	134	450	06.04.25	7755	000000	93999
769.684-022	FINAL INSPECTOR, SHUTTLE (woodworking)	3224	34433344355	LNNNNNNFFOONNNFNFONN	NNNN4NNNNNNNN	J,T	212	457	06.03.01	7820	480703	83005
769.684-026	OIL DIPPER (woodworking)	2113	44443534354	MNNNNNNFFOONNNFNFNON	NNNN4NNNNNNNN	R,T	151	457	06.04.25	7758	000000	93953

DOT #	DOT Title & Industry	Trng	Aptitude	Physical	Environment	Tempra	WkF	MPSMS	GOE	SOC	CIP	OES
769.684-030	PATCHER (woodworking)	2112	44443534354	MNNFNNNCCONNNNFNFNN	NNNN4NFNNNNNNNN	R,T	102	453	06.04.25	7740	000000	93956
769.684-034	REELER (woodworking)	2112	44444434354	HNNFFFNFFNNNNOONN	NNNN3NNNNNNNNN	R	102	457	06.04.25	7720	000000	93999
769.684-038	REPAIRER, ASSEMBLED WOOD PRODUCTS (woodworking)	3125	44443443353	MMNFNNNFFOONNNFNFFN	NNNN4NONNNNNNNN	V,T	221	460	05.10.01	6179	000000	85999
769.684-042	SAMPLE MAKER, VENEER (millwork-plywood)	2113	44434444454	LNNNNNNFFOONNNFNFON	NNNN4NNNNNNNNN	R,T	056	453	06.04.25	7753	000000	93926
769.684-046	SHUTTLE INSPECTOR (woodworking)	3224	34433433355	LNNNNNNFFONNNFNFONN	NNNN4NNNNNNNNN	J,T	212	457	06.03.01	7820	480703	83005
769.684-050	STOCK-PARTS FABRICATOR (ship-boat mfg.)	3113	34444434355	MNNONNNFFNNNNFNFNNN	NNNN4NNNNNNNNN	R,T	102	450	06.02.25	7753	000000	93926
769.684-054	WEAVER (wood. container)	2124	34433343255	SNNONNNCCCNNNNFNNNN	NNNN4NNNNNNNNN	R,T	164	454	06.04.34	7720	000000	93999
769.684-058	REPAIRER, VENEER SHEET (furniture)	2112	44432444354	MNNNNNNCCCNNNNCNNCCN	NNNN4NNONNNNNNN	R,T	061	453	06.03.02	6179	480702	85999
769.685-010	PANEL EDGE SEALER (millwork-plywood)	2112	44544544355	LNNNNNNCCONNNNFNNNN	NNNN4NNNNNNNNN	R,T	094	453	06.04.21	7669	000000	92953
769.687-010	BASKET GRADER (wood. container)	2112	44443444355	LNNNNNNCCCONNNNFNNNN	NNNF4NNNNNNNNN	R,T	212	454	06.03.02	7850	000000	83005
769.687-014	BOBBIN INSPECTOR (woodworking)	2112	44443444355	LNNNNNNFFOONNNFNNNN	NNNN4NNNNNNNNN	R,T	212	457	06.03.02	7820	480703	83005
769.687-018	CANOE INSPECTOR, FINAL (ship-boat mfg.)	2114	44444444355	LNNFNNNFFONNNNONONNN	NNNN4NNNNNNNNN	R,T	102	593	06.03.02	7820	000000	83005
769.687-022	FRAME TRIMMER II (wood prod., nec)	2112	44544544354	LNNNNNNFFOONNNFNONON	NNNN4NNNNNNNNN	R	051	457	06.04.25	7740	000000	93999
769.687-026	INSPECTOR (woodworking)	2223	34443444454	LNNFFNNFFFONONFNFFF	NNNN3NONNNNNNN	R,T	212	462	06.03.02	7820	000000	83005
769.687-030	INSPECTOR, PICTURE FRAMES (wood prod., nec)	2123	44444444354	LNNFNNNFFNNNNFNFNFN	NNNN4NNNNNNNNN	R,T	212	457	06.03.02	7820	000000	83005
769.687-034	PLUG SORTER (woodworking)	1111	44544544355	LNNNNNNFFOONNNNNFNNNN	NNNN4NNNNNNNNN	R,T	212	452	06.03.02	7850	000000	83005
769.687-038	PUTTY MIXER AND APPLIER (wood. container)	1111	44444544355	LNNNNNNFFOONNONNNNNN	NNNN4NNNNNNNNN	R	094	495	06.04.34	8769	000000	98999
769.687-042	SORTER II (wood prod., nec)	1112	44444444455	LNNNNNNFFONNNNFNFNNN	NNNN4NNNNNNNNN	R,T	212	459	06.03.02	7850	000000	83005
769.687-046	VENEER MATCHER (millwork-plywood)	3114	34443433353	LNNNNNNFFONNNNFNNCON	NNNN3NNNNNNNNN	J,T	212	453	06.03.02	7850	000000	83005
769.687-050	VENEER-STOCK GRADER (wood. container)	2112	44543544454	LNNNNNNCCNNNNNFNNNON	NNNN4NNNNNNNNN	R,T	212	457	06.03.02	7850	000000	83005
769.687-054	WOODWORKING-SHOP HAND (woodworking)	2112	44444444344	VNNFNFNFONNONFNFFON	NNNN4NFFNNNNNFN	R,T	102	460	06.04.25	8769	000000	98999
769.687-058	BRIAR-WOOD SORTER (fabrication, nec)	2112	44433444355	MNNNNNNCCCNNNNFNFNNN	NNNN3NNNNNNNNN	R	221	619	06.03.02	7850	000000	83005
770.131-010	JEWEL SUPERVISOR (clock & watch)	4347	33333343355	LNNNNNNFFOOFFNOONNN	NNNN3NNNNNNNNN	D,J,P	121	607	06.04.01	6700	470408	81008
770.131-014	SUPERVISOR, DIAMOND FINISHING (jewelry-silver.)	4338	33322443452	LNNNNNNFFNOONFNFFN	NNNN3NNNNNNNNN	D,J,T	051	613	05.05.14	6700	520205	81008
770.261-010	BRILLIANDEER-LOPPER (jewelry-silver.)	3226	33322523255	LNNNNNNFFFOONFNFNN	NNNN3NNNNNNNNN	J	051	613	05.05.14	6866	470408	89926
770.261-014	GIRDLER (jewelry-silver.)	3226	34322432255	SNNNNNNFFFOONFNFNN	NNNN3NNNNNNNNN	J,T	051	613	05.05.14	6866	470408	89926
770.267-010	DIAMOND EXPERT (jewelry-silver.)	4338	23322444452	SNNNNNNFFOOONFNOFN	NNNN3NNNNNNNNN	J,T	212	613	05.05.14	6881	470408	83002
770.281-010	DIAMOND SELECTOR (jewelry-silver.)	4238	33332433353	SNNNNNNCCCNNNNCNNFCN	NNNN3NNNNNNNNN	J,T	212	538	05.05.14	6866	470408	89926
770.281-014	GEM CUTTER (jewelry-silver.)	4336	34322433253	SNNNNNNCCFFNNNFNOOFN	NNNN3NNNNNNNNN	V,J,T	051	613	05.05.14	6866	470408	89126
770.381-010	BEAD MAKER (jewelry-silver.)	3227	33322432255	LNNNNNNFFCNNNNFNONNN	NNNO4NNNNNNNNN	R,J,T	132	611	01.06.02	6822	470408	89926
770.381-014	DIAMOND CLEAVER (jewelry-silver.)	3226	34433533354	SNNNNNNFFFNNNNFNNFNN	NNNN3NNNNNNNNN	V,J,T	051	613	05.05.14	6866	470408	89926
770.381-018	DIAMOND DRILLER (machine tools)	3225	34433433355	LNNNNNNFFONNNNFNONNN	NNNN3NNNNNNNNN	R,J,T	053	566	06.01.04	6866	000000	89926
770.381-022	DIAMOND-DIE POLISHER (machine tools)	3225	34433433355	LNNNNNNFFONNNNFNOONN	NNNN3NNNNNNNNN	R,J,T	051	566	06.01.04	6866	000000	89926
770.381-026	JEWEL BLOCKER AND SAWYER (clock & watch)	3226	34433533355	LNNNNNNFFONNNFNFNONN	NNNN4NNNNNNNNN	R,T	056	613	06.01.04	6866	470408	89926
770.381-030	JEWEL-BEARING MAKER (clock & watch)	4337	33322422355	LNNNNNNFFFNNNNFNFNN	NNNN3NNNNNNNNN	J	057	613	06.01.04	6866	470408	89926
770.381-034	OLIVING-MACHINE OPERATOR (clock & watch)	3225	34432422355	SNNNNNNCCFONNNCNNFNN	NNNN3NNNNNNNNN	J	051	613	06.01.04	6866	470408	89926
770.381-038	SAPPHIRE-STYLUS GRINDER (comm. equip.)	3225	33433443355	SNNNNNNFFOONNNFNFNNN	NNNN3NNNNNNNNN	J,T	051	585	06.01.04	6869	000000	89999
770.381-042	SPOTTER (machine tools)	4336	34433533354	LNNNNNNFFONNNNFNFOON	NNNN4NNNNNNNNN	V,J,T	241	613	05.05.14	6866	470408	89926
770.382-010	LATHE OPERATOR (jewelry-silver.)	3236	34433533354	LNNNNNNFFFONNNFNFONN	NNNN4NNNNNNNNN	R,J,T	056	613	06.02.08	6866	470408	89926
770.382-014	PHONOGRAPH-NEEDLE-TIP MAKER (comm. equip.)	3224	34433533355	LNNNNNNFFFONNNFNFONN	NNNN3NNNNNNNNN	J,T	051	613	06.02.30	7522	470408	92998
770.582-010	FACER (clock & watch)	3225	33433533355	LNNNNNNFFFONNNFNFONN	NNNN3NNNNNNNNN	R,J,T	051	613	06.02.30	7512	470408	92998
770.682-010	JEWEL-BEARING BROACHER (clock & watch)	3224	33433433355	LNNNNNNFFFONNNNFNFONN	NNNN3NNNNNNNNN	R,J,T	053	613	06.01.04	7512	470408	92998
770.682-014	JEWEL-BEARING DRILLER (clock & watch)	3224	34433433355	LNNNNNNFFFNNNNFNFONN	NNNN3NNNNNNNNN	R,J,T	051	613	06.02.08	7522	470408	92998
770.682-018	JEWEL-BEARING FACER (clock & watch)	3224	34433433355	LNNNNNNFFFNNNNFNFONN	NNNN3NNNNNNNNN	R,J,T	051	613	06.02.30	7512	470408	92998
770.682-022	JEWEL-BEARING TURNER (clock & watch)	3225	34433433355	LNNNNNNFFFNNNNFNFONN	NNNN4NNNNNNNNN	R,J,T	053	613	06.02.02	7518	470408	92998
770.682-026	JEWEL-HOLE DRILLER (clock & watch)	2125	44544533355	LNNNNNNCCFNNNNCNCNNN	NNNN4NNNNNNNNN	R,J,T	051	613	06.02.02	7758	470408	93953
770.684-010	JEWEL GRINDER II (clock & watch)	2113	44544533355	LNNNNNNCCFNNNNFNNFFNN	NNNN3NNNNNNNNN	R,J,T	051	613	06.04.30	7758	470408	92965
770.684-014	JEWEL-HOLE CORNERER (clock & watch)	2112	44544544355	LNNNNNNCCFFNNNNFNONNN	NNNN3NNNNNNNNN	R	051	613	06.02.30	7522	470408	93999
770.684-018	ROUGH OPENER, JEWEL HOLE (clock & watch)	2123	34433443355	LNNNNNNFFFNNNNFNFONN	NNNN3NNNNNNNNN	R,T	051	613	06.04.08	7522	000000	92965
770.685-010	FLAT SURFACER, JEWEL (clock & watch)	2123	44544533355	LNNNNNNFFFNNNNFNFONN	NNNN3NNNNNNNNN	R,J,T	051	613	06.04.08	7522	470408	92998
770.685-014	JEWEL GRINDER I (clock & watch)	2123	44544553355	LNNNNNNFFFNNNNFNFONN	NNNN3NNNNNNNNN	R,J,T	051	613	06.04.08	7522	470408	92998

DOT #	DOT Title & Industry	Trng	Aptitude	Physical	Environment	Tempra	WkF	MPSMS	GOE	SOC	CIP	OES
770.685-018	JEWEL-BEARING GRINDER (clock & watch)	3224	34433533355	LNNNNNNFFNNNNNFONN	NNNN3NNNNNNNNNN	R,J,T	051	613	06.04.08	7522	470408	92998
770.685-022	JEWEL-BEARING POLISHER (clock & watch)	3224	34433533355	LNNNNNNFFNNNNFNFONN	NNNN3NNNNNNNNNN	R,J,T	051	613	06.04.08	7522	470408	92998
770.685-026	JEWEL-CORNER-BRUSHING-MACHINE OPERATOR (clock & watch)	2113	44443533355	LNNNNNNFFNNNNFNFONN	NNNN3NNNNNNNNNN	R,J	051	613	06.04.08	7522	470408	92965
770.685-030	JEWEL-CUPPING-MACHINE OPERATOR (clock & watch)	2123	44443433345	LNNNNNNFFNNNNFNFNN	NNNN4NNNNNNNNNN	R,J	051	613	06.04.08	7518	470408	92965
770.685-034	TURNER, MACHINE (clock & watch)	3124	34433533355	LNNNNNNFFOONNNFNFNN	NNNN4NNNNNNNNNN	R,T	051	613	06.04.08	7522	470408	92965
770.687-010	ARTIFICIAL-PEARL MAKER (jewelry-silver.)	1112	44544544455	LNNNNNNFFNNNNNCNFNNN	NNNN3NNNNNNNNNN	R	054	611	06.04.33	7740	470408	93999
770.687-014	DIAMOND SIZER AND SORTER (clock & watch; jewelry-silver.)	3224	34343443455	SNNNNNNFFNNNNFNFNN	NNNN3NNNNNNNNNN	J,T	221	611	06.03.02	7850	470408	83005
770.687-018	JEWEL GAUGER (clock & watch)	3224	34432443355	SNNNNNNCCNNNNCNCNN	NNNN3NNNNNNNNNN	R,J,T	212	613	06.03.02	7850	470408	83005
770.687-022	JEWEL INSPECTOR (clock & watch)	3324	34324232355	SNNNNNNCCCNNNNCNNCNN	NNNN3NNNNNNNNNN	R,T	212	613	06.03.02	7850	470408	83005
770.687-026	JEWEL STRINGER (clock & watch)	2112	44543533255	SNNNNNNCCNNNNCNCNN	NNNN3NNNNNNNNNN	R	061	613	06.04.30	8769	000000	98999
770.687-030	PULVERIZER (jewelry-silver.)	2112	44554544354	LNNNNNNFFOONNNFNFNON	NNNN4NNNNNNNNNN	R	142	611	06.04.34	8769	470408	98999
770.687-034	ROCK BREAKER (retail trade; stonework)	2112	44443534354	LNNNNNNFFNNNNNFNFN	NNNN3NNNNNNNNNN	R,T	142	539	05.12.07	7759	000000	93999
771.137-010	SUPERVISOR, SLATE SPLITTING (stonework)	3225	33344344455	LONNNNNNFFNNFFNFNNNN	NNNN4NNNNNNNNNN	D,P,J	054	537	06.04.01	7100	000000	81008
771.281-010	STENCIL CUTTER (stonework)	4226	33432433355	MNNNNNNCCCNNNNCNNCNN	NNNN4NNNNNNNNNN	J,T	241	537	01.06.01	6862	000000	89908
771.281-014	STONE CARVER (stonework)	4448	23222322255	MNNOOONCCOFNNNNCNFCNN	NNNN4NCNNNNNNNNN	E,J	052	537	01.06.02	6861	000000	89905
771.381-010	STONECUTTER APPRENTICE, HAND (stonework)	4337	34422433255	MNNOOONCCFFNNNCNFONN	ONNN4FONNNNNNNN	J	052	537	05.05.01	6861	000000	89905
771.381-014	STONECUTTER, HAND (stonework)	4337	34422433255	MNNOOONCCFFNNNCNFONN	ONNN4FONNNNNNNN	J	052	537	05.05.01	6861	000000	89905
771.384-010	COPER, HAND (stonework)	3123	34434434355	HNNNNNNFFOONNNFNFNNN	NNNN4NNNNNNNNNN	J,T	052	537	06.02.30	7753	000000	93926
771.484-010	BEVELER (stonework)	3225	34433434355	HNNNNNNFFOONNNFNFNNN	NNNN4NNNNNNNNNN	R,T	051	537	06.02.30	7758	000000	93953
771.684-010	ROCK SPLITTER (stonework)	3116	34434534355	HNNNNNNCCOONNNNFNFNN	NNNN4FONNNNNNNN	J,T	053	537	05.12.07	7753	000000	93926
772.281-010	GLASS BLOWER, LABORATORY APPARATUS (glass products; inst. & app.)	4238	33322433343	MNNNNNNFFONNOFNOFN	NNNN3NOCNNNNNOO	V,T,J	133	531	05.05.11	6861	000000	89905
772.381-010	GLASS BENDER (fabrication, nec)	4338	33422422254	MNNNNNNFFONNNFNFNFN	NNNN3NNNNNNNNNN	J,T	133	531	01.06.02	6861	000000	89905
772.381-014	PATTERNMAKER (fabrication, nec)	4348	33332433354	LNNNNNNFFNNNNFFOON	NNNN3NNNNNNNNNN	J	241	559	01.06.03	6862	000000	89908
772.381-018	WARE FINISHER (glass mfg.)	3226	34433533355	LNNFNNNNFFNNNNFNFNNN	NNNN3NNNNNNNNNN	J	136	531	06.01.04	6861	000000	89905
772.381-022	GLASS BLOWER (glass mfg.)	3227	34433433344	LNNONNNNCCCNNNNFNFOO	NNFN4NNNNNNNNNF	J,T	136	531	06.01.04	6861	000000	89905
772.482-010	GLASS-BLOWING-LATHE OPERATOR (glass products)	3236	33322433233	LNNNNNNFFNNNNFNFNFN	NNFN3NNNNNNNNNF	R,T	136	531	06.02.08	7679	000000	92998
772.684-010	DEFECT REPAIRER, GLASSWARE (glass mfg.)	2123	44443433354	LNNFNNNNFFNNNNFNNNON	NNNN3NNNNNNNNNN	J,R,T	131	531	05.09.03	7755	000000	93999
772.684-014	HOT-WIRE GLASS-TUBE CUTTER (glass products)	2112	44444334355	LNNNNNNNFFONNNNFNFN	NNNN3NNNNNNNNNF	R	082	531	06.04.30	7755	000000	93999
772.684-018	WARM-IN WORKER (glass mfg.)	3113	44543534353	SNNNNNNFFNNNNFNFNFN	NNFN4NNNNNNNNNF	R,J,T	133	531	06.04.30	7754	489999	93944
772.684-022	WATCH-CRYSTAL MOLDER (glass products)	3114	34434544355	LNNNNNNFFFFFFFNFOON	NNFN3NNNNNNNNNN	R,T	132	532	06.02.32	7754	489999	93944
772.687-010	GLASS-WORKER, PRESSED OR BLOWN (glass mfg.)	2122	44443433344	SNNNNNNFFNNNNFNFNNN	NNFN4NNNNNNNNNF	R,T	132	535	06.02.30	7755	000000	93956
772.687-014	SPOTTER (glass mfg.)	2122	44443544355	LNNONNNNFFNNNNFNFNON	NNNO4NNNNNNNNNN	R,J	241	531	06.02.30	7755	000000	92998
773.131-010	PASTER SUPERVISOR (brick & tile)	4237	33433433353	MNNNNNNFFNNFFNNFNFN	NNNN4NNNNNNNNNN	V,D,P,J	061	534	06.03.01	7820	000000	83005
773.381-010	TILE DECORATOR (brick & tile)	3234	33333433353	LNNNNNNFFOONNNFNFNNN	NNNN4NNNNNNNNNN	T,J	212	535	06.04.30	7820	000000	83005
773.487-010	CLAY-STAIN MIXER (brick & tile)	3223	34344334353	MNNNNNNFFNNNNFNFNFN	NNNN4NNNNNNNNNN	R,J,T	143	496	06.04.34	7664	489999	92965
773.684-014	PASTER (brick & tile)	3234	34432433342	MNNONNNNFFNNNNFNFNN	NNNN3NNNNNNNNNN	R,T	153	534	01.06.03	7756	000000	93947
773.687-010	PASTING INSPECTOR (brick & tile)	2113	34433433353	MNNNNNNCCFNNNNFNFNN	NNNN4NNNNNNNNNN	R,T	061	534	06.04.30	7756	000000	93947
774.130-010	SUPERVISOR, CLAY SHOP (pottery & porc.)	2114	44444434353	LNNNNNNFFFFFFNFOON	NNNN4NNNNNNNNNN	R,J,T	063	534	06.03.02	7820	000000	83005
774.381-010	THROWER (pottery & porc.)	4337	33333333354	LNNNNNNFFFFFFNFOON	NNNF3NNNNNNNNNN	V,D,P,J	136	535	06.01.01	7100	000000	81008
774.382-010	POTTERY-MACHINE OPERATOR (pottery & porc.)	3237	34422522224	MNNNNNNFFONNNNFFNNN	NNNF3NNNNNNNNNN	R,J,T	136	535	06.02.30	6861	000000	89905
774.384-010	INSPECTOR II (pottery & porc.)	3225	34433433344	MNNNNNNFFONNNNFNFOON	NNNO4NNNNNNNNNN	R,J,T	136	535	06.02.08	6861	000000	92998
774.684-010	BISQUE CLEANER (pottery & porc.)	2115	33332333353	LNNFNNNNFFFFNNNNFOFN	NNNO4NNNNNNNNNN	T,J	212	535	06.03.01	7820	000000	83005
774.684-014	DIPPER (pottery & porc.)	2114	34433433354	LNNNNNNFFFFFNNNNFNFOON	NNNN3NNNNNNNNNN	R,J,T	051	535	06.04.30	7759	000000	93999
774.684-018	FINISHER (pottery & porc.)	3115	34433433354	LNNONNNNFFFONNNFNFNNN	NNNN3NNNNNNNNNN	R,T	151	535	06.02.30	7756	000000	93947
774.684-022	HANDLER (pottery & porc.)	2114	34434433354	LNNONNNNFFFONNNFNFN	NNFF4NFNNNNNNFN	R,T	051	535	06.04.30	7759	000000	93999
774.684-026	PLASTER-DIE MAKER (pottery & porc.)	3115	34443433355	LNNNNNNFFFFFNNNNFNFNNN	NNNF3NNNNNNNNNN	R,T	063	535	06.04.30	7720	000000	93999
774.684-030	SAGGER MAKER (pottery & porc.)	2113	44443534355	HNNONNNNFFFFNNNNFFNNN	NNNF3NNNNNNNNNN	R,T	132	536	06.02.30	7754	000000	93944
774.684-034	STICKER-ON (nonmet. min.)	2112	44543533355	LNNNNNNFFFONNNFNFNNN	NNNF3NNNNNNNNNN	R,T	061	535	06.04.30	7755	000000	93999
774.684-038	TURNER (pottery & porc.)	3226	34433434355	MNNNNNNFFONNNFNFNNN	NNNN3NNNNNNNNNN	R,J,T	055	535	06.02.30	7755	000000	93999
774.684-042	WARE DRESSER (pottery & porc.)	3114	34543533343	LNNNNNNCCFFNNNFNFOFN	NNNN4NNNNNNNNNNF	R,J,T	051	535	06.04.30	7677	000000	92965

DOT #	DOT Title & Industry	Trng	Aptitude	Physical	Environment	Tempra	WkF	MPSMS	GOE	SOC	CIP	OES
774.684-046	PATCHER (pottery & porc.)	2113	44443433454	LNNNNNNCCCNNNNNCNCNON	NNNO3NNNNNNNN	R	136	535	06.04.30	7720	489999	93999
774.687-010	BISQUE GRADER (pottery & porc.)	3233	44443444354	LNNNNNNCCCCNNNFNFON	NNNN2NNNNNNNN	R,T	221	535	06.03.02	7850	000000	83005
774.687-014	LACER (nonmet. min.)	2112	44543542355	SNNNNNNFFNNNNFNNN	NNNN3NNNNNNNN	R	136	535	06.04.30	7740	000000	93999
774.687-018	PRINT INSPECTOR (pottery & porc.)	3114	34333434353	LNNNNNNNFFNNNNFNFN	NNNO3NNNNNNNN	R,J,T	212	535	06.03.02	7820	000000	83005
774.687-022	WARE CLEANER (pottery & porc.)	2112	44543533454	LNNOONNFFFONNNFNFNON	NNNO3NNNNNNNN	R	031	535	06.04.30	8769	000000	98999
774.687-026	TESTER (pottery & porc.)	2112	44444444454	HNNONNNFFNNNNFNNNFN	NNNO3NNNNNNNN	R	212	525	06.03.02	7830	489999	83005
775.130-010	SUPERVISOR, FINISHING (glass mfg.)	4338	33433433355	LNNNNNNFFFNNFNNONN	NNNN3NNNNNNNN	D,J,P	051	531	06.02.01	7100	000000	81008
775.131-010	SUPERVISOR, CONCRETE-STONE FINISHING (concrete prod.)	4337	33333333344	LNNONONFFFOFFNFNONN	ONNN4NNNNNNNN	D,J,P	102	536	05.05.01	7100	000000	81008
775.134-010	CUTTING SUPERVISOR (glass products)	4436	33323333355	MNFNNNNFFFONNFNFNN	NNNN4NNNNNNNN	D,P,T,V	054	531	06.02.01	7100	000000	81008
775.281-010	SURFACE-PLATE FINISHER (stonework)	4437	34333433355	MNNNNNNFFFONNNFNFONN	NNNN3NNNNNNNN	J,T	051	537	05.05.01	6869	000000	92965
775.381-010	ENGRAVER (glass products)	3226	34442423355	MNNNONNNFFFONNNFNFNN	NNNN3NNNNNNNNF	J,T	183	531	01.06.01	6863	000000	89911
775.381-014	GLASS DECORATOR (glass mfg.; glass products)	4336	34323432255	LNNONNNFFFONONFNFFNN	NNNN4NNNNNNNN	T	051	531	01.06.01	6863	000000	89911
775.382-010	GLASS GRINDER, LABORATORY APPARATUS (glass products; inst. & app.)	3125	34333434345	LNNNNNNNFFONNNONFONN	NNNN3NNCNNNNN	T	051	531	06.02.08	7677	000000	93999
775.584-010	GLASS CALIBRATOR (glass products)	3223	33332433355	LNNNNNNFFFNNNNFNNN	NNNN3NNNNNNNN	V,T	182	531	06.02.31	7720	000000	93953
775.584-014	GLASS FINISHER, HAND (stonework)	2114	34433534354	MNNNNNNFFFNNNNFNFOON	NNNC4NCNNNNNN	R,T	051	537	06.04.30	7758	000000	93953
775.664-010	STONE POLISHER, HAND (stonework)	3225	34432434345	HNNONNNFFFNNNNFNNNN	NNNC4NCNNNNNNNC	J,R,T	051	531	06.02.30	7677	000000	92965
775.684-010	BEVELER (glass mfg.; glass products)	2222	34432434345	HNNFNNNFFFNNNNFNFFNN	NNNN4NNNNNNNN	R,T	051	531	06.04.30	7758	000000	93953
775.684-014	EDGER, HAND (glass mfg.; glass products)	2113	44443434355	HNNNNNNFFFNNFNFNNN	NNNN4NNNNNNNN	R,T	051	532	06.04.30	7677	000000	92965
775.684-018	EDGER, TOUCH-UP (glass products)	3114	34443433355	HNNONNNCCFNNONCNFFNO	NNNN3NNNNNNNNO	R,T	054	531	06.02.30	7753	469999	93926
775.684-022	GLASS CUTTER (any industry)	3225	34433534355	LNNNNNNFFFONNNFNFNNN	NNNN3NNNNNNNN	R,T	054	531	06.04.30	7753	469999	93926
775.684-026	GLASS FINISHER (glass products)	3226	34434534355	SNNNNNNNFFFNNNNFNFNNN	NNNN3NNNNNNNN	R,T	051	532	06.02.30	7677	000000	92965
775.684-030	GLASS GRINDER (glass products)	2222	44544544355	LNNFNNNFFFNNNNFNNN	NNNN3NNNNNNNN	R,T	051	531	06.04.30	7677	000000	93953
775.684-034	GLASS GRINDER (glass mfg.)	2123	44443434355	MNNNNNNNCCFNNNNFNNNN	NNNN3NNNNNNNNC	R,T	051	531	06.04.30	7758	000000	93953
775.684-038	GLASS POLISHER (glass mfg.)	2113	44443534355	MNNNNNNNFFFNNNNFNFONN	NNNF4NNNNNNNNF	R,T	051	531	06.04.30	7677	000000	92965
775.684-042	GLASS SANDER, BELT (glass products)	2123	44443433355	SNNNNNNNFFFNNNNFNFNNN	NNNN4NNNNNNNN	R,T	051	552	06.04.30	7753	000000	93926
775.684-046	LEVEL-VIAL MARKER (cutlery-hrdwr.)	3233	34433333355	MNNNNNNNFFFNNNNFNNN	NNNN4NNNNNNNN	V,J,T	241	531	06.02.31	7759	000000	93999
775.684-050	MARK-UP DESIGNER (glass mfg.)	1112	44543534345	MNNNNNNNCCOFNNNNFNNNN	NNNN4NCNNNNNNNC	R,T	051	537	06.04.30	7758	000000	93953
775.684-054	PATCH SANDER (stonework)	2114	44443434355	HNNONONFFFNNNNFNFNNN	NNNO4NNNNNNNNF	R,T	051	531	06.04.30	7677	000000	93953
775.684-058	POLISHER (glass mfg.; glass products)	2124	34434544355	SNNNNNNNFFNNNNNNNNN	NNNN4NNNNNNNN	R,T	051	532	06.04.30	7677	000000	93953
775.684-062	WATCH-CRYSTAL EDGE GRINDER (glass products)	2112	44444444345	LNNNNNNNFFONNNNNNNN	NNNN3NNNNNNNN	R	051	532	06.04.08	7678	000000	92944
775.685-010	CUTTING-MACHINE TENDER, DECORATIVE (glass mfg.)	2112	44533533354	MNNONNNFFOONNNFNFNON	NNNN3NNNNNNNN	R,T	031	538	06.04.30	7759	000000	93999
775.687-010	FINISHER (nonmet. min.)	2122	44443443355	LNNNNNNNFFNNNNFNNNNN	NNNN3NNNNNNNN	R,T	053	531	06.04.30	7759	000000	93999
775.687-014	GLASS DRILLER (glass mfg.)	2123	44443444355	HNNFNNNFFFNNNNFNFNN	NNNN4NNNNNNNN	R,T	054	531	06.04.30	8618	469999	98999
775.687-018	GLASS-CUTTER HELPER (any industry)	2112	44443433354	SNNNNNNNFFFNNNNFNNN	NNNN3NNNNNNNN	R	051	535	06.04.24	8769	000000	98999
775.687-022	GOLD BURNISHER (pottery & porc.)	3224	34443493354	MNNONNNFFFOONNNFNFNON	NNNN3NNNNNNNN	J,T	212	538	06.03.01	7820	000000	83005
776.487-010	GRINDING-WHEEL INSPECTOR (nonmet. min.)	3234	34443343355	LNNNNNNCCCFFNCNNNNNN	NNNN3NCNNNNNNN	J	212	538	06.03.02	7820	000000	83005
776.667-010	INSPECTOR (nonmet. min.)	2122	44444443355	MNNFNONFFFFNNNNFFNN	NNNN4NFNNNNNNN	R,T	054	538	06.04.34	7740	000000	93956
776.684-010	BELT MAKER (nonmet. min.)	2123	44543444355	MNNONNNCCFFNNNNFNNNN	NNNN4NFNNNNNNN	J,R	102	538	05.10.04	6140	000000	85128
776.684-014	POLISHING-WHEEL SETTER (any industry)	1111	44443443355	LNNNNNNFFFNNNNNFOONN	NNNN4NNNNNNNN	R,T	063	538	06.04.38	8620	000000	98999
776.687-010	BELT-MAKER HELPER (nonmet. min.)	4445	22323433353	MNNNNNNCCCNNNNFOFFNN	NNNN2NNNNNNNN	J,E	136	539	01.06.09	6861	000000	89908
777.081-010	MODELER (brick & tile)	4338	33322433355	MNNONNNFFFFFNNNNFFNN	NNNO3NNNNNNNN	V,D,P,J	132	536	06.01.01	7100	520205	81008
777.131-010	SUPERVISOR, MOLD SHOP (pottery & porc.)	5337	23322432254	LNNNNNNFFFNNNFONN	NNNN3NNNNNNNN	E,J	102	619	01.06.02	6861	489999	89908
777.261-010	MODEL MAKER I (any industry)	4227	23322422255	HNNNNNNNFFFNNNFFFNN	ONNN2NNNNNNNN	E,J	136	539	01.06.02	6861	000000	89908
777.281-010	CONCRETE SCULPTOR (concrete prod.)	4327	23322332255	LNNFOFNFFFNNNNFNONN	NNNO4NFNNNNNNN	J,E	136	535	01.06.02	6862	000000	89908
777.281-014	MODEL MAKER (pottery & porc.)	4447	23222333354	MOOOOOOFFOONNNFNOOON	NNNO4NFONONNFN	V,T,J	241	568	06.01.04	6862	000000	89908
777.281-018	PATTERNMAKER, PLASTER (aircraft mfg.)	4327	33322433254	MNNFOFNFFOONNNFNFOON	NNNN4NNNNNNNN	V,T,J	136	519	05.05.11	6862	000000	89908
777.361-010	EAR-MOLD LABORATORY TECHNICIAN (plastic prod.)	4338	33322433244	MNNNNNNFFFFNNNFNFOON	CNNN3NNNNNNNN	J,T	136	539	01.06.02	6862	000000	89908
777.381-010	MODEL MAKER, FIBERGLASS (concrete prod.)	4226	33322333255	LNNNNNNFFFNNNNFNNN	NNNN3NNNNNNNN	J,T	136	534	01.06.02	6862	000000	89908
777.381-014	MODEL-AND-MOLD MAKER (brick & tile)	4337	34432433355	LNNFOFNFFFNNNNFNONN	NNNF3NNNNNNNN	V,J,T	136	536	01.06.04	6861	000000	89908
777.381-018	MODEL-AND-MOLD MAKER, PLASTER (concrete prod.)	3127	34433433255	LNNNNNNFFFNNNNFNNNN	NNNN3NNNNNNNN	J,T	136	536	06.01.04	6861	000000	89905
777.381-022	MOLD MAKER II (jewelry-silver.)	4337	33333433355	MONFOONFFFONNNFNFNN	NNNN4NONNNNNNN	J,T	241	536	06.02.30	6861	470408	89905
777.381-034	PLASTER MOLDER I (foundry)	4337	33333433355	MONFOONFFFONNNFNFNN	NNNN4NONNNNNNN	J,T	241	536	06.02.30	6861	000000	89905

DOT #	DOT Title & Industry	Trng	Aptitude	Physical	Environment	Tempra	WkF	MPSMS	GOE	SOC	CIP	OES
777.381-038	PLASTER-PATTERN CASTER (machine tools)	4337	33332433254	MNNNNNFFNNNNFNNFNNFNFON	NNNN4NNNNNNNNNN	J,T	132	536	01.06.02	6861	000000	89905
777.381-042	RELIEF-MAP MODELER (any industry)	4336	33432433354	LNNNONFFFNNNNNFNNN	NNNN3NNNNNNNNNN	J,T	102	536	01.06.02	6862	000000	89908
777.381-046	SAND TESTER (foundry)	3226	34343333355	LONONONFFONNNFNNNN	NNNN4NNNNNNNNNN	J,T	212	345	06.01.05	6881	000000	83002
777.684-010	FORM MAKER, PLASTER (plastic prod.)	3224	44445354355	HNNNNNNFFONNNNNNNN	NNNO4NNNNNNNNNN	R,T	132	536	06.02.30	7667	000000	92971
777.684-014	MOLD MAKER (nonmet. min.)	3125	44443533355	LNNOOONFFOONNNFNFNNN	NNNO3NNNNNNNNNO	R,T	132	538	06.02.30	7754	489999	93944
777.684-018	MOLD MAKER (pottery & porc.)	3126	34433433355	HNNOOONFFONNNFNFFNN	NNNO3NNNNNNNNNO	J,T	132	536	06.02.30	7754	489999	93944
779.131-010	SUPERVISOR I (nonmet. min.)	4338	33323333354	LNNOOONFFOFFNFNFOON	NNNO3NNNNNNNNN	D,P,J,T	132	538	01.06.02	7100	000000	81008
779.281-010	CLAY MODELER (any industry)	4347	23322432254	LNNONNNFFNNNNFNFOON	NNNN3NNNNNNNNN	V,J,T	136	539	01.06.02	6861	000000	89908
779.381-010	GLAZIER, STAINED GLASS (glass products)	4337	33423433341	MNNFNNNFFONNNFNFOFN	NNNN3NNNNNNNNN	J,T	102	532	01.06.02	6862	469999	89908
779.381-014	MOSAIC WORKER (glass products; nonmet. min.)	3225	34433443353	LNNNNNNFFFNNNNFNFFN	NNNO3NNNNNNNNNNF	R,J,T	092	530	01.06.02	6863	000000	89911
779.381-018	REPAIRER, ART OBJECTS (any industry)	4337	33422442253	SNNNNNNFFFNNNNFNFOFN	NNNN2NNNNNNNNN	V,J,T	102	539	01.06.02	6179	000000	85999
779.381-022	TRACER (construction; stonework)	4337	33333433355	HNNONNNFFFNONNFNFONN	NNNN4NNNNNNNNNN	J,T	241	537	01.06.02	6863	000000	89911
779.387-010	FINAL INSPECTOR (glass products)	3225	34433444355	MNNONNNFFONNNFNFNNN	NNNN4NNNNNNNNNN	J	212	531	06.03.01	7820	000000	83005
779.387-014	INSPECTOR I (concrete prod.)	3226	34334344455	LONONONFFOONONFNQONN	NNNN4NNNNNNNNNN	J,T	212	536	06.03.01	7820	000000	83005
779.584-010	PATTERNMAKER (glass products)	3226	34433433354	LNNNNNNFFFNNNNFNFNNN	NNNN3NNNNNNNNN	R,T	241	532	06.02.31	7753	000000	93926
779.681-010	MICA SPLITTER (mine & quarry)	3234	34333432354	SNNNNNNCCFNNNNNQNFFON	NNNN3NNNNNNNNNNF	R,J,T	054	349	06.04.30	7753	000000	93926
779.684-010	CEMENT FITTINGS MAKER (concrete prod.)	2124	34433434355	HNNFOFNFFNNNNNONFNNN	NNNN3NNNNNNNNN	R,T	132	536	06.04.32	7754	000000	93944
779.684-014	CONCRETE-PIPE MAKER (concrete prod.)	2122	44554544335	HNNFFFOFONNNNNNOFNNN	CNNN4NNNNNNNNNN	R,T	132	536	06.04.32	7754	000000	93944
779.684-018	FETTLER (brick & tile)	2113	44443433355	LNNOOONFFOONNNFNCCNN	NNNN4NCNNNNNNN	R,T	051	534	06.04.30	7759	000000	93999
779.684-022	GLASS CUTTER, OVAL OR CIRCULAR (glass mfg.)	2123	44433534355	MNNONNNFFONNNNFNFNNN	NNNN3NNNNNNNNNF	R,T	054	531	06.04.30	7753	469999	93926
779.684-026	GLASS-LINED TANK REPAIRER (beverage)	3123	34433534355	LONOFFOFFONNNFOFNNNN	NONF3FNNNNNNNNN	R,T	102	539	05.10.01	6140	489999	85128
779.684-030	INSPECTOR-REPAIRER, SANDSTONE (stonework)	3223	34433433354	VNNNNNNFFOFNNNCNFNON	NNNN4NCNNNNNNN	R,J,T	051	537	05.10.01	7758	000000	93953
779.684-034	LEVEL-VIAL SEALER (cutlery-hrdwr.)	2112	44442433355	SNNNNNNFFFNNNNFNFONN	NNNN3NNNNNNNNNF	R,T	131	552	06.04.30	7759	000000	93999
779.684-038	MIRROR SPECIALIST (glass products; wood prod., nec)	2113	44444433355	HNNFNONFFOONNNNFOFNNN	NNNN4NNNNNNNNN	R,T	011	531	06.04.08	7678	000000	92944
779.684-042	PIPE FINISHER (brick & tile)	2113	34443434355	MNNNNNNFFFNNNNFNFNNN	NNNO4NNNNNNNNNN	R,T	051	534	06.04.30	7753	000000	93926
779.684-046	PLASTER MAKER (nonmet. min.)	3125	34443534354	MNNONONFFOONNNONONON	NNNF3NNNNNNNNNO	R,J,T	132	538	06.02.30	7759	489999	93944
779.684-050	PLASTIC MOLDER (fabrication, nec)	3123	34433533355	LNNNNNNFFFNNNNFNFNNN	NNNN3NNNNNNNNN	R,T	136	519	06.02.32	7754	000000	93944
779.684-054	SECOND CUTTER (glass mfg.)	2223	44443434355	MNNNNNNFFFONNNFNFONN	NNNN4NNNNNNNNN	R,J,T	054	531	06.04.30	7753	000000	93926
779.684-058	STONE REPAIRER (stonework)	3235	34433433354	LNNNNNNFFFONONFNFOOO	NNNN4NNNNNNNNNN	R,J,T	102	537	05.10.01	6413	460101	87305
779.687-010	BREAKER (glass products)	2112	44544534355	LNNNNNNFFFNNNNNCNFNNN	NNNN3NNNNNNNNC	R	054	531	06.04.30	7759	000000	93999
779.687-014	CARTRIDGE LOADER (elec. equip.)	1111	44554544455	LNNNFNONFFFNFNFNFFN	NNNN3NNNNNNNNN	R	041	583	06.04.34	7740	000000	93999
779.687-018	GLASS-BULB SILVERER (glass products)	1112	44554544455	SNNNNNNCCNNNNNNFNNNN	NNNN3NNNNNNNNN	R	151	532	06.04.33	7756	000000	93947
779.687-022	INSPECTOR, GLASS OR MIRROR (glass products)	3224	34442444355	MNNONONCCCONONCNFCNN	NNNN4NNNNNNNNNO	J,T	212	531	06.03.02	7820	000000	83005
779.687-026	MICA INSPECTOR (mine & quarry)	3224	34433433354	SNNNNNNCCCNNNNCNCNNN	NNNN4NNNNNNNNN	R,J,T	212	580	06.03.02	7820	000000	83005
779.687-030	MICA SIZER (mine & quarry)	2213	44443433355	MNNFFFNFFOFFNNNNFNNN	NNNN4NNNNNNNNN	R,T	054	580	06.04.30	7753	000000	93926
779.687-034	STOCK SHEETS CLEANER-INSPECTOR (glass products)	3224	44443433355	MNNFFFNFFONNNFNFNNF	NNNN4NNNNNNNNN	R,J,T	212	532	06.03.02	7759	000000	93999
779.687-038	WAXER (glass products)	1112	44544544355	SNNNNNNFFNNNNNFNNNN	NNNN3NNNNNNNNN	R	153	532	06.04.33	8769	000000	98999
780.131-010	SUPERVISOR, CUTTING-AND-SEWING DEPARTMENT (furniture)	4338	33333333353	MNNNNNNFFOFFNNNNFOFN	NNNN4NNNNNNNNNN	V,D,P,J	054	420	06.02.01	7100	200501	81008
780.131-014	SUPERVISOR, UPHOLSTERY DEPARTMENT (any industry)	4337	33332433253	LNNFNONFFFFNFNFFFN	NNNN3NNNNNNNNN	V,D,P	054	460	06.01.01	7100	000000	81008
780.134-010	SUPERVISOR, COVERING AND LINING (fabrication, nec)	4228	33433433344	MNNONONFFNFNFNNFNFOFN	NNNN4NNNNNNNNN	D,J	101	460	06.02.01	7100	520205	81008
780.134-014	SUPERVISOR, SPRING-UP (furniture)	4337	33443533354	MNNONONFFONOONFNNNON	NNNN4NNNNNNNNNO	R,T	102	619	06.02.01	7100	520205	81008
780.137-010	SUPERVISOR, MATTRESS AND BOXSPRINGS (furniture)	4227	33443434355	LNNNNNNFFOFFNNNOONN	NNNN4NNNNNNNNN	D,J,P,V	102	462	06.02.01	7100	200501	81008
780.381-010	AUTOMOBILE UPHOLSTERER (automotive ser.)	4236	33333433344	MNNFFFNFFOONNNFNNOON	NNNN3NNNNNNNNN	V,D,P,J	101	464	06.02.01	7100	520205	81008
780.381-014	AUTOMOBILE-UPHOLSTERER APPRENTICE (automotive ser.)	3236	33333433344	MNNFFFNFFONNNFNFOON	NNNN3NNNNNNNNN	R,T	101	591	05.05.15	6853	480303	89508
780.381-018	FURNITURE UPHOLSTERER (any industry)	4337	33322433253	MNNFOONFFFNNNNFFFN	NNNN4NNNNNNNNN	J,T	101	591	05.05.15	6853	200501	89508
780.381-022	FURNITURE-UPHOLSTERER APPRENTICE (any industry)	4337	33322433253	MNNFOONFFFNNNFNFFN	NNNN4NNNNNNNNN	J,T	101	460	05.05.15	6853	480303	89508
780.381-026	UPHOLSTERER, LIMOUSINE AND HEARSE (auto. mfg.)	3235	34333433345	MNNOOONFFFNNNNFNFNNN	NNNN3NNNNNNNNN	J,V	101	591	06.02.27	6854	480399	89511
780.381-030	PAD HAND (leather prod.)	3235	34433534354	LNNFOONFFNNNNFNFNFN	NNNN3NNNNNNNNN	R,T	102	529	06.02.32	6853	480399	92705
780.381-034	SLIPCOVER CUTTER (retail trade; tex. prod., nec)	3236	33333432353	LNNFOONFFNNNFNFNFN	NNNN3NNNNNNNNN	J,T	054	435	05.05.15	6853	480303	89508
780.381-038	UPHOLSTERER, INSIDE (furniture)	3336	34433433344	MNNFNONCCCFNNNFNFFFN	NNNN4NNNNNNNNN	J,T	101	460	06.02.27	6853	200501	89508
780.384-010	AUTOMOBILE-SEAT-COVER-AND-CONVERTIBLE-TOP INSTALLER (automotive ser.)	3336	34443433344	MNNFOONFFFONNNFNFNON	NNNN3NNNNNNNNN	J,T	101	591	05.05.15	7720	480303	93956

DOT #	DOT Title & Industry	Trng	Aptitude	Physical	Environment	Tempra	WkF	MPSMS	GOE	SOC	CIP	OES
780.384-014	UPHOLSTERER (aircraft mfg.)	3236	33343433343	MNNONNNFFNNNNFNOOON	NNNN4NNFNNNNNNNN	T,V	101	592	06.02.32	7654	000000	89508
780.587-010	SORTER, UPHOLSTERY PARTS (furniture)	2123	44443444354	MNNFNNNCCFNNNNFNNNFN	NNNN3NNNNNNNNNN	R	221	420	06.03.02	7850	200501	83005
780.682-010	SEWING-MACHINE OPERATOR (furniture)	3114	44435333344	LNNNNNNCCFNNNNCNFFON	NNNN4NNNNNNNNNN	R,T	171	464	06.02.05	7655	480303	92721
780.682-014	SLIP-COVER SEWER (tex. prod., nec)	3114	34433433445	LNNNNNNCCCNNNNCNFFNN	NNNN4NNNNNNNNNN	R,T	171	435	06.02.05	7655	480303	92721
780.682-018	UPHOLSTERY SEWER (any industry)	3224	34439433344	LNNONNNCCONNNNCNNNON	NNNN3NNNNNNNNNN	R,T	171	420	06.02.05	7655	200501	92721
780.684-010	BACK PADDER (furniture)	2112	44444534344	LNNNNNNFFFNNNNFNFNNN	NNNN4NNNNNNNNNN	R,T	102	462	06.04.27	7720	200501	93956
780.684-014	BAND-TOP MAKER (furniture)	2113	44445543355	LNNFNNNFFNNNNFNFNNN	NNNN4NNNNNNNNNN	R,T	073	464	06.04.22	7720	480303	93956
780.684-018	BOX-SPRING MAKER I (furniture)	2113	34443433355	MNNNNNNCCFNNNNFNFNNN	NNNN4NNNNNNNNNN	T	101	464	06.04.34	7720	480303	93956
780.684-022	BOX-SPRING MAKER II (furniture)	2113	44543533355	HNNNNNNFFNNNNFNFNNN	NNNN4NNNNNNNNNN	T	101	464	06.04.22	7720	480303	93956
780.684-026	CASKET COVERER (fabrication, nec)	2113	34433433354	MNNNNONCCFNNNFNFNON	NNNN3NNNNNNNNNN	R,T	101	619	06.04.27	7720	480303	93956
780.684-030	CASKET LINER (fabrication, nec)	3113	34433433354	HNNONNNCCFNNONFNFNON	NNNN4NNNNNNNNNN	R,T	101	619	06.02.22	7720	200501	93956
780.684-034	CHAIR UPHOLSTERER (furniture)	3225	34433543354	MNNFNNNFFONNNFNFNON	NNNN3NNNNNNNNNN	R,T	101	462	06.02.27	7720	200501	93956
780.684-038	COTTON DISPATCHER (furniture)	2112	44445434355	MNNONNNFFFNNNNCNNNNN	NNNN3NNNNNNNNNN	R,T	054	433	06.04.27	7720	480303	93999
780.684-042	CRUSHER (fabrication, nec)	2112	44443433355	MNNFNFNCCFONNNONNNNN	NNNN4NNNNNNNNNN	R,T	032	619	06.04.27	7720	480303	93999
780.684-046	CUSHION BUILDER (furniture)	2113	34444533355	LNNNNNNFFNNNNFNFNNN	NNNN4NNNNNNNNNN	R,T	102	462	06.04.22	7720	200501	93956
780.684-054	CUSHION MAKER I (furniture)	2114	44433443344	HNNNNNNFFFNONFNNNFN	NNNN4NNONNNNNNNN	R,T	101	433	06.04.23	7720	200501	93956
780.684-058	EDGE ROLLER (furniture)	2113	34444533355	LNNNNNNFFFNNNNFNFNNN	NNNN3NNNNNNNNNN	R	102	462	06.04.22	7720	480303	93999
780.684-062	FABRICATOR, FOAM RUBBER (any industry)	2112	44444434355	LNNFNNNFFNNNNFNFNNN	NNNN4NNNNNNNNNN	R,T	054	519	06.04.29	7740	200501	93956
780.684-066	FILLER (tex. prod., nec)	2112	44444534455	LNNNNNNFFOONNNFNNNN	NNNN3NFNNNNNNNN	R	041	433	06.04.23	7740	200501	93956
780.684-070	MATTRESS FINISHER (furniture)	3223	44443433355	MNNNNNNFFFNNNCNFNNN	NNNN3NNNNNNNNNN	R,T	171	464	06.02.27	7759	480303	93999
780.684-074	MATTRESS MAKER (furniture)	3124	34433433355	MNNNNNNFFFNNNNFNFONN	NNNN3NNNNNNNNNN	R,T	102	464	06.02.27	7720	480303	93956
780.684-078	PADDER, CUSHION (furniture)	2113	34443543344	LNNNNNNFFONNNNFNFNON	NNNN3NNNNNNNNNN	R,T	102	433	06.04.22	7720	480303	93956
780.684-082	PANEL COVERER, METAL FURNITURE (furniture)	2112	44444444354	LNNNNNNFONNNNFNFNON	NNNN4NNNNNNNNNN	R,T	102	466	06.04.22	7720	480303	93999
780.684-086	PANEL MAKER (furniture)	2113	44434444354	LNNNNNNCCONNNNFNFNNN	NNNN3NNNNNNNNNN	R,T	102	462	06.04.27	7720	480303	93956
780.684-090	POCKETED-SPRING ASSEMBLER (furniture)	2113	44443433355	LNNNNNNFFNNNNFNFNNN	NNNN3NNNNNNNNNN	R,T	101	464	06.04.27	7720	480303	93956
780.684-094	SLIP-SEAT COVERER (furniture)	2113	44444534355	MNNNNNNCCFNNNNNNNNN	NNNN4NNNNNNNNNN	R,T	101	462	06.04.27	7720	480303	93956
780.684-098	SPRING ASSEMBLER (furniture)	2112	44444533355	MNNONNNFFFNNNNFNFNNN	NNNN3NNNNNNNNNN	R	061	464	06.04.22	7720	480303	93956
780.684-102	SPRING CLIPPER (furniture)	2123	44444444355	LNNNNNNCCNNNNNONFNNN	NNNN4NNNNNNNNNN	R,T	054	460	06.04.24	7759	480303	93999
780.684-106	SPRINGER (furniture)	3124	34433443355	HNNFNNNCCFNNNNFNFNNN	NNNN4NNNNNNNNNN	R,T	101	460	06.02.32	7720	480303	93956
780.684-110	TESTER, CONVERTIBLE SOFA BEDSPRING (furniture)	3124	34534533355	MNNONNNFFFNNNNFNFONN	NNNN4NNNNNNNNNN	J,T	102	464	06.02.24	7759	480303	93999
780.684-114	TRIMMING ASSEMBLER (furniture)	3223	34433544453	LNNNNNNFFOONNFNFNFN	NNNN4NNNNNNNNNN	J,T	212	462	06.02.23	7720	200501	93956
780.684-118	UPHOLSTERER, OUTSIDE (furniture)	3125	34433433354	MNNFNNNFFFNNNFNFNFN	NNNN3NNNNNNNNNN	R,T	101	460	06.04.27	7720	200501	93956
780.684-122	UPHOLSTERY REPAIRER (furniture)	3116	34433343354	MNNOOONFFFNNNCNFNON	NNNN3NNNNNNNNNN	R,T	101	460	05.05.15	6853	200501	89508
780.684-126	UPHOLSTERY TRIMMER (furniture)	2123	44434433354	MNNONNNCCCNNNNFNFNON	NNNN4NNNNNNNNNN	R,T	101	462	06.04.22	7720	480303	93999
780.684-130	WEBBING TACKER (furniture)	2113	44544533355	HNNNNFNCCONNNNFNFNNN	NNNN4NNNNNNNNNN	R,T	101	462	06.04.27	7740	480303	93956
780.684-134	UPHOLSTERER, ASSEMBLY LINE (furniture)	2113	44434343354	LNNNNNNCCFONNNFNFON	NNNN3NNNNNNNNNN	R,T	101	462	06.04.20	7720	200501	93956
780.685-010	MATTRESS-FILLING-MACHINE TENDER (furniture)	2112	44543544345	MNNNNNNFFNNNNFNFNNN	NNNN4NNNNNNNNNN	R	061	464	06.03.02	7820	480303	83005
780.685-014	STUFFING-MACHINE OPERATOR (furniture)	2123	44444443355	MNNONNNFFNNNONONNN	NNNN4NNNNNNNNNN	R	101	591	06.04.36	7662	480303	92974
780.685-018	WIRE-BORDER ASSEMBLER (furniture)	2113	34443534345	LNNNNNNFFFNNNNFNNNN	NNNN4NNNNNNNNNN	R,T	061	464	06.04.22	7720	480303	93956
780.687-010	BORDER MEASURER AND CUTTER (furniture)	1111	44444544355	LNNNNNNFFFNNNNFNNNN	NNNN4NNNNNNNNNN	R	054	464	06.04.27	7740	480303	93999
780.687-014	CLIPPER AND TURNER (furniture)	1112	44554544355	MNNNNNNFFNNNNNFNNNN	NNNN4NNNNNNNNNN	R	054	464	06.04.24	7740	480303	93999
780.687-018	HASSOCK MAKER (tex. prod., nec)	2112	44543433354	MNNNNNNFFNNNNFNFNNN	NNNN3NNNNNNNNNN	R,T	102	433	06.04.34	7720	200501	93956
780.687-022	INSPECTOR II (furniture)	2124	44543544345	LNNNNNNFFFNNNNFNNNN	NNNN4NNNNNNNNNN	R	061	464	06.03.02	7820	480303	83005
780.687-026	MATTRESS STRIPPER (furniture)	1114	44554544355	MNNFNNNFFFNNNONONNN	NNNN3NNNNNNNNNN	R	101	464	06.04.27	8769	480303	98999
780.687-030	MATTRESS-SPRING ENCASER (furniture)	2112	44443534355	LNNONNNCCONNONNNNN	NNNN4NNNNNNNNNN	R	102	435	06.04.22	7720	480303	93956
780.687-034	PADDING GLUER (furniture)	2112	44454534355	HNNFNFNCCONNNNFNFNNN	NNNN4NNNNNNNNNN	R	063	462	06.04.27	7720	480303	93999
780.687-038	SPRING COVERER (furniture)	2112	44544544355	HNNONNNFFFNNNNFNFNNN	NNNN4NNNNNNNNNN	R,T	101	462	06.04.27	7720	480303	93956
780.687-042	STAPLER, HAND (furniture)	2112	44544534355	MNNFNNNFFFNNNNFNFNNN	NNNN3NNNNNNNNNN	R	062	464	06.04.22	7720	480303	93956
780.687-046	STUFFER (tex. prod., nec)	1111	44545544455	LNNNONNNCONNONNNNN	NNNN4NNNNNNNNNN	R	041	435	06.04.23	7740	200501	93999
780.687-050	TUFTER, HAND (furniture)	2112	44544543354	HNNNNNNFFFNNNNFNFNNN	NNNN4NNNNNNNNNN	R	171	464	06.04.27	7740	480303	93999
780.687-054	UPHOLSTERER HELPER (any industry)	2113	44433533354	HNNONNNFFFNNNNNNON	NNNN3NNNNNNNNNON	R	101	460	06.04.27	8619	480303	98999

DOT #	DOT Title & Industry	Trng	Aptitude	Physical	Environment	Tempra	WkF	MPSMS	GOE	SOC	CIP	OES
780.687-058	UPHOLSTERY CLEANER (furniture)	2112	44544544354	MNNNFNONFFFONNNFNNNFN	NNNN4NFNNNNNNNN	R	031	462	06.04.39	8769	480303	98999
780.687-062	BACK TUFTER (furniture)	1112	45544454354	MNNCNNNNCCCNNNNCNNNCN	NNNN3NNNNNNNNNN	R,U	062	435	06.04.27	7720	480303	93999
780.687-066	INSPECTOR I (furniture)	3226	34433344355	MNNFNNNFFNNNNFNFNNN	NNNN3NNNNNNNNNN	T,J	101	462	06.03.02	7820	480303	83005
780.687-070	SKIRT PANEL ASSEMBLER (furniture)	2223	44544444345	LNNNNNNNFFFNNNNFNNNFN	NNNN4NNNNNNNNNN	R,U	032	420	06.04.27	7720	480303	93999
781.131-010	SUPERVISOR, PATTERN MARKING (garment)	4337	33333333455	LNNNNNNNFFNFFNFNFNN	NNNN3NNNNNNNNNN	D,J	241	449	05.03.02	7100	200303	81008
781.134-010	SUPERVISOR, CUTTING DEPARTMENT (any industry)	4336	33333333354	LNNQNONFFFOFFNFNOOON	NNNN4NNNNNNNNNN	D,J,P,T	054	420	06.02.01	7100	200303	81008
781.287-010	CLOTHING-PATTERN PREPARER (garment)	4436	34323344455	SNNNNNNFFFNNNFNNNNN	NNNN3NNNNNNNNNN	J,T	241	489	06.02.31	7759	200303	93999
781.361-010	ASSISTANT DESIGNER (garment)	3237	33422432354	LNNNNNNFFFONOONFNFFN	NNNN3NNNNNNNNNN	J,T	171	443	06.02.31	6821	200303	89502
781.361-014	PATTERNMAKER (furniture; garment; tex. prod., nec)	4336	33322332354	LNNONNNFFFNOONFNOFON	NNNN3NNNNNNNNNN	J,T	241	489	05.03.02	6856	200303	89502
781.381-010	CARTOON DESIGNER (tex. prod., nec)	4337	33322334463	SNNNNNNFFFNNNNFNNFFN	NNNN3NNNNNNNNNN	J,T	241	432	01.02.03	6856	500402	89502
781.381-018	LEATHER STAMPER (leather prod.)	3115	34432532353	LNNNNNNFFFNNNNCNFFFN	NNNN3NNNNNNNNNN	R,T	183	520	01.06.02	6884	480399	89511
781.381-022	PATTERN GRADER-CUTTER (garment)	3336	34332433355	LNNNNNNFFFNNONCNNFNN	NNNN3NNNNNNNNNN	J,T	241	489	05.03.02	6856	200303	89502
781.381-030	SAIL-LAY-OUT WORKER (tex. prod., nec)	4328	33323433354	MNNOFFFFFNNNNFOFOON	NNNN4NNNNNNNNNN	J,T	241	752	05.05.15	6856	490306	89502
781.381-034	GRADER MARKER (garment)	3236	34332433355	LNNOOONFFONNNNFNFFNN	NNNN3NNNNNNNNNN	J,T	054	479	05.03.02	6856	200303	89502
781.384-014	MARKER I (any industry)	3224	34333433354	LNNONNNFFFNNNNFNOOON	NNNN3NNNNNNNNNN	R,T	241	440	06.02.31	7759	200303	93999
781.384-018	SAIL CUTTER (tex. prod., nec)	3224	34433443354	LNNOFOOFFFNNNFONOOOF	NNNN4NNNNNNNNNN	R,T	054	436	06.02.27	7753	490306	93926
781.484-010	PLEAT PATTERNMAKER (garment; tex. prod., nec)	3325	34333443355	LNNNNNNFFFNNNNFNNNNN	NNNN4NNNNNNNNNN	R,T	241	489	06.02.31	6856	200303	89502
781.667-010	ASSEMBLER (glove & mit.)	2122	44444444454	LNNNNNNFFFNOONFNNNFN	NNNN4NNNNNNNNNN	R	221	449	06.03.02	7850	200303	83005
781.682-010	TRIMMER, MACHINE (garment; knitting)	2112	44443534345	LNNNNNNNCCFNNNNFNFNFN	NNNN4NNNNNNNNNN	R,T	054	420	06.02.05	7654	200303	92705
781.684-010	CARPET CUTTER I (carpet & rug)	2224	34443444355	MNNFFOFCCONNNNFOFOONN	NNNN3NNNNNNNNNN	T	054	431	06.02.27	7753	000000	93932
781.684-014	CUTTER, MACHINE I (any industry)	3225	34433434354	MNNFNNNFFNNOONFNFFON	NNNN4NNNNNNNNNF	J,T	054	420	06.02.27	7753	200502	93928
781.684-018	CUTTER, ROTARY SHEAR (tex. prod., nec)	2123	34443443354	LNNNNNNFFFNNNNOFNFON	NNNN4NNNNNNNNNN	R	054	420	06.04.27	7753	000000	93926
781.684-022	CUTTING INSPECTOR (tex. prod., nec)	3113	34443443354	LNNNNNNNCCCNNNNNCNNNON	NNNN4NNNNNNNNNN	R,J,T	054	435	06.03.02	7820	200502	83005
781.684-026	DRAPER (garment; knitting)	3234	34433433354	LNNNNNNFFFNNNNFNNNNN	NNNN3NNNNNNNNNN	J,T	171	435	06.02.31	7820	200303	83005
781.684-030	DRAPERY-HEAD FORMER (retail trade)	2112	44443434354	LNNNNNNNFFFNNNONONON	NNNC3NNNNNNNNNN	R,T	032	435	06.04.27	7720	200502	93926
781.684-034	LAY-OUT-MACHINE OPERATOR (tex. prod., nec)	3114	34434433355	LNNNNNNNCCFNNNNFNFNNN	NNNN3NNNNNNNNNN	J,T	062	435	06.04.27	7850	200303	93999
781.684-038	NYLON-HOT-WIRE CUTTER (tex. prod., nec)	2213	44443433345	LNNNNNNNCCFNNNNFNFNNN	NNNN4NNNNNNNNNNF	R,U	054	439	06.04.27	7759	480303	93999
781.684-042	PERFORATOR (tex. prod., nec)	2113	44443433355	LNNNNNNNFFONNNFNOONN	NNNN3NNNNNNNNNN	R,T	192	489	06.04.26	7659	000000	92998
781.684-046	CUTTER, HAND I (any industry)	2223	44443533355	MNNONNNCCFONNNCNCFNN	NNNN3NNNNNNNNNN	R,T	054	431	06.04.27	7720	200303	93999
781.684-050	RUG CLIPPER (carpet & rug)	1112	45454544355	LNNNNNNFFFNNNNFNFFON	NNNN4NNNNNNNNNN	R	054	431	06.04.27	7753	000000	93926
781.684-054	RUG-SAMPLE BEVELER (carpet & rug)	2112	44444444355	LNNNNNNFFFNNNOFNFON	NNNN4NNNNNNNNNN	R	054	431	06.04.27	7740	000000	92944
781.684-058	TRIM-STENCIL MAKER (any industry)	2223	34433443355	LNNNNNNNCCONNNNNNONNN	NNNN3NNNNNNNNNN	R,T	054	446	06.04.26	7753	200501	93926
781.684-062	WASTE SALVAGER (garment)	3123	44443443354	LNNNNNNFFFONNNFNFNNN	NNNN3NNNNNNNNNN	J,T	241	489	06.04.26	7720	200303	93999
781.684-066	MATERIAL ASSEMBLER (furniture)	2224	34444444355	MNNONNNNFFONNNNONOONN	NNNN4NNNNNNNNNNO	R,J,T	054	420	06.02.27	7850	200303	83005
781.684-070	SAMPLE CUTTER (furniture)	2113	44433433353	MNNNNNNFFONNNFNNNNN	NNNN3NNNNNNNNNNO	R,U	011	462	06.04.27	7759	480303	93999
781.684-074	CUTTER, HAND I (any industry)	3124	44433433354	LNNONONFFFNNNFNFFN	NNNN3NNNNNNNNNN	R,T	241	420	06.02.27	7753	200501	93928
781.684-078	CUTTER APPRENTICE, HAND (any industry)	3124	44433433353	LNNONNNCCFNNNNFNFFFN	NNNN3NNNNNNNNNN	R,T	054	420	06.02.27	7753	200303	93926
781.685-010	SPREADER, MACHINE (any industry)	3223	34443433353	HNNFNNNFFFNNNNFNNFF	NNNN4NNNNNNNNNN	R,T	062	420	06.02.27	7659	480303	92998
781.687-010	ASSEMBLER (garment; glove & mit.)	2123	44444444453	LNNNNNNFFFNNNNFNFNFF	NNNN4NNNNNNNNNN	R,T	221	424	06.04.05	7850	200303	83005
781.687-014	CLOTH EXAMINER, HAND (textile)	2113	34443434353	LNNNNNNFFFNNNFFNOOFFN	NNNN4NNNNNNNNNN	J,T	054	420	06.03.02	7820	200303	83005
781.687-018	CLOTH TEARER (garment)	2113	44444433354	MNNNNNNFFNNNNONNNNN	NNNN3NNNNNNNNNN	R	054	420	06.03.02	8769	200303	98799
781.687-022	CUTTER HELPER (any industry)	2112	44444444455	LNNNNNNNFFONNNFNNNNN	NNNN3NNNNNNNNNN	R	054	420	06.04.27	8769	200303	98999
781.687-026	CUTTER, HAND II (any industry)	2112	44444444454	LNNNNNNCCFNNNNCNNCON	NNNN3NNNNNNNNNN	R,T	054	410	06.04.27	7753	200303	93926
781.687-030	CUTTER, HAND III (any industry)	2112	44543434355	MNNNNNNFFOONNNFNFNNN	NNNN4NNNNNNNNNNO	R	054	420	06.04.34	7753	200303	83005
781.687-034	GLOVE-PARTS INSPECTOR (glove & mit.)	1112	44443444353	LNNONNNFFFNNNFNFFN	NNNN4NNNNNNNNNNO	R,T	054	420	06.03.02	7820	200303	93926
781.687-038	GOODS LAYER (textile)	3124	44444433354	LNNONONFFFNNNFNFFN	NNNN3NNNNNNNNNN	J,T	054	529	05.09.02	8724	200303	83005
781.687-042	MARKER (garment; retail trade; tex. prod., nec)	2112	44444434344	LNNNONONCCFNNNNCNFNON	NNNN4NNNNNNNNNN	R,T	241	420	06.04.27	7759	200303	98799
781.687-046	MARKING STITCHER (garment)	2112	44545454455	LNNNNNNFFFNNNNONNNNN	NNNN4NNNNNNNNNN	R,T	054	420	06.04.27	8769	200303	93999
781.687-050	RIBBON CUTTER (narrow fabrics)	2112	44454343355	LNNNNNNFFFNNNNFNFFN	NNNN4NNNNNNNNNN	R	054	423	06.04.27	8769	000000	98999
781.687-054	RUG-BACKING STENCILER (carpet & rug)	2113	44443444354	MNNFFFCCNNNNNONNNNN	NNNN3NNNNNNNNNN	R,T	241	431	06.04.27	7756	000000	93947
781.687-058	SPREADER I (any industry)	2112	44544544344	MNNONNNCCFNNNNNNONNN	NNNN4NNNNNNNNNN	R	062	420	06.04.27	8769	200303	98999

DOT #	DOT Title & Industry	Trng	Aptitude	Physical	Environment	Tempra	WkF	MPSMS	GOE	SOC	CIP	OES
781.687-062	STAMPER I (tex. prod., nec)	2112	44544543455	LNNNNNNCCNNNONCNONNN	NNNN3NNNNNNNNNN	R,T	241	432	06.04.27	8769	200303	98999
781.687-066	STENCILER (garment; tex. prod., nec)	2112	44544544455	LNNNNNNCCNNNNNCNNNNN	NNNN3NNNNNNNNNN	R,T	191	440	06.04.27	8769	200303	98999
781.687-070	TRIMMER, HAND (any industry)	2112	44544544455	LNNNNNNCCNNNNNCNNNNN	NNNN4NNNNNNNNNN	R	054	430	06.04.27	7753	200303	89926
782.361-010	CORSET FITTER (retail trade)	3237	34333433345	LNNFOONFFFOOONFNFFNN	NNNN4NNNNNNNNNN	V,J,T	171	444	05.05.15	6859	200305	89502
782.361-014	EMBROIDERY PATTERNMAKER (retail trade; wholesale tr.)	4336	23322432343	LNNNNNNNFFNOONCNFOON	NNNN4NNNNNNNNNN	J,T	241	432	01.06.03	6856	200303	89599
782.381-010	HAT TRIMMER (laundry & rel.)	3125	34434532343	LNNNNNNNCCFONNNCNFOFN	NNNN3NNNNNNNNNN	R,T	171	440	06.02.27	6859	000000	89599
782.381-014	ORIENTAL-RUG REPAIRER (any industry)	4336	34432532352	MNNNNNNNFFNNNNFNFNFN	NNNN4NNNNNNNNNN	J,T	164	431	05.05.15	6859	000000	89599
782.381-018	RUG REPAIRER (laundry & rel.)	3236	34333432343	MNNNNNNCCCONNNCNNFNN	NNNN4NNNNNNNNNN	V,J,T	171	431	05.05.15	6859	000000	89599
782.381-022	WEAVER, HAND (personal ser.)	3225	34432433353	SNNNNNNCCCONNNCNNFNN	NNNN3NNNNNNNNNN	R,T	164	420	05.05.15	6859	200301	89599
782.487-010	NETTING INSPECTOR (tex. prod., nec)	2223	44443533354	LNNNNNNNFFNNNNFNFNON	NNNN4NNNNNNNNNN	R,T	165	439	06.03.02	7820	000000	83005
782.684-010	CANVAS REPAIRER (any industry)	2114	44443533344	HNNNNNNNFFNNNNFNFNON	NNNN4NNNNNNNNNN	R,T	171	436	06.04.27	6179	000000	85956
782.684-014	CROCHETER, HAND (knitting)	3125	44445322254	LNNNNNNNFFNNNNFNFNON	NNNN4NNNNNNNNNN	R,T	165	432	06.02.27	7759	200305	93956
782.684-018	EMBROIDERER, HAND (tex. prod., nec)	3125	44543532353	SNNNNNNNFCCFNNNCNNNON	NNNN4NNNNNNNNNN	R,T	171	432	06.02.27	7759	200303	93999
782.684-026	FISH-NET STRINGER (tex. prod., nec)	3113	34434533355	LNNNNNNNFFNNNNFNFNNN	NNNN3NNNNNNNNNN	R	165	439	06.04.27	7759	000000	93999
782.684-030	HOSIERY MENDER (knitting)	3113	34443433353	LNNNNNNNCCCNNNNFNFFN	NNNN4NNNNNNNNNN	R,T	171	446	06.02.27	7752	200303	93923
782.684-034	KNITTER, HAND (tex. prod., nec)	3325	33343322354	LNNNNNNNFFNNNNFNONON	NNNN4NNNNNNNNNN	R,J,T	165	424	06.02.27	7720	200305	93999
782.684-038	MATCH-UP WORKER (garment)	2114	34434433354	LNNNNNNNFFNNNNNFNFNN	NNNN4NNNNNNNNNN	R,T	221	440	06.04.27	6179	200303	85999
782.684-042	MENDER (carpet & rug; textile)	3124	34443433353	LNNONONFFFONNNFNFOON	NNNN3NNNNNNNNNN	J,T	164	420	06.02.27	7752	000000	93923
782.684-046	MENDER, KNIT GOODS (garment; knitting)	3113	44543533354	LNNONNNFFFNNNNNFNFFN	NNNN3NNNNNNNNNN	R,T	165	424	06.02.27	6179	200303	85956
782.684-050	PASSEMENTERIE WORKER (tex. prod., nec)	2114	44533533354	LNNNNNNCCCNNNNCNFNFN	NNNN4NNNNNNNNNN	R	171	432	06.04.27	7752	200303	93923
782.684-054	PINNER (tex. prod., nec)	2113	44443433455	LNNNNNNNFFNNNNFNFNNN	NNNN4NNNNNNNNNN	R,T	171	432	06.04.27	7756	200303	93947
782.684-058	SEWER, HAND (any industry)	2113	44443532354	LNNNNNNNCCCNNNONCNNFFN	NNNN3NNNNNNNNNN	J,R,T	171	440	06.04.27	7752	200305	93923
782.684-062	WEAVER, HAND (narrow fabrics; textile)	2123	34443433354	LNNNNNNNFFONNFNFNNNN	NNNN4NNNNNNNNNN	R,T	164	423	06.02.27	7759	000000	93999
782.687-010	BASTING PULLER (garment)	1112	44454544454	LNNNNNNNCCCNNNNCNNNNN	NNNN4NNNNNNNNNN	R	171	440	06.04.27	8769	000000	98999
782.687-014	BUTTONER (garment; knitting)	1111	44554543355	LNNNNNNNCCCNNNNCCFNNN	NNNN3NNNNNNNNNN	R	062	424	06.04.27	8769	200303	98999
782.687-018	CLOTH-BALE HEADER (textile)	1112	44544544455	MNNONNNFFFNNNNNNNNNN	NNNN4NNNNNNNNNN	R	171	436	06.04.27	7752	000000	93923
782.687-022	ELASTIC-TAPE INSERTER (garment)	2112	44443544455	LNNONNNFFFNNNNFNFNNN	NNNN3NNNNNNNNNN	R	062	440	06.04.27	7720	200303	93999
782.687-026	PINNER (garment; tex. prod., nec)	1112	44543543355	LNNNNNNNCCCNNNNFNNNNN	NNNN4NNNNNNNNNN	R	171	440	06.04.27	8769	000000	98999
782.687-030	PULLER-THROUGH (glove & mit.)	1111	44444533355	SNNNNNNNFFNNNNFNFNNN	NNNN3NNNNNNNNNN	R	062	449	06.04.27	8769	000000	98999
782.687-034	RAVELER (knitting)	1111	44544533355	LNNFNNNCCCNNNNCNNNNN	NNNN4NNNNNNNNNN	R	165	424	06.04.27	8769	200303	98999
782.687-038	RIPPER (garment; retail trade; tex. prod., nec)	2112	44544533355	LNNNNNNNFFFNNNNFNNNNN	NNNN3NNNNNNNNNN	R	171	420	06.04.27	8769	000000	98999
782.687-042	RUG BRAIDER, HAND (carpet & rug)	2112	44443433353	LNNFFFNFFFNNNFNNNFN	NNNN3NFNNNNNNNFN	R,T	164	431	06.04.27	7740	000000	93999
782.687-046	SACK REPAIRER (any industry)	2112	44545433345	SNNNNNNNFFFNNNNFFONN	NNNN4NNNNNNNNNN	R	054	436	06.04.27	7752	000000	92721
782.687-050	SECONDS HANDLER (knitting)	2112	44444543454	LNNNNNNNCCFNNNNNNNNFN	NNNN3NNNNNNNNNN	R	221	424	06.03.02	7850	200303	83005
782.687-054	TAPE STRINGER (garment; knitting)	1111	44445433355	LNNFNNNNCCCNNNNCNNNNN	NNNN4NNNNNNNNNN	R	061	424	06.04.27	7740	200303	93999
782.687-058	THREAD MARKER (garment)	2122	44544544355	LNNNNNNNFFNNNFNFNNNN	NNNN3NNNNNNNNNN	R	171	440	06.04.27	7752	200303	93923
783.131-010	SUPERVISOR, FURRIER SHOP (fur goods)	4347	23322343353	LNNONNNFFFONNNFNFNON	NNNN4NNNNNNNNNN	V,D,P,J	171	447	05.05.15	6700	200303	81008
783.132-010	SUPERVISOR (leather prod.)	4345	33333333343	LNNNNNNNCCNOONFFFFFF	NNNN4NNNNNNNNNN	D,J,P,V	054	524	06.02.01	7100	200303	81008
783.261-010	FURRIER (fur goods)	4338	22323423343	LNNNNNNNFFOOOONFNNFN	NNNN4NNNNNNNNNN	J	171	447	05.05.15	6859	200303	89599
783.361-010	CUSTOM-LEATHER-PRODUCTS MAKER (leather prod.)	3237	33422433343	LNNNNNNNFFNFNFFNNNFN	NNNN3NNNNNNNNNN	T,J	171	529	05.05.15	6854	480399	89511
783.381-010	FUR CUTTER (fur goods)	3327	34432433353	LNNNNNNNFFFNNNNFNFNN	NNNN3NNNNNNNNNN	J	054	447	06.02.27	6859	200303	89599
783.381-014	FUR FINISHER (fur goods)	3226	34433433344	LNNFNNNFFFNNNNFNNNON	NNNN4NNNNNNNNNN	J	171	447	05.05.15	6854	480399	89511
783.381-018	HARNESS MAKER (leather prod.; retail trade)	3337	34433423344	MNNNNNNNFFFNNNNFNFOON	NNNN4NNNNNNNNNN	J,T	102	529	05.05.15	6854	480399	89511
783.381-022	LUGGAGE MAKER (leather prod.)	3237	34433433344	MONFNNNFFONNNFNFNON	NNNN4NNNNNNNNNN	J,T	102	524	06.02.27	6854	000000	89511
783.381-026	SADDLE MAKER (leather prod.)	3338	34433423343	LNNNNNNNCCFNNNNNNNNO	NNNN3NNNNNNNNNN	V,J,T	102	529	05.05.15	6854	480399	89511
783.384-010	FUR SORTER (fur goods)	3127	23322542352	LNNNNNNNCCCNNNNCNNNCN	NNNN3NNNNNNNNNN	J	212	447	06.03.01	7850	200303	83005
783.387-010	FUR-REPAIR INSPECTOR (retail trade)	3228	34422432352	LNNOONNFFFONNNFNFNFN	NNNN3NNNNNNNNNN	V,J,T	241	447	05.05.15	7820	200301	83005
783.681-010	FUR BLENDER (leather mfg.)	3126	34422422252	LNNNNNNNCCCNNNNCNNNCN	NNNN3NNNNNNNNNN	J,T	153	521	01.06.02	7756	000000	93947
783.682-010	FUR-MACHINE OPERATOR (fur goods)	3226	34433433333	LNNNNNNNCCCNNNNNNFFON	NNNN4NNNNNNNNNN	J	171	447	06.02.05	7655	200303	92721
783.682-014	SEWING MACHINE OPERATOR (leather prod.)	3113	34433433344	LNNNNNNNCCNNNNNCNCFF	NNNN4NNFNNNNNNNN	R,T	171	524	06.02.05	7655	480304	92721
783.684-010	ASSEMBLER, LEATHER GOODS I (leather prod.)	3223	34443433343	LNNNNNNNCCCNNNNCNFFFN	NNNN4NNNNNNNNNN	R,T	102	524	06.02.27	7720	200303	93956

DOT #	DOT Title & Industry	Trng	Aptitude	Physical	Environment	Tempra	WkF	MPSMS	GOE	SOC	CIP	OES
783.684-014	FUR NAILER (fur goods)	3226	34433433353	LNMFNNNCCFNNNNNFNON	NNNN3NNNNNNNNNNN	J,T	241	447	06.02.31	7755	200303	93956
783.684-018	INSPECTOR-REPAIRER (leather prod.)	3223	44443343453	LNNNNNNCCCNNNNNFNN	NNNN4NNNNNNNNNNN	R,T	212	524	06.03.02	7820	200303	83005
783.684-022	LEATHER CUTTER (leather prod.)	3224	34433433355	LNNONONCCFNNNNCNFFN	NNNN4NNNNNNNNNNN	J,T	054	529	06.02.27	7753	480304	93926
783.684-026	LEATHER WORKER (leather prod.)	3225	44493433344	MNNNNNNNFFFNNNNFNON	NNNN4NNNNNNNNNNN	T,V	102	529	06.02.27	7720	480304	93999
783.684-030	UTILITY BAG ASSEMBLER (leather prod.)	2122	44443433344	LNNNNNNCCCNNNNFNFON	NNNN4NNNNNNNNNNN	J	102	529	06.04.23	7720	480304	93956
783.685-010	COVERING-MACHINE TENDER (leather prod.)	2112	44544533355	LNNNNNFFFNNNNFNFNNN	NNNN4NNNNNNNNNNN	R,T	134	529	06.04.20	7659	000000	92998
783.685-014	CREASER (leather prod.)	3124	34434432345	LNNNNNNCCCNNNNCNFNNN	NNNN4NNNNNNNNNNN	R,T	062	529	06.02.05	7659	200303	92998
783.685-018	DISK-AND-TAPE-MACHINE TENDER (leather prod.)	2112	44444433345	LNNNNNNCCCNNNNCNCNNN	NNNN4NNNNNNNNNNN	R,T	062	529	06.04.05	7659	000000	92998
783.685-022	LAMINATOR II (leather prod.)	2112	44544533355	LNNNNNNCCCNNNNNFNNN	NNNN4NNNNNNNNNNN	R,T	134	529	06.04.20	7659	200303	92998
783.685-026	MARKING-MACHINE TENDER (boot & shoe; leather prod.)	2112	44443433355	LNNNNNNCCFNNNNFNFNNN	NNNN4NNNNNNNNNNN	R,T	191	529	06.04.05	7659	200303	92998
783.687-010	ASSEMBLER, LEATHER GOODS II (leather prod.)	3122	44443433355	LNNNNNNCCCNNNNCNCNN	NNNN4NNNNNNNNNNN	R,T	102	524	06.04.23	7720	200303	93956
783.687-030	TABLE WORKER (leather prod.)	2123	44443533355	LNNNNNNFFFNNNNFNFNNN	NNNN3NNNNNNNNNNN	R,T	054	447	06.04.27	7753	200303	93926
783.687-014	FUR TRIMMER (fur goods)	3224	44444444454	LNNFNNNFFFNNNNFNNNFN	NNNN3NNNNNNNNNNN	J,T	221	521	06.03.02	7820	000000	83005
783.687-018	HIDE INSPECTOR (leather mfg.)	2123	44444343453	LNNNNNNCCCNNNCNNNCNN	NNNN4NNNNNNNNNNN	R,T	212	529	06.03.02	7850	000000	83005
783.687-022	MATCHER, LEATHER PARTS (leather prod.)	2112	44543543455	LNNNNNNFFNNNNNCNCNN	NNNN3NNNNNNNNNNN	R	063	529	06.04.23	7720	200303	93956
783.687-026	PASTER, HAND OR MACHINE (leather prod.)	1111	44544544455	LNNNNNNFFFFNNNNNFNNN	NNNN4NNNNNNNNNNN	R	061	529	06.04.27	8769	200303	98999
784.130-010	SUPERVISOR, CAP-AND-HAT PRODUCTION (hat & cap)	4337	33333433343	LNNNNNNFFFFFNFNNFF	NNNN3NNNNNNNNNNN	D,P,V	032	445	06.02.01	7100	200303	92717
784.132-010	SUPERVISOR (glove & mit.)	4337	33333433344	LNNONNNFFFOFFNFNFOON	NNNN3NNNNNNNNNNN	D,P,T	171	449	06.02.01	7100	200303	81008
784.261-010	MILLINER (retail trade)	4226	23433432352	LNNNNNNCCCNOONCNFNON	NNNN3NNNNNNNNNNN	E,T	171	445	01.06.02	6859	200303	89599
784.361-010	PATTERNMAKER (hat & cap)	4337	43433433354	LNNNNNNNFFNNNNFNFNON	NNNN3NNNNNNNNNNN	J,T	132	566	01.06.02	6856	200303	89502
784.387-010	INSPECTOR (hat & cap)	2113	44433443454	LNNNNNNCCFNNONCNNCON	NNNN3NNNNNNNNNNN	J,T	212	445	06.03.01	7820	200303	83005
784.387-014	LEATHER GRADER (glove & mit.)	3225	33433443353	MNNNNNNFFFNNNNFONFN	NNNN3NNNNNNNNNNN	J,T	212	529	06.03.01	7850	200303	83005
784.587-010	HAT-BODY SORTER (hat & cap)	2122	44444444454	LNNNNNNFFNNNNNFNNFN	NNNN4NNNNNNNNNNN	R,T	221	445	06.03.02	7850	200303	83005
784.682-010	GLOVE SEWER (glove & mit.)	3124	34443343345	LNNNNNNNFFFNNNNFOFFNN	NNNN4NNONNNNNNNN	R,T	171	449	06.02.05	7655	200303	92717
784.682-014	HAT-AND-CAP SEWER (hat & cap)	3113	44443353344	LNNNNNNCCCNNNNCNFFON	NNNN4NNNNNNNNNNN	R,T	171	445	06.02.05	7655	200303	92717
784.684-010	BOW MAKER (garment; hat & cap)	2113	44544433455	LNNNNNNNCCCNNONCNNNNN	NNNN4NNNNNNNNNNN	R,T	063	445	06.04.27	7753	200303	93926
784.684-014	BRIM IRONER, HAND (hat & cap)	2113	44444444355	LNNNNNNFFFNNONFNNFNN	NNNO4NNNNNNNNNNO	R,T	032	445	06.04.27	7759	200303	93999
784.684-018	CAP MAKER (hat & cap)	2124	44443533344	LNNNNNNNFFFNNNNFNFNON	NNNN4NNNNNNNNNNN	R,T	171	445	06.04.27	7755	200303	93956
784.684-022	DECORATOR (hat & cap)	2123	44444433354	LNNNNNNCCCNNONFNNNNN	NNNN3NNNNNNNNNNN	R,T	171	445	06.04.27	7752	200303	93923
784.684-026	FLANGER (hat & cap)	2123	44434434355	LNNNNNNNFFNNONONONNN	NNNN3NNNNNNNNNNN	R,T	032	445	06.04.27	7755	200303	93956
784.684-030	FOUNDATION MAKER (hat & cap)	2122	44543533345	SNNNNNNFFFFNNNNFNFNN	NNNN4NNNNNNNNNNN	R	171	445	06.04.34	7720	200303	93999
784.684-034	HARDENER (hat & cap)	2124	44445333345	LNNNNNNNFFFNNNNFNNNN	NNNO3NNNNNNNNNNN	R,T	147	432	06.04.27	7720	200303	93999
784.684-038	HAT BRAIDER (hat & cap)	2113	44443533355	LNNNNNNFFFNNNNFNNNN	NNNN3NNNNNNNNNNN	R,T	062	445	06.04.34	7720	200303	93956
784.684-042	HAT MAKER (hat & cap)	3125	34443532353	LNNNNNNCCFNNNNCNFNFN	NNNN3NNNNNNNNNNN	J,T	171	445	06.02.27	7752	200303	93923
784.684-046	MENDER (hat & cap)	2113	44535333353	SNNNNNNFFFNNNNFNFNON	NNNN3NNNNNNNNNNN	R,T	171	445	06.04.34	6179	200303	85956
784.684-050	ROUNDER, HAND (hat & cap)	2123	44444433354	LNNNNNNCCFNNONFNNFON	NNNN4NNNNNNNNNNN	R,T	054	445	06.04.27	7753	200303	93926
784.684-054	SIZER, HAND (hat & cap)	2113	44434434355	LNNNNNNNFFONNNNONONN	NNNO3NNNNNNNNNNN	R,T	152	432	06.04.27	7755	200303	93999
784.684-058	SIZER, MACHINE (hat & cap)	2112	44434434355	LNNNNNNFFONNNNNFNNNN	NNNF4NNNNNNNNNNN	R,T	062	445	06.04.16	7679	200303	92998
784.684-062	SLICKER (hat & cap)	2113	44443533345	LNNNNNNFFONONFNNNNN	NNNN4NNNNNNNNNNN	R,T	054	445	06.04.33	7759	200303	93999
784.684-066	SMOOTHER (hat & cap)	1112	45544444355	LNNNNNNCCCCNNNNCNFFON	NNNN4NNNNNNNNNNN	R,T	031	445	06.04.33	7759	200303	93956
784.684-070	STEAMER-BLOCKER (hat & cap; knitting)	2112	44544534344	LNNOONNFFFNNNNFNFON	NNFF3NNNNNNNNNNN	J	032	424	06.04.05	7654	200303	92705
784.684-074	TOP-HAT-BODY MAKER (hat & cap)	2113	34433434355	LNNNNNNFFFONNNNONFNN	NNNN3NNNNNNNNNNN	R,T	062	445	06.04.27	7720	200303	93956
784.684-078	TRIMMER (hat & cap)	2112	44434433344	LNNNNNNCCCONNNNCNNNN	NNNN4NNNNNNNNNNN	R,T	063	445	06.04.27	7720	200303	93956
784.685-010	BAND-AND-CUFF CUTTER (glove & mit.)	2112	44435444445	LNNNNNNFFONONFNNFON	NNNN4NNNNNNNNNNN	R,T	054	449	06.04.05	7654	200303	92705
784.685-014	BRIM STITCHER I (hat & cap)	2112	44543545354	LNNNNNNFFFONONFNNFON	NNNN4NNNNNNNNNNN	R,T	171	445	06.04.05	7655	200303	92721
784.687-010	BRIM RAISER (hat & cap)	2112	44543545355	LNNNNNNNFFNNONFNNNNN	NNNF3NNNNNNNNNNN	R,T	032	445	06.04.27	8769	200303	98999
784.687-014	CARROTER (hat & cap)	2113	44544544355	LNNNNNNFFFFNNNNFNNNN	NNNN3NNNNNNNNNNN	R	153	521	06.04.33	8769	000000	98999
784.687-018	CROWN POUNCER, HAND (hat & cap)	2113	44545444355	LNNNNNNFFFFNNNNFNNNN	NNNN3NNNNNNNNNNN	R,T	161	445	06.04.27	7759	200303	93999
784.687-022	EAR-MUFF ASSEMBLER (hat & cap)	2112	44445543354	LNNNNNNFFFNNNNFNFNNN	NNNN3NNNNNNNNNNN	R	061	445	06.04.23	7720	000000	93956
784.687-026	ENDBAND CUTTER, HAND (hat & cap)	2112	44433444355	SNNNNNNNFFNNNNNFNNNN	NNNN3NNNNNNNNNNN	R,T	054	445	06.04.27	8769	200303	98999
784.687-030	FLOORWORKER-DISTRIBUTOR (hat & cap)	2112	44444444354	LNNNNNNNFFNNNNNNNNON	NNNN4NNNNNNNNNNN	R,T	221	445	06.04.40	7870	490299	83005

DOT #	DOT Title & Industry	Trng	Aptitude	Physical	Environment	Tempra	WkF	MPSMS	GOE	SOC	CIP	OES
784.687-034	GLOVE PAIRER (glove & mit.)	2112	4444444354	LNNNNNNFFNNNNNFNFN	NNNNN4NNNNNNNNNN	R	221	449	06.03.02	7850	200303	83005
784.687-038	GLOVE TURNER (glove & mit.)	2113	44444434345	LNNONNNCCFFNNNCNNNNN	NNNNN4NNNNNNNNNN	R	062	449	06.04.27	8769	200303	98999
784.687-042	INSPECTOR-PACKER (hat & cap)	2122	44444444454	LNNNNNNNCCCONONCNNFFN	NNNNN3NNNNNNNNNN	R,T	212	445	06.03.02	8761	200303	98902
784.687-046	LINER (glove & mit.)	2112	44454534355	LNNNNNNNCCNNNNNNNNN	NNNNN3NNNNNNNNNN	R,T	061	523	06.04.27	7740	200303	93999
784.687-050	MATERIAL ASSEMBLER (hat & cap)	3123	44444443353	LNNNNNNNCCNNONFNNFFN	NNNNN3NNNNNNNNNN	R,T	054	445	06.03.02	7850	200303	83005
784.687-054	OPENER I (hat & cap)	2112	44544544355	LNNNNNNFFNNNNNNNNN	NNNNN3NNNNNNNNNN	R	054	445	06.04.27	8769	000000	98999
784.687-058	POWDERER (hat & cap)	2112	44544544354	LNNNNNNNFFNNONFNNNN	NNNNN4NNNNNNNNNN	R	153	445	06.04.33	8769	200303	98999
784.687-062	SINGER (hat & cap)	2112	44534534355	LNNNNNNNFFNNNNFNNNN	NNNOO4NNNNNNNNNNF	R,T	147	445	06.04.34	8769	200303	98999
784.687-066	SMOKE-ROOM OPERATOR (hat & cap)	1112	44544545455	MNNNNNNNFFNNNNNNNNN	NNNNN4NFNNNNNNNN	R	147	445	06.04.27	7759	000000	98999
784.687-070	STICKER (hat & cap)	1112	44544533355	LNNNNNNNFFNNNNFNFNNN	NNNNN4NNNNNNNNNN	R	063	432	06.04.27	7740	000000	93999
784.687-074	STRAW-HAT BRUSHER (hat & cap)	2112	44544544355	LNNNNNNNFFNNNNNFNNNN	NNNNN3NNNNNNNNNN	R	153	445	06.04.39	7759	200303	93999
784.687-078	STRAW-HAT-WASHER OPERATOR (hat & cap)	1111	44544544355	LNNNNNNNCCNNNNNNNNN	NNNF4NNNNNNNNNN	R	031	445	06.04.27	8769	200303	98999
784.687-082	WIRE INSERTER (hat & cap)	2112	44444443355	LNNNNNNNCCFNNNINFNNN	NNNN4NNNNNNNNNN	R,T	054	445	06.04.34	7720	200303	93956
784.687-086	HAT CONDITIONER (hat & cap)	1112	44544544455	LNNNNNNNFFNNNNNNNNN	NNNO4NNNNNNNNNN	R	152	445	06.04.27	8769	200303	85999
784.687-090	SWEATBAND SHAPER (hat & cap)	1112	44544534355	MNNNNNNNFFNNNNNNNNN	NNNNN4NNNNNNNNNN	R,U	032	445	06.04.27	8769	200303	85999
785.131-010	SUPERVISOR, ALTERATION WORKROOM (retail trade)	3336	33343333444	LNNNNNNNFFNNFFNFFON	NNNN3NNNNNNNNNN	D,J,P	171	440	05.05.15	7100	200305	81008
785.261-010	ALTERATION TAILOR (garment; personal ser.; retail trade)	4337	33323432343	LNNNNNNNFFCONNNNFNNN	NNNN3NNNNNNNNNN	J,T	171	440	05.05.15	6852	200305	89505
785.261-014	CUSTOM TAILOR (garment; personal ser.; retail trade)	4338	22323432343	LNNNNNNNFFCOFFNCNFOON	NNNN4NNNNNNNNNN	J	171	440	05.05.15	6852	200305	89505
785.261-018	TAILOR APPRENTICE, ALTERATION (garment; personal ser.; retail trade)	4337	33323432343	LNNNNNNNFFCONNNCNFOON	NNNN3NNNNNNNNNN	J,T	171	440	05.05.15	6852	200305	89505
785.261-022	TAILOR APPRENTICE, CUSTOM (garment; personal ser.; retail trade)	4338	22323422343	LNNNNNNNFFCOFFNCNFOON	NNNN4NNNNNNNNNN	J	171	440	05.05.15	6852	200305	89505
785.361-010	DRESSMAKER (any industry)	3337	33433433343	LNNOOONFFFOOONFNOON	NNNN3NNNNNNNNNN	V,J,T	171	443	05.05.15	6852	200305	89505
785.361-014	GARMENT FITTER (retail trade)	3226	34333332354	LONOONNFFFFFNFNFFN	NNNN4NNNNNNNNNN	J,T	171	440	05.05.15	6852	200305	89505
785.361-018	SAMPLE STITCHER (garment)	4336	33923432344	LNNNNNNNFFFOOONCNFOON	NNNN4NNNNNNNNNN	J,T	171	440	05.05.15	6852	200305	89505
785.361-022	SHOP TAILOR (garment; retail trade)	4337	33333433343	LNNNONNFFFOOONFOON	NNNN3NNNNNNNNNN	J,T	171	440	05.05.15	6852	200305	89505
785.361-026	SHOP TAILOR APPRENTICE (garment; retail trade)	4337	33333433343	LNNIOONNFFFOOONFOON	NNNN3NNNNNNNNNN	J,T	171	440	05.05.15	6852	200305	89505
786.132-010	SUPERVISOR, GARMENT MANUFACTURING (garment)	4236	33433433344	LNNNNNNNFFFNCNOOOON	NNNN4NNNNNNNNNN	D,P,V,J	171	440	06.02.01	7100	200303	81008
786.682-010	APPLIQUER, ZIGZAG (garment)	2113	44433532334	LNNNNNNNFCONNNCNFOON	NNNN4NNNNNNNNNN	R,T	171	440	06.02.05	7655	200303	92717
786.682-014	ARMHOLE BASTER, JUMPBASTING (garment)	2113	44433532335	LNNNNNNNCCNNNNCNOONN	NNNN4NNNNNNNNNN	R,T	171	440	06.02.05	7655	200303	92717
786.682-018	ARMHOLE FELLER, HANDSTITCHING MACHINE (garment)	2112	44433532334	LNNNNNNNCCNNNNCNNNNN	NNNN4NNNNNNNNNN	R,T	171	440	06.02.05	7655	200303	92717
786.682-022	ARMHOLE-SEW-AND-TRIM OPERATOR, LOCKSTITCH (garment)	2113	44433532334	LNNNNNNNCCCNNNNCNNOON	NNNN4NNNNNNNNNN	R,T	171	440	06.02.05	7655	200303	92717
786.682-026	BACK MAKER, LOCKSTITCH (garment)	2113	44433532334	LNNNNNNNCCNNNNCNNNNN	NNNN4NNNNNNNNNN	R,T	171	440	06.02.05	7655	200303	92717
786.682-030	BASTING-MACHINE OPERATOR (garment)	2113	44433532334	LNNNNNNNCCNNNNCNNNNN	NNNN4NNNNNNNNNN	R,T	171	440	06.02.05	7655	200303	92717
786.682-034	BINDER, CHAINSTITCH (garment)	2113	44433532334	LNNNNNNNCCNNNNCNNNNN	NNNN4NNNNNNNNNN	R,T	171	440	06.02.05	7655	200303	92717
786.682-038	BINDER, COVERSTITCH (garment)	2113	44433532334	LNNNNNNNCCNNNNCNNOON	NNNN4NNNNNNNNNN	R,T	171	440	06.02.05	7655	200303	92717
786.682-042	BINDER, LOCKSTITCH (garment)	2113	44433532334	LNNNNNNNCCNNNNCNNOON	NNNN4NNNNNNNNNN	R,T	171	440	06.02.05	7655	200303	92717
786.682-046	BLINDSTITCH-MACHINE OPERATOR (garment)	2112	44433532334	LNNNNNNNCCNNNNCNNNNN	NNNN4NNNNNNNNNN	R,T	171	440	06.02.05	7655	200502	92717
786.682-050	CANVAS BASTER, JUMPBASTING (garment)	2113	44433532334	LNNNNNNNCCNNNNCNNNNN	NNNN4NNNNNNNNNN	R,T	171	440	06.02.05	7655	200303	92717
786.682-054	CHAINSTITCH SEWING MACHINE OPERATOR (garment)	3123	44433432344	LNNNNNNNCCNNNNCNOOON	NNNN4NNNNNNNNNN	R,T	171	440	06.02.05	7655	200303	92717
786.682-058	COAT JOINER, LOCKSTITCH (garment)	2113	44433532334	LNNNNNNNCCNNNNCNNOON	NNNN4NNNNNNNNNN	R,T	171	440	06.02.05	7655	200303	92717
786.682-062	COLLAR BASTER, JUMPBASTING (garment)	2113	44433532334	LNNNNNNNCCNNNNCNNONN	NNNN4NNNNNNNNNN	R,T	171	440	06.02.05	7655	200303	92717
786.682-066	COLLAR FELLER, HANDSTITCHING MACHINE (garment)	2112	44433532334	LNNNNNNNCCNNNNCNNNNN	NNNN4NNNNNNNNNN	R,T	171	440	06.02.05	7655	200303	92717
786.682-070	COLLAR SETTER, LOCKSTITCH (garment)	2113	44433532334	LNNNNNNNCCNNNNCNNOON	NNNN4NNNNNNNNNN	R,T	171	440	06.02.05	7655	200303	92717
786.682-074	COLLAR SETTER, OVERLOCK (garment)	2113	44433532334	LNNNNNNNCCNNNNCNNOON	NNNN4NNNNNNNNNN	R,T	171	440	06.02.05	7655	200303	92717
786.682-078	COVERSTITCH-MACHINE OPERATOR (garment)	2112	44433532334	LNNNNNNNCCNNNNCNNOON	NNNN4NNNNNNNNNN	R,T	171	440	06.02.05	7655	200303	92717
786.682-082	CUP SETTER, LOCKSTITCH (garment)	2113	44433532334	LNNNNNNNCCNNNNCNNOON	NNNN4NNNNNNNNNN	R,T	171	440	06.02.05	7655	200303	92717
786.682-086	ELASTIC ATTACHER, CHAINSTITCH (garment)	2113	44433532335	LNNNNNNNCCNNNNCNNONN	NNNN4NNNNNNNNNN	R,T	171	440	06.02.05	7655	200303	92717
786.682-090	ELASTIC ATTACHER, COVERSTITCH (garment)	2113	44433532335	LNNNNNNNCCNNNNCNNONN	NNNN4NNNNNNNNNN	R,T	171	440	06.02.05	7655	200303	92717
786.682-094	ELASTIC ATTACHER, OVERLOCK (garment)	2113	44433532335	LNNNNNNNCCNNNNCNNONN	NNNN4NNNNNNNNNN	R,T	171	440	06.02.05	7655	200303	92717
786.682-098	ELASTIC ATTACHER, ZIGZAG (garment)	2113	44433532335	LNNNNNNNCCNNNNCNNONN	NNNN4NNNNNNNNNN	R,T	171	440	06.02.05	7655	200303	92717
786.682-102	FACING BASTER, JUMPBASTING (garment)	2113	44433532335	LNNNNNNNCCNNNNCNNONN	NNNN4NNNNNNNNNN	R,T	171	440	06.02.05	7655	200303	92717
786.682-106	FELLED-SEAM OPERATOR, CHAINSTITCH (garment)	2113	44433532334	LNNNNNNNFFNNNNCNFOON	NNNN4NNNNNNNNNN	R,T	171	440	06.02.05	7655	200303	92717

DOT #	DOT Title & Industry	Trng	Aptitude	Physical	Environment	Tempra	WkF	MPSMS	GOE	SOC	CIP	OES
786.682-110	FLATLOCK-SEWING-MACHINE OPERATOR (garment)	2113	44433532334	LNNNNNNCCCNNNNCNNOON	NNNN4NNNNNNNNNN	R,T	171	440	06.02.05	7655	200303	92717
786.682-114	FRONT MAKER, LOCKSTITCH (garment)	2114	44433532334	LNNNNNNCCCNNNNCNNOON	NNNN4NNNNNNNNNN	R,T	171	440	06.02.05	7655	200303	92717
786.682-118	FRONT-EDGE-TAPE SEWER, LOCKSTITCH (garment)	2114	44433532335	LNNNNNNCCCNNNNCNNONN	NNNN4NNNNNNNNNN	R,T	171	440	06.02.05	7655	200303	92717
786.682-122	FUR-MACHINE OPERATOR (garment)	3117	34433532334	LNNNNNNCCCNNNNCNNOON	NNNN4NNNNNNNNNN	R,T	171	440	06.02.05	7655	200303	92717
786.682-126	HEMMER, BLINDSTITCH (garment)	2112	44433532334	LNNNNNNCCCNNNNCNNOON	NNNN4NNNNNNNNNN	R,T	171	440	06.02.05	7655	200303	92717
786.682-130	HEMMER, CHAINSTITCH (garment)	2112	44433532334	LNNNNNNCCCNNNNCNNOON	NNNN4NNNNNNNNNN	R,T	171	440	06.02.05	7655	200303	92717
786.682-134	HEMMER, LOCKSTITCH (garment)	2112	44433532334	LNNNNNNCCCNNNNCNNOON	NNNN4NNNNNNNNNN	R,T	171	440	06.02.05	7655	200303	92717
786.682-138	HEMMER, OVERLOCK (garment)	2112	44433532334	LNNNNNNCCCNNNNCNNOON	NNNN4NNNNNNNNNN	R,T	171	440	06.02.05	7655	200303	92717
786.682-142	HEMSTITCHING-MACHINE OPERATOR (garment)	2112	44433533335	LNNNNNNCCCNNNNCNFNNN	NNNN4NNNNNNNNNN	R,T	171	440	06.02.05	7655	200303	92717
786.682-146	JUMPBASTING-MACHINE OPERATOR (garment)	2112	44433533335	LNNNNNNCCCNNNNCNNNNN	NNNN4NNNNNNNNNN	R,T	171	440	06.02.05	7655	200303	92717
786.682-150	LAPEL PADDER, BLINDSTITCH (garment)	2113	44433532334	LNNNNNNCCCNNNNCNNOON	NNNN4NNNNNNNNNN	R,T	171	440	06.02.05	7655	200303	92717
786.682-154	LINING BASTER, JUMPBASTING (garment)	2114	44433532335	LNNNNNNCCCNNNNCNNOON	NNNN4NNNNNNNNNN	R,T	171	440	06.02.05	7655	200303	92717
786.682-158	LINING FELLER, BLINDSTITCH (garment)	2113	44433532334	LNNNNNNCCCNNNNCNNOON	NNNN4NNNNNNNNNN	R,T	171	440	06.02.05	7655	200303	92717
786.682-162	LINING MAKER, LOCKSTITCH (garment)	2112	44433532335	LNNNNNNCCCNNNNCNNONN	NNNN4NNNNNNNNNN	R,T	171	440	06.02.05	7655	200303	92717
786.682-166	LINING SETTER, LOCKSTITCH (garment)	2113	44433532334	LNNNNNNCCCNNNNCNNOON	NNNN4NNNNNNNNNN	R,T	171	440	06.02.05	7655	200303	92717
786.682-170	LOCKSTITCH-MACHINE OPERATOR (garment)	3123	44433432344	LNNNNNNNFFNNONFNFNFN	NNNN4NNNNNNNNNN	R,T	171	440	06.02.05	7655	200303	92717
786.682-174	LOCKSTITCH-SEWING-MACHINE OPERATOR, COMPLETE GARMENT (garment)	3124	34433532334	LNNNNNNCCCNNNNCNNNNN	NNNN4NNNNNNNNNN	T	171	440	06.02.05	7655	200303	92717
786.682-178	MULTINEEDLE-CHAINSTITCH-MACHINE OPERATOR (garment)	2113	44433532334	LNNNNNNCCCNNNNCNFNON	NNNN4NNNNNNNNNN	R,T	171	440	06.02.05	7655	200303	92717
786.682-182	NECKTIE OPERATOR, POCKETS AND PIECES (garment)	2113	44433532334	LNNNNNNCCCNNNNCNNOCN	NNNN4NNNNNNNNNN	R,T	171	440	06.02.05	7655	200303	92717
786.682-186	NECKTIE-CENTRALIZING-MACHINE OPERATOR I (garment)	2113	44433532335	LNNNNNNCCCNNNNCNNOON	NNNN4NNNNNNNNNN	R,T	171	440	06.02.05	7655	200303	92717
786.682-190	NECKTIE-CENTRALIZING-MACHINE OPERATOR II (garment)	2113	44433532334	LNNNNNNCCCNNNNCNFNNN	NNNN4NNFNNNNNNN	R,T	171	440	06.02.05	7655	200303	92717
786.682-194	OVERLOCK-MACHINE OPERATOR, COMPLETE GARMENT (garment)	3124	44433532334	LNNNNNNCCCFNNNNCNFNON	NNNN4NNONNNNNNN	T	171	440	06.02.05	7655	200303	92717
786.682-198	PANTS OUTSEAMER, CHAINSTITCH (garment)	2113	44433532334	LNNNNNNCCCNNNNCNNOON	NNNN4NNNNNNNNNN	R,T	171	440	06.02.05	7655	200303	92717
786.682-202	PICKED-EDGE SEWING-MACHINE OPERATOR (garment)	2112	44433532334	LNNNNNNCCCNNNNCNNOON	NNNN4NNNNNNNNNN	R,T	171	440	06.02.05	7655	200303	92717
786.682-206	POCKET SETTER, LOCKSTITCH (garment)	3114	34433532334	LNNNNNNCCCNNNNCNNOON	NNNN4NNNNNNNNNN	R,T	171	440	06.02.05	7655	200303	92717
786.682-210	REPAIR OPERATOR (garment)	3123	44433532334	LNNNNNNFCCNNNNCNFOON	NNNN4NNNNNNNNNN	R,T	171	440	06.02.05	7655	200303	92717
786.682-214	SEAT JOINER, CHAINSTITCH (garment)	2113	44433532334	LNNNNNNCCCNNNNCNNOON	NNNN4NNNNNNNNNN	R,T	171	440	06.02.05	7655	200303	92717
786.682-218	SHOULDER JOINER, LOCKSTITCH (garment)	2112	44433532334	LNNNNNNCCCNNNNCNNOON	NNNN4NNNNNNNNNN	R,T	171	440	06.02.05	7655	200303	92717
786.682-222	SLEEVE MAKER, LOCKSTITCH (garment)	2114	44433532334	LNNNNNNCCCNNNNCNNOON	NNNN4NNNiNNNNNNN	R,T	171	440	06.02.05	7655	200303	92717
786.682-226	SLEEVE SETTER, LOCKSTITCH (garment)	2113	44433532334	LNNNNNNCCCNNNNCNNOON	NNNN4NNNNNNNNNN	R,T	171	440	06.02.05	7655	200303	92717
786.682-230	SLEEVE SETTER, OVERLOCK (garment)	2113	44433532334	LNNNNNNCCCNNNNCNNOON	NNNN4NNNNNNNNNN	R,T	171	440	06.02.05	7655	200303	92717
786.682-234	TOPSTITCHER, LOCKSTITCH (garment)	2113	44433532334	LNNNNNNCCCNNNNCNNOON	NNNN4NNNNNNNNNN	R,T	171	440	06.02.05	7655	200303	92717
786.682-238	TOPSTITCHER, ZIGZAG (garment)	3124	44433532334	LNNNNNNCCCNNNNCNNOON	NNNN4NNNNNNNNNN	T	171	440	06.02.05	7655	200303	92717
786.682-242	TUNNEL-ELASTIC OPERATOR, CHAINSTITCH (garment)	2113	44433532334	LNNNNNNCCCNNNNCNNOON	NNNN4NNNNNNNNNN	R,T	171	440	06.02.05	7655	200303	92717
786.682-246	TUNNEL-ELASTIC OPERATOR, LOCKSTITCH (garment)	2113	44433532334	LNNNNNNCCCNNNNCNNOON	NNNN4NNNNNNNNNN	R,T	171	440	06.02.05	7655	200303	92717
786.682-250	TUNNEL-ELASTIC OPERATOR, ZIGZAG (garment)	2113	44433532324	LNNNNNNCCCNNNNCNNNON	NNNN4NNNNNNNNNN	R,T	171	440	06.02.05	7655	200303	92717
786.682-254	ULTRASONIC-SEAMING-MACHINE OPERATOR (garment)	2122	44449533335	LNNNNNNCCCNNNNCNNNNN	NNNN3NNNNNNNNNN	R,T	171	440	06.02.05	7655	200303	92717
786.682-258	UTILITY OPERATOR (garment)	3124	44433532334	LNNNNNNCCCNNNNCNNNON	NNNN4NNNNNNNNNN	T	171	440	06.02.05	7655	200303	92717
786.682-262	WAISTBAND SETTER, LOCKSTITCH (garment)	2112	44433532334	LNNNNNNCCCNNNNCNNOON	NNNN4NNNNNNNNNN	R,T	171	440	06.04.05	7655	200303	92717
786.682-266	WAISTLINE JOINER, LOCKSTITCH (garment)	2113	44433532334	LNNNNNNCCCNNNNCNNOON	NNNN4NNNNNNNNNN	R,T	171	440	06.04.05	7655	200303	92717
786.682-270	WAISTLINE JOINER, OVERLOCK (garment)	2114	44433532324	LNNNNNNCCCNNNNCNNOON	NNNN4NNNNNNNNNN	R,T	171	440	06.04.05	7655	200303	92717
786.682-274	ZIGZAG-MACHINE OPERATOR (garment)	2112	44433532334	LNNNNNNCCCNNNNCNNOON	NNNN4NNNNNNNNNN	R,T	171	440	06.04.05	7655	200303	92717
786.682-278	ZIPPER SETTER, CHAINSTITCH (garment)	2113	44433532334	LNNNNNNFCFNNNNCNFNON	NNNN4NNNNNNNNNN	R,T	171	440	06.04.05	7655	200303	92717
786.682-282	ZIPPER SETTER, LOCKSTITCH (garment)	2112	44443433344	LNNNNNNCCCNNNNCNNOON	NNNN4NNNNNNNNNN	R,T	171	440	06.04.05	7655	200303	92717
786.682-286	BUTTON-SEWING-MACHINE OPERATOR (garment)	2112	44443434344	LNNNNNNCCCNNNNCNNOON	NNNN4NNNNNNNNNN	R,T	171	440	06.04.05	7655	200303	92717
786.685-010	BUTTONHOLE-MACHINE OPERATOR (garment)	2112	44443433344	LNNNNNNCCCOONNNCNFNON	NNNN4NNONNNNNNN	R,T	171	440	06.04.05	7655	200303	92717
786.685-014	EMBROIDERY-MACHINE OPERATOR (garment)	2112	44443433354	LNNNNNNFFFNNNNFNNNNN	NNNN4NNNNNNNNNN	R,T	171	440	06.04.05	7655	200303	92717
786.685-018	PIPED-POCKET-MACHINE OPERATOR (garment)	2112	44443433344	LNNNNNNFFFNNNNFNNFNON	NNNN4NNNNNNNNNN	R,T	171	440	06.04.05	7655	200303	92717
786.685-022	PROFILE-STITCHING-MACHINE OPERATOR (garment)	2113	44434434344	LNNNNNNFFFNNNNFNNNON	NNNN4NNNNNNNNNN	R,T	171	440	06.04.05	7655	200303	92717
786.685-026	SEWING-MACHINE OPERATOR, SEMIAUTOMATIC (garment)	2122	44443444344	LNNNNNNCCCNNNNFNFNON	NNNN4NNONNNNNNN	R,T	171	440	06.04.05	7655	200303	92717

DOT #	DOT Title & Industry	Trng	Aptitude	Physical	Environment	Tempra	WkF	MPSMS	GOE	SOC	CIP	OES
786.685-034	TACKING-MACHINE OPERATOR (garment)	2112	4443343344	LNNNNNNFFFONNNCNFOON	NNNN4NNNNNNNNN	R,T	171	440	06.04.05	7655	200303	92717
786.685-038	ULTRASONIC-SEAMING-MACHINE OPERATOR, SEMIAUTOMATIC (garment)	2111	4443533335	LNNNNNNFFNNNNNNNNNN	NNNN3NNNNNNNNN	R,T	171	443	06.04.05	7659	000000	92998
786.685-042	BUTTONHOLE-AND-BUTTON-SEWING-MACHINE OPERATOR (garment)	2122	4443544344	LNNNNNNFFNNNNNFNNOON	NNNN4NNNNNNNNN	R,T	171	440	06.04.05	7655	200303	92717
787.132-010	SEWING SUPERVISOR (any industry)	4336	3333343344	LNNONNNFFNFNFNFFON	NNNN4NNNNNNNNN	V,D,P	171	435	06.02.01	7100	200502	81008
787.132-014	SUPERVISOR, SEWING ROOM (fabrication, nec)	4235	3343343344	LNNNNNNFFFNFNFNOON	NNNN4NNNNNNNNN	D,P,J	171	421	06.02.01	7100	000000	81008
787.132-018	SUPERVISOR, STITCHING DEPARTMENT (tex. prod., nec)	4227	3343343344	LNNNNNNFFNOONFNOON	NNNN4NNNNNNNNN	V,D,P	171	432	06.02.01	7100	000000	81008
787.381-010	LAMP-SHADE SEWER (fabrication, nec)	3226	3343343344	LNNNNNNFFFONNNFNNN	NNNN4NNNNNNNNN	T	054	619	06.02.27	6859	000000	89599
787.682-010	BINDER (any industry)	3114	3443343344	LNNNNNNFFFNNNFNFCFN	NNNN4NNONNNNNNN	R,T	171	420	06.02.05	6859	200303	92721
787.682-014	CARPET SEWER (carpet & rug; retail trade)	3223	3443343344	LNNNNNNFFFNNNNFNCFN	NNNN4NFNNNNNNN	R,T	171	431	06.02.05	7655	000000	92721
787.682-018	DRAPERY OPERATOR (retail trade)	3124	3443343344	MNNNNNNNCCFNNNNNFNFOFN	NNNN3NNNNNNNNN	R,J,T	171	435	06.02.05	7655	200502	92721
787.682-022	EMBROIDERY-MACHINE OPERATOR (any industry)	3224	3443533343	LNNNNNNNCCNNNNNFNFOON	NNNN3NNNNNNNNN	R,J,T	171	420	06.02.05	7655	200303	92721
787.682-026	HEMMER (any industry)	3114	4443533343	LNNNNNNFFFNNNNNFNFFON	NNNN4NNNNNNNNN	R,T	171	435	06.02.05	7655	200502	92721
787.682-030	MENDER (any industry)	3124	3443353334	LNNNNNNNFCCFNONONCNNFCN	NNNN4NNONNNNNNN	R,T	171	420	06.02.05	6179	200301	85956
787.682-034	OVEREDGE SEWER (any industry)	3124	3444343344	LNNNNNNFFFNNNNNFNFOON	NNNN3NNNNNNNNN	R,T	171	440	06.02.05	7655	200502	92721
787.682-038	ROLL-OR-TAPE-EDGE-MACHINE OPERATOR (furniture)	2113	4443533344	MNNNNNNNCCFNNNNNFNFOON	NNNN4NNNNNNNNN	R,T	171	464	06.02.05	7655	000000	92721
787.682-046	SEWING-MACHINE OPERATOR (any industry)	3225	4443533344	LNNNNNNFFFNNNNNFNFOON	NNNN4NNNNNNNNN	R,T	171	420	06.02.05	7655	200502	92721
787.682-050	SEWING-MACHINE OPERATOR (knitting; protective dev.)	2113	4443533344	LNNONNNFCFNNONONCNFFON	NNNN4NNNNNNNNN	R,T	171	604	06.02.05	7655	000000	92721
787.682-054	SEWING-MACHINE OPERATOR (toy-sport equip.)	2113	4544553345	LNNNNNNNCCCNNNNCNFFNN	NNNN4NNNNNNNNN	R	171	615	06.02.05	7655	000000	92721
787.682-058	SEWING-MACHINE OPERATOR II (tex. prod., nec)	3224	3443343344	LNNNNNNCFNNONONONCON	NNNN4NFNNNNNNN	R,T	171	420	06.02.05	7655	200502	92721
787.682-066	SEWING MACHINE OPERATOR I (tex. prod., nec)	3223	3443343344	LNNNNNNCCNNONONCNFFFN	NNNN4NFNNNNNNN	R,T	171	435	06.02.05	7655	000000	92721
787.682-074	SEWING MACHINE OPERATOR (knitting)	2113	4443343344	LNNONNNCCNNONONCNOOON	NNNN4NNNNNNNNN	R,T	171	446	06.02.05	7655	200303	92717
787.682-078	SHIRRING-MACHINE OPERATOR (any industry)	2114	3443343344	LNNNNNNCCFNONONCNFFN	NNNN4NNNNNNNNN	R,T	171	432	06.02.05	7655	200303	92721
787.682-082	TUCKING-MACHINE OPERATOR (any industry)	3114	4443533345	LNNNNNNCCNNNNNCNFCON	NNNN4NNNNNNNNN	R,T	171	435	06.02.05	7655	200501	92721
787.682-086	ZIPPER SETTER (any industry)	3114	4444543354	LNNNNNNFFNNNNNFNFNON	NNNN4NNNNNNNNN	R,T	171	618	06.04.05	7655	000000	92721
787.685-014	FASTENER-SEWING-MACHINE OPERATOR (any industry)	2122	4444443354	LNNNNNNCCFNNNNNFNFOON	NNNN4NNNNNNNNN	R,T	171	435	06.04.05	7655	200502	92721
787.685-018	FOLDER-SEAMER, AUTOMATIC (any industry)	2123	4444543354	LNNONNNCCFNNNNFNFON	NNNN4NNNNNNNNN	R,T	171	420	06.04.05	7655	000000	92721
787.685-018	HEMMER, AUTOMATIC (tex. prod., nec)	3113	4543543354	LNNNNNNFFFNNNNNFNFFON	NNNN4NNNNNNNNN	R	171	464	06.04.05	7655	000000	92721
787.685-022	HEMMING-AND-TACKING-MACHINE OPERATOR (furniture)	2112	3443343344	LNNNNNNCCCNNNNNCNFFFN	NNNN4NNNNNNNNN	R,T	171	435	06.04.05	7655	200502	92721
787.685-026	PLEATER (tex. prod., nec)	3113	4443343344	LNNNNNNFFFONNNFNFOON	NNNN4NNNNNNNNN	R,T	171	420	06.04.05	7655	000000	92721
787.685-030	SERGING-MACHINE OPERATOR, AUTOMATIC (any industry)	3123	4443434344	LNNNNNNFFONNNNFNFOON	NNNN4NNNNNNNNN	R,T	171	618	06.04.05	7655	000000	92721
787.685-034	SEWING-MACHINE OPERATOR, ZIPPER (button & notion)	2112	4443533344	LNNNNNNFFONNNFNFFON	NNNN4NNNNNNNNN	R	171	435	06.04.05	7655	200502	92721
787.685-038	SHIRRING-MACHINE OPERATOR, AUTOMATIC (tex. prod., nec)	2113	4443543354	LNNNNNNFFONNNFNFFON	NNNN4NNNNNNNNN	R	171	435	06.04.05	7655	200303	92721
787.685-042	TACKING-MACHINE OPERATOR (any industry)	2113	4444343344	LNNNNNNCFNONONCNNFON	NNNN4NNNNNNNNN	R,T	171	420	06.04.05	7655	200303	92721
787.685-046	TOE-CLOSING-MACHINE TENDER (knitting)	2112	4444443345	LNNNNNNCCFNNNNFNFNONN	NNNN3NNNNNNNNN	R	171	446	06.04.05	7655	200303	92717
787.685-050	TRIMMING SEWER, AUTOMATIC (garment; tex. prod., nec)	2113	4444543354	LNNOONNFFONNNNOFNOON	NNNN4NNNNNNNNN	R	171	420	06.04.05	7655	200303	92721
787.685-054	SEWING-MACHINE OPERATOR, PAPER BAGS (paper goods)	2114	4444443355	LNNNNNNFFFNNNNNFNFNN	NNNN4NNNNNNNNN	R	171	474	06.04.04	7679	000000	92998
787.686-010	BAG SEWER (paper goods)	2112	4444543345	SNNNNNNNCCFONNNNNCNNNCN	NNNN3NNNNNNNNN	R	171	474	06.04.04	8725	000000	98502
788.131-010	SUPERVISOR (boot & shoe)	4437	3333333343	LNNNNNNFFFFONNFFONFNCFN	NNNN4NNNNNNNNN	D,J,P,T	102	604	06.02.01	7100	000000	81008
788.137-010	SUPERVISOR, PACKING (boot & shoe)	4437	3333334354	LNNNNNNFFOOFFNNFFN	NNNN4NNNNNNNNN	D,J	041	522	06.02.01	7100	520205	81008
788.222-010	INSTRUCTOR (boot & shoe)	4346	2322432244	LNNNNNNFFONFFNFNFNON	NNNN3NNNNNNNNN	J,P,V	296	522	06.02.01	2390	480304	31314
788.261-010	ORTHOPEDIC-BOOT-AND-SHOE DESIGNER AND MAKER (boot & shoe; protective dev.)	4347	2232432244	LNNFOONCCNOONCNCFON	NNNN4NOONNNNNN	J	102	604	05.05.15	6854	480304	89511
788.281-010	DESIGNER AND PATTERNMAKER (boot & shoe)	4437	2322232354	LNNNNNNCCNNNNCNCCON	NNNN4NNNNNNNNN	J,T	264	522	05.05.15	6856	480304	89502
788.381-010	COBBLER (boot & shoe)	3125	3453533344	MNNONNNNCCFNNNNFNFOON	NNNN4NNNNNNNNN	V,J,T	102	522	05.02.27	6854	480304	89511
788.381-014	SHOEMAKER, CUSTOM (boot & shoe)	4336	3333532254	LNNNNNNCCONNNCNFFON	NNNN4NNNNNNNNO	J,T	102	522	05.05.15	6854	480304	89511
788.384-010	INSPECTOR (boot & shoe)	3225	3333433343	MNNCNNNFFFONNCNFFON	NNNN4NNNNNNNNO	J,T	212	522	06.03.01	7820	480304	83005
788.387-010	UPPER-LEATHER SORTER (boot & shoe)	3224	3444344452	MNNNONNFFFNNNFNFFN	NNNN3NNNNNNNNN	J,T	221	522	06.03.01	7850	480304	83005
788.584-010	HEEL SORTER (boot & shoe)	3224	3444344454	SNNNNNNCCFONNNNCNNNN	NNNN3NNNNNNNNN	J,T	212	522	06.03.02	7820	480304	83005
788.584-014	MARKER, HAND (boot & shoe)	2112	4444434354	LNNNNNNCCCNNNNCNNNON	NNNN4NNNNNNNNN	T	241	522	06.04.27	7759	480304	93999
788.587-010	JOB PUTTER-UP AND TICKET PREPARER (boot & shoe)	3223	4444434354	MNNNONNNCCONNNNNCNFNN	NNNN4NNNNNNNNN	R,T	221	522	05.09.02	7850	480304	83005
788.667-010	ODD-SHOE EXAMINER (boot & shoe)	3113	4444444353	LNNNNNNCCONOONFNFFFN	NNNN4NNNNNNNNN	J,T	221	522	06.03.02	7820	480304	83005
788.684-010	ASSEMBLER FOR PULLER-OVER, HAND (boot & shoe)	3113	4454453355	LNNNNNNCCNNNFNFNNN	NNNN4NNNNNNNNN	R,T	063	522	06.04.27	7720	480304	93956

DOT #	DOT Title & Industry	Trng	Aptitude	Physical	Environment	Tempra	WkF	MPSMS	GOE	SOC	CIP	OES
788.684-014	ASSEMBLER, SANDAL PARTS (boot & shoe)	2122	44543543355	LNNNNNNCCFNNNNFNFFNN	NNNN4NNNNNNNN	R,T	063	521	06.04.27	7720	480304	93956
788.684-018	BINDING FOLDER, MACHINE (boot & shoe)	3124	44444444345	LNNNNNNCCFNNNNFNFNNN	NNNN4NNNNNNNN	R,T	062	522	06.04.27	7720	480304	93999
788.684-022	BLEMISH REMOVER (boot & shoe)	2114	44544533353	LNNNNNNCCFNNNNCNNNFN	NNNN4NNNNNNNN	R,T	153	522	06.04.33	6179	480304	85999
788.684-026	BOTTOM FILLER (boot & shoe)	2112	44544544345	MNNNONNNCCNNNNNNFNNNN	NNNN4NNNNNNNN	R,T	136	522	06.04.32	7720	480304	93956
788.684-030	BOTTOM WHEELER (boot & shoe)	2113	44443533355	LNNNNNNNFFNNNNNFNFNNN	NNNN4NNNNNNNN	R	192	522	06.04.27	7720	000000	93999
788.684-034	BOW MAKER (boot & shoe)	2112	45434543455	LNNNNNNCCCNNNNFNFNNN	NNNN3NNNNNNNN	R	062	522	06.04.27	7720	480304	93999
788.684-038	BUTTONHOLE MAKER (boot & shoe)	2113	45444543345	LNNNNNNFFNNNNNFNFNNN	NNNN4NNNNNNNN	R	171	522	06.04.27	7753	480304	93926
788.684-042	CRIPPLE WORKER (boot & shoe)	3113	34543433354	LNNNNNNCCCONNNNFNFFON	NNNN4NNNNNNNN	R,T	054	522	06.02.27	7753	480304	93926
788.684-046	FINGER COBBLER (boot & shoe)	3124	34543533353	LNNNNNNCCFNNNNFNNNFN	NNNN4NNNNNNNN	R,T	102	522	06.02.27	6179	480304	85999
788.684-050	FLAMER (boot & shoe)	2112	44544544355	MNNNNNNCCNNNNNCNNNNNO	NNNN4NNNNNNNNO	R,T	082	520	06.04.27	7759	480304	93923
788.684-054	HAND SEWER, SHOES (boot & shoe)	2112	44544533354	LNNNNNNCCFONNNNCNFFON	NNNO3NNNNNNNN	R,T	171	522	06.04.27	7752	480304	93923
788.684-058	HEEL ATTACHER, WOOD (boot & shoe)	2114	44543544355	LNNNNNNCCNNNNNFNFNNN	NNNN4NNFNNNNNN	R,T	063	522	06.04.34	7720	480304	93956
788.684-062	HEEL-SEAT FITTER, HAND (boot & shoe)	2114	44443534355	LNNNNNNCCFNNNNCNFNNN	NNNN3NNNNNNNN	R,T	054	522	06.04.34	7720	480304	93926
788.684-066	INKER (boot & shoe)	2112	44544544354	MNNNNNNCCFNNNNCNNNFN	NNNN4NNNNNNNN	R,T	153	522	06.04.33	7756	480304	93947
788.684-070	INTERLACER (boot & shoe)	2123	44543533355	SNNNNNNCCNNNNNFNFNNN	NNNN4NNNNNNNN	R	061	522	06.04.27	7759	480304	93999
788.684-074	LASTER, HAND (boot & shoe)	2112	44544533355	MNNNNNNCCFNNNNFNFNNN	NNNN4NNNNNNNN	R,T	102	522	06.04.27	7720	480304	93956
788.684-078	LASTING-MACHINE OPERATOR, HAND METHOD (boot & shoe)	2114	44443534355	LNNONONCCFNNNNFNFNNN	NNNN4NNNNNNNN	R,T	072	522	06.04.27	7753	480304	93956
788.684-082	OUTSIDE CUTTER, HAND (boot & shoe)	3224	34443423254	LNNNNNNCCCONNNNFNFNON	NNNN3NNNNNNNN	R,T	054	522	06.02.24	7720	480304	93926
788.684-086	PULLER AND LASTER, MACHINE (boot & shoe)	2123	44543544445	LNNNNNNCCOONNNNFNFONN	NNNN4NNNNNNNN	R,T	132	522	06.04.27	7720	480304	93956
788.684-090	PULLER OVER, MACHINE (boot & shoe)	2114	44443534345	LNNNNNNCCFNNNNNFNFNNN	NNNN4NNNNNNNN	R,T	072	522	06.04.27	7720	480304	93956
788.684-094	RASPER (boot & shoe)	2112	44544544345	LNNNNNNCCOFNNNNFNFNNN	NNNN3NNNNNNNN	R	051	522	06.04.27	7720	480304	93999
788.684-098	SAMPLE SHOE INSPECTOR AND REWORKER (boot & shoe)	3125	34533533353	LNNNNNNFFFNNNNFNFNONFN	NNNN3NNNNNNNN	R,T	032	522	06.03.02	7820	480304	85999
788.684-102	SCREW REMOVER (boot & shoe)	2112	44544544445	LNNNNNNFFNNNNNFNNONFN	NNNN4NNNNNNNN	R	071	522	06.04.27	7759	480304	93999
788.684-106	SLIP LASTER (boot & shoe)	2112	44533534355	LNNNNNNCCFNNNNNFNFNNN	NNNN4NNNNNNNN	R,T	061	522	06.04.27	7755	480304	92998
788.684-110	SOLE SEWER, HAND (boot & shoe)	3136	34433533355	LNNONONCCCONNNNCNCNNN	NNNN3NNNNNNNN	R,T	171	522	06.02.27	7752	480304	92723
788.684-114	THREAD LASTER (boot & shoe)	3123	44443543345	LNNNNNNCCNNNNNFNFNNN	NNNN4NNNNNNNN	R,T	171	522	06.04.05	7656	480304	92723
788.684-118	TREE DRILLER (boot & shoe)	2113	34443544455	LNNNNNNCCNNNNNFNFNNN	NNNN4NNNNNNNN	R,T	053	522	06.04.27	7759	480304	93999
788.684-122	UPPER-AND-BOTTOM LACER, HAND (boot & shoe)	2123	34543543355	LNNNNNNCCCNNNNNCNCNNN	NNNN4NNNNNNNN	R,T	171	522	06.04.27	7720	480304	93956
788.684-126	WOOD-HEEL FINISHER (boot & shoe)	2113	44543533355	SNNNNNNCCFONNNNFNFNNN	NNNN4NNNNNNNN	R,T	102	522	06.04.27	7759	480304	93999
788.684-130	WRINKLE CHASER (boot & shoe)	2112	44544534355	LNNNNNNCCCFONNNNFNFNNN	NNNN4NNNNNNNN	R,T	032	522	06.04.27	7755	480304	93956
788.685-010	FLARE BREAKER (boot & shoe)	1112	44544544355	LNNNNNNCCNNNNNCNCNNN	NNNN4NNNNNNNN	R,T	134	522	06.04.05	7679	480304	92998
788.685-014	FOLDING-MACHINE TENDER (boot & shoe)	2112	44544534345	LNNNNNNCCFNNNNFNFNNN	NNNN4NNNNNNNN	R	063	522	06.04.05	7679	480304	92998
788.685-018	STOCK FITTER (boot & shoe)	3116	34333433343	LNNONNNFFFNNNNNFNFONN	NNNN4NNNNNNNNO	V,J,T	102	522	06.02.27	7679	480304	92998
788.685-022	TONGUE PRESSER (boot & shoe)	2112	44544544355	LNNNNNNCCFNNNNFNFNNN	NNNN4NNNNNNNN	R,T	032	522	06.04.05	7679	480304	92998
788.685-026	TOP FORMER (boot & shoe)	2112	44534534345	LNNNNNNNCNNNNNNFNNNNN	NNNN4NNNNNNNN	R	134	522	06.04.05	7679	480304	92998
788.685-030	WRAP TURNER (boot & shoe)	1112	44544544345	LNNNNNNNCCNNNNNFNFNNN	NNNN4NNNNNNNN	R	061	522	06.04.05	7679	480304	92998
788.687-010	ANTISQUEAK FILLER (boot & shoe)	1112	44544544455	LNNNNNNFFNNNNNFNFNNN	NNNN4NNNNNNNN	R	153	522	06.04.33	7740	480304	93999
788.687-014	BOTTOM BLEACHER (boot & shoe)	1112	44544544354	LNNNNNNCCNNNNNFNFNNN	NNNN4NNNNNNNN	R	153	522	06.04.33	7740	480304	93953
788.687-018	BRUSHER (boot & shoe)	1112	44544544355	LNNNONONCCFNNNNFNFNNN	NNNN3NNNNNNNN	R	031	522	06.04.27	7758	480304	98999
788.687-022	BUCKLER AND LACER (boot & shoe)	1112	45544533355	SNNONNNCCCNNNNNNFNNNN	NNNN4NNNNNNNN	R	061	522	05.09.03	8769	490299	98999
788.687-026	CASER, SHOE PARTS (boot & shoe)	3223	34444444354	MNNNONNNFFONNONFNNFFN	NNNN3NNNNNNNN	R,T	221	522	06.04.27	7870	480304	83005
788.687-030	CEMENTER, HAND (boot & shoe)	1112	44544533355	LNNNNNNNCCONNONONFNNN	NNNN4NNNNNNNN	R	063	522	06.03.02	7850	480304	83005
788.687-034	COLOR MATCHER (boot & shoe)	2214	44544444352	SNNONNNNCCNNNNNCNNNNCN	NNNN4NNNNNNNN	J,T	212	522	06.04.27	7740	480304	93956
788.687-038	DRESSER (boot & shoe)	2112	44544534354	LNNONONCCFNNNNNFNFNNN	NNNN3NNNNNNNN	R	153	522	06.03.02	7820	480304	83005
788.687-042	FINISHING TRIMMER (boot & shoe)	2112	44544543355	LNNNNNNCCFNNNNNFNFNNN	NNNN4NNNNNNNN	R	054	522	06.04.33	7758	480304	93953
788.687-046	FLOORWORKER, LASTING (boot & shoe)	2122	44444444455	LNNNNNNFFFNNNNNFNFNNN	NNNN4NNNNNNNN	R	221	522	06.04.27	8769	480304	98999
788.687-050	FOLDER, HAND (boot & shoe)	2112	44534543355	LNNNNNNCCCFNNNNCNNNFN	NNNN3NNNNNNNN	R	062	522	06.04.27	7870	480304	83005
788.687-054	GOLF-SHOE-SPIKE ASSEMBLER (boot & shoe)	2112	44543533355	MNNNNNNCCCNNNNNCNNNNN	NNNN4NNNNNNNN	R,T	071	522	06.03.02	7720	480304	93999
788.687-058	HEEL DIPPER (boot & shoe)	1112	44544544455	LNNNNNNFFONNONFNNFNNN	NNNN3NNNNNNNN	R	151	522	06.04.33	8769	480304	98999
788.687-062	INSOLE-AND-HEEL-STIFFENER (boot & shoe)	1112	44544544355	LNNNNNNCCNNNNNFNFNNN	NNNN4NNNNNNNN	R	151	522	06.04.27	8769	480304	98999
788.687-066	LABORER, BOOT AND SHOE (boot & shoe)	2112	44544544455	MNNNONONCCFNNNNONNNNNN	NNNN4NNNNNNNN	R,V	011	522	06.04.40	8769	480304	98999

DOT #	DOT Title & Industry	Trng	Aptitude	Physical	Environment	Tempra	WKF	MPSMS	GOE	SOC	CIP	OES
788.687-070	LACER I (boot & shoe)	1112	44544544455	LNNNNNNCCNNNNNNNNNN	NNNN4NNNNNNNNNNN	R	062	522	06.04.27	8769	480304	98999
788.687-074	LACING-STRING CUTTER (boot & shoe)	1111	45544544455	LNNNONNNCCNNNNNNNNNN	NNNN3NNNNNNNNNNN	R	054	522	06.04.27	8769	000000	98999
788.687-078	LAST CHALKER (boot & shoe)	2112	44444543345	LNNNNNNCFNNNNNNNNNN	NNNN4NNNNNNNNNNN	R,T	151	522	06.04.33	8769	480304	98999
788.687-082	LAST CLEANER (boot & shoe)	1111	44544544455	LNNNNNNCCNNNNNNNNNN	NNNN4NNNNNNNNNNN	R	051	522	06.04.39	8750	000000	98905
788.687-086	LAST PULLER (boot & shoe)	2112	44544544345	LNNNNNNCCNNNNNNNNNN	NNNN4NNNNNNNNNNN	R	061	522	06.04.27	8769	480304	98999
788.687-090	LEATHER SOFTENER (boot & shoe)	2112	44444444355	MNNONNNCCONNNNNONNN	NNNO4NNNNNNNNNNN	R	152	522	06.04.27	8769	480304	98999
788.687-094	MOLDER, SHOE PARTS (boot & shoe)	2112	44544534355	LNNNNNNCCNNNNNNNNNN	NNNN4NNNNNNNNNNN	R	136	522	06.04.32	7740	480304	93956
788.687-098	PAINTER, BOTTOM (boot & shoe)	1112	44544544354	LNNNONNNCCNNNNNNNNON	NNNN4NONNNNNNNNNN	R	153	522	06.04.33	7756	480304	93947
788.687-102	PEGGER (boot & shoe)	2112	44443533355	LNNNNNNCCCNNNNNCNCNN	NNNN4NNNNNNNNNNN	R,T	072	522	06.04.27	7740	480304	93999
788.687-106	SCRAP SORTER (boot & shoe)	1112	44544544454	LNNNNNNFFNNOONFNNNON	NNNN3NNNNNNNNNNN	R	221	529	06.03.02	7850	000000	83005
788.687-110	SHANK INSPECTOR (boot & shoe)	2112	45554544355	LNNNNNNFFFNNNCNNNNN	NNNN4NNNNNNNNNNN	R,T	212	522	06.03.02	7820	480304	83005
788.687-114	SHANK TAPER (boot & shoe)	1112	44544543355	SNNNNNNCCNNNNNNNNNN	NNNN4NNNNNNNNNNN	R	063	522	06.04.27	8769	480304	98956
788.687-118	SHANK-PIECE TACKER (boot & shoe)	1112	44544543354	MNNNNNNCCNNNNNFNNNN	NNNN3NNNNNNNNNNN	R	072	522	06.04.27	7740	480304	98999
788.687-122	SHOE CLEANER (boot & shoe)	2112	44544543354	LNNNONONCCCNNNNNNNNN	NNNN4NONNNNNNNNNN	R	031	522	06.04.39	8769	480304	98999
788.687-126	SHOE COVERER (boot & shoe)	1112	44444544355	LNNNNNNCCNNNNNNNNNN	NNNN4NNNNNNNNNNN	R	041	522	06.04.27	8769	480304	98999
788.687-130	SHOE TURNER (boot & shoe)	2112	44544534345	LNNNNNNCCNNNNNNNNNN	NNNN4NNNNNNNNNNN	R	062	522	06.04.27	8769	480304	98999
788.687-134	SOLE SCRAPER (boot & shoe)	1112	45554544355	MNNNNNNCCNNNNNNNNNN	NNNN4NNNNNNNNNNN	R	031	522	06.04.27	8769	000000	98999
788.687-138	STEEL-BOX-TOE INSERTER (boot & shoe)	2112	44544533355	MNNNNNNCCNNNNNFNFNNN	NNNN4NNNNNNNNNNN	R,T	061	522	06.04.27	7720	480304	93999
788.687-142	TABLE WORKER (boot & shoe)	2112	44444433355	LNNONNNCCFNNNNNFNNNN	NNNN4NNNNNNNNNNN	R	063	522	06.04.27	7740	480304	93999
788.687-146	TACK PULLER (boot & shoe)	1112	44544544455	LNNNNNNCCNNNNNFNNNN	NNNN4NNNNNNNNNNN	R	072	522	06.04.27	8769	000000	98999
788.687-150	TRIMMER, HAND (boot & shoe)	2112	44544543345	LNNNNNNCCFNNNNFNNNN	NNNN4NNNNNNNNNNN	R	054	522	06.04.05	7753	480304	93926
788.687-154	VAMP CREASER (boot & shoe)	1112	44544544345	LNNNNNNCCFNNNONFNNN	NNNN4NNNNNNNNNNN	R	134	522	06.04.27	7740	480304	93999
788.687-158	VAMP-STRAP IRONER (boot & shoe)	2112	44544544345	SNNNNNNNFFONNNNNFNNN	NNNN4NNNNNNNNNNN	R	032	522	06.04.27	8769	480304	93926
788.687-162	WELT-BUTTER, HAND (boot & shoe)	2112	44544544455	LNNNNNNCCNNNNNNCNNNN	NNNN4NNNNNNNNNNN	R	054	522	06.04.27	7753	480304	93926
788.687-166	WHITE-SHOE RAGGER (boot & shoe)	1112	44544544455	SNNNNNNCCNNNNNNNNNN	NNNN4NNNNNNNNNNN	R	153	522	06.04.33	7756	480304	93947
789.132-010	SUPERVISOR IV (tex. prod., nec)	3326	33333343344	LNNNNNNFFONFFNFNNNFN	NNNN3NNNNNNNNNNN	D,T	054	435	06.02.01	7100	200502	81008
789.132-014	SUPERVISOR I (tex. prod., nec)	4336	33333434345	LNNOONFFNNFFNFNNNNN	NNNN4NNNNNNNNNNN	D,P,V	062	436	06.02.01	7100	000000	81008
789.132-018	SUPERVISOR III (tex. prod., nec)	4337	33333443354	LNNNNNNFFNFNNONOOFO	NNNN4NNNNNNNNNNN	D,P,T	171	436	06.02.01	7100	000000	81008
789.132-022	SUPERVISOR, NET MAKING (toy-sport equip.)	4337	33333433345	LNNNNNNFFNFNFNNOONN	NNNN4NNNNNNNNNNN	D,J,P	062	616	06.02.01	7100	000000	81008
789.132-026	SUPERVISOR, PARACHUTE MANUFACTURING (tex. prod., nec)	4237	33332332344	LNNNNNNFFNFFNFNFNON	NNNN4NNNNNNNNNNN	D,J,T	171	439	06.02.01	7100	000000	81008
789.134-010	SUPERVISOR II (tex. prod., nec)	4237	33333443354	LNNNNNNFFONCCNFFNON	NNNN4NNNNNNNNNNN	D,P,J,T	062	432	06.02.01	7100	000000	81008
789.134-014	SUPERVISOR II (protective dev.)	4347	33333333355	MNNNNNNFFFNFFNONFNNN	NNNN3NNNNNNNNNNN	D,P,J	164	604	06.02.01	7100	520205	81008
789.137-010	BOXING-AND-PRESSING SUPERVISOR (knitting)	4336	33333344454	LNNNNNNOOONFFNNONNN	NNNN3NNNNNNNNNNN	D,P	221	424	06.02.01	4525	200303	51002
789.137-014	SUPERVISOR, WEBBING (tex. prod., nec)	4337	33333344455	LNNNNNFFONNFFNFNFNNN	ONNN4NNNNNNNNNNN	V,D,P,J	164	439	06.02.01	7100	000000	81008
789.222-010	INSTRUCTOR, APPAREL MANUFACTURE (textile)	4336	32333333344	LNNNNNNFFNFFNFNFNON	NNNN4NNNNNNNNNNN	V,D,P	296	420	06.02.01	2390	000000	31314
789.261-010	BOAT-CANVAS MAKER-INSTALLER (tex. prod., nec)	3336	33333343345	MOOFFOOFFNOONFNOONN	ONNN3NNNNNNNNNNN	V,J,T	102	436	05.05.15	6859	490306	89599
789.381-010	BEADWORKER (fabrication, nec)	3126	33432432242	LNNNNNNFFNNNFNFOFN	ONNN3NNNNNNNNNNN	J	171	610	01.06.03	6859	200303	89599
789.381-014	PATTERN CHART-WRITER (paper goods)	3225	33333443355	LNNNNNNFFNNNFNFNFN	NNNN3NNNNNNNNNNN	J	242	752	05.03.02	6856	000000	89502
789.381-018	TRAWL NET MAKER (tex. prod., nec)	3236	34433434344	MNNNNNNFFFNNNNFNFNON	NNNN4NNNNNNNNNNN	J,T	165	439	06.01.04	6859	000000	89599
789.382-010	CLICKING-MACHINE OPERATOR (boot & shoe; glove & mit.; leather prod.)	3225	34433434353	MNNONNNCCFONNNCNNCON	NNNN4NNFNNNNNNNN	J,R,T	054	520	06.02.05	7654	480304	92944
789.387-010	QUALITY-CONTROL CHECKER (garment)	3235	34433344453	LNNNNNNFFNNNFNNNFFN	NNNN3NNNNNNNNNNN	J,T	212	440	06.03.01	7830	200303	83005
789.387-014	SAMPLE SELECTOR (tex. prod., nec)	2114	34433343353	SNNNNNNFFFNNNNFNFN	NNNN3NNNNNNNNNNN	J,T	221	439	06.02.27	7759	000000	93999
789.484-010	DIAGRAMMER AND SEAMER (carpet & rug)	4435	34333434354	MNNOOOFFONNNNFNFFON	NNNN4NNNNNNNNNNN	J,T	241	431	06.02.31	7753	469999	93932
789.484-014	FINISHER, HAND (tex. prod., nec)	3125	34443433354	MNNOOONFFFNNNFOFOOO	NNNN4NNFNNNNNNNN	R,T	171	436	06.02.27	7752	000000	93923
789.487-010	PLEAT TAPER (tex. prod., nec)	1112	44544544454	LNNNNNNFFNNNFNNNNNN	NNNN3NNNNNNNNNNN	R,T	062	420	06.03.01	7850	200303	83005
789.587-010	BOXING INSPECTOR (garment)	2123	44443444354	LNNNNNNFFFNNNNFNNNN	NNNN3NNNNNNNNNNN	R,J,T	171	440	06.03.02	7820	200303	83005
789.587-014	INSPECTOR, FABRIC (any industry)	3123	34443443453	LNNNNNNCCFNNNCNNNCN	NNNN3NNNNNNNNNNN	R,J,T	212	420	06.03.02	7820	200502	83005
789.587-018	PARACHUTE MARKER (tex. prod., nec)	2112	44434434355	MNNNNNNFFFNNNFNNNNN	NNNN4NNNNNNNNNNN	R,T	062	439	06.04.27	8769	000000	98999
789.587-022	RUG INSPECTOR II (carpet & rug)	3224	34443444353	LNNOOOFFFNNNNFNFFFN	NNNN4NNNNNNNNNNN	R,T	212	431	06.03.02	7820	000000	83005
789.587-026	SAMPLE CLERK (textile)	2113	44443444353	LNNONNNFFFNNNFNFNFN	NNNN3NNNNNNNNNNN	R,T	054	420	06.04.27	7720	000000	93999
789.684-010	BOW MAKER (any industry)	2123	44444543455	LNNNNNNCCCNNNNONONNN	NNNN3NNNNNNNNNNN	R,T	062	618	06.04.27	7755	200303	93999

DOT #	DOT Title & Industry	Trng	Aptitude	Physical	Environment	Tempra	WkF	MPSMS	GOE	SOC	CIP	OES
789.684-014	BUFFING-WHEEL FORMER, HAND (tex. prod., nec)	2113	44443434355	LNNNNNCCFNNNNNONNN	NNNN4NNNNNNNNN	R,T	062	538	06.04.27	7755	000000	93999
789.684-018	CANOPY STRINGER (tex. prod., nec)	3224	34443533354	LNNNNNNCCONNNNNONNN	NNNN4NNNNNNNNN	R,T	061	439	06.02.27	7720	000000	93999
789.684-022	HAIR CLIPPER, POWER (leather mfg.)	2112	44544534355	LNNNNNCCONNNNFNFNNN	NNNC3NCNNNNNNNN	R	054	529	06.04.34	7753	000000	93926
789.684-026	MOLDER, SHOULDER PAD (garment)	2112	44443534345	LNNNNNCCNNNNNFNFNNN	NNNN3NNNNNNNNN	R,T	032	439	06.04.27	7755	000000	93999
789.684-030	NET MAKER (tex. prod., nec)	2113	34434433355	LNNNNNNFFNNNNNFNNNN	NNNN4NNNNNNNNN	R,T	165	439	06.04.27	7720	000000	93999
789.684-034	PARACHUTE FOLDER (tex. prod., nec)	2113	44433533355	HNNNNNNCCFNNONONNNNN	NNNN4NNNNNNNNN	R,T	061	439	06.04.27	7759	000000	93999
789.684-038	PARACHUTE MENDER (tex. prod., nec)	3113	44443533355	LNNNONONFFFNNNNFNNN	NNNN3NNNNNNNNN	R,T	171	439	05.10.04	6179	000000	85956
789.684-042	RAWHIDE-BONE ROLLER (leather prod.)	2112	44454543355	LNNNNNNFFNNNNONONNN	NNNN3NNNNNNNNN	R,T	061	529	06.04.27	7755	000000	93999
789.684-046	RIGGER (tex. prod., nec)	2112	44445533355	MNNFNNNFFNNNNONNNNN	NNNN4NNNNNNNNN	R	102	436	06.04.34	7759	000000	93926
789.684-050	THREAD CUTTER (any industry)	2112	44544534354	LNNNNNNFFNNNNNFNNON	NNNN4NNNNNNNNN	R	054	420	06.04.27	7753	200303	93926
789.684-054	ELECTRIC BLANKET WIRER (tex. prod., nec)	2113	44543423255	MNNOONNCCCNNNNFNNNNN	NNNN4NNNNNNNNN	U	061	435	06.02.27	7759	000000	93999
789.685-010	ORNAMENT SETTER (garment; tex. prod., nec)	2123	44443533444	SNNNNNNFFNNNNNFNFNON	NNNN4NNNNNNNNN	R,T	062	432	06.04.34	7679	000000	92998
789.687-010	BAG CUTTER (tex. prod., nec)	2112	44544534355	LNNFNFNCCNNNNNNNNNNN	NNNN4NNNNNNNNN	R	054	436	06.04.27	7850	200303	83005
789.687-014	BAG LINER (tex. prod., nec)	1112	44544544355	LNNNNNCCNNNNNNNNNNN	NNNN3NNNNNNNNN	R	062	436	06.04.27	8769	000000	98999
789.687-018	BONER (garment; protective dev.)	2112	44454543455	LNNNNNNCCFONNNCNNNNN	NNNN4NNNNNNNNN	R	061	444	06.04.34	8769	000000	83005
789.687-022	BUFFING TURNER-AND-COUNTER (tex. prod., nec)	1112	44443443455	SNNNNNNFCCNNNNFNFNNN	NNNN4NNNNNNNNN	R	061	421	06.03.02	7740	480303	83005
789.687-026	BUFFING-WHEEL INSPECTOR (tex. prod., nec)	2112	44443444355	LNNNNNNCCNNNNNFNNNN	NNNN4NNNNNNNNN	J,T	062	538	06.03.02	7820	000000	83005
789.687-030	CLIPPER (any industry)	1112	44444533355	LNNOONNCGFOONNNFNNNNN	NNNN4NNNNNNNNN	R	054	424	06.03.02	8769	200303	98999
789.687-034	CLOTH-STOCK SORTER (tex. prod., nec; textile)	2122	44444444354	LNNNNNCCONNNNFNNNNFN	NNNN3NNNNNNNNN	R	221	420	06.03.02	7850	000000	83005
789.687-038	COVER INSPECTOR (furniture)	3223	34443444354	LNNNNNNFFFNNONCNNNNFN	NNNN4NNNNNNNNN	R,T	212	433	06.03.02	7820	000000	83005
789.687-042	EXAMINER (glove & mit.)	2113	34443444354	LNNNNNNFFONNNNNFNNNFN	NNNN4NNNNNNNNN	R,J,T	212	449	06.03.02	7820	200303	83005
789.687-046	FINAL ASSEMBLER (garment)	2112	44443433354	LNNONNNFCFNNNNFNFNON	NNNN3NNNNNNNNN	R	061	440	06.04.27	8769	200303	98999
789.687-050	FINISHER (tex. prod., nec)	2112	44443433354	LNNNNNCCFNNNNNNNNFN	NNNN4NNNNNNNNN	R,T	031	432	06.03.02	7820	200303	83005
789.687-054	FLOCKER (tex. prod., nec)	2112	44444444455	LNNNNNNCCNNNNNNNNNNN	NNNN4NNNNNNNNN	R	161	439	06.04.33	7740	200303	93956
789.687-058	FOLDER (tex. prod., nec)	1112	44544434355	LNNONNNCCNNNNNNNNNNN	NNNN3NNNNNNNNN	R	062	436	06.04.27	8769	000000	98999
789.687-062	FRINGER (carpet & rug; tex. prod., nec)	1112	44444443455	LNNNNNNFFNNONCNNNNFN	NNNN3NNNNNNNNN	R	054	435	06.03.02	8769	000000	98999
789.687-066	GARMENT FOLDER (garment; knitting)	1112	44444433355	LNNNNNNCCCNNNNFNNNNN	NNNN3NNNNNNNNN	R	062	440	06.04.38	8769	200303	98999
789.687-070	GARMENT INSPECTOR (any industry)	2123	44443433354	LNNFNNNFFNNONFNFFN	NNNN4NNNNNNNNN	R,T	212	424	06.03.02	7820	200303	83005
789.687-074	GARMENT TURNER (garment; knitting)	1112	44544544345	LNNONNNCCONNNNNNNNNN	NNNN4NNNNNNNNN	R	062	424	06.04.27	8769	200303	98999
789.687-078	GARMENT-ALTERATION EXAMINER (retail trade)	3114	34443444354	LNNNNNNFFNNNNNFNONON	NNNN3NNNNNNNNN	R,T	171	440	05.05.15	7820	200301	83005
789.687-082	HARNESS RIGGER (tex. prod., nec)	2212	34443533355	LNNNNNNCCNNNNNCNNNON	NNNN3NNNNNNNNN	R,T	061	439	06.04.27	7720	000000	83005
789.687-086	HARNESS-AND-BAG INSPECTOR (tex. prod., nec)	2122	44443444354	LNNNNNCCFNNNNCNNOON	NNNN4NNNNNNNNN	J,T	171	439	06.03.02	7820	000000	83005
789.687-090	LABORER, CANVAS SHOP (tex. prod., nec)	2112	44445444354	MONOOONFFFNNNNFNOOON	NNNN4NNNNNNNNN	V	171	436	06.04.39	8769	000000	98999
789.687-094	LACER (protective dev.)	2112	44545433455	LNNNNNNFFFNNNNNFNNNON	NNNN3NNNNNNNNN	R	061	604	06.04.27	7759	000000	93999
789.687-098	MIXER II (tex. prod., nec)	1112	45555544355	LNNFNNNCCFFNNNNNNNNN	NNNN4NNNNNNNNN	R	143	419	06.04.27	7740	000000	93926
789.687-102	MONOGRAM-AND-LETTER PASTER (tex. prod., nec)	2112	44444444454	LNNNNNNFFONNNNNNFNFN	NNNN4NNNNNNNNN	R,T	063	432	06.04.27	7740	200303	93956
789.687-106	MOPHEAD TRIMMER-AND-WRAPPER (tex. prod., nec)	1112	44444444355	LNNFNNNCCFNNNNONFNNN	NNNN3NNNNNNNNN	R	041	619	06.04.38	8761	000000	98902
789.687-110	PAIRER (tex. prod., nec)	1111	44545534355	LNNNNNFFNNNNNNNNNNN	NNNN4NNNNNNNNN	R	062	435	06.04.27	8769	000000	98999
789.687-114	PARACHUTE INSPECTOR (tex. prod., nec)	2112	44443444354	LNNNNNNCCNNNNNCNNNON	NNNN4NNNNNNNNN	J,T	171	439	06.03.02	7820	000000	83005
789.687-118	PARACHUTE-LINE TIER (tex. prod., nec)	2212	44443533355	MNNONNNCCCNNNNNNNNNN	NNNN4NNNNNNNNN	R,T	062	439	06.04.27	8769	000000	98999
789.687-122	PILLOW CLEANER (tex. prod., nec)	2112	44443444354	LNNNNNNFFNNNNNNNNNNN	NNNN4NNNNNNNNN	R	031	435	06.04.27	8769	000000	98999
789.687-126	POMPOM MAKER (knitting)	1111	44445444354	LNNNNNNFFNNNNNNNNNON	NNNN3NNNNNNNNN	R	163	424	06.04.27	7753	000000	93926
789.687-130	QUILT STUFFER (tex. prod., nec)	2112	44544534355	LNNNNNNFFONNNNNNNNNN	NNNN4NNNNNNNNN	R,T	041	435	06.04.23	7740	000000	93999
789.687-134	RAG SORTER AND CUTTER (tex. prod., nec)	1112	44544534354	LNNONNNFFFNNNNNFNNNN	NNNN3NNNNNNNNN	R	054	429	06.03.02	8769	000000	98999
789.687-138	RAKER (carpet & rug)	1112	44544544455	LNNNNNNFFNNNNNNNNNNN	NNNN4NNNNNNNNN	R	161	431	06.04.27	8769	000000	98999
789.687-142	REDYE HAND (knitting)	3113	34443433453	LNNNNNNCCFNNNNNFNNFN	NNNN3NNNNNNNNN	R,T	212	446	06.03.02	7850	200303	83005
789.687-146	REMNANT SORTER (textile)	2112	44444434354	LNNFNFNFFFNNNNNNFN	NNNN3NNNNNNNNN	R,T	062	420	06.03.02	7850	000000	98999
789.687-150	REMNANT'S CUTTER (textile)	1111	44545534355	LNNNNNFFFNNNNNNNFN	NNNN3NNNNNNNNN	R	054	420	06.04.27	8769	200303	93956
789.687-154	RIVETER, HAND (garment)	2112	44443533354	LNNNNNNFFNNNNNNFNNN	NNNN4NNNNNNNNN	R,T	062	440	06.04.27	7740	000000	83005
789.687-158	RUG-INSPECTOR HELPER (carpet & rug)	2113	44545444455	MNNOOONFFFNNNNFNFNNN	NNNN4NNNNNNNNN	R,T	011	431	06.04.40	8620	000000	98999
789.687-166	SEAM STEAMER (garment)	1111	44454534355	LNNNNNNNFFFNNNNNNNNNN	NNFN3NNNNNNNNN	R	032	424	06.04.27	8769	200303	98999

DOT #	DOT Title & Industry	Trng	Aptitude	Physical	Environment	Tempra	WkF	MPSMS	GOE	SOC	CIP	OES
789.687-170	STEAMER (tex. prod., nec)	1112	44545544455	MNNNNNFFNNNNNNNN	NNNC4NNNNNNNNNN	R	032	420	06.04.16	7740	200303	93999
789.687-174	THREAD SEPARATOR (tex. prod., nec)	1112	45544534355	SNNNNNFFNNNNFNNNN	NNNN3NNNNNNNNN	R	163	432	06.04.27	8769	000000	98999
789.687-178	TIE PRESSER (knitting)	2112	44454534355	LNNNNNNFFNNNNNNNN	NNFN3NNNNNNNNN	R	032	424	06.04.27	8769	200303	98999
789.687-182	TURNER (any industry)	1112	44444444355	LNNONNNCCONNNNFNNNNN	NNNN4NNNNNNNN	R	062	420	06.04.27	8769	200303	98999
790.134-010	SUPERVISOR, CIGAR MAKING, HAND (tobacco)	3236	33433343353	LNNNNNNFFNFFNFNNNN	NNNN4NNNNNNNN	D,P,T	136	409	06.04.01	7100	000000	81008
790.381-010	TOBACCO BLENDER (retail trade)	3226	33433343353	MNNNONOFFFNNNFNOFFN	NNNN3NNNNNNNN	J,T	143	403	05.10.08	6879	000000	89899
790.684-010	BUNCH MAKER, HAND (tobacco)	2214	44443533355	LNNNNNNCCCNNNCNFNNN	NNNN3NNNNNNNN	R,T	041	402	06.04.28	7755	000000	93999
790.684-014	CIGAR MAKER (tobacco)	2225	44443533355	LNNNNNNCCCNNNCNFNNN	NNNN3NNNNNNNN	R,T	041	402	06.04.28	7755	000000	93999
790.684-018	PATCH WORKER (tobacco)	2113	44443433353	LNNNNNNCCCNNNCNNNNFN	NNNN4NNNNNNNN	R,T	063	402	06.04.28	7759	000000	93999
790.684-022	ROLLER, HAND (tobacco)	2225	44443533355	LNNNNNNFFNNNNFNNNNN	NNNN3NNNNNNNN	R,T	041	402	06.04.28	7755	000000	98999
790.687-010	CANDY CUTTER, HAND (sugar & conf.)	2112	44443433355	LNNNNNNFFONNNFNNNNFN	NNNN3NNNNNNNN	R	054	393	06.04.28	8769	000000	98999
790.687-014	CIGAR PACKER (tobacco)	2123	34434433353	LNNONNNFFNNNNFNNNNN	NNNN3NNNNNNNN	R,J,T	041	402	06.04.28	7850	000000	83005
790.687-018	LUMP INSPECTOR (tobacco)	2112	44443444455	LNNNNNNFFNNNNFNNNN	NNNN3NNNNNNNN	R,T	041	403	06.03.02	7820	000000	83005
790.687-022	MOLD PRESSER (tobacco)	2112	44454434355	MNNONNNFFNNNNNNNNN	NNNN3NNNNNNNN	R	011	403	06.04.28	8769	000000	98999
790.687-026	REJECT OPENER (tobacco)	2113	44443434355	LNNNNNNCCCNNNONNNNN	NNNN3NNNNNNNN	R,T	041	403	06.04.28	7850	000000	83005
790.687-030	TWISTER, HAND (tobacco)	1112	44544543355	LNNNNNNCCCNNNONNNNN	NNNN3NNNNNNNN	R	136	403	06.04.28	8769	000000	98999
794.684-010	BAG REPAIRER (paper goods)	2112	44434543355	LNNOONNNFFNNNNFNFNNN	NNNN3NNNNNNNN	R,T	062	474	06.04.26	6179	000000	85999
794.684-014	BOX MAKER, PAPERBOARD (any industry)	2112	44433533355	MNNNONNNFFNNNNFNFNNN	NNNN4NNNNNNNN	R,T	062	475	06.04.26	7720	000000	93956
794.684-018	EXPANSION ENVELOPE MAKER, HAND (paper goods)	2112	44444444355	LNNNNNNNCCCNNNNNNNNNN	NNNN4NNNNNNNN	V	062	474	06.04.26	7720	000000	93999
794.684-022	PAPER-NOVELTY MAKER (paper goods)	2112	44444543355	LNNNNNNNCCCONNNFNFNNN	NNNN3NNNNNNNN	R,T	063	474	06.02.26	7720	000000	93999
794.684-026	PAPIER MACHE MOLDER (fabrication, nec)	3224	34433543355	LNNNNNNFFFNNNNNNNNNN	NNNO3NNNNNNNN	R,T	136	538	06.02.26	7720	000000	93999
794.684-030	SAMPLE MAKER, HAND (paper goods)	2123	44443443355	SNNNNNNCCCFNNNNFNONN	NNNN3NNNNNNNN	R	054	474	06.04.26	7720	000000	93956
794.687-010	ASSEMBLER, PRINTED PRODUCTS (print. & pub.)	2112	44443533354	LNNNNNNCCCNNNONFNOONN	NNNN4NNNNNNNN	R	062	480	06.04.26	7720	000000	93956
794.687-014	COLOR-CARD MAKER (paint & varnish)	2112	45454543454	LNNOONNCCOONNNFNFNFN	NNNN3NNNNNNNN	R,T	054	479	06.04.26	7740	000000	93999
794.687-018	COUNTER, HAND (paper goods)	2123	44344433354	LNNOONNNCCFONNNNFNNNON	NNNN4NNNNNNNN	J,T	221	474	06.03.02	7850	000000	83005
794.687-022	FOLDER, HAND (paper goods)	2113	44453533355	LNNNNNNNFFNNNNNFNONN	NNNN4NNNNNNNNF	R	062	474	06.04.26	7740	000000	93999
794.687-026	FORWARDER (print. & pub.)	2113	45453544355	LNNNNNNFFNNNNNNNNN	NNNN4NNNNNNNNF	R,T	054	486	06.04.26	7740	480299	93956
794.687-030	GLUER AND SLICER, HAND (paper goods)	2112	44444544355	HNNFNNNNFFNNNNNNNNN	NNNN4NNNNNNNN	R	063	474	06.04.26	7740	480299	93956
794.687-034	PAPER-PATTERN FOLDER (paper goods)	1111	44454544455	LNNNNNNNCCFNNNNNNNNN	NNNN3NNNNNNNN	R,T	062	489	06.04.26	8761	000000	98902
794.687-038	PATTERN RULER (tex. prod., nec)	1112	44544544455	LNNNNNNNCCCNNNNCNNNNN	NNNN3NNNNNNNN	R,T	062	420	06.04.27	8769	000000	98999
794.687-042	PUNCHBOARD ASSEMBLER I (paper goods)	2112	44544543454	LNNNNNNNCCCNNNNNFNFON	NNNN4NNNNNNNN	R	061	474	06.04.23	7720	000000	93956
794.687-046	PUNCHBOARD ASSEMBLER II (paper goods)	1111	44544543355	LNNNNNNNCCCNNNNNNNNN	NNNN3NNNNNNNN	R,T	061	474	06.04.23	7720	000000	93956
794.687-050	SCRAPPER (paper goods)	2112	44444443345	HNNFNNNNFFNNNNFNFNNN	NNNN4NNNNNNNNF	R	054	475	06.04.39	8769	000000	98999
794.687-054	STRINGER (paper goods)	1111	44554543355	LNNNNNNNFFNNNNFNFNNN	NNNN4NNNNNNNN	R,T	062	474	06.04.23	7740	000000	93999
794.687-058	TABBER (paper goods)	1111	44544553355	LNNNNNNNFFNNNNFNFNNN	NNNN3NNNNNNNN	R	061	474	06.04.23	7740	000000	93999
794.687-062	TRIMMER, HAND (paper goods)	1111	44544543354	SNNNNNNNFFNNNNCFNNNNN	NNNN3NNNNNNNN	R	063	474	06.04.26	7753	000000	93926
795.684-014	EDGE STRIPPER (paper goods; wood. container)	2124	44543543354	LNNNNNNFFNNNNFNNNN	NNNN4NNNNNNNN	R,T	054	454	06.04.26	7759	000000	93999
795.684-018	GLOBE MOUNTER (print. & pub.)	2113	44453543455	LNNNNNNFFNNNNFNNNN	NNNN3NNNNNNNN	T	063	486	06.04.26	7759	000000	93956
795.684-022	TIPPER (print. & pub.)	2213	44444434454	LNNNNNNNFFONNNNONOONN	NNNN3NNNNNNNN	R	063	486	06.04.26	7759	480299	93956
795.684-026	WADER-BOOT-TOP ASSEMBLER (rubber goods)	2122	44443433355	LNNFNFNCCFNNNNFNFNNN	NNNN4NNNNNNNN	R,T	063	512	06.04.29	7720	000000	93956
795.687-010	COVERER, LOOSELEAF BINDER (print. & pub.)	2214	44434534455	LNNNNNNFFNNNNNFNNNN	NNNN3NNNNNNNN	R,T	063	486	06.04.27	7661	000000	92956
795.687-014	GLUER (any industry)	1112	44544543355	LNNNNNNNFFFONONFNNNNN	NNNN4NNNNNNNN	R	063	610	06.04.34	7740	000000	93999
795.687-018	GLUER, WET SUIT (plastic prod.)	2112	44443443355	LNNNNNNNFFNNNNFNNNN	NNNN3NNNNNNNN	R,T	063	519	06.04.29	7720	000000	93956
795.687-022	LINING CEMENTER (hat & cap)	1111	44454544355	LNNNNNNFFNNNNNNNNN	NNNN3NNNNNNNN	R	063	445	06.04.27	7740	000000	93956
795.687-026	TENNIS-BALL COVERER, HAND (toy-sport equip.)	2112	44543533355	LNNNNNNFFNNNNNNNNN	NNNN3NCNNNNNNN	R	063	616	06.04.27	7720	000000	93956
795.687-030	TENNIS-BALL-COVER CEMENTER (toy-sport equip.)	1112	44544534355	LNNNNNNFFNNNNNNNNN	NNNN3NNNNNNNN	R	063	616	06.04.34	7740	000000	93956
800.662-010	RIVETER, HYDRAULIC (any industry)	3115	34433433335	MONNNNNCCFNNFNFONNN	NNNN4NNNNNNNNF	J,T	073	590	06.02.02	7529	480501	92198
800.682-010	RIVETER, PORTABLE PINCH (any industry)	3114	34433343355	MFNNNNNCCFNNNNFONNN	NNNN4NNNNNNNNF	T	073	360	06.02.02	7529	480501	92198
800.684-010	RIVETER (railroad equip.)	3114	34433434345	MONFOOOFFFOOONFNFONN	NNNN4NNNNNNNNF	T	073	592	05.10.01	7529	480501	92198
800.684-014	RIVETER, PNEUMATIC (any industry)	3114	34443434335	HONFONNFFNNNNFNFNNN	ONNN4NNNNNNNNO	T	073	360	05.10.01	7529	480501	92198
800.687-010	RIVETER HELPER (any industry)	2113	44534544355	HFNFNNNFFNNNNFNFNNN	NNNN4nFNNNNNNNF	J,T	073	360	05.12.12	8611	480501	98999

DOT #	DOT Title & Industry	Trng	Aptitude	Physical	Environment	Tempra	WkF	MPSMS	GOE	SOC	CIP	OES
801.131-010	SUPERVISOR, CHIMNEY CONSTRUCTION (construction)	4328	33332433224	LFOOOONFFNFFNFOFOON	FNNN4NNNNNNNNF	V,D,P,S,J	102	369	05.05.01	6312	520205	81005
801.131-014	SUPERVISOR, FITTING (any industry)	4438	33223433355	LONNNNMFFNFFNFNFNN	NNNN4NNNNNNNNN	D,P,J,T	102	554	06.02.01	7100	520205	81008
801.131-018	SUPERVISOR, RIDE ASSEMBLY (amuse. & rec.)	4227	33324443345	MNNNOOOFFFOFFNFONN	FNNN4NNNNNNNNN	D,P,J,T	121	360	05.12.15	7100	000000	81008
801.134-010	SUPERVISOR, REINFORCED-STEEL-PLACING (construction)	4338	33322433355	LFNFFNFFNFFNFOFONO	NNNN4NNNNNNNNNO	V,D,P,J	121	360	05.05.06	7100	520205	81008
801.137-010	SUPERVISOR, ASSEMBLY (agric. equip.)	4327	33332344455	LNNOOONFFONFFNFNONN	NNNN4NNNNNNNNN	V,D,P,J	121	562	06.02.01	7100	010204	81008
801.137-014	SUPERVISOR, INSPECTION (agric. equip.)	4337	33332344454	LNNNNNNFFONFFNFNOOON	ONNN4NNNNNNNNN	D,P,J,T	211	562	06.01.01	7100	010204	81008
801.261-010	ASSEMBLER, MINING MACHINERY (machinery mfg.)	4437	33323334345	MONFFNFFFNOONFNFONN	NNNN4NFNNNNNNF	J,T	121	564	05.05.09	6812	470399	93105
801.261-014	FITTER I (any industry)	4427	33323444334	HOOOOONCCONOONFOFOON	NNNN3NONNNNNNN	J,T	102	594	05.05.06	6812	480501	93108
801.261-018	ROTARY-ENGINE ASSEMBLER (engine-turbine)	4346	23322333244	HNNNNNNFFNOONFNFFON	NNNN4NNNNNNNNN	J,T	121	551	06.02.22	6812	470303	93105
801.361-010	BLOWER AND COMPRESSOR ASSEMBLER (machinery mfg.)	4336	33332433245	HNNOOONFFNNNNFFNONN	CNNN4NFNNNNNNF	J,T	121	568	06.02.22	6812	480503	93105
801.361-014	STRUCTURAL-STEEL WORKER (construction)	3237	33323433325	HFFFFFFOOFFNFOFONO	CNNN4NFNNNNNNF	J,S,T	102	360	05.05.06	6473	000000	87814
801.361-018	STRUCTURAL-STEEL-WORKER APPRENTICE (construction)	3237	33323433325	HFFFFFFOOFFNFOFONO	FNNN4NNNFNNNN	J,S,T	102	360	05.05.06	6473	000000	87814
801.361-022	TANK SETTER (petrol. & gas)	4227	34433443335	MOOOOONFFFNFFNFNFNNN	FNNN4NNNNNNNNN	J,T	102	369	05.12.12	6473	000000	87814
801.381-010	ASSEMBLER, METAL BUILDING (construction)	3226	33323434345	MFFFFFFFFNNNNFFFONF	NNNN4NNNNNNNNN	J,T	102	361	05.12.15	6473	000000	87814
801.381-014	FITTER (machine shop)	3327	33322332255	MNNNONFFFNNNNFNFONN	NNNN4NNNNNNNNN	V,J,T	102	554	05.05.06	6812	480501	93108
801.381-018	MAJOR-ASSEMBLY INSPECTOR (agric. equip.)	3226	33332443355	MNNNOOONFFNNNNFNFNN	NNNN4NNNNNNNNN	V,J,T	212	562	06.03.02	6881	010204	83002
801.384-010	ASSEMBLER, WIRE-MESH GATE (metal prod., nec)	3114	34433434355	MNNNONONFFFNNNNFNONNO	NNNN4NNNNNNNNN	J,T	102	212	06.02.22	7720	000000	93956
801.663-010	ASSEMBLY-INSPECTOR HELPER (agric. equip.)	2113	44444433435	MNNNNNNCCNNOONNNNNNN	NNNN4NNNNNNNNN	R	211	562	06.03.02	8620	010204	98999
801.664-010	LINER REPLACER (mine & quarry; smelt. & refin.)	2113	44434434345	MNNNNNNFFONNNNFNFNNN	NNNN4NNNNNNNNN	R,T	071	564	05.12.12	8620	000000	98999
801.664-014	UTILITY WORKER, MERCHANT MILL (steel & rel.)	2125	34434543345	MNNNNNNFFONNNNFNFNNN	NNON4NNNNNNNNN	R,T	121	568	05.12.12	6140	000000	85128
801.664-018	ROLL BUILDER (steel & rel.)	3235	34434434355	MFFNNNNFFNOONFNFNNN	NNNN4NNNNNNNNN	R,T,J	102	568	05.05.06	6140	480599	93956
801.667-010	INSPECTOR, SHIPPING (agric. equip.)	3114	34434444454	LNNOOOOFFONOONFNONON	NNNN4NNNNNNNNN	J,T	212	562	06.03.02	7820	000000	83005
801.684-010	JIG FITTER (machinery mfg.)	3215	33333443355	MNNOOONFFONNFNFNNN	NNNN4NNNNNNNNN	J,T	061	567	06.02.24	7720	000000	93999
801.684-014	PATTERN GATER (foundry)	2114	44435544355	MNNNNNNFFONNNFONNN	NNNN4NNNNNNNNN	R,T	102	566	06.04.24	7759	480501	93999
801.684-018	PLAYGROUND-EQUIPMENT ERECTOR (retail trade)	3113	34434433335	HNNFNFNFFONNNNNFNNNN	FNNN4NNNNNNNNNO	J,T	102	616	05.12.12	6479	000000	87899
801.684-022	PROGRESSIVE ASSEMBLER AND FITTER (agric. equip.)	2113	44434433355	MNNFNFOONFFNNNNNFONNN	NNNN4NNNNNNNNN	J,T	121	562	06.04.22	7720	010204	93902
801.684-026	REINFORCING-METAL WORKER (construction)	3116	34434543345	HFNFFOFFNNNNNFNFNNF	CNNN4NONNNNNNNF	J,T	102	360	05.05.06	6473	469999	87314
801.687-010	ASSEMBLER HELPER, INTERNAL COMBUSTION ENGINE (engine-turbine)	2112	44444434355	HNNFNFNFFONNNNNNFONNN	NNNN4NNNNNNNNN	R	011	561	06.04.40	7720	470604	93999
801.687-014	FITTER HELPER (any industry)	2113	44445444345	HFNFOONFFNNNNNFOFNNN	NNNN4NFNNNNNNF	V	102	550	05.12.12	8619	480501	98999
801.687-018	TANK-SETTER HELPER (petrol. & gas)	2112	44434444345	MOOOOONFFNFFNFFONNN	FNNN4NNNNNNNNN	R	102	369	05.12.12	8619	000000	98999
804.281-010	SHEET-METAL WORKER (any industry)	4437	33323433345	MNNNOOONFFNFFNFNFNNN	NNNN4NONNNNNNO	V,J,T	102	554	05.05.06	6824	480506	89132
804.281-014	SHEET-METAL-WORKER APPRENTICE (any industry)	4437	33324433345	MNNNFNNNFFOONONFNONNN	NNFN4NNONNNNNN	V,J,T	102	554	05.05.06	6824	480506	89132
804.481-010	HOOD MAKER (tex. prod., nec)	4335	33333434355	MNNNFNFFNFNNNNNFFNNN	NNNN4NNONNNNNN	J,T	102	554	05.05.06	7529	480506	92198
804.684-010	CUTTER, ALUMINUM SHEET (ship-boat mfg.)	2112	43443533355	HOOFFNFOOFFNFNFONN	NNNN4NNNNNNNNN	R,T	056	593	06.04.24	7529	480506	92198
804.684-014	EXTRUSION BENDER (ship-boat mfg.)	3224	34443534355	HOOFOFOFFNOONFNFNNN	NNNN4NNNNNNNNN	J,T	102	593	06.02.24	7720	490000	93999
805.131-010	SUPERVISOR, BOILERMAKING (struct. metal)	4438	33333334355	MONOOONFFNFFNFNFONN	ONNN4NONNNNNNO	V,D,P,J	102	554	05.05.06	6000	000000	98002
805.137-010	SUPERVISOR, BOILER REPAIR (any industry)	4338	33333334455	MNNOOONFFNFFNFNFNNN	NNFN4NNNNNNNNN	D,P,J,T	102	568	05.05.06	6000	520205	81002
805.261-010	BOILERMAKER APPRENTICE (struct. metal)	4437	33323433355	HOOFFNFFNFFNFNFNNN	FNNN4NNNNNNNNN	V,J,T	102	554	05.05.06	6814	000000	89135
805.261-014	BOILERMAKER I (struct. metal)	4437	33323433355	MNNFNNNFFNNNNNFNNNN	FNNN4NNNONNNNF	V,J,T	102	554	05.05.06	6814	000000	89135
805.361-010	BOILER HOUSE MECHANIC (any industry)	4337	33333433255	MONOONFFNOONFNFONN	NNON4NNNNONNNO	V,J,T	102	554	05.05.06	6814	000000	89135
805.361-014	BOILERMAKER FITTER (struct. metal)	4327	33333433345	HOOFOFOFFNOONFNOOON	ONNN4NNNNNNNNF	V,J,T	102	554	05.05.06	6814	000000	89135
805.381-010	BOILERMAKER II (struct. metal)	3227	33333434355	MONOOOFFNNNNNFNFNNN	ONNN4NNNNNNNNF	J,T	102	554	05.05.06	6814	000000	89135
805.664-010	BOILERMAKER HELPER II (struct. metal)	2225	34433533355	HOOOOONFFNOONFNNNNN	NNNN4NONNNNNNN	V	102	561	05.12.12	8619	000000	98999
805.667-010	BOILER HOUSE INSPECTOR (any industry)	3116	44444544455	LNNNNNNNNFFOFFNFNOONN	NNFN4NNNNNNNNN	J,T	102	568	05.07.01	7820	490306	83005
805.687-010	BOILERMAKER HELPER I (struct. metal)	2112	44445444355	HFFOOOOFFNNNNNNNNNN	ONNN4NNNNNNNNF	V	102	554	05.12.12	8769	000000	98999
806.130-010	SUPERVISOR, ENGINE ASSEMBLY (engine-turbine)	4328	33333433345	LNNNNNNFFOFFNFNOONN	NNNN4NNNNNNNNN	D,P,J,T	121	561	06.01.01	7100	000000	81008
806.131-010	SUPERVISOR, ALUMINUM BOAT ASSEMBLY (ship-boat mfg.)	4338	33333433354	MNNOOONFFNFFNFNFOON	NNNN4NNNNNNNNN	D,P,J,T	102	593	06.01.01	7100	490306	81008
806.131-014	SUPERVISOR, ASSEMBLY (motor-bicycles)	4338	33333333344	LNNNONNNFFNFFNFNFNNF	NNNN4NNNNNNNNN	J	121	595	06.02.01	7100	000000	81008
806.131-018	SUPERVISOR, BOAT OUTFITTING (ship-boat mfg.)	4328	33333433354	LOONNNNNFFOOFFNFNFNN	NNNN4NNNNNNNNO	D,P,J,T	102	593	06.02.01	7100	490306	81008
806.131-022	SUPERVISOR, ERECTION SHOP (railroad equip.)	4338	33333333454	MFNFOOOFFOFFNFNOOON	NNNN4NNNNNNNNN	D,P,J,T	102	594	06.02.01	7100	000000	81008
806.131-026	SUPERVISOR, INSPECTION AND TESTING (motor-bicycles)	4338	33333333334	LNNONONFFFOFFNFNFONN	NNNN4NNNNNNNNN	D,P,J,T	121	595	06.01.01	7100	520205	81008

DOT #	DOT Title & Industry	Trng	Aptitude	Physical	Environment	Tempra	WKF	MPSMS	GOE	SOC	CIP	OES
806.131-030	SUPERVISOR, RIGGER (ship-boat mfg.)	4328	33334334345	LNNNNNFFNFNFFNNN	FNNN4NNNNNNNNNN	D,J,P	102	593	05.05.06	7100	490306	81008
806.131-034	SUPERVISOR, SHIPFITTERS (ship-boat mfg.)	4338	3333333354	MFOOOOOFFFOFFNFOFONN	FNNN4NNNNNNNNNN	D,J,P,T	102	593	05.05.06	6700	490306	81008
806.131-038	SUPERVISOR, INSPECTION (aircraft mfg.)	4447	23333333354	LNNOOONFFFOFFNFNOON	NNNN4NNNNNNNNNN	D,P,T,V	212	592	06.01.01	7100	000000	81008
806.131-042	SUPERVISOR, PRODUCTION DEPARTMENT (aircraft mfg.)	4448	22223343344	MONOOONFFOOFFNFNONON	NNNN4NONONNNNN	V,D,P,J,T	102	592	06.01.01	7100	520205	81008
806.134-010	SUPERVISOR, MOTOR VEHICLE ASSEMBLY (auto. mfg.)	4447	22323344454	LNNNNNNFFNFNFFFOF	NNNN3NNNNNNNNNN	D,V,T,P,J	102	591	06.02.01	7100	000000	81008
806.134-014	SUPERVISOR, FIBERGLASS BOAT ASSEMBLY (ship-boat mfg.)	4338	33333433334	MOOOONNOOOOONONOOON	NNNN4NONNNNNNN	D,P,T,V	102	593	06.02.01	7100	490306	81008
806.137-010	SUPERVISOR, CAR INSTALLATIONS (railroad equip.)	4327	33333333344	LFOFOONFFNFNFNFOFOON	NNNO4NONNNNNNN	D,J,P	121	594	06.02.01	7100	000000	81008
806.137-014	SUPERVISOR, ORDNANCE TRUCK INSTALLATION (ordnance)	4337	33333344455	LNNNNNNFFOFFNFNFONN	NNNN4NNNNNNNNNN	D,P,J,T	102	370	05.10.01	7100	000000	81008
806.137-018	SUPERVISOR, SHIPPING TRACK (railroad equip.)	4337	33333433354	LFNFNNNFFNFNFFFFOC	NNNN4NNNNNNNNNF	D,P,T,V	102	594	06.02.01	7100	000000	81008
806.137-022	QUALITY ASSURANCE SUPERVISOR (auto. mfg.)	4347	22322344454	LNNNNNNFFNFFNFFFON	NNNN3NNNNNNNNNN	D,T,P,J	212	591	06.01.01	7100	470604	81008
806.261-010	INTERNAL-COMBUSTION-ENGINE INSPECTOR (engine-turbine)	4347	33323332355	MNNOOONFFFNFFNFNFFNN	NNNN4NNNNNNNNNN	V,J,T	121	561	06.01.05	7100	470604	83002
806.261-014	RIGGER (ship-boat mfg.)	4227	33323433225	HOOOOOOFFOOOONFFNNO	ONNN4NNNNFNNNO	J,T	102	593	05.05.06	6177	490306	85935
806.261-018	RIGGER APPRENTICE (ship-boat mfg.)	4227	33323433225	HOOOOONFFNOOOFFFONO	ONNN4NNNNFNNNO	J,T	102	593	05.05.06	6177	490306	85935
806.261-022	TESTER, ROCKET MOTOR (aircraft mfg.)	4448	33323333354	MONOOONFFNOOOFNONON	OOON4NNOOONOON	T,J	211	596	06.01.05	6812	000000	83002
806.261-026	MARINE-SERVICES TECHNICIAN (ship-boat mfg.)	4337	23433433222	HOOOOONFFFNFFNFNNOFN	FNNN4NOONNNNNN	J,T,V	121	593	05.05.02	6179	490306	85116
806.261-030	INSPECTOR, ASSEMBLIES AND INSTALLATIONS (aircraft mfg.)	4447	33322233344	MOOOOOOFFOOOONFOOOO	NNNN4NNOOONNNNN	T,J	102	592	06.01.05	6881	000000	83002
806.261-034	INSPECTOR, MATERIAL DISPOSITION (aircraft mfg.)	4447	23323444354	MOOOOONFFOOOONNOOON	NNNN4NNONONNNN	T,J	211	592	06.01.05	6881	000000	83002
806.261-038	INSPECTOR, MISSILE (aircraft mfg.)	4447	22223333354	LONOOONFFONOOOFNONON	ONNN4NOOOONNNN	T,J	211	596	06.01.05	6881	150801	83002
806.261-042	INSPECTOR, OUTSIDE PRODUCTION (aircraft mfg.)	4447	23322333355	LNNNOONFFONOONFNOONN	ONNN3NNNNONNNN	T,J	211	592	06.01.05	6881	000000	83002
806.261-046	INSPECTOR, PLASTICS AND COMPOSITES (aircraft mfg.)	4447	23322443354	MOOOOONFFOOOONFOOON	NNNN4NONNNNNNN	T,J	211	592	06.01.05	6881	000000	83002
806.261-050	OPERATIONAL TEST MECHANIC (aircraft mfg.)	4338	33332443355	MOOOOOOFFNNNNFNNNNN	NNNN5NNOOONNNNN	T,J,V	211	592	06.01.05	6881	000000	83002
806.264-010	HULL INSPECTOR (ship-boat mfg.)	4228	33332344355	LOOOOONOOFFNNNNFNNN	FNNN3NNNNNNNNNN	J	212	593	05.07.01	7820	490306	83005
806.264-014	INSPECTOR, AIRCRAFT LAUNCHING AND ARRESTING SYSTEMS (government ser.)	4446	23222344354	MNNNNNNFFNFNFNFOON	ONFN4NNNNNNNNNF	J,T	212	379	05.07.01	7820	000000	83005
806.281-010	DYNAMOMETER TESTER, ENGINE (auto. mfg.)	4336	33433433355	MNNNNNNFFNNNONFNFNN	NNNN3NNNNNNNNNN	J,T	121	591	06.01.05	6881	000000	83002
806.281-014	EXPERIMENTAL MECHANIC, ELECTRICAL (motor-bicycles)	4437	33334492354	LNNNNNNFFFNFNFNFOON	NNNN4NNNNNNNNNN	V,J,T	111	595	05.05.10	6869	470606	83002
806.281-018	FINAL INSPECTOR, MOTORCYCLES (motor-bicycles)	4227	33323334333	LNNNNNNFFFNFNFNFOFN	ONNN4NNNNNNNNNN	J,T	121	595	06.01.05	6881	470606	83002
806.281-026	INSPECTOR, PRECISION ASSEMBLY (aircraft mfg.)	4437	33322433354	LNNNONNFFFNNNNFOON	NNNN4NNNNNNNNNN	T	212	592	06.01.05	6881	000000	83002
806.281-058	CARPENTER, PROTOTYPE (ship-boat mfg.)	4337	23323433345	HFNFFFOFFONNNFNNNN	NNNN4NNONNNNNN	J,T	102	593	05.05.02	6422	460201	87102
806.283-010	TEST DRIVER II (auto. mfg.)	4337	33333433234	LNNNNNNFFONNONOFFFOF	NNNN4NNNFFFFF	J	212	591	05.07.02	7830	000000	83005
806.283-014	TEST DRIVER I (auto. mfg.)	3236	33433434334	LNNNNNNFFONNFNFFFFF	NNNN3NNNNNNNNNN	J,T	212	591	06.03.01	6881	000000	83002
806.361-010	ASSEMBLER-INSTALLER, GENERAL (aircraft mfg.)	4336	33333433344	MOOOOOOFFOOONFOFOON	NNNN4NNFNONNNN	T	102	592	06.02.22	6812	470608	93102
806.361-018	FINAL INSPECTOR, TRUCK TRAILER (auto. mfg.)	4348	33333433354	LOOOOONFFFOONFNFFON	NNNN3NNNNNNNNNN	J,T	212	591	06.01.05	6881	480501	83002
806.361-022	INSPECTOR, FABRICATION (aircraft mfg.)	4436	23332333354	MNNOOONFFOOONNFNFON	NNNN4NNNNNNNNNN	T,J	211	592	06.01.05	6881	000000	83002
806.361-026	NEW-CAR GET-READY MECHANIC (automotive ser.; retail trade)	3226	33433434334	MNNOOONFFOOOONFNFOO	ONNN4NNNNNNNNNN	J,T	121	591	05.10.02	6111	470604	85302
806.361-030	AIRCRAFT MECHANIC, ARMAMENT (aircraft mfg.)	4337	33322433244	HFNFFFOFFONNNFNFNNN	ONNN4NOOONONOO	T,S	111	592	06.01.04	6812	470607	93102
806.364-010	UTILITY WORKER, LINE ASSEMBLY (auto. mfg.)	3335	33333333345	LNNNNNNFFNNOONFNFNN	NNNN3NNNNNNNNNN	J,T	121	591	06.03.01	7870	490299	83005
806.367-010	QUALITY ASSURANCE GROUP LEADER (auto. mfg.)	3234	34444443355	MNNNNNNFFFONNNFNNN	NNNN4NNNNNNNNNN	V,T,P,J	102	591	06.04.01	7870	490299	83005
806.367-014	QUALITY ASSURANCE MONITOR (auto. mfg.)	3235	33433344454	LNNNNNNFFONFFNFNFNN	NNNN3NNNNNNNNNN	V,T,P,J	212	591	06.03.02	7820	000000	83005
806.367-018	QUALITY ASSURANCE MONITOR (auto. mfg.)	3235	34443344444	LNNNNNNFFONOONFFFOO	NNNN3NNNNNNNNNN	T,J,V,P	212	591	06.03.02	7820	000000	92197
806.380-010	RIVETING MACHINE OPERATOR, AUTOMATIC (aircraft mfg.)	4336	33333433355	MONONNNFFONNNNFNFNN	NNNN5NNONNNNNN	T	102	592	06.01.03	7339	000000	89121
806.381-014	AIRCRAFT MECHANIC, ENVIRONMENTAL CONTROL SYSTEM (aircraft mfg.)	4337	33333433345	HFFFFOOFFOONNFNFNNN	NNNN4NNFNONNNN	T	121	592	06.01.04	6812	470607	93102
806.381-018	AIRCRAFT MECHANIC, RIGGING AND CONTROLS (aircraft mfg.)	4436	33344334334	MOOOOOOFFOONNNNFOONN	NNNN4NNONONNNN	T	102	592	06.01.04	6812	470608	93102
806.381-022	ASSEMBLER, AIRCRAFT POWER PLANT (aircraft mfg.)	3236	33333333254	MOOOOONFFOONNNFOFON	NNNN4NNONONNNN	T	121	592	06.02.22	6812	470608	93105
806.381-026	ASSEMBLER, AIRCRAFT, STRUCTURES AND SURFACES (aircraft mfg.)	4336	33323433344	MOOOOOOFFONNNFNFOON	NNNN4NNONONNNN	T	102	592	06.01.04	6812	470607	93102
806.381-034	ASSEMBLER, TUBING (aircraft mfg.)	3336	33333433354	MNNNONNFFONNNFNFOON	NNNN4NOONNNNNN	T	102	592	06.01.04	6812	000000	93102
806.381-042	CABLE ASSEMBLER AND SWAGER (aircraft mfg.)	3336	33333433345	MNNNONNFFONNNNFNFNNN	NNNN4NNFNNNNNN	T	102	592	06.02.22	6869	000000	89999
806.381-046	SHIPFITTER (ship-boat mfg.)	4328	33329423235	HFFFFOOFFOONNFNFNNN	FNNN4NNNNNNNNNF	J,T	102	593	05.05.06	6821	490306	89121
806.381-050	SHIPFITTER APPRENTICE (ship-boat mfg.)	4328	33323423235	HFFFFOOFFOONNFNFNNN	FNNN4NNNNNNNNNF	J,T	102	593	05.05.06	6821	490306	89121
806.381-058	TRAILER ASSEMBLER (auto. mfg.)	3223	34433433334	MFOOOONFFFNNNFNFFN	NNNN4NNONNNNNN	J,T	102	591	06.02.22	6812	480501	93197
806.381-062	INSTALLER, ELECTRICAL, PLUMBING, MECHANICAL (ship-boat mfg.)	3337	33323433344	MFNFFFFFNNNNFNFFN	NNNN4NNOONNNNN	T,J,V	121	593	05.05.05	6432	460302	87202
806.381-066	AIRCRAFT MECHANIC, PLUMBING AND HYDRAULICS (aircraft mfg.)	3337	33333433355	MOOOOOOFFNNNNFNFONN	NNNN4NNONONNNN	T	121	592	06.02.22	6812	470607	93102

DOT #	DOT Title & Industry	Trng	Aptitude	Physical	Environment	Tempra	WkF	MPSMS	GOE	SOC	CIP	OES
806.381-070	CUSTOM VAN CONVERTER (auto. mfg.; automotive ser.)	4335	33333433344	MNNOOONFFNNNNFNOOON	NNNN3NNNNNNNNN	J,T	102	591	05.05.02	6422	460201	85999
806.381-074	INSPECTOR, PROCESSING (aircraft mfg.)	3335	33333244353	LNNNOOONFFNNNNFNOON	NNNN3NNNNNNNNN	T,J	211	592	06.01.05	7820	000000	83002
806.381-078	INSTALLER, INTERIOR ASSEMBLIES (aircraft mfg.)	4336	34434443344	MONOOOOFFFONNNFNFOON	NNNN4NNOONNNNNN	J,T	102	592	06.01.04	7720	000000	93197
806.381-082	PRECISION ASSEMBLER (aircraft mfg.)	4447	33322332254	MNNONNNFFFONNNNFNFOON	NNNN4NNOONNNNNN	V,T,J	102	592	06.01.04	6812	470105	93102
806.383-010	ROADABILITY-MACHINE OPERATOR (auto. mfg.)	3234	33433434345	LNNNNNNFFNNNNNFFNF	NNNN4NNNNNNNNN	T	212	591	06.01.05	7830	000000	83005
806.384-014	INSPECTOR, RETURNED MATERIALS (auto. mfg.)	3235	33333443355	MNNONONFFNNNNFNOFNN	NNNN3NNNNNNNNN	J,T	102	591	06.03.01	7820	000000	83005
806.384-022	ROCKET-TEST-FIRE WORKER (ordnance)	3115	34344443334	MNNNNNNFFNNNNNFNOF	ONNN5NNNNNNNNF	T	011	379	05.11.04	8319	490299	97989
806.384-030	ASSEMBLER, METAL BONDING (aircraft mfg.)	3235	33433443355	MNNOOONFFFONNNFNFNN	NNNN4NOONNNNNON	T	102	592	06.02.24	7720	000000	93956
806.384-034	ASSEMBLER, SUBASSEMBLY (aircraft mfg.)	3235	33434443354	MNNONOONFFONNNNFNFOON	NNNN5ONONNNNNNN	J,T	102	592	06.02.22	7720	470607	93956
806.384-038	PRESSURE SEALER-AND-TESTER (aircraft mfg.)	3234	33433433344	LOOOOOOFFFONONONFNON	NNNN4NFNNONNNNN	T	102	592	06.02.24	6116	470607	85323
806.387-014	WHEEL INSPECTOR (r.r. trans.)	3228	33323234455	LNNOOONFFFNFNFNNN	NNNN4NNNNNNNNN	J	212	594	05.07.01	7820	000000	83005
806.464-010	BOAT RIGGER (retail trade; ship-boat mfg.)	3214	34433444354	MOOOOOOFFNOONONFNON	ONNN4NNNNNNNNN	J,T	102	593	05.10.01	7720	490306	93956
806.481-010	ASSEMBLER, ALUMINUM BOATS (ship-boat mfg.)	3225	33333433355	MNNOOONFFFONNNFNNOON	NNNN4NNNNNNNNN	J,T	102	593	06.02.22	6812	490306	93197
806.481-014	ASSEMBLER, INTERNAL COMBUSTION ENGINE (engine-turbine)	4336	33334443255	MONFFNFOFFFONNNFNFNN	NNNN4NNNNNNNNN	J,T	121	561	06.02.22	6812	470604	93105
806.667-010	HELPER, METAL HANGING (mfd. bldgs.)	1112	44545544455	LNNFNNNCCNNOONONONNN	NNNN3NNNNNNNNN	R	011	554	06.04.22	8620	000000	98999
806.684-010	ASSEMBLER, MOTOR VEHICLE (auto. mfg.)	2122	44444444354	MNNONONFFONNNFNFFON	NNNN4NNNNNNNNN	R,T,U	102	591	06.04.22	7720	470604	93956
806.684-014	ASSEMBLER, BICYCLE I (motor-bicycles)	2114	44435533344	LNNNNNNNFCFONNNFNFNON	NNNN4NNNNNNNNN	T	121	595	06.04.22	7720	470499	93956
806.684-018	ASSEMBLER, CAMPER (vehicles, nec)	3223	34433433355	MMNFNNNCCFNNNNFNFNN	NNNN4NNNNNNNNN	J,T	102	597	06.04.22	7720	000000	93956
806.684-022	ASSEMBLER, DECK AND HULL (ship-boat mfg.)	3113	34433533355	HNNFOFNFFNNNNFNFNN	NNNN3NNNNNNNNN	T	102	593	06.02.22	7720	490306	93956
806.684-026	ASSEMBLER, INSULATION AND FLOORING (ship-boat mfg.)	2113	44344433345	MNNOONFFFNNNNFNFNN	NNNN3NNNNNNNNN	T	102	593	06.04.34	7720	490306	93956
806.684-038	AUTOMOBILE-ACCESSORIES INSTALLER (automotive ser.)	2124	34433433354	MNNFNFOFFFNNNNONFNON	NNNN4NNNNNNNNN	V,J,T	102	591	05.10.02	6111	470604	85302
806.684-046	CAR TRIMMER (railroad equip.)	3213	34444544355	HFNFOONFFNNNNNFFNNN	NNNN4NNNNONNNNF	T	102	594	06.04.22	7720	490306	93956
806.684-050	DOOR ASSEMBLER (mfd. bldgs.; vehicles, nec)	3213	34434434355	MNNONONFFFNNNNFNFNNN	NNNN4NNNNNNNNN	J,T	102	554	06.02.22	7720	480703	93956
806.684-054	FIBERGLASS LAMINATOR (ship-boat mfg.; vehicles, nec)	3214	34433444355	MMNFFFNFFNNNNONFNNNN	NNNN3NFNNNNNNNN	R,T	102	593	06.02.32	7720	490306	93956
806.684-066	INSTALLER-INSPECTOR, FINAL (vehicles, nec)	3224	34443433355	LNNNNNNNCCFNNNNNFNNN	NNNN4NNNNNNNNN	J,T	102	597	06.03.02	7820	000000	83005
806.684-070	INSTALLER, METAL FLOORING (railroad equip.)	2114	34434434355	HNNFFNNFFONNNNNFNFNNN	FNNN3NNONONNNNN	T	061	594	05.12.12	7720	000000	93999
806.684-074	INSTALLER, MOVABLE BULKHEAD (railroad equip.)	3114	34434533355	HFNFNNNCCFNNNNCNFNNN	FNNN4NNNNNNNNNF	T	102	594	05.10.01	7720	000000	93999
806.684-082	TRAILER ASSEMBLER II (auto. mfg.)	3223	34434433355	HNNNNNNFFNNNNNFFNN	NNNN3NNNNNNNNN	R,T	102	591	06.02.22	7720	480501	93956
806.684-086	MOLD LAMINATOR (concrete prod.; ship-boat mfg.)	3114	34433533354	MNNNNNNFFNNNNNFNNON	NNNN4NFNNNNNNNN	J,T	136	593	06.02.32	7755	000000	93999
806.684-090	MOTORCYCLE ASSEMBLER (motor-bicycles)	3115	34433433345	MNNOOONFFFONNNFNFFON	NNNN4NNNNNNNNN	T	121	595	06.04.22	7720	470606	93956
806.684-094	MOTORCYCLE SUBASSEMBLER (motor-bicycles)	3215	34433433354	HNNFNNNFFFONFNFNFON	NNNN4NNNNNNNNN	T	121	595	06.04.22	7720	470606	93956
806.684-098	ORDNANCE TRUCK INSTALLATION MECHANIC (ordnance)	3213	34434443335	MMNFFFNFFNNNNNFFNNN	NNNN3NNNNNNNNN	T	102	593	06.02.22	6179	480501	85999
806.684-102	OUTFITTER, CABIN (ship-boat mfg.)	3225	34434443345	MOOOOONFFFNNNNFNNNN	NNNN4NNNNNNNNN	J,T	102	593	06.04.22	7720	490306	93956
806.684-106	OVERLAY PLASTICIAN (ship-boat mfg.)	2114	34434543355	MMNFFFNFNNNNFNFNNN	ONNN4NFNNNNNNNN	T	063	593	06.04.24	7720	470607	93999
806.684-114	RAILROAD-CAR-TRUCK BUILDER (railroad equip.)	3113	34433533355	HNNFNNONFFONONFNFNN	NNNN4NNNNNNNNNF	T	121	594	06.04.22	7720	000000	93956
806.684-118	REPAIRER, GENERAL (auto. mfg.)	3224	34433432244	MNNONONFFFONNNNFNFFON	NNNN3NNNNNNNNN	T	121	591	06.04.22	7720	470603	93999
806.684-122	RIGGER HELPER (ship-boat mfg.)	3115	34434443355	HFFFFFOFFNNNNNNNNN	FNNN4NNNNNNNNNF	R	102	593	05.05.06	8637	490306	98102
806.684-126	ROOF FITTER (railroad equip.)	3214	34543533355	HFNOONFFNNNNNCFNNNN	FNNN4NFNNONNNF	T	102	594	06.02.22	7720	000000	93956
806.684-130	SKIN-LAP BONDER (aircraft mfg.)	3233	33444433345	MONOOOOFFONNNNNFNNNN	NNNN4NONNONNNON	T	063	592	06.04.24	7720	470607	93999
806.684-134	TRANSMISSION TESTER (auto. mfg.)	3234	34433443345	LNNNNNNFFONONNFNFNN	NNNN4NOCNNNNNNN	J,T	212	591	06.03.02	7830	000000	83005
806.684-142	RUNNING RIGGER (ship-boat mfg.)	3324	34433433354	MOONNNNNFFONNNNNFNN	NNNN3NNNNNNNNN	R,U	061	593	06.02.32	7759	490306	93999
806.684-146	BOAT OUTFITTER (ship-boat mfg.)	3224	34433433354	MONFOONFFONNNNFNNON	NNNN4NNNNNNNNN	J,R,T	102	593	05.10.01	7720	490306	93956
806.684-150	ROUTER OPERATOR, HAND (aircraft mfg.; railroad equip.)	3124	34443434355	MNNFOFNFFOONNNFNNNN	NNNN4NOCNNNNNNN	R,T	055	592	06.02.24	7720	470607	93926
806.687-010	ASSEMBLER, BICYCLE II (motor-bicycles)	1112	44445544355	LNNNNNNFFNNNNFNNNN	NNNN3NNNNNNNNN	R	121	595	06.04.22	7820	490306	93999
806.687-018	FINAL INSPECTOR (auto. mfg.)	3234	33433433354	LNNNNNNFFONNNFNFFN	NNNN3NNNNNNNNN	J,T	212	591	06.03.02	7820	470603	83005
806.687-022	HELPER, METAL BONDING (aircraft mfg.)	2223	44443444345	MNNONONFFONNNNONFNON	NNNN4NOONNNNON	V,U	011	592	06.04.24	8620	000000	98999
806.687-026	INSPECTOR, ALUMINUM BOAT (ship-boat mfg.)	2123	44443434355	MNNFNNNFFONNNNFNONN	NNNO5NNNNNNNNN	R	073	593	06.03.02	7830	490306	83005
806.687-030	INSPECTOR, BICYCLE (motor-bicycles)	2112	34533434354	LNNNNNNFFFNNNNNNNN	NNNN4NNNNNNNNN	J,T	212	595	06.03.02	7820	470499	83005
806.687-034	INSTALLER, DOOR FURRING (railroad equip.)	2112	44445544355	HNNNNNNCCNNNNNCNFNNN	FNNN4NFNNNNNNNF	R	102	594	06.04.22	7759	000000	93999
806.687-042	OUTBOARD-MOTOR INSPECTOR (engine-turbine)	3224	33442444453	LNNNNNNFFFNFNFNFN	NNNN4NNNNNNNNN	J,T	121	561	06.03.02	7820	490306	83005
806.687-046	ROLLER (ship-boat mfg.)	2113	44444444345	MNNCNNNFFFNNNNONNNN	NNNN4NCNNNNNNNN	R	063	593	06.04.27	7720	490306	93999

DOT #	DOT Title & Industry	Trng	Aptitude	Physical	Environment	Tempra	WkF	MPSMS	GOE	SOC	CIP	OES
806.687-050	SHIPFITTER HELPER (ship-boat mfg.)	2112	4444454445	HOOFFOOFFNNNNFNNNNN	FNNN4NNNNFNNNN	R	102	593	05.12.12	8619	490306	98999
807.137-010	SUPERVISOR, AUTOMOBILE BODY REPAIR (automotive ser.)	4337	33332344454	LNNNNNNNFONFNFNFOON	NNNN4NNNNNNNNN	V,D,P,T	102	591	05.05.06	7100	520205	81002
807.261-010	AIRCRAFT BODY REPAIRER (air trans.)	4337	33322434345	MONOOONFFONFFNFNNNN	NNNN4NOFNNNNNN	J,T	102	572	05.05.06	6116	470607	85323
807.267-010	SHOP ESTIMATOR (automotive ser.)	4336	33333344454	LNNOOONFFFOFFNFNFOON	NNNN4NNNNNNNNN	J,P	212	591	05.07.01	6115	470603	85305
807.281-010	TRUCK-BODY BUILDER (auto. mfg.; automotive ser.)	3325	33333433344	MOOOONNFFNNNNFNFFON	NNNN4NNNNNNNN	J,T	102	591	05.06.06	6115	470603	85305
807.361-010	AUTOMOBILE-BODY CUSTOMIZER (automotive ser.)	3226	33322433354	MNNOOONFFOOONFNFFON	NNNN4NNNNNNNNNN	V,J,T	102	591	05.05.06	6115	470603	85305
807.361-014	BOAT REPAIRER (ship-boat mfg.)	4337	33332433344	MOOFFFOFFFOONFNFON	ONNN4NNNNNNNNO	J	102	593	05.05.02	6179	490306	85999
807.381-010	AUTOMOBILE-BODY REPAIRER (automotive ser.)	3337	34433433354	MNNFFFOFFONONFNFNON	NNNN4NNNNNNNN	V,J,T	102	591	05.05.06	6115	470603	85305
807.381-014	BONDED STRUCTURES REPAIRER (aircraft mfg.)	3236	33332443345	MOOOONFFFONNNFNFNON	NNON4NOONONNOO	J,T	102	592	06.02.32	6116	470607	85323
807.381-018	FRAME REPAIRER (motor-bicycles)	3217	34433433344	HNNNNNNFFNNNNFNFNON	NNNN4NNNNNNNNN	J,T	121	595	05.10.01	6115	470603	85305
807.381-022	SERVICE MECHANIC (auto. mfg.)	3236	33443343355	MNNNNNNFFONNNNFNFNON	NNNN4NNNNNNNN	V,J	102	591	05.10.01	6115	470603	85305
807.381-026	STREETCAR REPAIRER (railroad equip.)	4226	33433434454	HONOOONFFONNNFNFNON	ONNN3NNNNNNNNN	J,T	102	594	05.10.04	6117	000000	85317
807.381-030	AUTO-BODY REPAIRER, FIBERGLASS (automotive ser.)	3227	33332433255	MNNFFFNNFFNNNFNFNN	NNNN4NOONNNNNN	T,J	102	591	05.10.01	6115	470603	85305
807.484-010	FRAME STRAIGHTENER (motor-bicycles)	3225	34433434345	HNNNNNNFFNNNNFNFNON	NNNN4NNNNNNNN	J,T	102	595	05.10.01	6115	000000	85305
807.664-010	MUFFLER INSTALLER (automotive ser.)	3224	34433433355	MNNOOONFFNOONFNFNON	NNNN4NNNNNNNN	J,T	102	591	05.10.01	6111	470604	85302
807.667-010	FLATCAR WHACKER (saw. & plan.)	2113	44435544355	HFNNNNNNFFNOONFFFNN	ONNN4NNNNNNNN	J,T	102	594	05.12.12	8769	000000	98999
807.684-010	AUTOMOBILE-BUMPER STRAIGHTENER (automotive ser.)	2113	34433544355	HNNONNNFFONNNNFNFNN	NNNN4NNNNNNNN	R,T	102	591	05.12.12	6115	470603	85305
807.684-014	BOAT PATCHER, PLASTIC (ship-boat mfg.)	3114	34443433353	MNNFFFNFFFNNNFNFNN	ONNN4NNNNNNNN	T	102	593	06.02.24	6179	490306	85999
807.684-018	AIRCRAFT SKIN BURNISHER (aircraft mfg.)	3123	44443443354	LONOOONFFOFNNNFNFNFN	NNNN4NONNONNON	T	051	592	06.04.24	6116	470607	85323
807.684-022	FLOOR SERVICE WORKER, SPRING (automotive ser.)	2114	44544534355	HNNOOONFFONNNNONONNN	ONNN4NNNNNNNNNF	R,T	102	591	05.12.12	6111	470604	85302
807.684-026	INSTALLER, SOFT TOP (automotive ser.)	2122	44443433355	NNNNNNNFFNNNNNFNFNN	NNNN4NNNNNNNN	R,T	121	591	06.04.22	7720	470603	93956
807.684-034	WATER LEAK REPAIRER (auto. mfg.)	2123	44444434355	LNNONNNNFFNNNNFNNNNN	NNNN4NNNNONNN	R,J,T	102	591	06.03.02	7830	000000	83005
807.687-010	AUTOMOBILE-BODY-REPAIRER HELPER (automotive ser.)	2112	44543544355	MNNONONNFFONNNNNONONNN	NNNN4NNNNNNNN	R	102	591	05.12.12	8632	470603	98102
807.687-014	STREETCAR-REPAIRER HELPER (railroad equip.)	2113	44444534355	HONONNNFFNNNNNFNFNNN	ONNN3NNNNNNNN	R	102	594	05.12.12	8632	000000	98102
809.130-010	SUPERVISOR, ASSEMBLY DEPARTMENT (struct. metal)	4337	33323333355	LNNONONFFONFFNFONONN	NNNN4NNNNNNNN	D,P,J,T	102	554	06.02.01	7100	520205	81008
809.130-014	SUPERVISOR, METAL FABRICATING (any industry)	4338	33333433344	MNNOOONFFFOFFNFNFNN	NNNN4NNNNNNNN	D,J,T	102	554	05.10.01	7100	520205	81008
809.131-010	SUPERVISOR, FABRICATION AND ASSEMBLY (toy-sport equip.)	4337	33333433355	MNNONNNCCNNNNNFNFNN	NNNN4NNNNNNNN	D,J,T	102	616	06.02.01	6812	480501	93197
809.131-014	SUPERVISOR, STRUCTURAL-STEEL ERECTION (construction)	4338	33322433354	MOOFFFNNFFNNFFNNFN	CNNN4NNNNNNNN	D,J,P	102	554	06.02.31	7100	000000	81008
809.131-018	SUPERVISOR, STRUCTURAL IRONWORKING (construction)	4338	33323433224	MFFFFNFFOFFNFFOOF	FNNN4NNFNNNNNF	V,D,P,S,J	102	562	05.05.09	6318	000000	81005
809.134-010	SUPERVISOR, GRINDING AND SPRAYING (struct. metal)	4335	33324334354	HNNONNNFFNFNFNFNON	NNNN4NNNNNNNNO	D,P	102	554	06.02.01	7100	000000	81008
809.134-014	SUPERVISOR, METAL HANGING (mfd. bldgs.)	4337	33333433355	HNNNNNNFFNFFNFNFNON	NNNN4NNNNNNNN	D,P,J,T	102	554	06.02.01	7100	520205	81008
809.261-010	ASSEMBLER, GROUND SUPPORT EQUIPMENT (aircraft mfg.)	4337	33323422255	MOOOONFFONOONFNONNN	ONNN3NNONONNNN	J,T	102	560	05.05.06	6869	480501	89999
809.281-010	LAY-OUT WORKER I (any industry)	4438	33222433355	MMNFNNNFFNNNNFNFFNN	NNNN4NNNNNNNN	J,T	241	554	05.05.06	6821	000000	89117
809.381-010	FABRICATOR-ASSEMBLER, METAL PRODUCTS (any industry)	3225	33333433345	MNNONNNFFFNONFNFFNN	NNNN4NNNNNNNN	J,T	102	550	06.02.24	6812	480501	93197
809.381-014	LAY-OUT WORKER II (any industry)	3325	34433433355	MNNNONNNCCNNNNCFFNNN	NNNN4NNNNNNNN	J,T	241	554	06.02.31	6821	480501	89117
809.381-018	MILKING-SYSTEM INSTALLER (agric. equip.; retail trade)	4336	33324433355	HONOOONFFNOONFNONNN	NNNN3NNNNNNNN	J,T	121	562	05.05.09	6869	010204	89999
809.381-022	ORNAMENTAL-IRON WORKER (construction)	4337	34333443355	HFONFFFNNFFNNNFFFNNN	FNNN4NOONONNNN	V,J,T	102	554	05.05.06	6479	000000	87899
809.381-026	ORNAMENTAL-IRON-WORKER APPRENTICE (construction)	4337	33333433235	HFONFFFNNFFNNNFFFNNN	FNNN4NOONONNNN	V,J,T	102	554	05.05.06	6479	000000	87899
809.381-030	PNEUMATIC-TOOL OPERATOR (ship-boat mfg.)	3227	33423434343	MOOOOONFFNNNNNFNFNNN	ONNN4NNNNNNNNN	J,T	102	593	05.05.06	6829	490306	89199
809.381-034	SOLAR-FABRICATION TECHNICIAN (machine shop)	3324	34322333244	HNNNONONFFNNNNFNFFON	NNNN4NNNNNNNN	V,T	102	553	06.02.24	6829	480503	93197
809.382-010	BALANCING-MACHINE SET-UP WORKER (any industry)	4337	33333343355	MNNNNNNFFNNNNNFNFFON	NNNN4NNNNNNNN	J,T	121	561	06.03.01	7479	150403	92997
809.484-010	AWNING-FRAME MAKER (tex. prod., nec)	3215	34333443355	MNNNNNNCCFNNNNCFFNNN	ONNN4NNNNNNNN	J,T	102	554	05.10.01	7720	480501	93956
809.484-014	TEMPLATE MAKER, TRACK (any industry)	3213	34434434355	LNNNNNNNFFNNNNNFNFNN	NNNN4NNNNNNNN	J,T	102	554	05.10.01	7720	480501	93956
809.664-010	ALUMINUM-POOL INSTALLER (construction)	3214	34434434355	MOOOOONFFONOONONFNNN	CNNN4NNNNNNNN	R	102	369	05.10.01	6479	000000	87899
809.667-010	HULL AND DECK REMOVER (ship-boat mfg.)	2113	44544534355	HNNFNONFFONOONFNFNNN	NNNN4NNNNNNNN	R	102	593	06.04.34	7740	490306	93956
809.681-010	ASSEMBLER, UNIT (struct. metal)	3224	34433443355	MNNOOONFFONNNNNFNNNNF	NNNN4NNNNNNNN	J,T	102	554	06.02.22	7720	480501	93956
809.684-010	ASSEMBLER, PRODUCTION LINE (struct. metal)	2113	44434533345	MNNFNFNCCFNNNNFNFNNN	NNNN4NNNNNNNN	R,T	102	554	06.04.22	7720	480501	93956
809.684-014	CASKET ASSEMBLER, METAL (fabrication, nec)	3114	34433534344	MONOOONFFONNNNFNFNON	NNNN4NNNNNNNN	J,T	102	619	06.04.34	7529	480503	92198
809.684-018	DRILLER, HAND (any industry)	2112	44443544355	MOOFFFNFFONNNONFNNNO	NNNN4NFNNNNNN	J,T	053	610	06.04.34	7720	480501	93953
809.684-022	FINISHER, FIBERGLASS BOAT PARTS (ship-boat mfg.)	2223	44443343345	MOOFFNFFONNONFNNNNO	NNNN4NFNNNNNN	R	102	593	06.04.34	7758	490306	93953
809.684-026	GRINDER-CHIPPER II (any industry)	2113	34443534355	HOOFOONFFNNNNNFNNNNF	NNNN4NFNNNNNNF	J,T	051	554	06.04.24	7758	480599	93953

DOT #	DOT Title & Industry	Trng	Aptitude	Physical	Environment	Tempra	WkF	MPSMS	GOE	SOC	CIP	OES
809.684-030	METAL HANGER (mfd. bldgs.; vehicles, nec)	3224	34334343345	MONOOONFFONNNFNFNNN	NNNN4NNNNNNNNNN	J,T	102	554	06.02.22	7720	469999	93999
809.684-034	REPAIRER, FINISHED METAL (any industry)	3115	34443434345	HNNNNNNFCNOOONCNFNNN	NNNN4NFFNNNNNNN	J,T	102	583	06.02.24	6179	470603	85999
809.684-038	WHEEL ASSEMBLER (mfd. bldgs.; vehicles, nec)	2112	34443434345	MNNFFOFFNNNNNONONNN	NNNN4NNNNNNNNNN	R	102	554	06.04.22	7720	000000	93956
809.684-042	PANEL LAMINATOR (struct. metal)	2113	34443433354	HNNONONFFFNNNNNFOFN	NNNN4NNNNNNNNNN	R,U	063	467	06.04.22	7720	480501	93956
809.687-010	DUCT MAKER (construction; mfd. bldgs.)	2122	44443444355	LNNNNNNFFONNNNNFNNN	NNNN4NNNNNNNNNN	R	062	369	06.04.24	7753	000000	93926
809.687-014	HELPER, MANUFACTURING (aircraft mfg.)	2112	44444344454	MOOOONFFOONNNNONONNN	NNNN4NNONNNNNNN	R,U	102	592	06.04.34	8620	470607	98999
809.687-018	INSPECTOR AND TESTER (struct. metal)	2123	44443444454	LNNNNNNFFFFNNNFNNNN	NNNN4NNNNNNNNNN	J	102	554	06.03.02	7820	480501	83005
809.687-022	LABORER, SHIPYARD (ship-boat mfg.)	2112	44544544455	HNNOOONFFNNNNNONONNN	FNNF4NNNNNNNNN	R	011	593	05.12.03	8769	000000	98999
809.687-026	MOLD PREPARER (ship-boat mfg.)	2112	44544544455	LNNOOONFFNNNNNFNNNN	NNNN4NFNNNNNNN	R	153	593	06.04.39	8750	490306	98905
810.382-010	WELDING-MACHINE OPERATOR, ARC (welding)	4436	34343434344	MNNONONFFNNNNNFFNON	NNNN4NNNNNNNNNF	J,T	081	554	06.02.19	7332	480508	91702
810.384-010	WELDER APPRENTICE, ARC (welding)	4435	34433433354	HOOOOOOCCFNNFNFNFFN	NNNN4NFNNNNNNN	J,T	081	540	05.05.06	7714	480508	93914
810.384-014	WELDER, ARC (welding)	4435	34433433354	HOOOOOOCFNNFNFNFFN	NNNN4NFNNNNNNN	J,T	081	540	05.05.06	7714	480508	93914
810.664-010	WELDER, GUN (welding)	2222	44444433354	MFNONONFFNOONFNFFON	NNNN4NCFFNNNNN	R,T	081	540	06.04.31	7714	480508	93914
810.684-010	WELDER, TACK (welding)	3225	44444333354	HOOFOFOFFONNFNFOFNON	FNNN4NFNNNNNNN	R,T	081	540	05.10.01	7714	480508	93914
811.482-010	WELDING-MACHINE OPERATOR, GAS (welding)	3326	34333433354	MNNONNNFFNNNNNFNON	NNNN4NFNNNNNNN	J,T	081	540	06.02.19	7332	480508	91702
811.684-010	WELDER APPRENTICE, GAS (welding)	3335	34333433354	MNNOOONFFNNNNNFNOON	NNNN4NFFNNNNNN	J,T	081	550	05.05.06	7714	480508	93914
811.684-014	WELDER, GAS (welding)	3335	34333433354	MNNOOONFFNNNNNFNOON	NNNN4NFFNNNNNN	J,T	081	540	06.01.02	7332	480508	91702
812.682-010	WELDING-MACHINE OPERATOR, RESISTANCE (welding)	4437	33222433334	MNNONNNCCFNNONCNCNON	NNNN3NNNNNNNNN	J,T	081	540	06.02.19	7332	480508	91702
813.360-010	BRAZING-MACHINE SETTER (welding)	4436	34443433344	MNNONONFFNOONFNFNON	NNNN4NNNNNNNNN	V,J,T	083	540	06.01.02	7333	480508	91708
813.360-014	SETTER, INDUCTION-HEATING EQUIPMENT (welding)	4437	33223433333	LNNNNNNFFNOONFNFNON	NNNN4NNNNNNNNN	J,T	083	373	06.01.02	7333	480508	91708
813.382-010	BRAZER, INDUCTION (welding)	3335	34433433355	MNNNNNNFFNNNNFNFFNN	NNNN4NNNNNNNNN	J,T	083	540	06.02.10	7333	480508	91708
813.382-014	BRAZING-MACHINE OPERATOR (welding)	3325	34334343343	MNNONNNFFNNNNFNFFON	NNFN4NFNNNNNNN	J,T	083	540	06.02.19	7533	480508	91711
813.482-010	BRAZER, FURNACE (welding)	3234	34335544353	MNNNNNNFFNNNNFNFNNN	NNFN4NFNNNNNNF	J,T	083	540	06.02.10	7533	480508	91711
813.682-010	BRAZER, RESISTANCE (welding)	3224	34433433343	MNNNNNNFFNNNNFNFNNN	NNNN4NNNNNNNNN	J,T	083	540	06.02.19	7714	480508	93914
813.684-010	BRAZER, ASSEMBLER (welding)	4335	34434433354	MNNNNNNCCFNNNNFNFNON	NNNN4NFNNNNNNN	J,T	083	540	06.02.22	7714	480508	93914
813.684-014	SOLDERER-ASSEMBLER (welding)	3234	34334434353	MNNNNNNFFNNNNNFNFN	NNNN3NFNNNNNNN	J,T	083	540	06.02.22	7717	480508	93917
813.684-018	SOLDERER-DIPPER (welding)	2222	44444544454	LNNNNNNFFNNNNNFNFFN	NNNN3NFNNNNNNF	R,T	083	540	06.04.31	7717	480508	93917
813.684-022	SOLDERER, PRODUCTION LINE (welding)	2222	44444544454	LNNNNNNFFNNNNNFNFN	NNNN4NFNNNNNNF	R,T	083	540	06.04.31	7717	480508	93917
813.684-026	SOLDERER, TORCH I (welding)	2223	34444433354	LNNONNNFFNNNNNFNFNN	NNNN4NONNNNNNO	R,T	083	591	06.04.31	7717	480508	93917
813.684-030	SOLDERER, ULTRASONIC, HAND (welding)	2223	44444544354	LNNNNNNFFONNNNFNFFNN	NNNN4NNNNNNNNN	R,T	083	591	06.04.31	7717	480508	93917
813.685-010	BRAZER, CONTROLLED ATMOSPHERIC FURNACE (welding)	3234	34444434354	LNNONONFFNNNNNFNFNON	NNNN4NFNNNNNNN	R,T	083	540	06.02.19	7533	480508	91711
814.382-010	WELDING-MACHINE OPERATOR, FRICTION (welding)	3325	34333434354	LNNNNNNFFONNNNFNFNN	NNNN4NNNNNNNNN	J,T	081	550	06.02.19	7532	480508	91705
814.682-010	WELDING-MACHINE OPERATOR, ULTRASONIC (welding)	3334	34333433355	MNNNNNNFFNNNNFNFFNN	NNNN3NNNNNNNNN	J,T	081	554	06.02.19	7532	480508	91705
814.684-010	WELDER, EXPLOSION (welding)	3325	34344434354	MNNNNNNFFONNNNNFFON	NNNN4NNNNNNFNN	J,T	081	540	06.02.24	7532	480508	91705
815.380-010	WELDER SETTER, ELECTRON-BEAM MACHINE (welding)	4336	33333434354	LOONNNNFFNNNFNFNON	NNNN3NNNNNNNNN	J,T	081	591	06.01.02	7332	480508	91702
815.382-010	WELDING-MACHINE OPERATOR, ELECTRON BEAM (welding)	4336	33333433344	MONOOOOFFONNNFNFFON	NNNN4NFNNNNFNN	J,T	081	540	06.02.19	7332	480508	91702
815.382-014	WELDING-MACHINE OPERATOR, ELECTROSLAG (welding)	3334	34433433355	HNNNNNNFFNNNNNFNFNN	NNNN4NONONNNNN	J,T	081	566	06.02.19	7532	480508	91705
815.682-010	LASER-BEAM-MACHINE OPERATOR (welding)	3334	33333333455	LNNNNNNFFONNNNFNFNN	NNNN4NNNNNNNFNN	T	081	566	06.02.19	7532	480508	91705
815.682-014	WELDING-MACHINE OPERATOR, THERMIT (welding)	3333	33343434455	MNNNNNNFFNNNNFNFNN	NNNN4NNNNNNNNF	J,T	081	550	05.10.01	7532	480508	91705
816.364-010	ARC CUTTER (welding)	3335	44433433353	MNNFFONFFNOONFNFNON	NNNN4NFNNNNNNN	J,T	082	540	05.05.06	7714	480508	93914
816.464-010	THERMAL CUTTER, HAND I (welding)	3335	34433434243	HNNNNNNFFNNNNNNFFNNN	ONNN4NFNNNNNNF	J,T	082	540	05.10.01	7714	480508	93914
816.482-010	THERMAL-CUTTING-MACHINE OPERATOR (welding)	3335	34333433354	MNNFNONFFNNNNNFFNON	ONNN4NFNNNNNNN	J,T	082	540	06.02.19	7339	480506	92197
816.682-010	SCARFING MACHINE OPERATOR (steel & rel.)	3225	34433434353	MNNOOONFFNNNNNOFFNFN	NNON4NFNNNNNNN	T,J	082	541	06.02.02	7329	480508	92197
816.684-010	THERMAL CUTTER, HAND II (welding)	2112	44544544343	HFNFNNNFFNNNNNFNNNF	ONNN3NFNNNNNNF	R	082	540	05.12.11	7714	480508	93914
819.131-010	LEAD-BURNER SUPERVISOR (welding)	4337	33332333244	MONOOONFFNFFNFNNON	ONNN4NFNNNNNNO	V,D,P,J	102	540	05.05.06	7100	520205	81008
819.131-014	WELDING SUPERVISOR (welding)	4438	33322334354	LNNOOONFFFNFFFFON	ONNN4NFNNNNNNO	V,D,P,T	081	540	06.02.01	7100	150699	81008
819.132-010	SUPERVISOR, FLAME CUTTING (steel & rel.)	4337	33343434354	LNNNNNFFONFNFNNCOFN	NNNN4NFNNNNNNN	D,J,T,P	082	541	06.02.01	7100	480508	81005
819.281-010	LEAD BURNER (welding)	4337	33323433344	MNNOOONFFNNNNNNFNON	ONNN4NFNNNNNNF	V,J,T	081	550	05.05.06	7714	480508	93914
819.281-014	LEAD-BURNER APPRENTICE (welding)	4337	33323433344	MNNOOONFFNNNNNNFNON	ONNN4NFNNNNNNF	V,J,T	081	550	05.05.06	7714	480508	93914
819.281-018	WELD INSPECTOR I (welding)	4437	33322344453	MOOOOOOFFONNNNFNFNON	ONNN3NONNNNNNO	J,T	081	540	06.01.05	6881	150699	83002

DOT #	DOT Title & Industry	Trng	Aptitude	Physical	Environment	Tempra	WkF	MPSMS	GOE	SOC	CIP	OES
819.281-022	WELDER, EXPERIMENTAL (welding)	4438	33332433344	LNNOOONFFNNNNFNNFFON	NNNN3NFNNNNNNNF	J	081	379	05.05.06	7714	150699	93914
819.361-010	WELDER-FITTER (welding)	4337	33322433244	MOOFOFNFFNOONFOFNON	ONNN4NFNNNNNNNF	J,T	081	550	05.05.06	7714	480508	93914
819.361-014	WELDER-FITTER APPRENTICE (welding)	4337	33322433244	MOOFOFNFFNOONFOFNON	ONNN4NFNNNNNNNF	J,T	081	550	05.05.06	7714	480508	93914
819.381-010	WELDER-ASSEMBLER (machinery mfg.)	3326	34333434355	MOOFFFNFFNNNNFNFNNN	NNNN4NNNNNNNNNF	J,T	102	564	05.05.06	7714	480508	93914
819.384-010	WELDER, COMBINATION (welding)	4336	34333433354	MNNONONFFNNNNFNFNON	ONFN4NNNNNNNNNO	J,T	081	550	05.05.06	7714	480508	93914
819.384-014	WELDER APPRENTICE, COMBINATION (welding)	4336	34333433354	MNNONONFFNNNNFNFNON	ONFN4NNNNNNNNNO	J,T	081	550	05.05.06	7714	480508	93914
819.664-010	PLATE CONDITIONER (steel & rel.)	2224	44434434355	LNNFNNNFFNNFFNFNNNN	NNNN4OFNNNNNNNN	R,T	102	541	06.04.24	7758	480508	93953
819.666-010	MACHINE HELPER (welding)	2122	44444444455	HNHFNNNFFNNNNNFNONN	NNON4NFONNNNNON	R	081	559	05.12.11	8620	480508	98999
819.684-010	WELDER, PRODUCTION LINE (welding)	2222	44444434354	MNNONONFFNNNNNFNFNON	NNNN4NNNNNNNNNN	R,T	081	540	06.04.31	7714	480508	93914
819.685-010	WELDING-MACHINE TENDER (welding)	2112	44444434345	MNNONONCCONNONFNFNNN	NNNN4NNNNNNNNNN	R,T	081	540	06.04.02	7532	480508	91705
819.686-010	MACHINE FEEDER (welding)	2112	44444544455	LNNFNNNFFNNNNNFNFNNN	NNFN4NFNNNNNNNF	R	081	559	06.04.31	8725	480508	98502
819.687-010	WELD INSPECTOR II (welding)	3224	44443444355	LNNNNNNCCNNNNNCNFFNN	NNNN4NNNNNNNNNN	J,T	081	550	06.03.02	7830	480508	83005
819.687-014	WELDER HELPER (welding)	2112	44444544454	HNNOOONFFNNNNNFNFNON	ONON4NFNNNNNNNF	R	081	540	05.12.11	8620	010201	98999
820.131-010	ELECTRICIAN SUPERVISOR, SUBSTATION (utilities)	4448	23322333343	LOOOOONFFFNFFNFNFOFN	FNNN4NNNONNNNNN	V,D,P,S,J	111	581	05.05.05	7100	520205	81008
820.137-010	TRANSFORMER ASSEMBLY SUPERVISOR (elec. equip.)	4447	23332344454	MNNNNNNNFFFNFNFFNNN	NNNN4NNNNNNNNNN	D,J,P	295	581	06.02.01	7100	520205	81008
820.261-010	ELECTRICIAN APPRENTICE, POWERHOUSE (utilities)	4438	23322433234	MOOOOOOFFNOONFNFNFN	ONNN4NNOFONNNNN	J,T,V	111	580	05.05.05	6153	470501	85721
820.261-014	ELECTRICIAN, POWERHOUSE (utilities)	4438	23322433234	MOOOOOOFFNOONFNFNFN	ONNN4NNOFONNNNN	J,T,V	111	580	05.05.05	6153	470501	85721
820.261-018	ELECTRICIAN, SUBSTATION (utilities)	4438	33332333234	MOOOOONFFNOONFNFNFN	ONNN4NNNFNNNNNN	V,J,T	111	581	05.05.05	6153	470501	85721
820.361-010	CORROSION-CONTROL FITTER (pipe lines; utilities)	4337	33333334333	MONFNNNFFNOONFNFNFON	CNNN3NNNNNNNNNN	J,T	111	584	05.05.05	6869	470501	89999
820.361-014	ELECTRIC-MOTOR-AND-GENERATOR ASSEMBLER (elec. equip.)	4446	33333433254	MNNONNNCCCNOONFNFOON	NNNN4NNOONNNNNN	V,J,T	111	582	06.01.04	6867	470199	93105
820.361-018	REGULATOR INSPECTOR (utilities)	4437	33332433354	MFFFFNNFFNFNFNFNFNN	NNNN4NNFNNNNNNN	V,J,T	111	581	05.05.05	6881	470501	83002
820.381-010	BATTERY MAINTAINER, LARGE EMERGENCY STORAGE (utilities)	3336	34433443344	LNNNNNNFFNNNNFNFNON	NNNN4NNNNNNNNNN	J,T	111	589	05.10.03	6153	460302	85721
820.381-014	TRANSFORMER ASSEMBLER I (elec. equip.)	4436	33332433354	MNNNNNNNFFNNNNFNFNON	NNNN4NNNNNNNNNN	V,J,T	111	581	06.01.04	6867	470199	93114
820.662-010	MOTOR-ROOM CONTROLLER (utilities)	3123	34433432244	HNNNNNNNFFONONFNFNON	NNNN4ANNONNNNNN	V,J,T	021	871	05.06.01	6932	470501	95028
820.684-010	TRANSFORMER ASSEMBLER II (elec. equip.)	4448	33322333354	LNNNNNNFFFNFFNFNFOON	FNNN3NNNNNNNNNN	R,T	111	581	06.02.22	7720	000000	93905
821.131-010	ELECTRICAL-INSTALLATION SUPERVISOR (utilities)	4448	33332433354	LNNNNNNFFFNFNFOFONN	FNNN3NNNNNNNNNN	V,D,P,J	111	581	05.05.05	6000	520205	81002
821.131-014	LINE SUPERVISOR (utilities)	4448	33332433344	LOOOOONFFFNFFNFNOOON	FNNN4NNNFNNNNNN	V,D,P,J	111	581	05.05.05	6000	520205	81002
821.131-018	SERVICE SUPERVISOR II (utilities)	4447	33333333344	LFFNNNNFFNFFNFNNNNN	FNNN3NNNNNNNNNN	V,D,P,J	102	584	05.05.05	7100	520205	81008
821.131-022	STEEL-POST-INSTALLER SUPERVISOR (utilities)	4448	33333333354	LNNNNNNNFFNFNFNNNON	ONNN4NNNNNNNNNN	V,D,P,J	111	581	05.05.05	6000	520205	81002
821.131-026	WIREWORKER SUPERVISOR (utilities)	4448	33344334343	HOOOOONFFONONOOOOOO	NNNN3NNNNNNNNNN	V,D,P,J	111	586	05.05.05	6000	520205	81002
821.261-010	CABLE TELEVISION LINE TECHNICIAN (radio-tv broad.)	3336	33434433343	MFOFFFFFFOONFNFFN	NNNN3NNNNNNNNNN	T,J	111	586	05.05.05	6151	460303	85599
821.261-014	LINE MAINTAINER (any industry)	4437	33433423224	LFFNNNFFNOONFFNON	FNNN3NNNNNNNNNN	J,T	111	581	05.05.05	6433	460303	85723
821.261-018	RELAY TECHNICIAN (utilities)	4438	23222333344	LFFNNNNFFNNNNFNNNNN	ONNN4NFNNNNFNNNF	J,S,T	111	581	05.05.05	6153	460303	85721
821.261-022	SERVICE RESTORER, EMERGENCY (r.r. trans.)	4237	34324333324	HOOOOONFFONNNNFFFOF	FNNN3NNNNNNNNNO	V,S,J,T	111	594	05.05.05	6159	460303	85723
821.261-026	TROUBLE SHOOTER II (utilities)	4438	33333323224	MFFFFOFFFOFFNFFON	FNNN4NNNFFNNNN	V,S,J,T	102	581	05.05.05	6433	460303	85723
821.281-010	CABLE TELEVISION INSTALLER (radio-tv broad.)	4435	33323433344	HOOOOONFFONNONOOOOOO	OOOO3NNNNFNNNN	S,J,T	102	586	05.10.03	6151	460303	85702
821.361-010	CABLE INSTALLER-REPAIRER (utilities)	4327	33422333334	MNFFFNFFNNNNFNNNN	CNNN4NNNFFNNNN	T,J	111	581	05.05.05	6152	460303	85723
821.361-014	ELECTRIC-METER INSTALLER I (utilities)	4438	33322433344	LNNOOONFFNOONFFNON	FNNN3NNNNNNNNNN	V,S,J,T	111	581	05.10.02	6175	000000	85911
821.361-018	LINE ERECTOR (construction; utilities)	4437	33433423224	LFFNNNFFNOONFFNON	FNNN3NNNNNNNNNN	J	111	581	05.05.05	6433	460303	85723
821.361-022	LINE INSTALLER, STREET RAILWAY (r.r. trans.)	4437	33432433324	MOOOOONFFNOONFNFNON	FNNN3NNNONNNNNN	S,J,T	102	584	05.03.06	7820	150701	83005
821.361-026	LINE REPAIRER (utilities)	4447	33433423224	HFFFFNFFNFNFFNFFNON	CNNN4NNNFFFNNNN	P,J	111	581	05.05.05	6433	460303	85723
821.361-030	LINE-ERECTOR APPRENTICE (construction; utilities)	4337	33433423224	HFFFFNFFNOONFFFNON	CNNN4NNNFFNNNN	J,T	111	581	05.05.05	6433	460303	85723
821.361-034	POWER-TRANSFORMER REPAIRER (utilities)	4327	33322333345	MFNFFNFFNNNNNFNNNN	OOOO3NNNNFNNNN	J,T	111	586	05.05.05	6152	470501	85714
821.361-038	TOWER ERECTOR (construction; utilities)	4327	33433423224	MFFFFONFFNNNNNFFNON	ONNO3NNNNNNNNN	V,J,T	102	581	05.05.05	6433	460303	85723
821.364-010	UTILITIES SERVICE INVESTIGATOR (utilities)	4436	33442444444	LNNOOONFFNOONFFNON	FNNN3NNNNNNNNNN	J,S,T,V	271	581	05.10.02	7820	000000	83005
821.367-010	CONSTRUCTION CHECKER (utilities)	4436	33333433335	MFFONNNFFNOONFNFNON	FNNN3NNNNNNNNNN	J,S,T,V	111	581	05.05.05	6433	460303	83005
821.367-014	SAFETY INSPECTOR (utilities)	4338	33433444444	LNNFFFNFFNFNFNFNON	FNNN3NNNNNNNNNN	S,J,T	111	581	05.03.06	6881	470501	83002
821.381-010	ELECTRIC-METER TESTER (utilities)	4437	33332333344	LFFNNNFFNNNONFNNON	NNNN3NNNNNNNNNN	J,T	111	581	05.05.10	6881	460303	83002
821.381-014	VOLTAGE TESTER (utilities)	4437	33443333324	MFFFFNFFNNNNNFFFNFN	FNNN4NNFFNNNNN	S,J,T	111	581	05.05.05	6433	470501	85714
821.381-018	WIND-GENERATING-ELECTRIC-POWER INSTALLER (construction; utilities)	4338	33323433354	HFFFONFFNNNNFNNNON	ONNO3NNNNNNNNN	S,T	111	871	05.05.05	6433	470501	85714
821.564-010	LABORATORY HELPER (utilities)	2223	44543434344	MNNOOONFFNNFFNNNNNN	ONNN3NNNONNNNN	R,T	111	581	05.12.16	8635	460302	98102

DOT #	DOT Title & Industry	Trng	Aptitude	Physical	Environment	Tempra	WkF	MPSMS	GOE	SOC	CIP	OES
821.667-010	HELPER, ELECTRICAL (utilities)	2223	44544443334	HFFFFNFFNFFNFNFNON	FNNN4NNNNNNNNNN	R	111	580	05.12.16	8643	460303	98319
821.684-010	ELECTRIC-METER INSTALLER II (utilities)	3324	34443444344	LFFNNNNFFNNNFNFNON	FNNN3NNNNNNNNNN	T	111	581	05.10.03	6175	000000	85911
821.684-014	TOWER ERECTOR HELPER (construction; utilities)	3225	34443543355	VNNNOOOFFONNNNNFNON	CNNN4NNNNNNNNNF	R,T	102	369	05.10.01	8643	460303	98313
821.684-018	WIRER, STREET LIGHT (utilities)	3223	44445453354	LNNNOFNNFFNNNNFNFNON	FNNN4NNNNNNNNNN	R,T	111	584	05.12.16	7720	460303	93999
821.684-022	TROLLEY-WIRE INSTALLER (mine & quarry)	3223	34433434334	HNNNNNNFFFNNNNNFNFNON	NNNN4NNNNNNNNNF	R,A,U	111	364	05.10.04	6433	470399	85723
821.687-010	STEEL-POST INSTALLER (utilities)	2223	44544444445	MNNNNNNFFNNNNNFNFNNN	FNNN3NNNNNNNNNN	R	102	362	05.12.12	6433	460303	85723
822.131-010	CENTRAL-OFFICE-REPAIRER SUPERVISOR (tel. & tel.)	4447	22333343333	LONONNNFFNFFNFNFNOFN	NNNN3NNNNNNNNNN	V,D,P,J	111	586	05.05.05	7100	520205	81002
822.131-014	CUSTOMER-FACILITIES SUPERVISOR (tel. & tel.)	4447	23334422223	LOONNNNOOFNFFNNNOOOOOO	NNNN3NNNONNNNNN	D,V,T,P,J	111	586	05.05.05	6000	520205	81002
822.131-018	LINE SUPERVISOR (tel. & tel.)	4447	23333343353	LOOOOOOFFNFFNFNFNOON	FNNN4NNNNNNNNNN	V,D,P,J	111	586	05.05.05	6000	520205	81002
822.131-022	PROTECTIVE-SIGNAL SUPERINTENDENT (business ser.)	4447	22233333344	LOOOOOFFFNFFONOON	NNNN4NNNNNNNNNN	D,J,P,T	242	586	05.02.02	7100	000000	81008
822.131-026	SIGNAL SUPERVISOR (r.r. trans.)	4437	23333433355	LOOOOOOFFNFFNFNFNON	CNNN4NNNNNNNNNN	D,P,J,T	111	586	05.05.05	7100	520205	81008
822.131-030	TEST-DESK SUPERVISOR (tel. & tel.)	4337	23333333355	SNNNNNNFFFNFFNFNFNNN	NNNN3NNNNNNNNNN	D,P,J,T	111	586	05.05.05	7100	520205	81008
822.261-010	ELECTRICIAN, OFFICE (tel. & tel.)	4337	33332443244	LONOOONFFFNFNFNFNFN	NNNN3NNNNNNNNNN	J,T	111	586	05.05.05	6151	470103	85599
822.261-014	EQUIPMENT INSPECTOR (tel. & tel.)	4438	23323344455	LNNNNNNFFONOONFNFFNN	NNNN3NNNNNNNNNN	P,J,T	212	586	05.07.01	6881	150303	83002
822.261-018	MAINTENANCE INSPECTOR (tel. & tel.)	4338	33333333355	MNNNNNNFFNOONFNFFNN	NNNN3NNNNNNNNNN	J	212	586	05.07.03	6881	150303	83002
822.261-022	STATION INSTALLER-AND-REPAIRER (tel. & tel.)	4437	33333333334	LOOFFNFFNNOONFNFN	ONNN3NNNNNNNNNN	V,P,J,T	111	586	05.05.05	6158	470103	85726
822.261-026	TESTING-AND-REGULATING TECHNICIAN (tel. & tel.)	4337	33333443454	LOONNNNNFFNFNFNNOOFN	NNNN3NNNNNNNNNN	V,J,T	111	586	05.05.05	6881	470103	83002
822.267-010	LINE INSPECTOR (tel. & tel.)	4337	23333444455	LOOOOOOFFFNFFNFNFNNN	ONNN3NNNNNNNNNN	J	212	586	05.07.03	7820	460303	83005
822.281-010	AUTOMATIC-EQUIPMENT TECHNICIAN (tel. & tel.)	4337	33333443354	MONOOONFFFNNNNNFNFFN	NNNN4NNNNNNNNNN	V,J,T	111	586	05.05.05	6151	150403	85508
822.281-014	CENTRAL-OFFICE REPAIRER (tel. & tel.)	4337	33333332234	LFFFFNFFNNNNNFNFNOON	NNNN4NNNNNNNNNN	V,J,T	111	586	05.05.05	6151	470103	85502
822.281-018	MAINTENANCE MECHANIC, TELEPHONE (any industry)	4437	33332433333	LNNNNNNFFNFNFNFNOFN	NNNN4NNNNNNNNNN	J,T	111	586	05.05.05	6158	470103	85726
822.281-022	PRIVATE-BRANCH-EXCHANGE REPAIRER (tel. & tel.)	4237	33433343344	MOOFFNFFNNNNNFNFNN	NNNN3NNNNNNNNNN	V,J,T	111	586	05.05.05	6151	470103	85502
822.281-026	SIGNAL MAINTAINER (r.r. trans.)	4337	33332433344	MOOFFNFFNNOONFNFN	FNNN4NNNNNNNNNN	J,T	111	586	05.05.05	6151	460302	85511
822.281-030	TECHNICIAN, PLANT AND MAINTENANCE (radio-tv broad.)	4337	33333443344	MONFFFNNOONFNOOON	FNNN4NNNNNNNNNN	J,T	111	586	05.05.05	6151	000000	85599
822.281-034	TECHNICIAN, SUBMARINE CABLE EQUIPMENT (tel. & tel.)	4337	33333432353	MONOOONFFFNNNFNFNNN	NNNN4NNNNNNNNNN	V,J,T	111	586	05.05.05	6151	470103	85599
822.361-010	CABLE TESTER (tel. & tel.)	4337	33333443434	MOOOOOOFFFNNNFNFNNNON	FNNN3NONNNNNNNN	V,J,T	111	586	05.05.05	6151	460303	83002
822.361-014	CENTRAL-OFFICE INSTALLER (tel. & tel.)	4337	34333433234	MONOOONFFNNNNNFNFNON	NNNN3NNNONNNNNN	V,J,T	111	586	05.05.05	6151	470103	85502
822.361-018	PROTECTIVE-SIGNAL INSTALLER (business ser.)	4327	33332343344	MOOFFFFNFFNFNFNOOON	NNNN3NNNONNNNNN	J,T	111	586	05.05.05	6432	460302	87202
822.361-022	PROTECTIVE-SIGNAL REPAIRER (business ser.)	4337	33332443244	MOOFFNFNFONOONFNFOON	ONNN3NNNFNNNNNN	V,J,T	111	586	05.05.05	6432	460302	87202
822.361-026	TRANSMISSION TESTER (tel. & tel.)	4236	33332443354	LNNNNNNFFNNNNNFNNNON	NNNN3NNNNNNNNNN	J,T	212	863	05.07.03	6151	470103	83002
822.361-030	TROUBLE LOCATOR, TEST DESK (tel. & tel.)	4236	33443333454	SNNNNNNCCFNFFNFNNNON	NNNN3NNNNNNNNNN	J,T	111	586	05.06.01	6881	470103	83002
822.381-010	EQUIPMENT INSTALLER (tel. & tel.)	4337	33333333344	MOOOOOOFFFNNFNFNNON	NNNN4NNNNNNNNNN	V,J,T	111	586	05.05.05	6151	470103	85508
822.381-014	LINE INSTALLER-REPAIRER (tel. & tel.)	4337	33344444344	HFFFFFNFFNNNFNFNOFN	NNNN4NNNONNNNNN	V,J,T	111	586	05.05.05	6157	460303	85702
822.381-018	PRIVATE-BRANCH-EXCHANGE INSTALLER (tel. & tel.)	4327	33432422234	MFFOOONFFNFNFNFNOON	NNNN3NNNNNNNNNN	V,J,T	111	586	05.05.05	6151	470103	85502
822.381-022	TELEGRAPH-PLANT MAINTAINER (tel. & tel.)	4337	33333333344	HOOFFNFFNONFNFNNFOON	FNNN4NNNNNNNNNN	V,T	111	586	05.05.05	6151	470103	85502
822.664-010	PROTECTIVE-SIGNAL-INSTALLER HELPER (business ser.)	3225	44343443344	MFFFFFOFFNFNFNFNOON	FNNN3NNNNNNNNNN	R,T	111	586	05.10.03	8643	460302	98319
822.684-010	FRAME WIRER (tel. & tel.)	3334	34333433334	MFFFFNCCCNNFNFNNNFN	ONNN3NNNFNNNNNN	J,T	111	586	05.10.03	6151	460303	85505
822.684-014	PROTECTIVE-SIGNAL-REPAIRER HELPER (business ser.)	3226	33449443344	MFFFFFOFFNFNFNFNOON	FNNN3NNNFNNNNNN	R,T	111	586	05.10.03	8643	460302	98319
822.684-018	SIGNAL MAINTAINER HELPER (r.r. trans.)	2223	44445433345	HOOOOONFFNFFNNOONFFN	NNNN4NNNONNNNNF	R,T	111	586	05.12.16	8635	460303	98102
823.131-010	COMMUNICATIONS ELECTRICIAN SUPERVISOR (any industry)	4447	23322333353	HOOONNNOOOFFNNOOOOOO	ONNN3NNNNNNNNNN	D,V,T,P,J	111	586	05.05.06	6000	150303	81002
823.131-014	RIGGER SUPERVISOR (radio-tv broad.; tel. & tel.)	4337	23333433334	LOOOOOOFFFOOONFNOOON	ONNN3NNNNNNNNNN	V,D,P,T	111	586	05.05.05	7100	520205	81008
823.131-018	SUPERVISOR, AVIONICS SHOP (air trans.)	4448	23322333353	LOFOOOOFFOOFFNFNFFN	ONNN5NNOOOONNNN	D,J,P	111	586	05.05.10	6000	150801	81002
823.131-022	SUPERVISOR, RADIO INTERFERENCE (electron. comp.)	4448	23333444344	LNNNNNNFFNFFNFNNNON	NNNN4NNNNNNNNNF	V,D,P,J	271	869	05.05.10	6000	100104	81002
823.131-026	SUPERVISOR, SOUND TECHNICIAN (business ser.)	4337	23333433353	LNNNNNNFFNFFNFNFNOON	NNNN4NNNONNNNNN	D,T,V,J,P	111	587	05.05.10	6000	470103	81002
823.261-010	PUBLIC-ADDRESS SERVICER (any industry)	4327	33333433343	MFFOOONFFNFFNFNFNOON	FNNN4NNNNNNNNNN	J	111	585	05.05.10	6153	000000	85599
823.261-014	RADIO INTERFERENCE INVESTIGATOR (electron. comp.)	4437	33443443344	LNNNNNNFFNFNFNFNNNN	ONNN4NNNNNNNNNN	J,T	271	586	05.05.05	6151	470103	85723
823.261-018	RADIO MECHANIC (any industry)	4336	33322333244	MONOOOOFFNOONFNFFFN	FNNN3NNNNONNNNN	V,T,J	111	586	05.05.10	6151	470103	85514
823.261-022	ANTENNA INSTALLER, SATELLITE COMMUNICATIONS (any industry)	3336	33323333355	MOOFFFNCCCNONNNFNFFN	FNNN3NNNNNONNNN	T,V,J	111	592	05.05.10	6151	470103	85599
823.261-026	AVIONICS TECHNICIAN (aircraft mfg.; air trans.)	4446	23322433244	LOOOOOOFFFOOONFNOOON	NNNN4NNNOOONNNO	V,T,J	111	586	05.05.10	6151	470607	93102
823.261-030	DATA COMMUNICATIONS TECHNICIAN (any industry)	4347	23333323354	MONOOONFFFOOONFOONON	NNNN3NNNNNNNNNN	T,J	111	586	05.05.05	6151	000000	85599
823.281-014	ELECTRICIAN, RADIO (any industry)	4437	33332443253	LNNOOONFFFNFNFNFNOFN	NNNN3NNNONNNNNN	V,J,T	111	586	05.05.05	6151	470103	85514

DOT #	DOT Title & Industry	Trng	Aptitude	Physical	Environment	Tempra	WKF	MPSMS	GOE	SOC	CIP	OES
823.281-018	METEOROLOGICAL-EQUIPMENT REPAIRER (any industry)	4337	33222333253	MNNNNNNFFNNNNFNFOFN	FNNN3NNNNNNNNNN	V,J,T	111	602	05.05.10	6171	470105	85905
823.281-022	RIGGER (radio-tv broad.)	4337	34333433324	MOOOONFFNNNNFNFNON	CNNN3NNNNNNNNN	J,T	111	586	05.05.06	6151	460303	85599
823.361-010	TELEVISION INSTALLER (any industry)	3336	33433443345	MOOFFNFFNOONFNFNNN	FNNN3NNNFNNNNN	R,J,T	111	585	05.10.03	6155	470103	85708
823.684-010	ANTENNA INSTALLER (any industry)	3224	34533533324	MFFNFNFFNNNNNFNFNON	ONNN3NNNFNNNNN	R,T	111	584	05.12.16	6479	470103	87899
824.137-010	ELECTRICIAN, CHIEF (motion picture)	4337	23334444455	LNNNNNNOOONFNFNNNNN	ONNN3NNNNNNNNNN	V,D,P,J	111	911	05.05.05	7100	520205	81008
824.137-014	STREET-LIGHT-SERVICER SUPERVISOR (utilities)	4337	33333344454	LOONNNNFFNFFNFNONON	FNNN3NNNNNNNNNN	D,P,V	111	584	05.05.05	7100	520205	81008
824.261-010	ELECTRICIAN (construction)	4437	23223433344	MOOOOOOFFONOONFNNON	NNNN4NNNFNNNNN	J,T,V	111	580	05.05.05	6432	460302	87202
824.261-014	ELECTRICIAN APPRENTICE (construction)	4437	23322433343	MOOOOOOFFONOONFNOFFN	NNNN4NNNFNNNNN	J,T,V	111	580	05.05.05	6432	460302	87202
824.281-010	AIRPORT ELECTRICIAN (air trans.)	4437	23322433344	MOOOOONFFNNNNNFOFOON	ONNN3NNNFNNNNN	V,J,T	111	584	05.05.05	6432	460302	87202
824.281-014	ELECTRIC-DISTRIBUTION CHECKER (construction; utilities)	4338	33343444344	LOOFFNFFNNNNNFNNOFON	FNNN3NNNFNNNNN	V,J,T	111	581	05.05.05	6881	460302	83002
824.281-018	NEON-SIGN SERVICER (fabrication, nec)	4227	33443433343	MFFNNNNFFNNNNNFNFNFN	FNNN3NNNFONNNN	V,J,T	111	589	05.05.10	6432	460302	87202
824.381-010	STREET-LIGHT SERVICER (utilities)	4337	33433433334	MFFNNONNFFNNNNFNONON	FNNN3NNNFFNNNNN	J,T	111	584	05.05.05	6432	460302	87202
824.664-010	STREET-LIGHT-SERVICER HELPER (utilities)	3234	34434433354	MONONONFFNFNNFNONNN	FNNN4NNNONNNNNO	R,T	111	871	05.12.16	8635	460302	98102
824.681-010	ELECTRICIAN (mfd. bldgs.)	3234	33433433354	LOOOOONFFNNNNFNFNON	NNNN4NNONNNNNN	J,T	111	584	05.05.05	6432	460302	87202
824.683-010	NIGHT-PATROL INSPECTOR (fabrication, nec)	2122	44443444443	LNNNNNNFFNNNNNFFFNFF	ONNN3NNNNNNNNN	R,J	212	896	05.08.03	7820	000000	83005
824.684-010	NEON-TUBE PUMPER (fabrication, nec)	3225	34444533353	LNNNNNNFFNNNNFNNNNON	NNNN3NNNFNNNNN	J,T	014	589	05.05.10	7720	000000	93999
825.131-010	ELECTRICIAN SUPERVISOR (ship-boat mfg.)	4338	33333333344	MNNNNNNFFNFFNFNFOFN	ONNN3NNNFNNNNN	V,D,P,J	111	593	05.05.05	6314	520205	81005
825.131-014	ELEVATOR-CONSTRUCTOR SUPERVISOR (construction)	4338	33333433334	MOOOONFFNFFNFNFOON	NNNN3NNNNNNNNO	V,D,P,J	121	565	05.05.09	6000	150403	81002
825.137-010	SUPERVISOR, LINE DEPARTMENT (r.r. trans.)	4337	33323344455	LNNNNNNFFOFFNFONNNN	ONNN3NNNNNNNNN	V,D,J	111	584	05.05.05	7100	520205	81008
825.261-010	ELECTRIC-TRACK-SWITCH MAINTAINER (r.r. trans.)	4437	33333333234	MOOOOONFFNOONFNOOON	NNNN3NNNFNNNNN	V,J,T	111	594	05.05.05	6151	460303	85511
825.261-014	ELEVATOR EXAMINER-AND-ADJUSTER (aircraft mfg.; air industry)	4338	23922433234	LONFFFNFFNNNNFNNFNNF	NNNN3NNNNNNNNF	V,J,T	212	565	05.07.03	6176	150403	85932
825.261-018	ELEVATOR REPAIRER (aircraft mfg.; air industry)	4337	32333443254	MOOOOOOFFOOOOFNFOON	OONN5NNNOONNNN	T,J	111	592	05.05.06	6159	000000	85932
825.361-014	ELEVATOR CONSTRUCTOR (construction)	4337	33329433353	LOOOOONFFNNNNFNNFFN	NNNN3NNNFNNNNN	V,J,T	111	854	05.05.05	6152	470199	85714
825.281-014	ELECTRICIAN (water trans.)	4337	33332533354	LNNFFFNFFONNNFNFOON	NNNN3NONNNNNNN	V,J,T	111	591	05.05.10	6159	470604	85728
825.281-022	ELECTRICIAN, AUTOMOTIVE (automotive ser.)	4337	23222433344	MOOOOONFFNNNNNFNFOON	ONNN4NNNNNNNNN	V,J,T	111	594	05.05.05	6159	460302	85728
825.281-026	ELECTRICIAN, LOCOMOTIVE (railroad equip.)	4337	33322443244	MFFFFFNFFNNONFNOON	NNNN3NNNONNNNNO	V,J,T	111	565	05.05.05	6176	470303	85932
825.281-030	ELEVATOR REPAIRER (any industry)	4337	33323443244	MFFFFFNFFNNONFNONON	NNNN3NNONNNNNO	J,T	111	565	05.05.05	6176	470303	85932
825.281-034	ELEVATOR-REPAIRER APPRENTICE (any industry)	4337	32344433254	MOOOOOOFFONNNNFNOONON	FNNN4NNNNNNNNN	J,T	102	601	05.05.05	6179	150801	85999
825.281-038	EXPERIMENTAL-ROCKET-SLED MECHANIC (aircraft mfg.)	4337	33323433344	HOOFFFNFFNNNNFNOFNON	NNNN3NNNONNNNN	V,J,T	111	565	05.05.06	6176	460302	85932
825.361-010	ELEVATOR CONSTRUCTOR (construction)	3336	33342333355	LNNNNNNFFNNNNFFNNONN	NNNN3NNNONNNNN	R,J,T	111	567	06.01.05	6881	000000	83002
825.361-014	VIBRATOR-EQUIPMENT TESTER (machinery mfg.)	4337	32233443253	MOOOOOOOOOOONFNFOON	NNNN3NNOOONNNN	T	111	592	06.02.23	6159	470607	85728
825.381-010	AIRCRAFT MECHANIC, ELECTRICAL AND RADIO (aircraft mfg.)	3334	34433533354	LNNNNNFFNNNNFNOOON	NNNN3NNNNNNNNN	J,T	111	589	05.10.03	6159	000000	85302
825.381-014	AUTOMATIC-WINDOW-SEAT-AND-TOP-LIFT REPAIRER (automotive ser.)	4337	33334444354	MNNOONFFFNNNNNFNFFN	ONNN3NNNNNNNNN	V,J,T	212	584	05.05.05	6159	460302	85728
825.381-018	CONTROLLER REPAIRER-AND-TESTER (railroad equip.)	4337	33333433354	MNONONNFFONNNNNFNFNON	NNNN3NNNNNNNNN	T	212	592	06.01.05	6881	470607	83002
825.381-026	ELECTRICAL INSPECTOR (aircraft mfg.; air trans.)	4338	33332443233	MFFFFFOFFNNNNFNFNON	NNNN3NNNONNNNN	V,J,T	111	593	05.05.05	6432	490306	87202
825.381-030	ELECTRICIAN (ship-boat mfg.)	4338	33332443233	MFFFFFOFFNNNFNFFN	NNNN3NNNNNNFFFN	V,J,T	111	582	06.02.01	7100	460302	81008
825.381-034	ELECTRICIAN APPRENTICE (ship-boat mfg.)	3225	34443533355	MFFFFFNFFNNNNFNFNNN	ONNN3NNNONNNNN	J,T	111	606	05.05.13	6159	460303	85914
825.381-038	THIRD-RAIL INSTALLER (r.r. trans.)	3223	33433533445	HOOOONFFNNONFNFNNO	NNNN4NNNNNNNNO	R,T	102	582	06.01.04	8637	000000	98102
825.664-010	ELEVATOR-CONSTRUCTOR HELPER (construction)	2222	44444533355	MNNNNNNFFNNNNFNFNON	NNNN3NNNNNNNNN	R	111	591	05.12.12	8632	470604	98313
825.684-010	ELECTRICIAN HELPER, AUTOMOTIVE (automotive ser.)	3223	44445333335	HOOFFOFFNNNNNFNFFN	ONNN3NNNNNNNNO	R,T	111	565	05.12.15	8637	000000	98102
825.684-014	ELEVATOR-REPAIRER HELPER (any industry)	2213	44443544355	MNNONNNFFONNNNNFNFNON	NNNN4NNNNNNNNN	R,T	111	589	05.12.16	8769	470302	98999
825.684-018	BATTERY CHARGER (any industry)	4447	33333333353	LNNOOONFFNNFFNFNFOON	CNNN3NNNONNNNN	V,D,P,J	111	582	05.05.05	7100	520205	81008
826.131-010	ELECTRICAL SUPERVISOR (petrol. & gas)	4447	33332443233	LNNNNNNFFFFNFNFFON	NNNN4NNNONNNNN	D,J,P	111	582	06.02.01	6432	460302	87202
826.131-014	SUPERVISOR, ELECTRICAL ASSEMBLIES (elec. equip.; machinery mfg.)	4438	22334433344	LNNOOOOFFOOONFNFOON	ONNN3NNNNNNNNN	J	121	606	05.05.13	6159	460303	85728
826.361-010	FIELD-SERVICE ENGINEER (photo. appar.)	4336	34333433254	MOOOONFFNOONFNFOFN	NNNN4NNNNNNNNNO	V,T,J	111	582	06.01.04	6867	470105	93114
826.381-010	ASSEMBLER AND WIRER, INDUSTRIAL EQUIPMENT (elec. equip.; machinery mfg.)	3336	34433433354	HNNFFNFFNNNNFNFFON	NNFN3NNNNNNNNNO	V,J,T	102	568	05.10.01	6869	460302	89999
826.384-010	CELL REPAIRER (chemical)	3225	34344344345	HNNOOONFFNNNNFNFNNN	NNFN3NFNNNNNNN	R,J,T	132	589	06.02.32	7720	000000	85714
826.684-010	ANODE BUILDER (chemical)	3224	34344344345	HNNOOONFFNNNNFNFNNN	NNNN3NFNNNNNNN	T	111	589	05.10.03	6140	000000	85128
826.684-014	CELL CHANGER (chemical)	3225	34343443345	HOOOOONFFNOONFNFON	NNFN3NFNNNNNNN	J,T	111	589	05.12.12	6140	000000	85128
826.684-018	CELL INSTALLER (chemical)	3226	34433443355	MNNOOONFFNNNNNNNNNNNN	NNFN3NNNNNNNNN	R,J,T	111	589	05.12.12	7720	000000	85128
826.684-022	POT BUILDER (chemical)	3224	34433443345	HNNNNNNFFNNNNFNFNNN	NNNN3NONNNNNNN	J,T	111	589	05.10.03	7720	000000	93956

DOT #	DOT Title & Industry	Trng	Aptitude	Physical	Environment	Tempra	WkF	MPSMS	GOE	SOC	CIP	OES
827.131-010	ELECTRICAL-APPLIANCE-SERVICER SUPERVISOR (any industry)	4447	33333333253	LNNNNNNFFNFFNFNONON	NNNN3NNNNNNNNN	V,D,P,J	111	583	05.10.03	6000	520205	81002
827.131-014	SUPERVISOR, MAJOR APPLIANCE ASSEMBLY (house. appl.)	4447	23333344454	LNNOOONFFNFFNFNFNON	NNNN4NNNNNNNNN	D,J,P	111	583	06.02.01	7100	520205	81008
827.131-018	SUPERVISOR, AIR-CONDITIONING INSTALLER (any industry)	4447	23333334334	LNNOOONFFFNFFNFOOOON	NNNN4NNNNNNNNN	D,P,J	121	573	05.10.04	6000	470201	81002
827.261-010	ELECTRICAL-APPLIANCE SERVICER (any industry)	4337	33333433254	MNNFFFOFFFNOONFOOOON	NNNN3NNNNNNNNN	V,J,T	111	583	05.05.10	6156	470106	85711
827.261-014	ELECTRICAL-APPLIANCE-SERVICER APPRENTICE (any industry)	4337	33333433254	MNNFFFOFFFNOONFOOOON	NNNN3NNNNNNNNN	V,J,T	111	583	05.05.10	6156	470106	85711
827.361-010	AIR-CONDITIONING-UNIT TESTER (svc. ind. mach.)	3226	33444434355	LNNNNNNFFNOONFNNNNN	NNNO3NNNNNNNNN	R,J,T	102	583	06.01.05	6881	470201	83002
827.361-014	REFRIGERATION MECHANIC (svc. ind. mach.)	4337	33333433355	HOOOOONFFNOONFNNNN	NNNO3NNNNNNNNN	V,J,T	121	583	05.05.09	6160	470106	85902
827.381-010	CONTROL-PANEL TESTER (elec. equip.)	4437	23332433353	LNNNNNNFFNNNNFNOFON	NNNN3NNNNNNNNN	J,T	212	582	06.01.05	6881	470105	83002
827.384-010	REFRIGERATOR TESTER (svc. ind. mach.)	4437	33444444345	LNNNNNNNFFONNNNFNOONN	NNNN3NNNNNNNNN	J,T	211	583	06.03.01	7830	470106	83005
827.485-010	GAS CHARGER (svc. ind. mach.)	3235	33454444455	MNNNNNNFFONNNNFNNNN	NNNN3NNNNNNNNN	J,T	014	583	06.04.36	7665	470201	92928
827.584-010	ELECTRICAL-APPLIANCE PREPARER (any industry)	2222	34444444354	HNNOOONFFNNNNFNOOON	NNNN3NNNNNNNNN	R,T	061	583	05.12.16	7720	470106	93956
827.584-014	GAS-LEAK TESTER (svc. ind. mach.)	2223	44444444454	LNNNNNNFFONNNNFNNNN	NNNN3NNNNNNNNN	R,J	211	583	06.03.02	7830	470201	83005
827.585-010	FOAM CHARGER (svc. ind. mach.)	2112	34344443354	MNNNNNNFFNNNNONNNON	NNNN3NNNNNNNNN	J	014	583	06.04.36	7679	470201	92998
827.661-010	HOUSEHOLD-APPLIANCE INSTALLER (any industry)	2223	34344434344	HOOOOONFFNNNNNONNNON	NNNN3NNNNNNNNN	R,T	121	583	05.10.04	6156	470106	85711
827.684-010	APPLIANCE ASSEMBLER, LINE (house. appl.; svc. ind. mach.)	3336	44443434354	MNNNNNNFFNNNNFNOOON	NNNN4NNNNNNNNN	R,T	111	583	06.02.22	7720	470106	93956
828.131-010	SUPERVISOR, ELECTRONIC CONTROLS REPAIRER (engine-turbine)	3223	33222322254	MNNOOONFFNFFNFNNNN	NNNN3NNNNNNNNN	T,P,J	111	580	05.05.10	6000	470605	81002
828.161-010	SUPERVISOR, ELECTRONICS SYSTEMS MAINTENANCE (any industry)	4438	22222242343	LNNNNNNFFNFFNFNOON	ONNN3NNNNNNNNN	V,D,P,J	111	586	05.05.05	6000	150303	81002
828.251-010	ELECTRONIC-SALES-AND-SERVICE TECHNICIAN (profess. & kin.)	5548	22222322244	MNNNNNNFFNOONFNOOON	NNNN3NNNNNNNNN	V,J,T	244	703	05.05.05	6153	150303	85717
828.261-010	ELECTRONIC-ORGAN TECHNICIAN (any industry)	4337	23323443344	LNNFNONFFNNFNFNFON	NNNN3NNNNNNNNN	J	111	614	05.05.12	6155	470404	85708
828.261-014	FIELD SERVICE ENGINEER (profess. & kin.)	4336	22222333344	LOOOOOOONFFNFOOOON	ONNN3NNNNNNNNN	D,J,P,T,V	111	571	05.05.05	6153	470104	85705
828.261-018	SENIOR TECHNICIAN, CONTROLS (pipe lines)	4447	33222433354	LNNNOONFFNFFNFNNOON	NNNN4NNNNNNNNN	J,T	111	581	05.01.08	3711	150303	22505
828.261-022	ELECTRONICS MECHANIC (any industry)	4447	23224432253	MONOOONFFNOONFNOFN	ONNN3NNNNNNNNN	J,T,V	111	580	05.05.10	6153	470105	85717
828.261-026	ELECTRONICS-MECHANIC APPRENTICE (any industry)	4447	23224432253	MONOOONFFNOONFNOFN	ONNN3NNNNNNNNN	J,T,V	111	580	05.05.10	6153	150402	85717
828.281-018	MISSILE FACILITIES REPAIRER (military ser.)	3334	33333433334	VFFNNNNFFNOONFOONN	FNNN3NNNNNNNNN	J,T	111	586	05.10.01	6179	150402	85999
828.281-022	RADIOACTIVITY-INSTRUMENT MAINTENANCE TECHNICIAN (petrol. & gas)	4447	23222433253	LNNNNNNFFNNNNFNNFN	NNNN3NNNNNNNNN	V,J,T	111	601	05.05.11	6153	000000	85717
828.281-026	COMPUTERIZED ENVIRONMENTAL CONTROL INSTALLER (electron. comp.)	4447	23222322254	LNNOONCCCNOONFNNFON	NNNN3NNNNNNNNN	V,T,J	111	589	05.05.05	6159	150403	85799
828.381-010	EQUIPMENT INSTALLER (any industry)	4337	33333443344	MNNOOONFFONNNFNFOON	FNNN3NNNONONNNN	V,J,T	111	596	05.10.04	6159	460302	85728
828.381-018	ASSEMBLER, ELECTROMECHANICAL (aircraft mfg.; electron. comp.; inst. & app.)	4337	33322443344	MNNOOONFFONNNFNFOON	NNNN4NNOONNNNN	T	111	580	06.01.04	6812	000000	93111
829.131-010	CABLE SUPERVISOR (construction; tel. & tel.; utilities)	4338	33332444353	LOOOONFFONFFNFNONON	FNNO3NFNFNNNNN	V,D,P,J	111	580	05.05.05	7100	520205	81008
829.131-014	ELECTRICIAN SUPERVISOR (any industry)	4338	33333333354	LOOOOONFFNFFNFNOOON	ONNN4NNNONNNNN	V,D,P,J,T	111	580	05.05.05	6314	520205	81005
829.131-018	IN-FLIGHT REFUELING SYSTEM REPAIRER (military ser.)	4338	33324433345	LNNNNNNFFONFFNFNNNN	NNNN3NNNNNNNNN	V,D,P,J	111	616	05.05.09	7100	000000	81008
829.131-022	INSTALLATION SUPERINTENDENT, PIN-SETTING MACHINE (construction)	4338	23322333344	HOOOOONFFNNNNFNNNN	NNNN3NNNNNNNNN	D,J,P	111	580	05.05.05	6000	520205	81002
829.137-010	SUPERVISOR, ELECTRICAL REPAIR AND TELEPHONE LINE MAINTENANCE (utilities)	4338	33333333334	LNNFFFNFFNOONFNOFON	FNNN3NNNONONNN	J,T	111	584	05.05.05	6881	470501	83002
829.261-010	COMPLAINT INSPECTOR (utilities)	4337	33333433354	MNNOONFFONOONFNONON	NNNN3NNNNNNNNN	J	111	604	05.10.02	6179	150401	85908
829.261-014	DENTAL-EQUIPMENT INSTALLER AND SERVICER (wholesale tr.)	4436	33324433354	MOOOOOFFFOOOOFNOOON	NNNN4NNOOONNNN	T,J	111	560	05.05.05	6153	460302	87202
829.261-018	ELECTRICIAN, MAINTENANCE (any industry)	4448	23222333234	MOOFFNFFNNNNFNOONN	NNNN3NNNONNNNN	V,J,T	111	580	05.10.03	6175	470303	85928
829.281-010	AUTOMATIC-DOOR MECHANIC (construction)	3226	33332433354	LNNNNNNFFNNNNFNNNN	NNNN3NNNNNNNNN	V,J,T	212	586	05.10.02	6159	000000	85799
829.281-018	IN-FLIGHT REFUELING SYSTEM REPAIRER (military ser.)	3337	33323322234	HOOOOONFFNNNNFNOOON	NNNN3NNNNNNNNN	V,J,T	111	586	05.05.05	6151	470103	85599
829.281-022	SOUND TECHNICIAN (any industry)	4336	44433443345	LFFOOONFFNOONFNOFON	FNNN3NNNONONNN	V,J,T	111	580	05.05.05	6157	460303	85723
829.361-010	CABLE SPLICER (construction; tel. & tel.; utilities)	4337	44433535345	LFFOOONFFNOONFNOFON	FNNN3NNNONONNN	J,T	111	580	05.05.05	6157	460303	85723
829.361-014	CABLE-SPLICER APPRENTICE (construction; tel. & tel.; utilities)	4337	33332332333	LNNNNNNFFNNNNFNOFN	NNNN3NNNONNNNN	J,T	212	580	06.01.05	6881	470105	83002
829.361-018	CIRCULATING PROCESS INSPECTOR (elec. equip.)	3336	34332433354	MNNOONFFNNNNFNNNN	FNNN3NNNNNNNNN	J,T	111	616	05.10.03	6881	470199	85599
829.381-010	PINSETTER ADJUSTER, AUTOMATIC (toy-sport equip.)	4336	34434443345	MOOOOONFFNNNNNFNNNN	FNNN3NNNNNNNNN	J,T	111	580	05.12.16	6881	460303	83002
829.667-010	CABLE-SPLICER HELPER (construction; tel. & tel.; utilities)	2223	44454544455	MOOOOONFFNNNNNFNNNN	FNNN4NNNNNNNNN	R	111	580	05.12.16	6635	470199	98102
829.667-014	PINSETTER-MECHANIC HELPER (any industry)	2222	44443535345	HONNNNNFFNNNNNNN	FNNN4NNNNNNNNN	R	121	616	05.12.15	6637	470199	98102
829.684-010	BATTERY INSPECTOR (railroad equip.; r.r. trans.)	3334	34334434354	LNNONONFFNNNNONNNON	NNNN3NNNNNNNNN	R,T	121	594	05.10.03	6152	460302	85714
829.684-014	BODY WIRER (vehicles, nec)	3234	34434433353	LNNOOONFFNNNNFNNNN	NNNN3NNNNNNNNN	R,T	111	584	05.05.05	6159	470604	85728
829.684-018	CABLE PULLER (construction; utilities)	2114	44454544335	HFFFFFFFNNNNNN	FNNN3NNNNNNNNN	R	111	871	05.12.16	7720	010299	93999
829.684-022	ELECTRICIAN HELPER (any industry)	3223	34433433344	MOOFFFOFFONNNNNFOON	NNNN3NNNONNNNN	T	111	580	05.12.16	8643	460302	98313
829.684-026	ELECTRICIAN HELPER (ship-boat mfg.)	2113	34434345253	MFFFFOFFNNNNFNNNFN	NNNN3NNNNNFNNNNN	R,T	111	593	05.10.07	8643	010299	98313
840.131-010	SUPERVISOR, PAINTING (construction)	4338	33333433342	MOONOONFFNFNFFNNNN	ONNN3NFNNNNNNN	D,V,T,P,J	102	360	05.10.07	6315	520205	81005
840.131-014	SUPERVISOR, PAINTING, SHIPYARD (ship-boat mfg.)	4338	33333433343	LOOOOONFFONFNFNOOON	ONNN3NFNNNNNNN	V,D,P,J	102	593	05.10.07	6315	520205	81005

DOT #	DOT Title & Industry	Trng	Aptitude	Physical	Environment	Tempra	WkF	MPSMS	GOE	SOC	CIP	OES
840.381-010	PAINTER (construction)	3227	34344343343	MOOFOONFFOOOONFOONFN	ONNN3NONNONNNN	T,J	102	360	05.10.07	6442	460408	87402
840.381-014	PAINTER APPRENTICE, SHIPYARD (ship-boat mfg.)	3227	33333433332	MFFFFNFFONNNNFNNNFN	FNNN3NFNNNNNNNO	J,T	153	593	05.10.07	6442	490306	87402
840.381-018	PAINTER, SHIPYARD (ship-boat mfg.)	3227	34333433332	MFFFFNFFONNNNFNNNFN	FNNN3NFNNNNNNNO	J,T	153	593	05.10.07	6442	460408	87402
840.681-010	PAINTER, STAGE SETTINGS (motion picture)	3217	34333434344	LFFFFNFFNNNNFNNNFN	NNNN3NCNNNNNNN	J,T	153	361	01.06.03	6442	460408	87402
840.684-010	GLASS TINTER (glass products)	2125	34433434344	MOONNNNFFONNNNONNNON	FNNN3NNNNNNNNN	R,T	153	531	06.04.33	6442	460408	87402
840.687-010	PAINTER HELPER, SHIPYARD (ship-boat mfg.)	2213	44444443344	MOOFFNFFNNNNNFNNNON	FNNN4NONNNNNNO	R,T	102	593	05.12.12	8644	460408	98314
841.137-010	SUPERVISOR, BILLPOSTING (business ser.)	4236	33333433243	LONOOONFFONFFNFOONON	FNNN3NNNNONNNN	D,P,J	063	896	05.12.01	6315	090201	81005
841.381-010	PAPERHANGER (construction)	4227	33333433243	MOOOOONFFFONNNCNFOFN	NNNN3NNNNNNNNN	J	102	361	05.05.04	6443	460408	87402
841.684-010	BILLPOSTER (business ser.)	2112	44533433344	LOOOOONFFFNNNNONFNON	FNNN3NNNFNNNN	R,T	063	896	05.12.14	6443	460408	98999
842.131-010	SUPERVISOR, DRY-WALL APPLICATION (construction)	4337	33333433345	VFNFFNFFNFFNFONN	NNNN3NNNNNNNNF	D,P,J	102	361	05.05.04	6313	520205	81005
842.131-014	SUPERVISOR, LATHING (construction)	4338	33333433345	MOOFFNFFNFFNFNNN	ONNN4NNNNNNNNN	V,D,P,J	102	361	05.10.01	6313	520205	81005
842.131-018	SUPERVISOR, PLASTERING (construction)	4337	33333434344	LONOOONFFOFFFNFNON	FNNN3NNNNNNNNO	D,P,J	091	360	05.05.04	6315	520205	81005
842.134-010	SUPERVISOR, TAPING (construction)	4336	33343433335	MOOFFNFFNNOONFNNNN	NNNN3NFNNNNNNO	D,P,J,T	094	361	05.10.01	6313	520205	81005
842.361-010	LATHER (construction)	3226	33433433345	MOOFFNFFNNNNNFNNN	NNNN3NNNNNNNNN	J,T	102	361	05.10.01	6424	469999	87114
842.361-014	LATHER APPRENTICE (construction)	3226	33433433345	MOOFFNFFNNNNNFNNN	NNNN3NNNNNNNNN	J,T	102	361	05.10.01	6424	469999	87114
842.361-018	PLASTERER (construction)	3227	33443434334	MOOFFNFFNNOONFOFNOO	ONNF3NNNNONNNO	J,T	091	361	05.05.04	6444	469999	87317
842.361-022	PLASTERER APPRENTICE (construction)	3227	33443434334	MOOFFFNFFNNOONFOFNOO	ONNF3NNNNONNNO	J,T	091	361	05.05.04	6444	469999	87317
842.361-026	PLASTERER, MOLDING (concrete prod.; construction)	4237	33322423234	MOOFFNFFNNOONFOONOO	NNNF3NONNNNNNO	V,J,T	102	536	05.05.04	6444	469999	87108
842.361-030	DRY-WALL APPLICATOR (construction)	3337	34333433333	VOOOOOOFFNOFNFOON	NNNN4NFNNONNNF	D,J,T	102	361	05.05.04	6424	469999	87108
842.381-014	STUCCO MASON (construction)	4337	33342533245	MOOOOONFFNNNNFNOONN	FNNF3NNNNNNNNO	J	091	361	05.05.04	6444	469999	87317
842.664-010	TAPER (construction; mfd. bldgs.)	3225	34433434344	MOOOOOOCOOOONFNNOOO	NNNN4NFNNONNNN	R,T	102	361	05.10.01	6424	469999	87111
842.665-010	PLASTER-MACHINE TENDER (construction)	2114	44544544445	LOOOONFFONNNNNNNNN	ONNF4NNNNNNNNN	R	014	536	05.12.06	6479	469999	87899
842.684-010	DRY-WALL SPRAYER (mfd. bldgs.)	3214	34443533345	MNNONNNFFNNNNNNFNNN	NNNN4NFNNNNNNN	J,T	153	455	06.04.33	7756	460408	93947
842.684-014	DRY-WALL APPLICATOR (construction; mfd. bldgs.)	2226	34433433345	MOOFFNFFNNONFNFONN	NNNN3NNNNNNNNN	J,T	102	361	05.10.01	6424	469999	87108
843.134-010	SUPERVISOR, DOPING (construction)	4237	33443444445	LNNNNNNFFONFFNFNNNN	NNNN3NONNNNNNN	V,D,P,J	092	364	05.10.07	7100	000000	81008
843.137-010	SUPERVISOR, WATERPROOFING (construction)	4337	34433444445	LFFFNNNFFONFFNFNNN	FNNN3NNNFNNNN	V,D,P,J	153	360	05.10.07	7100	520205	81008
843.384-010	WOOD CAULKER (ship-boat mfg.)	2113	34443533345	MFFOOONFFNNNNNFNNN	ONNN3NNNNNNNNN	J,T	094	593	05.12.14	7759	490306	93999
843.482-010	METAL SPRAYER, CORROSION PREVENTION (any industry)	3225	34343434344	MNNOOONFFONNNNFOFNON	NNNN4NFNNNNNNFF	J,T	153	360	05.12.14	7543	000000	91926
843.684-010	STEEL-PLATE CAULKER (any industry)	2114	34544534345	MOOFFONFFONNNNNNNNN	ONNN4NNNNNNNNN	R	094	554	05.12.14	7759	000000	93999
843.684-014	UNDERCOATER (automotive ser.)	2113	44533544345	LNNFFFNFCCNOONNFNNNO	NNNN3NFNNNNNNO	R,T	153	961	05.12.14	7756	470603	93947
844.364-010	CEMENT MASON (construction)	3227	34433434344	HOOFFNCCNOONFNFOON	FNNF3NNNNNNNNO	R,T	102	360	05.05.01	6463	469999	87311
844.364-014	CEMENT-MASON APPRENTICE (construction)	3327	34433434344	HOOFFNCCNOONFNFOON	FNNF3NNNNNNNNO	R,T	102	360	05.05.01	6463	469999	87311
844.461-010	CONCRETE-STONE FINISHER (concrete prod.)	4337	34433433344	MNNFFNFFNNNNNFNFOON	FNNF3NNNNNNNNN	J,T	102	530	05.05.01	6463	469999	87311
844.681-010	CELL MAKER (chemical)	3225	34443533345	MNNFFFNFFNNNNNFOFNNN	NNNN4NNNNNNNNN	J	102	536	06.02.30	7754	000000	93944
844.684-010	CONCRETE RUBBER (concrete prod.)	3115	34443543355	MNNOOONCCCFNNNFNOONN	FNNO3NNNNNNNNN	J,T	102	360	05.10.01	6463	469999	87311
844.687-010	CEMENT SPRAYER HELPER, NOZZLE (concrete prod.; construction)	1112	44544544435	HOOOONNFFNNNNNNNNN	FNNN4NNNNNNNNO	R	091	360	05.12.09	8648	469999	98319
845.381-010	PAINTER APPRENTICE, TRANSPORTATION EQUIPMENT (aircraft mfg.; air trans.; automotive ser.)	3236	33333433342	MOOOOONFFONNNFNFOFN	ONNN3NCNNONONNN	J,T	153	591	05.10.07	7669	470603	92947
845.381-014	PAINTER, TRANSPORTATION EQUIPMENT (aircraft mfg.; air trans.; automotive ser.)	3236	33434433342	MOOOOONFFONNNFNFOFN	ONNN3NCNNONONNN	J,T	153	591	05.10.07	7669	470603	92947
845.381-018	PAINT SPRAYER, SANDBLASTER (concrete prod.)	3214	34434433353	MOOOONNFFFNNNNFNFFN	NNNN4NNONNNNN	T,V	051	495	05.10.07	7756	470302	85305
845.681-010	RAILROAD-CAR LETTERER (r.r. trans.)	4337	34433433344	LOONNNNFFNNNNFNFNN	FNNN3NNNNNNNNN	J,T	262	594	01.06.03	6442	000000	87402
845.684-010	CAR SCRUBBER (railroad equip.)	2113	44444534355	MOOFFNFFONNNNFNFNNN	FNNN4NFNNNNNNN	R	031	594	05.12.18	8750	000000	98905
845.684-014	PAINTER HELPER, AUTOMOTIVE (automotive ser.)	2114	44543544354	MNNFFFNFFNNFFNNNFN	NNNN3NFNNNNNNN	R,T	102	591	05.12.12	8618	470603	98999
849.137-010	DISPATCHER (construction)	4336	34334444455	LNNNNNFFONFFNFNNNN	NNNN4NNNNNNNNN	D,P,J,T	013	536	05.09.01	7100	000000	81008
849.381-010	AIRPLANE COVERER (aircraft mfg.; air trans.)	3227	34923432244	MOOOONNCCFNNNNFNNON	NNNN3NFNNNNNNN	V,J,T	153	592	06.01.04	6859	470607	89599
849.484-010	BOILER RELINER, PLASTIC BLOCK (foundry)	2214	34433434355	LNNNNNNFFNNNNFNNNN	FNNN4NNONNNNNN	R,T	102	530	05.12.06	7759	480599	85126
849.665-010	PUMP TENDER, CEMENT BASED MATERIALS (concrete prod.; construction)	2114	44444444355	LNNOOONFFONOONFOONNN	FNNN4NNONNNNNN	R	014	533	05.12.06	6479	469999	87899
849.684-010	BOAT BUFFER, PLASTIC (ship-boat mfg.)	1113	44543534455	MNNOOOONFFNNNNNFNNNN	NNNN3NNNNNNNN	R	051	593	06.04.24	7758	000000	93953
850.133-010	SUPERVISOR, RECLAMATION (mine & quarry)	4347	23333334454	LNNNNNNFFNFNFFOOO	FNNN4NFNNNNNNN	D,P,J,T	005	341	05.11.02	6318	150901	81005
850.137-010	SUPERVISOR, CORE DRILLING (construction)	4337	33333234454	LNNNNNNFFNNNNFNNNON	FNNN4NNNNNNNNN	V,D,P,J	005	340	05.11.01	6318	490202	81005
850.137-014	SUPERVISOR, LABOR GANG (construction)	4236	33334444445	MOOOOONOOONFNFOONNO	FNNN4NNNNNNNNN	V,D,P,J	011	369	05.12.01	7100	490202	81008
850.137-018	SUPERVISOR, RIPRAP PLACING (construction)	4326	34333444445	LNNNNNNFONFFNFFNNN	FNNN4NNNNNNNNN	D,P,J,T	011	365	05.12.01	7100	490202	81008

DOT #	DOT Title & Industry	Trng	Aptitude	Physical	Environment	Tempra	WkF	MPSMS	GOE	SOC	CIP	OES
850.381-010	MINER (construction)	4327	33333533325	HFNFFNFFNNNNFNFNNN	NNNF4NFNNNNNNNO	S,J,T	005	363	05.11.01	6530	000000	87905
850.387-010	INSPECTOR OF DREDGING (water trans.)	4336	33334345445	LNNNANNNFFNNNFNFNNN	FNNN4NNNNNNNNNN	J	211	365	05.07.01	1472	460403	21908
850.467-010	GRADE CHECKER (construction)	3224	34333444455	LFFFFNNCONOONOFFNNN	CNNN4NCNNNANNNN	J,T	243	362	05.03.01	1472	490202	21908
850.662-010	HORIZONTAL-EARTH-BORING-MACHINE OPERATOR (construction)	3225	34433544345	MOOOONFFNNOONFNFNNN	CNNN4NNNNNNNNNNN	J,T	005	369	05.11.01	6474	490202	87902
850.662-014	ROCK-DRILL OPERATOR II (construction)	3115	33333433235	HFNOOONFFNOONFNFNNN	NNNF5NCNNNNNNNO	J,T	005	360	05.11.01	6474	490202	87902
850.663-010	DREDGE OPERATOR (construction; mine & quarry)	3225	33433433335	MOONNNNCCNOONFFFNNF	FNNF4NNNNNNNNNN	R,T	014	345	05.11.01	8316	490202	97928
850.663-014	ELEVATING-GRADER OPERATOR (construction)	3116	34433534335	MONNNNNCCONNNNOFFNNF	NNNN4NONNNNNNN	J,T	011	360	05.11.01	8317	490202	97938
850.663-018	LOCK TENDER II (construction)	3114	34443434344	LNNNONFFNNOONOFNNOO	NNNO4NONNNNNNN	R,T	011	363	05.11.01	8239	490202	97399
850.663-022	MOTOR-GRADER OPERATOR (construction)	3115	34433434324	MONNNNNCCOONNFFONOF	CNNN4NONNNNNNN	J,T	011	362	05.11.01	8317	490202	97938
850.663-026	STRIPPING-SHOVEL OPERATOR (mine & quarry)	3115	34534534335	MOONNNNNCONNNNOFFNNF	NNNN4NNNNNNNNN	R,T	011	340	05.11.02	8316	490299	97923
850.682-010	SHIELD RUNNER (construction)	3115	34433544345	LNNNNNNFFONNNNNNNNN	NNNN4NNNNNNNNNO	J,T	005	363	05.11.01	6540	490299	87949
850.683-010	BULLDOZER OPERATOR I (any industry)	3225	34434434335	HONONONCOONFNOFFNNF	CNNN3CNNNNNNNNO	J,T	007	360	05.11.01	8317	010204	97938
850.683-014	DITCHER OPERATOR (r.r. trans.)	3114	34434434334	LONNNNNCCNOONNCCNOC	CNNN4NNNNNNNNN	R	011	360	05.11.01	8317	490202	97938
850.683-018	DRAGLINE OPERATOR (any industry)	3225	34434534335	MONOOONCCNNNNNNCCNNC	ONNN4NNNNNNNNNN	J,T	011	340	05.11.04	8316	490299	97926
850.683-022	FORM-GRADER OPERATOR (construction)	3214	34433444345	LNNNNNNNFFNNNNNFFNNN	CNNN4NNNNNNNNN	J,T	011	362	05.11.01	8317	490202	97938
850.683-026	MUCKING-MACHINE OPERATOR (construction)	3113	34433444345	LNNOONFFNNOONFFNNNF	NNNO4NONNNNNNN	J,T	011	363	05.11.01	8316	490202	97923
850.683-030	POWER-SHOVEL OPERATOR (any industry)	3115	44434434334	MONNNNNCCFNNNNNFFNOF	CNNN4FNNNNNNNN	R,T	011	340	05.11.01	8316	490202	97923
850.683-034	ROCK-DRILL OPERATOR I (construction)	3225	34433433345	LNNOONCCFNNNNFFNFNN	CNNN4NNNNNNNNN	J	005	360	05.11.01	6474	490202	87902
850.683-038	SCRAPER OPERATOR (construction)	3125	34433534335	MNNNNNNCCONNNNNFFNNF	CNNN4NONNNNNNN	J,T	011	360	05.11.01	8317	490202	97938
850.683-042	TOWER-EXCAVATOR OPERATOR (construction)	3115	34433534334	LONNNNNCCNNNNOFFNOO	NNNN4NNNNNNNNN	R,T	011	360	05.11.04	8316	490202	97923
850.683-046	UTILITY-TRACTOR OPERATOR (construction)	3114	34433533335	LNNNNNNCCFNNNNOFFNNF	CNNN4NCNNNNNNN	J,T	011	360	05.11.01	8317	490202	97938
850.684-010	EXCAVATOR (any industry)	3113	34533533345	HNNOOOOCCCNNNNCNNONN	CNNN3NNNNNNNNN	R,T	011	340	05.12.03	6479	000000	87899
850.684-014	HORIZONTAL-EARTH-BORING-MACHINE-OPERATOR HELPER (construction)	2112	34544534345	HONOOONFFNNNNFNNNNN	CNNF4NNNNNNNNO	R,T	005	369	05.12.02	8648	490299	98319
850.684-018	STRIPPING-SHOVEL OILER (mine & quarry)	3116	34433433334	HONOOONFFOONNNNNNON	ONNN4NNNFNNNNON	J,T	033	564	05.12.08	6140	470399	85128
851.137-010	BANK BOSS (construction)	4337	33333344444	LNNNOONOOONFFNONNNNN	CNNN4NNNNNNNNNNO	V,D,P,J	102	340	05.12.01	7100	000000	81008
851.137-014	SUPERVISOR, SEWER MAINTENANCE (government ser.)	4336	33333344444	LNNNOONOOONFFNONOON	FNNO3NONNNNNNNN	V,D,P,J	102	364	05.12.01	7100	000000	81008
851.262-010	SEWER-LINE REPAIRER, TELE-GROUT (sanitary ser.)	4327	33333344354	LFNFFNFFNNFFNFNFFON	ONNN3NNNNNNNNO	D,J	211	364	05.10.01	6881	000000	83002
851.362-010	SEWER-LINE PHOTO-INSPECTOR (sanitary ser.)	3225	33433443344	MFNFFFNNFFNFNFNFON	ONNN4NNNNNNNNNO	J,T	211	364	05.07.01	6882	000000	34023
851.383-010	IRRIGATION SYSTEM INSTALLER (construction)	3225	34344433335	MNNNNNFFFNNNNOOFFNNO	CNNN3NNNNNNNNN	J,T	102	369	05.11.01	6479	010299	87899
851.663-010	SEPTIC-TANK INSTALLER (construction)	3224	34433434335	MNNNOOONCCFNNNNFFONF	CNNN4NNNNNNNNN	J,T	102	364	05.11.01	8316	490202	97923
853.133-010	SUPERVISOR, ASPHALT PAVING (construction)	4338	33333444445	LNNNONNFFNFFNFFONNN	FNNN4NNNNNNNNN	V,D,P,J	095	362	05.11.01	7100	520205	81008
853.133-010	SUPERVISOR, MIXING PLACE (construction)	4327	33333444455	LNNNNNFFNFNFFNFFNNNF	FNNN4NNNNNNNNN	V,D,P,J	091	362	05.10.01	7100	520205	81008
853.663-010	ASPHALT-PAVING-MACHINE OPERATOR (construction)	3115	34533534335	MONOOONFFNOONOCCNNC	CNNN4NCNNNNNNN	J,T	095	362	05.11.01	6466	490202	87708
853.663-014	CONCRETE-PAVING-MACHINE OPERATOR (construction)	3113	34433534335	MONOOONFFNOONFFNNNN	CNNN4NNNNNNNNN	R,T	095	362	05.11.01	6466	490202	87708
853.663-018	ROAD-OILING-TRUCK DRIVER (construction)	3115	34444334335	LNNNNNNCCNNOONFFNNF	ONNN4NNNNNNNNN	J,T	153	362	05.11.01	6466	490202	87708
853.663-022	STONE-SPREADER OPERATOR (construction)	3115	34444434335	LONNNNCCNNOONFFFNNN	CNNN4NCNNONNNNN	R,T	095	362	05.11.01	6466	490202	87899
853.665-010	ASPHALT-DISTRIBUTOR TENDER (construction)	2212	34443434355	LFFONONCCNNFFNFFNNF	CNNN4NCNNNNNNNF	R,T	095	362	05.12.14	6466	490202	87708
853.683-010	CURB-MACHINE OPERATOR (construction)	3214	34433534335	HOOFNNNCCNNNNNFFNNF	CNNN4NONNNNNNN	J,T	135	362	05.11.01	6466	490202	87708
853.683-014	HEATER-PLANER OPERATOR (construction)	3113	34443534335	MONNNNNCCNNNNNNCNNC	CNNN4NFNNNNNNN	R,T	095	362	05.11.01	8317	490202	97938
853.683-018	JOINT-CLEANING-AND-GROOVING-MACHINE OPERATOR (construction)	3114	34443434345	MNNFNNNFFNNNFNFFNNF	CNNN4NNNNNNNNN	J,T	056	362	05.11.01	6466	490202	87708
853.685-010	ASPHALT-HEATER TENDER (construction)	2113	44444444345	LONOOONFFNNNNNFNNNNC	CNFN4NCNNNNNNC	R	131	502	05.12.10	6466	490202	87899
859.133-010	SUPERVISOR, RIGHT-OF-WAY MAINTENANCE (utilities)	4337	33334433334	LNNNNNFFNFNFNFNFON	CNNN4NNNNNNNNNO	D,V,P,J	102	362	05.12.01	6318	000000	81005
859.137-010	SUPERVISOR, GRADING (construction)	4337	33333344445	LONNNNFFNFFNFFFNNF	FNNN4NNNNNNNN	V,D,P,J	102	360	05.11.01	8120	490202	81011
859.137-014	SUPERVISOR, PILE DRIVING (construction)	4338	33333334445	LOONNNNFFNFNFFONN	FNNN4NFNNNNNNN	V,D,P,J	102	360	05.11.01	6318	490202	81005
859.137-018	SUPERVISOR, TUNNEL HEADING (construction)	4337	33332444445	LNNNNNNFFFNFNFFFONN	NNNC4NCNNNNNNNO	V,D,P,J	102	363	05.12.01	6311	490299	81005
859.261-010	BLASTER (any industry)	4447	33333433334	HONFOOOFFOOONFFNON	NNNN5NONNNNNNC	S,J	005	360	05.10.06	6530	000000	87905
859.267-010	STREET-OPENINGS INSPECTOR (utilities)	4338	33332444344	LOOOOOOFFONOONFNFNON	CNNN4NNNNNNNNO	V,D,J	102	364	05.07.01	7820	460403	83005
859.281-010	GRAVEL INSPECTOR (construction)	4335	33343433445	LNNNNNNNFFFFNNFFFNN	NNNN4NNNNNNNNN	J,T	212	345	05.11.03	7820	470399	83005
859.362-010	WELL-DRILL OPERATOR (construction)	4337	33333334334	HOOOONNFFFOOOONOOFNON	FNNO4NONNNNNNNO	J	005	369	05.11.01	6474	490299	87902
859.682-010	EARTH-BORING-MACHINE OPERATOR (construction; utilities)	3114	34434534345	MNNNNNFFFNNNNONFNNN	FNNN4NNNNNNNN	R,T	005	369	05.11.01	6474	490299	87902
859.682-014	FOUNDATION-DRILL OPERATOR (construction)	3225	34432434335	LONONNNCCNNNFNONFNNN	CNNN4NFNNNNNNN	J	005	365	05.11.01	6474	490202	87902

DOT #	DOT Title & Industry	Trng	Aptitude	Physical	Environment	Tempra	WkF	MPSMS	GOE	SOC	CIP	OES
859.682-018	PILE-DRIVER OPERATOR (construction)	3225	33434534335	MONNNNNCCNNNNNNNFFNNN	CNNN5NNNNNNNNNN	J,T	102	360	05.11.01	6476	490202	87705
859.683-010	OPERATING ENGINEER (construction; mine & quarry)	3126	34433434334	MONOOONCCNNNNONOFFNOF	FNNN5NONNNNNNNNO	J,T,V	007	360	05.11.01	8312	490202	97956
859.683-014	OPERATING-ENGINEER APPRENTICE (construction; mine & quarry)	3126	34433434334	MONOOONCCNNNNONOFFNOF	FNNN5NONNNNNNNNO	J,T,V	007	360	05.11.01	8312	490202	97956
859.683-018	RAILWAY-EQUIPMENT OPERATOR (r.r. trans.)	3224	34434433335	MONOOOFFNNNNNOFFNNF	CNNN4NFNNNNNNNN	J,T	102	367	05.11.01	6466	490202	87714
859.683-022	REINFORCING-STEEL-MACHINE OPERATOR (construction)	3114	34434434335	LNNNNNNFFNNNNNFNFNNN	CNNN4NNNNNNNNNN	R,T	102	362	05.11.01	6466	469999	87708
859.683-026	ROAD-MIXER OPERATOR (construction)	3115	34443534334	LONNNNNCCFNNNNNOFFNOC	ONNN4NFNNNNNNNN	J,T	143	362	05.11.01	6466	490202	87708
859.683-030	ROAD-ROLLER OPERATOR (construction)	2113	34543534335	LONONNNCNNNNNNNFFNNF	FNNN4NONNNNNNNN	J,T	095	362	05.11.01	6466	490202	87708
859.684-010	LANE-MARKER INSTALLER (construction)	2213	44434433344	MNNFNFNCCFNNFNOONNON	CNNN4NFNNNNNNNF	J,T	063	362	05.12.14	6479	000000	87899
859.687-010	BLASTER HELPER (any industry)	2113	44434544445	HONFFONFNNNNONFNNNN	FNNN5NNNNNNNNNF	R,T	005	360	05.12.02	8650	000000	98319
860.131-010	SUPERVISOR, ACOUSTICAL TILE CARPENTERS (construction)	4438	33333433345	HFONNNNFFFOFFNFNFNN	NNNN3NNNNNNNNNN	V,D,P,J	102	361	05.10.01	6313	520205	81005
860.131-014	SUPERVISOR, BOATBUILDERS, WOOD (ship-boat mfg.)	4337	34333433345	LONOOONFFFOFFNFOFONN	ONNN4NNNNNNNNNN	V,D,P,J,T	102	593	05.05.02	6313	520205	81005
860.131-018	SUPERVISOR, CARPENTERS (construction)	4438	33323433344	MOOOOONFFFOFFNFFFOON	FNNN4NNNNNNNNNN	V,D,P,J	102	360	05.05.02	6313	520205	81005
860.131-022	SUPERVISOR, JOINERS (ship-boat mfg.)	4438	33323433354	LNNOOONFFFOFFNFNFNON	NNNN4NNNNNNNNNN	V,D,P,J	102	593	05.05.02	6313	520205	81005
860.131-026	SUPERVISOR, MOLD CONSTRUCTION (concrete prod.)	4337	33323433345	MONONNNFFNFNNFNFFNN	ONNN4NNNNNNNNNN	D,P,J,T	102	450	06.01.01	6313	520205	81005
860.137-010	CARPENTER-LABOR SUPERVISOR (construction)	4337	33333444445	LONOOONFFFFNFFNFNNN	FNNN4NNNNNNNNNN	V,D,P,J	102	360	05.12.01	7100	520205	81008
860.261-010	CARPENTER INSPECTOR (any industry)	4237	33333444334	MONOOONFFFOFFNFFOON	ONNN4NNNNNNNNNO	V,J,T	212	361	05.07.01	6881	460201	83002
860.281-010	CARPENTER, MAINTENANCE (any industry)	4337	33323433344	MFFFONNFFFNNONFOOON	ONNN4NOFNONNNNNN	T,J,V	102	361	05.05.02	6422	460201	87102
860.281-014	CARPENTER, SHIP (ship-boat mfg.)	4337	33323433344	MOOOOONFFFONNNFFFOON	FNNN4NNNNNNNNNN	V,J,T	102	450	05.05.02	6422	460201	87102
860.361-010	BOATBUILDER, WOOD (ship-boat mfg.)	3326	34333433345	MOOOOONFFFNOONFNFNNN	NNNN4NONNNNNNNN	J,T	102	593	05.05.02	6422	490306	87102
860.361-014	BOATBUILDER APPRENTICE, WOOD (ship-boat mfg.)	3326	34333433345	MOOOOONFFFNOONFNFNNN	NNNN4NONNNNNNNN	J,T	102	593	05.05.02	6422	490306	87105
860.381-010	ACOUSTICAL CARPENTER (construction)	4327	33333433345	MFNOOONFFFNNONFNFNON	NNNN3NONNNNNNNN	V,J,T	102	361	05.05.02	6422	460201	87102
860.381-022	CARPENTER (construction)	4337	33333433344	MOOOOONFFFONONFOFOON	ONNN4NONNONNNNN	V,J,T	102	360	05.05.02	6422	460201	87102
860.381-026	CARPENTER APPRENTICE (construction)	4337	33333433345	MOOOOOOFFFONONFOFOON	ONNN4NONNONNNNN	V,J,T	102	360	05.05.02	6422	460201	87102
860.381-030	CARPENTER, BRIDGE (r.r. trans.)	4227	33333433345	MNNFFFNFFFNNNFNNNN	FNNN4NNNNNNNNNN	J,T	102	363	05.05.02	6422	460201	87102
860.381-034	CARPENTER, MOLD (brick & tile; concrete prod.)	4337	33323433345	MNNFFFNFFFNNONFNFNNN	ONNN4NNNNNNNNNN	J,T	102	450	05.05.02	6422	460201	87102
860.381-038	CARPENTER, RAILCAR (railroad equip.)	4337	34333433345	MFNFFFNFFNNNFNFONN	FNNN4NONNNNNNNN	V,J,T	102	450	05.05.02	6422	460201	87102
860.381-042	CARPENTER, ROUGH (construction)	4427	34333433335	HOOFFNFFNNNONFNFONN	FNNN4NNNNNNNNNF	J,T	102	360	05.05.02	6422	010201	87102
860.381-046	FORM BUILDER (construction)	4327	33333433345	HOOFOONFFFNNNNFFFNNN	FNNN4NNNNNNNNNN	J,T	102	369	05.05.02	6422	490306	87102
860.381-050	JOINER (ship-boat mfg.)	4336	34333433344	MOOFOONFFFONONFNFNON	ONNN4NNNNNNNNNO	J,T,V	102	450	05.05.02	6422	460201	87102
860.381-054	JOINER APPRENTICE (ship-boat mfg.)	4336	34333433344	MOOFOONFFFONONFNFNON	ONNN4NNNNNNNNNO	J,T,V	102	450	05.05.02	6422	460201	87102
860.381-058	SHIPWRIGHT (ship-boat mfg.)	4438	33333433234	MOOOOOOFFFNNNNFFFOON	FNNN4NNNNONNNNF	V,J,T	102	593	05.05.02	6422	490306	87102
860.381-062	SHIPWRIGHT APPRENTICE (ship-boat mfg.)	4438	33333433234	MOOOOOOFFFNNNNFFFOON	FNNN4NNNNONNNNF	V,J,T	102	593	05.05.02	6422	490306	87102
860.381-066	TANK BUILDER AND ERECTOR (construction)	4337	34333433345	MOOFFONFFFNNNNFFFONN	FNNN4NNNNNNNNNN	J,T	102	454	05.05.02	6422	460201	87102
860.381-070	TANK ERECTOR (construction)	4337	33323433345	VFFFFFNFFFNNNNNFFFONN	FNNN4NNNNNNNNNN	V,J,T	102	454	05.05.02	6422	460201	87102
860.664-010	CARPENTER I (mfd. bldgs.)	3224	34444433355	MOOOOONFFFNOONFFFONN	CNNN3NNNNNNNNNN	R,T	102	455	05.10.01	6422	460201	98799
860.664-014	JOINER HELPER (ship-boat mfg.)	3222	34434534345	MOOOOONFFONOONFNFNNO	ONNN4NNNNFNNNNN	R,T	102	450	05.10.01	8642	490306	98319
860.664-018	SHIPWRIGHT HELPER (ship-boat mfg.)	2114	44445534345	HOOOOONFFFNNOONNNNNNN	FNNN4NONNNNNNNN	R,T	102	593	05.12.12	8642	490306	98319
860.681-010	CARPENTER II (mfd. bldgs.)	3225	34433433345	MONONNNFFFNNNNNFNFONN	NNNN4NNNNNNNNNN	J,T	102	455	06.02.22	6422	460201	87102
860.684-010	BUILDER, BEAM (mfd. bldgs.)	3223	34443433355	MNNFNNNFFFNNNNNFFFOON	NNNN4NFNNNNNNNN	R,T	102	455	06.04.25	6422	460201	87102
860.684-014	SIDER (mfd. bldgs.)	3123	34444433355	HOOONONFFFNONNNFNFNNN	NNNN4NNNNNNNNNN	R,T	102	455	05.10.01	6422	460201	98799
860.684-018	CAR BLOCKER (any industry)	2223	34433434355	MFFFNNNFFONNNNFNFNNN	NNNN3NNONONNNNN	R,U,T	102	457	05.12.12	8726	460201	98799
860.684-022	DISPLAY FABRICATOR (fabrication, nec)	3222	44433433354	HNNFNNNFFFNNNNFNNFFN	NNNN4NONNNNNNNN	R,T	102	619	06.04.22	7720	480703	93956
861.131-010	BRICKLAYER SUPERVISOR (construction)	4338	33333433334	MOOFFNFFFNFFNFFFONON	FNNN4NONNFNNNNN	V,D,P,J	091	360	05.05.01	6312	460101	81005
861.131-014	CHIMNEY SUPERVISOR, BRICK (construction)	4338	33333433224	MOOONONFFFOFFNFNFNON	FNNN4NNNNNNNNNN	V,D,P,S,J	091	361	05.05.01	6312	520205	81005
861.131-018	STONEMASON SUPERVISOR (construction)	4338	33323433344	LOOOONFFFNNNNFFFONN	FNNN4NFNNNNNNNN	V,D,P,J	091	360	05.05.01	6312	520205	81005
861.131-022	SUPERVISOR, MARBLE (construction)	4338	33333333344	HFNFFNFFFNFNFNFOFN	FNNN4NFNNNNNNNN	V,D,T	091	361	05.05.01	6312	520205	81005
861.131-026	SUPERVISOR, TERRAZZO (construction)	4338	33333433343	MNNCFFNFFONFFNFNFFN	ONNN3NNNNNNNNNN	V,D,T	091	361	05.05.01	6312	520205	81005
861.134-010	SUPERVISOR, SMOKE CONTROL (steel & rel.)	4337	33334433445	LONNNNNFFONFFNFOOONF	NNNN3NONNNNNNNF	D,T,P,J	211	369	06.04.01	7100	150599	81002
861.361-010	COMPOSITION-STONE APPLICATOR (construction)	3227	34443434344	LFFFFNFFNNOONFNFNON	FNNN4NNNNNNNNNN	V,J,T	092	361	05.05.01	6413	460101	87305
861.361-014	MONUMENT SETTER (construction)	4237	33433444355	HNNFFFNFFNOONFNFNNN	FNNN3NNNNNNNNNN	J,T	091	537	05.05.01	6413	460101	87305
861.381-010	ACID-TANK LINER (construction)	4337	33333433335	MFNFFFOFFFONNNFNFNNN	NNNN4NNNNNNNNNN	J,T	102	551	05.05.01	6412	460101	87302

DOT #	DOT Title & Industry	Trng	Aptitude	Physical	Environment	Tempra	WkF	MPSMS	GOE	SOC	CIP	OES
861.381-014	BRICKLAYER (brick & tile)	3228	33333434335	MOOOOONFFNNNNNFNNN	ONFN3NNNNNNNNNN	J,T	091	361	05.05.01	6412	460101	87302
861.381-018	BRICKLAYER (construction)	4338	33333433334	HFOFFNFFONNNNFNOOON	FNNN4NONNFNNNN	J,T	091	360	05.05.01	6412	460101	87302
861.381-022	BRICKLAYER APPRENTICE (construction)	4338	33333433334	FNNNANONNFNNNN	FNNN4NONNFNNNN	J,T	091	360	05.05.01	6412	460101	87302
861.381-026	BRICKLAYER, FIREBRICK AND REFRACTORY TILE (construction)	3326	33333433345	MFFFFFOFFNNNONFNONN	ONFN4NFNNNNNNF	V,T,J	102	568	05.05.01	6412	460101	87302
861.381-030	MARBLE SETTER (construction)	4237	34433434344	HFNFFNFFONNNNFNFNON	FNNN4NONNNNNON	J,T	091	361	05.05.01	6413	460101	87305
861.381-034	SOFT-TILE SETTER (construction; retail trade)	4237	34433434344	LOOFFNFFFNNNNFNFN	NNNN3NNNNNNNNN	J,T	092	361	05.05.01	6462	460101	87605
861.381-038	STONEMASON (construction)	4337	34433433334	MOOFFNFFFNNNNFNFNON	FNNN4NNNNNNNNF	J,T	091	360	05.05.01	6413	460101	87305
861.381-042	STONEMASON APPRENTICE (construction)	4337	34433433334	MOOFFNFFFNNNNFNFNON	FNNN4NNNNNNNNF	J,T	091	360	05.05.01	6413	460101	87305
861.381-046	TERRAZZO WORKER (construction)	4237	34433433344	MNNFFNFFONNNNFNFOON	ONNF4NNNNNNNNO	V,J,T	091	361	05.05.01	6463	460101	87311
861.381-050	TERRAZZO-WORKER APPRENTICE (construction)	4237	34433433344	MNNNFFFONNNNFNFOON	ONNF4NNNNNNNNO	V,J,T	091	361	05.05.01	6463	000000	87311
861.381-054	TILE SETTER (construction)	4337	34433433354	MONFFNNCCFNNNNFNFOON	ONNN4NNNNNNNNO	J,T	092	361	05.05.01	6414	460101	87308
861.381-058	TILE SETTER APPRENTICE (construction)	4337	34433433354	MONFFNNCCFNNNNFNFOON	ONNN4NNNNNNNNO	J,T	092	361	05.05.01	6414	460101	87308
861.381-062	TILE-CONDUIT LAYER (construction)	3226	34433433355	MNNFFFOFFNNNNFNFNNN	FNNN3NNNNNNNNN	R,J,T	092	369	05.10.01	6479	460101	87508
861.664-010	MARBLE FINISHER (construction)	2115	44333434344	VOOFFFFOCCOOOONFOFOOC	FNNO4NNONNNNON	R,J	011	361	05.05.01	6479	460101	98311
861.664-014	TERRAZZO FINISHER (construction)	2125	44444434334	VOOFFFOCCOOOONFOFOFO	ONNO4NNOONNNON	J,R	011	361	05.05.01	6479	000000	98319
861.664-018	TILE FINISHER (construction)	2125	44444434344	VOOFOFNCCONOONFOFOOO	ONNO4NNONNNNON	R,T	102	361	05.05.01	6479	460101	98311
861.684-010	CUPOLA PATCHER (foundry)	3114	34433434345	MONFFFNFFNNNNFNFNNN	NNNN4NNNNNNNNN	R,T	091	534	05.05.01	6412	460101	87302
861.684-014	PATCHER (steel & rel.)	2114	44444343354	HONFFFNFFNNNNFNFNNN	ONFN4NFNNNNNNN	R,T	091	534	05.10.01	6412	460101	87302
861.684-018	TILE SETTER (mfd. bldgs.)	2122	34444434354	MNNOOONFFNOONFNFNON	NNNO4NNNNNNNNN	R,T	092	361	05.05.01	6414	460101	87308
861.684-022	REPAIRER, KILN CAR (brick & tile)	2123	34444344355	MONOOONFFNNNNFNFNNN	NNON4NNNNNNNNN	R,T	033	567	05.12.08	6412	460101	85999
861.687-010	BRICKLAYER HELPER, FIREBRICK AND REFRACTORY TILE (construction)	2113	44444344355	HOOOOOOFFNNNNNNNNNN	ONNN4NONNNNNNO	R	091	568	05.12.08	8641	460101	98311
861.687-014	PATCHER HELPER (steel & rel.)	1112	44444434355	HFFFFNFFNNNNNNNNNN	FNON4NFNNNNNNO	R	091	534	05.12.09	8641	460101	98319
862.131-010	PIPE-FITTER SUPERVISOR (construction)	4338	33323433345	MFFFFFOFFNFNFNFNNN	ONNN4NNNNNNNNN	V,D,P,J	102	364	05.05.03	6316	520205	81005
862.131-014	PIPE-FITTER SUPERVISOR (ship-boat mfg.)	4338	33333433355	MOOOOOOFFNFFNFNFNNN	ONNN4NNNNNNNNN	V,D,P,T	102	593	05.05.03	6316	520205	81005
862.131-018	PLUMBER SUPERVISOR (construction)	4338	33333344355	MOOOOONFFNFFNFNFONN	OONF4NNNNNNNNN	D,P,J,T	102	364	05.05.03	6316	000000	81005
862.131-022	SUPERVISOR, PIPELINES (petrol. & gas)	4337	33333434355	LOOFFFOFFONFFNNNNN	FNNN4NNNNNNNNN	V,D,P,J	102	564	05.05.03	6316	520205	81005
862.132-010	WELL-POINT PUMPING SUPERVISOR (construction)	4337	33333434335	LNNNNNNFFNFFNFNFNNN	FNNN4NNNNNNNNN	V,D,P,J	014	369	05.11.01	7100	520205	81008
862.134-010	SUCTION-DREDGE-PIPELINE-PLACING SUPERVISOR (construction)	4337	33333433335	HNNFFNFFNFFNFNFNNN	FNNF4NNNNNNNNN	V,D,P,J	102	369	05.12.01	7100	520205	81008
862.134-014	SUPERVISOR, WATER SOFTENER SERVICE (business ser.)	4348	33323433255	LNNONONFFNFFNFNONNN	NNNN4NNNNNNNNN	V,D,P,T	102	369	05.05.03	6316	520205	81005
862.137-010	MAINS-AND-SERVICE SUPERVISOR (utilities)	4337	33332344444	LNNOOONFFNNNONFNNFN	ONNN4NONNNNNNO	V,D,P,T	102	364	05.10.01	7100	520205	81008
862.137-014	STEAM-DISTRIBUTION SUPERVISOR (utilities)	4337	29333344444	LONOOONFFNFFNFNFNNN	FNNO4NNNNNNNNN	V,D,P,J	102	364	05.05.03	7100	520205	81008
862.137-018	WATER-AND-SEWER-SYSTEMS SUPERVISOR (waterworks)	4437	33333443355	MNNFNNFFOONNNONFFNNN	FNNN4NONNNNNNN	V,P,J,T	102	364	05.05.03	6316	520205	81008
862.261-010	PIPE FITTER (ship-boat mfg.)	4238	33434433235	HOOOOONFFNONNFNFONN	ONNN4NONNNNNNN	J,T	102	593	05.05.05	6450	460501	87502
862.281-010	COPPERSMITH (ship-boat mfg.)	4238	33333433355	MNNNOOONFFONNFNFNNN	ONNN4NONNNNNNN	V,T	102	593	05.05.03	6450	460501	85902
862.281-014	COPPERSMITH APPRENTICE (ship-boat mfg.)	3127	33433433353	MNNNFFNFFNOONFNFONN	ONNN4NONNNNNNO	V,T	102	593	05.05.03	6450	460501	87502
862.281-018	OIL-BURNER-SERVICER-AND-INSTALLER (any industry)	4337	33333433345	HFNFFFOOOONFNNNN	CNNN4NONNNNNNN	J,T	102	553	05.05.03	6160	470201	85902
862.281-022	PIPE FITTER (construction)	4237	33333433345	HNNFOFNFFNNNNNFFNN	NNNN3NNONNNNNO	T,J	102	364	05.05.03	6450	460501	87502
862.281-026	PIPE-FITTER APPRENTICE (construction)	4237	33333443355	HONFFFNFFNNNNFNFNN	NNNN3NNONNNNNN	T,J	102	364	05.05.03	6450	460501	87502
862.361-010	FURNACE INSTALLER (utilities)	4237	33333433254	HOOOOONFFNNNNNNFNON	NNNN3NNNNNNNNN	V,J,T	102	553	05.05.03	6160	470201	85902
862.361-014	GAS-MAIN FITTER (utilities)	4337	33333433355	HOOOOONFFONNNNFNFOON	CNNN4NFNNNNNNF	V,T	102	364	05.05.03	6450	460501	87502
862.361-018	PIPE FITTER, DIESEL ENGINE I (engine-turbine)	4336	33332333354	LNNNNNNFFNFNNNNNN	NNON4NNNNNNNNO	V,T	121	561	05.07.01	6881	460501	87502
862.361-022	STEAM SERVICE INSPECTOR (utilities)	3226	34433444345	LNNOOOOFFNNNNFNNNNN	ONNN3NNNNNNNNN	R,T	031	564	05.11.01	6479	490202	87899
862.381-014	INDUSTRIAL-GAS FITTER (utilities)	3227	33333434344	MNNFOONFFNNNNNFFNN	CNNN4NFNNNNNNN	J,T	102	568	05.10.01	6450	460501	87502
862.381-022	PIPE FITTER, DIESEL ENGINE II (engine-turbine)	4237	33333433235	HONFFFNFFNNNNFNFONN	NNNN4NNNNNNNNN	V,T	121	561	05.05.03	6450	460501	87502
862.381-030	PLUMBER (construction)	4337	33333433244	HOOOOOONFFONNNNNFOON	ONNN4NONNNNNNO	V,J,T	102	364	05.05.03	6450	460501	87502
862.381-034	PLUMBER APPRENTICE (construction)	4337	33333433244	HOOOOONFFONNNNFNFOON	ONNN4NONNNNNNO	V,J,T	102	364	05.05.03	6450	460501	87502
862.381-038	THREAD INSPECTOR (petrol. & gas)	3226	33332333354	LNNNNNNFFFONNNNNNN	ONNN3NNNNNNNNN	J,T	212	564	05.07.01	6881	460501	83002
862.662-010	PIPE-CLEANING-AND-PRIMING-MACHINE OPERATOR (construction)	3226	34433444345	LNNOOOOFFNNNNFNNNNN	CNNN4NFNNNNNNN	R,T	031	364	05.11.01	6479	490202	87899
862.681-010	PLUMBER (mfd. bldgs.)	3226	33433433355	MNNFOONFFNNNNFNFOON	NNNN4NNNNNNNNN	J,T	102	364	05.05.03	6450	460501	87502
862.682-010	PIPE CUTTER (mfd. bldgs.)	4234	34434443355	MNNONONFFNNNNFNFONN	NNNN4NNNNNNNNN	J,T	054	550	06.02.02	6450	460501	87502
862.682-014	PIPE-WRAPPING-MACHINE OPERATOR (construction; pipe lines)	3125	34433434345	LNNNNNNFFONNNNFNFNNN	CNNN4NONNNNNNO	R,J,T	153	364	05.11.01	6479	490202	87899

DOT #	DOT Title & Industry	Trng	Aptitude	Physical	Environment	Tempra	WkF	MPSMS	GOE	SOC	CIP	OES
862.684-010	JUNCTION MAKER (brick & tile)	2125	34443433355	MNNONONFFNNNFNFNNON	NNNN3NNNNNNNNNNN	R,T	061	534	06.02.30	7759	460501	93999
862.684-014	LABORER, CONSTRUCTION OR LEAK GANG (utilities)	2114	44444434334	HONFFOOFFNNNNNONNNON	FNNN4NNNNNNNNNNN	V	102	364	05.12.12	8710	460501	98999
862.684-018	PIPE-FITTER HELPER (ship-boat mfg.)	3125	34443533345	HFFFOFNOFFONNNNNNNNNN	ONON4NNNNNNNNNNF	R,T	102	593	05.12.12	8645	460501	98315
862.684-022	PIPE-FITTER HELPER (construction)	2123	44433444345	HFNOOONFFNNNNNFNFNNN	ONNN4NNNNNNNNNNO	R,T	102	364	05.12.12	8645	460501	98315
862.684-026	PLUMBING ASSEMBLER-INSTALLER (mfd. bldgs.)	3124	34433433355	MOOOOONFFFNONFNFNNF	NNNN4NNNNNNNNNNN	R,T	102	364	06.02.22	6479	460501	87899
862.684-030	WATER REGULATOR AND VALVE REPAIRER (waterworks)	3225	34443433355	MOOFNFNFFFNNNNFNFNNN	FNNF4NNNNNNNNNNN	J,T	121	873	05.10.02	6175	470303	85928
862.684-034	WATER-SOFTENER SERVICER-AND-INSTALLER (business ser.)	3224	33434433355	HNNONONFFONNNNFNFONN	NNNO3NNNNNNNNNNN	T	102	969	05.10.01	6450	000000	87502
862.687-010	COOLING-PIPE INSPECTOR (construction)	3125	34443444454	LOOOOONFFONNNNFNFNON	FNNF4NNNNNNNNNNN	R,J	212	369	05.07.01	7820	460501	83005
862.687-014	HOLIDAY-DETECTOR OPERATOR (construction)	2122	44444544455	LNNONONFFFNNONFNFNNN	CNNN3NNNNNNNNNNN	R,T	212	364	05.07.01	7830	000000	83005
862.687-018	HYDRO-PNEUMATIC TESTER (any industry)	3224	44444444355	LNNNONFFFNNONFNFNNN	OONNF4NNNNNNNNNN	J,T	212	550	06.03.02	7830	460501	83005
862.687-022	OIL-BURNER-SERVICER-AND-INSTALLER HELPER (any industry)	1112	44544444455	HNNOOONFFNNNNNNNNNNN	NNNN4NNNNNNNNNNN	R	102	553	05.12.12	8637	470201	98102
863.134-010	BUILDING-INSULATION SUPERVISOR (construction)	4337	33333433345	LOOOOOOFFNFFNFNFNNN	ONNN4NONNNNNNNNN	V,D,P,J	102	361	05.10.01	7100	520205	81008
863.134-014	SUPERVISOR, INSULATION (construction)	4338	34333443345	MOOONNFFFFFFFNFNNN	FNNN4NFNNNNNNNNO	D,P,J	102	538	05.10.01	6318	520205	81005
863.364-010	INSULATION-WORKER APPRENTICE (construction)	3236	34433433345	MNNOOONCCFNNNNFNFNNN	FNNN3NONNONNNNN	J	092	361	05.10.01	6465	469999	87802
863.364-014	INSULATION WORKER (construction)	3236	34433433345	MNNOOONCCFNNNNFNFNNN	FNNN3NONNONNNNN	J	092	361	05.10.01	6465	469999	87802
863.381-010	CORK INSULATOR, REFRIGERATION PLANT (construction)	3227	34433433345	LOOOOONFFNNNNFNFNNN	NNNN4NNNNNNNNNNO	J,T	102	361	05.10.01	6465	469999	87802
863.381-014	PIPE COVERER AND INSULATOR (ship-boat mfg.)	4238	34333443345	MOOOOOOFFNNNNNFNFNNN	NNNN4NNNNNNNNNNO	J,T	102	538	05.10.01	6465	469999	87802
863.664-010	BLOWER INSULATOR (railroad equip.; retail trade; wholesale tr.)	2115	34434433345	MOFFOOOFFNNNNNOFFNNN	FNON4NFNNONNNNO	J,T	094	361	05.12.14	6465	469999	87802
863.664-014	COMPOSITION-WEATHERBOARD APPLIER (construction)	2114	44444433344	MOOOOONFFFNNNNFNFNON	CNNN4NNNNNNNNNNO	R,T	102	509	05.12.12	6422	469999	87102
863.684-014	SIDER (construction; mfd. bldgs.; retail trade)	3224	34343433335	MFFFOONFFNNNNFFFNNN	CNNN4NNNNNNNNNNF	R,T	102	538	05.10.01	6479	460201	87899
863.685-010	INSULATION-POWER-UNIT TENDER (construction; retail trade; wholesale tr.)	2114	44444544445	LNNFNNNFFNNNNNONNNNN	CNNN4NCNNNNNNNNN	R	094	538	05.11.01	6465	469999	87802
864.381-010	CARPET LAYER (retail trade)	3227	33333433353	HNNFFFFFFFFNNNNOOOON	NNNN3NNNNNNNNNNN	J,T	092	431	05.10.01	6462	469999	87602
864.481-010	FLOOR LAYER (construction; retail trade)	3226	33333433344	MOOFFOFFNNNNNFNFOON	NNNN3NNNNNNNNNNO	V,T	092	361	05.10.01	6462	469999	87605
864.481-014	FLOOR-LAYER APPRENTICE (construction; retail trade)	3226	33333433344	MOOFFOFFNNNNNFNFOON	NNNN3NNNNNNNNNNO	V,T	092	361	05.10.01	6462	469999	87605
864.684-010	FLOOR AND WALL APPLIER, LIQUID (construction)	3124	34443434344	MNNFNONFFONONFNFNNN	NNNN4NNNNNNNNNNF	R,T	092	452	05.10.07	6479	469999	87899
864.687-010	CARPET-LAYER HELPER (retail trade)	2123	44444444355	HNNFFFFFFFNNNONOOON	NNNN3NNNNNNNNNNN	R	092	460	06.02.22	8648	469999	98319
865.131-010	GLAZIER SUPERVISOR (construction)	4337	33333433335	LOOOOONFFOFFNFNFNNN	FNNN4NNNNNNNNNNN	V,D,P,J	102	531	05.10.01	6318	520205	81005
865.361-010	MIRROR INSTALLER (construction)	3226	34433433335	HFFFFNFFONNNNNFFFNN	NNNN3NNNNNNNNNNO	T	102	532	05.10.01	6464	469999	87811
865.381-010	GLAZIER (construction)	3227	34433433345	MFFOONFFNNNNNFNFNNN	FNNN4NNNNNNNNNNN	V,J,T	102	360	05.10.01	6464	469999	87811
865.381-014	GLAZIER APPRENTICE (construction)	3227	34433433345	MFFFOONFFNNNNNFNFNNN	FNNN4NNNNNNNNNNN	V,J,T	102	360	05.12.14	6464	469999	87808
865.684-010	GLASS INSTALLER (automotive ser.)	3124	34433433355	LFNFFNFFNNNNNFNFNON	CNNN4NNNNNNNNNNN	R,T	153	360	05.10.01	6115	470603	85305
865.684-014	GLASS INSTALLER (woodworking)	2123	34443443344	MNNFNONFFONONFNFNNN	NNNN4NNNNNNNNNNF	D,T	102	592	06.04.30	7720	469999	93999
865.684-018	GLAZIER, METAL FURNITURE (furniture)	3125	33333433344	LOOFOONFFFOFFNFONON	FNNN4NNNNNNNNNNN	R,T	102	360	05.05.01	7720	469999	93911
865.684-022	FIELD-ASSEMBLY GLAZIER (svc. ind. mach.)	3124	34444434355	MFNFFNFFNFFNFNFNNN	FNNN4NNNNNNNNNNN	R,T	102	455	06.02.22	7720	000000	93911
866.131-010	REFRIGERATOR GLAZIER (mfd. bldgs.)	4237	33333433335	HOOOOOOFONFNNFFFFONN	FNNN4NNNNNNNNNNN	R,T	102	460	05.10.01	7100	520205	81008
866.131-018	ROOFING SUPERVISOR (construction)	3227	34433433345	MONFFNFFNFFFONFFFONN	FNNN4NNNNNNNNNNF	D,P,T	092	573	06.02.01	6468	469999	87808
866.381-010	ROOFER (construction)	3126	34433444334	MOFFFNFFNNNNNNFOFNNN	CNFN4NFNFNFNNNNF	J,T	092	361	05.10.01	6468	469999	87808
866.381-014	ROOFER APPRENTICE (construction)	3126	34433433345	LFNFFNFFNNNNNNFNFNON	CNNN4NNNNNNNNNNF	R,T	102	369	05.10.01	6468	469999	87808
866.684-010	ROOFER APPLICATOR (construction)	4337	33332433345	LOOFOONFFOFFNFOFNON	FNNN4NNNNNNNNNON	V,D,P,J	102	361	05.12.14	6318	469999	81005
869.131-010	CABIN-EQUIPMENT SUPERVISOR (air trans.)	3126	33332433344	LOOFOONFFFOFFNFNFNON	FNNN4NNNNNNNNNNN	V,D,T	102	361	05.05.01	6318	520205	81005
869.131-014	CONCRETING SUPERVISOR (construction)	4337	33333433344	MONOOONFFFNFNNNNFN	CNNO3NNNNNNNNNNN	V,D,P,J	102	592	05.10.01	6318	520205	81005
869.131-018	FIELD-ASSEMBLY SUPERVISOR (mfd. bldgs.)	4337	33333433345	MFNFFNFFNFFNFNFNNN	FNNN4NNNNNNNNNNN	V,D,P,J	102	360	05.10.01	7100	000000	81005
869.131-022	HOUSE-MOVER SUPERVISOR (construction)	4337	33333434345	HOOOOOOFONFNFFFFONN	FNNN4NNNNNNNNNNN	V,D,P,T	102	455	05.10.01	7100	520205	81008
869.131-026	STEEL-PAN-FORM-PLACING SUPERVISOR (construction)	4337	33333433335	MONFFNFFNFFFONFFFONN	FNNN4NNNNNNNNNNN	V,D,P,J	102	369	06.02.01	6468	469999	87808
869.131-030	SUPERVISOR, MANUFACTURED BUILDINGS (mfd. bldgs.; vehicles, nec)	4337	33333334354	MONOOONFFFNFFONFFFOON	NNNN4NNNNNNNNNNN	V,D,P,J	102	455	05.05.06	6318	000000	81005
869.131-034	TANKAGE SUPERVISOR (construction)	4337	33333433335	MFFONNNFFNNFFNFNFNNN	FNNN4NNNNNNNNNNN	V,D,P,J	102	369	05.05.06	6318	520205	81005
869.131-038	SUPERVISOR, SWIMMING-POOL MAINTENANCE (construction)	4337	33324423342	MONOOONFFFNFNFNFNNN	CNNO3NNNNNNNNNNN	D,V,T,J	102	369	05.02.02	6318	520205	81005
869.133-010	CLEARING SUPERVISOR (construction)	4337	33333343445	LNNNNNNFFNFFNFFFFNN	FNNN4NNNNNNNNNNN	V,D,P,J	102	360	05.11.01	7100	000000	81008
869.134-010	FENCE-ERECTOR SUPERVISOR (construction)	4337	33333343444	LONNNNNFFONNNFFFFNN	ONNN4NNONNNNNNN	D,P,J,T	102	361	05.10.01	7100	520205	81008
869.134-014	SUPERVISOR, ADJUSTABLE-STEEL-JOIST-SETTING (construction)	4337	33333334445	LOOFOOFOONFFFNFNFONF	CNNN4NNONNNONN	V,D,P,J	102	364	05.05.06	7100	520205	81008
869.134-018	SUPERVISOR, PIPELINE MAINTENANCE (pipe lines)	4338	33333334345	LOOFOOFOONFFFNFNFONF	CNNN4NNONNNONN	V,D,P,J	102	364	05.12.01	7100	520205	81008
869.134-022	TRACK-LAYING SUPERVISOR (construction)	4347	33332444345	LNNOOONFFNFFFFNFFFONN	FNNN4NNNNNNNNNNN	D,P,J,T	102	367	05.11.01	7100	000000	81008

DOT #	DOT Title & Industry	Trng	Aptitude	Physical	Environment	Tempra	WkF	MPSMS	GOE	SOC	CIP	OES
869.134-026	SUPERVISOR, ASBESTOS REMOVAL (construction)	3336	33333333335	MOOOOOOFFFNFNFNNNNN	ONNN4NNNONNONNOO	D,S,T,P,J	031	360	05.10.01	6318	150701	81005
869.137-010	TRAFFIC-MAINTENANCE SUPERVISOR (government ser.)	4337	33323433344	MNNOOONFFFNFNFOFNON	FNNN4NNNNNNNNNNO	V,D,P,J	102	584	05.10.01	7100	000000	81008
869.137-014	WRECKING SUPERVISOR (construction)	4337	33433444445	LOOOOONFFFNFNFNFFONN	FNNN4NFNNANNNNNNO	D,P,J	102	360	05.11.01	7100	490202	81008
869.261-010	HOUSE MOVER (construction)	4336	33433433345	HOOFFFOFFNOONOOFNNN	CNNN4NNNNNNNNNNO	J,T	011	361	05.10.01	6479	000000	87899
869.261-014	MECHANICAL-TEST TECHNICIAN (inst. & app.)	4337	33323433253	MNNFNFNFFNFNFOFFFN	FNNN4NNNNNNNNNNO	V,J,T	121	602	05.05.06	6881	150404	83002
869.261-018	POURED-CONCRETE-WALL TECHNICIAN (construction)	4337	33322433344	HOOOOONFFNOONFONOON	ONNN4NONNNNNNNNO	J,T,V	102	361	05.10.01	6479	469999	87899
869.261-022	REPAIRER, RECREATIONAL VEHICLE (vehicles, nec)	4336	33382433444	MNNFFFNFFNFFNNFOFON	NNNN3NNNNNNNNNNN	J,T,V	102	591	05.10.01	6179	460401	85938
869.261-026	WIND TUNNEL MECHANIC (aircraft mfg.)	4447	22223433344	MOOOOONFFFOOONFOOON	NNNN5NOOOONNNNN	V,T,J	102	601	05.10.04	3719	000000	22599
869.281-010	FURNACE INSTALLER-AND-REPAIRER, HOT AIR (any industry)	4337	33333433344	MNNFFFNFFNNNNFNFOON	NNNN3NNNNNNNNNNN	V,T,J	102	553	05.05.09	6160	470201	85902
869.281-014	HOUSE BUILDER (construction)	3337	33333433334	MFFFFNFFFNONFFFOON	FNNN4NNNNNNNNNNF	V,J,T	102	361	05.05.02	6479	470401	87899
869.281-018	YARD INSPECTOR (ship-boat mfg.)	4337	34333444455	LOOOOOOFFFNNNNFNFONN	ONNN4NNNNNNNNNNN	J,T	212	593	05.07.01	6881	490306	83002
869.287-010	BRIDGE INSPECTOR (r.r. trans.)	4437	22322244445	MOOOOOOFFONNNFOFONN	FNNN4NNNNNNNNNNN	V,J,T	212	360	05.07.01	7820	460403	83005
869.361-010	CONDUIT MECHANIC (construction; utilities)	3337	33333433345	HOOOOOOFFNFFNFNFONN	CNNN4NNNNNNNNNNN	J,T	102	369	05.05.06	6479	469999	87899
869.361-014	HYDRAULIC-JACK ADJUSTER (construction)	3337	33433443325	HOOFOONFFNOONFNNN	FNNN4NNNNNNNNNNF	J,T	102	360	05.05.06	6479	490202	87899
869.361-018	SIGN ERECTOR-AND-REPAIRER (fabrication, nec)	3226	34433433324	MFFOOONFFNOONFFOFN	FNNN4NNNNNNNNNNN	S,J,T	102	559	05.05.06	6422	460201	87102
869.367-010	ASSISTANT CONSTRUCTION SUPERINTENDENT (construction)	3337	33344344454	LOOOOONFFNOONFOOOON	FNNN4NNNNNNNNNNN	D,P,V	102	563	05.02.02	6311	490202	81005
869.367-014	MEASURER (retail trade)	3223	34333334345	MFFFOFNFFNOONFNFNNN	FNNN3NNNNNNNNNNN	J,T	231	554	05.09.02	4490	460403	83005
869.367-018	PIPELINE CONSTRUCTION INSPECTOR (construction)	3337	33332244355	LONOOONFFNFFNFFFFNN	CNNN4NNNNNNNNNNN	J	102	364	05.07.01	7820	460403	87102
869.381-010	HOUSE REPAIRER (construction)	4938	33332433344	MFFFFFFFFFNONFFFOON	FNNN4NNNNNNNNNNF	V,J,T	102	361	05.10.04	6422	460201	85938
869.381-014	LABORATORY-EQUIPMENT INSTALLER (construction)	3337	33333433244	VOOOOOOFFNNNNFNFNON	NNNN4NNNNNNNNNNO	J,T	102	601	05.10.01	6869	460201	89999
869.381-018	PIPE INSTALLER (construction; utilities)	3237	34333433345	HFNFFNFFFNNNNNFOFON	ONNN4NNNNNNNNNNF	J,T	102	584	05.10.01	6450	460302	87899
869.381-022	SAFE-AND-VAULT SERVICE MECHANIC (business ser.; retail trade; tex. prod., nec; wholesale tr.)	3337	33333444335	HONFFFNFFNNNNFFFONN	ONNN4NNNNNNNNNNN	V,J,T	102	559	05.05.06	6173	470403	85923
869.381-026	SIGN ERECTOR I (fabrication, nec)	4237	34333444335	MFFNNNNFFFNNNNFFONN	FNNN4NNNNNNNNNNN	V,J	102	559	05.05.06	6869	000000	89999
869.381-030	STEEPLE JACK (construction)	3337	34432433224	MFFFFNFFFNNNNONFNOF	CNNN4NFNNFNNNNF	S,T	102	369	05.05.06	6479	460101	87899
869.381-034	TIMBER FRAMER (mine & quarry)	3226	34323433245	HONFFNFFONNNNFNFNNN	NNNN5NFNNNNNNNC	V,S,J,T	102	369	05.05.02	6422	460201	87102
869.384-010	REPAIRER, MANUFACTURED BUILDINGS (mfd. bldgs.; vehicles, nec)	3224	34434433354	HOOFOFOFFONNNFNFNOO	NNNN4NNNNNONNNO	R,T	231	361	05.10.01	6179	460401	85938
869.387-010	POLE INSPECTOR (utilities)	3225	33444344444	MFFNNNNFFONFNFNFNON	FNNN3NNNNNNNNNNF	V,J,T	102	452	05.07.01	7820	460303	83005
869.463-010	SWIMMING POOL INSTALLER-AND-SERVICER (construction)	4448	33332434335	VNNFFNFNNNNNFFNNNN	FNNO3NNNNNNNNNN	J	211	369	05.10.01	6479	000000	87899
869.481-010	AWNING MAKER-AND-INSTALLER (furniture; retail trade)	3325	34333433344	HFFNNNNFFNNNNFNFNON	FNNN3NNNNNNNNNNN	V,T	007	369	05.10.01	6869	460201	89999
869.484-010	AWNING HANGER (construction; retail trade; tex. prod., nec)	3224	34433433344	HFFOOONFFFNNNNFFONN	FNNN4NNNNNNNNNNN	J,T	102	554	05.10.01	6479	460201	87899
869.484-014	DRAPERY HANGER (retail trade)	3225	34334434355	MOOOOONFFFNNNNONONNN	NNNN2NNNNNNNNNN	J,T	102	435	05.10.01	6479	200502	87899
869.484-018	VENETIAN-BLIND INSTALLER (furniture; retail trade)	3224	34433444344	MFFONNNFFNNNNFNFNON	NNNN3NNNNNNNNNNN	V,J	102	467	05.12.12	6479	000000	87805
869.487-010	MEASURER (struct. metal)	3224	34433444455	MNNOOONFFFFNNNNFNNN	FNNN3NNNNNNNNNNN	R,T,V	102	554	05.12.12	6479	460201	87511
869.564-010	LINE WALKER (petrol. & gas; petrol. refin.; pipe lines)	3234	34434343344	LNNFNFNFONOOOFFFNOF	FNNN4NONNONNNNN	R,T	293	364	05.07.01	7820	470501	83005
869.567-010	SURVEYOR HELPER (any industry)	3124	44444444345	MNNFFNFFNNNNFFFFON	NNNN3NNNNNNNNNNN	R,T	243	310	05.12.02	8646	000000	98319
869.662-010	LIFT-SLAB OPERATOR (construction)	4237	33334533335	MOOOOONFFFNFFNFNNN	FNNN4NNNNNNNNNNF	J,T	011	360	05.12.04	6479	490202	87899
869.664-010	CONCRETE-BUILDING ASSEMBLER (mfd. bldgs.)	2224	44344434345	HONOOONFONFFNFNFNNN	CNNN4NNNNFNNNNN	R,T	102	361	05.12.04	6479	469999	87899
869.664-014	CONSTRUCTION WORKER I (construction)	3334	34333433344	MNNOONNFFNNNNNNNNN	CNNN4NNNNNNNNNNN	J,T	102	369	05.10.01	6479	469999	87899
869.664-018	SEWER-LINE REPAIRER (sanitary ser.)	3226	33323433344	HFNFFFFFFNFNFNFOFON	CNNN4NONNNNNNON	R,T,V	102	369	05.12.12	6479	200502	87899
869.665-010	AUXILIARY-EQUIPMENT TENDER (construction)	3226	34433444355	HNNFFNFFFNNNNNNNNN	CNNN5NNNNNNNNNF	R	021	871	05.11.01	6479	000000	87899
869.667-010	COLUMN PRECASTER (mfd. bldgs.)	2112	44544444445	HNNOOONFFONNNNNNNNN	NNNN4NNNNNNNNNNN	R,T	132	536	06.04.32	8314	470501	87899
869.667-014	SIGNALER (construction)	2122	44434544455	LNNNNNNFFNFNNNFFNNF	FNNN4NNNNNNNNNNN	R	011	565	05.12.04	8710	490202	98999
869.681-010	CONCRETE-FENCE BUILDER (construction)	3126	34334433345	HNNFFNNFFNNNNNFNFON	CNNN4NNNNNNNNNNN	J,T	011	536	05.05.01	6479	469999	87899
869.682-010	CIRCULAR SAW OPERATOR (construction)	3125	34433433345	MNNFFNNFFNNNNNNNNN	CNNN4NNNNNNNNNNO	R,T	056	870	05.10.01	6479	490202	87899
869.682-014	CORE-DRILL OPERATOR (construction)	3125	44544534355	MNNOONNFFNNNNNNNNN	NNNN4NNNNNNNNNNN	R,T	053	361	05.11.03	6479	490202	87899
869.683-010	FORM-TAMPER OPERATOR (construction)	2123	44544534355	HNNFNFFFNFFNNNNNNN	CNNN4NNNNNNNNNNN	R	102	369	05.11.01	6466	490202	87899
869.683-014	RIGGER (construction)	3124	34433544345	HNNFFNFFNNNNNNNNNN	CNNN5NNNNNNNNNF	R,T	011	565	05.11.01	8314	490202	97941
869.683-018	TAMPING-MACHINE OPERATOR (construction)	3125	34433544345	LNNNNNNFFONNNNNNNN	FNNN4NNNNNNNNNNN	R,T	095	362	05.11.01	6466	490202	87708
869.684-010	ASSEMBLER (mfd. bldgs.; vehicles, nec)	3224	34434433355	MOOOOONFFFONONFNFNNN	NNNN4NNNNNNNNNNO	R,T,J	102	455	06.02.22	7720	460201	93956
869.684-014	ASSEMBLER, SKYLIGHTS (plastic prod.)	2123	44544544354	MNNNNNNFFNNNNNNNNN	NNNN4NNNNNNNNNNN	R,T	102	619	06.04.24	7720	000000	93956
869.684-018	ASSEMBLER, SUBASSEMBLY (mfd. bldgs.; vehicles, nec)	3223	34433434345	MNNONNNCCOONNNONFNNF	NNNN4NNNNNNNNNNN	R,T	102	455	06.04.22	6422	460201	87102

DOT #	DOT Title & Industry	Trng	Aptitude	Physical	Environment	Tempra	WkF	MPSMS	GOE	SOC	CIP	OES
869.684-022	FENCE ERECTOR (construction)	3225	34433433344	HNNFFNFFNNNFOFNON	FNNN4NNNNNNNNO	R,T	102	369	05.10.01	6479	010201	87817
869.684-026	INSTALLER (mfd. bldgs.; vehicles, nec)	3224	33334434354	MONOOONFFFOOONFNOON	NNNN4NNNNNNNNNN	R,T	102	361	06.02.22	7720	000000	93956
869.684-030	LAWN-SPRINKLER INSTALLER (construction)	3225	34433443345	MNNNONONFFOOONFNOON	CNNN4NNNNNNNNNN	J,T	102	369	05.10.01	6479	010605	87899
869.684-034	LAY-OUT WORKER (mfd. bldgs.)	3226	34344433355	MNNONONFFNNNNFNONN	NNNN4NNNNNNNNNN	J,T	102	361	06.02.31	6422	460201	87102
869.684-038	PANEL INSTALLER (mfd. bldgs.)	2112	44444434345	MONNONNCCNNNNNNONNN	NNNN4NNNNNNNNNN	R,T	102	361	06.04.22	6422	460201	87899
869.684-042	ROOF ASSEMBLER I (mfd. bldgs.)	3123	34444534355	MONOFONFFNNNNFNFNNN	NNNN4NNNNNNNNNN	R,T	102	455	06.04.22	6422	460201	87102
869.684-046	ROUSTABOUT (petrol. & gas)	3125	34434433355	HNNNOONFFNNNNFNFNNN	FNNN4NNNNNNNNNO	R,T	102	564	05.10.01	6560	470399	87921
869.684-050	SHEETROCK APPLICATOR (mfd. bldgs.)	2113	44444433355	MNNFNNNCCFNNNNNONNN	NNNN4NNNNNNNNNN	R,T	102	455	06.04.34	6424	469999	87108
869.684-054	SIGN ERECTOR II (fabrication, nec)	3223	34434433345	HNNFNNNCCFNNNONONNN	FNNN4NNNNNNNNNN	R	102	559	05.10.01	6479	460201	87899
869.684-058	STOPPING BUILDER (mine & quarry)	3125	34433343345	HOOFFFOFFNNNNFFNNN	NNNN5NFNNNNNNNF	J,T	102	369	05.12.12	6422	460201	87121
869.684-062	STULL INSTALLER (concrete prod.)	2112	44434534355	MNNFNFNFFNNNNNNNNN	FNNN4NNNNNNNNNF	R	102	369	05.10.01	6479	460201	87899
869.684-066	TRIMMER (mfd. bldgs.)	2112	44444544345	MOOOONFFONNNNFNONN	NNNN3NNNNNNNNNN	R	102	361	06.04.25	6479	460201	87899
869.684-074	UTILITY WORKER (mfd. bldgs.; vehicles, nec)	3225	34334344344	MONQOONFFFONNNFNFNOO	NNNN4NNNNNNNNNO	T,V	102	361	06.02.22	7720	480503	93999
869.684-078	VENEER STAPLER (ship-boat mfg.)	3124	34444434355	MNNNNNNFFONNNFNFNNN	ONNN3NNNNNNNNNN	R,T	102	593	06.04.25	7720	490306	93999
869.684-082	ASBESTOS REMOVAL WORKER (construction)	3222	33444434325	HFFOOOOFFONNNNONNNN	ONNN4NONONONNON	S,T	031	360	05.10.01	6479	150701	87899
869.685-010	KETTLE TENDER (construction)	1112	44544444445	MNNFOFNFFONNNNNONNN	CNFN4NFNNNNNNNF	R	131	502	05.12.10	6479	000000	87899
869.687-010	AWNING-HANGER HELPER (construction; retail trade: tex. prod., nec)	2113	44454544345	HFFOONNFFNNNNNNNNN	FNNN4NNNNNNNNNN	R	102	436	05.12.12	8648	460201	98319
869.687-014	CAMOUFLAGE ASSEMBLER (ordnance)	1112	44554544455	LNNNNNNFFNNNNNNNNNN	NNNN3NNNNNNNNNN	R	061	379	06.04.34	7720	000000	93956
869.687-018	CLEANER (mfd. bldgs.)	2112	44444444454	MOOOOONFFONNONFNFNON	NNNN4NNNNNNNNNN	R	031	455	05.12.18	8710	200604	98999
869.687-022	CONCRETE-FLOAT MAKER (concrete prod.)	2112	44444544355	MNNFOFNFFNNNNNNNNNN	ONNN4NNNNNNNNNN	R,T	102	536	05.12.12	7720	469999	93999
869.687-026	CONSTRUCTION WORKER II (construction)	2112	44444544345	VOOFFFOFONNONNNFNNF	FNNN4NONNNNNNNF	R	011	360	05.12.03	8710	010201	98311
869.687-030	FURNACE-INSTALLER-AND-REPAIRER HELPER, HOT AIR (any industry)	2112	44445544355	HNNFFNFFONNNNNNNNNN	NNNN4NFNNNNNNNN	R	102	553	05.12.12	8637	470201	98102
869.687-034	HOUSE-MOVER HELPER (construction)	1112	44543534455	HNNNNNNCCNNNNNNONNN	CNNN3NNNNNNNNNN	R	011	361	05.12.04	8648	000000	98319
869.687-038	INSPECTOR (mfd. bldgs.)	3236	34433444354	LNNOONFFOONNNCNFNON	NNNN4NNNNNNNNNN	J,T	212	361	06.03.02	7820	460403	83005
869.687-042	TIMBER-FRAMER HELPER (mine & quarry)	2113	44435544345	HONFFNFFNFFNNONFNNN	NNNF4NNNNNNNNNF	R	102	369	05.12.12	8642	460201	98319
891.131-010	DOCK SUPERVISOR (ship-boat mfg.)	4337	33333344355	LOOOOOOFFNFFNFOFONO	FNNN4NNNNNNNNNN	V,D,P,J	031	593	05.12.18	6000	490306	81002
891.137-010	MAINTENANCE SUPERVISOR (any industry)	4337	23323333344	LOOOONFFNFFNFFOOON	ONNN3NOONNNNNN	D,V,T,P,J	102	361	05.02.02	7100	000000	81008
891.137-014	SUPERVISOR, AIRCRAFT CLEANING (air trans.)	4337	33334344354	LOOONONFFOFFNFOFNON	NNNN4NNNNNNNNNN	V,D,P	031	855	05.12.01	8500	200604	81017
891.137-018	SUPERVISOR, TANK CLEANING (water trans.)	4337	33334433355	MOOONONFFFNFFOFOFNN	FNOO4NONNNNNNNO	D,P,V,T	031	854	05.12.01	8500	000000	81017
891.564-010	PIPE CHANGER (mine & quarry)	2123	44434434345	HONFFNFFNFFNONFNNN	FNNN4NNNNNNNNNN	R,T	102	364	05.12.12	6140	460501	85128
891.685-010	STEAM-CLEANING-MACHINE OPERATOR (construction)	2123	44444433345	HOOOOONFFNNNNNONFNNN	FNNN3NFNNNNNNNF	R	031	593	05.12.18	6179	490306	98999
891.684-010	DOCK HAND (ship-boat mfg.)	3334	34433433344	MFNFFNFFNFFNONFNNN	FNNN4NFNNNNNNNN	J,T	121	519	05.10.01	6140	470201	85128
891.684-014	RUBBER AND PLASTICS WORKER (military ser.)	3124	34433433344	MOOFFOFFNNNNNONNNN	ONNN4NFNNNNNNNN	R	031	369	05.11.01	6179	000000	85999
891.684-018	SWIMMING-POOL SERVICER (any industry)	3224	34433433345	MONFFFNFFNNNNFNFNNN	FNNF3NNNNNNNNNN	R,T	031	361	05.10.04	6179	000000	85999
891.684-022	BUILDING CLEANER (any industry)	3224	34433433345	HONONNFFONNNNFNNNN	FNNO3NFNNFNNON	R,T	031	568	05.10.01	6479	000000	87899
891.687-030	TUBE CLEANER (any industry)	2114	44544534355	LNNNNNNFFNNNNNNONNNN	ONFF4NFNNNNNNNN	R	021	550	05.11.01	6479	200604	87899
899.130-010	SUPERVISOR, CANAL-EQUIPMENT MAINTENANCE (waterworks)	4338	33333333344	MOOOOONFFFFNFFFNFNON	FNNN4NNNNNNNNNN	V,D,P,T	102	369	05.06.03	6000	000000	81002
899.131-010	LABOR-CREW SUPERVISOR (construction; utilities)	4338	33333333345	LFNFNFNFFNFFFFNF	FNNN4NONNNNNNNO	V,D,P,J	102	360	05.12.01	6311	520205	81005
899.131-014	LOCK MAINTENANCE SUPERVISOR (construction)	4438	33333433345	HFOFFFOFFOFFNNFNNN	FNNN4ONOOFNNNN	V,D,P,T	102	360	05.10.04	6000	000000	81002
899.131-018	UTILITIES-AND-MAINTENANCE SUPERVISOR (any industry)	4338	33323433354	LONOONNFFNFFNFFOOOO	NNNN3NNNNNNNNNN	D,V,T,P,J	111	870	05.06.02	6311	460401	81005
899.131-022	UTILITY SUPERVISOR, BOAT AND PLANT (ship-boat mfg.)	4337	33333433345	MOOOOONFFNNOONFOFNO	NNNN4NNOONNNN	V,D,P,T	102	593	06.01.01	8500	490306	81017
899.133-010	SUPERVISOR, LABOR GANG (any industry)	4338	33333334344	MONOOONFFFNFFFOFOOO	FNNN4NNNNNNNNNO	V,D,P,J	102	362	05.12.01	7100	520205	81008
899.134-010	HIGHWAY-MAINTENANCE SUPERVISOR (government ser.)	4337	32333333455	MONOOONFFNFFFNFNON	FNNN4NNNNNNNNNO	D,P,T	102	362	05.11.01	6311	520205	81005
899.137-010	AIRPORT-MAINTENANCE CHIEF (air trans.)	4337	33333334445	LONOOONFFNFFNFOOONO	FNNN4NNNNNNNNNN	V,D,P,J	102	362	05.10.04	7100	520205	81008
899.137-014	SUPERINTENDENT, TRACK (construction)	4336	33333334445	LNNNNNNFFNFFOOONN	FNNO3NNNNNNNNN	V,D,P,J	102	310	05.12.01	7100	520205	81008
899.137-018	SUPERVISOR, MAINTENANCE (petrol. refin.)	4337	33333334445	LOOOOONFFNFFNFOFONO	FNNN4NONNNNNNNF	D,P,T	031	568	05.12.01	7100	520205	81008
899.261-010	DIVER (any industry)	4337	33323433325	HNNFFFOFFFFNFNFONN	CFNF3NNNNNNNNNF	V,S,T	102	365	05.10.01	6179	490304	85999

DOT #	DOT Title & Industry	Trng	Aptitude	Physical	Environment	Tempra	WkF	MPSMS	GOE	SOC	CIP	OES
899.261-014	MAINTENANCE REPAIRER, INDUSTRIAL (any industry)	4438	33322433244	HOOOOOOFFFOOONFFOON	NNNNN4NNOOONNNN	V,T,J	102	560	05.05.09	6100	460401	85132
899.281-010	CANAL-EQUIPMENT MECHANIC (waterworks)	3336	33333343345	HFOFOFOFFONNNFOFNNN	FNNN4NNNNNNNNNF	V,J,T	102	369	05.10.01	6130	000000	85119
899.364-010	CHIMNEY REPAIRER (business ser.)	3225	34333433345	MFFOOONFONOONONFNNN	FNNN3NONNFNNNF	R,T	031	361	05.10.01	6412	460101	87302
899.364-014	ARTIFICIAL-FOLIAGE ARRANGER (retail trade)	3225	33322333343	MNNFFNFFNNOONFNNNFN	NNNN3NNNNNNNNNN	T,J	264	618	05.12.12	6479	080503	87899
899.381-010	MAINTENANCE REPAIRER, BUILDING (any industry)	4337	33322433244	MOOOOONFFONNNNFNFNON	FNNN4NNNNNNNNNN	V,T	102	360	05.10.01	6179	010201	85132
899.384-010	TRANSPORTATION-EQUIPMENT-MAINTENANCE WORKER (museums)	3235	34333433343	MONONONNFFNNNNFNFOON	ONNN4NNNNNNNNNN	V,J	031	590	05.05.06	6179	000000	85999
899.484-010	MOBILE-HOME-LOT UTILITY WORKER (retail trade)	3126	34434434344	HNNOONNFFNNNNFNFNON	FNNN3NNNNNNNNNN	R,T	102	597	05.10.04	7720	460401	93956
899.487-010	TESTER (rubber goods)	2123	44444444355	LNNNNNNNFFFNNNNFFNN	NNNN4NNNNNNNNNN	R,T	212	519	06.03.01	7830	000000	83005
899.664-010	DIVER HELPER (any industry)	3123	34443434355	MNNFFNFFFOFFNOFNNN	CNNN3NNNNNNNNNN	R,T	102	330	05.12.12	8648	490304	93319
899.664-014	SEWER-PIPE CLEANER (business ser.)	3123	34423434355	MOOOOONFFNNOONOFNNN	FNNN3FNNNNNNNO	R,T	102	364	05.12.12	6479	460501	87511
899.682-010	DIVER PUMPER (construction; fishing & hunt.)	3114	33444434355	MNNNNNNNFFNNNNONNNNN	CNNN4NNNNNNNNNN	R,T	014	875	05.12.06	7679	000000	92998
899.684-010	BONDACTOR-MACHINE OPERATOR (foundry)	3113	34433434354	MFFOOOFFNNNONFNFNON	NNFN4NFNNNNNNNN	R,T	153	568	05.12.14	6479	480599	85126
899.684-014	HIGHWAY-MAINTENANCE WORKER (government ser.)	3123	34444444445	MNNFFNFFNNNNFNFNNN	FNNN3NNNNNNNNNN	R,T	102	362	05.12.12	6479	000000	87711
899.684-018	LAMINATOR (rubber goods)	2123	34443433355	MNNNNNNNFFNNNNFNNN	NNNN4NNNNNNNNNN	R,T	063	519	06.02.22	6479	000000	93956
899.684-022	MAINTENANCE-REPAIRER HELPER, INDUSTRIAL (any industry)	3125	34433433344	HOOOOOOFFONNNFNFFON	NNNN4NNOOONNNN	V,T	102	360	05.10.04	8633	460401	98102
899.684-026	PIPELINER (pipe lines)	3125	34443434355	HOOOOOOFFONNNFNFNNN	CNNN4NFNNNNNNN	V,T	102	364	05.10.04	6479	470501	87899
899.684-030	PORTABLE SAWYER (railroad equip.)	3213	34443534355	MNNNNNNNFFNNNNFNFNNN	NNNN4NFNNNNNNN	R,T	056	594	06.02.25	7753	480703	93926
899.684-034	SHAFT MECHANIC (mine & quarry)	3125	34433434335	HFFFFFNFFONNNNFNFNNN	FNNN4NONNNNNNN	V,S,J,T	102	369	05.10.01	6560	490299	87999
899.684-038	STRIPPER AND TAPER (rubber goods)	2113	34443434345	MNNNNNNNFFNNNNFNFNNN	NNNN3NNNNNNNNNN	R,T	063	519	06.04.29	7759	000000	93999
899.684-042	WINDOW REPAIRER (any industry)	2114	34443444355	MNNFOFNFFNNNNFNFNNN	NNNN4NNNNNNNNNN	R,T	102	554	05.12.12	6179	460201	85999
899.684-046	MAINTENANCE WORKER, MUNICIPAL (government ser.)	3235	34433433335	HONONONFFNFFNFNOONN	FNNO4NOOOONNNN	V,U	102	360	05.12.12	6479	010605	87711
899.687-010	DECORATOR, STREET AND BUILDING (any industry)	2114	44444433354	VFFFFNFFNNNNFNFNON	FNNN3NNNFNNNNF	R,T	102	360	05.12.12	6479	000000	87899
899.687-014	LABORER, AIRPORT MAINTENANCE (air trans.)	2112	34434434334	MNNOOOONFFONNNNOOFFNNO	NNNN5NNNNNNNNNN	R	031	360	05.08.01	8769	460401	98999
900.683-010	CONCRETE-MIXING-TRUCK DRIVER (construction)	3113	34434434334	MNNNNNNNFFONNNNFFNNO	ONNN4NNNNNNNNNN	R	013	853	05.08.01	8213	490205	97102
902.683-010	DUMP-TRUCK DRIVER (any industry)	3112	34434434334	MNNFNNNFFONNNNFFNNF	MNNN4NNNNNNNNNN	R	013	853	05.08.01	8213	490205	97102
903.683-010	EXPLOSIVES-TRUCK DRIVER (ordnance)	3123	33434343334	MNNINNNFFONNNNFFNNF	ONNN3NNNNNNNNNN	R,S	013	499	05.08.01	8213	490205	97102
903.683-014	POWDER-TRUCK DRIVER (ordnance)	3123	34343434334	MONFNNNFFONNNNFFNNF	ONNN4NNNNNNNNNNC	R,S	013	499	05.08.01	8213	490205	97102
903.683-018	TANK-TRUCK DRIVER (petrol. refin.; retail trade; wholesale tr.)	3123	34423334334	MONFNNNFFONNNNFFNNF	FNNN4NNNNNNNNNF	R	013	853	05.08.01	8213	490205	97102
904.383-010	TRACTOR-TRAILER-TRUCK DRIVER (any industry)	3234	34424434334	MOOONONFFONNONFFNFF	ONNN4NNNNNNNNNO	A,J	013	451	05.08.01	8212	490205	97102
904.683-010	LOG-TRUCK DRIVER (logging)	3124	34424334334	MOOOOONFFONNNNFFNFF	ONNN4NONNNNNNNN	R	013	383	05.08.01	8213	490205	97102
905.483-010	MILK DRIVER (dairy products)	3223	34433434334	MOONNNNFFNNONNFFNFF	ONNN4NONNNNNNNN	R	013	874	05.08.03	8213	490205	97102
905.663-010	GARBAGE COLLECTOR DRIVER (motor trans.)	3113	34434434334	MNNONNNFFNOONFFNFF	MNNN4NNNNNNNNNN	R	013	853	05.08.03	8213	490205	97102
905.663-014	TRUCK DRIVER, HEAVY (any industry)	3224	33434433334	MONONONFFONONNFFNFF	MONON4NNNNNNNNNN	R	013	853	05.08.03	8212	490205	97102
905.663-018	VAN DRIVER (motor trans.)	3234	33434334334	VNNFNFNFONOONFFNFF	VNNFN4NFNNNNNNN	P,J	011	853	05.08.03	8213	490205	97102
905.683-010	WATER-TRUCK DRIVER II (construction; petrol. & gas)	3123	44434434334	MONNNNNFFONNNNFFNFF	ONNN4NNNNNNNNNN	R	013	859	05.08.01	8213	490205	97102
905.687-010	TRUCK-DRIVER HELPER (any industry)	2112	44444433355	HFOFNFNFFNNNONNNNN	FNNN4NNNNNNNNNN	R	013	853	05.08.01	8213	490205	98799
905.687-014	VAN-DRIVER HELPER (motor trans.)	2113	44434344345	VOONFNFFNNNNONNNNN	ONNN4NNNNNNNNNN	R	011	853	05.12.03	8726	490205	98799
906.683-010	FOOD-SERVICE DRIVER (hotel & rest.)	2113	44433434334	MOONNNNFFNOONFFNFF	ONNN4NFNNNNNNNN	R	011	853	05.12.03	8726	490205	98799
906.683-014	LIQUID-FERTILIZER SERVICER (agriculture)	3113	44433343335	MNNNNNNNFFNNNNFFNFF	ONNN4NFNNNNNNNN	R,T	013	497	05.08.03	8214	490205	97105
906.683-018	TELEPHONE-DIRECTORY-DISTRIBUTOR DRIVER (business ser.)	2123	44443434334	LNNOOONFFONNNNFFNFF	ONNN4NFONNNNNNN	R	013	859	05.08.03	8214	490205	97105
906.683-022	TRUCK DRIVER, LIGHT (any industry)	3223	33434333334	MONOOONFFONONNFFNFF	ONNN4NNNNNNNNNN	R	013	853	05.08.03	8219	490205	97105
909.127-010	SAFETY COORDINATOR (motor trans.)	4337	32333344333	LONNNNNNFFFFNFFFFF	ONNN4NNNNNNNNNN	V,D,P,J	296	853	11.10.05	1342	430201	15023
909.137-010	DRIVER SUPERVISOR (motor trans.)	4347	22344344445	LNNNNNNNFFNFFNFNNO	FNNN4NNNNNNNNNN	V,D,P,J	013	859	05.08.01	8769	490205	98999
909.137-014	GARBAGE-COLLECTION SUPERVISOR (motor trans.)	4336	33343344455	LONONONFFFNFNFOFNNN	FNNN4NNNNNNNNNN	D,V,P,J	013	853	05.12.01	4525	080709	51002
909.137-018	TRUCK SUPERVISOR (motor trans.)	4348	33333444455	LNNNNNNNNFFNFNFNOO	FNNN4NNNNNNNNNN	D,P,J	031	594	05.12.01	8500	200604	81017
909.663-010	HOSTLER (motor trans.)	3224	34244433334	MFNOONNFFONOONFFNOF	ONNN4NNNNNNNNNN	D,P,V	011	853	05.12.01	8500	000000	81011
909.687-014	LABORER, GENERAL (motor trans.)	1112	44544544455	HNFFFNFFNNNNNNNNN	FNNN4NNNNNNNNNN	R,J	013	859	05.08.03	8219	490205	97102
910.137-010	BAGGAGE-AND-MAIL AGENT (r.r. trans.)	4336	33333344455	LONONONFFFNFNFOFNNN	FNNN4NNNNNNNNNN	R	031	851	05.12.18	8769	490205	98999
910.137-014	CAR-CLEANING SUPERVISOR (r.r. trans.)	3336	33343344455	LONONONFFFNFNFOFNNN	FNNN4NNNNNNNNNN	D,V,P,J	031	594	05.12.01	4525	080709	51002
910.137-018	CIRCUS-TRAIN SUPER (amuse. & rec.)	4336	33433444445	LNNNNNNOOONFFNFNFNNO	ONNN4NNNNNNNNNN	D,P,V	011	919	05.12.01	8500	200604	81017
910.137-022	CONDUCTOR, YARD (r.r. trans.)	4336	33433333344	LOOONONFFFNFNFFFNOF	FNNN4NNNNNNNNNN	D,P,V	013	851	05.08.02	8113	000000	81011

DOT #	DOT Title & Industry	Trng	Aptitude	Physical	Environment	Tempra	WkF	MPSMS	GOE	SOC	CIP	OES
910.137-026	FREIGHT-LOADING SUPERVISOR (r.r. trans.)	4336	33433344455	LNNONONFFNFNFNNNN	FNNN4NNNNNNNNN	V,D,P,J	221	851	05.12.01	8500	520903	81017
910.137-034	ROAD SUPERVISOR OF ENGINES (r.r. trans.)	4347	22323433344	LNNNNNNFFNOONFFNFF	ONNN4NNNNNNNNNN	V,D,P,J	013	851	05.08.02	7100	000000	81011
910.137-038	STATION AGENT I (r.r. trans.)	4346	22343234455	LNNNNNNFFNFNFFNFNN	NNNN3NNNNNNNNNN	V,D,P	282	851	07.01.02	4514	520408	51002
910.137-046	YARD MANAGER (any industry)	4346	33334433445	LNNNNNNFFFNFFNFFNOF	FNNN4NNNNNNNNN	V,D,P,J	013	851	05.12.01	7100	520903	81011
910.167-010	CAR CHASER (beverage)	3236	33334343443	LNNNNNNFFFNFNFNNNN	CNNN4NNNNNNNNNN	D,J	231	594	05.09.03	8113	490299	81011
910.167-014	TRAIN DISPATCHER, ASSISTANT CHIEF (r.r. trans.)	4237	23444344355	SNNNNNNFFONFFNFNNNN	NNNN3NNNNNNNNNN	D,T,P	281	851	05.09.02	4751	520903	58005
910.263-010	RAIL-FLAW-DETECTOR OPERATOR (r.r. trans.)	4336	22242343344	LONNNNNFFNOONFNNFON	FNNN4NNNNNNNNN	J,T	211	367	05.07.01	8280	000000	83008
910.362-010	TOWER OPERATOR (r.r. trans.)	3235	33433334354	LONNNNNFFONFFNFFNFN	NNNN3NNNNNNNNNN	J,T	013	851	05.03.03	8239	000000	97399
910.363-010	FIRER, LOCOMOTIVE (r.r. trans.)	4236	33433344344	LONNNNNOOONFFNOFFNON	NNNN4NNNNNNNNNN	J	013	851	05.08.02	8232	000000	97311
910.363-014	LOCOMOTIVE ENGINEER (r.r. trans.)	4237	33433334344	LNNNNNNFFNFFNFFNOF	NNNN4NNNNNNNNNN	D,V,J	013	851	05.08.02	8232	000000	97305
910.363-018	YARD ENGINEER (r.r. trans.)	3235	33433343344	LOONNNNFFFNNONFFNON	ONNN4NNNNNNNNNN	J	013	851	05.08.02	8232	000000	97308
910.364-010	BRAKER, PASSENGER TRAIN (r.r. trans.)	3234	33443343334	LNONNNNFFONFFNFOOOOO	NNNN3NNNNNNNNNN	V,P	013	851	09.01.04	8233	000000	97317
910.367-010	BRAKE COUPLER, ROAD FREIGHT (r.r. trans.)	3234	33442434334	MOOOOONFFONOONFFOOOF	FNNN4NNONONNNO	V,J	013	851	05.12.05	8233	470302	97317
910.367-014	CAR DISTRIBUTOR (r.r. trans.)	4235	33434434455	SNNNNNNFFNFFNFNNNNN	NNNN3NNNNNNNNNN	D,P	013	851	07.04.05	4759	000000	58099
910.367-018	ENGINE DISPATCHER (r.r. trans.)	3234	33444344355	SNNNNNNFFONFFNFNNNN	NNNN4NNNNNNNNNN	V,J	221	851	05.09.02	4751	000000	58005
910.367-022	LOCOMOTIVE OPERATOR HELPER (r.r. trans.)	2223	33433444344	LOONNNNOOONFFNOFOOOO	NNNN4NNNNNNNNNN	J,T	282	851	05.12.20	8233	000000	97317
910.367-026	PASSENGER SERVICE REPRESENTATIVE (r.r. trans.)	3234	33334344445	LNNNNNNOOONFFNNNNNN	NNNN4NNNNNNNNNN	P,J	291	851	09.01.04	5257	080709	68028
910.367-030	WAY INSPECTOR (r.r. trans.)	3235	33442344444	LOOOOONFFNOONFNOFON	FNNN3NNNNNNNNNN	D,J,T	211	367	05.07.01	8280	000000	83008
910.382-010	CAR-RETARDER OPERATOR (r.r. trans.)	3235	33433334354	SNNNNNNFFONNNNFFOFF	NNNN4NNNNNNNNNN	J,T	013	851	05.12.05	8239	000000	97399
910.384-010	TANK-CAR INSPECTOR (petrol. refin.)	3234	34433444355	MOOOOONFFONNNFNOONN	NNNN3NNNNNNNNNN	J,T	121	594	05.10.02	8280	000000	83008
910.387-010	PERISHABLE-FRUIT INSPECTOR (wholesale tr.)	3235	33442334343	LNNNNNNFFONNFNNOON	NFNNN3NNNNNNNNNN	J,T	211	305	05.10.08	8280	000000	83008
910.387-014	RAILROAD-CAR INSPECTOR (r.r. trans.)	3235	33442344444	LOOOONFFFNNNNNFNFOON	FNNN3NNNNNNNNNN	J	211	594	05.07.01	8280	000000	83008
910.583-010	LABORER, CAR BARN (r.r. trans.)	3224	34433334335	LNNNNNNFFFNNNNFFNNF	ONNN3NNNNNNNNNN	J	013	852	05.08.02	8239	000000	97308
910.663-010	TRACK-MOVING-MACHINE OPERATOR (construction; mine & quarry)	3224	34434434335	VNNFFNCCNNOONOOFNNN	CNNN4NNNNNNNNNN	R,J,T	011	367	05.11.01	6467	490202	87714
910.664-010	YARD COUPLER (r.r. trans.)	3224	33434434335	LNNNNNNOOONFFNNOONN	CNNN4NNCNONNNNN	V,J	013	851	05.12.05	8233	000000	97317
910.667-010	CAR INSPECTOR (railroad equip.)	3234	34443444354	MNNNNNNFFNFFNFNONNN	NNNN4NNNNNNNNNN	R,T	211	594	05.07.01	8280	000000	83008
910.667-014	CONDUCTOR (r.r. trans.)	3224	34434434334	LNNNNNNOOONNNOONFONNN	ONNN4NNNNNNNNNN	R,P	282	852	09.05.08	5257	000000	97308
910.667-018	LOADING INSPECTOR (r.r. trans.)	3234	34433434334	LOOOOOOOONOONFFONNN	FNNN4NNNNNNONN	J	211	594	05.08.02	8232	490299	97314
910.667-022	PERISHABLE-FREIGHT INSPECTOR (r.r. trans.)	3224	33434434345	LNNNNNNOOONFFNNOONN	ONNN4NNNNNNNNNN	R,J	013	852	05.07.01	8280	000000	83008
910.667-026	SWITCH TENDER (r.r. trans.)	2122	44444434335	MNNNNNNFFNNOONFFNFNOF	CNNN4NNNNNNNNNN	J,T	231	367	05.12.01	8280	000000	98799
910.667-030	TRANSFER-TABLE OPERATOR HELPER (railroad equip.; r.r. trans.)	2113	44434434345	HNNFNFNFFNNOONNFFNNN	FNNN4NNNNNNNNNN	T	013	851	05.12.04	8726	000000	98799
910.677-010	PASSENGER SERVICE REPRESENTATIVE II (r.r. trans.)	2122	43443444354	LONNNNNFFNFFNFFNNNN	ONNN4NNNNNNNNNN	R,P	292	851	09.05.08	5257	000000	97308
910.683-010	HOSTLER (r.r. trans.)	3224	34434434334	LNNNNNNOOONNNNOFNNN	NNNN4NNNNNNNNNN	J	013	594	05.08.02	8232	000000	97314
910.683-014	MOTOR OPERATOR (r.r. trans.)	3225	34433434334	LNNNNNNOOONNNNOFNNON	NNNN4NNNNNNNNNN	R,J	013	852	05.11.01	6467	490202	87714
910.683-018	TRACK-SURFACING-MACHINE OPERATOR (construction)	3223	34433434345	VNNFFFNCCNNOONNFFNNN	FNNN4NNNNNNNNNN	R,J,T	091	367	05.11.04	6467	490202	97399
910.683-022	TRANSFER-TABLE OPERATOR (railroad equip.; r.r. trans.)	3123	34434434335	MNNONNNFFNNNNNFNFNNN	ONNN4NNNNNNNNNN	T	011	594	05.10.01	6467	490202	87714
910.684-010	GRINDING-MACHINE OPERATOR, PORTABLE (r.r. trans.)	2223	44433433345	MNNCNCNCCNNNNNFNFNNN	CNNN4NNNNNNNNNN	R,T	051	594	05.12.01	6467	480503	87714
910.684-014	TRACK REPAIRER (r.r. trans.)	3224	34434434345	HNNFFFNCCFNNONONONNN	FNNN4NNONNNNNNN	V,T	102	367	05.12.12	6467	490202	87714
910.687-010	BAGGAGE HANDLER (r.r. trans.)	2112	34444434335	HNNFFNFFNFNNNNNNNN	NNNN3NNNNNNNNNN	R	011	851	05.12.03	8769	080709	98999
910.687-014	CAR COOPER (any industry)	2112	44444444345	MFNFNFNFFNNNNNNFNNN	NNNN3NNNNNNNNNN	R	031	851	05.12.18	8750	000000	98905
910.687-018	CAR ICER (food prep., nec; meat products)	2112	44444534345	HFNFNNFNFFNNNNNNFNNN	FFNN3NNNNNNNNNN	R	011	399	05.12.03	8769	000000	98899
910.687-022	FREIGHT-CAR CLEANER, DELTA SYSTEM (r.r. trans.)	2112	44443534345	HOOOOOOFFONNNNFNNNNN	FNNN4NOONNNNNNN	J,R	031	851	05.12.18	8750	000000	98905
910.687-026	TRACK OILER (r.r. trans.)	2112	44544544345	LNNFFNFNFNNNNNONFNNN	CNNN3NNNNNNNNNN	R	031	852	05.12.18	8769	000000	98999
911.131-010	BOATSWAIN (water trans.)	4237	33433444334	HFFFOFNFFONFFNONNOON	FNNF4NNNNNNNNNN	D,V	031	854	05.12.18	7100	490309	81011
911.131-014	LOCK TENDER, CHIEF OPERATOR (water trans.)	4337	33333233334	MOOOOONFFONFNFFFFOOF	ONNN3NONONNNNNO	D,P,J	013	854	05.05.09	8245	490309	97802
911.133-010	CADET, DECK (water trans.)	4436	33333234334	LOOOOONOOONOONOOOOO	ONNN3NONNNNNNO	V,D,P,J,T	013	854	05.04.02	8241	490309	97505
911.137-010	BARGE CAPTAIN (water trans.)	4336	33433444345	MNNNNNFNFFONFFFNOONN	FNNN3NNNNNNNNNN	D	011	854	05.12.01	8242	490399	97502
911.137-014	DERRICK-BOAT CAPTAIN (water trans.)	4337	33333444345	LNNNNNNOOONFFNOFONNO	FNNN3NNNNNNNNNN	D,P,J	011	854	05.12.01	8242	490399	97502
911.137-018	HEADER (water trans.)	3336	33333444345	LOOONNNFFONFFONFFNNN	FNNN3NNNNNNNNNN	D,P,J	011	854	05.12.01	8120	490299	81011
911.137-022	SUPERINTENDENT, STEVEDORING (water trans.)	4337	33323344355	LNNNNNNOOONFFNNOOONF	FNNN3OFNNNNNNNF	V,D,P,J	011	853	05.11.04	7100	520903	81011
911.137-026	SUPERVISOR, FERRY TERMINAL (water trans.)	4345	33334344455	LNNONNNFFONFFNFNFNNNN	ONNN3NNNNNNNNNN	D,J,P,V	232	854	11.11.03	8242	080709	81011

DOT #	DOT Title & Industry	Trng	Aptitude	Physical	Environment	Tempra	WkF	MPSMS	GOE	SOC	CIP	OES
911.167-010	DISPATCHER, TUGBOAT (water trans.)	4346	33434344455	SNNNNNNFFNFNNNNN	NNNN3NNNNNNNNNN	D,V,P,J	013	593	07.04.05	4751	490399	58005
911.263-010	DEEP SUBMERGENCE VEHICLE OPERATOR (military ser.)	3227	34434433354	LONNONFFFFNFFOOOF	NNNF4NNNNNNNNNNN	D,J,P,S	013	593	05.04.02	8242	490304	97505
911.362-010	LOCK OPERATOR (water trans.)	3225	33433444334	LNNONONFFFNFNONONON	FNNN3NNNNNNNNNN	V,T,J	013	854	05.11.04	8245	000000	97802
911.363-010	FERRYBOAT OPERATOR (water trans.)	3226	34433434344	LONNNNNFFNFFNOFFOOF	FNNN3NNNNNNNNNN	D,J	013	854	05.04.02	8242	490399	97502
911.363-014	QUARTERMASTER (water trans.)	3336	33333334344	LOONNNNFFONFNFFFNFN	ONNN3NNNNNNNNNN	J,T	013	854	05.04.02	8243	490399	97514
911.364-010	ABLE SEAMAN (water trans.)	3225	34433433324	HFFOOONFFONOONNFNON	FNNN3NFNNNNNNNN	J,T	013	854	05.12.03	8243	490309	97514
911.364-014	BOAT LOADER I (water trans.)	2223	34433433345	MNOOOONFFFNNNFONNNN	FNNN3NFNNNNNNNN	J	014	854	05.12.06	8243	490299	97989
911.584-010	MARINE OILER (water trans.)	3224	44443433355	MOONNNNFFNNNNFNNNNN	FNNN4NNNNNNNNNN	J	033	560	05.12.08	8242	490306	97517
911.663-010	MOTORBOAT OPERATOR (any industry)	3235	34433434334	MNNNNNFFNFFNOFFFF	NNNN3NNNNNNNNNN	J	013	854	05.08.04	8242	490399	97511
911.663-014	STEVEDORE I (water trans.)	3225	34434434335	MONOOONFFONNNNOFONNO	FNNN3NNNNNNNNNN	J	011	854	05.11.04	8313	490299	97902
911.664-010	FERRYBOAT OPERATOR, CABLE (water trans.)	2223	34433444355	MNNNNNNFFNNOONFNNNN	FNNN3NNNNNNNNNN	D	013	854	05.12.03	8242	000000	97502
911.664-014	SAILOR, PLEASURE CRAFT (water trans.)	3225	33333434333	HOOOOOOFFOOONNFNOON	FNNN3NNNNNNNNNN	J	031	593	05.12.18	8243	490309	97517
911.667-010	FERRYBOAT-OPERATOR HELPER (water trans.)	2222	44434434345	HNNOOONFFNNOONFNNNN	FNNN3NNNNNNNNNN	R	013	854	05.12.03	8726	000000	98799
911.667-014	HATCH TENDER (water trans.)	2112	44434544455	LNNNNNNFFNNNNFNONNO	CNNN3NNNNNNNNNN	R	011	854	05.12.04	8769	490309	98999
911.667-018	SOUNDER (any industry)	3222	44434344345	MNNOOONFFONNNNNFNNN	FNNN3NNNNNNNNNN	R	243	716	05.12.05	8646	490309	98319
911.677-010	TICKET TAKER, FERRYBOAT (water trans.)	2222	33444444354	MNNOOONFFFFNNNNNN	FNNN3NNNNNNNNNN	R,P	291	854	05.12.04	8769	490299	98999
911.687-010	BOAT-LOADER HELPER (water trans.)	2112	44444444344	VOOOOONFFONNNNNOFNON	ONNN3NNNNNNNNNN	R	014	854	05.12.06	8769	490299	98999
911.687-014	CLEANER III (any industry)	2112	44444444345	MNNFNNNFFNNNNNNNNN	FNFN4NFNNNNNNNF	R	031	341	05.12.18	8750	490306	98905
911.687-018	COAL TRIMMER (water trans.)	2113	44544544345	HNNNNNNFFNNNNNNNNNN	FNNN3NNNNNNNNNN	R	011	341	05.12.04	8314	490299	97941
911.687-022	DECKHAND (water trans.)	2114	33434544334	HOOFNFNFFNNNNNFNNON	FNNF4NNNNNNNNNN	J	013	854	05.08.04	8243	490309	97517
911.687-026	LINES TENDER (water trans.)	2112	44544544435	LNNNNNNFFONNNNNNNNN	FNNN3NNNNNNNNNN	R	011	854	05.12.03	8769	490309	98999
911.687-030	ORDINARY SEAMAN (water trans.)	3114	34434434334	MOOOOONFFONNNNOFNNFN	FNNO3NNNNNNNNNN	J	013	854	05.12.18	8243	490309	97517
912.167-010	DISPATCHER (air trans.)	5448	22243244453	SNNNNNNFFONFFNNFNON	NNNN3NNNNNNNNNN	D,P,S,J	211	855	05.03.03	3920	490105	39002
912.364-010	AIRPORT ATTENDANT (air trans.)	3235	33433334344	MOOOOONFFONOONONOON	FNNN5NNNNNNNNNN	V,J	111	855	05.10.04	5269	000000	67099
912.367-010	FLIGHT-INFORMATION EXPEDITER (air trans.)	4445	33343334454	LNNNNNNFFONFNFNNNN	NNNN3NNNNNNNNNN	J	231	855	07.04.05	4752	490105	58008
912.367-014	TRANSPORTATION AGENT (air trans.)	3335	33344333344	LNNNNNNFFFFNFNNNNON	ONNN5NNNNNNNNNN	P,V	281	855	07.05.01	4758	520499	58011
912.662-010	IN-FLIGHT REFUELING OPERATOR (military ser.)	4336	33322433355	SNNOOFFFFNFNNFFNNF	NNNN4NNNNNNNNNN	T,S	014	501	05.06.03	9100	000000	00000
912.663-010	AIRPORT UTILITY WORKER (air trans.)	3234	33233334334	HFFOOONFFNNOFFNNOO	FNNN5NONNNNNNNN	V,T	013	855	05.12.06	8700	000000	97899
912.682-010	AIRCRAFT LAUNCH AND RECOVERY TECHNICIAN (military ser.)	4335	34334434325	HNNFFFOFFONOONFONNOO	FNNN5NFNNNNNNNN	S,V,T	014	850	05.10.02	9100	000000	00000
912.684-010	PARACHUTE RIGGER (air trans.)	3225	34432433355	MNNNNNNCCNNOONFFFNFF	NNNN4NNNNNNNNNN	P,J	013	852	06.04.38	7759	000000	93999
912.687-010	LINE-SERVICE ATTENDANT (air trans.)	3222	34444434345	MNNNNNNCCONFFNOCCFFC	FNNN5NFNNNNNNNN	R,P	062	439	05.12.06	8726	470607	98799
913.133-010	ROAD SUPERVISOR (motor trans.)	4346	33393334334	MFFNNNNFFONNNNFNFNNN	FNNN4NNNNNNNNNN	J	041	855	09.03.03	7100	080709	81011
913.133-014	SUPERVISOR, CAB (motor trans.)	4347	33334434334	LNNNNNNFFONFNFNFNFF	NNNN4NNNNNNNNNN	D,P,J	013	852	09.03.03	7100	520903	58011
913.167-010	BUS DISPATCHER, INTERSTATE (motor trans.)	4335	33344444455	LNNNNNNFFONFFNFNNNN	NNNN3NNNNNNNNNN	D,P,J	013	852	07.04.05	4751	000000	58005
913.167-014	DISPATCHER, BUS AND TROLLEY (motor trans.)	4347	22343444455	LNNNNNNFFNFFNFNNONN	NNNN4NNNNNNNNNN	V,D,P,J	013	852	07.04.05	8111	080709	81011
913.167-018	SCHEDULE MAKER (motor trans.)	4345	34434344455	LNNNNNNFFOFFNFNFNON	NNNN4NNNNNNNNNN	J	013	850	07.05.01	4752	000000	58008
913.363-010	BUS DRIVER, DAY-HAUL OR FARM CHARTER (agriculture)	3223	33333434334	MNNNNNNCCNNOONFFFNFF	NNNN4NNNNNNNNNN	P,J	013	852	09.03.01	8215	010501	97108
913.367-010	TAXICAB STARTER (motor trans.)	3223	33344434355	SNNNNNNFFNNFFNNNNNF	FNNN3NNNNNNNNNN	R,P	013	852	07.04.05	4751	000000	58005
913.463-010	BUS DRIVER (motor trans.)	3224	33434434334	MNNNNNNCCONFFNOCCNFC	NNNN4NNNNNNNNNN	P,J	013	852	09.03.02	8216	490205	97108
913.463-014	STREETCAR OPERATOR (r.r. trans.)	3223	33334434334	MNNONNNCCONFFNOCCNFC	NNNN4NNNNNNNNNN	P,J	013	852	09.03.02	8216	490205	97114
913.463-018	TAXI DRIVER (motor trans.)	3223	34434434334	LNNONONFFONOONFFNOF	FNNN3NNNNNNNNNN	R	013	852	09.03.01	8215	490205	97108
913.663-010	CHAUFFEUR (any industry)	3223	34434434334	LNNNNNNFFONFNFNONN	NNNN4NNNNNNNNNN	P,J	013	852	09.03.01	8215	490205	97314
913.663-014	MOBILE-LOUNGE DRIVER (motor trans.)	3223	34434434334	LNNNNNNFFONNNFFNOF	NNNN4NNNNNNNNNN	R	013	852	09.03.01	8215	490205	97105
913.663-018	DRIVER (motor trans.)	2223	34434344335	MNNONNNCCONOONFCCNNC	NNNN4NNNNNNNNNN	R,P	013	852	09.03.01	8232	000000	97105
913.683-010	AMBULANCE DRIVER (medical ser.)	3224	34434434334	VOONNNNFFNNNNFNFNFF	NNNN4NNNNNNNNNN	P,S	013	929	05.08.03	5233	000000	66023
914.131-010	SUPERVISOR, PUMPING (smelt. & refin.)	4347	23333333255	LNNNNNNFFNFFFNFNOONN	ONNN4NNNNNNNNNN	V,D,P,J	014	364	06.01.01	7100	000000	81011
914.132-010	COMPRESSOR-STATION ENGINEER, CHIEF (pipe lines)	4348	23334444455	LNNNNNNNFFONFFNNOONN	FNNN4NONNNNNNNN	V,D,P,J	014	500	05.02.01	8120	520205	81011
914.132-014	STATION ENGINEER, CHIEF (pipe lines)	4348	23334334355	LOOOONFFNFNNFFNOONN	NNNN4NONNNNNNNN	V,D,P,J	014	856	05.06.03	8120	520205	81011
914.132-018	SUPERVISOR, CELLARS (beverage)	4227	33343433354	LNNNNNNFFOFFNFNFNON	NFNO3NNNNNNNNNN	V,D,P,J	014	395	05.12.01	7100	520205	97105
914.132-022	SUPERVISOR, FIELD PIPELINES (pipe lines)	4347	23333333355	LOOOONFFNFFNNONONN	FNNN4NONNNNNNNN	V,D,P,J	014	501	05.02.01	7100	520205	81011
914.134-010	GAUGER, CHIEF (petrol. & gas; petrol. refin.; pipe lines)	4347	23343344355	LNNNNNNFFNFFNFNNOONN	ONNN4NONNNNNNNN	V,D,P,J	221	501	05.06.03	7100	520205	81011

DOT #	DOT Title & Industry	Trng	Aptitude	Physical	Environment	Tempra	WkF	MPSMS	GOE	SOC	CIP	OES
914.137-010	DISTRIBUTION SUPERVISOR (pipe lines; wholesale tr.)	4346	23343344455	SNNNNNNFFONFFNFNNNNN	NNNN3NNNNNNNNNN	D,P,J,T	232	850	05.09.01	8111	080709	81011
914.137-014	LOADING-RACK SUPERVISOR (petrol. refin.)	4347	33333344445	LFNONONFFNFFNFNNNN	FNNN4NNNNNNNNNNN	V,D,P,J	014	850	05.12.01	7100	520205	81011
914.137-018	SUPERVISOR, DOCK (petrol. refin.; pipe lines)	4347	33334344344	LFOOONFFNFFNFFNOF	FNNN4NFNNNNNNNNF	V,D,P,J	014	854	05.12.01	7100	520205	81011
914.167-010	DISPATCHER, CHIEF II (petrol. & gas; petrol. refin.; pipe lines)	4347	23344344355	SNNNNNNFFONFFNFNNOON	NNNN3NNNNNNNNNN	V,D,J	231	342	05.02.01	7100	520205	81011
914.167-014	DISPATCHER, OIL (petrol. & gas; petrol. refin.; pipe lines)	4447	23233344454	SNNNNNNFFNFFNFNNOON	NNNN3NNNNNNNNNN	D,J,P	295	856	05.02.01	4751	150903	58005
914.362-010	COAL PIPELINE OPERATOR (pipe lines)	3334	34343334354	LNNNNNNFFNOONCNNFON	NNNN4NNNNNNNNNN	J,T	142	341	06.02.18	6960	470501	95099
914.362-014	CONSTRUCTION-AND-MAINTENANCE INSPECTOR (petrol. refin.)	3335	33444344345	LFONNNNFFONFFNFNNN	FNNN4NNNNNNNNNN	J,T	211	501	05.07.01	8280	000000	83008
914.362-018	STATION ENGINEER, MAIN LINE (pipe lines)	3237	33333334344	LOOOOONFFNOONFONNFO	ONNN4NONNNNONN	J,T	014	501	05.06.03	8319	470501	97914
914.382-010	OIL PUMPER (petrol. & gas)	3336	33333334344	LFFOOONFFNNNNFNONON	CNNN4NONNNNNON	J,T	014	342	05.06.03	8319	470399	97908
914.382-014	PUMPER-GAUGER (chemical; petrol. refin.; pipe lines)	4337	33323333444	MONONONFFNNNNFNOOON	FNNN4NNNNNNNNN	J,T	014	499	05.06.04	8319	470399	97905
914.382-018	PUMPER-GAUGER APPRENTICE (chemical; petrol. refin.; pipe lines)	4337	33323333444	MONONONFFNNNNFNOOON	FNNN4NNNNNNNNN	J,T	014	499	05.06.04	8319	150903	97905
914.382-022	PUMPER, HEAD (petrol. & gas)	3337	33334334355	LNNOOONFFNNNNFFFNNN	FNNN3NFNNFNNFN	V,T	014	342	05.06.03	8319	470399	97911
914.384-010	GAUGER (petrol. & gas; petrol. refin.; pipe lines)	3336	33333334344	MFFFOFOFFNNNNFNOOON	FNNN3NFNNFNNFN	J,T	014	501	05.06.03	6950	470399	95017
914.485-010	BARREL FILLER II (beverage)	2213	33343344355	HNNNNNNFFNNNNFNFNNN	ONNN3NNNNNNNNNN	R,T	395	501	06.04.37	7662	470501	97953
914.585-010	GAS-TRANSFER OPERATOR (chemical)	2222	44434433335	LNNNNNNFFNNOONCNNFON	CNNN4NNNNNNNNNN	T	014	491	06.04.12	8319	470501	97989
914.665-010	PIGMENT PUMPER (rubber reclaim.)	2114	44444434355	MONONNNFFNNOONFNFNNN	FNNN4NFNNNNNNNN	R,T	014	490	05.12.06	8319	470501	97953
914.665-014	PUMPER, BREWERY (beverage)	3223	34343434355	MONFFFNFFONOONFNNNN	NNNN4NNNNNNNNNN	R	395	395	06.04.40	8319	470501	97953
914.667-010	LOADER I (any industry)	3225	34433334344	MOOONONFFNOONFNFNON	FNNN4NFNNNNNNNN	R,T	014	380	06.04.40	8319	470399	97953
914.682-010	PUMPER (any industry)	3235	33334334355	MOOFOONFFNNNNFNNONN	FNNO2NNNNNNNNN	J,T	014	568	05.06.03	8319	470399	97989
914.685-010	FISH BAILER (fishing & hunt.)	1112	44544544455	MNNNNNNFFNNNNNNNNNN	FNNF4NNNNNNNNN	R	014	331	03.04.03	8319	000000	97989
914.687-010	LABORER, PIPELINES (pipe lines)	2112	44454544345	HOOOONFFOONNNNNNNNN	FNNN4NONNONNNN	V	011	364	05.12.03	8769	470399	98999
914.687-014	LOADER HELPER (any industry)	2113	44445544345	MFFFFNFFNNNNNNNNNN	CNNN4NFNNNNNNF	R,T	014	490	05.12.06	8726	470501	98799
914.687-018	PUMPER HELPER (any industry)	2112	44544544355	MONOOONFFNNNNNONOONN	FNNO4NNNNNNNNNO	R	014	568	05.10.02	8618	470399	98999
915.133-010	SUPERVISOR, PARKING LOT (automotive ser.)	3224	44444444455	LNNNNNNFFONFFNFFFNF	FNNN4NNNNNNNNN	D,P	291	961	09.04.02	8500	000000	81017
915.134-010	TIRE-SERVICE SUPERVISOR (automotive ser.)	4336	33333333355	LNNFFFNFFFFNFNNN	ONNN3NNNNNNNNNN	V,D,P,J	121	511	05.12.01	7100	520205	81011
915.137-010	CAR-WASH SUPERVISOR (automotive ser.)	3225	33333334355	LNNNNNNFFNFFNFNNNNN	NNNN4NNNNNNNNNN	D,V,P,J	031	961	05.12.01	8500	081209	81017
915.467-010	AUTOMOBILE-SERVICE-STATION ATTENDANT (automotive ser.)	3223	33343444355	MNNOOONFFNCNCNNINNN	FNNO4ONNNNNNNNO	V,P	292	591	05.10.02	8730	081209	97805
915.473-010	PARKING-LOT ATTENDANT (automotive ser.)	2112	44444444335	LNNNNNNFFNOONFFFFNF	FNNN4NNNNNNNNN	R,P	291	961	09.04.02	8740	080902	97808
915.477-010	AUTOMOBILE-SELF-SERVE-SERVICE-STATION ATTENDANT (automotive ser.)	3223	33344344454	LNNFNNNFFNOONONNOON	FNNO4NFNNNNNNN	V,P	292	961	09.04.02	8740	081209	97805
915.583-010	LOT ATTENDANT (retail trade)	3233	33443334334	LNNNNNNFFONNNNFONONF	FNNN3NNNNNNNNNN	R,T	231	961	05.08.03	8740	081203	97808
915.587-010	GAS-AND-OIL SERVICER (motor trans.)	2112	44444434355	LNNNNNNFFONNNNFONOOF	FNNN3NNNNNNNNNN	R,J	231	961	05.12.06	8730	081209	97805
915.667-010	CAR-WASH ATTENDANT, AUTOMATIC (automotive ser.)	2212	44444434355	LNNNNNNFFONNNONFNNN	ONNO4NNNNNNNNNN	R	031	961	09.04.02	8750	081209	98905
915.667-014	PARKING LOT SIGNALER (automotive ser.)	2112	44544544355	LNNNNNNFFNNOONNFNNN	CNNN4NNNNNNNNNN	R,U	282	961	09.04.02	8740	000000	97808
915.684-010	TIRE REPAIRER (automotive ser.)	2113	44433434345	HNNFFNFFFFNONFNFFN	FNNN4NFNNNNNNN	R,T	121	511	05.12.15	6179	470604	85953
915.687-010	AUTOMOBILE-SEAT-COVER INSTALLER (automotive ser.)	2112	44544543354	MNNFFNNFFFFNNNFNNNON	NNNN3NNNNNNNNNN	R	061	591	05.12.12	7720	480303	93956
915.687-014	GARAGE SERVICER, INDUSTRIAL (any industry)	2113	34444444355	MNNOOONFFONNNNFNNONN	NNNN4NNNNNNNNNN	R,U	033	591	05.12.08	8730	000000	97805
915.687-018	LUBRICATION SERVICER (automotive ser.)	2114	34444434355	MNNFOFNCCNNNONOOOONO	NNNN4NNONNNNNN	J,T	013	961	05.12.18	8750	470302	97805
915.687-022	PORTER, USED-CAR LOT (retail trade; wholesale tr.)	2112	44444444355	MNNFFFFNFNNNNNNONNN	OONNO3NNNNNNNNNN	R	031	961	05.12.18	8750	000000	98905
915.687-026	STEAM CLEANER (automotive ser.)	2112	44545545355	MNNFNNNFFNNNNNONONNN	ONNN4NNNNNNNNNN	R	033	961	05.12.18	8750	470303	98905
915.687-030	TAXI SERVICER (motor trans.)	2112	44444444355	MNNFNNNFFNNNNNONFNNN	ONNN4NONNNNNNNN	R	031	960	05.12.18	8769	470604	98999
915.687-034	AUTOMOBILE DETAILER (automotive ser.)	2112	44454544454	MMNFOFNFFNNNNFNFFON	OONNO4NONNNNNNNN	R	031	852	07.04.05	4751	000000	98905
919.162-010	DISPATCHER, TRAFFIC OR SYSTEM (motor trans.; r.r. trans.)	4337	22444234355	SNNNNNNFFNFFNFNNNNN	NNNN4NNNNNNNNNN	D,P,J	281	852	09.03.03	2390	490205	58005
919.223-010	INSTRUCTOR, BUS, TROLLEY, AND TAXI (motor trans.; r.r. trans.)	4336	22333333334	LNNNNNNFFONFFNFFNFF	NNNN4NNNNNNNNNN	D,P,J	296	852	09.03.03	8280	470604	31314
919.363-010	NEW-CAR INSPECTOR (motor trans.)	3224	33435334334	LNNNNNNFFONFNFFNFF	FNNN3NNNNNNNNNN	J	212	591	06.03.01	8280	490205	97114
919.363-010	DELIVERER, CAR RENTAL (automotive ser.; retail trade)	2223	33435334334	LNNOOONFFOOOONONONN	FNNO3NNNNNNNNNN	R	013	859	05.08.03	8216	000000	97308
919.663-010	DINKEY OPERATOR (any industry)	3224	34433343334	LONOOONCCONOONCCCNOC	NNNN4NNONNNNNN	R	013	851	05.11.04	8232	490299	97102
919.663-014	DINKEY OPERATOR (any industry)	3114	34433434334	MNNONONFFNOONOFFFFF	ONNN3NNNNNNNNNN	R	013	571	05.08.03	8213	490205	97105
919.663-018	DRIVER-UTILITY WORKER (auto. mfg.; automotive ser.)	2122	44444434334	SNNNNNNFFNNNNFNFFFF	NNNN3NNNNNNNNNN	R	013	859	05.08.03	8214	000000	97102
919.663-022	ESCORT-VEHICLE DRIVER (motor trans.)	2123	34434434334	MNNFFOFFQNOONOFFNFF	FNNN4NNNNNNNNNN	J	011	961	05.08.03	8213	490205	97102
919.663-026	TOW-TRUCK OPERATOR (automotive ser.)	2113	44544543445	MONFNFNFFNNOONNFFNF	CNNN3NONNNNNNO	R,T	013	859	03.04.05	8319	490299	97989
919.664-010	TEAMSTER (any industry)	3224	34423343345	LNNNNNNOONNNNNOOONNO	NNNN3NNNNNNNNNN	J,T	011	859	05.11.04	8245	000000	97802

DOT #	DOT Title & Industry	Trng	Aptitude	Physical	Environment	Tempra	WkF	MPSMS	GOE	SOC	CIP	OES
919.683-010	DOCK HAND (air trans.)	2224	33434433335	HNFOONNFFNNNNNOFFNNN	FNNF4NFNNNNNNO	P	013	855	05.08.04	8242	000000	97511
919.683-014	DRIVER (auto. mfg.; automotive ser.)	2112	34434434334	LNNNNNFFNNNNFFFOF	NNNN3NNNNNNN	R	013	591	05.08.03	8216	000000	97114
919.683-018	RAIL-TRACTOR OPERATOR (steel & rel.)	3224	34434534345	LNNNNNNFFNNNNNFFNNF	ONNN4NFNNNNNN	R	013	851	05.11.04	8239	490299	97399
919.683-022	STREET-SWEEPER OPERATOR (government ser.)	2113	44434534445	LNNNNNNCCONNNNCCNNC	ONNO4NNNNNNNN	R	031	362	05.11.01	8219	490202	97399
919.683-026	TRACKMOBILE OPERATOR (any industry)	2123	34434434335	MFFNNNNFFONNNNFFFNNF	NNNN4NNNNNNNN	R,T	013	859	05.08.02	8239	000000	97399
919.683-030	DRIVER, STARTING GATE (amuse. & rec.)	2112	44434434435	LNNNNNNCCNNNNNFFFNNF	NNNN3NNNNNNN	R,U	013	919	05.08.03	8219	000000	97399
919.687-010	CHECKER (motor trans.)	1112	44444544355	LNNNNNNFFONNNNFNFNNN	NNNN4NNNNNNNNF	R	221	859	05.09.01	4753	000000	58028
919.687-014	CLEANER II (any industry)	2111	33434434344	MONOONNCCNNNNNNNNNNN	FNNC4NNNNNNNN	R	031	960	05.12.18	8750	200604	98905
919.687-018	SAFETY INSPECTOR, TRUCK (automotive ser.; motor trans.)	3224	34434343344	LNNOOOOFFONNNNNFNFON	FNNN4NNNNNNNN	J,T	212	853	05.07.01	8280	470605	83008
919.687-022	SUPPLIES PACKER (any industry)	3225	34434434355	HNNONONFFNNNNNNFNNNN	COOO3NONNNNNNO	R	013	859	03.04.05	8726	490299	98799
920.130-010	SUPERVISOR, PACKING (sugar & conf.)	4336	33344334355	LNNNNNNFFONFFNFNFNNN	NNFN4NNNNNNNN	D,P,J	041	392	06.04.01	7100	000000	81008
920.132-010	PACKAGING SUPERVISOR (any industry)	4236	33332334343	LNNNNNNFFONFFNFNONFN	NNFN4NNNNNNNN	D,P,J,T	041	568	06.04.01	7100	000000	81008
920.132-014	SUPERVISOR, CARTON AND CAN SUPPLY (beverage)	4337	33333333354	LNNNNNNFFNNCCNFNFNNN	NNNN4NNNNNNNN	D,P,J	062	551	06.02.01	7100	000000	81008
920.137-010	PACKING-HOUSE SUPERVISOR (agriculture; wholesale tr.)	4336	33344344353	LNNNNNFFFFFNFFFFF	NONF4NNNNNNNN	D,P,J,V	041	300	06.02.01	7100	080799	81008
920.137-014	SORTING SUPERVISOR (brick & tile)	4236	33433444343	MONOOONFFONFFNFOFNFN	NNNN3NNNNNNNN	D,P,J	212	534	06.02.01	7100	000000	81008
920.137-018	SUPERVISOR (sugar & conf.)	4335	33443445455	LNNNNNNFFNNFFNNFFOONN	NNNN3NNNNNNNN	D,P,J	041	393	06.02.01	7100	000000	81008
920.137-022	SUPERVISOR, FILLING-AND-PACKING (paint & varnish)	3235	33344344444	LNNOOONFONFNFNNNFN	NNNN4NNNNNNNN	D,P,J,V	041	495	06.04.01	7100	520205	81017
920.137-026	SUPERVISOR, PACKING AND WRAPPING (any industry)	4237	33333434344	MNFNNNNFFFFNFNFOON	NNNN4NNNNNNNN	D,V,T,P	041	460	06.04.01	7100	000000	81008
920.380-010	SETTER, JUICE PACKAGING MACHINES (can. & preserv.)	4336	34423433355	MNNONNNFFNNNNNFNFNNN	NNNN4NNNNNNNN	T,J	121	567	06.01.02	7462	470303	92997
920.387-010	INSPECTOR, PACKAGING MATERIALS (pharmaceut.)	3324	33343333354	LNNNNNNFFNNNNNNFFON	NNNN3NNNNNNNN	J,T	212	474	06.03.01	7820	000000	83005
920.482-010	ICICLE-MACHINE OPERATOR (dairy products)	3224	34433444354	LNNNNNNFFONNNNONONON	NNNN4NNNNNNNN	R,T	041	383	06.02.15	7662	000000	92974
920.586-010	MASKING-MACHINE FEEDER (plastic-synth.)	2112	44443444354	MNNNNNNFFONNNNFNFNNN	NNNN4NNNNNNNN	R	011	492	06.04.02	8725	000000	98502
920.587-010	CLOTH-BOLT BANDER (textile)	2112	44444444455	MNNNNNNFFNNNNNFNNNN	NNNN4NNNNNNNN	R	041	420	06.04.38	8761	000000	98902
920.587-014	LABEL CODER (any industry)	2112	33444344444	LONONNNFFNNNNFNNNNN	NNNN4NNNNNNNN	R,T	054	470	06.04.26	8769	000000	98999
920.587-018	PACKAGER, HAND (any industry)	2122	44554343455	MNONNNNCCCNNONONONON	NNFN4NFNNNNNN	R	041	898	06.04.38	8761	000000	98902
920.587-022	SAMPLE CLERK, HANDKERCHIEF (garment)	2122	44443444455	LNNNNNNFFFNNNNNFNNNN	NNNN3NNNNNNNN	R,T	041	449	06.04.38	8761	080102	98902
920.587-026	MARKER, SEMICONDUCTOR WAFERS (electron. comp.)	2122	44434444455	LNNNNNNCCNNOONFNNNN	NNNN4NNNNNNNN	R,U	183	587	06.04.37	8769	000000	98999
920.665-010	CARTON-PACKAGING-MACHINE OPERATOR (tobacco)	2112	44443544345	MNNNNONFFNNOONFNFNNN	NNNN4NNNNNNNN	J,T	041	401	06.04.38	7662	000000	92974
920.665-014	RACK-ROOM WORKER (beverage)	2112	44443444354	MNNNNONFFNOONFNFNNN	NNNF4NNNNNNNN	R,T	041	395	06.04.38	7820	000000	83005
920.667-010	CIGARETTE-PACKAGE EXAMINER (tobacco)	2124	44443444354	LNNNNNNFFOONFNNNON	NNNN4NNNNNNNN	R,T	041	401	06.03.02	7820	000000	83005
920.667-014	SNUFF-CONTAINER INSPECTOR (tobacco)	2123	34433444455	LNNNNNNCCFNOONFNOONN	NNNN4NNNNNNNN	J,T	212	403	06.03.02	7820	000000	83005
920.680-010	FILLING-MACHINE SET-UP MECHANIC (food prep., nec)	3123	34433433354	LNNNNNNFFNNNNNNFOON	NNNN4NNNNNNNN	J,T	041	567	06.01.02	7462	000000	92997
920.684-010	CRATER (any industry)	3223	44544544345	MNNONFNFFONNNNFNFNNN	NNNN3NONNNNNN	R,T	041	454	06.04.38	8761	000000	98902
920.685-010	BALING-MACHINE TENDER (any industry)	2112	44544544345	HNNFNFNFFONNNNFNFNNN	NNNN4NNNNNNNN	R	041	410	06.04.38	7667	000000	92974
920.685-014	BANDER-AND-CELLOPHANER, MACHINE (tobacco)	2112	44445544355	LNNNNNNFFFNNNFNFNNN	NNNN4NNNNNNNN	R	041	402	06.04.38	7662	000000	92974
920.685-018	BB SHOT PACKER (ordnance)	2112	44444433355	LNNNNNNFFONNNNONONNN	NNNN4NNNNNNNN	R	041	374	06.04.38	7662	000000	92974
920.685-022	BLOCKER (tex. prod., nec)	2112	44544544345	MNNNNNNFFONNNNFNFNNN	NNNN4NNNNNNNN	R	061	474	06.04.38	7740	000000	93999
920.685-026	BOTTLE PACKER (beverage)	2112	44443544354	LNNNNNNFFFNNNFNFNNN	NNNN4NNNNNNNN	R	041	395	06.04.38	7662	000000	92974
920.685-030	CANDLE WRAPPING-MACHINE OPERATOR (fabrication, nec)	2112	44543544355	LNNNNNNCCNNNNCNONON	NNNN4NNNNNNNN	R	041	619	06.04.38	7662	000000	92974
920.685-034	CARDER (any industry)	2112	44545544355	LNNNNNNFFONNNNONONN	NNNN4NNONNNNN	R	041	618	06.04.38	7662	000000	92974
920.685-038	CASE PACKER AND SEALER (tobacco)	2123	44444433355	LNFNNNNFFONNNNFNFNNN	NNNN4NNNNNNNN	R,T	171	409	06.04.38	7662	000000	92974
920.685-042	CASE-LOADER OPERATOR (beverage)	2112	44443433355	LNNNNNNFFONNNNFNFNNN	NNNN4NNNNNNNN	R	041	585	06.04.37	7651	000000	92705
920.685-046	CIGAR BRANDER (tobacco)	2112	44543534455	MNNNNNNFFONNNNNONONN	NNNN4NNNNNNNN	R	041	401	06.04.38	7662	000000	92974
920.685-050	CIGARETTE-PACKING-MACHINE OPERATOR (tobacco)	2123	44543444345	LNNNNNNFFNNNFNFNNN	NNNN4NNNNNNNN	R	191	567	06.04.37	7662	000000	92974
920.685-054	COTTON-ROLL PACKER (protective dev.)	2112	44543544355	LNNNNNNFFNNNNONONNC	NNNN4NNNNNNNN	R,T	041	401	06.04.38	7662	000000	92974
920.685-058	FEED WEIGHER (grain-feed mills)	2112	44545544355	LNNNNNNFFNNNNNONFNNN	NNNN4NNONNNNN	R	041	604	06.04.38	7662	000000	92974
920.685-062	HYDRAULIC-PRESS OPERATOR (tobacco)	2122	44444444355	HNNNNNNFFONNNNONONNN	NNNN4NNONNNNN	R,T	041	381	06.04.38	7662	000000	92974
920.685-066	LABELING-MACHINE OPERATOR (recording)	2112	44444444455	LNNFNONNFFNNNNNFNFNNN	NNNN4NNNNNNNN	R	041	409	06.04.38	7662	000000	92974
920.685-070	LACE-ROLLER OPERATOR (leather prod.)	2123	44543534455	MNNNNNNFFONNNNFNFNNN	NNNN4NNNNNNNN	R	063	585	06.04.37	7662	000000	92705
920.685-074	PACKAGE SEALER, MACHINE (any industry)	2112	44544343345	MNNFNONFFNNONFNNN	NNNN4NNNNNNNN	R	163	529	06.04.38	7662	000000	92974
920.685-078	PACKAGER, MACHINE (any industry)	2112	44444433344	MNNONNNFCFONONFOFOON	NNNN4NNNNNNNN	R	041	551	06.04.38	7662	000000	92974

DOT #	DOT Title & Industry	Trng	Aptitude	Physical	Environment	Tempra	WkF	MPSMS	GOE	SOC	CIP	OES
920.685-082	PACKER OPERATOR, AUTOMATIC (tobacco)	2112	44444434355	LNNNNNNFFNNNNNFNFNNN	NNNN4NFNNNNNNN	R,T	041	409	06.04.15	7662	000000	92974
920.685-086	PACKING-MACHINE-PILOT CAN ROUTER (tobacco)	2112	44544544455	LNNNNNNFFNNNNNNNNNNN	NNNN4NNNNNNNNN	R	041	403	06.04.38	7662	000000	92974
920.685-090	ROLL FINISHER (paper & pulp)	2112	44544444355	HNNOONNFFNNNNNFNFNNN	NNNN4NNNNNNNNO	R	041	470	06.04.38	7662	000000	92974
920.685-094	SNUFF-PACKING-MACHINE OPERATOR (tobacco)	2112	44544444455	LNNNNNNFFONNNNONONNN	NNNN4NFNNNNNNN	R	041	403	06.04.38	7662	000000	92974
920.685-098	TOBACCO-PACKING-MACHINE OPERATOR (tobacco)	2123	34544544355	LNNNNNNFFNNNNNONFNNN	NNNN4NNNNNNNNN	R,T	041	403	06.04.38	7662	000000	92998
920.685-102	WRAPPER (metal prod., nec)	2123	44444444355	LNNONONFFNNNNNFNNNNN	NNNN4NNNNNNNNN	R	163	557	06.04.38	7679	000000	92974
920.685-106	CUBING-MACHINE TENDER (concrete prod.)	2112	44433434355	HONONNNFFONNNNFFFNNF	NNNN4NNNNNNNNN	R	041	536	06.04.38	7662	000000	92974
920.685-110	BUNDLE TIER AND LABELER (saw. & plan.)	2112	44444544345	MNNNNNNCCNNONONONNN	NNNN3NONNNNNNN	R	041	452	06.04.38	7662	000000	92974
920.685-114	COTTON BALER (agriculture)	2223	34444434355	MNNNNNFFONOONONONNN	NNNN4NFNNNNNNN	R,T	041	302	03.04.01	7662	000000	92974
920.686-010	BANDER-AND-CELLOPHANER HELPER, MACHINE (tobacco)	2112	44544544455	LNNNNNNFFONNNNNONFNNN	NNNN4NNNNNNNNN	R	041	402	06.04.38	8618	000000	98999
920.686-014	COTTON-BALL BAGGER (protective dev.)	2112	44444433355	LNNNNNNFFNNNNNFNFNNN	NNNN4NNNNNNNNN	R	041	604	06.04.05	8725	000000	98502
920.686-018	FOLDING-MACHINE FEEDER (tex. prod., nec)	1112	44544534355	LNNNNNNFFOFNNNOFNNNN	NNNN4NNNNNNNNN	R	062	420	06.04.36	8725	000000	98502
920.686-022	ORDER FILLER, LINSEED OIL (oils & grease)	2112	44444444345	MNNNNNFFNNNNNONFNNN	NNNN4NNNNNNNNN	R	041	499	06.04.40	8725	000000	98502
920.686-026	PACKING-FLOOR WORKER (tobacco)	2112	44444444355	MNNNNNNCCFNNNNNNNNNN	NNNN3NNNNNNNNN	R	011	402	06.04.38	8725	000000	98502
920.686-030	PACKING-MACHINE CAN FEEDER (tobacco)	2112	44444434355	MNNNNNNCCFNNNNNNONN	NNNN4NNNNNNNNN	R	041	409	06.04.09	8725	000000	98502
920.686-034	PAD-MACHINE FEEDER (saw. & plan.)	1112	44444434354	LNNNNNNFFNNNNNNNNNNN	NNNN4NONNNNNNN	R	041	459	06.04.38	8725	000000	98502
920.686-038	POLY-PACKER AND HEAT-SEALER (protective dev.)	2112	44444434355	LNNNNNNFFFNNNONFNNN	NNNN4NNNNNNNNN	R,T	041	604	06.04.38	8725	000000	98502
920.686-042	PRESS BUCKER (any industry)	1111	44444443355	HNNNNNNFFNNNNNFNFNNN	NNNN4NNNNNNNNN	R	163	414	05.12.03	8725	000000	98502
920.686-046	SPOOLER, SEQUINS (plastic prod.)	2112	44544533345	LNNNNNNFFNNNNNFNFNNN	NNNN3NNNNNNNNN	R	041	510	06.04.38	8725	000000	98502
920.686-050	TRAY FILLER (tobacco)	2112	45444543455	LNNNNNNFFNNNNNFNNNN	NNNN3NNNNNNNNN	R	041	402	06.04.38	8725	000000	98902
920.687-010	APPLE-PACKING HEADER (agriculture)	2112	44544544455	LNNNNNNFFNNNNNONOONN	ONNN4NNNNNNNNN	R	041	305	09.05.10	8724	080601	98799
920.687-014	BAGGER (retail trade)	1111	44444433355	MNNFNNNFFNNNNONOONN	ONNN3NNNNNNNNN	R	041	881	06.04.35	8761	200301	98902
920.687-018	BAGGER (garment; laundry & rel.)	1112	44444544355	MNNNNNFFFNNNNFNFNNN	NNNN4NNNNNNNNN	R	041	906	06.04.38	8761	000000	98902
920.687-022	BALE SEWER (agriculture)	1111	44444433355	MNNNNNFFFNNNFNFNNN	NNNN4NNNNNNNNN	R	062	309	06.04.38	8761	000000	98902
920.687-026	BANDER, HAND (paper goods)	1111	44443443355	LNNONNNFFNNNNNNNNNNN	NNNN4NNNNNNNNN	R	041	474	06.04.38	8761	000000	98902
920.687-030	BANDER, HAND (tobacco)	2112	44454443355	SNNNNNNCCNNNNCNNNNNN	NNNN4NNNNNNNNN	R	041	402	06.04.38	8761	000000	98902
920.687-034	BANDOLEER PACKER (ordnance)	1111	44444433355	LNNNNNNCCFNNNNONOFNNN	NNNN4NNNNNNNNN	R	041	374	06.04.26	8761	480103	98902
920.687-038	BLUEPRINT TRIMMER (any industry)	2112	44443443354	LNNFNNNFFNNNNNFNFNNN	NNNN4NNNNNNNNN	R	041	897	06.04.38	8761	000000	98902
920.687-042	BOTTLING-LINE ATTENDANT (beverage)	1111	44443443455	MNNNNNNFFNNNNNFNFNFN	NNNN4NNNNNNNNN	R	041	531	03.04.04	8769	010603	98999
920.687-046	BUNDLER, SEASONAL GREENERY (forestry)	2112	44444444355	MNNFOONFFFNNNNNFNFN	FNNN4NNNNNNNNN	R	041	312	06.03.02	7820	000000	83005
920.687-050	CAN INSPECTOR (beverage; can. & preserv.)	2123	44444433355	LNNNNNNFFNNNNNFNFON	NNNN4NNNNNNNNN	R,T	212	551	06.04.28	7840	000000	83005
920.687-054	CAN PATCHER (can. & preserv.)	2222	44444433355	LNNNNNNCCFNNNNCNFNNN	NNNN3NNNNNNNNN	R	212	551	06.03.02	8769	000000	99999
920.687-058	CAN RECONDITIONER (can. & preserv.)	2123	44543544354	LNNONNNFFNNNNFNFNON	NNNN4NFNFNNNNN	R,T	031	446	06.04.27	8769	000000	98999
920.687-062	CARDBOARD INSERTER (knitting)	1111	44544544354	LNNNNNNCCONNNNNNNNNN	NNNN3NNNNNNNNN	R	041	604	06.04.38	8769	000000	98999
920.687-066	CARRIER PACKER (protective dev.)	2112	44544544355	MNNNNNFFNNNNNONFNNN	NNNN3NNNNNNNNN	R	041	475	06.04.38	8761	000000	98902
920.687-070	CARTON INSPECTOR (tobacco)	2112	34443444454	LNNNNNNCCFNNNNNNNNON	NNNN4NNNNNNNNN	R,T	212	302	06.03.02	7820	000000	83005
920.687-074	COTTON TIER (agriculture)	2223	44534534345	MNNNNNNCCFNNNNNNNNON	NNNN3NNNNNNNNN	R	041	460	03.04.01	8761	000000	98902
920.687-078	CRATE LINER (furniture)	1112	44543543455	MNNNNNNFFNNNNNFNFNNN	NNNN3NNNNNNNNN	R	061	604	06.04.34	8761	000000	98902
920.687-082	DENTAL FLOSS PACKER (protective dev.)	2112	44443443354	LNNNNNNFFNNNNNFNFNNN	NNNN4NNNNNNNNN	R,T	041	331	06.04.28	8761	000000	98902
920.687-086	FISH PACKER (can. & preserv.)	2112	44444443455	HNNONNNFFNNNNNONFNON	NNNN4NNNNNNNNN	R	041	393	06.04.38	8761	000000	98902
920.687-090	FLOOR WORKER (sugar & conf.)	2112	44455543344	LNNNNNNCCFNNNNNONNNN	NNNN4NNNNNNNNN	R	041	319	06.04.38	8761	010603	98902
920.687-094	GREENS TIER (wholesale tr.)	1111	44453533355	MNNNNNNCCFNNNNNNNNON	NNNN3NNNNNNNNN	R	062	449	06.04.27	8761	200303	98999
920.687-098	HANDKERCHIEF FOLDER (garment)	2112	44444434355	LNNNNNNFFFNNNNNNFNNN	NNNN4NNNNNNNNN	R	041	409	06.04.28	8769	000000	98902
920.687-102	HOGSHEAD OPENER (tobacco)	2122	44545533355	LNNNNNNCCNNNNNNNNNNN	NNNO4NONNNNNNN	R	041	531	06.04.39	8769	000000	98902
920.687-106	LABEL REMOVER (beverage)	2112	44444533355	MONONNNFFNNNNNFNFNNN	NNNN4NNNNNNNNN	R	031	454	06.04.38	8761	000000	98902
920.687-110	LINE-OUT WORKER I (tobacco)	2122	43444344454	HONONNNFFNNNNNNONNNN	NNNN4NNNNNNNNN	R	072	409	06.04.38	8761	000000	98902
920.687-114	LINE-OUT WORKER II (tobacco)	2112	44444543355	LNNNNNNCCFNNNNFNONON	NNNN4NNNNNNNNN	R	041	440	05.09.01	8761	000000	99999
920.687-118	LINEN-SUPPLY LOAD-BUILDER (laundry & rel.)	2122	44444543355	LNNNNNNCCFNNNNCNONON	NNNN4NNNNNNNNN	R	221	440	05.09.01	8761	000000	98902
920.687-122	MACHINE-PACK ASSEMBLER (ordnance)	1112	44444444354	LNNNNNNCCONNONONOOON	NNNN4NNNNNNNNN	R	061	374	06.04.37	8769	000000	98999
920.687-126	MARKER II (any industry)	2112	44443433355	LNNNNNNCCONNONONOOON	NNNN4NNNNNNNNN	R	192	541	06.04.38	8761	000000	98902
920.687-130	PACKER (tobacco)	2112	44443433355	MNNONNNCCFNNNNFNFNNN	NNNN4NNNNNNNNN	J,T	041	403	06.04.38	8761	000000	98902

DOT #	DOT Title & Industry	Trng	Aptitude	Physical	Environment	Tempra	WkF	MPSMS	GOE	SOC	CIP	OES
920.687-134	PACKER, AGRICULTURAL PRODUCE (agriculture)	2112	4444443353	MNNFNFNFFONNNNONON	NNNN3NNNNNNNNN	R	041	300	03.04.01	8761	010401	98902
920.687-138	PAPER INSERTER (glass mfg.)	1112	44545522255	LNNFNNNFFNNNNNNNN	NNNN4NNNNNNNNN	R	041	531	06.04.38	8769	000000	98999
920.687-142	PRIZER (tobacco)	2112	44454445445	MNNNNNNNCCNNNNFNFNNN	NNNN4NFNNNNNNNN	R	041	403	06.04.38	8761	000000	98902
920.687-146	REPACK-ROOM WORKER (beverage)	2122	44445344445	LNNOOONCCNNNNFNFNNN	NNNN4NNNNNNNNNN	R	041	395	06.04.38	8761	000000	98902
920.687-150	ROSIN-BARREL FILLER (chemical)	1111	44544544455	LNNNNNFFNNNNNNFNNN	NNNN4NNNNNNNNNN	R	041	496	06.04.36	8761	000000	98902
920.687-154	SAMPLE WORKER (any industry)	3123	34444433354	LNNNNNNCCNNNNFNNFON	NNNN2NNNNNNNNN	R,T	062	420	06.04.38	4754	000000	58017
920.687-158	SHINGLE PACKER (saw. & plan.)	2112	45444534355	HNNNNNNCCONNNNNNOONN	NNNN4NFNNNNNNNN	R	041	452	06.04.38	8761	000000	98902
920.687-166	SHOE PACKER (boot & shoe)	2112	44444444355	LNNNNNNCCNNNNFNFNNN	NNNN3NNNNNNNNN	R	041	522	06.04.38	8761	480304	98902
920.687-170	SHOT BAGGER (ordnance)	2112	44544544355	LNNNNNFFNNNNNONNNN	NNNN3NNNNNNNNN	R	041	374	06.04.36	8761	000000	98902
920.687-174	SNUFF-BOX FINISHER (tobacco)	2112	44444544455	LNNNNNNCCNNNNCNONONNN	NNNN3NNNNNNNNN	R	063	403	06.04.38	8761	000000	98902
920.687-178	STENCILER (any industry)	1112	44444544354	LONNNNNCCNNNNNFNNNON	ONNN3NONNNNNNNN	R	191	898	06.04.37	7756	000000	93947
920.687-182	STERILIZER (beverage)	2112	44544544355	HNNNNNFFNNNNNNONFNNN	NNNN3NFNNNNNNNN	R	031	459	06.04.39	8750	000000	98905
920.687-186	TABLE-COVER FOLDER (tex. prod., nec)	2112	44543534355	LNNNNNNNCCNNNNNNNNN	NNNN3NNNNNNNNN	R	062	435	06.04.27	8769	000000	98999
920.687-190	TIE BINDER (garment)	2112	44544544355	LNNNNNNNCCNNNNNNNN	NNNN4NNNNNNNNN	R	041	442	06.04.38	8769	200303	98999
920.687-194	VACUUM TESTER, CANS (can. & preserv.)	1112	44544544455	LNNONNNCCNNNCNONONNN	NNNN3NNNNNNNNN	R,T	221	380	06.03.02	7830	000000	83005
920.687-198	WOOL SACKER (agriculture)	2112	44544544445	MMNFNFNFFNNNNNNFNNN	NNNN4NFNNNNNNNN	R	041	414	03.04.01	8761	000000	98902
920.687-202	WORM PACKER (agriculture)	1111	45444533355	LNNNNNNNFFONNNNNNNNN	NNNN3NNNNNNNNN	R	041	329	03.04.01	5617	000000	79999
921.130-010	RIGGING SUPERVISOR (construction)	4338	33333333345	MFFOOONFFOFFNFFFNNF	FNNN4NNNNNNNNNF	V,D,P,J	011	567	05.11.01	6000	490202	81002
921.131-010	HOOK TENDER (logging)	3227	33324444445	LFFFFFNFFONFFNFFNNF	CNNN4NNNNNNNNNNF	V,D,P,S,J	011	451	05.12.04	5710	030405	72002
921.132-010	TRACK SUPERVISOR (grain-feed mills)	3224	33434444355	LONNNNNFFONFFNOFFONO	NNNN4NFNNNNNNNN	D,P	011	565	05.12.01	8120	490299	81011
921.133-010	CRANE-CREW SUPERVISOR (any industry)	4237	33333334355	LNNNNNNOOONFFNFFFFNF	FNNN4NNNNNNNNNN	V,D,P,J,T	011	565	05.11.04	7100	490202	81008
921.133-014	LOAD-OUT SUPERVISOR (mine & quarry)	3234	33344444445	MFNOOONOOONFFNOFFNNF	FNNN4NNNNNNNNNN	V,D,P,J	011	345	05.12.01	8120	490299	81011
921.133-018	MATERIAL-HANDLING SUPERVISOR (any industry)	4237	*33334334355	LNNNNNNFFONFFOOONO	ONNN4NNNNNNNNNN	V,D,P,J	011	565	05.12.01	7100	490299	81008
921.137-010	COAL-YARD SUPERVISOR (any industry)	4338	33333344455	LNNNNNNFFFNFFNFFNNF	NNNN4NFNNNNNNNN	V,D,P,J	011	341	05.12.01	7100	490299	81008
921.137-014	MATERIAL-CREW SUPERVISOR (construction; mfd. bldgs.)	4237	33433444345	MONONNNNFFONONFNNF	FNNN4NNNNNNFNNF	V,D,P,J	221	554	05.11.04	8319	490299	81008
921.260-010	RIGGER (any industry)	4226	33433443345	HFOFFOOFFONOONFFNOF	FNNN4NNNNNNNNNF	V,T	011	565	05.11.04	6177	490202	85635
921.364-010	RIGGING SLINGER (logging)	3125	33434534345	MFFONNNFFNFFNFFFNNF	CNNN4NNNNNNNNNF	J,P,S	011	451	05.12.04	5790	030405	73099
921.365-010	GRAIN RECEIVER (grain-feed mills)	2212	34343344355	LFNNNNNFFOOONFNNNN	NNNN4NFNNNNNNNN	J,T	212	301	06.03.01	7840	490299	83005
921.382-010	CONVEYOR OPERATOR, PNEUMATIC SYSTEM (food prep., nec)	3224	33344433444	LONOOOFFFNNNNFNFNON	ONNN4NNNNNNNNNN	J,T	014	567	05.06.04	8319	490299	83005
921.563-010	COKE LOADER (steel & rel.)	3225	33433434454	MOOOONNFFNNOONFFNON	NNNN4NFNNNNNNNN	V,T	011	505	05.11.04	8319	490299	97989
921.565-010	CEMENT LOADER (cement)	2112	44444444345	HFNOONFFNOONFNNNN	ONNN4NFNNNNNNNN	V,T	014	533	06.04.40	8319	490299	97989
921.583-010	TRANSFER-CAR OPERATOR, DRIER (nonmet. min.)	2112	44444434335	HNNONNNFFFNOONFFNNN	NNON3NFNNNNNNNN	R,T	011	538	05.11.04	8318	490299	97947
921.662-010	CAR-DUMPER OPERATOR (beverage)	3114	34444434355	LONONNNFFNOONFFNNN	ONNN4NNNNNNNNNN	R	011	381	05.11.04	8319	490299	97989
921.662-014	CHARGE-MACHINE OPERATOR (chemical)	3235	33444443455	LONONNNFFFNFFNFNNF	NNNN3NNNOONNNN	J,T	011	559	06.02.11	8319	000000	97989
921.662-018	CONVEYOR-SYSTEM OPERATOR (any industry)	3223	33444334455	MNNNNNNFFONFFONNNO	NNNN4NNNNNNNNNN	R,T	011	300	05.12.04	8319	490202	97951
921.662-022	MARINE RAILWAY OPERATOR (ship-boat mfg.)	3224	34434534355	HOOOOOFFNNNFFNNNNO	NNNN4NNNNNNNNNN	R,T	011	593	05.11.04	8314	490299	97951
921.663-010	OVERHEAD CRANE OPERATOR (any industry)	3225	34434534335	LONONONFFONOOONFCNNF	FNNN4NNNNNNFNNF	R	011	452	05.12.04	8315	490202	97944
921.663-014	CHERRY-PICKER OPERATOR (construction)	2113	44434434345	MNNNNNNFFNOONFNNNN	NNNF4NFNNNNNNNF	R,S	011	969	05.11.04	8315	000000	97944
921.663-018	CHIP UNLOADER (paper & pulp)	2113	44434434345	MFONNNNFFNOONFFNNNF	FNNN4NNNNNNNNNN	R,T	011	459	05.11.01	8319	490299	97989
921.663-022	DERRICK OPERATOR (mine & quarry)	3114	34434534335	MONNNNNCNNNNNNCCNNC	ONNN4NNNNNNNNNN	R,T	011	565	05.11.02	8315	490299	97941
921.663-026	HOIST OPERATOR (mine & quarry)	3124	34434534334	MMNNNNNCCNNOONFFNOF	NNNN3NNNNNNNNN	R,T	011	565	05.11.02	8314	490202	97941
921.663-030	HOISTING ENGINEER (any industry)	3114	34434534334	MONOONFFONOONFFNOF	ONNN4NNNNNNNNNN	R,T	011	586	05.11.04	8314	490202	97941
921.663-034	IRRADIATED-FUEL HANDLER (chemical)	3115	34433433345	MMNONNNFFNNMMOFFNNF	NNNN4NFNNNNNNNN	R,T	011	559	05.11.04	8319	490202	97989
921.663-038	LOCOMOTIVE-CRANE OPERATOR (any industry)	3125	34434534335	MONOONOFFOOOONOFFNNF	ONNN4NONNNNNNNF	R,T	011	563	05.11.04	8315	000000	97944
921.663-042	MONORAIL CRANE OPERATOR (any industry)	2113	34434434334	LVNONONNFFNOONOFFNOF	NNNN4NNNNNNNNNN	R,T	011	565	06.04.40	8315	490202	97944
921.663-046	PNEUMATIC-HOIST OPERATOR (construction; mfd. bldgs.)	2113	44433534345	VONOOONFFFNNNVNFNNN	NNNN4NNNNNNNNNC	R,T	011	361	05.11.01	8314	490202	97941
921.663-050	SCRAPER-LOADER OPERATOR (mine & quarry)	3124	34434534334	HONFOFNFFNNNNNOFFNON	ONNN4NFNNNNNNNN	R,T	011	565	05.11.02	8314	490202	97941
921.663-054	TOWER-CRANE OPERATOR (construction)	3125	34434533335	LONNNNNFFNNNNOCFNNN	NNNN3NNNNNNNNNN	R,T	011	565	05.11.01	8315	490202	97944
921.663-058	TRACTOR-CRANE OPERATOR (any industry)	3114	34434434335	MONNNNNCNNNNNOCCNNC	ONNN4NNNNNNNNNN	R,T	011	563	05.11.04	8315	490202	97944
921.663-062	TRUCK-CRANE OPERATOR (any industry)	3115	34434534335	MONNNNNCCONOONOFFNNF	ONNN4NONNNNNNNN	R,T	011	565	05.11.04	8315	490202	97944

DOT #	DOT Title & Industry	Trng	Aptitude	Physical	Environment	Tempra	WkF	MPSMS	GOE	SOC	CIP	OES
921.663-066	YARDING ENGINEER (logging)	3126	33433433335	LONNNNNCCFNNCNFFNNF	NNNN4NNNNNNNNN	J	011	451	05.11.04	8314	030405	97941
921.663-070	TRUCK LOADER, OVERHEAD CRANE (nonfer. metal)	2124	44444434345	MNNNNNNFFNNNNNNOFFNNF	NNNN4NNNNNNNNN	R	011	544	05.11.04	8315	490299	97944
921.664-010	LINE MOVER (railroad equip.)	3113	44434534355	MNNNONNNFFNNFNNNNFFNNN	FNNN4NNNNNNNNN	R,T	011	594	05.12.04	8319	490299	97989
921.664-014	RIGGER (logging)	3225	34435544345	VFFFFNFFNNNNNNFFNNF	CNNN4NNFNNNNNNN	R,T	011	451	05.12.04	5790	030405	85935
921.665-010	CEMENT-BOAT-AND-BARGE LOADER (cement)	2112	44433444345	VNNNFFNFFNNNNNNNNNN	CNNN3NNNNNNNNN	R	014	533	05.12.06	8319	490299	97989
921.667-010	BOAT-HOIST-OPERATOR HELPER (retail trade)	1112	44444534355	HNNOOOOFFNNOONNOONNO	CNNN4NNNNNNNNN	R	011	593	05.12.04	8769	490299	98999
921.667-014	CHASER (logging)	2113	44544534335	HFFFFFNFFNNFFNNFFNNF	CNNN4NCNNNNNNNC	R,S	011	451	05.12.04	5790	030405	73099
921.667-018	DUMPER (any industry)	2112	44434534344	HFNFNFNFFONOONFFFNOF	FNNN4NFNNNNNNN	R	011	859	05.12.03	8726	490299	97989
921.667-022	LABORER, HOISTING (any industry)	2113	44544544335	MFOFOONFFNFFNOFFNNF	FNNN4NNNNNNNNN	R	011	541	05.12.04	8726	490299	98799
921.667-026	WHARF WORKER (water trans.)	1112	44544544335	MNNNNNNNFFNNOONNFFNNF	CNNN4NNNNNNNNN	R	011	301	05.12.03	8726	000000	98799
921.682-010	LOADER, MALT HOUSE (beverage)	2113	34433533335	MONOOONFFONNNNNFFNNN	NNFO3NFNONNNN	V	011	395	05.12.04	8319	490299	97989
921.682-014	PALLETIZER OPERATOR I (any industry)	3114	33433444355	LNNONNNFFNNNNFNFNNN	NNNN4NNNNNNNNN	J,T	011	565	06.04.40	8319	490299	97951
921.682-018	STACKER-AND-SORTER OPERATOR (saw. & plan.)	2113	44434534345	MNNNNNNCCNNNNNNFNON	NNNN4NNNNNNNNN	R	011	450	05.12.04	8319	490299	97941
921.682-022	TRANSFER CONTROLLER (saw. & plan.)	2113	44444534334	MNNNNNNCCNNNNNNFFNON	CNNN3NNNNNNNNN	R,T	011	593	05.11.04	8314	490299	97941
921.683-010	BOAT-HOIST OPERATOR (retail trade)	3113	34434434335	HONOOOOFFONNNNOFFNNF	FNNN4NFNNNNNNN	R,T	011	593	05.11.04	8319	000000	97941
921.683-014	BOOM-CONVEYOR OPERATOR (any industry)	2113	34434434355	LONNNNNFFNNONNFFNNF	FNNN4NFNNNNNNN	T	011	351	05.12.04	8319	490299	97951
921.683-018	CANTILEVER-CRANE OPERATOR (water trans.)	3225	34434534335	LONNNNNFFNNNNFFFNNF	ONNN4NNNNNNNNN	R,T	011	565	05.11.04	8315	490299	97944
921.683-022	COAL-EQUIPMENT OPERATOR (utilities)	3234	33434434335	MONNNNNFFONNONFFFNNF	FNNN4NFNNNNNNNF	R	011	341	05.11.02	8319	490299	97989
921.683-030	CUPOLA HOIST OPERATOR (foundry)	3124	34534534335	LNNNNNNCCNNNNNNCCNNC	NNON4NNNNNNNNN	R,T	011	350	06.04.40	8314	490299	97941
921.683-034	DERRICK-BOAT OPERATOR (water trans.)	3125	34434534335	HNNONNNCCNNNNNCCNNNC	ONNN4NNNNNNNNN	R,T	011	565	05.12.04	8315	490299	97944
921.683-038	ELEVATOR OPERATOR, FREIGHT (any industry)	2112	44444444445	LNNNNNNFFNNNNNFFFNNN	NNNN4NNNNNNNNN	R	011	969	05.12.04	5245	490299	67011
921.683-042	FRONT-END LOADER OPERATOR (smelt. & refin.)	2113	34434333335	MONNNNNCCONNONOFOFNC	FNNN4FCONNNNNNN	R,T	011	456	05.11.04	8318	490299	97947
921.683-046	HYDRAULIC-BOOM OPERATOR (any industry)	2113	44434534355	MONNNNNCCONNNNNNCCNNN	NNNN4NCONNNNNNN	R	011	565	06.04.40	8314	490299	97941
921.683-050	INDUSTRIAL-TRUCK OPERATOR (any industry)	2113	44434434334	MONONONCCFNNONOFFOOF	FNNN4NNNNNNNNO	R,T	011	450	06.04.40	8318	490299	97947
921.683-054	JAMMER OPERATOR (logging)	2113	34534534435	LNNNNNNCCNNNNNNCCNNN	CNNN4NNNNNNNNN	R	011	451	05.11.04	8314	030405	97941
921.683-058	LOG LOADER (logging)	3124	34434535335	LNNNNNNCCNNNNNNOCCNNC	NNNN4NFCNNNNNNN	R,T	011	451	05.11.04	8314	030405	97941
921.683-062	SKIP OPERATOR (steel & rel.)	2224	34433434335	LNNNNNNFFNNNNNFFFNNF	ONON4NFNNNNNNN	R,T	011	350	05.11.04	8319	490299	97989
921.683-066	SORTING-GRAPPLE OPERATOR (logging)	3126	33434434335	LONNNNNCCONNCNOCCNOC	NNNN4NNNNNNNNN	J,T	011	565	06.04.40	8315	030404	97944
921.683-070	STRADDLE-TRUCK OPERATOR (any industry)	2113	44434434335	LONNNNNFFNNNNNFFNNF	FNNN4NNNNNNNNN	R	011	341	06.04.40	8319	490299	97947
921.683-074	TOWER-LOADER OPERATOR (water trans.)	3235	44434334335	LNNNNNNFFNNNNFFFNNN	ONNN4NNNNNNNNN	R,T	011	341	05.11.04	8315	490299	97944
921.683-078	TRANSFER-CAR OPERATOR (brick & tile)	2112	44534544335	MNNNNNNFFONNNNNNOONNO	NNNN3NNNNNNNNN	R	011	534	05.11.04	8319	490299	97947
921.683-082	WINCH DRIVER (water trans.)	3124	34434434355	LNNNNNNFFNNNNNFFNNF	CNNN3NNNNNNNNN	R	011	565	05.11.04	8314	490299	97941
921.683-086	YARD WORKER (ship-boat mfg.)	2114	34434434355	MFNFNNNFFNNNNFNFNNN	FNNN4NNNNNNNNN	R,T	011	593	05.12.04	8314	490202	97941
921.685-010	BOAT LOADER II (water trans.)	2113	34434434355	MNNNNNNFFONNNNOFFNNN	CNNN4NNNNNNNNN	R,T	011	351	05.12.04	8314	490299	97941
921.685-014	BULL-CHAIN OPERATOR (saw. & plan.)	2112	44444444455	LNNNNNNFFONNNNNFNNNN	NNNN4NNNNNNNNN	R	011	452	05.12.04	8319	030404	97989
921.685-018	CAGER OPERATOR (can. & preserv.)	2113	44444444455	MOOOONFFNNNNNNOFFFNNN	ONNN4NNNNNNNNN	R,T	011	387	06.04.40	8315	030404	97944
921.685-022	CHIP-BIN CONVEYOR TENDER (chemical; paper & pulp)	1112	44434534355	MOONNNNNFFONNNNNFFNNO	NNNN4NNNNNNNNO	R	011	451	06.04.40	8319	490299	97951
921.685-026	CONVEYOR TENDER (any industry)	2112	44434434345	MONNNNNNFFONNNNFNFNNN	NNNN4NNNNNNNNN	R	011	340	06.04.40	8319	490299	97951
921.685-030	COOKER LOADER (oils & grease)	1112	44544444455	LNNONNNFFNNNNNFNFNNN	NNNF4NFNNNNNNN	R	011	499	06.04.40	8319	490299	97951
921.685-034	DRIER-TAKE-OFF TENDER (elec. equip.)	2112	34434434355	LNNFNNNFFNNNNNONONNO	NNNN3NNNNNNNNN	R	011	589	06.04.40	8319	490299	97989
921.685-038	DUMP OPERATOR (any industry)	2113	44434434345	LNNONNNFFNNNNNFNFNNN	ONNN4NNNNNNNNN	R	011	300	05.11.04	8319	490299	97989
921.685-042	ELECTRIC-FORK OPERATOR (agriculture)	1112	44534544355	HONFOFNFFNNNNNNFNNF	CNNN4NNNNNNNNN	R	011	303	03.04.01	8314	490299	97941
921.685-046	FRUIT DISTRIBUTOR (agriculture)	2112	44434535445	MNNONNNNOONNNNNFFNNF	NNNN4NNNNNNNNN	R,T	011	304	05.12.04	8319	010401	97951
921.685-050	PRODUCTION-SUPPLY-EQUIPMENT TENDER (food prep., nec)	3124	34333444355	MNNONNNFFONNNNNNFNNN	NNNN4NNNNNNNNN	R,T	011	301	06.04.15	8319	490299	97951
921.685-054	SORTER OPERATOR (saw. & plan.)	2114	34433443354	LNNNNNNFFFONNNFNFNON	FNNN4NNNNNNNNN	J	212	452	05.07.06	7850	030404	83005
921.685-058	SPOUT TENDER II (chemical)	2113	44534544445	LFFNNNNFFNNNNNNFFNNF	OOOO4NCNNFNNCN	J,T	011	347	05.12.04	8319	490299	97989
921.685-062	STACKER TENDER (millwork-plywood)	2113	44433444455	LNNNNNNFFONNNNNNFFFNNN	NNNN4NNNNNNNNN	R,T	011	453	06.04.40	8319	030404	97951
921.685-066	TRANSFER OPERATOR (paper & pulp)	2113	34433544344	MNNNNNNFFNNNNNNNNON	NNNN4NNNNNNNNN	R,T	011	451	06.04.40	7639	030404	92998
921.685-070	UNSCRAMBLER (can. & preserv.)	1112	44444444355	MNNNNNNFFONNNNFNNNN	NNNN4NNNNNNNNN	R,T	011	551	06.04.40	8319	000000	97951
921.686-010	CARTON-COUNTER FEEDER (tobacco)	1112	44544534454	LNNNNNNCCONNNNNNNNCN	NNNN4NNNNNNNNN	R	011	401	06.03.02	8725	000000	98502
921.686-014	CONVEYOR FEEDER-OFFBEARER (any industry)	1112	44444545255	MNNONNNFFCNNNNNNNONNN	NNNN4NNNNNNNNN	R	011	450	06.04.40	8725	000000	98502

DOT #	DOT Title & Industry	Trng	Aptitude	Physical	Environment	Tempra	WkF	MPSMS	GOE	SOC	CIP	OES
921.686-018	LOG-HAUL CHAIN FEEDER (paper & pulp; saw. & plan.)	2112	44544544535	HOOONONFFNNNNNNFNNN	CNNN3NNNNNNNNF	R	011	451	05.12.04	8725	000000	98502
921.686-022	POND WORKER (millwork-plywood; paper & pulp; saw. & plan.)	1112	44534534334	HNFFOFNFFNNNNNNFFNOF	CNNF3NNNNNNNNF	R	011	451	05.12.04	8725	030405	98502
921.687-010	CAR-DUMPER-OPERATOR HELPER (beverage)	2112	44444534355	MNNFNFNFFNNNNNNNNNN	ONNN3NFNNNNNNN	R	011	301	05.12.04	8726	000000	98799
921.687-014	CHOKE SETTER (logging)	1112	44544534335	VFFFFFFFNNNCNFNNF	CNNN4NNNNNNNNNF	R,S	011	451	05.12.04	5790	000000	73005
921.687-018	LOADER (mfd. bldgs.)	2123	44443444355	MOONFNNFFNNNNNFNONNN	ONNN3NNNNNNNNC	R	011	455	05.12.04	5790	490299	98799
921.687-022	LOG LOADER HELPER (logging)	1112	44534544445	MFFFFNFFNNNNNNFFNNF	CNNN4NCNNNNNNNC	R	011	451	05.12.04	8726	030405	98999
921.687-026	RIGGER HELPER (any industry)	2113	44544544445	HNNOOONFFNNNNNNFNFNF	FNNN4NNNNNNNNNF	R	011	360	05.12.04	8637	030405	98102
921.687-030	RIGGER, THIRD (logging)	1112	44544544445	VFFFFFNFFNNNNNNNFNNF	CNNN4NNNNNNNNNF	R	011	451	05.12.04	5790	030405	73099
921.687-034	WOOD HANDLER (paper & pulp)	1112	44434544355	MNNONNNFFNNNNNNNNNNN	CNNN3NNNNNNNNN	R	011	451	05.12.04	8769	000000	98999
922.137-010	SENIOR-COMMISSARY AGENT (air trans.)	4337	33344334355	MNNFFNFFONFFNFONNNN	NNNN3NNNNNNNNN	D,P,T,V	221	855	05.09.01	4525	000000	51002
922.137-014	SUPERVISOR, HIDE HOUSE (leather mfg.)	3227	33343433353	MNNONNNFFFFFNFNFOFN	NNNN3NCNNNNNNN	V,D,P,J	212	521	06.02.01	7100	000000	81008
922.137-018	SUPERVISOR, LOADING AND UNLOADING (any industry)	4226	33333344454	MNNNNNNFFFNFNFNNNN	ONNN4NNNNNNNNN	V,D,P,J	221	898	05.12.01	7100	490299	81008
922.137-022	SUPERVISOR, OPEN-HEARTH STOCKYARD (steel & rel.)	4228	33344344455	MNNNNNNFFNFNFNNNN	FNON4NFNNNNNNN	V,D,P,J	221	350	05.12.01	7100	490299	81008
922.137-026	WAREHOUSE TRAFFIC SUPERVISOR (wholesale tr.)	3225	33444444455	LNNNNNNFFFNFNFNNF	FNNN4NNNNNNNNN	D,P	011	302	05.12.01	8120	081199	81011
922.137-030	YARD SUPERVISOR (forestry)	3226	33333344454	LNNNNNNFFFNFNFNFNON	FNNN4NNNNNNNNN	V,D,P,J	221	312	05.09.01	7100	030404	81008
922.587-010	PRIMING-MIXTURE CARRIER (ordnance)	2122	44444344455	LNNNNNFFFNNNNNNFNNN	NNNN4NNNNNNNNNC	R	011	374	05.12.03	8769	490299	98999
922.665-010	FLUMER I (sugar & conf.)	2113	44444344355	LNNNNNFFNNOONNNNNNN	CNNF4NNNNNNNNN	R	011	309	06.04.40	8319	000000	97989
922.665-014	BIN TRIPPER OPERATOR (steel & rel.)	2113	44544544355	LNNNNNNFFFNFNFNNNN	NNON4NONNNNNNN	R	011	340	06.04.40	8319	490299	97989
922.667-010	YARD WORKER, USED BUILDING MATERIALS (retail trade)	2223	33443444445	MNNFOONFFONOONFNFNNN	FNNN4NNNNNNNNNF	R,T	221	530	05.09.01	8769	490299	98902
922.684-010	LOCKER-PLANT ATTENDANT (retail trade; wholesale tr.)	3124	34443443354	MNNNNNNFFFNNNNNFNFN	NFNN3NNNNNNNNF	V,T	221	380	05.09.01	8761	080799	98902
922.686-010	DUMPER (chemical)	1111	44544544345	HNNFNNNCCNNNNNNNNNN	ONNN3NNNNNNNNNC	R	011	499	06.04.40	8725	000000	98502
922.686-014	LOWERATOR OPERATOR (fabrication, nec)	1112	44444444355	MNNNNNNFFFNNNNFNNNN	NNNN3NNNNNNNNN	J,T	212	619	06.03.02	8725	000000	98502
922.687-010	BIN FILLER (tobacco)	1112	44545544455	LNNNNNNCCNNNNNNNNNN	NNNN3NNNNNNNNN	R	041	409	06.04.38	8761	000000	98902
922.687-014	BINDER-AND-WRAPPER PACKER (tobacco)	2112	44544544455	MNNNNNNFFNNNNNFNNN	NFNN3NNNNNNNNN	R	041	409	06.04.38	8761	000000	98902
922.687-018	BOBBIN SORTER (glass mfg.; plastic-synth.; textile)	2112	44544544455	LNNNNNNFFNNNNNFNNNN	NNNN4NNNNNNNNN	R,T	221	567	06.03.02	7850	000000	83005
922.687-022	BOLT LOADER (saw. & plan.)	1112	45545545445	MNNFNNNFFNNNNNNNNNN	CNNN4NNNNNNNNN	R	011	452	06.04.40	8726	000000	98799
922.687-026	BULL-GANG WORKER (tobacco)	1112	44544544455	VNNNNNNFFNNNNNNNNNN	NNNN4NNNNNNNNN	R	011	409	06.04.40	8726	000000	98799
922.687-030	CAN FILLER (tobacco)	1111	45544544455	MNNNNNNFFNNNNNNNNNN	NNNN3NNNNNNNNN	R	041	409	06.04.36	8769	000000	98999
922.687-034	CAR PINCHER (steel & rel.)	1111	44544544455	HNNFOONFFNNNNNNNNNN	CNNN4NNNNNNNNN	R	011	594	05.12.03	8726	000000	98799
922.687-038	COAL SAMPLER (utilities)	2112	44444544355	LFFNNNFFOONNNNNONONN	FNNN4NFNNNNNNN	R	041	341	05.12.03	7840	000000	83005
922.687-042	COTTON SAMPLER (agriculture; textile)	2112	44444444455	LNNONNNCCONNNNNNNNN	NNNN3NNNNNNNNN	R	221	414	06.04.27	7840	000000	58017
922.687-046	ICER (wholesale tr.)	1111	44444554355	HNNNNNNFFFNNNNNFNNN	NNNF3NNNNNNNNN	R	041	399	05.12.03	8761	000000	98902
922.687-050	INSTALLER (museums)	2112	44534534345	HOOONONFFONNNNFNNNN	NNNN3NNNNNNNNN	R	011	969	05.12.03	8726	000000	98799
922.687-054	LABORATORY-SAMPLE CARRIER (any industry)	2112	44444444354	LONOOONFFONNONOOONOO	ONNN3NNNNNNNNN	R	221	898	05.09.03	7840	000000	83005
922.687-058	LABORER, STORES (any industry)	2112	44444444444	MONFOFNFFNNONFNFOON	NNNN3NNNNNNNNN	R	221	898	05.09.01	8769	490299	98999
922.687-062	LABORER, WHARF (can. & preserv.)	1112	44444534345	HONONNNCCNNNNNNNNNN	OONF3NFNNNNNNN	R	011	386	06.04.40	8769	000000	98999
922.687-066	LAST PUTTER-AWAY (boot & shoe; rubber goods)	1112	44444444455	MNNONONFFNNNNNNFNNNN	NNNN4NNNNNNNNN	R	221	457	05.09.01	8769	480304	98999
922.687-070	LUMBER HANDLER (woodworking)	1112	44444444355	HNNFOONCCONNONNNNNNN	ONNN4NNNNNNNNN	R	011	451	05.12.03	8726	000000	98799
922.687-074	LUMBER SORTER (woodworking)	1112	44434444354	MNNFFNFFOFFNFNFNON	ONNN4NNNNNNNNNF	R	011	450	05.12.03	8724	000000	73099
922.687-078	PAPER STRIPPER (paper goods; print. & pub.)	1112	45435544454	MNNFFNNFFNNNNNFNNON	ONNN4NNNNNNNNN	J,T	212	450	06.03.02	7850	000000	83005
922.687-082	PULP PILER (logging)	1112	44434444354	HNNNNNNFFNNNNNFNNON	NNNN4NNNNNNNNNF	R	041	451	05.12.19	8724	000000	98799
922.687-086	RETURNED-GOODS SORTER (textile)	2122	44444444355	LNNFNNNFFNNNNNNNNNN	NNNN3NNNNNNNNN	R	011	420	06.03.02	7850	000000	83005
922.687-090	STEVEDORE II (water trans.)	2112	44544544335	VOOFOFNFFNNNNNNNNNN	FNNN4NNNNNNNNN	R	011	854	05.12.03	8723	490299	98702
922.687-094	TIMBER PACKER (saw. & plan.)	1112	44544544345	HFOONONFFNNNNNFNNNN	FNNN4NNNNNNNNN	R	011	450	05.12.03	8761	490299	98702
922.687-098	TIN STACKER (tinware)	1111	44544544345	HNNFNFNFFNNNNNNNNNN	NNNN5NNNNNNNNN	R	011	541	06.04.40	8726	000000	98799
929.131-010	YARD LABORER (paper & pulp)	1111	44544544345	HOOONNNFFNNNNNNFNNN	ONNN4NNNNNNNNNO	R	011	450	05.12.03	8769	000000	98999
929.131-014	SUPERVISOR, SALVAGE (petrol. refin.)	4337	33333333354	LNNFFONFFOFFNFNFNON	FNNN3NONNNNNNN	V,D,P,J	221	559	05.10.01	7100	000000	81008
929.132-010	SUPERVISOR, REACTOR FUELING (chemical)	4336	33333444444	LNNONNNFFOFONFNNON	NNNN4NONNNNNNN	D,J,P	011	543	05.12.01	8120	000000	81011
929.133-010	YARD SUPERVISOR (woodworking)	4337	33333334354	HNNNNNNFFOFOOO	CNNN4NNNNNNNNN	V,D,P,T	221	898	05.12.01	7100	490299	83005
929.137-010	GENERAL-HANDLING SUPERVISOR (smelt. & refin.)	4226	23233244455	LNNNNNNFFNFNFNFNNNN	FNNN3NNNNNNNNN	V,D,P,J	221	898	05.12.01	7100	490299	81008
929.137-014	POLEYARD SUPERVISOR (utilities)	4237	33333345445	LNNNNNNFFNFNFNFNNNN	FNNN4NNNNNNNNN	V,D,P,J	102	450	05.12.01	7100	000000	81008

DOT #	DOT Title & Industry	Trng	Aptitude	Physical	Environment	Tempra	WkF	MPSMS	GOE	SOC	CIP	OES
929.137-018	WAREHOUSE SUPERVISOR (motor trans.)	4337	34334434345	LNNOONNFFNFFNFNFNNN	NNNN3NNNNNNNNNNNN	V,D,P,J	011	853	05.12.01	7100	081199	81008
929.137-022	WAREHOUSE SUPERVISOR (any industry)	4337	33333344455	LNNONONFFNFFNFONONN	NNNN4NNNNNNNNNNN	V,D,P	221	898	05.09.01	7100	081199	81008
929.137-026	YARD SUPERVISOR (smelt. & refin.)	4237	22333244455	LNNNNNNFFNFFNFFONN	ONNN4NNNNNNNNNNN	V,D,P,J	221	898	05.12.01	7100	000000	81008
929.137-030	YARD SUPERVISOR, BUILDING MATERIALS OR LUMBER (retail trade; wholesale tr.)	4437	33343333345	MNNONONFFOFFNFOFONO	FNNN4NNNNNNNNNNN	V,D,P,J	221	450	05.12.01	7100	089999	81008
929.137-034	YARD SUPERVISOR, COTTON GIN (agriculture)	4336	33333334355	LNNNNNNFFNFNFNNNN	FNNN3NNNNNNNNNN	D,J	011	414	05.12.01	5621	000000	72002
929.367-010	PRESERVATION INSPECTOR, MARINE EQUIPMENT (government ser.)	4226	32433444454	MNNNNNNFFNOONFNFOON	NNNN3NNNNNNNNNN	J	151	379	05.03.09	7820	000000	83005
929.381-010	CARPET CUTTER (retail trade)	3225	34333433353	HNNFFFFFFNNNFNFFFN	NNNN3NNNNNNNNN	J,T	054	431	05.10.01	7753	469999	93332
929.382-010	LOAD-TEST MECHANIC (aircraft mfg.)	3236	34433433355	HOOOOONFFONNNFNFNNN	ONNN4NNFNONNNN	T	211	565	06.03.01	7830	000000	83005
929.583-010	YARD WORKER (agriculture)	3213	34434344335	MONONNNFFNNNFNFNNO	FNNN4NNNNNNNNN	R	013	302	05.11.04	8318	000000	97947
929.587-010	NUT-AND-BOLT ASSEMBLER (nut & bolt)	1112	44444533355	LNNOONNFFFNNNNNNNNN	NNNN4NNNNNNNNNN	R	061	555	06.04.38	8761	000000	98902
929.663-010	LOGGING-TRACTOR OPERATOR (forestry; logging; saw. & plan.)	3114	34434534334	MONOOONCCONOONOCCNOC	CNNN4NNNNNNNNNF	R,T	011	451	03.04.02	8318	030405	73008
929.683-014	TRACTOR OPERATOR (any industry)	3223	34433444335	MONOOONFFONNONFFFNNF	FNNN4NNNNNNNNN	R,T	003	562	05.11.04	8318	490202	97947
929.684-010	PACKER (ordnance)	2123	34433444344	MNNNONNFFNNNNONFNON	NNNN4NNNNNNNNN	R,T	041	372	06.04.38	8761	490299	98902
929.685-010	CRATE OPENER (furniture)	2112	44544544455	HNNNNNNFFONNNNNNNNN	NNNN3NNNNNNNNN	R	041	464	06.04.24	7667	490299	92971
929.685-014	TYING-MACHINE OPERATOR (paper goods; tex. prod., nec)	1112	44544444455	LNNNNNNFFNNFNNFFNNN	NNNN3NNNNNNNNN	R	041	436	06.04.38	7662	490299	92974
929.685-018	TYING-MACHINE OPERATOR, LUMBER (woodworking)	2112	44434434335	HONONONFFNNNNFNFNNN	NNNN4NNNNNNNNN	R	041	450	06.04.38	7662	490299	92974
929.686-014	BAND SALVAGER (agriculture)	1111	44544544455	LNNONONFFNNNNNNNNNN	NNNN4NNNNNNNNN	R	054	414	06.04.24	8769	000000	98999
929.686-018	CRAYON-SORTING-MACHINE FEEDER (pen & pencil)	2112	44444444453	LNNNNNNFFONNNFNFNFN	NNNN4NNNNNNNNN	R	041	617	06.04.09	8725	000000	98502
929.686-022	FEED-IN WORKER (grain-feed mills)	1112	45454544355	HNNNNNNFFNNNNNNNNNN	NNNN4NFNNNNNNNN	R	011	381	05.12.03	8725	000000	98502
929.687-010	CUTTER, BANANA ROOM (wholesale tr.)	2112	44444544344	MNNNNNNFFNNNNNNFNFN	NNNN4NNNNNNNNN	R	054	305	06.04.28	8769	000000	98999
929.687-014	KILN DRAWER (brick & tile)	2112	44443434344	HONFNNNFFOONNFNFNON	NNON4NONNNNNNNN	R	011	534	05.12.03	8769	490299	98999
929.687-018	LABORER, HIGH-DENSITY PRESS (agriculture)	1112	44544444455	LNNNNNNFFNNNNNNNNNN	NNNN4NNNNNNNNN	R	011	414	06.04.40	8769	000000	98999
929.687-022	LABORER, SALVAGE (any industry)	2112	44444444353	MNNFOFNFFNNNNFNFNN	NNNN4NONNNNNNN	R	221	898	06.04.40	8769	490299	98999
929.687-026	LINER INSERTER (tobacco)	1112	44544544355	LNNNNNNCCONNNNNNFNNN	NNNN3NNNNNNNNN	R	061	475	06.04.38	8769	490299	98999
929.687-030	MATERIAL HANDLER (any industry)	2113	44444444444	HOOOOOOFFNNONFNFNON	FOOO4NNNNNNNNNO	R	011	898	05.12.03	8726	490299	98799
929.687-034	MUNITIONS HANDLER (ordnance)	2112	44444444355	HNNFNONCCNNNNNONFNNN	ONNN4NNNNNNNNNC	R	011	370	06.04.40	8726	490299	98799
929.687-038	RETURNED-CASE INSPECTOR (beverage)	1112	44543544355	LNNFNNNFFNNNNNNNNN	NNNN5NFNNNNNNF	R,T	031	454	06.04.39	8769	000000	98999
929.687-042	ROLL COVERER, BURLAP (textile)	1112	44544544354	MNNFNNNFFNNNNNNNNN	FNNN4NNNNNNNNN	R	041	436	06.04.38	8761	000000	98902
929.687-046	SCALER-PACKER (meat products)	2123	44444444354	MNNNNNNFFNNNNNNNONN	CNNN4NNNNNNNNN	R,T	212	382	06.03.02	7840	490299	83005
929.687-050	WRAPPER COUNTER (tobacco)	2112	45444444455	LNNNNNNFFNNNNFNFNNN	FNNN4NNNNNNNNN	R	041	404	06.04.38	7850	490299	98902
929.687-054	PALLETIZER (nonfer. metal)	2222	44444434355	LNNNNNNFFOONNFNFNNN	ONNN3NNNNNNNNN	R,U	041	544	06.04.38	8761	490299	98902
929.687-058	BANDER, HAND (any industry)	2222	44444444455	HNNFFONCCONNNNNFFFN	NNNN4NONNNNNNN	R	041	453	06.04.38	8761	490299	98902
929.687-062	WEIGHER, PRODUCTION (any industry)	2123	44444444355	MNNNNNNFFNNONFNFONN	NNNN3NNNNNNNNN	R,T	212	490	06.03.02	6320	000000	83005
930.130-010	TOOL PUSHER (petrol. & gas)	4238	33333333355	LOONNNNFFNFFNFOFNNN	FNNN4NNNNNNNNN	V,D,P,J	005	564	05.02.05	6320	150903	81005
930.131-010	FIELD SUPERVISOR, OIL-WELL SERVICES (petrol. & gas)	4337	33333344355	LOONNNNFFNFFNFNFNNN	ONNN4NNNNNNNNN	V,D,P,J	005	564	05.02.05	6320	150903	81005
930.134-010	QUARRY SUPERVISOR, DIMENSION STONE (mine & quarry)	4336	44444444444	HFFNNNNFFNNFFFNON	FNNN5NFNNNNNNF	D,J,S	005	343	05.11.02	6320	000000	81005
930.167-010	TECHNICAL OPERATOR (petrol. & gas)	4336	22223344455	LNNOONNFFNNFFFNFNNN	FNNN4NNNNNNNNN	D,J	244	342	05.03.04	3833	150903	24511
930.261-010	FISHING-TOOL TECHNICIAN, OIL WELL (petrol. & gas)	4337	22223344355	LNNNNNNFFNFFNFNFNNN	CNNN4NNNNNNNNN	J	005	342	05.03.02	6560	150903	83002
930.261-014	FORMATION-TESTING OPERATOR (petrol. & gas)	4336	33333343354	LNNOONFFNOONFNFNFN	FNNN4NNNNNNNNN	V,J,T	212	342	05.07.05	6881	470399	83005
930.267-010	OIL-PIPE INSPECTOR (petrol. & gas)	4346	33333343354	LNNNNNNFFNOONFNFNON	ONNN3NNNNNNNNNO	J,T	005	564	05.07.01	7820	470399	83005
930.361-010	SERVICE-UNIT OPERATOR, OIL WELL (petrol. & gas)	3227	33333333355	LNNOONNFFNOONFNFNNN	FNNN4NNNNNNNNNO	J,T	005	342	05.11.03	6560	000000	87917
930.363-010	CLEAN-OUT DRILLER (petrol. & gas)	3225	33433234343	MNNOOONFFONONNFNFNO	CNNN5NNNNNNNNNF	R,T	212	369	05.07.01	8314	000000	97941
930.364-010	OIL-PIPE-INSPECTOR HELPER (petrol. & gas)	3215	33333334355	HNNFOFNFFONNNNFNFNN	FNNN5NFNNNNNNNF	R,T	342	342	05.07.01	8620	470399	98999
930.382-010	DRILLER, MACHINE (construction; mine & quarry)	3225	34434434345	HNNFOFNFFONNNNFNFNON	CNNN5NCNNNNNNNO	R,J	005	340	05.11.02	6540	490202	87943
930.382-014	PIPE TESTER (petrol. & gas)	3325	33333334334	MNNNNNNFFNNNNNNFFON	ONNN5NNNNNNNNNF	J,T	212	564	05.07.01	7830	470399	83005
930.382-018	PROSPECTING DRILLER (petrol. & gas)	3326	33333334344	MNNNNNNFFNNNNNFOFNOO	FNNN5NNNNNNNNF	J,T	005	342	05.11.03	6520	470399	87911
930.382-022	ROTARY DERRICK OPERATOR (petrol. & gas)	3225	33333433335	MFFONOOFFOONNNFOFNNO	CNNN4NNNNNNNNNF	V,T	005	342	05.11.03	6520	470399	87914
930.382-026	ROTARY DRILLER (petrol. & gas)	3226	33333433334	MOOONNNOFFFNNNNFNFNNO	CNNN5NNNNNNNNNF	J,T	005	342	05.11.03	6520	470399	87911
930.382-030	WELL PULLER (petrol. & gas)	3225	33333334355	HONNOONFFOONNNOFFNNO	CNNN5NONNNNNNNF	R,J,T	011	564	05.11.03	8314	470399	97941
930.383-010	CHANNELING-MACHINE RUNNER (mine & quarry)	3214	34434434334	MNNNNNNFFNNNNFNFFON	ONNN5NNNNNNNNF	J,T	052	343	05.11.02	6540	490299	87943
930.482-010	DRILLING-MACHINE OPERATOR (mine & quarry)	3216	34333434335	MNNOOOOFFNNNNFFNNF	NNNN5NFNNNNNNNF	J,T	005	340	05.11.02	6540	490299	87943

DOT #	DOT Title & Industry	Trng	Aptitude	Physical	Environment	Tempra	WkF	MPSMS	GOE	SOC	CIP	OES
930.662-010	LONG-WALL SHEAR OPERATOR (mine & quarry)	3225	34433534335	HNNOOONFFNNFFNNNCNNC	NNNN4NCNNNNNNNC	R	005	341	05.11.02	6540	490299	87943
930.663-010	SHALE PLANER OPERATOR (mine & quarry)	3234	33433534344	MONOOONFFFNNNNNFFNON	CNNF4NNNNNNNNNN	R	005	534	05.11.02	6540	490299	87943
930.664-010	CASER (petrol. & gas)	1113	44445534345	VOOOONNFFNNOONNNFNNN	CNNN5NNNNNNNNNC	R,S	102	369	05.12.12	6560	470399	87999
930.664-014	CLEAN-OUT-DRILLER HELPER (petrol. & gas)	2113	34433444355	HNNFFFNFFFNOONNNFNNN	CNNO5NNNNNNNNNN	R	005	369	05.12.02	8650	470399	87949
930.665-010	LONG-WALL-MINING-MACHINE TENDER (mine & quarry)	3225	44434433344	LNNNNNNFFNOFNFNFNFN	NNNN5NFNNNNNNNF	R,J,T	005	341	05.11.02	6540	490299	87949
930.666-010	DRILLER HELPER (construction; mine & quarry)	2222	44543534345	HONFFNNFFNNOONONFNNN	CNNN5NNNNNNNNNN	R	005	340	05.12.02	8650	490299	98319
930.666-014	TAILER (mine & quarry)	2113	44433534354	LNNNNNNFFFNFFNNNFNON	NNNN5NFNNNNNNNF	R,T	005	341	05.12.02	8650	490299	98323
930.667-010	SHALE PLANER OPERATOR HELPER (mine & quarry)	2112	44544544355	HOONFNNNFFNNOONNNNNNN	CFNF4NNNNNNNNNN	R,T	005	534	05.12.02	8650	490299	98319
930.682-010	CORE-DRILL OPERATOR (any industry)	3226	34443434345	MNNFOFNFFONNNNFNFNNN	FNNN4NNNNNNNNNN	R,T	005	340	05.11.02	6474	470399	87902
930.683-010	CONTINUOUS-MINING-MACHINE OPERATOR (mine & quarry)	3225	34443434345	MNNOOOOCCFNNNNFFFONF	NNNN5NCNNNNNNNN	R,S,T	005	341	05.11.02	6540	490299	87941
930.683-014	CUTTER OPERATOR (mine & quarry)	3226	34434434335	MNNFFFNFFNNNNNNFFNNN	NNNN5NCNNNNNNNF	R,T	005	341	05.11.02	6540	490299	87943
930.683-018	DERRICK WORKER, WELL SERVICE (petrol. & gas)	2113	44424544345	HFFFNFNFFNNNNNFFFNNN	NNNN5NCNNNNNNNF	R	011	342	05.11.03	8314	470399	97941
930.683-022	HARVESTER OPERATOR (chemical)	3114	44443534335	LNNNNNNFFONNNNFNFNNN	ONNN4NNNNNNNNNN	R,T	011	499	05.11.04	8316	470399	97923
930.683-026	ROOF BOLTER (mine & quarry)	3114	34433534335	MNNFNNNNFFFNNNNFFNNF	NNNN5NCNNNNNNNC	R,T	102	369	05.11.02	6560	490299	87923
930.684-010	FLAME CHANNELER (construction; mine & quarry)	2114	34433434355	MNNNNNNFFONNNNFNFFNN	CNNN5NCNNNNNNNC	J,T	005	340	05.11.02	6540	490299	87943
930.684-014	FLOOR WORKER, WELL SERVICE (petrol. & gas)	2113	44424544355	HNNFNFNFFNNNNNFNFNNN	CNNN5NNNNNNNNNN	R	121	342	05.12.02	6560	470399	87999
930.684-018	JACKHAMMER OPERATOR (mine & quarry)	2212	45544544345	HOOFOONFFNNNNNOOFNNF	FNNN5NFNNNNNNNF	R,T	005	340	05.12.02	6475	490202	87702
930.684-022	QUARRY PLUG-AND-FEATHER DRILLER (mine & quarry)	2114	34434444355	HOOFOONNFFNNNNNOOFNNF	CNNN5NCNNNNNNNN	R,T	005	343	05.12.02	6475	490299	87908
930.684-026	ROTARY-DRILLER HELPER (petrol. & gas)	2114	34434334344	HOOOOONFFOONNNFONNOF	CNNN5NCNNNNNNNNC	R,T	005	342	05.12.02	8650	490299	98323
930.685-010	MUD-PLANT OPERATOR (petrol. & gas)	3224	34344434355	HNNONONFFONNNNFNFNNN	CNNN4NNNNNNNNNN	R,T	143	345	05.11.03	7664	470399	92965
930.687-010	BOTTOM-HOLE-PRESSURE-RECORDING-OPERATOR HELPER (petrol. & gas)	2213	44544544355	MNNNNNNFFFNNNNFFNNF	FNNN3NNNNNNNNNN	R	011	602	05.12.03	8650	470399	98319
930.687-014	CORE-DRILL-OPERATOR HELPER (any industry)	2222	34444444355	HNNNNNNFFNNNNFNFNNN	FNNN4NNNNNNNNNN	R	005	340	05.12.02	8648	490299	98319
930.687-018	CUTTER-OPERATOR HELPER (mine & quarry)	2112	44544534345	HNNFOFNFFNNNNNNNNNNN	NNNN4NFNNNNNNNF	R,S	005	340	05.12.02	8769	490299	98999
931.261-010	BLASTER (mine & quarry)	4327	34434433344	MOOFFOFFNOONFFFOOF	FNNN5NFNNNNNNNF	J,S,T	005	342	05.10.06	6530	490299	87905
931.361-010	SAMPLE-TAKER OPERATOR (petrol. & gas)	3215	33333333333	MOONOOONFFNOONFNNON	FNNN4NNNNNNNNNN	R,T	005	342	05.12.02	6530	470399	87905
931.361-014	SHOOTER (petrol. & gas)	3226	33433433354	LNNNNNNNFFNFFNFNNNF	CNNN5NNNNNNNNNN	J,S,T	005	342	05.10.06	6530	470399	87905
931.361-018	SHOOTER, SEISMOGRAPH (petrol. & gas)	3226	33333334344	MNNOOOOFFNFNNFNFOFONN	FNNN5NNNNNNNNNN	V,S,T	005	342	05.10.06	6530	470399	87905
931.382-010	PERFORATOR OPERATOR, OIL WELL (petrol. & gas)	3226	33433434345	HONFOFOFONNNNFNFFON	FNNN3NNNNNNNNNO	V,J,T	005	369	05.11.03	6530	470399	87905
931.384-010	GUN-PERFORATOR LOADER (petrol. & gas)	3225	34433444345	VNNFFONFFNNNNFNFNNN	NNNN3NNNNNNNNNF	R,S,T	005	499	05.10.06	6560	470399	87999
931.664-010	TIER-AND-DETONATOR (mine & quarry)	2222	44444534445	MNNFONNFFNOONFFFNNN	CNNN5NON:NNNNNC	J	005	352	05.12.02	6530	490299	87905
931.667-010	POWDER LOADER (mine & quarry)	2222	44434434345	MNNFONNFFNOONFFFNNN	CNNN4NONNNNNNNN	J,T	005	352	05.12.02	8710	490299	98999
931.684-010	DUMPER-BAILER OPERATOR (petrol. & gas)	3215	33334434345	HONOOONFFFNNNFNFNNN	CNNN5NNNNNNNNNN	R,T	011	369	05.11.03	6560	470399	87999
932.132-010	BANK BOSS (mine & quarry)	4337	34433444355	LNNOOONFFFFNFFFNOFNNO	FNNN4NNNNNNNNNN	D,P	005	341	05.11.04	6320	150901	81005
932.132-014	SURFACE SUPERVISOR (mine & quarry)	4348	23322434455	LNNNNNNFFONFFNOFNNN	FNNN4NNNNNNNNNN	D,P,V	005	341	05.11.02	6320	150901	81005
932.167-010	DISPATCHER (mine & quarry)	4336	33334434454	LNNNNNNFFNFFNNNNFN	NNNN4NNNNNNNNNN	D,P,T	013	340	07.04.05	4751	150901	58005
932.363-010	HOIST OPERATOR (petrol. & gas)	3225	34433444335	MOOFFFOFFONOONFFFNOF	FNNN4NNNNNNNNNO	R,T	011	565	05.11.02	8314	470399	97941
932.664-010	BRAKE HOLDER (any industry)	2113	44444444355	MNNOOONFFNNOONNFFNNF	FNNN4NNNNNNNNNF	R	013	851	05.12.03	8233	490202	97317
932.664-014	SPOUT TENDER I (chemical)	2122	44434533345	MNNNNNNFFFNOONNFFNNN	CNNN4NNNNNNNNNN	R	011	349	05.12.03	8769	490299	98999
932.667-010	BOTTOMER I (mine & quarry)	2222	44444444445	HNNNNNNFFFNNFNONFNNN	FNNN4NFNNNNNNNF	R	011	340	05.12.04	8726	490299	98799
932.667-014	LOADING-SHOVEL OILER (mine & quarry)	2113	44544554345	MONFFFOFFNNNNNNFNNN	FNNN4NCNNNNNNNN	R	011	340	05.12.08	6140	470399	85128
932.683-010	CAR DROPPER (mine & quarry)	2113	44433434445	MFFOONFFNNNNNNNFFNNF	FNNN4NFNNNNNNNN	R	033	340	05.12.03	8726	490299	98799
932.683-014	LOADING-MACHINE OPERATOR (mine & quarry)	3225	34434344344	MNNOOOOFFFNNNONFFFNOF	NNNN5NCNNNNNNNN	R	011	564	05.11.02	8726	490299	98799
932.683-018	MECHANICAL-SHOVEL OPERATOR (mine & quarry)	3225	34534534345	MNNOOONFFNNOONNFFNNF	NNNN5NCNNNNNNNC	R	011	340	05.11.03	8316	490299	97932
932.683-022	SHUTTLE-CAR OPERATOR (mine & quarry)	3224	34424434335	MNNNONNFFONNNONOFFNNF	NNNN5NCNNNNNNNC	R	013	340	05.11.02	8319	490299	97935
932.685-010	AERIAL-TRAM OPERATOR (mine & quarry)	2113	34534544445	LNNNNNNFFFNNFNOFFNNN	FNNN4NNNNNNNNNN	R,T	011	340.	05.11.04	8316	490299	97923
932.687-010	CHUTE LOADER (mine & quarry)	1111	45444554355	MOOOOONFFFNNNNNFNNN	FNNN4NFNNNNNNNN	R,T	011	340	05.12.03	8769	000000	98999
933.664-010	CRUSHER SETTER (mine & quarry)	2113	34334534355	MNNNNNNFFNNOONFNNNN	NNNN4NNNNNNNNNN	R,T	142	351	06.01.02	6560	490299	92997
933.687-010	GRIZZLY WORKER (mine & quarry; smelt. & refin.)	1112	44544544355	HNNFOOONFFNNNNNNNNNO	ONNN5NFNNNNNNNO	R	142	340	05.12.07	8769	490299	98999
934.685-010	CONE OPERATOR (mine & quarry)	2113	44443444455	LNNONONFFFNNNNNFNNF	NNNN4NCNNNNNNNN	R	145	340	05.12.07	7666	490299	92962
934.685-014	SAND PLANT ATTENDANT (concrete prod.; mine & quarry)	2212	44443534353	MOOOOOOFFFNNNNNFNFF	CNNO4NNNNNNNNNN	R,T	145	345	05.12.07	6960	490299	95099
934.685-018	SHAKER TENDER (concrete prod.: mine & quarry)	2213	44443444355	MONOONNFFONNNNNFNNNF	ONNN4NCNNNNNNNN	R,T	145	341	05.12.07	7666	490299	92962

DOT #	DOT Title & Industry	Trng	Aptitude	Physical	Environment	Tempra	WkF	MPSMS	GOE	SOC	CIP	OES
934.685-022	SPIRAL RUNNER (mine & quarry)	2114	3443543355	MNNNNNFFNNNNFNNNN	NNNN4NNNNNNNNNN	R,T	145	341	05.12.07	7666	490299	92962
934.687-010	FOOT WORKER (chemical)	2112	4454544355	MNNNNNNFFNNNNNNNN	NNNN3NNNNNNNNNN	R	145	499	05.12.07	8769	490299	98999
939.130-010	SUPERVISOR, POND (chemical)	4337	33334934355	LNNNNNNFFNFFNFNNNN	FNNN4NNNNNNNNNN	V,D,P,J	014	389	05.12.01	7100	150901	81008
939.131-010	QUARRY SUPERVISOR, OPEN PIT (mine & quarry)	4337	33433333345	LONOOOOFFNFFNFONNO	CNNN5NONNNNNNNF	V,D,P,J	005	340	05.02.05	6320	150901	81005
939.131-014	SUPERVISOR, PRODUCTION (petrol. & gas)	4338	23343333355	LONONONFFNFFNFOFONO	FNNN5NNNNNNNNN	V,D,P,J	145	342	05.02.02	7100	150903	81008
939.131-018	WELL PULLER, HEAD (petrol. & gas)	4337	33333333355	HONNNNNFFNFFNFFNNF	FNNN4NNNNNNNNNF	V,D,P,J	005	342	05.12.02	8120	150903	81011
939.132-010	DREDGE OPERATOR SUPERVISOR (mine & quarry)	4337	33434444355	MONNNNNNFFONFFNFFNNO	FNNN4NNNNNNNNN	D,P,J	005	340	05.11.01	6320	490399	81005
939.132-014	OIL-WELL-SERVICES SUPERVISOR (petrol. & gas)	4338	23333334454	LOOOOONFFNFFNFNONON	FNNN4NNNNNNNNN	D,P,J	005	342	05.11.03	6320	150903	81005
939.137-010	CHIEF DISPATCHER (petrol. & gas)	4447	23244344454	SNNNNNNFFNFFNFNNOON	NNNN3NNNNNNNNN	D,P,V	281	969	07.04.05	7100	150903	81008
939.137-014	PIT SUPERVISOR (mine & quarry)	4337	23322344345	LNNOOONFFONFFNFOFNNF	FNNN5NONNNNNNNF	D,J,P	005	340	05.02.05	7100	490299	81008
939.137-018	SECTION SUPERVISOR (mine & quarry)	4337	23322344345	MONOOONFFFNFFNFNNNO	FNNN5NFNNNNNNNF	D,P,J	005	340	05.02.05	6320	150901	81005
939.137-022	SUPERVISOR, HARVESTING (chemical)	4335	33334444355	LNNNNNNFFNFFNFNONNN	FNNF4NNNNNNNNN	D,P,T,V	011	499	05.12.01	7100	490299	81008
939.167-010	CONTROLLER, COAL OR ORE (mine & quarry)	3336	33333334454	SNNNNNNFFNFFNFFNNFON	ONNN4NCNNNNNNNC	D,J,T	005	340	05.12.01	6320	150901	81005
939.281-010	MINER I (mine & quarry)	4326	34333433235	VONFFFOFFONNNNFOFNNF	NNNN4NCNNNNNNNC	J,S,T	005	340	05.11.02	6560	490299	87999
939.362-010	DISPATCHER, OIL WELL SERVICES (petrol. & gas)	3335	33444344454	SNNNNNNFFNFFNFNFON	NNNN3NNNNNNNN	R,P	281	342	07.04.05	4751	470399	58005
939.362-014	PANELBOARD OPERATOR (mine & quarry; smelt. & refin.)	4335	33334334354	LONOOOOFFFOOONFFNOF	ONNN4NCNONNNNN	J,T	147	340	06.02.18	6960	490299	95099
939.364-010	OBSERVER HELPER, SEISMIC PROSPECTING (petrol. & gas)	2214	33434434345	MNNFOFNFONOONFFOOF	FNNN4NNNNNNNNF	R,T	011	342	05.12.03	8650	470399	98319
939.382-010	DRY-PLACER-MACHINE OPERATOR (mine & quarry)	3214	33434444344	MNNNNNNFFONNNNFNFNON	CNNN4NNNNNNNNN	V,T	145	354	05.11.02	6540	490299	87949
939.462-010	OIL-WELL-SERVICE OPERATOR (petrol. & gas)	4336	33333444344	HOOFFNFFONOOONOFFNOO	CNNN4ONNNNNNNF	J,T	102	369	05.11.03	8319	470399	87989
939.485-010	SANDFILL OPERATOR (mine & quarry)	2213	44433444355	MONONONOOONNNNONONNN	ONNN3NNNNNNNNF	R,T	143	350	05.12.07	8319	490299	97989
939.585-010	DUST SAMPLER (mine & quarry)	2223	44434434455	LNNNNNNFFNFFNFNNFON	NNNN4NCNNNNNNN	R,T	212	341	05.07.04	7840	490299	83005
939.663-010	OBSERVER HELPER, GRAVITY PROSPECTING (petrol. & gas)	2213	34444444355	MNNOOONFFNOONFFFNNF	FNNN3NNNNNNNNN	R	013	564	05.08.03	8650	470399	98319
939.667-010	CAGER (mine & quarry)	2123	34344444345	HNNONNNFFNNOONNNNNN	FNNN4NNNNNNNNN	R	011	340	05.12.04	8726	490299	98799
939.667-014	QUARRY WORKER (mine & quarry)	2112	44544534345	HFFFOFNFFNNOONNFNNN	CNNN4NFNNNNNNN	R	011	344	05.12.03	6560	490299	87999
939.667-018	SHORE HAND, DREDGE OR BARGE (construction; mine & quarry)	2114	35534534345	HONOOONFFNNNNNNNNNN	CNNF4NNNNNNNNN	J	011	354	05.12.04	8726	490299	98799
939.682-010	MONITOR CAR OPERATOR (mine & quarry)	3216	34434433454	LNNNNNNFFNNNNFFNON	NNNN4NNNNNNNNO	J,R,T	143	347	06.02.18	8319	470399	97989
939.682-014	PNEUMATIC-JACK OPERATOR (petrol. & gas)	3225	34433444355	HOOOOONFFNNNOOONNO	CNNN4NNNNNNNNN	J,T	011	342	05.11.03	8319	470399	87999
939.684-010	JACK SETTER (mine & quarry)	3114	44433534344	MNNONONFFNNNNNFNFNNN	NNNN3NNNNNNNNC	R,J,T	005	341	05.12.02	6560	490299	87923
939.684-014	MINER, PLACER (mine & quarry)	3225	35535544344	HOOFFFNFFFNNNNOFFONF	CNNO3NNNNNNNNN	R,J,T	005	350	05.12.02	6560	490299	87999
939.684-018	OIL-WELL-SERVICE-OPERATOR HELPER (petrol. & gas)	3225	34433444335	HOOFFNFFFNNNNOFFONF	CNNN4ONNNNNNNN	R,T	143	369	05.12.07	8319	470399	97989
939.685-010	POND TENDER (mine & quarry)	2214	34444344355	MNNNNNNFFNNNNNFNNNN	FNNF4NNNNNNNNN	R,J	145	499	05.12.06	7676	490299	92962
939.687-022	LATRINE CLEANER (mine & quarry)	2223	44544534354	LNNNNNNOOONNNNNFFNOF	NNNN4NNNNNNNNN	R	145	345	05.12.07	7666	490299	92962
939.687-026	ROCK-DUST SPRAYER (mine & quarry)	2113	44544534344	MNNNOONFFFNNNNNNNNO	NNNN4NCNNNNNNNC	R,T	005	341	05.12.02	8319	490299	97989
939.687-030	SAMPLE WASHER (petrol. & gas)	1112	44543533455	LONNNNNCCNNNNNNCNNN	NNNN4NNNNNNNNN	R	145	342	05.12.07	7850	470399	83005
939.687-034	SAND FILLER (mine & quarry)	2112	44454544355	MONOOOOFFNNNNNONFNNN	ONNF3NNNNNNNNF	R	014	345	05.12.03	8769	490299	98999
950.131-010	REFRIGERATING ENGINEER, HEAD (any industry)	4347	33334344355	LONOOONFFONFFNFNOONN	NFNN4NNNNNNNNN	V,D,P,J	021	875	05.06.02	6700	520205	81008
950.131-014	STATIONARY-ENGINEER SUPERVISOR (any industry)	3337	33333434344	LONOOOOFFNFFNFNFNON	NNNN4NNNNNNNNN	V,D,P,J	021	560	05.06.02	6700	520205	81008
950.362-010	ENGINEER, EXHAUSTER (steel & rel.)	3337	33334344344	LONONOONFFONOOONFOOONO	NNNN4NFNNNNNNN	J,T	014	499	05.06.04	8319	470501	97989
950.362-014	REFRIGERATING ENGINEER (any industry)	4337	33334344344	MFOOOOOFFONNNNNNFFN	NNNF4NNNNNNNNN	J,T	021	875	05.06.02	6931	150501	95032
950.382-010	BOILER OPERATOR (any industry)	4337	33334344354	MFOOOOOFFONNONFNOFON	NNCN4NNNNNNNNN	J,T	021	875	05.06.02	6931	470201	95032
950.382-014	GAS-COMPRESSOR OPERATOR (any industry)	4337	34434344355	MONOOONFFONNNMFNFFN	NNNN4NFNNNNNNN	J,T	021	872	05.06.02	8319	470501	97921
950.382-018	GAS-ENGINE OPERATOR (any industry)	3226	33344344355	MONOOONFFFNNNNNFFNN	OFNF4NFNNNNNNN	J,T	021	871	05.06.01	6931	470501	95032
950.382-022	ROTARY-RIG ENGINE OPERATOR (petrol. & gas)	4337	33334434355	MOOONOOFFONNNOOONNO	CNNN4NNNNNNNNN	V,T	021	870	05.06.02	6932	470399	95032
950.382-026	STATIONARY ENGINEER (any industry)	4437	33334344355	MONONONFFONNNONFNNNN	NNOO4NFNNNNNNN	J,T,V	021	870	05.06.02	6931	150403	95032
950.382-030	STATIONARY-ENGINEER APPRENTICE (any industry)	4437	33334344355	MONONONFFONNONFNNNN	NNOO4NFNNNNNNN	J,T,V	021	870	05.06.02	6931	150501	95032
950.485-010	HUMIDIFIER ATTENDANT (textile; tobacco)	3226	44444434355	LFFNNNNCCFNNNNFNNNN	NNNN4NNNNNNNNN	J,T	021	875	05.06.02	7679	470201	95099

DOT #	DOT Title & Industry	Trng	Aptitude	Physical	Environment	Tempra	WkF	MPSMS	GOE	SOC	CIP	OES
950.562-010	PANELBOARD OPERATOR (chemical)	4447	23233333344	LNNNNNFFNFNFNNFFN	NNNN3NNNNNONNN	J,T	021	875	05.06.04	6960	410205	95099
950.585-010	VENTILATION EQUIPMENT TENDER (any industry)	3234	34434444345	LNNONONFFONNNNFNFONN	NNNN4NONNNNNNN	J,T	021	870	05.06.02	7679	470201	95099
950.585-014	BOILER-OPERATOR HELPER (sugar & cont.)	3234	34444444454	LNNNNNFFNNNNNFNFNNON	NNON4NNNNNNNNNF	R,T,U	021	875	05.06.02	7668	000000	92926
950.685-010	AIR-COMPRESSOR OPERATOR (any industry)	3225	34444444355	MNNONONFFNNNNNNFFNNN	NNNN4NNNNNNNN	J,T	021	875	05.06.02	7679	470501	92998
950.685-014	BOILER-ROOM HELPER (any industry)	2224	44444434355	LOOOOONFFNNNNNOONNNO	NNCO4NNNNNNNNN	R,J	021	875	05.06.02	7668	470201	92926
951.685-010	FIRER, HIGH PRESSURE (any industry)	3235	44444444344	MONFFNNFFNNNNNOOFOON	NNFN4NNNNNNNNO	J,T	021	875	05.06.02	6960	470501	95099
951.685-014	FIRER, LOW PRESSURE (any industry)	2225	44444444354	MFNFNNNFFONNNNFFONON	NNFF4NNNNNNNNN	T,J	021	875	05.06.02	7668	470501	92926
951.685-018	FIRER, MARINE (water trans.)	3335	44434434355	MONFNNNFFNNNNFNNNNN	NNFN4NNNNNNNNO	J,T	021	854	05.06.02	7668	470501	92926
951.686-010	FUEL-HOUSE ATTENDANT (saw. & plan.)	2112	44444534355	MNNNNNNCCNNNNNFNNNNN	NNCN4NONNNNNNN	R	021	875	05.12.04	8725	490299	98502
952.131-010	SUBSTATION OPERATOR, CHIEF (utilities)	4338	33343344354	LNNNNNNFFNFFNFFFOFO	ONNN4NNNNNNNNN	V,D,P,J	021	871	05.06.01	6700	520205	81008
952.132-010	OPERATIONS SUPERVISOR, NUCLEAR POWER PLANT (utilities)	5558	11133233444	LOOOOONFFNFFNFOOOOF	NNNN3NNNNNONNN	D,P,J,T	021	871	05.06.01	6700	000000	81008
952.137-010	CHIEF LOAD DISPATCHER (utilities)	4347	22333344455	LNNNNNNFFNFNFNFONN	NNNN4NNNNNNNNN	V,D,P,J	021	871	05.06.01	7100	520205	81008
952.137-014	HYDROELECTRIC-STATION OPERATOR, CHIEF (utilities)	4337	22333344455	LFFNNNNFFNFNFFFONF	NNNN4NNOONNNNN	V,D,P,J	021	871	05.06.01	6700	520205	81008
952.137-018	SUPERINTENDENT, LOCAL (utilities)	4337	33323344454	LNNNNNNFFONFFNFNOOON	ONNN3NNNNNNNNN	D,P,J,T	021	870	05.05.05	7100	520205	81008
952.137-022	TURBINE OPERATOR, HEAD (utilities)	4337	22333344455	LNNNNNNFFONFFNFNNNNN	NNNN4NNNNNNNNN	V,D,J	021	871	05.06.01	6700	520205	81008
952.137-026	SUPERVISOR, OPERATIONS (utilities)	4347	22333333444	LOOOOONFFNNNFFNFNNOON	NNNN4NNNNNNNNN	V,D,P,J	021	871	05.06.01	6700	470501	81008
952.167-010	DISPATCHER, SERVICE OR WORK (utilities)	4337	33334244454	SNNNNNNFFNFFNFNNNON	NNNN3NNNNNNNNN	P,J	111	580	07.04.05	4751	000000	58005
952.167-014	LOAD DISPATCHER (utilities)	4338	33333333344	LNNNNNNFFNFFNFFFFF	NNNN4NNNNNNNNN	D,J,P	021	871	05.06.01	6932	470501	95028
952.261-010	SUBSTATION INSPECTOR (utilities)	4337	34343444344	LFFFFFFFFNFFFF	FNNN4NNNNNNNNF	J,T	111	581	05.06.01	6881	470501	83002
952.362-010	AUXILIARY-EQUIPMENT OPERATOR (utilities)	3235	34343444344	MFNOOONFFOOFFFNNNFN	ONON4NNNONONON	J,T,V	021	871	05.06.01	6932	470501	95023
952.362-014	FEEDER-SWITCHBOARD OPERATOR (utilities)	3226	34433344354	LNNNNNNFFNOONFNFFON	NNNN4NNNFNNNNN	J,T	021	871	05.06.01	6932	470501	95028
952.362-018	HYDROELECTRIC-STATION OPERATOR (utilities)	4337	33344343354	LFFNNNNFFNNOONFFFFF	NNNN4NNNONNNNN	J	021	871	05.06.01	6932	470501	95021
952.362-022	POWER-REACTOR OPERATOR (utilities)	4337	22333344344	MNNNNNNFFONFFNFNNOOFN	NNNN3NNNNNONNN	V,S,J,T	021	871	05.06.01	6932	410205	95026
952.362-026	SUBSTATION OPERATOR (utilities)	4337	33343344344	LNNNNNNFFONOONFNNOON	NNNN4NNNONNNNN	J,T	021	871	05.06.01	6932	470501	95028
952.362-030	SUBSTATION OPERATOR APPRENTICE (utilities)	4337	33334344354	LNNNNNNFFONOONFNNOON	NNNN4NNNONNNNN	J,T	021	871	05.06.01	6932	470501	95028
952.362-034	SWITCHBOARD OPERATOR (utilities)	4337	33343334354	LNNNNNNFFNFNFFFFF	NNNN4NNNNNNNNN	J,T	021	871	05.06.01	6932	470501	95028
952.362-038	SWITCHBOARD OPERATOR (chemical)	4337	34333434354	LNNNNNNFFONNNNNFFFON	NNNN4NNNNNNNNN	J,T	021	879	05.06.01	6932	470501	95028
952.362-042	TURBINE OPERATOR (utilities)	4337	33333334354	LNNNNNNFFNFNFNNFNN	NNNN4NNNNNONNN	J,T	021	871	05.06.01	6932	470501	95021
952.364-010	TROUBLE SHOOTER I (utilities)	3225	34434444354	LFFOOONFFOFFNFFFFF	FNNN4NNNFNNNNF	J,T	111	871	05.10.03	6432	460303	87202
952.367-010	LOAD CHECKER (utilities)	3336	33343444354	LNNNNNNFFNFNFNNNFON	ONNN3NNNNNNNNN	R,J	221	580	05.09.01	7820	470501	83005
952.367-014	SWITCHBOARD OPERATOR ASSISTANT (utilities)	3337	33433344324	MFFNNNNCCCNNNNNFNFON	NNNN3NNNNNNNNN	J,T	021	871	05.06.01	6932	470501	95021
952.381-010	SWITCH INSPECTOR (utilities)	3235	34444433224	LNNNNNNFFNNNNFFNNNN	CNNN4NNNFFNNNN	J,T	021	871	05.10.03	6432	470501	87202
952.382-010	DIESEL-PLANT OPERATOR (utilities)	4336	33343334355	LNNNNNNFFNNNNNFNNOONN	NNNN4NNNONNNNN	J,T	021	871	05.06.01	6932	470501	95021
952.382-014	SUBSTATION-OPERATOR HELPER (utilities)	3327	34334343354	MNNNNNNFFONFFNNNNONFNON	NNNN4NNFNNNNNN	J,T	021	861	05.06.01	6932	470501	95021
952.382-018	POWER-PLANT OPERATOR (utilities)	4448	33333444354	MNNNNNNFFNFNFNFNFFFF	NNNN3NNNNNNNNN	J,T	111	871	05.06.01	6932	470501	95021
952.464-010	CABLE MAINTAINER (utilities)	3335	33334443344	LFFFFFFFFNNNNFNFON	CNNF4NNNFNNNNN	J,T	021	872	05.06.01	6175	470501	85928
952.567-010	TURBINE ATTENDANT (utilities)	3234	34343334354	LNNNNNNFFNOONFNNNON	NNNN4NNNNNNNNN	J,T	231	871	05.09.03	7820	470501	83005
952.665-010	LABORER, POWERHOUSE (utilities)	2113	44444444345	HFOFFNNCCNNOONOOOONN	FNNN4NFFNFNNNN	V	021	870	05.12.04	8769	470501	98999
952.667-010	STREET-LIGHT CLEANER (utilities)	2112	44444444334	LFFNNNNFFNOONFFNFF	CNNF3NNNNNNNNF	R	061	871	05.12.18	8769	000000	98999
952.687-010	HYDROELECTRIC-PLANT MAINTAINER (utilities)	2113	44545544345	MOOOOOOFFNNNNNNFNFNF	FNNN4NNNNNONNN	R	031	870	05.12.18	5244	470501	67005
952.687-014	SUBSTATION-OPERATOR HELPER (utilities)	2115	44444444344	LFFNNNNFFONNNNNONFNON	NNNN4NNFNNNNNN	J	021	871	05.06.01	8619	520205	98999
953.132-010	SUPERVISOR, LIQUEFACTION-AND-REGASIFICATION (utilities)	4348	22333344455	LNNNNNNFFONFFNFNOONN	NNNN4NNNNNNCNN	P,J	147	872	05.06.04	6700	520205	81008
953.137-010	GAS-PUMPING-STATION SUPERVISOR (utilities)	3335	33334443354	LNNNNNNFFONFFNFNNNNN	ONNN3NNNNNNNNN	D,P,J	014	872	05.06.03	8120	520205	81011
953.137-014	PRESSURE SUPERVISOR (utilities)	4337	33332344454	LNNNNNNFFONFFNFNNNNN	FNNN3NNNNNNNNN	V,D,P,J	014	872	05.06.03	7100	000000	81008
953.137-018	SERVICE SUPERVISOR I (utilities)	4337	33333444444	LNNNNNNFFNFNFNFFFFF	FNNN4NNNNNNNNN	V,D,P,J	121	872	05.10.02	7100	520205	81008
953.167-010	GAS DISPATCHER (pipe lines; utilities)	4338	22333344444	SNNNNNNFFONFFNFNNNNN	NNNN4NNNNNNNNN	V,D,J,T	014	872	05.06.03	4751	470501	58005
953.281-010	FIELD-MECHANICAL-METER TESTER (petrol. refin.; pipe lines; utilities)	4448	22333433354	MOOFFFNFFONNNFOFOOO	FNNN4NNNNNNNNO	V,J,T	121	856	05.05.09	6175	150403	85928
953.362-010	FUEL ATTENDANT (any industry)	3225	34443344344	LNNNNNNFFONONNNFNNNN	NNON4NNNNNNNNN	V,J,T	021	872	05.06.02	6920	470501	95005
953.362-014	LIQUEFACTION-AND-REGASIFICATION-PLANT OPERATOR (utilities)	4337	33334344354	MNNNNNNFFONFFNFNNNNN	ONNN4NNNNNNNON	V,J,T	342	871	05.06.04	6920	470501	95005
953.362-018	PRESSURE CONTROLLER (utilities)	3337	33334433345	MONNNNNNFFNNOONFNNNNN	FNNN3NNNNNNNNN	J,T	014	872	05.06.03	6920	470501	95005
953.364-010	GAS-METER INSTALLER (utilities)	3236	33433433344	MFFFFNFFONOONOFFNFF	ONNN4NNNNNNNNN	J,T	121	872	05.10.02	6450	460501	85928

DOT #	DOT Title & Industry	Trng	Aptitude	Physical	Environment	Tempra	WkF	MPSMS	GOE	SOC	CIP	OES
953.367-010	GAS-LEAK INSPECTOR (pipe lines; utilities)	3225	33443434343	LNNOONNFFNFFFNNNFN	FNNN3NFNNNNNNNNN	J,T	212	364	05.07.01	7820	460501	83005
953.367-014	GAS-METER CHECKER (utilities)	3225	34443444354	LNNNNNNFFONOONFNNNFN	FNNN3NONNNNNNNNN	J	212	872	05.07.01	7820	000000	83005
953.367-018	HOUSE-PIPING INSPECTOR (utilities)	3235	33433444344	LNNFFNFFONNNNFNNNON	FNNN3NNNNNNNNNN	J,T	212	364	05.07.01	7820	470501	97917
953.382-010	GAS-PUMPING-STATION OPERATOR (utilities)	3235	33443444355	LNNNNNNFFONNNNFNNNNN	ONNN3NNNNNNNNNN	J,T	014	872	05.06.03	8319	470501	81008
953.387-010	CYLINDER INSPECTOR-AND-TESTER (chemical)	3334	34443333345	MNNNNNNFFNNNNFNFFNN	NNNN4NNNNNNNNNN	J,T	212	551	06.03.01	7820	000000	83005
953.583-010	DRIP PUMPER (pipe lines; utilities)	3223	34434434354	LNNNNNNFFONNNNONNNFN	FNNN3NNNNNNNNNN	R	014	856	05.11.03	8213	490205	97102
953.584-010	HELPER, LIQUEFACTION-AND-REGASIFICATION (utilities)	3235	34434434344	LOOFFFNFFONNNNFNFNFN	FNNN3NNNNNNCNN	R,J	121	872	05.10.02	8619	470501	98999
953.667-010	GAS-LEAK INSPECTOR HELPER (pipe lines; utilities)	3334	44443444354	MNNFFNFFNNNNOOOOFF	FNNN3NNNNNNNNNN	R,J	212	872	05.07.01	8620	460501	98999
953.684-010	GAS-PUMPING-STATION HELPER (utilities)	2124	44443444355	MOOFFFNFFONNNNONONNN	FNNN4NNNNNNNNNN	R,J	014	872	05.12.06	8319	470501	97989
953.687-010	GAS-METER-INSTALLER HELPER (utilities)	2122	44443444355	MOONFFNFFNNNNNFONNO	ONNN3NNNNNNNNNN	R,J	121	872	05.12.15	8645	460501	98319
954.130-010	SUPERVISOR, PUMPING STATION (waterworks)	4437	33333333355	LOONNNNFFOFFNFFFNNF	ONNN4NNNNNNNNNN	V,D,P,J	014	873	05.06.03	6700	520205	81008
954.131-010	SUPERVISOR, WATER TREATMENT PLANT (waterworks)	4336	33333333345	LOONNNNFFNOONFFOONN	NNNN4NFNNNNNNNN	D,T,P,J	145	873	05.02.01	6910	150506	81008
954.132-010	SUPERVISOR, WATER TREATMENT PLANT (waterworks)	4334	33333344334	MNNONNNFFONOONFFOOON	CNNF4NNNNNNNNNN	V,J,T	014	873	05.06.03	8319	010299	97989
954.362-010	DITCH RIDER (waterworks)	3234	33444334355	LNNNNNNFFONFFNFNNNN	NNNN3NNNNNNNNNN	R,P	281	873	07.04.05	4751	000000	58005
954.367-010	WATER-SERVICE DISPATCHER (waterworks)	3235	34433434355	LOOOONNFFFONNNFOOOOO	ONNN4NNNNNNNNNN	J,T	014	873	05.06.03	6910	470501	95002
954.382-010	PUMP-STATION OPERATOR, WATERWORKS (waterworks)	3335	34343434354	MNNOOONFFONNONFNOOON	ONNO4NONNNNNNNNN	J,T	147	873	05.06.04	6910	470501	95002
954.382-014	WATER-TREATMENT-PLANT OPERATOR (waterworks)	3225	33333444355	LNNONNNFFNNNNFNNNNN	FNNO3NNNNNNNNNN	J,T	014	873	05.06.03	6960	470501	95099
954.382-018	WATERSHED TENDER (waterworks)	3224	44444444325	MONONNNFFONNNNFNNNNN	FNNO4NNNNNNNNNNO	V,J	145	873	05.12.07	7676	470501	92962
954.385-010	BASIN OPERATOR (waterworks)	3224	34433444355	MNNFFONFFONOOONFOFNNN	FNNF4NNNNNNNNNN	J	121	873	05.10.01	6450	460501	85928
954.564-010	WATER-METER INSTALLER (waterworks)	2112	44443444355	MONFOONFFONNNNONNNNNN	FNNF3NNNNNNNNNN	R	031	873	05.12.18	8750	000000	98905
954.587-010	WATER-FILTER CLEANER (waterworks)	4447	33333334344	LONOOOOFFFNFFNFOOOON	FNNF3NFNNNNNNNNN	V,D,P,J	145	874	05.02.01	6700	150506	81008
955.130-010	SUPERVISORY WASTEWATER-TREATMENT-PLANT OPERATOR (sanitary ser.)	4225	33333433355	LFOONONFFNFFNNNNNN	NNON3NFNNNNNNNNN	D,T,P	021	874	05.06.04	6700	520205	81008
955.131-010	SUPERVISOR, INCINERATOR PLANT (sanitary ser.)	4337	33334444455	LNNNNNNFFONFFNFNONN	FNNN3NFNNNNNNNNN	D,P,V	013	874	05.11.01	6318	000000	81008
955.133-010	SANITARY-LANDFILL SUPERVISOR (sanitary ser.)	4336	33333344455	MNNNNNOOONFFNONNNNNN	ONNO3NNNNNNNNNN	V,D,P,J	011	874	05.11.01	6910	410205	81008
955.137-010	SNOW-REMOVING SUPERVISOR (government ser.)	4447	22333334354	LNNNNOONFFONFFNCNOON	ONNN3NNNNNNNNNF	J	295	499	06.01.01	4751	410205	58005
955.167-010	DISPATCHER, RADIOACTIVE-WASTE-DISPOSAL (chemical)	4336	33343334344	LNNNNNNFFONFFNFNONON	NNNN3NNNNNNNNNN	D,J,P	296	874	05.06.04	6910	150506	31314
955.222-010	INSTRUCTOR, WASTEWATER-TREATMENT PLANT (sanitary ser.)	4436	33333334354	LNNNNNNFFONFFNFOOOOO	FNNC4NFNNNNNFFN	V,J,T	145	874	05.06.04	6910	470501	95002
955.362-010	WASTEWATER-TREATMENT-PLANT OPERATOR (sanitary ser.)	3234	33343344345	LOOOOONFFOOOONFOOOOO	NNON4NONNNNNNNNN	T,J	021	874	05.06.04	6960	150506	95099
955.362-014	INCINERATOR OPERATOR II (sanitary ser.)	3224	33343344354	MFNONONFFNNNNNNNON	NNNN4NONNNNNNNNN	J,T	147	874	06.02.16	6910	470501	95002
955.382-010	CLARIFYING-PLANT OPERATOR (textile)	4446	33343334344	LNNNOONFFFNNNNFNONON	NNNN4NNNNNNNNNF	J,T	147	499	06.02.11	6910	410205	95002
955.382-014	WASTE-TREATMENT OPERATOR (chemical)	3225	33443334344	HNNNONNFFONNNNFFNFF	FNNF4NFNNNNNNNN	V,S,T	011	520	05.12.03	8319	000000	97989
955.383-010	WASTE-DISPOSAL ATTENDANT (any industry)	1111	44544544445	LNNFOONCCNNNNNNFFNNN	FNNN4NNNNNNNNNN	R	031	874	05.11.01	8317	490202	97938
955.463-010	SANITARY LANDFILL OPERATOR (sanitary ser.)	2115	34434334345	MNNNNNNFFNNNNNFFNNF	ONNN4NONNNNNNNNN	R,U	011	874	05.12.07	6910	470501	95002
955.585-010	WASTEWATER-TREATMENT-PLANT ATTENDANT (sanitary ser.)	3224	34434443355	MFNNNNNFFONNNNNFOFONO	FNNF4NFNNONONNON	J	145	874	05.07.01	6910	470501	83005
955.667-010	INCINERATOR PLANT LABORER (sanitary ser.)	2111	44545544455	MNNONNNFFNNOONNNNNNN	NNON4NONNNNNNNNN	R	282	871	05.06.02	8769	150501	92923
955.685-010	INCINERATOR OPERATOR I (sanitary ser.)	2112	44544544445	MNNNNNNFFONOONFNNNN	NNON4NONNNNNNNNN	R,U	021	871	05.12.20	8769	520205	51002
955.687-010	SEWAGE-DISPOSAL WORKER (sanitary ser.)	4337	33344243355	HONFFNFNFNNNNFNNNNO	FNNF4NFNNNNNNNN	R	031	874	05.12.18	7675	000000	98905
955.687-014	SNOW SHOVELER (government ser.)	4236	33344344455	SNNNNNNNFFONFFNFNNNN	NNNN3NNNNNNNNNN	R	031	959	05.12.18	8726	000000	98799
955.687-018	STREET CLEANER (government ser.)	4346	33344344455	LNNFOONCCNNNNNNFFNNN	CNNN3NNNNNNNNNO	R	031	959	05.12.18	8769	000000	98999
955.687-022	GARBAGE COLLECTOR (motor trans.)	1111	44544544445	VFNFNFNFFNNNNNNNNNN	CNNN4NFNNNNNNNN	R	011	874	05.12.03	8722	000000	98705
956.267-010	INSPECTOR, CHIEF (utilities)	4437	33332344444	MNNNNNNNFFONOOONFOON	NNON4NNNNNNNFOON	J,T	121	364	05.07.01	7820	470501	83005
956.387-010	BUILDING-EQUIPMENT INSPECTOR (any industry)	3326	33333344444	LNNNNNNFFOONNFNFFON	ONON3NNNNNNNNNN	J,T	121	364	05.06.02	7820	150501	83005
959.131-010	HEATING-PLANT SUPERINTENDENT (any industry)	4338	33333343354	LNNNNNNFFONFFNFNON	NNON3NNNNNNNNNN	V,D,P,J	021	875	05.06.02	6700	150501	81008
959.137-010	DISPATCHER, CHIEF, SERVICE OR WORK (utilities)	4337	33344343355	LNNNNNNFFONFFNFFNN	NNNN3NNNNNNNNNN	D,P,S,J	111	871	07.04.05	6700	520205	51002
959.137-014	DISPATCHER, SERVICE, CHIEF (utilities)	4337	33334343355	SNNNNNNFFONFFNFNFNN	NNNN3NNNNNNNNNN	D,J,P	231	870	07.04.05	4525	000000	51002
959.137-018	ORDER DISPATCHER (utilities)	4236	33344344455	SNNNNNNNFFONFFNFNNNN	NNNN3NNNNNNNNNN	D,P,V	231	872	07.05.01	4525	520204	51002
959.137-022	SUPERVISOR, HOME-ENERGY CONSULTANT (utilities)	4346	32344344455	SNNNNNNOONFFNFFNNNN	NNNN3NNNNNNNNNN	D,P,V	231	870	05.02.01	1343	150503	15023
959.167-010	DISPATCHER, SERVICE (utilities)	4334	32344344455	SNNNNNNOOFNCCNONNONN	NNNN3NNNNNNNNNN	D,P,J	231	869	07.04.05	4751	000000	58005
959.361-010	CUSTOMER SERVICE REPRESENTATIVE (utilities)	3236	33443343355	LNNFFNFFFNNNNONOONN	NNNN3NNNNNNNNNN	J,T	271	871	05.10.04	6175	470501	85928
959.367-010	ELECTRIC POWER LINE EXAMINER (utilities)	3236	33433443334	LFFNNNNFFONOONOFFNOO	CNNN4NNNNFNNNNN	R,J	212	871	05.07.01	6433	470501	85723
959.367-014	FACILITY EXAMINER (tel. & tel.)	3236	33433443324	LNNNNNNFFNNNNFNNNON	FNNN3NNNNNNNNNN	V,P,J,T	271	861	05.05.05	6151	470103	49999
959.367-018	ENERGY-CONSERVATION REPRESENTATIVE (utilities)	3333	33344344445	MOOFFFFFFNNNFFNFFNN	ONNO4NNNNNNNNNN	T,J,P	212	870	05.07.01	1473	150503	21911

DOT #	DOT Title & Industry	Trmg	Aptitude	Physical	Environment	Tempra	WkF	MPSMS	GOE	SOC	CIP	OES
959.574-010	SERVICE REPRESENTATIVE (utilities; waterworks)	3223	34444344355	MNNFOONCCONOONFFFONF	FNNO4NNNNNNNNN	J,T	014	870	05.10.01	6175	470501	85928
959.684-010	POLE FRAMER (utilities; wood prod., nec)	2123	44433444345	MOONNNNFFFNNNNFNFNNN	CNNN4NNNNNNNNN	J	053	452	05.12.12	7639	000000	92998
960.132-010	CHIEF PROJECTIONIST (motion picture)	4238	33432334453	SNNNNNNFFONFFNFNFFFN	NNNN3NNNNNNNNN	D,P,J	281	911	05.10.05	7100	500602	81008
960.362-010	MOTION-PICTURE PROJECTIONIST (amuse. & rec.; motion picture)	4226	33333343353	LNNNNNNFFFNONOFNNFN	NNNN4NNNNNNNNNO	J,T	281	921	05.10.05	7479	500602	92905
960.382-010	AUDIOVISUAL TECHNICIAN (any industry)	4333	33434343354	LNNNONONFFFNNFNFONNO	NNNN3NNNNNNNNN	J,T	281	939	05.10.05	7479	100101	92905
961.364-010	DOUBLE (motion picture; radio-tv broad.)	3123	33534634445	LOOOOOOFFNNOONNOONNO	FNNN3NNNNNNNNN	E	297	911	01.08.01	3240	000000	34056
961.367-010	MODEL, PHOTOGRAPHERS' (any industry)	3114	34544343343	LOONONNFFNFFNFNFFN	FNNN3NNNNNNNNN	E,P	291	885	01.08.01	4450	000000	49032
961.667-010	MODEL ARTISTS' (any industry)	3113	34545544444	LNNONNNOONNNONNNNNNN	NNNN3NNNNNNNNN	E,P	291	750	01.08.01	4450	000000	49032
961.667-014	STAND-IN (motion picture; radio-tv broad.)	2112	44544555555	LOOOOOOONNOONOOOONNN	FNNN3NNNNNNNNN	R	297	911	01.08.01	3280	000000	34056
962.132-010	SUPERVISING FILM-OR-VIDEOTAPE EDITOR (motion picture; radio-tv broad.)	5358	22233343453	MNNONONFFFNFNONOOFN	NNNN3NNNNNNNNN	D,V,E,P,J	211	864	01.01.01	3312	000000	34032
962.134-010	RECORDIST, CHIEF (motion picture)	4347	22333344455	LNNNNNNFFONFFNFNOFN	NNNN3NNNNNNNNN	D,P,J,T	111	911	05.10.05	7100	100104	81008
962.137-010	GRIP BOSS (motion picture)	4348	33333444454	LNNNNNNNFFFNNFNFFFN	FNNO3NNNNNNNNN	V,D,P,J	295	911	05.12.01	7100	000000	81008
962.137-018	SUPERVISOR, COSTUMING (motion picture; radio-tv broad.)	4347	33333344453	SNNNNNNFFONFFNFOOOFN	NNNN3NNNNNNNNN	V,D,P,J	295	911	01.02.03	7100	000000	81008
962.137-022	SUPERVISOR, PROP-MAKING (motion picture)	4438	22333344453	LNNOONNCCONFNCNFFFN	ONNN4NNNNNNNNN	V,D,P,J	102	911	01.06.02	7100	500602	81008
962.137-026	SUPERVISOR, PROPERTIES (motion picture)	4348	22333444453	LNNNNNNFFONFFNFNOOFN	NNNN3NNNNNNNNN	V,D,P	102	911	05.12.01	7100	500602	81008
962.162-010	DIRECTOR, TECHNICAL (radio-tv broad.)	5248	22332443452	LNNNNNNFFFNFFNNNFFFN	NNNN3NNNNNNNNN	D,V,T,J	281	864	05.02.04	1341	100104	15023
962.167-010	MANAGER, SOUND EFFECTS (radio-tv broad.)	5457	22432443455	SNNNNNNOOONFFNONNNNN	NNNN3NNNNNNNNN	D,P,J	297	860	01.06.02	3719	100104	22599
962.167-014	PROGRAM ASSISTANT (radio-tv broad.)	4235	33333344454	LNNNNNNFFFNNFNNFNOOF	NNNN3NNNNNNNNN	D,V,P	282	863	01.03.01	3240	100104	34056
962.167-018	PROPERTY COORDINATOR (amuse. & rec.; radio-tv broad.)	4137	33434444355	VFFFFFNFFNFFNFNOONNO	NNNN3NNNNNNNNN	V,D,P,T	221	912	05.02.06	3240	100104	59999
962.261-010	PLANETARIUM TECHNICIAN (museums)	4447	23222322333	MQOONONFFFNQONFNNOFN	NNNN3NNNNNNNNN	J,T	111	606	05.10.05	3990	100101	39999
962.261-014	STAGE TECHNICIAN (amuse. & rec.)	4347	23323232324	HOOOOOOFFNOONOOOOON	NNNN4NNNONNNNN	V,T,J	111	919	05.10.04	3990	460201	39999
962.262-010	FILM OR VIDEOTAPE EDITOR (motion picture; radio-tv broad.)	5248	22332443353	LNNNNNNFFFNNFNONNNFN	NNNN3NNNNNNNNN	E,T,J	261	864	01.01.01	3312	100103	34032
962.267-010	SIGHT-EFFECTS SPECIALIST (amuse. & rec.)	4338	33233344453	LNNNNNNFFONFFNFNFNFN	NNNN4NNNNNNNNN	D,P,J,E	111	912	05.10.03	3990	500602	89502
962.281-010	PROP MAKER (amuse. & rec.; motion picture)	4447	33224342243	MNNNNNFFFNNNFFFFF	ONNN3NNONNNNNN	V,J,T	102	911	01.06.02	6422	460201	87102
962.281-014	SOUND-EFFECTS TECHNICIAN (radio-tv broad.)	4336	33333533333	MOOOOOOFFNONFFFFFF	NNNN3NNNNNNNNN	V,E	297	863	01.06.02	3990	100104	39999
962.281-018	SPECIAL EFFECTS SPECIALIST (amuse. & rec.; motion picture; radio-tv broad.)	4336	33343333353	MOOOOONFFFNNNNNFFFF	ONNN4NONNNNNNNN	V,J,T	121	910	01.06.02	3990	000000	39999
962.361-010	OPTICAL-EFFECTS LAYOUT PERSON (motion picture)	3336	33343333353	LNNNONONFFFNNNNNFFFN	NNNN3NNNNNNNNN	T,J	241	911	01.06.02	6868	500602	89914
962.362-010	COMMUNICATIONS TECHNICIAN (education)	4237	33332333343	LNNNNNNFFNOONFNONFN	FNNN4NNNNNNNNN	J	281	911	01.03.01	3990	100101	39999
962.362-014	LIGHT TECHNICIAN (motion picture; radio-tv broad.)	4237	33333433353	LONNNNNNOOFNFNNNNNFN	NNNN3NNNNNNNNN	J,T	111	864	05.10.03	3990	500602	39999
962.381-010	DRAPER (motion picture)	3227	33333432233	MFFNNNNFFFNNFFNFOFN	ONNN3NNNNNNNNN	J,T	241	911	05.05.15	6859	200502	89502
962.381-014	LIGHTING-EQUIPMENT OPERATOR (amuse. & rec.)	4236	33433343343	LNNONNNFFNNNNFFFNFF	NNNN3NNNNNNNNN	V,J,T	102	912	05.12.16	3990	000000	39999
962.381-018	MINIATURE-SET CONSTRUCTOR (motion picture)	4437	23222422252	LNNNNNNCCFNNNFNFFFF	NNNN3NNNNNNNNN	E,J	102	619	01.06.02	6862	000000	89908
962.382-010	RECORDIST (motion picture)	3226	33343443355	LNNNNNNFFFNNCNONONN	ONNN4NNNNNNNNN	J	281	911	05.10.05	3990	100199	22599
962.382-014	SOUND CUTTER (motion picture)	4346	33343433355	LNNNNNNFFFNQONFNFFN	NNNN3NNNNNNNNN	R,J,T	231	911	01.06.02	3719	100199	22599
962.384-010	MICROPHONE-BOOM OPERATOR (motion picture; radio-tv broad.)	3125	33434434345	LNNNNNNOOONONNNNNFFNN	NNNN3NNNNNNNNN	T,U	281	864	05.10.05	3990	500602	39999
962.687-010	HIGH RIGGER (amuse. & rec.; radio-tv broad.)	3226	34433433334	VFFFFOFFFOOONFFFNOF	NNNN3NNNNNNFNNN	V,J,T	102	912	05.10.01	6177	000000	85935
962.664-014	RECORDING STUDIO SET-UP WORKER (recording)	3114	34444334355	MNNFNNNFFONOONFNOONN	NNNN3NNNNNNNNN	R,T	281	869	05.12.03	8726	100199	98799
962.665-010	DUBBING-MACHINE OPERATOR (motion picture; radio-tv broad.)	3113	34434433354	MNNNNNNFFOFFNFNOON	NNNN4NNNNNNNNN	R,T	281	911	05.10.05	7679	100199	92998
962.684-010	ACROBATIC RIGGER (amuse. & rec.)	3116	34344534335	HFFNNNFFONNNNNFFFNNF	NNNN3NNNNFNNNN	R,T	102	913	05.10.01	6177	000000	85935
962.684-014	GRIP (amuse. & rec.; radio-tv broad.)	3225	34424434325	VFFFNFNFFNNNNFFFFN	NNNN4NNNNFNNNN	R,T	102	864	05.10.01	8769	000000	85999
962.684-018	MOTOR-POWER CONNECTOR (motion picture)	3115	34344433355	VFFFNFFFNFFONFNFNONN	NNNN4NNNNNNNNN	V,T	111	911	05.10.03	3990	000000	39999
962.684-022	PROP ATTENDANT (amuse. & rec.)	3232	34434444444	MFNFFFNFFNNFFFNNFF	NNNN4NNNNNNNNN	R,T	111	912	05.12.16	3990	000000	39999
962.687-010	DOLLY PUSHER (radio-tv broad.)	2112	44544534345	VNNNNNNCCNNNFNNFNNNN	NNNN3NNNNFNNNN	R	011	864	05.12.03	8769	000000	98999
962.687-014	FILM LOADER (motion picture)	2112	44445444455	MNNNNNNFFONNONFNFNNN	NNNN3NNNNFNNNN	R	011	911	05.12.04	8769	000000	98999
962.687-018	FLYER (amuse. & rec.; radio-tv broad.)	2113	43544534334	HFFFFFNFFFNNNFFFOFF	ONNN4NNNNNNOONN	V	011	912	05.12.04	8726	000000	98799
962.687-022	GRIP (motion picture; radio-tv broad.)	2125	34434433334	LNNNNNNFFONFFNFNFNN	NNNN3NNNNFNNNN	R	011	919	05.12.01	7100	000000	81008
969.137-010	SUPERVISOR, CIRCUS (amuse. & rec.)	4226	22333434455	LNNNNNNOOOONFNFNNNNN	NNNN4NNNNNNNNN	R	011	919	01.03.01	3290	520901	39999
969.137-014	SUPERVISOR, SHOW OPERATIONS (amuse. & rec.)	4446	22333343354	MNNNNNNFFFFFFNFNOOON	NNNN3NNNNNNOON	D,V,P	297	919	05.09.01	4754	000000	58023
969.367-014	CUSTODIAN, ATHLETIC EQUIPMENT (amuse. & rec.)	3225	33344333354	LNNNNNNCCFFNNNNFNNN	NNNN3NNNNNNNNN	V,P,T	221	913	05.09.07	6859	200305	39999
969.381-010	WARDROBE-SPECIALTY WORKER (motion picture; radio-tv broad.)	3327	34333432333	LNNNNNNCCFFNNNFNFNNN	NNNN3NNNNNNNNN	V,J,T	171	440	05.05.15	6859	000000	39599
969.664-010	FIREWORKS DISPLAY SPECIALIST (chemical)	4225	33333533354	MNNOOOOFFNOONFNOFFN	CNNN4NNNNNNFFNN	J,T	102	499	05.10.06	3990	000000	39999

DOT #	DOT Title & Industry	Trng	Aptitude	Physical	Environment	Tempra	WkF	MPSMS	GOE	SOC	CIP	OES
969.685-010	SNOWMAKER (amuse. & rec.)	2112	44534544335	HNNFFNFFNNNNNFFNNNN	FFNO4NNNNONNNN	R,U	143	910	05.12.18	7665	000000	92998
969.687-010	CIRCUS LABORER (amuse. & rec.)	2112	44445534445	MNNFNNNFNNNNNFNNNN	NNNN4NNNNNNNNNN	R	031	919	05.12.18	8769	000000	98999
969.687-014	ICE MAKER, SKATING RINK (amuse. & rec.)	2122	44544544435	MONNNNNFONNNNNNNNN	NFNO4NNNNNNNNNN	R	131	913	05.12.18	8769	000000	98999
970.131-014	SUPERVISOR, ARTIST, SUSPECT (government ser.)	4337	33322323252	LNNNNNNFFNFFNCNCCCN	NNNN2NNNNNNNNNN	D,V,E,P,J	264	752	01.06.01	3250	000000	34035
970.137-010	SUPERVISOR, SIGN SHOP (fabrication, nec)	4348	33322344452	LNNONNNNFFOFFNFFOFO	NNNN4NONNNNNNNN	D,V,E,P,J	102	619	05.10.04	7100	500402	81005
970.281-010	AIRBRUSH ARTIST (profess. & kin.)	4237	33322432352	SNNNNNNFFFNNNNFNFFN	NNNN3NNNNNNNNNN	J,T	262	752	01.02.03	6863	500402	89914
970.281-014	DELINEATOR (profess. & kin.)	4337	23211232353	SNNNNNNFFFNNNNFNFFN	NNNN3NNNNNNNNNN	J	262	752	01.02.03	6863	500402	89911
970.281-018	PHOTOGRAPH RETOUCHER (photofinishing)	4236	33432422352	SNNNNNNCCCNNNNCNCCCN	NNNN3NNNNNNNNNN	J,T	262	897	01.06.03	6868	100103	89914
970.281-022	SIGN WRITER, HAND (any industry)	4335	33433333352	SNNNNNNFFFNNNNFNFFN	NNNN4NNNNNNNNNN	J,T	262	889	01.06.03	6863	080299	89911
970.281-026	SKETCH MAKER, PHOTOENGRAVING (print. & pub.)	4337	23322422352	SNNNNNNNFFFNNNNFNFFN	NNNN3NNNNNNNNNN	J,T	242	752	01.02.03	6842	480205	89911
970.361-010	FORM DESIGNER (print. & pub.)	3336	33322324455	LNNNNNNCCFNOONCNCONN	NNNN3NNNNNNNNNN	J	264	474	01.06.01	6863	480205	89911
970.361-014	REPEAT CHIEF (print. & pub.)	4337	33332433353	SNNNNNNFFFNOONFNFFN	NNNN3NNNNNNNNNN	J,T	262	752	05.10.05	6863	480206	89712
970.361-018	ARTIST, SUSPECT (government ser.)	4336	23322232352	LNNNNNNNFFFNFFNCNCCCN	NNNN2NNNNNNNNNN	V,E,P,J	264	752	01.06.01	3250	000000	34035
970.381-010	COLORIST, PHOTOGRAPHY (photofinishing)	3126	33442343452	SNNNNNNCCFNNNNCNCCCN	NNNN3NNNNNNNNNN	J,T	262	897	01.06.03	6868	100103	89914
970.381-014	DECORATOR, MANNEQUIN (fabrication, nec)	3226	34432422353	LNNNNNNFFFNNNNFNFOFN	NNNN3NNNNNNNNNN	J,E,T	262	619	01.06.03	6863	500402	89706
970.381-018	LAY-OUT FORMER (business ser.)	4237	23322343352	SNNNNNNFFFNNNNCOFFFN	NNNN3NNNNNNNNNN	J,E	241	896	01.06.03	6863	500402	89911
970.381-022	PAINTER, HAND (any industry)	4237	34422542452	SNNNNNNFFFNNNNFNFFN	NNNN3NNNNNNNNNN	J,T,E	262	889	01.06.03	6863	500402	89911
970.381-026	PAINTER, SIGN (any industry)	4337	33332432232	LFNFNNNCCCNNNNCNFFFN	ONNN4NNNNNNNNNO	J	262	889	01.06.03	6863	500402	89911
970.381-030	RETOUCHER, PHOTOENGRAVING (print. & pub.)	3337	33332322352	SNNNNNNFFCNNNNCNNCCN	NNNN3NNNNNNNNNN	J,T	262	752	01.06.01	6842	480205	89712
970.381-034	SPOTTER, PHOTOGRAPHIC (photofinishing)	3215	34442432452	SNNNNNNFFFNNNNFNFFN	NNNN3NNNNNNNNNN	J,T	262	897	01.06.03	6868	100103	89914
970.381-038	STENCIL CUTTER (railroad equip.)	4337	33332432242	LNNFNNNFFFNNNNFNFFN	NNNN4NNNNNNNNNO	J,T	241	889	01.06.03	6863	500402	89911
970.381-042	TYPE COPYIST (machinery mfg.)	4337	33332222354	SNNNNNNFFFNNNNFNOOON	NNNN2NNNNNNNNNN	T,J	262	752	01.06.03	6863	500402	89911
970.581-010	MUSIC GRAPHER (print. & pub.)	3236	33492332255	SNNNNNNCCCNNNNCNCCNN	NNNN3NNNNNNNNNN	J,T	191	489	01.06.03	6863	000000	89911
970.661-010	ENGROSSER (profess. & kin.)	3228	33322332352	SNNNNNNFFFNNNNFNFFN	NNNN3NNNNNNNNNN	J,E	264	752	01.06.03	6863	500402	89911
970.661-014	LETTERER (profess. & kin.)	3226	33332322352	SNNNNNNCCCNOONCNFFFN	NNNN3NNNNNNNNNN	J	262	752	01.06.03	6863	500402	89911
970.664-010	PAINTER HELPER, SIGN (any industry)	3235	34443533343	LOONNNNFFNOONFNFNFN	FNNN3NNNNNNNNNF	J,T	262	896	01.06.01	8619	500402	98999
970.681-010	BEN-DAY ARTIST (print. & pub.)	3126	34432433353	LNNNNNNFFFNNNNFNFFN	NNNN3NNNNNNNNNN	J,T	191	752	01.06.03	6863	480205	89717
970.681-014	COLORER (print. & pub.)	3124	33433432352	SNNNNNNFFFNNNNFNFFN	NNNN3NNNNNNNNNN	J,T	262	752	01.06.03	7756	500402	93947
970.681-018	INKER AND OPAQUER (motion picture)	3117	34442432253	SNNNNNNFFFNNNNFNFFFN	NNNN3NNNNNNNNNN	J,T	262	752	01.06.03	6863	500402	89911
970.681-022	MANUGRAPHER (fabrication, nec)	3224	34432433453	SNNNNNNFFFNNNNFNFFN	NNNN3NNNNNNNNNN	T	262	896	01.06.03	6863	500402	89911
970.681-026	PAINTER, ANIMATED CARTOONS (motion picture; radio-tv broad.)	3114	34543432353	SNNNNNNFFFNNNNFNFFN	NNNN3NNNNNNNNNN	T	262	752	01.06.03	6863	500402	89911
970.681-030	PAINTER, PLATE (print. & pub.)	3126	33332333354	LNNNNNNFFNFNFNFFFN	NNNN3NNNNNNNNNF	D,P,J,T	191	752	01.06.01	6700	480299	81008
971.131-010	SUPERVISOR, PHOTOENGRAVING (print. & pub.)	4338	33332333354	MNNNNNNFFOFFNFNFFON	NNNN3NNNNNNNNNO	D,P,J,T	191	567	05.10.04	6700	480299	81008
971.131-014	SUPERVISOR, SCREEN MAKING (textile)	4236	33432433353	MNNONONFFOOONFNFFFN	NNNN3NNNNNNNNNN	J,T	182	567	01.06.01	6823	480206	89712
971.261-010	ETCHER, HAND (print. & pub.)	4248	33332344352	LNNONNNFFFNNNNFNFFN	NNNN3NFNNNNNNNN	J,T	182	567	01.06.01	6842	480206	89712
971.381-010	ETCHER APPRENTICE, PHOTOENGRAVING (print. & pub.)	4248	33332433353	LNNONNNFFFNNNNFNFFN	NNNN3NFNNNNNNNF	J,T	182	567	01.06.01	6842	480206	89712
971.381-014	ETCHER, PHOTOENGRAVING (print. & pub.)	4338	33332433353	LNNONNNFFFNNNNFNFFON	NNNO3NFNNNNNNNO	J,T	191	752	01.06.01	6842	480206	89712
971.381-022	PHOTOENGRAVER (print. & pub.)	4338	33332433353	LNNNNNNFFFONNFNFNFFN	NNNO3NFNNNNNNNO	J,T	191	567	01.06.01	6842	480206	89712
971.381-026	PHOTOENGRAVER APPRENTICE (print. & pub.)	4338	33322422253	LNNNNNNFFFONNNFNNFFN	NNNN3NNNNNNNNNN	J	191	567	01.06.01	6842	480206	89712
971.381-030	PHOTOENGRAVING FINISHER (print. & pub.)	4228	33332433254	LNNNNNNFFONNNFNONFFN	NNNO4NFNNNNNNNN	J,T	201	556	01.06.01	6842	480206	89712
971.381-034	PHOTOENGRAVING PRINTER (print. & pub.)	4228	33332344342	LNNNNNNFFFNNNNFNFFN	NNNN3NNNNNNNNNN	J,T	191	567	01.06.01	6842	480206	89712
971.381-038	PHOTOENGRAVING PROOFER (print. & pub.)	4228	33332433353	LNNNNNNFFFNNNNFNFFN	NNNN3NNNNNNNNNN	J,T	191	567	05.05.13	6842	480206	89712
971.381-040	PHOTOENGRAVING-PROOFER APPRENTICE (print. & pub.)	4228	33332344342	LNNNNNNFFFNNNNFNFFN	NNNN3NNNNNNNNNN	J,T	191	567	05.05.13	6842	480206	89712
971.381-046	SCREEN MAKER, TEXTILE (textile)	4227	33332433353	MNNNNNNFFFNNNNFNFFON	NNNO4NFNNNNNNNN	J	202	567	05.10.05	6869	480299	89999
971.381-050	STRIPPER (print. & pub.)	4238	33332432343	SNNONNNFFONNNFNFFN	NNNN3NNNNNNNNNN	J,T	191	567	01.06.01	6842	480206	89717
971.381-054	STRIPPER APPRENTICE (print. & pub.)	4238	33332433353	LNNONNNFFFNNNNFNFFN	NNNN3NFNNNNNNNN	J	201	567	01.06.01	7444	480206	89712
971.382-014	PHOTOGRAPHER, PHOTOENGRAVING (electron. comp.; print. & pub.)	4338	33332433353	LLNONNNFFFNNNNFNFFN	NNNN3NFNNNNNNNN	J	202	752	01.06.01	7644	480205	89712
971.382-018	REPEAT-PHOTOCOMPOSING-MACHINE OPERATOR (print. & pub.)	4337	33332433353	LNNFNNNFFFNNNNFNFFN	NNNN3NNNNNNNNNN	J,T	262	752	06.03.02	7756	480205	93947
971.684-010	BLOCKER II (print. & pub.)	3224	34433433355	SNNNNNNFFFNNNNFNFFNN	NNNN4NNNNNNNNNN	J,T	262	752	05.12.14	7756	480208	93947
971.685-010	ROLLER-PRINT TENDER (print. & pub.)	3213	34433434354	VNNFNFNFFONNNNFNFNON	NNNN3NNNNNNNNNN	R,J,T	202	567	05.10.05	7644	480208	92545

DOT #	DOT Title & Industry	Trng	Aptitude	Physical	Environment	Tempra	WkF	MPSMS	GOE	SOC	CIP	OES
971.687-010	ETCHER HELPER, HAND (print. & pub.)	2112	44544534355	HNNONONFFNNNNNNNNNN	NNNN4NFNNNNNNON	R	182	567	05.12.03	8619	480206	98999
972.137-010	SUPERVISOR, PREPRESS (print. & pub.)	4448	22332233353	LNNNNNOOONFNFOOOON	NNNN3NNNNNNNNNN	D,V,T,P,J	191	480	01.06.01	6700	000000	81008
972.281-010	DOT ETCHER (print. & pub.)	4328	33322422352	LNNNNNNNFFONNNNFNNFFN	NNNN4NNNNNNFNNN	J,T	262	752	01.06.01	6842	480205	89719
972.281-018	DOT ETCHER APPRENTICE (print. & pub.)	4328	33322422352	LNNNNNNNFFONNNNFNNFFN	NNNN4NNNNNNFNNN	J,T	262	752	01.06.01	6842	480205	89719
972.281-022	STRIPPER, LITHOGRAPHIC I (print. & pub.)	4338	33332233353	LNNNNNNNCCCNNONFNOOON	NNNN3NNNNNNNNNN	V,T,J	241	752	01.06.01	6868	480206	89717
972.282-010	SCANNER OPERATOR (print. & pub.)	4337	33333233352	LNNNNNNFFFNNNONFNOFFN	NNNN3NNNNNNNNNN	T,J	201	752	05.10.05	6868	480206	89715
972.282-018	ELECTRONIC MASKING SYSTEM OPERATOR (print. & pub.)	4338	33322233353	LNNFNNNCCFNNONCNOOFN	NNNN3ONFNNNNNN	T,J	241	752	01.06.01	7444	000000	89719
972.284-010	FILM FLAT INSPECTOR (print. & pub.)	4337	33322233353	LNNNNNNCCCNNNNFNOOON	NNNN2NNNNNNNNN	T,J	212	752	06.03.02	7820	000000	83005
972.381-010	LITHOGRAPHIC PLATEMAKER (print. & pub.)	4336	33333433355	LNNONNNFFFNNONFNFFNN	NNNN3NNNNNONON	T	201	567	01.06.01	6842	480206	89718
972.381-014	LITHOGRAPHIC-PLATE-MAKER APPRENTICE (print. & pub.)	4336	33333433355	LNNONNNFFFNNNONFNFFNN	NNNN3NNNNNONON	T	201	567	01.06.01	6842	480206	89718
972.381-018	SKETCH MAKER II (print. & pub.)	4227	33322232352	SNNNNNNFFNNNONFNFFFN	NNNO3NNNNNNNNN	J,T	241	752	01.06.01	6862	480206	89719
972.381-022	STRIPPER, LITHOGRAPHIC II (print. & pub.)	4337	33333333354	LNNNNNNCCCNNONFNOOON	NNNN3NFNNNNNNN	T	241	752	01.06.01	6868	480206	89717
972.381-026	TRANSFERRER (print. & pub.)	3116	34444443354	LNNNNNNFFFONNNNFNFNON	NNNN3NNNNNNNNN	T	201	567	01.06.01	6868	000000	89718
972.381-030	PASTE-UP ARTIST (print. & pub.)	4437	33322233355	LNNNNNNFFONNNONFNFNON	NNNN3NNNNNNNNN	T	241	752	01.06.01	6849	000000	89706
972.381-034	PROOFER, PREPRESS (print. & pub.)	3235	33333333353	LNNNNNNNCCFNNONFNOOFN	NNNN4NNNNNNCNNN	T	201	753	05.10.05	6868	000000	89799
972.381-038	PASTE-UP ARTIST APPRENTICE (print. & pub.)	4437	33322233355	LNNNNNNFFONNNONFNFFON	NNNN3NNNNNNNNNN	T	241	752	01.06.01	6868	000000	89706
972.382-010	PHOTOGRAPHER APPRENTICE, LITHOGRAPHIC (print. & pub.)	4237	33333433353	LNNNNNNFFNNFNNFNFNFON	NNNN3NNNNNNNNN	J,T	201	752	01.06.01	7444	480206	89713
972.382-014	PHOTOGRAPHER, LITHOGRAPHIC (print. & pub.)	4237	33333433353	LNNNNNNFFFNNFNNFNFFON	NNNN3NNNNNNNNN	J,T	201	752	01.06.01	7444	480206	89713
972.382-018	PHOTO MASK MAKER, ELECTRON-BEAM (electron. comp.)	3236	33333433355	LNNNNNNFOFNNONOFFFNN	NNNN3NNNNNNNNNN	T,J	201	587	05.10.05	6842	470105	89712
972.382-022	PHOTO MASK TECHNICIAN, ELECTRON-BEAM (electron. comp.)	3336	33332222355	LNNNNNNFOFINNNCNCNCNN	NNNN3NNNNNNNNNN	J,T	233	587	05.10.05	3990	470105	25105
972.384-014	PLATEMAKER, SEMICONDUCTOR PACKAGES (electron. comp.)	3234	33443334355	LNNNNNNFOFNNONONFFNN	NNNN4NNNNNNNON	R,T	201	753	05.10.05	7671	470105	92908
972.681-010	MUSIC ENGRAVER (print. & pub.)	3116	34433432255	SNNNNNNFFFNNNNFNFFNN	NNNN4NNNNNNNNN	J,T	183	567	01.06.01	6823	000000	89128
972.682-010	PLATE GRAINER (print. & pub.)	3237	34433434355	LNNONNNFFFNNNNFNFFNN	NNNF3NNNNNNNNNN	J,T	051	567	06.02.02	7644	480206	92549
972.682-014	PLATE-GRAINER APPRENTICE (print. & pub.)	3237	34433434355	LNNONNNFFFNNNNFNFFNN	NNNF3NNNNNNNNN	J,T	051	567	06.02.02	7644	480206	92549
972.687-010	PLATE INSPECTOR (print. & pub.)	3225	33432344453	LNNNNNNNFFONNONONCNOOON	NNNN3NNNNNNNNN	R,U,T	212	567	06.03.02	7820	000000	83005
973.137-010	SUPERVISOR, COMPOSING-ROOM (print. & pub.)	4237	33322344455	MNNNNNNFFFNNFNNNFNNNN	NNNN4NNNNNNNNNN	D,P,J,T	212	567	06.03.02	7100	520205	81008
973.381-010	COMPOSITOR (print. & pub.)	4238	23332232355	LNNONNNFFFNNFONNFNFNN	NNNN3NNNNNNNNNO	J,T	191	567	05.05.13	6841	480205	89702
973.381-014	COMPOSITOR APPRENTICE (print. & pub.)	4238	23332232355	LNNONNNFFFNNFONNFNFNN	NNNN3NNNNNNNNO	J,T	191	567	05.05.13	6841	480205	89702
973.381-018	JOB PRINTER (print. & pub.)	4238	23333332343	MNNONNNFFFNNNNFFNFFFN	NNNN4NNNNNNNNN	V,J,T	191	480	05.05.13	6841	480205	89705
973.381-022	JOB-PRINTER APPRENTICE (print. & pub.)	4238	23333332343	MNNONNNFFFNNNNFFNFFFN	NNNN4NNNNNNNNN	V,J,T	191	480	05.05.13	6841	480205	89705
973.381-026	MAKE-UP ARRANGER (print. & pub.)	4238	33422433355	MNNONNNFFFNNNNFNFFNN	NNNN3NNNNNNNNN	J,T	191	567	05.10.05	6841	480205	89702
973.381-030	PROOFSHEET CORRECTOR (print. & pub.)	4238	33432492355	LNNONNNFFFNNONNFNFNN	NNNN3NNNNNNNNN	J,T	191	567	05.05.13	6841	480205	89702
973.681-010	GALLEY STRIPPER (print. & pub.)	3225	33332422355	SNNNNNFFFNNNNNFNFFNN	NNNN2NNNNNNNNN	J,T	191	567	05.05.13	6863	480206	89717
974.131-010	SUPERVISOR, ELECTROTYPING AND STEREOTYPING (print. & pub.)	4338	33322444454	LNNONNNFFFNNNNFFNFFON	NNNN4NNNNNNNNN	D,P,J,T	191	567	05.10.05	6700	520205	81008
974.381-010	ELECTROTYPER (print. & pub.)	4238	23333432343	MNNONNNFFFNNNNNFFFON	NNNN4NNNNNNNNN	J,T	191	567	05.05.13	6841	480205	89799
974.381-014	ELECTROTYPER APPRENTICE (print. & pub.)	4238	33332433343	MNNONNNFFFNNNNNFFFON	NNNN4NONNNNNNN	J,T	191	567	05.05.13	6841	480205	89705
974.382-010	STEREOTYPER (print. & pub.)	4228	33333433254	LNNNNNNFFFNNFONNFNFON	NNNN4NONNNNNNN	J,T	191	567	05.05.13	6849	480206	89702
974.382-014	STEREOTYPER APPRENTICE (print. & pub.)	4228	33333433254	MNNNNNNFFFNNNNNFNFFON	NNNN4NNNNNNNNNN	J,T	191	567	05.05.13	6849	480206	89799
974.682-010	BLOCKER, METAL BASE (print. & pub.)	4227	33332433344	LNNFNFNFFNNNNFNFFON	NNFN4NFNNNNNNF	J,T	191	567	05.12.01	6849	480206	89799
976.131-010	LABORATORY CHIEF (photofinishing)	4238	33332433343	LNNONNNFFFFFNFFFON	NONN4NFNNNNNNF	V,D,P,J	202	567	05.10.05	7542	480208	92549
976.131-014	SUPERVISOR, FILM PROCESSING (motion picture; photofinishing; radio-tv broad.)	4337	33343343353	LNNNNNNFFFFNFFNFNNFFN	NNNN3NNNNNNNNN	V,D,P,J	202	897	06.01.01	7100	100103	81008
976.131-018	SUPERVISOR, MICROFILM DUPLICATING UNIT (business ser.)	4347	22343344454	LNNNNNNFFFFNFNFNNFFN	NNNN3NNNNNNNNN	V,D,P,T	202	911	05.10.05	7100	520205	81008
976.131-022	SUPERVISOR, QUALITY CONTROL (photofinishing)	4337	22332333341	LNNOOONFFNOONFNFNFN	NNNN3NNNNNNNNN	V,D,P,T	201	890	05.10.05	6700	100103	81008
976.131-026	SUPERVISOR, TYPE PHOTOGRAPHY (machinery mfg.)	4348	33332223354	LNNNNNNFFFFFNFNFNNOON	NNNN3NNNNNNNNN	V,D,J	202	897	05.10.05	7100	520205	81008
976.132-010	SUPERVISOR, FILM PROCESSING (photofinishing)	4336	33333333354	LNNOONNNFFFNFNFNNOON	NNNN2NNNNNNNNN	D,V,T,P,J	201	753	05.10.05	7100	100103	81008
976.134-010	SUPERVISOR, CUTTING AND SPLICING (motion picture; photofinishing)	4236	33333334454	LNNOONNFFOFFNFNFFON	NNNN3NNNNNNNNO	V,D,J	202	897	05.12.01	7100	100199	81008
976.137-014	SUPERVISOR, FINISHING DEPARTMENT (photofinishing)	4236	33343343454	LNNONNNFFFNFFFFNFFON	NNNN3NNNNNNNNN	D,P,J,T	212	897	05.09.01	7100	520205	81008
976.267-010	QUALITY-CONTROL TECHNICIAN (photofinishing)	4236	33433343353	LNNONNNFFFFNFNFNOOFN	NNNN3NNNNNNNNN	J,P	212	606	05.09.01	7820	100103	83005
976.360-010	PRINT CONTROLLER (photofinishing)	4326	33333333353	LNNNNNNFFFNFOFFNNFFN	NNNN3NNNNNNNNN	J,P	202	897	06.01.02	7479	100103	92997
976.361-010	REPRODUCTION TECHNICIAN (any industry)	4226	33322433342	LNNFNNNFFFOONFFFFN	NNNF3NFNNNNNNN	J,T	201	897	06.01.02	6868	100103	89914
976.362-010	FILM INSPECTOR (photofinishing)	4225	33332333352	LNNNNNNFFFOONFFFFN	NNNN3NNNNNNNNN	J	212	897	05.10.05	7820	100103	83005

DOT # DOT Title & Industry	Trng	Aptitude	Physical	Environment	Tempra	WkF	MPSMS	GOE	SOC	CIP	OES
976.380-010 COMPUTER-CONTROLLED-COLOR-PHOTOGRAPH-PRINTER OPERATOR (photofinishing)	3333	34343333343	SNNNNNNFFNNNNFNNFFN	NNNN3NNNNNNNNNN	J,T	202	753	05.10.05	7671	100103	89914
976.381-010 FILM LABORATORY TECHNICIAN I (motion picture)	4447	23232333352	LNNNNNNFFNNNNFNFFFN	NNNN3NNNNNNNNN	J	212	911	02.04.01	6868	100199	89914
976.381-014 MICROFICHE DUPLICATOR (business ser.)	4226	33322433345	LNNNNNNFFNNNNFNFFNN	NNNF3NFNNNONNF	J,T	201	890	05.10.05	6849	100103	89914
976.381-018 PROJECTION PRINTER (photofinishing)	3227	33333433353	LNNNNNNFFNNNNFNFFNN	NNNN3NONNNNNNO	J,T	212	897	05.10.05	6868	100103	89914
976.381-022 TEMPLATE REPRODUCTION TECHNICIAN (aircraft mfg.)	4237	33332433254	LNNNNNNFFONNNNFNOOON	NNNN3NNNNNNNNN	T	201	568	05.10.05	6868	000000	89914
976.382-010 CAMERA OPERATOR, TITLE (motion picture)	4337	34434443354	LNNNNNNFFNNNNCCCCCC	NNNN2NNNNNNNNN	R,T	201	911	05.10.05	7671	100103	92908
976.382-014 COLOR-PRINTER OPERATOR (photofinishing)	3223	33333444352	LNNNNNNCCNOONFNFFFN	NNNN3NNNNNNNNN	J,T	202	897	05.10.05	7671	100103	92908
976.382-018 FILM DEVELOPER (motion picture; photofinishing)	3116	34443433355	LNNNNNNFFFNNNNFNFNNN	NNNO4NNNNNNNNF	J,T	202	911	05.10.05	7671	100103	92908
976.382-022 PHOTOSTAT OPERATOR (any industry)	3225	33343434353	LNNNNNNFFNNNNFNFFFN	NNNF3NNNNNNNNN	J	201	897	05.10.05	6868	100103	89914
976.382-030 PHOTOGRAPHIC ALIGNER, SEMICONDUCTOR WAFERS (electron. comp.)	3224	34433433355	LNNNNNNFFNNNNFNFFNN	NNNN3NNNNNNNNN	J,T	201	587	06.02.18	7671	470105	92908
976.382-034 STEP-AND-REPEAT REDUCTION CAMERA OPERATOR (electron. comp.)	3225	33332333355	LNNNNNNFFNNNNFNFNNN	NNNN3NNNNNNNON	T,J	201	753	05.10.05	7444	500406	89713
976.382-038 PHOTO MASK PATTERN GENERATOR (electron. comp.)	3335	33322244455	LNNNNNNFFNNNNFNFNNNN	NNNN3NNNNNNNNN	T,J	201	587	05.10.05	7671	470105	89914
976.384-010 PHOTO TECHNICIAN (electron. comp.)	3234	33433333355	LNNNNNNFCCNNNNCNFFNN	NNNN3NNNNNNNNN	R,T	201	753	05.10.05	7671	470105	89914
976.384-014 PHOTO MASK PROCESSOR (electron. comp.)	3225	33433333354	LNNNNNNFFNNNNFNOOON	NNNN3NONNNNNNN	T	201	753	05.10.05	7671	470105	92908
976.385-010 MICROFILM PROCESSOR (business ser.)	3222	34433443355	LNNNNNNFFNNNNFNFNN	NNNN2NNNNNNNNN	T	202	897	05.10.05	7671	100103	92908
976.487-010 PHOTOGRAPH FINISHER (photofinishing)	2112	44344443354	LNNNNNNFFNNNNFNFNON	NNNN3NNNNNNNNN	R	054	897	05.10.05	7759	100103	93999
976.564-010 DETAILER, SCHOOL PHOTOGRAPHS (photofinishing)	3224	33333433353	LNNNNNNFFFNFFNFNFN	NNNN3NNNNNNNNN	V,J,T	282	897	07.05.03	4752	100103	58008
976.567-010 FILM-REPLACEMENT ORDERER (motion picture)	3233	34444433455	LNNNNNNFFNNNNFNFNNN	NNNN3NNNNNNNNN	R,T	231	911	07.07.03	4664	000000	55326
976.665-010 TAKE-DOWN SORTER (photofinishing)	3113	34333333353	LNNFNNNCCFFOONFNFNFN	NNNN3NNNNNNNNN	J,T	212	897	05.10.05	7671	100103	92908
976.667-010 PHOTOGRAPHER HELPER (any industry)	3224	34433433343	MNNOONNFFNOONFNFNFN	NNNF3NFNNNNNNN	V,T	202	753	01.02.03	7759	100103	93999
976.681-010 DEVELOPER (photofinishing)	3224	34433433354	LNNNNNNFFNOONFNFNFN	NNNF3NONNNNNNNO	J	202	897	05.10.05	6868	100103	89914
976.682-010 FILM PRINTER (motion picture)	3115	34433433353	LNNNNNNFFNNNNFNFOFN	NNNN3NNNNNNNNN	J,T	202	911	05.10.05	7671	100103	92908
976.682-014 PRINTER OPERATOR, BLACK-AND-WHITE (photofinishing)	3115	34443433355	SNNNNNNFFONNNFNFNNN	NNNN4NNNNNNNNN	R,T	202	897	05.10.05	7671	100103	92908
976.682-018 RECTIFICATION PRINTER (any industry)	3214	33343433355	LNNNNNNFFNNNNFNFNN	NNNN3NNNNNNNNN	R,T	202	897	05.10.05	7671	100103	92908
976.682-022 MICROFILM-CAMERA OPERATOR (business ser.)	3123	33443344344	LNNNNNNOFFONNNFNFOON	NNNN3NNNNNNNNN	R,T	201	897	05.10.05	7671	500406	92908
976.684-010 DENSITY CONTROL PUNCHER (motion picture)	3114	34433433354	LNNNNNNFFNNNNFNFNFN	NNNN3NNNNNNNNN	J,T	192	911	05.10.05	7759	100103	93999
976.684-014 FILM LABORATORY TECHNICIAN (motion picture; photofinishing)	3223	34433433354	SNNONNNFFOONNFNFFFN	NNNN3NNNNNNNNNO	J	054	911	05.10.05	7678	100103	92944
976.684-018 MOUNTER, HAND (photofinishing)	2112	44444433344	LNNNNNNFFOONNNFNFFON	NNNN3NNNNNNNNNN	R,T	054	897	06.04.34	7753	100103	93926
976.684-022 PRINT WASHER (photofinishing)	2113	44544453355	LNNNNNNFFOONNFNNNNN	NNNF3NNNNNNNNN	R	031	897	05.10.05	7759	100103	93999
976.684-026 SPLICER (photofinishing)	2112	44443443344	LNNNNNNFFNNNNFNFOFN	NNNN4NNNNNNNNN	R,T	062	897	06.04.34	7759	500406	93999
976.684-030 CONTACT PRINTER, PRINTED CIRCUIT BOARDS (electron. comp.)	2223	44434434355	LNNNNNNCFNNNNCNFFNN	NNNN2NNNNNONNN	R,T	201	587	05.10.05	7671	470105	92908
976.684-034 CONTACT PRINTER, PHOTORESIST (inst. & app.; optical goods)	3336	33333423355	LNNNNNNFFNNNNFNFNN	NNNN3NONNNNNNN	T	202	603	05.05.11	7757	150699	93951
976.684-038 CONTACT WORKER, LITHOGRAPHY (print. & pub.)	3226	33433433355	LNNNNNNFFONNONFNNNN	NNNN4NNNNNFNNN	R,T	201	753	05.10.05	7671	000000	92908
976.685-010 CUTTER (photofinishing)	2112	44434443354	LNNNNNNFFNNNNFNFNFN	NNNN4NNNNNNNNNO	R,T	054	897	06.04.09	7678	100199	92944
976.685-014 DEVELOPER, AUTOMATIC (photofinishing)	2112	44434433344	LNNNNNNFFFFFNFNFNNN	NNNN4NNNNNNNNNF	R,T	202	897	06.04.19	7671	100103	92908
976.685-018 FILM LABORATORY TECHNICIAN II (motion picture)	3225	34434553344	LNNNNNNFFOONNFNNOON	NNNN4NNNNNNNNN	V,J,T	153	911	05.12.14	7671	000000	92908
976.685-022 MOUNTER, AUTOMATIC (photofinishing)	2112	44443433355	LNNONNNFFNNNNFNFNNN	NNNN3NNNNNNNNN	R	054	897	06.04.20	7671	100103	92908
976.685-026 PRINT DEVELOPER, AUTOMATIC (photofinishing)	2114	44443443353	LNNONONFFNNNNFNFNFF	NNNN4NFNNNNNNNF	R,T	202	897	06.04.19	7671	100103	92908
976.685-030 UTILITY WORKER, FILM PROCESSING (photofinishing)	3123	33444433354	LNNNNNNFFNNNNFNFNNN	NNNN4NNNNNNNNNF	V	202	897	06.04.19	7671	100103	93951
976.685-034 DEVELOPER, PRINTED CIRCUIT BOARD PANELS (electron. comp.)	2222	44444444454	MNNNNNNCCONNNNCNCOFON	NNNO3NONNNNNNON	R,U	202	587	06.04.19	7671	470105	92908
976.685-038 PHOTOGRAPHIC PROCESSOR, SEMICONDUCTOR WAFERS (electron. comp.)	3122	44544443355	LNNNNNNFFONNONFNNNN	NNNN4NNNNNNNNN	R,U	202	587	06.04.19	7671	470105	92908
976.687-010 EDITOR, SCHOOL PHOTOGRAPH (photofinishing)	3125	34443443453	LNNNNNNFFNNNNFNFNFN	NNNN3NNNNNNNNN	J,T	212	897	01.06.03	7850	100103	83005
976.687-014 PHOTO CHECKER AND ASSEMBLER (photofinishing)	3114	34433444342	LNNONNNFFNNNNFNFFFN	NNNN3NNNNNNNNN	J,T	212	897	06.03.02	7671	100103	83005
976.687-018 PHOTOFINISHING LABORATORY WORKER (photofinishing)	2223	44444433354	LNNONNNFFNNNNFNFNFN	NNNN3NNNNNNNNN	R,J	221	897	06.03.02	4753	100103	58028
976.687-022 PRINT INSPECTOR (photofinishing)	3125	34453433352	MNNONNNFFNNONFNFFFN	NNNN3ONFNNNNNNN	J	212	897	06.03.02	7820	100103	83005
977.381-010 BOOKBINDER (print. & pub.)	3227	33433433343	MNNONNNFFNNONFNFFFN	NNNN3ONFNNNNNNN	V,T	102	480	05.05.15	6844	480299	89721
977.381-014 BOOKBINDER APPRENTICE (print. & pub.)	3227	33433433343	MNNONNNFFNNONFNFFFN	NNNN3ONFNNNNNNN	V,T	102	480	05.05.15	6844	480299	89721
977.684-010 BOOK REPAIRER (any industry)	2113	34433443354	LNNNNNNFFNNNNFNFNON	NNNN3NNNNNNNNN	J,T	102	486	05.12.19	6179	480299	85999
977.684-014 INLAYER (print. & pub.)	3114	34433443354	SNNNNNNFFNNNNFNFFON	NNNN3NNNNNNNNN	R,T	061	486	01.06.03	7756	480299	93947
977.684-018 PRESSER (print. & pub.)	2114	44434433335	LNNNNNNFFONNONONFNNNN	NNNN4NONNNNNNN	R,T	134	480	06.02.26	7667	480299	93956
977.684-022 STITCHER, HAND (print. & pub.)	2114	44434433354	LNNNNNNFFNNNNFNFFON	NNNN3NNNNNNNNN	R,T	171	486	06.04.26	7752	480299	93923

DOT #	DOT Title & Industry	Trng	Aptitude	Physical	Environment	Tempra	WkF	MPSMS	GOE	SOC	CIP	OES
977.684-026	BENCH WORKER, BINDING (print. & pub.)	2113	4444443354	LNNONNNFFFNNNNFNNNO	NNNN4NONNNNNNO	R,T,U	061	482	06.04.37	7759	000000	93999
977.687-010	COLLATOR, HAND (print. & pub.)	2113	4444443354	LNNNNNNNFFFNNNNFNFN	NNNN3NNNNNNNNN	R	061	486	06.04.26	7850	000299	83005
979.130-010	SUPERVISOR, BLUEPRINTING-AND-PHOTOCOPY (any industry)	4228	33343334353	LNNONONFFNFNFNFNFN	NNNN3NNNNNNNN	V,D,P,J	201	897	05.10.05	7100	520205	81008
979.130-014	SUPERVISOR, PRINTING-SHOP (print. & pub.)	4348	33332933353	LNNNNNNNFFFOFFNFNFFOOON	NNNN5OFFNNNNNN	V,D,P,J,T	191	480	05.05.13	7100	480208	81008
979.131-010	SUPERVISOR, PUBLICATIONS PRODUCTION (print. & pub.)	4248	22332433354	LNNNNNNNFFFOFFNFNFFN	NNNN3NNNNNNNN	D,P,J	264	752	01.02.03	7100	480205	81008
979.131-014	SUPERVISOR, ROLLER SHOP (textile)	4337	33224433354	HNNNNNNNFFFNFFNFNFN	NNNN4NNNNNNNN	D,P,J,T	212	567	06.02.01	6700	000000	81008
979.131-018	SUPERVISOR, SILK-SCREEN CUTTING AND PRINTING (any industry)	4338	33333433353	LNJNNNNNFFFNFNFNFFN	NNNN4NNNNNNNN	D,P,J	191	567	06.02.01	6700	520205	81008
979.132-010	SHIFT SUPERVISOR, FILM PROCESSING (print. & pub.)	4338	33322223251	LNNNNNNNFFFNFNFNFFN	NNNN3NNNNNNNN	D,P,V	202	753	05.10.05	6700	520205	81008
979.137-010	SUPERVISOR, FINISHING ROOM (print. & pub.)	4227	33333444454	LNNNNNNNFFFNFNFNFFON	NNNN3NNNNNNNN	D,P,J,T	061	489	06.02.01	7100	480299	81008
979.137-014	SUPERVISOR, INSPECTING (paper goods)	4227	33433334342	LNNNNNNNFFFOFNFNFFN	NNNN4NNNNNNNN	D,P,J,T	212	474	06.02.01	7100	000000	81008
979.137-018	SUPERVISOR, PRODUCTION (paper goods)	4226	33333334452	LNNNNNNNFFFNFNFNFFN	NNNN3NNNNNNNN	D,P,J,T	191	474	06.02.01	7100	520205	81008
979.137-022	SUPERVISOR, SAMPLE PREPARATION (textile)	4337	23333444452	LNNNNNNNFFFOFFNFNFN	NNNN3NNNNNNNN	D,P,J,T	191	567	06.02.01	7100	150699	81008
979.137-026	SUPERVISOR, TYPE-DISK QUALITY CONTROL (machinery mfg.)	4347	33332344354	LNNNNNNNFFFONFFNFNFON	NNNN3NNNNNNNN	D,V,T,P	191	567	06.01.01	6700	520205	81008
979.281-010	DIE MAKER (print. & pub.)	4337	23932422253	LNNNNNNNFFFONNNFNFFN	NNNN4NNNNNNNN	J,T	183	567	01.06.01	6823	000000	89128
979.281-014	ENGRAVER, BLOCK (print. & pub.)	4237	33323432254	LNNNNNNNFFFNNNFNFFON	NNNN3NNNNNNNNF	J	183	567	01.06.01	6823	480205	89128
979.281-018	ENGRAVER, PICTURE (print. & pub.)	4338	33322232354	LNNNNNNNCCCNNNNFNNFON	NNNN3NNNNNNNN	J	183	567	01.06.01	6823	480205	89128
979.282-010	ELECTRONIC PREPRESS SYSTEM OPERATOR (print. & pub.)	4337	33322323352	SNNNNNNNGFCNNNNCNNNCFN	NNNN2NNNNNNNN	R,T,J	262	752	01.06.01	6842	000000	89707
979.360-010	SCREEN-PRINTING-EQUIPMENT SETTER (paper goods)	4237	33332423352	LNNNNNNNFFFOONFNFFN	NNNN3NNNNNNNN	J	191	567	06.01.02	7449	480299	92524
979.361-010	DOCUMENT RESTORER (profess. & kin.)	4336	33333333333	MNNNNNNNFFFOONFNFFN	NNNN3NNNNNNNN	J	212	933	05.05.13	6849	000000	31511
979.362-010	INSTANT PRINT OPERATOR (print. & pub.)	3236	33333333353	MMNONNNFFONOONONNOON	NNNN4FFFNNNNNN	V,T,P	191	480	05.10.05	7643	000000	92543
979.380-010	PANTOGRAPH SETTER (print. & pub.)	4226	34434344344	MMNFNFNFONNNFNFFON	NNNN4NNNNNNNN	J,T	183	567	05.05.13	7449	000000	92529
979.381-010	ENGRAVER I (print. & pub.)	3125	34343433355	LNNNNNNNFFONNNFNFFN	NNNN3NNNNNNNN	J,T	183	567	05.10.05	6823	480205	89128
979.381-014	LINE-UP EXAMINER (print. & pub.)	3228	33332343353	LNNNNNNNFFNNNNFNFFN	NNNN3NNNNNNNN	J	191	567	01.06.01	6881	480205	83002
979.381-026	ROLLER REPAIRER (textile)	4227	34434422355	HNNNNNNNCCFFNNNFNFFN	NNNN3NNNNNNNN	J,T	183	567	01.06.01	6130	470303	85119
979.381-030	SIDEROGRAPHER (print. & pub.)	4326	33322343355	MNNNNNNNFFONNNNFNFFN	NNNN3NNNNNNNN	J,T	183	567	01.06.01	6823	480205	89128
979.381-034	SKETCH MAKER I (print. & pub.)	3114	34424433354	LNNNNNNNFFFNNNNFNFFN	NNNN3NNNNNNNN	J,T	241	752	01.06.01	6863	480205	89911
979.381-038	STENCIL MAKER (carpet & rug)	3226	34333433353	MMNFNNNNFFNNNNNFNFFN	NNNN3NNNNNNNN	T	241	752	01.06.02	6862	000000	89908
979.382-010	CLAMPER (print. & pub.)	3226	33322533345	MMNNNNNNFFFNNNNFNFFN	NNON4NNNNNNNN	J,T	192	752	05.05.13	7644	480208	92543
979.382-014	ENGRAVER, MACHINE (print. & pub.)	4228	33225533354	VNNONONFFNNNNFNFFN	NNNN4NNNNNNNN	J,T	192	567	05.10.05	7449	000000	92529
979.382-018	PRINTER (print. & pub.)	4235	34433433354	MNNONNNFFFNNONFNOONON	NNNN4NFONNONNNN	V,T,J	191	480	01.06.01	7449	480205	89799
979.382-022	PANTOGRAPHER (print. & pub.)	3114	34433343343	LNNNNNNNFFNNNNNFNFFN	NNNN3NNNNNNNN	J,T	183	567	01.06.01	7644	480299	92545
979.382-026	COMPUTER TYPESETTER-KEYLINER (print. & pub.)	4346	33332233354	SNNNNNNNFFNNONCNNFON	NNNN2NNNNNNNN	T	264	896	01.06.01	6849	000000	89799
979.384-010	SCREEN MAKER, PHOTOGRAPHIC PROCESS (any industry)	3224	34443434354	MNNNNNNNFFONNNNFNNOON	NNNO3NNNNNNNN	T	201	567	05.10.05	6868	480299	89914
979.581-010	ENGRAVER, RUBBER (print. & pub.)	3116	34433443354	SNNNNNNNFFFNNNNFNFFN	NNNN4NNNNNNNN	J,T	183	752	01.06.01	7757	480299	93951
979.667-010	INSPECTOR, SCREEN PRINTING (print. & pub.)	3223	34433444453	LNNONNNNFFONOONFNFFN	NNNN4NNNNNNNN	T,J	212	480	06.03.02	7820	480299	83005
979.681-010	LETTERER (machinery mfg.)	3116	33432243355	LNNNNNNNFFONNNNFNNFN	NNNN3NNNNNNNN	J,T	242	567	01.06.03	7759	500402	93999
979.681-014	PRINTER (glass products)	3125	34443443355	SNNNNNNNFFFNNNNNFNFFN	NNNN3NNNNNNNN	J,T	191	567	01.06.01	6849	480208	89799
979.681-018	ROLLER ENGRAVER, HAND (print. & pub.)	3227	34433433353	SNNNNNNNFFONNNNFNFFON	NNNN3NNNNNNNN	J,T	183	567	01.06.01	7757	480206	93951
979.681-022	SILK-SCREEN CUTTER (any industry)	3125	33433432354	LNNNNNNNFFONNNNFNFFN	NNNN3NNNNNNNN	J,T	191	567	01.06.01	6862	000000	89908
979.682-010	BLOCKER I (print. & pub.)	3227	33333534355	LNNNNNNNFFNNNNFNFFN	NNNN4NNFNNNNNN	V,J,T	102	567	06.02.09	7649	480104	92549
979.682-014	BLUEPRINTING-MACHINE OPERATOR (any industry)	3225	34443434354	LNNONNNNFFONNNFNNON	NNNN4NNNNNNNN	R,T	202	897	05.10.05	7644	480105	92545
979.682-022	ROLLER VARNISHER (print. & pub.)	3116	34443534355	LNNNNNNNFFFNNNNFNFFN	NNNN4NFNNNNNNN	R,T	151	567	06.02.21	7644	480206	92549
979.682-026	ROUTER (print. & pub.)	3115	33432243355	LNNNNNNNFFNNNNFNFFN	NNNN3NNNNNNNN	J,T	055	567	05.10.05	7757	000000	93951
979.684-010	CARBON PRINTER (print. & pub.)	3116	34433443355	LNNNNNNNFFNNNFNFFN	NNNN3NNNNNON	J,T	191	567	01.06.01	7757	480206	93999
979.684-014	ENGRAVER II (print. & pub.)	2123	34433433354	SNNNNNNNFFNNNFNFON	NNNN3NNNNNNNN	J,T	183	567	06.04.28	7759	480206	93951
979.684-018	LEGEND MAKER (fabrication, nec)	3225	34433533355	LNNNNNNNFFFNNNNNNNNN	NNNN3NNNNNNNN	R,T	061	619	06.04.26	7759	500402	93999
977.684-022	MAP-AND-CHART MOUNTER (print. & pub.)	2113	44444433345	MNNOOONFFNNNNNNNNNN	NNNN4NONNNNNNN	R,T	063	486	06.02.26	7679	500402	92998
979.684-026	PRINT-SHOP HELPER (print. & pub.)	3223	34443434354	LNNNNNNNFFFNNNNNNNN	NNNN4NFNNNNNNN	R	191	567	05.12.18	8616	480208	98999
979.684-030	SCREEN PRINTER (textile)	3115	34433434353	LNNNNNNNFFNNNFNFFN	NNNN3NNNNNNON	R,T	191	420	06.02.27	7757	480299	93951
979.684-034	SCREEN PRINTER (any industry)	2113	34433434353	LNNNNNNNCCCNOONFFFFN	NNNN3NNNNNON	R,T	191	480	06.04.34	7757	480299	93951
979.684-038	SILK-SCREEN REPAIRER (any industry)	3213	34433433354	LNNNNNNNFFNNNFNFFON	NNNN3NNNNNNNN	J	191	567	05.10.05	6179	480299	85999

DOT #	DOT Title & Industry	Trng	Aptitude	Physical	Environment	Tempra	WkF	MPSMS	GOE	SOC	CIP	OES
979.684-042	PRINTING SCREEN ASSEMBLER (electron. comp.)	2112	44544544355	LNNNNNNFFFNNNFNOONN	NNNNN3NNNNNNNNNN	R,U	061	610	06.04.34	7740	480299	93956
979.685-010	SILK-SCREEN PRINTER, MACHINE (any industry)	2123	44443434344	LNNNNNNFFFNNONFNOOON	NNNNN3NNNNNNNNNN	R,T,U	191	540	06.04.09	7643	480299	92543
979.687-010	EXAMINER (print. & pub.)	2124	44493444455	SNNNNNNCCCNNNNCNNCNN	NNNNN3NNNNNNNNNN	J	212	474	06.03.02	7820	480208	83005
979.687-014	PHOTOSTAT-OPERATOR HELPER (any industry)	2112	44444434355	LNNNNNNFFFNNNNFNOONN	NNNN3NNNNNNNNNN	R	201	606	05.12.19	8619	100103	98999
979.687-018	PLATE GAUGER (print. & pub.)	2123	44443443355	SNNNNNNFFFNNNNFNFFNN	NNNNN3NNNNNNNNNN	J,T	212	567	06.03.02	7820	480206	83005
979.687-022	SCREEN PRINTER HELPER (any industry)	2112	44544544454	MNNFNNNFFFONNNFNONON	NNNN4NNNNNNNNNO	R	191	752	06.04.34	8620	480299	98999
979.687-026	TYPE-COPY EXAMINER (machinery mfg.)	2112	44442344455	SNNNNNNFFFNNNNFNNFNN	NNNN3NNNNNNNNNN	T	211	567	06.03.02	7820	000000	83005
979.687-030	INSPECTOR, FURNITURE DECALS (furniture)	2112	44433444454	MNNNNNNCCCNNNNCNNCCN	NNNN3NFNNNNNNNN	R,T	212	752	06.03.02	7820	480299	83005
979.687-034	GENERAL WORKER, LITHOGRAPHIC (print. & pub.)	2221	44444433344	MONOOONFFFNNONOOOOOO	NNNO5OOONNNNON	V	191	480	06.03.02	8619	000000	98999

APPENDIX A:
DOT Occupational Categories, Divisions, and Groups

This provides a listing of the major groupings of occupations used by the U.S. Department of Labor. This system of organizing jobs is used in the *Dictionary of Occupational Titles* and is presented as the first three numbers of the DOT code number that is assigned to each occupation listed in the DOT. This appendix will allow you to interpret the specific meaning of these three DOT numbers.

ONE-DIGIT OCCUPATIONAL CATEGORIES

0/1 PROFESSIONAL, TECHNICAL, AND MANAGERIAL OCCUPATIONS

2 CLERICAL AND SALES OCCUPATIONS

3 SERVICE OCCUPATIONS

4 AGRICULTURAL, FISHERY, FORESTRY, AND RELATED OCCUPATIONS

5 PROCESSING OCCUPATIONS

6 MACHINE TRADES OCCUPATIONS

7 BENCHWORK OCCUPATIONS

8 STRUCTURAL WORK OCCUPATIONS

9 MISCELLANEOUS OCCUPATIONS

TWO-DIGIT OCCUPATIONAL DIVISIONS

00/01 OCCUPATIONS IN ARCHITECTURE, ENGINEERING, AND SURVEYING

02 OCCUPATIONS IN MATHEMATICS AND PHYSICAL SCIENCES

03 COMPUTER-RELATED OCCUPATIONS

04 OCCUPATIONS IN LIFE SCIENCES

05 OCCUPATIONS IN SOCIAL SCIENCES

07 OCCUPATIONS IN MEDICINE AND HEALTH

09 OCCUPATIONS IN EDUCATION

10 OCCUPATIONS IN MUSEUM, LIBRARY, AND ARCHIVAL SCIENCES

11 OCCUPATIONS IN LAW AND JURISPRUDENCE

12 OCCUPATIONS IN RELIGION AND THEOLOGY

13 OCCUPATIONS IN WRITING

14 OCCUPATIONS IN ART

15 OCCUPATIONS IN ENTERTAINMENT AND RECREATION

16 OCCUPATIONS IN ADMINISTRATIVE SPECIALIZATIONS

18 MANAGERS AND OFFICIALS, N.E.C.

19 MISCELLANEOUS PROFESSIONAL, TECHNICAL, AND MANAGERIAL OCCUPATIONS

20 STENOGRAPHY, TYPING, FILING, AND RELATED OCCUPATIONS

21 COMPUTING AND ACCOUNT-RECORDING OCCUPATIONS

22 PRODUCTION AND STOCK CLERKS AND RELATED OCCUPATIONS

23 INFORMATION AND MESSAGE DISTRIBUTION OCCUPATIONS

24 MISCELLANEOUS CLERICAL OCCUPATIONS

25 SALES OCCUPATIONS, SERVICES

26 SALES OCCUPATIONS, CONSUMABLE COMMODITIES

27 SALES OCCUPATIONS, COMMODITIES, N.E.C.

29 MISCELLANEOUS SALES OCCUPATIONS

30 DOMESTIC SERVICE OCCUPATIONS

31 FOOD AND BEVERAGE PREPARATION AND SERVICE OCCUPATIONS

32 LODGING AND RELATED SERVICE OCCUPATIONS

33 BARBERING, COSMETOLOGY, AND RELATED SERVICE OCCUPATIONS

34 AMUSEMENT AND RECREATION SERVICE OCCUPATIONS

35 MISCELLANEOUS PERSONAL SERVICE OCCUPATIONS

36 APPAREL AND FURNISHINGS SERVICE OCCUPATIONS

37 PROTECTIVE SERVICE OCCUPATIONS

38 BUILDING AND RELATED SERVICE OCCUPATIONS

40 PLANT FARMING OCCUPATIONS

41 ANIMAL FARMING OCCUPATIONS

42 MISCELLANEOUS AGRICULTURAL AND RELATED OCCUPATIONS

44 FISHERY AND RELATED OCCUPATIONS

45 FORESTRY OCCUPATIONS

46 HUNTING, TRAPPING, AND RELATED OCCUPATIONS

50 OCCUPATIONS IN PROCESSING OF METAL

51 ORE REFINING AND FOUNDRY OCCUPATIONS

52 OCCUPATIONS IN PROCESSING OF FOOD, TOBACCO, AND RELATED PRODUCTS

53 OCCUPATIONS IN PROCESSING OF PAPER AND RELATED MATERIALS

54 OCCUPATIONS IN PROCESSING OF PETROLEUM, COAL, NATURAL AND MANUFACTURED GAS, AND RELATED PRODUCTS

55 OCCUPATIONS IN PROCESSING OF CHEMICALS, PLASTICS, SYNTHETICS, RUBBER, PAINT, AND RELATED PRODUCTS

56 OCCUPATIONS IN PROCESSING OF WOOD AND WOOD PRODUCTS

57 OCCUPATIONS IN PROCESSING OF STONE, CLAY, GLASS, AND RELATED PRODUCTS

58 OCCUPATIONS IN PROCESSING OF LEATHER, TEXTILES, AND RELATED PRODUCTS

59 PROCESSING OCCUPATIONS, N.E.C.

60 METAL MACHINING OCCUPATIONS

61 METALWORKING OCCUPATIONS, N.E.C.

62/63 MECHANICS AND MACHINERY REPAIRERS

64 PAPERWORKING OCCUPATIONS

65 PRINTING OCCUPATIONS

66 WOOD MACHINING OCCUPATIONS

67 OCCUPATIONS IN MACHINING STONE, CLAY, GLASS, AND RELATED MATERIALS

68 TEXTILE OCCUPATIONS

69 MACHINE TRADES OCCUPATIONS, N.E.C.

70 OCCUPATIONS IN FABRICATION, ASSEMBLY, AND REPAIR OF METAL PRODUCTS, N.E.C.

71 OCCUPATIONS IN FABRICATION AND REPAIR OF SCIENTIFIC, MEDICAL, PHOTOGRAPHIC, OPTICAL, HOROLOGICAL, AND RELATED PRODUCTS

72 OCCUPATIONS IN ASSEMBLY AND REPAIR OF ELECTRICAL EQUIPMENT

73 OCCUPATIONS IN FABRICATION AND REPAIR OF PRODUCTS MADE FROM ASSORTED MATERIALS

74 PAINTING, DECORATING, AND RELATED OCCUPATIONS

75 OCCUPATIONS IN FABRICATION AND REPAIR OF PLASTICS, SYNTHETICS, RUBBER, AND RELATED PRODUCTS

76 OCCUPATIONS IN FABRICATION AND REPAIR OF WOOD PRODUCTS

77 OCCUPATIONS IN FABRICATION AND REPAIR OF SAND, STONE, CLAY, AND GLASS PRODUCTS

78 OCCUPATIONS IN FABRICATION AND REPAIR OF TEXTILE, LEATHER, AND RELATED PRODUCTS

79 BENCHWORK OCCUPATIONS, N.E.C.

80 OCCUPATIONS IN METAL FABRICATING, N.E.C.

81 WELDERS, CUTTERS, AND RELATED OCCUPATIONS

82 ELECTRICAL ASSEMBLING, INSTALLING, AND REPAIRING OCCUPATIONS

84 PAINTING, PLASTERING, WATERPROOFING, CEMENTING, AND RELATED OCCUPATIONS

85 EXCAVATING, GRADING, PAVING, AND RELATED OCCUPATIONS

86 CONSTRUCTION OCCUPATIONS, N.E.C.

89 STRUCTURAL WORK OCCUPATIONS, N.E.C.

90 MOTOR FREIGHT OCCUPATIONS

91 TRANSPORTATION OCCUPATIONS, N.E.C.

92 PACKAGING AND MATERIALS HANDLING OCCUPATIONS

93 OCCUPATIONS IN EXTRACTION OF MINERALS

95 OCCUPATIONS IN PRODUCTION AND DISTRIBUTION OF UTILITIES

96 AMUSEMENT, RECREATION, MOTION PICTURE, RADIO AND TELEVISION OCCUPATIONS, N.E.C.

97 OCCUPATIONS IN GRAPHIC ART WORK

THREE-DIGIT OCCUPATIONAL GROUPS

001 ARCHITECTURAL OCCUPATIONS

002 AERONAUTICAL ENGINEERING OCCUPATIONS

003 ELECTRICAL/ELECTRONICS ENGINEERING OCCUPATIONS

005 CIVIL ENGINEERING OCCUPATIONS

006 CERAMIC ENGINEERING OCCUPATIONS

007 MECHANICAL ENGINEERING OCCUPATIONS

008 CHEMICAL ENGINEERING OCCUPATIONS

010 MINING AND PETROLEUM ENGINEERING OCCUPATIONS

011 METALLURGY AND METALLURGICAL ENGINEERING OCCUPATIONS

012 INDUSTRIAL ENGINEERING OCCUPATIONS

013 AGRICULTURAL ENGINEERING OCCUPATIONS

014 MARINE ENGINEERING OCCUPATIONS

015 NUCLEAR ENGINEERING OCCUPATIONS

017 DRAFTERS, N.E.C.

018 SURVEYING/CARTOGRAPHIC OCCUPATIONS

019 OCCUPATIONS IN ARCHITECTURE, ENGINEERING, AND SURVEYING, N.E.C.

020 OCCUPATIONS IN MATHEMATICS

021 OCCUPATIONS IN ASTRONOMY

022 OCCUPATIONS IN CHEMISTRY

023 OCCUPATIONS IN PHYSICS

024 OCCUPATIONS IN GEOLOGY

025 OCCUPATIONS IN METEOROLOGY

029 OCCUPATIONS IN MATHEMATICS AND PHYSICAL SCIENCES, N.E.C.

030 OCCUPATIONS IN SYSTEMS ANALYSIS AND PROGRAMMING

031 OCCUPATIONS IN DATA COMMUNICATIONS AND NETWORKS

032 OCCUPATIONS IN COMPUTER SYSTEM USER SUPPORT

033 OCCUPATIONS IN COMPUTER SYSTEMS TECHNICAL SUPPORT

039 COMPUTER-RELATED OCCUPATIONS, N.E.C.

040 OCCUPATIONS IN AGRICULTURAL SCIENCES

041 OCCUPATIONS IN BIOLOGICAL SCIENCES

045 OCCUPATIONS IN PSYCHOLOGY

049 OCCUPATIONS IN LIFE SCIENCES, N.E.C.

050 OCCUPATIONS IN ECONOMICS

051 OCCUPATIONS IN POLITICAL SCIENCE

052 OCCUPATIONS IN HISTORY

054 OCCUPATIONS IN SOCIOLOGY

055 OCCUPATIONS IN ANTHROPOLOGY

059 OCCUPATIONS IN SOCIAL SCIENCES, N.E.C.

070 PHYSICIANS AND SURGEONS

071 OSTEOPATHS

072 DENTISTS

073 VETERINARIANS

074 PHARMACISTS

075 REGISTERED NURSES

076 THERAPISTS

077 DIETITIANS

078 OCCUPATIONS IN MEDICAL AND DENTAL TECHNOLOGY

079 OCCUPATIONS IN MEDICINE AND HEALTH, N.E.C.

090 OCCUPATIONS IN COLLEGE AND UNIVERSITY EDUCATION

091 OCCUPATIONS IN SECONDARY SCHOOL EDUCATION

092 OCCUPATIONS IN PRESCHOOL, PRIMARY SCHOOL, AND KINDERGARTEN EDUCATION

094 OCCUPATIONS IN EDUCATION OF PERSONS WITH DISABILITIES

096 HOME ECONOMISTS AND FARM ADVISERS

097 OCCUPATIONS IN VOCATIONAL EDUCATION

099 OCCUPATIONS IN EDUCATION, N.E.C.

100 LIBRARIANS

101 ARCHIVISTS

102 MUSEUM CURATORS AND RELATED OCCUPATIONS

109 OCCUPATIONS IN MUSEUM, LIBRARY, AND ARCHIVAL SCIENCES, N.E.C.

110 LAWYERS

111 JUDGES

119 OCCUPATIONS IN LAW AND JURISPRUDENCE, N.E.C.

120 CLERGY

129 OCCUPATIONS IN RELIGION AND THEOLOGY, N.E.C.

131 WRITERS

132 EDITORS: PUBLICATION, BROADCAST, AND SCRIPT

137 INTERPRETERS AND TRANSLATORS

139 OCCUPATIONS IN WRITING, N.E.C.

141 COMMERCIAL ARTISTS: DESIGNERS AND ILLUSTRATORS, GRAPHIC ARTS

142 ENVIRONMENTAL, PRODUCT, AND RELATED DESIGNERS

143 OCCUPATIONS IN PHOTOGRAPHY

144 FINE ARTISTS: PAINTERS, SCULPTORS, AND RELATED OCCUPATIONS

149 OCCUPATIONS IN ART, N.E.C.

150 OCCUPATIONS IN DRAMATICS

151 OCCUPATIONS IN DANCING

152 OCCUPATIONS IN MUSIC

153 OCCUPATIONS IN ATHLETICS AND SPORTS

159 OCCUPATIONS IN ENTERTAINMENT AND RECREATION, N.E.C.

160 ACCOUNTANTS, AUDITORS, AND RELATED OCCUPATIONS

161 BUDGET AND MANAGEMENT SYSTEMS ANALYSIS OCCUPATIONS

162 PURCHASING MANAGEMENT OCCUPATIONS

163 SALES AND DISTRIBUTION MANAGEMENT OCCUPATIONS

164 ADVERTISING MANAGEMENT OCCUPATIONS

165 PUBLIC RELATIONS MANAGEMENT OCCUPATIONS

166 PERSONNEL ADMINISTRATION OCCUPATIONS

168 INSPECTORS AND INVESTIGATORS, MANAGERIAL AND PUBLIC SERVICE

169 OCCUPATIONS IN ADMINISTRATIVE SPECIALIZATIONS, N.E.C.

180 AGRICULTURE, FORESTRY, AND FISHING INDUSTRY MANAGERS AND OFFICIALS

181 MINING INDUSTRY MANAGERS AND OFFICIALS

182 CONSTRUCTION INDUSTRY MANAGERS AND OFFICIALS

183 MANUFACTURING INDUSTRY MANAGERS AND OFFICIALS

184 TRANSPORTATION, COMMUNICATION, AND UTILITIES INDUSTRY MANAGERS AND OFFICIALS

185 WHOLESALE AND RETAIL TRADE MANAGERS AND OFFICIALS

186 FINANCE, INSURANCE, AND REAL ESTATE MANAGERS AND OFFICIALS

187 SERVICE INDUSTRY MANAGERS AND OFFICIALS

188 PUBLIC ADMINISTRATION MANAGERS AND OFFICIALS

189 MISCELLANEOUS MANAGERS AND OFFICIALS, N.E.C.

191 AGENTS AND APPRAISERS, N.E.C.

193 RADIO OPERATORS

194 SOUND, FILM, AND VIDEOTAPE RECORDING, AND REPRODUCTION OCCUPATIONS

195 OCCUPATIONS IN SOCIAL AND WELFARE WORK

196 AIRPLANE PILOTS AND NAVIGATORS

197 SHIP CAPTAINS, MATES, PILOTS, AND ENGINEERS

198 RAILROAD CONDUCTORS

199 MISCELLANEOUS PROFESSIONAL, TECHNICAL, AND MANAGERIAL OCCUPATIONS,

201 SECRETARIES

202 STENOGRAPHERS

203 TYPISTS AND TYPEWRITING-MACHINE OPERATORS

205 INTERVIEWING CLERKS

206 FILE CLERKS

207 DUPLICATING-MACHINE OPERATORS AND TENDERS

208 MAILING AND MISCELLANEOUS OFFICE MACHINE OPERATORS

209 STENOGRAPHY, TYPING, FILING, AND RELATED OCCUPATIONS, N.E.C.

210 BOOKKEEPERS AND RELATED OCCUPATIONS

211 CASHIERS AND TELLERS

213 COMPUTER AND PERIPHERAL EQUIPMENT OPERATORS

214 BILLING AND RATE CLERKS

215 PAYROLL, TIMEKEEPING, AND DUTY-ROSTER CLERKS

216 ACCOUNTING AND STATISTICAL CLERKS

217 ACCOUNT-RECORDING-MACHINE OPERATORS, N.E.C.

219 COMPUTING AND ACCOUNT-RECORDING OCCUPATIONS, N.E.C.

221 PRODUCTION CLERKS

222 SHIPPING, RECEIVING, STOCK, AND RELATED CLERICAL OCCUPATIONS

229 PRODUCTION AND STOCK CLERKS AND RELATED OCCUPATIONS, N.E.C.

230 HAND DELIVERY AND DISTRIBUTION OCCUPATIONS

235 TELEPHONE OPERATORS

236 TELEGRAPH OPERATORS

237 INFORMATION AND RECEPTION CLERKS

238 ACCOMMODATION CLERKS AND GATE AND TICKET AGENTS

239 INFORMATION AND MESSAGE DISTRIBUTION OCCUPATIONS, N.E.C.

241 INVESTIGATORS, ADJUSTERS, AND RELATED OCCUPATIONS

243 GOVERNMENT SERVICE CLERKS, N.E.C.

245 MEDICAL SERVICE CLERKS, N.E.C.

247 ADVERTISING-SERVICE CLERKS, N.E.C.

248 TRANSPORTATION-SERVICE CLERKS, N.E.C

249 MISCELLANEOUS CLERICAL OCCUPATIONS, N.E.C.

250 SALES OCCUPATIONS, REAL ESTATE, INSURANCE, SECURITIES AND FINANCIAL SERVICES

251 SALES OCCUPATIONS, BUSINESS SERVICES, EXCEPT REAL ESTATE, INSURANCE, SECURITIES, AND FINANCIAL SERVICES

252 SALES OCCUPATIONS, TRANSPORTATION SERVICES

253 SALES OCCUPATIONS, UTILITIES

254 SALES OCCUPATIONS, PRINTING AND ADVERTISING

259 SALES OCCUPATIONS, SERVICES, N.E.C.

260 SALES OCCUPATIONS, AGRICULTURAL AND FOOD PRODUCTS

261 SALES OCCUPATIONS, TEXTILE PRODUCTS, APPAREL, AND NOTIONS

262 SALES OCCUPATIONS, CHEMICALS, DRUGS, AND SUNDRIES

269 SALES OCCUPATIONS, MISCELLANEOUS CONSUMABLE COMMODITIES, N.E.C.

270 SALES OCCUPATIONS, HOME FURNITURE, FURNISHINGS, AND APPLIANCES

271 SALES OCCUPATIONS, ELECTRICAL GOODS, EXCEPT HOME APPLIANCES

272 SALES OCCUPATIONS, FARM AND GARDENING EQUIPMENT AND SUPPLIES

273 SALES OCCUPATIONS, TRANSPORTATION EQUIPMENT, PARTS, AND SUPPLIES

274 SALES OCCUPATIONS, INDUSTRIAL AND RELATED EQUIPMENT AND SUPPLIES

275 SALES OCCUPATIONS, BUSINESS AND COMMERCIAL EQUIPMENT AND SUPPLIES

276 SALES OCCUPATIONS, MEDICAL AND SCIENTIFIC EQUIPMENT AND SUPPLIES

277 SALES OCCUPATIONS, SPORTING, HOBBY, STATIONERY, AND RELATED GOODS

279 SALES OCCUPATIONS, MISCELLANEOUS COMMODITIES, N.E.C.

290 SALES CLERKS

291 VENDING AND DOOR-TO-DOOR SELLING OCCUPATIONS

292 ROUTE SALES AND DELIVERY OCCUPATIONS

293 SOLICITORS

294 AUCTIONEERS

295 RENTAL CLERKS

296 SHOPPERS

297 SALES PROMOTION OCCUPATIONS

298 MERCHANDISE DISPLAYERS

299 MISCELLANEOUS SALES OCCUPATIONS, N.E.C.

301 HOUSEHOLD AND RELATED WORK

302 LAUNDERERS, PRIVATE FAMILY

305 COOKS, DOMESTIC

309 DOMESTIC SERVICE OCCUPATIONS, N.E.C.

310 HOSTS/HOSTESSES AND STEWARDS/STEWARDESSES, FOOD AND BEVERAGE SERVICE, EXCEPT SHIP STEWARDS/STEWARDESSES

311 WAITERS/WAITRESSES, AND RELATED FOOD SERVICE OCCUPATIONS

312 BARTENDERS

313 CHEFS AND COOKS, HOTELS AND RESTAURANTS

315 MISCELLANEOUS COOKS, EXCEPT DOMESTIC

316 MEATCUTTERS, EXCEPT IN SLAUGHTERING AND PACKING HOUSES

317 MISCELLANEOUS FOOD AND BEVERAGE PREPARATION OCCUPATIONS

318 KITCHEN WORKERS, N.E.C.

319 FOOD AND BEVERAGE PREPARATION AND SERVICE OCCUPATIONS, N.E.C.

320 BOARDING-HOUSE AND LODGING-HOUSE KEEPERS

321 HOUSEKEEPERS, HOTELS AND INSTITUTIONS

323 HOUSECLEANERS, HOTELS, RESTAURANTS, AND RELATED ESTABLISHMENTS

324 BELLHOPS AND RELATED OCCUPATIONS

329 LODGING AND RELATED SERVICE OCCUPATIONS, N.E.C.

330 BARBERS

331 MANICURISTS

332 HAIRDRESSERS AND COSMETOLOGISTS

333 MAKE-UP OCCUPATIONS

334 MASSEURS AND RELATED OCCUPATIONS

335 BATH ATTENDANTS

338 EMBALMERS AND RELATED OCCUPATIONS

339 BARBERING, COSMETOLOGY, AND RELATED SERVICE OCCUPATIONS, N.E.C.

340 ATTENDANTS, BOWLING ALLEY AND BILLIARD PARLOR

341 ATTENDANTS, GOLF COURSE, TENNIS COURT, SKATING RINK, AND RELATED FACILITIES

342 AMUSEMENT DEVICE AND CONCESSION ATTENDANTS

343 GAMBLING HALL ATTENDANTS

344 USHERS

346 WARDROBE AND DRESSING-ROOM ATTENDANTS

349 AMUSEMENT AND RECREATION SERVICE OCCUPATIONS, N.E.C.

350 SHIP STEWARDS/STEWARDESSES AND RELATED OCCUPATIONS

351 TRAIN ATTENDANTS

352 HOSTS/HOSTESSES AND STEWARDS/STEWARDESSES, N.E.C.

353 GUIDES

354 UNLICENSED BIRTH ATTENDANTS AND PRACTICAL NURSES

355 ATTENDANTS, HOSPITALS, MORGUES, AND RELATED HEALTH SERVICES

357 BAGGAGE HANDLERS

358 CHECKROOM, LOCKER ROOM, AND REST ROOM ATTENDANTS

359 MISCELLANEOUS PERSONAL SERVICE OCCUPATIONS, N.E.C.

361 LAUNDERING OCCUPATIONS

362 DRY CLEANING OCCUPATIONS

363 PRESSING OCCUPATIONS

364 DYEING AND RELATED OCCUPATIONS

365 SHOE AND LUGGAGE REPAIRER AND RELATED OCCUPATIONS

366 BOOTBLACKS AND RELATED OCCUPATIONS

369 APPAREL AND FURNISHINGS SERVICE OCCUPATIONS, N.E.C.

371 CROSSING TENDERS AND BRIDGE OPERATORS

372 SECURITY GUARDS AND CORRECTION OFFICERS, EXCEPT CROSSING TENDERS

373 FIRE FIGHTERS, FIRE DEPARTMENT

375 POLICE OFFICERS AND DETECTIVES, PUBLIC SERVICE

376 POLICE OFFICERS AND DETECTIVES, EXCEPT IN PUBLIC SERVICE

377 SHERIFFS AND BAILIFFS

378 ARMED FORCES ENLISTED PERSONNEL

379 PROTECTIVE SERVICE OCCUPATIONS, N.E.C.

381 PORTERS AND CLEANERS

382 JANITORS

383 BUILDING PEST CONTROL SERVICE OCCUPATIONS

388 ELEVATOR OPERATORS

389 BUILDING AND RELATED SERVICE OCCUPATIONS, N.E.C.

401 GRAIN FARMING OCCUPATIONS

402 VEGETABLE FARMING OCCUPATIONS

403 FRUIT AND NUT FARMING OCCUPATIONS

404 FIELD CROP FARMING OCCUPATIONS, N.E.C.

405 HORTICULTURAL SPECIALTY OCCUPATIONS

406 GARDENING AND GROUNDSKEEPING OCCUPATIONS

407 DIVERSIFIED CROP FARMING OCCUPATIONS

408 PLANT LIFE AND RELATED SERVICE OCCUPATIONS

409 PLANT FARMING AND RELATED OCCUPATIONS, N.E.C.

410 DOMESTIC ANIMAL FARMING OCCUPATIONS

411 DOMESTIC FOWL FARMING OCCUPATIONS

412 GAME FARMING OCCUPATIONS

413 LOWER ANIMAL FARMING OCCUPATIONS

418 ANIMAL SERVICE OCCUPATIONS

419 ANIMAL FARMING OCCUPATIONS, N.E.C.

421 GENERAL FARMING OCCUPATIONS

429 MISCELLANEOUS AGRICULTURAL AND RELATED OCCUPATIONS, N.E.C.

441 NET, SEINE, AND TRAP FISHERS

442 LINE FISHERS

443 FISHERS, MISCELLANEOUS EQUIPMENT

446 AQUATIC LIFE CULTIVATION AND RELATED OCCUPATIONS

447 SPONGE AND SEAWEED GATHERERS

449 FISHERY AND RELATED OCCUPATIONS, N.E.C.

451 TREE FARMING AND RELATED OCCUPATIONS

452 FOREST CONSERVATION OCCUPATIONS

453 OCCUPATIONS IN HARVESTING FOREST PRODUCTS, EXCEPT LOGGING

454 LOGGING AND RELATED OCCUPATIONS

455 LOG GRADING, SCALING, SORTING, RAFTING, AND RELATED OCCUPATIONS

459 FORESTRY OCCUPATIONS, N.E.C.

461 HUNTING AND TRAPPING OCCUPATIONS

500 ELECTROPLATING OCCUPATIONS

501 DIP PLATING OCCUPATIONS

502 MELTING, POURING, CASTING, AND RELATED OCCUPATIONS

503 PICKLING, CLEANING, DEGREASING, AND RELATED OCCUPATIONS

504 HEAT-TREATING OCCUPATIONS

505 METAL SPRAYING, COATING, AND RELATED OCCUPATIONS

509 OCCUPATIONS IN PROCESSING OF METAL, N.E.C.

510 MIXING AND RELATED OCCUPATIONS

511 SEPARATING, FILTERING, AND RELATED OCCUPATIONS

512 MELTING OCCUPATIONS

513 ROASTING OCCUPATIONS

514 POURING AND CASTING OCCUPATIONS

515 CRUSHING AND GRINDING OCCUPATIONS

518 MOLDERS, COREMAKERS, AND RELATED OCCUPATIONS

519 ORE REFINING AND FOUNDRY OCCUPATIONS, N.E.C.

520 MIXING, COMPOUNDING, BLENDING, KNEADING, SHAPING, AND RELATED OCCUPATIONS

521 SEPARATING, CRUSHING, MILLING, CHOPPING, GRINDING, AND RELATED OCCUPATIONS

522 CULTURING, MELTING, FERMENTING, DISTILLING, SATURATING, PICKLING, AGING, AND RELATED OCCUPATIONS

523 HEATING, RENDERING, MELTING, DRYING, COOLING, FREEZING, AND RELATED OCCUPATIONS

524 COATING, ICING, DECORATING, AND RELATED OCCUPATIONS

525 SLAUGHTERING, BREAKING, CURING, AND RELATED OCCUPATIONS

526 COOKING AND BAKING OCCUPATIONS, N.E.C.

529 OCCUPATIONS IN PROCESSING OF FOOD, TOBACCO, AND RELATED PRODUCTS, N.E.C.

530 GRINDING, BEATING, AND MIXING OCCUPATIONS

532 COOKING AND DRYING OCCUPATIONS

533 COOLING, BLEACHING, SCREENING, WASHING, AND RELATED OCCUPATIONS

534 CALENDERING, SIZING, COATING, AND RELATED OCCUPATIONS

535 FORMING OCCUPATIONS, N.E.C.

539 OCCUPATIONS IN PROCESSING OF PAPER AND RELATED MATERIALS, N.E.C.

540 MIXING AND BLENDING OCCUPATIONS

541 FILTERING, STRAINING, AND SEPARATING OCCUPATIONS

542 DISTILLING, SUBLIMING, AND CARBONIZING OCCUPATIONS

543 DRYING, HEATING, AND MELTING OCCUPATIONS

544 GRINDING AND CRUSHING OCCUPATIONS

546 REACTING OCCUPATIONS, N.E.C.

549 OCCUPATIONS IN PROCESSING OF PETROLEUM, COAL, NATURAL AND MANUFACTURED GAS, AND RELATED PRODUCTS, N.E.C.

550 MIXING AND BLENDING OCCUPATIONS

551 FILTERING, STRAINING, AND SEPARATING OCCUPATIONS

552 DISTILLING OCCUPATIONS

553 HEATING, BAKING, DRYING, SEASONING, MELTING, AND HEAT-TREATING OCCUPATIONS

554 COATING, CALENDERING, LAMINATING, AND FINISHING OCCUPATIONS

555 GRINDING AND CRUSHING OCCUPATIONS

556 CASTING AND MOLDING OCCUPATIONS, N.E.C.

557 EXTRUDING OCCUPATIONS

558 REACTING OCCUPATIONS, N.E.C.

559 OCCUPATIONS IN PROCESSING OF CHEMICALS, PLASTICS, SYNTHETICS, RUBBER, PAINT, AND RELATED OCCUPATIONS, N.E.C.

560 MIXING AND RELATED OCCUPATIONS

561 WOOD PRESERVING AND RELATED OCCUPATIONS

562 SATURATING, COATING, AND RELATED OCCUPATIONS, N.E.C.

563 DRYING, SEASONING, AND RELATED OCCUPATIONS

564 GRINDING AND CHOPPING OCCUPATIONS, N.E.C.

569 OCCUPATIONS IN PROCESSING OF WOOD AND WOOD PRODUCTS, N.E.C.

570 CRUSHING, GRINDING, AND MIXING OCCUPATIONS

571 SEPARATING OCCUPATIONS

572 MELTING OCCUPATIONS

573 BAKING, DRYING, AND HEAT-TREATING OCCUPATIONS

574 IMPREGNATING, COATING, AND GLAZING OCCUPATIONS

575 FORMING OCCUPATIONS

579 OCCUPATIONS IN PROCESSING OF STONE, CLAY, GLASS, AND RELATED PRODUCTS, N.E.C.

580 SHAPING, BLOCKING, STRETCHING, AND TENTERING OCCUPATIONS

581 SEPARATING, FILTERING, AND DRYING OCCUPATIONS

582 WASHING, STEAMING, AND SATURATING OCCUPATIONS

583 IRONING, PRESSING, GLAZING, STAKING, CALENDERING, AND EMBOSSING OCCUPATIONS

584 MERCERIZING, COATING, AND LAMINATING OCCUPATIONS

585 SINGEING, CUTTING, SHEARING, SHAVING, AND NAPPING OCCUPATIONS

586 FELTING AND FULLING OCCUPATIONS

587 BRUSHING AND SHRINKING OCCUPATIONS

589 OCCUPATIONS IN PROCESSING OF LEATHER, TEXTILES, AND RELATED PRODUCTS,

590 OCCUPATIONS IN PROCESSING PRODUCTS FROM ASSORTED MATERIALS

599 MISCELLANEOUS PROCESSING OCCUPATIONS, N.E.C.
600 MACHINISTS AND RELATED OCCUPATIONS
601 TOOLMAKERS AND RELATED OCCUPATIONS
602 GEAR MACHINING OCCUPATIONS
603 ABRADING OCCUPATIONS
604 TURNING OCCUPATIONS
605 MILLING, SHAPING, AND PLANING OCCUPATIONS
606 BORING OCCUPATIONS
607 SAWING OCCUPATIONS
609 METAL MACHINING OCCUPATIONS, N.E.C.
610 HAMMER FORGING OCCUPATIONS
611 PRESS FORGING OCCUPATIONS
612 FORGING OCCUPATIONS, N.E.C.
613 SHEET AND BAR ROLLING OCCUPATIONS
614 EXTRUDING AND DRAWING OCCUPATIONS
615 PUNCHING AND SHEARING OCCUPATIONS
616 FABRICATING MACHINE OCCUPATIONS
617 FORMING OCCUPATIONS, N.E.C.
619 MISCELLANEOUS METALWORKING OCCUPATIONS, N.E.C.
620 MOTORIZED VEHICLE AND ENGINEERING EQUIPMENT MECHANICS AND REPAIRERS
621 AIRCRAFT MECHANICS AND REPAIRERS
622 RAIL EQUIPMENT MECHANICS AND REPAIRERS
623 MARINE MECHANICS AND REPAIRERS
624 FARM MECHANICS AND REPAIRERS
625 ENGINE, POWER TRANSMISSION, AND RELATED MECHANICS
626 METALWORKING MACHINERY MECHANICS
627 PRINTING AND PUBLISHING MECHANICS AND REPAIRERS
628 TEXTILE MACHINERY AND EQUIPMENT MECHANICS AND REPAIRERS
629 SPECIAL INDUSTRY MACHINERY MECHANICS
630 GENERAL INDUSTRY MECHANICS AND REPAIRERS
631 POWERPLANT MECHANICS AND REPAIRERS
632 ORDNANCE AND ACCESSORIES MECHANICS AND REPAIRERS
633 BUSINESS AND COMMERCIAL MACHINE REPAIRERS
637 UTILITIES SERVICE MECHANICS AND REPAIRERS
638 MISCELLANEOUS OCCUPATIONS IN MACHINE INSTALLATION AND REPAIR
639 MECHANICS AND MACHINERY REPAIRERS, N.E.C.
640 PAPER CUTTING, WINDING, AND RELATED OCCUPATIONS
641 FOLDING, CREASING, SCORING, AND GLUING OCCUPATIONS
649 PAPERWORKING OCCUPATIONS, N.E.C.
650 TYPESETTERS AND COMPOSERS
651 PRINTING PRESS OCCUPATIONS
652 PRINTING MACHINE OCCUPATIONS
653 BOOKBINDING-MACHINE OPERATORS AND RELATED OCCUPATIONS
654 TYPECASTERS AND RELATED OCCUPATIONS
659 PRINTING OCCUPATIONS, N.E.C.
660 CABINETMAKERS
661 PATTERNMAKERS
662 SANDING OCCUPATIONS
663 SHEARING AND SHAVING OCCUPATIONS
664 TURNING OCCUPATIONS
665 MILLING AND PLANING OCCUPATIONS
666 BORING OCCUPATIONS
667 SAWING OCCUPATIONS
669 WOOD MACHINING OCCUPATIONS, N.E.C.
670 STONECUTTERS AND RELATED OCCUPATIONS
673 ABRADING OCCUPATIONS
674 TURNING OCCUPATIONS
675 PLANING AND SHAPING OCCUPATIONS, N.E.C.
676 BORING AND PUNCHING OCCUPATIONS
677 CHIPPING, CUTTING, SAWING, AND RELATED OCCUPATIONS
679 OCCUPATIONS IN MACHINING STONE, CLAY, GLASS, AND RELATED MATERIALS, N.E.C.
680 CARDING, COMBING, DRAWING, AND RELATED OCCUPATIONS
681 TWISTING, BEAMING, WARPING, AND RELATED OCCUPATIONS
682 SPINNING OCCUPATIONS
683 WEAVERS AND RELATED OCCUPATIONS
684 HOSIERY KNITTING OCCUPATIONS
685 KNITTING OCCUPATIONS, EXCEPT HOSIERY
686 PUNCHING, CUTTING, FORMING, AND RELATED OCCUPATIONS
687 TUFTING OCCUPATIONS
689 TEXTILE OCCUPATIONS, N.E.C.
690 PLASTICS, SYNTHETICS, RUBBER, AND LEATHER WORKING OCCUPATIONS
691 OCCUPATIONS IN FABRICATION OF INSULATED WIRE AND CABLE
692 OCCUPATIONS IN FABRICATION OF PRODUCTS FROM ASSORTED MATERIALS
693 MODELMAKERS, PATTERNMAKERS, AND RELATED OCCUPATIONS
694 OCCUPATIONS IN FABRICATION OF ORDNANCE, AMMUNITION, AND RELATED PRODUCTS, N.E.C.
699 MISCELLANEOUS MACHINE TRADES OCCUPATIONS, N.E.C.
700 OCCUPATIONS IN FABRICATION, ASSEMBLY, AND REPAIR OF JEWELRY, SILVERWARE, AND RELATED PRODUCTS

701   OCCUPATIONS IN FABRICATION, ASSEMBLY, AND REPAIR OF TOOLS, AND RELATED PRODUCTS

703   OCCUPATIONS IN ASSEMBLY AND REPAIR OF SHEETMETAL PRODUCTS, N.E.C.

704   ENGRAVERS, ETCHERS, AND RELATED OCCUPATIONS

705   FILING, GRINDING, BUFFING, CLEANING, AND POLISHING OCCUPATIONS, N.E.C.

706   METAL UNIT ASSEMBLERS AND ADJUSTERS, N.E.C.

709   MISCELLANEOUS OCCUPATIONS IN FABRICATION, ASSEMBLY, AND REPAIR OF METAL PRODUCTS

710   OCCUPATIONS IN FABRICATION AND REPAIR OF INSTRUMENTS FOR MEASURING,

711   OCCUPATIONS IN FABRICATION AND REPAIR OF OPTICAL INSTRUMENTS

712   OCCUPATIONS IN FABRICATION AND REPAIR OF SURGICAL, MEDICAL, AND DENTAL INSTRUMENTS AND SUPPLIES

713   OCCUPATIONS IN FABRICATION AND REPAIR OF OPHTHALMIC GOODS

714   OCCUPATIONS IN FABRICATION AND REPAIR OF PHOTOGRAPHIC EQUIPMENT AND SUPPLIES

715   OCCUPATIONS IN FABRICATION AND REPAIR OF WATCHES, CLOCKS, AND PARTS

716   OCCUPATIONS IN FABRICATION AND REPAIR OF ENGINEERING AND SCIENTIFIC INSTRUMENTS AND EQUIPMENT

719   OCCUPATIONS IN FABRICATION AND REPAIR OF SCIENTIFIC AND MEDICAL APPARATUS, PHOTOGRAPHIC AND OPTICAL GOODS, HOROLOGICAL, AND RELATED PRODUCTS

720   OCCUPATIONS IN ASSEMBLY AND REPAIR OF RADIO AND TELEVISION RECEIVING SETS AND PHONOGRAPHS

721   OCCUPATIONS IN ASSEMBLY AND REPAIR OF MOTORS, GENERATORS, AND RELATED PRODUCTS

722   OCCUPATIONS IN ASSEMBLY AND REPAIR OF COMMUNICATIONS EQUIPMENT

723   OCCUPATIONS IN ASSEMBLY AND REPAIR OF ELECTRICAL APPLIANCES AND FIXTURES

724   OCCUPATIONS IN WINDING AND ASSEMBLING COILS, MAGNETS, ARMATURES, AND RELATED PRODUCTS

725   OCCUPATIONS IN ASSEMBLY OF LIGHT BULBS AND ELECTRONIC TUBES

726   OCCUPATIONS IN ASSEMBLY AND REPAIR OF ELECTRONIC COMPONENTS AND ACCESSORIES, N.E.C.

727   OCCUPATIONS IN ASSEMBLY OF STORAGE BATTERIES

728   OCCUPATIONS IN FABRICATION OF ELECTRICAL WIRE AND CABLE

729   OCCUPATIONS IN ASSEMBLY AND REPAIR OF ELECTRICAL EQUIPMENT, N.E.C.

730   OCCUPATIONS IN FABRICATION AND REPAIR OF MUSICAL INSTRUMENTS AND PARTS

731   OCCUPATIONS IN FABRICATION AND REPAIR OF GAMES AND TOYS

732   OCCUPATIONS IN FABRICATION AND REPAIR OF SPORTING GOODS

733   OCCUPATIONS IN FABRICATION AND REPAIR OF PENS, PENCILS, AND OFFICE AND ARTISTS' MATERIALS

734   OCCUPATIONS IN FABRICATION AND REPAIR OF NOTIONS

735   OCCUPATIONS IN FABRICATION AND REPAIR OF JEWELRY, N.E.C.

736   OCCUPATIONS IN FABRICATION AND REPAIR OF ORDNANCE AND ACCESSORIES

737   OCCUPATIONS IN FABRICATION OF AMMUNITION, FIREWORKS, EXPLOSIVES, AND RELATED PRODUCTS

739   OCCUPATIONS IN FABRICATION AND REPAIR OF PRODUCTS MADE FROM ASSORTED MATERIALS, N.E.C.

740   PAINTERS, BRUSH

741   PAINTERS, SPRAY

742   STAINING, WAXING, AND RELATED OCCUPATIONS

749   PAINTING, DECORATING, AND RELATED OCCUPATIONS, N.E.C.

750   OCCUPATIONS IN FABRICATION AND REPAIR OF TIRES, TUBES, TIRE TREADS, AND RELATED PRODUCTS

751   LAYING OUT AND CUTTING OCCUPATIONS, N.E.C.

752   FITTING, SHAPING, CEMENTING, FINISHING, AND RELATED OCCUPATIONS, N.E.C.

753   OCCUPATIONS IN FABRICATION AND REPAIR OF RUBBER AND PLASTIC FOOTWEAR

754   OCCUPATIONS IN FABRICATION AND REPAIR OF MISCELLANEOUS PLASTICS PRODUCTS

759   OCCUPATIONS IN FABRICATION AND REPAIR OF PLASTICS, SYNTHETICS, RUBBER, AND RELATED PRODUCTS, N.E.C.

760   BENCH CARPENTERS AND RELATED OCCUPATIONS

761   OCCUPATIONS IN LAYING OUT, CUTTING, CARVING, SHAPING, AND SANDING WOOD

762   OCCUPATIONS IN ASSEMBLING WOOD PRODUCTS, N.E.C.

763   OCCUPATIONS IN FABRICATION AND REPAIR OF FURNITURE, N.E.C.

764   COOPERAGE OCCUPATIONS

769   OCCUPATIONS IN FABRICATION AND REPAIR OF WOOD PRODUCTS, N.E.C.

770   OCCUPATIONS IN FABRICATION AND REPAIR OF JEWELRY, ORNAMENTS, AND RELATED PRODUCTS

771   STONE CUTTERS AND CARVERS

772   GLASS BLOWING, PRESSING, SHAPING, AND RELATED OCCUPATIONS, N.E.C.

773   OCCUPATIONS IN COLORING AND DECORATING BRICK, TILE, AND RELATED PRODUCTS

774   OCCUPATIONS IN FABRICATION AND REPAIR OF POTTERY AND PORCELAIN WARE

775   GRINDING, FILING, POLISHING, FROSTING, ETCHING, CLEANING, AND RELATED OCCUPATIONS

776 OCCUPATIONS IN FABRICATION AND REPAIR OF ASBESTOS AND POLISHING PRODUCTS

777 MODELMAKERS, PATTERNMAKERS, MOLDMAKERS, AND RELATED OCCUPATIONS

779 OCCUPATIONS IN FABRICATION AND REPAIR OF SAND, STONE, CLAY, AND GLASS PRODUCTS, N.E.C.

780 OCCUPATIONS IN UPHOLSTERING AND IN FABRICATION AND REPAIR OF STUFFED FURNITURE, MATTRESSES, AND RELATED PRODUCTS

781 LAYING OUT, MARKING, CUTTING, AND PUNCHING OCCUPATIONS, N.E.C.

782 HAND SEWERS, MENDERS, EMBROIDERERS, KNITTERS, AND RELATED OCCUPATIONS

783 FUR AND LEATHER WORKING OCCUPATIONS

784 OCCUPATIONS IN FABRICATION AND REPAIR OF HATS, CAPS, GLOVES, AND RELATED PRODUCTS

785 TAILORS AND DRESSMAKERS

786 SEWING MACHINE OPERATORS, GARMENT

787 SEWING MACHINE OPERATORS, NONGARMENT

788 OCCUPATIONS IN FABRICATION AND REPAIR OF FOOTWEAR

789 OCCUPATIONS IN FABRICATION AND REPAIR OF TEXTILE, LEATHER, AND RELATED PRODUCTS, N.E.C.

790 OCCUPATIONS IN PREPARATION OF FOOD, TOBACCO, AND RELATED PRODUCTS, N.E.C.

794 OCCUPATIONS IN FABRICATION OF PAPER PRODUCTS, N.E.C.

795 GLUING OCCUPATIONS, N.E.C.

800 RIVETERS, N.E.C.

801 FITTING, BOLTING, SCREWING, AND RELATED OCCUPATIONS

804 TINSMITHS, COPPERSMITHS, AND SHEET METAL WORKERS

805 BOILERMAKERS

806 TRANSPORTATION EQUIPMENT ASSEMBLERS AND RELATED OCCUPATIONS

807 STRUCTURAL REPAIRERS, TRANSPORTATION EQUIPMENT

809 MISCELLANEOUS OCCUPATIONS IN METAL FABRICATING, N.E.C.

810 ARC WELDERS AND CUTTERS

811 GAS WELDERS

812 RESISTANCE WELDERS

813 BRAZING, BRAZE-WELDING, AND SOLDERING OCCUPATIONS

814 SOLID STATE WELDERS

815 ELECTRON-BEAM; ELECTROSLAG; THERMIT; INDUCTION; AND LASER-BEAM WELDERS

816 THERMAL CUTTERS AND ARC CUTTERS

819 WELDERS, CUTTERS, AND RELATED OCCUPATIONS, N.E.C.

820 OCCUPATIONS IN ASSEMBLY, INSTALLATION, AND REPAIR OF GENERATORS, MOTORS, ACCESSORIES, AND RELATED POWERPLANT EQUIPMENT

821 OCCUPATIONS IN ASSEMBLY, INSTALLATION, AND REPAIR OF TRANSMISSION AND DISTRIBUTION LINES AND CIRCUITS

822 OCCUPATIONS IN ASSEMBLY, INSTALLATION, AND REPAIR OF WIRE COMMUNICATION, DETECTION AND SIGNALING EQUIPMENT

823 OCCUPATIONS IN ASSEMBLY, INSTALLATION, AND REPAIR OF ELECTRONIC COMMUNICATION, DETECTION, AND SIGNALING EQUIPMENT

824 OCCUPATIONS IN ASSEMBLY, INSTALLATION, AND REPAIR OF LIGHTING EQUIPMENT AND BUILDING WIRING, N.E.C.

825 OCCUPATIONS IN ASSEMBLY, INSTALLATION, AND REPAIR OF TRANSPORTATION AND MATERIAL-HANDLING EQUIPMENT

826 OCCUPATIONS IN ASSEMBLY, INSTALLATION, AND REPAIR OF INDUSTRIAL APPARATUS, N.E.C.

827 OCCUPATIONS IN ASSEMBLY, INSTALLATION, AND REPAIR OF LARGE HOUSEHOLD APPLIANCES AND SIMILAR COMMERCIAL AND INDUSTRIAL EQUIPMENT

828 OCCUPATIONS IN FABRICATION, INSTALLATION, AND REPAIR OF ELECTRICAL AND ELECTRONICS PRODUCTS, N.E.C.

829 OCCUPATIONS IN INSTALLATION AND REPAIR OF ELECTRICAL PRODUCTS, N.E.C.

840 CONSTRUCTION AND MAINTENANCE PAINTERS AND RELATED OCCUPATIONS

841 PAPERHANGERS

842 PLASTERERS AND RELATED OCCUPATIONS

843 WATERPROOFING AND RELATED OCCUPATIONS

844 CEMENT AND CONCRETE FINISHING AND RELATED OCCUPATIONS

845 TRANSPORTATION EQUIPMENT PAINTERS AND RELATED OCCUPATIONS

849 PAINTING, PLASTERING, WATERPROOFING, CEMENTING, AND RELATED OCCUPATIONS, N.E.C.

850 EXCAVATING, GRADING, AND RELATED OCCUPATIONS

851 DRAINAGE AND RELATED OCCUPATIONS

853 PAVING OCCUPATIONS, ASPHALT AND CONCRETE

859 EXCAVATING, GRADING, PAVING, AND RELATED OCCUPATIONS, N.E.C.

860 CARPENTERS AND RELATED OCCUPATIONS

861 BRICK AND STONE MASONS AND TILE SETTERS

862 PLUMBERS, GAS FITTERS, STEAM FITTERS, AND RELATED OCCUPATIONS

863 ASBESTOS AND INSULATION WORKERS

864 FLOOR LAYING AND FINISHING OCCUPATIONS

865 GLAZIERS AND RELATED OCCUPATIONS

866 ROOFERS AND RELATED OCCUPATIONS

869 MISCELLANEOUS CONSTRUCTION OCCUPATIONS, N.E.C.

891 OCCUPATIONS IN STRUCTURAL MAINTENANCE, N.E.C.

899 MISCELLANEOUS STRUCTURAL WORK OCCUPATIONS, N.E.C.

900 CONCRETE-MIXING-TRUCK DRIVERS

902 DUMP-TRUCK DRIVERS

903 TRUCK DRIVERS, INFLAMMABLES

904 TRAILER-TRUCK DRIVERS

905 TRUCK DRIVERS, HEAVY

906 TRUCK DRIVERS, LIGHT

909 MOTOR FREIGHT OCCUPATIONS, N.E.C.

910 RAILROAD TRANSPORTATION OCCUPATIONS

911 WATER TRANSPORTATION OCCUPATIONS

912 AIR TRANSPORTATION OCCUPATIONS

913 PASSENGER TRANSPORTATION OCCUPATIONS, N.E.C.

914 PUMPING AND PIPELINE TRANSPORTATION OCCUPATIONS

915 ATTENDANTS AND SERVICERS, PARKING LOTS AND AUTOMOTIVE SERVICE FACILITIES

919 MISCELLANEOUS TRANSPORTATION OCCUPATIONS, N.E.C.

920 PACKAGING OCCUPATIONS

921 HOISTING AND CONVEYING OCCUPATIONS

922 OCCUPATIONS IN MOVING AND STORING MATERIALS AND PRODUCTS, N.E.C.

929 PACKAGING AND MATERIALS HANDLING OCCUPATIONS, N.E.C.

930 EARTH BORING, DRILLING, CUTTING, AND RELATED OCCUPATIONS

931 BLASTING OCCUPATIONS

932 LOADING AND CONVEYING OPERATIONS

933 CRUSHING OCCUPATIONS

934 SCREENING AND RELATED OCCUPATIONS

939 OCCUPATIONS IN EXTRACTION OF MINERALS, N.E.C.

950 STATIONARY ENGINEERS

951 FIRERS AND RELATED OCCUPATIONS

952 OCCUPATIONS IN GENERATION, TRANSMISSION, AND DISTRIBUTION OF ELECTRIC LIGHT AND POWER

953 OCCUPATIONS IN PRODUCTION AND DISTRIBUTION OF GAS

954 OCCUPATIONS IN FILTRATION, PURIFICATION, AND DISTRIBUTION OF WATER

955 OCCUPATIONS IN DISPOSAL OF REFUSE AND SEWAGE

956 OCCUPATIONS IN DISTRIBUTION OF STEAM

959 OCCUPATIONS IN PRODUCTION AND DISTRIBUTION OF UTILITIES, N.E.C.

960 MOTION PICTURE PROJECTIONISTS

961 MODELS, STAND-INS, AND EXTRAS, N.E.C.

962 OCCUPATIONS IN MOTION PICTURE, TELEVISION, AND THEATRICAL PRODUCTIONS, N.E.C.

969 MISCELLANEOUS AMUSEMENT AND RECREATION OCCUPATIONS, N.E.C.

970 ART WORK OCCUPATIONS, BRUSH, SPRAY, OR PEN

971 PHOTOENGRAVING OCCUPATIONS

972 LITHOGRAPHERS AND RELATED OCCUPATIONS

973 HAND COMPOSITORS, TYPESETTERS, AND RELATED OCCUPATIONS

974 ELECTROTYPERS, STEREOTYPERS, AND RELATED OCCUPATIONS

976 DARKROOM OCCUPATIONS, N.E.C.

977 BOOKBINDERS AND RELATED OCCUPATIONS

979 OCCUPATIONS IN GRAPHIC ART WORK, N.E.C.

APPENDIX B:
DOT Industry
Abbreviations and Titles

To save space, a variety of abbreviations are used throughout this book and in other publications to refer to specific industries where an occupation may be found. While most of these abbreviations are easily understood, this appendix provides the full meaning of each industry abbreviation.

AGRIC. EQUIP.	AGRICULTURAL EQUIPMENT INDUSTRY
AGRICULTURE	AGRICULTURE AND AGRICULTURAL SERVICE
AIR TRANS.	AIR TRANSPORTATION INDUSTRY
AIRCRAFT MFG.	AIRCRAFT-AEROSPACE MANUFACTURING INDUSTRY
AMUSE. & REC.	AMUSEMENT AND RECREATION
ANY INDUSTRY	ANY INDUSTRY
AUTO. MFG.	AUTOMOBILE MANUFACTURING INDUSTRY
AUTOMOTIVE SER.	AUTOMOTIVE SERVICES
BAKERY PRODUCTS	BAKERY PRODUCTS INDUSTRY
BEVERAGE	BEVERAGE INDUSTRY
BOOT & SHOE	BOOT AND SHOE INDUSTRY
BRICK & TILE	BRICK, TILE, AND NONCLAY REFRACTORIES INDUSTRY
BUILD. MAT., NEC	BUILDING MATERIALS INDUSTRY, NOT ELSEWHERE CLASSIFIED
BUSINESS SER.	BUSINESS SERVICES
BUTTON & NOTION	BUTTON AND MISCELLANEOUS NOTIONS INDUSTRY
CAN. & PRESERV.	CANNING AND PRESERVING INDUSTRY
CARPET & RUG	CARPET AND RUG INDUSTRY
CEMENT	CEMENT INDUSTRY
CHEMICAL	CHEMICAL INDUSTRY
CLERICAL	CLERICAL AND KINDRED OCCUPATIONS
CLOCK & WATCH	CLOCKS, WATCHES, AND ALLIED PRODUCTS INDUSTRY
COMM. EQUIP.	RADIO, TELEVISION, AND COMMUNICATION EQUIPMENT INDUSTRY
CONCRETE PROD.	CONCRETE PRODUCTS INDUSTRY
CONSTRUCTION	CONSTRUCTION INDUSTRY
CUTLERY- HRDWR.	CUTLERY, HANDTOOLS, AND HARDWARE INDUSTRY
DAIRY PRODUCTS	DAIRY PRODUCTS INDUSTRY
DOMESTIC SER.	DOMESTIC SERVICE
EDUCATION	EDUCATION AND INSTRUCTION

ELEC. EQUIP.	ELECTRICAL EQUIPMENT INDUSTRY
ELECTRON. COMP.	ELECTRONIC COMPONENTS AND ACCESSORIES INDUSTRY
ELECTRO- PLATING	ELECTROPLATING INDUSTRY
ENGINE- TURBINE	ENGINE AND TURBINE INDUSTRY
ENGRAVING	ENGRAVING, CHASING, AND ETCHING INDUSTRY
FABRICATION, NEC	MISCELLANEOUS FABRICATED PRODUCTS, NOT ELSEWHERE CLASSIFIED
FINANCIAL	FINANCIAL INSTITUTIONS
FISHING & HUNT.	FISHING, HUNTING, AND TRAPPING
FOOD PREP., NEC	FOOD PREPARATIONS AND FOOD SPECIALTIES INDUSTRY, NOT ELSEWHERE CLASSIFIED
FORESTRY	FORESTRY INDUSTRY
FORGING	FORGING
FOUNDRY	FOUNDRY
FUR GOODS	FUR GOODS INDUSTRY
FURNITURE	FURNITURE AND FIXTURES INDUSTRY
GALVANIZING	GALVANIZING AND OTHER COATING INDUSTRY
GARMENT	GARMENT INDUSTRY
GLASS MFG.	GLASS MANUFACTURING INDUSTRY
GLASS PRODUCTS	GLASS PRODUCTS INDUSTRY
GLOVE & MIT.	GLOVE AND MITTEN INDUSTRY
GOVERNMENT SER.	GOVERNMENT SERVICES
GRAIN-FEED MILLS	GRAIN AND FEED MILLING INDUSTRY
HAT & CAP	HAT AND CAP INDUSTRY
HEAT TREATING	HEAT TREATING
HOTEL & REST.	HOTEL AND RESTAURANT INDUSTRY
HOUSE. APPL.	HOUSEHOLD APPLIANCES INDUSTRY
INST. & APP.	INSTRUMENTS AND APPARATUS INDUSTRY
INSURANCE	INSURANCE INDUSTRY
JEWELRY-SILVER.	JEWELRY, SILVERWARE, AND PLATED WARE INDUSTRY

KNITTING	KNITTING INDUSTRY
LAUNDRY & REL.	LAUNDRY, CLEANING, DYEING, AND PRESSING INDUSTRY
LEATHER MFG.	LEATHER MANUFACTURING INDUSTRY
LEATHER PROD.	LEATHER PRODUCTS INDUSTRY
LIBRARY	LIBRARY
LIGHT. FIX.	LIGHTING FIXTURES INDUSTRY
LOGGING	LOGGING INDUSTRY
MACHINE SHOP	MACHINE SHOP
MACHINE TOOLS	MACHINE TOOLS AND ACCESSORIES INDUSTRY
MACHINERY MFG.	MACHINERY MANUFACTURING INDUSTRY
MEAT PRODUCTS	MEAT PRODUCTS INDUSTRY
MEDICAL SER.	MEDICAL SERVICES
METAL PROD., NEC	FABRICATED METAL PRODUCTS, NOT ELSEWHERE CLASSIFIED
MFD. BLDGS.	MANUFACTURED BUILDINGS INDUSTRY
MILITARY SER.	MILITARY SERVICES
MILLWORK-PLYWOOD	MILLWORK, VENEER, PLYWOOD, AND STRUCTURAL WOOD MEMBERS INDUSTRY
MINE & QUARRY	COAL, METAL, AND NONMETAL MINING AND QUARRYING INDUSTRY
MOTION PICTURE	MOTION PICTURE INDUSTRY
MOTOR TRANS.	MOTOR VEHICLE TRANSPORTATION INDUSTRY
MOTOR-BICYCLES	MOTORCYCLES, BICYCLES, AND PARTS INDUSTRY
MUSEUMS	MUSEUMS, ART GALLERIES, AND BOTANICAL AND ZOOLOGICAL GARDENS
MUSICAL INST.	MUSICAL INSTRUMENTS AND PARTS INDUSTRY
NARROW FABRICS	NARROW FABRICS INDUSTRY
NONFER. METAL	NONFERROUS METAL ALLOYS AND PRIMARY PRODUCTS INDUSTRY
NONMET. MIN.	ABRASIVE, ASBESTOS, AND MISCELLANEOUS NONMETALLIC MINERAL PRODUCTS INDUSTRY
NONPROFIT ORG.	NONPROFIT MEMBERSHIP, CHARITABLE, AND RELIGIOUS ORGANIZATIONS
NUT & BOLT	SCREW MACHINE PRODUCTS AND BOLTS, NUTS, SCREWS, RIVETS, AND WASHERS INDUSTRY
OFFICE MACHINES	OFFICE, COMPUTING, AND ACCOUNTING MACHINES INDUSTRY
OILS & GREASE	ANIMAL AND VEGETABLE OILS, FATS, AND GREASE INDUSTRY
OPTICAL GOODS	OPTICAL GOODS INDUSTRY

ORDNANCE	ORDNANCE AND ACCESSORIES (EXCEPT VEHICLES AND GUIDED MISSILES) INDUSTRY
PAINT & VARNISH	PAINT AND VARNISH INDUSTRY
PAPER & PULP	PAPER AND PULP INDUSTRY
PAPER GOODS	PAPER GOODS INDUSTRY
PEN & PENCIL	PEN, PENCIL, MARKING DEVICE, AND ARTISTS' MATERIALS MANUFACTURING INDUSTRY
PERSONAL SER.	PERSONAL SERVICE
PETROL. & GAS	PETROLEUM AND NATURAL GAS PRODUCTION INDUSTRY
PETROL. REFIN.	PETROLEUM REFINING INDUSTRY
PHARMACEUT.	PHARMACEUTICALS AND RELATED PRODUCTS INDUSTRY
PHOTO. APPAR.	PHOTOGRAPHIC APPARATUS AND MATERIALS INDUSTRY
PHOTOFINISHING	PHOTOFINISHING INDUSTRY
PIPE LINES	PIPE LINES INDUSTRY
PLASTIC PROD.	FABRICATED PLASTIC PRODUCTS INDUSTRY
PLASTIC-SYNTH.	PLASTIC AND SYNTHETIC MATERIALS INDUSTRY
PLUMBING-HEAT.	PLUMBING AND HEATING SUPPLIES INDUSTRY
POTTERY & PORC.	POTTERY AND PORCELAIN WARE INDUSTRY
PRINT. & PUB.	PRINTING AND PUBLISHING INDUSTRY
PROFESS. & KIN.	PROFESSIONAL AND KINDRED OCCUPATIONS
PROTECTIVE DEV.	PERSONAL PROTECTIVE AND MEDICAL DEVICES AND SUPPLIES INDUSTRY
R.R. TRANS.	RAILROAD TRANSPORTATION INDUSTRY
RADIO-TV BROAD.	RADIO AND TELEVISION BROADCASTING INDUSTRY
RAILROAD EQUIP.	RAILROAD EQUIPMENT BUILDING AND REPAIRING INDUSTRY
REAL ESTATE	REAL ESTATE INDUSTRY
RECORDING	RECORDING INDUSTRY
RETAIL TRADE	RETAIL TRADE INDUSTRY
RUBBER GOODS	RUBBER GOODS INDUSTRY
RUBBER RECLAIM.	RUBBER RECLAIMING INDUSTRY
RUBBER TIRE	RUBBER TIRE AND TUBE INDUSTRY
SANITARY SER.	SANITARY SERVICES
SAW. & PLAN.	SAWMILL AND PLANING MILL INDUSTRY
SHIP-BOAT MFG.	SHIP AND BOAT MANUFACTURING AND REPAIRING INDUSTRY
SMELT. & REFIN.	SMELTING AND REFINING INDUSTRY
SOAP & REL.	SOAP, CLEANING, AND TOILET PREPARATION INDUSTRY

SOCIAL SER.	SOCIAL SERVICES	TOY-SPORT EQUIP.	TOYS, GAMES, AND SPORTS EQUIPMENT INDUSTRY
STEEL & REL.	BLAST FURNACE, STEEL WORK, AND ROLLING AND FINISHING MILL INDUSTRY	UTILITIES	UTILITIES (LIGHT, HEAT, AND POWER) INDUSTRY
STONEWORK	STONEWORK INDUSTRY	VEHICLES, NEC	MISCELLANEOUS VEHICLES AND TRANSPORTATION EQUIPMENT INDUSTRY, NOT ELSEWHERE CLASSIFIED
STRUCT. METAL	STRUCTURAL AND ORNAMENTAL METAL PRODUCTS INDUSTRY		
SUGAR & CONF.	SUGAR AND CONFECTIONERY PRODUCTS INDUSTRY	WATER TRANS.	WATER TRANSPORTATION INDUSTRY
SVC. IND. MACH.	REFRIGERATION AND SERVICE INDUSTRY MACHINERY INDUSTRY	WATERWORKS	WATERWORKS INDUSTRY
TEL. & TEL.	TELEPHONE AND TELEGRAPH INDUSTRY	WELDING	WELDING AND RELATED PROCESSES
TEX. PROD., NEC	TEXTILE PRODUCTS INDUSTRY, NOT ELSEWHERE CLASSIFIED	WHOLESALE TR.	WHOLESALE TRADE INDUSTRY
		WOOD PROD., NEC	WOOD PRODUCTS INDUSTRY, NOT ELSEWHERE CLASSIFIED
TEXTILE	TEXTILE INDUSTRY		
TINWARE	TINWARE AND OTHER METAL CANS AND CONTAINERS INDUSTRY	WOOD. CONTAINER	WOODEN CONTAINER INDUSTRY
		WOODWORKING	WOODWORKING
TOBACCO	TOBACCO INDUSTRY		

APPENDIX C:
Work Field Codes And Titles (WKF)

A 3-digit code number is used in Section 3 of this book to identify the Work Field (WKF) designation for each occupation. This appendix interprets these codes by providing the Work Field related to each of the 3-digit WKF code.

001 HUNTING-FISHING
002 ANIMAL PROPAGATING
003 PLANT CULTIVATING
004 LOGGING
005 MINING-QUARRYING-EARTH BORING
007 EXCAVATING-CLEARING-FOUNDATION BUILDING
011 MATERIAL MOVING
013 TRANSPORTING
014 PUMPING
021 STATIONARY ENGINEERING
031 CLEANING
032 SURFACE FINISHING
033 LUBRICATING
034 BUTCHERING-MEAT CUTTING
041 FILLING-PACKING-WRAPPING
051 ABRADING
052 CHIPPING
053 BORING
054 SHEARING-SHAVING
055 MILLING-TURNING-PLANNING
056 SAWING
057 MACHINING
061 FITTING-FOLDING
062 FASTENING
063 GLUING-LAMINATING
071 BOLTING-SCREWING
072 NAILING
073 RIVETING
081 WELDING
082 FLAME CUTTING-ARC CUTTING-BEAM CUTTING
083 SOLDERING-BRAZING
091 MASONING
092 LAYING-COVERING

094 CALKING
095 PAVING
101 UPHOLSTERING
102 STRUCTURAL FABRICATING INSTALLING-REPAIRING
111 ELECTRICAL-ELECTRONIC FABRICATING-INSTALLING-REPAIRING
121 MECHANICAL FABRICATING-INSTALLING-REPAIRING
131 MELTING
132 CASTING
133 HEAT CONDITIONING
134 PRESSING-FORGING
135 DIE SIZING
136 MOLDING
141 BAKING-DRYING
142 CRUSHING-GRINDING
143 MIXING
144 DISTILLING
145 SEPARATING
146 COOKING-FOOD PREPARING
147 PROCESSING-COMPOUNDING
151 IMMERSING-COATING
152 SATURATING
153 BRUSHING-SPRAYING
154 ELECTROPLATING
161 COMBING-NAPPING
162 SPINNING
163 WINDING
164 WEAVING
165 KNITTING
166 TUFTING
171 SEWING-TAILORING
182 ETCHING
183 ENGRAVING

191 PRINTING
192 IMPRINTING
201 PHOTOGRAPHING
202 DEVELOPING-PRINTING
211 APPRAISING
212 INSPECTING-MEASURING-TESTING
221 STOCK CHECKING
231 VERBAL RECORDING-RECORDKEEPING
232 NUMERICAL RECORDING-RECORDKEEPING
233 DATA PROCESSING
241 LAYING OUT
242 DRAFTING
243 SURVEYING
244 ENGINEERING
251 RESEARCHING
261 WRITING
262 ARTISTIC PAINTING-DRAWING
263 COMPOSING-CHOREOGRAPHING
264 STYLING
271 INVESTIGATING
272 LITIGATING
281 SYSTEM COMMUNICATING
282 INFORMATION GIVING
291 ACCOMODATING
292 MERCHANDISING-SALES
293 PROTECTING
294 HEALING CARING-MEDICAL
295 ADMINISTERING
296 TEACHING
297 ENTERTAINING
298 ADVISING-COUNSELING

APPENDIX D:
Materials, Products, Subject Matter, and Services Codes and Titles (MPSMS)

Section 3 of this book provides a 3-digit code that refers to the Material, Products, Subject Matter, and Services for each of the occupations listed. This appendix provides the meaning for each of these codes in numerical sequence.

Code	Title
300	PLANT FARM CROPS
301	GRAINS
302	FIELD CROPS, EXCEPT GRAIN
303	VEGETABLES & MELONS
304	CITRUS FRUITS
305	FRUITS, EXCEPT CITRUS
306	TREE NUTS
309	PLANT FARM CROPS, N.E.C.
310	HORTICULTURAL SPECIALTIES, FOREST TREES & FOREST PRODUCTS
311	FLORICULTURAL & RELATED NURSERY PRODUCTS
312	ORNAMENTAL TREES
313	STANDING TIMBER
314	FOREST NURSERY PRODUCTS
319	HORTICULTURAL SPEC., FOREST TREES, & FOREST PRODUCTS, N.E.C.
320	ANIMALS
321	CATTLE
322	HOGS
323	SHEEP & GOATS
324	POULTRY & OTHER FOWL
325	CAPTIVE FUR-BEARING ANIMALS
326	GAME & WILDLIFE
327	HORSES & OTHER EQUINES
329	ANIMALS, N.E.C.
330	MARINE LIFE
331	FINFISH
332	SHELLFISH
339	MARINE LIFE, N.E.C
340	RAW FUELS & NONMETALLIC MINERALS
341	COAL & LIGNITE
342	CRUDE PETROLEUM & NATURAL GAS
343	STONE, DIMENSION
344	STONE, CRUSHED & BROKEN
345	SAND & GRAVEL
346	CLAY
347	CHEMICAL & FERTILIZER MINERALS
349	RAW FUELS & NONMETALLIC MINERALS, N.E.C.
350	RAW METALLIC MINERALS
351	IRON ORES
352	COPPER ORES
353	LEAD & ZINC ORES
354	GOLD & SILER ORES
355	BAUXITE & OTHER ALUMINUM ORES
356	FERROALLOY ORES, EXCEPT VANADIUM
357	MERCURY ORES
358	URANIUM, RADIUM & VANADIUM ORES
359	RAW METALLIC MINERALS
360	STRUCTURES
361	BUILDINGS, EXCEPT PREFABRICATED
362	HIGHWAYS & STREETS
363	BRIDGES, TUNNELS, VIADUCTS, & ELEVATED HIGHWAYS
364	WATER, GAS, & SEWER MAINS
365	MARINE CONSTRUCTION
366	POWERPLANT PROJECTS
367	RAILROADS & SUBWAYS
368	OIL REFINERIES
369	STRUCTURES, N.E.C.
370	ORDNANCE
371	GUNS, HOWITZERS, MOTARS & RELATED EQUIPMENT
372	AMMUNITION, EXCEPT SMALL ARMS
373	SMALL ARMS
374	SMALL ARMS AMMUNITION
375	GUIDED MISSILES
379	ORDNANCE & ACCESSORIES, N.E.C.
380	FOOD STAPLES & RELATED
381	GRAIN MILL PRODUCTS
382	MEAT PRODUCTS, PROCESSED
383	DAIRY PRODUCTS
384	BAKERY PRODUCTS
385	OILS & FATS, EDIBLE
386	SEAFOOD, PROCESSED
387	FRUITS & VEGETABLES, PROCESSED
389	FOOD STAPLES & RELATED, N.E.C.
390	FOOD SPECIALTIES
391	COFFEE, TEA, & SPICES
392	SUGAR & SIRUP
393	CONFECTIONERY & RELATED PRODUCTS
394	FLAVORING EXTRACTS & FLAVORING SIRUPS
395	BEVERAGES, ALCOHOLIC
396	SOFT DRINKS & CARBONATED WATERS
397	MACARONI, SPAGHETTI, VERMICELLI, NOODLES
398	VINEGAR & CIDER
399	FOOD SPECIALTIES, N.E.C.
400	TOBACCO PRODUCTS
401	CIGARETTES
402	CIGARS
403	TOBACCO, CHEWING, SMOKING, & SNUFF
404	TOBACCO, STEMMED & REDRIED
409	TOBACCO PRODUCTS, N.E.C.
410	TEXTILE FIBERS & RELATED
411	YARN
412	THREAD
413	CORDAGE & TWINE
414	FIBER STOCK
419	TEXTILE FIBERS & RELATED, N.E.C.
420	FABRICS & RELATED
421	FABRICS, BROAD WOVEN COTTON
422	FABRICS, BROAD WOVEN WOOL
423	NARROW FABRICS & RELATED SMALLWARES

424 FABRICS, KNITTED

425 FABRICS, NONWOVEN

429 FABRICS & RELATED, N.E.C.

430 TEXTILE PRODUCTS

431 CARPETS & RUGS

432 TEXTILES, FANCY

433 PADDINGS & UPHOLSTERY FILLING

434 IMPREGNATED & COATED FABRICS

435 HOUSEFURNISHINGS

436 CANVAS & RELATED PRODUCTS

439 TEXTILE PRODUCTS, N.E.C.

440 APPAREL

441 MEN'S & BOY'S SUITS, COATS, & OVERCOATS

442 MEN'S & BOYS' FURNISHINGS, WORK CLOTHING

443 WOMEN'S, GIRLS' & INFANTS' OUTWEAR

444 WOMEN'S, GIRLS' & INFANTS' UNDERGARMENTS

445 HATS

446 HOSIERY

447 FUR GOODS

449 APPAREL, N.E.C.

450 LUMBER & WOOD PRODUCTS

451 LOGS & HEWN TIMBER PRODUCTS, UNTREATED

452 SAWMILL, PLANING MILL, & TREATED WOOD PRODUCTS

453 VENEER & PLYWOOD

454 WOOD CONTAINERS

455 PREFABRICATED WOOD BUILDINGS, MOBILE HOMES

456 PARTICLEBOARD

457 WOOD ARTICLES

459 LUMBER & WOOD PRODUCTS, N.E.C.

460 FURNITURE & FIXTURES

461 WOOD HOUSEHOLD FURNITURE, EXCEPT UPHOLSTERED

462 WOOD HOUSEHOLD FURNITURE, UPHOLSTERED

463 METAL HOUSEHOLD FURNITURE

464 MATTRESS, BEDSPRINGS, & SOFA BEDS

465 WOOD OFFICE, PUBLIC BUILDING, & RELATED FURNITURE

466 METAL OFFICE, PUBLIC BUILDING, & RELATED FURNITURE

467 WOOD & METAL FIXTURES

468 PLASTIC, GLASS, & FIBERGLASS FURNITURE & FIXTURES

469 FURNITURE & FIXTURES, N.E.C.

470 PAPER & ALLIED PRODUCTS

471 PULP

472 NONCONVERTED PAPER & PAPERBOARD

473 NONCONVERTED BUILDING PAPER & BUILDING BOARD

474 CONVERTED PAPER & PAPERBOARD PRODUCTS

475 PAPERBOARD CONTAINERS & BOXES

479 PAPER & ALLIED PRODUCTS, N.E.C.

480 PRINTED & PUBLISHED PRODUCTS

481 NEWSPAPERS

482 PERIODICALS

483 BOOKS & PAMPHLETS

484 MANIFOLD BUSINESS FORMS

485 GREETING CARDS

486 BLANKBOOKS, LOOSELEAF BINDERS, & RELATED PRODUCTS

489 MISCELLANEOUS PUBLISHED & PRINTED BOOKS

490 CHEMICAL & ALLIED PRODUCTS

491 CHEMICALS, INORGANIC

492 PLASTICS MATERIALS & SYNTHETIC RESINS & FIBERS

493 DRUGS

494 CLEANING PREPARATIONS, PERFUMES, & COSMETICS

495 PAINTS, ENAMELS, & ALLIED PRODUCTS

496 CHEMICALS, ORGANIC

497 AGRICULTURAL CHEMICALS

499 CHEMICAL & ALLIED PRODUCTS, N.E.C.

500 PETROLEUM & RELATED PRODUCTS

501 PETROLEUM PRODUCTS

502 PAVING MATERIALS

503 ROOFING MATERIALS

504 FUEL BRIQUETTES, PACKAGED FUEL, & POWDERED FUEL

505 COKE

509 PETROLEUM & RELATED PRODUCTS, N.E.C.

510 RUBBER & MISCELLANEOUS PLASTIC PRODUCTS

511 TIRES & TUBES

512 RUBBER & PLASTIC FOOTWEAR

513 RECLAIMED RUBBER

514 RUBBER & PLASTIC HOSE & BELTING

519 RUBBER & MISCELLANEOUS PLASTIC PRODUCTS, N.E.C.

520 LEATHER & LEATHER PRODUCTS

521 HIDES, SKINS, & LEATHER

522 FOOTWEAR, EXCEPT RUBBER

523 LEATHER GLOVES & MITTENS

524 LUGGAGE OF ANY MATERIAL

525 HANDBAGS & RELATED ACCESSORIES OF ANY MATERIAL

529 LEATHER & LEATHER PRODUCTS, N.E.C.

530 STONE, CLAY, & GLASS PRODUCTS

531 FLAT, PRESSED, OR BLOWN GLASS & GLASSWARE

532 GLASS PRODUCTS MADE OF PURCHASED GLASS

533 CEMENT, HYDRAULIC

534 STRUCTURAL CLAY PRODUCTS

535 POTTERY & RELATED PRODUCTS

536 CONCRETE, GYPSUM, & PLASTER PRODUCTS

537 CUT STONE & STONE PRODUCTS

538 ABRASIVE, ASBESTOS, & RELATED PRODUCTS

539 STONE, CLAY, & GLASS PRODUCTS, N.E.C

540 METAL, FERROUS & NONFERROUS

541 BLAST FURNACE, STEELWORKS

542 METAL CASTINGS

543 NONRERROUS METALS, SMELTED & REFINED

544 NONFERROUS METALS, ROLLED, DRAWN, & EXTRUDED

549 METAL, FERROUS & NONFERROUS, N.E.C.

550 FABRICATED METAL PRODUCTS

551 METAL CANS & CONTAINERS

552 CUTLERY, HANDTOOLS & GENERAL HARDWARE

553 NONELECTRIC HEATING EQUIPMENT

554 FABRICATED STRUCTURAL METAL PRODUCTS

555 SCREW-MACHINE PRODUCTS

556 METAL FORGINGS & STAMPINGS

557 FABRICATED WIRE PRODUCTS

559 FABRICATED METAL PRODUCTS, N.E.C.

560 MACHINERY & EQUIPMENT, EXCEPT ELECTRICAL

561 ENGINES & TURBINES

562 FARM & GARDEN MACHINERY & EQUIPMENT

563 CONSTRUCTION MACHINERY & EQUIPMENT

564 MINING & OIL-FIELD MACHINERY & EQUIPMENT

565 MATERIALS-HANDLING MACHINERY & EQUIPMENT

566 METALWORKING MACHINERY & EQUIPMENT

567 SPECIAL INDUSTRIAL MACHINERY

568 GENERAL INDUSTRIAL MACHINERY & EQUIPMENT

570 MACHINERY & EQUIPMENT, EXCEPT ELECTRICAL

571 OFFICE, COMPUTING & ACCOUNTING MACHINES

572 SERVICE-INDUSTRY MACHINERY

573 REFRIGERATION & AIR-CONDITIONING EQUIPMENT

579 MACHINERY & EQUIPMENT, EXCEPT ELECTRICAL, N.E.C.

580 ELECTRICAL & ELECTRONIC MACHINERY, EQUIPMENT & SUPPLIES

581 ELECTRICAL TRANSMISSION & DISTRIBUTION EQUIPMENT

582 ELECTRICAL INDUSTRIAL APPARATUS

583 HOUSEHOLD APPLIANCES

584 ELECTRIC LIGHTING & WIRING EQUIPMENT

585 HOME-ENTERTAINMENT ELECTRIC EQUIPMENT

586 COMMUNICATION & RELATED EQUIPMENT

587 ELECTRONIC COMPONENTS & ACCESSORIES

589 ELECTRICAL & ELECTRONIC MACHINERY, EQUIPMENT & SUPPLIES, N.E.C

590 TRANSPORTATION EQUIPMENT

591 MOTOR VEHICLES & MOTOR-VEHICLE EQUIPMENT

592 AIRCRAFT & PARTS

593 SHIPS & BOATS

594 RAILROAD EQUIPMENT

595 MOTORCYCLES, BICYCLES & PARTS

596 SPACE VEHICLES & PARTS

597 TRAVEL TRAILERS & CAMPERS

598 MILITARY TANKS & TANK COMPONENTS

599 TRANSPORTATION EQUIPMENT, N.E.C.

600 MEASURING, ANALYZING & CONTROLLING INSTRUMENTS

601 ENGINEERING, LABORATORY, SCIENTIFIC INSTRUMENTS

602 MEASURING & CONTROLLING INSTRUMENTS

603 OPTICAL INSTRUMENTS & LENSES

604 SURGICAL, MEDICAL & DENTAL INSTRUMENTS & SUPPLIES

605 OPHTHALMIC GOODS

606 PHOTOGRAPHIC EQUIPMENT & SUPPLIES

607 WATCHES, CLOCKS, CLOCKWORK-OPERATED DEVICES

609 MEASURING, ANALYZING & CONTROLLING INSTRUMENTS, N.E.C.

610 MISCELLANEOUS FABRICATED PRODUCTS

611 JEWELRY, PRECIOUS METAL

612 SILVERWARE, PLATED WARE, & STAINLESS STEEL WARE

613 JEWELERS' FINDINGS & MATERIALS

614 MUSICAL INSTRUMENTS & PARTS

615 GAMES & TOYS

616 SPORTING & ATHLETIC GOODS

617 PENS, PENCILS, & OTHER OFFICE & ARTISTS' MATERIALS

618 COSTUME JEWELRY & NOVELTIES

619 MISCELLANEOUS FABRICATED PRODUCTS, N.E.C.

700 ARCHITECTURE & ENGINEERING

701 ARCHITECTURAL ENGINEERING

702 AERONAUTICAL ENGINEERING

703 ELECTRICAL, ELECTRONIC ENGINEERING

704 CIVIL ENGINEERING

705 CERAMIC ENGINEERING

706 MECHANICAL ENGINEERING

707 CHEMICAL ENGINEERING

708 MINING & PETROLEUM ENGINEERING

710 ARCHITECTURE & ENGINEERING

711 METALLURGICAL ENGINEERING

712 INDUSTRIAL ENGINEERING

713 AGRICULTURAL ENGINEERING

714 MARINE ENGINEERING

715 NUCLEAR ENGINEERING

716 SURVEYING, CARTOGRAPHIC ENGINEERING

719 ARCHITECTURE & ENGINEERING, N.E.C.

720 MATHEMATICS & PHYSICAL SCIENCES

721 MATHEMATICS

722 ASTRONOMY

723 CHEMISTRY

724 PHYSICS

725 GEOLOGY & GEOPHYSICS

729 MATHEMATICS & PHYSICAL SCIENCES, N.E.C.

730 LIFE SCIENCES

731 AGRICULTURE, HORTICULTURE, & FORESTRY

732 BIOLOGICAL SCIENCES

733 PSYCHOLOGY

739 LIFE SCIENCES, N.E.C.

740 SOCIAL SCIENCES

741 ECONOMICS

742 POLITICAL SCIENCE

743 HISTORY

744 SOCIOLOGY

745 ANTHROPOLOGY

749 SOCIAL SCIENCES, N.E.C.

750 ARTS & LITERATURE

751 FINE ARTS

752 GRAPHIC ARTS

753 PHOTOGRAPHY

754 DRAMATICS

755 RHYTHMICS

756 MUSIC

757 LITERATURE & JOURNALISM

759 ARTS, N.E.C.

850 TRANSPORTATION SERVICES

851 INTERURBAN RAILROAD TRANSPORTATION

852 LOCAL & SUBURBAN TRANSIT & INTERURBAN BUSES

853 MOTOR FREIGHT TRANSPORTATION & WAREHOUSING

854 WATER TRANSPORTATION

855 AIR TRANSPORTATION

856 PIPELINE TRANSPORTATION

859 TRANSPORTATION SERVICES, N.E.C.

860 COMMUNICATION SERVICES

861 TELEPHONE COMMUNICATION

862 TELEGRAPH COMMUNICATION

863 RADIO BROADCASTING

864 TELEVISION BROADCASTING

867 BLUEPRINTING, PHOTOCOPYING, AND PHOTOFINISHING SERVICES

869 COMMUNICATION SERVICES, N.E.C.

870 ELECTRIC, GAS, & SANITARY SERVICES

871 ELECTRIC SERVICES

872 GAS PRODUCTION & DISTRIBUTION

873 WATER SUPPLY & IRRIGATION SERVICES

874 SANITARY SERVICES

875 STEAM SUPPLY

879 ELECTRIC, GAS, & SANITARY SERVICES, N.E.C.

880 MECHANDISING SERVICES

881 RETAIL TRADE

882 WHOLESALE TRADE

883 ROUTE SALES & DELIVERY SERVICES

884 AUCTIONEERING, VENDING, & RENTAL SERVICES

885 SALES PROMOTION SERVICES

889 MERCHANDISING SERVICES, N.E.C.

890 GENERAL BUSINESS, FINANCE, INSURANCE, & REAL ESTATE SERVICES

891 CLERICAL SERVICES, EXCEPT BOOKKEEPING

892 ACCOUNTING, AUDITING, & BOOKKEEPING SERVICES

893 GENERAL ADMINISTRATION

894 FINANCIAL SERVICES

895 INSURANCE & REAL ESTATE

896 ADVERTISING & PUBLIC RELATIONS SERVICES

897 BLUEPRINTING, PHOTOCOPYING, & PHOTOFINISHING SERVICES

898 PRODUCTION SERVICES

899 GENERAL BUSINESS SERVICES, N.E.C.

900 DOMESTIC, BUILDING, & PERSONAL SERVICES

901 DOMESTIC SERVICES

902 LODGING SERVICES

903 MEAL SERVICES, EXCEPT DOMESTIC

904 BEAUTY & BARBERING SERVICES

905 JANITORIAL & PORTERING SERVICES

906 APPAREL & FURNISHING SERVICES

907 FUNERAL & CREMATORY SERVICES

909 DOMESTIC, BUILDING, & PERSONAL SERVICES, N.E.C.

910 AMUSEMENT & RECREATION SERVICES

911 MOTION PICTURE SERVICES

912 THEATER SERVICES

913 SPORTS PARTICIPATION

914 SPORTS SERVICES

919 AMUSEMENT & RECREATION SERVICES, N.E.C.

920 MEDICAL & OTHER HEALTH SERVICES

921 PHYSICIAN SERVICES

922 DENTAL SERVICES

923 OPTOMETRIC, CHIROPRATIC, & RELATED SERVICES

924 NURSING, DIETETIC, & THERAPEUTIC SERVICES

925 HEALTH TECHNOLOGICAL SERVICES

926 MEDICAL ASSISTANT, AIDE, & ATTENDANT SERVICES

929 MEDICAL & OTHER HEALTH SERVICES, N.E.C.

930 EDUCATIONAL, LEGAL, MUSEUM, LIBRARY & ARCHIVAL SERVICES

931 EDUCATIONAL SERVICES

932 LEGAL SERVICES

933 MUSEUM, LIBRARY, & ARCHIVAL SERVICES

939 EDUCATIONAL, LEGAL, MUSEUM, LIBRARY & ARCHIVAL SERVICES, N.E.C

940 SOCIAL, EMPLOYMENT, & SPIRITUAL SERVICES

941 SOCIAL & WELFARE SERVICES

942 CHILD & ADULT RESIDENTIAL & DAY-CARE SERVICES

943 EMPLOYMENT SERVICES

944 SPIRITUAL SERVICES

949 SOCIAL, EMPLOYMENT, & SPIRITUAL SERVICES, N.E.C.

950 GOVERNMENT & RELATED SERVICES

951 PROTECTIVE SERVICES, EXCEPT MILITARY

952 MILITARY SERVICES

953 REGULATORY LAW INVESTIGATION & CONTROL SERVICES

954 POSTAL SERVICES

959 GOVERNMENT & RELATED SERVICES, N.E.C.

960 MISCELLANEOUS SERVICES

961 MOTOR-VEHICLE SERVICES

962 DEODORIZING, EXTERMINATING, & DECONTAMINATING SERVICES

969 MISCELLANEOUS SERVICES, N.E.C.

APPENDIX E:
Guide for Occupational Exploration (GOE) Interest Areas, Work Groups, Subgroups and Titles

The U.S. Department of Labor has developed a system of organizing occupations into 12 major Interest Areas and increasingly specific subgroups of related jobs. This system is used in the *Guide for Occupational Exploration* (GOE) and each of the occupations listed in Section 3 of this book includes a GOE number. This appendix presents the numerical system of GOE groupings along with their related group names and will help you better interpret the meaning of the GOE number assigned to each occupation in Section 3.

01 ARTISTIC
01.01 LITERARY ARTS
01.01.01 EDITING
01.01.02 CREATIVE WRITING
01.01.03 CRITIQUEING
01.02 VISUAL ARTS
01.02.01 INSTRUCTING AND APPRAISING
01.02.02 STUDIO ART
01.02.03 COMMERCIAL ART
01.03 PERFORMING ARTS: DRAMA
01.03.01 INSTRUCTING AND DIRECTING
01.03.02 PERFORMING
01.03.03 NARRATING AND ANNOUNCING
01.04 PERFORMING ARTS: MUSIC
01.04.01 INSTRUCTING AND DIRECTING
01.04.02 COMPOSING AND ARRANGING
01.04.03 VOCAL PERFORMING
01.04.04 INSTRUMENTAL PERFORMING
01.05 PERFORMING ARTS: DANCE
01.05.01 INSTRUCTING AND CHOREOGRAPHY
01.05.02 PERFORMING
01.06 CRAFTS ARTS
01.06.01 GRAPHIC ARTS AND RELATED CRAFTS
01.06.02 ARTS AND CRAFTS
01.06.03 HAND LETTERING, PAINTING, AND DECORATING
01.07 ELEMENTAL ARTS
01.07.01 PSYCHIC SCIENCE
01.07.02 ANNOUNCING
01.07.03 ENTERTAINING
01.08 MODELING
01.08.01 PERSONAL APPEARANCE

02 SCIENTIFIC
02.01 PHYSICAL SCIENCES
02.01.01 THEORETICAL RESEARCH
02.01.02 TECHNOLOGY
02.02 LIFE SCIENCES
02.02.01 ANIMAL SPECIALIZATION
02.02.02 PLANT SPECIALIZATION
02.02.03 PLANT AND ANIMAL SPECIALIZATION
02.02.04 FOOD RESEARCH
02.03 MEDICAL SCIENCES
02.03.01 MEDICINE AND SURGERY

02.03.02 DENTISTRY
02.03.03 VETERINARY MEDICINE
02.03.04 HEALTH SPECIALTIES
02.04 LABORATORY TECHNOLOGY
02.04.01 PHYSICAL SCIENCES
02.04.02 LIFE SCIENCES

03 PLANTS AND ANIMALS
03.01 MANAGERIAL WORK: PLANTS AND ANIMALS
03.01.01 FARMING
03.01.02 SPECIALTY BREEDING
03.01.03 SPECIALTY CROPPING
03.01.04 FORESTRY AND LOGGING
03.02 GENERAL SUPERVISION: PLANTS AND ANIMALS
03.02.01 FARMING
03.02.02 FORESTRY AND LOGGING
03.02.03 NURSERY AND GROUNDSKEEPING
03.02.04 SERVICES
03.03 ANIMAL TRAINING AND SERVICE
03.03.01 ANIMAL TRAINING
03.03.02 ANIMAL SERVICE
03.04 ELEMENTAL WORK: PLANTS AND ANIMALS
03.04.01 FARMING
03.04.02 FORESTRY AND LOGGING
03.04.03 HUNTING AND FISHING
03.04.04 NURSERY AND GROUNDSKEEPING
03.04.05 SERVICES

04 PROTECTIVE
04.01 SAFETY AND LAW ENFORCEMENT
04.01.01 MANAGING
04.01.02 INVESTIGATING
04.02 SECURITY SERVICES
04.02.01 DETENTION
04.02.02 PROPERTY AND PEOPLE
04.02.03 LAW AND ORDER
04.02.04 EMERGENCY REPORTING

05 MECHANICAL
05.01 ENGINEERING
05.01.01 RESEARCH
05.01.02 ENVIRONMENTAL PROTECTION
05.01.03 SYSTEMS DESIGN
05.01.04 TESTING AND QUALITY CONTROL
05.01.05 SALES ENGINEERING

06.02.10 EQUIPMENT OPERATION, METAL PROCESSING
06.02.11 EQUIPMENT OPERATION, CHEMICAL PROCESSING
06.02.12 EQUIPMENT OPERATION, PETROLEUM AND GAS PROCESSING
06.02.13 EQUIPMENT OPERATION, RUBBER, PLASTICS AND GLASS PROCESSING
06.02.14 EQUIPMENT OPERATION, PAPER AND PAPER PRODUCTS PROCESSING
06.02.15 EQUIPMENT OPERATION, FOOD PROCESSING
06.02.16 EQUIPMENT OPERATION, TEXTILE, FABRIC, AND LEATHER PROCESSING
06.02.17 EQUIPMENT OPERATION, CLAY AND COKE PROCESSING
06.02.18 EQUIPMENT OPERATION, ASSORTED MATERIALS PROCESSING
06.02.19 EQUIPMENT OPERATION, WELDING, BRAZING, AND SOLDERING
06.02.20 MACHINE ASSEMBLING
06.02.21 COATING AND PLATING
06.02.22 MANUAL WORK, ASSEMBLY LARGE PARTS
06.02.23 MANUAL WORK, ASSEMBLY SMALL PARTS
06.02.24 MANUAL WORK, METAL AND PLASTICS
06.02.25 MANUAL WORK, WOOD
06.02.26 MANUAL WORK, PAPER
06.02.27 MANUAL WORK, TEXTILE, FABRIC, AND LEATHER
06.02.28 MANUAL WORK, FOOD PROCESSING
06.02.29 MANUAL WORK, RUBBER
06.02.30 MANUAL WORK, STONE, GLASS, AND CLAY
06.02.31 MANUAL WORK, LAYING OUT AND MARKING
06.02.32 MANUAL WORK, ASSORTED MATERIALS
06.03 QUALITY CONTROL: INDUSTRIAL
06.03.01 INSPECTING, TESTING, AND REPAIRING
06.03.02 INSPECTING, GRADING, SORTING, WEIGHING, AND RECORDING
06.04 ELEMENTAL WORK: INDUSTRIAL
06.04.01 SUPERVISION
06.04.02 MACHINE WORK, METAL AND PLASTICS
06.04.03 MACHINE WORK, WOOD
06.04.04 MACHINE WORK, PAPER
06.04.05 MACHINE WORK, FABRIC AND LEATHER
06.04.06 MACHINE WORK, TEXTILES
06.04.07 MACHINE WORK, RUBBER
06.04.08 MACHINE WORK, STONE, GLASS, AND CLAY
06.04.09 MACHINE WORK, ASSORTED MATERIALS
06.04.10 EQUIPMENT OPERATION, METAL PROCESSING
06.04.11 EQUIPMENT OPERATION, CHEMICAL PROCESSING
06.04.12 EQUIPMENT OPERATION, PETROLEUM, GAS, AND COAL PROCESSING
06.04.13 EQUIPMENT OPERATION, RUBBER, PLASTICS, GLASS PROCESSING
06.04.14 EQUIPMENT OPERATION, PAPER MAKING
06.04.15 EQUIPMENT OPERATION, FOOD PROCESSING
06.04.16 EQUIPMENT OPERATION, TEXTILE, FABRIC, AND LEATHER PROCESSING
06.04.17 EQUIPMENT OPERATION, CLAY PROCESSING
06.04.18 EQUIPMENT OPERATION, WOOD PROCESSING
06.04.19 EQUIPMENT OPERATION, ASSORTED MATERIALS PROCESSING
06.04.20 MACHINE ASSEMBLING
06.04.21 MACHINE WORK, BRUSHING, SPRAYING, AND COATING
06.04.22 MANUAL WORK, ASSEMBLY LARGE PARTS
06.04.23 MANUAL WORK, ASSEMBLY SMALL PARTS
06.04.24 MANUAL WORK, METAL AND PLASTICS
06.04.25 MANUAL WORK, WOOD
06.04.26 MANUAL WORK, PAPER
06.04.27 MANUAL WORK, TEXTILE, FABRIC, AND LEATHER
06.04.28 MANUAL WORK, FOOD PROCESSING
06.04.29 MANUAL WORK, RUBBER
06.04.30 MANUAL WORK, STONE, GLASS, AND CLAY
06.04.31 MANUAL WORK, WELDING AND FLAME CUTTING
06.04.32 MANUAL WORK, CASTING AND MOLDING
06.04.33 MANUAL WORK, BRUSHING, SPRAYING, AND COATING
06.04.34 MANUAL WORK, ASSORTED MATERIALS
06.04.35 LAUNDERING, DRY CLEANING
06.04.36 FILLING
06.04.37 MANUAL WORK, STAMPING, MARKING, LABELING, AND TICKETING
06.04.38 WRAPPING AND PACKING
06.04.39 CLEANING
06.04.40 LOADING, MOVING, HOISTING, AND CONVEYING

07 BUSINESS DETAIL
07.01 ADMINISTRATIVE DETAIL
07.01.01 INTERVIEWING
07.01.02 ADMINISTRATION
07.01.03 SECRETARIAL WORK
07.01.04 FINANCIAL WORK
07.01.05 CERTIFYING
07.01.06 INVESTIGATING
07.01.07 TEST ADMINISTRATION
07.02 MATHEMATICAL DETAIL
07.02.01 BOOKKEEPING AND AUDITING
07.02.02 ACCOUNTING
07.02.03 STATISTICAL REPORTING AND ANALYSIS
07.02.04 BILLING AND RATE COMPUTATION
07.02.05 PAYROLL AND TIMEKEEPING
07.03 FINANCIAL DETAIL
07.03.01 PAYING AND RECEIVING
07.04 ORAL COMMUNICATIONS
07.04.01 INTERVIEWING
07.04.02 ORDER, COMPLAINT, AND CLAIMS HANDLING
07.04.03 REGISTRATION
07.04.04 RECEPTION AND INFORMATION GIVING
07.04.05 INFORMATION TRANSMITTING AND RECEIVING
07.04.06 SWITCHBOARD SERVICES
07.05 RECORDS PROCESSING
07.05.01 COORDINATING AND SCHEDULING
07.05.02 RECORD VERIFICATION AND PROOFING
07.05.03 RECORD PREPARATION AND MAINTENANCE
07.05.04 ROUTING AND DISTRIBUTION
07.06 CLERICAL MACHINE OPERATION
07.06.01 COMPUTER OPERATION
07.06.02 KEYBOARD MACHINE OPERATION
07.07 CLERICAL HANDLING
07.07.01 FILING
07.07.02 SORTING AND DISTRIBUTION
07.07.03 GENERAL CLERICAL WORK

08 SELLING
08.01 SALES TECHNOLOGY
08.01.01 TECHNICAL SALES
08.01.02 INTANGIBLE SALES
08.01.03 PURCHASING AND SALES

APPENDIX F:
Standard Occupational Classification (SOC) Codes and Titles

This appendix lists the numerical SOC code along with its interpretation.

1120 CHIEF EXECUTIVES AND GENERAL ADMINISTRATORS

1131 JUDICIAL, PUBLIC SAFETY AND CORRECTIONS ADMINISTRATORS

1132 HUMAN RESOURCES PROGRAM ADMINISTRATORS

1133 NATURAL RESOURCES PROGRAM ADMINISTRATORS

1134 RURAL, URBAN, AND COMMUNITY DEVELOPMENT PROGRAM ADMINISRATORS

1135 PUBLIC FINANCE, TAXATION, AND OTHER MONETARY PROGRAM ADMINISTRATORS

1139 OFFICIALS AND ADMINISTRATORS, PUBLIC ADMINSTRATION, NOT ELSEWHERE CLASSIFIED

1210 GENERAL MANAGERS AND OTHER TOP EXECUTIVES

1220 FINANCIAL MANAGERS

1230 PERSONNEL AND LABOR RELATIONS MANAGERS

1240 PURCHASING MANAGERS

1250 MANAGERS; MARKETING, ADVERTISING, AND PUBLIC RELATIONS

1260 MANAGERS; ENGINEERING, MATHEMATICS, AND NATURAL SCIENCES

1270 MANAGERS; SOCIAL SCIENCES AND RELATED FIELDS

1281 ADMINISTRATORS; COLLEGES AND UNIVERSITIES

1282 ADMINISTRATORS; ELEMENTARY AND SECONDARY EDUCATION

1283 ADMINISTRATORS; EDUCATION AND RELATED FIELDS, NOT ELSEWHERE CLASSIFIED

1310 MANAGERS; MEDICINE AND HEALTH

1320 PRODUCTION MANAGERS, INDUSTRIAL

1330 CONSTRUCTION MANAGERS

1341 COMMUNICATIONS OPERATIONS MANAGERS

1342 TRANSPORTATION FACILITIES AND OPERATIONS MANAGERS

1343 ELECTRICITY, GAS, WATER SUPPLY, AND SANITARY SERVICES MANAGERS

1344 POSTMASTERS AND MAIL SUPERINTENDENTS

1351 MANAGERS; FOOD SERVING AND LODGING ESTABLISHMENTS

1352 MANAGERS; ENTERTAINMENT AND RECREATION FACILITIES

1353 MANAGERS; PROPERTY AND LEASING

1354 MANAGERS; MEMBERSHIP ORGANIZATIONS

1359 MANAGERS; SERVICE ORGANIZATIONS, NOT ELSEWHERE CLASSIFIED

1360 MANAGERS; MINING, QUARRYING, WELL DRILLING, AND SIMILAR OPERATIONS

1370 MANAGERS; ADMINISTRATIVE SERVICES

1390 OFFICIALS AND ADMINISTRATORS; OTHER, NOT ELSEWHERE CLASSIFIED

1412 ACCOUNTANTS AND AUDITORS

1414 UNDERWRITERS

1415 LOAN OFFICERS

1419 OTHER FINANCIAL OFFICERS

1420 MANAGEMENT ANALYSTS

1430 PERSONNEL, TRAINING, AND LABOR RELATIONS SPECIALISTS

1442 BUYERS, WHOLESALE AND RETAIL TRADE, EXCEPT FARM PRODUCTS

1443 PURCHASING AGENTS AND BUYERS, FARM PRODUCTS

1449 PURCHASING AGENTS AND BUYERS, NOT ELSEWHERE CLASSIFIED

1450 BUSINESS AND PROMOTION AGENTS

1472 CONSTRUCTION INSPECTORS

1473 INSPECTORS AND COMPLIANCE OFFICERS, EXCEPT CONSTRUCION

1490 MANAGEMENT RELATED OCCUPATIONS, NEC

1610 ARCHITECTS

1622 AEROSPACE ENGINEERS

1623 METALLURGICAL AND MATERIALS ENGINEERS

1624 MINING ENGINEERS

1625 PETROLEUM ENGINEERS

1626 CHEMICAL ENGINEERS

1627 NUCLEAR ENGINEERS

1628 CIVIL ENGINEERS

1632 AGRICULTURAL ENGINEERS

1633 ELECTRICAL AND ELECTRONIC ENGINEERS

1634 INDUSTRIAL ENGINEERS

1635 MECHANICAL ENGINEERS

1636 COMPUTER ENGINEERS

1637 MARINE ENGINEERS AND NAVAL ARCHITECTS

1639 ENGINEERS, NOT ELSEWHERE CLASSIFIED

1643 LAND SURVEYORS

1644 CARTOGRAPHERS

1649 SURVEYORS AND MAPPING SCIENTISTS, NOT ELSEWHERE CLASSIFIED

1712 COMPUTER SYSTEMS ANALYSTS

1719 COMPUTER SCIENTISTS, NOT ELSEWHERE CLASSIFIED

1721 OPERATIONS RESEARCHERS AND ANALYSTS

1732 ACTUARIES

1733 STATISTICIANS

1739 MATHEMATICAL SCIENTISTS, NOT ELSEWHERE CLASSIFIED

1842 ASTRONOMERS

1843 PHYSICISTS

1845 CHEMISTS, EXCEPT BIOCHEMISTS

1846 ATMOSPHERIC AND SPACE SCIENTISTS

1847 GEOLOGISTS

1849 PHYSICAL SCIENTISTS, NOT ELSEWHERE CLASSIFIED

1852 FORESTRY AND CONSERVATION SCIENTISTS

1853 AGRICULTURAL AND FOOD SCIENTISTS

1854 BIOLOGICAL SCIENTISTS

1855 MEDICAL SCIENTISTS

1912 ECONOMISTS

1913 HISTORIANS

1914 POLITICAL SCIENTISTS

1915 PSYCHOLOGISTS

1916 SOCIOLOGISTS

1919 SOCIAL SCIENTISTS, NOT ELSEWHERE CLASSIFIED

1920 URBAN AND REGIONAL PLANNERS

2032 SOCIAL WORKERS

2033 RECREATION WORKERS

2042 CLERGY

2049 RELIGIOUS WORKERS, NOT ELSEWHERE CLASSIFIED

2110 LAWYERS

2120 JUDGES

2200 TEACHERS; COLLEGE, UNIVERSITY AND OTHER POSTSECONDARY INSTITUTION

2216 NATURAL SCIENCE TEACHERS,NOT ELSEWHERE CLASSIFIED

2232 HEALTH SPECIALTIES TEACHERS, NOT ELSEWHERE CLASSIFIED

2233 BUSINESS, COMMERCE AND MARKETING TEACHERS

2249 TEACHERS; POSTSECONDARY, NOT ELSEWHERE CLASSIFIED

2300 TEACHERS; EXCEPT POSTSECONDARY INSTITUTION

2310 PREKINDERGARTEN AND KINDERGARTEN TEACHERS

2320 ELEMENTARY SCHOOL TEACHERS

2330 SECONDARY SCHOOL TEACHERS

2350 TEACHERS; SPECIAL EDUCATION

2360 INSTRUCTIONAL COORDINATORS

2390 ADULT EDUCATION AND OTHER TEACHERS, NOT ELSEWHERE CLASSIFIED

2400 VOCATIONAL AND EDUCATIONAL COUNSELORS

2510 LIBRARIANS

2520 ARCHIVISTS AND CURATORS

2610 PHYSICIANS

2620 DENTISTS

2700 VETERINARIANS

2810 OPTOMETRISTS

2830 PODIATRISTS

2890 HEALTH DIAGNOSING AND TREATING PRACTITIONERS, NOT ELSEWHERE

2900 REGISTERED NURSES

3010 PHARMACISTS

3020 DIETITIANS

3031 RESPIRATORY THERAPISTS

3032 OCCUPATIONAL THERAPISTS

3033 PHYSICAL THERAPISTS

3034 SPEECH PATHOLOGISTS AND AUDIOLOGISTS

3039 THERAPISTS, NOT ELSEWHERE CLASSIFIED

3040 PHYSICIAN'S ASSISTANTS

3210 AUTHORS

3220 DESIGNERS

3230 MUSICIANS AND COMPOSERS

3240 ACTORS AND DIRECTORS

3250 PAINTERS, SCULPTORS, CRAFT-ARTISTS AND ARTIST-PRINTMAKERS

3260 PHOTOGRAPHERS

3270 DANCERS

3280 PERFORMERS, NOT ELSEWHERE CLASSIFIED

3290 WRITERS, ARTISTS, AND RELATED WORKERS; NOT ELSEWHERE CLASSIFIED

3312 EDITORS

3313 REPORTERS

3320 PUBLIC RELATIONS SPECIALISTS AND PUBLICITY WRITERS

3330 RADIO, TELEVISION AND OTHER ANNOUNCERS

3400 ATHLETES AND RELATED WORKERS

3620 CLINICAL LABORATORY TECHNOLOGISTS AND TECHNICIANS

3630 DENTAL HYGIENISTS

3640 HEALTH RECORD TECHNOLOGISTS AND TECHNICIANS

3650 RADIOLOGIC TECHNOLOGISTS AND TECHNCIANS

3660 LICENSED PRACTICAL NURSES

3690 HEALTH TECHNOLOGISTS AND TECHNICIANS, NOT ELSEWHERE CLASSIFIED

3710 ENGINEERING TECHNOLOGISTS AND TECHNICIANS

3711 ELECTRICAL AND ELECTRONIC ENGINEERING TECHNOLOGISTS

3712 INDUSTRIAL ENGINEERING TECHNOLOGISTS AND TECHNICIAN

3713 MECHANICAL ENGINEERING TECHNOLOGISTS AND TECHNICIAN

3719 ENGINEERING TECHNOLOGISTS AND TECHNICIANS, NEC

3720 DRAFTING OCCUPATIONS

3733 SURVEYING TECHNICIANS

3734 CARTOGRAPHIC TECHNICIANS

3739 SURVEYING AND MAPPING TECHNICIANS, NOT ELSEWHERE CLASSIFIED

3820 BIOLOGICAL TECHNOLOGISTS AND TECHNICIANS, EXCEPT HEALTH

3831 CHEMICAL TECHNOLOGISTS AND TECHNICIANS

3832 NUCLEAR TECHNOLOGISTS AND TECHNICIANS

3833 PETROLEUM TECHNOLOGISTS AND TECHNICIANS

3840 MATHEMATICAL TECHNICIANS

3890 SCIENCE TECHNOLOGISTS AND TECHNICIANS, NOT ELSEWHERE CLASSIFIED

3920 AIR TRAFFIC CONTROLLERS

3930 RADIO AND RELATED OPERATORS

3960 LEGAL TECHNICIANS

3971 PROGRAMERS, BUSINESS

3972 PROGRAMERS, SCIENTIFIC

3974 PROGRAMERS, NUMERICAL, TOOL AND PROCESS CONTROL

3980 TECHNICAL WRITERS

3990 TECHNICIANS, NOT ELSEWHERE CLASSIFIED

4010 SUPERVISORS; SALES OCCUPATIONS, INSURANCE, REAL ESTATE, AND BUSINESS SERVICES

4020 SUPERVISORS; SALES OCCUPATIONS, COMMODITIES EXCEPT RETAIL

4030 SUPERVISORS; SALES OCCUPATIONS, RETAIL

4100 INSURANCE, SECURITIES, REAL ESTATE AND BUSINESS SERVICE SALES

4122 INSURANCE SALES OCCUPATIONS

4123 REAL ESTATE SALES OCCUPATIONS

4124 SECURITIES AND FINANCIAL SERVICES SALES OCCUPATIONS

4152 BUSINESS SERVICE, EXCEPT ADVERTISING, SALES OCCUPATIONS

4153 ADVERTISING AND RELATED SALES OCCUPATIONS

4210 SALES ENGINEERS

4232 TECHNICAL SALES WORKERS, AIRCRAFT

4233 TECHNICAL SALES WORKERS, AGRICULTURAL EQUIPMENT AND SUPPLIES

4234 TECHNICAL SALES WORKERS, ELECTRONIC EQUIPMENT

4235 TECHNICAL SALES WORKERS, INDUSTRIAL MACHINERY, EQUIPMENT AND SUPPLIES

4236 TECHNICAL SALES WORKERS, MEDICAL AND DENTAL EQUIPMENT AND SUPPLIES

4237 TECHNICAL SALES WORKERS; CHEMICALS AND CHEMICAL PRODUCTS

4239 TECHNICAL SALES WORKERS, NOT ELSEWHERE CLASSIFIED

4242 SALES REPRESENTATIVES, COMMERCIAL AND INDUSTRIAL EQUIPMENT AND SUPPLIES

4243 SALES REPRESENTATIVES, GARMENTS AND RELATED TEXTILE PRODUCTS

4244 SALES REPRESENTATIVES, MOTOR VEHICLES AND SUPPLIES

4245 SALES REPRESENTATIVES; PULP, PAPER, AND PAPER PRODUCTS

4246 SALES REPRESENTATIVES; FARM PRODUCTS AND LIVESTOCK

4249 SALES REPRESENTATIVES; NOT ELSEWHERE CLASSIFIED

4342 SALESPERSONS; MOTOR VEHICLES, MOBILE HOMES, AND SUPPLIES

4343 SALESPERSONS; MUSICAL INSTRUMENTS AND SUPPLIES

4344 SALESPERSONS; BOATS AND MARINE EQUIPMENT AND SUPPLIES

4345 SALESPERSONS; SPORTING GOODS

4346 SALESPERSONS; GARMENTS AND TEXTILE PRODUCTS

4347 SALESPERSONS; BOOKS, STAMPS, COINS, AND STATIONERY

4348 SALESPERSONS; FURNITURE AND HOME FURNISHINGS

4351 SALESPERSONS, SHOES

4352 SALESPERSONS; RADIO, TELEVISION, HIGH FIDELITY, AND HOUSEHOLD APPLIANCES

4353 SALESPERSONS; HARDWARE

4354 SALESPERSONS; COSMETICS, TOILETRIES, AND ALLIED PRODUCTS

4356 SALESPERSONS; JEWELRY AND RELATED PRODUCTS

4359 SALESPERSONS; NOT ELSEWHERE CLASSIFIED

4362 SALES CLERKS

4363 COUNTER CLERKS

4364 CASHIERS

4365 NEWS VENDORS

4366 STREET VENDORS, DOOR-TO-DOOR SALES WORKERS, AND RELATED OCCUPATIONS

4367 SALESPERSONS; PARTS

4369 SALES OCCUPATIONS; SERVICES, NOT ELSEWHERE CLASSIFIED

4440 APPRAISERS AND RELATED OCCUPATIONS

4450 DEMONSTRATORS, PROMOTERS, AND MODELS

4460 SHOPPERS

4470 AUCTIONEERS

4490 SALES OCCUPATIONS; OTHER, NOT ELSEWHERE CLASSIFIED

4511 SUPERVISORS; GENERAL OFFICE OCCUPATIONS

4512 SUPERVISORS; COMPUTER AND PERIPHERAL EQUIPMENT OPERATORS

4513 SUPERVISORS; SECRETARIES, STENOGRAPHERS AND TYPISTS

4514 SUPERVISORS; INFORMATION CLERKS

4516 SUPERVISORS; CORRESPONDENCE CLERKS AND ORDER CLERKS

4519 SUPERVISORS; RECORD CLERKS

4521 SUPERVISORS; FINANCIAL RECORD PROCESSING OCCUPATIONS

4522 SUPERVISORS; DUPLICATING, MAIL AND OTHER OFFICE MACHINE OPERATORS

4523 CHIEF COMMUNICATIONS OPERATORS

4524 SUPERVISORS; MAIL AND MESSAGE DISTRIBUTION CLERKS

4525 SUPERVISORS; MATERIAL RECORDING, SCHEDULING, AND DISTRIBUTING CLERKS

4528 SUPERVISORS; ADJUSTERS, INVESTIGATORS, AND COLLECTORS

4529 SUPERVISORS; MISCELLANEOUS ADMINISTRATIVE SUPPORT OCCUPATIONS

4612 COMPUTER OPERATORS

4613 PERIPHERAL EQUIPMENT OPERATORS

4622 SECRETARIES

4623 STENOGRAPHERS

4624 TYPISTS

4630 GENERAL OFFICE OCCUPATIONS

4642 INTERVIEWING CLERKS

4643 HOTEL CLERKS

4644 RESERVATION AGENTS AND TRANSPORTATION TICKET CLERKS

4645 RECEPTIONISTS

4649 INFORMATION CLERKS, NOT ELSEWHERE CLASSIFIED

4662 CLASSIFIED-AD CLERKS

4663 CORRESPONDENCE CLERKS

4664 ORDER CLERKS

4692 PERSONNEL CLERKS, EXCEPT PAYROLL AND TIMEKEEPING

4694 LIBRARY CLERKS

4696 FILE CLERKS

4699 RECORD CLERKS, NEC

4712 BOOKKEEPING AND ACCOUNTING AND AUDITING CLERKS

4713 PAYROLL AND TIMEKEEPING CLERKS

4715 BILLING CLERKS

4716 COST AND RATE CLERKS

4718 BILLING, POSTING, AND CALCULATING MACHINE OPERATORS

4722 DUPLICATING MACHINE OPERATORS

4723 MAIL PREPARING AND HANDLING MACHINE OPERATORS

4729 OFFICE MACHINE OPERATORS, NOT ELSEWHERE CLASSIFIED

4732 TELEPHONE OPERATORS

4733 TELEGRAPHERS

4739 COMMUNICATIONS EQUIPMENT OPERATORS, NOT ELSEWHERE CLASSIFIED

4742 POSTAL CLERKS, EXCEPT MAIL CARRIERS

4743 MAIL CARRIERS, POST OFFICE

4744 MAIL CLERKS, EXCEPT POST OFFICE

4745 MESSENGERS

4751 DISPATCHERS

4752 PRODUCTION AND PLANNING CLERKS

4753 TRAFFIC, SHIPPING, AND RECEIVING CLERKS

4754 STOCK AND INVENTORY CLERKS

4755 METER READERS

4756 WEIGHERS, MEASURERS, AND CHECKERS

4757 SAMPLERS

4758 EXPEDITERS

4759 MATERIAL RECORDING, SCHEDULING, AND DISTRIBUTING CLERKS NOT ELSEWHERE CLASSIFIED

4782 INSURANCE ADJUSTERS, EXAMINERS, AND INVESTIGATORS

4783 INVESTIGATORS AND ADJUSTERS, EXCEPT INSURANCE

4784 CLERKS, SOCIAL WELFARE

4786 BILL AND ACCOUNT COLLECTORS

4787 LICENSE CLERKS

4791 BANK TELLERS

4792 PROOF READERS

4793 DATA ENTRY KEYERS

4794 STATISTICAL CLERKS

4795 TEACHER AIDES

4799 ADMINISTRATIVE SUPPORT OCCUPATIONS, INCLUDING CLERICAL NOT ELSEWHERE CLASSIFIED

5020 DAY WORKERS

5030 LAUNDERERS AND IRONERS

5040 COOKS, PRIVATE HOUSEHOLD

5050 HOUSEKEEPERS AND BUTLERS

5060 CHILD CARE WORKERS, PRIVATE HOUSEHOLD

5070 PRIVATE HOUSEHOLD CLEANERS AND SERVANTS

5090 PRIVATE HOUSEHOLD OCCUPATIONS, NOT ELSEWHERE CLASSIFIED

5111 SUPERVISORS; FIREFIGHTING AND FIRE PREVENTION OCCUPATIONS

5112 SUPERVISORS; POLICE AND DETECTIVES

5113 SUPERVISORS; GUARDS

5122 FIRE INSPECTION AND FIRE PREVENTION OCCUPATIONS

5123 FIREFIGHTING OCCUPATIONS

5132 POLICE AND DETECTIVES, PUBLIC SERVICE

5133 CORRECTIONAL INSTITUTION OFFICERS

5134 SHERIFFS, BAILIFFS AND OTHER LAW ENFORCEMENT OFFICERS

5142 CROSSING GUARDS

5144 GUARDS AND POLICE, EXCEPT PUBLIC SERVICE

5149 PROTECTIVE SERVICE OCCUPATIONS, NEC

5211 SUPERVISORS; FOOD AND BEVERAGE PREPARATION AND SERVICE OCCUPATIONS

5212 BARTENDERS

5213 WAITERS AND WAITRESSES

5214 COOKS, EXCEPT SHORT ORDER

5215 SHORT-ORDER COOKS

5216 FOOD COUNTER, FOUNTAIN AND RELATED OCCUPATIONS

5217 KITCHEN WORKERS, FOOD PREPARATION

5218 WAITERS'/WAITRESSES' ASSISTANTS

5219 MISCELLANEOUS FOOD AND BEVERAGE PREPARATION OCCUPATIONS

5232 DENTAL ASSISTANTS

5233 HEALTH AIDES, EXCEPT NURSING

5236 NURSING AIDES, ORDERLIES, AND ATTENDANTS

5241 SUPERVISORS; CLEANING AND BUILDING SERVICE WORKERS

5242 MAIDS AND HOUSEMEN

5244 JANITORS AND CLEANERS

5245 ELEVATOR OPERATORS

5246 PEST CONTROL OCCUPATIONS

5249 CLEANING AND BUILDING SERVICE OCCUPATIONS, NOT ELSEWHERE CLASSIFIED

5250 PERSONAL SERVICE OCCUPATIONS

5251 SUPERVISORS; PERSONAL SERVICE OCCUPATIONS

5252 BARBERS

5253 HAIRDRESSERS AND COSMETOLOGISTS

5254 ATTENDANTS, AMUSEMENT AND RECREATION FACILITIES

5255 GUIDES

5256 USHERS

5257 PUBLIC TRANSPORTATION ATTENDANTS

5258 WARDROBE AND DRESSING ROOM ATTENDANTS

5262 BAGGAGE PORTERS AND BELLHOPS

5263 WELFARE SERVICE AIDES

5264 CHILD CARE WORKERS, EXCEPT PRIVATE HOUSEHOLD

5269 PERSONAL SERVICE OCCUPATIONS, NOT ELSEWHERE CLASSIFIED

5512 GENERAL FARMERS

5513 CROP, VEGETABLE, FRUIT AND TREE NUT FARMERS

5514 LIVESTOCK, DAIRY, POULTRY AND FISH FARMERS

5515 HORTICULTURAL SPECIALTY FARMERS

5522 MANAGERS; GENERAL FARM

5523 MANAGERS; CROP, VEGETABLE, FRUIT AND TREE NUT FARM

5524 MANAGERS; LIVESTOCK, DAIRY, POULTRY AND FISH FARM

5525 MANAGERS; HORTICULTURAL SPECIALTY FARM

5611 SUPERVISORS; FARM WORKERS

5612 GENERAL FARM WORKERS

5613 FIELD CROP AND VEGETABLE FARM WORKERS (HAND)

5614 ORCHARD AND VINEYARD AND RELATED WORKERS (HAND)

5615 IRRIGATION WORKERS

5616 FARM MACHINERY OPERATORS

5617 LIVESTOCK WORKERS

5618 MARINE LIFE CULTIVATION WORKERS

5619 NURSERY WORKERS

5621 SUPERVISORS; RELATED AGRICULTURAL WORKERS

5622 GROUNDSKEEPERS AND GARDENERS, EXCEPT FARM

5624 ANIMAL CARETAKERS, EXCEPT FARM

5625 GRADERS AND SORTERS; AGRICULTURAL PRODUCTS

5627 INSPECTORS; AGRICULTURAL PRODUCTS

5710 SUPERVISORS; FORESTRY AND LOGGING WORKERS

5720 FORESTRY WORKERS, EXCEPT LOGGING

5730 TIMBER CUTTING AND RELATED OCCUPATIONS

5790 LOGGING OCCUPATIONS, NOT ELSEWHERE CLASSIFIED

5830 FISHERS

5840 HUNTERS AND TRAPPERS

6000 SUPERVISORS; MECHANICS AND REPAIRERS

6100 MECHANICS AND REPAIRERS

6111 AUTOMOBILE MECHANICS

6112 BUS AND TRUCK ENGINE, AND DIESEL ENGINE MECHANICS

6113 AIRCRAFT ENGINE MECHANICS

6114 SMALL ENGINE REPAIRERS

6115 AUTOMOTIVE BODY AND RELATED REPAIRERS

6116 AIRCRAFT MECHANICS (EXCEPT ENGINE SPECIALISTS)

6117 HEAVY EQUIPMENT MECHANICS

6118 FARM EQUIPMENT MECHANICS

6130 INDUSTRIAL MACHINERY REPAIRERS *

6140 MACHINERY MAINTENANCE OCCUPATIONS

6151 COMMUNICATIONS EQUIPMENT REPAIRERS

6152 ELECTRIC MOTOR, TRANSFORMER, AND RELATED REPAIRERS

6153 ELECTRICAL AND ELECTRONIC REPAIRERS, COMMERCIAL AND INDUSTRIAL EQUIPMENT

6154 DATA PROCESSING EQUIPMENT REPAIRERS

6155 ELECTRONIC REPAIRERS, HOME-ENTERTAINMENT EQUIPMENT

6156 HOUSEHOLD APPLIANCE AND POWER TOOL REPAIRERS

6157 TELEPHONE LINE INSTALLERS AND REPAIRERS

6158 TELEPHONE INSTALLERS AND REPAIRERS

6159 MISC ELECRICAL AND ELECTRONIC EQUIPMENT REPAIRERS

6160 HEATING, AIR-CONDITIONING, AND REFRIGERATION MECHANICS

6171 CAMERA, WATCH, AND OTHER PRECISION INSTRUMENT REPAIRERS

6172 MUSICAL INSTRUMENT REPAIRERS AND TUNERS

6173 LOCKSMITHS AND SAFE REPAIRERS

6174 OFFICE MACHINE REPAIRERS

6175 MECHANICAL CONTROLS AND VALVE REPAIRERS

6176 ELEVATOR INSTALLERS AND REPAIRERS

6177 RIGGERS

6178 MILLWRIGHTS

6179 MECHANICS AND REPAIRERS, NOT ELSEWHERE CLASSIFIED

6311 SUPERVISORS; OVERALL CONSTRUCTION

6312 SUPERVISORS; BRICKMASONS, STONEMASONS, AND HARD TILE SETTERS

6313 SUPERVISORS; CARPENTERS AND RELATED WORKERS

6314 SUPERVISORS; ELECTRICIANS AND POWER TRANSMISSION INSTALLERS

6315 SUPERVISORS; PAINTERS, PAPERHANGERS, AND PLASTERERS

6316 SUPERVISORS; PLUMBERS AND PIPEFITTERS AND STEAMFITTERS

6318 SUPERVISORS; OTHER CONSTRUCTION TRADES

6320 SUPERVISORS; EXTRACTIVE OCCUPATIONS

6412 BRICKMASONS

6413 STONEMASONS

6414 TILE SETTERS, HARD

6422 CARPENTERS

6424 DRYWALL INSTALLERS

6432 ELECTRICIANS

6433 ELECTRICAL POWER INSTALLERS AND REPAIRERS

6442 PAINTERS (CONSTRUCTION AND MAINTENANCE)

6443 PAPERHANGERS

6444 PLASTERERS

6450 PLUMBERS, PIPEFITTERS AND STEAMFITTERS

6462 CARPET AND SOFT TILE INSTALLERS

6463 CONCRETE AND TERRAZZO FINISHERS

6464 GLAZIERS

6465 INSULATION WORKERS

6466 PAVING, SURFACING, AND TAMPING EQUIPMENT OPERATORS

6467 RAIL AND TRACK LAYING EQUIPMENT OPERATORS

6468 ROOFERS

6473 STRUCTURAL METAL WORKERS

6474 DRILLERS, EARTH

6475 AIR HAMMER OPERATORS

6476 PILE DRIVING OPERATORS

6479 CONSTRUCTION TRADES, NOT ELSEWHERE CLASSIFIED

6520 DRILLERS, OIL WELL

6530 EXPLOSIVE WORKERS

6540 MINING MACHINE OPERATORS

6560 EXTRACTIVE OCCUPATIONS, NEC

6700 SUPERVISORS; PRECISION PRODUCTION OCCUPATIONS

6811 TOOL AND DIE MAKERS

6812 PRECISION ASSEMBLERS (METAL)

6813 MACHINISTS

6814 BOILERMAKERS

6816 PRECISION GRINDERS, FILERS, AND TOOL SHARPENERS

6817 PATTERNMAKERS AND MODEL MAKERS (METAL)

6821 LAY-OUT WORKERS

6822 PRECISION HAND MOLDERS AND SHAPERS (JEWELERS)

6823 ENGRAVERS

6824 SHEET METAL WORKERS

6829 MISCELLANEOUS PRECISION METAL WORKERS

6830 PRECISION WOODWORKERS

6831 PATTERNMAKERS AND MODEL MAKERS, WOOD

6832 CABINET MAKERS AND BENCH CARPENTERS

6835 FURNITURE FINISHERS

6839 MISCELLANEOUS PRECISION WOODWORKERS

6841 PRECISION TYPESETTERS

6842 PRECISION LITHOGRAPHERS AND PHOTOENGRAVERS

6844 BOOKBINDERS

6849 MISC PRECISION PRINTING OCCUPATIONS

6852 TAILORS AND DRESSMAKERS, HAND

6853 UPHOLSTERERS

6854 SHOEMAKERS AND LEATHER WORKERS AND REPAIRERS

6855 PRECISION LAUNDERING, CLEANING, AND DYEING OCCUPATIONS

6856 APPAREL AND FABRIC PATTERNMAKERS

6859 MISCELLANEOUS PRECISION APPAREL AND FABRIC WORKERS

6861 PRECISION HAND MOLDERS AND SHAPERS (EXCEPT JEWELERS)

6862 PRECISION PATTERNMAKERS, LAY-OUT WORKERS AND CUTTERS

6863 DETAIL DESIGN PAINTERS AND DECORATORS

6864 OPTICAL GOODS WORKERS

6865 DENTAL LABORATORY TECHNICIANS

6866 GEM AND DIAMOND WORKING OCCUPATIONS

6867 PRECISION ELECTRICAL AND ELECTRONIC EQUIPMENT ASSEMBLERS

6868 PHOTOGRAPHIC PROCESS WORKERS

6869 MISCELLANEOUS PRECISION WORKERS, NOT ELSEWHERE CLASSIFIED

6871 BUTCHERS AND MEAT CUTTERS

6872 BAKERS

6873 BATCHMAKERS (CANDYMAKERS, CHEESEMAKERS, ETC.)

6879 MISCELLANEOUS PRECISION FOOD WORKERS

6881 PRECISION INSPECTORS, TESTERS, AND GRADERS

6882 PRECISION ADJUSTERS AND CALIBRATORS

6910 WATER AND SEWAGE TREATMENT PLANT OPERATORS

6920 GAS PLANT OPERATORS

6931 STATIONARY ENGINEERS

6932 POWER PLANT AND SYSTEMS OPERATORS, EXC. STATIONARY ENGINEERS

6940 CHEMICAL PLANT OPERATORS

6950 PETROLEUM PLANT OPERATORS

6960 MISC PLANT OR SYSTEM OPERATORS

7100 SUPERVISORS; PRODUCTION OCCUPATIONS

7312 LATHE AND TURNING MACHINE SETUP OPERATORS

7313 MILLING AND PLANING MACHINE SETUP OPERATORS

7314 PUNCHING AND SHEARING MACHINE SETUP OPERATORS

7315 EXTRUDING AND DRAWING MACHINE SETUP OPERATORS

7316 ROLLING MACHINE SETUP OPERATORS

7317 PRESS AND BRAKE MACHINE SETUP OPERATORS

7318 DRILLING AND BORING MACHINE SETUP OPERATORS

7319 FORGING MACHINE SETUP OPERATORS

7322 GRINDING, ABRADING, BUFFING, AND POLISHING MACHINE SETUP OPERATORS

7324 LAPPING AND HONING MACHINE SETUP OPERATORS

7326 NUMERICAL CONTROL MACHINE SETUP OPERATORS

7329 MISCELLANEOUS METALWORKING AND PLASTIC WORKING MACHINE SETUP OPERATORS

7332 WELDING MACHINE SETUP OPERATORS

7333 SOLDERING AND BRAZING MACHINE SETUP OPERATORS

7339 MISCELLANEOUS FABRICATING MACHINE SETUP OPERATORS

7342 MOLDING AND CASTING MACHINE SETUP OPERATORS

7343 PLATING AND COATING MACHINE SETUP OPERATORS

7344 HEATING EQUIPMENT SETUP OPERATORS

7349 MISCELLANEOUS METAL AND PLASTIC PROCESSING MACHINE

7431 LATHE AND TURNING MACHINE SETUP OPERATORS

7432 ROUTER AND PLANER MACHINE SETUP OPERATORS

7433 SAWING MACHINE SETUP OPERATORS

7434 SANDING MACHINE SETUP OPERATORS

7435 SHAPING AND JOINING MACHINE SETUP OPERATORS

7439 MISCELLANEOUS WOODWORKING MACHINE SETUP OPERATORS

7443 PRINTING PRESS SETUP OPERATORS

7444 PHOTOENGRAVING AND LITHOGRAPHING MACHINE SETUP OPERATORS

7449 MISCELLANEOUS PRINTING MACHINE SETUP OPERATORS

7451 WINDING AND TWISTING MACHINE SETUP OPERATORS

7452 KNITTING AND WEAVING MACHINE SETUP OPERATORS

7459 TEXTILE MACHINE SETUP OPERATORS, NOT ELSEWHERE CLASSIFIED

7462 PACKAGING AND FILLING MACHINE SETUP OPERATORS

7463 EXTRUDING AND FORMING MACHINE SETUP OPERATORS

7467 COMPRESSING AND COMPACTING MACHINE SETUP OPERATORS

7472 ROASTING AND BAKING MACHINE SETUP OPERATORS

7474 FOLDING MACHINE SETUP OPERATORS

7476 STILL, CLARIFYING, AND PRECIPITATING MACHINE SETUP OPERATORS

7477 CRUSHING, GRINDING AND POLISHING MACHINE SETUP OPERATORS

7478 SLICING AND CUTTING MACHINE SETUP OPERATORS

7479 MISCELLANEOUS MACHINE SETUP OPERATORS

7500 MACHINE OPERATORS AND TENDERS

7512 LATHE AND TURNING MACHINE OPERATORS AND TENDERS

7513 MILLING AND PLANING MACHINE OPERATORS AND TENDERS

7514 PUNCHING AND SHEARING MACHINE OPERATORS AND TENDERS

7515 EXTRUDING AND DRAWING MACHINE OPERATORS AND TENDERS

7516 ROLLING MACHINE OPERATORS AND TENDERS

7517 PRESS AND BRAKE MACHINE OPERATORS AND TENDERS

7518 DRILLING AND BORING MACHINE OPERATORS AND TENDERS

7519 FORGING MACHINE OPERATORS AND TENDERS

7522 GRINDING, ABRADING, BUFFING AND POLISHING MACHINE OPERATORS AND TENDERS

7529 MISCELLANEOUS METALWORKING AND PLASTIC WORKING MACHINE OPERATORS AND TENDERS

7532 WELDING MACHINE OPERATORS AND TENDERS

7533 SOLDERING AND BRAZING MACHINE OPERATORS AND TENDERS

7539 MISCELLANEOUS FABRICATING MACHINE OPERATORS AND TENDERS

7542 MOLDING AND CASTING MACHINE OPERATORS AND TENDERS

7543 PLATING AND COATING MACHINE OPERATORS AND TENDERS

7544 HEATING EQUIPMENT OPERATORS AND TENDERS

7549 MISCELLANEOUS METAL AND PLASTIC PROCESSING MACHINE OPERATORS AND TENDERS

7631 LATHE AND TURNING MACHINE OPERATORS AND TENDERS

7632 ROUTER AND PLANER MACHINE OPERATORS AND TENDERS

7633 SAWING MACHINE OPERATORS AND TENDERS

7634 SANDING MACHINE OPERATORS AND TENDERS

7635 SHAPING AND JOINING MACHINE OPERATORS AND TENDERS

7636 NAILING AND TACKING MACHINE OPERATORS AND TENDERS

7639 MISCELLANEOUS WOODWORKING MACHINE OPERATORS AND TENDERS

7642 TYPESETTING AND COMPOSING MACHINE OPERATORS AND TENDERS

7643 PRINTING MACHINE OPERATORS AND TENDERS

7644 PHOTOENGRAVING AND LITHOGRAPHING MACHINE OPERATORS AND TENDERS

7649 PRINTING MACHINE OPERATORS AND TENDERS, NOT ELSEWHERE CLASSIFIED

7651 WINDING AND TWISTING MACHINE OPERATORS AND TENDERS

7652 KNITTING AND WEAVING MACHINE OPERATORS AND TENDERS

7654 TEXTILE CUTTING MACHINE OPERATORS AND TENDERS

7655 TEXTILE SEWING MACHINE OPERATORS AND TENDERS

7656 SHOE MACHINE OPERATORS AND TENDERS

7657 PRESSING MACHINE OPERATORS

7658 LAUNDERING AND DRY CLEANING MACHINE OPERATORS AND TENDERS

7659 MISCELLANEOUS TEXTILE MACHINE OPERATORS AND TENDERS

7661 CEMENTING AND GLUING MACHINE OPERATORS AND TENDERS

7662 PACKAGING AND FILLING MACHINE OPERATORS AND TENDERS

7663 EXTRUDING AND FORMING MACHINE OPERATORS AND TENDERS

7664 MIXING AND BLENDING MACHINE OPERATORS AND TENDERS

7665 COOLING AND FREEZING EQUIPMENT OPERATORS AND TENDER

7666 SEPARATING AND FILTERING MACHINE OPERATORS AND TENDERS

7667 COMPRESSING AND COMPACTING MACHINE OPERATORS AND TENDERS

7668 BOILER OPERATORS AND TENDERS (LOW PRESSURE)

7669 COATING, PAINTING, AND SPRAYING MACHINE OPERATORS AND TENDERS

7671 PHOTOGRAPHIC PROCESSING MACHINE OPERATORS

7672 ROASTING AND BAKING MACHINE OPERATORS AND TENDERS

7673 WASHING, CLEANING AND PICKLING EQUIPMENT OPERATORS AND TENDERS

7674 FOLDING MACHINE OPERATORS AND TENDERS

7675 FURNACE, KILN, AND OVEN OPERATORS AND TENDERS

7676 STILL, CLARIFIER AND PRECIPITATOR OPERATORS AND TENDERS

7677 CRUSHING, GRINDING AND POLISHING MACHINE OPERATORS AND TENDERS

7678 SLICING AND CUTTING MACHINE OPERATORS AND TENDERS

7679 MISC MACHINE OPERATORS AND TENDERS, NEC

7700 FABRICATORS, ASSEMBLERS AND HAND WORKING OCCUPATIONS

7714 WELDERS AND CUTTERS

7717 SOLDERERS AND BRAZERS

7720 ASSEMBLERS

7740 FABRICATORS, NOT ELSEWHERE CLASSIFIED

7752 HAND SEWING OCCUPATIONS

7753 HAND CUTTING AND TRIMMING OCCUPATIONS

7754 HAND MOLDING AND CASTING OCCUPATIONS

7755 HAND FORMING AND SHAPING OCCUPATIONS

7756 HAND PAINTING, COATING AND DECORATING OCCUPATIONS

7757 HAND ENGRAVING AND PRINTING OCCUPATIONS

7758 HAND GRINDING AND POLISHING OCCUPATIONS

7759 MISCELLANEOUS HAND WORKING OCCUPATIONS

7820 PRODUCTION INSPECTORS, CHECKERS AND EXAMINERS

7830 PRODUCTION TESTERS

7840 PRODUCTION SAMPLERS AND WEIGHERS

7850 GRADERS AND SORTERS, EXCEPT AGRICULTURAL

7870 PRODUCTION EXPEDITERS

8111 SUPERVISORS; MOTOR VEHICLE OPERATORS

8113 RAILROAD CONDUCTORS AND YARDMASTERS

8120 SUPERVISORS; MATERIAL MOVING EQUIPMENT OPERATORS

8212 TRUCK DRIVERS, TRACTOR-TRAILER

8213 TRUCK DRIVERS, HEAVY

8214 TRUCK DRIVERS, LIGHT (INCLUDING DELIVERY AND ROUTE DRIVERS)

8215 BUS DRIVERS

8216 TAXICAB DRIVERS AND CHAUFFEURS

8218 DRIVER-SALES WORKERS

8219 OTHER MOTOR TRANSPORTATION OCCUPATIONS, NOT ELSEWHERE CLASSIFIED

8232 LOCOMOTIVE OPERATING OCCUPATIONS

8233 RAILROAD BRAKE, SIGNAL, AND SWITCH OPERATORS

8239 RAIL VEHICLE OPERATORS, NOT ELSEWHERE CLASSIFIED

8241 SHIP CAPTAINS AND MATES

8242 BOAT AND BARGE OPERATORS

8243 SAILORS AND DECKHANDS

8244 MARINE ENGINEERS

8245 BRIDGE, LOCK, AND LIGHTHOUSE TENDERS

8250 AIRPLANE PILOTS AND NAVIGATORS

8280 TRANSPORTATION INSPECTORS

8312 OPERATING ENGINEERS

8313 LONGSHORE EQUIPMENT OPERATORS

8314 HOIST AND WINCH OPERATORS

8315 CRANE AND TOWER OPERATORS

8316 EXCAVATING AND LOADING MACHINE OPERATORS

8317 GRADER, DOZER, AND SCRAPER OPERATORS

8318 INDUSTRIAL TRUCK AND TRACTOR EQUIPMENT OPERATORS

8319 MISC MATERIAL MOVING EQUIPMENT OPERATORS

8500 SUPERVISORS; HANDLERS, EQUIPMENT CLEANERS, HELPERS,

8611 HELPERS; METALWORKING AND PLASTIC WORKING MACHINE OPERATORS AND TENDERS

8614 HELPERS; METAL AND PLASTIC PROCESSING MACHINE OPERATORS AND TENDERS

8615 HELPERS; WOODWORKING MACHINE OPERATORS AND TENDERS

8616 HELPERS; PRINTING MACHINE OPERATORS AND TENDERS

8617 HELPERS; TEXTILE, APPAREL AND FURNISHINGS MACHINE OPERATORS AND TENDERS

8618 HELPERS; MACHINE OPERATORS AND TENDERS, ASSORTED MATERIALS

8619 HELPERS; PRECISION PRODUCTION OCCUPATIONS AND SETUP OPERATORS

8620 HELPERS; FABRICATORS AND INSPECTORS

8632 HELPERS; VEHICLE AND MOBILE EQUIPMENT MECHANICS AND REPAIRERS

8633 HELPERS; INDUSTRIAL MACHINERY REPAIRERS

8635 HELPERS; ELECTRICAL AND ELECTRONIC EQUIPMENT REPAIRERS

8637 HELPERS; MISCELLANEOUS MECHANICS AND REPAIRERS

8641 HELPERS; BRICKMASONS, STONEMASONS, AND HARD TILE SETTERS

8642 HELPERS; CARPENTERS AND RELATED WORKERS

8643 HELPERS; ELECTRICIANS AND POWER TRANSMISSION INSTALLERS

8644 HELPERS; PAINTERS, PAPERHANGERS AND PLASTERERS

8645 HELPERS; PLUMBERS, PIPEFITTERS AND STEAMFITTERS

8646 HELPERS; SURVEYOR'S

8648 HELPERS, OTHER CONSTRUCTION TRADES

8650 HELPERS; EXTRACTIVE OCCUPATIONS

8700 HANDLERS, EQUIPMENT CLEANERS AND LABORERS

8710 CONSTRUCTION LABORERS

8722 GARBAGE COLLECTORS

8723 STEVEDORES

8724 STOCK HANDLERS AND BAGGERS

8725 MACHINE FEEDERS AND OFFBEARERS

8726 FREIGHT, STOCK, AND MATERIAL MOVERS, NOT ELSEWHERE CLASSIFIED

8730 GARAGE AND SERVICE STATION RELATED OCCUPATIONS

8740 PARKING LOT ATTENDANTS

8750 VEHICLE WASHERS AND EQUIPMENT CLEANERS

8761 HAND PACKERS AND PACKAGERS

8769 MANUAL OCCUPATIONS, NEC

9100 MILITARY OCCUPATIONS

9900 MISCELLANEOUS OCCUPATIONS

APPENDIX G:
Classification of Instructional Programs (CIP) Codes and Titles

Provides a listing of CIP codes in numerical order along with the related meaning for each.

00.0000 NO CODE AVAILABLE

01.0101 AGRICULTURAL BUSINESS AND MANAGEMENT, GENERAL

01.0102 AGRICULTURAL BUSINESS/AGRIBUSINESS OPERATIONS

01.0103 AGRICULTURAL ECONOMICS

01.0104 FARM AND RANCH MANAGEMENT

01.0199 AGRICULTURAL BUSINESS AND MANAGEMENT, OTHER

01.0201 AGRICULTURAL MECHANIZATION, GENERAL

01.0204 AGRICULTURAL POWER MACHINERY OPERATOR

01.0299 AGRICULTURAL MECHANIZATION, OTHER

01.0301 AGRICULTURAL PRODUCTION WORKERS AND MANAGERS, GENERAL

01.0302 AGRICULTURAL ANIMAL HUSBANDRY AND PRODUCTION MANAGEMENT

01.0303 AQUACULTURE OPERATIONS AND PRODUCTION MANAGEMENT

01.0304 CROP PRODUCTION OPERATIONS AND MANAGEMENT

01.0399 AGRICULTURAL PRODUCTION WORKERS AND MANAGERS, OTHER

01.0401 AGRICULTURAL AND FOOD PRODUCTS PROCESSING OPERATIONS AND MANAGEMENT

01.0501 AGRICULTURAL SUPPLIES RETAILING AND WHOLESALING

01.0505 ANIMAL TRAINER

01.0507 EQUESTRIAN/EQUINE STUDIES, HORSE MANAGEMENT AND TRAINING

01.0599 AGRICULTURAL SUPPLIES AND RELATED SERVICES, OTHER

01.0601 HORTICULTURE SERVICES OPERATIONS AND MANAGEMENT, GENERAL

01.0603 ORNAMENTAL HORTICULTURE OPERATIONS AND MANAGEMENT

01.0604 GREENHOUSE OPERATIONS AND MANAGEMENT

01.0605 LANDSCAPING OPERATIONS AND MANAGEMENT

01.0606 NURSERY OPERATIONS AND MANAGEMENT

01.0607 TURF MANAGEMENT

01.0699 HORTICULTURE SERVICES OPERATIONS AND MANAGEMENT, OTHER

01.0701 INTERNATIONAL AGRICULTURE

01.9999 AGRICULTURAL BUSINESS AND PRODUCTION, OTHER

02.0101 AGRICULTURE/AGRICULTURAL SCIENCES, GENERAL

02.0201 ANIMAL SCIENCES, GENERAL

02.0202 AGRICULTURAL ANIMAL BREEDING AND GENETICS

02.0203 AGRICULTURAL ANIMAL HEALTH

02.0204 AGRICULTURAL ANIMAL NUTRITION

02.0206 DAIRY SCIENCE

02.0209 POULTRY SCIENCE

02.0299 ANIMAL SCIENCES, OTHER

02.0301 FOOD SCIENCES AND TECHNOLOGY, GENERAL

02.0401 PLANT SCIENCES, GENERAL

02.0402 AGRONOMY AND CROP SCIENCE

02.0403 HORTICULTURE SCIENCE

02.0408 PLANT PROTECTION (PEST MANAGEMENT)

02.0409 RANGE SCIENCE AND MANAGEMENT

02.0499 PLANT SCIENCES, OTHER

02.0501 SOIL SCIENCES

02.9999 AGRICULTURE/AGRICULTURAL SCIENCES, OTHER

03.0101 NATURAL RESOURCES CONSERVATION, GENERAL

03.0201 NATURAL RESOURCES MANAGEMENT AND POLICY

03.0203 NATURAL RESOURCES LAW ENFORCEMENT AND PROTECTIVE SERVICES

03.0299 NATURAL RESOURCES MANAGEMENT AND PROTECTIVE SERVICES, OTHER

03.0301 FISHING AND FISHERIES SCIENCES AND MANAGEMENT

03.0401 FOREST HARVESTING AND PRODUCTION TECHNOLOGY/TECHNICIAN

03.0404 FOREST PRODUCTS TECHNOLOGY/TECHNICIAN

03.0405 LOGGING/TIMBER HARVESTING

03.0499 FOREST PRODUCTION AND PROCESSING, OTHER

03.0501 FORESTRY, GENERAL

03.0502 FORESTRY SCIENCES

03.0506 FOREST MANAGEMENT

03.0509 WOOD SCIENCE AND PULP/PAPER TECHNOLOGY

03.0599 FORESTRY AND RELATED SCIENCES, OTHER

03.0601 WILDLIFE AND WILDLANDS MANAGEMENT

03.9999 CONSERVATION AND RENEWABLE NATURAL RESOURCES, OTHER

04.0201 ARCHITECTURE

04.0301 CITY/URBAN, COMMUNITY AND REGIONAL PLANNING

04.0401 ARCHITECTURAL ENVIRONMENTAL DESIGN

04.0501 INTERIOR ARCHITECTURE

04.0601 LANDSCAPE ARCHITECTURE

04.0701 ARCHITECTURAL URBAN DESIGN AND PLANNING

04.9999 ARCHITECTURE AND RELATED PROGRAMS, OTHER

05.0101 AFRICAN STUDIES

05.0102 AMERICAN STUDIES/CIVILIZATION

05.0103 ASIAN STUDIES

2G   *The Worker Traits Data Book*

05.0104 EAST ASIAN STUDIES

05.0105 EASTERN EUROPEAN AREA STUDIES

05.0106 EUROPEAN STUDIES

05.0107 LATIN AMERICAN STUDIES

05.0108 MIDDLE EASTERN STUDIES

05.0109 PACIFIC AREA STUDIES

05.0110 RUSSIAN AND SLAVIC AREA STUDIES

05.0111 SCANDINAVIAN AREA STUDIES

05.0112 SOUTH ASIAN STUDIES

05.0113 SOUTHEAST ASIAN STUDIES

05.0114 WESTERN EUROPEAN STUDIES

05.0115 CANADIAN STUDIES

05.0199 AREA STUDIES, OTHER

05.0201 AFRO-AMERICAN (BLACK) STUDIES

05.0202 AMERICAN INDIAN/NATIVE AMERICAN STUDIES

05.0203 HISPANIC AMERICAN STUDIES

05.0204 ISLAMIC STUDIES

05.0205 JEWISH/JUDAIC STUDIES

05.0207 WOMEN'S STUDIES

05.0299 ETHNIC AND CULTURAL STUDIES, OTHER

05.9999 AREA, ETHNIC AND CULTURAL STUDIES, OTHER

08.0101 APPAREL AND ACCESSORIES MARKETING OPERATIONS, GENERAL

08.0102 FASHION MERCHANDISING

08.0103 FASHION MODELING

08.0199 APPAREL AND ACCESSORIES MARKETING OPERATIONS, OTHER

08.0299 BUSINESS AND PERSONAL SERVICES MARKETING OPERATIONS, OTHER

08.0301 ENTREPRENEURSHIP

08.0401 FINANCIAL SERVICES MARKETING OPERATIONS

08.0503 FLORISTRY MARKETING OPERATIONS

08.0601 FOOD PRODUCTS RETAILING AND WHOLESALING OPERATIONS

08.0701 AUCTIONEERING

08.0704 GENERAL BUYING OPERATIONS

08.0705 GENERAL RETAILING OPERATIONS

08.0706 GENERAL SELLING SKILLS AND SALES OPERATIONS

08.0708 GENERAL MARKETING OPERATIONS

08.0709 GENERAL DISTRIBUTION OPERATION

08.0799 GENERAL RETAILING AND WHOLESALING OPERATIONS AND SKILLS, OTHER

08.0809 HOME PRODUCTS MARKETING OPERATIONS

08.0810 OFFICE PRODUCTS MARKETING OPERATIONS

08.0899 HOME AND OFFICE PRODUCTS MARKETING OPERATIONS, OTHER

08.0901 HOSPITALITY AND RECREATION MARKETING OPERATIONS, GENERAL

08.0902 HOTEL/MOTEL SERVICES MARKETING OPERATIONS

08.0903 RECREATION PRODUCTS/SERVICES MARKETING OPERATIONS

08.0999 HOSPITALITY AND RECREATION MARKETING OPERATIONS, OTHER

08.1001 INSURANCE MARKETING OPERATIONS

08.1104 TOURISM PROMOTION OPERATIONS

08.1105 TRAVEL SERVICES MARKETING OPERATIONS

08.1199 TOURISM AND TRAVEL SERVICES MARKETING OPERATIONS, OTHER

08.1203 VEHICLE PARTS AND ACCESSORIES MARKETING OPERATIONS

08.1208 VEHICLE MARKETING OPERATIONS

08.1209 PETROLEUM PRODUCTS RETAILING OPERATIONS

08.1299 VEHICLES AND PETROLEUM PRODUCTS MARKETING OPERATIONS, OTHER

08.9999 MARKETING OPERATIONS MARKETING AND DISTRIBUTION, OTHER

09.0101 COMMUNICATIONS, GENERAL

09.0201 ADVERTISING

09.0401 JOURNALISM

09.0402 BROADCAST JOURNALISM

09.0501 PUBLIC RELATIONS AND ORGANIZATIONAL COMMUNICATIONS

09.0701 RADIO AND TELEVISION BROADCASTING

09.9999 COMMUNICATIONS, OTHER

10.0101 EDUCATIONAL/ INSTRUCTIONAL MEDIA TECHNOLOGY/TECHNICIAN

10.0103 PHOTOGRAPHIC TECHNOLOGY/TECHNICIAN

10.0104 RADIO AND TELEVISION BROADCASTING TECHNOLOGY/TECHNICIAN

10.0199 COMMUNICATIONS TECHNOLOGIES/ TECHNICIANS, OTHER

11.0101 COMPUTER AND INFORMATION SCIENCES, GENERAL

11.0201 COMPUTER PROGRAMMING

11.0301 DATA PROCESSING TECHNOLOGY/TECHNICIAN

11.0401 INFORMATION SCIENCES AND SYSTEMS

11.0501 COMPUTER SYSTEMS ANALYSIS

11.9999 COMPUTER AND INFORMATION SCIENCES, OTHER

12.0203 CARD DEALER

12.0204 UMPIRES AND OTHER SPORTS OFFICIALS

12.0299 GAMING AND SPORTS OFFICIATING SERVICES, OTHER

12.0301 FUNERAL SERVICES AND MORTUARY SCIENCE

12.0401 COSMETIC SERVICES, GENERAL

12.0402 BARBER/HAIRSTYLIST

12.0403 COSMETOLOGIST

12.0404 ELECTROLYSIS TECHNICIAN

12.0405 MASSAGE

12.0406 MAKE-UP ARTIST

12.0499 COSMETIC SERVICES, OTHER

12.0501 BAKER/PASTRY CHEF

12.0502 BARTENDER/MIXOLOGIST

12.0503 CULINARY ARTS/CHEF TRAINING

12.0504 FOOD AND BEVERAGE/RESTAURANT OPERATIONS MANAGER

12.0505 KITCHEN PERSONNEL/COOK AND ASSISTANT TRAINING

12.0506 MEATCUTTER

12.0507 WAITER/WAITRESS AND DINING ROOM MANAGER

12.0599 CULINARY ARTS AND RELATED SERVICES, OTHER

12.9999 PERSONAL AND MISCELLANEOUS SERVICES, OTHER

13.0101 EDUCATION, GENERAL

13.0201 BILINGUAL/BICULTURAL EDUCATION

13.0301 CURRICULUM AND INSTRUCTION

13.0401 EDUCATION ADMINISTRATION AND SUPERVISION, GENERAL

13.0402 ADMINISTRATION OF SPECIAL EDUCATION

13.0403 ADULT AND CONTINUING EDUCATION ADMINISTRATION

13.0404 EDUCATIONAL SUPERVISION

13.0405 ELEMENTARY, MIDDLE AND SECONDARY EDUCATION ADMINISTRATION

13.0406 HIGHER EDUCATION ADMINISTRATION

13.0407 COMMUNITY AND JUNIOR COLLEGE ADMINISTRATION

13.0499 EDUCATION ADMINISTRATION AND SUPERVISION, OTHER

13.0501 EDUCATIONAL/INSTRUC-TIONAL MEDIA DESIGN

13.0601 EDUCATIONAL EVALUATION AND RESEARCH

13.0603 EDUCATIONAL STATISTICS AND RESEARCH METHODS

13.0604 EDUCATIONAL ASSESSMENT, TESTING AND MEASUREMENT

13.0699 EDUCATIONAL EVALUATION, RESEARCH AND STATISTICS, OTHER

13.0701 INTERNATIONAL AND COMPARATIVE EDUCATION

13.0802 EDUCATIONAL PSYCHOLOGY

13.0901 SOCIAL AND PHILOSOPHICAL FOUNDATIONS OF EDUCATION

13.1001 SPECIAL EDUCATION, GENERAL

13.1003 EDUCATION OF THE DEAF AND HEARING IMPAIRED

13.1004 EDUCATION OF THE GIFTED AND TALENTED

13.1005 EDUCATION OF THE EMOTIONALLY HANDICAPPED

13.1006 EDUCATION OF THE MENTALLY HANDICAPPED

13.1007 EDUCATION OF THE MULTIPLE HANDICAPPED

13.1008 EDUCATION OF THE PHYSICALLY HANDICAPPED

13.1009 EDUCATION OF THE BLIND AND VISUALLY HANDICAPPED

13.1011 EDUCATION OF THE SPECIFIC LEARNING DISABLED

13.1012 EDUCATION OF THE SPEECH IMPAIRED

13.1099 SPECIAL EDUCATION, OTHER

13.1101 COUNSELOR EDUCATION COUNSELING AND GUIDANCE SERVICES

13.1201 ADULT AND CONTINUING TEACHER EDUCATION

13.1202 ELEMENTARY TEACHER EDUCATION

13.1203 JUNIOR HIGH/INTERMEDIATE/MIDDLE SCHOOL TEACHER EDUCATION

13.1204 PRE-ELEMENTARY EDUCATION/EARLY CHILDHOOD/KINDERGARTEN TEACHER EDUCATION

13.1205 SECONDARY TEACHER EDUCATION

13.1299 GENERAL TEACHER EDUCATION, OTHER

13.1301 AGRICULTURAL TEACHER EDUCATION (VOCATIONAL)

13.1302 ART TEACHER EDUCATION

13.1303 BUSINESS TEACHER EDUCATION (VOCATIONAL)

13.1304 DRIVER AND SAFETY TEACHER EDUCATION

13.1305 ENGLISH TEACHER EDUCATION

13.1306 FOREIGN LANGUAGES TEACHER EDUCATION

13.1307 HEALTH TEACHER EDUCATION

13.1308 HOME ECONOMICS TEACHER EDUCATION (VOCATIONAL)

13.1309 TECHNOLOGY TEACHER EDUCATION/INDUSTRIAL ARTS TEACHER EDUCATION

13.1310 MARKETING OPERATIONS TEACHER EDUCATION/MARKETING AND DISTRIBUTION TEACHER EDUCATION

13.1311 MATHEMATICS TEACHER EDUCATION

13.1312 MUSIC TEACHER EDUCATION

13.1314 PHYSICAL EDUCATION TEACHING AND COACHING

13.1315 READING TEACHER EDUCATION

13.1316 SCIENCE TEACHER EDUCATION, GENERAL

13.1317 SOCIAL SCIENCE TEACHER EDUCATION

13.1318 SOCIAL STUDIES TEACHER EDUCATION

13.1319 TECHNICAL TEACHER EDUCATION (VOCATIONAL)

13.1320 TRADE AND INDUSTRIAL TEACHER EDUCATION (VOCATIONAL)

13.1321 COMPUTER TEACHER EDUCATION

13.1399 TEACHER EDUCATION, SPECIFIC ACADEMIC AND VOCATIONAL PROGRAMS, OTHER

13.1401 TEACHING ENGLISH AS A SECOND LANGUAGE/FOREIGN LANGUAGE

13.1501 TEACHER ASSISTANT/AIDE

13.9999 EDUCATION, OTHER

14.0101 ENGINEERING, GENERAL

14.0201 AEROSPACE, AERONAUTICAL AND ASTRONAUTICAL ENGINEERING

14.0301 AGRICULTURAL ENGINEERING

14.0401 ARCHITECTURAL ENGINEERING

14.0501 BIOENGINEERING AND BIOMEDICAL ENGINEERING

14.0601 CERAMIC SCIENCES AND ENGINEERING

14.0701 CHEMICAL ENGINEERING

14.0801 CIVIL ENGINEERING, GENERAL

14.0901 COMPUTER ENGINEERING

14.1001 ELECTRICAL, ELECTRONICS AND COMMUNICATION ENGINEERING

14.1101 ENGINEERING MECHANICS

14.1201 ENGINEERING PHYSICS

14.1301 ENGINEERING SCIENCE

14.1401 ENVIRONMENTAL/ENVIRON-MENTAL HEALTH ENGINEERING

14.1501 GEOLOGICAL ENGINEERING

14.1601 GEOPHYSICAL ENGINEERING

14.1701 INDUSTRIAL/MANUFACTURING ENGINEERING

14.1801 MATERIALS ENGINEERING

14.1901 MECHANICAL ENGINEERING

14.2001 METALLURGICAL ENGINEERING

14.2101 MINING AND MINERAL ENGINEERING

14.2201 NAVAL ARCHITECTURE AND MARINE ENGINEERING

14.2301 NUCLEAR ENGINEERING

14.2401 OCEAN ENGINEERING

14.2501 PETROLEUM ENGINEERING

14.2701 SYSTEMS ENGINEERING

14.2801 TEXTILE SCIENCES AND ENGINEERING

14.9999 ENGINEERING, OTHER

15.0101 ARCHITECTURAL ENGINEERING TECHNOLOGY/TECHNICIAN

15.0201 CIVIL ENGINEERING/CIVIL TECHNOLOGY/TECHNICIAN

15.0301 COMPUTER ENGINEERING TECHNOLOGY/TECHNICIAN

15.0303 ELECTRICAL, ELECTRONIC AND COMMUNICATIONS ENGINEERING TECHNOLOGY/TECHN

15.0304 LASER AND OPTICAL TECHNOLOGY/TECHNICIAN

15.0399 ELECTRICAL AND ELECTRONIC ENGINEERING-RELATED TECHNOLOGIES/ TECHNICIANS

15.0401 BIOMEDICAL ENGINEERING-RELATED TECHNOLOGY/TECHNICIAN

15.0402 COMPUTER MAINTENANCE TECHNOLOGY/TECHNICIAN

15.0403 ELECTROMECHANICAL TECHNOLOGY/TECHNICIAN

15.0404 INSTRUMENTATION TECHNOLOGY/TECHNICIAN

15.0405 ROBOTICS TECHNOLOGY/TECHNICIAN

15.0499 ELECTROMECHANICAL INSTRUMENTATION AND MAINTENANCE TECHNOLOGIES/TECHNIC

15.0501 HEATING, AIR CONDITIONING AND REFRIGERATION TECHNOLOGY/TECHNICIAN

15.0503 ENERGY MANAGEMENT AND SYSTEMS TECHNOLOGY/ TECHNICIAN

15.0505 SOLAR TECHNOLOGY/TECHNICIAN

15.0506 WATER QUALITY AND WASTEWATER TREATMENT TECHNOLOGY/TECHNICIAN

15.0599 ENVIRONMENTAL CONTROL TECHNOLOGIES/ TECHNICIANS, OTHER

15.0603 INDUSTRIAL/MANUFACTURING TECHNOLOGY/TECHNICIAN

15.0607 PLASTICS TECHNOLOGY/TECHNICIAN

15.0611 METALLURGICAL TECHNOLOGY/TECHNICIAN

15.0699 INDUSTRIAL PRODUCTION TECHNOLOGIES/TECHNICIANS, OTHER

15.0701 OCCUPATIONAL SAFETY AND HEALTH TECHNOLOGY/TECHNICIAN

15.0702 QUALITY CONTROL TECHNOLOGY/TECHNICIAN

15.0799 QUALITY CONTROL AND SAFETY TECHNOLOGIES/ TECHNICIANS, OTHER

15.0801 AERONAUTICAL AND AEROSPACE ENGINEERING TECHNOLOGY/TECHNICIAN

15.0803 AUTOMOTIVE ENGINEERING TECHNOLOGY/TECHNICIAN

15.0805 MECHANICAL ENGINEERING/MECHANICAL TECHNOLOGY/TECHNICIAN

15.0899 MECHANICAL ENGINEERING-RELATED TECHNOLOGIES/ TECHNICIANS, OTHER

15.0901 MINING TECHNOLOGY/TECHNICIAN

15.0903 PETROLEUM TECHNOLOGY/TECHNICIAN

15.0999 MINING AND PETROLEUM TECHNOLOGIES/ TECHNICIANS, OTHER

15.1001 CONSTRUCTION/BUILDING TECHNOLOGY/TECHNICIAN

15.1102 SURVEYING

15.9999 ENGINEERING-RELATED TECHNOLOGIES/ TECHNICIANS, OTHER

16.0101 FOREIGN LANGUAGES AND LITERATURES, GENERAL

16.0102 LINGUISTICS

16.0301 CHINESE LANGUAGE AND LITERATURE

16.0302 JAPANESE LANGUAGE AND LITERATURE

16.0399 EAST AND SOUTHEAST ASIAN LANGUAGES AND LITERATURES, OTHER

16.0402 RUSSIAN LANGUAGE AND LITERATURE

16.0403 SLAVIC LANGUAGES AND LITERATURES (OTHER THAN RUSSIAN)

16.0499 EAST EUROPEAN LANGUAGES AND LITERATURES, OTHER

16.0501 GERMAN LANGUAGE AND LITERATURE

16.0502 SCANDINAVIAN LANGUAGES AND LITERATURES

16.0599 GERMANIC LANGUAGES AND LITERATURES, OTHER

16.0703 SOUTH ASIAN LANGUAGES AND LITERATURES

16.0901 FRENCH LANGUAGE AND LITERATURE

16.0902 ITALIAN LANGUAGE AND LITERATURE

16.0904 PORTUGUESE LANGUAGE AND LITERATURE

16.0905 SPANISH LANGUAGE AND LITERATURE

16.0999 ROMANCE LANGUAGES AND LITERATURES, OTHER

16.1101 ARABIC LANGUAGE AND LITERATURE

16.1102 HEBREW LANGUAGE AND LITERATURE

16.1199 MIDDLE EASTERN LANGUAGES AND LITERATURES, OTHER

16.1201 CLASSICS AND CLASSICAL LANGUAGES AND LITERATURES

16.1202 GREEK LANGUAGE AND LITERATURE (ANCIENT AND MEDIEVAL)

16.1203 LATIN LANGUAGE AND LITERATURE (ANCIENT AND MEDIEVAL)

16.9999 FOREIGN LANGUAGES AND LITERATURES, OTHER

19.0101 HOME ECONOMICS, GENERAL

19.0201 BUSINESS HOME ECONOMICS

19.0301 FAMILY AND COMMUNITY STUDIES

19.0401 FAMILY RESOURCE MANAGEMENT STUDIES

19.0402 CONSUMER ECONOMICS AND SCIENCE

19.0499 FAMILY/CONSUMER RESOURCE MANAGEMENT, OTHER

19.0501 FOODS AND NUTRITION STUDIES, GENERAL

19.0502 FOODS AND NUTRITION SCIENCE

19.0503 DIETETICS/HUMAN NUTRITIONAL SERVICES

19.0599 FOODS AND NUTRITION STUDIES, OTHER

19.0601 HOUSING STUDIES, GENERAL

19.0603 INTERIOR ENVIRONMENTS

19.0699 HOUSING STUDIES, OTHER

19.0701 INDIVIDUAL AND FAMILY DEVELOPMENT STUDIES, GENERAL

19.0703 FAMILY AND MARRIAGE COUNSELING

19.0704 FAMILY LIFE AND RELATIONS STUDIES

19.0705 GERONTOLOGICAL SERVICES

19.0799 INDIVIDUAL AND FAMILY DEVELOPMENT STUDIES, OTHER

19.0901 CLOTHING/APPAREL AND TEXTILE STUDIES

19.9999 HOME ECONOMICS, OTHER

20.0101 COMPREHENSIVE CONSUMER AND HOMEMAKING EDUCATION

20.0102 CHILD DEVELOPMENT, CARE AND GUIDANCE

20.0103 CLOTHING AND TEXTILES

20.0104 CONSUMER EDUCATION

20.0105 EXPLORATORY HOMEMAKING

20.0106 FAMILY/INDIVIDUAL HEALTH

20.0107 FAMILY LIVING AND PARENTHOOD

20.0108 FOOD AND NUTRITION

20.0109 HOME MANAGEMENT

20.0110 HOUSING, HOME FURNISHINGS AND EQUIPMENT

20.0199 CONSUMER AND HOMEMAKING EDUCATION, OTHER

20.0201 CHILD CARE AND GUIDANCE WORKERS AND MANAGERS, GENERAL

20.0202 CHILD CARE PROVIDER/ASSISTANT

20.0203 CHILD CARE SERVICES MANAGER

20.0299 CHILD CARE AND GUIDANCE WORKERS AND MANAGERS, OTHER

20.0301 CLOTHING, APPAREL AND TEXTILE WORKERS AND MANAGERS, GENERAL

20.0303 COMMERCIAL GARMENT AND APPAREL WORKER

20.0305 CUSTOM TAILOR

20.0306 FASHION AND FABRIC CONSULTANT

20.0309 DRYCLEANER AND LAUNDERER (COMMERCIAL)

20.0399 CLOTHING, APPAREL AND TEXTILE WORKERS AND MANAGERS, OTHER

20.0401 INSTITUTIONAL FOOD WORKERS AND ADMINISTRATOR, GENERAL

20.0404 DIETICIAN ASSISTANT

20.0405 FOOD CATERER

20.0409 INSTITUTIONAL FOOD SERVICES ADMINISTRATOR

20.0499 INSTITUTIONAL FOOD WORKERS AND ADMINISTRATORS, OTHER

20.0501 HOME FURNISHINGS AND EQUIPMENT INSTALLERS AND CONSULTANTS, GENERAL

20.0502 WINDOW TREATMENT MAKER AND INSTALLER

20.0599 HOME FURNISHINGS AND EQUIPMENT INSTALLERS AND CONSULTANTS, OTHER

20.0601 CUSTODIAL, HOUSEKEEPING AND HOME SERVICES WORKERS AND MANAGERS, GENERAL

20.0602 ELDER CARE PROVIDER/COMPANION

20.0604 CUSTODIAN/CARETAKER

20.0605 EXECUTIVE HOUSEKEEPER

20.0606 HOMEMAKER'S AIDE

20.0699 CUSTODIAL, HOUSEKEEPING AND HOME SERVICES WORKERS AND MANAGERS, GENERAL

20.9999 VOCATIONAL HOME ECONOMICS, OTHER

21.0101 TECHNOLOGY EDUCATION/INDUSTRIAL ARTS

22.0101 LAW (LL.B., J.D.)

22.0102 PRE-LAW STUDIES

22.0103 PARALEGAL/LEGAL ASSISTANT

22.0199 LAW AND LEGAL STUDIES, OTHER

23.0101 ENGLISH LANGUAGE AND LITERATURE, GENERAL

23.0301 COMPARATIVE LITERATURE

23.0401 ENGLISH COMPOSITION

23.0501 ENGLISH CREATIVE WRITING

23.0701 AMERICAN LITERATURE (UNITED STATES)

23.0801 ENGLISH LITERATURE (BRITISH AND COMMONWEALTH)

23.1001 SPEECH AND RHETORICAL STUDIES

23.1101 ENGLISH TECHNICAL AND BUSINESS WRITING

23.9999 ENGLISH LANGUAGE AND LITERATURE/LETTERS, OTHER

24.0101 LIBERAL ARTS AND SCIENCES/LIBERAL STUDIES

24.0102 GENERAL STUDIES

24.0103 HUMANITIES/HUMANISTIC STUDIES

24.0199 LIBERAL ART AND SCIENCES, GENERAL STUDIES AND HUMANITIES, OTHER

25.0101 LIBRARY SCIENCE/LIBRARIANSHIP

25.0301 LIBRARY ASSISTANT

25.9999 LIBRARY SCIENCE, OTHER

26.0101 BIOLOGY, GENERAL

26.0202 BIOCHEMISTRY

26.0203 BIOPHYSICS

26.0301 BOTANY, GENERAL

26.0305 PLANT PATHOLOGY

26.0307 PLANT PHYSIOLOGY

26.0399 BOTANY, OTHER

26.0401 CELL BIOLOGY

26.0402 MOLECULAR BIOLOGY

26.0499 CELL AND MOLECULAR BIOLOGY, OTHER

26.0501 MICROBIOLOGY/ BACTERIOLOGY

26.0601 ANATOMY

26.0603 ECOLOGY

26.0607 MARINE/AQUATIC BIOLOGY

26.0608 NEUROSCIENCE

26.0609 NUTRITIONAL SCIENCES

26.0610 PARASITOLOGY

26.0611 RADIATION BIOLOGY/RADIOBIOLOGY

26.0612 TOXICOLOGY

26.0613 GENETICS, PLANT AND ANIMAL

26.0614 BIOMETRICS

26.0615 BIOSTATISTICS

26.0699 MISCELLANEOUS BIOLOGICAL SPECIALIZATIONS, OTHER

26.0701 ZOOLOGY, GENERAL

26.0702 ENTOMOLOGY

26.0704 PATHOLOGY, HUMAN AND ANIMAL

26.0705 PHARMACOLOGY, HUMAN AND ANIMAL

26.0706 PHYSIOLOGY, HUMAN AND ANIMAL

26.0799 ZOOLOGY, OTHER

26.9999 BIOLOGICAL SCIENCES/LIFE SCIENCES, OTHER

27.0101 MATHEMATICS

27.0301 APPLIED MATHEMATICS, GENERAL

27.0302 OPERATIONS RESEARCH

27.0501 MATHEMATICAL STATISTICS

27.9999 MATHEMATICS, OTHER

28.0101 AIR FORCE R.O.T.C./AIR SCIENCE

28.0301 ARMY R.O.T.C./MILITARY SCIENCE

28.0401 NAVY/MARINE CORPS R.O.T.C./NAVAL SCIENCE

29.0101 MILITARY TECHNOLOGIES

30.0101 BIOLOGICAL AND PHYSICAL SCIENCES

30.0501 PEACE AND CONFLICT STUDIES

30.0601 SYSTEMS SCIENCE AND THEORY

30.0801 MATHEMATICS AND COMPUTER SCIENCE

30.1401 MUSEOLOGY/MUSEUM STUDIES

30.9999 MULTI/INTERDISCIPLINARY STUDIES, OTHER

31.0101 PARKS, RECREATION AND LEISURE STUDIES

31.0301 PARKS, RECREATION AND LEISURE FACILITIES MANAGEMENT

31.0505 EXERCISE SCIENCES/PHYSIOLOGY AND MOVEMENT STUDIES

31.9999 PARKS, RECREATION, LEISURE AND FITNESS STUDIES, OTHER

32.0101 BASIC SKILLS, GENERAL

32.0104 COMPUTATIONAL SKILLS

32.0105 JOB SEEKING/CHANGING SKILLS

32.0107 CAREER EXPLORATION/AWARENESS SKILLS

32.0108 READING, LITERACY AND COMMUNICATIONS SKILLS

32.0199 BASIC SKILLS, OTHER

33.0101 CITIZENSHIP ACTIVITIES, GENERAL

33.0102 AMERICAN CITIZENSHIP EDUCATION

33.0103 COMMUNITY AWARENESS

33.0104 COMMUNITY INVOLVEMENT

33.0199 CITIZENSHIP ACTIVITIES, OTHER

34.0102 BIRTHING AND PARENTING KNOWLEDGE AND SKILLS

34.0103 PERSONAL HEALTH IMPROVEMENT AND MAINTENANCE

34.0104 ADDICTION PREVENTION AND TREATMENT

34.0199 HEALTH-RELATED KNOWLEDGE AND SKILLS, OTHER

35.0101 INTERPERSONAL AND SOCIAL SKILLS, GENERAL

35.0102 INTERPERSONAL RELATIONSHIPS SKILLS

35.0103 BUSINESS AND SOCIAL SKILLS

35.0199 INTERPERSONAL AND SOCIAL SKILLS, OTHER

36.0101 LEISURE AND RECREATIONAL ACTIVITIES, GENERAL

36.0102 HANDICRAFTS AND MODEL-MAKING

36.0103 BOARD, CARD AND ROLE-PLAYING GAMES

36.0105 HOME MAINTENANCE AND IMPROVEMENT

36.0106 NATURE APPRECIATION

36.0107 PET OWNERSHIP AND CARE

36.0108 SPORTS AND EXERCISE

36.0109 TRAVEL AND EXPLORATION

36.0199 LEISURE AND RECREATIONAL ACTIVITIES, OTHER

37.0101 SELF-AWARENESS AND PERSONAL ASSESSMENT

37.0102 STRESS MANAGEMENT AND COPING SKILLS

37.0103 PERSONAL DECISION-MAKING SKILLS

37.0104 SELF ESTEEM AND VALUES CLARIFICATION

37.0199 PERSONAL AWARENESS AND SELF-IMPROVEMENT, OTHER

38.0101 PHILOSOPHY

38.0201 RELIGION/RELIGIOUS STUDIES

38.9999 PHILOSOPHY AND RELIGION

39.0101 BIBLICAL AND OTHER THEOLOGICAL LANGUAGES AND LITERATURES

39.0201 BIBLE/BIBLICAL STUDIES

39.0301 MISSIONS/MISSIONARY STUDIES AND MISOLOGY

39.0401 RELIGIOUS EDUCATION

39.0501 RELIGIOUS/SACRED MUSIC

39.0601 THEOLOGY/THEOLOGICAL STUDIES

39.0701 PASTORAL COUNSELING AND SPECIALIZED MINISTRIES

39.9999 THEOLOGICAL STUDIES AND RELIGIOUS VOCATIONS, OTHER

40.0101 PHYSICAL SCIENCES, GENERAL

40.0201 ASTRONOMY

40.0301 ASTROPHYSICS

40.0401 ATMOSPHERIC SCIENCES AND METEOROLOGY

40.0501 CHEMISTRY, GENERAL

40.0502 ANALYTICAL CHEMISTRY

40.0503 INORGANIC CHEMISTRY

40.0504 ORGANIC CHEMISTRY

40.0505 MEDICINAL/PHARMACEUTICAL CHEMISTRY

40.0506 PHYSICAL AND THEORETICAL CHEMISTRY

40.0599 CHEMISTRY, OTHER

40.0601 GEOLOGY

40.0602 GEOCHEMISTRY

40.0603 GEOPHYSICS AND SEISMOLOGY

40.0604 PALEONTOLOGY

40.0699 GEOLOGICAL SCIENCES, OTHER

40.0701 METALLURGY

40.0702 OCEANOGRAPHY

40.0703 EARTH AND PLANETARY SCIENCES

40.0799 MISCELLANEOUS PHYSICAL SCIENCES, OTHER

40.0801 PHYSICS, GENERAL

40.0802 CHEMICAL AND ATOMIC/MOLECULAR PHYSICS

40.0806 NUCLEAR PHYSICS

40.0807 OPTICS

40.0808 SOLID STATE AND LOW-TEMPERATURE PHYSICS

40.0899 PHYSICS, OTHER

40.9999 PHYSICAL SCIENCES, OTHER

41.0101 BIOLOGICAL TECHNOLOGY/TECHNICIAN

41.0204 INDUSTRIAL RADIOLOGIC TECHNOLOGY/TECHNICIAN

41.0205 NUCLEAR/NUCLEAR POWER TECHNOLOGY/TECHNICIAN

41.0299 NUCLEAR AND INDUSTRIAL RADIOLOGIC TECHNOLOGIES/TECHNICIANS, OTHER

41.0301 CHEMICAL TECHNOLOGY/TECHNICIAN

41.0399 PHYSICAL SCIENCE TECHNOLOGIES/TECHNICIANS, OTHER

41.9999 SCIENCE TECHNOLOGIES/TECHNICIANS, OTHER

42.0101 PSYCHOLOGY, GENERAL

42.0201 CLINICAL PSYCHOLOGY

42.0301 COGNITIVE PSYCHOLOGY AND PSYCHOLINGUISTICS

42.0401 COMMUNITY PSYCHOLOGY

42.0601 COUNSELING PSYCHOLOGY

42.0701 DEVELOPMENTAL AND CHILD PSYCHOLOGY

42.0801 EXPERIMENTAL PSYCHOLOGY

42.0901 INDUSTRIAL AND ORGANIZATIONAL PSYCHOLOGY

42.1101 PHYSIOLOGICAL PSYCHOLOGY/ PSYCHOBIOLOGY

42.1601 SOCIAL PSYCHOLOGY

42.1701 SCHOOL PSYCHOLOGY

42.9999 PSYCHOLOGY, OTHER

43.0102 CORRECTIONS/CORRECTIONAL ADMINISTRATION

43.0103 CRIMINAL JUSTICE/LAW ENFORCEMENT ADMINISTRATION

43.0104 CRIMINAL JUSTICE STUDIES

43.0106 FORENSIC TECHNOLOGY/TECHNICIAN

43.0107 LAW ENFORCEMENT/POLICE SCIENCE

43.0109 SECURITY AND LOSS PREVENTION SERVICES

43.0199 CRIMINAL JUSTICE AND CORRECTIONS, OTHER

43.0201 FIRE PROTECTION AND SAFETY TECHNOLOGY/TECHNICIAN

43.0202 FIRE SERVICES ADMINISTRATION

43.0203 FIRE SCIENCE/FIREFIGHTING

43.0299 FIRE PROTECTION, OTHER

43.9999 PROTECTIVE SERVICES, OTHER

44.0201 COMMUNITY ORGANIZATION, RESOURCES AND SERVICES

44.0401 PUBLIC ADMINISTRATION

44.0501 PUBLIC POLICY ANALYSIS

44.0701 SOCIAL WORK

44.9999 PUBLIC ADMINISTRATION AND SERVICES, OTHER

45.0101 SOCIAL SCIENCES, GENERAL

45.0201 ANTHROPOLOGY

45.0301 ARCHAEOLOGY

45.0401 CRIMINOLOGY

45.0501 DEMOGRAPHY AND POPULATION STUDIES

45.0601 ECONOMICS, GENERAL

45.0701 GEOGRAPHY

45.0702 CARTOGRAPHY

45.0801 HISTORY, GENERAL

45.0805 PUBLIC/APPLIED HISTORY AND ARCHIVAL ADMINISTRATION

45.0901 INTERNATIONAL RELATIONS AND AFFAIRS

45.1001 POLITICAL SCIENCE, GENERAL

45.1101 SOCIOLOGY

45.1201 URBAN AFFAIRS/STUDIES

45.9999 SOCIAL SCIENCES AND HISTORY, OTHER

46.0101 MASON AND TILE SETTER

46.0201 CARPENTER

46.0301 ELECTRICAL AND POWER TRANSMISSION INSTALLER, GENERAL

46.0302 ELECTRICIAN

46.0303 LINEWORKER

46.0399 ELECTRICAL AND POWER TRANSMISSION INSTALLERS, OTHER

46.0401 BUILDING/PROPERTY MAINTENANCE AND MANAGER

46.0403 CONSTRUCTION/BUILDING INSPECTION

46.0408 PAINTER AND WALL COVERER

46.0499 CONSTRUCTION AND BUILDING FINISHERS AND MANAGERS, OTHER

46.0501 PLUMBER AND PIPEFITTER

46.9999 CONSTRUCTION TRADES, OTHER

47.0101 ELECTRICAL AND ELECTRONICS EQUIPMENT INSTALLER AND REPAIRER, GENERAL

47.0102 BUSINESS MACHINE REPAIRER

47.0103 COMMUNICATION SYSTEMS INSTALLER AND REPAIRER

47.0104 COMPUTER INSTALLER AND REPAIRER

47.0105 INDUSTRIAL ELECTRONICS INSTALLER AND REPAIRER

47.0106 MAJOR APPLIANCE INSTALLER AND REPAIRER

47.0199 ELECTRICAL AND ELECTRONICS EQUIPMENT INSTALLER AND REPAIRER, OTHER

47.0201 HEATING, AIR CONDITIONING AND REFRIGERATION MECHANIC AND REPAIRER

47.0302 HEAVY EQUIPMENT MAINTENANCE AND REPAIRER

47.0303 INDUSTRIAL MACHINERY MAINTENANCE AND REPAIRER

47.0399 INDUSTRIAL EQUIPMENT MAINTENANCE AND REPAIRERS, OTHER

47.0401 INSTRUMENT CALIBRATION AND REPAIRER

47.0402 GUNSMITH

47.0403 LOCKSMITH AND SAFE REPAIRER

47.0404 MUSICAL INSTRUMENT REPAIRER

47.0408 WATCH, CLOCK AND JEWELRY REPAIRER

47.0499 MISCELLANEOUS MECHANICS AND REPAIRERS, OTHER

47.0501 STATIONARY ENERGY SOURCES INSTALLER AND OPERATOR

47.0603 AUTO/AUTOMOTIVE BODY REPAIRER

47.0604 AUTO/AUTOMOTIVE MECHANIC/TECHNICIAN

47.0605 DIESEL ENGINE MECHANIC AND REPAIRER

47.0606 SMALL ENGINE MECHANIC AND REPAIRER

47.0607 AIRCRAFT MECHANIC/TECHNICIAN, AIRFRAME

47.0608 AIRCRAFT MECHANIC/TECHNICIAN, POWERPLANT

47.0699 VEHICLE AND MOBILE EQUIPMENT MECHANICS AND REPAIRERS, OTHER

47.9999 MECHANICS AND REPAIRERS, OTHER

48.0101 DRAFTING, GENERAL

48.0102 ARCHITECTURAL DRAFTING

48.0103 CIVIL/STRUCTURAL DRAFTING

48.0104 ELECTRICAL/ELECTRONICS DRAFTING

48.0105 MECHANICAL DRAFTING

48.0199 DRAFTING, OTHER

48.0201 GRAPHIC AND PRINTING EQUIPMENT OPERATORS, GENERAL

48.0205 MECHANICAL TYPESETTER AND COMPOSER

48.0206 LITHOGRAPHER AND PLATEMAKER

48.0208 PRINTING PRESS OPERATOR

48.0299 GRAPHIC AND PRINTING EQUIPMENT OPERATORS, OTHER

48.0303 UPHOLSTERER

48.0304 SHOE, BOOT AND LEATHER REPAIR

48.0399 LEATHERWORKERS AND UPHOLSTERERS, OTHER

48.0501 MACHINIST/MACHINE TECHNOLOGIST

48.0503 MACHINE SHOP ASSISTANT

48.0506 SHEET METAL WORKER

48.0507 TOOL AND DIE MAKER/TECHNOLOGIST

48.0508 WELDER/WELDING TECHNOLOGIST

48.0599 PRECISION METAL WORKERS, OTHER

48.0701 WOODWORKER, GENERAL

48.0702 FURNITURE DESIGNER AND MAKER

48.0703 CABINET MAKER AND MILLWORKER

48.0799 WOODWORKERS, OTHER

48.9999 PRECISION PRODUCTION TRADES, OTHER

49.0101 AVIATION AND AIRWAY SCIENCE

49.0102 AIRCRAFT PILOT AND NAVIGATOR (PROFESSIONAL)

49.0104 AVIATION MANAGEMENT

49.0105 AIR TRAFFIC CONTROLLER

49.0106 FLIGHT ATTENDANT

49.0107 AIRCRAFT PILOT (PRIVATE)

49.0199 AIR TRANSPORTATION WORKERS, OTHER

49.0202 CONSTRUCTION EQUIPMENT OPERATOR

49.0205 TRUCK, BUS AND OTHER COMMERCIAL VEHICLE OPERATOR

49.0299 VEHICLE AND EQUIPMENT OPERATORS, OTHER

49.0303 FISHING TECHNOLOGY/COMMERCIAL FISHING

49.0304 DIVING (PROFESSIONAL)

49.0306 MARINE MAINTENANCE AND SHIP REPAIRER

49.0309 MARINE SCIENCE/MERCHANT MARINE OFFICER

49.0399 WATER TRANSPORTATION WORKERS, OTHER

49.9999 TRANSPORTATION AND MATERIALS MOVING WORKERS, OTHER

50.0101 VISUAL AND PERFORMING ARTS

50.0201 CRAFTS, FOLK ART AND ARTISANRY

50.0301 DANCE

50.0401 DESIGN AND VISUAL COMMUNICATIONS

50.0402 GRAPHIC DESIGN, COMMERCIAL ART AND ILLUSTRATION

50.0404 INDUSTRIAL DESIGN

50.0406 COMMERCIAL PHOTOGRAPHY

50.0407 FASHION DESIGN AND ILLUSTRATION

50.0499 DESIGN AND APPLIED ARTS, OTHER

50.0501 DRAMA/THEATER ARTS, GENERAL

50.0502 TECHNICAL THEATER/THEATER DESIGN AND STAGECRAFT

50.0601 FILM/CINEMA STUDIES

50.0602 FILM-VIDEO MAKING/CINEMATOGRAPHY AND PRODUCTION

50.0605 PHOTOGRAPHY

50.0699 FILM/VIDEO AND PHOTOGRAPHIC ARTS, OTHER

50.0701 ART, GENERAL

50.0703 ART HISTORY, CRITICISM AND CONSERVATION

50.0704 ARTS MANAGEMENT

50.0705 DRAWING

50.0706 INTERMEDIA

50.0708 PAINTING

50.0709 SCULPTURE

50.0710 PRINTMAKING

50.0711 CERAMIC ARTS AND CERAMICS

50.0712 FIBER, TEXTILE AND WEAVING ARTS

50.0713 METAL AND JEWELRY ARTS

50.0799 FINE ARTS AND ART STUDIES, OTHER

50.0901 MUSIC, GENERAL

50.0902 MUSIC HISTORY AND LITERATURE

50.0903 MUSIC-GENERAL PERFORMANCE

50.0904 MUSIC THEORY AND COMPOSITION

50.0999 MUSIC, OTHER

50.9999 VISUAL AND PERFORMING ARTS, OTHER

51.0101 CHIROPRACTIC (D.C., D.C.M.)

51.0202 AUDIOLOGY/HEARING SCIENCES

51.0203 SPEECH-LANGUAGE PATHOLOGY

51.0204 SPEECH-LANGUAGE PATHOLOGY AND AUDIOLOGY

51.0205 SIGN LANGUAGE INTERPRETER

51.0299 COMMUNICATION DISORDERS SCIENCES AND SERVICES, OTHER

51.0301 COMMUNITY HEALTH LIAISON

51.0401 DENTISTRY (D.D.S., D.M.D.)

51.0601 DENTAL ASSISTANT

51.0602 DENTAL HYGIENIST

51.0603 DENTAL LABORATORY TECHNICIAN

51.0699 DENTAL SERVICES, OTHER

51.0701 HEALTH CARE AND SERVICES ADMINISTRATION

51.0702 HOSPITAL/HEALTH FACILITIES ADMINISTRATION

51.0703 HEALTH UNIT COORDINATOR/WARD CLERK

51.0704 HEALTH UNIT MANAGER/ WARD SUPERVISOR

51.0705 MEDICAL OFFICE MANAGEMENT

51.0706 MEDICAL RECORDS ADMINISTRATION

51.0707 MEDICAL RECORDS TECHNOLOGY/TECHNICIAN

51.0799 HEALTH AND MEDICAL ADMINISTRATIVE SERVICES, OTHER

51.0801 MEDICAL ASSISTANT

51.0802 MEDICAL LABORATORY ASSISTANT

51.0803 OCCUPATIONAL THERAPY ASSISTANT

51.0805 PHARMACY TECHNICIAN/ASSISTANT

51.0806 PHYSICAL THERAPY ASSISTANT

51.0807 PHYSICIAN ASSISTANT

51.0808 VETERINARIAN ASSISTANT/ANIMAL HEALTH TECHNICIAN

51.0899 HEALTH AND MEDICAL ASSISTANTS, OTHER

51.0901 CARDIOVASCULAR TECHNOLOGY/TECHNICIAN

51.0902 ELECTROCARDIOGRAPH TECHNOLOGY/TECHNICIAN

51.0903 ELECTROENCEPHALOGRAPH TECHNOLOGY/TECHNICIAN

51.0904 EMERGENCY MEDICAL TECHNOLOGY/TECHNICIAN

51.0905 NUCLEAR MEDICAL TECHNOLOGY/TECHNICIAN

51.0907 MEDICAL RADIOLOGIC TECHNOLOGY/TECHNICIAN

51.0908 RESPIRATORY THERAPY TECHNICIAN

51.0909 SURGICAL/OPERATING ROOM TECHNICIAN

51.0910 DIAGNOSTIC MEDICAL SONOGRAPHY

51.0999 HEALTH AND MEDICAL DIAGNOSTIC AND TREATMENT SERVICES, OTHER

51.1001 BLOOD BANK TECHNOLOGY/TECHNICIAN

51.1002 CYTOTECHNOLOGIST

51.1003 HEMATOLOGY TECHNOLOGY/TECHNICIAN

51.1004 MEDICAL LABORATORY TECHNICIAN

51.1005 MEDICAL TECHNOLOGY

51.1099 HEALTH AND MEDICAL LABORATORY TECHNOLOGIES/ TECHNICIANS, OTHER

51.1101 PRE-DENTISTRY STUDIES

51.1102 PRE-MEDICINE STUDIES

51.1103 PRE-PHARMACY STUDIES

51.1104 PRE-VETERINARY STUDIES

51.1201 MEDICINE (M.D.)

51.1301 MEDICAL ANATOMY

51.1302 MEDICAL BIOCHEMISTRY

51.1307 MEDICAL IMMUNOLOGY

51.1308 MEDICAL MICROBIOLOGY

51.1312 MEDICAL PATHOLOGY

51.1313 MEDICAL PHYSIOLOGY

51.1314 MEDICAL TOXICOLOGY

51.1399 MEDICAL BASIC SCIENCES, OTHER

51.1501 ALCOHOL/DRUG ABUSE COUNSELING

51.1502 PSYCHIATRIC/MENTAL HEALTH SERVICES TECHNICIAN

51.1503 CLINICAL AND MEDICAL SOCIAL WORK

51.1599 MENTAL HEALTH SERVICES, OTHER

51.1601 NURSING (R.N. TRAINING)

51.1602 NURSING ADMINISTRATION (POST-R.N.)

51.1604 NURSING ANESTHETIST (POST-R.N.)

51.1606 NURSING, MATERNAL/CHILD HEALTH (POST-R.N.)

51.1610 NURSING, PSYCHIATRIC/MENTAL HEALTH (POST-R.N.)

51.1611 NURSING, PUBLIC HEALTH (POST-R.N.)

51.1612 NURSING, SURGICAL (POST-R.N.)

51.1613 PRACTICAL NURSE (L.P.N. TRAINING)

51.1614 NURSING ASSISTANT/AIDE

51.1615 HOME HEALTH AIDE

51.1699 NURSING, OTHER

51.1701 OPTOMETRY (O.D.)

51.1801 OPTICIANRY/DISPENSING OPTICIAN

51.1802 OPTICAL TECHNICIAN/ASSISTANT

51.1899 OPHTHALMIC/OPTOMETRIC SERVICES, OTHER

51.1901 OSTEOPATHIC MEDICINE (D.O.)

51.2001 PHARMACY (B.PHARM., PHARM.D.)

51.2101 PODIATRY (D.P.M., D.P., POD.D.)

51.2201 PUBLIC HEALTH, GENERAL

51.2203 EPIDEMIOLOGY

51.2207 PUBLIC HEALTH EDUCATION AND PROMOTION

51.2299 PUBLIC HEALTH, OTHER

51.2301 ART THERAPY

51.2302 DANCE THERAPY

51.2305 MUSIC THERAPY

51.2306 OCCUPATIONAL THERAPY

51.2307 ORTHOTICS/PROSTHETICS

51.2308 PHYSICAL THERAPY

51.2309 RECREATIONAL THERAPY

51.2310 VOCATIONAL REHABILITATION COUNSELING

51.2399 REHABILITATION/THERAPEUTIC SERVICES, OTHER

51.2401 VETERINARY MEDICINE (D.V.M.)

51.2601 HEALTH AIDE

51.2703 MEDICAL ILLUSTRATING

51.2801 DENTAL/ORAL SURGERY SPECIALITY

51.2802 DENTAL PUBLIC HEALTH SPECIALITY

51.2803 ENDODONTICS SPECIALITY

51.2804 ORAL PATHOLOGY SPECIALITY

51.2805 ORTHODONTICS SPECIALITY

51.2806 PEDODONTICS SPECIALITY

51.2807 PERIODONTICS SPECIALITY

51.2808 PROSTHODONTICS

51.2899 DENTAL RESIDENCY PROGRAMS, OTHER

51.2902 ALLERGIES AND IMMUNOLOGY RESIDENCY

51.2903 ANESTHESIOLOGY RESIDENCY

51.2909 COLON AND RECTAL SURGERY RESIDENCY

51.2913 DERMATOLOGY RESIDENCY

51.2915 DIAGNOSTIC RADIOLOGY RESIDENCY

51.2916 EMERGENCY MEDICINE RESIDENCY

51.2918 FAMILY MEDICINE RESIDENCY

51.2921 GENERAL SURGERY RESIDENCY

51.2922 GERIATRIC MEDICINE RESIDENCY

51.2924 HEMATOLOGY RESIDENCY

51.2928 INTERNAL MEDICINE RESIDENCY

51.2933 NEUROLOGICAL SURGERY/NEUROSURGERY RESIDENCY

51.2934 NEUROLOGY RESIDENCY

51.2936 NUCLEAR MEDICINE RESIDENCY

51.2937 NUCLEAR RADIOLOGY RESIDENCY

51.2938 OBSTETRICS AND GYNECOLOGY RESIDENCY

51.2941 OPHTHALMOLOGY RESIDENCY

51.2942 ORTHOPEDICS/ORTHOPEDIC SURGERY RESIDENCY

51.2943 OTOLARYNGOLOGY RESIDENCY

51.2944 PATHOLOGY RESIDENCY

51.2951 PEDIATRICS RESIDENCY

51.2952 PHYSICAL AND REHABILITATION MEDICINE RESIDENCY

51.2953 PLASTIC SURGERY RESIDENCY

51.2954 PREVENTIVE MEDICINE RESIDENCY

51.2955 PSYCHIATRY RESIDENCY

51.2958 RADIATION ONCOLOGY RESIDENCY

51.2961 SPORTS MEDICINE RESIDENCY

51.2962 THORACIC SURGERY RESIDENCY

51.2963 UROLOGY RESIDENCY

51.2999 MEDICAL RESIDENCY PROGRAMS, OTHER

51.9999 HEALTH PROFESSIONS AND RELATED SCIENCES, OTHER

52.0101 BUSINESS, GENERAL

52.0201 BUSINESS ADMINISTRATION AND MANAGEMENT, GENERAL

52.0202 PURCHASING, PROCUREMENT AND CONTRACTS MANAGEMENT

52.0204 OFFICE SUPERVISION AND MANAGEMENT

52.0205 OPERATIONS MANAGEMENT AND SUPERVISION

52.0299 BUSINESS ADMINISTRATION AND MANAGEMENT, OTHER

52.0301 ACCOUNTING

52.0302 ACCOUNTING TECHNICIAN

52.0399 ACCOUNTING, OTHER

52.0401 ADMINISTRATIVE ASSISTANT/SECRETARIAL SCIENCE, GENERAL

52.0402 EXECUTIVE ADMINISTRATIVE ASSISTANT/SECRETARY

52.0403 LEGAL ADMINISTRATIVE ASSISTANT/SECRETARY

52.0404 MEDICAL ADMINISTRATIVE ASSISTANT/SECRETARY

52.0405 COURT REPORTER

52.0406 RECEPTIONIST

52.0407 INFORMATION PROCESSING/DATA ENTRY TECHNICIAN

52.0408 GENERAL OFFICE/CLERICAL AND TYPING SERVICES

52.0499 ADMINISTRATIVE AND SECRETARIAL SERVICES, OTHER

52.0601 BUSINESS/MANAGERIAL ECONOMICS

52.0701 ENTERPRISE MANAGEMENT AND OPERATION, GENERAL

52.0801 FINANCE, GENERAL

52.0802 ACTUARIAL SCIENCE

52.0803 BANKING AND FINANCIAL SUPPORT SERVICES

52.0805 INSURANCE AND RISK MANAGEMENT

52.0807 INVESTMENTS AND SECURITIES

52.0901 HOSPITALITY/ADMINISTRATION MANAGEMENT

52.0902 HOTEL/MOTEL AND RESTAURANT MANAGEMENT

52.0903 TRAVEL-TOURISM MANAGEMENT

52.0999 HOSPITALITY SERVICES MANAGEMENT, OTHER

52.1001 HUMAN RESOURCES MANAGEMENT

52.1002 LABOR/PERSONNEL RELATIONS AND STUDIES

52.1003 ORGANIZATIONAL BEHAVIOR STUDIES

52.1099 HUMAN RESOURCES MANAGEMENT, OTHER

52.1101 INTERNATIONAL BUSINESS

52.1201 MANAGEMENT INFORMATION SYSTEMS AND BUSINESS DATA PROCESSING, GENERAL

52.1202 BUSINESS COMPUTER PROGRAMMING/ PROGRAMMER

52.1203 BUSINESS SYSTEMS ANALYSIS AND DESIGN

52.1205 BUSINESS COMPUTER FACILITIES OPERATOR

52.1299 BUSINESS INFORMATION AND DATA PROCESSING SERVICES, OTHER

52.1301 MANAGEMENT SCIENCE

52.1399 MANAGEMENT SCIENCE, OTHER

52.1401 BUSINESS MARKETING AND MARKETING MANAGEMENT

52.1402 MARKETING RESEARCH

52.1403 INTERNATIONAL BUSINESS MARKETING

52.1499 MARKETING MANAGEMENT AND RESEARCH, OTHER

52.1501 REAL ESTATE

52.1601 TAXATION

52.9999 BUSINESS MANAGEMENT AND ADMINISTRATIVE SERVICES, OTHER

APPENDIX H:
Occupational Employment Statistics (OES) Codes and Titles

Provides a listing of OES codes and their related meaning.

00000	OUTSIDE OES SURVEY
13002	FINANCIAL MANAGERS
13005	PERSONNEL, TRAINING, AND LABOR RELATIONS MANAGERS
13008	PURCHASING MANAGERS
13011	MARKETING, ADVERTISING, AND PUBLIC RELATIONS MANAGERS
13014	ADMINISTRATIVE SERVICES MANAGERS
13017	ENGINEERING, MATHEMATICAL, AND NATURAL SCIENCES MANAGERS
15002	POSTMASTERS AND MAIL SUPERINTENDENTS
15005	EDUCATION ADMINISTRATORS
15008	MEDICINE AND HEALTH SERVICES MANAGERS
15011	PROPERTY AND REAL ESTATE MANAGERS AND ADMINISTRATORS
15014	INDUSTRIAL PRODUCTION MANAGERS
15017	CONSTRUCTION MANAGERS
15021	MINING, QUARRYING, AND OIL AND GAS WELL DRILLING MANAGERS
15023	COMMUNICATIONS, TRANSPORTATION, AND UTILITIES OPERATIONS MANAGERS
15026	FOOD SERVICE AND LODGING MANAGERS
15031	NURSERY AND GREENHOUSE MANAGERS
15032	LAWN SERVICE MANAGERS
19002	PUBLIC ADMINISTRATION CHIEF EXECUTIVES, LEGISLATORS, AND GENERAL ADMINISTRATORS
19005	GENERAL MANAGERS AND TOP EXECUTIVES
19999	ALL OTHER MANAGERS AND ADMINISTRATORS
21102	UNDERWRITERS
21105	CREDIT ANALYSTS
21108	LOAN OFFICERS AND COUNSELORS
21111	TAX PREPARERS
21114	ACCOUNTANTS AND AUDITORS
21117	BUDGET ANALYSTS
21199	ALL OTHER FINANCIAL SPECIALISTS
21302	WHOLESALE AND RETAIL BUYERS, EXCEPT FARM PRODUCTS
21305	PURCHASING AGENTS AND BUYERS, FARM PRODUCTS
21308	PURCHASING AGENTS, EXCEPT WHOLESALE, RETAIL, AND FARM PRODUCTS
21502	CLAIMS TAKERS, UNEMPLOYMENT BENEFITS
21505	SPECIAL AGENTS, INSURANCE
21508	EMPLOYMENT INTERVIEWERS, PRIVATE OR PUBLIC EMPLOYMENT SERVICE
21511	PERSONNEL, TRAINING, AND LABOR RELATIONS SPECIALISTS
21902	COST ESTIMATORS
21905	MANAGEMENT ANALYSTS
21908	CONSTRUCTION AND BUILDING INSPECTORS
21911	COMPLIANCE OFFICERS AND ENFORCEMENT INSPECTORS, EXCEPT CONSTRUCTION
21914	TAX EXAMINERS, COLLECTORS, AND REVENUE AGENTS
21917	ASSESSORS
21921	CLAIMS EXAMINERS, PROPERTY AND CASUALTY INSURANCE
21999	ALL OTHER MANAGEMENT SUPPORT WORKERS
22102	AERONAUTICAL AND ASTRONAUTICAL ENGINEERS
22105	METALLURGISTS AND METALLURGICAL, CERAMIC, AND MATERIALS ENGINEERS
22108	MINING ENGINEERS, INCLUDING MINE SAFETY
22111	PETROLEUM ENGINEERS
22114	CHEMICAL ENGINEERS
22117	NUCLEAR ENGINEERS
22121	CIVIL ENGINEERS, INCLUDING TRAFFIC
22123	AGRICULTURAL ENGINEERS
22126	ELECTRICAL AND ELECTRONIC ENGINEERS
22127	COMPUTER ENGINEERS
22128	INDUSTRIAL ENGINEERS, EXCEPT SAFETY
22132	SAFETY ENGINEERS, EXCEPT MINING
22135	MECHANICAL ENGINEERS
22138	MARINE ENGINEERS
22199	ALL OTHER ENGINEERS
22302	ARCHITECTS, EXCEPT LANDSCAPE AND MARINE
22305	MARINE ARCHITECTS
22308	LANDSCAPE ARCHITECTS
22311	SURVEYORS AND MAPPING SCIENTISTS
22502	CIVIL ENGINEERING TECHNICIANS AND TECHNOLOGISTS
22505	ELECTRICAL AND ELECTRONIC ENGINEERING TECHNICIANS AND TECHNOLOGISTS
22508	INDUSTRIAL ENGINEERING TECHNICIANS AND TECHNOLOGISTS
22511	MECHANICAL ENGINEERING TECHNICIANS AND TECHNOLOGISTS
22514	DRAFTERS
22517	ESTIMATORS AND DRAFTERS, UTILITIES
22521	SURVEYING AND MAPPING TECHNICIANS

22599 ALL OTHER ENGINEERING AND RELATED TECHNICIANS AND TECHNOLOGISTS

24102 PHYSICISTS AND ASTRONOMERS

24105 CHEMISTS, EXCEPT BIOCHEMISTS

24108 ATMOSPHERIC AND SPACE SCIENTISTS

24111 GEOLOGISTS, GEOPHYSICISTS, AND OCEANOGRAPHERS

24199 ALL OTHER PHYSICAL SCIENTISTS

24302 FORESTERS AND CONSERVATION SCIENTISTS

24305 AGRICULTURAL AND FOOD SCIENTISTS

24308 BIOLOGICAL SCIENTISTS

24311 MEDICAL SCIENTISTS

24502 BIOLOGICAL, AGRICULTURAL, AND FOOD TECHNICIANS AND TECHNOLOGISTS, EXCEPT HEALTH

24505 CHEMICAL TECHNICIANS AND TECHNOLOGISTS, EXCEPT HEALTH

24508 NUCLEAR TECHNICIANS AND TECHNOLOGISTS

24511 PETROLEUM TECHNICIANS AND TECHNOLOGISTS

24599 ALL OTHER PHYSICAL AND LIFE SCIENCE TECHNICIANS AND TECHNOLOGISTS

25102 SYSTEMS ANALYSTS, ELECTRONIC DATA PROCESSING

25105 COMPUTER PROGRAMMERS

25108 COMPUTER PROGRAMMER AIDES

25111 PROGRAMMERS, NUMERICAL TOOL AND PROCESS CONTROL

25199 ALL OTHER COMPUTER SCIENTISTS

25302 OPERATIONS AND SYSTEMS RESEARCHERS AND ANALYSTS, EXCEPT COMPUTER

25312 STATISTICIANS

25313 ACTUARIES

25315 FINANCIAL ANALYSTS, STATISTICAL

25319 ALL OTHER MATHEMATICAL SCIENTISTS

25323 MATHEMATICAL TECHNICIANS

27102 ECONOMISTS, INCLUDING MARKET RESEARCH ANALYSTS

27105 URBAN AND REGIONAL PLANNERS

27108 PSYCHOLOGISTS

27199 ALL OTHER SOCIAL SCIENTISTS

27302 SOCIAL WORKERS, MEDICAL AND PSYCHIATRIC

27305 SOCIAL WORKERS, EXCEPT MEDICAL AND PSYCHIATRIC

27307 RESIDENTIAL COUNSELORS

27308 HUMAN SERVICES WORKERS

27311 RECREATION WORKERS

27502 CLERGY

27505 DIRECTORS, RELIGIOUS ACTIVITIES AND EDUCATION

27599 ALL OTHER RELIGIOUS WORKERS

28102 JUDGES AND MAGISTRATES

28105 ADJUDICATORS, HEARINGS OFFICERS, AND JUDICIAL REVIEWERS

28108 LAWYERS

28302 LAW CLERKS

28305 PARALEGAL PERSONNEL

28308 TITLE SEARCHERS

28311 TITLE EXAMINERS AND ABSTRACTORS

28399 ALL OTHER LEGAL ASSISTANTS AND TECHNICIANS, EXCEPT CLERICAL

31114 NURSING INSTRUCTORS, POSTSECONDARY

31117 GRADUATE ASSISTANTS, TEACHING

31202 LIFE SCIENCES TEACHERS, POSTSECONDARY

31204 CHEMISTRY TEACHERS, POSTSECONDARY

31206 PHYSICS TEACHERS, POSTSECONDARY

31209 ALL OTHER PHYSICAL SCIENCES TEACHERS, POSTSECONDARY

31210 SOCIAL SCIENCES TEACHERS, POSTSECONDARY

31212 HEALTH SPECIALTIES TEACHERS, POSTSECONDARY

31216 ENGLISH AND FOREIGN LANGUAGES TEACHERS, POSTSECONDARY

31218 ART, DRAMA, AND MUSIC TEACHERS, POSTSECONDARY

31222 ENGINEERING TEACHERS, POSTSECONDARY

31224 MATHEMATICAL SCIENCES TEACHERS, POSTSECONDARY

31226 COMPUTER SCIENCE TEACHERS, POSTSECONDARY

31299 ALL OTHER POSTSECONDARY TEACHERS

31302 TEACHERS, PRESCHOOL AND KINDERGARTEN

31305 TEACHERS, ELEMENTARY SCHOOL

31308 TEACHERS, SECONDARY SCHOOL

31311 TEACHERS, SPECIAL EDUCATION

31314 TEACHERS AND INSTRUCTORS, VOCATIONAL EDUCATION AND TRAINING

31317 INSTRUCTORS, NONVOCATIONAL EDUCATION

31321 INSTRUCTORS AND COACHES, SPORTS AND PHYSICAL TRAINING

31323 FARM AND HOME MANAGEMENT ADVISORS

31399 ALL OTHER TEACHERS AND INSTRUCTORS

31502 LIBRARIANS, PROFESSIONAL

31505 TECHNICAL ASSISTANTS, LIBRARY

31508 AUDIO-VISUAL SPECIALISTS

31511 CURATORS, ARCHIVISTS, MUSEUM TECHNICIANS, AND RESTORERS

31514 VOCATIONAL AND EDUCATIONAL COUNSELORS

31517 INSTRUCTIONAL COORDINATORS

31521 TEACHER AIDES, PARAPROFESSIONAL

32102 PHYSICIANS AND SURGEONS

32105 DENTISTS

32108 OPTOMETRISTS

32111 PODIATRISTS

32113 CHIROPRACTORS

32114 VETERINARIANS AND VETERINARY INSPECTORS

32199	ALL OTHER HEALTH DIAGNOSING AND TREATING PRACTITIONERS
32302	RESPIRATORY THERAPISTS
32305	OCCUPATIONAL THERAPISTS
32308	PHYSICAL THERAPISTS
32311	CORRECTIVE AND MANUAL ARTS THERAPISTS
32314	SPEECH-LANGUAGE PATHOLOGISTS AND AUDIOLOGISTS
32317	RECREATIONAL THERAPISTS
32399	ALL OTHER THERAPISTS
32502	REGISTERED NURSES
32505	LICENSED PRACTICAL NURSES
32508	EMERGENCY MEDICAL TECHNICIANS
32511	PHYSICIAN'S ASSISTANTS
32514	OPTICIANS, DISPENSING AND MEASURING
32517	PHARMACISTS
32518	PHARMACY TECHNICIANS
32521	DIETITIANS AND NUTRITIONISTS
32523	DIETETIC TECHNICIANS
32902	MEDICAL AND CLINICAL LABORATORY TECHNOLOGISTS
32905	MEDICAL AND CLINICAL LABORATORY TECHNICIANS
32908	DENTAL HYGIENISTS
32911	MEDICAL RECORDS TECHNICIANS
32914	NUCLEAR MEDICINE TECHNOLOGISTS
32917	RADIOLOGIC TECHNOLOGISTS
32921	RADIOLOGIC TECHNICIANS
32923	ELECTRONEURODIAGNOSTIC TECHNOLOGISTS
32925	CARDIOLOGY TECHNOLOGISTS
32926	ELECTROCARDIOGRAPH TECHNICIANS
32928	SURGICAL TECHNOLOGISTS AND TECHNICIANS
32931	PSYCHIATRIC TECHNICIANS
32951	VETERINARY TECHNICIANS AND TECHNOLOGISTS
32999	ALL OTHER HEALTH PROFESSIONALS, PARAPROFESSIONALS, AND TECHNICIANS
34002	WRITERS AND EDITORS
34005	TECHNICAL WRITERS
34008	PUBLIC RELATIONS SPECIALISTS AND PUBLICITY WRITERS
34011	REPORTERS AND CORRESPONDENTS
34014	BROADCAST NEWS ANALYSTS
34017	ANNOUNCERS, RADIO AND TELEVISION
34021	ANNOUNCERS, EXCEPT RADIO AND TELEVISION
34023	PHOTOGRAPHERS
34026	CAMERA OPERATORS, TELEVISION AND MOTION PICTURE
34028	BROADCAST TECHNICIANS
34032	FILM EDITORS
34035	ARTISTS AND RELATED WORKERS
34038	DESIGNERS, EXCEPT INTERIOR DESIGNERS
34041	INTERIOR DESIGNERS
34044	MERCHANDISE DISPLAYERS AND WINDOW TRIMMERS
34047	MUSIC DIRECTORS, SINGERS, COMPOSERS, AND RELATED WORKERS
34051	MUSICIANS, INSTRUMENTAL
34053	DANCERS AND CHOREOGRAPHERS
34056	PRODUCERS, DIRECTORS, ACTORS, AND OTHER ENTERTAINERS
34058	ATHLETES, COACHES, UMPIRES, AND RELATED WORKERS
39002	AIRPLANE DISPATCHERS AND AIR TRAFFIC CONTROLLERS
39005	TRAFFIC TECHNICIANS
39008	RADIO OPERATORS
39011	FUNERAL DIRECTORS AND MORTICIANS
39014	EMBALMERS
39999	ALL OTHER PROFESSIONAL, PARAPROFESSIONAL, AND TECHNICAL WORKERS
41002	FIRST-LINE SUPERVISORS AND MANAGER/SUPERVISORS, SALES AND RELATED WORKERS
43002	SALES AGENTS AND PLACERS, INSURANCE
43005	BROKERS, REAL ESTATE
43008	SALES AGENTS, REAL ESTATE
43011	APPRAISERS, REAL ESTATE
43014	SALES AGENTS, SECURITIES, COMMODITIES, AND FINANCIAL SERVICES
43017	SALES AGENTS, SELECTED BUSINESS SERVICES
43021	TRAVEL AGENTS
43023	SALES AGENTS, ADVERTISING
43099	ALL OTHER SALES REPRESENTATIVES AND SALESPERSONS, SERVICES
49002	SALES ENGINEERS
49005	SALES REPRESENTATIVES, SCIENTIFIC AND RELATED PRODUCTS AND SERVICES
49008	SALES REPRESENTATIVES, EXCEPT SCIENTIFIC AND RELATED PRODUCTS OR SERVICES
49011	SALESPERSONS, RETAIL
49014	SALESPERSONS, PARTS
49017	COUNTER AND RENTAL CLERKS
49021	STOCK CLERKS, SALES FLOOR
49023	CASHIERS
49026	TELEMARKETERS, DOOR-TO-DOOR SALES WORKERS, NEWS AND STREET VENDORS, AND RELATED SALES WORKERS
49032	DEMONSTRATORS, PROMOTERS, AND MODELS
49999	ALL OTHER SALES AND RELATED WORKERS
51002	FIRST-LINE SUPERVISORS AND MANAGER/SUPERVISORS, CLERICAL AND ADMINISTRATIVE
53102	TELLERS
53105	NEW ACCOUNTS CLERKS
53108	TRANSIT CLERKS
53111	LOAN INTERVIEWERS
53114	CREDIT AUTHORIZERS

53117	CREDIT CHECKERS
53121	LOAN AND CREDIT CLERKS
53123	ADJUSTMENT CLERKS
53126	STATEMENT CLERKS
53128	BROKERAGE CLERKS
53302	INSURANCE ADJUSTERS, EXAMINERS, AND INVESTIGATORS
53305	INSURANCE APPRAISERS, AUTO DAMAGE
53308	INSURANCE EXAMINING CLERKS
53311	INSURANCE CLAIMS CLERKS
53314	INSURANCE POLICY PROCESSING CLERKS
53502	WELFARE ELIGIBILITY WORKERS AND INTERVIEWERS
53505	INVESTIGATORS, CLERICAL
53508	BILL AND ACCOUNT COLLECTORS
53702	COURT CLERKS
53705	MUNICIPAL CLERKS
53708	LICENSE CLERKS
53802	TRAVEL CLERKS
53805	RESERVATION AND TRANSPORTATION TICKET AGENTS
53808	HOTEL DESK CLERKS
53902	LIBRARY ASSISTANTS AND BOOKMOBILE DRIVERS
53905	TEACHER AIDES AND EDUCATIONAL ASSISTANTS, CLERICAL
53908	ADVERTISING CLERKS
53911	PROOFREADERS AND COPY MARKERS
53914	REAL ESTATE CLERKS
55102	LEGAL SECRETARIES
55105	MEDICAL SECRETARIES
55108	SECRETARIES, EXCEPT LEGAL AND MEDICAL
55302	STENOGRAPHERS
55305	RECEPTIONISTS AND INFORMATION CLERKS
55307	TYPISTS, INCLUDING WORD PROCESSING
55314	PERSONNEL CLERKS, EXCEPT PAYROLL AND TIMEKEEPING
55317	CORRESPONDENCE CLERKS
55321	FILE CLERKS
55323	ORDER CLERKS, MATERIALS, MERCHANDISE, AND SERVICE
55326	PROCUREMENT CLERKS
55328	STATISTICAL CLERKS
55332	INTERVIEWING CLERKS, EXCEPT PERSONNEL AND SOCIAL WELFARE
55335	CUSTOMER SERVICE REPRESENTATIVES, UTILITIES
55338	BOOKKEEPING, ACCOUNTING, AND AUDITING CLERKS
55341	PAYROLL AND TIMEKEEPING CLERKS
55344	BILLING, COST, AND RATE CLERKS
55347	GENERAL OFFICE CLERKS
56002	BILLING, POSTING, AND CALCULATING MACHINE OPERATORS
56005	DUPLICATING MACHINE OPERATORS
56008	MAIL MACHINE OPERATORS, PREPARATION AND HANDLING
56011	COMPUTER OPERATORS, EXCEPT PERIPHERAL EQUIPMENT
56014	PERIPHERAL EDP EQUIPMENT OPERATORS
56017	DATA ENTRY KEYERS, EXCEPT COMPOSING
56021	DATA KEYERS, COMPOSING
56099	ALL OTHER OFFICE MACHINE OPERATORS
57102	SWITCHBOARD OPERATORS
57105	DIRECTORY ASSISTANCE OPERATORS
57108	CENTRAL OFFICE OPERATORS
57111	TELEGRAPH AND TELETYPE OPERATORS
57199	ALL OTHER COMMUNICATIONS EQUIPMENT OPERATORS
57302	MAIL CLERKS, EXCEPT MAIL MACHINE OPERATORS AND POSTAL SERVICE
57305	POSTAL MAIL CARRIERS
57308	POSTAL SERVICE CLERKS
57311	MESSENGERS
58002	DISPATCHERS, POLICE, FIRE, AND AMBULANCE
58005	DISPATCHERS, EXCEPT POLICE, FIRE, AND AMBULANCE
58008	PRODUCTION, PLANNING, AND EXPEDITING CLERKS
58011	TRANSPORTATION AGENTS
58014	METER READERS, UTILITIES
58017	WEIGHERS, MEASURERS, CHECKERS, AND SAMPLERS, RECORDKEEPING
58021	MARKING CLERKS
58023	STOCK CLERKS, STOCKROOM, WAREHOUSE, OR STORAGE YARD
58026	ORDER FILLERS, WHOLESALE AND RETAIL SALES
58028	SHIPPING, RECEIVING, AND TRAFFIC CLERKS
58099	ALL OTHER MATERIAL RECORDING, SCHEDULING, AND DISTRIBUTING WORKERS
59999	ALL OTHER CLERICAL AND ADMINISTRATIVE SUPPORT WORKERS
61002	FIRE FIGHTING AND PREVENTION SUPERVISORS
61005	POLICE AND DETECTIVE SUPERVISORS
61008	HOUSEKEEPING SUPERVISORS
61099	ALL OTHER SUPERVISORS AND MANAGER/SUPERVISORS, SERVICE WORKERS
63002	FIRE INSPECTORS
63005	FOREST FIRE INSPECTORS AND PREVENTION SPECIALISTS
63008	FIRE FIGHTERS
63011	POLICE DETECTIVES
63014	POLICE PATROL OFFICERS
63017	CORRECTION OFFICERS AND JAILERS
63021	PARKING ENFORCEMENT OFFICERS

63023 BAILIFFS

63026 UNITED STATES MARSHALLS

63028 CRIMINAL INVESTIGATORS, FEDERAL

63032 SHERIFFS AND DEPUTY SHERIFFS

63035 DETECTIVES AND INVESTIGATORS, EXCEPT PUBLIC

63038 RAILROAD AND TRANSIT POLICE AND SPECIAL AGENTS

63041 FISH AND GAME WARDENS

63044 CROSSING GUARDS

63047 GUARDS AND WATCH GUARDS

63099 ALL OTHER PROTECTIVE SERVICE WORKERS

65002 HOSTS AND HOSTESSES, RESTAURANT, LOUNGE, OR COFFEE SHOP

65005 BARTENDERS

65008 WAITERS AND WAITRESSES

65011 FOOD SERVERS, OUTSIDE

65014 DINING ROOM AND CAFETERIA ATTENDANTS AND BARTENDER HELPERS

65017 COUNTER ATTENDANTS, LUNCHROOM, COFFEE SHOP, OR CAFETERIA

65021 BAKERS, BREAD AND PASTRY

65023 BUTCHERS AND MEAT CUTTERS

65026 COOKS, RESTAURANT

65028 COOKS, INSTITUTION OR CAFETERIA

65032 COOKS, SPECIALTY FAST FOOD

65035 COOKS, SHORT ORDER

65038 FOOD PREPARATION WORKERS

65041 COMBINED FOOD PREPARATION AND SERVICE WORKERS

65099 ALL OTHER FOOD SERVICE WORKERS

66002 DENTAL ASSISTANTS

66005 MEDICAL ASSISTANTS

66008 NURSING AIDES, ORDERLIES, AND ATTENDANTS

66011 HOME HEALTH AIDES

66014 PSYCHIATRIC AIDES

66017 PHYSICAL AND CORRECTIVE THERAPY ASSISTANTS AND AIDES

66021 OCCUPATIONAL THERAPY ASSISTANTS AND AIDES

66023 AMBULANCE DRIVERS AND ATTENDANTS, EXCEPT EMERGENCY MEDICAL TECHNICIANS

66026 PHARMACY AIDES

66099 ALL OTHER HEALTH SERVICE WORKERS

67002 MAIDS AND HOUSEKEEPING CLEANERS

67005 JANITORS AND CLEANERS, EXCEPT MAIDS AND HOUSEKEEPING CLEANERS

67008 PEST CONTROLLERS AND ASSISTANTS

67011 ELEVATOR OPERATORS

67099 ALL OTHER CLEANING AND BUILDING SERVICE WORKERS

68002 BARBERS

68005 HAIRDRESSERS, HAIRSTYLISTS, AND COSMETOLOGISTS

68008 MANICURISTS

68011 SHAMPOOERS

68014 AMUSEMENT AND RECREATION ATTENDANTS

68017 GUIDES

68021 USHERS, LOBBY ATTENDANTS, AND TICKET TAKERS

68023 BAGGAGE PORTERS AND BELLHOPS

68026 FLIGHT ATTENDANTS

68028 TRANSPORTATION ATTENDANTS, EXCEPT FLIGHT ATTENDANTS AND BAGGAGE PORTER

68032 WARDROBE, AND LOCKER AND DRESSING ROOM ATTENDANTS

68035 PERSONAL AND HOME CARE AIDES

68038 CHILD CARE WORKERS

68041 FUNERAL ATTENDANTS

69999 ALL OTHER SERVICE WORKERS

72002 FIRST-LINE SUPERVISORS AND MANAGER/SUPERVISORS, AGRICULTURAL, FORESTRY

73002 FALLERS AND BUCKERS

73005 CHOKE SETTERS

73008 LOG-HANDLING EQUIPMENT OPERATORS

73011 LOGGING TRACTOR OPERATORS

73099 ALL OTHER TIMBER CUTTING AND RELATED LOGGING WORKERS

79002 FOREST AND CONSERVATION WORKERS

79005 NURSERY WORKERS

79008 LOG GRADERS AND SCALERS

79011 GRADERS AND SORTERS, AGRICULTURAL PRODUCTS

79015 ANIMAL BREEDERS

79016 ANIMAL TRAINERS

79017 ANIMAL CARETAKERS, EXCEPT FARM

79021 FARM EQUIPMENT OPERATORS

79030 GARDENERS AND GROUNDSKEEPERS, EXCEPT FARM

79033 PRUNERS

79036 SPRAYERS/APPLICATORS

79038 LAWN MAINTENANCE WORKERS

79806 VETERINARY ASSISTANTS

79855 GENERAL FARM WORKERS

79999 ALL OTHER AGRICULTURAL, FORESTRY, FISHING, AND RELATED WORKERS

81002 FIRST-LINE SUPERVISORS AND MANAGER/SUPERVISORS, MECHANICS, INSTALLERS,

81005 FIRST-LINE SUPERVISORS AND MANAGER/SUPERVISORS, CONSTRUCTION TRADES AND RELATED WORKERS

81008 FIRST-LINE SUPERVISORS AND MANAGER/SUPERVISORS, PRODUCTION AND OPERATIONS

81011 FIRST-LINE SUPERVISORS AND MANAGER/SUPERVISORS, TRANSPORTATION AND MATERIAL HANDLING

81017 FIRST-LINE SUPERVISORS AND MANAGER/ SUPERVISORS, HELPERS, LABORERS, AND RELATED WORKERS

83002 PRECISION INSPECTORS, TESTERS, AND GRADERS

83005 PRODUCTION INSPECTORS, TESTERS, GRADERS, SORTERS, SAMPLERS, AND WEIGHERS

83008 TRANSPORTATION INSPECTORS

85112 MACHINERY MAINTENANCE MECHANICS, TEXTILE MACHINES

85113 MACHINERY MAINTENANCE MECHANICS, SEWING MACHINES

85116 MACHINERY MAINTENANCE MECHANICS, MARINE EQUIPMENT

85117 UNDERGROUND MINE MACHINERY MECHANICS

85118 MACHINERY MAINTENANCE MECHANICS, WATER OR POWER GENERATION PLANT

85119 ALL OTHER MACHINERY MAINTENANCE MECHANICS

85123 MILLWRIGHTS

85126 REFRACTORY MATERIALS REPAIRERS, EXCEPT BRICKMASONS

85128 MACHINERY MAINTENANCE WORKERS

85132 MAINTENANCE REPAIRERS, GENERAL UTILITY

85302 AUTOMOTIVE MECHANICS

85305 AUTOMOTIVE BODY AND RELATED REPAIRERS

85308 MOTORCYCLE REPAIRERS

85311 BUS AND TRUCK MECHANICS AND DIESEL ENGINE SPECIALISTS

85314 MOBILE HEAVY EQUIPMENT MECHANICS, EXCEPT ENGINES

85317 RAIL CAR REPAIRERS

85321 FARM EQUIPMENT MECHANICS

85323 AIRCRAFT MECHANICS

85326 AIRCRAFT ENGINE SPECIALISTS

85328 SMALL ENGINE SPECIALISTS

85502 CENTRAL OFFICE AND PBX INSTALLERS AND REPAIRERS

85505 FRAME WIRERS, CENTRAL OFFICE

85508 TELEGRAPH AND TELETYPE INSTALLERS AND MAINTAINERS

85511 SIGNAL OR TRACK SWITCH MAINTAINERS

85514 RADIO MECHANICS

85599 ALL OTHER COMMUNICATIONS EQUIPMENT MECHANICS, INSTALLERS, AND REPAIRERS

85702 TELEPHONE AND CABLE TV LINE INSTALLERS AND REPAIRERS

85705 DATA PROCESSING EQUIPMENT REPAIRERS

85708 ELECTRONIC HOME ENTERTAINMENT EQUIPMENT REPAIRERS

85711 ELECTRIC HOME APPLIANCE AND POWER TOOL REPAIRERS

85714 ELECTRIC MOTOR, TRANSFORMER, AND RELATED REPAIRERS

85717 ELECTRONICS REPAIRERS, COMMERCIAL AND INDUSTRIAL EQUIPMENT

85721 POWERHOUSE, SUBSTATION, AND RELAY ELECTRICIANS

85723 ELECTRICAL POWER-LINE INSTALLERS AND REPAIRERS

85726 STATION INSTALLERS AND REPAIRERS, TELEPHONE

85728 ELECTRICAL INSTALLERS AND REPAIRERS, TRANSPORTATION EQUIPMENT

85799 ALL OTHER ELECTRICAL AND ELECTRONIC EQUIPMENT MECHANICS, INSTALLERS, AND RELATED REPAIRERS

85902 HEATING, AIR CONDITIONING, AND REFRIGERATION MECHANICS AND INSTALLERS

85905 PRECISION INSTRUMENT REPAIRERS

85908 ELECTROMEDICAL AND BIOMEDICAL EQUIPMENT REPAIRERS

85911 ELECTRIC METER INSTALLERS AND REPAIRERS

85914 CAMERA AND PHOTOGRAPHIC EQUIPMENT REPAIRERS

85917 WATCHMAKERS

85921 MUSICAL INSTRUMENT REPAIRERS AND TUNERS

85923 LOCKSMITHS AND SAFE REPAIRERS

85926 OFFICE MACHINE AND CASH REGISTER SERVICERS

85928 MECHANICAL CONTROL AND VALVE INSTALLERS AND REPAIRERS

85932 ELEVATOR INSTALLERS AND REPAIRERS

85935 RIGGERS

85938 INSTALLERS AND REPAIRERS, MANUFACTURED BUILDINGS, MOBILE HOMES, AND TRAILERS

85944 GAS APPLIANCE REPAIRERS

85947 COIN AND VENDING MACHINE SERVICERS AND REPAIRERS

85951 BICYCLE REPAIRERS

85953 TIRE REPAIRERS AND CHANGERS

85956 MENDERS, GARMENTS, LINENS, AND RELATED

85999 ALL OTHER MECHANICS, INSTALLERS, AND REPAIRERS

87102 CARPENTERS

87105 CEILING TILE INSTALLERS AND ACOUSTICAL CARPENTERS

87108 DRYWALL INSTALLERS

87111 TAPERS

87114 LATHERS

87121 BRATTICE BUILDERS

87202 ELECTRICIANS

87302 BRICKMASONS

87305 STONEMASONS

87308 HARD TILE SETTERS

87311 CONCRETE AND TERRAZZO FINISHERS

87314 REINFORCING METAL WORKERS

87317 PLASTERERS AND STUCCO MASONS

87402 PAINTERS AND PAPERHANGERS, CONSTRUCTION AND MAINTENANCE

87502 PLUMBERS, PIPEFITTERS, AND STEAMFITTERS

87505	PIPELAYING FITTERS
87508	PIPELAYERS
87511	SEPTIC TANK SERVICERS AND SEWER PIPE CLEANERS
87602	CARPET INSTALLERS
87605	FLOOR LAYERS, EXCEPT CARPET, WOOD, AND HARD TILES
87608	FLOOR SANDING MACHINE OPERATORS
87702	AIR HAMMER OPERATORS
87705	PILE-DRIVER OPERATORS
87708	PAVING, SURFACING, AND TAMPING EQUIPMENT OPERATORS
87711	HIGHWAY MAINTENANCE WORKERS
87714	RAIL-TRACK LAYING AND MAINTENANCE EQUIPMENT OPERATORS
87802	INSULATION WORKERS
87805	SHEET METAL DUCT INSTALLERS
87808	ROOFERS
87811	GLAZIERS
87814	STRUCTURAL METAL WORKERS
87817	FENCE ERECTORS
87899	ALL OTHER CONSTRUCTION TRADES WORKERS
87902	EARTH DRILLERS, EXCEPT OIL AND GAS
87905	BLASTERS AND EXPLOSIVES WORKERS
87908	ROCK SPLITTERS, QUARRY
87911	ROTARY DRILL OPERATORS, OIL AND GAS EXTRACTION
87914	DERRICK OPERATORS, OIL AND GAS EXTRACTION
87917	SERVICE UNIT OPERATORS
87921	ROUSTABOUTS
87923	ROOF BOLTERS
87941	CONTINUOUS MINING MACHINE OPERATORS
87943	MINE CUTTING AND CHANNELING MACHINE OPERATORS
87949	ALL OTHER MINING MACHINE OPERATORS
87999	ALL OTHER CONSTRUCTION AND EXTRACTIVE WORKERS, EXCEPT HELPERS
89102	TOOL AND DIE MAKERS
89105	PRECISION INSTRUMENT MAKERS
89108	MACHINISTS
89111	TOOL GRINDERS, FILERS, SHARPENERS, AND OTHER PRECISION GRINDERS
89114	PATTERN AND MODEL MAKERS, METAL
89117	PRECISION LAY-OUT WORKERS, METAL
89121	SHIPFITTERS
89123	JEWELERS AND SILVERSMITHS
89126	PRECISION HAND WORKERS, JEWELRY AND RELATED PRODUCTS
89128	PRECISION ETCHERS AND ENGRAVERS, HAND OR MACHINE
89132	SHEET METAL WORKERS
89135	BOILERMAKERS
89199	ALL OTHER PRECISION METAL WORKERS
89302	PATTERN AND MODEL MAKERS, WOOD
89305	PATTERN MARKERS, WOOD
89308	WOOD MACHINISTS
89311	CABINETMAKERS AND BENCH CARPENTERS
89314	FURNITURE FINISHERS
89399	ALL OTHER PRECISION WOODWORKERS
89502	FABRIC AND APPAREL PATTERNMAKERS AND LAY-OUT WORKERS
89505	CUSTOM TAILORS AND SEWERS
89508	UPHOLSTERERS
89511	SHOE AND LEATHER WORKERS AND REPAIRERS, PRECISION
89514	SPOTTERS, DRY CLEANING
89517	PRESSERS, DELICATE FABRICS
89521	PRECISION DYERS
89599	ALL OTHER PRECISION TEXTILE, APPAREL, AND FURNISHINGS WORKERS
89702	HAND COMPOSITORS AND TYPESETTERS
89705	JOB PRINTERS
89706	PASTE-UP WORKERS
89707	ELECTRONIC PAGINATION SYSTEM OPERATORS
89712	PHOTOENGRAVERS
89713	CAMERA OPERATORS
89715	SCANNER OPERATORS
89717	STRIPPERS
89718	PLATEMAKERS
89719	ALL OTHER LITHOGRAPHY AND PHOTOENGRAVING WORKERS
89721	BOOKBINDERS
89799	ALL OTHER PRECISION PRINTING WORKERS
89802	SLAUGHTERERS AND BUTCHERS
89805	BAKERS, MANUFACTURING
89808	FOOD BATCHMAKERS
89899	ALL OTHER PRECISION FOOD AND TOBACCO WORKERS
89902	PRECISION FOUNDRY MOLD AND COREMAKERS
89905	PRECISION MOLDERS, SHAPERS, CASTERS, AND CARVERS, EXCEPT JEWELRY
89908	PRECISION PATTERNMAKERS, MODEL MAKERS, LAY-OUT WORKERS, AND CUTTERS
89911	PRECISION DETAIL DESIGN DECORATORS AND PAINTERS
89914	PRECISION PHOTOGRAPHIC PROCESS WORKERS
89917	PRECISION OPTICAL GOODS WORKERS
89921	PRECISION DENTAL LABORATORY TECHNICIANS
89923	MEDICAL APPLIANCE MAKERS
89926	GEM AND DIAMOND WORKERS
89999	ALL OTHER PRECISION WORKERS
91102	SAWING MACHINE TOOL SETTERS AND SET-UP OPERATORS, METAL AND PLASTIC

91105 LATHE AND TURNING MACHINE TOOL SETTERS AND SET-UP OPERATORS, METAL AND PLASTIC

91108 DRILLING AND BORING MACHINE TOOL SETTERS AND SET-UP OPERATORS, METAL AND PLASTIC

91111 MILLING AND PLANING MACHINE SETTERS AND SET-UP OPERATORS, METAL AND PLASTIC

91114 GRINDING, LAPPING, AND BUFFING MACHINE TOOL SETTERS AND SET-UP OPERATORS, METAL AND PLASTIC

91117 MACHINE TOOL CUTTING OPERATORS AND TENDERS, METAL AND PLASTIC

91302 PUNCHING MACHINE SETTERS AND SET-UP OPERATORS, METAL AND PLASTIC

91305 PRESS AND PRESS-BRAKE MACHINE SETTERS AND SET-UP OPERATORS, METAL AND PLASTIC

91308 SHEAR AND SLITTER MACHINE SETTERS AND SET-UP OPERATORS, METAL AND PLASTIC

91311 EXTRUDING AND DRAWING MACHINE SETTERS AND SET-UP OPERATORS, METAL AND PLASTIC

91314 ROLLING MACHINE SETTERS AND SET-UP OPERATORS, METAL AND PLASTIC

91317 FORGING MACHINE SETTERS AND SET-UP OPERATORS, METAL AND PLASTIC

91321 FORMING MACHINE OPERATORS AND TENDERS, METAL AND PLASTIC

91502 NUMERICAL CONTROL MACHINE TOOL OPERATORS AND TENDERS, METAL AND PLASTI

91505 COMBINATION MACHINE TOOL SETTERS AND SET-UP OPERATORS, METAL AND PLASTIC

91508 COMBINATION MACHINE TOOL OPERATORS AND TENDERS, METAL AND PLASTIC

91702 WELDING MACHINE SETTERS AND SET-UP OPERATORS

91705 WELDING MACHINE OPERATORS AND TENDERS

91708 SOLDERING AND BRAZING MACHINE SETTERS AND SET-UP OPERATORS

91711 SOLDERING AND BRAZING MACHINE OPERATORS AND TENDERS

91714 METAL FABRICATORS, STRUCTURAL METAL PRODUCTS

91902 PLASTIC MOLDING AND CASTING MACHINE SETTERS AND SET-UP OPERATORS

91905 PLASTIC MOLDING AND CASTING MACHINE OPERATORS AND TENDERS

91908 METAL MOLDING, COREMAKING, AND CASTING MACHINE SETTERS AND SET-UP OPERATORS

91911 METAL MOLDING, COREMAKING, AND CASTING MACHINE OPERATORS AND TENDERS

91914 FOUNDRY MOLD ASSEMBLY AND SHAKE-OUT WORKERS

91917 ELECTROLYTIC PLATING AND COATING MACHINE SETTERS AND SET-UP OPERATORS, METAL AND PLASTIC

91921 ELECTROLYTIC PLATING AND COATING MACHINE OPERATORS AND TENDERS, METAL AND PLASTIC

91923 NONELECTROLYTIC PLATING AND COATING MACHINE SETTERS AND SET-UP OPERATORS, METAL AND PLASTIC

91926 NONELECTROLYTIC PLATING AND COATING MACHINE OPERATORS AND TENDERS, METAL AND PLASTIC

91928 HEATING EQUIPMENT SETTERS AND SET-UP OPERATORS, METAL AND PLASTIC

91932 HEAT TREATING, ANNEALING, AND TEMPERING MACHINE OPERATORS AND TENDERS, METAL AND PLASTIC

91935 FURNACE OPERATORS AND TENDERS

91938 HEATERS, METAL AND PLASTIC

92197 ALL OTHER METAL AND PLASTIC (CUTTING, FORMING, FABRICATING, OR PROCESS) MACHINE SETTERS

92198 ALL OTHER METAL AND PLASTIC (CUTTING, FORMING, FABRICATING, OR PROCESS) SET-UP OPERATORS

92302 SAWING MACHINE SETTERS AND SET-UP OPERATORS

92305 HEAD SAWYERS

92308 SAWING MACHINE OPERATORS AND TENDERS

92311 WOODWORKING MACHINE SETTERS AND SET-UP OPERATORS, EXCEPT SAWING

92314 WOODWORKING MACHINE OPERATORS AND TENDERS, EXCEPT SAWING

92512 OFFSET LITHOGRAPHIC PRESS SETTERS AND SET-UP OPERATORS

92515 LETTERPRESS SETTERS AND SET-UP OPERATORS

92519 ALL OTHER PRINTING PRESS SETTERS AND SET-UP OPERATORS

92521 PHOTOENGRAVING AND LITHOGRAPHING PHOTOGRAPHERS

92522 SPECIALTY MATERIALS PRINTING MACHINE SETTERS AND SET-UP OPERATORS

92524 SCREEN PRINTING MACHINE SETTERS AND SET-UP OPERATORS

92525 BINDERY MACHINE SETTERS AND SET-UP OPERATORS

92529 ALL OTHER PRINTING RELATED MACHINE SETTERS AND SET-UP OPERATORS

92541 TYPESETTING AND COMPOSING MACHINE OPERATORS AND TENDERS

92543 PRINTING PRESS MACHINE OPERATORS AND TENDERS

92545 PHOTOENGRAVING AND LITHOGRAPHING MACHINE OPERATORS AND TENDERS

92546 BINDERY MACHINE OPERATORS AND TENDERS

92549 ALL OTHER PRINTING, BINDING, AND RELATED MACHINE OPERATORS AND TENDERS

92702 TEXTILE MACHINE SETTERS AND SET-UP OPERATORS

92705 TEXTILE MACHINE OPERATORS AND TENDERS, WINDING, TWISTING, KNITTING

92708 EXTRUDING AND FORMING MACHINE OPERATORS AND TENDERS, SYNTHETIC OR GLASS

92711 TEXTILE DRAW-OUT MACHINE OPERATORS AND TENDERS

92714 TEXTILE BLEACHING AND DYEING MACHINE OPERATORS AND TENDERS

92717 SEWING MACHINE OPERATORS, GARMENT

92721 SEWING MACHINE OPERATORS, NONGARMENT

92723 SHOE SEWING MACHINE OPERATORS AND TENDERS

92726 LAUNDRY AND DRY-CLEANING MACHINE OPERATORS AND TENDERS, EXCEPT PRESSING

92728 PRESSING MACHINE OPERATORS AND TENDERS, TEXTILE, GARMENT, AND RELATED

92902 ELECTRONIC SEMICONDUCTOR PROCESSORS

92905 MOTION PICTURE PROJECTIONISTS

92908 PHOTOGRAPHIC PROCESSING MACHINE OPERATORS AND TENDERS

92911 TIRE BUILDING MACHINE OPERATORS

92914 PAPER GOODS MACHINE SETTERS AND SET-UP OPERATORS

92917 COOKING MACHINE OPERATORS AND TENDERS, FOOD AND TOBACCO

92921 ROASTING, BAKING, AND DRYING MACHINE OPERATORS AND TENDERS, FOOD AND TOBACCO

92923 FURNACE, KILN, OVEN, DRIER, OR KETTLE OPERATORS AND TENDERS

92926 BOILER OPERATORS AND TENDERS, LOW PRESSURE

92928 COOLING AND FREEZING EQUIPMENT OPERATORS AND TENDERS

92932 DAIRY PROCESSING EQUIPMENT OPERATORS, INCLUDING SETTERS

92935 CHEMICAL EQUIPMENT CONTROLLERS AND OPERATORS

92938 CHEMICAL EQUIPMENT TENDERS

92941 CUTTING AND SLICING MACHINE SETTERS AND SET-UP OPERATORS

92944 CUTTING AND SLICING MACHINE OPERATORS AND TENDERS

92947 PAINTERS, TRANSPORTATION EQUIPMENT

92951 COATING, PAINTING, AND SPRAYING MACHINE SETTERS AND SET-UP OPERATORS

92953 COATING, PAINTING, AND SPRAYING MACHINE OPERATORS AND TENDERS

92956 CEMENTING AND GLUING MACHINE OPERATORS AND TENDERS

92958 CLEANING, WASHING, AND PICKLING EQUIPMENT OPERATORS AND TENDERS

92962 SEPARATING, FILTERING, CLARIFYING, PRECIPITATING, AND STILL MACHINE OPERAT

92965 CRUSHING, GRINDING, MIXING, AND BLENDI MACHINE OPERATORS AND TENDERS

92968 EXTRUDING, FORMING, PRESSING, AND COMPACTING MACHINE SETTERS AND S OPERATORS

92971 EXTRUDING, FORMING, PRESSING, AND COMPACTING MACHINE OPERATORS AND TENDERS

92974 PACKAGING AND FILLING MACHINE OPERATORS AND TENDERS

92997 ALL OTHER MACHINE SETTERS AND SET-UP OPERATORS

92998 ALL OTHER MACHINE OPERATORS AND TENDERS

93102 AIRCRAFT STRUCTURE, SURFACES, RIGGING, AND SYSTEMS ASSEMBLERS, PRECISION

93105 MACHINE BUILDERS AND OTHER PRECISION MACHINE ASSEMBLERS

93108 FITTERS, STRUCTURAL METAL, PRECISION

93111 ELECTROMECHANICAL EQUIPMENT ASSEMBLERS, PRECISION

93114 ELECTRICAL AND ELECTRONIC EQUIPMENT ASSEMBLERS, PRECISION

93117 WATCH, CLOCK, AND CHRONOMETER ASSEMBLERS, ADJUSTERS, AND CALIBRATORS

93197 ALL OTHER PRECISION ASSEMBLERS

93902 MACHINE ASSEMBLERS

93905 ELECTRICAL AND ELECTRONIC ASSEMBLERS

93908 COIL WINDERS, TAPERS, AND FINISHERS

93911 GLAZIERS, MANUFACTURING

93914 WELDERS AND CUTTERS

93917 SOLDERERS AND BRAZERS

93921 PRESSERS, HAND

93923 SEWERS, HAND

93926 CUTTERS AND TRIMMERS

93928 PORTABLE MACHINE C

93932 CARPET CUTTERS,

93935 CANNERY WORK

93938 MEAT, POULT TRIMMERS

93941 METAL F

93944 MOL

93947 PA H

93951

93953

939

97
975
97702
97802
97805
97808
97899 P
97902 AL WO
97905 LON
97908 TANK
97911 OIL PU
97914 WELLHE
97917 MAIN-LINE
97921 GAS PUMPI
GAS COMPR

97102 TRUCK DRIVERS, HEAVY OR TRACTOR-TRAILER

97105 TRUCK DRIVERS, LIGHT, INCLUDE DELIVERY AND ROUTE WORKERS

97108 BUS DRIVERS, EXCEPT SCHOOL

97111 BUS DRIVERS, SCHOOL

97114 TAXI DRIVERS AND CHAUFFEURS

97117 DRIVER/SALES WORKERS

97199 ALL OTHER MOTOR VEHICLE OPERATORS

97302 RAILROAD CONDUCTORS AND YARDMASTERS

97305 LOCOMOTIVE ENGINEERS

97308 RAIL YARD ENGINEERS, DINKEY OPERATORS, AND HOSTLERS

97311 LOCOMOTIVE FIRERS

97314 SUBWAY AND STREETCAR OPERATORS

97317 RAILROAD BRAKE, SIGNAL, AND SWITCH OPERATORS

97399 ALL OTHER RAIL VEHICLE OPERATORS AND CONTROLLERS

97502 CAPTAINS, WATER VESSEL

97505 MATES, SHIP, BOAT, AND BARGE

97508 PILOTS, SHIP

97511 MOTORBOAT OPERATORS

97514 ABLE SEAMEN

97517 ORDINARY SEAMEN AND MARINE OILERS

97_21 SHIP ENGINEERS

97___ AIRCRAFT PILOTS AND FLIGHT ENGINEERS

____ BRIDGE, LOCK, AND LIGHTHOUSE TENDERS

____ SERVICE STATION ATTENDANTS

____ PARKING LOT ATTENDANTS

____ ALL OTHER TRANSPORTATION AND RELATED WORKERS

____ SHORE EQUIPMENT OPERATORS

____ CAR AND TRUCK LOADERS

____ PUMPERS, EXCEPT WELLHEAD

____ WELLHEAD PUMPERS

____ STATION ENGINEERS

____ PUMPING STATION OPERATORS

____ COMPRESSOR OPERATORS

97923 EXCAVATING AND LOADING MACHINE OPERATORS

97926 DRAGLINE OPERATORS

97928 DREDGE OPERATORS

97932 LOADING MACHINE OPERATORS, UNDERGROUND MINING

97935 SHUTTLE CAR OPERATORS

97938 GRADER, BULLDOZER, AND SCRAPER OPERATORS

97941 HOIST AND WINCH OPERATORS

97944 CRANE AND TOWER OPERATORS

97947 INDUSTRIAL TRUCK AND TRACTOR OPERATORS

97951 CONVEYOR OPERATORS AND TENDERS

97953 PUMP OPERATORS

97956 OPERATING ENGINEERS

97989 ALL OTHER MATERIAL-MOVING EQUIPMENT OPERATORS

98102 HELPERS, MECHANICS AND REPAIRERS

98311 HELPERS, BRICK AND STONEMASONS AND HARD TILE SETTERS

98312 HELPERS, CARPENTERS AND RELATED WORKERS

98313 HELPERS, ELECTRICIANS AND POWER-LINE TRANSMISSION INSTALLERS

98314 HELPERS, PAINTERS, PAPERHANGERS, PLASTERERS, AND STUCCO MASONS

98315 HELPERS, PLUMBERS, PIPEFITTERS, AND STEAMFITTERS

98316 HELPERS, ROOFERS

98319 HELPERS, ALL OTHER CONSTRUCTION TRADES WORKERS

98323 HELPERS, EXTRACTIVE WORKERS

98502 MACHINE FEEDERS AND OFFBEARERS

98702 STEVEDORES, EXCEPT EQUIPMENT OPERATORS

98705 REFUSE AND RECYCLABLE MATERIAL COLLECTORS

98799 ALL OTHER FREIGHT, STOCK, AND MATERIAL MOVERS, HAND

98902 HAND PACKERS AND PACKAGERS

98905 VEHICLE WASHERS AND EQUIPMENT CLEANERS

98999 ALL OTHER HELPERS, LABORERS, AND MATERIAL MOVERS, HAND

JIST's Essential Career References

Dictionary of Occupational Titles

U.S. Department of Labor

A standard reference describing 12,741 jobs. It is the primary source of information on most occupations and the best guide for specific job information.

Virtually all career reference products are cross-referenced to it.

Softcover (2 Volumes)
ISBN 1-56370-000-X
$39.00
Order Code DOT91

Hardcover (1 Volume)
ISBN 1-56370-006-9
$48.00
Order Code DOTH

Young Person's Occupational Outlook Handbook

Appropriate for children in grades 5 through 9, this exceptional new reference book covers the same 250 occupations as the adult edition, but in a simpler, graphically interesting way. Ideal to help young people explore the world of work.

ISBN 1-56370-201-0
$19.95
Order Code J2010

The Complete Guide for Occupational Exploration

Uses an intuitive occupational coding system developed by the U.S. Department of Labor to organize the 12,741 job titles in the **DOT** into 12 major "interest areas." A very good resource for career exploration.

Softcover
ISBN 1-56370-052-2
$39.95
Order Code CGOE

Hardcover
ISBN 1-56370-100-6
$49.95
Order Code CGOEH

The Enhanced Guide for Occupational Exploration, 2nd Edition

Organizes 2,800 of the most important jobs into 12 major interest areas with increasingly specific groupings of similar jobs. General information and specific job descriptions provided for each grouping.

Softcover
ISBN 1-56370-207-X
$34.95
Order Code J207X

Hardcover
ISBN 1-56370-244-4
$44.95
Order Code J2444

The Occupational Outlook Handbook

The best reprint available of the most widely used career reference in the country. Completely updated information on the 250 top jobs in our economy. Recommended for job seekers, students, career changers, and business people.

Softcover
ISBN 1-56370-277-0
$15.95
Order Code J2770

Hardcover
ISBN 1-56370-278-9
$21.95
Order Code J2789

Career Exploration Video

This unique video reviews all the essential career reference books described on this page, telling what they are and how to use them to best effect. This is a real time-saver for busy employment, training, and counseling professionals.

ISBN 1-56370-043-3
$99.00
Order Code CXV

Call 1-800-JIST-USA

JIST Provides the Resources That Help America Work!

JIST FAX:
1-800-547-8329